The
J.R.R. Tolkien
Companion
& Guide

The
J.R.R. Tolkien
Companion
& Guide

CHRISTINA SCULL
WAYNE G. HAMMOND

* *

Reader's Guide

HOUGHTON MIFFLIN COMPANY
BOSTON · NEW YORK
2006

For information about permission to reproduce selections
from this book, write to Permissions, Houghton Mifflin Company,
215 Park Avenue South, New York, New York 10003.

Visit our Web site: www.houghtonmifflinbooks.com.

Further copyright information is printed following the index.

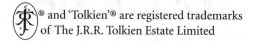® and 'Tolkien'® are registered trademarks
of The J.R.R. Tolkien Estate Limited

Library of Congress Cataloging-in-Publication Data
Scull, Christina.
The J.R.R. Tolkien companion & guide / Christina Scull,
Wayne G. Hammond.
v.   cm.
Includes bibliographical references and indexes.
Contents: 1. Chronology — 2. Reader's guide.
ISBN-13: 978-0-618-39102-8 (v. 1)
ISBN-10: 0-618-39102-9 (v. 1)
ISBN-13: 978-0-618-39101-1 (v. 2)
ISBN-10: 0-618-39101-0 (v. 2)
1. Tolkien, J. R. R. (John Ronald Reuel), 1892–1973 — Encyclopedias.
2. Middle Earth (Imaginary place) — Encyclopedias. 3. Fantasy liter-
ature, English — Encyclopedias. I. Hammond, Wayne G. II. Title.
III. Title: J.R.R. Tolkien companion and guide.
PR6039.O32Z833 2006
828'.91209 — dc22   2006025040

Set in Adobe Minion Pro and Gentium

Printed and bound in Italy by L.E.G.O SpA

1 2 3 4 5 6 7 8 9

In Memory of

RAYNER UNWIN

Mentor and Friend

Contents

Preface

THIS BOOK has been designed to serve as a reference of (at least) first resort for the study and appreciation of the works of J.R.R. Tolkien. It is meant to be a companion to his readers, and a basic guide to his writings and ideas, his life and times, his family, friends, and colleagues, and the places he knew and loved. It is not, despite a similarity of titles, a handbook of his invented lands and characters in the manner of Robert Foster's *Complete Guide to Middle-earth* or J.E.A. Tyler's *Complete Tolkien Companion*. Nor is it a substitute for standard works such as Humphrey Carpenter's *J.R.R. Tolkien: A Biography*, Christopher Tolkien's *History of Middle-earth*, and the present authors' *J.R.R. Tolkien: Artist and Illustrator* and *The Lord of the Rings: A Reader's Companion*, or for the vast body of critical literature about Tolkien. Although it often will be found useful by itself, in particular where it provides information newly gleaned from archives or collected from recent scholarship, its purpose is equally to point to other resources in which a subject is more fully considered or differing points of view are expressed.

The length of this work may surprise readers who, focused on *The Hobbit* and *The Lord of the Rings*, have been less aware of Tolkien's other writings, or who, perhaps misled by the biographies of our subject that have followed Carpenter (and are largely derived from his book), have thought that Tolkien lived in a simple circumscribed world in which little happened beyond his writing, his teaching, his immediate family, and the Inklings. In fact, his life was remarkably full, his circle of friends was wide and varied, and his tales of Bilbo and Frodo Baggins exist alongside other works of fiction and poetry, not least the vast 'Silmarillion' mythology, and next to significant contributions to Old and Middle English studies. In consequence, there is much to say about Tolkien, so much that we have had to divide our book into two volumes.

One of these is an extensive **Chronology** of Tolkien's life and works, which has allowed us reasonably to assemble – as a biographical essay would not have done, demanding more selection and brevity – many of the miscellaneous details about Tolkien we have gathered in the course of research, details which individually may be of little moment, but in relation to one another can be very illuminating. Altogether these form a picture of a extraordinarily busy man: Tolkien the scholar, Tolkien the teacher and administrator, Tolkien the husband and father, Tolkien the creator of Middle-earth. His critics have not always appreciated how busy he truly was – those who claim that he should have published more in his academic fields, and those who fault him for not completing *The Silmarillion* as if he had nothing else to do even in his retirement. One of our aims in this book is to show that Tolkien neither wasted his time nor shirked his responsibilities – to document how much, on a regular basis, duties in connection with his academic career (lectures, classes, supervision of postgraduate students, examinations, committee meetings, and so forth) occupied his waking hours; how often he and his family were beset by illness and injury; how, to pay doctors' bills in the years before the National Health Service was established (in 1948) and to provide for his children's education, he added to an already heavy workload; how he was almost constantly under the threat of deadlines, and if he did not meet them all it was not because he did too little, but because he did so much.

The Chronology also allows us to see when, as sometimes happened, Tolkien's many responsibilities came into collision. In April 1937, for instance, within the space of a day or two he received for correction proofs of both *The Hobbit* and his British Academy lecture, *Beowulf: The Monsters and the Critics*; while in the summer and autumn of 1953 he prepared simultaneously *The Lord of the Rings* for publication and his translation of *Sir Gawain and the Green Knight* for radio broadcast, and also wrote two talks to accompany the latter. We have not attempted, by any means (even if it were possible), a complete day-to-day reconstruction of Tolkien's complex life, but we have erred in the Chronology on the side of inclusion for the sake of a fuller picture. This is particularly so during the period from 18 January 1944 to early 1945, when Tolkien frequently described his daily chores, as well as the progress of *The Lord of the Rings*, in a series of letters to his youngest son, Christopher, then posted abroad in the Royal Air Force (see *Letters of J.R.R. Tolkien*, pp. 67 ff.).

Although the most private of Tolkien's surviving papers remain private, a great deal else has been open to us, published and unpublished, which we have found a rich mine of data. These papers have been useful not only in adding to our knowledge of J.R.R. Tolkien, but also in verifying details previously accepted as fact. We found, for instance, in assembling information for 1952 that there was no possible opportunity for Tolkien to travel to Kerry in Ireland that year, as authorities (even ourselves) have previously reported. This led, as we investigated further, to a vivid recollection by Tolkien's daughter Priscilla that the visit was, rather, in 1951, and that she herself had been a participant.

Sometimes, however, evidence has been lacking, and even when present is not always complete or clear-cut. To give only a few examples: we can say that Tolkien attended particular meetings of the Inklings because the facts are mentioned, chiefly in letters by his friend C.S. Lewis, in diaries kept by W.H. 'Warnie' Lewis, and in letters that Tolkien wrote to his son Christopher. We can list which lectures he was scheduled to give as an Oxford professor, because they were announced prior to each term in the *Oxford University Gazette*. We know that he was present at certain board and committee meetings because minutes are preserved, chiefly in the Oxford University archives. But we know about only some of the holidays he took, from a handful of letters and dated paintings and drawings, and about only some of the society meetings and other events he attended (or could have attended) at King Edward's School, Birmingham and at Oxford, through secretaries' minutes, magazine reports, and printed timetables. On occasion, his Oxford lectures were cancelled or rescheduled, but a published announcement of that fact has not always come to our attention; and as for the lectures Tolkien gave at Leeds, such schedules of these that survive in the Leeds University archives name only their subjects, not the lecturers themselves, in consequence of which we have indicated only those lectures that Tolkien seems likely to have given (based partly on the statement he wrote when he applied for the Rawlinson and Bosworth Professorship of Anglo-Saxon at Oxford in 1925). We know as well that Tolkien marked School Certificate papers for many years, to augment his professor's salary, and sometimes acted as an external university examiner, but these activities seem to be little documented.

We have also included in the Chronology references to some, but no more than a fraction (even of that portion known to us), of the personal and professional correspondence that consumed another large portion of Tolkien's time. He received many requests from colleagues for information, or for comments on their ideas; requests from colleagues or former students for references when applying for academic positions; and requests from publishers to give his opinion of books under consideration. He was often sent, in addition, offprints of scholarly papers and copies of books, most of which would have required at least an acknowledgement, if not reading and criticism: these amounted to hundreds of titles during his working life. And then, after the publication of *The Hobbit* and especially *The Lord of the Rings*, he received thousands of letters expressing appreciation, asking questions, or requesting his autograph. His publishers too were in frequent touch with him about various literary, financial, and legal matters. And all of this was in addition to letters he wrote to and received from his family and intimate friends.

Tolkien's correspondence with his publisher George Allen & Unwin in particular has been of immense value to us. In many of his letters he writes of his personal activities, of academic pressures, and of his or his family's health, as well as about business at hand. These documents, however, became less frequent in his later years, reflecting increased personal contact with publisher's staff and use of the telephone.

Perhaps our greatest difficulty in writing the Chronology has been to decide where to place events that cannot be firmly dated, such as the emergence of the Inklings. Many of Tolkien's works, moreover, can be placed only within a range of years, and only roughly in order of writing. In doing so, we have relied on internal as well as external evidence – on handwriting, paper, and typefaces, and on the state of development of the work in question. Where Christopher Tolkien as a result of his own extensive research into the history of his father's writings has been able to group works in a sequential order, we have placed the grouping at the start of the relevant time span, rather than insert the writings in question arbitrarily into the Chronology. We have also made use of dates of composition inscribed by Tolkien on his writings and art, keeping in mind that some of these were added after the fact, sometimes many years later, and that memory can err; but such statements by the creator of a work must hold weight, unless evidence is found to the contrary. In a few instances it is indeed the case that there is conflicting evidence for dates, most notably for the origin and writing of *The Hobbit*. In such cases we have made multiple entries in the

Chronology, with cross-references, and have discussed the matter at greater length in the other part of our *Companion and Guide*.

That volume, which we have called the **Reader's Guide**, complements the Chronology and vice versa. An asterisk (*) before names, titles, words, or phrases in the Chronology indicates that a corresponding entry may be found in the Guide; and in using the Guide, the reader will often wish to consult the Chronology for a more detailed view of a particular segment of time.

The Reader's Guide comprises a 'What's What', a 'Where's Where', and a 'Who's Who' of Tolkien, arranged in alphabetical order and in a single sequence. *Inter alia* it includes entries for:

¶ Tolkien's academic writings and his works of poetry and prose fiction, with summaries, concise backgrounds or histories, brief surveys of reviews and criticism (in so far as these exist), and miscellaneous commentary.

¶ Key ideas in Tolkien's writings, such as *eucatastrophe* and *sub-creation*, and general topics such as his religion, his views towards women, his reading, and disputes over the American copyright of *The Lord of the Rings*.

¶ Places that Tolkien lived, worked, or visited, the colleges and universities with which he was associated, pubs and bookshops he frequented, and so forth. It should be assumed by the reader that the places named in this book are in England unless otherwise stated, that English counties are referred to generally according to the names and boundaries that existed in Tolkien's lifetime (before the reorganization of local governments in the later twentieth century), and that while coverage is full, it is not exhaustive: we have not attempted to list every place in which Tolkien set foot. Nor have we attempted to account for every claim by British towns and regions to Tolkien's presence, or as an inspiration for *The Lord of the Rings*, put forth in recent years with the rise in his popularity: some of these are exaggerated, others dubious at best. In all cases, we have preferred to rely on documentary evidence such as letters, guest books, and diaries, rather than on assumptions and reported 'tradition'. It should be noted also that while some of the places described in this book are open to the public, others are not. Readers therefore who wish to follow in Tolkien's footsteps should take care not to trespass on private property, including college grounds when not open to visitors.

¶ Members of Tolkien's family; colleagues at Leeds and Oxford; fellow members of the Inklings and other groups or societies to which he belonged; publishers and editors; notable teachers and students; and major correspondents. Here too, our coverage is selective. Tolkien had many friends and acquaintances, some of whom figured mainly, or wholly, in his private life, and do not appear in published letters or biographies. Our aim has been to give an individual entry to anyone whom we know to have been particularly significant in Tolkien's life or to the production of his works, or for whom a biographical note gives us the opportunity to describe, more fully than in the Chronology, an important or particularly interesting aspect of Tolkien or his writings. Other persons with whom Tolkien was concerned are mentioned in passing, in various contexts in the *Companion and Guide*: references to these may be found in the comprehensive index at the end of each volume.

In the Chronology volume are also genealogical charts of the Tolkien and Suffield families; a bibliographical list of Tolkien's published writings; a list of his poems, published and unpublished, by title and first line; a list of his published paintings, drawings, doodles, and maps; and a list of his works with the languages into which they have been translated.

A bibliography, with full citations, of the books, articles, media, electronic resources, and archives we have used in the writing of the *Companion and Guide*, is included for convenience in both the Chronology and the Reader's Guide. In this list of sources we have indicated simply which, in our opinion, are the most important or essential for an understanding of J.R.R. Tolkien – a personal choice, but one informed by decades of familiarity with the subject, and which we feel may be welcomed especially by newer readers.

*

A few general notes are in order. J.R.R. Tolkien is sometimes referred to in this book as 'Ronald', to distinguish him from other Tolkiens or when reference by his surname seemed inappropriate in construction, and also generally for the young Tolkien, before he went up to Oxford in 1911. Titles of works are always given as found, except that we have regularized the capitalization of hyphenated titles where variation occurs in practice, e.g. *On Fairy-Stories*, *The Sea-Bell*. Titles of discrete works by Tolkien, including poems, essays, and the individual tales of *The Book of Lost Tales*, are italicized following Christopher Tolkien's example in *The History of Middle-earth*, while titles of chapters or other subsections of text are expressed in quotation marks. But it is to be understood that 'The Silmarillion', so expressed, refers to Tolkien's mythology in general, and *The Silmarillion*, so italicized, generally to the book edited by Christopher Tolkien and first published in 1977, though in a few instances (understood in context) to the book that Tolkien wished to complete. All other titles are given in italics or in roman within quotation marks, as appropriate, following common conventions of style, except that we have preferred not to distinguish titles of books *within* titles of books by reversion to roman or by quotation marks. Direct quotations generally follow their source in spelling and punctuation; but we have silently emended the occasional misspelled word or other minor error.

Because of the multiplicity of editions, *The Hobbit* and *The Lord of the Rings* are cited here only by chapter and by book and chapter, respectively; where we have quoted from these works, it has been from current corrected texts. For most books by Tolkien we have used and cited the first editions, unless otherwise stated. The same is true for two invaluable books by Humphrey Carpenter, his biography of Tolkien (1977) and his book on the Inklings (1978). *On Fairy-Stories* and *Leaf by Niggle*, however, have been quoted from the best edition of *Tree and Leaf*, first published by Unwin Hyman, London, in 1988, and works such as *Beowulf: The Monsters and the Critics* have been quoted most conveniently (as indicated) from *The Monsters and the Critics and Other Essays* (1983).

Contributions by Tolkien to books and periodicals, or discrete works by Tolkien otherwise contained in a larger work (for instance, as the *Ainulindalë* is contained within *The Silmarillion*), are cited in their separate entries in the Reader's Guide with inclusive page numbers according to (as a convenient point of reference) the first printing of the first edition.

We have assumed that our reader has some knowledge of *The Hobbit* and *The Lord of the Rings*, so that we may refer (say) to 'Bilbo' or 'Frodo' without further explanation. *The Silmarillion*, as the central work among Tolkien's writings on Middle-earth, should be as well known, but is not; nonetheless, it has not been feasible to gloss in the *Companion and Guide*, from entry to entry, every mention of every character or place in the mythology, these being legion. For assistance in this respect, we advise the reader to consult Robert Foster's invaluable *Complete Guide to Middle-earth*. We must also point out that in writing his stories Tolkien sometimes altered the names of characters, places, etc. from text to text, or applied multiple names within a story, e.g. *Melko > Melkor > Morgoth*, and that in our accounts of the history of Tolkien's fiction we refer to names as he used them in the particular text under discussion.

The titles of several books about Tolkien frequently referred to in the *Companion and Guide* are abbreviated for convenience:

J.R.R. Tolkien: Artist and Illustrator by Wayne G. Hammond and Christina Scull (1995; corrected edn. 1998) generally as *Artist and Illustrator*.

J.R.R. Tolkien: A Biography by Humphrey Carpenter (1977) as *Biography*.

Brothers and Friends: The Diaries of Major Warren Hamilton Lewis, edited by Clyde S. Kilby and Marjorie Lamp Mead (1982) as *Brothers and Friends*.

J.R.R. Tolkien: A Descriptive Bibliography by Wayne G. Hammond with the assistance of Douglas A. Anderson (1993) as *Descriptive Bibliography*.

The Inklings: C.S. Lewis, J.R.R. Tolkien, Charles Williams and Their Friends by Humphrey Carpenter (1978) as *The Inklings*.

Letters of J.R.R. Tolkien, selected and edited by Humphrey Carpenter, with the assistance of Christopher Tolkien (1981), as *Letters*.

J.R.R. Tolkien: Life and Legend by Judith Priestman for the Bodleian Library (1992) as *Life and Legend*.

Pictures by J.R.R. Tolkien, with a foreword and notes by Christopher Tolkien (1979; 2nd edn. 1992), as *Pictures*.

The Lord of the Rings: A Reader's Companion by Wayne G. Hammond and Christina Scull (2005) as *Reader's Companion*.

The Tolkien Family Album by John and Priscilla Tolkien (1992) as *The Tolkien Family Album*.

For all quotations, page references are given whenever possible.

Although selected cross-references are provided in the main sequence of boldfaced headings in the Reader's Guide, for full direction to the many names, titles, and topics mentioned in this book the reader is advised to consult the index in either volume.

In general we have applied the recommendations of the *Oxford Style Manual*, with a few exceptions guided by personal bibliographic or typographic taste. Quotations correspond to original text in wording, spelling, capitalization, and interior punctuation, except that on occasion, to suit construction, we have begun a quotation at a point within the original sentence or paragraph and have capitalized the first word to form a complete sentence. Omissions from quoted matter, except for brief extracts, are indicated by three spaced points (. . .); but quotations that are complete sentences end with full stops, or another terminal mark of punctuation as appropriate, even though the original text might continue beyond that point. In lengthier quotations we have indicated omission between two paragraphs by three spaced points following the full stop at the end of the matter quoted in the first, but (for simplicity's sake, the present book not being a rigorous textual study) not also with a mark of ellipsis when the succeeding paragraph begins at some point other than that in the original.

Our friends, at least, and our publisher especially, will be aware of how long a gestation this book has had, long years since we were asked to write for Tolkien a work of reference similar to that which Walter Hooper wrote for C.S. Lewis (*C.S. Lewis: A Companion & Guide*, 1996). In that time it grew far beyond its expected bounds, as new information was discovered, and as more aspects of Tolkien's life and works demanded explanation and expression. Other responsibilities, and other writings more time-sensitive (such as our fiftieth anniversary edition of *The Lord of the Rings* and its *Reader's Companion*), have also delayed the present book. Given still more time, two volumes could easily have become three, but in the end there must be limits. The Reader's Guide, indeed, had to be restrained to accommodate binding machinery as much as publishing schedules. Inevitably, as the length of this book and the labour to produce it have increased, the possibility for typographical errors and inconsistencies of practice or form has also become greater; and although we have made every possible effort to avoid them, we have no doubt that some are lurking in the text. If (or rather, when) in the process of using this book readers find that we have made errors or serious omissions, we would be glad to learn about them, and will endeavour to acknowledge such *addenda* and *corrigenda* in a public venue.

Unless otherwise stated, the opinions expressed in this book are our own.

*

As always, we are grateful to members of the Tolkien family for their assistance and support. Christopher Tolkien once again has acted as our mentor, a greater task than could be imagined when this book was first proposed (as a single volume), and with his sister Priscilla has shared memories of their father. Priscilla Tolkien has also read parts of the *Companion and Guide* in draft, and suggested valuable additions and improvements. Joanna Tolkien, Michael George Tolkien, and Simon Tolkien have also been of assistance.

For suggesting that we write for J.R.R. Tolkien the equivalent of Walter Hooper's excellent *C.S. Lewis: A Companion & Guide*, and for patiently awaiting its completion (in a somewhat different and considerably enlarged form), we would like to thank David Brawn at HarperCollins U.K. We are indebted also to Chris Smith, the current director of Tolkien projects at HarperCollins, who has been remarkably patient and diplomatic as we have brought this book to a close, and who has given us sound advice on matters of production.

Thanks are due as well to Cathleen Blackburn of Manches LLP, legal representatives of the Tolkien Estate, who has guided us in matters related to copyright and permissions to quote from Tolkien's writings.

We owe special thanks to Arden R. Smith, who kindly read most of this book in typescript and advised us especially on matters concerning Tolkienian linguistics; to Douglas A. Anderson, for reading parts of the *Companion and Guide*, for sharing with us information about Tolkien's early poetry, and for supplying other useful details; and to John Garth, for allowing us to read an early draft of part of his *Tolkien and the Great War* (2003) and for saving us time during our own early research in the National Archives by supplying us with pertinent reference numbers.

We are deeply grateful to the highly knowledgeable staff of many libraries and archives, including: Owen Dobbs, Blackwell's Bookshops; Neil Somerville, BBC Written Archives Centre, Caversham Park, Reading; Philippa Bassett, University of Birmingham Archives; Sandy Botha, Bloemfontein Cathedral; Judith Priestman, Colin Harris, and other staff of the Department of Special Collections and Western Manuscripts, Bodleian Library, Oxford; the staff of Duke Humfrey's Library, Bodleian Library; the staff of the Bodleian Law Library; Angela Pusey, British Academy; the staff of the Department of Manuscripts, British Library, London; John Wells, Department of Manuscripts and University Archives, Cambridge University Library; the staff of the Centre for Oxfordshire Studies, Oxford Central Library; Richard Hamer, Vincent Gillespie, and Judith Curthoys of the library of Christ Church, Oxford, for the Early English Text Society archive; the staff of Christie's, South Kensington; Thomas Lecky and Francis Wahlgren of Christie's, New York; Christine Butler, archives of Corpus Christi College, Oxford; Susan Usher, the English Faculty Library, Oxford; Paul Cavill, the English Place-Name Society; Lorise Topliffe and John Maddicott, Exeter College Library, Oxford; Natalie Milne, Glasgow University Archive Services; the staff of HarperCollins, London; Ólöf Dagný, Hið íslenska bókmenntafélag (Icelandic Literary Society), Reykjavík; Kerry York, King Edward's School, Birmingham; Ann Farr, Brotherton Library, the University of Leeds; Mark Shipway, Leeds University archives; Charles Elston, Matt Blessing, and their staff in the Department of Special Collections and University Archives, Marquette University, Milwaukee, Wisconsin; Fiona Wilkes and Sarah Bendall, Merton College Library, Oxford; Tony Cadogan, National Sound Archives, British Library, London; John Foley, National University of Ireland; Simon Bailey and Alice Blackford, Oxford University Archives; Martin Maw and Jenny McMorris, Oxford University Press Archives; Rob Wilkes, Oxford Theses (Humanities), Bodleian Library; Naomi Van Loo and Ellena J. Pike, McGowin Library, Pembroke College, Oxford; the staff of the National Archives, Kew (formerly the Public Record Office); the staff of the Radcliffe Science Library, Oxford; Michael Bott, Department of Archives and Manuscripts, University of Reading; Meic Pierce Owen, University of St Andrews Library; David Smith, St Anne's College Library, Oxford; Carolyn Warne, St Leonard's School, Fife; Claire Goodwin, Simmons College Archives, Boston, Massachusetts; Roger Dalrymple, Society for the Study of Mediaeval Languages and Literature; Sister Helen Forshaw, archives of the Society of the Holy Child Jesus; Phillip Errington, Sotheby's, London; the staff of the Staffordshire Archives Service; Lucy Wright, the library of University College, London; Kirsten Williams, Viking Society for Northern Research; Christopher Mitchell, Marjorie Mead, and the staff of the Marion E. Wade Center, Wheaton College, Illinois; the staffs of the Chapin Library of Rare Books and the Williams College Libraries, Williamstown, Massachusetts; and Joanna Parker, Worcester College Library, Oxford.

For assistance in ways both large and small, we are grateful to David Bratman; Hugh Brogan; Marjorie Burns; Raymond Chang; Joe R. Christopher; Michaël Devaux; John Ellison; Matt Fisher; Steve Frisby; Pauline Gasch; Christopher Gilson; Diana Pavlac Glyer; Mark Hooker; Carl F. Hostetter; Charles A. Huttar; Julia Margretts; Jeremy Marshall; Ed Meskys; Gregory Miller; Peter Miskech; John D. Rateliff; Alan and Louise Reynolds; Paolo Romeo; René van Rossenberg; William A.S. Sarjeant; Richard Sturch; Makoto Takahashi; Paul Edmund Thomas; George H. Thompson; Johann Vanhecke; Richard C. West; Diana and Barry Willson; and Susan Wood.

Most especially, we are indebted to the dedicatee of this book, the late Rayner Unwin, for advice in the writing of the *Companion and Guide* and for many years of friendship and encouragement.

Christina Scull & Wayne G. Hammond
Williamstown, Massachusetts
July 2006

Reader's Guide

Abercrombie, Lascelles (1881–1938). Lascelles Abercrombie read Science at the Owens College, Manchester, but after only two sessions (1900–2) he turned instead to journalism, poetry, and the study of literature. A major figure in the Georgian poets, his first book of verse, *Interludes and Poems*, was published in 1908, and his collected *Poems* in 1930. He also wrote critical studies, including *Thomas Hardy* (1912) and *The Epic* (1914), and works on aesthetic theory. From 1919 to 1922 he was Lecturer in Poetry at the University of Liverpool.

In 1922 Abercrombie became Professor of English Literature at the University of *Leeds, succeeding *George S. Gordon; Tolkien, then Reader in English Language at Leeds, was also a candidate for the chair. In 1925, when Tolkien applied for the Rawlinson and Bosworth chair of Anglo-Saxon at *Oxford, Abercrombie as his head of department at Leeds wrote a glowing letter of recommendation. He named Tolkien 'my principal colleague in the English Department', who 'has throughout acted as my advisor and collaborator in the conduct and policy of the department as a whole. . . . I have never consulted him without gaining an illumination that can penetrate as well as expatiate. But I must not omit to mention that I have gained at least as much from the keen artistic sensibility as from the science of his scholarship' (*An Application for the Rawlinson and Bosworth Professorship of Anglo-Saxon in the University of Oxford by J.R.R. Tolkien, Professor of the English Language in the University of Leeds, June 25, 1925*).

In 1929 Abercrombie left Leeds for the Hildred Carlile Professorship of English Literature at Bedford College, University of London. He remained there until 1935, when he was elected Goldsmiths' Reader in English at Oxford and a Fellow of Merton College.

Ace Books controversy. When *The Lord of the Rings* was first issued in the United States (1954–6) its publisher, the Houghton Mifflin Company of Boston (*Publishers), chose to import printed sheets from Great Britain for binding domestically, rather than newly typeset and print a separate edition. They had long imported copies of *The Hobbit* and *Farmer Giles of Ham*, and continued to do so for *The Lord of the Rings* through the 1950s and early 1960s. For a work as unusual as *The Lord of the Rings*, importation in the first instance presented less financial risk; but in the long run too at this time, it was more economical for Houghton Mifflin to import sheets than to print their own, and to the advantage of George Allen & Unwin (*Publishers) as well, as exporters of the books, and of Tolkien, because it lowered costs to both of his publishers and made his books more affordable to readers. This practice meant, however, that the number of imported copies soon exceeded that allowed by the so-called 'manufacturing clause' in United States copyright law. U.S. law from 1891 until 1986 sought to protect the American printing industry by limiting the importation of books printed abroad and by promoting domestic manufacture. Under the law as amended in 1949 and in effect at the time of first publication of *The Lord of the Rings*, an American publisher had six months in which to register *ad interim* copyright for a foreign work written in English, and then five years in which to typeset and print the book in the United States to qualify for full copyright; and in the meantime, no more than 1,500 copies printed abroad could be imported. In contrast, copyright in Great Britain and elsewhere under the Berne Convention (the international copyright agreement to which the United States, almost alone among nations, was not a signatory) was subject to fewer formalities, and was considered in force *ipso facto* for a living author.

Houghton Mifflin initially imported 1,500 copies of *The Fellowship of the Ring* and 1,000 copies of *The Two Towers*, numbers at or within the limit of the 'manufacturing clause'. They applied for and received *ad interim* copyright for these volumes, and included copyright notices in the first printing of each to reflect this protection. By the time *The Return of the King* was ready, however, there was so much demand for it that Houghton Mifflin imported 5,000 copies, in order to sell as many as possible without delay. Because more than 1,500 copies were imported in the first instance, *The Return of the King* could not receive *ad interim* copyright, and therefore did not include an American copyright notice in any printing. As soon as the total number of imported copies of *The Fellowship of the Ring* and *The Two Towers* exceeded 1,500, Houghton Mifflin omitted copyright notices in those volumes as well.

Knowing that they had passed the specified limit of imported copies, Tolkien's publishers began to be concerned about the validity of his American copyright of *The Hobbit* in the early 1960s, during discussions about the sale of film rights to that work (see *Adaptations). At this time also, the popularity of *The Lord of the Rings* having been well established, American reprint publishers sought to sublicense a paperback edition, but Houghton Mifflin rebuffed all such overtures. In part, this was because they did not wish to 'cheapen' a work which still sold well in hardcover, but also because they were unsure whether they had the authority to grant an exclusive license to publish a paperback edition, given the now questionable copyright status of *The Lord of the Rings* under U.S. law.

In January 1965 Houghton Mifflin advised Allen & Unwin that the U.S. copyrights of *The Hobbit* and *The Lord of the Rings* might be open to challenge. Although managers at both firms thought it unlikely that any reputable publisher would take advantage of the situation, they also felt that action should be taken to secure U.S. copyright for the two works beyond any doubt. On 8 February 1965 *Rayner Unwin of George Allen & Unwin explained the situation to Tolkien and asked him to provide revisions and extra material for *The Hobbit* and *The Lord of the Rings*, such as a long-promised index for the latter, so that the books could be newly submitted for copyright in the United States.

Before Tolkien could do so, however, Ace Books of New York, a well-known publisher of science fiction, issued their own edition of *The Lord of the Rings* beginning in May 1965, at the then very cheap price of seventy-five cents. Ace Books held that *The Lord of the Rings* was in the public domain in the United States, and therefore could be published by anyone without permission. Donald A. Wollheim, then chief editor at Ace Books, said in a contemporary article that it was 'no secret' to him that *The Lord of the Rings* had never been copyrighted in the United States. 'I had known it from the moment I'd first bought a copy of the Houghton Mifflin edition in a book store when it had first appeared in 1954. One glance at the page following the title page startled me. No copyright, no date of publication. Just the line "Printed in Great Britain" . . .' ('The Ace Tolkiens', *Lighthouse* 13 (August 1965), pp. 16–17). In fact, the first printing of the Houghton Mifflin *Fellowship of the Ring* had included a full statement of rights on the verso of its title-leaf, including 'Copyright, 1954, by J.R.R. Tolkien', and the American *Two Towers* likewise had included a proper notice in its first printing. Wollheim evidently had seen a later printing, and not 'when it [*The Fellowship of the Ring* only] had first appeared in 1954'. His concern about the inclusion of a copyright notice stemmed from a requirement for this in most books protected under U.S. copyright – but he overlooked an exception to the law as it then existed, for books protected by *ad interim* copyright.

In the same article, Wollheim refuted criticism that was already coming to his attention, within months of publication of the Ace Books edition, in regard to 'literary piracy' and the fact that Tolkien was receiving no royalties from Ace Books. Wollheim wrote that Tolkien 'should reserve his anger for the source of his deprival', meaning Houghton Mifflin, for failing to secure his U.S. copyright; and he stated that Ace Books was 'perfectly willing to pay the author for his work – and we've stated both publicly and in a message to Tolkien that we want to make an arrangement for such payments' ('The Ace Tolkiens', p. 18). A similar statement by Wollheim concerning payments to Tolkien also was quoted in other venues. On this point Tolkien wrote to Rayner Unwin on 11 September 1965: 'I do not believe that any such letter [offering royalties] was ever written to me. I certainly never received one. Had I done so, I should have at once sent the letter to you as . . . negotiators with Houghton Mifflin' (Tolkien-George Allen & Unwin archive, HarperCollins).

Tolkien sent material for a revised *Lord of the Rings* to Houghton Mifflin from July to September 1965. This was incorporated in an authorized and newly copyrighted paperback edition by Ballantine Books of New York (*Publishers) and first published in October 1965. By then Ballantine had already rushed *The Hobbit* into print without revisions (which Tolkien had not yet completed), to have a Ballantine-Tolkien presence in bookshops as quickly as possible and to forestall any unauthorized paperback of *The Hobbit* which might appear. A revised *Hobbit* was published by Ballantine finally in February 1966. Every copy of the Ballantine *Hobbit* and *Lord of the Rings* carried a statement by Tolkien in reply to Ace Books: 'This paperback edition, and no other, has been published with my consent and co-operation. Those who approve of courtesy (at least) to living authors will purchase it and no other.' And a new Foreword in the Ballantine *Lord of the Rings* conveyed Tolkien's view that it was 'a grave discourtesy, to say no more, to issue my book without even a polite note informing me of the project'. Privately he also undertook a campaign against Ace Books in correspondence with American readers, to whom he remarked on the nature of theft. Altogether this produced a groundswell of opinion in Tolkien's favour which seriously undercut sales of the Ace edition, even though the Ballantine *Lord of the Rings* was more expensive by twenty cents per volume.

Tolkien's authorized publishers expressed their point of view as well – firmly in opposition to Ace Books – in the popular press, which brought the 'war over Middle-earth' (as some writers called it) further to public attention. A legal challenge was ruled out, as Rayner Unwin recalled: 'Houghton Mifflin were not confident that they could enjoin Ace Books for breach of copyright, and from our general understanding of this complicated and untested branch of American law we [Allen & Unwin] agreed' (*George Allen & Unwin: A Remembrancer* (1999), p. 118).

Whether or not the Ace Books *Lord of the Rings* was legally a 'pirate', the ethical aspects of the issue were strong and recognized as such by Tolkien's fans. Some took it upon themselves to send him 'royalties'; others, such as Mrs Nan C. Scott, wrote directly to the managers of Ace Books to complain about their treatment of Tolkien. In reply to Mrs Scott, Donald Wollheim again denied 'piracy' and declared Ace Books willing to offer Tolkien 'some sort of royalty or honorarium, at our own volition' (quoted in Rayner Unwin, *George Allen & Unwin: A Remembrancer*, p. 120). Mrs Scott addressed this point in a letter to the *Saturday Review* of 23 October 1965 (p. 56, in response to an article on the Ace-Tolkien controversy), noting that the tone of Wollheim's reply to her 'was a mixture of the suavely apologetic and the insolent, and the letter contained the suggestion that, if I were in touch with Professor Tolkien, *I* ask *him* to write to Ace Books about arranging a royalty, though the firm had no obligation to pay one!' A letter by Wollheim himself in the same *Saturday Review* suggested that it was up to Tolkien to write to Ace Books if he was offended by their edition: 'It seemed correct to us to ask one of [his] correspondents [Nan C. Scott] to tell him of our interest, for he did not write us *nor did we even have his address*' (p. 56, italics ours).

Tolkien and his publishers on their part refused to countenance Ace Books' claims, and in November 1965 the Science Fiction Writers of America (SFWA) *Bulletin* supported Tolkien in an editorial. After quoting Donald Wollheim's views in *Lighthouse*, the *Bulletin* editor declared:

> To pretend that taking anything not nailed down is no robbery; or to protest, as Wollheim has done in another published statement (*Saturday Review*, Oct. 23 [1965]), that Ace is willing to pay Tolkien royalties but does not know his address; or to complain, with injured innocence, that Tolkien has failed to get in touch with Ace (as if the whole thing were

somehow the author's fault, and he really should apologize), is to adopt a distasteful attitude of wilful ignorance, bad faith and bad manners. Ace would earn more respect by admitting its fault; undertaking not to repeat it; and by making prompt and generous restitution to Professor Tolkien, whose address is: 76, Sandfield Road, Headington, Oxford, England.

Within a month of this pointed editorial, Donald Wollheim wrote to Tolkien (copied to the SFWA), offering to pay an unspecified royalty direct to the author (while continuing to claim no legal obligation to do so), or to use full royalties to establish an annual science-fantasy award through the Science Fiction Writers of America. Wollheim suggested that Ace Books were only now, in December 1965, in a position to know the financial return on their edition relative to their investment. Moreover, in comparing the Ace *Lord of the Rings*, with its low price and long print run (150,000 copies), to the more expensive and relatively scarce (but hardly unavailable) Houghton Mifflin hardcover edition, he implied that Ace Books had done Tolkien a significant favour in bringing his book to a larger audience.

Tolkien, however, had no interest in either establishing a 'Tolkien Award' or 'authorizing' the Ace edition in any way. He wrote to Rayner Unwin:

What would a skipper say to a pirate who (spying an ominous sail and ensign on the horizon) said 'Shake hands! If you feel sore about this, I can assure you that we shall spend all the profits of our loot on a hostel for poor sailors'? ...

I feel that there are only two ways of taking this offer: 1. Complete refusal to treat with Ace Books or countenance their edition. 2. Acceptance of royalties, if adequate, on the issue so far distributed, provided that Ace then retire from the competition. [29 December 1965, Tolkien-George Allen & Unwin archive, HarperCollins]

Unwin preferred the second alternative. After further negotiation, Tolkien and Ace Books came to an agreement by which he eventually received more than $9,000 in royalties on sales. This was formally announced by Ace Books in a press release issued in March 1966, which stated that the firm had 'been on record from the start as willing to pay royalties to Dr. [sic] Tolkien, but not to his publishers who had forfeited his copyrights in the United States'. The release also included a statement signed by Tolkien but in fact proposed by Donald Wollheim, expressing his happiness to accept Ace Books' 'voluntary offer to pay full royalties ... even though you have no legal obligation to do so' (quoted from a reproduction in the *Tolkien Journal* 2, no. 2 (Astron 1966), p. 4). On 23 February 1966 Tolkien wrote to W.H. Auden that he had 'signed an "amicable agreement"' with Ace Books 'to accept their voluntary offer under no legal obligation: to pay a royalty of 4 per cent. on all copies of their edition sold, and not to reprint it when it is exhausted (without my consent)' (*Letters*, p. 367). In a letter of 21 March 1966, sent to the trade magazine

Publishers Weekly (printed also, with date of writing, in *Tolkien Journal* 2, no. 2 (Astron 1966), p. 5), Rayner Unwin disagreed that Ace Books had been 'on record from the start as willing to pay royalties': 'Only after energetic protests from numerous quarters had been sustained for several months did Professor Tolkien receive, in December last, for the first time, a letter from Ace Books.' Unwin also remarked 'that the net result of this affair has been to distract an author of genius . . . from all creative work [i.e. on *The Silmarillion*]. Those who admire Professor Tolkien's books and clamour for more will draw their own conclusion.'

The Ace Books edition was never reprinted. In 1966-7 the number of copies returned was greater than the number sold, as the Ballantine Books edition became the one clearly preferred by readers.

In later years Donald Wollheim continued to argue that Ace Books had been in the right to issue its edition of *The Lord of the Rings*, and that Tolkien's authorized publishers had failed to protect his American copyrights. Some latter-day Tolkien enthusiasts also excuse the Ace Books edition, on the grounds that had the issue not been forced, Houghton Mifflin might never have allowed *The Lord of the Rings* to be published as inexpensive mass-market paperbacks. 'The Great Copyright Controversy' by Richard E. Blackwelder, published in *Beyond Bree* for September 1995, follows this line. Although Blackwelder's article is useful for its long (though by no means exhaustive) list of references to writings about the Ace Books controversy, he accepts Donald Wollheim's arguments uncritically. Wayne G. Hammond, F.R. Williamson, and Rayner Unwin offered rebuttals to Blackwelder in *Beyond Bree* for December 1995. See further, Rayner Unwin, *George Allen & Unwin: A Remembrancer*, ch. 5; and *Descriptive Bibliography*, notes for A5c.

The question of the validity of Tolkien's American copyrights continued to be challenged for more than a quarter-century after the Ace Books affair, and for the same reasons. At last in 1992 the issue was settled in U.S. District Court, Southern District of New York, in the case of Eisen, Durwood & Co. v. Christopher R. Tolkien et al. Eisen, Durwood, a book packager doing business as Ariel Books, sought a legal declaration that the original text of *The Lord of the Rings* – specifically, that of *The Fellowship of the Ring* and *The Two Towers* (*The Return of the King* was not considered due to 'differing circumstances') – was in the public domain in the United States due to the failure of Houghton Mifflin to include a copyright notice in a substantial number of the copies they had published. On the contrary, in a decision delivered on 6 April 1992 Judge Vincent L. Broderick found the Tolkien copyright of the first edition of *The Lord of the Rings* to be valid, and granted defendants' motion for summary judgement in their favour. He concluded that even though Houghton Mifflin had not included a notice of copyright in many copies of *The Lord of the Rings*, the law did not provide for the forfeiture of copyright because of the failure to include such a notice. Indeed, he found, the Copyright Act of 1909 as later amended did not require a copyright notice to be printed in books with subsisting *ad interim* protection, which was true of the Houghton Mifflin

Fellowship of the Ring and *Two Towers*. In presenting their case, Eisen, Durwood had abandoned any claim that excessive importation of copies printed abroad had resulted in loss of copyright through violation of the 'manufacturing clause'; but even if the plaintiff had not done so, the 1909 Act again nowhere stated that forfeiture of copyright would automatically result. Judge Broderick's decision was upheld on appeal in 1993.

This case immediately laid to rest any doubts about Tolkien's American copyright in the first edition of *The Lord of the Rings* or the legal correctness of his and his publishers' position (apart from its clear moral authority) during the Ace Books controversy. Six years later, the United States Congress passed the Copyright Extension Act in response to a new international agreement on copyright approved by the group formerly known as GATT (General Agreement on Tariffs and Trade), to which the United States was a signatory: this brought U.S. law regarding the length of copyright into line with the laws of its major trading partners, and provided, moreover, that if a work was validly in copyright in any of the signatory countries, it was also to be considered in copyright in all of the other countries party to the agreement. Under this authority, the Tolkien Estate acted to re-register Tolkien copyrights in the United States, reinforcing and extending their validity.

Copyrights of Tolkien's works, as well as trademark rights to the name 'Tolkien', his 'JRRT' personal monogram, and his signatures ('J.R.R. Tolkien' and 'Ronald Tolkien'), are administered chiefly by the Tolkien Estate, via Manches LLP, 9400 Garsington Road, Oxford Business Park, Oxford OX4 2HN U.K. (*www.manches.com*). The sale of film rights to *The Hobbit* and *The Lord of the Rings* (see *Adaptations) also conveyed certain merchandising and dramatic rights to characters, names, and other aspects of those works: these are currently owned by the Saul Zaentz Company, and controlled by its division Tolkien Enterprises (not connected with the Tolkien Estate) at 2600 Tenth Street, Berkeley, CA 94710 (*www.tolkien-ent.com*). Questions about reprinting work by Tolkien should be addressed to the permission departments of Tolkien's publishers (see *Publishers).

Acocks Green (Warwickshire). On 17 October 1966 Tolkien wrote to a group of primary school children in *Acocks Green, east of *Birmingham: 'I lived till I was 8 at *Sarehole and used to walk to A[cocks] G[reen] to see my uncle. It was all "country" then . . .' (quoted in Sotheby's, *English Literature, History, Children's Books and Illustrations*, London, 16 December 2004, p. 274). Acocks Green is some two miles north-east of Sarehole (now Hall Green). During Tolkien's years at Sarehole (1896–1900) Acocks Green was still one of three hamlets along the Warwick Road, though already developed into a middle-class suburb of Birmingham since the opening of a local railway station in 1852. Much of its rural landscape was obliterated with the construction of municipal housing beginning in the mid-1920s.

Acta Senatus. Report, in Latin, of a Latin debate at *King Edward's School, Birmingham, published in the *King Edward's School Chronicle* n.s. 26, no. 186 (March 1911), pp. 26–7. The work is not signed, but Tolkien's authorship is revealed in his papers.

Adaptations. Interest in dramatic adaptation of Tolkien's fiction was expressed at least as early as 1953, when Miss L.M.D. Patrick requested permission to perform a stage version of *The Hobbit* at St Margaret's School, Edinburgh. On that occasion Tolkien and George Allen & Unwin (*Publishers) approved a limited run; but another play based on *The Hobbit*, sent to Tolkien by early 1959, seemed to him 'a mistaken attempt to turn certain episodes . . . into a sub-*Disney farce for rather silly children. . . . At the same time it is entirely derivative' (letter to Charles Lewis, George Allen & Unwin, 30 April 1959, Tolkien-George Allen & Unwin archive, HarperCollins). He admitted to a prejudice against dramatization and any kind of 'children's theatre', but was willing to consent if an adaptation were 'good of its kind', or if the performance of the play were part of the normal processes of a drama school; but he felt strongly against the publication of such a work or its performance in a more public venue. Nonetheless, numerous versions of *The Hobbit* have been performed on stage, some with original songs.

In 1967 Paul Drayton, later director of music at New College School, Oxford, and Humphrey Carpenter, then an *Oxford undergraduate, with Tolkien's permission adapted *The Hobbit* for performance by eleven- to thirteen-year-old boys. Their essay, 'A Preparatory School Approach' in *Music Drama in Schools* (1971), explains how Drayton devised the songs and overall musical structure for the play, while Carpenter prepared the script with 'two main principles in mind. First, to retain the style and character of the book, and second, to impose dramatic shape upon it. The first simply involved using the existing dialogue wherever possible, and consciously adopting Tolkien's style when continuations and alterations had to be made.' The second principle was to omit 'incidents not absolutely vital to the plot – the trolls, the wolves, the eagles and Beorn. None of these occupy a strong place in the saga; they are trimmings, and easily disposed of.' Carpenter also imposed 'unity' by introducing Bard earlier than Tolkien does, and by killing Smaug at the Lonely Mountain 'in the centre of the action'; and he added references to *The Lord of the Rings* 'to extend the significance and importance of the ring in the play' (p. 18). The dragon 'flew overhead' by means of lighting effects.

Tolkien attended the final performance. 'He smiled a lot of the time,' Carpenter recalled, in particular at the boy who played Bilbo as a 'fussy middle-aged bachelor'. But towards the end of the play, with notable departures from his book, Tolkien 'did not approve of this tinkering with the story' ('". . . One Expected Him To Go on a Lot Longer": Humphrey Carpenter Remembers J.R.R. Tolkien', *Minas Tirith Evening-Star* 9, no. 2 (January 1980), pp. 10–11; see also report by Charles E. Noad of a talk by Humphrey Carpenter, *Amon Hen* 91 (May 1988), p. 14).

Other dramatizations of *The Hobbit* include those by the Oxford University Experimental Theatre Club, adapted by Graham Devlin, music by Michael Hinton (1971); Phoenix Arts, Leicester, adapted by Rony Robinson and Graham Watkins, music by Stephanie Nunn (1984); and the Children's Theatre Company of Minneapolis, adapted by Thomas W. Olson, music by Alan Shorter (1990).

The scripts of a dramatization by Patricia Gray and of a musical by Allan Jay Friedman, David Rogers, and Ruth Perry were published in 1968 and 1972 respectively by the Dramatic Publishing Company of Chicago, 'authorized by Professor J.R.R. Tolkien'. This imprimatur, however, was given only as part of a compromise between the publisher and George Allen & Unwin, at a time when the validity of the copyright of the first edition of *The Hobbit* in the United States, and therefore the ability to control or prevent dramatic adaptations, was seriously in question (see *Ace Books controversy, and further in the present entry). In fact, Tolkien disliked at least the version by Gray, and still less that he had little or no say in the matter. Through *Rayner Unwin he requested changes where the adapter had departed from the text without (as he felt) any dramatic necessity. Although the Dramatic Publishing Company held that they knew best what is needed for an effective stage play, they agreed to some of Tolkien's requests, and Unwin felt that these repaired 'a lot of the worst excesses and infelicities' (letter to Tolkien, 19 June 1968, Tolkien-George Allen & Unwin archive, HarperCollins). On 20 June Unwin wrote to H.N. Swanson, the American agent for Allen & Unwin, that 'neither Professor Tolkien nor I are concerned about the process of dramatization so long as it is a dramatization of the book in question and that intrusions from elsewhere conform to the spirit and style of the original'. Tolkien further agreed that 'the publication is with his authorization . . . [but] he would not wish it to be said that the dramatization has his *approval*' (George Allen & Unwin archive, University of Reading).

It is common in some dramatizations for characters to be changed or added to provide more female roles: thus the Elvenking may become an elven queen, or Bilbo Baggins may gain a sister who appears in the final scene. More simply, Thorin the chief dwarf, or even Bilbo, may be played by a female. The 'small cast version' of *The Hobbit* dramatized by Markland Taylor (1992) is an adaptation for only six actors with much doubling (there are twenty-three characters): in this the dwarves are reduced to only Thorin, and the Battle of Five Armies is only mentioned in a comment to the audience. Rob Inglis took the process even further with his adaptation for single performer, recorded in 1987 on the fiftieth anniversary of *The Hobbit*. There are also at least two operatic versions.

At perhaps the furthest extreme of adaptation of *The Hobbit* on stage was *Down in Middle Earth*, a musical for children by Fred Bluth performed in California in spring 1969. Bonniejean Christensen described this production as 'a fuzzy allegory' in which Bilbo undertakes a psychological quest to recover a stolen ring, accompanied by 'hip' talk, allusions to sexuality, and psychedelic lighting ('Report from the West: Exploitation of *The Hobbit*', *Orcrist* (1969–70), p. 15).

The Hobbit has also been dramatized on radio. In 1961 versions were made for the BBC radio programme *Children's Hour* and for the BBC Schools Department programme *Adventures in English*. In 1968 the BBC broadcast a dramatization by Michael Kilgariff, with music by David Cain; this was first issued as a commercial recording in 1988. Other recorded dramatizations include one for The Drama Project by the Marleybone Players (1975), and the 'Jabberwocky' or 'Mind's Eye' version by Bob Lewis (1979). An abridgement of *The Hobbit* by Brian Sibley, read by Michael Hordern, was broadcast on BBC radio in 1981. Abridged readings of *The Hobbit* by Nicol Williamson and Martin Shaw were first issued as commercial recordings in 1974 and 1993 respectively.

An illustrated fifteen-part serialization of *The Hobbit*, slightly abridged, appeared in the British magazine *The Princess* in 1964–5; Tolkien did not like the visual depiction of Gandalf. A graphic novel of *The Hobbit*, adapted by Charles Dixon and illustrated by David Wenzel, was first published in 1989–90 by Eclipse Books of Forestville, California.

The Lord of the Rings was first adapted for BBC radio in 1955–6, for the Third Programme, soon after its publication was complete. The producer Terence Tiller proposed an adaptation of its first part, *The Fellowship of the Ring*, on 25 January 1955, asking not only for Tolkien's permission to proceed, but also for preliminary suggestions from him, and promising to send him the draft scripts for approval. Tolkien replied on 26 January:

> I hope it will not seem too cool and cautious, if I ask whether you could (without much trouble) give me a general idea of what you have in mind as an 'adaptation', before I give my final approval.
>
> For instance: do you propose to use actual parts or passages with summarized narrative links? The proposed time to be allotted is 4½ hours [i.e. 45 minutes per episode]. The printed narrative, without preliminaries, occupies about 390 rather packed pages. . . .

Naturally he had 'some views and preferences'; but 'the "adapter" must, I think, work on his own lines. I should very much like to have some idea of what those are likely to be' (BBC Written Archives Centre).

Tiller proposed to preserve Tolkien's original dialogue as much as possible, which would be presented in a dramatic form with narration to link the scenes. Given time constraints, however, the original narrative and dialogue would need substantial reduction, and Tiller feared that many of Tolkien's songs and poems would have to be excised. Tolkien approved, though only because Allen & Unwin felt that the project would be good for sales of his book.

During the summer of 1955 Tiller sent Tolkien scripts for the first three episodes. Tolkien seems to have found room for improvement and suggested alterations, which Tiller seems to have accepted – the archive is vague and incomplete on this point, as on others. Moreover, Tiller wisely asked Tolkien's advice about accents for his characters' speech. Tolkien replied:

> I quite understand that the need for characterization, and making different speakers audibly recognizable, may well override my opinion. Also the skill of the actors may be inadequate to deal in nuances.
>
> The relative passages are Vol. III, pp. 408 and 411 [of *The Lord of the Rings*, first edition, both in Appendix F, 'On Hobbits' and the beginning of 'On Translation']. From these, and from the actual characterization in my text, I think it can be seen that the Hobbit 'gentry' should *not* be made rustical in actual tones and accents. Their divergence from High Speech is cast rather in forms of grammar and idiom: they just speak unstudied modern English. Merry and Pippin are the two young hobbits of the highest birth in the land (heirs of the Master and the Thain) and should at any rate *not* speak differently from Frodo. I am against anything more than the merest tinge of 'country' (if any) in their speech. (Frodo's superior linguistic skill would be exhibited only in Elvish.) The difference between 'gentlehobbits' and the Great is envisaged rather as one of period (in our terms) than dialect. The Great use a more archaic language (when functioning as the Great), and speak with greater solemnity and precision. The Hobbits just use our own rather slack colloquial.
>
> But Sam *and Butterbur* (for Breelanders, Men and Hobbits, were in the same linguistic position) may well be characterized by speaking with a 'country accent' of some kind – fairly but not too strongly marked.
>
> As for what kind of 'accent' – I do not think that matters very much, as long as it can be consistently maintained by the speakers. You say 'West-Country'. Well since Elizabethan days that seems to have been favoured as 'stage dialect', though not often with any local or historical accuracy. 'Accuracy' fortunately does not matter at all in this translation into modern terms of a vanished past, and as long as the 'accent' used is fairly consistent, and such as to seem to the average listener vaguely 'countrified', that will do.
>
> But you may note that I have deliberately avoided making the dropping or misuse of *h* a feature of any kind of hobbit-speech. I should prefer that this should be observed, though it is not, of course, vital (in the cases of Sam and Butterbur). Also I personally should prefer *not* to have any supposedly 'Zummerzet' z/v for s/f initially.
>
> If I might make a particular suggestion: I should use the pronunciation of *r* as a main characterizing detail. Hobbit-gentry should speak more or less as we do (at our most unstudied). Sam, in addition to a rustic tone and vowel-colouring, should use the burred (or reverted) *r*. The Great, and especially the Elves, should sound their *r*s as a trill (though not with a Scots extravagance) in *all* positions. It is a great enhancement of English, as well as (now) bearing an archaic flavour. However, that is by the way. Some people find it difficult to do!

I am sure the whole matter is safe in your hands; and only on the point of *not* making Meriadoc or Pippin rustic (nor indeed any of the 144 gentry at the party) do I place any final importance. [10 September 1955, BBC Written Archives Centre]

In late September 1955 Tiller finally was able to send Tolkien copies of all six scripts. In his covering note he warned that Tolkien would 'at first be a little shocked at the extent of the cutting: six half hours are pitifully brief [the running time per episode had been cut to only thirty minutes, rather than forty-five], and inevitably a great deal of the flavour of your work has been lost. Nevertheless, I think the addition of music, and of living voices, will do much to replace such losses' (21 September 1955, BBC Written Archives Centre). He telescoped certain incidents and simplified geographical details, but hoped that the main themes of the work were not totally obscured or mutilated. Tolkien replied that he was very interested in what Tiller had done, in an intellectual sense, as of course he had not yet heard the work performed on the air, and with music (by Anthony Smith-Masters); but the procedure had led him to some conclusions:

If a weakness of the book is the necessity of historical build-up concurrent with the tale of events – except for those who like the imaginary 'history' for its own sake – it is a greater weakness in a 'dramatic' form, in so far as this form still has to include a good deal of 'explanations'. But what chiefly interested me in reading your scripts – beyond the interest in noting what you had picked out and what you had cut – was the fact that the inevitable reduction of background and detail had tended to reduce the whole thing, making it much more of a 'fairy-tale' in the ordinary sense. The hobbits seem sillier and the others more stilted. Though, of course, living voices may make a great difference, as you say. Anyway, as an author, I was comforted by being confirmed in my opinion that there are actually few, if any, unnecessary details in the long narrative! The loss of any of them deprives the story of significance at some later point. [27 September 1955, BBC Written Archives Centre]

Tolkien next wrote again at length to Tiller on 8 December 1955, after the adaptation had begun to be broadcast (14 November–18 December), and following a discussion of it on the programme *The Critics* (14 November):

I am glad *The Times* was appreciative; even though that seemed to infuriate the precious self-styled 'critics'. I thought they were intolerable, with a superiority that only ignorance can maintain. You cannot expect to please many readers (or the author) at many points; but if it is any comfort to you I may say that I have a good many letters about the radio-version, and while some are adverse many 'readers' enjoy it, and also tell me that non-readers get a great deal out of it. . . . I do not agree with most of the criticisms myself . . . [such] as the one that wanted hobbits to pipe and squeak. Why should tones rise with fall in stature? Some of the silliest high-pitched voices I have heard belonged to people over six feet.

I liked Glóin's foreign accent – though it was perhaps a bit heavily laid on . . . : dwarves spoke the Common Tongue natively . . . ; but they had an uvular back R. But it does not matter. I was a bit disappointed that Bilbo sounded not only old but bored. The Elvish, and the names were managed excellently. But it was a pity that the preliminary announcer (unless I misheard) called Goldberry 'Bombadil's *daughter*' (!) and asserted that the evil willow was an ally of Mordor. Mordor is not the master of all things hostile to the 'humane'; and, so to say, there is much that seems evil to us that is not in league with the Devil!

I thought the cutting down of the difficult Chap. II of Book II (council [of Elrond]) was masterly, and got in all essentials without serious loss. [BBC Written Archives Centre]

Tiller for his part was not as unhappy about Bilbo as Tolkien, and noted that one or two letters sent to the BBC suggested that the Elves should have been more virile, while some maintained that Frodo was a good deal younger than the actor employed for the broadcast. Tiller admitted that it was his fault that Goldberry was described as Bombadil's daughter: the relationship between them was never definitely expressed, and Goldberry 'felt' to Tiller like a female and second-generation Bombadil. 'I really am sorry about this error', he wrote to Tolkien, 'but who *is* she?' (12 December 1955, BBC Written Archives Centre). Tolkien did not answer this question, but commented that he 'ought to remember that not all is in the "book", and it is asking a lot to expect even that to be known. I think I had quite forgotten that Bombadil's adventures as set out in the *Oxford Magazine* of 1934 (!) [see *The Adventures of Tom Bombadil*] were not included. . . . Authors are no doubt often peevish folk!' (letter to Tiller, 15 December 1955, BBC Written Archives Centre).

In other letters, however, Tolkien was more candid about his feelings. On 30 November he wrote to Molly Waldron: 'I think the book quite unsuitable for "dramatization", and have not enjoyed the broadcasts – though they have improved' (*Letters*, p. 228). On 8 December he wrote to *Naomi Mitchison: 'I think poorly of the broadcast adaptations. Except for a few details I think they are not well done, even granted the script and the legitimacy of the enterprise (which I do not grant). But they took some trouble with the names. I thought that the Dwarf (Glóin not Gimli, but I suppose Gimli will look like his father – apparently someone's idea of a German) was not too bad, if a bit exaggerated' (*Letters*, p. 229). To Rayner Unwin he wrote that he 'agreed with the "critics"' view of the radio adaptation', and that his 'correspondence is now increased by letters of fury against the critics and the broadcast' – 'but I suppose all this is good for sales' (8 December 1955, *Letters*, p. 229).

Given these opinions, it was probably for the sake of publicity, which translated to sales of *The Lord of the Rings*, that Tolkien let Tiller know that he was willing that adaptations also of *The Two Towers* and *The Return of the King* should go ahead, as the producer wished. Among the senior staff of the BBC Third Programme, however, all but one lacked any personal enthusiasm for *The Lord of the Rings*, and this fact seems to have carried more weight than the evident success of the *Fellowship* with listeners, and the apparent pride with which the BBC had announced that *The Fellowship of the Ring* was the first modern novel to be serialized on the Third Programme. Tiller was now told that the BBC would have great difficulty in placing another twelve episodes of *The Lord of the Rings* – six for each of the remaining two volumes, as for the *Fellowship* – but there could be six new episodes, each also of only thirty minutes, 'even though painful to the adapter' – thus only three hours in which to dramatize the rest of the work. It was suggested that this would be possible because 'Volume 2 is more homogeneous than Volume 1', and 'Volume 3 is not only shorter in itself than the other two, but could be made still shorter in adaptation by ending it with the victory and restoration of Gondor, the return to the Shire and final departure to the West being treated as an epilogue and either omitted altogether or disposed of in a few lines of narration' (letter from Christopher Holme, Chief Assistant, Third Programme, to Terence Tiller, 20 January 1956, BBC Written Archives Centre). Tiller was appalled at the cutting that would be necessary to achieve this scheme. He pointed out that several listeners had thought that, indeed, Volume 1 had been cut excessively at three hours. But he would accept the limitations imposed on him, rather than leave the radio version of *The Lord of the Rings* unfinished.

At the beginning of November 1956 Tiller sent Tolkien the first three scripts in the new series. 'Any listener who knows the books themselves will, I fear, be somewhat disappointed in the broadcasts', he wrote. 'I do feel, however, that other listeners will at least obtain the gist of the story and of its excitements' (letter to Tolkien, 1 November 1956, BBC Written Archives Centre). He had been forced on many occasions to script his own narration, rather than use Tolkien's. Should the Rohirrim speak with any particular accent? he asked. He proposed to make the Orcs sound as degraded and beastly as possible in their speech; but did Tolkien want them to have any particular accent, and should Sauron's and Saruman's Orcs be distinguished? Should the people of Minas Tirith have an accent? Tolkien replied at once:

> Taking 'accent' to mean . . . 'more or less consistent alterations of the vowels/consonants of "received" English': I should say that, in the cases you query, *no* accent-differentiation is needed or desirable. For instance, it would probably be better to avoid certain, actual or conventional, features of modern 'vulgar' English in representing Orcs, such as the dropping of aitches (these are, I think, *not* dropped in the text, and that is deliberate).
>
> But, of course, for most people, 'accent' as defined above is confused with impressions of different intonation, articulation, and tempo. You will, I suppose, have to use such means to make Orcs sound nasty!

I have no doubt that, if this 'history' were real, all users of the C[ommon] Speech would reveal themselves by their accent, differing in place, people, and rank, but that cannot be represented when C[ommon] S[peech] is turned into English – and is not (I think) necessary. I paid great attention to such linguistic differentiation as was possible: in diction, idiom, and so on; and I doubt if much more can be imported, except in so far as the individual actor represents his feeling for the character in tone and style.

As Minas Tirith is at the source of C[ommon] Speech it is to C[ommon] S[peech] as London is to modern English, and the standard of comparison! None of its inhabitants should have an 'accent' in terms of vowels &c.

The Rohirrim no doubt (as our ancient English ancestors in a similar state of culture and society) spoke, at least their own tongue, with a slower tempo and more sonorous articulation, than modern 'urbans'. But I think it is safe to represent them when using C[ommon] S[peech], as they practically always do (for obvious reasons) as speaking the best M[inas] T[irith]. Possibly a little too good, as it would be a learned language, somewhat slower and more careful than a native's. But that is a nicety safely neglected, and not always true: *Théoden* was born in Gondor and Common Speech was the domestic language of the Golden Hall in his father's day. . . . [2 November 1956, *Letters*, pp. 253–4]

A few days later, on 6 November, Tolkien wrote to Tiller about the three scripts, not with any criticisms of detail, but rather (one might say) with criticisms of principle. He acknowledged that Tiller had had a difficult task, and could not have done better under the circumstances. But he was sharply displeased with the compression and deletions necessary to fit the rest of *The Lord of the Rings* into such a short span of time:

As a private conversation between you and me, I could wish you had perhaps time to spare to tell me *why* this sort of treatment is accorded to the book, and what value it has – on [the] Third [Programme]. For myself, I do not believe that many, if any, listeners who do not know the book will thread the plot or grasp at all what is going on. And the text is (necessarily in the space) reduced to such simple, even simple-minded, terms that I find it hard to believe it would hold the attention of the Third [Programme's audience].

Here is a book very unsuitable for dramatic or semi-dramatic representation. If that is attempted it needs more space, a lot of space. It is sheerly impossible to pot the two books [*The Two Towers* and *The Return of the King*] in the allotted time – whether the object be to provide something in itself entertaining in the medium; or to indicate the nature of the original (or both). Why not then turn it down as unsuitable, if more space is not available?

I remain, of course, flattered and pleased that my book should receive this attention; but I still cannot help wondering: why this form? . . . I cannot help thinking that longer actual passages read, as a necklace upon a thread of narration (in which the narrator might occasionally venture an interpretation of more than mere plot-events) would, or might, prove both more interesting to listeners, and fairer to the author. But, as I have said, I lack experience in the medium, and this is in any case, no criticism of your text, but a sighing for something quite different – a moon no doubt. Final query: can a tale not conceived dramatically but (for lack of a more precise term) epically, be dramatized – unless the dramatizer is given or takes liberties, as an independent person? [*Letters*, pp. 254–5]

The preserved Tolkien-Tiller correspondence ends at that point; perhaps no reply was possible, nor is it known if Tolkien was sent the remaining three scripts. The new series of episodes was broadcast by the BBC from 19 November to 23 December 1956. By then a different version, or reading, of *The Lord of the Rings* had also been heard, in January–March 1956, in the BBC Schools Broadcast series *Adventures in English*; but of this adaptation, and any participation by Tolkien in its production, we have found no relevant papers.

In 1981 another BBC adaptation of *The Lord of the Rings*, by Brian Sibley and Michael Bakewell with music by Stephen Oliver, was broadcast on Radio 4; a commercial recording was first released in 1987. Sibley and Bakewell treated the book with great respect, utilizing Tolkien's words and style whenever possible, even as cuts were made, segments reorganized for dramatic effect in weekly episodes, and additional dialogue invented. The series was well received by listeners, if not without criticism. In reviewing the first episodes for the BBC Radio 4 programme *Kaleidoscope*, Humphrey Carpenter felt that radio reduced *The Lord of the Rings* to dialogue, that the production lacked the full flavour of the book, and that *The Lord of the Rings* could not be successfully translated into any medium other than print. See further, *Microphones in Middle Earth*, ed. Ian D. Smith (1982), and comments by Brian Sibley at *www.briansibley.com/Broadcasts/RingGoesEverOn.htm*.

For lack of broadcast time, Sibley and Bakewell omitted from their scripts (*inter alia*) the Tom Bombadil chapters from Book I of *The Lord of the Rings*, but in 1992 Sibley adapted these as one part of the BBC Radio series *Tales from the Perilous Realm*, together with dramatizations of Tolkien's *Farmer Giles of Ham*, *Leaf by Niggle*, and *Smith of Wootton Major*. This series too has been issued as a commercial recording (1993).

An American dramatization of *The Lord of the Rings*, by Bernard Mayes, was made in 1979. It has been heard on radio (as the 'Mind's Eye' or 'Radio 2000' version) and sold on commercial media.

According to Humphrey Carpenter, *Biography*, 'the first overtures from the film world' in regard to Tolkien's works 'came at the end of 1957 when Tolkien was approached by three American businessmen who showed him drawings for a proposed animated motion-picture of *The Lord of the Rings*. These gentlemen (Mr Forrest J. Ackerman, Mr Morton Grady Zimmerman, and Mr Al Brodax) also delivered to him a scenario or "Story Line" for the proposed film' (p. 226). Letters in the Allen & Unwin archive at the University of Reading (*Libraries and archives), however, seem to indicate that Al Brodax enquired about the film rights in May or June 1957, and Forrest J. Ackerman (on behalf of Morton Grady Zimmerman) independently in September of the same year.

At first Tolkien was willing (if not enthusiastic) to allow such a project to go forward. On 19 June 1957 he wrote to Rayner Unwin: 'As far as I am concerned personally, I should welcome the idea of an animated motion picture, with all the risk of vulgarization; and that quite apart from the glint of money, though on the brink of retirement that is not an unpleasant possibility. I think I should find vulgarization less painful than the sillification achieved by the B.B.C.' (*Letters*, p. 257). On 4 September he was visited in Oxford by Forrest J. Ackerman and associates, and was impressed by visualizations for the film prepared by artist Ron Cobb, whom Tolkien compared favourably to Arthur Rackham. But he was less pleased with the proposed story-line written by Morton Grady Zimmerman. He remarked to Rayner Unwin on 7 September that this was

> on a much lower level of art and perceptiveness than the pictorial material. It is in some points bad, and unacceptable, but is not irremediable, if the author of it . . . is open to criticism and direction. The ending is badly muffed . . . it reads like a production of haste, after a single reading, & without further reference to text. . . . Mr Ackerman's line of talk was that a big object to the group was 'pleasing the author'. I have indicated to him that will not be easy. Quite crudely: displeasing the author requires a cash equivalent. Only the prospect of a very large financial profit would make me swallow some of the things in this script! . . . An *abridgement* by selection with some good picture-work would be pleasant, & perhaps worth a good deal of publicity; but the present script is rather a *compression* with resultant over-crowding and confusion, blurring of climaxes, and general degradation: a pull-back towards more conventional 'fairy-stories'. People gallop about on Eagles at the least provocation; Lórien becomes a fairy-castle with 'delicate minarets', and all that sort of thing.
>
> But I am quite prepared to play ball, if they are open to advice – and if you decide that the thing is genuine, and worthwhile. [Tolkien-George Allen & Unwin archive, HarperCollins, partly printed in *Letters*, p. 261]

On 11 September Tolkien wrote to his son *Christopher: '*Stanley U[nwin] & I have agreed on our policy: *Art or Cash*. Either very profitable terms indeed; or absolute author's veto on objectionable features or alterations' (*Letters*, p. 261). To achieve this, Allen & Unwin negotiated with Ackerman through an agent in the United States knowledgeable about film contracts.

By the end of March 1958 Tolkien still had not given the story-line more concentrated attention. (See further, Todd Jensen, 'The Zimmerman Film Treatment of *The Lord of the Rings*', *Beyond Bree*, December 1995.) Rayner

Unwin pointed out the financial advantages to Tolkien if a film were eventually made; and it was agreed that Ackerman and company should have a free option on the film rights to *The Lord of the Rings* for six months from the date that Zimmerman received Tolkien's comments on the initial story-line, so that a new treatment could be produced which would be more agreeable to the author. Tolkien now applied himself to the task, but became even more dismayed. On 8 April 1958 he wrote to Rayner Unwin that the story-line

> as it stands, is sufficient to give me grave anxiety about the actual *dialogue* that (I suppose) will be used. . . . It seems to me evident that [Zimmerman] has skimmed through the [*Lord of the Rings*] at a great pace, and then constructed his s[tory] l[ine] from partly confused memories, and with the minimum of references back to the original. Thus he gets most of the names wrong in form – not occasionally by casual error but fixedly (always *Borimor* for *Boromir*); or he misapplies them: *Radagast* becomes an Eagle. The introduction of characters and the indications of what they are to say have little or no reference to the book. . . .
>
> I feel very unhappy about the extreme silliness and incompetence of Z[immerman] and his complete lack of respect for the original (it seems wilfully wrong without discernible technical reasons at nearly every point). [*Letters*, pp. 266–7]

In May, Tolkien commented that it was vital to secure, if possible,

> a revision of the story-line, with the object of removing its more wanton divergences from the book. Especially (for instance) reduction of eagles to their proper place; and amendment of such gross vulgarizations as the fairy-castle and minarets intruded into Lórien: and restoration of the vital scene at the end of the Ring in Chamber of Fire. [letter to Rayner Unwin, 16 May 1958, Tolkien-George Allen & Unwin archive, HarperCollins]

In June he addressed these issues at greater length in a letter to Forrest J. Ackerman, with an extensive commentary: these are partly printed in *Letters*, pp. 270–7. His chief points are presented more succinctly, though, in an unfinished letter to Ackerman (probably April or early May 1958) preserved at Marquette University:

> *The Lord of the Rings* is arranged in 6 sections or 'books'. Each section consists of a series of chapters or scenes; and the placing in sequence of these, as also of the sections themselves, is the result of purpose and thought. In the author's opinion this arrangement cannot be altered without serious damage.
>
> It must surely be obvious that the author could not be pleased or satisfied with any limitations that make the dislocation of his narrative and

its balance necessary; though he may, of course be made to understand the necessity for them, and put up with something less than pleasure or satisfaction.

In fact the whole construction, especially towards the end, has been extremely roughly handled; and I am not convinced that any limitations of time and space can really justify the confusion and violent alterations of the original narrative that are to be seen in the latter part of Series II and in Series III. The 'interleaving' of the events in the two main threads, Frodo-Sam and the War, which was deliberately avoided in the original with good reason, produces a jumble, that would be bewildering to any viewers not well acquainted with the book. The latter would not recognize the story as the one that I have told at all: the events, the characters, and the moral significance have all been altered and distorted. This is the crucial point, and I find Mr. Zimmerman's treatment quite unacceptable. (To instance two minor points: On page 40 we pass with a 'fade-out' from one set of persons in a tunnel, to another set in a tunnel, though the events are in the narrative separated in time, and in space by some 500 miles, and have no special connexion. What has happened to Frodo between his capture and the point where on p. 51 he ridiculously 'leaps through the air' and tears the Ring from Sam [who has abandoned Frodo in Shelob's lair and carried the Ring to Mount Doom himself]. I pass over the major matter: that the most important part of the whole work, the journey through Mordor and the martyrdom of Frodo, has been cut in preference for battles; though it is the chief point of the Lord of the Rings that the battles were of subordinate significance. Actually the skill of the artists could, I believe, have made the Mordor journey deeply impressive, and cuts elsewhere would have been justified, if they allowed them the opportunity.)

To speak frankly, the Story-line before me gives the impression of being hasty (and overheated). I am prepared to be told that it took Mr. Zimmerman weeks or months; but the impression will remain that it is nonetheless the product of a hasty reading of the original, which has failed to appreciate the tone and significance of the narrative. It appears to be based primarily on the memory of this reading (altered by the adapter's private imagination), and the resulting script does not seem to have been compared very carefully with the book.

This seems to me to be shown by various points, which I do not cite as of great importance in themselves, but as evidence for my opinion.

There is a constant needless alteration of points of detail. As I have pointed out many of these in the page by page notes there is no need to cite them here. I will point to only one significant case. On p. 48 we read: *He bends near to Eowyn and touches her lips lightly with his, then feeds her from a bowl of specially-prepared herbs.* Compare this with my Vol III p. 144 [e.g. 'Once more Aragorn bruised two leaves of *athelas* and cast them into steaming water; and he laved her [Éowyn's] brow with it, and her right arm lying cold and nerveless on the coverlet', bk. V, ch. 8]. The differences no doubt would be pictorially slight and unimportant; but I feel that they (especially the substitution of lips for brow in the circumstances) reveal insensitivity and/or haste – since this is only one instance out of a large number.

Events are coloured by anticipation of others later, to the destruction of carefully devised differences. For instance Rivendell is described as a 'shimmering forest', without any justification in the book (p. 10). This is a confusion with Lórien. (Mr. Zimmerman entirely misconceives Lórien and wilfully alters it to suit his own taste.) . . .

Granted the necessity for drastic reduction, I think that Mr. Z. is often mistaken in the methods that he employs for shortening. One may cut, or one may compress. In general, he prefers the more dangerous method of compression.

There are, of course, cuts – and the selection of the things to cut does not always meet the author's approval. But usually the adapter compresses in various ways: he merely flips or glances at an event or scene; he combines or confuses two distinct scenes; and most unsatisfactory, he compresses the time and/or space of the action.

There are plenty of events and scenes in the original. In less space the canvas would become overcrowded. The first method has this effect. There are fleeting glimpses of things that have lost all significance or function in the economy of the story. It is like flipping over the illustrations to a long tale that is half forgotten. [Special Collections and University Archives, John P. Raynor, S.J., Library, Marquette University]

In the letter as sent, Tolkien wrote that Zimmerman 'and/or others'

may be irritated or aggrieved by the tone of many of my criticisms. If so, I am sorry (though not surprised). But I would ask them to make an effort of imagination sufficient to understand the irritation (and on occasion the resentment) of an author, who finds, increasingly as he proceeds, his work treated as it would seem carelessly in general, in places recklessly, and with no evident signs of any appreciation of what it is all about. . . . The canons of narrative art in any medium cannot be wholly different; and the failure of poor films is often precisely in exaggeration, and in the intrusion of unwarranted matter owing to not perceiving where the core of the original lies. [*Letters*, p. 270]

On 16 June 1958 Tolkien wrote to Rayner Unwin that he did not want 'to kill the project, which I think promised well on the pictorial side' (Tolkien-George Allen & Unwin archive, HarperCollins), but he continued to be annoyed with it. Although he left matters in his publisher's hands, he felt that the proposal could not be accepted without ample payment in compensation. In the event, Ackerman allowed his option on a *Lord of the Rings* film to expire in early 1959.

By then at least one other enquiry had been made, and more soon followed. Among these the most promising was that by William L. Snyder, doing business as Rembrandt Films, who planned to make a feature-length motion picture of *The Hobbit*. Tolkien and Allen & Unwin reached an agreement with Snyder in April 1962. Negotiations were complicated, however, by questions that now arose about the validity of Tolkien's American copyright in *The Hobbit*, and 'in the end', as Rayner Unwin recalled, 'only the advance of $15,000 and a share of any profits earned in countries that were signatories of Berne [the Berne Convention] remained. But we were not in a strong position' (*George Allen & Unwin: A Remembrancer* (1999), p. 109). By contract, Snyder had a limited time to produce a motion picture of *The Hobbit*, and did so apparently before his deadline; but the result, running only about twelve minutes, was composed simply of cartoon stills or three-dimensional constructions, in which the only action was created by movement of the camera. The film story departs drastically from Tolkien's book. It omits all of the dwarves; instead, Bilbo is accompanied by Gandalf, a watchman, a soldier, and a princess on a quest to regain jewels stolen by the dragon Smaug from the town of Dale. Bilbo encounters Gollum, finds the magic ring, and himself kills the dragon.

In the late 1960s the Beatles planned to make a film of *The Lord of the Rings*, with themselves as Gollum (John), Frodo (Paul), Gandalf (George), and Sam (Ringo), but were unable to purchase the rights. Already by mid-1967 Allen & Unwin began to negotiate with United Artists, who wished to purchase film rights to both *The Lord of the Rings* and *The Hobbit* (though their interest was chiefly in the former work). A deal was struck at last in 1969. In the process, United Artists also secured any rights to a *Hobbit* film that might still be controlled by William L. Snyder: this avenue was deemed less expensive than litigation to decide whether Snyder's twelve-minute film had been too slight to fulfil his contract and the *Hobbit* rights had reverted to Tolkien.

In 1970 United Artists asked the director John Boorman to make a film of *The Lord of the Rings*. With Rospo Pallenberg, Boorman developed a two and one-half-hour script for a live action motion picture; but new management at United Artists chose not to pursue it, and it was eventually abandoned. Janet Brennan Croft has commented on the many liberties Boorman and Pallenberg took with Tolkien's book when writing the script: 'Characters, events, locations, themes, all are changed freely with no regard for the author's original intent. Situations are sexualized or plumbed for psychological kinks that simply do not exist in the book.' These include the seduction of Frodo by Galadriel, and the marriage of Aragorn and Éowyn. 'Pipeweed seems equivalent to marijuana in its effects, and the hobbits' beloved mushrooms are hallucinogenic' ('Three Rings for Hollywood: Scripts for *The Lord of the Rings* by Zimmerman, Boorman, and Beagle', unpublished paper (2004), p. 4).

In 1976 the Saul Zaentz Company acquired the film rights to *The Hobbit* and *The Lord of the Rings* in a complicated deal also involving the Metro-Goldwyn-Mayer studio. Zaentz now commissioned Ralph Bakshi, a sometimes controversial maker of animated feature films, to produce an animated version of *The Lord of the Rings*. Nominally following a screenplay by Chris Conkling and Peter S. Beagle, Bakshi adapted only *The Fellowship of the Ring* and part of *The Two Towers*. He planned a second film to complete the story, as well as one of *The Hobbit*; but his *Lord of the Rings* (1978 U.S.; 1979 U.K.), though often praised for its use of rotoscoping, was widely criticized on release as confusing and humourless, and among Tolkien enthusiasts has been derided for errors and inconsistencies. More recently, in the wake of Peter Jackson's *Lord of the Rings* film, some have looked back to Bakshi's effort in comparison and have found it the more faithful to Tolkien's book (if still wanting in many respects). It has been issued on videocassette and DVD.

At the time of Bakshi's *Lord of the Rings* the Saul Zaentz Company created a subsidiary, Tolkien Enterprises, to manage merchandising rights associated with the film. Tolkien Enterprises claims 'certain worldwide exclusive rights to the literary works *The Hobbit* and *The Lord of the Rings*' as enumerated at *www. tolkien-ent.com*.

In 1977 an animated motion picture of *The Hobbit* by Arthur Rankin, Jr. and Jules Bass, adapted by Romeo Muller, was first broadcast on American television. Sketches and finished paintings for the film were used to illustrate an edition of *The Hobbit*, first published by Harry N. Abrams, New York in the same year. An animated motion picture by the same producers based on *The Return of the King* was first shown on American television in 1980: Rankin-Bass maintained that the third part of *The Lord of the Rings* had fallen into the public domain in the United States, and therefore a film of the book could be undertaken without the consent of the Saul Zaentz Company or the Tolkien Estate. The latter parties disagreed, but an amicable settlement was reached. Both Rankin-Bass Tolkien films are often criticized for their acting, dialogue, and music. They have been made available as commercial video recordings (videocassette and DVD) in North America.

The most recent motion picture adaptation of *The Lord of the Rings* is that by Peter Jackson, Fran Walsh, and Philippa Boyens, directed by Jackson and released in three parts (2001–3). Filmed in live action but with extensive computer-generated characters and effects, it has been widely popular with audiences and critics, and has won prestigious awards. Tolkien enthusiasts, however, are sharply, even angrily divided over it (though the lines are often blurred). Some praise it highly; some accept its departures from its source as part of a legitimate interpretation of Tolkien's book, or as necessary changes to suit a different medium; and some feel that the film is a travesty as an adaptation and seriously flawed even when considered solely as a motion picture. Points frequently argued include the diminishing or other alteration of characters in the film relative to their portrayal in Tolkien's book, emphasis on violent action, the over-use of special effects, and the omission of scenes from the book while incidents invented by the screenwriters have been inserted. Criticism among Tolkien fans became more mixed as release of the three parts progressed, and has been complicated by extended/re-edited versions on DVD. See further, *Tolkien on Film: Essays on Peter Jackson's The Lord of the*

Rings, ed. Janet Brennan Croft (2004); and *Translating Tolkien: Text and Film*, ed. Thomas Honegger (2004). Heavily promoted, Peter Jackson's motion picture helped temporarily to increase sales of Tolkien's works to extraordinary levels, though it is arguable whether it inspired many new readers to become enthusiasts of Tolkien's book rather than devotees of the film. Numerous books about Tolkien were published to capitalize on the film's publicity: many were rushed into print, and some occasionally confused the film with its literary source.

Stage adaptations of *The Lord of the Rings* date from at least 1960, with a production by Joyce Biddell of Maidstone, Kent. A lavish musical treatment of the work was produced in Toronto in 2006. As he did for *The Hobbit*, Rob Inglis has performed a one-man adaptation of *The Lord of the Rings*, likewise much abbreviated.

Adaptations of Tolkien's work outside Britain and the United States have included stage productions of *The Hobbit* and *The Lord of the Rings* in Finland, *The Lord of the Rings* read on German radio by a full cast, a ballet based on part of *The Silmarillion* in Italy, and theatrical dramatizations of *Leaf by Niggle* and *Farmer Giles of Ham* in the Netherlands and Sweden respectively.

The Adventures of Tom Bombadil. Poem. The first of two published versions appeared in the *Oxford Magazine* 52, no. 13 (15 February 1934), pp. 464–5. This was reprinted in *Reader's Companion*, pp. 124–7, the first printing of which mistakenly omits the fifth verse, identical to the fifth verse of the later version (see below). In both versions, Tom Bombadil is 'a merry fellow' with a long beard, dressed in a bright blue jacket, yellow boots, and an old hat with a feather. On sunny days he wanders carefree in the meadows, or sits 'by the waterside for hours upon hours'. When he is happy he sings 'like a starling', 'Hey! come, derry-dol, merry-dol, my darling!' The poem relates his encounters with Goldberry, 'the Riverwoman's daughter' who playfully pulls him into the water; with Willow-man (Old Man Willow), a malevolent tree that traps him in a crack in its bole; with the Badgerfolk, who mean to hold him forever in their tunnels; and with Barrow-wight who threatens to take him 'under the earth' and make him 'pale and cold'. Tom dismisses them all: he is 'a clever fellow' whom 'none ever caught'. But in the final stanzas he himself catches Goldberry, and they have 'a merry wedding'.

Tolkien based at least the flamboyant clothing of Tom Bombadil on a Dutch doll, i.e. a jointed wooden doll, that belonged to his children (according to some sources; according to *Biography* it belonged to his second son, *Michael). Evidently in the late 1920s Tolkien told stories to his children about Tom Bombadil, but these were not written down. He seems to have written a version of his *Oxford Magazine* poem about the character *c.* 1931, the year to which a fine manuscript of the poem in Tengwar (*Writing systems) may be dated (reproduced in *Pictures*, no. 48).

In a letter to his publisher *Stanley Unwin of 16 December 1937, having been asked for a sequel to *The Hobbit*, Tolkien suggested instead a story in which

Tom Bombadil was the hero (and which Tolkien apparently had already begun and abandoned: see *Biography*, p. 162). 'Or is he, as I suspect,' Tolkien asked, 'fully enshrined in the enclosed verses [*The Adventures of Tom Bombadil* in the *Oxford Magazine*]? Still I could enlarge the portrait' (*Letters*, p. 26). As he had for *The Hobbit*, Unwin gave the poem to his young son *Rayner, who concluded that although it would make a good story, a better one would be that of Bullroarer Took, the hero of the Battle of the Green Fields mentioned in *The Hobbit*, chapter 1. 'This story could be a continuation of *The Hobbit*, for Bilbo could tell it to Gandalf and Balin in his hobbit hole when they visited him [as told at the end of that book]' (Tolkien-George Allen & Unwin archive, Harper-Collins).

So Stanley Unwin reported, quoting Rayner's review, in a letter of 20 December (Tolkien-George Allen & Unwin archive, HarperCollins). By then, however, Tolkien had written to C.A. Furth at George Allen & Unwin (*Publishers) that he had begun after all a new story about hobbits; but he did not forget *The Adventures of Tom Bombadil*. Tom and Goldberry, Old Man Willow and the Barrow-wight, and incidents and features of the poem reappear or are echoed in *The Lord of the Rings*. Tolkien 'wanted an "adventure" on the way', as he wrote to in a letter to Peter Hastings in September 1954 (*Letters*, p. 192) – that is, an adventure for the four hobbits in *The Lord of the Rings* as they travelled east from Hobbiton – and *The Adventures of Tom Bombadil*, though independently conceived, was at hand for inspiration.

Tom was now described in greater detail, and defined in part by his response to Sauron's Ring: alone among the characters in *The Lord of the Rings* he is unaffected by the One Ring, and does not desire it. But his precise nature is not wholly explained. When Frodo asks Goldberry 'who is Tom Bombadil' she replies, at most, that Tom 'is the Master of wood, water, and hill' (bk. I, ch. 7). At the end of *The Lord of the Rings* he remains an enigma – intentionally so, see *Letters*, p. 174. Some readers, however, have refused to accept this state, and have written widely about Tom's origin and meaning, in particular his place in the cosmology of *The Lord of the Rings* and *'The Silmarillion'.

In a letter to Stanley Unwin of 16 December 1937 Tolkien described Tom as 'the spirit of the (vanishing) Oxford and Berkshire countryside' (*Letters*, p. 26). Later he wrote to Peter Hastings:

> I don't think Tom needs philosophizing about, and is not improved by it. But many have found him an odd or indeed discordant ingredient [in *The Lord of the Rings*]. . . . I kept him in, and as he was, because he represents certain things otherwise left out. I do not mean him to be an *allegory – or I should not have given him so particular, individual, and ridiculous a name – but 'allegory' is the only mode of exhibiting certain functions: he is then an 'allegory', or an exemplar, a particular embodying of pure (real) natural science: the spirit that desires knowledge of other things, their history and nature, *because they are 'other'* and wholly independent of the enquiring mind, a spirit coeval with the rational

mind, and entirely unconcerned with 'doing' anything with the knowledge: Zoology and Botany not Cattle-breeding or Agriculture. . . . Also T[om] B[ombadil] exhibits another point in his attitude to the Ring, and its failure to affect him. [September 1954, *Letters*, p. 192]

In 1961–2 Tolkien slightly revised *The Adventures of Tom Bombadil* for publication in *The Adventures of Tom Bombadil and Other Verses from the Red Book* (1962), pp. 11–16. Tom is now said to live in the valley of the Withywindle, in the world of *The Lord of the Rings*. In his preface to the 1962 volume, writing as the 'editor' of the Hobbits' 'Red Book of Westmarch', Tolkien described the revised *Adventures of Tom Bombadil* as 'made up of various hobbit-versions of legends concerning Bombadil'. Also in that collection is a sequel, *Bombadil Goes Boating*. A third Bombadil poem, *Once upon a Time*, was published in 1965.

Tolkien recorded the revised *Adventures of Tom Bombadil* in 1967 for the album *Poems and Songs of Middle Earth* (1967, reissued in 2001 as part of *The J.R.R. Tolkien Audio Collection*); see further, *Recordings.

On the development of the Tom Bombadil episode in *The Lord of the Rings*, see Christopher Tolkien, *The Return of the Shadow* (1988), especially ch. 5–7. On Tom Bombadil as a Dutch doll, see Patricia Reynolds, 'The Real Tom Bombadil', *Leaves from the Tree: J.R.R. Tolkien's Shorter Fiction* (1991). The latter book also contains two other pertinent works, 'Tom Bombadil and *The Lord of the Rings*' by Christina Scull and 'The Natures of Tom Bombadil: A Summary' by Charles E. Noad; and see also Gene Hargrove, 'Who Is Tom Bombadil', *Mythlore* 13, no. 1, whole no. 47 (Autumn 1986), and Jeffrey Stevenson, 'T.B. or Not T.B.: That Is the Question', *Amon Hen* 196 (November 2005). See also *Reader's Companion*, pp. 124 ff.

The Adventures of Tom Bombadil and Other Verses from the Red Book. Poetry collection, first published in Great Britain by George Allen & Unwin, London, in November 1962, and in the United States by the Houghton Mifflin Company, Boston, in October 1963. See further, *Descriptive Bibliography* A6.

HISTORY

Tolkien's *Aunt Jane Neave wrote to him near the beginning of October 1961 to ask 'if you wouldn't get out a small book with Tom Bombadil at the heart of it, the sort of size of book that we old 'uns can afford to buy for Christmas presents' (quoted in *Biography*, p. 244). Tom Bombadil had featured in a poem, *The Adventures of Tom Bombadil*, published in 1934, and in Book I of *The Lord of the Rings* (1954). Tolkien replied that although he did not feel inclined to write any more about that character, the poem 'might make a pretty booklet of the kind you would like if each verse could be illustrated by *Pauline Baynes' (4 October 1961, *Letters*, p. 308). He had in mind a book with little text and many pictures in a small format, an 'interim amusement' until *The Silmaril-

lion could be completed; his publisher, *Rayner Unwin, suggested instead that it be fleshed out with other 'occasional verses', 'to make a book and not a pamphlet' (letters, 11 October and 2 November 1961, Tolkien-George Allen & Unwin archive, HarperCollins).

Between November 1961 and April 1962 Tolkien sifted through the poems he had written to date, even very early works such as *The Trees of Kortirion* and possibly *You & Me and the Cottage of Lost Play* (*The Little House of Lost Play: Mar Vanwa Tyaliéva*), looking for any that could be reprinted or revised. To Jane Neave he wrote that he had enjoyed himself very much 'digging out these old half-forgotten things and rubbing them up. All the more because there are other and duller things that I ought to have been doing' (22 November 1961, *Letters*, p. 309). Writing to Rayner Unwin, however, he regretted that there were few among his verses (he felt) that were compatible with *The Adventures of Tom Bombadil*, and few that fit well even with each other. He had particular misgivings about 'the vaguer, more subjective and least successful piece labelled *The Sea-Bell*' (letter to Rayner Unwin, 8 December 1961, Tolkien-George Allen & Unwin archive, HarperCollins). By 12 April 1962, as he told his publisher, he 'lost all confidence' in the poems under consideration,

> and all judgement, and unless Pauline Baynes can be inspired by them, I cannot see them making a 'book'. I do not see why she should be inspired, though I fervently hope that she will be. Some of the things may be good in their way, and all of them privately amuse me; but elderly hobbits are easily pleased.
>
> The various items . . . do not really 'collect'. The only possible link is the fiction that they come from the Shire from about the period of *The Lord of the Rings*. But that fits some uneasily. I have done a good deal of work, trying to make them fit better: if not much to their good, I hope not to their serious detriment. [*Letters*, pp. 314–15]

He now made an arrangement of sixteen poems: *The Adventures of Tom Bombadil*; *Bombadil Goes Boating*; *Errantry*; *Princess Mee*; *The Man in the Moon Stayed Up Too Late*; *The Man in the Moon Came Down Too Soon*; *The Stone Troll*; *Perry-the-Winkle*; *The Mewlips*; *Oliphaunt*; *Cat*; *Fastitocalon*; *Shadow-Bride*; *The Hoard*; *The Sea-Bell*; and *The Last Ship*. (Thus the order of contents in the first printing of the Allen & Unwin edition; see below.) Most were revised versions of earlier works, two (*The Man in the Moon Stayed Up Too Late* and *Oliphaunt*) were reprinted from *The Lord of the Rings*, one (*Cat*) had been written by Tolkien a few years earlier to amuse his granddaughter Joanna (see *Michael Tolkien), and one (*Bombadil Goes Boating*) was written for the collection, based on earlier workings. To these Tolkien added a preface, an extension of the fiction he had adopted in *The Hobbit* and *The Lord of the Rings* in which he posed as the editor of Hobbit manuscripts, including the 'Red Book of Westmarch': 'The present selection is taken from the older pieces [in the Red Book], mainly concerned with legends and jests of the Shire at the end of the Third Age, that appear to have been made by Hobbits, especially by Bilbo [Baggins] and his friends, or their immediate descendants' (1962 edn., p. 7).

Pauline Baynes, who had impressed Tolkien with her pictures for *Farmer Giles of Ham*, agreed to illustrate his new book. He advised her that the poems 'were conceived as a series of very definite, clear and precise, pictures – fantastical, or nonsensical perhaps, but not dreamlike! And I thought of you, because you seem able to produce wonderful pictures with a touch of 'fantasy', but primarily bright and clear visions of things that one might really see' (6 December 1961, *Letters*, p. 312). He approved of her new art, excepting only her full-page illustration for *The Hoard* (in which the dragon should have faced the mouth of the cave, the better to defend it) and the orientation of the original binding art in which the figure of Tom Bombadil is placed on the lower rather than the upper cover; these were published nonetheless.

With the second Allen & Unwin printing (and the first Houghton Mifflin printing) *Fastitocalon* and *Cat* were reversed in order, so that the first of these would not be bisected by an illustration for the second.

The Adventures of Tom Bombadil and Other Verses from the Red Book has been reprinted in *The Tolkien Reader* (1966), *Poems and Stories* (1980), and elsewhere. In 1967 Tolkien recorded *The Adventures of Tom Bombadil, The Mewlips, The Hoard, Perry-the-Winkle, The Man in the Moon Came Down Too Soon*, and *The Sea-Bell* for the album *Poems and Songs of Middle Earth* (1967). On the same album, *Errantry* is sung by baritone William Elvin, accompanied by *Donald Swann. Tolkien also recorded *Errantry* and *Princess Mee*, which, however, were issued only in 2001 as part of *The J.R.R. Tolkien Audio Collection* (incorporating *Poems and Songs of Middle Earth*; see *Recordings).

CRITICISM

With only a few exceptions, such as the anonymous critic in *Junior Bookshelf* (March 1963) who called it 'a pathetic pip-squeak of a book', reviewers approved of the *Adventures of Tom Bombadil* collection and found much to praise. Anthony Thwaite in 'Hobbitry' (*The Listener*, 22 November 1962, p. 831), for instance, described Tolkien's poems as 'by turns gay, pratling, melancholy, nonsensical, mysterious. And what is most exciting and attractive about them is their superb technical skill.' And the anonymous author of 'Middle Earth Verse' in the *Times Literary Supplement* for 23 November 1962 wrote that 'Tolkien is in fact a wordsmith, an ingenious versifier, rather than a discoverer of new insights. . . . Tom Bombadil himself is shown as a queer fellow, a little comical; but with something of the supernatural about him.' The rhymes 'invoke a mood rather than relate an anecdote. . . . These are clever verses, though they do not grip a reader as did all the tales of hobbits and elves [*The Hobbit* and *The Lord of the Rings*]' (p. 892).

On 28 November 1962 Tolkien wrote to *Stanley Unwin that he had seen the reviews in *The Listener* and the *Times Literary Supplement* and 'was agreeably surprised: I expected remarks far more snooty and patronizing. Also I was rather pleased, since it seemed that the reviewers had both started out not wanting to be amused, but had failed to maintain their Victorian dignity intact' (*Letters*, p. 322). On 19 December 1962 he remarked to his son *Michael that sales of *Tom Bombadil* were so good that Allen & Unwin had made him an advance, and that, 'even on a minute initial royalty, means more than is at all usual for anyone but [John] Betjeman to make on verse!' (*Letters*, p. 322).

Ae Adar Nín: The Lord's Prayer in Sindarin. Partial translation by Tolkien into Sindarin (*Languages, Invented), published with commentary in *Vinyar Tengwar* 44 (June 2002), pp. 21–30, 38, ed. Bill Welden. Tolkien wrote it during the 1950s on the verso of a postcard containing one of his Quenya translations of the Lord's Prayer (see *'Words of Joy'). The manuscript is reproduced on p. 23 of the *Vinyar Tengwar* article.

Ælfwine of England see **Eriol and Ælfwine**

Ainulindalë. The first component of *The Silmarillion* (1977), pp. 15–22, and the final version of Tolkien's tale of Creation, first told in *The Music of the Ainur* in *The Book of Lost Tales*.

SUMMARY

Tolkien described *The Music of the Ainur* as

> a cosmogonical myth . . . defining the relation of The One, the transcendental Creator, to the Valar, the 'Powers', the angelical First-created, and their part in ordering and carrying out the Primeval Design. It was also told how it came about that Eru, the One, made an addition to the Design: introducing the themes of the Eruhîn, the Children of God, The First-born (Elves) and the Successors (Men), whom the Valar were forbidden to try and dominate by fear or force. [letter to Christopher Bretherton, 16 July 1964, *Letters*, p. 345]

The tale is told to Eriol the mariner by Rúmil in the garden of the Cottage of Lost Play. Ilúvatar (Eru) describes to the Ainur (the First-created), whom he has sung into being, a design for the creation of a world and its history, and invites them to embellish it through their own music. They begin splendidly, with 'the harpists, and the lutanists, the flautists and the pipers, the organs and the countless choirs of the Ainur' fashioning 'the theme of Ilúvatar into great music; and a sound arose of mighty melodies changing and interchanging, mingling and dissolving amid the thunder of harmonies greater than the roar of the great seas . . .' (*The Book of Lost Tales, Part One*, p. 53). But one of the greatest of the Ainur, Melko, introduces ideas which destroy the harmony of the music. Twice Ilúvatar begins new themes, and twice Melko brings about discord. Ilúvatar stops the music and informs the Ainur that he has given shape and reality to all that they played and sung, and that even the discords introduced by Melko will in the end add to Ilúvatar's glory. Ilúvatar alone is responsible for the theme which introduces Elves and Men, 'nor, for they comprehended not fully when Ilúvatar first propounded their being, did any of the Ainur dare in their music to add anything to their fashion; and these races are for that reason named rightly the Children of Ilúvatar' (p. 57). Ilúvatar then shows the Ainur the world they have helped create, set in the void, and tells them: 'even now the world unfolds and its history begins as did my theme in your hands. Each one herein will find contained within the design that is mine the adornments and embellishments that he himself devised.... One thing only have I added, the fire that giveth Life and Reality' (p. 55).

As the Ainur watch the world, they have a vision of the beginning of its history, and many become so enthralled that they seek and are granted permission to dwell in the world, to guard its beauties and to instruct the Children. Among those who choose to do so, whom the Elves call the Valar, are Manwë and his spouse Varda, Aulë and Ulmo, and even Melko, who pretends that he wants to heal the ills he has introduced into the Music, but secretly plans to seize power from the other Ainur and to make war on the Children. From their participation in the Music and their vision of the beginning of the world's history, the Valar know much, but not all of the future. In telling this story to Eriol, Rúmil ends by reporting words concerning Elves and Men spoken by Ilúvatar after the departure of the Valar (see *'Of the Beginning of Days', in which this material appears in *The Silmarillion*).

HISTORY

The Creation is not mentioned in the *Sketch of the Mythology (c. 1926); it is summarized in one paragraph in the *Quenta Noldorinwa (c. 1930), and in one sentence in both the 'earliest' and 'later' *Annals of Valinor (early and mid-1930s respectively). But at some time in the mid-1930s, with *The Music of the Ainur* before him, Tolkien made a draft, followed by a fair copy, of a new version as a separate work with the title *Ainulindalë* (Quenya 'music of the Ainur'). He made extensive changes in word and phrase, and some additions, for instance that the Valar took the shape and form of the Children, but the story remained close to that in *The Music of the Ainur*. This new version was published in *The Lost Road and Other Writings (1987), presented as if a transcription or translation of a document written by Rúmil of Tûn.

In 1946 Tolkien made a draft (now lost) and then a typescript of a radical new version of the *Ainulindalë*. In this Ilúvatar shows the Ainur only a vision of what their Music had created, but aware of their desire for what they see, he speaks and by his words gives being to their vision. In earlier versions the Valar enter the world together and find it fully formed by the Music; now Melkor arrives before the others, who find the world unshaped and labour in it for ages to accomplish their vision. An account of the first conflicts in Arda between

Melkor and the other Valar, which had appeared in a later tale in *The Book of Lost Tales*, is now placed in the *Ainulindalë* (see 'Of the Beginning of Days'). Another significant change is to the cosmology: unlike the earlier version, the Sun exists from the beginning, and the Moon is made by Morgoth from a piece of the Earth, from which he observes what happens below, until he is cast out by the Valar. *Christopher Tolkien has called this a 'de-mythologizing' of the Sun and the Moon 'by removal from all association with the Two Trees' (again see *'Of the Beginning of Days'), and comments that 'it seems strange indeed that my father was prepared to conceive of the Moon – the Moon, that cherishes the memory of the Elves . . . – as a dead and blasted survival of the hatred of Melkor, however beautiful its light' (*Morgoth's Ring*, p. 43). Also the world (now called *Arda*) inhabited by the Valar and the Children was now only part of a much greater Creation.

By this time Tolkien had begun to doubt whether his invented cosmology should be contrary to scientific reality. In summer 1948 he lent to *Katharine Farrer the mid-1930s manuscript of the *Ainulindalë*, on which he wrote 'Flat World Version', and the 1946 typescript on which he wrote 'Round World Version'. In a letter written to Tolkien probably in October 1948 Mrs Farrer said that she preferred the 'Flat World' version, and between then and 1951 Tolkien extensively revised that manuscript in several layers and wrote much new material on blank versos. Although this was again a 'Flat World' version, without the Sun in existence from the beginning, Tolkien incorporated with revision much of the 1946 text, including the Ainur being shown a vision and not reality, and Arda as only a small part of creation, and he removed Melkor's earlier arrival in Arda and his making of the Moon. An added 'title-page' changes the work's history: it was now 'written by Rúmil of Túna and was told to Ælfwine in Eressëa (as he records) by Pengoloð the Sage' (*Morgoth's Ring*, p. 8).

From this now complex document Tolkien wrote a beautiful manuscript with illuminated capitals. It begins by following its predecessor closely, but diverges more in its later parts. In this Tolkien introduces the word *Ea* to mean the whole of Creation, the universe which Ilúvatar brings into reality with the words '*Ea!* Let these things Be!' (*Morgoth's Ring*, p. 31). The 1946 and later texts are published, in whole or in part, in *Morgoth's Ring* (1993).

The *Ainulindalë* in *The Silmarillion* is based on this final manuscript, incorporating emendations made both to it and to a later amanuensis typescript, and presented as straightforward narrative without reference to 'ancient sources'. Some of the material from the 1951 *Ainulindalë* was incorporated in 'Of the Beginning of Days', the first chapter of the *'Quenta Silmarillion': the account of the early conflicts in Arda and of the establishment of the Valar in Valinor, and in the final paragraphs, the words of Ilúvatar concerning Elves and Men, and comments on their differing fates. Two editorial changes made to the published *Ainulindalë* by Christopher Tolkien are noted by him in *The Lost Road and Other Writings*, p. 164, note 9, and in *Morgoth's Ring*, p. 40.

Although Tolkien wrote no later version of the *Ainulindalë*, towards the end of the 1950s he again began to consider whether myth and science could be reconciled. In one of several texts he wrote that in 'the oldest forms of the mythology' which were 'intended to be no more than another primitive mythology . . . it was consequentially a "Flat Earth" cosmogony (much easier to manage anyway): the Matter of Númenor had not been devised.' He had considered whether the best solution was to consider the earlier cosmology as representing confused and incorrect Mannish tradition, rather than truth known by the Elves:

> I was inclined to adhere to the Flat Earth and the astronomically absurd business of the making of the Sun and the Moon. But you can make up stories of that kind when you live among people who have the same general background of imagination, when the Sun 'really' rises in the East and goes down in the West, etc. When however (no matter how little most people know or think about astronomy) it is the general belief that we live upon a 'spherical' island in 'Space' you cannot do this any more. [*Morgoth's Ring*, p. 370]

CRITICISM

Several critics have remarked on the important role of music in the *Ainulindalë* as in other creation myths. In 'The "Music of the Spheres": Relationships between Tolkien's *The Silmarillion* and Medieval Cosmological and Religious Theory' in *Tolkien the Medievalist* (2003), Bradford Lee Eden writes:

> As a medievalist, Tolkien knew and recognized the importance of music as an anthropomorphic reality and creational material in many mythologies. The medieval concept of the 'music of the spheres' was grounded in ancient and classical philosophy, discussed and theorized by Plato and Aristotle, through the early Christian writers and the third-century pagan philosopher Plotinus, up to the eventual standardization by Boethius in the early sixth century . . . as a classicist and medievalist, the 'music of the spheres' concept would have been deeply ingrained in his educational training, and his Catholic background would also have influenced his thought and creative processes. [p. 181]

Eden also finds recalled in the *Ainulindalë* 'the medieval depiction of the various hierarchies of angels singing continuously around the throne of God' (p. 185).

Other commentators have suggested that Tolkien's Creation myth reflects ideas found in the writings of St Augustine. In 'Augustine and the *Ainulindalë*', *Mythlore* 21, no. 1, whole no. 79 (Summer 1995), John Houghton compares the *Ainulindalë* with Augustine's interpretations of Genesis:

This is, I submit, an Augustinian account of creation. . . . In both cases, God first creates the angels and then reveals to them the further elements of creation; the angels' own knowledge reflects ideas in the divine mind. In both cases, as well, after the revelation, God gives real existence to what the angels have perceived, upholding that existence in the void; yet that real existence has only the undeveloped potential of what it will become in the unfolding of time, and God reserves to God's self the introduction of elements unanticipated in the basic design.

Granted these similarities, however, the two schemata do contrast in two ways. First is the fact that the predominant musical images function in the *Ainulindalë* in the way that speech and light, taken together as intellectual illumination do in Augustine's reading of Genesis. Second is the way the Ainur act as sub-creators, developing the themes proposed to them by Eru Ilúvatar, whereas Augustine focuses on God as the sole creator. [p. 7]

Anne C. Petty in *Tolkien in the Land of Heroes: Discovering the Human Spirit* (2003) draws attention to the voice of the narrator of the *Ainulindalë*: 'Anyone looking for biblical parallels within *The Silmarillion* should make note of the highly formal, King James-style diction.' She also points out that this Creation myth 'is where the seeds of discord are first sown and where all the difficulties, conflicts, sorrows, and heroic efforts that infuse Tolkien's fantasy originate. Here's the starting point for the main theme of The Fall, as well as the first use of the signature imagery of music and water, light and shadow, that Tolkien used to carry this theme through all three of his major works' (p. 39).

Brian Rosebury in *Tolkien: A Cultural Phenomenon* (2003) finds the *Ainulindalë*

a success both in literary and philosophical terms. Its fundamental mythical conception, the world as a Great Music made visible, its history a fulfilment of creative purposes which proceed both directly from God and mediately from him, through the sub-creativity of created beings, dates from as early as 1918–20 . . . it is the key to much else in Tolkien's religious, moral and aesthetic vision. And its prose is at once appropriately 'scriptural' and distinctive of Tolkien. [p. 107]

He points out the similarities to Christian myth with Ilúvatar, the Ainur, and Melkor in place of God, the angels, and Lucifer, and notes that 'the basic Augustinian apparatus in which nothing is created evil, but evil arises from the free will of created beings, is in place'. He also discusses differences mainly arising because the Creation 'is carried out partly through intermediaries' (p. 187).

See also Howard Davis, 'The *Ainulindalë*: Music of Creation' in *Mythlore* 9, no. 2, whole no. 32 (Summer 1982).

Akallabêth: The Downfall of Númenor. The penultimate component of *The Silmarillion* (1977), pp. 259–82, and the last of three accounts of the island realm of *Númenor and its destruction at the end of the Second Age. Tolkien had previously told this story in *The Fall of Númenor* (c. 1936) and *The Drowning of Anadûnê* (first part of 1946).

Probably in the autumn of 1948 he wrote a new version, drawing on the earlier accounts; its original title was *The Fall of Númenor*, later changed to *The Downfall of Númenor*, but Tolkien always referred to it as the *Akallabêth* ('the downfallen' in the Númenórean language, Adûnaic).

Although he apparently wrote the *Akallabêth* in parallel with the Appendices of *The Lord of the Rings*, he seems to have intended that the history of Númenor and the Second Age should be part of 'The Silmarillion'. On 7 April 1948 he referred in a letter to *Hugh Brogan to 'The Silmarillion*, which is virtually a history of the Eldalië (or Elves . . .) from their rise to the Last Alliance, and the first temporary overthrow of Sauron . . .' (*Letters*, p. 129). He still hoped to publish that work, and indeed felt, as he wrote to *Stanley Unwin on 24 February 1950, that its publication was necessary to make *The Lord of the Rings* 'fully intelligible' (*Letters*, p. 137).

Before he began work on the *Akallabêth* Tolkien made an outline history of Númenor, with rough dates for the thirteen kings (most of them not named) who followed after the death of Elros in Second Age 460, and for significant events. He then produced a manuscript of twenty-three pages, rewriting and replacing several of them in the process, emended these, and made a typed copy. Probably in 1951 he took up and emended the typescript, altered some names and the sequence of some events, rewrote certain passages, and inserted a lengthy rider with more details of the history of the last Númenórean kings, in particular their growing hostility to the Eldar and the Valar and to the Faithful. *Christopher Tolkien notes in detail in *Sauron Defeated* (pp. 375–87) and *The Peoples of Middle-earth* (ch. 5) how this version of the *Akallabêth* derives from both *The Fall of Númenor* and *The Drowning of Anadûnê*. He also calculates that from 'the sailing to Anadûnê . . . no less than three-fifths of the precise wording of [the second version of the *Drowning*] was preserved in the *Akallabêth*', but from 'the same point . . . only three-eighths of the latter (again, in precisely the same wording) are present in [the second version of the *Drowning*]' (*Sauron Defeated*, p. 376).

The emended typescript text, with a few corrections added to a later amanuensis typescript, was published in *The Silmarillion* as the *Akallabêth*. When dealing with the *Akallabêth* in *The Peoples of Middle-earth* Christopher Tolkien noted only the differences between the published version and the earlier versions, and explained changes he made to the text for publication in *The Silmarillion*, some of which he came to regret. Earlier he noted other changes in the published text in *Unfinished Tales*, pp. 226–7.

For comment and criticism, see *Númenor.

Alcar mi Tarmenel na Erun: The Gloria in Excelsis Deo in Quenya. Translations of the opening verse of the *Gloria* (Luke 2:14) into Quenya (*Languages,
Invented), published with commentary and notes in *Vinyar Tengwar* 44 (June
2002), pp. 31–7, ed. Arden R. Smith. Five texts are extant, dating evidently from
the mid-1960s.

Aldarion and Erendis: The Mariner's Wife. Story, published with commentary and notes in *Unfinished Tales* (1980), pp. 173–217.

SUMMARY

Aldarion, son of Tar-Meneldur, fifth king of the island of Númenor, has a great
love for the sea, and from the age of twenty-five makes many voyages to Middle-earth. He forms a Guild of Venturers, and establishes in Middle-earth the
haven of Vinyalondë. He is welcomed by Gil-galad, the last High King of the
Noldorin Elves in Middle-earth, and by Círdan the Shipwright. In time, while
in Númenor Aldarion comes to live on board ship, and to spend much of his
time improving harbours, overseeing the building of ships, and planting and
tending trees to provide timber for ships. But 'Tar-Meneldur looked coldly
on the enterprises of his son, and cared not to hear the tale of his journeys,
believing that he sowed the seeds of restlessness and the desire of other lands
to hold' (*Unfinished Tales*, p. 176). At last the king commands his son to stay in
Númenor for a while, and in Second Age 800 proclaims him the King's Heir.
At a feast of celebration, Aldarion meets Erendis: she is immediately attracted,
and enters the queen's household.

After only six years, Aldarion resumes his voyages, dismissing his father's
plea that 'the need of the King's house is for a man who knows and loves this
land and people' (p. 178), and that Aldarion take a wife. Tar-Meneldur becomes
wrathful, and forbids his wife and daughters from setting upon Aldarion's ship
the Green Bough of Return, cut from the tree *oiolairë*; but Erendis takes the
bough in the queen's stead, and Aldarion for the first time looks on her with
love. Nonetheless many years pass before he seeks to marry her. He had not
wanted to be bound; but now Erendis hesitated, not for lack of love, but unwilling to share Aldarion with the Sea. Her mother believes that it is not so much
ships, the Sea, the winds, or strange lands that appeal to Aldarion, 'but some
heat in his mind, or some dream that pursues him'; to which the narrator of
the story adds: 'And it may be that she struck near the truth; for Aldarion was
a man long-sighted, and he looked forward to days when the people would
need more room and greater wealth; and whether he himself knew this clearly
or no, he dreamed of the glory of Númenor and the power of its kings, and he
sought for footholds whence they could step to wider dominion' (p. 191).

For a while Aldarion neglects ships and the Sea and, wooing Erendis, finds
'more contentment in those days than in any others of his life, though he did
not know it until he looked back long after when old age was upon him' (p.
182). Eventually he persuades Erendis to be his wife, but is seized again with

longing for the Sea. He suggests to Erendis that she sail with him; she refuses, having no desire to leave Númenor and fearing that she will die out of sight of land, but nonetheless places a bough on his ship. Aldarion finds Vinyalondë ruined and men in Middle-earth hostile to Númenóreans, and on his return voyage winds drive his ship into the icy North, where the bough of *oiolairë* withers. Despite his absence, the love between Aldarion and Erendis remains warm, and they are married at last in Second Age 870. Three years later, their daughter, Ancalimë, is born. But when she is only four, Aldarion again sails for Middle-earth, promising not to be away more than two years, contrary to custom that parents stay close to their children when they are very young. Ancalimë never forgets that father put her away firmly when she clung to him at this parting, and this time Erendis does not take or send a bough of *oiolairë* to Aldarion's ship. She leaves the home she had shared with him and retires to a house in the midst of Númenor, far from the sea, with only women about her. Aldarion is absent five years, during which time Erendis imparts to her daughter her bitterness against men. On his return Erendis receives Aldarion coldly, and he departs again the next day.

Aldarion brings to his father a letter from Gil-galad, who believes that a growing shadow in the east of Middle-earth is a servant of Morgoth, and seeks help from Númenor when the assault should come. Tar-Meneldur is in doubt what to do, and decides to resign the sceptre to Aldarion. This dismays Erendis, who refuses to leave her home to attend the proclamation of Aldarion as king.

At this point the manuscript ends, and no clear continuation emerges from Tolkien's notes. Tar-Aldarion as King makes other voyages to Middle-earth. Though his achievements there are transitory, they pave the way for the success of later rulers, and for the aid which Tar-Minastir sent to Gil-galad in Second Age 1700, which led to the temporary defeat of Sauron. But there are also unfortunate consequences: Aldarion's involvement in Middle-earth sets Númenor on the road which leads eventually to its Downfall, and Ancalimë's character suffers from her upbringing and her parent's differences. Though she is clever, she is also wilful and malicious, and her own marriage is also unhappy. In Second Age 1075 she becomes the first ruling Queen of Númenor, the rules of succession having been changed. The last mention of Erendis is that in old age in 985 she sought Aldarion, who was expected to return from a voyage, and 'perished in water' (p. 212).

HISTORY

This unfinished work was probably written in 1960; a sketch of a Númenórean helmet, with an inscription referring to Aldarion's Guild of Venturers, is dated 'March 1960' (a redrawn version was reproduced on the dust-jacket of the first British and American editions of *Unfinished Tales*). Tolkien began, but left unfinished, five sometimes contradictory texts, which as he wrote tended to move from annalistic plot outlines to full narrative. The fifth text, which extends for some sixty manuscript pages, has the title *The Shadow of the Shadow: The Tale of the Mariner's Wife: and the Tale of Queen Shepherdess*. A typescript was made from this, and at some time after January 1965 Tolkien began a new typescript, filling out the schematic beginning, but abandoned it after only two pages; this has the title *Indis i · Kiryamo 'The Mariner's Wife': A Tale of Ancient Númenórë, which Tells of the First Rumour of the Shadow*. Tolkien made a few notes and wrote some unconnected fragments of text for the unwritten part of the story, mainly concerning Ancalimë in later life, but little more about Aldarion and Erendis. *Christopher Tolkien notes that the work needed a considerable amount of 'editorial rehandling' to prepare it for publication; see *Unfinished Tales*, pp. 7–8, and also *The Peoples of Middle-earth*, pp. 155, 351.

CRITICISM

The story of the unhappy marriage of Tar-Aldarion, the sixth King of Númenor, and Erendis, and of their daughter Ancalimë, is of great interest, not only for the information it gives of Númenor during the eighth to thirteenth centuries of the Second Age, but also because it is Tolkien's most detailed study of a human relationship. The tale becomes increasingly sad in its depiction of two people of different interests and temperaments who love each other but cannot live the same life, until eventually love turns to bitterness. Tolkien gives a sympathetic depiction of both sides. (See also *Women.)

In a review of *Unfinished Tales* Thomas M. Egan wrote that *Aldarion and Erendis* 'really illustrates Tolkien's power as a story-teller' and

> answers his critics who have claimed he is insensitive to women, putting them up as plaster statues without real knowledge of their character and conflicts in the strains of married life. Using the structure of Númenor's idyllic realm, Tolkien explores the war of the sexes as husband and wife find love from their differing characters, then grow gradually isolated. . . . Isolation and loneliness for Erendis makes her want to punish her adventuresome husband, and her recorded dialogue strikes a strangely modern tone. The result, as Tolkien probes further, is the tragic hatred which grows until it poisons their daughter, and sets the stage for further marital conflict in the next generation. . . . ['Fragments of a World: Tolkien's Road to Middle-earth', *The Terrier* 48, no. 2 (Fall 1983), p. 10]

In another review, Peter S. Beagle called *Aldarion and Erendis*

> a haunting story out of Númenor which tells of a king and queen who loved and damaged one another, and their daughter as well. Moving even in its sketchiness, it is unlike anything else of Tolkien's that I know, and it nips strangely at the heart. The man understood more than the grandly heroic; he knew something about sorrow, and about possession, whether

by hunger or fury or dreams. ['A Fantasy Feast from Middle-earth', *San Francisco Examiner*, 19 October 1980, p. A14]

T.A. Shippey in *The Road to Middle-earth* compares Erendis's retreat to the centre of Númenor, and her statement that the bleating of sheep was sweeter to her ears than the mewing of gulls, to the story of 'Njǫrthr the sea-god and Skathi, daughter of the mountain-giant, in Snorri Sturluson's *Prose Edda*. Obliged to marry, these two tried taking turns to live in each other's homes. But the marriage was a failure. . . .' Njǫrthr complains: 'Hateful to me were the mountains, I was there no longer than nine nights; the howling of wolves seemed ugly to me against the song of the swans'. And Skathi 'replies with a complaint about the noise of the sea-mews' (2nd edn. 1992, p. 217).

Richard Mathews in 'The Edges of Reality in Tolkien's Tale of Aldarion and Erendis', *Mythlore* 18, no. 3, whole no. 69 (Summer 1992), discusses how pride and differences in interests and outlook lead step by step to the complete breakdown of the marriage, and describes 'Tolkien's refusal to allow the characters of the story to be portrayed in black and white' as 'a credit to the sophistication of emotion and mythos he conceives' (p. 29).

Aldershot (Hampshire). From 28 July to 6 August 1910 Tolkien attended a camp with the *King Edward's School Officers Training Corps (*Societies and clubs) and cadets from other schools at Aldershot, south-west of London. Their camp was pitched on a expanse of open land called Farnborough Common (now subsumed by the **Farnborough** airfield), and their exercises and inspections took place in the general vicinity. They were also taken in groups to visit a depot of military aeroplanes and airships in neighbouring Farnborough. Then as now, Aldershot was the centre of military training in England.

Allegory. In July 1947 *Rayner Unwin wrote of *The Lord of the Rings* (then still in manuscript) that 'the struggle between darkness and light' sometimes seemed to leave 'the story proper to become pure allegory' (quoted in *Letters*, pp. 119–20). Tolkien was quick to advise Rayner's father, publisher *Stanley Unwin, that he should

> not let Rayner suspect 'Allegory'. There is a 'moral', I suppose, in any tale worth telling. But that is not the same thing. Even the struggle between darkness and light (as he calls it, not me) is for me just a particular phase of history, one example of its pattern, perhaps, but not The Pattern; and the actors are individuals – they each, of course, contain universals, or they would not live at all, but they never represent them as such.
>
> Of course, Allegory and Story converge, meeting somewhere in Truth. So that the only perfectly consistent allegory is a real life; and the only fully intelligible story is an allegory. And one finds, even in imperfect human 'literature', that the better and more consistent an allegory is the more easily it can be read 'just as a story'; and the better and more

closely woven a story is the more easily can those so minded find allegory in it. But the two start from opposite ends. You can make the Ring into an allegory of our own time, if you like: an allegory of the inevitable fate that waits for all attempts to defeat evil power by power. But that is only because all power magical or mechanical does always so work. You cannot write a story about an apparently simple magic ring without that bursting in, if you really take the ring seriously, and make things happen that would happen, if such things existed. [31 July 1947, *Letters*, p. 121]

In a letter to *Milton Waldman, ?late 1951, Tolkien made it clear that for him, allegory was something deliberately introduced into a work by the author: 'I dislike Allegory – the conscious and intentional allegory – yet any attempt to explain the purport of myth or fairytale must use allegorical language' (*Letters*, p. 145). The *Oxford English Dictionary* agrees with this interpretation: *allegory* is the 'description of a subject under the guise of some other subject of aptly suggestive resemblance', or 'an instance of such description: a figurative sentence, discourse, or narrative, in which properties and circumstances attributed to the apparent subject really refer to the subject they are meant to suggest; an extended or continued metaphor.' The eighth edition of *The Concise Oxford Dictionary of Current English* (1990) defines the term more succinctly: 'a story, play, poem, picture, etc. in which the meaning or message is represented symbolically', or 'the use of such symbols'. But in the current tenth edition of the *Concise Oxford* (revised 2002) the definition has undergone a subtle change away from that of Tolkien: 'a story, poem or picture which can be interpreted to reveal a hidden meaning'. This seems to suggest that a work can be an allegory without the intent of its creator, if it is so in the opinion of the reader, and may reflect a tendency in contemporary literary criticism to prefer a critic's opinions to the author's intentions, or what he says were his intentions.

When *The Lord of the Rings* was first published, many readers wrote to ask Tolkien what the story meant, or to describe their own interpretations. These led to an autobiographical statement written in 1955, in which Tolkien felt it necessary to state that *The Lord of the Rings* 'is not "about" anything but itself. Certainly it has *no* allegorical intentions, general, particular, or topical, moral, religious, or political' (*Letters*, p. 220). He thought that many readers misunderstood the meaning of the word *allegory*, and *c.* 1955 wrote to G.E. Selby: 'There is, of course, no "allegory" at all in the work [*The Lord of the Rings*]. But people are very confused about this word, and seem to mix it us with "significance" or relevance' (quoted in Sotheby Parke Bernet, *Catalogue of Nineteenth Century and Modern First Editions, Presentation Copies, Autograph Letters and Literary Manuscripts*, London, 28–9 July 1977, p. 110). The word he came to prefer, to describe what readers saw, was *applicability*. In a letter to Herbert Schiro on 17 November 1957 he wrote: 'There is *no* "symbolism" or conscious allegory in my story. Allegory of the sort "five wizards = five senses" is wholly foreign to my way of thinking. . . . To ask if the Orcs "are" Communists is to me are sensible as asking if Communists are Orcs. That there is no allegory does not, of course, say there is no applicability. There always is' (*Letters*, p. 262).

Tolkien felt so strongly about the matter that in 1965 he devoted space to it in his Foreword to the second edition of *The Lord of the Rings*. There he explained at length that much of the work, which some critics had supposed to be inspired by the Second World War and in some respects an allegory of it, in fact had been written before the war began.

As for any inner meaning or 'message', it has in the intention of the author none. It is neither allegorical or topical . . . its main theme was settled from the outset by the inevitable choice of the Ring as a link between it and *The Hobbit*. The crucial chapter, 'The Shadow of the Past', is one of the oldest parts of the tale. It was written long before the foreshadow of 1939 had yet become a threat of inevitable disaster, and from that point the story would have developed along essentially the same lines, if the disaster had been averted. . . .

The real war does not resemble the legendary war in its process or its conclusion. If it had inspired or directed the development of the legend, then certainly the Ring would have been seized and used against Sauron; he would not have been annihilated but enslaved, and Barad-dûr would not have been destroyed but occupied. . . .

Other arrangements could be devised according to the tastes or view of those who like allegory or topical reference. But I cordially dislike allegory in all its manifestations, and always have done so since I grew old and wary enough to detect its presence. I much prefer history, true or feigned, with its varied applicability to the thought and experience of readers. I think that many confuse 'applicability' with 'allegory'; but the one resides in the freedom of the reader, and the other in the purposed domination of the author.

The fact that readers today can find relevance in *The Lord of the Rings* to current situations unknown to Tolkien emphasizes that *applicability* has a wider range than *allegory*, and can indeed originate in the mind of the reader. *C.S. Lewis approached the heart of the matter when, after reading part of Tolkien's *Lay of Leithian*, he wrote to him on 7 December 1929: 'The two things that come out clearly are the sense of reality in the background and the mythical value: the essence of a myth being that it should have no taint of allegory to the maker and yet should suggest incipient allegories to the reader' (quoted in *The Lays of Beleriand*, p. 151). And in a letter to Lucy Matthews about *The Lord of the Rings* he wrote: 'A strict allegory is like a puzzle with a solution: a great romance is like a flower whose smell reminds you of something you can't quite place. I think the something is "the whole *quality* of life as we actually experience it"' (11 September 1958, quoted in *Eglerio! In Praise of Tolkien*, ed. Anne Etkin (1978), p. 43).

Despite Tolkien's statement that he 'cordially dislike[d] allegory in all its manifestations', his stories *Leaf by Niggle and *Smith of Wootton Major seem to include allegorical elements, but it is not clear in either case that Tolkien set out consciously to write an allegory. His accounts of the writing of Leaf by Niggle suggest that it was entirely unplanned: 'I woke up one morning . . . with that odd thing virtually complete in my head. It took only a few hours to get it down, and then copy out. I am not aware of ever "thinking" of the story or composing it in the ordinary sense' (letter to Stanley Unwin, ?18 March 1945, Letters, p. 113). Much later he called the story 'not really or properly an "allegory" so much as "mythical". For Niggle is meant to be a real mixed-quality person and not an "allegory" of any single vice or virtue' (letter to *Jane Neave, 8–9 September 1962, Letters, pp. 320–1). And yet in a draft letter to Peter Hastings in September 1954 he wrote: 'I tried to show allegorically how that [*sub-creation] might come to be taken up into Creation in some plane in my "purgatorial" story Leaf by Niggle' (Letters, p. 195).

In regard to Smith of Wootton Major, as part of prefatory comments to a reading of the story at Blackfriars, Oxford, in October 1966, Tolkien wrote that the story 'is not an allegory – properly so called. Its primary purpose is itself, and any applications it or parts of it may have for individual hearers are incidental. I dislike real allegory in which the application is the author's own and is meant to dominate you. I prefer the freedom of the hearer or reader' (Tolkien Papers, Bodleian Library, Oxford). Probably at the beginning of 1967 he wrote to Clyde S. Kilby that Smith of Wootton Major is 'not an allegory (however applicable to this or that) in intention: certainly not in the "Fay" parts, and only fleetingly in the Human, where evidently The Cook and the Great Hall etc. represent The Parson and Church and their decay' (Marion E. Wade Center, Wheaton College, Wheaton, Illinois). And on 12 December 1967 Tolkien described it as 'an old man's book already weighted with the presage of "bereavement"' (letter to *Roger Lancelyn Green, Letters, p. 389), a statement which has been seized upon by critics who have sought to interpret the work as a personal allegory. Notable among these are T.A. Shippey, who has described Leaf by Niggle and Smith of Wootton Major as 'autobiographical allegories, in which Tolkien commented more or less openly on his own intentions, feelings and career' (J.R.R. Tolkien: Author of the Century (2000), pp. 265–6); and Paul H. Kocher, to whom Leaf by Niggle was 'an apparently simple but actually quite intricate vision of the struggles of an artist to create a fantasy world and of what happens to him and his work after death', and who was tempted to describe Smith of Wootton Major as 'Tolkien's personal farewell to his art' (Master of Middle-earth: The Fiction of J.R.R. Tolkien (1972), pp. 161, 203).

In Keble College Chapel on 23 August 1992, in his sermon delivered at the Tolkien Centenary Conference, *Father Robert Murray remarked that

> the power of stories to act as parables depends not on whether they are fictitious or factually true, but on whether they possess that potential universality which makes others find them applicable, through an imaginative perception of analogy, to other situations.

At this point you will have picked up one of Tolkien's memorable words, 'applicable'. He used it often when discussing the power of stories to suggest more to the reader than they say, without their being artificial allegories. . . . A good story need not have a 'message' yet Tolkien often acknowledged that most great stories, whether as wholes or in many particulars, abound in morally significant features which are applicable to the experience of readers far removed in time and place from the storyteller.

Tolkien had an ambivalent attitude to allegory, often expressing dislike of it; but he 'could not, however, refuse allegory some place, provided it were kept in it. It could serve in an argument; there he was quite prepared to make up allegories and call them such as, he did twice in two pages of his great lecture on Beowulf [*Beowulf: The Monsters and the Critics]' ('Sermon at Thanksgiving Service, Keble College Chapel, 23rd August 1992', Proceedings of the J.R.R. Tolkien Centenary Conference 1992 (1995), p. 18).

See also Tolkien's comments on the character Tom Bombadil relative to allegory, under *The Adventures of Tom Bombadil; and his views in regard to allegory and symbolism in the Middle English *Pearl.

The Alphabet of Rúmil see Writing systems

Aman. Originally the beginning of the introductory text to the *Athrabeth Finrod ah Andreth (c. 1959), Aman was removed from that work to stand alone. Only one manuscript is extant, written with little hesitation or correction. *Christopher Tolkien published it, with notes and commentary, as text XI in the section 'Myths Transformed' in *Morgoth's Ring (1993), pp. 424–31.

In this the Valian Year is redefined, in accordance with cosmogonic changes Tolkien contemplated making to the *'Silmarillion' in later life: it is no longer based on the waxing and waning of the Two Trees, but on the Valar's perception of the slow ageing of Arda. Elves are said to be able to live in Aman, the Blessed Realm of Tolkien's mythology, because their speed of growth was in accord with the slow rate with which other living things aged in Aman. 'For in Aman the world appeared to them as it does to Men on Earth, but without the shadow of death soon to come. Whereas on Earth to them all things in comparison with themselves were fleeting, swift to change and die or pass away, in Aman they endured and did not so soon cheat love with their mortality' (Morgoth's Ring, p. 426). In Middle-earth the Elves' hröar (bodies, singular hröa) weakened or faded, even if very slowly, until only their longeval fëar (spirit, singular fëa) remained, whereas in Aman these aged at the same rate, and 'the Eldar that remained in the Blessed Realm endured in full maturity, and in undimmed power of body and spirit conjoined for ages beyond our mortal comprehension' (p. 427).

Tolkien also considered, under the (later) subheading 'Aman and Mortal Men', what would have happened to a Man if he had been allowed to live in

Aman. The Valar could not alter his nature; he would remain mortal. Even in a life of a hundred years, little would seem to change or age in the land about him. His mortality would thus seem an even greater burden: 'he would become filled with envy, deeming himself a victim of injustice. . . . He would not value what he had, but feeling that he was among the least and most despised of all creatures, he would grow soon to contemn his manhood, and hate those more richly endowed. He would not escape the fear and sorrow of his swift mortality that is his lot upon Earth . . . but would be burdened by it unbearably to the loss of all delight' (p. 428).

Possibly the *hröa* of a man living in Aman might not wither and age, but the nature and doom of his *fëa* could not be changed and it must soon depart. 'The *hröa* being in full vigour and joy of life would cling to the *fëa*, lest its departure should bring death; and against death it would revolt. . . . But the *fëa* would be as it were in prison, becoming ever more weary of all the delights of the *hröa*, until they were loathsome to it, longing ever more and more to be gone. The Man would not be blessed, but accursed' (p. 429).

Ambarkanta: The Shape of the World. List of cosmographical words with explanations, and a description of the world of Tolkien's mythology (*'The Silmarillion') as it stood at the time of writing, published with commentary, notes, three diagrams, and two maps in *The Shaping of Middle-earth* (1986), pp. 235–61. The Earth is said to be globed within the Ilurambar, the transparent Walls of the World, impassable except by the Door of Night. On all sides of the Earth is Vaiya, the Enfolding Ocean – the seas and air – of which the Air is of two kinds, *Vista* which 'sustains birds and clouds' and *Ilmen* 'breathed by the Gods, and purified by the passage of the luminaries; for in Ilmen [the Vala] Varda ordained the courses of the stars, and later of the Moon and Sun' (*The Shaping of Middle-earth*, p. 236). Vaiya, Vista, and Ilmen are further defined in relation to Valinor and Middle-earth, and to the movements of the Sun and Moon. The creation of Valinor and the shaping of Middle-earth by the Valar are recounted; 'but the symmetry of the ancient Earth was changed and broken in the first Battle of the Gods . . . and the Earth was again broken in the second battle . . . and it has changed ever in the wearing and passing of many ages' (pp. 239–40).

When editing the *Ambarkanta* for *The Shaping of Middle-earth* *Christopher Tolkien believed that it belonged with his father's writings of the early 1930s. Later, however, he realized that it dated instead from the mid-1930s, following the 'later Annals' but preceding *The Fall of Númenor*; see *The Lost Road and Other Writings*, pp. 9, 108.

At the beginning of the six manuscript pages of the text is an alternate title, *Of the Fashion of the World*; the title *Ambarkanta* (Qenya *ambar* 'Earth' + *kanta* 'shape') and a subtitle, *The Shape of the World*, are given on a separate but related title-leaf. Two of the three diagrams accompanying the text are labelled 'The World from Númen (West) to Rómen (East)' and 'The World from Formen (North) to Harmen (South)'. The third, 'The World after the

Cataclysm and the ruin of the Númenóreans', is related to three sentences added by Tolkien to the original text of the *Ambarkanta*, which ended with the final words quoted above: these refer to the re-shaping of the world that occurred at the end of the Second Age, when the Númenóreans sailed West against the ban of the Valar: 'But the greatest change took place, when the First Design was destroyed, and the Earth was rounded, and severed from Valinor' (p. 240). Christopher Tolkien feels that this addition could date from 'much later; but . . . is far more likely to be contemporary, since the story of Númenor arose about this time' (*The Shaping of Middle-earth*, p. 261). The third diagram, twice marked with 'the Straight Path' (by which the Elves may seek Valinor, while mortals may follow only the curvature of the earth), seems to belong to the same period; a precursor, 'a very rough and hasty sketch, which shows a central globe . . . with two circles around it' in which 'a straight line' extends 'to the outer circle in both directions', is described in *The Lost Road and Other Writings*, p. 11.

The two related maps are inscribed 'The World about V[alian] Y[ear] 500 after the fall of the Lamps . . . and the first fortification of the North by Melko' and 'After the War of the Gods (Arvalin was cast up by the Great Sea at the foot of the Mts.' (*sic*, lacking a closing parenthesis).

Amroth and Nimrodel
see *Part of the Legend of Amroth and Nimrodel Recounted in Brief*

'Analysis of fragments of other languages found in *The Lord of the Rings*'.
Manuscript described in similar words by *Christopher Tolkien in *Morgoth's Ring* (1993), p. 387. In *The War of the Ring* (1990) he notes that after the publication of *The Lord of the Rings* 'my father began on an analysis of all fragments of other languages (Quenya, Sindarin, Khuzdul, the Black Speech) found in the book, but unhappily before he reached the end of [*The Fellowship of the Ring*] the notes, at the outset full and elaborate, had diminished to largely uninterpretable jottings' (p. 20; see *Languages, Invented). Christopher Tolkien quotes from this analysis several times in *The History of Middle-earth*: in *The Return of the Shadow*, p. 466, referring to Dwarf names associated with Moria; in *The War of the Ring*, p. 20, regarding Gimli's battle-cry; in *Sauron Defeated*, p. 73, regarding Treebeard's farewell to Galadriel and Celeborn; and in *Morgoth's Ring*, pp. 387–8, for a long note concerning the Song to Elbereth in the *Lord of the Rings* chapter 'Many Meetings' (bk. II, ch. 1).

It is possible that Tolkien was inspired to begin this analysis by lists sent to him by the librarian of the Central Lending Library in Scunthorpe, Lincolnshire, which seems to have included a certain amount of linguistic material. In a letter of 9 December 1959 to *Rayner Unwin, who had forwarded the lists to Tolkien, he asks to keep the lists for a while, as he 'should then be able to make them perhaps a little more useful by some corrections in the "tentative vocabulary". I think this is a very remarkable performance, especially considering the very scanty information provided in the book about the languages concerned'

(Tolkien-George Allen & Unwin archive, HarperCollins). And on 9 February 1960 he wrote to Rayner Unwin:

> I did sit down promptly and dutifully to the Scunthorpe lists, but I found that any attempt to correct them or explain them landed me in difficulty and actually revealed many points in the general structure of names etc. I will send them back fairly soon with only minor notes. Time has not been wasted. I have done a great deal of work on the Silmarillion largely as a consequence of thinking about the points raised. [Tolkien-George Allen & Unwin archive, HarperCollins]

Ancrene Riwle. A medieval guide or set of rules for anchoresses (female religious recluses), the *Ancrene Riwle* is the longest and best known of a group of religious prose works written or translated in the thirteenth century in the West Midlands of England, in all of which Tolkien took an interest. Its eight sections prescribe a daily routine of prayers, but also offer practical guidelines for the conduct of life. Written originally in English, it proved so popular that it was translated into French and Latin, and adapted for other audiences. Its language, Tolkien wrote in his preface to the Modern English translation by his former B.Litt. student *M.B. Salu,

> now appears archaic ... and it is also "dialectal" to us whose language is based mainly on the speech of the other side of England, whereas the soil in which it grew was that of the West Midlands and the Marches of Wales. But it was in its day and to its users a natural, easy, and cultivated speech, familiar with the courtesy of letters, able to combine colloquial liveliness with a reverence for the already long tradition of English writing. [*The Ancrene Riwle* (1955), p. v]

Tolkien was concerned with the *Ancrene Riwle* as early as 1920, while teaching at the University of *Leeds, most particularly with the example held at Corpus Christi College, Cambridge (MS CCCC 402), the only surviving manuscript of a revised version of the text (there called *Ancrene Wisse*). His interest was linguistic, as demonstrated in the several references to the *Ancrene Riwle* in his article *Some Contributions to Middle-English Lexicography* in the *Review of English Studies* for April 1925, and as he remarked in *Ancrene Wisse and Hali Meiðhad*, published in *Essays and Studies* in 1929. In November 1930 he wrote to *Kenneth Sisam of Oxford University Press (*Publishers), in regard to a proposed edition of the *Ancrene Riwle*, that he could produce a plain text, with a limited glossary, in a short time, once he completed work on the 'Clarendon Chaucer' (see *Geoffrey Chaucer); but a full text, with a complete glossary and grammar, would better serve the study of Middle English. He already had a set of rotographs (photographic facsimiles) of MS CCCC 402 for private study, and if he did not yet have it in mind to prepare an edition of that text, it seems to have occurred to him at this point.

In the next few years he worked with various students, notably an Oxford B.Litt. candidate, *M.E. (Elaine) Griffiths, to prepare a partial transcription of the Cambridge manuscript, a nearly complete glossary, and an index. He also prepared a complete vocabulary and grammar of 'AB' (a term coined by Tolkien), a variant of Middle English related to MS CCCC 402 and MS Bodley 34 – that is, to the *Ancrene Wisse* and the *Katherine Group. In late 1935 he was formally engaged by the Early English Text Society (EETS, see *Societies and clubs) to edit the *Ancrene Wisse* for publication, as part of a proposed series of editions of *Ancrene Riwle* texts. (For the history that follows, see also **Chronology**, especially entries from Autumn 1935, January 1936, 5 February 1956, and 30 March 1959 *et passim*.)

Almost at once, Tolkien entered into a dispute with the governing committee of the EETS as to whether the various manuscripts in the series should be transcribed line by line, exactly as written in the original text. The Committee argued that this approach was unnecessary and would take up too much space; a uniform page design was more important, for consistency and economy. Tolkien disagreed, in part because his transcription of the Cambridge manuscript, then much advanced, had been made line by line, and the thousands of references already in its glossary and index were keyed to folio and line in the manuscript, not to the typeset pages of the book planned by EETS. To alter these would have meant considerable expense of time and labour. But also, as he pointed out, a printed text which does not reproduce the precise order of its source will not serve a scholar interested in the finer points of the original manuscript. A line-by-line transcription, however, has

enormous advantages – in giving a clue to the relative vertical association of words in corrupt passages, as well as indicating the places where special alterations, paleogr[aphical] forms, omissions and other errors are likely. To this is added the facility of reference in those places where, however careful the present edition, a future worker will inevitably be obliged to collate with the manuscript. [draft letter to A.W. Pollard, *c.* 16 January 1936, Tolkien Papers, Bodleian Library, Oxford]

This argument continued for more than a year, the Secretary of the EETS, *Mabel Day (herself later an editor of one of the *Ancrene Riwle* texts) bearing much of the burden, until in May 1937 a subcommittee devoted to the *Ancrene Riwle*, and in August 1937 the full EETS Committee, their members perhaps weary of the debate (though still not without objection), at last agreed to follow Tolkien's view.

Tolkien hoped to quickly finish his transcription of the *Ancrene Wisse* from the set of rotographs and then collate it against the original manuscript at Cambridge. But he found it difficult to arrange access to the library at Corpus Christi College, and other matters demanded his attention, not least the publication of *The Hobbit* in September 1937. Before long, the Second World War halted many projects, although from 1942 to 1949 work on the *Ancrene Wisse* which had been abandoned by Elaine Griffiths was taken up by M.B. Salu, who completed the index as well as a successful thesis on the grammar and phonology of the text. Salu later made a Modern English translation of MS CCCC 402 which was published as *The Ancrene Riwle* (1955) with a brief preface by Tolkien. In Michaelmas Term 1946, now as the Merton Professor of English Language and Literature officially concerned with Middle English studies at Oxford, Tolkien began to lecture on the *Ancrene Wisse* and its language. In March 1948, faced with serious dental problems, he offered to hand over his still uncollated transcriptions of MS 402 if some other scholar would be willing to complete the edition of *Ancrene Wisse* for the EETS. In the event, he was not replaced, and except for the production of specimen pages in August 1948 no further action seems to have been taken for eight years. One assumes, from lack of evidence to the contrary, that Tolkien was simply left to get on with the work as best he could, though the continuing delay to its completion must have been an embarrassment to him, as he himself had been appointed to the EETS Committee in 1938 and to the *Ancrene Riwle* subcommittee in 1945.

By February 1956 Tolkien's edition of the *Ancrene Wisse* became the concern of *R.W. Burchfield, who had succeeded Mabel Day as EETS Secretary. At that time he was also officially a D.Phil. candidate under Tolkien's supervision, and the two were on friendly terms. At Tolkien's suggestion the EETS approached Oxford palaeographer *N.R. Ker to write an introduction to the *Ancrene Wisse*, while Tolkien himself was to aim to deliver his finished transcription by Michaelmas Term that year. Apart from other demands on his time, however, there was still too much work to be done on the manuscript in Cambridge to complete it by autumn, and arthritis had begun to make it hard for him to type or use a pen. In May 1957 Burchfield became concerned that several of the EETS editions of the *Ancrene Riwle* were delayed, not only Tolkien's, and suggested that deadlines be imposed. On 31 March 1958, at a meeting which Tolkien did not attend, the EETS Committee voted to require him to deliver his book by the end of the following June, or the Society would issue a straightforward facsimile of the Cambridge manuscript rather than his transcription. Spurred on by this decision, Tolkien devoted more concentrated attention to the task, in particular during the month of August 1958, though even so he did not deliver a typescript to the EETS until September of that year.

When acknowledging receipt of the book R.W. Burchfield now unfortunately took the opportunity to express his personal view, which he suggested would be held also by other officials in the EETS, that the *Ancrene Wisse* should be printed in the same style as the other editions of the *Ancrene Riwle* already issued by the Society, not in a line by line transcription. He carefully laid out his reasons, which had much to do with consistency and aesthetics, but apparently was unaware of the heated debate that had occurred long before he had become Secretary, or that it had been agreed twenty years earlier that the *Ancrene Wisse*, at least, should appear as its editor wished.

Tolkien replied to Burchfield at once and at length, evidently in more than one letter. A draft of what was surely the longest of these, accompanying three pages of comments on printer's specimen pages, contains a mass of detail and close argument, as well as calculations of spacing and lines per page, accompanied by fabrications of typeset pages made by Tolkien with his typewriter to illustrate his points. Although the finished version of his letter seems not to be extant, and typically in correspondence Tolkien restrained his final remarks having vented his feelings in draft, it is clear from comments that he and Burchfield later made, and from the effect of the document, that his argument was strongly worded, eloquent, and logical. He pointed out, *inter alia*, that the manuscripts of the *Ancrene Riwle* were inconsistent by nature; that the aesthetics of a printed text were in the eye of the beholder (for his part, he found much that was unattractive in the versions of the *Ancrene Riwle* published by the EETS thus far); and that contrary to Burchfield's view that line-end features of the manuscript could be dealt with in an introduction,

> the place of the line-ending is an important feature, palaeographical, textual, *and* linguistic, at least as important as other features carefully attended to. In any case I think it would be an advantage to have at least one version presented in a form bearing a closer relation to the manuscript arrangements; and the specially important and beautiful MS A [MS CCCC 402, the chief English manuscript of the *Ancrene Riwle*] seems a reasonable choice. [Tolkien Papers, Bodleian Library, Oxford]

On 27 September Burchfield gracefully withdrew his opposition and renewed the support of the EETS Committee for Tolkien's views.

On 22 March 1959 Burchfield informed Tolkien that his introduction to the *Ancrene Wisse* was now wanted by 28 May. It was not a good moment: Tolkien had recently had an operation for appendicitis, and his wife was also ill. Proofs of the text were now expected in June or July; but then the printers went on strike, and proofs did not reach Tolkien until a year later, in early June of 1960, by which time he was again occupied with other things. His introduction still was not ready on 24 June 1960, and when visited by his colleague *Norman Davis, now the Director of the EETS, Tolkien declared himself unable to complete it, and that he would give Davis his notes, to be passed on to N.R. Ker to use if he wished. Tolkien felt himself too unwell also to correct proof; but then he suddenly rallied. As he wrote to Rayner Unwin:

> I am in fact utterly stuck – lost in a bottomless bog. . . . The crimes of omission that I committed in order to complete the [*Lord of the Rings*] are being avenged. The chief is the *Ancrene Riwle*. My edition of the prime [manuscript] should have been completed *many years* ago! I did at least try to clear it out of the way before retirement, and by a vast effort sent in the text in Sept. *1958*. But then one of the misfortunes that attend on delay occurred; and my [manuscript] disappeared into the confusion of the Printing Strike. The proofs actually arrived at the beginning

of *this* June, when I was in full tide of composition for the *Silmarillion*, and had lost the threads of the M[iddle] E[nglish] work. I stalled for a while, but I am now under extreme pressure: 10 hours hard per diem day after day, trying to induce order into a set of confused and desperately tricky proofs, and notes. And then I have to write an introduction. [31 July 1960, *Letters*, pp. 301–2]

He sent Burchfield the corrected proofs at last at the end of August.

On 11 October 1960 Burchfield sent Tolkien an introduction on palaeo-graphical aspects of MS CCCC 402 that N.R. Ker had completed. One month later, Norman Davis lunched with Tolkien, and having judged that there was no prospect of anything further from him for the introduction, gave permission that this could now go to press. But Tolkien had merely been distracted by other business, and replied with six pages of comments on Ker's text early in the new year; these were accommodated, though the introduction was already set in type. Tolkien now also decided to write a supplementary introduction, which in the event became only a preface. During 1961 he made further comments on what Ker had written, correcting a serious error, and he proceeded to revise proofs under pressure of reminders from Burchfield. His progress was slowed by fibrositis and arthritis, but also by the unexpected discovery of editorial alterations, largely to do with capitalization, that Ker had made to the transcription of the Cambridge manuscript before it was set in type. When Tolkien finally delivered corrected proofs on 23 January 1962 he objected strongly to these changes, which had been made without his knowledge or consent. Burchfield defended Ker's actions, which had been done without consulting the editor for lack of time, but agreed that the finished book should follow Tolkien's instructions.

Because there had been so many delays already, Tolkien was not shown the final proofs as further revised. He was not to know also that the Early English Text Society wished to have the *Ancrene Wisse* in print in 1962 (it was published officially in December of that year) to coincide with the publication by George Allen & Unwin of a *Festschrift* in Tolkien's honour (**English and Medieval Studies Presented to J.R.R. Tolkien on the Occasion of His Seventieth Birthday*), a mark of the esteem with which he was held by his colleagues. Burchfield himself was a contributor.

Reviewers of Tolkien's *Ancrene Wisse* uniformly welcomed its appearance and noted its long gestation. It was greeted, however, with disagreement over its methods and manner of presentation, notably its retention of original line-endings, and some small errors were pointed out. Arne Zettersten in *English Studies* 47 (1966) noted 'a certain change or even improvement in editorial matters' relative to earlier editions of *Ancrene Riwle* texts published by the EETS (p. 291).

A useful introduction to the *Ancrene Riwle* and related texts is *Medieval English Prose for Women: Selections from the Katherine Group and Ancrene Wisse*, ed. Bella Millett and Jocelyn Wogan-Browne (rev. edn. 1992). See also

Arne Zettersten, 'The AB Language Lives', *The Lord of the Rings, 1954–2004: Scholarship in Honor of Richard E. Blackwelder* (2006).

Ancrene Wisse *see* **Ancrene Riwle**

Ancrene Wisse and Hali Meiðhad. Essay, published in *Essays and Studies by Members of the English Association* 14 (1929). Tolkien argues that the language of the *Ancrene Wisse* (Corpus Christi College, Cambridge MS 402, see **Ancrene Riwle*) is 'either a faithful transcript of some actual dialect of nearly unmixed descent [from Old English, unadulterated by the effects of the Norman conquest], or a "standard" language based on one' (p. 106). It is self-consistent and individual, and 'identical, even down to minute and therefore significant details, with the language of MS. Bodley 34' (p. 107) which contains the texts of the **Katherine Group, Hali Meiðhad* (an appreciation of 'holy maidenhood' or virginity) among them. Tolkien theorizes that 'the (English) originals of these works were in [a common] language ([which Tolkien called] AB), they both belonged to nearly the same time, one not far removed from that of the actual manuscripts' under consideration, 'and they both belonged to the same (small) area)', which he localizes to Herefordshire (p. 114). To support his argument, he intended to provide 'a sample of a minute comparison' of the texts, but this proved 'impossible of satisfactory accomplishment within a very little space'; instead he analyzes the manuscripts in regard to their treatment of 'the verbs belonging to the 3rd or "regular" weak class, descended from O[ld] E[nglish] verbs with infinitive in -*ian*, or conjugated on this model' (p. 117).

This essay may be a development of one Tolkien listed as forthcoming in his application for the Rawlinson and Bosworth Professorship of Anglo-Saxon at Oxford (June 1925), *The Second Weak Conjugation in the Ancren Riwle and the Katherine-Group*.

Annals of Aman *see* **Annals of Valinor**

Annals of Beleriand. The *Annals of Beleriand* exist in three versions. The first two, the 'earliest' *Annals* from the early 1930s, published with commentary and notes in **The Shaping of Middle-earth* (1986), pp. 294–341, and the 'later' *Annals* from the mid-1930s, published with commentary in **The Lost Road and Other Writings* (1987), pp. 124–54, chronicle events in Tolkien's mythology (**The Silmarillion*) east of the Sea from the first appearance of the Sun and Moon to the end of the First Age. The *Grey Annals* from *c.* 1951, published with commentary and notes in **The War of the Jewels* (1994), pp. 3–170, include events which happened in Middle-earth before the appearance of the Sun and Moon until the release of Húrin, at which point Tolkien left the manuscript unfinished.

In the internal context of the mythology the *Annals of Beleriand* (and the **Annals of Valinor*) 'were written by Pengolod the Wise of Gondolin, before its fall, and after at Sirion's Haven, and at Tavrobel in Tol Eressëa after his return unto the West, and there seen and translated by Eriol of Leithien, that is Ælfwine of the Angelcynn' (*The Shaping of Middle-earth*, p. 263); while the *Grey Annals* 'were made by the Sindar, the Grey Elves of Doriath and the Havens, and enlarged from the records and memories of the remnant of the Noldor of Nargothrond and Gondolin at the Mouths of the Sirion, whence they were brought back into the West' (*The War of the Jewels*, p. 5).

*Christopher Tolkien has speculated that his father's 'primary intention' in writing the 'earliest' *Annals of Beleriand* 'was the consolidation of the historical structure in its internal relations and chronology – the *Annals* began, perhaps, in parallel with the *Quenta* [*Quenta Noldorinwa*] as a convenient way of driving abreast, and keeping track of, the different elements in the ever more complex narrative web' of 'The Silmarillion' (*The Shaping of Middle-earth*, p. 294). The first manuscript of the 'earliest' *Annals* was apparently written at speed, much of it in a staccato style, then heavily emended, with many changes to the dates. At this stage the First Age lasted 250 years. Tolkien began a second text as a fair copy of the first, but this soon became a new work, with the Siege of Angband extended by a hundred years. This text was left unfinished, as was another version, in Old English, attributed to Ælfwine or Eriol, which corresponds in part to each of the other two texts but breaks off in mid-sentence just as the Siege of Angband begins.

Closely associated with the 'earliest' *Annals* are a series of genealogies of the Elven princes, of the Three Houses of the Fathers of Men, and of the Houses of the Eastern Men, together with a table of the divisions of the Quendi and a list of the many names by which the three divisions of the Elves were known; and a list of all the names in Tolkien's works concerned with the legends of the Elder Days. These were described in *The Lost Road and Other Writings*, pp. 403–4.

The 'later' *Annals of Beleriand* are 'not only fuller in matter but also more finished in manner': they were now 'becoming an independent work' though 'still annalistic, retaining the introductory *Here* of the year-entries (derived from the *Anglo-Saxon Chronicle*), and lacking connection of motive between events' (Christopher Tolkien, *The Lost Road and Other Writings*, p. 124). It is clear from various title-pages produced by Tolkien that he intended the *Annals of Beleriand* to be included in any published 'Silmarillion' following the *Quenta Silmarillion* (begun mid-1930s) and the *Annals of Valinor* (early and mid-1930s). The 'later' *Annals of Beleriand* are in a clear manuscript which Tolkien later emended, notably during the writing of the *Quenta Silmarillion* when he further extended the length of the First Age.

Tolkien began work on the *Grey Annals* by extensively revising the manuscript of the 'later' *Annals of Beleriand*, then writing a fuller version on the blank versos of the manuscript and some loose sheets. Before he had proceeded very far with this he began a new manuscript version, with the title *The Annals of Beleriand or the Grey Annals*. Although Tolkien never finished the *Grey Annals*, writing little beyond the death of Túrin, it is still a work of considerable length and substance: as in the contemporary *Annals of Aman* (see *Annals of Valinor*), here the annalistic form almost gives way to a 'fully fledged narrative' (Christopher Tolkien, *Morgoth's Ring*, p. 192). Indeed, Christopher Tolkien considered that 'for the structure of the history of Beleriand the *Grey Annals* constitutes the primary text', and he used 'much of the latter part . . . in the published *Silmarillion* with little change' (*The War of the Jewels*, p. 4).

Tolkien introduced a lengthy excursus on the languages of Beleriand into the first text of the *Grey Annals*, partially rewrote it for a second text, then replaced most of the latter and introduced a new conception.

For the part played by the *Annals* in the evolution of Tolkien's mythology, see entries for the separate chapters of *The Silmarillion*.

Annals of Valinor. The *Annals of Valinor* chronicle events in Tolkien's mythology (*The Silmarillion*) from the arrival of the Valar in Arda until the raising of the Sun and the Moon. They exist in three versions: the 'earliest' *Annals* from the early 1930s, published with commentary and notes in *The Shaping of Middle-earth* (1986), pp. 262–93; the 'later' *Annals* from the mid-1930s, published with commentary in *The Lost Road and Other Writings* (1987), pp. 109–23; and the *Annals of Aman* from c. 1951, published with commentary and notes in *Morgoth's Ring* (1993), pp. 47–138. Tolkien emended his manuscript of the 'earliest' *Annals* in at least two stages, with many changes of date and some additions. He also wrote four Old English versions of the *Annals of Valinor*, supposedly translations from the Elvish (*Languages, Invented) made by Ælfwine, of varying length and completeness. One may have preceded the Modern English version; another is unlikely to be earlier than c. 1937, and is written in a different form of Old English, that of ninth-century Mercia, used in glosses on the Vespasian Psalter (on which Tolkien lectured almost every year from 1932 to 1938).

The 'later' *Annals of Valinor* show little development from the 'earliest' *Annals*. The ending of the section written as if by Rúmil is clearly marked. This work was now considered part of 'The Silmarillion', to be placed between the *Quenta Silmarillion* and the *Annals of Beleriand*.

Tolkien began work on the *Annals of Aman* by heavily emending his manuscript of the 'later' *Annals of Valinor*. But before he had proceeded very far, he began a new manuscript, adding much material as he wrote. *Christopher Tolkien has noted that from the birth of Fëanor this new version 'bears no comparison with the cursory ["later" *Annals of Valinor*], and represents a wholly different impulse; indeed, in this section we see the annal form disappearing as a fully-fledged narrative emerges. As was often the case in my father's work, the story took over and expanded whatever restrictions of form he had set for it' (*Morgoth's Ring*, p. 102). Tolkien divided these annals into two sections, beginning a new reckoning with the creation of the Two Trees (Valian Year 3501 = Year 1 of the Trees). He made frequent changes to dates after the creation of the Trees; only the final form has been published. He also began a typescript of the work, making many changes of varying significance, but abandoned it before the awakening of the Elves.

A preamble to the 'earliest' *Annals of Valinor* states that both this work and the *Annals of Beleriand* were written by 'Pengolod the Wise of Gondolin, before its fall, and after at Sirion's Haven, and at Tavrobel in Tol Eressëa after his return unto the West, and there seen and translated by Eriol of Leithien, that is Ælfwine of the Angelcynn' (*The Shaping of Middle-earth*, p. 263); but by an addition, the original authorship of all of the entries up to and including the Doom of Mandos is transferred to Rúmil the Elfsage of Valinor. The preamble in Tolkien's typescript of the *Annals of Aman* gives a different 'provenance' for the work: 'Rúmil made them in the Elder Days, and they were held in memory by the Exiles. Those parts which we learned and remembered were then set down in Númenor before the Shadow fell upon it' (*Morgoth's Ring*, pp. 64–5). A section in the manuscript, 'Of the Beginning of Time and its Reckoning', is said to have been 'drawn from the work of [Eldarin loremaster] Quennar Onótimo' (*Morgoth's Ring*, p. 49); it was later transferred to *The Tale of Years*.

For the part played by the *Annals* in the evolution of Tolkien's mythology, see entries for the separate chapters of *The Silmarillion*.

Appearance. Photographs of Tolkien at school and university – see especially *Biography* and *The Tolkien Family Album* – show a serious young man of medium height, slender, clean-shaven, hair parted in the middle. By 1916, in Army uniform, he had a more conventional haircut and – briefly – a moustache. The image of Tolkien most familiar to his readers, however, is that of the author in his later years. Richard Plotz, who visited Tolkien in 1966, described him as 'a medium-sized man . . . [who] looks much younger than his seventy-four years. Like one of his creations, the Hobbits, he is a bit fat in the stomach . . .' ('J.R.R. Tolkien Talks about the Discovery of Middle-earth, the Origins of Elvish', *Seventeen*, January 1967, p. 92). In a letter of 8 February 1967, to interviewers Charlotte and Denis Plimmer, Tolkien stated that he was not 'tall, or strongly built. I now measure 5 ft 8 1/2, and am slightly built, with notably small hands. For most of my life I have been very thin and underweight. Since my early sixties I have become "tubby". Not unusual in men who took their exercise in games and swimming, when opportunities for these things cease' (*Letters*, p. 373). In 'The Man Who Understands Hobbits' (*Daily Telegraph Magazine*, 22 March 1968) the Plimmers noted that Tolkien had 'grey eyes, firm tanned skin, silvery hair and quick decisive speech' (p. 31).

When Tolkien was a pupil at *King Edward's School, Birmingham there was no uniform except for the school cap; but when he attended a function at the School in 1944 he found that some of his contemporaries remembered him for his taste in coloured socks. As an undergraduate at *Oxford, and later as a professor, he wore the appropriate gown when concerned with academic matters. Richard Plotz noted on his visit in 1966 that Tolkien 'wore a conservative English suit which fitted impeccably' ('J.R.R. Tolkien Talks . . .', p. 92). Clyde S. Kilby, who spent some time with Tolkien in the summer of 1966, noted that he 'was always neatly dressed from necktie to shoes. One of his favorite suits was a herringbone with which he wore a green corduroy vest [waistcoat]. Always there was a vest, and nearly always a sport coat. He did not mind wearing a very broad necktie which in those days was out of style' (*Tolkien and the Silmarillion* (1976), p. 24). He had a particular liking for decorative waistcoats: he told one correspondent that he had 'one or two choice embroidered specimens, which I sometimes wear when required to make a speech, as I find they so fascinate the eyes of the audience that they do not notice if my dentures become a little loose with excitements of rhetoric' (letter to Nancy Smith, 25 December 1963, Special Collections and University Archives, John P. Raynor, S.J., Library, Marquette University).

Interviewers have noted that Tolkien almost clung to his pipe, cradling it in his hand, or speaking with it in his mouth, sometimes making him difficult to understand. One of these, Richard Plotz, wrote that Tolkien 'took out a pipe as he entered his study, and all during the interview he held it clenched in his teeth, lighting and relighting it, talking through it; he never removed it from his mouth for more than five seconds' ('J.R.R. Tolkien Talks . . .', p. 92). See also *Smoking.

An Application for the Rawlinson and Bosworth Professorship of Anglo-Saxon in the University of Oxford by J.R.R. Tolkien, Professor of the English Language in the University of Leeds, June 25, 1925. Pamphlet, twelve pages privately printed for Tolkien, in which he conveys his credentials to the electors for the Rawlinson and Bosworth chair, accompanied by a list of his publications and testimonials by colleagues and university officials: *Lascelles Abercrombie, *Henry Bradley, *L.R. Farnell, *George S. Gordon, Allen Mawer, M.E. Sadler, and *Joseph Wright. Most of Tolkien's statement was printed in *Letters*, pp. 12–13.

Art. Tolkien learned to draw and paint at an early age. Although never more than an amateur artist, with a limited ability to draw the human figure, nonetheless he had a talent for rendering trees, flowers, and mountains; and though he sometimes complained that he could not draw, some of the illustrations he made for his own stories rival in quality the work of professionals.

His earliest art was inspired by places he visited, such as *Berkshire, *Cornwall, and *Lyme Regis, and reflects a concern for accuracy: some of the views and buildings he depicted can still be found today, almost exactly as he drew them. Between about December 1911 and summer 1913, however, while he was a student at the University of *Oxford, he made at least twenty 'visionary' pictures which he later collected into an envelope labelled *Earliest Ishnesses*. Although the derived word *ishness* appears as the final element in only two of the titles of his early drawings (*Undertenishness* and *Grownupishness*, see *Artist and Illustrator*, figs. 34–35), Tolkien applied it to all of his visual depictions of things symbolic and abstract, and later to any picture he drew from his imagination rather than from life. In January 1914 he wrote the title *The*

Book of Ishness on the cover of a sketchbook, in which he continued his series of imaginative drawings. These now included *The Land of Pohja* (*Artist and Illustrator*, fig. 41), related to the **Kalevala*, and pictures such as *Water, Wind and Sand, Tanaqui*, and *The Shores of Faery* (*Artist and Illustrator*, figs. 42–44), which are related to Tolkien's **'Silmarillion'* mythology. From this point painting and drawing became an additional outlet for his burgeoning imagination. Some aspects of his mythology emerged in writing and were then depicted in pencil, ink, and paints; but others began in pictorial form, and only later were put into words.

With the birth of his children Tolkien also used his skills as an artist to complement the stories he now invented for the entertainment of his sons and daughter. For many years he produced annual letters to his children, written, decorated, and illustrated as by Father Christmas and accompanied by facsimile stamps and envelopes from the 'North Pole' (**The 'Father Christmas'* letters). He also illustrated some of his longer stories, such as **Roverandom*, **The Hobbit*, and the picture book **Mr. Bliss*. When *The Hobbit* was accepted for publication, Tolkien convinced George Allen & Unwin (**Publishers*) that it should contain pictures, some based on those already in its 'home manuscript', others made by Tolkien especially for the book, as well as maps, among which *Thror's Map* is a 'facsimile' of an 'antique' map which figures in the story. He also designed the original binding for *The Hobbit*, and a dust-jacket – a decorative stylized landscape of mountains and trees – which is still used on some editions of the book with only minor revisions.

The first edition of *The Hobbit* contained only black and white art; but when colour illustrations were wanted for the American edition, Tolkien produced five paintings in July and August 1937: *The Hill: Hobbiton-across-the Water, Rivendell, Bilbo Woke Up with the Early Sun in His Eyes, Bilbo Comes to the Huts of the Raft-elves*, and *Conversation with Smaug* (*Artist and Illustrator*, figs. 98, 108, 113, 124, 133). These are some of his finest work, produced while Tolkien was 'divided between knowledge of my own inability [to draw] and fear of what American artists (doubtless of admirable skill) might produce', in particular 'the **Disney* studios (for all whose works I have a heartfelt loathing)' (letter to C.A. Furth, 13 May 1937, *Letters*, p. 17).

Despite the success of his *Hobbit* art, Tolkien referred to it almost always with self-effacement: it was 'indifferent', 'defective', 'not very good'. He lacked the time, while pressed with many academic and personal responsibilities, to practise and develop his painting and drawing to the point at which he might feel comfortable exposing it to public view. For his next book, **Farmer Giles of Ham*, he turned to a professional artist, **Pauline Baynes*, whose work he found a perfect complement to his text. After this Baynes became his illustrator of choice. He hoped that she might illustrate **The Lord of the Rings*, but its limited budget made little allowance for art. Tolkien however, while writing *The Lord of the Rings*, made numerous rough sketches and several finished coloured pencil drawings to help him visualize topography and architecture. His painstakingly rendered picture of the Doors of Durin (Book II, Chapter 4) was redrawn by a blockmaker's artist before publication; his even more elaborate 'facsimile' pages of the Dwarves' Book of Mazarbul, with genuine stab holes and burn marks, proved too costly to reproduce; and the three distinct dust-jacket designs he made for *The Lord of the Rings* were set aside in favour of a uniform design for all three volumes, each with Tolkien's Eye of Sauron-Ring inscription motif.

Although Tolkien did not study art as an academic subject, he was aware of styles or movements such as Symbolism and Art nouveau, and had a keen interest in decoration and handicraft. There are few references to the 'fine' arts of painting and sculpture in his writings (*Leaf by Niggle* notably excepted, in which the title character is a painter), but many to decorative art such as carving, weaving, jewellery, and metalwork (see especially *Smith of Wootton Major*), as well as *calligraphy and artistic lettering, in which Tolkien himself was skilled. Throughout his life he was drawn to decoration: most of his later art consists of brightly coloured patterns and devices, drawn purely for enjoyment; and among his papers are several versions of a decorated tree, the 'Tree of Amalion', bearing various shapes of leaves and many flowers. These are visual representations of 'the countless foliage of the Tree of Tales, with which the Forest of Days is carpeted', as Tolkien wrote in his essay *On Fairy-Stories* (*Tree and Leaf*, p. 52), and they are related also to Niggle's painting of a tree in *Leaf by Niggle* which had 'all of its leaves in the same style, and all of them different. . . . It had begun with a leaf caught in the wind, and it became a tree; and the tree grew, sending out innumerable branches, and thrusting out the most fantastic roots' (*Tree and Leaf*, pp. 75–6).

To date the best reproductions of Tolkien's paintings and drawings are those in *J.R.R. Tolkien: Artist and Illustrator* by Wayne G. Hammond and Christina Scull (1995). *Artist and Illustrator* mostly, but not entirely, supersedes *Pictures by J.R.R. Tolkien* (1979; 2nd edn. 1992), a collection of pictures which had appeared in a series of Tolkien calendars, with foreword and notes by Christopher Tolkien. Tolkien's art has been variously exhibited; see: *Catalogue of an Exhibition of Drawings by J.R.R. Tolkien* (1976, for an exhibition held successively at the Ashmolean Museum, Oxford, and the National Book League, London, 1976–7); *Catalogue of an Exhibit of the Manuscripts of JRRT* (Marquette University Library, 1984); *Drawings for 'The Hobbit' by J.R.R. Tolkien* (Bodleian Library, Oxford, 1987); *J.R.R. Tolkien: The Hobbit Drawings, Watercolors, and Manuscripts* (Patrick and Beatrice Haggerty Museum of Art, Marquette University, 1987); and *J.R.R. Tolkien: Life and Legend* (Bodleian Library, 1992).

A list of Tolkien's published art is contained in the **Chronology** volume of the *Companion and Guide*.

See also *Artist and Illustrator*; Priscilla Tolkien, 'My Father the Artist', *Amon Hen* 23 (December 1976); John Ellison, 'Tolkien's Art', *Mallorn* 30 (September 1993); Nancy-Lou Patterson, 'Tree and Leaf: J.R.R. Tolkien and the Visual Image', *English Quarterly* 7, no. 1 (Spring 1974); and *Descriptive Bibliography*, section E. On art inspired by Tolkien's works, see *Illustration.

Arthur and the Matter of Britain. Tolkien enjoyed stories of King Arthur in his childhood reading, and 'hoped that some of the creatures of fairy-story were true. . . . In particular I had a deep longing to see and speak to a Knight of Arthur's Court whom I should have regarded much as Peredur did. But that is a special case; for owing to the accident of the development of Arthurian Legend it was and is presented largely as History. It was not, which is not quite fair' (draft of *On Fairy-Stories*, Tolkien Papers, Bodleian Library, Oxford). Peredur is the protagonist of a Welsh romance, dating at least to the thirteenth century.

In the early 1930s Tolkien began to write a lengthy poem in alliterative verse called *The Fall of Arthur*. He may have been drawn to this subject because it is dealt with in two important Middle English poems: *Le Morte Arthur*, a four-teenth-century work written in a dialect said to belong to the northern border of the West Midlands, a region of particular linguistic interest to Tolkien; and the *Morte Arthure*, a long poem in alliterative verse with much specialized vocabulary, written probably *c.* 1400. Tolkien abandoned *The Fall of Arthur*, however, after 954 lines, though various outlines and drafts survive in addition to the final unfinished text. Humphrey Carpenter comments in *Biography* that in this work 'Tolkien did not touch on the Grail but began an individual rendering of the Morte d'Arthur, in which the king and Gawain go to war in "Saxon lands" but are summoned home by news of Mordred's treachery. . . . It is one of the few pieces of writing in which Tolkien deals explicitly with sexual passion, describing Mordred's unsated lust for Guinever (which is how Tolkien chooses to spell her name). . . .' But here Guinever 'is not the tragic heroine beloved by most Arthurian writers'; rather, she is a 'lady ruthless / fair as fay-woman and fell-minded, / in the world walking for the woe of men' (*Biography*, p. 168). Todd Jensen in 'Tolkien and Arthurian Legend', *Beyond Bree*, November 1988, suggests that this unflattering portrait of Guinever may derive from Layamon's *Brut*, the first account of the Arthurian story in English, written in alliterative verse at the beginning of the thirteenth century.

In ?late 1951 Tolkien explained in a letter to *Milton Waldman that one of the reasons he wrote *'The Silmarillion' was that he

> was from early days grieved by the poverty of my own beloved country: it had no stories of its own (bound up with its tongue and soil), not of the quality that I sought, and found (as an ingredient) in legends of other lands. There was Greek, and Celtic, and Romance, Germanic, Scandinavian and Finnish (which greatly affected me); but nothing English, save impoverished chap-book stuff. Of course there was, and is, all the Arthurian world, but powerful as it is, it is imperfectly naturalized, associated with the soil of Britain but not with English; and it does not replace what I felt to be missing. For one thing its 'faerie' is too lavish, and fantastical, incoherent and repetitive. For another and more important thing: it is involved in, and explicitly contains the Christian religion. [*Letters*, p. 144]

The Arthurian legends are 'associated with the soil of Britain' because they had their origins among the inhabitants of that land, and indeed, that whole body of legend is often referred to as the 'Matter of Britain'. The Romans, who invaded the island in 43 AD, called it 'Britannia', a version of 'Ynys Prydain', the name given it by its native Celtic inhabitants. When the last of the Roman troops were withdrawn in 410 AD the Romano-British peoples tried unsuccessfully to defend themselves against invasion by Germanic tribes, mainly Angles and Saxons, the ancestors of the English, and eventually held out only in western areas such as Wales and Cornwall; many fled across the channel into north-west Gaul and called their new settlement 'Brittany'. Although there is very little contemporary evidence, such as there is suggests that in the late fifth or early sixth century a *dux bellorum* or war-leader arose among the British and, in a series of battles, for a time managed to stem the Saxon advance and even to regain some territory. By the tenth century a body of literature about this leader, now given the name *Arthur*, developed among the remnants of the original British inhabitants in Wales and Brittany, written in the vernacular Welsh or Breton. ('Wales' and 'Welsh' are English names, derived from Germanic *walh*, *wealh*, used to describe speakers of Celtic languages, though as Tolkien points out in **English and Welsh* the same word was used to describe speakers of Latin.) The Arthurian legends arose in part to celebrate the successes, even if temporary, of the native British population against the English.

Those of the legends developed in Brittany were translated or retold in French, and new stories or versions of stories were written, introducing new characters such as Lancelot, changing Arthur's early companions (such as Bedivere, or Bedwyr) into chivalric knights of the Round Table, laying increasing emphasis on the Grail Quest, and sometimes reducing Arthur himself to an ineffectual figure. The Norman invaders who conquered England in 1066 introduced some of these new tales into England, and the Norman rulers tended to identify themselves with Arthur, who had also defeated the English. Thus for Tolkien, who strongly identified himself with **England and the English, the Arthurian legends were not only not themselves English (as opposed to British), but to some extent were identified with the Norman invaders who had had such a devastating effect on English language, traditions, and literature.

Tolkien's objection in his letter to Milton Waldman that the 'faerie' of Arthurian legend was 'too lavish, and fantastical, incoherent and repetitive' was probably directed mainly at the Welsh tales in the fourteenth- to fifteenth-century collection known as the *Mabinogion*. Earlier he had told **Stanley Unwin that he felt for Celtic things 'a certain distaste; largely for their fundamental unreason. They have bright colour, but are like a broken stained glass window reassembled without design. They are in fact "mad"' (16 December 1937, *Letters*, p. 26). In his letter to Waldman he said that while he would like his *legendarium* to have 'the fair elusive quality that some call Celtic (though it is rarely found in genuine, ancient Celtic things)', he also desired a 'tone and quality . . . somewhat cool and clear' (*Letters*, p. 144). As for the important role played by the Christian religion in Arthurian legend, he accepted that it was of major significance in *Sir Gawain and the Green Knight*, and in his W.P. Ker Lecture on that work in 1953 he discussed at length Gawain's conduct as a Christian. He may have felt that in some of the tales of Arthur the Christian content was treated superficially. But his main thought may have been regret that the heroic tales of the pre-Christian Anglo-Saxons are lost, only hinted at in such works as survived the Norman Conquest.

In spite of what Tolkien wrote to Milton Waldman, some critics have discerned influence from or echoes of Arthurian legends in Tolkien's own *legendarium*. The most obvious is the similarity of the wounded Frodo's departure from Middle-earth to Tol Eressëa in the West, at the end of *The Lord of the Rings*, to the departure of Arthur to the Isle of Avalon after the battle of Camlann, to be healed of his wounds. Tolkien himself recognized this in the summary of *The Lord of the Rings* that he sent to Waldman: 'To Bilbo and Frodo the special grace is granted to go with the Elves they loved – an Arthurian ending, in which it is, of course, not made explicit whether this is an "allegory" of death, or a mode of healing and restoration leading to a return' (*Morgoth's Ring*, pp. 365–6). A few years later, in a letter to *Naomi Mitchison, Tolkien was sure that there was no return for Frodo to Middle-earth as a mortal, 'since their "kind" cannot be changed for ever, this is strictly only a temporary reward: a healing and redress of suffering. They cannot abide for ever, and though they cannot return to mortal earth, they can and will "die" – of free will, and leave the world. (In this setting the return of Arthur would be quite impossible, a vain imagining)' (25 September 1954, *Letters*, pp. 198–9).

Various other parallels to or influences of Arthurian legend have been suggested, but many of these, such as the Quest motif, are not unique to the Matter of Britain. In a series of articles in *Beyond Bree* Todd Jensen has considered both similarities and differences between Tolkien's writings and Arthurian legend, noting that many of them may have been unintentional or are derived from a common source. See 'Hobbits at the Round Table: A Comparison of Frodo Baggins to King Arthur' (*Beyond Bree*, September 1988); 'Tolkien and Arthurian Legend' (November 1988); 'The Sons of Fëanor and the Sons of Lot' (July 1992); 'Mordred and Maeglin' (September 1992); 'Merlin and Gandalf' (November 1992); 'Aragorn and Arthur' (January 1993); 'The Historical Arthur' (March 1993); and 'Arthurian Britain and Middle-earth' (April 1993). See also Verlyn Flieger, 'J.R.R. Tolkien and the Matter of Britain', *Mythlore* 23, no. 1, whole no. 87 (Summer/Fall 2000).

Other writers have commented on parallels between the Arthurian wizard Merlin and Tolkien's Gandalf, and have come to different conclusions. Nikolai Tolstoy has said that

> there can be no doubt that the wizard Gandalf of *The Hobbit* (1937) and the trilogy [*sic*, i.e. *The Lord of the Rings*] which follows, is drawn from the Merlin of early legend.

Like Merlin, Gandalf is a magician of infinite wisdom and power; like

Merlin, he has a sense of humour by turns impish and sarcastic; and, like Merlin, he reappears at intervals, seemingly from nowhere, intervening to rescue an imperilled cosmos. Even minor aptitudes are openly appropriated, such as Merlin's propensity for appearing in the incongruous guise of a beggar, and his capacity for launching splendid displays of pyrotechnics. [*The Quest for Merlin* (1985; 1986 edn. cited), p. 40]

Miriam Youngerman Miller, however, concludes 'that Tolkien did not so much employ the model of any one wizard, be it Merlin or Odin, in his invention of Gandalf, but rather patterned his mage according to the characteristics which underlie the archetype of the magician as it developed in ancient Persia (and no doubt before) and as it persists to this day' ('J.R.R. Tolkien's Merlin: An Old Man with a Staff: Gandalf and the Magus Tradition', *The Figure of Merlin in the Nineteenth and Twentieth Centuries* (1989), p. 138).

In 'An Ethnically Cleansed Faery? Tolkien and the Matter of Britain', *Mallorn* 32 (September 1995), David Doughan notes that although Tolkien may have tried to avoid introducing an Arthurian element in his poetry and fiction, nonetheless it 'keeps breaking through', particularly in the influence of Welsh on names, though not necessarily on their meaning. Doughan cites (pp. 23–4) the use in the *Lay of Leithian* of 'Broseliande' (later 'Beleriand'), 'originally "Bro Celiddon" – the land of Caledonia, and the supposed place of one of Arthur's battles'; and, in *The Fall of Númenor*, 'Avallon' as a name for Tol Eressëa (in later versions 'Avallónë', a haven in that island), similar to Arthurian 'Avalon', though Avallon is so called because 'it is hard by Valinor' (*The Lost Road and Other Writings*, p. 24), and Arthurian *Avalon* is related to Welsh *afal* 'apple'.

Characters in *The Notion Club Papers* discuss Arthurian legend, possibly expressing Tolkien's own opinions. One member says:

Of course the pictures presented by legends may be partly symbolical, they may be arranged in designs that compress, expand, foreshorten, combine, and are not at all realistic or photographic, yet they may tell you something true about the Past. And mind you, there are also real details, what are called facts, accidents of land-shape and sea-shape, of individual men and their actions, that are caught up: the grains on which the stories crystallize like snowflakes. There was a man called Arthur at the centre of the cycle.

To which another answers: 'Perhaps! . . . But that doesn't make such things as the Arthurian romances real in the same way as true past events are real.' The first speaker comments that 'history in the sense of a story made up out of the intelligible surviving evidence (which is not necessarily truer to the facts than legend)' is not the same as '"the true story", the real Past' (*Sauron Defeated*, pp. 227–8, 230).

In *Farmer Giles of Ham* (1949), set in a time 'after the days of King Coel maybe, but before Arthur or the Seven Kingdoms of the English' (p. 8), Tolkien parodies and mocks both Arthurian legend and the critics who try to reconstruct its true history. The King in his tale is not at all glorious, and his knights are cowards. The story also contains anachronisms for the period in which it is set, 'though not really worse than all the medieval treatment of Arthurian matter', as Tolkien wrote to Naomi Mitchison (18 December 1949, *Letters*, p. 133).

Athrabeth Finrod ah Andreth. The 'converse of Finrod and Andreth', published in *Morgoth's Ring* (1993), pp. 303–66.

SUMMARY

An introductory section preceding the actual converse states that, though the Elves learned little from Men about their past, they discovered that some Men believed that they were not naturally short-lived, 'but had been made so by the malice of Melkor' (*Morgoth's Ring*, p. 304). The Elves were not certain whether Men meant by this a general result of the Marring of Arda, or a deliberate change in their nature.

Then follows a philosophical debate between the Noldorin Elf Finrod of Nargothrond, and Andreth, a Wise-woman of the House of Bëor. A record of this debate, which took place in the First Age during the long Siege of Angband (*c.* 409), was supposedly preserved in the lore of the Eldar and called in Sindarin *Athrabeth Finrod ah Andreth*. In this Andreth rejects the belief of the Elves that it was through Eru's design, or as a result of the general marring of Arda, that Men are short-lived. She says that some of the Wise among her people preserve a tradition that Men '"were not made for death, nor born ever to die. Death was imposed on us." And behold! the fear of it is with us always . . .' (p. 309). According to their lore, 'we knew that in our beginning we had been born *never to die*. And by that . . . we meant: *born to life everlasting, without any shadow of any end*' (p. 314). Finrod suggests that it is not death, but the fear of it, which comes from Melkor, and says that Elves too have died. Andreth points out that Elves do not die unless slain, and may return to life, while all Men die 'and we go out to no return. Death is an uttermost end, a loss irremediable' (p. 311). Finrod replies that although the Elves may endure as long as Arda, they do not know their fate beyond its end; and if Melkor has been able to change the very nature of Men, and 'that in Eru's despite' (p. 312), then he is far more powerful than the Elves believed. Finrod suggests that only Eru would be able to do such a thing, and asks what Men did to anger him. Andreth is unwilling to reply.

Finrod and Andreth discuss the manner in which the *hröar* (bodies, singular *hröa*) and *fëar* (spirits, singular *fëa*) of Elves and Men differ. This leads Finrod to speculate that Eru's original design for Man was that when his *fëa* departed from Arda it should 'have the power to uplift the *hröa*, as its eternal spouse and companion, into an endurance everlasting beyond Eä, and beyond Time'; and from this he propounds that Men, as 'heirs and fulfillers of all', were intended 'to heal the Marring of Arda, already foreshadowed before their devising; and to do more, as agents of the magnificence of Eru: to enlarge the Music and surpass the Vision of the World' (p. 318). When Finrod asks Andreth if Men have no hope, she says that some believe that 'the One will himself enter into Arda, and heal Men and all the Marring from the beginning to the end' (p. 321). Finrod then comments that only Eru has greater power than Melkor, and 'if He will not relinquish His Work to Melkor, who must else proceed to mastery, then Eru must come in to conquer him' (p. 322). Towards the end, the conversation having turned to the unfulfilled love between Andreth and Finrod's brother, Aegnor, Finrod explains that Aegnor turned away from Andreth not for lack of love, but from foresight that he would soon be slain.

The *Athrabeth* proper is followed by a commentary and lengthy notes, apparently (and unusually) written by Tolkien in his own persona, i.e. not presented as a text or edited text deriving from an 'original' within the *legendarium*. The *Athrabeth* 'is in fact simply part of the portrayal of the imaginary world of the *Silmarillion*, and an example of the kind of thing that enquiring minds on either side, the Elvish or the Human, must have said to one another after they became acquainted' (p. 329). The existence of Elves and the Valar within this world must be accepted as 'fact'. Tolkien outlines Finrod's basic beliefs, derived from 'his created nature; angelic instruction; thought; and experience' (p. 330), and states how these are affected by his conversation with Andreth. Among matters discussed are the Elvish view of the nature of Mankind, the necessary union of *hröa* and *fëa* for incarnates (Elves and Men), and the Elves' thoughts concerning their own fate at the ending of Arda. It is said that Finrod probably guessed that if Eru were to enter Arda he 'would come incarnated in human form' (p. 335), thus hinting at the coming of Christ. The notes, also written in an authorial voice, expand on certain points raised in the commentary, such as the place of 'Arda' (now referring to the solar system, but often used loosely so that the name seems to mean Earth) in 'Eä' (the universe), Elvish traditions of re-incarnation, and so forth, and relate them to the larger *legendarium*.

One of the notes to the commentary explains Andreth's unwillingness to say much about the past history and fall of Men:

> Partly by a kind of loyalty that restrained Men from revealing to the Elves all that they knew about the darkness in their past; partly because she felt unable to make up her own mind about the conflicting human traditions. Longer recensions of the *Athrabeth*, evidently edited under Númenórean influence, make her give, under pressure, a more precise answer. Some are brief, some longer. All agree, however, in making the cause of disaster the acceptance by Men of Melkor as King (or King and God). In one version a complete legend [the *Tale of Adanel*] . . . is given explicitly as a Númenórean tradition. . . . The legend bears certain resemblances to the Númenórean traditions concerning the part played

by Sauron in the downfall of Númenor. But this does not prove that it is entirely a fiction of post-downfall days. It is no doubt mainly derived from actual lore of the People of Marach, quite independent of the *Athrabeth*.

An addition to the note comments: 'Nothing is hereby asserted concerning its "truth" [i.e. the truth of the *Tale of Adanel*], historical or otherwise' (p. 344).

According to the attached *Tale of Adanel*, Men, near the beginning of their history, before any had died, turned away from the Voice which urged them to seek for answers, to the allegiance of a being who offered knowledge and gave many gifts. They revered him and obeyed him when he forbade them to listen to the Voice and ordered them to bow before him as their Master. The Voice then told them that the life it had given them would be shortened, and they began to die and suffer ills. Some rejected the Master but only a few escaped from his followers.

Tolkien also made a glossary or brief index of names and terms appearing in the *Athrabeth*, with definitions and some etymological information; this too was published in *Morgoth's Ring*.

HISTORY

Only part of a preliminary draft (itself probably based on an earlier lost draft) for the manuscript debate of *Athrabeth Finrod ah Andreth* survives. This differs considerably from the finished manuscript. In the draft, much of what Finrod deduces during the conversation is presented as being Mannish tradition. Also, whereas in the final text Finrod asks Andreth what Men did to anger Eru and she refuses to reply, in the draft she gives a brief account similar to the *Tale of Adanel*. Tolkien then made a clear manuscript of the introductory matter and the debate. At some date he detached the beginning of the introduction as a separate text and gave it the title **Aman*, and probably at the same time gave the remaining part of the manuscript the title *Of Death and the Children of Eru, and the Marring of Men*. He later added as another title or subtitle *The Converse of Finrod and Andreth*, an English rendering of Sindarin *Athrabeth Finrod ah Andreth*. Tolkien himself usually referred to the work as simply the *Athrabeth*.

Two separate amanuensis typescripts were made from the manuscript of the debate, except for introductory matter. Tolkien lightly emended these, and himself typed the introduction on the typewriter he used from the beginning of 1959, making some changes. After the amanuensis typescripts had been made, Tolkien drafted the commentary and notes, and made a typescript of these. The text and commentary of the *Athrabeth* were preserved in a folded newspaper of January 1960, inscribed 'Addit. Silmarillion | Athrabeth Finrod ah Andreth | Commentary' and 'Should be last item in an appendix' (to *The Silmarillion*). Christopher Tolkien is inclined to date the work to 1959, following **Laws and Customs among the Eldar* and **The Converse of Manwë and Eru*.

CRITICISM

In the commentary Tolkien says that the *Athrabeth* is

> a conversation, in which many assumptions and steps of thought have to be supplied by the reader. Actually, though it deals with such things as death and the relations of Elves and Men to Time and Arda, and to one another, its real purpose is dramatic: to exhibit the generosity of Finrod's mind, his love and pity for Andreth, and the tragic situations that must arise in the meeting of Elves and Men. . . . For as eventually becomes plain, Andreth had in youth fallen in love with Aegnor, Finrod's brother; and though she knew that he returned her love . . . he had not declared it, but had left her – and she believed that she was rejected as too lowly for an Elf. [p. 335]

But this is not the aspect which makes the greatest impression on most readers. For many the *Athrabeth* is a puzzling and somewhat startling work, in which Tolkien seems to introduce radical changes to some conceptions established in his earlier writings, and writes in more detail about matters either left untold or barely touched on previously.

In earlier writings, Man's mortal nature is considered a gift, not a punishment, little indication is given of Eru's intentions for Man's part in the history of Arda, and the Fall of Man is only hinted at, as having taken place long before Men arrive in Beleriand. In the summary of his *legendarium* that he sent to *Milton Waldman in ?late 1951 Tolkien wrote that 'the Doom (or the Gift) of Man is mortality, freedom from the circles of the world' and 'the first fall of Man . . . nowhere appears – Men do not come on the stage until all that is long past, and there is only a rumour that for a while they fell under the domination of the Enemy and that some repented' (*Letters*, pp. 147–8). In the same letter, he wrote that 'myth and fairy-story must, as all art, reflect and contain in solution elements of moral and religious truth (or error), but not explicit, not in the known form of the primary "real" world'; and he criticized Arthurian legend for explicitly containing the Christian religion (p. 144). In other letters, from 1954, Tolkien said that in his *legendarium* 'Men are essentially mortal and must not try to become "immortal" in the flesh' and that 'Mortality' is 'represented as a special gift of God' to Men and not 'a punishment for a Fall'; and 'Death – the mere shortness of human life-span – is not a punishment for the Fall but a biologically (and therefore also spiritually, since body and spirit are integrated) inherent part of Man's nature' (*Letters*, pp. 189, 205).

Of course, these statements were made in letters not intended for publication, and Tolkien therefore could have introduced any changes or new ideas that he wished into the still unpublished 'Silmarillion'. He would have to take into account, however, the statement made in Appendix A of *The Lord of the Rings* that although the Númenóreans had a longer life, 'they must remain mortal since the Valar were not permitted to take from them the Gift of Men (or the Doom of Men, as it was afterwards called)'. According to a note written on the wrapping in which it was preserved, Tolkien intended, at least at one time, to include the *Athrabeth* and associated commentary in 'The Silmarillion' as the last item in an appendix.

Another note shows that Tolkien hesitated to include an account of the Fall: 'Is it not right to make Andreth refuse to discuss any traditions or legends of the "Fall"? Already it is (if inevitably) too like a parody of Christianity. Any legend of the Fall would make it completely so?' (*Morgoth's Ring*, p. 354). Nonetheless, he included the *Tale of Adanel*. Christopher Tolkien writes that these remarks 'are evidence that [Tolkien] was in some way concerned about these new developments, these new directions, in the underlying "theology" of Arda, or at any rate their so explicit expression', and he saw a 'significant shift' from his father's earlier writings and from comments made in letters (p. 354). But Christopher was unable to interpret exactly what his father meant by them. He wonders if his father was referring to the suggestion that Eru himself would enter Arda, probably in human form: this, he says,

> surely is not parody, nor even parallel, but the extension – if only represented as vision, hope, or prophecy – of the 'theology' of Arda into specifically, and of course centrally, Christian belief; and a manifest challenge to my father's view in his letter of 1951 [to Milton Waldman] on the necessary limitations of the expression of 'moral and religious truth (or error)' in a 'Secondary World'. [p. 356]

Various interpretations have been made of the *Athrabeth* texts, influenced to some extent by how far the reader accepts the truth of what is said and written. In the debate, Finrod and Andreth report Elvish and Mannish traditions and beliefs, and express their own opinions and deductions, but none of these is necessarily actual truth, and even what is said may not (in the context of the invented world) have been correctly transmitted into later Elvish and Mannish tradition. The protagonists and the reader are within Tolkien's secondary world. Although the commentary and notes seem to have a greater authority, coming from the creator of the fiction, they confirm neither Adanel's account of the Fall nor Finrod's deductions concerning Eru's intentions for Man, nor Eru's future entry into Arda, leaving these as possibilities rather than facts.

Verlyn Flieger suggests in 'Whose Myth Is It?' in *Between Faith and Fiction: Tolkien and the Powers of His World* (1998), that Tolkien wrote the *Athrabeth* to explain his statement that death is a gift, because to maintain an inner consistency of reality 'Men had to come to terms with death and question the circumstance of their own mortality'. Tolkien handled 'what was clearly an ethically difficult, theologically risky problem for his sub-created world': he allowed 'the competing voices to speak for themselves, each to make its own case', but 'made sure that none of these competing voices spoke with final authority' (p. 35). He did not include the *Tale of Adanel* in the *Athrabeth*, only as an appendix to his commentary, and presented as lore rather than fact.

Nils Ivar Agøy argues in 'The Fall and Man's Mortality: An Investigation of Some Theological Themes in J.R.R. Tolkien's "Athrabeth Finrod ah Andreth"', also in *Between Faith and Fiction: Tolkien and the Powers of His World* (1998), that in his later writings Tolkien was aiming 'at "consonance" with Catholic theology in more and more contexts' (p. 17). The *Athrabeth* 'may have been intended as a kind of final statement' on Death and the Fall 'in the context of the legendarium, written at a time when the process of adjustment to Catholicism had gone so far that even the Revelation in Christ and the Incarnation were more than hinted at' (p. 18). Agøy notes that 'both Finrod and Andreth take for granted the view, essential in Christianity, that man is both body and soul. They reject the notion that the soul is the "real" human person, using the body only as a temporary habitation. . . . Their insistence that the soul cannot go on without the body is of course sound Catholic doctrine . . .' (p. 19).

Agøy calls attention to Tolkien's statement in a note to the commentary that mortals (such as Frodo) who passed 'oversea' did so by special grace, given 'an opportunity for dying according to the original plan for the unfallen: they went to a state in which they could acquire greater knowledge and peace of mind, and being healed of all hurts both of mind and body, could at last surrender themselves: die of free will, and even of desire, in *estel* [hope]' (*Morgoth's Ring*, p. 341). He points out that this supports the idea of 'an afterlife for humans', and that 'God's [Eru's] "original plan for the unfallen" involved dying' (Agøy, p. 20). He considers that Tolkien in the *Athrabeth* and in various letters is making the point 'that humanity had the wrong attitude towards Death': it is indeed a Gift, and 'accepting and welcoming death, giving up life voluntarily when the time was come, was a sign of "goodness" in Men' (pp. 20–1). As the focus of Tolkien's writings 'shifted more and more from "stories" to working out in detail the philosophical and metaphysical framework in which they existed, explicit Christianity in Roman Catholic form simply could not be avoided. Its presence was a logical consequence of the fact that Tolkien insisted that "Middle-earth is . . . this earth"' (p. 26).

In this regard, one might wonder if, as old age approached and despite his devout adherence to Catholic teaching, Tolkien needed to convince himself that death should not be feared. In the 1968 BBC television documentary *Tolkien in Oxford*, in a discussion of the importance of death in the human story, he quoted Simone de Beauvoir, from the Patrick O'Brian translation of *Une mort très douce*: 'There is no such thing as a natural death: nothing that happens to man is ever natural, since his presence calls the whole world into question. All men must die, but for every man his death is an accident and, even if he knows it and consents to it, an unjustifiable violation.'

In *J.R.R. Tolkien's Sanctifying Myth: Understanding Middle-earth* (2002) Bradley J. Birzer describes the *Athrabeth* as 'possibly Tolkien's most theological and profound writing in the entire legendarium, and it is essential to one's understanding of Tolkien's mythological vision'. On Andreth's statement of men's belief that they are '*born to life everlasting*', Birzer comments that 'she misinterprets it to mean the life of the body' (p. 56).

Maria Kuteeva in '"Old Human", or "The Voice in Our Hearts": J.R.R. Tolkien on the Origin of Language', in *Between Faith and Fiction: Tolkien and the Powers of His World* (1998), describes the *Tale of Adanel* as not only offering 'the most detailed account of the Fall of Man ever written by Tolkien', but also containing 'a fairly explicit account of the origin of human language' (p. 84). Andreth, telling the story, says: 'We understood the Voice in our hearts, though we had no words yet. Then the desire for words woke in us, and we began to make them' (*Morgoth's Ring*, p. 345).

In a comment on the work itself rather than on its theological content, David Bratman thinks that the *Athrabeth* 'stands with the Council of Elrond [*The Lord of the Rings*, Book II, Chapter 2] as one of the great conversations in Tolkien's work, and it certainly contains more dialogue, as opposed to narration, than anything else he wrote about the Elder Days' ('The Literary Value of *The History of Middle-earth*' in *Tolkien's Legendarium: Essays on The History of Middle-earth* (2000), p. 77).

Atlantis. From his youth Tolkien experienced dreams which he came to call his 'Atlantis-haunting' or 'Atlantic complex'.

> This legend or myth or dim memory of some ancient history has always troubled me. In sleep I had the dreadful dream of the ineluctable Wave, either coming out of the quiet sea, or coming in towering over the green inlands. It still occurs occasionally, though now exorcized by writing about it. It always ends by surrender, and I awake gasping out of deep water. I used to draw it or write bad poems about it. [letter to Christopher Bretherton, 16 July 1964, *Letters*, p. 347]

In a letter to W.H. Auden on 7 June 1955 Tolkien wondered if he might have inherited this dream from his parents, since he had then recently discovered that his son Michael, to whom he had never mentioned his own dreams, had similar experiences. At this time, Tolkien did not think that he had had the dream 'since I wrote the "Downfall of Númenor" as the last of the legends of the First and Second Ages', which bears strong similarities to the legend of Atlantis (*Letters*, p. 213; see also *Númenor); but his letter to Bretherton in 1964 suggests that the dream still occasionally recurred.

The story of Atlantis is recounted in two works by Plato (*c.* 429–347 BC), the *Critias* and the *Timaeus*, repeating one that Solon (*d. c.* 560/559 BC) is said to have heard in Egypt, told to him by an Egyptian priest. Thousands of years earlier, Plato says in the *Timaeus*, the powerful island realm of Atlantis was defeated in its attempt to extend its power to Greece and Egypt, 'but afterwards there occurred violent earthquakes and floods; and in a single day and night' Atlantis 'disappeared in the depths of the sea' (Benjamin Jowett translation, in *The Dialogues of Plato*, 1905 edn., vol. 2, p. 521). In the *Critias* Plato describes how Poseidon settled some of his offspring by mortal women on the island of Atlantis, and how the realm prospered and then lost the favour of the gods.

For many generations, as long as the divine nature lasted in them, they were obedient to the laws, and well-affectioned towards the gods, who were their kinsmen; for they possessed true and in every way great spirits, practicing gentleness and wisdom in the various chances of life, and in their intercourse with one another. They despised everything but virtue, not caring for their present state of life, and thinking lightly of the possession of gold and other property, which seemed only a burden to them. . . . But when this divine portion began to fade away in them, and became diluted too often and with too of the mortal admixture, and the human nature got the upper hand, then they, being unable to bear their fortune, became unseemly, and to him who had an eye to see, they began to appear base, and had lost the fairest of their precious gifts; but to those who had no eye to see the true happiness, they still appeared glorious and blessed at the very time when they were filled with unrighteous avarice and power. [Jowett translation, *The Dialogues of Plato*, 1905 edn., vol. 2, p. 607]

The work breaks off as Zeus decides that people of Atlantis must be punished, 'that they might be chastened and improved'.

Tolkien ended early versions of his *'Silmarillion'* mythology with the overthrow of Morgoth at the end the First Age. He said little of the fate of Men after that event, other than that by the judgement of the Valar the Outer Lands (Middle-earth) were to be for Mankind. Then, in 1936 or 1937, he extended his *legendarium* into a Second Age, centred on a new version of the Atlantis legend. As he told Christopher Bretherton: 'I began an abortive book of time-travel of which the end was to be the presence of my hero in the drowning of Atlantis. This [land] was to be called *Númenor*, the Land in the West' (16 July 1964, *Letters*, p. 347). Tolkien abandoned his time-travel story, *The Lost Road*, when he had written only part of the Atlantis-Númenor episode, and only a few rough and incoherent notes indicate how he might have continued it. But to provide background for this, he wrote *The Fall of Númenor*, a brief history of the island realm which has more than a few similarities with the story of Atlantis. Given by the Valar to Men as a reward for fighting against Morgoth, *Númenor lay in the West of the Great Sea; and there for nearly two thousand years its people flourished, becoming great mariners. Returning at times to Middle-earth, at first they sought to teach and help lesser men, but in their third millennium they sought instead dominion and tribute. Also they began to fear death, and at last defied a ban imposed by the Valar against sailing west beyond sight of Númenor. Vainly seeking immortality, the king's fleet invaded Valinor in the West, upon which the Valar appealed to a higher power, and Eru (God) changed the shape of the world, destroying Númenor and most of its peoples. (See further, entry for *Númenor.)

In *The Fall of Númenor* (*c.* 1936–7) it is said that

Valinor was sundered from the earth, and a rift appeared in the midst of Belegar [the Sea] ... and into this chasm the great seas plunged, and the noise of the falling waters filled all the earth and the smoke of the cataracts rose above the tops of the everlasting mountains. But all the ships of Númenor ... were drawn down into the great abyss and drowned. ...
    But Númenor being nigh upon the East to the great rift was utterly thrown down and overwhelmed in sea, and its glory perished. [*The Lost Road and Other Writings*, pp. 15–16]

In *The Drowning of Anadûnê* (end of 1945–mid-1946) Tolkien added portents warning the last king not to proceed with his invasion plans: 'the land shook under them, and a groaning as of thunder underground was mingled with the roaring of the sea; and smoke appeared upon the top of [Meneltarma, the holy mountain in the centre of Númenor]', and in the destruction of Númenor 'last of all the mounting wave, green and cold and plumed with foam took to its bosom Ar-Zimrahil the Queen' (*Sauron Defeated*, pp. 371, 373). This seems to be the first hint in Tolkien's writings that Meneltarma was volcanic. In the *Akallabêth* (*c.* 1948) the eruption of Meneltarma contributes to the destruction of Númenor: 'Then suddenly fire burst from the Meneltarma, and there came a mighty wind and a tumult of the earth, and the sky reeled, and the hills slid, and Númenor went down into the sea ...' (*The Silmarillion*, p. 279).
    Many of these details in Tolkien's fiction have counterparts in writings of the first half of the twentieth century in which the legend of Atlantis was tied to the history of the eastern Mediterranean. Sir Arthur Evans' excavations in the island of Crete from 1899 to 1945 revealed the existence there in the second millennium BC of a previously unknown civilization which he called 'Minoan', after Minos, king of Crete in Greek legend. Minoan Crete was revealed as a trading and maritime power which had suffered a sudden and unexplained disaster. Later K.T. Frost suggested in two articles that Plato's Atlantis preserved a memory of Minoan Crete and the sudden ending of its glory: 'The Lost Continent', *The Times* (London), 19 February 1909, and 'The Critias and Minoan Crete', *Journal of Hellenic Studies* 33 (1913), both cited in the 'Atlantis' entry in the *Encyclopædia Britannica* (14th edn. 1938). Then in 1939 Spyridon Marinatos put forward the theory that the sudden disaster which so damaged Minoan civilization was the cataclysmic eruption in the middle of the second millennium BC of the volcanic Cycladean island of Thera, north of Crete ('The Volcanic Destruction of Minoan Crete', *Antiquity* 13 (1939)). During the eruption, the greater part of Thera collapsed into the sea, huge tsunamis ravaged nearby Crete, and pumice and other debris covered the ground. From this point it was no great leap to link, as Marinatos did in 1950, the sinking of Thera, the disaster suffered by Minoan civilization, and the story of Atlantis as a reflection of actual events.
    In his 1955 letter to W.H. Auden Tolkien wrote that he had 'bequeathed' his

dream of the Great Wave to Faramir in *The Lord of the Rings*. In that work (Book VI, Chapter 5) Faramir tells Éowyn that the mountain of darkness they see from the walls of Minas Tirith reminds him of '[Númenor] that foundered and of the great dark wave climbing over the green lands and above the hills, and coming on, darkness inescapable'. Tolkien also mentioned to Bretherton that he 'used to draw [the wave] or write bad poems about it' (*Letters*, p. 347), possibly a reference to his poem *The Horns of Ylmir* and the drawing *Water, Wind & Sand* (*Artist and Illustrator*, fig. 42). Otherwise, there are only two drawings which might be connected with the wave among his art preserved in the Bodleian Library, Oxford (*Libraries and archives): one of them, a decorative frieze, was reproduced in *Artist and Illustrator* as fig. 59.

Attacks of Taste. Collection of statements by authors regarding the books they loved as teenagers, compiled and edited by Evelyn B. Byrne and Otto M. Penzler and published by the Gotham Book Mart, New York, in 1971. Tolkien briefly wrote (in a single paragraph) that during his teenage years he was not interested in 'literature' – perhaps forgetting the *Kalevala*, which he read at that time – but mostly in works of science, 'especially botany and astronomy' (p. 43). His 'most treasured volume' was *Flowers of the Field* by C.A. Johns, first published *c.* 1850.

Auden, Wystan Hugh (1907–1973). As an undergraduate at Christ Church, *Oxford, W.H. Auden had a special admiration for Old and Middle English poetry and attended at least one of Tolkien's lectures on *Beowulf*, an 'unforgettable experience': he recalled that 'the voice was the voice of Gandalf', the good wizard in *The Lord of the Rings* (quoted in *Biography*, p. 133). Tolkien later said that Auden possessed an ear for Old English poetry while others were deaf to it. But Auden's scholarship was wanting, and in 1928 he earned only a Third from a panel of examiners that included Tolkien and *David Nichol Smith. He was not interested in literary analysis, but in literature as art, and in whatever could help him become a great poet, a goal he confided to his tutor *Nevill Coghill. Indeed, Auden came to be considered one of the great poets of the twentieth century, as well as a distinguished playwright and critic. In 1939 he moved to the United States, where he lived until almost the end of his life.

Auden long admired Tolkien's *Hobbit*, and enthusiastically welcomed *The Lord of the Rings*. In 1954 he warmly reviewed *The Fellowship of the Ring* for the *New York Times* and the magazine *Encounter*, in 1955 gave a radio talk (which Tolkien disliked) on *The Lord of the Rings* on the BBC Third Programme, and in 1956 reviewed *The Return of the King* for the *New York Times* and the complete *Lord of the Rings* for *Commonweal*. Before writing about *The Return of the King* he sent Tolkien a series of questions and received a lengthy reply (*Letters*, pp. 211–17), the beginning of a long correspondence.

Also in 1956 Auden was elected Professor of Poetry at Oxford for a five-year term. He was required to give only three lectures per year, and usually spent only four weeks out of the year in Oxford. In his inaugural lecture, *Making,*

Knowing and Judging (1956), he described Tolkien as a magnificent reciter of *Beowulf*, and he singled out Old and Middle English poetry among his strongest personal influences. Undergraduates in the audience who objected to the inclusion of Old English in the Oxford syllabus were shocked, but Tolkien was greatly pleased.

In December 1965 Auden gave an impromptu talk at a gathering of the recently formed Tolkien Society of America in New York. According to newspaper reports, he said that Tolkien lived in 'a hideous house', and otherwise made remarks that Tolkien thought 'so fantastically wide of the mark that I should have to enter into a long correspondence in order to correct your notions of me sufficiently for the purpose' (letter to Auden, 8 April 1966, *Letters*, p. 368). Tolkien and his wife felt ridiculed, though he allowed that the press reports (of an account published in the *New Yorker* for 15 January 1966) might have been garbled.

Nor was he pleased to learn that Auden had agreed to collaborate on a book about him for the Wm. B. Eerdmans series *Contemporary Writers in Christian Perspective*, a project that did not proceed in the face of Tolkien's strong disapproval. 'I regard such things as premature impertinences', Tolkien wrote, 'and unless undertaken by an intimate friend, or with consultation of the subject . . . I cannot believe that they have a usefulness to justify the distaste and irritation given to the victim. I wish at any rate that any book could wait until I produce the *Silmarillion' (*Letters*, p. 367; cf. *Biographies). Auden yielded to Tolkien's wishes.

Although Tolkien sometimes disagreed with Auden's assessment of his works, the two remained on friendly terms. Auden sent his books to Tolkien, contributed a poem, 'A Short Ode to a Philologist', to the *Festschrift *English and Medieval Studies Presented to J.R.R. Tolkien on the Occasion of His Seventieth Birthday* (1962), and dedicated to Tolkien the Auden-Paul B. Taylor translation of the *Elder Edda* (1969). Tolkien in turn wrote an alliterative poem in Old and Modern English, **For W.H.A.*, for a special number of the magazine *Shenandoah* (Winter 1967) in honour of Auden. On 25 August 1971 Tolkien wrote to Robert H. Boyer that in recent years Auden's

> support of me and interest in my work has been one of my chief encouragements. He gave me very good reviews, notices and letters from the beginning when it was by no means a popular thing to do. He was, in fact, sneered at for it.
>
> I regard him as one of my great friends although we have so seldom met except through letters and gifts of his work. [*Letters*, p. 411]

Two standard references for Auden's life and works are *W.H. Auden: A Biography* by Humphrey Carpenter (1981) and *W.H. Auden: A Commentary* by John Fuller (1998).

'**Of Aulë and Yavanna**'. The second chapter of the *'Quenta Silmarillion', published in *The Silmarillion* (1977), pp. 43–6.

SUMMARY

Aulë, the great smith of the Valar, is eager to have pupils to whom he can teach his craft. Unwilling to wait until the Elves awake, he secretly fashions the Seven Fathers of the Dwarves. When Ilúvatar (Eru, the One) rebukes him, Aulë is prepared to destroy his creation, but because of his humility Ilúvatar gives the Dwarves life of their own, and Aulë stays his hand. The Dwarves, however, must sleep until the awakening of the Elves, who are to be the Firstborn of the Children of Ilúvatar. When Yavanna, the spouse of Aulë, learns of this, she fears that the Dwarves, and even the Children (Elves and Men), will harm the plants and trees that she loves. From Manwë, chief of the Valar, she seeks protection for what she holds dear, especially the trees: 'Long in the growing, swift shall they be in the felling, and unless they pay toll with fruit upon bough little mourned in their passing. . . . Would that the trees might speak on behalf of all things that have roots, and punish those that wrong them!' (*The Silmarillion*, p. 45).

Manwë has a vision of the Song of Creation, in which he perceives things he had not seen before. Eru speaks to him, saying: 'When the Children awake, then the thought of Yavanna will awake also, and it will summon spirits from afar, and they will go among the *kelvar* [animals, living things that move] and the *olvar* [growing things with roots in the earth], and some will dwell therein, and be held in reverence, and their just anger shall be feared' (p. 46). Some who enter the *kelvar* will become the great Eagles of the Lords of the West and others will walk in the forests as the Shepherds of the Trees (the Ents).

HISTORY

Aulë's creation of the Dwarves first appeared in the 'later' *Annals of Beleriand* of the mid-1930s, as reported by some of the wise in Valinor. But there is no intervention by Ilúvatar, and it is said that the Dwarves have 'no spirit indwelling, as have the Children of the Creator, and they have skill but not art; and they go back into the stone of the mountains of which they were made' (*The Lost Road and Other Writings*, p. 129). An early addition says that some believed 'that Aulë cares for them and that Ilúvatar will accept from him the work of his desire, so that the Dwarves shall not perish' (p. 146). Similar accounts were repeated in the *Lhammas* and the *Quenta Silmarillion*, written soon after the *Annals*.

In the earliest *'Silmarillion' narratives the Dwarves are portrayed as treacherous and unreliable. From the mid-1930s Tolkien began to take a less severe view; in this period he also wrote *The Hobbit*, in which the Dwarves become sympathetic characters as the story progresses. Although *The Hobbit* did not become demonstrably incorporated into the greater *legendarium* until Tolkien began to write *The Lord of the Rings*, nonetheless Thorin's dying words look forward to later writings: 'I go now to the halls of waiting to sit beside my fathers, until the world is renewed' (*The Hobbit*, ch. 18). The *Annals of Aman* (see *Annals of Valinor*), published in *Morgoth's Ring* (1993), and the *Grey Annals* (see *Annals of Beleriand*), published in *The War of the Jewels* (1994), both written c. 1950–1, repeat the original story. But the relevant part of the *Quenta Silmarillion*, as rewritten c. 1951, states that according to the traditions of the Dwarves, Aulë told their Fathers that Ilúvatar had accepted his work and 'will hallow them and give them a place among the Children in the End' (*The War of the Jewels*, p. 204). The Dwarves believed that when they died Aulë gathered them in special halls in Mandos where they practiced their crafts, and that after the Last Battle they would aid him in the re-making of Arda.

Probably towards the end of 1958, and perhaps in response to a query from his correspondent Rhona Beare (see *Letters*, p. 287), Tolkien decided that the story of the Dwarves needed expansion. He tried out various ideas before writing a two-page manuscript, followed by a fair copy, to replace most of the relevant section in the *Quenta Silmarillion*, and making emendations to the rest. This text provides the first part of 'Of Aulë and Yavanna' in *The Silmarillion*, with editorial changes noted in *The War of the Jewels*, p. 210.

The second part of 'Of Aulë and Yavanna', in which 'the Shepherds of the Trees' are mentioned, derives from a text of c. 1958–9 or later. See further, *Of the Ents and the Eagles*.

Barfield, Arthur Owen (1898–1997). Owen Barfield went up to Wadham College, *Oxford in 1919 on a Classical Scholarship. By mid-1921, when he received his B.A. and began work on a B.Litt., he was already a freelance contributor to periodicals such as the *New Statesman*, the *London Mercury*, and *New Age*. His first book was *The Silver Trumpet* (1925), a fairy-story which the Tolkien family enjoyed. This was followed by *History in English Words* (1926), concerning the history of language as the evolution of human consciousness, and *Poetic Diction: A Study in Meaning* (1928), based on his Oxford B.Litt. thesis, which was to have a profound influence on Tolkien.

Barfield had ambitions as a writer, but when at the end of the 1920s he had a family to support and his father needed help in his law practice, he resentfully became a solicitor. This experience, which lasted some three decades, found expression in *This Ever Diverse Pair* (1950, originally as by 'G.A.L. Burgeon'). During this period Barfield also produced *Romanticism Comes of Age* (1944), a collection of literary and philosophical essays first published in periodicals, and his own favourite among his books, *Saving the Appearances: A Study in Idolatry* (1957). Partial retirement in 1959, and full retirement in 1965, gave him greater freedom to write, and in the next twenty years he published many of his best works, including *Worlds Apart* (1963), *Unancestral Voice* (1965), *What Coleridge Thought* (1971), and *History, Guilt and Habit* (1979).

He also worked as an editor and translator, especially of the works of Rudolf Steiner. Most of Barfield's writings were informed by his embrace of

Anthroposophy and his study of Samuel Taylor Coleridge's thoughts on the Imagination.

In a brief note published in 1980 Barfield recalled that he was introduced to Tolkien 'somewhere back in the 'twenties' at dinner at the Eastgate Hotel in Oxford with their mutual friend *C.S. Lewis. 'For some reason Tolkien was in a ridiculously combative mood', for which Lewis afterwards privately apologized. But Barfield felt that the conversation was 'entirely good-humoured and enjoyable; and [Tolkien's] random belligerence had only made me laugh' ('Foreword', *Seven* 1 (March 1980), p. 9). In 1983 Barfield said in an interview that he had not known Tolkien very well, and had never had a conversation of any length alone with him; rather, they tended to meet in company with Lewis. Elsewhere Barfield recalled that he, Lewis, and Tolkien had 'quite a few meetings . . . in Lewis's room [at Magdalen College, Oxford] in the twenties', even before the circle of friends who gathered around Lewis became known as the *Inklings (quoted in G.B. Tennyson, 'Owen Barfield: First and Last Inklings', *The World and I* (April 1990), p. 548).

He came, however, to attend Inklings meetings so rarely, as his home and work were in London rather than Oxford, that he 'began to feel more like a visitor and less like a member. Moreover, since I had to leave early for London after a weekend with Lewis, I was excluded from all those auxiliary, and no doubt exhilarating, Tuesday morning luncheons at the Eagle and Child public house' (quoted in Tennyson, p. 548). He estimated that he attended no more than ten per cent of Inklings gatherings, and regretted that he never heard Tolkien read from *The Lord of the Rings* as it was being written – and yet Tolkien reported to his publisher that 'the audience that has so far followed The Ring, chapter by chapter' included 'a solicitor', by which he surely meant Barfield, among the Inklings (letter to Stanley Unwin, 31 July 1947, *Letters*, p. 122).

Tolkien once said that 'the only philological remark (I think) in *The Hobbit* is on p. 221 (lines 6–7 from end) [of the first edition, 1937; in ch. 12]: an odd mythological way of referring to linguistic philosophy, and a point that will (happily) be missed by any who have not read Barfield (few have) . . .' (letter to C.A. Furth, George Allen & Unwin, 31 August 1937, *Letters*, p. 22). The citation is to the sentence 'There are no words left to express his [Bilbo's] staggerment, since Men changed the language that they learned of elves in the days when all the world was wonderful', and the reference is to Barfield's *Poetic Diction*, whose arguments John D. Rateliff has summarized:

Imagination is as valid a tool as reason for the discovery of truth; the history of language is the history of human consciousness, showing a definite movement towards ever greater self-consciousness; many great poems and ancient texts cannot be properly understood unless we grasp that what looks to us like a word used in many different ways – some metaphorical, some literal – seemed to its author and original audience expressions of a single, unified meaning. For example, since we need different words for *spirit*, *inspiration*, and *respiration*, we miss the full meaning of the old word *spiritus* from which all three of these words and concepts descend. ['Owen Barfield: A Short Reading List', *C.S. Lewis and Owen Barfield: A Souvenir Book for the Centenary Celebration Held . . . by the Mythopoeic Society* (1998), p. 22]

Or, as Humphrey Carpenter has put it, 'in the dawn of language, said Barfield, speakers did not make a distinction between the "literal" and the "metaphorical" but used words in what might be called a "mythological" manner' (*The Inklings*, p. 41).

This idea ran counter to the theory propounded by the philologist Max Müller, who called mythology 'a disease of language'. Tolkien in his essay *On Fairy-Stories* turned Müller's phrase on its head by stating that 'languages . . . are a disease of mythology' (*Tree and Leaf*, p. 24). Not long after the publication of *Poetic Diction*, C.S. Lewis reported that Tolkien had told him that Barfield's 'conception of the ancient semantic unity had modified [Tolkien's] whole outlook and that he was always just going to say something in a lecture when your [Barfield's] conception stopped him in time. "It is one of those things," he said, "that when you've once seen it there are all sorts of things you can never say again"' (quoted in *The Inklings*, p. 42). Verlyn Flieger has written at length of Barfield's influence on Tolkien in her book *Splintered Light: Logos and Language in Tolkien's World* (1983; 2nd edn. 2002). Another treatment of this subject is '"The Language Learned of Elves": Owen Barfield, *The Hobbit* and *The Lord of the Rings*' by Stephen Medcalf, *Seven* 16 (1999).

Convenient collections of Barfield's short writings and of extracts from his books are *A Barfield Sampler*, ed. Jeanne Clayton Hunter and Thomas Kranidas (1993), and *A Barfield Reader*, ed. G.B. Tennyson (Hanover, New Hampshire: Wesleyan University Press/University Press of New England, 1999). *Evolution of Consciousness: Studies in Polarity*, ed. Shirley Sugerman (1976), is an important collection of works in appreciation of Barfield, with a bibliography by G.B. Tennyson.

A photograph of Owen Barfield is reproduced in *The Inklings*, pl. 4a.

Barnsley, Thomas Kenneth (*d.* 1917). T.K. Barnsley, known as 'Tea Cake', was a friend of Tolkien at *King Edward's School, Birmingham. A fellow member of the Debating Society, he was described in the *King Edward's School Chronicle* as 'a loyal upholder of the Society who has never failed to display his unusual fluency (as distinct from argument) and remarkable talent for personalities of amiable virulence' (n.s. 26, no. 187 (June 1911), p. 46). With Tolkien, *G.B. Smith, and *Christopher Wiseman he performed in *The Rivals* as produced by *R.Q. Gilson; and with them too he was a member of the *T.C.B.S., though not in its inner circle. He went on to read History at *Cambridge, where his high spirits and clever wit seem not to have been tempered by the discipline of study. In the First World War he joined the 1st Birmingham Battalion (later known as the 14th Battalion of the Royal Warwickshire Regiment), formed by his father, Lieutenant-Colonel (later Brigadier-General) Sir John Barnsley. In

1915 he transferred to the Coldstream Guards, in which he rose to the rank of Captain. In August 1916 he was buried alive by a trench mortar at Beaumont-Hamel and evacuated to England. He returned to France, and in July 1917 was killed in action near Ypres while consolidating a captured position.

Barnt Green (Worcestershire). After *Mabel Tolkien's death (1904) Ronald and *Hilary Tolkien spent some of their holidays with their *Incledon relatives in Barnt Green, a village south-east of *Birmingham. The area is now developed, and the Incledons' cottage, if it still exists, has not been located. Tolkien was at Barnt Green during the Christmas vacation in 1912, when his play *The Bloodhound, the Chef, and the Suffragette* was performed in the family's seasonal theatricals, and when upon reaching his twenty-first birthday on 3 January 1913 he wrote to Edith Bratt (*Edith Tolkien) proposing marriage. On another visit, in July 1913, he made several paintings and drawings, including *King's Norton from Bilberry Hill*, *Foxglove Year*, and *The Cottage, Barnt Green* (*Artist and Illustrator*, figs. 16–18). In July 1915 while at Barnt Green he worked on an early version of his poem *The Happy Mariners*.

Barrowclough, Sidney. A friend of Tolkien at *King Edward's School, Birmingham, S. Barrowclough was involved in many of the same activities: football, the School library and magazine, the Literary Society, the Debating Society (in which he is said to have had a cold, cynical, elegant style). He was also a fellow member of the *T.C.B.S., though not in its inner circle. In 1913 he went on to Cambridge to read Classics. In the First World War he joined the Royal Field Artillery, in which he rose to the rank of Lieutenant. He fought in the Somme and Salonica, was invalided home in 1916, returned to France in 1917, and due to injuries was placed on Home Service from June 1917 to January 1919.

The Battle of the Eastern Field. Poem, first published in the *King Edward's School Chronicle* n.s. 26, no. 186 (March 1911), pp. 22–6. It was reprinted in *Mallorn* 12 (1978), pp. 24–8. 'A curious fragment' of lofty antique verses which Tolkien, in the guise of 'G.A.B.', pretends to have found in a waste paper basket and deciphered for publication, in fact it is a parodic account of a rugby match and its aftermath: 'Ho, rattles sound your warnote! / Ho, trumpets loudly bray! / The clans will strive and gory writhe / Upon the field to-day.'

The Eastern (Road) Field was the playing grounds for *King Edward's School, Birmingham. References to other local places, and to persons well known to Tolkien and his fellow students, abound in the poem. The verses are interrupted by 'blots' in the supposed copy-text, and by 'editor's comments'. Jessica Yates was first to note that the poem is a parody of 'The Battle of the Lake Regillus' from *The Lays of Ancient Rome* by Thomas Babington Macaulay. 'G.A.B.' may be related to the young Tolkien's sometime schoolboy nickname 'Gabriel'.

The Battles of the Fords of Isen. Late, unfinished piece of 'historical analysis' related to *The Lord of the Rings*, published with notes and commentary in *Unfinished Tales* (1980), pp. 355–73. Written by Tolkien no earlier than 1969, it surveys in retrospect the situation in Rohan prior to the War of the Ring, examines Saruman's aims and strategy, and covers in detail the defending positions taken by the Rohirrim and the actual course of the battles. Associated material, also published in *Unfinished Tales*, gives particulars about the Marshals of the Mark and their duties at the time of the War. It also provides a short history of the Enedwaith beyond Gondor's western boundary at the Isen, and of the Tower of Orthanc in the Ring of Isengard.

Baynes, Pauline Diana (*b.* 1922). Pauline Baynes began to draw pictures for books and periodicals in the 1940s. She had almost no formal art training, but a natural talent for illustration and design. Her earliest published work includes pictures for three books by Victoria Stevenson (1944–50) and her own *Victoria and the Golden Bird* (1948).

On 10 August 1948 she was asked by Ronald Eames, art editor for George Allen & Unwin (*Publishers), to submit specimen illustrations for 'an adult fairy story (complete with dragon and giant!)' requiring 'some historical and topographical (Oxford and Wales) realism' in its setting: Tolkien's *Farmer Giles of Ham* (George Allen & Unwin archive, University of Reading). She replied at once, noting in jest, by way of credentials, that she had sketched in Oxford and picked potatoes in Wales. Around the beginning of October 1948 Tolkien looked at her portfolio and was charmed especially by ink and watercolour cartoons she had drawn after medieval manuscript illuminations, whose character perfectly complemented his mock-medieval story of Farmer Giles. Formally commissioned, Baynes quickly produced more than the required number of drawings. Tolkien found them to be in such perfect accord with his text that he declared: 'they are more than illustrations, they are a collateral theme. I showed them to my friends whose polite comment was that they reduced my text to a commentary on the drawings' (letter to Ronald Eames, 16 March 1949, *Letters*, p. 133).

After *Farmer Giles of Ham* (1949) Baynes was Tolkien's illustrator of choice for his own works. He wanted her to illustrate *The Lord of the Rings*, but its production budget made little allowance for art. Nonetheless, she fulfilled several related commissions for Allen & Unwin. She made a drawing of Aragorn's standard (cf. *The Lord of the Rings*, Book V, Chapter 7) for a newspaper advertisement (October 1955); she painted a triptych view of Middle-earth to cover the slipcase of a deluxe boxed set of *The Lord of the Rings* (1964; parts were reproduced on the cover of the first one-volume paperback, 1968); partly in collaboration with Tolkien, in so far as names were concerned, she drew a poster-map of Middle-earth with figures and scenes from *The Lord of the Rings* (1970); she depicted the scene of the last ship sailing from the Grey Havens (*The Lord of the Rings*, Book VI, Chapter 9) for the British poster edition of *Bilbo's Last Song* (1974); and for the book version of that poem (1990) she illustrated the final chapter of *The Lord of the Rings* in a series of painted vignettes.

In 1961 the first paperback edition of *The Hobbit* was published, with a wraparound cover by Baynes. In that same year she married **Fritz Otto Gasch** (1919–1988), a former German prisoner of war. Together they were good friends with Tolkien and his wife; letters were exchanged, and the Gaschs visited the Tolkiens in Bournemouth.

Late in 1961 Tolkien suggested that Baynes illustrate a selection of his poems. *The Adventures of Tom Bombadil and Other Verses from the Red Book*, first published in 1962, is enlivened by a variety of her pictures. Tolkien objected only to an illustration for *The Hoard* because of the way Baynes drew a knight, and because the dragon in the picture is facing away from the mouth of his cave – a poor position from which to defend his lair.

Baynes also illustrated Tolkien's *Smith of Wootton Major* (1967); she drew a second poster-map, *There and Back Again* (1974), based on *The Hobbit*; she painted new covers for the 1975 and 1976 editions (respectively) of *Smith of Wootton Major* and *Farmer Giles of Ham*; she produced the cover art for a paperback edition (1978) of Tolkien's translations of *Sir Gawain and the Green Knight, Pearl and Sir Orfeo*; she added new art to previous work in the reprint collection *Poems and Stories* (1980); and she contributed a map of the Little Kingdom to the fiftieth anniversary edition of *Farmer Giles of Ham* (1999). A painting made by Baynes in the mid-1970s, intended for a new edition of *Tree and Leaf*, was first published at last in 2003 as insert art for a compact disc recording of *Smith of Wootton Major* and *Leaf by Niggle*.

Art by Pauline Baynes has also appeared in a wide range of books other than those by Tolkien, including *Medieval Tales* by Jennifer Westwood (1967), *The Times Cookery Book* by Katie Stewart (1972), and *A Companion to World Mythology* by Richard Barber (1979). Her illustrations for *A Dictionary of Chivalry* by Grant Uden (1968) won her the coveted Kate Greenaway medal. Her most famous work, however, is her art for the seven volumes of the *Chronicles of Narnia* by Tolkien's friend *C.S. Lewis, first published in 1950–6.

See also Wayne G. Hammond, 'Pauline Baynes', *British Children's Writers, 1914–1960* (1996).

Bedford (Bedfordshire). Tolkien attended a class of instruction at Bedford, a town some fifty miles north of London, for about a month from 19 July 1915 before joining his Army battalion at *Lichfield. 'He was billeted in a house in the town with half a dozen other officers. He learnt to drill a platoon, and attended military lectures. He bought a motor bicycle which he shared with a fellow officer, and when he could get weekend leave he rode over to *Warwick to visit Edith [Bratt, his fiancée; see *Edith Tolkien]' (Humphrey Carpenter, *Biography*, p. 77). While at Bedford he wrote a poem, *Thoughts on Parade*, completed the poem *The Happy Mariners*, and revised another, *The Trumpets of Faerie*.

'Of the Beginning of Days'. The first chapter of the *'Quenta Silmarillion',
published in *The Silmarillion (1977), pp. 35–42.

SUMMARY

The chapter is divided roughly into three sections, concerning early events
in Arda; comments on the greatest of the Valar and their relationship with
the Elves; and the words concerning Elves and Men spoken by Ilúvatar after
the departure of the Ainur who chose to enter Arda. In the first section, the
attempts of the Valar to shape Arda are hindered by Melkor until Tulkas
comes to their aid, and Melkor is driven out of Arda for a time. To give light to
Middle-earth, Aulë builds two great lamps on pillars, one in the north and one
in the south, and in their light many growing things flourish (including trees,
but not flowers), and beasts (but not birds) come forth. The Valar dwell on the
Isle of Almaren in the midmost part where the light of the Lamps meets. There
they rest from their labours and hold a great feast at which Tulkas and Nessa
are wed. While they are thus occupied, Melkor looks down in envy and hatred
on the Spring of Arda. He returns in secret with spirits he has perverted to
his service, and begins to excavate a vast fortress, Utumno, under mountains
in the north. The Valar are unaware of his return until they see the blight of
his hatred on growing things, and beasts turning into monsters. They seek for
his hiding place, but before they find it Melkor throws down the pillars and in
their fall not only are the lamps broken, but the lands and seas rise in upheaval.
Melkor escapes to Utumno, and the Valar need all their strength to restrain
the tumult and save what they can of their labours. Once this is achieved, they
fear to rend the Earth in pursuit of Melkor, since they do not know where the
Children of Ilúvatar are sleeping.

The Isle of Almaren having been destroyed, the Valar establish new dwellings in Aman in the West across the Sea, in Valinor behind the protection of
the mountains of the Pelóri which they raise on the eastern shore. Valinor
becomes even more beautiful than Middle-earth in the Spring of Arda. It is
blessed and holy because the Valar live there. Nothing fades or withers, and
living things suffer no corruption or sickness. When Valinor is full-wrought,
the Valar gather around a green mound which Nienna waters with her tears,
and Yavanna sings into being the Two Trees, Telperion the elder, from whose
flowers fall 'a dew of silver light', and Laurelin from whose clustered flowers
spills 'a golden rain'. Each in turn 'waxed to full and waned again to naught;
and 'twice every day there came a gentle hour of softer light when both trees
were faint and their gold and silver beams were mingled' (p. 38). The Valar
reckon time by this waxing and waning.

In the second section, the Valar, with the exception of Yavanna and Oromë,
give little thought to Middle-earth, which lies in darkness. Then follow
descriptions of Aulë, his spheres of devising and making, and his later friendship with the Noldor; of Manwë, his powers, and his later love of the Vanyar;
and of Ulmo and his music which runs through all the waters of the world.

In the third section, after the Ainur depart to Arda, Ilúvatar declares that the Elves 'shall be the fairest of all earthly creatures, and they shall have and shall conceive and bring forth more beauty than all my Children; and they shall have the greater bliss in this world'. But to Men he gives a different gift: 'that the hearts of Men should seek beyond the world and should find no rest therein; but they should have a virtue to shape their life, amid the powers and chances of the world, beyond the Music of the Ainur, which is as fate to all things else; and of their operation everything should be, in form and deed, completed, and the world fulfilled unto the last and smallest' (pp. 41–2). He knows that Men will often stray, but prophesies that nonetheless all they do will redound to his glory. Elves have a greater love of the Earth and are fated not to die unless slain or wasted in grief, but to live on the Earth until the end of days. If slain, they may in time return. Men are short-lived: they die and 'depart soon whither the Elves know not' (p. 42). The Valar tell the Elves that Men will join in a second Music of the Ainur, but they do not know the fate of the Elves after the World's End.

HISTORY

Much of the content of the first section of this chapter was already present in the earliest version in *The Coming of the Valar and the Building of Valinor* in *The Book of Lost Tales* (c. 1919): there Melko reaches Arda before the other Ainur, causing tumult in the air and sea with his speed, and soon begins to delve for himself a stronghold, Utumna, in the North. There is no mention of where the Ainur dwell in Middle-earth. Melko is brought before the other Ainur but ingratiates himself with most of them, and at the request of Aulë builds two tall pillars on which Aulë places lamps to illuminate the earth, one with silver light, the other with gold. But Melko makes the pillars of ice, so that they melt from the heat of the lamps, which fall to the ground, causing floods and fires. The Ainur take refuge from the floods on an island which Ossë and water spirits draw across the Sea to a land in the west. There they create a secure dwelling place protected by mountains for themselves in the far West, which they call Valinor.

This first version of the creation of the Two Trees was much more elaborate than later texts, and less mythical, involving 'sympathetic magic'. In the pit where Silpion (Telperion) would grow

> they cast three huge pearls ... and a small star ... and they covered it with foams and white mists and thereafter sprinkled lightly earth upon it, but Lórien who loved twilights and flittering shadows, and sweet scents borne upon the evening winds, who is the lord of dreams and imaginings, sat night and whispered swift noiseless words, while his sprites played half-heard tunes beside him like music stealing out into the dark from distant dwellings. [*The Book of Lost Tales, Part One*, p. 71]

Laurelin, not Telperion, is there the elder tree. The chapter also includes lengthy description of the dwellings and mansions that Aulë built for each of the Valar, not carried forward into later texts.

The texts of the 1920s and 1930s are much shorter, and the absence of any element of the story does not necessarily might mean that it had been rejected, but rather merely omitted. In none of these versions is Melko, now usually referred to as *Morgoth*, said to have arrived before the other Valar. The *Sketch of the Mythology* (c. 1926), the *Quenta Noldorinwa* (c. 1930), and the first version of the *Quenta Silmarillion* (begun mid-1930s) do not mention Morgoth as having any part in the making of the pillars, stating only that he overthrew the lamps, which implies physical action. Yet Tolkien evidently had not abandoned the old story, for in both the 'earliest' and 'later' versions of the *Annals of Valinor* (early and mid-1930s) Morgoth is said to have destroyed the lamps by deceit, and in the *Ambarkanta* it is said that 'the pillars were made with deceit, being wrought of ice' (*The Shaping of Middle-earth*, p. 238). The *Sketch of the Mythology* says that when the lamps fall the (unnamed) isle where the Valar live is flooded, but nothing is said of its position. In the *Quenta Noldorinwa* the isle is said to be in the seas.

In the *Sketch of the Mythology* Yavanna 'plants the Two Trees' and 'they grow under her songs' (*The Shaping of Middle-earth*, p. 12). Telperion is described first, suggesting that it may already have become the elder of the Trees; this is specifically stated in the *Quenta Noldorinwa*. A replacement page in the *Quenta Noldorinwa* brings the description of the creation of the Trees closer to its final form, with Yavanna hallowing the mould with her song and Nienna watering the ground with her tears.

The version of the *Ainulindalë* written in 1946 contained a new account, not only of the Creation, but also of early events in Arda. Since the Sun exists from the beginning and provides light to the earth (round, not flat), the episode of the making of the pillars and their overthrow is omitted. Instead there is open strife between Melkor and the other Valar as he tries to corrupt or destroy all that they labour to achieve in fashioning the earth for the coming of Elves and Men. With the help of the newly arrived Tulkas, Melkor is put to flight for a while, but seizing a piece of the earth he creates the moon, and from it keeps watch on the earth below. In versions of the *Ainulindalë* written c. 1949–51 Tolkien reverted to his original conception of a flat world without a sun, but retained some aspects introduced in the round world version. The story now approaches more closely that told in *The Silmarillion*: Morgoth has no part in the making of the Lamps, and the Isle of Almaren is in a great lake in the middle of the earth; but some elements are introduced which do not appear in the published text. Flowers and birds are mentioned as appearing under the light of the Lamps. Melkor makes war on the Valar and throws down the Lamps, and has grown so strong that the Valar can neither overcome him nor take him captive. He escapes and builds a stronghold in the North, Utumno. A similar story is told in the chapter 'Of Valinor and the Two Trees' in the *Quenta Silmarillion* as revised c. 1951. The contemporary *Annals of*

Aman (see **Annals of Valinor*) introduce the account of the Valar resting on Almaren, and the wedding of Tulkas and Nessa.

Christopher Tolkien used material from all three of these closely contemporary texts – the *Ainulindalë*, the *Quenta Silmarillion*, and the *Annals of Aman* – to produce the first section of 'Of the Beginning of Days' in *The Silmarillion*. The beginning was taken mainly from the *Ainulindalë* with some phrases from the *Annals of Aman*; most of p. 36 and part of p. 37 were derived from the *Annals*, with a short section from the *Ainulindalë*; for the section on the establishment of Valinor and of the Two Trees, he drew on both the *Annals* and the *Quenta Silmarillion*.

The second section was drawn mainly from the *Ainulindalë*, *c.* 1949–51, which is a revision of a section of the earlier *Ainulindalë* of the mid-1930s, but Christopher Tolkien also incorporated a few phrases from the *Annals of Aman*.

The third section appeared first in the draft for *The Music of the Ainur* in *The Book of Lost Tales, Part One*. Ilúvatar's statement is generally similar in meaning to that in *The Silmarillion*, but there are subtle differences: the Elves have a deeper knowledge of beauty; and to Men he gives the gift of 'free will and the power of fashioning and designing beyond the original Music of the Ainu [*sic*, the plural form at this stage], that by reason of their operations all things shall in shape and deed be fulfilled, and the world that comes of the music of the Ainu be completed unto the last and smallest' (*The Book of Lost Tales, Part One*, p. 61). Although Men live only a short time in the world, they 'do not perish utterly for ever' (p. 59), and at the world's end will join in the Second Music of the Ainur. The Elves dwell for ever unless slain or wasted by grief, and should they die they are reborn in their children, but their fate after the ending of the world is not known even to the Valar.

In the fair copy that followed, Ilúvatar's gift to Men is worded differently, or perhaps more clearly defined: 'a free virtue whereby within the limits of the powers and substances and chances of the world they might fashion and design their life even beyond the original Music of the Ainur that is as fate to all things else' (p. 59). Similarly the Elves dwell in the world 'until the Great End' rather than 'for ever' (pp. 59, 61).

In the *Ainulindalë* of the mid-1930s Ilúvatar's words reach those in *The Silmarillion*. Though worded differently, the fates of Elves and Men remain the same. The 1946 *Ainulindalë* comments on the deep love of the Elves for the world to which they are bound, and in this text only it is said that Manwë knows the fate of Elves after the end of Arda. In the version of the *Ainulindalë* written *c.* 1949–51 was added, concerning Men, that 'Death is their fate, the gift of Ilúvatar unto them, which as Time wears even the Powers shall envy. But Melkor hath cast his shadow upon it, and confounded it with darkness, and brought forth evil out of good, and fear out of hope' (*Morgoth's Ring*, p. 21). From this version Tolkien then made a fine manuscript incorporating further revisions; it was this text that Christopher Tolkien used for the last part of 'Of the Beginning of Days' in *The Silmarillion*, but removed references to the tale being told by Pengolod, and the statement that Elves who die often return and are reborn in their children, since Tolkien abandoned this idea in his later writings.

In the late 1950s Tolkien again considered a major change in the cosmology of his *legendarium*. Some of his ideas of how this part of the story might be modified were published in 'Myths Transformed' in *Morgoth's Ring*; see especially pp. 375–85.

'Of Beleriand and Its Realms'. The fourteenth chapter of the **Quenta Silmarillion*', published in *The Silmarillion (1977), pp. 118–24. It describes the topography of the North-west of Middle-earth and the peoples that lived there after the Dagor Aglareb (see **'Of the Return of the Noldor'*).

In the development of the **'Silmarillion*' mythology this was a constantly shifting picture as Tolkien altered or added elements, moved places on the map, and changed names. The most significant texts in this sequence are: the **Quenta Noldorinwa* (*c*. 1930) in **The Shaping of Middle-earth*, pp. 103–4, 107–8; the 'earliest' **Annals of Beleriand* (early 1930s) in *The Shaping of Middle-earth*, pp. 296–7, 310, 330–5; the 'later' *Annals of Beleriand* (mid-1930s) in **The Lost Road and Other Writings*, pp. 127–9, 145–6; 'Of Beleriand and its Realms', Chapter 9 in the **Quenta Silmarillion* (mid-1930s–early 1938) in *The Lost Road and Other Writings*, pp. 258–72; and the *Grey Annals* (*c*. 1951, see **Annals of Beleriand*) in **The War of the Jewels*, pp. 38–9, 117. In the rewriting of the *Quenta Silmarillion c*. 1951, original Chapter 9 became Chapter 11, 'Of Beleriand and its Realms', renumbered as Chapter 14 in the amanuensis typescript of *c*. 1958.

'Of Beleriand and Its Realms' in *The Silmarillion* was taken almost entirely from the final version of the *Quenta Silmarillion*, but with a certain amount of editorial reordering. It also includes short passages from the *Grey Annals* and one or two names from **Of Maeglin: Sister-son of Turgon, King of Gondolin*.

Belgium. Tolkien went to Belgium at least four times, on professional business or to visit his colleague and former student *S.R.T.O. (Simonne) d'Ardenne. From 10 to 12 November 1950 he attended the Congrès du LXᵉ anniversaire des sections de Philologie romane et de Philologie germanique at the University of **Liège** as the official representative of the Oxford English School, and spoke on the teaching of philology and literature at *Oxford. After the conference, until 17 November, he stayed with Simonne d'Ardenne at **Solwaster** in the Ardennes, in her family's former hunting lodge. From 10 to 13 September 1951 he was in Liège for the Congrès International de Philologie Moderne, where he delivered a paper, **Middle English 'Losenger'*. On 2 October 1954 he received at the University of Liège an honorary D.Litt. (Doct. en Lettres et Phil.). He was again at Solwaster from 13 to 19 September 1957: on 17 September he wrote to *R.W. Burchfield that 'the rain on these moors and dark forests is continuous. "Water, water everywhere nor any drop to drink" is very applicable, as everything is deluged, but the chalybeate water [impregnated with iron salts] is nearly brick-red: a bath is like being in a dye-vat; to drink is nonsense' (Early English Text Society archive).

Bennett, Henry Stanley (1889–1972). Stanley Bennett was associated with the English School at Cambridge, as undergraduate and teacher, from its earliest days at the end of the First World War. He lectured on medieval subjects and on Shakespeare, was elected a Fellow of Emmanuel College in 1933, and for twenty-five years was its Librarian. His writings include *The Pastons and Their England* (1922), *Life on the English Manor* (1937), *Chaucer and the Fifteenth Century* (1947), and *English Books and Readers* (1952–70). His wife **Joan** (*née* Frankau, 1896–1986) was also at Cambridge, educated at Girton College, a lecturer in English from 1936 to 1964, a specialist in seventeenth-century English literature who also wrote on George Eliot and Virginia Woolf. Tolkien was acquainted with the Bennetts and with their children, whom he amused with his story **Farmer Giles of Ham* when he visited Cambridge in March 1939. In 1954 he corresponded at length with Stanley Bennett to encourage the election of **C.S. Lewis as Professor of Medieval and Renaissance English at Cambridge.

Bennett, Jack Arthur Walter (1911–1981). After reading English at Auckland University College, New Zealand, J.A.W. Bennett arrived at Merton College, **Oxford in 1933 to study philology and medieval literature. He attended Tolkien's lectures, and later would lend his notes on those of 1934–5 to **Alan Bliss for his edition of **Finn and Hengest* (1982). In 1938 Bennett was awarded a D.Phil. for his thesis *The History of Old English and Old Norse Studies in England from the Time of Junius till the End of the Eighteenth Century*, examined by Tolkien and **David Nichol Smith. Also in that year he was elected to a junior research fellowship by Queen's College, Oxford, but could not take it up until after the Second World War. In 1947 he was elected a Fellow at Magdalen College, Oxford, where he took over the teaching of Old and Middle English from **C.S. Lewis, and in the early 1960s was instrumental in the creation of the B.Phil. (later M.Phil.) in English studies. In 1964 he succeeded Lewis as Professor of Medieval and Renaissance Literature at Cambridge.

Bennett wrote widely on Middle English literature, most notably on **Chaucer (*The Parlement of Foules* (1957), *Chaucer at Oxford and at Cambridge* (1974), etc.), and was an editor of medieval and Tudor texts. With **G.V. Smithers he was co-editor of *Early Middle English Verse and Prose* (1966; 2nd edn. 1968). Twice the Oxford University Press considered him a candidate to take over the long-delayed 'Clarendon Chaucer' (see **Geoffrey Chaucer) from Tolkien: in the first instance, Tolkien himself was given another chance to complete the work, and in the second it was decided to delay the Chaucer until Tolkien had retired from his professorship, to avoid embarrassing him.

For many years Bennett was assistant or chief editor of *Medium Ævum*, the journal of the Society for the Study of Mediaeval Languages and Literature (**Societies and clubs). He also served, with Tolkien, on the Council of the

Early English Text Society. He contributed an essay, 'Climates of Opinions' (a history of the word *climate*), to the *Festschrift* **English and Medieval Studies Presented to J.R.R. Tolkien on the Occasion of His Seventieth Birthday* (1962), and another, '*Nosce te ipsum*: Some Medieval Interpretations', to *J.R.R. Tolkien, Scholar and Storyteller: Essays in Memoriam*, ed. *Mary Salu and Robert T. Farrell (1979).

On 15 August 1946 Tolkien brought Bennett to one of the regular Thursday evening meetings of the *Inklings. A week later Bennett showed up on his own, and soon became associated with the group despite initial misgivings by some of its members. *W.H. Lewis recorded in his diary that he found Bennett 'a dull dog' (*Brothers and Friends*, p. 193), and that *Hugo Dyson objected to Bennett because he was a Roman Catholic. In fact, Bennett was not received into the Catholic Church until more than a decade later, though he was inclined towards that faith and especially interested in the history of the liturgy.

Beowulf. The longest and most important surviving Old English poem, the work of a Christian of uncertain date, its earliest extant manuscript dates from around the year 1000. Briefly summarized – to say nothing of its richness as poetry – *Beowulf* concerns the exploits of the eponymous hero, a warrior of the Geats (a tribe of southern Sweden), endowed by God with superhuman strength. With his men he sails to Denmark, where a monster named Grendel is killing the warriors of the king, Hrothgar, in his hall Heorot. Beowulf slays Grendel in terrible combat. When Grendel's mother carries off one of Hrothgar's thanes, Beowulf follows her to the bottom of a lake in the midst of a fen and slays her as well. He then returns home, and after many years becomes king of his people. His fame as a warrior keeps his country free from invasion, and he increases its prosperity and happiness. After fifty years, however, a dragon appears, having been drawn from its hoard by the theft of a cup; although the beast wreaks havoc on the countryside, no warrior dares risk his life to confront it. The aged king takes up his sword and shield and, with the aid only of his retainer Wiglaf (his other companions having fled), defeats the dragon, but at the cost of his own life.

As an undergraduate at *Oxford, Tolkien took classes on *Beowulf* taught by *Kenneth Sisam and attended lectures on the work by *A.S. Napier. While at the University of *Leeds (1920–5), as the Rawlinson and Bosworth Professor of Anglo-Saxon at Oxford (1925–45), and occasionally later at Oxford he himself lectured on *Beowulf* as well as other works in Old English. From one set of his Oxford lectures he derived **Beowulf: The Monsters and the Critics*, a landmark work which he delivered to the British Academy in November 1936. Brief extracts from other lectures by Tolkien on *Beowulf* were published in **The Lost Road and Other Writings* (1987), pp. 93–6. Later thoughts on the poem, relative to the Old English *Battle of Maldon*, appear in the third part ('Ofermod') of his **Homecoming of Beorhtnoth Beorhthelm's Son* (1953).

At Leeds, Tolkien began, but left unfinished, an alliterative verse translation of *Beowulf* into Modern English, and also worked on a prose Modern English translation, which was complete by the end of April 1926; neither, however, was ever finished to his satisfaction. On 25 October 1932 he suggested to R.W. Chapman that his prose translation of *Beowulf* might be published by Oxford University Press (*Publishers), but that it should be preceded by introductory matter on the diction of Old English verse, its metre, and so forth, and include notes concerning particularly difficult problems in the text. Later George Allen & Unwin, publishers of *The Hobbit* and other works by Tolkien, expressed an interest in the translation, but it was never brought to the point of submission. Tolkien included a few lines of his verse translation in his preface to Clark Hall (see below), and others have appeared posthumously, the longest passage to date in *The Lost Road and Other Writings*, pp. 92–3.

Probably early in 1936, Allen & Unwin asked Tolkien if he would be interested in producing a new edition of John R. Clark Hall's Modern English translation (1901, 1911) of *Beowulf* and another work in Old English, the 'Finnesburg Fragment'. Clark Hall's text was ultimately revised by *C.L. Wrenn and published in 1940, with a long preface by Tolkien. His remarks, in two parts ('On Translation and Words' and 'On Metre'), are probably similar in content to the introductory matter Tolkien had earlier suggested should be included with his own Modern English translation. See further, *Prefatory Remarks on Prose Translation of 'Beowulf'.*

In January 1938 Tolkien gave a thirteen-minute talk on *Beowulf* and other Old English poetry in the BBC radio series 'Poetry Will Out'.

Beowulf was also an important influence on his own poetry and prose fiction. Probably at the end of 1922 he wrote the poem *Iumonna Gold Galdre Bewunden*, later revised as *The Hoard*, which was inspired by line 3052 in *Beowulf*, 'the gold of men long ago enmeshed in enchantment'. His unfinished poem *The Fall of Arthur* is in the *Beowulf* metre. In *The Hobbit* Bilbo's theft of a cup from Smaug's hoard in Chapter 12 is indebted to a similar episode in the final part of *Beowulf*, which likewise provokes a dragon's rampage. In February 1938, in reply to a query about his sources for *The Hobbit*, Tolkien wrote that *Beowulf* was among the most valued, 'though it was not consciously present to the mind in the process of writing, in which the episode of the theft [of a cup] arose naturally (and almost inevitably) from the circumstances. It is difficult to think of any other way of conducting the story at that point. I fancy the author of *Beowulf* would say much the same' (letter to *The Observer*, published 20 February 1938, *Letters*, p. 31).

Critics such as Jane Chance (*Tolkien's Art: A Mythology for England*, 1979; 2nd edn. 2001) have suggested other parallels between *The Hobbit* and *Beowulf*, but the major work in this respect is *Beowulf and The Hobbit: Elegy into Fantasy in J.R.R. Tolkien's Creative Technique* by Bonniejean Christensen (Ph.D. dissertation, University of Southern California, 1969; later reductions in article form). *Beowulf* is also often seen as an influence on *The Lord of the Rings*, especially in regard to the men and culture of Rohan and in the heroism of the hobbits; and it was an acknowledged source for the episode concerning

King Sheave in *The Lost Road ('I have been getting a lot of new ideas about Prehistory lately (via Beowulf and other sources of which I may have written) and want to work them into the long shelved time-travel story I began', letter to Christopher Tolkien, 18 December 1944, Letters, p. 105).

In the early 1940s Tolkien wrote a story, Sellic Spell (unpublished), as an attempt to reconstruct the Anglo-Saxon tale that lies behind the folk- or fairy-tale element in Beowulf (here 'Beewolf'). He felt, however, that in many points it was not possible to do so with certainty, and in some points the tale was not quite the same. The 'principal object' of Sellic Spell, Tolkien wrote in a late note, was 'to exhibit the difference of style, tone and atmosphere if the particular heroic or historical is cut out' (Tolkien Papers, Bodleian Library, Oxford). In 1945 Tolkien's friend *Gwyn Jones, Professor of English at the University College of Wales, Aberystwyth, saw Sellic Spell and remarked that it should be prescribed for all university students of Beowulf.

In September 1927 Tolkien painted in The Book of Ishness (*Art) a coiled dragon, inscribed 'hringboga heorte gefysed' (Artist and Illustrator, fig. 48). These words are derived from a passage in Beowulf, 'ða wæs hringbogan heorte gefysed / saecce tó séceanne' ('now was the heart of the coiling beast stirred to come out to fight'). In May 1928, also in The Book of Ishness, Tolkien drew an untitled watercolour sketch of a warrior with spear and shield facing a fire-breathing dragon (Artist and Illustrator, fig. 49); on 1 January 1938 he used this picture in a slide lecture at the University Museum, Oxford to illustrate how the king and his attendant fought the dragon at the end of Beowulf. In July 1928 Tolkien drew two pictures of Grendel's mere, each inscribed 'wudu wyrtum fæst' ('wood clinging by its roots'; Artist and Illustrator, figs. 50, 51).

Books and essays about Beowulf are legion. Among these, the present authors have found the following particularly helpful: A Beowulf Handbook, ed. Robert E. Bjork and John D. Niles (1997); Interpretations of Beowulf: A Critical Anthology, ed. R.D. Fulk (1991); A Critical Companion to Beowulf by Andy Orchard (2003); Beowulf by T.A. Shippey (1978); and Beowulf with the Finnesburg Fragment, ed. C.L. Wrenn, rev. W.F. Bolton (1973). Wrenn's preface to the latter credits Tolkien, together with *R.W. Chambers, with 'what is valuable in my approach to Beowulf' (p. 5). See also references cited in the entry *Beowulf: The Monsters and the Critics.

Beowulf: The Monsters and the Critics. The Sir Israel Gollancz Memorial Lecture for 1936, delivered by Tolkien to the British Academy in London on 25 November 1936, and to a meeting of the Manchester Mediaeval Society on 9 December 1936. It was first published in July 1937 as a separate booklet by Humphrey Milford, London, and in December 1937 within the annual volume of the Proceedings of the British Academy. See further, Descriptive Bibliography A2. It has been reprinted often; citations here are to its appearance in *The Monsters and the Critics and Other Essays (1983), pp. 5–48.

SUMMARY

Tolkien argues that critics of *Beowulf* to 1936 had viewed it 'as a quarry of fact and fancy far more assiduously than it has been studied as a work of art' (p. 5). It had not been considered as a poem, though it is 'in fact so interesting as poetry, in places poetry so powerful, that this quite overshadows the historical content' (p. 7). Nor have critics appreciated the importance to the poem of the monsters that Beowulf defeats: Grendel and the dragon. Quoting, *inter alia*, an influential statement by W.P. Ker that *Beowulf* has a 'radical defect, a disproportion that puts the irrelevances [the monsters] in the centre and the serious things [allusions to history and other stories] on the outer edges' (pp. 10–11), Tolkien remarks that while critics have praised the detail, tone, style, and total effect of *Beowulf*, they have felt that the talent of the *Beowulf*-poet 'has all been squandered on an unprofitable theme: as if Milton had recounted the story of Jack and the Beanstalk in noble verse' (p. 13). 'The high tone, the sense of dignity, alone is evidence in *Beowulf* of the presence of a mind lofty and thoughtful', he writes.

> It is, one would have said, improbable that such a man would write more than three thousand lines (wrought to a high finish) on matter that is really not worth serious attention. . . . Or that he should in the selection of his material, in the choice of what to put forward, what to keep subordinate 'upon the outer edges', have shown a puerile simplicity much below the level of the characters he himself draws in his own poem. [pp. 13–14]

The great critics of *Beowulf* have thought otherwise partly because they have been more concerned with 'research in comparative folk-lore, the objects of which are primarily historical or scientific', and because the allusions contained in *Beowulf* 'have attracted curiosity (antiquarian rather than critical) to their elucidation; and this needs so much study and research that attention has been diverted from the poem as a whole, and from the function of the allusions, as shaped and placed, in the poetic economy of *Beowulf* as it is' (pp. 14–15). Also there is 'a real question of taste . . . a judgement that the heroic or tragic story on a strictly human plane is by nature superior' (p. 15); but one must consider the ancient taste of the audience of the poem as well as the modern taste of its critics.

Beowulf, Tolkien claims, helps us to esteem 'the old heroes: men caught in the chains of circumstance or of their own character, torn between duties equally sacred, dying with their backs to the wall' (p. 17). Its poet has devoted his whole work to the theme of 'defeat inevitable yet unacknowledged . . . and has drawn the struggle in different proportions, so that we may see man at war with the hostile world, and his inevitable overthrow in Time' (p. 18). The monsters of the poem are essential to this, 'fundamentally allied to the underlying ideas of the poem' (p. 19). They are at a point of fusion between the Heroic

Age and Christendom, 'adversaries of God' but still 'mortal denizens of the material world, in it and of it' (p. 20). They are also connected to the theory of courage, for which Tolkien turns to 'the tradition of pagan imagination as it survived in Icelandic', in which men are allied with the Northern gods, able to share in the resistance to Chaos and Unreason, though defeat is inevitable. 'At least in this vision of the final defeat of the humane (and of the divine made in its image), and in the essential hostility of the gods and heroes on the one hand and the monsters on the other, we may suppose that pagan English and Norse imagination agreed' (p. 21). In *Beowulf* both the specifically Christian and the old gods were suppressed, but 'the heroic figures, the men of old . . . remained and still fought on until defeat. For the monsters do not depart, whether the gods go or come. A Christian was (and is) still like his forefathers a mortal hemmed in a hostile world. The monsters remained the enemies of mankind, the infantry of the old war, and became inevitably the enemies of the one God . . .' (p. 22).

Tolkien concludes that *Beowulf* is 'a poem by a learned man writing of old times, who looking back on the heroism and sorrow feels in them something permanent and something symbolical' (p. 25). 'It is essentially a balance, an opposition of ends and beginnings. In its simplest terms it is a contrasted description of two moments in a great life, rising and setting; an elaboration of the ancient and intensely moving contrast between youth and age, first achievement and final death' (p. 28). Tolkien analyzes and praises its structure and the harmony of this with its elements, language, metre, and theme. 'We have . . . in *Beowulf* a method and structure that within the limits of the verse-kind approaches rather to sculpture or painting. It is a composition not a tune' (p. 30).

HISTORY

The Sir Israel Gollancz Memorial Lecture is given biennially. Endowed in 1924, it deals with 'Old English or Early English Language and Literature, or a philological subject connected with the history of English, more particularly during the early periods of the language, or cognate subjects, or some textual study and interpretation'. The subject is left entirely to the chosen scholar, who is nominated by a specialist committee of Fellows of the British Academy, and is sent an invitation to deliver the lecture at least two years in advance of the event. Tolkien therefore would have received an invitation from the British Academy *c.* 1934.

He derived *Beowulf: The Monsters and the Critics* from a longer work, originally entitled *Beowulf with Critics*, later *Beowulf and the Critics*. The latter exists in two manuscripts, the second much enlarged from the first. Both have been transcribed and annotated by Michael D.C. Drout in *Beowulf and the Critics* (2002). Drout dates the two texts, on various grounds, to between August 1932 and 23 October 1935; the first of these dates refers to the composition of a poem by *C.S. Lewis which Tolkien quotes in full. Internal evidence and general prose style clearly mark the work as a series of lectures; and given its subject and presumed *terminus post quem*, its first text seems likely to have been prepared for the lecture series '*Beowulf*: General Criticism' which Tolkien was scheduled to give at *Oxford beginning in Michaelmas Term 1933. (At that time he also gave a series entitled 'The Historical and Legendary Traditions in *Beowulf* and Other Old English Poems', concerned, however, with the background of those works rather than their criticism. The manuscript of these lectures, the first page of which is dated at the time of writing 'October 1933', is preserved in the Bodleian Library, Oxford.) Tolkien produced the second, expanded manuscript of *Beowulf and the Critics* presumably for a later iteration of '*Beowulf*: General Criticism', scheduled again for Michaelmas Term 1934 and 1936. For delivery to the British Academy in November 1936, he revised the second manuscript into a much more concise and polished form; see comments in Drout, introduction to *Beowulf and the Critics* as published, and 'The Rhetorical Evolution of *Beowulf: The Monsters and the Critics*' by Drout in *The Lord of the Rings, 1954–2004: Scholarship in Honor of Richard E. Blackwelder* (2006).

In late 1936 or early 1937 Tolkien sent the text of *Beowulf: The Monsters and the Critics*, with an appendix and notes, to his friend and fellow *Beowulf* scholar *R.W. Chambers. On 2 February 1937 Chambers advised him to make no cuts, and to include the appendix (concerning Grendel's titles, Christian and pagan ideas of praise and judgement as expressed in *Beowulf*, and particular difficulties arising from lines 175–88 of the poem). On 6 February, apparently in reply to a nervous message by Tolkien, Chambers wrote to reassure him that his lecture held together well, and again that it should be printed in its entirety. After its first publication in July 1937, Tolkien received numerous letters of congratulations from his academic colleagues.

CRITICISM

Beowulf: The Monsters and the Critics changed the course of *Beowulf* studies. To quote Michael D.C. Drout, 'while it does not mark the moment that *Beowulf* was first studied as literature (W.P. Ker and R.W. Chambers, among others, had in fact already much advanced that study), it does begin the study of the poem and its workings as legitimate in their own right, as something worth studying to see how it worked rather than simply comparing it (unfavorably) with other literature' (*Beowulf and the Critics*, p. 1). *Kenneth Sisam wrote in his study *The Structure of Beowulf* (1965; corrected 1966) that Tolkien's lecture 'brought fresh ideas and has influenced all later writers' on the poem. 'Knowing well the detailed problems that occupy critics, he has withdrawn from them to give a general view of *Beowulf* as poetry, with a fineness of perception and elegance of expression that are rare in this field' (p. 20). T.A. Shippey has said that 'two of the qualities that made [the lecture] so influential are its aggression and its humour. In one allegory after another, Tolkien presents the poem as Cinderella taken over by a series of domineering fairy godmothers, as a victim of "the jabberwocks of historical and antiquarian research," and as a tower looking out on the sea. . . . The major achievement of Tolkien's essay was to insist on the poem's autonomy and its author's right to create freely, regardless of critical canons' ('Structure and Unity', in *A Beowulf Handbook* (1997), pp. 162–3). Reviews of the published lecture had little to say against it. R.W. Chambers, for instance, wrote in *Modern Language Review* 33, no. 2 (April 1938) that 'towards the study of *Beowulf* as a work of art, Professor Tolkien has made a contribution of the utmost importance.' However, 'instead of weaving them into his discourse' Tolkien 'has hidden away all too many of his good things in appendices and notes' (pp. 272, 273). T.A. Shippey, in a useful brief overview of the critical response to *Beowulf: The Monsters and the Critics*, notes that Tolkien's 'defence of the poem as something existing in its own right . . . was seized on eagerly, even gratefully, by generations of critics' ('Structure and Unity', p. 163). One of these was his former B.Litt. student Joan Blomfield (see *E.O.G. Turville-Petre), who built on his remarks on the structure of *Beowulf* in an essay for the *Review of English Studies* ('The Style and Structure of *Beowulf*', 1938). Another was the Swiss scholar Adrien Bonjour, who in his monograph *The Digressions in Beowulf* (1950) stated unequivocally that he followed Tolkien concerning the general structure of the poem:

> Professor Tolkien's interpretation seems to us indeed by far the most satisfactory dramatically as well as artistically. It is, at the same time, perfectly objective: it considerably heightens our appreciation of the poem by showing the grand simplicity of its original design, its real perspective, its structural force and permanent human element – and all this on a quite solid basis, all the more solid that it is devoid of the speculative element inherent in so many other tentative explanations. [p. 70]

The first major criticism of Tolkien's lecture did not appear until 1952. T.M. Gang, in his 'Approaches to *Beowulf*', *Review of English Studies* n.s. 3 (1952), disputed Tolkien's view that

> the dragon-fight symbolizes the tragedy of the human struggle against the forces of evil. . . . That Grendel, who is maddened by the sound of harps, should represent the outer darkness in all its active malevolence is plausible; but dragons were, after all, the natural guardians of treasures . . . unpleasant though they were, they were not accomplices of hell. Nor, for that matter, were they "things made by the imagination" for any purpose whatsoever; they were solid enough fact for the Anglo-Saxon Chronicle [pp. 7–8]

Gang argued that Tolkien 'never exactly claims that the poet's original audience would have interpreted it as he does', and that his 'reconstruction of the Anglo-Saxon view of the world, leaning heavily as it does on the extremely doubtful evidence of Norse poetry (of a later date than *Beowulf* and suggestive of a very different outlook on life) can hardly be accepted as objective, unbiased, or altogether convincing' (p. 11). This was answered by Adrien Bonjour, in defence of Tolkien, in 'Monsters Crouching and Critics Rampant: or The *Beowulf* Dragon Debated', *PMLA* 68 (March 1953). But Gang's views were echoed by J.C. van Meurs in '*Beowulf* and Literary Criticism', *Neophilologus* 39 (1955): he found it 'difficult to believe that the poem contains as much implicit symbolism as Tolkien ascribes to it' (p. 118), and worried that Tolkien's theory was so attractive 'that it is in danger of being taken as dogmatic truth by present-day *Beowulf* scholars' (p. 115).

A more concerted disagreement was put forth by Kenneth Sisam in *The Structure of Beowulf*. He took issue with Tolkien's 'explanation of the architecture of *Beowulf* as an artistic balance between the first two-thirds . . . and the last part' of the poem, and with 'his view that the central theme is the battle, hopeless in this world, of man against evil' (p. 21). According to Sisam,

> if the two parts of the poem are to be solidly bound together by the opposition of youth and age, it is not enough that the hero should be young in the one part and old in the other. The change in his age must be shown to change his ability to fight monsters, since these fights make the main plot. Instead, Beowulf is represented from beginning to end as the scourge of monsters, always seeking them out and destroying them by the shortest way. [p. 24]

Whereas for Tolkien the unifying theme of the poem is 'man at war with the hostile world and his inevitable overthrow in Time', in Sisam's view 'the monsters Beowulf kills are inevitably evil and hostile because a reputation for heroism is not made by killing creatures that are believed to be harmless or beneficent – sheep for instance.' The idea 'that Beowulf was defeated, that "within Time the monsters would win"' must be read into the text. 'There is no word of his defeat in the poem . . . according to the poet, the Dragon Fight was "his last victory" (2710). On the other hand, all the monsters are utterly defeated' (p. 25).

More recently George Clark in his *Beowulf* (1990), while agreeing with certain aspects of Tolkien's lecture and acknowledging its significance in the history of *Beowulf* studies, found fault with it for having marginalized Grendel's mother and trivialized the dragon 'into an emblem of malice, blaming the monster for being too symbolic, for not being "dragon enough," then graciously relenting with the comment "But for *Beowulf*, the poem, that is as it should be." But it is not so' (p. 10). He also rejected Tolkien's view of the *Beowulf*-poet, in part because 'the membrane separating Tolkien's critical and creative faculties was permeable in both directions' (p. 12) – that is, in Clark's opinion, Tolkien the writer of fiction influenced Tolkien the scholar: 'we have no evidence for an Anglo-Saxon poet like Tolkien's, indeed like Tolkien himself, a nostalgic re-creator of lost worlds, of pastiche' (p. 16). In response, one could argue that a scholar who is also a storyteller may have an advantage in

understanding the work of a 'mighty predecessor and kindred spirit', to quote
T.A. Shippey in *The Road to Middle-earth* (2nd edn. 1992). No one, Shippey
wrote, 'had understood *Beowulf* but Tolkien. The work had always been something personal, even freakish, and it took someone with the same instincts to
explain it. Sympathy furthermore depended on being a descendant, on living
in the same country and beneath the same sky, on speaking the same language . . .' (p. 44).

Although George Clark would place 'Tolkien's critical paradigm' firmly
among 'the literary, moral, and political convictions' of the period following
the First World War (p. 9), the influence of *Beowulf: The Monsters and the Critics* is still to be felt in *Beowulf* studies. Its lively prose remains effective despite
the passage of decades – untouched by the obfuscation that infects so much
writing on literary subjects today. Its advanced age, however, seems to have led
R.D. Fulk, editor of the anthology *Interpretations of Beowulf* (1991), to apologize for including Tolkien's lecture in that book. 'Any editor worth his salt',
he says in a preface,

> and with an adequate understanding of the changing critical winds in
> the profession, would no doubt remark . . . that Tolkien's lecture . . . has
> become the object of mindless veneration, is over-anthologized, hope-
> lessly retrograde, and much too long, and so can safely be set aside now
> to make way for more important matters. . . . No one denies the his-
> torical importance of this lecture as the first sustained effort at viewing
> the poem on its own terms, according to aesthetic guidelines discover-
> able in the work itself, thus opening the way to the formalist principles
> that played such a vital role in the subsequent development of *Beowulf*
> scholarship. But Tolkien's study is not just a pilgrims' stop on the road
> to holier shrines: his explanation of the poem's larger structure, though
> frequently disputed, has never been bettered, and the methodology
> inherent in his practice of basing claims about the macrostructural level
> on patterns everyone discerns in the microstructure remains a model
> for emulation. His view of the poet as an artist of an antiquarian bent
> remains enormously influential (and a major obstacle to dating the
> poem); and although the issue of the appropriateness of the monsters is
> not as pressing as it was in 1936, it is not superfluous in the context of
> some subsequent criticism. . . . [pp. xi–xii]

Peter S. Baker, editor of *Beowulf: Basic Readings* (1995), more directly counts
Beowulf: The Monsters and the Critics among those works 'that have long been
part of the standard reading list for a *Beowulf* course' which 'continue to be
influential and are still worth the student's attention' (p. xi).

It may be worth noting, as a measure (if unscientific) of the attention paid to
Tolkien's lecture, that in the copy of the 1936 *Proceedings of the British Academy*
shelved in the Upper Reading Room of the Bodleian Library, Oxford, *Beowulf:
The Monsters and the Critics* has been read to the point of soiled exhaustion,

with marks in pencil and blots of ink. The rest of the volume is comparatively clean.

'Of Beren and Lúthien'. The nineteenth chapter of the *'Quenta Silmarillion', published in *The Silmarillion* (1977), pp. 162–87.

SUMMARY

Barahir of the House of Bëor and a small band of men live as outlaws in their former homeland of Dorthonion, which was seized by Morgoth in the Battle of Sudden Flame. They are hunted until only Barahir, his son Beren, and eleven others remain. One of these, Gorlim, while visiting his ruined home is ensnared by a vision of his missing wife and captured by the enemy. Deceived by Sauron, he reveals his comrades' hiding place and is put to death. But Gorlim's shade appears to Beren, who is alone on an errand, and declares his treachery and death. Beren finds the others of his band slain, pursues their killers, and recovers from them the ring they had taken from his father, given by Felagund of Nargothrond with a promise of aid in need to Barahir who had rescued him from foes.

After four years Beren leaves Dorthonion and undertakes a terrible journey through Ered Gorgoroth and the region where the spider offspring of Ungoliant dwell. Eventually he comes to Doriath, 'and he passed through the mazes that Melian wove about the kingdom of Thingol, even as she had foretold; for a great doom lay upon him' (pp. 164–5). One summer evening he sees Lúthien, daughter of Thingol and Melian, 'the most beautiful of all the Children of Ilúvatar', dancing on the grass, and is enchanted by her. She disappears, and for long Beren seeks her. At last, near springtime, he hears her song which 'released the bonds of winter, and the frozen waters spoke, and flowers sprang from the cold earth where her feet had passed' (p. 165). He calls her *Tinúviel*, nightingale, and as she looks on him she loves him, but once more vanishes from sight. 'Thus he began the payment of anguish for the fate that was laid on him; and in his fate Lúthien was caught, and being immortal she shared his mortality, and being free received his chain . . .' (pp. 165–6). But she returns, and they meet secretly through the summer.

They are betrayed to Thingol by Daeron the minstrel, who also loves Lúthien. Lúthien refuses to tell her father anything unless he first promises not to slay Beren or imprison him. She then leads Beren before her father, who scornfully asks him what he seeks in Doriath. Beren, feeling almost as if the words are put into his mouth, says that Lúthien is the treasure he desires. Melian warns Thingol to be careful but, seeking a way to keep his promise and yet destroy Beren, Thingol says that he too desires a treasure: 'Bring to me in your hand a Silmaril from Morgoth's crown; and then, if she will, Lúthien may set her hand in yours' (p. 167). Beren accepts the challenge. Melian tells Thingol that he has doomed either his daughter or himself.

Beren makes his way to Nargothrond and seeks aid from Felagund according the promise the king had made to Barahir. But Celegorm and Curufin, two of Fëanor's sons who are living in Nargothrond, influence the Elves against giving aid to Beren. Felagund, therefore, removes his crown and with only ten faithful companions accompanies Beren on his quest. He disguises their band as Orcs, but Sauron is suspicious and has them brought to his stronghold. He and Felagund strive against each other with songs of power, but Sauron prevails, and their true forms are revealed. Refusing to tell their names and purposes, they are cast into a pit and one by one devoured by a werewolf.

Learning of Beren's plight from Melian, Lúthien wishes to go to his aid, but Daeron betrays her, and she is imprisoned by Thingol in a house high in a beech tree. By enchantment she grows her hair long, and from it weaves a dark robe to conceal her and a rope by which to escape, both charged with a spell of sleep. Meanwhile Celegorm and Curufin go hunting, hoping to hear news of Felagund, and take with them Huan, a wolfhound given to Celegorm by the Vala Oromë. It has been foretold that Huan can be overcome only by the greatest wolf ever whelped. They come upon Lúthien, and even her magic does not enable her to escape Huan. Brought to Huan's master, she tells her story and seeks help in rescuing Beren from Sauron's dungeons. But the brothers have no interest in doing so; they keep Lúthien a prisoner in Nargothrond, thinking to force her to marry Curufin. Huan, however, has loved Lúthien from the moment he saw her, and comes to her often. He understands all that she tells him about Beren, but is permitted to speak only three times before his death. He returns to her the magic cloak and, speaking for the first time, gives her counsel. They escape together, Lúthien riding on Huan's back.

At last among the captives only Felagund and Beren are left. When a wolf comes to devour Beren, Felagund manages to free himself from his bonds and kills it, but is himself slain. As Beren grieves, he hears Lúthien singing outside, and sings in reply. Sauron recognizes Lúthien's voice and thinks to capture her for Morgoth, but Huan slays all the wolves he sends, including Draugluin, greatest of werewolves, and even overcomes Sauron himself when he takes werewolf form. After Lúthien forces Sauron to yield the spells that control his tower, he flies away in the form of a vampire. The tower crumbles, Lúthien and Huan bring Beren forth, and together they bury Felagund's body.

Huan returns to his master. When the folk of Nargothrond hear of Felagund's fate Celegorm and Curufin are expelled. As they ride to join their brethren they come on Beren and Lúthien, who are arguing whether she should stay in safety or accompany him on his quest for a Silmaril. Curufin tries to abduct Lúthien, but Beren rescues her and is then himself rescued from Celegorm by Huan, who now rejects Celegorm as his master. Beren lets the brothers go free but takes Curufin's weapons, including the knife Angrist made by Telchar of Nogrod, and his horse. As the brothers flee on Celegorm's horse, Curufin fires two arrows: one is caught by Huan, but the other wounds Beren. Lúthien heals Beren and they reach the safety of Doriath. Beren steals away secretly while Lúthien is sleeping, not wishing her to accompany him into danger.

At the edge of the waste before Angband Beren sets Curufin's horse free and sings a Song of Parting, believing that he is going to his death. But Lúthien arrives riding Huan, by whose counsel they have collected from Sauron's ruined stronghold the wolf-skin of Draugluin and the bat-skin of Thuringwethil, a messenger of Sauron in vampire form. Huan speaks a second time and tells Beren that he cannot save Lúthien from 'the shadow of death ... for by her love she is now subject to it'. Beren can turn aside from his fate and they can live in exile for a while, 'but if you will not deny your doom, then either Lúthien being forsaken, must assuredly die alone, or she must with you challenge the fate that lies before you' (p. 179). Huan cannot accompany them further, but they may meet again in Doriath. Beren dons the skin of Draugluin and Lúthien that of Thuringwethil, and in this form reach the Gate of Angband.

They are challenged by Carcharoth, a whelp of the race of Draugluin raised by Morgoth on living flesh to be the doom of Huan, but Lúthien casts a spell of sleep on him. They make their way down to Morgoth's hall. Beren slinks beneath his throne. When Morgoth's gaze strips Lúthien of her disguise she 'named her own name, and offered her service to sing before him', and he conceives 'in his thought an evil lust' (p. 180). With her song, however, she casts him and all of his court into slumber, and his crown falls from his head. Using the knife Angrist Beren cuts one Silmaril from the crown, but the knife snaps when he tries to take a second. He flees with Lúthien. As they reach the gate, Carcharoth springs at them. Beren tries to daunt Carcharoth with the Silmaril, but the wolf devours the both Beren's hand and the jewel within it. The Silmaril burns his inward parts, and he runs off mad with pain. While Morgoth and his court begin to rouse, the eagle Thorondor and his vassals carry Beren and Lúthien to Doriath.

Huan, who comes to them, and Lúthien tend and heal Beren from the poisonous bite of Carcharoth. For a while they walk in the woods, but Beren, not wanting to withhold Lúthien from her father or to have her live in the wild, eventually persuades her that they should make their way to Thingol. The people of Doriath have sought in vain for Lúthien and grieved for her absence, and Daeron has strayed far away. Thingol has heard that Lúthien had been in Nargothrond but had fled. Just before Beren and Lúthien come to Thingol the king hears that messengers he had sent to Maedhros for aid in seeking Lúthien have been attacked by Carcharoth, who cannot be restrained by the power of Melian from entering Doriath. Beren kneels before Thingol and claims Lúthien as his own: he has fulfilled his quest. 'Even now a Silmaril is in my hand', but the hand is no longer on his arm. Thingol's heart is softened, and 'Beren took the hand of Lúthien before the throne of her father' (pp. 184, 185).

But Carcharoth is drawing ever nearer to Menegroth. Beren rides out with Thingol and his hunters, Mablung and Beleg, and with Huan to seek the dread beast. Carcharoth leaps on Thingol, and Beren receives a mortal wound while defending the king. Huan and Carcharoth fight and slay each other, but before dying Huan speaks for the third time, bidding Beren farewell. Mablung cuts the Silmaril from the belly of the wolf and places it in Beren's hand; 'and Beren was aroused by the touch of the Silmaril, and held it aloft, and bade Thingol receive it' (p. 186).

In Menegroth they are met by Lúthien who bids Beren wait for her beyond the Western Sea. And his spirit 'tarried in the halls of Mandos . . . until Lúthien came to say her last farewell'. The spirit of Lúthien herself 'fell down into darkness', and coming to Mandos sang before him 'the song most fair that ever in words was woven', in which she 'wove two themes . . . of the sorrow of the Eldar and the grief of Men. . . . And as she knelt before him her tears fell upon his feet . . . and Mandos was moved to pity, who never before was so moved, nor has been since' (pp. 186–7). Mandos lays the case before Manwë, who consults the will of Ilúvatar and offers Lúthien two choices: to dwell among the Valar where Beren cannot come, or to become mortal and return to Middle-earth with Beren for a short time, and like him be subject to death. She chooses the latter, 'that thus whatever grief might lie in wait', her fate and that of Beren 'might be joined, and their paths lead together beyond the confines of the world' (p. 187).

HISTORY

The first version of this story, *The Tale of Tinúviel* in *The Book of Lost Tales*, does not survive. Tolkien wrote it in pencil, probably in the second half of 1917, but overwrote it with a second version in ink and erased the pencil text, probably in summer 1919. References in other stories written in the intervening period, however, give some indication of what might have been in the original text. There, as in *The Silmarillion*, Beren was a Man, not an Elf. An allusion to 'Tevildo Prince of Cats' (*The Book of Lost Tales, Part One*, p. 47) suggests that Tevildo was already present in the first version. Elsewhere there are references to Lúthien's parents, Linwë Tinto (> Tinwelint > Thingol) and Tindriel (> Wendelin > Gwendeling > Melian), and to their meeting, foreshadowing that of Lúthien and Beren. They have two children, Timpinen and Tinúviel, who 'long after joined the Eldar again' (*The Book of Lost Tales, Part One*, pp. 106–7; it is impossible to guess what Tolkien meant by this phrase).

In the revised version of *The Tale of Tinúviel* Tinwelint and Gwendeling, who live in a deep cavern in a hidden realm in the forest of Artanor protected by the magic of Gwendeling, also have two children, Dairon the piper and Tinúviel (her real name, not that given her by Beren) whose greatest joy is dancing. One night in June Beren the Gnome (i.e. a Noldo Elf) sees Tinúviel dancing to Dairon's flute and is enchanted. As in the final version, she flees from Beren and he seeks her. There is no betrayal by Dairon, but Beren steps boldly before her and asks her to teach him to dance. She dances away, and leads Beren to her father's halls. There is no suggestion that she has already committed herself to him. Tinwelint, who distrusts the Noldoli, is not welcoming, but Tinúviel pleads for Beren because of his great appreciation of her dancing. When Tinwelint asks Beren what he seeks, Beren replies: 'thy daughter . . . for she is the fairest and most sweet of all the maidens I have seen or dreamed of'. Tinwelint laughs, and asks for a Silmaril from the Crown of Melko as the price of his daughter's hand. All present think that he is jesting, but Beren replies: 'Nay, but 'tis too small a gift to the father of so sweet a bride. . . . I . . . will fulfil thy small desire . . .' (*The Book of Lost Tales, Part Two*, p. 13). He leaves, and Tinúviel weeps, fearing that 'Melko will slay him, and none will look ever again with such love upon my dancing' (p. 14).

Beren, travelling towards Melko's stronghold, is captured by Orcs. He pretends that he is a trapper of small animals and birds who wishes to serve Melko. He is sent as a thrall to Tevildo, Prince of Cats, the mightiest of all cats and 'possessed of an evil sprite' (p. 16) with many cats subject to him. When Beren fails in the tasks Tevildo sets him, he is made a scullion in Tevildo's kitchen. As in the final version, Tinúviel learns of Beren's captivity, is betrayed by Dairon, and is imprisoned by her father. She achieves her escape in the same way, but the tale describes at length the spells by which she makes her hair grow and gives the cloak and rope made from it the power of compelling sleep. Dairon tries to follow her but becomes lost. On her journey north Tinúviel meets Huan, Captain of Dogs, a friend of Beren and great enemy of Tevildo, who devises a plan to rescue Beren. Tinúviel goes to Tevildo's stronghold, says that she has seen Huan lying sick in the woods, and offers to lead Tevildo to him. Through a hatch she catches a glimpse of Beren in the kitchen and speaks loudly so that he knows she is there. So deceived, Tevildo with two other cats follows Tinúviel to where Huan lies pretending to be sick. Huan kills one of the cats, Oikeroi, and the other two climb trees to escape him. Huan says that he will not let them come down until Beren is set free. Eventually Tevildo yields, throws down his gold collar as a token of authority to his followers, and reveals to Huan 'the secret of the cats and the spell that Melko had entrusted to him . . . words of magic whereby the stones of his evil house were held together, and whereby he held all beasts of the catfolk under his sway, filling them with an evil power beyond their nature . . .' (*The Book of Lost Tales, Part Two*, p. 28). Tinúviel returns to Tevildo's stronghold, speaks the spell, and rescues Beren.

Tinúviel wanders a long time in the woods with Beren and Huan, but 'grew at last to long sorely for Gwendeling'. She wishes to return home but does not want to leave Beren. He suggests that the only thing they can do is to find a Silmaril. They consult Huan (who has no restriction on his speech), who gives them the skin of Oikeroi which he had taken as a trophy; Tinúviel sews Beren into it and teaches him how to behave like a cat. They leave Huan and make their way to Melko's stronghold, Angband. Here the earlier story differs only in detail: Tinúviel pretends that she has been driven out by her father; Beren uses a knife from Tevildo's kitchen to prise the Silmaril from Melko's crown; and their escape is aided by Huan, not by eagles.

Beren feels that he should leave Tinúviel, since he has no Silmaril to give her father, but she persuades him to go in hope with her, for her father might have relented. They find that her father's realm has suffered in her absence, most recently by the incursion of Karkaras (the precursor of Carcharoth) who, driven mad by anguish, has run wild through the woods and killed many. When they come before Tinwelint Beren declares that he has a Silmaril in his hand, but shows that his hand is no longer on his arm. As in *The Silmarillion*, Tinwelint's heart is softened, and he accepts Beren; but in the revised *Tale of Tinúviel* Karkaras comes on the hunters while they are sleeping, with Beren keeping watch; Beren does not lose his life protecting Tinwelint; Tinwelint, not Huan, kills Karkaras; and Huan survives the fight. Tinúviel is not offered a choice, but Mandos allows both her and Beren to return into the world, warning them that 'it is not to any life of perfect joy that I dismiss you . . . and know ye that ye will become mortal even as Men, and when ye fare hither again it will be for ever, unless the Gods summon you indeed to Valinor' (*The Book of Lost Tales, Part Two*, p. 40). They return to dance in the woods and hills.

Since in this version both Beren and Tinúviel are Elves, the conflict between differing fates which becomes such an important element in later versions is absent. Here they are permitted a fate which differs from that usual for Elves who die. Instead of waiting in the Halls of Mandos and being reborn again in their children, they are sent back as themselves, but now as mortal as Men. In another tale Tolkien wrote that 'upon Beren and Tinúviel fell swiftly that doom of mortality that Mandos had spoken', and while their child was still young Tinúviel slowly faded, and Beren searched for her until he too faded (*The Book of Lost Tales, Part Two*, p. 240). Unfortunately it is not known how the matter was resolved in the lost first version, when Beren was a Man. *Christopher Tolkien has said that in this version of the story Tevildo and his castle occupy 'the same "space" in the narrative' as Sauron and Tol-in-Gaurhoth, but otherwise the two have nothing in common (*The Book of Lost Tales, Part Two*, p. 53; see his detailed comparison of *The Tale of Tinúviel* with 'Of Beren and Lúthien' in *The Silmarillion*, in *The Book of Lost Tales, Part Two*, pp. 51–60).

The names of Tinúviel's parents achieved their final form – *Thingol* and *Melian* – in a typescript which Tolkien began soon after the second version of the story, but abandoned after Tinúviel's meeting with Huan.

The earliest extant texts of the poem *Light as Leaf on Lindentree* were made in Leeds *c.* 1923–4, when also some introductory lines of alliterative verse were added. Tolkien inserted this poem and various references to the story of Beren and Tinúviel into the second version of his alliterative poem *The Children of Húrin*, probably *c.* 1924–5. These show some development in the story, though Tolkien still hesitated whether Beren should be a Man or an Elf. The elven princess was now called *Lúthien*, and *Tinúviel* is the name given her by Beren. Dairon is no longer her brother but in love with her, and being jealous of Beren, ceases to play his flute. Perhaps most significantly, the inserted poem stresses the immediacy of Lúthien's love for Beren when she first comes face to face with him.

In the brief *Sketch of the Mythology* (*c.* 1926) Tolkien was evidently still undecided about Beren: his father Barahir is a chieftain of Ilkorindi (Elves), but Beren himself is said to be mortal. More is said about Beren's earlier history: 'Barahir is driven into hiding, his hiding betrayed, and Barahir slain; his son Beren after a life outlawed flees south, crosses the Shadowy Mountains, and after grievous hardships comes to Doriath' (*The Shaping of Middle-earth*, p. 24). A statement that Barahir had been a friend of Celegorm of Nargothrond is not developed further, but foreshadows a major new element. Beren is given as a slave to Thû the hunter, not to Tevildo. Huan is killed in the fight with Carcaras while defending Beren. Events after Beren's death are uncertain: 'Some songs say that Lúthien went even over the Grinding Ice, aided by the power of her divine mother, Melian, to Mandos' halls and won him back; others that Mandos hearing his tale released him. Certain it is that he alone of mortals came back from Mandos and dwelt with Lúthien and never spoke to Men again . . .' (*The Shaping of Middle-earth*, p. 25). An addition made probably soon after this says that Mandos exacted in payment that Lúthien should become as mortal as Beren. The text was revised c. 1926–30 in response to the way the story was developing in the *Lay of Leithian*, so that Beren is definitely a Man and the Nargothrond element enters.

Tolkien began to write the *Lay of Leithian* in summer 1925, telling the story of Beren and Lúthien at length in octosyllabic couplets. At various points while this was in progress he made five synopses for parts of the story still to be written, which indicate how the story changed in stages and expanded as new ideas came to the author and were adopted or rejected. Tolkien finally decided that Beren was a Man, and in its final form the story told in the *Lay* approached very closely (if more briefly) that of *The Silmarillion*. Significant differences are few: Gorlim sees a phantom image of his missing wife by chance in a house and, believing her alive, deliberately seeks out Morgoth and betrays his comrades, hoping to be reunited with her; but he is killed by Morgoth. Beren, Felagund, and their companions are captured by Thû, Master of Wolves. After Beren steals away, Lúthien catches up with him first, and Huan comes later, having fetched the wolf coat and bat skin. Tolkien left the *Lay* unfinished in September 1931 at the point where Carcharoth devours Beren's hand and the Silmaril.

The fourth and fifth synopses, however, contain additional material concerning the unwritten part of the *Lay*. During their flight Beren and Lúthien are ensnared by great spiders, but Huan rescues them – an idea that did not survive into later versions. As foretold, Huan is killed by Carcharoth in the great wolf hunt. The fate of the lovers is close to that in the *Sketch*: 'Fading of Lúthien. Her journey to Mandos. The song of Lúthien in Mandos' halls, and the release of Beren. They dwelt long in Broseliand, but spake never more to mortal Men, and Lúthien became mortal' (*The Lays of Beleriand*, p. 312). One idea which is referred to several times in the *Lay* and synopses, but which Tolkien abandoned in later versions, is that Morgoth sent a war band under Boldog to capture Lúthien.

The *Quenta Noldorinwa*, written c. 1930 while Tolkien was still working on the *Lay of Leithian*, contains a brief account of the story based on the *Lay* to which it even refers. The latter part, roughly from the point where Beren is injured by Celegorm, was written before the corresponding part of the *Lay*. It follows the fourth synopsis in that Beren does not steal away from Lúthien after his recovery, but Huan, learning that they are not certain what to do, brings them the wolfskin and bat-garb and counsels them. Tolkien hesitated about the sequence of events at this point; in the fifth synopsis Beren leaves alone and is overtaken by both Lúthien and Huan, whereas in the *Lay* Lúthien reaches him first and Huan arrives later with the skins. There is no suggestion that Morgoth forces Lúthien to abandon her bat disguise. By an addition, Huan speaks for a third time ere he dies.

The story is given briefly in both the 'earliest' and the 'later' *Annals of Beleriand* (early and mid-1930s respectively). According to the 'earliest' *Annals* Barahir was slain in Year 160, and the whole story of Beren and Lúthien took place in 163–4. In the 'later' *Annals* Barahir's death takes place in 261, emended to 460; the deeds of Beren and Lúthien are spread over a longer period 263–5 [> 463–5].

When writing the *Quenta Silmarillion* (mid-1930s–early 1938) Tolkien found it difficult to keep the story of Beren and Lúthien to a length commensurate with the rest of the work, abandoning not only an unfinished draft when he realized it was too long, but also a shorter fair copy that followed at the point where Felagund and Beren are about to leave Nargothrond. He then rewrote the entire story more succinctly, closely following the *Lay of Leithian* with only a few changes. One of these, of the name *Thû* to *Sauron* as the servant of Morgoth who captures Beren and Felagund, was merely a change of name, as is clear in various contemporary versions of *The Fall of Númenor*. The evolution of the story of Beren and Lúthien was virtually complete by the end of 1937.

About 1950, Tolkien began to make a revision of the *Lay of Leithian* left unfinished nearly twenty years before, and a full prose version closely related to the revision. This work included a revision of the story of Gorlim, in which his treachery is less deep and deliberate. Tolkien also told the story of Beren and Lúthien in short in the *Grey Annals* (c. 1951, see *Annals of Beleriand*), adding a few details such as descriptions of the refuge of Barahir and his men.

The chapter 'Of Beren and Lúthien' in *The Silmarillion* was based for the most part on the texts of the *Quenta Silmarillion* of the 1930s, mainly on a rejected first fair copy as far as the point where Felagund gives the crown of Nargothrond to Orodreth, but with some elements from the complete fair copy which was the source for the rest of the chapter. Christopher Tolkien also took from the *Grey Annals* a short passage describing Barahir's refuge, and several short phrases which elucidated points of importance. He took the account of Gorlim's treachery from the revision of c. 1950, and inserted thirty-two lines from the *Lay of Leithian* describing the contest between Felagund and Sauron (covered in only one sentence in the *Quenta Silmarillion*). See further, discussion in *The Lost Road and Other Writings*, pp. 295–306; *The Lays of Beleriand*, p. 196; and *The Peoples of Middle-earth*, pp. 318 and 369, and p. 372, note 8.

BACKGROUND TO THE STORY

The story of Beren and Lúthien was inspired by an incident in Tolkien's life that occurred in late May or early June 1917, when *Edith Tolkien danced for her husband in a woodland glade. He described the event in a letter to his son Christopher in 1972:

> I never called Edith *Lúthien* – but she was the source of the story that in time became the chief part of the *Silmarillion*. It was first conceived in a small woodland glade filled with hemlocks at Roos in *Yorkshire (where I was for a brief time in command of an outpost of the Humber Garrison in 1917, and she was able to live with me for a while). In those days her hair was raven, her skin clear, her eyes brighter than you have seen them, and she could sing – and *dance*. [11 July 1972, *Letters*, p. 420]

What this meant to Tolkien is shown by the inscription on the stone in Wolvercote Cemetery, *Oxford, marking the burial place of Ronald and Edith Tolkien: *Edith Mary Tolkien, Lúthien, 1889–1971. John Ronald Reuel Tolkien, Beren, 1892–1973.*

Tolkien commented on the story in a letter to *Milton Waldman in ?late 1951:

> Here we meet, among other things, the first example of the motive . . . that the great policies of world history, 'the wheels of the world', are often turned not by the Lords and Governors, even gods, but by the seemingly unknown and weak – owing to the secret life in creation, and the part unknowable to all wisdom but One, that resides in the intrusions of the Children of God into the Drama. It is Beren the outlawed mortal who succeeds (with the help of Lúthien, a mere maiden, even if an elf of royalty) where all the armies and warriors have failed: he penetrates the stronghold of the Enemy and wrests one of the Silmarilli from the Iron Crown. Thus he wins the hand of Lúthien and the first marriage of mortal and immortal is achieved. [*Letters*, p. 149]

CRITICISM

Christina Scull has noted that the significance of the story became greater in later versions as the importance of the Silmarils grew in the *legendarium*, and the one recovered by Beren and Lúthien enabled Eärendel to reach Valinor and obtain help against Morgoth. She also has found that the love of Beren and Lúthien for each other 'becomes deeper in successive retellings, and seems at last foreordained in the Music of the Ainur' ('The Development of Tolkien's *Legendarium*: Some Threads in the Tapestry of Middle-earth', *Tolkien's Legendarium: Essays on The History of Middle-earth* (2000), p. 16).

T.A. Shippey in *The Road to Middle-earth* counts at least eight extant versions of the tale of Beren and Lúthien, varying in length, completeness, intrinsic merit, literary merit, and 'importance for understanding the development of the whole story. Yet the existence of all the versions together does more than merely provide one with more "ox-bones" for study. It also radically alters the flavour of the soup, creating something of the "flavour of deep-rootedness" which Tolkien so often detected and admired' (2nd edn. 1992, pp. 277–8; 'ox-bones' and 'soup' are references to *On Fairy-Stories). Shippey also discusses at length some small but significant details in the story, among them Beren's oath to Thingol:

> If one had only the *Silmarillion* version of this scene, its logic and development would seem perfectly clear. One irreducible fact about Beren is that he becomes . . . 'the One-Handed'. . . . Since this is an irreducible fact, surely it must all along have been part of the story that Beren, in the scene with Thingol, should find himself swearing an unknowingly ironic oath: in the words of the *Silmarillion* version, 'when we meet again my hand shall hold a Silmaril' – because of course when he and Thingol meet again his hand *will* be holding a Silmaril, but both will be in the belly of the wolf. With that established it would seem to be only plain sense for Thingol to have provoked the oath by setting up a hand for hand, jewel for jewel exchange, as again he so clearly does in the *Silmarillion*: bring me a jewel (the Silmaril) in your hand, and I will put in your hand a compensating jewel (Lúthien's hand). . . .
>
> Yet a glance at the [*Book of Lost Tales, Part Two*] version shows that in the beginning these connections were simply not there. Beren does say, in his *second* meeting with Thingol (there Tinwelint), 'I have a Silmaril in my hand even now' . . . but in the first meeting does not make the corresponding promise. His exact words are only 'I . . . will fulfil thy small desire': which, of course, at the time of their second meeting he has still *not done*. [p. 278]

Iwan Rhys Morus in 'The Tale of Beren and Lúthien', *Mallorn* 20 (September 1983), comments that this story is

> in many ways a turning-point in the mythology for in it many of the various strands of other narratives are brought together and combined to bring about the doom of the Eldar. Indeed I would argue that one of Tolkien's master-strokes in this tale is the irony of the fact that the Free People's greatest achievement against Morgoth – the taking of a Silmaril from the Iron Crown – is the seed that brings about their eventual utter downfall. [p. 19]

He discusses the influence of the episode at Roos on the story, and notes that this is not Tolkien's only use of the motif of the 'encounter in the woods', citing among others Aragorn and Arwen, Thingol and Melian, Eöl and Aredhel, and

Aldarion and Erendis. He suggests possible sources for elements of the story, in particular in the *Kalevala* 'the journey of Väinämöinen and Lemminkäinen to steal the Sampo, in which Väinämöinen's singing casts the whole of Pohja into deep slumber', and several wizards' singing-contests.

> Around this central core Tolkien has piled a plethora of mythic themes and motifs. The striking image of a hand in a wolf's mouth is straight from the Prose Edda: Fenris and the god Tyr. Lúthien with her escape via a rope of her own hair from prison is of course Rapunzel from Grimms' Fairy Tales. The hunting of Carcharoth recalls the great quest for the Twrch Trwyth in 'Culwch ac Olwen' whilst the great hound Huan reminds me strongly of the most faithful of wolfhounds: Gelert in the old Welsh legend. [p. 22]

Richard C. West in 'Real-world Myth in a Secondary World', *Tolkien the Medievalist* (2003), also comments on resonances from various sources which a reader might recognize and suppose to have influenced elements of the story. But he quite rightly points out that similarities do not necessarily mean influence, and that the differences are often far more marked than the similarities. As one example he cites 'Rapunzel', one of the *Märchen* collected by the Brothers Grimm, remarking that 'Lúthien lets her hair down not just to allow her lover to reach her but to enable *her* to reach *him*' (p. 263). Myth, legend, and fairy-tale 'were an integral part of [Tolkien's] mental furniture and imaginative make-up', and what we read 'over and over are echoes, even when we cannot pinpoint an exact source' (p. 264). West cites several works which may have provided 'echoes' for the story of Beren and Lúthien: Robin Hood and his outlaw band for Barahir; Tristan and Iseult living in the woods; the killing one by one of Finrod and Beren's companions 'is strongly reminiscent of the sons of King Völsung being killed one each night until only Sigmund survives'; Sauron's shape-shifting recalls the Norse god Loki and the Greek Nereus; Carcharoth biting off Beren's hand recalls Fenris Wolf and Tyr; Huan plays the same role as the magical helper in many fairy-tales; Lúthien in her pleading before Mandos 'reenacts the descent into the underworld of Orpheus in Greek mythology or of Ishtar in Babylonian to recover a loved one, but with a happier result: much as in the Middle English *Sir Orfeo . . .*' (p. 265).

Katharyn W. Crabbe in *J.R.R. Tolkien* (rev. and expanded edn. 1988) compares Beren as a hero to Túrin; like Túrin, he suffers loss and loneliness, but is motivated not by vengeance but by love. He is brave, and 'although his pride may lead him to attempt the seemingly impossible, it does not lead him to mindless violence. It is a productive rather than a destructive pride . . . unlike Túrin, whose pride leads him time after time to bad decisions and self-destructive behavior' (p. 194).

Verlyn Flieger devotes two chapters in *Splintered Light: Logos and Language in Tolkien's World* (1983; 2nd edn. 2002) to the story. She poses the questions: 'Can the *free will of Men alter the fate of Elves? Does the fate of the Elf entangle the Man who intersects it?' and finds that 'both fate and free will appear to be involved . . . in the lives of Beren, Lúthien, and Thingol' (p. 131). She examines their actions in this context, and in relation to the main theme of her book, that *The Silmarillion* is 'a story about light. Images of light in all stages – bright, dim, whole, refracted, clear or rainbow-hued – pervade the songs and stories of the fictive. It is a world peopled with sub-creators whose interactions with and attitudes toward the light shape their world and their own destinies within it' (p. 49).

See also Richard C. West, '"And She Named Her Own Name": Being True to One's Word in Tolkien's Middle-earth', in *Tolkien Studies* 2 (2005).

Berkshire. In summer 1912 Tolkien went on a walking tour in this county in the south-east of England, where he made several drawings and watercolours. He was especially interested in the local landscape and buildings, such as the church of St Michael, founded in Anglo-Saxon times but rebuilt in various periods, at **Lambourn** where King Alfred once had a manor. He drew its late Norman west doorway, a detail of its keystone, and a gargoyle above a Gothic window. (See *Artist and Illustrator*, figs. 11, 13.) He also went to **Eastbury**, where he drew the High Street and picturesque thatched cottages (*Artist and Illustrator*, fig. 12), one of which still stands. In later years he was attracted, with his family, to the **Vale of the White Horse** with its famous stylized figure of a horse, *c.* 374 feet long, cut into the grass on a chalk hillside *c.* 100 BC, and the ancient long-barrow known as Wayland's Smithy (*c.* 2000 BC).

All three of Tolkien's sons attended the Oratory School when it was located at **Caversham**, near Reading in Berkshire. When he returned to Oxford in 1972 after his wife's death he often visited his youngest son, *Christopher, who at that time lived with his wife and children in the village of **West Hanney** in Berkshire (since 1974 part of Oxfordshire).

In his poems and stories the character Tom Bombadil, he said, was 'the spirit of the (vanishing) Oxford and Berkshire countryside' (letter to Stanley Unwin, 16 December 1937, *Letters*, p. 26), and the Barrow-downs near Tom's home in *The Lord of the Rings* (Book I, Chapter 8) may be indebted to the many prehistoric graves found in Berkshire.

Bibliographies. The standard history of the publication of Tolkien's works is *J.R.R. Tolkien: A Descriptive Bibliography* by Wayne G. Hammond with the assistance of Douglas A. Anderson (1993; 2nd edn. forthcoming). Except for a few minor omissions it is a comprehensive account (to mid-1992) of Tolkien's books and the books to which he contributed, with details of content, binding, and textual changes in discrete editions and printings; of his contributions to periodicals, his published letters and art, interviews, recordings, and miscellanea; and of translations of his writings. Addenda and corrigenda to the *Bibliography*, as well as articles on Tolkien bibliography addressed to the serious enthusiast, have been published in the occasional magazine *The Tolkien Collector* (begun 1992). For concise checklists of Tolkien's principal works, and of his published art and poetry, see the **Chronology** volume of the *Companion and Guide*. Appendix C, 'The Published Writings of J.R.R. Tolkien', in Humphrey Carpenter's *Biography* (1977, revised 1987 and later, see *Biographies) is also a useful guide, as is the Internet site 'A Chronological Bibliography of the Writings of J.R.R. Tolkien' by Åke Bertenstam, at *www.geocities.com/SoHo/Bistro/9656/tbchron.html*.

The most important of the early bibliographies of writings about Tolkien, *Tolkien Criticism: An Annotated Checklist* by Richard C. West (1970, an expansion of a work that appeared in the journal *Extrapolation* for December 1968), today is useful chiefly for the picture it affords of Tolkien studies in their infancy. A list of everything of major interest on Tolkien published to that date, it also includes much less important material, but omits work published in fanzines. Entries considered by West to be of special note are marked with an asterisk. A second edition of *Tolkien Criticism* published in 1981 is much enlarged but also more selective, to keep its length within bounds, the literature about Tolkien having expanded greatly in the 1970s. Essays and reviews from three leading American fanzines (*Mythlore*, *Orcrist*, and the *Tolkien Journal*) were now cited. All entries in West's second edition are to be considered 'definitely of real importance' to Tolkien studies 'through the greater part of 1980, while what is excluded is much of what I consider peripheral' (p. xi).

For *Modern Fiction Studies* 50, no. 4 (Winter 2004) West produced 'A Tolkien Checklist: Selected Criticism 1981–2004', giving his subjective choices for 'some of the best critical studies' of Tolkien (p. 1015). Michael D.C. Drout and Hilary Wynne include an extensive bibliography, without annotations, in 'Tom Shippey's *J.R.R. Tolkien: Author of the Century* and a Look Back at Tolkien Criticism since 1982', *Envoi: A Review Journal of Medieval Literature* 9, no. 1 (Fall 2000). This has been continued in the journal *Tolkien Studies*.

J.R.R. Tolkien: Six Decades of Criticism by Judith A. Johnson (1986) is more expansive than West's bibliography in its coverage of fan as well as mainstream publications (through 1984), and in its annotations provides a welcome alternative point of view to West, but is otherwise less helpful as a guide to scholarship. Valuable writings about Tolkien are listed in the dubious company of Tolkien-inspired blank books and other 'Tolkieniana'. And whereas West's second edition is divided simply into two sections, Tolkien's own writings arranged chronologically, and critical works about Tolkien listed alphabetically by author or (when no author is given) by title, the entries in Johnson are organized in a difficult scheme of multiple chronological and alphabetical divisions and subdivisions. Johnson's book, moreover, suffers from errors and inconsistencies.

Åke Jönsson, later known as Åke Bertenstam, cast a wide net in compiling *En Tolkienbibliografi 1911–1980 = A Tolkien Bibliography 1911–1980* (1983; rev. edn. 1986). Despite the terminal date indicated in the title, Bertenstam also lists works by Tolkien, reviews of Tolkien's works, and reviews of books about Tolkien that were published later than 1980. Fan publications are included, and many more British and European works than are covered by West or Johnson. Alone among Tolkien bibliographers, Bertenstam provides an index by subject. Five supplements to his bibliography have appeared in the occasional Swedish Tolkien journal *Arda*, beginning with the number for 1982–83 (published 1986) and ending with that for 1988–91 (published 1994).

Bertenstam's experience illustrates the difficulties involved in maintaining a comprehensive bibliography of works by and about Tolkien, given the continual growth in that field, the rapidity of its expansion, and the cost of print publication (his final supplement occupied more than 200 pages, fully half of the 1988–91 *Arda*). Computer technology and the Internet would seem to offer a means to produce a less expensive and more easily updated Tolkien bibliography, though there remains the significant labour of gathering data. Michael D.C. Drout of Wheaton College, Massachusetts has begun such an online work with student assistance, at *acunix.wheatonma.edu/mdrout/TolkienBiblio/*. Intended to augment West and Johnson, and like those works omitting many fan-based sources, at the time of this writing it is still a work in progress.

Further information on early reviews of books by Tolkien, and on early articles and comments on Tolkien, may be found in a series of annotated bibliographies by George H. Thompson in various issues of *Mythlore* (Autumn 1984–Autumn 1987; errata, Autumn 1997). 'An Inklings Bibliography', a feature published in most issues of *Mythlore* between whole nos. 12 (June 1976) and 85 (Winter 1999), often included annotated citations to Tolkien *criticism, compiled by Joe R. Christopher and Wayne G. Hammond. Two checklists of dissertations concerned with Tolkien supplement West's *Tolkien Criticism*: Richard E. Blackwelder, 'Dissertations from Middle-earth' in *Beyond Bree*, March 1990, and Daniel Timmons, 'Tolkien-Related Dissertations and Theses in English' in *Tolkien Collector* 16 (July 1997).

No comprehensive, widely available bibliography of articles, reviews, and other writings about Tolkien that have appeared in fanzines has yet been published. One of the foremost experts on the subject, Sumner Gary Hunnewell, produced at least three relevant checklists in the early 1990s, but these are of limited scope and were printed in very small numbers. Occasional reviews by Hunnewell of Tolkien fan publications have appeared in the Tolkien Society bulletin *Amon Hen*. Lists, by a variety of hands, of Tolkien-inspired items such as calendars, posters, recordings, games, and collectible figures are occasionally published in the fanzine *Beyond Bree*; some of these were collected in the *List of Tolkienalia*, ed. Nancy Martsch (1992).

See also *Criticism.

The Bidding of the Minstrel, from the Lay of Eärendel. Poem, the latest version of which was published with commentary in *The Book of Lost Tales, Part Two* (1984), pp. 269–71. A minstrel is encouraged to sing of 'Eärendel the wandering', 'a tale of immortal sea-yearning / The Eldar once made ere the change of the light'. But the poet replies that 'the music is broken, the words half-forgotten', the song he can sing 'is but shreds one remembers / Of golden imaginings fashioned in sleep'.

The Bidding of the Minstrel survives in several versions, on one of which Tolkien noted that he wrote the poem in his rooms in St John Street, *Oxford in winter 1914. To its earliest finished text he later hastily added the title (as it appears to *Christopher Tolkien) *The Minstrel Renounces the Song*; later this became *Lay of Eärendel* and finally *The Bidding of the Minstrel, from the Lay of Eärendel*. In its original form it 'was much longer than it became' (Christopher Tolkien, *The Book of Lost Tales, Part Two*, p. 270): in early 1915 Tolkien divided its first part, *The Bidding of the Minstrel*, from its second, which he entitled *The Mermaid's Flute* (unpublished; see **Chronology**, entry for 17–18 March 1915 and later). He made slight revisions to *The Bidding of the Minstrel* in the period *c.* 1920–4.

The work is one of several early poems by Tolkien concerning the mariner Eärendel (variously spelled), who would figure prominently in *'The Silmaril-lion' (see *'Of the Voyage of Eärendil and the War of Wrath'). Here Eärendel wanders earthly seas, a figure of ancient lore whose tales are bound up with those of the Elves (earlier 'fairies'). On the back of one of the earliest workings of the poem is an outline of a great voyage by Eärendel to all points of the compass on earth, but also to 'a golden city' later identified as the Elvish city Kôr, before setting sail in the sky: see *The Book of Lost Tales, Part Two*, pp. 261–2.

Bilbo's Last Song (at the Grey Havens). Poem, first published in English by the Houghton Mifflin Company, Boston, as a poster in April 1974 (a Dutch translation appeared at the end of 1973), and by George Allen & Unwin, London, in September 1974. See further, *Descriptive Bibliography* A11.

The hobbit Bilbo Baggins, now near the end of his life ('Day is ended, dim my eyes'), bids farewell to his friends and to Middle-earth as he takes ship at the Grey Havens (at the end of *The Lord of the Rings*) and sails 'west of West' to 'fields and mountains ever blest'. The content and mood of the poem call to mind 'Crossing the Bar' (1889) by Alfred, Lord Tennyson. It was not, however, Tolkien's own farewell to Middle-earth, as some have interpreted it, nor is it wholly a later work. *Bilbo's Last Song* is a revision of a much earlier poem, *Vestr um haf* (Old Norse 'west over sea'), from the 1920s or 1930s. In this there is no connection with Bilbo Baggins or Middle-earth; and it could not have become *Bilbo's Last Song* until after Tolkien had conceived of the end of *The Lord of the Rings*, no later than November 1944 (see *Letters*, p. 104, letter to Christopher Tolkien, 29 November 1944: 'But the final scene will be the passage of Bilbo and Elrond and Galadriel through the woods of the Shire on their way to the Grey Havens. Frodo will join them and pass over the Sea. . . .'). But the poem was in its final form by October 1968, when Tolkien's occasional assistant, *Joy Hill, discovered its manuscript while helping him arrange his books after he had moved from *Oxford to *Poole. On 3 September 1970 he presented the poem, with its copyright, to Joy Hill as a token of gratitude for years of friendship and service.

In the original Houghton Mifflin issue *Bilbo's Last Song* was accompanied by a gauzy photograph of a river, for mood rather than as a depiction of the poem's events. George Allen & Unwin, London, published the poem in September 1974, also in poster form but with an illustration by *Pauline Baynes of Sam, Merry, and Pippin watching the Last Ship sail into the West. In 1990 *Bilbo's Last Song* was published in book form, accompanied by three series of illustrations by Pauline Baynes: one which tells the story of Bilbo's last days at Rivendell, his procession to the Grey Havens, and his departure for the Undying Lands; another which depicts Bilbo remembering his past adventures; and a third which tells the story of *The Hobbit*. The second of these was omitted in a new edition of *Bilbo's Last Song* published in 2002.

As a poster, *Bilbo's Last Song* was too slight to attract reviews, while the book version received (favourable) notice mainly for its illustrations.

Although it is not strictly part of *The Lord of the Rings*, the poem was smoothly incorporated into the 1981 BBC radio production of that work (*Adaptations) by Brian Sibley and Michael Bakewell. It has also been set to music (see *The Road Goes Ever On: A Song Cycle*) and recorded by *Donald Swann.

Biographies. Tolkien held qualified views on biography and its uses, in particular when he was to be the subject. On 24 June 1957 he wrote in response to a request from Caroline Everett, author of an M.A. thesis on his fiction: 'I do not feel inclined to go into biographical detail. I doubt its relevance to criticism. Certainly in any form less than a complete biography, interior and exterior, which I alone could write, and which I do not intend to write' (*Letters*, p. 257) – a biography, that is, which not only recorded 'exterior' facts such as those found in *Who's Who*, but also examined how (or whether) Tolkien's experiences had influenced his writings. Produced by anyone other than the subject himself, such a biography in its 'interior' aspects could be no more than speculation (notwithstanding critics who have argued that an author is the last person to understand what he writes). Elsewhere Tolkien wrote that 'only one's guardian Angel, or indeed God Himself, could unravel the real relationship between personal facts and an author's works' (letter to Deborah Webster, 25 October 1958, *Letters*, p. 288).

Even so, Tolkien was aware that many readers of *The Lord of the Rings* were interested to know more about him, and he was concerned that facts about his life be reported accurately, if they were to be reported at all. In 1955 he provided information about his life and work to the columnist Harvey Breit of the *New York Times Book Review*, 'out of sheer pity' to one of many such enquirers; but he felt that the result ('Oxford Calling', 5 June 1955, quoted in *Letters*, pp. 217–18) did not make sense. At the end of June 1955, anticipating a need for a succinct statement – part biography, part comment on issues related to *The Lord of the Rings* – he prepared one and sent it to his American publisher, the Houghton Mifflin Company (*Publishers; the statement, with annotations and corrections, appears in *Letters*, pp. 218–21). This was sent in turn to further enquirers at various times: a portion was quoted, for instance, in the article 'Tolkien on Tolkien' in the *Diplomat* for October 1966, together with three paragraphs from a letter Tolkien had written in 1963 to Mrs Nancy Smith (provided to the magazine by the recipient). But there too, errors were introduced: the letter was wrongly transcribed, with 'Deren' instead of 'Beren' (*'Of Beren and Lúthien'), and the episode at Roos (*Yorkshire) when Edith Bratt (*Edith Tolkien) danced in the woodland glade is said to have occurred while Tolkien 'was in the Humber Garrison in 1913' (*sic*, for 1917; in 1913 Tolkien was still an undergraduate); and the latter error was compounded when the *Diplomat* paragraphs were reprinted in *Letters* (p. 221), with the date '1913' wrongly emended to '1918'.

Accounts of Tolkien's life have continued to be plagued by such errors, by misinterpretations of facts, and even by outright invention. On 16 January 1961, translator Åke Ohlmarks having included biographical information in a preface to the Swedish *Lord of the Rings* (*Sagan om ringen*, 1959–61), Tolkien objected that he did 'not wish to have any biographical or critical material on myself inserted by the translator without my permission and without any consultation. The five pages of impertinent nonsense inserted by Mr Ohlmarks . . . could well have been spared' (letter to Alina Dadlez, foreign rights coordinator at George Allen & Unwin, Tolkien-George Allen & Unwin archive, Harper-Collins). On 24 January 1961 he wrote again:

> I do not object to biographical notice, if it is desirable (the Dutch [translation of *The Lord of the Rings*] did without it). But it should be correct, and it should be pertinent. . . .
>
> *Who is Who* is not a safe source in the hands of foreigners ignorant of England. From it Ohlmarks has woven a ridiculous fantasy. Ohlmarks is a very vain man . . . preferring his own fancy to facts, and very ready to pretend to knowledge which he does not possess. He does not hesitate to attribute to me sentiments and beliefs which I repudiate. Amongst them a dislike of the University of Leeds, because it was 'northern' and no older than the Victorian seventies. This is impertinent and entirely untrue. [letter to Alina Dadlez, *Letters*, p. 305]

Ohlmarks had also made numerous factual mistakes, such as that the Tolkien-Gordon edition of *Sir Gawain and the Green Knight* (1925) was first published in 1934.

On 23 February 1966 Tolkien wrote to *W.H. Auden, who planned to write a book about him, that he regarded 'such things as premature impertinences; and unless undertaken by an intimate friend, or with consultation of the subject (for which at present I have no time), I cannot believe that they have a usefulness to justify the distaste and irritation given to the victim. I wish at any rate that any book could wait until I produce the *Silmarillion*' (*Letters*, p. 367). Indeed, not until *The Silmarillion* was published in 1977 could one begin to appreciate Tolkien's life's-work, while today the biographer of Tolkien overlooks at his peril the long circuitous development of the mythology documented in *The History of Middle-earth* (1983–96).

And yet Tolkien did not veto a book about him published in 1968 by William Ready, the former Director of Libraries at Marquette University (*Libraries and archives) to which Tolkien had sold some of his literary papers. *The Tolkien Relation: A Personal Enquiry* by William Ready (reprinted as *Understanding Tolkien and The Lord of the Rings*) is 'personal' in the double sense that it is one man's view of his subject, and an enquiry into Tolkien's life and character relative to his fiction, primarily *The Lord of the Rings*. Ready evidently hoped to play on his subject's past acquaintance to gain his support and approval; and it may be that a sense of gratitude, for the interest Ready had shown in his work while at Marquette, prevented Tolkien from replying as forcefully as he had to W.H. Auden. Nonetheless he declined to supply personal information to Ready, once again citing a dislike of 'being written about', the results of which to that date 'have caused me both irritation and distaste.' And he hoped that Ready would make his treatment 'literary (and as critical of that aspect as you like)' rather than personal (letter to Ready, 2 February 1967, quoted in *The Tolkien Relation*, pp. 55–6).

Having seen Ready's book in print, Tolkien wrote to Clyde S. Kilby:

Though ill-written it is not entirely without value, since the man is intelligent. But he is a rogue.... Ready paid me a short visit [in April 1967].... A large part of the time he was with me he was talking about himself. I can now see his difficulty. If he had brought out a notebook and informed me of his object, I should have shown him out. He therefore had to rely on his own memory of the few remarks I made about my personal history. These he appears to have embroidered with wholly illegitimate deductions of his own and the addition of baseless fictions. [letter of 4 June 1968, Marion E. Wade Center, Wheaton College, Wheaton, Illinois]

Among these, Ready says that Tolkien's mother, Mabel Suffield (*Mabel Tolkien), before her marriage had 'worked with her sisters as a missionary among the women of the Sultan of Zanzibar' (*The Tolkien Relation*, p. 6); that she died in 1910, not 1904; that Tolkien gave the W.P. Ker Lecture in 1933 (in fact it was in 1953); and that one of the *Oxford pubs in which the *Inklings met was the 'Burning Babe', surely a mishearing of 'Bird and Baby', a nickname of the Eagle and Child. Mabel's service in Zanzibar, a story wholly without foundation, in particular has cast a long shadow over later biographies and biographical sketches.

The first full biography of Tolkien, *J.R.R. Tolkien: Architect of Middle Earth* by Daniel Grotta (or Grotta-Kurska), was published in 1976, three years after its subject's death. To its credit, far more than may be said for most later accounts, it is the product of appreciable research, in libraries and through personal contacts. Grotta was denied access to Tolkien's private papers, however, and according to his author's note (p. 160) the Tolkien family 'requested Tolkien's close friends and associates to refrain from giving me information, out of respect for Tolkien's memory' – by that time, Humphrey Carpenter had been commissioned to write an 'official' biography (see below), to which the Tolkien Estate gave preference. Grotta seems, moreover, to have been refused permission to publish some of the material he was able to glean nonetheless: there are omissions in his 1976 text, each with the label 'deleted for legal considerations'. Under these circumstances, he learned nothing of the *T.C.B.S., and wrongly concluded that Tolkien was referring to his fellow Oxford student Allen Barnett (rather than *Christopher Wiseman) when he said that all but one of his close friends had been killed in the First World War (*War). And since Grotta produced his biography too early to have read *The Silmarillion (published in 1977), he could say little of substance about that seminal work, and with no knowledge of its manuscripts he wrote a confused description of its history.

Omissions such as these limit the usefulness of Grotta's book, while its reliability is called into question by many careless errors, only a few of which need be mentioned. He mistakenly names as 'Tolkien's first tutor . . . a young Fellow named Joseph Wrighty, who had arrived at Oxford in the same year as Tolkien' (p. 38; the eminent *Joseph Wright had been at Oxford since 1888 and a professor since 1901). Grotta notes that Tolkien took a Second in 'Moderns (which included Anglo-Saxon, as opposed to Greek and Latin)' (p. 39), rather than Honour Moderations, an examination for those reading Classics. He names *Nevill Coghill rather than *Norman Davis as Tolkien's successor as Merton Professor of English Language and Literature (Coghill became the Merton Professor of English Literature in 1957, before Tolkien retired). And he describes the Ace Books edition of The Lord of the Rings as having 'neither index nor appendices' (p. 126), though it did include the latter.

In the second edition of his book, retitled The Biography of J.R.R. Tolkien, Architect of Middle-earth (1978), Grotta made a few minor alterations, having 'received much additional information from readers' (p. 175; Carpenter's Biography had appeared the previous year), but the greater number of errors from the previous text remained. One of these, in which Tolkien is said to have written a work called Númenor in the 1920s which preceded 'The Silmarillion' (the reverse of the actual sequence), is even compounded in Grotta's second edition, in a new 'epilogue' on The Silmarillion then recently published. The 1992 reprint of his book contains a new preface, but is otherwise unchanged.

J.R.R. Tolkien: A Biography by Humphrey Carpenter (in the United States, originally Tolkien: A Biography), first published in 1977, is much to be preferred to Grotta. Publisher *Rayner Unwin recalled that he

> had long worried that without an authorised biography there would inevitably be ill-informed and tendentious writings about Tolkien over which neither he nor we [his publishers] would have any control. In his lifetime Tolkien had brushed aside the fear, and for him it would indeed have been yet another distraction. But after his death it was one of the first matters that I raised with the [Tolkien] family. They accepted the

need for something to be done, but were doubtful about who could be entrusted with such a commission and what control there might be over what was written. As a stop-gap solution I suggested a pictorial biography, using family pictures for the most part, with extended captions as the text. . . . *Priscilla [Tolkien], who lived in Oxford, knew a young man that she thought might be suitable. He worked for Radio Oxford, and I agreed to meet him. Humphrey Carpenter . . . was personable, eager, and willing to throw up his job on the radio to undertake our project. I didn't think a mixture of photographs and extended captions needed any great qualifications so I agreed terms on the spot and encouraged him to get down to work. The material he needed for his research was stored in the converted barn next to the house that *Christopher [Tolkien] was then living in outside Oxford, and Humphrey found himself working closely alongside Christopher.

It soon became apparent that Humphrey had dug himself so enthusiastically into the project that a full-scale biography was in the making. Christopher seemed agreeable, and so was I. [*George Allen & Unwin: A Remembrancer*, pp. 248–9]

To date, only Carpenter among Tolkien's biographers has had full access to his subject's private papers. In addition, he was able to interview members of Tolkien's family and many friends and colleagues, and he remains unsurpassed in personal knowledge of Oxford and understanding of university life. Although 'authorized' by the Tolkien family, his book is by no means hagiography: it does not omit mention, for instance, of the younger Tolkien's occasional bouts of despair, or of tensions within his marriage. And having been vetted by Christopher Tolkien, it contains very few errors or misinterpretations. (We note occasional disagreements with Carpenter in the **Chronology** volume of this *Companion and Guide*, and in present volume under *Reading.) Comparatively short by later standards, only (in its first edition) 260 pages excluding appendices and index, the *Biography* serves its purpose well without verbosity. In later editions its useful checklist of Tolkien's published writings was expanded to include further posthumous works.

Tolkien: A Biography by Michael White (2001) is largely a retelling of the standard life. In order to provide 'a more colourful image of the creator of Middle-earth' (p. 6), White adopted a 'breezy' prose style and, to impart a sense of immediacy, often assumes knowledge of thoughts and feelings. The tone of his book is set at once, as he imagines Tolkien returning home on 'a warm early summer afternoon', kissing his wife, and greeting 'his baby daughter, five-month-old Priscilla' (pp. 7–8) – even though Priscilla Tolkien was born on 18 June 1929, and could not have been five months old in 'early summer'. In the same chapter White reports a 'legend' not substantiated anywhere else, that Tolkien was inspired to write the first line of *The Hobbit* when he noticed a hole in his study carpet. Such inventions or suppositions are frequent in White's book, together with many errors of fact.

Tolkien: Man and Myth by Joseph Pearce (1998) often has been referred to as a biography, though in truth it more narrowly explores the significance of Middle-earth and what it represented in Tolkien's thought, and the connection between his religious faith and his life and writings – 'internal' biography more so than 'external'. About a third of its text consists of long quotations by Tolkien himself and from writings about him, while several chapters are little more than a summary of Carpenter's *Biography*.

Tolkien and the Great War: The Threshold of Middle-earth by John Garth (2003) has an even narrower scope, largely from the end of Tolkien's days at *King Edward's School, Birmingham to his demobilization from the Army. But Garth examines those formative years (1911–19) much more fully than Carpenter was able to do, after the opening of pertinent First World War papers in the Public Record Office, and he makes more extensive use of correspondence by Tolkien's friends, in an attempt to relate Tolkien's military experiences and comradeship in the T.C.B.S. to his early poetry and the beginnings of his mythology.

J.R.R. Tolkien: A Biography by Leslie Ellen Jones (2003) is aimed specifically at an American schools audience. For the sake of the student reader, she frequently interrupts her narrative of Tolkien's life to explain about late nineteenth-century British society, English as a Germanic language, the causes of the First World War, and the like; and she often comments on matters of current social concern, such as class distinctions and the role of women. She devotes two chapters of her book to a discussion of *The Lord of the Rings*.

Seven shorter, illustrated biographies of Tolkien have also appeared, intended for younger or more casual readers: *J.R.R. Tolkien: Man of Fantasy* by Russell Shorto (1988); *J.R.R. Tolkien: Master of Fantasy* by David R. Collins (1992); *Myth Maker: J.R.R. Tolkien* by Anne E. Neimark (1996); *J.R.R. Tolkien: The Man Who Created The Lord of the Rings* by Michael Coren (2001); *J.R.R. Tolkien: Creator of Languages and Legends* by Doris Lynch (2003); *The Importance of J.R.R. Tolkien* by Stuart P. Levine (2004); and *J.R.R. Tolkien* by Edward Willett (2004). Each suffers to some degree from factual errors, and – Neimark and Coren's books especially – from a tendency to embroider or exaggerate for dramatic effect. Of these, Collins' account is to be preferred for balance and accuracy; but the young person who has read *The Lord of the Rings* successfully should be equally capable of reading Carpenter's *Biography*, with greater reward.

Among more miscellaneous books on Tolkien's life, *The Tolkien Family Album* by *John and Priscilla Tolkien, published for the Tolkien centenary in 1992, follows more or less the lines that Rayner Unwin had suggested (see above): 'a pictorial biography, using family pictures for the most part, with extended captions as the text'. It is interesting as a brief reminiscence of two of Tolkien's children, and for its collection of photographs not reproduced elsewhere. The Bodleian Library (*Libraries and archives) exhibition catalogue *J.R.R. Tolkien: Life and Legend* by Judith Priestman, also published in 1992, describes and reproduces letters, illustrations, and drawings by Tolkien, pages from his academic and literary manuscripts, and photographs of relevant people and places. These are placed in the context of Tolkien's life, 'to indicate something of the scope and variety of [his] achievements' (p. 7). Finally, the present authors' *J.R.R. Tolkien: Artist and Illustrator* (1995) provides extensive coverage of the place of painting and drawing in Tolkien's life and how his visual art relates to his fiction.

Most biographical writings about Tolkien since 1977 have been reductions or adaptations of Carpenter's *Biography*, often supplemented by reference to Tolkien's published letters (1981). And yet, as shown by John Garth in *Tolkien and the Great War* and in the present book, important biographical information remains to be gleaned from libraries and archives, and from a variety of published works. The assiduous Tolkien biographer must cast a wide net of research, but also must seek to understand what he finds, without assumptions based on his own age or culture – one finds, for instance, in many American accounts of Tolkien's life, a lack of comprehension of English universities and their customs.

Nor can the biographer afford to be uncritical of his sources. In the course of writing the *Companion and Guide* the present authors discovered errors and discrepancies even in standard published works, and inconsistencies in manuscripts and recorded reminiscences. A wealth of information is to be found in a series of recordings of Tolkien's family and friends made soon after his death by Ann Bonsor, and first broadcast on Radio Oxford in 1974; but in some of these, looking back to times long past, memory demonstrably failed. Nevill Coghill, for one, recalled how as secretary of the Exeter College Essay Club (*Societies and clubs) he had asked Tolkien to read a paper at one of their meetings. Tolkien agreed, and said that the subject of his paper would be 'the fall of Gondolin'. Coghill remembered that he then spent weeks searching in reference books in vain to find a mention of 'Gondolin', not realizing that it was the name of a city in Tolkien's mythology. Records show, however, that Coghill had not held any office in the Essay Club when Tolkien read *The Fall of Gondolin* (see *The Book of Lost Tales*) to its members, and in fact was elected to the Club only on 27 February 1920, less than two weeks before the event.

Even Tolkien himself sometimes nodded. In referring to his lecture *On Fairy-Stories* he twice gave an erroneous date for its delivery at the University of St Andrews ('1940' and '1938', in fact 1939), and in his Foreword to the second edition of *The Lord of the Rings* (1965) he wrote that the work 'was begun soon after *The Hobbit* was written and before its publication in 1937', though in fact he began the sequel between 16 and 19 December 1937, after publication of *The Hobbit* on 22 September 1937. The latter is clear from a reading of *Letters*, and yet occasionally one still sees it written in books about Tolkien that he began *The Lord of the Rings* before the publication of *The Hobbit*, uncritically accepting his misstatement of 1965.

'Bird and Baby' (*i.e.* **Eagle and Child**) *see* **Oxford and environs**

Birmingham and environs. Both of Tolkien's parents came from this major manufacturing centre in the English *West Midlands, and he himself spent sixteen of his early years in or near the city. His father (*Arthur Tolkien) and paternal grandparents (see *Tolkien family) lived at 'Beechwood' in **Church Road** in the southern suburb of **Moseley**, while his mother *Mabel and her family were from **Kings Heath** still further south. Tolkien himself came to Birmingham from *South Africa with his mother and brother at the end of April 1895; until summer 1896 they stayed at **9 Ashfield Road, Kings Heath** with Mabel Tolkien's parents and siblings (see *Suffield family). It was there in December 1895 that young Ronald Tolkien experienced his first wintry Christmas. In February 1896, however, his father died in Bloemfontein, and his mother decided that she and her sons should live independent of her parents' crowded home, and in the countryside where the boys could have fresh air. In summer 1896 Mabel rented a semi-detached cottage at **5 Gracewell Road** (today 264a Wake Green Road) in the hamlet of ***Sarehole** not far to the east of Kings Heath, now part of the suburb of Hall Green. It was an idyllic setting, or became so in Tolkien's memory, a rural paradise of fields, trees, and flowers, and a working mill. But the interlude there was brief.

In September 1900 Tolkien began to attend classes at *King Edward's School in New Street in the centre of Birmingham, some four miles distant, and at first walked most of the way between home and school since trams did not run as far as Sarehole and Mabel could not afford the train fare. It was a long walk for the family also to Sunday services at St Anne's, the Roman Catholic church in Alcester Street, Moseley, in which Mabel had been received into the faith the previous June. Mabel Tolkien now, in September 1900, briefly rented a small house at **214 Alcester Road, Moseley**, near a tram route into the city. After the pleasures of rural Sarehole Tolkien found it 'dreadful' to be in a built-up area with views only of houses and smoking factory chimneys (quoted in *Biography*, p. 25). Birmingham was a centre of the Industrial Revolution, known for its metal-working, and a focus of the railways. A contemporary observer called it 'a metropolis of machinery . . . exceedingly interesting as a consistently developed exemplification of the nineteenth-century spirit' (Harry Quilter, *What's What* (1902), p. 236). Inevitably there was pollution and traffic, and substantial development was already underway; but in residential suburbs such as Moseley factory smoke was less pronounced, and local industry supported the city's excellent schools and museums, including an art gallery with works by the Pre-Raphaelites.

At the end of 1900 or the beginning of 1901 Mabel, Ronald, and *Hilary moved once again, to **86 Westfield Road, Kings Heath**. She chose their new home because it was close to the Roman Catholic church of St Dunstan, then a building of wood and corrugated iron on the corner of Westfield Road and Station Road. Although it was a noisy location, near Kings Heath station, the slopes of the railway cutting behind the house were covered with grass and flowers, and (as today) there were fields on the other side of the line. Tolkien now first came into contact with the Welsh language, in names on passing coal-trucks. Mabel was not satisfied with St Dunstan's, however, and in looking for a new place of worship found the *Birmingham Oratory in the suburb of Edgbaston. In early 1902 she and the boys moved to **26 Oliver Road, Edgbaston** (the house no longer exists), conveniently near the Oratory church and its attached grammar school, St Philip's. There they stayed until April 1904, when Mabel was taken into hospital suffering from diabetes. Her boys lived for a while with relatives and then in *Rednal with their mother until her death on 14 November 1904.

Immediately after the loss of their mother Ronald and Hilary stayed with Laurence Tolkien, one of their father's brothers (see *Tolkien family), at **Dunkeld, Middleton Hall Road, Kings Norton**. By January 1905 *Father Francis Morgan, the priest whom Mabel had named her sons' guardian, placed them instead with their Aunt Beatrice Suffield at **25 Stirling Road, Edgbaston**, not far from the Oratory. Their room was on the top floor. Early in 1908, life with Aunt Beatrice having proved unhappy for the boys, Father Francis moved them to **37 Duchess Road, Edgbaston**, the home of the Faulkner family. Ronald and Hilary had a rented room on the second floor; on the first floor was another lodger, Edith Bratt (*Edith Tolkien), with whom they became friends. Edith played the piano and accompanied soloists at musical evenings given by Mrs Faulkner, but was discouraged from practising. Gradually Ronald and Edith fell in love. When their clandestine relationship came to the attention of Father Francis late in 1909 he took steps to end it. Ronald and Hilary were now removed to new lodgings with a Mrs MacSherry at **4 Highfield Road, Edgbaston**, at which address Tolkien lived until going up to Exeter College, *Oxford in October 1911.

During his years at King Edward's School Tolkien became familiar with central Birmingham and with some of its merchants. Among these were **Cornish's** bookshop in New Street, which Tolkien explored for books on *Philology; **E.H. Lawley & Sons** at 24 New Street, a jeweller at which Ronald and Edith bought each other presents in January 1910 (see *Life and Legend*, fig. 25); and **Barrow's Stores** in Corporation Street (north from New Street), until the 1960s a flourishing grocer's which had its origin in a shop founded in 1824 by John Cadbury (of Cadbury's cocoa). An engraving of Barrow's Stores is reproduced in *The Tolkien Family Album*, p. 26. Tolkien and some of his friends at King Edward's School, having formed a Tea Club, met regularly in Barrow's Tea Room. *Christopher Wiseman recalled that 'in the Tea Room there was a sort of compartment, a table for six, between two large settles, quite secluded; and it was known as the Railway Carriage. It became a favourite place for us, and we changed our title to the Barrovian Society after Barrow's Stores' (quoted in *Biography*, p. 46). The group ultimately combined and abbreviated their names, Tea Club and Barrovian Society, and called themselves the *T.C.B.S.

On 9 November 1916, having contracted trench fever during military service in France, Tolkien was admitted to the First Southern General Hospital, a converted facility of over one thousand beds at the then newly built

Birmingham University in Edgbaston. He was a patient there until 9 December 1916, when he was able to take sick leave. During these few weeks in hospital he may have begun to write *The Book of Lost Tales. At least in the period 1913–15, Tolkien occasionally visited his friend *Robert Q. Gilson at his family home in **Marston Green**, near Birmingham to the east.

When Tolkien lived in Birmingham, most of the buildings in the city centre were still of recent vintage, having been built or re-built within the previous fifty years. But some were replaced within the next half-century, to Tolkien's dismay. On 3 April 1944, having recently visited the new King Edward's School in Edgbaston Park Road, he wrote to his son *Christopher: 'Except for one patch of ghastly wreckage (opp[osite] my old school's site) [Birmingham] does not look much damaged: not by the enemy [in wartime bombing raids]. The chief damage has been the growth of great flat featureless modern buildings. The worst of all is the ghastly multiple-store erection on the old site' (*Letters*, p. 70).

Contemporary maps and descriptions of the places in and near Birmingham where Tolkien lived, and recent photographs of his former homes, are reproduced in the booklet *Tolkien's Birmingham* by Patricia Reynolds (1992). Photographs of Tolkien homes are included also in the article on Tolkien in *Some Moseley Personalities, Volume I* (1991). *Moseley and Kings Heath on Old Picture Postcards*, compiled by John Marks (1991), is a useful collection of photographs of those places dating from Tolkien's years in Birmingham.

Birmingham Oratory. The Oratory Order begun in Rome by St Philip Neri was formally recognized by Pope Gregory XIII in 1575. Its main mission is preaching, prayer, and the administration of the sacraments. John Henry Newman (later Cardinal Newman) introduced the order into England by founding the Oratorian Congregation in Birmingham in 1848. In 1852 the community moved to Hagley Road in the suburb of Edgbaston, where a house and church were built. (Their first chapel, in Alcester Road, Moseley, was replaced by St Anne's Church, which Tolkien, his mother, and his brother attended for a while; see *Birmingham and environs.) In 1859 Newman also founded St Philip's, a grammar school attached to the Oratory Church. The church was later extended, and beginning in 1903 a new building, designed by E. Doran Webb, was constructed over the old, in the style of the Church of San Martino in Rome as Newman had originally desired. A photograph of the old church is reproduced in *The Tolkien Family Album*, p. 23.

Tolkien's mother *Mabel, a recent convert to Catholicism seeking a satisfactory place of worship, discovered the Oratory in 1901, and early in 1902 moved with her sons to Edgbaston. *Father Francis Morgan, a member of the Oratory community then carrying out the duties of parish priest, became a close family friend and after Mabel's death the guardian of her children. Tolkien and his brother *Hilary briefly went to St Philip's School, because it offered a Catholic education at low cost and was convenient to home, until it became clear that it could not provide the quality of learning that young Ronald Tolkien needed. (Tolkien returned to *King Edward's School, which he had attended earlier; Hilary joined him after a period of tuition by their mother.)

As wards of Father Francis the Tolkien boys spend much of their time between 1904 and 1911 at the Oratory. Tolkien later recalled that he was 'virtually a junior inmate of the Oratory house, which contained many learned fathers (largely "converts"). Observance of religion was strict. Hilary and I were supposed to, and usually did, serve Mass before getting on our bikes to go to [King Edward's] school in New Street' (letter to his son Michael, 1967, *Letters*, p. 395). In these years they would have witnessed the transformation of the Oratory Church from old to new.

Blackwell, Basil Henry (1889–1984). Basil Blackwell was educated at Merton College, *Oxford and trained at Oxford University Press in London. From 1913, for six years, he worked with his father's publishing firm, B.H. Blackwell, which published Tolkien's early poem *Goblin Feet* in *Oxford Poetry 1915*; the series of annual *Oxford Poetry* volumes, begun in 1913, was Basil's idea. In 1919 Blackwell became an independent publisher, and in succeeding years expanded his operation. In 1924, on his father's death, he became head of the family bookselling business as well. During his long life he also presided over trade and scholarly associations, and held civic posts in Oxford. He received numerous honours, including a knighthood in 1956 and an honorary fellowship at Merton College in 1959.

For a few years, from 1926, Blackwell and Tolkien were neighbours in North Oxford, at 20 and 22 Northmoor Road respectively. When in 1929 Blackwell vacated no. 20, Tolkien purchased it; he moved his family into the comparatively larger house in 1930. Tolkien was also a frequent customer of Blackwell's Bookshop in Broad Street, *Oxford, where by 1942 his account was seriously overextended. Blackwell offered to reduce Tolkien's debt by publishing his translation of *Pearl* (which existed in a finished form since 1926) and applying the translator's payment against his account. The work was set in type, but Tolkien failed to write more than rough notes for an introduction, and in the end Blackwell abandoned the project with remarkable grace.

See also Rita Ricketts, *Adventurers All: Tales of Blackwellians, of Books, Bookmen, and Reading and Writing Folk* (2002).

Bliss, Alan Joseph (1921–1985). Having received his B.A. at King's College, the University of London, Alan Bliss studied at *Oxford for a B.Litt. from 1946 to 1948. His thesis, supervised by Tolkien, was an edition of the Middle English poem *Sir Orfeo*. In Hilary Term 1948 he delivered a series of lectures on that poem, and in Trinity Term 1948 he lectured on 'The West Saxon Dialect in Middle English', on both occasions acting on Tolkien's behalf. Bliss later taught at Malta and Istanbul before taking up appointments in Old and Middle English at University College, Dublin. He succeeded to the Chair of Old and Middle English at Dublin in 1974.

Revised for publication, his *Sir Orfeo* appeared in 1954 in the *Oxford English Monographs*, of which Tolkien was a general editor. In his introduction Bliss thanks Tolkien 'whose penetrating scholarship is an inspiration to all who have worked with him' (p. vi). Among other works which Bliss wrote or edited are *The Metre of Beowulf* (1957); *A Dictionary of Foreign Words and Phrases in Current English* (1966); *Spoken English in Ireland, 1600–1740* (1979); and *Finn and Hengest: The Fragment and the Episode* (1982), an edition of Tolkien's lectures on the 'Finnesburg Fragment' and the related episode in *Beowulf*. In his preface to *Finn and Hengest* Bliss relates that in 1966 Tolkien had offered him all of his material on the story, to use in preparing for publication a paper on 'Hengest and the Jutes'. Bliss did not receive the papers until 1979, however, after Tolkien's death; and when he read Tolkien's lectures 'it became obvious to me that I could never make use of his work in any work of my own: not only had he anticipated nearly all my ideas, but he had gone far beyond them in directions which I had never considered' (p. v). Bliss agreed instead, in response to a proposal by *Christopher Tolkien, to prepare Tolkien's lectures for publication, with added notes and comments.

Bliss contributed an essay, 'The Appreciation of Old English Metre', to the *Festschrift *English and Medieval Studies Presented to J.R.R. Tolkien on the Occasion of His Seventieth Birthday* (1962), and another, 'Beowulf Lines 3074–3075', to *J.R.R. Tolkien, Scholar and Storyteller: Essays in Memoriam*, ed. Mary Salu and Robert T. Farrell (1979).

Bloemfontein *see* **South Africa**

Blomfield, Joan Elizabeth *see* **Turville-Petre, Joan Elizabeth**

Bombadil Goes Boating. Poem, first published in *The Adventures of Tom Bombadil and Other Verses from the Red Book* (1962), pp. 17–23. A sequel to *The Adventures of Tom Bombadil*, the new poem follows merry Tom Bombadil as he rows a boat down stream on an autumn day, intending to meet his friend Farmer Maggot (from *The Lord of the Rings*). Once again, in the course of events, Tom is challenged by a variety of creatures – now a wren, a kingfisher, an otter, a swan, and the hobbit defenders of Buckland at Grindwall – but here the exchanges are light, laced with humour, without the menace that underlies most of the earlier poem. At length Tom meets Farmer Maggot in the Marish and goes home with him: at Maggot's farm 'songs they had and merry tales, the supping and the dancing', and they swap 'all the tidings / from Barrow-downs to Tower Hills'.

Tolkien developed and enlarged *Bombadil Goes Boating* for the 1962 volume from an earlier, isolated work which he called the 'germ of Tom Bombadil' ('Ho! Tom Bombadil / Whither are you going / With John Pompador / Down the River rowing?'), published in *The Return of the Shadow* (1988), pp. 115–16. In a letter to his publisher *Rayner Unwin on 12 April 1962 Tolkien allowed that an understanding of *Bombadil Goes Boating* required a knowledge of *The*

Lord of the Rings: 'at any rate it performs the service of further "integrating" Tom with the world of the *Lord of the Rings* into which he was inserted.' He felt that it tickled his 'pedantic fancy' because it contains an echo of the Norse Nibelung legends and 'one of the lines comes straight . . . from *The Ancrene Wisse* [*Ancrene Riwle]' (Letters, p. 315).* On 1 August 1962 he wrote to *Pauline Baynes that he had placed the fictional time of the poem 'to the days of growing shadow', that is, before Frodo's departure from Hobbiton in *The Lord of the Rings* (Letters, p. 319).

The Book of Lost Tales. Series of tales in which a traveller, Eriol, having come to the Lonely Island (or Isle) of the Elves, Tol Eressëa, is told of the Creation of the World and the history of the Elves until the time of his arrival in their midst. For convenience in *The History of Middle-earth*, the tales were published in two volumes, *The Book of Lost Tales, Part One* (1983) and *The Book of Lost Tales, Part Two* (1984): these follow the chronology of events within the mythology, but not the order of writing of the tales, nor necessarily Tolkien's original plan for the order of their telling. Each volume also includes descriptions and commentary by Christopher Tolkien, poems by Tolkien related to the tales, and appendices on the meanings of names within his invented languages. In the **Reader's Guide**, summaries of the tales and consideration of their place in the evolution of the mythology are dealt with in relation to the chapters of the published *Silmarillion* (1977); these are listed, with cross-references, in the separate entries for *Part One* and *Part Two*.

HISTORY

In *Christopher Tolkien's words, *The Book of Lost Tales* was 'the first substantial work of imaginative literature by J.R.R. Tolkien, and the first emergence in narrative of the Valar, of the Children of Ilúvatar, Elves and Men, of the Dwarves and the Orcs, and of the lands in which their history is set, Valinor beyond the western ocean, and Middle-earth, the "Great Lands" between the seas of east and west' (*The Book of Lost Tales, Part One*, p. 1). It was also the expression of the *'Silmarillion' mythology in prose. Poems, drawings, and references in letters from the years preceding its writing, however, show that many of its elements had already been developing in Tolkien's thoughts. Among the more significant of these poems were *The Voyage of Éarendel the Evening Star* (*Éalá Éarendel Engla Beorhtast*, September 1914); *The City of the Gods* (earlier *Kôr*, April 1915); *The Happy Mariners* (July 1915); and *Kortirion among the Trees* (November 1915, later *The Trees of Kortirion*). In 1915 Tolkien also made several watercolours which suggest that he was visualizing particular places: *Tanaqui* (*Artist and Illustrator*, fig. 43) almost certainly depicts Kôr. Most significant are a watercolour dated 10 May 1915, *The Shores of Faery* (*Artist and Illustrator*, fig. 44), with an accompanying poem, each showing or referring to Kôr and to the Sun and Moon forming from the Two Trees.

Tolkien may have begun to write *The Book of Lost Tales* while still in the

First Southern General Hospital in November 1916, or during his sick leave in Great Haywood from mid-December that year. There is no clear evidence for this, nor whether *The Cottage of Lost Play* or *The Fall of Gondolin* came first among the tales. Tolkien several times in later years referred to *The Fall of Gondolin* as being the first of these to be written; but he may not have considered *The Cottage of Lost Play* a tale. It introduces the framework of the tales, and Eriol who hears them (see *Eriol and Ælfwine); and although Eriol survived as a transmitter of documents and traditions in later versions of the mythology, the Cottage of Lost Play itself did not appear again after *The Book of Lost Tales*. This interpretation might seem to be strengthened by Tolkien's description of *The Fall of Gondolin* as 'the first real story of this imaginary world' in a letter to W.H. Auden (7 June 1955, *Letters*, p. 215); but a note by Tolkien, probably dating from 1919, which reads '*Link between Cottage of Lost Play and (Tale 2) Music of Ainur*' (*The Book of Lost Tales, Part One*, p. 45) suggests that at that early date he did consider the former a 'tale' (although *The Music of the Ainur* was certainly not the second tale written, it was the first told to Eriol).

Whenever he began it, Tolkien completed the first pencil version of *The Cottage of Lost Play* on loose sheets by early February 1917, when *Edith Tolkien wrote on the cover of the exercise book in which she made a fair copy 'her initials, E.M.T., and a date, Feb. 12th 1917' (*The Book of Lost Tales, Part One*, p. 13) – either the date she began the copy or the date she finished it. Either then or at some later date, Tolkien made a few emendations. As early as April 1915 he had written a poem, *You & Me and the Cottage of Lost Play* (**The Little House of Lost Play: Mar Vanwa Tyaliéva*), in which children meet and play in their sleep in the gardens of a cottage; but it cannot be known if, at that time, he foresaw the part the Cottage would play in *The Book of Lost Tales*. The main theme of the poem concerns two children, presumably Edith and Tolkien himself, meeting and playing together in dreams in the garden and surrounding area.

With no contemporary evidence to date the writing of the first (pencil) version of *The Fall of Gondolin* in two exercise books, one must rely on statements made by Tolkien decades later. He dated the writing of *The Fall of Gondolin* to the end of 1916 or to 1917, and sometimes mentioned having written it only while on sick leave, and sometimes while in hospital and on sick leave. Its writing could equally precede or follow *The Cottage of Lost Play*, or he may have worked on both at once. One factor in suggesting that it came second is that, with *The Cottage of Lost Play* completed by early February 1917, and the next tale not begun until June 1917 at the earliest, the writing (or most of the writing) of *The Fall of Gondolin* would fit well into the intervening period.

Tolkien substantially overwrote the pencil version of *The Fall of Gondolin* in ink, without erasing the pencilled text though in places striking it through. Christopher Tolkien has described this revision as 'by no means a complete recasting (still less a re-imagining)' (*The Book of Lost Tales, Part Two*, p. 146). From this emended state Edith Tolkien wrote out a fair copy, which Christopher Tolkien in *Unfinished Tales* (1980) believed was done 'apparently in 1917'

(p. 5). By the time he came to edit *The Book of Lost Tales, Part Two*, however, he came to think it 'improbable' that the revision and fair copy were made in 1917, and associated them more closely to his father's preparation of *The Fall of Gondolin* for public reading in spring 1920 (*Part Two*, p. 146). This later judgement seems to be supported by the evidence presented in the note on *The Fall of Gondolin* given below, item 23 in the sequence of texts.

The story after *The Fall of Gondolin*, *The Tale of Tinúviel*, was evidently not foreseen, but inspired by a contemporary event in Tolkien's own life, when his wife Edith danced for him in a woodland glade near Roos (*Yorkshire). Tolkien wrote about this event several times. In 1963, for instance, in a letter to Nancy Smith, he said: 'The kernel of the mythology, the matter of *Lúthien Tinúviel* and *Beren*, arose from a small woodland glade filled with "hemlocks" (or other white umbellifers) near Roos on the Holderness peninsula – to which I occasionally went when free from regimental duties while in the Humber Garrison in 1917' (*Letters*, p. 221, '1918' corrected by the present authors to '1917'; see *Tolkien on Tolkien*). And on 16 July 1964 he told Christopher Bretherton that he wrote *The Fall of Gondolin* in 1917, and later in the same year 'the original version of the "Tale of Lúthien Tinúviel and Beren" . . . founded on a small wood with a great undergrowth of "hemlock" . . . near Roos in Holderness . . .' (*Letters*, p. 345). Internal evidence in the tale and in later retellings suggest that the visit to the wood took place in early summer, probably in late May or early June. The flowering season for hemlocks and other umbellifers in England at its widest range is May to September; Tolkien also mentions chestnut trees in flower and white moths fluttering: chestnut trees usually flower in late May or early June, and moths are unlikely to be active outside the warmer months. In *The Tale of Tinúviel* Tolkien actually states that Beren first saw Tinúviel in 'June'. As for external evidence, Tolkien was certainly with the Humber Garrison between mid-April and mid-August 1917, except for a period at a signalling school. In a note to a letter to Christopher Tolkien of 11 July 1972, he said that 'the earliest form of the legend' was 'written in hospital', which would place all or part of the actual writing of the first pencil version to mid-August–October 1917 (*Letters*, p. 420).

Humphrey Carpenter in *Biography* dates the incident near Roos after the birth of the Tolkiens' first child on 16 November 1917, and, despite Tolkien's statement to Christopher Bretherton, places the writing of *The Tale of Tinúviel* after *The Tale of Turambar*, thus presumably in 1918. It seems unlikely, however, that Edith would have danced on the windy east coast of England in winter while still recovering from a difficult birth. And twice in the published *Book of Lost Tales* Christopher Tolkien has no hesitation in dating the original *Tale of Tinúviel* to 1917 and calling it 'the second' tale, after *The Fall of Gondolin*. It may be that Carpenter's placement of *Tinúviel* after *Turambar* was influenced by the fact that, although the original pencil version of *Tinúviel* preceded the original pencil text of *Turambar* (both lost when overwritten in ink in 1919 and the pencil texts erased), the ink version of *Turambar* preceded the ink text of *Tinúviel*; see *The Book of Lost Tales, Part One*, p. 10, and *Part Two*, pp. 3, 49, 69.

The seeds of *The Tale of Turambar* were planted early in Tolkien's thoughts, from his interest in the story of Kullervo in the *Kalevala*, and from that of Sigurd he had read as a boy. An early entry in the *Qenyaqetsa* suggests that he may have been planning some version of the story as early as 1915–16. With *Tinúviel* apparently in progress in late 1917, *Turambar* presumably followed at the end of 1917 or in 1918, with the bulk of its writing accomplished in the latter year. (There seems to be no evidence of work by Tolkien on any part of *The Book of Lost Tales* other than *Tinúviel* and *Turambar* in the period from summer 1917 to late 1918.) In an early outline of *Turambar*, the story and names differ considerably from the earliest surviving text, but it is impossible to say if this was also the case in the preceding pencil version, erased after being overwritten in ink.

On 16 July 1964 Tolkien wrote to Christopher Bretherton that while on the staff of the *Oxford English Dictionary* he 'wrote a cosmogonical myth, "The Music of the Ainur"' (*Letters*, p. 345). Since this tale seems to have been the next written, after *Turambar*, the continuation of work on *The Book of Lost Tales* can be dated to the end of 1918, after Tolkien returned to Oxford and joined the staff of the *OED*, or to his period of employment from the start of 1919 until mid-1920. There is some evidence, though, as detailed below, to suggest more narrowly that most of the rest of *The Book of Lost Tales* was completed by the end of June 1919.

There is no other exterior evidence to date the writing of individual tales, but internal clues give some indication of the sequence in which most of the stories and linking sections were written. Following is a possible order of original compositions and rewriting of the tales following *The Tale of Turambar*, with some alternatives noted, based on the published *Book of Lost Tales*. Texts which are no longer extant because of erasure, etc. are also included.

(1) Link between *Cottage of Lost Play* and *The Music of Ainur*. First draft in pencil, no longer extant; overwritten in ink and erased.

(2) *The Music of the Ainur* is told by Rúmil in the garden of the Cottage of Lost Play. A pencil draft, written in haste with many emendations.

(3) Link between *Cottage of Lost Play* and *The Music of Ainur* in which Eriol sleeps in the Cottage and the next morning meets Rúmil in the garden. Written in ink over the erased earlier pencil text, with the title 'Link between Cottage of Lost Play and (Tale 2) Music of Ainur'.

(4) *The Music of the Ainur*, told by Rúmil in the garden of the Cottage of Lost Play. Second version written in ink, closely based on the pencil version but with additions and emendations.

(5) Link between *The Music of the Ainur* and *The Coming of the Valar and the Building of Valinor*. First draft in pencil, not extant; overwritten in ink and erased. The ink version of *The Music of the Ainur*, in which Tolkien did not overwrite a pencil draft, was apparently followed at once by the pencil draft for this following link, which suggests that the ink text of *The Music of the Ainur* was already in existence.

(6) *The Coming of the Valar and the Building of Valinor*. First draft in pencil, no longer extant; overwritten in ink and erased.

(7) Link between *The Coming of the Valar and the Building of Valinor* and *The Chaining of Melko*. First draft in pencil, no longer extant; overwritten in ink and erased.

(8) *The Chaining of Melko* and *The Coming of the Elves and the Making of Kôr*. First draft in pencil, very rough and difficult to read. Most of this is no longer extant (overwritten in ink and erased), but towards the end the pencil text survives and was the only text made.

(9) Link in which Eriol returns to the Cottage of Lost Play and, after some days have passed, Lindo recounts *The Theft of Melko and the Darkening of Valinor* and *The Flight of the Noldoli*. Towards the end, Eriol asks a question, and after some conversation the tale is finished by Rumil, not Lindo. All of this is a continuous pencil draft following *The Coming of the Elves and the Making of Kôr*, with some emendations made at that time or later. On one page of the exercise book, part of *The Theft of Melko* is written around the earliest (or earliest surviving) map for the *legendarium*, a rough pencil sketch indicating features of importance to the early history of Arda: Valinor, the Great Sea, Utumna, but not at a particular time, since the map shows the positions both of the two Pillars and of the Two Trees. One section of *The Flight of Noldoli* was later struck through and replaced with a much longer text written carefully in ink on separate sheets, 'The Kinslaughter: (Battle of Kópas Alqalunten)'.

Tolkien probably wrote at least this far in pencil draft before he began to rewrite *The Coming of the Valar* and the following tales in ink. There is a close similarity of a passage of geographical description in the ink version of *The Coming of the Valar and the Building of Valinor* to a passage in the pencil draft of *The Coming of the Elves and the Making of Kôr*; Christopher Tolkien thinks it more logical that his father decided to include the description earlier, rather than that he decided to repeat it. The names *Habbanan* and *Harmalin* are used as late as the pencil text of *The Flight of the Noldoli*, whereas the later names *Eruman* and *Arvalin* appear *ab initio* part of the way through the ink text of *The Coming of the Elves*; but this is not as conclusive, as *Arvalien* (*sic*) appears once in *The Theft of Melko and the Darkening of Valinor*.

I Vene Kemen, a separate pencil drawing by Tolkien of the world in the form of a Viking ship, connected with the cosmology of *The Book of Lost Tales*, was made probably at this time. Christopher Tolkien thinks that the image may not have begun as a ship, but as a section of the world, and that his father later added mast, sail, and prow. The name *Harmalin* in the drawing suggests that it preceded the ink rewriting of *The Coming of the Elves and the Making of Kôr*.

For the following revisions of earlier tales (10–13), evidence of date is unfortunately lacking, but they may be conveniently described at this point:

(10) Link between *The Music of the Ainur* and *The Coming of the Valar and the Building of Valinor*, in which Eriol spends the day in the garden, and in

the evening in the Room of the Log Fire he asks to hear more about Valinor. Second version in ink, written over the earlier erased pencil text.

(11) *The Coming of the Valar and the Building of Valinor* is told by Rúmil in the Room of the Log Fire. Second version in ink, written over the earlier erased pencil text.

(12) Link between *The Building of Valinor* and *The Chaining of Melko*. Second version in ink, written over earlier erased pencil text. Eriol talks the next day with Vairë in the garden of the Cottage of Lost Play, and some days later is sent to visit Meril-i-Turinqui in Kortirion, who tells him the next tale.

(13) *The Chaining of Melko* and *The Coming of the Elves and the Making of Kôr*. Second version in ink, written over the erased earlier pencil text. A few small parts which were not completely erased and are still legible suggest that Tolkien made alterations as he wrote. He did not complete the rewriting, however, and the end of the tale exists only in the pencil draft.

From this point several texts, and rewritings and rearrangements, may be placed in two sequences, according to whether Ailios or Gilfanon is present or mentioned, Gilfanon having replaced Ailios in later writing and revision.

(14) Link between *The Flight of the Noldoli* and *The Tale of the Sun and Moon*. First draft in pencil, no longer extant (overwritten in ink and erased), but it presumably mentioned Ailios.

(15) *The Tale of the Sun and Moon*. First draft in pencil, no longer extant (overwritten in ink and erased) except at the end, with the ink manuscript continuing on fresh sheets. In the surviving part of the pencil draft Ailios is among those present, and the story is told by Lindo.

(16) Link between *The Tale of the Sun and Moon* and *The Hiding of Valinor*. Pencil draft of a conversation between Lindo and Ailios, which ends as Lindo begins the next tale.

(17) *The Hiding of Valinor*, told by Lindo. Pencil draft in which Ailios appears at the end.

(18) Pencil draft continuing from *The Hiding of Valinor*, in which another tale-telling is fixed for a week later on the day of Turuhalmë, the Logdrawing, after Ailios has returned from a journey.

(19) Rough draft describing the collection of firewood for Turuhalmë and the renewing of the fires. This ends with Ailios preparing to tell a tale and mentioning that when the Sun first rose there was 'travail and much sorrow' in the world due to Melko (*The Book of Lost Tales, Part One*, p. 230). For some reason Tolkien decided to delay the writing of that tale, which would have been *Gilfanon's Tale: The Travail of the Noldoli and the Coming of Mankind*.

(20) Instead he decided to rewrite *The Tale of Turambar*. On the same page as the continuation from *The Hiding of Valinor* he began anew, with a few lines referring to Ailios having finished a story on the first evening of Turuhalmë. Since Ailios is not there, on the next night Lindo asks one Eltas to tell a tale. This brief introduction leads into *The Tale of Turambar*.

(21) *The Tale of Turambar*, told by Eltas on the second day of Turuhalmë. Second version, written in ink over the erased pencil version. Some rejected sections of the text were replaced by riders, and the last part and two outlines which followed were struck through. The ending, which tells of the release of Úrin and his carrying of the treasure of the Rodothlim to Tinwelint, was rewritten on loose sheets. The rewriting of this tale preceded the rewriting of *The Tale of Tinúviel*; in *The Tale of Turambar* Beren is still a Man (as in the lost first version of *The Tale of Tinúviel*). After Beren became an Elf in the rewriting of *Tinúviel*, however, Tolkien similar emended the rewritten *Tale of Turambar*. Two outlines which followed the end of the tale and were struck through show Tolkien's early ideas for the tale of the *Nauglafring*, in particular his uncertainty as to how the treasure of the Rodothlim should be brought to Tintoglin/Tinwelint.

(22) The link to *Fall of Gondolin* continues from the rewritten end of *The Tale of Turambar*, also on loose sheets. In this, after Eltas has finished, there is some discussion of what should come next. Eltas mentions that the story of the Nauglafring would show how the evil of Glorund continued, but he refuses to tell it the next night, saying that it would be better to deal first with the tale of Tuor and the coming of Eärendel, or the tale of Beren. Since many of his listeners say that they know the story of Beren, Ilfiniol (Littleheart) is asked to tell of Tuor and Eärendel, but he replies that it is a mighty tale that would occupy seven evenings, being intertwined with the story of the Nauglafring and the Elf-march, and he would fain have the aid in the telling of 'Ailios here', and also Meril (*The Book of Lost Tales, Part Two*, p. 144, despite the fact that in the link to *The Tale of Turambar* Eltas had been the teller, because Ailios was not present). Messengers are sent to ask Meril to be present on the fourth night when this story-telling would begin. The link indicates that Ilfiniol/Littleheart should begin the tale of Gondolin.

(23) The second version of *The Fall of Gondolin* presumably followed. As noted above, the first version in pencil was written probably in the first half of 1917, then overwritten with a new version in ink, from which Edith Tolkien made a fair copy. Although Christopher Tolkien originally assigned the revision and copy to 1917, he came to prefer a later date for these. In *The Book of Lost Tales, Part Two* notes that the ink version mentions, 'by later addition', the Music of the Ainur, although that '*may* of course have been in my father's mind a good while before he wrote that tale in Oxford while working on the Dictionary [effectively late 1918–mid-1920] . . . , but it seems more likely that the revision' and therefore also the fair copy 'belongs to that period also' (p. 146). The presence of 'Ainur' as a plural form of the name in the ink version of *The Fall of Gondolin* also points to a later date, concurrent with the change from 'Ainu' to 'Ainur' as the plural form between the pencil and ink texts of *The Music of the Ainur*, not written before late 1918. Finally, since Tolkien rewrote the other early tales at this point, it seems likely that he would have done the same for *The Fall of Gondolin* when he provided the joining links (22, 24).

(24) Link between *The Fall of Gondolin* and *The Nauglafring: The Necklace of the Dwarves*. First draft in pencil, no longer extant; overwritten in ink and erased.

(25) *The Nauglafring: The Necklace of the Dwarves*. First draft in pencil. The first part of this was later overwritten in ink and erased. The pencilled text that survives seems be a primary composition written in haste, and although not entirely legible it shows that Ailios had been the teller of the tale. Tolkien rejected one section and rewrote it before the tale was finished. The ending makes it clear that the next tale after *The Nauglafring* would have been *The Tale of Eärendel*, but that was never written.

(26) Link between *The Fall of Gondolin* and *The Nauglafring: The Necklace of the Dwarves*. Second version in ink, over earlier erased pencil text. After Ilfiniol finishes telling *The Fall of Gondolin* there is discussion as to which story, that of Eärendel or of the Nauglafring, should come next, then Ailios begins to tell *The Nauglafring*.

(27) *The Nauglafring: The Necklace of the Dwarves*. Second version in ink, over earlier erased pencil text, extending only about a third of the way through the tale, which is told by Ailios. Tolkien was still uncertain about how the treasure of the Rodothlim reached Tinwelint, and heavily emended the ink rewriting.

At this point another series of texts began, in which Gilfanon replaced Ailios. The sequence is less clear than for the Ailios series, because Tolkien was uncertain where to place *The Tale of Tinúviel*, and for a time evidently intended to have it out of chronological order after *The Flight of the Noldoli*.

(28) Link to *The Tale of Tinúviel*. Written over an erased pencil text. The first brief section records a conversation between Lindo and Eriol after the former has finished telling *The Flight of the Noldoli*, beginning with a comment by Eriol: 'Great was the power of Melko for ill', and finishing with his 'sorrow at the destruction of those most fair Trees and the darkness of the world' (*The Book of Lost Tales, Part Two*, p. 3). This is followed by a longer section which says that in the days following the telling of *The Flight of the Noldoli* winter approached, and on a grey day Eriol was with the children in the Hall of Play Regained; and after he told them of his past life, one of the children, Vëannë, told *The Tale of Tinúviel*.

(29) *The Tale of Tinúviel*. The earliest surviving text, written in ink over the erased pencil version made in 1917 and continuous with the link. Two sections within the tale are on loose sheets placed within the note-book, probably because Tolkien expanded the story in rewriting and found himself short of space. The tale ends with a conversation between Eriol, Vëannë, and the other children, which is interrupted by the gong for the evening meal.

(30) A link between *The Tale of Tinúviel* and *The Tale of the Sun and Moon* follows *The Tale of Tinúviel* without a break. It describes how one evening Eriol asks for more information, in particular about the Sun and the Moon,

the coming of Men, and the deeds of the Elves beyond Valinor. Among those present is Gilfanon, a visitor to the Cottage from Tavrobel. Lindo tells Eriol that Gilfanon can tell him much of what he wants to know, but first he, Lindo, will tell of what happened in Valinor after the departure of the Noldoli. Gilfanon comments that Lindo is likely to make the tale last several nights, by which time he, Gilfanon, 'shall have fared long back to Tavrobel' (*The Book of Lost Tales, Part One*, p. 196).

(31) At this point or soon after, Tolkien changed his mind and decided that the tales should be told in their chronological order. He therefore struck through the conversation between Lindo and Eriol at the beginning of the link to *The Tale of Tinúviel*, and instead wrote it at the end of *The Flight of the Noldoli*, and followed it with a text based on the link to *The Tale of the Sun and Moon* at the end of *The Tale of Tinúviel*, presumably written over a lost link in which Ailios appeared. In this version Gilfanon is described as having long dwelled away from the Noldoli, faring with the Ilkorins in Hisilómë and Artanor, and having become a great friend and companion of the Children of Men. Lindo suggests that Eriol should visit Gilfanon, but Gilfanon says that he will be staying in Kortirion for a week and urges Lindo to tell another tale.

(32) *The Tale of the Sun and Moon*. Rewritten version; most of the tale is in ink over the erased pencil draft, but the latter part was written on new pages. In the part for which both pencil draft and ink versions survive, the differences between the two are slight. During the ink overwriting Lindo is interrupted at one point by Gilfanon, and during their conversation it is agreed that three nights hence they will have another tale-telling with great ceremony, when Gilfanon will tell of the travail of the Noldoli and the coming of Mankind. One section was rewritten later, but probably not much later, at greater length on a detached sheet.

(33) Link between *The Tale of the Sun and Moon* and *The Hiding of Valinor*. Second version, written in ink on new pages, in which Eriol asks for more information and Vairë continues with *The Hiding of Valinor*.

(34) *The Hiding of Valinor*, told by Vairë. Second version in ink on new pages, which considerably expands some parts of the draft and adds a new section on 'The Weaving of the Days and Months and Years'. Gilfanon appears at the end.

When all of this writing was done, Tolkien apparently made a preliminary outline of *Gilfanon's Tale*, and then an outline of the extant tales and a plan for the rest. In this the extant texts, including *The Tale of Tinúviel*, *The Tale of Turambar*, and *The Fall of Gondolin*, are dealt with in a cursory manner, while those tales not yet written are considered more fully: *Gilfanon's Tale: The Travail of the Noldoli and the Coming of Mankind*, which would have told of the awakening of Men and the history of the exiled Noldoli, including events only alluded to in the tales already written; and *The Tale of Eärendil*.

Following on the second version of *The Hiding of Valinor* Tolkien began a new tale, told by Gilfanon on the next night rather than three days hence as had been agreed in the interruption of *The Tale of the Sun and Moon*. Apparently based on the second outline (of the whole scheme), it begins with an account of the Elves who did not go to Valinor, and how one of these, Nuin, discovered the Fathers of Men still sleeping in a hidden vale. But it breaks off after only a few hastily pencilled pages, and with that Tolkien seems to have abandoned any new writing for *The Book of Lost Tales*. If he had finished *Gilfanon's Tale* it would have ended with a link to the rewritten *Tale of Tinúviel*, which in turn would probably have been followed by *The Tale of Turambar*, and so forth, with rewritten links.

Tolkien also began, but did not complete, a typescript of the story of Tinúviel, based on the manuscript but with some changes introduced. Originally *The Tale of Tynwfiel, Princess of Dor Athro*, its title became *The Tale of Tinúviel, the Dancer of Doriath*. The Lindo-Eriol conversation which began the link from the previous tale in the manuscript, but was then deleted (see text 31), was omitted in the typescript, indicating that Tolkien had abandoned the idea of *The Tale of Tinúviel* following *The Flight of the Noldoli*. In the rest of the link presented in the typescript Eriol gives a somewhat different account of his life from that in the manuscript. The heroine's name in the first part is typed *Tynwfiel*, but in the latter part *Tinúviel*, as it had been in the preceding manuscript, and earlier instances in the typescript were emended accordingly. The names of Tinúviel's parents, however, changed in the typescript from *Gwenethlin* to *Melian* and *Tinwelint* to *Thingol*.

Possibly at about the same time, Tolkien also emended, mainly for stylistic reasons, Edith's manuscript copy of *The Fall of Gondolin*, and began a typescript of the emended version while making further changes; but he abandoned the story shortly after the arrival of Tûr (the name spelled thus in typescript) in Gondolin. Tolkien further emended Edith's manuscript at a later date, probably early in 1920.

The rewritten *Tale of Tinúviel* and an unfinished typescript made from it were among the last texts to be written before Tolkien abandoned work on *The Book of Lost Tales*. When Humphrey Carpenter was writing his biography of Tolkien he discovered a short manuscript which Tolkien had written in the 'Alphabet of Rúmil' (see *Writing systems), which he had been using in his diary since the beginning of 1919 and changed frequently. When Carpenter transliterated this text, he found that it was close to a passage near the beginning of the rewritten *Tale of Turambar* and, because Tolkien changed the Alphabet so often, by comparison with the diary Carpenter felt that he could date the manuscript to June 1919. This also used some names which do not appear in the tales until the typescript of *The Tale of Tinúviel*. If Carpenter is correct, *The Tale of Turambar* and *The Tale of Tinúviel*, both manuscript and typescript, must have been rewritten by the end of June 1919. In the rewritten *Turambar* and *Tinúviel*, earlier forms of the name of Tinúviel's father are altered to *Tinwelint*; in the typescript, the name in the first part is *Tinwelint* (changed to *Thingol*), and later it is typed *Thingol*. In the two references in the Rumilian text this character is once called 'Tinwelint' and once 'Thingol'.

The Book of Lost Tales seems, then, to have been close to its final (incomplete) state by the end of June 1919, with a great deal of writing done during the first six months of the year but very little in the second half of 1919 or in early 1920. The most notable exception is Tolkien's adaptation of *The Fall of Gondolin* to read to a meeting of the Exeter College Essay Club (*Societies and clubs) on 10 March 1920: it was probably for that occasion that he made further emendations to Edith's manuscript, some of which postdate the rewriting of *The Tale of Tinúviel*, and made notes on possible cuts should the tale prove too long for the time allowed for reading. (A review of the event in the *Stapeldon Magazine* for June 1920 noted that 'Mr Tolkien entertained the Club with a reading from an unpublished work of his, an imaginative mythological fairy story after the manner of Lord Dunsany . . .' (p. 87). See further, **Chronology**, entry for 10 March 1920.)

In summer or early autumn 1919 Tolkien was asked to write the glossary (*A Middle English Vocabulary*) to the collection *Fourteenth Century Verse & Prose* being prepared by his former tutor *Kenneth Sisam for the Clarendon Press, the most prestigious imprint of Oxford University Press. Given this opportunity to do work which might help him obtain an academic post, he surely would have felt the need to give it close attention; and in these circumstances it is perhaps no wonder that *The Book of Lost Tales* was largely set aside. Lexicographers Peter Gilliver, Jeremy Marshall, and Edmund Weiner in *The Ring of Words: Tolkien and the Oxford English Dictionary* (2006) have said, in the absence of details of the time Tolkien spent in writing *A Middle English Vocabulary*, that 'it is difficult to imagine how it could have taken less than the equivalent of nine months' *full-time* work' (p. 36). In the event, Tolkien's work on the glossary was spread out much longer than nine months. To support himself and his family he remained on the staff of the *Oxford English Dictionary* and tutored students until summer 1920; and then his appointment to the Readership of English Language at the University of *Leeds from autumn 1920 made new demands upon his time. The *Vocabulary* was not published until May 1922.

Outlines of the *Lost Tales* show that Tolkien planned to take six more nights (i.e. six more tales) to tell the story of Eärendel and his voyages, of the march of the Elves from Valinor to the aid of their kin and of their settling on Tol Eressëa after the defeat of Melko, and the Valar's prohibition of their return to Valinor. But extant outlines and notes, often cryptic, show that while Tolkien had a general idea of what was to happen, the details were fluid and subject to change, and he would not have been able to write the remaining six tales easily or without much thought. But *The Book of Lost Tales* was not to end with those six, but to continue, with Eriol playing an active part in the history of the Elves and providing a link between them and England. The material dealing with Eriol is even less coherent than that dealing with Eärendel but he apparently came from the Continental home of the ancestors of the English; he was (in some accounts) to take part in, or even be responsible for a second unsuccessful march or Faring Forth of the Elves; they would be transported east across the Sea to the Great Lands on the island of Tol Eressëa, which would remain in its new position; later Eriol's sons, Hengist and Horsa, and their followers would settle on the island and Tol Eressëa would become England, the home of the English; and through Eriol and his sons the English would preserve the true tradition of the fairies. The appearance of Gilfanon in some of these outlines shows that they were made comparatively late.

Probably in 1920, but later than March when he referred to the mariner as 'Eriol' in his introductory remarks to the Exeter College Essay Club, Tolkien produced two outline schemes for *The Book of Lost Tales* in both of which the voyager who hears the stories is called *Ælfwine*. One scheme is very brief, while the other seems to project a revision of the whole work, preserving the general plan of the tales but with some recast or abridged, and with changes to the names of some of those who tell the tales. Ælfwine, the protagonist, was made an eleventh-century Anglo-Saxon who comes to Tol Eressëa and records the history of the Elves, but does not play an active part in it. In this revision there is no second Faring Forth of the Elves to the Great Lands, but still strong connections between the Elves and Tol Eressëa, and England. After the first march of the Elves from Valinor, many of them stay in the Great Lands, and especially in Luthany to which they retreat to escape evil men. Luthany is invaded several times, but the only Men with whom the Elves are able to dwell in peace and love are the English, from whom Luthany gains a new name, *England*. By Ælfwine's time most of the Elves have sailed away to Tol Eressëa, where they have named many places after those they had known in Luthany. When Ælfwine reaches Tol Eressëa he finds that the Elves understand English. The only part of this story that Tolkien wrote, however, is an account of Ælfwine's youth and his voyage to the Lonely Isle (see *Eriol and Ælfwine).

There are various antecedents for Tolkien's replacement of straightforward narrative with a series of tales told within a framework. Bocaccio's *Decameron* and *Chaucer's *Canterbury Tales* are perhaps the best known. Another is pointed out by Marjorie J. Burns, in 'Norse and Christian Gods: The Integrative Theology of J.R.R. Tolkien' in *Tolkien and the Invention of Myth: A Reader*: in 'The Beguiling of Gylfi' in Snorri Sturluson's prose *Edda* (c. 1300) it is told how King Gylfi of Sweden leaves home to seek knowledge, and finds lodging for the night in a strange hall, where he asks his three hosts questions about the gods and their halls, Creation, the structure of heaven and earth, and Ragnarok. Burns comments that similarly in *The Book of Lost Tales* Eriol is a traveller who finds lodging in a strange cottage, and 'here, too, a pattern of questions and answers begins, questions and answers that shape the storytelling through the remainder of the book' – stories of the Creation, the 'Valar, their powers, their dwellings, and the destruction that Melkor brings' (p. 165). Another analogue, itself possibly influenced by the *Edda*, is the long poem *The Earthly Paradise* by William Morris: in its Prologue certain wanderers set sail to find the Earthly Paradise, and eventually come to a Western land and 'a nameless city in a distant sea / White as the changing walls of faërie'. There each month one of the Elders of the city and one of the wanderers tells a story in verse to the assembled company, but these are derived from classical and medieval history, romance, and legend, and are not connected.

The framework of stories of the creation and history of the world being told to Eriol by those who had witnessed the events, or heard accounts told by others, disappeared in later texts of 'The Silmarillion'. But its various parts were often represented as records written and preserved by Elves, or copies of such records made by Eriol or Ælfwine, or copies of copies made in Númenor or Middle-earth. When Tolkien returned to 'The Silmarillion' after the publication of *The Lord of the Rings*, perhaps influenced by the impression made on readers of the latter work by its glimpses of ancient history, he again considered a framework for the tales, now in the context of *The Lord of the Rings* – selections, perhaps, from the three volumes of 'Translations from the Elvish' made by Bilbo Baggins from sources available to him at Rivendell.

While the basic story told in *The Book of Lost Tales* is similar to that of later versions, by the time the work was abandoned Tolkien had not yet managed to weave his ideas into a cohesive picture. Many conceptions which readers of *The Silmarillion* would consider to be the most significant and fundamental of the *legendarium* are lacking or only foreshadowed. In the *Lost Tales* the Silmarils are the most beautiful of the gems made by Fëanor, but are not the fateful holy gems of later texts. The second version of *The Tale of Tinúviel*, in which Beren is an Elf, lacks some of the poignancy of the tale as it became, the story of undying love between the mortal Beren and the immortal Lúthien; and it is only because Tinúviel tires of living in the forest and wants to return home that Beren decides to make another attempt to gain a Silmaril. Eärendel, meanwhile, is merely a great mariner, who plays no part in bringing aid from Valinor to the Elves in Middle-earth, nor does he become a celestial symbol of hope. The Valar seem closer to the gods and goddesses of Olympus or Asgard than to the more austere angelic Powers of later versions of the *legendarium*: they marry and have children, they use deceit to get Melko to leave his stronghold, Ulmo and Ossë quarrel in an undignified way; there is even a war god and a war goddess. Relationships and conflicts between the descendants of Finwë, so important in later texts, are also lacking, since Fëanor is not yet the son of the chief of the Noldoli, who indeed appears to have had only one son, Turgon, born after the return to Middle-earth.

The Book of Lost Tales is written in a somewhat ornate, but not overly archaic language. Compared to most of the later texts of the mythology, it contains much more, perhaps too much, detail about certain events – the creation of the Two Trees, the making of the Silmarils, the creation of the Sun and the Moon, Tinúviel's spell of lengthening – so that they seem less mythic than they might be. Yet the *Lost Tales* also contain almost humorous episodes, such as Beren being made a scullion to Tevildo, Prince of Cats, and his rescue by Tinúviel and Huan.

CRITICISM

The two volumes of *The Book of Lost Tales* were the only parts of *The History of Middle-earth* that were reviewed to a notable extent outside of specialist Tolkien publications. Thomas M. Egan in 'Tolkien's Son Compiles Fascinating "Book of Lost Tales, Part I"', *New York Tribune*, 8 March 1984, wrote that it

> reveals a side of Tolkien other than the one millions of readers have become used to. . . . It will disturb, even shock, many of the faithful in its 'rawer' themes and pagan associations of ancient folklore – but it retains its power to fascinate and inspire feelings of wonder in our imaginations. . . .
> The prose style is a quasi-Biblical archaic form of English which may scare off some readers. It is not as polished as the later *Silmarillion* turned out to be, but it is livelier in action-scenes and at times the prose – and the inserted poem-epics – is majestic enough to give us a feel of a lost elder world that has much to teach man, even modern man, about the search for honor and glory and self-worth. [p. 5B]

In his review of *Part Two*, 'Tolkien's Fantasy Universe Expands', *New York Tribune*, 25 March 1985, Egan commented:

> Despite their lack of sophistication as compared with Tolkien's later writings these stories have more than the gamut of unusual adventures and violent battle scenes that resound on every page. The language takes in an imagery of beauty and sorrow that are partners in the development of a world rather than opposites. Every tale seems to hammer home this point: this world even as 'Middle-earth' is a vale of tears. The joy we can gain, the courage we must exhibit before evil, the honor we must uphold are all surrounded by the thorns of life – chief among them the realization that nothing will last in this temporal realm. . . . [p. 5B]

Several reviewers rightly pointed out that *The Book of Lost Tales* probably would not appeal to the casual reader. As Norman Power wrote in his review of *Part One*, 'Mists of Middle Earth', *Birmingham Post*, 17 November 1983, 'it is for those who are already addicts and wish to study the origins of Tolkien's gigantic achievement. They will love it, and Christopher Tolkien's incredible industry has given them enough for a life-time of study'. Don Sakers wrote of *Part One* in 'It Isn't "Lord of the Rings" but It Is Tolkien', *The Sun* (Baltimore), 25 March 1984, that 'readers looking for another story like that of Frodo and Samwise will be disappointed by this new book'. 'The true devotee of Tolkien, however,' will find that 'many of the conceptions in the "Lost Tales"' have 'a power and depth of imagination . . . missing in later versions . . .' (p. C4).

Some critics did little more than quote a few paragraphs from Christopher Tolkien's Foreword and explain the background to the writing of the *Lost*

Tales. The view of the most hostile of these is summed up in a review by John Baxter, 'The Tolkien That Should Remain Decently Buried', *The Australian*, 11 February 1984: 'This is mostly dull stuff, the academic jottings of a nascent medievalist toying with fantasy worlds. You won't find the matter-of-fact hobbits here, the evil or the tragedy of the Ring books. The prose is choked with whimsy, and the occasional verses read like Tennyson's first drafts. It does Tolkien no service to exhume this rightly-forgotten juvenilia.'

Reviewers for journals and newsletters published by Tolkien enthusiasts, whose readers could be assumed to have a knowledge of Tolkien's works, were able to make more detailed comparisons. In *Mallorn* 21 (June 1984) Charles Noad wrote of *The Book of Lost Tales, Part One*:

> *The Book of Lost Tales* has the same relationship to the finished *Silmarillion* as a preliminary charcoal sketch has to the finished painting, or a rough-hewn block of marble to the finished sculpture. The general outline is there, but a great deal more work is needed to realise its full potential. Perhaps the most obvious difference between the earlier and the later work is simply that of *style*. That of *Lost Tales* is immature and unsophisticated: 'little' and 'magic' abound. Tolkien had not yet learnt restraint or subtlety. This, combined with . . . explicitness of detail in the narration, not to mention an excessive use of archaism (the book requires a glossary of archaic terms), gives the book an unsatisfactory feel. There is no sense of the numinous. This is not to deny the splendour of Tolkien's vision. The germ of that vision seems to have existed from the first; but the vision in its totality, together with the language and style best fitted to express it, did not arrive all at once: they had to take many years to come to full growth. . . .
>
> *The Book of Lost Tales* is, I think, of mainly 'archaeological' interest, and cannot be recommended to the casual reader of Tolkien. As an example of the primitive formulation of his mythology, however, it is of consuming interest. . . . [pp. 12, 13]

Christina Scull wrote of *Part Two* in *Beyond Bree* for November 1984 that 'while the basic outlines and much of the detail of *The Silmarillion* are already present in *The Book of Lost Tales*, Tolkien has not yet fully worked out the motifs and ideas which in connecting the various stories weld them into a unity and give them a sense of purpose in which one feels the pattern of the Music of the Ainur, the fulfilling of the design of Ilúvatar.' She cites as an example:

> In *The Silmarillion* the three Silmarils preserved the light of the Trees and were hallowed by Varda, 'and Mandos foretold that the fates of Arda, earth, sea, and air, lay locked within them (p. 67). It was for the recovery of the Silmarils that Fëanor and his sons swore their oath which again and again led to Elf attacking Elf in Middle-earth. It was the power of the

Silmaril which enabled Eärendil to reach Valinor, and its light by which he shone in the heavens. The other Silmarils were buried in the sea and the earth. In *The Book of Lost Tales* the Silmarils are only the most beautiful of the jewels made by Fëanor and have no special relationship to the Light of the Two Trees. . . . The Silmaril recovered by Beren. . . . is finally lost in the sea when Elwing drowned while seeking Eärendel. It therefore plays no part in enabling Eärendel to reach Valinor and it is by the light of the diamond dust which covered him when he trod the streets of Kôr (Tirion) that he shines in the heavens. [p. 2]

David Bratman wrote of *The Tale of Tinúviel* in *Mythprint* 21, no. 12, whole no. 55 (December 1984):

Like most of the Lost Tales, it's written with a liveliness and vividness that eludes the condensed, summarized style of *The Silmarillion*. The style reflects the content, as well. This is not a terse high tragedy so much as a true fairy tale. Huan the Hound speaks at will instead of being restricted to three utterances before his death. His antagonist, taking the place that Sauron was to fill in the later version, is the remarkable character of Tevildo, Prince of Cats. At points the conflict becomes a real cat-and-dog fight. It's things like this, along with a fey and sometimes uncouth quality to the Elves (Thingol, here called Tinwelent [*sic*], is a slightly threadbare miser – quite a contrast to the splendid Hidden King of the later story), that give *The Book of Lost Tales* its unique quality. [p. 2]

Few writers of books on Tolkien written since the publication of *The Book of Lost Tales* have devoted much, if any, attention to that work or considered it of more than historical interest. Brian Rosebury in *Tolkien: A Cultural Phenomenon* (2003), after remarking that he thought 'the later versions [of *The Silmarillion*] can generally be regarded as supplanting the earlier, incorporating almost everything of aesthetic value in them, and so rendering them superfluous except to the scholar' (p. 95), admits that it was worth looking at *The Fall of Gondolin* 'in which the vividly-imagined betrayal and destruction of the last Elvish city is narrated with ruthless energy, and an impressive capacity for evoking panic and disorder while maintaining narrative coherence' (p. 97). He spends almost a page analyzing the style of one paragraph from *The Flight of the Noldoli*, finding 'a sustained archaism, strongly reminiscent of the prose romances of William Morris' (p. 95). While there are 'no words which are archaic in the sense of requiring a glossary [and yet such a glossary is included in each volume of the *Lost Tales*], there is a persistent preference for forms which have no rationale except to push the language back into a generalised pre-twentieth-century idiom.' Among aspects that Rosebury feels obscure 'a potentially beautiful description' are 'unnecessary negatives', 'superfluous articles and particles', 'mannered tentativeness', and 'mishandled inversions'. He concludes:

Tolkien might have reflected that, since the legends belong to no specific period in the history of the English language, and therefore have no 'fitting' historical style, uniform archaism could only convey the impression of a lack of confidence in the communicability of his vision to a contemporary readership. 'High style' for especially exalted moments might be justified, but this is by no means an especially exalted moment and too much sublimity becomes self-defeating. (In fact I suspect Tolkien was still too bewitched by Morris's prose mannerisms to make this kind of independent compositional judgement.) [p. 96]

The Book of Lost Tales, Part One. The first of two parts of *The Book of Lost Tales* and the first volume of *The History of Middle-earth*, edited with notes and commentary by *Christopher Tolkien, first published in Great Britain by George Allen & Unwin, London, in October 1983, and in the United States by the Houghton Mifflin Company, Boston, in February 1984. See further, *Descriptive Bibliography* A21.

Part One contains the following tales, here listed (as appropriate) with references to entries in the present book where summaries, history, and analysis may be found:

The Cottage of Lost Play. Not included in later versions of the mythology; see *The Book of Lost Tales.*

The Music of the Ainur. See (in order of appearance in *The Silmarillion* (1977)) *Ainulindalë; *Valaquenta; *'Of the Beginning of Days'.

The Coming of the Valar and the Building of Valinor. See *'Of the Beginning of Days'.

The Chaining of Melko. See *'Of the Coming of the Elves and the Captivity of Melkor'.

The Coming of the Elves and the Making of Kôr. See *'Of the Coming of the Elves and the Captivity of Melkor'; *'Of Eldamar and the Princes of the Eldalië', and *'Of the Silmarils and the Unrest of the Noldor'.

The Theft of Melko and the Darkening of Valinor. See *'Of Fëanor and the Unchaining of Melkor'; *'Of the Silmarils and the Unrest of the Noldor'; *'Of the Darkening of Valinor'; *'Of the Flight of the Noldor'; *'Of the Sun and Moon and the Hiding of Valinor'.

The Flight of the Noldoli. See *'Of the Flight of the Noldor'.

The Tale of the Sun and Moon. See *'Of the Sun and Moon and the Hiding of Valinor'.

The Hiding of Valinor. See *'Of the Sun and Moon and the Hiding of Valinor'.

Gilfanon's Tale: The Travail of the Noldoli and the Coming of Mankind. See *'Of the Coming of the Elves and the Captivity of Melkor'; *'Of the Flight of the Noldor'; *'Of Men'; *'Of the Return of the Noldor'; *'Of the Noldor in Beleriand'; *'Of the Ruin of Beleriand and the Fall of Fingolfin'; *'Of the Fifth Battle: Nirnaeth Arnoediad'.

Part One also includes the earliest map of the world of the mythology, the diagram *I Vene Kemen*, and related poetry. See also *The City of the Gods*; *Habbanan beneath the Stars*; *The Man in the Moon Came Down Too Soon*'; *Over Old Hills and Far Away*; *A Song of Aryador*; *Tinfang Warble*; *The Trees of Kortirion*; and *The Little House of Lost Play: Mar Vanwa Tyaliéva*.

The Book of Lost Tales, Part Two. The second of two parts of *The Book of Lost Tales* and the second volume of *The History of Middle-earth*, edited with notes and commentary by *Christopher Tolkien, first published in Great Britain by George Allen & Unwin, London, in August 1984, and in the United States by the Houghton Mifflin Company, Boston, in November 1984. See further, *Descriptive Bibliography* A22.

Part Two contains the following tales, here listed with references to entries in the present book where summaries, history, and analysis may be found:

The Tale of Tinúviel. See (in order of appearance in *The Silmarillion* (1977)) *'Of the Sindar'; *'Of Beren and Lúthien'.

Turambar and the Foalókë (*The Tale of Turambar*). See *'Of the Fifth Battle: Nirnaeth Arnoediad'; *'Of Túrin Turambar'; *'Of the Ruin of Doriath'.

The Fall of Gondolin (*Tuor and the Exiles of Gondolin*). See *'Of Maeglin'; *'Of Tuor and the Fall of Gondolin'. Associated with this is a 'Name-list to *The Fall of Gondolin*' (pp. 148, 214–17, 335–49).

The Nauglafring: The Necklace of the Dwarves. See *'Of the Sindar'; *'Of the Ruin of Doriath'.

The Tale of Eärendel (not a connected text, but an assembly of various notes, etc. which indicate what Tolkien might have intended the tale to contain). See *'Of the Voyage of Eärendil and the War of Wrath'.

The History of Eriol or Ælfwine and the End of the Tales (not a connected text, but an assembly of notes and pieces of narrative). See *Eriol and Ælfwine.

Part Two also includes the poems *The Bidding of the Minstrel*; *The Happy Mariners*; *The Shores of Faery*; *Éalá Éarendel Engla Beorhtast* (*The Voyage of Éarendel the Evening Star*); and *The Wanderer's Allegiance*; and reproductions of one manuscript page each from *The Fall of Gondolin* and *The Tale of Tinúviel*.

The Boundaries of Lórien
see The History of Galadriel and Celeborn and of Amroth King of Lórien

Bournemouth (Hampshire). The resort town of Bournemouth on the south coast of England has long been a favourite winter residence or place of retirement for invalids and older people. It is noted for its fine situation on Poole Bay at the mouth of the river Bourne, its public parks and gardens, pleasant drives, and concerts in the Winter Garden. Tolkien seems to have visited Bournemouth as early as September 1913, staying at Devonshire House, accompanied by the two Mexican boys he had escorted to *France earlier that summer.

*Edith Tolkien began to take holidays in Bournemouth, without her husband, in the 1950s, staying at the Hotel Miramar in East Overcliff Drive; a photograph of the hotel is reproduced in *The Tolkien Family Album*, p. 82. Later, and especially after he retired, Tolkien began to accompany her. Edith's health improved in the gentler climate of Bournemouth, and in a hotel neither she nor her husband needed to undertake any of the *domestic duties that burdened them at home. On 20 January 1966 Tolkien wrote to *Rayner Unwin from the Miramar, where he was recovering from an infection: 'though virtually confined to quarters by weather . . . we are living in the height of comfort in what is practically our private house – a chef and a number of servants that we know personally to wait on us two and three others' (Tolkien-George Allen & Unwin archive, HarperCollins).

Over the years, as Edith's health and then Tolkien's declined, their visits to Bournemouth became more frequent. They became friends of the proprietors of the hotel, Douglas and Minna Steele, and of a local Catholic doctor and his wife, Denis and Jocelyn Tolhurst. Edith felt comfortable and on equal terms with the other elderly guests, unlike the academic society of Oxford with which she had never felt at home. Tolkien was less happy with the social life at Bournemouth and a lack of intellectual conversation, and although he sometimes managed to do some work or to write letters it was difficult without his books and papers to hand; but he was pleased that Edith was happy. Eventually, in 1968, he and Edith bought a bungalow in nearby *Poole and moved there from Oxford. Even then, they often entertained family and friends at the Miramar.

On 28 August 1973, after Edith had died and Tolkien had returned to Oxford, he travelled once again to Bournemouth to stay with the Tolhursts. There he fell ill, and on 31 August was admitted to a private hospital. He died in Bournemouth on 2 September 1973.

Bradley, Henry (1845–1923). For twenty years, while a clerk to a cutlery firm in Sheffield, Henry Bradley in his spare time read widely and gained a mastery of several languages. In 1884 he moved to London and devoted himself to reviewing and scholarship. Having published in the *Academy* in 1886 a knowledgeable review of the *Oxford English Dictionary*, he was hired to assist in that work (with the letter B), and in 1888 was appointed its second editor. He was senior editor from 1915 until his death in 1923, and supervisor to Tolkien while the latter was on the *Dictionary* staff.

In his appreciation *Henry Bradley, 3 Dec., 1845–23 May, 1923*, in the *Bulletin of the Modern Humanities Association* for October 1923, pp. 4–5, Tolkien wrote that he had once pictured the author of *The Making of English* (1904) as 'a young enthusiast', before he saw 'for the first time from far down the hall the grey beard of Bradley at Exeter high-table in the days before Magdalen claimed him. To see him working in the Dictionary Room at the Old Ashmolean and to work for a time under his wise and kindly hand was a privilege not at that time looked for' (p. 5). Bradley was 'one of the most kindly and friendly of men to even the merest beginner who in any small degree shared his enthusiasm; willing to talk, to teach and advise; to communicate his delight in discoveries, smaller or greater, of his own or others' making; to jest or cap a jest with enjoyment' (p. 4). Yet he had the gift, or curse, of 'uncanny instinct' whereby his eye was led always to omissions or defects in any work submitted to him.

Bradley on his part praised Tolkien in a letter of recommendation in support of Tolkien's candidacy for the post of Reader in English Language at Leeds (used again by Tolkien when applying for the Rawlinson and Bosworth Professorship in 1925): 'His work gives evidence of an unusually thorough mastery of Anglo-Saxon and of the facts and principles of the comparative grammar of the Germanic languages. Indeed, I have no hesitation in saying that I have never known a man of his age who was in these respects his equal' (*An Application for the Rawlinson and Bosworth Professorship of Anglo-Saxon in the University of Oxford by J.R.R. Tolkien, Professor of the English Language in the University of Leeds, June 25, 1925).

Bratt, Edith see **Tolkien, Edith Mary**

Braunholtz, Gustav Ernst Karl (1887–1967). Educated at Emmanuel College, Cambridge, and at Freiburg and Berlin, G.E.K. Braunholtz was a lecturer in Classics and in Indo-European Philology at Manchester University from 1913 to 1924, and Professor of Latin at University College of South Wales and Monmouthshire from 1924 to 1925. He went to *Oxford in 1925 as Professor of Comparative Philology, a post he held until 1952. *Joseph Wright, his predecessor in the chair, called him 'a firstrate Scholar and a kind of man who will easily make friends' at Oxford (quoted, sic, in E.M. Wright, *The Life of Joseph Wright* (1932), p. 483). Braunholtz took up his latter post at the same time that Tolkien returned to Oxford from *Leeds, and for many years they served together on the Committee for Comparative Philology and the panel of electors for the Jesus Professorship of Celtic. They were also fellow members of the Kolbítar (*Societies and clubs).

The 'girl of 12–13' to whom Tolkien refers in a letter of 31 August 1937 to C.A. Furth at George Allen & Unwin (*Letters*, p. 21), who read *The Hobbit* before it was given to *Rayner Unwin, may have been Mary Braunholtz, daughter of Professor Braunholtz.

Brett-Smith, Herbert Francis Brett (1884–1951). Educated at Corpus Christi College, Oxford, H.F.B. Brett-Smith became a lecturer and tutor in English at *Oxford just before the beginning of the First World War. From 1926 to 1939 he was the University Reader in English, and from 1939 to 1947 Goldsmiths' Reader in English. Tolkien was personally acquainted with him by Trinity Term 1924, when both men were examiners for the Oxford English School, Tolkien then an external examiner from *Leeds. After Tolkien returned to Oxford in 1925 he often served with Brett-Smith on Faculty committees. Brett-Smith edited the Halliwell Edition of the works of Thomas Love

Peacock (1924–34) and some of the *Percy Reprints* of Browning, Congreve, Shelley, et al. He was also an amateur poet – his *Poems of the North* was published by Blackwell in 1912 – and an accomplice of *H.C. Wyld in foisting upon the readers of the *Oxford Magazine* for 12 March 1925 the poem 'Gothique', a supposed translation into heroic couplets, by an eighteenth-century anti-quary, of the opening and closing passages of *Beowulf*. By then Tolkien had lent Brett-Smith some of his own poems – undoubtedly including some of his *'Silmarillion' verses – and in a letter of 22 July 1925 observed that 'the slim vir-tues of philology' had not eradicated his vice of writing poetry, 'or if you like the virtues of verse have not yet quite been stifled by the fumes of philology.' In another letter to Brett-Smith, of 8 August 1925, he remarked, prophetically, that if he were to publish a volume of such 'moonshine' it would cause his colleagues to look upon him with consternation. (Both quoted in David J. Holmes, Autographs *Catalogue 37* (1991), pp. 58–9.)

Brett-Smith's son, John, recalled Christmas parties at Tolkien's home which culminated in Tolkien donning a bearskin hearth-rug and chasing the chil-dren around the room (cf. *Biography*, p. 130).

Brewerton, George (1847?–1929). George Brewerton was a Classics master at *King Edward's School, Birmingham who also taught English literature. He joined the staff in 1871 and remained until his retirement in 1913. Tolkien was placed under him in the Sixth Class in autumn 1903. According to an obituary of Brewerton in the *King Edward's School Chronicle*, 'neither Latin nor Greek seemed much to interest him; his treatment of these subjects was inclined to be perfunctory. As an English master, on the other hand, he was probably in advance of his times' (March 1929, p. 4). Humphrey Carpenter describes him as one of only two masters at the school, together with *R.W. Reynolds, who 'made any serious attempt to teach English literature' (*Biography*, p. 47).

An accomplished amateur actor and singer, Brewerton brought a measure of theatricality to his teaching, along with strength of character and a ferocity that nervous boys feared. 'He demanded that his pupils should use the plain old words of the English language. If a boy employed the term "manure" Brew-erton would roar out: "Manure? Call it muck! Say it three times! *Muck, muck, muck!*" He encouraged his pupils to read *Chaucer, and he recited the *Canter-bury Tales* to them in the original Middle English' (*Biography*, pp. 27–8). When Tolkien showed an interest in *languages, Brewerton encouraged his studies with the loan of an Old English primer.

Brogan, Denis Hugh Vercingetorix (*b.* 1936). In 1944 or 1945, at the Dragon School, *Oxford, young Hugh Brogan heard *The Hobbit* read aloud by a teacher; and when, three years later, he bought a copy for himself he wrote almost at once to its author, begging him to write another book and asking to know more about the world in which *The Hobbit* is set. Tolkien responded warmly, beginning a long correspondence and friendship. In March 1949 Tolkien visited Brogan and his family in *Cambridge, and saw him again in

Cambridge in about 1967. In later years Brogan occasionally visited Tolkien in Oxford. In a letter to *Rayner Unwin of 15 December 1965 Tolkien called Brogan 'my most faithful fan since a small boy' (Tolkien-George Allen & Unwin archive, HarperCollins). By then Brogan was grown, and like his father, Professor D.W. Brogan of the University of Cambridge, had become a scholar of American history and political science. From 1963 to 1974 he was a Fellow of St John's College, Cambridge, where he had read History, and from 1974 until his retirement in 1998 he was a lecturer and reader, and finally R.A. Butler Professor of History, at the University of Essex. His publications in his primary field include *Tocqueville* (1973) and *The Longman History of the United States of America* (1985). He is also known for his *Life of Arthur Ransome* (1984) and as the editor of *Ransome's letters and two volumes of his shorter fiction.

Brogan's comments on *The Lord of the Rings*, written in various letters, elicited from Tolkien some of the author's most interesting thoughts about his work; see *Letters*, especially pp. 131–2 and 225–6. Tolkien did not always agree with his critic, and Brogan feared that in commenting he would be stupid or tactless; but 'you are welcome to let your pen run as it will', Tolkien wrote, 'since you give me such close attention, and sensitive perception' (14 December 1955, *Letters*, p. 230).

Brogan published two essays on Tolkien, 'Why Hobbits?' in the *Cambridge Review* for 23 January 1965, and 'Tolkien's Great War' in *Children and Their Books: A Celebration of the Work of Iona and Peter Opie* (1989). The first is a criticism of *The Lord of the Rings*, wrapped in a review of *Tree and Leaf* and in particular *On Fairy-Stories*. The second is concerned with Tolkien's place among the writers of his generation, and his success in communicating his experience of the First World War in his fiction. In a footnote to 'Tolkien's Great War' (p. 366) Brogan wonders whether Tolkien's protest in his Foreword to the second edition of *The Lord of the Rings*, that the penultimate chapter of that work ('The Scouring of the Shire') is not an allusion to the state of affairs in England immediately after the Second World War, was at least partially provoked by Brogan's 'unhappy' remark in 'Why Hobbits?' that 'some passages in *The Return of the King* were probably inspired by wartime and post-war experience of bureaucracy and shortage' (p. 205).

Brookes-Smith family. In summer 1911 Tolkien, his brother *Hilary, and their *Aunt Jane Neave travelled to *Switzerland with the Brookes-Smith family: James (1868–1952), his wife Ellen, their son Colin (1899–1982), and their daughters Phyllis (1895–1974) and Doris (*b.* 1897). At that time the Brookes-Smiths lived at The Lodge, Hurst Green, in Sussex. According to Humphrey Carpenter, in 1911 Hilary was working on a Sussex farm owned by the Brookes-Smiths, 'having left school early to take up agriculture' (*Biography*, p. 50). Colin Brookes-Smith, however, stated in an unpublished memoir (February 1982, Tolkien-George Allen & Unwin archive, HarperCollins) that the family became acquainted with the Tolkiens through Jane Neave when she was warden of the women's college at the University of St Andrews and the two Brookes-Smith daughters were at school nearby (we have been unable to confirm this). In 1913, according to Colin Brookes-Smith – but if so, before late March 1913 – his parents sold their country house in Sussex and bought Manor Farm and Phoenix Farm, both at *Gedling, east of Nottingham. Hilary Tolkien and Jane Neave came to live and work at Phoenix Farm, and Ronald Tolkien was an occasional visitor.

Colin Brookes-Smith eventually settled in Bloxham, north-west of *Oxford near Banbury. Tolkien corresponded with Colin's younger daughter, Jennifer Paxman.

Bryson, John Norman (1896–1976). John Bryson read English at Merton College, *Oxford; he received his B.A. in 1922, and in that year also was appointed a tutor and lecturer in English at Merton. In 1939 he became a Fellow and tutor of Balliol College, Oxford, and also served as College Librarian. He was a senior member of the Oxford University Dramatic Society and a founder member of the Oxford Playhouse Committee. His obituary in the *Times* (20 August 1976, p. 14) notes that during the 1920s and 30s his rooms in the High Street in Oxford 'were a meeting-place for friends, both old and young, who cared for art, music, and the theatre.' There, on occasion, the Kolbítar met (*Societies and clubs); Bryson at first was only a beginner in Old Icelandic and found it hard going. He later recalled, in conversation with Humphrey Carpenter, that 'when we were enrolled [in the Kolbítar] we never realised that it was going to be such a business' (*The Inklings*, p. 28).

Bryson and Tolkien for many years served together on the Faculty Board of the Oxford English School and on various committees, and were both members of The Society (*Societies and clubs). It was Bryson who, in 1952 as chairman of the English Faculty Board, nominated Tolkien to serve on a committee concerned with the O'Donnell Lectures (*English and Welsh*), and it was through an acquaintance of Bryson that the BBC in 1950 expressed an interest in broadcasting Tolkien's Modern English translation of *Sir Gawain and the Green Knight*.

Burchfield, Robert William (1923–2004). After receiving degrees at Victoria University College of Wellington, New Zealand, R.W. Burchfield went to Magdalen College, *Oxford as a Rhodes Scholar in 1949. His interest in words and their origins was already keen; now, in the Oxford English School, he was entranced by Tolkien's lectures and became one of 'his small band of true followers', undeterred by 'the speed of his delivery and the complexity of his syntax'. Burchfield was impressed most by Tolkien's lectures on the *Ormulum*, a late twelfth-century set of metrical homilies, and chose the vocabulary and phonology of that work as his D.Phil. subject under Tolkien's supervision. Although officially, Burchfield worked on his D.Phil. (not to completion) between Michaelmas Term 1951 and Hilary Term 1957, he recalled that he saw Tolkien only 'at weekly intervals in the academic years 1951–2 and 1952–3' ('My

Hero: Robert Burchfield on J.R.R. Tolkien', *Independent Magazine*, 4 March 1989, p. 50).

Beginning in 1952 Burchfield lectured at Oxford on medieval linguistics and on the history of the English language, and informally assisted *C.T. Onions, then editor of *Medium Ævum* and other works. From 1955 to 1968 he was the Honorary Secretary of the Early English Text Society (*Societies and clubs), and from 1968 to 1980 a member of its Council. In 1957 he was invited to edit a new supplement to the *Oxford English Dictionary* (published 1972–86), and with G.W.S. Friedrichsen was assistant editor of C.T. Onions' *Oxford Dictionary of English Etymology* (1966). From 1971 to 1984 he was also chief editor of the Oxford English Dictionaries, whose scope he broadened to include words from Australia, New Zealand, South Africa, and other lands.

Burchfield and Tolkien exchanged many letters in the 1950s and early 1960s in regard to the edition of *Ancrene Wisse* (*Ancrene Riwle*) that Tolkien prepared for the Early English Text Society and which was published only after many delays. Although the two men had differences of opinion about the project, their relationship was always one of friendship and mutual respect. Burchfield was instrumental in coordinating the publication of the *Ancrene Wisse* (by Oxford University Press, 1962) with that of the *Festschrift *English and Medieval Studies Presented to J.R.R. Tolkien on the Occasion of His Seventieth Birthday* (1962), and himself contributed an essay to the latter, 'Ormulum': Words Copied by Jan van Vliet from Parts Now Lost'. In 1969–70, in preparation for the *Oxford English Dictionary* supplement, Burchfield consulted Tolkien on the origin of the word *hobbit*.

Burchfield's other writings include *The English Language* (1985), *Studies in Lexicography* (1987), *Unlocking the English Language* (1989), and a controversial revision of H.W. Fowler's *Modern English Usage* (1996).

Calligraphy. Tolkien was exposed at a young age to ornamental handwriting. His maternal grandfather, John Suffield (*Suffield family), was a skilled amateur who wrote a fine copperplate script; while the penmanship of his mother (*Mabel Tolkien) tended to be exuberantly ornamental: see *Life and Legend*, pp. 8–10; *The Tolkien Family Album*, p. 17; and *Biography*, plate 1a. Tolkien's own early handwriting resembled his mother's in its eccentricities of form: see *The Tolkien Family Album*, p. 35. Later, however, Tolkien's everyday script changed to one more disciplined, even formal when written deliberately (but which, at speed, usually devolved into a scrawl): see, *inter alia*, *Life and Legend*, p. 46.

This change was almost certainly influenced by exposure to the 'foundational hand' promoted in *Writing & Illuminating, & Lettering* by Edward Johnston (first published 1906), or by one of the other writing manuals that appeared from Johnston or his students and imitators. The 'foundational hand' was based on tenth- and eleventh-century models, and could be written with any pen or pencil, though it was designed to be formed with a square-nib pen. Tolkien used all of these implements at one time or the other. Of course, as a philologist and scholar of Old and Middle English, Tolkien had many occasions to look at early manuscripts in the original; and he brought his own substantial visual imagination to the creation of letters as well as pictures. Among many examples are the floral alphabet, and the manuscript of the *Dangweth Pengoloð, published as figs. 197 and 198 respectively in *Artist and Illustrator*. The latter is decorated in a medieval manner, guided perhaps by Johnston's manual which is concerned with decorative capitals, and with working in black and red inks, as much as with calligraphy.

Tolkien utilized his talent for lettering in *The Hobbit, in drawing runes and other inscriptions on the dust-jacket and maps, and also in *The Lord of the Rings*, for instance in the decorative Ring-verse in Book I, Chapter 2. This and other inscriptions in the latter book are written in original alphabets by Tolkien (see *Writing systems), the *Tengwar* and the *Cirth*. Two versions of the 'King's Letter' he invented for the abandoned Epilogue to *The Lord of the Rings*, that is, a letter in Tengwar written by Aragorn, the King Elessar, to Sam Gamgee, are reproduced in *Sauron Defeated, and a third in *Artist and Illustrator*, fig. 199.

Tolkien also adapted scripts for special purposes, most notably those used in writing the *'Father Christmas' letters, in which different handwriting distinguishes different characters. The hand of ancient 'Father Christmas', for instance, appears to be shaky, while that of the elf Ilbereth is flowing and 'secretarial', and that of the North Polar Bear is thick and heavy, or (later) angular and rune-like. A variety of decorative scripts appeared on the letters, on their envelopes, and on accompanying pictures.

Cambridge (Cambridgeshire). Tolkien visited Cambridge, both the town and its venerable university some sixty-five miles north-east of Oxford, many times from at least March 1939. He had been there at least once in his youth, on 1 November 1910 for a *King Edward's School 1st XV football match against the Leys School; but he failed to attend a meeting of the *T.C.B.S. in Cambridge in March 1915 arranged by his close friends *Robert Q. Gilson and *Christopher Wiseman, then students at the University, and no evidence has come to light that he visited them there on other occasions. That he had not spent much time in Cambridge in his earlier years is suggested by a draft letter, c. 1939–40, in which he remarked on his first glimpse of King's College, whose chapel is one of the finest medieval buildings in England and a prominent landmark: '[I] am ashamed that it should have been my first [glimpse] though it made it all the more delightful' (Special Collections and University Archives, John P. Raynor, S.J., Library, Marquette University).

On some of his later visits he examined the important manuscript of the *Ancrene Wisse (*Ancrene Riwle) held in the library of Corpus Christi College; for this purpose he spent several weeks in Cambridge altogether, including the period 11–18 August 1952 when he stayed with his wife and daughter at the Garden House Hotel, Granta Place and Mill Lane. In May 1957 he attended a Perne Feast at Peterhouse, the oldest college of the University. On other occasions he attended dinners of the Ad Eundum intervarsity society (*Societies and clubs), which met several times per year alternately in Oxford and Cambridge. And at times he called on friends such as H.S. Bennett, whose family Tolkien amused with his story *Farmer Giles of Ham in March 1939, and his young admirer *Hugh Brogan and his family, with whom Tolkien had Sunday tea in March 1949.

In September 1947, while on a tour of Merton College (*Oxford) properties, he 'managed to visit Merton House and Pythagoras Hall in Cambridge, antiques that I had never seen before' (letter to Stanley Unwin, 30 September 1947, Tolkien-George Allen & Unwin archive, HarperCollins). Merton House on the Queen's Road was built c. 1800 and is owned by St John's College, Cambridge; but by 'Merton House' Tolkien may have meant Merton Hall, built in the fifteen-hundreds. This is on Northampton Street, next to the 'School of Pythagoras', built c. 1200, once owned by Merton College but sold to St John's College in 1959. (See further, J.A.W. Bennett, Chaucer at Oxford and at Cambridge (1974), Appendix C, 'Merton and Cambridge'.)

From 8 to 11 May 1954 Tolkien was in Cambridge for a meeting of electors to the newly established Chair of Medieval and Renaissance English (ultimately awarded to *C.S. Lewis). On this occasion he stayed again at the Garden House Hotel.

On 14 May 1961 he 'spent the whole of Sunday in the company of what appears to be quite a large club in Queens' College [Cambridge] devoted to my works' (letter to Rayner Unwin, 16 May 1961, Tolkien-George Allen & Unwin archive, HarperCollins). This may have been the occasion when he is reported to have read from his story of *Beren and Lúthien to a group of fans whose interest had been fostered by Henry St J. Hart, Dean of Queens' College.

Through the end of 1967, when passenger service on the line was discontinued, Tolkien would have travelled between Oxford and Cambridge by train more directly than is possible today. This is said never to have been a convenient service, requiring a change at **Bletchley**. Thus, probably, Tolkien's remark in his essay *On Fairy-Stories as revised for publication (1947): 'For my part, I cannot convince myself that the roof of Bletchley station is more "real" than the clouds. And as an artefact I find it less inspiring than the legendary dome of heaven. The bridge to platform 4 is to me less interesting than Bifröst guarded by Heimdall with the Gjallarhorn' (*Tree and Leaf, p. 57). The Victorian station building at Bletchley was demolished and replaced in the 1960s.

Campbell, Alistair (1907–1974). Having read English at the University of Birmingham, Alistair Campbell went to Balliol College, Oxford for postgraduate work. In 1931 he received his B.Litt.: his thesis, The Production of Diphthongs by 'Breaking' in Old English from 700 to 900, inspired an enthusiastic report from its examiners, Tolkien and *C.T. Onions. From 1946 to 1953 Campbell was Lecturer in English Language at Balliol, and from 1949 to 1963 University Lecturer in Medieval English at Oxford. In 1963 he became the Rawlinson and Bosworth Professor of Anglo-Saxon, succeeding *C.L. Wrenn. He visited Tolkien from time to time after the latter's retirement in 1959, one of the few contacts Tolkien continued to have with academic life in his final years.

Campbell wrote, among other works, *An Old English Grammar* (1959), long the standard book on the subject, and produced editions of *The Battle of Brunanburh* (1938), the *Encomium Emmae Reginae* (1949), and the Latin *Chronicle of Æthelweard* (1962). He contributed an essay, 'The Old English Epic Style', to the *Festschrift* *English and Medieval Studies Presented to J.R.R. Tolkien on the Occasion of His Seventieth Birthday* (1962).

Campbell, Ignatius Roy Dunnachie (1901–1957). On 3 October 1944, during a brief visit to *Oxford, the flamboyant author Roy Campbell encountered some of the *Inklings, including Tolkien, at the Eagle and Child pub:

> I noticed a strange tall gaunt man half in khaki half in mufti with a large wide-awake hat, bright eyes and a hooked nose sitting in the corner.... It was rather like Trotter at the Prancing Pony [in *The Lord of the Rings*], in fact very like. All of a sudden he butted in, in a strange unplaceable accent, taking up some point about Wordsworth. In a few seconds he was revealed as Roy Campbell (of *Flowering Rifle* and *Flaming Terrapin* [his first book, published in 1924]).... Here was a scion of an Ulster prot[estant] family resident in S. Africa ... who became a Catholic after sheltering the Carmelite fathers in Barcelona.... It was (perhaps) gratifying to find that this powerful poet and soldier desired in Oxford chiefly to see Lewis (and myself).... *Martin D'Arcy vouches for him, and told him to seek us out. [Tolkien, letter to Christopher Tolkien, 6 October 1944, *Letters*, pp. 95–6]

Campbell in fact was already acquainted with *C.S. Lewis, and with Oxford. He had briefly read Greek at Merton College, but preferred his own verses and the company of Moderns, notably *T.W. Earp. In 1944 Tolkien found him 'a rare character' and was taken with his 'picaresque stories' of his exploits. At least some of these were exaggerated: Campbell's poem *Flowering Rifle* (1939), for instance, wrongly suggested that he had fought in the Spanish Civil War. However, he had indeed, like Tolkien, converted ardently to Catholicism, and had come down on the side of Franco as a defender of the Catholic Church in Spain against Communism. These qualities in particular made an impression upon Tolkien, who remarked with some bitterness upon the fact that C.S. Lewis, an Ulster Protestant, held opposing religious and political views (*Letters*, p. 96).

By invitation, Campbell attended the Thursday evening meeting of the Inklings on 5 October 1944, at which Tolkien was also present. According to Humphrey Carpenter, Campbell 'reappeared at the Bird and Baby [Eagle and Child] once or twice' (*The Inklings*, p. 192). He also attended another Thursday Inklings meeting, some two years later on 28 November 1946.

See further, Peter Alexander, *Roy Campbell: A Critical Biography* (1982);

Joseph Pearce, *Bloomsbury and Beyond: The Friends and Enemies of Roy Campbell* (2001); Joe R. Christopher, 'Roy Campbell and the Inklings', *Mythlore* 22, no. 1, whole no. 83 (Autumn 1997); and J.S. Ryan, 'J.R.R. Tolkien, C.S. Lewis and Roy Campbell', *The Shaping of Middle-earth's Maker: Influences on the Life and Literature of J.R.R. Tolkien* (1992).

Carr, Charlie. Charlie Carr and his wife **Mavis** were on the domestic staff of Merton College, *Oxford. They looked after Tolkien after he returned to Oxford from *Bournemouth in March 1972 and took up residence at 21 Merton Street: legally part of the college, the flat included free domestic service. The Carrs lived in the basement. They attended to his flat, provided breakfast and occasionally other meals, depending on whether or not he felt like eating in college, and otherwise showed him much kindness and attention. Tolkien sometimes ate with them, and became a favourite of their young granddaughters. Tolkien's assistant *Joy Hill once became concerned when she could not reach him by phone, only to find that he had been watching Wimbledon tennis matches on the Carrs' television.

Carter, Douglas (1905–1991). Tolkien long had a close relationship with Father Douglas Carter, the parish priest of St Gregory's Church (St Gregory and St Augustine) in *Oxford. In letters to his son *Christopher he described the priest's sermons with enthusiasm (see *Letters*, pp. 80, 99–102). Tolkien and Father Carter corresponded as late as June 1972.

Cat. Poem, first published in *The Adventures of Tom Bombadil and Other Verses from the Red Book* (1962), p. 48, with an illustration on p. 50. With the second British printing (1962) and the first American printing (1963), the illustration and poem were made contiguous, pp. 50–1.

Tolkien wrote *Cat* in 1956 to please his granddaughter Joanna (Joan Anne; see *Michael Tolkien). 'The fat cat on the mat' dreams of mice or cream, or maybe of his feline kin, 'the giant lion with iron / claw in paw' or 'the pard dark-starred'. Although the dreaming cat is tame 'he does not forget' his fierce ancestors.

The Cat and the Fiddle: A Nursery Rhyme Undone and Its Scandalous Secret Unlocked see The Man in the Moon Stayed Up Too Late

Cecil, Edward Christian David Gascoyne (1902–1986). Lord David Cecil, the youngest son of the fourth Marquess of Salisbury, read History at Christ Church, *Oxford; he received his B.A. in 1924. In that year also he accepted a Fellowship at Wadham College, Oxford. He taught English Literature and History until the beginning of the 1930s, when he withdrew briefly from academic life to pursue literary work and to marry. In June 1938 he lost the election for the chair of Poetry at Oxford to the Reverend *Adam Fox, but later in June was named to a Fellowship in English Literature at New College, Oxford. In 1946, when *David Nichol Smith retired as Merton Professor of English Literature, Tolkien felt that the chair should go next either to Lewis or to David Cecil; in the event, it went to *F.P. Wilson, but in 1948 Cecil became the first Goldsmiths' Professor of English Literature.

By most accounts Cecil was a gifted teacher, and in his time was one of the most popular lecturers in the English School. He also had much success as a biographer and critic. The first of his many books was *The Stricken Deer* (1929), a life of the poet William Cowper. Later he wrote about English historical, literary, and artistic figures such as Lord Melbourne, Jane Austen, and Thomas Hardy, and on the art and pleasures of reading.

Humphrey Carpenter described Cecil as 'always a most welcome visitor' to meetings of the *Inklings 'whenever Lewis or Tolkien could persuade him to attend. "Visitor", perhaps, Cecil always remained, for his friendships were too wide-ranging and his literary tastes too broad to make him (so to speak) "spiritually an Inkling"' (*The Inklings*, p. 186). Cecil himself noted that

the meetings were also occasionally attended by persons who did not share The Inklings' distinctive point of view but who liked spending an evening in their company. I myself was one of these: I found such evenings enjoyable and stimulating; and all the more because the spirit of The Inklings was in piquant contrast to those of the Oxford circles in which I spent most of my time ['Oxford's Magic Circle', *Books and Bookmen*, January 1979, p. 10]

For additional, though only brief and miscellaneous, remarks by Cecil on the Inklings, as 'a school of ideas expressed through adventurous but learned fantasy', see his discussion with Rachel Trickett, 'Is There an Oxford "School" of Writing?' *Twentieth Century* (June 1955).

Celtic influences. The adjective *Celtic* refers to a group of West European peoples, including the pre-Roman inhabitants of Britain and Gaul (France) and their descendants; to a group of languages spoken by those peoples, which includes Breton, Cornish, Gaelic, and Welsh; and to related works of literature, among which are legends of King Arthur. (On all of these topics, see further, *Arthur and the Matter of Britain.)

Tolkien was first attracted to the Welsh language at the age of nine, by the strange Welsh names painted on coal-trucks that passed near his home in *Birmingham; and at about the same age he read *Celtic Britain* by John Rhys (first published 1882) which, in addition to historical matter, devotes attention to names and languages. While still at school he began to collect books on Celtic languages, among them Salesbury's *Dictionary in Englysche and Welshe* (1877), acquired on 9 May 1907. As an undergraduate he had access to books which enabled him to study Welsh more seriously, and he bought *A Welsh Grammar* by Sir John Morris-Jones. Joseph Wright, the Professor of Comparative Philology at Oxford, encouraged his interest, telling him: 'Go in for Celtic, lad; there's money in it' (though 'the last part of the admonition was hardly true'; Tolkien, *English and Welsh*, in *The Monsters and the Critics and Other Essays*, p. 163). In 1913, while in *France as a chaperon to three schoolboys, he was disappointed not to be able to see Celtic Brittany; but at other times, on holiday or professional business, he travelled to *Wales, *Scotland, and *Ireland, where Celtic traditions and language still survive.

While at *Leeds University in the early 1920s Tolkien continued to purchase books on Celtic languages and literature, as part of his professional working library. In 1924–5 he taught a course in Medieval Welsh. He also collected Celtic tales and legends, in their original languages and in translation, but felt some reservations about them. In the revised version of his paper on the *Kalevala* made in the early 1920s he wrote that though the 'unrestraint and exaggeration' in the *Kalevala* recalled the Welsh *Mabinogion* 'and other similar things in Welsh and Irish . . . in reality their cases are very different'. He found the Welsh tales both more and less absurd. 'They are more absurd for they are (when we get them) less fresh than they once were; there is in many places a thick dust of no longer understood tradition lying on them; strings of names and allusions that no longer have any meaning. . . .' He cites as an example the story of Kilhwch and Olwen. But 'on the other hand the Welsh stories are far *less* absurd for the pictures painted have far more technique; their colours are cleverly, even marvellously schemed; their figures are cunningly grouped.' He describes the *Mabinogion* as having a background of literary or artistic tradition

> full of the sense of long years of development and even of decay, which has resulted on the one hand, in the cumbering of the tales with forgotten traditional names and matter, and on the other has produced a field of the most excellently harmonised and subtly varied colours against which the figures of the action stand out – but they also harmonise with the surrounding colour-scheme and lose in startlingness if not in clearness. [Tolkien Papers, Bodleian Library, Oxford]

The opinion he expressed in a letter to *Stanley Unwin on 16 December 1937 was less favourable. He objected to Edward Crankshaw, a publisher's reader, having found Celtic influence behind the names and stories in *'Silmarillion' material submitted to George Allen & Unwin (*Publishers). 'I do know Celtic things (many in their original languages Irish and Welsh), and feel for them a certain distaste: largely for their fundamental unreason. They have bright colour, but are like a broken stained glass window reassembled without design. They are in fact "mad" as your reader says' (letter to Stanley Unwin, 16 December 1937, *Letters*, p. 26).

Nonetheless Tolkien did write several works influenced by Celtic literature. He began, but did not finish, a 'pseudo-Celtic fairy-story of a mildly satirical order, which is also amusing . . . called the *King of the Green Dozen*' (letter to C.A. Furth, 31 August 1938, *Letters*, p. 40). Humphrey Carpenter describes this as 'the story of the King of Iwerddon, whose hair and the hair of his descendant's twelve sons is coloured green. The story, which is set in Wales, parodies the "high" style of narrative' (*Letters*, p. 436). Also Tolkien copied the style of the Breton *lais* in his poem **The Lay of Aotrou and Itroun*, the first version of which was completed in 1930 and which he revised in 1941–2. The poem **Imram*, originally written as part of **The Notion Club Papers* (1945–6), was inspired by Irish tales of voyages to a deathless land in the West. And Tolkien considered whether to include an Irish episode in **The Lost Road*: 'Chapter IV "the Irish legend of Tuatha-de-Danaan – the oldest man in the world"' (**The Lost Road and Other Writings*, p. 78).

On 21 October 1955 in Oxford he gave the first of the O'Donnell Lectures, established to consider 'the British or Celtic element in the English language and the dialects of English Counties and the special terms and words used in agriculture and handicrafts and the British or Celtic element in the existing population of England'. In *English and Welsh* he expresses the view that 'English philologists . . . who have no first-hand acquaintance with Welsh and its philology lack an experience necessary to their business. As necessary, if not so obviously and immediately useful, as a knowledge of Norse or French' (*The Monsters and the Critics and Other Essays*, p. 163). He also makes a passing reference to **The Lord of the Rings* (*The Return of the King* was published the day before the lecture was delivered) as containing 'in the way of presentation that I find most natural, much of what I personally have received from a study of things Celtic' (p.162).

In 1967 he wrote: 'I have no liking at all for Gaelic from old Irish downwards, as a language, but it is of course of great historical and philological interest, and I have at various times studied it. (With alas! very little success)' (draft letter to Mr Rang, August 1967, *Letters*, p. 385).

Despite his denial to Stanley Unwin, elsewhere Tolkien admitted a certain Celtic influence on his writing. In a letter to Milton Waldman written in ?late 1951 he said that one element he wanted his mythology to possess was 'the fair elusive beauty that some call Celtic (though it is rarely found in genuine ancient Celtic things)' (*Letters*, p. 144). On 25 April 1954 he wrote to Naomi Mitchison that 'the living language of the Western Elves', Sindarin, had 'a linguistic character very like (though not identical with) British-Welsh: because that character is one that I find, in some linguistic moods, very attractive; and because it seems to fit the rather "Celtic" type of legends and stories told of its speakers' (*Letters*, p. 176).

Marjorie J. Burns, though considering Tolkien's world primarily influenced by the Scandinavian and Germanic North, pointed out that

> inevitably . . . the Celts would be there too, leaving their haunting and magical touch on incident, setting, character, and tome. It shows most clearly in *The Lord of the Rings*, particularly in the high elves, in their ability to live at once in both the world of spirits and the world of hobbits and men. Lothlórien, with its mystical bridging of time, is strongly Celtic

in tone, as are the Dead Marshes and the Paths of the Dead in a less comfortable way. ['J.R.R. Tolkien and the Journey North', *Mythlore* 15, no. 4,
whole no. 58 (Summer 1989), p. 6]

Marie Barnfield surveyed Celtic influences on the First and Second Ages
of Tolkien's mythology in two articles, 'Celtic Influences on the History of the
First Age', *Mallorn* 28 (September 1991), and 'More Celtic Influences: Númenor
and the Second Age', *Mallorn* 29 (August 1992). The first article concludes:

> The *Silmarillion* is rich in Celtic inspiration; indeed it is Celtic at its
> very core. The topography of its enchanted West, and the greatest of its
> Other-world treasures, the Two Trees of Valinor and the Silmarils that
> entrapped their light, have a provenance in the apple-trees of Avalon and
> Emain Ablach [Palace of the Apple Trees]. If it was from Teutonic myth
> that Tolkien took the name of the 'Elves', then it was from Irish legend
> that he drew their soul. From Irish legend too comes the history of their
> long defeat, the motive of the 'fading'. . . .
> There is a sense in which The *Silmarillion* is the broken stained-glass
> window of Celtic myth, reassembled *with* design. And the light that
> shines through it, the Light of the Blessed realm, is the very same that
> greeted St. Brendan as he emerged from the hedge of mist upon the
> shores of the Land of Promise. [pp. 5–6]

In the second article she notes that in attempting to provide an English
mythology Tolkien stated that 'through Eriol and his sons the *Engle* (i.e. the
English) have the true traditions of the fairies, of whom the *Íras* and *Wéalas*
(the Irish and Welsh) tell garbled things' (*The Book of Lost Tales, Part Two*,
p. 290). She comments: 'In one sense this statement reinforces the view that
Tolkien's mythology was to be specifically English and not Celtic. Looked at
the other way, however, he seems to have been suggesting that he planned to
tell the "true" version of stories told in garbled form by the Irish and Welsh
– *i.e.*, that the English mythology he is about to invent is to be at base a reconstruction of Celtic myth' (p. 7).

In a letter published in *Amon Hen* 42 (December 1979) Iwan Rhys Morus
points out similarities between elements in *The Lord of the Rings* and in the
Welsh 'Pwyll Pendefig Dyfed': between the hill Amon Hen and Gorsedel
Arberth 'from whose high seat wonders can be seen . . . and between the giant
hand which stole Pryderi and the Barrow-wight's hand in *The Lord of the Rings*
both of which were dealt with in the same way' (p. 18).

David Doughan's article 'Elvish and Welsh' in *Mallorn* 30 (September 1993)
provides a useful survey of differences between Celtic languages, and of elements that Tolkien incorporated in his created Elvish languages. He also
comments on the romantic view of a mystical 'Celtic twilight' prevalent in the
late nineteenth and early twentieth centuries (especially in the works of Yeats
and of William Sharp writing as 'Fiona Macleod'), and suggests that Tolkien's

conception of both the Elves and the Valar may owe more than a little to the Tuatha Dé Danaan, the divine race of Celtic mythology (which developed into the fairies of Irish tradition), in particular as they are depicted in Fiona Macleod's play *The Immortal Hour* (1900): 'The lordly ones / Who dwell in the hills, / In the hollow hills.' An operatic version by Rutland Boughton had an extraordinary success on the London stage in the early 1920s.

Chambers, Raymond Wilson (1874–1942). R.W. Chambers was associated with University College, London for most of his life, from his undergraduate days (B.A. 1894) almost until his death. Through his efforts as Librarian from 1901 to 1922 the University College collections approached in quality those at Oxford and Cambridge. In 1904 he was made Assistant Professor of English, and in 1922 Quain Professor of English Language and Literature, succeeding W.P. Ker. In 1925 he declined to accept the Rawlinson and Bosworth Professorship of Anglo-Saxon at Oxford, a chair for which he was himself an elector, and the honour went instead to Tolkien. He retired as Quain Professor in 1941, but continued as a Special Lecturer.

Chambers wrote widely on Old and Middle English poetry, and was an authority also on Shakespeare and Sir Thomas More. His study of *Widsith* (1912) was fundamental, his *Beowulf: An Introduction to the Study of the Poem* (1921; rev. 1932; 3rd edn., with supplement by *C.L. Wrenn, 1959) and his facsimile edition of the *Exeter Book* (with Max Förster and Robin Flower, 1933) equally important. His studies of *Piers Plowman* spanned his working life. A number of his essays and lectures were collected in 1939 as *Man's Unconquerable Mind*. Although Tolkien recommended (in unpublished lecture notes) as a student's *vade mecum* Klaeber's edition of *Beowulf over Chambers' revision of the edition by A.J. Wyatt (1914), he proclaimed Chambers' '*Beowulf* and the Heroic Age', the foreword to Strong's *Beowulf* (1925), 'the most significant single essay on the poem that I know' (*Beowulf: The Monsters and the Critics*, p. 12 in *The Monsters and the Critics and Other Essays*).

Chambers on his part admired Tolkien's British Academy lecture on *Beowulf*, despite small points of disagreement with his own writings on the subject, and praised it in *Modern Language Review* (April 1938). He was in fact 'an old and kindhearted friend' (letter to C.A. Furth, George Allen & Unwin, 31 August 1937, *Letters*, p. 20) with whom Tolkien corresponded and to whom he also sent his fiction and poetry for private review, including *The Hobbit* and *The Fall of Arthur* (*Arthur and the Matter of Britain). In 1933 Tolkien gave Chambers, as a Christmas present, a fine manuscript of *Doworst*, a verse satire on the subject of viva examinations at Oxford, written in the style and metre of *Piers Plowman*.

See further, C.J. Sisson and H. Winifred Husbands, 'Raymond Wilson Chambers, 1874–1942', *Proceedings of the British Academy* 30 (1945); Caroline Chabot, 'Raymond Wilson Chambers (1874–1942)', *Moreana* 24, nos. 93 (February 1987) and 94 (June 1987). See also Douglas A. Anderson, 'R.W. Chambers and *The Hobbit*', *Tolkien Studies* 3 (2006).

Chandler, Pamela (1928–1993). Pamela Chandler was a celebrated portrait photographer, based in London, from the 1950s through the early 1970s. When only thirty-one she was commissioned to photograph the then Prime Minister, Harold Macmillan. Her work also encompassed the ballet and theatre, the Royal Opera House, architecture, industry, dogs, and the countryside. Some of her portrait photographs are included in the permanent collection of the National Portrait Gallery, London.

In July 1961 Chandler asked permission to photograph Tolkien, as part of a larger project to photograph authors published by George Allen & Unwin (*Publishers), and on 17 August visited him and his wife *Edith at their home in Sandfield Road, *Oxford. She took a series of formal black and white photographs of Tolkien in his garage-study, and several informal black and white photographs of Tolkien and Edith in their garden or at the gate to their house. Tolkien found Pamela Chandler charming, though she 'inflicted such blistering lights on me, and held the poses until I was nearly stunned. So that I felt like a boiled or grilled owl, and think I look rather like one in most of the resulting pictures' (letter to Rayner Unwin, 22 October 1961, Tolkien-George Allen & Unwin archive, HarperCollins). The photographs in fact are very fine, and are frequently reproduced: one appears (misdated '1966') in *Biography*, pl. 13.

Chandler returned in August 1966 to take a series of less formal colour photographs: of Tolkien alone, of Tolkien and Edith in the garage-study, and of the Tolkiens in their garden. One particularly fine print from this session appears on the dust-jacket of *The Tolkien Family Album* (1992). Chandler hoped to take another set of informal photographs in 1967, to illustrate a newspaper article, but Tolkien felt that he could not spare the time, and had become tired of being photographed, even by someone whose work he admired.

A set of eight postcards, reproducing photographs of Tolkien by Chandler from 1961 and 1966, was published in 2002 by the Pamela Chandler Photography Collection.

Chaucer, Geoffrey (c. 1340–1400). The writings of Geoffrey Chaucer were long the concern of Tolkien as both scholar and teacher. Works such as *The Romaunt of the Rose*, *The Hous of Fame*, *The Parlement of Foules*, *Troilus and Criseyde*, and – most famously – the *Canterbury Tales* lie at the heart of Middle English literature as it has survived from the fourteenth century. And if Tolkien was chiefly interested in the language of Chaucer's works, he was closely familiar with them also as poetry and prose. He was introduced to Chaucer, in Middle English as well as in translation, already as a schoolboy; at university Chaucer's writings were set texts; and Tolkien himself lectured on them at *Leeds and later at *Oxford.

While Tolkien was at Leeds, plans were made to produce a volume of selections from the works of Chaucer, to be published by Oxford University Press (*Publishers) in their Clarendon English Series of books for younger students. It was to have emphasized Chaucer's writings other than the *Canterbury Tales*, and to have included an introduction, textual notes, a glossary, and extracts from the words of Chaucer's most important critics. A proof half-title refers to it as *Selections from Chaucer's Poetry and Prose*, but in surviving correspondence it is called the 'Clarendon Chaucer'. It was conceived in the first half of 1922 by *George S. Gordon in consultation with *David Nichol Smith, or the editorship was offered to Gordon around that time. Tolkien became co-editor of the book by 14 June 1923, when he is first named in pertinent letters between Gordon and *Kenneth Sisam, overseer of the project at Oxford University Press.

At first Gordon and Tolkien proposed to make a fresh text for the anthology, based on publications of the Chaucer Society. Sisam, however, preferred that they select from the existing edition by Professor Skeat, which was published by Oxford also as the *Student's Chaucer* and in their World's Classics series. Economy measures such as this, he insisted, had to be taken if the Clarendon Chaucer was to sell at a low price (as a school edition) and still make a profit; nor could its production be delayed for long without cost to the Press, who were attempting to strengthen their market share in Middle English texts and hoped to do well with this volume.

By autumn 1923, when proofs of the text proper of the Chaucer began to appear (the added matter was not yet ready for setting), time already had been lost. Tolkien had become gravely ill with pneumonia in March, followed by a recuperation of several months and then domestic difficulties; and there had been changes in the selection of works for the Chaucer, notably the substitution of the 'Reeve's Tale' for the 'Prioress's Tale' to avoid objections to anti-Semitism in the latter, and questions about the text of the General Prologue to the *Canterbury Tales* which were referred to David Nichol Smith. Tolkien was responsible for the glossary, but under the circumstances was not able to produce it as quickly as expected. (It may have been felt that he could do so easily, illness notwithstanding, having published only a year earlier his *Middle English Vocabulary* for Sisam's *Fourteenth Century Verse & Prose*.) Nor was he able to mark the first proofs of the text before late December 1923: these caused another delay, after Tolkien began to send corrected pages in early January 1924, as he suggested various alterations, feeling that Skeat was mistaken or inconsistent in some of his representations of words and lavish in his punctuation ('There are a dreadful lot of semi-colons!' letter to Kenneth Sisam, 5 January 1924, Oxford University Press archives). Sisam approved a few of these changes, but vetoed most on grounds of expense, 6d for each 'trifle'.

Sisam blamed Tolkien for the slow progress of the Chaucer. He was not unsympathetic to Tolkien's personal troubles or ignorant of his heavy academic duties at Leeds, but it was Sisam's responsibility to see that books under his charge were published in a timely manner, and so far Tolkien had neither delivered the Chaucer nor completed his work with *E.V. Gordon on a similarly delayed edition of *Sir Gawain and the Green Knight*. In May 1924 Sisam sought to remove him from the Chaucer, and Tolkien agreed to retire so that the project should not be held up any further. But in the following October he received from Oxford University Press two more sets of proofs of Chaucer text to read, which suggests that Sisam had a change of heart, or that he could find no one better suited to complete a job already well advanced.

In 1924–5, while George Gordon compiled the selection of criticism, Tolkien struggled to complete the glossary and to write textual notes. These were finished in draft by the end of 1925, but not to Sisam's satisfaction. He found the glossary much too long for reasons of cost, and its preface too elevated for the intended audience of schoolchildren (a 'chattier' version of the latter was supplied by Gordon). Also he cancelled emendations that Tolkien, still inclined to revise Skeat's text, had made in Chaucer's *Boethius* but with which Sisam disagreed, feeling that Tolkien did not understand his source.

During the next five years, while Tolkien settled into the Rawlinson and Bosworth Professorship of Anglo-Saxon at *Oxford, he seems to have done no further work on the Chaucer except to enlist George Gordon's help in reducing the notes, like the glossary too long for the purpose. Gordon, however, failed to assist in this respect, a fact about which Tolkien complained to Sisam on 21 November 1930:

> [Gordon's] elevation [as President of Magdalen College, Oxford in 1928] is some excuse, but when one thinks of the labour of the glossary disturbed by alteration in selection, the notes, and the text, which have all fallen to my share, there is some justification for my attitude – I will do no more unless I am given some help in the difficult task of selecting notes and reducing them to the somewhat narrow limits which are presumably contemplated. [Oxford University Press Archives]

Tolkien soon retrieved his notes, to which Gordon had added comments but which he had failed to reduce, and during 1931 and 1932 made some small further progress on the book, partly with the aid of Sisam's own edition (1927) of the 'Nun's Priest's Tale', snatching time for the Chaucer 'normally given to sleep or study' (letter to Kenneth Sisam, 22 January 1931, Oxford University Press archives). But despite sound advice from Sisam he managed neither to reduce the book to the desired length nor to simplify it for a younger audience. In the end only his research on the 'Reeve's Tale' proved useful, as an element in his paper *Chaucer as a Philologist* delivered to the Philological Society on 16 May 1931, and in a version of the tale performed by Tolkien himself (in the guise of Chaucer) in the Summer Diversions of 1939 (see *John Masefield).

The Clarendon Chaucer thus became a derelict at Oxford University Press and a concern of Sisam's successors. At one point it was suggested that E.V. Gordon might be given the chance to finish it off, and at another *J.A.W. Bennett was considered for the job; but hope remained for a long while that Tolkien would complete the work himself. He himself long hoped to do so, until in June 1949, with other obligations pressing upon him (including the late E.V. Gordon's edition of *Pearl*), he offered once again to hand over his materials for the Chaucer to Oxford University Press for someone else to complete. The Secretary of the Press, D.M. Davin, was glad to accept – though in the event, Tolkien did not deliver his papers until 8 June 1951. These included, as he wrote to Davin:

(1). Working copy made of galleys of *text*, with 2 copies of the resultant revises in page-proof (not themselves, I think, again corrected throughout). (2). The correct[ed] proofs of the *glossary*. (3). The draft of notes for *all* pieces but the last two (from *Monk's Tale* and *Nun's Priest's Tale*): the earlier items revised and reduced, the rest progressively in need of revision, and those for the *Reeve's Tale* possibly too illegible.

'I deeply regret the whole affair,' Tolkien said. 'The material contains much that is fresh and a prodigious amount of labour – esp[ecially] in the construction, reduction and revision of the glossary. But I was given the very sticky end of the stick, and need say no more' (Oxford University Press Archives).

Now that the papers were in Davin's hands, he could think of no suitable action to take. Despite the amount of labour that had gone into them to that date, there still remained a significant amount of work to be done, and as late as 1960 all of the likely candidates to complete the Chaucer were occupied with other things. Kenneth Sisam, who had retired from the Press in 1948 but kept in touch, advised that the book be left to lie fallow while Tolkien still held his professorship at Oxford, to avoid embarrassment.

Chaucer as a Philologist: The Reeve's Tale. Essay, published in the annual volume of *Transactions of the Philological Society* for 1934, pp. 1–70. Originally entitled *Chaucer's Use of Dialects*, it was derived by Tolkien in part from his work on the aborted 'Clarendon Chaucer' (see *Geoffrey Chaucer). He read it at a meeting of the Philological Society (*Societies and clubs) in *Oxford on 16 May 1931, but delayed publication, as he said in his preface to the work, 'principally due to hesitation in putting forward a study, for which closer investigation of words, and more still a much fuller array of readings from [manuscripts] of the *Reeve's Tale*, were so plainly needed.' In the event, he had no time to do so, and therefore published the paper 'with apologies, practically as it was read, though with the addition of a "critical text", and accompanying textual notes, as well as of various footnotes, appendices, and comments naturally omitted in reading' (p. 1).

Its subject is Geoffrey Chaucer's representation of Northern Middle English dialect as a linguistic joke in the 'Reeve's Tale', part of the *Canterbury Tales*: 'not mere popular ideas of dialect' but 'the genuine thing, even if he is careful to give his audience certain obvious features that they were accustomed to regard as funny' (p. 3). The elaborateness of the jests in the 'Reeve's Tale', and the fullness with which they are carried out, show that Chaucer must have possessed a knowledge of spoken and written dialect unusually great for his day, as well as a 'private philological interest' (p. 3). Tolkien felt that as far as treatment of himself [Chaucer] goes (and he had a well-formed opinion of the value of his own work), of all the words and ink posterity has spent or spilt over his entertaining writings, he would chiefly esteem the efforts to recover the detail of what he wrote, even (indeed particularly) down to forms and spellings, to recapture an idea of what it sounded like, to make certain what it meant. Let the source-hunter *have his swink to him reserved*. For Chaucer was interested in 'language', and in the forms of his own tongue. [p. 1]

*J.A.W. Bennett lamented in his *Chaucer at Oxford and at Cambridge* (1974) that because 'linguistics has elbowed philology out of the way' since Tolkien delivered his paper in 1934, no one had bothered to test or extend his 'findings on "Chaucer as a philologist"' in the light of new collations of the manuscripts or later place-name studies.' That being so, Bennett took 'these findings largely, though not entirely, on trust; merely noting that Tyrwhitt tentatively anticipated some of them' (i.e. Thomas Tyrwhitt, eighteenth-century editor of Chaucer; p. 100). *Norman Davis in his appreciation 'J.R.R. Tolkien' in the Merton College *Postmaster* (January 1976) remarked that *Chaucer as a Philologist* has 'never been surpassed in its exact knowledge of varieties of fourteenth-century English, or its delicate understanding of the elusive implications of jokes based on dialect' (p. 10). S.C.P. Horobin in 'J.R.R. Tolkien as a Philologist: A Reconsideration of the Northernisms in Chaucer's *Reeve's Tale*' (*English Studies* (Amsterdam, 2001) casts some doubt on Tolkien's conclusions, based on more recent Chaucer scholarship.

Cheddar Gorge and Caves (Somerset). Cheddar Gorge is an ancient geological formation over two miles long, with cliffs more than 400 feet high; and within these cliffs are many caves, some of them large, with quiet pools and limestone formations of great beauty. Tolkien and his wife *Edith visited Cheddar Gorge during their honeymoon at nearby *Clevedon in March 1916, and again with most of their children in early April 1940, while on holiday at *Weston-super-Mare. On 4 February 1971 Tolkien wrote to P. Rorke: 'I was most pleased by your reference [in a letter] to the description of the "glittering caves" [in *The Lord of the Rings*]. . . . It may interest you to know that the passage was based on the caves in Cheddar Gorge and was written just after I had revisited these in 1940 but was still coloured by my memory of them much earlier before they became so commercialized' (*Letters*, p. 407). See Gimli's description of the caverns of Helm's Deep in *The Lord of the Rings*, Book II, Chapter 8, with 'gems and crystals and veins of precious ore'.

Cheltenham (Gloucestershire). Her relationship with Tolkien forbidden by *Father Francis Morgan, in March 1910 Edith Bratt (*Edith Tolkien) moved to Cheltenham, where she lived with two elderly family friends whom she called Uncle and Auntie Jessop. There she took an active part in the Anglican church and became engaged to the brother of one of her school friends. On

8 January 1913 Tolkien, now twenty-one and free to contact Edith despite his guardian's objections, visited her in Cheltenham and persuaded her to marry him instead. A few months later, Edith told the Jessops that she had agreed to Tolkien's request that she convert to Catholicism; ordered to leave their house, she moved into lodgings in *Warwick.

Probably in late September 1917, while her husband was ill in hospital and the war continued, Edith returned to Cheltenham, which was thought to be safe from Zeppelin raids. Ronald and Edith's first child, *John Francis Reuel Tolkien, was born in a nursing home there on 16 November 1917. *May Incledon visited mother and son soon after the birth and wrote a reassuring letter to Tolkien, who was not able to travel to Cheltenham until almost a week later. Father Francis Morgan went there to perform the baptism.

On 18 July 1966 Tolkien wrote to a Mrs Webster in Cheltenham that he knew that place well: 'my wife lived there for many years, and we both occasionally still visit it' (Marion E. Wade Center, Wheaton College, Wheaton, Illinois).

See also *'Heraldic Devices of Tol Erethrin'.

Chesterton, Gilbert Keith (1874–1936). G.K. Chesterton was one of the most popular and influential authors of the early twentieth century, and is still highly regarded for his insight, wit, and vitality. A champion of orthodox Christianity, he also wrote prolifically about art, history, literature, politics, and social issues, as well as fiction and poetry. Among his many books are *The Napoleon of Notting Hill* (1904); *Heretics* (1905) and *Orthodoxy* (1908), copies of which Tolkien gave in 1909 to the library of *King Edward's School, Birmingham where he was a pupil; *The Man Who Was Thursday* (1908); *George Bernard Shaw* (1909); *The Ballad of the White Horse* (1911); the 'Father Brown' mysteries (1911 and later); *St Francis of Assisi* (1923); *The Everlasting Man* (1925), which influenced the thoughts and faith of Tolkien's friend *C.S. Lewis; *The Outline of Sanity* (1926); and *The Coloured Lands* (1938). Tolkien had most of these in his personal library, and according to his friend *George Sayer, knew poems from Chesterton's *The Flying Inn* (1914) well enough to recite them.

Critics have traced numerous parallels between Chesterton and Tolkien: notably, that Chesterton too was a devout convert to Catholicism (if not formally until 1922); that both men were concerned with the effects of industry and technology upon the world; and that they were both strongly patriotic, not for the British Empire but for 'the "little England" of rustic shires, small towns, with their eccentric customs and laws, their sense of propriety, their lack of ideology, their loyalty and love of hearth and home' (Thomas M. Egan, 'Chesterton and Tolkien: The Road to Middle-earth', *Seven* 4 (1983), p. 45). Also like Tolkien, Chesterton was an amateur artist of some talent. Some have detected Chestertonian influences on *The Lord of the Rings*, for instance that Hobbit society in the Shire might reflect the Distributism advocated by Chesterton and Hilaire Belloc. Joseph Pearce especially has argued at length that there are 'clearly discernible links of affinity between the two men' (*Tolkien: Man and Myth* (1998), p. 165), which may be seen not only in Tolkien's stories of Middle-earth but also in his shorter fiction, in particular *Farmer Giles of Ham*. In the event, however, such 'affinities' are easy to perceive but difficult to prove, and absent direct evidence, similarities between the works of two authors cannot be a sure sign that one was a source for the other. In 'The Shire & Notting Hill' (1997) Michael Foster rightly observes that Chesterton and Tolkien were 'unlike as much as like' (p. 45).

Nonetheless, and apart from references in his published letters, it is clear from his lecture *On Fairy-Stories* that Tolkien was closely familiar with Chesterton's writings. He quotes Chesterton or mentions him approvingly several times in the lecture, and seems to have drawn (at least) from Chesterton's 'Ethics of Elfland' in *Orthodoxy*, 'Science and the Savages' in *Heretics*, 'Man and Mythologies' in *The Everlasting Man*, 'The Wheel of Fate' in *The Outline of Sanity*, and parts of *The Coloured Lands*. Most of the specific references to Chesterton in *On Fairy-Stories* can be traced to the latter book, a posthumous collection of Chesterton's works previously unpublished, or published only in magazines and journals – and issued in this volume, moreover, only in November 1938, a matter of months before Tolkien delivered *On Fairy-Stories* in March 1939 at the University of St Andrews. Tolkien's famous description of '*Mooreeffoc*, or Chestertonian Fantasy', to give only one example, was undoubtedly drawn from the introduction to *The Coloured Lands* in which Maisie Ward summarizes an article by Chesterton in *The New Witness* for 10 June 1915:

> In Dickens, fantasy holds the next place to humour. But just as the humour is true human laughter, so the fantasy grows in that strange eerie twilight where trees and men have alien shapes that melt and merge back into realities. The things in Dickens that are most haunting are christened by Chesterton, 'Mooreeffocish' – and 'Mooreeffoc' is only 'coffee-room' read backwards as the child Dickens read it in the gloom and despondency of a foggy London night during his slavery at Murdstone and Grinby. Gloomy fantasy is truth read backwards. Cheerful fantasy is the creation of a new form wherein man, become creator, co-operates with God. [pp. 14–15]

In *On Fairy-Stories* Tolkien wrote that '*Mooreeffoc* is a fantastic word, but it could be seen written up in every town in this land. It is Coffee-room, viewed from the inside through a glass door, as it was seen by Dickens on a dark London day, and it was used by Chesterton to denote the queerness of things that have become trite, when they are seen suddenly from a new angle.' But he thought that 'recovery of freshness of vision is its only virtue', and that it has 'limited power' compared with 'creative fantasy' (*Tree and Leaf*, p. 54). In his rough drafts for the lecture Tolkien tried to include the concepts of 'cheerful' and 'gloomy' fantasy, but abandoned the attempt in his finished work. In fact, the surviving drafts for *On Fairy-Stories*, and the first published version of the lecture (1947, in *Essays Presented to Charles Williams*), include more references to Chesterton than the final version published in *Tree and Leaf* (1964). Chesterton's writings, however, were not always to Tolkien's liking, or did not remain so. In 1944, while trying to explain to his daughter *Priscilla some of the more obscure points of Chesterton's *Ballad of the White Horse*, Tolkien found the poem 'not as good' as he had remembered. 'The ending is absurd. The brilliant smash and glitter of the words and phrases (when they come off, and are not mere loud colours) cannot disguise the fact that G.K.C. knew nothing whatever about the "North", heathen or Christian' (letter to *Christopher Tolkien, 3 September 1944, *Letters*, p. 92).

Among several biographies of Chesterton, *Gilbert Keith Chesterton* by Maisie Ward (1943), *The Outline of Sanity: A Life of G.K. Chesterton* by Alzina Stone Dale (1982), and *Wisdom and Innocence: A Life of G.K. Chesterton* by Joseph Pearce (2001) are highly regarded.

Childe, Wilfred Rowland Mary (1890–1952). Educated at Magdalen College, *Oxford, Wilfred Childe joined the English School at the University of *Leeds in 1922. At that time he was one of three Lecturers, and of only five members of the English Faculty including Tolkien. He remained at Leeds for many years, serving as well in 1943–5 as Dean of the Faculty of Arts. He was also a poet: his first book of verse, *The Little City*, was published in 1911, and his *Selected Poems* in 1936. One of the so-called 'Oxford Group' of poets together with *T.W. Earp and Chaman Lall, he was an editor of *Oxford Poetry* in 1916 and 1917, and a contributor to several volumes in that series and to Lall's controversial periodical *Coterie*. His verses were frequently published also in *The Microcosm*, and together with poetry by Tolkien his work appeared in the collections *A Northern Venture* (1923) and *Leeds University Verse 1914–24* (1924).

In a letter to George Allen & Unwin (*Publishers) of 7 September 1937, regarding promotion of *The Hobbit*, Tolkien described Childe as 'specially interested in elves and related creatures. He was (once at any rate) a fairly well-known poet, and is still a good one; and is in close touch with various literary and journalistic sets & folk, in the North especially. He would probably do something, if he got a copy. He saw the [manuscript] and is well disposed' (Tolkien-George Allen & Unwin archive, HarperCollins). He was an old personal friend to Tolkien, a fellow Roman Catholic, and godfather to Tolkien's youngest son, *Christopher.

Children. We learn a great deal about Tolkien by considering his relationship with his children: *John, *Michael, *Christopher, and *Priscilla. Because he did much of his work at home – writing lectures, marking papers, tutoring students – his children saw more of their father than is often the case in families. Priscilla Tolkien has noted: 'Our father's study at home was in some ways the hub of the house. It was never forbidden territory to us, except when he was teaching, and on one occasion when I went in to show him my latest drawing, thinking he was alone, I was introduced with great courtesy to his pupil.'

She has also said that 'it was not until adult life that I gradually came to realize how continuously hard he worked. In order to take part in family life as he did and be so available to our needs and interests he often had to work far into the night when the household was quiet' ('Memories of J.R.R. Tolkien in His Centenary Year', *The Brown Book* (December 1992), p. 13).

Tolkien liked to spend leisure time with his children exploring the countryside and villages near *Oxford. Humphrey Carpenter describes

afternoons boating on the river Cherwell . . . floating in the family punt hired for the season down past the Parks to Magdalen Bridge, or better still poling up-river to Water Eaton and Islip, where a picnic tea could be spread on the bank. Walks across the fields to Wood Eaton to look for butterflies, and then back along by the river where Michael would hide in the crack of an old willow; walks when their father seemed to have a boundless store of knowledge about trees and plants. . . . Then there were . . . drives on autumn afternoons to the villages east of Oxford, to Worminghall or Brill or Charlton-on-Otmoor, or west into *Berkshire and up White Horse Hill to see the ancient long-barrow known as Wayland's Smithy. . . . [*Biography*, p. 160]

John and Priscilla Tolkien note that 'celebratory visits were sometimes made to take tea at country inns, like The Roof Tree at Woodstock, . . . The White Hart at Dorchester . . . and The George at Sandford-on-Thames. More often these expeditions were in search of wildlife' (*The Tolkien Family Album*, p. 63).

Family holidays were usually spent at the seaside, at *Filey in *Yorkshire while Tolkien was at *Leeds, and at *Lyme Regis, Lamorna Cove (*Cornwall), *Milford-on-Sea, or *Sidmouth after he moved to Oxford. According to John and Priscilla, on their several visits to Sidmouth the family would settle down to 'a routine of swimming, sitting on the beach, shopping in town, playing clock-golf . . . and making expeditions to more distant beaches to collect beautiful, rare shells like cowries' (*The Tolkien Family Album*, p. 65).

Since Priscilla refused to be parted from her large 'family' of soft toys, mainly bears, when she went on holiday, her indulgent father would drive the car to Sidmouth filled with the luggage and her toys, while other members of the family took the train or rode bicycles to their destination. On one occasion, Tolkien was asked if he was 'a travelling salesman in teddy bears' (*The Tolkien Family Album*, p. 64). Although he himself disliked railways for their 'noise and dirt and the despoiling of the countryside' (Humphrey Carpenter, *Biography*, p. 114), he supported Michael and Christopher's interest in them. In 1931 'Father Christmas' gave them additions to their track layout, which occupied one of the upstairs rooms in the Tolkien home, and their father took them to watch engines and draw the Great Western Railway locomotives. Tolkien was even 'persuaded on occasion to take them on expeditions to a distant station to watch the Cheltenham Flier pass through' (*Biography*, p. 114).

Priscilla Tolkien has recalled how her father also 'conveyed to all four of us as children his love of *stationery*: this meant large supplies of paper and pencil and a wonderful range of coloured chalks, paintboxes and coloured inks . . . we were all generously provided with these ourselves. . . . I can remember him showing me at the nursery table how to draw ordinary things like chairs and tables when I was in difficulties' ('My Father the Artist', *Amon Hen* 23 (December 1976), p. 6). But although Michael Tolkien as a boy made up stories, some in imitation of **The Hobbit*, and all of the children had active imaginations, none in adult life followed in their father's footsteps as a writer of fiction.

In 1920 Tolkien he produced the first of his ***Father Christmas' letters, for three-year old John. As the years passed, these story-letters became longer and more complex, and were discontinued only when Priscilla became too old for them; meanwhile, they were integral to Christmas excitement in the Tolkien household, and only one example of the storytelling that was an important part of Tolkien's relationship with his children. Priscilla recalls 'the story-telling presence of our father. . . . Stories at bed-time, whether invented or re-tellings of other more ancient stories, such as fairy stories, and reading aloud, especially when we were ill in bed, of our favourite books, such as Beatrix Potter's stories – these things he gave us in abundance' ('Memories of J.R.R. Tolkien in His Centenary Year', p. 13). Tales of 'Bill Stickers' and 'Major Road Ahead', inspired by notices seen in the street, were only told orally and so have been lost to posterity. Others began as oral tales but were eventually written down: **Roverandom*, first told to comfort Michael for the loss of a toy dog, and to keep the attention of his two elder sons from a storm raging outside; **Farmer Giles of Ham*, said by John to have been first told in an impromptu manner after a picnic; and eventually *The Hobbit*, part of the boys' 'winter reads'. **Mr Bliss*, uniquely, was not only written down but illustrated as a picture book. In these works Tolkien developed a different, freer style of writing than in his ***'Silmarillion' mythology, even if occasionally the mythology intruded into the stories or was borrowed for some purpose. **The Lord of the Rings*, begun as a children's-book sequel to *The Hobbit* (though not as a story by Tolkien strictly for his own children), combines elements of both kinds of storytelling, setting it apart from all of his other works.

Because Tolkien wanted the best for his children, he took on extra work as an external examiner at several universities, and marked School Certificate papers so that he could afford to give his sons and daughter the best schooling. Each of his three boys was sent to the Oratory boarding school near Reading when about the age of twelve; and all four of his children took degrees at Oxford. Priscilla Tolkien has commented on her father's 'complete belief in higher education for girls; never at any time in my early life or since did I feel that any difference was made between me and my brothers so far as our educational needs and opportunities were concerned. . . . It was . . . a source of pride and pleasure to him that he had a daughter as well as sons at the University' ('Memories of J.R.R. Tolkien in His Centenary Year', p. 12).

Tolkien continued to be close to his children in their adult life, his affection for them evident in numerous published letters. Humphrey Carpenter wrote that Tolkien and his wife were 'very proud when Michael won the George Medal in the Second World War . . . and they felt similar pride when John was ordained a priest in the Catholic Church. . . . Tolkien was immensely kind and expressive as a father, never shy of kissing his sons in public even when they were grown men, and never reserved in his display of warmth and love' (*Biography*, pp. 158–9).

In his later years he also played an important role in the lives of his grandchildren. He advised Michael's son, Michael George, about his studies, and enabled him to buy a cello. Michael's daughter, Joanna, has recalled 'being encouraged and helped by Grandfather in my interest of different species of plants, trees, birds and animals, particularly horses. He sent me two pocketbooks of British Birds, and an Encyclopaedia of horses so that I could study them further.' In 1956, when she was elected May Queen at her primary school, he sent her 'best wishes and salutations' and hoped that 'your Mayship' was the correct form of address. During the late 1950s and early 1960s, she spent Christmases at Sandfield Road with her grandparents, and later remembered 'the delight [Tolkien] took in decorating the tree, the crib and the house, and his insistence on my helping him, and our going together to midnight mass'. He 'always crossed my forehead before I went to bed, and before he gave me a goodnight hug' ('Joanna Tolkien Speaks at the Tolkien Society Annual Dinner, Shrewsbury, April 16, 1994' in *Digging Potatoes, Growing Trees*, vol. 2 (1998), pp. 33, 34). After Christopher and his wife Faith separated and divorced, Tolkien kept in close touch with their son, Simon. Simon stayed with his grandparents at the Hotel Miramar, *Bournemouth, on several occasions, and in 1972 went on holiday with Tolkien and Priscilla in Sidmouth.

TOLKIEN AND CHILDREN OTHER THAN HIS OWN

Tolkien enjoyed being with children, and in the 1920s and 1930s had a reputation as an entertainer at children's parties. One young friend remembered Christmas parties at which Tolkien would don a bearskin hearthrug, complete with head, and chase delighted children around the room. Priscilla Tolkien does not remember witnessing such an occasion, but has explained:

> For many years my parents shared Christmas parties with *Charles Wrenn and his wife, Agnes, who lived at 121 Woodstock Road. The bear rug occasion was famous because my father walked through the street in his costume. I think at that stage the party may have been held in the University Catholic Chaplaincy at the Old Palace in St Aldgate's which would account for my memory of being told that my father walked across Carfax in the small hours in costume! [private correspondence]

Priscilla also recalls that her father was often an entertainer at children's parties held in the summer and at Christmas at the Sacred Heart Convent, 11 Norham Gardens, Oxford.

According to *George Sayer, Tolkien once accompanied him and his wife to Mass while staying with them in *Malvern. There Tolkien helped some children who were trying to follow the service in a picture-book missal, and told stories about the Virgin Mary to the children and their mother. 'This again was typical: he loved children and had the gift of getting on well with them.' Sayer recalled that the last time he saw Tolkien in Merton Street, Oxford, after *Edith Tolkien's death, 'he was with children . . . playing trains: "I'm Thomas the Tank Engine. Puff. Puff. Puff." That sort of thing. I was conscripted as a signal' ('Recollections of J.R.R. Tolkien', *Proceedings of the J.R.R. Tolkien Centenary Conference 1992* (1995), pp. 24, 25).

From 1948 Tolkien carried on a notable correspondence with Hugh Brogan, then aged twelve and a Hobbit enthusiast (see *Letters*, pp. 129, 131–2, 185–6, 225–6, 230). Tolkien sent his young friend information about 'The Silmarillion' and the state of progress of *The Lord of the Rings*, and when the latter was finally published answered Brogan's questions. One Christmas, he sent Brogan greetings in runes and two versions of Fëanorian script. In 1965, when Paula Iley, a young family friend, sent him some of the poems she had written, he told her about his own early efforts at writing poetry, and sent her a five-page commentary on her verses. In 1969 *Rayner Unwin's daughter, Camilla, as part of a school project was told to write and ask 'What is the purpose of life?' to which Tolkien wrote the long and thoughtful reply (20 May 1969) published in *Letters*, pp. 399–400. In a covering letter to Rayner Unwin he said: 'If you write to children at all, I think you should not fob them off with something conventional. Better to shoot above their heads than that' (24 May 1969, Tolkien–George Allen & Unwin archive, HarperCollins).

HOW TO WRITE FOR CHILDREN AND WHAT THEY SHOULD READ

In 1959 Tolkien was asked to give his opinions on writing for children, with particular reference to his own works. In his lengthy draft reply he said:

> When I published *The Hobbit* . . . I was still influenced by the convention that 'fairy-stories' are naturally directed to children. . . . And I had children of my own. But the desire to address children, as such, had nothing to do with the story as such in itself or the urge to write it. But it had some unfortunate effects on the mode of expression and narrative method, which if I had not been rushed, I should have corrected. Intelligent children of good taste . . . have always, I am glad to say, singled out the points in manner where the address is to children as blemishes.
>
> I had given a great deal more thought to the matter before beginning the composition of *The Lord of the Rings*; and that work was not specially addressed to children or to any other class of people. But to any one who enjoyed a long exciting story. [letter to Walter Allen, *New Statesman*, April 1959, *Letters*, p. 297]

Elsewhere in the same letter he wrote: 'I think that *The Hobbit* can be seen to begin in what might be called a more "whimsy" mode, and in places even more facetious, and move steadily to a more serious or significant, and more consistent and historical [mode]' (p. 298).

But that letter was written over twenty years after the publication of *The Hobbit*, and an examination of the evidence suggests that it was only after Tolkien had begun *The Lord of the Rings* that his ideas about writing for children started to change. The earliest versions of the first few chapters of *The Lord of the Rings* are written in a style close to the facetious earlier part of *The Hobbit*, not to the more serious later chapters, and with the narrator's voice prominent. But as the writing progressed and the story took a more serious turn, 'the narrator was steadily becoming less of a presence, less intrusive, more self-effacing, and more inclined to show rather than tell the action. Some sections of these drafts are so highly conversational that the narrator almost vanishes altogether' (Paul Edmund Thomas, 'Some of Tolkien's Narrators', *Tolkien's Legendarium: Essays on The History of Middle-earth* (2000), p. 176). Even though Tolkien revised the early chapters of *The Lord of the Rings* several times, some readers still feel that these have a different tone to the rest of the work.

In a letter to his *Aunt Jane Neave on 22 November 1961 Tolkien explained how and why his opinions changed. After again stating that when writing *The Hobbit* he had not freed himself from contemporary ideas about what was suitable for children, he continued:.

> I had to think about it ... before I gave an 'Andrew Lang' lecture at St Andrews on Fairy-stories; and I must say I think the result was entirely beneficial to *The Lord of the Rings*, which was a practical demonstration of the views that I expressed. It was *not* written 'for children', or for any kind of person in particular, but for itself. (If any parts or elements in it appear 'childish', it is because I am childish, and like that kind of thing myself *now*.) I believe children do read it or listen to it eagerly, even quite young ones, and I am very pleased to hear it, though they must fail to understand most of it, and it is in any case stuffed with words that they are unlikely to understand – if by that one means 'recognize as something already known'. I hope it increases their vocabularies. [*Letters*, p. 310]

His Andrew Lang Lecture, *On Fairy-Stories*, was given in March 1939, and it is unlikely that Tolkien had done much research or writing for it when he began *The Lord of the Rings* in December 1937, demonstrably as a children's book, a sequel to *The Hobbit*. The change in tone which soon began to take place may have been due to his work on the lecture.

In regard to *The Hobbit*, it is hardly surprising that a story first told orally and later read aloud to the author's children should include authorial asides and explanations. They are not necessarily as intrusive as Tolkien thought them. The reader can, if he wishes, imagine himself sitting with Tolkien's sons on the floor in their father's study, listening to him tell the story. Nor were such interpolations by narrators unusual in the children's stories that Tolkien read as a child, or others contemporary with *The Hobbit* (for instance, George MacDonald in the Curdie books, Edith Nesbit in *Five Children – and It*, and E.A. Wyke-Smith in *The Marvellous Land of Snergs*; while in *Josephine: A Fairy Thriller* by Geoffrey Mure, also an Oxford don, the narrator actually converse with Janet, Mure's daughter to whom the story is told).

Tolkien did not believe in writing down to children, but thought that both children and adults should be stretched when reading. In *Roverandom*, originally told to his two elder sons when they were not quite eight and five, and probably written down when they were ten and seven, he used a vocabulary with long and unusual words. In the draft letter noted above he wrote:

> We all need literature that is above our measure – though we may not have sufficient energy for it all the time. But the energy of youth is usually greater. Youth needs then less than adulthood or Age what is down to its (supposed) measure. But even in Age I think we only are really moved by what is at least in some point or aspect above our measure, at any rate before we have read and 'taken it in'. Therefore do not write down to Children or to anybody. Not even in language. Though it would be a good thing if that great reverence which is due to children took the form of eschewing the tired and the flabby cliches of adult life. But an honest word is an honest word, and its acquaintance can only be made by meeting it in a right context. A good vocabulary is not acquired by reading books written according to some notion of the vocabulary of one's age-group. It comes from reading books above one. [*Letters*, pp. 298–9]

To Jane Neave he wrote similarly:

> Children are not a class or kind, they are a heterogeneous collection of immature persons, varying, as persons do, in their reach, and in their ability to extend it when stimulated. As soon as you limit your vocabulary to what you suppose to be within their reach, you in fact simply cut off the gifted ones from the chance of extending it. . . .
>   I think that this writing down, flattening, Bible-in-basic-English attitude is responsible for the fact that so many older children and younger people have little respect and no love for words, and very limited vocabularies – and alas! little desire left (even when they had the gift which has been stultified) to refine or enlarge them. [22 November 1961, *Letters*, pp. 310–11]

Nor did Tolkien think that the inclusion in stories of a certain amount of danger or even horror caused harm to children. In *On Fairy-Stories* he commented:

The beauty and horror of *The Juniper Tree* . . . with its exquisite and tragic beginning, the abominable cannibal stew, the gruesome bones, the gay and vengeful bird-spirit coming out of a mist that rose from the tree, has remained with me since childhood; and yet always the chief flavour of that tale lingering in the memory was not the beauty or horror, but distance and a great abyss of time. . . . Without the stew and the bones – which children are now too often spared in mollified versions of Grimm – that vision would largely have been lost. I do not think I was harmed by the horror *in the fairy-tale setting*, out of whatever dark beliefs and practices of the past it may have come. Such stories have now a mythical or total (unanalysable) effect, an effect quite independent of the findings of Comparative Folk-lore, and one which it cannot spoil or explain; they open a door on Other Time, and if we pass through, though only for a moment, we stand outside our own time, outside Time itself, maybe.

In a note, he added that children should not be spared the stew and bones 'unless they are spared the whole story until their digestions are stronger' (*Tree and Leaf*, p. 32). On 15 October 1937 he wrote to *Stanley Unwin about *The Hobbit*, that 'the presence (even if only on the borders) of the terrible is, I believe, what gives this imagined world its verisimilitude. A safe fairyland is untrue to all worlds' (*Letters*, p. 24).

The Children of Húrin. Alliterative poem, the various texts of which were published with notes and commentary in *The Lays of Beleriand* (1985), pp. 3–130. Tolkien referred to the work as *The Children of Húrin*; as published, it has the section and running title 'The Lay of the Children of Húrin'.

SUMMARY

In this work Tolkien set out to tell in verse the story of Túrin Turambar, which he had told already in prose (during 1918 and 1919) in one of the longest parts of *The Book of Lost Tales*, *The Tale of Turambar*. (See *'Of Túrin Turambar' for the part *The Children of Húrin* played in the development of the story of Túrin, and *'Of the Fifth Battle: Nirnaeth Arnoediad' for Morgoth's temptation of Húrin and curse on Húrin's children.) In his preface to *The Lays of Beleriand* *Christopher Tolkien describes this poem as 'the most sustained embodiment' of his father's

> abiding love of the resonance and richness of sound that might be achieved in the ancient English metre. It marks also an important stage in the evolution of the Matter of the Elder Days, and contains passages that strongly illumine his imagination of Beleriand; it was, for example, in this poem that the great redoubt of Nargothrond arose from the primitive caves of the Rodothlim in the *Lost Tales*, and only in this poem was Nargothrond described. [p. 1]

Tolkien is particularly successful in suggesting atmosphere and tension, as in the rescue of the unconscious Túrin from the Orc camp by Flinding and Beleg (pp. 44–5).

HISTORY

In a later note, Tolkien recorded that he began the poem *c.* 1921, but changed the date (with hesitation, Christopher Tolkien feels) to '1918'. Although one sheet of the earliest manuscript of the poem was written on a slip from the *Oxford English Dictionary* with the stamped date 'May 1918', this establishes only a *terminus a quo*, and the presence in the manuscript of the names *Melian* and *Thingol* points to a date no earlier than summer 1919: these were adopted only in the typescript of *The Tale of Tinúviel*, which can be dated to near the end of work on *The Book of Lost Tales*. The latter date is supported also by a fragment in Rúmilian script (*Writing systems) which contains a few lines of draft of the alliterative story of Túrin, datable to mid-1919 by comparison with another piece of Rúmilian writing dated by Humphrey Carpenter to *c.* June 1919. It seems possible that in summer 1919, following on *The Tale of Turambar* in prose, Tolkien began a new version of the story of Túrin in verse; but work at the *Oxford English Dictionary* and on *A Middle English Vocabulary*, then recently commissioned, left him little time to pursue his *legendarium* until after he was settled at *Leeds in autumn 1920 – thus his original note, '*c.* 1921', may have been closer to the mark.

The Children of Húrin exists in two unfinished versions, the second mainly an expansion of the first. Tolkien composed each of these first as a manuscript, emended it, and then produced a typescript, making other changes in progress. Christopher Tolkien thinks that the second version was not 'significantly later than the first; it is indeed possible, and would not be in any way uncharacteristic, that my father began work on [the second version] while he was still composing at a later point in [the first version]' (p. 4). Changing names indicate that at least for the first version, the typescript was begun while the manuscript was still developing.

The earliest manuscript is divided into two distinct parts numbered consecutively: the first 528 lines, a very rough draft with many alternative readings, written mainly on thirty-two small slips; and a second half in a more finished form mainly on large sheets of Leeds University examination paper, with the conclusion on *Oxford University examination paper. Christopher Tolkien points out that 'we have thus one sole text, not two, without any overlap' (p. 4), and if slips with rough drafting ever existed for the second part of the work, they have disappeared. If Tolkien did write any of the poem in Oxford in summer 1919, it would have been all or part of the early section on slips, with one sheet on *Dictionary* proof. Tolkien abandoned the manuscript abruptly with an unfinished sentence at line 2276, having just described the relationship of Túrin and Failivrin and begun to suggest the danger approaching Nargothrond. He made a typescript as far as line 2201, added a further seventy-five lines in manuscript on Oxford examination paper, again ending at line 2276. The use of Oxford paper dates the composition of the latter part of both texts to the second half of 1924 at the earliest, after Tolkien had been an external examiner at Oxford.

Tolkien gave no title to the manuscript of the first version; the typescript was originally called *The Golden Dragon*, but this was changed to *Túrin Son of Húrin & Glórund the Dragon*. The completed part of the poem is divided into an untitled prologue and three sections, 'Túrin's Fostering', 'Beleg', and 'Failivrin'. Tolkien made a further manuscript of lines 2005–2225 from the typescript and its continuation, as *Túrin in the House of Fuilin and His Son Flinding*. In *The Lays of Beleriand* Christopher Tolkien published the text of the typescript and its continuation, noted significant differences between it and the manuscript versions, and reproduced two pages of the manuscript.

The second version of the lay expands upon the first, especially in the prologue, but does not extend as far into the story. The manuscript, incomplete and in a rough state, extends to line 767; the typescript continues to line 817, and breaks off just before Túrin's quarrel with Orgof during a feast at Thingol's court, a point reached in 435 lines in the first version. After emending the typescript, Tolkien made another typed copy of the first ninety-four lines, emended it, and wrote out the same number of lines on Oxford examination paper, taking up the emendations and making further changes. A significant addition to the typescript was the introduction of the poem *Light as Leaf on Lindentree*, and other references to Lúthien. The rough manuscript has no title; the title of the complete typescript was changed from *Túrin* to *The Children of Húrin*. The text published in *The Lays of Beleriand* is that of the final manuscript for the first 94 lines, and then that of the typescript. Again Christopher Tolkien notes significant differences in the earlier texts.

Tolkien also separately developed lines 2082–2113 of *The Children of Húrin* in three manuscripts. The first, beginning 'The high summer / waned to autumn, // and western gales', remained closest to the lay. The second, entitled *Storm over Narog*, was more greatly changed and expanded. The third, retitled more descriptively *Winter Comes to Nargothrond*, contains only slight changes from the second. On the back of the latter Tolkien developed lines 1554–70 of *The Children of Húrin* to describe the River Sirion reaching the sea ('With the seething sea // Sirion's waters').

He seems to have abandoned work on *The Children of Húrin* early in 1925. In the early 1930s, however, he began another version of the story, in rhyming couplets. Christopher Tolkien says of this unpublished work, also entitled *The Children of Húrin*, that it 'extends only to 170 lines and breaks off abruptly, after a short prologue based on the opening of the alliterative Lay and an incomplete second section titled "The Battle of Unnumbered Tears and Morgoth's Curse"' (*The Lays of Beleriand*, p. 130). When Tolkien returned to work on 'The Silmarillion' *c.* 1950, after finishing *The Lord of the Rings*, for the story of Beren and Lúthien he began to revise the *Lay of Leithian*, but for Túrin he began a new account in prose.

See also *'Index of Names for *The Lay of the Children of Húrin*'.

CRITICISM

Writing in *Amon Hen* 75 (September 1985), John A. Ellison thought that, compared with the octosyllabic couplets of the later *Lay of Leithian*, the alliterative metre of *The Children of Húrin* provided Tolkien with

an instinctive, rather than artificial, means of expression. . . . At the same time, the difference of metre is important in another sense. The earlier poem can be viewed from the standpoint of an inhabitant of the Third Age of Middle-earth, as a 'text' of much earlier 'provenance' than its more sophisticated successor. This is one way of creating that sense of historical depth and perspective in relation to the mythology, to which Tolkien himself attached importance. [review of *The Lays of Beleriand*, p. 11]

Katharyn W. Crabbe in *J.R.R. Tolkien* (rev. and expanded edn. 1988) felt that certain aspects of Túrin's character receive more attention in this poem than in other versions:

The most striking feature of the poem is the intensity with which it presents two conflicting explanations for Túrin's tragedy. On the one hand, the 'Lay' seems to emphasize the importance of Túrin's character in determining the unhappy course of his life. On the other, Morgoth's omnipresence in the poem serves as a constant reminder that his curse is influencing Túrin's choices. Thus in this version of the story, Tolkien intensifies the debate he raises in other versions by bringing to the foreground the question of the relative importance of fate and free-will in the lives of men.

As a hero Túrin is flawed. A part of that flaw is attributable to Morgoth who has determined 'a weird of woe//woven darkly' for the children of Húrin, and it is perhaps the case that Morgoth's curse determines Túrin's character. Certainly the constant references to Morgoth and his curse in this poem encourage one to think so. [p. 184]

She finds Túrin 'the only weak child I can recall in Tolkien. He is also the closest thing to a real child.' When his mother sends him away 'he perceives at once that his world is hostile and that he is an exile: "The hills are hateful," he cries, "where hope is lost; . . . and my home is gone" [*The Lays of Beleriand*, p. 106]'; he feels 'alone and abandoned' (Crabbe, p. 184). She suggests that 'the poet thinks of Túrin as psychologically stunted' by "the sundering sorrow // that seared his youth" [*The Lays of Beleriand*, p. 116]' (p. 185). Although Túrin is 'brave and competent in battle' (p. 184), he is also impetuous, one might even say immature. In a fit of temper, he strikes Orgof and kills him. He declares himself to be an outlaw and alone in the world without waiting for the opinion of his king and foster father. . . . He kills his best friend, mistaking a rescuer for a torturer. None of these is a willful act of violence; but they are all characteristic. It is in his character to act unthinkingly. Furthermore he is usually unthinking because he is not fully conscious. . . .

What are the characteristics of this lack of awareness? First, it is part and parcel of a lack of 'mirth' or as it seems to mean here, joy. Túrin takes joy in nothing. . . . He is a singularly joyless character. Second, he is without hope. He is unhappy in the world and he sees no possibility of his situation's improving. Finally, he has become a machine of destruction rather than a vehicle of creation. [p. 185]

Círdan. Discussion, published with notes in *The Peoples of Middle-earth* (1996), pp. 385–7, 391–2. Círdan is said to be a Telerin Elf, 'one of the highest of those who were not transported to Valinor' (*The Peoples of Middle-earth*, p. 385), and akin to Olwë and Elwë, the leaders of the Teleri. In both *'The Silmarillion'* and *The Lord of the Rings* he is always called *Círdan*, 'shipwright' in Sindarin, but a name that could have been given to him only after he had become noted as a builder of ships. In one authorial note to this late text it is stated that even before Círdan and the Teleri came to Beleriand they developed the craft of boat-making, first on lakes near their first homes, and then during their journey to the Sea. According to another note there was a tradition that his original name 'was in archaic form *Nōwē*' (p. 392).

He was the leader of those who sought in vain for Elwë when he was lost, held spellbound by the singing of Melian, and thus Círdan came to the shores of the Great Sea too late to be transported to Valinor with Olwë and his followers. As he looked out to sea and cried out that he would follow in his own ship, he heard a voice which came from the Valar telling him to stay in Middle-earth for a work of utmost importance, then saw a vision of the ship which Eärendil would build with his advice and help. 'From that night onwards Círdan received a foresight touching all matters of importance, beyond the measure of all other Elves upon Middle-earth' (p. 386). He is described as being similarly endowed in the introduction to the 'Tale of Years' for the Third Age in *The Lord of the Rings* (Appendix B): 'Círdan saw further and deeper that any other in Middle-earth'. But there are subtle differences in the wording in this late work: it indicates that it was especially 'further and deeper' *into the future* that he saw, and it specifies that this ability was greater than that of all other Elves 'upon Middle-earth' (thus greater than the foresight of Elrond, Galadriel, and Celeborn, and of the Noldorin and Sindarin rulers of the First Age), rather than 'any other in Middle-earth'.

This text probably dates from the end of 1972 or from 1973.

Cirion and Eorl and the Friendship of Gondor and Rohan. Four fragmentary texts, published with commentary and notes in *Unfinished Tales* (1980), pp. 288–320, under a collective title assigned by *Christopher Tolkien. Together they provide greater detail than is given in the Appendices of *The Lord of the Rings* of the history of the Northmen, ancestors of the Rohirrim, their relations with Gondor, the ride of Eorl to the aid of Cirion, and the gift to him and his people of lands formerly part of the realm of Gondor.

SUMMARY

The first text, *The Northmen and the Wainriders*, relates background history of the Northmen and describes their alliances with kings of Gondor against the Wainriders in the Third Age, c. 1851–1944. This breaks off in mid-sentence, in the middle of an account of the battle against the Wainriders in T.A. 1944 in which King Ondoher of Gondor is slain. Christopher Tolkien summarizes his father's ideas for its continuation, which survive only in very rough notes.

The Ride of Eorl tells of events leading up to the Battle of the Field of Celebrant in Third Age 2510. Cirion, the Steward of Gondor, aware of an impending attack by men from the East, seeks aid from Eorl, the leader of the Northmen. Only one of six messengers manages to get through. Eorl musters all of his able men and rides south to the aid of Gondor. As they pass near Lórien, Galadriel protects them against attack from Dol Guldur. The text ends as the host is approaching the site of the battle, with a note that a description of the battle (never written) should follow.

Cirion and Eorl describes events after the victory. Cirion orders that an ancient, overgrown path to Amon Anwar, the 'Hill of Awe', in the White Mountains be opened. He leads Eorl and several witnesses along the path to the upper slopes of the hill, and there declares that as a reward for their aid he is granting to Eorl and his people (later known as the Rohirrim) the land of Calenardhon, the north-western region of Gondor, and in return requires only that 'they shall live in perpetual friendship with Gondor and its enemies shall be their enemies. . . . But the same bond shall be laid also on the people of Gondor' (*Unfinished Tales*, p. 303). They ascend to the summit and swear an oath of friendship by the tomb of Elendil, a site which had been chosen by his son, Isildur, because it was in the centre of the realm of Gondor.

The final text, *The Tradition of Isildur*, tells the history of Elendil's tomb. Since Amon Anwar was no longer the mid-point of Gondor after the grant of Calenardhon to Eorl, Cirion moved the casket containing Elendil's body to the Hallows in Minas Tirith. Nonetheless, Amon Anwar remained 'a place of reverence to Gondor and to the Rohirrim, who named it in their own tongue Halifirien, the Holy Mount' (p. 310).

Tolkien's own notes to these texts contain background information concerning such matters as the composition of the *éored* of the Rohirrim, the history of the Lords of Dol Amroth, and customs and wording associated with oath-taking.

HISTORY

The four texts are in early draft form, full of variants and ending in rapid jottings. Christopher Tolkien thinks that they were intended 'to form parts of a substantial history, developing in detail the summary accounts given in Appendix A to *The Lord of the Rings*' (*Unfinished Tales*, p. 10). Tolkien cites as 'sources' for these fragments 'The Chronicle of Cirion and Eorl', which begins with the first meeting of those rulers, and the 'lays and legends of the great ride of the Rohirrim from the North' preserved in Rohan and Gondor (p. 288).

Christopher Tolkien thinks that *Cirion and Eorl* was written probably soon after *The Rivers and Beacon-hills of Gondor*, which can be dated with certainty to summer 1969 or later. The idea of Elendil's tomb being on Halifirien evidently arose while Tolkien was writing that essay. See further, *The Rivers and Beacon-hills of Gondor* in *Vinyar Tengwar* 42 (July 2001), especially pp. 22–3, which also includes the text of a rejected page for *Cirion and Eorl* in which Cirion opened the tomb of Elendil on the day after the oath-taking.

The City of Present Sorrow
   see **The Town of Dreams and the City of Present Sorrow**

The City of the Gods. Poem, first published in *The Microcosm* (Leeds) 8, no. 1 (Spring 1923), p. 8. Tolkien wrote its first version on 30 April 1915 in his rooms in St John Street, *Oxford. In its two extant manuscript versions the poem is entitled *Kôr: In a City Lost and Dead* after its subject as it was then called, the shining city of the Elves in Eldamar in *The Book of Lost Tales*: 'marble temples white, and dazzling halls' upon 'a sable hill, gigantic, rampart-crowned'. Tolkien changed its title to *The City of the Gods* in a typescript copy, which also incorporated a minor emendation made already in manuscript. The published version was reprinted (with its earlier title) in *The Book of Lost Tales, Part One* (1983), p. 136.

In that volume Christopher Tolkien remarks that 'it seems possible, especially in view of the original subtitle, that the poem described Kôr after the elves had left it': 'There slow forgotten days for ever reap / The silent shadows counting out rich hours; / And no voice stirs . . .' (p. 136). In *Artist and Illustrator* we relate the poem to Tolkien's contemporary watercolour *Tanaqui* (fig. 43).

Clark Hall, John R. *see* **Prefatory Remarks on Prose Translation of 'Beowulf'**

Classical influences. Tolkien was first taught Latin by his mother (*Mabel Tolkien). At *King Edward's School, Birmingham, he studied both Latin and Greek, and gained an Open Classical Exhibition to Exeter College, *Oxford. He went up to Oxford in Michaelmas Term 1911, and during his first five terms prepared himself for Honour Moderations. He was required to read a considerable amount of classical literature, as well as learn about Greek and Roman history and culture. At Oxford his set texts for Honour Moderations included works by Virgil, Homer, Aeschylus, Sophocles, and Euripides. These studies contributed to the 'leaf-mould of the mind' (*Biography*, p. 126) from which Tolkien's creative writings grew, though their influence on his fiction and poetry was less than that of the literature of Northern Europe. For the drowning of *Númenor, for instance, Tolkien drew upon Plato's reports of the sinking of *Atlantis, combined with his own recurring dream of a 'Great Wave'. In his private mythology, Elendil and his sons escape the destruction of Númenor and found new cities just as in Virgil's *Aeneid* Aeneas flees the fall of Troy and establishes a new city in Italy.

On several occasions Tolkien described peoples or events in his stories as 'Homeric'. In a letter to *Milton Waldman he wrote that in Middle-earth in the Second Age 'the better and nobler sort of Men are in fact the kin of those that had departed to Númenor, but remain in a simple "Homeric" state of patriarchal and tribal life'. Later in the same letter he refers to the Rohirrim, usually noted only for Anglo-Saxon elements in their culture, as 'heroic "Homeric" horsemen' (?late 1951, *Letters*, pp. 154, 159). While writing *The Lord of the Rings* he referred to Homer's list of ships and men in the *Iliad*, Book II, in a note he wrote on an outline looking forward to the siege of Minas Tirith: 'Homeric catalogue. Forlong the Fat. The folk of Lebennin' (*The War of the Ring*, p. 229). In Book V, Chapter 1 of *The Lord of the Rings* this became the arrival of reinforcements from the fiefs and Outlands of Gondor which Pippin witnesses in the company of Bergil.

The Valar, especially in earlier versions of the *'Silmarillion' mythology where they are less remote and exhibit certain human flaws, seem to owe almost as much to the gods and goddesses of Greece and Rome as to the northern Æsir and Vanir.

In the later classical period various legends gathered around the figure of Alexander the Great. The earliest surviving text in Latin, *Alexander's Letter to Aristotle about India* (probably 7th century AD), actually contains elements which predate Alexander, derived from the 5th-century BC writings of Ctesias of Cnidos about Persia and India. From this Latin text, or the Old English translation of it, or a retelling of the (mythical) life of Alexander such as *The Story of Alexander* by Robert Steele (1894), Tolkien may have derived the idea for the Two Trees of Valinor. *Alexander's Letter* tells of two sacred trees, one of the Sun (male) and one of the Moon (female), which could prophecy, the tree of the Sun at sunset, and the tree of the Moon at moonrise. In the many retellings of this story, details were changed or added; Steele describes the trees as being 'not like others, but their boles and leaves shone like metal, and the tree of the sun was like gold, and the tree of the moon was like silver' (p. 165). Tolkien refers to these trees in *On Fairy-Stories*: 'in the Trees of the Sun and the Moon, root and stock, flower and fruit are manifested in glory' (*Tree and Leaf*, p. 55).

David Greenman in his article 'Aeneidic and Odyssean Patterns of Escape and Return in Tolkien's *The Fall of Gondolin* and *The Return of the King*', *Myth-*

lore 18, no. 2, whole no. 68 (Spring 1992), notes similarities and differences between Tolkien's account of the fall of Gondolin and the escape of Tuor and Eärendil from Gondolin, and Virgil's account in the *Aeneid* of the fall of Troy and the escape of Aeneas and his son, as well as, less convincingly, between the return of Frodo, Sam, Merry, and Pippin to the Shire in *The Lord of the Rings*, and the return of Odysseus to his native land in the *Odyssey*.

David Paul Pace in 'The Influence of Vergil's *Aeneid* on *The Lord of the Rings*', *Mythlore* 6, no. 2, whole no. 20 (Spring 1979), pp. 37–8, discusses similarities in character and events in the lives of Aeneas and Aragorn. He compares Aeneas's rejection of Dido and her suicide with Éowyn's attempt to find death in battle after being rejected by Aragorn; and Aeneas entering the Underworld to obtain the advice of his dead father with Aragorn taking the Paths of the Dead.

In *Evocation of Virgil in Tolkien's Art: Geritol for the Classics* (1986) Robert E. Morse, while recognizing that 'the importance of Vergil in the European literary heritage, as well as Tolkien's training in Classics, makes a Vergilian echo almost certain', notes that 'most commentators simply ignore the specifically Roman contribution. Where is the concept of duty the Romans called *pietas*? What about the theme of the founding of Rome and the Pax Augusti as a new spiritual ideal? What about Tolkien's own assertion about the relation of his work to the Holy Roman Empire?' (p. viii). Morse compares Frodo and Aeneas, noting that both are reluctant to leave home, and that 'Frodo's task like that of Aeneas has the aura of a mission around it. The first step involves flight and wandering which reveal the character's willingness to do his duty, i.e., to be *pius*' (p. 3). He suggests parallels rather than influences between the journey of Aeneas and that of Frodo, and concludes that 'the associations seem to permit the conclusion that Tolkien approved Vergil's description of leadership as a sacrifice of oneself for the future of the community' (p. 16). In a later chapter he compares Aragorn and Aeneas, citing the similarity of Aragorn's journey through the Paths of the Dead to Aeneas's descent into the Underworld, and notes that both leaders make a special journey to secure reinforcements for their besieged comrades, both sailing back with help and arriving at a critical moment. He points out that both Dido and Denethor in despair abandon their duty and commit suicide on a funeral pyre.

Others have found more general influences from classical literature in Tolkien's writings. Lin Carter, one of the first Tolkien critics to consider classical sources, in *Tolkien: A Look Behind 'The Lord of the Rings'* (1969) saw the early epics and cyclic poems as establishing a powerful literary tradition in which some of the elements visible in Tolkien's work can be seen: 'the world conception, a sprawling landscape with fantastic wars and imaginary places inhabited by ferocious and fantastic monsters and curious peoples, dominated by divinities of superhuman powers' (p. 107).

In 'Some Trees in Virgil and Tolkien', published in *Perspectives of Roman Poetry: A Classics Symposium* (1974), Kenneth Reckford aims 'to show, not so much that Virgil influenced Tolkien – although *The Lord of the Rings* evidently has western as well as northern roots – as that a deep affinity exists between Virgil's mind and Tolkien's and may be observed in the way they perceive life, in their sense of the relation between heroic choice and achievement, on the one hand, and time, change, loss, sadness, uncertainty, and suffering, on the other' (pp. 57–8). He does so chiefly by discussing similarities of mood and attitude.

The Clerke's Compleinte. Poem, first published as by 'N.N.' ('No Name'?) in *The Gryphon* (Leeds) n.s. 4, no. 3 (December 1922), p. 95. Tolkien plays on the General Prologue to the *Canterbury Tales* by *Geoffrey Chaucer ('Whan that Aprille with its shoures soughte / the drouth of Marche hath perced to the roote', etc.):

> Whanne that Octobre mid his schoures derke
> The erthe hath dreint, and wete windes cherke
> And swoghe in naked braunches colde and bare,
> And th' olde sonne is hennes longe yfare; [etc.]

Then folk 'from every schires ende / In al the North' of England seek a 'faire educacioun' at Leeds, where Tolkien at that time was Reader in English Language at the University. The 'clerke' describes the chaos of registration: he is one of a large number of prospective students, some of whom wish to learn old languages, though they have little Latin and less Greek, but are outnumbered by those interested in chemistry and physics and other sciences. Though 'maystres hadde I mo than thryes ten, / And wisdom of an heap of lerned men', the speaker cannot answer the questions put to him and is sent away. 'It is only appropriate', T.A. Shippey has said, 'that the whole poem should be in Middle English, for its imagined author is a throwback, speaking a language no-one can understand' and unable to understand practical questions 'however "expert and curious" he may be in other matters' ('The Clerkes Compleinte', *Arda 1984* (1988), p. 7).

No manuscript of the poem in the version published in *The Gryphon* is known to survive. There exist, however, a cutting of the published text emended in manuscript by Tolkien; a typescript made in Leeds, the text slightly altered from *The Gryphon* and itself emended; and a formal manuscript with the text slightly revised. The latter is written on paper used in Oxford examinations, unavailable to Tolkien until 1924, when he served as an external examiner at Oxford from Leeds; but a still later date, after Tolkien had formally returned to Oxford (in 1925, though he continued to teach at Leeds for two terms), is suggested by its description of Leeds as the 'derkest toune of Yorkeschire', whereas in earlier versions it was the 'fairest'. Tolkien also, at some unknown date, further emended and annotated the manuscript, changing the location from 'Leedes' to 'Oxenforde'.

The Clerke's Compleinte was reprinted (with some errors) with notes, commentary, and translations in *Arda 1984* (1988), pp. 1–10. The later manuscript was printed in facsimile in *Arda 1986* (1990), in the article '*The Clerkes Compleinte* Revisited', pp. 1–13, which examines the differences between the three versions of the poem.

Clevedon (Somerset). After their wedding on 22 March 1916 Tolkien and his wife *Edith stayed for a week in Clevedon, a quiet watering place on the Severn Estuary. During this time they also visited the nearby *Cheddar Gorge and Caves. They returned to Clevedon at least once, in September 1952, when they stayed at the Highcliffe Hotel, Wellington Terrace. On the latter occasion Tolkien wrote to his grandson, Michael George Tolkien, enclosing a map of the area where he and Edith were staying, and a drawing of the view from his window across the Severn Estuary with the coast of Wales in the distance. He also sent a sketch to his son Christopher, with the note: 'Not a vision of Tirion [a city of the Elves in his *'Silmarillion' mythology], but an attempt to catch Cardiff caught in a rainbow across the Severn Sea. . . . My window drops sheer into water at present as violent as the open Atlantic' (25 September 1952, quoted by Christopher Tolkien in private correspondence).

Coalbiters (Kolbítar) *see* **Societies and clubs**

Coghill, Nevill Henry Kendal Aylmer (1899–1980). Nevill Coghill read History and then, for an additional year, English at Exeter College, *Oxford. He was active in several of the student societies at Exeter, including the Essay Club (*Societies and clubs): he attended a meeting of the latter on 10 March 1920, at which Tolkien read *The Fall of Gondolin* (see *The Book of Lost Tales). From 1924 to 1957 he was a Fellow and Librarian at Exeter, and from 1957 to 1966 Merton Professor of English Literature at Oxford, succeeding his old tutor, *F.P. Wilson. In Hilary Term 1937 he joined Tolkien, *Hugo Dyson, *C.S. Lewis, and *C.L. Wrenn in giving a series of lectures on *Hamlet*. Coghill saw Tolkien also at meetings of the Kolbítar (*Societies and clubs) and the *Inklings.

Ahead of his time, Coghill realized that medieval literature, 'even as late as the days of Chaucer and [William] Langland, was still often intimately involved with oral performance, and that modern readers could often understand it better if it was read aloud' (Douglas Gray, introduction to *The Collected Papers of Nevill Coghill* (1988), pp. vii–x). He was famous for his contemporary English version of *Chaucer's *Canterbury Tales* (1951), which was published in book form and broadcast on radio. He was also closely involved with the Oxford University Dramatic Society, and founder of the Experimental Theatre Club, a more adventurous group than the OUDS and one which gave women equal opportunities: its first programme stated that the purpose of the Club was 'to give scope to all those lesser creative talents and crafts that are involved in the Art of Theatre . . . [and] to present the little-known masterpieces of the past.' The *'Summer Diversions', organized by Coghill together with *John Masefield and presented in 1937–9, had a similar aim.

Among his other achievements, Coghill wrote a general introduction to Chaucer and his works (*The Poet Chaucer* (1949), to which Tolkien contributed an emendation), and collaborated with *Christopher Tolkien on student editions of Chaucer's 'Pardoner's Tale', 'Nun's Priest's Tale', and 'Man of Law's Tale' in Middle English (1958, 1959, 1969). He is known as well for his writings on Shakespeare and on *Piers Plowman*; regarding the latter, he contributed an essay, 'God's Wenches and the Light That Spoke (Some Notes on Langland's Kind of Poetry)', to the *Festschrift *English and Medieval Studies Presented to J.R.R. Tolkien on the Occasion of His Seventieth Birthday* (1962).

After Tolkien's death Coghill was one of several friends and family members interviewed by Ann Bonsor for a series of programmes first broadcast on Radio Oxford in 1974. He recalled that it was he, as secretary of the Exeter College Essay Club, who asked Tolkien to read a paper to that group; and having been told that the subject of the paper was to be 'the fall of Gondolin', he spent weeks searching reference books, trying to find a mention of that (fictional) place. Records show, however, that Coghill had not held any office in the Essay Club when Tolkien read *The Fall of Gondolin* to its meeting, and in fact Coghill had been elected to the Club only on 27 February 1920, less than two weeks before Tolkien's reading on 10 March.

See further, Rowland Ryder, 'Nevill Coghill', *Exeter College Association Register 1992*; and *To Nevill Coghill from Friends*, collected by John Lawlor and W.H. Auden (1966).

Collecting and sales. The first and only major sale of manuscripts and typescripts by Tolkien occurred in 1957, by private treaty between Tolkien himself and Marquette University (*Libraries and archives). Librarian William Ready of Marquette, who was eager to build library collections for the University, worked through the London bookseller Bertram Rota to purchase from Tolkien working papers of *The Hobbit*, *The Lord of the Rings*, *Farmer Giles of Ham*, and *Mr. Bliss*. The total price was £1,500, a bargain in today's market even adjusting for inflation; but Tolkien on his part was satisfied with the amount. Despite the success of *The Lord of the Rings* (1954–5), his fame was not then such that his papers, or his published works, would command high prices from collectors, nor were they widely sought or sold. Not until 1977, the year in which both his long-awaited *Silmarillion* and Humphrey Carpenter's *Biography* were published, did the collectors' market for 'Tolkieniana' become significantly active. The animated feature film of *The Lord of the Rings* by Ralph Bakshi (1978; *Adaptations) also helped to generate interest.

In 1980 the first bookseller's catalogue devoted solely to Tolkien appeared: *Precious Stones* by Melissa and Mark Hime of Idyllwild, California. Prices ranged from $15 to $12,500, with $2,500 for an unsigned first edition of *The Lord of the Rings* perhaps a good benchmark (twenty years later, the same copy might bring four times that amount). Since that time one finds an increasing number of published works and minor manuscripts (usually letters) by Tolkien sold at auction and otherwise, and increasingly as investments to be held for later resale – not always at a profit, as the market in Tolkieniana has troughs as well as peaks.

For much of the 1980s prices for good Tolkien material were artificially high, raised by a dealer who bid high at auction in order to create sale records to 'justify' high prices in the general market. In the end he was overtaken by values dropping to a saner level. But in the 1990s prices for Tolkien's works, ephemera, and memorabilia rose again, eventually to record levels, driven by growth of sales venues on the Internet, especially online auctions such as eBay which allowed private sellers easy access to the market, by a burgeoning economy, and by widespread publicity surrounding the live-action films of *The Lord of the Rings* directed by Peter Jackson (2001–3; *Adaptations). Even lesser editions and later printings of books by Tolkien began to command prices in at least three figures, with first editions of his major works valued often in the high five or even low six figures. By late 2002, however, the market now saturated with Tolkieniana and the world economy in retreat, the pace of sales began to moderate, and in some respects even to decline.

Upon Tolkien's death in 1973 hundreds of offprints, reprints, and spare copies of scholarly works in Tolkien's professional library were sold by his estate *en bloc* to a dealer who then dispersed them into the general market. Many of these bear a 'Tolkien Library' label, inserted posthumously. Books given by Tolkien to family members also occasionally appear in booksellers' catalogues and at auction, as do books from his personal library which he was forced to reduce drastically in size when he retired from his *Oxford chair in 1959, gave up his college rooms, and had insufficient space in his home to absorb all of the books he had kept in Merton. Copies of Tolkien's own works containing his autograph are less scarce in the market than commonly supposed, but some copies offered as such are of questionable authenticity, and in others his signature has been inserted, having been excised from a less marketable work in Tolkien's library in which he had written his name.

Some of the miscellaneous sales of letters and autographed books by Tolkien through mid-1992 are noted in *Descriptive Bibliography*. News of sales of Tolkien's works have been reported in the occasional magazine *The Tolkien Collector* (begun 1992), edited and published by Christina Scull.

'Of the Coming of the Elves and the Captivity of Melkor'. The third chapter of the *'Quenta Silmarillion', published in *The Silmarillion* (1977), pp. 47–54.

SUMMARY

The Valar dwell in the light of the Trees in Aman, and except for Oromë and Yavanna seldom visit Middle-earth, now lit only by the stars. Yavanna sets a sleep on the many things that had arisen in the Spring of Arda, until a time of awakening should come. The power of Morgoth spreads over Middle-earth from his northern fortress, Utumno, where he gathers to himself the Balrogs and breeds monsters. He builds a second fortress, Angband, further west, commanded by Sauron. At length the Valar are troubled by news of Middle-earth brought by Yavanna and Oromë, and wonder if they should leave in darkness the lands where the Children of Ilúvatar are to awake. But Mandos declares that although the Children will come soon, it is decreed that they should awaken in darkness, under the stars. Varda therefore creates more stars, and as she finishes her labours the Elves awake 'by the starlit mere of Cuiviénen ... and while they dwelt yet silent by Cuiviénen their eyes beheld first of all things the stars of heaven. Therefore they have ever loved the starlight, and have revered Varda Elentári above all the Valar' (*The Silmarillion*, p. 48). The Elves dwell long in Cuiviénen, in the north-east of Middle-earth, and begin 'to make speech and give names to all things' (p. 49).

Oromë comes upon them by chance as he hunts in Middle-earth, but already Melkor has become aware of the Elves, and his spies have seized or pursued those who stray. Therefore the Elves fear Oromë, but most are soon drawn to him. The fate of those seized by Melkor is not known, but in after days the wise believe that they were 'by slow arts of cruelty ... corrupted and enslaved', and from them Melkor bred 'the hideous race of the Orcs' (p. 50).

Oromë swiftly brings news of the awakening of the Children to Valinor, then returns to Cuiviénen. Manwë seeks the counsel of Ilúvatar, who decides that the Elves must be freed from the shadow of Melkor. The Valar besiege Melkor in Utumno. In the conflicts that follow, the shape of Middle-earth is changed. At last Utumno is broken, Melkor is bound by the great chain Angainor, and the Valar imprison him in the fastness of Mandos for three ages. Neither Utumno nor Angband are completely destroyed, however, and many evil things, including Sauron, remain free. After debate, the Valar choose to summon the Elves to Valinor rather than leave them in Middle-earth. At first the Elves are unwilling to go, but after three ambassadors, Ingwë, Finwë, and Elwë, are brought by Oromë to Valinor so that they might report its glory, many accept the summons.

Thus comes the sundering of the Elves, into the Eldar who accept the invitation and the Avari, the Unwilling, who prefer to remain in the starlight of Middle-earth. Guided by Oromë, the Elves begin a long march west: first the Vanyar, the smallest host, led by Ingwë; then the Noldor, led by Finwë; and finally the Teleri, the greatest host, led by Elwë and Olwë. Not all who set out reach the shores of Middle-earth, and some who do, mainly of the Teleri, decide to stay there and not cross the Sea. Others of the Teleri, led by Lenwë, leave the host and settle in the lands east of the Misty Mountains, becoming the Nandor. The Vanyar and the Noldor pass through Beleriand and reach the Sea while the Teleri are still in eastern Beleriand. Oromë leaves the Elves to seek counsel from Manwë.

HISTORY

The earliest account of the events in this chapter was written as part of one tale in *The Book of Lost Tales* probably early in 1919. As published in *The Book of

Lost Tales, Part One, it is divided between two tales, *The Chaining of Melko* and *The Coming of the Elves and the Making of Kôr*. A small part of the chapter in *The Silmarillion* derives ultimately from material in the unfinished *Gilfanon's Tale: The Travail of the Noldoli and the Coming of Mankind*.

The story in *The Chaining of Melko* differs greatly from that in *The Silmarillion*. In *The Book of Lost Tales* the Lamps, on their pillars of ice, fall before much growth has taken place in Middle-earth, and Yavanna then sows seeds in the following darkness. But what grows is corrupted by Melko, who considers the Great Lands (Middle-earth) to be his domain, and

> caused the Earth to quake and split and his lower fires to mingle with the sea. Vaporous storms and a great roaring of uncontrolled sea-motions burst upon the world, and the forests groaned and snapped. The sea leapt upon the land and tore it, and wide regions sank beneath its rage or were hewn into scattered islets, and the coast was dug into caverns. The mountains rocked and their hearts melted, and stone poured like liquid fire down their ashen sides and flowed even to the sea.... [*The Book of Lost Tales, Part One*, p. 100]

The Valar decide that they will try to dissuade Melko from his deeds, but if that fails, 'to overcome him by force or guile, and set him in a bondage from which there should be no escape' (p. 101). For this purpose, Aulë forges a great chain, Angaino, with manacles and fetters of six metals plus a seventh with all the properties of the other six. The Valar arm themselves and travel to Utumna, but Melkor refuses to come out, and will only allow two of the Valar to enter to speak with him.

The Valar therefore resort to trickery. They send a herald to tell Melko that they seek his pardon for past actions, and beg him, the greatest and mightiest of the Valar, to dwell with them in Valinor. Melko demands that all, including Manwë, lay aside their arms and pay homage, but he will not receive Tulkas, who had played a major role in opposing him in earlier conflicts. Manwë replies that they will come before Melko, and deliver Tulkas to him in chains. The Valar descend into Utumna, Tulkas bearing Angaino about his neck and arms. As Manwë advances to pay homage, Tulkas, Aulë, and Oromë restrain Melko with Angaino. They take him to Valinor, where he is sentenced to be chained for three ages in the house of Mandos, and then live for four ages in the house of Tulkas as a servant. After Melko's imprisonment growth begins again in the Great Lands.

The beginning of *The Coming of the Elves and the Making of Kôr* relates that Manwë, from his high seat in Valinor, sees lights in the lands east of the Sea and knows that the Elves have awakened. On hearing the news, Varda places more stars in the heavens. Oromë returns from the Great Lands, saying that he has seen and heard the Elves, as has also Yavanna. The Valar send their herald (not Oromë) to invite representatives of the Elves to come to Valinor to speak with them. The three ambassadors who volunteer to return with him are Isil

Inwë, leader of the Teleri (later called the Vanyar); Finwë Nólemë, leader of the Noldoli (later called the Noldor); and Tinwë Linto (later called Elwë and Thingol), leader of the Solosimpi (in later texts called the Teleri). In Valinor the ambassadors are dazzled by the light of the Trees and filled with awe at the sight of the Valar. In this version only Manwë questions them concerning their coming into the world, but they can remember nothing. After much debate, in which even Melko takes part (having been released early from Mandos), the Valar decide to invite the Elves to dwell with them in Valinor. The ambassadors persuade their peoples to do so, Oromë leads them on the march, and they depart in the same order as in *The Silmarillion*. The Elves who refuse the invitation, or who are lost or turn aside on the journey, are mentioned in Gilfanon's unfinished tale.

Although the brief *Sketch of the Mythology* (c. 1926) omits much of this matter, it also introduces some major changes in the story. The most significant change is that the Valar do not attack Morgoth (Melko) until the Elves awaken, when their coming reminds the Valar that it is their duty to govern the earth for the two races 'who should come each in appointed time' (*The Shaping of Middle-earth*, p. 13). Nothing is said of how they capture Melko, and this change in chronology means that it is not until the Elves have been living in Valinor for a great time that Melko is released from Mandos. Also, growth begins under the Lamps but is checked when they fall. The awakening of the Elves when Varda makes the stars is introduced, with the suggestion that these were the first stars. There is no mention of Manwë seeing the Elves' lights or of Yavanna also discovering them. In this 'synopsis' no mention is made of the ambassadors, or that not all of the Elves accepted the invitation to Valinor.

In the *Quenta Noldorinwa* (c. 1930) Tolkien reintroduced a few details from *The Book of Lost Tales*. It is now stated that it was because of the Elves that the Valar attacked Morgoth, and 'this he never forgot'. And it seems clear that the Valar used force, not deceit: 'Little do the Elves or Men know of that great riding of the power of the West against the North and of the war and tumult of the battle of the Gods [i.e. the Valar]. Tulkas it was who overthrew Morgoth and bound him captive' (*The Shaping of Middle-earth*, p. 84). Morgoth is said to have made the Orcs 'of stone, but their hearts of hatred' (p. 82).

The 'earliest' *Annals of Valinor* (early 1930s) added a time frame for these events. Originally both Varda's star-making and the awakening of the Elves were recorded for Valian Year 2000, but by amendment Varda begins to make the stars in Valian Year 1900 and spends fifty Valian Years (500 years of the Sun) doing so, and the Elves awake with her last creation, the Sickle of the Gods. Morgoth is imprisoned for 900 Valian Years (changed to 700). The Elves begin their journey to the Sea thirty Valian Years after they awake, and it takes them about ten Valian Years to complete. There is an oblique suggestion that some of the Elves refused the invitation, as in *The Book of Lost Tales*, but this is not mentioned in the intervening texts. The 'later' *Annals of Valinor* follow the account in the 'earliest' *Annals*, except that these say that Yavanna visited Middle-earth during the time of its darkness 'and the slow growth of the forests was begun' (*The Lost Road and Other Writings*, p. 111), and it is made clear that Oromë finds the Elves thirty Valian Years after they awake, and ten Valian Years later they reach the Sea.

In the *Quenta Silmarillion*, begun in the mid-1930s, Tolkien enlarged the account told in the *Quenta Noldorinwa* with more detail, as the first part of a chapter called 'Of the Coming of the Elves'. A temporary change in the story is that only Manwë among the Valar has any foreknowledge of the coming of the Children of Ilúvatar, and he reveals the will of Ilúvatar that the Valar should take up their duty to govern the world for the Children. The Elves awaken with the first stars, not at the completion of Varda's work. Melkor makes the Orcs only after seeing the Elves, in mockery of the Children. The chain Angainor, used to bind Morgoth, re-enters the story. The three ambassadors of the Elves, omitted from the intervening texts (probably due to compression rather than rejection), are mentioned for the first time since *The Book of Lost Tales*, and in this part the story now approached *The Silmarillion*.

The story moved further towards the published text in revisions made to the *Quenta Silmarillion c.* 1951. Yavanna and Oromë report the evil spread in Middle-earth by Melkor, and Yavanna begs Manwë to provide light for the Children (of whom they now have foreknowledge) when they awake. But Mandos says that the Elves are ordained to waken in darkness under the stars. Therefore Varda not only makes new stars, but gathers others she had created long before, and sets them as signs in the heavens. Again the Elves wake at the end of her star-making; and now Melkor makes Orcs in mockery of the Elves. When Oromë brings news that the Children have come, Manwë consults Ilúvatar as to what action the Valar should take. The Nandor who failed to complete the journey now enter the tale.

In the *Annals of Aman* (also *c.* 1951, see *Annals of Valinor*) Tolkien made adjustments to the dating and time-spans in the *Annals of Valinor*, took up some of the new material into the *Annals of Aman*, and added new details. Yavanna now sets a sleep on the growth that had begun in the Spring of Arda. An addition to the original text introduces Melkor's early discovery of the Elves and his breeding of Orcs from those he captured, for which reason the Elves are at first suspicious of Oromë. Since in these *Annals* a new reckoning begins from the creation of the Trees, the chronology differs, and there are also additions. Varda's star-making lasts fifty years from (in the new reckoning of the Trees) 1000–1050. Oromë finds the Elves in 1085, the Valar decide to attack Melkor in 1090, and the siege of Utumno begins in 1092. After many battles its gates are broken and Melkor takes refuge in its uttermost pit; there in 1099 he stands alone against Tulkas, who casts him down and binds him with Angainor. Melkor is taken to Valinor and brought before Manwë and the other Valar. He begs for pardon, but is sentenced to be imprisoned in Mandos for three ages of the Valar (300 Valian Years, i.e. 3,000 years of the Sun). The three ambassadors are brought to Valinor in 1102 and return to Cuiviénen in 1104. In this text only, the leaders of the Avari are named, and it is suggested that they were reluctant to go to Valinor because they had not seen Oromë and believed the lies about him spread by the servants of Melkor. The description of the journey of the Elves to the shores of the Sea is expanded to include references to parts of Middle-earth which appear in *The Lord of the Rings. It now takes the Elves ten Valian Years to reach the River Anduin, and a further ten before the Vanyar and the Noldor reach the Sea. Some years later Tolkien inserted references to the birth of Fëanor, son of Finwë and Indis, during the journey, and to the death of Indis while crossing the mountains, but then struck them out. An entry in the Grey Annals (see *Annals of Beleriand), written soon after the Annals of Aman, adds the information that the spies of Melkor discovered the Elves about five Valian Years before Oromë first saw them; another entry returns to the earlier time-scheme in that it took the Elves ten years to reach the Sea.

The text of the Silmarillion chapter was compiled by Christopher Tolkien from a complex interweaving of phrases, parts of paragraphs, and whole paragraphs, taken from both the revised Quenta Silmarillion and the Annals of Aman. The report of rumours concerning Melkor (pp. 49–50) and the account of the journey of the Elves (pp. 53–4) were taken almost entirely from the Annals, and the description of the three hosts of the Elves (pp. 52–3) mainly from the Quenta Silmarillion. Part of the description of changes in Arda as a result of the battle with Melkor (p. 51), and a short piece in the penultimate paragraph, were taken from the Grey Annals.

'Of the Coming of Men into the West'. The seventeenth chapter of the *'Quenta Silmarillion', published in *The Silmarillion (1977), pp. 140–9.

SUMMARY

Over three hundred years after the Noldor have returned to Middle-earth, Finrod Felagund, while travelling in Ossiriand in the east of Beleriand, comes upon Men of the kindred and following of Bëor who have travelled west across the Blue Mountains and believe they have now escaped from the perils and fear that threatened them in the East. Finrod takes up Bëor's harp and plays music of great beauty and wisdom. He dwells with them for a time and teaches them true knowledge. They love him and take him as their lord. Since Finrod can 'read in the minds of Men such thoughts as they wished to reveal in speech', and Men have learned much of their speech from the Dark Elves whose tongue ultimately had the same origin as all other elven tongues, Finrod is soon able to converse with Bëor. He can learn little of Men's past, except that 'a darkness lies behind us . . . and we have turned our backs upon it, and we do not desire to return thither even in thought. Westwards our hearts have been turned, and we believe that there we shall find Light' (The Silmarillion, p. 141). But Elves later believe that Morgoth soon learned of the waking of Men, and went himself into the East planning to corrupt or destroy them, and to use them against the Eldar, but returned to Angband before fully achieving his aim.

Bëor tells Felagund that other groups of Men are also moving westward, including the Haladin and a numerous people led by Marach. The Green-elves of Ossiriand do not want strangers in their land, and speak of this to Felagund. On his advice Bëor and his people move across the river Gelion to a place called Estolad. When Felagund returns home to Nargothrond, Bëor goes with him, leaving his son to rule his people. Not long after this, the Haladin enter Beleriand and settle in Thargelion, and a year later Marach and his people also reach Beleriand and settle near the people of Bëor. The Elves call these three kindreds of Elf-friends the Edain. The Noldor welcome them and see them as allies. In the following years many of these Men move further west and dwell near or among the Elves. Thingol of Doriath, annoyed because he is not consulted in this and is troubled by dreams, refuses to allow any Men into Doriath; but Melian tells Galadriel that one man will enter despite the girdle of protection she has set round Doriath, 'for doom greater than my power shall send him' (p. 144).

But many Men still remain in Estolad, some of whom do not trust the Elves, and Morgoth fosters dissent among them. The leaders of the discontented are Bereg of the House of Bëor, and Amlach, a grandson of Marach. A council is held to discuss the different views. The Elf-friends declare that Morgoth is the source of all the evils experienced by Men, that he seeks dominion over Middle-earth and is restrained only by the Elves. But an agent of Morgoth, appearing in the shape of Amlach, responds by questioning Elvish lore of the Valar, and saying that it is the Elves who seek dominion. Even when Amlach denies having made this speech, some are of the opinion that Men only increase Morgoth's hostility to them by supporting the Elves, and return east or travel south out of Beleriand.

Morgoth feels even greater hostility towards those who remain, and he sends an army of Orcs against the Haladin. They resist bravely until rescued by an elven host under Caranthir. Haleth, the daughter of their slain leader, leads the survivors west, and Felagund obtains permission from Thingol for them to settle in the forest of Brethil, on condition that they guard the Crossings of Teiglin. The Elf-kings, 'seeing that it was not good for Elves and Men to live mingled together without order, and that Men needed lords of their own kind, set regions apart where Men could live their own lives, and appointed chieftains to hold these lands freely. They were allies of the Eldar in war, but marched under their own leaders' (p. 147). Hador, a descendant of Marach, holds the lordship of Dor-lomin of King Fingolfin, while that of Dorthonion is given to the descendants of Bëor. Most Men who live among the Elves learn the Sindarin tongue and, though it is the only tongue spoken in House of Hador, his people also remember their own speech.

Then follows a brief summary of some of the most prominent figures among Men in the later history of Beleriand: Barahir and his son Beren; Galdor and his sons Húrin and Húor, and their sons Túrin and Tuor, and Húrin's wife Morwen of the House of Bëor. The chapter ends with a description of the physical appearance and character of Men of the Three Houses, and the grief and wonder of the Elves at the short life of Men, especially of Felagund when Bëor dies of old age at ninety-three after serving him forty-four years.

HISTORY

There is no 'tale' in *The Book of Lost Tales (c. 1916–20) corresponding to this chapter. Tolkien abandoned Gilfanon's Tale: The Travail of the Noldoli and the Coming of Mankind after only a few pages, and what he did write has no connection with later versions other than to show that the early corruption of some men by Melkor was part of the story from the beginning. The *Sketch of the Mythology (c. 1926) says that Men who awake in the far East with the first rising of the Sun learn speech and other things from the Ilkorindi (Elves who had refused the summons to Valinor) and spread west and north. It is not clear from the extremely compressed form of this text whether Men and Ilkorindi are already warring with Morgoth when the Noldoli return from Valinor: 'The Gnomes [Noldoli] march forward and beleaguer Angband. They meet Ilkorins and Men. At that time Men already dwelt in the woods of the North, and Ilkorins also. They long warred with Morgoth. Of Ilkorin race was Barahir and his son Beren. Of mortal race was Húrin son of Gumlin, whose wife was Morwen; they lived in the woods upon the borders of Hithlum. These come after into the tales'. This was later emended to make Barahir and Beren also mortal, with Huor added as another son of Gumlin. When Morgoth breaks the siege, Men, Noldoli, and Ilkorin are scattered, and his emissaries spread lies to promote distrust 'of each to each' (*The Shaping of Middle-earth, p. 23).

Tolkien expanded and changed this account in the *Quenta Noldorinwa (c. 1930). There Men definitely do not arrive in Broseliand (later Beleriand) until after the return of the Noldoli from Valinor. It is only during the time of the Siege of Angband that Felagund discovers Bëor and his people, and as in the final version plays Bëor's harp. Bëor and his son Barahir become friends of Felagund and his brothers, but rather than dying of old age Bëor is slain in the war against Morgoth. Hador and his people arrive next. His sons, Haleth and Gumlin, and Gumlin's sons Huor and Húrin are noted as being allied to the House of Fingolfin. The sons of Huor and Húrin, Tuor and Túrin, are also mentioned. 'All these were tangled in the fates of the Gnomes and did mighty deeds which the Elves still remember among the songs of the deeds of their own lords and kings' (The Shaping of Middle-earth, p. 104). A rough note added later seems to be the first reference to the Haladin, the third house of Men, at this point led by Haleth the Hunter.

The 'earliest' *Annals of Valinor and the 'earliest' *Annals of Beleriand, both of the early 1930s, give some indication of the chronology of events as Tolkien envisaged them at this time. According to the former source, Men awake in Year 1 of the Sun. According to the latter, Bëor is born in the East in Year 70. He and his men wander west into Beleriand and are found by Felagund in Year 100. Haleth and Hador are born in 88 and 90, and both enter Beleriand in Year 120. Men join the Noldoli in the Siege of Angband. Most of the more important descendants of Bëor and Hádor mentioned in the *Silmarillion* chapter now emerge, though, since at this stage Tolkien only imagined the First Age lasting 250 years, they are separated by only a few generations from the first Men to arrive in Beleriand. The annal for Year 150 records Bëor's death of old age and that 'the Elves see for the first time the death of weariness, and sorrow over the short span allotted to Men' (*The Shaping of Middle-earth*, p. 298). The *Annals of Beleriand* also include a brief description of the physical characteristics of the three houses of Men.

In works that followed Tolkien gradually lengthened the duration of the Siege of Angband – by a hundred years in a second version of the 'earliest' *Annals of Beleriand*, and then a further two hundred years by emendation in the 'later' *Annals of Beleriand* (mid-1930s) and the *Quenta Silmarillion* (mid-1930s–early 1938), each time increasing all of the dates noted above by the same amount so that Bëor is born in Year 370, meets Felagund in 400, and dies in 450. In the 'later' *Annals of Beleriand* more information is given about the folk of Haleth: that they 'wandered much, owning allegiance to none, but they held most to the woods of Brethil between Taiglin and Sirion' (*The Lost Road and Other Writings*, p. 130, with emendation p. 146, note 21). It is also said that the folk of Hádor abandon their own Mannish tongue and speak only the Elvish language. The chapter 'Of Men and Dwarfs' in the *Quenta Silmarillion* contains a more extensive account of the arrival of Men in the West of Middle-earth, but this is mainly by expansion of detail and description, as in the description of the differing appearances and characteristics of the folk of the three houses, rather than by significant addition.

When Tolkien returned to the history of the First Age after completing *The Lord of the Rings*, in work on the *Quenta Silmarillion c.* 1951, he rewrote the part of 'Of Men and Dwarfs' dealing with dwarfs (as then spelled) and gave the chapter a new title, 'Of the Naugrim and the Edain'; but at this stage he made few changes to the part dealing with Men. In the *Grey Annals* (*c.* 1951, see *Annals of Beleriand*), on the other hand, he added many new details: the account of Thingol's decree against Men entering Doriath, and Melian's words of foresight to Galadriel. On a replacement sheet he added the story of Morgoth leaving Angband and his intention to corrupt Men, and of the darkness the Elves saw lying on the hearts of Men.

In *c.* 1958–60 Tolkien turned again to the *Quenta Silmarillion*, struck through the part of the chapter 'Of the Naugrim and the Edain' dealing with Men, and replaced it with a new version as a separate chapter entitled 'Of the Coming of Men into the West and the Meeting of the Edain and the Eldar' (or, on a separate title-page, 'Of the Coming of the Edain & Their Houses and Lordships in Beleriand'). *Christopher Tolkien describes this new chapter as 'a massive extension of and departure from the "traditional" history of the Edain' (*The War of the Jewels*, p. 215). In addition to the introduction of greater detail, there were now significant changes. Bëor and his people come into the West ninety years earlier, in Year 310, but since later events and dates remained unchanged Tolkien had to provide intervening generations for the houses of

Bëor and Hador. Bëor remains as the leader of his people into Beleriand, with four generations inserted between him and Barahir, originally his son; but Hador remains the great-grandfather of Tuor and Túrin, becoming fourth in descent from Marach, who replaces him as the man who led his people into Beleriand. In the *Grey Annals* Haleth the Hunter still leads the Haladin, but in the rewritten *Quenta Silmarillion* they are led by Haldad and, after his death, by his daughter Haleth.

The text of *The Silmarillion* chapter is mainly that of the *c.* 1958–60 rewritten chapter of the *Quenta Silmarillion*, but Christopher Tolkien made editorial emendations to bring the text into accord with his father's latest writings and thoughts, including changes of names (e.g. *Finrod* to *Finarfin*, *Felagund* to *Finrod Felagund*, *Hador Glorindol* to *Hador Lórindol*). He also introduced passages from the *Grey Annals*, including those about Morgoth's early dealings with Men and the resulting darkness on their hearts, and about Thingol's reaction to the coming of Men and Melian's foresight. See further, notes on pp. 226–8 of *The War of the Jewels*. Some of Tolkien's late thoughts on the movement of Men westwards, their appearance, and their languages appear in *Of Dwarves and Men in *The Peoples of Middle-earth (pp. 303–9, 324–6) and in a note to *The Problem of Ros (The Peoples of Middle-earth, pp. 373–4, note 13).

Concerning Galadriel and Celeborn
see *The History of Galadriel and Celeborn and of Amroth King of Lórien*

The Converse of Manwë and Eru. Late work, of which the first part only of the first version is published in *Morgoth's Ring (1993), pp. 361–6, as an appendix to the *Athrabeth Finrod ah Andreth.

Manwë consults Eru as to what should be done concerning the houseless *fëar* (spirits) of Elves killed in Middle-earth, and of Míriel who had 'died' in Aman. Eru gives Manwë and the Valar the power of rehousing the *fëar* in *hröa* (bodies) identical to those they inhabited before death. Eru also tells Manwë that if any *fëar* prefer to be reborn as a child, and Manwë judges them fit for re-birth, he should submit them to Eru for consideration. According to *Christopher Tolkien, the unfinished second part of the work is 'an elaborate philosophical discussion of the significance and implications' of the first, in the form of 'a commentary by Eldarin loremasters' (*Morgoth's Ring*, pp. 361, 363).

The unfinished typescript of *The Converse of Manwë and Eru* was followed by a new expanded version in manuscript, abandoned after only two pages. This work shows that Tolkien beginning to abandon the idea concerning the fate of the Elves who died; hitherto they had re-entered the world only through rebirth as a child. In addition he had 'come to think that before the death of Míriel there had not been any "re-housing" of the *fëar* of the Dead, and that it was only in response to the appeal of Manwë that Eru decreed such a possibility and the modes by which it might be brought about' (p. 362). Christopher Tolkien places the writing of this text after *Laws and Customs among the Eldar and before *Reincarnation of Elves and the commentary on the *Athrabeth, within the period late 1958–1960.

Copyright *see* **Ace Books controversy**

Cornwall. In August 1914 Tolkien visited the **Lizard** in Cornwall, an area south of the Helford River to the southern headland, Lizard Point, in the south-west corner of England. While there he stayed at the home of the mother of his travelling companion, *Father Vincent Reade of the *Birmingham Oratory. He described in a letter to his fiancée, Edith Bratt (*Edith Tolkien), how he

> walked over the moor-land on top of the cliffs to **Kynance Cove**. . . . The sun beats down on you and a huge Atlantic swell smashes and spouts over the snags and reefs. The sea has carved weird wind-holes and spouts into the cliffs which blow with trumpety noises or spout foam like a whale, and everywhere you see black and red rock and white foam against violet and transparent seagreen. [quoted in *Biography*, p. 70]

During this holiday Tolkien made the drawings *Cadgwith, Cornwall, Caerthilian Cove & Lion Rock* (*Artist and Illustrator*, fig. 20), and *Cove near the Lizard* (*Artist and Illustrator*, fig. 21). **Cadgwith**, drawn by Tolkien from a vantage point on the steep road descending to the picturesque fishing village, has changed little in the intervening years. Lion Rock is so called because it looks like a crouching lion; Tolkien drew it while standing on **Pentreath Beach** – the view today is almost unchanged – from which Caerthilian Cove would have been behind a promontory at his back.

In November–December 1914, inspired by his visit to Cornwall, Tolkien rewrote and greatly extended a poem he had composed in 1912, *The Grimness of the Sea*. The version dated 4 December, entitled *The Tides*, is inscribed 'On the Cornish Coast'. (See *The Horns of Ylmir*.)

In summer 1932 Tolkien, together with his wife and children, his colleague *C.L. Wrenn, and Wrenn's wife and daughter, spent a month at **Lamorna Cove** on the Cornish coast near Penzance, 'then wild and fairly inaccessible' (letter to Christopher Bretherton, 16 July 1964, *Letters*, p. 347). John and Priscilla Tolkien recalled that 'it was a delightful, carefree holiday, with walks as far as **Land's End**, bathing in the cove, and complete isolation from the outside world' (*The Tolkien Family Album*, p. 62, with photograph). Humphrey Carpenter reports that 'Wrenn and Tolkien held a swimming race wearing panama hats and smoking pipes while they swam' (*Biography*, p. 160). During this holiday Tolkien met 'a curious local character, an old man who used to go about swapping gossip and weather-wisdom and such like. To amuse my boys I named him Gaffer Gamgee, and the name became part of family lore to fix on old chaps of that kind' (letter to Bretherton, *Letters*, p. 348). A 'Gaffer Gamgee' appears briefly in *Mr. Bliss* (pp. 36–7), and the name is given to Sam Gamgee's father in *The Lord of the Rings*.

Corrected Names of Chief Valar. List, arranged according to familial group-ings, of secondary names of the Valar, in Qenya (*Languages, Invented) written near the end of *The Coming of the Valar and the Building of Valinor* in ***The Book of Lost Tales*, probably in the first half of 1919. It is described by *Christopher Tolkien in ***The Book of Lost Tales, Part One* (1983), p. 93, and information from it is included in that volume in the appendix 'Names in the *Lost Tales*'. See also *Parma Eldalamberon* 14 (2003), p. 11–15, for a description of the list and a consideration of its contents in association with *'Names of the Valar'.

Craigie, William Alexander (1867–1957). W.A. Craigie was educated at the University of St Andrews and at Balliol and Oriel colleges, *Oxford, and also went to Copenhagen to enlarge his knowledge of Scandinavian languages. On his return from studies he took up an appointment at St Andrews as Assistant and Lecturer in Humanity, a post he held from 1893 to 1897. In the latter year he joined the staff of the *Oxford English Dictionary*; there he assisted *Henry Bradley with the letter G, and James A.H. Murray with I–K, before becoming the third editor of the *Dictionary* in 1901. From 1905 to 1916 he was Lecturer in the Scandinavian Languages at the Taylor Institution, *Oxford, during which time Tolkien as an undergraduate attended his lectures and was tutored by him in Old Icelandic (Old Norse) as a Special Subject. *C.L. Wrenn recalled that

> to have made one's first steps in the study of an Anglo-Saxon or an Old Norse text under Craigie, was to acquire almost imperceptibly the ambi-tion to become a keen and exact puzzle-solver. In his small seminars . . . many were stimulated to lifelong interests. He would make each stu-dent produce a careful short paper on a given problem or text, and then, after only the kindliest criticism, give his own view in precise and clear language enlivened by an occasional very Scots reminiscence; and his summary presentation and solution of the question at issue invariably seemed right and final. [*Times* (London), 9 September 1957, p. 10]

Tolkien carried Craigie's example with him to the English school at *Leeds, where he too promoted the study of Old Norse.

In 1916 Craigie became the Rawlinson and Bosworth Professor of Anglo-Saxon. Tolkien succeeded him in that chair in 1925, after Craigie resigned to take a post as professor of English at the University of Chicago and to edit the *Dictionary of American English on Historical Principles* (published 1936–44) – at the same time, continuing his work on the *Oxford English Dictionary* until its first supplement was completed in 1933. Craigie also produced *Icelandic Sagas* (1913), *A Dictionary of the Older Scottish Tongue* (1931 to date, ed. Craigie through the letter *I*), and the *Sýnisbók Islenzkra Rímna* (*Specimens of the Ice-landic Metrical Romances*, 1952), among many other works of substance and value. He was knighted in 1928.

Tolkien felt indebted to Craigie, both for his tutelage and for having in late

1918 arranged a post for Tolkien, then a young scholar just returned from the war, on the staff of the *Oxford English Dictionary*. See further, J.M. Wyllie, 'Sir William Craigie, 1867–1957', *Proceedings of the British Academy* 48 (1962).

The Creatures of the Earth. Table of names of beings, published with commentary and notes within 'Early Qenya Fragments' in *Parma Eldalamberon* 14 (2003), pp. 5–10, ed. Patrick Wynne and Christopher Gilson. A 'later elaboration and refinement of material appearing on the *"Early Chart of Names"', it was made subsequent to the ink version of the *Gnomish Lexicon* in 1917 and may be contemporary with work on *The Book of Lost Tales* after Tolkien moved to *Oxford at the end of 1918. The original list, in pencil, was of Qenya forms (*Languages, Invented) glossed in English, with some Gnomish (Goldogrin) forms added in blue crayon. It lists subdivisions of the Eldar or Elves, Úvanimor or monsters (demons, goblins, balrogs, ogres, trolls), Earthlings (wood-giants, mountain-giants, dwarves, pygmies), Fays, Children of the Gods, and Children of Men, and concludes with a 'hierarchical reordering of the seven categories of beings' (p. 7). A related sheet lists 'various types of fays and folk of the Valar arranged according to the elemental categories of Air, Earth, Water, and Fire' (p. 7).

Criticism. The critical response to Tolkien's works has been divided for the most part – more extensive studies such as T.A. Shippey's *The Road to Middle-earth* (1982; 2nd edn. 1992) excepted – between criticism of his scholarly writings and consideration of his fiction. The former is much the smaller category, but includes the earliest notices of Tolkien's achievements. Judith A. Johnson in *J.R.R. Tolkien: Six Decades of Criticism* (1986) dates these from 1922, when Margaret L. Lee praised *A Middle English Vocabulary* in *The Year's Work in English Studies*. The edition of *Sir Gawain and the Green Knight* by Tolkien and *E.V. Gordon, and Tolkien's British Academy Lecture *Beowulf: The Monsters and the Critics*, in particular were widely reviewed on first publication. Over the years their acceptance by scholars has waxed and waned, according to movements in Old and Middle English studies and changing trends in critical approaches. The *Beowulf* lecture, for instance, was not seriously opposed in scholarly journals until the 1950s; while in 1991 R.D. Fulk felt it necessary, in his preface to the anthology *Interpretations of Beowulf* (1991), to defend *Beowulf: The Monsters and the Critics* from the view that it had become no more than a milestone on the road of *Beowulf* studies which could be left behind in favour of newer scholarship.

Criticism of Tolkien's fiction began in 1937 with the publication of *The Hobbit*. Most reviewers welcomed that book to the ranks of children's literature, though some found it difficult to classify, either in terms of its literary pedigree or according to the age of its appropriate readers. (See Åke Bertenstam, 'Some Notes on the Reception of *The Hobbit*', *Angerthas* 23 (16 August 1988).) *Farmer Giles of Ham* (1949), in contrast, went largely unremarked, a circumstance Tolkien regretted. In 1954 and 1955 *The Lord of the Rings* was widely noticed, but put reviewers on their mettle: what were they to make of something so new and different, but compared by advance readers to Spenser, Mallory, and Ariosto, or called, uniquely, 'super science fiction'? Some suspected *allegory, which Tolkien denied in his Foreword to the second edition of *The Lord of the Rings* (1965). Praise for originality was set against objections about style and characterization. Among the puzzlement was much positive comment; and yet, in his review of the final volume of *The Lord of the Rings* *W.H. Auden observed: 'I rarely remember a book about which I have had such violent arguments. Nobody seems to have a moderate opinion: either, like myself, people find it a masterpiece of its genre or they cannot abide it . . .' ('At the End of the Quest, Victory', *New York Times Book Review*, 22 January 1956, p. 5).

Notorious among critics in the latter category were Edmund Wilson, who in 'Oo, Those Awful Orcs!', *The Nation*, 14 April 1956, took *The Lord of the Rings* to task for everything from clumsy dialogue to a lack of imagination; and Philip Toynbee, who in 'Dissension among the Judges', *The Observer* (London), 6 August 1961, badly misread the signs and proclaimed that 'the Hobbit fantasies of Professor Tolkien . . . dull, ill-written, whimsical and childish . . . have passed into a merciful oblivion'. (Catharine R. Stimpson, in her derogatory *J.R.R. Tolkien* (1969), similarly felt (p. 45) that 'Frodo lives, on borrowed time'.) In 1962 Edmund Fuller commented that the critical acclaim with which *The Lord of the Rings* was received was so great as to carry in it 'an inevitable counterreaction – a natural hazard of any work unique in its time that kindles a joy by its very freshness' ('The Lord of the Hobbits: J.R.R. Tolkien', rev. reprint in *Tolkien and the Critics*, ed. Neil D. Isaacs and Rose A. Zimbardo (1968), p. 36). Tolkien himself, who read reviews of his works as they came to him, wrote in the Foreword to the second edition of *The Lord of the Rings*:

> The prime motive was the desire of a tale-teller to try his hand at a really long story that would hold the attention of readers, amuse them, delight them, and at times maybe excite them or deeply move them. As a guide I had only my own feelings for what is appealing or moving, and for many the guide was inevitably often at fault. Some who have read the book, or at any rate have reviewed it, have found it boring, absurd, or contemptible; and I have no cause to complain, since I have similar opinions of their works, or of the kinds of writing that they evidently prefer.

In 1968 Neil D. Isaacs wrote in 'On the Possibilities of Writing Tolkien Criticism', *Tolkien and the Critics: Essays on J.R.R. Tolkien's The Lord of the Rings* (1968): 'This is surely a bad time for Tolkien criticism.' Due to the *Ace Books controversy an inexpensive paperback edition of *The Lord of the Rings* had been published in the United States, sold widely, and attracted a 'cult' following (see *Fandom). Numerous stories about Tolkien in popular magazines, 'to say nothing of the feverish activity of the [Tolkien] fanzines,' Isaacs felt, did 'not produce a climate for serious criticism. Nor does the fact that *The Lord of the Rings* and the domain of Middle-earth are eminently suitable for faddism and fannism, cultism and clubbism encourage scholarly activity' (p. 1). Thirteen years later, in 'On the Need for Writing Tolkien Criticism', *Tolkien: New Critical Perspectives* (1981), Isaacs continued to complain that 'the distinctions between the stuff of a cult and the objects of critical literary investigation should be brought sharply into focus' (p. 1). And further, 'it seems . . . important to try to distinguish those efforts produced by and for Tolkien *fans* from those which have value for serious students (or readers) of literature' (p. 2). In 2004, in a third comment, 'On the Pleasures of (Reading and Writing) Tolkien Criticism' in *Understanding The Lord of the Rings: The Best of Tolkien Criticism*, Isaacs confessed to having shown 'ill temper' in his *New Perspectives* essay. He felt that the publication of *The Silmarillion*, some four years earlier, 'had altered both the public perception of, and the critical climate for, Tolkien's work', and that 'critics with negative attitudes toward *The Lord of the Rings* used *The Silmarillion* to bolster their positions, disregarding the wholly different natures of the two works and illogically applying their distaste for the latter to the former' (p. 5).

Many readers, however, even those sympathetic to Tolkien, took particular note of the differences between *The Silmarillion* and *The Lord of the Rings*, and criticized the former because it was not more like the latter. Not a few readers, then and now, found *The Silmarillion* difficult, dense with history and nomenclature over great spans of years, set on a higher plane. Neil D. Isaacs himself complained in a review that it was 'persistently Biblical' (quoted in 'On the Pleasures of (Reading and Writing) Tolkien Criticism', p. 6). Eric Korn in the *Times Literary Supplement* ('Doing Things by Elves', 30 September 1977, p. 1097), to cite another instance, felt that Tolkien had 'crossed the boundary between mythology and scripture, and lost its head entirely. . . . [There are] too many exotic names for pleasure: not the Horns of Elfland faintly blowing but a garrulous station announcer for Finnish State Railways.' The lack of hobbits, which in *The Lord of the Rings* 'mediate' between the common reader and Tolkien's fantasy world, was especially noticed. Jessica Yates, writing in *British Book News* for January 1978, perceptively observed that 'lovers of the *Rings* . . . will miss the humour, suspense and variety of the earlier book, but they will still appreciate the romance and beauty of the descriptions and names. . . . *The Silmarillion* will create admirers and enemies, neither of whom will listen to the other.' (On these and other points, see further, *Christopher Tolkien, Foreword to *The Book of Lost Tales, Part One*, pp. 1–5.)

If *The Silmarillion* was found to be difficult, *Unfinished Tales* (1980) and *The History of Middle-earth*, which document in extensive detail the development of the *legendarium*, were thought by mainstream critics suitable only for 'Tolkien addicts', and after the two volumes of *The Book of Lost Tales* were rarely reviewed. In this the critics were on relatively safe ground, since *The History of Middle-earth*, at least, was intended for an audience whose interest in Tolkien was already keen and who was eager to study his works and the process of his imagination in depth. Some reviewers have complained that Tolkien's posthumous works, even the more popular *'Father Christmas' letters, *Mr. Bliss, and *Roverandom, are products of a 'Tolkien industry', published to capitalize on the popularity of *The Hobbit* and *The Lord of the Rings*.

Bruce Beatie in 'The Tolkien Phenomenon: 1954–1968', *Journal of Popular Culture* 3, no. 3 (Spring 1970), described three stages of Tolkien criticism from 1954 to 1968, that is from the first publication of *The Lord of the Rings*: 1954–1956, characterized by reviews and questions of the genre to which *The Lord of the Rings* belongs; 1957–1964, in which scholars reacted to the work; and 1965–1968, at the time of the *Ace Books controversy, in which there was general reader and 'cult' reaction accompanying increased sales. But none of these stages is mutually exclusive in scope, and they depend upon artificial distinctions between reviews and scholarship, and between scholars and general readers. Judith A. Johnson in *J.R.R. Tolkien: Six Decades of Criticism* (1986) presented her more expansive study in four parts: 'The First Three Decades: 1922–1953; Before and After *The Hobbit*'; 'The Fourth Decade: 1954–1963: *The Lord of the Rings*, Phase One'; 'The Fifth Decade: 1964–1973; All Is Controversy'; and 'The Sixth Decade, 1974–1984; The Work Goes Ever On'. These are natural divisions, marked by the first publication of *The Lord of the Rings* in 1954–5, the first publication of *Tree and Leaf* in 1964 and the second edition of *The Lord of the Rings* in 1965, and Tolkien's death in 1973.

As a children's book *The Hobbit* received little scholarly notice until long after its first publication, when it began to be viewed in relation to its sequel. *The Lord of the Rings* was the first of Tolkien's works of fiction to be seriously regarded by scholars, beginning c. 1956 with authors such as Douglass Parker ('Hwaet We Holbytla . . .', *Hudson Review* 9 (Winter 1956)), and has remained their central focus in Tolkien studies. The earliest Master's thesis devoted to Tolkien, however, *The Imaginative Fiction of J.R.R. Tolkien* by Caroline Whitman Everett at Florida State University (1957), looked at a larger picture, even to the point of discussing Tolkien's statements about fantasy expressed in *On Fairy-Stories*. In the following year Clinton W. Trowbridge completed apparently the first doctoral dissertation to discuss Tolkien at length, *The Twentieth Century British Supernatural Novel* (University of Florida), in which Tolkien is treated together with authors such as *C.S. Lewis and *Charles Williams. Other theses and dissertations followed, and occasional scholarly articles, some of which were influential and have remained of value, such as Patricia Meyer Spacks, 'Ethical Pattern in *The Lord of the Rings*' in *Critique* 3 (Spring–Fall 1959), reprinted as 'Power and Meaning in *The Lord of the Rings*' in *Tolkien and the Critics* (1968), and 'The Quest Hero' by W.H. Auden in *Texas Quarterly* 4, no. 4 (Winter 1961), also reprinted in *Tolkien and the Critics*. Also important in the early years of Tolkien studies was *Mankato Studies in English* 2 (February 1967), a collection of papers for the most part read at the Tolkien Symposium in Mankato, Minnesota in 1966.

Unlike articles and papers, book-length studies of Tolkien were slow to develop. Among the earliest of these were *Tolkien: Cult or Culture?* (1969) by

J.S. Ryan, *J.R.R. Tolkien* by Robley Evans (1971), and *Master of Middle-earth: The Fiction of J.R.R. Tolkien* (1972) by Paul H. Kocher. In this period Tolkien was also often studied in conjunction with his fellow *Inklings, as in *Shadows of Imagination: The Fantasies of C.S. Lewis, J.R.R. Tolkien, and Charles Williams* (1969), ed. Mark R. Hillegas, and *Romantic Religion: A Study of *Barfield, Lewis, Williams, and Tolkien* (1971) by R.J. Reilly. Some of these early works, Kocher's *Master of Middle-earth* in particular, still offer valuable insights for a study of Tolkien, though they were written before the publication of *The Silmarillion* and important resources such as Carpenter's *Biography* (1977) and Tolkien's selected letters (1981).

It is important to note, in a history of Tolkien criticism, that such works as those by Spacks and Auden, published in respected journals, until recent years have been far fewer in number than articles of substance in fan-produced publications such as *The Tolkien Journal, Orcrist, Mallorn,* and *Mythlore*; and of all of these works of criticism, the majority have been published in the United States. Tolkien's popularity has been as great, or greater, in Britain as in America, but the universities of his ancestral land long omitted popular contemporary authors as subjects of serious study. A thesis wholly concerned with Tolkien was not accepted at a university in Britain until 1988: *A Study of the Fictional Works of J.R.R. Tolkien* by Deirdre M. Greene, M.Litt., Oxford. Although this practice is not unknown in the United States, American academics have tended to be (for better or worse) more open to the acceptance of popular culture as an element of scholarly research and of curriculum. Papers concerning Tolkien have become a common feature of academic conferences, such as those sponsored by the International Association for the Fantastic in the Arts and by the International Congress on Medieval Studies. Works presented at the latter event are now regularly collected in volumes ed. by Jane Chance.

In 1971 J.R. Watson, in 'The Hobbits and the Critics', *Critical Quarterly* 13, no. 3 (Autumn 1971), noted that while sales of *The Lord of the Rings* went 'on and on' 'from the shores of the Pacific to the grey waters of the North Sea',

> the academics find themselves on the wrong foot, thrown off balance by the fact that (unlike Tolkien's earlier work) this is a large scale undertaking by one of their own colleagues of great distinction, which has been commended by other colleagues of great distinction . . . ; yet finding, as they examine it, that the work is a fairy-story and surprisingly resistant to modern critical techniques. Above all, there is the question of its awful popularity, the great fear (after *Ulysses* [by James Joyce] and *The Waste Land* [by T.S. Eliot]) that nothing so widely liked can really be *good*. . . .
> [p. 252]

Later T.A. Shippey summarized in *J.R.R. Tolkien: Author of the Century* (2000) that the 'deep and seemingly compulsive antipathy' of *literati*, professional intellectuals, towards Tolkien's works is a reflex of the ongoing language/literature war which has preoccupied university departments of English for a century: this is perhaps too narrow an explanation. Patrick Curry argues in his *Defending Middle-earth* [1997] that it stems from a kind of generation war, as a group devoted to 'modernism', and to thinking themselves up-to-date, find themselves pushed aside by 'postmodernism' . . . but Curry's definition of 'postmodernism' is a personal and tactical one. . . . Joseph Pearce's 1997 book *Tolkien: Man and Myth* implies that the antipathy is a reaction if not to Tolkien's Catholicism specifically, then to his 'religious sensibility': again not impossible, but not often overtly mentioned. . . . [pp. 308–9]

In his earlier book, *The Road to Middle-earth*, Shippey commented that next to the 'sheer success' of *The Lord of the Rings* 'the thing that irritated reviewers most was their author's obstinate insistence on talking about language as if it might be a subject of interest' (2nd edn. 1992, p. 22). And further: 'If one reads very much at all of what has been written on Tolkien, one cannot help concluding that there is an enormous 'culture-gap' between him and his critics, which they cannot bridge and usually have not noticed' (p. 291). But 'the real horror for Tolkien would probably have come when he realised that there were people writing about him who could not tell Old English from Old Norse, and genuinely thought the difference didn't matter' (p. 292). See also Patrick Curry, 'Tolkien and His Critics: A Critique', in *Root and Branch: Approaches towards Understanding Tolkien* (1999).

In 'J.R.R. Tolkien: The "Monstrous" in the Mirror', *Journal of the Fantastic in the Arts* 9, no. 3 (1998), as elsewhere, Daniel Timmons argues a contrary point of view, that there has been 'relatively little criticism which disparages' Tolkien. He seeks to distinguish between critical antipathy – expressions of distaste for Tolkienian fantasy, heroic literature, and other aspects of his works such as the sense of religious joy – and negative criticism, and to emphasize those responses to Tolkien's works which have been thoughtful and positive. See further, Timmons, *Mirror on Middle-earth: J.R.R. Tolkien and the Critical Perspectives*, Diss., University of Toronto, 1998; and his comments in the introduction to *J.R.R. Tolkien and His Literary Resonances: Views of Middle-earth*, ed. George Clark and Daniel Timmons (2000). Even so, there can be no denying that fiercely negative responses to Tolkien exist, that they have been put forward by critics of note, indeed that they persist despite a more widespread acceptance of Tolkien's writings, particularly *The Lord of the Rings*, as serious literature: see also the section 'Popularity' in our entry for *The Lord of the Rings*.

In considering Tolkien criticism John Ellison has made a useful distinction between 'Tolkien studies' and 'Middle-earth studies'. The former is 'the student's proper concern', while the latter is derivative, concerned to operate within Tolkien's invented world, as when a writer speculates about the population of the Shire or the industry of Gondor ('Editorial', *Mallorn* 31 (December 1994), p. 5). Richard C. West, in 'The Status of Tolkien Scholarship', *Tolkien*

Journal [4, no. 4], whole no. 15 (Summer 1972), similarly commented that 'one possible response' to Tolkien's fiction 'is to pretend that the subcreated world is the primary one, and examine its geography, geology, systems of coinage, and so on. [But] this is not criticism ... for it does nothing to enrich our appreciation of the text; nor is it scholarship, since it does not provide relevant background information.' West also observed, at that point in the history of Tolkien scholarship, that 'most of the attempts ... to criticize Tolkien's art take a rather limited number of approaches. Myth criticism seems to be far the most popular. It is used to examine sources and narrative patterns for [*The Lord of the Rings*], as well as to explain Tolkien's widespread vogue by reference to his offering a mythic wholeness and resonance that deeply satisfies our fragmented and symbol-starved society.' The critics, he felt, tended to concentrate too exclusively on northern European sources for Tolkien's writing. 'Another common approach is to place [*The Lord of the Rings*] in what I like to call the "twentieth-century medieval renaissance" and consider its adaptation of much medieval material for a modern audience.' But 'we must not forget' that *The Lord of the Rings* 'is, in the final analysis, a contemporary book'. He argued that 'the criticism of Tolkien's fiction has been largely favorable, even adulatory. Where it is seriously adverse, it has usually been due, in my opinion, to bewilderment at the teeming variety of Middle-earth. Some critics will focus on one strand of the story ... not just to discuss one important aspect at length, but because they take everything else for mere trimming' (p. 21).

In 1972 it was easily possible to know intimately most, even all, of Tolkien's works that had appeared to that point, as well as most of the relevant critical literature. But with his death in 1973 circumstances changed, as a succession of his unfinished works, drafts, and miscellaneous writings soon began to appear – *The Silmarillion, Unfinished Tales, The History of Middle-earth*, and scholarly essays among them, more than were published in the author's lifetime – all of which need to be considered for a thorough understanding of Tolkien's achievement. At the same time, scholars began to approach Tolkien's writings from a greater number of orientations, including folklore studies, philology, and Jungian psychology. The study of Tolkien's invented languages has made particularly notable progress, aided by the measured publication of the author's own papers on this subject in the journals *Parma Eldalamberon* and *Vinyar Tengwar*.

Judith A. Johnson has calculated that in the decade following Tolkien's death 'over 650 items of critical response were published, well over twice the number (258) found for the fourth decade, 1954–1963' (*J.R.R. Tolkien: Six Decades of Criticism*, p. 135). And a far greater number than that have appeared to the present day. So substantial has this growth become that bibliographers have been unable to document new Tolkien criticism on a timely basis (see *Bibliographies). A large number of books concerned with Tolkien, or using Tolkien as an excuse to discuss religion, philosophy, or some other subject in a wider context, were published during and immediately after the release of the *Lord of the Rings* films in 2000–2003; but of these, few are of lasting value.

At least in the United States, the films seem to have spurred scholars to examine Tolkien's writings who have not previously taken an interest. The present authors find with regret, however, that too many recent critics appear not to have a genuine feeling for their subject, that they tend to overlook or ignore much of the wealth of resources contained in posthumous works such as *The History of Middle-earth*, that they have little familiarity also with the existing literature of Tolkien studies and thus revisit certain topics without adding comments of worth, and that the jargon of current scholarly discourse sometimes makes their writings impenetrable, or at least uninviting.

In addition to fan magazines and journals of long standing, and newer journals such as *Tolkien Studies*, outlets for Tolkien criticism abound on the Internet. Some articles indeed have appeared only in electronic form. Discussions of Tolkien's life and works are held continuously on numerous Web sites. The value of such materials varies considerably, though perhaps no more so than among printed writings about Tolkien. The nature of the Internet, fast and 'free', unfortunately encourages comments made in haste and uncritically, and too many writers online tend to prefer online resources to those in print, though the latter include most of the best writings to date. Michael D.C. Drout and Hilary Wynne, in 'Tom Shippey's *J.R.R. Tolkien: Author of the Century* and a Look Back at Tolkien Criticism since 1982', *Envoi: A Review Journal of Medieval Literature* 9, no. 1 (Fall 2000), complain that 'the sheer glut of materials on Tolkien now in the MLA [Modern Language Association] database makes searching for Tolkien bibliography an exceptionally difficult task: since everything ever published [within the MLA parameters of selection] is in the database, good articles are missed due to the bad signal-to-noise ratio' (p. 104). The same is true of Tolkien resources on the Internet, as they may be retrieved through search engines.

It is an advantage of the Internet, and of computer applications such as desktop publishing and print-on-demand, that easier publication is permitted of what Colin Duriez has called 'people's commentary' ('Survey of Tolkien Literature', *Seven* 20 (2003), p. 107), writings not subject to review in the often contentious world of academic publication; for it has long been true that useful Tolkien scholarship has been produced by writers who belong to no college or university faculty, or whose academic credentials lie in the Sciences rather than the Humanities. Though Drout and Wynne are correct when they write (p. 104) that some fan-produced 'newsletters and pamphlets . . . contain much that is trivial or silly admixed with the occasional important essay or note', others, most notably *Beyond Bree*, contain more than occasional material of value to Tolkien research.

See also Jane Chance and David D. Day, 'Medievalism in Tolkien: Two Decades of Criticism in Review', *Studies in Medievalism* 3, no. 3 (Winter 1991); Wayne G. Hammond, 'The Critical Response to Tolkien's Fiction', *Proceedings of the J.R.R. Tolkien Centenary Conference 1992* (1995); and Joseph Pearce, *Tolkien: Man and Myth* (1998), Chapter 8, 'The Well and the Shallows: Tolkien and the Critics'.

Cromer (Norfolk). A seaside resort town, north of Norwich, fashionable in Edwardian times and known for its medieval church. Tolkien visited Cromer in 1914, an occasion which inspired an unpublished poem, *The Lonely Hare-bell.*

Cuivienyarna. 'The legend of the Awaking of the Quendi', published with commentary in **The War of the Jewels* (1994), pp. 420–4. According to a note by Tolkien, it was 'actually written (in style and simple notions) to be a surviving Elvish "fairytale" or child's tale, mingled with counting-lore' (*The War of the Jewels*, p. 421). The three Elf-fathers who woke first of all the Elves in Cuiviénen in the east of Middle-earth 'are named in the ancient tales *Imin, Tata,* and *Enel* . . . and from them, say the Eldar, the words for one, two, and three were made: the oldest of all numerals' (p. 421). Imin, Tata, and Enel then woke their wives who lay beside them, and after some time had passed discovered other groups of Elves who were just waking. Imin claimed the first group of twelve to be his companions, and the next two groups (eighteen and twenty-four) were claimed by Tata and Enel respectively. But Imin noted that each group they found was larger than the one before, so that he had fewer companions than the others. He therefore did not claim the next two groups they come upon (thirty-six and forty-eight), hoping that the sixth group would be the greatest of all; but no more Elves were found. Thus Imin and his followers remained the smallest group by far (fourteen), from whom came the Vanyar. From Tata and his followers came the Noldor, and from Enel and his followers the Teleri, the most numerous of the Elven-kindreds.

Although brief and simple, the *Cuivienyarna* nonetheless contains powerful and mythopoeic images, such as the Elf-fathers' first sights upon waking:

> The first thing that they saw was the stars, for they woke in the early twilight before dawn. And the next thing they saw was their destined spouses lying asleep in the green sward beside them. Then they were so enamoured of their beauty that their desire for speech was immediately quickened and they began to 'think of words' to speak and sing in. And being impatient they could not wait but woke up their spouses. Thus, the Eldar say, the first thing that each elf-woman saw was her spouse, and her love for him was her first love; and her love and reverence for the wonders of Arda came later. [p. 421]

The text exists only as a single typescript and carbon copy, made *c.* late 1959 or early 1960. The legend is mentioned also in **Quendi and Eldar*, with further information about the relative sizes of the various kindreds in later history (see *The War of the Jewels*, pp. 380–1).

Cullis, Colin (1892–1919). A close friend of Tolkien during their under-graduate years at Exeter College, *Oxford, Colin Cullis was a fellow member of student organizations such as the Apolausticks, the Stapeldon Society, and the Exeter College Essay Club (*Societies and clubs). As President and Secretary of the Stapledon Society respectively for Hilary Term 1914, Tolkien and Cullis suggested amendments to the Society's rules. They were also instrumental in the formation of the Chequers Clubbe (*Societies and clubs). In October 1914 they took rooms together at 59 St John Street, Oxford. Declared unfit for military service, nonetheless Cullis died young, in the influenza pandemic of 1918–19.

Cullis appears in a photograph of the Apolausticks, May 1912, reproduced in *Biography*, pl. 6b.

Dagnall, Margery Kathleen Mary, known as Susan (1910–1952). Susan Dagnall read English at *Oxford as a member of the Society of Oxford Home-Students, contemporary with *M.E. Griffiths and probably a resident of the same hostel for Roman Catholics at Cherwell Edge (*Oxford and environs). In 1933, after receiving her B.A., she joined George Allen & Unwin (*Publishers) as a volunteer worker. *Stanley Unwin, then head of the firm, 'was never keen on employing graduates: he much preferred to recruit school leavers, claiming that their application was greater and their expectations less. But Miss Dagnall ... evidently worked her passage and was appointed to the permanent staff – and presumably paid – six months later. Her job was ill-defined, but vaguely editorial' (Rayner Unwin, *George Allen & Unwin: A Remembrancer* (1999), p. 74).

By 1936 Dagnall seems to have been managing the Allen & Unwin advertising department, but also still occupied with editorial concerns. At some time that year she visited Oxford, probably to discuss the revision of the Clark Hall translation of *Beowulf* with M.E. Griffiths, whom Tolkien had recommended for the job. In some manner, Dagnall learned that Tolkien had written a children's story, *The Hobbit*, and borrowed it to read. Impressed with the work, she convinced Tolkien that it deserved to be published, and helped to see it through the press. She also was in touch with Tolkien about the Clark Hall project, and received and read other works by him on behalf of Allen & Unwin, including *Mr. Bliss, *The Lost Road, and early draft chapters of *The Lord of the Rings.

Dagnall continued to work for George Allen & Unwin for several years, then devoted herself to marriage and children as Mrs Richard Grindle. She died in an automobile accident at Weybridge, England.

Dangweth Pengoloð. Text, subtitled 'the answer of Pengoloð to Ælfwine who asked him how came it that the tongues of the Elves changed and were sundered', published with commentary and notes in *The Peoples of Middle-earth* (1996), pp. 395–402. Ælfwine wonders why there are many elven tongues 'akin indeed and yet unlike', since Elves do not die and 'their memories reach back into ages long past' (*The Peoples of Middle-earth*, p. 396). Pengoloð replies at length, noting that all things change in Eä (here meaning the universe), and that though the Elves may be immortal within Eä 'they are no more changeless than the great trees, neither in the forms that they inhabit, nor in the things that they desire or achieve by means of those forms. Wherefore should they not then change in speech, of which one part is made with tongues and received by ears?' (p. 397). Also the Elves 'being skilled and eager in art will readily make things new, both for delight to look on, or to hear, or to feel, or for daily use: be it in vessels or raiment or in speech' (p. 398). And the kindreds of the Elves had been widely sundered over long ages, during which their speech had also grown apart 'swifter or slower, yet ever inescapably'. The Elves now dwelling in Eressëa have the greater part of their being in memory 'so that now we preserve rather than make anew . . . here at last in Eressëa our tongues are steadfast . . .' (p. 401).

*Christopher Tolkien states that this work cannot have been written before 1951 and probably no later than the end of 1959; he is inclined to place it earlier rather than later in the decade. Tolkien followed his original clear handwritten text with a second version in which he made a few changes: an illuminated manuscript written in a decorative hand. The first page of the manuscript is reproduced in colour as the frontispiece to the HarperCollins hardback edition of *The Peoples of Middle-earth* (later in black and white in the HarperCollins paperback, but omitted in Houghton Mifflin editions), and as fig. 198 in *Artist and Illustrator*.

Darbishire, Helen (1881–1961). Except for brief periods Helen Darbishire spent most of her life in *Oxford and in association with Somerville College, first as an undergraduate, then – after a few years as a Lecturer at Royal Holloway College, London – as tutor in English from 1908, Fellow from 1922, and Principal from 1931 to 1945. From 1927 to 1931 she was also a University Lecturer in English at Oxford. Administrative duties frequently put her in contact with Tolkien, on the English Faculty Board (of which she was the first woman chairman) and on the Library Committee. In 1945 she left Somerville to pursue research. Milton and Wordsworth (and his circle) were her special interests, the definitive editions of their poetical works the most notable results of her labours. A collection of her shorter writings, *Somerville College Chapel Addresses and Other Papers*, was published in 1962.

See further, Basil Willey, 'Helen Darbishire, 1881–1961', *Proceedings of the British Academy* 47 (1961).

D'Arcy, Martin Cyril (1888–1976). Father Martin D'Arcy entered the Jesuit Order in 1906, and in 1912, after preliminary training in the priesthood, went up to *Oxford to read Classical Literature and History. He was ordained in 1921. He taught for a time at Stonyhurst College, then went to the Gregorian University, Rome for further study. In 1927 he returned to Oxford as a Lecturer at Campion Hall on Aristotle and Moral Philosophy. He was appointed Master of Campion Hall in 1933. In 1945 he again left Oxford to become Provincial of the English Province of the Society of Jesus. His numerous writings include *The Nature of Belief* (1931) and *The Mind and the Heart of Love* (1945).

During his years at Oxford, and before the older kind of English Roman Catholicism he represented began to go out of favour after the Second World War, Father D'Arcy was a prominent figure, brilliant and cultured, a vigorous defender of his faith and church. He was associated with many Catholic writers and artists: it was he, for instance, who directed the poet *Roy Campbell to seek out the *Inklings. Like Tolkien, Father D'Arcy was a member of the Oxford Dante Society (*Societies and clubs).

D'Ardenne, Simonne Rosalie Thérèse Odile (1899–1986). The Belgian scholar S.R.T.O. (sometimes seen as S.T.R.O.) d'Ardenne was admitted to the B.Litt. program in the Oxford English School in February 1932. Tolkien was appointed her supervisor and approved her thesis subject, an edition of the Middle English *Liflade ant te Passiun of Seinte Iuliene* (*The Life and Passion of St Juliene*, see *Katherine Group). At first, as a member of the Society of Oxford Home-Students, d'Ardenne stayed at Cherwell Edge (*Oxford and environs), but around October 1932 she joined the Tolkien household at 20 Northmoor Road for about a year as 'a sort of unofficial aunt' (*The Tolkien Family Album*, p. 68). The English Faculty Board having allowed her to count two vacation terms towards her residency requirement, she rapidly qualified for her B.Litt., which she received in 1933. On returning to *Belgium she earned, based on her work on *Seinte Iuliene*, a doctoral degree at the University of Liège. She became Professor of Comparative Grammar at Liège in 1938, and Emerita Professor in 1970.

Seinte Iuliene as published (1936; with corrigenda, 1961) bears d'Ardenne's name alone as editor, because it was her thesis. But for that it would have appeared as her joint work with Tolkien, as she referred to it in correspondence. *E.V. Gordon, aware of the collaboration, praised Tolkien for having contributed greatly to its success. *Norman Davis, writing in the Merton College magazine *Postmaster* (January 1976, p. 11), likewise noted that the edition of *Seinte Iuliene* owes a great deal to Tolkien, indeed it 'presents more of Tolkien's views on early Middle English than anything he himself published'. And *G.V. Smithers wrote in the margin of his copy of the book, concerning a point on p. 154: 'if this isn't Tolkienian, nothing is!' (private collection). (There the text reads:

> The special use of *grá-r* in Norse is regarded as due to the frequent application of *grár* to the wolf. But when so applied the adjective refers solely to colour, not temper, and provides actually no link between *grár* grey and *grályndr*. It would seem that the notions of 'grim' and 'grey' were associated in Germanic from an early period, and one may suspect the influence of some accident of homophony: alliteration probably played a greater part than wolves.

Tolkien and d'Ardenne began to prepare as well an edition of *Seinte Katerine*, another medieval manuscript in the same group as *Seinte Iuliene*, which they offered in 1936 to submit to the Early English Text Society (*Societies and clubs) for publication. They completed most of the preliminary work on the book by spring 1939. D'Ardenne meanwhile also wrote scholarly articles and reviews, some of which she sent to Tolkien for comment and improvement, and by November 1937 she produced a French translation of his *Farmer Giles of Ham* (published 1975). On the strength of the latter Tolkien recommended her to George Allen & Unwin (*Publishers) as a possible translator of *The Hobbit*.

During the Second World War the village in Belgium where d'Ardenne lived came under German control, and her correspondence with Tolkien was interrupted. At great risk to herself she assisted in the escape of Allied servicemen from occupied territory. In March 1945 she was able to contact Tolkien again and came to Oxford at the end of that year on a British Council grant, eager to resume work on *Seinte Katerine*. In subsequent years she saw Tolkien several times, in Oxford and in Belgium, and they wrote to each other often. Although d'Ardenne hoped for a continued collaboration, and even arranged that the Early English Text Society would publish editions of *Seinte Katerine* and *Sawles Warde* under both their names, together she and Tolkien completed only two articles as joint authors, *'Iþþlen' in Sawles Warde* in the journal *English Studies* (Amsterdam, December 1947) and *MS. Bodley 34: A Re-Collation of a Collation* in *Studia Neophilologica* (Uppsala, 1947–8). The last of these refers to an edition of the whole of MS Bodley 34 by Tolkien and d'Ardenne as still a possibility: 'This edition begun long ago was interrupted in 1938–45, when we were otherwise engaged. It is now, however, nearly completed on the basis of a careful review of the manuscript itself, and will, we hope, shortly be in print' (p. 72). In the event, no such edition ever appeared.

D'Ardenne completed an edition of *Seinte Katerine* (1981) at last in collaboration with *E.J. Dobson. The editors acknowledge in their preface that

> when S.R.T.O. d'A. first planned this edition, over forty years ago, she had hoped to have the collaboration of J.R.R. Tolkien, the academic supervisor of her work on *Seinte Iuliene*, but in the event (initially because of the war of 1939–45) he took no part in it; nevertheless she and her eventual co-editor wish to express their great sense of obligation to and their admiration of his teaching and inspiration. [p. vii]

By then she had already published (1977) a transcript of MS Bodley 34, following Tolkien's favoured principle of recording the text line-for-line, as it stands in the manuscript. She contributed an essay, 'A Neglected Manuscript of British History' (on MS Liège University Library 369 C, with a miniature of Woden), to the *Festschrift *English and Medieval Studies Presented to J.R.R. Tolkien on the Occasion of His Seventieth Birthday* (1962), and a reminiscence, 'The Man and the Scholar', to *J.R.R. Tolkien: Scholar and Storyteller: Essays in Memoriam* (1979). Among her other writings is 'The Editing of Middle English Texts' in *English Studies Today* (1951), an engaging imaginary conversation among the authors and scribes of Middle English texts, commenting on the errors and foolish practices of modern-day editors.

A photograph of Simonne d'Ardenne is reproduced in *The Tolkien Family Album*, p. 68.

'Of the Darkening of Valinor'. The eighth chapter of the *'Quenta Silmaril-lion', published in *The Silmarillion*, pp. 73–7.

SUMMARY

On hearing the news that the Teleri have seen Melkor turning north, Oromë and Tulkas pursue him, but fail to find any trace of him in the North; for before the pursuit began Melkor had secretly made his way south to the dark region of Avathar, east of the mountains of the Pelóri. In that region lives Ungoliant, a being in spider form, who devours light and from it spins darkness. With her Melkor plots revenge, and offers Ungoliant whatever she wants if she will do his bidding. She weaves a cloak of darkness about them, and using her webs they cross the Pelóri and descend onto the plains of Valinor. In this they are unobserved, for it is a time of festival to celebrate the gathering of fruits, and the Vanyar and the Noldor of Tirion are assembled with the Valar and the Maiar on Taniquetil. At this festival it is the custom of the Valar 'to clothe themselves as in a vesture in the forms of the Children of Ilúvatar' (*The Silmarillion*, p. 74). Manwë hopes at this feast to heal the divisions that have arisen among the Noldor but, although Fëanor and his half-brothers are formally reconciled, Finwë does not attend, and Fëanor does not wear the Silmarils to the feast.

Melkor and Ungoliant came to the Two Trees of Valinor at the time of the mingling of their lights. Morgoth wounds each Tree with his spear, and Ungoliant's bite poisons them, so that they wither and die. As she drinks the sap and stored light of the Trees, Ungoliant belches forth black vapour. Darkness falls on Valinor, a darkness 'more than loss of light. . . . made by malice out of Light, and it had power to pierce the eye, and to enter heart and mind, and strangle the very will' (p. 76). Looking down from Taniquetil, Varda sees the Shadow soaring upwards. All song ceases, and the only sound is the wailing of the Teleri. Manwë alone can see a greater Darkness which marks the passage north of Melkor and Ungoliant. Oromë and Tulkas lead the pursuit, but are blinded and dismayed.

HISTORY

The earliest version of the destruction of the Two Trees is included in the tale of *The Theft of Melko and the Darkening of Valinor* in *The Book of Lost Tales, Part One*. This exists only as a rough pencil manuscript, dating probably from early 1919. Tolkien never wrote a finished version of this tale. The order of events differs in this early version: there the theft of the Silmarils and of Fëanor's other jewels (not mentioned until the next chapter in *The Silmarillion*) precedes the destruction of the Two Trees. The feast, which is described in great detail, is held to celebrate the anniversary of coming of the Elves to Valinor. On the day of the feast, when all are assembled on Taniquetil, Melko with the assistance of spirits he has perverted attacks the dwellings of the Noldoli, slaying the guards left there, including the father of Fëanor (not yet the son of the leader of the Noldoli), and steals all the jewels, including the Silmarils. Melko and his assistants escape south on stolen horses. The Noldoli cry for vengeance, especially for those slain, but Manwë coldly points out that had they not placed such a value on their treasure as to need guards, and all had come to the Feast, none would have been slain.

Melko sends a messenger to the Valar, declaring himself ruler of the world and demanding compensation for the ills done to him. Manwë rejects these demands; and against Manwë's wishes Tulkas, helped by some of the Elves, slays the herald. The Noldoli are given permission to return to Kôr, but Fëanor and others choose to stay in their place of exile. Fëanor tries in vain to make more jewels like the Silmarils. He broods on his father's death and persuades many of the Noldoli to ask Manwë to let them return to Middle-earth. When Manwë tells them that Men will soon awaken there, and that he fears strife between Men and Elves, Fëanor declares that the Valar have robbed the Elves of their rightful heritage in favour of Men. Meanwhile in the south, Melko seeks the great spider, Ungoliont, and offers her all the jewels he has stolen, save only the Silmarils, in return for her help. While Valinor is still in uproar they steal across the plains. The Valar and the Elves notice the darkness, but think it some work of Ossë. Melko and Ungoliont arrive when Silpion is shining and Laurelin sleeping. Melko smites Laurelin with a sword (not a spear), which is consumed by the radiance of the Tree, and Ungoliont sucks the sap. Melko takes a knife to strike at Silpion, but a Noldo intervenes, attacking and wounding Ungoliont. Melko kills the Noldo with his knife and thrusts the Noldo's blade, stained with Ungoliont's blood, into Silpion, and its light dies from the poison. The pursuit begins, but Melko escapes to the north and Ungoliont returns to the south.

The story moved closer to its final form in the next narrative, the *Sketch of the Mythology* (c. 1926): Tulcas pursues Morgoth, who flees south and plots revenge with Ungoliant. They destroy the Two Trees: Morgoth stabs both with a poisoned sword, and Ungoliant drinks their sap with venomous lips. Morgoth's attack on Fëanor's treasuries and his murder of Finn now follow the destruction of the Trees. There is no mention of where Fëanor is at the time of the attack, but following it, he summons the Gnomes (Noldoli) to Tûn in breach of the exile imposed upon him. Morgoth and Ungoliant escape the pursuit. Only after the account of Morgoth's escape is it mentioned that he had chosen to attack on a day of festival when the Valar and most of the Elves, except the Teleri, were assembled on Taniquetil. This is also mentioned in the unfinished poem *The Flight of the Noldoli from Valinor*, which may predate the *Sketch*.

In the *Quenta Noldorinwa* (c. 1930) the attack on the Trees takes place at the mingling of their lights; after sucking the juice from the Trees Ungoliant belches forth black clouds; and Varda, looking down from Taniquetil, sees all hidden in a mist. The festival is still mentioned after the account of Morgoth's escape, and following this the wailing of the Teleri in the darkness enters the story. It is now stated that Fëanor and his sons are not present when Morgoth plunders the treasuries of the Gnomes, but he is not yet said to be attending the festival.

The 'earliest' *Annals of Valinor*, written in the early 1930s, added little to the story but give a time-span for events. As originally written, in Valian Year 2950 Fëanor is deposed from the leadership of the Noldoli, and the Valar fail to capture Morgoth, who flees to Arvalin. By emendation, after his part in sowing dissension among the Noldoli is discovered in 2900, Morgoth hides in the North, his whereabouts known only to Finwë and Fëanor, and it is not until 2950 (500 of our years later) that he flees south when the Valar try to capture him. Morgoth destroys the Trees in 2990–1, seizes the jewels of the Noldoli, and escapes to Middle-earth. A pencil emendation places the destruction of the Trees to 2998, but in the 'later' *Annals of Valinor* of the mid-1930s the date is 2990. These annals explain that the Valar try to apprehend Morgoth in 2950 because they hear tidings of him.

In the *Quenta Silmarillion*, also from the mid-1930s, in the latter part of Chapter 4, 'Of the Silmarils and the Darkening of Valinor', the festival and absence of everyone on the mountain of Manwë are now mentioned, before the destruction of the Trees, and Morgoth uses a black spear rather than a sword to stab them. Fëanor is now stated to have been present at the festival.

According to the *Annals of Aman* (see *Annals of Valinor*), written c. 1951, in which the years are reckoned from the creation of the Trees, Morgoth and Ungoliantë destroy the Trees in 1495. The festival which occupies the attention of Valar and Elves is now said to have been held to celebrate the gathering of fruits, and that at this festival it was the custom of the Valar to assume the forms of the Children. Manwë's intention to use the festival to try to heal dissension among the Noldor now enters, along with his disappointment that Finwë refuses to attend while Fëanor is banned from Tûna. Fëanor comes as he has been commanded, but does not wear the Silmarils or any festive attire, and he and Fingolfin are formally reconciled. Manwë sees the Darkness moving over the land as Melkor flees north.

Tolkien made only a few slight changes to this part of the *Quenta Silmarillion* during his revisions of c. 1951, but at the end of the 1950s he typed a greatly expanded version of this chapter, bringing it in many respects close to the *Annals of Aman*. New details include that the Valar believe that Melkor was hidden in the north because he was seen moving in that direction by the Elves, and the words spoken at the reconciliation of Fëanor and Fingolfin. But he also made some significant changes, not all of which were incorporated into the published *Silmarillion*. Melkor now has great difficulty in gaining Ungoliantë's aid, and has to persuade her with shining gems. When Ungoliantë looks out

over Valinor she sees 'the dome of Varda' and only she descends from the
mountains and attacks the Two Trees. At the same time, Morgoth makes his
own way north through the gap in the Pelóri, and in the Ring of Doom 'defiled
the judgement seat of Manwë and threw down the thrones of the Valar' (*Morgoth's Ring*, p. 288). *Christopher Tolkien thinks that the reason for this new
form of the story is that Melkor did not want Ungoliantë with him when he
seizes the Silmarils. The 'dome of Varda' is mentioned because of a change that
Tolkien had made in the cosmology of his *legendarium*, making the world
round and lit by the sun from the beginning. According to 'Myths Transformed III' (*Morgoth's Ring*, pp. 385–7) Aman had been covered by a dome lit
by stars which excluded the light of the defiled sun.

The chapter published in *The Silmarillion* was taken by Christopher Tolkien
from both the *Annals of Aman* (especially for Melkor's attack on the Trees)
and the latest version of the *Quenta Silmarillion* (especially the reconciliation
of Fëanor and Fingolfin, and Melkor persuading Ungoliantë to help him). In
places the *Quenta Silmarillion* was emended so that Melkor and Ungoliantë
travelled together from the south. Some paragraphs are in any case similar in
both works. Even where a paragraph was taken almost entirely from one, an
addition from, or change dependent on, the other was often incorporated.

Davis, Norman (1913–1989). After taking his degree at the University of Otago
in New Zealand, Norman Davis read English at Merton College, *Oxford as
a Rhodes Scholar. There a second B.A. (1936) was followed by a Diploma in
Comparative Philology. Tolkien proved a sympathetic and inspiring teacher,
and became a lifelong friend. In later years Davis and his wife took lunch every
week with Ronald and *Edith Tolkien at a country hotel.

For about a decade from 1937, except during the Second World War, Davis
lectured in English at several universities in England and on the continent.
Among the students he tutored at Oriel and Bracenose Colleges, Oxford, from
1947 was *Rayner Unwin. In 1948–9 he was Lecturer in Medieval English at
Oxford, and from 1949 to 1959 held the chair of English Language at the University of Glasgow. He returned to Oxford in 1959 as Tolkien's successor to the
Merton Professorship of English Language and Literature, and remained in
that post until his own retirement in 1980.

Among his more notable publications are a thorough revision of Sweet's
Anglo-Saxon Primer for its ninth edition (1953); editions of the Paston letters
and papers (1958, etc.); the glossary for *Early Middle English Verse and Prose*,
ed. *J.A.W. Bennett and *G.V. Smithers (1966; 2nd edn. 1968); a revision of
Sir Gawain and the Green Knight, ed. Tolkien and *E.V. Gordon (1967); and
Non-Cycle Plays and Fragments (1970). With *C.L. Wrenn he co-edited the
Festschrift *English and Medieval Studies Presented to J.R.R. Tolkien on the
Occasion of His Seventieth Birthday* (1962), to which he himself contributed the
essay 'Man and Monsters at Sutton Hoo'. He also served for many years as co-editor of the *Review of English Studies* and as Honorary Director of the Early
English Text Society. In the latter capacity he was concerned with the extrac-

tion from Tolkien of his edition of the *Ancrene Wisse* (**Ancrene Riwle*), whose publication had been long delayed.

Dawkins, Richard MacGillivray (1871–1955). After reading Classics at Cambridge, R.M. Dawkins entered the British School of Archaeology at Athens to pursue a career in Dialectology. From 1906 to 1914 he was Director of the School and in charge of notable excavations, while also collecting linguistic data in the Greek islands. C.M. Bowra recalled that 'Dawkins' first and strongest love was for language. . . . He liked to discover rare words and enjoyed all variations of dialect . . .' (*Memories, 1898–1939* (1966), pp. 250–1). In addition to Greek dialects, he was familiar with Sanskrit, Italian, German, Irish, Finnish, and Icelandic. His first book, *Modern Greek in Asia Minor*, appeared in 1916, and his edition of the medieval *Chronicle* of Makhairas in 1932.

In 1920 Dawkins was elected to the Bywater and Sotheby Chair of Byzantine and Modern Greek Language and Literature at *Oxford. He retired in 1939 but continued to reside in Oxford and to work industriously, in particular in the field of Greek folk-tales. His *Modern Greek Folk-Tales* was published in 1953, and *More Greek Folk-Tales* in 1955. While at Oxford he was a member of the Kolbítar (*Societies and clubs) and served with Tolkien on the Committee for Comparative Philology. On 15 October 1937 Tolkien told *Stanley Unwin that 'the professor of Byzantine Greek' (Dawkins) had bought a copy of *The Hobbit*, '"because first editions of 'Alice' are now very valuable"' (*Letters*, p. 25).

Day, Mabel (*d.* 1964). Mabel Day spent her working life at King's College, London, as the lieutenant of Sir Israel Gollancz. From 1921 to 1949 she was Assistant Director and Secretary of the Early English Text Society (*Societies and clubs), as well as a member of its Council until 1960, in which capacity she corresponded with Tolkien about his edition of the *Ancrene Wisse* (**Ancrene Riwle*). A scholar of Middle English, she edited or co-edited several works for the Early English Text Society, including *The English Text of the Ancrene Riwle* (Cotton Nero MS A. XIV), published in 1952.

Death *see* **Mortality and Immortality**

A Description of the Island of Númenor. Account of the land of Men in the West prominent in the Second Age of Tolkien's mythology (see further, *Númenor): its topography, settlements, trees, plants, means of travel, crafts, and interest of its people in the sea. Selections were published with commentary and notes in *Unfinished Tales (1980), pp. 165–72, together with a map redrawn by *Christopher Tolkien from a rapid sketch made by his father. A passage omitted from *Unfinished Tales* was included in **The Peoples of Middle-earth* (1996), pp. 144–5; and in that volume also Christopher Tolkien notes (p. 351) an editorial change he made to the *Description* in *Unfinished Tales*.

Tolkien almost certainly wrote the *Description* in 1960, contemporary with and closely related to the tale **Aldarion and Erendis*: see *The Peoples of Mid-*

dle-earth, p. 351, amending Christopher Tolkien's statement in *Unfinished Tales* where he dated the *Description* to 1965. On 30 August 1960 Tolkien wrote to the American zoologist George Lewis Hersch that the latter might be interested in a description of the flora and fauna of Númenor supposed to be 'derived from documents of a merely descriptive and unscientific kind' (Michael Silverman, *Catalogue No. 2* (1998), item no. 43). The *Description* is said to be 'derived from descriptions and simple maps that were long preserved in the archives of the Kings of Gondor' (*Unfinished Tales*, p. 165; see also **The Lord of the Rings*).

The Devil's Coach-horses. Article, published in the *Review of English Studies* (London) 1, no. 3 (July 1925), pp. 331–6. Tolkien discusses Old English *eafor* 'boar', Middle English *aver*, based on a passage in *Hali Meiðhad*, MS Bodley 34 (see *Katherine Group), called to his attention by *C.T. Onions. The passage in question refers to *þe deofles eaueres*, 'the devil's boars', which the Devil is said to ride and spur to do his will. Tolkien argues that

> we have in Middle English a word *aver* (West Midland *eaver*) meaning 'cart-horse'. . . . Further, from its form alone this word is of native origin and must have existed in Old English in the forms *afor* and *eafor*. . . . In mediaeval Latin, French, and English, the *aver*, though usually distinguished, expressly or by implication, from cattle, was also distinguished from horses for riding. The devil appears to have ridden his coach-horses like a postillion. [p. 337]

The Disaster of the Gladden Fields. Account of the ambush by Orcs of Isildur and his Guard as they marched north after the defeat of Sauron at the end of the Second Age, published with notes in **Unfinished Tales* (1980), pp. 271–85. Tolkien refers to the event briefly in the narrative of **The Lord of the Rings* and in 'The Tale of Years' (Appendix B; Third Age 2); here he explains the background to the event, giving life to a character who, elsewhere in Tolkien's fiction, is only a name from the past. Although the work proper is brief, it is supported by numerous, sometimes lengthy author's notes, which *inter alia* provide details about Númenórean battle strategy and the organization of long marches, the topography of Middle-earth, and the Battle of the Last Alliance. The text explains the sources for Isildur's story as it was known in the Third Age, but continues with evidence found by King Elessar at Orthanc in the beginning of the Fourth Age.

The *Disaster of the Gladden Fields* was written no earlier than 1969. It survives in two typescripts, the first a rough draft, the second incorporating many changes but incomplete: it continues only to the point at which Elendur urges his father, Isildur, to flee.

See also **Númenórean Linear Measures*.

Disney Studio. Tolkien's opinion of the animated films produced by the Disney Studio, as expressed in extant letters, was consistently negative. Most famously he wrote to C.A. Furth at George Allen & Unwin (*Publishers) on 13 May 1937, in regard to illustrations for the first American edition of *The Hobbit*: 'It might be advisable, rather than lose the American interest, to let the Americans do what seems good to them – as long as it was possible (I should like to add) to veto anything from or influenced by the Disney studios (for all whose works I have a heartfelt loathing)' (*Letters*, p. 17). As late as 15 July 1964, in a letter to Jane Louise Curry at Stanford University (herself later an author of children's books), Tolkien said that although he recognized Walt Disney's talent, 'it has always seemed to me hopelessly corrupted. Though in most of the "pictures" proceeding from his studios there are admirable or charming passages, the effect of all of them is to me disgusting. Some have given me nausea . . .' (quoted in Sotheby's, *English Literature, History, Children's & Illustrated Books & Drawings*, London, 10 July 2001, p. 123).

Jessica Yates has shown that at the time of Tolkien's earliest recorded comment on this subject he could have seen only the early 'funny animal' cartoons by Disney, not yet feature films such as *Snow White* and *Pinocchio*; see her 'The Other 50th Anniversary', *Mythlore* 16, no. 3, whole no. 61 (Spring 1990). *Snow White and the Seven Dwarfs* had its United States premiere in December 1937, seven months after Tolkien's letter to Furth, and was not released in England until 1938, where (as elsewhere) it was enormously popular. Tolkien's friend *C.S. Lewis saw it at the beginning of 1939, and was struck by the filmmakers' 'good unoriginality in the drawing of the queen . . . the very archetype of all beautiful, cruel queens' but 'bad originality in the bloated, drunken, low comedy faces of the dwarfs. Neither the wisdom, the avarice, nor the earthiness of true dwarfs were there, but an imbecility of arbitrary invention' (*A Preface to Paradise Lost* (1942), p. 56). According to *George Sayer, Lewis saw the film twice, the second time accompanied by Tolkien who 'thought that Snow White was rather beautiful, but the dwarfs were dreadful' ('A Dialogue: Discussion by Humphrey Carpenter, Professor George Sayer and Dr. Clyde S. Kilby, Recorded Sept. 29, 1979, Wheaton, Illinois', *Minas Tirith Evening Star* 9, no. 2 (January 1980), p. 18).

On 7 December 1946 Tolkien remarked to *Stanley Unwin that certain German illustrations for *The Hobbit* were 'too "Disnified" for my taste: Bilbo with a dribbling nose, and Gandalf as a figure of vulgar fun rather than the Odinic wanderer that I think of' (*Letters*, p. 119); and on 7 February 1959, in a letter to Charles Lewis at Allen & Unwin, he hoped that if an animated film of *The Hobbit* were made, the dwarves would not be made 'ridiculous' in the 'Disney manner' (Tolkien-George Allen & Unwin archive, HarperCollins).

In 1966 *Joy Hill at Allen & Unwin, who promoted Tolkien's works in media, sent *The Lord of the Rings* to Disney to consider as the basis of a film. The studio declined, judging that such a film would be too expensive to make. In his letter to Miss Curry two years earlier, Tolkien said that he was himself 'not innocent of the profit-motive', though 'I should not have given any pro-

posal from Disney any consideration at all. I am not all that poor . . .' (quoted
in Sotheby's catalogue, 10 July 2001, p. 123).

Dobson, Eric John (1913–1984). E.J. Dobson read English both at Sydney
University and at Merton College, *Oxford. Having received his B.A. in 1937,
he began a study of the pronunciation of English in the sixteenth and seventeenth centuries, work towards his D.Phil. which he undertook while, in turn,
Harmsworth Scholar at Merton College, Lecturer in English at the University
of Reading, a member of the wartime staff of Naval Intelligence, and Lecturer
in English at Jesus College and St Edmund Hall, Oxford. He completed his
work at last in 1951; his thesis, *English Pronunciation 1500–1700 According to the
Evidence of the English Orthoepists* (i.e. those who study the correct pronunciation of words), was examined by Tolkien and *C.L. Wrenn and later published
(1957; 2nd edn. 1968). In 1954 Dobson was made Reader (later Professor) in
English Language at Oxford, as well as a Professorial Fellow of Jesus College.

Like Tolkien, Dobson had an abiding interest in the *Ancrene Riwle* and
related manuscripts. In 1962 he contributed an essay, 'The Affiliations of the
Manuscripts of *Ancrene Wisse*', to the *Festschrift *English and Medieval Studies Presented to J.R.R. Tolkien on the Occasion of His Seventieth Birthday*; in
1966 he delivered a British Academy Lecture on 'The Date and Composition
of *Ancrene Wisse*'; in 1972 the Early English Text Society published his edition
of the Cotton Cleopatra manuscript of the *Ancrene Riwle*; and his *Origins of
'Ancrene Wisse'* was published in 1976. In 1981 he produced an edition of *Seinte
Katerine* (see *Katherine Group) in collaboration with *S.R.T.O. d'Ardenne.

Domestic duties. It was only when Tolkien returned to *Oxford at the end of
1918 that he, his wife *Edith, and baby *John were able to begin to live as an
ordinary family in their own home. Earlier Edith had lived in rooms with her
cousin, *Jennie Grove, and Tolkien spent time with her when his military obligations permitted. In summer 1919 Tolkien's income allowed them to rent a
house in Oxford instead of rooms, and they were even able to afford to hire a
cook-housemaid. Jennie remained with them until the family moved to Leeds
at the beginning of 1921.

In Leeds the Tolkiens were able to employ both a maid and a nurse for their
growing family, though it was not always easy to find the right person. One
maid employed by the Tolkiens proved to be a thief. Edith's accounts for the
week 27 February–4 March 1922 (published in *The Tolkien Family Album*,
p. 46) show that out of a total expenditure of £8 9s 6d she paid £2.6s.8d in
wages to Mary (? a maid) who actually left during that week, and £2.5s on 1
March to Nurse (presumably for the children). In their early years at 22 Northmoor Road, Oxford, the Tolkiens had a succession of Icelandic *au pair* girls
rather than a nurse to help them look after the children. According to Humphrey Carpenter, there were endless difficulties over servants until the arrival
of Phoebe Coles as daily help, probably in 1929. In his reconstruction of a day
in Tolkien's life in 1931 Carpenter describes Phoebe as wearing a housemaid's

cap and, after arriving in time to prepare breakfast, working in the house all day. Even with this help, Tolkien himself undertook domestic tasks such as cleaning out and lighting the stove in his study in the morning. Gardening also made demands on his time, though this was something he enjoyed and in which he was assisted by his children. In *The Tolkien Family Album* John and *Priscilla Tolkien wrote: '20 Northmoor Road was as much loved for its garden as for the house. John and Ronald worked at landscaping and redesigning the garden over many years, turning the rather decrepit tennis court at the top into a vegetable garden' (p. 55). Photographs in that book show the family relaxing and picnicking in the garden. John Tolkien and his father erected a trellis in front of 20 Northmoor Road in 1933 to make the garden more private from the view of passers-by.

The Second World War brought many changes. It was impossible to get any domestic help, and 20 Northmoor Road was a large house for Edith to manage alone. On 7 December 1942 in a letter to *Stanley Unwin Tolkien referred to 'trebled official work' and 'quadrupled domestic work' (*Letters*, p. 58). Some of this was a direct result of the war, such as having to put up blackout curtains every evening and remove them in the morning. On 18 April 1944 'the afternoon was squandered on plumbing (stopping overflow) and cleaning out fowls', i.e. the hens the Tolkiens kept for eggs. 'The grass grows so quick that I feel like a barber faced with a never-ending queue (& not a chinaman's either, to be trimmed with one snip)' (letter to *Christopher Tolkien, *Letters*, p. 73). Part of his time in the days before 11 May 1944 was spent in work about the house and garden, 'very exigent just now: lawns, hedges, marrow-beds, weeding' (letter to Christopher Tolkien, *Letters*, p. 79). On 7–8 November 1944 he wrote of doing 'one of the foulest jobs. I grease-banded all the trees (apple) tying 16 filthy little pantalettes on. It took 2 hours, and nearly as long to get the damned stuff off hands and implements. I neglected it last year, and so lost ½ a glorious crop to "moth"' (letter to Christopher Tolkien, *Letters*, p. 102). On 26 December he 'spent the day (after chores . . .) out of doors, well wrapped up in old rags, hewing old brambles and making a fire' (letter to Christopher Tolkien, 28 December 1944, *Letters*, p. 107). On 29 January 1945 he had to deal with a leaking scullery tap and a blocked sink, and the following morning, after a snowstorm, he spent the early part of the morning and part of the afternoon digging out coal, coke, and fowls and clearing drains – giving a lecture in between. In several of his letters to Christopher between 1944 and 1945 he mentions shopping, often time-consuming and involving queuing, e.g. 'the morning was wrecked by shopping and queuing: result one slab of pork-pie' (letter to Christopher Tolkien, 3 April 1944, *Letters*, p. 69).

Tolkien also took on much of the responsibility for taking care of the hens. Priscilla remembered her father 'cleaning out the hens, all the while smoking a large and pungent pipe' (*The Tolkien Family Album*, p. 55). On 26 April 1944 he 'arrived back to find Biddy had broken another egg . . . so, despairing that the "henwife" would attend to it, I have spent an agreeable time catching her (i.e. the bird), cleaning her, trimming her and disinfecting her – and then disinfecting myself. Grr! The fourth lawn will have to wait' (letter to Christopher Tolkien, 24–6 April 1944, *Letters*, p. 74). A month later he made a 'hen-coop and chick-run' to replace 'the untidy box and jumbled net which did duty on the lawn' (letter to Christopher Tolkien, 25 May 1944, *Letters*, p. 82). On 7 July 1944 he spent from 5.00 to 8.00 p.m. 'enlarging the [hen] house, with bits of old wood and salvaged nails, for the new hen-folk' (letter to Christopher Tolkien, 7–9 July 1944, *Letters*, p. 87).

By the end of the war only Priscilla among the children still lived at home, and although this may have meant less work, there were fewer hands to do it. In 1947 Tolkien, Edith, and Priscilla moved to a much smaller house, which Tolkien hoped would 'solve the intolerable domestic problems that thieve so much of the little time that is left over [from his academic work]' (letter to Stanley Unwin, 7 December 1946, *Letters*, p. 119). But Edith was beginning to suffer from arthritis and other problems which made chores increasingly difficult for her, and it was still difficult to find domestic help. In a letter to Moira Sayer (see *George Sayer) in August 1952 Tolkien said that he was 'moderately and cheerfully domesticated, though no cook' (quoted in Christie's, *20th-century Books and Manuscripts*, London, 13 November 2001, p. 25).

In 1953 Tolkien and Edith moved to 76 Sandfield Road, Headington. They were able to find a 'help' who came in to do some of the domestic work, but in autumn 1961 she had to retire because of ill health. Nearly a year later, a replacement still had not been found, and Tolkien wrote to his *Aunt Jane Neave: 'If ever you pray for temporal blessings for us, my dear, ask for the near-miracle of finding some help. Oxford is probably one of the hardest places even in this England, to find such a thing.' In the same letter he noted that Edith did 'all of the cooking, most of the housework, and some of the gardening' (18 July 1962, *Letters*, p. 316). Humphrey Carpenter commented that

> as the nineteen-sixties advanced and [Edith] came closer to her eighti-
> eth birthday it was clear that she could not manage for much longer. A
> daily help generally came in for a few hours, but it was not a small house
> and there was much to be done.... Tolkien himself did what he could
> to help, and since he was good with his hands he could mend broken
> furniture or repair fuses; but he too was becoming increasingly stiff. ...
> [*Biography*, p. 245–6]

With Tolkien undertaking more duties in the house as well as the garden, he found it difficult to spend much uninterrupted time on *'The Silmarillion' or other works. On 8 November 1965 he wrote to his publisher *Rayner Unwin that he needed domestic rather than secretarial help.

In 1968 Tolkien and Edith moved to a bungalow in *Poole which was much easier to manage. In addition they found assistance in the form of a Mrs Parke, who acted as driver and general help for several hours a week, though on occasion she herself was ill. When after Edith's death Tolkien returned to Oxford to live in Merton College, he had the services of a College scout, *Charlie Carr.

Doworst. Humorous verse 'report', relating remarkable errors committed by nervous students in oral English examinations at the University of *Oxford. The first page of a manuscript version was reproduced in *A Elbereth Gilthoniel!* (newsletter of the fan group The Fellowship of Middle Earth, Monash University, Victoria, Australia) 1, no. 2 [?Summer 1978], p. 3.

The work is in the style and metre of the fourteenth-century alliterative poem *Piers Plowman*. The poet witnesses the Oxford *vivas* at the end of Trinity Term: 'In a summer season when sultry was the sun / with lourdains & lubbers I lounged in a hall', etc. Students are summoned 'to an assize to be held / by four clerks very fell whom few could appease', where they will 'doworst', i.e. do their worst in answering the examiners' questions. Two of the 'four clerks' are intended to be Tolkien and *C.S. Lewis.

Tolkien wrote out the work as a decorated manuscript in a medieval manner, headed 'Visio Petri Aratoris de Doworst' (the vision of Piers Plowman of Doworst). In December 1933 he gave it to his friend *R.W. Chambers at University College, London. On Chambers' death it passed to his friend and colleague Winifred Husbands; and when Husbands retired from University College she gave the manuscript to Arthur Brown, an old student of Chambers who had become Professor of English at Monash University. In summer 1953 Tolkien gave a revised manuscript of *Doworst* to his Oxford colleague *Kathleen Lea.

The Dragon's Visit. Poem, one of the series *Tales and Songs of Bimble Bay*, set in an imaginary part of England. Its first version was published in the *Oxford Magazine* 55, no. 11 (4 February 1937), p. 342. A dragon is found in Mr Higgins' cherry trees; the fire brigade is summoned to evict the creature but succeeds only in provoking him to destruction. He eats Mr Higgins and his neighbours in Bimble Bay, 'Box, / Miss Biggins, and old Tupper', as well as fireman Captain George, then muses that 'the world is getting duller' and flies home far away over the sea.

The Dragon's Visit dates perhaps from 1928 and was revised in 1937, according to a late note by Tolkien on the first typescript of the poem, which followed two fair copy manuscripts with differing texts. The original version was reprinted in *The Annotated Hobbit*, pp. 262–3 (1988), 309–11 (rev. and expanded edn. 2002). On 15 November 1961 Tolkien sent a copy of the poem, with other verses, to *Rayner Unwin as a candidate for the poetry collection *The Adventures of Tom Bombadil and Other Verses from the Red Book* (1962). In the event, it was omitted; Douglas A. Anderson has speculated that this was 'both because Tolkien found it deficient and because he found it impossible to remodel and bring it into the world of *The Hobbit* and *The Lord of the Rings*' (*The Annotated Hobbit*, rev. and expanded edn., p. 311). But it was later revised and expanded for publication in *Winter's Tales for Children 1*, edited by Caroline Hillier and with an illustration by Hugh Marshall (London: Macmillan; New York: St Martin's Press, 1965), pp. 84–7 (see further, *Descriptive Bibliography* B27). In its revised ending (also reprinted in *The Annotated*

Hobbit) Miss Biggins stabs the dragon, with regret because he is 'a very splendid creature' but she will not stand for 'wanton damage'.

Dragons. Dragons entered Tolkien's consciousness early in life and inspired in him an interest in fantasy. In *On Fairy-Stories* he confessed that as a child he had enjoyed more than any other tale that of 'the nameless North of Sigurd of the Völsungs, and [Fáfnir] the prince of all dragons', in *Andrew Lang's Red Fairy Book* (first published 1890).

> Such lands were pre-eminently desirable. I never imagined that the dragon was of the same order as the horse. And this was not solely because I saw horses daily, but never even the footprint of a worm [i.e. dragon]. The dragon had the trade-mark *Of Faërie* written plain upon him. In whatever world he had his being it was an Other-world. Fantasy, the making or glimpsing of Other-worlds was the heart of the desire of Faërie. I desired dragons with a profound desire. Of course, I in my timid body did not wish to have them in the neighbourhood, intruding into my relatively safe world, in which it was, for instance, possible to read stories in peace of mind, free from fear. But the world that contained even the imagination of Fáfnir was richer and more beautiful, at whatever cost of peril. [*Tree and Leaf*, p. 40]

Almost certainly it was this tale which inspired him, when he was about six or seven as he recalled, to write a poem or story about a 'green great dragon', only to be told by his mother that he must say 'great green dragon' instead. And it was an inclination which persisted in the adult writer, who included dragons in his more mature fiction and poetry. Most notable among these are the one called successively Glorund, Glórund, Glórung, Glómund, and Glaurung in 'The Silmarillion' (see *Of Túrin Turambar*), Chrysophylax in *Farmer Giles of Ham*, and Smaug in *The Hobbit*, each with a distinct personality. Less developed dragons figure in the story of *Roverandom*, the poem *The Dragon's Visit*, and one of the *'Father Christmas'* letters. Glórund and Smaug also appear in Tolkien's paintings and drawings, and the Great White Dragon in a picture for *Roverandom*.

DRAGONS IN 'THE SILMARILLION'

In *The Book of Lost Tales* (composed c. 1916–19) Tolkien wrote an account of the dragons that Melko (Morgoth) bred to aid him in his wars against Elves and Men.

> Now those drakes and worms are the evillest creatures that Melko has made, and the most uncouth, yet of all are they the most powerful, save it be the Balrogs only. A great cunning and wisdom have they, so that it has long been said amongst Men that whosoever might taste the heart

of a dragon would know all the tongues of Gods or Men, of birds or beasts, and his ears would catch whispers of the Valar or of Melko such as never had he heard before. Few have there been that ever achieved a deed of such prowess as the slaying of a drake, nor might any even of such doughty ones taste their blood and live, for it is as a poison of fires that slays all save the most godlike in strength. Howso that may be, even as their lord these foul beasts love lies and lust after gold and precious things with a great fierceness of desire, albeit they may not use or enjoy them. [*The Book of Lost Tales, Part Two, p. 85]

There is no corresponding passage to this in the later texts from which the published *Silmarillion (1977) was formed, but many of the draconic characteristics described in it are present in its account of Glaurung, the most evil of Morgoth's dragons, and his slayer Túrin Turambar comes closest in Tolkien's writings to the conventional hero.

Glaurung is a wingless firedrake. As he crawls on the ground, he leaves a trail of destruction. He dominates Túrin with his glance: 'Glaurung withheld his blast, and opened wide his serpent-eyes and gazed upon Túrin. Without fear Túrin looked in them as he raised up the sword; and straightway he fell under the binding spell of the lidless eyes of the dragon, and was halted moveless' (The Silmarillion, p. 213). Glaurung spares Túrin not from pity, but out of malice; his lies lead Túrin to abandon the captives taken from Nargothrond to their fate, and Glaurung thus furthers Morgoth's curse on the children of Húrin. Glaurung then gathers all the riches of Nargothrond to form his bed in the manner of legendary dragons. Túrin's sister, Nienor, also meets Glaurung and 'having learned who she was [Glaurung] constrained her to gaze into his eyes, and he laid a spell of utter darkness and forgetfulness upon her, so that she could remember nothing that had ever befallen her, nor her own name, nor the name of any other thing' (p. 218). Unaware of her own identity, she meets and marries Túrin, who has not seen her since she was a child.

Later Túrin sets out with two companions to slay Glaurung. One deserts him, recalling the companions of Beowulf who likewise abandoned their leader (see *Beowulf). The other is killed by a falling stone, thus leaving Túrin to kill the dragon unaided. As Glaurung is dragging his great body across a ravine, Túrin climbs a cliff on the far side and stabs upwards into the dragon's soft belly. As Túrin draws his sword from the dying dragon 'a spout of black blood followed it, and fell on his hand, and the venom burned it. And thereupon Glaurung opened his eyes and looked upon Turambar with such malice that it smote him as a blow; and by that stroke and the anguish of the venom he fell into a dark swoon, and lay as one dead . . .' (The Silmarillion, p. 222). With his last breath Glaurung reveals to the distraught Nienor that her husband is in fact her brother.

Glaurung conveys an impression of utmost malice without any redeeming feature. Tolkien does not describe him in The Silmarillion other than to call him 'Glaurung the golden' (p. 151) and to indicate that he clearly breathed fire and had no wings. Tolkien did, however, depict Glaurung (or Glórund, as he was called in earlier writings) in a watercolour painting made in 1927 (*Artist and Illustrator*, fig. 47). He is shown as mainly golden, with four legs and a serpent's tongue, and flames coming from his mouth or nostrils. His frontal pose, strong legs ending in claws, and mask-like face suggest strength and ferocity.

It is noteworthy that Morgoth's dragons were bred by him to be used as a weapon in war, whereas the dragons faced in legend by Sigurd and Beowulf seem to be acting only in their own interests.

BEOWULF: THE MONSTERS AND THE CRITICS

In his British Academy Lecture *Beowulf: The Monsters and the Critics*, presented in November 1936, Tolkien rebuked critics who thought that the *Beowulf*-poet had paid too much attention to monsters rather than to things which interested the critics themselves:

A dragon is no idle fancy. Whatever may be his origins, in fact or invention, the dragon in legend is a potent creation of men's imagination, richer in significance than his barrow is in gold. Even to-day (despite the critics) you may find men not ignorant of tragic legend and history, who have heard of heroes and indeed seen them, who yet have been caught by the fascination of the worm. . . .

Beowulf's dragon, if one wishes really to criticise, is not to be blamed for being a dragon, but rather for not being dragon enough, plain pure fairy-story dragon. There are in the poem some vivid touches of the right kind . . . in which this dragon is real worm, with a bestial life and thought of his own, but the conception, none the less, approaches *draconitas* rather than *draco*: a personification of malice, greed, destruction (the evil side of heroic life), and of the undiscriminating cruelty of fortune that distinguishes not good or bad (the evil aspect of all life). But for *Beowulf*, the poem, that is as it should be. In this poem the balance is nice, but it is preserved. The large symbolism is near the surface, but it does not break through, nor become allegory. Something more significant than a standard hero, a man faced with a foe more evil than any human enemy of house or realm, is before us, and yet incarnate in time, walking in heroic history, and treading the named lands of the North.
[*The Monsters and the Critics and Other Essays*, pp. 16–17]

T.A. Shippey has observed that in this lecture Tolkien was concerned with the question of what the dragon meant to the *Beowulf*-poet, not to readers in later ages, and that the poet lived at a time when the dragons in which his ancestors believed as creatures that might actually have to be faced, had not yet become allegories of the devil or the like. 'He [the poet] was indeed phenomenally lucky in his freedom to balance exactly between "dragon-as-simple-beast" and "dragon-as-just-allegory", between pagan and Christian worlds, on a pinpoint of literary artifice and mythic suggestion' (*The Road to Middle-earth* (2nd edn. 1992), p. 44).

Among Tolkien's drawings of dragons is one labelled with the Old English words *hrinȝboȝa heorte ȝefýsed*, 'the heart of the coiling beast', derived from a passage late in *Beowulf*. In this (*Artist and Illustrator*, fig. 48) the beast has coiled itself into a knot; it has four legs, but only tiny wings which would seem unable to support it in flight. Unlike the perilous dragon in *Beowulf* it seems merely playful and decorative.

SMAUG IN THE HOBBIT

In *The Hobbit* (1937) Smaug is a winged firedrake who lies under the Lonely Mountain on a hoard stolen from Dwarves. Although he is still a dangerous beast, he does not convey the same impression of utter evil and malice as Glaurung. He comes, rather, from the fairy-story dragon traditions, most evident in the description of Smaug in the first edition of *The Hobbit* (ch. 1) as devouring 'many maidens of the valley' rather than 'many of the dwarves and men of Dale' as in later editions. In Chapter 12 Smaug is said to be 'a vast red-golden dragon, fast asleep; a thrumming noise came from his jaws and nostrils, and wisps of smoke; but his fires were low in slumber. Beneath him, under all his limbs and his huge coiled tail, and about him on all sides . . . lay countless piles of precious things. . . . Smaug lay, with his wings folded like an immeasurable bat, turned partly on one side, so that the hobbit could see his underparts and his long pale belly crusted with gems and fragments of gold. . . .' Tolkien painted an illustration of Smaug lying awake on his hoard (*Artist and Illustrator*, fig. 133), with a long jaw and a thin, flexible body and tail. He also made several drawings of Smaug flying around the Lonely Mountain after he discovers that Bilbo has stolen a cup from his hoard, a motif taken from *Beowulf* (*Artist and Illustrator*, figs. 134–136).

When Bilbo returns inside the mountain, wearing the magic ring that makes him invisible, Smaug can smell his presence. The conversation that follows shows Smaug to be a wily beast, susceptible to flattery, who enjoys the riddling talk with which Bilbo conceals his name, similar to Sigurd's conversation with Fafnir. Tolkien as narrator comments: 'This of course is the way to talk to dragons, if you don't want to reveal your proper name (which is wise), and don't want to infuriate them by a flat refusal (which is also very wise). No dragon can resist the fascination of riddling talk and of wasting time trying to understand it.' But Bilbo gives away more information than he realizes, and 'whenever Smaug's roving eye, seeking for him in the shadows, flashed across him, he trembled, and an unaccountable desire seized hold of him to rush out and reveal himself and tell all the truth to Smaug. In fact he was in grievous danger of coming under the dragon-spell' (ch. 12).

After this encounter Smaug flies off to burn Lake-town, but is slain by Bard the Bowman's arrow which pierces an unprotected spot in the dragon's breast. Tolkien also made a drawing of this scene (*Artist and Illustrator*, fig.

137), with Smaug seen from below, his four legs clearly visible. Although in an early outline Tolkien considered whether to let Bilbo himself kill Smaug, in the published book the hobbit is only the means by which Bard learns of an unprotected patch on Smaug's breast. The death of Smaug is unusual in accounts of dragon-slaying in that he is not slain by the chief protagonist, but by Bard who enters the story only as Smaug attacks Lake-town, as the organizer of its defence. Yet in some ways, as T.A Shippey notes, 'Bard is a figure from the ancient world of heroes. He prides himself on his descent, from Girion Lord of Dale.... The proof of his descent lies in an inherited weapon to which he speaks as if it were sentient. . . . And it is this arrow . . . shot by Bard . . . which kills the dragon, in a way not entirely dissimilar to Sigurth [sic] or Beowulf' (*J.R.R. Tolkien: Author of the Century* (2000), pp. 39–40).

LECTURE ON DRAGONS

It was probably as a result of the success of *The Hobbit*, and the emphasis on the dragon Tolkien had placed in *Beowulf: The Monsters and the Critics*, that soon after the publication of these works (in September and July 1937 respectively) he was invited to give a lecture on dragons to children in the University Museum, *Oxford, on 1 January 1938. The text of this largely unpublished lecture reveals Tolkien's thoughts on aspects of dragon-lore not discussed elsewhere in his works, and provides a yardstick for the consideration of dragons in his writings (all quotations from the Tolkien Papers, Bodleian Library, Oxford).

He began by discussing whether dragons had ever actually existed. He showed slides of pictures of dinosaurs, comparing them to conceptions of dragons. He pointed out that dinosaurs died out long before men evolved, but perhaps men had developed their visions of dragons from fossils of these creatures. But while the dragon might not live in *Natural History* it had a definite place in *Legendary History*, man-made, founded on creatures that man knew, serpents and lizards, but made more terrible. He described the history of the word *dragon*, and of *drake* and other words such as *wyrm* or *worm* used for the same creature. He then spoke of 'the fabulous dragon, the *old worm*, or *great drake*', illustrating his points with slides of his own drawings of Glórund, the 'coiled dragon', and others (see *Artist and Illustrator*, p. 53). This was

> a serpent creature but with four legs and claws; his neck varied in length but had a hideous head with long jaws and teeth or snake-tongue. He was usually heavily armoured especially on his head and back and flanks. Nonetheless he was pretty bendable (up and down or sideways), could even tie himself in knots on occasion, and had a long powerful tail. . . . The swish of the dragon's tail was dangerous. Some had wings – the legendary kind of wings that go together with front legs (instead of being front legs 'gone queer'). The winged kind was, of course, specially alarming; though some of the direst and most evil of these monsters had no

wings. Of course, *size* is also a consideration. . . . A respectable dragon should be twenty feet or more.

The true dragon at his least was sufficiently large to be a terrible foe. . . . It was the function of dragons to tax the skill of heroes; and still more to tax other things, especially courage. . . .

But though the *dragon* might be of a primordial and immeasurable size beyond the power of a hero – his real dread did not lie in his armour, or in his teeth, or in his size. The dragon may have been 'founded on worm' but he was more terrible than any *dinosaur*. Because he was filled with a horrible spirit. The legend-makers put it in him. He was filled with malice. Not only the mere animal fierceness that fights for food and mate, or to defend a coveted hole, but with hatred of other living things as such. A dragon made a desert. He rejoiced in destruction, and his wicked heart was fired by a smouldering and envious guess at the work of the things destroyed. Legend had filled him with evil, and he grew strong on that terrible gift: he was cunning, deadly, bitter and piercingly keen. . . . His glance has a terrible effect if it holds yours. He may seek to bind your will. At least that was the way of old dragons who had lived long in wickedness. Also he will probably try to find out your name. For dragons also deal in evil magic, and even when defeated may (if they have your name) curse you as they die. . . .

Dragons . . . loved to possess beautiful things – though they could not use or enjoy them. They hoarded them. But they were terribly keen-scented after thieves. The hottest thief-haters and the cruellest thief-pursuers are usually those who possess large wealth which they cannot enjoy, but only lose. Such were dragons. Greed and hatred inspired them. That is, I suppose, why they were often so hot. There often were flaming dragons, *fire-drakes*; their breath was flame and venom, and withered what it touched. . . .

And how can you withstand a dragon's flame, and his venom, and his terrible will and malice, and his great strength? How can you pierce his armour? . . . It needs first of all courage. For the most remarkable thing about the great dragons of legend is that their legends mostly tell of their overthrow. . . . Dragons can only be defeated by brave men – usually *alone*. Sometimes a faithful friend may help, but it is rare; friends have a way of deserting you when a dragon comes. Dragons are the final test of heroes.

Tolkien continued with a discussion of how heroes in legend and literature have overcome dragons, finding a weak spot, cutting upwards with a sword or firing an arrow into the soft belly. He described at length Beowulf's encounter in old age with the dragon, and mentioned that dragon's blood is supposed to make your skin hard and sword-proof, and eating a dragon's heart to enable one to understand the language of birds and beasts. He gave an account of 'the greatest of all the old northern dragon stories', that of the Völsung Sigurd who killed the dragon Fafnir by concealing himself in a pit and stabbing from below as the dragon passed overhead; how Sigurd concealed his name from the dying dragon by speaking in riddles but revealed it when he was accused of concealing it out of fear; how Fafnir cursed the gold and foretold that it would be Sigurd's death; and how when Sigurd tasted fat from the heart of Fafnir he understood what birds were singing. Tolkien also recounted the legend of Thórr and the *Midgardsorm*, and referred briefly to Chinese dragons, to Merlin and the red and white dragons in Geoffrey of Monmouth's *History of the Kings of Britain*, and to St George.

CHRYSOPHYLAX DIVES IN FARMER GILES OF HAM

Although superficially Chrysophylax has some resemblance to dragons of legend – he is a winged firedrake with a hoard in a cave – his fire seems less terrible than that of Smaug and he is, in fact, a coward. As a character he owes a great deal to the humorous treatment of dragons in stories for children of the late nineteenth and early twentieth centuries by writers such as Kenneth Grahame (*The Reluctant Dragon*), Edith Nesbit (*The Dragon Tamers, The Last of the Dragons*, etc.), and Noel Langley (*The Land of Green Ginger*). (See further, Christina Scull, 'Dragons from Andrew Lang's Retelling of Sigurd to Tolkien's Chrysophylax', in *Leaves from the Tree: J.R.R. Tolkien's Shorter Fiction* (1991).) In *Farmer Giles of Ham* (1949), a mock-heroic story set in early medieval times, dragons have become scarce, a mock dragon's tail made of cake, almond-paste, and icing sugar has replaced a real dragon's tail at the King's Christmas feast, and the King's knights are afraid to go into battle. Chrysophylax too is less brave than earlier dragons: 'He was cunning, inquisitive, greedy, well-armoured, but not over bold' (*Farmer Giles of Ham*, p. 25). He is too cowardly to fight Farmer Giles, who has a magic sword, and through misadventure is forced to carry a large part of his treasure back to Giles's village, his back loaded with 'boxes and bags till he looked like a royal pantechnicon. There was no chance of flying for his load was too great, and Giles had tied down his wings' (p. 64). In this story the dragon is not slain, but tamed and used as a beast of burden.

Jonathan Evans in 'The Dragon-Lore of Middle-earth: Tolkien and Old English and Old Norse Tradition', in *J.R.R. Tolkien and His Literary Resonances: Views of Middle-earth* (2000), discusses at length the medieval sources Tolkien knew and his use of both these and the work of his immediate predecessors. He considers that Tolkien's works

reveal rich and powerful realizations of the narrative possibilities inherent in the dragon as a motif and the dragon-slayer story as a narrative type. Tolkien was conscious and explicit about this both in his fiction writing and in his critical scholarship, and in both we can find a dependence upon medieval developments of the motif and narrative type that preserves and highlights aspects of the tradition and at the same time extends them beyond the limitations already imposed by Tolkien's medieval predecessors – going so far, in some instances, as to introduce new motifs. Further, through artful recombination of themes contributed by his immediate literary forebears Andrew Lang and *William Morris, Tolkien advances fantasy narratives of dragons and dragon slayers to a level of literary achievement which in the end would dwarf the popular, and arguably the scholarly, appeal of the writers he drew from. [p. 22]

See also Anne C. Petty, *Dragons of Fantasy* (2004).

Drama. The earliest professional dramatic performance Tolkien attended seems to have been *Peter Pan*, in a *Birmingham theatre in April 1910. He wrote of it in his diary: 'Indescribable but shall never forget it as long as I live' (quoted in *Biography*, p. 47). Later, during his many years in *Oxford, attending plays, whether performed by professional actors or by college or university dramatic societies, was a part of social life. Among these were productions of the Oxford University Dramatic Society, with which Tolkien's friend *Nevill Coghill was closely involved. Early in 1940 Tolkien and *C.S. Lewis saw Shakespeare's *Midsummer Night's Dream* at the Oxford Playhouse, after which Lewis recorded that *Elaine Griffiths, who was also present, commented how nice it was to see that play indoors, away from the discomforts of the open air (where *A Midsummer Night's Dream* is often staged). In letters written in 1944 Tolkien mentioned having attended two performances of *Hamlet*, and one of *Arms and the Man* by George Bernard Shaw. To judge from a draft for Note F to *On Fairy-Stories*, he also saw more than one performance of J.M. Barrie's play *Mary Rose*: one of these, *Priscilla Tolkien recalls, was probably in the late 1940s, when she joined both of her parents in the audience at the Playhouse.

In *On Fairy-Stories* Tolkien mentions several occasions on which he took his children to the theatre. He did not always approve of what he saw:

Men dressed up as talking animals may achieve buffoonery or mimicry, but they do not achieve Fantasy. This is, I think, well illustrated by the failure of the bastard form, pantomime. The nearer it is to 'dramatized fairy-story' the worse it is. It is only tolerable when the plot and its fantasy are reduced to a mere vestigiary framework for farce, and no 'belief' of any kind in any part of the performance is required or expected of anybody. This is, of course, partly due to the fact that the producers of drama have to, or try to, work with mechanism to represent either Fantasy or Magic. I once saw a so-called 'children's pantomime', the straight story of *Puss-in-Boots*, with even the metamorphosis of the ogre into a mouse. Had this been mechanically successful it would either have terrified the spectators or else have been just a turn of high-class conjuring. As it was, though done with some ingenuity of lighting, disbelief had not so much to be suspended as hung, drawn, and quartered. [*Tree and Leaf*, p. 47]

He was equally vociferous about a performance of *Toad of Toad Hall*, A.A. Milne's 1929 dramatization of *The Wind in the Willows*, finding it remarkable that Milne,

> so great an admirer of this excellent book, should have prefaced to his dramatized version a 'whimsical' opening in which a child is seen telephoning with a daffodil. Or perhaps it is not very remarkable, for a perceptive admirer (as distinct from a great admirer) of the book would never have attempted to dramatize it. Naturally only the simpler ingredients, the pantomime, and the satiric beast-fable elements, are capable of presentation in this form. The play is, on the lower level of drama, tolerably good fun, especially for those who have not read the book; but some children that I took to see *Toad of Toad Hall*, brought away as their chief memory nausea at the opening. For the rest they preferred their recollections of the book. [*Tree and Leaf*, pp. 66–7]

*Christopher Tolkien remembers this performance, and thinks that it took place around 1930.

Humphrey Carpenter notes in *Biography* that Tolkien's children recalled 'visits to the theatre, which their father always seemed to enjoy, although he declared he did not approve of Drama' (p. 159). He bases the latter part of this statement on various comments by Tolkien, which can be divided roughly into two groups. First, in principle Tolkien opposed dramatizations of his own works (see *Adaptations), thinking them unsuitable for such presentation. On 11 September 1964 he wrote to *Joy Hill at George Allen & Unwin (*Publishers) that he had replied to an enquirer 'that I was personally averse to any dramatization of my works, especially *The Lord of the Rings*' (Tolkien-George Allen & Unwin archive, HarperCollins). Other comments, however, suggest that he made a careful distinction between the studying of 'Drama' as part of the English syllabus, and seeing plays performed on the stage. He told Peter Alford in a letter of 14 January 1956 that '"drama" is a wholly different art from literature, though it may use words; as different as (say) sculpture from painting' (quoted in Sotheby's, *Valuable Printed Books and Manuscripts*, London, 13 December 2001, p. 260). He presumably felt that a play could be fully understood and appreciated only when seen as intended, performed on the stage. On 28 July 1944 he wrote, after seeing a performance of *Hamlet*, that this

> emphasised more strongly than anything I have ever seen the folly of reading Shakespeare (and annotating him in the study), except as a concomitant of seeing his plays acted. It was a very good performance, with a young rather fierce Hamlet; it was played fast without cuts; and came out as a very exciting play. Could one have seen it without ever having read it or knowing the plot, it would have been terrific. It was well produced except for a bit of bungling over the killing of Polonius. But to my surprise the part that came out as the most moving, almost intolerably

so, was the one that in reading I always found a bore: the scene of mad Ophelia singing her snatches. [letter to Christopher Tolkien, *Letters* p. 88].

Tolkien's preference for seeing a play rather than reading it depended, however, on the play itself as well as the performance. It was not only in plays for children that he found that supernatural or fantasy elements worked better when read than when staged:

> In *Macbeth*, when it is read, I find the witches tolerable: they have a narrative function and some hint of dark significance; though they are vulgarized, poor things of their kind. They are almost intolerable in the play. They would be quite intolerable, if I were not fortified by some memory of them as they are in the story as read. . . . To be dissolved, or to be degraded, is the likely fate of Fantasy when a dramatist tries to use it, even such a dramatist as Shakespeare. [*Tree and Leaf*, pp. 47–8]

In a draft for *On Fairy-Stories* he refers to the differences between drama and narrative, and how the attention paid to the former affected understanding of the latter, because

> the characters and even the places are in Drama not imagined but actually seen – Drama is, even though it uses similar material (words, verse, plot) . . . fundamentally different from narrative art. Thus, if you prefer Drama, as so many 'literary' critics seem to do, or are dominated by the excellencies of Shakespeare, you are apt to misunderstand pure story-making, and to measure its aims and achievement by the limitations of plays. [Tolkien Papers, Bodleian Library, Oxford]

In a letter written in 1965 he said that Drama usurped 'too much attention' among the arts (letter to Miss Jaworski, 9 December 1965, quoted in Sotheby Parke Bernet, *Catalogue of Autograph Letters, Literary Manuscripts and Historical Documents*, London, 16 October 1978), and in the letter to Peter Alford cited above, he expressed his opinion that the attention paid to Drama as literature was due mainly to the 'dominant position' accorded Shakespeare among English writers – a playwright about whom Tolkien had notably ambivalent feelings.

Tolkien probably first read Shakespeare when he was in George Brewerton's class at *King Edward's School, Birmingham, between autumn 1903 and summer 1905. Many years later, he told *W.H. Auden that at school he had 'learned English. Not English Literature! Except Shakespeare (which I disliked cordially)' (7 June 1955, *Letters*, p. 213). One of the plays he read at school was *Macbeth*: he later said that he thought the part played by the Ents in *The Lord of the Rings* was due 'to my bitter disappointment and disgust from school-days with the shabby use made in Shakespeare of the coming of "Great Birnam

wood to High Dunsinane hill": I longed to devise a setting in which the trees
might really march to war' (letter to Auden, *Letters*, p. 212). *Macbeth* seems
to have made a particular impression on Tolkien, probably influencing other
parts of *The Lord of the Rings* as well. The deceiving prophecy that 'none of
woman born shall harm Macbeth' (Act IV, Scene 1), for instance, is similar to
that in which the Witch-king trusts that 'no living man may hinder me' (bk. V,
ch. 6); and Edward the Confessor's healing ability, stressed in *Macbeth*, Act IV,
Scene 3, is recalled by the healing hands of Aragorn, the rightful king.

Even though Tolkien had chosen to specialize in the language side of the
*Oxford English School, he still had to study Shakespeare: one paper of his
final examinations in 1915 was devoted to that author. The set plays were *Love's
Labour's Lost, Henry IV: Part 1, Henry IV: Part 2, Hamlet,* and *Antony and Cleopatra,* but candidates were also required to do background reading and be
able to answer questions such as 'Give some account of the acting company
of which Shakespeare was a member. What are the indications that in writing his plays he sometimes thought of the special abilities of the actors?' and
'Show how Shakespeare's dramas reflect the experiences, and the reading of
his school-days.' After Tolkien returned to Oxford as Rawlinson and Bosworth
Professor of Anglo-Saxon, he played a major role in 1930–1 in the revision of
the syllabus of the English School, after which students on the language side
no longer had to take a paper on Shakespeare.

In later years Tolkien held Shakespeare responsible to a great extent for the
debasement of the concept of elves and fairies as diminutive beings, in particular in *A Midsummer Night's Dream.* In a letter to Milton Waldman, ?late
1951, after referring to his use of the word *Elves* in his *legendarium* he added:
'Intending the word to be understood in its ancient meanings, which continued as late as [Edmund] Spenser – a murrain on Will Shakespeare and his
damned cobwebs' (*Letters*, p. 143 note). In 1954 he deeply regretted 'having
used *Elves*, though this is a word in ancestry and original meaning suitable
enough. But the disastrous debasement of this word, in which Shakespeare
played an unforgiveable part, has really overloaded it with regrettable tones,
which are too much to overcome' (letter to *Hugh Brogan, 18 September 1954,
Letters, p. 185, italics added). But Tolkien himself had once accepted the diminutive aspect of fairies or elves, and only gradually came to reject it; it appears
in some of his early poems, such as **The Princess Ní* and **Goblin Feet.* Early
'Silmarillion' texts indicate that he intended that his Elves should fade and
diminish into beings of the sort depicted by Shakespeare: 'After the Battle of
Rôs the Elves faded with sorrow . . . and ever as Men wax more powerful and
numerous so the fairies fade and grow small and tenuous, filmy and transparent. . . . At last Men, or almost all, can no longer see the fairies' (**The Book of
Lost Tales, Part Two*, p. 283).

T.A. Shippey points out in *J.R.R. Tolkien: Author of the Century* (2000) that
'in Tolkien's professional lifetime Shakespeare had a status which approached
the holy, and it seemed indefensibly Philistine to many critics that Tolkien
should have had the nerve to be dissatisfied with him; but Tolkien usually saw

things from a different angle than his literary colleagues, and often expressed only half of his opinion at a time' (p. 192). He thinks that Tolkien 'was guardedly respectful of Shakespeare' (p. 194), but 'the trouble with Shakespeare (Tolkien might have said) was that he was too much a dramatist. He dealt by choice with single events closely related to the fortunes of particular characters, tightly contextualized' (p. 195).

Nonetheless Tolkien recognized Shakespeare as a great writer. In a draft letter of 1954 he mentioned Shakespeare among some of the great names of world literature whose works he certainly respected: 'There are, I suppose, always defects in any large-scale work of art; and especially in those of literary form that are founded on an earlier matter which is put to new uses – like Homer, or Beowulf, or Virgil, or Greek or Shakespearian tragedy! In which class, as a class not as a competitor, *The Lord of the Rings* really falls . . .' (letter to *Robert Murray, 4 November 1954, *Letters*, p. 201).

TOLKIEN AS PERFORMER

At King Edward's School it was the custom for a Greek play to be performed in the original language as part of the entertainment on Speech Day at the end of the school year. In July 1910 Tolkien played the part of the Inspector in *The Birds* by Aristophanes, and in July 1911 he was 'a spirited Hermes' in *The Peace* by Aristophanes ('Speech Day', *King Edward's School Chronicle* n.s. 26, no. 189 (October 1911), p. 72). Much later he recalled that after the latter performance, at the end of his years at King Edward's School, 'the school-porter was sent by waiting relatives to find me. . . . He reported that my appearance might be delayed. "Just now," he said, "he's the life and soul of the party." Tactful. In fact, having just taken part in a Greek play, I was clad in a himation and sandals, and was giving what I thought a fair imitation of a frenzied Bacchic dance' (quoted in *Biography*, p. 49). He returned to the School at the end of his first term at Oxford, on 21 December 1911, to play Mrs Malaprop in a performance of *The Rivals* by Richard Brinsley Sheridan. It is ironic to think of the future philologist playing the part of the character who gave a new word to the English language because of her constant *misuse* of words. A review in the *King Edward's School Chronicle* reported that his Mrs Malaprop 'was a real creation, excellent in every way and not least so in make-up' ('The Musical and Dramatic Society', n.s. 27, no. 191 (March 1912), p. 10).

In their youth, Tolkien and his brother *Hilary often spent Christmas holidays with the family of their late mother's sister May Incledon (*Incledon family), who had the custom of producing amateur theatricals. Tolkien took part, and had a hand in writing, some of these, including the farce *Cherry Farm* at Christmas 1911 and *The Bloodhound, the Chef, and the Suffragette* at Christmas 1912. In the latter, he played the leading part of

> 'Professor Joseph Quilter, M.A., B.A., A.B.C., alias world-wide detective Sexton Q. Blake-Holmes, the Bloodhound', who is searching for a lost

heiress named Gwendoline Goodchild. She meanwhile has fallen in love with a penniless student whom she meets while they are living in same lodging-house, and she has to remain undiscovered by her father until her twenty-first birthday in two days' time, after which she will be free to marry. [Humphrey Carpenter, *Biography*, p. 59]

The family audience on this occasion probably was unaware how topical the subject of the play was to its author: on his twenty-first birthday on 3 January 1913 he would be free to renew contact with *Edith Bratt whom he hoped to marry.

For two years Tolkien took part in the Summer Diversions organized by *John Masefield and *Nevill Coghill, reciting with the original pronunciation or a modified version of it, Chaucer's 'Nun's Priest's Tale' in 1938, and his *'Reeve's Tale' in 1939. The *Oxford Mail* reported on 4 August 1938:

> Prof. Tolkien, wearing a beard and the resplendent robes of the 14th century and speaking into a 20th-century microphone, was a spectacle in himself.
>
> One can only stand amazed at his bravery in reciting without manuscript a Canterbury Tale, slightly cut, it is true, but still fraught with endless perils and difficulties for the speaker.
>
> The audience were at first a little scared of Chaucer's Middle English, but not for long. Prof. Tolkien spoke his lines magnificently, and there can have been none present who were unable to enjoy the beauty and the subtlety and the wit of the first Poet Laureate's work. ['"Gammer Gurton" at Oxford Diversions: With Chaucer's "Nonnes Preestes Tale," Spoken in Middle English by Prof. J.R.R. Tolkien', p. 6]

In 1939 Tolkien managed without a microphone: 'He did it superbly, and it is a lasting tribute to him that he barely once faltered' ('Canterbury Tale and Ballet: Oxford Performances of Summer Diversions', *Oxford Mail*, 29 July 1939, final page).

Tolkien occasionally liked to be dramatic when lecturing. When he began a series of lectures on *Beowulf*,

> he would come silently into the room, fix the audience with his gaze, and suddenly begin to declaim in a resounding voice the opening lines of the poem in the original Anglo-Saxon, commencing with a great cry of '*Hwaet!*' (the first word of this and several other English poems). . . . It was not so much a recitation as a dramatic performance, an impersonation of an Anglo-Saxon bard in a mead hall, and it impressed generations of students because it brought home to them that *Beowulf* was not just a set text to be read for the purposes of an examination but a powerful piece of dramatic poetry. As one former pupil, the writer J.I.M. Stewart, expressed it: 'He could turn a lecture room into a mead hall in which

he was the bard and we were the feasting, listening guests.' [*Biography*, p. 133]

Tolkien's acting ability can be judged to a certain extent from the *recordings he made of excerpts from *The Lord of the Rings*, and especially in his dramatic reading of part of Chapter 5 of *The Hobbit*, in which he differentiates the voices of Gollum and Bilbo. Also preserved on tape is his reading of *The Homecoming of Beorhtnoth Beorhthelm's Son*, in which he not only played both parts (Torhthelm and Tídwald) but also provided background noises.

Dramatizations *see* **Adaptations**

The Drowning of Anadûnê. Version of the story of the destruction of *Númenor, written in close association with *The Notion Club Papers*, published with commentary and notes in *Sauron Defeated* (1992), pp. 331–440.

Before beginning the first version of *The Drowning of Anadûnê*, Tolkien evidently made some emendations to the third version of *The Fall of Númenor* written about five years earlier. He also made a series of three successive 'Sketches', written at speed, in which he seems to have been working out ideas for telling the history of Men and especially of Númenor from a new perspective. The first of these has the title 'The theory of this version'.

Tolkien composed the first rough version of *The Drowning of Anadûnê* on a typewriter; later he added in pencil the title *The Drowning of Númenor*. He began to correct this, but found that he had left insufficient space to do so, and did not proceed very far. He then made a second, fair copy typescript, developing the story and incorporating more detail. After making changes to this, including rewritten or extended passages typewritten on slips of paper, he produced a third typescript, taking up the alterations and additions and making further changes. He emended this in turn, then made a fourth typescript, taking up the new emendations but introducing little further change.

Textual evidence suggests that Tolkien worked on both *The Drowning of Anadûnê* and Part Two of *The Notion Club Papers* in overlapping stages, with the texts of each of the two works influencing the other. He began work on *The Notion Club Papers* during the Christmas vacation 1945, read the third or fourth version of *The Drowning of Anadûnê* to *Christopher Tolkien in the summer of 1946, and probably read the fourth version to the *Inklings on 22 August 1946.

Although *The Drowning of Anadûnê* tells a story similar to that of the earlier *Fall of Númenor*, it is an entirely new work which in many ways contradicts the traditions established in the (then still unpublished) 'Silmarillion'. Christopher Tolkien believes that his father had begun 'to be concerned with questions of "tradition" and the vagaries of tradition, the losses, confusions, simplifications and amplifications in the evolution of legend, as they might apply to his own', and in *The Drowning of Anadûnê* portrayed 'a tradition of Men, through long ages become dim and confused' (*Sauron Defeated*, p. 406).

The Drúedain see Of Dwarves and Men

Dundas-Grant, James Harold (1896–1985). James Dundas-Grant served in the Royal Navy in the First World War, and was recalled into service at the beginning of the Second. In October 1944, appointed commander of the Oxford University Naval Division, he took up residence in Magdalen College. There he met *C.S. Lewis, who was also his tutor in a wartime course in Philosophy. Sometimes he visited Lewis in his rooms, and in this manner came to meet Tolkien, 'tall, sweptback grey hair, restless. He read to us parts of his manuscript for *Lord of the Rings*, asking for criticism' (Dundas-Grant, 'From an "Outsider"', C.S. *Lewis at the Breakfast Table and Other Reminiscences* (new edn. 1992), p. 230).

After the war Dundas-Grant and his wife settled in *Oxford, where they took charge of a residential house for Roman Catholic undergraduates. Eventually Dundas-Grant was invited to join the *Inklings at their Tuesday meetings in the Eagle and Child pub (*Oxford and environs): 'We sat in a small back room with a fine coal fire in winter. Back and forth the conversation would flow. Latin tags flying around. Homer quoted in the original to make a point' ('From an "Outsider"', p. 231).

A photograph of Dundas-Grant is reproduced in *The Inklings*, p. 10.

Of Dwarves and Men. Essay, the greater part of which was published with commentary and notes in *The Peoples of Middle-earth* (1996), pp. 295–330, as *Of Dwarves and Men*, a title assigned by *Christopher Tolkien based on one found in a rough synopsis; but parts were published earlier in *Unfinished Tales* (1980).

Tolkien described the essay as

> an extensive commentary and history of the interrelation of the languages in *The Silmarillion* and *The Lord of the Rings*, arising from consideration of the Book of Mazarbul, but attempting to clarify and where necessary to correct or explain the references to such matters scattered in *The Lord of the Rings*, especially in Appendix F and in Faramir's talk in LR II [i.e. Book IV, Chapter 5]. [*The Peoples of Middle-earth*, p. 295]

The surviving text (the first page is missing) begins with a discussion of the Common Speech, where it was spoken and by whom, and continues with information about the languages and writing systems used by the Dwarves. From this Tolkien proceeds to a discussion of the Book of Mazarbul and his 'facsimiles' of the three damaged leaves in runes or Fëanorian script, partially deciphered by Gandalf in *The Lord of the Rings*, Book II, Chapter 5. The Dwarves were supposed to have written these in the Common Speech, which in *The Lord of the Rings* is represented by English. Tolkien had also used English for the text of these fragments, not taking into account, however, that

English was not the actual language used by the Dwarves. He now described this as 'an erroneous extension of the general linguistic treatment. It is one thing to represent all the dialogue of the story in varying forms of English: this must be supposed to be done by "translation".... But it is quite another thing to provide *visible* facsimiles or representations of writings or carvings supposed to be of the date of the events in the narrative' (*The Peoples of Middle-earth*, p. 299).

Discussing the representation of the actual runic inscription on Balin's tomb, Tolkien notes that the names *Balin* and *Fundin* were, of course, not the real 'outer' names of those Dwarves, but the Norse names chosen to represent the 'outer' names in *The Lord of the Rings*. In discussing runes used by the Dwarves of Moria, Tolkien refers to their association in the Second Age with the Elves of Eregion, and describes the Elven-smith Celebrimbor as 'a Sinda who claimed descent from Daeron' (p. 297). Christopher Tolkien examines his father's development of Celebrimbor at length (pp. 317–19, note 7).

In the section headed '[I.] Relations of the Longbeard Dwarves and Men', Tolkien gives some account of the history of both races, mainly from the Dwarves' point of view. In earlier times 'Men became the chief providers of food, as herdsmen, shepherds, and land-tillers, which the [Longbeard] Dwarves exchanged for work as builders, roadmakers, miners, and the makers of things of craft . . .' (p. 302). Tolkien comments on the Longbeards' use of Mannish languages, their refusal to reveal their personal names to people of other kin, their adoption of Mannish 'outer' names, and that they also assigned 'similar names to Dwarves remembered in their annals long before the meeting of Dwarves and Men' (p. 304). Among the latter was *Durin*, the name of the prime ancestor of the Longbeards. 'The Elvish loremasters held that in the matter of language the changes in speech . . . of the Speaking Peoples were far slower in the Elder Days than they later became. The tongue of the Eldar changed mainly by design; that of the Dwarves resisted change by their own will; the many languages of Men changed heedlessly in the swift passing of their generations' (p. 305).

The next section, 'II. The Atani and Their Languages', gives an account of Men and their movements in the First Age (with some differences from Tolkien's earlier writings and the account in *The Silmarillion*) and of the physical characteristics and languages of their three peoples, the Folk of Bëor, Hador, and Haleth.

Most of the third section, 'III. The Drúedain (Púkel-men)', was published in *Unfinished Tales* as *The Drúedain*, introduced by the description of the Folk of Haleth that concludes section II. Here it is said that among the Folk of Haleth were 'a people of a wholly different kind', the Drûgs, called *Drúedain* by the Eldar. They were 'unlovely in looks' to Elves and other Men, with 'deep and guttural' voices and 'rich and rolling' laughter which affected all who heard it; but they were 'relentless enemies' and had great skill as trackers (*Unfinished Tales*, pp. 377–8). They also had a talent for carving in wood or stone, and often carved images of themselves which they placed 'at the entrances to

tracks or at turnings of woodland paths. These they called "watch-stones" . . .'
(p. 379) which the Orcs feared and avoided. The Drúedain had a 'capacity of
utter silence and stillness, which they could at times endure for many days on
end' (p. 379), and might be mistaken by Men as being one of the images they
made. Among tales of the Drûgs told by the Folk of Haleth, who believed that
they had magical powers, was *The Faithful Stone*, in which a watch-stone set by
a Drûg saves a family of Men from an attack by Orcs.

A comparison of the Drúedain and the Hobbits is given in curtailed form
in *Unfinished Tales*, but in full in *The Peoples of Middle-earth* (cf. the latter, pp.
326–7, note 51). In *Unfinished Tales* Christopher Tolkien also gathered together
miscellaneous notes made by his father concerning the Drúedain, Púkel-men,
and Ghân-buri-Ghân (pp. 382–4, 387).

Without a new heading, the essay turns to a discussion of Faramir's classification of men into the High Men or Númenóreans, the Middle Men, and the
Men of Darkness (cf. *The Lord of the Rings*, Book IV, Chapter 5), the reasons
and history behind this classification, and languages spoken by the various
peoples. Much is said about the languages spoken in Númenor, and of the
relationship between the Númenóreans and the various groups of Men they
encountered when they returned to Middle-earth in the Second Age and after
the Downfall. A part of this section, relating the first meeting of Númenórean
mariners with Men of Eriador early in the Second Age, was earlier published
in *Unfinished Tales* (pp. 213–14, note 3); cf. *The Peoples of Middle-earth*, note
71, pp. 329–30. The essay turns finally to the languages spoken in Arnor and
Gondor, and the development of the Common Tongue or Westron from the
Adûnaic of the Númenóreans, before ending abruptly.

Tolkien wrote *Of Dwarves and Men* no earlier than late 1969. He began it in
manuscript, but after three and a half pages composed the rest of the twenty-
eight-page text on his typewriter. In this as in many of his late writings, the text
is accompanied by extensive notes by the author.

Within the notes for *Of Dwarves and Men*, p. 318, is a section from a late
text (not before 1968) on Eldarin words for 'hand' (**Eldarin Hands, Fingers &
Numerals*).

Dyson, Henry Victor Dyson (1896–1975). 'Hugo' Dyson read English at Exeter College, *Oxford, where as a member of the Essay Club (*Societies and
clubs) he heard Tolkien read *The Fall of Gondolin* (**The Book of Lost Tales*) on
10 March 1920. He took his B.A. in 1921, and in 1924 his B.Litt. From 1924 to
1945 he was a lecturer and tutor at University College, Reading (from 1926 the
University of Reading), especially concerned with Shakespeare, Dryden, Pope,
and Dickens. He also lectured at Oxford in University Extension Courses and
gave classes for the Workers' Educational Association. In Hilary Term 1937
he joined Tolkien, *Nevill Coghill, *C.S. Lewis, and *C.L. Wrenn in giving a
series of lectures on *Hamlet*. In 1945 he was elected Fellow and tutor of English
Literature at Merton College, Oxford, where he remained until his retirement
in 1963. (On 11 October 1945 Tolkien, who had just been installed himself at

Merton College, wrote to his son *Christopher: 'I walked round [Merton] this afternoon with Dyson who was duly elected yesterday, and is now ensconced in the rooms I hoped for, looking out over the meadows!' (*Letters*, p. 116).)

Dyson published only a handful of works, most notably *Augustans and Romantics, 1689–1830* (with John Butt et al., 1940) and a British Academy Lecture, *The Emergence of Shakespeare's Tragedy* (1952, read in 1950). His preference was always for talk: he loved to engage in conversation, often with a bellowing, booming voice. He is uniformly described as exuberant, gregarious, and outgoing. He revelled in company, though as one of the *Inklings he appeared only rarely at their Thursday meetings. *W.H. Lewis enjoyed his friendship, and included many anecdotes about him in his diaries (*Brothers and Friends*, ed. Clyde S. Kilby and Marjorie Lamp Mead (1982)); but even he found Dyson sometimes to be irritating, a noisy fellow who liked to dominate a conversation and, at meetings of the Inklings, preferred talk to the readings that were part of the group's purpose. He was famously impatient with readings from *The Lord of the Rings*, then a work in progress, and was allowed to veto them when he was present. According to A.N. Wilson, Tolkien 'could not be sure that his readings would not be interrupted by Dyson . . . snorting, grunting and exhaling – "Oh **** not another elf!"' (*C.S. Lewis: A Biography* (1990), p. 217). (The phrase is often mistakenly attributed to Lewis.)

Fellow Inkling *John Wain later wrote that no circle of which Dyson was a member

> could be said to remain the same. He was a *raconteur*, a barnstormer, a wit if your definition of wit includes knock-down-and-drag-out, a performer to his fingertips. I always felt that he was driven by inward nightmares into an endless routine of conviviality, and indeed his experiences in the First World War trenches had been enough to give a man nightmares for life if he lived a hundred years. The removal of Williams [at his death in 1945] dimmed the radiance of the Inklings' meetings; the accession of Dyson rekindled it, but with a smokier light. ['Push Bar to Open', *Oxford Magazine*, Hilary Term 1988, p. 4]

And yet he was also a man of intellect and insight, who had a notable influence on the life of C.S. Lewis. On 19 September 1931 Dyson and Tolkien had dinner with Lewis at Magdalen College, Oxford, and after the meal discussed metaphor and myth long into the night. It was this talk, Lewis said, that led him to progress from a mere belief in God to an acceptance of Christianity, having been convinced by Tolkien and Dyson that the story of Christ was a 'true myth' (see *The Inklings*, pp. 42–5).

Photographs of Hugo Dyson are reproduced in *The Inklings*, pl. 6b and 11a. See further, David Bratman, 'Hugo Dyson: Inkling, Teacher, Bon Vivant', *Mythlore* 21, no. 4, whole no. 82 (Winter 1997).

Tha Eadigan Saelidan *see* **The Happy Mariners**

Eagle and Child *see* **Oxford and environs**

Éalá Éarendel Engla Beorhtast. Poem, the latest version of which was published under this title, with commentary and divergent readings of the earliest extant version, in **The Book of Lost Tales, Part Two* (1984), pp. 267–9. Éarendel is the planet Venus crossing the night sky, but depicted as if a mariner in a sailing ship, launched 'like a silver spark / From the last and lonely sand'. He passes 'many a star / In his gleaming galleon', 'On an endless quest through the darkling West / O'er the margin of the world'.

The first eight lines of its original version, called *The Voyage of Éarendel the Evening Star*, were printed in *Biography*, p. 71, and (with one difference in capitalization) in *The Book of Lost Tales, Part Two*, p. 268. According to Christopher Tolkien, 'there are some five different versions, each one incorporating emendations made in the predecessor, though only the first verse was substantially rewritten.' The date of its latest version 'cannot be determined, though the handwriting shows it to be substantially later than the original composition' (*The Book of Lost Tales, Part Two*, p. 267). The title of the poem was changed in a later copy to *Éalá Éarendel Engla Beorhtast*.

That phrase comes from the Old English *Crist*, a group of poems in the medieval *Exeter Book*: 'Eala Earendel engla beorhtast / ofer middangeard monnum sended' ('Hail Earendel, brightest of angels, / above the middle-earth sent unto men'). In *Biography* Tolkien is quoted as writing, long afterwards, that on reading these lines he 'felt a curious thrill, as if something had stirred in me, half wakened from sleep. There was something very remote and strange and beautiful behind those words, if I could grasp it, far beyond ancient English' (p. 64. In August 1967 Tolkien explained in a draft letter to a Mr Rang that the name *Eärendil*, as it appears in **The Lord of the Rings*, was derived from Old English *earendel* – defined in Bosworth and Toller's dictionary as 'a shining light, ray', but in the *Crist* poem clearly with some special meaning. 'I was struck', Tolkien wrote,

> by the great beauty of this word (or name), entirely coherent with the normal style of A[nglo]-S[axon], but euphonic to a peculiar degree in that pleasing but not 'delectable' language. Also its form strongly suggests that it is in origin a proper name and not a common noun. This is borne out by the obviously related forms in other Germanic languages; from which amid the confusions and debasements of late traditions it at least seems certain that it belonged to astronomical-myth, and was the name of a star or star-group. To my mind the A[nglo]-S[axon] uses seem plainly to indicate that it was a star presaging the dawn (at any rate in English tradition): that is what we now call *Venus*: the morning-star [or sometimes evening star] as it may be seen shining brilliantly in the dawn, before the actual rising of the Sun. That is at any rate how I took it. Before 1914 I wrote a 'poem' upon Earendel who launched his ship like a bright spark from the havens of the Sun. I adopted him into my mythol-

ogy – in which he became a prime figure as a mariner, and eventually as a herald star, and a sign of hope to men. [Quenya] *Aiya Eärendil Elenion Ancalima* [in *The Lord of the Rings*, Book IV, Chapter 9] 'hail Earendil brightest of Stars' is derived at long remove from *Éala Éarendel engla beorhtast*. [*Letters*, p. 385]

In fact, the manuscript of the earliest extant version of the poem is dated 24 September 1914, when Tolkien was staying at Phoenix Farm, east of Nottingham, with his friends the *Brookes-Smith family. He read the poem to members of the Exeter College Essay Club (*Societies and clubs) on 27 November that same year.

Upon seeing a copy of *The Voyage of Éarendel the Evening Star*, Tolkien's friend *G.B. Smith asked what it was about, to which Tolkien is said to have replied: 'I don't know. I'll try to find out' (*Biography*, p. 75). His 'investigation' contributed to the evolution of the great *'Silmarillion' mythology that was to occupy him for the rest of his life. In this Eärendel (variously spelled) became an important character (see further, *'Of the Voyage of Eärendil and the War of Wrath'); and he appeared also in other early poems (*The Bidding of the Minstrel*, *The Shores of Faery*).

In *Biography* Humphrey Carpenter calls the poem 'the beginning of Tolkien's own mythology' (p. 71), and in one sense that is true: the work contains elements which also figure in the *legendarium*. But *The Voyage of Éarendel the Evening Star* was not at its writing intended to be part of a larger conception. Indeed it was later revised and recast, in one version, entitled *Classical*, with 'Phosphorus' in place of 'Éarendel'. (See also note for *The Shores of Faery*.)

Carl F. Hostetter discusses the poem at length in 'Over Middle-earth Sent unto Men: On the Philological Origins of Tolkien's Eärendel Myth', *Mythlore* 17, no. 3, whole no. 65 (Spring 1991).

Earendel at the Helm. Poem, first published in *The Monsters and the Critics and Other Essays* (1983), pp. 216–17, within the autobiographical lecture *A Secret Vice* (written ?Autumn 1931). *Earendel at the Helm* is the English-language version of the same work in Qenya (*Languages, Invented), called more simply *Earendel*, included in the lecture as an example of the author's 'vice' of language invention and its outlet in poetry. The mariner Earendel (Eärendil), a significant figure in *'The Silmarillion', here pilots his 'white ship in the sea gliding' along a 'road going on for ever ... / To havens in the West'. The poem celebrates the action of sailing, 'White froth at the prow spuming / Glistening in the sun'.

In his notes to *A Secret Vice* *Christopher Tolkien refers to a variant copy of the poem with Tolkien's later emendations.

'Early Chart of Names'. Chart of names in early forms of Tolkien's 'Elvish' languages (*Languages, Invented), published with commentary within 'Early Noldorin Fragments' in *Parma Eldalamberon* 13 (2001), pp. 98–9, ed. Christopher Gilson, Bill Welden, Carl F. Hostetter, and Patrick Wynne. Tolkien wrote the chart in the same notebook as the *Poetic and Mythologic Words of Eldarissa*, with which it is associated. 'All the names are given with an Eldarissa or Qenya version on the left, followed by an explanation or gloss in English, and for most items a Gnomish equivalent is given at the right' (p. 98). Its purpose seems to have been 'to outline the kinds of beings that appear in the poems and stories that Tolkien was writing' (p. 98) or had written at the time the *Qenyaqetsa* was substantially complete. It probably predates the composition of the *Gnomish Grammar* and *Gnomish Lexicon*.

See also *Parma Eldalamberon* 12 (1998), p. xx, and *Parma Eldalamberon* 14 (2003), pp. 5–6.

'Early Noldorin Grammar'. Unfinished grammar of the early 'Elvish' language Noldorin (*Languages, Invented), published with commentary within 'Early Noldorin Fragments' in *Parma Eldalamberon* 13 (2001), pp. 119–32, ed. Christopher Gilson, Bill Welden, Carl F. Hostetter, and Patrick Wynne. Entitled *Lam i·Ngolthor*, changed to *Lam na·NGoluith*, it 'begins with a brief description of the definite article, which leads into a detailed discussion. Following this is a description of the ways of forming plural nouns and adjectives, and a brief discussion of noun phrases. The document, mainly handwritten, ends, incomplete, after a final section on the comparison of adjectives' (p. 119). There are also two closely related pages of verb conjugations. Tolkien wrote the work on examination paper from the University of *Leeds, thus *c.* 1921–5. The editors comment that 'the grammar of the noun shows a considerable development' (p. 119) from the *Gnomish Grammar* accompanying the *Gnomish Lexicon*.

'Early Qenya Grammar'
 see **Qenya: Descriptive Grammar of the Qenya Language**

'Early Qenya Pronouns'. Fragments of series of tables of Qenya (*Languages, Invented) pronouns and pronominal prefixes and suffixes, published with commentary and notes in *Parma Eldalamberon* 15 (2004), pp. 41–58, ed. Christopher Gilson. Tolkien wrote these on sheets of paper later torn into slips, some of which were reused in compiling an English–Old English dictionary, and the remainder presumably discarded. Internal evidence seems to suggest that the pronominal forms 'represent a conceptual stage of the language intermediary between' the *Qenyaqetsa* (*c.* 1915–*c.* 1919) and *Qenya: Descriptive Grammar of the Qenya Language* (*c.* 1923).

Earp, Thomas Wade (1892–1958). T.W. Earp attended Exeter College, *Oxford contemporary with Tolkien, and was a fellow member of its Essay Club and Stapeldon Society (*Societies and clubs). His path crossed Tolkien's from time to time: in October 1914, as Tolkien wrote to Edith Bratt (*Edith Tolkien), 'I went and had an interesting talk with that quaint man Earp I have told you of and introduced him (to his great delight) to the *"Kālevalā" the Finnish ballads' (*Letters*, p. 7). But they seem never to have been more than acquaintances. Earp moved in more rarefied circles. He was elegant and cosmopolitan, the son of a wealthy banker, the friend of artists and writers, at the centre of undergraduate life at Oxford but also with connections to the wider world. He held office in student societies, including the Oxford Union; *Roy Campbell, a contemporary at university, called him 'the uncrowned King of Oxford' (*Light on a Dark Horse: An Autobiography (1901–1935)* (1952), p. 165). He was also an amateur poet: some of his verses were published in the *Stapeldon Magazine* and in *Oxford Poetry* from 1914 to 1918. He was co-editor of *Oxford Poetry* for 1915, for which he selected Tolkien's *Goblin Feet* – together with six works of his own, all of a modern character and relatively unimaginative. On 22 December 1915 *G.B. Smith wrote to Tolkien disparaging Earp's poems in *Oxford Poetry 1915*, compared with those by himself, Tolkien, and Smith's friend *H.T. Wade-Gery, 'much the best contributors' to the volume (Tolkien Papers, Bodleian Library, Oxford).

Later Earp was one of the 'Oxford Group' of poets with *Wilfred Childe, and a contributor to the important if short-lived periodical *Coterie* (1919–20). He had ties to Bloomsbury and to Lady Ottoline Morrell's *salon* at Garsington, Oxfordshire. He was concerned since his younger days with the relationship between art and society, and was well placed to study it. He became an art critic of long standing for the *Daily Telegraph*, and published several books, most notably works on Augustus John and Vincent Van Gogh (both 1934), and *French Painting* (1945).

Eddas *see* Northernness

Eddison, Eric Rucker (1882–1945). Educated at Trinity College, *Oxford, E.R. Eddison for most of his life was a civil servant, until his retirement in 1938 employed by the British Board of Trade in a variety of posts. In private life he taught himself Old Norse, translated *Egil's Saga* into Modern English (1930), and produced romances in archaic prose, some of which today are considered classics of fantasy fiction. His most famous book is *The Worm Ouroboros* (1922), concerned with the struggle between the lords of Demonland and the Witches of Carcë, and featuring characters such as Goldry Bluszco, Brandoch Daha, and the Lord Gro. Eddison also wrote the adventure *Styrbiorn the Strong* (1926) and two novels of 'Zimiamvia' (a land glimpsed in the *Worm*), *Mistress of Mistresses* (1935) and *A Fish Dinner in Memison* (1941). A third 'Zimiamvia' book, *The Mezentian Gate*, was assembled from notes and published posthumously in 1958.

The Worm Ouroboros is often set beside *The Lord of the Rings*, though an apt comparison, as Douglas E. Winter has said, does not extend beyond 'their narrative ambition and epic sweep' (foreword to *The Worm Ouroboros*, 1991 edn., p. xii). And yet this and other works by Eddison, because of their strength of story and skill in the telling, appealed to Tolkien and to friends such as *C.S.

Lewis. After reading the *Worm* in 1942, Lewis invited Eddison to a meeting of the *Inklings: this took place on 18 February 1943 at Magdalen College, with Tolkien present. On 8 June 1944 Eddison attended a second Inklings meeting, at which he read from *The Mezentian Gate* as a work in progress. On that occasion Tolkien found Eddison to be 'of undiminished power and felicity of expression' (letter to Christopher Tolkien, 10 June 1944, *Letters*, p. 84). Tolkien later wrote that he read Eddison's works

long after they appeared . . . with great enjoyment for their sheer literary merit. My opinion of them is almost the same as that expressed by Mr. Lewis on p. 104 of the *Essays Presented to Charles Williams* [in 'On Stories': 'You may like or dislike his invented worlds (I myself like that of *The Worm Ouroboros* and strongly dislike that of *Mistress of Mistresses*) but there is no quarrel between the theme and the articulation of the story.']. Except that I disliked his characters (always excepting the Lord Gro) and despised what he appeared to admire more intensely than Mr. Lewis at any rate saw fit to say of himself. Eddison thought what I admire 'soft' (his word: one of complete condemnation, I gathered); I thought that, corrupted by an evil and indeed silly 'philosophy', he was coming to admire, more and more, arrogance and cruelty. Incidentally, I thought his nomenclature slipshod and often inept. In spite of all of which, I still think of him as the greatest and most convincing writer of 'invented worlds' that I have read. But he was certainly not an 'influence' [on Tolkien]. [letter to Caroline Everett, 24 June 1957, *Letters*, p. 258]

The best editions of *The Worm Ouroboros* and the 'Zimiamvia' novels (collected as *Zimiamvia: A Trilogy*) were published by Dell, New York, in 1991 and 1992 respectively, introduced and annotated by Paul Edmund Thomas.

'Of Eldamar and the Princes of the Eldalië'. The fifth chapter of the *'Quenta Silmarillion', published in *The Silmarillion* (1977), pp. 57–62.

SUMMARY

Oromë leads the Elves to the shores of Beleriand. When the hosts of the Vanyar and Noldor arrive, they embark on an island uprooted by Ulmo, who draws it across the sea to Valinor. The Teleri who dwell far inland hear the summons late and are left behind; when they reach the sea they dwell long near the mouths of the River Sirion, and the Maia Ossë teaches them 'all manner of sea-lore and sea-music' (*The Silmarillion*, p. 58). Elwë's brother Olwë becomes their king. After many years, at the request of Finwë and the Noldor in Valinor, Ulmo returns to bring the Teleri to Valinor. Ossë is grieved, 'for his care was for the seas of Middle-earth and the shores of the Hither Lands, and he was ill-pleased that the voices of the Teleri should be heard no more in his domain' (p. 58). He persuades some to remain in Middle-earth: these are the

Elves of Falas, whose lord is Círdan the Shipwright. Those still seeking Elwë (Thingol) also remain, and when he awakes dwell with him and Melian in the woods of Beleriand.

Ossë follows after the host of Olwë, and in response to his voice the Teleri beg Ulmo to halt their voyage; thus the island on which they are ferried is anchored in the Bay of Eldamar. Ulmo grants this request 'the more readily, for he understood the hearts of the Teleri,' and had counselled against bringing the Elves to Valinor. The Teleri live long on this island, Tol Eressëa, the Lonely Isle, within sight of Valinor, and their speech becomes sundered from that of the Vanyar and Noldor. Light from the Two Trees reaches the western shore of the Lonely Isle through the Calacirya, a gap the Valar made in the mountains protecting Valinor so that the Vanyar and Noldor could build in it a city – Tirion on the hill of Túna – which received the light of the Trees from the west, but also looked east to the sea and the stars. In the courts of Tirion beneath the Tower of Ingwë is planted Galathilion, a tree 'like to a lesser image of Telperion' (p. 59), made for them by Yavanna. A sapling (Celeborn) from this tree will later grow on Tol Eressëa, and from Celeborn will come 'Nimloth, the White Tree of Númenor' (p. 59).

Manwë and Varda love most the Vanyar, but Aulë loves the Noldor whom he teaches much. The Noldor have a great thirst for knowledge: they love words, changing and developing their speech; they are great builders; and they cut and shape gems they find in the ground.

Then follows a list of the princes of the Noldor, descendants of Finwë: Fëanor his son by his first wife, Míriel, and Fëanor's seven sons; and Finwë's two sons by Indis his second wife – Fingolfin, and his sons Fingon and Turgon and daughter Aredhel; and Finarfin, who with his wife Eärwen, daughter of Olwë, has four sons, Finrod, Orodreth, Angrod, and Aegnor, and one daughter, Galadriel.

The desire of the Teleri for the light of Valinor and to see their kindred again having grown, Ossë teaches them the craft of shipbuilding and sends swans to draw their ships to Valinor. They settle on the shores of Eldamar and build the harbour of Alqualondë. The Noldor give them many jewels, and they themselves find pearls in the sea.

After ages have past, the Vanyar, desiring the full light of the Trees, leave Tirion to dwell on Taniquetil or on the plains and woods of Valinor. The Noldor remain in Tirion though they, especially Fëanor and his sons, often journey elsewhere.

HISTORY

The earliest version of this chapter, written probably in early 1919, forms the second part of *The Coming of the Elves and the Making of Kôr* in *The Book of Lost Tales* (c. 1916–20). In this the story is told at much greater length and with more detail, and differs in several respects. There are several differences in nomenclature: for instance, the Vanyar, Noldor, and Teleri are here respectively the Teleri, the Noldoli, and the Solosimpi. Also the character of the Valar is less elevated, less dignified, and the Noldorin genealogy is little developed. Ossë, in this stage of the evolution of the mythology a Vala, objects when Ulmo, eager to bring the Elves to Valinor, without consulting him ferries them on the island Ossë had used to transport the Valar. The Teleri and Noldoli are conveyed across the Great Sea separately, on the island drawn by Ulmo's greatest fish and his mightiest whale, Uin. The Solosimpi come last to the shores of Middle-earth and wait long for Ulmo's return, which Ossë hinders with storms. When they have crossed less than half of the Great Sea Ossë, with the aid of his spouse Ónen, anchors the island to the sea bed and Ulmo is unable to move it: 'Vainly doth Ulmo trumpet and Uin with the flukes of his unmeasured tail lash the seas to wrath, for thither Ossë now brings every kind of deep sea creature that buildeth itself a house and dwelling of stony shell; and these he planted about the base of the island: corals there were of every kind and barnacles and sponges like stone' (*The Book of Lost Tales, Part One*, p. 120). The Lonely Isle is thus situated in the midst of the Great Sea, not close to Valinor, but because it has twice come close enough to Valinor to receive light from the Trees it is fair and fertile. Thus isolated, the speech and customs of the Solosimpi develop differently from those of the Elves in Valinor.

Manwë's love for the Teleri and Aulë's for the Noldoli, who had a great desire for knowledge, are already present, but it also said that from Manwë and Ómar (a Vala who appears only in *The Book of Lost Tales*) the Teleri learn the craft of song and poesy. The city of Kôr (later Tirion) is described in greater detail:

> Upon the hill-top the Elves built fair abodes of shining white – of marbles and stone quarried from the Mountains of Valinor that glistened wondrously, silver and gold and a substance of great hardness and white lucency that they contrived of shells melted in the dew of Silpion [Telperion], and white streets there were bordered with dark trees that wound with graceful turns or climbed with flights of delicate stairs up from the plain of Valinor to topmost Kôr . . . till the house of Ingwë was reached that was the uppermost, and had a slender tower shooting skyward like a needle, and a white lamp of piercing ray was set therein that shone upon the shadows of the bay, but every window of the city on the hill of Kôr looked out toward the sea. [*The Book of Lost Tales, Part One*, p. 122]

The Valar give shoots of the Trees to Inwë, leader of the Teleri, and to Finwë Nólemë, leader of the Noldoli.

Ossë introduces many seabirds to Tol Eressëa, especially swans, and the Solosimpi who have already built rafts to use on the lakes of the island harness the birds to draw their craft. Ulmo, who wants the Solosimpi brought to Valinor, brings Aulë and Oromë to Tol Eressëa where they make great boats in the shape of swans, and in these drawn by birds they escort the Solosimpi to Valinor. Then follows a description of the various isles in the Great Sea, and of the shores of Valinor.

The Solosimpi are welcomed by the Teleri and Noldoli and choose to dwell on the shores. From Ulmo they learn much lore and the love of music. They fare on the sea in swanships and find many pearls. How the Noldoli gather together fair materials and fashion the first gems is described in great detail. Nothing is said here of the descendants of Nólemë, nor much elsewhere in *The Book of Lost Tales*: Fëanor is not his son, though Fëanor's seven sons appear in some outlines for the later, unfinished tales. The only children of Nólemë are his son Turgon, who becomes king of Gondolin, and his daughter Isfin.

The genealogy of the rulers of the Noldoli began to evolve, however, in the various works that Tolkien wrote in the first half of the 1920s. In an untitled prose fragment ('*The Gnomes Come to the Great Lands*') Gelmir (possibly another name for Finn/Finwë Nólemë), the king of the Gnomes (Noldoli) who returns to Middle-earth, has three sons, Golfin, Delin, and Lúthien, but is unrelated to Fëanor. The unfinished *Lay of the Fall of Gondolin* refers to Gelmir's heir, Fingolfin, whose children are Turgon and Isfin. During the writing of the alliterative *Children of Húrin* (c. 1919–25) and by emendation, Fingolfin becomes the son of Finwë and has two sons, Finweg (changed to *Fingon*) and Turgon; and the seven sons of Fëanor are named. In the poem *The Flight of the Noldoli from Valinor* Fëanor is called 'Finn's son' (*The Lays of Beleriand*, p. 133).

In the *Sketch of the Mythology* (c. 1926) the Quendi (formerly the Teleri) and the Noldoli are transported together. The Teleri (formerly the Solosimpi) during their long wait for Ulmo to return have grown to love the Sea. When they are eventually being ferried on an island to Valinor, Ossë now anchors it not in the middle of the sea but 'far out in the bay of Faërie whence the Mountains of Valinor could dimly be seen' (*The Shaping of Middle-earth*, pp. 13–14). The city of the Elves in Valinor is now called Tûn, on the hill of Côr. The Noldoli still 'invent' and 'make' gems. Fëanor becomes one of the two sons of Finwë or Finn, originally the younger, but by emendation the elder. The other son is Fingolfin, whose son is Finnweg. A passage added later also mentions Turgon and Isfin as children of Fingolfin, and by emendation Felagund, Orodreth, Anrod, and Egnor as the sons of Finrod. Eventually attracted by the distant light of Valinor and wishing to travel there, the Teleri are taught to build boats by Ulmo, and by Ossë are given swans to draw their ships.

The *Quenta Noldorinwa* (c. 1930), expanding upon the *Sketch*, describes how Ossë grew to love the Teleri as they waited on the shores of Middle-earth, and that he persuaded some to stay there. On an inserted slip Tolkien introduced the removal of the Lindar (i.e. the Quendi, Vanyar) from the city of Kôr to live in the full light of the Trees on the plains of Valinor.

The 'earliest' *Annals of Valinor*, written in the early 1930s, give a time span for these events. Originally the making of the stars, the waking of the Elves, and the arrival of the Quendi and Noldoli in Valinor all seem to have taken place in Valian Year 2000. The Teleri remain on the shores of Beleriand from 2000 to 2100 (100 Valian years = 1,000 of our years), spend a further one hundred Valian Years on Tol Eressëa, and come to Valinor only in 2200. The

Noldoli begin to make their gems at about 2500. By emendations, possibly not all at the same time, the Elves awake in 1950 and begin their march in 1980, the Quendi and Noldoli reach Valinor in 2000, the Teleri leave Beleriand in 2010, and they reach Valinor in 2111. In an Old English version of the tale, Finrod's eldest son became *Inglor Felagund*. The dates remained unchanged in the 'later' *Annals of Valinor*, probably written a few years later in the mid-1930s. The Noldoli there became the Noldor, and the Quendi the Lindar.

In the *Quenta Silmarillion*, also of the mid-1930s, material relevant to the *Silmarillion* chapter is part of a long third chapter, 'Of the Coming of the Elves', mainly from the subheading 'Of Kôr and Alqualondë'. Movements towards the final *Silmarillion* text include Oromë leading the Elves to the land near the River Sirion, Ossë instructing the Teleri on the shores of Middle-earth, and that those persuaded to stay there became the Elves of the Falas. It is now said that ages passed before the Vanyar left Túna to dwell near Manwë; that the Noldor were changeful of speech; that Fëanor and his sons rarely stayed long in one place, but travelled widely in Valinor; that it was in response to a request from the Teleri wishing to take leave of Ossë and look their last on a sky filled with stars that Ulmo halted the movement of the island; and that Ossë seized the opportunity and anchored the island in the Bay of Elvenhome. But in contradiction to his feelings as described in *The Silmarillion*, Ulmo is said to have been angry at their request, and was later responsible for teaching them to build ships.

When Tolkien revised the *Quenta Silmarillion c.* 1951 the last part of Chapter 3 in the 1930s text, 'Of Kôr and Alqualondë', became Chapter 5 with the title 'Of Eldanor [*sic*] and the Princes of the Eldalië'. In this Tolkien mainly emended the old text and did little rewriting, but more significant changes include the description of the tree Yavanna made for the Noldor as one 'in all things like a lesser image of Telperion, save that it did not give light of its own being' (*Morgoth's Ring*, p. 176). Ulmo's displeasure at the Teleri's request to halt their voyage now disappeared, and it is on his orders that Ossë anchors Tol Eressëa near the shore of Aman. It is now also stated that Ulmo had opposed the decision of the Valar to summon the Elves to Valinor. In a later addition, instead of contriving the fashioning of gems the Noldor, quarrying for stone, discover them in the earth and carve and fashion them 'in shapes of bright beauty' (*Morgoth's Ring*, p. 181). By later emendation Finrod became *Finarphin*, and Inglor became *Finrod*.

In the *Annals of Aman* (*c.* 1951, see *Annals of Valinor*), in which the years are reckoned from the creation of the Trees, the first Elves now reach the shores of the Great Sea in Year 1125; the Vanyar and the Noldor embark on the island in 1132, reach Valinor in 1133, and finish Tirion upon Túna in 1140. Also in 1140 Ingwë and many of the Vanyar leave Tirion to live with the people of Manwë. In 1142 Yavanna gives Galathilion, the image of Telperion, to the Noldor. In 1149 Ulmo goes to fetch the Teleri, and in 1150 begins to ferry those who are willing to leave. Círdan the Shipwright is now named as the lord of those who choose to remain by the shores of Middle-earth. Kinsfolk and friends of Elwë also stay. Ossë anchors Tol Eressëa near Aman in 1151. The Teleri stay on Tol Eressëa only for one hundred years of our reckoning, and reach Valinor in 1161. By emendation it is Ossë, not Ulmo, who teaches them to build ships. In 1165 the last of the Vanyar leave Tirion. In 1179 Fëanor is born and (by emendations) the Noldor discover earth-gems.

The entries for marriages and births in the House of Finwë originally showed little change apart from the introduction of Galadriel from *The Lord of the Rings* as the daughter of Finrod. Later additions and emendations introduce the root of so much dissension arising from the remarriage of Finwë after the passing of his first wife, Míriel, and Fëanor's resentment of his half-brothers. Some of these dates, with similar entries, also appear in the *Grey Annals* (*c.* 1951, see *Annals of Beleriand*).

The text published in *The Silmarillion* was derived from the *Annals of Aman*, the *Grey Annals*, and the *c.* 1951 *Quenta Silmarillion*, taking up some later emendations and additions. The earlier part depends mainly on the two *Annals*, and the later part almost entirely on the *Quenta Silmarillion*. *Christopher Tolkien evidently made some editorial changes to replace usages such as 'gods' (for the Valar) and to introduce later important developments in the Noldorin genealogy and nomenclature. Some of these changes were made by Tolkien when he was working on other chapters of the *Quenta Silmarillion* in 1959. Probably in association with this work, in December 1959 Tolkien made a set of four Elvish genealogies, mainly of the descendants of Finwë, which he emended in later years, especially when writing about Finwë's descendants in 1968 or later in *The Shibboleth of Fëanor*. Christopher Tolkien mentions these genealogies in *The War of the Jewels*, p. 229, but discusses them further in *The Peoples of Middle-earth*, pp. 349–51 and p. 359, n. 26.

Eldarin Hands, Fingers & Numerals. Essay, published with commentary and notes as part of '*Eldarin Hands, Fingers & Numerals* and Related Writings' in *Vinyar Tengwar* 47 (February 2005), pp. 3–42, ed. Patrick H. Wynne. It is described by *Vinyar Tengwar* editor Carl F. Hostetter as

an account of the Common Eldarin words for 'hand' and their descendants in Quenya, Telerin, and Sindarin [*Languages, Invented], followed by a brief discussion of Elvish ambidexterity. The essay then details the Eldarin names for the fingers (and toes), including children's 'play-names' that treat the fingers as members of an imaginary family . . . ; and it concludes by showing how the finger-names were closely connected with the development of numerical stems in Common Eldarin. [Then follows] a related [untitled] text on the invention of the Common Eldarin stems for *neter* 9, *kanat* 4, and *enek* 6, which serves as a sort of alternative ending to the essay. [p. 2]

Both texts, a nine-page typescript emended in manuscript and three manuscript pages respectively, date from *c.* 1968. The editorial notes draw extensively from Tolkien's unpublished writings, including a revised version of the beginning of the third section ('The Fingers') of the first text. Patrick H. Wynne comments that Christopher Tolkien quoted two sentences from the first text in *The Shaping of Middle-earth*, p. 187, giving the legendary origin of the Sindarin name *Mablung*, and almost the whole of the entry for *quár* 'fist' in relation to Celebrimbor in *The Peoples of Middle-earth*, p. 318.

See also *'Synopsis of Pengoloð's *Eldarinwe Leperi are Notessi*'.

The Elessar
see *The History of Galadriel and Celeborn and of Amroth King of Lórien*

'**Elvish Reincarnation**'. 'Discussion of the question of Elvish reincarnation' within Tolkien's mythology, but the extract published in *The Peoples of Middle-earth* (1996), pp. 382–4, is concerned rather with the Dwarves' belief that the spirits of their Seven Fathers were occasionally reborn in their kindreds. The Longbeard Dwarves reported that their successive rulers named Durin 'retained memory of their former lives as Kings, as real, and yet naturally as incomplete as if they had been consecutive years of life in one person' (p. 383).

The work exists in two versions, the first a rough draft, partly written on one of the manuscripts of *Glorfindel*, probably from 1972–3. A brief account of Aulë's making of the Dwarves (see *'Of Aulë and Yavanna') is omitted from the extract in *The Peoples of Middle-earth* apart from its conclusion, noting the Dwarves' belief that Aulë had gained for them the privilege that the spirit of each of the Fathers, after a long life, would fall asleep, 'then lie in a tomb of his own body, at rest, and there its weariness and any hurts that had befallen it should be amended. Then after long years he should arise and take up his kingship again' (p. 383). The second text suggests, however, that this is not a case of rebirth 'but of the preservation of the *body* of a former King Durin (say) to which at intervals his spirit would return' (p. 384).

*Christopher Tolkien notes that in this discussion, as in *Reincarnation of Elves*, his father discussed the idea that Elvish reincarnation might be achieved by 'rebirth' but rejected it because of physical and psychological difficulties. The idea, Tolkien wrote, 'must be abandoned, or at least noted as a false notion, e.g. probably of Mannish origin, since nearly all the matter of *The Silmarillion* is contained in myths and legends that have passed through Men's hands and minds . . .' (p. 390, note 17).

Elvish Song in Rivendell. Poem, published in *The Annotated Hobbit* (rev. and expanded edn. 2002), pp. 92–3. Its writing appears to date from the early 1930s, thus contemporary with at least part of the writing of *The Hobbit*. Of its two extant manuscripts, the earliest also contains a version of *Shadow-Bride*. The 'elvish song' is one of homecoming ('Come home, come home, ye merry folk!') as the sun sets, 'the shades of evening loom', and 'the early stars now spring'. Its hearty encouragement to 'Sing merrily, sing merrily, sing all together!' recalls the last of the three elf-songs published in *The Hobbit* in 1937 ('Sing all ye joyful, now sing all together!').

Emery, Augustine. Father Augustine Emery was the Roman Catholic priest in the Staffordshire village of *Great Haywood when Tolkien's wife *Edith moved there in April 1916. He welcomed the Tolkiens and gave them a special nuptial blessing at Sunday Mass, as they had not had one after their marriage service in March. *Priscilla Tolkien has recalled that her mother, a fine pianist, spoke of 'the comfort and pleasure she had during this time from making music with Fr. Emery, who played the violin' ('J.R.R. Tolkien and Edith Tolkien's Stay in Staffordshire 1916, 1917 and 1918', *Angerthas* 34 (July 1993), p. 4). 'Uncle Gus' became a close family friend, and godfather to the Tolkiens' second son, *Michael. In spring 1931 the family spent a holiday at *Milford-on-Sea, Hampshire, where Father Emery now lived.

The End of the Third Age: The History of The Lord of the Rings, Part IV. The first part of *Sauron Defeated* (1992), with draft texts, etc. for *The Lord of the Rings*, Book VI and the unpublished Epilogue, together with notes and commentary by *Christopher Tolkien. It has been published both as a separate volume and as part of a set with the other volumes of *The History of Middle earth* devoted to the writing of *The Lord of the Rings* (*The Return of the Shadow*, *The Treason of Isengard*, *The War of the Ring*).

England. Tolkien considered himself to be *English* rather than *British*. He wrote to his son *Christopher on 9 December 1943: 'I love England (not Great Britain and certainly not the British Commonwealth (grr!))' (*Letters*, p. 65). In 1946, when he stayed at New Lodge, *Stonyhurst, he filled in his nationality in the guest book as 'English', breaking a line of dittos under the topmost entry, 'British'.

Years after his return from a holiday in Italy in 1955, Tolkien wrote:

As the train carried me from the seaport back into the heart of my own land, suddenly I saw it as I had not seen it since I was very young, when nothing (not even grass) had become familiar. The trees were nobler and taller than tired memory had made them, the grass was greener, the very way in which the land was shaped, or had been ordered and laid out by my own people was beautiful, loveable, fair, dear as being homelike, but seen with unfamiliar eyes. I knew then that I had missed the quiet richness, the soft distances, the gentle skies, the cool shadows and pale gold of Southern England, and back at last in my own small garden . . . I stopped suddenly to hear the voices of birds – natives like myself of this land, and not afraid to declare it. In the land that I had visited they are silent and furtive. [from a draft preface to 'The Golden Key' by *George MacDonald (see *Smith of Wootton Major*), Tolkien Papers, Bodleian Library, Oxford]

His deepest loyalty was to the *West Midlands, in particular to the area around Evesham, the area from which his mother's family, the *Suffields, came. On 18 March 1941 he wrote to his son *Michael: 'Though a Tolkien by name, I am a Suffield by tastes, talents, and upbringing, and any corner of that county [Worcestershire] (however fair or squalid) is in an indefinable way "home" to me, as no other part of the world is' (*Letters*, p. 54). On 12 December 1963 he wrote to Nancy Smith that his '"patriotism" generally embraces most of Europe, but its heart is the March-counties, especially Hereford, Shropshire, Worcester, and Staffordshire, and the rest of this island I regard as somewhat alien & inferior (especially linguistically). A fact which has some bearing on the placing of Hobbiton & Michel Delving in the West Farthing' (Special Collections and University Archives, John P. Raynor, S.J., Library, Marquette University).

In this Tolkien referred to the counties almost certainly as he knew them in his youth. As David Bratman notes in his article 'In Search of the Shire: Tolkien and the Counties of England', *Mallorn* 37 (December 1999), whereas it is of great interest to Tolkien enthusiasts to know the location of the counties associated with him, 'this is not as easy as it may seem . . . unless one is familiar with the history of local government in the U.K.' (p. 5). County boundaries have changed over the years, for administrative reasons or as urban areas have spread into the countryside. For instance, when Tolkien lived in *Sarehole it was in Worcestershire, but in 1911 was annexed by Birmingham, becoming nominally part of Warwickshire, and in 1973 became part of the West Midlands urban county.

Tolkien's feelings for England were expressed also in the special position it occupied in his *legendarium*. He told Milton Waldman in ?late 1951:

I was from early days grieved by the poverty of my own beloved country: it had no stories of its own (bound up with its tongue and soil), not of the quality that I sought, and found (as an ingredient) in legends of other lands . . . nothing English, save impoverished chap-book stuff. . . .
Once upon a time . . . I had a mind to make a body of more or less connected legend, ranging from the large and cosmogonic, to the level of romantic fairy-story . . . which I could dedicate simply to: to England; to my country. It should possess the tone and quality that I desired, somewhat cool and clear, be redolent of our 'air' (the clime and soil of the North West, meaning Britain and the hither parts of Europe . . . it should be 'high', purged of the gross, and fit for the more adult mind of a land long now steeped in poetry. [*Letters*, pp. 144–5]

In the unfinished *Book of Lost Tales* Eriol (*Eriol and Ælfwine), a mariner from the ancestral lands of the Anglo-Saxons, finds his way to the Lonely Isle, Tol Eressëa, and hears from the Elves who live there a series of tales concerning their history and the creation of the world. Notes by Tolkien for tales left unwritten suggest that the Elves would attempt to rescue their kin in the lands to the East, transported thither on the Lonely Isle, which would actually become England; and the descendants of Eriol, the English, would preserve the true tradition of the Elves (or Fairies), one more true than that found in Celtic lore. In a useful survey of the relationship between Tolkien's mythology and England, Sarah Beach wrote of the moving of Tol Eressëa: 'With this stroke of geopoesis, Tolkien has made his true land of Faery, the land of the Elves, into the England he loves. He has done it on a mythic level, involving the god-like personages of Ulmo and Ossë. This geographical relocation (from the West of his imagination to the actual, "real-world", position of England) is merely the beginning of his creating a unity of identity between Tol Eressëa and England' ('A Myth for Angle-land: J.R.R. Tolkien and Creative Mythology', *Mythlore* 15, no. 4, whole no. 58 (Summer 1989), p. 33).

Later Tolkien abandoned the physical link of Tol Eressëa becoming England, but continued a special relationship between the Elves and Anglo-Saxons or English. The Elves' name for England was *Luthany*, meaning 'friendship'. Tolkien's notes for *The Book of Lost Tales* tell of Luthany as 'the only land where Men and Elves once dwelt an age in peace and love', and 'How Old English became the sole mortal language which an Elf will speak to a mortal that knows no Elfin' (*The Book of Lost Tales, Part Two*, p. 304). Still later, the link became even less close, but most of the 'lost tales' were supposed to have been learned from the Elves or read in their records by Ælfwine, an Anglo-Saxon who succeeded in reaching Tol Eressëa.

On hearing the reference to *Earendel* in the Old English *Crist*, Tolkien felt 'as if something had stirred in me, half wakened from sleep. There was something very remote and strange and beautiful behind those words, if I could grasp it, far beyond ancient English' (quoted in *Biography*, p. 64; see **Éalá Éarendel Engla Beorhtast*). In 'And the Word Was Made Flesh', *Mallorn* 32 (September 1995), Clive Tolley comments:

> One thing that stands out in Tolkien's use of *earendel* is his dramatic description of his imaginative encounter with the word itself and its context in Old English: vistas opened up of the lost mythological and literary wealth of Germania, things that might have been, had our records been more profuse. Tolkien is inspired above all by fragments that can be reassembled through comparative philology and mythology. He did not however reassemble them into what they had been, by means of academic research, but into something new: he builds a new tower out of the stray bricks of the old, to use the metaphor he employed in his great article on *Beowulf*. [p. 9]

In *Biography* Humphrey Carpenter speculates that Tolkien may have been inspired by the **Kalevala*, a nineteenth-century collection of traditional poems organized into a more or less continuous narrative and supplemented with new verse by Elias Lönnrot, which became the mythology of Finland, to try to do something similar: to create a 'mythology for England' (p. 59).

Compared with Lönnrot, Tolkien had very little older material to use, and the
*'Silmarillion' is almost entirely his own work. The *Kalevala* may indeed have
inspired Tolkien to write *The Book of Lost Tales* (begun late 1916), but the quotation from Tolkien's paper on the *Kalevala* which Carpenter cites to support
his speculation ('I would that we had more of it [mythological ballads] left –
something of the same sort that belonged to the English', p. 59) does not appear
in the manuscript of the paper (written 1914–15), only in the typescript version
Tolkien made in the early 1920s, after *The Book of Lost Tales* was abandoned.

Tolkien did include, at least in early versions of the *Lost Tales*, elements
derived from Anglo-Saxon history and literature. Tom Shippey has said
of these: 'Clearly . . . the idea was to fit in all the little bits and pieces which
philologists during the 19th and 20th centuries had uncovered from the English stories which would have made a mythology for England, if only it had
not all got lost' ('Long Evolution: *The History of Middle-earth* and Its Merits', *Arda* 1987 (1992), p. 24). And Carl F. Hostetter and Arden R. Smith have
demonstrated, 'through an examination of five figures of Tolkien's mythology,
Eärendil, Ermon and Elmir, Ælfwine, and Ingwë . . . that English geography,
language, and mythology are all incorporated into Tolkien's creation. Thus
even as Tolkien developed a mythology for his Elvish languages [*Languages,
Invented], he encompassed in it a mythology for England' ('A Mythology for
England' in *Proceedings of the J.R.R. Tolkien Centenary Conference 1992* (1995),
p. 282). Eventually *The Lord of the Rings* also was drawn into its scope: originally a sequel to *The Hobbit*, it soon became an extension of the *'Silmarillion',
recognized by Tolkien in a draft reply to a 'Mr Thompson', who had written a
'kind and encouraging letter' about *The Lord of the Rings*, then recently published: 'Having set myself a task, the arrogance of which I fully recognized
and trembled at: being precisely to restore to the English an epic tradition and
present them with a mythology of their own: it is a wonderful thing to be told
that I have succeeded, at least with those who have still the undarkened heart
and mind' (14 January 1956, *Letters*, pp. 230–1).

In *The Lord of the Rings* the culture of the Rohirrim is closely based on that
of the Anglo-Saxons, except for their use of horses. T.A. Shippey has pointed
out that their names and the fragments of their language are in what is thought
to have been the Mercian form of Old English spoken in the *West Midlands.
Also, as Tolkien wrote to his publishers on 12 December 1955, 'the Shire . . . is
in fact more or less a Warwickshire village of about the period of the Diamond
Jubilee' (*Letters*, p. 230). It was for such reasons that he was unhappy when
translators of *The Lord of the Rings* wished to change its English names, and
that he fought so hard, if in vain, to preserve the Englishness of his creation
(see *Translations). On 3 July 1956 he wrote to Rayner Unwin:

> But, of course, if we drop the 'fiction' of long ago, 'The Shire' is based on
> rural England and not any other country in the world – least perhaps of
> any in Europe on Holland. . . . The toponymy of *The Shire* . . . is a 'parody'
> of that of rural England, in much the same sense as are its inhabitants:

they go together and are meant to. After all the book is English, and by an Englishman, and presumably even those who wish its narrative and dialogue turned into an idiom that they understand, will not ask of a translator that he should deliberately attempt to destroy the local colour. [*Letters*, p. 250]

On 11 September 1959 he wrote to Allen & Unwin in response to queries from the Polish translator: 'As she perceives, this is an English book and its Englishry should not be eradicated. That the Hobbits actually spoke an ancient language of their own is a pseudo-historical assertion made necessary by the nature of the narrative' (*Letters*, p. 299). In a letter to Mrs L.M. Cutts on 26 October 1958 he was equally emphatic: if *The Lord of the Rings* 'is "English" – (not British, please) – that is because I am English' (quoted in Sotheby's, *English Literature, History, Fine Bindings, Private Press Books, Children's Books, Illustrated Books, and Drawings*, London, 10 July 2003, p. 297).

See also *English language.

English and Medieval Studies Presented to J.R.R. Tolkien on the Occasion of His Seventieth Birthday. A *Festschrift* in honour of Tolkien, in recognition of his 'great contributions to English philology and medieval literature', by 'twenty-two former pupils, friends and colleagues' (jacket blurb). Edited by *Norman Davis and *C.L. Wrenn, it was prepared in secret and published by George Allen & Unwin (*Publishers) near the end of 1962. A specially bound copy was presented to Tolkien on 5 December 1962 at a small dinner party at Merton College, *Oxford arranged by Davis. Tolkien had heard about the book almost a month earlier; on 19 November he wrote to *Rayner Unwin: 'The "gunpowder plot", in which you have been implicated, was exposed almost (Nov[ember] 9) on the correct date. My spies and agents failed me, or I should have become aware of it some time ago. But benevolent as this was in object – to 'blow me up' in NED [*New English Dictionary*, i.e. *Oxford English Dictionary*] sense 23 not 24 – it came as a shock. That I should be treated to a "festschrift" had never occurred to me. I must say that it was a very great added pleasure that "Allen & Unwin" had taken it on' (Tolkien-George Allen & Unwin correspondence, HarperCollins).

English and Welsh. Lecture, first published in *Angles and Britons: O'Donnell Lectures* (1963), pp. 1–41. Reprinted in *The Monsters and the Critics and Other Essays* (1983, cited here for convenience), pp. 162–97.

SUMMARY

Tolkien discusses the interrelationship of the English and Welsh languages and peoples, their effects upon each other, and the influence upon both by peoples and languages outside Britain. Of particular interest to Tolkien are English and Welsh surnames and place-names. He wishes chiefly to illustrate the value of a

study of Celtic languages, especially Welsh, to the study of English, stating that
a first-hand acquaintance with Welsh and its philology is essential to the English philologist, 'as necessary, if not so obviously and immediately useful, as a
knowledge of Norse or French' (p. 163). Further, he feels, one may take pleasure in knowing Welsh:

> Most English-speaking people . . . will admit that *cellar door* is 'beauti-
> ful', especially if dissociated from its sense (and from its spelling). More
> beautiful than, say, *sky*, and far more beautiful than *beautiful*. Well then,
> in Welsh for me *cellar doors* are extraordinarily frequent, and moving
> to the higher dimension, the words in which there is pleasure in the
> contemplation of the association of form and sense are abundant. [pp.
> 190–1]

Each person, he argues, has a 'native language', by which he means 'inherent linguistic predilections', which is not the same as the 'cradle-tongue' one
first learns to speak. In a significant autobiographical passage (pp. 191–2) he
remarks on his own 'cradle-tongue', English, 'with a dash of Afrikaans', and on
his experiences with other languages. Gothic was the first of these to take him
'by storm, to move my heart'; and 'of all save one among them the most overwhelming pleasure was provided by Finnish' – Welsh being the exception. 'My
college, I know, and the shade of Walter Skeat, I surmise, was shocked when
the only prize I ever won [as an undergraduate] . . ., the Skeat Prize for English
at Exeter College, was spent on Welsh [*A Welsh Grammar* by Sir John Morris-
Jones].'

HISTORY

Presented by Tolkien at *Oxford University on 21 October 1955, *English and
Welsh* was the first of the annual O'Donnell Lectures, a series established by
the bequest of Charles James O'Donnell to promote the study of the 'British
or Celtic element in the English language and the dialects of English Counties and the special terms and words used in agriculture and handicrafts and
the British or Celtic element in the existing population of England'. Although
O'Donnell died in 1934, his wish to establish a series of lectures was not
addressed in earnest until late in 1952. Probably in November of that year
*John Bryson, then Chairman of the English Faculty Board, nominated Tol-
kien as one of two representatives from Oxford to a committee to discuss the
basis of the O'Donnell Lectures. The committee, comprising representatives
from the universities of Oxford, Wales, and Edinburgh (but not the National
University of Ireland or Trinity College, Dublin, also named in O'Donnell's
will), first met on 10 January 1953 at the Senate House, University of London.
Tolkien reported on this meeting to the boards of the faculties of English Language and Literature and of Medieval and Modern Languages at Oxford. On
16 October 1953 he was appointed by the English Faculty Board to the Board

of Electors for the O'Donnell Lectureship in Celtic Studies until Michaelmas Term 1958; he remained an elector until 1963.

It seems to have been decided at once that Tolkien would give the first O'Donnell Lecture, but more than two years passed before he was able to do so. In his introductory remarks to *English and Welsh* he felt that his audience might have expected 'a less dilatory performance': 'But the years 1953 to 1955 have for me been filled with a great many tasks, and their burden has not been decreased by the long-delayed appearance of a large "work", if it can be called that, which contains, in the way of presentation that I find most natural, much of what I personally have received from the study of things Celtic' (p. 162). The final volume of *The Lord of the Rings* was published on 20 October 1955, just one day before the delivery of the lecture. On 12 October Tolkien had written to Philip Unwin of George Allen & Unwin (*Publishers) begging him in jest not to fail to publish *The Return of the King* on the 20th, in the hope that 'a large part of my audience' at the O'Donnell Lecture 'will be so bemused by sitting up late the night before that they will not so closely observe my grave lack of equipment as a lecturer on a Celtic subject. Anyway, I want to tactfully allude to the book, since a part of what I wish to say is about "Celticness" and in what that consists as a linguistic pattern' (*Letters*, p. 227).

Tolkien worked on his lecture until the eleventh hour. On 27 September he was still researching a point, made early in the lecture, regarding King Henry VIII and his attempt to eliminate the Welsh language. On 8 December 1955 he wrote to *Naomi Mitchison that he had composed *English and Welsh* 'with "all the woe in the world", as the Gawain-poet says of the wretched fox with the hounds on his tail. All the more woe, since I am the merest amateur in such matters, and Celtic scholars are critical and litigious; and more woe since I was smitten with laryngitis' (*Letters*, pp. 228–9).

The collection of O'Donnell Lectures for *Angles and Britons* began probably in 1961. Tolkien had page proofs in hand by 18 February 1962, on which date he wrote to the University of Wales Press that he had found it necessary to make serious alterations to his lecture in four places. Revised proofs were sent to him on 17 August 1962. It was probably one copy of these that Tolkien sent to his *Aunt Jane Neave, then living in Wales. On 8–9 September he wrote to her, apparently in reply to a positive review:

> I was a bit afraid that I had overstepped the mark with that lecture: much of it rather dull except to dons. It is not really 'learned': my task was to thread together items of common (professional) knowledge in an attempt to interest English people. The only 'original' things in it, are the autobiographical bits, and the reference to 'beauty' in language; and the theory that one's 'native language' is not the same as one's 'cradle-tongue'.
> [*Letters*, p. 319]

English language. Tolkien's feelings about *England were bound up with the history of the English language, in particular Old English and Middle English. One of his masters at *King Edward's School, Birmingham, George Brewerton, 'encouraged his pupils to read Chaucer and he recited the *Canterbury Tales* to them in the original Middle English. To Ronald Tolkien's ears this was a revelation . . .' (Humphrey Carpenter, *Biography*, p. 28). Brewerton was pleased with his pupil's interest in early English, and lent him an Anglo-Saxon primer.

Tolkien now began to read Old English literature in the original, as well as works in Middle English such as *Sir Gawain and the Green Knight*, the latter in a dialect spoken in the *West Midlands, from which his *Suffield forebears had come. Later he told W.H. Auden: 'I am a West-midlander by blood (and took to early west-midland Middle English as a known tongue as soon as I set eyes on it)' (7 June 1955, *Letters*, p. 213). And in an autobiographical statement sent to the Houghton Mifflin Company (*Publishers) in 1955 he wrote: 'I am indeed in English terms a West-midlander at home only in the counties upon the Welsh Marches; and it is, I believe, as much due to descent as to opportunity that Anglo-Saxon and Western Middle English and alliterative verse have been both a childhood attraction and my main professional sphere' (*Letters*, p. 218). Other works about which Tolkien taught and wrote professionally, such as *Pearl* and the *Ancrene Wisse* (*Ancrene Riwle*), are also in Middle English from the West Midlands.

Tolkien's antagonism to *France, the French, and the French language was due in large part to his regret that English culture was dislocated and nearly destroyed following the conquest of England by French-speaking Normans in 1066. Anthony Curtis recalled that during the first class he and other Cadets attended at Oxford during the Second World War, Tolkien as their teacher gave them sample passages of medieval English. One of them was an English translation of the first verses of the Gospel according to John. '"You see," he said triumphantly, "English was a language that could move easily in abstract concepts when French was still a vulgar Norman patois"'('Remembering Tolkien and Lewis', *British Book News*, June 1977, p. 429). On 20 March 1969 Tolkien wrote to his friend Amy Ronald that one unfortunate result of the Norman invasion was 'the adulteration of our own language with the consequence that we have a large Franco-Latin ingredient largely floating about like oil – specially used when we are being "adult", stuffy or professional' (quoted in Christie's, *Autograph Letters and Printed Books, including First Editions*, London, 19 May 2000, p. 37).

And yet he did not welcome the worldwide spread of English. On 9 December 1943 he wrote to his son *Christopher: 'Col. Knox says ⅛ of the world's population speaks "English", and that is the biggest language group. If true, damn shame – say I. May the curse of Babel strike all their tongues till they can only say "baa baa". It would mean much the same. I think I shall have to refuse to speak anything but Old Mercian [the dialect of Old English spoken in much of the West Midlands]' (*Letters*, p. 65).

'**English-Qenya Dictionary**'. Approximately 120 entries for an English–Qenya dictionary, published with commentary and notes in *Parma Eldalamberon* 15 (2004), pp. 65–84, edited by Arden R. Smith and Christopher Gilson. Tolkien's own title, written in Valmaric script (*Writing systems), was *i·Lambe n·Eldalion | Qenya | i·Lambe n·Valion* ('the tongue of the Eldar; Qenya; the tongue of the Valar'). Most of the Qenya (*Languages, Invented) glosses 'are written in Valmaric script, and usually (though not always) transcribed in Roman letters' (p. 65). Tolkien wrote this material in a loose-leaf notebook, which he seems to have begun to use for a projected English–Old English dictionary, but after only a few entries began an English–Qenya dictionary with sixteen items beginning with 'A'; these were apparently derived from entries in the *Qenyaqetsa*. Later he deleted all of these entries and began a third series, closely associated with *Qenya: Descriptive Grammar of the Qenya Language* (c. 1923).

Associated with the notebook are several slips on which Tolkien began to compile a Noldorin–English dictionary, which can be dated after 16 April 1932.

Enigmata Saxonica Nuper Inventa Duo. Two riddles, based on traditional sources but original compositions by Tolkien in Old English, first published in the *Leeds English School collection *A Northern Venture* (1923), p. 20. The Latin title means 'two Saxon riddles newly discovered'.

The first 'enigma', which begins 'Meolchwitum sind marmanstane', is an adaptation of the familiar rhyme beginning 'In marble halls as white as milk, / Lined with a skin as soft as silk', as Douglas A. Anderson notes in *The Annotated Hobbit*; the solution is 'an egg' (cf. one of Bilbo's riddles in *The Hobbit*, Chapter 5). It was written no later than 26 June 1922, when Tolkien sent a copy to *Henry Bradley for his amusement. The version in *A Northern Venture* has very slight differences, mainly in punctuation.

The second riddle begins 'Hæfth Hild Hunecan hwite tunecan, / ond swa read rose hæfth rudige nose' ('Hild Hunic has a white tunic / And like a red rose, a ruddy nose'); its solution is 'a lighted candle'. Douglas A. Anderson has compared it to the nursery rhyme 'Little Nancy Etticoat / In a white petticoat'. The riddles were reprinted in *The Annotated Hobbit* (rev. and expanded edn. 2002), pp. 124–5.

Of the Ents and the Eagles. Text which *Christopher Tolkien used to form the second part of the chapter *'Of Aulë and Yavanna' in *The Silmarillion* (1977). An account of its writing is given in *The War of the Jewels* (1994), pp. 340–1. The title refers to the 'Shepherds of the Trees' and the 'Eagles of the Lords of the West'; see further, the entry for 'Of Aulë and Yavanna'.

Tolkien invented the Ents no later than the beginning of 1942, while writing Book III of *The Lord of the Rings*. *Of the Ents and the Eagles* was written no earlier than 1958–9, and is probably a close contemporary to a note on the same subject written by Tolkien in September 1963. The original draft, with the title *Anaxartamel*, was written at speed on two sides of a sheet of paper.

Tolkien then expanded this in an untitled typescript and made emendations. Two amanuensis typescripts followed, on one of which Tolkien wrote the title *Of the Ents and the Eagles*, but on the other *Anaxartaron Onyalië*. In *The War of the Jewels* Christopher Tolkien notes some differences between the manuscript and the typescript and lists a few editorial emendations that he made in the work as published.

Environment. One of Tolkien's concerns, and a frequent subject for comment in his writings and correspondence, was what we would now call the Environment, but in the widest sense of that word: both the natural world, and what Man has done to it and to his immediate surroundings. He was particularly aroused by Man's ever-increasing use of machines of all sorts, and the resulting pollution and noise. And yet, he was no Luddite; he was born into an industrial age and lived within it. He himself bought a car in 1933, and gave it up only with the introduction of petrol rationing at the start of the Second World War. In later life he was driven by car between Oxford and Bournemouth. Though he regretted their mark upon the landscape, he used trains regularly. Despite his great dislike of aeroplanes, he flew to Dublin in 1965. At Sandfield Road (*Oxford and environs) he and his wife *Edith had no central heating, no washing machine or dishwasher, no television; but in the last years of his life he enjoyed watching televised sports. He and Edith listened to the radio, especially during the Second World War, but he commented to his son *Christopher that he had been better off in the First World War, before the days of public 'wireless' broadcasting. 'I daresay it had some potential for good, but it has in fact become a weapon for the fool, the savage, and the villain to afflict the minority with, and to destroy thought. Listening in has killed listening' (18 April 1944, *Letters*, p. 72). He used a typewriter and the telephone, and after some hesitation a tape recorder. But he did not welcome each new invention as some of his contemporaries did. In *On Fairy-Stories* he quoted approvingly *G.K. Chesterton's comment 'that, as soon as he heard that anything "had come to stay", he knew that it would be very soon replaced – indeed regarded as pitiably obsolete and shabby' (*Tree and Leaf*, p. 56).

THE MACHINE

Tolkien felt that machines often created far more problems than they solved: that men invented and used machines to try to achieve their dreams, or to save time, or to provide more freedom, but often in vain. Flying in an aeroplane is not the same as achieving the flight of birds; labour-saving for some often leads to soulless labour in ugly factories for others; using cars to escape the pollution of towns and cities leads to the pollution of the countryside; and machines are often perverted and used for the wrong purposes. He referred to the Second World War as 'the first War of the Machines', and to it 'leaving, alas, everyone the poorer, many bereaved or maimed and millions dead, and only one thing triumphant: the Machines. As the servants of the Machines are becoming a privileged class, the Machines are going to be enormously more powerful. What's their next move?' (letter to Christopher Tolkien, 30 January 1945, *Letters*, p. 111). 'Unlike art', he said, 'which is content to create a new secondary world in the mind, [the machine] attempts to actualize desire, and so create power in this World; and that cannot really be done with any real satisfaction' (letter to Christopher Tolkien, 7 July 1944, *Letters*, pp. 87–8).

In this same regard, he remarked on the dropping of atom bombs on Hiroshima and Nagasaki: 'The news ... is so horrifying one is stunned. The utter folly of these lunatic physicists to consent to do such work for war-purposes: calmly plotting the destruction of the world! Such explosives in men's hands, while their moral and intellectual status is declining, is about as useful as giving out firearms to all inmates of a gaol and then saying that you hope "this will ensure peace"' (letter to Christopher Tolkien, 9 August 1945, *Letters*, p. 116).

He regretted very much that Christopher was in the Royal Air Force, training to be a pilot. Although he admired and was grateful to the pilots of the British forces, he considered 'the aeroplane of war ... the real villain' (letter to Christopher Tolkien, 29 May 1945, *Letters*, p. 115). To begin with, they produced noise. 'The heavens are full of roar and riot', he wrote on 30 April 1944. 'You cannot even hold a shouting conversation in the garden now, save about 1 a.m. and 7 p.m. – unless the day is too foul to be out. How I wish the "infernal combustion" engine had never been invented. Or (more difficult still since humanity and engineers in special are both nitwitted and malicious as a rule) that it could have been put to rational uses – if any' (letter to Christopher Tolkien, *Letters*, p. 77). Also during the war the countryside was destroyed in many places to provide military airfields. 'The heart has gone out of the Little Kingdom', he wrote to *Stanley Unwin c. 18 March 1945, referring to the country around Oxford as depicted in *Farmer Giles of Ham*, 'and the woods and plains are aerodromes and bomb-practice targets' (*Letters*, p. 113). Towards the end of his life 'he crossed a cheque for a large sum payable to the tax authorities with the words "Not a penny for Concorde"' (i.e. for development of the commercial supersonic aeroplane; Humphrey Carpenter, *Biography*, p. 244).

In unused drafts for *On Fairy-Stories* he wrote of the aeroplane:

It was fledged just in time to be baptized in blood, to become the chief exemplar in our time of the dreadful potency of Original Sin. Clumsy and, in spite of its growing complexity, inefficient machine in comparison with its high object, it has taken the menacing shape not of birds but of fishlike or saurian monsters, and it defies and overrides all privacies, and scatters over all quietudes the deadly roar of its parent den; at unawares it may fall in ruins on the frail houses of men, burning and crushing them at play, or by their hearths, or working in their gardens. This 'in peace'. War, it has raised to a mass-production of slaughter. [Tolkien Papers, Bodleian Library, Oxford]

Someone once said to Tolkien that if his child could be saved only by being flown to a specialist in America, he would then welcome an aeroplane. 'So to save the life of that hypothetical child by the supposed skill of an imaginary specialist (who might not succeed)', he continued in the *On Fairy-Stories* draft,

> hundreds of thousands of men, women, and children are to be blown to rags and burned, and half the remaining beautiful things of saner centuries with them. It would seem rather more economical to have a few more doctors more handily placed. It would be too brutally 'realistic' to suggest that the poor child must die, if it can only be saved by a machine with so terrible a potential of murder. It is all right if it is done by a machine. It might be regarded as odd if I sacrificed even one man on an altar to gain the favour of the Gods. The question to be asked, of course, is not 'would you try to save your child's life by using an aeroplane now – in a situation that you did not make or will?' but 'would you will such a situation to save your child's life?' The answer to the first question is: 'Yes, let Moloch turn doctor for once, if he can.' The answer to the second is just: no. [Tolkien Papers, Bodleian Library, Oxford]

As for the motor-car, he felt that although 'it may have some practical uses', he doubted that it is essential. It is 'fundamentally a mechanical toy that has run off the nursery floor', 'the chief and most futile piece of "escape" mechanism'.

> For, of course, it would not be bought or made in 'mass', nor millions made out of it, but for its invention at a time when we have made our towns impossible to live in. The motor-car attracts because it enables people [to] live far away from their horrible 'works', or to fly from their depressing dormitories to the 'country'. But the motor works and all the subsidiaries and garages destroy that 'country' like locusts. [*On Fairy-Stories*, Tolkien Papers, Bodleian Library, Oxford]

Oxford having been a centre of the motor industry, Tolkien saw the urban sprawl of factories and dormitory suburbs for workers. In the 1950s he objected strongly to a proposed ring road intended to enable traffic to move more easily through the city, but which would have destroyed much of value, including Christ Church Meadow.

Near the end of *Roverandom, conceived in 1925, as the dog Rover makes his way home after his adventures 'motor after motor racketed by, filled (Rover thought) with the same people, all making all speed (and all dust and all smell) to somewhere. "I don't believe half of them know where they are going to, or why they are going there, or would know it if they got there," grumbled Rover as he coughed and choked; and his feet got tired on the hard, gloomy road' (p. 87). Probably in the early 1960s he wrote *The Bovadium Fragments*, a satirical 'parable of the destruction of Oxford (*Bovadium*) by the *motores* manufactured by the *Daemon* of *Vaccipratum* (a reference to Lord Nuffield and his motor-works at Cowley) which block the streets, asphyxiate the inhabitants, and finally explode' (*Biography*, p. 163).

Meredith Veldman in *Fantasy, the Bomb, and the Greening of Britain: Romantic Protest, 1945–1980* (1984) places Tolkien's feelings on these matters in relation to those of precursors such as John Ruskin and *William Morris, contemporaries such as *C.S. Lewis, and the political movements of Tolkien's day (see *Political thought):

> Lewis and Tolkien swam against the currents of contemporary Britain, but their protest flowed within the deeper stream of British romanticism. They viewed romantics such as William Morris as their literary forebears and, like Morris, revolted against the industrial world. Their fantasies articulated a rejection of materialism and empiricism deeply rooted in segments of British middle-class culture. [p. 38]

Veldman suggests that 'the lifeless, mechanical, tyrannical Mordor [in *The Lord of the Rings*] became for Tolkien a powerful symbol of what was wrong with twentieth-century England. Rooted in a world view that reduces people to objects, Mordor glorifies technology and the power it confers as the unquestionable and ultimate good'. Also, Tolkien's 'equation of modernity with Mordor stemmed from more than just a crochety distaste for a too-quickly changing world. His antimachinery, antitechnology stance grew out of the soil of his world view: his religious belief in a fallen world and the consequent necessity of limiting the power of fallen human beings' (p. 87; see *The Fall). *The Lord of the Rings*, Veldman says, belongs

> in the tradition of romantic protest. In its pages Tolkien protested against the basic assumptions of industrial Britain. He refused to draw the boundaries of reality at the material world and endeavoured to assert the individual's right and responsibility to participate in and help shape the decisions and structures that determined his life. . . . Decades ahead of the Greens, he denounced the exaltation of mechanization and the narrow definition of economic progress that resulted in the degradation of the natural environment, and he did so in romantic terms. In Tolkien's Middle-earth, nature expressed a reality beyond human comprehension and worthy of human respect. Through his creation of Middle-earth, Tolkien offered a vision of an alternative reality, one that he believed could never be achieved because of the sinfulness of humankind, but one that both drew on and nourished the romantic protest tradition. [pp. 89–90]

Patrick Curry in *Defending Middle-earth: Tolkien, Myth and Modernity* (1997) says that in his works Tolkien has 'made it possible for his readers to unselfconsciously combine Christian ethics and a neo-pagan reverence for nature, together with . . . a liberal humanist respect for the small, the precarious and apparently mundane. This is a fusion which couldn't be more relevant to resisting the immense and impersonal forces of runaway modernity' (p. 29).

MAN-MADE LANDSCAPE

Tolkien wrote to his son Christopher on 6 October 1944: 'It is not the *not-man* (e.g. weather) nor *man* (even at a bad level), but the *man-made* that is ultimately daunting and insupportable. If a ragnarök would burn all the slums and gas-works, and shabby garages, and long arc-lit suburbs, it [could] for me burn all the works of art – and I'd go back to trees' (*Letters*, p. 96). He liked the countryside, but all too often found that spoiled by the felling of trees, the introduction of heavy farm machinery, or debris of bottles and wrapping paper. He enjoyed seaside holidays but hated commercialized resorts and the litter dropped by visitors. In the poem **Progress in Bimble Town* he describes the seaside litter: orange-rind, banana-skins, paper, bottles, packets, tins.

But time and 'progress' were often more devastating. After a visit in September 1933 to *Sarehole, the idyllic hamlet near *Birmingham where he had lived for a few formative years as a child, Tolkien wrote in his diary that his old cottage was

> now in the midst of a sea of new red-brick. The old mill still stands, and Mrs Hunt's still sticks out into the road as it turns uphill; but the crossing beyond the now fenced-in pool, where the bluebell lane ran down into the mill lane, is now a dangerous crossing alive with motors and red lights. The [miller's] house ... is become a petrol station, and most of Short Avenue and the elms between it and the crossing have gone. How I envy those whose precious early scenery has not been exposed to such violent and peculiarly hideous change. [quoted in *Biography*, pp. 124–5]

*King Edward's School, which Tolkien had attended as a boy, by 1944 had also changed, having left crowded buildings in central Birmingham for new construction in nearby Edgbaston. After Tolkien visited Birmingham in that year he commented to Christopher that the 'chief damage' in the city was not from enemy bombs, but 'the growth of great flat featureless modern buildings. The worst of all is the ghastly multiple-store erection on the old site [of King Edward's School]'. He felt that the new school buildings were 'ghastly utterly third-rate. . . . If you can imagine a building better than most Oxford colleges being replaced by what looks like a girls' council school, you've got it and my feelings' (3 April 1944, *Letters*, p. 70). Such feelings carried over into *The Lord of the Rings*, in Tolkien's description of what the hobbits found when they returned to the Shire (bk. VI, ch. 8).

In 1953 Tolkien left the house in Holywell Street, Oxford, in which he and his wife had been living, partly because, as he told *Rayner Unwin, it had become 'uninhabitable – unsleepable-in, unworkable-in, rocked, racked with noise, and drenched with fumes. Such is modern life. Mordor in our midst'

(24 October 1952, *Letters*, p. 165). He moved to Sandfield Road, then a quiet cul-de-sac but soon opened up, and for a time used by lorries as an unofficial bypass. Later it was used as a car park by people attending home games of the Oxford United football team. Tolkien told Christopher Bretherton that 'the actual inhabitants' of Sandfield Road did 'all that radio, tele[vision], dogs, scooters, buzzbikes, and cars of all sizes but the smallest, can do to produce noise from early morn to about 2 a.m. In addition in a house three doors away dwells a member of a group of young men who are evidently aiming to turn themselves into a Beatles Group. On days when it falls to his turn to have a practice session the noise is indescribable' (16 July 1964, *Letters*, p. 345).

Eriol and Ælfwine. In Tolkien's *legendarium* (*'The Silmarillion') the name of the man who is the means by which Elvish stories and traditions are transmitted to mankind is successively *Eriol* ('one who dreams alone') and *Ælfwine* ('Elf-friend').

In the completed part of *The Book of Lost Tales*, the stories are heard and recorded by Eriol, a man of northern Europe in the period preceding the Anglo-Saxon invasions of Britain. According to an early outline, his original name was *Ottor*, but he called himself *Wǽfre* ('restless, wandering') and lived with his wife and two sons, Hengest and Horsa, on the island of Heligoland in the North Sea. But within the story itself, Eriol tells children in the Cottage of Lost Play that he grew up in an inland town, yet a love of the sea that he had never seen was in his bones. Both of his parents die in a cruel siege of that town, but Eriol escapes, seeks the shore of the Western Sea, and becomes a sailor. When he is wrecked on an island he is sheltered by 'an ancient sailor' who tells him 'strange tales of things beyond the Western Seas, of the Magic Isles and that most lonely one that lay beyond' (*The Book of Lost Tales, Part Two*, p. 5). After much seeking, Eriol eventually reaches the Lonely Isle, Tol Eressëa, and meets the Fairies (or Elves) who dwell there. He hears and records the stories they tell him of the history of the world. According to notes and outlines for the unwritten end of *The Book of Lost Tales* as reconstructed by *Christopher Tolkien ('The History of Eriol or Ælfwine', in *The Book of Lost Tales, Part Two*), he takes part in an unsuccessful expedition by the Elves to the aid of their kin, during which Tol Eressëa is 'drawn east back across the ocean and anchored off the coasts of the Great Lands ... in the geographical position of England'. Evil men and Orcs follow the retreating Elves to Tol Eressëa, and after another defeat the Elves fade. Then 'the sons of Eriol, Hengest, Horsa, and Heorrenda, conquered the island and it became "England". They were not hostile to the Elves, and from them the English have "the true tradition of the Fairies"' (p. 293). By introducing Hengest and Horsa, named in early records as two of the leaders of the Germanic invasions of Britain in the mid-fifth century AD, as the sons of Eriol, Tolkien provides a link between his tales and the history of *England.

While several tales still remained to be told, Tolkien abandoned his original conception for the end of *The Book of Lost Tales* and made an outline for a revised version with a new framework. No earlier than February 1920, and probably after March of that year when he referred to 'Eriol' in remarks to the Exeter College Essay Club (*Societies and clubs), he renamed the mariner Ælfwine and changed his history. Now he was said to be an Anglo-Saxon born in the centre of England, who inherited a sea-longing from his mother who came from the West. One note indicates that he lived no earlier than the reign of Alfred of Wessex (late ninth century), and Christopher Tolkien concludes more specifically from an addition to this note that 'he is apparently a man of eleventh-century Wessex' (*The Book of Lost Tales, Part Two*, p. 302). Tolkien wrote three accounts of Ælfwine's early life and his voyage to Tol Eressëa: a plot outline (notes 29, 31, 39, 42, on pp. 330–3), a substantial narrative with the title *Ælfwine of England*, part of it on letters dated February 1920, and a fair copy introducing many changes and much new material.

Ælfwine's early story has similarities to that of Eriol, but the besieged town is now identified as Kortirion (i.e. *Warwick), and his father is 'Déor the singer', the name of a minstrel in an Old English poem. Ælfwine is enslaved by the victorious Forodwaith (Vikings) but eventually escapes and makes his way to the shore of the Western Sea, from which Elves still remaining in England set sail. He learns 'all that a man may of the craft of ships and of the sea', and desiring to find 'the Magic Isles of the songs of Men' (pp. 315, 316) sets sail into the west with such companions as he can find willing to undertake such a voyage. Swept overboard, he comes upon an island where an old Man of the Sea dwells. From him Ælfwine hears more of what lies further west, including the Lonely Island and the Bay of Faëry. With the old man's aid he acquires another ship, and is reunited with his comrades from England or finds new companions. After untold adventures in the West they are about to turn for home when they catch a momentary glimpse of lights in the harbour of the Elves and hear music 'laden with unimagined longing'. Then 'the mists of time veiled the shore, and nothing could they see and nought more hear save the sound of the surf of the seas in the far-off pebbles of the Lonely Isle' (p. 321–2). Ælfwine leaps into the sea, never to be seen again. Presumably Tolkien meant him to reach Tol Eressëa, and the reorganized *Book of Lost Tales* to follow (though in the second version, surprisingly he remains on the ship and is driven back across the sea by a fierce wind).

Tolkien wrote no more at length of Ælfwine's story, but notes make it clear that the only expedition of the Elves to the Great Lands had taken place long before, and when it failed the Elves had retreated first to England and then to Tol Eressëa. Ælfwine finds that the Elves understand English, from the time they lived in England, 'the only land where men and Elves once dwelt an age in peace and love' (p. 304). Unlike Eriol, he has no active role in the history of the Elves: 'his part is only to learn and to record' (Christopher Tolkien, p. 301).

Even though this second framework of *The Book of Lost Tales* was also abandoned, Tolkien continued to cite Ælfwine as the intermediary source for many of his 'Silmarillion' texts: he is supposed to have written them down after hearing them in Tol Eressëa from the wise elf Pengolod.

In the early 1930s Tolkien decided to combine Eriol and Ælfwine into one character. *Eriol* became the name given by the Elves to Ælfwine, who remains an Anglo-Saxon and even translates into Old English some documents recording Elvish history. He is called 'Eriol of Leithien, that is Ælfwine of the Angelcynn' (*The Shaping of Middle-earth*, p. 206).

Tolkien's unfinished time-travel story, *The Lost Road*, written 1936–?1937, concerns a father and son of the present day, Alboin and Audoin Errol (*Alboin* is a Lombardic name corresponding to Old English *Ælfwine*, and *Errol* is possibly to be associated with *Eriol*). They are to travel back in time by way of similarly named fathers and sons in historical and legendary times, and ultimately reach *Númenor not long before its destruction. A projected chapter concerns a tenth-century Ælfwine who is to sail with his son Eadwine on the Straight Road (see *Road) and catch just a glimpse of Tol Eressëa. In the only part written, Ælfwine chants to King Edward the Elder (AD 900–924) and his men, first of his sea-longing, then a long account of the legend of Sheaf.

This led Tolkien to consider a new introduction to *The Book of Lost Tales* in which Ælfwine would find himself on the Straight Road to Tol Eressëa and Valinor after the shape of the world was changed in the destruction of Númenor. Christopher Tolkien comments that this note shows his father 'combining the old story of the voyage of Ælfwine to Tol-eressëa and the telling of the *Lost Tales* with the idea of the World Made Round and the Straight Path, which entered at this time' (*The Lost Road and Other Writings*, p. 78). Also,

> with the entry at this time of the cardinal ideas of the Downfall of Númenor, the World Made Round, and the Straight Road, into the conception of 'Middle-earth', and the thought of a 'time-travel' story in which the very significant figure of the Anglo-Saxon Ælfwine would be both 'extended' into the future, into the twentieth century, and 'extended' also into a many-layered past, my father was envisaging a massive and explicit linking of his own legends with those of many other places and times: all concerned with the stories and dreams of the peoples who dwelt by the coasts of the great Western Sea. [p. 98]

In *The Notion Club Papers (written end of 1945–mid-1946) Alwin Lowdham in a dream or vision finds himself in the time of Edward the Elder and in the persona of Ælfwine. He recites the same verse of sea-longing as in *The Lost Road*, and his friend Wilfred Trewin Jeremy (as an Anglo-Saxon, Tréowine) tells the story of Sheaf. Although *The Notion Club Papers* was left unfinished, brief outlines indicate that Ælfwine and Tréowine were to set sail, find the Straight Road, and see the Book of Stories. Verlyn Flieger has given much thought to the significance of Eriol and Ælfwine, in all of their incarnations, in *A Question of Time: J.R.R. Tolkien's Road to Faërie* (1997):

The importance of the name 'Elf-friend', the English equivalent of Anglo-Saxon *Ælfwine* ... should not be underestimated. . . . The name and the concept behind it grew with the mythology and put out branches.

Ælfwine is Tolkien's later name for one of his earliest characters, Eriol the mariner who in *The Book of Lost Tales* comes to Tol Eressëa, the Lonely Isle, where he hears the tales of the Ainur and the Valar. Both the name and the character underwent complicated modifications as Tolkien's vision grew and changed. . . . The epithet 'Elf-friend', as well as the concept behind the character, became one of most recurrent elements in the mythology. Over the long length of Tolkien's work on his mythology, the name *Ælfwine* and the character who bore it became the emblem and embodiment of some of his most deeply rooted attitudes toward myth, language, history, and the participation of the unconscious in all these. [pp. 64–5]

Flieger also discusses the role of Ælfwine and other 'elf-friends' in Tolkien's writings in 'The Footsteps of Ælfwine', in *Tolkien's Legendarium: Essays on The History of Middle-earth* (2000): 'These figures have widely different characteristics and fulfill a variety of different plot functions in the stories in which they appear, but the important position they all share is that of the link, the connector or mediator between the "real" or natural world and the world of Faërie – the supernatural world of myth and the imagination' (p. 185).

In *The Road to Middle-earth* (2nd edn. 1992) T.A Shippey comments that 'one extremely unexpected aspect of Tolkien's early writings is his determined identification of England with Elfland', and that 'England must be the most de-mythologised country in Europe, partly as a result of 1066 (which led to near-total suppression of native English belief . . .), partly as a result of the early Industrial Revolution. . . . If Tolkien was to create an English mythology', as he told *Milton Waldman in ?late 1951,

he would first (given his scholarly instincts) have to create a context in which it might have been preserved.

His earliest attempts to do this centre on the figure of Ottor 'Wæfre', Ottor the Wanderer, also known as Eriol: as it were a dual ancestral figure, a point from which two chains of transmission ran, the one authentic, the other invented, but both determinedly native and English. In Tolkien's thinking, Ottor/Eriol was by his first wife the father of Hengest and Horsa, in early but authentic legend the invaders of Britain and the founders of England. But by his second wife he was to be the father of Heorrenda, a harper of English (and Norse) legend, about whom nothing else is known – an image, therefore, of the fantastic 'lost' tradition which Tolkien was about to invent. [pp. 268–9]

Carl F. Hostetter and Arden R. Smith in 'A Mythology for England', *Proceedings of the J.R.R. Tolkien Centenary Conference 1992* (1995), comment that no discussion of Tolkien's creation of a mythology for England would be complete without at least a cursory discussion of the story of Ælfwine, which is without a doubt its fullest, most complex, and most remarkable expression. Though the details of the role and significance of Ælfwine varied considerably as Tolkien developed and refined his mythology ... he serves throughout as an ambassador between Tolkien's mythology and English legend, the agent through whom the English receive, in Anglo-Saxon, what Tolkien calls 'the true tradition of the fairies'. . . . [p. 286]

They note that although Ælfwine's role is less prominent after *The Book of Lost Tales*,

the mere fact that it is a man of Anglo-Saxon England who throughout receives the 'true tradition' of the Elves demonstrates that Tolkien did not completely abandon his ambition of creating a mythology for England. Moreover, while English geographical and mythological elements are manifest in the story of Ælfwine, the role of Ælfwine as translator into Old English of the Elvish legends shows that the crucial third element of Tolkien's criteria for a true English mythology, the linguistic element, is also present, since it demonstrates that Old English and the Elvish tongues coexisted in Tolkien's mythology. [p. 287]

Errantry. Poem. The first of its two finished versions was published in the *Oxford Magazine* 52, no. 5 (9 November 1933), p. 180. A revised text, with only a few differences of wording and rhyme, was first published in *The Adventures of Tom Bombadil and Other Verses from the Red Book* (1962), pp. 24–7.

Each version concerns 'a merry passenger, / a messenger, a mariner' who wanders alone in 'a gilded gondola', across rivers, through meadow-lands, 'and under hill and over hill'. He begs a butterfly to marry him, but is spurned; he catches her, and gives her gifts, but they quarrel and he wanders on. He goes to war and triumphs, then tarries 'for a little while / in little isles', until he recalls the message and errand with which he started out – and departs again.

The long, involved history of *Errantry* as set forth by Christopher Tolkien occupies most of Chapter 5 of *The Treason of Isengard* (1989), but may be summarized as follows. The earliest extant manuscript of the poem was written without hesitation or correction, and seems to be its first complete text, possibly that which Tolkien is known to have read to the original *Inklings in the early 1930s; its preliminary workings have been lost. This version was published in *The Treason of Isengard*, together with a reprint of the *Oxford Magazine* text and different readings in four intermediate versions. In a letter to *Donald Swann of 14 October 1966 Tolkien described *Errantry* as 'a piece of verbal acrobatics and metrical high-jinks ... intended for recitation with great variations of speed.' Having finished, 'the reciter was supposed at once to begin repeating (at even higher speed) the beginning, unless somebody cried

"Once is enough".' The piece, he said, was 'an attempt to go on with the model that came unbidden into my mind: the first six lines, in which, I guess, *D'ye ken the rhyme to porringer* [from a nursery rhyme] had a part. Later I read it to an undergraduate club that used to hear its members read unpublished poems or short tales, and voted some of them into the minute book' (quoted in *The Treason of Isengard*, p. 85).

In 1952 Tolkien was intrigued to receive two inquiries concerning *Errantry*, which had entered oral tradition, apparently from a typescript made at the time it was read to the Inklings. In response to one of these inquiries Tolkien remarked that the poem is 'in a metre I invented (depending on trisyllabic assonances or near-assonances, which is so difficult that except in this one example I have never been able to use it again – it just blew out in a single impulse)' (letter to Rayner Unwin, 22 June 1952, *Letters*, p. 162). On 13 November 1966 Donald Swann, who was then setting *Errantry* to music (see **The Road Goes Ever On: A Song Cycle*), informed Tolkien that he had been given a copy of the poem *c.* 1949, taken from a school magazine where it had been published anonymously, and had himself caused it to be reprinted in a law students' magazine called *Glim*. Only later did he learn its authorship.

Errantry also evolved separately, from its *Oxford Magazine* version, in the 1940s to become Bilbo's song at Rivendell, 'Eärendil was a mariner', in Book II, Chapter 1 of **The Lord of the Rings*. The history of this line is particularly complex, containing fifteen manuscript and typescript versions in two groups, one of which followed the idea of a 'merry messenger', while the other – possibly after a long interval – became more serious and linked (in the event, imperfectly) to the ***Silmarillion' mythology. Tolkien developed the latter through three versions, of which the last was published in *The Fellowship of the Ring* in 1954 – mistakenly so, evidently because three later texts, including that with the ultimate development of the poem as *The Short Lay of Eärendel: Eärendillinwë*, could not be found when wanted for the printer. Pertinent texts from this line of composition, in both groups, are likewise published in *The Treason of Isengard*.

In his preface to *The Adventures of Tom Bombadil and Other Verses from the Red Book* Tolkien, anticipating that readers would notice a similarity between the two, invented a plausible connection between Bilbo's song in *The Lord of the Rings* and *Errantry* as revised for the new collection, there presented for the first time as a Hobbit poem:

It [*Errantry*] was evidently made by Bilbo. This is indicated by its obvious relationship to the long poem recited by Bilbo, as his own composition, in the house of Elrond. In origin a 'nonsense rhyme', it is in the Rivendell version found transformed and applied, somewhat incongruously, to the High-elvish and Númenorean legends of Eärendil. Probably because Bilbo invented its metrical devices and was proud of them. They do not appear in other pieces in the Red Book. . . . Though the influence of Elvish traditions is seen, they are not seriously treated, and the names used . . . are mere inventions in the Elvish style, and are not in fact Elvish at all. [1962 edn., p. 8]

A manuscript of *Errantry* written *c.* 1931 in the Elvish script Tengwar (*Writing systems) was reproduced in *Pictures*, no. 48. Donald Swann's setting of *Errantry*, sung by baritone William Elvin accompanied by the composer, was recorded for the album *Poems and Songs of Middle Earth* (1967, *Recordings). Tolkien also recorded the poem, in spoken form, but his reading was issued only in 2001 as part of *The J.R.R. Tolkien Audio Collection* (*Recordings).

Escape. One of the criticisms most frequently made of Tolkien's writings, and of fantasy fiction in general, is that it is 'escapist', that is, that the writer or the reader of such works is not mature enough, or strong enough, to face the real world. Tolkien was well aware of such criticism and answered it in *On Fairy-Stories*:

> I have claimed that Escape is one of the main functions of fairy-stories, and since I do not disapprove of them, it is plain that I do not accept the tone of scorn or pity with which 'Escape' is now so often used: a tone for which the uses of the word outside literary criticism give no warrant at all. In what the misusers are fond of calling Real Life, Escape is evidently as a rule very practical, and may even be heroic. In real life it is difficult to blame it, unless it fails; in criticism it would seem to be the worse the better it succeeds. Evidently we are faced by a misuse of words, and also by a confusion of thought. Why should a man be scorned, if, finding himself in prison, he tries to get out and go home? Or if, when he cannot do so, he thinks and talks about other topics than jailers and prison-walls? The world outside has not become less real because the prisoner cannot see it. In using Escape in this way the critics have chosen the wrong word, and what is more, they are confusing, not always by sincere error, the Escape of the Prisoner with the Flight of the Deserter. [*Tree and Leaf*, pp. 55–6]

For Tolkien the so-called 'escape from the real world' might be a valid form of protest and revolt against what was wrong with the contemporary world: ugliness in design, mass production, pollution, weapons of mass destruction. But he also recognized that men might also wish to escape from 'other things more grim and terrible . . . hunger, thirst, poverty, pain, sorrow, injustice, death' (p. 60). (See also *Mortality.)

Tolkien thought that temporary 'escape' could bring *'Recovery' and a clearer way of seeing and facing things in the real world. In a letter to his son *Christopher on 10 June 1944 he described how writing had helped him during and after the First World War: 'I took to "escapism": or really transforming experience into another form and symbol with Morgoth and Orcs and the

Eldalië (representing beauty and grace of life and artefact) and so on; and it has stood me in good stead in many hard years since and I still draw on the conceptions then hammered out' (*Letters*, p. 85). On 2 April 1958 he wrote to Professor Jongkees that 'fantasy at its best is founded on love and respect for the real world', and that the writing of **The Lord of the Rings* had 'no connection with "day-dreaming" of which some psychologists or pseudopsychologists have accused me' (R.M. Smythe, *Spring Autograph Auction*, 10 May 2001, item 579).

He did not himself 'opt out' of life; nor indeed do most of the characters in *The Lord of the Rings*. Instead they do their utmost, even in the face of what seems almost inevitable defeat. **C.S. Lewis, after reading a typescript of the completed *Lord of the Rings* in 1949, wrote to Tolkien: 'No romance can repell the charge of "escapism" with such confidence. If it errs, it errs in precisely the opposite direction: the sickness of hope deferred and the merciless piling up of odds against the heroes are near to being too painful' (27 October 1949, *Collected Letters*, vol. 2 (2004), p. 990).

Unfortunately the popularity of *The Lord of the Rings* among hippies in the 1960s led some critics to accuse all of its readers of 'escapism' in the sense of 'dropping out' of the real world, an allegation often repeated in later years, in particular by many 'literary' critics when *The Lord of the Rings* came first in readers' polls. In a letter published in the *Daily Telegraph* on 1 February 1997, defending *The Lord of the Rings* against such criticism after it won the Waterstone's and Channel 4's poll for the greatest book of the twentieth century, Professor Jeffrey Richards of Lancaster University praised Tolkien's work for its 'evocation of such invaluable virtues as loyalty, service, comradeship and idealism'. Referring to Angus Wilson's statement 'that most modern novels are about adultery in Muswell Hill', Richards argued that 'it was an exaggeration, but a pardonable one, for it drew attention to the tyranny of realism, narrowness, self-absorption and "relevance" that holds too many modern writers and critics in thrall. Tolkien is an antidote to all that' ('Tiptop Tolkien?' p. 11).

T.A. Shippey points out in *The Road to Middle-earth* (2nd edn. 1992) that 'when people start appealing to "truth", "experience" and "reality", still more to "the fundamental character of reality", they imply very strongly that they know what these things *are*, an insight not likely to be shaken by argument' (p. 123). In *On Fairy-Stories* Tolkien reported an Oxford don as having declared 'that he "welcomed" the proximity of mass-production robot factories, and the roar of self-obstructive mechanical traffic, because it brought his university into "contact with real life"'. But the suggestion that 'motor-cars . . . are more "real" than, say, horses is pathetically absurd' (*Tree and Leaf*, p. 57). Shippey argues further that

> if it is the function of works of literature to enlarge their readers' sympathies and help them understand what their own experience may not have taught them, then Tolkien's fictions qualify on all counts. Certainly they are about 'creatures who never existed'. Most novels

are about 'people who never existed'. The cry that fantasy is 'escapist' compared to the novel is only an echo of the older cry that novels are 'escapist' compared with biography, and to both cries one should make the same answer: that the freedom to invent outweighs loyalty to mere happenstance, the accidents of history; and good readers should know how to filter a general applicability from a particular story. [p. 251]

Stephen Lawhead in 'J.R.R. Tolkien: Master of Middle-earth', in *Tolkien: A Celebration* (1999), notes that 'the best of fantasy offers not an escape away from reality, but an escape to a heightened reality – a world at once more vivid and intense and real, where happiness and sorrow exist in double measure, where good and evil war in epic conflict, where joy is made more potent by the possibility of universal tragedy and defeat' (p. 167).

Verlyn Flieger in *A Question of Time: J.R.R. Tolkien's Road to Faërie* (1997) declares that Tolkien was not the only writer after the First World War to turn to fantasy: so too did David Lindsay, E.R. Eddison, and Mervyn Peake: 'All look away from the visible world to a more engaging – though not necessarily more pleasant, and certainly not contemporary – country of the mind. This retrogression is as much illusory as it is real. It is just as contemporary a response to cultural forces as that of the avant-garde: whether backward or forward, the very act of escape acknowledges that which it flees, and nostalgia, like modernism, must have a ground from which to turn away' (pp. 16–17). Later she points out that Tolkien 'knew that real escape is impossible. We are where we are, and we cannot go back to where we were; we can only long to', then let go and move on (p. 112).

Essays Presented to Charles Williams see **On Fairy-Stories**

Etymologies. The most frequently cited of Tolkien's linguistic texts (see also *Languages, Invented), published with commentary in **The Lost Road and Other Writings* (1987), pp. 341–400. *Christopher Tolkien describes the *Etymologies*, or *Beleriandic and Noldorin Names and Words: Etymologies*, as the nearest his father 'ever came to a sustained account of Elvish vocabulary', but 'not in the form of nor intended to serve as a dictionary in the ordinary sense but . . . an etymological dictionary of word-relationships: an alphabetically-arranged list of primary stems or "bases", with their derivatives' (pp. 342–3). In producing this Tolkien apparently began at the beginning of the alphabet, and made changes to earlier parts as he progressed; and when he reached the end, he returned to the beginning and re-wrote clearly the entries beginning A B, and D, destroying the earlier text for A and B; there was no text for C. The work seems to be contemporary with the **Quenta Silmarillion*, that is, begun in the mid-1930s, with some additions or changes which may be dated to late 1937 or early 1938, and a few more additions, not made systematically, during the first few years of the writing of **The Lord of the Rings*. The result, Christopher Tolkien comments, was among the most difficult of all the unique material his father left. 'In some sections the maze of forms and cancellations is so dense, and for the most part made so quickly, that one cannot be sure of what my father's intention was: in these parts he was working out potential connections and derivations on the spot, by no means setting down already determined histories' (*The Lost Road and Other Writings*, p. 343). The editor's task was made even more difficult by the poor physical condition in which the manuscript survives.

Christopher Tolkien's object in presenting the *Etymologies* in *The Lost Road and Other Writings* in particular, he wrote, 'is rather an indication of the development, and mode of development of the vocabularies of the Elvish languages at this period than as a first step in the elucidation of the linguistic history; and also because they form an instructive companion to the narrative works of this time' (p. 343). In their introduction to 'Addenda and Corrigenda to the *Etymologies*', in *Vinyar Tengwar* 45–6 (November 2003 and July 2004), Carl F. Hostetter and Patrick H. Wynne observe that because Christopher Tolkien's purpose in editing the *Etymologies* was 'as much *textual* and *literary* as it was linguistic . . . the *Etymologies* providing either explicit translations or obvious component elements for most of the names in the mythology as it then stood', there was no need for him 'to present every variant or dubious reading in the manuscript, or every deleted form or entry . . . even had there been no constraints of time or space imposed by the plan of publication'. But given a 'vast increase in the amount of linguistic material' available since 1987, which 'provides scholars with a far more comprehensive picture of the external evolution of the Elvish languages from their earliest forms', Hostetter and Wynne 'note the contents of the *Etymologies* in greater detail' and 'correct typographical errors and misreadings of Tolkien's difficult handwriting' (no. 45, p. 3).

Hostetter and Wynne include reproductions of three pages of Tolkien's manuscript (no. 45, pp. 10, 31; no. 46, p. 5). An appendix to the 'Addenda and Corrigenda' in *Vinyar Tengwar* 46, 'The Tengwar in the *Etymologies*' by Arden R. Smith, notes that the *Etymologies* is also 'a valuable source for vocabulary pertaining to the Fëanorian letters or *tengwar*', and in manuscript provides an 'unexpected wealth of *tengwar* and *tengwa*-names', many of them different from those given in *The Lord of the Rings*, Appendix E (pp. 29, 30).

Eucatastrophe. A word coined by Tolkien to describe

> the consolation of fairy-stories, the joy of the happy ending: or more correctly of the good catastrophe, the sudden joyous 'turn' (for there is no true end to any fairy-tale): this joy, which is one of the things which fairy-stories can produce supremely well, is not essentially 'escapist', nor 'fugitive'. In its fairy-tale – or otherworld – setting, it is a sudden and miraculous grace: never to be counted on to recur. It does not deny the existence of *dyscatastrophe*, of sorrow and failure: the possibility of these is necessary to the joy of deliverance; it denies (in the face of much

evidence, if you will) universal final defeat and in so far is *evangelium*, giving a fleeting glimpse of Joy, Joy beyond the walls of the world, poignant as grief. [*On Fairy-Stories*, in *Tree and Leaf*, p. 62]

'The *eucatastrophic* tale', he wrote, 'is the true form of fairy-tale, and its highest function' (p. 62). Further in *On Fairy-Stories* Tolkien considered the function of eucatastrophe in the writings of creators of secondary worlds, and in the Christian Story, calling the Birth of Christ 'the eucatastrophe of Man's history' and the Resurrection 'the eucatastrophe of the story of the Incarnation' (p. 65).

He found a real-life example of eucatastrophe in an incident described by *Father Douglas Carter in 1944: a little boy who had not been cured at Lourdes, sadly returning home with his parents and two nurses, saw the Grotto from the train and suddenly recovered. Tolkien commented in a letter to his son *Christopher on 7–8 November 1944:

At the story of the little boy . . . with its apparent sad ending and then its sudden unhoped-for happy ending, I was deeply moved and had that peculiar emotion we all have – though not often. It is quite like any other sensation. And all of a sudden I realized what it was: the very thing that I have been trying to write about and explain [in *On Fairy-Stories*]. . . . For it I coined the word 'euctasatrophe'. . . . And I was there led to the view that it produces its peculiar effect because it is a sudden glimpse of Truth, your whole nature chained in material cause and effect, the chain of death, feels a sudden relief as if a major limb out of joint had suddenly snapped back. [*Letters*, p. 100]

In the same letter he cites a 'lesser' example in one of his own works: 'I knew I had written a story of worth in "The Hobbit" when reading it (after it was old enough to be detached from me) I had suddenly in a fairly strong measure the "eucatastrophic"' emotion at Bilbo's exclamation: "The Eagles! The Eagles are coming!"' (*Letters*, p. 101, referring to *The Hobbit*, ch. 17). Another instance occurs in *The Lord of the Rings*, Book VI, Chapter 4, when Sam wakes after the destruction of the Ring and is greeted by Gandalf, whom he thought dead: 'But Sam lay back, and stared with open mouth, and for a moment, between bewilderment and great joy, he could not answer. At last he gasped: "Gandalf! I thought you were dead! But then I thought I was dead myself. Is everything sad going to come untrue?"'

An Evening in Tavrobel. Poem, a glimpse of fairies ('gleaming spirits') dancing among flowers by day and dewdrops by night, published in *Leeds University Verse 1914–24* (1924), p. 56. Originally the first of a pair of poems (the second unpublished), together *Two Eves in Tavrobel*, derived by Tolkien from a still longer work, *A Dream of Coming Home*, composed in France from 4 to 8 July 1916.

Tavrobel in *The Book of Lost Tales* is the place in Tol Eressëa where Eriol stays for a while listening to the stories of the Elves; but in the earliest conception of the mythology, Tol Eressëa was to become England at the end of the book, and Tavrobel was to become the Staffordshire village of *Great Haywood. See also *The Grey Bridge of Tavrobel.

Everett, Dorothy (1894–1953). Educated at Girton College, Cambridge, Bryn Mawr in the United States, and Royal Holloway College, London (where she was also an Assistant Lecturer), Dorothy Everett came to *Oxford in 1921 as a tutor at St Hugh's College. In 1926, after a temporary appointment as Lecturer in English at Somerville College, she became tutor in English Language and Literature, and in 1928 a Fellow, at Lady Margaret Hall. Among her students in later years was Tolkien's daughter *Priscilla. In 1930 she was made a University Lecturer in Middle English and a member of the English Faculty Board, on which she served with Tolkien. In 1948 she was named Reader in English at Oxford.

An authority on the works of *Chaucer, Everett delivered the 1950 Sir Israel Gollancz Memorial Lecture at the British Academy, 'Some Reflections on Chaucer's "Art Poetical"'. In 1951 Tolkien suggested her to the Oxford University Press as a candidate to complete the 'Clarendon Chaucer' (see *Geoffrey Chaucer) he had begun with *George S. Gordon but which was long delayed. For many years Everett contributed reviews of Middle English scholarship to Medium Ævum and The Year's Work in English Studies. With Tolkien she served on the *Ancrene Riwle subcommittee of the Early English Text Society, and was a fellow member of the first Executive Committee of the Society for the Study of Mediaeval Languages and Literature (*Societies and clubs).

Examinations. In July 1910, while at *King Edward's School, Birmingham, Tolkien sat the precursor of the School Certificate examination, the Oxford and Cambridge Higher Certificate, in five subjects: Latin, Greek, Elementary Mathematics, Scripture Knowledge (Greek Text), and History. He also satisfied the examiners in English Essay. This was set and marked by the Oxford and Cambridge Schools Examination Board, established in 1873. In 1917 the Oxford and Cambridge Higher Certificate was superseded by the introduction of the School Certificate, generally taken at age 16 or 17, 'a higher standard in which, under certain conditions, [the pupil] qualifies for the matriculation in entrance to the university', and the Higher School Certificate, generally taken at age 18 or 19 'in a more limited number of subjects' (Encyclopædia Britannica, 14th edn. (1938), vol. 8, p. 937).

Oxford University was one of the recognized examining boards for the new certificates, and Tolkien for many years was one of the examiners. According to Humphrey Carpenter, Tolkien undertook this task 'annually in pre-war years' (Biography, p. 136). When he and his family spent several weeks at *Filey on the Yorkshire coast in summer 1922, Tolkien 'had to spend a good deal of time marking School Certificate examination papers, a chore he now undertook annually to earn some extra money' (Biography, pp. 105–6). It seems likely that at least from the time of his election to a chair at Oxford he marked English examination papers for the Oxford board, probably for the Higher School Certificate.

On 22 July 1925 Tolkien told *H.F.B. Brett-Smith that he had 'done 200 answers on Caesar's ghost' (letter, quoted in David J. Holmes Autographs, *Catalogue 37* (December 1991), p. 58): one of the set books for the School Certificate examination was Shakespeare's *Julius Caesar*. On 7 August 1925 he wrote to *R.W. Chambers that he had only just finished with that year's school examinations, which helped to pay family medical bills, and jokingly hoped that he had not done himself any permanent damage. On 8 August he wrote again to Brett-Smith, who was evidently marking the same papers and had remarked on Tolkien's habit of scribbling on those he read: Tolkien commented on the low standard of the answers, and that scribbling saved him from apoplexy.

The *Encyclopædia Britannica* (1938) in its section on examinations in Britain gives a general description of methods of marking which probably applies to both the School Certificate and University examinations. Because of the greater number of candidates taking the former, no one examiner could mark or even survey all of the papers, and the examiners and candidates were unknown to each other. For examinations at a university, most of the examiners were drawn from that institution, but to provide an objective view and monitor standards there was usually one examiner appointed from outside. The aim was to ensure that all candidates were treated equally and fairly:

> The chief examiner usually sets the papers of questions and marks some of the scripts; the assistant examiners mark scripts. The preliminary stages in marking are usually occupied with the determination of a schedule of marks. All markers read a sample batch of scripts and then meet to discuss what the particular batch of candidates have done with the particular paper. The chief examiner has provided a provisional schedule of marking, and this schedule is modified in the light of the experience gained from reading the samples of scripts. The marking thus tends to be objective and to become merely a grading of the candidates against each other. The markers in conference determine upon a revised schedule of marks which is strictly followed thereafter; they disperse and, later, supply the chief examiner with samples of their marking. Markers, being human and being required to work under pressure against a time limit inevitably err; many of their vagaries occur in mechanical matters such as totalling marks. The marking of simple questions is merely a matter of eyesight. When the questions are more complex, or are of the kind which require essay-type answers, marking becomes more difficult; human judgment in these cases does not always act consistently, and inconsistencies of marking are inevitable. It is the function of the chief examiner to standardize the work of several examiners engaged on the same paper. [vol. 8, p. 941]

On 7 June 1955 Tolkien wrote to W.H. Auden regarding the origin of *The Hobbit*: 'All I remember . . . is sitting correcting School Certificate papers in the everlasting weariness of that annual task forced on impecunious academics with children. On a blank leaf I scrawled: "In a hole in the ground there lived a hobbit"' (*Letters*, p. 215).

There are many other references in his letters to the burden of examining, but few specific details other than those relating to his duties as an examiner within the English School at Oxford (see *Oxford English School). According to Humphrey Carpenter, Tolkien did a great deal of work as an external examiner to universities. 'During the nineteen-twenties and thirties he made frequent visits to many of the British universities as an examiner, and spent countless hours marking papers. After the Second World War he restricted this activity to examining regularly for the Catholic [or National] University of *Ireland' (*Biography*, p. 136). After *Stanley Unwin wrote to Tolkien suggesting that he write a sequel to the successful *Hobbit*, Tolkien replied on 15 October 1937 that he had 'spent nearly all the vacation times of seventeen years examining, and doing things of that sort, driven by immediate financial necessity. . . . Writing stories in prose or verse has been stolen, often guiltily, from time already mortgaged. . . . I may perhaps now do what I much desire to do, and not fail of financial duty' (*Letters*, p. 24).

His correspondence from earlier in the 1930s gives some idea of how busy he was as an examiner. On 22 January 1931 he wrote to *Kenneth Sisam that 'P[ass] Mod[eration]s [at Oxford] and 4 Universities will leave me no leisure before August'; and on 18 December 1932 that in addition to being an examiner in the Oxford English Honour School (with a new syllabus) in the coming year 'I am obliged to examine . . . Manchester and Reading, for the meeting of ends, this coming year; and probably P. Mods at the end of it' (Oxford University Press archives). Manchester and Reading were probably two of the four unnamed universities in 1931. Correspondence with E.V. Gordon in 1936 concerning dates for vivas (oral examinations) shows that he was examining in Manchester also that year, and very probably had been an examiner in the intervening years.

In one of these letters, dated 11 June 1936, Gordon indicates that Tolkien had undertaken a four-year commitment as an examiner for the University of London's M.A. degree, including students outside Britain. Gordon explains that there were four examiners, each apparently serving four years, who in their final two years were responsible for vivas as well as marking papers.

On 13 October 1938 Tolkien wrote to Stanley Unwin that 'even the Christmas vacation will be darkened by New Zealand scripts, as my friend [E.V.] Gordon died in the middle of their Honours Exams, and I had to finish setting the papers' (*Letters*, p. 41). On 2 February 1939 he wrote to C.A. Furth at George Allen & Unwin (*Publishers) that he had not been able to touch *The Lord of the Rings* since the beginning of December:

Among many other labours and troubles that the sudden death of my friend Professor Eric Gordon bequeathed to me, I had to clear up the

New Zealand examinations, which occupied nearly all last vacation. . . . But I have other heavy tasks ahead. I am at the 'peak' of my educational financial stress, with a second son clamouring for a university and the youngest wanting to go to school . . . , and I am obliged to do exams and lectures and what not. . . .

I may get part of the Easter Vac[ation] free. Not all – I shall have some papers to set. . . . [*Letters*, p. 42]

In 1939 Tolkien was not an examiner for the Oxford English Honour School, but he was concerned with examinations held by the Civil Service Commissioners for prospective entrants to the Civil Service, mentioned by Tolkien in a letter to *John Masefield on 14 July 1939.

For examinations taken by students at the University of Oxford, see the subsection 'Miscellaneous' in the entry for *Oxford.

Fairford (Gloucestershire). From 11 to 14 December 1945 Tolkien visited the town of Fairford with *R.E. Havard, *C.S. Lewis, and *W.H. Lewis for a 'Victory Inklings' gathering to celebrate the end of the war. Fairford and its 'Bull' inn were familiar to the Lewis brothers from a visit in September 1945; it is known in particular for the late-Perpendicular church of St Mary with its series of 16th-century stained-glass windows. Tolkien and his friends also visited hamlets and villages in the vicinity of Fairford, including **Coln St Aldwyn, Hatherop, Horcott, Meysey Hampton, Quenington, Sunhill,** and **Whelford.**

Fairy-stories. It is clear from his Andrew Lang Lecture (*On Fairy-Stories*) and from his letters that Tolkien was familiar with fairy-stories from many sources (see also *Reading), but generally preferred more traditional tales, such as those collected by the Brothers Grimm in Germany, by Asbjørnsen and Moe in Scandinavia, and by Campbell in Scotland, to the more 'literary' compositions written in seventeenth-century France by Perrault, Madame d'Aulnoy, and others, or in nineteenth-century Denmark by Hans Christian Andersen. He wrote in *On Fairy-Stories*: 'Important as I now perceive the fairy-story element in early reading to have been, speaking for myself as a child, I can only say that a liking for fairy-stories was not a dominant characteristic of early taste. A real taste for them awoke after "nursery" days, and after the years, few but long-seeming, between learning to read and going to school' (*Tree and Leaf*, p. 40). This was written by Tolkien not only in retrospect, but following immersion in fairy-stories and related critical literature as preparation for writing On Fairy-Stories for delivery in 1939. In later years he attributed the pronounced change in style between *The Hobbit* and *The Lord of the Rings* to this study, conducted during the same period (1938) that the sequel to *The Hobbit* was in its earliest stage of formation.

A comment that Tolkien wrote about the creation of *The Lord of the Rings* should always be borne in mind in any consideration of 'sources' or 'influence' on his writings: 'One writes such a story not out of the leaves of trees still to be observed, nor by means of botany and soil-science; but it grows like a seed in the dark out of the leaf-mould of the mind: out of all that has been seen or thought or read, that has long ago been forgotten, descending into the deeps' (quoted in *Biography*, p. 126). Motifs from fairy-tales may emerge in recognizable form, even if not consciously used, but they may also arrive transformed into something new, or intermingled with a leaf from another source. The 'leaf-mould' of Tolkien's mind was very rich, and in it fairy-story became mixed with epic, saga, quest, and romance – all words which commentators have used in their efforts to categorize his writings. Tolkien recognized this himself in his reply (*Observer*, 20 February 1938) to a query about the sources of *The Hobbit*: it was 'derived from (previously digested) epic, mythology, and fairy-story' (*Letters*, p. 31). In a letter to *Stanley Unwin on 16 December 1937 Tolkien described the dwarves in *The Hobbit* as 'conventional and inconsistent Grimm's fairy-tale dwarves' (*Letters*, p. 26), but he took most of their names (and that of Gandalf) from the *Elder Edda*, and in his letter to *The Observer* he commented that 'these dwarves are not quite the dwarfs of better known lore'. The trolls in *The Hobbit* who turn to stone when the sun rises belong to Scandinavian folk and fairy tradition, almost certainly a conscious reuse of a motif, introduced to please the Tolkien children who had been told tales about trolls by Icelandic *au pair* girls. Hence the narrator's comment: 'for trolls as you probably know, must be underground before dawn, or they go back to the stuff of the Mountains they are made of, and never move again' (*The Hobbit*, ch. 2).

In 'Real-world Myth in a Secondary World: Mythological Aspects in the Story of Beren and Lúthien', in *Tolkien the Medievalist* (2003), Richard C. West describes how Lúthien is imprisoned by her father to prevent her following Beren:

He has a comfortable prison built for her in the great beech Hirilorn . . . a tree house that can only be reached by long ladders that are taken away when not in use to bring her daily needs. She contrived to include magical ingredients among her daily needs. She sings a spell to lengthen her dark hair so that it reaches to the ground, and then she cuts it off and weaves from it a cloak and a cord. She uses the cloak to shroud herself in darkness – and so go about invisible – and the long cord, which she drops, to put a sleeping spell on the guards below. Then she climbs down the cord and dances away into the hinterlands.

Is there anyone who isn't reminded of Rapunzel? . . . Tolkien was familiar with the *Märchen* of the Brothers Grimm. Nevertheless the differences are far more marked than the similarities. Nowadays we are quite accustomed to what Jay Williams called 'the practical princess' who does not sit around waiting to be rescued, but this must have been unusual [when Tolkien first wrote the story]. Lúthien lets her hair down not just to enable her lover to reach her but to enable *her* to reach him.

The situation is full of resonances from other tales: the enchanted sleep of such stories as *Sleeping Beauty*: the cloak of invisibility in *The Twelve Dancing Princesses*. . . . [pp. 263–4]

One of the more common themes in fairy-tales, as also in romance and epic, is that of the *Quest, which can take many forms: to win the hand of a princess by performing a difficult task set by her father; to rescue someone (often a princess) imprisoned or held under a spell; to find something that has been lost; or just to make one's fortune. The hero or heroine may be set apparently impossible tasks, which they usually accomplish with the aid or advice of helpers, sometimes in the form of talking animals, or with the aid of gifts or objects with special powers. If a hero or heroine ignores a prohibition or warning, danger and hardship usually ensue.

Various types of quests occur in Tolkien's writing. In *The Silmarillion*, when the human Beren asks the Elven-king Thingol for the hand of his daughter Lúthien, Thingol, bound by a promise to his daughter that he would 'neither slay Beren nor imprison him', instead sets him a task which he believes impossible to fulfil and certain to lead to Beren's death: 'Bring to me in your hand a Silmaril from Morgoth's crown; and then, if she will, Lúthien may set her hand in yours' (pp. 166, 167). In *The Lord of the Rings* the story of Beren and Lúthien is echoed in their descendants when Elrond refuses to let his daughter, Arwen, wed Aragorn unless he regains the crowns of Gondor and Arnor. In *The Hobbit* the dwarves and Bilbo set out on a quest to recover treasure from a dragon, but in *The Lord of the Rings* Tolkien reversed the quest motif: Frodo does not set out to gain something, but to destroy the Ring. Both stories include instances of the inadvisability of ignoring prohibitions. In *The Hobbit* Bilbo and the dwarves find trouble when they disobey Gandalf's warning not to leave the path in Mirkwood; and in *The Lord of the Rings* Gandalf warns Frodo not to use the Ring, but when Black Riders attack under Weathertop he is unable the resist the temptation to put it on, and is wounded.

Also in *The Hobbit*, without the magic ring which Bilbo finds under the Misty Mountains it is unlikely that the quest would have succeeded: its power of making the wearer invisible enables Bilbo to escape from the goblins, to rescue the dwarves from the spiders and the Elvenking's halls, and to approach the dragon Smaug. When Tolkien decided to make this ring the link between *The Hobbit* and *The Lord of the Rings*, in the larger tale it acquired supreme significance, moving outside the usual boundary of fairy-tale. Other magical objects or features are also mentioned in *The Hobbit*: Gandalf had once given the Old Took 'a pair of magic diamond studs that fastened themselves and never came undone till ordered' (ch. 1); the trolls had a purse which could talk (like them, with a cockney accent); and in Mirkwood there is an enchanted river which induces drowsiness and forgetfulness. In *Farmer Giles of Ham* the sword, Tailbiter, sent to Giles by the King 'will not stay sheathed, if a dragon is within five miles' (p. 34) and does most of the fighting for Giles when he meets the dragon: 'Tailbiter did the best it could in inexperienced hands' (p. 44).

In *The Lord of the Rings* Frodo and his companions are given gifts with powers similar to those of the simple magic objects of fairy-stories, but as with the Ring these have been transformed and reshaped, and provided with a history which explains not only their powers but gives them a greater significance to the story as a whole. The cloaks that help conceal the company are not magic cloaks of invisibility but 'Elvish robes'. The knife with which Merry helps destroy the Witch-king of Angmar is not just a magic knife, but the 'work of Westernesse', 'wrought . . . slowly long ago in the North-kingdom when the Dúnedain were young, and chief among their foes was the dread realm of Angmar and its sorcerer king. No other blade, not though mightier hands had wielded it, would have dealt that foe a wound so bitter, cleaving the undead flesh, breaking the spell that knit his unseen sinews to his will' (bk. V, ch. 6). And in the crystal phial which she gives to Frodo, Galadriel has 'caught the light of Eärendil's star, set amid the waters of my fountain' – the light of the Silmaril worn by Eärendil which preserves the unsullied light of the Two Trees of Valinor. 'It will shine still brighter when night is about you. May it be a light to you in dark places, when all other lights go out' (bk. II, ch. 8).

In *The Hobbit*, to enable them survive the long journey through Mirkwood, Beorn gives Bilbo and the dwarves iron rations of 'twice-baked cakes that would keep a long time, and a little of which they could march far' (ch. 7). In *The Lord of the Rings* the elves of Lothlórien give the Company something far more significant, indeed numinous: '*lembas* or waybread . . . more strengthening than any food made by Men' (bk. II, ch. 8). As the story proceeds, it becomes clear that *lembas* (see *Of Lembas*) is more than mere food, it also has other virtues, especially a power to feed the will and give it strength to endure.

In *On Fairy-Stories* Tolkien wrote: 'Beasts and birds and other creatures often talk like men in real fairy-stories. In some part (often small) this marvel derives from one of the primal "desires" that lie near the heart of Faërie: the desire of men to hold communion with other living beings' (*Tree and Leaf*, p. 19). Variations of this motif include a human character being able to speak the actual language of other living beings or to understand the meaning of their natural utterances, or animals being able to understand human speech. Instances in Tolkien's writings include Tevildo the cat who holds Beren prisoner, Huan the hound, Glaurung the dragon, and Thorondor the eagle, in various *'Silmarillion'* texts; the old grey mare, Garm the dog, and Chrysophylax the dragon in *Farmer Giles of Ham*; eagles, wolves, Beorn's horses, dogs, and sheep (who not only understand what Beorn says, but also seem to do much of the housekeeping), spiders, Smaug, a thrush, and Roäc the raven in *The Hobbit*. In fairy-tales a character may receive important advice or information from a beast or bird 'helper', or is warned of impending danger by overhearing and understanding a conversation. In *The Hobbit* the thrush, having overheard Bilbo describing Smaug's unprotected soft spot, informs Bard the bowman, who uses the information to kill the dragon.

The earliest version of the story of Beren and Lúthien in *The Book of Lost Tales* (*'Of Beren and Lúthien'*) is much more like a fairy-tale than later versions. When Beren is captured by agents of Melko (Morgoth) he is made thrall to Tevildo Prince of Cats, who tests his abilities as a hunter by demanding that he catch three mice – the kind of task sometimes imposed on a heroine in a fairy-tale, and one that Beren fails. Huan, Captain of Dogs, suggests a ruse by which Tinúviel rescues Beren, and after defeating Tevildo in a fight takes from him a collar of gold in which lay 'a great magic of strength and power' (*The Book of Lost Tales, Part Two*, p. 29). In later versions of the story it is not Tevildo but Sauron who holds Beren prisoner, and though Lúthien plays a greater part in freeing Beren, Huan still overcomes Sauron, who attempts to escape by shifting into the form first of a werewolf, then a serpent. Huan is also raised in status, becoming a wolfhound of Valinor, originally given by the Vala Oromë to Celegorm, one of the sons of Fëanor. Huan comprehends the speech of 'all things with voice', but is permitted to speak 'only thrice with words' (*The Silmarillion*, p. 173). He loves Lúthien from the hour of their meeting, and aids her escape from Celegorm to rescue Beren, fights and defeats Sauron, brings a healing herb to Lúthien when Beren is wounded, and counsels them in their quest for a Silmaril.

In *The Lord of the Rings* speaking animals or birds do not appear, with the exception of the eagles: Gwaihir who bears Gandalf, and the eagle who brings news of victory to Minas Tirith. But as in *The Silmarillion*, the eagles are the messengers of Manwë, chief of the Valar. There are hints that birds act as spies for Saruman, and they may be the means by which Gildor informs Tom Bombadil, Aragorn, and Rivendell that Frodo has set out, but nothing is said of their speaking. Magic horses who can speak, or have great speed, or even fly are a standard element in fairy-stories, but Shadowfax is more than this: although he does not speak, he evidently understands the words not only of Gandalf but also of Pippin. He can outrun other horses, and 'alone among the free horses of the earth' can endure the terror of the Witch-king (bk. V, ch. 4). But then, as Tolkien wrote to Miss A.P. Northey, 'Shadowfax came of a special race, being as it were an Elvish equivalent of ordinary horses; his "blood" came from "West over Sea"' (*Letters*, p. 354). The 'thinking' fox in Book I, Chapter 3 belongs rather to *The Lord of the Rings* as it was first conceived, closer to the fairy-tale mode of *The Hobbit* to which the greater story is a sequel.

In fairy- or folk-tales it is often the least-regarded character, the youngest son or daughter, who unexpectedly succeeds where others fail. Tolkien uses this device in *Farmer Giles of Ham* and *The Hobbit*: at first sight neither Farmer Giles nor Bilbo Baggins seem to have the making of a hero, but unusually, both are reluctant heroes. Katharyn W. Crabbe points out that

> despite his reluctance to fight giants and dragons, Farmer Giles is a traditional fairy-tale hero. His heroic attributes are not obvious or conventional – he is not braver or stronger, or wiser, or more handsome than other men. . . . What virtues he has are, like Bilbo's, the virtues of the powerless: prudence (in loading his blunderbuss and covering his ring mail with a cloak), discretion (in agreeing to leave part of the treasure for

Chrysophylax in return for the dragon's protection), and reverence for the past (in his appreciation of Tailbiter). However, as the narrator notes, his most important characteristics are luck and wits. [*J.R.R. Tolkien* (rev. and expanded edn. 1988), pp. 148–9]

Bilbo, as described in a blurb written by Tolkien, is almost an archetypal hero of this sort: 'a humble hero (blessed with a little wisdom and a little courage and considerable good luck)' (George Allen & Unwin *Summer Announcements* (1937), and the dust-jacket of early editions of *The Hobbit*).

In *The Lord of the Rings*, although Frodo in some ways resembles Bilbo, the idea of the humble hero is given greater and more universal significance. Elrond says of the quest to destroy the Ring that it 'may be attempted by the weak with as much hope as the strong. Yet such is oft the course of deeds that move the wheels of the world: small hands must do them, while the eyes of the great are elsewhere' (bk. II, ch. 2). This was a theme dear to Tolkien, who wrote in 1956: 'I loved [the hobbits] myself, since I love the vulgar and simple as dearly as the noble, and nothing moves my heart (beyond all the passions and heartbreaks of the world) so much as "ennoblement" (from the Ugly Duckling [by Hans Christian Andersen] to Frodo)' (*Letters*, p. 232).

In his letter to *The Observer* Tolkien cited *George MacDonald as the exception to the rule that Victorian fairy-stories had not had much influence on *The Hobbit*. He acknowledged the debt his Goblins and Orcs owed to MacDonald's *The Princess and the Goblin* (1872) and *The Princess and Curdie* (1883) on several occasions, notably in a draft of *On Fairy-Stories* where he wrote: 'George MacDonald, in that mixture of German and Scottish flavours (which makes him so inevitably attractive to myself) has depicted what will always be to me the classic goblin. By that standard I judge all goblins, old or new' (Tolkien papers, Bodleian Library, Oxford). It should be noted, however, that the Goblins in *The Hobbit*, written for the Tolkien children, differ greatly from the Orcs in 'The Silmarillion', though identified as the same beings in *The Lord of the Rings*.

In fact, there was at least one other Victorian writer who seems to have a considerable influence on Tolkien's writings, though perhaps subconsciously. When Tolkien was trying to establish for the supplement to the *Oxford English Dictionary* whether he had, as he thought, invented the word *hobbit*, or whether, as had been suggested in a letter to *The Observer* in 1938, it had appeared in an old collection of fairy-tales, he consulted his friend *Roger Lancelyn Green: 'One cannot exclude the possibility that buried childhood memories might suddenly rise to the surface long after. . . . I used (before 1900) to be read to from an 'old collection' – tattered and without cover or title-page – of which all I can now remember was that . . . [it] contained one story I was then very fond of called "*Puss Cat Mew*"' (8 January 1971, *Letters*, p. 407). Green identified the book in question as *Stories for My Children* (1869) by E.H. Knatchbull-Hugessen. In 'Puss-Cat Mew' (as it is spelled in the book) the hero, Joe, sets out to rescue his wife (Puss-Cat Mew) who is being held prisoner by ogres. A fox gives him several gifts to aid him on his quest, including a left-hand glove which makes its wearer invisible. While he is invisible he provokes two ogres and their dwarf servant to attack each other, each believing the other is responsible for Joe's blows and taunts – rather in the way that Gandalf foments dispute among the trolls in *The Hobbit* – with the result that they injure each other so badly that Joe is able to kill all three. While he is invisible in the ogres' castle he overhears two dwarf servants mention the prisoner, Puss-Cat Mew, follows them, and discovers her prison. In a similar way in *The Hobbit* the invisible Bilbo hears the guards talking and learns that Thorin is a prisoner in the Elvenking's palace. At one point Joe is in great danger, because when wearing the glove, 'as ill luck would have it, a nail in the doorpost caught his glove, which fell from his hand, and as he rushed from the yard the Ogre saw him' (p. 60); the 'accident' foreshadows the tricky behaviour of the One Ring which tended to slip from the wearer's finger in moments of crisis.

In this story there is also a possible influence on *The Lord of the Rings*: the description of an ogre, who had taken on the appearance of a tree, may have contributed to the Giant Treebeard, a creature in league with the enemy who in early drafts of *The Lord of the Rings* was to hold Gandalf captive, or to be encountered by Frodo, who thought one of his legs was 'the stem of a monstrous oaktree' (*sic*; *The Return of the Shadow*, p. 384). Joe sees 'an old dead Oak, with two great branches, with scarce a leaf upon them, spreading out left and right. . . . Gradually . . . the bark of the tree appeared to become the skin of a living body, the two dead limbs became the gigantic arms of a man, a head popped up from the trunk, and an enormous Ogre stood before the astonished traveller' (p. 4). Even when the unfriendly giant was transformed into Treebeard the Ent, some similarity remained: Merry and Pippin see 'one old stump of a tree with only two bent branches left: it looked almost like the figure of some gnarled old man' (bk. III, ch. 4). In the illustration of this scene the tree-ogre has a very Entish look, and Joe would make a good Hobbit.

In 'Ernest', another story in the Knatchbull-Hugessen collection, a boy goes down a well to recover his ball and meets an enormous toad smoking a large cigar. Their encounter in some respects seems to foreshadow Bilbo's meeting with Smaug: the toad calls Ernest a presumptuous fool for daring to come down the well. Ernest 'replied, with the lowest bow which circumstances enabled him to make. "Presumptuous, sir, I may possibly be, but it can hardly be the act of a fool which has brought one into the presence of so noble and handsome a Toad as yourself." "Not so bad," replied the Toad; "I see you have been taught manners"' (p. 74). In *The Hobbit*, Chapter 12, Bilbo similarly flatters Smaug, who comments on his manners. In *Stories for My Children* there is also an illustration for the scene in which the bowing Ernest and the head of the toad smoking his cigar, which has similarities to Tolkien's painting *Conversation with Smaug* (*Artist and Illustrator*, fig. 133). See further, Christina Scull, 'The Fairy-Tale Tradition', *Mallorn* 23 (Summer 1926).

In *On Fairy-Stories* Tolkien rejected the commonly held view that children were 'the natural or the specially appropriate audience for fairy-stories', asking: 'Is there any *essential* connexion between children and fairy-stories?' He suggested rather that 'if a fairy-story as a kind is worth reading at all it is worthy to be written for and read by adults. They will of course put more in and get more out than children can' (*Tree and Leaf*, pp. 33, 34). Later he wrote to Michael Straight that *The Lord of the Rings* 'is a "fairy-story", but one written – according to the belief I once expressed in an extended essay "on Fairy-stories" that they are the proper audience – for adults. because I think that fairy story has its own mode of reflecting "truth", different from allegory, or (sustained) satire, or "realism", and in some ways more powerful' (probably January or February 1956, *Letters*, pp. 232–3; see also *Children). The Lord of the Rings* having begun as a sequel to *The Hobbit* and intended for children, Tolkien wrote its early chapters at first in the same facetious style he used for much of the earlier book. Its style changed gradually as the story took a more serious turn, but this seems to have come from the demands of the story, rather than imposed from without, according to the author's notion of his audience.

Fairy-stories, Tolkien said,

> are not in normal English usage stories *about* fairies or elves, but stories about Fairy, that is *Faërie*, the realm or state in which fairies have their being. *Faërie* contains many things besides elves and fays, and besides dwarfs, witches, trolls, giants, or dragons: it holds the seas, the sun, the moon, the sky; and the earth, and all things that are in it: tree and bird, water and stone, wine and bread, and ourselves, mortal men, when we are enchanted.
>
> Stories that are actually concerned primarily with 'fairies', that is with creatures that might also in modern English be called 'elves' are relatively rare, and as a rule not very interesting. Most good 'fairy-stories' are about the *aventures* of men in the Perilous Realm or upon its shadowy marches. Naturally so; for if elves are true, and really exist independently of our tales about them, then this also is certainly true: elves are not primarily concerned with us, nor we with them. Our fates are sundered, and our paths seldom meet. [*On Fairy-Stories*, in *Tree and Leaf*, p. 14]

Among Tolkien's stories, **Smith of Wootton Major* is the only one which exactly fits the above description. Smith is given a star which enables him to cross the borders of Faërie and to see and experience various wonders. 'Fairies' (later Elves) do appear in Tolkien's earliest 'Silmarillion' stories, but only because 'the old word was indeed the only one available, and was once fitted to apply to such memories of this people as Men preserved, or to the makings of Men's minds not wholly dissimilar. But it has been diminished, and to many it may now suggest fancies either pretty or silly, as unlike to the Quendi of old as are butterflies to the falcon' (*The Lord of the Rings*, Appendix F). Tolkien's Elves inhabit Middle-earth with Men, and in the First Age fight together against Morgoth. By the end of the Third Age the few elves that remain in Middle-earth live in Rivendell, Lothlórien, northern Mirkwood, and the Grey Havens, and have little to do with Men. Lothlórien, which comes closest to the traditional concept of Faërie, is viewed with suspicion by the men of Gondor and Rohan. Boromir says that 'of that perilous land we have heard in Gondor, and it is said that few come out who once go in; and of that few none have escaped unscathed' (*The Lord of the Rings*, bk. II, ch. 6).

Tolkien blamed writers such as William Shakespeare (see *Drama) and Michael Drayton for transforming 'the glamour of Elfland into mere finesse, and invisibility into a fragility that could hide in a cowslip or shrink behind a blade of grass', and referred to the 'flower-fairies and fluttering sprites with antennae that I so disliked as a child' (*Tree and Leaf*, pp. 11–12). Nonetheless, some of his earliest writings, such as the poems *Goblin Feet and *The Princess Ní, portray similar diminutive beings, and it was his intention in *The Book of Lost Tales* that in the future the Elves would actually fade and diminish and become transparent, and so become the 'fairies' as commonly conceived. Years later he wrote of *Goblin Feet*: 'I wish the unhappy little thing, representing all that I came (so soon after) to fervently dislike, could be buried for ever' (quoted in *The Book of Lost Tales, Part One*, p. 32). The elves at Rivendell in *The Hobbit* with their silly songs are not much better. In contrast, the elves whose deeds are related in the mythology and those that appear in *The Lord of the Rings* are powerful beings of great ability, and hardly diminutive. Tolkien told William Cater that 'elves were large, formidable . . . Spenser wrote about knights who were elves. By writing about elves as tall as men I am restoring tradition, trying to rescue the word from the nursery' ('Lord of the Hobbits', *Daily Express*, 22 November 1966, p. 10). There is little doubt that Tolkien succeeded, and that today most people are likely to visualize elves as they appear in his created world.

Towards the end of *On Fairy-Stories* Tolkien defined what he thought should be the values and functions of fairy-stories as literature for adults: 'if written with art' their 'prime value . . . will simply be that value which, as literature, they share with other literary forms. But fairy-stories offer also, in a peculiar degree or mode, these things: Fantasy, Recovery, Escape, Consolation, all things of which children have, as a rule, less need than older people' (*Tree and Leaf*, p. 44; see also *Escape, *Eucatastrophe, *Recovery).

The Fall. A devout Roman Catholic (*Religion), Tolkien believed in a Fall of Man from which came much of the evil and unhappiness in the world. Because of his fallen nature, whatever Man touched or made, even with good intentions, was likely to turn out other, or less good, than he hoped (see *Good and Evil). Tolkien wrote to his son *Christopher on 7 July 1944: 'Labour-saving machinery only creates endless and worse labour. And in addition to this fundamental disability of a creature, is added the Fall, which makes our devices not only fail of their desire but turn to new and horrible evil. So we come inevitably from Daedalus and Icarus to the Giant Bomber' (*Letters*, p. 88). In regard to human relationships, Tolkien wrote to his son *Michael that 'the dislocation of sex-instinct is one of the chief symptoms of the Fall. The world has been "going to the bad" all down the ages. The various social forms shift, and each new mode has its special dangers: but the "hard spirit of concupiscence" has walked down every street, and sat leering in every house, since Adam fell.' 'The essence of a *fallen* world', he continued, 'is that the *best* cannot be attained by free enjoyment, or by what is called "self-realization" (usually a nice name for self-indulgence, wholly inimical to the realization of other selves); but by denial, by suffering' (6–8 March 1941, *Letters*, pp. 48, 51). He suggested that in the idea of a man and a women '"destined" for one another, and capable of a very great and splendid love' as told in so many stories, usually with a tragic outcome, 'we catch a vision . . . of marriage as it should have been in an unfallen world' (p. 52).

Tolkien's view of Man and the world as 'fallen' at times led to pessimism. In a letter to Amy Ronald on 15 December 1956 he wrote: 'Actually I am a Christian, and indeed a Roman Catholic, so that I do not expect "history" to be anything but a "long defeat" – though it contains (and a legend may contain more clearly and movingly) some samples or glimpses of final victory' (*Letters*, p. 255). Verlyn Flieger comments in *Splintered Light: Logos and Language in Tolkien's World* (2nd edn. 2002) that

pessimism is disappointed optimism, but a Christian acceptance of the Fall leads inevitably to the idea that imperfection is the state of things in this world and that human actions, however hopeful, cannot rise above that imperfection. . . .

The world, then, must be seen as a place of defeat and disappointment, and man must be seen as born to trouble. . . . Tolkien's enclosure of the word 'history' in quotation marks suggests that he means history in contrast to eternity and that the 'long defeat' has to do with humanity's work in this world, not its expectations in the next. [p. 4]

In a letter to Christopher on 30–1 January 1945 Tolkien expressed reservations of the Fall taking place precisely as told in Genesis, but had no doubt that there had once been an Eden from which Man had been exiled.

As for Eden, I think most Christians, except the v[ery] simple and uneducated or those protected in other ways, have been rather bustled and hustled now for some generations by the self-styled scientists, and they've sort of tucked Genesis into a lumber-room of their mind as not very fashionable furniture, a bit ashamed to have it about the house. . . . In consequence they have indeed (myself as much as many), as you say, forgotten the beauty of the matter even 'as a story'. . . . But partly as a development of my own thought on my lines and work (technical and literary), partly in contact with [*C.S. Lewis], and in various ways not least the firm guiding hand of Alma Mater Ecclesia, I do not now feel either ashamed or dubious on the Eden 'myth'. It has not, of course, historicity of the same kind as the N[ew] T[estament], which are virtually contemporary documents, while Genesis is separated by we do not know how many sad exiled generations from the Fall, but certainly there was an Eden on this very unhappy earth. We all long for it, and we are constantly glimpsing it: our whole nature at its best and least corrupted, its gentlest and most humane, is still soaked with the sense of 'exile'. . . . As far as we can go back the nobler part of the human mind is filled with the thoughts of . . . peace and goodwill, and with the thought of its *loss*. [*Letters*, pp. 109–10]

In a letter to *Milton Waldman Tolkien wrote that 'there cannot be any "story" without a fall – all stories are ultimately about the fall – at least not for human minds as we know them and have them' (?late 1951, *Letters*, p. 147). In his *'Silmarillion' mythology the fall of some of the Ainur (Melkor, Aulë, Sauron) takes the place that the fall of Satan and rebel angels occupies in Christian myth. Melkor 'fell' because he tried to pervert the Music of Creation to his own ends and turned his powers 'to evil purposes, and squandered his strength in violence and tyranny. For he coveted Arda and all that was in it, desiring the kingship of Manwë and dominion over the realms of his peers' (*The Silmarillion*, p. 31). Sauron, his chief servant, had a part in all of the deceits of Melkor (Morgoth) and 'in after years rose like a shadow of Morgoth and a ghost of his malice, and walked behind him on the same ruinous path down into the Void' (p. 32).

A lesser fall in these legends is that of the Vala Aulë, who creates the Dwarves because he is too impatient to wait for Elves and Men to awake. When Ilúvatar rebukes him, he repents and seeks pardon, prepared even to destroy his creation; but because of his repentance Ilúvatar takes the Dwarves into his own design.

But 'The Silmarillion' is largely concerned with 'the fall of the most gifted kindred of the Elves, their exile from Valinor (a kind of Paradise, the home of the Gods) in the furthest West. . . . The Fall of the Elves comes about through the possessive attitude of Fëanor and his seven sons to [the Silmarils].' When these gems are seized by Morgoth,

> the sons of Fëanor take a terrible and blasphemous oath of enmity and vengeance against all or any, even of the gods, who dares to claim any part or right in the Silmarilli. They pervert the greater part of their kindred, who rebel against the gods, and depart from paradise, and go to make hopeless war upon the Enemy. The first fruit of their fall is war in Paradise, the slaying of Elves by Elves, and this and their evil oath dogs all their later heroism, generating treacheries and undoing all victories. [letter to Milton Waldman, ?late 1951, *Letters*, p. 148]

In Tolkien's *legendarium* as it stood for most of his life, 'the first fall of Man . . . nowhere appears – Men do not come on the stage until all that is long past, and there is only a rumour that for a while they fell under the domination of the Enemy [Morgoth] and that some repented' (letter to Waldman, *Letters*, pp. 147–8). In *The Silmarillion*, all Bëor will tell Finrod is that 'a darkness lies behind us . . . and we have turned our backs on it' (p. 141).

Anne C. Petty comments on 'The Myth of the Fall' at length in *Tolkien in the Land of Heroes: Discovering the Human Spirit* (2003). She points out that the two falls in Christian tradition, that of Satan who rebelled against God and was expelled from Heaven, and that of Adam and Eve who broke a ban, 'provided Tolkien with all the raw ingredients . . . for his universe of fallen heroes and civilizations'. His 'use of the fall from grace as an important plot device is interwoven throughout his history of Middle-earth, injecting the tales with dramatic tension and a sense of peril as well as a pervading tone of sadness and loss' (pp. 30–1). Petty concludes that

> Ilúvatar's decision to allow the creation of Eä to go forward out of the divine music, flaws and all, opens the door for a world much more complex and difficult than was first designed. When the direct effects of Melkor's evil take hold in Middle-earth, we can see just how much ruin and grief comes into the world in spite of all the positive works the Valar accomplish as guardians of Arda. . . . We are left, then, with a flawed, fallen world that contains both beauty and horror within its borders, which might be said of the world we live in as well. [p. 94]

The Fall of Númenor. Story, the first two versions of which were published with commentary in **The Lost Road and Other Writings* (1987), pp. 11–35, and a third with commentary in *Sauron Defeated (1992), pp. 331–40. A summary of *The Fall of Númenor* and a description of the further development of the history of Númenor and its significance for **The Lord of the Rings* are given in the present book under *Númenor.

In 1936 or 1937 Tolkien and *C.S. Lewis agreed that they would each try to write a book of the sort they themselves liked to read, but did not find as often as they wished. Tolkien's attempt, ultimately abandoned, was *The Lost Road, in which he transformed the legendary island of *Atlantis into Númenor, a land in the West of the Great Sea given by the Valar to Men who fought against Morgoth during the First Age. Before beginning *The Lost Road*, however, Tolkien felt it necessary to work out the history of Númenor. A single-page outline of the fall of *Númar* or *Númenos* was followed by a rough untitled narrative of the history of Númenor from its creation to its destruction; many corrections were made to this in the course of writing. Tolkien may have written part of the Númenórean episode in *The Lost Road* next; the second version of the history of Númenor was either written concurrently with the episode, or immediately after. In this more finished manuscript, later entitled *The Last Tales: The Fall of Númenor*, he greatly expanded the earlier part of the history and made many changes otherwise.

These versions of *The Fall of Númenor* can only be roughly dated to 1936 or possibly 1937. Some of the names used in the work indicate that it is later than the *Ambarkanta*, but a sketch within the outline seems to be a forerunner of a diagram of the World Made Round after the destruction of Númenor which accompanies the *Ambarkanta*. An amanuensis typescript, taking up emendations Tolkien made to the second version, was produced not long after the manuscripts. Some years later, after he had written much of *The Lord of the Rings*, but before February 1942, Tolkien used this typescript as a basis for further change, and also drafted new versions of parts of the text on a loose sheet. He then produced a third version, a fine manuscript, with the title *The Last Tales: 1. The Fall of Númenor*, incorporating changes made to the typescript and others worked out in the new versions, and making other improvements as he wrote. Tolkien later made additions and changes to this manuscript when working on *The Drowning of Anadûnê*, the next version of the Númenor story.

In a letter written to Christopher Bretherton on 16 July 1964 Tolkien said that he never finished *The Lost Road* because his 'real interest' was only in the Númenórean part, 'so I brought all the stuff I had written on the originally unrelated legends of Númenor into relation with the main mythology' (*Letters*, p. 347). But Christopher Tolkien could find no evidence that his father had written anything about Númenor before the brief outline preceding *The Fall of Númenor*, which was already fully integrated with the mythology; see *The Lost Road and Other Writings*, pp. 7–10.

Fandom. Tolkien began to receive fan letters soon after *The Hobbit* was first published in September 1937. Some writers simply expressed their delight in the book, while others wanted to know more about the world in which it was set. Tolkien himself acknowledged most of these; but with the publication of *The Lord of the Rings* in 1954–5, he was inundated with mail, and able to send personal replies to only a few of the many thousands who wrote to him. Secretarial help, and finally George Allen & Unwin (*Publishers), provided assistance in this regard. (It is a measure of the popularity of *The Lord of the Rings* that Tolkien was forced to use printed form replies to fans even before the work appeared in paperback in 1965.) As Tolkien fandom grew, he also received uninvited visitors at his house and unwanted telephone calls, some of the latter from American enthusiasts who had not considered the time difference between the U.S.A. and England. Together with letters, admirers sent Tolkien gifts of all sorts: in a letter to Sterling Lanier, 21 November 1972, for instance, he noted that he had received a drinking goblet from a fan, only to find that it was 'of steel engraved with the terrible words seen on the Ring [of Sauron in *The Lord of the Rings*]. I of course have never drunk from it, but use it for tobacco ash' (*Letters*, p. 422).

Tolkien eventually removed his telephone number from the Oxford directory, and when he moved to *Poole took care that his new address was not published, all correspondence being directed c/o Allen & Unwin. When he returned to Oxford after his wife's death, his privacy was again protected. Although Tolkien appreciated the attention his readers gave him, it was more than he could bear, and he was often irritated, or at least puzzled, by readers' interpretations of his works: 'guesses at the "sources" of the nomenclature, and theories or fancies concerning hidden meanings' (draft letter to Mr Rang, August 1967, *Letters*, p. 379). In a draft letter to Carole Batten-Phelps, autumn 1971, he wrote of the 'horrors of the American scene' which 'have given me great distress and labour' (*Letters*, p. 412), and in a letter to Norman Davis he referred to 'my deplorable cultus' (quoted in *Biography*, p. 231).

ORGANIZED TOLKIEN FANDOM

Appreciation of *The Lord of the Rings* first entered into discussions of British and American Science Fiction fans in the late 1950s, when Fantasy was not yet considered a separate literary (or publishing) genre. In 1960, at the World Science Fiction Convention in Pittsburgh, a group of fans from Los Angeles formed a Tolkien club, The Fellowship of the Ring. The first number of their magazine *I Palantir* was published in August of that year. The activities of the Fellowship were limited during its six years of existence, however, and *I Palantir* lasted only four issues. Another short-lived fanzine, *Entmoot*, was published at about the same time, but was independent of any formal organization. Tolkien-related articles and news also appeared in the early sixties in *Niekas*, published by Ed Meskys. In May 1961 Tolkien spent a day in the company of a large club at Queen's College, Cambridge devoted to the reading and study of his works.

In early 1965 Richard (Dick) Plotz, then a high school student attending classes at Columbia University in New York, invited fellow Tolkien enthusiasts to meet as a 'Tolkien club' on the University campus, and also placed an advertisement in the *New Republic* magazine: 'Discuss hobbit lore and learn Elvish'. Thus was born the New York Tolkien Society. In May 1965 Plotz published the first number (Spring 1965) of the *Tolkien Journal*, in which he said that the 'basic aim' of the Society was 'to further communication among all the Tolkien enthusiasts everywhere' (p. 1). It was a fateful moment, for in ?May–?July of that year Ace Books published their unauthorized edition of *The Lord of the Rings*, which touched off a 'war over Middle-earth', as Ace Books, Tolkien's authorized *publishers Houghton Mifflin and Allen & Unwin, and Tolkien himself argued whether the Ace edition was or was not an act of 'piracy' (see *Ace Books controversy). By the second number of the *Tolkien Journal* (Winterfilth 1965, adopting a term from the Hobbit calendar), the New York Tolkien Society had become the Tolkien Society of America (or TSA), reflecting the growth it had experienced in the interim.

Dick Plotz wrote to Tolkien probably in early September 1965, inviting him to become a member of the Society and asking him questions. By then Tolkien had already heard about the group; he wrote to *W.H. Auden on 4 August 1965 that 'real lunatics don't join' such organizations, 'but still such things fill me too with alarm and despondency' (*Letters*, p. 359). Tolkien replied to Plotz on 12 September 1965 that he was 'much interested to hear of the formation of the "Tolkien Society", and very grateful for the compliment. I do not, how-ever, see how I can become a "member" of a society inspired by liking for my works and devoted (I suppose) to study and criticism of them, as at least part of their activities.' But he would 'be pleased to be associated with you in some informal capacity', willing to offer advice 'or provide information not yet in print' (*Letters*, p. 359). Probably referring especially to Dick Plotz, who then signed himself 'Frodo' and was the 'Thain' or president of the Society, Tolkien suggested that it was 'a mistake to give names of characters (or offices) in the story' (*Letters*, p. 360). The *Tolkien Journal* quickly became an organ of support for Tolkien's campaign against Ace Books, helping to encourage the purchase of the Ballantine Books edition instead of one that was not authorized by Tolkien and did not pay him royalties.

The Tolkien Society of America grew quickly, having been mentioned in publicity surrounding the Ace Books affair. Subscriptions and letters over-whelmed Dick Plotz, who handed over direction of the Society to Ed Meskys in September 1967. The *Tolkien Journal* continued for a while (Meskys also still issued *Niekas* and a TSA newsletter, *The Green Dragon*), for three issues part-nered with *Orcrist*, the fanzine of the University of Wisconsin Tolkien Society (founded 1966, edited by Richard C. West), and for one with *Mythlore*, the journal of the Mythopoeic Society.

The latter group was founded in September 1967 by Glen GoodKnight of Los Angeles, who earlier that year had formed a Tolkien society at California State University and now wished to extend its membership and focus. The Mythopoeic Society from the start was devoted to *C.S. Lewis and *Charles Williams as well as Tolkien. Meetings took place in members' homes, and discussion groups were encouraged. Following a one-day Narnia Conference in 1969, a Mythopoeic Conference ('Mythcon') has been an annual event. A Society bulletin was published beginning in January 1968, succeeded by *Myth-print* in 1970; the quarterly journal *Mythlore* began in 1969. Other Society periodicals (*Mythril, Mythellany, Mythic Circle*) have been devoted to creative writing and poetry. In 1972 Ed Meskys, having lost his sight, arranged for the Tolkien Society of America to merge with the Mythopoeic Society.

Notable among many other, mostly ephemeral Tolkien fan groups in the United States have been the National Tolkien League, founded in 1972, pub-lisher of *Frodo Fortnightly*; the American Tolkien Society, founded in 1975 in the Midwest by Paul Ritz, David Dettman, and Philip and Marci Helms (its fanzine, *Minas Tirith Evening-Star*, existed from 1967); the American Hobbit Association, founded in 1977 by Michael Dorman, Greg Everitt, and Renee Alper, who published *Annúminas* (later *Rivendell Review*); the Tolkien Fellow-ships, begun in 1977 by Bernie Zuber, who published the *Westmarch Chronicle*; and the New England Tolkien Society, begun by Sumner Gary Hunnewell in Maine in 1979 (and later moved to Missouri, with no change of name), with its fanzine *Ravenhill*. Hunnewell became one of the leading experts on Tolkien fandom and fanzines. *Beyond Bree*, edited and published from California by Nancy Martsch, nominally as the organ of the Tolkien special-interest group

of American MENSA, has enjoyed a long run (remarkably for a Tolkien fanzine, mostly on schedule) and remains perhaps the most generally informative
magazine for Tolkien fans.

The first regular Tolkien-related magazine in Britain, the *Middle Earth-
worm*, began publication in January 1969, under the direction of Archie
Mercer, the U.K. agent of the TSA. Although a Hobbit Society was in existence
at University College, London, since before 1967, there was not yet in 1969 a
general Tolkien Society in the manner of the TSA and the Mythopoeic Society.
The formation of such a group was taken in hand at last by Vera Chapman,
who wished 'to rescue the appreciation of Tolkien from what she felt to be
the gross abuse of his name and works to be found in certain quarters, especially the drugs-oriented writings of hippiedom' (Charles E. Noad, 'The Early
Days of the Tolkien Society', *A Long-expected Party: Progress Report* 1 (1990),
p. 10). She announced the conception of a Tolkien Society in Britain through
the personal column of the *New Statesman* magazine for 6 November 1969,
and further publicized it in her own publication, *Belladonna's Broadsheet*, for
December 1969. (Like other Tolkien fans of the period, Vera Chapman took a
Tolkienian pseudonym: hers was Belladonna Took, mother of Bilbo Baggins.
She was ever after known to friends as 'Bella'.) The inaugural meeting of the
Tolkien Society occurred in January 1970. The Society continues to flourish: it
hosts an annual 'Oxonmoot', a general meeting, and a seminar, and publishes
a bulletin, *Amon Hen* (previously *Anduril* and *Henneth Annûn*), and a journal,
Mallorn. In 1992 the Tolkien Society joined with the Mythopoeic Society to
organize the Tolkien Centenary Conference held at Oxford; and in summer
2005 it was the principal sponsor of a major Tolkien gathering at *Birmingham.

A Tolkien fan society, the Forodrim, was founded in Sweden in 1972. Other
national Tolkien groups have been slower to form, but today are active in most
countries of Europe, as well as in Russia and Japan. Perhaps the most exotic of
Tolkien fan organizations was the 'North Borneo Frodo Society' in Malaysia:
one of its membership cards is reproduced in *The Tolkien Family Album*, p. 85.

TOLKIEN FANDOM AND THE INTERNET

*Adaptations of Tolkien's works for radio, television, and film have always
been catalysts for the formation of Tolkien fan groups, and for (at least temporary) increases in membership for existing societies, because of attendant
publicity. The Peter Jackson films of 2001–3 in particular led to a resurgence
of fans taking Tolkienian names and attending conventions and other events
in costume, phenomena which (along with talking in 'Elvish') further attract
media attention and detract from serious fan activities in the realm of scholarship. The most important influence on the course of Tolkien fandom, however,
has been the Internet, which has provided an outlet for discussion, and a
source of information and news, independent of formal societies and with a
far greater number of readers than any printed fanzine. In some respects this

has been a positive development, in that e-mail and the Web easily and swiftly bring together many individuals of like interests.

But it has also made it easier for heated arguments to occur, inhibiting others from joining discussions lest they too be 'flamed'; and the culture of the Internet, emphasizing speed and convenience, has tended to discourage Tolkien research in sources other than those available online – where, moreover, material of significance is often buried in an abundance of triviality.

Many of the Tolkien fan sites currently on the Internet were formed in response to the 2001–3 films, such as *www.theonering.net* and *www.lotrplaza. com*. A few, however, such as the newsgroup *rec.arts.books.tolkien*, have a longer history, and special-interest sites, such as *www.elvish.org*, home of the Elvish Linguistic Fellowship (ELF, successor to the Mythopoeic Linguistic Fellowship, an offshoot of the Mythopoeic Society), proceed deliberately from Tolkien's works rather than from adaptations, though the latter is not excluded from discussion. The ELF exemplifies Tolkien fan activities in transition, providing both print publications *Parma Eldalamberon* and *Vinyar Tengwar*, an online journal *Tengwestië*, and an electronic forum, *Lambengolmor*.

From the Internet has come the coinages *Ringer*, 'fan of *The Lord of the Rings*'; *Tolkienist* (or *Tolkienite*) 'one who studies the work of Tolkien'; and *purist*, variously 'one who dislikes attempts to adapt or expand Tolkien's works (in film, fiction, or linguistics)'. But not all fans approve of these labels, and such attempts to categorize the varieties of opinion in Tolkien fandom are ultimately misguided.

Farmer Giles of Ham. Story, first published in Great Britain by George Allen & Unwin, London, in October 1949, and in the United States by the Houghton Mifflin Company, Boston, in October 1950. See further, Christina Scull and Wayne G. Hammond, introduction to the fiftieth anniversary edition of *Farmer Giles of Ham* (1999); and *Descriptive Bibliography* A4.

SUMMARY

Ægidius de Hammo, or Giles, a farmer of the village of Ham 'in the midmost parts of the Island of Britain' (p. 9), is awakened one night by his dog Garm, who warns of an approaching giant. Giles drives off the giant by firing a blunderbuss loaded with old nails and other rubbish. Although this deed is accomplished more by luck than skill – the giant thinks that he has been stung by insects – Giles is acclaimed a hero and is given a disused sword by the King. Months later, the kingdom is menaced by a dragon, Chrysophylax, whom the King's knights are reluctant to fight. The people of Ham turn to Giles, especially when they learn that his old sword is Tailbiter, a famous weapon of dragon-slayers. Dressed in makeshift armour, Giles captures the dragon and returns with it to Ham; but Chrysophylax gains his freedom by falsely promising to give the villagers all of his wealth. The King, claiming that the dragon's fortune belongs to himself as lord of the land, sends his knights, together with

Farmer Giles, into the country to hunt Chrysophylax. The dragon kills or scatters the knights, but Giles once again is victorious, aided by his sword and his grey mare. He forces Chrysophylax to carry an enormous load of treasure back to Ham, and with the aid of the dragon defies the King. As the years pass, Giles' rank increases, until he becomes a king with knights of his own.

HISTORY

*John Tolkien once said that his father invented *Farmer Giles of Ham* as an impromptu tale after a picnic, when he and his family were caught in a rainstorm and took shelter under a bridge. Precisely where and when (or if) this event occurred, it is impossible to say. But because *Farmer Giles of Ham* is set largely in the country around *Oxford, it is most likely to have been first told after the Tolkien family moved to that city in 1926, and the style and tone of its earliest extant manuscript, akin to *Roverandom* (written down probably in late 1927) and to the early parts of *The Hobbit* (begun *c.* 1928–30), also suggest that the work dates originally from the late twenties.

In that earliest written version the narrator has a distinctly parental voice – indeed, the story is told by 'Daddy', as to a child who interrupts his father to ask the meaning of 'blunderbuss'. It contains traditional fairy-story imagery ('once there was a giant') and is often put in a personal context that a child would enjoy ('if [the giant] had trodden on *our* garden', 'if he had bumped into *our* house'; 1999 edn., p. 81); it lacks most of the philological jokes and scholarly allusions that would appear in the published book of 1949, as well as all of the Latin references, most of the nomenclature, and other features also later included; and it is given no historical background, and only a vague setting until the end, when Giles takes the surname *Worming* and builds a fine hall in Ham – *Worminghall* being a village a few miles from Oxford. A transcription of this manuscript was published in the fiftieth anniversary edition of *Farmer Giles of Ham.*

A second version of the story, only slightly revised and with the narrator now 'the family jester', existed in typescript by the early to mid-1930s. Its events were now definitely placed in the past, and distances and times compressed: for instance, Giles' magic sword leaps from its sheath if a dragon is within two miles' distance, rather than one hundred miles as in the earlier version. Tolkien's friend from Belgium, *S.R.T.O. d'Ardenne, translated this version of *Farmer Giles* into French, most likely when she lodged with the Tolkien family in Oxford in 1932–3, but before November 1937 when Tolkien mentioned the translation in a letter.

In late 1936 Tolkien submitted *Farmer Giles* to George Allen & Unwin (*Publishers) along with other works for consideration, his *Hobbit* already having been accepted by the publisher. In January 1937 it was read by young *Rayner Unwin, who found it 'a well written and amusing book' which 'should appeal to every English boy or girl' (1999 edn., p. v). His father, publisher *Stanley Unwin, felt that the tale was not long enough to make a book by itself, unaccompanied by other stories, and after *The Hobbit* was published in September 1937 he wanted to capitalize on its success with a sequel.

Tolkien therefore began to write a 'new Hobbit' (*The Lord of the Rings*); but progress was slow, against many other pressures, and by the end of July 1938 he was temporarily at a loss to know how to continue with it, or failing to continue, how to fulfil his obligations. 'For my own sake as well as yours I would like to produce something,' he wrote to C.A. Furth, production manager at Allen & Unwin (24 July 1938, *Letters*, p. 39). He needed extra income to pay for his children's education and medical care, and he was mindful that Allen & Unwin expected him to write another book for children, indeed that they had expected to have one from him already, for sale at Christmas 1938.

He offered them *Mr. Bliss*, though the expense of reproducing its colour illustrations was prohibitive; and more hopefully, he put forward a third version of *Farmer Giles of Ham*. In January 1938 he rewrote the story, enlarging it by some fifty per cent, for reading on 14 February 1938 to the Lovelace Society, an essay club at Worcester College, Oxford. He now added many proper names, jokes, and allusions, and developed characters and settings more fully. Ham, in the 'Little Kingdom', was now the precursor of the modern town of Thame, and *Worminghall* the vernacular form of *Aula Draconaria*, the name of the house that the twelve likely lads, who had helped bring the captive dragon back to Ham, built for themselves on the spot where Giles first met Chrysophylax. The Lovelace Society approved. 'It took nearly twice as long as a proper "paper" to read aloud,' Tolkien wrote to Allen & Unwin, but 'the audience was apparently not bored – indeed they were generally convulsed with mirth.' They were the ideal audience, in fact, for references to the 'Four Wise Clerks of Oxenford' (transparently the editors of the *Oxford English Dictionary*) and for bogus place-name etymologies. However, Tolkien added, 'I am afraid that means [the work] has taken on a rather more adult and satiric flavour. Anyway I have not written the necessary two or three other stories of the Kingdom to go with it!' (letter to C.A. Furth, 24 July 1938, *Letters*, p. 39).

By late summer 1938, however, he had arranged for the Academic Copying Office, Oxford, to make a professional typescript of *Farmer Giles*, working from a home-made copy of the third version (referred to in correspondence through 1949, then lost from the archival record; see letter to Stanley Unwin, ?18 March 1945, *Letters*, p. 113). On 31 August 1938 Tolkien sent C.A. Furth the professional typescript, 'for your consideration in its rather altered scope and tone' (*Letters*, p. 40). Then, despite 'difficulties of all kinds, including ill-health' (2 February 1939, *Letters*, p. 42) Tolkien managed to make limited progress with the *Hobbit* sequel. Furth was encouraged: he returned the typescript of *Farmer Giles of Ham* and optimistically hoped that Tolkien would be able to finish *The Lord of the Rings* by the middle of June 1939. Tolkien agreed to meet this new deadline, but wondered:

Did *Farmer Giles* in the enlarged form meet with any sort of approval? Is it worth anything? Are two more stories, or any more stories of the

Little Kingdom, worth contemplating? For instance the completion in the same form of the adventures of Prince George (the farmer's son) and the fat boy Suovetaurilius (vulgarly Suet), and the Battle of Otmoor. [letter to C.A. Furth, 10 February 1939, *Letters*, p. 43]

Furth replied that although personally he liked *Farmer Giles of Ham* very much, it presented 'a difficult selling problem', because it did not fall into a firm category. As it now stood, it was neither a children's book nor a novel – 'hence rather bewildering to the [book] trade' (letter to Tolkien, 11 February 1939, Tolkien-George Allen & Unwin archive, HarperCollins). Allen & Unwin did not reject the work, but wished to postpone its publication until after the sequel to *The Hobbit* had appeared.

In the event, Tolkien would not complete *The Lord of the Rings* until several more years had passed. And as the sequel was further delayed, he promoted *Farmer Giles of Ham* in the interim. 'He [the text] is at least finished, though very slender in bulk,' Tolkien wrote to Stanley Unwin. 'But he amuses the same people, although Mr Furth seemed to think he has no obvious public. He has mouldered in a drawer since he amused H.S. Bennett's children when I was in Cambridge last March. Admittedly they are bright children . . .' (19 December 1939, *Letters*, p. 44). Glimmers of hope for its publication during the war were dashed by paper rationing and by Unwin's sustained opinion that *Farmer Giles of Ham*, even in its enlarged form, needed to be part of a collection. By early 1945 Tolkien still had only plotted its sequel: 'The heart has gone out of the Little Kingdom, and the woods and plains are aerodromes and bomb-practice targets,' he wrote to Unwin, referring to the countryside around Oxford (*c.* 18 March 1945, *Letters*, p. 113).

In summer 1946 Stanley Unwin's son David, the children's writer 'David Severn', read *Farmer Giles of Ham* and gave it a good report. Encouraged by his publisher's renewed interest, Tolkien summed up the situation:

I should, of course, be delighted if you see your way to publish 'Farmer Giles of Ham'. In its present form it was revised from its primitive nursery form and read to the Lovelace Society at Worcester College, and *Cyril Wilkinson (the old war-horse [and dedicatee of *Farmer Giles*]) has always been at me to publish it. He returned to the charge on September 3rd when we met at the Election of Nichol Smith's successor to the Merton Chair of Literature – a tiresome business which has gone far to destroy my chances of 'writing' this summer. All the same I feel, as you seem to do, that [*Farmer Giles*] is rather a short long and really needs some company. . . .

I think I once planned a volume of 'Farmer Giles' with (say) three other probably shorter stories interleaved with such verse as would consort with them from the *Oxford Magazine*: *'Errantry', *'[The Adventures of] Tom Bombadil', and possibly *'The Dragon's Visit'. Of the stories one only is written ['Sellic Spell', see *Beowulf*] – and might not seem to suitable though I have been urged to publish it. I send you a copy. The other 'The King of the Green Dozen' [an unfinished comic fairy story, see *Letters*, p. 113; see *Celtic influences] would exactly consort, but is only half-written. The third an actual sequel to 'Farmer Giles' is a mere plot. My verse story [*The Lay of Aotrou and Itroun] . . . might not be felt to go with it. As *'Leaf by Niggle' certainly would not? Well there it is: if you decide to publish the 'Farmer' I shall be delighted. With leisure I could give him company, but I am in a tough spot academically and domestically, and see no hope of leisure until the various new professors come along [to reduce his wartime burden in the Oxford English School]. I could not promise to complete anything soon. . . . [letter to Stanley Unwin, 30 September 1946, Tolkien-George Allen & Unwin archive, HarperCollins; partly printed in *Letters*, p. 118]

Allen & Unwin at last decided to publish *Farmer Giles of Ham* by itself, but to flesh out its length with illustrations. Tolkien now made still more alterations to the text, 'for the better (I think and hope) in both style and narrative' (5 July 1947, *Letters*, p. 119). Around this time he also added a foreword, or rather a mock foreword, in which Tolkien pretends to be the editor and translator of an ancient text, 'a legend, perhaps, rather than an account' of the history of the 'Little Kingdom' (*Farmer Giles of Ham*, p. 7). In this he places the events of *Farmer Giles of Ham* between the end of the third century and the early part of the sixth; however, the foreword is really no more than a *jeu d'esprit*, added to a story otherwise set in 'a "no-time" in which [seventeenth-century] blunderbusses or anything might occur' (Tolkien to *Naomi Mitchison, 18 December 1949, *Letters*, p. 133).

The artist first chosen to illustrate the story, Milein Cosman, was slow to produce specimens, and those pictures that she eventually delivered in January and July 1948 did not please either Tolkien or his publisher. The commission was transferred to *Pauline Diana Baynes, whose drawings for *Farmer Giles of Ham*, produced with speed, skill, and sensitivity to the subject, Tolkien found 'the perfect counterpart to the text (or an improvement on it)' (letter to Ronald Eames, Allen & Unwin art director, 10 December 1948, Tolkien-George Allen & Unwin archive, HarperCollins). Baynes' art has appeared also in later editions. The editions of 1990–1, published by Unwin Hyman and Houghton Mifflin, were illustrated by Roger Garland.

Farmer Giles of Ham has been reprinted in *The Tolkien Reader* (1966), *Poems and Stories* (1980), and elsewhere. A commercial recording of the work, read by Derek Jacobi, was first issued in 1999, as part of *Farmer Giles of Ham and Other Stories*. In 1992 a dramatization of *Farmer Giles of Ham* by Brian Sibley was broadcast on BBC Radio as one part of the series *Tales from the Perilous Realm*, first issued as a commercial recording in 1993.

Tolkien only briefly sketched a sequel to *Farmer Giles of Ham*: Prince George, Giles' son, was to be 'a stout young man, good with horses and dogs but not much at figures or at the Book-latin.' He would have been taken prisoner and held for ransom, but would escape and fall in with the giant driven off by Farmer Giles at the beginning of the earlier story. George would then have been rescued from the giant by the 'pig boy' Suet and Chrysophylax, and all together would have come to the aid of King Giles and his knights in battle. Tolkien's notes for the sequel were published in the fiftieth anniversary edition of *Farmer Giles of Ham* mentioned above, pp. 101–3.

CRITICISM

At first *Farmer Giles of Ham* did not sell as well as Allen & Unwin had hoped. 'Rather a donnish little squib after all?' Tolkien wondered. 'I cannot discover that he [the book] has been widely heard of. He does not seem to have been very forcibly brought to notice' (letter to Stanley Unwin, 10 March 1950, *Letters*, pp. 138–9). By the standard of the day it did indeed receive few reviews, and those were very brief – but after all it was a slim book, difficult to categorize (as C.A. Furth had warned), and not of the same calibre as *The Hobbit*.

Its critics were quick to see that it was not expressly a book for children. Gwendolen Freeman in the *Spectator* (18 November 1949, p. 718), for instance, who found Tolkien's humour 'dry rather than extravagant', felt that *Farmer Giles* 'would be appreciated by adolescents who have read something of the tales of chivalry', while Marcus Crouch remarked in *Junior Bookshelf* (January 1950, pp. 14–15) that 'children are inclined to take their dragons seriously and they may not fancy Chrysophylax, that cowardly, obsequious monster who is small beer indeed after Smaug [in *The Hobbit*]. I fancy they will like Giles himself, and they will love his craven dog. The mannerisms, the learned allusions, as well as the stylized decorations by Miss Baynes, are for adults only.' However, Crouch judged it also 'a delightful book, exquisitely written and full of charming touches of humour' which 'should certainly form part of any children's library. One must not be disappointed, however, if the children's reactions are slow.' Most reviewers judged Pauline Baynes' pictures well suited to the text, an asset rather than a liability.

Later criticism of *Farmer Giles of Ham* is sparse, as for all of Tolkien's shorter works, eclipsed by his famous tales of Middle-earth; and writers about *Farmer Giles* often read more into that brief and humorous work than its author is likely to have meant. Katharyn W. Crabbe, however, in her *J.R.R. Tolkien* (rev. and expanded edn. 1988) provides useful comments on the fairy-story aspects of *Farmer Giles*: 'Despite his reluctance to fight giants and dragons, Farmer Giles is a traditional fairy-tale hero. His heroic attributes are not obvious or conventional – he is not braver or stronger, or wiser, or more handsome than other men – but he is a hero nonetheless. What virtues he has are, like Bilbo's [in *The Hobbit*], the virtues of the powerless': prudence, discretion, and reverence for the past. 'However, as the narrator notes, his most important characteristics are luck and wits. Like traditional fairy tales, "Farmer Giles of Ham" suggests that, with these two qualities, what appears to be a perfectly ordinary person might well be a real prince' (pp. 148–9). And Steve Linley in his 'Farmer Giles: Beowulf for the Critics?', Amon Hen 98 (July 1989), and 'Farmer Giles of Ham', Anor 28 (1996), reasonably argues that in Farmer Giles Tolkien wrote a lighthearted reply to the scholars he criticized in his essay *Beowulf: The Monsters and the Critics, those who approached Beowulf as a quarry of historical or philological information rather than as a work of art.

In our introduction to the fiftieth anniversary edition of Farmer Giles of Ham (1999) we trace the evolution of the story through its several versions and note (p. xi) that the work 'did not become a classic of children's literature like The Hobbit. However, it has appealed to readers of all ages for half a century. It is a lively story, told with intelligence and wit. Also it is interesting as one of the few works of fiction by Tolkien that is wholly distinct from the "matter of Middle-earth" – he kept it apart from his invented mythology "with an effort" (Letters, p. 136).'

The geography of England that lies behind Farmer Giles of Ham is helpfully discussed by Brin Dunsire in his 'Of Ham, and What Became of It', Amon Hen 98 (July 1989), and by Alex Lewis in 'The Lost Heart of the Little Kingdom', contained in Leaves from the Tree: J.R.R. Tolkien's Shorter Fiction (1991).

Farnell, Lewis Richard (1856–1934). During Tolkien's undergraduate years at *Oxford L.R. Farnell was University Lecturer in Classical Archaeology (1903– 14), Senior Tutor at Exeter College, and Rector of the College from 1913 to 1928. Farnell was himself a product of Exeter College, having graduated with honours in 1878. He returned in 1880 with an Open Fellowship, after which he was closely involved with teaching and administration. From 1920 to 1923 he was also Vice-Chancellor of the University. An authority on Greek religion, Farnell also had a wide knowledge of Classical archaeology. His publications include The Cults of the Greek States (1896–1909), a translation of the writings of Pindar (1930), and a memoir, An Oxonian Looks Back (1934). From 1911 to 1913 Tolkien almost certainly attended Farnell's lectures on set texts such as Agamemnon by Aeschylus and the Odyssey by Homer.

When Tolkien earned only a Second Class in Honour Moderations, but an 'alpha' on his paper on Comparative Philology, his tutors suggested that he change his course of study from Classics to the language side of the English Honour School. Due to the influence of Farnell, who had a great respect for philology, Exeter College generously allowed Tolkien to keep his Classics exhibition. In 1925 Farnell wrote a letter in support of Tolkien's application for the Rawlinson and Bosworth Professorship of Anglo-Saxon at Oxford:

> I was most impressed with his enthusiasm and special aptitude for Philology, a quality which is becoming increasingly rare among our younger students; and I believe he has now reached a leading position in the sphere of philological study and will prove himself of high value to the University in this department. I believe him also to possess not only a special linguistic but a real literary interest in the earliest monuments of our literature. [*An Application for the Rawlinson and Bosworth

Professorship of Anglo-Saxon in the University of Oxford by J.R.R. Tolkien, Professor of the English Language in the University of Leeds, June 25, 1925]

Farrer, Katharine Dorothy (1911–1972). When Tolkien and his family lived at 3 Manor Road, *Oxford from March 1947 to May 1950, his neighbours included the writer Katharine Farrer and her husband, the theologian **Austin Marsden Farrer** (1904–1968). Katharine Farrer (*née* Newton) read Classics and Greats at Oxford as a member of the Society of Oxford Home-Students. She published her first stories in the student magazine *The Cherwell*. Later, after a course in education, she taught Classics and Scripture at Gerrard's Cross. In 1949 her translation of Gabriel Marcel's *Etre et avoir* was published as *Being and Having*. She then wrote the three detective novels for which she is best known: *The Missing Link* (1952), *The Cretan Counterfeit* (1954), and *Gownsman's Gallows* (1957).

Austin Farrer was a distinguished Classical Scholar at Balliol College, and from 1929 a priest in the Church of England. In 1931 he returned to Oxford as Chaplain and tutor of St Edmund Hall. From 1935 to 1960 he was Fellow and Chaplain of Trinity College, Oxford, and from 1960 until his death Warden of Keble College, Oxford.

In November 1947 Tolkien sent Katharine Farrer a postcard in runes, agreeing to sign her copy of *The Hobbit* (see *Letters*, p. 125). In response to the welcome interest she expressed in his mythology and in *The Lord of the Rings* (then in progress), he lent her some of his manuscripts: among these were, apparently, the *Quenta Silmarillion* and both the 'flat world' and 'round world' versions of the creation story *The Music of the Ainur* (*Ainulindalë*). On 15 June [?1948] Tolkien wrote to Farrer that he had never found anyone else, except for his son *Christopher and *C.S. Lewis (with whom the Farrers were also friends), who wanted to read *'The Silmarillion' and related manuscripts. Possibly in October 1948 Katharine Farrer sent Tolkien 'illuminating and deeply enthusiastic remarks' about his writings, in which she said that she liked the 'Flat Earth versions best. The hope of Heaven is the only thing which makes modern astronomy tolerable: otherwise there must be an East and a West and Walls: aims and choices and not an endless circle of wandering' (quoted, with comments by Christopher Tolkien, in *Morgoth's Ring*, p. 6). Tolkien seems to have taken this to heart, for he temporarily abandoned the attempt to include modern astronomical views, such as a round earth, in 'The Silmarillion'.

Tolkien continued to correspond with Katharine Farrer through at least the late 1950s, in part about the progress and reception of *The Lord of the Rings*.

Fastitocalon. Tolkien wrote two poems with this title. The earliest is one of the *Adventures in Unnatural History and Medieval Metres, Being the Freaks of Fisiologus*, published as by 'Fisiologus' in the *Stapeldon Magazine* (Exeter College, *Oxford) 7, no. 40 (June 1927), pp. 123–5. It was composed probably not long before its publication. Together with a companion, *Iumbo* (the precursor of *Oliphaunt*), and two other (unpublished) animal poems, *Reginhardus, the Fox* and *Monoceros, the Unicorn, Fastitocalon* was inspired by the medieval bestiary, in particular the *Physiologus* ('Naturalist') poems in the Exeter Book, which describe the characteristics of animals and draw from them Christian morals. Tolkien followed this model but added elements of contemporary culture.

'Fastitocalon' in the *Stapeldon Magazine* poem is a great whale. At times he 'wallows on a bed of slime / In the Ocean's deep and weedy clime', welcoming fish into 'the portals of His jaws'; but when 'He finds the depths devoid of rest' he floats on the surface of the sea, as if a 'sunny island', and drowns unsuspecting visitors

> who land on HIM,
> And patent stoves proceed to trim,
> Or make incautious fires
> To dry your clothes or warm a limb,
> Who dance or prance about the glim –
> 'Tis just what He desires.

The notion that a whale could be mistaken for an island, on which sailors land only to die when the beast dives to escape the heat of their fire, comes from the *Physiologus*, and figures also in the medieval *Voyage of St Brendan* (see *Imram*). In the bestiary the Whale represents Satan, who attracts men weak in their faith and drags them down to Hell; but in Tolkien's poem, written with tongue in cheek, the monster teaches us that 'perils lurk in wait' for those who trespass or pry, 'or dance on floors / Too early or too late / with jazz.'

In a letter to Mrs Eileen Elgar of 5 March 1964 Tolkien wrote that the name *Fastitocalon* seems to have been originally

> *Aspido-chelōne* 'turtle with a round shield (of hide)'. Of that *astitocalon* is a corruption no worse than many of the time [in the bestiaries]; but I am afraid the F was put on by the versifier simply to make the name alliterate, as was compulsory for poets in his day, with the other words in his line. . . . The notion of the treacherous island that is really a monster seems to derive from the East: the marine turtles enlarged by myth-making fancy. . . . But in Europe the monster becomes mixed up with whales. . . . [*Letters*, pp. 343–4]

By the time of this letter, Tolkien had revised and abbreviated *Fastitocalon* for publication in *The Adventures of Tom Bombadil and Other Verses from the Red Book* (1962), pp. 49, 51 (first British printing, bisected by an illustration for *Cat*), 48–9 (second British printing, first American printing). In the process he removed anachronisms such as jazz music and patent stoves, centred the work on the beast as 'an island good to land upon', and transformed the whale of the first version into a giant turtle – thus correct according to the etymology of its name. The poem now became, in the fictional context of the Hobbits' 'Red Book of Westmarch' put forward in the preface to the 1962 collection, a verse by Sam Gamgee of *The Lord of the Rings*, 'though at most Sam can only have touched up an older piece of the comic bestiary lore of which Hobbits appear to have been fond' (p. 7).

The 'Father Christmas' letters. Illustrated serial. An abridged selection edited by Baillie Tolkien (see *Christopher Tolkien) was published as *The Father Christmas Letters* in Great Britain by George Allen & Unwin, London, in September 1976, and in the United States by the Houghton Mifflin Company, Boston, in October 1976. A briefer selection was first published as miniature volumes in Great Britain by HarperCollins, London, in 1994. Some of the letters (or parts of letters) and envelopes were published in a volume of facsimiles, but with three previously unpublished pictures, as *Letters from Father Christmas* in Great Britain by HarperCollins, and in the United States by the Houghton Mifflin Company, in 1995. The texts of all of the surviving letters (none are extant for 1921 and 1922), reproductions of some of the original manuscripts and envelopes, and most of the pictures that accompanied them were published in an enlarged edition (also as *Letters from Father Christmas*) in 1999, again by HarperCollins and Houghton Mifflin. The edition of 2004 (with the same title) was a reduction in content as well as size. For editions of the letters published through 1992, see *Descriptive Bibliography* A14; for subsequent editions, see issues of *The Tolkien Collector*. See also *Artist and Illustrator*, chapter 3.

HISTORY

At Christmas 1920 Tolkien's son *John, aged three, asked his father what Father Christmas is like and where he lives. Tolkien responded by writing a letter as if from Father Christmas himself, which 'arrived' at the Tolkien home in an envelope bearing a 'North Pole' stamp and 'postmark', together with a double picture of Father Christmas and his house (*Artist and Illustrator*, fig. 64). This was the first in a long series of letters to the Tolkien children in which 'Father Christmas' and some of his helpers wrote of their lives and adventures. For his children's sake Tolkien took pains to make the 'Father Christmas' letters appear to be genuine, and to sustain the fiction on which they were based. 'Sometimes the envelopes, dusted with snow and bearing Polar postage stamps, were found in the house on the morning after his visit; sometimes the postman brought them; and the letters that the children wrote [to Father Christmas] themselves vanished from the fireplace when no one was about' (Baillie Tolkien, *Letters from Father Christmas* (1999), p. 5; see also *Children). Each 'author' of the letters wrote in a distinct visual style: old Father Christmas (aged 1,927 in 1923) had a very shaky hand; his chief assistant, the North Polar Bear, usually printed with thick strokes, because he had a fat paw, or in angular 'Arktik' letters resembling runes; while the elf Ilbereth used a flowing secretarial script. Often letters written by one character also contained comments by another.

The earliest of the surviving letters, from 1920 and 1923, are relatively brief, and are concerned mainly with Father Christmas himself or with presents he will bring. But with the letter of 1925 Tolkien began to enlarge and embroider the fantasy, until Father Christmas was at the centre of a populous Northern country with its own history and mythology. Polar Bear, also called Karhu (Finnish 'bear'), is faithful, well-meaning, and valiant but comically prone to accidents. In 1925, for instance, he broke the North Pole (a large inverted icicle), smashing Father Christmas's house; in 1929 he opened a window in the midst of a gale, upsetting papers and inks; and in 1936 he allowed his bath to overflow into the English Delivery Room – all good reasons why the Tolkien children did not receive particular gifts, or why Father Christmas drew not with ink but with coloured pencils. If a letter was late, it might be because Polar Bear forgot to post it. Tolkien's daughter *Priscilla has described Polar Bear as 'the *enfant terrible*, always involved in crises. His somewhat irreverent attitude to authority gave us particular pleasure' ('News from the North Pole', *Oxford Today* (Michaelmas 1992), p. 9).

As the letters progressed – and as the Tolkien family itself grew – Father Christmas and Polar Bear were joined by Karhu's young nephews Paksu and Valkotukka (Finnish 'stout' and 'white-hair'), red and green elves, Snowmen ('the only sort of people that live near – not of course men made of snow', 1930), penguins visiting from the South Pole (1940), even (in 1927) the Man in the Moon, whose absence from his post allowed dragons to obscure the moon with smoke – surely a reference to the lunar eclipse of 8 December 1927, related to an incident in *Roverandom*. In 1932 Polar Bear found goblins in nearby caves, probably inspired by those in *The Hobbit* or in *The Princess and the Goblin* by *George MacDonald: these became a recurring menace, but Father Christmas and his friends always defeated them heroically ('Polar Bear was squeezing, squashing, trampling, boxing and kicking goblins skyhigh, and roaring like a zoo, and the goblins were yelling like engine whistles', 1933).

Tolkien designed each of the 'Father Christmas' letters, envelopes, and accompanying pictures as a decorative 'artifact', more or less elaborate depending upon how much time he could afford to devote to it. He used a variety of black and coloured inks, watercolours, coloured pencils, and sealing wax on white and toned papers, varying his approach each year. Most of the pictures are 'by' Father Christmas, but Polar Bear and Ilbereth also contributed, each in his own style. Those for 1932 are of particular note (*Artist and Illustrator*, fig. 63): 'Father Christmas' himself called them 'specially nice pictures this year'. On one ornamented sheet four panels depict, in turn, Father Christmas and his reindeer flying over Oxford at night; an Arctic landscape; Father Christmas in the Goblin caves; and his party on St Stephen's Day. Another sheet is meant to contain copies of ancient paintings in the caves, made by 'cave bears' long ago, in fact based by Tolkien on real cave art. And a third is a letter from Polar Bear written in a pictographic 'Goblin alphabet'.

Alongside fantasy elements like these were allusions to the world at large. Priscilla Tolkien has recalled in particular

> the Letter for Christmas 1934 when Father Christmas writes: 'We have brought a tree all the way from Norway and planted it in a pool of ice', and there is a picture to illustrate this. . . . There are also references to comets and in 1929 to the Aurora Borealis or Northern Lights being 'specially good'. Much astronomy is brought into the fantasy. This was of great interest to my father and I can recall how my brother Christopher and I were encouraged to learn about the stars and planets and eclipses of the sun and moon. . . . These references give a great sense of reality to Father Christmas's world. ['News from the North Pole', p. 9]

After 1938 the tone of the letters became sombre, as the 'horrible war' in the real world intruded even at the North Pole. Father Christmas reported in 1939 that he was 'very busy and things are very difficult this year. . . . Many of my messengers have never come back.' In 1941 the Goblins attacked again in force, thinking 'that with so much war going on this was a fine chance to recapture the North'; they were defeated as always, but with remarkable violence. In 1942 Polar Bear 'spent lots of time . . . making fresh gunpowder – just in case of trouble.' The letter of 1943 was the last: Priscilla, Tolkien's youngest child, was now thirteen, and Father Christmas supposed that she would 'be hanging up your stocking just once more. . . . After this I shall have to say "goodbye", more or less.' He assured Priscilla that he was 'still very much alive, and shall come back again soon, as merry as ever', after the grimness of the war. Priscilla has recalled that she was 'about ten when I realised that the letters were written by my father and that there was no Father Christmas. . . . There was a friendly conspiracy of silence in the family and the older ones kept quiet because they enjoyed it all so much themselves' ('Priscilla Tolkien Talks to Shirley Lowe', *Over 21*, December 1976, p. 32).

In *The Father Christmas Letters* (1976) the 'last letter' is a conflation of most of the letter for 1941 and part of that for 1943. The 1999 *Letters of Father Christmas* also includes notes by 'Father Christmas' sent to the Tolkien children in reply to letters they (or their toy bears) sometimes wrote well in advance of the holidays.

A commercial recording of *Letters from Father Christmas*, read by Derek Jacobi, John Moffatt, and Christian Rodska, was first issued in 1997.

CRITICISM

The Father Christmas Letters (1976) was widely reviewed, almost universally with enthusiasm. A small minority of reviewers grumbled that the book was only another product of the growing 'Tolkien industry'. Terry Pratchett, writing in the *Bath and West Evening Chronicle* (18 September 1976, p. 7), hoped that the private world Tolkien created for his children would 'appeal to any

1976 kids whose appreciation of new worlds hasn't been blighted by Action Man and enlightened schoolteachers'.

'Of Fëanor and the Unchaining of Melkor'. The sixth chapter of the *'Quenta Silmarillion', published in *The Silmarillion* (1977), pp. 63–6.

SUMMARY

In the Noontide of the Blessed Realm the Noldor 'advanced ever in skill and knowledge' and devised many new things, and Rúmil of Tirion conceived 'fitting signs for the recording of speech and song, some for graving upon metal or in stone, others for drawing with brush or with pen' (*The Silmarillion*, p. 63). During this time Fëanor is born in Tirion, the son of Finwë, King of the Noldor, and his wife Míriel. Míriel is exhausted by the birth, and finds no healing even in the garden of the Vala Lórien. She falls asleep, and her spirit departs to Mandos and refuses to return. Finwë devotes himself to Fëanor, who grows up to become 'of all the Noldor . . . the most subtle in mind and the most skilled in hand' (p. 64). He improves on Rúmil's system of letters, and discovers how to make greater and brighter gems than those found in the earth. While still young he marries Nerdanel and they have seven sons, but Fëanor and his wife become estranged because his deeds grieve her. He is not pleased when his father, Finwë, takes as his second wife Indis of the Vanyar, even though he still has the first place in his father's heart. He feels no affection for Indis or for his half-brothers, Fingolfin and Finarfin. The anonymous author of *The Silmarillion* comments that many thought that if Finwë had endured his loss and not remarried, much evil and sorrow might have been prevented; but the children and descendants of Finwë and Indis were also great and glorious.

Melkor completes his sentence of three ages confined in the Halls of Mandos, and is brought before the Valar. He envies their glory and lusts after their bright gems, but abases himself before Manwë and sues for pardon. He declares that, if freed, he will aid the Valar, especially in healing the harm he has done. With Nienna's intercession he is pardoned, but at first must stay within Valmar, the City of the Valar. He puts on an appearance of seeking to do good, and indeed provides both the Valar and the Eldar with aid and good counsel. Ulmo and Tulkas are not deceived, but Manwë, who is free from evil and does not comprehend it in others, believes that Melkor has indeed reformed. Although Melkor pretends love for the Eldar, in reality he hates them because they are fair and joyful, and especially because it was to protect them that the Valar had attacked him in Middle-earth. The Vanyar reject his friendship, and he pays little heed to the Teleri, but focuses his attention on the Noldor who delight in the knowledge he teaches them. Melkor later falsely claims that Fëanor secretly learned much from him, especially in the achievement of his greatest works.

HISTORY

There is no tale in *The Book of Lost Tales* that corresponds to this chapter. In that work Fëanor is not the son of Finwë, King of the Noldoli, merely a crafts-man of that people. His sons are referred to in *The Tale of the Sun and Moon*, and are numbered seven in an outline for the unwritten *Gilfanon's Tale: The Travail of the Noldoli and the Coming of Mankind*. Turgon is the only son of Finwë mentioned. Melko had already been released from Mandos when the first Elves arrived in Valinor, and indeed had spoken in favour of them being invited to dwell there. In the tale of *The Theft of Melko and the Darkening of Valinor* it is said that Melko hated the Eldar and desired the gems invented and fashioned by the Noldoli, begged them as gifts, and perhaps hoped to discover the secret of their making.

In works written during the first half of the 1920s the descendants of Finwë began to emerge and become important. In an untitled prose fragment (*'The Gnomes Come to the Great Lands'*) Gelmir, the King of the Gnomes (Noldoli) who return to Middle-earth, has three sons, Golfin, Delin, and Lúthien, but is unrelated to Fëanor; *Gelmir* is possibly another name for Finn/Finwë Nólemë. The unfinished *Lay of the Fall of Gondolin* refers to Gelmir's heir, Fingolfin, whose children are Turgon and Isfin. During the writing of the alliterative *Children of Húrin* (c. 1919–25) and by emendation, Fingolfin became the son of Finwë and had two sons, Finweg (changed to *Fingon*) and Turgon. In the poem *The Flight of the Noldoli from Valinor* Fëanor is called 'Finn's son' (*The Lays of Beleriand*, p. 133).

In the *Sketch of the Mythology* (c. 1926) Fëanor becomes Finn's second son, but by emendation replaces Fingolfin as the elder son. There is no suggestion that Fëanor and Fingolfin are other than full brothers, and no mention is made of their mother(s). A later note on the descendants of Finwë added a third son, Finrod (later renamed Finarfin). In addition to the developing genealogy, the basic story told in *The Silmarillion* appears: Morgoth is released after seven ages in the prisons of Mandos, and 'looks with greed and malice on the Eldar ... and lusts especially after the jewels'. He 'dissembles his hatred and desire for revenge' (*The Shaping of Middle-earth*, p. 15) and is eventually permitted free movement in Valinor, but Ulmo and Tulkas are suspicious of his intent. He appears to help the Elves, but attempts to destroy their contentment with lies. He succeeds with the Noldoli, but not with the Qendi (Vanyar) and Teleri. As in *The Book of Lost Tales*, the Noldoli of the *Sketch* invent and make gems.

In the *Quenta Noldorinwa* (c. 1930) Tolkien added only a few extra details to the account in the *Sketch*, such as Morgoth humbling himself and seeking pardon at the feet of Manwë. In this there is a slight shift in Melkor's relations with the Elves: the Quendi, warned by Ulmo, mistrust him and refuse his offers of help, but the Gnomes 'delight in the many things of hidden and secret wisdom that he could tell to them, and some harkened to things which it had been better that they never heard ' (*The Shaping of Middle-earth*, p. 90).

The 'earliest' *Annals of Valinor*, written in the early 1930s, give some indication of the time-span of events. At about Valian Year 2500 the Noldoli begin to fashion gems, and in the same year Fëanor makes the Silmarils. Morgoth is pardoned in Valian year 2900 (4,000 of our years later); during the course of writing the date of his release was changed to Valian Year 2700. Nienna intercedes for him, and he is described as coveting the gems of the Noldoli and lusting for the Silmarils.

Nothing of significance was added in works of the mid-1930s, the 'later' *Annals of Valinor* and the *Quenta Silmarillion*. In work towards the end of his revisions to the *Quenta Silmarillion c.* 1951 Tolkien wrote a new version of Chapter 4, with the title 'Of the Silmarilli and the Darkening of Valinor' changed to 'Of Fëanor and the Silmarilli and the Darkening of Valinor'. This describes Fëanor's mother, Míriel Serindë, and her skill in needlework, but her death and Finwë's second marriage are still absent. Fëanor devises new letters ' bettering the work of Rúmil' (*Morgoth's Ring*, p. 185). By an addition Fëanor is the first of the Noldor to discover how to make gems greater and brighter than those found in the earth.

Much of this new material also appears in the *Annals of Aman* (see *Annals of Valinor*), *c.* 1951. According to a new reckoning of years from the creation of the Trees, by an early emendation Fëanor, the eldest son of Finwë, is born in Tirion in Valian Year 1179. Fingolfin is born in 1190 and Finrod in 1230. In 1250 Fëanor devises new letters. Morgoth is pardoned in 1400 but not until 1410 is he permitted freedom outside Valmar.

Several years later, probably in autumn 1958, Tolkien returned to the history of Finwë, Míriel, Fëanor, and Indis in the *Quenta Silmarillion*. He added this important element to the mythology with a rider to the *c.* 1951 *Quenta Silmarillion*, describing Míriel's passing to Mandos after the birth of Fëanor, Finwë's second marriage, and Fëanor's resentment. But this also describes the rules laid down by Manwë concerning remarriage among the Eldar, which *Christopher Tolkien did not include in *The Silmarillion*. At the same time, Tolkien made changes and additions to the *Annals of Aman*: Valian Year '1179' became '1169', the birth of Fëanor; 1170 'Míriel falls asleep and passes to Mandar'; 1172 'Doom of Manwë concerning the espousals of the Eldar' (p. 101); 1179 marriage of Finwë and Indis of the Vanyar. The rider to the *Quenta Silmarillion* was followed by a lengthy essay concerning Elvish marriage with particular reference to Finwë, Míriel, and Indis, *Laws and Customs among the Eldar, and three successive versions culminating in a new typescript of the chapter 'Of the Silmarils and the Darkening of Valinor', the first part with the subtitle 'Of Finwë and Míriel'. See also *The Shibboleth of Fëanor.

The chapter 'Of Fëanor and the Unchaining of Melkor' in *The Silmarillion* was pieced together by Christopher Tolkien from both the *c.* 1951 version and the final text (*c.* 1958–60) of the *Quenta Silmarillion*; from the part of *Laws and Customs among the Eldar* which tells the story of Finwë and Míriel; and for the release of Melkor, a small part from the *Annals of Aman*.

The Fellowship of the Ring see **The Lord of the Rings**

'Of the Fifth Battle: Nirnaeth Arnoediad'. The twentieth chapter of the
*'Quenta Silmarillion', published in *The Silmarillion (1977), pp. 188–97.

SUMMARY

Beren and Lúthien return to Middle-earth 'as living man and woman'.
Lúthien heals her father's winter. Melian looks into her daughter's eyes, reads
her choice to become a mortal, and knows 'that a parting beyond the end of
the world had come between them'. Beren and Lúthien dwell in Ossiriand, and
their son Dior is born there. No mortal man speaks with Beren after his return,
and none see Beren and Lúthien 'leave the world' (*The Silmarillion*, p. 188).
Maedhros, eldest son of Fëanor, plans a new union of forces against
Morgoth. Orodreth refuses to join him because of the deeds of Celegorm
and Curufin, and from Nargothrond comes only a small company led by
Gwindor, seeking to avenge his brother Gelmir lost in the Battle of Sudden
Flame. Thingol also refuses aid, because the sons of Fëanor had demanded the
Silmaril won by Beren and Lúthien, but he permits Mablung and Beleg to join
the company of Fingon. But Maedhros has the help of the Naugrim, and of
the Men of Bór and Ulfang, and can rely on Fingon and Men of the House of
Hador. The People of Haleth in the forest of Brethil also prepare for war. News
of this comes to Turgon in Gondolin.

Maedhros attacks before his plans are fully made, and though he drives
the Orcs out of the north of Beleriand, Morgoth is warned of his plans by the
attack, by spies, and by faithless men among the allies of the sons of Fëanor.

Maedhros plans to advance from the east and draw out Morgoth's armies,
which Fingon will attack from the west. A beacon is to be fired as a signal.
Fingon surveys his army as he waits on the appointed morning and sees
Turgon and the army of Gondolin arrive unexpectedly. While Uldor son of
Ulfang treacherously delays Maedhros, Morgoth sends an army to entice
Fingon's host into premature action. As Fingon holds firm, the leaders of
Morgoth's host bring forth Gelmir of Nargothrond, blind him, then kill him in
sight of Fingon's army. Gwindor leaps forward, and others follow him. Fingon's
host sweeps to the gates of Angband and some, including Gwindor, make their
way inside. But then Morgoth sends forth his main force, and Fingon retreats
with great losses.

Then begins 'Nirnaeth Arnoediad, Unnumbered Tears, for no song or tale
can contain all its grief' (p. 192). Most of the Men of Brethil fall, and Fingon
is surrounded. Turgon and his army, who have been guarding the Pass of
Sirion, come to his aid, and the host of Maedhros arrives at last. But Morgoth sends forth Balrogs and dragons including Glaurung. Yet still Morgoth
might not have prevailed but for the treachery of Men. Many of the Easterlings in the army of Maedhros flee, and others led by the sons of Ulfang attack
Maedhros and his forces. The Dwarves of Belegost stand firm and even attack
the dragons, but when their lord is slain they leave the battle carrying his body.
The elven armies are utterly defeated and the survivors put to flight. Fingon

THE J.R.R. TOLKIEN COMPANION AND GUIDE

is killed by Gothmog, Lord of Balrogs. Húrin and Huor, Men of the House of Hador who serve Fingon, urge Turgon to retreat: Huor prophecies to Turgon that if Gondolin survives but a while, 'then out of your house shall come the hope of Elves and Men . . . from you and from me a new star shall arise' (p. 194). They guard his retreat, and he reaches Gondolin safely; but Huor is killed, and Húrin is taken captive by the command of Morgoth. None of the Elves of the host of Fingon, nor the Men of the House of Hador, return home. Because of the treachery of some men, the Elves no longer trust others except for those of the three Houses of the Edain.

Such Elves as remain, even the sons of Fëanor, are scattered. Others are enslaved by Morgoth. Men loyal to Morgoth are given the lands that had belonged to Fingon and Húrin. A few Men survive in Brethil. Orcs and wolves roam freely. Many Elves flee to the Havens, but in the 'next year Morgoth captures these, from which only a few escape to the Isle of Balar. Turgon sends more messengers to seek help in the West, but only one returns. For a time Morgoth pays little attention to Doriath and Nargothrond which remain free, but concentrates his thought on Gondolin, because he fears and hates the House of Fingolfin. He tries to discover the whereabouts of Gondolin from Húrin, and when Húrin refuses, Morgoth curses him and his family, and sets him in a high place from which he must see the curse working on those he loves.

Morgoth commands his servants to pile the bodies and weapons of those slain in the battle in a great mound. Grass grows on the mound alone in the midst of the desolation of Anfauglith, and afterwards no creature of Morgoth dares tread on that hill.

HISTORY

Although Tolkien never completed *Gilfanon's Tale: The Travail of the Noldoli and the Coming of Mankind* in *The Book of Lost Tales* (*c.* 1916–20), outlines for the unwritten part indicate that much of the framework was in place, if with a very different time-span and some differences in the leading players. In this, apparently not long after the Noldoli return to Middle-earth Fingolma Nólemë (the later Finwë) leads an army against Melko, but is attacked or deserted by treacherous Men. Then follows the Battle of Unnumbered Tears in which Nólemë is slain. Among Men the sons of Úrin stand fast until slain, and Úrin is taken prisoner. Turgon and many with him escape, and he goes to Gondolin (which is apparently founded *after* the battle). Most other survivors are taken captive by Melkor. Thereafter there is distrust between Men and Elves. The sons of Fëanor arrive after the battle, drive off those despoiling the bodies, bury Nólemë, and build a cairn over his body and the others slain.

The beginning of the second version of *The Tale of Turambar* tells of the captivity of Úrin, his refusal to seek for Turgon as a spy for Melko, and Melko's curse on the life of Úrin's son Túrin, and his condemnation of Úrin to watch all that happens. The Battle of Unnumbered Tears is also referred to in the second version of *The Tale of Tinúviel*. These last two tales were probably rewritten in mid-1919. An addition to *The Fall of Gondolin* made probably in 1919 says that the people of Gondolin 'were that kin of the Noldoli who alone escaped Melko's power when at the Battle of Unnumbered Tears he slew and enslaved their folk...' (*The Book of Lost Tales, Part Two*, p. 157). In *The Tale of Turambar* Tinwelint (Thingol) says that he did not go to the battle 'of the wisdom of my heart and the fate of the Valar' (p. 73). The return of Beren and Lúthien is told briefly at the end of the same tale, but does not have the same poignancy, since in the surviving version Beren is an Elf rather than a mortal Man.

Tolkien began to tell the story of Túrin at length in the alliterative *Children of Húrin* (c. 1919–25) in two successive versions. Both begin with an account of the treachery of Men, the capture of Húrin at the Battle of Unnumbered Tears, and a detailed account of his refusal to tell Morgoth how to find Turgon, who 'then cursed him for ever // and his kin and seed' (*The Lays of Beleriand*, p. 8). In the first version by inference, and in the second as told, the elven leader killed in the battle is not Nólemë but his grandson Finweg (Fingon).

The story began to take its final shape in the *Sketch of the Mythology* (c. 1926). After their return from Mandos, Beren (now a Man) and Lúthien dwell in the woods of Doriath and in the Hunter's Wold, and Beren never speaks to Men again. Maidros, son of Fëanor, organizes an alliance against Morgoth. At this point in the evolution of the story his brothers, Curufin and Celegorm, who (before later emendation) are founders and rulers of Nargothrond, do not send as large a host as they had promised, and Thingol does not send help from Doriath because of the demand by Maidros for the Silmaril, but permits Noldoli living in Doriath to join the conflict. Finweg of his own accord leads his host in attack, and pursuing a defeated army of Orcs is overwhelmed by new hordes from Angband. The Battle of Unnumbered Tears follows, in which Finweg falls. Most Men, corrupted by Morgoth, flee, but Húrin and his kin, acting as a rearguard, enable Turgon and part of his people to escape. They then found Gondolin. Húrin is taken prisoner on Morgoth's orders but refuses to lead an army against Turgon. Maidros, Curufin, and Celegorm arrive late for the main battle, but in time to rescue some elves before being repulsed by their foes. Morgoth's host piles the slain in a great hill in the desert before Angband, but grass grows on the hill.

Tolkien emended the *Sketch* in the light of developments in the second half of the 1920s in the *Lay of Leithian*, so that Curufin and Celegorm are not the rulers of Nargothrond, but had lived there for a time, and were expelled because of their opposition to Felagund. It is for this reason that Orodreth, the ruler of Nargothrond, sends no aid. The planned division into two hosts appears, one under Maidros and Maglor, and the other under Finweg and Turgon, but less from strategy than from bad feeling between factions of the Noldoli. Another addition mentions the presence of the dragon Glómund at the battle.

Tolkien made some changes to this in the *Quenta Noldorinwa* (c. 1930) and introduced further detail. On their return Beren and Lúthien wander in

Broseliand (emended to *Ossiriand*). More is said of the preparations of Maidros and also that he attacks before the major assault. The Dwarves refuse to aid either side, though they are willing to make weapons for the Elves – for a price. From Doriath only Mablung and Beleg take part in the battle. The battle plan now becomes clearer. Finweg and Turgon in the west wait long for a sign of the army of Maidros advancing from the east, and send heralds to challenge Morgoth. In response to the slaughter of one of these by Morgoth's agents, Finweg's army attacks prematurely. But the background for the later version of this event is now also present. Orodreth of Nargothrond allows a small company to join the army of Finweg, among whom is Flinding who, without the later personal motive of his brother's slaughter, still bursts into Angband and is taken prisoner. Maidros now arrives as Finweg's army is surrounded, but the Men in his army flee or change sides and attack him. Finweg falls and his army retreats. Maidros and his army retreats before Glómund and the other dragons that Morgoth sends forth. Orcs roam freely in Beleriand, and Men who aided Morgoth are given lands once belonging to Finweg and his allies. Though the text is considerably shorter than the corresponding chapter in *The Silmarillion*, almost all of the elements of the final story were now present, and even some of the actual phrasing. Some later emendations introduced the foundation of Gondolin before the battle, the assembly of Turgon and his host with Fingon before the battle began, and Maidros delayed by the machinations of Uldor the Accursed.

According to the chronology of the 'earliest' *Annals of Beleriand* (early 1930s) the Siege of Angband ended in Year 155, Maidros organized the union against Morgoth during 165–70, and the Battle of Unnumbered Tears took place in 172. Gondolin was founded in Year 50, and Turgon arrived unexpectedly to take part in the battle as Fingon was driven back from Angband by fresh forces of Morgoth. Of significance is the addition earlier in the *Annals* that Húrin had visited Gondolin, thus providing a better reason for Morgoth's order that he be taken alive. In a brief, unfinished second version of the 'earliest' *Annals* Tolkien extended the period of the Siege of Angband by a hundred years so that it ended in 255; had the *Annals* reached that far, the Battle of Unnumbered Tears would have taken place in Year 272.

In the 'later' *Annals of Beleriand* (mid-1930s), by emendation, Tolkien again extended the Siege of Angband so that it ended in 455, and the Battle of Unnumbered Tears took place in 472. The writing of the sixteenth chapter in the *Quenta Silmarillion*, 'Of the Fourth Battle: Nírnaith Arnediad', can be securely dated to the end of 1937 since it is part of the manuscript that Tolkien wrote while the main *Quenta Silmarillion* manuscript was with George Allen & Unwin (*Publishers) for consideration. Tolkien now added extra detail, but the basic story of the battle changed little from the preceding versions. As *Christopher Tolkien points out, however, his father produced 'a most uncharacteristic incoherence' (*The Lost Road and Other Writings*, p. 314) in his account of Turgon's part in the Battle, deriving details from the incompatible stories of both the *Quenta Noldorinwa* and the *Annals of Beleriand*: some elements derive from the later changes to the *Quenta Noldorinwa* in which Turgon arrives some time before the battle begins, and others from the *Annals* in which he does not arrive until Fingon is in retreat. But the story seems to move towards the final text in which, although Turgon arrives before the battle, he and his host are positioned to guard the Pass of Sirion and enter the fray only when Fingon is forced to retreat.

Tolkien hardly touched this chapter in the *Quenta Silmarillion* when he returned to the mythology after completing *The Lord of the Rings*, but in the *Grey Annals* (*c.* 1951, see *Annals of Beleriand*) he told the story more as narrative than annal, drawing on both the 'later' *Annals* and the *Quenta Silmarillion* and adding new details. With the addition of an early battle before the return of the Noldor, the Nírnaeth Arnediad became the Fifth Battle. Maidros begins to organize his union against Morgoth in Year 468 and foolishly reveals himself with a trial of strength in 469. In the same year is entered the probable return of Beren and Lúthien, with the description of Melian's grief when she realizes her daughter's choice. The Dwarves not only make weapons and armour but take part in the battle, and are the only ones able to attack the dragons. The treachery of Uldor is related in greater detail, and Turgon's actions clarified. The prisoner killed to taunt Fingon's host into battle is now Gwindor's brother Gelmir, who had been captured in a previous battle. Huor's words to Turgon about a new star rising in Gondolin now enter. In 473 Morgoth attacks the Havens, those who escape sail to the Isle of Balar, and Turgon tries to send messengers into the West.

Some years later, Tolkien produced another account of the Battle of Unnumbered Tears, intended to be part of the *Narn i Chîn Húrin*. In most respects this follows the *Grey Annals* closely, but differs in that there is no mention of Uldor delaying Maedros, who is, however, attacked by a second army sent by Morgoth to prevent him joining with Fingon. This army defeats Maedros, then joins in the attack on Fingon and Turgon. (See *The War of the Jewels*, pp. 165–9.)

Christopher Tolkien used several sources to produce this chapter in *The Silmarillion*, as he explains in *The War of the Jewels*, p. 165. His primary source was the *Grey Annals*, but he also used elements from Chapter 16 of the *Quenta Silmarillion*, written in late 1937, and several short sections from the later account of the Battle intended for the *Narn* (but not its variant account of the actual battle). For the confrontation between Morgoth and Húrin he also derived some material from the part of the *Narn* published in *Unfinished Tales* (pp. 66–8).

Filey (Yorkshire). A popular resort town on the north-east coast of England, convenient to *Leeds, Filey has long attracted visitors to its beaches and entertainments. Tolkien and his family took summer holidays there in 1922 and 1925, each visit lasting a few weeks. On the second of these, in August–September 1925, the family stayed in a rented cottage built on a cliff. From this vantage point on two or three beautiful evenings young *John Tolkien watched the full moon rise out of the sea and shine a silver 'path' across the water. The family walked a long way to see the remains of a German submarine sunk in the First World War near **Flamborough Head**, and Tolkien taught his elder boys, John and *Michael, to skim stones from the beach into the sea. In spare moments he wrote lines 649–757 of the *Lay of Leithian*.

The holiday was marred, however, by the loss of Michael's beloved toy dog, and by a terrible storm which began to strike Filey in the afternoon of 5 September. Waves leapt over the sea wall onto the promenade, and high winds littered the beach with wood. To keep their minds off the storm, and to console Michael for the loss of his toy, Tolkien told John and Michael a story about the adventures of a dog named Rover who is turned into a toy by a wizard and then lost by a small boy on the beach. As later written down *Roverandom* includes glimpses of Filey as Tolkien would have seen it: a beach where 'the sand was clean and yellow, and the shingle white, and the sea blue with silver foam' (p. 10), and a town with cigarette and chocolate shops, bathing-tents and vans, and people hurrying places in their motor-cars: 'Motor after motor racketed by, filled (Rover thought) with the same people, all making all speed (and all dust and all smell) to somewhere)' (p. 87).

According to Humphrey Carpenter, Tolkien considered Filey 'a very nasty little suburban seaside resort' (quoted in *Biography*, p. 105), and it may have inspired his poems collectively known as *Tales and Songs of Bimble Bay* (but written, probably, c. 1928).

Finn and Hengest: The Fragment and the Episode. Lectures on the Old English 'Finnesburg Fragment' (or *The Fight at Finnesburg*) and a related episode in *Beowulf*, edited with commentary by *Alan Bliss, first published in Great Britain by George Allen & Unwin, London, in January 1983, and in the United States by the Houghton Mifflin Company, Boston, in ?October 1983 (announced for May 1983).

THE 'FINNESBURG' MATTER

The 'Finnesburg' in question (variously spelled, e.g. also *Finnsburg* and *Finnsburh*, cf. modern *Finsbury*) was the citadel of Finn, ruler of the Frisians. His wife was Hildeburh, from a tribe closely connected with the Danes (though, like her husband, of Jutish origin); her marriage to Finn had seemingly settled a feud between their two peoples. But it came to pass that Hildeburh's brother Hnæf, together with sixty warrior retainers, paid a visit to her, and while they were sleeping they were attacked by Finn's men. Hnæf and many other warriors on both sides were killed. What remained of Hnæf's Danes were outnumbered, but in too strong a position to be defeated without greater loss than Finn could risk. Hengest, now leader of the Danes, proposed a truce, which Finn accepted: both sides would have a funeral for their dead, and at least for the approaching winter (during which no sea voyage to their homes was possible) the Danes would become Finn's followers. But at the end of the winter Hengest and his men, though conflicted between their duty to exact revenge for Hnæf's death and their oath to Finn under the truce, chose the former, killed Finn and all his men, and returned Hildeburh to her homeland. This is a bare summary of a tale partly expressed in an Old English lay, of which only a fragment of forty-seven lines survives, and that in a questionable transcription of a later version, first published in 1705. The fragment begins part way into the text though near the beginning, with Hnæf responding to a sentry that the light he sees is neither the dawn, nor a dragon, nor fire, but reflection from weapons. His warriors rise and take up their arms. Battle is joined, and continues for five days with no losses among the Danes. The fragment ends with Hnæf, or perhaps Finn, asking how the warriors are surviving their wounds. The action of the poem is rapid and compressed.

A later part of the tale, concerning the truce, the funeral of Hnæf and of Hildeburh's son who was also slain, and Hengest's revenge upon Finn, is related by Hrothgar's bard in the so-called 'Finn Episode' in *Beowulf*. There the story is referred to as the *Freswæl*, and is told so allusively that the *Beowulf*-poet must have assumed prior knowledge of it among his listeners. Both Finn and Hnæf are also mentioned in the Old English poem *Widsith*.

HISTORY

In the early 1960s Alan Bliss read a paper to the Dublin Mediæval Society, 'Hengest and the Jutes'. Later he learned from colleagues that Tolkien had anticipated most of his conclusions in lectures on the story of Finn and Hengest delivered at *Oxford for more than two decades from the 1920s, and again by special arrangement in 1963. Feeling that he could not publish his paper without reference to the lectures, in 1966 Bliss explained his situation to Tolkien, his former B.Litt. supervisor at Oxford, and 'with characteristic generosity' Tolkien agreed to lend to Bliss 'all his material on the story of Finn and Hengest, to make what use of it I wished. The material was in disorder, and when Tolkien died in 1973 he had still not sorted it out; eventually, through the kindness of Mr *Christopher Tolkien, it came into my hands in 1979' (Bliss, *Finn and Hengest*, p. v).

On reading the lectures Bliss found that not only had Tolkien anticipated nearly all of his ideas, he had explored avenues which Bliss had not considered. Now Bliss felt that he could not write about Hengest without making use of Tolkien's thoughts, and it seemed to him 'that the lectures ought to be published, since they displayed to a high degree the unique blend of philological erudition and poetic imagination which distinguished Tolkien from other scholars' (p. v). Persuaded by Christopher Tolkien, he agreed to edit the lectures and related materials himself. The most substantial part of the papers, he found, contained

a study of the proper names in the Fragment and the Episode, arranged in the order in which they occur; notes on the text of the Fragment; notes on the text of the Episode; and a reconstruction of the story underlying the remains. The first of these four parts also exists in a much longer and fuller version: this may have been prepared for publication, since it is more carefully penned in a more formal style, and is liberally supplied with footnotes. Another set of lecture-notes on the Episode . . . seems to have been extracted from the lectures on *Beowulf* delivered [by Tolkien] during the war-years. . . . Finally there is a bundle of 'Later Material' . . . [which] includes two versions of a translation of the Episode and an additional reconstruction. [p. vi]

In a letter of 25 October 1932 to R.W. Chapman at Oxford University Press (*Publishers) Tolkien wrote: 'I have (in size already a large volume) a work on Hengest and Finn but that will require a good deal of work to make printable, and is in any case intricate and special' (Oxford University Press archives). But although he worked on this material at least through 1962 – at the last, presumably for his lectures in 1963, when he came briefly out of retirement to substitute for the absent Professor *C.L. Wrenn – when Bliss wrote to him about the material in 1966 he realized that, at his time of life, he would never put it into publishable order.

Bliss felt that 'in many ways the easiest thing to do would have been to write a new book based on Tolkien's ideas' (p. vii). Instead he produced a consistent text in Tolkien's own words, including: a general introduction to the matter; notes on the texts; glossaries of names; commentary on the texts; a Modern English prose translation of the episode; Tolkien's reconstruction of the events described or suggested by the fragment and episode; and two appendices, 'The Danes' and 'The Dating of Healfdene and Hengest'. Besides his preface and other preliminary matter, Bliss contributed an introduction, a translation of the fragment, a third appendix ('The Nationality of Hengest'), and occasional notes.

In his editor's introduction Bliss notes that

Tolkien's most important contribution to the interpretation of the story was what he refers to several times as the 'Jutes-on-both-sides' theory. In the lecture notes he revised in the early 1940s he stated his position as follows: 'My *private and patent* solution, derived from the text, and not solely devised in order to get round the difficulties of other views, is that *Jutes were on both sides in the quarrel*; on Finn's side, and on Hengest's side: it was a *Jutish feud*.' [p. 5]

Although Tolkien never published this view, as Bliss remarks it was referred to in print several times by C.L. Wrenn (see, for instance, his edition of *Beowulf with the Finnesburg Fragment* (1953; 3rd edn. rev. 1973), pp. 44–5, and his *Study of Old English Literature* (1967), p. 90). Bliss comments that Wrenn did not do so 'in terms consistent with the details of Tolkien's theory', but it seems likely from the similarities between Tolkien's argument and Wrenn's that the two friends and colleagues discussed the issues and were at least generally in agreement. Bliss himself, in his appendix 'The Nationality of Hengest', accepts without dispute Tolkien's (and Wrenn's) identification of the Hengest of the 'Finnesburg' matter with the Hengest of the *Anglo-Saxon Chronicle* without dispute, though not Tolkien's assertion that Hengest of the *Freswæl* was a Jute.

CRITICISM

In reviewing *Finn and Hengest* for *Amon Hen* 61 (May 1983), Joe Houghton commented that although it was marketed to 'admirers of *The Lord of the Rings*', the book held 'little if any common ground ... between the Middle-earth devotee, and the serious student of Old English'. Not already conversant with its subject matter, he found it 'almost unreadable' (p. 4). Kathleen Herbert in *Mallorn* 20 (September 1983) also found the book to be difficult, and was concerned that the reader begin with the preface, editor's introduction, and Modern English translations before proceeding with the texts proper. 'It is not a story but a work-book for specialists and for students in the process of specializing' (p. 12). In his review 'Fragmentary Glimpses', *Mythlore* 11, no. 1, whole no. 39 (Summer 1984), Thomas M. Egan expressed regret that although Tolkien's writings in medieval studies 'played a strong influence in the characterization of the mythic culture he created' in his fiction, 'regrettably ... his writing [in works of scholarship] tends to be turgid, over-stuffy, and hard to grasp in its importance to later writings.' He too found *Finn and Hengest* 'a specialized study, not for everyone' (p. 37). In *Amon Hen* 66 (March 1984) Anders Stenström (Beregond) published an alternative review, arguing (in contrast to Joe Houghton) that the book does not presuppose knowledge by the reader, finding links with the 'matter of Middle-earth', and commenting on names in the 'Finnesburg' material.

Tom Shippey remarks on names, and on Tolkien's views on the material in the context of history, in 'A Look at *Exodus* and *Finn and Hengest*', *Arda* 3 (1986, for 1982–83). In his later *J.R.R. Tolkien: Author of the Century* (2000) Shippey notes in regard to *Finn and Hengest*:

> Considering that this was only Tolkien's second publication on *Beowulf* [after **Beowulf: The Monsters and the Critics*], and that his first has remained the most influential and frequently-cited publication on the poem of all time, it might seem amazing that it has had no academic impact at all – no one ever cites it. But it is extremely hard to follow, detail-crammed past ready comprehension. [p. 267]

The most extensive review of *Finn and Hengest* seems to be that by Malcolm Godden in the *Times Literary Supplement* for 8 July 1983 ('From the Heroic to the Allegorical', p. 736). Godden is fascinated by Tolkien's 'extensive use of story-making' in the lectures, and especially in the 'reconstruction', in which he builds a tale from stones which 'are few and jumbled'. Godden describes how Tolkien focuses on the Jutes as 'crucial figures' in the background to the 'Finnesburg' matter, and on the figure of Hengest, who – identified with the person of the same name who was a leader of the first Anglo-Saxon invasion of England – took up with the British king Vortigern and turned on him as he had with Finn. 'The tragic hero of this drama is Finn, caught up in conflicts not of his own making and destroyed by his own generosity. The Machiavel is Hengest, who appears first in the service of the Danes, the supposed enemies of the Jutes, and thereafter switches allegiances rapidly. But it is the place of the story in the history of nations which Tolkien is keenest to establish.'

Godden finds this 'a powerful story, and when first delivered in 1928', not so long after the First World War, 'it can have lost nothing from its echoes of recent events, with its picture of two great powers anxious to maintain peace but dragged into ruinous conflict by resentful exiles from smaller nations, pursuing their old vendettas'. Nonetheless, Godden does not find the argument very plausible: 'the scraps of evidence are forcefully exploited, but they will not really prove, with any degree of conviction, the date or historical context that Tolkien suggests' or his argument that the two Hengests were one and the same.

Firiel *see* **The Last Ship**

Firth, Charles Harding (1857–1936). C.H. Firth read History at New College and Balliol College, *Oxford; he received his B.A. in 1878. For a few years he taught at Firth College in Sheffield, founded by his uncle, industrialist Mark Firth, then in 1883 returned to Oxford to conduct research – the Civil War and the Protectorate were special interests on which he published widely – and in 1887 obtained a History tutorship at Pembroke College. He resigned in 1893 in protest against the College's refusal to establish a Scholarship in History. In 1901 he was elected a Fellow of All Souls' College, Oxford, and in 1904 became Regius Professor of Modern History, with a fellowship at Oriel College, a post he held until 1925. He received a knighthood in 1922.

During his years as Regius Professor of Modern History (a chair originally responsible for the teaching of European languages), and as Emeritus Professor from 1925, Firth was closely concerned with the development of the Oxford English School. His main object was the promotion of standards and facilities for research. In this he worked in particular alongside *A.S. Napier, *Walter Raleigh, and *Joseph Wright, but was more vociferous than they as a university politician. He also lectured in the English School, on ballads, Milton, the Restoration, and the relationship between history and literature. He is recorded as present at Oxford English Faculty Board meetings, together with Tolkien, as late as 1930.

The Five Wizards. Discussion, arising from Tolkien's consideration of the history of Glorfindel, partly published under this assigned title, with commentary, in *The Peoples of Middle-earth* (1996), pp. 384–5.

*Christopher Tolkien summarizes the first part, headed 'Note on the landing of the Five Wizards and their functions and operations', in which Tolkien rejects the possibility of any of the Istari being Eldar. The following section, published in *Unfinished Tales* (1980), p. 394, states that the Istari were 'all Maiar, that is persons of the "angelic" order . . . sent by the Valar at a crucial moment in the history of Middle-earth to enhance the resistance of Elves of the West . . . and of uncorrupted Men of the West. . . .' It touches briefly on the different powers and stature of Saruman, Gandalf, and Radagast.

The other two Wizards are mentioned only briefly, but more information is given in almost illegible notes on the verso, mentioned in *Unfinished Tales* and published in *The Peoples of Middle-earth*. These are concerned with establishing the time and order of the arrival of the Istari, but one suggests a history for the 'other two': they came in the Second Age and 'their task was to circumvent Sauron' (p. 385).

These texts probably date from the end of 1972 or from 1973.

Fletcher, Ronald Frank William (1890–1950). After reading English at Lincoln College, *Oxford, R.F.W. Fletcher took holy orders. From 1915 to 1923 he served as chaplain and teacher in a series of schools, then returned to Oxford as Chaplain and tutor at St Edmund Hall. From 1930 to 1942 he was also rector of the Oxfordshire village of Broughton Pogis, until wartime transport problems led him to resign. His work in the Oxford English School often brought him in contact with Tolkien. From 1946 until his death in October 1950 Fletcher was chairman of the English Faculty Board. In November 1950 Tolkien took his place as representative of the Oxford English School at the Congrès du LXe anniversaire des sections de Philologie romane et de Philologie germanique in Liège (*Belgium).

'Flight of the Gnomes'. Isolated outline, published as the third prose fragment in the first chapter of *The Shaping of Middle-earth* (1986), pp. 9–10. Written in the early 1920s, it seems to show an intermediate stage in the development from the story in *The Book of Lost Tales* to that in the *Sketch of the Mythology* with the emergence of Finweg and Fingolfin who oppose Fëanor, but also includes allusions to events or actions not taken up in later versions.

The Flight of the Noldoli from Valinor. Poem in alliterative verse related to *'The Silmarillion', published with commentary and notes in *The Lays of Beleriand* (1985), pp. 131–41. In its third and final (but unfinished) form, extending 146 lines, the work begins with the destruction of the Two Trees and ends just after Fëanor and his sons have sworn their Oath before the Noldoli in Côr. Two earlier versions bear the titles *The Flight of the Gnomes as Sung in the Halls of Thingol* and *The Flight of the Gnomes*. The changes made in the successive texts are almost all metrical or verbal, and each version ends at the same point, except that the first has three additional draft lines in which Fingolfin speaks against the urging of Fëanor.

The poem probably dates from early 1925, after Tolkien laid aside *The Children of Húrin*, and before he began the *Lay of Leithian*. For the part *The Flight of the Noldoli from Valinor* played in the development of *'The Silmarillion', see *'Of the Flight of the Noldor'.

'Of the Flight of the Noldor'. The ninth chapter of the *'Quenta Silmarillion', published in *The Silmarillion* (1977), pp. 78–90.

SUMMARY

After the destruction of the Trees, their light survives only in the Silmarils, but with a little of that light Yavanna could recall the Trees to life. Fëanor refuses her the gems, for to release their light they would have to be broken, and he could never make their like again, nor would his heart bear their breaking. Nienna mourns the Trees and washes away the poison of Ungoliant with her tears.

A messenger brings news that Melkor has attacked Fëanor's dwelling at Formenos, killed his father Finwë, and stolen the Silmarils along with other jewels. Fëanor curses Melkor, naming him *Morgoth*, the Black Foe, and also Manwë for summoning Fëanor to the festival, else he would have been at Formenos to protect his father and property. 'The Silmarils had passed away, and all one it may seem whether Fëanor had said yea or nay to Yavanna; yet had he said yea at the first, before the tidings came from Formenos, it may be that his after deeds would have been other than they were' (p. 79).

Morgoth and Ungoliant escape to Middle-earth across the Helcaraxë, the northern part of the Great Sea, frozen to grinding ice. Ungoliant demands the promised payment, and devours the lesser jewels Morgoth gives her, but is not satisfied and asks for the Silmarils. Despite the fact that even in their casket they have begun to burn him, Morgoth refuses. Ungoliant attacks, but Balrogs come to Morgoth's rescue out of the remains of Angband. Ungoliant flees into Beleriand and mates with spiders living in the valley of Nan Dungortheb, producing hideous offspring, before travelling further south. Her final fate is not known. Morgoth builds Angband anew, and gathers to him beasts, demons, and Orcs. He sets the Silmarils in a great iron crown, though they cause him constant pain. Rarely does he leave his stronghold, but exerts power through his armies.

In Tirion Fëanor claims the kingship of the Noldor and swears hatred and vengeance on Morgoth. A master of words, he urges the Noldor to leave darkened Valinor and win realms across the sea. He accuses the Valar of holding the Elves captive so that Men might rule in Middle-earth, and declares that once the Noldor have recovered the Silmarils 'we alone shall be lords of the unsullied Light, and masters of the bliss and beauty of Arda'. He and his seven sons swear a terrible oath, vowing 'to pursue with vengeance and hatred to the ends of the World Vala, Demon, Elf or Man as yet unborn . . . whoso should hold or take or keep a Silmaril from their possession' (p. 83). Although some of his kin disagree, Fëanor prevails; yet not all will accept him as leader, and the Noldor set out as two hosts, the greater with Fingolfin. Only a tenth of the Elves refuse to leave. Through a messenger Manwë urges the hosts against departure, warning that Morgoth is beyond their ability to overcome. The Valar will neither help nor hinder the Elves' quest, but because of his oath Fëanor is exiled. Fëanor refuses to listen, and accuses Manwë of sitting idle in grief.

Fëanor goes to Alqualondë to urge the Teleri to join the Noldor, partly to swell their numbers, but mainly because he needs their ships to cross the sea to Middle-earth. They refuse him aid 'against the will of the Valar' (p. 86): Olwë, their lord, declares that their ships, made with their own hands, are as dear to the Teleri as gems are to the Noldor. Fëanor takes the ships by force, and in bitter fighting many on both sides are killed – the Kinslaying of Alqualondë.

As the Noldor travel, some in ships and some on land, to the North where the sea dividing Aman and Middle-earth is narrowest, a figure appears to them, said to be Mandos. He speaks a curse and prophecy against those who will not stay and seek pardon: they will weep 'tears unnumbered', and Valinor shall be fenced against them. The wrath of the Valar lies on the House of Fëanor and on its followers. 'Their Oath shall drive them, and yet betray them, and ever snatch away the very treasures that they have sworn to pursue. To evil end shall all things turn out that they begin well; and by treason of kin unto kin, and the fear of treason, shall this come to pass. The Dispossessed shall they be for ever.' Because they have shed the blood of their kindred, they will dwell in Death's shadow, and though fated not to die through sickness or age they may be slain, 'and slain ye shall be: by weapon and by torment and by grief; and your houseless spirits shall come then to Mandos. . . . And those that endure in Middle-earth . . . shall grow weary of the world as with a great burden, and shall wane, and become as shadows of regret before the younger race that cometh after' (p. 88). Fëanor counters that he and his people are not cowards, and their deeds will be sung while Arda lasts. Finarfin, but not his sons, and many others in the host now turn back and are pardoned by the Valar.

Then follows the first treachery among the Noldor. Some of the followers of Fingolfin begin to murmur against Fëanor. Since there are not enough ships to carry all of the host, Fëanor and his forces depart secretly in those ships that they have and reach Middle-earth; but instead of sending ships back for Fingolfin and his followers, they burn them. Fingolfin, seeing the fires from afar, knows what has been done and is filled with bitterness. He and those with him pass further north and cross the Helcaraxë. It is a desperate journey and many are lost, including Turgon's wife, Elenwë. Little love is felt for Fëanor.

HISTORY

The earliest version of this story, a single tale in *The Book of Lost Tales* (c. 1916–20), is divided between two chapters – *The Theft of Melko and the Dark-*

ening of Valinor and *The Flight of the Noldoli* – in **The Book of Lost Tales, Part One* (1983). It exists only as a hastily written, unrevised pencil draft. In *The Theft of Melko and the Darkening of Valinor* Melko's murder of Fëanor's father Bruithwir (not the leader of the Noldoli) and the theft of the jewels and the Silmarils (not yet as significant as they would become) take place a considerable time before the destruction of the Trees. Manwë gives permission for Fëanor and those who accompanied him into exile to return to Kôr, but Fëanor rejects this. He fails to make more jewels like the Silmarils and broods on his wrongs. He urges the Noldoli to return to Middle-earth to make war on Melko. Accompanied by some of the Noldoli, he asks Manwë that they be taken back to Middle-earth; but Manwë tells them that Men will soon wake in Middle-earth, that Men are destined to rule there, and that he fears conflict between Men and Elves. Fëanor believes that the Valar are depriving the Elves of their rightful inheritance. After the destruction of the Trees there is, of course, no request for Fëanor to give up the Silmarils.

In *The Flight of the Noldoli* Fëanor exhorts his people to leave darkened Valinor and return to Middle-earth. Finwë Nólemë, the leader of the Noldoli, urges that they speak first to Manwë but, when Fëanor prevails, joins the rest of his folk. Since the genealogy of Finwë's descendants has not yet emerged, nothing is said about other divided sentiments. In the first account of events the Noldoli only steal the ships of the Solosimpi, most of whom are absent hunting Melko, and there is apparently no bloodshed; but in a replacement text, 'The Kinslaughter (Battle of Kópas Alqalunten)', when Fëanor arrives and the Solosimpi deny him their ships he and the Noldoli take them by force. The Solosimpi do not attack until the Noldoli begin to sail away, but are then themselves attacked by another host of the Noldoli, and many are killed. As the Noldoli travel north, some by sea and some by land, they meet a servant of Mandos whom they answer scornfully when he asks them to return. He prophesies evil for them, and declares 'Great is the Fall of Gondolin' (*The Book of Lost Tales, Part One*, p. 167), though none know what his words mean. This text contains more description of the terrors of the Helkaraksë and the adjoining sea, and of the loss of one of the ships in a great eddy. Nonetheless, very few of the Noldoli seek to return, and those who do are not welcomed. When winter comes and the ice is packed more firmly, they abandon the ships and reach Middle-earth across the ice, though many are lost.

Other tales also touch upon the story. At the beginning of *The Tale of the Sun and Moon* the eagle Sorontur tells Manwë that he has seen a fleet of white ships drifting empty on the sea, some on fire, and a host of Elves on the far side of the Helkaraksë. In the unfinished *Gilfanon's Tale: The Travail of the Noldoli and the Coming of Mankind* the Seven Sons of Fëanor swear their oath against any who should hold a Silmaril, but this is done in Middle-earth after the death of their father. In *The Tale of Tinúviel* it is said that Melko wore the Silmarils in an iron crown.

In the brief *'Flight of the Gnomes', probably written in the early 1920s, Fëanor is still not the son of Finwë, but some of his future kin emerge. 'Finweg & Fingolfin speak against him' (*The Shaping of Middle-earth, p. 9). This outline also includes ideas which were not developed further, such as that the Noldoli repent when they reach Fangros, and burn the boats, and that they are apparently cursed by Gilfanon, one of the Teleri of Alqualondë. In the alliterative poem *The Flight of the Noldoli from Valinor, begun probably in early 1925, after the destruction of the Trees and the resulting darkness in Valinor, the Noldoli gather in Côr. Fëanor, now the son of Finn (Finwë) who has been slain by Melko, calls on the assembled Noldoli to leave Valinor and join him in pursuit of Morgoth. He swears a binding oath to hunt endlessly for the Silmarils. Immediately his seven sons swear their oath of vengeance against anyone who should seize, steal, or keep a Silmaril. A few draft lines indicate that the Noldorin genealogy is beginning to develop.

In the *Sketch of the Mythology (c. 1926), prior to the point at which this chapter begins in The Silmarillion, significant development took place in Fëanor's family relationships. He and Fingolfin are now both sons of Finwë, and when Fëanor is banished from Tûn because of his hostility to Fingolfin and to Fingolfin's son Finweg, Finwë leaves with him, and Fingolfin rules in Tûn in his place. The final order of events is present: on the day of festival Melkor and Ungoliant destroy the Trees, and fleeing north they attack Fëanor's treasury, killing Finwë and stealing the Silmarils and other jewels. Noldoli bring news of the attack to the Valar. Morgoth and Ungoliant dispute the plunder, he is rescued by Balrogs, and she flees south. Morgoth rebuilds Angband and makes an iron crown in which he sets the Silmarils, though they burn his hands and cause him pain. Fëanor summons the Noldoli to Tûn despite his banishment, and makes his speech. Fingolfin and his son Finweg (Fingon) speak against Fëanor, but when the Noldoli vote to depart, join them and are in command of half of those that set out. The fight with the Teleri now begins before the seizing of the ships. A curse is pronounced against the Noldoli at Swanhaven (Alqualondë) that they will suffer treachery of their own kindred and fear of treachery, and later an emissary of Mandos speaks the 'Prophecy of Mandos', of war against one another when they refuse to return. The treachery of Fëanor in stealing and burning the boats now enters. Tolkien is still uncertain about the rest; as originally written, some of the Elves under Fingolfin return to seek pardon of the Valar, and the rest cross the ice led by Finweg. Some later changes are themselves subsequently changed when Finwë's third son, Finrod (Finarfin), enters the story: Finrod tries to calm the Noldoli after Fëanor's speech, though his sons side with Fëanor; he does not leave Tûn > he is killed at Alqualondë trying to stop the fighting > he and his sons are not present at Alqualondë, but they do leave Tûn, though reluctantly, and arrive after the burning of the ships; he (rather than Fingolfin) leads some of the Noldoli back to seek pardon of the Valar. Fingolfin, not his son, leads those who cross the ice. Lines 1584–1643 of the *Lay of Leithian, written at the end of March 1928, also describe the Oath of Fëanor and his sons, but add nothing of significance.

In the *Quenta Noldorinwa (c. 1930) the only Noldoli who do not leave with

Fëanor are those who are absent at the time. Of those who do leave, not all of Fingolfin's host take part in the Kinslaying, and none of those who arrive last with Finrod are involved in the deed. The curse pronounced at Alqualondë has disappeared, but Mandos or his messenger declares the Prophecy of Mandos, the content of which moves closer to that in the published *Silmarillion*. Fëanor sails away in all of the ships because he is annoyed by the murmurings and grumblings of many in Fingolfin's host. Finrod's host still arrives after the burning of the ships; in a pencil addition he returns to Kôr after hearing the Prophecy.

The 'earliest' *Annals of Valinor* (early 1930s) give some indication of the span of time during which the pertinent events took place. The destruction of the Trees, the theft of the Silmarils, and Melkor's escape to Middle-earth occur in Valian Years 2990–1. Fëanor makes his speech in 2991, and the march of the Noldoli begins in 2992 after long preparation. The Valar forbid the march but do not hinder it. The Kinslaying takes place *c.* 2992. The Prophecy or Doom of Mandos is delivered in 2993. Finrod and many others return to Valinor and are pardoned, but find that they have lost the friendship of Aulë and the Teleri. Those who continue with Fëanor and Fingolfin, including all of the sons of Finrod, reach the North in 2994. Fëanor seizes the ships, which are too few to carry all of the Noldoli, and sails to Middle-earth, reaching it *c.* 2995, then burns the ships. It is not until 3000 that the rest of the Noldoli arrive after the perilous crossing of the Helkaraksë. A Valian Year being the equivalent of ten of our years, a considerable time (about a century) elapses between the destruction of the Trees and the arrival of the second host of the Noldoli in Middle-earth. Pencil emendations shorten this time, however. The Trees are destroyed in 2998, in which year also Fëanor incites the Noldoli to follow him from Valinor. Preparations for the flight begin in 2999, and Fingolfin arrives in Middle-earth in Valian Year 3000. An additional reckoning, according to Sun Years, places the Battle of Alqualondë in 29991, the Doom of Mandos in 29992, the burning of the ships in 29994, and the landing of Fëanor in Middle-earth in 29995. Some new ideas in these *Annals* and the nearly contemporary 'earliest' *Annals of Beleriand* are only temporary: in both, three of Finrod's sons are given passage in the ships because of their friendship with the sons of Fëanor, and in the *Annals of Beleriand* Morgoth only 'devises' Balrogs and Orcs after his return to Middle-earth.

The dates in the 'later' *Annals of Valinor* of the mid-1930s are the same as the original dates in the 'earliest' *Annals*, except that the events entered for 2990–1 are placed in 2990. *Christopher Tolkien has suggested that his father may have deliberately rejected the shorter time-span introduced into the earlier *Annals* by emendation. The name *Noldor* now replaced *Noldoli*.

In 'Of the Flight of the Noldor', the fifth chapter of the *Quenta Silmarillion* (begun in the mid-1930s) and forerunner of the chapter of the same title in *The Silmarillion*, the Balrogs are again pre-existing, as they come to Morgoth's aid in his conflict with Ungoliantë, but only on his return does he make Orcs, out of stone, in mockery of Elves. Fëanor sends messengers to the Teleri asking them to join the Noldor in their return to Middle-earth, but they refuse to either join them or to give or sell them ships; it is suggested that the figure who speaks the prophecy of the North may be Mandos; Fëanor seizes the ships because, fearing treachery, none of the Noldor are willing to stay behind to wait for the ships' return; he now takes two of Finrod's sons with him.

When Tolkien rewrote or emended parts of the *Quenta Silmarillion c.* 1951 he made few changes to this chapter. Galadriel was now noted among the descendants of Finwë who hear and react to Fëanor's speech. Also *c.* 1951 Tolkien wrote the *Annals of Aman* (see *Annals of Valinor*) in a more fuller, more narrative style than the earlier *Annals*, and with changes similar to those in the *Quenta Silmarillion*. Yavanna requests the Silmarils of Fëanor and he refuses; and he gives Melkor his new name, *Morgoth* 'the Dark Enemy'. The suggestion is now made that Morgoth may have produced Orcs from captive and corrupted Elves. In the *Annals of Aman*, according to the new reckoning which entered with the creation of the Trees, Morgoth's attack on the Trees and all events of this chapter up to and including the Kinslaying take place in Year 1495, and the Noldor journey North in 1496–7.

Further work on the *Quenta Silmarillion c.* 1958–60 included a more detailed account of Ungoliantë's demand for payment and Morgoth's refusal to give her the Silmarils. The comment that Fëanor's later deeds might have been different if he had agreed to give up the Silmarils now entered. One change that was not taken into *The Silmarillion* was that the sons of Fëanor brought the news of Melkor's attack on Formenos and described what happened there in detail. Also at this time both the *Quenta Silmarillion* and the *Annals of Aman* were emended with changes in names introduced in the late 1950s: *Finrod* became *Finarphin* and his son *Felagund* (or *Inglor*) became *Finrod*. Probably at this time additions were made to the *Annals of Aman*, stipulating that Finrod (probably Felagund) and Galadriel fought against Fëanor at Alqualonde; and that among those lost during the crossing of the Helcaraxë was Turgon's wife, Elenwë.

In *The Shibboleth of Fëanor* (1968 or later) Tolkien gave another reason for Fëanor's treachery towards Fingolfin: Fingolfin had prefixed the name *Finwë* to his existing name before the Noldor reached Middle-earth. 'This was in pursuance of his claim to be the chieftain of all the Noldor after the death of Finwë, and so enraged Fëanor that it was no doubt one of the reasons for his treachery in abandoning Fingolfin and stealing away with all the ships' (*The Peoples of Middle-earth*, p. 344; see also p. 361, n. 33). This text also develops a story only hinted at in a late addition to the *Annals of Aman*, that one of Fëanor's youngest twin sons was burnt with the ships (see *Morgoth's Ring*, p. 128; *The Peoples of Middle-earth*, pp. 353–5).

The text published in *The Silmarillion* was taken mainly from the *Annals of Aman*. In the first pages the part of the *Quenta Silmarillion* rewritten *c.* 1958–60 is of equal importance (though in places the text differs only slightly). In the latter part some small sections or phrases were also taken from the *Quenta Silmarillion*, but that text had been little emended since the mid-1930s. Christopher Tolkien used the *c.* 1958–60 version of the quarrel between Morgoth and Ungoliant over the Silmarils but had to make adjustments to make it fit, when it referred to the later story (not used in *The Silmarillion*) that Morgoth was not present at the destruction of the Trees, and tried to keep Ungoliant from Formenos).

Folkestone (Kent). In summer 1912 Tolkien spent a fortnight encamped with the King Edward's Horse on Dibgate Plateau, near the ancient town of Folkestone on the south-east coast of England. In June 1916 Folkestone was his port of embarkation when joining the British Expeditionary Force in *France.

Food and drink. While an undergraduate at *Oxford Tolkien was instrumental in founding two societies, the Apolausticks and the Chequers Clubbe (*Societies and clubs), among whose activities dining featured prominently. On 1 June 1912 members of the Apolausticks enjoyed an elaborate dinner of many courses, apparently prepared in a French manner. Whatever Tolkien felt about French cooking as a young man, in later years he expressed a pronounced dislike for it, in comparison with 'good plain food' (letter to Deborah Webster, 25 October 1958, *Letters*, p. 288). *John and *Priscilla Tolkien recalled that 'there was a considerable difference between' their father's 'sophisticated taste in wine and his dislike of foreign or 'messed about' food. He attended many college dinners over the years and increasingly his antipathy towards French food and culture became more pronounced' (*The Tolkien Family Album*, p. 78).

In many of the societies to which he belonged in adult life the members regularly dined together, sometimes preceding a paper given by one of them, but often just for the pleasure of meeting. Among the more relaxed occasions were the 'ham feasts' given by *C.S. Lewis (see **Chronology** for 11 March 1948). Tolkien also regularly dined at high table in his various colleges, on occasions with a guest, or he himself might be invited to dine at high table in other colleges.

He mentions in a letter during the Second World War having breakfast of toast and home-made marmalade in bed. He tells Nancy Smith in a letter written at the end of 1963 that like Gollum he is fond of fish.

In his diary of a visit to Italy in 1955 he recorded details of several meals, from which it is clear that he enjoyed Italian cooking. On arrival in Venice he and Priscilla enjoyed a 'fabulous' dinner – 'ham and melon, roast veal and stuffed tomatoes, Bel Paese, real Pêche Melba, and abundant fruit. We arrived just at peach time, and I ate more peaches in fourteen days than in all my days before together.' He also spoke highly on this occasion of the excellent ordinary table wines, which he found 'most refreshing diluted'. On one day for lunch he ate fish, smoked salmon, and scampi, again with a 'pleasant wine' (Tolkien Papers, Bodleian Library, Oxford).

He liked to drink beer in a pub with friends, especially the *Inklings. In a letter of 31 October 1970 he told his friend Amy Ronald, who evidently had sent him a voucher to spend on alcohol: 'My palate has never learned to appreciate [brandy] as it deserves. But I have laid in some burgundy – some port which we [Tolkien and his wife] both like, and some good sherry, some liqueurs, and one bottle of champagne (with a view to Christmas).' The burgundy, he added, was 'not "vintage". But I like port (v[ery] much) as a mid-morn[ing] drink: warming, digestible, and v[ery] good for my throat, when taken (as I think it should be) by itself or with a dry biscuit, and *not* after a full meal, nor (above all) with dessert!' (*Letters*, p. 405). He purchased a stock of wine, port, and rum for Inklings meetings to be held in his room in Merton College (*Oxford), but on one occasion at least he also served green tea.

In his *George Allen & Unwin: A Remembrancer* (1999) *Rayner Unwin recalled that the last meal he gave Tolkien – at the Garrick Club in London – 'consisted of smoked salmon, a kipper and stilton cheese' (p. 45).

As Marjorie Burns points out in *Perilous Realms: Celtic and Norse in Tolkien's Middle-earth* (2005), 'the greatest pleasures' in *The Hobbit and *The Lord of the Rings 'are the pleasures of food and drink' (p. 156). The Hobbit especially has frequent images of food, from the seed-cakes, raspberry jam and apple-tart, mince-pies and cheese, pork-pie and salad, eggs, cold chicken, and so forth of the 'unexpected party' (Chapter 1) to Bilbo's dreams of food when he is in the wild. The theme of plenty is carried into *The Lord of the Rings*, with the 'yellow cream and honeycomb, and white bread, and butter; milk, cheese, and green herbs and ripe berries' on the table of Tom Bombadil and Goldberry (bk. I, ch. 7), and the meal served at the *Prancing Pony* in Bree, 'hot soup, cold meats, a blackberry tart, new loaves, slabs of butter, and half a ripe cheese: good plain food, as good as the Shire could show, and homelike' (bk. I, ch. 9). Against such imagery Tolkien later contrasts the privations of Frodo and Sam in Mordor.

For W.H.A. Poem in parallel Old and Modern English, first published in *Shenandoah: The Washington and Lee University Review* (Lexington, Virginia) 18, no. 2 (Winter 1967), pp. 96–7. It is a 'tardy tribute and token of thanks' to *W.H. Auden on his sixtieth birthday, praising his poetry, his learning, and his friendship.

A Fourteenth-Century Romance. Article on the Middle English poem *Sir Gawain and the Green Knight*, published in the *Radio Times*, 4 December 1953 (with programmes for the week December 6–12), p. 9, but only in the edition not marked as for one of the broadcast regions. The article was meant to serve as a printed introduction to the broadcast in four parts of Tolkien's translation of *Sir Gawain* into Modern English, beginning 6 December.

Tolkien describes the poem as 'one of the best examples of the art of narrative in verse that has survived from the fourteenth century'. It is a 'romance', 'in fact a fairy-story, but one written at a time when that kind was (happily) not yet associated with children'. Its roots are 'deep in the almost forgotten pagan past of northern Europe, and in Ireland and Britain in particular'. 'The reshaping of the inherited material by a mind of the fourteenth century, concerned with the problems and ideals of conduct at that period, is as interesting to observe as is, say Shakespeare's in similar cases, such as *King Lear*.'

Sir Gawain is 'the chief surviving work of the Alliterative Revival' in the West Midlands and North-west of England, but its language 'was, to London ears and eyes,' exemplified by *Chaucer, 'dialectal, strange in grammar and vocabulary'. The object of Tolkien's translation was 'to preserve the original metre' of the poem, 'so essential to the total effect, and at the same time to reproduce the language in modern terms, showing it to be not, as it may appear to a superficial glance, queer, crabbed, and rustic, but as it was for the people to whom *Sir Gawain* was addressed: Western maybe, and conservative, yet truly English, and above all courtly, wise and well bred.'

Tolkien probably had little more than a week in which to write his article, having been sent a request by Lionel Simmons, Assistant to the Literary Editor of the *Radio Times*, only on 18 November.

Fourteenth Century Verse & Prose *see* **A Middle English Vocabulary**

Fox, Adam (1883–1977). Educated at University College, *Oxford, Adam Fox took holy orders in the Church of England in 1911. From 1906 to 1929 he served in turn as Assistant Master at Lancing College, West Sussex, as Warden of Radley College, Abingdon, Oxfordshire, and as Assistant Master of the Diocesan College, Rondebosch, South Africa. From 1929 to 1942 he was a Fellow and Dean of Divinity of Magdalen College, Oxford, and from 1942 to 1963 Canon of Westminster Abbey. Long a friend of *C.S. Lewis, Fox joined the *Inklings, though his visits became rare and ended in 1942 when he left Oxford for London.

In 1938 Tolkien and *C.S. Lewis nominated Fox to the chair of Poetry at Oxford, and successfully campaigned on his behalf against E.K. Chambers, the Shakespearian scholar, and *Lord David Cecil (who himself was later welcomed into the Inklings). Lewis argued that the Professor of Poetry should be a practising poet – though Fox was hardly that, notwithstanding his award of the Sacred Poem Prize at Oxford in 1929 and his long narrative poem, *Old King Coel*, published in 1937.

Among other writings by Adam Fox are *Plato for Pleasure* (1945), *English Hymns and Hymn Writers* (1947), and *Meet the Greek Testament* (1952).

France. In the summer holidays of 1913 Tolkien took the job of escorting two Mexican boys to **Paris**, to join another boy and two aunts. He enjoyed Paris, and 'later in life . . . would entertain the family with his expert mimicry of the accents of Paris errand-boys and their gutter talk' (*The Tolkien Family Album*, p. 36); but contact with its people did nothing to change the poor opinions he had already formed of almost everything French. He wrote to Edith Bratt (*Edith Tolkien) about 'the vulgarity and the jabber and spitting and the indecency' (quoted in *Biography*, p. 67). He was pleased when the aunts decided to visit **Brittany**, since he was interested in Celtic languages, but disappointed when he discovered that their destination was **Dinard**, a popular seaside resort. He wrote to Edith: 'Brittany! . . . And to see nothing but trippers and dirty papers and bathing machines' (quoted in *Biography*, p. 67). The visit was cut short when one of the aunts was killed in a traffic accident (see further, **Chronology**, 13 August 1913 etc.).

When Tolkien next crossed the English Channel to France it was as a member of the British Expeditionary Force in the midst of war. From 6 June to 8 November 1916 he was present at **Abbeville, Acheux-en-Amiénois, Albert, Amiens, Auchonvillers, Beaumont-Hamel, Beauquesne, Beauval, Bertrancourt, Bouzincourt, Bus-lès-Artois, Calais, Colincamps, Englebelmer, Étaples, Forceville, Franqueville, Gézaincourt, Hédauville, La Boiselle, Le Havre, Le Touquet, Léalvillers, Mailly-Maillet, Ovillers, Puchevillers, Rubempré, Senlis, Thiepval**, and **Warloy-Baillon**. The main battleground of the actions in which he took part during this period, altogether known as the Battle of the Somme, is conveniently described by J.C. Latter in his *History of the Lancashire Fusiliers, 1914–1918* (1949, p. 130). That country lay between the two main rivers that flow through the plain of Artois, the Somme and the Ancre:

> It is mainly open, hedgeless and undulating, somewhat reminiscent of the Yorkshire Wolds, and has a chalk subsoil. It is cut into by a number of small streams which find their way into one or other of the two rivers. These streams, flowing some south, some north, rise in a long ridge running east-south-east from the River Ancre at Thiepval to the northern slopes of the valley of the River Somme near Pèronne. Between these streams lie smaller ridges, jutting out into the valleys from the main ridge, like the branches of a fir tree. In some places the main ridge rises to a height of 300 feet above the River Somme. The country was then freely dotted with picturesque little villages and contained a few large woods.

A more detailed description of this area is provided by Gerald Gliddon in *The Battle of the Somme: A Topographical History* (corrected edn. 1996).

See also *Food and drink; *Languages.

Fraser, John (1882–1945). Educated at Aberdeen, Cambridge, and Jena, John Fraser was from 1907 Assistant to the Professor of Humanity and Lecturer in Comparative Philology at Aberdeen University, before becoming in 1921 the Jesus Professor of Celtic at *Oxford. There he was one of the dons invited to membership in Tolkien's informal society the Kolbítar (*Societies and clubs). Fraser's writings placed him in the front rank of Celtic scholars.

Free will and Fate. To many readers who came to *The Lord of the Rings* before the publication of *The Silmarillion* in 1977 it seemed clear that some events were guided by Providence, and that characters were free to choose whether to accept a role for which they were chosen. The nature of that Providence, however, was barely hinted at. There are only two references to the One in *The Lord of the Rings*, both in Appendix A: 'When Ar-Pharazôn set foot upon the shores of Aman the Blessed, the Valar laid down their Guardianship and called upon the One, and the world was changed' (in *The Númenórean Kings*); and 'If this is indeed, as the Eldar say, the gift of the One to Men, it is bitter to receive' (Arwen's words concerning death, near the end of *The Tale of Aragorn and Arwen*). There are other references to the Valar, as a group or individually, who clearly have power, but far less than the One. The Elves sing to Elbereth, and Frodo and Sam are inspired to call on her (bk. I, ch. 11; bk. IV, ch. 10), while Damrod calls on the Valar to turn the Mûmak aside (bk. IV, ch. 4). In Appendix A it is said (but only from the second edition) that Fëanor left the Blessed Realm 'against the will of the Valar', and by allusion the Valar gave help which led to the overthrow of Morgoth; as 'Guardians of the World' they granted the isle of Númenor to the Edain, but laid on the Númenóreans the 'Ban of the Valar' that they not sail west out of sight of Númenor or attempt to reach the Undying Lands. 'For though a long span of life had been granted to them . . . they must remain mortal, since the Valar were not permitted to take from them the Gift of Men. . . .'

At any rate, in *The Lord of the Rings* there is very evidently a plan, or plans, underlying events of the story, to which there are many allusions. In Book I, Chapter 2, Gandalf tells Frodo that in the finding of the Ring by Bilbo (in *The Hobbit*) 'the Ring was trying to get back to its master', but was 'picked up by the most unlikely person imaginable. . . . Behind that there was something else at work, beyond any design of the Ring-maker. I can put it no plainer than by saying that Bilbo was *meant* to find the Ring, and *not* by its maker. In which case you also were *meant* to have it.' Gandalf also knows that Bilbo's *pity in sparing Gollum's life (in *The Hobbit*) was important: 'Even the very wise cannot see all ends. I have not much hope that Gollum can be cured before he dies, but there is a chance of it. And he is bound up with the fate of the Ring. My heart tells me that he has some part to play yet, for good or ill, before the end; and when that comes, the pity of Bilbo may rule the fate of many – yours not least.' In the third version of *The Quest of Erebor*, probably written in 1954 for inclusion in the Appendices but abandoned for lack of space, Gandalf has premonitions even before he meets Bilbo in the first chapter of *The Hobbit*. Although the Dwarves are reluctant to include Bilbo in their company, Gandalf urges it: 'And suddenly I felt that I was indeed in hot earnest. This queer notion of mine was not a joke, it was *right*. It was desperately important that it should be carried out' (*Unfinished Tales*, p. 334; *Annotated Hobbit* (rev. and expanded edn. 2002), p. 374). When Frodo wonders why he was chosen to receive the Ring, Gandalf replies: 'Such questions cannot be answered. . . . You may be sure that it was not for any merit that others do not possess: not for power or wisdom at any rate. But you have been chosen, and you must therefore use such strength and heart and wits as you have.' Having explained the situation to Frodo, he does not tell him what to do, but instead says: 'And now . . . the decision lies with you. But I will always help you. . . . I will help you bear this burden, as long as it is yours to bear. But we must do something, soon' (bk. I, ch. 2). Frodo may be *meant* to bear the Ring, but his course of action is left to him.

Richard L. Purtill comments in *J.R.R. Tolkien: Myth, Morality and Religion* (1984) that 'an author may attempt . . . to show the *interplay* of fate and free will, as Tolkien does. Bilbo was *meant* to find the Ring, but whether he is strong enough to pass it on to Frodo is genuinely in doubt. It is Frodo's destiny to be the Ring-bearer, but he may shirk that destiny, either by refusing it at the beginning or by failing to carry out his mission' (p. 116). Paul H. Kocher in *Master of Middle-earth: The Fiction of J.R.R. Tolkien* (1972) deduces from the few hints given in *The Lord of the Rings* that 'the future is the property of the One who plans it'. But he asks: 'Yet is it fixed in the sense that every link in the chain is foreordained? . . . It cannot be, because in his encounter with Gollum Bilbo's choice to kill or not to kill is genuinely free, and only after it has been made is it woven into the guiding scheme. Tolkien leaves it at that. Human . . . free will coexists with a providential order and promotes this order, not frustrates it' (p. 36).

'The Council of Elrond', Book II, Chapter 2, likewise indicates the working of some higher power. By chance or otherwise, Legolas from Mirkwood, Galdor from the Grey Havens, Glóin and Gimli from Erebor, and Boromir from Gondor arrive at Rivendell at about the same time as Frodo and the Ring. Elrond says near the beginning of the Council, after hearing Glóin's story:

> What shall we do with the Ring, the least of rings, the trifle that Sauron fancies? That is the doom that we must deem.
>
> 'That is the purpose for which you are called hither. Called, I say, though I have not called you to me, strangers from distant lands. You have come and are here met, in this very nick of time, by chance as it may seem. Yet it is not so. Believe rather that it is so ordered that we, who sit here, and none others, must now find counsel for the peril of the world.

After an exchange of information and a discussion of alternatives, Elrond says that it is clear that they 'must send the Ring to the Fire', and comments that it is a 'quest which may be attempted by the weak with as much hope as the strong'. Bilbo thinks that Elrond is directing this statement at him, but when Gandalf says that the Ring has passed on, Bilbo asks: 'Who are they to be [those who are to carry the Ring to Mordor]? That seems to me what this Council has to decide, and all that it has to decide.' Frodo feels 'a great dread', as if 'awaiting the pronouncement of some doom'. At last he speaks, volunteering to take the Ring, wondering 'to hear his own words, as if some other will was using his small voice'. Elrond replies: 'If I understand aright all that I have heard . . . I think that this task is appointed for you, Frodo; and that if you do not find a way, no one will. . . . But it is a heavy burden. So heavy that none could lay it on another. I do not lay it on you. But if you take it freely, I will say that your choice is right. . . .' The choice of whether to take up the *quest is left to Frodo. Though there is a hint of 'some other will', it is clear in context that he has already made up his mind. After this, he rejects all opportunities offered to abandon the quest, even when it seems the most hopeless.

Also of relevance in this chapter is the dream that brings Boromir to Rivendell, one which came several times to his brother Faramir, and finally to Boromir himself, telling them in riddling words to seek the heir of Elendil in Rivendell, where the Ring would be revealed and 'counsels taken stronger than Morgul-spells'. Much comment has been made about whether it was the One or the Valar who sent this prophetic dream, and whether it was the intent that Faramir rather than Boromir should travel to Rivendell. It has been suggested that whoever sent the dream knew enough of Boromir's character to be sure that he would insist on being the one to make the journey, and even that perhaps he was not telling the truth when he said he had also experienced the dream. The possibility that Faramir was intended to make the journey raises intriguing questions, for it seems unlikely that he would have tried to take the Ring, as Boromir does in Book II, Chapter 10, propelling Frodo to the decision to turn east without the others. Even if Frodo had made his decision without that impetus, who would have aided him in Ithilien? In the end, Tolkien's emphasis on Frodo being *meant* to have the Ring and *chosen* for the quest suggests that the same end would have been reached, even if by a different path. And if Frodo had not accepted the burden, it may be that someone else would have done so, perhaps later rather than sooner, and by some different means, in quite a different story, brought about Sauron's end. *The Silmarillion* seems to point to Eru, the One, as the source of the dream rather than the Valar, for he was solely responsible for the creation of Elves and Men, and he alone knew the whole history of Arda and could intervene at will.

Another question concerns the return of Gandalf after his fall into the abyss with the Balrog. He tells Aragorn, Legolas, and Gimli in Fangorn: 'Darkness took me, and I strayed out of thought and time, and I wandered far on roads I will not tell. Naked I was sent back – for a brief time, until my task is done' (bk. III, ch. 5). It was only in Tolkien's draft letter to Robert Murray of 4 November 1954, published in *Letters* in 1981, that readers learned who had sent Gandalf back to complete his task, and more about Tolkien's hints of a higher power:

> [In *The Lord of the Rings*] I have purposely kept all allusions to the highest matters down to mere hints, perceptible only by the most attentive, or kept them under unexplained symbolic forms. So God and the 'angelic' gods, the Lords or Powers of the West, only peep through in such places as Gandalf's conversation with Frodo: 'behind that there was something else at work, beyond any design of the Ring-maker's'. . . .
>
> Gandalf really 'died', and was changed. . . . . But G. is not, of course, a human being (Man or Hobbit). . . . I [would] venture to say that he was

an *incarnate* 'angel' . . . an emissary from the Lords of the West, sent to Middle-earth as the great crisis of Sauron loomed on the horizon. . . . But in this 'mythology' all the 'angelic' powers concerned with this world were capable of many degrees of error. . . . The 'wizards' were not exempt. . . . Gandalf alone fully passes the tests, on a moral plane anyway (he makes mistakes of judgement). For in his condition it was for him a *sacrifice* to perish on the Bridge in defence of his companions, less perhaps than for a mortal Man or Hobbit, since he had a far greater inner power than they; but also more, since it was a humbling and abnegation of himself in conformity to 'the Rules': for all he could know at that moment he was the *only* person who could direct the resistance to Saruman successfully, and all *his* mission was vain. He was handing over to the Authority that ordained the Rules, and giving up personal hopes of success.

That I should say is what the Authority wished, as a set-off to Saruman. The 'wizards', as such, had failed; or if you like: the crisis had become too grave and needed an enhancement of power. So Gandalf sacrificed himself, was accepted, and enhanced, and returned. . . . He was sent by a mere prudent plan of the angelic Valar or governors; but Authority had taken up this plan and enlarged it, at the moment of its failure. 'Naked I was sent back – for a brief time, until my task is done'. Sent back by whom, and whence? Not by the 'gods' whose business is only with this embodied world and its time; for he passed 'out of thought and time'. [*Letters*, pp. 201–3]

Although Tolkien does not specifically say that the 'Authority' who sent Gandalf back was Eru (the One, Ilúvatar), this must be so if, as he states, it was not the Valar ('the gods').

Throughout *The Lord of the Rings* there is an emphasis on the offering of choice and of making the right choice. The other members of the Company all choose freely to join Frodo, and not to leave him until he leaves them. On several occasions a character chooses what seems right rather than obey an order: Éomer when he aids Aragorn, Legolas, and Gimli; Háma when he allows Gandalf to keep his staff; Faramir when he aids Frodo and Sam; Merry and Éowyn when they ride to war; Beregond when he leaves his post to save Faramir. Gandalf and Galadriel refuse the Ring when it is offered to them; Elrond and Aragorn never seem to have been tempted. Gandalf twice offers Saruman the chance to repent; both Gandalf and Théoden offer Wormtongue a chance to redeem himself; Denethor refuses to carry out his duties as the ruler of Gondor. Gandalf, Éomer, and Théoden refuse to be persuaded by the voice of Saruman. Tolkien commented that Saruman did not use hypnotism; 'it was always open to one to reject, *by free will and reason*, both his voice while speaking and its after impression' (letter to Forrest J. Ackerman, 9 June 1958, *Letters*, p. 277).

Richard L. Purtill comments in *J.R.R. Tolkien: Myth, Morality and Religion* that 'Tolkien often gives us pairs of characters faced with basically the same problem and shows one handling the problem in the right way, the other in the wrong way': Théoden and Denethor, Frodo and Gollum, Gandalf and Saruman, Boromir and Faramir. 'The fact that one character fails and the other does not, in what is essentially the same situation, is one way of dramatizing in fiction the idea of genuine free will, the idea that a person can make choices that are not determined by his or her character or circumstances' (p. 115).

Paul H. Kocher in *Master of Middle-earth* describes Tolkien's technique for suggesting 'the mysterious hand . . . guiding events' without taking away 'from the people acting them out the capacity for moral choice'. He also lets 'most of the major characters voice premonitions or prophecies, seeming to entail a definite foreseeable future', yet keeps these 'either misty in content or tentative in tone, so loosening their fixity and hinting that the routes are various by which they may come true' (p. 40). See further, Kocher's Chapter 3, 'The Cosmic Order'.

Even before the publication of *The Silmarillion*, some theologically-minded readers had queried the suggestions in *The Lord of the Rings* that Sauron (or Morgoth) might be able to create sentient living beings. In a draft letter to Peter Hastings in September 1954, Tolkien discussed the freedom of *sub-creation granted by Eru to the Ainur, even to the extent of allowing Morgoth's corruption of Arda, and the exercise of free will by men.

> The right to 'freedom' of the sub-creator is no guarantee among fallen men that it will not be used as wickedly as is Free Will. . . .
>   To conclude: having mentioned Free Will, I might say that in my myth I have used 'subcreation' in a special way . . . to make visible and physical the effects of Sin or misused Free Will by men. Free Will is derivative, and is therefore only operative within provided circumstances; but in order that it may exist, it is necessary that the Author should guarantee it, whatever betides: sc. when it is 'against His Will', as we say, at any rate as it appears on a finite view. He does not stop or make 'unreal' sinful acts and their consequences. So in this myth, it is 'feigned' (legitimately whether this is a feature of the real world or not) that He gave special 'sub-creative' powers to certain of His highest created beings: that is a guarantee that what they devised and made should be given the reality of Creation. Of course within limits, and of course subject to certain commands or prohibitions. But if they 'fell', as the Diabolus Morgoth did, and started making things 'for himself, to be their Lord', these would then 'be', even if Morgoth broke the supreme ban against making other 'rational' creatures like Elves or Men. They would at least 'be' real physical realities in the physical world, however evil they might prove, even 'mocking' the Children of God. [*Letters*, pp. 194–5]

The publication of *The Silmarillion* in 1977 finally informed readers of what lay behind Tolkien's 'allusions to the highest matters', and at the same time provided them with one of the most difficult problems in the whole of Tolkien's *legendarium*: Eru's words concerning his gift to Men. 'He willed that Men should seek beyond the world and should find no rest therein; but they should have a virtue to shape their life, amid the powers and chances of the world, beyond the Music of the Ainur, which is as fate to all things else . . .' (p. 41). This immediately raised the question of what happened when Elves, governed by the Music through which the world and its story were created, met and interacted with Men who had virtue to shape their life – free will. The wording differs in some earlier texts of *'The Silmarillion'*, but not the main intent.

In *The Book of Lost Tales* it is said that Ilúvatar 'devised that Men should have a free virtue whereby within the limits of the powers and substances and chances of the world they might fashion and design their life beyond even the original Music of the Ainur that is as fate to all things else'. But this is followed by a comment by the Elves which did not survive into the latest texts: 'Even we Eldar have found to our sorrow that Men have a strange power for good or ill and for turning things despite Gods [Valar] and Fairies [Elves] to their mood in the world; so that we say: "Fate may not conquer the Children of Men, but yet are they strangely blind, whereas their joy should be great"' (*The Book of Lost Tales, Part One*, p. 59). In the *Ainulindalë* of the mid-1930s the words of Eru are those in *The Silmarillion*, but the comment of the Elves becomes: 'We, Elves, have found to our sorrow that Men have a strange power for good or ill, and for turning things aside from the purpose of Valar or of Elves; so that it is said among us that Fate is not master of the children of Men . . .' (*The Lost Road and Other Writings*, p. 163). The final passage, with the comment of the Elves, survived into the final text of the *Ainulindalë* (*c.* 1951) but was struck through, and does not appear in *The Silmarillion*.

The free will of Men to choose 'for good or ill' is evident throughout the chapters of 'The Silmarillion' in which Men are present. The story of Túrin (*'Of Túrin Turambar'*) presents a series of bad decisions by Túrin, his mother Morwen, and his sister Nienor, but here the situation is complicated by Morgoth's curse on Húrin, Morwen, and their children. Does his curse override the free will granted to Men by Eru? Does Morgoth influence every fatal decision from that of Morwen refusing Thingol's invitation to join her son in Doriath through pride? Is it nurture, character, or curse which leads Túrin almost always to choose wrongly? See further, comments by Thomas M. Egan cited in the entry for the *Narn i Chîn Húrin*, and those by Katharyn W. Crabbe in the entry for *The Children of Húrin*.

But if Elves were bound to the Music of the Ainur, were they responsible for their actions, or were those laid down by the Music? On occasion, Tolkien seems to suggest that events could have fallen out otherwise. When Ungoliant poisons the Two Trees, Yavanna asks Fëanor to give her the Silmarils with which she could recall their light, but he refuses. Neither knew that Morgoth had already seized the gems. 'The Silmarils had passed away, and all one it may seem whether Fëanor had said yea or nay to Yavanna; yet had he said yea at the first, before the tidings came from Formenos, it may be that his after deeds would have been other than they were' (*The Silmarillion*, p. 79). But Fëanor's actions were partly driven by feelings resulting from the early death of his mother, and from his father Finwë's remarriage. It should be noted that in the debate of the Valar *Laws and Customs among the Eldar* (late 1950s), concerning whether Finwë should be allowed to remarry, Mandos prophesies that the children of Finwë's second marriage shall be great,

and the Tale of Arda more glorious because of their coming. And from them shall spring things so fair that no tears shall dim their beauty; and in whose being the Valar, and the Kindreds both of Elves and of Men that are to come shall all have part, and in whose deeds they shall rejoice. So that, long hence when all that here is, and seemeth yet fair and impregnable, shall nonetheless have faded and passed away, the Light of Aman shall not wholly cease among the free peoples of Arda until the End. 'When he that shall be called Eärendil setteth foot upon the shores of Aman, ye shall remember my words. [*Morgoth's Ring*, p. 247]

Apparently the destruction of the Two Trees and the deeds of Feanor's half-brothers were part of the Music. In the *Valaquenta* it is said that Mandos 'knows all things that shall be, save only those that lie still in the freedom of Ilúvatar' (*The Silmarillion*, p. 28).

In the making of the Music, Melkor introduced discords, and had the mastery until Ilúvatar introduced the third theme:

It seemed at first soft and sweet, a mere rippling of gentle sounds in delicate melodies; but it could not be quenched, and it took to itself power and profundity. And it seemed at last that there were two musics progressing at one time before the seat of Ilúvatar, and they were utterly at variance. The one was deep and wide and beautiful, but slow and blended with an immeasurable sorrow, from which its beauty chiefly came. The other had now achieved a unity of its own; but it was loud, and vain, and endlessly repeated; and it had little harmony, but rather a clamorous unison as of many trumpets braying upon a few notes. And it essayed to drown the other music by the violence of its voice, but it seemed that its most triumphant notes were taken by the other and woven into its own solemn pattern. [*The Silmarillion*, pp. 16–17]

Ilúvatar says 'that no theme may be played that hath not its uttermost source in me, nor can any alter the music in my despite. For he that attempteth this shall prove but mine instrument in the devising of things more wonderful, which he himself hath not imagined' (*The Silmarillion*, p. 17). This seems to suggest that from the very beginning, the themes introduced by Ilúvatar were compensating for, and transforming, the discords of Melkor.

Of course Tolkien did not produce a final, comprehensive 'Silmarillion', and it is dangerous to quote from texts of different dates and to assume that all statements necessarily have equal weight. Nonetheless, the idea of Men having freedom 'to shape their life . . . beyond the Music, which is as fate to all things else' remained unchanged for over forty years. Readers and commentators have struggled with the problem of how much choice or free will Men had, if the actions of the Elves were ordained. It may be that the actions of Men were sketched in the Music, but subject to change if a Man chose a path other than that laid down. When Thingol declares that no Man should enter Doriath, Melian foretells that 'one of Men, even of Bëor's house, shall indeed come, and the Girdle of Melian shall not restrain him, for doom greater than my power shall send him; and the songs that shall spring from that coming shall endure when all Middle-earth is changed' (*The Silmarillion*, p. 144). And so Beren (*'Of Beren and Lúthien')* does come to Doriath, presumably in accordance with the Music. When asked by Thingol what he seeks, he asks for Lúthien, 'above all gold and silver, and beyond all jewels. Neither rock, nor steel, nor the fires of Morgoth, nor all the powers of the Elf-kingdoms, shall keep from me the treasure that I desire' (p. 166). Thingol replies that he will grant Beren his jewel, Lúthien, in return for the treasure Thingol himself desires, a Silmaril from Morgoth's crown. Significantly, when Beren makes his demand 'it seemed to him that words were put into his mouth' (p. 166). One might suggest that the story of Beren and Lúthien was part of the Music, but if Beren had deliberately resisted the 'words put into his mouth', either using other words prompting a different reply, or not asking for Lúthien, then things might have occurred differently. Eru did not say that Men *would* go beyond the Music, only that they *could*.

Anne C. Petty comments in *Tolkien in the Land of Heroes: Discovering the Human Spirit* (2003) that in Tolkien's writings we 'find ourselves continually stumbling over contradictory elements such as doom vs. redemption or free will vs. fate. . . . These seemingly disparate elements are not totally reconciled in Tolkien's world, and I don't think that he ever intended that they should be. This paradox has fascinated and confounded Tolkien readers for decades' (p. 33). Verlyn Flieger in *Splintered Light: Logos and Language in Tolkien's World* (2nd edn. 2003) spends much space exploring this problem:

> Tolkien through his god-figure has conferred another power on man-
> kind: the virtue to 'shape their life' beyond the creational design of the
> Music 'which is as fate to all things else.' In bestowing this capability
> on mortals while withholding it from the immortal Elves, Tolkien has
> deliberately introduced a paradox, a world guided by both fate and free
> will, thus increasing the tension inherent in intersecting lives and their
> possible effect on one another and on events. At several points in *The Sil-
> marillion* Tolkien presents situations in which Elves appear to be given a
> choice between good and evil or in which the decisions of Men have the
> power to affect the fates of Elves. A possible distinction between them
> may be that Men are given the power to *act* beyond the Music (that is,
> to alter external events or circumstances), while Elves, though bound by

the Music, have the freedom to make internal choices, to alter some attitude toward themselves of other creatures or Eru. They may have power over their own natures, though not over external happenings. [pp. 52-3]

She cites Tolkien's letter to Michael Straight (end of 1955) in which he declares that both races were 'rational creatures of free will in regard to God' (*Letters*, p. 236), and suggests that

> the key may lie in the phrase 'in regard to God,' suggesting that in the sub-created world God, Eru, who proposed the theme but had the Ainur make the Music, is himself beyond and above it. This implies a kind of Boëthian concept in which the mind of God encompasses any design perceivable by any of his creatures and is explicit in such statements by Eru to the Ainur, as 'no theme may be played that hath not its uttermost source in me, nor can any alter the music in my despite'. . . . [p. 53]

Also in the letter to Michael Straight, Tolkien says that 'the One retains all ultimate authority, and (or so it seems as viewed in serial time) reserves the right to intrude the finger of God into the story: that is to produce realities which could not be deduced even from complete knowledge of the previous past, but which being real become part of the effective past for all subsequent time . . .' (p. 235).

   Kathleen E. Dubs in 'Providence, Fate and Chance: Boethian Philosophy in *The Lord of the Rings*', *Tolkien and the Invention of Myth: A Reader* (2004), suggests the influence of the *Consolation of Philosophy* (AD 542) by Boethius, one of the most influential works in Europe throughout the Middle Ages and into the Renaissance. Dubs comments that if Tolkien did not know the original Latin text, he surely knew King Alfred's translation into Old English (excerpts from Alfred's translation were included in the set texts for Tolkien's final English examinations). She summarizes Lady Philosophy's statement to Boethius, distinguishing between Providence and Fate, thus: 'Providence is the divine reason itself, the unfolding of temporal events as this is present to the vision of the divine mind; fate is this same unfolding of events as it is worked out in time, as we perceive it in the temporal world. We as human beings are unable to know providence. All we can know is fate' (p. 135). Asked about the relationship between freedom of will and divine providence, Lady Philosophy says that 'you can indeed alter what you propose to do, but, because the present truth of Providence sees that you can, and whether or not you will, you cannot frustrate the divine knowledge . . .' (p. 137). As Verlyn Flieger says, the divine knowledge is all-encompassing. After citing various examples which 'join inextricably the concepts of providence, fate, chance and often free will' in *The Lord of the Rings*, Dubs concludes that

> seeming contradictions can be resolved by following Boethius in distinguishing providence, which orders the universe; fate the temporal

manifestation of that order; chance, that 'fate' which occurs not according to our expectations, and for causes of which we are unaware; and, of
course, freedom of will, which operates as part of this providential order.
It is the fusion of all these concepts that gives complexity to Tolkien's
fantasy, and which in large part accounts for its continuing intellectual
and imaginative appeal. For the very fusion of the paradoxical elements
. . . gives an impression of authenticity to the work. As readers, on the
one hand, we identify with Tolkien's characters, sharing their uncertainty. . . . On the other hand we follow an omniscient author, and sense
his repeated – though often subtle – assurances that . . . all will turn out
well. [p. 141]

See also Patricia Meyer Spacks, 'Power and Meaning in *The Lord of the Rings*'
in *Tolkien and the Critics: Essays on J.R.R. Tolkien's The Lord of the Rings* (1968),
and Matthew Dickerson. *Following Gandalf: Epic Battles and Moral Victory in
The Lord of the Rings* (2003), especially Chapters 4, 5, and 9.

   Outside of Tolkien's *legendarium*, there is a curious echo near the end of
Smith of Wootton Major. On Smith's last visit to Faery, the Queen bids him
farewell, and says that if he meets the King (of Faery), he should give him the
message: 'The time has come. Let him choose' – that is, choose who should be
the next wearer of the star that gives entry to Faery. Smith meets Alf the Prentice, and after taking off the star, finally recognizes Alf as the King. Because he
gives up the star freely, Smith is allowed to choose the next bearer. He chooses
Tim Nokes, and Alf says that he had already chosen Tim. Smith asks him why,
then, had he asked him to choose? Alf replies, because the Queen wished it,
and 'if you had chosen differently I should have given way' (p. 48).

From the Many-Willow'd Margin of the Immemorial Thames. Brief, untitled
poem (the first line is cited here), published as by 'J.' in the *Stapeldon Magazine* (Exeter College, Oxford) 4, no. 20 (December 1913), p. 11. Tolkien wrote
this ode to Oxford as seen from the River Thames, 'many-mansion'd, tower-
crownèd in its dreamy robe of grey', in October 1911. It was the first of two
stanzas, together entitled *From Iffley* (a village three miles south-east of
Oxford), but the editor of the *Stapeldon Magazine* lost the second part, and
only the text of the first survives. Later Tolkien slightly revised the surviving
lines and gave them a new title, *Valedictory*.

Gale, St Teresa (1873–1951). The daughter of the British Minister to the Royal
Court of Wurttemberg at Stuttgart, the Reverend Mother St Teresa Gale was
educated at Newnham College, Cambridge, where she read Medieval and
Modern Languages. While at university she converted to Roman Catholicism.
She was received into the Church in 1894, and in 1896 entered the Society of
the Holy Child Jesus. The greater part of her life was spent between London,
Oxford, and Paris, but her greatest work was in Oxford. She was sent there
first as Superior in 1907 to establish at the convent at Cherwell Edge (*Oxford

and environs) a house of studies to bring the Society into contact with Oxford University standards of education. A chapel and a large residential block were subsequently added to the house, the latter to serve as a hostel for Catholic women in the Society of Oxford Home-Students.

Mother St Teresa left Oxford in 1910 but returned in 1930. Before her second departure in 1939 she made Cherwell Edge a centre of Catholic action in Oxford. An able administrator, she was respected by students and University authorities alike. *M.E. Griffiths was one of her lodgers, respectful of Mother St Teresa and somewhat in awe of her. Tolkien was a good friend and supporter of Cherwell Edge and its mission, and it was apparently through these connections that Mother St Teresa was lent a copy of *The Hobbit in typescript. It may have been through her that the work came to the attention of *Susan Dagnall, also formerly a resident of the hostel, and was subsequently published by Dagnall's firm, George Allen & Unwin.

Gardner, Helen Louise (1908–1986). Having read English at St Hilda's College, Oxford, Helen Gardner taught at the University of Birmingham and at Royal Holloway College, London, before returning to St Hilda's as tutor in English Literature (1941–54) and a Fellow (1942–66). In 1954 she declined the chair of Medieval and Renaissance English at Cambridge in favour of *C.S. Lewis; but in that year she was named Reader in Renaissance Studies at Oxford and took on more administrative responsibility in the planning, maintenance, and control of courses for the degrees of B.Litt., B.Phil., and D.Phil. By that time she was already active on the Oxford English Faculty Board, on which Tolkien also served. In 1966, on the retirement of *Nevill Coghill, she was elected Merton Professor of English Language and Literature. From 1959 until her retirement from the chair in 1975 she was also a Delegate to the Oxford University Press, and for a while was a co-editor with Tolkien of the *Oxford English Monographs* series. In 1967 she received the DBE. Gardner's distinguished publications include *The Art of T.S. Eliot* (1949), *The Divine Poems of John Donne* (1952; 2nd edn. 1978), and *A Reading of Paradise Lost* (1965).

Gedling (Nottinghamshire). Apparently early in 1913 the *Brookes-Smith family bought Manor Farm and Phoenix Farm at Gedling, a village east of Nottingham. Much of the land there was devoted to market gardening. *Hilary Tolkien and his *Aunt Jane Neave worked at Phoenix Farm, and Ronald Tolkien was an occasional visitor. A postcard forwarded to Tolkien at Phoenix Farm on 25 March 1913 indicates that he spent part of his Easter vacation there. He probably visited again later in 1913: in one of his sketchbooks is a distant view of the farm, not dated but almost certainly drawn during the summer. A closer view of the farm by Tolkien (*Artist and Illustrator*, fig. 15) most likely dates from 1914, in which year he certainly stayed at Phoenix Farm at the end of the Oxford long vacation. During that visit he wrote the poem *The Voyage of Éarendel the Evening Star* (*Éalá Éarendel Engla Beorhtast*).

Tolkien went to Phoenix Farm now and then also in 1915–16, while stationed at camps in *Staffordshire. Colin Brookes-Smith recalled that early one morning he was allowed to ride up the road and back on the motor cycle Tolkien shared with another officer; that Tolkien made a cobblestone path near the house; that he fell while playing a game of hide-and-seek on a picnic by the River Trent, and his face landed in a large cowpat; and that he may have helped to repel a raid on the farm's orchards by miners from Gedling colliery (unpublished memoir, Tolkien-George Allen & Unwin archive, HarperCollins).

Most of the area on which Manor Farm and Phoenix Farm stood is now a housing estate in a Nottingham suburb. When one of the authors of this book visited Gedling in 1994 Manor Farm was still there, or rather there was a house in the correct vicinity with that name and of similar design to the building Tolkien drew at Phoenix Farm.

'Gerald of Wales on the Survival of Welsh'. An essay by W. Rhys Roberts, published in the *Transactions of the Honourable Society of Cymmrodorion: Session 1923–1924* (1925), pp. 46–60, concerning a prophecy by Gerald of Wales (Giraldus de Barri, Giraldus Cambrensis, c. 1146–1223) that Wales and the Welsh tongue will survive until Judgement Day. Included, on pp. 58–9, is a version of the prophecy in late twelfth-century English of the South-west Midlands, prepared by Tolkien for Roberts, a former colleague at the University of *Leeds (Professor of Classics, retired 1923).

See further, Douglas A. Anderson, 'J.R.R. Tolkien and W. Rhys Roberts's "Gerald of Wales on the Survival of Welsh"', *Tolkien Studies* 2 (2005).

Gilson, Robert Cary (1863–1939). Robert Cary Gilson was educated at Cambridge, where he earned Firsts in the Classical Tripos and in Natural Sciences. Later he read for the Bar, but abandoned Law for a career in Education. From 1887 to 1900 he was in turn Classical Lecturer at Newnham College, Cambridge, Sixth Form Master at Haileybury, and Composition Master at Harrow. In 1900 he became Chief Master at *King Edward's School, Birmingham, a post he held until Easter 1929. Under Gilson's direction, marked by a light rein but strong personal authority, the School thrived academically, with a record number of university distinctions, as well as in games and other activities.

In spring term 1907 Tolkien entered the Second Class at King Edward's School, and in autumn 1907 the First Class, both under Gilson and his assistant A.E. Measures. With the permission of his Roman Catholic guardian Tolkien also attended the Chief Master's classes on the New Testament in Greek. Humphrey Carpenter has said that when teaching, Gilson 'encouraged his pupils to explore the byways of learning and to be expert in everything that came their way: an example that made a great impression on Ronald Tolkien' (*Biography*, p. 34). He had other qualities as well: he was fluent in several modern languages; he was an amateur inventor with a home laboratory and workshop; and he was an experienced mountain climber, elected to the Alpine Club in 1891.

Although on many occasions Gilson imposed on him the writing of lines – 'punctuality is the soul of business' or 'brevity is the soul of wit' (manuscript fragment, Special Collections and University Archives, John P. Raynor, S.J., Library, Marquette University) – for one infraction or another, Tolkien like so many other pupils admired the Chief Master and corresponded with him after leaving King Edward's School. Their relationship was strengthened by Tolkien's close friendship with Gilson's son, *Robert Quilter Gilson, who often invited Tolkien to the family home in Marston Green (*Birmingham and environs).

Photographs of Robert Cary Gilson are reproduced in T.W. Hutton, *King Edward's School, Birmingham, 1552–1952* (1952), plate facing p. 81, and in Anthony Trott, *No Place for Fop or Idler: The Story of King Edward's School, Birmingham* (1992), p. 86.

Gilson, Robert Quilter (1893–1916). R.Q. 'Rob' Gilson was one of Tolkien's closest friends during his years at *King Edward's School, Birmingham and immediately following. The son of *Robert Cary Gilson, the Chief Master of King Edward's School, he was active in the Musical and Dramatic Society, the Literary Society, the Debating Society, the Officers' Training Corps, and the Shooting Club. He concerned himself also with the School library (run by senior boys) and with the School magazine, and served as a Prefect. An amateur artist, he was fond of sketching churches, and took a particular interest in Renaissance painting. His enthusiasm for the eighteenth century led to a performance at King Edward's School of *The Rivals* by Sheridan, with Gilson, *G.B. Smith, *Christopher Wiseman, and Tolkien all taking parts. These four friends were also the core members of the *T.C.B.S., whose intellectual discussions Gilson found invigorating.

After leaving King Edward's School in 1912 Gilson went to Trinity College, Cambridge on a Classics exhibition. Although he seems not to have been an assiduous student, distracted by spirited friends such as *T.K. Barnsley and *R.S. Payton, in 1914 he won a First Class in Division 3 of the Classical Tripos, Part I. During this period he and Tolkien saw each other occasionally, the latter always being welcome at the Gilson family home at Marston Green near Birmingham, and they corresponded. In late November 1914, a few months after the outbreak of war in France, Gilson succumbed to guilt at not yet having volunteered for war service, abandoned his studies, and joined the Cambridgeshire (11th) Battalion, Suffolk Regiment as a second lieutenant. On 25–6 September 1915 he joined his T.C.B.S. friends in Lichfield (*Staffordshire), the last meeting of Tolkien, Gilson, Smith, and Wiseman together.

Gilson sailed for France on 8 January 1916. He was more aesthete than soldier, horrified by war and the responsibility of command, but he was friendly with his fellow officers and popular with his men. He expressed his thoughts and fears in letters home and to Estelle King, a Birmingham friend to whom he had proposed marriage; extracts from these were published in *Tolkien and the Great War* by John Garth (2003). Near La Boiselle on 1 July 1916, the first day of the Battle of the Somme, Gilson was killed by a bursting shell while leading his platoon into No Man's Land. He was buried in Becourt Cemetery, France.

Glip. Poem, first published in the second edition of *The Annotated Hobbit* (2002), p. 119. Glip is 'a slimy little thing' with 'two round eyes' that gleam in the dark; he lives in 'a little cave of stone' below the cliffs of Bimble Bay. At night he listens to a 'wicked mermaid' draw ships onto the rocks with her song, and there Glip steals the bones of dead men on which to gnaw. Even so, 'there are darker and wickeder things that prowl / On Bimble rocks at night.' Tolkien wrote *Glip* probably around 1928, as one of a series of poems he called **Tales and Songs of Bimble Bay*. Two nearly identical manuscripts of the poem are extant.

Douglas A. Anderson comments in *The Annotated Hobbit* that Glip closely anticipates the character Gollum introduced in Chapter 5 of **The Hobbit*, a work contemporary (or nearly contemporary) with the poem.

Glorfindel. Discussion, published with commentary in **The Peoples of Middle-earth* (1996), pp. 377–82. In this Tolkien considers whether the Glorfindel who appears in **The Lord of the Rings* was the same as the Glorfindel of Gondolin who died in battle in the First Age, and if so, how he returned to Middle-earth. The first of two manuscripts (lacking its first page) suggests that the Glorfindel of Gondolin, after purging his sins in Mandos, was re-embodied and lived in Valinor until he returned to Middle-earth with Gandalf about Third Age 1000. In a note written between this version and the second manuscript, Tolkien suggested that Glorfindel might have returned in the Second Age in a Númenórean ship.

Tolkien began a second, five-page manuscript with a discussion of the name *Glorfindel*, which had originally appeared in *The Fall of Gondolin* (**The Book of Lost Tales*), written in 1916–17: 'It was intended to mean "Golden-tressed"', and 'its use in *The Lord of the Rings* is one of the cases of the somewhat random use of names found in the older legends . . . which escaped reconsideration in the final published form of *The Lord of the Rings*. This is unfortunate, since the name is now difficult to fit into Sindarin, and cannot possibly be Quenyarin' (*The Peoples of Middle-earth*, p. 379). He summarizes what was already written about Glorfindel, published and unpublished, and finally rejects the 'simplest solution' that the two Glorfindels were different persons. 'No other major character in the Elvish legends . . . has a name borne by another Elvish person of importance' (p. 380). He notes that the identification of the two would serve to explain why Glorfindel appears as such a powerful figure in *The Lord of the Rings*. He then proceeds to explain why after his re-embodiment Glorfindel was allowed to remain in Valinor (minimizing his part in the rebellion of the Noldor, and emphasizing his self-sacrifice defending the fugitives from Gondolin), and decides that he must have returned to Middle-earth to aid Gil-galad and Elrond in the Second Age before the World was changed.

In notes to these manuscripts, Tolkien also discusses two uses of the name *Galdor* (probably the same person, pp. 387–8, notes 1 and 3). Both manuscripts probably date from the end of 1972 or from 1973. Part of a draft on the related topic of *'Elvish Reincarnation' is written on the manuscript of the first version.

Nothing is said of Glorfindel's history in *The Lord of the Rings*, but in the summer of 1938, in a note related to the then still unwritten account of the Council of Elrond, Tolkien included the phrase 'Glorfindel tells of his ancestry in Gondolin', making it clear that this was not quite the random re-use of a name as suggested in this late text. (See *The Return of the Shadow*, pp. 214–15, and *Reader's Companion*, pp. 192–4.) It is significant that even late in his life, when he became concerned with the problem of *how* Glorfindel returned to Middle-earth, Tolkien apparently never chose to change the name of the Elf of Gondolin, which had not yet appeared in a published work.

'The Gnomes Come to the Great Lands'. Untitled prose fragment, published with commentary in *The Shaping of Middle-earth* (1986), pp. 5–9. Hastily written in pencil probably in the early 1920s, it shows a stage between the unfinished *Gilfanon's Tale: The Travail of the Noldoli and the Coming of Mankind* of *The Book of Lost Tales* and the story as it had developed by the mid-1920s. Fëanor is here a 'gem-smith' and the father of seven sons, but not related to the leader of the Noldor in Middle-earth, here called Gelmir (which may be another name for Finwë). The fragment ends as some of the Elves are about to have their first encounter with Orcs (though not so named).

Gnomish Grammar. Grammar of the Gnomish language, i.e. of the language of the Gnomes, the Second Kindred of the Elves later called the *Noldor*; eventually this language, called successively Goldogrin or Gnomish and Noldorin, developed into Sindarin, but with a completely new history (see *Languages, Invented). The title *Gnomish Grammar* was assigned by its editors for convenience, to a work called by Tolkien *Lam na nGoldathon* ('tongue of the Gnomes'), *In the dialect of Tol Erethrin or Dor Faidwen* ('Lonely Isle', 'Land of Release'). The work was published with commentary and notes in *Parma Eldalamberon* 11 (1995), edited by Christopher Gilson, Patrick Wynne, Arden R. Smith, and Carl F. Hostetter.

Contemporary with the writing of *The Book of Lost Tales (c. 1916–20), the *Gnomish Grammar* was written by Tolkien in pencil in the notebook in which he wrote *The Nauglafring: The Necklace of the Dwarves* (see *The Book of Lost Tales*), but from the back with the notebook turned upside down. According to the editors, it 'presents a concise but thorough account of the inflexions and syntax of the article, noun, and adjective', and 'was written and abandoned *before* work on the [*Gnomish Lexicon*] was completed' (p. 5); it may have been contemporary with the earliest pencil layer of that work. Cross-references in the *Lexicon* to the *Grammar* indicate planned material which was never written.

Gnomish Lexicon. Lexicon of the 'Gnomish' (Elvish) language 'Goldogrin' (*Languages, Invented, see also *Gnomish Grammar*), called for convenience by *Christopher Tolkien the *Gnomish Lexicon*, but by his father *I·Lam na·Ngnoldathon* and dated 1917. The Gnomish title means 'the tongue of the Gnomes', i.e. of the Second Kindred of the Elves, later called the *Noldor*. Some material from this lexicon was included in appendices on names in *The Book of Lost Tales*, published in *The Book of Lost Tales, Part One* (1983) and *The Book of Lost Tales, Part Two* (1984).

Christopher Tolkien notes that the *Gnomish Lexicon* 'is not arranged historically, by roots (though occasionally roots are given), but rather, in plan at least, as a conventional dictionary'. He found it difficult to transcribe because of the 'intensity' his father devoted to the 'diminutive book' in which the *Lexicon* is written, 'emending, rejecting, adding, in layer upon layer, so that in places it has become very hard to interpret. Moreover later changes to the forms in one entry were not necessarily made in related entries; thus the stages of a rapidly expanding linguistic conception are very confused in their representation.' It is a work in progress, 'by no means the setting-out of finished ideas'. Contemporary with *The Book of Lost Tales* in the period *c*. 1916–*c*. 1919, it shows (together with the *Qenyaqetsa*) 'in the clearest possible way how deeply involved were the developments in the mythology and in the languages' (*The Book of Lost Tales, Part One*, p. 247).

The complete *Gnomish Lexicon* was published with commentary and notes in *Parma Eldalamberon* 11 (1995), ed. Christopher Gilson, Patrick Wynne, Arden R. Smith, and Carl F. Hostetter. There the titling is transcribed from the manuscript in full as: 'I·Lam na·Ngoldathon "Goldogrin" di Sacthoðrin, Eriol Sarothron whom else is called *Angol*, but in his own folk Ottor Wæfre. Tol Withernon (ar lim gardhin arthi)'. It is explained that 'the phrase *di Sacthoðrin* refers to the fact that the Goldogrin is being rendered into English' (or rather, Old English), and that 'authorship of the work is ascribed to *Eriol Sarothron* ("voyager, seafarer"), clearly the Eriol of *The Book of Lost Tales*' (see *Eriol and Ælfwine). *Tol Withernon* and *ar lim gardhin arthi* ('and many places besides') 'apparently describes where the work was completed' (*Parma Eldalamberon* 11, pp. 3–4). The name *Tol Withernon*, which does not occur elsewhere in Tolkien's *legendarium*, may be a personal reference, inspired by *Withernsea*, the name of a place near which Tolkien was stationed during part of 1917.

The editors describe in more detail the notebook and the stages of composition of the *Gnomish Lexicon*:

The text ... was composed in layers, which can be separated chronologically because Tolkien ... began compiling the lexicon in pencil, and apparently it had progressed significantly when he switched to ink, revising a few existing entries and adding some new ones. At this point, while still using ink, Tolkien decided to rewrite the entire lexicon, in the process erasing most of the earlier pencil layer, and struck through (and replaced elsewhere) the earliest ink entries. [p. 2]

This rewriting seems to have been 'primarily a matter of reorganizing and taking stock of what had already been devised', but later deletions, alterations, and additions in blue crayon 'seem to represent changes in Tolkien's ideas about the historical phonology of Gnomish' (p. 3).

Probably *c.* 1919–June 1920, at least a year after the ink text of the *Gnomish Lexicon* was written, Tolkien compiled notes about the language on ten loose proof slips for the *Oxford English Dictionary*, mostly glosses in similar style to, and following the order of, the *Lexicon*. This material was published as 'The Gnomish Lexicon Slips' within 'Early Noldorin Fragments' in *Parma Eldalamberon* 13 (2001), pp. 106–18, ed. Christopher Gilson, Bill Welden, Carl F. Hostetter, and Patrick Wynne.

Goblin Feet. Poem, first published in the anthology *Oxford Poetry 1915* (1915), pp. 64–5. The poet is 'off down the road / Where the fairy lanterns glowed / And the little pretty flittermice are flying'. He sees and hears the fairy-folk, the goblins or gnomes, follows in their train, and exults in the experience ('O! the magic! O! the sorrow when it dies').

Tolkien wrote *Goblin Feet* in Oxford between 27 and 28 April 1915, together with *You & Me and the Cottage of Lost Play* (*The Little House of Lost Play: Mar Vanwa Tyaliéva*), to please his fiancée, Edith Bratt (*Edith Tolkien) who liked 'spring and flowers and trees, and little elfin people' (quoted in *Biography*, p. 74). In later years, when he had become known for *The Hobbit* and *The Lord of the Rings*, and requests were received to reprint *Goblin Feet*, Tolkien wished that 'the unhappy little thing, representing all that I came (so soon after) to fervently dislike, could be buried for ever' (quoted in *The Book of Lost Tales, Part One*, p. 32); for he had long ago abandoned in his writings the idea of diminutive fairies or elves. And yet at the time of its composition, Tolkien thought well enough of *Goblin Feet* to offer it to *T.W. Earp, the chief editor of *Oxford Poetry 1915*, and was pleased when it was accepted for publication.

Oxford Poetry 1915 was the third in a series of annual volumes of verse written by undergraduates or graduates of Oxford (the first covered 1910–13) and published in Oxford by B.H. Blackwell (*Publishers). The 1915 volume, ed. Gerald Crow and T.W. Earp, includes fifty-two poems by twenty-five authors. Among the latter, in addition to Tolkien himself, are several poets who had or were later to have personal connections: T.W. Earp, Naomi M. Haldane (*Naomi Mitchison), *Leonard Rice-Oxley, *G.B. Smith, and *H.T. Wade-Gery. Other contributors include Aldous Huxley; Dorothy L. Sayers; and H.R. Freston, soon to die in the Somme, about whose poems Tolkien delivered a paper to an Oxford student society in May 1915.

Goblin Feet was reprinted as early as 1920, in *The Book of Fairy Poetry*, ed. Dora Owen, with an illustration by Warwick Goble. Today it is most conveniently found in *The Annotated Hobbit* (1988, p. 77; rev. and expanded edn. 2002, p. 113).

Gollins, Annie. Annie Gollins was a maidservant at the home of Mrs Faulkner at 37 Duchess Road, Edgbaston, *Birmingham, where the young Ronald Tolkien, his brother *Hilary, and Edith Bratt (*Edith Tolkien) were lodgers *c.* 1908. Annie was enlisted by Edith to smuggle food from the kitchen to the hungry Tolkien brothers on the second floor, by means of a basket lowered from a window. She remained in touch with the Tolkiens until after the Second World War, and named her own children after Ronald and Edith.

Good and Evil. Edmund Wilson in 'Oo, Those Awful Orcs', *The Nation* 182 (14 April 1956), described *The Lord of the Rings* as 'a simple confrontation – in more or less the traditional terms of British melodrama – of the Forces of Evil with the Forces of Good, the remote and alien villain with the plucky little home-grown hero' (p. 313). Other critics, assuming an absolute division of 'sides' in *The Lord of the Rings*, have felt that Tolkien did not adequately explain why one is 'good' and the other is not. The anonymous reviewer of *The Lord of the Rings* (nominally of the third volume) in the *Times Literary Supplement* wrote:

> Throughout Middle Earth there is an eternal conflict between Good and Evil, in which Evil is usually the more powerful. It is in considering the attributes of these antagonists that difficulties of interpretation arise. The Lord of Evil is black and ugly, and his followers are bad-mannered and quarrelsome creatures who in general give off a bad smell; they torture their prisoners, and take pleasure in destroying pleasant woodlands and fair buildings. But save for their cruelty in war (and the Good do not as a rule grant quarter) we are never told exactly in what their wickedness consists. It cannot be anything to do with the worship of false gods, for in the whole of this lengthy composition no character, good or bad, performs an act of worship in honour of any kind of divinity. The Good are beautiful, intelligent and artistic. They are all craftsmen who make lovely objects, or industrious farmers. They always find suitable mates, and their domestic lives, when they are not fighting Evil, are entirely delightful. But save for the chivalrous courage and devotion to duty which they all display (and the followers of Evil have their fair share of this) there seems to be nothing outstandingly virtuous in their behaviour. They build no temples, though some of their valued possessions are endowed with supernatural influence. ['The Saga of Middle-earth', 25 November 1955, p. 704]

In reply, David Masson commented:

> Does wickedness reside, as appears to be implied, in the worship of false gods, or virtue in the building of temples? Surely the contrast in the story is absolute: it is that between love and hatred. . . . Common men, hobbits, dwarves, are clearly imperfect. But any of the truly good elves, hobbits,

men, or wizards, spares no pains to help his fellow-beings, and when he can, creates. An orc or troll, egoist run mad, stops at nothing in injuring his fellow-beings, and destroys . . . and *all* beings *while* possessed by [Sauron's] will or his Ring, exhibit an insane ambition or hatred. ['*The Lord of the Rings*', *Times Literary Supplement*, 9 December 1955, p. 743]

To which the reviewer responded in the same number: 'Throughout the book the good try to kill the bad, and the bad try to kill the good. We never see them doing anything else. Both sides are brave. Morally there seems nothing to choose between them' (p. 743).

*W.H. Auden more thoughtfully wrote in a review of *The Return of the King* that Tolkien's world includes 'elves, beings who know good and evil but have not fallen', 'Sauron, an incarnation of absolute evil', and 'orcs who are corrupt past hope of redemption'. He thought that 'to present the conflict between Good and Evil as a war in which the good side is ultimately victorious is a ticklish business', for 'wars are won by the stronger side, just or unjust. At the same time most of us believe that the essence of the Good is love and freedom so that Good cannot impose itself by force without ceasing to be good.' He points out that although Sauron has greater power than his opponents, he has one weakness, inferior imagination. 'Good can imagine the possibility of becoming evil . . . but Evil, defiantly chosen, can no longer imagine anything but itself', and therefore Sauron cannot foresee that his opponents will not use the Ring ('At the End of the Quest, Victory', *New York Times Book Review*, 22 January 1956, p. 5). At this time, well before *The Silmarillion* was published (1977), no one could have known – unless told directly by Tolkien – that elves had indeed fallen within the invented history that lay behind *The Lord of the Rings*. Only in *The Silmarillion* does it become clear that there is no absolute Good or Evil in the world, though Morgoth and Sauron are effectively embodiments of Evil for purposes of *The Silmarillion* and *The Lord of the Rings* respectively.

Although Tolkien himself stated in a letter to *Naomi Mitchison on 25 April 1954 that *The Lord of the Rings* 'is cast in terms of a good side, and a bad side, beauty against ruthless ugliness, tyranny against kingship, moderated freedom with consent against compulsion that has long lost any object save mere power, and so on' (*Letters*, pp. 178–9), a few months later he wrote:

Some reviewers have called the whole thing [*The Fellowship of the Ring*] simple-minded, just a plain fight between Good and Evil, with all the good just good, and the bad just bad. Pardonable, perhaps (though at least Boromir has been overlooked) in people in a hurry, and with only a fragment to read, and, of course without the earlier written but unpublished Elvish histories. But the Elves are *not* wholly good or in the right. Not so much because they had flirted with Sauron; as because with or without his assistance they were 'embalmers'. They wanted to have their cake and eat it: to live in the mortal historical Middle-earth because they had become fond of it (and perhaps because they there had the advantages of a superior caste), and so tried to stop its change and history, stop its growth, keep it as a pleasaunce, even largely a desert, where they could be 'artists' – and they were overburdened with sadness and nostalgic regret. In their way the Men of Gondor were similar: a withering people whose only 'hallows' were their tombs. But in any case this is a tale about a war, and if war is allowed (at least as a topic and a setting) it is not much good complaining that all the people on one side are against those on the other. Not that I have made even this issue quite so simple: there are Saruman, and Denethor, and Boromir; and there are treacheries and strife even among the Orcs. [letter to Naomi Mitchison, 25 September 1954, *Letters*, p. 197]

In *The Fellowship of the Ring* the treachery of Saruman is made known, and Boromir is shown to be both a hero, in the defence of Gondor and the West, but also subject to the temptation of the Ring, which in a moment of weakness he tries to take from Frodo. Tolkien suggested to Naomi Mitchison that the earliest reviewers of *The Lord of the Rings*, before the second and third volumes were published, might at least have taken this in. *The Two Towers* and *The Return of the King* added the figure of Smeágol-Gollum, torn between loyalty to Frodo and overwhelming desire for the Ring, between wanting to do good – indeed at one point (Book IV, Chapter 8) on the verge of repentance – and unable to resist his darker side; and finally, even hobbits who turn on their own kind and collaborate with Ruffians who have invaded the Shire.

On the question of giving quarter, the Rohirrim spare the Dunlendings who took part in Saruman's attack on Helm's Deep, and after the overthrow of Sauron, Aragorn 'pardoned the Easterlings that had given themselves up, and sent them away free, and he made peace with the peoples of Harad; and the slaves of Mordor he released and gave to them all the lands about Lake Núrnen to be their own' (bk. VI, ch. 5). At no point in *The Lord of the Rings*, however, or in *The Silmarillion*, does Tolkien show an orc surrendering or seeking pardon, or even being taken prisoner. But in theory, at least, he thought that they should be treated as other rational beings. The Orcs

> might have become irredeemable (at least by Elves and Men), but they remained within the Law. That is, that though of necessity, being the fingers of the hand of Morgoth, they must be fought with the utmost severity, they must not be dealt with in their own terms of cruelty and treachery. Captives must not be tormented, not even to discover information for the defence of the homes of Elves and Men. If any Orcs surrendered and asked for mercy, they must be granted it, even at a cost. This was the teaching of the Wise, though in the horror of the War it was not always heeded. [*Morgoth's Ring*, p. 419]

Many critics of *The Lord of the Rings* have overlooked Elrond's statement that 'nothing is evil in the beginning. Even Sauron was not so' (bk. II, ch. 2). Tolkien reiterated this point several times, and stressed that evil could arise out of good intentions. In a draft letter to Peter Hastings in September 1954 he wrote: 'Sauron was of course not "evil" in origin. He was a "spirit" corrupted by the Prime Dark Lord ... Morgoth. He was given an opportunity of repentance, when Morgoth was overcome, but could not face the humiliation of recantation, and suing for pardon; and so his temporary turn to good and "benevolence" ended in a greater relapse, until he became the main representative of Evil in later ages' (*Letters*, p. 190). In his comments on Auden's review of *The Return of the King* Tolkien wrote:

> In my story I do not deal in Absolute Evil. I do not think there is such a thing, since that is Zero. I do not think that at any rate any 'rational being' is wholly evil. Satan fell. In my myth Morgoth fell before Creation of the physical world. In my story Sauron represents as near an approach to the wholly evil will as is possible. He had gone the way of all tyrants: beginning well, at least on the level that while desiring to order all things according to his own wisdom he still at first considered the (economic) well-being of other inhabitants of the Earth. [*Letters*, p. 243]

David Harvey in *The Song of Middle-earth: J.R.R. Tolkien's Themes, Symbols and Myths* (1985) notes that 'Tolkien's starting point' in his mythology (*'The Silmarillion') 'is that nothing was bad in the beginning. How could it be. In the beginning was Ilúvatar. All things came from him. All things were good and those things that flowed from the themes of Ilúvatar continued to be good until such time as evil took a hold of them.' In Harvey's opinion,

> Orcs, trolls, wargs and the other minions of Sauron and Morgoth cannot really be termed evil. They are the slaves of evil and have no minds of their own. They cannot choose for good. They have been under the aegis of evil from their beginning and were perverted from the previously created beauty of Ilúvatar. ... The tragedy for Orcs and trolls is that they cannot know good. They are mindless and committed to an evil course through no choice of their own. [p. 56]

T.A. Shippey, however, in 'Orcs, Wraiths, Wights: Tolkien's Images of Evil', *Tolkien and His Literary Resonances: Views of Middle-earth* (2000), concludes from various conversations between orcs in *The Lord of the Rings* 'that orcs are moral beings, with an underlying morality much the same as ours. But if that is true, it seems that an underlying morality has no effect at all on actual behaviour. How, then, is an essentially correct theory of good and evil corrupted?' (p. 184). He finds that Orcs 'recognize the idea of goodness, appreciate humour, value loyalty, trust, group cohesion, and the ideal of a higher cause than themselves, and condemn failings from these ideals in others. So, if they know what is right, how does it happen that they persist in wrong?'

(p. 186). He concludes that Orcish behaviour is also human behaviour, 'and their inability to judge their own actions by their own moral criteria is a problem all too sadly familiar' (p. 189).

In *The Road to Middle-earth* (2nd edn. 1992) Shippey sees *The Lord of the Rings* 'as an attempt to reconcile two views of evil'. The first is that of orthodox Christianity which finds 'its clearest expression' in the sixth-century *De Consolatione Philosophiae* by Boethius: this holds that Evil is the absence of Good, that it 'cannot itself create' and 'was not in itself created (but sprang from a voluntary exercise of free will by Satan, Adam and Eve, to separate themselves from God)', and that ultimately it will 'be annulled or eliminated' (p. 128). Tolkien himself held that Evil could not create 'a race of "rational incarnate" creatures', even such beings of such ill-intent as Orcs (letter to Peter Hastings, September 1954, *Letters*, p. 190). As Frodo says to Sam: 'The Shadow that bred them [Orcs] can only mock, it cannot make real new things of its own. I don't think it gave life to the Orcs, it only ruined them and twisted them' (*The Lord of the Rings*, bk. VI, ch. 1; see further, *Orcs). Against this, says Shippey, is the philosophy by which Evil is not merely an absence of Good, but an actual force which can (indeed, must) be resisted. 'The danger of this opinion is that it tends towards Manichaeanism, the heresy which says that Good and Evil are equal and opposite and the universe is a battlefield . . .' (Shippey, p. 128). Tolkien presents 'this philosophical duality . . . through the Ring', which offers temptation leading to wickedness (p. 129).

> If evil were only the absence of good . . . then the Ring would never be anything other than a psychic amplifier; it would not 'betray' its possessors, and all they would need do is put it aside and think pure thoughts. . . . However if evil were merely a hateful and external power without echo in the hearts of the good, then someone might have to take the Ring to the Cracks of Doom, but it need not be Frodo: Gandalf could be trusted with it, while whoever went would have only to distrust his enemies, not his friends and not himself. [pp. 132–3]

As a Catholic, Tolkien had no doubt that Evil could not be banished in our fallen world. He wrote in a draft letter to Robert Murray on 4 November 1954: 'Of course the Shadow will arise again in a sense [after the events of *The Lord of the Rings* . . . , but never again . . . will an evil daemon be incarnate as a physical enemy; he will direct Men and all the complications of half-evils, and defective goods, and the twilights of doubt as to sides, such situations as he most loves . . . : those will be and are our more difficult fate' (*Letters*, p. 207).

See further, W.H. Auden, 'Good and Evil in *The Lord of the Rings*', *Tolkien Journal* 3, no. 1 (1967); Anne C. Petty, 'The Persistence of Evil' in *Tolkien in the Land of Heroes: Discovering the Human Spirit* (2003), pp. 99–137; T.A. Shippey, *J.R.R. Tolkien: Author of the Century* (2000), ch. 3. See also *Fall, *Magic, *Political thought, *Possessiveness, *Power, *Prejudice and Racism, *War.

Gordon, Eric Valentine (1896–1938). E.V. Gordon was educated at Victoria College and McGill University College in British Columbia, and in 1915 went to University College, *Oxford to read English as a Rhodes Scholar. His first tutors were *Kenneth Sisam and *Percy Simpson; but war service soon forced a hiatus in his studies. When he returned to Oxford in 1919 he was tutored by Tolkien. After receiving his B.A. in 1920 he began to study for a B.Litt., but left his work uncompleted in January 1922 when he took up a post as Assistant Lecturer in English at *Leeds. Tolkien himself was at Leeds by this time, and welcomed Gordon as a valued colleague. He wrote in his diary: 'Eric Valentine Gordon has come and got firmly established and is my devoted friend and pal' (quoted in *Biography*, p. 104). In 1923, when Tolkien became ill with pneumonia and could not write a commissioned review-essay on Philology for *The Year's Work in English Studies 1922*, Gordon did so as his substitute.

Gordon worked closely with Tolkien to improve and promote the language side of the Leeds English curriculum. To make English Language study more popular, they formed a Viking Club (*Societies and clubs) for undergraduates, who met to drink beer, read sagas, and sing comic songs in Old English, Old Norse, and other languages; Tolkien and Gordon wrote some of these verses, which were later published in *Songs for the Philologists*. They collaborated also in preparing a standard edition of the Middle English poem *Sir Gawain and the Green Knight* (first published 1925): Gordon was responsible for the greater part of the notes, and was principal contact with their editor at Oxford University Press, Kenneth Sisam. Tolkien found Gordon 'an industrious little devil' (quoted in *Biography*, p. 105), and maintained an active working relationship with him even after Tolkien left Leeds for Oxford. In 1926 Gordon succeeded Tolkien to the chair of English Language at Leeds, and in the next few years further distinguished himself in the promotion of Icelandic studies. In 1931 he became Smith Professor of English Language and Germanic Philology at the University of Manchester. He also served for many years as an external examiner at other universities, including Oxford, in the course of which he and Tolkien often met. In 1934 Tolkien and Gordon were co-examiners of the Oxford B.Litt. thesis of *E.O.G. Turville-Petre.

Gordon was indeed an industrious writer and scholar. He produced numerous articles, reviews, and poems, and several notable books in addition to *Sir Gawain and the Green Knight*. In 1927 he published *An Introduction to Old Norse* (2nd edn., rev. A.R. Taylor, 1957), for which Tolkien read proof and made suggestions and corrections concerning its grammar, and whose illustration of a Viking hall inspired Tolkien's picture *Beorn's Hall* for *The Hobbit (Artist and Illustrator*, figs. 114–116). In the early 1930s he assisted and advised his scholar-friend Eugène Vinaver in work towards an edition of Malory's *Morte d'Arthur* (published 1947). In 1933 an introduction by Gordon appeared in *The Saga of Hrolf Kraki*, a translation by his former student *Stella M. Mills, dedicated to Gordon, Tolkien, and C.T. Onions. Gordon himself translated *Scandinavian Archaeology* by Haakon Shetelig and Hjalmar Falk, published in 1937, and also in that year published an edition of the Old English *Battle of Maldon*, for which Tolkien also read proof, 'made many corrections and contributions', and provided the solution to many of its textual and philological problems (p. vi). Tolkien and Gordon planned to collaborate as well on editions of the Middle English *Pearl* and the Old English elegies *The Wanderer* and *The Seafarer*, but Tolkien's other commitments left him time to do no more than advise and consult, and then in 1938 Gordon died, aged only forty-two.

Tolkien at once stepped into the breach to help in the settling of his friend's affairs and academic obligations, including the setting of papers for the 1938 New Zealand Honours examinations and revisions to the edition of *Pearl*. In the event, the latter was accomplished primarily by Gordon's widow, **Ida Lilian Gordon** (*née* Pickles, b. 1907), whom he had married in 1930. A former Leeds student of E.V. Gordon (B.A. honours 1928, Ph.D. 1930), she herself became a distinguished scholar, and like her late husband a teacher at the University of Manchester. *Pearl* was published at last in 1953, with warm acknowledgements to Tolkien for his assistance. Ida Gordon intended to bring her late husband's work on *The Wanderer* and *The Seafarer* also into a final form, but by the time she was free to begin to do so

> there had been a revolution in the study of these poems. Articles had been published which threw new light on their themes and opened up new fields of investigation. And it soon became clear that the approach would have to be very different from that of the original draft, and that the treatment also would have to be much fuller, since many conflicting theories had been offered, which in themselves raised new problems of interpretation. [*The Seafarer* (1960), p. vii]

And because the series for which the poems were intended dictated that the book be of a small size, Ida Gordon chose to concern herself only with *The Seafarer* 'for its more challenging theme' (p. vii). The edition appeared, in 1960 (new edn. 1996), only under her name, because of the substantial changes she made to it relative to the original draft, but it 'incorporates much of the original material, especially in the Notes' (p. vii). For this too, Tolkien's work and assistance were generously acknowledged.

Photographs of E.V. Gordon are reproduced in *Biography*, p. 8b, and *The Tolkien Family Album*, p. 47. See also Douglas A. Anderson, '"An Industrious Little Devil": E.V. Gordon as Friend and Collaborator with Tolkien', in *Tolkien the Medievalist* (2002).

Gordon, George Stuart (1881–1942). George S. Gordon distinguished himself as a student of Classics both at the University of Glasgow, where he encountered *Walter Raleigh, the Professor of English Literature, and at Oriel College, *Oxford. He also spent a year in Paris to enlarge his knowledge of modern history and politics. In 1907, though he was still only an amateur in the subject, he was elected to a prize fellowship in English Literature at Magdalen College, Oxford (to which Raleigh had moved), and in 1913 he became

Professor of English Language and Literature at the University of *Leeds. The latter post was offered to him with a free hand to develop the programme of English studies, but war service postponed his initiatives until mid-1919. He then applied himself to the task in earnest, remodelling the Leeds English syllabus on the University of *Oxford model and building a small but excellent staff. By June 1920, when Tolkien met him during an interview for the post of Reader in English Language, Gordon was 'not only God's Own Head of a Department, but Dean of the Faculty, Chairman of the Board of Arts, a Member of Council, O/C O.T.C., President of the Association of University Teachers, &c., &c.' (Gordon, letter to R.W. Chapman, 26 June 1920, *The Letters of George S. Gordon, 1902–1942* (1943), p. 136).

As Tolkien later wrote, Gordon's 'kindness and encouragement' began at their first meeting.

> He rescued me from the barren waiting-room [at the station], and took me to his house. I remember we spoke of Raleigh on the tram. As . . . a stiff-necked young philologist, I did not in fact think much of Raleigh – he was not, of course, a good lecturer; but some kind spirit prompted me to say that he was 'Olympian'. It went well; though I only really meant that he reposed gracefully on a lofty pinnacle above my criticism.
>
> I was extraordinarily fortunate. And if I speak so of myself, instead of directly and impersonally of Gordon, it is because my prime feeling and first thoughts of him are always of personal gratitude, of a friend rather than of an academic figure. It is not often in 'universities' that a Professor bothers with the domestic difficulties of a new junior in his twenties; but G. did. He found me rooms himself, and let me share his private room at the University. I do not think that my experience was peculiar. *He was the very master of men.* Anyone who worked under him could see (or at least suspect) that he neglected some sides of his own work: finding, especially, the sort of half-baked 'research', and dreary thesis-writing by the serious minded but semi-educated hunters of the M.A., of which there was far too much, an exceeding weariness, from which he sometimes took refuge in flight. Yet he created not a miserable little 'department', but a team. A team fired not only with a departmental esprit de corps, determined to put 'English' at the head of the Arts departments, but inspired also with a missionary zeal. . . . [draft letter to R.W. Chapman, 26 November 1941, *Letters*, pp. 56–7]

Gordon's success in reshaping the Leeds English School, even with Tolkien's assistance on the linguistic side of the syllabus, is all the more notable for the brevity of the time in which he achieved it: already in 1922 he returned to Oxford as the Merton Professor of English Literature, succeeding Raleigh. In 1928 he became President of Magdalen College as well, and in 1933 the Professor of Poetry. From 1938 to 1941 he served also as Vice-Chancellor of the University.

He is said to have earned the Merton Professorship on the strength of well admired leaders he wrote for the *Times Literary Supplement*. He took pains even with shorter works, and like Tolkien was a perfectionist in his writing. R.W. Chapman has written of Gordon that 'it was hard to persuade him that even a lecture was fit to be printed; if he parted with the manuscript, he clung to the proof. Of anything much more than a lecture his friends learned to despair. The sum of his occasional publications is none the less substantial, and they are some index of the range of his knowledge and the scope of his thinking' (*Dictionary of National Biography 1941–1950*, p. 308). Gordon's wife Mary stated that 'the curiosity of his mind, always open to a new venture in literature or scholarship, the boundless diversity of his interests, and the increase in his administrative duties, all united to frustrate his plans for his *oeuvres de longue haleine*. He was, therefore, led to express himself in essays and papers written under the spur of some special occasion' (preface to George Gordon, *The Discipline of Letters* (1946), p. v). He wrote briefly but effectively on a range of authors from Shakespeare and Charles Lamb to Andrew Lang and Robert Bridges. For several years, beginning in 1922, he collaborated with Tolkien on a book of selections from *Chaucer for Oxford University Press, ultimately abandoned. This was an ironic combination, from which the result was almost inevitable: both were eager to work but unwilling to hand over an inferior product, and both had too many responsibilities, as teacher or administrator, and too few extended opportunities for writing and research. On 26 April 1922 Gordon wrote to his friend *David Nichol Smith: 'I am indeed full of schemes: I wish I were fuller of performance. Nothing can keep my mind from working – but those vacant intervals, when plans long conceived are put on the anvil and hammered to a finish – I hardly ever get them here [Leeds] . . .' (*The Letters of George S. Gordon, 1902–1942*, p. 150).

In 1925 Gordon praised his former colleague in support of his application for the Rawlinson and Bosworth Professorship at Oxford:

> Of Mr. Tolkien's published work I cannot claim to be an expert critic; but something of its rare quality is discernible by others than experts. It is as conscientious as it is original, and it is always alive. . . . There is no philological (or literary) scholar of his generation from whom I have learned so much, with whom I have worked more happily, or from whom, in my opinion, greater things may be expected. [*An Application for the Rawlinson and Bosworth Professorship of Anglo-Saxon in the University of Oxford by J.R.R. Tolkien, Professor of the English Language in the University of Leeds, June 25, 1925*]

After Tolkien's return to Oxford he and Gordon worked closely together in the Oxford English School, serving on numerous committees and conducting examinations. Both were members of the Kolbítar (*Societies and clubs), and Gordon was one of several friends to whom Tolkien sent a complimentary copy of *The Hobbit upon publication.

Photographs of George S. Gordon appear in *Biography*, pl. 8a, and in *The Tolkien Family Album*, p. 47. See also J.S. Ryan, 'Tolkien and George Gordon: or, A Close Colleague and His Notion of "Myth-maker" and of Historiographic Jeux d'esprit', in *The Shaping of Middle-earth's Maker: Influences on the Life and Literature of J.R.R. Tolkien* (1992).

Grahame, Kenneth (1859–1932). Frustrated in his desire to enter *Oxford University for lack of funds, Kenneth Grahame became a clerk in the Bank of England. Soon he rose through the ranks to positions of responsibility, but his true desire was to write. He excelled at essays, which began to be published in 1887: these tended to follow the theme of escape from everyday life, whether through walking in the countryside, or eating and drinking, or other comforts. Some of his essays were collected, together with six stories about children, as *Pagan Papers*, first published in 1893. In 1895 more stories were added to these six and published as *The Golden Age*; a sequel, *Dream Days*, appeared in 1898. These books established him as a writer about (if not for) children. Nonetheless, Grahame remained at the Bank, where for a while he had secure employment, though he was also drawn to a wayfaring life, much like Mole in Grahame's masterpiece, *The Wind in the Willows*.

That book, published in 1908, grew out of tales told by Grahame to his son. Some enjoy it for the antics of Mr Toad, while others respond to the love of nature, of life in the country and on the river, which Grahame felt and expressed with all his heart, all the more so because that idyllic English rural life was already passing. In a draft of *On Fairy-Stories* Tolkien called *The Wind in the Willows* 'an almost perfect blend, at the russet stage of many pigments: a beast-fable, satire, comedy, *Contes des Fées* (or even pantomime), wild-woodland rivers of Oxfordshire – with just in one corner that colour too much the beautiful colour in itself that muddies the exquisite hue. Pan [as in the chapter "The Piper at the Gates of Dawn"] has no business here: at least not explicit and revealed' (Tolkien Papers, Bodleian Library, Oxford).

Tolkien's interest in Grahame's book is shown also in his eagerness, expressed on 1 August 1944 to his son *Christopher (*Letters*, p. 90), to obtain a copy of *First Whisper of 'The Wind in the Willows'* by Kenneth Grahame's widow, Elspeth. First published in July 1944, *First Whisper* contains Grahame's story 'Bertie's Escapade' and transcriptions of the original story-letters to his son Alistair in which he introduced Toad, Mole, Rat, and Badger.

The Hobbit has often been compared to *The Wind in the Willows*, perhaps first by *C.S. Lewis in his reviews of Tolkien's children's book for the *Times* and *Times Literary Supplement* in 1937. Wayne G. Hammond draws parallels between the homes of Mole and Badger in Grahame's book and Bilbo's hobbit-hole, in 'All the Comforts: The Image of Home in *The Hobbit* and *The Lord of the Rings*', *Mythlore* 14, no. 1, whole no. 51 (Autumn 1987). Lois R. Kuznets in 'Tolkien and the Rhetoric of Childhood', in *Tolkien: New Critical Perspectives* (1981), comments that the geography of *The Wind in the Willows* is 'roughly similar' to that in *The Hobbit*: in Grahame's book 'the safe field and rich river cultures oppose the Wild Wood, which lies on the other side of The River. Such simple geography not only emblematically indicates outside good and evil but also represents inner states and relative psychic disturbance' (p. 152). In *Reader's Companion*, p. 96, we note similarities between *The Wind in the Willows* and both *The Hobbit* and **The Lord of the Rings* in their images of the open road; and in our introduction to the fiftieth anniversary edition of **Farmer Giles of Ham* (1999), we find that Tolkien's story recalls Grahame's 'The Reluctant Dragon', first published in 1898 in *Dream Days*.

See further, Peter Green, *Kenneth Grahame, 1859–1932: A Study of His Life, Work and Times* (1959); Alison Prince, *Kenneth Grahame: An Innocent in the Wild Wood* (1994); and Roger Sale, *Fairy Tales and After: From Snow White to E.B. White* (1978), ch. 7.

Great Haywood (Staffordshire). At the end of his honeymoon in March 1916 Tolkien returned to his battalion encamped on Cannock Chase near Stafford (*Staffordshire), while his wife *Edith moved with her cousin *Jennie Grove from *Warwick to Great Haywood, only a few miles east of Stafford, where they rented furnished rooms from a Mrs Kendrick. There Edith and her husband became friends with the local Catholic priest, *Father Augustine Emery. Edith and Jennie stayed in Great Haywood after Tolkien was sent to *France with the British Expeditionary Force in early June 1916. In December of that year Tolkien returned to Great Haywood while on sick leave. He and Edith lived in the village until the end of February 1917, when Tolkien was sent for further medical treatment in *Harrogate.

During the winter that he lived in Great Haywood Tolkien either began or continued to write **The Book of Lost Tales*, in particular *The Cottage of Lost Play* and *The Fall of Gondolin*. At this early stage of his mythology he intended that Tol Eressëa, the Lonely Isle where Eriol hears stories from the Elves, should become England at the end of the tales, and Tavrobel, where Eriol stays for a while on the island, should become Great Haywood. The name *Tavrobel* is said in the *Gnomish Lexicon to mean 'wood-home' (for this place, see also **An Evening in Tavrobel* and **The Grey Bridge of Tavrobel*). (See also *'Heraldic Devices of Tol Erethrin'.)

In *The Tale of the Sun and Moon* Tolkien wrote of Gilfanon, an Elf who came from 'that region of the isle [Tol Eressëa] where stands the Tower of Tavrobel beside the rivers . . .' (**The Book of Lost Tales, Part One*, p. 174). These 'rivers', later named Taiglin and Sirion, come together at Tavrobel, not unlike the Sow and Trent which reach a confluence at Great Haywood; and they are crossed by a bridge just as the Essex Bridge crosses the Sow and Trent at their point of merging.

Tolkien also wrote of the 'ancient house' of Gilfanon, 'the House of the Hundred Chimneys, that stands nigh the bridge of Tavrobel' (*The Book of Lost Tales, Part One*, p. 175). Shugborough Hall, a National Trust property in Great Haywood, has been suggested as the inspiration for Gilfanon's house; but although it has eighty chimneys, they are not visually prominent, nor is the neoclassical design of the building, with eight giant Ionic columns, particularly 'elvish'. Also, as Nils Ivar Agøy has pointed out ('In Search of Tolkien's Roots', *Angerthas in English* 2 (1992)), it is very difficult to see Shugborough Hall from Essex Bridge because of the trees (at least, as they stood when Agøy visited in 1988). Mr John Vaughan, a senior guide at Shugborough Hall, has suggested Ingestre Hall (also with many, and more notable chimneys), not far to the north of Shugborough Hall, as another possible precursor of Gilfanon's house – though it too cannot be seen from the bridge.

Green, Roger Gilbert Lancelyn (1918–1987). Roger Lancelyn Green read English at Merton College, *Oxford from 1937 to 1940. He attended Tolkien's lectures on *Beowulf*, which Green would recall with pleasure; but he did not meet Tolkien until years later. Poor health having exempted him from war service, Green remained at Oxford to study for a B.Litt. under *David Nichol Smith. His thesis, *Andrew Lang as a Writer of Fairy Tales and Romances*, was examined by Nichol Smith and Tolkien in March 1943. While impressed, Nichol Smith and Tolkien felt that it needed improvements, in particular that it should include more about *fairy-stories. For this purpose, in October 1943, Tolkien became Green's supervisor for an additional term, and admitted that it was his fault that Green's thesis was referred back: 'I wanted to know more about the Fairies!' This led Green to write an additional chapter, 'of which I treasure the original draft written all over by Tolkien with comments and suggestions' (Green, 'Recollections', *Amon Hen* 44 (May 1980), p. 7). Possibly at this time, Green confessed to Tolkien that he had written a fairy-story himself, *The Wonderful Stranger*. Tolkien insisted on reading and criticizing it – Green thought that he did not care for it much – and in return lent Green his own story to read, *Farmer Giles of Ham*, then still in draft. In March 1944 Tolkien and Nichol Smith approved Green's resubmitted thesis. It was published as *Andrew Lang: A Critical Biography* in 1946.

After leaving Oxford, Green worked variously as a teacher, an antiquarian bookseller, and a part-time professional actor. From 1945 to 1950, while Deputy Library of Merton College, he met Tolkien frequently. He became friends also with *C.S. Lewis and sometimes met members of the *Inklings for a drink at the King's Arms or at their meetings in the Eagle and Child (*Oxford and environs). In 1947, on the death of his father, Green became Lord of the Manors of Poulton-Lancelyn and Lower Bebington of The Wirral, in Cheshire. From 1950 to 1952 he was a William Nobel Research Fellow in English Literature at Liverpool University.

His story *The Wonderful Stranger* was published in 1950, and was followed by other works for children, including *The Land beyond the North* (1958), *The Land of the Lord High Tiger* (1958), and *The Luck of Troy* (1961). He also wrote a work of fantasy for adults, *From the World's End* (1948). Green is best known, however, for his many writings about authors for (or read by) children, such as J.M. Barrie, Lewis Carroll, Arthur Conan Doyle, Rudyard Kipling, and Mrs Molesworth, in addition to Andrew Lang. His classic study of children's literature, *Tellers of Tales*, was first published in 1946; its revised edition of 1953 added coverage of Lewis and Tolkien. *C.S. Lewis: A Biography* (1974; rev. edn. 2002), written by Green and Walter Hooper, remains one of the best books on its subject. Green last met Tolkien at a Merton Gaudy in March 1972.

Grey Annals *see* **Annals of Beleriand**

The Grey Bridge of Tavrobel. Poem, published probably in the mid-1920s; Tolkien preserved a copy of the leaf on which it was printed (p. 32). A holograph list of his poems by Tolkien indicates the name of the publication as 'I U Mag'; John Garth in *Tolkien and the Great War* (2003) is correct that this was the *Inter-University Magazine*, published by the University Catholic Societies' Federation of Great Britain. See also **Tinfang Warble*, also published in the *Inter-University Magazine*, though not in the same issue.

According to a later inscription by Tolkien, *The Grey Bridge of Tavrobel* was written in 'Brooklands', the officers' hospital in Hull (*Yorkshire), in mid- to late August or September 1917. At 'an old grey bridge in Tavrobel' the speaker asks a 'damozelle' why she is smiling. She replies that it is because the speaker came after she had 'waited, waited, wearily / To see you come a-homing' from 'beyond the rivers'. 'Long and long I have been away,' the speaker says, 'Dreaming always of the day / Of my returning hither.' The poem almost certainly echoes Tolkien's reunion with his wife after months of separation, while he was on active service in *France in 1916, but is composed in terms of his mythology. As it was then conceived, the island of Tol Eressëa was to become England at the end of **The Book of Lost Tales*, and Tavrobel, where Eriol (*Eriol and Ælfwine) stays for a while listening to the stories of the Elves, was to become the Staffordshire village of *Great Haywood. The bridge in the poem, near 'two rivers running fleetly', may be compared to 'the valley of the two rivers where the grey bridge leaps the joining waters' in *The History of Eriol or Ælfwine* (**The Book of Lost Tales, Part Two*, p. 288). See also **An Evening in Tavrobel*.

Griffiths, Mary Elaine (1909–1996). Elaine Griffiths read English at *Oxford as a member of the Society of Home-Students. A Roman Catholic, she lived in the hostel at Cherwell Edge. In late 1933 she began work on a B.Litt. thesis under Tolkien's supervision, *Notes and Observations on the Vocabulary of Ancrene Wisse MS CCCC 402*. By this time Tolkien was planning an edition of the *Ancrene Wisse* (**Ancrene Riwle*), and had acquired a set of rotographs (photographic facsimiles) of MS CCCC 402 for private study. Griffiths now became his *de facto* assistant, made a diplomatic transcript of the manuscript, and made a nearly complete glossary and index. At the same time, she gave informal tuition in English to undergraduates at Cherwell Edge. She became a close friend of Tolkien and his family, and was one of the intimates allowed to read **The Hobbit* in typescript. Her acquaintance with *Susan Dagnall of George Allen & Unwin (*Publishers) appears to have led to the publication of

The Hobbit by that firm. Tolkien later referred to Griffiths, who was herself of small stature, as 'queen of Hobbits' when inscribing her copy of *The Lord of the Rings* ('Elainen tárin Periandion ar meldenya anyáran' – 'To Elaine, queen of Hobbits and my very old friend'; Bonhams, *Printed Books & Maps* (online), 24 February 2004, lot 601).

She continued to work on her B.Litt. until Trinity Term 1936, but never completed her thesis. Probably early in that year, when Tolkien was asked by Allen & Unwin to produce a revised edition of John R. Clark Hall's Modern English translation of *Beowulf* and the 'Finnesburg Fragment' (*Prefatory Notes on Prose Translation of Beowulf*), he suggested that Griffiths undertake the work instead. Although she made some progress, she was not able to complete the revision, and at the end of June 1938 asked to be released from her contract. In the 1950s she began work on an edition of the Old English *Judith* but was pre-empted by another scholar. Her historical essay 'King Alfred's Last War' was published in the *Festschrift *English and Medieval Studies Presented to J.R.R. Tolkien on the Occasion of His Seventieth Birthday* (1962).

Griffiths' primary interest, however, was not in publication but in teaching and service to students. In 1938 she became a Fellow and tutor in English in the Society of Oxford Home-Students, and until her retirement in 1976 held, at one time or another, nearly every office in what became St Anne's Society (in 1942) and then St Anne's College (in 1952). Her efforts to improve the College's physical facilities are particularly notable. At Oxford she also served as chairman of the English Faculty Board and as a member of the General Board, and was a University Lecturer in English.

A photograph of Elaine Griffiths is reproduced in *The Tolkien Family Album*, p. 69.

Grove, Jennie (1864–1938). Jennie Grove spent her early years in Blundell Sands near Liverpool. Later she came to live with her cousin Edith Bratt (*Edith Tolkien) in *Warwick, and together they moved from place to place following Ronald Tolkien's Army postings. She also lived with Ronald and Edith when Tolkien returned to *Oxford after the First World War, and until the Tolkiens moved to *Leeds in 1921. Known in the family as 'Auntie Ie', based on young *John Tolkien's early attempts to pronounce her name, she was a substitute mother to Edith and like a grandmother to the Tolkien children. Having had an accident to her back as a child, she grew to only four feet eight inches in height, 'but she was a doughty character' (John and *Priscilla Tolkien, *The Tolkien Family Album*, p. 36), one of the first recipients of the 1906 Liberal Government's Old Age Pensions at 5s. per week. She also received some financial help from the Tolkiens, and paid long visits to them, but maintained her independence and managed to live comfortably on a small income, in one room in a house in *Birmingham until the last week of her life.

A photograph of Jennie Grove is reproduced in *The Tolkien Family Album*, p. 36. A portrait of her drawn by Tolkien is reproduced in *Artist and Illustrator*, fig. 24.

Guide to the Names in *The Lord of the Rings* see **Nomenclature of *The Lord of the Rings***

Habbanan beneath the Stars. Poem with brief prose introduction, first published in **The Book of Lost Tales, Part One* (1983), pp. 91–2. The poet speaks of the moon and stars in the night sky, then perceives that the men answering the stars with music are 'His wandering happy sons / Encamped upon those aëry leas / Where God's unsullied garment runs / In glory down His mighty knees.' In the prose introduction it is said that 'Habbanan is that region where one draws nigh to the places that are not of Men.' In **The Book of Lost Tales*, *Habbanan* is a name of the region later called Eruman or Arvalin, near the home of the Valar, the gods or powers in Tolkien's mythology (**'The Silmarillion'*); and there, after death and judgement, some Men 'wander in the dusk, camping as they may, yet are they not utterly without song, and they can see the stars, and wait in patience till the Great End come' (*The Book of Lost Tales, Part One*, p. 77).

Tolkien composed *Habbanan beneath the Stars* evidently in June 1916 in Étaples, *France, where he was encamped as a soldier in the First World War before going to the front. Three texts are extant; on a revised manuscript Tolkien substituted 'Eruman' for 'Habbanan', and inscribed the poem 'insp[ired] Brocton [i.e. Brocton Camp, see *Staffordshire] Dec 1915, written Étaples June 1916'. *Christopher Tolkien has suggested that the notion in *The Book of Lost Tales* of men 'ferried by the death-ship to (Habbanan) Eruman, where they wander in the dusk and wait in patience till the Great End' is a 'reflection of Purgatory' (*The Book of Lost Tales, Part One*, p. 92).

Haggard, Henry Rider (1856–1925). The English novelist H. Rider Haggard gained early fame with *King Solomon's Mines* (1885) and *She* (1887). Each combines adventure with elements of fantasy, and was based in part on knowledge of Africa gained by Haggard as a young man. Among his many other novels are the sequels *Allan Quatermain* (1887), *Ayesha: The Return of She* (1905), *She and Allan* (1921), and *Wisdom's Daughter* (1923), and *The World's Desire* (1890), a collaboration with *Andrew Lang. Haggard was also noted for service on several government commissions, for which he was knighted in 1912.

In an interview with Henry Resnik Tolkien said that as a boy *She* interested him 'as much as anything – like the Greek Shard of Amynatas [*i.e.* Amenartas], which was the kind of machine by which everything got moving' ('An Interview with Tolkien', *Niekas* 18 (Spring 1967), p. 40). He evidently also read *King Solomon's Mines*, as he judged it a suitable book to buy in Paris in August 1913 to occupy the minds of Mexican boys in his care (see **Chronology**). Both novels, and their sequels, have been examined by commentators on Tolkien as sources of possible influences on his works. Even *Christopher Tolkien has said that while there is no external evidence for the name of the Elven city of *Kôr* in Valinor, in the *'Silmarillion' mythology, being derived from the same name for a city in *She*, 'it can hardly be doubted. In this case it might be

thought that since the African Kôr was a city built on the top of a great mountain standing in isolation the relationship was more than "phonetic"' (*The
Book of Lost Tales, Part Two, p. 329).

Stephen Linley in 'Tolkien and Haggard: Some Thoughts on Galadriel',
Anor 23 (1991), and John D. Rateliff in 'She and Tolkien', Mythlore 8, no. 2,
whole no. 28 (Summer 1981), both compare Ayesha, 'She-Who-Must-Be-
Obeyed', in Haggard's writings and Galadriel in *The Lord of the Rings (bk. II,
ch. 7–8). Though it seems unlikely that Tolkien deliberately modelled Galadriel
on the much more ambiguous and egotistic Ayesha, it is entirely possible that
resonances from Haggard's books became embedded in Tolkien's consciousness and contributed to his portrait of Galadriel. The following descriptions
of Ayesha seem particularly pertinent: 'Though the face before me was that of
a young woman of certainly not more than thirty years, in perfect health, and
the first flush of ripened beauty, yet it had stamped upon it a look of unutter-
able experience, and of deep acquaintance with grief and passion' (She, ch. 13);
and 'she began slowly to stroke her abundant hair, then her breast and body.
Wherever her fingers passed the mystic light was born, until in that darkened
room . . . she shimmered from head to foot like the water of a phosphores-
cent sea, a being glorious yet fearful to behold. Then she waved her hand, and,
save for the gentle radiance on her brow, became as she had been' (Ayesha:
The Return of She, ch. 19). Both Ayesha and Galadriel have a mirror or basin
filled with water in which visions appear: Ayesha's is described as 'a vessel like
a font cut in carved stone, also' full of pure water', and when Holly gazes in it
'the water darkened. Then it cleared', and he sees a vision of himself and his
companion on their journey to Kôr. The visions in Ayesha's mirror are
restricted to the past and to events known by her and the viewer, or taking
place in her country, but like Galadriel she does not claim that the mirror is
magic: 'It is no magic, that is a fiction of ignorance. There is no such thing as
magic, though there is such a thing as knowledge of the secrets of Nature. That
water is my glass; in it I see what passes if I care to summon up the pictures . . .'
(She, ch. 13).

Stephen Linley notes other similarities, but also significant differences in
character. 'Both live amidst a culture of preservation; Ayesha, however, preserves only herself, for selfish reasons. . . . She treats all other human beings
as a lesser species . . . and she is prepared to destroy mercilessly any who cross
her. . . . Ayesha actively seeks power and world domination. . . .' Galadriel,
on the other hand, exhibits generosity and rejects the power to be achieved
through the Ring. But, Linley points out, had she accepted the Ring from
Frodo 'the reader familiar with She might recognise that Galadriel would come
to resemble Ayesha more closely in respect of her less appealing characteristics' (pp. 13–14). He comments further:

> I do not wish to claim that Tolkien simply copied Haggard; rather that
> the various characteristics of Ayesha made a deep impression on him,
> and that he used various elements in a creative way. It is, to my mind,

typically Tolkienian that Galadriel is reminiscent of Ayesha while being obviously different, and that the differences are all the more strongly emphasized as a result of that surface similarity. I would suggest that what we have here is an example of literary allusion whereby Tolkien gives his characters greater depth and resonance in the same way that, for example, Vergil uses references to sundry Greek literature in order to highlight certain features of the characters in the *Aeneid*. [p. 15]

John D. Rateliff in his article compares the setting of the ruined city of Kôr in *She* with Tolkien's hidden city of Gondolin rather than with Kôr in Valinor. Haggard's Kôr

> stands in the center of a green plain which is completely surrounded by circular mountains. . . . The way to reach the ruined city is to go through a long tunnel which has a stream flowing through it. In addition, there is a secret, hidden path over the surrounding mountains which the heroes use as an escape route at the end of the book [*She*, ch. 11, 28]. This description of Kôr would also be an excellent description of the hidden vale of Tumladen and the city of Gondolin, which in *The Silmarillion* is built on a low hill in the centre of a green plain . . . surrounded by the Encircling Mountains. Gondolin can only be reached by 'a deep way under the mountains delved in the darkness of the world by waters that flowed out to join the streams of Sirion' (*The Silmarillion*, p. 125). When Gondolin is finally attacked and destroyed, the survivors of the battle escape by a secret path over the mountains (*Silmarillion*, p. 242–3). [p. 7]

Among other similarities between *She* and *The Lord of the Rings*, Rateliff notes that

> both Haggard and Tolkien claimed that they were only editing tales written by the characters themselves . . . their heroes cross swamps filled with 'corpse candles' [*She*, ch. 10; *The Lord of the Rings*, bk. IV, ch. 2]. . . . Both *She* [ch. 18] and *The Lord of the Rings* [bk. V, ch. 2, 9] contain descriptions of the March of the Dead, and the description of She's sudden aging and death [ch. 26] is very similar to the sudden aging of Saruman's body after he is killed by Gríma Wormtongue [*The Lord of the Rings*, bk. VI, ch. 8]. [p. 7]

Rateliff also points out that an antecedent of the One Ring as kept by Frodo, who is unable to discard or destroy it, appears in *She and Allan*. There Allan Quatermain wears a magic amulet on a chain around his neck and hidden under his shirt, which he has been warned to keep safe. When a magician tells him that he will not be able to throw the amulet away, he tries to take it from around his neck, but finds first his pipe and then his collar in the way, and 'then a pang of rheumatism to which I was accustomed from an old injury, developed of a sudden in my left arm, and lastly I grew tired of bothering about the thing' (ch. 1).

William H. Green in *The Hobbit: A Journey into Maturity* (1994) suggests a similarity between the battle plan adopted for the defence of the Lonely Mountain in *The Hobbit* and the battle at the end of *King Solomon's Mines*: 'In both books . . . the narrator stands in the thick of the fight but avoids fighting, an alien in the midst of a strange but admirable army. Knocked senseless at a desperate moment, he is later told the outcome of the battle. . . . Both battles are decided by giant fighters compared to Norse berserks . . .' (pp. 105–6, referring to *King Solomon's Mines*, ch. 13–14). William N. Rogers and Michael R. Underwood in 'Gagool and Gollum: Exemplars of Degeneration in *King Solomon's Mines* and *The Hobbit*', in *J.R.R. Tolkien and His Literary Resonances* (2000), explore other, more general similarities between the same two works: 'an unheroic and unassuming narrator who is both resourceful and brave when faced by crisis; a band of questers whose journey has comic elements . . . perilous wanderings in caves with an immense treasure as the goal; and a return to a pastoral landscape of peace and contentment.' They note, however, that Haggard himself drew 'on already-existing formulaic elements and patterns' (p. 124). They argue at length (pp. 124 ff.) for an 'intimate connection' between Gollum and the ancient 'wizened monkey-like figure' (*King Solomon's Mines*, ch. 9) of Gagool, noting similarities between Gagool and Gollum as he appears in the (second edition) *Hobbit* and *The Lord of the Rings*, most of which are not apparent in the Gollum of the first edition *Hobbit*.

On Tolkien and Haggard, see also Clive Tolley, 'Tolkien and the Unfinished', *Scholarship & Fantasy: Proceedings of* The Tolkien Phenomenon, *Turku, May 1992* (1993).

Halsbury, John Anthony Hardinge Giffard, Earl of (1908–2000). Lord Halsbury, as he was when Tolkien knew him (succeeded to the earldom in 1943), studied Physics and Chemistry at Chelsea Polytechnic, after which he became an accomplished research chemist and administrator. He was also the first Chancellor of Brunel University and chairman of many committees, including the Decimalization Committee in the 1960s. As a fellow member of the Ad Eundem dining society (*Societies and clubs) he became acquainted with Tolkien and expressed an interest in his writings. In 1955 he suggested that the then unfinished *Silmarillion (mentioned in Appendix A of *The Lord of the Rings*) might be published by subscription, if George Allen & Unwin (*Publishers) were unwilling to do so commercially. In 1957 he read by the author's invitation several parts of *The Silmarillion* in manuscript, and wrote to Tolkien: 'Thank you for the privilege of seeing this wonderful mythology. I have never read anything like it and can hardly wait for its publication. You *must* get it published while your sales of *The Lord of the Rings* are still actively developing.' Tolkien was pleased to interpret this 'as an indication that . . . this Silmarillion stuff would have at least some audience' (letter to *Rayner Unwin, 7 December 1957, quoting from a letter by Lord Halsbury, *Letters*, p. 262).

Lord Halsbury visited Tolkien periodically after the latter returned to *Oxford in 1972, and attended the dinner in Tolkien's honour given at the Garrick Club, *London the night before Tolkien received his CBE. In a letter dated 4 August 1973 Tolkien wrote to Lord Halsbury:

> When you retire I shall certainly beg your help. Without it, I begin to feel that I shall never produce any part of *The Silmarillion*. When you were here on July 26, I became again vividly aware of your invigorating effect on me. . . . For over and above all the afflictions and obstacles I have endured since *The Lord of the Rings* came out, I have lost confidence. May I hope that perhaps . . . you could come again before so very long and warm me up again? I particularly desire to hear you read verse again, and especially your own: which you make come alive for me. [*Letters*, pp. 430–1]

The Happy Mariners. Poem, first published in the *Stapeldon Magazine* (Exeter College, Oxford) 5, no. 26 (June 1920), pp. 69–70. The poet, looking out from a window 'that opens on celestial seas', describes 'a white tower builded in the Twilit Isles' that 'glimmers like a spike of lonely pearl', and 'fairy boats' that 'go by to gloaming lands'. He admires the 'happy mariners' upon their journey 'To those great portals on the Western shores / Where, far away, constellate fountains leap, / And dashed against Night's dragon-headed doors / In foam of stars fall sparkling in the deep'.

Tolkien dated the earliest extant manuscript of *The Happy Mariners* to 24 July 1915. A later version is inscribed 'Barnt Green July 1915 and Bedford and later', and another 'July 24 [1915], rewritten Sept. 9', which suggests that he began the poem at *Barnt Green and continued it after he went to *Bedford for army training beginning 19 July 1915. Part of the poem is written on the verso of a letter sent to Tolkien by a Mr How, dated 11 July 1915.

Elements and imagery in the poem are enlarged upon in *The Book of Lost Tales*. In *The Cottage of Lost Play* Tolkien refers to 'the Sleeper in the Tower of Pearl that stands far out to west in the Twilit Isles' (*The Book of Lost Tales, Part One*, p. 15). And in *The Hiding of Valinor* it is told that radiance spilled from the Sun and Moon into the sea 'escaped to linger as secret sparks. . . . These have many elfin divers, and divers of the fays, long time sought beyond the outmost East, even as is sung in the song of the Sleeper in the Tower of Pearl' (*The Book of Lost Tales, Part One*, p. 215). Earendel (so spelled), a significant figure in the *'Silmarillion' mythology, is mentioned in the poem, in passing, as a 'shining mariner' (*The Book of Lost Tales, Part Two*, p. 274).

The Happy Mariners was reprinted, with very minor alterations, in the *Leeds English School collection *A Northern Venture* (1923), pp. 15–16, as *Tha Eadigan Saelidan: The Happy Mariners*. Many years later, Tolkien rewrote the poem, and still later revised it further, adding the date '1940?' The first and last of its several texts were published with notes and commentary in *The Book of Lost Tales, Part Two* (1984), pp. 273–7.

Hardie, Colin Graham (1906–1998). Colin Hardie read Classics at Balliol College, *Oxford, and continued his studies there as a Junior Research Fellow in 1928–9. From 1930 to 1933 he was a Fellow and Classical tutor at Balliol, and from 1933 to 1936 the Director of the British School in Rome. He returned to Oxford in 1936 as a Fellow and tutor in Classics at Magdalen College, where he remained until 1973. In 1945 he was received into the Roman Catholic Church. From 1967 to 1973 he was also Public Orator at Oxford University, and in that capacity provided the Latin address when Tolkien received an Honorary Doctorate of Letters from Oxford in June 1972. (A photograph of Hardie and Tolkien at this ceremony is reproduced in *The Inklings*, pl. 13a.)

Hardie's particular academic interests were Homer and Virgil among the Classics, and Dante among later writers. He served for thirty years as secretary of the Oxford Dante Society (*Societies and clubs), of which Tolkien was also a member. At Magdalen Hardie became friends with *C.S. Lewis, and through him joined the *Inklings. His later claim to have been 'only on the fringe of that informal group' ('A Colleague's Note on C.S. Lewis', *Inklings-Jahrbuch* 3 (1985), p. 177) is in contrast to the numerous times he is noted in attendance at Inklings meetings by W.H. Lewis (*Brothers and Friends*).

Photographs of Colin Hardie are reproduced in *The Inklings*, pl. 10 and 13a.

Harrogate (Yorkshire). At the end of February 1917 Tolkien was sent by an Army medical board to the Furness Auxiliary Hospital in Harrogate to continue his recovery from trench fever. After one month's treatment he was given three weeks' leave, but stayed in this spa town with his wife *Edith and her cousin *Jennie Grove, who had taken lodgings at **95 Valley Drive**. Tolkien's friend *Christopher Wiseman visited them in Harrogate on 17–18 April 1917.

Havard, Robert Emlyn (1901–1985). R.E. Havard read Chemistry at Keble College, *Oxford, but moved to Queen's College, Oxford for his B.M. and B.Chem. after he became a Roman Catholic, a faith prohibited at Keble until the 1940s. His continued his studies in London, then returned to Oxford as an Assistant House Surgeon at the Radcliffe Infirmary and Demonstrator in the Biochemistry Department. Later he taught in the Biochemistry Department of the University of *Leeds, until taking over a surgery in Headington and St Giles', Oxford in 1934. *C.S. Lewis became one of his patients, and it was through friendship with Lewis that he joined the *Inklings. Within that group *Hugo Dyson gave Havard the nickname 'Humphrey', and after Havard had grown a ruddy beard while at sea, Lewis called him 'the Red Admiral'. He was also known to his friends affectionately as 'the UQ' (Useless Quack).

From about the time of the Second World War he was also the Tolkien family doctor. Havard recalled that his first meeting with Tolkien must have been early in 1935, at an Inklings session in C.S. Lewis's rooms in Magdalen College, Oxford.

I gradually became aware of a smallish slender man settled in the depths of an armchair, with a pipe always in his mouth. . . . I was impressed by the breadth of his learning and the sharp edge of his wit, also by the way that neither was ever paraded or used to inflict pain. I was in awe of his standing as a Professorial Fellow of Merton [College], and soon became aware of his international reputation as a philologist, and also that, in spite of this, he was extremely good company. But we were, I felt, worlds apart in outlook, apart from our common religion. ['Professor J.R.R. Tolkien: A Personal Memoir', *Mythlore* 17, no. 2, whole no. 64 (Winter 1990), p. 61]

Havard later lived near the Tolkiens' house on Sandfield Road and went to the same church. He often sat next to Tolkien at Mass on Sundays, and sometimes drove him home. Early in 1943 Tolkien became godfather to Havard's youngest son, David. Havard retired from his medical practice in September 1968 and went to live on the Isle of Wight. He ceased to see much of the Tolkiens, but made at least two visits to their bungalow in *Poole.

Health. On 27 October 1916, with the Battle of the Somme continuing, Second Lieutenant Tolkien of the 11th Battalion of the *Lancashire Fusiliers reported sick. He was found to have a temperature of 103 degrees, and was diagnosed as suffering from trench fever, a highly infectious disease carried by the lice with which most soldiers were infested. The illness usually began with a headache, giddiness, and muscular pain especially in the shins, and sometimes lasted only a few days, followed by a remission and then a relapse, or often a series of relapses and remissions. Tolkien was sent from the trenches in *France to hospital in *Birmingham, where he stayed there over a month before he was found fit enough to be granted sick leave. His recovery was slow and he suffered several setbacks. He spent the rest of the First World War in *England, in various hospitals, on sick leave, and in camps preparing for a return to France. If he had been fit enough to rejoin his battalion, he might well not have survived the war: the 11th Battalion, after taking part in various campaigns, was annihilated at Haut Voisins, Romain, on 28 May 1918.

Although he recovered at last from trench fever, he was prone to illness for the rest of his days (see mentions of various ailments such as shingles, influenza, and virus infections throughout **Chronology**). A remarkable number of the letters he wrote to George Allen & Unwin (*Publishers) and to other correspondents begin with or contain comments on his health, often by way of explanation why he had not written sooner, or had failed to do something. As *Rayner Unwin has said, ill-health for Tolkien was an 'insidious distraction':

> It is difficult to judge from our intermittent correspondence and meetings to what extent his unspecific complaints – 'drained and nervous state' . . . 'under the weather' . . . 'laid up for a few days' – that became something of a threnody in successive letters, disguised some specific ill-

ness or were, at least in part, a defence against his failure to achieve some rashly-promised goal. But, apart from this, he did suffer a great number of much more specific illnesses and accidents that certainly interrupted his concentration, and often distracted him from work that required calm and patience to complete. . . .

In his letters, especially to me as he came to regard me more and more as a friend, his catalogue of physical woes grew year by year. As his retirement approached there was a crescendo, and thereafter illness was never far away. There was no particular pattern to these ailments. Sometimes the less specific complaints seem to have been associated with worry, but for the most part they were far from psychosomatic. He was struck by the usual germs like bronchitis and influenza, but with increasing frequency there were physical troubles as well. Teeth had to be extracted, lumbago inexorably increased, his shoulder and right arm became so painful that for a period he could scarcely write, and, for unspecified reasons, he was taken briefly into hospital. None of these ailments was life-threatening, but they were certainly distractions. [*George Allen & Unwin: A Remembrancer* (1999), pp. 114–15]

'Occasionally I might have suspected that he was protesting too much [about his own or his wife's health] to be taken entirely seriously,' Unwin continues, 'or that he was exploiting his afflictions as a shelter for non-performance. I now believe that although he always appeared to be in good health when we met, he was more liable than most men to minor ailments and less able to cope with the distractions they caused to his daily life, and the burden they added to his intellectual labours' (pp. 116–17).

On 10 February 1949 Tolkien requested a period of leave from his professorial duties, mainly to complete various professional writing projects, but also for 'the minor medical object of having all my teeth, which are said to be poisoning me, removed' (letter to Douglas Veale, University Registrar, Oxford University Archives FA 9/2/875). In the event he did not take leave in 1949, and his teeth were not removed until the following year. In a letter to *Stanley Unwin on 14 April 1950 he apologized for not replying sooner: 'I have been troubled by dentist and doctors since you wrote. I do not yet know the full report of the specialist and X-ray; but I gather that my throat is in a bad way. Still when all my teeth are at last out (four more went today) it may improve a little, and I may hope to escape any immediate operation. That is at any rate a more cheerful prospect than I had begun to envisage' (Tolkien-George Allen & Unwin archive, HarperCollins).

On 15 October 1953 he wrote somewhat dramatically to *P.H. Newby that he was 'laid up at the moment, afflicted simultaneously with laryngitis, lumbago, and (worst) sciatica. The last is very immobilizing and not improving very rapidly. The first is improving, but my voice such as it is, is in poor shape . . . at the moment even sitting is not a comfortable process' (BBC Written Archives Centre). These indispositions prevented him from attending some of the rehearsals for broadcasts of his translation of *Sir Gawain and the Green Knight*, and the laryngitis led to several postponements of the recording of his introduction and talk on the poem. In October 1955 laryngitis prevented him from delivering several university lectures, but on 21 October 1955, though not fully recovered, he managed to give the first O'Donnell Lecture (*English and Welsh*).

Tolkien used a variety of names to describe the physical pains he suffered as he advanced in years, and it is not always clear how he applied them. On 2 December 1953 he apologized to *Robert Murray for typing rather than handwriting a letter, commenting that his hand 'has to be spared as it quickly gets tired and painful' (*Letters*, p. 173). On 6 March 1955 he told W.N. Beard at Allen & Unwin that he was almost incapacitated with lumbago and confined to quarters. On 9 May 1957 he wrote to Rayner Unwin: 'I have not been very well lately, and am beginning to be affected by arthritis which makes long sitting painful' (*Letters*, p. 256). On 20 September 1960 he explained to *Robert Burchfield that he could attend the Early English Text Society (*Societies and clubs) Council meeting the next day, as he had 'been laid up and immobile with "fibrositis" for some weeks, which has not yet yielded to treatment' (Early English Text Society archive). Towards the end of August 1961, Tolkien noted that he was being treated for arthritis and fibrositis, which were painful after long hours at a desk, in fact their chief cause. On 18 June 1962 he wrote to his Aunt Jane Neave: 'I had some treatment last September, and have been more or less free and easy on the legs since, though my usual lumbago afflicted me in June' (*Letters*, p. 316).

He began a long reply on 18 April 1963 to a letter about *The Lord of the Rings* but could not complete it until 6 May because he was afflicted with fibrositis in the right side and arm, which made writing or typing difficult. The problem with his right arm continued, though in his letter to Colonel Worskett on 20 September 1963 he attributed it to rheumatism. On 5 October 1963 he told Stanley Unwin: 'I am afraid that I am falling behind with things that I should do; but it has not been a good year. It was not until the end of August that I got relief from the trouble with my shoulder and right arm. I found not being able to use a pen or pencil as defeating as the loss of her beak would be to a hen' (*Letters*, p. 335). On 8 February 1967 he apologized to Charlotte and Denis Plimmer for walking around while being interviewed; he explained: 'I suffer from arthritis and my knees give me pain if I sit for long' (*Letters*, p. 372). On 2 January 1969 he told his son, Christopher, that he now had 'horrible arthritis in the *left* hand' (*Letters*, p. 397). On 1 October 1969 he wrote to Pauline Baynes that he had 'developed (or re-developed) an acutely painful arm which makes writing difficult and typing almost so' (Marion E. Wade Center, Wheaton College, Wheaton, Illinois).

On 21 September 1967 Tolkien was taken ill with a severe virus infection. His secretary Phyllis Jenkinson wrote to *Joy Hill that the doctor's report was not encouraging, and it might be some weeks before Tolkien would be fit again. He told Clyde S. Kilby in a letter written at the beginning of December 1967 that his illness was 'serious enough to require the daily visits of an anxious doctor for a month, and left me an emaciated wreck. It was 8 weeks before I could walk about' (Marion E. Wade Center, Wheaton College, Wheaton, Illinois). In a letter to Rayner Unwin on 4 October, *Edith Tolkien wrote: 'Ronald is a little better, though still has a good deal of pain in his eyes, ears, head and neck. The temperature has been most persistent for nearly a fortnight – so he's weak and Dr Havard won't let him get up – except to just come down for lunch' (Tolkien-George Allen & Unwin archive, Harper-Collins). Miss Jenkinson helped all that she could with letters, but other business had to wait. On 11 October Tolkien travelled with Edith to the Hotel Miramar, *Bournemouth, where he stayed in bed for a further week. On 25 October he was still weak and suffering from headaches, and had problems with his eyes. On 30 October he wrote to Joy Hill that he was 'recovering – but slowly. . . . I was very run-down before the "virus" assailed me, and it took a month before I had overcome it, by which time I resembled Gollum in appearance' (Tolkien-George Allen & Unwin archive, HarperCollins).

Tolkien was admitted to hospital for surgery at least twice. In late February 1959 he had his appendix removed; on 17 April 1959 wrote to Allen and Unwin that he had only just returned from convalescence. On 17 June 1968, just before he was about to move from Sandfield Road (*Oxford) to *Poole, he fell downstairs and injured his leg. He was taken to hospital where he stayed some weeks, and never returned to Sandfield Road. On 16 July he left hospital, in plaster from foot to waist, and was driven to the Hotel Miramar, Bournemouth. He wrote to Joy Hill on 3 August 1968 that although he was feeling better he was 'pretty completely frustrated. I am ceasing to notice the great weight of plaster, but a straight unbendable leg makes all things difficult; dressing is a problem, and cannot ride in a car, except laid out on the back seat. . . . Also – a natural result this and the shock of the accident – I still find concentration even on simple letters very difficult. And crutches give me stiff tired hands' (collection of René van Rossenberg).

In a letter to Joy Hill on 12 August 1968 he said: 'I am physically very tired, since the ordinary things of daily life are exhausting. Dressing and undressing are the equivalent to an hour's hard work; and 100 yards on crutches equals (calculation of Professor Duthee) a four mile walk for the uninjured. Both my hands are permanently weary' (collection of René van Rossenberg). On 29 September 1968 he wrote to Frau Carroux: 'I returned to hospital in Oxford on September 8, and I was kept there until the 20th under medical treatment owing to my blood-condition after my long immobility. I am still under daily treatment, and am finding attention to business difficult' (Tolkien-George Allen & Unwin archive, HarperCollins).

His accident also had other consequences. Since he was unable to supervise the move to Poole, nor to pack his books and papers, the resulting chaos took months to sort out and prevented any work on *'The Silmarillion'. He told Joy Hill in his letter of 3 August 1968: 'Even with great effort I cannot do anything useful to reorder the complete confusion of my books, files, and papers – mostly still quite inaccessible.' In October 1968 he wrote to his son Michael: 'Also I am still – since no one seems able to help me, and I have been too lamed to help myself for long without weariness – searching for vanished or scattered notes; and my library is still a wilderness of disordered books' (*Letters*, pp. 395–6). It was not until 2 January 1969 that he could write to his son Christopher: 'My library is now in order; and nearly all the things that I thought were lost have turned up' (*Letters*, p. 397).

In mid-1969 he began to suffer from a series of intermittent abdominal and gastric complaints. Though apparently no cause for these was discovered, periodically dietary restrictions were prescribed. On 31 July 1969 he wrote to Christopher that he had been 'assailed by very considerable pain and depression which no ordinary remedy would relieve'. His doctor diagnosed 'an inflamed/ or diseased gall-bladder. Took me at once off all fats (including butter) and all alcohol.' But X-rays having found nothing, he was allowed butter and alcohol after all, 'in moderation'; and 'I feel quite well: i.e. as well as I did before the outset' (*Letters*, p. 401). In early October 1971 he contracted a virus infection, and lost over fourteen pounds in a week. On 24 May 1973 he wrote to *Christopher Wiseman: 'I have had a longish bout of poor health since my 81st birthday party on Jan 3rd (a mere sequel in time & not due to the party!). After having my inside X-rayed extensively (with on the whole v[ery] g[ood] reports) I am now deprived of the use of *all* wines, and on a somewhat restricted diet; but am allowed to smoke & consume the alcoholic products of barley, as I wish' (*Letters*, p. 429).

By 25 August 1973 the restrictions on Tolkien's diet had been lifted, and a few days later he went to visit friends in Bournemouth. He did not feel well on 30 August, began to suffer pain during the night, and on 31 August was taken to hospital where an acute bleeding gastric ulcer was diagnosed. He died early on 2 September 1973.

The Heirs of Elendil. Chronology, published with commentary and notes in *The Peoples of Middle-earth* (1996), pp. 188–224. It is the primary document for the history of the Númenórean kingdoms in Middle-earth (see *Númenor'), from which *The Realms in Exile* in Appendix A of *The Lord of the Rings* was derived.

The Heirs of Elendil survives in three manuscripts, each heavily emended, and in an amanuensis typescript made from the corrected text. The manuscripts date from *c.* 1948–1950, when Tolkien was finishing *The Lord of the Rings*, and they influenced alterations in the larger work. The typescript appears to date from *c.* 1958.

Henry Bradley, 3 Dec., 1845–23 May, 1923 *see* **Bradley, Henry**

'Heraldic Devices of Tol Erethrin'. Three drawings by Tolkien on a loose leaf found within the notebooks of *The Book of Lost Tales*, discussed and reproduced in Christopher Gilson, Bill Welden, Carl F. Hostetter, and Patrick

Wynne, 'Early Noldorin Fragments', *Parma Eldalamberon* 13, pp. 93–6. In style heraldic or otherwise emblematic, they represent three places associated by Tolkien with his wife *Edith: *Great Haywood, *Warwick, and *Cheltenham. He drew them possibly while on sick leave at Great Haywood in the winter of 1916–17. In the left margin is a phrase in Goldogrin (an early form of Noldorin, see *Languages, Invented), 'i·glin grandin a·Dol Erethrin Airi', possibly translated 'the fair town of holy Tol Eressea'. *Dol* (= *Tol*) *Erethrin* is 'the Lonely Isle', in Quenya *Tol Eressëa*.

The first device features three trees above a bridge with three arches, and the words 'Tram Nybol' and 'Tavrobel' (*Tram* is 'bridge' in Tolkien's invented Goldogrin language, an early form of Noldorin; the name *Tavrobel* is said in the *Gnomish Lexicon* to mean 'wood-home'). The second, labelled 'Cortirion' (i.e. Kortirion, a city of the Elves in Tolkien's mythology; see *The Trees of Kortirion*), includes a tall tower and a peacock, references to the great tower of Warwick Castle and the peacocks that still wander about its grounds – two trees, the sun, and stars. The third device, labelled 'Celbaros', 'depicts a fountain, to the left of which is a spike-like mountain surmounted by the sun, while to the right is a weeping willow, and overarching these are the forms *Ranon* above the mountain and *Ecthelin* above the willow. Written under this device is *bod'ominthadriel*, with two interlinked rings in the middle of the words' ('Early Noldorin Fragments', p. 96). *Bod'ominthadriel*, like the other inscriptions derived mainly from Goldogrin, probably means 'coming together again, reunion' (Tolkien was reunited with Edith in Cheltenham after a separation of three years). *Ranon* may be associated with 'moon' or 'month', and *Ecthelin* probably with 'fount, fountain' (a spa, Cheltenham has many fountains). It seems likely that *Ranon* and *Ecthelin* were meant to stand for 'Ronald' and 'Edith'. *Celbaros* may be derived from an alternate etymology for the elements of the place-name *Cheltenham*.

Hill, Margaret Joy (1936–1991). Joy Hill recalled that she began to work for George Allen & Unwin (*Publishers) in her late teens, as a secretary to *Rayner Unwin, and at once began to type letters to Tolkien, whose surname she at first misspelled and of whom she had never heard. (No reference to her appears in the preserved Tolkien-Allen & Unwin correspondence, however, until the beginning of 1959, when she was in her twenties.) One day she was asked to visit Tolkien in *Oxford, to take him letters and parcels sent to him by admirers, and to deal with any of his replies. On this occasion, 'because my hands were full, the packers in the warehouse tied the parcels with great loops of twine and hung them on my arms under my cape' (Joy Hill, 'Echoes of the Old Ringmaster', *Times* (London), 10 December 1990, p. 16). Upon seeing her, Tolkien remarked to his wife (*Edith Tolkien) that Rayner Unwin had sent him a walking Christmas tree.

Joy Hill frequently came to visit the Tolkiens in Oxford, usually bearing gifts from readers. One day, as Tolkien 'cut the string on a packet, he said: "If I find this is a gold bracelet studded with diamonds, it is to be yours." Of course it wasn't, but the bracelet became a joke between us' ('Echoes of the Old Ring-master', p. 16).

Early in the 1960s Hill became responsible at Allen & Unwin for handling subsidiary rights and permissions concerning Tolkien. She worked hard to promote his interests, as she did for other Allen & Unwin authors, such as Thor Heyerdahl. Her letters, retained in the Allen & Unwin archives, bristle with energy. She took a particular interest in *Donald Swann's musical settings for Tolkien poems (*The Road Goes Ever On: A Song Cycle*), and introduced Swann to William Elvin, with whom he performed the song cycle in concert and on the recording *Poems and Songs of Middle Earth* (*Recordings). Tolkien appreciated her efforts on his behalf, though sometimes he found them so numerous as to be overwhelming. By mid-1965 she also helped him to deal with fan mail, which arrived in huge quantities. 'I love them and I hate them', she wrote in 1968 of his fan letters; 'I am fascinated by them, I am appalled by them, I won't be without them for they are part of my office life, I am utterly sick of them, yet they make my working day' ('Daily Life on Middle Earth', *The Bookseller*, 3 August 1968, p. 374). 'She was not as orderly or as forceful as some of his Oxford secretaries had been,' Rayner Unwin recalled, 'but she was never intrusive and her devotion was so palpable that both Tolkien and his wife came to regard her almost as a daughter' (*George Allen & Unwin: A Remembrancer* (1999), p. 122).

After Tolkien broke his leg at the time of his move to *Poole in 1968, he invited Hill to help him set up an office and library in his new home. She stayed for a week at the Hotel Miramar nearby in *Bournemouth. 'One day,' she recalled, 'as I picked up a pile of books in my arms and put them on the shelf, something dropped out from between two of them. It was an exercise book: just the covers with a single sheet between, and on the page a poem' ('Echoes of the Old Ringmaster', p. 16). This was *Bilbo's Last Song. Later Tolkien gave her the manuscript, together with its copyright, as the 'gold bracelet' that never arrived in one of the parcels she continued to bring him.

Hill also visited Tolkien in Oxford after his return. She last saw him probably in August 1973, not long before his death: they went to the Oxford Botanic Garden, walked by the river, then returned to the Botanic Garden, visiting Tolkien's favourite trees.

In 1973 Hill was made redundant by Allen & Unwin, though she remained good friends with Rayner Unwin. She took on a variety of other work, including positions at publishers Penguin and Faber & Faber. For a while she was employed at Imperial College, London, and for the Duke of Edinburgh's Award Scheme in which she took a keen interest. She loved to embroider, and hoped to take a degree course at the Royal College of Needlework, but was prevented from doing so by illness. Towards the end of her life she befriended the present authors, to whom she related warm memories of Tolkien as she knew him, of his sometimes mischievous sense of humour, their occasional storms of disagreement, his wide range of reading and interests.

A photograph of Joy Hill is reproduced in *The Tolkien Family Album*, p. 83.

Historical and cultural influences. History was one of the subjects that Tolkien studied at *King Edward's School, Birmingham, and in July 1910 one of five subjects he took and passed in the Oxford and Cambridge Higher Certificate examinations. The *Literae Humaniores* or Classics curriculum at *Oxford, which he followed for five terms, included Classical History. His early interest in *Philology and his transfer to the Language side of the English School at Oxford necessarily involved a study of the history of the late Roman and Medieval periods, in that the evolution of the *English language was affected by its contact with other languages, in particular stemming from invasions of England. On 23 February 1958 he wrote to his son *Christopher: 'I like history, and am moved by it, but its finest moments for me are those in which it throws light on words and names.' (*Letters*, p. 264).

History indeed, as Tolkien was aware, was visibly present all around him in Britain: prehistoric barrows such as Wayland's Smithy, and circles such as the Rollright Stones; modern roads whose straightness indicate that they follow courses established by the Romans; the remains of pre-Roman and medieval fortifications, and later buildings that have survived (if not wholly unchanged) for centuries. Tolkien was interested in such things, and that interest is evident in his fiction and in his paintings and drawings. Readers perceive, consciously or subconsciously (see *Source-hunting), that behind his stories lie backgrounds of legend and history, at least parts of which seem familiar. The Middle-earth of *The Hobbit, *The Lord of the Rings, and *'The Silmarillion' is, in fact, 'this earth, the one in which we now live, but the historical period is imaginary. The essentials of that abiding place are all there (at any rate for inhabitants of N[orth] W[est] Europe), so naturally it feels familiar, even if a little glorified by the enchantment of distance in time' (Tolkien, note on a review by *W.H. Auden, 1956, *Letters*, p. 239).

PREHISTORY

Tolkien's description of the Barrow-downs in *The Lord of the Rings*, with their standing stones and ancient burials, brings to mind many areas in southern *England, especially the *Berkshire Downs near Oxford which Tolkien knew well. The burial mounds of the Kings of Rohan, 'seven mounds upon the left, and nine upon the right' (bk. III, ch. 6), similarly recall prehistoric structures: William Stukeley's *Stonehenge: A Temple Restor'd to the British Druids* (1740) includes a plate which shows a view of barrows in a line at right angles to the Avenue at Stonehenge, with descriptions 'The 7 Kings Barrows' to the left of the Avenue, and 'The 6 Old Kings Barrows' to the right (p. 18, tab. X or p. 52, tab. XXVII). In this Tolkien also might have been influenced by Anglo-Saxon burial mounds at Sutton Hoo in Suffolk, or by Viking graves at Vendel or Uppsala in Sweden.

In two of his pictures of Nargothrond (*'The Silmarillion') and two of the entrance to the Elvenking's halls in *The Hobbit* (*Pictures*, nos. 12, 33, and *Artist and Illustrator*, figs. 57, 120, 121) Tolkien shows another prehistoric, megalithic construction, often found at the entrance to a burial chamber: two upright stones set at a slight inward angle, on which rests a horizontal capstone. In *The Notion Club Papers* Michael George Ramer refers to 'the Great Door, shaped like a Greek π with sloping sides', and in a variant text to 'the Door π of the Megalithic' (*Sauron Defeated*, pp. 206, 221). A similar gateway appears in Tolkien's early 'visionary' drawing *Before* (*Artist and Illustrator*, fig. 30).

Lake Town (Esgaroth) in *The Hobbit* is described as not being built on the shore 'but right out on the surface of the lake . . . on huge piles made of forest trees' (ch. 10). It was almost certainly inspired by the Stone and Bronze Age lake villages found in many parts of Europe, including *Switzerland and England. Tolkien's illustrations of Lake Town (*Artist and Illustrator*, figs. 126, 127) bear are remarkably similar to one of a reconstruction of a lake village (after A. de Mortillet) in Robert Munro's 1908 *Les Stations lacustres d'Europe* (see *Artist and Illustrator*, fig. 125). In this regard, see also notes by Douglas A. Anderson in *The Annotated Hobbit* (rev. and expanded edn. 2002), pp. 244–5, and mentions of lake dwellings in M.C. Burkitt, *Prehistory* (see below).

The page illustrating some of the cave paintings found by Father Christmas, Polar Bear, and Cave-Bear which accompanied Tolkien's 1932 *'Father Christmas' letter was based on real examples in Europe. In *Artist and Illustrator* we suggested that Tolkien might have referred to *The Art of the Cave-Dweller* by Baldwin Brown (1928, reprinted 1932), but we have since been informed by *Christopher Tolkien that all of the 'Father Christmas' cave images appear in a book which had once belonged to his father, *Prehistory: A Study of Early Cultures in Europe and the Mediterranean Basin* by M.C. Burkitt (2nd edn. 1925): the single mammoth and the dark bear, from the cave of Les Combarelles, Dordogne, and the horse, from La Pasiega, Cantabria, appear in plate XI; the bison, from Altamira, Cantabria, in plate XII; the line of three mammoths, based on a mammoth from Font-de-Gaume, Dordogne, in plate XV; the woolly rhinoceros with a glint in its eye, from La Colombière, and the galloping boar and stag below it to the left, from Altamira, in plate XXVII; the stag at middle left, from Valltorta (Castellón), and the human figure to the right of the bison, from the rock shelter of Tortosilla in south-eastern Spain, in plate XXXIV. Many of the human figures and stylized derivatives (from various Spanish sites) are reproduced in plate XXXVIII. Other human figures on horseback come from Bronze Age sites in Sweden, and the multi-oared boat at top left from a site near Lake Onega in Russia.

NÚMENÓR AND ANTIQUITY

On 14 October 1958 Tolkien wrote to Rhona Beare that the Númenóreans of Gondor in *The Lord of the Rings*

> were proud, peculiar, and archaic, and I think are best pictured in (say)
> Egyptian terms. In many ways they resembled 'Egyptians' – the love of,
> and power to construct, the gigantic and massive. And in their great

interest in ancestry and in tombs. . . . I think the crown of Gondor (the S[outh] Kingdom) was very tall, like that of Egypt, but with wings attached, not set straight back but at an angle.

The N[orth] Kingdom had only a *diadem*. . . . Cf. the difference between the N. and S. kingdoms of Egypt. [*Letters*, p. 281]

Within the letter he drew an illustration of the crown of Gondor, clearly based on the White Crown of Upper or Southern Egypt; the Red Crown of Lower or Northern Egypt had a different shape. Tolkien's references to the 'gigantic and massive' probably refer both to architecture and to statuary. The worn Colossi of Memnon, two seated worn figures built at the entrance to the now vanished Mortuary Temple of Amenophis III, 1417–1379 BC, come to mind from Tolkien's description of the Argonath as it appeared to Frodo:

Great pillars rose like towers to meet him. Giants they seemed to him, vast grey figures silent but threatening. Then he saw that they were indeed shaped and fashioned: the craft and power of old had wrought upon them, and still they preserved through the suns and rains of forgotten years the mighty likenesses in which they had been hewn. Upon great pedestals . . . stood two great kings of stone: still with blurred eyes and crannied brows they frowned upon the North. . . . Great power and majesty they still wore, the silent wardens of a long-vanished kingdom. [bk. II, ch. 9]

Also in *The Lord of the Rings*, the headless statue at the Cross-roads with its head lying on the ground (Book IV, Chapter 7) in turn recalls the famous statue of Rameses II at the Ramesseum, originally some 66 feet (20 m) high, but with its fallen head and shoulders now lying beside the remains of its lower part. It was this statue which inspired Percy Bysshe Shelley's poem 'Ozymandias'.

Tolkien's Númenóreans resemble the ancient Egyptians also in the building of tombs and the science of embalming bodies. It is said of the Númenóreans in the *Akallabêth* that 'they began to build great houses for their dead, while their wise men laboured unceasingly to discover if they might the secret of recalling life, or at the least of the prolonging of Men's days. Yet they achieved only the art of preserving incorrupt the dead flesh of Men, and they filled all the land with silent tombs . . .' (*The Silmarillion*, p. 266). These customs were continued in Gondor, in which (as Faramir describes, Book IV, Chapter 5) 'kings made tombs more splendid than houses of the living'.

But the Númenóreans in exile also bear similarities to the Romans and their empire. Like the Romans, they built roads and bridges, including the Great East-West Road in the North, and in Gondor the road south through Ithilien, though in places by the end of the Third Age these were in poor repair. In comparison with Roman roads, which are known for their straight courses, that in Ithilien was made in a long lost time. . . . The handiwork of Men of old could still be seen in its straight sure flight and level course: now and again it cut its way through hillside slopes, or leaped over a stream upon a wide shapely arch of enduring masonry; but at last all signs of stonework faded. . . . It dwindled at last to a country cart-road little used; but it did not wind: it held on its own sure course and guided them by the swiftest way. [bk. IV, ch. 4]

In Britain the Romans also built walls with forts at intervals to protect the northern border, the most extensive and best known of which was that built by order of the Emperor Hadrian after his visit in AD 122, extending for seventy miles from the east coast to the west. This or later works, such as Offa's dyke built in the eighth century to protect the western frontier of the Anglo-Saxon kingdom of Mercia, provided prototypes for the fortifications of the Weather Hills 'the forts along the walls' referred to by Aragorn in *The Lord of the Rings*, Book I, Chapter 11.

In the days of the decline of the Roman Empire its rulers granted land near its borders to relatively civilized tribes, such as the Ostrogoths, in return for protecting the Empire against more barbaric invaders, and similarly the British ruler Vortigern invited the Anglo-Saxons to Britain. This resembles the grant of Calenardhon by Cirion of Gondor to Eorl and the Rohirrim, though in that case the consequences were much happier than occurred in our own world.

The history of Númenórean kingdoms in exile, divided after the death of Elendil, resembles that of the late Roman Empire, in which the Western Empire had its capital in Rome and the Eastern Empire was ruled from the newly founded city of Constantinople. The Western Empire soon fell, and its territory was divided among tribes from outside the Empire, but Byzantium endured for almost another thousand years. Similarly Arnor, the northern Númenórean kingdom, soon declined and finally fell, while Gondor enjoyed great power before it too waned. Tolkien summarized for *Milton Waldman in ?late 1951: 'In the north Arnor dwindles . . . and finally vanishes. . . . In the south Gondor rises to a peak of power . . . and then fades slowly to decayed Middle Age, a kind of proud, venerable, but increasingly impotent Byzantium' (*Letters*, p. 157).

NORTHERN CIVILIZATION

The hall in the citadel at Minas Tirith (*The Lord of the Rings*, Book V) in its use of stone and vaulting, and with its columns and aisles, incorporates some of the elements of a Roman basilica or court of justice. In contrast, Meduseld (Book III, Chapter 6) seems to be based on a type of Northern mead-hall described in *Beowulf*, as befits the dwelling of the ruler of the Rohirrim, a people originally from the North of Middle-earth. Beorn's hall in *The Hobbit* is of a similar kind, but less elaborate; Tolkien made several drawings of it. J.S. Ryan points out in 'Two Oxford Scholars' Perceptions of the Traditional Germanic Hall', *Minas Tirith Evening-Star* 19, no. 1 (Spring 1990), that the illustration *Beorn's Hall* which appears in most editions of *The Hobbit* is closely related to a reconstruction of the interior of a Norse hall in *E.V. Gordon's *Introduction to Old Norse* (1927). But a drawing which Tolkien made, but abandoned for the published *Hobbit*, is even closer: see *Artist and Illustrator*, figs. 114, 115, and further, Douglas A. Anderson, *The Annotated Hobbit* (rev. and expanded edn. 2002), p. 171.

The Lord of the Rings includes sly allusions to Anglo-Saxon history at least in the names of Marcho and Blanco, the Fallohide brothers who led the colonization of the Shire, which are a deliberate parallel to *Hengest* and *Horsa*, the names of two Germanic chieftains who came to Britain in the early fifth century, the first of the invading Anglo-Saxons; all four names are Old English for 'horse' or derived from Old English words with that meaning. The division of the Hobbits into three tribes may in turn reflect the usual division of the Germanic invaders of Britain into Jutes, Angles, and Saxons.

One must be careful, however, not to press such similarities too far. Tolkien invariably in his fiction transformed anything he drew from history or legend. The Rohirrim, for instance, are frequently compared to the Anglo-Saxons, but Tolkien notes in Appendix F of *The Lord of the Rings* that, although he made the language of Rohan 'to resemble ancient English', this 'does not imply that the Rohirrim closely resembled the ancient English otherwise, in culture or art, in weapons or modes of warfare, except in a general way due to their circumstances: a simpler and more primitive people living in contact with a higher and more venerable culture, and occupying lands that had once been part of its domain'.

See further, Christina Scull, 'The Influences of Archeology and History on Tolkien's World', *Scholarship and Fantasy* (2003), and *Reader's Companion*, *passim*.

The History of Galadriel and Celeborn and of Amroth King of Lórien.

Miscellaneous writings, collected and discussed under this assigned title by *Christopher Tolkien in *Unfinished Tales* (1980), pp. 228–67.

'A history of Galadriel', he comments, 'can only be a history of my father's changing conceptions' (*Unfinished Tales*, p. 9); and 'it must be admitted that there are severe inconsistencies "embedded in the traditions"; or, to look at the matter from another point of view, that the role and importance of Galadriel only emerged slowly, and that her story underwent continual refashionings' (p. 228; cf. *Reader's Companion*, pp. 314–19). Christopher summarizes details given in *The Lord of the Rings*, *The Road Goes Ever On: A Song Cycle*, *The Silmarillion*, and a letter of 1967 (to Mr Rang; cf. *Letters*, p. 386), and interweaves these with accounts from other sources as described below (but see also notes 2, 5, and 7, *Unfinished Tales* pp. 252–4).

THE SHIBBOLETH OF FËANOR

The extract from a 'very late and primarily philological essay' on pp. 229–31 of *Unfinished Tales* was also published, in the context of a complete document, in *The Peoples of Middle-earth* (1996). See *The Shibboleth of Fëanor*.

'GALADRIEL'

In an untitled account, pp. 231–3, Tolkien emphasizes Galadriel's commanding stature in Valinor, 'the equal if unlike in endowments of Fëanor' (p. 231), and decides (or perhaps 'discovers') that she played no part in Fëanor's rebellion (in *'The Silmarillion') and 'was in every way opposed to him. She did indeed wish to depart from Valinor and to go into the wide world of Middle-earth for the exercise of her talents' (p. 232), but had not yet received permission from Manwë. While staying at Alqualondë she meets Celeborn, and they plan to sail to Middle-earth together. They fight in the defence of Alqualondë against Fëanor, and despairing of darkened Valinor, sail to Middle-earth without Manwë's leave. Thus Galadriel 'came under the ban set upon all departure, and Valinor was shut against her return' (p. 232), as it was also for Celeborn. In Middle-earth Galadriel and Celeborn take no part in the war against Angband, which they think a hopeless cause, and reject permission of the Valar to return into the West after the overthrow of Morgoth.

Christopher Tolkien describes this note as 'the last writing of my father's on the subject of Galadriel and Celeborn, and probably the last on Middle-earth and Valinor set down in the last month of his life [August 1973]' (p. 231). Tolkien was either writing or about to write this note when he told Lord Halsbury in a letter on 4 August 1973:

> I meant right away to deal with Galadriel, and with the question of Elvish child-bearing – to both of which I have given much thought. . . .
> Galadriel was 'unstained': she had committed no evil deeds. She was an enemy of Fëanor. She did not reach Middle-earth with the other Noldor, but independently. Her reasons for desiring to go to Middle-earth were legitimate, and she would have been permitted to depart, but for the misfortune that before she set out the revolt of Fëanor broke out, and she became involved in the desperate measures of Manwë, and the ban on all emigration. [*Letters*, p. 431]

Christopher notes that this new story 'is profoundly at variance with all that is said elsewhere. It arose from "philosophical" (rather than "historical") considerations, concerning the precise nature of Galadriel's disobedience in Valinor on the one hand, and her status and power in Middle-earth on the other. That it would have entailed a good deal of alteration in the narrative of *The Silmarillion* is evident; but that my father doubtless intended to do' (*Unfinished Tales*, p. 232). Christopher could not take into account 'merely projected revisions' when preparing *The Silmarillion* after his father's death, but had to form the book 'from completed narratives' (p. 233).

CONCERNING GALADRIEL AND CELEBORN

Concerning Galadriel and Celeborn, pp. 233–40 of *Unfinished Tales*, is 'almost the sole narrative source for the events in the West of Middle-earth up to the defeat and expulsion of Sauron from Eriador in the year 1701 of the Second Age' (p. 233). In this there is no mention of a ban against Galadriel returning into the West at the end of the First Age (cf. *Reader's Companion*, pp. 316–19); she stayed in Middle-earth because of her love for Celeborn, who was unwilling to leave, and perhaps also for reasons of pride. At the beginning of the Second Age Galadriel and Celeborn, with a following of Elves, settle in northern Eriador. About the year 700 they establish the (mainly Noldorin) Elvish realm of Eregion, west of the Misty Mountains, near the Dwarves of Khazad-dûm. Although Celeborn has no love for Dwarves, Galadriel is sympathetic, and sees them as allies against the evil she has begun to sense in the East. She also establishes relations with Lórinand, the realm of the Green-elves east of the Misty Mountains.

About the year 1200 Sauron comes to Eregion, posing as an emissary of the Valar, and persuades the powerful society of smiths, led by Celebrimbor, to seize control. At this Galadriel travels with her children through Khazad-dûm to Lórinand and becomes its ruler; but Celeborn, who will not enter the dwarf-mansions, stays behind. Sauron leaves Eregion and forges the ruling Ring. When Celebrimbor discovers this, he consults Galadriel, and by her counsel the Three Rings of the Elves are hidden. As Sauron's army approaches, Celeborn escapes and joins Elrond at the head of a force sent to the aid of Eregion by Gil-galad. But Sauron takes Eregion, seizes the Nine and lesser rings, kills Celebrimbor when he refuses to reveal the whereabouts of the Three, and turns his army upon Elrond. Elrond's lesser forces are saved by Dwarves from Khazad-dûm and Elves from Lórinand attacking the enemy from the rear. Elrond retreats and founds the stronghold of Imladris (Rivendell). Sauron attacks Lindon, seeking the Three Rings, but the King of Númenor sends a great navy to the aid of Gil-galad. Sauron is defeated and flees to Mordor.

Though sea-longing grows in Galadriel, she deems it her duty to remain in Middle-earth until Sauron is conquered. But wishing to live closer to the sea, she entrusts the rule of Lórinand to her son, Amroth, and with her daughter, Celebrían, joins Celeborn in Imladris. Some time later Galadriel, Celeborn, and Celebrían move to Belfalas where they are joined by Elves from Lórinand and visited at times by Amroth. Galadriel stays until Third Age 1981, returning to Lórinand only when it is in peril after the loss of Amroth.

Written some time after the publication of *The Lord of the Rings*, perhaps at the end of the 1950s, *Concerning Galadriel and Celeborn* is a 'short and hasty outline, very roughly composed' and 'much emended, and it is not always possible to see what belongs to the time of composition of the manuscript and what is indefinitely later' (*Unfinished Tales*, pp. 233, 234). For the purposes of *Unfinished Tales*, to create a readable narrative, Christopher Tolkien retold the material, selectively and with occasional interspersed comments, but applied the title given by his father to the outline. The history of Galadriel and Celeborn was 'greatly modified afterwards' (p. 240); see below, and related comments in *The War of the Jewels*, pp. 352–3.

PART OF THE LEGEND OF AMROTH AND NIMRODEL RECOUNTED IN BRIEF

In this tale, so titled by Tolkien but published in *Unfinished Tales* (pp. 240–8) with related materials under the section title 'Amroth and Nimrodel', it is said that Amroth, a Sindarin Elf, was the ruler of Lórien after the death of his father Amdír in the Battle of Dagorlad near the end of the Second Age. His love for Nimrodel, a Silvan Elf, was returned, but she would not become his wife because she regretted the return of the Elves from the West. When terror came out of Moria, she fled south, Amroth followed, and she agreed to marry if he would take her to a land of peace. They set out to cross the Sea into the West and, as Legolas sang on the borders of Lothlórien in *The Lord of the Rings* (bk. II, ch. 6), became separated. After failing to find Nimrodel, Amroth made his way to the Haven in Gondor where he found only one ship left. Still Nimrodel did not come; but a great autumn storm tore the ship from its moorings and drove it out to sea. Amroth leapt overboard and swam back to shore. 'No eyes of Elves or Men ever saw him again in Middle-earth. Of what befell Nimrodel nothing is said here, though there were many legends concerning her fate' (*Unfinished Tales*, p. 242).

Christopher Tolkien dates this tale to 1969 or later, an offshoot of the essay *The Rivers and Beacon-hills of Gondor* in which it is suggested that Nimrodel rested for a while by the River Gilrain when she became separated from Amroth. In a note to *Amroth and Nimrodel* Christopher Tolkien comments on the differences of detail between this account and that contained in *Concerning Galadriel and Celeborn*, such as the parentage of Amroth.

The second part of this section includes extracts from various unspecified sources: one ('elsewhere') concerning the movements of Celeborn and Galadriel in the Second and Third Ages (p. 245); an explanation of the name *Amroth* in 'another [late] etymological discussion' (pp. 245–6), which also gives information about *flets* (wooden platforms in the trees of Lothlórien); a 'discussion of linguistic and political interrelations in Middle-earth (dating from 1969 or later)' (pp. 246–7), concerning an Elvish settlement on the Bay of Belfalas; extracts from an 'unfinished scrap on the origin of the name *Belfalas*' (p. 247), the whole of which note is published in *Vinyar Tengwar* 42 (July 2001), pp. 15–16; a note written in December 1972 or later (pp. 247–8) with 'a discussion of the Elvish strain in Men' observed in their beardlessness; and a note concerning the Elvish strain in the house of Dol Amroth (p. 248), also printed in *The Peoples of Middle-earth* (p. 220) with a genealogy of the line of

Dol Amroth, both note and genealogy being part of workings for the Appendices to *The Lord of the Rings*.

THE RIVERS AND BEACON-HILLS OF GONDOR

The greater part of this etymological discussion (see separate entry) was published in *Vinyar Tengwar* 42 (July 2001), omitting the extracts already published in *Unfinished Tales*. The latter, listed in the order in which they appear in the complete essay, are an excerpt and note concerning the name *Glanduin* (*Unfinished Tales*, pp. 264–5); an entry on the name *Gwathló* (pp. 261–3); and a large part of an entry on the river Gilrain, including an account of Lothlórien in the late Second Age and in the Third Age (pp. 242–5, and note on p. 255). The first two of these are included in Appendix D to *The History of Galadriel and Celeborn*, 'The Port of Lond Daer' (see below). *Vinyar Tengwar* also records authorial deletions not noted in the extracts published in *Unfinished Tales*, as well as editorial changes or omissions.

THE ELESSAR

In a brief work entitled *The Elessar*, pp. 248–52, Tolkien seeks to provide a history for 'the great stone of a clear green, set in a silver brooch that was wrought in the likeness of an eagle', which Galadriel gives to Aragorn as the Fellowship prepare to leave Lothlórien (*The Lord of the Rings*, bk. II, ch. 8). There Galadriel says that she gave it to her daughter Celebrían, who gave it to *her* daughter Arwen, who has sent it to her grandmother to give to Aragorn as a token of hope.

According to *The Elessar*, Enerdhil, a jewel-smith in Gondolin, made the Elessar for Idril, the king's daughter. It was a green jewel within which the clear light of the sun was imprisoned. 'It is said that those who looked through this stone saw things that were withered or burned healed again or as they were in the grace of their youth, and that the hands of one who held it brought to all that they touched healing from hurt' (*Unfinished Tales*, p. 249). Idril took it with her when she fled to the Havens, and it passed to her son Eärendil who wore it on his breast when he sailed into the West. In later ages there was again an Elessar: some say that it was the original stone which Olórin (Gandalf) brought with him when he came to Middle-earth in the Third Age and gave to Galadriel, but for her to hold only for a while. 'You shall hand it on when the time comes. For before you grow weary, and at last forsake Middle-earth one shall come who is to receive it, and his name shall be that of the stone: Elessar he shall be called' (p. 250). But another tale held that Galadriel's Elessar was made for her by Celebrimbor, chief of the Elven-smiths of Eregion who had been a friend of Enerdhil in Gondolin, to alleviate her grief for the falling leaves and fading flowers of Middle-earth. Celebrimbor set his Elessar in a brooch of silver in the likeness of an eagle. Then 'wielding the Elessar all things grew fair about Galadriel. . . . But afterwards when Nenya, chief of the

Three [Rings], was sent to her by Celebrimbor, she needed it (as she thought) no more, and she gave it to Celebrían her daughter, and so it came to Arwen and to Aragorn who was called Elessar' (p. 251). A note at the end declares that Celebrimbor made both Elessars, displacing Enerdhil (who appears in no other writing).

The first story agrees with Galadriel's statement in *The Lord of the Rings* that the name *Elessar* had been foretold for Aragorn, but not with her gift of the jewel to her daughter Celebrían: thus the tale seems to suggest that there was a breach of trust, in that Galadriel did not keep the Elessar for the one destined to receive it. The second story, however, dovetails neatly with the published *Lord of the Rings*: cf. *Reader's Companion*, pp. 337–8.

The Elessar exists in one text only, described by Christopher Tolkien as a four-page manuscript in the first stage of composition. He dates it to about the same time as *Concerning Galadriel and Celeborn*, after the publication of *The Lord of the Rings*.

APPENDICES

Appendix A, 'The Silvan Elves and Their Speech', *Unfinished Tales* pp. 256–7, quotes from two unnamed late works, 'a late etymological discussion of the names Galadriel, Celeborn, and Lórien' which tells something of the history of the Silvan Elves of Mirkwood and Lórien and the languages they spoke; and 'a linguistic-historical discussion dating from the same late period'. The latter includes a general statement concerning the dialects of the Silvan Elves, and concludes that by the end of the Third Age Silvan Elvish had ceased to be spoken in Lórien and in Thranduil's realm in Mirkwood.

Appendix B, 'The Sindarin Princes of the Silvan Elves', pp. 257–60, quotes from two unnamed texts from Tolkien's 'late philological writings' (p. 258). An extract from an essay gives information about the Silvan Elves in Greenwood and their Sindarin rulers during the Second and Third Ages, including the part they played in the Last Alliance at the end of the Second Age. 'Another passage written at the same time' tells how the Silvan Elves under Thranduil retreated north and underground when the Shadow fell on Southern Greenwood. This also says that the few Sindar among them adopted the Silvan language and merged with the Silvan Elves. Christopher Tolkien notes that this latter statement contradicts what is said in an extract quoted in 'The Silvan Elves and Their Speech'.

Appendix C, 'The Boundaries of Lórien', pp. 260–1, quotes from a 'late writing on the interrelations of the languages of Middle-earth' and an extract from another essay. These include descriptions of the terrain of Lothlórien, and an account of an early meeting between Fangorn (Treebeard) and the King of the Galadhrim.

Appendix D, 'The Port of Lond Daer', pp. 261–5: see above.

Appendix E, 'The Names of Celeborn and Galadriel', pp. 266–7, summarizes the name-giving of the Eldar in Valinor and discusses the various names of

Celeborn and Galadriel, citing some of Tolkien's 'latest philological writings' (p. 266).

The History of Middle-earth. Twelve volumes of writings by J.R.R. Tolkien in various formats relating to *'The Silmarillion', and drafts and early versions of *The Lord of the Rings, edited with notes and commentary by *Christopher Tolkien:

I. *The Book of Lost Tales, Part One (1983)
II. *The Book of Lost Tales, Part Two (1984)
III. *The Lays of Beleriand (1985)
IV. *The Shaping of Middle-earth: The Quenta, The Ambarkanta and the Annals Together with the Earliest 'Silmarillion' and the First Map (1986)
V. *The Lost Road and Other Writings (1987)
VI. *The Return of the Shadow: The History of The Lord of the Rings, Part One (1988)
VII. *The Treason of Isengard: The History of The Lord of the Rings, Part Two (1989)
VIII. *The War of the Ring: The History of The Lord of the Rings, Part Three (1990)
IX. *Sauron Defeated: The End of the Third Age (The History of The Lord of the Rings, Part Four); The Notion Club Papers and The Drowning of Anadûnê (1992)
X. *Morgoth's Ring: The Later Silmarillion, Part One: The Legends of Aman (1993)
XI. *The War of the Jewels: The Later Silmarillion, Part Two: The Legends of Beleriand (1994)
XII. *The Peoples of Middle-earth (1996)

HISTORY

The History of Middle-earth is not a history of events in Middle-earth within Tolkien's fiction, but an account of his writings concerned with that invented land, or more widely with the world (Arda) of which Middle-earth is a part. The series grew out of Christopher Tolkien's experience in editing *The Silmarillion (1977) for publication. Designated his father's literary executor, he had three choices in regard to 'The Silmarillion' as it came to him on his father's death:

> I could withhold it indefinitely from publication, on the ground that the work was incomplete and incoherent between its parts. I could accept the nature of the work as it stood, and, to quote my Foreword to the book, 'attempt to present the diversity of the materials – to show "The Silmarillion" as in truth a continuing and evolving creation extending over more than half a century'; and that, as I have said in Unfinished

Tales (p. 1), would have entailed 'a complex of divergent texts interlinked by commentary' – a far larger undertaking than those words suggest. In the event, I chose the third course, 'to work out a single text, selecting and arranging in such a way as seemed to me to produce the most coherent and internally self-consistent narrative'. [*The Book of Lost Tales, Part One*, p. 6]

At that time (1973–7) there could have been no doubt that a single coherent account of the legends of the Elder Days, such as Tolkien had long promised, was the best solution. But as Christopher Tolkien also commented, such a book could not include an 'exposition of the complexities of its history' (p. 6).

Some of those complexities became evident in 1980, with the appearance of *Unfinished Tales* – a precursor to *The History of Middle-earth*, containing works which would have been included in the series had they not been already published; and by the same token, in some cases sections of a work omitted in *Unfinished Tales* were published in the later volumes. In his introduction to *Unfinished Tales* Christopher Tolkien considered the difficult problems

> that confront one given responsibility for the writings of a dead author. . . . Some persons in this position may elect to make no material whatsoever available for publication, save perhaps for work that was in a virtually finished state at the time of the author's death. In the case of the unpublished writings of J.R.R. Tolkien this might seem at first sight the proper course; since he himself, peculiarly critical and exacting of his own work, would not have dreamt of allowing even the more completed narratives in this book to appear without much further refinement. [p. 1]

On the other hand, Christopher acknowledged, even his father's abandoned stories contain much of interest, and have 'a value greater than the mere uncovering of curious detail' (p. 2). Although he does not say so explicitly, it would become clear in *The History of Middle-earth* that the chief value of publishing such materials lies in the view they permit the reader into the author's process of writing and literary (or linguistic) invention.

In the first volume of *The History of Middle-earth* Christopher Tolkien remarked that his father's

> vision of his own vision underwent a continual slow shifting, shedding and enlarging: only in *The Hobbit* and *The Lord of the Rings* did parts of it emerge to become fixed in print, in his own lifetime. The study of Middle-earth and Valinor is thus complex; for the object of the study was not stable, but exists, as it were 'longitudinally' in time (the author's lifetime), and not only 'transversely' in time, as a printed book that undergoes no essential further change. By the publication of 'The Silmarillion' the 'longitudinal' was cut 'transversely', and a kind of finality imposed. [*The Book of Lost Tales, Part One*, pp. 7–8]

The purpose of *The History of Middle-earth* is to present the 'longitudinal' view, to document the evolution of Tolkien's mythology from its earliest expression in narrative (**The Book of Lost Tales*) to its final miscellaneous writings in the period following the publication of *The Lord of the Rings*. Christopher Tolkien presents the most significant of various texts, in chronological order as far as that could be determined, together with expert commentary, glossaries, diagrams, and maps. This was, as we have said elsewhere, a Herculean task. 'Simply reading J.R.R. Tolkien's hasty script can be an exhausting experience; while the organization of Tolkien's texts, sometimes with multiple layers of emendation, was a test of his son's endurance as well as of his intelligence and skill' ('The History of Middle-earth', *Seven* 12 (1995), p. 106).

*Rayner Unwin recalls in his brief essay 'Early Days of Elder Days', in *Tolkien's Legendarium: Essays on The History of Middle-earth* (2000), that when Christopher Tolkien first proposed *The History of Middle-earth* to George Allen & Unwin (*Publishers) they talked of four volumes, and were confident of sufficient sales to meet costs, but did not expect it to be commercially rewarding.

> That it would be rewarding in other ways has now become self-evident. Not four but twelve volumes have appeared at regular annual intervals. I cannot now remember how we drifted beyond the four that the contract originally laid down. It didn't really matter: we trusted each other, and to my surprise reprints and paperback editions were called for; and although, as usual, literary reviewers studiously ignored *The History of Middle-earth*, the sales of volume after volume were remarkably stable. [p. 5]

In his introduction to *Unfinished Tales*, referring specifically to **The History of Galadriel and Celeborn* but in words generally applicable to *The History of Middle-earth*, Christopher Tolkien explains that one of the consequences of publishing his father's 'unfinished narratives and sketches of narrative' is

> the acceptance of the history not as a fixed, independently-existing reality which the author 'reports' (in his 'persona' as translator and redactor), but as a growing and shifting conception in his mind. When the author has ceased to publish his works himself, after subjecting them to his own detailed criticism and comparison, the further knowledge of Middle-earth to be found in his unpublished writings will often conflict with what is already 'known'; and new elements set into the existing edifice will in such cases tend to contribute less to the history of the invented world itself than to the history of its invention. [p. 3]

CRITICISM

In this regard we have commented in *Seven*:

> Some readers have suggested that *The History of Middle-earth* should never have been published, that it is a disservice to Tolkien to display his missteps and false starts. Others have rejected it on false grounds of 'canonicity': although written by Tolkien, he did not approve these texts for publication, and the ideas they contain are not 'fixed – preventing their 'authoritative' use in role-playing games, Middle-earth encyclopedias, or the like. It disconcerts some readers that they will never have definitive answers to many questions about Tolkien's stories, because the author himself could not always make up his mind. Such critics entirely miss the point. *The History of Middle-earth* was conceived to illustrate not a fixed design, but a living creation, and the process by which Tolkien gave it life. It is a unique opportunity to view the creative spark, a fascinating insight into the work of one of the most imaginative and influential writers of the twentieth century. ['The History of Middle-earth', pp. 108–9]

David Bratman remarks in 'The Literary Value of *The History of Middle-earth*', in *Tolkien's Legendarium: Essays on The History of Middle-earth* (2000), that the series has been 'thought of primarily as a mine for scholarly research, a huge collection of background material for secondary-world study of J.R.R. Tolkien's sub-creation or *legendarium*, and for helping place into context for the other major published works of the sub-creation, *The Lord of the Rings* and the book called *The Silmarillion*'. It has also 'been treated as a giant artifact to stare at in wonder at one man's creativity and industry. And indeed *The History of Middle-earth* is these things' (p. 69), Bratman concludes, but it is also literature to be read and enjoyed. That some readers have difficulty with it, and with some volumes more than others (depending on taste and inclination), is not surprising, for, as Bratman says,

> *The History of Middle-earth* was not designed by its editor for casual reading, and only scattered parts of it have the potential for the kind of widespread popularity that came to *The Hobbit* and *The Lord of the Rings*. But there is much of it that can be read as straightforward narrative, ignoring the textual notes, by a reader with a sympathetic attitude towards the author's and the editor's intent. And of course it is a tremendously rich resource for scholarly study. [p. 87]

Some readers of Tolkien, he feels, 'will not get much out of *The History of Middle-earth*. Those who consider the post-Tolkien epic fantasies of Robert Jordan, Terry Brooks, Dennis McKiernan, and David Eddings to be equal in appeal to *The Lord of the Rings* will probably not enjoy Tolkien's posthumous works.' But 'those who find something special in Tolkien's writing above that of other fantasists can choose from a variety of material, catering to a variety of tastes', which Bratman lists as recommended approaches to the series (p. 88). Among the latter group of readers, the critic Katharyn W. Crabbe found in *The History of Middle-earth*, when less than half of the volumes were yet published,

> the richness of Tolkien's creative vision . . . reflected in the variation of forms he employed in telling and retelling the same stories. In these works we can see him transform material from one genre, say fairy tale, to a second, say alliterative verse, to a third, say heroic romance. Not surprisingly, his language varies, too, from the archaic to the contemporary, from the poetic to the flat factual prose of the historical saga. [*J.R.R. Tolkien* (rev. and expanded edn. 1988), pp. 172–3]

It may be difficult for those somewhat younger than the present authors to imagine what it was like to read Tolkien before the publication of, successively, *The Silmarillion*, *Unfinished Tales*, *Letters*, and the twelve volumes of *The History of Middle-earth*. Each of those works opened new vistas of understanding and appreciation. Those who rushed to buy *The Silmarillion* in 1977, after waiting patiently (or impatiently), first for Tolkien himself and then for Christopher Tolkien to finish the work, had no idea of the vast quantity of material that was still to be published. One can, of course, be sad that Tolkien himself did not bring 'The Silmarillion' to a finished form, and in particular that writings such as his later accounts of the stories of Tuor and Túrin were left unfinished, but then, if he had published a version of *The Silmarillion* in his lifetime we might never have seen the discarded earlier versions that lay behind it. It was because the publication of 'The Silmarillion' was left to his son, and because Christopher Tolkien was not certain how best to fulfil that trust, that we now have both a coherent, 'finished' *Silmarillion* and, for those who wish to look behind and beyond, the 'Silmarillion' texts on which Tolkien worked for most of his adult life.

The importance that Tolkien placed on these is evident in a letter he wrote on 23 February 1966 to *W.H. Auden, on hearing that Auden was planning to write a book about him. He thought this 'premature', and wished that any such book 'could wait until I produce the *Silmarillion*' (*Letters*, p. 367). Even so, *The Silmarillion* alone could not have given Tolkien's biographers or his readers a true picture of the significance of the *legendarium* in his life or the magnitude of the work as a whole. As Rayner Unwin has said, Christopher Tolkien, 'and probably only Christopher, knew what [his father's voluminous box files] contained, and believed that a true vision of Middle-earth was incomplete if the serious pilgrim could not be guided along all the paths, and variants, and blind ends of his father's creation' ('Early Days of Elder Days', p. 5).

See also other contributions to Verlyn Flieger and Carl F. Hostetter, eds., *Tolkien's Legendarium: Essays on The History of Middle-earth* (2000); and T.A. Shippey, *The Road to Middle-earth* (2nd edn. 1992), ch. 9.

The History of The Lord of the Rings. A subset of **The History of Middle-earth*, comprising volumes 6–8 (**The Return of the Shadow*, **The Treason of Isengard*, **The War of the Ring*) and the first part of volume 9 (*Sauron Defeated, as *The End of the Third Age*).

See also Part One of **The Peoples of Middle-earth*, which traces the writing of the Prologue and Appendices to *The Lord of the Rings*.

The Hoard. Poem, first published in this revised form, and with the stated title, in **The Adventures of Tom Bombadil and Other Verses from the Red Book* (1962), pp. 53–6. In ages past the Elves 'wrought many fair things'. But at last 'their doom fell, and their song waned, / by iron hewn and by steel chained'. In turn a dwarf, a dragon, and a warrior come to possess the Elves' treasure, each new owner killing the old in succession, and each himself becoming enslaved by greed. In the end 'the old hoard' lies forgotten 'while earth waits and the Elves sleep'.

*Pauline Baynes remarked to Tolkien that *The Hoard* was her favourite among the poems sent to her for illustration in the *Adventures of Tom Bombadil* collection. Tolkien was interested in her choice, because *The Hoard* 'is the least fluid [of that selection of poems], being written in [a] mode rather resembling the oldest English verse – and was in fact inspired by a single line of ancient verse: *iúmonna gold galdre bewunden*, "the gold of men of long ago enmeshed in enchantment" (*Beowulf, l. 3052)' (letter to Pauline Baynes, 6 December 1961, *Letters*, p. 312). In fact, *The Hoard* is the last in a series of related poems which began with *Iúmonna Gold Galdre Bewunden*, written possibly at the end of 1922 and published in *The Gryphon* (Leeds) n.s. 4, no. 4 (January 1923), p. 130. The latter was heavily revised and the result newly published, under the same title, in the *Oxford Magazine* 55, no. 15 (4 March 1937), p. 473; and this became *The Hoard* with only a few small additional emendations. *Iúmonna Gold Galdre Bewunden* as it appeared in *The Gryphon* was reprinted in *The Annotated Hobbit*, pp. 288–9 (1988), 335–7 (rev. and expanded edn. 2002). The 1923 and 1937 versions were reprinted in *Beowulf and the Critics* (**Beowulf: The Monsters and the Critics*), pp. 201–5, together with an intermediate version on pp. 110–12, in final form almost identical with that of 1937 but less so before emendation (see notes, pp. 385–7).

A close comparison of the different versions of the poem is included in 'The Versions of "The Hoard"' by Tom Shippey, *Lembas* 100 (2001). In this Shippey also notes parallels between the 'bewilderment' caused by the riches of the dragon's hoard in Tolkien's poem and the adverse effects of Smaug's hoard on Thorin and the Master of Lake-town in *The Hobbit. An analysis of the final version comprises Part 1 of 'The Use of Language in Tolkien's Poetry' by Nancy Martsch, in *Beyond Bree* for December 2003.

Tolkien recorded *The Hoard* in 1967 for the album *Poems and Songs of Middle Earth* (1967, reissued in 2001 as part of *The J.R.R. Tolkien Audio Collection*); see *Recordings.

The Hobbit. Story, first published in Great Britain by George Allen & Unwin, London, in September 1937, and in the United States by the Houghton Mifflin Company, Boston, in March 1938. See further, *Descriptive Bibliography* A3.

SUMMARY

The work introduces a race called Hobbits, little people about half the height of Men. 'They are inclined to be fat in the stomach; they dress in bright colours (chiefly green and yellow); wear no shoes, because their feet grow natural leathery soles and thick warm brown hair like the stuff on their heads (which is curly); have long clever brown fingers, good-natured faces, and laugh deep fruity laughs (especially after dinner, which they have twice a day when they can get it)' (ch. 1). 'Long ago in the quiet of the world' a very well-to-do hobbit, Bilbo Baggins, is comfortably settled in his hobbit-hole at Bag-End, a luxurious underground dwelling in the village of Hobbiton, until he is visited by a wizard named Gandalf and thirteen dwarves. The leader of the dwarves, Thorin Oakenshield, tells how his people were driven out of their underground halls in the Lonely Mountain far to the east by a dragon, Smaug, who now sleeps there upon a mound of treasure. The dwarves seek to revenge themselves upon Smaug and regain their fortune, and Gandalf has chosen Bilbo to go with them, as a 'burglar'.

As the company travels east it encounters trolls; takes a short rest with elves in the hidden valley of Rivendell, where the master, Elrond, reads the 'moon-letters' on an old chart (*Thror's Map*); and nearly meets disaster when attacked by goblins beneath the Misty Mountains. Bilbo is separated from the dwarves; in a deep cavern he finds a ring lying upon the ground and puts it in his pocket, and he meets Gollum, a slimy, wretched creature who lives on fish from an underground lake and on any goblins he can catch – he would eat Bilbo too if the hobbit were not armed with a sword from the trolls' cave. Bilbo and Gollum have a riddle contest, which Bilbo wins by accident. 'What have I got in my pocket?' Bilbo asks, and Gollum cannot guess that it is the ring that he himself has long kept but does not know he has lost, a ring which makes the wearer invisible. Bilbo puts on the ring and escapes from the goblin caves to rejoin Gandalf and the dwarves. (On the revision of the riddle-game episode in the second edition of *The Hobbit*, see below.)

With the aid of eagles the company escapes from goblins and wild wolves. They rest in the home of Beorn, a 'skin-changer' or were-bear; then, Gandalf having left them (to deal 'off-stage' with 'the Necromancer'), Bilbo and the dwarves pass into the forest of Mirkwood. Using his ring of invisibility and his sword Sting, Bilbo rescues his friends from giant spiders and helps them escape from Wood-elves by riding in empty barrels down the Forest River to Lake-town, a dwelling of Men near the Lonely Mountain. At the Mountain Bilbo enters the dragon's lair by a secret door, arousing Smaug to anger. The dragon finally is so enraged that he flies to Lake-town and sets it on fire, but is killed by the archer Bard. With Smaug dead, the thoughts of men and elves turn to the hoard he had gathered, a treasure Thorin and company claim as their own and prepare to defend as other dwarves rush to their aid. Battle is about to be joined when goblins and wargs attack, and dwarves, men, and elves band together to defeat their common enemy. Bilbo returns home at last with a share of the dragon's treasure, a coat of mail, his sword, and the magic ring.

HISTORY

The history of the writing of *The Hobbit* cannot be recounted with complete certainty. The physical evidence is incomplete; and although Tolkien addressed the history of *The Hobbit*, or at least its origin, in numerous letters and interviews, he could never recall precisely when he wrote its famous first words, nor did he ever provide a clear account of its subsequent development. On 7 June 1955 he wrote to *W.H. Auden:

> All I can remember about the start of *The Hobbit* is sitting correcting School Certificate papers in the everlasting weariness of that annual task [during the summer months] forced on impecunious academics with children [see *Examinations]. On a blank leaf I scrawled: 'In a hole in the ground there lived a hobbit.' I did not and do not know why. I did nothing about it, for a long time, and for some years I got no further than the production of Thror's Map. But it became *The Hobbit* in the early 1930s. . . . [*Letters*, p. 215]

'For a long time' and 'for some years' suggest a significant gap between the initial inspiration for *The Hobbit* and the major part of its writing; while 'it became *The Hobbit* in the early 1930s' could mean (among other interpretations) that the work did not take substantial shape until that decade, 'some years' after its first workings. However, in a letter to his American publisher, the Houghton Mifflin Company (*Publishers), written at the end of June 1955, Tolkien remarked more specifically that he had 'once scribbled "hobbit" on a blank page of some boring school exam[ination] paper in the early 1930s. It was some time before I discovered what it referred to!' (*Letters*, p. 219). Thus he assigned both the origin of *The Hobbit* and its subsequent development to the 1930s (most of the work apparently was complete by 1933: see below), a belief he continued to assert. In a note preserved in the Bodleian Library, undated but almost certainly, from the style of handwriting and references to *The Lord of the Rings*, written after that work (published 1954–5) had appeared, he said that *The Hobbit*

> took long in first writing and then typing (by myself). I am not sure but I think the Unexpected Party [the first chapter of *The Hobbit*] was hastily written before 1935 but certainly after 1930 when I moved to 20 Northmoor Road (from 22!). I can remember sitting one summer with a pile

of dreary exam papers in a chair near the front window of my study in 20 Northmoor Road. I came across a blessed blank page and scrawled on it (without conscious reflection or effort of invention) *In a hole in the ground lived a Hobbit.* The story that grew from that unfolded itself gradually, but gradually entered the world of the *Silmarillion* (in which I had been engaged since 1917). Its first contact was with the name *Elrond*, with references to *Gondolin*. The 'Necromancer' [Sauron in *The Lord of the Rings*] had yet no part to play but I remember 'feeling' that he was important, more important than the Dragon. [Tolkien Papers, Bodleian Library, Oxford]

In 1968, when interviewed about *The Hobbit* for the BBC television programme *Tolkien in Oxford*, he told much the same story of its origin, but was even more emphatic that he could 'very clearly . . . still see the corner of my house in 20 Northmoor Road where it happened.'

It is evident, then, that despite some confusion Tolkien was convinced by the 1950s that he had begun *The Hobbit* no earlier than 1930. Indeed he had pointed (roughly) to this date as early as 31 August 1937, just before *The Hobbit* was published: in a letter to C.A. Furth of George Allen & Unwin (*Publishers) he wrote that 'my eldest boy was thirteen when he heard the serial. It did not appeal to the younger ones who had to grow up to it successively' (*Letters*, p. 21). *John Tolkien was thirteen in 1930–1.

Against these recollections by the author, however, must be set the memories of John Tolkien and his brother *Michael. John Tolkien said in interviews and in conversation with the present authors that his father began *The Hobbit* in 1926 or 1927. He remembers having heard the story told to him and his brothers in their father's study in 22 Northmoor Road – thus before 1930 – in portions of perhaps two, three, or four chapters each Christmas. Michael Tolkien likewise, as his younger brother *Christopher has written,

recorded long after his recollection of the evenings when my father would stand with his back to the fire in his small study of the house in North Oxford (22 Northmoor Road) and tell stories to my brothers and me; and he said that he remembered with perfect clarity the occasion when my father said that he was going to start telling us a long story about a small being with furry feet, and asked us what he should be called – then answering himself, said 'I think we'll call him a "Hobbit".' Since my family moved from that house at the beginning of 1930, and since my brother preserved stories of his own, in imitation of *The Hobbit*, which he dated '1929', he was convinced that *The Hobbit* 'began' at any rate no later than that year. His opinion was that my father had written the opening sentence . . . in the summer before he began telling us the story; and that he repeated those opening words 'as if he had invented them on the spur of the moment.' He also remembered that I (then between four and five years old) was greatly concerned with petty consistency as the story unfolded, and that on one occasion I interrupted: 'Last time, *you said* Bilbo's front door was blue, and *you said* Thorin had a golden tassel on his hood, but you've just said that Bilbo's front door was green and that Thorin's hood was silver', at which my father muttered 'Damn the boy', and then strode across the room to his desk to make a note. [foreword to *The Hobbit* (Unwin Hyman, 1987), pp. vi–vii]

Christopher himself retains no memory of his father telling the story of *The Hobbit*; however, in December 1937 he wrote in a letter to Father Christmas that 'Daddy' had written *The Hobbit* 'ages ago, and read it to John, Michael, and me in our winter "reads" after tea in the evening' (quoted in *The Hobbit* (Unwin Hyman, 1987), p. vii).

From this tangled web of evidence one may conclude at least that Tolkien told *The Hobbit* to his sons in parts, and if the younger two 'had to grow up to it successively' it must have been told over a period of years. The beginning of this span cannot be earlier than 1926, when Tolkien and his family moved to Northmoor Road in Oxford – all accounts agree that Tolkien wrote the first words of *The Hobbit* after he had returned to Oxford from Leeds – and there is an additional consideration which suggests a date not before 1927 or 1928. In his letter to W.H. Auden of 7 June 1955 Tolkien remarked parenthetically that his sons did not like *The Hobbit* any better than *The Marvellous Land of Snergs* by E.A. Wyke-Smith, which was published in September 1927: 'Seeing the date, I should say that this was probably an unconscious source-book! for the Hobbits, not of anything else' (*Letters*, p. 215). If that was so, it would seem that the telling of *The Hobbit* (if not the writing of its apparently independent first sentence) must have followed the publication of *The Marvellous Land of Snergs*, thus not before Christmas 1927. This would agree with Michael Tolkien's memories, which point to *The Hobbit* having been told at the end of the 1920s, perhaps in 1928 or 1929, when Christopher Tolkien was four and five years old; and together these better accommodate Tolkien's assertion that his younger sons had to 'grow up' to the story: for by 1930, when John, the eldest, was thirteen, Michael was already ten and Christopher six, ages at which *The Hobbit* has since pleased countless readers or listeners, let alone two boys who appear to have been notably intelligent and creative. But then – even so – there remain Tolkien's own recollections of having begun *The Hobbit* after January 1930, in 20 rather than 22 Northmoor Road, and one may wish to give extra weight to declarations by the author himself.

The course of composition of *The Hobbit* is difficult to discern partly because Tolkien's comments on the history of the work tend to be vague when expressing the passage of time. The examples of 'for a long time' and 'for some years' in his letter to W.H. Auden have been noted already. The phrase 'It was some time before I discovered what [the word *hobbit*] referred to' in his 1955 letter to Houghton Mifflin could refer to years, months, or only weeks. In his Bodleian Library note, probably from the end of the 1950s or from the 1960s, 'the story . . . unfolded itself gradually' leaves us in the dark as to what he considered 'gradual'. In a letter of February 1938 to the newspaper *The Observer* he said that 'the tale halted in the telling for about a year at two separate points' (*Letters*, p. 32), without specifying which points or which year. In a 1957 interview with Ruth Harshaw ('Carnival of Books') he said that it was only 'some months later' when he thought that the opening words of *The Hobbit* were

> too good to leave just on the back of an examination [paper]. . . . I wrote the first chapter first – then I forgot about it, then I wrote another part. I myself can still see the gaps. There is a very big gap after they [Bilbo, the wizard, and the dwarves] reach the eyrie of the Eagles. After that I really didn't know how to go on. [private transcription]

But in a 1967 interview with Charlotte and Denis Plimmer he said of 'In a hole in the ground there lived a hobbit': 'I knew no more about the creatures [Hobbits] than that, and it was years before his [Bilbo's] story grew' ('The Man Who Understands Hobbits', *Daily Telegraph Magazine*, 22 March 1968, p. 32). And in a 1966 interview with Richard Plotz the hiatus between inspiration and first manuscript seems to vanish entirely:

> I was doing the dull work of correcting examination papers when I came upon a blank page that someone had turned in. A blank page is a boon to all examination markers, and I was overjoyed. I turned over the paper and wrote on the back – 'In a hole in the ground there lived a Hobbit.' I had no idea what a Hobbit was. Or perhaps I did sense it was a little creature of some sort. But I had never heard the word and had never used it. Then I decided, here is the beginning of a good book for my children, and I began to write. ['J.R.R. Tolkien Talks about the Discovery of Middle-earth, the Origins of Elvish', *Seventeen*, January 1967, p. 92]

At least, he invented a story, whether or not he began by writing it out on paper. The evidence of stories such as *Roverandom* and *Farmer Giles of Ham* suggests that, like these, *The Hobbit* most likely began as an oral tale. Indeed, as Humphrey Carpenter reported in 1977, John and Michael Tolkien 'are not certain that what they were listening to [in the study of 22 Northmoor Road in the late 1920s] was necessarily a *written* story: they believe that it may well have been a number of impromptu tales which were later absorbed into *The Hobbit* proper' (*Biography*, p. 177). It may be that the greater part of *The Hobbit* was not set on paper until the early 1930s, or was not developed at length until then, and that this is what Tolkien remembered when he dated the origin of the work. But the young Christopher Tolkien seems to have known *The Hobbit* as a written story, and to have described it as such in his 1937 letter to Father Christmas, as a work *read* to the Tolkien boys; and it must be acknowledged that *The Hobbit* was, or became as it grew, a longer and more complex children's story than Tolkien had written before, perhaps too long and too complex to be told (and retold) wholly from memory.

The earliest extant manuscript of any part of *The Hobbit* consists of only six pages on three leaves. On the last of these leaves, for a long time separated from the others and reproduced in the 1987 fiftieth anniversary edition of *The Hobbit*, Tolkien later wrote: 'Only page [i.e. leaf] preserved of the first scrawled copy of *The Hobbit* which did not reach beyond the first chapter.' Even the three surviving leaves, however, are incomplete, lacking the text from the beginning of the story until just after the dwarves sing about their 'long-forgotten gold', the dragon's hoard beneath the Lonely Mountain; the fragment commences: 'As they sang the hobbit felt the love of beautiful things made by hands and by cunning and by magic moving through him . . .' and continues almost to the end of Chapter 1 as finally published. (For convenience, here we will refer to portions of *The Hobbit* by their published chapter divisions.) This is perhaps part of the initial draft to which Tolkien referred in his letter to W.H. Auden – 'for some years I got no further than the production of Thror's Map' – described in these words because a sketch of *Thror's Map* is drawn on the 'only page' Tolkien wrongly thought to be still extant, and is discussed in the accompanying dialogue. The three leaves bear no date, but are clearly from an early stage, when the wizard was called 'Bladorthin' (later 'Gandalf'), the chief dwarf was 'Gandalf' (later 'Thorin'), and the dragon was 'Pryftan' (later 'Smaug').

The earliest typescript of *The Hobbit*, also a fragment, fortunately begins with the first words of the book and (in so far as the typescript and the manuscript fragment overlap) suggests that the original manuscript may not have been substantially different, although Tolkien made many improvements in revision. The whole of this typescript comprises eighteen leaves, but of these the first twelve, on a different paper stock and numbered in pencil rather than in the typewriter, are obviously of a separate and certainly early making. On p. 12 the dragon was named 'Pryftan' as typed, which Tolkien changed by hand to 'Smaug'; and almost precisely from the point at which this page ends, in mid-sentence, he began a new manuscript, numbered from '13' to continue the sequence of pages. In this the name 'Smaug' (together with 'Bladorthin' the wizard and 'Gandalf' the chief dwarf) appears *ab initio*.

From this later manuscript Humphrey Carpenter concluded

> that the actual writing of the main part of the story [to the death of Smaug] was done over a comparatively short period of time: the ink, paper, and handwriting style are consistent, the pages are numbered consecutively, and there are almost no chapter divisions. It would appear that Tolkien wrote the story fluently and with little hesitation, for there are comparatively few erasures or revisions. [*Biography*, pp. 177–8]

In fact, the principal manuscript is not so straightforward. Folios 13 through 50, that is, through the first few paragraphs of Chapter 5, were indeed written fluently, or rather are in a quick but almost casual script, without substantial emendation: of course, the earliest part of the book had been worked out already in manuscript and typescript, and it may be that the first episodes of the story were already so well established in oral form that writing them down took little effort. Near the end of manuscript folio 50, however, there was a definite break: a slight gap in the text, and then fresh writing in a darker ink. The script, especially from folio 51, shows a distinct change of mood by the writer. Moreover, the text for most of two difficult chapters, 5 and 6 (including the riddle contest between Bilbo and Gollum, and the escape of the company from goblins and wolves), was now more frequently emended, clearly in the process of writing.

Tolkien claimed in the 'Carnival of Books' interview that there was a 'very big gap' after Bilbo, the wizard, and the dwarves reach the eagles' eyrie at the end of Chapter 6: and indeed, there is an apparent change of script from folio 80, after the wizard has told the company of his intention to leave them, and before he introduces them to Medwed (later 'Beorn'). But there is no compelling physical or textual evidence of as large a gap as Tolkien recalled, and indeed one finds small changes in Tolkien's handwriting throughout the *Hobbit* manuscript, which may mean no more than that the author briefly rested his hand. The next obvious break in the work does not occur until roughly the beginning of Chapter 9, just as the dwarves are captured by the wood-elves: folios 119 and following of the manuscript, for the equivalent of some five chapters, are on a different paper, ruled rather than plain, on which Tolkien now wrote on only one side rather than two.

At this point he also paused to make notes, to determine the outcome of the story – here, remarkably, he thought to have Bilbo kill the dragon and ride to safety in a golden bowl carried on a river of dragon's blood – and he decided to change the names of the chief dwarf and the wizard. On manuscript folio 125 the dwarf 'Gandalf' enters a barrel in the wood-elves' halls, but on folio 131, in Lake-town, he emerges as 'Thorin'; and when the wizard is again mentioned by name, much later in the tale, he is 'Gandalf' rather than 'Bladorthin'. What, if anything, Tolkien's sons thought about the sudden renaming of important characters by their father in the midst of telling the story, in particular the confusing transferral of the name 'Gandalf' from one character to another, is nowhere recorded and is now beyond recollection.

This section of the manuscript apparently continued through the episode ('Fire and Water', published as Chapter 14) in which Smaug attacks Lake-town and is killed by Bard, just to the point at which the dragon falls from the sky. (As explained below, 'Not at Home', published as Chapter 13, did not yet exist.) That Tolkien then ceased to work on the story for a period of time, after manuscript folio 155, seems almost certain. Changes in script and paper are evident from folio 156, and there are also marked differences in tone from the point that Bard reappears, when Tolkien at once introduces weighty issues of property, politics, and war. It may be noted as well that in the complete master typescript of *The Hobbit* that Tolkien began to prepare concurrent with this phase of writing (the wizard is 'Gandalf' and the chief dwarf is 'Thorin' throughout) there is an obvious gap in the typing near the end of 'Fire and

Water', after the sentence 'And that was the end of Smaug and Esgaroth, but not of Bard'; and whereas the sheets of typescript to this point were numbered in the typewriter, the remainder of the book, 'Not at Home' (later inserted) and Chapters 15–19, is distinguished by folio numbers added in pencil.

According to Humphrey Carpenter, Tolkien abandoned the story after describing the death of Smaug because his sons 'were growing up and no longer asked for "Winter Reads", so there was no reason why *The Hobbit* should ever be finished' (*Biography*, pp. 179–80); and yet as late as 1936 *Owen Barfield's children's book *The Silver Trumpet* was reported to be a great success among Tolkien's sons and daughter. In his December 1937 letter to Father Christmas, Christopher Tolkien wrote that when his father read *The Hobbit* to his sons 'the ending chapters were rather roughly done, and not typed out at all' (quoted in *The Hobbit* (Unwin Hyman, 1987), p. vii). Carpenter, expanding upon this statement, asserts that the final chapters 'were not even written in manuscript', that for the benefit of his children Tolkien only narrated an impromptu conclusion to the story (*Biography*, p. 179). If so, it was an incomplete work, relative to its published form, which Tolkien lent to his friend *C.S. Lewis in early 1933, and which prompted these comments by Lewis in a letter of 4 February in that year: 'Since term began [15 January] I have had a delightful time reading a children's story Tolkien has just written. . . . Whether it is really *good* (I think it is until the end) is of course another question: still more, whether it will succeed with modern children' (*They Stand Together: The Letters of C.S. Lewis to Arthur Greeves (1914–63)* (1979), p. 449). Here Lewis seems to describe a completed work – at least, he makes no overt mention that it was yet to be finished (neither, of course, does he make overt mention of *The Hobbit* by name, but it could be no other work at this time). His comment 'whether it is really *good* (I think it is until the end)' may refer to a conclusion, at the death of Smaug, with many aspects of the story still unresolved; but the letter is too imprecise to know definitely what Lewis meant.

In any event, thanks to the *terminus ad quem* provided by this letter, the period of initial development of *The Hobbit* can be delimited to only two and a half years, if one accepts Tolkien's date of 1930 for its first inspiration, or to six and a half years at the extreme bounds of possibility (1926–32). In addition, one may assume that by the beginning of 1933 Tolkien had also finished, to the same extent as the *Hobbit* manuscript, the master typescript of the book, 'made in the small neat typeface of the Hammond machine [Tolkien's typewriter], with italics for the songs, [which] was shown to favoured friends, together with its accompanying maps (and perhaps already a few illustrations)' (*Biography*, p. 180). He took pains to make this presentable, correcting or deleting words and passages neatly in ink, and typing out corrected passages on slips and pasting them precisely over earlier text – clearly it was produced to be read by others, and it was surely this, rather than the manuscript with its occasional rough workings and superseded forms of names, that Tolkien lent to friends ('though strictly it was forced on the friends by me', letter to C.A. Furth, 31 August 1937, *Letters*, p. 21). That it already included illustrations seems beyond question, though which of the surviving original *Hobbit* pictures were among them can be only a matter of conjecture. Likely candidates include *Mirkwood, The Hill: Hobbiton, Trolls' Hill, Riding Down into Rivendell, The Misty Mountains Looking West from the Eagles' Eyrie towards Goblin Gate, Firelight in Beorn's House,* an untitled view of the entrance to the Elvenking's halls, *Esgaroth,* and *The Front Gate* (see *Artist and Illustrator,* figs. 88, 92, 99, 104, 110, 115, 117, 126, 135).

Between 1933 and 1936 the *Hobbit* typescript 'wandered' to other readers (*Letters,* p. 21), including *M.E. (Elaine) Griffiths, a B.Litt. student under Tolkien's supervision; the *Reverend Mother St Teresa Gale, Mother Superior at Cherwell Edge (*Oxford and environs), a convent of the Society of the Holy Child Jesus to which was attached a hostel for Catholic women in the Society of Oxford Home-Students; and most importantly, *Susan Dagnall, a member of the staff of the publisher George Allen & Unwin. Tolkien gave several accounts of how *The Hobbit* came to the attention of Allen & Unwin: he had lent it to Elaine Griffiths, or to the Reverend Mother, and one or the other of these women in turn lent it to Susan Dagnall (see especially *Letters,* pp. 215, 346, and 374) – the details vary and cannot all be accurate, but it is not of much moment which account is the most factual. Suffice it to say that Susan Dagnall visited Oxford, probably early in 1936, almost certainly on professional business, to see Elaine Griffiths, who had been commissioned by Allen & Unwin to revise the Modern English translation by John R. Clark Hall of *Beowulf* and the 'Finnesburg Fragment'; and while visiting Griffiths, who at the time lodged at Cherwell Edge, she saw the *Hobbit* typescript or was encouraged by Griffiths to borrow it from Tolkien – on whom Dagnall may have intended to call in any case, because he had agreed to supervise Griffiths' work on the Clark Hall book and to write a brief introduction. By whatever route, Dagnall read *The Hobbit,* was impressed by what she read, and convinced its author that the book should be published. According to Humphrey Carpenter, Dagnall 'sent the typescript back to Tolkien, asking him if he would finish it, and preferably soon, so that the book could be considered for publication in the following year' (*Biography,* p. 180; this, however, cannot be confirmed by publisher's records, in which there is no relevant correspondence from before October 1936).

Tolkien now (as it seems) returned to *The Hobbit* at the point where he had left off some three years earlier, at the death of Smaug. He wrote 'Not at Home', originally as Chapter 14, and the first part of 'The Gathering of the Clouds' (published Chapter 15), but then decided that the structure of the story would be improved if 'Not at Home' preceded 'Fire and Water', so that in the former chapter neither Bilbo and the dwarves nor the reader can know whether the dragon will suddenly return to his lair. (In the previous order of chapters, the reader knew that Smaug was already dead when the company ventured into and out of the Mountain.) 'Fire and Water' now became Chapter 14, and was neatly given a new sentence at the beginning to make the episode a flashback. Tolkien added text to the end of the chapter as well, and typed a small part of it in a blank space on the final sheet of the existing typescript. From this point he worked out the remaining text in a new manuscript, and added this to the master typescript to send to Allen & Unwin. (He also produced, assisted by his son Michael, another complete typescript of *The Hobbit*, but by accident or design it was the earlier typescript that he sent to Allen & Unwin, perhaps because it was already proofread and corrected, and its pages were already numbered.) On 10 August 1936 Tolkien wrote to his son Christopher that '*The Hobbit* is now nearly finished, and the publishers [are] clamouring for it' (quoted in *Biography*, p. 180) – whether a reference to the completion of the final chapters, or to the preparation of the final typescript, it is impossible to say. It may be guessed, however, that he did not turn back to *The Hobbit* until the summer vacation of 1936, after the end of Trinity Term on 20 June. He submitted the finished typescript to Allen & Unwin on 3 October.

PUBLICATION

According to the publisher's receipt book (George Allen & Unwin archive, University of Reading) *The Hobbit* now was read by *Stanley Unwin, chairman of the firm, and by the noted children's poet and author Rose Fyleman, at that time a freelance reader and translator for Allen & Unwin. Then, as he had done with other children's books under consideration, Unwin passed the typescript to his ten-year-old son *Rayner, and on 30 October 1936 received the following report (*sic*):

> Bilbo Baggins was a hobbit who lived in his hobbit-hole and *never* went for adventures, at last Gandalf the wizard and his dwarves perswaded him to go. He had a very exiting time fighting goblins and wargs. at last they got to the lonley mountain; Smaug, the dragon who gawreds it is killed and after a terrific battle with the goblins he returned home – rich!
> This book, with the help of maps, does not need any illustrations it is good and should appeal to all children between the ages of 5 and 9. [quoted in *Biography*, pp. 180–1]

Stanley Unwin accepted *The Hobbit* for publication officially on 2 December 1936. By then the wheels of production were already turning. On 4 December Susan Dagnall sent Tolkien a specimen typeset page for his approval. On 8 December Tolkien wrote, by invitation, a descriptive paragraph about the book for his publisher's 1937 summer announcements brochure. The production of maps to accompany *The Hobbit* also began quickly and in earnest. Tolkien's original plan was to include five maps which, with one exception, would trace Bilbo's journey from Hobbiton to the Lonely Mountain. He laboured on *Thror's Map* in particular: he wanted it to appear in the book as if a facsimile of an actual document, with the 'moon-letters' mentioned by Elrond in Chapter 3 printed as a mirror-image on the reverse side of the sheet, so that they would read correctly through the paper when held to a light. In the event, only *Thror's*

Map and the more general map, *Wilderland*, were published, and for reasons of economy were printed as endpapers rather than inserted sheets, the former with runes necessarily on the same side as the rest of the art.

Although Rayner Unwin had concluded in his reader's report that *The Hobbit* did not need illustrations other than maps, Tolkien had already drawn several pictures for the 'home manuscript' (so called in *Letters*, p. 14, probably the master typescript described above) and continued to think of *The Hobbit* as an illustrated book during the early stages of its production. On 4 January 1937 he submitted to Allen & Unwin four redrawn illustrations, and six more on 17 January. The publisher in fact had not allowed any cost margin for these, but was charmed by Tolkien's pictures and agreed to include them – much to the book's advantage. They enhance the text, providing details of landscape and architecture the author does not describe in words. (See further, *Artist and Illustrator*, ch. 4.) Tolkien also provided art and lettering for the original dust-jacket – an enduring design still (with small modifications) reproduced on some editions – and he was consulted by the publisher about the design of the original binding and about the book's interior typography. 'I marvel (but am not entirely surprised)', Rayner Unwin said many years after the event,

> that George Allen & Unwin really thought they were economising by using the author as an amateur designer-cum-illustrator. But in those happy days cost-benefit analysis had scarcely been invented. I believe that the overall standards of editing and production were probably higher than they are now, but I know of no editor in any publishing company today who would be allowed to indulge an author to the extent that [production manager] Charles Furth and Susan Dagnall indulged Tolkien. [*George Allen & Unwin: A Remembrancer* (1999), p. 78]

Tolkien received proofs of *The Hobbit* in February 1937. He noted 'very few divergences from copy . . . but I ought to have given the manuscript a revision – in places there were considerable confusions of narrative and geography!' (letter to C.A. Furth, ?10 March 1937, Tolkien-George Allen & Unwin archive, HarperCollins). His corrections were heavy, sometimes to entire blocks of text, which made hard work for the printers. He corrected the revised proofs in April, this time more lightly, 'to rectify narrative errors that escaped my previous care' and other errors 'that descended from copy and also escaped' (letter to Allen & Unwin, 13 April 1937, Tolkien-George Allen & Unwin archive, HarperCollins). Among other changes in proof, he removed several references to the primary world of the reader rather than the fairy-tale world of the hobbit: 'squirrels' for example, in Bilbo's question about the 'skin-changer' Beorn in Chapter 7 ('What! a furrier, a man that calls rabbits conies, when he doesn't turn their skins into squirrels?') was originally 'arctic fox', and most remarkably, 'the wild Were-worms in the Last Desert' in Chapter 1 at first were 'the Wild Wireworms of China' (Special Collections and University Archives, John P. Raynor, S.J., Library, Marquette University).

The Hobbit was published on 21 September 1937. In December of that year, Tolkien submitted to Allen & Unwin a list of new emendations, too late, however, to correct the second printing which already had been rushed to press to satisfy a strong demand for the book. Four of five colour illustrations by Tolkien were first added to this printing (lacking *Bilbo Woke Up with the Early Sun in His Eyes*, see *Artist and Illustrator*, fig. 113), though they had been commissioned by the Houghton Mifflin Company of Boston (*Publishers); a different selection of four was published in the first American edition in 1938 (including *Bilbo Woke*, but lacking *Bilbo Comes to the Huts of the Raft-elves*, see *Artist and Illustrator*, fig. 124). A third Allen & Unwin printing, incorporating several corrections, was delayed by wartime conditions until 1943, although dated '1942'. A fourth printing, dated '1946', appeared in 1947.

LATER EDITIONS

In September 1947 Tolkien sent Stanley Unwin further corrections to *The Hobbit*, and '(for the possible amusement of yourself and Rayner) a specimen of re-writing of Chapter V of that work, which would simplify, though not necessarily improve, my present task' (letter to Stanley Unwin, 21 September 1947, *Letters*, p. 124) – the writing of a sequel to *The Hobbit*, *The Lord of the Rings* (see below). Unwin took the 're-writing' as another correction and handed on to his production department. Three years later, when another printing of *The Hobbit* was needed, Allen & Unwin addressed the corrections Tolkien had sent in 1947 and reset Chapter 5 as revised. Tolkien was astonished when he received new proofs:

> The thing took me much by surprise. It is now a long while since I sent in the proposed alteration ... and tentatively suggested the slight remodelling of the original *Hobbit*. . . . I never heard any more about it at all; and I assumed that alteration of the original book was ruled out. . . . If I had had warning I could possibly have shortened and tightened the revision; but if you are (as appears) content, and prepared to make the necessary changes in pagination etc. then I am quite content also. [letter to W.N. Beard, 1 August 1950, Tolkien-George Allen & Unwin archive, Harper-Collins; partly printed in *Letters*, p. 141]

In Chapter 5 as it was first published Gollum, although willing to kill and eat Bilbo, nonetheless treats the riddle contest as sacred; and when he loses and cannot give Bilbo the present he had promised him (the magic ring that confers invisibility), he apologizes and shows the hobbit a way out of the caverns. But in *The Lord of the Rings* Gollum's ring is revealed to be an object of great power, the One Ring made by the Dark Lord, Sauron, which exerts a corrupting hold on its bearer and which would not have been easily given away as a 'present'; while Gollum himself is shown to be exceedingly treacherous, not likely to be courteous or to honour the terms of a riddle game. In revised

Chapter 5, first published in the printing of 1951, Gollum promises not a 'present' but to show Bilbo a way out, should the hobbit win their contest; and when Bilbo does win, Gollum intends to kill him with the aid of the ring. Even without the ring, he attempts to do so, once he realizes that the object is now in Bilbo's possession. As revised, the chapter was now in better accord with the history and nature of the One Ring as it had developed in the sequel; but rather than ignore the original version of the chapter, Tolkien cleverly decided to embrace it as the story that Bilbo first told to Gandalf and the dwarves and that he wrote in his memoirs. In *The Lord of the Rings* it is made clear that the Ring, as part of its attempt to return to its malevolent creator, established an unhealthy hold on Bilbo from the moment he found it (or, as may be, the Ring found him), causing the otherwise honest hobbit to lie to his companions.

Since, however, *The Lord of the Rings* was not yet due to be published, in the meantime Tolkien explained the differences in the Gollum episode between the first and second editions in an author's note added with the *Hobbit* printing of 1951. In this he also addressed a discrepancy that had been noted by readers, concerning the dwarf-kings Thrain and Thror, relative to *Thror's Map*, and he made a few additional revisions, to Bilbo's account of the riddle-game, in Chapter 6 to accord with Chapter 5.

By now Tolkien had rejected the children's book as a form in which he could tell further stories of Middle-earth – as the lands in which *The Hobbit* is set, but there not named, came to be called in *The Lord of the Rings*. Indeed, one may see him moving in this direction already in the final chapters of *The Hobbit*, as Paul Edmund Thomas has observed (see below). C.S. Lewis also wrote of this 'very curious shift in tone' late in *The Hobbit*: 'As the humour and homeliness of the early chapters, the sheer "Hobbitry", dies away we pass insensibly into the world of epic' ('On Stories', *Essays Presented to Charles Williams* (1947), p. 104). At the end of 1937, when Tolkien at the request of Stanley Unwin began to write a sequel to *The Hobbit*, he approached *The Lord of the Rings* at first very much in the same children's-story manner and tone in which he had written the earlier parts of *The Hobbit*, no doubt because he still felt that this approach was expected in a book wanted, once again, for the children's market. But he found that this mode of writing was no longer to his taste and could not be sustained, and from time to time he expressed regret that he had employed it in *The Hobbit*. In a letter to Walter Allen in April 1959, to give only one instance, he wrote that

> [*The Hobbit*] was overtly addressed to children for two reasons: I had at that time children of my own and was accustomed to making up (ephemeral) stories for them; I had been brought up to believe that there was a real and special connexion between children and fairy-stories. Or rather to believe that this was a received opinion of my world and of publishers. I doubted it, since it did not accord with my personal experience of my own taste, nor with my observation of children (notably my own). But the convention was strong. [*Letters*, p. 298]

Apparently in 1960 Tolkien began to revise *The Hobbit* more substantially, recasting it in language not 'overtly addressed to children'. But before long he abandoned this text – recognizing, perhaps, that for better or worse, he had created *The Hobbit* as a children's book and a fairy-tale, and to make it otherwise would be to deny its essential nature and destroy much of its charm. Although he might have pleased critics who have found *The Hobbit* as written to be 'filled with a whimsy few adults can accept with pleasure' (Randel Helms, *Tolkien's World* (1974), p. 19) and marred by an intrusive 'parental' narrator, he surely would have displeased those readers who are gladly drawn into the book, as written and as it remains, by its style and by the personality of its narrator, drawn as it were into the company of the Tolkien children listening to their father tell them a story.

In the revision of 1960 Tolkien also enlarged and emended Chapter 2, adding an episode of Bilbo and company fording a river, partly to harmonize the journey of Bilbo and his companions with the geography of *The Lord of the Rings*; this was read at the 1987 Mythopoeic Society conference in Milwaukee, Wisconsin by Christopher Tolkien. But since the revised text was never used, inconsistencies remain between *The Hobbit* and its sequel in regard to distances and time taken to travel through the same territory.

Tolkien emended *The Hobbit* again for the American and British editions of 1966, the former in part to ensure the validity of his copyright in the work in the United States (*Ace Books controversy). On 24 August 1965 he wrote to Rayner Unwin regarding the new Unwin Books edition of *The Hobbit* (published 1966):

> I have (I hope) resisted the inclination to 'improve' *The Hobbit* – except for removing the 'author-to-reader' asides in some places: very irritating to intelligent children (as some have said). There are some correction[s] due to the actual errors and discrepancies in the tale itself; some that try to make things clearer. But since in order to spot these things – including printer's errors that still survive! – one has to read the whole with line-to-line care, it seemed to me a pity not to get rid of a few happy-go-lucky passages that are quite out of joint. *The Hobbit* is taken as a prologue to *The Lord of the Rings* and though no one expects consistency between the two to be exact, it is a pity that some passages in *The Hobbit* should be completely impossible in *The Lord of the Rings*. [Tolkien-George Allen & Unwin archive, HarperCollins]

Other editions and printings of *The Hobbit* also sometimes have been corrected or otherwise emended, for good but not always inarguable reasons, and with each resetting misprints have been introduced as well as repaired. Most famously, the 1961 Puffin (Penguin) Books edition, the first paperback, altered Tolkien's preferred *dwarves* to *dwarfs*, etc.; see further, **Chronology**. At this writing, the most accurate text of *The Hobbit* is contained in *The Annotated Hobbit*, ed. Douglas A. Anderson (rev. and expanded edn. 2002).

Many of the changes made to *The Hobbit* in its complex history are set forth in detail in *The Annotated Hobbit*, and in *Descriptive Bibliography*, pp. 15 ff. The implications of Tolkien's revisions to Chapter 5 are discussed at length by Bonniejean Christensen in her 'Gollum's Character Transformation in *The Hobbit*', in *A Tolkien Compass* (1975). In regard to the issue of Thrain and Thror, see Christopher Tolkien, **The Treason of Isengard*, pp. 159–60. Other analyses of note are Constance B. Hieatt, 'The Text of *The Hobbit*: Putting Tolkien's Notes in Order', *English Studies in Canada* 7, no. 2 (Summer 1981); David Cofield, 'Changes in Hobbits: Textual Differences in Editions of *The Hobbit*', *Beyond Bree*, April 1986; and Christopher Tolkien, 'Notes on the Differences in Editions of *The Hobbit* Cited by Mr. David Cofield', *Beyond Bree*, July 1986.

In 1952 Tolkien privately tape recorded revised Chapter 5 of *The Hobbit* while a guest at the home of his friend *George Sayer. This recording was first issued commercially in 1975, with other material, as *J.R.R. Tolkien Reads and Sings His The Hobbit and The Fellowship of the Ring*, and reissued in 2001 as part of *The J.R.R. Tolkien Audio Collection*; see further, *Recordings. A recording of the complete *Hobbit*, read by Rob Inglis, was first issued in 1991. Abridged readings of *The Hobbit* by Nicol Williamson and Martin Shaw were first issued as commercial recordings in 1974 and 1993 respectively. An abridgement by Brian Sibley, read by Michael Hordern, was broadcast on BBC radio in 1981. See also *Adaptations.

CRITICISM

Most reviews of *The Hobbit* on its first publication welcomed it enthusiastically, not a few even immediately to the ranks of classic children's books. Not all were intelligent appraisals of the book: some reviewers seem not to have ventured much beyond its first chapter, and many relied overmuch on the publisher's blurb, which said that Tolkien had written *The Hobbit* for his four children (thus including Priscilla, not born until 1929), and which compared the work to *Alice's Adventures in Wonderland*, Tolkien and Lewis Carroll having both been Oxford dons. (For Tolkien's own comments on the blurb, see *Letters*, pp. 20–2.) Other critics, however, rejected this comparison but offered many analogues of their own in attempts to put *The Hobbit* into literary perspective.

Of its earliest reviewers two are particularly notable. The anonymous writer in the *Times Literary Supplement* of 2 October 1937 – in fact Tolkien's friend C.S. Lewis – pointed out that both *The Hobbit* and *Alice* 'belong to a very small class of books which have nothing in common save that each admits us to a world of its own – a world that seems to have been going on before we stumbled into it but which, once found by the right reader, becomes indispensable to him.' Among these are also *Flatland* by Edwin A. Abbott, *Phantastes* by George MacDonald, and *The Wind in the Willows* by *Kenneth Grahame. 'Though all is marvellous,' Lewis continued, 'nothing is arbitrary:

all the inhabitants of Wilderland seem to have the same unquestionable right
to their existence as those of our own world, though the fortunate child who
meets them will have no notion – and his unlearned elders not much more
– of the deep sources in our blood and tradition from which they spring'
(p. 714). Lewis also wrote a short review of *The Hobbit* for the London *Times*
of 8 October 1937, alluding again to *The Wind in the Willows* (Bilbo 'is as
prosaic as Mole') and remarking that 'in this book a number of good things,
never before united, have come together: a fund of humour, an understanding
of children, and a happy fusion of the scholar's with the poet's grasp of mythology' (p. 20).

Richard Hughes in 'Books for Pre-Adults' (*New Statesman and Nation*, 4
December 1937) observed that Tolkien does not serve up 'Nordic mythology'
at second-hand,

> rather he contributes to it at first hand: and thus his wholly original story
> of adventure among goblins, elves and dragons, instead of being a *tour-
> de-force*, a separate creation of his own, gives rather the impression of a
> well-informed glimpse into the life of a wide other-world; a world wholly
> real, and with a quite matter-of-fact, supernatural natural-history of its
> own. [pp. 944, 946]

To those adults who think that parts of *The Hobbit* are too terrifying for reading to a child,

> I myself think this caution is a mistaken one. For a child has a natural
> capacity for terror which it is next to impossible to curtail; and if you
> withhold from him such proper objects of terror as goblins, trolls, and
> dragons, he will work himself just as frantic over an odd-shaped bed-
> post – or the over-hearing of such a frightful piece of news as that *there is
> a barrister pleading in the court*. [p. 946]

Hughes had earlier conveyed much the same sentiment in a letter to Stanley
Unwin. Tolkien was 'particularly interested' to read it, and flattered by Hughes'
compliments. But the 'snag' that Hughes foresaw, 'that many parents ... may
be afraid that certain parts of [*The Hobbit*] would be too terrifying for bedside
reading', 'appears in everything', Tolkien said: 'though actually the presence
(even if only on the borders) of the terrible is, I believe, what gives this imagined world its verisimilitude. A safe fairy-land is untrue to all worlds' (letter to
Stanley Unwin, 15 October 1937, *Letters*, p. 24).

The Hobbit was nominated in Britain for the prestigious Carnegie Medal for
1937, awarded by the Library Association to the outstanding children's book
of the year. It lost to *The Family from One End Street* by Eve Garnett, but in
America it won the *New York Herald Tribune* Children's Spring Book Festival contest for the best children book published in the United States between
1 January and 1 June 1938. Today it is well established among classic works for

children, and is mentioned in every major survey of children's literature in English, perhaps most memorably by *Roger Lancelyn Green in his *Tellers of Tales: Children's Books and Their Authors from 1800 to 1964* (rev. edn. 1965): 'It is a breathtaking book both for its adventures and for its power of transporting us into a clear, keen world of legend come to life, where, as we read, we seem to feel the cold invigorating wind of the North blowing away all the cobwebs of civilization that keep us from venturing out into that bright morning world of high adventure' (pp. 276–7).

And yet it is not universally loved. Jonathan Keates, for example, in his 'Just a Bash at Bilbo' (*The Observer*, 15 March 1987) confessed that he has always hated *The Hobbit*: 'As a work of literature it appears insufferably arch, suffused with the bogus winsomeness of a pampered child at a fancy-dress party.' One suspects that many late judgements of *The Hobbit* such as this have been coloured by antagonism towards its sequel. Certainly with the publication of *The Lord of the Rings* in 1954–5 *The Hobbit* came to be seen often as no more than its 'prelude', a lesser work in the shadow of a masterpiece, although when *The Hobbit* was written *The Lord of the Rings* was not yet conceived. Of this attitude the most extreme instance is that of Brian Rosebury in his *Tolkien: A Critical Assessment* (1992) who relegates *The Hobbit* (and even *The Silmarillion*) to the category of 'minor works'. In his *Tolkien: A Cultural Phenomenon* (2003) he no longer applies that label, but says in similar words:

> For Tolkien's hostile critics, patting *The Hobbit* on the head has become something of a tradition: the critic indicates a benevolent receptiveness towards 'fantasy' (when confined to the marginal world of children's books) before proceeding to ridicule the ambitious scale and implied adult readership of *The Lord of the Rings*. *The Hobbit* seems to me, on the contrary, to be a likeable patchwork of accomplishments, blunders, and tantalising promises of the Middle-earth to come: flawed by inconsistencies of tone and conception, it is essentially a transitional work, a stopping-off point on Tolkien's creative journey from the rudimentary forms of bedtime story-telling to the richly 'realistic' narrative of *The Lord of the Rings*, a journey that converges in that work with the progressive abandonment of the mannered archaism of the early mythical writings. [pp. 113–14]

Already in 1974 Randel Helms had said much the same in his *Tolkien's World*, describing *The Hobbit* as a necessary stage in Tolkien's development as a writer which culminated in *The Lord of the Rings* – *The Hobbit* 'writ large', with greater intricacy and stature. Tolkien had to write *The Hobbit* to learn that if a fairy-story is to be worth reading, 'it is worthy to be written for and read by adults', and then he had to write the essay *'On Fairy-Stories' (1939, from which this quotation is drawn), to work out critically what his discovery meant. 'In his children's story [Tolkien] discovered his theme, learned what he had to say and how the fairy story could say it; captured by that theme, he was drawn irresistibly into a world that would make it credible' (Helms, p. 20). Although this argument is not without merit, the reader may wish to consider it in light of sources unavailable to earlier critics, especially *Roverandom* and the *'Father Christmas' letters, as other stages in the development of Tolkien's craft, and the early workings of *The Lord of the Rings* published in *The Return of the Shadow* (1988).

Helms concluded that, 'taken in and for itself, Tolkien's children's story deserves little serious, purely literary criticism' (p. 52); and this thought seems to have been shared by other writers, for there has been much less critical literature concerned primarily with *The Hobbit* than with *The Lord of the Rings*, and a comparatively narrower range of approaches to the work. The chief (and almost self-evident) critical view of *The Hobbit* regards Bilbo's journey as a 'coming of age' story, as it were from childhood to maturity. Many writers have also investigated Tolkien's sources for *The Hobbit*, genuine or presumed: in this heavily worked vein Bonniejean Christensen, *Beowulf and The Hobbit: Elegy into Fantasy in J.R.R. Tolkien's Creative Technique* (Ph.D. dissertation, University of Southern California, 1969); Christina Scull, 'The Fairy Tale Tradition', *Mallorn* 23 (Summer 1986); Christina Scull, '*The Hobbit* Considered in Relation to Children's Literature Contemporary with Its Writing and Publication', *Mythlore* 14, no. 2, whole no. 52 (Winter 1987); and Marjorie J. Burns, 'Echoes of William Morris's Icelandic Journals in J.R.R. Tolkien', *Studies in Medievalism* 3, no. 3 (Winter 1991), as well as *The Annotated Hobbit*, ed. Douglas A. Anderson, are particularly useful. Among other notable writings on *The Hobbit* are Lois R. Kuznets, 'Tolkien and the Rhetoric of Childhood' in *Tolkien: New Critical Perspectives* (1981), which places Tolkien's book firmly within the tradition of the British children's classic and makes cogent points concerning his visual imagination; and Paul Bibire, 'By Stock or by Stone: Recurrent Imagery and Narrative Pattern in *The Hobbit*' in *Scholarship & Fantasy: Proceedings of The Tolkien Phenomenon, Turku, May 1992* (1993).

William H. Green in *The Hobbit: A Journey into Maturity* (1995) provides a selective account of the critical reception of *The Hobbit* from its first reviews through *The Road to Middle-earth* by T.A. Shippey (1982). Åke Bertenstam, 'Some Notes on the Reception of *The Hobbit*', *Angerthas* 23 (1988), should also be consulted.

THE HOBBIT AND 'THE SILMARILLION'

One of the most debated questions about *The Hobbit* concerns its original relationship to its author's existing 'Silmarillion' mythology. In a letter to C.A. Furth of 13 May 1937 Tolkien referred to 'the mythology on the outskirts of which the Hobbit [Bilbo Baggins] had his adventures' (*Letters*, p. 17). On 31 August 1937 he wrote again to Furth, noting 'the mythology into which Mr Baggins intrudes', but also that 'the magic and mythology and assumed "history" and most of the names [in *The Hobbit*] (e.g., the epic of the Fall of Gondolin) are, alas!, drawn from unpublished inventions. . . . I believe they give the narrative an air of "reality" and have a northern atmosphere' (*Letters*, p. 21). In a letter to Stanley Unwin of 16 December 1937 Tolkien wrote that *The Hobbit* 'began as a comic tale among conventional and inconsistent Grimm's fairy-tale dwarves, and got drawn into the edge of [the "Silmarillion" mythology] – so that even Sauron the terrible peeped over the edge [as the Necromancer]' (*Letters*, p. 26). On 24 July 1938, as he struggled to write *The Lord of the Rings*, Tolkien told C.A. Furth that his 'mind on the "story" side is really preoccupied with the "pure" fairy stories or mythologies of the *Silmarillion*, into which even Mr Baggins got dragged against my original will . . .' (*Letters*, p. 38). And – not to belabour the point much further – on 7 June 1955 Tolkien wrote to W.H. Auden that '*The Hobbit* was originally quite unconnected [to the mythology], though it inevitably got drawn in to the circumference of the greater construction; and in the event modified it' (*Letters*, p. 215). Indeed, as late as 16 July 1964, in a letter to Christopher Bretherton, Tolkien said that

by the time *The Hobbit* appeared (1937) this 'matter of the Elder Days' [the 'Silmarillion' mythology] was in coherent form. *The Hobbit* was not intended to have anything to do with it. I had the habit while my children were still young of inventing and telling orally, sometimes of writing down, 'children's stories' for their private amusement – according to the notions I then had, and many still have, of what these should be like in style and attitude. . . . *The Hobbit* was intended to be one of them. It had no necessary connexion with the 'mythology', but naturally became attracted towards this dominant construction in my mind, causing the tale to become larger and more heroic as it proceeded. Even so it could really stand quite apart, except for the references (unnecessary, though they give an impression of historical depth) to the Fall of Gondolin . . . ; the branches of the Elfkin . . . , and the quarrel of King Thingol, Lúthien's father, with the Dwarves. . . . [*Letters*, p. 346]

The Hobbit, he told Bretherton, provided the sequel with the magic ring (the central connection between the two books),

the matter of the Dwarves, Durin their prime ancestor, and Moria; and Elrond. The passage in Ch. iii relating him to the Half-elven of the mythology was a fortunate accident, due to the difficulty of constantly inventing good names for new characters. I gave him the name Elrond casually, but as this came from the mythology . . . I made him half-elven. Only in *The Lord* [*of the Rings*] was he identified with the son of Eärendel, and so the great-grandson of Lúthien and Beren, a great power and a Ringholder. [*Letters*, pp. 346–7]

And yet, in a letter to *The Observer* published on 16 January 1938, Tolkien said that *The Hobbit* was 'not consciously based on any other book – save one, and that is unpublished: the "Silmarillion", a history of the Elves, to which frequent allusion is made' (*Letters*, p. 31). On 31 July 1947 he told Stanley Unwin that *The Hobbit* 'was torn rather at random out of a world in which it already existed' (*Letters*, p. 122). Probably late in 1951 he explained to Milton Waldman that the work was 'taken by me as a matter from the great cycle ["The Silmarillion"] susceptible of treatment as a "fairy-story", for children' (*Letters*, p. 159) – and in the same letter, that

> *The Hobbit* ... was quite independently conceived: I did not know as I began it that it belonged [to the mythology]. But it proved to be the discovery of the completion of the whole, its mode of descent to earth, and merging into 'history'. As the high Legends of the beginning are supposed to look at things through Elvish minds, so the middle tale of the Hobbit takes a virtually human point of view – and the last tale [*The Lord of the Rings*] blends them. [*Letters*, p. 145]

And in the Foreword to the second edition of *The Lord of the Rings* (1965) Tolkien made the following statement which could well be interpreted to mean that the cited references to his mythology had been inserted as if *The Hobbit* were its extension:

> [*The Lord of the Rings*] was drawn irresistibly towards the older world [of 'The Silmarillion'], and became an account, as it were, of its end and passing away before its beginning and middle had been told. The process had begun in the writing of *The Hobbit*, in which there were already some references to the older matter: Elrond, Gondolin, the High-elves, and the orcs, as well as glimpses that had arisen unbidden of things higher or deeper or darker than its surface: Durin, Moria, Gandalf, the Necromancer, the Ring.

The question, therefore, is whether Tolkien set *The Hobbit* in the world of 'The Silmarillion' from (or soon after) the former's conception; or whether the *Hobbit* world became that of the mythology only retroactively when *The Lord of the Rings* was conceived as a sequel to *The Hobbit*, and the sequel set consciously in the line of 'The Silmarillion'. To this there can be no simple answer. Randel Helms in *Tolkien and the Silmarils* (1981) argues that Tolkien apparently

> never recognized the extent to which *The Silmarillion* served as a source of *The Hobbit*. Tolkien's Foreword to *The Lord of the Rings* indicates only that *The Hobbit* contains 'some references to the older matter' of *The Silmarillion*, such as Elrond, the orcs [goblins], and the Necromancer. He has forgotten, or more likely never understood, that more than merely containing references to the world of *The Silmarillion*, *The Hobbit* is in fact a retelling of parts of its story. ... [p. 80]

There is a fundamental progression, Helms maintains, from 'The Silmarillion' to *The Hobbit* to *The Lord of the Rings*: '*The Hobbit* stands in large part as a version for children of some portions of *The Silmarillion*, and that *The Lord of the Rings* is virtually an enlarged retelling of its predecessor *The Hobbit*' (p. 73). As proof, he describes parallels between, for instance, the dragon Glaurung in 'The Silmarillion' laying waste to the underground kingdom of Nargothrond in which he then lives upon a hoard of treasure, and Smaug in *The Hobbit* similarly invading the dwarves' realm under the Lonely Mountain; and between the 'Silmarillion' story of the Nauglamír, the Necklace of the Dwarves, and the *Hobbit* story of the Arkenstone.

To this we are inclined to reply that *dragons traditionally cause havoc and lie upon hoards, and that some motifs, such as that of the treasure among treasures, may recur in myths and fairy-stories without being consciously based one upon another. It must be remarked as well that an author may legitimately borrow from himself without intending to evoke another work, no less than a composer may use a segment from an earlier work, especially an unpublished manuscript, in a later composition. Thus in *Roverandom* the whale Uin carries the title character to within sight of Elvenhome in the far West – a clear reference to Aman, the home of the Valar in Tolkien's mythology – and yet *Roverandom* just as clearly does not belong to 'The Silmarillion' but merely touches it in passing. Nor, most strikingly, are the jolly elves of Rivendell in *The Hobbit* (or, for that matter, the North Pole elves of the 'Father Christmas' letters) very like the noble and tragic race of Elves in Tolkien's legends of the Elder Days (or of *The Lord of the Rings*), although they share the same name.

In addition, it must be understood that when Tolkien wrote the new Foreword to *The Lord of the Rings* he was concerned to present that work and *The Hobbit* as part of a continuous story – for so they were, as soon as *The Lord of the Rings* was conceived and despite lingering inconsistencies between them; and that earlier, when he wrote of 'The Silmarillion', *The Hobbit*, and *The Lord of the Rings* to Milton Waldman, Tolkien was attempting to convince Waldman, of the firm Collins, to accept the first and last of these works for publication. *The Hobbit* was their link, a known (and successful) quantity, and by now an integral part of the 'stuff that is connected with my imaginary world' (*Letters*, p. 143).

Christopher Tolkien notes in his foreword to *The Return of the Shadow* that his father clearly (one may say, very forcefully) expressed his view of *The Hobbit* in relation to 'The Silmarillion' in a letter to G.E. Selby of 14 December 1937:

> I don't much approve of *The Hobbit* myself, preferring my own mythology (which is just touched on) with its consistent nomenclature – Elrond, Gondolin, and Esgaroth *have escaped out of it* – and organized history, to this rabble of Eddaic-named dwarves out of Völuspá [in the *Elder Edda*], newfangled hobbits and gollums (invented in an idle hour) and Anglo-Saxon runes. [*The Return of the Shadow*, p. 7; added italics ours]

Christopher concludes that 'the importance of *The Hobbit* in *the history of the evolution* of Middle-earth lies then . . . in the fact that it was published, and that a sequel to it was demanded. As a result, from the nature of *The Lord of the Rings* as it evolved, *The Hobbit* was *drawn into* Middle-earth – and transformed it; but as it stood in 1937 it was not a part of it' (*The Return of the Shadow*, p. 7).

One must not overlook, however, the strong influence that 'The Silmarillion' exerted generally upon Tolkien. As he wrote to Stanley Unwin on 24 February 1950, 'the *Silmarillion* and all that has refused to be suppressed. It has bubbled up, infiltrated, and probably spoiled everything (that even remotely approached "Faery") which I have tried to write since. . . . Its shadow was deep on the later parts of *The Hobbit*' (*Letters*, p. 136). Paul Edmund Thomas in 'Some of Tolkien's Narrators', in *Tolkien's Legendarium: Essays on The History of Middle-earth* (2000), indeed has detected this 'shadow' on the final chapters of *The Hobbit*. If, as Tolkien said in his letter to Christopher Bretherton (*Letters*, p. 346), 'the tale became "larger and more heroic" as it progressed, because of the influence of "The Silmarillion," it follows that the narrator had to follow suit by becoming more serious and by making utterances more appropriate to a heroic tale than to a children's story'. Thomas demonstrates, through a catalogue of direct addresses in *The Hobbit*,

> that no obvious addresses to the reader occur in the last six chapters of the novel. Also, in Chapter 14 ['Fire and Water'], which recounts the attack of Smaug and his death, Bilbo and the dwarves are omitted entirely, and the narrator presents the action from more points of view than in any other chapter. . . . These constitute major changes in the narrative voice. It is no coincidence that these changes occur as the language of the dialogue becomes more elevated and focused on subjects like the debate over the property claims to Smaug's treasure and the debate over political rights in Esgaroth. It is no coincidence that these changes occur as the plot turns to violent action and swells from the onslaught of Smaug towards the Battle of Five Armies. And it is no coincidence that these changes occur as the scope of the narrator's view abandons the domestic and provincial perspective of Bilbo and begins to sweep over great distances. . . . This is the narrator of a prose epic. This is a whisper from the narrator who speaks in full voice in *The Lord of the Rings*. [pp. 178–9]

Holy Maidenhood. Review of *Hali Meidenhad: An Alliterative Prose Homily of the Thirteenth Century*, revised by F.J. Furnivall from the edition by the Reverend O. Cockayne (Early English Text Society, 1923), published in the *Times Literary Supplement* for 26 April 1923, p. 281. The review is not signed, but Tolkien's authorship is revealed in his diary.

Furnivall died before completing his work on the Middle English *Hali Meiðhad* from MS Bodley 34 (see *Katherine Group), and 'it may be doubted,' Tolkien wrote, 'whether . . . the best service has been rendered to [Furnivall], or to English scholarship, by publishing work that might have been revised and supplemented at many points without very great labour.' Tolkien regrets the lack of an introduction, the paucity of notes, faults in translation, and errors in the glossary. But he extols the importance of *Hali Meiðhad* and related works such as the *Ancrene Riwle*: 'the language of this group, and of other works closely related linguistically ... was in its day no mere archaic survival of a dying tradition, but was in the closest touch with the living colloquial speech, and in addition to its great interest for linguistic students is well worthy of attention from students of literature. ...'

The Homecoming of Beorhtnoth Beorhthelm's Son. Dramatic dialogue with criticism, first published in *Essays and Studies 1953* by John Murray, London, for the English Association, in October 1953, pp. 1–18. See further, *Descriptive Bibliography* B21.

SUMMARY

The alliterative verse-drama *The Homecoming of Beorhtnoth Beorhthelm's Son* is set following the Battle of Maldon in Essex in August 991. In that conflict the local defence force, commanded by Beorhtnoth (or Byrhtnoth), son of Beorhthelm and ealdorman of Essex, opposed a host of invading Vikings camped on the opposite side of an arm of the river Pante (Blackwater) which could be crossed at low tide only by a causeway. The narrow path might have been held by determined men; but Beorhtnoth agreed to the Vikings' request to be allowed to cross so that a fair fight could be joined. Outnumbered by their foes, he and the men of his household were slain, and the English routed. An Old English poem, *The Battle of Maldon*, of which only a large fragment survives, tells this tale. Beorhtnoth's body was recovered, except for the head, and buried in the abbey of Ely.

In Tolkien's work two servants of Beorhtnoth go to the battlefield to retrieve their master's corpse; neither had been in the fighting itself. One, Tídwald ('Tída'), is an old farmer, seasoned in battle, while his younger companion Torhthelm ('Totta') is the son of a minstrel. As they search in darkness among the slain they find the remains of men they knew, some notably young. Torhthelm is affected with emotion and offers the fine words of one who, enamoured of old stories of Northern heroes, tends to romanticize war without any personal knowledge of it. Tídwald points out that Torhthelm's time will come, 'and it'll look less easy than lays make it' (*Essays and Studies*, p. 5). Tídwald faces his task with grimness and resignation. He knows why the Vikings won the battle: Beorhtnoth was 'too proud, too princely!'

> He let them cross the causeway, so keen was he
> to give minstrels matter for mighty songs.
> Needlessly noble. It should never have been:
> bidding bows be still, and the bridge opening,

> matching more with few in mad handstrokes!
> Well, doom he dared, and died for it. [p. 10]

When at last they find Beorhtnoth's body Tídwald offers a silent prayer, and Torhthelm a chant of praise ('His head was higher than the helm of kings / with heathen crowns', etc., p. 6) such as rulers of old would have received. Disturbing Englishmen stripping corpses, Torhthelm kills one, though Tídwald tells him that 'a wallop on the nose, / or a boot behind' (p. 8) would have sufficed. Torhthelm is alternately brazen and fearful. Riding back to Ely, he drowses, and in a dream echoes the words of the English retainer Beorhtwold near the end of *The Battle of Maldon*:

> Heart shall be bolder, harder be purpose,
> more proud the spirit as our power lessens!
> Mind shall not falter nor mood waver,
> though doom shall come and dark conquer. [p. 12]

The work ends with Latin chanting of monks as Tídwald and Torhthelm approach Ely: 'Dirige, Domine, in conspectu tuo viam meam' (p. 13).

For its publication in *Essays and Studies* Tolkien augmented the drama proper with an introduction, 'Beorhtnoth's Death', providing historical background and brief comments on the relation of the dialogue to *The Battle of Maldon*, and an afterword, 'Ofermod' (Old English for overmastering pride or spirit, used in condemnation), in which he argues that heroic excess was Beorhtnoth's downfall and comments on the similar quality expressed in *Beowulf* and *Sir Gawain and the Green Knight*. He notes that *The Battle of Maldon* 'has usually been regarded rather as an extended comment on, or illustration of the words of the old retainer Beorhtwold' ('Heart shall be bolder', etc.), 'the best-known lines of the poem, possibly of all Old English verse', 'the finest expression of the northern heroic spirit'. But these were of less interest to him than 'lines 89, 90 of the original [poem]: *ða se eorl ongan for his ofermode alyfan landes to fela laþere ðeode*, "then the earl in his overmastering pride actually yielded ground to the enemy, as he should not have done"' (p. 13). These, Tolkien held in contradiction of earlier scholars, were meant to be lines 'of *severe* criticism, though not incompatible with loyalty, and even love' (pp. 15–16).

HISTORY

Tolkien conceived *The Homecoming of Beorhtnoth Beorhthelm's Son* at least as early as the period ?1931–Trinity Term 1933, at first in rhyming rather than alliterative verse. A portion of a draft survives on the verso of the earliest extant manuscript of *Errantry*, and was published in *The Treason of Isengard* (1989), pp. 106–7. There the speakers are named 'Pudda' and 'Tibba'. *Christopher Tolkien comments that 'this text is extremely rough, one would say in the first stage of composition, were there not another text still rougher, but in very much the same words', preserved in the Bodleian Library, Oxford (*Libraries and archives).

According to Humphrey Carpenter (*Biography*, p. 214), *Beorhtnoth* 'was in existence by 1945', presumably as further developed. Numerous manuscript and typescript versions survive, with the speakers called 'Tudda' and 'Totta' before acquiring their final names. The earliest of these were still rhymed and much shorter than the final text. The present authors have found no mention of the work in Tolkien's correspondence until October 1952, after he had agreed to send a contribution to *Essays and Studies* and was labouring to complete it (among much else). He sent the dramatic dialogue, now with the accompanying texts, to *Essays and Studies* in ?February or March 1953 for publication that October. By 3 May 1954 he made a private recording of the drama proper, speaking all of the voices and making his own sound effects – he made the sound of waggon wheels, for instance, by moving furniture in his study. He thought this good enough to suggest, while writing on another matter to *P.H. Newby at the British Broadcasting Corporation, that it would be suitable to broadcast in August 1954 on the anniversary of the Battle of Maldon. In one of several letters written to BBC producer Rayner Heppenstall in the following months, during the development of the work for reading by a small cast, Tolkien advised that the difference between the voices used for Tídwald and Torhthelm should be 'one of temper, and matter' rather than 'class'. 'In a period when "dialect" merely marked place and not rank or function, and at any rate details of grammar and vowels had no social implications, it would be best to avoid any modern rusticity' (22 September 1954, *Letters*, p. 187). *Beorhtnoth* was broadcast on the Third Programme on 3 December 1954, and repeated on 17 June 1955. Tolkien found the production 'incompetent' (letter to Philip Unwin, 29 January 1955, Tolkien-George Allen & Unwin archive, Harper-Collins).

Tolkien long thought to reprint *Beorhtnoth* together with **Beowulf: The Monsters and the Critics* and **On Fairy-Stories*, 'three things that to my mind really do flow together' (unlike, in his view, *On Fairy-Stories* and **Leaf by Niggle*). 'The [*Beowulf* essay] deals with the contact of the "heroic" with fairy-story; [*On Fairy-Stories*] primarily with fairy-story; and [*Beorhtnoth*] with "heroism and chivalry"' (letter to Anne Barrett, 7 August 1964, *Letters*, p. 350). When in 1966 Ballantine Books (*Publishers) proposed to publish a 'Tolkien Reader' with a selection of his shorter works, Tolkien recommended in particular the inclusion of *Beorhtnoth*, which, 'with the accompanying essay on "Heroism" ["Ofermod"] . . . is very germane to the general division of sympathy exhibited in **The Lord of the Rings*' (letter to Rayner Unwin, 25 April 1966, Tolkien-George Allen & Unwin archive, HarperCollins).

Beorhtnoth has been reprinted in **The Tolkien Reader* (1966), **Poems and Stories* (1980), and elsewhere. A separate edition was published in August 1991 by Anglo-Saxon Books, Pinner, Middlesex, but with numerous deviations from the *Essays and Studies* text. Tolkien's private recording of *The Homecom-*

ing of Beorhtnoth Beorhthelm's Son, with a brief introduction, 'Beorhtnoth's Death', and 'Ofermod' recorded by *Christopher Tolkien, was issued as an audio cassette tape by HarperCollins, London, in a complimentary limited edition for the Tolkien Centenary Conference at Oxford in 1992.

CRITICISM

As Richard C. West points out in 'Túrin's *Ofermod*: An Old English Theme in the Development of the Story of Túrin', *Tolkien's Legendarium: Essays on The History of Middle-earth* (2000), Tolkien's views expressed in 'Ofermod' 'have had a decided mixed reception from other critics of *Maldon* and of *Beowulf*' (p. 236). Some have argued that the heroic excess displayed by Beorhtnoth was considered admirable by medieval peoples, not a quality to be criticized, while others find Tolkien's reading of *The Battle of Maldon* to be persuasive. T.A. Shippey, in his 'Boar and Badger: An Old English Heroic Antithesis?', *Leeds Studies in English* 16 (1985), considers many of Tolkien's theses in *The Homecoming of Beorhtnoth* 'tendentious and personal to a marked degree', and feels that 'once one begins to unwind Tolkien's skein of argument, very little of it can bear much weight' (p. 233). He returns to the subject more briefly in *J.R.R. Tolkien: Author of the Century* (2000): Tolkien's opinion that the *Battle of Maldon* poet intended severe criticism of Beorhtnoth 'seems to be challenged . . . if not outright denied' in the *Maldon* poem itself by the words of Beorhtwold ('Heart shall be bolder', etc.), who offers no criticism of his lord. 'Tolkien deals with this problem in the verse-dialogue – and this is entirely personal, quite without scholarly warrant – by taking the lines away from their context on the battlefield, putting them into a dream, and adding to them'. In adding Torhthelm's words 'Mind shall not falter nor mood waver, / though doom shall come and dark conquer', Shippey argues, Tolkien made the expression 'clearly pagan, indeed Manichaean' (p. 295).

In 'Tolkien and "The Homecoming of Beorhtnoth"', *Leaves from the Tree: J.R.R. Tolkien's Shorter Fiction* (1991), Shippey argues that Tolkien deliberately and in several ways blackens the character of Torhthelm, who 'in a sense represents the tradition of Old English poetry. He is mesmerised by words . . . [his] mind is presented as in some sense addled by Old English poetry. He is unable to understand plain language or to see events plainly because Old English poetry has confused him. . . .' Beorhtnoth too had listened to minstrels, and so allowed the Danes to fight on even terms.

> Tolkien's suggestion is that Beorhtnoth made his mistake out of diabolical pride; but that that diabolical pride was actually created by heroic tradition as expressed in Old English poetry. Beorthnoth wanted to be a hero. He was prepared to sacrifice his own life for that. But he was also prepared to sacrifice the lives of the Essex levy. Tolkien's view was that he had no right to expend the lives of his men as well as his own. But since piety prevents one from criticising the dead in Beorhtnoth, Tolkien has

created a character to represent the bad qualities of Old English poetry in Torhthelm: and the criticism which might be directed at Beorhtnoth is directed at Torhthelm instead. [pp. 10–11]

Shippey suggests that Tolkien at the same time was presenting 'a veiled attack' on his late colleague *E.V. Gordon, who had produced an edition of *The Battle of Maldon*: 'the main drive of Tolkien's piece is to say that Gordon is wrong . . . in seeing this poem as the supreme example of the northern heroic spirit' (p. 13). According to Shippey, Tolkien held that *The Battle of Maldon* 'was an attack on the northern heroic spirit which had led to Beorhtnoth's act of disastrous folly; but this had not been understood by modern critics like Gordon, who had preferred in a way to revive that heroic spirit by praising retainers like Beorhtwold instead of criticising leaders like Beorhtnoth' (p. 14). Indeed, says Shippey, Torhthelm and Beorhtwold and critics such as Gordon 'had to be put incontrovertibly in the wrong over the heroic spirit in order to give Tolkien himself permission to write a work [*The Lord of the Rings*] embodying a different and non-heathen version of that heroic spirit' (p. 15).

In *Master of Middle-earth: The Fiction of J.R.R. Tolkien* (1972) Paul H. Kocher observes that Tolkien lived through two world wars, and 'had most of a lifetime in which to think long thoughts about war', some of which were expressed in *Beorhtnoth*. 'By putting the reader right among the corpses on the battlefield after night fall it drives home with utter immediacy the horror of a carnage that need never have taken place' (p. 187). Tídwald and Torhthelm repeatedly lament 'on the youth and worth of the slain men. Tídwald, particularly, thinks it ". . . a wicked business / to gather them ungrown"' (pp. 188–9). All of the deaths in the battle were needless, as is that of the corpse stripper whom Torhthelm kills. Kocher points to a subtheme of the work: 'Torhthelm's gradual and by no means uninterrupted discovery that the heroic grandeur he sees in his sagas is not compatible with the unheroic reality he is finding on the Essex battlefield' (p. 190). But Kocher thinks that Torhthelm never fully takes in Tídwald's attempt to explain Beorhtnoth's action, 'the key to a proper understanding of the meaning of the battle' (p. 191).

Hope and Despair. Of the Christian virtues, Hope is the most prominent in Tolkien's writings. In *The Lord of the Rings* it is a constant thread, always in tension with the denial of hope, despair. Although Tolkien does not present these opposites implicitly in Christian terms – virtue and sin – they are moral choices to be made by the various characters in different circumstances, on which the outcome of the story hinges. Moreover, Tolkien uses the frequent opposition of hope and despair to emphasize the near impossibility of the task faced by the Company of the Ring, especially Frodo, while keeping open the possibility of ultimate victory – of *eucatastrophe. To a first-time reader the quest of the Ring seems almost bound to fail, while anyone reading the book again will know how many hopes are actually fulfilled, not by a *deus ex machina* but by the determination of most of the characters to carry on against all odds, ultimately embracing hope when logic would lead them to despair and, in turn, the failure of the West against Sauron, an embodiment of Evil (see also *Good and Evil).

Near the beginning of the Council at Rivendell (bk. II, ch. 2) Elrond tells Gimli that all that the Dwarves can do if Sauron attacks Erebor and Dale is to 'resist, with hope or without it'. Near the end of the debate he defines the quest: 'It seems to me now clear which is the road that we must take. . . . Now at this last we must take a hard road, a road unforeseen. There lies our hope, if hope it be. To walk into peril – to Mordor. We must send the Ring to the Fire.' He also says: 'The road must be trod, but it will be very hard. And neither strength nor wisdom will carry us far upon it. This quest may be attempted by the weak with as much hope as the strong. Yet such is oft the course of deeds that move the wheels of the world: small hands do them because they must, while the eyes of the great are elsewhere.' Thus he defines the two main strands of the strategy against Sauron: open resistance in battle against a vastly superior foe, and a desperate, surreptitious attempt to overthrow Sauron by reaching Mount Doom and destroying the Ring, each apparently hopeless and certainly fraught with difficulty.

The Company of the Ring, and later Frodo and Sam alone, face many set-backs on their roads to Mordor, but ultimately succeed by refusing to give in to despair. After the Company are prevented by the snowstorm from crossing the Misty Mountains (bk. II, ch. 4) Frodo wishes that he was back in Riven-dell, but feels that he cannot return without shame unless there is truly no other way. Gandalf confirms that 'to go back is to admit defeat, and face worse defeat to come'. After the loss of Gandalf in Moria Aragorn cries: 'What hope have we without you?' (bk. II, ch. 6), but immediately turns to the Company and declares they that they must continue on their way without hope. Not one of them accepts Celeborn's offer to stay in Lothlórien; all are resolved to continue with the quest. As he sits in the Seat of Seeing on Amon Hen (bk. II, ch 10) Frodo feels hope when he sees the strength of Minas Tirith, but then his gaze is drawn past Minas Morgul and Mount Doom, to 'Barad-dûr, Fortress of Sauron. All hope left him.' Nonetheless he decides that that is where he must go, and turns east. Sam insists on accompanying him. Neither has much hope of a successful outcome: the paths are unknown to them, and Sam worries whether their supply of food is sufficient for the journey to Mount Doom, let alone for their return. Frodo tells him: 'I don't know how long we shall take to – to finish. . . . But . . . I do not think we need give thought to what comes after that, To *do the job* as you put it – what hope is there that we ever shall? And if we do, who knows what will come of that? If the One goes into the Fire, and we are at hand?' (bk. IV, ch. 2).

At the Morannon Frodo, knowing no other route, is determined to attempt to enter Mordor by that formidable gate. Sam knows that it is hopeless to try to persuade him otherwise: 'And after all he [Sam] never had any real hope in the affair from the beginning; but being a cheerful hobbit he had not needed hope, as long as despair could be postponed. Now they were come to the bitter end' (bk. IV, ch. 3). Faramir, whom they meet on the journey south, gives them what help is within his power to give, though he tells them: 'I do not hope to see you again on any other day under this Sun. . . . If ever beyond hope you return to the lands of the living and we re-tell our tales, sitting by a wall in the sun, laughing at old grief, you shall tell me then [of Gollum and the Ring]' (bk. IV, ch. 6). As Frodo and Sam turn east to Mordor and approach the Cross-roads (bk. IV, ch. 7), Sam tries to encourage Frodo by citing the (real world) proverb, *where there's life there's hope*, but with the Gaffer's hobbitish addition: *and need of vittles*.

When Sam cannot revive Frodo after Shelob's attack (bk. IV, ch. 10) he realizes that in his vision in the Mirror of Galadriel he saw Frodo 'Not asleep, dead! And as he said it, as if the words had set the venom to its work again, it seemed to him that the hue of the face grew livid green. And then black despair came down on him. . . .' In a letter to his son *Christopher on 7–8 November 1944, Tolkien wrote that he hoped that when Christopher received and read the chapter he would note 'that Frodo's face goes livid and convinces Sam that he's dead, just when Sam gives up *hope*' (*Letters*, p. 101). But although Sam gives up hope of Frodo being alive, he does not abandon the quest. The song he later sings to help him find where Frodo is being held captive in the Tower of Cirith Ungol illustrates his refusal to despair:

> Though here at journey's end I lie
>   in darkness buried deep,
> beyond all towers strong and high,
>   beyond all mountains steep,
> above all shadows rides the Sun
>   and Stars for ever dwell:
> I will not say the Day is done,
>   nor bid the Stars farewell. [bk. VI, ch. 1]

Later, in Mordor, as Sam keeps guard while Frodo sleeps:

> Far above the Ephel Dúath in the West the night-sky was still dim and pale. There, peeping among the cloud-wrack above a dark tor high up in the mountains, Sam saw a white star twinkle for a while. The beauty of it smote his heart . . . and hope returned to him. For like a shaft, clear and cold, the thought pierced him that in the end the Shadow was only a small and passing thing: there was light and high beauty for ever beyond its reach. His song in the Tower had been defiance rather than hope. . . . Now, for a moment, his own fate, and even his master's ceased to trouble him. [bk. VI, ch 2]

After the attack by Shelob and his captivity, Frodo takes a more passive role. In Mordor Sam is the real leader: whatever the setbacks and difficulties, he refuses to give up. Soon after their escape from the file of orcs he calculates the journey still ahead and accepts the bitter truth that, at best, he and Frodo have enough provisions only to reach their goal. After that they will be 'alone, houseless, foodless, in the midst of a terrible desert'.

> But even as hope died in Sam, or seemed to die, it was turned to a new strength. Sam's plain hobbit-face grew stern, almost grim, as the will hardened in him, and he felt through all his limbs a thrill, as if he was turning into some creature of stone and steel that neither despair nor weariness nor endless barren miles could subdue. [bk. VI, ch. 3]

The words used to describe Sam's determination to carry on recall Tolkien's translation and reuse in *The Homecoming of Beorhtnoth Beorhthelm's Son* of two lines from the Old English poem *The Battle of Maldon* which embody the Northern ethic of endurance and resistance. In the introductory section of the work he translates the lines as 'Will shall be sterner, heart the bolder, spirit the greater as our strength lessens', but within the verse-play they become: 'Heart shall be bolder, harder be purpose, / more proud the spirit as our power lessens! / Mind shall not falter nor mood waver, / though doom shall come and dark conquer' (*Essays and Studies 1953* (1953), pp. 3, 12). Tolkien comments that the lines from *The Battle of Maldon* 'have been held to be the finest expression of the northern heroic spirit, Norse or English; the clearest statement of uttermost endurance in the service of indomitable will' (p. 13). See further, *Northernness.

In Fangorn (bk. III, ch. 5) Gandalf says to Aragorn, Gimli, and Legolas that there is still hope for a successful outcome, if Frodo and Sam are able to slip into Mordor unseen while Sauron's thoughts are busy elsewhere, and in Edoras he looks east and tells Théoden – whom Gandalf has brought out of the depths of despair created by Wormtongue – and tells him 'that way lies our hope, where sits our greatest fear. Doom hangs still on a thread. yet hope there is still, if we can but stand unconquered for a little while' (bk. III, ch. 6).

In his conversation with Pippin on the battlement of Minas Tirith (bk. V, ch. 1) Beregond wonders who will stand if Gondor falls, and both he and Pippin feel despair when a winged Nazgûl passes overhead. But Pippin sees the sun still shining and says: 'No, my heart will not yet despair. Gandalf fell and has returned and is with us. We may stand, if only on one leg, or at least be left still upon our knees.' Beregond applauds his speech and says that even if Minas Tirith is taken, 'there are still other fastnesses, and secret ways of escape into the mountains. Hope and memory shall live still in some hidden valley where the grass is green.'

Denethor, who thinks Gandalf's hope of defeating Sauron by the destruction of the Ring 'a fool's hope' (bk. VI, ch. 4), is deceived by what he sees in the *palantír*, gives way to despair, and takes his life. In the debate after the Battle of the Pelennor Fields (bk. V, ch. 9) Gandalf outlines the policy to draw Sauron's attention and give Frodo time to accomplish the quest:

His Eye is now straining towards us, blind almost to all else that is moving. So we must keep it. Therein lies all our hope. . . . Without [the Ring]
we cannot by force defeat his force. But we must at all costs keep his Eye
from his true peril. We cannot achieve victory by arms, but by arms we
can give the Ring-bearer his only chance, frail though it be. . . .
    We must march out to meet him at once. We must make ourselves the
bait, though his jaws should close on us. . . .

Aragorn comments: 'We now come to the very brink, where hope and despair
are akin.'

    Aragorn, who was given the name *Estel* ('Hope') as a child, is the centre of
a complex of allusions to 'hope' in *The Lord of the Rings*. When Elrond reveals
his lineage to him, 'he sang, for he was full of hope and the world was fair'. For
many years 'he laboured in the cause against Sauron and . . . became at last
the most hardy of living Men. . . . His face was sad and stern because of the
doom that was laid on him, and yet hope dwelt ever in the depths of his heart,
from which mirth would arise at times like spring from the rock.' When he
plights his troth with Arwen, she foretells that he will be among those who will
destroy the Shadow. Aragorn, who cannot foresee it, says that with her hope he
will hope (Appendix A, 'The Tale of Aragorn and Arwen'). At the parting feast
before the Company leaves Lórien (bk. II, ch. 8), Galadriel gives to Aragorn a
green stone set in a silver brooch in the form of an eagle, sent by Arwen to him
as 'a token of hope'. Arwen also sends to Aragorn a standard she has wrought
for him, with the message: 'The days now are short. Either our hope cometh or
all hope's end' (bk. V, ch. 2). And their hope is realized. But when after a long
reign Aragorn feels that the time has come for him to lay down his life, Arwen
tries to dissuade him. He refuses, but speaks words of hope beyond death: 'let
us not be overthrown in the final test, who of old renounced the Shadow and
the Ring. In sorrow we must go, but not in despair. Behold! we are not bound
for ever to the circles of the world, and beyond them is more than memory'
(Appendix A, 'The Tale of Aragorn and Arwen'). And yet, in one of the most
curious turns in *The Lord of the Rings*, albeit in an appendix, Arwen, who had
been a focus of hope for Aragorn through all his labours, herself after her
husband's death seems to give way to grief and despair.

    Edea A. Baldwin in her online essay 'The Flag of Middle-earth: Tolkien's
Use of Chesterton to Illustrate Hope and Despair in *The Lord of the Rings*'
(2003) comments that

    Tolkien carries the theme of hope in the face of despair throughout [*The
    Lord of the Rings*], from the devastated Fellowship's departure from
    Moria, to its fracturing at Amon Hen, to a vastly outnumbered army on
    the walls of Helm's Deep, to Aragorn's return from the Paths of the Dead
    with a mighty army, and to Samwise Gamgee, carrying his defeated
    master up the slope of Mount Doom and then leading him to safety as
    Mordor crumbles around them. Some characters, like Frodo and the

Elves, give up hope for themselves in order to secure it for others. Others, like Denethor, can no longer bear to live under the flag of the world [a phrase in *Orthodoxy* by *G.K. Chesterton], and they give themselves over to despair. . . .

See also Matthew Dickerson, *Following Gandalf: Epic Battles and Moral Victory in* The Lord of the Rings (2003), ch. 7; and Anne C. Petty, *Tolkien in the Land of Heroes* (2003), ch. 8.

Hope plays a lesser role in the darker *'Silmarillion' mythology. One notable exception is the potent image of Eärendil, who after his mission to the Valar is set to sail his ship Vingilot as a star in the sky, with a Silmaril bound on his brow. When the people of Middle-earth saw Vingilot rise 'they took it for a sign, and called it Gil-Estel, the Star of High Hope' (*The Silmarillion*, p. 250). Another is Andreth's reply to Finrod in the *Athrabeth*, when he asks her if Men have no hope. She says that some believe that 'the One will himself enter into Arda, and heal Men and all the Marring from the beginning to the end' (p. 321).

The Horns of Ylmir. Poem, the latest version of which was published with commentary and notes in *The Shaping of Middle-earth* (1986), pp. 213–18. The poet, in 'the Land of Willows', hears the conch-horns of Ylmir, i.e. the Vala Ulmo, lord of waters, and the trumpets of Ossë, vassal of Ulmo. This 'immortal music' wails around the poet as he sits 'on the ruined margin of the deep-voiced echoing sea'. Wind and waves crash against the shore, described first with imagery of war, of armies and 'billowed cavalry' and songs of wrath.

Deep hollows hummed and fluted as they sucked the sea-winds in;
Spumes and great white spoutings yelled shrilly o'er the din;
Gales blew the bitter tresses of the sea in the land's dark face
And wild airs thick with spindrift fled on a whirling race
From battle unto battle. . . . [*The Shaping of Middle-earth*, p. 216]

The ocean then is described in terms of music, like an 'organ whose stops were the piping of gulls and the thunderous swell', the waves singing, voices 'rolling to the caves' (p. 217). Slumber takes the poet. The tides go out, the wind dies, 'and I woke to silent caverns and empty sands and peace' (p. 217). But he will hear the Horns of Ylmir till his death.

The earliest extant version of the poem is entitled *The Grimness of the Sea* and later inscribed 'original nucleus of "The Sea-song of an Elder Day" (1912) (St Andrews)'. If the inscription is correct, Tolkien wrote it while visiting St Andrews, *Scotland, probably during the summer vacation but possibly at Easter. Another manuscript, with the same title, is inscribed '1912 (sometime)', but with added lines dated 'Nov 27 1914'. A third bears a new title, *The Tides*, with the inscriptions 'Dec. 4 1914' and 'On the Cornish Coast', the latter evidently inspired by Tolkien's visit to *Cornwall that August. In March 1915 he wrote a new, extended version, now entitled *Sea-Chant of an Elder Day*, and that month read a further revision to the Essay Club of Exeter College, Oxford (*Societies and clubs). He now sent a copy, with the title changed to *Sea-Song of an Elder Day*, to his friend *G.B. Smith; and probably at the same time, he painted in his *Book of Ishness* (see *Art) a watercolour entitled *Water, Wind & Sand* (*Artist and Illustrator*, fig. 42). On the facing page of the sketchbook he wrote: 'Illustration to Sea-Song of an Elder Day'.

A small figure enclosed in a white sphere in the foreground of the painting may be the seed from which Tolkien developed the idea that now attached the poem to his *'Silmarillion' mythology, with which it originally had no contact. Against the second text of *Sea-Chant of an Elder Day* he wrote: 'This is the song that Tuor told to Eärendel his son what time the Exiles of Gondolin dwelt awhile in Dor Tathrin the Land of Willows after the burning of their city.' Tuor (see *'Of Tuor and the Fall of Gondolin'), introduced in *The Book of Lost Tales*, is the first Man to see the Ocean, but is guided by Ulmo to the hidden city of Gondolin as a messenger; there he marries and has a son, Eärendel. After the fall of Gondolin Tuor, Eärendel, and other survivors rest in the Land of Willows, where Tuor sings to his son of his meeting with Ulmo. Later, when Tuor reaches old age, he hears the call of the sea and sails away.

In spring 1917 Tolkien revised *Sea-Song of an Elder Day* as *The Horns of Ulmo*. Later he emended the title to *The Horns of Ylmir*, using instead the Gnomish form of the name *Ulmo*.

Hove (Sussex). For a few months from April 1904, while his mother (*Mabel Tolkien) was in hospital, Tolkien lived with his *Aunt Jane Neave and her husband Edwin in Hove, a town on the south coast of England west of Brighton. Four drawings by Tolkien document this time: in *'For Men Must Work' as Seen Daily at 9 am* Ronald and Edwin are seen striding along the promenade to the Guardian Fire Insurance office where Edwin worked as a clerk; *Working Overtime S.P.Q.R.* depicts Edwin sitting at a tall desk with a Guardian Fire Insurance calendar on the wall; *They Slept in Beauty Side by Side* (*Artist and Illustrator*, fig. 4) apparently shows Jane and Edwin in bed; and in *What is Home without a Mother (or a Wife)* (*Life and Legend*, p. 14) Ronald is sewing a button on his trousers while Edwin darns his socks – the forced result, apparently, of Jane having gone alone to *Birmingham to visit her sister.

The Hunt for the Ring. Miscellaneous writings related to *The Lord of the Rings*, concerning Sauron's hunt to recover the One Ring and especially the part played in this by the Black Riders in Third Age 3018, collected and discussed by *Christopher Tolkien under the assigned title *The Hunt for the Ring* in *Unfinished Tales* (1980), pp. 337–54.

The first of its three sections, headed 'Of the Journey of the Black Riders according to the account that Gandalf gave to Frodo', is 'the most finished as a narrative' (*Unfinished Tales*, p. 341). It describes Gollum's capture by Sauron, his release, his capture by Aragorn, and Sauron's strategy in summer and autumn 3018 when he tried to recapture Gollum, openly attacked Osgiliath, and sent the Nazgûl secretly to find the land of the Halflings and the One Ring. The movements of the Nazgûl are described, including their encounter with Saruman at Isengard two days after Gandalf had escaped; Saruman's lies to them that he did not know the location of the Shire, but Gandalf did; and their meeting first with Wormtongue, who told them of the whereabouts of the Shire, and then with one of Saruman's spies from whom they obtained charts. (See *Unfinished Tales*, pp. 337–41, and p. 353, note 2.)

In the second section, headed 'Other Versions of the Story', Christopher Tolkien notes that 'there is much other writing that bears on these events, adding to or modifying the story in important particulars' (p. 341), but with 'precise dates . . . slightly at variance both with each other and with those given in the Tale of Years [i.e. Appendix B in *The Lord of the Rings*]' (p. 345). He included some extracts in *Unfinished Tales*, while further material is quoted and summarized in Wayne G. Hammond and Christina Scull, *The Lord of the Rings: A Reader's Companion* (2005).

A second version of the story is similar to the first, but includes more about Aragorn's journey north with the captive Gollum, and 'more consideration is given to Sauron's doubts about the use of the Ringwraiths in the search for the Ring' (p. 342), and to the movements of the Black Riders in and near the Shire (text or summary, pp. 342–4, 348; author's notes, p. 353, notes 3, 6). A third manuscript says more about Gollum's part in events, especially his movements after he escaped from the Elves (*Unfinished Tales*, two extracts, pp. 342, 345; author's notes, p. 353, notes 11, 12; *Reader's Companion*, p. 285).

Yet another text, headed 'Official & final' and 'Concerning the Escape of Gandalf, His Ride and the Ride of the Black Riders', is probably the latest in composition and introduces some changes in the story. Gandalf is still a prisoner when the Nazgûl arrive at Isengard; Saruman reacts with fear, resolves to beg for Gandalf's pardon and aid, but finding him gone convinces the Nazgûl that Gandalf has confessed the location of the Shire, on the borders of the Elvish country to the north-west. The Nazgûl still meet one of Saruman's spies, but not Wormtongue. The complete text is summarized at length in *Unfinished Tales* (pp. 346–8; author's note, p. 354, note 18). Lengthy extracts concerning Gandalf's escape and visit to Rohan, the Black Riders' visit to Isengard, and Gandalf's ride north are quoted in *Reader's Companion*, pp. 249–50, 251–2, with briefer extracts on pp. 145, 247.

Extensive extracts from another, rough manuscript, which shows Tolkien working out a solution to a chronological problem, appear in *Reader's Companion*, pp. 241–3. Tolkien had realized that if the Black Riders crossed the Anduin only on 20 June, there was insufficient time for Saruman to find out about them and send Radagast with a message to Gandalf, and for Radagast to find Gandalf by Midyear's Day. Christopher Tolkien mentions yet another text, 'notes recounting in detail the movements of the Black Riders' (*Unfinished Tales*, p. 352, note 1). A large part of this lengthy manuscript was published in *Reader's Companion*, but in sections appropriate to the development of the story (see pp. 97, 99, 116, 145, 164–5, 166, 166–7, 180–1, 194, 195–6, 262–3) and adapted to make it more comprehensible in this form, i.e. with descriptive phrases substituted for the letters ABCDEFGHI used by Tolkien to identify the individual Black Riders.

The third section of *The Hunt for the Ring*, headed 'Concerning Gandalf, Saruman and the Shire', contains texts which note variously that Saruman's interest in the Shire arose from his jealousy and suspicion of Gandalf, and describe a meeting of the White Council at which Saruman mocks Gandalf for smoking and for his interest in 'childish folk'. These differ in their accounts of Saruman's reactions and Gandalf's purpose.

Tolkien wrote all of the *Hunt for the Ring* texts after *The Fellowship of the Ring* was in page proof at the end of September 1953, and before *The Return of the King* was completed for press – probably, then, in late 1954 or early 1955. They may have been written as supplements to *The Lord of the Rings*, but omitted when problems arose about the length of the Appendices. On 20 September 1963 Tolkien commented to Colonel Worskett that there are 'quite a lot of links between *The Hobbit* and [*The Lord of the Rings*] that are not clearly set out. They were mostly written or sketched out, but cut out to lighten the boat: such as Gandalf's exploratory journeys, his relations with Aragorn and Gondor; all the movements of Gollum, until he took refuge in Moria' (*Letters*, p. 334).

Illustration. Tolkien usually spoke deprecatingly of his own artistic ability, and of the illustrations and dust-jacket designs he produced for his own work (see *Art). But he would complain if his own illustrations were misused. He described the dust-jacket for the first American edition of *The Hobbit* (1938) as 'appalling' (letter to *Rayner Unwin, 13 May 1954, *Letters*, p. 181): Houghton Mifflin's (*Publishers) designer had covered parts of Tolkien's illustrations *The Hill: Hobbiton-across-the-Water* and *Converation with Smaug* with white bands printed with blurbs, over which projected respectively the tower of the Hobbiton mill and Smaug's head, completely destroying any sense of depth (see *The Annotated Hobbit* (rev. and expanded edn. 2002), p. 18). Tolkien also thought that Houghton Mifflin had 'spoilt the Rivendell picture [the colour plate *Rivendell* in *The Hobbit*], by slicing the top and cutting out the ornament at the bottom' (letter to *Stanley Unwin, 4 March 1938, *Letters*, p. 34). If a publisher wanted to commission more illustrations for *The Hobbit* by another artist, Tolkien did not object, but thought that his own should be omitted, as 'professional pictures would make my own amateurish productions look rather silly' (letter to C.A. Furth, 13 May 1937, *Letters*, p. 17). When he saw other people's illustrations, and particularly dust-jacket designs, for his books, however, he was often very critical, and judged them not only as good or pleasing art but whether they were good *illustrations* of the story, true to the text.

Tolkien described the dust-jacket of the Foyle's Children's Book Club edition of *The Hobbit* (1942) as 'hideous' (see *The Annotated Hobbit*, rev. and expanded edn., p. 384), and thought that the paper could have been better used for the maps, which were omitted (letter to Stanley Unwin, *c.* 18 March 1945, Tolkien-George Allen & Unwin archive, HarperCollins). Later he commented to Stanley Unwin on illustrations for *The Hobbit* by Horus Engels: 'He has sent me some illustrations (of the Trolls and Gollum) which despite certain merits, such as one would expect of a German, are I fear too "Disnified" [i.e. like the work of the *Disney Studio] for my taste: Bilbo with a dribbling nose, and Gandalf as a figure of vulgar fun rather than the Odinic wanderer that I think of' (7 December 1946, *Letters*, p. 119). (For the Engels illustrations, see *The Annotated Hobbit*, rev. and expanded edn., p. 6 of the colour plates. Some of Engels' illustrations for the first German translation are reproduced in *The Annotated Hobbit*, rev. and expanded edn., pp. 175, 223, 232.)

Tolkien also disliked the illustrations for the Swedish *Hobbit* (1947) by Torbjörn Zetterholm and Charles Sjöblom (see *The Annotated Hobbit*, rev. and expanded edn., pp. 44, 73, 112, 212, 248). On 18 January 1948 he wrote to 'Rosemary' that the edition had 'some dreadful pictures which make Gollum look simply huge. But he was not much bigger than Bilbo, only thin and very wiry, and he had of course large flabby-sticky hands and feet' (*Mallorn* 36 (November 1998), p. 34). In a letter of 15 February 1960 to Alina Dadlez in the George Allen & Unwin (*Publishers) foreign rights department, Tolkien said that he hoped that the illustrations would not be used in a new edition: 'with one or two exceptions they were frightful, quite out of tune with the tone of the text; and in the matter of Gollum, who is made some kind of monster, the text was wholly neglected' (Tolkien-George Allen & Unwin, archive, Harper-Collins). He was no happier with the cover art of the Swedish *Fellowship of the Ring* (1959): in a draft letter on 14 January 1961, probably to Alina Dadlez, he described it as containing 'pink nudes [which] appear to be fighting some blue nudes of similar shape (in black bathing costumes). Three of the pink nudes are riding horses and have spears; those on foot have axes. Two of the blue men are on oxen; the blues have swords or bows. To what people or incidents in the Tale at any point can this have any conceivable reference?' (Tolkien Papers, Bodleian Library, Oxford).

He noted of the dust-jacket on the Dutch translation of *The Fellowship of the Ring* (1956) that 'among other sins [it] got my initials wrong', i.e. his name was printed as 'J.J.R. Tolkien'. He told Alina Dadlez that he found the illustrations in the Polish *Hobbit* (1960) 'Mordoresque', and felt that the covers of the Polish *Return of the King* (1963) were 'of a Mordor hideousness' (letters dated 16 December 1956, 23 November 1960, 1 November 1963, Tolkien-George Allen & Unwin archive, HarperCollins).

In 1963 Houghton Mifflin proposed to produce a sumptuous edition of *The Hobbit* with illustrations by an artist other than the author. Although all parties agreed in principle, they found it hard to choose an illustrator. Rayner Unwin thought that the artist should attend scrupulously to detail, while Austin Olney of Houghton Mifflin held that the new art should maintain the mood of Tolkien's original pictures. They obtained a sample picture from the renowned science fiction illustrator Virgil Finlay, who depicted the dwarves and Bilbo being rescued by eagles (reproduced in *The Annotated Hobbit*, rev. and expanded edn., p. 154). When this was shown to Tolkien he said that although

> it gives prospects of a general treatment rather heavier and more violent and airless than I should like – I thought it was good, and actually I thought Bilbo's rather rotund and babyish (but anxious) face was in keeping with the character (up to that point). After the horrors of the 'illustrations' to the translations [of *The Hobbit*] Mr Finlay is a welcome relief. As long (as seem likely) as he will leave 'humour' to the text, and pay reasonable attention to what the text says, I shall I expect, be quite happy. One point: if he includes any illustration of *Gollum* it should be noted that G. is *not* a monster, but a slimy little creature no larger than Bilbo. [letter to *Joy Hill, 11 October 1963, Tolkien-George Allen & Unwin archive, HarperCollins]

Finlay seems to have abandoned the project, however, and in his place Houghton Mifflin chose the successful children's book artist Maurice Sendak. More than three years passed before Sendak was able to produce a sample drawing, of Gandalf meeting Bilbo outside Bag End. Tolkien saw this on 16 February 1967, and on 20 February Rayner Unwin wrote to Houghton Mifflin that Tolkien was unhappy about the relative sizes of its figures: he thought that Bilbo was drawn too large compared to Gandalf (which however can be excused by the perspective). Sendak unfortunately suffered a heart attack a few weeks later, and although he recovered his health he never returned to *The Hobbit*, and the project was abandoned.

Tolkien did not like a design made for the first American edition of *Tree and Leaf* (1965), and on 10 September 1964 expressed his displeasure to Houghton Mifflin: 'I find the block on p. iii very distasteful. . . . The lettering is, to my taste, of a bad kind and ill-executed, and though no doubt this is deliberate, I do not like it any the better for that. The fat and apparently pollarded trunk, with no roots, and feeble branches, seems to me quite unfitting as a symbol of Tale-telling, or as a suggestion of anything that Niggle could possibly have drawn!' (*Letters*, pp. 351–2). Both Tolkien's criticism and one written to Joy Hill at Allen & Unwin the following day ('a ghastly thing, like a cross between a fat sea-anemone and a pollarded Spanish chestnut, plastered with lettering of indecent ugliness'; Tolkien-George Allen & Unwin archive, HarperCollins), seem more apt to the design on the published American jacket than that on published p. iii (the title-page), which presumably differed in proof.

Perhaps the cover design which upset Tolkien the most was that of Barbara Remington for the first Ballantine Books (*Publishers) edition of *The Hobbit* (1965), which showed a lion and (apparently) emus in a strange landscape. When neither Houghton Mifflin nor Ballantine seemed to understand Tolkien's objections to this, he poured out his feelings to Rayner Unwin on 12 September 1965:

I wrote to [Houghton Mifflin] expressing (with moderation) my dislike of the cover for *The Hobbit*. It was a short hasty note by hand, without a copy, but it was to this effect: I think the cover ugly; but I recognize that a main object of a paperback cover is to attract purchasers, and I suppose that you are better judges of what is attractive in USA than I am. I therefore will not enter into a debate about taste – (meaning though I did not say so: horrible colours and foul lettering) – but I must ask this about the vignette: what has it got to do with the story? Where is this place? Why a lion and emus? And what is that thing in the foreground with pink bulbs? I do not understand how anybody who has read the tale (I hope you are one) could think such a picture would please the author. [*Letters*, p. 362]

These queries were never answered, but Mrs Ballantine had a 'longish' telephone conversation with Tolkien. She seemed to him 'impermeable'. When he made the same points to her that he had done in his letter, she exclaimed that the artist 'hadn't TIME to read the book! . . . With regard to the pink bulbs she said as if to one of complete obtusity: "they are meant to suggest a Christmas Tree". . . . I begin to feel that I am shut up in a madhouse' (p. 363). All that Tolkien's protests achieved was the removal of the lion in later printings: see *The Annotated Hobbit*, rev. and expanded edn., p. 384.

When the Japanese translation of *The Hobbit* was published in 1965 Tolkien was sent a presentation copy signed by the translator and the illustrator. He commented in a letter to Rayner Unwin on 15 December: 'Much could be said about the pictures: in many ways astonishing' (Tolkien-George Allen & Unwin archive, HarperCollins). Clyde S. Kilby recalled that when he visited Tolkien in the summer of 1966 Tolkien 'showed me with particular pleasure the frontispiece which portrayed Smaug falling convulsively over Dale [*sic*]' (*Tolkien & The Silmarillion* (1976), p. 23). Ryûichi Terashima, the illustrator of the Japanese *Hobbit* and later of *The Lord of the Rings*, paid great attention to the text and to Tolkien's own illustrations (see *The Annotated Hobbit*, rev. and expanded edn., pp. 96, 105, 121, 176, 202, 234, 265, 297). Tolkien also told Kilby that the illustrations in the Portuguese *Hobbit* were 'horrible' (Kilby, p. 23; for examples, see *The Annotated Hobbit*, rev. and expanded edn., pp. 37, 71, 278).

In 1964 *The Hobbit* was serialized in *The Princess*, a magazine for girls, with illustrations by Ferguson Dewar. Tolkien commented in a letter to Joy Hill on 14 August 1964 that he wished at least 'that Gandalf was less fussy and overclad and had some dignity' (Tolkien-George Allen & Unwin archive, HarperCollins). At the beginning of January 1967 he was sent a copy of *The Children's Treasury of Literature in Colour*, an anthology edited by Bryna and Louis Untermeyer and illustrated by various artists, in which the first chapter of *The Hobbit* was included with illustrations by Robert J. Lee. Tolkien wrote to Joy Hill on 5 January: 'I think a great many of the illustrations are very good, including some of the modern ones. Illustrations to *The Hobbit* extract seem to me the worst of all, vulgar, stupid, and entirely out of keeping with the text which Robert J. Lee does not seem to have read with any care' (collection of René van Rossenberg).

But Tolkien liked the work of a Dutch artist, Cor Blok, and even bought two of his illustrations of *The Lord of the Rings*: *The Battle of the Hornburg* and *The Dead Marshes*. On 23 May 1961 he wrote to Rayner Unwin, after seeing five examples of Blok's work:

> I thought them most attractive. . . . I should very much like to see some more, in the hope that some more will be as good as The Battle of the Hornburg. The other four I thought were attractive as pictures, but bad as illustrations. But I suppose it is impossible to hope, nowadays, that one might come across an artist of talent who could, or would even try to depict the noble and the heroic. [Tolkien-George Allen & Unwin archive, HarperCollins]

In 1965 some of Blok's illustrations were used on the covers of the three-volume paperback edition of the Dutch translation of *The Lord of the Rings*, and later on a one-volume hardback edition.

Tolkien disapproved of the sample illustrations submitted by Milein Cosman, the first artist chosen to illustrate **Farmer Giles of Ham*, not only because he did not like her style and technique, but because of her pictures' 'lack of resemblance to the text' (letter to Robert Eames, 5 August 1948, Tolkien-George Allen & Unwin archive, HarperCollins). He was much happier with samples by *Pauline Baynes, who was eventually chosen in place of Cosman. Tolkien thought that her illustrations exactly suited the text of *Farmer Giles of Ham*: 'They seem to me the perfect counterpart to the text (or an improvement on it) and to accord exactly in mood' (letter to Robert Eames, 10 December 1948, Tolkien-George Allen & Unwin archive, HarperCollins). *Farmer Giles of Ham* was the first of many Tolkien commissions carried out by Pauline Baynes. As recently as 1999 she supplied a map for the fiftieth anniversary edition of *Farmer Giles of Ham*.

With the failure of Houghton Mifflin's plans for a new illustrated edition of *The Hobbit*, only Tolkien's own pictures appeared in editions by his two main English language publishers until 1984, when both Allen & Unwin and Houghton Mifflin published large format editions with colour illustrations by Michael Hague. In 1997 HarperCollins and Houghton Mifflin produced a new edition of *The Hobbit* with full-page colour illustrations and monochrome vignettes by Alan Lee. In 1991 both HarperCollins and Houghton Mifflin published new editions of *The Lord of the Rings* with fifty colour illustrations by Alan Lee. Twenty colour pictures by Ted Nasmith appeared in an edition of *The Silmarillion* in 1998, and forty-five by the same artist in another edition in 2004.

For each of these titles the Folio Society produced an edition with black and white illustrations, mainly at chapter headings: for *The Lord of the Rings* in 1977 these are by 'Ingahild Grathmer', i.e. H.M. Queen Margrethe II of

Denmark, redrawn by Eric Fraser; for *The Hobbit* in 1979 the pictures are wholly by Eric Fraser; and for *The Silmarillion* in 1997 the illustrations were supplied by Francis Mosley.

A variety of artists have produced covers of Tolkien's works issued by his official publishers, and a series of Tolkien calendars, most notably Inger Edelfeldt, Roger Garland, the Brothers Hildebrandt, John Howe, Michael Kaluta, Alan Lee, Tim Kirk, and Ted Nasmith. These represent only a small fraction of the art inspired by Tolkien's works since the mid-twentieth century, which may be found in countless places: within and on the covers of translations, on role-playing game cards, in fan magazines, on posters, etc.

Immortality *see* **Mortality and Immortality**

Imram. Poem, first published in *Time and Tide* (London) for 3 December 1955, p. 1561. It was reprinted in *Sauron Defeated* (1992), pp. 296–9.

St Brendan, at his life's end, tells of a time when he and his companions 'sailed for a year and a day and hailed / no field nor coast of men'. They came under a cloud and to 'a shoreless mountain' with a 'smoking hood', then with sail and oar 'came to a starlit strand' and rowed 'through gates of stone . . . and left the sea'. In a 'hidden land' they found 'a Tree more fair than ever I deemed / in Paradise might grow', broad, tall, and 'white as winter'. The tree shook, its leaves flying; on high they heard a song, maybe by 'a third fair kindred'. At last Brendan saw a star,

> a light on the edge of the Outer Night
>   beyond the Door of Days,
> where the round world plunges steeply down,
>   but on the old road goes,
> as an unseen bridge that on arches runs
>   to coasts that no man knows.

The Irish monk Brendan, called 'the Navigator', who lived from about 486 to 575, is the subject of the best known of the tales of sea voyages, or *imrama*, told of early Irish saints. The *Navigatio Sancti Bendani*, first written down in the ninth or tenth century and widely copied, tells of Brendan's wondrous voyage to the Land of Promise in the West, a green country filled with light and precious stones. That Tolkien was aware of the story is evident from his mentions of Brendan in *The Nameless Land* (composed 1924, published 1927; 'Such loveliness to look upon / Nor Bran nor Brendan ever won'), and in notes for *The Lost Road* (written 1936–?7; 'the holy Brendan'). He drew upon it more extensively in a poem within *The Notion Club Papers* (1945–6), originally with the title *The Ballad of St Brendan's Death*, later called *The Death of St Brendan*. Although this closely approached its final form already in its earliest text, Tolkien produced four finished manuscript versions following its initial working, and then four typescripts. The latest versions have the title *Imram*.

Imram is notable for imagery shared with Tolkien's mythology (*'The Silmarillion'), especially the 'old road' that continues on, though 'the round world plunges steeply down', 'to coasts that no man knows': a Straight Road to the Blessed Land (see also *Road). Norma Roche discusses these aspects, and the legendary and historical background of *Imram*, in 'Sailing West: Tolkien, the Saint Brendan Story, and the Idea of Paradise in the West', *Mythlore* 17, no. 4, whole no. 66 (Summer 1991).

Incledon family. Edith Mary Suffield, called 'May' (?1866–1936; see also *Suffield family), sister of *Mabel Tolkien, married Walter Incledon (*b.* ?1850), a *Birmingham merchant. In 1893, shortly after Ronald Tolkien's first birthday, May and Walter Incledon, with their daughter Marjorie (1891–1973), visited Mabel and *Arthur Tolkien in *South Africa, where Walter had business interests. A second daughter, Mary, was born in 1895 (in the 1901 Census she is listed as 'Frieda'). May returned to England with her daughters probably in 1899, leaving Walter to follow. By now she had decided, like her sister Mabel, to become a Roman Catholic, and received instruction at St Anne's, Moseley. Her husband, however, was a staunch Anglican; when he returned to Birmingham he forbade her to enter a Catholic church ever again. Eventually she turned instead to spiritualism. Walter Incledon had earlier provided financial help for Mabel after Arthur's death in 1896, but discontinued it after her own conversion to Catholicism.

By 1901 the Incledons were living in Kings Norton, near Birmingham; Walter was then a commercial manager of a wrought iron tube works. By *c.* 1907 the family moved to *Barnt Green in Worcestershire. Ronald and Hilary Tolkien often visited them during the holidays. At Christmas the Incledons enjoyed amateur theatricals: in 1912 Ronald wrote a play for the occasion, *The Bloodhound, the Chef, and the Suffragette*, in which he also played the leading role of 'Professor Joseph Quilter, M.A., B.A., A.B.C., alias world-wide detective Sexton Q. Blake-Holmes, the Bloodhound' (quoted in *Biography*, p. 59). Marjorie and Mary made up a private language, 'Animalic', constructed principally from animal names; and after Marjorie lost interest in that, Mary collaborated with Ronald to invent a more sophisticated language, 'Nevbosh' (*Languages, Invented).

Mary Incledon later became godmother to Ronald's eldest son, *John. For many years she lived alone in a London flat near Westminster Cathedral, having herself converted to Roman Catholicism. After her early death from cancer in 1940, she was found to have left a large number of shares in her father's business to the Catholic Archbishop of Liverpool, to help in the building of a new cathedral. Her father, still anti-Catholic, bought back the shares at great expense.

Marjorie Incledon became a gifted artist in watercolours and oils, specializing in landscapes and portraits. In late middle age she trained at the Brighton School of Art, and exhibited more than once in the Royal Academy Summer Exhibition. She lived for a number of years with her widowed father at

Rottingdean in Sussex, except for about four years during the Second World War, when because of the threat of invasion they were evacuated to Worcester. After his death she moved to Ditchling, where she continued to paint in her studio until the age of eighty, when she dispersed her collection and retired to live in a quasi-religious community in the same neighbourhood. One of her cousin Ronald Tolkien's last visitors, she stayed with him in Oxford in August 1973.

'Index of Names for *The Lay of the Children of Húrin*'. Index of names occurring in *The Children of Húrin*, published with commentary and notes in *Parma Eldalamberon* 15 (2004), pp. 59–64, ed. Bill Weldon and Christopher Gilson. Dating from the period of composition of the poem (?1921–4), this includes proper names in Noldorin (*Languages, Invented) and English from the first forty lines of the poem (but not necessarily in the first form used in those lines), more or less in the order of occurrence, and is annotated by Tolkien with explanations of the names, relationships, and other miscellaneous other information. Some emendations made to the list follow developments in the genealogy of the princes of the Noldor. Also on one of the sheets are some tables 'apparently summarizing the developments of diphthongs in Noldorin' (p. 64).

The Inklings. Literary and social group of which Tolkien was a leading member. It played such an important part in his life that it is unfortunate that so little evidence exists to document its history. Although several of its members shared their memories in interviews or publications in later years, such accounts are mainly anecdotal and have sometimes been shown to be inaccurate or contradictory. The period during the Second World War and the late 1940s, when the group was most active, is partially documented in the letters that *C.S. Lewis wrote to his brother, Major *W.H. 'Warnie' Lewis, at the beginning of the war; in Tolkien's letters to his son *Christopher during 1943–5; and in Warnie Lewis's diary in the years following the war, supplemented by a few references in other letters. For earlier meetings of the Inklings (or of what might be called a proto-Inklings) there are only a few contemporary references, and the situation is the same for the group in the years of its decline.

The earliest known contemporary use of the name *Inklings* is in a letter from C.S. Lewis to *Charles Williams on 11 March 1936, in which he says that he, his brother, *Nevill Coghill, and Tolkien had all enjoyed Williams' book *The Place of the Lion*: 'So there are three dons and one soldier all buzzing with excited admiration. We have a sort of informal club called the Inklings; the qualifications (as they have informally evolved) are a tendency to write, and Christianity' (*Collected Letters*, vol. 2 (2004), p. 183). Tolkien gave a brief account of the origins of the group and its name in a letter to William Luther White on 11 September 1967, but pointed out he was relying on memory, for 'the Inklings had no recorder and C.S. Lewis no Boswell':

The name was not invented by C.S.L. (nor by me). In origin it was an undergraduate jest, devised as the name of a literary (or writers') club [see *Societies and clubs]. The founder was an undergraduate at University College, named Tangye-Lean. . . . In the event both C.S.L. and I became members. . . .

The club soon died . . . but C.S.L. and I at least survived. Its name was then transferred (by C.S.L.) to the undetermined and unelected circle of friends who gathered about C.S.L., and met in his rooms in Magdalen [College, *Oxford]. Although our habit was to read aloud compositions of various kinds (and lengths!), this association and its habit would in fact have come into being at that time, whether the original short-lived club had ever existed or not. C.S.L. had a passion for hearing things read aloud, a power of memory for things received in that way, and also a facility in extempore criticism, none of which was shared (especially not the last) in anything like the same degree by his friends.

I called the name a 'jest' because it was a pleasantly ingenious pun in its way, suggesting people with vague or half-formed intimations and ideas plus those who dabble in ink. [*Letters*, pp. 387–8]

C.S. Lewis surely would not have transferred the name while the earlier Inklings still in existence; and it seems unlikely that the earlier club lasted later than the summer of 1933, when Tangye Lean graduated and left Oxford.

Tolkien's letter implies that the group around C.S. Lewis already existed before the name was applied. The roots of what became the Inklings go back a considerable time, even if Lewis's frequent meetings with various friends did not coalesce into the regular gathering, twice a week, of a larger group until the mid-1930s. Lewis and *Owen Barfield probably first met in 1919 (though there is no contemporary evidence) and began 'a lifelong friendship that would be both social and intellectual' in which they deeply agreed and disagreed with each other on important questions and enjoyed 'the stimulation of *intellectual* combat and exchange' (George B. Tennyson, 'Owen Barfield: First and Last Inklings', *The World & I* (April 1990), pp. 541, 542). The first documented meeting of Lewis and Tolkien (mentioned by Lewis in his diary) was at an Oxford English Faculty 'tea' at Merton College on 11 May 1926. From the autumn of 1926 they met regularly outside Faculty business at the *Kolbítar founded by Tolkien (*Societies and clubs), a group which met socially to read and discuss the sagas and Eddas and to enjoy a drink while doing so. One evening in late November 1929 Tolkien accompanied Lewis back to Magdalen after some meeting, and they spent three hours talking of gods and giants and Asgard in Norse mythology, and not long after that Tolkien lent Lewis his unfinished *Lay of Leithian* to read. Lewis was delighted with it, but also sent him a detailed criticism as if written centuries later by a group of scholars. As Tolkien recalled in his letter to William Luther White, discussion (often quite heated), reading, and criticism of each other's works were characteristic components of meetings of the Inklings.

Lewis liked to bring his friends together. Owen Barfield recalled that Lewis introduced him to Tolkien in the 1920s when dining at the Eastgate Hotel. 'For some reason Tolkien was in a ridiculously combative mood', for which Lewis afterwards privately apologized. But Barfield felt that the conversation was 'entirely good-humoured and enjoyable; and [Tolkien's] random belligerence had only made me laugh' ('Foreword', *Seven* 1 (March 1980), p. 9). Barfield also recalled 'quite a few meetings – enough to constitute a "series" – in Lewis's room in the twenties between Lewis, Tolkien, and myself, sometimes together with *Colin Hardie [though Hardie later wrote that he did not attend meetings in Lewis's rooms until after the Second World War] and at least one with Nevill Coghill. I think it was these foregatherings that ultimately turned into the Inklings, though it may well be that the name was not adopted until 1933 . . .' ('The Inklings Remembered', *The World & I* (April 1990), p. 548). Another 'proto-Inklings' meeting was on 19 September 1931, when Tolkien and *H.V.D. 'Hugo' Dyson dined with Lewis and the conversation which followed dinner led to Lewis's acceptance of Christianity. Two months later, on 22 November, Lewis wrote to his brother that the custom had developed for Tolkien to call on him at Magdalen on Monday mornings for conversation and to drink a glass: 'Sometimes we talk English school politics; sometimes we criticise one another's poems: other days we drift into theology or "the state of the nation" . . .' (*Collected Letters*, vol. 2 (2004), p. 16).

Meetings at which members read works finished or in progress were well established by 1938. On 18 February of that year Tolkien told *Stanley Unwin that he had heard Lewis's *Out of the Silent Planet* 'read aloud to our local club (which goes in for reading things short and long aloud). It proved an exciting serial, and was highly approved. But of course we are all rather like-minded' (*Letters*, p. 29). And in a letter to Unwin on 4 June 1938: 'the Rev. *Adam Fox was elected Professor of Poetry . . . a member of our literary club of *practising poets* – before whom the *Hobbit*, and other works (such as *the Silent Planet*) have been read' (*Letters*, p. 36).

The meetings settled into a general pattern, if not as fixed as some commentators have assumed. The Inklings met in a pub, usually the Eagle and Child (called 'the Bird and Baby') in St Giles' late on Tuesday mornings before lunch. Lewis, Tolkien, and others on the Oxford English Faculty found the Eagle and Child especially convenient in wartime when most English lectures were given in the nearby Taylor Institution (and scheduled suitably). These meetings in a pub were for discussion and exchange of news, *not* for reading aloud works written by members, as is often wrongly stated. There are references, however, to meetings on other days of the week and in other pubs. It was at Inklings meetings in C.S. Lewis's rooms in Magdalen, after dinner on Thursdays, that members read their offerings, among which were sections of Tolkien's *Lord of the Rings*. These gatherings sometimes continued into the small hours, and in the war years members would have had to make their way home in the blackout. There is evidence that at some periods during the war some of the meetings at Magdalen took place on other days, especially in the autumn of 1943 when Tuesday seems to have been the usual day. Tolkien often still visited Lewis at Magdalen on a morning when neither of them was lecturing, not necessarily on Mondays, and they were sometimes joined by Charles Williams, whom Lewis had brought into the Inklings in late 1939. In general, between 7 October 1947 and 4 March 1948 (at least) Thursday meetings were hosted alternately by Lewis at Magdalen and Tolkien at Merton.

The number of members present at meetings varied, and some could attend only infrequently. Members turned up when they were able, but did not need to advise Lewis (or later Tolkien) in advance, or to send apologies when they could not attend. There was no formal organization or official election of proposed members, though evidence suggests that in later years, at least, there was some discussion among existing members before inviting someone to join the group. On 9 October 1945 Tolkien wrote to his son Christopher that the Inklings had proposed 'to consider you a *permanent member*, with right of entry and what not quite independent of my presence or otherwise' (quoted in Humphrey Carpenter, *The Inklings* (1978), p. 205). At a meeting on 23 October 1947 Warnie Lewis suggested *C.E. Stevens as a new member, and those present agreed. On the other hand, it proved difficult to remove self-invited members. Warnie Lewis wrote in his diary on 22 August 1946: 'J. [his brother, C.S. 'Jack' Lewis] and I much concerned this evening by the gate crashing of [*J.A.W.] B[ennett]; Tollers [Tolkien], the ass, brought him here last Thursday, and he has apparently now elected himself an Inkling. Not very clear what one can do about it' (*Brothers and Friends*, p. 194). Lewis later recalled in his edition of *Letters of C.S. Lewis* (1966):

> Properly speaking [the Inklings] was neither a club nor a literary society, though it partook of the nature of both. There were no rules, officers, agendas, or formal elections. . . . Proceedings neither began nor terminated at any fixed hour, though there was a tacit agreement that ten-thirty was as late as one could decently arrive. From time to time we added to our original number, but without formalities: someone would suggest that Jones be asked to come in of a Thursday, and there could either be general agreement, or else a perceptible lack of enthusiasm and a dropping of the matter. [p. 13]

In addition to those already mentioned, the following are also considered to have been Inklings: *Lord David Cecil, *Commander James Dundas-Grant, *R.E. Havard, *Father Gervase Mathew, *R.B. McCallum, *John Wain, and *Charles Wrenn. Special guests, such as *E.R. Eddison and *Roy Campbell, might be invited to the Thursday evenings. Some early members such as Barfield, Coghill, Fox, and Wrenn attended rarely or not at all when they moved from Oxford or became involved in other activities. Williams died in 1945. They were succeeded, however, by others who become members after the Second World War, including Hardie, McCallum, Christopher Tolkien, and Wain. Many of the Inklings were Oxford academics, mainly from the English

School, but McCallum was a historian and Hardie a Classics tutor; but other professions were represented. Barfield was a solicitor, Dundas-Grant a Lloyd's insurance underwriter and in the Royal Naval Reserve, Fox in Holy Orders (later a Canon of Westminster Abbey), Havard a medical doctor, Warnie Lewis a professional soldier, Mathew a Dominican priest, and Williams an editor at Oxford University Press who also wrote and lectured. As Lewis wrote to Williams, most of these were practising Christians. In addition to the Tolkiens and Mathew, Dundas-Grant, Havard, Wrenn, and Hardie after his marriage in 1940 were Catholics; Dyson, Fox, the Lewises, and Williams were Anglicans; Barfield was an Anthroposophist, a follower of Rudolf Steiner, and from 1949 a member of the Anglican Church; and Cecil was Anglo-Catholic (High Anglican). Although Warnie Lewis referred to J.A.W. Bennett in his diary in 1946 as a Roman Catholic, in fact Bennett was not received into the Catholic Church until the early 1960s.

Humphrey Carpenter in Part 3, Chapter 4 of *The Inklings*, 'A Fox That Isn't There', considers and rejects various theories put forward by others which hold that the Inklings were more than a group of friends: that they constituted a movement intended to alter the course of literature; that as 'Oxford Christians' they shared a common academic and religious point of view; that some at least represented 'a conscious attempt to present religion through the medium of romanticism' (p. 154), or that they had a common attitude to various aspects of life, including a dislike of much contemporary literature. He concludes the chapter: 'One day Tolkien, in a letter to his son Christopher, referred to the Inklings as "the Lewis seance", and there was more than an element of truth in this. They were Lewis's friends: the group gathered round him, and in the end one does not have to look any further than Lewis to see why it came into being. He himself is the fox' (p. 171).

David Cecil, in reviewing Carpenter's *Inklings*, pointed out that the individual Inklings had different opinions on many matters, including the form of Christianity they followed.

> The qualities, then, that gave The Inklings their distinctive personality were not primarily their opinions; rather it was a feeling for literature, which united, in an unusual way, scholarship and imagination. Their standard of learning was very high ... they were academic in the best sense of the word. But ... they also read imaginatively. The great books of the past were to them living in the same way as the work of a contemporary. ... Yet they did not try to bring them up-to-date. Simply they read their books in the spirit in which they were written. And they could communicate their sense of this spirit to their hearers. ... ['Oxford's Magic Circle', *Books and Bookmen* 24, no. 4 (January 1979), p. 10]

Among the longer works read at meetings of the Inklings were Tolkien's *Hobbit*, *Lord of the Rings*, and **Notion Club Papers*, C.S. Lewis's *Out of the Silent Planet*, *Perelandra*, *The Problem of Pain*, and *The Great Divorce*, Williams' *All*

Hallows' Eve, and W.H. Lewis's *Splendid Century: Some Aspects of French Life in the Reign of Louis XIV*. Other offerings were much shorter – a single poem, or Havard's paper on his clinical experience of pain. The Inklings also discussed current affairs, literature, and a wide variety of topics such as ghosts, cremation, and hymns.

In *The Inklings*, Part 3, Chapter 3, Humphrey Carpenter includes a reconstruction of a typical Thursday meeting, for which he interviewed many of the surviving Inklings. But probably the most vivid picture of the sort of no-holds-barred discussion that took place appears in *The Notion Club Papers*, especially in the earlier parts before the myth of Númenor begins to intrude. In his 'Memoir' included in his edition of his brother's letters, Warnie Lewis describes the beginning of a meeting:

> When half a dozen or so had arrived, tea would be produced, and then when pipes were well alight Jack [C.S. Lewis] would say, 'Well, has nobody got anything to read us?' Out would come a manuscript, and we would settle down to sit in judgement upon it – real unbiased judgement, too, since we were no mutual admiration society: praise for good work was unstinted, but censure for bad work – or even not-so-good work – was often brutally frank. To read to the Inklings was a formidable ordeal. . . . [*Letters of C.S. Lewis* (1966), pp. 13–14]

On several occasions during the years of austerity and rationing after the Second World War, an American admirer of C.S. Lewis sent him a large ham, and Lewis gave a ham supper for a select group of the Inklings at Magdalen.

Just as the Inklings seem to have gradually come together, so that no definite date can be given for its beginning, so the bonds linking the group gradually loosened, and no date can be given for its demise. Some have concluded from W.H. Lewis's entry in his diary on 27 October 1949, 'No one turned up after dinner' (*Brothers and Friends*, p. 230), that the last Magdalen meeting was that of 20 October 1949; but a ham supper attended by several Inklings is recorded on 7 February 1952.

Various reasons have been put forth for the gradual decline of the Inklings, but given the informal nature of the group, it is perhaps more surprising that it lasted so long than that it eventually faded away. One reason that has been suggested is the perceived cooling of the relationship between Tolkien and C.S. Lewis: see further under *Lewis. The fact that the Thursday meetings ceased much earlier than those in the Bird and Baby may be significant. It was at the evening meetings that members read works in progress as well as talked. Possibly some members began to dislike criticism, though this had not caused problems in the past. From Warnie Lewis's diaries it seems possible that a contributory factor may have been the behaviour of Hugo Dyson, who disliked any readings, but *The Lord of the Rings* in particular. Readings and criticism of work in progress had distinguished the Thursday meetings from other social occasions, and without them the main reason for the gatherings was gone.

It may also be that the evening meetings had been fostered in wartime and post-war austerity, when people drew closer together and there was less competition for the members' time. The pub meetings continued and were eventually moved to Mondays when C.S. Lewis was elected to a Cambridge chair in 1954, and thereafter divided his time between Cambridge and Oxford. When changes to the Eagle and Child made that pub less attractive to the group, meetings took place in the Lamb and Flag on the other side of St Giles'.

Tolkien's last recorded presence at such a meeting was on 9 November 1954. He may have attended later meetings, but after his retirement from the Merton professorship at the end of Trinity Term 1959, attendance would have entailed a special journey into the centre of Oxford from Headington. A few remaining members tried to continue the Monday morning meetings at the Lamb and Flag after C.S. Lewis's death in November 1963.

Two papers in the *Proceedings of the J.R.R. Tolkien Centenary Conference 1992* (1995) consider the influence of various Inklings on Tolkien's writings: 'Tolkien and the Other Inklings' by Colin Duriez (who also considers Tolkien's influence on C.S. Lewis) and 'More than a Bandersnatch: Tolkien as a Collaborative Writer' by Diana Lynne Pavlac. Both agree that perhaps the most important debt Tolkien owed to C.S. Lewis and other Inklings was encouragement, without which he might not have finished *The Lord of the Rings*. Pavlac cites instances noted by Christopher Tolkien in the relevant volumes of *The History of Middle-earth* where criticism by Lewis or Williams led to changes: Lewis's comments that there was too much hobbit talk in the earlier chapters (a point also made by *Rayner Unwin), and changing Treebeard's exclamation from 'Crack my timbers' to 'Root and twig' in response to criticism from Williams. The influence of Barfield's *Poetic Diction* (1928) on Tolkien's thinking and writing is explored in depth in Verlyn Flieger's *Splintered Light: Logos and Language in Tolkien's World* (1983; 2nd edn. 2002).

Ireland, Republic of (Eire). From 1949 Tolkien travelled frequently to Ireland, largely on business but also for pleasure. In 1949–51, 1954, and 1958–9, typically in late June to early July and in late September or October, he went as required to **Dublin, Cork, Galway**, and **Maynooth** as an external examiner for the National University of Ireland. On 8 October 1958 he wrote to *Robert Burchfield:

> I have covered 1500 miles since I left home on 23 September. On Sept. 24th I was involved in an alarming tempest at sea. . . . I arrived 5 hours overdue in Dublin at noon on 25th, rather battered; and I have since crossed Eire (E–W, and N–S) about 6 times, read 130 lbs (avd) of theses, assisted in the exams of 4 colleges, and finally presided at fellowship-vivas in Dublin before re-embarking (doubled up with lumbago). [Early English Text Society archive]

On 20 July 1954 the National University awarded him an Honorary D.Litt.

In August 1951 Tolkien went on holiday in Ireland with his wife and daughter (*Edith Tolkien, *Priscilla Tolkien). They stayed first in Cork, having sailed there from Fishguard in Wales. After several days they travelled to the remote village of **Castle Cove** in the west part of **Kerry** on the north bank of the Kenmare River, near the point where it flows into the Atlantic. There they stayed in a hotel run by the Misses O'Flaherty; another sister or sisters ran the village shop-cum-bar. Their brother, who operated the local taxi service, drove the Tolkiens to Mass in the nearby village of **Derrynane**. Tolkien drew nine views of the Kerry landscape with special emphasis on the sky and weather; one is reproduced in *Artist and Illustrator*, fig. 29 (misdated 1952).

On another holiday in Ireland, in early September 1965, Tolkien flew from Birmingham to Dublin – his first and probably only journey in an aeroplane. As on many of his visits to Ireland, he was accompanied by his son *Christopher, who arranged the flight and drove them from Dublin to Galway. Tolkien described this occasion in a letter to his grandson, Michael George:

> I enjoyed my holiday (or high-speed raid) in Ireland, where I have a good many friends, and am treated as sort of Irish-by-adoption, sealed by the possession of a Dublin degree. We had good weather: 1 damp day and half a wet morning is very little (even in a good year) out of 7 days in Ireland largely spent in the extreme west. But the country is now much more expensive to 'tour' in than it was, and something of its curious shabby, happy-go-lucky, tumbledown charm has gone. Motor-cars are (of course) the main agents of ruin, but within a few miles of Dublin motoring is still actually a pleasure: quick, safe, and often entirely unhindered. [16 September 1965, British Library MS Add. 71657]

On 8 January 1971 he wrote to Michael George:

> Of course I was also delighted to hear about your walking tour in Ireland although in fact you were a little bit further North than the parts which I know well of which the best are Galway, **Clare** and Cork. I am always happy when I am in Eire (except, of course, the North, where I have never been) and am now suffering from acute Eire-starvation, but I see no immediate chance of getting back there again. [British Library MS Add. 71657]

The Istari. Miscellaneous writings, collected and discussed under this assigned title by *Christopher Tolkien in *Unfinished Tales* (1980), pp. 388–402.

'THE ESSAY ON THE ISTARI'

Untitled work, pp. 388–91, written by Tolkien in 1954 in association with his unfinished index for *The Lord of the Rings*. He discusses the suitability of using the word *wizard* to translate Quenya *istar*, 'one of the members of an "order" . . . claiming to possess, and exhibiting, eminent knowledge of the history and nature of the World' (*Unfinished Tales*, p. 388). The Istari arrived in Middle-earth at about Third Age 1000 in the guise of Men, old but hale, and were perceived as such by Men of Middle-earth until it was noted that the Istari did not die and aged little. In fact, they came from Valinor, members of the same high order as the Valar, sent by them to Middle-earth with the consent of Eru when the shadow of Sauron began to grow again. They were 'forbidden to reveal themselves in forms of majesty, or to seek to rule the wills of Men or Elves by open display of power, but coming in shapes weak and humble were bidden to advise and persuade Men and Elves to good, and to seek to unite in love and understanding all those whom Sauron . . . would endeavour to dominate and corrupt' (p. 389). Five of this order came to the North of Middle-earth, notably Mithrandir (Gandalf) to whom Círdan gave the ring Narya, having perceived him to have 'the greatest spirit and the wisest' (p. 389). Gandalf arrived last, and alone remained faithful to his charge.

Christopher Tolkien compares this essay with what is said about the Istari in Appendix B of *The Lord of the Rings* and in *Of the Rings of Power and the Third Age*.

MISCELLANEOUS NOTES

Christopher Tolkien describes 'a brief and very hasty sketch of a narrative' in which a council of the Valar resolves 'to send out three emissaries to Middle-earth' (p. 393). Only two volunteer, Curumo (Saruman) and Alatar, sponsored by Aulë and Oromë respectively. Manwë commands a reluctant Olórin to be the third. Curumo and Alatar each take a companion, that of Curumo being Aiwendil (Radagast). With this are a 'page of jottings' concerning Curuno being obliged by Yavanna to take Aiwendil (Radagast), and a table relating the Istari to various Valar. An extract from notes on the Istari, probably written in 1972 (p. 394), was also published in the context of a complete document in *The Peoples of Middle-earth* (1996). See *The Five Wizards*.

WRITINGS CONCERNED WITH GANDALF

On the verso of the sketch concerning the council of the Valar is a discussion (*Unfinished Tales*, pp. 395–6) concerning the Last Alliance and the part played by the Elves in the final overthrow of Sauron at the end of the Third Age. The statement that the Istari, including Gandalf, were emissaries from Valinor leads into a discussion of 'Who was "Gandalf"?' and rejects the theory that he was Manwë. It concludes with a short alliterative poem on Manwë ('Wilt thou learn the lore // that was long secret'), mentioning the Istari, and (pp. 396–7) two notes on *Olórin*, one of the names of Gandalf.

These are followed, pp. 397–9, by a long note dating from before the publication of the second edition of *The Lord of the Rings* in 1966 'to elucidate the passage in *The Two Towers* IV 5 [i.e. bk. IV, ch. 5] where Faramir' reports what Gandalf had said concerning his many names (p. 397). This considers the meaning of the names in relation to Gandalf's travels in Middle-earth. Finally, pp. 399–400, is a note written in 1967 which gives 'a wholly different view' of Gandalf's travels and the etymology of his name *Incánus* (p. 399).

QUEEN BERÚTHIEL

In note 7 of *The Istari*, pp. 401–2, Christopher Tolkien cites his father's statement in 1956 that 'the cats of Queen Berúthiel and the names of the other two wizards' are the only things referred to in *The Lord of the Rings* which he can recollect as having no other existence in his sub-creation. He then summarizes with brief quotations a 'primitive outline' of the story of Queen Berúthiel. (See further, *Reader's Companion*, pp. 283–4.)

Italy. Tolkien first visited Italy with his daughter *Priscilla from late July to early August 1955 (see further, **Chronology**). Travelling by train via Milan, they arrived in **Venice** in the north of Italy on 31 July. For a few days they explored the city, built on more than one hundred islands. On one 'beautiful, balmy night' Tolkien found it 'incredibly, elvishly lovely – to me like a dream of Old Gondor, or Pelargir of the Númenórean ships, before the return of the Shadow' (travel diary, Tolkien Papers, Bodleian Library, Oxford, as for other quotations in this entry). He went twice to the Basilica di San Marco (St Mark's Basilica, mainly from the eleventh century), on one side of the great Piazza San Marco, but was disappointed to find most of its splendid interior hidden by scaffolding while under repair. On the island of Torcello he found the church of Santa Fosca (*c.* 1000) sad and dusty, but was impressed by the cathedral of Santa Maria Assunta, begun in the seventh century, in which many early carvings and mosaics are preserved. 'It was here,' Tolkien recorded, 'that in a corner, neglected except by excursionists, centuries past its days of wealth, that I first had the feeling that haunted me during the rest of my short visit to Italy: that of having come to the heart of Christendom; an exile from the borders and far provinces returning home, or at least to the home of his fathers.'

The 'great church of the Frari' about which Tolkien wrote at length in his travel diary is the Franciscan Chiesa di Santa Maria Gloriosa dei Frari (St Mary of the Friars), founded *c.* 1250, enlarged and rebuilt from 1340. Tolkien found it

> probably once beautiful, but now deformed by additions and by monu-
> ments (of doges and other notables), many of which are of a tastelessness
> on a crushing scale hardly to be rivalled in Westminster Abbey. The
> preposterous monument to a seventeenth-century Doge over the north
> door ... was beaten only by the appalling Canova monument. After
> these Titian looked homely and modest. I found the whole place deeply
> depressing, though a few old men collected chairs in the middle of the
> nave and had a pleasant evening chat.

The 'preposterous monument' is an elaborate work, probably designed by Baldassare Longhena and made by Antonio Canova to honour Giovanni Pesaro. After Canova's death his followers erected a pyramid-shaped monument to him, depicting St Mark's lion paying him homage, in fact a design Canova had made for a monument to the great painter Titian, who is also buried in the basilica.

The church of 'San Giorgio' which Tolkien found 'hideous' on 2 August 1955 is probably the well-known San Giorgio Maggiore, rebuilt in the late sixteenth to early seventeenth centuries to plans by Andrea Palladio, and generally considered one of his greatest works.

On 2 August Tolkien and Priscilla also visited two factories on the island of Murano, centre of the Venetian glassmaking industry since the late thirteenth century. Most of the products they saw were 'remarkable for their incredible vulgarity and hideous tastelessness. . . . Yet there was some lovely glass to be found, beautiful in shape and colour. . . .' On 4 August they spent two hours in the Galleria dell'Accademia di Belle Arti which houses a fine collection of Venetian art. Tolkien was especially moved by paintings by Tintoretto and a picture of St Jerome by Bassano. On 5 August they saw an exhibition of work by Giorgione at the Palazzo Ducale (Doges' Palace) beside San Marco. Once the home of the Doge, the elected leader of Venice, most of the present building dates from the fourteenth century.

On 6 August Tolkien and Priscilla took a series of trains via Florence, Terentola, and Perugia to **Assisi**. This hill town in central Italy is best known as the birthplace of St Francis (or Francesco) of Assisi, the founder of the Franciscan Order, and of his follower St Clare (or Chiara), the founder of the order of nuns known as the Poor Clares. Although its history extends back to Etruscan and Roman times, little of that period remains, most notably six Corinthian columns from the Tempio di Minerva built in the time of Augustus and preserved in the church of Santa Maria. But many medieval buildings have been preserved.

From 7 to 12 August 1955 Tolkien and Priscilla explored Assisi: the Public Gardens which they found dreary; the impressive Rocca Maggiore, a ruined castle on a high point above the town; the Capella dei Pellegrini, all that remains of a fifteenth-century hospice for pilgrims; and especially the town's many churches, as worshippers as well as tourists. Among these are the Basilica di San Francesco, begun in 1228 to house the tomb of St Francis and decorated with frescoes by leading artists of the thirteenth and fourteenth centuries; the church of San Pietro, built in the twelfth century by the Benedictines, which was near the convent where Tolkien and his daughter stayed in Assisi, and which Tolkien loved for its 'bareness and antiquity'; the Duomo di San Ruffino, where Saints Francis and Clare were baptized, with 'a beautiful ancient [twelfth-century] façade, but inside sombre and lugubrious baroque: much of it actually hideous . . .'; the church of Santa Chiara, with St Clare's tomb in the crypt, built in 1257–65 with some late fourteenth-century additions; and the Chiesa di San Damiano, just outside the town walls, where

St Francis in 1205 renounced the world and in 1212 accepted Chiara as his follower. San Damiano became the first house of the Poor Clares.

Tolkien visited Italy again while on a cruise with his wife *Edith in 1966. On the way to the eastern Mediterranean the ship called at Civitavecchia near Rome, but there is no evidence that Tolkien went ashore. Priscilla Tolkien, in correspondence with the authors, is certain that her father did not take the opportunity to visit Rome. On the return voyage the ship docked at Venice from 27 to 28 September 1966: on this occasion Tolkien went ashore and attended mass in St Mark's.

'Iþþlen' in Sawles Warde. Note, written in collaboration with *S.R.T.O. d'Ardenne, published in *English Studies* (Amsterdam) 28, no. 6 (December 1947), pp. 168–70. Its subject is the corrupted or misread word *iþþlen* in printed editions of the Bodleian Library version of the Middle English homily *Sawles Warde* (MS Bodley 34, see *Katherine Group), and the actual reading of the word in all surviving manuscripts of the work.

Iumbo, or ye Kinde of ye Oliphaunt see Oliphaunt

J.R.R. Tolkien: Artist and Illustrator. The standard account of Tolkien's paintings, drawings, and designs, written by Wayne G. Hammond and Christina Scull, first published in Great Britain by HarperCollins, London, in September 1995, and in the United States by the Houghton Mifflin Company, Boston, in October 1995. A corrected paperback edition was first published by Harper-Collins in 1998.

Included in this book are the most faithful reproductions to date of nearly 200 images by Tolkien, among which are all of his major illustrations and pictures made for reference or inspiration while writing his works of fiction. For the most part *Artist and Illustrator* supersedes *Pictures by J.R.R. Tolkien* (1979; 2nd edn. 1992), though a small number of images in the latter were not reproduced also in the former.

A list of Tolkien's art published in *Artist and Illustrator* is included as an appendix in the **Chronology** volume of the *Companion and Guide*. See also *Art.

Jennings, Elizabeth Joan (1926–2001). Elizabeth Jennings was one of two daughters of Dr Henry Cecil Jennings and his wife Mary; the family moved to Oxfordshire when Elizabeth was young. In North *Oxford they attended the same parish church as the Tolkiens, and became acquainted with them in the early thirties. *Priscilla Tolkien has recalled her memories of Elizabeth Jennings when they were young: 'We shared a neighbourhood, a culture, both religious and secular, and the friendship that grew between our families, both parents and siblings' ('Beginnings and Endings', *PN Review* 31, no. 1 (September–October 2004), p. 9). In 1937 Tolkien sent the Jennings family two complimentary copies of *The Hobbit*.

While reading English at St Anne's College, Oxford, Elizabeth counted among her friends Philip Larkin and Kingsley Amis, and when some of her own early poems were published in *Oxford Poetry* for 1949, and later in Robert Conquest's influential anthology *New Lines* (1956), she became associated with the 'Movement' school, a comparison to which she objected: as a woman and a Roman Catholic she was immediately different, but also, her poetry was too individual to be classified.

From 1950 to 1958 she was a librarian in the Oxford City Library, then spent three years as an editorial assistant at the publishers Chatto and Windus. She was also a freelance writer and poetry critic for *The Scotsman*, and an editor of anthologies. She published several books of her own poetry, beginning with *Poems* (1953), and including *Recoveries* (1961) and *The Mind Has Mountains* (1966) which dealt with a mental breakdown she had suffered. Her *Collected Poems* appeared in 1967, and *Collected Poems 1953–85* in 1986. Of her work, Tolkien read at least *A Way of Looking* (1955): he wrote to her on 3 December 1955 to congratulate her on its appearance, and again on 21 December with specific comments and criticisms. If he did not necessarily understand Jennings' poems (as he admitted), he appreciated them, in particular 'New Worlds', which concerns *Atlantis as a dream of 'swelling waters' to 'be ignored forever', losing even its name, now that one knows actual 'countries in space'.

The Jerusalem Bible. First published in Great Britain by Darton, Longman & Todd, London, and in the United States by Doubleday, Garden City, New York. Prepared by Roman Catholic scholars in Great Britain, *The Jerusalem Bible* was based on *La Sainte Bible*, more popularly called *La Bible de Jérusalem* because it was produced at the Dominican Biblical School in Jerusalem. *La Sainte Bible* was published, in French, by Les Éditions du Cerf, Paris, in fascicles between 1945 and 1955, and in one volume in 1956. For the English *Jerusalem Bible*, general editor Alexander Jones explained,

> in the case of a few books the initial draft was made [translated] from the French and was then compared word for word with the Hebrew or Aramaic by the General Editor and amended where necessary to ensure complete conformity with the ancient text. For the much greater part, the initial drafts were made from the Hebrew or Greek and simultaneously compared with the French when questions of variant reading or interpretation arose. [p. v]

Its purpose was to counter 'two of the principal dangers facing the Christian religion today. The first is the reduction of Christianity to the status of a relic – affectionately regarded, it is true, but considered irrelevant to our times. The second is its rejection as a mythology, born and cherished in emotion with nothing at all to say to the mind.' While Christianity had changed 'without betrayal' to meet the needs of changing times, it was felt that the Bible 'is of its nature a written charter guaranteed (as Christians believe) by the Spirit of

God, crystallised in antiquity, never to be changed – and what is crystallised may be thought by some to be fossilised' (p. v). *The Jerusalem Bible* therefore was intended to be both a faithful translation of the ancient texts and a literary expression of 'contemporary' English, in order to appeal to 'the mind of today' (p. vi).

On 30 January 1957, impressed with *The Lord of the Rings*, Jones wrote to Tolkien and asked him to contribute to *The Jerusalem Bible*. He offered Tolkien almost any book, or books, of the Bible to translate, few having been apportioned at that time. He hoped that Tolkien would agree to translate, from the French, the earliest books of the Old Testament, the Pentateuch (Genesis, Exodus, Leviticus, Numbers, Deuteronomy), but also held out the very brief Book of Jonah (only three pages in the printed *Jerusalem Bible*) as a possibility if Tolkien were pressed for time, even with one or two years in which to do the work. Tolkien replied that he did have many commitments, and moreover, was no French scholar (see *France; *Languages); but Jones wanted him as a collaborator primarily for his command of English. By 20 February 1957 Tolkien sent Jones a sample translation from the Book of Isaiah (1:1–31). By 7 March he finished a draft of Jonah, and had entered into correspondence with Jones about approaches to translation, in particular the use of archaisms in a work for contemporary readers. On 12 March 1957 Jones returned to Tolkien his translation of Jonah, with comments, for Tolkien to correct at leisure; and he sent also the Book of Joshua (in French), so that it would be on hand should Tolkien be moved, and have the time, to translate that also. (So one may learn, or deduce, from Jones's letters to Tolkien, preserved in the Tolkien Papers in the Bodleian Library, Oxford. Tolkien's letters to Jones are apparently no longer extant.)

On 24 April 1957 Tolkien wrote to his grandson Michael George (see *Michael Tolkien):

> I am hoping when I retire to get included in a new Bible-translation team that is brewing. I have passed the test: with a version of the Book of Jonah. Not from Hebrew direct! Incidentally, if you ever look at the Old Testament, and look at *Jonah* you'll find that the 'whale' – it is not really said to be a whale, but a big fish – is quite unimportant. The real point is that God is much more merciful than 'prophets', is easily moved by penitence, and won't be dictated to even by high ecclesiastics whom he has himself appointed.) [British Library MS Add. 71657]

Jones visited Tolkien in Oxford on 2 July 1957. The two agreed that it would be two years before Tolkien could consider giving much more time to *The Jerusalem Bible*, though that did not exclude his completing work on Jonah, plus Joshua and Judges and perhaps even the Books of Samuel. Tolkien did not agree to become a literary editor of *The Jerusalem Bible*, as Jones seems to have hoped, even after the end of two years, but he did not mind if Jones were to occasionally send him draft translations into English for comment. On 26

January 1958 Jones solicited Tolkien's opinions of a first draft of most of the Book of Job. Tolkien revised his translation of Jonah by 25 April 1961.

The history of *The Jerusalem Bible* is recalled by Anthony Kenny, nephew of Alexander Jones, in his autobiography *A Path from Rome* (1985). According to Kenny, Tolkien was asked to translate Judges and Jonah: 'He proved a difficult collaborator – I once visited him with Alec [Alexander Jones] in an attempt to iron out some of the difficulties – and in the end he contributed only a version of Jonah, leaving Judges to Walter Shewring' (p. 117). According to a letter from Darton, Longman & Todd quoted by Jessica Kemball-Cook (Jessica Yates) in *Amon Hen* 26 (May 1977), p. 12, Tolkien provided the initial draft of Job and played an important part in establishing its final text, but we have not been able to verify this from archival sources.

Jones, Gwyn (1907–1999). Educated at University College, Cardiff, where his M.A. thesis was on the Icelandic sagas, Gwyn Jones became a schoolmaster in 1929, then Lecturer in English at University College, Cardiff, from 1935 to 1940, and Professor of English Language and Literature at the University College of Wales, Aberystwyth, from 1940 to 1964. One of his students at Aberystwyth remembered him as 'a Bardic figure who bestrode the narrow universe like some Cymric colossus' (Jim Henderson, 'Dear PROM: Memories of Plyn', 2001, *www.prom-aber.com*). In 1965 he returned to University College, Cardiff, as Professor of English Language and Literature, a post he held until his retirement in 1975.

Jones was a major figure in the study of Anglo-Welsh Literature. He edited books such as *Welsh Legends and Folk-Tales* (1955), *The Oxford Book of Welsh Verse in English* (1977), and volumes of Welsh short stories, and with his colleague Thomas Jones he produced the standard English translation of *The Mabinogion* (1948). In 1939 he founded the *Welsh Review*, of which he was editor until 1948; Tolkien's **Lay of Aotrou and Itroun* appeared in the December 1945 number of that journal. Jones and Tolkien were acquainted in part because Tolkien was an external examiner at Aberystwyth. In June 1945 Tolkien lent him *Aotrou and Itroun* and *Sellic Spell* (**Beowulf*): Jones thought that the latter should be prescribed reading for all university students of *Beowulf*.

In early 1947 Jones and Tolkien discussed **Sir Gawain and the Green Knight* by correspondence: Tolkien lent Jones his draft Modern English translation of that work, which Jones praised, and which influenced him in producing his own translation, published in 1952. Among his other works are *A History of the Vikings* (1968; rev. edn. 1984), *Kings, Beasts and Heroes* (1972), and many popular novels, beginning with *Richard Savage* (1935).

On 24 April 1947 Tolkien brought Jones with him to a meeting of the **Inklings. **W.H. Lewis recorded that the other members were annoyed at Tolkien for bringing a stranger with him, 'but he turned out to be capital value; he read a Welsh tale of his own writing, a bawdy humorous thing told in a rich polished style which impressed me more than any new work I have come across for a long time' (*Brothers and Friends*, p. 200).

Kalevala. During the nineteenth century Dr Elias Lönnrot, among others, began to collect traditional songs of the Finns. His earliest compilation, known as the *Proto-Kalevala*, was not published; but in 1835 he issued an arrangement of songs as a continuous story in thirty-two *runos* (cantos), the *Old Kalevala*, and in 1849 an expanded text of fifty *runos*. The latter is the work generally referred to by the *Kalevala*, for which Lönnrot wrote extra material to provide necessary links between its component tales. Some of the traditional songs thus collected were narratives preserving ancient myths, while others were sung at weddings or were charms to protect cattle: these Lönnrot inserted at suitable places. Because of multiple sources, there are variant versions of some tales, and even inconsistencies within a single version, on which Tolkien would later comment.

Nonetheless, the *Kalevala* was the first significant work of literature written in Finnish. It made the Finns aware of a past and a cultural tradition of which they could be proud. From the twelfth century, Finland (Suomi) had been ruled by Sweden, but its eastern province, Karelia, was ceded to Russia in 1721, and the rest of the country in 1809. While under Russian rule, Finland enjoyed semi-independence as a grand duchy with a local senate and the Tsar as Grand Duke, to the extent that a Finnish 'nationalist' party now began to assert itself. In these circumstances, Lönnrot gathered his songs and the *Kalevala* took shape. Although it has been called the national epic of Finland, the *Kalevala* is not one in the same sense as the Greek *Iliad*, the French *Chanson de Roland*, or the German *Nibelungenlied*. As Francis Peabody Magoun has said, all of these epics 'possess a more or less unified and continually moving plot with actors who are wealthy aristocratic warriors performing deeds of valor . . . on a rather large stage'; but the *Kalevala* 'is essentially a conflation and concatenation of a considerable number and variety of traditional songs, narrative, lyric, and magic, sung by unlettered singers, male and female, living to a great extent in northern Karelia in the general vicinity of Archangel' (*The Kalevala, or Poems of the Kaleva District* (1963), p. xiii).

Tolkien discovered the *Kalevala* in W.F. Kirby's English verse translation (1907) during his final year at *King Edward's School, Birmingham. A few years later, he said that when one discovers the *Kalevala* 'you are at once in a new world and can revel in an amazing new excitement. You feel like Columbus on a new Continent, or Thorfinn in Vinland the Good' (Tolkien Papers, Bodleian Library, Oxford). By then the stories of the *Kalevala* had inspired him to creation in several modes. In September 1911 he wrote a poem, *The New Lemminkäinen*, a parody of part of Kirby's translation, and in Michaelmas Term 1914 he began *The Story of Kullervo*, a retelling in prose and verse of one of the components of the *Kalevala*. He wrote a paper, *On 'The Kalevala' or Land of Heroes* (quoted above), which he delivered first to the Sundial Society at Corpus Christi College, *Oxford, on 22 November 1914, and then to the Exeter College Essay Club (*Societies and clubs) in February 1915. On 27 December 1914 he painted an elaborate watercolour, *The Land of Pohja* (*Artist and Illustrator*, fig. 41), inspired by another story in the *Kalevala*. And in the early 1920s he made a revised version of most of his lecture, which he delivered probably to an audience at *Leeds.

In *J.R.R. Tolkien: A Biography* Humphrey Carpenter wrote that in 'a paper on the *Kalevala* [read] to a college society' Tolkien

> began to talk about the importance of the type of mythology found in the Finnish poems. 'These mythological ballads,' he said, 'are full of that very primitive undergrowth that the literature of Europe has on the whole been steadily cutting and reducing for many centuries with different and earlier completeness among different people.' And he added: 'I would that we had more of it left – something of the same sort that belonged to the English.' An exciting notion; and perhaps he was already thinking of creating that mythology for England himself [p. 59]

The implication is that these words come from the paper Tolkien that wrote and delivered at Oxford in 1914 and 1915 – words which have been frequently quoted in association with the earliest poems of his *'Silmarillion' mythology, and as written before he commenced *The Book of Lost Tales* in which the history of the Elves has close ties with England. Although a variant of his first sentence ('These mythological ballads . . .') is in the paper as first written, the second appears only in the version of the 1920s, after Tolkien had written and abandoned *The Book of Lost Tales*. He *may*, then, have *thought* about creating a 'mythology for England' in 1914, but he did not *write* 'I would that we had more of it left – something of the same sort that belonged to the English' until nearly a decade later. Whatever his thought or intent, Tolkien had much less to work on than Lönnrot, and his 'Silmarillion' is almost an entirely new creation, incorporating only a few fragmentary remains of lost English tales and legends. Its main connection with England is the recording and transmission of the history of the Elves by a man of Anglo-Saxon race and, temporarily, Tol Eressëa physically becoming England (see further, entries for *The Book of Lost Tales* and *England).

Tolkien's watercolour *The Land of Pohja* illustrates the episode near the end of the *Kalevala* in which the old magician Väinämöinen fills Pohja, or Pohjola, in the North of Finland with music so sweet that the Moon settles in a birch-tree and the Sun in a fir-tree, so that they may hear it better. Louhi, the evil mistress of the land, captures the Moon and the Sun and hides them away. Then (in Kirby's translation) 'was the night unending, / And for long was utter darkness'. It seems likely that this was a precursor of the 'Silmarillion' tale of the destruction of the Two Trees, the theft of the Silmarils, the Darkening of Valinor, and the creation of the Sun and Moon from the last fruit and flower of the Trees. In May 1915, in another watercolour, *The Shores of Faery*, Tolkien depicted the Sun and Moon growing on two almost leafless trees (*Artist and Illustrator*, fig. 44), and in a poem with the same title, written then or a few months later, he referred to 'naked trees' bearing 'Night's silver bloom' and 'the globed fruit of Noon'.

The mysterious magical object called in the *Kalevala* the Sampo has similarities to the Silmarils of Fëanor. Forged by Ilmarinen and given by him to
Louhi as part of a bride-price for her daughter, it grinds out grain, salt, and
coins, but its possession is disputed and leads to conflict. In 'The *Kalevala* and
The Silmarillion' Clive Tolley wrote:

> The Sampo was forged by the greatest smith, Ilmarinen, a task of which
> he alone was capable, for the purpose of winning the maid of Pohja. Also,
> the materials needed could apparently only be procured once; the Sampo
> made its environs prosperous, which may be compared with the Silmaril
> on Tol Galen; like the Silmarilli, the Sampo was kept hidden away in
> an impregnable mountain in the north . . . in Pohjola, which resembles
> Angband in many respects. [*Mallorn* 15 (September 1980), p. 14]

Tolley compares 'the contest of song and magic between Felagund and
Sauron' with that between Väinämöinen and Joukahainen, or 'between
the Master of Pohja and Lemminkäinen', and notes that 'Lúthien's chants to
Morgoth in Thangorodrim resemble Väinämöinen's singing on his lyre in
Pohja, by the power of which he casts a spell of sleep over all Pohja, and then
steals the Sampo. . . .' But 'Tolkien changes his sources and uses them only
cursorily. so that what is used is welded inextricably into the story, and the
result is essentially original' (pp. 14–15).

David Elton Gay sees Väinämöinen, often described as 'old', as a source for
Tom Bombadil in *The Lord of the Rings*. For both,

> power comes from their command of song and lore rather than from
> ownership and domination. Väinämöinen spends his time in endless
> singing, not singing songs of power, however, but rather songs of know-
> ledge. Indeed, it would appear that he, like Tom Bombadil, sings for the
> simple pleasure of singing. . . .
> To have power over something in the mythology of the *Kalevala* one
> must know its origins and be able to sing the appropriate songs and
> incantations concerning these origins. Great power in the world of the
> *Kalevala* requires great age and great knowledge, and Väinämöinen has
> both. A large part of his power comes from the fact that as the oldest
> of all living things he saw the creation of things, heard their names, and
> knows the songs of their origins, and it was his works which helped give
> shape to the land. The same is clearly true of Tom Bombadil. ['J.R.R. Tol-
> kien and the *Kalevala*: Some Thoughts on the Finnish Origins of Tom
> Bombadil and Treebeard', *Tolkien and the Invention of Myth: A Reader*
> (2004), pp. 298–9]

KULLERVO AND TÚRIN TURAMBAR

But the *Kalevala* story which had the most influence on Tolkien was that of Kullervo. In a letter to *W.H. Auden Tolkien explained that he 'was immensely attracted by something in the air of the Kalevala, even in Kirby's poor translation', and that the beginning of 'The Silmarillion' and all that followed was 'an attempt to reorganize some of the Kalevala, especially the tale of Kullervo the hapless, into a form of my own' (7 June 1955, *Letters*, p. 214). That story eventually was a major influence on *The Tale of Turambar* (*'Of Túrin Turambar'), one of the earliest written parts of *The Book of Lost Tales* and a story which became of increasing importance to Tolkien in his later years.

In the 1849 *Kalevala* Untamo attacks the house of his brother, Kalervo, killing all his people except one girl, who is pregnant with Kalervo's child. Kullervo, the son she bears in captivity, grows so fast that at three months he is knee-high and threatens to avenge his father's death and his mother's tears. Untamo tries three times to kill the child (putting him in a barrel pushed out into the water, casting him on a burning pyre, and hanging him from an oak tree), but each time Kullervo is found unharmed. When Kullervo is older, Untamo sets him to work, but every task he is given has disastrous results. Untamo therefore sells him to the smith Ilmarinen as a slave. Ilmarinen's wife orders Kullervo to take her cows out to pasture, and maliciously gives him a cake to eat in which she has inserted a stone. When Kullervo tries to cut the cake, his knife, his only heirloom from his father, breaks. In revenge, he drives the cattle into the marshes and takes back a herd of wolves and bears. When Ilmarinen's wife goes to milk them, she is torn to pieces. Despite her pleading, Kullervo refuses to save her.

Kullervo runs away and decides to avenge his family's wrongs on Untamo. He finds, however, that his father and mother are both still alive, though a sister has disappeared while gathering berries. When he attempts various tasks, all end disastrously, because he exerts too much strength. Finally he is sent to pay the family taxes, and on his homeward journey tries to entice a maiden into his sleigh. When she declines, he uses force and then seduces her compliance with silver and rich clothing. Later, she enquires who he is, and realizes that he is her brother. She reveals this to him, then flings herself into a river. Kullervo laments her death and wishes he had never been born.

He still wishes to seek vengeance, however, and rejects his mother's pleading not to leave his family. His father, and a surviving sister and brother who have suddenly appeared, declare that they will not weep if they hear of his death, and he responds in kind. As he makes his way to Untamo, messengers bring news of the deaths of his father, brother, sister, and mother, but he shows no sorrow except for the last. After slaughtering Untamo and all his people, Kullervo returns to his father's house and finds all dead as he had been told. He goes into the forest, taking with him the family dog, Musti (first mentioned at this point). When he comes to the place where his sister killed herself, he asks his sword if it is willing to slay him, and it replies:

Wherefore at thy heart's desire
Should I not thy flesh devour,
And drink up thy blood so evil?
I who guiltless flesh have eaten
Drank the blood of those who sinned not?
[Kirby trans., vol. 2, p. 124]

Kullervo sets his sword in the ground and throws himself upon it.

There are inconsistencies evident in this account, and the arrangement in the *Old Kalevala* is different again. Lönnrot notes in a revised preface to the *Old Kalevala* that 'the Kullervo runes [runos] were particularly confused. First, a number of variants relate that his parents had been killed by Untamo – while he himself, yet unborn, was taken into captivity inside his mother's womb. Still others tell of his bidding farewell to his parents, and others describe his departing for war' (trans. by Pentikäinen, cited below, p. 40).

The most obvious similarities between the stories of Kullervo and Túrin Turambar are that each unwittingly commits incest with his sister (though in very different circumstances), and each commits suicide after having asked his sword to slay him, to which the sword replies that having drunk guiltless blood it will not hesitate to take the life of a master who has sinned (Kullervo) or killed others unjustly (Túrin). In addition, both Kullervo and Túrin are torn from their families, both achieve feats of great strength, both seem ill-fated, with much that they do turning out disastrously, and both seek revenge for evil treatment of their family (Kullervo on Untamo, and Túrin on Brodda). Kullervo, however, is a less sympathetic character, seeming to care little for anyone. The revenge he takes on Ilmarinen's wife is out of proportion, and he uses force followed by gifts to have his way with his sister; whereas Túrin's sister, Nienor, who has lost her memory, is his willing wife, and Morgoth's malice is seen to be working constantly against Túrin.

In comparing the story of Túrin with that of Kullervo, Jonathan B. Himes says that

> the effect of tragedy is heightened by tainting Túrin's destiny with inescapable doom. Though imperfect, he is more a victim of Melkor's subtle designs than an evil-doer. Instead of omitting the killing and incest, Tolkien makes them the integral result of Túrin's indomitable yet unwitting youth, while suppressing his spite and pettiness.
>
> Whereas Kullervo lashes out with malice to kill Ilmarinen's wife and Untamo's household, Túrin attacks too rashly, inadvertently killing Saeros upon extreme provocation, and later mortally wounding his friend Beleg in the confusion of his rescue from Morgoth. . . . Kullervo's incest is the result of chasing maidens in his sleigh, but for Túrin it is a marriage doomed by the amnesia cast over his sister by Glaurung the dragon. ['What J.R.R. Tolkien Really Did with the Sampo?' *Mythlore* 22, no. 4, whole no. 86 (Spring 2000), p. 73]

See also Marie Barnfield, 'Túrin Turambar and the Tale of the Fosterling', *Mallorn* 31 (December 1994).

THE STORY OF KULLERVO

Between reading the *Kalevala* and writing various accounts of the story of Túrin, Tolkien began *The Story of Kullervo* in 1914. In October of that year he wrote to his fiancée, Edith Bratt (*Edith Tolkien): 'I am trying to turn one of the stories [of the *Kalevala*] – which is really a very great story and most tragic – into a short story somewhat on the lines of [*William] Morris's romances with chunks of poetry in between' (*Letters*, p. 7). He left it unfinished, but later considered its writing a step leading to 'The Silmarillion'. It is also significant as his first attempt to write a work of literature mainly in prose. His choice of words depends heavily on Kirby, and the story he tells is basically that in the *Kalevala*, but he removes the inconsistencies, and some of the changes he makes look forward to the story of Túrin. In Tolkien's version, Untamo slays Kalervo before the eyes of his pregnant wife, and carries her and her son and daughter into bondage. She bears twins, Kullervo and a daughter whose name *Wanona* meant 'weeping' (compare the name given to Túrin's sister, *Nienor* 'Mourning'). Kullervo and Wanona are dear to each other, and he also tries to comfort his mother, who weeps for Kalervo. Kullervo's early affection and loving relationship with Wanona foreshadow Túrin's affection for Lalaith in the *Narn i Chîn Húrin*, though it was with Nienor that he committed unwitting incest.

When Kullervo is sold to the smith, here called Asemo, he grieves to leave his sister. Another change, foreshadowing Morgoth's curse on Túrin, is that Asemo's wife, as she dies, curses Kullervo and foretells that his end will be more awful than hers, and remembered for ever as a tale of horror. Kullervo sets out to revenge himself and his family on Untamo, but meets a maiden in a clearing in the forest. Tolkien suggests that it is the curse of Asemo's wife that leads Kullervo to desert his quest and make advances to the maiden. These are not as forceful as in the *Kalevala*, but still she flees him like a wild thing (foreshadowing the flight of Nienor in 'The Silmarillion'). He catches her, and here Tolkien's wording is ambiguous: it is not clear if she ceases to resist him (because of the curse) before or after he takes her. Only after the two have lived together for a while in the forest (like Túrin and Nienor) does she ask about his family, and realize from his reply that he is her brother. She throws herself over a waterfall, as does Nienor in early versions of the story in the *legendarium*. At this point the narrative ends.

While Tolkien's Kullervo is still in many ways an unattractive character, he is more sympathetic than his namesake in the *Kalevala*; nonetheless (like Túrin), everything he does turns out badly, and at times he overreacts to events. Tolkien also enhances the role of the hound, Musti (sometimes called Mauri), whom Kullervo meets while he is still living in Untamo's house. Musti warns Kullervo against Untamo, and gives him three hairs, telling him that if he is ever in danger, he should take one and call on him. Almost immediately, Untamo makes three attempts on Kullervo's life, and each time Kullervo is saved by the magic of Musti, whose wisdom and power Tolkien stresses. Musti did not survive into Túrin's story, but Huan the hound in the tale of Beren and Lúthien (*'Of Beren and Lúthien') was perhaps his successor.

The verse translation of the *Kalevala* by W.F. Kirby, *Kalevala: The Land of Heroes* (1907), which Tolkien knew was long available in the Everyman's Library series. For a more modern, prose translation, see that by Magoun cited above, and his *The Old Kalevala and Certain Antecedents* (1969). *Kalevala Mythology* by Juha Y. Pentikäinen, translated and edited by Ritva Poom (expanded edn. 1999), provides a detailed background to the sources and compilation of the *Kalevala*.

Katherine Group. A group of five religious works in prose contained in MS Bodley 34 in the Bodleian Library, Oxford: *Seinte Katerine, Seinte Margarete, Seinte Iuliene, Hali Meiðhad*, and *Sawles Warde*. The first three are lives of virgin saints, Katherine of Alexandria (from which the group of works takes its name), Juliana of Nicomedia, and Margaret of Antioch. The epistle *Hali Meiðhad* (sometimes *Hali Meidenhad*, 'Holy Maidenhood') attempts to persuade women to choose, or to remain in, a religious life of virginity rather than life in the world. *Sawles Warde* ('The Custody of the Soul') is a homily on the human being as if a household under the overlordship of God. Written in the early thirteenth century in the West Midlands of England, these works are contemporary with and thematically related to the **Ancrene Riwle*. They also share features of the same literary dialect of Middle English, with which Tolkien was long concerned and whose study he advanced. See **Holy Maidenhood* (1923), a review by Tolkien of the Early English Text Society edition of *Hali Meiðhad*; the article **Some Contributions to Middle-English Lexicography* (1925), half of which is devoted to notes on the glossary of the Early English Text Society (**Societies and clubs*) edition of *Hali Meiðhad*; **Ancrene Wisse and Hali Meiðhad* (1929), an essay on the relationship between those works; **'Iþþlen' in Sawles Warde* (1947), an article written with S.R.T.O. d'Ardenne; and **MS. Bodley 34: A Re-Collation of a Collation* (1947–8), also written with S.R.T.O. d'Ardenne.

Tolkien and d'Ardenne produced an edition of *Þe Liflade ant te Passiun of Seinte Iuliene* (*The Life and Passion of St Juliene*), in the first instance as d'Ardenne's **Oxford B.Litt.* thesis and the basis for her doctoral degree from Liège (**Belgium*): as such, it bears only her name. It was published in 1936, and reissued with corrigenda in 1961. They also began to prepare an edition of *Seinte Katerine*. Although Tolkien and d'Ardenne evidently planned an edition of the whole of MS Bodley 34, their joint efforts progressed only so far. D'Ardenne herself published a transcript of the complete manuscript in 1977 (*The Katherine Group*), and with **E.J.* Dobson completed an edition of *Seinte Katerine* (*Seinte Katerine: Re-Edited from MS Bodley 34 and the Other Manuscripts*, 1981).

Tolkien also assisted *W. Meredith Thompson in preparing an edition of a related manuscript, Þe Wohunge of Ure Lauerd ('The Wooing of Our Lord'), one of the so-called 'Wooing Group' of monologues or prayers.

A useful collection of Katherine Group texts, with translations and notes, is *Medieval English Prose for Women: Selections from the Katherine Group and Ancrene Wisse*, ed. Bella Millett and Jocelyn Wogan-Browne (rev. and corrected edn. 1992).

Ker, Neil Ripley (1908–1982). The noted palaeographer N.R. Ker at first read Philosophy, Politics, and Economics at *Oxford, but on the advice of *C.S. Lewis changed his study to English Language and Literature. His B.Litt. thesis, *A Study of the Additions and Alterations in MSS Bodley 340 and 342*, was examined by Tolkien and *Kenneth Sisam in 1933. From 1935 Ker gave regular lectures at Oxford on Old English manuscripts, and from 1941 to 1968 was successively Lecturer and Reader in Palaeography. From 1945 he was also a Fellow of Magdalen College. His catalogues of English manuscripts and other writings, most notably *Medieval Libraries of Great Britain* (1941; 2nd edn. 1964) and the series *Medieval Manuscripts in British Libraries* (begun 1969), are numerous and renowned.

In 1956 Tolkien suggested Ker to write an introduction to Tolkien's edition of the Ancrene Wisse (*Ancrene Riwle*) for the Early English Text Society (*Societies and clubs); this was not published until 1962, by which time Ker had contributed descriptions of the relevant manuscripts to other editions of Ancrene Riwle issued by the EETS. Although Tolkien and Ker disagreed about certain points regarding the transcription and presentation of the manuscript of the Ancrene Wisse, they seem to have remained on friendly terms. Ker contributed an essay, 'The Bodmer Fragment of Ælfric's Homily for Septuagesima Sunday', to the Festschrift *English and Medieval Studies Presented to J.R.R. Tolkien on the Occasion of His Seventieth Birthday* (1962), and in 1970 Ker sent Tolkien a copy of an article he had written on *A.S. Napier which Tolkien found deeply interesting.

King Edward's School, Birmingham. King Edward's School, named after King Edward VI, was founded in 1552 in response to a petition from citizens of *Birmingham. As usual for a grammar school at that time, its syllabus was devoted almost entirely to Latin and Greek. Towards the end of the seventeenth century a Petty School or English School was established as a preparatory school to the grammar school, where pupils were taught reading and writing and some arithmetic. From the mid-eighteenth century, in response to a demand for a syllabus more relevant to the needs of the youth of Birmingham, now of growing importance as a centre of industry and trade, subjects such as geography, French, and drawing were added. In 1839 an English School or 'Modern Side' devoted to modern languages, arts, and sciences was established in the then recently rebuilt school alongside and equal to the Grammar or Classical School, each with about 220 boys. At first the two sides were taught separately except for a few shared classes, and functioned almost as separate schools. By the time Tolkien attended King Edward's School, from September 1900, the Classical and English Schools had been formally united except for the different syllabi they offered, and even the Classical School studied a wider range of subjects. (A High School for Girls was established by the Governors of King Edward's School in 1883. One of its earliest pupils was Tolkien's *Aunt Jane Neave.)

In Tolkien's day the School was in New Street in the centre of Birmingham, near the New Street railway station (the School song refers to 'our smoke-encrusted precinct'). The School building, completed in 1838, was designed in the Gothic Revival style by Charles Barry, best known as the architect of the present Houses of Parliament. An exterior photograph of the old school is reproduced in *The Tolkien Family Album*, p. 25. Rectangular and built around two courtyards, it was designed according to the teaching systems of the early nineteenth century, when it was customary for several classes to be conducted simultaneously in one large room. By the early twentieth century the rooms intended to provide accommodation for the Chief Master and the Second Master at each end of the building had been converted into classrooms, as had the 102-foot-long room on the first floor at the front of the building originally used by the English School. The 'Big School', a room 104 feet long and 30 feet wide built on the first floor at the back of the building, survived and was used mainly for prayers and assembly; a photograph is reproduced in *Life and Legend*, p. 15. Other photographs are included in T.W. Hutton, *King Edward's School, Birmingham, 1552–1952* (1952), and Anthony Trott, *No Place for Fop or Idler: The Story of King Edward's School, Birmingham* (1992).

At that time the Thirteenth Class was the lowest and the First Class the highest, but after the Eighth Class there were three unnumbered classes: Lower Remove, Upper Remove, and Transitus. Pupils were organized into sets for Mathematics. According to the School curriculum published in July 1906,

the nine Classes from the 13th upwards to the Transitus, inclusive, receive instruction in the ordinary elementary subjects of a liberal education, *viz.* Arithmetic and Elementary Mathematics, Scripture, English, History, Geography, French, Latin and Drawing. The boys are also (as far up as Class 8) instructed in Botany, with the intention of training their powers of observation and evoking an interest in the objects and phenomena of nature. In the Removes and Transitus, Botany is replaced by the beginning of a systematic course in Physics and Chemistry. All boys throughout the School are required to take physical exercises in the Gymnasium, unless forbidden to do so by a medical man.

Above the Transitus the School was divided into a Classical (or Literary) Side and a Modern (or Scientific) Side: boys intending to go to Oxford or Cambridge took the Classical Side, which included Greek but not Science (except in a Voluntary Class). The Classical Side did not include a Seventh

Class. Both sides spent the same amount of time on Mathematics, and both studied Modern Languages.

The number of boys in each class varied; the average was about twenty. There was no school uniform other than the school cap.

At first, entry to the School was by nomination by one of its Governors, but after 1866 most places were obtained by competitive examination, which could be taken at various ages for admission to different classes. Pupils did not spend a specific time in each class, and the more able would move up the classes more speedily, or might even skip classes. Those boys who intended to go on to university stayed longer than those who did not. (Tolkien's brother *Hilary left King Edward's School in July 1910 at the age of 16; Tolkien himself left in 1911 at the age of 19, though he would have done so a year earlier had he obtained an Oxford scholarship in December 1909.)

Tolkien's father (*Arthur Tolkien) had attended King Edward's School, which enjoyed a deserved reputation for academic excellence. Tolkien himself sat the entrance examination in autumn 1899 and failed, but was successful in his second attempt in the following year. He entered the School in September 1900 and was placed with twenty other pupils in the Eleventh Class under W.H. Kirkby. A sympathetic uncle paid the fees, then £12 per year. By autumn term 1901 Tolkien had advanced to the Eighth Class, under A.W. Adams. In 1902 he briefly attended St Philip's School, attached to the *Birmingham Oratory, but after winning a foundation scholarship returned to King Edward's in spring term 1903, where he remained a pupil until the end of the 1911 summer term.

At the beginning of 1903 Tolkien was in the Lower Remove, where he was taught by R.H. Hume. In autumn term 1903 he moved into the Sixth Class on the Classical Side under *George Brewerton. He stayed there until the end of summer term in 1905, when he received a prize for placing first in the class. In autumn term 1905 he entered the Fifth Class under C.H. Heath, where he first met *Christopher Wiseman. He spent probably only one term in Heath's class, and entered the Fourth Class under *R.W. Reynolds in spring or summer term 1906. In autumn term 1906 he entered the Third Class under A.E. Measures. After only one term he then entered the Second Class taught by the Chief Master, *Robert Cary Gilson, together with A.E. Measures. In autumn term 1907 he moved into the First Class, also under Gilson and Measures.

King Edward's School encouraged many activities beside study (*Societies and clubs). Tolkien belonged to the Debating Society from at least October 1909, and was its Secretary during his final year (1910–11). He took part in the annual Latin debates, in which he displayed his skill with languages (Greek, Gothic, and Old English as well as Latin) and a flair for the dramatic. He was probably also a member of the Literary Society, to which he read a paper on the Norse sagas in February 1911. The Musical and Dramatic Society provided an Annual Open Concert. A Cadet Corps, later the Officers Training Corps, was begun at King Edward's School in 1907; in January 1911 Tolkien was a corporal. On Speech Day at the end of the summer prizes were awarded and entertainment was provided by the boys, including dramatic performances in English and Greek. Tolkien took part in the Greek performances in 1910 and 1911.

Games at King Edward's School were not compulsory; pupils could choose whatever attracted them most. There was rugby football in winter and cricket in summer, as well as fives, swimming, and shooting. By Tolkien's time each of the boys was allotted to one of four houses, which competed in games against each other in addition to matches played against teams from other schools or institutions. Tolkien was in Measures' House. From October 1909 he was a member of the 1st XV Rugby Football team, and in his last year at the School was Football Secretary and Captain of his house team. The School playing fields were some three miles away, on Bristol Road at the corner of Eastern Road. Tolkien's early poem *The Battle of the Eastern Field, published in the King Edward's School Chronicle for March 1911, is a satirical account of a football match. Towards the end of the summer term each year there were two days of Athletic Sports, which most of the boys probably attended. Tolkien is recorded as having been placed in the One Mile Flat Race Open on two occasions.

The King Edward's School Chronicle, written and produced mainly by the boys themselves, carried reports of school and sporting events, academic successes, and the activities of student societies. As Secretary of the Debating Society, Tolkien probably contributed the unsigned reports of meetings to the numbers for November and December 1910, February 1911, and June 1911: these can be attributed to him with some confidence on the basis of style and content. Acta Senatus, a report by Tolkien in Latin of one of the Latin debates, was published in the Chronicle for March 1911; it is not signed, but Tolkien's authorship is noted in his papers. As Football Secretary he may also have written the unsigned reports of matches published in November and December 1910, and February and March 1911. He served as Editor of the Chronicle for June and July 1911, and presumably wrote the editorials for those months. (On Tolkien's publications in the King Edward's School Chronicle, see further, Descriptive Bibliography, C1–8 and preliminary note to Section C.) In his final year he was also in charge of the School library, much of the administration of which was left to the senior boys.

During Christmas break in his first year at Oxford Tolkien returned to King Edward's School to take part in a production of Sheridan's play The Rivals. He also returned on several occasions to join in the Old Boys' Debate, to play for the Old Boys against a School Fifteen, or to attend the Old Edwardians' annual dinner.

As a result of the reform of the King Edward's School governing board towards the end of the nineteenth century, the Hebdomadal Council of Oxford University nominated one of the School's twenty-one governors. On 23 November 1937 Tolkien was selected for this position, to serve until 5 May 1940. He was subsequently reappointed to serve until 1947, but resigned on

1 January 1941, probably because his administrative burden at Oxford did not allow him sufficient time to devote to the extra duty.

By the turn of the century Barry's building, despite its magnificence, no longer provided sufficient or suitable space for King Edward's School, nor by the 1930s could it satisfy safety regulations. In 1936 it was demolished, the pupils and staff having moved to temporary quarters. A new building, designed by Old Edwardian H.W. Hobbiss, was subsequently constructed in Edgbaston Park Road close to the School playing fields. On 1 April 1944 Tolkien attended a lunch at the new school, and on 3 April wrote to his son *Christopher: 'I won't weary you with impressions of the ghastly utterly third-rate new school buildings. But if you can imagine a building better than most Oxford colleges being replaced by what looks like a girls' council school, you've got it and my feelings' (*Letters*, p. 70).

King Edward's School remains today an outstanding independent day school for boys.

Knocking at the Door see *The Mewlips*

Kolbítar see **Societies and clubs**

Kortirion among the Trees see *The Trees of Kortirion*

Lancashire Fusiliers. Regiment in which Tolkien served during the First World War. Founded on 5 November 1688 by Sir Richard Peyton, it was first known as Peyton's Regiment of Foot or Peyton's Own. In 1752 it became the 20th Regiment Foot, and in 1782 the 20th East Devon Regiment of Foot, based in Exeter. In 1881 its name was changed again, to the 20th Lancashire Fusiliers, and it was based at Wellington Barracks in Bury. During its long history it took part in many battles and campaigns, including most notably: the Battle of the Boyne in Ireland between supporters of William III and Mary II and the deposed James II at the beginning of July 1690; the Battle of Dettingen against the French on 16 June 1743; the Battle of Culloden in Scotland against Charles Edward Stuart 'the Young Pretender' on 16 April 1748; the Battle of Minden against the French in the Seven Years' War on 1 August 1759; in Egypt against Napoleon in 1801; in the Peninsula War in Spain, 1808–14, from 1809 under Sir Arthur Wellesley (later Duke of Wellington); in Washington, D.C. in 1814, when they were part of the force that occupied the city and burned down the White House on 24 August; in the Crimean War, 1854–5; in India in 1857, when they helped relieve the Siege of Lucknow; in Sudan, where they were part of the forces that won the battle of Omdurman on 2 September 1898, and relieved Khartoum on 5 September; and during the Boer War, in which they took part in the battles of Spion Kop on 24–25 January 1900 and the Relief of Ladysmith on 28 February.

During the period 1870–74 when he was Secretary of State for War, Edward Cardwell introduced several reforms in the organization of British forces, notably in 1872 the system by which each regiment should be composed of no fewer than two Regular battalions of professional soldiers, one of which was always abroad and the other at home. In the period following the Boer War the British Army underwent further changes in organization and administration. The system introduced by Lord Cardwell was retained,

> but the forces at home were no longer regarded as primarily available for home defence and draft-finding, and came to be looked upon . . . as a potential striking force, capable of being employed at short notice in a foreign theatre of war. With this object they were so organized as to be capable of taking the field overseas as an Expeditionary Force within a very short period after mobilization. . . . The old Militia, a survival from Napoleon's days, gave way to the Special Reserve, to which was expressly assigned the function of furnishing drafts to the Regular forces in the field. Finally, the Volunteers were transformed into the Territorial Force, and reorganized into fourteen divisions, each complete with the necessary artillery and divisional troops. To this new force was assigned the task of home defence, thus setting free the Regular forces for operations overseas. [Major-General J.C. Latter, *The History of the Lancashire Fusiliers 1914–1918* (1949), vol. 1, p. 1]

At the outbreak of the First World War on 4 August 1914 the Lancashire Fusiliers had two Regular battalions, the 1st stationed in Karachi, India (now in Pakistan), and the 2nd in Dover as part of the 12th Infantry Brigade in the 4th Division. It also had two Special Reserve units, the 3rd and 4th Battalions with their headquarters at Wellington Barracks in Bury, where there was also a Depot organization of Regular troops; and four Territorial Force battalions, the 5th and 6th stationed at Rochdale, and the 7th and 8th in Salford (both in Lancashire), these last four forming the Lancashire Fusiliers Infantry Brigade.

At 4.00 p.m. on 4 August 1914 the British Government gave orders for the mobilization of the Army. Within a very short time all but a few of the reservists had reported to Wellington Barracks. After being equipped, the greater proportion were drafted to join the 2nd Battalion at Dover and the rest to join the 3rd Battalion, which then moved to its war station at Hull while the 4th Battalion moved to Barrow-in-Furness. By the evening of 8 August, mobilization was complete. The 2nd Battalion at Dover, in accordance with a system introduced in October 1913,

> was organized in four companies (each commanded by a mounted officer), a machine-gun section, a transport section and a signalling section. . . . The troops were clothed in the regulation khaki service dress uniform, and they were also issued with full dress of scarlet tunic and blue trousers, which was withdrawn on mobilization. They were armed with the Lee-Enfield short magazine rifle, Mark IV, which had been introduced after the South African War. . . .

The machine-gun section was armed with two Vickers machine-guns, which were carried in a general service limber wagon. . . . A second limber wagon was available for the carriage of ammunition. The machine-gun officer was mounted.

The regimental first-line transport consisted of four general service limber wagons, which were used for the carriage of ammunition, entrenching tools and light stores. Two pack animals were available for each company to carry additional supplies of ammunition. There were also authorized four travelling kitchens, one of which was allotted to each company, though these were in fact not issued till March, 1915. The establishment of horses was 12 heavy draught, 18 light draught, 12 riding and 8 pack animals – a scale afterwards increased. Two water-carts with filtering apparatus formed part of the mobilization stores; a maltese cart was provided for the medical officer's stores and comforts, and a light cart for the use of the officers' mess.

The band instruments were withdrawn on mobilization and the members of the band, all of whom had been trained in First Aid duties, were distributed amongst the companies as stretcher-bearers. [Latter, vol. 1, p. 5]

Although foreign service was not obligatory for Territorial units, almost all the men volunteered when asked. The response from the four Lancashire battalions was overwhelming. They were posted to Egypt to train and relieve troops there for active service, arriving on 25 September 1914.

The 2nd Battalion of the Lancashire Fusiliers, as part of the 4th Division, arrived at Boulogne in France as part of the British Expeditionary Force early on 23 August 1914. It fought in the Battle of Le Cateau on 26 August, then in the general retreat from Mons in late August and early September. It remained in France throughout the war, taking part in a series of actions, and notably suffering severe casualties in a gas attack on 2 May 1915.

The 1st Battalion left India in October and, after a spell of garrison duty at Aden, arrived back in England early in 1915. On 16 March, as part of the 29th Division, it embarked to take part in the campaign against the Turkish control of the Dardanelles. The Lancashire Fusiliers were given the task of landing first on the Gallipoli peninsula early on 25 April 1915, and then to cover the disembarking of the rest of the Division. The peninsula was strongly defended, and British forces suffered heavy casualties; but the Fusiliers distinguished themselves. The Commander-in-Chief, General Sir Ian Hamilton, wrote in his official dispatch on 20 May:

> It is my firm conviction that no finer feat of arms has ever been achieved by the British soldier – or any other soldier – than the storming of these trenches from open boats on the morning of 25th April. The landing at W [i.e. 'W' Beach] had been entrusted to the 1st Battalion Lancashire Fusiliers . . . and it was to the complete lack of the senses of danger or

of fear of this daring battalion that we owed our astonishing success. . . . Gallantly led by their officers, the Fusiliers literally hurled themselves ashore and, fired at from right, left and centre, commenced hacking their way through the wire. A long line of men was at once mown down as by a scythe, but the remainder were not to be denied. . . . [quoted in Latter, vol. 1, p. 53]

Six Victoria crosses were awarded to men who took part in the landing. In the next few days various problems prevented the British troops from making much progress, and the delay was fatal, allowing the Turks to strengthen their defences. Despite the arrival of reinforcements, including the four Territorial Battalions of the Lancashire Fusiliers (5th, 6th, 7th, 8th) in early May, and a newly formed 9th Battalion in early August, the invasion force made little progress. In December 1915 it was gradually withdrawn. During the Gallipoli campaign the Lancashire Fusiliers suffered losses of 88 officers and 1,728 other ranks, killed or died of wounds or disease.

Back in England, the British Army was expanding rapidly. Eventually the Lancashire Fusiliers grew to thirty battalions, though not all were in existence at the same time. Of these the battalions that were of the most significance to Tolkien were the 13th, a reserve training unit to which he was assigned in July 1915 and with whom he was stationed until he was sent to France; the 11th, with which he served in France from June to October 1916; the 3rd, to which he was assigned while recovering his strength after suffering trench fever; and the 19th, in which his friend *G.B. Smith served.

The 13th Battalion was formed as an offshoot of the 3rd Battalion at Hull on 5 December 1914, and was stationed at Chesterfield. In April 1915 it became a Reserve Battalion, a draft-finding unit, and moved first to Lichfield, then to Rugeley in November 1915 and to Brocton in Staffordshire in December 1915.

The 11th (Service Battalion) was formed in September 1914, one of the 'Kitchener' or New Army battalions, recruited mainly from the Lancashire area (Burnley, Oldham, Bolton, Wigan, Preston, and Blackburn), though some of its number came from South Wales, many of them miners. The recruits were sent to Codford in Wiltshire for training. In July 1915 the battalion moved to Aldershot, where it formed part of the forces inspected by King George V and by Lord Kitchener. On 25 September 1915 the 11th Battalion crossed to France as part of the 74th Infantry Brigade, 25th Division, going almost immediately into the front line at Le Touquet, near Armentières. In April the battalion moved into the Vimy area and took part in a successful action on Vimy Ridge, 15–19 May. Under the command of Lieutenant-Colonel L.G. Bird, it was one of twelve battalions from the Lancashire Fusiliers in the Battle of the Somme, 1 July–18 November 1916, an attempt to drive the German army from the area between the rivers Somme and Ancre. It was not in action on the first day of the Somme, but took part in the attacks on Ovillers, 7–10 and 14–17 July, and in the battle for Thiepval Ridge, 28–29 September, and successfully achieved its objectives on 21–22 October in the battle for Ancre Heights. These periods of fighting were interspersed with training, or with stretches of quieter yet still dangerous trench duty.

On 27 October 1916 Tolkien reported sick, and was eventually sent home to England suffering from trench fever. On 29 October the 11th Battalion was sent to a different part of the front, to Ploegsteert in Belgium, and 'spent a winter and spring of routine in and out of the trenches there and at Neuve Eglise' (Latter, vol. 1, p. 206). From 5–9 June it successfully took part in the battle for the main road between Messines and Ypres; in the battle for Passchendaele Ridge, in particular during 5–11 August; and in rear guard actions during the German offensive in 1918, especially 21–6 March and 9–17 April. In the latter action the casualties were so high that the survivors of the 11th Lancashire Fusiliers, the 9th Loyal North Lancashire Regiment, and the 74th Trench Mortar Battery were formed into a composite battalion, which was in action again on 26–27 April. On 6 May it was moved south, to an area south-east of Soissons in France, reportedly a quiet area for rest and training of new recruits, but in fact the target of a new German attack on 27 May. Early on 28 May 1918, while defending a ridge near Haut Voisins, the battalion was annihilated except for the party left in reserve, not sufficient to reconstitute the battalion which was officially disbanded on 12 August.

After its move to Hull on 8 August and thence to other locations in the vicinity, the 3rd Battalion finally settled at Thirtle Bridge in November 1916. It was a Reserve unit, but in addition to furnishing drafts to the Regular battalions it also carried out coastal defence duties.

The 19th (Service) Battalion (3rd Salford) was formed in Salford in January 1915 with Lieutenant-Colonel (Brevet-Colonel) L.C.H. Stainforth, formerly of the Indian Army, as its first Commanding Officer. While in training it was stationed at various places in England and Wales, including Catterick Bridge, 21 June–28 July, and Codford, Salisbury Plain, 25 August–20 November. It went to France on 21 November 1915 as part of the 96th Infantry Brigade, 32nd Division, but shortly afterward was transferred into the 14th Infantry Brigade, 32nd Division, and sent to an area near Albert where it stayed for most of the period until G.B. Smith's death on 3 December 1916. Tolkien's battalion was sent to the same area in summer 1916. The 19th Battalion took part in the attack on Thiepval on 1 July 1916, the first day of the Battle of the Somme. On 7 August 1916 the 19th Battalion was converted into a pioneer (path-finding) battalion and made part of the 49th (West Riding) Division, with which it remained until disbanded at the end of the war.

On 23 April 1968 the four regiments of the Lancashire Fusiliers, the Northumberland Fusiliers, the Warwick Fusiliers, and the Royal Fusiliers were amalgamated to create the Royal Regiment of Fusiliers.

Lang, Andrew (1844–1912). Scottish writer, educated at the Edinburgh Academy, St Andrews, Glasgow University, and Balliol College, Oxford. At Oxford in 1866 he earned a First Class in Honour Moderations, and again in 'Greats' (Literae Humaniores, i.e. Classics, Philosophy, and Ancient History) in 1868.

In the latter year he was also awarded the Open Fellowship at Merton College; in 1870 he became a full Fellow. He remained at Merton until 1875, but soon after his marriage that year moved to London to pursue a career in journalism.

He is perhaps best known today for his series of twelve 'colour' books of fairy-tales for children, published between 1889 and 1910, but he also wrote poetry, novels, biographies, history, and literary criticism, translated and wrote about Homer – Tolkien had copies of his translations of the *Odyssey* (1879, in collaboration with S.H. Butcher) and the *Iliad* (1883, in collaboration with Walter Leaf and Ernest Myers) – and produced much else besides. His fiction includes original fairy-stories such as *Prince Prigio* and *Prince Ricardo* (1889 and 1893, later published together as the *Chronicles of Pantouflia*, 1932), and *The Gold of Fairnilee* inspired by the ballads 'Thomas the Rhymer' and 'Tam Lin'. His novel *The World's Desire* (1891), about Helen of Troy and Odysseus in Egypt, was written in collaboration with *H. Rider Haggard.

Lang's collections of *fairy-stories for children were mainly by-products of a serious study of myth, folklore, and ritual in which he radically changed generally accepted ideas of their origins and history. His major publications on this subject were *Custom and Myth* (1884), *Myth, Ritual, and Religion* (1887, 2nd rewritten edn. 1899), *Modern Mythology* (1897), and *The Making of Religion* (1898). But his ideas were first published as early as May 1973 in an article 'Mythology and Fairy-tales' in the *Fortnightly Review*. Salomon Reinach described this as 'the first full refutation of Max Müller's mythological system based on the Veda, and the first full statement of the anthropological method applied to the comparative study of myths'. He also said that 'Lang has taught us that folklore is not, what it still was for Grimm's school, the debased residue of a higher mythology, but that higher or literary mythology rests on the foundation of folklore. He who demonstrated that and made it a key to the darkest recesses of classical mythology has conferred a benefit on the world of learning, and was a genius' ('Andrew Lang', *Quarterly Review* (London) 218, no. 435 (April 1913), pp. 311, 318).

On 1 December 1927, following the endowment of an Andrew Lang Lecturership at St Andrews, *George S. Gordon, presenting the first annual lecture, referred to the way Lang had reversed accepted ideas about mythology and folklore. He described the philological school of comparative mythology which had grown up around Max Müller and 'was concerned to derive our folk-tales from the Aryan cradle, and to represent them as the debris of a higher and literary mythology of which the key-words in course of time had been forgotten. The Frog of the fable only talks and goes a-wooing through a linguistic misunderstanding, because in that nobler Aryan civilization the word for Frog once meant the Sun God.' Lang 'was the first man in this country to see and say plainly that folk-lore is not the debris of a higher mythology, but the foundation on which mythology rests . . .' ('Andrew Lang', in *The Discipline of Letters* (1946), p. 136).

Lang also discussed particular fairy-stories and myths in his introduction to Mrs Hunt's translation of *Grimm's Household Tales* (1884), and his introductory treatises to *Cupid and Psyche* (1887), *Perrault's Popular Tales* (1888), and Robert Kirk's *Secret Commonwealth of Elves, Fauns and Fairies* (1893). Lang was a founder and later president of the Folk-lore Society.

He was similarly a founder and president of the Society for Psychical Research. Another of his publications was *The Book of Dreams and Ghosts* (1897) 'which set out mainly to tell in strictly historical form, all the best attested psychical stories, from classical times to contemporary parallels', which he had learned from a cousin who lived in the South Seas. He also developed from his 'careful study of Australian creeds and legends' a theory that 'the earliest and most natural belief of primitive man was in a single God the Creator, the righteous Maker and Judge of men, and that degradation rather than evolution had followed in the wake of the earliest stages of evolution' (*Roger Lancelyn Green, *Andrew Lang: A Critical Biography* (1946), pp. 72, 73). But this theory found less acceptance than his repudiation of Müller's.

Tolkien first encountered Lang in the fairy books, and as a boy was especially impressed by the *Story of Sigurd* (adapted by Lang himself from the *William Morris translation of the *Völsunga Saga*) in the *Red Fairy Book*. When he was invited to give the eleventh Andrew Lang Lecture at St Andrews he chose to speak on fairy-stories: he delivered *On Fairy-Stories* at St Andrews on 8 March 1939. In that lecture he refers frequently, directly, and indirectly to Andrew Lang. His text, extensive notes, and drafts reveal a close study of some of Lang's works, and other related material. Tolkien later declared that his work on this lecture developed and changed his ideas about what qualities fairy-stories and fantasy should have, and the correct way to write for children. See further, *Fairy-stories and *Children.

In a draft of his discussion of the origins of fairy-stories, Tolkien called it 'a subject in which Andrew Lang was deeply interested and wrote brilliantly and originally'. He commented on Lang's part in the overthrow of Max Müller's theories:

> Philology has been dethroned from the high place it once had in this court of inquiry; *and it was Andrew Lang who played a part in the revolution*. Max Müller's view of mythology as a 'disease of language' can be abandoned without regret. Mythology is not a disease at all, though it may like all human things become diseased. You might as well say that thinking is a disease of the mind. It would be more near the truth to say that languages, especially modern European languages, are a disease of mythology *and the folk-tale is often nearer to the roots than the legend or myth*. [*Tree & Leaf*, p. 24; the italicized phrases appear only in drafts in the Tolkien Papers, Bodleian Library, Oxford]

Tolkien also noted that there had been much debate concerning the relationship of myth and folk-tale, or as 'higher or lower mythology as A[ndrew L[ang] called them' (Tolkien Papers, Bodleian Library, Oxford).

At one time it was a dominant view that all such matter was derived from 'nature-myths'. The Olympians were *personifications* of the sun, of dawn, of night, and so on, and all the stories told about them were originally *myths* (*allegories* would have been a better word) of the greater elemental changes and processes of nature. Epic, heroic legend, saga, then localized these stories in real places and humanized them by attributing them to ancestral heroes, mightier than men and yet already men. And finally these legends, dwindling down, became folk-tales, *Märchen*, fairy-stories – nursery tales. [*Tree and Leaf*, p. 25]

Tolkien rejected the dominant view, commenting that it seemed 'to be the truth almost upside down' (p. 25) and in his drafts noted that Lang also opposed it.

For his lecture Tolkien surveyed the stories chosen by Lang for the twelve colour fairy books (though most of the stories were actually retold, translated, or adapted by Lang's wife), the prefaces he wrote for them, and the introductions to the *Blue Fairy Book* and the *Red Fairy Book*, the latter included only in the large paper editions. In his drafts for *On Fairy-Stories* Tolkien noted that the first of the series, the *Blue Fairy Book*, contained mainly stories from French sources, but also

> six stories from Grimm.... There are also four from popular tales of Scandinavia: an ingredient not readily obtained, except in the Andrew Lang books, by English people (or at any rate by their children), but one which I specially liked in childhood. (I specially disliked the sophisticated (even bogus) form of it in Hans Andersen, which was constantly pressed upon me. Aunts seemed quite incapable of distinguishing the spurious article from the genuine thing, and I was then incapable of doing more than tasting the difference. ...) As for the other main ingredients of the *Blue Book*: three are drawn from *The Arabian Knights*; there are a couple of English chap-book tales (*Jack the Giant-Killer*, and *Dick Whittington*); and a couple of traditional Scottish tales (*The Black Bull of Norroway* and *The Red Etin*). [Tolkien Papers, Bodleian Library, Oxford]

He thought that some of the stories included in the volumes were not really fairy-stories, and mentioned specifically *A Voyage to Lilliput* in the *Blue Fairy Book*, probably included because the Lilliputians were small, and *The Monkey's Heart* in the *Lilac Fairy Book*, which he considered a beast-fable.

He quoted approvingly Andrew Lang's criticism in the preface to the *Lilac Fairy Book* of the tales of tiresome contemporary authors: 'they always begin with a little boy or girl who goes out and meets the fairies of polyanthuses and gardenias and apple-blossom. ... These fairies try to be funny and fail; or they try to preach and succeed' (*Tree and Leaf*, p. 12).

He took issue with Lang about children's taste for fairy-tales, and that children have, as Lang wrote, an 'unblunted edge of belief, a fresh appetite for marvels' (introduction to the *Blue Fairy Book*; quoted in *Tree and Leaf*, p. 36). He also disagreed with Lang's statement in the preface to the *Violet Fairy Book* that children's 'taste remains like the taste of their naked ancestors thousands of years ago; and they seem to like fairy-tales better than history, poetry, geography, or arithmetic'. Tolkien pointed out that we know little about these ancestors or their tastes, and 'if it is assumed that we have fairy-stories because they did, then probably we have history, geography, poetry, and arithmetic because they liked these things too' (*Tree and Leaf*, pp. 38–9). He argued from his own experience as a child that 'a liking for fairy-stories was not a dominant characteristic of early taste' (p. 40), and that for him 'fairy-stories were plainly not primarily concerned with possibility, but desirability' (p. 39).

There appears to be no evidence that Tolkien read Lang's *Prince Prigio* and *Prince Ricardo* as a child, but scattered references in *On Fairy-Stories* (drafts and published text) show that he read those works closely in preparing the lecture. He found *Prince Prigio* flawed with redeeming features, but considered *Prince Ricardo* bad. He thought that 'too often [Andrew Lang] had an eye on the faces of other clever people over the heads of his child-audience – to the very grave detriment of the *Chronicles of Pantouflia*' (*Tree and Leaf*, p. 41). In drafts he commented that the names in *Prince Prigio* were neither apt nor beautiful. Yet despite its weaknesses it had the 'turn' or *eucatastrophe he considered the mark of a good fairy-story.

> When 'each knight came alive and lifted his sword and shouted "long live Prince Prigio"', the joy has a little of that strange mythical fairy-story quality, greater than the event described. It would have none in Lang's tale, if the event described were not a piece of more serious fairy-story 'fantasy' than the main bulk of the story, which is in general more frivolous, having the half-mocking smile of the courtly, sophisticated *Conte*. [*Note by Tolkien:* This is characteristic of Lang's wavering balance. On the surface the story is a follower of the 'courtly' French *conte* with a satiric twist, and of Thackeray's *Rose and the Ring* in particular – a kind which being superficial, even frivolous, by nature, does not produce or aim at producing anything so profound; but underneath lies the deeper spirit of the romantic Lang.] [p. 63]

But in a draft of the lecture Tolkien expressed the view that *Prince Prigio* had the germ of the faults which destroyed *Ricardo*: too much use of wishing caps, seven-league boots, invisible cloaks, and magic spyglasses, as well as the intrusion of real history.

He criticized Lang's comments in his preface to the *Lilac Fairy Book*, directed to the parents and guardians whom he hoped might be influenced to buy his own original fairy stories, *Prince Prigio*, *Prince Ricardo*, and *Tales of a Fairy Court*. Lang wrote:

I take this opportunity of recommending these fairy books – poor things, but my own. . . . They are rich in romantic adventure, and the Princes always marry the right Princesses and live happy ever afterwards; while the wicked witches, stepmothers, tutors and governesses are *never* cruelly punished, but retire to the country on ample pensions. I hate cruelty: I never put a wicked stepmother in a barrel and send her toboganing down a hill. It is true that Prince Ricardo *did* kill the Yellow Dwarf; but that was in fair fight, sword in hand, and the dwarf, peace to his ashes! *died in harness*. [*Lilac Fairy Book*, p. vi; partly quoted in *Tree and Leaf*, p. 42]

Tolkien commented that although Lang protested that he hated cruelty and that the Yellow Dwarf was killed 'in a fair fight, sword in hand', nonetheless 'it is not clear that "fair fight" is less cruel than "fair judgement"; or that piercing a dwarf with a sword is more just than the execution of wicked kings and evil stepmothers – which Lang abjures: he sends the criminals (as he boasts) to retirement on ample pensions. That is mercy untempered by justice' (*Tree and Leaf*, p. 43).

Tolkien did not believe that the horror and violence in traditional fairy-stories harmed children, and felt strongly that such stories should not be 'mollified' to suit a young audience. Rather, children should wait to read them 'until their digestions are stronger' (p. 32).

Languages. Tolkien was introduced to languages other than *English in his youth. His mother (*Mabel Tolkien) began his education in Latin, French, and German; and he studied Latin and Greek at *King Edward's School, Birmingham. As was usual at that time in any school that aimed at academic excellence, the Classical languages formed a major part of the syllabus. They were also central to Tolkien's initial education at *Oxford, where for five terms he studied Latin, Greek, *Philology, and other requirements for the first examination, Honour Moderations, at the end of Hilary Term 1913.

By then his interest in languages, and knowledge of several, was already broad. He had been introduced to Old and Middle English at King Edward's School, and began to teach himself other languages, such as Gothic and Old Icelandic (Old Norse). According to Humphrey Carpenter, in spring term 1910 Tolkien 'delivered to the First Class at King Edward's a lecture with the weighty title: "The Modern Languages of Europe – Derivations and Capabilities". It took three one-hour lessons to read, and even then the master in charge stopped him before he could reach the "Capabilities"' (*Biography*, p. 48). Tolkien also discovered and was intrigued by Welsh, and then by Finnish, languages which were to influence two of his own invention, Sindarin and Quenya (see *Languages, Invented), though it was not until he went to Oxford that he was able to study Welsh or Finnish to any extent.

His months on the staff of the *Oxford English Dictionary* in 1919–20 allowed him even greater freedom to work with languages. In his entry for the word *wasp*, for instance, he cited comparable forms in 'Old Saxon, Middle Dutch, Modern Dutch, Old High German, Middle Low German, Middle High German, Modern German, Old Teutonic, primitive pre-Teutonic, Lithuanian, Old Slavonic, Russian, and Latin' (*Biography*, p. 101). Which is not to say that he was fluent in all of these languages, as too many readers have assumed; nor is there any evidence that he was expert in Sanskrit, Hebrew, or various African languages, as we have seen stated as fact at one time or another. He took a great interest in translations of his works and liked to be consulted about them, but, as he wrote to *Rayner Unwin on 3 April 1956, 'my linguistic knowledge seldom extends, beyond the detection of obvious errors and liberties, to the criticism of the niceties required' (*Letters*, p. 249). In his *Nomenclature of The Lord of the Rings*, in which he is concerned only with the translation of names which he feigns are English translations of names in 'Westron' (the 'Common Speech'), he cites or refers to Danish, Dutch, French, German, Icelandic, Middle English, Middle High German, Norwegian, Old English, Old High German, Old Norse, Old Swedish, and Scandinavian.

OLD AND MIDDLE ENGLISH

In *Biography* Humphrey Carpenter describes how *George Brewerton, one of the masters at King Edward's School, introduced Tolkien to the works of *Chaucer and lent him a primer of **Old English** (Anglo-Saxon). This

> was familiar and recognisable to him as an antecedent of his own language, and at the same time was remote and obscure. The primer explained the language clearly in terms that he could easily understand, and he was soon making light work of translating the prose examples at the back of the book. He found that Old English appealed to him though it did not have the aesthetic appeal of Welsh. This was rather a historical appeal, the attraction of studying the ancestor of his own language. And then he began to find real excitement when he progressed beyond the simple passages in the primer and turned to *Beowulf*. Reading this first in a translation and then in the original language he found it to be one of the most extraordinary poems of all time. [pp. 34–5]

He also began to read works in **Middle English**, and discovered *Sir Gawain and the Green Knight*. He was delighted to find that its dialect was related to that spoken by his mother's *West Midlands ancestors.

He found Old English easy to learn. In a letter to his son *Michael on 1 November 1963 he said: 'I cannot understand why Anglo-Saxon should seem difficult – not to people able to learn any language (other than their own) at all. It is certainly not harder than German, and vastly simpler than say mod. French. And as for Latin and Greek! . . . it does seem that "A-S" is a kind of "touchstone" distinguishing the genuine linguists (the students and lovers of Language) from the utilitarians' (*Letters*, p. 340). In a letter to *W.H. Auden on 7 June 1955 he described the language as 'beautifully co-ordinated and patterned (if simply patterned)' (*Letters*, p. 214). But in a draft letter to a Mr Rang in August 1967 he wrote that when he was studying Old English as an undergraduate and came across the word *éarendel* 'I was struck by the great beauty of this word (or name) entirely coherent with the normal style of A-S, but euphonic to a peculiar degree in that pleasing but not "delectable" language' (*Letters*, p. 385).

OTHER LANGUAGES

Afrikaans. In his lecture **English and Welsh* Tolkien commented that his 'cradle-tongue was English (with a dash of Afrikaans)' (**The Monsters and the Critics and Other Essays*, p. 191), that is, the official language of the Orange Free State (now part of *South Africa), developed from Dutch. Whatever the source of the 'dash' – picked up from his parents' servants, from his nurse, or from employees at his father's bank, or a deliberate effort by his parents intending that he should grow up bilingual – Tolkien left the land of his birth when he was only three, and in his mind 'there would remain no more than a few words of Afrikaans' (*Biography*, p. 15).

Danish. A stray comment in a letter on 22 September 1954 to the BBC radio producer of **The Homecoming of Beorhtnoth Beorhthelm's Son*, that the modern East Anglian English accent depends on fusion of Danish and English elements, suggests that Tolkien had some knowledge of the impact of the language of Danish invaders during the Anglo-Saxon period on the development of the English language. Later he concerned himself with Danish translations of names in his **Nomenclature of The Lord of the Rings*.

Dutch. After the Dutch *Fellowship of the Ring* was published, but before he received a copy, Tolkien wrote to Rayner Unwin on 24 November 1956: 'My knowledge of Dutch is not really adequate for general praise or blame. Nomenclature was a different and easier matter' (Tolkien-George Allen & Unwin archive, HarperCollins). After receiving a copy and making notes to be sent to the publisher, Tolkien wrote in a covering letter to Rayner Unwin on 3 February 1957: 'I hope I have been sufficiently polite. After all, they cannot expect me not to notice actual errors – and a close examination would show these to be fairly numerous; whereas only a thorough knowledge of Dutch (which I do *not* possess) would enable me to appreciate any positive virtues' (Tolkien-George Allen & Unwin archive, HarperCollins). On 24 April 1957 he wrote to his grandson Michael George (see **Michael Tolkien*): 'The Dutch edition and translation are going well. I have had to swot at Dutch; but it is not a really nice language' (British Library, MS Add. 71657).

Finnish. Tolkien first read the *Kalevala*, often described as the Finnish national epic, in his final year at King Edward's School, in W.F. Kirby's English translation. On 25 November 1911, not long after arriving in Oxford, he borrowed *A Finnish Grammar* (1870) by C.N.E. Eliot from the Exeter College Library. He borrowed it again on 11 November 1914, either to help him in writing an essay presented that year, *The Finnish National Epic* (or *On 'The Kalevala' or Land of Heroes*), or to assist him while writing a version of the *Kalevala* story of *Kullervo*.

Tolkien described his first encounter with the Finnish language in a letter to *W.H. Auden:

> It was like discovering a complete wine-cellar filled with bottles of an amazing wine of a kind and flavour never tasted before. It quite intoxicated me; and I gave up the attempt to invent an 'unrecorded' Germanic language, and my 'own language' – or series of invented languages – became heavily Finnicized in phonetic pattern and structure. . . . I never learned Finnish well enough to do more than plod through a bit of the original, like a schoolboy with Ovid; being mostly taken up with its effect on 'my language'. . . . [7 June 1955, *Letters*, p. 214]

For Finnish influence on Quenya, see Helena Rautala, 'Familiarity and Distance: Quenya's Relation to Finnish', in *Scholarship & Fantasy: Proceedings of The Tolkien Phenomenon* (1993). Later in the same letter, Tolkien ascribed his poor performance in Honour Moderations at Oxford in March 1913 to spending too much time on Finnish and writing his own version of the story of Kullervo derived from the *Kalevala*. Since evidence shows that he was writing *Kullervo* in the autumn of 1914, it seems likely that it was his interest in Finnish rather than *Kullervo* that affected his work in Classics.

In a letter to *Naomi Mitchison on 25 April 1954 Tolkien wrote that Finnish and Greek gave him '"phonaesthetic" pleasure' (*Letters*, p. 176). In *English and Welsh* he said that of all the languages he had studied ('"tasted" would be better'), except for Welsh, 'the most overwhelming pleasure was provided by Finnish, and I have never quite got over it' (*The Monsters and the Critics and Other Essays*, p. 192). In a letter written to a Miss Morley on 8 November 1971, Tolkien said that he had never been to *Suomi* (Finland) or mastered the Finnish language, 'though its word-forms and linguistic style gave and give me great aesthetic pleasure' (eBay, March 2005).

French. Tolkien was first taught some French by his mother, after she introduced him to Latin. He liked French 'less, not for any particular reason; but the sounds did not please him as much as the sounds of Latin or English' (Humphrey Carpenter, *Biography*, p. 22). At least in Tolkien's early years at King Edward's School, French formed part of the syllabus. He evidently had not achieved much fluency in the language by summer 1913, when he escorted some Mexican boys in France, since 'he found . . . his French deserted him

when he was faced with the necessity of speaking it' (*Biography*, p. 67). But
*John and *Priscilla Tolkien report that 'later in life he would entertain the
family with his expert mimicry of the accents of Paris errand-boys and their
gutter talk' (*The Tolkien Family Album*, p. 36). In a letter to his son Michael
on 1 November 1963 he wrote that Old English was a 'vastly simpler' language
to learn 'than say mod[ern] French' (*Letters*, p. 340). Although he admitted
that he was no scholar in the language, in his three articles entitled *Philology:
General Works* in *The Year's Work in English Studies* for 1923, 1924, and 1925 he
was able to review works written in French.

In *English and Welsh* Tolkien remarked that 'French and Latin together
were my first experience of second-learned language. Latin – to express now
sensations that are still vivid in memory though inexpressible when received
– seemed so *normal* that pleasure or distaste was equally inapplicable. French
has given to me less of this pleasure than any other language with which I
have sufficient acquaintance for this judgement' (*The Monsters and the Critics and Other Essays*, p. 191). To the published lecture Tolkien added a note:
'I refer to Modern French; and I am speaking primarily of word-forms, and
those in relation to meaning, especially in basic words' (p. 197). Apart from
the fact that Tolkien did not find French an aesthetically pleasing language,
he also resented the impact on Old English of the French spoken by the
Normans who conquered England in 1066. On 4 November 1910 he spoke at
a meeting of the King Edward's School Debating Society on the motion: 'This
House deplores the occurrence of the Norman Conquest'. In the *King Edward's
School Chronicle* it was reported that Tolkien in his speech attempted 'to return
to something of Saxon purity of diction ("right English goodliness of speech-
craft"?) deplored before "the worshipful fellows of the speechguild," the influx
of polysyllabic barbarities which ousted the more honest if humbler native
words' ('Debating Society', n.s. 26, no. 184 (December 1910), p. 95). One of the
Songs for the Philologists (1936), *Frenchmen Froth*, begins: 'Though Frenchmen froth with furious sound / And fill our frousty mansion, / And gurgling
uvulas are ground, / And tremblers pay "attention"' (p. 24).

Anthony Curtis, who as an RAF cadet in the Second World War was taught
medieval English by Tolkien, recalled that among the samples of Old English
handed out at the first class was an English translation of the beginning of the
Gospel according to John, and that Tolkien commented: 'You see ... English was a language that could move easily in abstract concepts when French
was still a vulgar Norman patois' ('Remembering Tolkien and Lewis', *British
Book News*, June 1977, p. 429). In a letter to Amy Ronald on 20 March 1968 Tolkien wrote that perhaps the most unfortunate result of the Norman invasion
was the 'adulteration' of English with a 'large Franco-Latin ingredient largely
floating about like oil', often used when 'when we are being "adult", stuffy,
or professional' (quoted in Christie's, *Autograph Letters and Printed Books,
including First Editions*, London (South Kensington), 19 May 2000, p. 37).

Gaelic (including Old Irish). On 18 December 1949 Tolkien wrote to Naomi Mitchison that 'in spite of efforts I have always been rather heavily defeated by Old Irish, or indeed its modern descendants' (*Letters*, p. 134). In an autobiographical statement he sent to the Houghton Mifflin Company (*Publishers) in summer 1955 he wrote that he found 'both Gaelic and the air of Ireland wholly alien – though the latter (not the language) is attractive' (*Letters*, p. 219). He told Deborah Webster in a letter of 25 October 1958 that he found the Irish language 'wholly unattractive' (*Letters*, p. 289). In his draft letter to Mr Rang in August 1967, in which he admits that *nazg* ('ring' in his invented Black Speech) might have been influenced subconsciously by Gaelic, Tolkien wrote that he had

> no liking at all for Gaelic from Old Irish downwards, as a language, but it is of course of great historical and philological interest, and I have at various times studied it. (With alas! very little success). It is thus probable that *nazg* is actually derived from it, and this short, hard and clear vocable, sticking out from what seems to me (an unloving alien) a mushy language, became lodged in some corner of my linguistic memory. [*Letters*, p. 385]

Nonetheless, in a letter to *Stanley Unwin of 16 December 1937 Tolkien said that 'I do know Celtic things (many in their original languages Irish and Welsh)' (*Letters*, p. 26), and he owned books on the Irish language and literary texts in the original (*see Reading).

German. Tolkien told Charlotte and Denis Plimmer that his taste for Germanic languages had no connection with his Germanic ancestors on the Tolkien side (*Tolkien family), but from his *Suffield mother who 'knew German, and gave me my first lessons in it. She was also interested in etymology and aroused my interest in this . . .' (8 February 1967, *Letters*, p. 377). He continued to study German on his own at King Edward's School, where he was runner-up on the Classical side for the German prize at Speech Day and prize-giving on 26 July 1909; the following year, he was the winner. At Oxford his original intention to read Classics gave way to interest in Philology and the Germanic languages and literature, with emphasis on the early forms of English. These remained the focus of his professional life. During the First World War Tolkien had some occasion to use German conversationally: in France he 'spoke to a captured [German] officer who had been wounded, offering him a drink of water; the officer corrected his German pronunciation' (Humphrey Carpenter, *Biography*, pp. 84–5).

*Henry Bradley, his supervisor on the *Oxford English Dictionary*, wrote of Tolkien: 'His work gives evidence of an unusually thorough mastery of Anglo-Saxon and of the facts and principles of the comparative grammar of the Germanic languages. Indeed I have no hesitation in saying that I have never known a man of his age who was in these respects his equal' (7 June 1920, *An

Application for the Rawlinson and Bosworth Professorship of Anglo-Saxon in the University of Oxford by J.R.R. Tolkien, Professor of the English Language in the University of Leeds, June 25, 1925). On 1 May 1962 Tolkien replied to enquiries from Paul Bibire, then a prospective university student:

> I do not think I can safely advise you about German: a very good knowledge of any European language is very useful to a literary student or philologist. . . . As far as English philology is concerned the prime use of German is an ability to read and use German dictionaries and technical books. For medieval literature you would require a knowledge of Middle High German which is another matter best left till later. [Tolkien–George Allen & Unwin archive, HarperCollins]

Gothic. While still at King Edward's School Tolkien discovered Gothic, the language once spoken by the eastern Germanic peoples on the fringes of the Roman Empire. Only a few short texts in Gothic survive. Tolkien described his first contact with the language in a letter to Zillah Sherring, who had written to him after purchasing Tolkien's copy of *The Fifth Book of Thucydides* in which he had written a Gothic inscription in 1910.

> I had come across this admirable language a year or two before 1910 in *Joseph Wright's Primer of the Gothic Language. . . .* I was fascinated in Gothic in itself: a beautiful language, which reached the eminence of liturgical use, but failed owing to the tragic history of the Goths to become one of the liturgical languages of the West. At the time I had only the Primer with its small vocabulary, but I had learned from it some of the technique necessary for converting the words of other Germanic languages into Gothic script. I often put 'Gothic' inscriptions in books, sometimes Gothicizing my Norse name and German surname as Ruginwaldus Dwalakōneis. [20 July 1965, *Letters*, p. 357]

In *English and Welsh* Tolkien said that

> Gothic was the first [language] to take me by storm, to move my heart. It was the first of the old Germanic languages that I ever met. I have since mourned the loss of Gothic literature. I did not then. The contemplation of the vocabulary in *A Primer of the Gothic Language* was enough: a sensation at least as full of delight as first looking into Chapman's *Homer*. Though I did not write a sonnet about it. I tried to invent Gothic words. [*The Monsters and the Critics and Other Essays*, pp. 191–2]

In another letter, to W.H Auden on 7 June 1955, Tolkien wrote that he discovered in Gothic 'not only modern historical philology, which appealed to the historical and scientific side, but for the first time the study of a language out of mere love: I mean for the acute aesthetic pleasure derived from a language for its own sake, not only free from being useful but free even from being the "vehicle of a literature"' (*Letters*, p. 213).

Humphrey Carpenter comments that Tolkien moved from inventing Gothic words 'to the construction of a supposedly unrecorded but historical Germanic language' (*Biography*, p. 37). He also reports that Tolkien, during a Latin debate at King Edward's School, 'astonished his schoolfellows when, in the character of a barbarian envoy, he broke into fluent Gothic' (p. 48). Among the songs that Tolkien wrote for the Viking Club is one in Gothic, *Bagme Bloma* (see *Songs for the Philologists*). His friend *George Sayer recalled that before he recorded extracts from *The Hobbit* and *The Lord of the Rings* on Sayer's tape recorder Tolkien 'said whimsically that he ought to cast out any devil that might be in it by recording a prayer, the Lord's Prayer in Gothic' (Sayer, sleeve notes to *J.R.R. Tolkien Reads and Sings His The Hobbit and The Fellowship of the Ring* (1975)). *Robert Murray recalled that at a lunch with Tolkien in summer 1973

> Ronald was maintaining with great vigour over the luncheon table that one of the greatest disasters of European history was the fact that the Goths turned Arian: but for that, their languages, just ready to become classical, would have been enriched not only with a great bible version but also on Byzantine principles, with a vernacular liturgy, which would have served as a model for all the Germanic peoples and would have given them a native Catholicism which would never break apart. And with that he rose and in splendidly sonorous tones declaimed the Our Father in Gothic. ['A Tribute to Tolkien', *The Tablet*, 15 September 1973, pp. 879–80]

See further, Arden R. Smith, 'Tolkienian Gothic', *The Lord of the Rings, 1954–2004: Scholarship in Honor of Richard E. Blackwelder* (2006).

Greek. Tolkien began to learn Greek in the Sixth Class at King Edward's School in autumn 1903. In a letter to her mother-in-law at Christmas 1903, Mabel Tolkien wrote that Ronald 'is going along at a great rate at school – he knows far more Greek than I do Latin' (quoted in *Biography*, p. 28). He not only studied classical Greek, but later, with special permission from *Father Francis Morgan, attended the Headmaster's classes on the Greek New Testament. During one of the Latin debates at school Tolkien, 'taking the role of Greek Ambassador to the Senate ... spoke entirely in Greek' (Humphrey Carpenter, *Biography*, p. 48). He also twice took part in performances of a Greek play, traditionally part of an entertainment on the last day of the summer term at King Edward's School. In 1910 he played the part of the Inspector in Aristophanes' *The Birds*, and in 1911 that of Hermes in Aristophanes' *The Peace*.

Tolkien wrote of his first encounter with the language: 'The fluidity of

Greek, punctuated by hardness, and with its surface glitter, captivated me, even when I met it first only in Greek names, of history or mythology . . . ; but part of the attraction was antiquity and alien remoteness (from me): it did not touch home' (*English and Welsh*, in *The Monsters and the Critics and Other Essays*, p. 191). He told Robert Murray in a letter of 2 December 1953 that it was not in English literature but in Homer (in the original) that he 'first discovered the sensation of literary pleasure' (*Letters*, p. 172). In July 1910 he successfully passed five subjects in examinations for the Oxford and Cambridge Higher Certificate, two of which were Greek and Scripture Knowledge (Greek Text).

Tolkien went up to Oxford to study Classics in Michaelmas Term 1911. He spent five terms concentrating on Latin and Greek, before switching to the English School in Trinity Term 1913. During these terms he studied Greek philology with Joseph Wright. He only achieved a Second in Honour Moderations, but generally seems to have done better in his Greek papers than in Latin. (See **Chronology** for details of the works Tolkien studied.)

In a letter to *Father Douglas Carter of ?6 June 1972 Tolkien wrote: 'In dealing with Greek I feel like a renegade, resident wilfully for long years among "barbarians", though I once knew something about it. Yet I prefer Latin' (*Letters*, p. 419).

Hebrew. Tolkien wrote to his grandson Michael George on 24 April 1957: 'I am at present immersed in Hebrew. If you want a beautiful but idiotic alphabet, and a language so difficult that it makes Latin or even Greek seem footling – but also glimpses into a past that makes Homer seem recent – then that is the stuff.' He hoped that when he retired he could take part in the *Jerusalem Bible* project. 'I have passed the test: with a version of the Book of Jonah. Not from the Hebrew direct!' (British Library, MS Add. 71657).

Old Icelandic (Old Norse). As a child Tolkien greatly enjoyed 'The Story of Sigurd' in *Andrew Lang's *Red Fairy Book*. At King Edward's School, after embarking on teaching himself Old English and Middle English, Tolkien looked at Old Norse and began to read the *Völsunga Saga*, the work from which Lang had adapted his story. On 17 February 1911 he read a paper on 'Norse Sagas' at a meeting of the King Edward's School Literary Society, and in Trinity Term 1913 presented the same, or a revision, to the Essay Club of Exeter College, Oxford (*Societies and clubs). When Tolkien transferred to the Oxford English School in that term, he chose Scandinavian Philology as his Special Subject: according to the *Regulations*, this included special reference to Icelandic, together with a special study of sections of the *Prose Edda* and the *Völsunga Saga*, as well as the *Hallfreðar Saga*, *Þorfinns Saga Karlsefnis*, and *Hrafnkels Saga*.

Tolkien taught Old Icelandic at Leeds, and noted in his application for the Oxford Rawlinson and Bosworth chair that at Leeds 'Old Icelandic has been a point of special development, and usually reaches a higher standard than the other special subjects' (*Letters*, p. 13). Two of the activities of the mainly undergraduate Viking Club at Leeds, founded by Tolkien and *E.V. Gordon to encourage interest in Old Icelandic, were the reading of sagas and the singing of comic songs (see *Songs for the Philologists). At Oxford in Hilary Term 1926 Tolkien founded the more serious Kolbítar (*Societies and clubs), in which the members, all dons, by the mid-1930s achieved the aim of translating all of the major sagas as well as the Prose Edda and the Poetic Edda.

Although his chair at Oxford from 1925 was nominally devoted to Anglo-Saxon, in fact Tolkien was also mainly responsible for Old Icelandic until his former student, *E.O.G. Turville-Petre, was appointed to the newly instituted Vigfússon Readership in Ancient Icelandic Literature and Antiquities in 1941. On 11 June 1933 Sigurður Nordal nominated Tolkien as an honorary member of Hið íslenzka bókmenntafélag (the Icelandic Literary Society).

In a letter to Naomi Mitchison on 18 December 1949 Tolkien said: 'I know Icelandic pretty well' (Letters, p. 134). On 5 June 1973 he wrote to Ungfrú Aðalsteinsdottir that he was very pleased to hear of a forthcoming Icelandic translation of The Hobbit. 'I had long hoped that some of my work might be translated into Icelandic, a language which I think would fit it better than any other I have any adequate knowledge of' (Letters, p. 430).

Italian. According to Humphrey Carpenter, Tolkien spent some of his time in hospital in the summer of 1918 'improving his Italian' (Biography, p. 98), though he had made no previous mention of Tolkien studying the language. On 7 June 1955 Tolkien commented in a letter to W.H. Auden, on the 'linguistic-aesthetic satisfaction' he found in Welsh and Spanish, that 'it is not quite the same as the mere perception of beauty: I feel the beauty of say Italian . . .' (Letters, p. 214).

In his private account of his visit to Venice and Assisi (*Italy) with his daughter Priscilla in August 1955 Tolkien notes several times his lack of fluency in Italian. 'We made the acquaintance of a charming Italian, Sr. Gardin, who had some English but was incredibly gracious and patient with our attempts upon his own language. I received a linguistic shock at the discovery that, contrary to legend and my belief, Italians . . . dislike exaggeration, superlatives, and adjectives of excessive praise. But they seem to answer to colour and poetic expression, if justified.' Both the sisters and the guests at the convent in Assisi where he and Priscilla stayed were mainly French-speaking; Tolkien found that 'the attempt to switch from my embryonic Italian to my weak French destroys both'.

Just before they left the country, he wished that he 'could have come to Italy long ago and learned Italian while there was still a chance of doing it properly' (Tolkien Papers, Bodleian Library, Oxford). He wrote to his son Christopher on 15 August 1955, after returning from his visit to Italy: 'I remain in love with Italian, and feel quite lorn without a chance of trying to speak it. We must keep it up' (Letters, p. 223).

Latin. According to Humphrey Carpenter, when Tolkien was about five or six his mother 'introduced him to the rudiments of Latin, and this delighted him. He was just as interested in the sounds and shapes of words as in their meanings . . .' (*Biography*, p. 22). Tolkien says in *English and Welsh* that 'French and Latin together were my first experience of second-learned language. Latin – to express now sensations that are still vivid in memory though inexpressible when received – seemed so *normal* that pleasure or distaste was equally inapplicable' (*The Monsters and the Critics and Other Essays*, p. 191). He continued his Latin studies at King Edward's School. A comment in his letter to W.H. Auden on 7 June 1955 shows that pupils were expected to try to translate English poetry into Latin. In a letter to his son Michael in 1967 Tolkien wrote that he had grown up 'in a two-front state, symbolizable by the Oratorian Italian pronunciation of Latin', heard in the *Birmingham Oratory to which his guardian, Father Francis Morgan, was attached, 'and the strictly "philological" pronunciation at that time introduced into our Cambridge dominated school' (*Letters*, p. 395). Tolkien took part in the school's Latin debates, though he sometimes adopted the *persona* of a Greek or Gothic ambassador and spoke in those languages instead. For his first five terms at Oxford, as a Classics scholar, Latin language and literature formed a significant part of his studies. Even in the English School, however, to which he transferred and in which he spent most of his professional career, it was essential to understand the influence of Classical and Medieval Latin on the development of the English language and its literature.

For the greater part of his life, the Roman Catholic religious services and ceremonies Tolkien attended were conducted in Latin. When the best-known and loved Latin phrases were replaced by the vernacular after the second Vatican Council, he mourned their passing. His son John, a Catholic priest, commented that his father 'very strongly couldn't see any point in abandoning Latin. He used to try and struggle with using the Latin missal with the English Mass' (*J.R.R.T.: A Portrait of John Ronald Reuel Tolkien, 1892–1973* (1992)). Latin was, however, still used in various Oxford ceremonies: *Colin Hardie, for instance, made a speech in Latin in the ceremony on 3 June 1972 when Oxford University conferred an honorary Doctorate of Letters upon Tolkien.

Latin as well as Finnish influenced one of his two chief invented languages, Quenya. He wrote to Naomi Mitchison on 25 April 1954 that the archaic 'Elvish' 'language of lore is meant to be a kind of "Elven-latin", and by transcribing it into a spelling closely resembling that of Latin . . . the similarity to Latin has been increased ocularly. Actually it might be said to be composed on a Latin basis with two other (main) ingredients that happen to give me "phonaesthetic" pleasure: Finnish and Greek' (*Letters*, p. 176).

Polish. Tolkien wrote to his son Christopher on 18 January 1944: 'I can't write Russian and find Polish rather sticky yet. I expect poor old Poptawski [a Polish officer who had consulted Tolkien] will be wondering how I am getting on, soon. It will be a long time before I can be of any assistance to him in devising a new technical vocabulary!!! The vocab[ulary] will just happen along anyway (if there are any Poles and Poland left)' (*Letters*, pp. 67–8).

On 3 July 1959 Tolkien commented to Alina Dadlez at Allen & Unwin that a translation into such a language, as Polish, 'quite alien to English . . . is rather a different situation to that presented by the Dutch translation' (Tolkien-George Allen & Unwin archive, HarperCollins).

Russian. According to Humphrey Carpenter, while in hospital in summer 1918 Tolkien taught himself a little Russian. But he evidently did not get far, for on 18 January 1944 he wrote in a letter to his son Christopher: 'I can't write Russian' (*Letters*, p. 67). On 2 December 1953 he wrote to Robert Murray that he had 'had a go at many tongues in my time, but I am in no ordinary sense a "linguist"; and the time I once spent on trying to learn **Serbian** and Russian have left me with no practical results, only a strong impression of the structure and word-aesthetic' (*Letters*, p. 173).

Spanish. Tolkien's half-Spanish guardian, Father Francis Morgan, spoke Spanish fluently. Tolkien 'often begged to be taught the language, but nothing came of it' (Humphrey Carpenter, *Biography*, p. 37). Tolkien did try to learn it, however, from books owned by Father Francis, and Spanish influenced one of his earliest invented languages, Naffarin. When he escorted two Mexican boys to France in 1913 he found his Spanish 'only rudimentary' (*Biography*, p. 67). Carpenter notes that Tolkien spent some of his time in hospital in summer 1918 improving his fluency.

In his letter To W.H. Auden on 7 June 1955 Tolkien commented that Spanish, along with Welsh, gave him an 'abiding linguistic-aesthetic satisfaction'. Spanish was 'the only Romance language that gives me the particular pleasure of which I am speaking – it is not quite the same as the mere perception of beauty . . . it is more like the appetite for a needed food' (*Letters*, pp. 213–14). In *English and Welsh* he said 'Spanish came my way by chance and greatly attracted me. It gave me strong pleasure, and still does – far more than any other Romance language' (*The Monsters and the Critics and Other Essays*, p. 191). His attraction to Spanish is borne out also in several of his other published letters.

Swedish. Tolkien was much irritated by Åke Ohlmarks, the Swedish translator of *The Lord of the Rings* (*Translations). He wrote to Rayner Unwin on 7 December 1957: 'I hope my inadequate knowledge of Swedish . . . tends to exaggerate the impression I received' (*Letters*, p. 263). Nonetheless, he had enough Swedish to detect several errors in Ohlmarks' translation, and to translate Ohlmarks' semi-fictional account of Tolkien's life at the beginning of the first two volumes (see *Letters*, pp. 304–7).

Welsh. Tolkien described his feelings about Welsh in *English and Welsh*, given at Oxford on 21 October 1955. After discussing his feelings about other languages, he continued:

> But all the time there had been another call – bound to win in the end, though long baulked by sheer lack of opportunity. I heard it coming out of the west. It struck me in the names on coal-trucks; and drawing nearer, it flickered past on station-signs, a flash of strange spelling and a hint of a language old and yet alive; even in an *adeiladwyd 1887*, ill-cut on a stone slab, it pierced my linguistic heart. 'Late Modern Welsh' (bad Welsh to some). Nothing more than an 'it was built'. . . . It was easier to find books to instruct one in any far alien tongue of Africa or India than in the language that still clung to the western mountains and the shores that look out to Iwerddon. . . . [*The Monsters and the Critics and Other Essays*, p. 192]

It was during the few months that Tolkien lived at 86 Westfield Road in Kings Heath (*Birmingham and environs), at about the time he reached his ninth birthday, that he first saw the coal-trucks with Welsh names. Later in *English and Welsh* he said that his pleasure in the language was 'not solely concerned with any word, any "sound pattern + meaning", by itself, but with its fitness also to the whole style' (p. 192); 'it is the ordinary words for ordinary things that in Welsh I find so pleasing'; 'this pleasure is most immediately and acutely felt in the moment of association: that is in the reception (or imagination) of a word-form which is felt to have a certain style, and the attribution to it of a meaning which is not received through it'; and 'if I were pressed to give any example of a feature of this style, not only as an observable feature but as a source of pleasure to myself, I should mention the fondness for nasal consonants, especially the much favoured *n*, and the frequency with which word-patterns are made with the soft and less sonorous *w* and the voiced spirants *f* and *dd* contrasted with the nasals . . .' (pp. 192, 193–4).

Although Tolkien wrote to W.H. Auden on 7 June 1955 that he 'did not learn any Welsh until I was an undergraduate' (*Letters*, p. 13), an inscription in one of his books, now in the English Faculty Library, Oxford, shows that as early as 9 May 1907 he had acquired a copy of W. Salesbury's *Dictionary in Englyshe and Welshe* (1877 edn.). Later he built a substantial library of books on Welsh language and literature. At Oxford he certainly had more opportunity to study Welsh, in particular Medieval Welsh, and when he won the Skeat Prize for English he spent part of it on Sir John Morris-Jones's *Welsh Grammar*. At Leeds Tolkien taught a course in Medieval Welsh, but at Oxford Welsh fell within the province of the Jesus Professor of Celtic.

Sindarin, one of his two main Elvish languages, was influenced by Welsh. Tolkien told Naomi Mitchison on 25 April 1954 that Sindarin was 'derived from an origin common to it and *Quenya*; but the changes have been deliberately devised to give it a linguistic character very like (though not identical with) British-Welsh: because that character is one that I find, in some linguistic moods, very attractive; and because it seems to fit the rather "Celtic" type of legends and stories told of its speakers' (*Letters*, p. 176). In the autobiographical statement he sent to Houghton Mifflin in summer 1955 he wrote that Sindarin was 'in fact constructed deliberately to resemble Welsh phonologically and to have a relation to High-elven [Quenya] similar to that existing between British (properly so-called, sc. the Celtic languages spoken in this island at the time of the Roman Invasion) and Latin' (*Letters*, p. 219).

Artificial. In the late nineteenth and early twentieth centuries several serious attempts were made to create a new language, easy to learn and free from nationalistic interests, which might serve to foster international communication. These languages included *Volapük*, devised by Johann Martin Schleyer in 1879, *Esperanto*, devised by L.L. Zamenhof in 1887, *Ido*, based on Esperanto and put forward by the Delegation for the Adoption of an International Language in 1907, and *Novial*, devised by Otto Jespersen in 1928. Tolkien was interested in these languages, especially Esperanto, though his views on them seem to have changed over the years.

He learned a certain amount of Esperanto while at school, and in 1909 used it together with English in a notebook he called *Book of the Foxrook*. One page of this is reproduced in *Life and Legend*, together with an entry which says that the notebook 'contains a code-alphabet and commentary in a language based on Esperanto and Spanish' (p. 18). Arden R. Smith and Patrick Wynne, however, state in 'Tolkien and Esperanto' (*Seven* 17 (2000)) that 'the language in Foxrook is in fact straightforward Esperanto, with no particular Spanish influence' (p. 31). They describe Esperanto as 'a language closely resembling those of the Indo-European family in grammatical structure, with a basic vocabulary drawn primarily from Latin and Romance languages, but also containing elements from German, Russian, English, and Polish' (p. 28).

In 1931 Tolkien began his paper **A Secret Vice* by referring to the Esperanto Congress held in Oxford in July 1930. 'Personally', he wrote,

> I am a believer in an 'artificial' language, at any rate for Europe – a believer, that is, in its desirability, as the one thing antecedently necessary for uniting Europe, before it is swallowed up by non-Europe; as well as for many other good reasons – a believer in its possibility because the history of the world seems to exhibit, as far as I know it, both an increase in human control of (or influence upon) the uncontrollable, and a progressive widening of the range of more or less uniform languages. Also I particularly like Esperanto, not least because it is the creation ultimately of one man, not a philologist, and is therefore something like a 'human language bereft of the inconveniences due to too many successive cooks' – which is as good a description of the ideal artificial language (in a particular sense) as I can give. [*The Monsters and the Critics and Other Essays*, p. 198]

In 1932 he became a member of the Board of Honorary Advisors to the Education Committee of the British Esperanto Association. Extracts from a letter that he wrote to the Secretary of the Committee were published in the May 1932 issue of the *British Esperantist* (28, no. 325) as 'A Philologist on Esperanto'. In this he expressed his interest in 'the international-language movement', especially Esperanto, but pointed out that he was not a 'practical Esperantist':

> I can neither write nor speak the language. I know it, as a philologist would say, in that 25 years ago I learned and have not forgotten its grammar and structure, and at one time read a fair amount written in it, and, since I am trained to that sort of thing, I feel competent to have an opinion concerning its defects and excellencies. That being so, I feel that I could make no useful contribution, except as a philologist and critic. . . .
>
> Esperanto seems to me beyond doubt, taken all round, superior to all present competitors, but its chief claim to support seems to me to rest on the fact that it has already the premier place, has won the widest measure of practical acceptance, and developed the most advanced organisation.

But he felt that the temptation to try to improve what already exists could be counter-productive:

> Actually it seems to me, too, that technical improvement of the machinery, either aiming at greater simplicity and perspicuity of structure, or at greater internationality, or what not, tends . . . to destroy the 'humane' or aesthetic aspect of the invented idiom. This apparently unpractical aspect appears to be largely overlooked by theorists; though I imagine it is not really unpractical, and will have ultimately great influence on the prime matter of universal acceptance. N[ovial] for instance, is ingenious, and easier than Esperanto, but hideous – 'factory product' is written all over it, or rather, 'made of spare parts' – and it has no gleam of the individuality, coherence, and beauty, which appear in the great natural idioms, and which do appear in a considerable degree (probably as high a degree as is possible in an artificial idiom) in Esperanto – a proof of the genius of the original author. [p. 182]

It seems, however, that Tolkien's view of artificial languages changed over the years. Christopher Tolkien notes that the manuscript of *A Secret Vice* 'was later hurriedly revised here and there, apparently for a second delivery of the paper' at the end of the 1940s, as a reference to Tolkien having abandoned Nevbosh (*Languages, Invented) 'more than 20 years' became 'almost 40 years' (p. 203). In a draft probably connected with this revision Tolkien said he was 'no longer so sure that [an artificial language] would be a good thing', and that 'at present I think we should be likely to get an *inhumane* language without any cooks at all – their place being taken by nutrition experts and dehydrators' (*The Monsters and the Critics and Other Essays*, p. 219).

On 14 January 1956, in a draft letter to a Mr Thompson, he wrote that he had

> made the discovery that 'legends' depend on the language to which they
> belong; but a living language depends equally on the 'legends' which it
> conveys by tradition. (For example, that the Greek mythology depends
> far more on the marvellous aesthetic of its language and so of its nomen-
> clature of persons and places and less on its content than people realize,
> though of course it depends on both. And *vice versa*. Volapük, Esperanto,
> Ido, Novial, &c &c are dead, far deader than ancient unused languages,
> because their authors never invented any Esperanto legends.) [*Letters*,
> p. 231]

Languages, Invented. Tolkien's keen interest in language in general (*Languages), manifest already in his youth, led him to invent languages of his own.
'The linguistic faculty', he would later write, 'is sufficiently latent' in all children for them to learn at least one language, as a practical object.

> It is more highly developed in others, and may lead not only to polyglots
> but to poets; to savourers of linguistic flavours, to learners and users of
> tongues, who take pleasure in the exercise. And it is allied to a higher art
> ... for which life is not long enough, indeed: the construction of imagin-
> ary languages in full or outline for amusement, for the pleasure of the
> constructor or even conceivably of any critic that might occur. [*A Secret
> Vice*, in *The Monsters and the Critics and Other Essays*, p. 202]

Tolkien's cousins Marjorie and Mary Incledon (see *Incledon family) devised a
conversational language, 'Animalic', constructed largely from English animal,
bird, and fish names. Later, Marjorie having lost interest in Animalic, Tolkien
and Mary developed 'Nevbosh', or 'New Nonsense', the vocabulary of which he
could still recall decades later (see example, *Biography*, p. 36, or *A Secret Vice*,
p. 203). But both of these languages were dominated by either the words or the
structure of *English. Around Autumn term 1907 at *King Edward's School,
Birmingham, Tolkien created 'Naffarin', a private language influenced by Latin
and Spanish ('O Naffarínos cutá vu navru cangor', etc.; *A Secret Vice*, p. 209).
While still at school, he also attempted for a while to create an 'unrecorded'
Germanic language, probably inspired by his interest in Gothic.

Such language-construction, as Tolkien later reflected, was a hobby
intended to express his particular linguistic aesthetics, which varied over time.
In *A Secret Vice* (?autumn 1931) he wrote that he was 'personally most interested perhaps in word-form in itself, and in word-form in relation to meaning
(so-called phonetic fitness) than in any other department'. But there were
other interests as well:

> There is the purely philological (a necessary part of the completed whole
> though it may be developed for its own sake): you may, for instance,

construct a pseudo-historical background and deduce the form you have actually decided on from an antecedent and different form (conceived in outline); or you can posit certain tendencies of development and see what sort of form this will produce. In the first case you discover what sort of general tendencies of change produce a given character; in the second you discover the character produced by given tendencies. Both are interesting, and their exploration gives one a much greater precision and sureness in construction – in the technique in fact of producing an effect you wish to produce for its own sake. [*The Monsters and the Critics and Other Essays*, pp. 211–12]

His 'Elvish' language 'Qenya' (also 'Eldarissa', later 'Quenya') was 'the one language which has been expressly designed to give play to my own most normal phonetic taste' (p. 212). The Germanic language that Tolkien began to invent in school may have contributed to it in its early stages: Christopher Gilson, et al. have pointed out that some words in the *Qenyaqetsa*, a phonology and lexicon of Qenya, begun *c.* 1915, 'are Germanic in inspiration' (*Parma Eldalamberon* 12 (1998), p. xi). Later the language was strongly influenced by Finnish in its phonetic pattern and structure, by way of Tolkien's enthusiasm for the *Kalevala* and study of *A Finnish Grammar* by C.N.E. Eliot (1890), which as an undergraduate he borrowed from the Exeter College library. (See further, Helena Rautala, 'Familiarity and Distance: Quenya's Relation to Finnish', *Scholarship & Fantasy: Proceedings of The Tolkien Phenomenon, May 1992, Turku, Finland* (1993).)

To speak of Quenya as 'one language', however, is a simplification, no less than it is, for Tolkien, to refer only to language-construction. In *A Secret Vice* he wrote that

for perfect construction of an art-language it is found necessary to construct at least in outline a mythology concomitant. Not solely because some pieces of verse will inevitably be part of the (more or less) completed structure, but because the making of language and mythology are related functions; to give your language an individual flavour, it must have woven into it the threads of an individual mythology, individual while working within the scheme of natural human mythopoeia, as your word-form may be individual while working within the hackneyed limits of human, even European, phonetics. The converse indeed is true, your language construction will *breed* a mythology. [*The Monsters and the Critics and Other Essays*, pp. 210–11]

Later he wrote that 'the invention of languages is the foundation [of his fiction of Arda and Middle-earth]. The "stories" were made rather to provide a world for the languages than the reverse' (letter to the Houghton Mifflin Company, 30 June 1955, p. 219). In practice, however, both activities proved of equal importance, and each reinforced the other.

At the same time that Tolkien was developing Qenya, he also invented a second 'Elvish' language, influenced by his study of Welsh. The first form of this was called 'Goldogrin' or 'Gnomish' or 'Noldorissa', and expressed in a grammar and lexicon dated 1917, called by Tolkien *I·Lam na·Ngoldathon 'Goldogrin'* but by Christopher Tolkien, for convenience, the *Gnomish Lexicon*. Like Qenya, Goldogrin underwent constant evolution while Tolkien lived. It was subsequently renamed 'Noldorin', and still later, as further developed, became 'Sindarin'. In 1955, in a footnote to an autobiographical statement, Tolkien stated that he constructed Sindarin 'deliberately to resemble Welsh phonologically and to have a relation to High-elven [Quenya] similar to that existing between British (properly so-called, sc. the Celtic languages spoken in this island at the time of the Roman Invasion) and Latin' (*Letters*, p. 219). (See also Christopher Gilson, 'Gnomish Is Sindarin: The Conceptual Evolution of an Elvish Language', *Tolkien's Legendarium: Essays on The History of Middle-earth* (2000).)

As Christopher Gilson and Patrick Wynne have said, the elven tongues 'grew and developed over the course of Tolkien's entire lifetime. Sometimes their development was as gradual as the slow growth of an oak; at other times there were sudden flowerings of new forms and grammatical features, or even new languages' ('The Growth of Grammar in the Elven Tongues', *Proceedings of the J.R.R. Tolkien Centenary Conference 1992* (1995), p. 187). It is important to acknowledge that (for instance) although Goldogrin, Noldorin, and Sindarin share a common thread of evolution, they are not the same language merely renamed or with minor changes. Each is distinct; and even two examples of (say) Quenya, or two of Sindarin, separated by a distance of time, may express a different 'linguistic aesthetic' though they are called by the same name. 'Finality and completion' of Tolkien's languages was 'not only never achieved, it was not even a goal', as Carl F. Hostetter writes.

> Indeed, to the extent that we can speak accurately of Quenya and Sindarin as single entities at all, it is only as continuities of change over time, not only within their fictional internal histories (continual change being of course also a feature of primary-world languages), but also across Tolkien's lifetime. All of the writings concerning his invented languages that Tolkien left behind are, then, essentially a chronological sequence of individual snapshots, of greater or lesser scope, of stages in a lifelong process of invention and reinvention in accordance with changes in Tolkien's linguistic aesthetic, and of which the endeavor itself and not its achievement was the purpose. ['"Elvish as She Is Spoke"', *The Lord of the Rings, 1954–2004: Scholarship in Honor of Richard E. Blackwelder* (2006), pp. 235–6]

The development of the invented languages, as Hostetter indicates, was on historical principles, of the same sort which operate on languages in our own world. As Christopher Tolkien has said, 'every element in the languages, every element in every word, is in principle historically "explicable" – as are the elements in languages that are not "invented". . . . "Invention" was thus altogether distinct from "artificiality". Tolkien did not

'invent' new words and names arbitrarily: in principle, he devised them from within the historical structure, proceeding from the 'bases' or primitive stems, adding suffix or prefix or forming compounds, deciding (or, as he would have said, 'finding out') when the word came into the language, following through the regular [phonological and orthographical] changes of form that it would thus have undergone, and observing the possibilities of formal or semantic influence from other words in the course of its history. Such a word would then exist for him, and he would know it. As the whole system evolved and expanded, the possibilities for word and name became greater and greater. [introduction to the *Etymologies, in *The Lost Road and Other Writings, pp. 341, 342]

Such attention to detail in matters of language, applying actual mechanisms of historical linguistic development rather than arbitrarily 'making up' words and (especially) nomenclature, is the feature of Tolkien's fiction which, perhaps most of all, distinguishes his works of fantasy from all others. Moreover, as Carl Hostetter points out, besides their external history of development, by their real-world creator, Tolkien's languages have an internal history, within the fiction. This too changed over the years, from text to text. Already (for instance) in The Music of the Ainur in the early *Book of Lost Tales there is a reference to the 'many speeches of the Eldar' (Elves). The sage Rúmil comments on

that tongue to which the Noldoli cling yet – and aforetime the Teleri, the Solosimpi, and the Inwir had all their differences. Yet these were slighter and are now merged in that tongue of the island Elves. . . . Still are there the lost bands too that dwell wandering sadly in the Great Lands, and maybe they speak very strangely now, for . . . 'twas but the long wandering of the Noldoli about the Earth and the black ages of their thraldom while their kin dwelt yet in Valinor that caused the deep sundering of their speech. [*The Book of Lost Tales, Part One, p. 48]

In other words, the Noldoli brought their speech to Middle-earth, where it changed over time. But in The Silmarillion it is said that whereas the High Speech of Valinor, Quenya, was brought to Middle-earth by the Noldor, it did not change, but was abandoned (except among 'the lords of the Noldor' and 'as a language of lore', p. 129) in favour of the Sindarin tongue of the Grey-elves of Beleriand, who had never been to Valinor, and whose speech became separate early in Elvish history.

Quenya and Sindarin nonetheless were of common origin. In the later history, they derived ultimately from the 'Primitive Quendian' devised by the original Elvish speakers (Quendi), which became a 'Common Eldarin' (common to all the Eldar) before undergoing division. In *The Silmarillion* it is said that the Elves dwelled long by their first home 'and they walked the Earth in wonder; and they began to make speech and to give names to all things that they perceived. Themselves they named the Quendi, signifying those that speak with voices; for as yet they had met no other living things that spoke or sang' (p. 49). In the earlier history, the Elvish tongues derived ultimately from Valarin, the language of the Valar; and in the *Lhammas* it is told how the first of the Elves were found by the Vala Oromë,

> and of him they learned after their capacity the speech of the Valar; and all the tongues that have been derived thence may be called Oromian or Quendian. The speech of the Valar changes little, for the Valar do not die; and before the Sun and Moon it altered not from age to age in Valinor. But when the Elves learned it, they changed it from the first in the learning, and softened its sounds, and they added many words to it of their own liking and devices even from the beginning. For the Elves love the making of words, and this has ever been the chief cause of the change and variety of their tongues. [*The Lost Road and Other Writings*, p. 168]

At this time (?mid-1930s), in addition to a description in the *Lhammas*, Tolkien showed the intricate relationships among the Elvish languages as they had 'evolved' within his fictional history, and with those of Dwarves, Goblins (Orcs), and Men, graphically in the *Tree of Tongues*, reproduced in *The Lost Road and Other Writings*, pp. 169, 170. The Elvish tongues during this period included not only Qenya and Noldorin, but also less fully elaborated languages such as Telerin, Ilkorin, Doriathrin, Danian, Leikvian, and Ossiriandeb.

The Dwarves, made by the Vala Aulë, learned the speech he devised for them (*Khuzdul*), which was 'cumbrous and unlovely' to the Elves, 'and few ever of the Eldar have achieved the mastery of it' (*The Silmarillion*, p. 92); but the Dwarves eagerly learned the Elvish tongue, as well as Westron, the Common Speech (*Sóval Phárë*) of Men.

In the *Lhammas* it is said that 'the languages of Men were from their beginning diverse and various; yet they were for the most part derived remotely from the language of the Valar', taught to wandering Men by the Dark-elves; but 'the tongue of the folk of Bëor and Haleth and Hádor . . . was greatly influenced by the Green-elves, and it was of old named *Taliska*. . . .' Some Men of Beleriand, however, 'forsook the daily use of their own tongue and spoke and gave even names unto their children in the language of the Gnomes. Yet other Men there were, it seems, that remained east of Eredlindon, who held to their speech, and from this, closely akin to Taliska, are come after many ages of change languages that live still in the North of the earth' (*The Lost Road and Other Writings*, p. 179). This linguistic diversity continued to be reflected in Tolkien's later account, 'Of Men', in *The Lord of the Rings*, Appendix F, where it is said that the ancestral tongue of the Númenóreans, *Adûnaic*, in time 'mingled with many words of the languages of lesser men [and] became a Common Speech that spread thence along the coasts [of Middle-earth] among all that had dealings with Westernesse'. The languages of 'most of the Men of the northern regions of the West-lands' were 'related to the Adûnaic, and some still preserved a likeness to the Common Speech', including the tongues of the Beornings, the Woodmen of Western Mirkwood, the Men of the Long Lake and of Dale, and the Rohirrim. The Hobbits 'in ancient days ... seem always to have used the languages of Men near whom, or among whom, they lived' (Appendix F, 'Of Hobbits'). But the speech of the Wild Men of Drúadan Forest and of the Dunlendings were alien to these, or 'only remotely akin'.

See further, Christopher Gilson, 'Elvish and Mannish', *Vinyar Tengwar* 33 (January 1994); Patrick Wynne and Carl F. Hostetter, '"Verbs, Syntax! Hooray!": A Preliminary Assessment of Adunaic Grammar in *The Notion Club Papers*', *Vinyar Tengwar* 24 (July 1992), pp. 14–38; and 'An Adunaic Dictionary' compiled by Carl F. Hostetter and Patrick Wynne, *Vinyar Tengwar* 25 (September 1992), pp. 8–26. An historical grammar of Taliska exists, but is not yet published.

Tolkien also says in Appendix F that the Orcs

> had no language of their own, but took what they could of other tongues and perverted it to their own liking; yet they made only brutal jargons, scarcely sufficient even for their own needs, unless it were for curses and abuse. And these creatures ... quickly developed as many barbarous dialects as there were groups or settlements of their race, so that their Orkish speech was of little use to them in intercourse between different tribes.

The Black Speech, such as used in the inscription on the One Ring, is said to have been devised by Sauron as a common language for his servants, but failed in the purpose.

For many years, the study of Tolkien's invented languages rested largely upon the limited information given in Appendices E and F of *The Lord of the Rings*, and in matter appended to *The Road Goes Ever On: A Song Cycle* (1967), supplemented by close examination of the words in Quenya, Sindarin, Silvan Elvish, Khuzdul, the Black Speech, and Westron contained in the Appendices and *The Lord of the Rings* proper. The merest scrap of text was welcome as a further example to analyze, let alone a letter such as Dick Plotz received from Tolkien in 1966 or 1967, and which became widely circulated, concerning the declension of the nouns *cirya* and *lasse* in 'classical' or 'book' Quenya as known to Númenórean scholars (see Jorge Quiñonez, 'A Brief Note on the Background of the Letter from J.R.R. Tolkien to Dick Plotz Concerning the Declension of the High-elvish Noun', *Vinyar Tengwar* 6 (July 1989)). Useful work was done even thus, particularly in journals such as *Mythlore* and *Parma Eldalamberon*, some of which was collected in *An Introduction to Elvish* (1978), ed. Jim Allan, still a useful reference though it was dated even on publication.

Beginning in 1977 with *The Silmarillion*, which includes an appendix of 'elements in Quenya and Sindarin names', a substantial amount of additional material concerning Tolkien's invented languages has appeared, most notably in volumes of *The History of Middle-earth*, in *Letters of J.R.R. Tolkien*, and in the journals *Vinyar Tengwar* and *Parma Eldalamberon* (see part VII of the bibliography of Tolkien's works contained in the **Chronology** volume of the *Companion and Guide*). See especially the appendices of names in both volumes of *The Book of Lost Tales* (drawn from the *Qenyaqetsa* and the *Gnomish Lexicon*); the *Lhammas* and *Etymologies* in *The Lost Road and Other Writings*; *The Notion Club Papers* and *Lowdham's Report on the Adunaic Language*, in the volume *Sauron Defeated*, with extensive commentary; the 'excursus on the languages of Beleriand' within the *Grey Annals* (*Annals of Beleriand*) and *Quendi and Eldar* in *The War of the Jewels*; and the *Dangweth Pengoloð*, *The Problem of* Ros, and *The Shibboleth of Fëanor* in *The Peoples of Middle-earth*.

Besides works cited above, see also entries in the present volume: *'Analysis of fragments of other languages found in *The Lord of the Rings*'; *Ae Adar Nín: The Lord's Prayer in Sindarin*; *Corrected Names of Chief Valar*; *The Creatures of the Earth*; *'Early Chart of Names'; *'Early Qenya Pronouns'; *Eldarin Hands, Fingers & Numerals*; *'English–Qenya Dictionary'; *Gnomish Grammar*; *'Index of Names for *The Lay of the Children of Húrin*'; *'Matar and Tulir'; *'Name-list to *The Fall of Gondolin*'; *Names and Required Alterations*; *'Names of the Valar'; *Narqelion*; *Nieninque*; *'Noldorin Dictionary'; *'Noldorin Word-lists'; *Notes on Óre*; *Official Name List*; *'Otsan and Kainendan'; *Poetic and Mythologic Words of Eldarissa*; *Qenya: Descriptive Grammar of the Qenya Language*; *Quendi and Eldar*; *The Quenya Verb Forms*; *The Rivers and Beacon-hills of Gondor*; *'Sí Qente Feanor'; *'Synopsis of Pengoloð's *Eldarinwe Leperi are Notessi*'; *'Variation D/L in Common Eldarin'; and *'Words of Joy'.

Interest in Tolkien's invented languages has always been a significant component of Tolkien *fandom, from which have emerged various reference books, such as *A Dictionary of Quenya and Proto-Eldarin and Ante-Quenya* (1982, rev. 1983) by J.C. Bradfield and a series of lexicons, glossaries, and indexes by Paul Nolan Hyde; instructional materials such as the *Basic Quenya* course devised by Nancy Martsch (1992, originally 'Quenya Language Lessons' in *Beyond Bree*, 1988–90); and extended treatments such as *A Gateway to Sindarin* (2004) by David Salo. A more concerted and systematic analysis of Tolkien's languages, however, has been supported by the Tolkien Estate, with the release of relevant papers and authorized publication through a limited body of scholars, primarily in *Parma Eldalamberon* and *Vinyar Tengwar*. The progress of this work is necessarily slow, given the complexity of the material, the occasional difficulty of Tolkien's handwriting, and the desire to proceed (for the most part) historically, beginning with the earliest relevant texts and fragments.

Some Tolkien enthusiasts have objected to this approach, and to so deliberate a pace of publication: those interested only, or chiefly, in the languages as they stood at the time of *The Lord of the Rings*, and those who wish to use Tolkien's languages, particularly Quenya and Sindarin, for their own writing and conversation. Unfortunately, as Carl Hostetter has observed, there is little 'conversational Elvish' in Tolkien's writings, and even the most developed of the languages are incomplete. Those who seek to converse extensively in Elvish, therefore, must themselves invent nouns, verbs, and other elements, in the process creating a 'Neo-Quenya' or 'Neo-Sindarin' which is no longer a language by Tolkien but only based on one.

This division of emphasis in Tolkienian linguistics, between those who approach the field as a matter of historical study and those who wish to use Tolkien's languages for, say, tattoos or wedding invitations, is reflected in numerous Web sites. Two of the more substantive of these are *www.elvish.org*, home of the Elvish Linguistic Fellowship (ELF), and *www.uib.no/People/hnohf* (Ardalambion). Each of these provides useful links, e.g. to the ELF online journal *Tengwestië* and to relevant Internet forums.

See also *Writing systems.

Lascelles, Mary Madge (1900–1995). Mary Lascelles, for many years a colleague of Tolkien in the *Oxford English School, herself read English at Lady Margaret Hall, Oxford beginning in 1919. In 1922 she began work on a B.Litt. supervised by *George S. Gordon; her thesis was published as 'Alexander and the Earthly Paradise in Mediaeval English Writings' in *Medium Ævum* in 1936. Later her professional interests turned to Shakespeare, Samuel Johnson, Jane Austen, and Sir Walter Scott.

After teaching for brief periods at St Leonard's School in St Andrews, Scotland, and at Royal Holloway College, London, Lascelles returned to Lady Margaret Hall for two terms as a substitute. In 1931, following the elevation of *Helen Darbishire to Principal, Lascelles was appointed tutor in English at Somerville College, Oxford. She became a Fellow of Somerville in 1932, and remained a tutor until 1960 when she became a University Lecturer in English Literature. From 1947 to 1960 she was also Vice-Principal of Somerville. In 1966 she became a Reader in the University and a Professorial Fellow of Somerville.

Both a literary scholar and a practising poet, her publications include *Jane Austen and Her Art* (1939), *The Adversaries and Other Poems* (1971), *Notions and Facts: Collected Criticism and Research* (1972), and *Further Poems* (1982).

The Last Ark. Poem, first published in *The Monsters and the Critics and Other Essays* (1983), pp. 213–15, 220–3, within the autobiographical lecture *A Secret Vice* (written ?Autumn 1931). *The Last Ark* is the English language version of the same work in Qenya (*Languages, Invented), *Oilima Markirya*, included in the lecture as an example of the author's 'vice' of language invention and its outlet in poetry. Its sentimental reflection on things past or passing ('Who shall see a white ship / leave the last shore', 'Who shall see the last evening?') recalls the 'ubi sunt' motif of Old English poems such as *The Wanderer*.

Several manuscripts of *Oilima Markirya* and *The Last Ark* are extant. These are discussed with variants in *Christopher Tolkien's notes to *A Secret Vice*. At one stage *The Last Ark* was called *The Last Ship*, not to be mistaken for the poem of that title (*q.v.*) first published in 1962.

The Last Ship. Poem, first published in this form in *The Adventures of Tom Bombadil and Other Verses from the Red Book* (1962), pp. 61–4. At dawn by the river, Fíriel hears singing 'like wind-voices keen and young'; a splendid boat arrives, rowed by 'fair folk out of Elvenland'. They are 'on the last road faring', 'back to Elvenhome', forsaking Middle-earth. They ask Fíriel to join them, but 'deep in clay her feet sank', and she declines, for she was 'born Earth's daughter'. She returns 'under the house-shadow' to her home and work. The years pass, 'but never more / westward ships have waded / in mortal waters as before / and their song has faded'.

In his preface to the *Tom Bombadil* collection, in which he pretends that its contents are examples of Hobbit poetry, Tolkien describes *The Last Ship* as 'derived ultimately from Gondor . . . based on the traditions of Men, living in shorelands and familiar with rivers running into the Sea.' 'Fíriel', he says, is a 'Gondorian name, of High-elvish form', meaning 'mortal woman'.

The Last Ship is a revision and reduction of an earlier poem, *Firiel*, published in the *Chronicle of the Convents of the Sacred Heart* 4 (1934), pp. 30–2. Tolkien submitted it to that journal in ?October 1933 (he received an acknowledgement dated 2 November 1933), through the Oxford branch of the Convents, and probably wrote it around that time: its style, relative to other, dated works, is consistent with Tolkien's poems from the early 1930s.

References to Middle-earth aside, *Firiel* and *The Last Ship* are very similar. In the earlier work, however, it is more explicit that Firiel's 'heart misgave and shrank' when she dares to step towards the Elves' boat; and there the poem ends not with the sense of an opportunity lost forever, with Fíriel returned home to merely a plain existence, but with a vision of a bright and cheerful world, 'like an anthill dizzy' but with 'voices loud and merry'.

T.A. Shippey argues in *The Road to Middle-earth* (2nd edn. 1992) that *The Last Ship* 'is an unprecedented reversal' of the ballad-genre 'in which the elves steal away a human man or woman to live with them in delight in "elf-hill".' Fíriel refuses to go; but 'she also turns from glamour to dullness and oblivion' (p. 248).

Laws and Customs among the Eldar. Late essay, published in *Morgoth's Ring* (1993), pp. 207–53, deriving from a new reason for the conflict between the sons of Finwë which Tolkien introduced into the *Quenta Silmarillion c.* 1958–60.

The title of its first version, a manuscript, was *Of the Marriage Laws and Customs of the Eldar, Their Children, and Other Matters Touching Thereon*, but for an unfinished typescript revision this became *Of the Laws and Customs among the Eldar Pertaining to Marriage and Other Matters Related Thereto:*

Together with the Statute of Finwë and Míriel and the Debate of the Valar at Its Making. The revised text follows the first closely but with some important differences. The published text is that of the typescript as far as that continues, with notes on significant variations from the first text, and then that of the manuscript.

Tolkien decided that not long after Fëanor's birth, his mother, Míriel, fell asleep, and her spirit departed to Mandos but refused to return to her body; and that her husband, Finwë, eventually married a second time, taking Indis of the Vanyar as his wife. This idea greatly enhanced the story Tolkien was telling, providing anl explanation for the divisions among the Noldorin princes. But it also posed ethical problems for a Roman Catholic writer who did not accept divorce, but could recognize as valid the remarriage of one partner after the death of the other. Since Míriel's body had not been destroyed, by the nature of Elvish reincarnation it would have been open to her spirit to return to it at any time, in which case, given Finwë's remarriage, he would then have two wives alive at the same time. This quandary led Tolkien to consider the nature of the Eldar and to incorporate his conclusions in a lengthy essay, which he then revised, but abandoned the revision when it was less than half complete.

In an introductory section marked as 'Ælfwine's Preamble', he describes how the children of the Eldar grew and matured in comparison with those of Men. An untitled section describes betrothal and marriage customs and ceremonies, the begetting and bearing of children, and differences in interests, skills, and tasks between male and female. Then follows 'Of Naming', describing the various names given to children of the Elves. The next section, entitled 'Of Death and the Severance of *Fëa* and *Hröa*', points out that although the Eldar were intended to be immortal within Arda (see *Mortality and Immortality), as a result of the marring of Arda their bodies, or *hröar*, might be destroyed, leaving their *fëar* (spirits) unhoused. The disembodied *fëar* would be summoned to Mandos, and those that obeyed might in time be reborn.

Another section, 'Of Re-birth and Other Dooms of Those That Go to Mandos', discusses rebirth as a newborn child and the gradual recovery of memories of the first life, rare cases in which the original body was still whole and might be reinhabited, what happened to the *fëar* of corrupted Eldar, and the fate of those who refused the summons to Mandos. 'Of the Severance of Marriage' deals with the effect of death and rebirth on marriage among the Elves: 'Permanent marriage was in accordance with elvish nature, and they never had need of any law to teach this or to enforce it; but if a "permanent" marriage was in fact broken, as when one of the partners was slain, then they did not know what should be done or thought' (*Morgoth's Ring*, p. 225). They therefore sought counsel from Manwë, who delivered through Mandos a pronouncement called the 'Doom of Finwë and Míriel': marriage, he ruled, involves both *fëa* and *hröa*, and therefore is not ended with the death of the body of one of the partners. A marriage can be ended only if the Dead are unwilling ever to return to life in the body, or not permitted to do so. Tolkien's typescript ends in the middle of series of commentaries on this ruling, based on explanations given by the Valar in response to questions, and on later reasoning of the Eldar.

The manuscript continues, with more questions and answers on the ruling which in this text is called 'The Statute of Finwë and Míriel'. One answer states that a *fëa* released from Mandos would naturally desire to return to its state in its former life and therefore to its former marriage; indeed, 'none of the Dead will be permitted by Mandos to be reborn, until and unless they desire to take up life again in continuity with their past' (p. 233). In discussing where and into what families the *fëa* might be reborn, the text defines the closeness of kin within which marriage did not take place.

Another answer defines the three kinds of dooms uttered by Mandos. For the first two of these – 'the decisions of Manwë, or of the Valar in conclave' and 'the decisions and purposes of others who are under his jurisdiction, who are the Dead, in grave matters that affect justice and the right order of Arda' – time must pass between the decision and Mandos uttering the doom which is binding. A note comments that 'in the case of a decision never to return to life by a *fëa* of the Dead, the least time of interval appointed by Mandos was ten Valian years. During this period the decision could be revoked' (p. 235). The third kind are 'the dooms of Mandos that proceed from Mandos himself, as judge in matters that belong to his office as ordained from the beginning. He is the judge of right and wrong, and of innocence or guilt . . .' (p. 235).

Then follows a detailed account of Míriel's *fëa* leaving her body after the birth of Fëanor and refusing to return, of Finwë's appeal to Manwë, and Manwë's decision, and of the doom spoken by Mandos after ten years. It is said that three years after that, Finwë took Indis as his second wife, to the displeasure of his son Fëanor. 'In those unhappy things which afterward came to pass . . . many saw the effects of this breach in the house of Finwë, judging that if Finwë had endured his loss and been content with the fathering of his mighty son, the courses of Feanáro would have been otherwise, and much sorrow and evil would never have been' (p. 239). The work concludes with an account of the debate of the Valar concerning Finwë and Míriel (and in particular whether her unnatural death resulted from the Marring of Arda) between the decision of Manwë and Mandos declaring it as a binding doom. During the debate Mandos says that he foresees the 'Tale of Arda' made 'more glorious' (p. 247) by the children of Indis, and prophesies the coming of Eärendil.

When Finwë was slain by Morgoth, however, his *fea* met that of Míriel in the Halls of Mandos. She recognized her error, and expressed the wish 'to set the Tale of our people and of thee and thy children in a tapestry of many colours, as a memorial brighter than memory' (pp. 249). Mandos accepted Finwë's offer that his *fëa* abide for ever with Mandos and not seek reincarnation, in return for which the *fëa* of Míriel was released and took up her body again. But rather than returning to her own people, Míriel became the chief handmaid of Vairë the Weaver, the spouse of Mandos, 'and all the tidings of the Noldor down the years from their beginning were brought to her, and she wove them in webs historical' (p. 250).

*Christopher Tolkien describes *Laws and Customs among the Eldar* as an important work by his father,

> a comprehensive (if sometimes obscure, and tantalising in its obscurity) declaration of his thought at that time on fundamental aspects of the nature of the Quendi, distinguishing them from Men: the power of the incarnate *fëa* (spirit) in relation to the body; the 'consuming' of the body by the *fëa*; the destiny of Elvish spirits, ordained by Eru, 'to dwell in Arda for all the life of Arda'; the meaning of death for such beings, and of existence after death; the nature of Elvish re-birth; and the consequences of the Marring of Arda by Melkor. [*Morgoth's Ring*, p. 209]

He also comments that 'it is not easy to see from what fictional perspective' the work was composed. 'There is a reference to Elves who linger in Middle-earth "in these after days"' (p. 233), but the writer also 'speaks as if the customs of the Noldor were present and observable. . . . It is clear in any case that it is presented as the work, not of one of the Eldar, but of a Man. After the manuscript was complete, Tolkien 'wrote "Ælfwine's Preamble"' in the margin against the opening of the text', but did not indicate where the Preamble ended. In the typescript the first two paragraphs are clearly marked as 'Ælfwine's Preamble', and a later bracketed passage of observation ends: 'So spoke Ælfwine' (p. 208).

See also *The Shibboleth of Fëanor* in *The Peoples of Middle-earth*, which contains a brief account of the story of Finwë, Míriel, and Indis, and summarizes the judgement of the Valar. This was written after a gap of several years in 1968 or later, by which time Tolkien had abandoned the idea of Elvish reincarnation through rebirth, in favour of the healing or restoration of the original body through the power of the Valar.

The Lay of Aotrou and Itroun. Poem, published in the *Welsh Review* (Cardiff) 4, no. 4 (December 1945), pp. 254–66. A childless lord of Britany, Aotrou, obtains a potion from a Corrigan, or witch, and gives it to his wife, Itroun, who gives birth to a boy and a girl. Aotrou having offered to grant Itroun's 'lightest wish', she dreams 'for water cool and clear / and venison of the greenwood deer, / for waters crystal-clear and cold / and deer no earthly forests hold'. Aotrou pursues a white doe in 'the green boughs of Broceliande', and there comes upon the witch, who demands his love in payment for the potion: 'thou shalt wed / anew with me, or stand as stone / and wither lifeless and alone.' He refuses, and is doomed to die. Itroun looks for him but finds no sign; then, hearing mourning bells, she learns of his death. She herself soon dies of grief.

The earliest extant texts of *The Lay of Aotrou and Itroun* – an incomplete manuscript, a complete fair copy, and a typescript – date from mid-1930. The fair copy is dated at the end 23 September 1930; its composition interrupted the writing of Canto X of the *Lay of Leithian*. Tolkien heavily revised the typescript, probably in late 1941: some rough workings for the revision are on the back of a synopsis for 'The Breaking of the Fellowship' (*The Lord of the Rings*, bk. I, ch. 12). In June 1945, when he was in Wales as an external examiner at the University in Aberystwyth, he lent the revised version to his friend *Gwyn Jones, editor of the *Welsh Review*.

The influence of Breton lays upon *Aotrou and Itroun* was noted as early as 1972, by Paul H. Kocher (*Master of Middle-earth: The Fiction of J.R.R. Tolkien*). Jessica Yates in 'The Source of "The Lay of Aotrou and Itroun"', in *Leaves from the Tree: J.R.R. Tolkien's Shorter Fiction* (1991), argues that Tolkien did not decide to write a poem in the form of a Breton lay, then cast about for a subject; rather, he wanted to write a version of the 'Clerk Colvill' story about a young man and a water-nymph, was intrigued by the translations he found of the analogous Breton 'Lord Nann' ballad in F.J. Child's *Ballads* (1882–98), and used them as the source for his poem, in the octosyllabic form of a Breton lay. Yates shows how Tolkien reshaped the versions of 'Lord Nann' in a collection by Hersart de la Villemarqué to suit his own ends.

T.A. Shippey comments further, in *J.R.R. Tolkien: Author of the Century* (2000), that Aotrou's refusal of the witch, her curse, and his death 'are there in the Breton ballad; but in Tolkien alone the death is deserved, or at least prompted by Aotrou's attempt to sway Providence by supernatural forces', rather than humbly submit to their fate. The poem ends:

> God keep us all in hope and prayer
> from evil rede [advice] and from despair,
> by waters blest of Christendom
> to dwell, until at last we come
> to joy of Heaven where is queen
> the maiden Mary pure and clean.

Shippey says that 'Tolkien's moral is clear and unequivocal. Aotrou's sin lay not in submitting to the Corrigan – he defied her as successfully as Sir Gawain warded off the Green Knight's lady [*Sir Gawain and the Green Knight*], and with a firm profession of Christian faith – it lay in having any dealings with her at all' (pp. 293–4).

'Lay of Eärendel'. Fragment of an alliterative poem, published under this title in *The Lays of Beleriand* (1985) with notes and commentary, pp. 141–4. In thirty-eight lines, references are made to the escape of refugees led by Tûr (Tuor) from the burning city of Gondolin, to Glorfindel's battle with a balrog, and to the survivors' arrival in the Land of Willows. Tolkien wrote the name *Eärendel* in various forms at the end, from which *Christopher Tolkien thinks it 'extremely likely, even almost certain, that this poem was to be a Lay of Eärendel' (p. 141). Its single rough manuscript was written on *Leeds examination paper, and therefore dates from the same time as other alliterative poems, *The Children of Húrin* and *The Flight of the Noldoli from Valinor*.

The fragment is of interest mainly because it seems to identify Tûr with Wade of the Helsings, a mysterious figure who appears in the Old English poem *Widsith*. Christopher Tolkien notes that Wade's ship was called *Guingelot*, from which he is sure that Eärendel's ship *Wingelot* derived its name.

Lay of Leithian. Poem in octosyllabic couplets, published with commentary and notes in **The Lays of Beleriand* (1985), pp. 150–363. It tells the greater part of the story of Beren and Lúthien (**'Of Beren and Lúthien'*) more extensively and in more detail than any other version, but ends abruptly as Carcharoth devours Beren's hand holding the Silmaril.

THE FIRST VERSION

In the course of writing, Tolkien would begin a section of the poem with rough drafts, and when he was satisfied with what he had written would add the text to a fair copy. From this he made a typescript in stages, incorporating emendations and insertions, and making further changes. A note in his diary indicates that he began the typescript by 16 August 1926 at the latest. On the covering page of the rough workings is written *Tinúviel*, used by Tolkien in early references to the poem. The manuscript itself has no title, but the typescript is called elaborately *The Gest of Beren Son of Barahir and Lúthien the Fay Called Tinúviel the Nightingale, or the Lay of Leithian, Release from Bondage*. In *The Lays of Beleriand* *Christopher Tolkien presents the typescript, but in his notes records significant differences in the manuscript. He also explains editorial problems he faced, his decisions, and resulting inconsistencies: see especially pp. 152–3.

Tolkien wrote in his diary that he began the *Lay of Leithian* during the period of the summer examinations in 1925. Almost certainly this was after he had abandoned unfinished various works in alliterative verse, including the substantial *Children of Húrin*. Since, unusually, Tolkien at intervals wrote dates on the manuscript as it progressed, the *Lay of Leithian* is perhaps the best documented of the components of 'The Silmarillion'. These dates show that he did most of the writing during vacations, and often left the manuscript untouched for over a year at a time. The first 757 lines, begun during the examinations of 1925 (probably June or July), were completed by September that year; lines 758–3030 probably (1161–2929 definitely) were written during the Easter vacation of 1928, including 1,768 lines in nine days; lines 3031–75 were written in November 1929; lines 3076–(probably) 3880 were written in September and on 1 October 1930; and the rest of the work, from *c.* line 3881 to 4228, was composed in September 1931, this last section written into the typescript. At some date Tolkien also wrote a 22-line passage headed 'a piece from the end of the poem'. A page with lines 3994–4027 written in Tengwar (*Writing systems) is reproduced in black and white in *The Lays of Beleriand*, p. 299.

During the six-year period that Tolkien worked on the *Lay of Leithian*, not only did he expand and evolve the story of Beren and Lúthien but also had many new ideas for his *legendarium* (*'The Silmarillion') in general. At intervals he made five successive synopses or outlines for the part of the poem still to be written, usually more detailed close to the point already reached, less so towards the end of the story. As further ideas came to him which changed the story, he made another synopsis beginning at the point reached. Some ideas appear only in a synopsis, overtaken by later thoughts. All of these synopses are included in *The Lays of Beleriand*, and together with the poem itself, the partly contemporary *Sketch of the Mythology*, and Christopher Tolkien's notes and commentary, provide insight into the evolution of the story.

The synopses are not given as complete texts; rather, the relevant part of each appears in the commentary after each Canto. Synopsis I begins part way through Canto IV, with Beren and Lúthien dancing together (pp. 197, 209, 219–21, 244, 256–8, 270, 282, 304). Synopsis II, much emended in parts, begins part way through Canto VI, as Beren comes to Nargothrond, but was probably written before Tolkien began the Canto itself (pp. 221, 233, 245–6, 256–8, 270, 282, 304). Synopsis III begins part way through Canto IX, as Huan overcomes Thû (pp. 257–8, 270–2, 282–3, 293–4, 304–5). Synopsis IV begins near the beginning of Canto X, as Beren decides to leave Lúthien safe in Doriath (pp. 272–4, 283, 294, 304, 311–12). Synopsis V may lack earlier pages, but in its extant form begins part way through Canto X, as Huan brings a herb to heal Beren's wound (pp. 273, 283, 294, 305, 309, 310, 311–14). Synopses IV and V provide information about the proposed content of the unwritten part of the poem.

Towards the end of 1929 Tolkien lent the typescript of the *Lay of Leithian*, as far as it had progressed, to his friend *C.S. Lewis. On 7 December, having spent the previous evening reading as far as about line 2017, Lewis wrote to Tolkien: 'I can quite honestly say that it is ages since I have had an evening of such delight. . . . The two things that come out clearly are the sense of reality in the background and the mythical value: the essence of a myth being that it should have no taint of allegory to the maker and yet should suggest incipient allegories to the reader' (p. 151). Probably in 1930, Lewis sent Tolkien fourteen pages of detailed criticism of the poem as far as line 1161, described by Christopher Tolkien as in the form of 'a heavily academic commentary on the text, pretending to treat the Lay as an ancient and anonymous work extant in many more or less corrupt manuscripts, overlaid by scribal perversions in antiquity and the learned argumentation of nineteenth-century scholars; and thus entertainingly took the sting from some sharply expressed judgements, while at the same time in this disguise expressing strong praise for particular passages' (p. 151). Christopher Tolkien notes that his father marked for revision in typescript most of the passages criticized, and thinks that Tolkien also made replacement typescripts of parts of Cantos I and IV in response to Lewis's comments. Most of Lewis's commentary are also included in *The Lays of Beleriand* (pp. 315–29), with notes by Christopher Tolkien on his father's reactions and the changes he made.

In October 1937 Tolkien submitted the *Lay of Leithian*, among other works, to George Allen & Unwin (*Publishers) for consideration as a successor to *The Hobbit*. The publisher's reader, Edward Crankshaw, was at a loss to know what to do with it, and in fact presumed that it was an authentic Celtic *geste*. 'In any case', he wrote, 'authenticity apart ... would there be any market for a long, involved, romantic verse-tale of Celtic elves and mortals? I think not. Especially as this particular verse is of a very thin, if not always downright bad, quality, and the tale in this retelling has been spread out almost to nothingness' (Tolkien-George Allen & Unwin archive, HarperCollins).

THE SECOND VERSION ('THE LAY OF LEITHIAN RECOMMENCED')

After completing *The Lord of the Rings* Tolkien turned again to 'The Silmarillion', and *c.* 1949–50 to the *Lay of Leithian*. He began to revise Canto I on the typescript made many years before; and by the time he reached Canto II he was virtually writing a new poem, expanding the original 302 lines to 500 and subdividing the work into two cantos (given arabic numerals, 2 and 3, by Christopher to distinguish them from the roman numerals of the cantos in the earlier version of the poem). This expansion extended into old Canto III (new Canto 4), at which point the poem was some 660 lines long. Tolkien made preliminary drafts for at least part of this rewriting, then wrote the new version partly on the typescript and partly on inserted new pages or slips. From this 'now extremely chaotic text' (p. 330) he then made a fine, decorated manuscript, with some additional changes. An amanuensis typescript, top copy, and carbon copy were made at a later date. Several years later, Tolkien again looked at the poem and made still more emendations, some drafted on the early typescript, but most incorporated into the amanuensis typescript, as typed additions or replacement sections.

The text as published in *The Lays of Beleriand* is that of the manuscript, incorporating authorial emendations made to the amanuensis typescript, together with a short section found only in draft. The first page of Canto 2 in the decorated manuscript is reproduced as a frontispiece, in colour in the Allen & Unwin first edition, and in black and white in the Houghton Mifflin first edition.

In her review of *The Lays of Beleriand* in *Beyond Bree*, November 1985, Christina Scull comments on 'the evolution from the somewhat superficial and fairytale-like version' of the story of Beren and Lúthien 'in *The Book of Lost Tales* to the much more deeply felt and mythopoeic version of the *Lay*' (p. 1), and that 'the greatest change' in the story is the characters' deepening relationship. Charles Noad, in his review of *The Lays of Beleriand* in *Mallorn* 23 (Summer 1986), writes concerning the *Lay of Leithian*:

> The story is much the same as in *Lost Tales* although with many minor differences. But there is a major difference in Tolkien's general treatment of the theme. If the *Lost Tales* showed a coherent but out-of-focus view of the myth, then here in the *Lays* it as though the lens through which we perceive has been suddenly turned, and all become clearer and sharper. This is because Tolkien knew his own material better. By the time the

Lays had come to be written he had lived with his mythology for some years, and his increasing understanding of and sensitivity to it allowed him greatly to refine it, both as tales in themselves and in the language used to express those tales. [p. 15]

Of the later version of the poem Noad comments: 'Insofar as the revised lay represents, as I think it does, the peak of Tolkien's mature poetic style, it is another tragedy of unfulfilled beginnings that was never completed' (p. 15).

Brian Rosebury in *Tolkien: A Cultural Phenomenon* (2003) considers the *Lay of Leithian*, 'though unfinished and seriously flawed ... to contain the most rewarding work Tolkien produced before the 1930s, and to be much the best account of the Beren and Lúthien story' (p. 98).

RELATED PROSE VERSION

At the same time that Tolkien returned to the *Lay of Leithian*, c. 1950, he also began to write another (unpublished) prose 'saga' concerning Beren and Lúthien. Christopher Tolkien describes this in *The Lost Road and Other Writings* as 'a substantial text, though its story goes no further than the betrayal by Dairon to Thingol of Beren's presence in Doriath, and it is so closely based on the rewritten form of the [*Lay of Leithian*] as to read in places almost as a prose paraphrase of the verse' (p. 295). Written on blank verso pages of the 'later' *Annals of Beleriand*, it follows several earlier attempts by Tolkien to tell the story of Beren and Lúthien in the *Quenta Silmarillion* at a suitable length. Christopher Tolkien argues in *The War of the Jewels* (p. 129) that this new version, which was not known to him when he prepared *The Silmarillion* for publication, preceded the much shorter versions of the story in the *Grey Annals* (see *Annals of Beleriand*).

The Lay of the Children of Húrin see **The Children of Húrin**

The Lay of the Fall of Gondolin. Poem in rhyming couplets, extracts of which were published with commentary in *The Lays of Beleriand* (1985), pp. 144–9. *Christopher Tolkien believes that this unfinished work was his father's first attempt to tell in verse a story from the unfinished *Book of Lost Tales*. 'So far as it goes' it 'has undergone virtually no development from the prose tale of *The Fall of Gondolin*' (p. 145), and for that reason the poem is not given *in extenso* in *The Lays of Beleriand*. Apparently 'not conceived on a large scale,' the narrative reaches 'dragon-fire arising over the northern heights' of Gondolin 'already within 130 lines' (pp. 144–5). It contains, however, the earliest account of the story of Isfin, Eöl, and Meglin (see *'Of Maeglin'*).

The poem probably dates from the beginning of the 1920s, after Tolkien moved to *Leeds.

The Lays of Beleriand. The third volume of *The History of Middle-earth*, edited with notes and commentary by *Christopher Tolkien, first published in Great Britain by George Allen & Unwin, London, in August 1985, and in the United States by the Houghton Mifflin Company, Boston, in November 1985. See further, *Descriptive Bibliography* A23.

The *Lays of Beleriand* contains poetic works from the *'Silmarillion' mythology, written primarily in the period ?mid-1919 to 1931, after Tolkien had ceased to work seriously on the unfinished *Book of Lost Tales*:

Part One, *The Lay of the Children of Húrin*, contains two versions of an unfinished alliterative poem, *The Children of Húrin*, and poems developed from it: *Winter Comes to Nargothrond, Storm over Narog*, and an untitled poem about the River Sirion ('With the seething sea // Sirion's waters'); a discussion of the poem *Light as Leaf on Lindentree*; and a brief description of an unpublished *Children of Húrin* in rhyming couplets.

Part Two, 'Poems Early Abandoned', contains *The Flight of the Noldoli from Valinor*, a fragment of an alliterative *'Lay of Eärendel', and *The Lay of the Fall of Gondolin*.

Part Three is the first, abandoned version of the *Lay of Leithian* from 1925 to 1931, together with a commentary on the poem by *C.S. Lewis.

Part Four, 'The *Lay of Leithian* Recommenced', contains revisions and expansion of the poem, *c.* 1949–50 and later.

Appended to the volume is a note on the original submission of the *Lay of Leithian* and 'The Silmarillion' to George Allen & Unwin (*Publishers) in 1937.

The Allen & Unwin hardback edition of *The Lays of Beleriand* includes as a frontispiece a colour reproduction of a page from a fine manuscript of the *Lay of Leithian* recommenced. This is reproduced in black and white in the Houghton Mifflin hardback, but omitted in paperback editions. Both British and American editions reproduce in black and white two manuscript pages from *The Children of Húrin* and a page of the original *Lay of Leithian* written in Tengwar.

CRITICISM

Compared to the two volumes of *The Book of Lost Tales*, *The Lays of Beleriand* received little attention in general newspapers and journals, and opinions were mixed. Jan Murphy in the *San Francisco Chronicle*, 10 November 1985 ('Another Fairy Tale for Adults'), thought that even if Tolkien was not always successful, 'the best moments are splendid', and noted that in *The Children of Húrin* 'Túrin's grief at discovering that he has killed not his enemy but his friend Beleg is very moving.' Beth Ann Mills wrote in *Library Journal* for December 1985 that 'while the power of Tolkien's central characters – tragic, cursed Túrin; the lovers Beren and Lúthien – shines through these poems, they are of interest chiefly in showing the development of a writer's ideas'

(p. 114). Even reviews in specialist Tolkien publications tended to devote most of their space to a description of the contents of the book and comment on developments in the *story* since *The Book of Lost Tales* and in relation to *The Silmarillion and **The Lord of the Rings*. Among exceptions, Charles Noad wrote in a review in *Mallorn* 23 (Summer 1986):

> Tolkien's poetry as exemplified in the *Lays* succeeds quite well at what it sets out to do. There is little to displease the ear (I suspect that [the poems] were written with the possibility in mind that they would be read aloud) or to pain the sensibility. There are some, if not a great many, heights and few depths. If we are to consider the present lays as poetry in the same sense as the kind of thing written by a Blake or a Keats is poetry, then we shall consider in vain; but to see them as narratives in metrical form shows how well they succeed in that form. Tolkien's grasp of language, especially regarding choice of appropriate words, has advanced considerably from *Lost Tales*.... [pp. 15–16]

And David Bratman wrote in *Mythprint* 22, no. 12, whole no. 67 (December 1985), pp. 2–3):

> In general, the reader of these lays will find a world much closer to the final Silmarillion than is that of the Lost Tales. Many familiar names and story elements first appear here, and the Elves have developed from the fey, shabby creatures of the Lost Tales into something much more like the majestic beings of *The Silmarillion*....
>
> I am not enormously fond of narrative poetry, and in any case Tolkien was not a master of it – he was right to drop these poems in favor of a prose Silmarillion closer to the form we have today. However, there are some passages and images in these poems that we are fortunate that Tolkien wrote and preserved. And as a step in the series of books tracing the development of the concept of Middle-earth, *The Lays of Beleriand* is invaluable. [p. 3]

See also notes on criticism in entries for *The Children of Húrin* and the *Lay of Leithian*.

Lea, Kathleen Marguerite (1903–1995). After reading English at Lady Margaret Hall, *Oxford, Kathleen Lea taught at Wycombe Abbey and Westfield College, London, and wrote a book on the *commedia del arte, Italian Popular Comedy* (1934). In 1936 she returned to Lady Margaret Hall as tutor in English. She was elected a Fellow in 1937, and from 1947 to 1971 was Vice-Principal. In the 1950s her administrative duties at Oxford, including examining in the English Final Honour School, occasionally brought her into contact with Tolkien. After the examinations of 1953 Tolkien send her a calligraphic manuscript of a revision of his poem *Doworst; Miss Lea sent him some sherry in return.

Leaf by Niggle. Story, first published in the *Dublin Review* for January 1945, pp. 46–61. It was first reprinted, with minor revisions, together with *On Fairy-Stories* in *Tree and Leaf* (1964). See further, *Descriptive Bibliography* C32 and A7.

SUMMARY

Niggle is a painter, but not very successful, partly because he has many other things to do, such as helping his lame neighbour, Mr Parish, with odd jobs. Visitors come to his house in the country for tea, and hint that his garden is 'rather neglected'. Few of them know, or would care, about one of his pictures with which he has become particularly concerned: 'begun with a leaf caught in the wind', it has become a tree;

> and the tree grew, sending out innumerable branches, and thrusting out the most fantastic roots. Strange birds came and settled on the twigs and had to be attended to. Then all round the Tree, and behind it, through the gaps in the leaves and boughs, a country began to open out; and there were glimpses of a forest marching over the land, and of mountains, tipped with snow.

Niggle has lost interest in his other pictures, or has 'tacked them on to the edges of his great picture'. But he is often interrupted, and the painting is not yet finished when he is called away on a long journey. Arriving at a railway station, he falls ill and is put in a workhouse infirmary. He is made to do manual labour, or to lie in the dark, for what seems like centuries, until two Voices appraise his virtues and he is allowed to 'go on to the next stage'. Travelling to green fields, he finds the tree he had been painting, finished and alive, in a landscape he had only glimpsed in his imagination. He is drawn to a distant forest, where he finds his neighbour, Parish; together they build a small house and garden. At length Niggle leaves Parish in order to explore the larger country, 'to learn about sheep, and the high pasturages, and look at a wider sky, and walk ever further and further towards the Mountains, always uphill.' Of his unfinished painting in the world he left behind, 'one beautiful leaf' remains intact and is hung in a museum; 'but eventually the Museum was burnt down, and the leaf, and Niggle, were entirely forgotten in his old country.'

HISTORY

On ?18 March 1945 Tolkien wrote to *Stanley Unwin that *Leaf by Niggle* 'was the only thing I have ever done which cost me absolutely no pains at all. Usually I compose only with great difficulty and endless rewriting. I woke up one morning (more than two years ago) with that odd thing virtually complete in my head. It took only a few hours to get down, and then copy out' (*Letters*, p. 113). On 8–9 September 1962, in a letter to his *Aunt Jane Neave, Tolkien tentatively recalled having written *Leaf by Niggle* just before the Second World War began, 'though I first read it aloud to my friends early in 1940. I recollect nothing about the writing, except that I woke one morning with it in my head, scribbled it down – and the printed form in the main hardly differs from the first hasty version at all' (*Letters*, p. 320). His introductory comment in *Tree and Leaf* concurs: both *Leaf by Niggle* and *On Fairy-Stories*, he says, 'were written in the same period (1938–9), when **The Lord of the Rings* was beginning to unroll itself and to unfold prospects of labour and exploration in yet unknown country as daunting to me as to the hobbits.' In a postcard written to the poet Alan Rook on 21 April 1943, however, Tolkien hopes that Rook will one day (metaphorically) paint a 'great picture', and promises to send him a story relevant to 'pictures' that Tolkien 'wrote this time last year' (reproduced on eBay online auctions, October 2001). This must surely refer to *Leaf by Niggle*, and therefore would date its writing to around April 1942.

On 6 September 1944 T.S. Gregory, editor of the Roman Catholic *Dublin Review*, wrote to Tolkien asking for a contribution of verse or narrative. Tolkien sent him *Leaf by Niggle* on 12 October 1944, and it was published in the number for January 1945 (not 1947, as Tolkien recalled in *Tree and Leaf*). It reached a wider audience only with its appearance in *Tree and Leaf* in 1964, but little immediate critical response, as reviewers found it less interesting to discuss than the seminal essay *On Fairy-Stories*.

The bare summary of *Leaf by Niggle* given above hardly captures its flavour, let alone its autobiographical elements. On 24 June 1957 Tolkien wrote to Caroline Everett that 'in addition to my tree-love (it was originally called *The Tree*), it arose from my own pre-occupation with *The Lord of the Rings*, the knowledge that it would be finished in great detail or not at all, and the fear (near certainty) that it would be "not at all". The war had arisen to darken all horizons' (*Letters*, p. 257). In his letter to Jane Neave of 8–9 September 1962 Tolkien commented more fully that *Leaf by Niggle*

> is not really or properly an 'allegory' so much as 'mythical'. For Niggle is meant to be a real mixed-quality *person* and not an 'allegory' of any single vice or virtue.... Of course some elements are explicable in biographical terms.... There was a great tree – a huge poplar with vast limbs – visible through my window even as I lay in bed. I loved it, and was anxious about it. It had been savagely mutilated some years before, but had gallantly grown new limbs...; and now a foolish neighbour was agitating to have it felled [fearing that it would fall on her house in a high wind].... Also, of course, I was anxious about my own internal Tree, *The Lord of the Rings*. It was growing out of hand, and revealing endless new vistas – and I wanted to finish it, but the world was threatening. [*Letters*, pp. 320–1]

In September 1954, however, in a draft letter to Peter Hastings, Tolkien wrote that he 'tried to show allegorically how [*sub-creation, examined in **On*

Fairy-Stories] might come to be taken up into Creation in some plane in my "purgatorial" story *Leaf by Niggle* . . . to make visible and physical the effects of Sin or misused Free Will by men' (*Letters*, p. 195).

A commercial recording of *Leaf by Niggle*, read by Derek Jacobi, was first issued in 1999 as part of *Farmer Giles of Ham and Other Stories*. It was later re-issued only with **Smith of Wootton Major*. In 1992 a dramatization of *Leaf by Niggle* by Brian Sibley was broadcast on BBC Radio as one part of the series *Tales from the Perilous Realm*. This series was first issued as a commercial recording in 1993.

CRITICISM

On its more general publication in *Tree and Leaf* in 1964–5, in Britain and the United States, *Leaf by Niggle* attracted brief, complimentary notices from reviewers, who for the most part were more interested in its companion piece, *On Fairy-Stories*. Typical of these is Peter Sykes' comments in the *Oxford Mail*, 28 May 1964: *Leaf by Niggle* 'is a didactic little tale . . . told with the economy of phrase and quiet assurance which stamp all Prof. Tolkien's writing and provides impressive credentials for his authority to discuss the subject' (p. 6).

In *The Road to Middle-earth* (2nd edn. 1992) T.A. Shippey describes *Leaf by Niggle* as provable **allegory: thus Niggle's journey is (or can be equated to) death; Niggle the painter is Tolkien the writer, a perfectionist and easily distracted; his 'leaf' is **The Hobbit*, his 'tree' *The Lord of the Rings*, 'the "country" that opens from it = Middle-earth, and the "other pictures . . . tacked on to the edges of his great picture" = the poems and other works which Tolkien kept on fitting into his own greater one. Meanwhile the garden which Niggle does not keep up looks ominously like Tolkien's professorial duties' (p. 40) – that is, his obligation as the holder of an **Oxford chair to publish works of scholarship. Shippey expands this argument further in *J.R.R. Tolkien: Author of the Century* (2000), pp. 266–77, where he calls *Leaf by Niggle* 'autobiographical allegory'.

In *Tolkien's Art: A Mythology for England* (rev. edn. 2001) Jane Chance also proposes an allegorical basis for *Leaf by Niggle*, but one strongly linked to Christian symbolism. She interprets Niggle's tree as a symbol of the biblical Tree of Knowledge of Good and Evil, and holds that 'it is ironic that Niggle captures in oils a single leaf that is eventually destroyed by that mutability that resulted from [our first parents'] original sin' (p. 87). In her view, Tolkien reworked in *Leaf by Niggle* 'the Christian convention of good works into a fairy-story framework' as well as 'the Christian convention of the earthly conflict between soul and body. . . . Niggle and Parish personify the two sides of humankind that inevitably clash in this world because each is pulled in a different direction, although they eventually enjoy a harmonious "collaboration" (resurrection) in the other world after the fantasy equivalent of "death"' (p. 89).

The religious implications of *Leaf by Niggle* have not been lost on other critics as well, such as Richard L. Purtill, who explores in *J.R.R. Tolkien: Myth,*

Morality, and Religion (1984) the theme of Niggle as Everyman (or Every artist), and Katharyn W. Crabbe, who writes in *J.R.R. Tolkien* (rev. and expanded edn. 1988) that *Leaf by Niggle* 'is plainly a story that reflects a deeply religious turn of mind. That is, while the story is not *about* Christianity, it celebrates certain Christian values: responsibility for one's neighbor . . . ; the replacement of justice by mercy . . . ; and the importance of grace over works.' Even so, these values and attitudes do not 'suggest that the story is a religious allegory. The story is not about God; it is about an artist whose ability to be a sub-creator means that parallels exist between him and the creator of the universe' (p. 163).

Paul H. Kocher comments in *Master of Middle-earth: The Fiction of J.R.R. Tolkien* (1972) that *Leaf by Niggle* gave 'literary form' to Tolkien's views about sub-creation and *eucatastrophe, and expanded upon the symbols of 'tree' and 'leaf' as they connect *Leaf by Niggle* and *On Fairy-Stories*:

> 'Leaf' of course refers literally to any leaf in the foliage of Niggle's Tree, and also more specifically to the particular painted Leaf rescued from the destruction of the picture as a whole and hung in the Museum. . . . Figuratively, it stands for any single story taken out of a greater connected body of narratives; and also for this one story of Tolkien's . . . seen in detachment from the whole body of his writing. The other symbol, 'Tree,' stands sometimes for that same whole body of Tolkien writing, but more often for the living, growing tradition of fairy stories in general, which the essay 'On Fairy-stories' calls the 'Tree of Tales.' [p. 162]

In *On Fairy-Stories* (first published in 1947, after a lecture in 1938) Tolkien wrote that

> it is easy for the student [of fairy-stories] to feel that with all his labour he is collecting only a few leaves, many of them now torn or decayed, from the countless foliage of the Tree of Tales, with which the Forest of Days is carpeted. It seems vain to add to the litter. Who can design a new leaf? The patterns from bud to unfolding, and the colours from spring to autumn were all discovered by men long ago. But that is not true. The seed of the tree can be replanted in almost any soil. . . . Each leaf, of oak and ash and thorn, is a unique embodiment of the pattern. . . . [*Tree and Leaf*, p. 52]

John A. Ellison, in his perceptive essay 'The "Why", and the "How": Reflections on "Leaf by Niggle"' in *Leaves from the Tree: J.R.R. Tolkien's Shorter Fiction* (1991), examines Tolkien's story as

> a fable directly concerned with the processes involved in the translation of artistic inspiration into physical reality. Its subjects are skill, craftsmanship, technique; the essentials of bringing any large artwork to

completion, be it painting, building, symphony, or *The Lord of the Rings*
... it deals with the 'How', as well as the 'Why', of sub-creation. It is concerned, in both these senses, with that perennial topic of Romanticism,
the predicament of the individual artist. [p. 24]

Leeds (Yorkshire). In autumn 1920 Tolkien took up a teaching post in Leeds,
an industrial city in the north of England long known for its textile mills. His
wife *Edith and their first son, *John, remained in *Oxford until after the birth
of their second son, *Michael that October, while Tolkien lived in a Leeds
bedsitter at **21a St Michael's Road, Headingley** and visited his family on week-
ends.

In March 1921 he found suitable furnished rooms to rent in Leeds as a temporary home at **5 Holly Bank, Headingley,** a house owned by Miss Moseley, a
niece of Cardinal Newman; a photograph of the house ('Hollybank') is reproduced in *The Tolkien Family Album*, p. 44. The Tolkiens moved there probably
towards the end of April. Near the end of 1921 they relocated to **11 St Mark's
Terrace, Woodhouse Lane**, near the University (*Leeds, University of). John
and *Priscilla Tolkien have described the neighbourhood, now built over, as
'dingy and soot-covered. Chemicals in the air rotted the curtains within six
months, and baby *Michael was covered in smuts if he was left outside in his
pram for any length of time; and Ronald found that he had to change his collar
three times a day!' (*The Tolkien Family Album*, p. 45, with a photograph). John
later recalled visiting the ruins of Kirkstall, a chiefly twelfth-century abbey
built by the Cistercians, not far to the west of Headingley.

In early 1924 Tolkien and Edith bought a three-storey house at **2 Darnley
Road, West Park** and moved there by 5 March. In October of that year Tolkien
was promoted from Reader to Professor of English Language at Leeds, and in
November his third son, *Christopher, was born. On Darnley Road the Tolkiens were on the north-west edge of the city, near open fields where Tolkien
took the children for walks.

Tolkien was elected Rawlinson and Bosworth Professor of Anglo-Saxon
at Oxford University in July 1925, but because his old and new appointments
overlapped he continued to teach at Leeds as well as at Oxford for two terms.
His wife and children remained in Leeds until early 1926, when the family
moved to 22 Northmoor Road, Oxford.

During his years at Leeds, despite a heavy academic schedule, Tolkien
completed work on *A Middle English Vocabulary* (published 1922); with E.V.
Gordon, he prepared an edition of *Sir Gawain and the Green Knight* (1925);
he began work on the 'Clarendon Chaucer' (see *Geoffrey Chaucer), and on
translations of *Beowulf* and *Pearl*; and he contributed essays, notes, and
reviews to several professional journals. At the same time, he wrote poetry,
including most or perhaps all of *The Children of Húrin*, as well as parts of
The Lay of the Fall of Gondolin, a *'Lay of Eärendel', *The Flight of the Noldoli
from Valinor*, and *The Nameless Land*. Several of his shorter poems were
published in the Leeds journal *The Gryphon*, in *Yorkshire Poetry*, and in two

Leeds English School anthologies, *A Northern Venture and *Leeds University Verse 1914–24.

John Tolkien remembers his father telling him stories at Darnley Road when he could not sleep; one of these was The Orgog (unpublished), to which one of Tolkien's drawings, A Shop on the Edge of the Hills of Fairy Land, may be connected. Tolkien later inscribed this: 'Drawn for John, Darnley Road, Leeds 1924.'

Leeds, University of. The University of Leeds was formed in 1904 out of the Leeds School of Medicine (founded 1831) and the former Yorkshire College of Science (1874). Despite its historical emphasis on scientific and technical subjects, the University already had upon its creation a Faculty of Arts, and in 1913 named *George S. Gordon, late of the University of *Oxford, to the Professorship of English Language and Literature with a view to the development of English studies. Gordon was given a free hand to remodel the English Department on his own terms; war service, however, prevented him from doing so at once.

In 1920, when Tolkien was appointed Reader in English Language at Leeds, Gordon had only just begun to revise the English syllabus by adopting that of Oxford, according to which undergraduates were offered specialized courses in medieval English language and literature or post-Chaucerian literature. But he was also concerned, as he wrote in a letter of recommendation for Tolkien, 'to bring the linguistic and literary interests of the Department into more natural and friendly association: the hardest task, as a rule, which such Departments present.' He wished 'to encourage the formation, within the Department, of a School of English philology, and here Mr. Tolkien was given a free hand. Students of philological aptitude are not infrequent in Yorkshire, but they take some finding out; for philology, it is well known, is an unworldly pursuit' (*An Application for the Rawlinson and Bosworth Professorship of Anglo-Saxon in the University of Oxford by J.R.R. Tolkien, Professor of the English Language in the University of Leeds, June 25, 1925). Tolkien himself noted that he

began with five hesitant pioneers out of a School (exclusive of the first year) of about sixty members. The proportion today is 43 literary to 20 linguistic students. The linguists are in no way isolated or cut off from the general life and work of the department, and share in many of the literary courses and activities of the School; but since 1922 their purely linguistic work has been conducted in special classes, and examined in distinct papers of special standard and attitude. The instruction offered has been gradually extended, and now covers a large part of the field of English and Germanic philology. Courses are given on Old English heroic verse, the history of English*, various Old English and Middle English texts*, Old and Middle English philology*, introductory Germanic philology*, Gothic, Old Icelandic (a second-year* and third-year course), and Medieval Welsh*. All these courses I have from time to time given myself; those that I have given personally in the past year are marked*. During this last session a course of voluntary reading of texts not specially considered in the current syllabus has attracted more than fifteen students, not all of them from the linguistic side of the department.

Philology, indeed, appears to have lost for these students its connotations of terror if not of mystery. An active discussion-class has been conducted, on lines more familiar in schools of literature than of language, which has borne fruit in friendly rivalry and open debate with the corresponding literary assembly. A Viking Club [*Societies and clubs] has even been formed, by past and present students of Old Icelandic, which promises to carry on the same kind of activity independently of the staff. Old Icelandic has been a point of special development, and usually reaches a higher standard than the other special subjects, being studied for two years and in much the same detail as Anglo-Saxon.

Considered absolutely, our results in scholarship, in these five years, are of course small. Of the twelve linguistic candidates examined since 1922 five obtained first class honours; one of these is now on the staff of the *Oxford English Dictionary*, and another promises to be an able recruit to the *Survey of English Place-Names* [begun 1924]. Although a special subject rather than a dissertation is encouraged at the B.A. stage, some interesting dissertations have recently been presented: notably a study of the place-names of Richmondshire, and a translation of the Saga of Hrolfr Kraki [probably *The Saga of Hrolf Kraki*, translated by *Stella M. Mills (1933)].... [*An Application for the Rawlinson and Bosworth Professorship . . .* ; partly printed in *Letters*, pp. 12–13]

Much later Tolkien wrote of the students at Leeds that they 'are/were probably England's most (at least apparently) dullest and stodgiest students: Yorkshire's young men and women of sub-public school class and home backgrounds bookless and cultureless.... A surprisingly large proportion prove "educable": for which a primary qualification is the willingness *to do some work* (to learn)' (letter to *Christopher Tolkien, 15 December 1969, *Letters*, p. 403).

Under the so-called Scheme B in the Leeds English School special attention was paid to Language, although students in that programme also attended some courses on later literature; but Scheme A students, who concentrated on Literature, were also required to attend a number of Language classes. The University *Calendar* for 1920–1 describes the syllabus that the students who opted for Language would have followed during Tolkien's first year at Leeds: 'Under both schemes a competent knowledge of one classical and at least one modern European language, and of the outlines of English social and political history, shall be required for the attainment of high Honours' (p. 146). All students took an intermediate examination at the end of their first year and thereafter proceeded to an Honours Course in English or to an Ordinary degree of Bachelor of Arts. For Scheme B,

Candidates shall be required to attend the following courses in the subjects of the School: (i) during three academic years courses in English Language, including the History of the Language, Early English prose and verse, and Gothic, such courses amounting to not less than three hours a week for the first year, and not less than four hours a week for the second and third years; (ii) during three academic years courses of three hours a week on periods of English Literature; (iii) during one academic year a course on the Outlines of English Literary History.

Candidates shall also be required

(1) *either* (*a*) to attend approved courses in *two* of the following subjects: Old Icelandic, Old High German, Old French (with special reference to Anglo-Norman), Elementary Palaeography; *or* (*b*) or to present a dissertation on a subject approved by the Board of the Faculty of Arts;

(2) to attend for two years approved courses of two hours a week in History, Mediaeval *or* Modern; for two years approved courses in French *or* German; and for a third year an approved course in the History of the French Language and Literature, *or* in the History of the German Language and Literature. They are further required to attend during the first year, an approved course in Latin *or* Greek. [p. 148]

Most or all of the courses in (2) were not taught by the English Faculty.

The syllabus also listed the papers the students would take in their final examinations:

Essay, one paper.

Translation of unseen passages in Old and Middle English, with literary and linguistic questions, one paper.

Selected texts in Old and Middle English, with literary, historical, and linguistic questions, one paper.

Outlines of the History of English Literature, with selected texts, two papers.

Grammar of Old and Middle English dialects, with illustrative passages for translation or comment, two papers.

History of English, with reference to general principles of linguistic development, one paper.

Gothic, one paper.

Either two of the following: Old Icelandic, one paper; Old High German, one paper; Old French (with special reference to Anglo-Norman), one paper; Elementary Palaeography, one paper; *or* a dissertation on a subject approved by the Board of the Faculty of Arts. [pp. 148–9]

There was also an oral examination.

From 1921 to 1926 the English syllabus was adjusted year by year, as the Faculty sought better balances of courses and papers, and as differing opinions

502 THE J.R.R. TOLKIEN COMPANION AND GUIDE

of what should be taught were accommodated. For instance, for 1921–2 Gothic became an optional rather than a required subject, and one of the papers on the grammar of Old and Middle English dialects was replaced by a paper on *Chaucer; for 1923–4 only one paper on Outlines of the History of English Literature was required, but also a new paper on an English author (usually Shakespeare) or a selected subject from English literature; for 1924–5 Medieval Welsh was added to the list of optional subjects; and for 1925–6 there was a new paper on Old and Middle English philology. A note in the *Calendar* for 1924–5 states that Old Icelandic and Gothic courses were given every year, but anyone wishing to take the other options were required to make arrangements with Tolkien. (For the courses that Tolkien may have taught each year at Leeds, see **Chronology**.)

Tolkien attributed much of the success of the English School during these formative years to George Gordon:

> Gordon found 'English' in Leeds a departmental subject (I rather fancy you could not get a degree in it alone) and left it a school of studies (in bud). When he arrived he shared a box of glazed bricks, mainly furnished with hot water pipes, with the Professor of French, as their private room. Mere assistants possibly had a hat-peg somewhere. When he left we had 'English House', where every member had a separate room (not to mention a bathroom!) and a common room for students: and with this centre the growing body of students became a cohesive unit, and derived some of the benefits (or distant reflections of them) that we associate with a university rather than a municipal college. It would not have been difficult to build on this foundation. But I fancy that, after he left, the thing just 'ran on', and did not fall into hands of the same quality. In any case numbers fell and finances changed. And Vice-Chancellors. [draft letter to R.W. Chapman, 26 November 1941, *Letters*, pp. 57–8]

Gordon left Leeds to return to Oxford in 1922; he was succeeded by the poet and critic *Lascelles Abercrombie. When Tolkien became Reader in English Language at Leeds in 1920 the staff of the English School, besides himself and Gordon, consisted of two Assistant Lecturers, G.H. Cowling and R.S. Knox, and a tutor in English composition, H.J. Davis. In 1924 Tolkien was made Professor of English Language, opposite Abercrombie's Professorship of English Literature. In 1925, when Tolkien exchanged his Leeds professorship for one at Oxford (though he continued to teach at Leeds for two more terms), G.H. Cowling had been made Reader, *E.V. Gordon was a Lecturer, and *Wilfred R. Childe was Assistant Lecturer.

A photograph of some of the buildings of the University of Leeds, *c.* 1920, is reproduced in *The Tolkien Family Album*, p. 43.

Leeds University Verse 1914–24. Collection of poems 'written by members of the University [of *Leeds] during the past ten years', 'compiled and edited by the English School Association [of the University]' and published by the Swan Press, Leeds, in May 1924. It includes three works by Tolkien: see *An Evening in Tavrobel, *The Lonely Isle, and *The Princess Ní. Other contributors to the volume include *Lascelles Abercrombie, *Wilfred R. Childe, *E.V. Gordon, and *A.H. Smith.

Of Lembas. The answer of Pengoloð to Ælfwine's question, 'What is the coimas [lembas] of the Eldar?' It was published with commentary and notes in *The Peoples of Middle-earth (1996), pp. 403–5, together with the *Dangweth Pengoloð in a section to which *Christopher Tolkien gave the title Teachings of Pengoloð.

According to the Elves, lembas, a food made from a kind of corn grown in Aman, was sent to them by Yavanna to sustain them on their Great Journey into the West. They later learned to make it themselves. Pengoloð describes the sowing of the corn, the harvesting of the ears by hand, and the fashioning of baskets from the stalks in which to store the grain. Because the corn came originally from Yavanna, only certain elven-women called maidens of Yavanna were permitted to handle the ears, and knew the secret of making the wafers, and only 'the queen, or highest among the elven-women of any people, great or small, had the keeping and gift of the lembas' (p. 404). It was given only to those undertaking a long journey in the wild or whose life was in peril, as its name indicates 'Lembas is the Sindarin name . . . from the older form lenn-mbass "journey-bread". In Quenya it was most often named coimas which is "life-bread"' (p. 404).

The text exists only as a finely written manuscript (similar but not as fine as that of the Dangweth Pengoloð) with decoration in red ballpoint pen, perhaps added later. It cannot be dated more closely than between 1951 and 1959, but according to Christopher Tolkien, is more likely from earlier in this period than later.

The Letters of J.R.R. Tolkien. Selection of Tolkien's letters, edited by Humphrey Carpenter with the assistance of *Christopher Tolkien, first published in Great Britain by George Allen & Unwin, London, in August 1981, and in the United States by the Houghton Mifflin Company, Boston, in October 1981. (See further, Descriptive Bibliography Dia–c.) The British edition (now published by HarperCollins) from 1999, and the American edition from 2000, contains a new, more extensive index by Christina Scull and Wayne G. Hammond.

Letters contains 354 letters, drafts, or extracts from letters, selected primarily for content regarding Tolkien's fiction. These are only a fraction of the 'immense number of letters' that survive (p. 1). The volume omits 'the very large body of letters' Tolkien wrote to his fiancée, Edith Bratt (*Edith Tolkien), as well as most of his academic and business correspondence, but includes some of his letters to his children, most notably a long series written to

Christopher Tolkien during the Second World War, and many others which reveal his character and thoughts.

Eighty-seven additional sources of letters are cited in *Descriptive Bibliography*, section Dii, and many others have come to light since the publication of that book in 1993. Letters by Tolkien frequently appear for sale at auction, and are quoted or reproduced in catalogues or online. Significant portions of the correspondence between Tolkien and his publishers, preserved largely in the Tolkien-George Allen & Unwin archive now held by HarperCollins in London, and other letters by Tolkien, have been quoted in works by the present authors, especially *Descriptive Bibliography*, *Reader's Companion*, and this *Companion and Guide*. Altogether we have recorded some 1,500 letters by Tolkien which survive in archives, libraries, and private collections, and more continue to come to light.

Tolkien claimed, however, in a letter to his son *Michael on 1 November 1963, to have 'a dislike of letter-writing.... I think we both like writing letters *ad familiares*; but are obliged to write so much in the way of "business", that time and energy fail' (*Letters*, p. 336). As a resource for Tolkien studies his letters are indispensable, though it must be understood that each may reflect Tolkien's thoughts or opinions only at a particular moment in time.

Lewis, Clive Staples (1898–1963). C.S. Lewis, known to his friends as 'Jack', was born in Belfast, Northern Ireland, and raised as a Protestant. Even as a boy, he wrote stories; some of his earliest work has been published as *Boxen* (1985). At school he came to value the friendship of a few rather than the society of many; he discovered the joys of *'Northernness' he would later share with Tolkien, including a love of the *Eddas* and Norse sagas; and he became an apostate. While briefly at Malvern College (1913–14) he met Arthur Greeves, with whom he would correspond for almost fifty years (see *They Stand Together: The Letters of C.S. Lewis to Arthur Greeves, 1914–1963* (1979), ed. Walter Hooper). In 1914, unsuited to Malvern, Lewis was sent for private tuition to W.T. Kirkpatrick, a strict retired headmaster from whom Lewis learned discipline of thought and the pleasures of logic and reason. Having won a classical scholarship to University College, *Oxford, Lewis went up in April 1917 for one term before entering military service in France. In April 1918 he was wounded in the Battle of Arras. After the war he shared a series of houses in Oxford with Mrs Janie King Moore (*d.* 1951), the mother of a friend killed in 1918, and her daughter Maureen, settling finally at 'The Kilns'. They were joined by Lewis's brother *Warren after his retirement from the Army.

In 1919 he returned to University College, and also published his first book of poetry, *Spirits in Bondage* (1919). In 1920 he took a First Class in Honour Moderations, in 1922 a First in *Literae Humaniores*, and in 1923 a First in English Language and Literature. After a year as a deputy lecturer at University College, he was made a Fellow in English at Magdalen College, where he remained until 1954. His colleague *Helen Gardner has written that 'there were so few men reading English at Magdalen' during Lewis's first years there, to make up his tutorial hours, he taught Political Science to Magdalen men reading History and Modern Greats. He also assisted *Percy Simpson in teaching textual criticism to research students in English. Lewis was not a born tutor, and though some of his undergraduate pupils have given testimony to the stimulus of his teaching, others found their tutorial hours uncomfortable; but he was a born lecturer. ['Clive Staples Lewis, 1898–1963', *Proceedings of the British Academy* 51 (1965), p. 422]

His popularity among students was such that he could fill the largest lecture hall at Oxford, and his presence at the Socratic Club, in which questions of religion and philosophy were discussed, energized that undergraduate body which Lewis had helped to found.

In 1926 Lewis's long poem *Dymer* was published; and in that same year, on 11 May, occurred the earliest recorded meeting of Lewis and Tolkien, at a meeting of the English Faculty at Merton College. At first they appeared to be potential opponents in any argument about the relative importance of Literature and Language in the *Oxford English School, but they soon found that they had interests in common, and by the end of the decade were working together to effect a successful reform of the syllabus. Their friendship was close and firm. In his autobiography *Surprised by Joy: The Shape of My Early Life* (1955) Lewis wrote that friendship with Tolkien 'marked the breakdown of two old prejudices. At my first coming into the world I had been (implicitly) warned never to trust a Papist, and at my first coming into the English Faculty (explicitly) never to trust a philologist. Tolkien was both' (pp. 204–5). Although he could be blunt and argumentative, Lewis was also warm and outgoing. In Tolkien's words, he possessed a 'great generosity and capacity for friendship' (letter to Dick Plotz, 12 September 1965, *Letters*, p. 362). Much to the dismay of some of his later, more conservative admirers, he openly smoked and drank. On 1 March 1944 Tolkien wrote to his son *Christopher that Lewis 'put away three pints in a very short session we had this morning, and said he was "going short for Lent"' (*Letters*, p. 68).

On 19 September 1931 Tolkien dined in Magdalen with Lewis and their friend *H.V.D. 'Hugo' Dyson. After dinner, they strolled in the College grounds, discussing metaphor and myth, then retired to Lewis's rooms and talked further. By that date Lewis had progressed from atheism to theism; now, within the month, he came to accept Christ, whose story Tolkien and Dyson described that night as a 'true myth'. Tolkien's poem *Mythopoeia* is partly based on his conversation with Lewis on that occasion. Later Tolkien wrote in his diary: 'Friendship with Lewis compensates for much, and besides giving constant pleasure and comfort has done me much good from the contact with a man at once honest, brave, intellectual – a scholar, a poet, and a philosopher – and a lover, at least after a long pilgrimage, of Our Lord' (quoted in *Biography*, p. 148).

Lewis and Tolkien met frequently in pubs and in Lewis's rooms for long conversations; Tolkien lent Lewis works such as the *Lay of Leithian* and *The

Hobbit to read for comment; and they saw each other also at meetings of the Kolbítar (*Societies and clubs). Fellow members as well of Edward Tangye Lean's 'Inklings' society (*Societies and clubs), they later carried its name to a new group of friends centred mainly around Lewis (*The Inklings). In the mid-1930s, Tolkien often attended 'beer and *Beowulf* ' evenings Lewis held in his rooms with undergraduates. One of Lewis's students, E.L. Edmonds, recalled that 'it was very obvious that [Tolkien and Lewis] were great friends – indeed, they were like two young bear cubs sometimes, just happily quipping with one another' ('C.S. Lewis, the Teacher', *In Search of C.S. Lewis* (1983), p. 45).

Tolkien and Lewis agreed, *c.* 1936, that there were too few stories of the kind they themselves liked to read, and that they would try to write some. It was also agreed that Lewis would write a 'space-travel' story, and Tolkien one on 'time-travel'. The effort by Lewis resulted in *Out of the Silent Planet*, finished by October 1937 and published the following year. Tolkien failed to complete his story, *The Lost Road, but found time to write to George Allen & Unwin (*Publishers) on behalf of *Out of the Silent Planet*, then under consideration (but published, in the event, by John Lane, The Bodley Head). Tolkien liked its sequel, *Perelandra* (1943), even more, but felt that the third book in the 'space trilogy' (or 'cosmic trilogy'), *That Hideous Strength* (1945), was less good, spoiled by the influence of the Arthurian-Byzantine mythology of fellow Inkling *Charles Williams. The philologist Elwin Ransom, who appears in all three books, was probably modelled on Tolkien at least in part, and Lewis drew from Tolkien's *'Silmarillion', parts of which he had read or heard read to him, in character or place-names such as *Numinor* (from *Númenor*).

In his letter of 12 September 1965 to Dick Plotz Tolkien wrote that 'the unpayable debt' he owed to Lewis 'was not "influence" as it is ordinarily understood, but sheer encouragement. He was for long my only audience. Only from him did I ever get the idea that my "stuff" could be more than a private hobby. But for his interest and unceasing eagerness for more I should never have brought *The* [*Lord of the Rings*] to a conclusion' (*Letters*, p. 362). Lewis also helped to promote Tolkien's books. He wrote two reviews of *The Hobbit*, in *The Times* and the *Times Literary Supplement*, of which Tolkien wrote to *Stanley Unwin: 'Both [reviews were] written by the same man, and one whose approval was assured: we started with common tastes and reading, and have been closely associated for years. . . . I believed him to be the best living critic until he turned his attention to me, and no degree of friendship would make him say what he does not mean: he is the most uncompromisingly honest man I have met!' (15 October 1937, *Letters*, p. 23). For *The Lord of the Rings* Lewis supplied an enthusiastic (if perhaps excessive) blurb, comparing Tolkien to Ariosto, and in 1954 and 1955 he reviewed the work in *Time and Tide*.

On 3 March 1955, after *The Lord of the Rings* had begun to be published, Tolkien remarked to Dora Marshall that Lewis, 'being a man of immense power and industry', finished his 'space trilogy' 'much sooner amidst much other work; but at last my slower and more meticulous (as well as more indolent and less organized) machine has produced its effort' (*Letters*, p. 209). Lewis's output, of academic writings as well as fiction, indeed was copious in contrast to Tolkien's. His other works to this date included *The Pilgrim's Regress* (1933), a semi-autobiographical allegory; *The Allegory of Love: A Study in Medieval Tradition* (1936), which considers allegory in relation to courtly love; *A Preface to 'Paradise Lost'* (1942), based on lectures Lewis gave at the University College of North Wales in 1941; *The Screwtape Letters* (1942, dedicated to Tolkien), a series of communications from a devil, Screwtape, to his nephew Wormwood, an inexperienced tempter; *The Abolition of Man* (1943), collecting the Riddell Lectures given at Durham that same year; the novel *The Great Divorce* (1945); the important essay 'On Stories' in *Essays Presented to Charles Williams* (1947), a volume edited by Lewis (see *On Fairy-Stories*); and most of *The Chronicles of Narnia*.

The seven 'Narnia' books for children, from *The Lion, the Witch, and the Wardrobe* (1950) to *The Last Battle* (1956), are perhaps his most famous writings. Works of fantasy set in a land in which animals talk and magic is real, they have a religious foundation, with the lion Aslan representing Christ. Such Christian elements are not overt, however, and some readers do not notice them. Part of the popularity of the series, as Lewis himself acknowledged, was due to its delicate illustrations by *Pauline Baynes. *The Last Battle* won the Carnegie Medal for 1956. On 11 November 1964 Tolkien wrote to David Kolb, S.J.: 'It is sad that "Narnia" and all that part of C.S.L.'s work should remain outside the range of my sympathy, as much of my work was outside his' (*Letters*, p. 352). In 1949, when Lewis read part of *The Lion, the Witch, and the Wardrobe* to *Roger Lancelyn Green, he remarked that he had read the story also to Tolkien, who 'disliked it intensely'. Shortly afterward, Tolkien complained about it to Green: 'It really won't do, you know!' (reported in Green and Walter Hooper, *C.S. Lewis: A Biography* (rev. and expanded edn. 2002), p. 307). Tolkien did not approve of the book's combination of diverse elements such as the White Witch, Mr and Mrs Beaver, and Father Christmas. George Sayer wrote that Tolkien 'so strongly detested Jack's assembling figures from various mythologies in his children's books that he soon gave up trying to read them. He also thought they were carelessly and superficially written. His condemnation was so severe that one suspects he envied the speed with which Jack wrote and compared it with his own laborious method of composition' (*Jack: A Life of C.S. Lewis* (2nd edn. 1994), p. 313). And yet, his granddaughter Joanna (see *Michael Tolkien) recalled that when she was a girl, staying with her grandparents in Oxford, she was handed from Tolkien's bookshelf the Narnia books, together with *The Borrowers* by Mary Norton and the fairy-stories of *Andrew Lang. 'The fact that he directed me to reading these other books before *The Lord of the Rings* is perhaps an indication of his humility . . .' ('Joanna Tolkien Speaks at the Tolkien Society Annual Dinner, Shrewsbury, April 16, 1994', *Digging Potatoes, Growing Trees*, vol. 2 (1998), p. 34).

Tolkien was also privately critical of the extent to which Lewis had, by now, become a well-known Christian apologist, beginning with *The Problem of Pain* (1940) and especially through a series of broadcasts on BBC radio in 1941–4. These were initially collected in *Broadcast Talks* (1942), *Christian Behaviour* (1943), and *Beyond Personality* (1944), and with revisions and added chapters were published as the perennial Christian bestseller *Mere Christianity* (1952). In 1943 Tolkien drafted a comment on Lewis's views of Christian marriage and divorce expressed in *Christian Behaviour*: see *Letters*, pp. 59–62. As a devout Roman Catholic, whose faith (*Religion) was bound to the structure of his church, he did not approve of Lewis as a lay theologian, at least not to the extent that he preached, as it were, to the masses (with more fame, Tolkien commented, than was comfortable even for Lewis himself). Moreover, Lewis's Northern Irish Protestant bias against Catholics occasionally surfaced in unguarded moments, to Tolkien's distress. On 30 August 1964 Tolkien wrote to Anne Barrett: 'C.S.L. of course had some oddities and could sometimes be irritating. He was after all and remained an Irishman of Ulster. But he did nothing for effect; he was not a professional clown, but a natural one, when a clown at all. He was generous-minded, on guard against all prejudices, though a few were too deep-rooted in his native background to be observed by him' (*Letters*, p. 350). Of Lewis's *Letters to Malcolm: Chiefly on Prayer*, published posthumously in 1964, Tolkien wrote to David Kolb that he found it 'a distressing and in parts horrifying work. I began a commentary on it, but if finished it would not be publishable' (11 November 1964, *Letters*, p. 352).

Lewis's fame was (and still is) especially pronounced in the United States. He received many letters from American admirers, one of whom was Joy Gresham, born Helen Joy Davidman in New York City. An educated and uninhibited woman, teacher, and poet, she was once an atheist and Communist. In 1942 she married William Gresham, with whom she had two sons, David and Douglas; in 1948 they became Christians, but in 1954 were divorced. Joy began to correspond with Lewis in 1950. In 1952 they met in Oxford, and a friendship grew between them. In 1955 she moved with her sons to Oxford; but in the following year found that she was unable to have her visa renewed. In order that she and her sons might stay in England, Lewis married Joy in a registry office in April 1956. Later that year, he published *Till We Have Faces*, a retelling of the story of Cupid and Psyche, in the writing of which Joy assisted; and she was found to have cancer. In March 1957 Joy and Lewis married again, in a Christian ceremony, and in April she and her sons took up residence at The Kilns. By the autumn, her cancer went into remission, but in late 1959 it returned, and Joy died in July 1960. Lewis expressed his sadness at her passing in *A Grief Observed* (1961).

Lewis's marriage came as a surprise to Tolkien, who learned about it eight months after the fact, and only through a notice in *The Times*. Lewis had been a confirmed bachelor for most of his life, and even critical of those of his friends, like Tolkien, whose time was not entirely their own, because of responsibilities to wife and family. Now, as Humphrey Carpenter puts it, Lewis expected his friends to 'pay court to his new wife'. Carpenter suggests that

Tolkien 'felt betrayed by the marriage, resented the intrusion of a woman into his friendship with Lewis – just as *Edith [Tolkien] had resented Lewis's intrusion into her marriage'. Moreover, Lewis had married a divorced woman, which ran counter to Tolkien's Roman Catholic beliefs. 'Ironically', says Carpenter, 'it was Edith who became friends with Joy Davidman' (*Biography*, p. 237) – though the friendship was no more than casual, having been formed only one month before Joy's death, when she and Edith were both patients in the Acland Nursing Home in Oxford. That, indeed, may have been the only occasion when Tolkien himself met Joy, when he encountered Lewis at the nursing home when they were both visiting their wives.

When Lewis supplied his blurb for *The Lord of the Rings* in late 1953 or early 1954, he warned Tolkien that even if Allen & Unwin, and Tolkien himself, 'approve my words, think twice before using them: I am certainly a much, and perhaps an increasingly, hated man whose name might do you more harm than good' (quoted in *Biography*, p. 219). Animosity towards Lewis was already evident in 1946, when he was passed over for the Merton Professorship of English Literature at Oxford in favour of his old tutor, *F.P. Wilson. Although Helen Gardner found him to be, in the early 1940s, 'by far the most impressive and exciting person in the Faculty of English',

a suspicion had arisen that Lewis was so committed to what he himself called 'hot-gospelling' that he would have had little time for the needs of what had become a very large undergraduate school and for the problems of organization and supervision presented by the rapidly growing numbers of research students in English Literature. In addition, a good many people . . . disliked the thought of a professor of English Literature winning fame as an amateur theologian; and, while undoubtedly there were a good many people in Oxford who disliked Christian apologetics *per se*, there were others who were uneasy at Lewis's particular kind of apologetic, disliking both its method and its manner. ['Clive Staples Lewis, 1898–1963', p. 425]

In 1947, when the Goldsmiths' Professorship of English Literature was established at Oxford, again Lewis was not elected, the chair going instead to his friend *Lord David Cecil; and in 1950 he narrowly lost the Professorship of Poetry to C. Day Lewis despite impressive support from his colleagues. Instead, he worked on (among other projects) the volume of the *Oxford History of English Literature* devoted to works of the sixteenth century excluding drama, which he had been commissioned to write. In 1954, however, the year his *Oxford History* volume was published, a chair of Medieval and Renaissance English was created at Cambridge and was offered to Lewis. At first he was reluctant to accept, but one of the electors to the chair was Tolkien, who worked strenuously behind the scenes and overcame Lewis's doubts, convincing him in particular that he would have to spend only four days per week in Cambridge, otherwise returning to The Kilns. Lewis accepted a fellowship

510 THE J.R.R. TOLKIEN COMPANION AND GUIDE

at Magdalene College, Cambridge, and taught there almost until his death, though illness came to restrict his lecturing and supervision. Among his publications in these last years were *The Four Loves* (1960), *Studies in Words* (1960), *A Grief Observed* (1961), and *An Experiment in Criticism* (1961). The *Discarded Image: An Introduction to Medieval and Renaissance Literature*, based on lectures at both Oxford and Cambridge, was published posthumously in 1964.

Much has been written about the 'cooling' of Tolkien's friendship with Lewis in their later years. It is sometimes called, misleadingly, a 'rift', though there does not appear to have been any major argument or disagreement to cause a division. Humphrey Carpenter writes of 'a gradual cooling on Tolkien's part. It is impossible to say precisely why. Lewis himself probably did not notice it at first, and when he did he was disturbed and saddened by it. Tolkien continued to attend Inklings meetings. . . . But although Tolkien could regularly be seen in the "Bird and Baby" [Eagle and Child pub] on Tuesday mornings there was not the same intimacy as of old between him and Lewis' (*Biography*, p. 200). Carpenter suggests that this 'decay' in friendship may have been hastened by criticisms Lewis made of *The Lord of the Rings*, particularly its verses; and, on Tolkien's part, by his dislike of the Narnia stories, and resentment of Lewis's popularity as a theologian and his speed as a writer. On 12 September 1960, Tolkien commented to his son Christopher on *Studies in Words* that Lewis's 'ponderous silliness is becoming a fixed manner'. Tolkien had supplied Lewis with a long linguistic analysis, of which little remained and some was dismissed. In late 1962 or early 1963, persuaded by Christopher to call on Lewis at The Kilns, the two had 'an awkward meeting, like an encounter between estranged members of a family', in which neither had much to say to each other (A.N. Wilson, from information by Christopher Tolkien, reported in *C.S. Lewis: A Biography* (1990), p. 294). Lewis was not well, however: on 20 November 1962 he wrote to Tolkien that he now wore a catheter, lived on a low protein diet, and went early to bed. He had contributed an essay, 'The Anthropological Approach', to *English and Medieval Studies Presented to J.R.R. Tolkien on the Occasion of His Seventieth Birthday*, but his health did not allow him to attend a dinner in December at Merton College marking the publication of the *Festschrift*.

In November or December 1963, after Lewis's death on 22 November, Tolkien wrote to his son *Michael (in draft) that 'many people' still regarded him as one of Lewis's 'intimates'. 'Alas! that ceased to be so some ten years ago. We were separated first by the sudden apparition of Charles Williams [in 1939, when he moved to Oxford], and then by his [Lewis's] marriage. Of which he never even told me; I learned of it long after the event. But we owed each a great debt to the other, and that tie with the deep affection that it begot, remains' (*Letters*, p. 341). Tolkien and Lewis did not cease to see each other, or to be friendly when they did. But friends often drift apart through no fault of their own or for particular reasons. Lewis's marriage was no doubt a contributing factor; so was Edith Tolkien's frailty, which was her husband's constant concern, and Tolkien's professorial responsibilities, and his obligations to publishers; and of course, Lewis's professorship in Cambridge, and his own illness.

On 26 November 1963, the day of Lewis's funeral, Tolkien wrote to his daughter *Priscilla: 'So far I have felt the normal feelings of a man of my age – like an old tree that is losing all its leaves one by one: this feels like an axe-blow near the roots. Very sad that we should have been so separated in the last years; but our time of close communion endured in memory for both of us' (*Letters*, p. 341).

Photographs of C.S. Lewis are reproduced in *Biography*, pl. 10b, and *The Tolkien Family Album*, p. 66.

See further, Roger Lancelyn Green and Walter Hooper, *C.S. Lewis: A Biography* (rev. and expanded edn. 2002); George Sayer, *Jack: A Life of C.S. Lewis* (2nd edn. 1994); and A.N. Wilson, *C.S. Lewis: A Biography* (1990). The last of these is sometimes controversial, addressing for instance the nature of Lewis's relationship with Mrs Moore, and was later revised. Green and Sayer knew Lewis well, and Hooper for a brief time, so have personal recollections and points of view. A more recent biography, by Alan Jacobs, *The Narnian: The Life and Imagination of C.S. Lewis* (2005), presents a fresh view though the author draws upon his predecessors. Tolkien is mentioned frequently in all of these sources, and also in Lewis's *Collected Letters* (2000 etc.). *C.S. Lewis* (1987) by Joe R. Christopher remains a useful introductory book on Lewis's writings. *The C.S. Lewis Readers' Encyclopedia* (1998), ed. Jeffrey D. Schultz and John G. West, Jr., was a handy reference for the present article, but some of its entries suffer from brevity and editorial agenda. The central references for Lewis studies are *C.S. Lewis: A Companion & Guide* (1996) by Walter Hooper and *The Inklings: C.S. Lewis, J.R.R. Tolkien, Charles Williams, and Their Friends* by Humphrey Carpenter (1978).

Lewis, Warren Hamilton (1895–1973). W.H. 'Warnie' Lewis was the elder brother of *C.S. Lewis. Educated at Malvern College, where he first won praise as a writer, he later trained at the Royal Military Academy, Sandhurst, in a shortened course due to the wartime need for officers. He was commissioned in the Royal Army Service Corps in 1914, and until his retirement in 1932 served in France, West Africa, and China, rising to the rank of Captain. He was recalled to active service in 1939, but in 1940 was transferred to the Reserve of Officers and for the duration of the war, promoted to Major, served as a private soldier with the 6th Oxford City Home Guard Battalion.

Although he lived in the shadow of his famous brother and from 1943 acted as his secretary, W.H. Lewis himself achieved distinction as a historian of seventeenth- and eighteenth-century France, in works such as *The Splendid Century: Some Aspects of French Life in the Reign of Louis XIV* (1953), *The Sunset of the Splendid Century: The Life and Times of Louis Auguste de Bourbon, Duc du Maine, 1670–1736* (1955), and *The Scandalous Regent: The Life of Philippe, Duc d'Orléans, 1674–1723, and of His Family* (1961). After his brother's death Warren edited the *Letters of C.S. Lewis* (1966), with a memoir. His diaries, held at the Marion E. Wade Center of Wheaton College, Wheaton, Illinois (*Libraries and archives), are a trove of information about Tolkien and the other members of the *Inklings, of which group Warren was one of the most active. Selections from his diaries were published as *Brothers and Friends*, ed. Clyde S. Kilby and Marjorie Lamp Mead (1982). See further, Richard C. West, 'W.H. Lewis: Historian of the Inklings and of Seventeenth-century France', in *Seven* 14 (1997).

*John Wain wrote of Warren Lewis in *Sprightly Running: Part of an Autobiography* (1962) that he was 'the most courteous [man] I have ever met – not with mere politeness, but with a genial, self-forgetful considerateness that was as instinctive to him as breathing' (p. 184). Tolkien often had the pleasure of his company on visits to pubs, at meals, and on country walks, as well as at Inklings meetings; see **Chronology**, entries for 25 January 1933 etc.

Photographs of W.H. Lewis are reproduced in *The Inklings*, pl. 1a, 2b, and 12.

The Lhammas. Essay on languages in Tolkien's mythology, the two later versions of which (of three) were published with commentary in *The Lost Road and Other Writings* (1987), pp. 167–98.

The work begins with brief comments on the language of the Valar which the Elves learned from Oromë, and from which derived all later Elvish languages (see *Languages, Invented), and a summary of the history of the Elves, explaining events which led to the development of the various Elvish tongues both in Valinor and in Middle-earth. It deals briefly with the language of the Orcs derived from Morgoth, and with the language that Aulë devised for the Dwarves. The languages of Men are said to derive from contact with Dark Elves who did not go to Valinor, with Orcs, and with Dwarves. *Taliska*, the language spoken by Men of the houses of Bëor, Haleth, and Hádor, is said to have been greatly influenced by the language of the Green-elves. The essay concludes with a summary of the state of languages at the time within the mythology at which Pengoloð was writing.

All three *Lhammas* texts survive in clear manuscripts. The title of the first was probably 'The *Lammas* or "Account of Tongues" that Pengolod of Gondolin wrote afterward in Tol-eressëa, using in part the work of Rúmil the sage of Kôr' (*The Lost Road and Other Writings*, p. 167). The second version, which closely follows the first, is entitled *The 'Lhammas'* and inscribed (adding another stage to the transmission): 'This is the "Account of Tongues" which Pengoloð of Gondolin wrote in later days in Tol-eressëa, using the work of Rúmil the sage of Tûn. This account Ælfwine saw when he came into the West.' The third text is shorter than its predecessors, and indeed is entitled *The Shorter Account of Pengoloð: or Lammasethen: Of the Elvish Tongues*; Tolkien later wrote on this, then erased, 'Sketch of a corrected version'. On most points it agrees with the second text, but has a different account of the origin of Quenya.

None of the versions can be precisely dated, but probably were written in the mid-1930s, before the *Quenta Silmarillion* but after the 'later' *Annals of Valinor* and 'later' **Annals of Beleriand.* Tolkien considered the *Lhammas* an integral part of a published ***'Silmarillion', to be placed after the *Quenta Silmarillion* and the *Annals.*

Each version of the *Lhammas* contains a 'genealogical' table, *The Tree of Tongues,* showing the 'descent' of languages. Associated with these texts is also another 'genealogical tree', *The Peoples of the Elves.* These too are published in *The Lost Road and Other Writings,* together with comments by *Christopher Tolkien on differences between the three *Lhammas* texts, and on his father's evolving ideas of the history of the Elves and of their languages.

Libraries and archives. The bulk of Tolkien's literary papers, other than those still in the physical possession of the Tolkien family, are housed at Marquette University in Milwaukee, Wisconsin, and at the University of *Oxford.

MARQUETTE UNIVERSITY LIBRARY

The J.R.R. Tolkien Collection, now in the Department of Special Collections and University Archives, John P. Raynor, S.J., Library, Marquette University, was established during Tolkien's lifetime. William B. Ready, Director of Libraries at Marquette, had been charged with the collection of material to support research at the University, and recognized the importance of **The Lord of the Rings* as literature soon after its publication (1954–6 in the United States). Probably at the end of 1956 or the beginning of 1957 he inquired, through the offices of the London bookseller Bertram Rota, if Tolkien would be willing to sell to Marquette the manuscripts of **The Hobbit* and *The Lord of the Rings.* Tolkien replied in the affirmative, and after a brief period of negotiation in which the manuscripts of **Farmer Giles of Ham* and the then unpublished **Mr. Bliss* were added to the agreement, accepted £1,500 in payment – a fair sum at the time (May 1957), when Tolkien had not yet achieved fame as a writer of fiction.

Files of papers concerning *The Hobbit, Farmer Giles of Ham,* and *Mr. Bliss* went to Marquette via Bertram Rota in June 1957, but the *Lord of the Rings* files, or rather some of them, were not sent until the following year. 'The reason for this', *Christopher Tolkien explains in his Foreword to **The Return of the Shadow,*

> was that my father had undertaken to sort, annotate, and date the multifarious manuscripts of *The Lord of the Rings,* but found it impossible at that time to do the work required. It is clear that he never did so, and in the end let the papers go just as they were; it was noted when they reached Marquette that they were 'in no order'. Had he done so, he must have seen at that time that, very large though the manuscript collection was, it was nonetheless incomplete. [p. 1]

In his posthumous autobiography *Files on Parade* (1982) William Ready claimed that Tolkien struck up a correspondence with him after Ready wrote a favourable review of *The Lord of the Rings*; that Ready then arranged for Tolkien a speaking tour of the United States, which Tolkien had to cancel due to his wife's illness; and that to make amends for the cancelled tour he agreed to sell Marquette University his literary papers. Although it is true that Tolkien planned to visit America at that time, the correspondence between Ready and Bertram Rota held at Marquette shows clearly that he was directly approached to sell his papers, and did not himself suggest their sale.

The *Hobbit* papers include more than 1,500 pages of manuscript, typescript, and corrected proofs, as well as a preliminary design for the dust-jacket of *The Hobbit* in pencil, ink, and watercolour (*Artist and Illustrator*, fig. 143), but not the art for Tolkien's text illustrations. More than 200 pages of manuscript, typescript, and proofs are held for *Farmer Giles of Ham*, including the earliest version but omitting notes for its unfinished sequel, which are in the Bodleian Library. The illustrated calligraphic manuscript of *Mr. Bliss* is complete on more than 60 pages. The largest part of the Marquette Tolkien holdings, the *Lord of the Rings* papers, comprises more than 9,200 pages of material, documenting different stages of writing, revision, and initial printing. Drafts of the abandoned Epilogue to *The Lord of the Rings* are also included, but with only a few minor exceptions, none of Tolkien's working drawings for the book.

Additional manuscripts of *The Lord of the Rings* were given to Marquette by the Tolkien Estate in later years. According to Christopher Tolkien in *The Return of the Shadow*, when sending the *Lord of the Rings* papers to Marquette in 1958 his father gathered together 'largely [those] of the earliest phase of composition, although in some cases ... successive revisions found among these papers bring the narrative to an advanced state. In general, however, it was only the initial notes and earliest drafts, with outlines for the further course of the story, that remained in England when the great bulk of the papers went to Marquette.' Christopher Tolkien thinks it likely that when the time came to send the papers his father was defeated by their chaotic state: 'inextricably complex, disorganised, and dispersed'. Nonetheless it 'must have been my father's intention at the time of the original sale' that the separated manuscripts of *The Lord of the Rings* be joined together, which Christopher has facilitated (p. 2).

In the decades since the first Tolkien papers were received, Marquette has acquired, by gift and purchase, a growing collection of Tolkien's published works, of works about him, and of miscellaneous ephemera. To these have been added, to date and *inter alia*, several private Tolkien collections, autograph letters, and papers related to the Morton Grady Zimmerman screen treatment of *The Lord of the Rings* (see *Adaptations) with Tolkien's annotations.

Inquiries should be directed to the Department of Special Collections and University Archives, John P. Raynor, S.J., Library, Marquette University, 1355 W. Wisconsin Ave., P.O. Box 3141, Milwaukee, WI 53201-3141. Some of the Marquette holdings are recorded in the University online public access catalogue; others are described on part of the Special Collections and University Archives website, at *www.marquette.edu/library/collections/archives/tolkien. html.*

BODLEIAN LIBRARY, OXFORD

After Tolkien's death in 1973 substantial collections of his papers were transferred by the Tolkien Estate to the Department of Special Collections and Western Manuscripts in the Bodleian Library, Oxford. These include, among much else, files concerning *The Adventures of Tom Bombadil and Other Verses from the Red Book*, *Beowulf: The Monsters and the Critics*, *The Book of Lost Tales* and other parts of *'The Silmarillion'*, *English and Welsh*, *Farmer Giles of Ham* (exclusive of the papers sold to Marquette), the *'Father Christmas' letters*, *The Homecoming of Beorhtnoth Beorhthelm's Son*, *Leaf by Niggle*, *On Fairy-Stories*, *The Road Goes Ever On: A Song Cycle*, *Roverandom*, *A Secret Vice*, *Smith of Wootton Major*, and *Tree and Leaf*; Tolkien's translations of *Beowulf* and *Sir Gawain and the Green Knight*; lecture notes from Tolkien's years as an Oxford professor; essays and notes written by Tolkien while an undergraduate; other personal papers; and a collection of Tolkien's original paintings, drawings (*Art), and *calligraphy. Some of these materials, especially those of a more sensitive nature, particularly fragile, or susceptible to damage by light or handling, are specially restricted.

Inquiries should be directed to the Department of Special Collections and Western Manuscripts, New Bodleian Library, University of Oxford, Broad Street, Oxford OX1 3BG U.K. General details and conditions of access are given on the department website, at *www.bodley.ox.ac.uk/dept/scwmss.* Permissions to view Tolkien papers may also be required from the Tolkien Estate, via Manches LLP, 9400 Garsington Road, Oxford Business Park, Oxford OX4 2HN U.K. (*www.manches.com*).

The Tolkien Estate itself preserves some of Tolkien's papers, including the diaries that Humphrey Carpenter used in *Biography* and the majority of Tolkien's writings on invented languages (*Languages, Invented).

OTHER LIBRARIES AND ARCHIVES

Among other relevant holdings in Oxford are the libraries of **Exeter**, **Merton**, **Pembroke**, and **Worcester** colleges, with miscellaneous letters from Tolkien and records of student and Faculty meetings in which he took part; the **Oxford English Faculty Library**, with minutes of the Library Committee on which Tolkien served for many years, some of which are in his hand while chairman and secretary, and a collection of books that Tolkien once owned, some of them dated or annotated; the **Oxford University Archives** at the Bodleian Library, with records of the English Faculty Board, the General Board, the committees and the panels of electors and examiners on which Tolkien served, postgraduate students he supervised, and his elections to Oxford professorships; and the archives of **Oxford University Press** (*Publishers), with papers concerning Tolkien's work for the *Oxford English Dictionary*, the Tolkien-*E.V. Gordon edition of *Sir Gawain and the Green Knight*, and other projects. Recorded interviews with Tolkien's family and friends, made soon after Tolkien's death, are available in the **Oxford Central Library**, together with useful local history materials.

The **University of Reading** holds most of the archives of Tolkien's publisher George Allen & Unwin (*Publishers). These include production ledgers, account books, records of manuscripts received, reader's reports, and letters to and from printers, booksellers, contributors, etc. concerning Tolkien's works. At one time or another, however, probably when Allen & Unwin moved its corporate offices, some parts of its archive were lost, or were pruned of materials apparently felt not to be of lasting value to the firm; thus the archive now contains, for instance, no letters concerning the first interest of Allen & Unwin in *The Hobbit* in the mid-1930s, nor are there any records after the late sixties. Access to the surviving material is aided by records in the University of Reading online public access catalogue.

Most of the correspondence directly between Tolkien and publisher's staff is not kept at Reading, but has been retained separately for ease of reference by Allen & Unwin and its successors, currently **HarperCollins** in London (*Publishers). It is not normally accessible to the public.

Smaller numbers of letters by Tolkien are held in various libraries, notably the **British Library**, London, which also contains, in the National Sound Archive, recorded interviews of Tolkien produced by the British Broadcasting Corporation, and **King's College, the University of London**, which holds the archive of the Early English Text Society (*Societies and clubs; formerly at Christ Church, Oxford). Written and printed material concerning Tolkien and the BBC, including much about the early adaptations of Tolkien's works for radio, is at the **BBC Written Archives Centre** at Caversham Park near Reading.

Records of Tolkien's military service in World War One may be seen at the **National Archives** (formerly the Public Record Office) at Kew. Other archives containing papers relevant to a study of Tolkien's life are at *King Edward's School, Birmingham** and the **University of *Leeds**.

The **Marion E. Wade Center** at Wheaton College, Wheaton, Illinois, founded by Clyde S. Kilby, contains substantial numbers of books by Tolkien and materials about him, a small collection of Tolkien letters, relevant oral histories, and notable collections concerned with fellow members of the *Inklings.

Both the **Tolkien Society** in Great Britain (*www.tolkiensociety.org*) and the **Inklings-Gesellschaft** in Germany (*www.inklings-gesellschaft.de*) maintain libraries and archives which include Tolkien materials, deposited respectively at the Surrey History Centre, Woking, and the Universitätsbibliothek Eichstätt.

Some holdings of Tolkien manuscripts in Britain may be found through the *Location Register of 20th-century English Literary Manuscripts and Letters*, originally published in 1988, later updated and mounted online at *www.library. rdg.ac.uk/colls/projects/locreg.html*. See further, Wayne G. Hammond, 'Special Collections in the Service of Tolkien Studies', in *The Lord of the Rings, 1954– 2004: Scholarship in Honor of Richard E. Blackwelder* (2006).

Readers interested in consulting any of the materials described in this entry should ensure that they have contacted the relevant library or archive in advance and met its requirements for admission and use.

Light. Light was an essential element in Tolkien's mythological thought since at least his early poem *The Voyage of Éarendel the Evening Star* (**Éalá Éarendel Engla Beorhtast*). In **'The Silmarillion'* it has different manifestations which underlie the various tales and provide motivating force. The biblical division of light from darkness, given importance early in Genesis, has several analogues in Tolkien's mythology, such as the labours of the Valar (the Gods) to illuminate their own lands and Middle-earth. In **The Book of Lost Tales*, when the Valar reach the world it is not entirely dark: 'Those were the days of Gloaming . . . for light there was, silver and golden, but it was not gathered together but flowed and quivered in uneven streams about the airs, or at times fell gently to the earth in glittering rain and ran like water on the ground; and at that time Varda in her playing had set but a few stars within the sky.' To provide light, Aulë persuades Melko to build two pillars, one in the North and one in the South, which rise 'up through the lower air even to Ilwë and the stars', and on these Aulë places two lamps he has made, filled with light which Manwë and Varda have gathered, 'silver to the North and golden to the South' (**The Book of Lost Tales, Part One*, p. 69). But Melko has treacherously made the pillars out of ice, which soon melts, and the lamps fall to earth. In later texts, both lamps and pillars are made by the Valar, and Melkor overthrows them by force. In the published **Silmarillion* (1977) 'the light of the Lamps of the Valar flowed out over the Earth, so that all was lit as it were in a changeless day', but Melkor casts them down, marring the world with 'destroying flame', 'so that the first designs of the Valar were never after restored' (pp. 35, 37).

After the destruction of the lamps, as described in *The Book of Lost Tales*, the Ainur labour to raise protecting mountains and to build dwellings. Varda wishes to gather light from that remaining in the air, and from pools and lakes of light spilled from the lamps, and to set a beacon on Taniquetil, the highest mountain.

> But Manwë suffered not more radiance to be gleaned from heaven, for that the dark was already that of night, but at his asking Ulmo rose from his deeps and fared to the blazing lakes and pools of brilliance. Therefrom he drew rivers of light into vast vessels, pouring back waters in their place, and with these he got him back to Valinor. There was all the light poured into two great cauldrons that Aulë fashioned in the gloom against his return, and those are called Kulullin and Silindrin.

Now in the midmost vale they digged two great pits. . . . In the one did Ulmo set seven rocks of gold . . . and a fragment was cast thereafter of the lamp that had burned awhile upon Helkar in the South. Then was the pit covered with rich earths that Palúrien [Yavanna] devised, and Vána . . . sang . . . the song of spring upon the mound, and danced about it, and watered it with great streams of that golden light that Ulmo had brought from the spilled lakes. . . .

But in the other pit they cast three huge pearls . . . and a small star Varda cast after them, and they covered it with foams and white mists and thereafter sprinkled lightly earth upon it, but Lórien who loveth twilights and flittering shadows . . . sat nigh and whispered swift noiseless words . . . ; and the Gods poured upon that place rivers of the white radiance and silver light which Silindrin held even to the brim. . . . [*The Book of Lost Tales, Part One*, pp. 70–1]

Only after all of this sympathetic magic does Palúrien sing and weave spells about the two places. First a golden tree, Laurelin, arises, and even before it flowers the light it gives is 'wide and fair', but then it 'put forth blossom in exceeding great profusion, so that all its boughs were hidden by long swaying clusters of gold flowers . . . and light spilled from the tips of these . . .' (p. 72). Some hours later, the white tree Silpion (Telperion) begins to grow: 'its blossoms did not hang in clusters but were like separate flowers growing each on fine stems that swung together, and were as silver and pearls and glittering stars and burnt with a white light; and it seemed as if the tree's heart throbbed, and its radiance wavered thereto . . .' (p. 72). Each tree waxes and wanes in turn, so that only one at a time gives light, except that as one fades and the other comes to life there is 'a wondrous gloaming of gold and silver and mingled lights' (p. 73).

In later texts this event is given greater weight of significance. By c. 1951 it is said in the *Annals of Aman* (see *Annals of Valinor*) that 'from those Trees there came forth a great light, and all Valinor was filled with it. Then the bliss of the Valar was increased; for the light of the Trees was holy and of great power, so that, if aught was good or lovely or of worth, in that light its loveliness and its worth were fully revealed; and all that walked in that light were glad at heart' (*Morgoth's Ring*, p. 55). Probably in late 1951 Tolkien wrote to *Milton Waldman: 'As far as all this has symbolical or allegorical significance, Light is such a primeval symbol in the nature of the Universe, that it can hardly be analysed. The Light of Valinor (derived from light before any fall) is the light of art undivorced from reason, that sees things both scientifically (or philosophically) and imaginatively (or subcreatively) and "says they are good" – as beautiful' (*Letters*, p. 148).

While Valinor rejoices in the changing light of the Two Trees, the lands east of the sea are lit only by the stars. In *The Book of Lost Tales* it is said that in the time before the raising of the Lamps 'Varda in her playing had set but a few stars within the sky' (*The Book of Lost Tales, Part One*, p. 69). When Aulë hears

of the awakening of the Elves, he flings his hammer down, by chance striking some silver ingots, from which seven sparks become stars in the sky. This
inspires Varda to take the radiance of Telimpë (Silindrin), which Aulë has in
a bowl, and mingle it with molten silver; then she sets 'stars about the firmament in very great profusion, so that the skies grew marvellously fair and their
glory was doubled' (*The Book of Lost Tales, Part One*, p. 113). Three of the Elves,
'whose eyes knew only the dusk and yet had seen no brighter things than
Varda's stars', are brought to Valinor, at which Inwë, seeing the Valar and the
Trees, is filled 'with a desire for light' (p. 116).

Works subsequent to *The Book of Lost Tales*, until the *Annals of Aman*, make
no mention of star-making by Varda before that which preceded the waking of
the Elves. These texts lay more emphasis on her great achievement with less
explicit detail of the materials used, and on the awakening of the Elves under
the stars. In the *Annals of Aman* Yavanna foretells that the Elves will awaken
soon, and asks Manwë to give light to Middle-earth for their comfort and
as a hindrance to the evil deeds of Melkor, but Mandos declares that it was
ordained that the Elves 'should come in the darkness and look first upon the
Stars'.

> Now Varda took the light that issued from Telperion and was stored in
> Valinor and she made stars newer and brighter. And many other of the
> ancient stars she gathered together and set as signs in the heavens of
> Arda....
>   Last of all Varda made the sign of bright stars that is called the Vala-
> kirka, the Sickle of the Gods, and this she hung about the North as a
> threat unto Utumno and a token of the doom of Melkor....
>   By the Waters of Awakening, Kuiviénen, [the Elves] rose from the
> sleep of Ilúvatar and their eyes beheld first of all things the stars of
> heaven. Therefore they have ever loved the starlight, and have revered
> Varda Elentárië above all the Valar. [*Morgoth's Ring*, p. 71]

Such aspects of light – lamps, Trees, and stars – lead in 'The Silmarillion'
to the gems fashioned by the Elf Fëanor, whose theft and pursuit inform the
rest of the mythology. In *The Book of Lost Tales* the Silmarils are made from
'a great pearl ... an urn full of the most luminous phosphor-light gathered
of foam in dark places', the glint of other gems 'by the light of white lamps
and silver-candles, and ... the sheen of pearls and the faint half-colours of
opals'. All of these Fëanor bathes 'in phosphorescence and the radiant dew of
Silpion, and but a tiny drop of the light of Laurelin' and gives 'all those magic
lights a body to dwell in of ... perfect glass' (*The Book of Lost Tales, Part One*,
p. 128). In works written during the 1920s and 1930s Tolkien gradually enlarged
the significance of the Silmarils, until in the *Quenta Silmarillion* of the mid-
1930s–early 1938 they are described thus:

A living fire burned within them that was blended of the light of the Two Trees. Of their own radiance they shone even in the dark; yet all lights that fell upon them, however faint, they took and reflected in marvellous hues to which their own inner fire gave a surpassing loveliness. No mortal flesh, nor flesh unclean, could touch them, but was scorched and withered. These jewels the Elves prized beyond all their works, and Manwë hallowed them; but Varda foretold that the fate of the World was locked within them. [*The Lost Road and Other Writings, p. 227]

The light of Sun and Moon enters the tales with the bearing of one last fruit and one last flower by the Trees, from which the greater lights of heaven are fashioned. The description of the making of the Sun and Moon in The Book of Lost Tales is more physical and less mythical than in later accounts, and the light of the Sun in particular is incredibly bright and hot. In the *Quenta Noldorinwa (c. 1930) it becomes clear, however, that the Sun and Moon produce a light of a lesser quality than that of the Two Trees: 'their light is not the light which came from the Trees before ever Ungoliant's poisonous lips touched them' (The Shaping of Middle-earth, p. 99). As Tolkien wrote to Milton Waldman:

There was the Light of Valinor made visible in the Two Trees of Silver and Gold. These were slain by the Enemy . . . and Valinor was darkened, though from them, ere they died utterly, were derived the lights of Sun and Moon. (A marked difference here between these legends and most others is that the Sun is not a divine symbol, but a second-best thing, and the 'light of the Sun' (the world under the sun) become terms for a fallen world, and a dislocated imperfect world.)

But the chief artificer of the Elves (Fëanor) had imprisoned the Light of Valinor in the three supreme jewels, the Silmarilli, before the Trees were sullied or slain. This Light thus lived thereafter only in these gems. [Letters, p. 148]

Nonetheless, Tolkien connected both the Sun and the Moon closely with Elves and Men, 'for the Sun was set as a sign for the awakening of Men and the waning of the Elves; but the Moon cherishes their memory' (earlier Quenta Silmarillion, in The Lost Road and Other Writings, p. 240).

At length, however, Tolkien came to feel uneasy about a 'Silmarillion' cosmology that was contrary to scientific fact. In the version of the *Ainulindalë he wrote c. 1946–8 the Sun is present from the beginning of the world, and neither it nor the Moon has any connection with the Two Trees. The Moon is made by Melkor, who seizes a portion of the Earth and sets it in the sky as a place from which he can observe what happens below. Even after the Valar cast him from the Moon, it suffers 'both blinding heat and cold intolerable, as might be looked for in any work of Melkor, but now at least it is clean, yet utterly barren' (Morgoth's Ring, p. 42), and it shines silver by the light of the

Sun. Because the Sun is already exists to shed light upon the earth, no longer is the making of lamps among the early works of the Valar. It seems in this instance, and again when he considered radical changes to his cosmology in the late 1950s, that Tolkien had no compunction about abandoning both the lamps and the making of the Sun and Moon from the last fruit and flower of the Two Trees. But texts published in *Morgoth's Ring* make it clear that he wanted nonetheless to retain in 'The Silmarillion' the purity and significance of light as provided by the Two Trees, its preservation in the Silmarils, and the wakening of the Elves under stars.

In contrast, *The Lord of the Rings* is comparatively straightforward in its use of light. The phial given by Galadriel to Frodo, which contains 'the light of Eärendil's star' (in fact the light of a Silmaril), is a helpful device, particularly in the darkness of Cirith Ungol. 'It will shine still brighter when night is about you. May it be a light to you in dark places, when all other lights go out' (bk. II, ch. 8). But Lothlórien itself is a metaphorical light in the darkness. Paul H. Kocher comments in *Master of Middle-earth: The Fiction of J.R.R. Tolkien* (1972):

> Just across the river Sauron's stronghold of Dol Guldur broods on its stony heights above twisted, rotting trees. But the darkness it generates can make no headway against its opposite, the light of Lórien. Tolkien has arranged the confrontation with a purpose, of course. The elf Haldir speaks for him in seeing in the combat between light and darkness large implications for the theme underlying the whole War of the Ring: 'In this high place you may see,' he points out to Frodo . . . 'the two powers that are opposed to one another; and ever they strive in thought, but whereas the light perceives the very heart of the darkness, its own secret has not been discovered. Not yet.' [p. 95]

Anne C. Petty comments in *Tolkien in the Land of Heroes: Discovering the Human Spirit* (2003) that

> light in the dark appears many times in [*The Silmarillion* and *The Lord of the Rings*], both figuratively and literally. Hope is literally offered as a light in dark places (for example Galadriel's phial). . . .
> In one sense, Tolkien envisioned light as the personification and actual embodiment of the Creator, Eru, the One, such that objects in Middle-earth containing that Light (the Lamps of Arda, the Two Trees of Valinor, and eventually the Silmarils) are sacred and the closest one is likely to get to actual contact with the deity. [p. 291]

The most extensive study of light in Tolkien's writings is *Splintered Light: Logos and Language in Tolkien World* by Verlyn Flieger (2nd edn. 2003). In this Flieger builds upon *Owen Barfield's theory of the fragmentation of meaning in language, relating it to an image of light, from Tolkien's poem *Mythopoeia, 'splintered from the original White "to many hues" as it is refracted through the prism of the sub-creative human mind' (p. 43). She argues that

the task of the Valar [in *The Silmarillion*] is to shape and light the world, but the whole concept belongs to Eru alone. In fulfilling his purpose the Valar are already at one remove from his wholeness, for they bring to the world not light, but lights, a variety of lights of differing kinds and progressively lessening intensities. Each light that comes is dimmer than the one before it, splintered by Tolkien's sub-creators.

This extended image of light diminished from its primal brilliance, yet still and evermore faintly illuminating the world, is paralleled by Tolkien's presentation of the peoples of that world and of their language. Increasingly as the story progresses, we are shown, through character, deed, and word, that Elves and Men are in their different ways drawn to the light and yet separated from it. The whole work is permeated by an air of deepening sorrow, a sense of loss, of estrangement, and ever-widening distance from the light and all that it signifies. Tolkien has imagined a world and its peoples through which he can explore the meaning and consequence of the *Fall – the long separation of humanity from the light of God. [p. 60]

Light as Leaf on Lindentree. Poem, first published in *The Gryphon* (Leeds) n.s. 6, no. 6 (June 1925), p. 217. Variously entitled *Light as Leaf on Lind* and *As Light as Leaf on Lindentree*, the poem is the first expression in print of the story of Beren and Lúthien (see *'Of Beren and Lúthien'), one of the central elements in Tolkien's mythology (*'The Silmarillion'). Beren 'from the wild country' comes 'wayworn sorrowing' to 'the tangled woods of Elfinesse' and sees an 'elfin maid', Luthien (*sic*), called 'Tinúviel', dancing to the flute of Dairon. He joins the dance, and the others flee 'on nimble fairy feet'; but he seeks for them, 'Still hearkening for the imagined sound / Of lissom feet upon the leaves, / For music welling underground / In the dim-lit caves of Doriath'. At last he catches Tinúviel and they fall in love. Henceforth, 'till moonlight and till music dies' Beren and Lúthien 'dance in the starlight of her eyes / In the forest singing sorrowless.'

Tolkien later noted on one of the three extant typescripts of this work that it had its 'first beginnings' in 1919–20, at his home in Alfred (now Pusey) Street in *Oxford, thus between late summer 1919 and September 1920; of this earliest version nothing survives. The same typescript is also inscribed 'Leeds 1923, retouched 1924'; two more were made with the same purple ribbon as the first, and date from the same period. Tolkien revised the latest of these after publication in *The Gryphon*. A small manuscript page, with reworkings of the penultimate stanza, is also extant.

In addition to its separate publication Tolkien incorporated *Light as Leaf on Lindentree* into the second version of **The Children of Húrin*, as the song Halog sings to Túrin when they are lost in the forest of Doriath, having already told him the story of Beren and Lúthien. In this context the poem was published in *The Lays of Beleriand* (1985), pp. 108–10, with a detailed textual history by *Christopher Tolkien, pp. 120–3. This episode in *The Children of Húrin* is the direct precursor of Aragorn's tale of Beren and Lúthien in Book I, Chapter 11 of *The Lord of the Rings*, sung and told to comfort his companions before the attack of the Ringwraiths at Weathertop. His poetic 'tale of Tinúviel' ('The leaves were long, the grass was green' etc.) is based closely upon *Light as Leaf on Lindentree* but incorporates, in its final stanza, aspects of the story as it developed later in 'The Silmarillion'. See also *The Return of the Shadow*, pp. 179–82.

Lincoln (Lincolnshire). Tolkien visited Lincoln in September 1947 while on an official tour of estates owned by Merton College (*Oxford and environs) in Lincolnshire, Cambridge, and Leicestershire. Able to see Lincoln Cathedral for the first time, he remarked that a notice over the tomb of Little Saint Hugh (a child supposed to have been murdered by Jews in Lincoln, c. 1255) claimed that St Hugh's story was told in *Chaucer's *Canterbury Tales* by the Prioress: in fact, her story was set in Asia.

The Line of Elros: Kings of Númenor. Account of the kings of *Númenor, published in *Unfinished Tales* (1980), pp. 218–27. Dates of birth, surrender of the sceptre, and death are given for each ruler, with annotations of important events in each reign. Tolkien wrote *The Line of Elros* probably in 1960, and made many emendations to the manuscript. In *Unfinished Tales*, pp. 224–5, *Christopher Tolkien notes some discrepancies between its latest form and Appendix B (*The Tale of Years*) in *The Lord of the Rings*, and refers to late writings by his father in which he reconsidered the life-spans of Elros, his descendants, and other Númenóreans. See also *The Peoples of Middle-earth*, p. 155, where Christopher Tolkien notes a change he made to a name.

The Little House of Lost Play: Mar Vanwa Tyaliéva. Poem, the earliest and latest versions of which were published with notes, variant readings, and commentary in *The Book of Lost Tales, Part One* (1983), pp. 27–32. The poet reminisces of days gone by, when in sleep 'a dark child and a fair' would wander 'shyly hand in hand' on the beach or in the flower gardens of 'the Little House of Play' (or 'Cottage of Lost Play'), where folk played and danced and sang. Chiefly descriptive of this wondrous place, in its final lines the poem returns to the 'little pair': 'and what they said, / ere Waking far apart them led, / that only we now know' (final version).

According to inscriptions on its earliest extant manuscript and a later typescript, Tolkien first composed this work on 27–8 April 1915 in his rooms at 59 St John Street, *Oxford. Its original title, *You & Me and the Cottage of Lost Play*, ties it to the introduction to *The Book of Lost Tales* of 1916–17, entitled *The Cottage of Lost Play*. In this the story is told to the mariner Eriol (*Eriol and Ælfwine) of a cottage in Valinor, near Kôr, which was visited by children who arrived on the *Olórë Mallë* or Path of Dreams. Much as in the poem, 'for the most part the children did not often go into the house, but danced and played in the garden, gathering flowers or chasing the golden bees and butterflies with embroidered wings that the Eldar set within the garden for their joy.' But that was long ago, at 'the Cottage of the Children, or of the Play of Sleep, and not of Lost Play, as has wrongly been said in song among Men – for no play was lost then, and here alas only and now is the Cottage of Lost Play' (*The Book of Lost Tales, Part One*, p. 19): that is, the cottage in Tol Eressëa visited by Eriol, the Mar Vanwa Tyaliéva of the Gnomes (later Noldorin Elves).

Several versions of the poem exist, as *Christopher Tolkien explains, 'each modified in detail from the preceding one, and the end of the poem was twice entirely rewritten' (*The Book of Lost Tales, Part One*, p. 27). Later its title became *Mar Vanwa Tyaliéva, The Cottage of Lost Play*, and finally *The Little House of Lost Play: Mar Vanwa Tyaliéva*.

Christopher Tolkien finds lines in the first version reminiscent of verse by Francis Thompson (the poem *Daisy*), and suspects that the latest version 'was very much later – and may indeed have been one of the revisions made to old poems when the collection *The Adventures of Tom Bombadil [and Other Verses from the Red Book]* (1962) was being prepared . . .' (p. 27). Brian Rosebury in *Tolkien: A Cultural Phenomenon* (2003) detects in the poem 'hints of Christina Rossetti' and of William Allingham's 'The Fairies',

> but also a deeper resemblance in mood to the nostalgic nineteenth-century ballads of which [Thomas] Hood's 'I remember, I remember' and [Thomas Love] Peacock's 'Love and Age' ('I played with you 'mid cowslips blowing / When I was six and you were four') are examples. Evidently it is a homage, deliberately projected backwards in time and transformed into fairy-tale mode, to an aspect of Tolkien's adolescent romance with his fellow-orphan Edith Bratt [*Edith Tolkien]. [p. 92]

Elsewhere in his commentary Christopher Tolkien states that 'the conception of the coming of mortal children in sleep to the gardens of Valinor [in *The Book of Lost Tales*] was soon to be abandoned in its entirety, and in the developed mythology there would be no place for it . . .' (pp. 31–2). But Tolkien wrote of a similar garden where children come to play, the garden of the Man-in-the-Moon, in his story *Roverandom*, first conceived in 1925 (published 1998): 'Grey fountains were there, and long lawns; and children everywhere, dancing sleepily, walking dreamily, and talking to themselves. Some stirred as if just waking from deep sleep; some were already running wide awake and laughing: they were digging, gathering flowers, building tents and houses, chasing butterflies, kicking balls, climbing trees; and all were singing' (p. 42).

London. Tolkien visited London on many occasions, perhaps for the first time as one of eight members of the *King Edward's School Officers Training Corps who were chosen to line the route for the coronation of King George V. The cadets encamped in Lambeth Park on 21 June 1911. On 22 June they marched to Constitution Hill adjoining Buckingham Palace, and were near the Palace also on 23 June before returning to *Birmingham.

Tolkien was again in London on 20 February 1912, for the seventh annual dinner of the Old Edwardian Association at the Holborn Restaurant, and from 12 to 13 December 1914, at the home of *Christopher Wiseman at 33 Routh Road, Wandsworth Common, for an important meeting of the *T.C.B.S. The latter was the 'Council of London' at which the four members discussed their aims and literary ambitions. Tolkien later wrote that after this meeting he found 'a voice for all kind of pent up things and a tremendous opening up of everything for me: – I have always laid that to the credit of the inspiration that even a few hours with the four brought to us' (letter to *Geoffrey Bache Smith, 12 August 1916, *Letters*, p. 10).

Most of Tolkien's visits to London however were on professional or literary business. On 25 November 1936 he delivered his lecture *Beowulf: The Monsters and the Critics* at the British Academy in Burlington House, Piccadilly. He consulted manuscripts in the British Museum in Great Russell Street (these are now in the British Library in St Pancras). He attended meetings at the Senate House, University of London, north of the British Museum, to discuss arrangements for the O'Donnell Lectures (*see* *English and Welsh*). And he visited his *publishers, George Allen & Unwin, who until Autumn 1987 had their offices in Ruskin House at 40 Museum Street just south of the British Museum. On 14 March 1968 he attended a reception given by Allen & Unwin at Crosby Hall, Chelsea, to launch the British edition of *The Road Goes Ever On: A Song Cycle*, at which *Donald Swann and singer William Elvin performed.

On 27 March 1972 Tolkien, with his children *John and *Priscilla, stayed at Brown's Hotel in Albemarle Street, and was given a private dinner by *Rayner Unwin at the Garrick Club in Covent Garden. On 28 March he went to Buckingham Palace where he was presented with the C.B.E.

When Tolkien travelled to London from Oxford by train he arrived at Paddington Station. In drafts for his lecture *On Fairy-Stories* he referred not to the roof of Bletchley station (see *Cambridge) but to the roof of Paddington, a much admired piece of engineering: 'The roof of Paddington Station is not more real than the sky; and as an artifact it is less interesting than the legendary dome of heaven' (Tolkien Papers, Bodleian Library, Oxford).

The Lonely Isle. Poem, published in *Leeds University Verse 1914–24* (1924), p. 57. Its earliest, undated manuscript has the title *Tol Eressëa*, but later versions are entitled *The Lonely Isle* and dedicated 'For England'. On one of these Tolkien later wrote, but not long after the fact, 'Étaples Pas de Calais June 1916'. In 1941 Tolkien recalled to his son Michael that he wrote *The Lonely Isle* on the occasion of his crossing the English Channel en route to 'the carnage of the Somme' (6–8 March 1941, *Letters*, p. 53; Tolkien sailed for France as a soldier in the British Expeditionary Force on 6 June 1916). The work is appro-

priately one of farewell to home, a 'glimmering island set sea-girdled and alone
... / A gleam of white rock over sundering seas'. The poet longs 'for thee and
thy fair citadel' with its 'lighted elms at eve'.

The latter is a reference to the city of *Warwick and the tower of Warwick
Castle. But at this time Warwick was bound up for Tolkien with his mythology in *The Book of Lost Tales, so that the 'fair citadel' with its elms also refers
to the 'fairy' city of Kortirion in Alalminórë ('land of elms'). The Lonely Isle,
by the same token, is Tol Eressëa ('lonely island' in Tolkien's invented 'elvish'
tongue), which was to have become England at the end of The Book of Lost
Tales, according to the earliest conception of that work; see further, comments
by Christopher Tolkien, *The Book of Lost Tales, Part One, pp. 24–5.

The Lonely Isle was reprinted in John Garth, Tolkien and the Great War
(2003), p. 145.

Looney see *The Sea-Bell*

The Lord of the Rings. Story, first published in Great Britain by George Allen
& Unwin, London, in three volumes, in July 1954 (Books I–II, The Fellowship
of the Ring), November 1954 (Books III–IV, The Two Towers), and October
1955 (Books V–VI and Appendices, The Return of the King); and in the United
States by the Houghton Mifflin Company, Boston, in October 1954 (The
Fellowship of the Ring), April 1955 (The Two Towers), and January 1956 (The
Return of the King). A detailed history of the writing of the work was published
in *The Return of the Shadow (1988), *The Treason of Isengard (1989), *The War
of the Ring (1990), the first part of *Sauron Defeated (1992), and the greater
part of *The Peoples of Middle-earth (1996), vols. 6–9 and 12 of The History of
Middle-earth by Christopher Tolkien. See further, Descriptive Bibliography
A5; The Tolkien Collector, especially nos. 20–22; Artist and Illustrator, ch. 5;
and Reader's Companion, in which part of this entry first appeared as a 'Brief
History'.

SUMMARY

The Lord of the Rings begins fifty-nine years after the events related in *The
Hobbit. Bilbo Baggins, the hero of that book, hosts a 'long-expected party' to
celebrate his 'eleventy-first' birthday (111) as well as the coming of age of his
adopted nephew, Frodo. During the party Bilbo disappears by means of the
magic ring he had found years earlier in Gollum's cave; and leaving the ring
and his home, Bag End, to Frodo, he departs from the Shire (as the land of the
Hobbits is now named). The wizard Gandalf the Grey, suspecting that the ring
is more powerful than it appears, urges Frodo to keep it safe and secret.

Several years later, Gandalf confirms his fear: that the ring in fact is that
forged long ago by the Dark Lord, Sauron, to rule the peoples of Middle-earth.
He tells Frodo the history of the One Ring and of the other Rings of Power:
three the Elves kept unsullied and hidden from Sauron; seven were held by

the Dwarf-kings, of which Sauron has recovered three and the rest have been consumed by dragons; and nine were given by Sauron to Men, who in consequence have become the Nazgûl, or Ringwraiths, 'shadows under his great Shadow, his most terrible servants' (bk. I, ch. 2). The Ring had been cut from Sauron's finger by a man, Isildur, son of Elendil, but was not destroyed. It was kept and then lost by Isildur, only to be found long after by Déagol, a creature of hobbit-kind, who was killed for it by his friend Sméagol, later known as Gollum; and from Gollum the Ring passed to Bilbo Baggins, and from Bilbo to Frodo. Now Sauron knows that the Ring has been found, he is searching for it, and he has heard about *hobbits* and *the Shire*.

On Gandalf's advice Frodo leaves Bag End, intending to make for the Elvish stronghold Rivendell; but he does so reluctantly, while Gandalf is inexplicably absent. With his servant Samwise (Sam) Gamgee and his cousin Peregrin (Pippin) Took he travels to Buckland on the eastern edge of the Shire. Along the way they escape discovery by a Ringwraith in the guise of a Black Rider, and are joined by another friend, Meriadoc (Merry) Brandybuck. The four hobbits travel east together. Attacked by the malevolent Old Man Willow and by a Barrow-wight, in each case they are saved by the enigmatic Tom Bombadil (**The Adventures of Tom Bombadil*). At the village of Bree they meet a friend of Gandalf, a weather-beaten man called Aragorn, also known as Strider, who offers them his protection. On the hill called Weathertop they are attacked by Black Riders; Frodo is gravely wounded but defiant. As the Black Riders press their attack at the Ford of Bruinen, the river rises in wrath and sweeps them away.

In Rivendell Frodo is healed by Elrond Half-elven, master of lore. He is reunited with Bilbo and Gandalf, and attends a feast at which is also Arwen, daughter of Elrond and beloved of Aragorn. With representatives of Elves, Dwarves, and Men Frodo attends a council to determine what course of action should be taken in regard to the Ring. Gandalf explains that he was betrayed and imprisoned in the tower of Orthanc at Isengard by his fellow wizard Saruman the White, who wants to seize the Ring for himself, but Gandalf escaped with the aid of a great eagle. Aragorn is revealed as the direct descendant of Isildur and heir to the kingdoms of Arnor and Gondor. The council concludes that the Ring cannot be kept hidden from Sauron and his forces, and is too dangerous to be used, lest it corrupt the user. Frodo volunteers to take it to Mordor, Sauron's land in the south-east of Middle-earth, for only there, in the fire-mountain Orodruin or Mount Doom, can the Ring be unmade. Sam, Merry, and Pippin choose to go on this quest as well; and to accompany them, Elrond selects Gandalf, Aragorn, Legolas (an elf), Gimli (a dwarf), and Boromir, a man of Gondor.

Together these nine, the Fellowship or Company of the Ring, journey south, but snow blocks their passage of the Misty Mountains. Instead they travel underground through Moria, an abandoned city of the Dwarves: there they are attacked by evil creatures called orcs (in *The Hobbit* called goblins), and by a more ancient and deadly evil, a balrog, with whom Gandalf falls in battle.

The remaining members of the Company escape into the forest of Lothlórien, ruled by the elves Celeborn and Galadriel. After a rest, the Company travel down the river Anduin, until each must choose whether to follow Frodo and the Ring east into Mordor, or to turn west with Boromir to the defence of Gondor. After Boromir attempts to take the Ring by force, Frodo departs alone; but Sam guesses his plan, and together he and Frodo cross the river into the land of Ithilien. While Aragorn, Legolas, and Gimli search for Frodo, Merry and Pippin are captured by orcs. Boromir, repentant, is killed trying to defend the two hobbits.

With the fate of the Ringbearer now out of their hands, Aragorn, Legolas, and Gimli pursue the orcs carrying Merry and Pippin into the land of Rohan. They encounter horsemen led by Éomer, nephew of the king of Rohan, and find signs that the hobbits have escaped their captors; the orcs, indeed, have been slain by Éomer and his men, and Merry and Pippin, fleeing into Fangorn Forest, have met Treebeard, one of a race of giant beings called Ents, protectors of trees. As Aragorn, Legolas, and Gimli continue to search for the hobbits they are met by Gandalf, now clad in white, and hear of his victory over the balrog and his return from death. Together they ride to Edoras in Rohan, where Gandalf frees the king, Théoden, from black despair fostered by his traitorous counsellor Gríma, also called Wormtongue, who is in league with Saruman. Théoden banishes Wormtongue and sends his people to the fastness at Dunharrow, led by his niece Éowyn; then he rides to meet the threat of Saruman on the northern border of Rohan. But Saruman has already sent his army south. The men of Rohan defeat their enemy at Helm's Deep; meanwhile, the Ents march on Saruman at Isengard and are also victorious. There Merry and Pippin are reunited with their comrades. Saruman is made powerless except for his persuasive voice; with Wormtongue he is imprisoned in Orthanc by the Ents. Pippin having looked in a *palantír* or seeing-stone and been observed by Sauron from afar in the Dark Tower, Gandalf takes the hobbit into his care and rides with him to Minas Tirith, the chief city of Gondor.

Frodo and Sam, meanwhile, have begun their journey to Mount Doom. They are soon joined by Gollum, who has followed them since Moria, seeking to recover the Ring for himself. Subdued by the hobbits, Gollum swears on the Ring, his 'Precious', that he will be Frodo's guide into Mordor. The three cross the Dead Marshes to the Black Gate, but finding the way barred, they agree to follow another, secret path known to Gollum, to the high pass of Cirith Ungol near the city of the Ringwraiths, Minas Morgul. Before they can do so, however, they are captured by men of Gondor, Rangers of Ithilien, led by Faramir, Boromir's brother. Faramir gives Frodo and Sam refuge for a time, and supplies to aid their journey. The hobbits then proceed towards Mordor with Gollum, who leads Frodo and Sam into peril from Shelob, a huge spider-like creature. Sam drives off Shelob, but not before Frodo is stung and apparently killed.

Gandalf and Pippin reach Minas Tirith, where they speak with the Steward,

Denethor, father of Boromir and Faramir. Pippin offers his service to Denethor and is made an esquire. In Rohan, Aragorn uses the *palantír* of Orthanc to reveal himself to Sauron, drawing the Dark Lord's eye away from Frodo and Sam in Mordor; and in the process sees a new and urgent peril. With Gimli, Legolas, and men from among his own people in the North he rides to Dunharrow: there, despite entreaties by Éowyn, Aragorn and his Grey Company take the Paths of the Dead through the mountains. It is the shortest route to the south, where Aragorn has seen a threat to Minas Tirith, but is fraught with darkness and fear, home of the restless ghosts of men who long ago had broken a pledge of service to Isildur in the fight against Sauron. Aragorn now commands the Dead to follow him and fulfill their oath to Isildur's heir. Merry has remained in Rohan, and has sworn his service to Théoden; but the king having mustered his men to ride to the relief of Minas Tirith, he orders Merry to remain behind and serve the Lady Éowyn, who is to govern the folk of Rohan in the king's stead. But when the warriors depart, Merry rides with them in secret with a rider called Dernhelm.

Faramir returns to Minas Tirith with news of Frodo and Sam in Ithilien. Gandalf suspects treachery by Gollum in leading the hobbits to Cirith Ungol. With the siege of Gondor imminent, Faramir rides to Osgiliath to command its defense. Sauron's forces drive the men of Gondor back to the city; in the retreat Faramir is wounded by the Witch-king, captain of the Nazgûl. With Boromir dead and Faramir near death, Denethor despairs, and orders that a pyre be prepared for Faramir and himself: they will burn before Sauron is victorious.

The warriors of Rohan ride to Minas Tirith, guided on secret paths by Wild Men of the woods. They battle with Sauron's forces on the Pelennor fields. Théoden falls, mortally wounded. Dernhelm is revealed to be Éowyn, who kills the Witch-king, aided by Merry, but they too are gravely hurt. Ships of the Corsairs of Umbar come to landings near the city, but they are manned by men led by Aragorn, the Dead having fulfilled their oath in fighting in the south of Gondor. The forces of Sauron at Minas Tirith are now killed or routed. Gandalf, Pippin, and the soldier Beregond save Faramir from death; but Denethor kills himself on the pyre, revealing as he does so that he too has looked into a *palantír*, through which Sauron fed the Steward's despair. Aragorn comes into the city and heals Faramir, Éowyn, Merry, and others.

To further draw Sauron's attention from his own land, as long as there is hope that Frodo might succeed in his quest, Aragorn, Gandalf, Gimli, Legolas, Pippin, and forces from Gondor and Rohan ride to the Black Gate, and speak with Sauron's lieutenant; but this parley is only the prelude to a trap. In the meantime, Sam has rescued Frodo, who was not killed but only immobilized by Shelob, and then captured by orcs. They escape from Minas Morgul and cross Mordor with much hardship. The Ring becomes a terrible burden to Frodo as they reach Mount Doom. Gollum attacks, but is beaten off by Sam while Frodo enters the Sammath Naur, the Chambers of Fire. There he succumbs at last to temptation and claims the Ring for his own. Gollum wrestles with Frodo and bites off his finger, along with the Ring. Dancing with exultation, Gollum falls into the chasm of fire. The Ring is destroyed, the Dark Tower falls, and Mount Doom erupts. Sauron rises like a great shadow but is blown away by the wind.

With the fall of Sauron, the company from Minas Tirith is victorious. Gandalf flies with three eagles to the rescue of Frodo and Sam from Mount Doom; they are brought back to Ithilien in honour. Word is sent to Minas Tirith, where Faramir and Éowyn have fallen in love. Aragorn returns to the city and is proclaimed king. Arwen and Aragorn are married.

After a time, the survivors of the Company of the Ring journey back to the North, through Rohan and Isengard. Treebeard reveals that he has released Saruman and Wormtongue from Orthanc. At last Frodo, Sam, Merry, and Pippin return to their own land and find it oppressed by ruffians, who have cut down trees, fouled air and water, and raised ugly buildings. The four hobbits raise the Shire and drive out the Men. Coming to Bag End, they learn that the Men have been under the command of Saruman. He tries to kill Frodo, but is himself killed by Wormtongue, who is then killed by hobbits.

Before long, the Shire is restored. Sam marries Rose Cotton. Pippin and Merry are renowned among their people. But Frodo's wounds do not heal. At last he takes ship into the West, a gift from Arwen who has given up her Elvish immortality to wed the mortal Aragorn. Frodo is accompanied by Bilbo, Gandalf, Elrond, and Galadriel.

HISTORY

Tolkien began to write *The Lord of the Rings* in December 1937, not, as he erroneously recalled in the Foreword to its second edition (1965), and as numerous critics have repeated, 'soon after *The Hobbit* was written and before its publication' (that is, between late 1936 and September 1937). Indeed, he might never have written his masterpiece if *The Hobbit* had not been an immediate success, and publisher *Stanley Unwin had not encouraged him to produce a sequel. Within only a few weeks of the publication of *The Hobbit* on 21 September 1937, Unwin warned Tolkien that 'a large public' would be 'clamouring next year to hear more from you about Hobbits!' (quoted in *Letters*, p. 23). Tolkien was flattered, but 'a little perturbed. I cannot think of anything more to say about *hobbits.* . . . But I have only too much to say, and much already written, about the world into which the hobbit intruded' (letter to Stanley Unwin, 15 October 1937, *Letters*, p. 24). For more than twenty years he had been concerned with the development of his private mythology, *'The Silmarillion'; and now, with *The Hobbit* in print, he wished to return to his 'secret vice', the creation of languages (*Languages, Invented) and stories set in the world of Arda and the lands of Middle-earth. But Unwin aroused in him 'a faint hope. . . . I have spent nearly all the vacation-times of seventeen years examining, and doing things of that sort, driven by immediate financial necessity (mainly medical and educational)' – that is, earning money to supplement his teaching salaries from the universities of *Leeds and *Oxford, the better to support his family. 'Writing stories in prose or verse has been stolen, often guiltily, from time already mortgaged, and has been broken and ineffective. I may perhaps now do what I much desire to do, and not fail of financial duty' (letter to Stanley Unwin, 15 October 1937, *Letters*, p. 24). On 19 October 1937 Unwin wrote again with encouragement ('You are one of those rare people with genius', quoted in *Letters*, p. 25), to which Tolkien replied: 'I will start something soon, & submit it to your boy [*Rayner Unwin, who had enjoyed *The Hobbit*] at the earliest opportunity' (23 October, *Letters*, p. 25). But he did not do so at once. On 15 November he met Stanley Unwin in London, handed over for consideration by George Allen & Unwin (*Publishers) parts of 'The Silmarillion' and other stories, among them *Farmer Giles of Ham*, then continued to work on his mythology.

On 15 December Stanley Unwin told him that 'The Silmarillion' contained 'plenty of wonderful material' which might be mined to produce 'further books like *The Hobbit* rather than a book in itself' (quoted in *The Lays of Beleriand*, p. 366), but what Allen & Unwin needed was another *Hobbit*, or failing that, a volume of stories like *Farmer Giles of Ham*. On 16 December Tolkien replied that it was now clear to him that 'a sequel or successor to *The Hobbit*' was called for, to which he promised to give thought and attention. But it was difficult with 'the construction of elaborate and consistent mythology (and two languages)' occupying his mind, and the Silmarils in his heart. Hobbits, he said, 'can be comic, but their comedy is suburban unless it is set against things more elemental' (*Letters*, p. 26). He did not need to add, for Unwin knew it already, that his academic and administrative duties in the *Oxford English School consumed many hours of his time, and he had responsibilities also to his wife and children. Nonetheless, inspiration seems to have struck at once – and by good fortune, at a free moment during the Christmas vacation – for on 19 December he informed C.A. Furth of George Allen & Unwin that he had 'written the first chapter of a new story about Hobbits – "A long expected party"' (*Letters*, p. 27).

In this as first conceived, Bilbo Baggins, the hero of *The Hobbit*, gives a magnificent party to celebrate his seventieth (not yet 'eleventy-first') birthday, then disappears from Hobbiton. The treasure he had gained in *The Hobbit* is now depleted, and he has a renewed desire to travel again outside his own land. But Tolkien did not yet know what adventures might be in store for Bilbo, or whether his new story would be about Bilbo or one of Bilbo's descendants. After five pages he abandoned this version of the opening chapter, though many aspects, even some of its phrasing, survived with little change into the published book. He then wrote a second version, closely based on the first, with much new material, including the presence of the wizard Gandalf; but after heavy emendation he left this draft unfinished. A third version soon followed, in which the party is given not by Bilbo, who has left his homeland, but by his son Bingo (so called, perhaps, because Tolkien's children owned a 'family' of stuffed koala bears, the 'Bingos'), and then a fourth, in which the party is given by Bilbo's adopted cousin Bingo Bolger-Baggins. On 1 February 1938 Tolkien wrote to C.A. Furth: 'Would you ask Mr Unwin whether his son [Rayner], a very reliable critic, would care to read the first chapter of the sequel to *The Hobbit*? . . . I have no confidence in it, but if he thought it a promising beginning, could add to it the tale that is brewing' (*Letters*, p. 28).

A few jottings from this time reveal the ideas that Tolkien was now considering. In one he noted: 'Make return of ring a motive', that is, the magic ring that Bilbo found in *The Hobbit* and which in the third and fourth versions of the new chapter is Bilbo's parting gift to Bingo (**The Return of the Shadow*, p. 41). In another memo Tolkien began to consider the nature of the ring:

> *The Ring*: whence its origin. Necromancer [an evil figure mentioned but not seen in *The Hobbit*]? Not very dangerous, when used for good purpose. But it exacts its penalty. You must either lose it, or *yourself.* Bilbo could not bring himself to lose it. He starts on a holiday handing over ring to Bingo. But he vanishes. Bingo worried. Resists desire to go and find him – though he does travel round a lot looking for news. Won't lose ring as he feels it will ultimately bring him to his father.
>
> At last he meets Gandalf. Gandalf's advice. You must stage a *disappearance*, and the ring may then be cheated into letting you follow a similar path. But you have got to *really disappear* and give up the past. Hence the 'party'.
>
> Bingo confides in his friends. Odo, Frodo, and Vigo (?) [> Marmaduke] insist on coming too. . . . [*The Return of the Shadow*, p. 42]

From these and similar thoughts Tolkien began to write a tale in which the hobbits Bingo, Frodo, and Odo set out for Rivendell. On the road they are overtaken by a rider wrapped in a great cloak and hood, who after a moment of tension is comically revealed to be Gandalf. But Tolkien immediately abandoned this idea, already beginning to conceive a story much darker than *The Hobbit*, and instead decided that Bingo and company were being pursued by Black Riders. He began the chapter anew, and much as in the finished *Lord of the Rings* (if with many differences of detail) brought the hobbits to a meeting with elves in the Woody End, to Farmer Maggot's house, and to a house in Buckland with their friend Marmaduke (precursor of Merry) Brandybuck. On 4 March 1938 Tolkien wrote to Stanley Unwin: 'The sequel to *The Hobbit* has now progressed as far as the end of the third chapter. But stories tend to get out of hand, and this has taken an unpremeditated turn' (*Letters*, p. 34). 'Beyond any doubt', *Christopher Tolkien has said, that turn was 'the appearance of the Black Riders' (*Return of the Shadow*, p. 44). But it would be some time yet before their nature and purpose became clear.

After a pause, from the end of August to mid-September 1938 Tolkien continued *The Lord of the Rings* as far as the middle of Bingo's conversation with the dwarf Glóin during the feast at Rivendell (the equivalent of published Book II, Chapter 1). During this period the story continued to change and evolve, and new ideas arose in the process. When Tolkien reached the point at which the hobbits are captured by a Barrow-wight, he made a rough plot outline for the story as far as the hobbits' arrival at Rivendell, and already foresaw a journey to the Fiery Mountain (Mount Doom). But he had doubts about some of the story he had written to date, and considered possible changes. The character Trotter, a hobbit 'ranger' who joins Bingo and company in Bree, was a particular mystery; and as Tolkien considered the powers and history of Bingo's ring, the idea that it is the Ruling Ring began to emerge.

From probably late September to the end of 1938 Tolkien altered the cast of hobbits, introducing Sam Gamgee, and added a new second chapter, 'Ancient History' (later 'The Shadow of the Past', published Book I, Chapter 2), in which Gandalf tells Bingo about the Ring and Gollum, and advises Bingo to leave the Shire. Also added was an account of the Black Riders' attack on Crickhollow. Tolkien now made a new fair copy manuscript of the work as far as the conversation between Frodo (the name now replacing *Bingo*) and Glóin out of existing drafts, incorporating many small changes and moving generally closer to the published text. Here in places, as in later workings, he tried out several versions of new or revised material before he was satisfied. He also wrote a new text to provide background information about Hobbits – the precursor of the Prologue – and drew a first selection of Hobbit family trees.

On 31 August he had written to C.A. Furth that *The Lord of the Rings* was 'getting quite out of hand' and progressing 'towards quite unforeseen goals' (*Letters*, p. 40). On 13 October he wrote to Stanley Unwin that the work was 'becoming more terrifying than *The Hobbit*. It may prove quite unsuitable [for its original intended audience of children]. It is more "adult".... The darkness of the present days [as *war with Germany was an evident possibility] has had some effect on it. Though it is not an *"allegory"' (*Letters*, p. 41). The *Lord of the Rings* now ran to over 300 manuscript pages, and according to the author's overly optimistic estimate, required at least another 200 to complete. He was eager to finish it. 'I am at the "peak" of my educational financial stress,' he wrote to C.A. Furth on 2 February 1939, 'with a second son [*Michael] clamouring for a university and the youngest [Christopher] wanting to go to school (after a year under heart-specialists), and I am obliged to do exams and lectures and what not.' *The Lord of the Rings* was 'in itself a good deal better than *The Hobbit*,' he felt, 'but it may not prove a very fit sequel. It is more grown-up – but the audience for which *The Hobbit* was written [his children] has done that also.' Although his eldest son (*John) was enthusiastic about the new work, 'it would be a relief to me to know that my publishers were satisfied.... The writing of *The Lord of the Rings* is laborious, because I have been doing it as well as I know how, and considering every word' (*Letters*, p. 42). On 10 February he wrote again to Furth, vowing to make a special effort to complete *The Lord of the Rings* before 15 June; but other duties occupied his time, and later that summer he had an accident which resulted in concussion and required stitches.

Tolkien's injury left him unwell for a long time, 'and that combined with the anxieties and troubles that all share [with the outbreak of war], and with the lack of any holiday, and with the virtual headship of a department in this bewildered university have made me unpardonably neglectful', he wrote to Stanley Unwin on 19 December 1939 (*Letters*, p. 44). Nonetheless, during the second half of the year Tolkien produced rough 'plot-outlines, questionings, and portions of the text' which show the author temporarily 'at a halt, even at a loss, to the point of a lack of confidence in radical components of the narrative structure that had been built up with such pains' (Christopher Tolkien, *The Return of the Shadow*, p. 370). He considered, *inter alia*, a version of the story once more with Bilbo as the hero, that the hobbit Trotter was actually Bilbo's well-travelled cousin Peregrin Boffin, that a dragon should invade the Shire, and that Frodo should meet the 'Giant Treebeard'; and he accurately foresaw final elements of the story yet to be written: a snowstorm in the pass over the mountains, the Mines of Moria, the loss of Gandalf, a siege, that Frodo would find himself unable to destroy the Ring, that Gollum would seize it and fall, the devastation of the Shire.

Tolkien now, after several false starts, completed a version of 'The Council of Elrond' (published Book II, Chapter 2), still far from its final form, in which the Company of the Ring consisted of Gandalf, Boromir, and five hobbits, one of whom was Peregrin Boffin (alias Trotter). He then wrote first drafts of 'The Ring Goes South' (Book II, Chapter 3) and 'The Mines of Moria' (later 'A Journey in the Dark', Book II, Chapter 4), and substantially revised his account of the journey to Rivendell told in Book I in order to clarify Gandalf's part in events. To this end he made many outlines, notes, and time-schemes co-ordinating events and the movements of Gandalf, the Black Riders, and Frodo and his companions. In the process, he decided that Trotter was not a Hobbit but a Man, whose true name was Aragorn.

In his Foreword to the second edition of *The Lord of the Rings* (1965) Tolkien said that in writing the story he suffered delays because of his academic duties, which were

increased by the outbreak of war in 1939, by the end of which year the tale had not yet reached the end of Book I. In spite of the darkness of the next five years I found that the story could not now be wholly abandoned, and I plodded on, mostly by night, till I stood by Balin's tomb in Moria. There I halted for a long while. It was almost a year later when I went on and so came to Lothlórien and the Great River late in 1941.

But in his letter to Stanley Unwin of 19 December 1939 (*Letters*, p. 44) Tolkien wrote that he had 'never quite ceased work' on *The Lord of the Rings*, which had 'reached Chapter XVI' – a clear indication that he was at work on 'The Mines of Moria' (published as 'A Journey in the Dark'), and in Book II, during 1939. From this Christopher Tolkien has convincingly argued that his father's hiatus in writing must have begun in that year rather than 1940 as the Foreword implies. He comments in *The Return of the Shadow* (p. 461): 'I feel sure . . . that – more than a quarter of a century later – [my father] erred in his recollection of the year' – a memory, perhaps, of his revision of the Moria episode rather than of its initial writing.

Tolkien returned to *The Lord of the Rings* evidently in late August 1940, continued to work on it probably until the beginning of Michaelmas Term at Oxford in October of that year, picked up the story again during the Christmas vacation, and returned to it again at times during 1941. It is not possible to date his writing or revision during this period more precisely except for a narrative outline, headed 'New Plot. Aug. 26–27, 1940': in this Tolkien decided that Gandalf's unexplained absence in Book I was caused by the wizard Sarumond (> Saramund > Saruman), who betrayed Gandalf to the Black Riders. He also wrote an account of Gandalf and the hobbit Hamilcar (later Fredegar 'Fatty') Bolger telling Frodo in Rivendell of their adventures, and of Gandalf's rescue of Hamilcar from Black Riders, and added other passages to agree with this account, but in the end rejected the episode.

Various decisions that Tolkien now made entailed considerable emendation and rewriting, especially of the second part of 'At the Sign of the Prancing Pony' (later 'Strider', Book I, Chapter 10). He also revised 'Many Meetings' (Book II, Chapter 1), with an addition in which Bilbo tells Frodo of Aragorn's background, and the third of ultimately fifteen versions of the poem Bilbo recites at Rivendell (evolved in stages from Tolkien's *Errantry*). At least three new versions of 'The Council of Elrond' date from this time as well, as Tolkien worked out additional material to be discussed, mainly arising from the position of Aragorn as the heir of Elendil. At this stage the chapter included material that was later removed to the Appendices, or that became the basis of the separate work *Of the Rings of Power and the Third Age*.

Having settled most of his doubts and made necessary changes in Book I and the beginning of Book II, Tolkien revised the account already written of the journey of the Company of the Ring from Rivendell as far as Balin's tomb. He wrote a fresh manuscript of 'The Ring Goes South' (Book III, Chapter 3), advancing confidently and making changes in the process, and rewrote the first part of the Moria episode. At last he moved the story beyond the discovery of Balin's tomb until the surviving members of the Company emerged from Moria. It was probably not until towards the end of 1941 that he wrote of the Company in Lothlórien and their farewell from that golden land (published Book II, Chapters 6–8, 'Lothlórien', 'The Mirror of Galadriel', and 'Farewell to Lórien'): here too, the story evolved as it progressed, requiring many emendations to earlier parts of the episode. 'By this time,' Christopher Tolkien has said, 'it had become my father's method to begin making a fair copy before a new stretch of the narrative had proceeded very far' (*The Treason of Isengard*, p. 267), built up in stages as different parts of the draft text were completed. During the writing of the chapters set in Lothlórien, Tolkien temporarily rejected *Aragorn* as Trotter's true name in favour first of *Elfstone* (and replaced the name *Aragorn* with *Elfstone* haphazardly in earlier text as far back as the chapter at Bree and the fifth version of the Council of Elrond), then rejected

Elfstone for *Ingold*, before returning to *Elfstone*. He also drafted a substantial outline of subsequent chapters in which he imagined Boromir's encounter with Frodo, his attempt to seize the Ring, Frodo's flight, and Frodo and Sam's journey in Mordor.

Tolkien then continued *The Lord of the Rings* with a new chapter, 'The Scattering of the Company' (later divided into 'The Great River' and 'The Breaking of the Fellowship', published Book II, Chapters 9–10). Uncertain as to whether time moved at a different pace, or no time passed at all, while the Company was in Lothlórien, he wrote several versions of the conversation on the subject (ultimately in 'The Great River') and devised variant time-schemes. At the end of 1941 and the beginning of 1942 he finished Book II and began to write Book III, completing Chapters 1–4 ('The Departure of Boromir', 'The Riders of Rohan', 'The Uruk-hai', and 'Treebeard') around the end of January. The next two chapters ('The White Rider' and 'The King of the Golden Hall') were written probably by midsummer, along with two outlines of the course of the story foreseen from Fangorn, though Tolkien still had not conceived many significant parts of the story yet to be told. He devoted spare time in summer and autumn 1942 to the remainder of Book III ('Helm's Deep', 'The Road to Isengard', 'Flotsam and Jetsam', 'The Voice of Saruman', and 'The Palantír'), which he seems to have worked on as a whole rather than bringing each part to a developed state before beginning work on the next.

As he developed the story of Helm's Deep in successive drafts, its fortifications became more elaborate and the account of its defence more complex. He completed 'The Road to Isengard' (Book III, Chapter 8) only after writing seven versions of Théoden and Gandalf's conversation about riding to Saruman's fortress, and four of Merry's lecture on pipe-weed, besides much other preliminary drafting. Apparently satisfied at last, he made a fair copy, but removed most of the material on pipe-weed into a preliminary section that became the Prologue; then he rejected much of what he had written and began to draft again, with a different chronology and changes in the route to Isengard. In 'The Voice of Saruman' (Book III, Chapter 10) he completed the interview with Saruman only after several drafts. And when he came to 'The Palantír' (Book III, Chapter 11) the appearance of that object was unexpected, and he did not know immediately how to use it in the story. As he later wrote: 'I knew nothing of the *Palantíri*, though from the moment the Orthanc-stone was cast from the window, I recognized it, and knew the meaning of the "rhyme of lore" that had been running through my mind: *seven stars and seven stones and one white tree*' (letter to *W.H. Auden, 7 June 1955, *Letters*, p. 217).

On 7 December 1942 Tolkien wrote to Stanley Unwin, wondering if, because of the war, it was 'of any use, other than private and family amusement, to endeavour to complete the sequel to *The Hobbit*. I have worked on it at intervals since 1938, all such intervals in fact as trebled official work, quadrupled domestic work, and "Civil Defence" have left. It is now approaching completion' (*Letters*, p. 58). He hoped to have free time to work on *The Lord of the Rings* during the Christmas vacation, and thought that he might finish it early in 1943. It had now reached 'Chapter 31' (i.e. 'The Palantír'), and Tolkien believed that it needed at least six more chapters to be finished, which were already sketched. But he did no further work on the book until spring 1944.

On 3 April 1944 he wrote to his son Christopher that he had begun 'to nibble at [the] Hobbit again' (*The Lord of the Rings*) and had 'started to do some (painful) work on the chapter which picks up the adventures of Frodo and Sam again; and to get myself attuned have been copying and polishing the last written chapter (Orthanc-Stone ['The Palantír'])' (*Letters*, p. 69). Apart from occasional revisions to earlier parts of the tale, during the rest of April and May Tolkien brought Frodo, Sam, and Gollum through the Dead Marshes, into Ithilien and a meeting with men of Gondor, to Shelob's Lair and the pass of Kirith (later Cirith) Ungol. Christopher's keen interest in the story, while in South Africa for training in the Royal Air Force, encouraged his father to work on his book, as did the enthusiasm of friends such as *C.S. Lewis. During this period Tolkien had chapters typed and sent them to Christopher by post; and his frequent letters to Christopher allow us to date the progress of *The Lord of the Rings* for a while with some precision.

On 6 May 1944 Tolkien informed Christopher that a new character had come on the scene: '(I am sure I did not invent him, I did not even want him, though I like him, but there he came walking into the woods of Ithilien): Faramir, the brother of Boromir' (*Letters*, p. 79). By 21 May he struck a difficult patch: 'All that I had sketched or written before proved of little use, as times, motives etc., have all changed. However at last with v[ery] great labour, and some neglect of other duties, I have now written or nearly written all the matter up to the capture of Frodo in the high pass on the very brink of Mordor' (letter to Christopher Tolkien, *Letters*, p. 81). 'The matter' comprised the final three chapters of Book IV ('The Stairs of Cirith Ungol', 'Shelob's Lair', and 'The Choices of Master Samwise'), in which Tolkien decided to alter the sequence of events as the hobbits and Gollum climbed to the pass, from a stair, then a tunnel, then a stair to stair, stair, and tunnel. On 15 May he wrote to Christopher that he was 'now coming to the nub, when the threads must be gathered and the times synchronized and the narrative interwoven; while the whole thing has grown so large in significance that the sketches of concluding chapters (written ages ago) are quite inadequate, being on a more "juvenile" level' (*Letters*, pp. 80–1). On 31 May he reported that he had just spent all the time he could spare in a 'desperate attempt to bring "The Ring" to a suitable pause, the capture of Frodo by the Orcs in the passes of Mordor, before I am obliged to break off by examining', and achieved this only 'by sitting up all hours' (letter to Christopher Tolkien, 31 May 1944, *Letters*, p. 83). On 12 August 1944 he wrote that he was now 'absolutely dry of any inspiration for the Ring [*The Lord of the Rings*] and am back where I was in the Spring, with all the inertia to overcome again. What a relief it would be to get it done' (*Letters*, p. 91).

He returned to the story in October 1944, with abortive beginnings of 'Minas Tirith' and 'The Muster of Rohan' (published Book V, Chapters 1 and 3).

He now mistakenly thought that Book V would be the final part of *The Lord of the Rings*, and again was uncertain of events to come. On 16 October he wrote to Christopher that he had 'been struggling with the dislocated chronology of the Ring,' that is, the timeline of *The Lord of the Rings* as a whole, 'which has proved most vexatious, and has not only interfered with other more urgent and duller duties, but has stopped me getting on. I think I have solved it all at last by small map alterations, and by inserting [in Books III and IV] an extra day's Entmoot, and extra days into Trotter's chase and Frodo's journey' (*Letters*, p. 97). In fact, some of his changes to the chronology required substantial emendation to the text. And it was probably at this point that he made a new, elaborate working time-scheme which shows the actions of all the major characters synoptically from 19 January, the fifth day of the voyage of the Company down the Anduin, until 8 February.

Tolkien remained optimistic about Book V into the next spring. On ?18 March 1945 he told Stanley Unwin that given 'three weeks with nothing else to do – and a little rest and sleep first' he probably would be able to finish *The Lord of the Rings*, but 'I don't see any hope of getting them'. He remembered that he had promised to let Unwin see part of what was written, but

> it is so closely knit, and under a process of growth in all its parts, that I find I have to have all the chapters by me – I am always, you see, hoping to get at it. And anyway only one copy (home-typed or written by various filial hands and my own), that is legible by others, exists, and I've feared to let go of it; and I've shirked the expense of professional typing in these hard days, at any rate until the end, and the whole is corrected. [*Letters*, pp. 113–14]

But he made little or no further progress until the middle of the following year. On 21 July 1946 he wrote to Stanley Unwin:

> I have been ill, worry and overwork mainly, but am a good deal recovered; and am at last able to take some steps to see that at least the overwork, so far as it is academic, is alleviated. For the first time in 25 years, except the year I went on crutches (just before *The Hobbit* came out, I think), I am free of examining, and though I am still battling with a mountain of neglects . . . and with a lot of bothers in this time of chaos and 'reconstruction', I hope after this week actually to – write.

But after a long gap since he had last worked on *The Lord of the Rings* 'I shall now have to study my own work in order to get back into it. But I really do hope to have it done before the autumn term, and at any rate before the end of the year' (*Letters*, pp. 117–18).

Around the end of September 1946 he returned to Book V, now with more developed ideas than two years previously. He completed it probably by the end of October 1947, with the usual succession of drafts and fair copies, and uncertainties as to how to proceed. As first written, the whole of Aragorn's journey from Helm's Deep to Minas Tirith was told in retrospect on the day following the Battle of the Pelennor Fields. At a later date, Tolkien decided to tell the first part of this tale, as far as the Stone of Erech, as narrative in a new chapter preceding 'The Muster of Rohan' (Book V, Chapter 3).

Also during the period 1946–7 Tolkien made further revisions to Books I and II, and wrote as a 'specimen' a revised account of Bilbo's encounter with Gollum in Chapter 5 of *The Hobbit*, which he sent to Allen & Unwin on 21 September 1947. In the first edition of *The Hobbit* Gollum offers the Ring to Bilbo as a 'present'; but this was now unlikely, given the dark possessive nature of the Ring as conceived in *The Lord of the Rings*, as well as the more sinister personality of Gollum in the sequel. Tolkien changed the episode so that Gollum offers to show Bilbo the way out of the goblin-caves if the hobbit should be successful at the riddle-game.

Tolkien completed *The Lord of the Rings* at last, at least in draft, in the period 14 August to 14 September 1948 in the quiet of his son Michael's home at Payables Farm, Woodcote, while Michael and his family were away on holiday. Some parts of Book VI were achieved, for once, with little difficulty. As Christopher Tolkien has said about 'Mount Doom' (Book VI, Chapter 3), for instance, it

is remarkable in that the primary drafting constitutes a completed text, with scarcely anything in the way of preparatory sketching of individual passages, and while the text is rough and full of corrections made at the time of composition it is legible almost throughout; moreover many passages underwent only the most minor changes later. It is possible that some more primitive material has disappeared, but it seems to me . . . that the long thought which my father had given to the ascent of Mount Doom and the destruction of the Ring enabled him, when at last he came to write it, to achieve it more quickly and surely than almost any earlier chapter in *The Lord of the Rings*. [*Sauron Defeated*, p. 37]

But other parts were not so easy to write. Tolkien seems to have felt his way in 'The Scouring of the Shire' (Book VI, Chapter 8), with much revision and significant changes. Although he realized that Saruman was behind the troubles in the Shire, it was only after several false starts that he made the character actually present among the Hobbits. Christopher Tolkien has said that 'it is very striking that here, virtually at the end of *The Lord of the Rings* and in an element in the whole that my father had long meditated, the story when he first wrote it down should have been so different from its final form (or that he so signally failed to see "what really happened"!)' (*Sauron Defeated*, p. 93). Also at this stage Tolkien conceived Book VI as ending not with the present final chapter, 'The Grey Havens', but with an Epilogue featuring Sam and his children reading from the Red Book, ultimately omitted (but published in *Sauron Defeated*).

Over the next year Tolkien made fair copies and typescripts of *The Lord of the Rings*, finishing the complete work in October 1949. In doing so he incorporated late changes and additions already in draft, and made new changes as well. Not until this late date was the name of Elrond's daughter changed from *Finduilas* to *Arwen Evenstar*, and Frodo's role in the Scouring of the Shire made passive rather than active. Tolkien also now further developed background and ancillary material for the Prologue and Appendices, concerning the history, peoples, languages, alphabets, and calendars of Middle-earth.

PUBLICATION

Although he had written *The Lord of the Rings* nominally for publication by Allen & Unwin, at length Tolkien began to resent their rejection of 'The Silmarillion' in 1937 and came increasingly to feel that *The Lord of the Rings* and 'The Silmarillion' should be published together – indeed, that the former needed the latter to make its full impact. Thus when in autumn 1949 he was introduced to *Milton Waldman, a senior editor at the London publisher Collins, and Waldman expressed an interest in publishing both books if 'The Silmarillion' could be finished, Tolkien responded eagerly. The question now arose, however, whether Tolkien had any moral or legal commitment to Allen & Unwin. In a draft letter to Waldman of 5 February 1950 Tolkien wrote that he believed himself to have no legal obligation, 'since the clause in *The Hobbit* contract with regard to offering the next book seems to have been satisfied either (a) by their rejection of *The Silmarillion* or (b) by their eventual acceptance and publication of *Farmer Giles*' (*Letters*, p. 135). But he had friendly relations with Stanley and Rayner Unwin, and since *The Lord of the Rings* had always been considered a sequel to *The Hobbit*, he thought that he might have a moral obligation to the publisher of the earlier work. On 24 February 1950 he wrote to Stanley Unwin about *The Lord of the Rings*, deliberately putting it in a poor light:

> And now I look at it, the magnitude of the disaster is apparent to me. My work has escaped from my control, and I have produced a monster: an immensely long, complex, rather bitter, and very terrifying romance, quite unfit for children (if fit for anybody); and it is not really a sequel to *The Hobbit*, but to *The Silmarillion*. My estimate is that it contains, even without certain necessary adjuncts, about 600,000 words.... I can see only too clearly how impracticable this is. But I am tired. It is off my chest, and I do not feel that I can do anything more about it, beyond a little revision of inaccuracies. Worse still: I feel that it is tied to the *Silmarillion*....
>
> Ridiculous and tiresome as you may think me, I want to publish them both – *The Silmarillion* and *The Lord of the Rings* – in conjunction or in connexion ... that is what I should like. Or I will let it all be. I cannot contemplate any drastic re-writing or compression.... But I shall

not have any just grievance (nor shall I be dreadfully surprised) if you decline so obviously unprofitable a proposition. . . . [*Letters*, pp. 136–7]

Unwin replied on 6 March that it would be difficult to publish both 'The Silmarillion' and *The Lord of the Rings*, especially with the costs of book production three times what they were before the war. Would there be any possibility, he asked, of breaking the work into, say, 'three or four to some extent self-contained volumes' (quoted in *Letters*, p. 137)? 'A work of great length can, of course, be divided artificially', Tolkien replied on 10 March.

> But the whole Saga of the Three Jewels and the Rings of Power has only one natural division into two parts . . . : *The Silmarillion* and other legends; and *The Lord of the Rings*. The latter is as indivisible and unified as I could make it.
>   It is, of course, divided into sections for narrative purposes (six of them), and two or three of these, which are of more or less equal length, could be bound separately, but they are not in any sense self-contained. [*Letters*, p. 138]

He wondered, moreover, if many beyond his friends would read, or purchase, so long a work. He understood the financial barriers to publication, and said that he would not feel aggrieved should Allen & Unwin decline.

Stanley Unwin did not reply at once, but on 3 April informed Tolkien that he was still studying the problem of how *The Lord of the Rings* might be published. To print 2,500 copies in two large volumes, each of 1392 pages, 'would involve an outlay of well over £5,000, and each volume would actually cost for paper, printing, and binding, without allowing anything for overheads, author or publisher, about 22/-' (Tolkien-George Allen & Unwin archive, HarperCollins). Rayner Unwin by now also supplied an opinion, requested by his father, which the elder Unwin sent to Tolkien though it had never been intended for Tolkien's eyes:

> *The Lord of the Rings* is a very great book in its own curious way and deserves to be produced somehow. *I* never felt the lack of a *Silmarillion* when reading it. But although he claims not to contemplate any drastic rewriting, etc., surely this is a case for an editor who would incorporate any *really* relevant material from *The Silmarillion* into *The Lord of the Rings* without increasing the enormous bulk of the latter and, if feasible, even cutting it. Tolkien wouldn't do it, but someone whom he would trust and who had sympathy (one of his sons?) might possibly do it. If this is not workable I would say publish *The Lord of the Rings* as a prestige book, and after having a second look at it, drop *The Silmarillion*. [quoted in *Biography*, p. 210]

This infuriated Tolkien, who on 14 April demanded that Unwin give an immediate answer to his proposal for publication of both works. Unwin replied on 17 April that he was sorry that Tolkien felt it necessary to present an ultimatum,

> particularly one in connection with a manuscript which I have never seen in its final and complete form. We have not even had an opportunity of checking whether it does in fact run to one million, two hundred thousand words. . . . As you demand an *immediate* 'yes' or 'no' the answer is 'no'; but it might well have been yes given adequate time and the sight of the complete typescript. [Tolkien-George Allen & Unwin archive, HarperCollins; partly quoted in *Letters*, p. 141]

Tolkien now was able to tell Milton Waldman that *The Lord of the Rings* was free of any entanglements. But once Collins' staff considered the work in earnest, Waldman informed Tolkien that it would have to be cut for publication. Dismayed, Tolkien said that he would try to comply, but appears never to have begun to do so; indeed, he continued to expand Appendix A. Waldman then left England for Italy where he lived for much of the year, and also fell ill, leaving *The Lord of the Rings* and the still unfinished 'Silmarillion' in the hands of colleagues who did not share Waldman's enthusiasm for what Tolkien had written. Probably in late 1951 and apparently at Waldman's suggestion, Tolkien wrote a long letter, about 10,000 words, explaining the two works and demonstrating his view that they are interdependent and indivisible. (See *Letters*, pp. 143–61, and *Reader's Companion*, pp. 742–9.)

Stanley Unwin meanwhile had written to Tolkien, taking note of his problems with Collins and letting him know that the door had not closed for him at Allen & Unwin. Then on 22 June 1952 Tolkien wrote humbly to Rayner Unwin, in reply to a query:

> As for *The Lord of the Rings* and *The Silmarillion*, they are where they were. The one finished (and the end revised), the other still unfinished (or unrevised), and both gathering dust. I have been both off and on too unwell, and too burdened to do much about them, and too downhearted. Watching paper-shortages and costs mounting against me. But I have rather modified my views. Better something than nothing! Although to me all are one, and the 'L[ord] of the Rings' would be better far (and eased) as part of the whole, I would gladly consider the publication of any part of this stuff. Years are becoming precious. And retirement (not far off) will, as far as I can see, bring not leisure but a poverty that will necessitate scraping a living by 'examining' and such like tasks.
>
> When I have a moment to turn round I will collect the *Silmarillion* fragments in process of completion – or rather the original outline which is more or less complete, and you can read it. My difficulty is, of course, that owing to the expense of typing and the lack of time to do my own (I typed nearly all of *The Lord of the Rings*!) I have no spare copies to let

out. But what about *The Lord of the Rings*? Can anything be done about that, to unlock gates I slammed myself? [*Letters*, p. 163, corrected from the Tolkien-George Allen & Unwin archive, HarperCollins]

Rayner quickly replied, asking to see a copy of the complete *Lord of the Rings* to 'give us a chance to refresh our memories and get a definite idea of the best treatment for it'. The capital outlay would be great, he advised, but less serious if Allen & Unwin did not publish *The Lord and the Rings* and 'The Silmarillion' all at once. 'We do *want* to publish for you – it's only ways and means that have held us up. So please let us have the Ring now, and when you are able the Silmarillion too (I've never read it at all you see) and by the time you are freer we shall be ready to discuss it' (1 July 1952, Tolkien-George Allen & Unwin archive, HarperCollins, partly quoted in *Letters*, pp. 163–4).

Tolkien now retreated again to his son Michael's home, at Chapel Cottage, Woodcote, to read through and correct *The Lord of the Rings*. Since he had written the work over such a long span of years, he found that some of its elements needed to be changed, and even in later parts Tolkien needed to ensure that all of the adjustments consequent upon changes in the story's chronology had been made.

In early November 1952, having obtained cost estimates for printing *The Lord of the Rings*, Rayner Unwin sent a telegram to his father, who was in the Far East. Rayner admitted that publication of *The Lord of the Rings* would be a big risk for their firm, and believed that Allen & Unwin might lose up to a thousand pounds in the process; but in his opinion, Tolkien had written a work of genius. He asked his father if he might offer Tolkien a contract. Stanley Unwin famously cabled in reply: '*If* you believe it is a work of genius, *then* you may lose a thousand pounds' (quoted in Rayner Unwin, *George Allen & Unwin: A Remembrancer* (1999), p. 99). Allen & Unwin minimized their risk, however, by offering Tolkien a profit-sharing agreement, by which no royalties would be paid to him until all of the publisher's costs had been recovered, but thereafter he would receive half-profits. Tolkien quickly agreed.

By 17 November 1952 Allen & Unwin decided that the most economical way to publish *The Lord of the Rings* was in three volumes, at a price not exceeding 25s each. This unfortunately has led many of its readers to speak of it as three separate but interconnected works, a 'trilogy', though it is no such thing (see below). Tolkien himself considered its important division to be its six books, to each of which he had given a title, not the three volumes into which these were artificially broken. He wrote to Rayner Unwin on 24 March 1953:

I have given some thought to the matter of sub-titles for the volumes, which you thought were desirable. But I do not find it easy, as the 'books', though they must be grouped in pairs, are not really paired; and the middle pair (III/IV) are not really related.

Would it not do if the 'book-titles' were used: e.g. *The Lord of the Rings*: Vol. I *The Ring Sets out* and *The Ring Goes South*; Vol. II *The*

Treason of Isengard, and *The Ring goes East*; Vol. III *The War of the Ring*, and *The End of the Third Age*?

If not, I can at the moment think of nothing better than: I *The Shadow Grows* II *The Ring in the Shadow* III *The War of the Ring* or *The Return of the King*. [*Letters*, p. 167]

(Alternate book titles are preserved in a galley proof of the combined tables of contents of the three volumes, Marquette University MSS 4/2/16: Book I *The First Journey*; Book II *The Journey of the Nine Companions*; Book III *The Treason of Isengard*; Book IV *The Journey of the Ring-bearers*; Book V *The War of the Ring*; Book VI *The End of the Third Age*. All of these were ultimately abandoned.)

On 11 April 1953 Tolkien reported to Rayner Unwin that he had 'at last completed the revision for press – I hope to the last comma – of Part I: *The Return of the Shadow*: of *The Lord of the Rings*, Books I and II' (*Letters*, p. 167). He was also prepared to send his Foreword, but still had not decided what would appear in the Appendices, or what he would be able to provide in the time remaining before publication. By now he had proposed that the book contain a facsimile of the burnt pages of the Book of Mazarbul (which figures in Book II, Chapter 5), but expensive halftones were ruled out. Allen & Unwin also suggested economies for the picture of the Doors of Durin in Book II, Chapter 4, and for the three maps that Tolkien thought necessary. Although Tolkien had originally hoped that *The Lord of the Rings* could contain illustrations, the cost was prohibitive, given the great length of the book and the difficulties of Britain's postwar economy. In the event, only a few essential blocks could be included, and all in line. In the process of writing *The Lord of the Rings*, however, Tolkien drew a number of quick sketches to aid his thoughts, such as a diagram of Helm's Deep, different conceptions of Saruman's fortress Orthanc and of Minas Tirith, and a plan of Farmer Cotton's house. He also made several more finished drawings in coloured pencil, of Old Man Willow, Moria Gate, Lothlórien, Dunharrow, and Barad-dûr – not all of which are actual scenes from *The Lord of the Rings*, or accord in every detail with the final text. (See further, *Artist and Illustrator*, Chapter 5.)

Galley proofs began to arrive for Tolkien's attention in July 1953. On 4 August he wrote to his son Christopher:

> There seem such an endless lot of them; and they have put me very much out of conceit with parts of the Great Work, which seems, I must confess, in print very long-winded in parts. But the printing is very good, as it ought to be from an almost faultless copy; except that the impertinent compositors have taken it upon themselves to correct, as they suppose, my spelling and grammar: altering throughout *dwarves* to *dwarfs*; *elvish* to *elfish*; *further* to *farther*; and worst of all, *elven-* to *elfin*. [*Letters*, p. 169]

He complained, and his original readings were restored.

On 28 July Rayner Unwin pressed Tolkien that each of the three volumes needed a title, and made his own suggestions; among these, he felt that *The Lord of the Rings* could be applied to Volume 1, and did not propose an overall title for the complete work. Tolkien countered that he preferred *The Lord of the Rings* for the whole, with *The Return of the Shadow*, *The Shadow Lengthens*, and *The Return of the King* for the volumes. After further discussion, on 17 August he proposed

> as titles of the *volumes*, under the overall title of *The Lord of the Rings*: Vol. I The Fellowship of the Ring. Vol. II The Two Towers. Vol. III The War of the Ring (or, if you still prefer that: The Return of the King).
>
> The Fellowship of the Ring will do, I think; and fits well with the fact that the last chapter of the Volume is The Breaking of the Fellowship. The Two Towers gets as near as possible to finding a title to cover the widely divergent Books 3 and 4; and can be left ambiguous – it might refer to Isengard and Barad-dûr, or to Minas Tirith and B[arad-dûr]; or to Isengard and Cirith Ungol. On reflection I prefer for Vol. III The War of the Ring, since it gets in the Ring again; and also is more non-committal, and gives less hint about the turn of the story: the chapter titles have been chosen also to give away as little as possible in advance. But I am not set in my choice. [*Letters*, pp. 170–1]

Rayner agreed, but preferred *The Return of the King* for Volume III.

During the rest of 1953, through 1954, and for the first half of 1955 Tolkien worked with Allen & Unwin on production of *The Lord of the Rings*. Proofs arrived at intervals for correction. Frequent correspondence was needed to deal with these, to arrange the completion of miscellaneous art (for the most part redrawn by a printer's copyist after Tolkien's originals), to transmit and correct the three maps (drawn by Christopher Tolkien; see 'The Maps of *The Lord of the Rings*' in *Reader's Companion*), and to settle the dust-jacket designs. Probably during 1953 Tolkien began to prepare a glossary-index to *The Lord of the Rings*, as promised in the original Foreword to *The Fellowship of the Ring*, and continued to work on it at least into 1954, but completed only a list of place-names. And in the second half of 1954 and early 1955 he wrote additional material for the Appendices, but had to omit most of this for lack of space: it included the works now known as **The Quest of Erebor* and **The Hunt for the Ring*.

Early in the process he was asked by Allen & Unwin to write, for publicity purposes, a description of *The Lord of the Rings* in not more than 100 words, with biographical details of the author. He felt that he could not write so brief a sketch, but provided one in 300 words. His friend *George Sayer, English Master at Malvern, also agreed to help, and himself provided 95 words. The publisher then drafted a final blurb for Tolkien's approval, drawing mainly upon his effort, with a reduced comment by Sayer about poetry in *The Lord of the Rings*.

LATER EDITIONS

Far from losing a thousand pounds, as Rayner Unwin had feared, *The Lord of the Rings* proved a commercial success. The cautiously short initial print runs of 3,000 and 3,250 copies respectively for *The Fellowship of the Ring* and *The Two Towers* (plus 1,500 and 1,000 further copies for the American edition) sold quickly, and new printings had to be put in hand without delay. As a matter of course, Allen & Unwin had instructed its printer to keep the (metal) type of the three volumes standing, ready for additional impressions; but the printer had failed to do so for *The Fellowship of the Ring*, and on receiving an order for more copies quickly reset that volume so that it would appear to be identical to the original setting. This was done, however, without notifying either Allen & Unwin or Tolkien, thus without fresh proofreading by publisher or author, and in the process numerous errors were introduced, mainly the substitution of a word with a similar word, a change in the order of words, or a change in punctuation. The fact of the resetting was not discovered until 1992.

By the time Tolkien completed *The Return of the King*, the popularity of *The Lord of the Rings* was such that Allen & Unwin ordered 7,000 copies of the first printing of the final volume, plus 5,000 copies for the Houghton Mifflin (*Publishers) edition.

Small corrections were made to *The Lord of the Rings* in its early printings, before the standing type was cast into more durable printing plates for subsequent impressions. Then in 1965 Tolkien learned that his American copyright in *The Lord of the Rings*, and in *The Hobbit*, could be open to legal challenge. He was asked to revise both works so that new U.S. copyrights could be obtained. But before he could act, Ace Books of New York, a well-known publisher of science fiction, issued their own paperback edition of *The Lord of the Rings* at the cheap price of seventy-five cents. Ace Books held that *The Lord of the Rings* was in the public domain in the United States, due to improper attention to details of copyright (a claim later taken up by others, and at last disproved in court). See further, *Ace Books controversy.

From July to September 1965 Tolkien sent material for a revised *Lord of the Rings* to the Houghton Mifflin Company; this was incorporated in an authorized paperback edition by Ballantine Books of New York (*Publishers) and first published in October 1965. These revisions were then made to the Allen & Unwin second edition of 1966, which in turn was the basis for the Houghton Mifflin second edition of 1967. Further emendations were made to later Ballantine printings, and notably to the second printing of the Allen & Unwin second edition in 1967 – Tolkien had continued to work on the text beyond his deadline for changes in 1965. In the process, however, errors and omissions were variously made, and the texts of these different editions diverged.

With each resetting of the text, new errors have been introduced. In 1987 Douglas A. Anderson, working with Christopher Tolkien, encouraged Houghton Mifflin to bring its standard edition of *The Lord of the Rings* (unchanged since 1966) into line with the standard British edition (to which emendations had been made from time to time), and to make additional corrections to the text as needed. For several years this was the most accurate edition available. Then in 1994 HarperCollins, successor to Allen & Unwin (and its successor, Unwin Hyman) as Tolkien's primary publisher, reset *The Lord of the Rings* again, now in electronic form for ease of correction; but in doing so, once again errors were made, which in turn were carried into later printings and into other editions (by HarperCollins, Houghton Mifflin, and Ballantine Books) based on the 1994 setting. Some of these errors were corrected in the HarperCollins edition of 2002, others not until the HarperCollins edition of 2004 (also published by Houghton Mifflin) and its further corrected reprint of 2005. (See further, *Reader's Companion*, pp. xl–xliv, for an account of the editing of the 2004–5 fiftieth anniversary *Lord of the Rings*.)

In 1952 Tolkien privately tape recorded selections from *The Lord of the Rings* while a guest at the home of George Sayer. This recording was first issued commercially in 1975, with other material, as *J.R.R. Tolkien Reads and Sings His The Hobbit and The Fellowship of the Ring* and *J.R.R. Tolkien Reads and Sings His The Lord of the Rings: The Two Towers/The Return of the King*, and reissued in 2001 as part of *The J.R.R. Tolkien Audio Collection*; see further, *Recordings. An unabridged recording of *The Lord of the Rings*, including among the Appendices only Appendix A (*Annals of the Kings and Rulers*), was made by Rob Inglis and first issued in 1991.

See also *Adaptations; *Nomenclature of The Lord of the Rings; *Translations.

LATER WRITINGS

With the success of *The Lord of the Rings*, Tolkien was able to return to work on 'The Silmarillion', now with the blessing and active encouragement of Allen & Unwin. His aim was to compile the variant tales he had written since 1916 and to revise them in light of *The Lord of the Rings*, in which some of the mythology had become 'fixed' in print. Before his death in 1973 Tolkien was able to accomplish some of this task, but in the process also created new texts, some of which were effectively extensions of *The Lord of the Rings*, which itself was an integral part of the *legendarium*. See *The Battles of the Fords of Isen; *Cirion and Eorl and the Friendship of Gondor and Rohan; *The Disaster of the Gladden Fields; *The History of Galadriel and Celeborn and of Amroth King of Lórien; and *The Rivers and Beacon-hills of Gondor.

REVIEWS

The initial critical response to *The Lord of the Rings* was mixed, but on the whole mostly positive, a state of affairs which has continued to the present day. Some of its first reviewers were puzzled: it was not the sort of book they were accustomed to read, nor the sort they might have expected from Tolkien, whose two previous works of fiction (*The Hobbit* and *Farmer Giles of Ham*) had been marketed for children, nor could it be read complete until 1955 (in America, 1956). Some were put off by comments on the dust-jacket by its advance readers, who compared it grandly to Spenser, Malory, and Ariosto. But not a few were impressed by what they read.

The anonymous reviewer of *The Fellowship of the Ring* for the *Times Literary Supplement*, describing Hobbits, wrote that 'it is as though these Light Programme types had intruded into the domain of the Nibelungs'. He felt, however, that Tolkien had just managed to pull off the difficult 'change of key' within the first volume; and yet 'the plot lacks balance. All right-thinking hobbits, dwarfs, elves and men can combine against Sauron, Lord of Evil; but their only code is the warrior's code of courage, and the author never explains what it is they consider the Good.' Perhaps, he thought, 'this is the point of a subtle allegory', of the West against the Communist East. In any case, '*The Fellowship of the Ring* is a book to be read for sound prose and rare imagination' ('Heroic Endeavour', *Times Literary Supplement*, 27 August 1954, p. 541). In contrast, Peter Green in the *Daily Telegraph* ('Outward Bound by Air to an Inappropriate Ending', 27 August 1954, p. 8) remarked that Tolkien had 'written, with the interminable prosiness of a bazaar story-teller, an adventure yarn about magic rings and Black Riders which should prove immensely popular with those 10-year-olds who don't prefer space-fiction. . . . It's a bewildering amalgam of Malory, Grimm, the Welsh *Mabinogion*, T.H. White and "Puck of Pook's Hill". The style veers from pre-Raphaelite to Boy's Own Paper.' But even so, he concluded, 'this shapeless work has an undeniable fascination'. In the *New Statesman and Nation* Naomi Mitchison praised Tolkien's book for its details of geography and language, but regretted that certain aspects of its world were not worked out, and that there were 'uncertainties on the scientific side. But on the fully human side, from the standpoint of history and semantics, everything is there' ('One Ring to Bind Them', 18 September 1954, p. 331).

Much firmer and unequivocal support for *The Fellowship of the Ring* came from Tolkien's friend C.S. Lewis (who had read the work or heard it read to him in draft) in a review for *Time and Tide* ('The Gods Return to Earth', 14 August 1954):

> This book is like lightning from a clear sky: as sharply different, as unpredictable in our age as *Songs of Innocence* [by William Blake] were in theirs. To say that in it heroic romance, gorgeous, eloquent, and unashamed, has suddenly returned at a period almost pathological in its anti-romanticism, is inadequate. To us, who live in that odd period, the return – and the sheer relief of it – is doubtless the important thing. But in the history of Romance itself – a history which stretches back to the *Odyssey* and beyond – it makes not a return but an advance or revolution: the conquest of new territory. [p. 1082]

With the publication of *The Two Towers* the *Times Literary Supplement* proclaimed the work to be 'a prose epic in praise of courage', and noted that 'within his imagined world the author continually unveils fresh countries of the mind, convincingly imagined and delightful to dwell in.' But 'large sectors of this mythic world are completely omitted; women play no part; no one does anything to get money; oddly enough, no one uses the sea, though that may come in the final volume. And though the allegory is now plainer there is still no explanation of wherein lies the wickedness of Sauron' ('The Epic of Westernesse', 17 December 1954, p. 817). Maurice Richardson in the *New Statesman and Nation* thought that *The Two Towers* would 'do quite nicely as an allegorical adventure story for very leisured boys, but as anything else . . . it has been widely overpraised'. The work had begun as 'a charming children's book' but 'proliferated into an endless worm', its fantasy 'thin and pale'. He liked its scenes of battle and the 'atmosphere of doom and danger and perilous night-riding', though, and thought that the allegory (as he perceived it to be) raised 'interesting speculations' as to whether the Ring related to the atomic nucleus, and Orcs perhaps with materialist scientists ('New Novels', 18 December 1954, pp. 835–6).

The *Times Literary Supplement* praised the completion of *The Lord of the Rings* upon the appearance of *The Return of the King*: 'At last the great edifice shines forth in all its splendour, with colonnades stretching beyond the ken of mortal eye, dome rising behind dome to hint at further spacious halls as yet unvisited.' The reviewer felt that *The Lord of the Rings* was 'not a work that many adults will read right through more than once; though even a single reading will not be quickly forgotten' ('The Saga of Middle Earth', 25 November 1955, p. 704). But he thought that Tolkien could have distinguished Good and Evil better. In response to a reader's letter, the reviewer wrote, with an astonishing lack of perception, that 'throughout the book the good try to kill the bad, and the bad try to kill the good. We never see them doing anything else. Both sides are brave. Morally there seems nothing to choose between them' (*TLS*, 9 December 1955, p. 743). C.S. Lewis answered such criticism in his combined review of *The Two Towers* and *The Return of the King* for *Time and Tide* ('The Dethronement of Power', 22 October 1955): 'Since the climax of Volume I was mainly concerned with the struggle between good and evil in the mind of Boromir', it was not easy to see how anyone could complain that the characters in *The Lord of the Rings* 'are all either black or white'; and even those who do complain

> will hardly brazen it out through the two last volumes. Motives, even in the right side, are mixed. Those who are now traitors usually began with comparatively innocent intentions. Heroic Rohan and imperial Gondor are partly diseased. Even the wretched Sméagol, till quite late in the story, has good impulses; and (by a tragic paradox) what finally pushes him over the brink is an unpremeditated speech by the most selfless character of all [Sam]. [p. 1373]

By now *The Lord of the Rings* had been widely reviewed, and the critical climate was such that W.H. Auden would later write: 'I rarely remember a book about which I have had such violent arguments. Nobody seems to have a moderate opinion; either, like myself, people find it a masterpiece of its genre or they cannot abide it' ('At the End of the Quest, Victory', *New York Times Book Review*, 22 January 1956, p. 5). He himself had given it high praise. On the other hand, there was (most famously) Edmund Wilson, who wrote of *The Lord of the Rings* in *The Nation* ('Oo, Those Awful Orcs!' 14 April 1956, pp. 312–13) that there was little in the book 'over the head of a seven-year-old child', that it dealt with 'a simple confrontation – of the Forces of Evil with the Forces of Good, the remote and alien villain with the plucky little home-grown hero', that Tolkien's 'poverty of imagination' was so pathetic that to have critics such as C.S. Lewis, Naomi Mitchison, and Richard Hughes pay tribute to *The Lord of the Rings* (on the original dust-jackets) could be explained only by the 'lifelong appetite' that 'certain people – especially, perhaps, in Britain – have . . . for juvenile trash'. In 1962 Edmund Fuller observed that the critical acclaim with which *The Lord of the Rings* was received was so great as to carry in it 'an inevitable counterreaction – a natural hazard of any work unique in its time that kindles a joy by its very freshness' ('The Lord of the Hobbits: J.R.R. Tolkien', *Tolkien and the Critics: Essays on J.R.R. Tolkien's The Lord of the Rings* (1968), p. 36). Or, as Tolkien himself put it,

> *The Lord of the Rings*
> is one of those things:
> if you like it you do:
> if you don't, then you boo!

(quoted in *Biography*, p. 223). He took note of criticism as it came to his attention. On 9 September 1954, following the first reviews of *The Fellowship of the Ring*, he wrote to Rayner Unwin:

> As for the reviews they were a great deal better than I feared, and I think might have been better still, if we had not quoted the Ariosto remark, or indeed got involved at all with the extraordinary animosity that C.S. L[ewis] seems to excite in certain quarters. . . . All the same many commentators seem to have preferred lampooning his remarks or his review to reading the book.
>
> The (unavoidable) disadvantage of issuing in three parts has been shown in the 'shapelessness' that several readers have found, since that is true if one volume is supposed to stand alone. . . . There is too much 'hobbitry' in Vol. I taken by itself; and several critics have obviously not got far beyond Chapter I.
>
> I must say that I was unfortunate in coming into the hands of the D[aily] Telegraph, during the absence of [John] Betjeman. My work is not in his line, but he at any rate is neither ignorant nor a gutter-boy.

Peter Green seems to be both. I do not know him or of him, but he is so rude as to make one suspect malice. . . .

I am most puzzled by the remarks on the style. I do not expect, and did not expect, many to be amused by hobbits, or interested in the general story and its modes, but the discrepancy in the judgements on the style (which one would have thought referable to standards independent of personal liking) are very odd – from laudatory quotation to 'Boys Own Paper' (which has no one style)! [*Letters*, p. 184]

POPULARITY

The Lord of the Rings has remained continuously in print since its first publication, and for much of that time in multiple formats: in one, three, even seven volumes, sold separately or slipcased, in hardback and paperback, in de luxe and illustrated editions. It brought Tolkien world-wide fame (see *Fandom) and has been translated into at least forty languages. By no means did it need the film adaptations of 2001–3 to find a readership; it was already in a leading position among the most popular books of the twentieth century. In the Waterstone's-BBC Channel 4 *Book Choice* programme readers' poll of 1996 to name the greatest book of the century, *The Lord of the Rings* not only topped the list, but had one-third more votes (from 25,000 voters) than the runner-up, George Orwell's *Nineteen Eighty-Four*. *The Hobbit* came nineteenth. Many literary critics were horrified, and some suggested that Tolkien fans had organized heavy voting. The Chief Inspector of Schools in Britain said that the choice of *The Lord of the Rings* as the nation's favourite book was an example of low cultural expectation. Newspapers published articles and letters supporting or attacking the result, explaining why the book was popular, or why it ought not to be popular. The *Daily Telegraph* repeated the poll, and again *The Lord of the Rings* won. Then the Folio Society held a poll of the ten books of all time that had most inspired, influenced, or affected its members, and from 10,000 voters *The Lord of the Rings* came first, defeating not only twentieth-century rivals, but also works by Jane Austen, Charles Dickens, William Shakespeare, Leo Tolstoy, Dante, and Homer, even the Bible. In 2003 it won a BBC poll for the best-loved novel from any country or date. (See further, Wayne G. Hammond and Christina Scull, 'J.R.R. Tolkien: The Achievement of His Literary Life', *Mythlore* 22, no. 3 [whole no. 85] (Winter 1999); Joseph Pearce, *Tolkien: Man and Myth* (1998), Chapter 1; and T.A. Shippey, *J.R.R. Tolkien: Author of the Century* (2000), pp. xx–xxiv.)

These polls (such as they are) and the reaction to them show that *The Lord of the Rings* is very popular with a large part of the general public, but less so with some academics and literary critics, at least a few of which seem to view it with almost pathological distaste. The response of the latter group, in fact, suggests that *The Lord of the Rings* might also come near the top of a poll for the most disliked or over-rated book. But those who like *The Lord of the Rings* often read it again and again, discovering new depths with each reading.

Many join societies, or write to Internet forums, to meet others who share their tastes. Some are even inspired to read and study the works of early literature that inspired Tolkien. No one explanation will account for this.

But several reasons are commonly given by readers when asked why they like *The Lord of the Rings*. To begin with, it is an exciting story; on first reading, many are unable to put the book down, wanting to know what happens next. (Allen & Unwin were inundated with letters from anguished readers when there was a publication gap of nearly a year between *The Two Towers* and *The Return of the King*.) Another reason is the unequalled richness of Tolkien's invention – new beings such as Hobbits and Ents, a history going back thousands of years, languages, geography – some aspects drawn in detail, some only hinted at, yet all (within the frame of the book) seemingly real. Readers are attracted to this world and want to know more about it; many in Tolkien's day wrote to him asking for more information.

Tolkien took great care in crafting the work and achieving consistency. Its action is carefully paced, beginning slowly, then moving more quickly. Chapters depicting tension, action, and fear are balanced by interludes of rest, peace, and beauty, each by contrast enhancing the impact made by the other. The style of the work is varied to suit the occasion and the speaker. Most of the story is seen through the eyes of the hobbits, with whom readers can easily identify. And all of it was written by one of the twentieth century's masters of the English language.

It has also been suggested that readers turn to *The Lord of the Rings* because they are not interested in modern novels praised by literary critics as dealing with 'real life', novels about the dysfunctional lives and petty relationships of uninteresting and unpleasant people whom most readers would prefer not to actually meet. Fantasy or *fairy-story can deal with much more fundamental problems, more applicable to our own lives, and still be an enjoyable read. Tolkien wrote to Dora Marshall on 3 March 1955 that 'it remains an unfailing delight to me to find my own belief justified: that the 'fairy-story' is really an adult genre, and one for which a starving audience exists' (*Letters*, p. 209). The same 'starving' reaction seems to have been at work in the current popularity of J.K. Rowling's 'Harry Potter' series, which in addition to exciting narratives presents issues of loyalty, courage, and resistance to Evil. The latter aspect is of special importance in a world where ethics and morality no longer seem clear-cut, where one feels helpless to influence events for the better. In such a case, readers may welcome a book where *Good and Evil are more clearly defined, and where even the weak are shown as having an important role to play.

Some of Tolkien's academic colleagues were less than enthusiastic about *The Lord of the Rings* because they felt that its author should have spent his time producing scholarly works on Old and Middle English literature. Yet Tolkien probably did more to encourage Old English studies by writing *The Lord of the Rings* than if he had produced dozens of learned articles. It has inspired many of its readers to study Old English, even towards the end of the twentieth century while many universities were revising their English syllabi to make

Old English an optional rather than a required study, or removing it altogether. T.A. Shippey has suggested that some of the hostility to Tolkien shown by literary critics stems from the fact that Tolkien was a philologist, from the Language side of the English school, not from the Literature side, and moreover, not one of the writers (or like any of the writers) that the critics had backed.

For some critics of *The Lord of the Rings* it is not enough to say that it is not the type of work that appeals to them: they seem to feel threatened by its very existence. Some are prejudiced simply because the work is popular, and so a large and easy target. Others oppose it because it is fantasy and therefore necessarily 'escapist' (see *Escapism) and unconnected with 'real life'. Some admit shamefully that they liked *The Lord of the Rings* in adolescence, but 'grew out of it' – a legitimate reaction, except that on occasion one feels that the critic did not have a true change of heart, but only felt the need to think like his peers. Some clearly have judged it not from their own reading but from the reviews of others, or have abandoned it after only a few pages. Many have paid little attention while reading, misspelling names in reviews, making no attempt to understand what Tolkien is trying to convey, declaring that every character is either good or evil, that most of the characters never develop, or that everything ends happily – despite the theme of *loss that underlies the work. Others have complained that it has few female characters – though the story does not demand them, and their absence has not deterred female readers, who seem as numerous as male – or have objected to Sam's 'servile' attitude, or a lack of sex, or to perceived homosexual undertones in the relationship of Frodo and Sam.

Against these, Tolkien has had many defenders, notably Patrick Curry (*Defending Middle-earth: Tolkien, Myth and Modernity* (1997)) and T.A. Shippey. In his *J.R.R. Tolkien: Author of the Century* (2000) Shippey writes that 'the continuing appeal of Tolkien's fantasy' is not 'a mere freak of popular taste, to be dismissed or ignored by those sufficiently well-educated to know better'. It rests 'on a deeply serious response to . . . the major issues of his century: the origin and nature of evil . . . ; human existence in Middle-earth, without the support of divine Revelation; cultural relativity; and the corruptions and continuities of language' (p. ix). Charles Dickens was once thought an unsuitable author for those reading English at university: commercially popular, 'he had been downgraded from being "a novelist" to being "an entertainer". The opinion was reversed as critics developed broader interests and better tools' – but the same, Shippey argues, has not 'for the most part' occurred for Tolkien. 'Too many critics have defined "quality" in such a way as to exclude anything other what they have been taught to like. To use the modern jargon, they "privilege" their own assumptions and prejudices . . . against the reading choices of their fellow-men and fellow-women . . .' (p. xix). They refuse to allow Tolkien 'to be even a part of "English literature"', and 'while the hostility is open enough, the reasons for it often remain unexpressed, hints and sneers rather than statements. Many critics are very ready to express their anger, to call Tolkien childish and his readers retarded; they are less ready to explain or defend their judgements' (p. 305).

See further, entry for *Criticism. See also the accounts by sixteen writers inspired by Tolkien and *The Lord of the Rings* in *Meditations on Middle-earth*, ed. Karen Haber (2001).

FURTHER CRITICISM

Among all of Tolkien's works, *The Lord of the Rings* has been not only the most popular, but also the subject or main focus of the greatest number of books and essays. Their number is legion, and continually growing. Our list of 'Works Consulted' in *Reader's Companion* (pp. 815–29) includes many of the most useful resources for a study of *The Lord of the Rings*; we would refer readers also to the resources cited in the present book under *Bibliographies. Space does not permit us here even to begin to cite, with any degree of fairness, the many inspired writings on *The Lord of the Rings* that have appeared in academic and fan-produced journals, and more recently on the Internet. But among general books and collections concerned (at least in large part) with *The Lord of the Rings*, some of them now dated but still significant, the serious reader may wish to consult *Strategies of Fantasy* by Brian Attebery (1992); *The Lord of the Rings: The Mythology of Power* by Jane Chance (rev. edn. 2001); *J.R.R. Tolkien* by Katharyn W. Crabbe (rev. and expanded edn. 1988); *The Lord of the Rings, 1954–2004: Scholarship in Honor of Richard E. Black-welder*, ed. Wayne G. Hammond and Christina Scull (2006); *Tolkien and the Critics: Essays on J.R.R. Tolkien's The Lord of the Rings*, ed. Neil D. Isaacs and Rose A. Zimbardo (1968); *Tolkien: New Critical Perspectives*, ed. Isaacs and Zimbardo (1981); *Master of Middle-earth: The Fiction of J.R.R. Tolkien* by Paul H. Kocher (1972); *A Tolkien Compass*, ed. Jared Lobdell (first published 1975); *Tolkien: A Cultural Phenomenon* by Brian Rosebury (2003); *The Road to Middle-earth* by T.A. Shippey (first published 1982); and *J.R.R. Tolkien: Author of the Century* by T.A. Shippey (2000). See also works cited in the entry *Religion.

Other essential references are *A Tolkien Thesaurus* by Richard E. Black-welder (1990; rather, a concordance to *The Lord of the Rings*, useful though coverage is incomplete); *The Complete Guide to Middle-earth: From The Hobbit to The Silmarillion* by Robert Foster (2003); *The Atlas of Middle-earth* by Karen Wynn Fonstad (rev. edn. 1991); *The Lord of the Rings: A Reader's Companion* by Wayne G. Hammond and Christina Scull (2005); and *Journeys of Frodo: An Atlas of J.R.R. Tolkien's The Lord of the Rings* by Barbara Strachey (1981).

NOT A TRILOGY

Although sometimes called a 'trilogy', *The Lord of the Rings* in fact is a single work, often divided into three volumes for reasons of economics, marketing, or convenience. A *trilogy*, to quote *A Handbook to Literature* by William Flint Thrall and Addison Hibbard (rev. and enlarged by C. Hugh Holman, 1960), is 'a literary composition, more usually a novel or a play, written in three parts, *each of which is in itself a complete unit'* (p. 494, italics ours). A good example is the 'space (or cosmic) trilogy' by *C.S. Lewis. Each volume of *The Lord of the Rings*, in contrast, is not a complete unit in itself.

Among notes sent by Tolkien in June 1955 to the Houghton Mifflin Company, he wrote that *The Lord of the Rings* 'is *not* of course a "trilogy". That and the titles of the volumes was a fudge thought necessary for publication, owing to length and cost. There is no real division into three, nor is any one part intelligible alone. The story was conceived and written as a whole and the only natural divisions are the "books" I–VI (which originally had titles)' (*Letters*, p. 221). Occasionally, however, out of politeness Tolkien allowed the misuse of the word to stand.

Loss. As a boy and young adult, Tolkien was profoundly affected by loss, beginning with the death of his father when Tolkien was only four, and then his mother when he was not quite thirteen. Humphrey Carpenter speculates in *Biography* that the latter event led to a new side to Tolkien's personality, in which a naturally cheerful person was now capable of bouts of despair. 'More precisely . . . when he was in this mood he had a deep sense of impending loss. Nothing was safe. Nothing would last. No battle would be won for ever' (p. 31). This feeling was reinforced by the First World War in which close friends were killed, beyond the general horror of death, injury, and devastation. Even in England, of which he had happy memories of quiet countryside unspoiled by motor-cars and industry (or relatively so), change occurred noticeably, and in Tolkien's opinion not for the better (see further, *Environment). In his Foreword to the second edition of *The Lord of the Rings* (1965) he wrote: 'The country in which I lived in childhood was being shabbily destroyed before I was ten, in days when motor-cars were rare objects. . . . Recently I saw in a paper a picture of the last decrepitude of the once thriving corn-mill beside its pool that long ago seemed to me so important.'

In his professional life, meanwhile, Tolkien regretted the incalculable amounts of knowledge and literature that have been lost to time. Two works to which he devoted much attention, *Beowulf* and *Sir Gawain and the Green Knight*, for instance, survive each in only a single copy, their authors unknown, while many other works are known to have existed only from fragments or brief references. In an unpublished lecture, *The Goths*, Tolkien wrote: 'In vain we regret the past, or speculate on what might have been. Yet it is inevitable that we should regret. . . . In dealing with the Goths – regret cannot be avoided, if not regret for what might have been, at any rate regret for our altogether scanty records of what was . . . the vanishing of their tradition, literature, history, and most of their tongue.' In this he also deplored the Roman conquest, which led to 'the ruin of Gaul and the submergence of its native language (or languages) arts and traditions . . . dooming to obscurity and debate the history of perhaps the most remarkable of the Cymric speaking peoples' (Tolkien Papers, Bodleian Library, Oxford.)

Tolkien's *religion fostered his pessimism about events, but also gave him hope. He wrote to Amy Ronald on 15 December 1956: 'Actually I am a Christian, and indeed a Roman Catholic, so that I do not expect "history" to be anything but a "long defeat" – though it contains . . . some samples or glimpses of final victory' (*Letters*, p. 255).

Such feelings inevitably found their way into Tolkien's fiction. Loss and defeat pervade *'The Silmarillion' in all its versions. The conclusion to the published *Silmarillion* refers (using words which originally ended the last version of the *Valaquenta*) to it being the 'fate of Arda Marred' to pass 'from the high and the beautiful to darkness and ruin' (p. 255). Although Melkor/Morgoth is defeated at the last, his evil deeds leave their mark on the world. All are tragic, though not described by Tolkien to the same degree of significance. Melkor's overthrow of the Lamps, in which 'the shape of Arda and the symmetry of its waters and its lands were marred in that time, so that the first designs of the Valar were never after restored' (*The Silmarillion*, p. 37), is less affecting than the destruction of the Two Trees and their light, an act of which 'no song or tale could contain all the grief and terror that then befell' (p. 76).

> Varda looked down from Taniquetil, and beheld the Shadow soaring up in sudden towers of gloom; Valmar had foundered in a deep sea of night. Soon the Holy Mountain stood alone, a last island in a world that was drowned. All song ceased. There was silence in Valinor, and no sound could be heard, save only from afar there came on the wind through the pass of the mountains the wailing of the Teleri like the cold cry of gulls. For it blew chill from the East in that hour, and the vast shadows of the sea were rolled against the walls of the shore. [p. 77]

Loss upon loss occurs in *The Silmarillion*, too numerous to mention. The realms of Men and Elves are conquered, armies are slaughtered, families are broken by death and separation. And yet, as Anne C. Petty declares in *Tolkien in the Land of Heroes: Discovering the Human Spirit* (2003), 'the dilemmas of impermanence, mortality, loss, and longing are what gives Tolkien's world its heart and soul' (p. 179).

In Tolkien's mythology the First Age ends with the destruction of Beleriand and the departure of most of the Elves into the West. Near the end of the Second Age, the great island realm of *Númenor is destroyed. Most of the events of *The Lord of the Rings* take place at the end of the Third Age, a 'darkling and ominous' time (Foreword, 1st edn.) in which the shadow of Sauron threatens the whole of Middle-earth. Although Sauron is defeated and the Free Peoples saved from his domination, victory is not achieved without loss, and the ending is bittersweet rather than 'happy'. *The Lord of the Rings* ends in a minor key as most of the remaining Elves leave Middle-earth and the Age of Man begins, in which other evils will come. Tolkien wrote in a letter to *Milton Waldman that he did not finish *The Lord of the Rings* with the celebrations on the field of Cormallen because it was 'the function of the longish *coda* to show the *cost* of victory (as always)' (?late 1951, *Reader's Companion*, p. 748).

At the beginning of the story the Hobbits and the Shire seem safe and comfortable, but the elf Gildor points out to Frodo that 'others dwelt here before hobbits were; and others will dwell here again when hobbits are no more' (bk. I, ch. 3). The attentive reader will recall indications in the Prologue that the Hobbits have already declined: they were 'more numerous formerly than they are today'; they have 'dwindled' in height; and they now only 'linger' in the regions where they once lived.

On their southward journey the Company of the Ring pass through two former realms. Eregion, where the Noldor lived in the Second Age and made the Rings of Power, is now empty, but Legolas says: 'The Elves of this land were of a race strange to us of the silvan folk, and the trees and the grass do not now remember them. Only I hear the stones lament them: *deep they delved us, fair they wrought us, high they builded us; but they are gone. They are gone. They sought the Havens long ago*' (bk. II, ch. 3). Khazad-dûm, the once splendid kingdom of the Dwarves, is now dark, but Gimli says that its former glory is remembered in song. Where all now is dark once 'The light of sun and star and moon / In shining lamps of crystal hewn / Undimmed by cloud or shade of night / There shone for ever fair and bright' (bk. II, ch. 4).

Lothlórien, however, still survives and is inhabited. But even as the hobbits (and the reader) are enchanted by its beauty, they learn that it is unlikely to endure much longer. Haldir does not believe that the Shadow will draw back and peace return, nor 'that the world about us will ever again be as it was of old, or the light of the Sun as it was aforetime. For the Elves, I fear, it will prove at best a truce, in which they may pass to the Sea unhindered and leave the Middle-earth for ever. Alas for Lothlórien that I love! It would be a poor life in a land where no mallorn grew' (bk. II, ch. 6). Galadriel tells the Company of herself and Celeborn that 'ere the fall of Nargothrond or Gondolin I passed over the mountains, and together through ages of the world we have fought the long defeat'. She tells Frodo that 'the Love of the Elves for their land and their works is deeper than the deeps of Sea, and their regret is undying and cannot ever wholly be assuaged. Yet they will cast all away rather than submit to Sauron' (bk. II, ch. 7). Later, when she gives Sam his gift, she tells him that if he uses it well 'then you may remember Galadriel, and catch a glimpse far off of Lórien, that you have seen only in our winter. For our Spring and our Summer are gone by, and they will never be seen on earth again save in memory' (bk. II, ch. 8).

As they ride to Isengard Théoden says to Gandalf, who has told Théoden that he should be glad to know he has allies: 'Yet also I should be sad. . . . For however the fortune of war shall go, may it not so end that much that was fair and wonderful shall pass for ever out of Middle-earth?' Gandalf replies: 'It may. . . . The evil of Sauron cannot be wholly cured. nor made as if it had not been. But to such days we are doomed' (bk. III, ch. 8).

Matthew Dickerson comments in *Following Gandalf: Epic Battles and Moral Victory in The Lord of the Rings* (2003) that 'it is hard to read either *The Silmarillion* or *The Lord of the Rings* and not come away with a profound sense of sorrow and loss'. He cites Galadriel's words about fighting 'the long defeat' and Treebeard's words to Aragorn: 'Forests may grow. . . . Woods may spread. But not Ents. There are no Entings'; and to Celeborn and Galadriel: 'It is sad that we should meet only thus at the ending. For the world is changing. I feel it in the water, I feel it in the earth, and I smell it in the air. I do not think we shall meet again' (bk. VI, ch. 6). This, Dickerson continues,

> is a clear picture of loss: no Entwives; no Entings; no future. Tolkien leaves the reader with the knowledge that the Ents are doomed to disappear from Middle-earth, and with them something good and wonderful is forever lost. Likewise, we also learn from Celeborn that his own doom is to be parted from Galadriel, while Galadriel's doom is to see . . . the subsequent loss of all that she had worked for in Loth-lórien. . . . There is also the grievous parting of Arwen from Elrond her father. 'None saw her last meeting with Elrond her father, for they went up into the hills and there spoke long together, and bitter was there parting that should endure beyond the end of the world' (bk. VI, ch. 6). [pp. 212–13]

See also W.A. Senior, 'Loss Eternal in J.R.R. Tolkien's Middle-earth', *J.R.R. Tolkien and His Literary Resonances: Views of Middle-earth* (2000).

The Lost Road. Story, published with commentary and notes in *The Lost Road and Other Writings* (1987), pp. 36–98.

SUMMARY

Tolkien was inspired to write *The Lost Road* by a conversation with *C.S. Lewis, c. 1936. As he later recalled:

> L[ewis] said to me one day: 'Tollers, there is too little of what we really like in stories. I am afraid we shall have to try and write some ourselves.' We agreed that he should try 'space-travel', and I should try 'time-travel'. . . . My effort, after a few promising chapters, ran dry: it was too long a way round to what I really wanted to make, a new version of the Atlantis legend. The final scene survives as *The Downfall of Númenor*. [letter to Charlotte and Denis Plimmer, 8 February 1967, *Letters*, p. 378]

The legend of *Atlantis had haunted Tolkien since boyhood. 'This legend or myth or dim memory of some ancient history has always troubled me. In sleep I had the dreadful dream of the ineluctable wave, either coming out of the quiet sea, or coming in towering over the green inlands. It still occurs occasion-ally, though now exorcized by writing about it. It always ends by surrender, and I awake gasping out of deep water' (letter to Christopher Bretherton, 16 July 1964, *Letters*, p. 347). For a broader view of the development of Tolkien's

'Atlantis' legend, the story of Númenor, in his writings, including *The Lost Road*, see *Númenor. The importance of the Atlantis element in *The Lost Road* is shown by the fact that Tolkien wrote an outline of the history of Númenor, then a fuller narrative, the draft for *The Fall of Númenor*, before he wrote any of the time-travel framework.

The Lost Road was to comprise a series of episodes at different points in historical and legendary time. Its connecting thread, Tolkien wrote to Christopher Bretherton,

> was to be the occurrence time and again in human families . . . of a father and son called by names that could be interpreted as Bliss-friend and Elf-friend. These no longer understood are found in the end to refer to the Atlantid-Númenórean situation and mean 'one loyal to the Valar, content with the bliss and prosperity within the limits prescribed' and 'one loyal to friendship with the High-elves. It started with a father-son affinity between Edwin and Elwin of the present, and was supposed to go back into legendary time by way of an Eädwine and Ælfwine of circa A.D. 918, and Audoin and Alboin of Lombardic legend, and so to the traditions of the North Sea concerning the coming of corn and culture heroes, ancestors of kingly lines, in boats (and their departure in funeral ships). One such Sheaf, or Shield Sheafing, can actually be made out as one of the remote ancestors of the present Queen. In my tale we were to come at last to Amandil and Elendil leaders of the loyal party in Númenor, when it fell under the domination of Sauron. Elendil 'Elf-friend' was the founder of the Exiled kingdoms in Arnor and Gondor. [16 July 1964, *Letters*, p. 347]

In fact, none of the characters in *The Lost Road* are called *Edwin* or *Elwin*, but have other names with the meanings mentioned by Tolkien in his letter. Three generations of the Errol family appear in the first two chapters. The name *Errol* perhaps owes something to Eriol of *The Book of Lost Tales* (see *Eriol and Ælfwine), which would be appropriate since *Eriol* is defined as meaning 'one who dreams alone' (*The Book of Lost Tales, Part One*, p. 14), and the two members of the Errol family, Alboin and Audoin, certainly dream, and indeed dreaming is to be their method of time-travel. The first two chapters of *The Lost Road* before the time-travel begins are of particular interest, as each of the three Errols seems to have share something of Tolkien's special interests in language and myth.

The first chapter begins with a conversation between Oswin (*ós* 'god' + *wine* 'friend'), a widower, and his young son Alboin. Oswin tells his son stories of the Lombards and Gepids of early medieval history, and explains why he chose the name *Alboin* ('Elf-friend') for his son. Later that evening, as Alboin looks out of the window he sees dark clouds coming out of the West over the sea:

'They look like the eagles of the Lord of the West coming upon Númenor,' Alboin said aloud, and he wondered why. . . . In those days he often made up names. Looking on a familiar hill, he would see it suddenly standing in some other time or story. . . .

Some of these names were really made up, to please himself with their sound (or so he thought); but others seemed 'real', as if they had not been spoken first by him. So it was with *Númenor*. 'I like that,' he said to himself. 'I could think of a long story about the land of *Númenor*.' [p. 38]

He dreams in his sleep that night, but 'when he woke the dream slipped beyond recall, and left no tale or picture behind, only the feeling that these had brought: the sort of feeling Alboin connected with long strange names' (p. 39).

At school he learns Latin and Greek, but when he is about fifteen, like Tolkien, Alboin develops an interest in the older Northern languages: Old English, Norse, Welsh, Irish. He likes their flavour and

got to know a bit about linguistic history, of course . . . sound-changes were a hobby of his. . . . But, although he had some idea of what were supposed to be the relationships of European languages, it did not seem to him quite all the story. The languages he liked had a definite flavour – and to some extent a similar flavour which they shared. It seemed, too, in some way related to the atmosphere of the legends and myths told in the languages. [p. 39]

When he is nearly eighteen Alboin tells his father at length about his feeling for 'language-atmosphere' and the echoes of words that seem to come into his mind from two different, but related, languages, which he calls *Eressëan* or *Elf-Latin* and *Beleriandic*. Oswin warns him not to let such interests interfere with his need to win a scholarship if he is to go to university. After this conversation, Alboin's dreams cease.

The beginning of the second chapter gives a brief history of Alboin's undergraduate career. Apparently, like Tolkien, he wins a scholarship only at his second attempt, moves from Classics after 'Honour Mods' to a different school, and achieves a First in his final examinations – although Alboin changes to History, while Tolkien moved to the Language side of the *Oxford English School. Just before Alboin begins to take his final examinations, his dreams return and take a new direction. In a conversation not long before Oswin's death, he tells his father that he has not been hearing much Elf-Latin lately, but instead some old form of Germanic. He quotes a phase which he translates as 'a straight road lay westward, now it is bent' (p. 43).

The story then leaps forward many years. Alboin is now a professor (though, unlike Tolkien, 'only in a small southern university', p. 44) and is himself a widower with one son, Audoin, who shares many of his father's interests and is glad that his name is *Audoin*, not *Edwin*. Alboin is still hearing Eressëan and Beleriandic in his dreams, and has a growing longing *to go back.* To walk in Time, perhaps, as men walk on long roads; or to survey it, as men may see the world from a mountain, or the earth as a living map beneath an airship. But in any case to see with eyes and to hear with ears: to see the lie of old and even forgotten lands, to behold ancient men walking, and hear their languages as they spoke them, in the days before the days, when the tongues of forgotten lineage were heard in kingdoms long fallen by the shore of the Atlantic. [p. 45]

One night, Alboin dreams a whole passage in Eressëan, describing the downfall of Númenor, after which all roads were bent. The next night, he is restless and longs for a machine so that he could travel back in time. In his sleep Elendil of Númenor appears to him and offers him the chance to go into the past, but only under certain conditions: he cannot choose the halts or return at will, and he must take his son with him. Also he is warned that there may be danger. In the morning, Alboin is uncertain what to say to his son, who goes out for a lonely walk. That evening, still undecided, Alboin falls asleep again and finds himself making the choice to go back in time. Then follows a brief account of Audoin's thoughts during his walk. He also dreams, but sees pictures rather than hearing words: pictures of towers, of battles with swords, and – particularly ominous – of 'the great temple on the mountain, smoking like a volcano. And that awful vision of the chasm in the seas, a whole land slipping sideways, mountains rolling over; dark ships fleeing into the dark' (p. 52). On his return he finds his father asleep in his chair, and the adventure begins.

Tolkien wrote the Númenórean episode to follow immediately, but later decided that it should come last (as mentioned in his letter to Christopher Bretherton). It takes place in the final days of Númenor, when its king is under the influence of Sauron and has become hostile to the Elves and the Valar. He is preparing to invade Aman, hoping thereby to gain immortality, while those who oppose his wishes and remain faithful to tradition are persecuted and in danger. Tolkien's description of the political situation in Númenor, written *c.* 1936–7, seems to reflect then current events in Nazi Germany. We are given a rare glimpse of Númenor as Elendil, one of the leaders of the faithful, ponders the situation and discusses it with his son, Herendil, who is rather attracted by new ideas put forward by Sauron. During the discussion much is said of the history of Arda and of Númenor. Elendil tells his son that he must choose between his father and Sauron. Although the manuscript ends with Herendil choosing to stay and hear more, it is not clear how the episode was to continue. Notes made by Tolkien suggest that he was uncertain himself, and that possibly it was to end badly for both father and son. Christopher Tolkien thinks, however, that these notes may have preceded the extant chapters, and that Herendil's decision suggests a more hopeful outcome.

HISTORY

Some of Tolkien's earliest, very rough workings for *The Lost Road* survive, but do not form a continuous text. The manuscript which followed these workings was still fairly rough, and much emended. Tolkien submitted it to George Allen & Unwin (*Publishers) on 15 November 1937 for their consideration as one of several possible successors to *The Hobbit. Allen & Unwin had a typescript of the text made for easier reading, and returned the manuscript to Tolkien on 30 November. Later he was also sent the typescript, which breaks off at the beginning of the second Númenórean chapter. Christopher Tolkien thinks that this was because the rest of the chapter is very confusing, not because his father had not written any more. Tolkien later emended a few of the typist's errors. At some point later than the submission of the manuscript to Allen & Unwin, Tolkien re-wrote at greater length a section of the fourth chapter of *The Lost Road*, in which Elendil summarizes history in speaking to his son.

Some of Tolkien's early notes for *The Lost Road* include 'an English story of the man who got on the Straight Road', with an added note that 'this would do best of all for introduction to the Lost Tales'. Christopher Tolkien comments that this note shows his father 'combining the old story of the voyage of Ælfwine to Tol-eressëa and the telling of the *Lost Tales* with the idea of the World Made Round and the Straight Path, which entered at this time' (*The Lost Road and Other Writings*, p. 78). Other ideas included '"Lombard story?"; "a Norse story of ship burial (Vinland)"; "a Tuatha-de-Danaan story, or Tirnan-Og" . . . ; "a story concerning 'painted caves'"; "the Ice Age – great figures in ice", and "Before the Ice Age: the Galdor Story"; "post-Beleriand and the Elendil and Gil-galad story of the assault on Thû"; and finally "the Númenor story"' (pp. 77–8).

Tolkien's latest ideas for the intervening chapters, before Alboin and Audoin reach Númenor, are probably indicated by an outline which he submitted with the completed chapters to Allen & Unwin. 'Chapter III was to be called *A Step Backward: Ælfwine and Eadwine* – the Anglo-Saxon incarnation of the father and son, and incorporating the legend of King Sheave; Chapter IV "the Irish legend of Tuatha-de-Danaan – the oldest man in the world"; Chapter V "Prehistoric North: old kings found buried in the ice"; Chapter VI "Beleriand"; Chapter VIII (presumably a slip for VII) "Elendil and Herendil in Númenor"' (p. 78). Lombardic legend was no longer an ingredient.

Of these projected chapters, Tolkien wrote only an outline for, and part of, the story of Ælfwine and Eadwine set in tenth-century England, in the time when the king, Edward the Elder, was defending the south of the country against invading Danes. According to Tolkien's outline, the story was to open with the attack of the Danes on Porlock. Both Ælfwine and Eadwine are tired of war, and after a discussion of tales of men who sailed west, they were to set sail, find themselves on the Straight Road, and glimpse Eressëa before falling back into the real sea and returning to port. Tolkien wrote only a small part of this episode: Ælfwine, a minstrel who has been a great traveller, wakes suddenly in a hall where King Edward and many of his men are assembled. When he is called upon to sing for the king, he first chants a verse about his longing to journey over the sea, derived from the Old English poem *The Seafarer*. But this does not appeal to most of the men in the hall – and so the story ends. Christopher Tolkien is sure that Ælfwine would then have recited a long verse telling the story of King Sheave.

Tolkien began to write a rough draft of the (real world) legend of Sheaf in prose: how he arrived as a child in a boat with a sheaf of corn and the people made him their king; how he taught them much, so that the land and its people prospered greatly in a golden age; and how he became the forefather of many kings. But in old age Sheaf returned whence he came, laid on his bed in a ship surrounded by treasures, and was borne away into the West: some say that he found the Straight Road. Tolkien began to turn this draft into alliterative verse, changing or adding details, but left it unfinished, probably deciding to omit the account of Sheaf's departure. Christopher Tolkien discusses his father's references to the Sheaf legend and others in literature and history in the lectures he gave at Oxford, and quotes from them. He comments:

> With the entry at this time of the cardinal ideas of the Downfall of Númenor, the World Made Round, and the Straight Road, into the conception of 'Middle-earth', and the thought of a 'time-travel' story in which the very significant figure of the Anglo-Saxon Ælfwine would be both 'extended' into the future, into the twentieth century, and 'extended' also into a many-layered past, my father was envisaging a massive and explicit linking of his own legends with those of many other places and times: all concerned with the stories and the dreams of peoples who dwelt by the coasts of the great Western Sea. [p. 98]

In the Christmas vacation 1945 Tolkien began another time-travel story, *The Notion Club Papers*, in which he developed and re-used elements from *The Lost Road*, in particular the Anglo-Saxon episode with Ælfwine and the story of King Sheave.

The reader's report on *The Lost Road* for George Allen & Unwin, dated 17 December 1937, is signed 'SD', almost certainly for *Susan Dagnall. She said, on the basis of the fragment submitted, that the work seemed 'a hopeless proposition', but continued: 'It is immensely interesting as a revelation of the personal enthusiasms of a very unusual mind, and there are passages of beautiful descriptive prose.' After briefly summarizing the contents (which makes it clear that Tolkien had already decided to place the Númenórean episode last), Dagnall said that 'it is difficult to imagine this novel when completed receiving any sort of recognition except in academic circles. It is almost certain that the best part of the book, certainly the finest writing, – would come in the middle and later chapters. Perhaps the whole should be seen, but one could not hold out to the author a promise of popular success or large sales as an inducement to finish it' (Tolkien-George Allen & Unwin Archive, HarperCollins, partly quoted in *The Lost Road and Other Writings*, p. 97, where Christopher Tolkien calls it 'perceptive').

The Lost Road also contains four poems which are part of the actual text: *Thus Cwæth Ælfwine Wídlást* in Old English (p. 44, where it is also translated; see also *The Notion Club Papers*, p. 224, in **Sauron Defeated*); *Ilu Ilúvatar en Káre Eldain a Fírimoin* in Eressëan or Quenya (mentioned and partially quoted on pp. 62–3, and given in full with translation and comment on pp. 71–2); *Monað Modes Lust mid Mereflode* in Old English (derived from the Old English *Seafarer*, p. 84 with translation; see also *The Notion Club Papers*, pp. 243–4 in *Sauron Defeated*); and *King Sheave* in alliterative verse (pp. 85–91; but see also *The Notion Club Papers*, pp. 273–6 in *Sauron Defeated*, where Tolkien again uses *King Sheave*, and Christopher Tolkien in note 103, pp. 294–5, revises what he wrote in *The Lost Road and Other Writings*, pp. 86–7).

CRITICISM

By the time *The Lost Road and Other Writings* was published, little attention was being paid to **The History of Middle-earth* except in specialist magazines. The volume was reviewed in the *Times Literary Supplement*, 23–9 December 1988, by Stephen Medcalf, who wrote of *The Lost Road*:

> The four opening chapters which are all that was ever completed . . . have an urgency which Tolkien's detractors at any rate would not expect. They are made both haunting and poignant by the presence in them of two earnest feelings: Tolkien's special longing for a road into the lost world which was hidden, he believed, in the history of language, and any father's anxiety about his relationship with his children.

He comments that when the story moves to Númenor, there is no escapism, but 'an intelligent frontal attack on the diseases – religious, epistemological and political – of the twentieth century' ('The Anxious Longing', p. 1414).

David Bratman writes in 'The Literary Value of *The History of Middle-earth*', *Tolkien's Legendarium: Essays in The History of Middle-earth* (2000), concerning both *The Lost Road* and *The Notion Club Papers*: 'Here we have something not otherwise found in Tolkien's fiction – stories with an explicitly modern setting, which displays the author's own aesthetic reactions to language. . . . Not even in his essay **A Secret Vice* did Tolkien so vividly convey what the imagination of language meant to him' (p. 81).

In *A Question of Time: J.R.R. Tolkien's Road to* Faërie (1997) Verlyn Flieger writes that *The Lost Road* 'marked the clear introduction into Tolkien's work of the idea of time as a road between the worlds of past and present, of everyday and Faërie, of waking and dream. It also conveyed the vision of the lost paradise and the longing to return to it that is embryonic in some of his earliest efforts and that became a more and more powerful element in his later fiction.'

Although he abandoned the story, 'the ideas remained and found their way into much that came after. . . . These ideas and their treatment in his work were the outward expression of a developing inner concern, a philosophical and psychological exploration of the relationship between the exterior, so-called "real" world and time and the interior, illimitable, but no less real time and space of the imagining, remembering, dreaming mind' (p. 19). In Chapter 3, 'Strange Powers of the Mind', she discusses *The Lost Road* at length, including its relation to Tolkien himself and to the theories of time by J.W. Dunne.

See also John D. Rateliff, '*The Lost Road, The Dark Tower,* and *The Notion Club Papers*: Tolkien and Lewis's Time Travel Triad', *Tolkien's Legendarium: Essays on The History of Middle-earth* (2000).

The Lost Road and Other Writings. The fifth volume of **The History of Middle-earth*, edited with notes and commentary by *Christopher Tolkien, first published in Great Britain by George Allen & Unwin, London, in August 1987, and in the United States by the Houghton Mifflin Company, Boston, in November 1987. See further, *Descriptive Bibliography* A25.

In Christopher Tolkien's words, *The Lost Road and Other Writings* 'completes the presentation and analysis of my father's writings on the subject of the First Age up to the time at the end of 1937 and the beginning of 1938 when he set them for long aside. The book provides all the evidence known to me for the understanding of his conceptions in many essential matters at the time when **The Lord of the Rings* was begun' (p. 1). The volume contains a variety of works from the 1930s:

*The Fall of Númenor: the original outline and two versions in which Tolkien worked out the history of Númenor as background to the Númenórean chapters in *The Lost Road*.

*The Lost Road: Tolkien's unfinished time-travel story, and notes for unwritten parts. Included as an integral part of the story are four poems: *Thus Cwæth Ælfwine Wídlást, Monað Modes Lust mid Mereflode, Ilu Ilúvatar en Káre Eldain a Fírimoin,* and *King Sheave*. Also included is an earlier poem, **The Nameless Land*, which seems to anticipate some elements of the work. In discussing the unwritten or partly written chapters Christopher Tolkien quotes from his father's unpublished prose translation of **Beowulf* (pp. 92–3) and unpublished lectures on Sheave and *Beowulf* (pp. 93–6).

The 'later' **Annals of Valinor*.
The 'later' **Annals of Beleriand*.
*Ainulindalë.
*The Lhammas: two versions, and the shorter *Lammasethen*.
*Quenta Silmarillion: the text prior to *The Lord of the Rings*.
*The Etymologies.
'The Genealogies' (see **Annals of Beleriand*).
A 'List of Names' (see **Annals of Beleriand*).
The second 'Silmarillion' Map (see **'The Silmarillion'*).

Lyme Regis (Dorset). A fishing port and bathing resort town on the south coast of England, with steep streets and a curving stone pier known as the Cobb, Lyme Regis was popular already in the nineteenth century when it featured in Jane Austen's novel *Persuasion*. *Father Francis Morgan took his wards, Ronald and *Hilary Tolkien, there for summer holidays. The hotel in which they stayed, the Three Cups in Broad Street, once one of best in Lyme Regis, is now disused.

During these holidays Tolkien liked to hunt for fossils in the cliffs along the shore (still subject to landslips). He later said, in a lecture on dragons, that he 'once as a boy found a saurian jaw myself with nasty teeth at Lyme Regis – and thought I had stumbled on a bit of petrified dragon' (delivered at the University Museum, Oxford, 1 January 1938; Tolkien Papers, Bodleian Library, Oxford). In August 1906 he made a drawing, *Lyme Regis Harbour from the Drawing Room Window of the Cups Hotel* (*Artist and Illustrator*, fig. 8). On one of his visits he painted views of the cliffs, including one looking east towards Golden Cap (*Artist and Illustrator*, fig. 6, location identified by the late William A.S. Serjeant).

Tolkien returned to Lyme Regis with his family in September 1927 and at the end of July and beginning of August 1928. During the first of these visits he again made several drawings and paintings: these include two related to his mythology, *Mithrim* and *Glorund Sets Forth to Seek Túrin*, a watercolour miniature of a coiled dragon, and at least three drawings for *Roverandom* (*Artist and Illustrator*, figs. 46–47, 48, and 73–75 respectively). The latter suggest that Tolkien was inspired on this occasion to retell the story of 'Roverandom' he had conceived in *Filey two years earlier. For the 1928 holiday the Tolkiens were joined by Father Francis Morgan, whom *John Tolkien recalled 'producing a pile of marshmallows on top of an ant-hill as if by magic' (*The Tolkien Family Album*, p. 61, with photographs). Tolkien made at least three topographical pictures on this occasion – *View from Mr Wallis' Broad Street, Lyme*; *Tumble Hill near Lyme Regis* (*Artist and Illustrator*, figs. 26–27); and a sketch of roofs and chimneys – as well as several fine illustrations for his mythology, including *Halls of Manwë on the Mountains of the World above Faerie* and *Taur-na-Fúin* (*Artist and Illustrator*, figs. 52, 54).

Tolkien visited Lyme Regis again later, at an undetermined date, apparently while on a walking tour with *C.S. Lewis. On 24 April 1957 he wrote to his grandson, Michael George, that 'the last really long walk I did (years ago) was from Lyme Regis to **Minehead**, largely cross-country. Not in one day!' (British Library MS Add. 71657).

McCallum, Ronald Buchanan (1898–1973). As a student at Worcester College, *Oxford, R.B. McCallum read Modern History; he received his B.A. in 1922. After a brief period as a lecturer in History at the University of Glasgow, he was elected a Fellow and tutor in History at Pembroke College, Oxford: he arrived there in 1925, when Tolkien also became associated with Pembroke as Rawlinson and Bosworth Professor of Anglo-Saxon. He served in most offices in the College; from 1955 to 1967 he was Master of Pembroke. From 1967 to 1971 he was Principal of St Catharine's, Cumberland Lodge, Windsor Great Park, and also played a role in the creation of Nuffield College, Oxford. His writings include *Asquith* (1936) and *England and France, 1939–1943* (1944); and he was twice editor of the *Oxford Magazine*.

McCallum was introduced by Tolkien to the *Inklings. According to Humphrey Carpenter, McCallum's 'manner was too formally "donnish" to make him an entirely congenial member of the group. Indeed McCallum was among those who to some extent invited themselves to be Inklings, rather than waiting for the invitation' (*The Inklings*, p. 186). Although he never became part of the 'inner ring' of the group, his company was generally welcomed by the other members. He is first mentioned in the diary of *W.H. Lewis in 1948. He was unable to attend many of the Thursday evening sessions of the Inklings, but was often present when members met Tuesdays at the Eagle and Child pub (*Oxford and environs).

See further, David Bratman, 'R.B. McCallum: The Master Inkling', *Mythlore* 23, no. 3, whole no. 89 (Summer 2001).

MacDonald, George (1824–1905). Writer and poet, educated at King's College, Aberdeen, and Highbury Theological College. From 1845 he lived mainly in England, but also spent time in Italy for the sake of his health. Among his circle of friends and acquaintances were many of the notable figures of the day, including Lewis Carroll, John Ruskin, and Edward Burne-Jones. The author of a series of contemporary novels set mainly in his native Scotland (and sometimes including a great deal of Scots dialect), today MacDonald is best remembered for his two fantasy novels for adults, *Phantastes* (1858) and *Lilith* (1895), and for the stories he wrote for children – he himself was the father of eleven. His children's books *At the Back of the North Wind* (1871), *The Princess and the Goblin* (1872), and its sequel *The Princess and Curdie* (1883) are recognized as classics, as are some of his shorter tales including 'The Golden Key', 'The Light Princess', 'Little Daylight', and 'The History of Photogen and Nycteris' (sometimes called 'The Day Boy and the Night Girl').

MacDonald for a time was a Congregationalist minister, and introduced a moral overtone into many of his works. In his writing for children he often adopted the kind of narrator's voice that Tolkien used in *The Hobbit* and later regretted. But children and even adults often do not notice, or are not put off by, these faults (if they are faults), as they are swept away by the breadth of MacDonald's imagination and the haunting mythical and symbolic elements that are a major element in his writing. *C.S. Lewis wrote that his own imagination 'was in a sense baptized' after reading *Phantastes* (*Surprised by Joy*, ch. 11). In a rejected beginning to his Andrew Lang Lecture, *On Fairy-Stories*, Tolkien wrote: 'For me at any rate fairy-stories are especially associated with Scotland ... by reason of the names of *Andrew Lang and George MacDonald. To them in different ways I owe the books which most affected the background of my imagination since childhood' (Tolkien Papers, Bodleian Library, Oxford).

In notes for *On Fairy-Stories*, Tolkien says that he introduced his own children to works he himself liked, such as *The Princess and the Goblin*. That work, and *The Princess and Curdie*, are set in an imaginary kingdom and feature goblins which Tolkien acknowledged as an influence on those in *The Hobbit*. In reply to a letter from 'Habit' in *The Observer* of 16 January 1938, asking about sources of *The Hobbit*, Tolkien wrote that fairy-story had been one influence, 'not, however, Victorian in authorship, as a rule to which George Macdonald [*sic*] is the chief exception' (*Letters*, p. 31). In a letter to *Naomi Mitchison on 25 April 1954 he supposed that his orcs owe 'a good deal to the goblin tradition (*goblin* is used as a translation in *The Hobbit* . . .), especially as it appears in George MacDonald, except for the soft feet [i.e. in *The Princess and the Goblin* Curdie stamps on goblins' feet, their only vulnerable part] which I never believed in' (*Letters*, p. 178). He wrote in a draft for *On Fairy-Stories*, delivered in 1939, that 'George MacDonald, in that mixture of German and Scottish flavours (which makes him so inevitably attractive to myself) has depicted what will always be to me the classic goblin. By that standard I judge all goblins, old or new' (Tolkien Papers, Bodleian Library, Oxford).

MacDonald describes his goblins as having been human originally, but become misshapen and grown in cunning and mischief. Unlike the goblins in *The Hobbit* ('*Clap! Snap! the black crack! / Grip, grab! Pinch, nab! / And down down to Goblin-town / You go, my lad!*' etc., ch. 4) they do not sing, and indeed cannot bear to hear others singing, especially the doggerel songs Curdie sings in *The Princess and the Goblin* to annoy and repel them. These bear a resemblance to the songs sung by Tolkien's goblins as they carry their captives to their chief. When Curdie is held prisoner by the goblins (ch. 21) he sings: '*Jabber, bother, smash! / You'll have it all in a crash. / Jabber, smash, bother! / You'll have the worst of the pother / Smash, bother, jabber!*'

MacDonald's *At the Back of the North Wind* contains a poem, 'The True History of the Cat and the Fiddle', which seems to prefigure Tolkien's own rewritings of nursery rhymes, *The Man in the Moon Stayed Up too Late* and *The Man in the Moon Came Down Too Soon*, and the short tale 'Little Daylight', elements of which resemble Beren's first sight of Lúthien Tinúviel (*'Of Beren and Lúthien*'). In the latter, a prince who has been driven out of his country comes upon an enchanted princess in a neighbouring land. 'All at once he spied something in the middle of the grass . . . a girl dressed in white, gleaming in the moonshine. . . . He crept behind a tree and watched, wondering. . . . All at once she began singing like a nightingale, and dancing to her own music. . . .' After resting, 'again she began dancing to her own music, and danced away into the distance' (*At the Back of the North Wind* (Dent edn. 1956), pp. 227–8).

Tolkien presumably read, or read again, MacDonald's works in 1934 when he was an examiner of the B.Litt. thesis of Mary M. McEldowney, *The Fairy Tales and Fantasies of George MacDonald*. Later, while writing *On Fairy-Stories* for delivery at St Andrews, he wrote a memo: 'get out B.Litt. on Macdonald [*sic*]', i.e. refer to McEldowney's thesis (Tolkien Papers, Bodleian Library,

Oxford). Some of the ideas Tolkien put forward in *On Fairy-Stories* recall some advanced by MacDonald in 'The Fantastic Imagination', first published in 1893. MacDonald pointed out that because there is no English word corresponding to German *Märchen*, we are driven 'to use the word *Fairytale*, regardless of the fact that the tale may have nothing to do with any sort of fairy' (*Fantasists on Fantasy: A Collection of Critical Reflections*, ed. Robert H. Boyer and Kenneth J. Zahorski (1984), p. 14; compare *Tree and Leaf*, p. 14). He also wrote:

> The natural world has its laws, and no man must interfere with them in the way of presentment and more than in the way of use; but they themselves may suggest laws of other kinds, and man may, if he pleases, invent a little world of his own, with its own laws . . . – which is the nearest, perhaps, he can come to creation. . . .
>
> His world once invented, the highest law that comes next into play is, that there shall be harmony between the laws by which the new world has begun to exist; and in the process of his creation, the inventor must hold by those laws. The moment he forgets one of them, he makes the story, by its own postulates, incredible. To be able to live a moment in an imagined world, we must see the laws of its existence obeyed. Those broken, we fall out of it. The imagination in us, whose exercise is essential to the most temporary submission to the imagination of another, immediately, with the disappearance of Law, ceases to act. . . . A man's inventions may be stupid or clever, but if he do not hold by the laws of them, or if he make one law jar with another, he contradicts himself as an inventor, he is no artist. [p. 15–16; compare *Tree and Leaf*, pp. 36–7, 46]

Frank Bergman in 'The Roots of Tolkien's Tree: The Influence of George MacDonald and German Romanticism upon Tolkien's Essay "On Fairy-Stories"', *Mosaic* 10, no. 2 (Winter 1977), thinks that MacDonald praised Friedrich de la Motte Fouqué's *Undine* above all fairy tales because, as

> the story of the soul, *Undine* is the story of man's fallibility and God's justice and forgiveness. It is the story of 'good death' that marks MacDonald's fantasy work and leads Tolkien to observe in 'On Fairy-Stories' that 'Death is the theme that most inspired George MacDonald.' Tolkien derives from MacDonald – and MacDonald's German sources – the insight that the richest fairy tales do not end with the perpetuation of the hero's presumably carefree *terrestrial* life ('and they lived happily ever after'). [p. 11; cf. *Tree and Leaf*, p. 62]

Apart from general influence, Tolkien mentions specific works by MacDonald several times both in the published *On Fairy-Stories* and in his drafts and notes. He refers to MacDonald's use in 'The Giant's Heart' of the traditional folk-lore motif that 'the life or strength of a man or creature may reside in some other place or thing; or in some part of the body (especially the heart) that can be detached and hidden in a bag, or under a stone, or in an egg' (*Tree and Leaf*, p. 20). Also, in his description of the three faces of fairy-stories, 'the Mystical towards the Supernatural; the Magical towards Nature; and the Mirror of scorn and pity towards Man', he notes that

> the essential face of Faërie is the middle one, the Magical. But the degree in which the others appear (if at all) is variable. . . . The Magical, the fairy-story, may be used as a *Mirour de l'Omme*; and it may (but not so easily) be made a vehicle of Mystery. This at least is what George Mac-Donald attempted, achieving stories of power and beauty when he succeeded, as in *The Golden Key* (which he called a fairy-tale); and even when he partly failed, as in *Lilith* (which he called a romance). [p. 28]

A rough note made while preparing the lecture, referring to 'The Golden Key', seems to read: 'a gem – of the kind *constructed* with consc[ious] alleg[ory] but well done that it remains true. This is due to Macdonald's [*sic*] background. (He often fails as [in the] Second part of Curdie.)' On other pages he wrote: 'And beside *The Princess and the Goblin*, and *The Princess and Curdie*, and other things he wrote shorter fairy-stories, some with a tone (not at all for their good) of addressing children, some whatever their tone, not at all for children (like Photogen & Nycteus) and one (I think) nearly perfect tale (in his kind and style) which is not for children though children do read it with pleasure: *The Golden Key*.' Also: 'Death is the theme that most inspired George Mac-Donald whether in fairy stories such as the Princess and Curdie, or the Golden Key; or in what he called the "romance of Lilith"' (Tolkien Papers, Bodleian Library, Oxford).

In a letter written to Mrs L.M. Cutts on 26 October 1958 Tolkien commented on the Ents in *The Lord of the Rings* as an expression of his love of trees, 'with perhaps some remote influence from George MacDonald's *Phantastes*', even though Tolkien did not much like that work (quoted in Sotheby's, *English Literature, History, Fine Bindings, Private Press Books, Children's Books, Illustrated Books and Drawings*, London, 10 July 2003, p. 297). In *Phantastes* the Ash, the Beech, and the Alder take human form.

In 1964, when asked by Pantheon Books to write a preface to a new edition of 'The Golden Key', Tolkien agreed, commenting in his reply on 7 September: 'I am not as warm an admirer of George MacDonald as C.S. Lewis was; but I do think well of this story . . .' (letter to Michael di Capua, *Letters*, p. 351). But when he re-read 'The Golden Key', and other works by MacDonald, he found that 'a highly selective memory had retained only a few impressions of things that moved me, and re-reading G[eorge] M[acDonald] critically filled me with distaste. I had, of course, never thought of ['The Golden Key'] as a story for children (though apparently G. McD did)' (Tolkien Papers, Bodleian Library, Oxford). See further, *Smith of Wootton Major*.

Clyde S. Kilby recalled that during his visits with Tolkien in 1966 the latter 'was making frequent wholesale attacks on [MacDonald]. He called

him an "old grandmother" who preached instead of writing. He thought
MacDonald would have done better to retain his native dialect in some of
his writings. He did not like the way in which MacDonald wrote of trees etc.'
(*Tolkien and the Silmarillion* (1976), p. 31). It may be that Tolkien no longer felt
the same about some of MacDonald's stories because he now noticed far more
clearly than as a child, or even in the 1930s, their didactical and moral bent,
and the strong voice of the narrator which he criticized also in his own earlier
writings.

See further, William Raeper, *George MacDonald* (1987).

McFarlane, Kenneth Bruce (1903–1966). Bruce McFarlane read History at
Exeter College, *Oxford; he received his B.A. in 1925. In 1927 he was elected
a Fellow by Examination at Magdalen College, and around this time also
was associated with the Kolbítar (*Societies and clubs), the informal group
founded by Tolkien who met to read and discuss the Icelandic sagas and the
Eddas. In 1928 McFarlane became, and remained, an Official Fellow and tutor
at Magdalen. Near the end of his life he was also appointed University Reader
in Medieval History. His writings include *John Wycliffe and the Beginnings of
English Non-conformity* (1953) and the Raleigh Lecture *The Wars of the Roses*
(1964). His collected essays, *England in the Fifteenth Century*, were published
posthumously in 1981.

The Machine *see* **Environment**

Madlener, Josef (1881–1967). The German artist Josef Madlener studied in
Munich at the Kunstgewerberschule and the Akademie der Bildenden Künste.
After working for some years as an illustrator for newspapers and magazines,
he turned to painting, especially rural scenes from his native Amendingen
and pictures with religious themes. He is notable in connection with Tolkien
by virtue of a colour postcard reproduction of his painting *Der Berggeist*
('The Mountain Spirit'), numbered 'A 4102', found among Tolkien's effects
wrapped in a paper inscribed by him at some later date: 'Origin of Gandalf'.
In an unpublished late manuscript (Tolkien Papers, Bodleian Library, Oxford)
Tolkien said that his 'personal vision' of Gandalf 'was largely derived' from

> a picture postcard acquired years ago – probably in Switzerland. It is one
> of a series of six taken from the work of a German artist J. Madelener
> [*sic*], called *Gestalten aus Märchen und Sage* ['Figures from Story and
> Legend']. Alas! I only got one called *Der Berggeist*. On a rock under a
> pinetree [*sic*] is seated a small but broad old man with a wide-brimmed
> round hat and a long cloak talking to a white fawn that is nuzzling his
> upturned hands. He has a humorous but also compassionate expression
> – his mouth is visible and smiling because he has a white beards but no
> hair on his upper lip. The scene is a woodland glade (pine, fir, and birch)
> beside a rivulet with a glimpse of rocky mountain-towers in the distance.

An owl and four other smaller birds are looking on from the branches of the trees. The Berggeist has a green hat, and a scarlet cloak, blue stockings and light shoes. I altered the colours of hat and cloak to suit Gandalf, a wanderer in the wild, but I have no doubt that when at ease in a house he wore light blue stockings and shoes.

Humphrey Carpenter described this postcard in *Biography*, misspelling the artist's name, and stated as fact that Tolkien bought the postcard during his visit to Switzerland in 1911. But when Manfred Zimmermann contacted the artist's daughter, he learned that the picture was not painted before 1925–6, and that 'a postcard version of *Der Berggeist* was published in the late twenties by Ackermann Verlag München, in a folder with three or four similar pictures with motifs drawn from German mythology . . .' ('The Origin of Gandalf and Josef Madlener', *Mythlore* 23, no. 4, whole no. 34 (Winter 1983), pp. 22). As Zimmermann points out, this later dating suggests that the postcard came into Tolkien's hands at about the time he began to write **The Hobbit*.

The postcard is reproduced in colour in *The Annotated Hobbit* (rev. and expanded edn. 2002). The original painting of *Der Berggeist*, long thought to be lost, was sold at Sotheby's, London on 12 July 2005; the auction catalogue, *English Literature, History, Children's Books and Illustrations*, contains a full-page reproduction of the painting in colour.

See further, Eduard Raps, *Josef Madlener 1881 bis 1967* (1981).

'Of Maeglin'. The sixteenth chapter of the *'Quenta Silmarillion', published in **The Silmarillion* (1977), pp. 131–9.

SUMMARY

Aredhel Ar-Feiniel, daughter of Fingolfin, wearies of life in the hidden city of Gondolin and seeks permission to leave from her brother Turgon. He gives it unwillingly, and on condition that she join their brother Fingon, in Hithlum to the west. But she disobeys and, seeking her cousins Celegorm and Curufin in the East, becomes separated from her escort. Her cousins are absent when she arrives and, after a while, she grows restless and often rides out alone. On one occasion she enters the wood of Nan Elmoth, and by enchantments is led to the dwelling of the Dark Elf Eöl, an able smith who has learned much from the Dwarves. Eöl makes Aredhel his wife, not entirely against her will. They have a son, Maeglin, who is more like his Noldor kindred in appearance, but 'in mood and mind' (*The Silmarillion*, p. 144) like his father. Like Eöl he learns much from the Dwarves, especially the craft of finding metals. He loves to hear his mother's stories of her kin, and as she tells him of Gondolin she begins to desire to return there herself. Maeglin is especially interested in the fact that Turgon of Gondolin has no heir, except for a daughter, Idril.

Eöl is unwilling for his wife or son to have any contact with the Noldor, and forbids his son to speak with the sons of Fëanor as he wishes to do. One midsummer, while Eöl is absent, on Maeglin's suggestion he and his mother ride to Gondolin. Eöl returns sooner than they had expected, and follows them, thinking that they have gone to visit Curufin and Celegorm. After meeting these brothers, and exchanging words with them, he realizes that Aredhel and Maeglin are making for Gondolin. Following, he sees the secret way they take to reach the hidden city. Aredhel and Maeglin are allowed to pass through the Seven Gates to Gondolin and are welcomed by Turgon. Maeglin is immediately attracted to Idril.

As Eöl tries to enter the city he is captured and brought before the king. Eöl is welcome in Gondolin but according to law can never leave; indeed for Eöl and Maeglin the only choices are to stay in Gondolin or to die. Crying 'the second choice I take and for my son also! You shall not hold what is mine!' (p. 138) Eöl hurls a javelin at Maeglin, but Aredhel leaps in front of her son and is killed instead. Sentenced to be cast down from the walls of the city, Eöl says to Maeglin that as he has failed his father, so may his own hopes fail and he die the same death.

Maeglin becomes great in Gondolin and in high favour with Turgon, and fights fearlessly in the Nirnaeth Arnoediad. Yet his love for Idril is an inward grief, for as kin they are too close to wed, and she mistrusts him and thinks his love for her 'strange and crooked' (p. 139).

HISTORY

Only the slightest foreshadowings of this story appear in *The Book of Lost Tales* (c. 1916–20). In the tale *The Fall of Gondolin* Meglin (spelled thus) is 'nephew to the king by his mother the king's sister Isfin; and that tale of Isfin and Eöl may not here be told' (*The Book of Lost Tales, Part Two*, p. 165). Meglin, whose sign is a sable mole and who is less attractive than most of the Elves of Gondolin, seeks Idril's hand, but as she is unwilling, Turgon denies the suit. There is no suggestion that Meglin and Idril are too closely related for marriage. Tolkien wrote an outline for a story of Isfin, but it says no more than that Isfin was 'loved from afar by Eöl of the Mole-kin of the Gnomes. He is strong and in favour with [her father] and with the sons of Fëanor (to whom he is akin) because he is leader of the Miners and searches after hidden jewels, but he is illfavoured and Isfin loathes him' (*The Book of Lost Tales, Part Two*, p. 220). *Christopher Tolkien thinks that this outline, elements of which resemble the story of Meglin and Idril, may be even earlier than the writing of *The Fall of Gondolin*.

In *The Lay of the Fall of Gondolin* (?early 1920s) Isfin, daughter of Fingolfin, wanders astray with her mother in the dark woods of Doriath, seeking Fingolfin. Eöl, the Dark Elf, captures Isfin and makes her his unwilling wife. Later she sends her son Meglin to Gondolin where he wins lordship, but 'little was his mirth and dark he was and secret' (*The Lays of Beleriand*, p. 146). The story becomes clearer in the *Sketch of the Mythology* (c. 1926): there Isfin, sister of Turgon, is lost in Taur-na-Fuin after the Battle of Unnumbered Tears and trapped by the Dark Elf Eöl. She later sends their son Meglin to Gondolin where he is accepted 'although half of Ilkorin blood, and treated as a prince' (*The Shaping of Middle-earth*, p. 35). The story advances in the *Quenta Noldorinwa* (c. 1930) with Isfin taking advantage of Eöl being lost in Taur-na-Fuin to escape and travel with her son to Gondolin, where Meglin again is treated like a prince. He is described as 'swart but comely, wise and eloquent, and cunning to win men's hearts and minds' (*The Shaping of Middle-earth*, p. 141).

The 'earliest' *Annals of Beleriand* (early 1930s) provided a chronological framework for events and advanced the story. In Year 171 Isfin, sister of Turgon, 'strays out of Gondolin and is taken to wife by Eöl a Dark-elf' (*The Shaping of Middle-earth*, p. 301), but Tolkien reverts to the earlier story when in Year 192 Meglin goes alone to Gondolin. In the 'later' *Annals of Beleriand* (mid-1930s) there is no change in the story, but as a result of Tolkien lengthening the extent of the Siege of Angband Isfin strays from Gondolin in Year 271 > 471, and Meglin is sent to Gondolin in 292 > 492.

Tolkien did not reach this part of the mythology in the unfinished *Quenta Silmarillion* begun in the mid-1930s, and his work on that text c. 1951 was confined to emending or rewriting chapters already written. In the *Grey Annals* (see *Annals of Beleriand*), c. 1951, as first written Isfin still leaves Gondolin in 471 'against the will and counsel of Turgon' (*The War of the Jewels*, p. 47) because she is weary of the city and wants to see her other brother, Fingon, again. She strays and is found by Eöl. In 492 she sends her son to Gondolin. Also in 1951 Tolkien wrote the story of Isfin and Meglin at length (twelve sides of manuscript), apparently (according to a later note) not for inclusion in the *Quenta Silmarillion* but as part of a projected long retelling of the Fall of Gondolin.

In late 1951 or 1952 Tolkien emended the *Grey Annals*, incorporating the most significant developments in the twelve-page manuscript. He replaced the annal for 471 with one dated 316 in which Isfin is not lost but deliberately disobeys Turgon, and instead of going to Fingon seeks out Celegorm and his brethren, but becomes parted from her escort and is found by Eöl. A new annal notes the birth of Maeglin in 320. The annal for 492 is replaced by one for 400 which records briefly the flight of Isfin and Maeglin to Gondolin and subsequent events as told in *The Silmarillion*.

An amanuensis typescript was made from the manuscript c. 1970 with the title *Of Maeglin: Sister-son of Turgon, King of Gondolin*. Tolkien then used this typescript as a basis for further emendation. The basic story remained much the same, except that details were added (especially of the routes and timings of various journeys) and some names were changed (e.g. *Meglin* to *Maeglin*, and *Isfin* variously to *Areðel, Aredhel, Rodwen, Feiniel, Ar-Feiniel*).

Christopher Tolkien derived the chapter 'Of Maeglin' in *The Silmarillion* from the manuscript of 1951 or 1952 and the later typescript with its emendations, but omitted material which seemed too detailed or out of place. See further, the chapter 'Maeglin' in *The War of the Jewels*, pp. 316–39.

Of Maeglin: Sister-son of Turgon, King of Gondolin. The first account to any degree of the story of Isfin (Aredhel), Eöl, and their son Meglin (Maeglin), to a large extent used by *Christopher Tolkien for the chapter *'Of Maeglin' in *The Silmarillion (1977). An account of the writing of this work was published in **The War of the Jewels* (1994) in the chapter 'Maeglin', pp. 316–39, but not the work itself. Instead Christopher Tolkien, using 'Of Maeglin' as a reference, concentrated on variations from the published text and on late additions to the original text which include 'notable features that of their nature could have no place' in *The Silmarillion* (p. 317). Among the latter are names and name changes, rejected sketches of Eöl's history in which he had been a captive of Morgoth, and a detailed discussion of the motives behind the actions of Celegorm and Curufin (printed in full in *The War of the Jewels*, pp. 327–9). Christopher Tolkien also describes associated writings concerned with geography and times and distances of journeys, and related photocopies of parts of the second 'Silmarillion' map on which his father made new entries to record emerging topographical details. He quotes suitable extracts from this 'complicated and confused' matter, and reproduces a redrawn version of the relevant part of the emended map.

Tolkien wrote the original text, a twelve-page manuscript, in 1951, and subsequently emended it. The title *Of Meglin* was added later, at length changed to *Of Isfin and Glindûr*. From this, possibly as late as 1970, an amanuensis typescript and carbon copy were made, taking up the emendations and bearing the title *Of Maeglin: Sister-son of Turgon, King of Gondolin*. Tolkien emended both the ribbon and carbon copies, but in different ways, and into the ribbon copy added further manuscript material, some of it written on publisher's notices dated 19 January 1970. He also wrote on the ribbon copy: 'An enlarged version of the coming of Maeglin to Gondolin, to be inserted in [*The Fall of Gondolin*] in its place' (p. 317). Christopher Tolkien assumes that this note refers to the abandoned *Of Tuor and the Fall of Gondolin* (**Of Tuor and His Coming to Gondolin* in *Unfinished Tales (1980)), and that the typescript was made to serve as a basis for further substantial work on the story.

Christopher Tolkien comments that

> this development of the story of Maeglin from the form in which he had written it twenty years before seems to have been the last concentrated work that my father did on the actual narratives of the Elder days. Why he should have turned to this legend in particular I do not know; but one sees in his minute consideration of the possibilities of the story, from the motives of the actors to the detail of the terrain, of roads, of the speed and endurance of riders, how the focus of his vision of the old tales had changed. [p. 337]

Magic. In the first paragraph of *On Fairy-Stories as published in *Essays Presented to Charles Williams* (1947) Tolkien says that as an Englishman being asked to talk about fairy-stories in Scotland (i.e. in giving the Andrew Lang

Lecture at the University of St Andrews), he feels 'like a conjurer who finds himself, by some mistake, called upon to give a display of magic before the court of an elf-king' (p. 39). *Conjuring*, that is, is only the appearance of magic, produced by trickery, in contrast to the 'real' magic associated with elves, fairies, and the like, and with the 'Perilous Realm' (Faërie) in which they live. Faërie indeed 'may perhaps most nearly be translated by Magic – but it is magic of a peculiar mood and power, at the furthest pole from the vulgar devices of the laborious, scientific, magician' (*Tree and Leaf*, p. 15). The virtue of such magic

> is in its operations: among these are the satisfaction of certain primordial human desires. One of these desires is to survey the depths of space and time. Another is . . . to hold communion with other living beings. A story may thus deal with the satisfaction of these desires, with or without the operation of either machine or magic, and in proportion as it succeeds it will approach the quality and have the flavour of fairy-story. [p. 17]

Later in the essay, however, Tolkien decides that *magic* should not be used to indicate the 'elvish craft' of making, within a story, a 'Secondary World' commanding 'Secondary Belief' (see *Sub-creation).

> Magic should be reserved for the operations of the Magician. Art is the human process that produces by the way (it is not its only or ultimate object) Secondary Belief. Art of the same sort, if more skilled and effort-less, the elves can also use . . . but the more potent and specially elvish craft I will . . . call Enchantment. Enchantment produces a Secondary World into which both designer and spectator can enter, to the satis-faction of their senses while they are inside; but in its purity it is artistic in desire and purpose. Magic produces, or pretends to produce, an alter-ation in the Primary World. It does not matter by whom it is said to be practised, fay or mortal, it remains distinct from the other two; it is not an art but a technique; its desire is *power* in this world, domination of things and wills. [pp. 49–50]

Fantasy, Tolkien says, is a human art which aspires to the Elvish craft of Enchantment, but 'which (however much it may outwardly resemble it) is inwardly wholly different from the greed for self-centred power which is the mark of the mere Magician'. The creative desire, if uncorrupted, 'does not seek delusion, nor bewitchment and domination; it seeks shared enrichment, part-ners in making and delight, not slaves' (p. 50).

In a letter to his son *Christopher on 7 July 1944 Tolkien wrote of the 'tragedy and despair' of machinery, which 'unlike art which is content to create a new secondary world in the mind . . . attempts to actualize desire, and so create power in this World . . .' (*Letters*, p. 87; cf. *Environment, *Power). Later, in a letter to *Milton Waldman, he wrote of the desire for Power, for making the will more quickly effective, – and so to the Machine (or Magic). By the last I intend all use of external plans or devices (apparatus) instead of the development of the inherent inner powers or talents – or even the use of these talents with the corrupted motive of dominating: bulldozing the real world or coercing other wills. The Machine is our more obvious modern form though more closely related to Magic than is usually recognised. [?late 1951, *Letters*, pp. 145–6]

This relationship between 'machines' and magic was already evident in his fiction. In stories for his children Tolkien introduced several simple magic objects of the type common to fairy tales, without much, if any, discussion of their moral use. Farmer Giles's sword, Caudimordax (Tailbiter), for instance, 'will not stay sheathed, if a dragon is within five miles' (*Farmer Giles of Ham*, p. 34) and 'did the best it could' (p. 44) to fight Chrysophylax, even in Giles's inexperienced hands; and in *The Hobbit* are 'the magic diamond studs that fastened themselves and never came undone until ordered' and the talking purse that Bilbo steals from the trolls (*The Hobbit*, Chapters 1, 2).

When *The Hobbit* was written Bilbo's ring was not much different: its power of conferring invisibility served only to enhance the ability of the small, and not very powerful, hobbit to deal with difficult situations. Even so, it did offer opportunities for misuse: even Bilbo recognized this, and gave a necklace from Smaug's treasure to the Elvenking as a return for the food and wine he had consumed while living invisible in the king's halls. But when the Ring became the link between *The Hobbit* and its sequel, *The Lord of the Rings*, and both entered the world of *'The Silmarillion'*, it became, as Bradley J. Birzer comments in his *J.R.R. Tolkien's Sanctifying Myth: Understanding Middle-earth* (2002), 'the ultimate symbol of magic and the machine . . . into which Sauron poured much of his spirit and will. He made it to dominate the other rings of power. . . . Indeed the sole purpose of the One Ring is to re-order the world in Sauron's image, to mock, to corrupt, and to pervert Ilúvatar's creation' (p. 104).

Tolkien told Milton Waldman that one of the functions of the Elves in his tales was to demonstrate their 'magic', which is 'Art, delivered from many of its human limitations: more effortless, more quick, more complete (product, and vision in unflawed correspondence). And its object is Art not Power, sub-creation not domination and tyrannous reforming of Creation.' Galadriel, in responding to Sam's remark in *The Lord of the Rings* that he would like to see some Elf-magic, felt it necessary to point out that Hobbits seemed to use the same word, *magic*, 'both for the devices and operations of the Enemy, and for those of the Elves' (*Letters*, p. 146).

Tolkien returned to the point in a draft letter to Naomi Mitchison in September 1954. There he calls upon an old distinction between *magia* (charms, spells) and *goeteia* (cheatery; cf. obsolete English *goety* 'witchcraft or magic performed by the invocation and employment of evil spirits; necromancy' (*Oxford English Dictionary*)).

I do not intend to involve myself in any debate whether 'magic' in any sense is real or really possible in the world. But I suppose that, for the purposes of the tale [*The Lord of the Rings*], some would say that there is a latent distinction such as once was called the distinction between *magia* and *goeteia*. . . . *Magia* could be, was, held good (per se), and *goeteia* bad. Neither is, in this tale, good or bad (per se), but only by motive or purpose or use. Both sides use both, but with different motives. The supremely bad motive is (for this tale, since it is specially about it) domination of other 'free' wills. The Enemy's operations are by no means all goetic deceits, but 'magic' that produces real effects in the physical world. But his *magia* he uses to bulldoze both people and things, and his *goeteia* to terrify and subjugate. Their *magia* the Elves and Gandalf use (sparingly): a *magia* producing real results (like fire in a wet faggot) for specific beneficent purposes. Their goetic effects are entirely *artistic* and not intended to deceive: they never deceive Elves (but may deceive or bewilder unaware Men) since the difference is to them as clear as the difference to us between fiction, painting, and sculpture, and 'life'.

Both sides live mainly by 'ordinary' means. The Enemy, or those who have become like him, go in for 'machinery' – with destructive and evil effects – because 'magicians', who have become chiefly concerned to use *magia* for their own power, would do so (do do so). The basic motive for *magia* . . . is immediacy: speed, reduction of labour, and reduction also to a minimum (or vanishing point) of the gap between the idea or desire and the result or effect. But the *magia* may not be easy to come by, and at any rate if you have command of abundant slave-labour or machinery (often only the same thing concealed), it may be as quick or quick enough to push mountains over, wreck forests, or build pyramids by such means. [*Letters*, pp. 199–200]

Malvern (Worcestershire). This name is given to a group of seven villages beneath the Malvern Hills, many with medicinal springs. The chief among them, **Great Malvern**, is the home of Malvern College, a public school at which *C.S. Lewis was a pupil during 1913–14. Maureen, the daughter of Lewis's friend Mrs Moore, married Leonard Blake, Director of Music at Malvern College from 1945, and one of Lewis's pupils, *George Sayer, was Senior English Master at Malvern from 1949 to 1974.

In August 1947 Lewis and his brother *Warren exchanged houses with Maureen and Leonard Blake so that she could be with her mother in Oxford. Tolkien accompanied the Lewises for part of their stay in Malvern, arriving by train with them on 5 August 1947. The Blakes' house was at no. 4, The Lees. Between then and the morning of 9 August Tolkien joined the Lewises in cross-country walks and visiting pubs: the Camp, the Wych, the Foley, the County, and the Unicorn. W.H. Lewis complained in his diary that Tolkien preferred to stroll rather than walk; 'however, we managed two good days with him, including one to the top of the Camp [the British Camp, said to have been defended by Caractacus against the Romans in 75 A.D., on the Herefordshire Beacon or Camp Hill, 1114 feet high], where I was more than ever impressed with the beauty of the northward view.' At 'the old cab rank in Pring Rd.' Tolkien christened its 'mysterious and ornate little green and silver doors' as 'Sackville-Baggins's' (*Brothers and Friends*, pp. 207–8).

Tolkien again stayed in Malvern for a few days in late August 1952, in the home of George Sayer and his wife Moira. The Sayers had read in typescript *The Lord of the Rings* which Tolkien had lent to them; now, with George Sayer's encouragement, Tolkien recited extracts from *The Lord of the Rings*, as well as Chapter 5 of *The Hobbit*, into a tape recorder, after reciting the Lord's Prayer in Gothic to 'exorcise' any devils in the machinery. 'It was easy to entertain [Tolkien] by day,' Sayer recalled.

> He and I tramped the Malvern Hills which he had often seen during his boyhood in Birmingham or from his brother's house [*Hilary Tolkien] on the other side of the Severn River valley. He lived the book [*The Lord of the Rings*] as we walked, sometimes comparing parts of the hills with, for instance, the White Mountains of Gondor. We drove to the Black Mountains on the borders of Wales, picked bilberries and climbed through the heather there. . . . When he saw signs of industrial pollution he talked of orcs and orcery. [liner notes accompanying the issue of Tolkien's tape recordings by Caedmon Records (1975); see *Recordings]

The Man in the Moon Came Down Too Soon. Poem, first published in *The Adventures of Tom Bombadil and Other Verses from the Red Book* (1962), pp. 34–8. The Man in the Moon, tired and lonely in his pale home of white and grey and silver, comes to Earth on 'a mad adventure'. He yearns for the rich colours and life of the world. But he arrives in the middle of the night, when the town is asleep and 'Only the knell of one slow bell / high in the Seaward Tower / announced the news of his moonsick cruise / at that unseemly hour'. For food he finds only 'porridge cold and two days old' bought from a surly cook.

The poem was derived, in the first instance, from a nursery rhyme well known (with variations) by the nineteenth century:

> The man in the moon
> Came down too soon,
> And asked his way to Norwich;
> He went by the south,
> And burnt his mouth
> With supping cold plum porridge.

This is reflected more clearly in earlier versions of Tolkien's poem, one of which was published in the *Leeds English School collection *A Northern Venture* (1923), pp. 17–19, and another in *The Book of Lost Tales, Part One*

(1983), pp. 204–6, both as *Why the Man in the Moon Came Down Too Soon*. The work was originally written on 10–11 March 1915 as *Why the Man in the Moon Came Down Too Soon (An East Anglian Phantasy)*. Later its subtitle was omitted and the words *A Faërie* added before the title proper. In the 1923 version, among many differences, the Man takes 'a foamy bath / In the Ocean of Almain' and is picked up by 'a Yarmouth boat' and taken to 'Norwich town'; whereas in the version of 1962 he is found by 'a fisherman's boat' in 'the windy Bay of Bel' and carried simply 'back to land'. Tolkien revised the poem for the *Adventures of Tom Bombadil* collection to fit within the context of *The Lord of the Rings: thus it is said to be 'derived ultimately from Gondor . . . based on the traditions of Men, living in shore-lands and familiar with rivers running into the Sea. [The poem] actually mentions *Belfalas* (the windy bay of Bel), and the Sea-ward Tower, *Tirith Aear*, of Dol Amroth' (preface to *The Adventures of Tom Bombadil and Other Verses from the Red Book*, 1962 edn., p. 8).

Four lines from the first (1915) manuscript of *Why the Man in the Moon Came Down Too Soon* are also found in *The Book of Ishness* (*Art), opposite an illustration by Tolkien of the Man in the Moon sliding towards the earth on a thread of 'spidery hair' (*Artist and Illustrator*, fig. 45).

Tolkien recorded *The Man in the Moon Came Down Too Soon* in 1967 for the album *Poems and Songs of Middle Earth* (1967, reissued in 2001 as part of *The J.R.R. Tolkien Audio Collection*); see *Recordings.

Thomas Honegger in his 'The Man in the Moon: Structural Depth in Tolkien', *Root and Branch: Approaches towards Understanding Tolkien* (1999), suggests that there are parallels also between Tolkien's poem and one published in 1839–40 by an 'Undergraduate of Worcester College, London; and of the Inner Temple, London'. In the latter the Man in the Moon was similarly tired 'Of living so long in the land of dreams; / 'Twas a beautiful sphere, but nevertheless, / Its lunar life was passionless.' He too arrives on earth like 'a falling star' (cf. Tolkien's 'like a meteor') and makes his way to a sleeping city. But whereas Tolkien's Man in the Moon retains his folk tradition attributes, the character in the 1839–40 verses is depicted as an angel in search of love 'in an imperfect, sinful and fallen [mortal] world' (Honegger, p. 37).

The Man in the Moon appears in several of Tolkien's works, conceived in different ways. In *The Tale of the Sun and Moon* in *The Book of Lost Tales* he is an aged Elf who stows away on the vessel of the moon when it is placed in the sky, and there he dwells in a white turret. In *The Man in the Moon Came Down Too Soon* he lives in a 'minaret / Of tall moonstone that towered alone / on a lunar mountain set'. The Man in the Moon in *Roverandom similarly remarks (p. 40) on the lack of 'real colour' in his home. See also *The Man in the Moon Stayed Up Too Late.

Comments on the structure and vocabulary of the poem are included in Part 2 of 'The Use of Language in Tolkien's Poetry' by Nancy Martsch, in *Beyond Bree* for April 2004.

The Man in the Moon Stayed Up Too Late. Poem, first published without a title as Frodo's song in the Prancing Pony in *The Lord of the Rings*, Book I, Chapter 9 (1954), reprinted with the stated title in *The Adventures of Tom Bombadil and Other Verses from the Red Book* (1962), pp. 31–3. In 'a merry old inn . . . they brew a beer so brown' that one night the Man in the Moon comes down to drink it. He drinks so much that he falls asleep, and only with the help of the ostler (stableman) and the landlord is he returned to the Moon before dawn. The ostler's 'tipsy cat' meanwhile plays a fiddle, exciting the landlord's dog 'that is mighty fond of jokes' and a 'hornéd cow' whose head is turned by music. As the cat plays ever more quickly, 'the dog began to roar, / The cow and the horses stood on their heads; / The guests all bounded from their beds / and danced upon the floor'. The cow at last jumps over the moon, 'the little dog laughed to see such fun', and 'the Saturday dish went off at a run / with the silver Sunday spoon'.

An earlier version was published in *Yorkshire Poetry* (Leeds) 2, no. 19 (October–November 1923), pp. 1–3, as *The Cat and the Fiddle: A Nursery-Rhyme Undone and Its Scandalous Secret Unlocked*; a still earlier text, with a few minor differences relative to that in *Yorkshire Poetry*, was published in *The Return of the Shadow* (1988), pp. 145–7. The earliest extant version is a manuscript probably written in the period 1919–20, entitled *Nursery Rhymes Undone*.

The poem is obviously indebted to the nursery rhyme 'Hey Diddle Diddle'. But George Burke Johnston in his essay 'The Poetry of J.R.R. Tolkien', *Mankato State University Studies* 2, no. 2 (February 1967), suggests that Tolkien was inspired also by a similar poem by *George MacDonald in *At the Back of the North Wind* (1870, ch. 24), 'The True History of the Cat and the Fiddle', in which the nursery rhymes 'Hey Diddle Diddle' and 'The Man in the Moon Came Down Too Soon' (cf. entry for Tolkien's poem of that name, above) are combined. See also Paul Nolan Hyde, 'Mythos: The Daughter of Mountains, the Mother of Pearls', *Mythlore* 16, no. 1, whole no. 59 (Autumn 1989).

Tolkien may have had *The Man in the Moon Stayed Up Too Late* in mind when he wrote his 'Father Christmas' letter (*The 'Father Christmas' letters) for December 1927 in which the Man in the Moon visits the North Pole and falls asleep after drinking too much brandy. In his absence dragons on the moon cause an eclipse with their smoke, and the Man hurries back only just in time to set things right.

MS. Bodley 34: A Re-Collation of a Collation. Article, written in collaboration with *S.R.T.O. d'Ardenne, published in *Studia Neophilologica* (Uppsala) 20, nos. 1–2 (1947–8), pp. 65–72. Tolkien and d'Ardenne respond to an article by Ragnar Furuskog, 'A Collation of the *Katherine Group* (MS. Bodley 34)' (*Studia Neophilologica* 19, nos. 1–2 (1947), pp. 119–66), noting its inaccuracies 'partly due to insufficient acquaintance with the work and habits of this particular scribe. Mr. Furuskog appears, moreover, to have relied on photostats only, and these are not for such meticulous work a satisfactory substitute for the manuscript: they appear to have misled him on several points' (p. 66).

Masefield, John Edward (1878–1967). John Masefield went to sea at age fourteen, and for several years trained and apprenticed in sailing ships; but at seventeen, impressed by the poetry of *Geoffrey Chaucer, he developed a passion for writing which proved his true calling. He contributed to various periodicals and newspapers, and in 1907 began work on the *Manchester Guardian*. By then he was already an established poet, his *Salt-Water Ballads* having appeared in 1902. His reputation was confirmed by later works such as *The Everlasting Mercy* (1911) and *The Widow in the Bye Street* (1912). His *Collected Poems* were published in 1923. In 1930 he was named Poet Laureate, succeeding Robert Bridges. He also wrote fiction, including *Sard Harker* (1924) and two popular works for children, *The Midnight Folk* (1927) and *The Box of Delights* (1935). His *Gallipoli* (1916) and *The Old Front Line* (1917, on the battleground of the Somme) are evocative accounts of events in the First World War, though produced for the British War Propaganda Bureau.

In the 1920s Masefield gave a series of recitations in Oxford. Tolkien heard at least one of these, in which Masefield performed Chaucer's 'Monk's Tale' from the *Canterbury Tales* using 'a modified modern pronunciation' (Tolkien, letter to Masefield, 27 July 1938, *Letters*, p. 40). Following on from these, in summers from 1923 until 1929 there were competitions in Oxford to encourage 'the beautiful speaking of poetry'; then in the 1930s the competitive element was abandoned and the annual event became a festival, the 'Summer Diversions' organized by Masefield and *Nevill Coghill. For the August 1938 'Diversions' Masefield invited Tolkien to read Chaucer's 'Nun's Priest's Tale' pronounced in a supposed fourteenth-century manner; Masefield himself introduced Tolkien, and also read from his own *Letter from Pontus* (1936), which Tolkien enjoyed hearing. In July 1939 Masefield invited Tolkien to perform once again: on this occasion Tolkien read a reduced version of the *'Reeve's Tale'. Masefield felt that 'Tolkien knows more about Chaucer than any living man: and sometimes tells the [Canterbury] Tales superbly, inimitably, just as though he were Chaucer returned' (*Letters to Reyna* (1983), p. 72).

On 9 January 1965 Tolkien wrote to his son *Michael that if he wanted 'a perfect specimen of bad verse ... I could [not] find you a better than poor old John Masefield's 8 lines on [T.S.] Eliot in *The Times* of Friday Jan. 8: "East Coker". Almost down/up to Wordsworth's zero-standard' (*Letters*, p. 353).

'*Matar* and *Tulir*'. Table of forms of the Qenya (*Languages, Invented) verbs *mat-* 'eat' and *tul-* 'bring, come', published with commentary and notes within 'Early Qenya Fragments' in *Parma Eldalamberon* 14 (2003), pp. 23–4, ed. Patrick Wynne and Christopher Gilson. The editors believe that this table predates or is contemporary with *The Qenya Verb Forms*.

Mathew, Anthony Gervase (1905–1976). Father Gervase Mathew was an expert on English medieval history and a distinguished authority on Byzantine art. Having joined the Dominican Order in 1928, at which time he took the name Gervase, he was ordained a priest in 1934 and spent practically all of his life at Blackfriars, the Oxford Dominican house of studies. He lectured regularly at *Oxford in the faculties of Modern History, Theology, and English. He recalled that 'for nine years my lectures for the English faculty were coordinated with' those of *C.S. Lewis, 'and, when he went to Cambridge, he arranged that I should take on his course "Prolegomena to Medieval Literature"' ('Orator' in *C.S. Lewis at the Breakfast Table and Other Reminiscences* (new edn. 1992), p. 97). From 1947 to 1971 Father Mathew was University Lecturer in Byzantine Studies, and took part in archaeological surveys in Africa and the Middle East. His writings include *The Reformation and the Contemplative Life*, in collaboration with his brother, Archbishop David Mathew (1934); *Byzantine Painting* (1950); *Byzantine Aesthetics* (1963); *The Court of Richard II* (1968); and 'Marriage and *Amour Courtois* in Late Fourteenth-Century England' in *Essays Presented to Charles Williams* (1947).

Desirous to be 'in touch with spheres of influence', as Humphrey Carpenter reports, Father Mathew sought out the *Inklings and virtually elected himself a member, 'not that he was unwelcome' (*The Inklings*, p. 186, for this and subsequent quotations). He began to attend Inklings meetings around 1939 (according to Father Mathew, via Walter Hooper; he is not mentioned as present at an Inklings gathering in the diaries of *W.H. Lewis until 1946). He 'smoked a continual succession of cigarettes in a nicotine-stained holder and talked in a kind of breathless mutter, speaking at such speed that even Tolkien, until then the champion among the Inklings for haste and inaudibility, was left far behind.' Tolkien wrote of him:

> The Rev. Mathew (Gervase)
> Made inaudible surveys
> Of little-read sages
> In the dark Middle Ages.

Father Mathew took pleasure in assisting his friends. In Tolkien's case, he suggested to his friend and fellow Catholic, *Milton Waldman of the publisher Collins, that he should read the then-unpublished *Lord of the Rings*.

Melkor Morgoth. Brief work, published with notes and commentary as text VI in the section 'Myths Transformed' of *Morgoth's Ring* (1993), pp. 390–4.

Here Tolkien introduces new ideas on the comparative powers and motivations of Melkor and Manwë. 'Melkor must be made *far more powerful* in original nature. . . . The greatest power under Eru (sc. the greatest created power). (He was to make / devise / begin; Manwë (a little less great) was to improve, carry out, complete.)' (p. 390). The Valar undertake a war against Melkor's stronghold Utumno with little hope of victory, 'but rather as a covering action to get the Quendi [Elves] out of his sphere of influence' (p. 390). But he has already begun to disperse some of his personal force into his agents, and when Manwë and Melkor come face to face, both realize that Manwë now has the greater 'personal force'. Melkor considers and rejects repentance, but feigns it, first to avoid being chained, then with the idea of penetrating and ruining Valinor. Manwë does not see through the wish Melkor expresses to help to repair 'all the evils and hurts he has done' (p. 392).

The text was written on four slips of paper, probably at the end of the 1950s, after the *Athrabeth Finrod ah Andreth existed in some form. It is entitled *Melkor*, with *Morgoth* written beneath, thus *Melkor Morgoth* as given in *Morgoth's Ring*.

'Of Men'. The twelfth chapter of the *'Quenta Silmarillion', published in *The Silmarillion* (1977), pp. 103–5.

SUMMARY

The Valar sit in peace in Valinor; in Middle-earth only the Noldor oppose Morgoth. From this time date the Years of the Sun, in which 'the air of Middle-earth became heavy with the breath of growth and mortality, and the changing and ageing of all things was hastened exceedingly; life teemed upon the soil and in the waters of the Second Spring of Arda, and the Eldar increased, and beneath the new Sun Beleriand grew green and fair' (*The Silmarillion*, p. 103). Men wake when the Sun first rises in the West. The Elves call them by many names, often deriving from the different abilities and fates of Men; and 'of Men little is told' in *The Silmarillion*, 'save of those fathers of men, the Atanatári' (p. 103). No Vala comes to guide Men when they wake, but Ulmo speaks to them through his waters, though they do not understand his messages. They move west and come into contact with the Dark Elves, from whom they learn much, and eventually with the returning Noldor. In their early years the lands are safer, for Morgoth has not long returned from Valinor, and the spread of his power has been halted by the light of the Sun. But 'now the time drew on to the great wars of the powers of the North, when Noldor and Sindar and Men strove against the hosts of Morgoth Bauglir, and went down in ruin' (p. 104). To this end the lies of Morgoth, the curse resulting from the Kinslaying, and the oath of Fëanor and his sons were ever at work.

Elves and Men are said to be of like stature and strength, but the Elves, especially those who have lived in Valinor, have greater wisdom, skill, and beauty. The Elves are immortal, and Men are mortal; only Mandos and Manwë know where their spirits go after death. In later years Elves and Men became estranged, and the Elves who remained in Middle-earth became shadows and memories while Men took their place. But in the early years described in *The Silmarillion* some Men became great among the Noldor, and from alliances between the two races came the Half-elven.

HISTORY

There is no equivalent account of Men in *The Book of Lost Tales* (c. 1916–20). The unfinished *Gilfanon's Tale: The Travail of the Noldoli and the Coming of*

Mankind, however, includes an account of the Dark Elf Nuin, who comes upon Men before they wake, and hurries to inform the wizard-king Tû (or Túvo). Outlines show that Nuin was to wake two of the sleepers and teach them speech, and that they alone of Men were to see the first rising of the Sun. But some Men are corrupted by agents of Melko in the beginning of days, while others become allies of the Elves. Although most of this story did not appear again in 'The Silmarillion', the conception that some Men are faithful and others treacherous persisted. Various references indicate that Elves who stayed in the Great Lands (Middle-earth) after the events told in the tales would 'fade and grow small and tenuous, filmy and transparent' (*The Book of Lost Tales, Part Two*, p. 283).

The *Sketch of the Mythology* (*c.* 1926) already contained (with some variations of detail and omissions) much of the material and even some phrasing of the latter part of the *Silmarillion* chapter (see *The Shaping of Middle-earth*, p. 21). An addition to the *Quenta Noldorinwa* (*c.* 1930) reintroduces an idea of Elves who stayed in Middle-earth 'fading'. The various annals of the 1930s say little. The *Quenta Silmarillion* of the mid-1930s adds much of the first part of the *Silmarillion* text to that already existing, and gives the whole the title 'Of Men'. The names Men were called by the Elves appears there as a footnote. Refinements to the latter part move the text closer to the published version.

When Tolkien revised the *Quenta Silmarillion c.* 1951 he made few changes to this chapter. The *Grey Annals* (also *c.* 1951, see *Annals of Beleriand*) record for Year 1 the awakening of Men, and the speeding of time under the Sun. The entry for Year 60 notes that Morgoth soon hears of the awakening of Men, and leaves Angband to see for himself. It also hints at a fall, that 'a darkness lay upon the hearts of Men' (*The War of the Jewels*, p. 37), and at the schemes of Morgoth to corrupt Men or use them against the Elves. An entry for the period 60–445 records early contacts between Men and Dark Elves, and the repentance of some Men. Not all of this was taken up into the *Silmarillion* chapter.

Most of the chapter 'Of Men' in *The Silmarillion* was taken by *Christopher Tolkien from the *Quenta Silmarillion* manuscript of the 1930s as emended *c.* 1951, omitting a passage dealing more extensively with the immortal nature of the Elves. For the earlier part of the chapter, some short sections derive from the *Grey Annals*.

When Tolkien considered changing his cosmology in his later writings, it was no longer possible for Men to awake with the first rising of the Sun. Tolkien then experimented with the idea that Morgoth 'darkens the world' with great clouds, and that there are great floods, and 'Men awake in an Isle amid the floods and therefore welcome the Sun which seems to come out of the East' (*Morgoth's Ring*, pp. 377–8). But this conception does not appear in *The Silmarillion*.

The Mewlips. Poem, first published in *The Adventures of Tom Bombadil and Other Verses from the Red Book* (1962), pp. 45–6. The 'Mewlips', whatever they may be, dwell in darkness and damp cellars 'over the Merlock Mountains a long and weary way, / In a mouldy valley where the trees are grey', and apparently feed upon hapless visitors.

Although *The Mewlips* is said in the *Tom Bombadil* collection to have come from the Hobbits' Red Book of Westmarch, originally it had no connection with Middle-earth. Tolkien based it on an earlier, similar poem, *Knocking at the Door*, subtitled 'Lines Induced by Sensations When Waiting for an Answer at the Door of an Exalted Academic Person', which he wrote possibly in 1927 and published as by 'Oxymore' in the *Oxford Magazine* 55, no. 13 (18 February 1937), p. 403. *Knocking at the Door* seems to be a comment on the trepidation of a student calling on a professor; transformed into *The Mewlips* and divorced from its original meaning, it is a work purely of mood and imagination.

Tolkien recorded *The Mewlips* in 1967 for the album *Poems and Songs of Middle Earth* (1967, reissued in 2001 as part of *The J.R.R. Tolkien Audio Collection*); see *Recordings.

Middle English 'Losenger'. Essay, published in *Essais de philologie moderne (1951)* (Paris: Société d'édition 'Les belles lettres', 1953), pp. 63–76. See further, *Descriptive Bibliography* B20.

In November 1950 Tolkien attended the first of two conferences in Liège (*Belgium) to mark the sixtieth anniversary of the Departments of Germanic and Romance Philology at the University of Liège: the Congrès du LXe anniversaire des sections de Philologie romane et de Philologie germanique. On that occasion he delivered an address (in English) explaining the syllabus and aims of the Oxford English School. For the second conference, held in September 1951, Tolkien chose to present a 'sketch of an etymological and semantic enquiry' into the Middle English word (of French origin) *losenger* because 'a fresh scrutiny of its etymology may afford a glimpse (if no more) into the complexities of the contacts of Germanic and Latin in Northern Gaul' (p. [63]).

He had first encountered the word in Chaucer's *Legend of Good Women*, with 'that dubious character the *losengeour*' (p. 64). 'Who and what was he? What was his function or mischief in the Court of Love? A *flatterer* as the editors and glossaries say . . . , or a *slanderer*, a *backbiter*, a *liar*, as the context in this Chaucerian passage . . . seems rather to require?' (p. 65). Tolkien traces the word into Old French, with reference also to Old English, Old Saxon, Old Frisian, Gothic, and Old Norse. In doing so he may have drawn upon research shared by his Belgian colleague *S.R.T.O. d'Ardenne, who in 1946 sent him a draft article on the word *losenge*.

A Middle English Vocabulary. Tolkien's first book and first academic publication, a glossary designed for use with the collection *Fourteenth Century Verse & Prose*, ed. *Kenneth Sisam. It was first published as a separate volume by the Clarendon Press, Oxford, in May 1922. In June 1922 it was first published, also by the Clarendon Press, together in one volume with the texts edited by Sisam. See further, *Descriptive Bibliography* A1 and B3.

HISTORY

Fourteenth Century Verse & Prose, a volume of specimens of Middle English texts, began as a joint effort between Kenneth Sisam and Professor *A.S. Napier of the Oxford English School. It was intended to be 'for the use of language students . . . with an apparatus strictly linguistic', as Sisam recalled in his introduction (p. xliii). It was abandoned when Napier died (in 1916) and Sisam (in 1917) took a wartime post in the Ministry of Food; but as the First World War ended, students returned in great numbers to university, and Oxford University Press (of which 'Clarendon Press' is an imprint for books of special distinction; see also *Publishers) examined their offerings of textbooks in Middle English in order to dominate that section of the market. Sisam now revived the anthology he and Napier had planned, as an introduction for newcomers to fourteenth-century English literature, brought into it an excerpt from *Sir Gawain and the Green Knight*, and drew upon Napier's lecture notes for interpretation.

In *The Ring of Words: Tolkien and the Oxford English Dictionary* (2006) Peter Gilliver, Jeremy Marshall, and Edmund Weiner note that it had become apparent by June 1919 that Sisam was not going to have the time himself to compile a glossary for *Fourteenth Century Verse & Prose* 'as he had originally planned, and Tolkien was asked to help out' (p. 33). Tolkien had joined the staff of the *Oxford English Dictionary (OED) at the beginning of 1919 and was doing impressive work, news of which perhaps reached Sisam, who although still a civil servant was also an important consultant to Oxford University Press. In any case, Sisam was already familiar with Tolkien: he had been his tutor at Oxford, and had recognized and encouraged his pupil's philological talents.

Tolkien's contract for the glossary cannot be found; but he received the commission in summer or autumn of 1919, and was already working on it before the winter of 1919–20. He recorded in his diary that he was then 'still pegging away at tutoring in Oxford, still with the glossary hanging over me' (*Christopher Tolkien, private correspondence). Gilliver, Marshall, and Weiner comment that it was

> characteristic of Tolkien that, although he was commissioned to compile
> a relatively straightforward glossary – and, crucially, to do so quickly,
> so that it could be published as part of Sisam's volume – the project
> increased in size and elaborateness to the point that Sisam had to ask
> [Oxford University Press] to give Tolkien time off from his work on the
> *OED* to work on it, and that even then he failed to complete it before
> leaving for Leeds. [p. 33]

And yet he made progress during the latter part of 1919 – apparently setting aside for the most part work on *The Book of Lost Tales* – and before he ceased to be employed on the *OED* staff at the end of May 1920. Gilliver, Marshall, and

Weiner point to marginal annotations made by Tolkien in office copies of the *OED*, the majority of which were derived from his work on the Middle English glossary. During the second half of 1920 Tolkien was preoccupied with his appointment to a Readership at *Leeds, and with the birth of his second son, *Michael, to the extent that *A Middle English Vocabulary* was hardly touched.

On 12 February 1921, however, he was able to hand over some material for the glossary to Oxford University Press, and on 14 February sent in a revision, calling the work a 'mole-hill glossary (grown into a mountain by accumulated domestic distractions)' (letter to John Johnson, University Printer, Oxford University Press archives). By now Sisam's book was in progress; the editor was correcting proof at the end of April 1921. An edition of *Fourteenth Century Verse & Prose* was published in October 1921, without the glossary, while Tolkien was still completing his work. He sent his full manuscript to Oxford University Press at last early in 1922, received proofs at the beginning of March, and returned the bulk of them to the Press, heavily corrected, on 11 March. It was first published in May 1922 as a separate volume for the benefit of purchasers of Sisam's book in its original form, before being combined with the texts themselves in a single volume; and for a while both books continued to be available separately as well as conjoined.

As he later wrote to Elizabeth Wright (*Joseph Wright), Tolkien 'lavished an amount of time' on the glossary 'which is terrible to recall, and long delayed the Reader [i.e. *Fourteenth Century Verse & Prose*] bringing curses on my head; but it was instructive' (13 February 1923, *Letters*, p. 11). According to Gilliver, Marshall, and Weiner's count, the texts in *Fourteenth Century Verse & Prose* contain some 43,000 words, each of which Tolkien would have had to consider for inclusion in the glossary, and that the finished *Middle English Vocabulary* contains some 4,740 entries, nearly 6,800 definitions, almost 15,000 references to places in the texts where the meaning of a word occurs, and some 1,900 cross-references to different forms of the same word, as well as a list of 236 proper names mentioned in the texts. 'No details are available of the time Tolkien spent on the job, but it is difficult to imagine how it could have taken less than the equivalent of nine months' *full-time* work' (*The Ring of Words*, p. 36). As Gilliver, Marshall, and Weiner observe, Sisam had checked his texts against the original manuscripts and had sometimes made emendations, so Tolkien could not simply borrow material from existing editions, nor did there exist at that time a reliable or detailed dictionary of Middle English. Tolkien had to rely on the *OED* – so far as it had then progressed – but otherwise to do original research.

It is true, however, that Tolkien made more of the project than Sisam and others at Oxford University Press had expected. Not content with simply glossing words from the relevant texts, Tolkien held that

a good working knowledge of Middle English depends less on the possession of an abstruse vocabulary than on familiarity with the ordinary machinery of expression – with the precise forms and meanings that common words may assume; with the uses of such innocent-looking little words as the prepositions *of* and *for*; with idiomatic phrases, some fresh-minted and some worn thin, but all likely to recur again and again in an age whose authors took no pains to avoid usual or hackneyed turns of expression. These are the features of the older language which an English reader is predisposed to pass over, satisfied with a half-recognition: and space seldom permits of their adequate treatment in a compendious general dictionary or the word-list to a single text. So in making a glossary for use with a book itself designed to be a preparation for the reading of complete texts, I have given exceptionally full treatment to what may rightly be called the backbone of the language. [*A Middle English Vocabulary*, p. 3]

CRITICISM

Margaret L. Lee commented in *The Year's Work in English Studies* 1920–1 (1922) that Tolkien had 'worthily completed a piece of work which can hardly be praised too highly by teachers whom experience has brought to realize the underlying unity of all literary and linguistic study worthy of the name.' The *Vocabulary* 'devotes much space and care to the various meanings of the preposition *to*, and the various forms of the pronoun *he*, or the verb *habben*, rather than to suggested etymologies of the rare and obscure words contained in his texts.' The result has 'a value independent of the extracts to which it is appended – comparable indeed in fullness and interest with Heyne's Glossary to *Beowulf* and a few others like it' (pp. 42–3).

In his 'Tolkien's Academic Reputation Now', *Amon Hen* 100 (November 1989), Tom Shippey observed that *A Middle English Vocabulary* 'has been part of a standard student work-book for more than sixty years' (p. 19). *Fourteenth Century Verse & Prose* long remained in print from Oxford University Press. More recently it was also re-issued as *A Middle English Reader and Vocabulary* (New York: Dover, 2005), with Tolkien's name given added prominence.

See also Carl F. Hostetter, 'Revisions to Sisam's *Fourteenth Century Verse and Prose* Due to Tolkien', an appendix to 'Tolkien's Middle English *Sir Orfeo*', in *Tolkien Studies* 1 (2004).

Milford-on-Sea (Hampshire). In spring 1931 the Tolkien family went on holiday to this resort on the south coast of England, almost opposite the westernmost point of the Isle of Wight. *Father Augustine Emery, who had been the priest at *Great Haywood in 1916, was now living in Milford in a bungalow with a chapel that served as the local Catholic church. *John Tolkien recalled that during this holiday he walked with his father along the shingle spit to Hurst Castle, a fort which had been built by King Henry VIII to guard the entrance to the Solent and where King Charles I had been imprisoned.

Mills, Stella Marie. One of Tolkien's students at *Leeds, Stella Mills became a close friend of the Tolkien family. With Tolkien's assistance she secured employment on the staff of the *Oxford English Dictionary* under *C.T. Onions. Later she was on the staff of St Joseph's Catholic Primary School in *Oxford. In 1933 she published *The Saga of Hrolf Kraki*, with an introduction by *E.V. Gordon and dedicated to Gordon, Tolkien, and Onions.

Mr. Bliss. Picture book, first published in Great Britain by George Allen & Unwin, London, in September 1982, and in the United States by the Houghton Mifflin Company, Boston, in January 1983. See further, *Descriptive Bibliography* A18.

SUMMARY

Mr Bliss lives in a tall house, wears tall hats, and keeps a girabbit, a creature like a rabbit with a giraffe's markings and long neck. On impulse he buys a motor-car, leaving his bicycle as security for later payment; runs down Mr Day and Mrs Knight, damaging their barrow and donkey-cart; and is accosted by three bears. Together they crash into the midst of a picnic held by the Dorkins family. The bears having stolen Mr Day's cabbages and Mrs Knight's bananas, Mr Bliss, Mr Day, Mrs Knight, and the Dorkinses pursue them. Frightened away, Mr Bliss abandons his car in the bears' wood, and coming upon the motor-car shop retrieves his bicycle without leaving payment. Upon returning home, he finds that the Girabbit has entered his house and eaten its way up the chimney. The motor-car dealer, Mr Day, Mrs Knight, the Dorkinses, and the bears demand money for breakage caused by Mr Bliss and his bad driving; but the Girabbit frightens away all but the bears, who leave an itemized bill for damages. Mr Bliss later has his revenge when the Girabbit eats all the food in the bears' house, breaks their pantry window, bites the tops off every tree in the Dorkinses' orchard, and makes an enormous hole in the middle of their best lawn.

HISTORY

Mr. Bliss is so curious a story that this brief summary can only begin to suggest its eccentricities, both verbal and visual. It is unusual among Tolkien's works in that it is a picture book for children, in which words and art are equally important, rather than a story with illustrations; and it is unique among his finished works in that no drafts of the writing and only two preliminary sketches are known to survive. Humphrey Carpenter asserts in *Biography* that Tolkien was inspired to write *Mr. Bliss* after he bought a car in 1932 and had mishaps while driving. The telling of the story by Tolkien to his three sons was recorded, however, in a diary kept by *Michael Tolkien which dates its origin to no later than summer 1928; and according to a letter written by Joan (Mrs Michael) Tolkien to the *Sunday Times* (10 October 1982, p. 25) *Mr. Bliss* 'was inspired by a toy car complete with driver which was then *Christopher [Tolkien]'s most cherished toy.' The bears of the story are the teddy bears that belonged to the three Tolkien boys. Christopher Tolkien (who does not now recall the toy car referred to above) has said that his father's handwriting in the finished manuscript suggests the 1930s rather than the 1920s; but we have argued (*Artist and Illustrator*, p. 86) that the work

> was so obviously planned and executed as a unity that it must have been accomplished in one short period, probably during a long summer vacation, when Tolkien was freed from many of his academic duties. The summer of 1928 was one of his most productive periods for drawing and painting, and would have been more so if he had produced *Mr. Bliss* then as well. But the summers of 1929–31 are more likely candidates for the work, when Christopher was still young enough to enjoy the story. . . .

Another clue, however, may be the fleeting appearance, on pp. 36–7, of a 'Gaffer Gamgee'. Tolkien recalled that when he and his family visited Lamorna Cove in *Cornwall in summer 1932 'there was a curious local character, an old man who used to go about swapping gossip and weather-wisdom and such like. To amuse my boys I named him Gaffer Gamgee, and the name became part of family lore to fix on old chaps of the kind' (letter to Christopher Bretherton, 16 July 1964, *Letters*, pp. 347–8), including Sam Gamgee's father in *The Lord of the Rings*. *Gaffer* is an old word for an elderly rustic, and *Gamgee* 'was caught out of childhood memory, as a comic word or name' in *Birmingham for cotton-wool. The (unanswerable) question, therefore, is whether Tolkien used the name first in *Mr. Bliss* before the holiday at Lamorna Cove, or first at Lamorna Cove before conceiving *Mr. Bliss*. His letters (see also *Letters*, p. 88) would suggest the latter, and thus a later rather than an earlier date.

Certainly the illustrated manuscript of *Mr. Bliss* was in existence by late 1936, when Tolkien submitted it to George Allen & Unwin (*Publishers) as a possible successor to *The Hobbit*. C.A. Furth, the publisher's production manager, wrote to Tolkien on 7 January 1937 that although *Mr. Bliss* was in a class with *Alice's Adventures in Wonderland*, its delicate illustrations, drawn with coloured pencils and inks, could be reproduced (given the technology of that time) only at a prohibitive cost, relative to the need to sell the book at a reasonable price. Tolkien offered to make his pictures less elaborate and so less expensive to reproduce, and consulted Furth to this end. But in the event he had no time to revise his art in a more limited colour scheme, and for many years the cost of reproduction remained an obstacle to publishing the book.

By late 1964 the manuscript of *Mr. Bliss* came to the attention of Clyde S. Kilby of Wheaton College, Wheaton, Illinois, who proposed that it be published. Tolkien by this time had come to dislike *Mr. Bliss* except as a private joke, and decided that it would be best for his reputation if it were published posthumously. It was not until after several American firms had inquired about the book that *Mr. Bliss* was published at last in 1982, a facsimile of the illustrated manuscript with a typeset transcription of Tolkien's calligraphy on each facing page.

CRITICISM

Mr. Bliss was launched with fanfare by a colour feature article in the *Sunday Times* for 19 September 1982. For the most part, however, the book received only very brief notices, apparently (from the repetition of phrases) inspired less by *Mr. Bliss* itself than by its publisher's press release. Among more assiduous critics, Jessica Yates in *Amon Hen* (December 1982, p. 6) compared *Mr. Bliss* to the work of Beatrix Potter 'with its high ratio of picture to text, in its rural English setting, and [with its] mix of human and animal characters. Also [with] its unpatronising attitude to children, who are credited with a decent vocabulary and grasp of plot. . . .' Humphrey Carpenter (*Biography*, p. 163) similarly felt that *Mr. Bliss* 'owes a little to Beatrix Potter in its ironical humour and to Edward Lear in the style of its drawings, though Tolkien's approach is less grotesque and more delicate than Lear's.' Jared Lobdell in '*Mr. Bliss*: Notes on the Manuscript and Story' (*Selections from the Marquette J.R.R. Tolkien Collection* [1987]) also compares the work to Lear – 'certainly one could make an argument that Lear's *Book of Nonsense* is among Mr. Bliss's spiritual progenitors' (p. 7) – and to *The Wind in the Willows* by Kenneth Grahame, with Mr Toad's misadventures in a motor-car. T.A. Shippey ('Blunt Belligerence', *Times Literary Supplement*, 26 November 1982, p. 1306) describes *Mr. Bliss* as a celebration, in the spirit of *The Wind in the Willows*, of 'a vanished vulgar England where everybody did – and spoke – exactly as he pleased, and life was consequently a series of amiable abrupt collisions, feebly refereed by the police in the shape of Sergeant Boffin.' Although the book 'ought to feel dated, from its pounds, shillings and pence, its language-jokes, its assumptions about class, and its whole ethos of anarchic independence within a rigid framework of law, or convention', it does not: 'dating has done little harm to Tom Kitten or Mr Badger, and there seems no reason why it should here.'

Mitchison, Naomi Mary Margaret (1897–1999). Naomi Mitchison was raised in *Oxford, where her father, the noted physiologist and philosopher J.S. Haldane, was a Fellow of New College. She herself was educated at Oxford, as a member of the Society of Home-Students. In 1916 she married a barrister, Gilbert Richard Mitchison, but for a time when she believed in 'open marriage' she had a relationship as well with *H.T. Wade-Gery. Active in the Labour Party and the Fabian Society, Mitchison was a radical in religion and politics and an ardent feminist. While at Oxford she contributed verse to *Oxford Poetry* for 1915 and 1916 (in the former, in company with Tolkien's *Goblin Feet*). Later she wrote thousands of articles and letters, and books at a rate of more than one per year: these include historical novels such as *The Conquered* (1923), the fantasies *Travel Light* (1952) and *Graeme and the Dragon* (1954, illustrated by *Pauline Baynes), the Arthurian story *To the Chapel Perilous*

(1955, which Tolkien found not to his taste), and the collection of Scottish tales and verse *Five Men and a Swan* (1957), as well as drama, biographies, travel books, and practical philosophy. She was created a Life Peer in 1964 but refused to be called 'Lady Mitchison'.

Long a devotee of Tolkien's works, Mitchison sent him letters, gifts, and remembrances, at least as early as 1949 after reading *Farmer Giles of Ham. She asked many questions, to which Tolkien replied at length. Knowing of her keen interest, Tolkien's publisher, George Allen & Unwin (*Publishers), sent her advance proofs of the first two volumes of *The Lord of the Rings*, and used a quotation from one of her letters as a blurb on the dust-jacket of the first edition ('It's really super science fiction, but it is timeless and will go on and on. It's odd, you know. One takes it completely seriously: as seriously as Malory'). She praised *The Fellowship of the Ring* also in a review in the *New Statesman and Nation* ('One Ring to Bind Them', 18 September 1954), which Tolkien thought 'perceptive': 'Yours is the only comment that I have seen that, besides treating the book as "literature", at least in intent, and even taking it seriously (and praising or ridiculing it accordingly), also sees it as an elaborate form of the *game* of inventing a country . . .' (letter to Mitchison, 25 September 1954, *Letters*, p. 196). But she was negative about *Smith of Wootton Major* when reviewing it for the *Glasgow Herald* ('Why Not Grown-ups Too?', 25 November 1967), and by October 1977, when she reviewed Carpenter's *Biography* and *The Silmarillion* for *Books and Bookmen* ('Maps of Middle Earth'), she was 'increasingly critical of the later volumes [of *The Lord of the Rings*] where the style tends to tilt over from the grand into the grandiose.' She also noticed, on re-reading that work, 'as I had earlier', a deficiency of female characters and relationships. 'All the great friendships are man to man, but oh so pure' (p. 29). By then she no longer had an 'addiction' to Tolkien, and which she supposed would be required to read *The Silmarillion* with pleasure: she herself found it simplistic.

See further, Jill Benton, *Naomi Mitchison: A Biography* (1990).

The Monsters and the Critics and Other Essays. Collection, edited and with a foreword by *Christopher Tolkien, first published in Great Britain by George Allen & Unwin, London, in March 1983, and in the United States by the Houghton Mifflin Company, Boston, in April 1984. See further, *Descriptive Bibliography* A19.

The volume conveniently assembles seven essays and lectures by Tolkien: *Beowulf: The Monsters and the Critics*; On Translating Beowulf (*Prefatory Remarks on Prose Translation of 'Beowulf'*); the 1953 W.P. Ker Memorial Lecture on *Sir Gawain and the Green Knight*; *On Fairy-Stories*; *English and Welsh*; *A Secret Vice*; and *Valedictory Address to the University of Oxford*. The lecture on *Sir Gawain* and *A Secret Vice* were published here for the first time. The included *Valedictory Address* was taken from a different manuscript, with alterations, than that published earlier in *J.R.R. Tolkien, Scholar and Storyteller: Essays in Memoriam*, ed. *Mary Salu and Robert T. Farrell (1979).

Morgan, Francis Xavier (1867–1935). Father Francis Morgan of the *Birmingham Oratory was of Welsh and Anglo-Spanish descent. He attended the Oratory School, and the higher studies institute of Monsignor Capel in London, and spent time in Louvain, before returning to the Oratory as a novice. Ordained at the age of twenty-five, he devoted his early years in the priesthood to parish and school work. In early 1902 he called on *Mabel Tolkien and her sons after they moved to Edgbaston (*Birmingham and environs). He 'was not a man of great intellect, but he had an immense fund of kindness and a flamboyance that was often attributed to his Spanish connections. Indeed, he was a very noisy man, loud and affectionate, embarrassing to small children at first but hugely lovable when they got to know him. He soon became an indispensable part of the Tolkien household' (Humphrey Carpenter, *Biography*, p. 27). When Mabel Tolkien came out of hospital in 1904, following treatment for diabetes, Father Francis arranged for her to convalesce at *Rednal, near the Oratory retreat. He paid the family many visits, and took young Ronald and *Hilary kite-flying. 'He kept a dog at Rednal named "Lord Roberts", and he used to sit on the ivy-covered verandah of the Oratory House smoking a large cherrywood pipe; "the more remarkable", Ronald recalled, "since he never smoked except there. Possibly my own later addiction to the Pipe derives from this"' (*Biography*, p. 30). He was at Mabel's bedside when she died in November 1904, and under her will became her sons' legal guardian.

In that capacity he was generous with his support: he had a private income from his family's sherry business in southern Spain, which he used to augment Mabel's legacy of invested capital. In the years immediately after her death, although Ronald and Hilary did not live with Father Francis, they were often in his company. They served Mass for him in the Oratory Church before school, and ate breakfast in the refectory. In the summers he took the boys on holiday to *Lyme Regis. As Ronald progressed in school, Father Francis was concerned that he work without distractions towards a university scholarship, and so was hurt when he learned, near the end of 1909, of Ronald's clandestine romance with Edith Bratt (*Edith Tolkien). He demanded that it be broken off. In early 1910, Ronald and Edith having continued to meet secretly, Father Francis forbade Ronald to meet or write to Edith until he was twenty-one. On 26 February, after an accidental encounter with Edith, Ronald received 'a dreadful letter from Fr. F[rancis] saying I had been seen with a girl again, calling it evil and foolish. Threatening to cut short my University career if I did not stop. . . . I owe all to Fr. F and so must obey' (Tolkien, diary, quoted in *Biography*, p. 43).

In January 1913 Ronald and Edith became engaged. Father Francis gave his blessing, if not with enthusiasm. 'This was as well, for although the priest was no longer Ronald's legal guardian, he still gave him much-needed financial support; so it was essential that he tolerate the engagement' (*Biography*, p. 62). Father Francis sometimes came to visit Tolkien in Oxford, once acting as chaperon for Edith. On the latter occasion he insisted on buying Banbury cakes when their train stopped at that town: the grease from these local delicacies, Edith later recalled, 'got everywhere and caused considerable confusion' (*The Tolkien Family Album*, p. 35). Even so, it was not until only a fortnight before his wedding to Edith in 1916 that Ronald could bring himself to inform Father Francis of the event, mindful of the latter's opposition six years earlier; and although Father Francis offered to perform the ceremony himself in the Oratory Church, by then arrangements were already made for the wedding to take place in *Warwick.

In 1928 Father Francis joined Ronald and Edith, now with three sons of their own, on a holiday to Lyme Regis. *John Tolkien remembered that he produced 'a pile of marshmallows on top of an ant-hill as if by magic' (*The Tolkien Family Album*, p. 61).

On 6 January 1965 Tolkien wrote to his grandson Michael George (see *Michael Tolkien) of Father Francis: 'he was an upper-class Welsh-Spaniard Tory, and seemed to some just a pottering old snob and gossip. He was – and he was *not*. I first learned charity and forgiveness from him; and in the light of it pierced even the 'liberal' darkness out of which I came . . .' (*Letters*, p. 354).

Photographs of Father Francis Morgan appear in *Biography*, pl. 3b, and in *The Tolkien Family Album*, pp. 24 and 61. A pictorial code-letter (rebus) drawn by Tolkien on 8 August 1904, inviting his guardian to visit him, is reproduced in *Life and Legend*, p. 17 (page one), and *The Tolkien Family Album*, p. 22 (page two).

Morgoth's Ring: The Later Silmarillion, Part One: The Legends of Aman. The tenth volume of *The History of Middle-earth*, edited with notes and commentary by *Christopher Tolkien, first published in Great Britain by HarperCollins, London, in September 1993, and in the United States by the Houghton Mifflin Company, Boston, in December 1993. See further, *Tolkien Collector* 5 (November 1993), p. 6, and *Tolkien Collector* 7 (June 1994), p. 5.

SUMMARY

Morgoth's Ring contains most of Tolkien's writings concerning the Elder Days up to and including the Hiding of Valinor, written between from the time when *The Lord of the Rings* was nearly complete and Tolkien's death in 1973:

Part One contains three texts of the *Ainulindalë*, one dated from *c.* 1946 and the others from *c.* 1948–51, developed from and on the manuscript of that work written in the 1930s.

Part Two contains the *Annals of Aman* from *c.* 1950–1, a much expanded version of the *Annals of Valinor*. A plate at the front of *Morgoth's Ring* reproduces in colour the first page of a calligraphic, decorated manuscript of *The Tale of Years* which includes the beginning of a text originally part of the *Annals of Aman*.

Part Three, 'The Later *Quenta Silmarillion*', is devoted to the development of the *Quenta Silmarillion* in two phases. In the first, *c.* 1951, Tolkien revised the whole of the text covering the earlier period of the Elder Days, though the amount of new writing and emendation varied from chapter to chapter. Eight chapters are treated in *Morgoth's Ring*: 'Of the Valar'; 'Of Valinor and the Two Trees'; 'Of the Coming of the Elves'; 'Of Thingol and Melian'; 'Of Eldanor and the Princes of the Eldalië'; 'Of the Silmarils and the Darkening of Valinor'; 'Of the Flight of the Noldor'; and 'Of the Sun and Moon and the Hiding of Valinor'. In the second phase, *c.* late 1958–60, Tolkien's revisions and additions were focused on specific parts. The first chapter was expanded in two successive texts and made into a separate work, the *Valaquenta*; since that work (in its later version) was published in *The Silmarillion* (1977), neither text is printed in *Morgoth's Ring*, but Christopher Tolkien notes differences between the texts and editorial changes that he made in *The Silmarillion*. Much of the rest of the work on the *Quenta Silmarillion* in this phase arose from Tolkien's development of the story of Finwë and Míriel and their descendants, and a consequent consideration of the nature of Elves and their marriage customs. Included in this material is *Laws and Customs among the Eldar*, not part of the *Quenta Silmarillion* but a lengthy work which considers marriage, death, and re-birth among the Elves.

Part Four contains the *Athrabeth Finrod ah Andreth*, with a commentary and the *Tale of Adanel*; and as an appendix, part of *The Converse of Manwë and Eru* and a summary of *Reincarnation of Elves*.

Part Five, 'Myths Transformed', contains eleven short works and miscellaneous notes mainly arising from Tolkien's attempts at the end of the 1950s and later to make fundamental changes in his mythology. These include:

I. Two slips attached to a typescript of *The Annals of Aman*. In this Tolkien seems to be considering abandoning the idea that the Earth was originally flat and the Sun and Moon later creations, which could only be untrue 'Mannish' tradition: the Elvish loremasters, he reasoned, must have known the truth. He notes some of the dramatic losses this alteration would entail.

II. A proposal for the 'regeneration' of the mythology and an abandoned narrative, which seem to precede Tolkien's commentary on the *Athrabeth*. He tries to work out how the Elves could still be 'Star-folk' if the Sun and Moon were in existence when they woke.

III. 'What happened in Valinor after death of Trees?' Tolkien decides that Valinor had been protected from the light of the Sun defiled by Melkor by the Dome of Varda, lit with stars, and when the Trees were destroyed the Dome was removed.

IV. Christopher Tolkien quotes relevant entries in an *'analysis (in intention) of all fragments of other languages found in The Lord of the Rings' (Morgoth's Ring*, p. 387) which relate to the idea of a Dome and the part played by Varda in the creation of the stars.

V. *Sun The Trees Silmarils*.

VI. *Melkor Morgoth*.

VII. *Notes on Motives in the Silmarillion, and a related text, Some Notes on the 'Philosophy' of the Silmarillion.

VIII. *Orcs.

IX. An untitled note on the origin of Orcs (see *Orcs).

X. A four-page typescript, also entitled Orcs (see *Orcs), attached to *Quendi and Eldar.

XI. *Aman.

The title of the volume derives from a passage in a note by Tolkien 'in which he contrasted the nature of Sauron's power, concentrated in the One Ring, with that of Morgoth, enormously greater, but dispersed or disseminated into the very matter of Arda: "the whole of Middle-earth was Morgoth's Ring"' (Christopher Tolkien, Morgoth's Ring, p. ix).

CRITICISM

Morgoth's Ring, like the later volumes of The History of Middle-earth in general, was not widely reviewed. But readers were struck by its revelation that Tolkien was willing to alter the basis of his mythology so radically in his later years. A typical comment was made by Kaj André Apeland in 'On Entering the Same River Twice: Mythology and Theology in the Silmarillion Corpus', in Between Faith and Fiction: Tolkien and the Powers of His World (1998):

> According to a saying attributed by Plato to Heraclitus, no man can enter the same river twice: the man will not be the same man, and the river will not be the same river. The truth of this statement struck me forcibly last year when I turned to Morgoth's Ring. . . . I read this book with grow-ing discomfort as I realized what it revealed. The first ominous sign was Tolkien's intention of abolishing his 'Flat world' cosmology and replac-ing it with one in which the earth had been round from the start. At this stage Tolkien was evidently submitting his legendarium to reality test-ing; in other words, he was evaluating the work according to standards that were extrinsic to the mythology itself. This clearly demonstrates that he was no longer in the river; he was now observing it from the bank. I propose that the Silmarillion corpus was no longer a flowing creative process in which he was immersed; it had now become a collection of texts with which he was not entirely comfortable.
>
> It is not difficult to determine the theological considerations involved in Tolkien's own censure of his early texts. I would like to point out, how-ever, that these considerations were ex post facto. . . . The alterations to make the Silmarillion theologically 'correct' were not products of the mythopoeic imagination [involved in the initial phase of the writing of *'The Silmarillion']. They were the results of the misgivings of an elderly man worrying about the sins of his youth. [p. 48]

Morris, William (1834–1896). While at Marlborough College from 1848 to 1851 William Morris developed an interest in English Gothic by reading books and visiting nearby examples of the style. In January 1853 he went up to Exeter College, *Oxford, intending to take holy orders. He immediately established a close friendship with Edward Burne-Jones, and with him and other undergraduates formed a circle called the Brotherhood. Morris abandoned plans to enter the church, and in January 1856 was articled to George Edmund Street, a prominent architect of the Gothic Revival. A year later, influenced by Dante Gabriel Rossetti, Morris abandoned architecture for painting, and ultimately became a major figure in the Arts and Crafts movement.

On his marriage in 1859 Morris, together with the architect Philip Webb, designed and furnished Red House, Bexley Heath, as a home for Morris and his wife Jane Burden, a favourite model of the Pre-Raphaelite painters. In 1861 he founded Morris, Marshall, Faulkner and Company (from 1875, Morris & Company), manufacturers and decorators whose products revolutionized both church and domestic interior decoration in England. Emphasizing hand craftsmanship over mass production, the firm produced furniture, wallpapers, textiles, tapestries, carpets, tiles, stained glass, and so forth, with designs by Morris and his associates, often inspired by nature or by medieval models. At the same time, his interest in preserving the architecture of the past led Morris in 1877 to found the Society for the Protection of Ancient Buildings. He wrote in 'How I Became a Socialist': 'Apart from the desire to produce beautiful things, the leading passion of my life has been and is hatred of modern civilization' (*Justice*, 16 June 1884; reprinted in *William Morris: Selected Writings and Designs* (1962), p. 36).

As a boy he found great pleasure in the medieval illuminated manuscripts at Canterbury Cathedral, and as an undergraduate at Oxford and in later life studied the collections at the Bodleian Library, Oxford and in the British Museum. These inspired him to collect early manuscripts and printed books himself, and to produce manuscripts with scripts and decorations influenced by medieval and Renaissance originals, but also informed by the interpretation of those sources prevalent among the Pre-Raphaelites. In 1890 he founded the Kelmscott Press, at which he published some of his own books as well as classic works, rejecting current styles of printing for his own typefaces adapted from early books, ornamented with letters and borders also of his own design.

Such activities had a profound influence on the decorative arts in England in the late nineteenth and early twentieth centuries, during which Tolkien was born and raised: his own love for ornament and talent for *calligraphy were products of that era. In *Artist and Illustrator* we comment that Tolkien observed the decorative work of the Arts and Crafts period, which was widespread, and that it was 'a lasting inspiration to him', evident in works such as the borders of some of his *Hobbit* paintings and the ornamental patterns he drew in his later years. 'It seems clear, too, that he agreed with the underlying philosophy of Morris and his followers, which looked back to a much earlier time: that the "lesser" arts of handicraft embodied truth and beauty no less than the "fine" arts of painting and sculpture. One looks for the latter almost in vain in Tolkien's writings (*Leaf by Niggle* excepted), but finds a wealth of references to crafts' (p. 10).

Much of the poetry Morris wrote, such as *The Defence of Guinevere and Other Poems* (1858), *The Life and Death of Jason* (1867), and *The Earthly Paradise* (1868–70), retells classical and medieval tales. His translations of the *Aeneid* and the *Odyssey* appeared in 1875 and 1887 respectively. He was particularly interested in the literature of medieval Iceland, and translated with Eiríkr Magnússon several Icelandic sagas and tales, including the *Grettis Saga* (1869), the *Eyrbyggja Saga* (1892), and *Heimskringla* (3 vols., 1893–5). By himself he translated the *Volsunga Saga* (1870), on which he based his own poetic version of the legend, *The Story of Sigurd the Volsung and the Fall of the Nibelungs* (1876). He visited Iceland in 1871 and 1873; the intriguing journals he kept on those occasions were published in 1911. He also wrote several prose works, generally described as romances (in the sense of narratives dealing with events set in the distant past, often concerned with chivalry and legendary heroes), many of which, including *The Wood beyond the World* (1894) and *The Well at the World's End* (1896), are set in invented worlds, or at least in unknown parts of our own world in a vaguely medieval time. Two other works by Morris, in prose interspersed with verse, are *A Tale of the House of the Wolfings* (1889) and *The Roots of the Mountains* (1889), set in northern Europe in the early medieval period and depicting (unhistorical) wars of idealized Goths against the Romans and the Huns.

Morris was also active politically. His Utopian ideals led to him becoming a leading light in the Socialist movement. He wrote two romances fostering these ideals, *The Dream of John Ball* (1888) and *News from Nowhere* (1891).

Tolkien himself acknowledged specific instances of influence by Morris on his own works, and others may be deduced. 'The Story of Sigurd' in *The Red Fairy Book* (first published 1890), which made such an impression on him as a boy, had been adapted by *Andrew Lang from the Morris translation of the *Völsunga Saga*, as Tolkien noted in his drafts for *On Fairy-Stories*. As a pupil at *King Edward's School, Birmingham, Tolkien may have attended the meeting of its Literary Society on 26 November 1909, at which one of the masters, the Rev. E.W. Badger, gave a talk, 'William Morris, Artist, Craftsman and Poet'. And while a student at Exeter College, Oxford, which Morris and Burne-Jones had also attended, although as a Catholic Tolkien would not have been obliged to attend services in the College Chapel, he surely visited it, and saw there the tapestry *The Adoration of the Magi* (1890) designed by Burne-Jones and made under Morris's supervision at Morris & Company's tapestry works at Merton Abbey.

In spring 1914, when he was awarded the Skeat Prize, Tolkien used part of it to buy three works by Morris: the long poem *The Life and Death of Jason*, the translation of the *Völsunga Saga*, and *The House of the Wolfings*. Of these the most immediately influential was the last: in the autumn of 1914 Tolkien began, as he described it in a letter to his fiancée (*Edith Tolkien), 'a short story somewhat on the lines of Morris' romances with chunks of poetry in between' (October 1914, *Letters*, p. 7). This was a retelling of an episode, the story of Kullervo from the Finnish *Kalevala*, which he had read at school in W.F. Kirby's verse translation.

The Earthly Paradise may have influenced the framework of Tolkien's *Book of Lost Tales*, and perhaps the city of the Elves in Valinor. In Morris's work wanderers seeking the Earthly Paradise find in the west 'a nameless city in a distant sea / White as the changing walls of faërie' (prologue). There each month in turn one of them and one of the elders of the city tells a story, whereas *The Book of Lost Tales* has a framework in which Eriol (*Eriol and Ælfwine) hears a succession of stories. The archaic style of *The Book of Lost Tales*, less elevated than some later versions of *'The Silmarillion', may also owe something to Morris's romances: the minute book of the Exeter College Essay Club records that *The Fall of Gondolin* which Tolkien read to members on 10 March 1920 'marked him out as a staunch follower of tradition, a treatment indeed in the manner of such typical Romantics as William Morris, George MacDonald, de la Motte Fouqué, etc.' (Exeter College archives).

In a letter written at the end of 1960 to Professor L.W. Forster about the sources of *The Lord of the Rings*, Tolkien said that he thought the only influence of the two great wars evident in his book was possibly on the landscape. 'The Dead Marshes and the approaches to the Morannon owe something to Northern France after the Battle of the Somme. They owe more to William Morris and his Huns and Romans, as in *The House of the Wolfings* or *The Roots of the Mountains*' (*Letters*, p. 303). The former work certainly uses the name *Mirkwood*, and a clearing in the wood where many men dwelt is called Midmark (compare *The Mark*, i.e. Rohan), but Tolkien told his grandson Michael George Tolkien (see *Michael Tolkien, and *Letters*, pp. 369–70) that *Mirkwood* at least was derived from medieval sources, on which Morris probably also drew. Also in *The House of the Wolfings*, the Wolfings are summoned to war against the Romans by the war-horn of the Elkings heard in the distance, and by a messenger who carried 'the token of the war-arrow ragged and burnt and bloody' (ch. 2), which may be compared to the summoning of the Rohirrim in *The Lord of the Rings*. The social organization of the people of Brethil and the Folkmoot in *The Wanderings of Húrin* have a similar flavour as well to that of *The House of the Wolfings* and *The Roots of the Mountains*.

Richard Mathews in *Fantasy: The Liberation of Imagination* (1997) says that *Christopher Tolkien told him that 'his father owned nearly all of Morris's works and . . . he has a distant but clear recollection of having been read *The House of the Wolfings* by his father' (p. 87). Tolkien bequeathed to Christopher eleven books by Morris, including *The House of the Wolfings*, *The Roots of the Mountains*, and *The Sundering Flood* (1898), as well as the *Life of William Morris* by J.W. Mackail and *William Morris: His Work and Influence* by A. Clutton-Brock. Other works known to be in Tolkien's library by the mid-1920s are *The Earthly Paradise*, *The Defence of Guinevere and Other Poems*, *The Story of Sigurd the Volsung and the Fall of the Nibelungs*, Morris's translation of *Beowulf* (1895, originally a Kelmscott Press publication), his translation with Eiríkr Magnússon of *Grettis Saga*, and *Three Northern Love Stories and Other Tales* (1875), which includes *The Saga of Gunnlaug the Worm-tongue and Rafn the Skald*. The name 'Gunnlaug the Worm-tongue' is recalled, perhaps, in 'Gríma Wormtongue' of *The Lord of the Rings* (see *Reader's Companion*, p. 400). Mathews thinks that

> Tolkien found in Morris something of a kindred spirit or inspiration; the spark or connection helped advance a new fantasy tradition. The Western romance tradition staunchly reasserted itself in Britain at the great watershed of the twentieth century, and the modern romance hero was first clearly shaped in the 10 fantasy novels Morris wrote between 1886 and 1896. A quarter century later Tolkien began to craft a related but original heroic pattern of his own. . . . The two authors, sharing many influences and values, nonetheless developed markedly distinct heroic types. . . . [p. 87]

In *Biography* Humphrey Carpenter thought that Tolkien enjoyed *The House of the Wolfings* because

> Morris's view of literature coincided with his own. In this book Morris had tried to recreate the excitement he himself had found in the pages of early English and Icelandic narratives. . . . Many elements in the story seem to have impressed Tolkien. Its style is highly idiosyncratic, heavily laden with archaisms and poetic inversions in an attempt to recreate the aura of ancient legend. Clearly Tolkien took note of this, and it would seem that he also appreciated another facet of the writing: Morris's aptitude, despite the vagueness of time and place in which the story is set, for describing with great precision the details of his imagined landscape. Tolkien himself was to follow Morris's example in later years. [*Biography*, p. 70]

Tom Shippey comments in an introduction to *The Wood beyond the World* (Oxford, 1980) that

> almost certainly J.R.R. Tolkien remembered *The Roots of the Mountains* when he created Gollum; probably *The Wood beyond the World* was an element in the making of Lothlórien, or better still Fangorn, where also characters wander in a network of lies and glimpses and coincidences. . . . However Tolkien could read sagas and romances as well as Morris . . . so that when one sees similarity it may not be descent from one to another, but rather descent of both from some centuries-old common source. [p. xvii]

Marjorie Burns in 'Echoes of William Morris's Icelandic Journals in J.R.R. Tolkien' thinks that Morris's influence on Tolkien can be seen

> in the emphasis both men give to the mythology and social structure of an idealized medieval North, a world which emphasizes independence, directness, and simple artistic form. Northern elements in Morris's romances (hall life in *The Glittering Plain* or the Germanic sense of enemy and battle in *The House of the Wolfings*) have their counterparts throughout *The Hobbit* and *The Lord of the Rings*, as do Morris's poetry and translations from the Icelandic sagas and tales. [*Studies in Medievalism* 3, no. 3 (Winter 1991), pp. 367–73, p. 367]

In this essay and in her *Perilous Realms: Celtic and Norse in Tolkien's Middle-earth* (2005) Burns explores resemblances between Morris's experiences during his two visits to Iceland as recorded in his journals, and incidents in *The Hobbit* and *The Lord of the Rings*. 'In *The Lord of the Rings*, influence from the *Journals* is mostly a matter of similarities in wasteland or mountain scenes. In *The Hobbit*, however, certain of Bilbo's adventures not only come remarkably close to experiences Morris described during his first Icelandic visit but Bilbo himself, in a number of ways, closely resembles the *Journal* persona that Morris chose to assume' (*Perilous Realms*, p. 75). She summarizes the troll adventure in *The Hobbit* as beginning 'with rain, a startled pony, lost equipment, a fire that won't light, a weariness . . . with mutton' (p. 81); then during the next days, as Bilbo and the dwarves continue their journey, Bilbo thinks longingly of home, unexpected valleys open before them, Bilbo nods off and bumps his nose on his pony as they near Rivendell (*The Hobbit*, ch. 3). The entry by Morris in his Icelandic journal for 1 August 1871 contains many of the same elements:

> I groaned and got up and went out into the bitterest morning, the wind north-west and plenty of it and of rain; Magnússon and I made a desperate attempt at a fire, and failed of course . . . well, we decamped and packed, and walked up and down eating our breakfast of cold mutton bones and cold water. . . . As we rode now we could not see a rod in front of us, the rain, or hail, or sleet . . . was driven in a level sheet into our faces. . . . I did at last in the early part of the day fairly go to sleep as I rode, and fall to dreaming of people at home: from which I was woke up by a halt, and Magnússon coming to me and telling me that my little haversack was missing. . . . A little after we came to the brow of a steep slope over which we looked into a very deep narrow valley, cleft down from the wilderness by a biggish stream. . . . The country we were riding over was high upland-looking ground with no indication of this terrible gorge [their destination, Vatnasdalur or Water Dale] till one was quite on the edge of it. . . . [*Icelandic Journals* (1996 edn.), pp. 68–70]

Burns notes a similarity between 'Tolkien's comfort-loving, untried Bilbo Baggins and the somewhat inept persona Morris created for himself in his *Icelandic Journal* accounts. . . . Morris in Iceland often chooses to place himself in a comic light and to exaggerate his own ineptitude . . .' (*Perilous Realms*, p. 87). She reproduces (p. 88) Edward Burne-Jones's drawing of Morris on pony back, describes it as 'one of several similar cartoons poking fun at a friend', and comments that 'these exaggerated portrayals make excellent models for Tolkien's hobbit as he rushes "very puffed" to the Green Dragon or jogs behind Gandalf and the dwarves on his journey into the Wild' (p. 88).

Nancy Martsch in 'Tolkien and William Morris', *Beyond Bree*, September 1997, considers similarities between Morris's early story 'Gertha's Lovers' (1856) and *The Lord of the Rings*. Among these are a siege and a changing wind which enables a relieving force to arrive.

Meredith Veldman in *Fantasy, the Bomb, and the Greening of Britain: Romantic Protest, 1945–1980* (1994) comments that Tolkien and *C.S. Lewis 'viewed romantics such as William Morris as their literary forebears and, like Morris, revolted against the industrial world. Their fantasies articulated a rejection of materialism and empiricism deeply rooted in segments of British middle-class culture' (p. 38). Tolkien tended to be conservative rather than socialist, but was also suspicious of the way power can corrupt those who wield it. His Shire, where such officials as there were did not have an onerous job because there was little crime and little need for administration, is similar to some of the ideals of the socialists. Veldman notes: 'It may seem odd that Tories such as Lewis and Tolkien should find Morris, the revolutionary Marxist, so appealing, but the common quest for community overcame these political barriers. . . . They found in Morris's romantic fantasies, however, the spiritual enrichment and the sense of community for which they longed' (p. 53).

Chester N. Scoville in 'Pastoralia and Perfectability in William Morris and J.R.R. Tolkien', in *Tolkien's Modern Middle Ages* (2005), comments that Morris and Tolkien 'shared a deep and abiding love for the Middle Ages and saw in them clues to an alternative way of living, different from the shabby, materialist, and industrialized world around them. . . . Morris's self-description as a man "with a deep love of the earth and the life on it, and a passion for the history of the past of mankind" could as easily apply to Tolkien . . .' (p. 94). But he also notes, having described Morris's *News from Nowhere* as 'an account of the final defeat of both bourgeois England and mechanized State Socialism', and as such 'a fundamentally optimistic work', that 'for Tolkien, no such earthly paradise could exist, at least not after the Fall of Man. The Shire, which bears so much superficial resemblance to Morris's Nowhere, is not a utopia and never could be one; nor is it an Arcadia, despite its rural setting. . . . Its people are neither perfect nor perfectible but, for all their love of peace and harmony, live in a sublunar, fallen world' (pp. 98, 100).

In 1935 Tolkien examined an Oxford thesis entitled *William Morris's Treatment of His Icelandic Sources*, and in 1952 another, *The Icelandic Episode in the*

Life and Work of William Morris. In Michaelmas Term 1941 he delivered a lecture entitled *William Morris: The Story of Sigurd and the Fall of the Nibelungs*, presumably dealing at least in the first instance on Morris's poem based on the *Völsunga Saga*.

See also Fiona MacCarthy, *William Morris: A Life for Our Time* (1994), and Linda Parry, ed., *William Morris* (1996).

Mortality and Immortality. In Tolkien's created world the mortal nature of Man is contrasted with the 'immortal' nature of the Elves, as determined by Ilúvatar, the One, in the Music of Creation.

MEN AND MORTALITY

In the draft of *The Music of the Ainur* in **The Book of Lost Tales* Ilúvatar says: 'to Men I will appoint a task and give a great gift' (**The Book of Lost Tales, Part One*, p. 61), but in the fair copy he gives Men 'a new gift, and a greater' (p. 59). Then, according to Rúmil, who is telling the tale, Ilúvatar further 'devised that Men should have a free virtue whereby within the limits of the powers and substances and chances of the world they might fashion and design their life beyond even the original Music of the Ainur that is as fate to all things else. This he did that of their operations everything should in shape and deed be completed, and the world fulfilled unto the last and smallest' (p. 59). Rúmil also comments: 'It is however of one with this gift of power that the Children of Men dwell only a short time in the world alive, yet do not perish utterly for ever', and that 'the Sons of Men will after the passing of things of a certainty join in the Second Music of the Ainur . . .' (pp. 59–60).

This does not say that Men leave the world after death, and it may be that at this early stage Tolkien had not fully conceived that idea. Indeed, in the tale *The Coming of the Valar and the Building of Valinor* in *The Book of Lost Tales* Tolkien described a life after death for Men within the world, waiting for the Great End. Men who die or are slain come to the Halls of Fui, wife of Mandos, in Aman 'to hear their doom', and she reads their hearts.

> Some then she keeps in Mandos . . . and some she drives forth . . . and Melko seizes them and bears them to Angamandi, or the Hells of Iron, where they have evil days. Some too, and these are many, she sends aboard the black ship Mornië. . . .
> Then, when she is laden, of her own accord she spreads her sable sails and before a slow wind coasts down those shores. Then do all aboard as they come South cast looks of utter longing and regret to that low place amid the hills where Valinor may just be glimpsed upon the far off plain. . . . No more do they ever see of that bright place, but borne away dwell after on the wide plains of Arvalin. There do they wander in the dusk, camping as they may, yet are they not utterly without song, and they can see the stars, and wait in patience till the Great End come.

Few are they and happy indeed for whom at a season doth Nornorë the herald of the Gods set out. Then they ride with him in chariots or upon good horses down into the vale of Valinor and feast in the halls of Valmar, dwelling in the houses of the Gods until the Great End come. [p. 77]

*Christopher Tolkien comments that this account is 'in deep contradiction to the central thought of the later mythology. . . . We are far away here from the Gift of Ilúvatar, whereby Men are not bound to the world, but leave it, none know where' (*The Book of Lost Tales, Part One*, p. 90). In *The Silmarillion*, based on the latest text (cf. *Morgoth's Ring*, p. 37), the wording that follows Ilúvatar's announcement is:

But the sons of Men die indeed, and leave the world; wherefore they are called the Guests, or the Strangers. Death is their fate, the gift of Ilúvatar, which as Time wears even the Powers shall envy. But Melkor has cast his shadow upon it, and confounded it with darkness, and brought forth evil out of good, and fear out of hope. Yet of old the Valar declared to the Elves in Valinor that Men shall join in the Second Music of the Ainur. . . . [*The Silmarillion*, p. 42]

The *Book of Lost Tales* account is related to an early poem by Tolkien, *Habbanan beneath the Stars*, and an entry in an early word-list which connects Habbanan with a place of purgatory. Christopher Tolkien comments that these 'offer a rare and very suggestive glimpse of the mythic conception in its earliest phase; for here ideas that are drawn from Christian theology are explicitly present. It is disconcerting to perceive that they are still present in this tale.' He points out that 'the fates of dead Men after judgement in the black hall of Fui Nienna' in which they are ferried to Habbanan, seized by Melko, or dwell with the Gods in Valinor, seem to be 'a reflection of Purgatory, Hell, and Heaven' (*The Book of Lost Tales, Part One*, p. 92). He finds this account 'extraordinary' when compared with the concluding passage of *The Music of the Ainur*. He notes that that passage does not say, as in *The Silmarillion*, that Men 'leave the world'. 'Even so, it seems clear that this central idea, the Gift of Death, was already present.' In the end he is forced to leave the matter 'as a conundrum that I cannot solve' (p. 93).

There are, however, other difficulties with *The Book of Lost Tales*. In the surviving version of *The Tale of Tinúviel* both Beren and Tinúviel (*'Of Beren and Lúthien') are Elves, but when Mandos hears Tinúviel's plea he allows her and Beren to return to life, and tells them: 'Ye will become mortal even as Men, and when ye fare hither again it will be for ever, unless the Gods summon you indeed to Valinor' (*The Book of Lost Tales, Part Two*, p. 40). And at the end of *The Tale of Turambar* (*'Of Túrin Turambar'), it is said that after the death of Túrin Turambar and his sister-wife Nienóri

Turambar indeed had followed Nienóri along the black pathways to the doors of Fui, but Fui would not open to them, neither would Vefántur [Mandos]. Yet now the prayers of Úrin and Mavwin [later Húrin and Morwen] came even to Manwë, and the Gods had mercy on their unhappy fate, so that those twain Túrin and Nienóri entered into Fôs'Almir, the bath of flame . . . and so were all there sorrows and stains washed away, and they dwelt as shining Valar among the blessed ones. . . . But Turambar indeed shall stand beside Fionwë in the Great Wrack, and Melko and his drakes shall curse the sword of Mormakil. [*The Book of Lost Tales, Part Two*, pp. 115–16]

It may be that when Tolkien was writing *The Book of Lost Tales* he already had a clear idea what immortality meant in respect to the Elves (see below), but had not yet thought deeply about Men, except that they were mortal and did not return after death.

In the works that followed *The Book of Lost Tales* this picture gradually became clearer. In the *Sketch of the Mythology* (*c.* 1926) Tolkien first wrote that the Elves did not know what happened to the spirits of Men who were slain or died: 'They did not go to the halls of Mandos, and many thought their fate was not in the hands of the Valar after death. Though many, associating with Eldar, believed that their spirits went to the western land, this was not true. Men were not born again' (*The Shaping of Middle-earth*, p. 21). But this passage was replaced with: 'They went to the halls of Mandos, but not the same as the halls of awaiting where the Elves were sent. There they too waited, but it was said that only Mandos knew whither they went after the time in his halls – they were never reborn on Earth, and none ever came back from Mandos, save only Beren . . . who thereafter spoke not to mortal Men. Their fate after death was perchance not in the hands of the Valar' (p. 22). It is still said that when Morgoth returns, Túrin will fight him, and even slay him. The *Quenta Noldorinwa* (*c.* 1930) says that in the Last Battle, when Melko returns, Túrin will fight with Tulkas and Fionwë against him, and will kill him, and be named 'among the Gods' (*The Shaping of Middle-earth*, p. 165). Emendations to this text say that Túrin will come 'to the fight from the halls of Mandos' and will be named 'among the sons of the Gods' (p. 166). Christopher Tolkien comments that he can say no more than that 'Túrin Turambar, though a mortal Man, did not go . . . to a fate beyond the world' (p. 205). In the 'earliest' *Annals of Beleriand* (early 1930s) it is first mentioned that with the death of Bëor 'the Elves see for the first time the death of weariness, and sorrow over the short span allotted to Men' (p. 298).

In the *Ainulindalë* (mid-1930s) Tolkien says of Men that they 'dwell only a short space in the world alive, and yet are not bound to it, nor shall perish utterly for ever', and 'it is said that they will join in the Second Music of the Ainur . . .' (*The Lost Road and Other Writings*, p. 163). But *c.* 1936, in association with his time-travel story *The Lost Road*, Tolkien developed a Second Age for his mythology in *The Fall of Númenor*, in which Men are the main focus of attention, and in which they desire the immortality enjoyed by Elves and try to obtain it by force. Tolkien now began to develop more clearly the idea that mortality was inherent in the nature of Men, and could not be changed even by the Valar, and that after death their spirits left the world. In the very earliest outline for *The Fall of Númenor* 'the Gods will not allow them [Men] to land in Valinor – and though they become long-lived because many have been bathed in the radiance of Valinor from Tol-eressëa – they are mortal and their span brief. They murmur against this decree' (*The Lost Road and Other Writings*, p. 11). In the last text of *The Fall of Númenor* in this period it is said that 'Elrond [at that time the first King of *Númenor] and all his folk were mortal; for the Valar may not withdraw the gift of death, which cometh to Men from Ilúvatar'. In time the Númenóreans 'began to hunger for the undying bliss of Valinor', but 'though the Lords [the Valar] had rewarded them with long life, they could not take from them the weariness of the world that cometh at last; and they died . . .' (pp. 25–6). Men who escaped the destruction of Númenor preserved a tradition 'that the fate of Men was not bounded by the round path of the world [the world made round at the destruction of Númenor], nor destined for the straight path [to Valinor]. For the round is crooked and has no end but no escape; and the straight is true, but has an end within the world, and that is the fate of the Elves. But the fate of Men, they said, is neither round nor ended, and is not complete within the world' (pp. 18, 28).

In the tale of Beren and Lúthien given in the *Quenta Silmarillion*, written towards the end of 1937, the spirit of the mortal Beren tarries in the halls of Mandos until Lúthien comes to say her last farewell upon. The choice offered them in the draft *Quenta Silmarillion* is that 'they should dwell now in Valinor until the world's end in bliss, but in the end . . . each must go unto the fate appointed to their kind when all things are changed', or else return to Middle-earth as mortals. They choose the latter, that 'their fates might be joined and their paths lead together beyond the confines of the world' (*The Lost Road and Other Writings*, pp. 303–4). As Christopher Tolkien points out,

> if the first choice were accepted Beren and Lúthien must finally part, even though that parting is cast into a future indefinitely remote – the end of the world; and that parting would proceed from the different principles of their being, leading inevitably to a different final destiny or doom. Beren could not *finally* escape the necessity imposed upon him by his 'kind', the necessity of leaving the Circles of the World, the Gift of Ilúvatar that cannot be refused, though he may dwell – by unheard-of privilege, as an unheard-of reward – in Valinor until the End. The union of Beren and Lúthien 'beyond the world' could only be achieved by acceptance of the second choice, whereby Lúthien herself should be permitted to change her 'kind', and 'die indeed'. [*The Lost Road and Other Writings*, p. 304]

But in the fair copy, and in *The Silmarillion*, the first choice offered Lúthien, an immortal Elf, is that she may dwell in Valinor until the world's end, but 'thither Beren could not come. For it was not permitted to the Valar to withhold death from him, which is the gift of Ilúvatar to Men' (*The Silmarillion*, p. 187). Yet the special position of Túrin in the Last Battle still survived in the *Quenta Silmarillion* as an anomaly, though he was now said to be 'coming from the halls of Mandos' (*The Lost Road and Other Writings*, p. 333). The anomaly survives in emendations to the *Quenta Silmarillion* of *c.* 1951, where he 'returns from the Doom of Men at the ending of the world' (**The War of the Jewels*, p. 247). But in a note to **The Problem of* Ros (*c.* 1968) his return is qualified both as a Mannish tradition or prophecy and by Túrin eventually leaving the Circles of the World: 'unless the prophecy of Andreth the Wise-woman should prove true, that Túrin in the Last Battle should return from the Dead, and before he left the Circles of the World for ever should challenge the Great Dragon of Morgoth, Ancalagon the Black, and deal him the death-stroke' (**The Peoples of Middle-earth*, p. 374) – although, as Christopher Tolkien notes, Andreth seems to be referring to the Last Battle at the end of the First Age, in which Eärendil kills Ancalagon.

Thus when Tolkien began **The Lord of the Rings* at the end of 1937 the fate of Men in Middle-earth had reached much the same position as in our own world: they were mortal and must die; they are not bound to the world and only God knows their fate after death. But there was one great difference: in Judaic and Christian tradition death is (or is sometimes seen as) God's punishment for Adam and Eve's disobedience, but in Tolkien's *legendarium* death is a gift from God, though Men grow to fear it through the lies of Morgoth. ('Death is their fate, the gift of Ilúvatar, which as Time wears even the Powers shall envy. But Melkor has cast his shadow upon it, and confounded it with darkness, and brought forth evil out of good, and fear out of hope', *The Silmarillion*, p. 42.) On 4 November 1954 Tolkien wrote in a draft letter to Robert Murray that

> the view of the myth [in the *legendarium*] is that Death – the mere shortness of human life-span – is not punishment for the **Fall, but a biologically (and therefore also spiritually, since body and spirit are integrated) inherent part of Man's nature. The attempt to escape it is wicked because 'unnatural', and silly because Death in that sense is the Gift of God (envied by the Elves), release from the weariness of Time. Death, in the penal sense, is viewed as a change in attitude to it: fear, reluctance. [*Letters*, p. 205]

In a draft letter to Peter Hastings in September 1954 Tolkien stressed that only Ilúvatar could make any change: 'Immortality and Mortality being the special gifts of God to [Elves and Men] (in whose conception and creation the Valar had no part at all) it must be assumed that no alteration of their fundamental kind could be effected by the Valar even in one case: the cases of

Lúthien (and Túor) and the position of their descendants was a direct act of God' (*Letters*, p. 194). In a draft letter to Rhona Beare on 14 October 1958 Tolkien elaborated that

> *mortality*, that is a short life-span having no relation to the life of Arda, is spoken of as the given nature of Men: the Elves called it the *Gift of Ilúvatar* (God). But it must be remembered that *mythically* these tales are Elf-centred, not anthropocentric, and Men only appear in them, at what must be a point long after their Coming. This is therefore an 'Elvish' view, and does not necessarily have anything to say for or against such beliefs as the Christian that 'death' is not part of human nature, but a punishment for sin (rebellion), a result of the 'Fall'. It should be regarded as an Elvish perception of what *death* – not being tied to the 'circles of the world' – should now become for Men, however it arose. A divine 'punishment' is also a divine 'gift', if accepted, since its object is ultimate blessing, and the supreme inventiveness of the Creator will make 'punishments' (that is changes of design) produce a good not otherwise to be attained: a 'mortal' Man has probably (an Elf would say) a higher if unrevealed destiny than a longeval one. [*Letters*, pp. 285–6]

At about this period (late 1958–60) Tolkien was apparently working on the *Athrabeth Finrod ah Andreth*, in which the Wise-woman Andreth tells the Elf Finrod that some Men believe that they 'were not made for death, nor born ever to die. Death was imposed on us' (*Morgoth's Ring*, p. 309). According to their lore, 'we knew that in our beginning we had been born *never to die*. And by that . . . we meant: *born to life everlasting, without any shadow of any end*' (p. 314). Men also believed that they had begun to suffer death only after worshipping Morgoth. It is not clear whether Tolkien was envisioning a major change to the original nature of Man in his *legendarium*, bringing the whole more in accord with Christian belief, or whether, as in *The Drowning of Anadûnê*, he was recording Mannish lore and legends.

After the publication of *The Lord of the Rings* Tolkien was asked if the departure of Frodo and Bilbo from Middle-earth with the Elves meant that were granted immortality in the West. He wrote to *Naomi Mitchison on 25 September 1954:

> In this story it is supposed there may be certain rare exceptions or accommodations (legitimately supposed? there always seem to be exceptions); and so certain 'mortals', who have played some great part in Elvish affairs, may pass with the Elves to Elvenhome. Thus Frodo (by the express gift of Arwen) and Bilbo, and eventually Sam . . . and as a unique exception Gimli the Dwarf, as friend of Legolas and 'servant' of Galadriel.
>
> I have said nothing about it in this book, but the mythical idea underlying is that for mortals, since their 'kind' cannot be changed for ever,

this is strictly only a temporary reward: a healing and redress of suffering. They cannot abide for ever, and though they cannot return to mortal earth, they can and will 'die' – of free will, and leave the world. [*Letters*, pp. 198–9]

In a letter to *Milton Waldman Tolkien wrote that the longer life granted to the Númenóreans 'is their undoing – or the means of their temptation. Their long life aids their achievements in art and wisdom, but breeds a possessive attitude to these things, and desire awakes for more *time* for their enjoyment' (?late 1951, *Letters*, p. 154), but their nature could not, in fact, have endured immortality. To this he added 'that each "Kind" has a natural span, integral to its biological and spiritual nature. This cannot really be *increased* qualitatively or quantitatively; so that prolongation in time is like stretching a wire out ever tauter, or "spreading butter ever thinner" – it becomes an intolerable torment' (p. 155). In his draft letter to Robert Murray on 4 November 1954 he pointed out that the Blessed Realm in the West 'does not confer immortality. The land is blessed because the Blessed dwell there, not vice versa, and the Valar are immortal by right and nature, while Men are mortal by right and nature' (*Letters*, p. 205).

In this draft Tolkien also wrote that 'a good Númenórean died of free will when he felt it to be time to do so' (p. 205). In *Unfinished Tales* Christopher Tolkien cites writing by his father after the publication of *The Lord of the Rings* which explains that Númenóreans matured at the same rate as other Men, then enjoyed a longer period 'of vigour of mind and body'. But

the first approach of 'world-weariness' was . . . a sign that their period of vigour was nearing its end. When it came to an end, if they persisted in living, then decay would proceed, as growth had done, no more slowly than among other Men. Thus a Númenórean would pass quickly, in ten years maybe, from health and vigour of mind to decrepitude and senility. In the earlier generations [the Númenóreans] did not 'cling to life', but resigned it voluntarily. 'Clinging to life', and so in the end dying perforce and involuntarily, was one of the changes brought about by the Shadow and the rebellion of the Númenóreans. . . . [*Unfinished Tales*, p. 225]

Thus in *The Lord of the Rings*, when he feels old age approaching, Aragorn as the descendant and heir of the royal house of Númenor chooses to give up his life. He tells Arwen that he is 'the last of the Númenóreans and the latest King of the Elder Days; and to me has been given not only a span thrice that of Men of Middle-earth, but also the grace to go at my will, and give back the gift. . . . I speak no comfort to you, for there is no comfort for such pain within the circles of the world.' 'In sorrow we must go,' he adds, 'but not in despair. Behold! we are not bound for ever to the circles of the world, and beyond them is more than memory' (Appendix A, *The Tale of Aragorn and Arwen*).

There is no indication from Tolkien's correspondence from the time he began *The Lord of the Rings* that he had any intention that Death should be its main theme, or even one of its main themes. He told C. Ouboter on 10 April 1958 that he had been primarily concerned to write an exciting story, and it was only later,

> in reading the work myself (with criticisms in mind) that I become aware of the dominance of the theme of Death. (Not that there is any original 'message' in that: most human art & thought is similarly preoccupied.) But certainly Death is not an Enemy! I said, or meant to say, that the 'message' was the hideous peril of confusing true 'immortality' with limitless serial longevity. Freedom from Time, and clinging to Time. The *confusion* is the work of the Enemy, and one of the chief causes of human disaster. [*Letters*, p. 267]

In the television documentary *Tolkien in Oxford* (1968) Tolkien said that 'if you really come down to any large story that interests people – holds the attention for a considerable time . . . human stories are practically always about one thing, aren't they? Death. The inevitability of death.' In this regard he cited a quotation from Simone de Beauvoir which he felt put the matter in a nutshell: 'There is no such thing as a natural death. Nothing that happens to man is ever natural, since his presence calls the whole world into question. All men must die, but for every man his death is an accident, and even if he knows it and consents to it, an unjustifiable violation.' To this he added: 'Well, you may agree with the words or not, but those are the keyspring of *The Lord of the Rings*.'

Richard L. Purtill writes in *J.R.R. Tolkien: Myth, Morality and Religion* (1984) that 'from the language used [by Tolkien] about human deaths, it is clear that the person is thought of as continuing to exist, but that nothing is known or believed about what happens to the person. . . . But underlying Tolkien's writing on the subject is a firm belief that there *is* something after death and that we can trust in the wisdom and goodness of God to ensure that whatever comes after death will be not only just but generous' (pp. 131–2). Grant C. Sterling similarly comments in '"The Gift of Death": Tolkien's Philosophy of Mortality', *Mythlore* 21, no. 4, whole no. 82 (Winter 1997):

> So behind the fictional story of Middle-earth lies a clear message, a Christian message. As Tolkien saw it, although God intends that we love the world . . . yet He also intends that we see death, in its appropriate time, as a blessing, for through it we may escape the world and serve Him in other ways, and receive from Him a greater reward. The immortals do not die, but it is also true that they are bound to the world for better and for worse. Mortal men must die and venture into the unknown, but they should see that Ilúvatar does not do anything without a purpose. [p. 18]

ELVES AND IMMORTALITY

In *The Music of the Ainur* Ilúvatar declares that the Elves 'will be the fairest and most lovely of all things by far; and deeper in the knowledge of beauty and happier than Men', and that they will 'dwell till the Great End unless they be slain or waste in grief . . .' (*The Book of Lost Tales, Part One*, p. 59). Thus they will be reborn in their children, and their strength will not diminish with age. But 'what Ilúvatar has devised for the Eldar beyond the world's end he has not revealed even to the Valar . . .' (p. 60). In his correspondence Tolkien was careful to distinguish between true immortality as enjoyed by the Ainur, and the limited immortality within the life of Arda granted to the Elves. He wrote to Michael Straight in late 1955 that the Elves are '"immortal". *Not* "eternally", but to endure with and within the created world, while its story lasts. When "killed", by the injury or destruction of their incarnate form, they do not escape from time, but remain *in* the world, either discarnate, or being re-born. This becomes a great burden as the ages lengthen . . .' (*Letters*, p. 236). On 14 October 1958 he told Rhona Beare that in his 'mythical "prehistory" *immortality*, strictly longevity co-extensive with the life of Arda, was part of the given nature of the Elves; beyond the End nothing was revealed' (*Letters*, p. 285); and again to Rhona Beare, on 25 June 1963:

> Even in these legends we see the Elves mainly through the eyes of Men. It is in any case clear that neither side was fully informed about the ultimate destiny of the other. The Elves were sufficiently longeval to be called by Man 'immortal', But they were not unageing or unwearying. Their own tradition was that they were confined to the limits of this world (in space and time), even if they died, and would continue in some form to exist in it until 'the end of the world'. But what 'the end of the world' portended for it or for themselves they did not know (though they no doubt had theories). Neither had they of course any special information concerning what 'death' portended for Men. They believed that it meant 'liberation from the circles of the world', and was in that respect to them enviable. And they would point out to Men who envied them that a dread of ultimate loss, though it may be indefinitely remote, is not necessarily the easier to bear if it is in the end ineluctably certain: a burden may become heavier the longer it is borne. [*Letters*, p. 325]

In the *Athrabeth* the Elf Finrod makes exactly this point to the human Andreth:

> Now none of us know . . . the future of Arda, or how long it is ordained to endure. But it will not endure for ever. It was made by Eru, but He is not in it. The One only has no limits. Arda [the world], and Eä [the material universe] itself, must therefore be bounded. You see us, the Quendi [Elves], still in the first ages of our being, and the end is far off.

As maybe among you death may seem to a young man in his strength; save that we have long years of life and thought already behind us. But the end will come. That we all know. And then we must die; we must perish utterly, it seems, for we belong to Arda (in *hröa* and *fëa* [body and soul]). And beyond that what? 'The going out to no return,' as you say; 'the uttermost end, the irremediable loss'? . . .

It is not clear that a foreseen doom long delayed is in all ways a lighter burden than one that comes soon. [*Morgoth's Ring*, pp. 311–12]

This burden is made even greater and more sorrowful by the Elves' love of the world and its beauty. Their doom, as Tolkien wrote to Milton Waldman, was to bring the world 'to full flower with their gifts of delicacy and perfection, to last while it lasts, never leaving it even when "slain", but returning – and yet, when the Followers [Men] come, to teach them, and make way for them, to 'fade' as the Followers grow and absorb the life from which both proceed.' Bound to the world, the Elves were 'concerned rather with the griefs and burdens of deathlessness in time and change, than with death' (?late 1951, *Letters*, pp. 147, 146). Tolkien considered this point further in his late essay *Aman, originally closely connected with the *Athrabeth*: in Aman the world appeared to the Elves

as it does to Men on Earth, but without the shadow of death soon to come. Whereas on Earth to them all things in comparison with themselves were fleeting, swift to change or die or pass away, in Aman they endured and did not so soon cheat love with their mortality. On Earth while an elf-child did but grow to be a man or a woman, in some 3000 years, forests would rise and fall, and all the face of the land would change, while birds and flowers innumerable would be born or die . . . under the wheeling Sun. [*Morgoth's Ring*, p. 426]

In *The Lord of the Rings*, Legolas tells the other members of the Fellowship that 'for the Elves the world moves, and it moves both very swift and very slow. Swift, because they themselves change little, and all else fleets by: it is a grief to them. Slow, because they need not count the running years, not for themselves. The passing seasons are but ripples ever repeated in the long long stream' (bk. II, ch. 9).

That Elves who were slain or died of grief would, or could, be reborn in their children long remained Tolkien's conception of Elvish reincarnation, though from the beginning it included the idea of a time of meditation and recollection before rebirth. In *The Book of Lost Tales* it is said that Elves who died went to the Halls of Mandos, and 'there Mandos spake their doom, and there they waited in the darkness, dreaming of their past deeds, until such time as he appointed when they might again be born into their children, and go forth to laugh and sing again' (*The Book of Lost Tales, Part One*, p. 76). But in his later years Tolkien began to see problems in such a method of reincarnation, and considered other alternatives (see *The Converse of Manwë and Eru; *'Elvish Reincarnation'; Laws and Customs among the Eldar; *Reincarnation of Elves). As Christopher Tolkien summarizes, he saw

> the difficulties at every level (including practical and psychological) in the idea of the reincarnation of the fëa as the newborn child of second parents, who as it grows up recaptures the memory of its previous life: 'the most fatal objection' being that 'it contradicts the fundamental notion that fëa and hröa were each fitted to the other: since hröar have a physical descent, the body of rebirth, having different parents, must be different'.... [Morgoth's Ring, p. 363]

Tolkien ultimately abandoned the idea of reincarnation through rebirth for the Elves, and instead decided that the fëa retained in memory 'an imprint, of its hröa . . . so powerful and precise that the reconstruction of an identical body can proceed from it' (Morgoth's Ring, p. 363).

Murray, Robert Patrick Ruthven (b. 1925). Robert Murray, grandson of Sir James A.H. Murray of the *Oxford English Dictionary, read Classics at Corpus Christi College, Oxford from 1944 to 1948. At the beginning of this period he began a close friendship with Tolkien and his family, which in 1945–6 helped to lead Murray to convert to the Roman Catholic faith. In 1949 he joined the Society of Jesus, and in 1959 was ordained. From 1961 to 1963 he attended the Gregorian University in Rome, where he earned a Doctorate in Sacred Theology. From 1963 he has been on the Faculty of Heythrop College in Oxfordshire and London. He has written many articles and essays on subjects such as the Bible and related literature, Syriac Christianity and literature, theology of the Church, Jewish-Christian relations, and ecology. From 1971 to 1983 he edited the Heythrop Journal. His books include Symbols of Church and Kingdom: A Study in Early Syriac Theology (1975) and The Cosmic Covenant: Biblical Themes of Justice, Peace and the Integrity of Creation (1992).

Murray was privileged to read *The Lord of the Rings as a work in progress and in proof. In 1953 and 1954 he commented about it in letters to Tolkien, who replied at length, especially about the religious and Catholic nature of The Lord of the Rings, and about religious aspects of his larger mythology (see Letters, pp. 171–3, 200–7). Correspondence also ensued about other subjects, and he and Tolkien saw each other on occasion. On 1 August 1959 Tolkien served Father Robert Murray's first Mass, 'in full academic dress, excitement making him clumsy as a small boy' (Robert Murray, 'A Tribute to Tolkien', The Tablet, 15 September 1973, p. 880). On 6 September 1973 Father Robert Murray assisted in a requiem Mass for Tolkien in the Church of St Anthony of Padua in Headington, Oxford. Later he wrote of his friendship with Tolkien in an obituary and tribute in the Tablet, and in a sermon of thanksgiving at the Tolkien Centenary Conference, Keble College, Oxford in August 1992.

Music. On 16 August 1964 Tolkien wrote to Carey Blyton, who had asked permission to compose a *Hobbit Overture*:

> I have little musical knowledge. Though I come of a musical family, owing to defects of education and opportunity as an orphan, such music as was in me was submerged (until I married a musician), or transformed into linguistic terms. Music gives me great pleasure and sometimes inspiration, but I remain in the position in reverse of one who likes to read or hear poetry but knows little of its technique or tradition, or of linguistic structure. [*Letters*, p. 350]

Humphrey Carpenter notes in *Biography* that Tolkien's mother 'tried to interest him in playing the piano, but without success. It seemed rather as if words took the place of music for him, and that he enjoyed listening to them, reading them, and reciting them, almost regardless of what they meant' (p. 22). Tolkien evidently made an unsuccessful attempt to learn to play the violin: in a letter to *Robert Murray, who was learning to play the cello, he wrote: 'Anyone who can play a stringed instrument seems to me a wizard worthy of respect. I love music, but have no aptitude for it; and the efforts spent trying to teach me the fiddle in youth, have left me only with a feeling of awe in the presence of fiddlers' (2 December 1953, *Letters*, p. 173). *Priscilla Tolkien has said that

> the love of music was . . . deep between my parents, but I believe that for much of his external working life this love . . . was overlaid in my father. Perhaps no one, however talented, can attend to more than two of the arts fully and my father was certainly active in the pursuits of writing and drawing and painting. He later expressed real regret that he did not practise the violin as a boy, so that his guardian, understandably, removed the instrument, which was valuable, and discontinued the lessons. Hence the power and beauty of music [in his writings] may . . . represent the feeling of unsatisfied longing in my father. ['Talk Given at the Church House Westminster on 16.9.77 by Priscilla Tolkien', *Amon Hen* 29 (?November 1977), p. 5]

Tolkien would have attended at least some of the musical performances given during his time at *King Edward's School, Birmingham, though there is no record of him taking part. The School Choir usually performed on Speech Days. There was also an Annual Open Concert: the *King Edward's School Chronicle* for June 1910 described one of these as having attracted over 300 people. Tolkien may also have accompanied his friend *Christopher Wiseman to public performances; years later Wiseman recalled having attended orchestral concerts in Birmingham Town Hall, in the days when the city orchestra was celebrated and its conductors included Hans Richter and Artur Nikisch.

Early in 1908 Tolkien and his brother *Hilary moved into a room let by a Mrs Faulkner. Another lodger was Edith Bratt (*Edith Tolkien), Tolkien's future wife, an able pianist who had spent several years as a boarder at the Dresden House School, which specialized in music. Mrs Faulkner gave musical soirées at which Edith played the piano and accompanied soloists. Edith could also sing, and the episode in the wood at Roos (*Yorkshire) when she sang and danced inspired the story that became what Tolkien considered the central part of the *'Silmarillion'.

At Exeter College, *Oxford, concerts and other events were a part of undergraduate life. Tolkien was present on many such occasions, sometimes obtaining signatures of participants on printed programmes. In Michaelmas Term each year there was the Freshman's Wine to welcome new undergraduates, at which the programme included songs (mainly light and popular), piano solos, and recitation. Smoking Concerts were more ambitious, with the College Orchestra and Choir playing an important part, sometimes with guest vocalists. On these occasions the entertainment was usually a mixture of popular classical music (such as the overture to Bizet's *Carmen*), parts of oratorios, and popular or traditional songs.

Edith continued to play at home until her hands became stiff with age and she gave her piano to her daughter, *Priscilla. In 1918, in a sheet of vignettes by Tolkien entitled *High Life at Gipsy Green* (*Artist and Illustrator*, fig. 23), is a view of Edith playing a piano. Priscilla Tolkien still owns some of the albums in which Edith copied music, 'showing her taste ranging from classical music to the lighter ballads of the time' (*The Tolkien Family Album*, p. 30). Tolkien knew popular songs and tunes well enough to suggest pre-existent tunes for the verses he wrote for the Viking Club at Leeds University, noting them either on the original duplicated typescripts or on one of his copies of *Songs for the Philologists* (1936).

Tolkien attended an opera at Covent Garden at least once in the 1930s, when he and *C.S. Lewis heard part of Wagner's *Der Ring des Nibelungen*. Priscilla Tolkien thinks that the opera in question was *Siegfried*. In 1955, during their visit to *Italy, Tolkien and Priscilla attended an open-air performance of *Rigoletto* in Venice. He had not seen this opera before, and bought a libretto to read before each act. He recorded in his diary that the work had 'a good dramatic plot, though both the handling by Piave and Verdi's music dragged in places', not however through any fault of the singers. He was particularly impressed by the tenor singing the part of the Duke of Mantua, and commented:

> I have never before in opera had the fortune to see a young man who *looked* young gallant handsome and wilful, was beautifully dressed, acted excellently and sang superbly. He swept both P[riscilla] and me off our feet, together with Gilda and Maddalena, though we knew all about his wickedness. The moment when his voice in the background is heard repeating the *la donna è mobile*, just as Rigoletto is gloating over his supposed mantled corpse, is or was on this occasion, a great dramatic thrill. This is a lot for one to say, who is not dramatic or operatic in taste. [Tolkien Papers, Bodleian Library, Oxford]

Priscilla Tolkien has said that her father 'had had hitherto little opportunity to enjoy opera. This performance . . . was a revelation to him' (foreword to *A Tribute to J.R.R. Tolkien* (1992), p. viii).

In the 1968 BBC television documentary *Tolkien in Oxford* (*Interviews) Tolkien commented that he had always been extremely fond of the music of Carl Maria von Weber (1786–1826). Weber is known as one of the earliest composers of romantic opera, and in particular for works such as *Der Freischütz* and *Oberon* with supernatural elements. In 1960, when a composer asked his permission to compose an operetta on the subject of *The Hobbit*, Tolkien wrote to *Rayner Unwin: 'I should not disapprove out of hand until I have seen some of the results. Though of course I am prejudiced against operettas in general [presumably as opposed to opera] and the use of *The Hobbit* for this purpose in particular. And I prefer to monkey with my own songs' (9 September 1960, Tolkien-George Allen & Unwin archive, HarperCollins).

Tolkien disliked most contemporary popular music. In a letter to his son *Christopher on 31 July 1944 he foresaw that 'music will give place to jiving: which as far as I can make out means holding a "jam session" round a piano (an instrument properly intended to produce the sounds devised by, say, Chopin) and hitting it so hard that it breaks. This delicately cultured amusement is said to be a "fever" in the U.S.A.' (*Letters*, p. 89). On 30 January 1945 he replied to a letter from Christopher complaining about certain aspects of his life in the Air Force in South Africa: 'I read eagerly all details of your life, and all the things you see and do – and suffer, Jive and Boogie-Woogie among them. You will have no heart-tug at losing that (for it is essentially vulgar, music corrupted by the mechanism, echoing in dreary unnourished heads) . . .' (*Letters*, p. 111). In 1964 he complained in a letter to Christopher Bretherton how noisy the area around his house in Sandfield Road had become: 'in a house three doors away dwells a member of a group of young men who are evidently aiming to turn themselves into a Beatle Group. On days when it falls to his turn to have a practice session the noise is indescribable' (16 July 1964, *Letters*, p. 345). At the end of 1968 there were reports that the Beatles might be involved with a proposed film of *The Lord of the Rings*. On 7 January 1969 *Joy Hill wrote a memo to Rayner Unwin after a visit to Tolkien: 'Professor Tolkien is getting more and more furious about this . . . because it seems that the Beatles are announcing plans in connection with the film. . . . He is livid that the Beatles have done this and loathes them anyway. . . . Particularly . . . he seem to have a thing against John Lennon' (Tolkien–George Allen & Unwin archive, HarperCollins).

But Tolkien enjoyed most of *Donald Swann's musical settings of Tolkien's verse. Swann visited Oxford on 30 May 1965 to play these to Tolkien. In his foreword to *The Road Goes Ever On: A Song Cycle* (1967) Swann describes Tolkien's reaction:

> After he had heard the six songs Professor Tolkien approved five but bridled at my setting for 'Namárië.' He had heard it differently in his

mind, he said, and hummed a Gregorian chant. I made a note of it, and in the following week I played it over many times to the Elvish words. There was no doubt that this monodic line from a remote musical tradition expressed the words ideally, in particular the sadness of the title word 'Namárië' and the interjection "Ai!' For my song cycle it would make a pleasant variation for the piano to stop, and then return for the next song. So I added only the introduction, interlude and coda. [p. vi]

Tolkien and Edith were delighted when Donald Swann and the baritone William Elvin offered to perform the song-cycle at Merton College on 23 March 1966 as part of their Golden Wedding celebration.

MUSIC IN TOLKIEN'S WRITINGS

In the 'Silmarillion' mythology music is frequently present and often a manifestation of power. Creation is achieved through the Music the Ainur make before Ilúvatar, into which Evil enters through the discords of Melkor. Yavanna sings the Two Trees into being. Melian's singing fills Thingol's heart with such 'wonder and desire' that he forgets his people. Fingon uses song to contact the captured Maedhros. Finrod Felagund discovers Men who have just arrived in Beleriand when he hears them singing 'because they were glad, and believed that they had escaped from all perils and had come at last to a land without fear'; he takes up a harp and plays to them, and 'wisdom was in the words of the Elven-king, and the hearts grew wiser that hearkened to him; for the things of which he sang, of the making of Arda, and the bliss of Aman beyond the shadows of the Sea, came as clear visions before their eyes. . . .' The song of Lúthien releases 'the bonds of winter'. The battle between Finrod and Sauron is depicted as a contest of songs of power. Lúthien sings to contact the imprisoned Beren, and to challenge Sauron; and before Morgoth she sings 'a song of such surpassing loveliness, and of such blinding power, that he listened perforce, and a blindness came upon him. . . .' And by 'the song most fair that ever in words was woven, and the song most sorrowful that ever the world should hear' Lúthien moved to pity Mandos 'who never before was so moved, nor has been since' (*The Silmarillion*, pp. 55, 140, 140–1, 165, 180, 186–7).

Music and song appear also in *The Hobbit* and *The Lord of the Rings*, and although not depicted as having such power as in 'The Silmarillion' are more varied in tone and style. In *The Hobbit* are playful songs such as that of the dwarves threatening to break Bilbo's crockery, and of the elves in Rivendell; the enticing song of the dwarves which rouses in Bilbo a 'love of beautiful things' and a wish 'to go and see the great mountains, and hear the pine-trees and the waterfalls and explore the caves, and wear a sword instead of a walking-stick' (ch. 1); and the humorously threatening songs of the goblins, and of Bilbo when taunting the spiders. In *The Lord of the Rings* there are carefree songs such as the walking song ('Upon the hearth the fire is red'), the bath-song at Crickhollow, and Frodo's song in the Prancing Pony; the haunting beauty of Elvish singing on the road to Woody End, and at Rivendell and Loth-lórien; the many songs of Tom Bombadil, some nonsensical or descriptive, but others revealing his power over Old Man Willow and the Barrow-wight; the heroic song recording the ride of the Rohirrim from Dunharrow to the relief of Minas Tirith; the laments for Boromir and for those slain on the Pelennor Fields; and the song of praise for Frodo and Sam on the Field of Cormallen.

In 'The "Music of the Spheres": Relationships between Tolkien's *The Silmarillion* and Medieval Cosmological and Religious Theory', in *Tolkien the Medievalist* (2003), Bradford Lee Eden discusses influence of the medieval concept of the 'music of the spheres' on Tolkien's mythology. He summarizes the idea as 'grounded in ancient and classical philosophy' (p. 183) and eventually standardized by Boethius (*c.* AD 480–524) in his treatise *De institutione musica*. Boethius stated that 'music was divided into three specific kinds, in order of priority and importance: the music of the universe, human music (vocal), and instrumental music. The first kind . . . is embodied in the movement of celestial bodies, the harmony of the four elements, and the four season' (p. 184). Eden relates the creation story of the *Ainulindalë* to this first kind of music, and comments: 'That music is the creational and binding force that sets in motion the entire drama of Middle-earth . . . not only emphasizes the importance of the first type of music . . . but also binds Tolkien in the rest of his mythological work to construct and illustrate music's power through the other two types of music as well' (p. 186). Concerning the second type, vocal music, and citing Thingol and Melian and examples from the story of Beren and Lúthien, he comments that 'many examples exist within *The Silmarillion* itself that music is the generational force out of which much of the drama of Middle-earth develops' (p. 187). He considers that 'the intensity with which Tolkien slowly yet intentionally weaves cosmological and human/vocal music throughout his mythology, in individual stories and dramas as well as through the ages of Middle-earth . . . is a testimony to his understanding, knowledge, and indeed belief in music as a creational and cosmological power' (p. 188). He notes that in *The Silmarillion* there is no direct reference to the third type, instrumental music, except possibly the two minstrels, Maglor and Daeron, and suggests that this may not be a coincidence. Both vocal and instrumental music are more common in *The Hobbit* and *The Lord of the Rings*, but there songs seem to have less power: 'Elves and Men are farther away in both time and space from the "music of the spheres" and closer to the third and lower type of music in the Third Age' (p. 191).

Gill Gleeson comments in 'Music in Middle-earth' (*Mallorn* 16, May 1981) that 'all types of musical instrument are found in Middle-earth except for bellows and keyboard'. The Elvish 'religious song'

> *Namárië*, is like an improvisatory plainsong for voice and (melodic) instrument; a self-contained unharmonised melody. How strange the Dwarvish ensembles must have sounded to a people used to this; and how rarefied the Elvish chants, to the Dwarves. . . .

The Ents had entwined in their language a complex harmonic system within which the voice of each one could be heard and fashioned in ever-changing relationships with the others, until one concord was reached. Perhaps all the different styles of music represented different facets of the original Great Music of Creation, as did the creatures they belonged to: yet of all of them it is the music of the Ents that gives me a vision of what the *Ainulindalë* must have been like. [p. 30; see *The Lord of the Rings*, bk. III, ch. 4]

MUSIC INSPIRED BY TOLKIEN

Tolkien's works have inspired original music since at least the mid-1960s. One of the foremost authorities on Tolkien-related music, Chris Seeman, has counted thousands of artists who have set Tolkien's words to music, written new lyrics based on Tolkien's stories, and created instrumental, orchestral, and choral compositions using his works as a foundation or point of departure. Among these, popular musicians are the most numerous, and among the earliest of them perhaps the best known is Bo Hansson from Sweden (*Sagan om ringen* or *Music Inspired by The Lord of the Rings*, 1970). Classical composers inspired by Tolkien include Johan de Meij (*Symphony No. 1, 'The Lord of the Rings'*); Aulis Sallinen (*Symphony No. 7 'The Dreams of Gandalf'*, op. 71, and *Lohikäärmevuori* ('The Dragon Mountain'), op. 78, based on *The Hobbit*; Craig Russell (*Middle Earth*); and the aforementioned Carey Blyton (*Hobbit Overture*). Donald Swann's settings of Tolkien verse are in a class by themselves, most of them having been heard and approved by the author.

Notable music for *adaptations of Tolkien's writings for other media include that composed by Stephen Oliver for the 1981 BBC radio play of *The Lord of the Rings*, and the score for the 2001–3 film adaptation of *The Lord of the Rings*, composed by Howard Shore.

See also *The Tolkien Music List* by Chris Seeman at *www.tolkien-music.com*.

Myth and legend *see* **Arthur and the Matter of Britain; Atlantis; Celtic influences; England; Fairy-stories;** *Kalevala***; Lang, Andrew; Northernness; Quest**

'Mythology for England' *see* **England; Eriol and Ælfwine**

Mythopoeia. Poem, first published in its entirety in *Tree and Leaf*, Unwin Hyman, London, 1988, and Houghton Mifflin, Boston, 1989, pp. 97–101. The poet addresses 'one who said that myths were lies and therefore worthless, even though "breathed through silver"', in fact *C.S. Lewis. He describes 'great processes' of Nature, seen in terms of science ('for trees are "trees"', and 'a star's a star, some matter in a ball / compelled to courses mathematical') or as creations of God. Yet trees, beasts, stars were not so, to Man, until he sees them in spirit as well as sense.

> He sees no stars who does not see them first
> of living silver made that sudden burst
> to flame like flowers beneath an ancient song,
> whose very echo after-music long
> has since pursued. There is no firmament,
> only a void, unless a jewelled tent
> myth-woven and elf-patterned; and no earth,
> unless the mother's womb whence all have birth.

Man, in this sense, is a 'sub-creator', 'the refracted light / through whom is splintered from a single White / to many hues, and endlessly combined / in living shapes that move from mind to mind'. The poet blesses men of imagination, of faith, 'the legend-makers with their rhyme / of things not found within recorded time'. He 'will not walk with your progressive apes', before which 'gapes / the dark abyss to which their progress tends', or accept a world in which 'the little maker' (the sub-creator) has no part in the 'maker's art' (the creations of God).

Mythopoeia was inspired by a discussion among Tolkien, C.S. Lewis, and *'Hugo' Dyson at Magdalen College, Oxford on 19–20 September 1931. After dinner, they strolled in the College grounds, talking of metaphor and myth; and later, to escape the wind, continued in Lewis's rooms. Lewis appreciated the power of myth, and delighted in certain myths, such as that of the dying Norse god Balder, but held that such stories were nonetheless not true – lies, though 'breathed through silver'. Tolkien disagreed, and apparently – the event as described by Humphrey Carpenter in *The Inklings* is merely a paraphrase of *Mythopoeia* – argued successfully that in making a myth, Man exercises an imaginative invention which must originate with God (see *Sub-creation), and therefore must 'reflect something of eternal truth' (*The Inklings*, p. 43).

It can only be guessed when Tolkien first composed *Mythopoeia*. Seven versions of the poem exist. On the fifth and sixth, Tolkien inscribed 'J.R.R.T. for 'C.S.L.' On the last he added two marginal notes which *Christopher Tolkien has dated to 'November 1935 or later', in one of which Tolkien commented that he referred to trees in the opening lines of the poem ('You look at trees and label them just so, / (for trees are "trees", and growing is "to grow"') 'because they are at once easily classifiable and innumerably individual; but as this may be said of other things, then I will say, because I notice them more than most other things (far more than people). In any case the mental scenic background of these lines is the Grove and Walks of Magdalen at night' (*Tree and Leaf*, p. 7). Also on the seventh version is the inscription 'Written mainly in the Examination Schools during Invigilation', which suggests a date between June 1932 and June 1933, those years between 1931 and 1935 when Tolkien acted as an examiner in the *Oxford English School.

Tolkien quoted a small portion of *Mythopoeia* in *On Fairy-Stories* (first published 1947), as if 'a letter I once wrote to a man who described myth and fairy-story as "lies"' (*Tree and Leaf*, p. 50). The existence of the longer work was not generally known, however, until revealed by Humphrey Carpenter in *Biography*. Following Carpenter, the earliest comment on the poem, based on a view of the manuscript, was in 'The Coincidence of Myth and Fact' by Stephen Medcalf, in *Ways of Reading the Bible* (1981); in this Medcalf, like Carpenter in *The Inklings*, related the events that inspired *Mythopoeia* to the return of C.S. Lewis to belief in Christianity. Medcalf further commented on the poem, in relation to ideas of language expressed by *Owen Barfield, in '"The Language Learned of Elves": Owen Barfield, *The Hobbit* and *The Lord of the Rings*', *Seven* 16 (1999). In 'Tolkien's "Essay on Man": A Look at *Mythopoeia*', *Inklings-Jahrbuch für Literatur und Ästhetik* 10 (1992), Clive Tolley finds notable parallels between *Mythopoeia* and Alexander Pope's *Essay on Criticism* and *Essay on Man*, as well as Sir Philip Sidney's *Apologie for Poetrie* and Owen Barfield's *Poetic Diction*.

'Name-list to *The Fall of Gondolin*'. Unfinished compilation of names in Qenya and Gnomish (Noldorin, later Sindarin; see *Languages, Invented) occurring in *The Fall of Gondolin* in *The Book of Lost Tales* as 'set forth by Eriol at the teaching of Bronweg's son . . . Littleheart' (*The Book of Lost Tales, Part Two*, p. 148). Tolkien evidently compiled this list in more or less alphabetical order from the *Official Name List* (?1917–?1919), but it extends only as far as the letter *L*. *Christopher Tolkien incorporated information from the list in the Appendices ('Names in the *Lost Tales*') to *The Book of Lost Tales, Part One* and *The Book of Lost Tales, Part Two*. The complete list was published with commentary and notes in *Parma Eldalamberon* 15 (2004), pp. 19–30, ed. Christopher Gilson and Patrick H. Wynne.

In the original list the word are listed by letter of the alphabet, but within entries for each letter in the order in which they occur in *The Fall of Gondolin*. The section in *Parma Eldalamberon* also publishes another projected list, abandoned after only three entries (p. 19; *The Book of Lost Tales, Part Two*, p. 202), probably the beginning of a list for names in *The Cottage of Lost Play* (*The Book of Lost Tales*).

The Name 'Nodens'. Note, published as Appendix I in the *Report on the Excavation of the Prehistoric, Roman, and Post-Roman Site in Lydney Park, Gloucestershire* by R.E.M. Wheeler and T.V. Wheeler (1932), pp. 132–7.

The report is concerned with excavations in 1928–9 of a promontory fort or small embanked hill-town of five acres, established at Lydney in or shortly before the first century BC. 'Soon after A.D. 364–7 a temple, dedicated to the otherwise unknown deity Nodens, was built within the earthwork, and with the temple, which was of unusual plan, were associated a guest-house, baths, and other structures, indicating that the cult was an important centre of pilgrimage' (Wheeler and Wheeler, p. 1). Tolkien observes in his note that *Nodens* occurs in three inscriptions; otherwise, 'from the same place and presumably roughly contemporary, there is in early Keltic [Celtic] material no trace of any such name or stem' (p. 132). He relates *Nodens* to *Núadu* (later *Núada*)

Argat-lám, the king of the Túatha dé Danann, 'the possessors of Ireland before the Milesians' (p. 133), and to other Nuadas in Irish. 'It is possible to see a memory of this figure in the medieval Welsh Lludd Llaw Ereint ("of the Silver Hand") – the ultimate original of King Lear – whose daughter Creiddylad (Cordelia) was carried off, after her betrothal to Gwythyr vab Greiddawl, by Gwynn vab Nudd, a figure having connexions with the underworld' (p. 133). The normal Welsh form of *Nuada* or *Nodens* is *Nudd*.

Tolkien researched the name *Nodens* and wrote a note on the subject probably in 1929 or 1930, at the request of R.E.M. (later Sir Mortimer) Wheeler, Keeper and Secretary of the London Museum. Wheeler had the finished note in hand apparently well before 2 December 1931, when he informed Tolkien that a report on the Lydney Park excavations was to be issued by the Society of Antiquaries, including Tolkien's note, and enclosed a proof. Tolkien replied to Wheeler by 9 December, evidently having had related thoughts on the possible evolution of the name *Lydney* out of *Lludd*. He wrote at once to his colleague Allen Mawer, then Director of the Survey of English Place-names, about the history of *Lydney*, but the data Mawer could supply were indeterminate.

Tolkien wrote a paragraph on the subject nonetheless, commenting on the obscurity of the origin of the place-name *Lydney*, and that it did not shed light on the problem of *Nodens*. Lydney was an English settlement, not the site of the temple to Nodens, though Tolkien thought that it might contain a pre-English name with a different original focus. Because of the uncertainty of this argument, however, or because production was already too far advanced to permit an addition, the note was omitted from the published report by Wheeler and Wheeler.

The Nameless Land. Poem, first published in *Realities: An Anthology of Verse* (Leeds: Swan Press, 1927), ed. G.S. Tancred for the benefit of the Queen's Hospital for Children, Hackney, London, pp. 24–5. The 'nameless land' is Eressëa, the land of the Elves in the True West of the world. The poet speaks of its golden 'lingering lights', its 'grass more green than in gardens here', its 'dells that immortal dews distill / And fragrance of all flowers that grow'. It is unattainable, 'a thousand leagues' distant, a land 'without a name / No heart may hope to anchor near', more fair than Tir-nan-Og (the land of youth in Irish legend) and 'more faint and far' than Paradise, a 'shore beyond the Shadowy Sea'. The poet dreams that he sees 'a wayward star' – the mariner Eärendel (or Eärendil) sailing the heavens – and refers to 'beacon towers in Gondobar' ('city of stone'), one of the Seven Names of Gondolin.

According to a note on one of its typescripts, Tolkien wrote *The Nameless Land* at his home in Darnley Road, *Leeds, in May 1924, 'inspired by reading *Pearl* for examination purposes'. Like that medieval poem, *The Nameless Land* has both rhyme and alliteration, and the last line of each stanza is echoed in the first line of the next ('And the woods are filled with wandering fire. / The wandering fires the woodland fill'). On 18 July 1962 Tolkien wrote to his *Aunt Jane Neave (*Letters*, p. 317):

The poem [*Pearl*] is very well-known to mediaevalists; but I never agreed to the view of scholars that the metrical form was almost impossibly difficult to write in, and quite impossible to render in modern English. NO scholars (or, nowadays, poets) have any experience in composing themselves in exacting metres. I made up a few stanzas in the metre to show that composition in it was not at any rate 'impossible' (though the result might today be thought bad). . . . I send you the original stanzas of my own – related inevitably as everything was at one time with my own mythology.

Tolkien later revised *The Nameless Land* as *The Song of Ælfwine (on Seeing the Uprising of Eärendel)*, with the intermediate title *Ælfwine's Song Calling upon Eärendel*, tying the poem more explicitly to his mythology. Ælfwine, a mortal mariner who finds the sea-path to Eressëa, figures in *The Book of Lost Tales*, *The Lost Road*, and *The Notion Club Papers*; see *Eriol and Ælfwine. Many texts of *The Song of Ælfwine* survive in manuscript and typescript. Two of these were published, together with *The Nameless Land*, in *The Lost Road and Other Writings* (1987); see further in that volume, pp. 98–104.

Names. On 4 January 1892, the day after his son was born, *Arthur Tolkien wrote to his mother: 'The boy's first name will be "John" after his grandfather, probably John Ronald Reuel altogether. Mab [*Mabel Tolkien] wants to call it Ronald and I want to keep up John and Reuel' (quoted in *Biography*, p. 12). Arthur chose 'John' for his own father (see *Tolkien family), but in fact Mabel's father was also a John (John Suffield, see *Suffield family). Tolkien explained the choice of names in a letter to Amy Ronald on 2 January 1969:

> I was called John because it was the custom for the eldest son of the eldest son to be called John in my family. My father was Arthur, eldest of my grandfather John Benjamin's second family; but his elder half-brother John had died leaving only 3 daughters. So John I had to be. . . .
> My father favoured John Benjamin Reuel (which I should now have liked); but my mother was confident that I should be a daughter, and being fond of more 'romantic' (& less O[ld] T[estament] like) names decided on Rosalind. When I turned up . . . Ronald was substituted. . . .
> Reuel . . . was (I believe) the surname of a friend of my grandfather. The family believed it to be French (which is formally possible); but if so it is an odd chance that it appears twice in the O[ld] T[estament] as an unexplained other name for Jethro Moses' father-in-law. All my children, and my children's children, and their children, have the name.
> [*Letters*, pp. 397–8]

In an autobiographical statement written in 1955 Tolkien explained his surname as 'a German name (from Saxony), an anglicization of *Tollkiehn*, i.e. *tollkühn*. But, except as a guide to spelling, this fact is as fallacious as all facts in the raw. For I am neither 'foolhardy' [= *tollkühn*] nor German, whatever some remote ancestors may have been' (*Letters*, p. 218). Tolkien's aunt Grace Mountain (see *Tolkien family) alleged that their surname had originally been *von Hohenzollern*, after that district of the Holy Roman Empire from which the family had come. 'A certain George von Hohenzollern had, she said, fought on the side of the Archduke Ferdinand of Austria at the Siege of Vienna in 1529. He had shown great daring in leading an unofficial raid against the Turks and capturing the Sultan's standard. This (said Aunt Grace) was why he was given the nickname *Tollkühn*, "foolhardy"; and the nickname stuck' (Humphrey Carpenter, *Biography*, pp. 18–19). The story was also told of a French variation of the surname, *du Téméraire*, but may be no more than family lore.

On a copy of a George Allen & Unwin (*Publishers) press release, not before 1968, Tolkien wrote his surname phonetically and gave instructions for its pronunciation: '(tôl kēn) *tŏlkeen* (sc. *tolk* does not rhyme with *yolk*; the division is tol–keen in which *tol* rhymes with *doll* and *kien* (NOT KEIN) = *keen* as *ie* in *field* and many other words' (Tolkien-George Allen & Unwin archive, HarperCollins). It was, and is, frequently misspelled *Tolkein*. Tolkien complained of this in a letter to Graham Tayar in June 1971, 'in spite of all my efforts to correct this – even by my college-, bank-, and lawyer's clerks!' (*Letters*, p. 410). On 12 October 1966 he wrote to Joy Hill at Allen & Unwin about a document from the Performing Rights Society: 'I wish producers of documents would see to it that they give me my correct name. My third name appears as Revel twice in each of the Deeds. My surname is Tolkein on one of them' (Tolkien-George Allen & Unwin archive, HarperCollins). Even on his tombstone *Reuel* at first was carved *Revel*.

Arthur and Mabel Tolkien called their son by his second name, *Ronald*, as did his other relatives and his wife. In his letter to Amy Ronald, Tolkien said that when he was a boy in England *Ronald* was a much rarer name than it later became: it was shared by none of his contemporaries at school or university 'though it seems now alas! to be prevalent among the criminal and other degraded classes. Anyway I have always treated it with respect, and from earliest days refused to allow it to be abbreviated or tagged with. But for myself I remained John. Ronald was for my near kin. My friends at school, Oxford and later have called me John (or occasionally John Ronald or J. Rsquared)' (*Letters*, p. 398). Tolkien occasionally signed himself 'John' to Edith Bratt (*Edith Tolkien) when they were courting.

To intimates such as Edith or his *Aunt Jane Neave he would sign his letters 'Ronald'. To friends such as *Katharine Farrer and *Donald Swann he signed 'Ronald Tolkien', and to C.S. Lewis 'J.R.R.T'. His formal signature was 'J.R.R. Tolkien'. In 1964, when Allen & Unwin wanted to include a facsimile signature on the title-page of *Tree and Leaf, as was their custom for publications in their 'U Books' series, and sent Tolkien a sample with 'Ronald Tolkien', he wrote to Ronald Eames at Allen & Unwin: 'I do not and never have used the signature "Ronald Tolkien" as a public or auctorial signature and I do not think it suitable for the purpose' (3 February 1964, Tolkien-George Allen & Unwin archive,

HarperCollins). In letters from his *T.C.B.S. friends Tolkien was called variously 'Gabriel', 'Gab', 'Cludhari' – nicknames whose origin is obscure and not mentioned in surviving correspondence – but mainly 'John Ronald', with isolated instances of 'Ronald' or 'JRRT'. His few surviving letters to the T.C.B.S. are signed 'John Ronald'. In a letter to *Joy Hill of 26 December 1971 he noted that his contemporaries used to write his initials as 'JR²T' and pronounce them 'to rhyme with *dirt*' (collection of René van Rossenberg).

According to Humphrey Carpenter, when Tolkien 'was an adult his intimates [presumably other than family] referred to him (as was customary at the time) by his surname, or called him "Tollers", a hearty nickname typical of the period. To those not so close, especially in his later years, he was often known as "J.R.R.T."' (*Biography*, p. 13).

The correspondence between Tolkien and the publishing Unwins, *Stanley and *Rayner, is an interesting lesson in the nuances of methods of address. In 1937 Tolkien wrote to 'Dear Mr Unwin' and signed himself 'J.R.R. Tolkien'; Stanley Unwin replied to 'Dear Professor Tolkien'. During 1944 they wrote to 'Dear Unwin' and 'Dear Tolkien'. In 1946, after Stanley Unwin received a knighthood, Tolkien began his letters 'Dear Sir Stanley', while Unwin continued to write to 'Dear Tolkien'. Despite the fact that he had been addressing letters to 'Dear Tolkien' for some time, on 28 July 1947 Stanley Unwin wrote: 'Dear Tolkien (If I may thus address you in the hope that you will call me "Unwin")' (Tolkien-George Allen & Unwin archive, HarperCollins). Tolkien replied: 'Dear Unwin, I will certainly address you so, cum permissu [with permission], though it hardly seems a fair exchange for the loss of "professor", a title one has rather to live down than to insist on' (*Letters*, p. 120).

When Rayner Unwin began to correspond with Tolkien in 1952 he addressed him as 'Dear Professor Tolkien', and Tolkien replied to 'My dear Rayner' or 'Dear Rayner'. At first Tolkien signed his letters 'J.R.R. Tolkien', but by about 1960 he began to sign 'Ronald Tolkien'. On 15 December 1965 Tolkien wrote to Rayner Unwin:

> Do you think you could mark the New Year by dropping the *Professor*? I belong to a generation which did not use Christian names outside the family, but like the dwarves [in his mythology] kept them private, and for even their intimates used surnames (or perversions of them), or nicknames, or (occasionally) Christian names that did not belong to them. Even C.S. Lewis never called me by a Christian name (or I him). So I will be content with a surname. I wish I could get rid of the "professor" altogether, at any rate when not writing technical matter. It gives a false impression of "learning", especially in "folklore" and all that. It also gives a probably truer impression of pedantry, but it is a pity to have my pedantry advertised and underlined, so that people sniff it even when it is not there. [*Letters*, pp. 365–6]

From that point Rayner wrote to 'Dear Tolkien'. Seven years later, on 30

March 1972, Tolkien wrote to Rayner Unwin: 'Would it be possible for you to use my Christian name? I am now accepted as a member of the community here [Merton College] – one of the habits of which has long been the use of Christian names, irrespective of age or office – and as you are now a v[ery] old friend, and a very dear one, I should much like also to be a "familiaris"' (*Letters*, p. 418).

He did not care whether he was addressed as 'Professor' or 'Mr'; on 12 December 1955 he wrote to Mr Smith at Allen & Unwin that 'there is no need to alter "Mr" to "Professor". In proper Oxford tradition professor is not a title of address – or was not, though the habit has drifted in from places where "professors" are powerful little domestic potentates' (*Letters*, p. 230).

Names and Required Alterations. Parallel list of names in Qenya (*Languages, Invented) from *The Cottage of Lost Play* (**The Book of Lost Tales*), with equivalents in Gnomish (Goldogrin, later Sindarin), published with commentary and notes in *Parma Eldalamberon* 15 (2004), pp. 5–18, ed. Patrick H. Wynne. This appears to date from the period ?1917–?1919. Following the list is an appendix 'which assembles a variety of isolated words, linguistic notes, and phonological charts from the Lost Tales [*Book of Lost Tales*] notebooks that could not be conveniently presented in previous issues of *Parma Eldalamberon*' (p. 6).

'Names of the Valar'. List of the names of the Valar, arranged by gender, published with commentary and notes within 'Early Qenya Fragments' in *Parma Eldalamberon* 14 (2003), pp. 11–15, ed. Patrick Wynne and Christopher Gilson. Originally written only in Qenya (*Languages, Invented), Gnomish (Goldogrin, later Sindarin) forms were added later. It is contemporary with **The Book of Lost Tales*, but probably later than *Corrected Names of Chief Valar*, i.e. from the ?first half of 1919.

Napier, Arthur Sampson (1853–1916). A.S. Napier, educated at Owens College, Manchester and Exeter College, Oxford, taught at Berlin and Göttingen before becoming the Merton Professor of English Language and Literature at Oxford in 1885. In 1903 he became, as well, Rawlinsonian Professor of Anglo-Saxon. Napier's appointment to the Merton Professorship, on the establishment of that chair, strengthened the language side of English studies at Oxford – he was one of three professors of Philology, together with John Earle and F. Max Müller – much to the regret of those who pictured the philologists 'lecturing simultaneously on *Beowulf* to empty benches, while there was no one to lecture on Shakespeare and Milton' (D.J. Palmer, *The Rise of English Studies* (1965), p. 87). In fact, Napier would later play a key role, with *Walter Raleigh, in bifurcating the Oxford English syllabus to make it more attractive to students whose primary interest was literature rather than language (from 1908 only four out of ten papers were required in common of all students reading English, with the other six oriented to suit the language or literature specialty).

Never robust, during the last ten years of his life Napier was frequently in ill health, but was ably assisted by *Kenneth Sisam, whose B.Litt. thesis Napier supervised. Tolkien later recalled meeting Napier when, as an undergraduate at Oxford, he changed his course of study from Classics to English Language and Literature: 'I recall that I was ushered into a very dim room and could hardly see Napier. He was courteous, but said little. He never spoke to me again. I attended his lectures, when he was well enough to give them' (letter to *N.R. Ker, 22 November 1970, *Letters*, p. 406). These definitely included, in Michaelmas Term 1913, lectures on English Historical Grammar and on Old English Dialects, and in Michaelmas Term 1914 and Hilary Term 1915, on *Pearl* and *Beowulf* (see further, **Chronology**).

Narn i Chîn Húrin. Prose narrative of the story of Túrin (see *'Of Túrin Turambar'), published with notes and commentary in *Unfinished Tales* (1980), pp. 57–162, as *Narn i Hîn Húrin: The Tale of the Children of Húrin* (see below). Some sections of draft and further commentary were included in the account of the *Grey Annals* in *The War of the Jewels* (1994).

When *Christopher Tolkien edited *Unfinished Tales* he was under the impression that the whole of the *Narn* was a work of the late 1950s, but after extensive work on his father's papers during the writing of *The History of Middle-earth* he realized that the latter part of the *Narn*, from the section headed 'The Return of Túrin to Dor-lómin' to 'The Death of Túrin' (*Unfinished Tales*, pp. 104–46), was written *c.* 1951 and in close association with the *Grey Annals* (*Annals of Beleriand*). 'The manuscript was headed (later) "The Children of Húrin: last part", and at the top of the first page my father wrote "Part of the 'Children of Húrin' told in full scale"' (*The War of the Jewels*, p. 144). Up to the point where the Men of Brethil discuss what action to take against Glaurung, preliminary drafting for the manuscript text 'consists of little more than scribbled slips. From here on . . . there are in effect two manuscripts', one of which Christopher Tolkien calls 'the draft manuscript', being a 'continuation of the original, which became so chaotic with rewriting' that Tolkien made a fair copy (*The War of the Jewels*, p. 152). In his comments on the relevant portion of the *Grey Annals* in *The War of the Jewels* (pp. 144–65) Christopher Tolkien includes comparisons of various versions of the story of Túrin, lengthy extracts from drafts for the *Narn*, and synopses for the end of the story which show Tolkien hesitating over the dénouement.

Tolkien possibly chose to begin this prose account part way through the story because he had already written a lengthy account of Túrin's earlier life in alliterative verse in the 1920s (*The Children of Húrin*), but nothing at length of his later life since *The Book of Lost Tales*. The part of the *Narn* dealing with Túrin's earlier life, however, is a work of the late 1950s. In *The War of the Jewels* Christopher Tolkien describes 'a twelve-page typescript composed *ab initio* by my father and bearing the title "Here begins the tale of the Children of Húrin, *Narn i Chîn Húrin*, which Dírhaval wrought"' (p. 314). This provided the text for the first part of the *Narn* (*Unfinished Tales*, pp. 57–65), but two passages describing the sojourn of Húrin and Huor in Gondolin and an account of the Nirnaeth Arnoediad were omitted, since similar texts taken from the *Grey Annals* had appeared in **The Silmarillion*. Christopher Tolkien comments at length on differences between these passages in the *Narn* and the *Grey Annals*, and his use of elements from both in *The Silmarillion* (*The War of the Jewels*, pp. 165–70, 314–15). He noted in *Unfinished Tales* that the next section

> (to the end of Túrin in Doriath) required a good deal of revision and selection, and in some places some slight compression, the original texts being scrappy and disconnected. But the central section (Túrin among the outlaws, Mîm the Petty-dwarf, the land of Dor-Cúarthol, the death of Beleg at Túrin's hand, and Túrin's life in Nargothrond) constituted a much more difficult editorial problem. The *Narn* is here at its least finished, and in places diminished to outlines of possible turns in the story. My father was still evolving this part when he ceased to work on it. . . .
>
>   For the first part of this central section, as far as the beginning of Túrin's sojourn in Mîm's dwelling on Amon Rûdh, I have contrived a narrative, in scale commensurate with other parts of the *Narn*, out of the existing materials (with one gap . . .). [p. 6]

But from that point he found the task of compiling a continuous narrative impossible, and instead published a series of disconnected fragments and notes as an Appendix.

In **The Lost Road and Other Writings* Christopher Tolkien explains that in *Unfinished Tales* he 'improperly' replaced [Elvish] *Chîn* with *Hîn* 'because I did not want *Chîn* to be pronounced like Modern English *chin*' (p. 322; in Exilic Noldorin *ch* is pronounced as in Scottish *loch*). In *The War of the Jewels* (pp. 142, 145, 146, 149, 151) he notes editorial changes he made in the text published in *Unfinished Tales*, as well as authorial emendations.

Tolkien also wrote two versions of an introductory note to the *Narn*, probably *c.* 1958, which explains its origins within the context of the **'Silmarillion'* mythology. A brief summary appeared in *Unfinished Tales* (p. 146); both texts, under the title *Ælfwine and Dírhaval*, were published with commentary and notes in *The War of the Jewels*, pp. 311–15. The *Narn* began as a lay in an Elvish mode of verse written in Sindarin by Dírhaval, a Man who lived at the Havens towards the end of the First Age and gathered all the information he could about the House of Hador. According to the first version, Ælfwine (see **Eriol and Ælfwine*) translated the lay into the English of his time as a prose narrative, from which the Modern English version is said to have been made. The second version is purported to be written by Ælfwine himself, explaining that he did not feel able to translate the work into verse.

The first version is a manuscript with the title *Túrin Turumarth*; the second is an untitled, much shorter typescript which Tolkien attached to the twelve-page typescript he had made of the opening of the *Narn*.

CRITICISM

In his review of *Unfinished Tales* ('Dug Out of the Dust of Middle-earth', *Maclean's*, 26 January 1981) Guy Gavriel Kay wrote that

> Túrin Turambar is Tolkien's most tragic character – perhaps his only tragic figure. His story is told in *The Silmarillion*: victim of the curse of a fallen god, condemned to bring evil on those who aid him, tangled in a web that leads to a bitter ending of unwitting incest with a long-lost sister and ultimate suicide. Here the same tale is retold, at three times the length and in detail that would have overwhelmed the spare narrative style and the overriding shape of *The Silmarillion*. The story was inspired by a part of the Finnish myth-cycle, **The Kalevala*, but in the fated inevitability of its conclusion, Túrin's saga moves and feels like something out of Greek tragedy. The reader's affinity for the longer or the shorter version will depend on whether he prefers his tragedy austere or baroque. [p. 46]

Thomas M. Egan in his review ('Fragments of a World: Tolkien's Road to Middle-earth', *Terrier* 48, no. 2 (Fall 1983) wrote:

> Adventure tales like 'Narn I Hîn Húrin' . . . grip us with the moral drama of Good and Evil involved. The language . . . is almost always quasi-Biblical, elegant in tone and forcing us to slow down in our reading habits. It is the context the author uses to explore a human soul, when it ultimately finds despair and loss, rather than the optimistic triumph of the Ring heroes [in **The Lord of the Rings*]. . . . The mood is sometimes bitter but never cynical. Incest, rape, murder are all here as Tolkien explores his version of the modern anti-hero. Túrin Turambar seems cursed by fate. . . . But Tolkien adds the depths of his convictions to the tale. The respect for the power of human free will, that which links the soul to God (Eru) Himself . . . appears here as always operating. Even when it is denied or misused, the author always puts in the concrete details of other characters or situations to remind us that things could have gone so differently – if the dominating figure was willing to curb his pride, chastise his lust for revenge (even when severely provoked) and especially, learn the elusive art of possessions (rather than letting things control the individual). [p. 10]

Narqelion. Poem in Qenya (Quenya, see *Languages, Invented), a lament to autumn, with passing references to Eldamar and the Gnomes (a kindred of the Elves) from the **'Silmarillion' mythology, inspired by the poem *Kortirion among the Trees* (**The Trees of Kortirion*). (Compare Quenya *Narquelië* 'sun-fading', the name of the tenth month given in *The Lord of the Rings*, Appendix D.) A single text survives, apparently begun in November 1915 and completed in March 1916. Four lines were published in *Biography* (1977). The complete poem was first published, with a commentary, in 'Narqelion: A Single, Falling Leaf at Sun-fading' by Paul Nolan Hyde, *Mythlore* 15, no. 2, whole no. 56 (Winter 1988), pp. 47–52. The poem, with extracts from Hyde's article, was reprinted in *Vinyar Tengwar* 6 (July 1989), pp. 12–13.

A fuller linguistic analysis of the poem, 'Bird and Leaf: Image and Structure in *Narqelion*' by Patrick Wynne and Christopher Gilson, was published in *Parma Eldalamberon* 3, no. 1, whole no. 9 (1990); it includes an English translation from the Qenya. A facsimile of the manuscript of *Narqelion* was published (p. 5) in *Vinyar Tengwar* 40 (April 1999), which number also includes '*Narqelion* and the Early Lexicons: Some Notes on the First Elvish Poem' by Christopher Gilson, a new linguistic analysis made in light of Elvish lexicons published in 1995 and 1998 (see **Gnomish Lexicon* and **Qenyaqetsa*). Gilson provides both a literal translation of the poem into English prose and a fresh translation in verse.

Nature. Tolkien's love of and delight in all aspects of the natural world – plants, trees, birds, weather, sky, the changing seasons – as they appear in a rural or even a town landscape, is made abundantly clear in his correspondence. To quote only a few examples from letters to his son *Christopher: 'A lovely morning dawned.... A mist like early Sept[ember] with a pearl-button sun ... that soon changed into serene blue, with the silver light of spring on flower and leaf. Leaves are out: the white-grey of the quince, the grey-green of the young apple, the full green of hawthorn, the tassels of flower even on the sluggard poplars. The narcissuses are a marvellous show...' (18 April 1944, *Letters*, p. 73); 'The most marvellous sunset I have seen for years: a remote pale green-blue sea just above the horizon, and above it a towering shore of bank upon bank of flaming cherubim of gold and fire, crossed here and there by misty blurs like purple rain' (22 August 1944, *Letters*, p. 92);

> It froze hard with a heavy fog, and so we have had displays of Hoarfrost such as I only remember once in *Oxford before ... and only twice before in my life. One of the most lovely events of Northern Nature. We woke ... to find all our windows opaque, painted over with frost-patterns, and outside a dim silent misty world, all white, but with a light jewelry of rime; every cobweb a little lace net, even the old fowls' tent a diamond-patterned pavilion.... The rime was yesterday even thicker and more fantastic. When a gleam of sun ... got through it was breathtakingly beautiful: trees like motionless fountains of white branching spray against a golden light and, high overhead, a pale translucent blue. It did not melt. About 11 p.m. the fog cleared and a high round moon lit the whole scene with a deadly white light: a vision of some other world or time. [28 December 1944, *Letters*, p. 107]

Towards the end of his life, in a letter to *Rayner Unwin, Tolkien described a more formal display in the Fellows' Garden at Merton College: 'The great bank . . . looks like the foreground of a pre-Raphaelite picture: blazing green starred like the Milky Way with blue anemones, purple/white/yellow crocuses, and final surprise, clouded-yellow, peacock, and tortoiseshell butterflies flitting about' (16 March 1972, *Letters*, p. 417). And his delight in watching birds is shown in another letter to Christopher:

> There is a family of bullfinches, which must have nested in or near our garden, and they are very tame, and have been giving us entertainment lately by their antics feeding their young, often just outside the dining-room window. Insects on the trees and sowthistle seeds seem their chief delight. I had no idea they behaved so much like goldfinches. Old fat father, pink waistcoat and all, hangs absolutely upside down on a thistle-spray, tinking all the while. [7 July 1944, *Letters*, p. 87]

In turn Tolkien applied his keen interest in the world around him, observed in minute detail and vividly described, to the invented landscapes of his fiction, giving them the substance of reality. *The Lord of the Rings* is particularly rich in this regard, from Goldberry's gown 'green as young reeds, shot with silver like beads of dew' and her belt 'of gold, shaped like a chain of flag-lilies set with the pale-blue eyes of forget-me-nots' (bk. I, ch. 7), to *elanor*, *athelas*, *niphredil*, and *mallorn*, to landscapes like that in Book I, Chapter 6, where the four hobbits approach the River Withywindle:

> Coming to the opening they found that they had made their way down through a cleft in a high steep bank, almost a cliff. At its feet was a wide space of grass and reeds; and in the distance could be glimpsed another bank almost as steep. A golden afternoon of late sunshine lay warm and drowsy upon the hidden land between. In the midst of it there wound lazily a dark river of brown water, bordered with ancient willows, arched over with willows, blocked with fallen willows, and flecked with thousands of faded willow-leaves. The air was thick with them, fluttering yellow from the branches; for there was a warm and gentle breeze blowing softly in the valley, and the reeds were rustling, and the willow-boughs were creaking.

The scene is not unlike that Tolkien would have found on the banks of the River Cherwell near Oxford, which he and his family would occasionally explore. Cerin Amroth, on the other hand, has no analogue in our world, but Tolkien permits his reader to stand in its midst through vivid description of its natural features:

> They were standing in an open space. To the left stood a great mound, covered with a sward of grass as green as Springtime in the Elder Days. Upon it, as a double crown, grew two circles of trees: the outer had bark

of snowy white, and were leafless but beautiful in their shapely naked-
ness; the inner were mallorn-trees of great height, still arrayed in pale
gold. . . . At the feet of the trees, and all about the green hillsides the grass
was studded with small golden flowers shaped like stars. Among them,
nodding on slender stalks, were other flowers, white and palest green:
they glimmered as a mist amid the rich hue of the grass. Over all the sky
was blue, and the sun of afternoon glowed upon the hill and cast long
green shadows beneath the trees. [bk. II, ch. 6]

Above all, Tolkien felt a deep affection for trees. Photographs often show
him in their company: of these the most notable are Lord Snowdon's portrait
of Tolkien reclining against the roots of a great tree behind his home in *Poole,
and the last photograph of him taken by his grandson Michael George (see
*Michael Tolkien) on 9 August 1973, in the Botanic Garden, Oxford, stand-
ing with his hand on the trunk of a *Pinus nigra*, one of his favourite trees. *Joy
Hill recalled that the last time she visited him in August 1973 he did not want
to work, but took her on a long walk. They visited the Botanic Garden, walked
by the river to look at willows, then went through the Botanic Garden again.
He asked her to bring a camera on her next visit, so that he could have photographs of the trees.

Tolkien was saddened to see so many trees ill-treated or felled in both
countryside and town. He wrote in an autobiographical note for the Houghton
Mifflin Company in the summer of 1955: 'I am (obviously) much in love with
plants and above all trees, and always have been; and I find human maltreatment of them as hard to bear as some find ill-treatment of animals' (*Letters*,
p. 220). His friend *George Sayer noted that Tolkien, during walks in the
country while on a visit to *Malvern in 1947, 'liked to stop to look at the trees,
flowers, birds and insects that we passed', but

> his greatest love seemed to be for trees. . . . He would often place his hand
> on the trunks of ones that we passed. He felt their wanton or unnecessary
> felling almost as murder. The first time I heard him say 'ORCS' was when
> we heard not far off the savage sound of a petrol-driven chain saw. 'That
> machine,' he said, 'is one of the greatest horrors of our age.' He said that
> he had sometimes imagined an uprising of the trees against their human
> tormentors. ['Recollections of J.R.R. Tolkien', in *Proceedings of the J.R.R.
> Tolkien Centenary Conference 1992* (1995), p. 22]

By 1947 Tolkien had already written the chapters in *The Lord of the Rings*
dealing with the march of the Ents on Isengard. Many readers have found the
Ents, the shepherds of the trees, among Tolkien's most original and most vivid
creations. The chapter 'Treebeard' (bk. III, ch. 4), he said, seemed to write
itself; and there the Ent Quickbeam's lament for the rowan trees cut down
by Saruman's orcs certainly echoes Tolkien's feelings. In a letter to the *Daily
Telegraph* he wrote:

In all my works I take the part of trees as against all their enemies. Loth-lórien is beautiful because there the trees were loved; elsewhere forests are represented as awakening to consciousness of themselves. The Old Forest was hostile to two legged creatures because of the memory of many injuries. Fangorn Forest was old and beautiful, but at the time of the story tense with hostility because it was threatened by a machine-loving enemy. Mirkwood had fallen under the domination of a Power that hated all living things but was restored to beauty and became Green-wood the Great before the end of the story. [30 June 1972, *Letters*, pp. 419–20]

In the same letter he commented on 'the destruction, torture and mur-der of trees perpetuated by private individuals and minor official bodies' (p. 420). Was he thinking of the poplar tree which was an inspiration for his story *Leaf by Niggle? He told his *Aunt Jane Neave that 'there was a great tree – a huge poplar with vast limbs – visible through my window even as I lay in bed. I loved it, and was anxious about it. It had been savagely mutilated some years before, but had gallantly grown new limbs – though of course not with the unblemished grace of its former natural self; and now a foolish neighbour was agitating to have it felled. Every tree has its enemy, few have an advocate' (8–9 September 1962, *Letters*, p. 321). At the end of *Leaf by Niggle* the great tree that Niggle had attempted to paint, but could reproduce his vision only imper-fectly, is made real, whole and glorious.

Trees figured prominently in Tolkien's imagination no less than in Niggle's. In *'The Silmarillion' the Two Trees that lit Valinor with their unsullied light are of primary mythical importance; the light provided by the Sun and Moon, created from the fruit and flower of the Trees after they had been defiled, is of lesser kind. In *On Fairy-Stories Tolkien refers to a symbolic 'Tree of Tales', which he himself drew several times (the 'Tree of Amalion', see *Artist and Illustrator*, pp. 64–5). He described it to Rayner Unwin on 23 December 1963 as 'a 'mythical "tree", which ... bears besides various shapes of leaves many flowers small and large signifying poems and major legends' (*Letters*, p. 342). In *Smith of Wootton Major* a birch tree protects Smith from the Wind and is stripped of all its leaves. In *The Lord of the Rings* there are also the Party Tree at Bag End, the Old Forest and Old Man Willow, the holly trees at the entrance to Moria and the crescent moon-bearing trees on the doors of the west gate, Fan-gorn Forest, the woods of Ithilien, the White Tree embroidered on Aragorn's banner and found by him as a sapling, and finally the trees felled by Saruman in the Shire and replaced by Sam.

Dylan Pugh discusses trees in myth and history in relation to Tolkien's writings in 'The Tree of Tales', *Mallorn* 21 (June 1984). In 'Tolkien's Trees', *Mallorn* 35 (September 1997), Claudia Riiff Finseth comments that Tolkien gives us in his fiction all kinds of forests and groves in which to find adventure – and he does more. He ascribes to his individual trees and forests a fantastic variety of meanings and possibilities by drawing from and adding to the rich symbolism of trees that has developed throughout the history of litera- ture. Tolkien describes the trees with which we are familiar – oak, birch, willow – so that we see them with a fresh eye. He creates new trees for us such as we have never seen growing on our earth. He gives us a chance to look at things from a treeish point of view, which is to say a fresh point of view, and from there he can give an added dimension to his human characters, who define themselves in part through their attitude towards trees.

Indeed, she comments that 'as a lover of trees and a man who abhorred the needless destruction of them, Tolkien the writer often defined his characters as good or evil by their feelings about trees' (p. 37). Verlyn Flieger, however, in 'Taking the Part of Trees: Eco-Conflict in Middle-earth', in *J.R.R. Tolkien and His Literary Resonances* (2000), points out some inconsistencies in Tolkien's attitude to trees. She notes that the 'well-ordered, well-farmed countryside' of the Shire (*The Lord of the Rings*, Prologue) and even 'Frodo's peaceful sun- lit garden ... must at some earlier time have been wrested from what Tom Bombadil calls the "vast forgotten woods" [bk. I, ch. 7] of which the Old Forest is the sole survivor' (p. 150). And she discusses whether there is any difference between hobbits cutting down and burning trees to prevent the Old Forest advancing into the Shire, and Saruman's orcs felling trees in Fangorn, and between the Ents' anger at the Orcs and the hostility towards Hobbits from Old Man Willow and trees in the Old Forest.

In *Tolkien in the Land of Heroes: Discovering the Human Spirit* (2003) Anne C. Petty comments that

> Tolkien's love of the outdoors and the wildness of the natural world took hold early and continued throughout his life. His role as a crusader for nature in the face of mechanized progress seems to have been triggered when his mother moved the family from rural Sarehole to industrial Birmingham, and escalated after his return from the war – an attitude you can see developing if you read his collected letters sequentially. Nature itself becomes a sentient character in Tolkien's writings, and its destruction in his tales serves as a grand symbol for what he felt was wrong with society (whether modern-day industrialists or corrupted wizards).
>
> The forces of evil are frequently associated with scenarios that demon- strate the horrible things done to the natural world, especially to trees. But rather than just creating ongoing lament for the death of trees Tolkien takes advantage of the printed page to provide an outlet for revenge. He creates champions and personifications of nature who can take up the crusade for him, righting the wrongs inflicted on hill and tree

by those who mar the landscape with evil intent. Although his stance on defending nature and trees in particular, was notoriously embraced by the 'green' activists of the sixties and several more aggressive ecology movements since then, you won't find any evidence that he supported these groups. . . . But the dismantling of Isengard by Ents and Huorns is one of the most satisfying acts of retribution committed to paper. In this sense Tolkien's pen was definitely mightier than any sword he might have waved trying to stop the felling of trees or building of parking lots. [pp. 219–20]

She explores this theme further in the rest of the chapter 'In Defense of Nature', pp. 219–43.

In *On Fairy-Stories* Tolkien wrote of 'the desire of men to hold communion with other living things. . . . Other creatures are like other realms with which Man has broken off relations, and sees now only from the outside at a distance, being at war with them, or on the terms of an uneasy armistice' (*Tree and Leaf*, pp. 19, 60–1). In his fiction men and animals often exist in close relationship. Huan the hound and Carcharoth the wolf are important to the 'Silmarillion' tale of Beren and Lúthien (*'Of Beren and Lúthien'). Among Tolkien's writings for children, Mr Bliss (*Mr. Bliss*) interacts with bears, Farmer Giles (*Farmer Giles of Ham*) with his dog Garm, Father Christmas (*The 'Father Christmas' letters) with the North Polar Bear, Beorn of *The Hobbit* with his animal servants. Birds, some of which can speak with humans, take active roles in *The Hobbit* and *The Lord of the Rings*. And in the latter book, horses are featured as characters in their own right, particularly Shadowfax and Bill the Pony. Animals are also the subjects of several of Tolkien's poems, such as *Fastitocalon* and *Oliphaunt*, drawn partly from the medieval bestiary tradition. Unusually, *Roverandom* is told from the viewpoint of an animal, a dog who converses with other dogs, the gull Mew, and the whale Uin.

Some of Tolkien's paintings and drawings made from nature – his talents as a pictorial artist were in landscape rather than portraiture – are also memorable, though often one feels that, like Niggle, Tolkien caught only a shadow of what his inner eye was seeing. On the other hand, it would be difficult to think of any painter who could capture visually the Mallorn trees of Lothlórien (*Artist and Illustrator*, fig. 157) which Tolkien described so hauntingly with words. Nor could his watercolour of Taur-na-Fuin (*Artist and Illustrator*, fig. 54) fully convey the claustrophobic picture of those woods Tolkien describes in *The Tale of Turambar*: 'a dark and perilous region so thick with pines of giant growth that none but the goblins might find a track, having eyes that pierced the deepest gloom' (*The Book of Lost Tales, Part Two*, p. 78). Some of his more successful illustrations celebrating aspects of nature and landscape are *The Gardens of the Merking's Palace* (*Artist and Illustrator*, fig. 76), with its depiction of an underwater world full of colour; 'Mr Bliss on the Hillside' (*Artist and Illustrator*, fig. 83), with a view into the distance similar to many in the Cotswolds Tolkien knew so well; four watercolours for *The Hobbit* with contrasting landscapes – the well tended sunny fields of *The Hill: Hobbiton-across-the-Water*, the deep valley of *Rivendell*, the wildness of the Misty Mountains in *Bilbo Woke Up with the Early Sun in His Eyes* inspired by Tolkien's 1911 visit to Switzerland, and the light glimpsed through an avenue of trees in *Bilbo Comes to the Huts of the Raft-Elves* (*Artist and Illustrator*, figs. 98, 108, 113, 124); and the stylized late *The Hills of the Morning* (*Artist and Illustrator*, fig. 1). Tolkien also made topographical drawings and watercolours which suggest weather, season, or time of day: the detailed view of the garden at 20 Northmoor Road in *Spring 1940*, the rainstorm in the background of *Lambourn, Berks*, the light filtered through the trees in *Foxglove Year*, and the sky, clouds, and shadows in *Summer in Kerry* are particularly noteworthy (*Artist and Illustrator*, figs. 3, 11, 17, 29).

See also *Environment.

Neave, Emily Jane (*née* Suffield, 1872–1963). From 1885 to April 1892 Emily Jane Suffield, commonly known as 'Jane', attended King Edward VI High School for Girls in *Birmingham. The convenience of the School to New Street Station allowed Jane to pass private messages from her elder sister Mabel (*Mabel Tolkien) to *Arthur Tolkien on the railway platform, before their father (see *Suffield family) would permit Mabel to be formally betrothed. In 1892 Jane entered Mason College, the predecessor of the University of Birmingham. She received a Bachelor of Science degree in 1895, under the examinations of the University of London, and subsequently became a school-teacher (as she is listed in the 1901 Census).

In spring 1895 Mabel Tolkien brought her two sons to England from *South Africa. She taught her boys many things, but it was Jane who instructed her young nephew Ronald Tolkien in geometry. At this time, and for the next few years, Jane still lived in the Suffield family home in the Birmingham suburb of Kings Heath. There she met a lodger, **Edwin Neave** (1872–1909), now or later a clerk for Guardian Fire Insurance: he would sit 'on the stairs singing "Polly-Wolly-Doodle" to the accompaniment of a banjo and making eyes at Jane. The family thought him common, and they were horrified when she became engaged to him' (Humphrey Carpenter, *Biography*, p. 18). After 1901, but by the spring of 1904, Jane and Edwin were married and living in *Hove. Ronald Tolkien stayed with them temporarily while his mother was in hospital. Their marriage was cut short, however, by Edwin's early death in 1909.

In summer 1911 Jane Neave joined her nephews Ronald and *Hilary on a visit to *Switzerland organized by James and Ellen *Brookes-Smith; their son, Colin Brookes-Smith, recalled long after the event that his parents had met Jane Neave in St Andrews, Scotland, where she was the warden of a women's college and the Brookes-Smith daughters attended school. Although we have been unable to confirm this, it seems reasonable to think that Tolkien's visits to St Andrews in 1910 or 1911 and again in 1912 (see **Chronology**) were to visit his aunt, of whom he was especially fond; and by extension, that Jane Neave went to St Andrews soon after her husband died, to continue her career in education.

By 1914, however, she was living in Nottinghamshire, working at Phoenix Farm at *Gedling which was owned by the Brookes-Smiths. Ronald's brother *Hilary was also there, having chosen a life in agriculture. By 1923 Jane left Nottinghamshire and took a farm at Dormston, Inkberrow, Worcestershire, at the end of a lane local people referred to as 'Bag End'. Her father, John Suffield, spent much time with her there in his final years, until his death in 1930. Jane was still at the same address in 1937 when Tolkien sent her a copy of *The Hobbit. In her later years she lived in a caravan on Hilary's land at Blackminster, near Evesham (*West Midlands), and then in Wales with her younger cousin Frank Suffield.

Tolkien wrote about his Aunt Jane to Joyce Reeves on 4 November 1961: 'The professional aunt is a fairly recent development, perhaps; but I was fortunate in having an early example: one of the first women to take a science degree. She is now ninety, but only a few years ago went botanizing in Switzerland' (Letters, p. 308). Asked by Jane earlier that year 'if you wouldn't get out a small book with Tom Bombadil at the heart of it, the sort of book that we old 'uns can afford to buy for Christmas presents', Tolkien assembled *The Adventures of Tom Bombadil and Other Verses from the Red Book (1962). It was published just in time to delight Jane Neave, a few months before her death.

Nesbit, Edith (1858–1924). Despite the death of her father when she was three, the English writer E. Nesbit enjoyed a generally happy childhood with her mother and siblings: she was the youngest of five surviving children. Her marriage in 1880 to Hubert Bland was unconventional, to say the least: both had lovers, and Bland's two illegitimate children were brought up together with the three surviving children of the marriage. Hubert and Edith were also founding members of the Fabian Society, formed to propagate evolutionary socialism. After Hubert's death Nesbit married an old friend, Tommy Tucker, with whom she lived the rest of her life.

To supplement the family income Edith sold poems and juvenile and adult fiction to magazines, much of it hack-work. It was not until she was almost forty that she wrote the first of the children's stories that brought her fame. Her stories of the Bastable family began to appear in 1897, and were published in book form as The Story of the Treasure Seekers in 1899. Tales of children trying to find ways to make money to amend the fortunes of their impoverished family, they were appreciated by readers of all ages. Further books about the Bastables followed, including The Would-be-Goods (1901) and The New Treasure Seekers (1904). *Roger Lancelyn Green notes in Tellers of Tales: Children's Books and Their Authors from 1800 to 1964 (rewritten and rev. edn. 1965) that it was from her own 'holiday life that Edith derived the joyous recollections of childhood' evident in her work (p. 208). 'She had, as perhaps no other author has quite possessed it, the power of becoming a child again, of thinking and inventing with her child characters, speaking and writing from their point of view – but with the skill and discrimination of a practised author' (p. 206). *The Railway Children*, probably her best known story about ordinary children and their leisure activities, was first published (in book form) in 1906.

In 1900 eight short stories which had appeared in *Strand Magazine* in 1899 were collected in *The Book of Dragons* (1900). In writing of many of these dragons, comic figures that are no match for their child opponents, Nesbit may have been influenced by 'The Reluctant Dragon' by *Kenneth Grahame (1898). Grahame's story and Nesbit's collection may have contributed in turn to the character of Chrysophylax in *Farmer Giles of Ham* (1949).

Nesbit also wrote two stories about children travelling into their family's past, *The House of Arden* (1908) and *Harding's Luck* (1909), and a series of books in which contemporary children experience a series of magical adventures. Of the latter the most generally admired are *Five Children – and It* (1902), *The Phoenix and the Carpet* (1904), and *The Story of the Amulet* (1906). Roger Lancelyn Green's comment on the opening of the first of Nesbit's dragon stories is also applicable to these: 'And so straight into the realm of magic, with the prosaicness of everyday life that makes it absolutely real and acceptable; the mixture of fancy and observation which is the real child-world, the game come to life and the day-dream that stands up to the clear light of noon' (p. 211).

On 31 August 1939 Tolkien wrote to C.A. Furth at George Allen & Unwin (*Publishers) that Nesbit was 'an author I delight in' (courtesy of Christopher Tolkien), and in drafts for *On Fairy-Stories* he wrote of the 'triumphant formula that E. Nesbit found in the Amulet and the Phoenix and the Carpet' (Tolkien Papers, Bodleian Library, Oxford). From *The Story of the Amulet*, and earlier *Five Children – and It* Tolkien borrowed the Psammead for his own *Roverandom* (1998). In *Five Children – and It*, while digging a hole in a gravel-pit the children find in sand at the bottom a strange creature: 'Its eyes were on long horns like a snail's eyes, and it could move them in and out like telescopes; it had ears like a bat's ears, and its tubby body was shaped like a spider's and covered with thick soft fur; its legs and arms were furry too, and it had hands and feet like a monkey's (1912 printing, p. 14). It is a Psammead, or sand-fairy. It likes to sleep in warm sand, dislikes getting wet, and if disturbed can be rather gruff. Like Gandalf at the beginning of *The Hobbit* it plays with the meaning of words and conventional phrases: when one of the children says that 'now one comes to look at you' she can see that it is a sand-fairy, the Psammead replies, with literal correctness, 'You came to look at me several sentences ago' (p. 16). The Psammead magically grants the children a series of wishes, almost all of which have unfortunate consequences, but luckily the magic lasts only until sunset. Similarly in *Roverandom* the dog Rover, who has been turned into a toy, meets a 'sand-sorcerer' called Psamathos Psamathides, 'an excellent magician' who 'liked to lie buried in warm sand when the sun was shining, so that not more than the tip of one of his long ears stuck out' (p. 11; 'long ears' was an emendation from 'long horns'), 'certainly was ugly' (p. 13), and had 'a fat tummy' (p. 16) and 'legs like a rabbit' (p. 57). Psamathos saves

Rover from the incoming tide, and sends him on excursions to the Moon and to the mer-king's palace under the sea. In the earliest text of *Roverandom* the sand-sorcerer is actually called a *psammead*.

See also Julia Briggs, *A Woman of Passion: The Life of E. Nesbit, 1858–1924* (1987).

Netherlands. Tolkien visited the Netherlands from 28 to 31 March 1958, at the invitation of the Rotterdam booksellers Voorhoeve en Dietrich (the Dutch edition of *The Lord of the Rings* had been published in 1956–7). He arrived by sea at the Hook of Holland early on 28 March, then went by train to **Rotterdam**. Together with a representative of his Dutch publisher, Het Spectrum, he 'saw a good deal of the depressing world of ruined and half-rebuilt [post-war] Rotterdam ... with its gigantic and largely dehumanized reconstruction' (letter to Rayner Unwin, 8 April 1958, *Letters*, p. 265). In the evening he attended, as guest of honour, a 'Hobbit Maaltijd' or hobbit-themed dinner at the Flev-restaurant in Rotterdam. On 29 March he went with his friend, Professor Piet Harting of Amsterdam University, to the Mauritshuis at **The Hague**, and then to **Amsterdam** for a private dinner. On 30 and 31 March Tolkien visited Amsterdam and the University; there he was joined by students of the English department and 'made an extremely hobbit-like expedition to [the distillery] Wynand Fockink' (letter to Rayner Unwin, 8 April 1958, Tolkien-George Allen & Unwin archive, HarperCollins).

See further, René van Rossenberg, 'Tolkien's Exceptional Visit to Holland: A Reconstruction', *Proceedings of the Tolkien Centenary Conference 1992* (1995).

New English Dictionary see *Oxford English Dictionary*

A New Glossary of the Dialect of the Huddersfield District.
Written by Walter E. Haigh and published by Oxford University Press in January 1928, with a foreword by Tolkien (pp. xiii–xviii), the *Glossary* concerns the dialect spoken in South Yorkshire 'in the geographical basin, measuring some ten to fifteen miles across, which lies in the south-west corner of the West Riding, close under the main ridges of the Pennines' (p. vii). Tolkien first became acquainted with the book in 1923, 'when Mr. Haigh had already lavished endless time and care upon it; almost my only contribution since has been to urge him to go on, and to assure him of the value of his work, not only to local patriotism, but to English philology generally' (p. xiii). He compliments Haigh for having compiled a complete, not selective, glossary, which is essential for the full understanding of a dialect. Because it includes all types of words, including those of more recent times, it more nearly approaches 'a true and lively picture of its dialect, and is of much greater value to philologists, than if it had dealt only with those rare or venerable words which are imagined to interest such people specially' (p. xiv).

Tolkien commends the work also for 'the excellence, humour, and idiomatic raciness of its illustrative quotations, which bear the mark of the native speaker.' Dialect words are dead when isolated from 'colloquial instances' (p. xiv). A 'foreigner' to the district, Tolkien is interested in its speech because

> even if not a student of dialect generally, ... his attention is at once aroused by this dialect because of the very region to which it belongs – the North-West ... the field of dialectal competition and mingling at a particularly important boundary, the borders of the Northern and the (Western) Midland, and the scene of the swaying fortunes of different types of English since very early times. ... [p. xv]

He also remarks that

> the North-West became later, in the fourteenth century, the centre of a revival of writings in vernacular speech, of which the most interesting examples preserved are poems in an alliterative metre descended from the old verse of Anglo-Saxon times, though clothed in a language now difficult to read because of its strong Scandinavian element and its many other peculiar and obscure dialectal words. ... [p. xvi]

Books such as Haigh's *Glossary* 'throw valuable light on the meanings or forms of words' in old poems, including *Sir Gawain and the Green Knight*, *Pearl*, and the *Wars of Alexander* (p. xvi).

The New Shadow. Abandoned sequel to *The Lord of the Rings*, published with commentary and notes in *The Peoples of Middle-earth* (1996), pp. 409–21. The brief text is set during the reign of Eldarion, son of King Elessar. Borlas, son of Beregond, now an old man, is visited by Saelon (in earlier versions Egalmoth or Arthael), whom he had rebuked as a boy not only for stealing good fruit, but also for destroying unripe fruit, calling his action 'Orcs' work'. The two discuss that occasion, the roots of evil in Men ('the roots of Evil lie deep, and from far off comes the poison that works in us', *The Peoples of Middle-earth*, p. 414), and 'rumours' they have heard. Saelon invites Borlas, if he would know more, to come with him that evening. It is not clear if Saelon is working with or against a barely suggested conspiracy.

In a letter to Colin Bailey, 13 May 1964, Tolkien comments that he began 'a story placed about 100 years after the Downfall [of Mordor], but it proved both sinister and depressing', showing 'the most regrettable feature' of human nature,

> quick satiety with good. So that the people of Gondor in times of peace, justice and prosperity, would become discontented and restless – while the dynasts descended from Aragorn would become just kings and governors. ... I found that even so early there was an outcrop of revolutionary plots, about a centre of secret Satanic religion; while Gondorian boys were playing at being Orcs and going round doing damage. I could

have written a 'thriller' about the plot and its discovery and overthrow – but it would be just that. Not worth doing. [*Letters*, p. 344]

Compare his letter to Father Douglas Carter, ?6 June 1972, *Letters*, p. 419.

It seems unlikely that Tolkien began to write *The New Shadow* until after the publication of *The Lord of the Rings* (1954–5), but there is evidence that its first versions were in existence by late 1958. The first draft opening of the story extends for two sides of a sheet and is accompanied by other manuscript material. Tolkien then wrote a clear manuscript, followed by a typescript in which he made minor emendations and improvements; both manuscript and typescript end at the same point, at the farthest point the story ever reached. The typescript and an amanuensis typescript based upon it were both produced on the machine that Tolkien used up to the end of 1958. The first page of the amanuensis typescript was made on the typewriter he used from the beginning of 1959. Several years later, probably at the beginning of 1968, Tolkien made another typescript with many emendations, none of significance to the story: this did not reach as far as the earlier versions.

Newby, Percy Howard (1918–1997). P.H. Newby was a prolific writer of novels, including *A Journey to the Interior* (1945) and *The Picnic at Sakkara* (1955). His *Something to Answer For* (1968) was the first winner of the Booker Prize. He also wrote non-fiction books, such as *The Warrior Pharaohs* (1980). In 1946–8 he lectured in English literature at Fouad I University in Cairo. In 1949 he joined BBC radio as a producer in the Talks Department; in that capacity, in June–July 1953, he expressed an interest in broadcasting Tolkien's Modern English translation of *Sir Gawain and the Green Knight*. Tolkien and Newby met for tea at Merton College, Oxford on 31 July 1953 to discuss how the work should be read and introduced. Although Tolkien wanted to do this himself, Newby felt that he was not good enough to read the whole poem; and in the event, it was read by several voices.

Newby and Tolkien later discussed other possible topics for radio talks, such as the eighteenth-century Grammarians, fairy-stories, and Tolkien's old teacher *Joseph Wright; but none came about, at least not with Tolkien in the broadcast. Newby was also instrumental in fostering interest at the BBC in Tolkien's verse dialogue of the Battle of Maldon, *The Homecoming of Beorhtnoth Beorhthelm's Son* (1953). He was not impressed, however, with *Smith of Wootton Major*, which Tolkien stipulated that it should not be cut, or with Tolkien's offer to read it himself.

Late in 1958, Newby became Controller of the BBC Third Programme, and at the end of 1971 rose to the position of Director of Programmes, Radio. He retired in 1978.

A photograph of P.H. Newby is reproduced in *The Envy of the World* by Humphrey Carpenter (1996), pl. following p. 274.

Nichol Smith, David (1875–1962). Educated at the University of Edinburgh and the Sorbonne, D. Nichol Smith held posts at the University of Glasgow (as assistant to Professor *Walter Raleigh) and at Armstrong College, Newcastle upon Tyne, before his election as Goldsmiths' Reader in English at *Oxford in 1908. Raleigh had preceded Nichol Smith to Oxford, as Professor of English Literature, and now together again, they made significant contributions to the development of the fledgling English School. 'If Raleigh's brilliance as a lecturer and his undogmatic and stimulating mind gave the new school much of its distinction, his "indifference to system" might have retarded its growth, if the calm and orderly mind of Nichol Smith had not been available with suggestion and criticism' (James Sutherland, 'David Nichol Smith, 1875–1962', *Proceedings of the British Academy* 48 (1962), p. 453). In particular Nichol Smith helped to improve the B.Litt. course, making it more rigorous and methodical. In 1929 he became Merton Professor of English Literature, a chair he held until 1946.

His special interest was the eighteenth century, and on critical attitudes of the eighteenth century towards earlier literature. His publications include *Eighteenth-Century Essays on Shakespeare* (1903) and *Some Observations on Eighteenth-Century Poetry* (1937), and editions of Dryden, Johnson, Swift, among other authors of the period. As an undergraduate Tolkien certainly attended lectures by Nichol Smith on Samuel Johnson and his friends, and possibly also his lectures on Dryden, and on English literature from Caxton to Milton. Upon Tolkien's election to the Rawlinson and Bosworth Professorship of Anglo-Saxon in 1925 he and Nichol Smith became colleagues, and served together on the English Faculty Board and numerous committees.

Nichol Smith was also an adviser on English literature to the Oxford University Press, its chief adviser in that field after the death of Raleigh in 1922 and a confidant to *Kenneth Sisam. He was also consulted by *George S. Gordon when Gordon and Tolkien agreed to produce for the Press the 'Clarendon Chaucer' (see *Geoffrey Chaucer), and later by Tolkien in a vain attempt to reduce his mass of notes for that book. From *c.* 1938 Nichol Smith was one of the first three editors of the *Oxford English Monographs* series, together with Tolkien and *C.S. Lewis.

Nieninque. Poem in Qenya (*Languages, Invented), concerning the maiden Niéle 'like a snowdrop (Nieninqe), to whom the air gives kisses'. It was first published in *The Monsters and the Critics and Other Essays* (1983), pp. 215–16, within the autobiographical lecture *A Secret Vice, as an example of the author's 'vice' of language invention and its outlet in poetry.

'Of the Noldor in Beleriand'. The fifteenth chapter of the *Quenta Silmarillion*, published in *The Silmarillion* (1977), pp. 125–30.

SUMMARY

Inspired by the Vala Ulmo, Turgon of Nevrast discovers the hidden Vale of Tumladen, a suitable place for a refuge. After the Dagor Aglareb he sends some of his people to build a city there, while he himself remains in Nevrast. Fifty-two years later, the city of Gondolin is completed. Ulmo tells Turgon it that will endure longest of the realms of the Noldor, and when a time of peril draws near, one will come to warn him, wearing armour which Turgon is directed to leave behind in Nevrast. Turgon and all of his people, both Noldor and Sindar, make their way secretly to Gondolin. In that fair city the inhabitants remain concealed for over 350 years, not leaving until they take part in the Nirnaeth Arnoediad.

Meanwhile, Finrod Felagund prepares the refuge of Nargothrond, and his sister Galadriel dwells with her kinsman Thingol and with Melian in Doriath. Pressed for information by Melian, who sees that some shadow lies on her and her kin, Galadriel tells her of the theft of the Silmarils and the death of Finwë, but not of the Oath or the Kinslaying. Melian foresees the significance of the Silmarils, and warns Thingol against the sons of Fëanor, but he still sees them and the Noldor as allies against Morgoth.

Rumours of the deeds of the Noldor in Valinor, perhaps spread and enhanced by Morgoth, come to the ears of Círdan, who reports them to Thingol at a time when Finrod and his brothers are visiting Doriath. When Thingol accuses the brothers of concealing the matter from him, they plead their innocence in the Kinslaying and tell of Fëanor's treachery against them. Thingol is prepared to forgive them, as well as Fingolfin and his people, but forbids the language (Quenya) of those who had slain his kin at Alqualondë to be spoken in his realm. The Sindar obey his decree, and the Noldor begin to use Sindarin for their daily speech. Otherwise Quenya is spoken only by Noldorin lords among themselves, or used as a language of lore.

Finrod celebrates the completion of Nargothrond with a feast. When Galadriel, who is staying with him, asks Finrod why he has no wife, foresight comes upon him that he will be bound by an oath, and his realm will not endure for a son to inherit. But Amarië of the Vanyar, whom he loved, had stayed behind in Valinor.

HISTORY

Only isolated threads of this chapter can be found in *The Book of Lost Tales* (c. 1916–20), which says little directly of the early years of the Noldor in Beleriand. An outline for the unwritten part of *Gilfanon's Tale: The Travail of the Noldoli and the Coming of Mankind* refers to Turgon founding Gondolin *after* the Battle of Unnumbered Tears (the Nirnaeth Arnoediad), but there is nothing between this and the first written of the *Lost Tales*, *The Fall of Gondolin*, which takes place when the city is nearing its end. Turgon's former dwelling at Nevrast, and the armour left there, do not appear in the tale. Although Gondolin is a hidden secret city, it is not so cut off; some Noldoli manage to find their way to it. The caves inhabited by the Rodothlim, refugee Noldoli led by Orodreth, in *The Tale of Turambar* are a precursor of Nargothrond, but in *The Book of Lost Tales* Finrod Felagund has not yet been introduced. Artanor (Doriath) is ruled by Tinwelint and Gwendeling, less noble versions of the later Thingol and Melian. Galadriel does not enter the history of the First Age until after the writing of *The Lord of the Rings*.

In *The Children of Húrin* (c. 1919–25) the rulers of Doriath are Thingol and Melian, and the Noldorin stronghold of Nargothrond has replaced the more humble caves of the Rodothlim. Although two of Fëanor's sons, Celegorm and Curufin, establish Nargothrond, at the time of the events of *The Children of Húrin* it is ruled by Orodreth, who seems to be unrelated to Finwë. *Christopher Tolkien has suggested, as an explanation of the change of ruler, that when writing the early part of the lay his father thought of Nargothrond as being founded after the Battle of Unnumbered Tears by Celegorm and Curifin, but as the writing progressed he decided that it was founded before that battle, but afterwards the brothers settled elsewhere, and Orodreth became the ruler of Nargothrond.

The first consecutive, if brief, account of the matter of this chapter appeared in the *Sketch of the Mythology* (c. 1926). At this stage Thingol willingly accepts the Noldor in his realm. Turgon still builds Gondolin *after* the Battle of Unnumbered Tears, inspired by Ylmir (Ulmo), who foretells that it will last the longest of elven refuges. As written, Celegorm and Curufin establish Nargothrond, but are replaced in an emendation by Felagund and his brothers (Felagund, Orodreth, Angrod, and Egnor having already appeared by emendation earlier in the story as the sons of Finrod (later Finarfin) and grandsons of Finwë). This same development took place during the writing of the *Lay of Leithian* in the second half of the 1920s. In the *Quenta Noldorinwa* (c. 1930) Felagund founds Nargothrond after the Battle of Sudden Flame, in which his brothers Angrod and Egnor were slain. Christopher Tolkien comments that, though in the *Quenta Noldorinwa* Gondolin is still established after the Battle of Unnumbered Tears, the description of its building suggests a much longer period than the chronology allows.

The 'earliest' *Annals of Beleriand* (early 1930s) provide a chronological framework for the events. In the entry for Year 50 Tolkien introduced the idea that Turgon and Felagund were inspired by dreams and foreboding to build their strongholds, which both do immediately: thus Gondolin is founded before the Battle of Unnumbered Tears, which takes place in Year 172, when for the first time since its founding Turgon and his people leave Gondolin. In an incomplete second version of these annals, Turgon finds the site of Gondolin in Year 50, but does not lead his people there until the following year, after the Dagor Aglareb. The building of both Nargothrond and Gondolin is complete at about Year 102. Although Tolkien did not finish this version, it is clear that the Battle of Unnumbered Tears would have taken place in Year 272. In the 'later' *Annals of Beleriand* of the mid-1930s Turgon delays his departure until Year 52 (emended to Year 64). The *Quenta Silmarillion* (begun mid-1930s) seems to tell the same story.

In the *Grey Annals* (c. 1951, see *Annals of Beleriand*), moving from annal to narrative form, Tolkien added much new material, including the various conversations between Galadriel, Melian, Thingol, and Inglor (= Felagund, Finrod); Thingol's ban on the language of the Noldor; and Turgon remaining at Nevrast while Gondolin is being built. He moves to Gondolin in 116, and as instructed, leaves armour at Nevrast to be found by Ulmo's messenger. At about the same time or a little later, while revising the *Quenta Silmarillion*, Tolkien added a short chapter (three pages of manuscript), 'Of Turgon and the Building of Gondolin', partly new and partly copied almost word for word from the *Grey Annals*, replacing the original text there with a 'short notice' (*The War of the Jewels*, p. 199).

The first part of 'Of the Noldor in Beleriand' in *The Silmarillion*, concerning Gondolin, was taken from this new chapter, incorporating a few emendations made by Tolkien. The second part, concerning Galadriel, her brothers, Melian, and Thingol, was taken from the *Grey Annals*.

'Noldorin Dictionary'. Brief dictionary of the early 'Elvish' language Noldorin (*Languages, Invented), published with commentary within 'Early Noldorin Fragments' in *Parma Eldalamberon* 13 (2001), pp. 157–65, ed. Christopher Gilson, Bill Welden, Carl F. Hostetter, and Patrick Wynne. Tolkien based this unfinished work on his *'Noldorin Word-lists' and organized it on principles similar to those underlying the *Gnomish Lexicon*, with etymologically related words grouped together, 'with derivatives listed under the more basic Noldorin word from which they derive, with the Old Noldorin form of words indicated (where different from the "modern" form) as well as prehistoric reconstructions, and with listings of cognates in Qenya, Telerin, and Ilkorin' (p. 157). This complex scheme seems to have been devised as Tolkien proceeded, working on slips of paper in manuscript and typescript, probably c. summer 1923. Most of the paper (from the University of *Leeds) bears a printed date, 16 April 1923.

'Noldorin Word-lists'. Lists of words, names, and components of words in the early 'Elvish' language Noldorin (*Languages, Invented), published with commentary within 'Early Noldorin Fragments' in *Parma Eldalamberon* 13 (2001), pp. 133–56, ed. Christopher Gilson, Bill Welden, Carl F. Hostetter, and Patrick Wynne. Tolkien compiled these typed lists, with additions and revisions in manuscript, c. 1921–3, reflecting his work on *The Book of Lost Tales* and *The Children of Húrin* and closely associated with the *'Early Noldorin Grammar' and slips added to the *Gnomish Lexicon*.

Nomenclature of *The Lord of the Rings*. A guide to names in **The Lord of the Rings*, prepared by Tolkien for the use of translators. It grew out of his objections to the alteration of names in the first *translations of *The Lord of the Rings*, in Dutch (*In de ban van de ring*) and Swedish (*Sagan om ringen*), published in 1956–7 and 1959–61 respectively. On 3 July 1956 he wrote to his publisher *Rayner Unwin concerning the version in Dutch:

> *In principle* I object as strongly as is possible to the 'translation' of the *nomenclature* at all (even by a competent person). I wonder why a trans-lator should think himself called on or entitled to do any such thing. That this is an 'imaginary' world does not give him any right to remodel it according to his fancy, even if he could in a few months create a new coherent structure which it took me years to work out.

The correct way to translate *The Lord of the Rings*, he felt, 'is to leave the maps and nomenclature alone as far as possible, but to substitute for some of the least-wanted Appendices a glossary of names (with meanings but no ref[erence]s.). I could supply one for translation. May I say at once that I will *not* tolerate any similar tinkering with the *personal nomenclature*. Nor with the name/word *Hobbit*' (*Letters*, pp. 249–51). But he was only partly success-ful in having his way with the Dutch edition, despite lengthy correspondence. Later he had a similar experience with the Swedish *Lord of the Rings*, all the more distressing because the translator of the first Swedish **Hobbit* (*Hompen*, 1947) had also taken liberties with the text. On 7 December 1957 Tolkien wrote to Rayner Unwin: 'I do hope that it can be arranged, if and when any further translations are negotiated [after the Dutch and Swedish], *that I should be con-sulted at an early stage*. . . . After all, I charge nothing, and can save a translator a good deal of time and puzzling; and if *consulted* at an early stage my remarks will appear far less in the light of peevish criticisms' (*Letters*, p. 263).

At last Tolkien himself took the initiative. He continued to prefer that *The Lord of the Rings* in translation preserve the essential *Englishness* of many of its personal and place-names; but he came to accept that other translators were likely to take a line similar to those of the Dutch and Swedish editions, who had sometimes misunderstood their source, and instead of insisting on *no* translation of nomenclature, he attempted to influence the translator through an explanatory document. On 7 December 1957 he had also written to Rayner Unwin:

> I see now that the lack of an 'index of names' [in *The Lord of the Rings*] is a serious handicap in dealing with [questions of translation]. If I had an index of names (even one with only reference to Vol. and chapter, not page) it would be a comparatively easy matter to indicate at once all names suitable for translation (as being themselves according to the fiction 'translated' into English), and to add a few notes on points where (I know now) translators are likely to trip. So far, though both eager to

translate the toponymy into other terms, and deliberately to efface the references to England (which I regard as integral and essential) neither appear to be at all conversant with English toponymy, or even to be aware that there is anything to know. Nor do they consult large dictionaries when faced by anything that is not current. [Tolkien-George Allen & Unwin archive, HarperCollins, partly printed in *Letters*, pp. 263–4]

Such an index was compiled for him, through the offices of George Allen & Unwin (*Publishers), by May 1958. On 11 September 1959, after considering difficulties facing the translator of the Polish *Lord of the Rings*, Tolkien asked his publisher for a spare copy of the index of names, so that he could mark on it all of those that are not English and therefore, in his view, should not be translated. He seems to have done nothing more with this, however, until around the beginning of December 1966: on 12 December he wrote to Alina Dadlez, of the Allen & Unwin foreign rights department:

> When I was reading the specimens of the proposed German translation, I began to prepare an annotated name list based on the index: indicating those names that were to be left unchanged and giving information of the meaning and origin of those that it was desirable to render into the language of translation, together with some tentative advice on how to proceed. I hope soon to complete this and be able to send you a copy or copies for the use of translators. . . . [Tolkien-George Allen & Unwin archive, HarperCollins]

On 2 January 1967 he wrote to Otto B. Lindhardt, of the Danish publisher Gyldendals Bibliotek, who were planning to publish *The Lord of the Rings* in Danish, that 'experience in attempting to help translators or in reading their versions has made me realize that the nomenclature of persons and places offers particular difficulty', but is important 'since it was constructed with considerable care, to fit with the supposed history of the period described. I have therefore recently been engaged in making, and have nearly completed, a commentary on the names in this story, with explanations and suggestions for the use of a translator, having especially in mind Danish and German' (Tolkien-George Allen & Unwin archive, HarperCollins). On 16 January he wrote to *Joy Hill at Allen & Unwin:

> I have completed and Miss Jenkinson [his secretary] has typed out a commentary on the names in *The Lord of the Rings*, especially devised to be (I hope) useful to anyone translating the book into German or Danish. . . . I think it would save me a considerable amount of time when the German and Dutch projects go forward, and also enable the translators to avoid a lot of the mistakes, and in some cases nonsense, that I now discover in the extant translations. [Tolkien-George Allen & Unwin archive, HarperCollins]

Tolkien's 'commentary' for many years was photocopied by Allen & Unwin and sent to translators of *The Lord of the Rings* as an aid to their work. After Tolkien's death it was edited by his son *Christopher and published in *A Tolkien Compass* (ed. Jared Lobdell, 1975), pp. 153–201, as *Guide to the Names in The Lord of the Rings*. In 2005 Wayne G. Hammond and Christina Scull made a fresh transcription of the *Nomenclature* from the professional typescript as corrected by Tolkien, with reference also to an earlier version in manuscript and typescript; this was published in *The Lord of the Rings: A Reader's Companion* (2005), pp. 750–82. (In the first printing of the *Reader's Companion* entries for *Mathom* and *Smials* were inadvertently omitted from the *Nomenclature*. These were absent in the editors' copy-text, but present in *A Tolkien Compass*.)

A Northern Venture. Collection of 'verses by members of the *Leeds University English School Association', published by the Swan Press, Leeds, in June 1923. It includes three poems by Tolkien: see *Enigmata Saxonica Nuper Inventa Duo*, *The Happy Mariners*, and *The Man in the Moon Came Down Too Soon*. Other contributors to the volume include *Wilfred R. Childe, *E.V. Gordon, and *A.H. Smith.

Northernness. Tolkien considered himself a man of north-eastern Europe, and in his professional life was mainly concerned with the languages, literature, and culture of that region. As he wrote to his son *Michael on 9 June 1941:

> I have spent most of my life, since I was your age, studying Germanic matters (in the general sense that includes England and Scandinavia). There is a great deal more force (and truth) than ignorant people imagine in the 'Germanic' ideal. I was much attracted by it as an undergraduate ... in reaction against the 'Classics'.... I have in this [Second World] War a burning private grudge ... against that ruddy little ignoramus Adolf Hitler.... Ruining, perverting, misapplying, and making for ever accursed, that noble northern spirit, a supreme contribution to Europe, which I have ever loved, and tried to present in its true light. Nowhere, incidentally, was it nobler than in England, nor more early sanctified and Christianized. [*Letters*, pp. 55–6]

During the nineteenth century many scholars in Northern Europe began to discover and take pride in a common 'Northern' heritage, recognizing a culture and literature which they could place beside, and contrast with, the long-established Classical traditions of Greece and Rome. Comparative Philology showed the roots and interrelationship of Germanic and Scandinavian languages. The literature of Iceland, previously little known, was seen as a major contribution to the 'Northern' heritage, and there was also an interest in that country's early form of democracy. An article in the *Oxford Magazine* applauding the establishment of the Vigfússon Readership in Ancient Icelandic Literature and Antiquities in 1941 hailed 'this new link . . . forged between Iceland and England: the lands of thousand-year-old Althing and venerable Parliament; the lands of two ancient European vernacular literatures, through the splendid fragments of whose combined traditions we can look beyond the Middle Age[s] and glimpse the far past of the North' ('The Vigfússon Readership', *Oxford Magazine* 60, no. 5 (13 November 1941), p. 65).

But this interest in the North was not confined to scholars. Marjorie J. Burns notes in 'J.R.R. Tolkien and the Journey North', *Mythlore* 15, no. 4, whole no. 58 (Summer 1989), that

> by 1892, when Tolkien was born, English popular thought had for some time been turning from the classical world. Southern tastes and southern considerations, particularly from mid-century onward, had been increasingly replaced by Northern ideals. Britain's Nordic ancestry was taken up like a banner and pointed to as indicative of all that the nation should hold in highest esteem. . . .
>
> The English, who had previously played down their Northern ties, now chose to deny their Southern past, to see the South as un-English, as decadent, feeble, and lacking in vigor or will. . . . Neither position is just, of course. Culturally, linguistically, racially, England's heritage is mixed; but Northern Romanticism, and that human knack of ignoring what doesn't appeal, now allowed the English to see themselves basically as Norsemen only slightly diluted in race, as Vikings only slightly tempered by time. [p. 5]

For a study in depth of this fascination with the North, see Andrew Wawm, *The Vikings and the Victorians: Inventing the Old North in 19th-Century Britain* (2000).

Tolkien says in *On Fairy-Stories* that of all his childhood reading he enjoyed most 'the nameless North of Sigurd of the Völsungs, and the prince of all dragons. Such lands were pre-eminently desirable' (*Tree and Leaf*, p. 40). The version he read, 'The Story of Sigurd' in *Andrew Lang's Red Fairy Book* (1890), was written for children, based on the translation by *William Morris of the Icelandic *Völsunga Saga*. The legend of Sigurd provides a good example of the common heritage of Northern Europe: it appears in medieval works written in different languages and places, including the *Poetic Edda*, the *Völsunga Saga*, and Snorri Sturluson's prose *Edda* (Icelandic); Þidreks Saga (a Norwegian translation of northern German heroic tales); and the *Nibelungenlied* (a southern German or Austrian heroic epic). A version was also known to the Anglo-Saxons, shown by a reference in *Beowulf* to Sigemund slaying a dragon guarding a hoard (in most other versions Sigemund is the father of Sigfrid, and not a dragon-slayer).

While still at school, as part of a general interest in German *languages, including Old English and Gothic, Tolkien also began to learn Old Norse so that he could read the story of Sigurd in the original. He shared his appreciation of Icelandic literature with his fellow pupils at *King Edward's School, Birmingham in a paper on 'Norse Sagas' which he read to the school Literary Society on 17 February 1911. According to a report in the *King Edward's School Chronicle*, Tolkien described a saga as a

> story of things which happened indeed but so long ago that marvels and miracles of the strange old Northern brand have crept into the tale. The best sagas are those of Iceland, and for pictures of human life and character they can hardly be bettered in any literature.... They tell how brave men – of our own blood, perhaps – lived and loved, and fought, and voyaged, and died.
>
> One of the best ... is the Völsunga Saga – a strange and glorious tale. It tells of the oldest of treasure hunts: the quest of the red gold of Andvari, the dwarf. It tells of the brave Sigurd Fafnirsbane, who was cursed by the possession of this gold, who, in spite of his greatness, had no happiness from his love for Brynhild. The Saga tells of this and many another strange and thrilling thing. It shows us the highest epic genius struggling out of savagery into complete and conscious humanity. ['Literary Society', n.s. 26, no. 186 (March 1911), pp. 19–20]

Tolkien also praised the story of *Burnt Njal*, and thought *Howard the Halt* the best among shorter works. He concluded with a sketch of the Norse religion and quotations from various sagas. The *Chronicle* reporter thought that the passages Tolkien read aloud constituted one of the charms of the paper.

'NORTHERN' STUDIES AT OXFORD AND LEEDS

When Tolkien transferred from Classics to the English School at *Oxford in Trinity Term 1913 he chose for his Special Subject 'Scandinavian Philology', which included a study of the literature. In that same term he read a paper on the Norse sagas to the Exeter College Essay Club (*Societies and clubs), perhaps the same as or similar to the paper he gave in Birmingham two years earlier; the brief report in the *Stapeldon Magazine* (June 1913) gives no details apart from noting that the audience (again) enjoyed the quotations with which Tolkien ended his talk. Reports in the *Stapeldon Magazine* and the Essay Club minutes note a similar response to a paper on the *Elder Edda* which Tolkien, now Rawlinson and Bosworth Professor of Anglo-Saxon, read to the Club on 17 November 1926: 'The reader, after sketching the character and historical background of the Edda, described certain of the poems. He also gave a number of translations and readings from the Icelandic which demonstrated the peculiar poetic and musical qualities of the language' ('Essay Club', *Stapeldon Magazine* 7, no. 39 (December 1926), p. 96).

At the University of *Leeds he was concerned with the teaching of Old Icelandic, which was studied in much the same detail as Old English; and as an adjunct, he helped to form a 'Viking Club' (*Societies and clubs) which comprised past and present students of Old Icelandic. On his return to Oxford Tolkien established the Kolbítar (*Societies and clubs), a group of dons who met to read in the original and translate all of the major Icelandic Sagas and both Eddas.

During most of his time as Rawlinson and Bosworth Professor of Anglo-Saxon at Oxford (1925–45) Icelandic studies were part of Tolkien's responsibilities: lecturing on all aspects of Old Icelandic language and literature, and often acting as a supervisor or examiner for any B.Litt. or D.Phil. theses on the subject. This was recognized in Iceland, when in 1933 Tolkien was made a honorary member of Hið íslenska bókmenntafélag (the Icelandic Literary Society; *Societies and clubs). In 1931 he served on an English Faculty Board committee which proposed, among the main needs of the Faculty, 'the endowment of a Readership or Lecturership in (medieval) Scandinavian languages'. Their justification was that 'Norse literature and philology are of central importance in the medieval curriculum of the English School. Adequate provision for the teaching of these subjects, and for the direction of advanced studies is urgently required. No provision for Scandinavian studies has been made by the Faculty of Medieval and Modern Languages since 1916' (Oxford University Archives FA 4/5/2/3). The request was rejected by the General Board, but made again in 1939. A bequest ultimately enabled the founding of the Vigfússon Readership in Ancient Icelandic Literature and Antiquities, first held by Tolkien's former B.Litt. student *E.O.G. Turville-Petre. With the Vigfússon Readership established, Tolkien was no longer responsible for Icelandic studies, and although Turville-Petre was called to war work almost as soon as he became Reader on 1 October 1941, Tolkien was not scheduled to give any lectures or classes on Icelandic studies after Michaelmas Term 1941 for the rest of his time in the Rawlinson and Bosworth chair. See also J.S. Ryan, 'The Work and Preferences of the Professor of Old Norse at the University of Oxford from 1925 to 1945', *Angerthas* 27 (May 1990).

NORTHERN INFLUENCES ON TOLKIEN'S FICTION

Among many influences from Northern literature on Tolkien's works, *Beowulf* not only provides the cup stolen from Smaug in *The Hobbit*, but also contributes to the Anglo-Saxon culture of the Rohirrim in *The Lord of the Rings*, in particular the reception of Gandalf, Aragorn, Legolas, and Gimli at Edoras (Book III, Chapter 6), which is based on that of Beowulf at Heorot. It also seems likely that Unferþ in *Beowulf* provided a prototype which Tolkien reworked as Gríma Wormtongue (see Clive Tolley, 'And the Word Was Made Flesh', *Mallorn* 32 (September 1995)). Most of the Dwarf-names in *The Hobbit*, and the name *Gandalf* (originally the name of the dwarf later called Thorin), are taken from the *Völuspá* in the *Elder Edda*. Even *Middle-earth* and *Mirkwood* are derived from early Germanic languages where they appear in various forms (see *Letters*, pp. 220, 369–70). The figure of Gandalf, as Tolkien himself recognized (*Letters*, p. 119), embodies some aspects of the god Odin in Norse mythology (see further, Marjorie Burns, *Perilous Realms: Celtic and Norse in Tolkien's Middle-earth* (2005), pp. 95–106). A dragon guarding a hoard, as in *The Hobbit* and Tolkien's poem **The Hoard*, appears in both *Beowulf* and the story of Sigurd. Tolkien also drew upon the latter for the story of Túrin Turambar in *The Silmarillion* (**'Of Túrin Turambar'*), who kills the dragon Glaurung as Sigurd kills Fáfnir, by striking the beast's soft belly from below. Also in *The Silmarillion*, the slaying of the companions of Finrod and Beren at intervals by a werewolf echoes the account in the *Völsunga Saga* of the slaying of nine of the ten fettered sons of King Volsung, one by one, on consecutive nights by a she-wolf. Beorn in *The Hobbit* who shape-changes into a great bear in the Battle of the Five Armies owes much to the berserk warriors of Northern tradition who fought with frenzied fury, and whose name according the most accepted interpretation described them as wearing bear skins. Verlyn Flieger comments that although 'ljösalfar (light elves) and döckalfar (dark elves) are part of the world of the Icelandic *Prose Edda* and its source, the *Poetic* or *Elder Edda*, Tolkien carries the concept [of Light Elves and Dark Elves] beyond mere naming to create a context in which the differences that underlie the distinction can be explained and justified' (*Splintered Light: Logos and Language in Tolkien's World* (2nd edn. 2002), p. 83).

After discussing the fragmentary remains of early Germanic writings, especially in Old English and Gothic, Paul Bibire observes in 'Sægde se þe cuþe: Tolkien as Anglo-Saxonist', *Scholarship and Fantasy* (1993), that

> Tolkien manifestly felt the imaginative pull of these lost literatures, of what must have been. His scholarly caution . . . warned him against confusing what is with what might have been. . . . He is also remarkably careful to dissociate his recreative from his scholarly activities, and the legends of the Rohirrim and their ancestors and cousins of Mirkwood are not those of the early English, or of their continental Gothic or Norse cousins: rather, he creates an analogue of such a body of legends, as it might have developed in the different cultural and geographical circumstances of Rohan and Gondor. [pp. 124–5]

Tolkien commented on this separation of his re-creative and scholarly activities in an unpublished essay concerning his thoughts on translating poetry:

> I must protest that I have never attempted to 're-create' anything. My aim has been the basically more modest, and certainly the more laborious one of trying to make something new. No one would learn anything valid about the 'Anglo-Saxons' from any of my lore, not even that concerning the Rohirrim; I never intended that they should. Even the lines beginning 'Where now the horse and the rider' [*The Lord of the Rings*, bk. III, ch. 6], though they echo a line in [the Old English poem] 'The Wanderer' . . . are certainly *not* a translation, re-creative or other wise. They are integrated (I hope) in something wholly different . . . they are

particular in reference, to a great hero and his renowned horse, and they are supposed to be part of the song of a minstrel of a proud and undefeated people in a hall still populous with men. Even the sentiment is different: it laments the ineluctable ending and passing back into oblivion of the fortunate, the full-lived, the unblemished and beautiful. To me that is more poignant than any particular disaster, from the cruelty of men or the hostility of the world. But if I were to venture to *translate* 'The Wanderer' – the lament of the lonely man withering away in regret, and the poet's reflexions upon it – I would not dare to intrude any sentiment of my own, nor to disarrange the order of word and thought in the old poem, in an impertinent attempt to make it more pleasing to myself, and perhaps to others. That is not 're-creation' but destruction. At best a foolish misuse of a talent for personal poetic expression; at worst the unwarranted impudence of a parasite. [Tolkien Papers, Bodleian Library, Oxford]

Tolkien did, however, give a version of part of the Old English poem *The Seafarer* a significant place in **The Lost Road* and **The Notion Club Papers*, though he placed and used it in an entirely different context: a sea-longing to seek the land of the Elves. He also wrote, probably in the late 1920s or 1930s, *Völsungakviða en nýja* ('The New Lay of the Völsungs'), an unpublished poem of 339 eight-line stanzas. On 29 March 1967 he wrote to **W.H. Auden, who had sent him part of the *Elder Edda* that he and Paul B. Taylor had translated into Modern English: 'In return again I hope to send you ... a thing I did many years ago when trying to learn the art of writing alliterative poetry: an attempt to unify the lays about the Völsungs from the *Elder Edda*, written in the old eight-line *fornyrðislag* stanza' (*Letters*, p. 379). A companion poem, *Guðrúnarkviða en nýja* ('The New Lay of Gudrún'), of 166 eight-line stanzas, dates to the same time. Each survives only in a fair copy manuscript and a postwar amanuensis typescript.

In the Old English poem *The Battle of Maldon* the old retainer Beorhtwold, prepared to die in a last desperate stand, proclaims: 'Will shall be the sterner, heart the bolder, spirit the greater as our strength lessens'. These words, Tolkien comments, 'have been held to be the finest expression of the northern heroic spirit, Norse or English; the clearest statement of uttermost endurance in the service of indomitable will' (**The Homecoming of Beorhtnoth Beorhthelm's Son*, in *Essays and Studies* (1953), p. 13). They exemplify as well an ideal which Tolkien applied frequently in **'The Silmarillion'* and *The Lord of the Rings*. To name only one instance in the former, in the Nirnaeth Arnoediad the Men of the House of Hador stand firm against the forces of Morgoth until only Húrin remains:

> Then he cast aside his shield, and wielded an axe two-handed; and it is sung that the axe smoked in the black blood of the troll-guard of Gothmog until it withered, and each time he slew Húrin cried: '*Aurë*

entuluva! Day shall come again!' Seventy times he uttered that cry; but they took him at last alive . . . for the Orcs grappled him with their hands, which clung to him still though he hewed off their arms; and ever their numbers were renewed, until at last he fell buried beneath them. [*The Silmarillion*, p. 195]

Likewise, in *The Lord of the Rings*, Book V, Chapter 6, Éomer lets 'blow the horns to rally all men to his banner that could come thither; for he thought to make a great shield-wall at the last, and stand, and fight there on foot till all fell, and do deeds of song on the fields of Pelennor, though no man should be left in the West to remember the last King of the Mark'. On a non-military level, the same spirit is expressed by Frodo, and especially Sam, as they struggle across the desolation of Mordor to Mount Doom, and he realizes that

> at best their provision would take them to their goal; and when the task was done, there they would come to an end, alone, houseless, foodless in the midst of a terrible desert. There could be no return.
> 'So that was the job I felt I had to do when I started,' thought Sam: 'to help Mr. Frodo to the last step and then die with him? Well, if that is the job then I must do it. . . .'
> But even as hope died in Sam, or seemed to die, it was turned to a new strength. Sam's plain hobbit-face grew stern, almost grim, as the will hardened in him. . . . [bk. VI, ch. 3]

*Priscilla Tolkien once said of her father and his works of fiction:

> When thinking of his imagination I feel that like his scholarship it was overwhelmingly *Northern European* in every detail of his deepest loves and fears. The ideas aroused by the sufferings of long, hard, cruel winters, the dazzling beauty of the short flowering of Spring and Summer, and the sadness of seeing this once more pass back into the darkness; the symbolism of darkness and light is continual in [*The Silmarillion*] for good and evil, despair and hope. Such a climate also nourished the virtues which he held in such high regard: heroism and endurance, loyalty, and fidelity, both in love and in war. ['Talk Given at Church House, Westminster on 16.9.77 by Priscilla Tolkien', *Amon Hen* 29 [?November 1977], p. 4]

On this subject, see also 'Norse Mythological Elements in *The Hobbit*' by Mitzi M. Brunsdale, *Mythlore* 9, no. 4, whole no. 34 (Winter 1983); Marjorie Burns, *Perilous Realms: Celtic and Norse in Tolkien's Middle-earth* (2005); Fredrik J. Heinemann, 'Tolkien and Old Icelandic Literature', *Scholarship and Fantasy* (1993); Gloria St. Clair, 'An Overview of the Northern Influences on Tolkien's Works' and '*Volsunga Saga* and Narn: Some Analogies', both in *Proceedings of the J.R.R. Tolkien Centenary Conference 1992* (1995); and

Tom Shippey, 'Tolkien and Iceland: The Philology of Envy' (2002), *www2.hi.is/ Apps/WebObjects/HI.woa/wa/dp?detail=1004508&name=nordals_en_greinar_ og_erindi.*

The Northmen and the Wainriders
   see *Cirion and Eorl and the Friendship of Gondor and Rohan*

'Note on the landing of the Five Wizards
   and their functions and operations' see *The Five Wizards*

Notes on Motives in the Silmarillion. Essay, published with notes and commentary as text VII in the section 'Myths Transformed' of **Morgoth's Ring* (1993), pp. 394–408.

The work, probably from the late 1950s, exists in two versions. The earlier is a four-page manuscript inscribed 'Some notes on the "philosophy" of the Silmarillion', described by *Christopher Tolkien as 'rapidly expressed' and without 'a clear ending' (*Morgoth's Ring*, p. 394). The later version, greatly expanded and more carefully expressed, was left unfinished in mid-sentence after twelve manuscript pages.

The 'notes' compare Sauron and Morgoth, their characters and motives, their relative power at various times, and the way they used it. 'Morgoth had no "plan": unless destruction and reduction to *nil* of a world in which he had only a *share* can be called a "plan"' (p. 397). But 'Sauron had never reached this stage of nihilistic madness. He did not object to the existence of the world, so long as he could do what he liked with it' (p. 396). Then follows a discussion of the reasons why the Valar were reluctant 'to come into open battle with Morgoth', concluding that Morgoth's power and being were disseminated throughout the world – 'the whole of "middle-earth" was Morgoth's Ring' – and to try to destroy him 'might well end in reducing Middle-earth to chaos, possibly even all Arda'; whereas 'the final eradication of Sauron . . . was achievable by the destruction of the Ring' into which his power had been concentrated (p. 400).

In a section developed fully only in the second text Tolkien suggests reasons for the apparent inaction of the Valar against Morgoth during the First Age, and that their eventual intervention was precisely timed, Manwë with his knowledge of the Music and 'power of *direct* recourse to and communication with Eru . . . must have grasped with great clarity . . . that it was the essential mode of the process of "history" in Arda that evil should constantly arise, and that out of it new good should constantly come' (p. 402). The second version ends soon after turning its attention to the resistance to Sauron in later ages, but the published text continues with the first version, from the point where the two texts diverge, with a brief philosophical consideration of the future of Arda.

Finally Tolkien turns to the question of the origin of Orcs: 'Part of the Elf-Man idea gone wrong. Though as for Orcs, the Eldar believed Morgoth had actually "bred" them by capturing Men (and Elves) early [i.e. in the early days of their existence] and increasing to the utmost any corrupt tendencies they possessed' (p. 406). (See also *Orcs.)

Christopher Tolkien comments that 'despite its incomplete state ... this is the most comprehensive account that my father wrote of how, in his later years, he had come to "interpret" the nature of Evil in his mythology ...' (p. 406). See also *Good and Evil.

Notes on Óre. A single typescript sheet, apparently the beginning of a substantial essay on the common Eldarin root 3OR and its descendants, edited with notes by Carl F. Hostetter and published in *Vinyar Tengwar* 41 (July 2000), pp. 11–19. In *The Lord of the Rings* Appendix E Quenya óre is glossed 'heart (inner mind)', as used in a phrase such as 'my heart tells me', but '"heart" is not suitable, except in brevity, since óre does not correspond in sense to any of the English confused uses of "heart". . . .' The essay was to have discussed 'what the óre was for Elvish thought and speech, and the nature of its counsels' (p. 11) but does not proceed very far. The sheet was found between the typescript of the finished part of *The Shibboleth of Fëanor and the manuscript draft for an unwritten excursus on the names of the sons of Fëanor. It seems unconnected with that work, though probably contemporary with it, 1968 or later.

Pages of manuscript draft material give some indications of how the essay might have continued. Among these is an interesting note, more concerned with the *Athrabeth than etymology. The writer is not identified, but seems to be a Man of a later period. After summarizing the Athrabeth it continues: 'For (as far as we can now judge [from]) the legends (mainly of Elvish origin probably, though coming down to us through Men) it would seem clear that Men were not intended to have Elvish longevity, limited only by the life of the Earth', but were intended to enjoy a much greater life-span before passing from the circles of the world. The Elves believed that the life-span of Men had been shortened as a result of some rebellion against Eru in the form of accepting Melkor as God, after which 'only the wisest of Men could distinguish between [?his] evil promptings and true óre' (p. 14).

On Eldarin and Quenya, see *Languages, Invented.

The Notion Club Papers. Story, published with commentary and notes in *Sauron Defeated (1992), pp. 145–327.

SUMMARY

The heart of *The Notion Club Papers* is presented as the surviving part of a record of meetings of an *Oxford society during 1986 and 1987 (some forty years in the future when Tolkien wrote the work). Following some preliminaries, the first of its two parts (as originally conceived) begins with a brief report of a meeting in November 1986, notes the omission of 'one or two minor entries', and continues with an account of the meeting of 20 February 1987. Michael Ramer, one of the members of the club, has finished reading a space-travel story he has written. This leads to discussion of the credibility of the machine or other device used by writers of space stories to take characters to their destination. Another member, Rupert Dolbear, says that the problem with Ramer's work is that it is out of keeping with its frame-machinery, and challenges Ramer to say how *he* got to the place described in the story. At the next meeting, Ramer explains that he has considered methods of space-travel both for a story and for himself, and that he has tried to train his mind to travel in his dreams. He describes various dream experiences, some inspired by stories he had written long ago, some fragmentary, such as a Green Wave towering over fields, and visions of the planets of our solar system as well as unknown worlds. When he mentions the names of his worlds, the members discuss language and the weak methods of communication common in space-travel stories. Ramer says he has more dreams about *Atlantis than about space, and mentions the Wave towering over the land, a Great Door, and the Elvish En-keladim (all aspects of Tolkien's mythology, in which *Númenor is associated with Atlantis and his own dreams of a great wave). Ramer ends his account by describing a vision of a disorderly planet, then of an area in which the inhabitants and their buildings spread like ringworm; but as he came closer, he realized that he had been watching a speeded-up history of the Thames Valley and Oxford.

The second part of the work records a series of meetings following directly on the first part, in which the matter of Númenor becomes of prime importance. It seems likely that Tolkien originally intended Part Two to proceed differently, since an outline for it begins: 'Do the Atlantis story and abandon Eriol-Saga, with Loudham, Jeremy, Guildford and Ramer taking part' (*Sauron Defeated*, p. 281). But there is no indication of how the 'Eriol-Saga' was to be introduced. Since Arundel Loudham (changed to *Lowdham* during the writing of the first version of Part Two) was to play an important role in the 'Atlantis story', Tolkien made additions to Part One to suggest Lowdham's interest in the myth. A link is provided by a fragmentary entry reporting the end of a meeting on 13 March, when Lowdham tells Ramer and Guildford that he has been having strange experiences. As the story proceeds, it becomes clear that he is haunted subconsciously by Númenor, and is reminded of the temple Sauron built there when he sees what appears to be smoke coming from the lantern of the Radcliffe Camera.

At the first meeting of the Club in Trinity Term 1987, on 8 May, the members discuss neologisms (the use of new words or expressions), the misuse of established words, and the way that language changes and evolves. They also talk about legends of origin and cultural myths, and whether, if one could go back in time, one would find that myth dissolves into history, or real history becomes more mythical. At some point Lowdham becomes upset, curses 'Zigûr', and cries out: 'Behold the Eagles of the Lords of the West! They are coming over Númenór!' Ramer says that *Númenór* is his name for Atlantis, and fellow member Wilfrid Trewin Jeremy says that he also has some recollection of hearing the name. At the meeting on 22 May Lowdham comments on his strange names *Alwin Arundel*, chosen when his mother objected to the *Ælfwine Éarendel* his father, Edwin, had wanted to give him. He tells how his father set out in his ship *The Éarendel* (in the first text *Éarendel Star*) one day in 1947 and was never seen again. Lowdham remembers his father keeping a diary in a strange script, and that after his disappearance Lowdham had found a sheet in the same script but could not decipher it. The members discuss the meanings of the names *Ælfwine* and *Éadwine*, and historical figures with those and related names. (See also *Eriol and Ælfwine.)

This in turn leads to a discussion of the name *Éarendel* in the lines from the Old English *Crist*: *Éalá Éarendel engla beorhtost / ofer middangeard monnum sended*. Lowdham says that he has heard the similar *ëarendil* in another language, 'where it actually means Great Mariner, or literally Friend of the Sea; though it also has, I think, some connexion with the stars' (p. 237). When he is asked 'what language?' he tells the members that since he was about ten he has had 'words, even occasional phrases', ringing in his ears; 'both in dream and waking abstraction. They come into my mind unbidden, or I wake to hear myself repeating them. Sometimes they seem to be quite isolated, just words or names. . . . It was a long time before I began to piece the fragments together' (pp. 237–8). He recorded these, and after removing Anglo-Saxon or related elements, most of the remainder seem to belong to two languages which he had never come across. He associates both languages with a place called *Númenór* in the first language (which he calls *Avallonian*, in fact Quenya; see *Languages, Invented), and *Anadûnê* in the second (which he calls *Adunaic*). He discusses other words, and notes that even those in Old English came to him before he began to learn that language. Among the longer passages of Old English are a line which means 'a straight way lay westward, now it is bent', and some verses, one of which includes lines Lowdham translates as: 'There is many a thing in the west of the world unknown to men; marvels and strange beings, [a land lovely to look on,] the dwelling place of the Elves and the bliss of the Gods' (pp. 243, 244).

By the next meeting, in Ramer's rooms on 12 June 1987, Lowdham has heard a much longer passage in his two unidentified languages. His incomplete translation shows that it is an account of the Fall of Númenor – the coming of Sauron, the attempt to invade the land of the Lords of the West, the drowning of Númenor, and the changing of the shape of the world so that there is no longer a straight path to the West. He mentions the name *Sauron*, and its Adunaic equivalent *Zigûr*, at which Wilfrid Trewin Jeremy reacts strangely. Both he and Lowdham seem to relive the destruction of Númenor, as dark clouds roll over the sky from the West and a violent thunderstorm breaks. Lowdham addresses Jeremy as 'Voronwë', and Jeremy addresses Lowdham as 'Elendil'; both rush out into the freak storm. During the evening, Lowdham mentions again the sheet with the strange script he had found among his father's papers, intending to say something about it later, but does not. The other members leave when the storm subsides, and Ramer picks up a sheet of paper and puts it in a drawer.

On 26 June a brief letter from Lowdham and Jeremy is read to the Club, saying they 'were cast up far away when the wind fell' (p. 254) and are now doing research. Ramer produces the sheet dropped by Lowdham at the last meeting. Since Lowdham had mentioned that some of the words he received were in Old English, on the chance that this was the language of the strange script, Ramer took the sheet to old Professor Rashbold of Pembroke, who deciphered it and positively identified the language as 'Old English of a strongly Mercian (West Midland) colour, ninth century' (p. 257). Translated into Modern English, it turns out to be another, longer account of the last days of Númenor.

The next meeting, on 25 September 1987, begins with Philip Frankley, another member affected by the resonances of Númenor, reading a poem, *The Death of St Brendan* (see *Imram*), which includes allusions to Tolkien's mythology (*'The Silmarillion'). He woke 'four days ago with the thing largely fixed' in his mind (p. 265). The members discuss possible influences from real accounts of St Brendan, but note there seems no source for the lines describing 'the round world' plunging 'steeply down' while 'the old road' goes on 'as an unseen bridge . . . on arches' (p. 264). Lowdham and Jeremy then describe their travels around the western coasts of Britain and Ireland, and the rumours they heard of huge phantom waves. They recount that while staying in Porlock (in Somerset on the coast of the Bristol Channel) they both dreamed themselves back to tenth century England in a hall crowded with warriors who had come to join Edward the Elder's fight against the invading Danes. In that dream Lowdham, now the minstrel Ælfwine, was called upon to entertain those in the hall, and recited a verse about his sea-longing, while Jeremy, now Tréowine from the Marches, told the story of King Sheave. They finish their account for that evening as these Anglo-Saxon personas leave the hall and promise to tell the members more at the next meeting.

At that point, however, Tolkien abandoned *The Notion Club Papers*. Only a few notes and fragments indicate how the story might have continued. One note suggests that Tréowine and Ælfwine were to sail west, find the Straight Path, and see the round world below, then be driven back. Another has 'sojourn in Númenor before and during the fall ends with Elendil and Voronwë fleeing on a hill of water into the dark with the Eagles and lightning pursuing them', and 'At the end . . . Lowdham and Jeremy have a vivid dream of the Fall of Númenor' (p. 279).

ASSOCIATED 'PAPERS'

In addition to this inner core of the minutes of the Notion Club, as part of their fictional 'frame', Tolkien also produced associated 'papers'. The layer nearest the core is the framework of the book *Leaves from the Notion Club Papers*, subdivided into Part One and Part Two, supposedly edited by one Howard Green and published in 2014, for which Tolkien produced a facsimile title-page (*Sauron Defeated*, p. 154). According to the 'editor's' foreword, Green found the Club's papers 'after the Summer Examinations of 2012 on the top of one of a number of sacks of waste paper in the basement of the Examination Schools in Oxford . . .' (p. 155), but was unable to discover how they had got there. They appear to be the incomplete reports of the meetings of an Oxford club from approximately 1980 to 1990, with references to an event as late as 1987, apparently prepared for publication with notes; but 'Brown' could find no trace of the existence of a Notion Club. He describes the surviving papers, including a list of members.

Another layer is a 'Note to the Second Edition' of the book, in which Howard Green quotes the opinions of Mr W.W. Wormald and Mr D.N. Borrow that the paper and style of writing suggest that the materials date to during or just after the 'Six Years' War' (i.e. the Second World War, 1939–45). Green, who had earlier suggested that if the future events described in the papers were 'foreseen' by their author, concludes: 'If . . . any such club existed at that earlier period, the names remain pseudonyms. The forward dating might have been adopted as an additional screen. But I am now convinced that the Papers are a work of fiction; and it may well be that the predictions (notably the Storm), though genuine and not coincidences, were unconscious . . .' (p. 158).

THE INKLINGS

An important element of the minutes are references or allusions made by the members of the Notion Club to members of the *Inklings and their works. These include criticism of the methods of transporting Elwin Ransom to Mars and Venus in *Out of the Silent Planet* (1938) and *Perelandra* (1943) by *C.S. Lewis. One of the members has lectured on Lewis and *Charles Williams with the title *Public House School*. *The Allegory of Love* (1936) by Lewis and Williams' *House of the Octopus* (1945) are mentioned as probably the only works by those authors still remembered at all. A few 'read C.R. [*Christopher] Tolkien's little books of memoirs: *In the Roaring Forties*, and *The Inns and Outs of Oxford*' but only three members of the Club 'bothered with Tolkien père and all that elvish stuff' (p. 219). In the first manuscript of Part Two Jeremy remembers finding in a secondhand shop a manuscript, *Quenta Eldalien, being the History of the Elves* by John Arthurson (= John R.R. Tolkien, son of *Arthur Tolkien), in which he found the name *Númenor* [sic]. Other members then recall C.S. Lewis's use of 'Numinor'. Professor Rashbold of Pembroke, who deciphers and translates the Old English text (written in Tengwar; see *Writing systems) is another sly allusion to Tolkien himself (see *Names).

There are also 'external' associations with the Inklings, provided in editorial apparatus. A rejected first page of Part One bears the title *Beyond Lewis or Out of the Talkative Planet*, and continues: 'Being a fragment of an apocryphal Inklings' Saga, made by some imitator at some time in the 1980s'. Its replacement has the title *Beyond Probability or Out of the Talkative Planet*', a play on the titles of two of C.S. Lewis's works, *Out of the Silent Planet* and *Beyond Personality* (1944), and suggests that the work was 'written after 1989, as an apocryphal imitation of the *Inklings Saga Book*' (pp. 148–9). The real Inklings regrettably kept no such record of their meetings, but *The Notion Club Papers* probably conveys some of the atmosphere of their discussions. An early list of members of the Notion Club, identifying some with individual Inklings, shows that Tolkien began with such a scheme, but he seems to have abandoned the idea almost immediately. Although some Notion Club members seem to portray aspects of certain of the Inklings, exact equivalences were soon rejected.

The first pages mentioned above continue with 'Preface to the Inklings' (rejected version) and 'aside to the audience' (second) version): 'I beg of the present company not to look for their own faces in this mirror. For the mirror is cracked, and at the best you will only see your countenances distorted, and adorned maybe with noses (and other features) that are not your own, but belong to other members of the company – if to anybody' (pp. 148–9). Christopher Tolkien thinks it likely that his father's first idea 'was far less elaborate than it became; intending perhaps, so far as the form was concerned, no more than a *jeu d'esprit* for the entertainment of the Inklings – while the titles seem to emphasize that it was to be, in part, the vehicle of criticism and discussion of aspects of Lewis's "planetary" novels' (p. 149). He sees no indication that his father envisaged Part Two as written, until after he completed Part One.

HISTORY

Tolkien wrote to *Stanley Unwin on 21 July 1946 that he had 'in a fortnight of comparative leisure round about last Christmas written three parts of another book, taking up in an entirely different frame and setting what little value in the inchoate *Lost Road* . . . and other things beside. I hoped to finish this in a rush, but my health gave way after Christmas' (*Letters*, p. 118). Christopher Tolkien is undoubtedly correct that it would have been impossible for his father to produce *The Notion Club Papers*, and all of its associated material (*The Drowning of Anadûnê*, Adunaic language, facsimiles) in a fortnight. He thinks, rather, that his father continued to work on it through the first half of 1946. This seems to be confirmed by the fact that Tolkien read *The Drowning of Anadûnê* (probably the final version) to the Inklings on 22 August 1946, and in recording this in his diary *W.H. Lewis implied that *The Notion Club Papers* had previously been read to the Inklings. Christopher suggests that during Christmas 1945 his father probably wrote only the first two manuscripts of Part One and the manuscript of Part Two.

The earliest, roughly written manuscript of Part One was apparently followed by an expanded version with many changes and additions. Christopher Tolkien thinks that after some rough drafting, his father produced the first, manuscript, version of Part Two (in which the two languages which come to Lowdham are unnamed, but clearly Quenya and Noldorin/Sindarin), but left it unfinished to make some preliminary sketches and outlines for, and the first version of, *The Drowning of Anadûnê*. He then made a fair copy of Part One, abandoning it just before the end, and then a typescript, one section of which seems to have been done before the fair copy. He began a typescript of Part Two (in which Adunaic replaced Sindarin), but stopped after completing the entry for 22 May to make typescripts of three successive versions of *The Drowning of Anadûnê*. Probably when all or most of this was finished, he returned to *The Notion Club Papers* and began another typescript of Part Two at a point near the beginning of the minutes for 22 May. He replaced the relevant part of the first typescript, and continued as far as the manuscript extended. Christopher Tolkien notes that his father apparently changed his mind about the division into two parts, deleting 'Part I / The Ramblings of Michael Ramer / *Out of the Talkative Planet*' from the first page of the last version of Part One, and providing no heading at the beginning of the typescript of Part Two, whereas on the title-page for the previous manuscript appears 'II / The Strange Case of Arundel Lowdham' (p. 153).

The final texts of both parts of *The Notion Club Papers* were published in *Sauron Defeated*, with readings from earlier versions where they differ significantly. Notes explain some of the allusions and references in the text. Some of the names that appear in *The Notion Club Papers* are explained in **The War of the Jewels*, p. xi.

Christopher Tolkien admits that he does not know why his father abandoned *The Notion Club Papers*. 'It may be that he felt that the work had lost all unity, that "Atlantis" had broken apart the frame in which it had been set. . . . But I think also that having forced himself to return to *The Lord of the Rings*, and having brought it to its end, he was then deflected into the very elaborate further work on the legends of the Elder Days that preceded the actual publication of *The Lord of the Rings*' (p. 152). Later he wonders, too, if the conception had not become too 'intricate' for his father to continue (p. 282).

Another reason, surely, is that Tolkien became distracted by ideas for a new language, Adunaic (later *Adûnaic*, see **Languages, Invented*), as spoken in Númenor, and interested in working out a new study of the fall of Númenor, in a Mannish tradition: **The Drowning of Anadûnê*. He spent considerable time on Adunaic, producing a seventeen-page typescript, said to be a report written by Lowdham to present to the Notion Club. This begins by describing the probable history of the language, and continues with an elaborate but incomplete account of its phonology. Tolkien also spent hours making 'facsimiles' of Lowdham's Adunaic fragments and two of Lowdham's father's Old English texts written in Tengwar (**Writing systems*); these are reproduced in *Sauron Defeated*. The transcriptions and translation of the fragments that Lowdham produces at the meeting of 12 June are reproduced as two colour plates at the beginning of the HarperCollins and Houghton Mifflin hardback editions.

CRITICISM

In 'Tolkien's Experiment with Time: *The Lost Road*, "The Notion Club Papers", and J.W. Dunne', *Proceedings of the J.R.R. Tolkien Centenary Conference 1992* (1995), Verlyn Flieger finds that *The Notion Club Papers* show

> a considerable advance in technical sophistication over *The Lost Road*. Tolkien's handling of his material is surer, and his sense of story better developed. There is an increase in narrative tension through a carefully-orchestrated sequence of psychological aberrations, a judicious sprinkling of plot-teasers in the first part of the story, and a gothic use of weather, culminating in the story's violent climax in a night of storm. The tone of this second narrative is more energetic and its setting more clearly contemporary, more conspicuously grounded in time and place, than that of the earlier story. The argumentative, rumbustious members of the Notion Club are a distinct improvement over the rather quiet Errols, while Tolkien's earliest drafts make it clear that the wit, rough badinage, and often heated exchanges were drawn from life – specifically the Inklings. [p. 42]

See also Flieger's *A Question of Time: J.R.R. Tolkien's Road to Faërie* (1997), especially Chapter 5.

David Bratman wrote in 'The Literary Value of *The History of Middle-earth*', *Tolkien's Legendarium: Essays on The History of Middle-earth* (2000), that in *The Lost Road* and *The Notion Club Papers* 'we have something not otherwise found in Tolkien's fiction – stories with explicitly modern setting, which display the author's own aesthetic to language so extensively that his biographer quoted from them for that purpose. . . . Not even in his essay *A Secret Vice* did Tolkien so vividly convey what the imagination of language meant to him' (p. 81). He also remarks that

> The club may best be thought of as the Inklings viewed through Tolkien's eyes and idealized to his tastes. . . . He knew his men intimately . . . and his imaginary conversations have all the freshness, repartee, and meanderings into intellectual byways that one would expect of a transcription of the real Inklings meetings. The opening discussions are wide-ranging considerations of secondary-world literature that in style must be very similar to actual Inklings meetings, though the content is tinged heavily by Tolkien's own ideas and interests. [p. 82]

See also John D. Rateliff, 'The Lost Road, The Dark Tower, and The Notion Club Papers: Tolkien and Lewis's Time Travel Triad', *Tolkien's Legendarium: Essays on The History of Middle-earth* (2000).

Númenor. The story of Númenor apparently sprang from a chance conversation between Tolkien and *C.S. Lewis around 1936. As Tolkien recalled in a letter to Charlotte and Denis Plimmer: 'L[ewis] said to me one day: "Tollers, there is too little of what we really like in stories. I am afraid we shall have to try and write some ourselves." We agreed that he should try "space-travel", and I should try "time-travel".... My effort, after a few promising chapters, ran dry: it was too long a way round to what I really wanted to make, a new version of the Atlantis legend' (8 February 1967, *Letters*, p. 378). In an earlier letter, Tolkien wrote that he and Lewis 'tossed up' to decide who should take which theme (letter to Christopher Bretherton, 16 July 1964, *Letters*, p. 347). Whether choice or chance, the time-travel theme allowed Tolkien to plan a story, *The Lost Road*, in which he could incorporate a version of the *Atlantis myth which had haunted him since childhood. He told Christopher Bretherton: 'This legend or myth or dim memory of some ancient history has always troubled me. In sleep I had the dreadful dream of the ineluctable wave, either coming out of the quiet sea, or coming in towering over the green inlands. It still occurs occasionally, though now exorcized by writing about it. It always ends by surrender, and I awake gasping out of deep water' (*Letters*, p. 347). In a letter to Mrs E.C. Ossendrijver on 5 January 1961 he said that 'Númenor, shortened form of Númenórë' was his own invention. Its legends 'are my own use for my own purposes of the *Atlantis* legend, but not based on special *knowledge*, but on a special personal concern with this tradition of the culture-bearing men of the Sea, which so profoundly affected the imagination of peoples of Europe with westward-shores' (*Letters*, p. 303).

Early texts of the *'Silmarillion' mythology say little about the fate of the Men who fought with the Elves against Morgoth in the First Age. *The Book of Lost Tales* never reached that point. The *Sketch of the Mythology* (*c.* 1926) says only that the Valar assigned Middle-earth to Men, and that Elves who did not leave those lands would fade. The first version of the *Quenta Noldorinwa* (*c.* 1930) states that Men of the race of Hador and Bëor were to be allowed to depart with the Elves for the West if they wished, but of these Men only Elrond was left, and he elected to remain in Middle-earth. In the second version, the permission for Men to leave was omitted. *Christopher Tolkien thinks that this passing idea in the *Quenta Noldorinwa* nonetheless represents 'the first germ of the story of the departure of the survivors of the Elf-friends to Númenor' (*The Shaping of Middle-earth*, p. 200).

The subsequent evolution of Númenor in Tolkien's writings was complex. It has roots in his mythology of the First Age and in real world myths; and in the quarter-century following his agreement with Lewis, Tolkien not only brought Númenor into two unfinished works of time-travel, *The Lost Road* and *The Notion Club Papers*, but also wrote three narrative accounts of the island's story, *The Fall of Númenor, *The Drowning of Anadûnê*, and the *Akallabêth*, as well as *A Description of the Island of Númenor*; he developed and extended its history to provide a vital background to *The Lord of the Rings*; and he began (but did not complete) two other narrative works, one (*Aldarion and

Erendis) set in Númenor and telling the story of one of the earlier kings, the other (**Tal-Elmar*) in which Númenóreans are seen from the point of view of men of Middle-earth.

THE LOST ROAD AND THE FALL OF NÚMENOR

Tolkien described his plans for *The Lost Road* in his letter to Christopher Bretherton: 'the end was to be the presence of my hero in the drowning of Atlantis. This was to be called *Númenor*, the Land in the West.' A father and son would enter into various historic and legendary times and

> come at last to Amandil and Elendil leaders of the loyal party in Númenor, when it fell under the domination of Sauron. Elendil 'Elf-friend' was the founder of the Exiled kingdoms in Arnor and Gondor. But I found my real interest was only in the upper end, the *Akallabêth* or *Atalantie* ('Downfall' in Númenórean and Quenya [see *Languages, Invented]), so I brought all the stuff I had written on the originally unrelated legends of Númenor into relation with the main mythology. [16 July 1964, *Letters*, p. 347]

Christopher Tolkien, however, can find no evidence that Númenor/Atlantis ever existed independent of the mythology: 'there was never a time when the legends of Númenor were "unrelated to the main mythology". My father erred in his recollection (or expressed himself obscurely, meaning something else); the letter cited above was indeed written nearly thirty years later' (**The Lost Road and Other Writings*, p. 10).

It also seems evident that the conception of Númenor and of its destruction arose only as part of Tolkien's plans for his time-travel story. The importance he attached to this part of *The Lost Road* is confirmed by the preliminary work he did on the Númenórean background before he began to write the story proper. He wrote a quick outline of the history of Númenor, then a fuller, untitled draft narrative: the first version of *The Fall of Númenor*. After this he wrote four chapters of *The Lost Road*, two introductory chapters which end as the first instance of time-travel is about to take place, and two which narrate the beginning of the episode in Númenor. There the manuscript ends, except for brief notes for other episodes and part of a chapter set in tenth-century England. Probably after composing the two chapters set in Númenor, Tolkien wrote a second version of *The Fall of Númenor*.

Although later writings extended the history of Númenor, and added or changed many details, the basic story was already present in the first outline. After the defeat of Morgoth at the end of the First Age, the Valar reward Men who had helped to bring this about with an island in which to dwell, variously called *Atalantë*, *Númenor*, and *Andúnië*. The Númenóreans grow in wisdom and become great mariners. They sail around the shores of Middle-earth and see the Gates of the Morning in the East at the edge of the world (in Tolkien's mythology originally conceived as flat). Lesser men living in Middle-earth take the Númenóreans as gods. In early versions of the story, the Valar, the 'Lords of the West', permit the people of Númenor to sail west to Tol Eressëa, the Lonely Isle where many Elves live, but not further west to Valinor, home of the Valar themselves.

The Númenóreans are granted longer lives than other Men, but are still mortal. Later generations begin to resent this limitation, and to believe that in Valinor they would gain immortal life (*Mortality and Immortality). They are encouraged in this by Thû (the name of Sauron in some early versions of the mythology), once a follower of Morgoth, who comes to Númenor in the likeness of a bird and gains such influence that the king builds a temple to Morgoth and eventually attempts to invade Valinor with a great fleet. In this crisis the Valar, empowered by Ilúvatar, sunder Valinor from the earth, the edges of which are bent back so that it becomes a globe, while a rift opens in which the Númenórean fleet and Númenor itself are destroyed.

The Númenóreans who escape this disaster by sailing to Middle-earth become lords and kings of men. Many still seek in vain to prolong life, but manage only to preserve the bodies of the dead. Their descendants preserve a confused memory of a land in the West ruled by the Gods, to which the dead might come. From this arises a custom among those who dwell on the west coast of Middle-earth of placing their dead on ships and sending them out to sea. Some Númenóreans are able to see, or partly see, a path or bridge rising above the world and leading to the True West; but when they try to find this path they succeed only in sailing around the world. Only the Elves are still able to reach Valinor along the Straight Road.

Amroth, who had continued to honour the Valar, is one of those who escape the destruction of Númenor. He becomes a king in Middle-earth and allies with Elrond, son of Eärendel, and with Elves who had stayed in Middle-earth in an attack on Thû's fortress. Although they are victorious, Amroth is slain. Thû is driven out and flees to a dark forest.

Having established this history, Tolkien was able to begin to write *The Lost Road*. The first two chapters, set in more or less contemporary *Cornwall, introduce the main protagonist, Alboin Errol, who from boyhood has heard in his dreams echoes of strange languages, which he calls Eressëan or Elf-latin and Beleriandic, including a passage in Eressëan describing the downfall of Númenor. He finds himself suddenly declaring that some dark clouds 'look like the eagles of the Lords of the West coming upon Númenor'. Then Elendil of Númenor appears to him and offers him the chance to go back in time, if he takes his son with him. (These two chapters are described at greater length in the entry for *The Lost Road*.)

The two Númenórean chapters take place forty-four years after the arrival of Sauron (now so named) in Númenor. Elendil (replacing Amroth) is the leader of a party faithful to the old ways and beliefs, while his son, Herendil, has been half won over to the opinion of those supporting Sauron. The kings of Númenor are now descended from Eärendel, and the last king, Tarkalion, in his pride, summons Sauron to Númenor, demanding homage from him. Elendil, who is trying to persuade Herendil to his own point of view, says that men now covet the lands of others, influenced by Sauron; they build metal-clad ships, strong fortresses, and many weapons. Those who displease the king disappear, and there are spies, prisons, torments, and evil rites. Sauron has built a temple to Morgoth on the mountain holy to Ilúvatar, and is encouraging the Númenóreans to abandon the Elvish Eressëan language and revive the ancestral speech of Men. Elendil foresees that Sauron will encourage the ageing king to invade Valinor in a useless bid for immortality. He asks his son to choose between his father and Sauron, and with Herendil's choice for his father the narrative ends.

The picture Tolkien draws of Númenor under the influence of Sauron, a once great nation in decay, almost certainly owes something to then-current events in Nazi Germany. Christopher Tolkien comments:

> From Elendil's words at the end of *The Lost Road* there emerges a sinister picture: the withdrawal of the besotted and aging king from the public view, the unexpected disappearance of people unpopular with the 'government', informers, prisons, torture, secrecy, fear of the night; propaganda in the form of the 'rewriting of history' . . . ; the multiplication of weapons of war, the purpose of which is concealed but guessed at; and behind all the dreadful figure of Sauron. . . . Moreover, Númenor is seen by the young as over-populous, boring, 'over-known' . . . ; and this cause of discontent is used, it seems, by Sauron to further the policy of 'imperial' expansion and ambition that he presses on the king. When at this time my father reached back to the world of the first man to bear the name 'Elf-friend' he found there an image of what he most condemned and feared in his own. [*The Lost Road and Other Writings*, p. 77]

The second version of *The Fall of Númenor* probably followed, or was contemporary with, the writing of *The Lost Road*, for it includes details introduced in that work. Elrond, son of Eärendel, is now named as the first ruler of Númenor. The Númenóreans adopt the speech of the Elves of the Blessed Realm and Tol Eressëa. Elendil, who escapes the downfall, becomes a king in Beleriand and allies with Gil-galad, the Elf-king, against Sauron, whose stronghold, Mordor, is now named. Although Sauron is overthrown, both Elendil and Gil-galad are slain. A later addition states that Tol Eressëa as well as Valinor is removed from the world.

On 15 November 1937 Tolkien submitted the unfinished manuscript of the *Quenta Silmarillion* to George Allen & Unwin (*Publishers). In the following month, while the work was being considered, he leaped ahead in it and wrote an account of the end of the First Age which includes information relevant to the story of Númenor. Eärendel now has two sons who are allowed by Manwë to choose freely whether to be accounted among the immortal Elves or mortal Mankind. One son, Elrond, chooses to be of Elf-kind but remains in Middle-earth rather than accompany the Elves returning into the West; but the other, Elros, chooses the fate of Men. At some time after this, in an amanuensis type-script of the second version of *The Fall of Númenor*, Tolkien substituted *Elros* for *Elrond* as the first king of that realm.

THE LORD OF THE RINGS

Further developments in the Númenor story occurred intermittently during the writing of *The Lord of the Rings* as it began to play an increasingly import-ant role in the background history to that work, and finally as an essential strand. Tolkien began to write *The Lord of the Rings* in December 1937, but it was some time before he developed the Necromancer of *The Hobbit* into the maker of the One Ring, and eventually identified him with Sauron, the servant of Melkor in the First Age, responsible for the destruction of Númenor near the end of the Second Age. It was not until late summer and early autumn 1938 that relevant allusions began to appear in the text: Trotter (the precursor of Aragorn) remarks of land the company is passing through that evil people once lived there, who 'came under the sway of the Dark Lord. It is said that they were overthrown by Elendil, as King of Western Men, who aided Gil-galad, when they made war on the Dark Lord' (*The Return of the Shadow*, pp. 192–3). The idea emerged that Bilbo's ring is more powerful than other rings, and that it was 'taken from the Lord [Sauron] himself when Gilgalad wrestled with him, and taken by a flying Elf' (*The Return of the Shadow*, p. 226). The 'flying Elf' was soon replaced by Isildur, son of Elendil, who cuts the One Ring from Sauron's hand but then loses it in the river Anduin when he is attacked. Tolkien also considered making the Rangers 'the last remnant of the kingly people from beyond the Seas' (*The Return of the Shadow*, p. 331).

In autumn 1939 the Númenórean realms in exile began to emerge with the mention of *Ond* (later *Ondor* > *Gondor*) in early versions of the Council of Elrond (bk. II, ch. 2). Trotter becomes a man rather than a hobbit, described in Gandalf's letter to Frodo as 'Aragorn son of Celegorn, of the line of Isildur Elendil's son' (*The Treason of Isengard*, p. 50). Eventually Aragorn becomes the last descendant of Elendil and the rightful heir to the realms Elendil founded. Tolkien tried out several ideas for the establishment and early history of these realms before he was satisfied. The story that eventually emerged was that Elendil the Tall and his sons Isildur and Anárion sailed first to the North, where they were befriended by Gilgalad and Elendil established the kingdom of Arnor. His sons then sailed south and founded the realm of Gondor, close to Mordor. When Sauron attacks and takes Isildur's city, Minas Ithil, Isildur joins his father in the North, and Elendil and Gilgalad form the Last Alliance against Sauron.

THE NOTION CLUB PAPERS AND THE DROWNING OF ANADÛNÊ

During Christmas vacation 1945 and the first half of 1946, with *The Lord of the Rings* still unfinished, Tolkien began to transform some of the material from *The Lost Road* into a new work, *The Notion Club Papers*, again involving time-travel and the final days of Númenor. As part of this work he also wrote *The Drowning of Anadûnê*, a new account of *The Fall of Númenor*. Apparently it was only after completing the first part of *The Notion Club Papers* that he decided that the second part should deal with Númenor, writing a note: 'Do the Atlantis story and abandon Eriol-Saga' (*Sauron Defeated*, p. 281).

In the second part of *The Notion Club Papers*, two members of the titular society, Alwin Arundel Lowdham and Wilfrid Trewyn Jeremy, evidently having inherited memories from remote ancestors, have experiences like those of Alboin Errol in *The Lost Road*. Both are stirred by the name *Éarendel*, both dream of hearing fragments of strange languages (Quenya and Sindarin) or of seeing manuscripts written in strange scripts, and report these at meetings of the Club. Lowdham remembers that his father kept a diary in a strange script, and that after his father's disappearance in his boat *Éarendel Star* he found a sheet in the same script but could not decipher it. During one meeting, a thunderstorm rages outside, and both Lowdham and Jeremy seem to have a vision of, or to experience, the destruction of Númenor. They cry out:

> The ships have set sail at last. . . . Behold, the mountain smokes and the earth trembles! . . . Woe to this time and the fell counsels of Sauron! Tarkalion hath set forth his might against the Lords of the West. . . . The Lords have spoken to the Maker . . . and the fate of the world is overturned. . . . The ships of the Númenóreans are drowned in the abyss. They are lost for ever. See now the eagles of the Lords overshadow Númenor. The mountain goes up to heaven in flame and vapour; the hills totter, slide, and crumble: the land founders. The glory has gone down into the deep waters. [p. 251, emended from notes 63–4, p. 290]

Lowdham addresses Jeremy as 'Voronwë', and Jeremy addresses Lowdham as 'Elendil'. Both rush into the freak storm and do not return for some months. Then they begin to tell of their travels round the western coasts of Britain and Ireland, and of a shared dream in which they were in tenth-century England, Lowdham as the minstrel Ælfwine, Jeremy as Tréowine from the Marches.

Tolkien abandoned *The Notion Club Papers* with this account only partly told. Only a few notes and fragments indicate how the story might have continued. One note suggests that Tréowine and Ælfwine were to sail west, find the Straight Road, see the round world below, then be driven back. Another has 'sojourn in Númenor before and during the fall ends with *Elendil* and *Voronwë* fleeing on a hill of water into the dark with the Eagles and lightning pursuing them', and 'at the end . . . Lowdham and Jeremy have a vivid dream of the Fall of Númenor' (p. 279).

In association with *The Notion Club Papers* Tolkien wrote a new account of the fall of Númenor, *The Drowning of Anadûnê*. This differs significantly from *The Fall of Númenor*, which had ended with the words: 'And here endeth the tale of the ancient world as it is known to the Elves' (*The Lost Road and Other Writings*, p. 29). There is no reason to doubt that when Tolkien wrote those words he intended that the Elves' knowledge of the world and its history, deriving from the Valar and their own experiences, should reflect what actually occurred. Nothing is said about if, and how, this Elvish tradition was passed on to Men. *The Drowning of Anadûnê* is intended to show how events in the First Age and the history of Númenor might have been remembered in the traditions of Men after being passed down through many generations: filtered, changed, distorted, and with much forgotten. But this was also a time when Tolkien began to doubt whether he should include in his mythology elements contrary to scientific knowledge, such as a flat world made round, and considered whether to make fundamental changes, or alternatively, changes in perception and knowledge, even writing a version of the *Ainulindalë* in which the world was round from Creation. In *The Fall of Númenor* a flat world is made round at the time of the Downfall, but in *The Drowning of Anadûnê* the world was always round.

Tolkien made three rough preliminary sketches before beginning *The Drowning of Anadûnê*, then produced four successive typescripts. There are considerable differences in the story told in these texts, and Christopher Tolkien concludes 'that the marked differences in the preliminary sketches reflect my father's shifting ideas of what the "Mannish tradition" might be, and how to present it; he was sketching rapidly possible modes in which the memory, and the forgetfulness, of Men in Middle-earth, descendants of the Exiles of Númenor, might have transformed their early history' (*Sauron Defeated*, p. 407). The confusions and obscurities are even deeper in the *Drowning of Anadûnê* texts. If one assumes that the Elvish traditions of events in the First Age recounted in the *Quenta Silmarillion*, the *Annals of Beleriand*, and *The Fall of Númenor* record what actually happened, then it is clear that these versions of 'Mannish tradition' preserve only faint and erroneous memories of events. They are particularly confused about the Valar and the Elves, sometimes making no distinction between them, and uncertain about their dwelling places in the West.

In the preliminary sketches and in *The Drowning of Anadûnê* Tolkien pays much attention to what the Númenóreans thought or were told about the shape of the world. Although he made no authorial statement on this matter, a careful study of internal evidence suggests that this world was round from the beginning. In the first sketch the Númenóreans 'believe the world flat, and that "the Lords of the West" (Gods) dwell beyond the great barrier of cloud hills – where there is no death and the Sun is renewed and passes under the world to rise again' (*Sauron Defeated*, p. 400), but are told by the Elves that the world is round. By emendations it is Sauron, not the Elves, who tells the Númenóreans that the world is round, but in the third sketch (in a section later struck through) 'the ancient Númenóreans knew (being taught by the Eledāi [= Elves]) that the Earth was round; but Sauron taught them that it was a disc and flat . . .' (p. 404). In the first version of *The Drowning of Anadûnê* the Avalāi (= confused mixing of the Valar and the Elves), who live in Avallondē, tell the Númenóreans that the world is round 'and that if they sailed into the utmost West, yet would they but come back again to the East and so to the places of their setting out, and the world would seem to them but a prison' (p. 345); while Sauron 'bade them think that the world was not a closed circle; and that therein there were many lands for their winning . . . ; and even yet, when they came to the end thereof, there was the Dark without, out of which came all things' (p. 347). A note written beside the text says that after the disaster, the Númenóreans continued to believe Sauron's lies that the world was flat until their fleets, seeking for the remains of Númenor, sailed around the world. In the second and later versions of *The Drowning of Anadûnê* the Valar send messengers to the last king (now called Ar-Pharazôn) and tell him that 'the fashion of the Earth is such that a girdle may be set about it. Or as an apple . . . it is round and fair, and the seas and lands are but the rind of the fruit . . .' (p. 364). But Zigûr (= Sauron) refutes this with similar words as in the first version. There is no reference in any of the texts to the Númenóreans seeing the Gates of Morning, as there was in *The Fall of Númenor*.

The sketches refer only briefly to the cataclysm that destroyed Númenor and its aftermath. In various texts of *The Drowning of Anadûnê* men do not *know* exactly what happened, for there were no surviving human witnesses of anything but the destruction of Númenor itself. In the first version, 'those that are wisest in discernment aver' that when the Númenórean fleets sail into the West the Avalāi (= Valar) 'laid down their governance of Earth. And Eru overthrew its shape, and a great chasm was opened in the sea' into which the fleets fall, and Avallondē and Númenor are destroyed, 'and the Avalāi thereafter had no local habitation on earth . . .' (*Sauron Defeated*, p. 351). The second version says that men later heard from the Nimri (= Elves) that Eru 'changed the fashion of the world; and a great chasm opened in the sea between Anadûnê and the Deathless Land [= Aman, the home of the Valar] . . . and the world was shaken'. The Númenórean fleet fell into the abyss, and Aman and Númenor which stood on either side of it were destroyed (pp. 372–3).

In neither version is there any suggestion that the world was ever anything but round, nor is there any mention of a Straight Road. But in both the Númenóreans think that some blessed with a special sight might be able to see, in some fashion, the lands that once had been, and they comment that all the ways are crooked that once were straight (pp. 352, 374). In the third version, Tolkien made an addition to explain this:

> For in the youth of the world it was a hard saying to men that the Earth was not plain [flat] as it seemed to be, and few even of the Faithful of Anadûnê had believed in their hearts this teaching; and when in after days, what by star-craft, what by the voyages of ships that sought out all

the ways and waters of the Earth, the Kings of Men knew that the world was indeed round, then the belief arose among them that it had so been made only in the time of the great Downfall, and was not thus before. Therefore they thought that, while the new world fell away, the old road and the path of the memory of the Earth went on towards heaven. . . . [p. 392]

There were rumours of mariners who found this road and reached the Land of Aman. Christopher Tolkien points out that whereas 'the author of *The Fall of Númenor* knows that "of old many of the exiles of Númenor could still see, some clearly, and some more faintly, the paths to the True West", but for the rationalising author (as he may seem to be) of *The Drowning of Anadûnê* the Straight Road was a belief born of desire and regret' (p. 395).

In emendations made at this time to the latest version of *The Fall of Númenor* (a fine manuscript written in the early 1940s), and in the sketches and especially successive versions of *The Drowning of Anadûnê*, Tolkien added a great deal of information about Númenor and its history, much of which survived into the *Akallabêth* and *The Lord of the Rings* and was evidently not intended to represent distorted later tradition. Among its more significant features is a strengthening of the ban against the Númenóreans sailing west: they are now forbidden to sail out of sight of the west coast of Númenor. In early years they offer first-fruits to Ilúvatar on the mountain in the centre of Númenor, the Pillar of Heaven; and they visit Middle-earth, where they teach the men they find there language, agriculture, and crafts, and to reject the rule of the followers of Morgoth. But even before they are corrupted by Sauron, the Númenóreans begin to resent their mortality and murmur against the Valar. Ar-Pharazôn, the last king, no longer invites Sauron to Númenor but takes a great army to Middle-earth and demands that Sauron pay him homage. Sauron feigns submission, and is taken back to Númenor as a hostage, where he soon gains ascendancy over the king. Most Númenóreans cease to honour Ilúvatar, and instead human sacrifices, often of those who were faithful to the old ways, are offered to Morgoth in the temple built by Sauron. Those who sail east to Middle-earth now do so as cruel conquerors and enslavers. Among the Faithful are Amardil, his son Elendil, and Elendil's sons Anárion and Isildur, who are descended from Earendil through a junior line. In despair at the king's plans to invade Valinor, Amardil decides to follow the example of Earendil and sail into the West to seek aid of the Valar. He is never seen again. The eruption of the Pillar of Heaven, which is volcanic, contributes to the destruction of Númenor, which slides into the sea and is overwhelmed by gigantic waves. The ships of Elendil are driven east by the winds and carried on great waves to Middle-earth.

Tolkien evidently had clear pictures in his mind of events in the latter part of *The Drowning of Anadûnê*, which he transformed into passages of brilliant and memorable descriptive writing:

And now the fleets of the Adûnâi [Númenóreans] darkened the sea upon the west of the land, and they were like an archipelago of a thousand isles; their masts were as a forest upon the mountains, and their sails were like a brooding cloud; and their banners were black and golden like stars upon the fields of night. And all things now waited upon the word of Ar-Pharazôn; and Zigûr withdrew into the inmost circle of the Temple, and men brought him victims to be burned. Then the Eagles of the Lords of the West came up out of the dayfall, and they were arrayed as for battle, advancing in a line the end of which could not be seen. [etc.; p. 371, as emended from p. 391]

In the first version, the Númenóreans abandon their own language and adopt that of the Avalâi (Elvish). In the second version, most Númenóreans continue to speak their own Mannish tongue, Adûnaic, and only kings and princes learned the Elvish language. In the last two versions of *The Drowning of Anadûnê*, most of the names are in Adûnaic.

THE AKALLABÊTH AND APPENDICES A AND B TO THE LORD OF THE RINGS

Probably in the autumn of 1948, while working on material to be published in *The Lord of the Rings*, Tolkien wrote yet another account of the fall of Númenor, entitled *The Downfall of Númenor*, but always referred to it as the *Akallabêth*. In writing this work, he drew on both *The Fall of Númenor* and *The Drowning of Anadûnê*. He evidently intended it not for *The Lord of the Rings*, but for inclusion in a published 'Silmarillion'. Neither *The Fall of Númenor* nor *The Drowning of Anadûnê*, however, suited that purpose. *The Fall of Númenor* is less than half the length of *The Drowning of Anadûnê*, which includes much fine description and new matter not found in the earlier account. But the parts of *The Drowning of Anadûnê* in which confused later 'Mannish tradition' is predominant made it unsuitable to accompany the other 'Silmarillion' texts derived from 'true' Elvish traditions. Also, apparently influenced by the preference his friend *Katharine Farrer expressed in the autumn of 1948 for the 'Flat World' version of the *Ainulindalë* over the 'Round World' version, Tolkien, for a time at least, seems to have decided to retain the cosmology of the world being originally flat as it was in *The Fall of Númenor*. In addition, some new material needed to be added to the story of Númenor to take account of various matters introduced in *The Lord of the Rings*. Christopher Tolkien thinks that a note his father wrote many years later explains how he regarded the different accounts: *The Fall of Númenor* relates 'Elvish tradition', *The Drowning of Anadûnê* 'Mannish tradition', and the *Akallabêth*, which draws on both of the others, 'Mixed Dúnedanic tradition' (*Sauron Defeated*, pp. 406–7).

Before starting work on the *Akallabêth*, Tolkien made an outline history of Númenor with rough dates for the thirteen kings (most not named) who followed after the death of Elros in Second Age 460, and for some significant events (e.g. the fourteenth and last king, Tarkalion or Arpharazôn, challenges

Sauron in Second Age 3125, and the Downfall of Númenor takes place in 3319). The first text, a manuscript, is addressed to Ælfwine, presumably by Pengoloð, an Elf of Tol Eressëa, and begins with two new paragraphs summarizing the Elvish tradition of the coming of Men into the world, their falling under the dominion of Morgoth, the repentance of the Edain who fought with the Eldar against Morgoth, and the voyage of Eärendil into the West to speak to the Valar on behalf of Elves and Men. The text then briefly follows the third version of *The Fall of Númenor* for an account of the defeat of Morgoth, the summoning of the Elves into the West to the Isle of Eressëa whose haven was Avallónë, and the creation of Númenor for Men.

From that point the *Akallabêth* follows mainly *The Drowning of Anadûnê*, but takes or revises some passages from *The Fall of Númenor*. The language spoken by most of the Númenóreans is still Adûnaic, but most names are in the Elvish languages, either that which their kings and lords had learned during their alliance with the Elves (here called Noldorin) or the High Eldarin tongue (Quenya) which their lore-masters learn. The Númenóreans are forbidden by the Valar to sail west out of sight of the shores of Númenor, but they know that Eressëa lies to the west, and beyond that is the Blessed Realm. The Eldar from Eressëa visit and bring gifts, including a seedling of the White Tree of Eressëa, itself a seedling of Telperion, one of the Two Trees of Valinor. The seedling is planted in the courts of the king. The Númenórean mariners again see the Gates of Morning in the East. The Númenóreans' resentment of their mortality begins earlier, and it is to Tar-Atanamir, the seventh king, that the Valar send messengers, who now say nothing about the shape of the world but tell him that even if he came to Aman it would not profit him. 'For it is not the land of Manwë that makes its people deathless, but the Deathless that dwell therein have hallowed the land; and there you would but wither and grow weary the sooner' (*The Silmarillion*, p. 264).

More detail is given of the growing obsession of the Númenóreans with death, building great tombs, and seeking to prolong life, but discovering only how to preserve bodies of the dead. Most cease to show any devotion to Eru. Even before Sauron comes to power, they make settlements in Middle-earth, mainly in the south, and instead of teaching and helping those living there, they seek wealth and dominion. The Faithful sail mainly to the North-west, establish a haven at Pelargir, and help Gil-galad against Sauron. Some of this, and much else of the added material, derived from *The Lord of the Rings*. In the *Akallabêth* it is during the reign of Tar-Atanamir that Sauron completes the building of Barad-dûr and begins his campaign for domination of Middle-earth. He is said to hate the Númenóreans because they aided Gil-galad against him. Three of the nine Men whom Sauron snares with rings are great lords of Númenórean race, and he uses them (the Ringwraiths) to attack Númenórean strongholds by the sea. When he comes to Númenor, Sauron urges the king to cut down the White Tree growing in his courts, but before the king consents, Isildur manages to steal a fruit, and the sapling grown from this fruit and the Seven Stones given to them by the Eldar are included in the treasure the Faithful put aboard their ships (cf. the rhyme in *The Lord of the Rings*, bk. III, ch. 11). Sauron says nothing about the shape of the world except that many lands lie east and west. As in *The Fall of Númenor*, when the fashion of the world is changed Aman is not destroyed, and Aman and Eressëa are 'taken away and removed from the circles of the world beyond the reach of Men for ever' (*The Peoples of Middle-earth*, p. 157). Although it is not stated in the account of the actual Downfall in what way the fashion of the world is changed, other than that new lands and seas are made, it is implied in the later statement 'in after days, what by the voyages of ships, what by lore and star-craft, the kings of Men knew that the world was indeed made round, and yet the Eldar were permitted still to depart and to come to the Ancient West and to Avallónë, if they would. Therefore the loremasters of Men said that a Straight Road must still be, for those that were permitted to find it' (*The Silmarillion*, p. 281).

Probably in 1951 Tolkien took up a typescript he had made from the manuscript of the *Akallabêth* and emended it, altering some names and the sequence of certain events, rewriting a few passages, and adding a lengthy rider giving much more detail of the history of the last Númenórean kings, and in particular their growing hostility to the Eldar and the Valar and to those who remained faithful. The White Tree is no longer a descendant of Telperion, but of a memorial of that tree given to the Elves of Túna. Messengers from the Valar still come to Tar-Atanamir, but he is now the thirteenth king. The nineteenth king chooses a name in Adûnaic rather than in the Elven-tongue – Adûnakhor, Lord of the West – a title belonging to the Valar, and forbids the use of the Elven-tongues in his hearing. Emphasis is laid the status of the Lords of Andúnië descended from Silmarien, the daughter of the fourth king, who, as his eldest child, would have been queen according to a rule of succession introduced later – thus stressing the royal descent of Amandil and his son Elendil, and ultimately of Aragorn. Although the Lords of Andúnië are loyal to the kings, they hold to the old ways and try to protect the Faithful. The twenty-second king forbids the use of the Elven-tongues and any contact with the Eldar of Eressëa, but his wife is a close relative of the Lords of Andúnië and herself one of the Faithful. Their elder son, influenced by his mother, repents, takes the elven name Tar-Palantir, and again pays reverence to Eru. On his death, his daughter Míriel should become queen, but her cousin forces her to marry him and usurps the sceptre for himself, taking the name Ar-Pharazôn and becoming the twenty-fourth ruler. He persecutes the Faithful and seeks homage from Sauron.

Having written this rider, Tolkien seems to have hesitated as to whether Míriel was indeed the unwilling wife of Ar-Pharazôn, and sketched some ideas for a different story. In these he considered the possibilty that Míriel was loved by, and possibly even betrothed to, Amandil's brother Elentir, but then fell in love with Pharazôn.

Tolkien's early work on the Appendices for *The Lord of the Rings* reflect developments which also appear in the *Akallabêth*. The earliest versions of Appendix B (*The Tale of Years*) for the Second Age briefly cover events in

Middle-earth and Númenor; an enlarged fair copy version was in existence in 1950. In these Tolkien constantly made changes to dates and to the number of kings who ruled in Númenor, as well as adding or emending entries. It eventually evolved that Númenor was founded in Second Age 50; the great voyages of the Númenóreans began in 1700; the Shadow fell on Númenor, and Men began to murmur against the ban, *c.* 2000; Sauron submitted to Ar-Pharazôn, the twenty-fifth king of Númenor, in 3125; Amandil sailed west to seek help in 3310; the Downfall took place in 3319; the realms in exile lasted 110 years before the war with Sauron; and the Second Age ended in 3441 after a seven-year siege and the overthrow of Sauron. In 1954–5, while preparing the Appendices for publication, Tolkien made further additions and changes, some reflecting revisions made to the *Akallabêth c.* 1951. Among the more significant dates as published are S.A. 32 for the arrival of Men in Númenor; 600, the return to Middle-earth of the first Númenórean ships; 1200, the Númenóreans begin to establish havens in Middle-earth; 1700, the king of Númenor sends a navy to aid Gil-galad against Sauron; from *c.* 1800, the Númenóreans establish dominions on the coasts of Middle-earth; 2251, Tar-Atanamir becomes king, during whose reign 'rebellion and division of the Númenóreans begins', and the Ringwraiths first appear. Ar-Pharazôn seizes the sceptre in 3255; Sauron is taken to Númenor as a prisoner in 3262; Ar-Pharazôn breaks the ban of the Valar and Númenor is destroyed in 3319; Sauron is overthrown and the Second Age ends in 3441.

Quite late in his work on the Appendices, probably when the space allotted to them was more than doubled, Tolkien decided to include a brief narrative account of the history of Númenor – section I (i) of Appendix A – and wrote two versions, the second of which (with some changes and omissions) was published. Some of the omitted material was published in *The Peoples of Middle-earth.*

*The Heirs of Elendil, contemporary with the versions of the *Akallabêth*, also includes an account of the last years of Númenor, the establishment of the realms in exile and the overthrow of Sauron, but adds nothing to the other texts. Probably in 1960 Tolkien compiled **The Line of Elros: Kings of Númenor*, which gives dates of birth, surrender of the sceptre, and death for each ruler, with annotations of important events in each reign. He made many emendations to the manuscript, the latest form of which was published in *Unfinished Tales.*

The story of the glory of Númenor and its Downfall is of significance as the only part of Tolkien's *legendarium* in which Men are the main, indeed almost the only, focus of attention. Among the questions of importance to Tolkien dealt with in this work are the imperfect and fallen nature of Man (see *The Fall), and the necessity for men to accept their mortal nature. While various 'falls' of the Elves are recounted in the *Quenta Silmarillion*, almost nothing is said about the first Fall of Man. There are only hints: the Eldar knew nothing of Morgoth's dealings with Men, but they perceived 'that a darkness lay upon the hearts of Men (as the shadow of the Kinslaying and the Doom of

Mandos lay upon the Noldor)' (*The Silmarillion*, p. 141). The beginning of the *Akallabêth* is more informative: 'It is said by the Eldar that Men came into the world in the time of the Shadow of Morgoth, and they fell swiftly under his dominion; for he sent his emissaries among them, and they listened to his evil and cunning words, and they worshipped the Darkness and yet feared it' (p. 259). But some Men repented and assisted the Elves against Morgoth, and were rewarded by the Valar with the island of Númenor. Although details of Man's first Fall were hidden in the past, in the story of Númenor the second Fall is dealt with at centre stage and, as with the story of Eden, involves the breaking of a Ban. In a letter to *Milton Waldman in ?late 1951 Tolkien said that this second Fall was 'partly the result of an inner weakness in Men – consequent . . . upon the first Fall . . . , repented but not finally healed'. Their reward of an extended life 'is their undoing – or the means of their temptation. Their long life aids their achievements in art and wisdom, but breeds a possessive attitude to these things, and desire awakes for more *time* for their enjoyment.' He describes 'three phases in their fall from grace. First acquiescence, obedience that is free and willing, though without complete understanding. Then for long they obey unwillingly, murmuring more and more openly. Finally they rebel . . .' (*Letters*, pp. 154–5). In a draft letter to Peter Hastings in September 1954 Tolkien wrote that his '*legendarium*, especially the "Downfall of Númenor" . . . is based on my view: that Men are essentially mortal and must not try to become "immortal" in the flesh' (*Letters*, p. 189).

CRITICISM

Randel Helms devotes an entire chapter to the *Akallabêth* in *Tolkien and the Silmarils* (1981). He notes that the work involves Tolkien in 'one of his favorite literary tricks, the creation of the "real" source or origin of a famous tale' (p. 64). But it is also 'Tolkien's first full-scale brief epic of men as opposed to elves, presenting his deepest thinking about death, the Gift of Men'. He had prepared for it in the *Quenta Silmarillion*, where it is said 'that the hearts of Men should seek beyond the world and should find no rest therein', but they would be able to 'shape their life'. The price they pay 'for this freedom of will and ability to yearn toward Ilúvatar' is that 'though their longings be immortal, their bodies are not'.

> Here . . . Tolkien sets a major theme of *Akallabêth*, showing as well his grasp of human psychology. Always to yearn for what we do not have, to seek beyond the confines of our world, is our destiny, and one resulting directly from our freedom. Because of this combination of desire and liberty, unique in the mortal creatures of Arda, man is peculiarly susceptible to temptation, and men long for what they can never have, immortality in the flesh.

Tolkien thus uses Plato's story of Atlantis, but deepens its themes. The Atlanteans desired conquest and empire. . . . The Númenóreans desired not merely conquest – though that was indeed one of their aims – they wanted an attribute of divinity itself, eternity. They wanted to be as gods – knowing not good and evil only, but endlessness – for Tolkien has blended Plato's legend of Atlantis with the Bible's story of the Fall of Man, to produce a tale of great resonance. [pp. 66–7]

David Harvey in *The Song of Middle-earth: J.R.R. Tolkien's Themes, Symbols and Myths* (1985) likewise relates the fall of the Númenóreans to 'a Fall in the theological sense. The actions of Ar-Pharazôn are in direct opposition to a stated Ban imposed by superhuman powers and derived from the authority and decree of the One' (p. 41).

In 'Aspects of the Fall in *The Silmarillion*', *Proceedings of the J.R.R. Tolkien Centenary Conference 1992* (1995), Eric Schweicher points out that in Tolkien's *legendarium* Man's mortality is 'neither a punishment nor a direct consequence of their [first] Fall. The condition of Man . . . was determined long before the world was created, in the Great Music of the Ainur. . . . Yet there is a fear of death on Middle-earth, which is paradoxical if one considers death as a gift.' Therefore he suggests that 'the Fall must have had an influence on the attitude of Man towards death, and there one must see Melkor's influence, which lures Men into believing that what they had been given as a gift is but a bitter fruit' (p. 169). Thus the desire of the Númenóreans for immortality, and Ar-Pharazôn's attempt to gain it by conquest, are directly related to the first Fall.

Anne C. Petty, in *Tolkien in the Land of the Heroes: Discovering the Human Spirit* (2003), thinks that

the passage in the 'Akallabêth' that describes the coming of the first Númenóreans to their new land contains some of Tolkien's most inspired saga-style language, conjuring images of dragon ships and seascapes straight out of such Old English poems as *The Seafarer*. He balances this vision of wonder with an equally stark vision of horror that concludes the account. This is something Tolkien does better than anyone: he presents the reader with a vision of incredible beauty, and then allows it to be ruined to equally incredible depths, making the end result all the more poignant and devastating. [p. 82]

Númenórean Linear Measures. Series of notes from various manuscripts, published as an appendix to *The Disaster of the Gladden Fields* in *Unfinished Tales* (1980), pp. 285–7, under a collective title devised by *Christopher Tolkien. These concern the relationship of Númenórean measurements to British units (leagues, yards, feet), and the stature of Númenóreans (especially Elendil), the Eldar (especially Galadriel), the Rohirrim (with a note on Morwen, wife of Thengel), the Hobbits, and the Dúnedain.

Of . . . *such titles are entered by the first significant word following 'Of'*

Official Name List. List of names in early 'Elvish' languages (*Languages, Invented) which appear in *The Fall of Gondolin* in *The Book of Lost Tales*, published with commentary within 'Early Noldorin Fragments' in *Parma Eldalamberon* 13 (2001), pp. 100–5, ed. Christopher Gilson, Bill Welden, Carl F. Hostetter, and Patrick Wynne. It is arranged with Eldarissa (Qenya) names on the left and Noldorissa (Gnomish, later Sindarin) names on the right. A few names are translated into English. The names come from the original manuscript of *The Fall of Gondolin* as revised by Tolkien, but before *Edith Tolkien made a fair copy. This list was written in the same note-book as the *Poetic and Mythologic Words of Eldarissa*; the *'Name-list to *The Fall of Gondolin*' was derived from the *Official Name List*. A short table of abbreviations indicates that Tolkien probably intended to list names from all of the 'Lost Tales'.

See also *Parma Eldalamberon* 12 (1998), p. xx.

Oilima Markirya *see **The Last Ark***

The Old English Apollonius of Tyre. Edition of the Old English version of *Apollonius* (Corpus Christi College, Cambridge MS 201) prepared by Peter Goolden, published by Oxford University Press in November 1958 with a brief prefatory note by Tolkien. Goolden was admitted as a B.Litt. student in the Oxford English School in May 1950 and received his degree in 1953; his thesis, *The Old English Version of the Story of Apollonius of Tyre*, was supervised by *C.L. Wrenn. In 1954 Goolden submitted his thesis to Oxford University Press and was informed that although the Press would not publish it independently (it was not judged to be a mature work of learning), it might be suitable for publication in the series *Oxford English Monographs*, of which Tolkien was then chief among three general editors (with *F.P. Wilson and *Helen Gardner). Tolkien received a copy of Goolden's thesis in February 1954 but could not consider it until later in the year. It was approved for inclusion in the series, pending revision.

At the beginning of March 1956 Goolden lost the manuscript of his work in a fire and had to start revision again with a second copy of his thesis. He seems to have completed this in short order. Already on 14 May 1956 the Delegates of Oxford University Press approved the publication of his book, supported by Tolkien and Wrenn; but Tolkien took more than a year to look over and approve the manuscript, and the finished work was not sent to the printers until the end of August 1957. Wrenn complained to Oxford University Press about Tolkien's delay, which was the more unfortunate because a German work with the same text of *Apollonius* (ed. Josef Raith) had been published in 1956. In his prefatory note Tolkien wrote that 'the [series] editors feel justified . . . in publishing Mr. Goolden's work, since it is independent, and differs from Dr. Raith's edition in treatment and in some points of opinion,' and because it was specifically designed for English students and 'provides a conflated text of the Latin source, notes, and glossary' (p. iii).

In his preface Goolden thanks C.L. Wrenn as 'the prime mover of the work', and 'Professor J.R.R. Tolkien who kindly suggested revisions in presentation and style' (p. vi).

The Old English Exodus. Edition of the Old English poem *Exodus*, with a Modern English translation and commentary, assembled from Tolkien's lecture notes and other papers by his former B.Litt. student *Joan Turville-Petre, published by the Clarendon Press, Oxford in 1982 (despite imprint and copyright dates of 1981). The Old English *Exodus* is a free paraphrase of that portion of the Old Testament book (ch. 13–14) which deals with the passage of the Israelites through the Red Sea and the destruction of Pharaoh's host. A single instance of the work survives, in an eleventh-century manuscript, Junius 11 in the Bodleian Library, Oxford (*Libraries and archives). It is considered one of the most difficult Old English texts to interpret, in part because it is incomplete, and it contains many words that are otherwise unrecorded.

Tolkien lectured on the Old English *Exodus* at *Oxford for many years, beginning in Michaelmas Term 1926. Joan Turville-Petre comments that his papers concerning the poem were 'never intended as an edition, although the lecturer scrupulously drew up an edited text as the basis of his commentary. It is an interpretation of the poem, designed to reconstruct the original (as far as that is possible), and to place it in the context of Old English poetry' (p. v). And yet, on 25 October 1932 Tolkien noted in a letter to R.W. Chapman at Oxford University Press that

both *Elene* [a poem by Cynewulf] and *Exodus* will remain set books in the English School. They both need editing. I have commentaries to both. I should like very much after *Beowulf* [i.e. after he completes his Modern English translation of *Beowulf*] to tackle a proper edition of O.E. *Exodus*. The Routledge edn. of Ms. Junius 11 by Krapp [*The Junius Manuscript*, 1931] is thoroughly bad, and virtually negligible for our students, though admittedly better than nothing. Sedgefield is of course merely laughable (he does a large chunk of Exodus in his miserable Anglo-Saxon verse-book [*An Anglo-Saxon Verse Book* (1922)]). [Oxford University Press archives]

Tolkien's surviving lecture notes on *Exodus* represent 'the discourse of a teacher among a small group of pupils, expressing his understanding of the text in the circumstances of that time.' Joan Turville-Petre therefore reduced 'diffuse comments and some basic instruction ... such as observations on phonology and morphology' (p. v).

A manuscript page by Tolkien showing the opening of the Old English *Exodus*, with his notes, is reproduced in *Life and Legend*, p. 81.

In *Notes and Queries* for June 1983 Peter J. Lucas harshly criticized *The Old*

English Exodus for its manner of presentation, lack of an introduction and glossary, numerous errors and omissions, and unnecessary emendations. 'As an editor Tolkien emerges as an inveterate meddler who occasionally had bright ideas' (p. 243). Nonetheless, Lucas was himself indebted to Tolkien in his own edition of *Exodus* (1977; rev. edn. 1994): 'In the preparation of this edition I have had access to notes taken from lectures given by J.R.R. Tolkien at Oxford. Two of the emendations adopted in the text . . . were, as far as I know, first suggested by him in these lectures. . . . His comments or suggestions are also incorporated in the Commentary from time to time . . .' (p. x).

In another review, D.C. Baker commented in *English Language Notes* for March 1984 that 'lesser mortals, in their preparation for lecturing undergraduate students, do not prepare themselves in this way; they do not edit the texts on which they are to expound; they do not provide a commentary exhaustive in its learning together with original criticisms and suggestions. These are the work of a master, a master of all he surveyed' (p. 59).

See also T.A. Shippey, 'A Look at *Exodus* and *Finn and Hengest*', *Arda* 3 (1986, for 1982–83), pp. 72–82.

Oliphaunt. Poem, first published in *The Lord of the Rings*, Book IV, Chapter 3, and reprinted with the title *Oliphaunt* (i.e. an elephant) in *The Adventures of Tom Bombadil and Other Verses from the Red Book* (1962), p. 47. In the former work Sam Gamgee describes it as 'a rhyme we have in the Shire. Nonsense maybe, and maybe not.' Tolkien included it, with three minor textual differences, as 'a hobbit nursery-rhyme' in a letter to his son Christopher, 30 April 1944 (*Letters*, p. 77). Although in another letter, to Mrs Eileen Elgar, 5 March 1964, he wrote that *Oliphaunt* was 'my own invention entirely', unlike *Fastitocalon* which was 'a reduced and rewritten form, to suit hobbit fancy, of an item in old "bestiaries"' (*Letters*, p. 343), in fact *Oliphaunt* had a similar origin. An earlier and much longer version, *Iumbo, or ye Kinde of ye Oliphaunt*, composed probably in the 1920s, was published as one of the *Adventures in Unnatural History and Medieval Metres, Being the Freaks of Fisiologus*, as by 'Fisiologus' in the *Stapeldon Magazine* (Exeter College, *Oxford) 7, no. 40 (June 1927), pp. 125–7; and like an earlier version of *Fastitocalon* and two other animal poems, *Reginhardus, the Fox* and *Monoceros, the Unicorn*, it was inspired by the medieval bestiary, in particular the *Physiologus* ('Naturalist') poems in the Exeter Book, which describe the characteristics of animals and draw from them Christian morals.

Tolkien followed this model but added elements of contemporary culture. *Iumbo* (i.e. Jumbo) describes the elephant as 'a moving mountain, a majestic mammal', whose nose 'Performs the functions of a rubber hose / Or vacuum cleaner as his needs impose.' His vice is not drink but drugs: 'the dark mandragora's unwholesome root', a notion from the bestiary. This fills him 'with sudden madness', and he 'blindly blunders thumping o'er the ground', crushing villages in his path. When he tires he leans against a tree, but hunters who know of this habit cut the trunk so that the tree will collapse, and the elephant with it – who, according to the bestiary, cannot rise again of his own accord. In the *Physiologus* the elephant falling to the ground because of a tree is related to Adam's fall.

Oliphaunt in turn is a reduction of *Iumbo*, made much simpler and cleansed of anachronisms. In *The Lord of the Rings* it is meant to be traditional verse, and indeed is in the form of nursery rhymes with which readers in English are familiar: it retains the essential characteristics of the elephant in a concise form and in a rhyme that is easy to remember ('Grey as a mouse, / Big as a house', etc.). These qualities have made the poem a popular choice to include in anthologies for children.

A private tape recording of *Oliphaunt*, made by Tolkien in 1952, was issued on the album *J.R.R. Tolkien Reads and Sings His The Lord of the Rings: The Two Towers/The Return of the King* (1975, reissued in 2001 as part of *The J.R.R. Tolkien Audio Collection*); see *Recordings.

On Fairy-Stories. Lecture, first published in Great Britain in *Essays Presented to Charles Williams* by Oxford University Press, December 1947, pp. 38–89. A slightly revised text was first published in Great Britain by George Allen & Unwin, London, in May 1964, and in the United States by the Houghton Mifflin Company, Boston in March 1965, in *Tree and Leaf*. See further, *Descriptive Bibliography* B19, A7. References here are to its appearance in the 1988 edition of *Tree and Leaf*.

SUMMARY

Tolkien attempts to explain what a fairy-story (or fairy-tale) is, turning to the *Oxford English Dictionary* but finding its definitions too narrow. He rejects the notion of *fairies* as 'supernatural beings of diminutive size', propagated by works such as Shakespeare's *Midsummer Night's Dream* (c. 1595–6) and Michael Drayton's *Nymphidia* (1627), and notes that although '*fairy* as a noun more or less equivalent to *elf*' (p. 12) was hardly found until the late fifteenth century, *faërie*, meaning the realm of fairies or 'Elfland', appeared in John Gower's *Confessio Amantis* (c. 1390). Tolkien also rejects the definition of *fairy-story* (or *fairy-tale*) as simply 'a tale about fairies, or generally a fairy legend'.

> Fairy-stories are not in normal English usage stories *about* fairies or elves, but stories about Fairy, that is *Faërie*, the realm or state in which fairies have their being. *Faërie* contains many things besides elves and fays, and besides dwarfs, witches, trolls, giants, or dragons: it holds the seas, the sun, the moon, the sky; and the earth, and all things that are in it: tree and bird, water and stone, wine and bread, and ourselves, mortal men, when we are enchanted.
>
> Stories that are actually concerned primarily with 'fairies', that is with creatures that might also in modern English be called 'elves' are relatively rare, and as a rule not very interesting. Most good 'fairy-stories' are

about the *aventures* of men in the Perilous Realm or upon its shadowy marches. [p. 14]

Tolkien would exclude from a list of 'fairy-stories' traveller's tales such as Swift's *Gulliver's Travels* (1726), dream-fiction such as Lewis Carroll's *Alice's Adventures in Wonderland* (1865), and beast-fables such as *Reynard the Fox*, although the latter has a connection with fairy-story in that it 'derives from one of the primal "desires" that lie near the heart of Faërie: the desire of men to hold communion with other living things' (p. 19).

Considering the origin or origins of fairy elements in stories, Tolkien finds little value in folklorists' relation of tales according to similar motives. 'It is precisely the colouring the atmosphere, the unclassifiable individual details of a story, and above all the general purport that informs with life the undissected bones of the plot, that really count' (pp. 21–2). Using Sir George Webbe Dasent's words, he says that 'we must be satisfied with the soup that is set before us, and not desire to see the bones of the ox out of which it has been boiled. . . . By the "the soup" I mean the story as it is served up by its author or teller, and by "the bones" its sources or material – even when (by rare luck) those can be with certainty discovered. But I do not, of course, forbid criticism of the soup as soup' (pp. 22–3).

He notes various theories concerning the origin and history of fairy-stories, '*independent evolution* (or rather *invention*) of the similar; *inheritance* from a common ancestry; and *diffusion* at various times from one or more centres', of which the first 'is the most important and fundamental' (p. 23). *Philology is no longer thought to be of such significance; nonetheless, the human mind and language have played a part.

> The mind that thought of *light, heavy, grey, yellow, still, swift*, also conceived of magic that would make heavy things light and be able to fly, turn grey lead into yellow gold, and the still rock into swift water. . . . Or we may cause woods to spring with silver leaves and rams to wear fleeces of gold, and put hot fire into the belly of the cold worm [dragon]. But in such 'fantasy', as it is called, new form is made; Faërie begins; Man becomes a sub-creator. [pp. 24–5; see *Sub-creation]

After a discussion of mythology and religion related to folk- and fairy-tales, and of the magical face of fairy-story (notably in 'The Golden Key' by *George MacDonald), Tolkien comments that 'new bits' have been continually added to the constantly boiling 'Pot of Soup, the Cauldron of Story' (p. 28), and shows how fairy-tale elements may become attached to 'the great figures of Myth and History', such as Arthur (*Arthur and the Matter of Britain). The antiquity of some of these elements opens 'a door on Other Time, and if we pass through, though only for a moment, we stand outside our own time, outside Time itself, maybe' (p. 32). Tolkien thinks that such story elements have survived because they produce so profound a 'literary effect' (p. 33).

Children, he observes, are generally thought to be the natural or most appropriate audience for fairy-stories. But this was not always the case: such tales were once read by adults, and having become 'old-fashioned' in our 'modern lettered world' (p. 34) were relegated to the nursery. 'In fact only some children, and some adults, have any special taste' for fairy-stories; 'and when they have it, it is not exclusive, nor even necessarily dominant' (p. 35). Tolkien rejects a suggestion implicit in the introduction by *Andrew Lang to the large paper edition of his *Blue Fairy Book* (1889), that 'the teller of marvellous tales to children' appeals to a supposed desire to believe 'that a thing exists or can happen in the real (primary) world', and trades on a child's 'lack of experience which makes it less easy . . . to distinguish fact from fiction' (p. 36). Instead, 'what really happens is that the story-maker proves a successful "sub-creator". He makes a Secondary World which your mind can enter. Inside it, what he relates is "true": it accords with the laws of that world. You therefore believe it, while you are, as it were, inside. The moment disbelief arises, the spell is broken; the magic, or rather the art, has failed' (pp. 36–7).

As for himself as a child, his reactions to stories were not those described by Lang:

> Belief depended on the way in which stories were presented to me, by older people, or the authors, or on the inherent tone and quality of the tale. But at no time can I remember that the enjoyment of a story was dependent on belief that such things could happen, or had happened in 'real life'. Fairy-stories were plainly not primarily concerned with possibility, but with desirability. If they awakened *desire*, satisfying it, while often whetting it unbearably, they succeeded. [p. 39]

Some children may like fairy-stories, he argues, not because they are children, but because they are human, and fairy-stories are a natural though not a universal human taste. But 'if fairy-story as a kind is worth reading at all it is worthy to be written for and read by adults' (p. 43).

Tolkien finds four particular values and functions in fairy-stories as adult reading. The first is *Fantasy*, which he uses to describe the successful achievement of 'the inner consistency of reality' (p. 44), which commands belief in a Secondary World. To succeed in making such a world demands much labour and skill, and is best achieved by words, not by visible arts such as painting, or by drama. Tolkien defends Fantasy from those who call it childish folly by quoting from his poem *Mythopoeia*, an extract in which he declares the right of Man, made in the image of his Creator, to sub-create in turn and fill the world with Elves, Goblins, dragons, and so forth.

The second value is *Recovery*. Man is heir 'in enjoyment or in practice of many generations of ancestors in the arts. In this inheritance of wealth there may be a danger of boredom or of anxiety to be original . . .' (p. 53). Fairy-story and Fantasy help us to achieve Recovery, because they allow us to look again at things we think we know, see them in a new way, regain a freshness of vision.

Escape is another important function of fairy-story, but many critics who describe fairy-stories as 'escapist' use that term in a derogatory sense, and consider those who read such tales as unable to face 'real life'. Tolkien argues that such critics 'are confusing, not always by sincere error, the Escape of the Prisoner with the Flight of the Deserter' (p. 56). They consider a tale worthwhile only if it embraces all of the details of modern life: factories, ugly street-lamps, the noise of traffic, the latest and soon obsolete invention. Tolkien points out that a desire to escape from such transitory things to the more enduring is often accompanied by other emotions, 'Disgust, Anger, Condemnation, and Revolt' (p. 56). He remarks sarcastically: 'How real, how startlingly alive is a factory chimney compared with an elm-tree: poor obsolete thing, insubstantial dream of an escapist!' (p. 57). The 'oldest and deepest desire' of all is the Escape from Death, and yet fairy-stories teach the burden of 'immortality, or rather endless serial living' (p. 62; see *Mortality and Immortality).

But the most important value offered by fairy-stories is the Consolation of the Happy Ending. Tolkien coins a new word to describe it: *Eucatastrophe*, 'the joy of the happy ending; or more correctly of the good catastrophe, the sudden joyous 'turn'. . . . In its fairy-tale – or otherworld – setting, it is a sudden and miraculous grace: never to be counted on to recur' (p. 62).

In an 'epilogue' Tolkien suggests that a work which achieves an 'inner consistency of reality' must in some way 'partake of reality', and 'the peculiar quality of the "joy" in successful Fantasy can thus be explained as a sudden glimpse of the underlying reality or truth. . . . It may be a far-off gleam or echo of *evangelium* in the real world' (p. 64). Tolkien applies this to the story of Christ: 'the Gospels contain a fairy-story, or a story of a larger kind which embraces all the essence of fairy-stories', one which 'has entered History and the primary world; the desire and aspiration of sub-creation has been raised to the fulfilment of Creation. The Birth of Christ is the eucatastrophe of Man's History' (p. 65).

HISTORY

Probably towards the end of 1937, Tolkien was invited by the Lovelace Society, an essay club at Worcester College, *Oxford, to read a paper at a meeting of 14 February 1938. In a letter to C.A. Furth of George Allen & Unwin (*Publishers) on 24 July 1938, Tolkien said that he had rewritten *Farmer Giles of Ham* the preceding January 'and read it to the Lovelace Society in lieu of a paper "on" fairy stories' (*Letters*, p. 39). It seems likely that he did not give a paper on fairy-stories on that occasion because he found that he did not have enough time to write one, or to finish writing, and it was easier in the event to revise *Farmer Giles of Ham*, a version of which was already in hand. Just over a year later, however, on 8 March 1939, Tolkien delivered the Andrew Lang Lecture for 1938–9 at the University of St Andrews in Scotland, on a subject chosen by himself: *On Fairy-Stories*. There seems to be no record of when the invitation to lecture was sent to Tolkien; at any rate, on the evidence of the abandoned paper for the Lovelace Society, the subject of fairy-stories was engaging his interest as early as the beginning of 1938.

Two versions of *On Fairy-Stories* are evident among its earliest extant manuscripts. The first presumably dates to 1938, following or simultaneous with substantial reading for background, as shown by the many tales and authorities cited in the work. Both this and a second version, derived from the first and dating presumably to 1938–9, are heavily marked with revisions. That Tolkien worked on the lecture until at least the final months before March 1939 is revealed by the inclusion of references to *The Coloured Lands* by G.K. Chesterton, a book not published until November 1938; and it seems likely that a comment in the second version was inspired by a letter of 11 February 1939 to Tolkien from C.A. Furth at George Allen & Unwin (*Publishers), who found *Farmer Giles of Ham* hard to categorize for a prospective market. ('Grown-ups writing fairy-stories for grown-ups', Tolkien wrote, 'are not popular with publishers or book-sellers. They have got to find a niche. To call their works *fairy-tales* places them at once as *juvenilia*; but if a glance at their contents shows that that *will* not do, then where are you? This is what is called a "marketing problem".' – Tolkien Papers, Bodleian Library, Oxford.)

The rough script and frequent emendation of the *On Fairy-Stories* papers, which include miscellaneous interspersed notes and memoranda of various date, make it hard to trace the history of writing. It clear only that the composition did not come smoothly to Tolkien. On the face of it, none of the earlier manuscripts in the Bodleian Library (*Libraries and archives) seem fit to have been reading copy for the lecture at St Andrews; and if not, then the text as delivered in March 1939 apparently has not survived. One can say for sure, as Tolkien does in an introductory paragraph to *On Fairy-Stories* in *Essays Presented to Charles Williams*, only that the 1939 text was 'abbreviated' relative to that of 1947. The earlier papers contain nothing about *eucatastrophe*, or any of the material contained in the published epilogue. Indeed it may be significant that a lengthy summary of the lecture in the *St Andrews Citizen* for 11 March 1939 makes no mention of 'eucatastrophe' or any reference to Christianity ('Andrew Lang's Unrivalled Fairy Stories: Oxford Professor's St Andrews Address', p. 6).

Much evidence exists, both among and outside of the Tolkien Papers, to show that Tolkien returned to *On Fairy-Stories* only a few years later. It may be that he was inspired to look at it again after being appointed on 4 December 1942 an examiner of the B.Litt. thesis of *Roger Lancelyn Green, *Andrew Lang as a Writer of Fairy Tales and Romances*. He drafted the new introductory paragraph on an unused calendar page for 16–22 August 1943, where it is said that only 'some part' of the lecture 'was actually delivered [at St Andrews]. Its present form is somewhat enlarged . . . and . . . made longer and I hope clearer than the lecture' (Tolkien Papers, Bodleian Library, Oxford). Another piece of manuscript is on the verso of a sheet referring to cadets that Tolkien taught at Oxford beginning in spring 1943, and the new text explicitly mentions the period 1940–1943 (changed to 1940–1945 in the published essay, p. 29). Once Tolkien had written out a fair copy of the revised lecture, now with its epilogue, *Charles Williams arranged for it to be typed by his friend Margaret Douglas. Douglas mentioned the work in a letter of 5 August 1943, and that she found it hard to read Tolkien's handwriting.

In late 1944, with the prospect that Williams would soon be leaving Oxford for the London-based office of Oxford University Press, Tolkien and *C.S. Lewis began to organize a *Festschrift* to honour Williams' work for Oxford University. When Williams died unexpectedly on 15 May 1945, the *Festschrift* became a memorial volume, with proceeds to go to Williams's widow. Tolkien's contribution, *On Fairy-Stories*, needed only a few emendations to the carbon copy of the typescript made by Margaret Douglas.

Tolkien felt that the ideas he developed in *On Fairy-Stories* had influenced the writing of *The Lord of the Rings*, and said so in letters at least as early to correspondents including Peter Hastings (September 1954) and Dora Marshall (3 March 1955). In a letter to *W.H. Auden on 7 June 1955 he complained that Oxford University Press had 'most scurvily' allowed the lecture (in *Essays Presented to Charles Williams*) to go out of print (*Letters*, p. 216). But Allen & Unwin were eager publish it themselves, perhaps as a small book if Tolkien could expand it by about half and remove references that revealed its origin as a lecture. In August 1959 Tolkien signed a contract with Allen & Unwin for publication of an expanded version of *On Fairy-Stories*, which he hoped to have ready by the end of the year; in the event, the idea lay dormant until 1963, when Tolkien and *Rayner Unwin discussed the possibility of publishing *On Fairy-Stories* to keep Tolkien's name in the public eye while he continued to work on *The Silmarillion*. At length it was decided to publish the lecture together with the story *Leaf by Niggle* in a new volume, *Tree and Leaf*.

CRITICISM

Published on 4 December 1947, *Essays Presented to Charles Williams* received few reviews. The anonymous reviewer in the *Times Literary Supplement* commented that 'some of the contributors . . . present their ideas of what story should be. None of them hazards a definition, although Mr. J.R.R. Tolkein [*sic*], who has a decided conception of what a fairy-story should be, gets nearest to a prescription' ('Telling Stories', 19 June 1948, p. 345).

On Fairy-Stories received much more attention in 1964 when it was published in *Tree and Leaf*, and since then has been widely cited (if not extensively discussed) in most books concerning Tolkien, as well as in writings about children's literature and fantasy fiction. Folklore scholar K.M. Briggs disagreed with Tolkien's 'belief, which is shared by a good many well-informed people, that the tiny fairies came into folk-tradition from literature in the sixteenth century. It was actually the other way round, and they first entered literature from that time; but he is of course right in maintaining that diminutiveness is not an essential part of fairy nature' (*Folklore* 75 (Winter 1964), pp. 293–4).

When Tolkien expresses his distrust of 'the classification of tales' he 'puts his finger upon an insensitiveness to the essence of a story which is apt to overtake the classifier, anxious to find a home for the rebellious original theme'. Some form of classification of the thousands of stories is needed, but in 'our anxious efforts to preserve, to classify, let us not forget that the stories we study were invented and handed down for the sake of delight and enlargement of spirit. Such an essay as this of Professor Tolkien's is a timely and permanent reminder of the delight that lies behind our occupation' (p. 294).

See also Robert J. Reilly, 'Tolkien and the Fairy Story', *Tolkien and the Critics: Essays on J.R.R. Tolkien's The Lord of the Rings* (1968); Chris Seeman, 'Tolkien's Revision of the Romantic Tradition', *Proceedings of the J.R.R. Tolkien Conference 1992* (1995); and James V. Schall, S.J., 'On the Realities of Fantasy', *Tolkien: A Celebration: Collected Writings on a Literary Legacy* (1999). On the background to the study of folk- and fairy-tales as touched on in *On Fairy-Stories*, see Verlyn Flieger, '"There Would Always Be a Fairy-tale": J.R.R. Tolkien and the Folklore Controversy', *Tolkien the Medievalist* (2003).

See also *Escape; *Eucatastrophe; *Fairy-stories; *Recovery; *Sub-creation.

On Translating Beowulf
see Prefatory Remarks on Prose Translation of 'Beowulf'

Once upon a Time. Poem, first published in *Winter's Tales for Children 1*, ed. Caroline Hillier (London: Macmillan; New York: St Martin's Press, 1965), pp. 44–5. See further, *Descriptive Bibliography* B27. In the first of three stanzas, 'once upon a day on the fields of May', Goldberry is 'blowing away a dandelion clock' and 'stooping over a lily-pool'. In the second, 'once upon a night in the cockshut light', Tom walks 'without boot or shoe, / with moonshine wetting his big brown toes'. In the third, 'once upon a moon on the brink of June', Tom speaks to the 'lintips', but they are 'the only things that won't talk to me, / say what they do or what they be.'

Goldberry and Tom (Bombadil) first appeared in the 1934 poem **The Adventures of Tom Bombadil*, and later more famously in **The Lord of the Rings* (1954–5). *Once upon a Time* evidently was written at least after the first of these, and probably after the latter. Readers have failed to identify a source of the 'lintips', which may be no more than undefined invented creatures like those in **The Mewlips*.

Onions, Charles Talbut (1873–1965). Following education at Mason College (later the University of Birmingham), C.T. Onions joined the staff of the **Oxford English Dictionary* in 1895 as assistant first to Sir James A.H. Murray and then to **Henry Bradley. He was co-editor from 1914 to 1933, during which period he and **Sir William Craigie brought the original *OED* to completion. Some of Tolkien's work for the *Dictionary* was done under Onions' supervision. In his **Valedictory Address to the University of Oxford* Tolkien recalled his 'first glimpse of the unique and dominant figure of Charles Talbut Onions, darkly surveying me, a fledgling prentice in the Dictionary Room' in 1919. Onions was also responsible for the *Shorter Oxford English Dictionary* (1933) and the *Oxford Dictionary of English Etymology* (1966, with the assistance of *R.W. Burchfield), and produced a *Shakespeare Glossary* (1911, etc.) which was an offshoot of his work on the *OED*.

He was no less valuable to the Oxford University Press as an advisor and editor concerned with Old and Middle English texts and readers: he revised Sweet's *Anglo-Saxon Reader* (1922, 1946, etc.), urged Tolkien to undertake an edition of **Sir Gawain and the Green Knight* (1925), and supported Tolkien and his collaborator *E.V. Gordon in disputes with the Press on the length and contents of *Sir Gawain*. From 1932 to 1956 he was editor of the distinguished journal of medieval studies *Medium Ævum* (latterly with *J.A.W. Bennett), and from 1944 to 1957 served on the Council of the Early English Text Society (*Societies and clubs), from 1945 as its Honorary Director.

Onions was also on the Faculty of the Oxford English School, as Lecturer in English (1920–27) and Reader in English Philology (1927–49). He had therefore the added responsibilities of lectures to be delivered in term, notably on Middle English texts, and (often in company with Tolkien) administrative duties on the English Faculty Board and various committees. In 1923 he was made a Fellow of Magdalen College. In 1925 he was an Elector for the Rawlinson and Bosworth Professorship when Tolkien was chosen for that chair. As a member of the Kolbítar (*Societies and clubs) Onions, like Tolkien, had the advantage of existing knowledge of Icelandic in translating the sagas and *Eddas*.

On 9 January 1965 Tolkien wrote to his son Michael: 'My dear old protector, backer, and friend Dr C.T. Onions died on Friday at 91 1/3 years. I had not seen him for a long while. [Excepting Kenneth Sisam] he was the last of the people who *were* "English" at Oxford and at large when I entered the profession' (*Letters*, p. 353).

See further, J.A.W. Bennett, 'Charles Talbut Onions, 1873–1965', *Proceedings of the British Academy* 65 (1979).

Orcs. Two essays, a note, and an extract, published with notes and commentary as texts VIII, IX, and X in the section 'Myths Transformed' of **Morgoth's Ring* (1993), pp. 408–24.

Text VIII is a short essay, entitled *Orcs*, which *Christopher Tolkien describes as 'very much a record of "thinking with the pen"' (*Morgoth's Ring*, p. 409). The Orcs posed a major problem for Tolkien as he recognized at the beginning of the essay: 'Their nature and origin require more thought. They are not easy to work into the theory and system. . . . As the case of Aulë and the Dwarves shows [see *'Of Aulë and Yavanna'], only Eru could make creatures with independent wills, and with reasoning powers. But Orcs seem to have both . . .' (p. 409). In September 1954 Tolkien had written to Peter Hastings that because Eru had given special 'sub-creative' powers to certain of His highest created beings: that is a guarantee that what they devised and made should be given the reality of Creation. Of course within limits, and of course subject to certain commands or prohibitions. But if they 'fell', as the Diabolus Morgoth did, and started making things 'for himself, to be their Lord', these would then 'be' real physical realities in the physical world, however evil they might prove. . . . They would be . . . creatures begotten of Sin, and naturally bad. (I nearly wrote 'irredeemably bad'; but that would be going too far. Because by accepting or tolerating their making – necessary to their actual existence – even Orcs would become part of the World, which is God's and ultimately good.) But whether they could have 'souls' or 'spirits' seems a different question; and since in my myth at any rate I do not conceive of the making of souls or spirits, things of an equal order if not an equal power to the Valar, as a possible 'delegation', I have represented at least the Orcs as pre-existing real beings on whom the Dark Lord has exerted the fullness of his power in remodelling and corrupting them, not making them. [*Letters*, p. 195]

In other words, the Orcs were not 'made' by Morgoth but only corrupted and, as Tolkien describes them elsewhere in the letter, 'fundamentally a race of "rational incarnate" creatures' (p. 190). The only question was whom or what had Morgoth corrupted to produce them.

Up until at least 1954 Tolkien's solution was that Morgoth transformed captured Elves into Orcs. Towards the end of the 1950s his opinion seems to have shifted, however, to the idea that Orcs had been bred from both Elves and Men, but primarily Men (see *Notes on Motives in the Silmarillion*, another of the texts in 'Myths Transformed'). Probably at this time he also added a note in the *Annals of Aman* (*Annals of Valinor*), originally written *c.* 1951, beside a statement that Orcs were believed to be corrupted Elves: 'Alter this. Orcs are not Elvish' (*Morgoth's Ring*, p. 80). In the present essay, which dates probably from 1959, he now considered other possibilities for the origin of Orcs, and ultimately decided that '"talking" is not necessarily the sign of the possession of a "rational soul"', and therefore Orcs were '*beasts* of humanized shape (to mock Men and Elves) deliberately perverted/converted into a more close resemblance to Men' (p. 410) – though possibly there was an Elvish or Mannish strain also.

In the untitled text IX, undated but probably from also from the late 1950s, Tolkien reiterated: 'One point only is certain: Melkor could not "create" living "creatures" of independent wills' (p. 413). He decided that Orcs had a mixed origin, not only from corruptions of Elves and Men, but also from corrupted minor spirits.

Text X contains the first two paragraphs of Appendix C of *Quendi and Eldar*, 'Elvish Names for Orcs', and another essay entitled *Orcs*. Both probably date from 1959–60. Deliberately bypassing the question of the ultimate origin of Orcs, the extract describes them as bred by Morgoth in 'mockery of the Children of Ilúvatar, wholly subservient to his will, and nursed in an unappeasable hatred of Elves and Men'. Nonetheless they are 'living creatures, capable of speech and of some crafts and organization, or at least capable of learning such things from higher creatures or from their Master' (p. 416). But it was unlikely that the Eldar had met any Orcs before they began their march into the West.

This seems to have led Tolkien to compose on his typewriter a four-page essay on Orcs, which he attached to *Quendi and Eldar*. Prior to Tolkien's proposed revision of the cosmology of Arda in the late 1950s, Men awoke only with the rising of the Sun, formed from the last fruit of the tree Laurelin after the destruction of the Two Trees, and therefore could not have been corrupted to form Orcs, who were abundant in Middle-earth before this event. But once the Sun was conceived as having been in existence since the beginning, the awakening of Men could be placed far back in the history of Middle-earth, though not, Tolkien decided, before most of the Elves followed Oromë on the Great March to the West. This, however, also posed a chronological problem, since Melkor had been taken prisoner to Aman before the March began. Orcs, like Men, were short-lived; and 'it became clear in time that undoubted Men could under the domination of Morgoth or his agents in a few generations be reduced almost to the Orc-level of mind and habits' (p. 418).

In the essay Tolkien seems also to be trying to explain why Orcs were treated differently from other servants of Morgoth or Sauron:

> Though of necessity, being fingers of the hand of Morgoth, they must be fought with the utmost severity, they must not be dealt with in their own terms of cruelty and treachery. Captives must not be tormented, not even to discover information for the defence of the homes of Elves and Men. If any Orcs surrendered and asked for mercy, they must be granted it, even at a cost. (*[footnote:]* Few Orcs ever did so in the Elder Days, and at no time would any Orc treat with any Elf. . . .] [p. 419]

The essay continues with a discussion of Orcs in the Second and Third Ages under Sauron, who 'achieved even greater control over his Orcs than Morgoth had done' (p. 419). This suggests a solution to the chronological problem: the idea of breeding Orcs came from Morgoth, but the accomplishment was left to Sauron, who was able to continue with the programme in the long years of Morgoth's captivity in Aman.

Accompanying one copy of the typescript of text X are two notes written almost a decade later on versos of papers dated 10 November 1969. One discusses the spelling *orc* versus *ork*, the other the ability of Morgoth to reduce Orcs to 'puppets' but at a great expense of his power, and therefore this was the case for only a small part of their numbers.

Ósanwe-kenta *see* **Quendi and Eldar**

Otley (Yorkshire). From mid-April to mid-May 1916 Tolkien took an army course at the Northern Command and Ripon Training Centre Signalling School, based in Farnley Park, Otley, a market town north-west of *Leeds. Within the park is Farnley Hall, built in 1581 with an eighteenth-century addition.

'Otsan and Kainendan'. Two lists, detailing the week as defined by the Elves and the fortnight as defined by 'the Valar, Eldar, etc.', published with commentary and notes within 'Early Qenya Fragments' in *Parma Eldalamberon* 14 (2003), pp. 16–22, ed. Patrick Wynne and Christopher Gilson. These are entitled respectively 'The *Otsan* or *Otsola* of the Elves' and 'The *Kainendan, Kainella* of the Valar'.

In the first, the Qenya (*Languages, Invented) names for a seven-day week, derived from terms in the *Qenyaqetsa*, are equated to English names, and each is also associated with names and domains of responsibility of the Valar (or Children of the Valar). Wednesday, the first day of the week, is linked to Manwë and Varda, perhaps 'to create an association between Manwe, Lord of the Valar, and Woden (Odin), chief of the Germanic gods after whom Wednesday is named . . . while still according Manwe the honour of having his day come first in the week' (pp. 19–20).

In the second list 'the names of the fourteen days of the *Kainendan* are all compounds derived from particular names of the Valar together with the element *-san* or *-ran*' (p. 18), meaning 'day', with some alternatives.

Over Old Hills and Far Away. Poem, published in *The Book of Lost Tales, Part One* (1983), pp. 108–10. The poet is lured from his bed by the sound of a flute. He finds Tinfang Warble (cf. *Tinfang Warble*) 'dancing there, / Fluting and tossing his old white hair, Till it sparkled like frost in a winter moon'; but the piper slips 'through the reeds like a mist in the glade'. The poet follows 'the hoot' of a 'twilight flute' 'over old hills and far away / Where the harps of the Elvenfolk softly play' (*The Book of Lost Tales, Part One*, pp. 109–10).

Tolkien composed *Over Old Hills and Far Away* at Brocton army camp, *Staffordshire, in January–February 1916, to judge by an apparently contemporaneous note on the earliest manuscript of the poem. (A later manuscript is inscribed 'Brocton Camp, Christ[mas]–Jan[uary] 1915–16'.) Tolkien rewrote it in Oxford in 1927. The poem exists in five texts, the latest of which is published in *The Book of Lost Tales, Part One* together with selected earlier readings.

Oxford and environs. The city of Oxford, where Tolkien lived and worked for most of his life, lies north-west of London at the meeting place of two rivers, the Cherwell and the Isis (as the upper part of the Thames is known locally). A settlement existed there as early as the eighth century, by a ford used for oxen, hence *Oxford*. A town was established at this location by the year 912; Oxford received its charter in 1155. It became an important crossroads, and trade flourished. The University of Oxford grew up there in the twelfth century.

The importance of Oxford in Tolkien's life has demanded that it be treated in detail, and it has been most convenient to divide coverage into three parts: one concerned with Tolkien's homes in Oxford; a second with buildings, businesses, colleges, and other features within central Oxford; and a third with places that Tolkien knew near Oxford but outside the city proper. The history and operation of the University of Oxford are discussed in a separate entry (*Oxford, University of).

TOLKIEN'S OXFORD HOMES

Tolkien went up to Exeter College in Michaelmas Term 1911. Until the end of Trinity Term 1914 he lived in a building called 'Swiss Cottage', which looked out on **Turl Street** – see his sketch *Turl Street, Oxford* in *Artist and Illustrator*, fig. 19, and his cover for an 'Exeter College Smoker' programme reproduced in *Life and Legend*, p. 26, and *The Tolkien Family Album*, p. 32. He had a bedroom and a sitting-room at no. 9 on the no. 7 staircase, on which he paid rent as well as a fee for the hire of furniture. 'Swiss Cottage' was later replaced by the building today occupied by the specialist art bookshop operated by Blackwell's.

During the academic year 1914–15 Tolkien shared rooms at **59 St John Street** with his friend *Colin Cullis. St John Street connects Wellington Square with Beaumont Street, west of and parallel to St Giles'. Tolkien found living there 'a delicious joy compared with the primitive life of college' (quoted in *Biography*, p. 72). It was at this address that he wrote, at least, the poems *You & Me and the Cottage of Lost Play* (*The Little House of Lost Play: Mar Vanwa Tyaliéva*) and *Goblin Feet*.

In late 1918, Tolkien having accepted an offer to join the staff of the *New English Dictionary* (*Oxford English Dictionary*), he and his wife *Edith, their son *John, and Edith's cousin *Jennie Grove moved into rooms at **50 St John Street** let by a Miss Mahon. From there it was only a short walk to the Old Ashmolean in Broad Street, where the *Oxford English Dictionary* editorial offices were located.

In late summer 1919, his income at last sufficient to rent a small house, Tolkien moved with his family to **1 Alfred Street (Pusey Street)**. Alfred Street connects St John Street and St Giles'; it was renamed Pusey Street in 1925. A photograph of 1 Alfred Street at that time is reproduced in *The Tolkien Family Album*, p. 43. John Tolkien recalled the boyhood sight of elephants in the St Giles' Fair taken down Alfred Street for morning exercise: as they passed the Tolkiens' dining-room window 'they blocked out the light' (*The Tolkien Family Album*, p. 43). In early 1921 the family moved to *Leeds, Tolkien having taken up the Readership in English Language at the University in October 1920.

Although Tolkien became Rawlinson and Bosworth Professor of Anglo-Saxon at Oxford as of Michaelmas Term 1925, it was not until 7 January 1926 that he and his family moved into their next Oxford home. This was at **22 Northmoor Road** in North Oxford, 'L-shaped and of pale brick, with one wing running towards the road' (Humphrey Carpenter, *Biography*, p. 113).

Photographs taken in its garden are reproduced in *The Tolkien Family Album*, pp. 50–2. A small sketch by Tolkien of the front of 22 Northmoor Road is reproduced in *Artist and Illustrator*, fig. 77. The Oxford bookseller and publisher *Basil Blackwell lived next door at no. 20.

Edith Tolkien always thought no. 22 too small for their growing family, and with the arrival of a daughter, *Priscilla, in 1929 a larger house became a necessity. Fortunately in that year Basil Blackwell's house became available, and on 14 January 1930 the Tolkiens moved next door to **20 Northmoor Road**. 'This second house was broad and grey, more imposing than its neighbour, with small leaded windows and a high slate roof' (*Biography*, pp. 113–14). Its rooms were not large, but there were many of them. The most exciting room in the house, as far as the Tolkien children were concerned, was their father's study:

> The walls were lined with books from floor to ceiling, and it contained a great black lead stove, the source of considerable drama every day. . . . The study was very much the centre of Ronald's home life and the centre of his study was his desk. Over the years the top of his desk continued to show familiar landscapes: his dark brown wooden tobacco jar, a Toby jug containing pipes, and a large bowl into which the ash from his pipe was regularly knocked out,

as well as inks, sealing wax, coloured pencils, and tubes of paint (*The Tolkien Family Album*, pp. 55–6). Humphrey Carpenter wrote that Tolkien's study contained 'a tunnel of books formed by a double row of bookcases, and it is not until the visitor emerges from this that the rest of the room becomes visible. There are windows on two sides, so that the room looks southwards towards a neighbouring garden and west towards the road. Tolkien's desk is in the south-facing window' (*Biography*, p. 116). Because he snored and kept late hours, Tolkien slept apart from his wife, in a bathroom-cum-dressing-room which looked east over the garden.

John and Priscilla Tolkien wrote that no. 20

> was as much loved for its garden as for the house. John and Ronald worked at landscaping and redesigning the garden over many years, turning the rather decrepit tennis court at the top into a vegetable garden: an important asset during the war years that were to follow. Over the years we lived there the trees planted by the Blackwells grew almost to forest height. In a side garden, Edith had an aviary, in which budgerigars, canaries and other exotic birds lived during the summer months, being taken indoors for the winter. In war-time, the aviary was turned into a hen-house. . . . [*The Tolkien Family Album*, p. 55]

A photograph of the hens at 20 Northmoor Road is reproduced in *The Tolkien Family Album*, p. 72. In 2004 the house was given protected status as a Grade II listed building, on the basis of Tolkien's importance.

In 1933 Tolkien and his son John built a trellis in front of 20 Northmoor Road to at least partly screen their garden from the view of passers-by. In spring 1940 Tolkien drew a picture of the garden, with daffodils and a flowering Victoria Plum tree (*Artist and Illustrator*, fig. 3).

On 14 March 1947 the Tolkiens moved to a small house at **3 Manor Road** owned by Merton College, of which Tolkien became a Fellow in 1945. By this time, with only Priscilla among the children still living with her parents, 20 Northmoor Road had become too large and too costly to maintain. But at 3 Manor Road Tolkien and Edith 'found both house and garden cramped and claustrophobic after the spaciousness' they had enjoyed (*The Tolkien Family Album*, p. 74). Tolkien described their Manor Road home in a letter to Sir Stanley Unwin as 'a minute house near the centre of this town' (5 May 1947, Tolkien-George Allen & Unwin archive, HarperCollins). For lack of space he no longer had a proper study: he later remarked to his *Aunt Jane Neave that he had typed out the whole of *The Lord of the Rings* twice, 'mostly on my bed in the attic of the tiny terrace-house to which war had exiled us from the house in which my family grew up' (8–9 September 1962, *Letters*, pp. 321–2). A photograph of Tolkien, Priscilla, *Christopher, and Edith in the garden of 3 Manor Road in 1949 is reproduced in *The Tolkien Family Album*, p. 74. Austin and *Katharine Farrer were neighbours at 7 Manor Road.

In May 1950 Tolkien, Edith, and Priscilla moved to a larger Merton College house at **99 Holywell Street** which dated from the seventeenth and eighteenth centuries. 'The house had a small step up from the street and lay back at an angle. . . . Its small garden contained a hawthorn tree that attracted nuthatches and tree creepers, and the high wall at the back, dividing it from the gardens of New College, was part of the medieval wall of the city' (*The Tolkien Family Album*, p. 74; photographs, pp. 74, 75). Tolkien again had room for a study, and could see his postgraduate students at home as well as in college. But after the war Holywell Street became a major traffic route in Oxford. On 24 October 1952 Tolkien wrote to *Rayner Unwin that his 'charming house has become uninhabitable – unsleepable-in, unworkable-in, rocked, racked with noise, and drenched with fumes. Such is modern life. Mordor in our midst' (*Letters*, p. 165).

On 30 March 1953 Tolkien and Edith moved to **76 Sandfield Road** in Headington, east of the centre of Oxford; Priscilla by now had taken her degree and had left Oxford for Bristol. Holywell Street was abandoned in part on doctor's orders: Edith's increasing ill health required that she live in 'a house on high dry soil and in the quiet' (Tolkien, letter to Rayner Unwin, 24 March 1953, *Letters*, p. 166). Humphrey Carpenter describes 76 Sandfield Road in *Biography* as it looked in spring 1967: it was a long way down 'a residential street of two-storey brick houses, each with its tidy front garden. . . . The house is painted white and is partially screened by a tall fence, a hedge, and overhanging trees.' One entered through an arched gate – a photograph of Tolkien and Edith at the gate is reproduced in *Biography*, pl. 13 – and along a short path between rose bushes. The entrance hall was 'small and tidy and contains nothing that one would not expect in the house of a middle-class elderly couple. *W.H. Auden, in an injudicious remark quoted in the newspapers, has called the house "hideous", but that is nonsense. It is simply ordinary and suburban' (*Biography*, pp. 3–4).

The house was small; it could not hold comfortably all of Tolkien's books, most of which he had kept at Merton College but which on his retirement in 1959 he was obliged to remove. When he had filled his upstairs study-bed-room, he converted the (unoccupied) garage into a library-office. Humphrey Carpenter described the latter:

> The shelves are crammed with dictionaries, works on etymology and philology, and editions of texts in many languages, predominant among which are Old and Middle English; but there is also a section devoted to translations of *The Lord of the Rings* . . .; and the map of his invented 'Middle-earth' is pinned to the window-ledge. On the floor is a very old portmanteau full of letters, and on the desk are ink-bottles, nibs and pen-holders, and two typewriters. The room smells of books and tobacco-smoke. [*Biography*, p. 4]

Tolkien himself wrote about it to Charlotte and Denis Plimmer on 8 February 1967:

> May I say that it is not a 'study', except in domestic slang. . . . It was a hastily contrived necessity, when I was obliged to relinquish my room in college and provide a store for what I could preserve of my library. Most of the books of value have since been removed, and the most important contents are the rows of orderly files kept by my part-time secretary. She is the only regular user of the room. I have never written any literary matter in it. [*Letters*, p. 373]

Since there were only two rooms on the ground floor besides the kitchen, Tolkien converted a smaller bedroom into a study where he did his writing.

The chief disadvantage of 76 Sandfield Road was that it was almost two miles from Oxford centre, a long journey for Tolkien while he was still the Merton Professor of English Language and Literature – and the same for family and friends to visit Sandfield Road. The size of the house was also a problem, demanding too many domestic chores of people in advanced years, even with daily help. Nor did the quiet that Tolkien and Edith found there in 1953 last more than a few years. As Tolkien wrote to Christopher Bretherton on 16 July 1964:

> Sandfield Road was a cul-de-sac when I came here, but was soon opened at the bottom end, and became for a time an unofficial lorry by-pass, before Headley Way was completed. Now it is a car-park for the field of 'Oxford United' at the top end. While the actual inhabitants do all that

radio, tele, dogs, scooters, buzzbikes, and cars of all sizes but the smallest, can do to produce noise from early morn to about 2 a.m. In addition
in a house three doors away dwells a member of a group of young men
who are evidently aiming to turn themselves into a Beatle Group. On
days when it falls to his turn to have a practice session the noise is indescribable. . . . [*Letters*, pp. 344–5]

In mid-July 1968 Tolkien and Edith moved to a bungalow in *Poole, near
*Bournemouth. Edith died in Bournemouth in November 1971. Before
the end of the year Tolkien began to look for a place in Oxford, and in mid-
January 1972 Christopher Tolkien wrote on behalf of his father to the Warden
of Merton to ask if the College had any housing available. The Warden called
a special meeting of Merton's Governing Body, which unanimously voted that
Tolkien should be invited to become a residential Fellow. In this manner he
was offered a set of rooms at **21 Merton Street**, which proved an ideal arrangement, if short-lived: they were Tolkien's final Oxford home before his death in
1973. On 24 January 1972 he wrote to his son Michael:

Merton has now provided [me] with a very excellent flat, which will
probably accommodate the bulk of my surviving 'library'. But wholly
unexpected 'strings' are attached to this! (1) The rent will be 'merely
nominal' – which means what it implies: something extremely small
in comparison with actual market-value. (2) All or any furniture
required will be provided *free* by the college – and a large Wilton carpet has already been assigned to me, covering the whole floor of a sitting
room. . . . (3) Since 21 M[erton] St. is legally part of the college, domestic
service is provided *free*: in the shape of a resident care-taker and his wife
as housekeeper [*Charlie and Mavis Carr]. (4) I am entitled to *free* lunch
and dinner throughout the year when in residence: both of a very high
standard. This represents – allowing 9 weeks absence – an actual emolument of between £750 and £900 a year which the claws of the I[ncome]
Taxgatherers have so far been driven off. (5) The college will provide free
of rent two telephones: (a) for *local* calls, and calls to extensions, which
are *free*, and (b) for long distance calls, which will have a private number
and be paid by me. This will have the advantage that business and private
calls to family and friends will not pass through the overworked lodge;
but it will have the one snag that it will have to appear in the Telephone
book, and cannot be ex-directory. . . . (6) No rates, and gas and electri-
city bills at a reduced scale. (7) The use of 2 beautiful common-rooms
(at a distance of 100 yards) with free writing paper, free newspapers, and
mid-morning coffee. It all sounds too good to be true – and of course it
all depends on my health. . . . [*Letters*, pp. 415–16]

On 16 March 1972 Tolkien wrote to Rayner Unwin: 'I am now at last . . . IN but
not "settled" in [at 21 Merton Street]. . . . The great bank in the Fellows' Garden

looks like the foreground of a pre-Raphaelite picture: blazing green starred like the Milky Way with blue anemones, purple/white/yellow crocuses, and final surprise, clouded-yellow, peacock, and tortoiseshell butterflies flitting about' (*Letters*, p. 417).

A photograph of the façade of 21 Merton Street is reproduced in *The Tolkien Family Album*, p. 87.

CENTRAL OXFORD

Blackfriars. Blackfriars, the Priory of the Holy Spirit at 64 St Giles, was established in 1929 by Father Bede Jarrett as a House of Studies for the English Province of the Order of Preachers, better known as the Dominicans. The Order had arrived in Oxford as early as August 1221, only five years after its founding in 1216, and there established a priory and school of teaching. The school flourished during the thirteenth and fourteenth centuries, but had declined by 1538 when the Order was suppressed by Henry VIII. The chapel and priory were designed by Edwin Doran Webb, the architect of the *Birmingham Oratory; the chapel was consecrated on 20 May 1929, but the priory buildings were not completed until 1954, though sufficiently advanced in 1929 for a small number of friars to take up residence. *Father Gervase Mathew was a member of the community.

On at least one occasion, in 1945, Tolkien served during Mass in the chapel. On 26 October 1966 he read his still unpublished *Smith of Wootton Major* to so large an audience at Blackfriars 'that the Refectory (a long hall as long as a church) had to be cleared and could not contain it. Arrangements for relay to passages outside had to be hastily made. I am told that more than 800 people gained admittance' (letter to Michael George Tolkien (see *Michael Tolkien), 28 October 1966, *Letters*, pp. 370–1).

Blackwell's Bookshop. The most famous of Oxford booksellers, founded in 1879. Since 1883 its main shop has been at 50 Broad Street, later expanded into nos. 48 and 49 and other buildings nearby. Tolkien was a frequent customer. In 1942 the chairman of the firm, *Basil Blackwell, gracefully helped him settle an overdue account (see *Pearl*). Tolkien also bought books from the now defunct Parker and Son, once in Broad Street at the present site of Blackwell's art bookshop.

Bodleian Library. One of the oldest and most important libraries in the world, opened in 1602 through the generosity of Sir Thomas Bodley but on a foundation of books given to the University of Oxford from the early fourteenth century. It is one of six deposit libraries entitled to receive a copy of every book published in the United Kingdom. Its oldest buildings are located south of the Sheldonian Theatre and the Clarendon Building, around the Schools Quadrangle. A doorway on the west leads from the Quadrangle to the Proscholium, a vestibule, now the Bodleian shop, from which general visitors may see the

Divinity School, constructed from about 1420 through most of the fifteenth century. Above these rooms are Duke Humfrey's Library (begun 1444, completed 1488, refitted 1598–1602, named for the collection of manuscripts given by Humfrey, Duke of Gloucester) and its extensions Arts End (completed 1612) and Selden End (completed 1637), where rare books and early manuscripts are read. The Schools Quadrangle (built 1613–19) was originally a series of lecture-rooms with a picture gallery on the top floor, but was taken over by the Library for additional book storage and reading rooms beginning in 1789.

Tolkien used the Bodleian holdings on many occasions. Some of the works he consulted for *On Fairy-Stories* are listed with the Bodleian shelfmarks in his notes for that essay. Among the Library's rich manuscript holdings, MS Bodley 34 was of particular interest to Tolkien: this contains works in the Middle English *Katherine Group. As a member of the English Faculty Library Committee Tolkien advised the Bodleian Library regarding the purchase of foreign books and periodicals on English.

The **Radcliffe Camera**, a large circular building in Radcliffe Square south of the Schools Quadrangle, was designed by James Gibbs after Nicholas Hawksmoor and built as a general library in 1737–49 with money bequeathed by Dr John Radcliffe. It became a reading room of the Bodleian Library in 1862. Tolkien refers to the 'Camera' with its lofty dome in *The Notion Club Papers*: it seems to remind Lowdham of the circular, domed temple that Sauron built in Númenor (as described in *The Drowning of Anadûnê* and the *Akallabêth*).

The New Bodleian Library, designed by Sir Giles Gilbert Scott, was built on the corner of Broad Street and Parks Road in 1937–9. This more modern building (not open to tourists) provides book storage, reading rooms, and staff offices to supplement the 'old' Bodleian across the street. Due to the Second World War it was not opened officially until 24 October 1946, by King George VI and Queen Elizabeth. *Priscilla Tolkien recalled that her father was present on that occasion, when the ceremonial key broke in the lock and someone had to open the door from the other side. The Department of Western Manuscripts in the New Bodleian holds one of the two major collections of Tolkien manuscripts (see *Libraries and archives), including his academic working papers, some printed books from his personal library, family papers and correspondence, paintings and drawings, and manuscripts of most of his literary works except for those at Marquette University.

Botanic Garden. Founded in 1621 as the Oxford Physick Garden for the Faculty of Medicine, the Botanic Garden is located south of High Street across from *Magdalen College. In its grounds and greenhouses are a wide variety of cultivated plants, including some 150 trees of botanical interest. Tolkien's rooms in Merton Street near the end of his life overlooked the Garden, to which he was a frequent visitor. In August 1973 he was photographed by his grandson Michael George (see *Michael Tolkien) next to one of his favourite trees, a *Pinus nigra* (Black or Austrian pine, see *Biography*, pl. 14b); and that month also he twice walked in the Garden with his friend *Joy Hill.

Cherwell Edge. Built in 1886–7 in St Cross Road, Cherwell Edge was originally a private house, designed by J.W. Messenger. In 1905 it became a convent of the Society of the Holy Child Jesus. In 1907 the Reverend Mother *St Teresa Gale established at Cherwell Edge a house of studies to bring the Society into contact with Oxford University standards of education. Under her guidance it became a centre of Catholic action in Oxford. A chapel and a large residential block (designed by Basil Champneys) were subsequently added to the house, the latter to serve as a hostel for Catholic women in the Society of Oxford Home-Students. *Susan Dagnall and *M.E. Griffiths, among many others, lodged there, and Tolkien is said to have been a friend and supporter of the establishment. In 1977 Cherwell Edge became part of Linacre College, and was later altered and further enlarged.

Clarendon Building. As a member of various boards and committees at Oxford Tolkien attended numerous meetings in the Clarendon Building in Broad Street, opposite *Blackwell's Bookshop. The building (not open to tourists) was designed by Nicholas Hawksmoor and built in 1712–13 for the Oxford University Press (*Publishers); it was used for that purpose until 1829. During Tolkien's time at Oxford the Clarendon Building contained University offices. It is now part of the *Bodleian Library.

Corpus Christi College. Founded in 1517, Corpus Christi College is located on the south side of Merton Street, to the west of Merton College. Tolkien stayed at Corpus Christi in December 1909 when he first sought to win a scholarship or exhibition to Oxford. His friend *G.B. Smith became an exhibitioner at Corpus Christi in Michaelmas Term 1913. On 22 November 1914 Tolkien read a paper, *The Finnish National Epic*, to the Sundial Society at Corpus Christi. On 7 June 1947 he was one of the members of a committee appointed by the English Faculty Board who met at Corpus Christi to draft an outline proposal for an English Preliminary Examination.

Eagle and Child. Public house, located at 49 St Giles' since 1650, named for the family crest of the Earl of Derby (a coronet with eagle and child) but popularly known as the 'Bird and Baby'. From about 1939 until the early 1950s the *Inklings met informally on Tuesdays (later, Mondays) for conversation and refreshment, usually at the Eagle and Child. *C.S. Lewis liked its traditional character, as well as its landlord, Charlie Blagrove (*d.* 1948); and it was conveniently close to the Taylor Institution where many English School lectures were given during the Second World War. The Inklings usually assembled in late morning in the pub's small back room. According to *John Wain, Lewis preferred the open tavern, and deeply regretted that Tolkien later arranged for them to meet in the Blagrove family's private parlour. In 1962, when the parlour was opened to the public and joined on to the main bar, the Inklings moved across St Giles' to the Lamb and Flag.

There are many references to the Eagle and Child in *Letters* and in the diaries of *W.H. Lewis (*Brothers and Friends*). See also John Wain, 'Push Bar to Open', *Oxford Magazine*, Eighth Week, Hilary Term (1988). A photograph of the Eagle and Child is reproduced in *The Inklings*, p. 8b.

Eastgate Hotel. The Eastgate Hotel at 73 High Street was built in 1899–1900 and later enlarged. It is close to Magdalen College where *C.S. Lewis was a Fellow, and to Merton College, where Tolkien was Professor of English Language and Literature from 1945 to 1959. For many years Tolkien and Lewis would meet in Lewis's rooms in Magdalen on Monday morning, and then take a drink together in the Eastgate. It was often favoured by Tolkien for lunch or dinner when he had guests to entertain.

Examination Schools. Designed in a neo-Jacobean style by Thomas Graham Jackson and constructed in 1876–82, the Examination Schools in the High Street are used for lectures as well as examinations. Tolkien knew the 'Schools' as an undergraduate, and taught and examined in them as an Oxford professor. He gave most of his lectures in the Examination Schools, except during the Second World War when the building was used as a military hospital; the English Faculty Library, normally housed in the Schools, was then moved to the Taylor Institution and later to its new building in Manor Road.

Exeter College. Bounded by Turl Street, Broad Street, and Brasenose Lane, Exeter College was founded in 1314 as Stapeldon Hall by Walter de Stapeldon, Bishop of Exeter. Most of its present architecture dates from the seventeenth century, notably the Hall built in 1618, or from the nineteenth century, including two Gothic Revival buildings by Sir George Gilbert Scott, the library (1855–6) and the chapel (1856–9). In the latter is a fine tapestry designed by Edward Burne-Jones and *William Morris. A photograph of Exeter College before the First World War is reproduced in *Life and Legend*, p. 24.

Tolkien won a Classical Exhibition to Exeter in December 1910 and came up to the College in Michaelmas Term 1911. His rooms until Trinity Term 1914 were in an Exeter building called Swiss Cottage (on the site of the present Blackwell's art bookshop), which looked out on Turl Street – see his sketch *Turl Street, Oxford* in *Artist and Illustrator*, fig. 19, and his cover for an 'Exeter College Smoker' programme reproduced in *Life and Legend*, p. 26, and *The Tolkien Family Album*, p. 32. He usually had breakfast in his rooms, brought to him by his scout (college servant), and dinner in the Hall. In February 1913 he sent his fiancée (*Edith Tolkien) a postcard with a view of the Hall and an 'X' marking the spot where he usually sat: see *Life and Legend*, p. 35. He had to pay weekly for any food and drink brought to his room. Surviving battels (re-used by Tolkien for notes) show that he was charged for tea, coffee, milk and cream, sugar, dry toast, butter, jam, marmalade and honey, anchovy and buttered toast, cakes, crumpets and muffins, porridge, eggs, fruit, potted meat and pickles, sardines, chutney and sauce, cider and claret cup and mulled claret, and lemon squash, as well as tobacco and cigarettes.

Tolkien took part actively in College life, joining *inter alia* the Exeter College Essay Club and the Stapeldon Society (*Societies and clubs), in both of which he held office. He was a member of the committee appointed by the Stapeldon Society to organize the elaborate dinner held 6 June 1914 at which the Junior Common Room entertained the Senior Common Room to celebrate the Sexcentenary of the College's foundation. He also often attended social events such as concerts and the annual Freshman's Wine. For part of his time at Oxford he played on the Exeter College rugby team; see photograph, *Life and Legend*, p. 25. From Hilary Term 1919 until Trinity Term 1920, while he was working in Oxford after the war, Tolkien was an honorary member of the Essay Club, to whom he read *The Fall of Gondolin* (*The Book of Lost Tales*) on 10 March 1920. At a meeting of the Club in November 1926, after his return to Oxford from *Leeds, Tolkien read a paper on the *Elder Edda*.

On 26 July 1933 Tolkien and *Hugo Dyson invited *C.S. Lewis and *W.H. Lewis to dine at Exeter. W.H. Lewis on that occasion described the college as 'a delightful place, the chief feature being the garden – a quiet oblong of close shaven, walled and treed fringed grass, ending in a little paved court with a sunk pond where a small fountain plays on water lilies: this court is overlooked from a terrace or rampart which is approached by a flight of stone steps from the lawn.' From the terrace Lewis found 'a most unusual view of Oxford: the terrace is perhaps fifteen feet above the square in which the Bodleian stands . . . it looked wonderfully dignified, backed by St Mary's and a pale yellow afterglow of sunset' (*Brothers and Friends*, pp. 105–6).

Tolkien retained an affection for Exeter, although as a professor he was later attached to Pembroke and Merton colleges. His daughter *Priscilla remembered a 'conflict of loyalties' one year during the annual college Boat Races, 'when Exeter were rowing against Pembroke: whilst having tea with us . . . on the Pembroke [spectators'] barge, he shouted for their opponents!' (*The Tolkien Family Album*, p. 77).

Exeter College made Tolkien an Honorary Fellow in 1958.

King's Arms. A public house at 41 Holywell Street, opened in 1607. Most of the present building dates from the eighteenth century. It is close to the Bodleian Library, and therefore much used by readers and employees. On 22 August 1944 Tolkien wrote to his son *Christopher: 'This morning I . . . found the Bird and Baby [Eagle and Child] closed; but was hailed in a voice that carried across the torrent of vehicles that was once St Giles', and discovered the two Lewises [*C.S. and *W.H.] and *C[harles] Williams, high and very dry on the other side. Eventually we got 4 pints of passable ale at the King's Arms – at a cost of 5/8' (*Letters*, p. 92). *Roger Lancelyn Green recalled that during one summer, *c.* 1949–50, he 'was doing research work in the Bodleian and would meet C.S. Lewis . . . and he would say in a conspiratorial whisper "King's Arms! 12.30!" and we would meet there for a drink and a talk in the yard behind the hotel. There Tolkien usually joined us, and frequently Hugo Dyson, plus occasionally others of the "Inklings"' ('Recollections', *Amon Hen* 44 (May 1980), pp. 7–8).

Lady Margaret Hall. Founded in 1878 to accommodate women desiring to study at Oxford, Lady Margaret Hall was named after Lady Margaret Beaufort, mother of King Henry VII and a patron of learning. Its buildings range from the original grey brick villa built in 1879 (extended in 1881) to a neo-Georgian block by Raymond Firth, constructed 1963-6. Gardens stretch east to the Cherwell. During Tolkien's day Lady Margaret Hall was one of five women's colleges in Oxford (men began to be admitted in 1979), and according to his daughter *Priscilla, an undergraduate there between 1948 and 1951, 'probably the one he knew best' ('Memories of J.R.R. Tolkien in His Centenary Year', *The Brown Book* (December 1992), p. 12).

Lamb and Flag. A public house at 12 St Giles', almost opposite the Eagle and Child, opened towards the end of the seventeenth century. Some of the original building survives. When the Eagle and Child was modernized in 1962 and its inner parlour opened to the public, the *Inklings met instead in the Lamb and Flag.

Magdalen College. The college of St Mary Magdalen, founded in 1458 by William Waynflete, is one of the wealthiest and most spacious colleges in Oxford. Its original quadrangle was built in 1474-80, its landmark tower in 1492-1505. To the north is the New Building of 1733, largely designed by Edward Holdsworth; behind it is Magdalen Grove, a deer park. South-east of New Building a bridge leads over the River Cherwell to a meadow enclosed by a path called Addison's Walk. (A photograph of Addison's Walk is reproduced in *The Inklings*, p. 4b.)

As an undergraduate Tolkien attended lectures and classes given by *Sir Walter Raleigh at Magdalen. During the First World War part of the College was commandeered; for a short time in spring 1915 *G.B. Smith was billeted there with the Oxford and Bucks Light Infantry.

*C.S. Lewis became a Fellow of Magdalen in 1925: he occupied rooms no. 3 on staircase 3 of New Buildings. On 19 September 1931 Tolkien dined with Lewis and *Hugo Dyson at Magdalen, then strolled along Addison's Walk and through Magdalen Grove discussing myth, a conversation which led to C.S. Lewis accepting Christianity. On 22 November 1931 Lewis wrote to his brother that it had become a regular custom for Tolkien to call on him at Magdalen on Monday mornings 'and drink a glass. This is one of the pleasantest spots of the week. Sometimes we talk English school politics; sometimes we criticise one another's poems: other days we drift into theology or "the state of the nation" . . .' (*Letters of C.S. Lewis* (rev. edn. 1988), p. 292). When Charles Williams came to Oxford in September 1939 he often joined Lewis and Tolkien at Magdalen, and the three would read their works aloud. Lewis recalled the occasion when Williams read the first chapters of his *Figure of Arthur*: 'Picture to yourself, then, an upstairs sitting-room with windows looking north into the "grove" of Magdalen College on a sunshiny Monday Morning in vacation at about ten o'clock. The Professor [Tolkien] and I, both on the chesterfield, lit our pipes and stretched out our legs. Williams in the arm-chair opposite to us threw his cigarette into the grate . . . and began . . .' (Charles Williams, *Arthurian Torso* [1948], p. 2).

From some time in the 1930s the *Inklings met in the same sitting-room after dinner on Thursday evenings, often not leaving until at least midnight. Humphrey Carpenter has described the room (*The Inklings*, pp. 128–9) as shabby and in need of cleaning; but there Tolkien, and later his son *Christopher, read aloud much of * *The Lord of the Rings* as it was written, and in turn heard the other Inklings read their works. In addition to C.S. Lewis, Inklings who were Fellows of Magdalen were *Adam Fox, *C.E. Stevens, *Colin Hardie, and *J.A.W. Bennett. During the Second World War part of Magdalen was again commandeered by the military: on that occasion *James Dundas-Grant, commanding the Oxford University Naval Division, resided there and became an Inkling. Two other friends of Tolkien associated with Magdalen were *George S. Gordon, President of the College from 1928 to 1942, and *C.T. Onions, Fellow and Librarian.

Tolkien attended several meetings of the Early English Text Society (*Societies and clubs) committee or council at Magdalen between 1945 and 1963. At the end of August 1950 he was present at the Conference of University Professors of English held at Magdalen which led to the formation of the International Association of University Professors of English.

Merton College. Merton College was founded in 1264 by Walter de Merton, Chancellor of England and later Bishop of Rochester. Its statutes are the oldest in Oxford. It is bounded on the north by Merton Street and on the south originally by the city wall, now by Merton Field and Christ Church Meadow. Many of its medieval buildings survive, alongside later construction and renovation. Its thirteenth-century Hall was rebuilt by Sir George Gilbert Scott in 1874.

When Tolkien was elected Merton Professor of English Language and Literature in 1945 he also became a Fellow of Merton College, which had endowed the chair in 1885. Tolkien felt more comfortable at Merton than he had at Pembroke College: Merton gave him spacious rooms in which he could receive postgraduate students and entertain friends, and in which until his retirement he kept most of his library. He was scheduled to give seminars and classes at Merton from Trinity Term 1947 to Hilary Term 1951, and morning lectures there in Michaelmas Term 1957. On occasion he stayed overnight in college, while his wife *Edith was on holiday or in hospital. From at least autumn 1947 he hosted meetings of the *Inklings at Merton, sharing that duty with *C.S. Lewis at Magdalen College. He also invited friends to dine with him at Merton: on one such occasion, *W.H. Lewis recalled in his diary, 'as I waited for him in his room, I was struck by the absolute silence of Merton compared with the perpetual hum that floats in through Magdalen windows. We dined in common room [term was not yet in session] by candle light a party of seven. . . . A good dinner, and a glass of better port than Magdalen gives one' (22 August 1946, Marion E. Wade Center, Wheaton College, Wheaton, Illinois).

Tolkien described his first impressions of Merton to his son *Christopher in letters written on 11 October and 22 October 1945:

> I was duly admitted yesterday at 10 a.m. and then had to endure the most formidable College Meeting I have ever seen – went on till 1.30 p.m. without cessation and then broke up in disorder. The Warden talked almost unceasingly. I lunched in Merton and made a few arrangements, putting my name down at the Estates Bursary on the housing list; and getting a Master Key to all gates and doors. It is incredible belonging to a real college (and a very large and wealthy one). . . . I walked round this afternoon with [*Hugo] Dyson who was duly elected yesterday, and is now ensconced in the rooms I hoped for, looking out over the meadows! [*Letters*, p. 116]

> I dined for the first time at Merton high table on Thursday, and found it very agreeable; though odd. For fuel-economy the common room is not heated, and the dons meet and chat amiably on the dais, until some-one thinks there are enough there for grace to be said. After that they sit and dine, and have their port, and coffee, and smoke and evening news-papers all at high table in a manner that if agreeably informal is rather shocking to one trained in the severer ceremonies and strict precedence of mediaeval Pembroke. [*Letters*, pp. 116–17]

He was allotted new rooms, part of set 6, staircase 4, in the Fellows Quadrangle on 24 June 1947, overlooking Christchurch Meadow, and moved to even better rooms in May 1954.

Tolkien and his wife lived successively in two houses owned by Merton College, at 3 Manor Road and 99 Holywell Street, after they could no longer afford to stay at 20 Northmoor Road. After Edith's death in 1971, when Tolkien wished to return to Oxford, Merton made him a Resident Fellow and provided a set of rooms at 21 Merton Street.

During his years at Merton Tolkien played an active part in college life. He attended most College meetings, an average of eleven per year. He was a member of the Library Committee in 1946–49 and 1952–3, of the Wine Com-mittee in 1947–59, and of the Stipends Committee in 1948–59. He was also on various committees set up to consider specific matters: in 1948, for instance, to recommend a suitable inscription on a commemorative tablet to be placed in the College Chapel. The most onerous of his several College offices was that of Sub-Warden, from 1 August 1953 to 21 June 1955: in this capacity he was *ex officio* a member of the Finance Committee, and of any other committee set up during his term of office, of which there were many. In September 1947, as Fellow attending on the estates progress, Tolkien spent four days with the Warden and Bursar inspecting the College's extensive holdings of land in Leicestershire and *Lincolnshire. *John and *Priscilla Tolkien have noted that their father 'enjoyed warm relationships with the College's domestic staff.

He was their champion, often arguing that they should enjoy better working conditions . . .' (*The Tolkien Family Album*, p. 79). In December 1963 Tolkien was elected to an emeritus Fellowship, and in May 1973 an Honorary Fellow. A memorial service was held for him on 17 November 1973 in Merton College Chapel.

A photograph of Merton College from a distance is reproduced in *The Tolkien Family Album*, p. 78.

Mitre Hotel. Located at the corner of High Street and Turl Street, the Mitre was founded in 1300, and from the seventeenth to the early nineteenth century was a major coaching inn. Its present buildings date from *c.* 1630 with some later additions. Although still called a hotel, it now functions only as a restaurant. In 1926 its stables were converted into a separate bar. The Mitre was one of the places where the *Inklings met during the Second World War.

Old Ashmolean. Now the Museum of the History of Science, the Old Ashmolean was built in 1679–83, probably to the design of Oxford master mason Thomas Wood, to house a collection of natural curiosities inherited by Elias Ashmole as well as a scientific lecture room and a chemical laboratory. Much of the Ashmole collection was transferred to the University Galleries (the Ashmolean Museum; see *Taylor Institution, below) in Beaumont Street at the end of the nineteenth century. The *Oxford English Dictionary* editorial offices were located in the Old Ashmolean when Tolkien was on the *OED* staff (1919–20).

Pembroke College. Pembroke College, founded in 1624 by King James I and named after the then Chancellor of the University, William Herbert, third Earl of Pembroke, lies to the west of St Aldgate's. Most of its buildings date from the nineteenth or twentieth centuries; its few earlier buildings have been mostly remodelled. Tolkien became a non-stipendiary Professorial Fellow of Pembroke in 1926. In that year the recommendations of the Royal Commission on Oxford and Cambridge (Asquith Commission) came into force, by which (*inter alia*) each professor was made *ex officio* a fellow and member of the governing body of a college; the Rawlinson and Bosworth Professorship was thus attached to Pembroke, in fact imposed upon the college, and in these circumstances Tolkien seems to have felt that he was not entirely welcome. Also he found the atmosphere at Pembroke rigid and formal: when he moved to Merton College in 1945 he commented to his son *Christopher that dining at Merton 'if agreeably informal is rather shocking to one trained in the severer ceremonies and strict precedence of mediaeval Pembroke' (*Letters*, p. 117). Even so, Tolkien attended over half of the College meetings while he was attached to Pembroke, an average of seven per year.

In the *Pembroke Record* for 1966–7 *R.B. McCallum noted that in 1925 the College consisted of the Master, a professional full-time Bursar, three teaching Fellows, and about 125 undergraduates. Pembroke was one of the smaller colleges at Oxford, and one of the poorest. But it kept a good table, the menu being rather old English in its flavour, and our port was, and remains, the best in Oxford. On the undergraduate side Pembroke was known for a remarkably strong beer. . . . The Fellows after some time passed a limiting order which reduced the quantity anyone could have at one time in Hall. Professor Tolkien, in a minority of one, protested against this enactment, alluding derisively to the continued potations of our very formidable port in the Senior Common Room. . . . ['Pembroke 1925–1967', *Pembroke Record*, pp. 14–15]

Tolkien seems to have dined regularly at Pembroke, usually on Thursdays, and occasionally entertained guests.

He gave some of his classes at Pembroke, and seems to have hosted at the College some meetings of committees set up by the English Faculty Board. During the Second World War Pembroke was partly taken over by the Army and the Ministry of Agriculture. 'At lunch one day Ronald reported that a notice on the College Lodge now read: PESTS: FIRST FLOOR' (*The Tolkien Family Album*, p. 71).

Even after he became *Merton Professor of English Language and Literature in 1945 Tolkien continued to be an honorary member of the Senior Common Room at Pembroke and occasionally dined there. The College announced his election as an Honorary Fellow in March 1972.

Randolph Hotel. Oxford's largest and most prestigious hotel, the Randolph is on the corner of Magdalen and Beaumont streets. It was designed by William Wilkinson in the Victorian Gothic style and opened to the public in 1866. On 1 June 1912 Tolkien enjoyed a nine-course dinner in the hotel as a member of the Apolaustics (*Societies and clubs). In late July 1924 he dined there with *George S. Gordon and three visitors from Canada. On 20 January 1965 he waited in the hotel foyer for Denys Gueroult before being interviewed by him for the BBC.

St Aloysius, Church of. A Roman Catholic church at 25 Woodstock Road, designed by Joseph Hansom for the Jesuits and completed in 1875. St Aloysius was one of the churches that Tolkien attended while an undergraduate, and while living in Northmoor Road from 1926 to 1947. His eldest son, John, a Roman Catholic priest, said his first Mass in the church in February 1946.

St Anthony of Padua, Church of. A Roman Catholic church at 115 Headley Way, Headington, built in 1960 after a hall in Jack Straw's Lane, in which Mass was held, became inadequate for the numbers attending. Tolkien was a parishioner both while he lived in Sandfield Road (until 1968) and after his return to Oxford in 1971. He was driven by taxi to St Anthony's from Merton Street every Sunday. On 6 September 1973 a Requiem Mass was held for him at St Anthony's, conducted by his son *John, assisted by *Robert Murray and the parish priest Monsignor Wilfrid Doran.

St Gregory and St Augustine, Church of. A Roman Catholic church at 322 Woodstock Road, designed by Ernest Newton in 1912. Tolkien sometimes attended this church while living in Northmoor Road. He had a long and close relationship with the parish priest, *Father Douglas Carter. Tolkien's eldest son, *John, was ordained a priest in the church in February 1946.

Sheldonian Theatre. The Sheldonian, on the south side of Broad Street, was designed by Sir Christopher Wren and built in 1664–7 at the expense of Gilbert Sheldon, Warden of All Souls (later Archbishop of Canterbury). It provides a venue for various University ceremonies, including meetings of Convocation and, in June, Encaenia when honorary degrees are presented and speeches are made in Latin. Tolkien sat his English Honour School examinations in the Sheldonian in June 1915, as the Examination Schools had been commandeered, and received his B.A. there on 16 March 1916. An honorary Doctorate of Letters was conferred on Tolkien himself in the Sheldonian on 3 June 1972.

Taylor Institution. The Taylor Institution or 'Taylorian' at the corner of Beaumont Street and St Giles' is the centre for the study of modern European languages and literatures at Oxford, established with a bequest from the architect Sir Robert Taylor. Its building was designed by Charles Robert Cockerell and constructed in 1841–4, originally to house both the Taylor Institution and the University Galleries; the latter were enlarged at the end of the nineteenth century and became the Ashmolean Museum. An extension to the Taylorian along St Giles' was completed in 1938.

As an undergraduate Tolkien attended lectures at the Taylor Institution, in particular those by *Joseph Wright on Gothic and on Greek and Latin, and by *W.A. Craigie on Scandinavian Philology and Old Icelandic. Two series of Tolkien's own lectures were delivered there in Hilary Term 1932, and during the Second World War, when the Examination Schools were commandeered as a military hospital, English Faculty lectures moved to the Taylorian along with most of the English Faculty Library.

Trinity College. This college with a narrow entrance in Broad Street and another in Parks Road was founded by Sir Thomas Pope in 1555. Some fifteenth-century buildings survive from the earlier Durham College which stood on the same site, but most of the present buildings are from later times. Two of Tolkien's sons, *Michael and *Christopher, were undergraduates at Trinity, in each case interrupted by service in the Second World War. Christopher returned as a postgraduate to work on a B.Litt. *Rayner Unwin was stationed at Trinity College as a Naval Cadet for six months in 1944, and returned as an undergraduate. When Tolkien heard from *Stanley Unwin of Rayner's arrival in 1944 he asked if a visit would be welcome. Rayner later recalled: 'He did roll into my room at Trinity. I was somewhat abashed: a Professor was a revered figure in Oxford in those days. But Tolkien was considerate and quite prepared to do most of the talking. The difficulty was to follow the thread of his conversation' (*George Allen and Unwin: A Remembrancer* (1999), pp. 87–8). Austin Farrer, Fellow and Chaplain of Trinity College 1935–60, and his wife *Katharine were friends of the Tolkien family.

University Museum. Housed in a Gothic Revival building designed by Benjamin Woodward under the influence of John Ruskin and constructed in Parks Road in 1855–60, the Museum preserves the University's collections of zoological, entomological, mineralogical, and geological specimens. There, on 1 January 1938, Tolkien gave a lecture on dragons, one of a series of Christmas lectures for children sponsored by the Museum.

University Parks. An extensive area to the north of central Oxford, bounded to the east by the River Cherwell. Tolkien drilled in the Parks as an undergraduate member of the Officer Training Corps. In 1992 two trees were planted in the Parks to mark the centenary of his birth, a silver-leaved maple and a false acacia, chosen to represent Telperion and Laurelin, the Two Trees of Valinor in Tolkien's mythology.

The White Horse. A public house at 52 Broad Street, next to Blackwell's Bookshop. A pub has stood on this site since at least 1591, and has been called 'White Horse' since at least 1750. Although the interior is old, the façade was rebuilt in 1951. Tolkien met *C.S. Lewis, his brother Warren (*W.H. Lewis), and *Charles Williams at the White Horse at least twice in 1944.

Wolvercote Cemetery. Originally a village to the north-west of Oxford, Wolvercote was absorbed into the expanding city in 1929. Here Tolkien and his wife *Edith are buried, in the area reserved for Roman Catholics on the western side of the Corporation cemetery. Their grave is marked by a grey granite stone inscribed, at Tolkien's instruction, 'Edith Mary Tolkien, Lúthien, 1889–1971' and 'John Ronald Reuel Tolkien, Beren, 1892–1973', after characters in his mythology. Their son *John is buried nearby. Tolkien visited Edith's grave every Sunday after attending Mass in Headington.

Worcester College. Worcester College was established by royal charter in 1714 and built slowly from 1720 onward, on the site and incorporating parts of the former Gloucester College for Benedictine monks (founded 1283) and its successor, Gloucester Hall. Parts of the medieval buildings survive. On 14 February 1938 Tolkien read *Farmer Giles of Ham* to members of the Lovelace Society, an essay club at Worcester College. *C.H. Wilkinson, Dean of Worcester College, later urged Tolkien to publish the story, and was made its dedicatee.

PLACES NEAR OXFORD

The county of **Oxfordshire** in central southern England is bounded by Buckinghamshire, *Berkshire, Gloucestershire, Warwickshire, and Northamptonshire. After their move to Oxford in 1926 Tolkien, his wife *Edith, and their children made many excursions into the surrounding countryside, especially after Tolkien purchased a car in 1932: Humphrey Carpenter mentions 'the drives on autumn afternoons to the villages east of Oxford, to Worminghall or Brill or Charlton-on-Otmoor, or west into Berkshire and up White Horse Hill to see the ancient long-barrow known as Wayland's Smithy' (*Biography*, p. 160). **Worminghall** is a village in Buckinghamshire a few miles east of Oxford. *John and *Priscilla Tolkien recalled the excitement one year when they found a rare bee orchid in the countryside near Worminghall. The village also figures in *Farmer Giles of Ham*. **Brill**, a hilltop village about twelve miles north-east of Oxford, is appropriately if doubly named: *Brill* is derived from Welsh *bree* ('hill') and English *hill*; see T.A. Shippey, *The Road to Middle-earth* (1982; rev. edn. 1992), p. 99, and compare *Bree* in *The Lord of the Rings*. A mile or so further east is Wotton Underwood, one of several Wottons or Woottons (from the Old English for 'homestead' or 'village in or by a wood') in Oxfordshire, whose name is echoed in the setting of *Smith of Wootton Major*. **Charlton-on-Otmoor** is a village about eight miles north-east of Oxford, with a fine Gothic church.

The Tolkien family also enjoyed punting on the **Cherwell**, which was not far from their home in Northmoor Road, 'down past the Parks to Magdalen Bridge, or better still . . . up-river towards **Water Eaton** and Islip [see below] where a picnic tea could be spread on a bank' (Humphrey Carpenter, *Biography*, p. 160). The river winds along the eastern boundary of the University Parks and through the grounds of Magdalen College until it joins the **Isis** (Thames) to the south of Christ Church Meadow. The family also went on 'walks across the fields to **Wood Eaton** [north of Oxford] to look for butterflies . . . walks when their father seemed to have a boundless store of knowledge about trees and plants' (*Biography*, p. 160).

John and Priscilla Tolkien note in *The Tolkien Family Album* that 'celebratory visits were sometimes made to take tea at country inns, like The Roof Tree at Woodstock (now long since gone), The White Hart at Dorchester (now a very grand restaurant) and The George at Sandford-on-Thames' (p. 63). **Woodstock** is about eight miles north-west of Oxford. Its royal manor built by Henry I no longer exists, but the king's deer park is part of the grounds of Blenheim Palace. *Chaucer's House in Woodstock is said to have belonged to the poet's son. Tolkien stayed at The Bear in Woodstock in April 1946 for about ten days with his son *Christopher while Edith was away. On 2 April *W.H. Lewis and *R.E. Havard joined them there for lunch, and on 11 April there was an *Inklings dinner and meeting at The Bear. **Dorchester** is about ten miles south of Oxford, once a Roman station and an important Anglo-Saxon town, at times the cathedral city of Wessex or Mercia. The Augustinians established a house here in 1140, and their fine church, with parts built from the twelfth to the fourteenth century, still survives. **Sandford-on-Thames** is just beyond the southern edge of Oxford, along the towpath of the river below **Iffley**. In the second half of October 1911, while he was an undergraduate, Tolkien wrote a poem, *From Iffley* (*From the Many-Willow'd Margin of the Immemorial Thames*), describing Oxford as seen from the river at that village.

Before the Second World War Tolkien also often visited **Deddington**, about sixteen miles north of Oxford. On 14 December 1956 he made a speech at the dedication of the new town library, and was entertained to tea by the Domestic Science Department in the local secondary school.

Several places in Oxfordshire are mentioned or alluded to in *Farmer Giles of Ham* and its projected sequel, including Islip, Oakley, Otmoor, the Rollright Stones (the Standing Stones), Thame, and Worminghall. **Islip** is a village seven miles north of Oxford, the birthplace of Edward the Confessor. **Oakley** is a small village about five miles north-east of Oxford, originally called Quercetum; a church was first recorded in Oakley in 1142. In *Farmer Giles of Ham* the parson of Oakley is eaten by the dragon Chrysophylax. **Otmoor** is a wild moorland east of the city, one of the boundaries of Giles' 'Little Kingdom'. It was once a great marshy area, and is so described by Tolkien in notes for the sequel to *Farmer Giles*. The **Rollright Stones** are a prehistoric monument about twenty-four miles north-east of Oxford on the Warwickshire border, near the village of Little Rollright: they consist of a small stone circle about 100 feet in diameter, with a large isolated 'King's Stone' probably dating from the early Bronze Age, about 1500 BC. A group of five additional large stones about a quarter of a mile distant, known as 'The Whispering Knights', is probably the remains of a late Stone Age long barrow built *c.* 2000 BC. **Thame** is an old market town thirteen miles east of Oxford, named for the River Thame, which flows into the Thames. Despite its spelling, *Thame* is pronounced 'Tame'. In *Farmer Giles of Ham* Tolkien pretends that the name derives from a conflation of its 'original' name *Ham* and Giles' titles 'Lord of Ham' and 'Lord of the Tame Worm'. **Worminghall** has been mentioned already; its name, pronounced 'wunnle', figures in *Farmer Giles of Ham* as that of the hall built by the twelve Draconarii or Wormwardens on the spot where Giles first met the dragon (or worm, from Old English *wyrm* 'serpent'). The true if more prosaic origin of *Worminghall*, according to Eilart Ekwall, *Concise Oxford Dictionary of Place-names* (1960), may be 'Wyrma's halh' (Old English *halh* or *healh*, 'nook, recess').

In later years Tolkien mourned the destruction of much of the 'Little Kingdom' – that is, the countryside around Oxford. In ?March 1945 he wrote to *Stanley Unwin: 'The heart has gone out of the Little Kingdom, and the woods and plains are aerodromes and bomb-practice targets' (*Letters*, p. 113).

Tolkien also associated Tom Bombadil, of *The Adventures of Tom Bombadil* and *The Lord of the Rings*, partly with Oxfordshire. On 16 December 1937, in a letter to Stanley Unwin, he called Tom Bombadil 'the spirit of the (vanishing) Oxford and Berkshire countryside'; and on 25 June 1962 he wrote to *Pauline

Baynes, who was to illustrate *The Adventures of Tom Bombadil and Other Verses from the Red Book*, that 'one might say that the "landscape" envisaged is southern English, and in particular South Oxfordshire and Berkshire' (quoted in Sotheby's, *Valuable Printed Books and Manuscripts*, London, 13 December 2001, p. 260).

For several years after the Second World War Michael Tolkien was a master at the Oratory School at **Woodcote** in southern Oxfordshire. At times in July and early August 1948, and from 14 August to 14 September of that year, Tolkien went into 'retreat' at Michael's home, then Payables Farm in Woodcote, where he 'succeeded at last in bringing the "Lord of the Rings" to a successful conclusion' (letter to Hugh Brogan, 31 October 1948, *Letters*, p. 131). Michael and his family later moved to a house on the School grounds. On 29 August 1952 Tolkien wrote to *Rayner Unwin: 'I am now going to devote some days to correcting [*The Lord of the Rings*] finally. For this purpose, I am retiring tomorrow from the noise and stench of Holywell [see above, Tolkien's Oxford homes] to my son's cottage on Chilton-top while he is away with his children: Chapel Cottage, the Oratory School, Woodcote, near Reading' (Tolkien-George Allen & Unwin archive, HarperCollins). In a letter to his grandson, Michael George, on 24 September 1952 Tolkien wrote: 'I enjoyed staying in your house; and I used your desk' (British Library MS Add. 71657).

Oxford, University of. The University of Oxford was of paramount importance in Tolkien's life, with only brief interruptions, from his days as an undergraduate at Exeter College until his death. Colleges and other features of the University (and of the city of Oxford) are considered in this volume under *Oxford and environs. The following notes on the University, its institutions and administration, though expressed usually in the present tense (to harmonize with quotations from contemporary sources), are intended to be generally applicable to Oxford as it was when Tolkien was an undergraduate or professor, and do not necessarily take account of reforms and changes made since his retirement in 1959.

HISTORY

The origins of the University of Oxford can be traced to the late twelfth century, when groups of scholars began to gather in Oxford around masters who lectured on Canon and Roman Law, Liberal Arts, and Theology. Some scholars lived in a house or 'academic hall' hired by the master. The young university received royal support and 'prospered, gradually gaining a large measure of independence under a Chancellor elected by the masters, whose interests were represented by the Proctors and whose collective decisions were made known in Convocation' (*The Encyclopædia of Oxford*, ed. Christopher Hibbert (1988), p. 471). During the thirteenth century the first colleges were founded, including University (1249), Balliol (1263), Merton (1264), and Exeter (1314). These gradually replaced the less organized 'academic halls'. The Reformation brought many changes, including the confiscation of the property of some Oxford institutions linked to religious communities such as the Dominicans, Franciscans, Carmelites, and Benedictines, as well as changes in curriculum. By the seventeenth century most students belonged to a college, and a smaller number to the few remaining academic halls; but the University continued to teach and examine.

From the end of the eighteenth century various reforms have been made, often as a result of special commissions intended to make the organization of the University and the colleges more democratic and to abolish vested interests; to raise academic standards and make the syllabi of the various schools more appropriate to national needs; and to broaden the student body by removing restrictions by religion or gender, and providing financial assistance for those whose families could not afford the cost of a university education. Much reform has also been directed at ensuring the proper use of the colleges' income from property and endowments, and strengthening the role of the professoriate, both as a teaching body and in the government of the University.

From 1874 *fellows* – elected senior members of a college – were allowed to marry, and many became only nominally resident. During the second half of the nineteenth century women students were admitted to lectures and the first women's colleges were founded: Lady Margaret Hall and Somerville, both in 1879. Although women students were allowed to sit some University examinations in 1884, and from 1894 even the B.A. final examination, it was not until 1920 that they were allowed to matriculate, become full members of the University, and receive degrees.

Oxford (like *Cambridge) differs from other British (and American) universities in that its colleges, established from the medieval period onwards, have remained largely independent self-governing bodies within the University, and 'membership in [the University] is acquired and retained only through membership in a College, Hall or other recognized society, which is itself a federated member of the University' (L.A. Crosby, 'The Organization of the University and Colleges', *Oxford of Today: A Manual for Prospective Rhodes Scholars* (1927), p. 29). The colleges have charitable status and elect their own (often resident) fellows, who are responsible for the administration of the college and of its property. When Tolkien went up to Oxford in 1911 there were twenty-five colleges, varying in size and wealth. By the time he retired in 1959 there were twenty-nine, but three of the additions (St Edmund Hall, St Anne's, and St Peter's) had existed in other guises prior to 1911. After the Second World War the number of undergraduates at Oxford, and of graduates reading for higher degrees, increased dramatically, many of them from less privileged backgrounds as a result of the introduction of state aid for higher education.

The *University* is responsible for various functions which are distinct from those of the colleges:

First, to examine and to grant degrees, and for this purpose to lay down courses, syllabuses, and regulations, and to exercise a general supervision over the lectures and other methods of study. Second, to provide, through its professors and other teachers, its scientific departments and special research institutes, such teaching and guidance as the colleges cannot or do not customarily offer. Third, to maintain discipline and order, to represent the assembly of colleges in relation to outside authorities or persons, to collect and distribute central finances, to extend the activities of the University beyond its local habitation, and to lay down the general conditions under which colleges and halls may be created, and they and their members conduct their life. Fourth, to create and maintain such institutions as libraries, laboratories, museums, parks, printing presses, and so on, which it would be wasteful or otherwise improper for the several colleges to maintain. [J.L. Brierly and H.V. Hodson, 'The Constitution of the University', *Handbook to the University of Oxford* (1933), p. 92]

The *colleges*, in contrast, are self-governing bodies with charitable status, owning their own buildings. Some have substantial endowments. In general, the governing body of a college

is composed of Fellows, who, if they are not administrators such as bursars, are statutorily required to teach or to research. Most of the tutors and lecturers in a college will be Fellows, and so will the professors attached to the college. The chairman of the governing body is the Head of the College (Master, President, Warden, Principal, Provost, Rector) elected by the Fellows to hold office until he reaches the statutory retiring age. . . . The Fellows form a close corporation, save for the appointment of professors, having otherwise the independent and unchallenged right to choose new Fellows within the bounds set by their statutes. The Fellows are nowadays usually elected for a term of years, but . . . they are commonly re-elected. . . .

The colleges are entirely responsible for discipline within their walls. . . . The colleges also possess the extremely important privilege of admission to the University. No candidate can be matriculated if he is not sponsored by a college, while the University accepts without veto all those put forward by the colleges, subject to the condition that candidates for matriculation . . . must have passed or be exempt from Responsions, the University entrance examination. [Brierly and Hodson, pp. 97–8]

In Tolkien's day as now, colleges played a major role in the teaching of undergraduates, and also provided rooms for their students, who were usually resident for most of their time at Oxford, moving in their third or fourth year into outside lodgings or 'digs'. College manservants, known as *scouts*, looked after the undergraduates and other residents, performing services such as laying fires, bringing breakfast and lunch and washing up afterwards, and making beds. When Tolkien returned to Merton College in 1972 *Charlie Carr and his wife performed many of these duties for him. There were strict rules governing behaviour, in particular the time in the evening by which undergraduates had to be within college, the only official entrance to which was through the *Porter's lodge*.

UNIVERSITY INSTITUTIONS AND OFFICIALS

The University legislative body known as **Convocation** consists of all recipients of the degrees of Master of Arts, Doctor of Divinity, Doctor of Medicine, or Doctor of Civil Law whose names are on the college books – thousands all told. Unless the business at hand is controversial, however, only a few resident members of the University attend meetings of Convocation, and almost all of the functions of that body have passed over time to *Congregation*. Notable exceptions are the responsibilities to elect the *Chancellor* and the Professor of Poetry, and to consider statutes, and decrees containing a preamble, which have passed Congregation with a majority of less than two-thirds.

From 1913 voting rights in **Congregation** were restricted to academic residents, so that this body includes the teaching and administrative staff of the University and colleges, rather than past graduates in other occupations who had proved unsympathetic to various academic reforms. 'Every enactment, whether general or particular, and most appointments to administrative offices, have to be approved by Congregation; reports and accounts are submitted to it; it elects members to the chief financial and executive committees of the University, and in particular it elects eighteen members to the Hebdomadal Council [see below], which is, roughly speaking, the Cabinet of this Parliament' (Brierly and Hodson, p. 80). The initiation of a statute or a decree is the province of the *Hebdomadal Council*, a member of which introduces the measure to Congregation.

A statute always, and occasionally ... a decree, contains a preamble stating shortly the principle of the measure. The preamble is submitted separately to the House [Congregation]; if it is passed the enacting clauses are submitted later. The clauses of a statute, but not those of a decree, may be amended by the House. ...

Congregation elects eighteen of the twenty-three members of the [Hebdomadal] Council, and three of the twelve Curators of the [University] Chest; its approval is required for the election of the three chief university officers, the Registrar, the Secretary of the Faculties, and the Secretary to the Curators of the Chest. Congregation also has power, which it seldom exercises, to address questions to such university boards of curators and other bodies as are compelled to present annual reports to it, and it is required to approve the annual financial statement prepared by the Curators of the Chest. [Brierly and Hodson, pp. 83–4]

The **Hebdomadal Council** 'proposes legislation for Congregation and in general constitutes the University cabinet, being responsible for the administration of the University and for the management of its finances and property' (Hibbert, p. 169). During the time that Tolkien taught at Oxford the membership of the Hebdomadal Council was composed of the Chancellor (though he did not attend meetings), the *Vice-Chancellor*, two *Proctors*, either the previous Vice-Chancellor for the year following his vacation of office, or the future Vice-Chancellor, and eighteen members elected by Congregation, six every two years.

> The business of [the Hebdomadal] Council covers the whole field of university affairs, and varies from trivial matters such as the terms of admission to the University of some particular student to vital questions of principle. It is largely organized by means of *ad hoc* or standing committees, which investigate each question in detail and report to the Council for decision. Besides its key power of legislative initiation, the Council has valuable rights of appointment to the various committees, including boards of electors to university teaching posts, and it also nominates the Registrar, subject to the approval of Congregation. [Brierly and Hodson, p. 85]

The handling of University finances was one of the duties of the Vice-Chancellor until 1868, when it was given over to a committee, the **Curators of the University Chest**. The University Chest derives its name from an actual chest in which University money was kept secure in medieval times. The Curators

> are the Vice-Chancellor and the Proctors, two nominees of the Chancellor . . . , a member of Convocation elected by [the Hebdomadal] Council, three members of Council, and three members of Congregation elected by those bodies. . . .
>
> The Curators of the Chest collect the revenues and pay the administrative expenses of the University; they have charge of its public buildings, estates, and other property, except whatever is specially provided for. They advise Council and other bodies on financial matters and prepare financial statements, returns, and reports. . . . An application by some university body for specific expenditure is made in the first place to the Hebdomadal Council, but has to be referred to the Curators of the Chest, whose sanction is likewise necessary for schemes contemplated by the Council itself. The Curators also have to prepare for Council an annual budget forecast. They appoint their Secretary, subject to the approval of Congregation. [Brierly and Hodson, p. 86]

The **General Board of the Faculties** was formed in 1912 and 'later became the main forum for coordinating academic policy' (Janet Howarth, 'The Self-Governing University', *The History of the University of Oxford, Vol. VII*:

Nineteenth-Century Oxford, Part 2 (2000), p. 600). The General Board took over from the Hebdomadal Council its 'functions in drafting curriculum changes and also the administration of the C[ommon] U[niversity] F[und]' (Howarth, p. 608). Its composition was adjusted at various times; it always included the Vice-Chancellor and the Proctors, but the number elected by the several Faculty boards and faculties as a whole, and by the Hebdomadal Council, has varied. In 1933 the other members were 'two members of [the Hebdomadal] Council elected by Council, one member of Convocation elected by Council subject to the approval of Congregation, three persons elected by the Faculties of Science (voting together), and six by the Faculties of the Humanities (voting together) in either case from among their own members. Elected members hold office for three years' (Brierly and Hodson, p. 90).

'As one of its chief functions, the General Board is charged with the co-ordination and supervision of the work of the several Boards of Faculties' (Hibbert, p. 152). It

> exercises a general advisory supervision over the lecture lists. . . . It receives and makes proposals for the provision of facilities for advanced work and research, and for the maintenance of an adequate staff in all subjects; and it frames statutes and decrees on these matters for consideration by [the Hebdomadal] Council and the University. The Statutes lay upon the General Board certain further special duties in the same connexion, including the transmission to Council of any reports of the Boards of Faculties, with comments and recommendations, the appointment of most University readers, the advising of Council upon the regulations concerning the salaries of teachers, laboratory finances, duties of professors, &c.; and it is comprehensively authorized 'to exercise a general supervision over the studies and examinations of the University'. [Brierly and Hodson, p. 90]

Tolkien served as an elected member of the General Board in 1929–32 and 1938–44. During 1944–7 he was on the Board not as an elected member, but on the nomination of the Vice-Chancellor and the Proctors, presumably because of the difficult circumstances during the Second World War and the postwar period.

When Tolkien returned to Oxford from *Leeds in 1925 there were eight *faculties* in the University. In 1926 English Language and Literature, previously part of Medieval and Modern Languages and Literature, including English, became a separate ninth Faculty with its own executive Faculty Board. By 1945 there were fourteen faculties at Oxford. All teachers of the subjects of a Faculty were considered members of that body, regardless of individual position or rank.

The *faculty boards* were required to meet at least once each term. The membership in 1925 comprised an equal number who served *ex officio* (professors and most readers) and members elected by the Faculty; the board could also co-opt members. Elected members served two-year terms but could usually be re-elected twice. The 1945 statutes of Oxford lists the *ex officio* members of the **English Faculty Board** as the Rawlinson and Bosworth Professor of Anglo-Saxon, the Merton Professor of English Literature, the Merton Professor of English Language and Literature, the Professor of Poetry (though he rarely if ever attended), the Goldsmith's Reader in English, the Vigfússon Reader in Icelandic Literature and Antiquities, and, by a decree in 1931, Dr C.T. Onions as long as he held the post of University Reader in English Philology.

The responsibilities of the English Faculty Board (as appropriate for the *Oxford English School) were defined in the 1945 statutes as the supervision, studies, and examinations on which it reported to and advised the General Board of Faculties; the preparing of lecture lists; receiving and considering reports and representations from the Faculty and boards of examiners; presenting an annual report on its work in the previous year to the General Board of Faculties; appointing University Lecturers, and recommending to the General Board appointments of such University Readers who were not elected; making recommendations to the General Board on subjects such as the payment of University Lecturers, and the provision of Faculty rooms and libraries; appointing members of various boards of electors to professorships; the general supervision of examinations, and suggesting changes in the regulations governing them (either major changes in syllabus or changes in some set book or books). On such questions the Board usually consulted the entire Faculty and had to submit proposals to the General Board for approval.

The nominal head of the University of Oxford is the **Chancellor**, but his duties are now mainly ceremonial. He presides over occasions such as *Encaenia*. His former, more powerful functions, are vested instead in the Vice-Chancellor. The Chancellor is elected for life by members of Convocation, and is not required to be resident in the University. Most of the chancellors during Tolkien's time at Oxford had studied there themselves, after which they pursued successful political careers.

The office of the **Vice-Chancellor** was originally, as the name suggests, that of a temporary deputy acting for the Chancellor when he was absent, but from the early sixteenth century he became the chief executive officer of the University. Although from the seventeenth century he was nominated annually by the Chancellor, by convention the office went to whichever head of the various colleges or halls had seniority of appointment. From 1923, following the report of the Asquith Commission, no Vice-Chancellor could hold office for more than three years. 'Besides being Chairman of the [Hebdomadal] Council, of the Board of Curators of the Chest, and of all the chief boards, committees, and delegacies, the Vice-Chancellor can veto a statute or decree, though he does so only on rare occasions in order to prevent legislative errors, and he has statutory powers to rule as to their interpretation' (Brierly and Hodson, p. 85).

*L.R. Farnell, who had been Rector of Exeter during part of Tolkien's time as an undergraduate, was Vice-Chancellor from 1920 to 1923. The Vice-Chancellor who took part in the 1925 election of Tolkien to the Rawlinson and

Bosworth Professorship of Anglo-Saxon was Joseph Wells, Warden of Wadham. From 1938 to 1941 the office was held by *George S. Gordon, President of Magdalen and Tolkien's former colleague at Leeds. The Vice-Chancellor at the time of Tolkien's election to the Merton chair was Sir Richard Livingstone, President of Corpus Christi.

The **Registrar of the University** is nominated by the Hebdomadal Council, subject to the approval of Congregation. He is 'secretary of [the Hebdomadal] Council, Congregation, and Convocation, and he has to keep, besides their minutes and other papers, a large number of registers and records, and see that the Statutes are regularly published. He is not secretary to the Vice-Chancellor, nor answerable to him, but to Council' (Brierly and Hodson, p. 93). The position is subject to a statutory retirement age, but otherwise permanent. He is

> aided by an assistant registrar appointed by Council after consultation with [the Registrar], and if the consent of Congregation is obtained he may also be provided from time to time, with other assistant officers. The assistant registrar is charged with attending such meetings as the Registrar, with the approval of the Vice-Chancellor, may direct, to prepare their business and to keep minutes of their proceedings. He is thus an important instrument for co-ordinating the work of the various committees. [Brierly and Hodson, p. 93]

Both the **Secretary of the Faculties** and the **Secretary to the Chest** are also permanent positions, subject only to a statutory retirement age, nominated by the General Board subject to the approval of Congregation. The Secretary of the Faculties is secretary both of the General Board and of the several boards of faculties, while the Secretary to the Chest keeps the University accounts as well as the records of the meetings of the Curators of the University Chest.

Two **Proctors**, elected annually in rotation by the colleges, sit on all University boards and committees. In Tolkien's time they still retained many of their disciplinary powers over students when the latter were found to be breaking rules outside of their colleges.

> The Proctors are primarily a co-ordinating link in University administration, and their main function is to serve as co-adjutors of the Vice-Chancellor on all the more important administrative boards, committees, and delegacies, besides representing the University at the conferment of degrees and on similar ceremonial occasions. But this side of their activities is not spectacular, and is of little interest to the undergraduate, who sees them only as ministers of admonition and correction. They regularly patrol the streets at night, accompanied by minions who have been known throughout the ages as 'bull-dogs'. . . . They wear a distinctive costume, and the effect of their presence in public places is cautionary rather than minatory; but it is their duty to challenge any member of the University, being *in statu pupillari* [in general, students

who have not yet received their Bachelor of Arts degree], who is failing to wear a gown [academic dress] after nightfall – or a violation of (a somewhat liberally interpreted) propriety. . . . The delinquent is required, with the utmost politeness, to call upon the Proctor at a stated time, when his defence is heard and judgement delivered. [Brierly and Hodson, p. 113]

Professorial *chairs* (professorships) were established at Oxford from the early sixteenth century. In Britain the term *Professor* specifically applies to the holder of a professorship; it is not used, as in the United States, to refer to any teacher at a university. At Oxford the teaching staff consists of University *Professors, readers, lecturers*, and *demonstrators*, and of college *fellows, tutors*, and *lecturers*. Professors 'are the principal means whereby the university, as distinct from the colleges that compose it, teaches [through lectures and classes] and directs study' (Brierly and Hodson, p. 90). Each professor is selected by a special board of *electors*,

composed, as a rule, of the Vice-Chancellor, the Head of the college to which the professorship is attached and another member appointed by that college, a person nominated by the Hebdomadal Council and one by every board of Faculty concerned, and occasionally one or two outside persons. The professors do not ordinarily give tutorial teaching though they may voluntarily open small seminar classes or informal discussions. Their statutory duties include original work by the professors themselves, and the general supervision of research and advanced work in their subjects or departments. Every professor must give to students in their studies by advice, informal instruction, examination or otherwise. [Brierly and Hodson, p. 91]

During the nineteenth century the number of professors at Oxford increased from twenty-one to fifty-four. Among reforms made in that century aimed at strengthening the University, from 1877 the colleges were required to make contributions out of their revenues to the Common University Fund for University purposes, including the support of existing professorships and the founding of new ones. From 1925, following the report of the Asquith Commission, the University also received a government grant. Other changes made as a result of the Asquith Commission were that from 1926 'every professor appointed by the university was to be found a place in a college and every tutor appointed by a college would . . . receive an appointment as a university lecturer' (John Prest, 'The Asquith Commission, 1919–1922', *The History of the University of Oxford, Vol. VIII: The Twentieth Century* (1994), p. 41). Some chairs were already attached to a particular college, but the Rawlinson and Bosworth Professorship of Anglo-Saxon held by Tolkien was not: it was assigned to Pembroke College. Also, professors, heads, and fellows of colleges now had to retire on reaching the statutory retirement age of sixty-five, but were to receive a pension.

Tolkien became the Rawlinson and Bosworth Professor of Anglo-Saxon in 1925, with the responsibility to 'lecture and give instruction on the Anglo-Saxon Language and Literature, and on the other old Germanic Languages, especially Gothic and Old Icelandic' (*Statuta Universitatis Oxoniensis* (1925), p. 117). At that time there were only two other chairs in the English School: the Merton Professorship of English Language and Literature, with responsibility for the History of the English Language, and the History of English Literature through the period of Chaucer, and the Merton Professor of English Literature, responsible for post-medieval literature. No more chairs were added in the School until the Goldsmith's Readership in English Language was converted into the Goldsmith's Chair of English Literature in 1948. The Professor of Poetry is also attached to the English School, but has minimal duties. Since Tolkien's retirement other chairs have been established, among them the J.R.R. Tolkien Professorship of English Literature and Language, in the field of Medieval English Literature and Language in the period 1100–1500.

Professors generally were required to give at least thirty-six lectures or classes in each year, though the statutes for 1925 state that the Rawlinson and Bosworth Professor had to 'lecture and give instruction for six hours in each week, and for a period not less in any Term than six weeks, nor less in the whole year than twenty-one weeks' (pp. 117–18), thus a minimum of 126 hours.

Next in importance after professors are **readers**, either elected by the University or appointed by the General Board to hold office for a specified number of years with the duty of lecturing and giving instruction. They are perhaps closest to the associate or assistant professors in American colleges and universities, positions which do not exist in Britain. In the Oxford English School during Tolkien's day there was a Goldsmith's Readership in English Language, until its conversion to a chair devoted to English Literature in 1948, when it was replaced by a new Readership in English Language; a Readership in English Philology from 1927 until *c.* 1950; the Vigfússon Readership in Ancient Icelandic Literature and Antiquities, from 1941; and the Readership in Textual Criticism from 1948.

Although professors, readers, fellows, and tutors usually give lectures, 'the separate boards of faculties have power to appoint to the status and title of university lecturers any recognized teachers in their faculties, as and when they may think fit, subject to the approval of the General Board and of Congregation' (Brierly and Hodson, p. 92). These **lecturerships** were another result of the report of the Asquith Commission in 1922. Since the Commission also wanted to make it possible for college tutors and other teachers to undertake 'specialized work of study and research in addition to their activities in College teaching, by freeing them from an excessive burden of teaching in term and from the necessity of seeking paid work in the vacation', the University used the Common University Fund to create fifty lecturerships 'for tutors who undertook to do specific research and limit their other commitments' (J.P.D. Dunbabin, 'Finance since 1914', *The History of the University of Oxford, Vol. VIII: The Twentieth Century* (1994), p. 652, partly quoting from the

Commission report). These lecturers remained college tutors, but restrictions were placed on the number of hours they could spend teaching. The scheme having proved very successful, the number of CUF lecturers was gradually increased. In 1949, when their number had more than doubled, the Vice-Chancellor proposed that 'all 286 "inter-collegiate lecturers"' should be included in the scheme, and he managed to persuade the University Grants Committee to provide state support on the ground that the public 'lecturing which was done in most Universities by persons employed by the University was, in Oxford, done by the College teachers' (quoted in Dunbabin, p. 653). This went into effect in January 1950.

The Faculty boards are responsible for scheduling the lectures given by both University and college teachers. 'Practically all lectures, even those held in college lecture rooms, are open to all members of the University without conditions or payment of special fees. . . . No record is kept of attendance, but an undergraduate is expected to attend such lectures as may be recommended by his tutor' (L.A. Crosby, 'The Oxford System of Education', *Oxford of Today* (1927), pp. 48–9). The most important form of study for the undergraduate, however, is the *tutorial*.

> Immediately on arrival in the University, each undergraduate is assigned by his College to a tutor . . . a Fellow, Tutor, or Lecturer of his or some other College, subject to whose guidance, the undergraduate will pursue his studies (or 'reading', in the Oxford phrase) during terms and vacations throughout his course at the University. The tutor directs the student's work, advises him to attend certain lectures, and to read certain books. One or twice weekly the student spends an hour or more in conference with the tutor; at which time he usually reads an essay or essays embodying the results of his reading since the last conference. The essay is followed by the tutor's comments and criticism, and an informal discussion, in which the tutor aims to assist the undergraduate in the analysis and correct statement of the matter involved. [Crosby, pp. 49–50]

MISCELLANEOUS

Tolkien entered Exeter College as an undergraduate by virtue of having earned an Open Classical Exhibition offered by that college. (An *exhibition* is less prestigious, and usually of less value, than a *scholarship*.) But a student could not *matriculate*, or enrol in the University, without first having passed **Responsions**, an entrance examination in four subjects, or having already obtained (as had Tolkien) School Certificate passes in relevant subjects. The choice of these varied, but in earlier years Greek and Latin were essential. Responsions was converted into a University entrance examination in 1926. Later a student had to pass the **First Public Examination**, either **Honour Moderations** or **Pass Moderations** (with a choice of subjects), generally taken not earlier than the third term after matriculation, before continuing his studies. Until 1932 a student also had to pass an **Examination in Holy Scripture** ('Divvers Prelim'). Since Tolkien was entered to study *Literae Humaniores* ('more humane letters'), also called 'Greats' (i.e. Classics), he took Classical Honour Moderations, but had he intended to study English from the beginning he could have taken Pass Moderations. It was not until Michaelmas Term 1948 that a First Public Examination specifically for the English Honour School was enabled.

At the end of his time at Oxford the student took the **Second Public Examination**, or Final Examination, in one of a number of Honour Schools or in a Pass School. In Tolkien's time candidates were awarded first-, second- third- or fourth-class Honours.

The Oxford academic year begins with **Michaelmas Term** from early to mid-October through about the middle of December. Next, after a vacation of six weeks (Christmas vacation), is **Hilary Term** (sometimes called Lent Term), from around mid-January to mid-March. Finally, after another six-week (Easter) vacation, is **Trinity Term** (or Summer Term), from late April or the beginning of May until late June. Final Honours Examinations are taken at the end of Trinity Term of the student's final year at the school, followed after an interval by a public *viva voce* (oral) examination, or 'viva'. Between the end of Trinity Term and the beginning of Michaelmas Term is the 'long vacation' (or 'long vac'). The *Handbook to the University of Oxford* warns that although the year is thus divided almost equally between term and vacation, 'it is an essential part of the Oxford system that the undergraduate shall do a great deal of his reading in vacation, and anybody who relies solely on his work during term will certainly meet with disaster in his examinations' (Carleton Kemp Allen, 'College Life' (1933), p. 121).

As an undergraduate Tolkien would have been expected to wear **academic dress** – a black gown and cap – at lectures and during tutorials, in the presence of University officials, at ceremonies, and during examinations, as well as on other occasions. Later, as a Master of Arts, Tolkien wore 'a full-style black gown ... reaching below the calf ... with a full gathered yoke behind and closed sleeves with a crescent-shaped cut at the bottom and an opening at the elbow' with a hood 'made from black corded silk or art silk edged and lined with crimson or shot crimson silk or art silk' and a square cap (D.R. Venables and R.E. Clifford, *Academic Dress of the University of Oxford* (8th edn. 1998), p. 30). As an Honorary D.Litt. his full academic dress was 'a scarlet robe with bell-shaped sleeves, of which the body is made from scarlet cloth with facings and sleeves of grey silk' (p. 18). At examinations and formal occasions, men were required to wear *sub-fusc* clothing underneath the gown: a dark suit, socks, and footwear, and a white shirt, collar, and tie. When lecturing Tolkien wore his gown, but over ordinary clothes.

Technically **Encaenia** is a meeting of Convocation, held in the Sheldonian Theatre on the Wednesday of the ninth week in Trinity Term, which is presided over by the Chancellor and at which honorary degrees are conferred and prize compositions read. In the morning before the ceremony the Chancellor, those being honoured (the *honorands*), Doctors, Heads of colleges, and other University dignitaries in full academic dress are entertained in the college of the Vice-Chancellor to enjoy strawberries and champagne provided by the benefaction of Lord Crewe in the early eighteenth century. They then walk in procession to the Sheldonian. The honorands wait in the Divinity School, and after the Chancellor has opened the proceedings are escorted into the Theatre, where each is introduced by the Public Orator with a speech in Latin and admitted to his or her new degree. The Orator then delivers the Creweian Oration on events of the past year, and either he or the Professor of Poetry commemorate the University's benefactors. In the afternoon is an Encaenia garden party.

See further, *The Encyclopædia of Oxford*, ed. Christopher Hibbert (1988); *Handbook to the University of Oxford*, first published 1932; *The History of the University of Oxford, Vol. VII: Nineteenth-Century Oxford, Part 2*, ed. M.G. Brock and M.C. Curthoys (2000); *The History of the University of Oxford, Vol. VIII: The Twentieth Century*, ed. Brian Harrison (1994); and *Oxford of Today: A Manual for Prospective Rhodes Scholars*, ed. Laurence A. Crosby, Frank Aydelotte, and Alan C. Valentine (1927). See also *Examinations; *Libraries and archives; *Oxford English School; *Societies and clubs. The **Chronology** volume of the *Companion and Guide* illustrates by example the flow of the Oxford academic year and Tolkien's duties on the college and University levels.

Oxford English Dictionary. The *New English Dictionary on Historical Principles*, or *Oxford English Dictionary (OED)* to give it its later and more familiar title, traces the meaning and usage of English words from their earliest appearance and illustrates them with quotations. Work on it began in 1860, under Herbert Coleridge (1830–61) and F.J. Furnivall (1825–1910) successively, along lines suggested in 1857 by Richard Chenevix Trench, then the Dean of Westminster. Its most eminent editor, James A.H. Murray (1837–1915), succeeded Furnivall in 1873, and the first fascicle of the dictionary, *A–Ant*, was published at last in 1879. Murray was followed at his death by his associate *Henry Bradley, who was later joined by *William Craigie and *C.T. Onions. The dictionary proper was completed in 1928. This has been followed by supplements and by shorter and concise versions, as well as new editions in print and electronic form.

At the end of October or the beginning of November 1918, Tolkien returned to *Oxford following military service, not yet demobilized from the Army but authorized to seek civilian employment. Prospects of an academic appointment were poor; but within a short time, his former tutor in Old Icelandic, William Craigie, promised him work on the staff of the *OED*. Tolkien was placed, however, not under Craigie himself (who kept his staff small, the better to supervise) but as an assistant to Henry Bradley.

Salary records in the Oxford University Press archives suggest that Tolkien began work on the *OED* at or near the start of 1919, having settled with his family at 50 St John Street in late 1918. The offices of the *Dictionary* were only a short walk away, in the Old Ashmolean building in Broad Street. Within them was the Dictionary Room, a 'great dusty workshop, that brownest of brown studies', as Tolkien called it in his appreciation of Bradley after the latter's death. One of his earliest duties there was to take illustrative quotations in Old and Middle English submitted to the *Dictionary* by volunteer researchers, against which he would write the forms of words to be defined. Later he drafted dictionary entries themselves, detailing pronunciation, spelling, and etymology, writing definitions, and selecting and copy-editing quotations. His work was then examined and, as necessary, revised by Bradley.

Tolkien contributed to entries for words beginning with the letter *W*, such as *waggle, waistcoat, wallop, walnut, walrus, wampum, warm, wasp, weald, wild*, and *wold*. As Simon Winchester has said, *W* is 'reckoned an interesting letter – there are essentially no Greek or Latin derivatives that begin with *W*, and its words are generally taken, as Bradley put it, "from the oldest strata of the language"' (*The Meaning of Everything* (2003), p. 206). The original fascicles of the *OED* pertinent to Tolkien's work are *W–Wash* (published October 1921), *Wash–Wavy* (May 1923), *Wavy–Wezzon* (August 1926), *Whisking–Wilfulness* (November 1924), and *Wise–Wyzen* (April 1928). Peter M. Gilliver has determined, in his thorough 'At the Wordface: J.R.R. Tolkien's Work on the *Oxford English Dictionary*', *Proceedings of the J.R.R. Tolkien Centenary Conference 1992* (1995), that the first bundle of word-slips with which Tolkien was concerned was sent to press on 3 April 1919.

On the whole, Bradley was pleased with his assistant's work. He singled out *walnut, walrus*, and *wampum* in his introduction to the fascicle *W–Wash* as containing 'etymological facts or suggestions not given in other dictionaries'. And he wrote of Tolkien in support of the latter's application for the Rawlinson and Bosworth Professorship of Anglo-Saxon (succeeding Craigie): 'His work gives evidence of an unusually thorough mastery of Anglo-Saxon and of the facts and principles of the comparative grammar of the Germanic languages. Indeed, I have no hesitation in saying that I have never known a man of his age who was in these respects his equal' (**An Application for the Rawlinson and Bosworth Professorship of Anglo-Saxon in the University of Oxford by J.R.R. Tolkien, Professor of the English Language in the University of Leeds, June 25, 1925*). But Tolkien and his editor did not always agree. In a review of the *Whisking–Wilfulness* fascicle of the *Dictionary* for the **Year's Work in English Studies* for 1924, Tolkien noted that in the etymology of *wild* 'the connexion with **walþus* (*wold, weald*, forest) is rejected . . .' (p. 48). He had asserted this connection in his draft of the entry for *wild*, and would not be dissuaded.

While Tolkien's work for the *Oxford English Dictionary* lasted, it was a fruitful experience for one who loved language. He once said that he 'learned more in those two years than in any other equal period of my life' (quoted in *Biography*, p. 101) – although in fact, according to official records, it was a term of fewer than eighteen months. It must also have been a great relief to him, after years in the Army and months in military hospitals, to be again among people with similar interests, and doing something that he enjoyed: digging among the roots of words. But he did not earn enough from this work to support his family, and therefore accepted English students for tutoring (it was common for *OED* staff to function also within the University). Before long, evidently by the end of May 1920, he earned enough in tuition to give up his post at the *Dictionary*. By now, he was also writing the glossary, *A Middle English Vocabulary*, for *Kenneth Sisam's *Fourteenth Century Verse & Prose*.

In the course of his research for *A Middle English Vocabulary* Tolkien found uses of words antedating the earliest illustrative quotations given in the *OED*. He also suggested, for future addition to the *Dictionary*, at least a quotation from *Sylvie and Bruno* by Lewis Carroll, illustrating the word *smirkle*. These and other notes left by Tolkien, some in the working copies of the *OED* used by staff, have aided, or will someday aid, the lexicographers who prepare supplements to the *Dictionary*. In 1969–71, in correspondence with *R.W. Burchfield, Tolkien was concerned with the definition of *hobbit* to be published in the second supplement to the *OED*.

On 20 January 1922, at the University of *Leeds, Tolkien gave a lecture on the *Dictionary* to a joint meeting of the Yorkshire Dialect Society and the English Association (*Societies and clubs). The *Transactions of the Yorkshire Dialect Society* for January 1922 reported that 'the lecture was extraordinarily interesting, and the attendance of members of the Yorkshire Dialect Society was unaccountably poor. Members are not to be congratulated on missing this opportunity of hearing an account of the aims of the "N.E.D." by one who was until lately a distinguished member of its staff of philologists' (p. 5).

For comic effect in his story *Farmer Giles of Ham* (1949), Tolkien quoted the *Oxford English Dictionary* definition of *blunderbuss*, attributing it to the 'Four Wise Clerks of Oxenford'. The reference is presumed to be to the *OED* editors Murray, Bradley, Craigie, and Onions.

J.S. Ryan has noted in 'Lexical Impacts', *Amon Hen* 76 (November 1985) and 77 (January 1986), that numerous quotations from Tolkien's writings are used as illustrative examples in the *Supplement to the Oxford English Dictionary* (1972–1982), ed. R.W. Burchfield. Deirdre Greene has argued that Tolkien's predilection for historical lexicography influenced the plot structures and logic of *The Hobbit* and *The Lord of the Rings*: see her 'Tolkien's Dictionary Poetics: The Influence of the *OED*'s Defining Style on Tolkien's Fiction', *Proceedings of the J.R.R. Tolkien Centenary Conference 1992* (1995).

On Tolkien's work on the *OED*, and his passion for words reflected in his fiction, see further, Peter Gilliver, Jeremy Marshall, and Edmund Weiner, *The Ring of Words: Tolkien and the Oxford English Dictionary* (2006).

Oxford English Monographs. Oxford University Press series established in the 1930s, under the aegis of Faculty in the Oxford English School, for the publication of B.Litt. (today D.Phil.) theses of outstanding merit. The Press had earlier disdained the publishing of theses, considering them unprofitable. Tolkien served as a general editor from the beginning of the series through 1958, originally with *D. Nichol Smith and *C.S. Lewis, later with *F.P. Wilson and

*Helen Gardner. By 1954 he is referred to in correspondence as chief editor, though there is evidence that he acted in this capacity as early as 1938, when *Víga-Glúms Saga* was in press. Altogether he is named as a general editor in seven volumes, in order of publication:

Víga-Glúms Saga, ed. *(E.O.) G. Turville-Petre (1940), was originally a thesis produced under Tolkien's supervision. In this Turville-Petre wrote: 'It would be difficult to overestimate all that I owe to Professor Tolkien; his sympathy and encouragement have been constant and, throughout the work, I have had the benefit of his wide scholarship' (p. vi).

Elizabethan Acting by B.L. Joseph (1951) includes a brief acknowledgement to Tolkien, among others.

Þorgils saga ok Hafliða, ed. Ursula Brown (1952), thanks Tolkien and *Alistair Campbell for 'valuable criticism and advice' (p. vi). The chief guide of the original thesis was Gabriel Turville-Petre.

Sir Orfeo, ed. *A.J. Bliss (1954), records a debt to Tolkien, the editor's B.Litt. supervisor, 'whose penetrating scholarship is an inspiration to all who have worked with him' (p. vi).

The Peterborough Chronicle 1070–1154, ed. Cecily Clark (1958), includes no acknowledgement to Tolkien, but correspondence indicates that he was concerned with its publication.

The Old English Apollonius of Tyre, ed. Peter Goolden (1958), for which Tolkien wrote a brief prefatory note, includes thanks to Tolkien for suggesting 'revisions in presentation and style', though the 'prime mover of the work' was *C.L. Wrenn (p. vi).

Sonnets by William Alabaster, ed. G.M. Story and Helen Gardner (1959), includes no acknowledgement to Tolkien.

Oxford English School. A chair of Anglo-Saxon was established at the University of *Oxford as early as 1795; from 1873 English was among the subjects that could be taken in the lesser pass examination; from 1881 English Language and Literature was one of the special examinations for women; and in 1885 the Merton Professorship of English Language and Literature was created. It was not until 1894, however, that an English Final Honour School was established by statute. Several earlier attempts had failed, partly because of the competing interests of *Philology and Literature, resulting in different views as to what the School should teach. There was a deep feeling that the study of English Literature might be a 'soft' option compared to other subjects, and therefore Philology and Language studies, which would provide a more exacting discipline, should form a substantial part of the English syllabus. The statute that eventually established the English School laid down that only those who had already obtained Honours in another school, or had passed the First Public Examination (either Classical Honour Moderations or Pass Moderations) would be admitted. D.J. Palmer points out in *The Rise of English Studies* (1965) that this 'meant in effect that apart from the women candidates, the English School recruited largely from undergraduates who had passed Honour Moderations' (p. 112). This was still the case when Tolkien transferred to the Oxford English School after taking Honour Moderations in 1913.

The syllabus introduced in 1894 was intended to provide a balance between Language and Literature. All candidates were required to take papers on Old English Texts; Middle English Texts; *Chaucer and *Piers Plowman*; Shakespeare; Authors from 1700 to 1832; History of English Literature to 1800 (including criticism); History of the English Language; and (together) Gothic and unseen translations from Old and Middle English. Only two papers devoted to Special Subjects allowed any choice. The first Honour Examination was held in 1896. The committee that drafted the syllabus had hoped that at least some of the examination papers would cover both literary and linguistic matters (e.g. literary as well as linguistic aspects of *Beowulf*), but in most cases this did not happen. In 1898 History of English Literature to 1800 (including criticism) was replaced by two papers devoted to a general History of English Literature (including criticism) before and after 1700.

Palmer notes that the new school was dominated by philologists who did not adapt their teaching to the wider view encompassed by the syllabus, and for many years there was only one teacher on the Literature side, due to lack of support by the University and the colleges. It was not until the appointment of *Walter Raleigh in 1904 to a newly created Professorship of English Literature that there was any real development of the Literature side. Raleigh also introduced an important change in the syllabus which came into effect in 1908, and

> recognized the *de facto* division between 'literature' and 'language' created by the nature of the available teaching, and which therefore abandoned the original principle that literature and language should not be identified with modern and medieval periods respectively. Raleigh's notion . . . was that those who wished to specialize in either literature or language should be allowed to take separate papers. . . . [Palmer, p. 128]

In submitting proposals to the Board of Studies Raleigh and his colleague *A.S. Napier stated that 'the [Oxford English] School has to provide for the needs of two classes of students – those who are primarily students of language, and those who are primarily students of literature. Experience has shown that the existing scheme is too rigid, and does not allow sufficient freedom for the development of excellence in either branch of the subject' (quoted in Palmer, p. 129). Palmer calls this division 'a recognition of defeat so far as a genuine combination of "English Language and Literature" was concerned', and places the blame mainly on 'the failure of the philologists to treat medieval texts as literature . . . their neglect of literature after the age of Chaucer, and . . . the inadequate provision of teaching on the literature side' (pp. 129–30).

Four papers on *Beowulf* and Old English texts, *Sir Gawain and the Green Knight* and other Middle English texts, Chaucer, and Shakespeare remained compulsory. Otherwise students could choose to take papers devoted to Literature (with the exception of a compulsory paper on the History of the English

Language) or to Language (with the exception of a compulsory paper on the History of English Literature). With minor adjustments, this scheme was the one that Tolkien followed as an undergraduate.

To deal with the lack of suitable tuition provided by the colleges, a Committee of English Studies was formed, which put forward a proposal to establish a 'pool' of teachers who would provide adequate lectures, classes, and tutorials in return for the payment of a fee for each student of English by his college. Most colleges welcomed this offer, and the English Fund was established. During the years that Tolkien was an undergraduate, those lecturing and teaching in the English School included *H.F.C. Brett-Smith, lecturer and tutor in English; *W.A. Craigie, Taylorian Lecturer in Scandinavian Languages, for those who chose Scandinavian Philology as a special subject; *George S. Gordon, Fellow of Magdalen College; A.S. Napier, Merton Professor of English Language and Literature and Rawlinson Professor of Anglo-Saxon; *David Nichol Smith, Goldsmiths' Reader in English; Sir Walter Raleigh, Professor of English Literature, from 1914 attached to Merton College; *Percy Simpson, lecturer in English; Napier's assistant *Kenneth Sisam; and *Joseph Wright, Professor of Comparative Philology.

From its inception the English School had also been intended to foster graduate studies. It attracted a considerable number of B.Litt. students, and from 1917, when the degree was introduced, a smaller number of students working towards the D.Phil. David Nichol Smith defined the difference between the B.Litt. and the D.Phil. in his paper 'The Degree of Doctor of Philosophy' delivered to the Fourth Congress of the Universities of the British Empire in Edinburgh on 8 July 1931:

> All B.Litt. Probationers attend classes in such subjects as Elizabethan handwriting, the relation of manuscripts, the establishment of texts, the history of English editing of English Studies, bibliography, the resources of the Bodleian. In these classes they are instructed in the use of their tools, and after three terms' instruction they are examined. They have then to submit a specimen piece of prentice work – their dissertation. They have to pass this double test before they get the B.Litt. in English Literature.
>
> A very good man who has been placed in 1st Class in an Oxford Honour School, or who comes with high qualifications from another University, may start on his work for the D.Phil. in English without taking what we now regard as the preliminary degree, but he is well advised to attend the preliminary course of instruction. . . . The man who gains the B.Litt. is understood to be competent to research, the man who gains the D.Phil. has researched so successfully as to have made contributions to his subject which deserve to be made known to other scholars. [offprint of *Proceedings* of the Congress, in Oxford University Archives FA 4/5/2/1]

Napier died in 1916, but his successor to the Merton Professorship of English Language and Literature, another philologist, *Henry Cecil Wyld, did not take the chair until 1920. Also in 1920 *C.T. Onions was appointed to a new lecturership in English, and in 1927 became Reader in English Philology. The number of students in the English School increased greatly after the First World War (fifty men and fifty-two women took the Final Honour Examination in 1923, versus twelve men and twenty-five women in 1913), and gradually the colleges began to provide their own teachers in the discipline.

On his return to Oxford in 1925, after being elected to the Rawlinson and Bosworth Professorship of Anglo-Saxon, Tolkien found among his colleagues several who had taught him as an undergraduate. Over the years many of his own students also became colleagues, and by the time he retired in 1959 a considerable number of the English Faculty had studied under him at Oxford as undergraduates or had been supervised or examined by him for the B.Litt. or D.Phil.

In 1925 the English School was still part of the Faculty of Medieval and Modern Languages and Literature, but in Michaelmas Term 1926 became a separate Faculty, of English Language and Literature, with its own Board. One of the Board's first actions, in an attempt to improve the quality of the Language papers submitted in the Final Honour Examination, was to request a separate English First Public Examination. A committee which included Tolkien suggested that this should include papers on English History; Old English and Chaucer; Greek or Latin set books; books to be prescribed by the same Board; unprepared translation from not fewer than two nor more than three languages (Greek, Latin, French, German, Italian, Spanish). Although the request for a separate examination was refused, in 1930 a paper in Old English and one on English History and Literature from 1603 to 1688 were added to the existing Pass Moderations.

By then the division of the course of study into a Language side (which attracted about ten per cent of the students) and a Literature side was not working as well as had been hoped, and Tolkien was the leading force in working for a change in the syllabus which would provide a greater choice. He put forward various suggestions to this end to the English Faculty Board in February 1930, and promoted them in his article *The Oxford English School, published in the Oxford Magazine for 29 May 1930. In the latter he noted that 'owing to the accidents of history, the distinction between philology and literature is notoriously marked'. He thought the titles 'language' and 'literature' loosely used to define these were inaccurate, and 'A and B would be preferable'. He pointed out that

> in current use 'language', A, must, if one refers to what is studied under that head, mean (i) *anything* concerned with English letters before A.D. 1300 – whether literary, historical, critical or linguistic; and (ii) exclusively *one thing* after 1400, linguistic history. The fourteenth century remains an awkward moment in our national history. On the other hand,

'literature,' B, would appear to mean (i) a cursory, sometimes reluctant, notice of the first six hundred years of recorded English – so cursory in fact that it must perforce be either almost entirely linguistic or deplorably inaccurate; and (ii) a purely 'literary' – perhaps best defined as a 'consciously non-linguistic' – interest in the remaining centuries, or some of them. This is further modified by a required, but seldom achieved, knowledge of the outlines of the history of the English language during twelve centuries, an enormous field as intricate at least as the whole history of the literature, examined in one paper. . . .

The 'literature' student may learn a little Anglo-Saxon and Middle English, but it is precisely at the point of his linguistic effort that his literary effort is least or absent. He is not allowed by the regulations to take a paper in literature up to 1300, even if he wishes to. That is a 'language' subject. (On the other hand, a real study of the history of the modern language is [compulsory for] the 'language,' A, student, who is scarcely required to study any 'books' in the modern period.

The divergence of interests is such that no one person can be expected to deal adequately with both of the 'sub-schools'. [pp. 778–9]

Tolkien suggested for B that the literature of the nineteenth century should be replaced by 'a scholarly study of worthy Anglo-Saxon and Middle-English texts, with a paper of unseen translation, for the extracts and the meagre "philology"', though nineteenth-century literature might be an additional subject. For A he suggested that the history of the language from 1400 to 1900 be abandoned, pointing out that

> philology goes hand in hand with as full a study from all points of view of the old and mediæval periods as is possible in two years. The centre of the curriculum is actually Anglo-Saxon and parts of Middle English; while the place occupied by the additional cognate language or languages is probably increasing, and rightly so. Among the latter Old Icelandic is naturally and deservedly most prominent. [p. 779]

He admitted that few first-class Anglo-Saxon texts survive, and among the advantages of studying Old Icelandic was the language's 'philological value of an intimate relationship with English' and its 'literary and historical value of the highest rank' (p. 779). In support of Gothic, he said that it 'introduces its student to many diverse things, the textual history of the Gospels, Greek, the history of Italy, and of north-eastern Europe, and the background of Gothic legend and tradition which was a main source of the poetic inspiration of ancient England and the North' (pp. 779–80).

After discussion and negotiations during English Faculty Board meetings in 1931, significant changes were made in the syllabus, which was first examined in 1933. This allowed candidates more choice in the nine papers to be taken, with basically three main areas of study. Candidates who wished to do so could also take a tenth paper. Here we describe this syllabus in detail, since with minor changes it remained in force for most of Tolkien's working life at Oxford, and it expresses his ideas of what English studies should cover.

SYLLABUS

Course I was aimed at those whose interest was mainly in Medieval Philology, but also covered Literature in the period up to Chaucer. Students took papers on Old English Philology; Middle English Philology; Old English Texts – *Beowulf*, *The Fight at Finnesburg* (**Finn and Hengest*), *Deor's Lament*, and *Exodus* (**The Old English Exodus*); Old English Literature; Middle English Texts – *The Owl and the Nightingale*, *Sawles Warde* (**Katherine Group*), *Havelok*, **Sir Orfeo*, and **Pearl*; Middle English Literature; Chaucer, Langland, and Gower; and had a choice of two papers, each devoted to a subsidiary language: Gothic, Old Saxon, Old High German, Middle High German, Old Norse and Old Norse Texts (two papers), or Old French and Old French Texts (two papers). Candidates wanting to offer a tenth paper could take another of the subsidiary Language papers, or choose from the following Special Subjects: Elements of Comparative Indo-European Philology; Old English Palaeography; Runic Epigraphy; Old Norwegian and Old Icelandic Literature; Old French Literature to *c*. 1400; an historical subject studied in relation to linguistic history (Germanic Origins; the English Conquest of Britain; the Scandinavian invasions of England; the Norman Conquest; Mediaeval London); or a literary subject studied in relation to political or social history.

Course II was a more modern philological course which also covered Literature up to Milton. Candidates had to take the same papers on Old English Philology, Middle English Philology, Old English Texts, Middle English Texts, and Chaucer, Langland, and Gower as in Course I. They also took papers on Modern English Philology from *c*. 1400 to *c*. 1800; English Literature from 1400 to 1550; Shakespeare and Contemporary English Dramatists; and another paper chosen from Old English Literature, Middle English Literature, Spenser and Milton, Old Norse, or Old French. Candidates wishing to offer a tenth paper could choose a second from the first three options for their ninth paper, or one of the first, second, or sixth Special Subjects listed for Course I.

Course III was for those whose main interest was literature. Candidates took papers on Modern English; on Old English and Middle English with set texts different than those in Courses I and II; Chaucer and his contemporaries; Shakespeare and Contemporary English Dramatists; Spenser and Milton; and three papers covering English Literature from 1400 to 1830. Candidates wishing to offer a tenth paper could choose from English Literature from 1830 to 1900; a literary subject studied in relation to political or social history; Greek Literary Criticism; Virgil and his relation to English Literature; Roman Satire; the influence of Italian Literature on English Literature in the sixteenth century; or French Classical Drama.

After the Second World War there was again pressure on the English School for a change of syllabus. Jose Harris comments that

> the faculty of English . . . was dominated by the principle that the evolution of English both as a living and a literary language should be studied from its earliest roots in the Anglo-Saxon period. This principle generated a powerful and fertile school of Old and Middle English scholarship; but it also led to an undergraduate degree course dominated by philology and language studies, within which even the most 'literary' options included no writing after 1830. Moreover the rise of the powerful new genre of twentieth-century literary criticism was virtually ignored. . . . ['The Arts and Social Sciences, 1939–1970' in *The History of the University of Oxford*, vol. 8: *The Twentieth Century* (1994), p. 239]

Harris points out that *C.S. Lewis in particular firmly set himself against the new criticism. His

> towering personality exerted great influence over colleagues and students alike, but from the start of the post-war period there were murmurings of dissent, partly against the monopoly of philology, partly against the exclusion from the syllabus of any echo of the new criticism, partly against the permeation of the faculty's intellectual life by values that were deemed not literary but religious and moral. [p. 240]

In the years immediately after the war the English Faculty Board again sought to create a Preliminary Examination in English Language and Literature (First Public Examination). This was finally established by statute coming into force in Michaelmas Term 1948. Tolkien was a member of the committee that drafted the statute, and dealt with various emendations. In a reply to the General Board in March 1948 the committee said that 'the English Preliminary is as wide as any examination of this kind can be for it asks for a knowledge of a classical, a medieval and a modern language (other than English) as well as a study of some important critical problems' (Oxford University Archives FA 4/5/1/2).

In 1954 there was an attempt to make 'English Literature from 1830 to 1920' a compulsory rather than optional paper for students taking Course III in the Final Honour Examination. A committee comprising Tolkien, *J.N. Bryson, *Lord David Cecil, Humphry House, and *F.P. Wilson considered the question and recommended the change, but the proposal was rejected at a meeting of the English Faculty on 18 May 1954 (see entry in **Chronology** for that date, and note to the entry). Another committee, of which Tolkien was not a member, was set up on 21 January 1955 to discuss both the Final Honour School and the Preliminary Examination. Its report eventually led to changes in the syllabus, but these came into effect after Tolkien's retirement.

During the latter half of the twentieth century Philology and the Language side of the Oxford English School gradually declined in popularity. Although a campaign to abolish compulsory Old English for students on the Literature side failed in 1991, it was eventually successful. Old English ceased to be a compulsory part of the First Public Examination for students who matriculated in Michaelmas Term 2002.

FACULTY

From a series of reports or submissions made by Tolkien and others on behalf of the English Faculty Board, the Oxford English School seems to have been chronically short of lecturers and tutors, imposing a heavy burden on all its members. In May 1928 Tolkien typed and was one of five signatories to the report of the Committee on Tuition in Linguistic Subjects in the English School.

> The Committee desire to point out that at present neither the University nor the colleges are able to provide for Male candidates special tuition in the linguistic subjects of the English School that is comparable in range or thoroughness to that given in literature, or sufficient in amount or quality to enable these candidates to satisfy the minimum requirements of the statutes.
>
> The lack of such tuition has been responsible in the past for the low standard of philological knowledge shown by candidates in the examinations: a serious defect to which the examiners have repeatedly drawn the attention of the Board. . . .
>
> The Committee wish to record, also, the view that the linguistic and literary subjects of the curriculum are intended to be simultaneous and complementary studies, and that, it is very undesirable that candidates should be allowed to relegate either the one or the other (according to their specialization) to a brief portion only of the period of their reading, whatever may be, now or in the future, the practical necessities of tutorial arrangements. [Oxford University Archives FA 4/5/2/1]

On 20 May 1929 Tolkien seems to have been involved with H.C. Wyld and C.T. Onions in drafting a request to the General Board of Faculties for the appointment of a lecturer to teach English Language for the Honour School of English Language and Literature.

> The official teachers of these subjects are at present three: the Merton Professor of English Language and Literature, the Rawlinson and Bosworth Professor of A-S, and the Reader in English Philology. The two Professors normally give from two to three times the amount of public instruction required by statute, not infrequently dealing with elementary parts of their subjects. The Reader from time to time also gives courses beyond the statutory requirements, as he is doing, by special request, in

the present Trinity Term. All three, if they are to consider the needs of the School, are obliged to neglect considerable sections of the subjects which ought to be adequately represented in the University, and still the linguistic syllabus of the School is not covered. [Oxford University Archives FA 4/5/2/1]

*C.L. Wrenn was appointed Lecturer in English Philology for one year from 1 October 1930, and then to a University Lecturership in English Language for five years from 1 October 1931; and *Dorothy Everett to a University Lecturership in the Middle English for five years from 1 October 1930.

On 15 May 1931 Tolkien and Nichol Smith submitted to the English Board a draft on the needs of the English Faculty for submission to the General Board. As submitted after emendation this listed three main needs: the establishment of a statutory University Lecturership in English Literature; the endowment of a readership or lecturership in (medieval) Scandinavian languages; and a new building for the English Faculty library. Tolkien surely drafted the justification for the second request, for the burden of Scandinavian studies fell on him: 'Norse literature and philology are of central importance in the mediaeval curriculum of the English School. Adequate provision for the teaching of these subjects, and for the direction of advanced studies is urgently required. No provision for Scandinavian studies has been made by the Faculty of Medieval and Modern Languages since 1916' (Oxford University Archives FA 4/5/2/3). It was not until 1941 that the first election to the newly created Vigfússon Readership in Ancient Icelandic Literature and Antiquities relieved Tolkien of those duties.

The Second World War produced added problems and burdens. There might have been fewer male students in Oxford, but several members of the English Faculty left to take up war work, and University restrictions made replacing them difficult. In addition, the English Faculty were asked to provide short courses for Naval and RAF cadets during their training, which not only needed new lectures but successive courses continued through traditional university vacations; and a special course for undergraduates who took part of their course of study before military service, and would later return to complete their degree.

With the end of the war in sight, Tolkien submitted on 26 March 1945 a statement on the 'Needs of the English Faculty' drawn up by himself and Nichol Smith to H.M. Margoliouth, Secretary of Faculties. They asked for more University Lecturerships and pointed out that the English School

receives small support in the way of fellowships from the men's colleges as a whole, least of all in linguistic and mediaeval subjects; and it can never count on reappointment in the same subject, if one of its few male teachers that hold fellowships either retires or dies. An important part of the lecturing has in recent years been provided without fee or emolument.

In spite of this shortage the tendency appears to be to reduce the number of men supported either by fellowship or university appointment, and those that remain are over-worked. In order to conduct a Cadet Course all the resident men, fellows and professors (with the exception of the late Professor Wyld, whose sight and health were failing), had to take part, and most of these have now had no break in teaching and examining since January 1943.

At present there are not enough men and women with a fellowship or appointment to provide for the proper relief and change of examiners in those examinations of which the English Board has charge.... The Professor of Anglo-Saxon [i.e. Tolkien] has for years been obliged to take a large share in the examination of Pass Moderations and Sections. [Oxford University Archives FA 4/5/2/7]

*Lord David Cecil and *Dorothy Whitelock were appointed to University Lecturerships from 1 October 1946.

The report of a committee (of which Tolkien was a member) on the needs of the Faculty for the quinquennium 1947–1952, approved by the English Faculty Board in October 1946, addressed

the immediate and pressing need of the School of English ... for an increase in teaching staff. This has never been adequate; it is now gravely deficient. There are not enough teaching members of the Faculty to cover the linguistic and literary tuition, or the supervision of advanced students, or the requisite changes of examiners in the preliminary and final examinations.

When the Faculty of English was separated from Modern Languages in 1926 the School possessed: 3 Professors: 1 English Literature; 1 Language; 1 Anglo-Saxon. 1 Goldsmiths' Reader. 4 University Readers: 3 Literature; 1 Language.

In spite of the growth of the School the provision remains much the same. Instead of the 4 University Readerships the School now has:

1 University Reader. Language.

1 Statutory Lecturer. Language.

*1 Lecturer. Literature. [Lord David Cecil].

*1 Lecturer. Mediaeval English. [Dorothy Whitelock]

(* These last two have only recently been established. For most of the intervening period the School has been deprived of the equivalent of 2 of the Readerships with which it started its independent existence.)

The only increase has been the recent appointment of Mr Ker as Reader in Palaeography. His services, mainly in the graduate ('postgraduate') department, are shared with History.

A Readership in Ancient Icelandic was established in 1940 (by a legacy) and attached to the English School. This has been of assistance to the professor of Anglo-Saxon, whose work has very greatly increased since 1926; but Scandinavian studies are a separate subject, of which the English School has become the caretaker.

In addition to the general growth of the School, in scope and numbers, there has been a considerable growth in the department of advanced ('post-graduate') studies. For the last twenty years this department has had the services, at small cost, of Mr S.R. Gibson. If the bibliographical work is to be maintained, the loss of his services will have to be replaced.

Since 1926 a few of the men's colleges have assisted the School by tutorial fellowships and lectureships (other than those held by Readers and Lecturers). There has recently been (balanced against losses) some slight increase in this assistance. It is still inadequate, even on the tutorial side, and there appears to be small prospect of any substantial increase. A large part of the tuition, lecturing, and supervision, will still have to be provided by the School independently. . . . [Oxford University Archives FA 4/5/2/8]

The Board asked for the Goldsmiths' Readership to be upgraded to a second chair of English Literature, and for two additional lecturerships in English Literature and one in Old and Middle English, and a readership or lecturership in Textual Criticism.

TOLKIEN AND THE OXFORD ENGLISH SCHOOL

The *Statuta Universitatis Oxoniensis* (1925 edn.) defines the general duties of a professor as 'to give instruction to Students, assist the pursuit of knowledge and contribute to the advancement of it, and aid generally the work of the University'. It further states that the lectures he gives must conform to the Regulations specific to his Chair, and 'it shall be his duty to give to Students attending his Ordinary Lectures assistance in their studies by advice, informal instruction, by occasional or periodical examination, and otherwise, as he may judge to be expedient. For receiving Students who desire such assistance he shall appoint stated times in every week in which he lectures' (p. 61). Most professors were required to reside within the University for at least six months in each academic year, between the first day of September and the following first day of July, and to lecture in each term (by 1945 this span had become between 1 October and the following 1 August). The Vice-Chancellor of the University could grant dispensation from this requirement for a short time for reasons of health or some other urgent cause. Any leave of absence or dispensation from statutory duties, whether for ill-health or travel for the purpose of research, had to be approved by the Visitatorial Board.

By 1945 a change in the *Statuta* included among the duties of a professor 'original work by the Professor himself and the general supervision of research and advanced work in his subject and department' (p. 41).

According to the 1925 *Statuta* the Rawlinson and Bosworth Professor of Anglo-Saxon – thus Tolkien between 1925 and 1945 – was required to 'lecture and give instruction on the Anglo-Saxon Language and Literature, and on the other Old Germanic Languages, especially Gothic and Old Icelandic ... [to] lecture and give instruction for six hours in each week, and for a period not less in any Term than six weeks, nor less in the whole year than twenty-one weeks' (p. 117–18): a minimum of 126 hours per academic year. The announcement of the forthcoming election to the chair on 12 June 1925 in the *Oxford University Gazette* (following the resignation of W.A. Craigie) said that the successful candidate would be required to 'give not less than forty-two lectures in the course of the academical year; six at least of such lectures shall be given in each of the three University Terms, and in two at least of the University Terms he shall lecture during seven weeks not less than twice a week' (supplement, p. 745). Presumably the remaining hours required of him were devoted to instruction and the supervision of post-graduate students. According to the *Oxford University Gazette*, in the second year after his election (when he was fully resident in Oxford and had no duties at *Leeds) Tolkien was scheduled to give seven lectures and classes each week in Michaelmas Term 1926 and Hilary Term 1927, and three each week in Trinity Term 1927 (see **Chronology**).

By 1945, when Tolkien vacated the Rawlinson and Bosworth chair, the requirement had been reduced to only thirty-six lectures or classes per academic year, of which at least twenty-eight had to be lectures. The same requirement applied to the Merton Professorship of English Language and Literature, to which Tolkien was elected in 1945 and which he held until 1959. The Merton Professor of English Language and Literature was required to lecture and give instruction in the History of the English Language, and in the History of English Literature through the period of Chaucer.

Opinions about Tolkien as a lecturer vary. He himself said in his 1959 *Valedictory Address to the University of Oxford* that he had not given an inaugural address on his election to the Merton chair, because 'my ineffectiveness as a lecturer was already well known, and well-wishers had made sure (by letter or otherwise) that I should know it too; so I thought it unnecessary to give a special exhibition of this unfortunate defect' (*The Monsters and the Critics and Other Essays*, p. 224). But in a letter to his son *Michael in October 1968 he wrote: 'I have only *since* I retired learned that I was a successful professor. I had no idea that my lectures had such an effect – and, if I had, they might have been better. My "friends" among dons were chiefly pleased to tell me that I spoke too fast and might have been interesting if I could be heard. True often: due in part to having too much to say in too little time, in larger part to diffidence, which such comments increased' (*Letters*, p. 396).

At least one of his students at Leeds retained pleasant memories of Tolkien's lectures. On 22 December 1937 K.M. Kilbride, to whom he had sent a copy of *Beowulf: The Monsters and the Critics*, wrote that in reading it she was pleased to find the sense of humour that she recalled from Tolkien's language lectures, which had made them entertaining as well as informative. *Roger Lancelyn Green, who matriculated at Oxford in 1937, described the first lecture by Tolkien that he attended in 1938:

He strode to the rostrum, his gown wrapped tightly round him, his cap pulled low over his brows, scowling fiercely. After taking off his cap and bowing slightly to us, he barked out: 'Take notes. I will give you the headings of what I propose to deal with this term.'

Accordingly we took down twelve headings of aspects of *Beowulf*, and he finished: 'And that's what I intend to discuss'. Then suddenly his face broke into the utterly charming smile which we were soon to know so well, and he added, in a burst of confidence: 'But I don't suppose we'll get through *half* of it!' . . . Nor did we, as he was for ever wandering off into side issues – usually more entertaining than the rather philological-slanted study of the epic itself.

I think it was on this occasion, while we relaxed with restrained titters over the beautiful timing of his last remarks, that he suddenly shouted out the first words of the poem: 'HWAET we Gardena. . . .' And then remarked 'That made you jump! Well, that's what the author intended – so that the skald could suddenly silence his would-be audience as they sat at the end of the feast drinking their beer or mead.' ['Recollections', *Amon Hen* 44 (May 1980), p. 6]

Another former student, *J.I.M. Stewart, wrote that Tolkien 'could turn a lecture room into a mead hall in which he was the bard and we were the feasting, listening guests'. And *W.H. Auden wrote to Tolkien many years after hearing him lecture: 'I don't think I have ever told you what an unforgettable experience it was for me as an undergraduate, hearing you recite *Beowulf*. The voice was the voice of Gandalf' (both quoted in *Biography*, p. 133).

*Robert Burchfield, who came to Oxford in 1949, was another student who enjoyed Tolkien's lectures, but his account of them perhaps explains why others were less happy:

I was entranced by the arguments that he presented to largely bewildered audiences of undergraduates in the Examination Schools. The mobs, many of them doubtless already devoted to hobbitry and all that, were soon driven away by the speed of his delivery and the complexity of his syntax. By the third week of term his small band of true followers remained. . . . ['My Hero: Robert Burchfield on J.R.R. Tolkien', *Independent Magazine*, 4 March 1989, p. 50]

According to *George Sayer, Tolkien

was known mainly as, frankly, a very bad lecturer. He muttered and spoke very quietly. He had a very poor speaking voice. . . .
Very few people went to his lectures, because they couldn't hear unless they were in the first three rows. The material, which was Old English poetry, was often excellent, especially the footnotes. The things he muttered and added to the typed text. You might often have only twenty

people who went to listen to him.... ['Tales of the Ferrograph', *Minas Tirith Evening-Star* 9, no. 2 (January 1980), p. 2]

An increasingly demanding part of Tolkien's work was the supervision of B.Litt., and to a lesser extent D.Phil., students, most of whom would have visited him for an hour once per week or once each fortnight. Before the Second World War he generally supervised one or two such students, but after the war he was frequently responsible for six or more. *R.F.W. Fletcher, then chairman of the English Faculty Board, described a B.Litt. supervisor's duties in a paper dated 15 January 1947 which was circulated to members of the English Faculty:

> Students for the B.Litt. course in English are admitted in the first instance as Probationers and are neither expected nor even encouraged to define their thesis at this stage. As Probationers they are expected to attend lectures on such subjects as the History of English Studies, Bibliography, Textual Criticism, &c., and have to pass an examination thereon within a year. Supervision of Probationers involves seeing that they pursue this probationary course, and discussing with them the field for a thesis and the choice of subject for submission for the Board's approval....
>
> The supervision of a Full Student, whose subject for a thesis has been approved by the Board, naturally involves more advanced and more technical discussion of research for the approved subject. The discussion must, however, be limited to advice and general guidance (i.e. the supervisor must not shape the thesis or direct it in detail)....
>
> The amount of supervision needed varies with different students but as a whole it should be enough for the supervisor to see a student once a fortnight in Full Term. Sometimes it will be more convenient to see little of him in term and to concentrate on him in the vacation. [Oxford University Archives FA 4/5/2/8]

Some fifty students supervised by Tolkien are listed in **Chronology**, over thirty of these in the period 1945–59. In addition, Tolkien generally interviewed all prospective B.Litt. and D.Phil. students wishing to write a thesis on a language or medieval literature subject, and as a member of the Applications Committee he took part in allocating supervisors, approving subjects of theses, and appointing examiners of the completed theses. Each thesis was considered by two examiners, first as a written text and then in a *viva* (*viva voce*). Tolkien examined over thirty theses during his time at Oxford. Roger Lancelyn Green wrote that he first met Tolkien

> when he and David Nichol Smith were putting me through the oral examination for my B.Litt. Degree, my thesis being on *Andrew Lang and the Fairy Tale*. The thesis was 'referred back' to me – which Nichol Smith, who had been my supervisor, kindly explained was no reflection on its

merits, in fact rather the reverse as it was obviously nearly good enough to be the basis of a published book but could be improved; and that I must spend another term over it – with Tolkien as my supervisor.

Accordingly, once a week for that term I made my way to 20 North-moor Road [*Oxford] for a delightful hour with Tolkien. 'It was my fault that your thesis was referred back – you must blame me!' were his first words. 'But I wanted to know more about the Fairies!' In consequence of which, besides a good deal of revision, I wrote an additional chapter on the Fairies – of which I treasure the original draft written all over by Tolkien with comments and suggestions. ['Recollections', *Amon Hen* 44 (May 1980), pp. 6–7]

Early in 1946, when John Lawlor returned to Oxford after war service to work on an edition of Julian of Norwich as a B.Litt. thesis, Tolkien was appointed his supervisor. Lawlor wrote that his 'first and abiding impression' of Tolkien 'was one of immediate kindness. Tutored by [C.S.] Lewis I had expected to be tested with a few falls, so to speak. But the gentle creature who sucked his pipe and gazed meditatively along its stem seemed interested only in what he could do to help' (*C.S. Lewis: Memories and Reflections* (1998), pp. 30–1). Robert Burchfield began, but did not complete, a D.Phil. on the *Ormulum* under Tolkien:

I saw Tollers (as he was known) at weekly intervals in the academic years 1951–2 and 1952–3, sometimes in Merton College, sometimes at his home in Holywell. He puffed at his pipe while I told him of my work. He made many acute observations. I followed them all up. He beamed when I made some discoveries. Now and then he mentioned the hobbits, but he didn't press them on me, spotting that my interest lay in the scraped-out o's and double consonants of the *Ormulum* rather than in dwarves . . . Orcs, and Mr Bilbo Baggins. ['My Hero: Robert Burchfield on J.R.R. Tolkien', p. 50]

In a long letter to a Mr Burns on 15 November 1952 Tolkien remarked that he had been able to write at a greater length because of 'unexpected freedom and exhilaration. I was "cut" by two researchers this morning who normally occupy between them over two hours of every Saturday morning: freedom' (private collection).

Since Tolkien was a professor employed by the University and not by a college, he did not have to undertake the tutorial work that imposed a heavy burden on members of colleges. He did, however, teach classes, includ-ing those established during the Second World War for Naval and Air Force cadets. Anthony Curtis, an RAF cadet, contrasted Tolkien and C.S. Lewis:

At the end of an hour with Lewis I always felt a complete ignoramus; no doubt an accurate impression but also a rather painful one; and if you did venture to challenge one of his theories the ground was cut away from beneath your feet with lightning speed. It was a fool's mate in three moves with Lewis smiling at you from the other side of the board in unmalicious glee at his victory. By contrast Tolkien was the soul of affability. He did all the talking, but he made you feel you were his intellectual equal. Yet his views beneath the deep paternal charm were passionately held. At the first of these classes he handed round some sample passages of medieval English he had typed out. One of them was an English translation of the first verses of the Gospel According to John. 'You see,' he said triumphantly, 'English was a language that could move easily in abstract concepts when French was still a vulgar Norman patois.' ['Remembering Tolkien and Lewis', *British Book News*, June 1977, p. 429]

Another major demand on Tolkien's time was examining, mainly the Final Honour School papers, but also Pass Moderations, and in the Second World War examinations set for cadets. He was an examiner in the Final Examinations in 1927–9, 1932–3, 1940–2, and 1952–3, and several times was chairman of the examiners. The papers were usually set by the examiners in the spring, then from about mid-June to the end of July examining involved 'a 7-day week, and a 12-hour day' (letter to *Rayner Unwin, 22 June 1952, *Letters*, p. 162).

In addition to lecturing, teaching, supervising, and examining Tolkien carried a heavy administrative burden. By virtue of his successive professorships he was always a member of the English Faculty Board which met twice a term. At almost every other meeting he was appointed to a subcommittee to consider some matter, such as changes to the syllabus or set books, candidates for a lecturership, and the need for more staff. The subcommittee was usually required to report at the next meeting of the Board, and no doubt meetings of the subcommittee were required in the interim. Tolkien was elected chairman of the Board at the beginning of Michaelmas Term 1939, and in the difficulties imposed by the war was re-elected several times, serving until Michaelmas Term 1946. On the unexpected death of the chairman (R.F.W. Fletcher) in October 1950, Tolkien served a further two years, from 1950 to 1952. The chairman of the Board was always also a member of the English Faculty Library Committee, and *ex officio* of any English Faculty Board subcommittees. During the academic years 1929–32 and 1938–47 Tolkien also served on the General Board, which met about every two weeks in term time, but from Michaelmas Term 1946 every week.

To these duties were added many other calls on Tolkien's time: organizing lecture lists, writing references for colleagues and former students, taking part in elections to various chairs and readerships, answering questions sent to him by his colleagues, and thanking those who sent him offprints of articles they had written, *inter alia*.

In letters to his sons Tolkien commented generally about Oxford University, teaching, and students. On 1 November 1963 he wrote to Michael:

I remember clearly enough when I was your age (in 1935). I had returned 10 years before (still dewy-eyed with boyish illusions) to Oxford, and now disliked undergraduates and all their ways, and had begun really to know dons. Years before I had rejected as disgusting cynicism by an old vulgarian the words of warning given me by old Joseph Wright. 'What do you take Oxford for, lad?' 'A university, a place of learning.' 'Nay, lad, it's a factory! And what's it making? I'll tell you. It's making *fees*. Get that in your head, and you'll begin to understand what goes on.'

Alas! by 1935 I now knew that it was perfectly true. At any rate as a key to dons' behaviour. Quite true, but not the whole truth.... I was stonewalled and hindered in my efforts (as a schedule B professor on a reduced salary, though with schedule A duties) for the good of my subject and the reform of its teaching, by vested interests in *fees* and fellowships....

The devotion to 'learning', as such and without reference to one's own repute, is a high and even in a sense spiritual vocation; and since it is 'high' it is inevitably lowered by false brethren, by tired brethren, by the desire of money (or even the legitimate *need* of money), and by pride: the folk who say 'my subject' & do not mean the one I am humbly engaged in, but the subject I adorn, or have 'made my own'. Certainly this devotion is generally degraded and smirched in universities. But it *is* still there. [*Letters*, pp. 336–7]

On 15 December 1969 he wrote to Christopher:

I had once a considerable experience of what are/were probably England's most (at least apparently) dullest and stodgiest students: Yorkshire's young men and women of sub-public school class and home backgrounds bookless and cultureless. That does not, however, necessarily indicate the actual innate mental capacity – largely unawakened – of any given individual. A surprisingly large proportion proved 'educable': for which a primary qualification is the willingness *to do some work* (to learn) (at any level of intelligence). Teaching is a most exhausting task. But I would rather spend myself on removing the 'dull' from 'stodges' – providing some products of β to β + quality that retain some sanity – a hopeful soil from which another generation with some higher intelligence could arise. Rather – rather than waste effort on those of (apparently at any rate) higher intelligence that have been corrupted and disintegrated by school, and the 'climate' of our present days. Teaching an organized subject is simply not the instrument for their rehabilitation – if anything is. [*Letters*, pp. 403–4]

The Oxford English School. Essay, published in the *Oxford Magazine* 48, no. 21 (29 May 1930), pp. 778–80, 782, one of a series by a variety of authors concerned with different schools at the University of *Oxford. In this Tolkien took the opportunity to examine the failings of the English syllabus as it stood at the time (see *Oxford English School), and to suggest improvements. His comments were 'purely personal', and if one part of the English School receives more notice, it is because it was Tolkien's

> principal concern, not because I regard it as the most important – though I do not measure importance by counting heads in final examinations. The length of the comment may be excused by those who reflect that the position of an English School in an English-speaking University is peculiar, and presents special problems too seldom considered. . . .
>
> 'English' plainly belongs by nature to a group of schools whose primary concern is with 'books', written in one of the literary languages of Europe, ancient, medieval or modern, and with that language itself. Yet its 'books' are not in a foreign tongue, the language is the vernacular – although it may be held that for all the related schools the fact that the language studied is precisely not English is of fundamental importance.
>
> The divergence between the two 'sides' of the English School, its 'sub-schools', may be regarded as the result of different attempts at solving the special problem of an English English School. [p. 778]

He notes that the two sides are generally dubbed, not entirely accurately, as 'language' and 'literature', the latter more popular being preferred by more than ninety per cent of the English students. He proceeds to criticize the current regulations of the School, which mean that the 'literature' student who wishes to gain a knowledge of Old and Middle English (a 'language' subject) cannot do so in depth, while a 'language' student is 'scarcely required to study any "books" in the modern period.' 'No one person', therefore, 'can be expected to deal adequately with both of the "sub-schools"' (pp. 778–9).

Tolkien surmises that the 'literature' curriculum 'is felt unsatisfactory by all' because it allows for only an elementary linguistic component; though 'it is probable that some would prefer its equivalent (e.g., "Latin and Greek without tears") rather than its re-ordering and revival.' Personally he favours

> curtailing the thousand years at the modern end, jettisoning certainly the nineteenth century (unless parts of it could appear as an 'additional subject'); and the substitution of a scholarly study of worthy Anglo-Saxon and Middle English texts, with a paper of unseen translation, for the extracts and the meagre 'philology.' If real philology is required it should deal with the periods also studied as literature, and be examined in the same connection; otherwise it is valueless. [p. 779]

In contrast, he praises the 'language' curriculum and extols the importance of a study of Old English, Middle English, and Old Icelandic (Old Norse): Philology 'is essential to the critical apparatus of student and scholar' and 'language is more important than any of its special functions, such as literature.

Its study is profound and fundamental' (p. 780). Old Icelandic, Tolkien believes, should 'be prescribed for all and made more central.' Texts in the three languages should be increased, with definite books prescribed. 'The specialised history, especially the phonetic history, of modern English should disappear as a compulsion from this branch of the School.' Chaucer should be recovered as a mediaeval author, 'and part of his works become once more the subject of detailed and scholarly study. The pretence that no "English" curriculum is humane which does not include Shakespeare must naturally be abandoned, since that author lies quite outside the purview of such a course' (p. 782).

Oxford Letter. Letter apparently written at the editor's request, published as by 'Oxon' in the *King Edward's School Chronicle* n.s. 28, no. 202 (December 1913), pp. 80–1. Tolkien's authorship is revealed in his papers. The letter contains news of Old Edwardians (former pupils at *King Edward's School, Birmingham) now at the University of *Oxford. *G.B. Smith is prominently mentioned.

The Palantíri. Various writings concerning the *palantíri*, made by Tolkien while revising *The Lord of the Rings* for its second edition, formed by *Christopher Tolkien into a continuous essay and published with notes in *Unfinished Tales* (1980), pp. 403–15.

The Palantíri expands upon the history and nature of the seeing-stones, how they were used and what could be seen in them, why they were forgotten in the latter part of the Third Age, what was known to the White Council and what Saruman concealed from it. It reveals that no thought had been given to the use Sauron might make of the Ithil-stone if he had seized it when Minas Ithil fell, and explains that while riding to Minas Tirith with Pippin and answering his questions about the Orthanc-stone, Gandalf was pondering the possibility that Denethor had used the Anor-stone and might have fallen, which was one reason for Gandalf's haste. The essay points out also that Gandalf could not *know* when Denethor began to use the Anor-stone, and presumed that Denethor had not used it until peril grew great; but in fact Denethor had been using it since he succeeded to the Stewardship. Tolkien discusses how Denethor used the stone, and how the use affected him. Denethor is said to have withstood Sauron's domination partly because of his character, but also because, as a Steward for the heirs of Elendil, he had a lawful right to use the Anor-stone.

Since changes consequent on these were not incorporated into *The Lord of the Rings* until the second printing (1967) of the Allen & Unwin second edition, they date probably from 1966 or early 1967.

Part of the Legend of Amroth and Nimrodel Recounted in Brief
see *The History of Galadriel and Celeborn and of Amroth King of Lórien*

Payton, Ralph S. (*d.* 1916). R.S. Payton, known as 'the Baby', was a friend of Tolkien at *King Edward's School, Birmingham, and a fellow member of the *T.C.B.S. Like his elder brother *Wilfrid, Ralph Payton was involved in a wide range of school activities – football, the Shooting Club, the School magazine, the Debating Society – and in most of these he held office. As Debating Secretary he 'performed with great energy' the 'less pleasant duties' of the office, 'especially the finding of new speakers. In his own speeches he is more successful as a humorist, and does not often contrive to be serious without being dull' ('Characters, 1911–12', *King Edward's School Chronicle* n.s. 27, no. 193 (June 1912), p. 41). But he was outwardly modest, and his delivery in debate was often faulted. He also served as Prefect, Sub-Treasurer, and School Captain and General Secretary. In 1913 he followed his brother to Cambridge, on an Open Scholarship for Classics at Christ's College. In the First World War he joined the 1st Birmingham Battalion, in which he rose to the rank of Lieutenant, in charge of machine gunners. He was killed in the Somme in July 1916.

Payton, Wilfrid Hugh. W.H. Payton, known as 'Whiffy', was a friend of Tolkien at *King Edward's School, Birmingham, and a fellow member of the *T.C.B.S. Like his younger brother *Ralph, Wilfrid Payton was involved in a wide range of school activities – football, the Shooting Club, the School library and magazine, the Debating Society, the Literary Society – in most of which he held office and was highly regarded. He also served as Prefect, Sub-Treasurer, and School Captain and General Secretary. In 1911 he went up to Trinity College, Cambridge, on an Open Exhibition for Classics. In the First World War he joined the Indian Reserve of Officers and rose to the rank of Captain. He was attached to the 1st Gurkha Rifles, and later to the Khyber Rifles, on the Afghan frontier.

Pearl. Alliterative poem in Middle English. It is attributed to the same anonymous late fourteenth-century poet who wrote *Sir Gawain and the Green Knight*, another of four works preserved in the same manuscript (British Library MS Cotton Nero A.x, with the poems *Patience* and *Cleanness*).

The subject of *Pearl* (or *The Pearl*) is the poet's daughter, who died as a child. As he wanders in the garden in which his child is buried, the poet slips, 'and to sudden sleep was brought, / O'er that precious pearl'. He has a vision of a fair land of marvels and splendour, of a deep stream beyond which lies Paradise, and of 'a gentle maid of courtly grace' arrayed in pearls: his daughter grown to maturity. 'Lament alone by night I made,' he tells her, 'Much longing I have hid for thee forlorn, / Since to the grass you from me strayed.' She upbraids him for excessive grief, and explains that she is in a blissful state of grace, the bride of Christ. Headlong her father plunges into the stream, eager to join her, but 'right as I rushed then to the shore / That fury made my dream to fade', and he wakes from his trance. If, he says, it is true that his daughter is 'set at ease, / Then happy I, though chained in care, / That you that Prince indeed do please' (translation by Tolkien).

The excellence of the poem is observed by *Kenneth Sisam in his *Fourteenth Century Verse & Prose* (1921):

> If [the contemporary poem] *Piers Plowman* gives a realistic picture of the drabness of mediaeval life, *Pearl*, more especially in the early stanzas, shows a richness of imagery and a luxuriance in light and colour that seem scarcely English. Yet they have their parallels in the decorative art of the time – the elaborate carving in wood and stone; the rich colouring of tapestries, of illuminated books and painted glass; the designs of the jewellers, goldsmiths, and silversmiths, which even the notaries who made the old inventories cannot pass without a word of admiration. The *Pearl* reminds us of the tribute due to the artists and craftsmen of the fourteenth century. [p. 57]

Tolkien first encountered the work while still at *King Edward's School, Birmingham, as part of his private study of early English literature. A few years later, it was part of his required reading as a student in the English School at *Oxford. Tolkien attended lectures on *Pearl* by *A.S. Napier, and very probably a class on the work taught by Sisam. The West Midlands dialect of Middle English in which *Pearl* was written was a subject of special interest to Tolkien; see *English language and *A Fourteenth-Century Romance.

Pearl was also part of the curriculum at *Leeds when Tolkien was on the staff of the University's English School, and also at Oxford. In May 1924 Tolkien wrote a poem, *The Nameless Land*, inspired by reading *Pearl* for examination papers (see *Examinations).

MODERN ENGLISH TRANSLATION

After the publication of their *Sir Gawain and the Green Knight* in 1925, Tolkien and his colleague *E.V. Gordon began work on an edition of *Pearl* in Middle English. But Tolkien made little or no contribution to it for many years; instead he prepared, in spare moments during ?1925–6, a Modern English translation of the poem. On 26 April 1926 he sent a copy of this to Kenneth Sisam, for whose *Fourteenth Century Verse & Prose* he had prepared a glossary (*A Middle English Vocabulary). At some time by summer 1936 Tolkien offered the translation to the publisher J.M. Dent: it was rejected, but was seen by Guy Pocock, who having joined the staff of BBC Radio arranged for part of the translation to be read, with Tolkien's permission, in August 1936 on London regional radio. In October 1936 *Stanley Unwin, of the firm George Allen & Unwin (*Publishers), expressed an interest in publishing the translation; but with the success of *The Hobbit the following year, his main desire was soon for a sequel to that work.

By August 1942 the translation apparently had been lent to the Oxford bookseller and publisher *Basil Blackwell. He wrote to Tolkien, expressed his delight in the work, and asked if Tolkien would write, for publication with the poem, an introduction to *Pearl* aimed at the lay reader rather than the student. He offered to purchase the copyright to the translation, with the sum placed against Tolkien's outstanding account at Blackwell's Bookshop. Tolkien agreed, and proofs of the poem were ready in late March 1943. The introduction, however, was not forthcoming at once; and in September 1944 Blackwell, wondering if Tolkien's delay was caused by objection to giving up copyright, now suggested that publication proceed instead on the basis of a royalty. Tolkien certainly wished to proceed: in a letter of 23–5 September 1944 he wrote to his son *Christopher: 'I must try and get on with the Pearl and stop the eager maw of Basil Blackwell' (*Letters*, p. 94). Six months later, *c*. 18 March 1945, he was still 'in trouble with Blackwell who has set up my translation of *Pearl*, and needs corrections and an introduction', as he wrote to Stanley Unwin (*Letters*, p. 114).

In the event, Tolkien never finished this work for Blackwell. In late 1950 Stanley Unwin again enquired about *Pearl*, in conjunction with Tolkien's Modern English translation of *Sir Gawain and the Green Knight*, but it was not until August 1959, after the completion and successful publication of *The Lord of the Rings*, that plans for Allen & Unwin to publish both *Pearl* and *Sir Gawain* were actively discussed. On 24 August Tolkien met with Basil Blackwell, who magnanimously relinquished any rights in the translation of *Pearl* and refused any compensation for the cost of the abortive typesetting. On finding the Blackwell galley proofs for *Pearl* in his son Christopher's library, Tolkien felt less guilty about Blackwell's sacrifice, as 'inspection showed them to have been of an astonishing badness; so that the cost of correction of about a thousand fatuous mistakes (from reasonable copy), which would have arisen if I had proceeded with the publication, was at any rate spared' (letter to *Rayner Unwin, 25 August 1959, Tolkien-George Allen & Unwin archive, Harper-Collins). On 27 August Tolkien wrote to Rayner Unwin of his desire

to get *Gawain* and *Pearl* into your hands as soon as possible. The spirit is indeed willing; but the flesh is weak and rebellious. It has contracted lumbago, from amongst its weapons of delay – with the colourable excuse that an old man, robbed of helpers by mischance, should not shift bookcases and books unaided. Every book and paper I possess is now on the floor, at home and in college, and I have only a table to type on. When the turmoil will subside, I do not know for certain; nor in what state of weariness I shall then be. [Tolkien-George Allen & Unwin archive, HarperCollins]

Although he now felt that the translations did not need very much work to finish, again Tolkien was delayed in attending to them, partly because he could not decide on the form of the general introduction and commentary that were needed to accompany the poems. 'On the one hand', Christopher Tolkien has said, he undoubtedly sought an audience without any knowledge of the original poems; he wrote of his translation of *Pearl*: 'The *Pearl* certainly deserves to be heard by lovers of English poetry who have not the opportunity or the desire to master its difficult idiom. To such readers I offer this translation.' But he also wrote: 'A translation may be a useful form of commentary; and this version may possibly be acceptable even to those who already know the original, and possess editions with all their apparatus.' He wished therefore to explain the basis of his version in debatable passages; and indeed a very great deal of unshown editorial labour lies behind his translations, which not only reflect his long study of the language and metre of the originals, but were also in some degree the inspiration of it. As he wrote: 'These translations were first made long ago for my own instruction, since a translator must first try to discover as precisely as he can what his original means, and may be led by ever closer attention to understand it better for its own sake. Since I first began I have given to the idiom of these texts very close study, and I have certainly learned more about them than I knew when I first presumed to translate them.'

But the commentary was never written, and the introduction did not get beyond the point of tentative beginnings. [*Sir Gawain and the Green Knight, Pearl and Sir Orfeo* (1975), p. 7]

Tolkien mentioned in a letter to his *Aunt Jane Neave that a translation of *Pearl* attracted him because of the poem's 'apparently insoluble metrical problems' (18 July 1962, *Letters*, p. 317). Later, in a letter to his grandson Michael George (see *Michael Tolkien) he wrote that '*Pearl* is, of course, about as difficult a task as any translator could be set. It is impossible to make a version in the same metre close enough to serve as a "crib". But I think anyone who reads my version, however learned a Middle English scholar, will get a more direct impression of the poem's impact (on one who knew the language)' (6 January 1965, *Letters*, p. 352).

Tolkien's translation of *Pearl* was published at last in 1975, posthumously in *Sir Gawain and the Green Knight, Pearl and Sir Orfeo*, edited by Christopher Tolkien. A three-part version of the translation was broadcast in Britain on Radio 3 from 19 May 1978, adapted by Kevin Crossley-Holland and read by Hugh Dickson. An commercial recording of Tolkien's *Pearl* read (with *Sir Orfeo*) by Terry Jones was first issued in 1997.

EDITION IN MIDDLE ENGLISH

By summer 1937 E.V. Gordon completed work on the edition of *Pearl* in Middle English begun in 1925. He had given up hope of any contribution by Tolkien, though he told Kenneth Sisam at Oxford University Press (*Publishers) that he would still welcome Tolkien's participation, for the good of the book; but he did not want long delays, as he had other commitments and *Pearl* was due to replace *Sir Gawain* on the Oxford English syllabus in 1938, offering opportunities for sales of the new edition. Therefore, by the start of September 1937, he sent his manuscript to Tolkien for comment and revision, and suggested a date by which the work should be done. (Gordon's actions in this paragraph, and much else in our account of the edition of *Pearl*, are documented in correspondence held in the Oxford University Press archives, Oxford.)

Sisam, Gordon's editor, thought that the edition needed cutting. Gordon, reasoning that it is much easier to cut someone else's work than to reduce one's own, hoped that Tolkien would be willing to do so with *Pearl*. In December 1937 Tolkien replied that he was willing to attempt to reduce its length, but was opposed to the drastic reduction that had been suggested. It was agreed that Gordon and Tolkien together would work on the revision; but Gordon wrote to Sisam that he feared it would take a long time.

On 29 July 1938 E.V. Gordon died. Tolkien then began to help in the settling of his friend's affairs and academic obligations, as far as he was able to do so. Among these was the edition of *Pearl*, which was still in abeyance when Tolkien wrote to Stanley Unwin *c.* 18 March 1945 that he was 'in trouble with the widow of Professor E.V. Gordon of Manchester, whose posthumous work on *Pearl* I undertook, as a duty to a dead friend and pupil, to put in order; and have failed to do my duty' (*Letters*, p. 114). By mid-1947 Gordon's widow, Ida, a scholar of Middle English in her own right (see entry for *E.V. Gordon), herself took over the task of completing the edition of *Pearl* for publication. As she later wrote in its preface, at the time of her husband's death 'the edition was complete – complete, that is, in that no part was missing and all had been put into form, if not final form' (p. iv). On *c.* 22 July 1947 Tolkien sent Mrs Gordon a revised introduction to the work, and by early August sent her related linguistic matter as well as general comments and suggestions. In a return letter, she asked for Tolkien's advice about preparing the manuscript for publication, and he agreed to assist her further. He did not do so at once, however, much to the consternation of Mrs Gordon and Oxford University Press. Kenneth Sisam warned her that Tolkien was a perfectionist, and so he was; but his busy Oxford schedule, and matters such as the completion of *The Lord of the Rings*, also contributed to delay. On 13 June 1949 Tolkien advised D.M. Davin at Oxford University Press that only half of the glossary for *Pearl* remained to be done – referring, presumably, to his review of the glossary for revision. Probably in June 1950 Tolkien at last completed his revisions. In her preface Mrs Gordon wrote: 'Many factors combined to delay publication, and . . . I started the work of final revision in 1950 . . .' (p. iv).

On 19 August Ida Gordon sent the manuscript, now finished except for the introduction, to Oxford University Press; in this she incorporated Tolkien's suggestions and corrections, as well as notes left by her husband. She herself made emendations to the text, restored one reading on Tolkien's advice, and in general brought order to the material. Tolkien also suggested two changes of punctuation, and wrote one note that Mrs Gordon could not read. During September 1950 Tolkien replied to further queries about the work. On 13

September Mrs Gordon wrote to Tolkien that she was still worried about the introduction to *Pearl*, though a section which Tolkien had rewritten simplified the task considerably; and in other sections she felt that there may be some unnecessary detail, which she would try to reduce.

But more drastic cuts were called for by the publisher. On 6 June 1951 Ida Gordon commented to D.M. Davin at Oxford University Press that although she could understand some of the suggestions he sent her in regard to *Pearl*, she felt that the work would suffer if its associated matter were cut in half, as Davin had asked on the advice of Kenneth Sisam. The section Davin targeted in particular, including a discussion of problems involved with the work ('Form and Purpose', pp. xi–xix), was contributed by Tolkien, and was already a reduced revision. Davin discussed Mrs Gordon's letter with Tolkien, who was happy to give her a free hand to condense or omit any parts of his contribution, in the interests of brevity; it is not known if any change was made in Tolkien's text, though some parts of the introduction were omitted from the published work. Mrs Gordon stated in her preface that she wished to reduce the length of the book 'in a way that would sacrifice as little as possible of the original material', and that this 'made it necessary to make extensive alterations in the form' (p. iv).

Later, when the question arose about whether his name should appear on the title-page of *Pearl*, Tolkien declined, giving full credit to his late friend; nor did Ida Gordon sign her name except to the Preface. The edition was published at last at the Clarendon Press, Oxford, in June 1953; see further, *Descriptive Bibliography* B22. It is still well respected as a standard text.

'FORM AND PURPOSE'

A central feature of Tolkien's part of the introduction to *Pearl* is a discussion of allegory and symbolism in relation to the poem. 'It is proper, or at least useful,' he writes, 'to limit allegory to narrative, to an account (however short) of events; and symbolism to the use of visible signs or things to represent other things or ideas. . . . To be an "allegory" a poem must *as a whole*, and with fair consistency, describe in other terms some event or process; its entire narrative and all its significant details should cohere and work together to this end.' *Pearl* contains 'minor allegories'; 'but an allegorical description of an event does not make that event itself allegorical' (pp. xi–xii). In the poet's day

> visions . . . allowed marvels to be placed within the real world . . . while providing them with an explanation in the phantasies of sleep, and a defence against critics in the notorious deception of dreams. . . . We are dealing with a period when men, aware of the vagaries of dreams, still thought that amid their japes came visions of truth. And their waking imagination was strongly moved by symbols and the figures of allegory. . . . [pp. xiv–xv]

This text was later reprinted as part of the introduction to *Sir Gawain and the Green Knight, Pearl and Sir Orfeo*, pp. 18–23.

The Peoples of Middle-earth. The twelfth and final volume of *The History of Middle-earth*, edited with notes and commentary by *Christopher Tolkien, first published in Great Britain by HarperCollins, London, in September 1996, and in the United States by the Houghton Mifflin Company, Boston, in December 1996. See further, *Tolkien Collector* 14 (October 1996), pp. 7–8, and *Tolkien Collector* 15 (February 1997), pp. 5–6.

Part One, 'The Prologue and Appendices to *The Lord of the Rings*', is divided into nine parts: 'The Prologue'; 'The Appendix on Languages'; 'The Family Trees'; 'The Calendars'; 'The History of the *Akallabêth*'; 'The Tale of Years of the Second Age'; 'The Heirs of Elendil'; 'The Tale of Years of the Third Age'; and 'The Making of Appendix A' ('The Realms in Exile', 'The Tale of Aragorn and Arwen', 'The House of Eorl', 'Durin's Folk'). Christopher Tolkien did not realize when he brought the story of *The Lord of the Rings* to an end in *Sauron Defeated* (1992) that his father had done much work on the Prologue and the Appendices possibly even while writing the final chapters of *The Lord of the Rings* in the summer of 1948, and certainly immediately after that time, until by the middle of 1950 he had a series of fair copy texts which might provide the necessary background to the story. He probably did little more with this until 1952, when he began to prepare *The Lord of the Rings* for publication, and most of the final work on the Appendices was accomplished in 1954–5.

Part Two, 'Late Writings', contains works from the final years of Tolkien's life, *c.* 1967–1973: *Of Dwarves and Men*; *The Shibboleth of Fëanor*; *The Problem of* Ros; *Glorfindel, together with extracts from two versions of a discussion of the Dwarves' tradition that the spirits of their Seven Fathers were from time to time reborn (drawn from a larger discussion mainly on the reincarnation of Elves, hence see *'Elvish Reincarnation'); *The Five Wizards ('Note on the landing of the Five Wizards and their functions and operations'); and *Círdan. This was a time, Christopher Tolkien comments, when his father 'was moved to write extensively, in a more generalised view, of the languages and peoples of the Third Age and their interrelations, closely interwoven with discussion of the etymology of names' (*The Peoples of Middle-earth*, p. 293); cf. *The History of Galadriel and Celeborn and of Amroth King of Lórien* in *Unfinished Tales* (1980). These 'historical-philological' essays

> are not developments and refinements of earlier versions, and they were not themselves subsequently developed and refined. . . . Almost all of this work was etymological in its inspiration, which to a large extent accounts for its extremely discursive nature; for in no study does one thing lead to another more rapidly than in etymology, which also of its nature leads out of itself in the attempt to find explanations beyond the purely linguistic evolution of forms. [p. 294]

Part Three, 'Teachings of Pengoloð', contains two works of the 1950s, the *Dangweth Pengoloð and *Of Lembas.

Part Four, 'Unfinished Tales', contains *The New Shadow, an aborted sequel to The Lord of the Rings begun c. late 1958, and the story *Tal-Elmar, also from the 1950s.

Perry-the-Winkle. Poem, first published in *The Adventures of Tom Bombadil and Other Verses from the Red Book (1962), pp. 41–4. A lonely troll, whose 'heart is soft', 'smile is sweet', and 'cooking good enough', leaves his home in the hills and wanders through Michel Delving in the Shire. Despite good manners, he frightens everyone he meets, except for the lad Perry-the-Winkle. The troll carries him home 'to a fulsome tea', which becomes a Thursday tradition. In time, Perry-the-Winkle grows 'so fat . . . / his weskit bust, and never a hat / would sit upon his head'; and he becomes a great baker, though not so good as the troll.

Perry-the-Winkle is a revision of The Bumpus (unpublished), one of a series of poems called *Tales and Songs of Bimble Bay. In the Adventures of Tom Bombadil collection it is overtly a Hobbit poem, with references to the Shire and Bree, and in Tolkien's preface to that volume is ascribed to Sam Gamgee (from *The Lord of the Rings).

Tolkien recorded Perry-the-Winkle in 1967 for the album Poems and Songs of Middle Earth (1967, reissued in 2001 as part of The J.R.R. Tolkien Audio Collection); see *Recordings.

Philology. The first definition of philology given in the original *Oxford English Dictionary (section compiled c. 1906) is: 'Love of learning and literature; the study of literature in a wide sense, including grammar, literary criticism and interpretation, the relation of literature and written records to history etc.; literary or classical scholarship; polite learning'; but this is noted as 'now rare in general sense'. The first documented use in this sense is by *Geoffrey Chaucer, c. 1386. The first definition of philologist is: 'One devoted to learning or literature; a lover of letters or scholarship; a learned or literary man; a scholar, especially a classical scholar. Now less usual.' These remained the primary senses in the United States, but in Britain during the eighteenth and nineteenth centuries the words began to be more commonly used in a narrower sense: philologist as 'a person versed in the science of language; a student of language; a linguistic scholar' and philology as 'the study of the structure and development of language; the science of language; linguistics. (Really one branch of sense 1).' In the 1972–86 supplement to the OED this definition of philology is further qualified: 'In Britain now usu[ally] restricted to the study of the development of specific languages or language families, esp[ecially] research into phonological and morphological history based on written documents. . . . Linguistics is now the more usual term for the study of the structure of language, and, with qualifying adjective or adjective phrase, is replacing philology even in the restricted sense.' For comment on these and later definitions, see *The Ring of Words: Tolkien and the Oxford English Dictionary* by Peter Gilliver, Jeremy Marshall, and Edmund Weiner (2006).

During the nineteenth century the discovery of similarities between Sanskrit and Greek and Latin led to the recognition of the Aryan or Indo-European family of languages, and the rise of Comparative Philology. More detailed study of existing languages and their history followed, as philologists sought to discover relationships between languages by comparison of their forms past and present, noting regular shifts and changes in sound and spelling over the years and deducing by analogy not only earlier lost forms, but also a common ancestral language from which the Indo-European family developed. From these relationships and fragmentary memories in later writings, some attempted to throw light on the history of the speakers of the languages, in particular the dark period towards the end of the Roman Empire when Germanic and other tribes pressed against its borders.

In England this led to a greater interest in Old English and its relationship with other Germanic languages. A chair in Anglo-Saxon was established at *Oxford as early as 1795 (see *Oxford English School), but during the nineteenth century the responsibilities of its holder were gradually extended to include Old Low German dialects and the antiquities of northern Europe. German scholars played a major role in defining new philological methods, which were fostered at Oxford by the creation of a Chair of Comparative Philology for Max Müller. The first holder of the Merton Professorship of English Language and Literature, established in 1885, was *A.S. Napier, who had trained as a philologist in Germany and previously occupied a chair at the University of Göttingen. There was as yet no Honour School of English at Oxford, and those who had hoped that the Merton chair would go to someone more interested in Literature than Philology were disappointed. One of the major attacks on Philology came from John Churton Collins, who wrote that

as an instrument of culture it ranks – it surely ranks – very low indeed. It certainly contributes nothing to the cultivation of the taste. It as certainly contributes nothing to the education of the emotions. The mind it neither enlarges, stimulates, nor refines. On the contrary, it too often induces or confirms that peculiar woodenness and opacity, that singular coarseness of feeling and purblindness of moral and intellectual vision, which has in all ages been the characteristic of mere philologists. . . . Instead of encouraging communion with the noblest manifestations of human energy, with the great deeds of history, or with the masterpieces of art and letters, it tends, as Bacon remarks, to create habits of unintelligent curiosity about trifles. It too often resembles that rustic who, after listening for several hours to Cicero's most brilliant conversation, noticed nothing and remembered nothing but the wart on the great orator's nose. [*The Study of English Literature* (1891), quoted in D.J. Palmer, *The Rise of English Studies* (1965), pp. 83–4]

A different, more moderately expressed point of view was put forward by Henry Nettleship. Philology, he wrote, 'can never, from the nature of the case, be hostile to literature, whatever temporary misunderstandings may arise between them. I believe also that philology is a necessary adjunct to the academical study of literature; that the academical study of literature, without philology, is a phantom which will vanish at the dawn of day' (*The Study of Modern European Languages and Literature* (1887), quoted in Palmer, *The Rise of English Studies*, p. 104). But as D.J. Palmer has pointed out, however reasonable this might seem, it avoided consideration of various practical factors and vested interests:

> Exactly what literature was to be studied in an English School? The pabulum of philologists was solidly medieval; linguistic interest did not, except by chance, coincide with literary quality; and on modern literature philologists had little to say that was of interest to literary critics. Moreover, even if the principle were conceded that philology was 'a necessary adjunct' to literary study, was it any more so than history, or philosophy, or rhetoric, or comparative literature? These issues would directly affect the actual organization of an English School and the definition of its scope and flexibility. [*The Rise of English Studies*, p. 105]

In the background of this debate was the opinion held by some that the study of English literature, and especially of more recent works, would be a 'soft' option compared to other schools, and that Philology, a precise and demanding discipline, would provide some 'stiffening'. Thus even before an English School was established at Oxford in 1894 there were competing interests and ideas of what its syllabus should cover, and what part, if any, Philology should play in it.

T.A. Shippey has noted that even philologists were divided in how they approached or used their subject:

> At one extreme scholars were drawing conclusions from the very *letters* of a language: they had little hesitation is ascribing texts to Gothic or Lombardic authors, to West Saxons and Kentishmen or Northumbrians, on the evidence of sound-changes recorded in spelling. At the other extreme they were prepared to pronounce categorically on the existence or otherwise of nations and empires on the basis of poetic tradition or linguistic spread. They found information, and romance, in songs and fragments everywhere. [*The Road to Middle-earth* (2nd edn. 1992), pp. 16–17]

Philology was able to identify the changed names of leaders and heroes in later poetry with earlier writings, and in some cases these did preserve memories of actual people and events. Shippey comments: 'The change of viewpoint marks an enormous if temporary shift of poetic and literary interest from Classical to native. It also shows how philology could seem to some, the "noblest of sciences", the key to "spiritual life", certainly "something much greater than a misfit combination of language plus literature"' (*The Road to Middle-earth*, 2nd edn., p. 17, quoting Leonard Bloomfield and Holger Pedersen). Also,

> the thousands of pages of 'dry as dust' theorems about language-change, sound-shifts and ablaut-gradations were, in the minds of most philologists, an essential and natural basis for the far more exciting speculations about the wide plains of 'Gothia' and the hidden, secret traderoutes across the primitive forests of the North, *Myrkviðr inn ókunni*, 'the pathless Mirkwood' itself. You could not have, you would never have *got* the one without the other. [p. 19]

Tolkien's interest in words manifested itself while he was still a child. When his mother (*Mabel Tolkien) introduced him to Latin it 'delighted him. He was just as interested in the sounds and shapes of the words as in their meanings. . . .' He liked French less: 'the sounds did not please him as much as the sounds of Latin and English [*Languages]. She also tried to interest him in playing the piano, but without success. It seemed rather as if words took the place of music for him, and that he enjoyed listening to them, reading them, and reciting them, almost regardless of what they meant' (Humphrey Carpenter, *Biography*, p. 22). On several occasions in later life Tolkien referred to the effect the sound of certain words had on him. On 7 June 1955 he wrote to *W.H. Auden: 'It has been always with me: the sensibility to linguistic pattern which affects me emotionally like colour or music . . .' (*Letters*, p. 212). On 22 November 1961 he wrote to his *Aunt Jane Neave: 'As for *plenilune* and *argent* [in his poem *Errantry*], they are beautiful words *before* they are understood – I wish I could have the pleasure of meeting them for the first time again! – and how is one to know them till one does meet them?' (*Letters*, p. 310).

In his lecture *English and Welsh*, given in 1955, he commented that 'most English-speaking people . . . will admit that *cellar door* is "beautiful", especially if dissociated from its sense (and from its spelling). More beautiful than, say, *sky*, and far more beautiful than *beautiful*' (*The Monsters and the Critics and Other Essays*, p. 190). He continued, concerning Welsh, the language which influenced his 'Elvish' language Sindarin (*Languages, Invented): 'In Welsh for me *cellar doors* are extraordinarily frequent, and moving to the higher dimension, the words in which there is pleasure in the contemplation of the association of form and sense are abundant' (*The Monsters and the Critics*, pp. 190–1). He wrote in his letter to Auden of discovering Finnish, which influenced his 'Elvish' language Quenya, that 'it was like discovering a complete wine-cellar filled with bottles of an amazing wine of a kind and flavour never tasted before. It quite intoxicated me . . .' (*Letters*, p. 214).

Tolkien also described to Auden how he developed his interest in languages while still at school:

I went to King Edward's School and spent most of my time learning Latin and Greek; but I also learned English. . . . I learned Anglo-Saxon at school (also Gothic, but that was an accident quite unconnected with the curriculum though decisive – I discovered in it not only modern historical philology, which appealed to the historical and scientific side, but for the first time the study of language out of mere love: I mean for the acute aesthetic pleasure derived from a language for its own sake, not only free from being useful but free even from being the 'vehicle of a literature'). [*Letters*, p. 213]

According to Humphrey Carpenter, *Robert Cary Gilson, the Chief Master at King Edward's School,

encouraged his pupils to explore the byways of learning and to be expert in everything that came their way: an example that made a great impression on Ronald Tolkien. But though he was discursive, Gilson also encouraged his pupils to make a detailed study of classical linguistics. This was entirely in keeping with Tolkien's inclinations; and, partly as a result of Gilson's teaching, he began to develop an interest in the general principles of language.

It was one thing to know Latin, Greek, French and German; it was another to understand *why* they were what they were. Tolkien had started to look for the bones, the elements that were common to them all: he had begun, in fact, to study philology, the science of words. [*Biography*, p. 34]

To assist his studies he began to buy books on Philology, including a copy of *Chambers's Etymological Dictionary* in which he noted in February 1973: 'This book was the beginning of my interest in Germanic Philology (& Philol. in general' (*Life and Legend*, p. 16). At Oxford Tolkien took Comparative Philology as a special subject for Honour Moderations, then abandoned Classics for the Language side of the English School.

As Rawlinson and Bosworth Professor of Anglo-Saxon (1925–45) he was required to teach not only literary aspects of works such as *Beowulf, but also the philological aspects of Old English. He gave lectures on such subjects as Old English Dialects, The Common Germanic Consonant-Changes, and Old English Historical Grammar (Inflexions). That he had a deep interest in such matters is shown in the languages he himself devised, especially Quenya and Sindarin, which underwent shifts and changes similar to those of real world languages, which could be 'traced' back to a common and original 'Quendian' tongue and developed in different branches according to events explained in *The Silmarillion'.

Although words and language remained of prime importance to him, Tolkien thought the divide between Language and Literature unfortunate and unnatural, and as a teacher at *Leeds and Oxford he tried to bridge it in the English syllabi. In his application for the Rawlinson and Bosworth chair of Anglo-Saxon at Oxford he promised 'to advance . . . the growing neighbourliness of linguistic and literary studies, which can never be enemies except by misunderstanding or without loss to both . . .' (27 June 1925, *Letters*, p. 13). In his lecture **Beowulf: The Monsters and the Critics* he objected to critics who mined *Beowulf* for miscellaneous information, historical as well as philological, and did not study it for itself, as a work of literature. In a draft letter to a Mr Thompson on 14 January 1956 he described himself as 'a philologist by nature and trade (yet one always primarily interested in the aesthetic rather than the functional aspects of language)' (*Letters*, p. 231). But he was also interested in Philology for the light it could shed on the darker, forgotten corners of history and the peoples who had spoken earlier forms of languages, and whose stories and legends had been mainly lost. He gave lectures on subjects such as 'Legends of the Goths' and 'The Historical and Legendary Traditions in *Beowulf* and Other Old English Poems'. In a letter written to his son *Christopher after hearing him lecture on 'Barbarians and Citizens', Tolkien said that he had

suddenly realized that I am a *pure* philologist. I like history, and am moved by it, but its finest moments for me are those in which it throws light on words and names! Several people (and I agree) spoke to me of the art with which you made the beady-eyed Attila on his couch almost vividly present. Yet oddly, I find the thing that really thrills my nerves is the one you mentioned casually: *atta, attila* [diminutive of Gothic *atta* 'father']. Without those syllables the whole great drama both of history and legend loses savour for me – or would. [21 February 1958, *Letters*, p. 264]

Tolkien also had an associated interest in place-names. He joined the English Place-Name Society (*Societies and clubs) at its inception on 27 April 1923 and remained a member until his death. **The Name 'Nodens'*, which he wrote as an appendix to the *Report of the Excavation of the Prehistoric, Roman, and Post-Roman Site in Lydney Park, Gloucestershire* (1932), discusses not only philological aspects of the word but also history, legend, and mythology. The story **Farmer Giles of Ham*, purporting to explain the names of some of the places near Oxford that Tolkien and his family used to visit, not only provides an 'historical' source for *Thame* and *Worminghall* but also explains why those names are not pronounced as written.

For a general discussion of Philology and the division in English studies, see T.A. Shippey, *The Road to Middle-earth*, especially the chapter 'Lit. and Lang.' Both that book and Shippey's *J.R.R. Tolkien: Author of the Century* (2000) are useful references for studying the influence of Tolkien's philological interests on his literary works. *The Ring of Words: Tolkien and the Oxford English Dictionary* by Peter Gilliver, Jeremy Marshall, and Edmund Weiner (2006) is also essential reading on Tolkien and Philology.

Pictures by J.R.R. Tolkien. Collection of paintings, drawings, and designs by Tolkien, with foreword and notes by *Christopher Tolkien, first published in Great Britain by George Allen & Unwin, London, and in the United States by the Houghton Mifflin Company, Boston, both in November 1979. The images first appeared in a series of Tolkien calendars published by Allen & Unwin from 1973 to 1979, excepting 1975. A revised edition was published in 1992. The book was allowed to go out of print after the publication of *J.R.R. Tolkien: Artist and Illustrator* (1995) by Wayne G. Hammond and Christina Scull, in which most (but not all) of the images in *Pictures by J.R.R. Tolkien* were also reproduced, with greater definition.

A list of Tolkien's art published in *Pictures by J.R.R. Tolkien* is included in an appendix to the **Chronology** volume of the *Companion and Guide*. See also *Art.

Pity and Mercy. In *The Lord of the Rings* the pity of Bilbo, Frodo, and Sam, each of whom spares Gollum's life, is clearly shown as having led to the ultimate success of the *quest. In the account of Bilbo's encounter with Gollum under the Misty Mountains it is said that, as Bilbo fled from Gollum, who suspected that Bilbo had found his ring, the Ring slipped on Bilbo's finger, making him invisible, and that Bilbo followed Gollum until they came to an opening that led to the lower gates: 'There Gollum crouched at bay, smelling and listening; and Bilbo was tempted to slay him with his sword. But pity stayed him, and though he kept the ring, in which his only hope lay, he would not use it to help him kill the wretched creature at a disadvantage. In the end, gathering his courage, he leaped over Gollum in the dark, and fled away . . .' (Prologue). In Book I, Chapter 2, when Frodo learns that through Gollum Sauron has probably discovered the whereabouts of the Ring, he cries: 'What a pity that Bilbo did not stab that vile creature, when he had the chance!' To which Gandalf replies: 'Pity? It was Pity that stayed his hand. Pity, and Mercy: not to strike without need. And he has been well rewarded, Frodo. Be sure that he took so little hurt from the evil, and escaped in the end, because he began his ownership of the Ring so. With Pity.'

There are several points to be made about these passages. One is the use of 'pity' in the conventional phrase 'what a pity', often used to indicate regret or disappointment about comparatively minor events or mishaps; but this is not the focus of the present article. That usage is clearly different from the 'pity' shown by Bilbo, which falls within the second definition of the word in the *Oxford English Dictionary*: 'a feeling or emotion of tenderness aroused by the suffering, distress or misfortune of another, and prompting a desire for its relief; compassion; sympathy'. The first definition in the OED, 'the quality of being pitiful; the disposition to mercy or compassion; clemency, mercy, mildness, tenderness', is noted as obsolete, or merged into the second. The definitions of *pitiful* include an obsolete use, 'characterized by piety, pious', and among modern usages 'full of pity, compassionate, merciful'. It is clear that one can feel compassion, without mercy being a necessary concomitant, though in some uses it is implied. The *Oxford English Dictionary* defines *mercy* as 'forbearance and compassion shown by one person to another who is in his power and has no claim to receive kindness; kind and compassionate treatment in a case where severity is merited or expected'. 'It was Pity that stayed [Bilbo's] hand. Pity, and Mercy'.

It is, however, an interesting fact that until the second edition of *The Hobbit* (1951) Bilbo showed neither of these to Gollum, nor was any needed. In the original version of *The Hobbit*, Chapter 5, Gollum offered Bilbo a present if he won the riddle contest, but when Gollum lost and went to get his ring, he could not find it, and therefore agreed to show Bilbo the way out instead. He led him through the tunnels as far as he dared, then 'Bilbo slipped under the arch, and said good-bye to the nasty miserable creature'. The revised version of Chapter 5 was probably written in August or September 1947, and until summer 1950 Tolkien thought that Allen & Unwin were unwilling to make the change. Yet during the writing of *The Lord of the Rings* Bilbo's, and later Frodo's, pity for Gollum are of the same major significance in the story, even in the earliest account of Bingo's (Frodo's) conversation with Gandalf, written in autumn 1938, though with some contortion: 'What a pity Bilbo did not stab the beastly creature when he said goodbye'. . . . 'What nonsense you do talk sometimes, Bingo. . . . Pity! It was pity that prevented him. And he could not do so, without doing wrong. It was against the rules. If he had done so he would not have had the ring, the ring would have had him at once' (**The Return of the Shadow*, p. 81). It is clear that Tolkien knew almost from the beginning that without pity and mercy being shown to Gollum, the quest would end in failure.

In the published text Frodo responds to Gandalf's comment on Bilbo's pity: 'I am frightened; and I do not feel any pity for Gollum. . . . He deserves death.' Gandalf points out that Frodo has not seen Gollum, and it may be that Gollum does deserve death; but

> many that live deserve death. And some that die deserve life. Can you give it to them? Then do not be too eager to deal out death in judgement. For even the very wise cannot see all ends. I have not much hope that Gollum can be cured before he dies, but there is a chance of it. And he is bound up with the fate of the Ring. My heart tells me that he has some part to play yet, for good or ill, before the end; and when that comes, the pity of Bilbo may rule the fate of many – yours not least. In any case we [his captors] did not kill him: he is very old and very wretched. The Wood-elves have him in prison, but they treat him with such kindness as they can find in their wise hearts.

Already not only Bilbo, but Gandalf and the Wood-elves, have felt pity for Gollum. Because the Wood-elves did not have 'the heart to keep him ever in dungeons under the earth' (bk. II, ch. 2) Gollum was able to escape, and to play a part such as Gandalf foresaw.

When, in Book IV, Chapter 1, Frodo and Sam capture Gollum at the foot of the Emyn Muil and he begs for mercy, Frodo seems to hear the words spoken by Gandalf in their conversation at Bag End, and says: 'I will not touch the creature. For now that I see him, I do pity him.' Frodo's pity for a while seems to bring about a change in Gollum. At the pool of Henneth Annûn Frodo is offered an easy way out as he approaches Gollum and hears his murmuring about the Precious, nasty hobbits, nasty Men: 'We hates them. . . . Throttle them, precious.'

> So it went on. . . . Frodo shivered, listening with pity and disgust. He wished it would stop, and that he never need hear that voice again. Anborn was not far behind. He could creep back and ask him to get the huntsmen to shoot. . . . Only one true shot, and Frodo would be rid of the miserable voice for ever. But no, Gollum had a claim on him now. The servant has a claim on the master for service, even service in fear. They would have foundered in the Dead Marshes but for Gollum. Frodo knew, too, somehow, quite clearly that Gandalf would not have wished it. [bk. IV, ch. 6]

Faramir, against the command that he slay any he find in Ithilien without leave, allows Frodo, for whom he feels 'pity and honour' (bk. IV, ch. 5), to continue on his journey. He also shows mercy (but perhaps not pity) in not killing Gollum, allowing him to leave with Frodo.

On Mount Doom Gollum attacks first Frodo and then Sam, and despite Gollum's treachery, even Sam at last comes to feel pity for him:

> It would be just to slay this treacherous, murderous creature, just and many times deserved; and also it seemed the only safe thing to do. But deep in his heart there was something that restrained him: he could not strike this thing lying in the dust, forlorn, ruinous, utterly wretched. He himself, though only for a little while, had borne the Ring, and now dimly he guessed the agony of Gollum's shrivelled mind and body, enslaved to that Ring, unable to find peace or relief ever in life again. [bk. VI, ch. 3]

At the last, Frodo admits that but for Gollum, 'I could not have destroyed the Ring. The Quest would have been in vain, even at the bitter end. So let us forgive him! For the Quest is achieved . . .' (bk. VI, ch. 3).

After the publication of *The Lord of the Rings* some readers wrote to Tolkien commenting on the honour given to Frodo despite his 'failure'. In a letter to Michael Straight, written probably at the end of 1955, Tolkien said that

> the 'salvation' of the world and Frodo's own 'salvation' is achieved by his previous *pity* and forgiveness of injury. At any point any prudent person would have told Frodo that Gollum would certainly betray him, and

could rob him in the end. To 'pity' him, to forbear to kill him, was a piece of folly, or a mystical belief in the ultimate value-in-itself of pity and generosity even if disastrous in the world of time. He did rob him and injure him in the end – but by a 'grace', that last betrayal was at a precise juncture when the final evil deed was the most beneficial thing any one c[oul]d have done for Frodo! By a situation created by his 'forgiveness', he was saved himself, and relieved of his burden. [*Letters*, p. 234]

On 27 July 1956 he wrote to Amy Ronald:

It is possible for the good, even the saintly, to be subjected to a power of evil which is too great for them to overcome – in themselves. In this case the cause (not the 'hero') was triumphant because by the exercise of pity, mercy, and forgiveness of injury, a situation was produced in which all was redressed and disaster averted. Gandalf certainly foresaw this [in Book I, Chapter 2]. Of course, he did not mean to say that one must be merciful, for it may prove useful later – it would not then be mercy or pity, which are only truly present when contrary to prudence. Not ours to plan! But we are assured that we must be ourselves extravagantly generous, if we are to hope for the extravagant generosity which the slightest easing of, or escape from, the consequences of our own follies and errors represents. And that mercy does sometimes occur in this life. [*Letters*, pp. 252–3]

In a draft letter to Mrs Eileen Elgar in September 1963, Tolkien explained his thoughts on

that strange element in the World that we call Pity or Mercy, which is also an absolute requirement in moral judgement (since it is present in the Divine nature). In its highest exercise it belongs to God. For finite judges of imperfect knowledge it must lead us to the use of two different scales of 'morality'. To ourselves we must present the absolute ideal without compromise, for we do not know our own limits of natural strength (+ grace), and if we do not aim at the highest we shall certainly fall short of the utmost that we could achieve. To others, in any case of which we know enough to make a judgement, we must apply a scale tempered by 'mercy': that is, since we can with good will without the bias inevitable in judgements of ourselves, we must estimate the limits of another's strength and weigh this against the force of particular circumstances. [*Letters*, p. 326]

There are other examples of mercy and pity in *The Lord of the Rings*; indeed, the opponents of Sauron generally seem eager to offer mercy to all except Orcs. Wormtongue, who has betrayed his king, is allowed to depart unhindered by both Théoden and Gandalf. After the Battle of Helm's Deep, the hillmen beg for mercy; the Rohirrim disarm them, set them to bury the dead, and then set them free to return to their own land, asking only that they swear an oath not to pass the Fords of Isen in arms again or aid the enemies of Rohan. As the host of the West nears the desolation before the Morannon, the horror of the place unmans some among the men. Aragorn looks at them, and with 'pity in his eyes rather than wrath' he suggests another task that they might attempt 'and so be not wholly shamed' (bk. V, ch. 10). After his coronation Aragorn pardons and frees the Easterlings who have surrendered, and makes peace with Harad, and pronounces a judgement on Beregond which combines 'mercy and just-ice' (bk. VI, ch. 5). Gandalf offers to let Saruman go free on certain conditions, Treebeard releases him, hating to keep any live thing caged, and Frodo spares him despite all the harm he has done to the Shire and Saruman's attempt to kill him. Other examples of pity are concerned with compassion rather than mercy: when, for instance, Faramir first sees Éowyn, 'being a man whom pity deeply stirred, it seemed to him that her loveliness amid her grief would pierce his heart'; but later she tells him 'I desire no man's pity', and he replies: 'Do not scorn the pity that is the gift of a gentle heart. . . . But I do not offer you my pity. . . . I love you. Once I pitied your sorrow. But now, were you sorrowless, without fear or any lack, were you the blissful Queen of Gondor, still I would love you' (bk. VI, ch. 5).

Katharyn W. Crabbe in *J.R.R. Tolkien* (rev. and expanded edn. 1988) comments that in *The Lord of the Rings* 'to be able to pity others who suffer distinguishes the heroic from the villainous. In fact, Tolkien was no doubt making use of the philological fact that *pity*, in the general sense of "a feel-ing of compassion"' did not exist as separate from its specific religious sense of *piety* until well after 1600: until then the ability to feel pity was a mark of piety' (p. 81). In the 'instances of heroic mercy' shown by Gandalf, Treebeard, and Frodo to Saruman, by Frodo to Gollum, and by Aragorn to the faint-hearted,

> there is an existential side . . . for in *The Lord of the Rings* mercy seems to mean the refusal to accept any being's less than perfect state as his essen-tial nature. Justice would pay each according to what he has done; mercy pays him according to what he might do – according to the ideal. . . . In a sense, the act of mercy works to preserve the free will of the receiver, giving him the chance to become the better being that is within his capa-bility. Thus mercy is an essentially creative act – it leaves the possibilities for a recreation of the self open as does any healing process. As the hero shares with a divine being the quality of mercy, he shares with him his creative power. [p. 82]

Instances of pity and mercy are less frequent and less prominent in *The Silmarillion*. There the Vala Nienna, who 'is acquainted with grief, and mourns for every wound that Arda has suffered . . . does not weep for herself; and those who hearken to her learn pity, and endurance in hope' (p. 28). When Mandos, the Doomsman of the Valar, hears the song of Lúthien, he is 'moved to pity, who never before was so moved, nor has been since' (p. 187). Eärendil, as representative of Elves and Men, stands before the Valar and asks pardon 'for the Noldor and pity for their great sorrows, and mercy upon Men and Elves and succour in their need. And his prayer was granted' (p. 249).

Paul H. Kocher in *Master of Middle-earth: The Fiction of J.R.R. Tolkien* (1972) comments on the more overtly religious concept of mercy in *Leaf by Niggle*, specifically in the dialogue between two voices discussing what is to be done with Niggle,

> one voice insisting on justice, the other pleading for mercy. Here the resemblance is to the debate between the four daughters of God – Righteousness and Truth against Mercy and Peace – at the judging of souls, a favorite theme in medieval drama and poetry. . . . That Tolkien should employ techniques and ideas drawn from the literature of a period he knew so well is not surprising. But his success in acclimatizing them to our times is remarkable. Again we are justified in stressing that they were, and still are, Catholic. [p. 164–5]

Poems and Stories. Collection of shorter works by Tolkien, illustrated by *Pauline Baynes, first published (in de luxe form) by George Allen & Unwin, London, in May 1980. See further, *Descriptive Bibliography* A16. Trade editions were published by HarperCollins, London, in 1992 and by the Houghton Mifflin Company, Boston, in 1994.

The volume contains the poems of *The Adventures of Tom Bombadil and Other Verses from the Red Book*; *The Homecoming of Beorhtnoth Beorhthelm's Son*; *On Fairy-Stories*; *Leaf by Niggle*; *Farmer Giles of Ham*; and *Smith of Wootton Major*.

The Poetic and Mythologic Words of Eldarissa. List of words in Eldarissa, i.e. Qenya, the language of the Eldar (*Languages, Invented). Information from this early source, indicated by 'PME', was incorporated in relevant entries from the dictionary portion of the *Qenyaqetsa* (the 'Qenya Lexicon') as published in *Parma Eldalamberon* 12 (1998), ed. Christopher Gilson, Carl F. Hostetter, Patrick Wynne, and Arden R. Smith. The list, dating from ?1917–?1918 and entitled variously *Vocab[ulary]* and *The Poetic and Mythologic Words of Eldarissa*, is contained in a notebook with the title *Names and Lang[uage] to Book of Lost Tales*, later altered to *Notebook B, being Names to the Book of Lost Tales*.

The alphabetical order of the words suggests that Tolkien used the *Qenyaqetsa* to compile this list. On four pages in the middle of the list Tolkien interposed 'a chart outlining the different kindreds of Elves and other races of beings in his mythological world, giving the terms for them in both Qenya and Gnomish' (p. xx), and the names of few prominent characters (*'Early Chart of Names'); and a list of names from the 'Story of Tuor' in Qenya and Gnomish (*Official Name List).

The *Parma Eldalamberon* editors comment that the title *The Poetic and*

Mythologic Words of Eldarissa 'suggests that Tolkien's intention was to prepare a basic vocabulary list to accompany his poems and mythological tales, and explain the significance of the names and other Elvish words included in them' (p. xx).

Poetry. Tolkien recalled in *On Fairy-Stories* that as a child he was 'insensitive to poetry, and skipped it if it came in tales. Poetry I discovered much later in Latin and Greek and especially through being made to try and translate English verse into classical verse' (*Tree and Leaf*, p. 41). Robert Browning's *Pied Piper*, at least, 'failed with me even as a child, when I could not yet distinguish the shallow vulgarity of Browning from the general grown-uppishness of things I was expected to like' (letter to his *Aunt Jane Neave, 22 November 1961, *Letters*, p. 311). Nonetheless the young Tolkien may have tried to write a poem himself, about a dragon, when he was six or seven years old. In later years he could not recall if it was a poem or a story, only that his mother told him that he must write 'great green dragon', not 'green great dragon' (*Letters*, pp. 214, 221).

Tolkien's earliest surviving poem appears to be *Morning*, which he included in a letter to Edith Bratt (*Edith Tolkien) written on 26 March 1910. Many of his early verses celebrate his feelings for *nature and landscape, or copy (or parody) poetic styles. *The Battle of the Eastern Field* (1911), for instance, is a description of a rugby football match written in the style of one of Lord Macaulay's *Lays of Ancient Rome*. Tolkien also looked for inspiration to the Finnish *Kalevala* and the works of *Geoffrey Chaucer (see *The Clerke's Compleinte*) and William Langland (*Piers Plowman*; see *Doworst*). For several years, verse was his chosen form of literary composition, except for papers to be read to various societies, and some of those were on poetry or poets – the *Kalevala*, Francis Thompson, H.R. Freston (1891–1916).

Tolkien believed that his poetic voice was stimulated by the meeting of the *T.C.B.S. in London on 12–13 December 1914. He wrote to his friend *G.B. Smith on 12 August 1916 of 'the hope and ambitions . . . that first became conscious at the Council of London. That Council was as you know followed in my own case with my finding a voice for all kinds of pent up things and a tremendous opening up of everything for me: – I have always laid that to the credit of the inspiration that even a few hours with the four [core members of the T.C.B.S.] always brought to all of us' (*Letters*, p. 10). Smith was himself an amateur poet of some talent; also, poetry had long been a pursuit by which young men of a literary bent sought to make their names.

In the months following the 'Council of London' Tolkien began to write poems even more prolifically, and shared them with his T.C.B.S. friends (G.B. Smith, *R.Q. Gilson, and *Christopher Wiseman) and with a former schoolmaster, *R.W. Reynolds, for comment and criticism. He made fair copies of his poems and had them typed, arranging them for possible publication. The prospect of death for a young officer during the war gave such activity a special urgency. With no time for Tolkien to establish himself by publishing individual poems in magazines, he submitted a collection of his verse, with the title *The Trumpets of Faerie*, to Sidgwick & Jackson of London early in 1916; but it was rejected.

By now his poem *Goblin Feet* had appeared in *Oxford Poetry 1915*, and he had also written verses such as *You & Me and the Cottage of Lost Play* (April 1915, see *The Little House of Lost Play: Mar Vanwa Tyaliéva*) and *The Princess Ní* (July 1915). Although Tolkien later came to dislike his early depictions of diminutive beings with 'fairy lanterns' and 'little pretty flittermice', they were not uncommon in poetry of his day. 'Fairy poetry' had been popular since the nineteenth century, promoted by the likes of Christina Rossetti and William Allingham. Fairies also featured often in pictorial art. John Garth in *Tolkien and the Great War* (2003) cites *The Piper of Dreams* (1914), a painting by Estella Canziani, as a possible influence on Tolkien's poem *Tinfang Warble*. Some of his fairy poetry – which R.W. Reynolds felt to be his strong suit – foreshadows the fairies and elves of his *'Silmarillion'* mythology, while other verses of the period, such as *Kortirion among the Trees* (November 1915, see *The Trees of Kortirion*), are more clearly within its framework. Tolkien wrote on one version of *The Shores of Faëry* (July 1915, illustration May 1915, see *Artist and Illustrator*, fig. 44) 'first poem of my mythology'.

In other respects, Tolkien the poet was like many other men faced with the challenge of war, who found a voice to express feelings of nostalgia for England left behind, so different from life in the trenches, or about the war itself. Verses of this sort by G.B. Smith appeared after his death in *A Spring Harvest* (1918), edited by Tolkien; of Tolkien's own poems, *The Lonely Isle* and *The Town of Dreams and the City of Present Sorrow* have been published, but not *A Dream of Coming Home*, *A Memory of July in England*, and *Companions of the Rose* (dedicated to the memory of Gilson and Smith), among others.

In the years following his return from service in France, Tolkien continued to write new poetry and to revise earlier work, but until he went to *Leeds in 1920 the greater part of his literary writing was *The Book of Lost Tales*, in prose. While at Leeds he retold the story of Túrin Turambar (*'Of Túrin Turambar'*) from *The Book of Lost Tales* at length in alliterative verse as *The Children of Húrin*, though unfortunately this was left unfinished. Several of his shorter poems were published in magazines and collections. He also wrote poems and songs in English and other Northern languages to be sung at meetings of the Leeds Viking Club (*Songs for the Philologists*). During this time, while he taught Old and Middle English poetry, Tolkien also made verse translations into Modern English of part of *Beowulf* and probably the whole of *Pearl*. The complex metre of the latter work inspired him to write an original poem, *The Nameless Land* (1924). In 1962 he wrote of this to Jane Neave:

> I never agreed with the view of scholars that the metrical form [of *Pearl*] was almost impossibly difficult to write in, and quite impossible to render in modern English. NO scholars (or, nowadays, poets) have any experience in composing themselves in exacting metres. I made up a few

stanzas in the metre to show that composition in it was not at any rate 'impossible' (though the result today might be thought bad). [*Letters*, p. 317]

In summer 1925 Tolkien began the *Lay of Leithian*, a lengthy treatment of the tale of Beren and Lúthien (*'Of Beren and Lúthien') written in octosyllabic couplets, but this too he left unfinished. He revised and rewrote parts of it *c.* 1950. *Christopher Tolkien quotes the remarks of an unnamed critic who wrote to his father that in 'the staple octosyllabic couplet of romance' he had chosen one of the most difficult of forms 'if one wishes to avoid monotony and sing-song in a very long poem. I am often astonished by your success, but it is by no means consistently maintained' (quoted in *The Lays of Beleriand*, p. 1).

Clearly Tolkien liked to try his hand at poetry with complex metrical demands, including alliteration, the repetition of words, and rhyming schemes, often inspired by styles of the past. He wrote to *W.H. Auden on 29 March 1967 that many years earlier, 'when trying to learn the art of writing alliterative poetry', he composed a poem in which he attempted 'to unify the lays about the Völsungs from the Elder Edda, written in the old eight-line fornyrðislag stanza' (*Letters*, p. 379; see *Northernness). Most of the riddles in Chapter 5 of *The Hobbit, all of them Tolkien's own work, in style and method were modelled on old literary riddles. Poems such as *Iumbo* and its descendent *Oliphaunt, and *Fastitocalon were inspired by the medieval bestiary. *The Lay of Aotrou and Itroun is in the style of a Breton *lai*, and the poem *Imram was inspired by Irish tales and legends of voyages. Tolkien wrote the first version of *The Homecoming of Beorhtnoth Beorhthelm's Son in rhyming verse, but later rewrote it in alliterative verse, a form he wrote with pleasure, and used also for his unfinished poem *The Fall of Arthur* (*Arthur and the Matter of Britain) and in *The Lord of the Rings to mark the Anglo-Saxon affinities of the Rohirrim.

The poems and songs found in *The Lord of the Rings*, Tolkien wrote to Margaret Carroux, who was translating the work into German,

> are an integral part of the narrative (and of the delineation of the characters) and not a separable 'decoration' like pictures by another artist. . . .
> I myself am pleased by metrical devices and verbal skill (now out of fashion), and am amused by representing my imaginary historical period as one in which these arts were delightful to poets and singers, and their audiences. But otherwise the verses are all impersonal; they are as I say dramatic, and fitted with care in style and content to the characters and the situations in the story of the actors who speak or sing. [29 September 1968, Tolkien-George Allen & Unwin archive, HarperCollins]

In October 1968 he wrote to his son *Michael that his poetry had 'received little praise – comment even by some admirers being as often as not contemptuous. . . . Perhaps largely because in the contemporary atmosphere – in which "poetry" must only reflect one's personal agonies of mind or soul, and exterior things are only valued by one's own "reactions" – it seems hardly ever recognized that the verses in *The [Lord of the Rings]* are all dramatic . . .' (*Letters*, p. 396). Both William Reynolds in 'Poetry as Metaphor in *The Lord of the Rings*', *Mythlore* 4, no. 4, whole no. 16 (June 1977), and T.A. Shippey in *J.R.R. Tolkien: Author of the Century* (2000) examine two poems from *The Lord of the Rings* – *The Road Goes Ever On* (bk. I, ch. 1, 2; bk. VI, ch. 6) and *Upon the Hearth the Fire Is Red* (bk. I, ch. 3; bk. VI, ch. 9) – and how by subtle changes Tolkien uses them to reveal character, emotion, and situation.

From the beginning Tolkien often revised and rewrote his poems, sometimes after gaps of many years, improving, changing emphasis, or transforming to fit into one of his narrative works. The most extraordinary example of this is how **Errantry* evolved through many stages to become the poem 'Eärendil was a mariner' which Bilbo recites at Rivendell in *The Lord of the Rings*, Book II, Chapter 1. By that time, only one line survived from the version of *Errantry* published in 1933. The poem, Tolkien said, is 'in a metre I invented (depending on trisyllabic assonances or near-assonances, which is so difficult that except in this one example I have never been able to use it again – it just blew out in a single impulse)' (letter to Rayner Unwin, 22 June 1952, *Letters*, pp. 162–3).

When he needed a theme for the mostly light-hearted collection published as **The Adventures of Tom Bombadil and Other Verses from the Red Book* (1962), Tolkien was able to pretend that the contents were Hobbit poetry, and even attributed some of them to characters in *The Lord of the Rings*. He told **Pauline Baynes, who was illustrating the book, that the poems 'were conceived as a series of very definite, clear and precise, pictures – fantastical, or nonsensical perhaps, but not dreamlike!' and were, he thought, 'dexterous in words, but not very profound in intention'. **The Hoard* was an exception, 'written in [a] mode rather resembling the oldest English verse – and was in fact inspired by a single line of ancient verse' from *Beowulf* (6 December 1961, *Letters*, p. 312).

TRANSLATION OF POETRY

Tolkien probably first undertook the translating of poetry at **King Edward's School, Birmingham, where pupils were required to translate English verse into Latin. In the early 1920s, while employed at the University of Leeds, he translated the traditional song 'The Mermaid' ('It was in the broad Atlantic') into Old English to be recited or sung by the Viking Club (**Societies and clubs). But his most important translations are those that he made of Old and Middle English poems into Modern English. In these he took pains to preserve as far as possible the original metre, rhyming pattern, alliteration, and style. In reply to a letter from Professor John Leyerle, who had obviously expressed different ideas, he wrote on 28 April 1967: 'You of course go clean contrary to my own views on translation of works of a former time in your remarks about "aping features that are anachronistic today". If the taste and sympathies of the present day are to be the criterion, why bother to present to moderns things that are anachronistic in feeling and thought?' (Tolkien Papers, Bodleian Library, Oxford).

In an unpublished essay concerning his thoughts on the translation of poetry, written after reading *Poems from the Old English* translated by Burton Raffel (1960), Tolkien points out first the value of making such translations without intention to publish them: 'The making of translations should be primarily for private amusement, and profit. The profit, at any rate, will be found in the increased and sharpened understanding of the language of the original which the translator will acquire in the process, and can acquire no other way.' He then considers how some of the impact of the work on its original audience might be achieved not only for those who could not read the original, but also for those whose appreciation of the texts had been spoiled because they were objects of study:

First of all by absolute allegiance to the thing translated: to its meaning, its style, technique, and form. The language used in translation is, for this purpose, merely an instrument, that must be handled so as to reproduce, to make audible again, as nearly as possible, the antique work. Fortunately modern (modern literary, not present-day colloquial) English is an instrument of very great capacity and resources, it has long experience not yet forgotten, and deep roots in the past not yet all pulled up. It can, if asked, still play in modes no longer favoured and remember airs not now popular; it is not limited to the fashionable cacophonies. I have little sympathy with contemporary theories of translation, and no liking for their results. In these the allegiance is changed. Too often it seems given primarily to 'contemporary English', the present-day colloquial idiom as if being 'contemporary', that most evanescent of qualities, by itself guaranteed its superiority. In many the primary allegiance of the 'translator' is to himself, to his own whims and notions, and the original author is evidently considered fortunate to have aroused the interest of a superior writer. This attitude is often a mask for incompetence, and for ignorance of the original idiom; in any case it does not encourage close study of the text and its language, the laborious but only sure way of acquiring a sensitive understanding and appreciation, even for those of poetic temperament, who might have acquired them, if they had started with a more humble and loyal allegiance. [Tolkien Papers, Bodleian Library, Oxford]

Tolkien remarked to Jane Neave that translations which follow the original closely are more difficult to create than original verse, since the translator does not have the freedom of the original poet. By example, he described the complexities of *Pearl*, the rhyming pattern of its twelve-line stanzas, its internal alliteration of line, and its requirement that certain words and lines be echoed from stanza to stanza. The translation of *Pearl* attracted him because of the poem's 'apparently insoluble metrical problems' (18 July 1962, *Let-*

ters, p. 317). Later, in a letter to his grandson Michael George (see *Michael Tolkien), he wrote that '*Pearl* is, of course, about as difficult a task as any translator could be set. It is impossible to make a version in the same metre close enough to serve as a "crib". But I think anyone who reads my version, however learned a Middle English scholar, will get a more direct impression of the poem's impact (on one who knew the language)' (6 January 1965, *Letters*, p. 352).

For Tolkien, translation not only made a work of the past available to modern readers who could not read the older language, it was also a means by which the translator could study the poem and get close to the thought of its author, and could by the words he chose for the translation provide a commentary on the original. Tolkien had begun translations of *Pearl* and of *Sir Gawain and the Green Knight* for his own instruction, since 'a translator must first try to discover as precisely as he can what his original means, and may be led by ever closer attention to understand it better for its own sake. Since I first began I have given to the idiom of these texts very close study, and I have certainly learned more about them than when I first presumed to translate them' (*Sir Gawain and the Green Knight, Pearl and Sir Orfeo*, p. 7). His translations of *Sir Gawain and the Green Knight, Pearl*, and *Sir Orfeo* were published together in 1975; but his unfinished verse and completed prose translations of *Beowulf* are still unpublished except for brief extracts. Tolkien also began a translation of the Middle English *Owl and the Nightingale*, but probably did not complete it. In 1967 he wrote to Professor Leyerle: 'I have at present given up the task. . . . It comes off well enough in certain passages, but in general octo-syllabic couplets are defeating for a translator; there is no room to move' (Tolkien Papers, Bodleian Library, Oxford).

Political thought. Tolkien's political views on the whole were conservative, in that he supported the Conservative Party rather than the Labour Party, but also in that he wanted to conserve what was good, and not to assume that new ideas or inventions were good merely because they were new. He understood that power could corrupt, and mistrusted those who sought it. He applauded the medieval ideal of *nolo episcopari*: that only the man who does not want to be a bishop is fit to be a bishop – by extension, that those who seek power are unfit to wield it. Letters he wrote to his son *Christopher during the Second World War are enlightening on all of these issues. His feelings were undoubtedly sharpened by the situation around him – the use of machines (*Environment) leading to destruction and loss of life, incompetency and corruption, controls and restrictions – and he found some relief in writing about them. On 29 November 1943 he wrote to Christopher, with deliberate overemphasis to make his point:

My political opinions lean more and more to Anarchy (philosophically understood, meaning abolition of control not whiskered men with bombs) – or to 'unconstitutional' Monarchy. I would arrest anybody who uses the word State (in any sense other than the inanimate realm of England and its inhabitants, a thing that has neither power, rights nor mind); and after a chance of recantation, execute them if they remained obstinate! If we could get back to personal names, it would do a lot of good. Government is an abstract noun meaning the art and process of governing and it should be an offence to write it with a capital G or so as to refer to people. If people were in the habit of referring to 'King George's council, Winston [Churchill] and his gang', it would go a long way to clearing thought, and reducing the frightful landslide into They-ocracy. Anyway the proper study of Man is anything but Man; and the most improper job of any man, even saints (who at any rate were at least unwilling to take it on), is bossing other men. Not one in a million is fit for it, and least of all those who seek the opportunity. [*Letters*, pp. 63–4]

In a draft letter to Michael Straight at the end of 1955 he explained: 'I am not a "socialist" in any sense – being averse to "planning" . . . most of all because the "planners", when they acquire power, become so bad . . .' (*Letters*, p. 235). In another draft letter, to Joanna de Bortadano in April 1956, Tolkien explained his doubts about 'democracy' as necessarily an ideal method of government: 'I am *not* a "democrat" only because "humility" and equality are spiritual princi-ples corrupted by the attempt to mechanize and formalize them, with the result that we get not universal smallness and humility, but universal greatness and pride, till some Orc gets hold of a ring of power – and then we get and are getting slavery' (*Letters*, p. 246). In other words, he could see that the ideals of democracy are all too rarely achieved: those elected may abuse the power they achieve in the interests of themselves or their friends, or for various reasons may not represent the whole population but only a section of it – great land-owners, or those with inherited wealth or political connections.

Tolkien loved *England and applauded true patriotism, but was against any form of imperialism or colonialism, whether political or cultural. In a letter to Christopher Wiseman on 16 November 1914, not long after the beginning of the First World War, he discussed matters that he felt to be of supreme import-ance, including 'the duty of patriotism and a fierce belief in nationalism'. He concluded: 'I am not of course a militarist. I no longer defend the Boer War! I am a more & more convinced Home Ruler. . . . I don't defend "Deutschland über alles" but certainly do the Norwegian "alt for Norge" which translates itself (if I have it right?)' (Tolkien Papers, Bodleian Library, Oxford). On 9 December 1943 he wrote to his son Christopher: 'I love England (not Great Britain and certainly not the British Commonwealth (grr!)), and if I was of military age, I should, I fancy, be grousing away in a fighting service, and will-ing to go on to the bitter end . . .' (*Letters*, p. 65). On 29 May 1945, after the end of the war in Europe but while it still continued in the Far East, he wrote to Christopher: 'As I know nothing about British or American imperialism in the Far East that does not fill me with regret and disgust, I am afraid I am not even supported by a glimmer of patriotism in this remaining war. I would not subscribe a penny to it, let alone a son, were I a free man. It can only benefit America or Russia: prob[ably] the latter' (*Letters*, p. 115).

He was patriotic but not blindly so – patriotic to his country but not necessarily to its government's policies or propaganda. He expressed this in historical terms in another letter to Christopher, on 31 July 1944:

> I should have hated the Roman Empire in its day (as I do), and remained a patriotic Roman citizen, while preferring a free Gaul and seeing good in Carthaginians. *Delenda est Carthago* [Plutarch, 'Carthage must be destroyed']. We hear rather a lot of that nowadays. I was actually taught at school that that was a fine saying; and I 'reacted' . . . at once. There lies still some hope that, at least in our beloved land of England, propaganda defeats itself, and even produces the opposite effect. [*Letters*, p. 89]

Tolkien recognized that *good and evil are not all on one side, even if he felt that perhaps there was more evil, or more evil men, in the Second World War among the Germans and Japanese. When he read an article in a local paper 'seriously advocating systematic exterminating of the entire German nation as the only proper course after military victory: because, if you please, they are rattlesnakes, and don't the difference between good and evil!' he wondered if the writer himself knew the difference, and commented to Christopher: 'The Germans have just as much right to declare the Poles and Jews exterminable vermin, subhuman, as we have to select Germans: in other words, no right, whatever they have done. Of course there is still a difference here. The article was answered, and the answer printed' (23–5 September 1944, *Letters*, p. 93). In the same letter he objected to propaganda on the BBC and in newspapers, which he supposed was produced by the Ministry of Information,

> that the German troops are a motley collection of sutlers and broken men, while yet recording the bitterest defence against the finest and best equipped armies . . . that have ever taken the field. The English pride themselves, or used to, on 'sportsmanship' (which included 'giving the devil his due'). . . . But it is distressing to see the press grovelling in the gutter as low as [Nazi propagandist Joseph] Goebbels in his prime, shrieking that any German commander who holds out in a desperate situation . . . is a drunkard, and a besotted fanatic. [*Letters*, p. 93]

It has been alleged that Tolkien was not interested in current affairs, and hardly ever read a newspaper. He told Henry Resnik in an interview in 1966, however, that he and his wife took three newspapers, and 'I read them when I'm interested. I take a strong interest in what is going on, both in the university and in the country and in the world' ('An Interview with Tolkien', *Niekas* 18 (Spring 1967), p. 39). The sinister picture of *Númenor under the influence of Sauron in *The Lost Road* (written c. 1936–7), for instance, almost certainly reflects knowledge of the contemporary rise of Nazi Germany. This includes the withdrawal of the besotted and aging king from the public view, the unexplained disappearance of people unpopular with the 'government', informers, prisons, torture, secrecy, fear of the night; propaganda in the form of the 'rewriting of history'. . . ; the multiplication of weapons of war, the purpose of which is concealed but guessed at. . . . The teaching of Sauron has led to the invention of ships of metal that traverse the seas without sails . . . ; to the building of grim fortresses and unlovely towers; and to missiles that pass with a noise like thunder to strike their targets many miles away. Moreover, Númenor is seen by the young as over-populous, boring, 'over-known' . . . and this cause of discontent is used, it seems, by Sauron to further the policy of 'imperial' expansion and ambition that he presses on the king. When at this time my father reached back to the world of the first man to bear the name 'Elf-friend' he found there an image of what he most condemned and feared in his own. [*The Lost Road and Other Writings, p. 77]

That Tolkien was well aware of anti-Semitism in Nazi Germany (*Prejudice and Racism) is shown by his reaction to a request by the proposed publisher of a German translation of The Hobbit, for a declaration of Tolkien's 'arisch' origin. He pointed out the correct meaning of Aryan and regretted that he had no Jewish blood. In addition, Christopher Tolkien remembers *Father Vincent Reade visiting his father in Oxford not long before the Second World War and describing the maltreatment of Jews in Germany, which he had recently visited (correspondence with the authors).

In the mid-1950s Tolkien made references in letters comparing the disintegration of Frodo's will under the influence of the Ring in *The Lord of the Rings to brainwashing, and though he did not specify, obviously to the treatment of some prisoners of war by North Korea. In a draft letter to Michael Straight at the end of 1955, he said that Frodo did indeed fail at the end of his *quest, and one correspondent had said that Frodo should have been executed as a traitor. 'Believe me, it was not until I read this that I had myself any idea how "topical" such a situation might appear. . . . I did not foresee that before the tale was published we should enter a dark age in which the technique of torture and disruption of personality would rival that of Mordor and the Ring and present us with the practical problem of honest men of good will broken down into apostates and traitors' (Letters, p. 234). In a draft to Miss J. Burn on 26 July 1956 he wrote: 'In the case of those who now issue from prison "brainwashed", broken, or insane, praising their torturers, no such immediate deliverance is as a rule to be seen. But we can at least judge them by the will and intentions with which they entered the Sammath Naur; and not demand impossible feats of will, which could only happen in stories unconcerned with real moral and mental probability' (Letters, p. 252).

He also objected to cultural 'colonialism' and the standardization that often follows, regretting the loss of diversity, including diversity of language with the spread of English:

The bigger things get the smaller and duller or flatter the globe gets. It is getting to be all one blasted little provincial suburb. When they have introduced American sanitation, morale-pep, feminism, and mass production throughout the Near East, Middle East, Far East, U.S.S.R., the Pampas, el Gran Chaco, the Danubian Basin, Equatorial Africa, Hither Further and Inner Mumbo-land, Gondhwanaland, Lhasa, and the villages of darkest Berkshire, how happy we shall be. At any rate it ought to cut down travel. There will be nowhere to go. So people will (I opine) go all the faster. Col. ['Collie'] Knox says ⅙ of the world's population speaks 'English', and that is the biggest language group. If true, damn shame – say I. May the curse of Babel strike all their tongues till they can only say 'baa baa'. It would mean much the same. I think I shall have to refuse to speak anything but old Mercian.

But seriously : I do find this Americo-cosmopolitanism very terrifying. . . . I am not really sure that its victory is going to be so much better for the world as a whole and in the long run than the victory of —— [sic].
[letter to Christopher Tolkien, 9 December 1943, *Letters*, p. 65]

In yet another letter to Christopher, on 31 July 1944, Tolkien wondered what the end of the war would bring, 'but I suppose the one certain result of it all is a further growth in the great standardised amalgamations with their mass-produced notions and emotions' (*Letters*, p. 89).

Poole (Dorset). Tolkien and his wife *Edith in their later years frequently visited *Bournemouth on the south coast of England. Eventually they decided to move to the area permanently. Tolkien seems to have made up his mind as soon as he saw the property at **19 Lakeside Road** in Poole that it was what he and Edith wanted. On 14 May 1968 he wrote to *Rayner Unwin: 'I have discovered a very admirable and commodious bungalow in the borough of Poole (with of course a correspondingly ample price)' (George Allen & Unwin archive, University of Reading). Their possessions were removed from *Oxford to Poole in mid-July 1968, but in Tolkien's absence due to a leg injury in June.

In Poole the Tolkiens 'lived in greater luxury than they had ever known, for despite the wealth from his writings, they both retained a great simplicity in the way they lived. Now, for the first time they enjoyed the comforts of central heating and a bathroom each; while Edith was as excited as a young bride at the sophistication of their new kitchen' (John and Priscilla Tolkien, *The Tolkien Family Album*, p. 83, with photograph). There was also a sitting-room, a dining-room, a bedroom each, a room for Tolkien to use as a study, a veranda where he and Edith could sit, and a large garden; and since it was a bungalow, there were no stairs for its aged owners to negotiate. The building was plain and modern, but a private gate led to the wooded Branksome Chine, where Lord Snowdon photographed Tolkien leaning against the roots of a great tree, and down to the sea. As at Sandfield Road in Oxford, a double garage was converted into a library and office. *Joy Hill of George Allen

& Unwin (*Publishers) often came to help Tolkien with his fan mail and other correspondence. His new address and telephone number were kept secret to avoid unwelcome intrusions by fans such as he had suffered in Oxford. Tolkien lived in Poole until Edith's death on 29 November 1971. In March 1972 he returned to Oxford.

Possessiveness. In Tolkien's writings possessiveness is a major sin, and usually leads to the loss of the desired object and evil consequences. This is a recurring motif particularly in *'The Silmarillion'.

Fëanor is possessive about the Silmarils, ignoring the fact that, although he has made them, much of their glory is due to the light of the Two Trees created by Yavanna and Nienna, which has been captured in the jewels. He wears the Silmarils at great feasts, but 'at other times they were guarded close, locked in the deep chambers of his hoard in Tirion. For Fëanor began to love the Silmarils with a greedy love, and grudged the sight of them to all save to his father and his seven sons; he seldom remembered now that the light within them was not his own' (*The Silmarillion, p. 69). When he is summoned by the Valar to a reconciliation with his brother, 'he denied the sight of the Silmarils to the Valar and the Eldar, and left them locked in Formenos in their chamber of iron' (p. 75). But Melkor is able to seize them when he attacks Formenos after destroying the Two Trees. Fëanor refuses Yavanna's request for the Silmarils to try to revive the Two Trees with their light, neither knowing that the jewels have already been seized by Melkor. The writer of *The Silmarillion* comments that 'all one it may seem whether Fëanor had said yea or nay to Yavanna; yet had he said yea at the first . . . it may be that his after deeds would have been other than they were' (p. 79). Fëanor and his sons then swear 'a terrible oath . . . to pursue with vengeance and hatred to the ends of the World' any being 'whoso should hold or take or keep a Silmaril from their possession' (p. 83). From this follows war and treachery, so that at the end of the First Age Eönwe, the herald of Manwë, refuses to give two Silmarils to the two surviving sons, telling them 'that the right to the work of their father . . . had now perished, because of their many and merciless deeds, being blinded by their oath . . .' (p. 253).

In the story of the mortal Beren and the Elf Lúthien Tinúviel (*'Of Beren and Lúthien) Thingol, King of Doriath, is so possessive of his daughter Lúthien that to send her lover, Beren, to his death and yet keep the promise he has made to Lúthien not to harm Beren, he demands as the price of his daughter's hand that Beren bring him a Silmaril from Morgoth's crown. Beren comments: 'For little price do Elven-kings sell their daughters: for gems, and things made by craft' (*The Silmarillion, p. 168), implying that Thingol is treating his daughter like a possession. Later, when he has the Silmaril, 'Thingol's thought turned unceasingly to the jewel of Fëanor, and became bound to it, and he liked not to let it rest even behind the doors of his inmost treasury; and he was minded now to bear it with him always, waking and sleeping' (p. 232). His resulting commission to the Dwarves to place it in a necklace, the Nauglamír, leads to the ruin of his realm.

In the story *'Of Tuor and the Fall of Gondolin' the message that Tuor brings from the Vala Ulmo to Turgon, King of Gondolin, is 'that the Curse of Mandos now hastened to its fulfilment, when all the works of the Noldor should perish; and he bade him depart, and abandon the fair and mighty city that he had built. . . .' Turgon remembers words spoken to him long before by Ulmo: 'Love not too well the work of thy hands and the devices of thy heart; and remember that the true hope of the Noldor lieth in the West, and cometh from the Sea' (*The Silmarillion*, p. 240). But out of love for the city he has built, and trust in its strength, Turgon does not heed the message, and Gondolin is destroyed.

In *The Hobbit* Tolkien describes the dragon Smaug's reactions when he discovers that one cup from his hoard had been stolen. 'His rage passes description – the sort of rage that is only seen when rich folk that have more than they can enjoy suddenly lose something that they have long had but have never before used or wanted' (ch. 12). Later the dwarf Thorin is unwilling to share any of the treasure of the dragon's hoard, even though he knows that not all of it originally had been the property of the his people. The Dwarves were particularly prone to the sin of possessiveness, and 'used their rings only for the getting of wealth; but wrath and an overmastering greed of gold were kindled in their hearts, of which evil enough after came . . .' (*The Silmarillion*, pp. 288–9).

Tolkien's cautionary poem *The Hoard* relates how doom fell on the Elves; the treasure they had made is hoarded in a dark cave by an old dwarf; he is killed by a dragon who lies on the hoard, only to be killed in turn by a young warrior. And although the warrior becomes a king, as he grows old he can think only 'of his huge chest . . . / where pale gems and gold lay hid'. An enemy invades, his kingdom is lost, and the hoard lies hidden under a mound 'while earth waits and the Elves sleep' (*The Adventures of Tom Bombadil and Other Verses from the Red Book*, p. 54).

In *Smith of Wootton Major* Smith receives a star which gives him entry to Faery. After many years he meets the Queen of Faery face to face: she says farewell and lays her hand on his head, 'and a great stillness came on upon him; and he seemed to be both in the World and in Faery, and also outside them and surveying them, so that he was at once in bereavement, and in ownership, and in peace' (p. 38). He leaves sadly, and meets Alf the Prentice, actually the King of Faery, who tells him that it is time to give up the star. At first Smith is unwilling: 'Isn't it mine? It came to me, and may a man not keep things that come to him so, at least as a remembrance?' Alf replies: 'Some things. Those that are free gifts and given for remembrance. But others are not so given. They cannot belong to a man for ever, nor be treasured as heirlooms. They are lent. You have not thought, perhaps, that someone else may need this thing. But it is so' (pp. 41, 44). Because Smith then gives up the star freely, he is allowed to choose who shall be the next bearer of the star.

In his letter to *Milton Waldman of ?late 1951 Tolkien found fault with the Elves who chose to stay in Middle-earth at the end of the First Age:

In [*Of the Rings of Power and the Third Age] we see a sort of second fall or at least 'error' of the Elves. There was nothing wrong essentially in their lingering against counsel. . . . But they wanted to have their cake without eating it. They wanted the peace and bliss and perfect memory of 'The West', and yet to remain on the ordinary earth where their prestige as the highest people . . . was greater than at the bottom of the hierarchy in Valinor. They thus became obsessed with 'fading', the mode in which the changes of time (the law of the world under the sun) was perceived by them. . . . With the aid of Sauron's lore they made *Rings of Power*. . . . The chief power (of all the rings alike) was the prevention or slowing of *decay* (i.e. 'change' viewed as a regrettable thing), the preservation of what is desired or loved, or its semblance – this is more or less an Elvish motive. But also they enhanced the natural powers of a possessor – thus approaching 'magic', a motive easily corruptible into evil, a lust for domination. [*Letters*, pp. 151–2]

In *The Lord of the Rings*, at the end of the Third Age Elrond and Galadriel accept that the power of their rings must pass, and therefore aid the Ringbearer in his quest to destroy the One Ring (which, however, is also their only hope of preventing Sauron from regaining the ruling ring). Elrond never seems to consider the possibility of using the One Ring, and Galadriel refuses it when it is offered to her.

The possessive attitude of the various owners of the One Ring – Isildur, Gollum, Bilbo, Frodo – as expressed in *The Lord of the Rings* is a different matter, since their behaviour towards it arises not wholly from innate character, but from the insidious influence of the Ring towards possessiveness. Ominously Isildur, Gollum, and Bilbo each use the word 'precious' in relation to the Ring.

Paul H. Kocher notes that in the section on *Recovery in *On Fairy-Stories* Tolkien says that it is necessary to provide a clear view of things which seem trite: because we know them so well, we no longer look at them, but keep them locked in our memory as in a hoard. This, says Kocher, explains much of Tolkien's feelings about correct attitudes and sources of evil. 'We are not to be like dragons hoarding in our dens whatever we can snatch from the living world around us. People and things are not meant to be our property, they belong to themselves. . . . We are possessed, captured, by what we think we possess, says Tolkien. And if we believe we can wholly possess anything we delude ourselves' (*Master of Middle-earth: The Fiction of J.R.R. Tolkien* (1972), pp. 66–7).

Power. Several of Tolkien's correspondents thought that the main theme of *The Lord of the Rings* was power and its misuse. In his replies Tolkien admitted its importance, but generally rejected the idea that it was the most significant or predominating theme in the work. In a letter to G.E. Selby soon after the publication of *The Lord of the Rings* was complete (?late 1955 or ?1956) he wrote: 'The story is for me about Mercy and Hope/Death, to which "Power" (which most people fasten on) is subsidiary' (quoted in Sotheby's, *Fine Books and Manuscripts: Including English and American Literature*, New York, 16–17 May 1984, lot 703). On 17 November 1957 he told H. Schiro that 'the tale is not really about Power and Dominion: that only sets the wheels going; it is about Death and the desire for deathlessness. Which is hardly more than to say it is a tale written by a Man!' (*Letters*, p. 262). And to Rhona Beare on 14 October 1958 he wrote that 'if the tale is "about" anything (other than itself) it is not as seems widely supposed about "power". Power-seeking is only the motive-power that sets events going, and is relatively unimportant, I think. It is mainly concerned with Death, and Immortality [*Mortality and Immortality]; and the 'escapes': serial longevity, and hoarding memory' (*Letters*, p. 284).

In a draft letter to Joanna de Bortadano in April 1956 Tolkien wrote more fully:

> Of course my story is not an allegory of Atomic power, but of *Power* (exerted for Domination). . . . [But] I do not think that even Power or Domination is the real centre of my story. It provides the theme of a war, about something dark and threatening enough to seem at that time of supreme importance, but that is mainly a 'setting' for characters to show themselves. The real theme for me is about something much more per-manent and difficult: Death and Immortality. . . . I am *not* a 'democrat' only because 'humility' and equality are spiritual principles corrupted by the attempt to mechanize and formalize them, with the result that we get not universal smallness and humility, but universal greatness and pride, till some Orc gets hold of a ring of power. . . . [*Letters*, p. 246]

Tolkien was aware of the corrupting effect that power could have on those who wield it, and indeed that those who seek power are often the least fit to have it. He wrote to his son *Christopher on 29 November 1943 that 'the most improper job of any man, even saints (who at any rate were at least unwill-ing to take it on), is bossing other men. Not one in a million is fit for it, and least of all those who seek the opportunity. . . . The mediævals were only too right in taking *nolo episcopari* ["I do not wish to be made a bishop"] as the best reason a man could give to others for making him a bishop' (*Letters*, p. 64). He undoubtedly agreed with John Emerich Edward Dalberg, the first Baron Acton (1834–1902), who wrote that 'power tends to corrupt and absolute power corrupts absolutely', and with William Pitt, Earl of Chatham (1708–1778), who said in the House of Lords in 1770 that 'unlimited power is apt to corrupt the minds of those who possess it'.

Tolkien objected especially to the use of power to dominate the wills of others, even 'knowing what was best for them' and to the use of *magic or machines (see *Environment) to enforce or impose one's own will. In a letter to *Milton Waldman in ?late 1951 he noted that even a sub-creator (*Sub-creation) 'may become possessive, clinging to the things made as "its own"' (as did Fëanor in *'The Silmarillion'), and wish to be the Lord and God of his private creation. He will rebel against the laws of the Creator – especially against mortality. Both of these (alone or together) will lead to the desire for Power, for making the will more quickly effective, – and so to the Machine (or Magic). By the last I intend all use of external plans or devices (apparatus) instead of the development of the inherent inner powers or talents – or even the use of these talents with the corrupted motive of dominating: bulldozing the real world, or coercing other wills. . . .

The Enemy [Melkor/Morgoth in 'The Silmarillion'] in successive forms is always 'naturally' concerned with sheer Domination, and so the Lord of magic and machines; but the problem: that this frightful evil can and does arise from an apparently good root, the desire to benefit the world and others – speedily and according to the benefactor's own plans – is a recurrent motive. [*Letters*, pp. 145–6]

It is noteworthy in *The Lord of the Rings* that most of those who oppose Sauron reject using the One Ring as a weapon against him, and will not even accept it as a gift. Gandalf tells Frodo:

With that power I should have power too great and terrible. And over me the Ring would gain a power still greater and more deadly. . . . Do not tempt me! For I do not wish to become like the Dark Lord himself. Yet the way of the Ring to my heart is by pity, pity for weakness and the desire of strength to do good. Do not tempt me! I dare not take it, even to keep it safe, unused. The wish to yield it would be too great for my strength. I shall have such need of it. Great perils lie before me. [bk. I, ch. 2]

Tolkien commented in a draft letter to Mrs Eileen Elgar in September 1963, that 'Gandalf as Ring-Lord would have been far worse than Sauron. He would have remained "righteous", but self-righteous. He would have continued to rule and order things for "good", and the benefit of his subjects according to his wisdom . . .' (*Letters*, pp. 332–3).

In 'The Silmarillion' the Valar reject the use of force to bring all of the Elves to Aman, and though they warn, they take no steps to prevent the Noldor returning to Middle-earth. In the Third Age the Valar send the Istari to Middle-earth as messengers 'to contest the power of Sauron, and to unite all those who had the will to resist him; but they were forbidden to match power with power, or to seek to dominate Elves or Men by force or fear' (*The Lord of the Rings*, Appendix B). Saruman falls, and his words as he tempts Gandalf to join him seem to embody the deceits, lies, and corruption of those who will do anything to obtain power or to gain the attention of those who have power:

A new Power is rising. . . . We may join with that Power. It would be wise, Gandalf. There is hope that way. Its victory is at hand; and there will be rich reward for those who aided it. As the Power grows, its proved friends will also grow; and the Wise, such as you and I, may with patience come at last to direct its courses, to control it. We can bide our time, we can keep our thoughts in our hearts, deploring maybe evils done by the way, but approving the high and ultimate purpose: Knowledge, Rule, Order; all the things that we have so far striven in vain to accomplish, hindered rather than helped by our weak or idle friends. There need not be, there would not be, any real change in our designs, only in our means. [bk. II, ch. 2]

In a late work, *Notes on Motives in the Silmarillion*, Tolkien commented that Morgoth had 'a vast demiurgic lust for power and the achievement of his own will and designs, on a great scale'. When 'confronted by the existence of other inhabitants of Arda, with other wills and intelligences, he was enraged by the mere fact of their existence, and his only notion of dealing with them was by physical force, or the fear of it. His sole ultimate object was their destruction.' He endeavoured 'to break wills and subordinate them to or absorb them into his own will and being, before destroying their bodies. This was sheer nihilism, and negation its one ultimate object' (*Morgoth's Ring*, pp. 395–6). In contrast, 'Sauron had never reached this stage of nihilistic madness. He did not object to the existence of the world, so long as he could do what he liked with it' (p. 396). He desired to dominate the 'minds and wills' of the 'creatures of earth' (p. 395). Sauron's corruption of the Númenóreans, which led to the destruction of *Númenor, was 'a particular matter of revenge upon Ar-Pharazôn', for his humiliation of Sauron. But 'Sauron (unlike Morgoth) would have been content for the Númenóreans to exist, *as his own subjects*, and indeed he used a great many of them that he corrupted to his allegiance' (p. 398).

In *Tolkien: A Cultural Phenomenon* (2003) Brian Rosebury comments, regarding the despotism of both Saruman and Sauron, that the 'keynote' of evil is 'aggrandisement of self and negation of not-self', achieved

through the enslavement and torture of other persons and the destruction of growing things. There is only one form of political order, a military despotism which terrorises its own soldiery as well as its enemies; sexuality is loveless, either diverted into sadism or confined to the organised breeding of warriors; economic life is based on slavery, and is devoted not to the cultivation, but to the exploitation, and ultimately the destruction of resources. Industrial processes are developed solely for the purposes of warfare and deliberate pollution. [p. 45]

Katharyn W. Crabbe comments in *J.R.R. Tolkien* (rev. and expanded edn. 1988) on the power shown by Sauron that it

goes beyond the simple acquisitiveness of *The Hobbit* to include the ultimate control – control over being. Sauron's power, or the power he seeks, is a power that parodies the power of the creator. Rather than create, Sauron will destroy; rather than set free, he will enslave; rather than heal, he will harm. The desire of Sauron to make everything in Middle-earth less than it is capable of being is clear in his repeated threats to 'break' captives, in the ruined and desolate lands that were once fertile and productive. . . . [p. 86]

Meredith Veldman points out in *Fantasy, the Bomb, and the Greening of Britain: Romantic Protest 1945–1980* (1994) that

> Saruman's faith in 'a lot of slaves and machines and things' reflects his failure to see other beings in their wholeness and individuality. The Mordor spirit reduces individuals to an undifferentiated mass in need of regimentation. Saruman's fall begins with his desire for power in order to do good, but he demands to be able to dictate to others the timing, scope, and scale of this goodness. . . . Such a desire to dictate, even for the good, stems from the urge to dominate, the 'will to mere power' embodied in the Ring and triumphant in Mordor. . . .
>
> Because it regards other creatures as slaves rather than allies, the 'will to mere power' incarnate in Sauron annihilates individual freedom and choice. Sauron reduces those in his power to mere pawns to satisfy his own insatiable hunger for total domination. In contrast, the good achieve victory by recognizing the importance of individual choice and action. The corrupted Saruman would have 'the Wise' determine the course of events, but the unfolding of *The Lord of the Rings* reveals the significance of the actions of small and weak individuals. [pp. 83–4]

Anne C. Petty discusses use of innate and external power at length in the chapter 'The Use and Abuse of Power' in her *Tolkien in the Land of Heroes: Discovering the Human Spirit* (2003). She notes that 'as a talisman of power, the Ring is both actual and symbolic. It represents what happens when concentrated power (especially in a technological sense) takes our imaginations in frightening directions. The inference to weapons and industries of war in our technological age is applicable, although not allegorical. For Tolkien, the Ring served as a symbol of desire for pure power, wielded through deception . . . and technology . . .' (p. 155).

Prefatory Remarks on Prose Translation of 'Beowulf'. Essay, first published by George Allen & Unwin, London, in July 1940 in *Beowulf and the Finnesburg Fragment*, a new edition of Modern English translations by John R. Clark Hall of the Old English poems **Beowulf* and the 'Finnesburg (or Finnsburg) Fragment'. These translations had been published originally in 1901 and 1911; for 1940 they were completely revised, with notes and an introduction, by *C.L. Wrenn, and newly prefaced by Tolkien's essay. In 1983 the *Prefatory Remarks* were reprinted as *On Translating 'Beowulf'* in **The Monsters and the Critics and Other Essays*, pp. 49–71. See further, *Descriptive Bibliography* B17, A19.

SUMMARY

In the first of the essay's two parts, 'On Translation and Words', Tolkien warns that although Clark Hall's text is a 'competent translation' of *Beowulf* it is no substitute for reading the poem itself – a great poem whose 'specially poetic qualities' cannot be caught in prose, and which in Modern English may lose the shades of meaning present in the original Old English. 'For many Old English poetical words there are (naturally) no precise modern equivalents of the same scope and tone: they come down to us bearing echoes of ancient days beyond the shadowy borders of Northern history.' Thus, for instance, Old English *eacen*, rendered by Clark Hall variously as 'stalwart', 'broad', 'huge', and 'mighty', originally meant 'not "large" but "enlarged"', an *addition* of power, beyond the natural, whether it is applied to the superhuman thirtyfold strength possessed by Beowulf . . . or to the mysterious magical powers of the giant's sword and the dragon's hoard imposed by runes and curses' (pp. 49, 50). Another difficulty for the translator is Old English descriptive compounds such as *sundwudu* 'flood-timber' (i.e. 'ship') and *swan-rad* 'swan's-road' ('sea'), which are 'generally foreign to our present literary and linguistic habits' (p. 51).

Tolkien warns the translator against 'colloquialism and false modernity'. 'If you wish to translate, not re-write, *Beowulf*, your language must be literary and traditional: not because it is now a long while since the poem was made, or because it speaks of things that have since become ancient; but because the diction of *Beowulf* was poetical, archaic, artificial (if you will), in the day that the poem was made.' But 'words should not be used merely because they are "old" or obsolete' (p. 54). (For a related discussion by Tolkien of deliberate 'archaism' in **The Lord of the Rings*, see his letter to *Hugh Brogan, September 1955, *Letters*, pp. 225–6.)

In the second part of the essay, 'On Metre', Tolkien discusses metre and alliteration in Old English poetry.

HISTORY

Probably early in 1936 Tolkien himself was asked by George Allen & Unwin (*Publishers) if he would be interested in revising Clark Hall's translations. Feeling that he did not have the time to spare to undertake the work himself, Tolkien suggested that it be given to *M.E. Griffiths, then a B.Litt. student under his supervision. He, however, would read what she produced, and write a preface or introduction to the book. In the event, Griffiths could not complete the revision, and at the end of June 1938 asked to be released from her contract. By then Tolkien had not yet written his own contribution: 'I would quickly write my brief introductory note, if I saw the book complete,' he told *Stanley Unwin on 4 June 1938. 'It would be brief for I do not wish to anticipate the things I should say in a preface to a new [Modern English] translation [by himself]' (Tolkien-George Allen & Unwin archive, HarperCollins). He had completed a prose translation already by the end of April 1926, and had begun an alliterative verse translation of *Beowulf*, but never finished either of these to his satisfaction. A few lines from the prose translation, however, are included in the *Prefatory Remarks*.

On Griffiths' withdrawal Tolkien still did not wish to deal with the whole of the book, but on 24 July 1938, presumably feeling an obligation to Allen & Unwin, he offered to 'put the thing into such order as is now possible, for such remuneration as seems good to you, with a title to be devised.... My concern would be primarily to put *the text* into reasonable working order, as far as can be contrived without too great or too costly cutting up of the version now in type' (letter to C.A. Furth, Tolkien-George Allen & Unwin archive, HarperCollins). His offer was accepted; but he soon found that other commitments, and problems of health, prevented him from doing the required work. He recommended that he relinquish the revision, therefore, to his Oxford colleague C.L. Wrenn, himself a formidable scholar of Old English, who was ready to complete the project in short order.

Indeed, Wrenn finished the revision months before Tolkien wrote his promised note. In a letter of 19 December 1939 to Stanley Unwin, having received several inquiries from his publisher, Tolkien apologized: 'I will try and collect my weary wits and pen a sufficient foreword to the "Beowulf" translation, *at once*' (*Letters*, p. 44). But ill health, the war, domestic troubles, and academic duties made writing difficult. In early 1940 he was again pressed for a note: 'a word or two' would be enough. He replied to Stanley Unwin on 30 March 1940:

> I knew that a 'word or two' would suffice (though could not feel that any words under my name would have any particular value unless they said something worth saying – which takes space). But I believed that more was hoped for.... For a fairly considerable 'preface' is really required. The so-called 'Introduction' does not exist, being merely an argument [or summary, with ten lines concerning the *Beowulf* manuscript, much less than Clark Hall had included in the previous edition]: there is no reference whatever to either a translator's or a critic's problems. I advised originally against any attempt to bring the apparatus of the old book up to date – it can be got by students elsewhere. But I did not expect a reduction to 10 lines, while the 'argument' (the least useful part) was rewritten at length.
>
> That being so I laboured long and hard to compress (and yet enliven) such remarks on *translation* as might both be useful to students and of interest to those using the book without reference to the original text. But the result ran to 17 of my [manuscript] pages (of some 300 words each) – not counting the metrical appendix, the most original part, which is as long again! [*Letters*, p. 45]

Tolkien now sent all that he had done to Stanley Unwin, suggesting that Unwin might care to consider it for inclusion later in a further edition, or that 'it might make a suitable small booklet for students' (p. 46); or certain passages might be removed for the sake of length. In the event, Unwin printed Tolkien's manuscript in full, though it increased the length of the book. Tolkien corrected proofs of the *Prefatory Notes* in April 1940.

At his suggestion and with Wrenn's approval, the spelling of 'Finnsburg', used in earlier editions of the book, was changed to 'Finnesburg'. (On this poem, see also *Finn and Hengest*.)

Another edition of *Beowulf and the Finnesburg Fragment* was published by Allen & Unwin, and distributed in the United States by Barnes & Noble, New York, in 1950; in this the scholarship of the work proper was revised again, a new introduction was provided, the notes were greatly enlarged, and misprints were corrected in the translations and in Tolkien's *Prefatory Remarks*, which were otherwise unchanged.

Prejudice and Racism. The letters that Tolkien wrote in 1938 to his publisher *Stanley Unwin and to Rütten & Loening, the proposed publisher of a German translation of *The Hobbit*, in response to a request from the latter that he confirm his 'arisch' (Aryan) origin, clear him of any suggestion of anti-Semitism. He objected to the request, and wrote to Stanley Unwin on 25 July:

> Personally I should be inclined to refuse to give any *Bestätigung* [confirmation] . . . and let a German translation go hang. In any case I should object strongly to any such declaration appearing in print. I do not regard the (probable) absence of all Jewish blood as necessarily honourable; and I have many Jewish friends, and should regret giving any colour to the notion that I subscribed to the wholly pernicious and unscientific race-doctrine. [*Letters*, p. 37]

With this he sent two possible replies, and left it to Stanley Unwin to decide which to send to Germany. Only one remains in the Allen & Unwin archive, presumably the one not sent, possibly the more strongly worded of the two. In this Tolkien displays his knowledge of the correct use of the word *Aryan* as opposed to the Nazi misuse: 'I regret I am not clear as to what you intend by *arisch*. I am not of *Aryan* extraction: that is Indo-iranian; as far as I am aware none of my ancestors spoke Hindustani, Persian, Gypsy, or any related dialects. But if I am to understand that you are enquiring whether I am of *Jewish* origin, I can only reply that I regret that I appear to have *no* ancestors of that gifted people' (*Letters*, p. 37).

In 1944, in response to a comment made in a letter by his son *Christopher about apartheid in *South Africa, where he was training to be a pilot, Tolkien wrote on 18 April: 'As for what you say or hint of "local" conditions: I knew of them. I don't think they have much changed (even for the worse). I used to hear them discussed by my mother; and have ever since taken a special interest in that part of the world. The treatment of colour nearly always horrifies anyone going out from Britain & not only in South Africa. Unfort[unately] not many retain that generous sentiment for long' (*Letters*, p. 73).

During the Second World War Tolkien wrote to Christopher on 23–25 September 1944, objecting to racist propaganda about the enemy:

> I cannot understand the line taken by BBC (and papers, and so, I suppose, emanating from M[inistry] O[f] I[nformation]) that the German troops are a motley collection of sutlers and broken men. . . . The English pride themselves, or used to, on 'sportsmanship' (which included 'giving the devil his due'). . . . But it is distressing to see the press grovelling in the gutter as low as Goebbels in his prime, shrieking that any German commander who holds out in a desperate situation . . . is a drunkard, and a besotted fanatic.

It is clear that he considered revilement of the enemy, just because he was the enemy, as much an exhibition of racism as segregation or anti-Semitism – that patriotism did not justify racism. He continued in his letter that a recent article had called for the extermination of the German people because 'they are rattlesnakes, and don't know the difference between good and evil'. If one were to accept that idea, said Tolkien, then 'the Germans have just as much right to declare the Poles and the Jews exterminable vermin, subhuman, as we have to select the Germans: in other words, no right, whatever they have done' (*Letters*, p. 93).

Those who see evidence of racism in Tolkien's works, whether conscious or unconscious, draw attention to descriptions which suggest that the various races of men that fought for Morgoth, Sauron, or Saruman (in **The Silmarillion'* or **The Lord of the Rings*) are of Asian or African origin, while those on the 'good' side have European features. They also point to the existence of the race of Orcs, apparently irredeemably evil (**Good and Evil). Charles Moseley in *J.R.R. Tolkien* (1997) sums up some of the points:

> Tolkien's texts do reveal values that are Eurocentric, white, middle-class, patriarchal – those of the majority of his generation in England, in fact. They are values embedded in the very vocabulary of his work. The Black Speech of the Dark Tower . . . echoes the consonantal patterns of Turkish; the Orcs' curved swords and their cruelty recall ancient legends, and illustrations, of the heathen East. The Southerners who come up the Greenway or fight in Mordor's host are ugly, slant-eyed and swart, emblematic of a culturally embedded racial stereotype of evil, the enemy; while the forces ranged against them, so far as we can see, are clean-limbed, white, dark-haired, grey-eyed examples of Northern European excellence [p. 63]

Mosley does not mention Tolkien's sympathetic treatment of Ghân-buri-Ghân and the Woses, but he does also point out that 'no fiction can satisfy every orthodoxy, least of all those that are differently historically conditioned from those of its own time' (p. 63).

Such critics tend to make no allowance for the fact that, although Tolkien meant Middle-earth to represent our world in fictional earlier ages, it is in fact a Secondary World which cannot be judged by events in our own particular history; that Tolkien as author had the right to change the parameters; and that what he states as the truth *is true within that world*. Morgoth, Sauron, and Saruman, who seek to obtain dominion by force and fear, are indeed rebels against the Creator, Eru, and his vicegerents the Valar, and the Elves and Men who oppose them have learned the truth directly or indirectly from the Valar. Nor, indeed, do some critics note how many episodes in *The Lord of the Rings* plead for the abandonment of old prejudices, for tolerance and understanding, and show this being achieved through knowledge, and greater appreciation of 'the other'.

Virginia Luling in 'An Anthropologist in Middle-earth', *Proceedings of the J.R.R. Tolkien Centenary Conference 1992* (1995), notes that although Faramir's explanation to Frodo that the lore of Gondor divides Men into 'the High, or Men of the West, which were Númenóreans; and the Middle Peoples, Men of the Twilight, such as are the Rohirrim . . . ; and the Wild, the Men of Darkness' (*The Lord of the Rings*, bk. IV, ch. 5) may sound 'like the classic Victorian evolutionary sequence of Savagery – Barbarism – Civilisation, which was around in Tolkien's youth. . . .' But on closer look,

the resemblance is only superficial; the whole structure of assumption underlying the two schemes is quite different. For the anthropology of Middle-earth is not evolutionary at all. The 'high' civilisations of Gondor and its predecessor Númenor have not developed by their own interior dynamic out of societies like that of the Rohirrim; they owe their arts and wisdom to their contact with the Elves. . . . The Rohirrim, too, owe their 'twilight' status to being descended from the Elf-friends of old. The 'Men of Darkness' are those who have not enjoyed the influence of the Elves. . . .

If we have something here that looks outwardly like what in our world we know as 'racism', we can dismiss that appearance, not only because Tolkien in his non-fictional writing several times repudiated racist ideas, but because . . . in his sub-creation the whole intellectual underpinning of racism is absent. The Haradrim and the Variags of Khand are corrupt not because they are biologically inferior but because they are human and therefore corruptible. In any case, though they are politically subject to Sauron it is uncertain . . . how far they are corrupt as individuals (unlike Orcs, who are a separate problem, and one that Tolkien himself never really solved). The men of Gondor and their allies are 'nobler', not by their intrinsic nature but because they have had the luck to inherit from their ancestors the mediated tradition – the faith – of Aman, and more or less held on to it – though they are constantly in danger of letting go. (As far as actual descent goes, they are ultimately the same as the Rohirrim.) [pp. 54–6]

Tolkien was writing out of the 'leaf-mould' of his own experience, and as he pointed out, 'a man of the North-west of the Old World will set his heart and the action of his tale in an imaginary world of that air, and that situation: with the Shoreless Sea of his innumerable ancestors to the West, and the endless lands (out of which enemies mostly come) to the East' (letter to *W.H. Auden, 7 June 1955, *Letters*, p. 212). The invaders who gained the most lasting reputation for savagery were the Huns, a warlike Asiatic nomadic people, who under Attila menaced both Constantinople and Rome. They suffered a major defeat in AD 451 at a battle on the Catalaunian plains, a recorded incident which may have influenced the depiction of Théoden's death on the Pelennor Fields (see *Reader's Companion*, p. 563). Europe also saw invasions by – *inter alia* – Arabs, whose drive into France was halted only at the Battle of Tours in AD 732, and who were not entirely expelled from Spain until 1492; the Ottoman Turks, who took Constantinople in 1453, tried to take Malta in 1565, and besieged Vienna as late as 1683; and pirates from the north African coast and Turkey, who threatened ships in the Mediterranean and inspired the Corsairs of Umbar in *The Lord of the Rings*. This is not to say that the Europeans did not engage in internal conflict and in conquests of their own, but for them the invader from Asia or Africa was viewed with particular horror because he was an 'infidel'.

Any discussion of racism and prejudice in Middle-earth is complicated by the fact that within those lands are not only several races of Men, but also other species – Elves, Dwarves, Hobbits, Ents, Drúedain (Woses), even Ainur – and the relations between these must also be considered. In 'The Silmarillion' a series of interspecies marriages are of great significance, obviously fated, and necessary to achieve the overthrow of Morgoth: those between Melian the Maia and Thingol the Elf, between their daughter Lúthien and the Man Beren, between the Man Tuor and the Elf Idril, and between their son Eärendil and Idril, the granddaughter of Beren and Lúthien. Although many of the different species in Middle-earth do get on reasonably well, and sometimes are closely allied, very rarely do two species live together; but this seems to be by choice, not because of imposed segregation, with each species preferring to retain its own traditions and way of life. Even when two species do live in close contact, such as Men and Hobbits in Bree, this is still the case: 'the Big and Little Folk (as they called one another) were on friendly terms, minding their own affairs in their own ways, but both rightly regarding themselves as necessary parts of the Bree-folk. Nowhere else in the world was this peculiar (but excellent) arrangement to be found' (bk. I, ch. 9).

Slavery is always depicted by Tolkien as evil. Elves captured by Morgoth are forced to work, and some are perhaps corrupted and refashioned as Orcs; followers of Morgoth oppress and enslave the remnants of the People of Hador; in their decline, and under the influence of Sauron, the Númenóreans 'came no longer as the bringers of gifts, but as men of war. And they hunted the men of Middle-earth and enslaved them and took their goods' (*Sauron Defeated*, p. 348); Sauron has many slaves to supply the needs of his armies in 'the great slave-fields away south' (*The Lord of the Rings*, bk. VI, ch. 2); and the Haradrim use captured men of Gondor to row their ships. Most of these examples of slavery are closer to that known in European history (the enslavement of the defeated by Greeks and Romans, or Irish or Viking raids on Britain for captives) than to 'plantation' slavery in the American South.

Rohan and Gondor do not enslave their defeated enemies. When the Rohirrim overwhelm Saruman's army at Helm's Deep, they disarm the hillmen of Dunland and tell them that if, after helping to bury the dead and repairing the damage Saruman's army had done to Helm's Deep, they are willing to take an oath never to attack Rohan again, they will be allowed to return, free, to their own land. 'The Men of Dunland were amazed, for Saruman had told them that the men of Rohan were cruel and burned their captives alive' (bk. III, ch. 8). At the end of the War of the Ring, Aragorn pronounces his judgement on those who have fought in Sauron's armies and attacked the forces of the West: 'And embassies came from many lands and peoples, from the East and the South, and from the borders of Mirkwood, and from Dunland in the West. And the King pardoned the Easterlings that had given themselves up, and sent them away free, and he made peace with the peoples of Harad; and the slaves of Mordor he released and gave to them all the lands about Lake Núrnen to be their own' (bk. VI, ch. 5).

Since strife and open warfare are major elements in both 'The Silmarillion' and *The Lord of the Rings*, there is a certain amount of the nationalistic fervour expressed as hatred and even vilification of the opponent which Tolkien criticized in the letter he wrote to Christopher in September 1944. In Ithilien, both Mablung and Damrod curse the Southrons who are coming to reinforce Sauron's armies. But this is balanced by Sam's thoughts about the Southron killed in the ambush, seeing him as a person rather than an enemy: 'He was glad he could not see the dead face. He wondered what the man's name was and where he came from; and if he was really evil of heart, or what lies or threats had led him on the long march from his home; and if he would not really rather have stayed there in peace' (bk. IV, ch. 4).

Tolkien rarely described the physical features of the enemy in any detail. The Swarthy Men or Easterlings who entered Beleriand after the Dagor Bragollach are said to be 'short and broad, long and strong in the arm; their skins were swart or sallow, and their hair was dark as were their eyes' (*The Silmarillion*, p. 157). A Mediterranean type was probably intended; some of these men betrayed their alliance with Maedhros, but others proved as faithful as the men of the Three Houses of the Edain. There are only a few brief descriptions of the men allied to Sauron in *The Lord of the Rings*: Gollum describes those about to enter the Morannon: 'They have black eyes and long black hair, and gold rings in their ears. . . . And some have red paint on their cheeks' (bk. IV, ch. 3). The fallen Southron seen by Sam had 'black plaits braided with gold', and his 'brown hand still clutched the hilt of a broken sword' (bk. IV, ch. 4). In the Battle of the Pelennor Fields the Southron chieftain wields a scimitar, which suggests a Saracen or Turk; and 'out of Far Harad' came 'black men like half-trolls with white eyes and red tongues' (bk. V, ch. 6). Since they come from the far South, these may be intended to suggest Africans, but as Virginia Luling points out, since Sauron's armies were recruited mainly from the South and East it was natural that Tolkien should draw 'on inherited images of "paynims" and other enemies' ('An Anthropologist in Middle-earth', pp. 56–7), and it is only because they fight for Sauron that they are seen as enemies.

There are some examples of prejudice among Elves in *The Silmarillion*, but it always seems to suggest a character defect. The sons of Fëanor in their pride look down on the Elves who had remained in Middle-earth; Caranthir says to Angrod, in response to a message from Thingol, 'Let not the sons of Finarfin run hither and thither with their tales to this Dark Elf in his caves!' (*The Silmarillion*, p. 112); and later Curufin calls Eöl 'Dark Elf', and tells him that 'those who steal the daughters of the Noldor and wed them without gift or leave do not gain kinship with their kin' (pp. 135–6). When Thingol learns of the slaying of his kin at Alqualondë by some of the Noldor, he bans the use of the Noldorin tongue in his realm.

Even within the small area of the Shire, there are prejudices among the Hobbits. Christina Scull wrote in 'Open Minds, Closed Minds in *The Lord of the Rings*', *Proceedings of the J.R.R. Tolkien Centenary Conference 1992* (1995): 'The Hobbits were . . . doubtful about other Hobbits, not those of a different breed, but also those who lived in a different part of the Shire. In this Tolkien probably intended to reflect the attitudes of the inhabitants of the English countryside in the days before travel was common, when areas beyond the next village or market town were considered "foreign" and the people "different"' (p. 151). While the Hobbits in the *Ivy Bush* and the Gaffer think the hobbits in Buckland 'queer', Farmer Maggot in the Marish has the same opinion of those who live in Hobbiton. Sam is suspicious of any hobbit who lives far from Hobbiton, and the Shire Hobbits refer to those of Bree as 'Outsiders' and consider them dull and uncouth. By the end of the story, however, some hobbits have learned greater toleration for others, and there is hope that attitudes will change.

The one clear example of prejudice in *The Lord of the Rings* is the persecution of Ghân-buri-Ghân and the Woses or Wild Men of the Woods, and this is ended within the story. This people seems to have been an unplanned element which arose in Tolkien's mind only just before their meeting with the Rohirrim. Ghân-buri-Ghân is described as 'a strange squat shape of a man, gnarled as an old stone, and the hairs of his scanty beard straggled on his lumpy chin like dry moss. He was short-legged and fat-armed, thick and stumpy and clad only with grass about his waist' (bk. V, ch. 5). The Woses communicate by beating drums, and are 'woodcrafty'. As Virginia Luling says, they 'are a sort of identikit Savage' ('An Anthropologist in Middle-earth', p. 55). Even though they have evidently been persecuted, they want to help the enemies of

Sauron. Ghân-buri-Ghân offers to lead the Rohirrim by a hidden road to avoid an ambush, asking in return only that if the Rohirrim prevail, they will leave the Wild Men alone in the woods and no longer hunt them like beasts. Although Ghân-buri-Ghân seems strange to the Riders, he wins their trust. After the victory against Sauron, Aragorn gives the Forest of Drúadan 'to Ghân-buri-Ghân and to his folk, to be their own for ever; and hereafter let no man enter it without their leave' (bk. VI, ch. 6).

Tolkien's sympathy for the Woses led him in later years to write about their remote ancestors, the Drúedain, in the First Age. The Drúedain live in close contact with the People of Haleth, but again with a certain separation: 'The strangest of all the customs of the Folk of Haleth was the presence among them of a people of a wholly different kind. . . . They were not many, a few hundreds maybe, living apart in families or small tribes, but in friendship, as members of the same community' (*Unfinished Tales*, p. 377). Although their appearance is unlovely to Elves and ordinary Men, nonetheless they are much loved and are recognized by the Elves as belonging to the race of Men.

In *The Silmarillion* it is the aim of Morgoth to foster division, mistrust, and hatred among those who oppose him, and after the defeat of the Noldor and their human allies in the Nirnaeth Arnoediad 'great was the triumph of Morgoth, and his design was accomplished in a manner after his own heart; for Men took the lives of Men, and betrayed the Eldar, and fear and hatred were aroused among those that should have been united against him. From that day the hearts of the Elves were estranged from Men, save only those of the Three Houses of the Edain' (p. 195). More notable still, as an example of interspecies prejudice and hostility, is the division between Elves and Dwarves, after the sacking of the Elvish stronghold of Menegroth by Dwarves in the First Age. For this reason, the King of the Wood-elves in *The Hobbit* is suspicious of Dwarves; Glóin in *The Lord of the Rings* refers to old grudges at the Council of Elrond; there is tension between Legolas the Elf and Gimli the Dwarf in the Company of the Ring during the first part of its journey south; the elven guards on the borders of Lórien at first are unwilling to admit Gimli, and Celeborn gives him only a grudging welcome. But when Galadriel greets him, Gimli 'looked up and met her eyes; and it seemed to him that he looked suddenly into the heart of the enemy and saw there love and understanding' (bk. II, ch. 7). 'From that moment he gave his heart to her and loved her in a way that echoes the courtly love of the Middle Ages. And because he loves her, he loves her people and wants to bring a reconciliation between Dwarves and Elves. . . . From that time on, friendship grows between Gimli and Legolas' (Scull, p. 153). Tolkien suggests that old prejudices and hatreds can be overcome with greater understanding. In this light, it is ironic that his own opinion of Dwarves, depicted usually as 'treacherous' in early 'Silmarillion' texts, changed after he wrote about them in *The Hobbit*.

Only the Orcs are treated as an exception. Portrayed as naturally evil, the 'good' side in *The Lord of the Rings* shows them no mercy and makes no attempt to understand them – though it might be argued that knowing that an Orc was evil was understanding enough. In comments written in June 1958 on the proposed story-line for a film of *The Lord of the Rings*, Tolkien said that 'the Orcs are definitely stated to be corruptions of the "human" form seen in Elves and Men. They are (or were) squat, broad, flat-nosed, with wide mouths and slant eyes: in fact degraded and repulsive versions of the (to Europeans) least lovely Mongol-types' (*Letters*, p. 274). In *On Fairy-Stories* Tolkien commented that 'to us evil and ugliness seem indissolubly allied. We find it difficult to conceive of evil and beauty together' (*Tree and Leaf*, p. 59). He therefore gave the Orcs a (to him) unlovely appearance, but implicitly allowed that this was not an absolute standard of beauty, and others might judge differently. If he were writing today, at a time of greater appreciation (or at least discussion) of diversity and racial sensitivity, he might well have chosen a more fantastic description which could not be related to any actual people. One might ask why Tolkien even included such a race of beings in his mythology; to which T.A. Shippey has replied: 'there can be little doubt that the orcs entered Middle-earth originally just because the story needed a continual supply of enemies over whom one need feel no compunction' (*The Road to Middle-earth* (2nd edn. 1992), p. 207).

In 'Tolkien the Anti-Totalitarian', *Proceedings of the J.R.R. Tolkien Centenary Conference 1992* (1995), Jessica Yates sums up a correspondence she had with Robert Westall in which she defended Tolkien against various accusations:

> I argued that we were not meant to identify any one race in the real world with the orc. Orcish tendencies are twofold: to vandalism and crude violence, and to blind fanaticism. Orcs follow their leaders because they have been brainwashed. Tolkien symbolises in the orc all mindless crowds who chant slogans and are ready to kill other people because their leader tells them to. . . . It is the orcs, not the Westerners, who are filled with unreasoning hate for others who are different. In distancing the orcs from his other created races, Tolkien indicated that they symbolised human tendencies – and surely it cannot be denied that what is recorded of humans is far worse than what Tolkien describes of orcish behaviour. [pp. 235–6]

Helen Armstrong in 'Good Guys, Bad Guys, Fantasy and Reality', *Proceedings of the J.R.R. Tolkien Centenary Conference 1992* (1995), argues that 'it is clear that Tolkien has humans at least partly in mind when he writes about orcs. They have individual self-interest. They enjoy inflicting damage and cruelty, but can hold back in the pursuit of other goals. . . . The inhabitants of fairyland are the denizens of our dreams, but we dream mainly of what we already know. Orcs are rather like humans because humans can be rather like orcs' (pp. 247–8). She points out that characters who encounter an orc 'do not ask whether it is friend or foe; they either run, hide, or attempt to kill it. They know that, unless they pursue one of these three options, they can themselves expect to be killed, or worse.' She cites examples of human violence, including incidents of massacre, rape, and mutilation in former Yugoslavia, and says that in such cases 'the common humanity between abuser and victim must seem very remote'.

All of this behaviour is cruel: much of it goes far beyond anything that can be explained as a necessity of war. This is not the time to tell the victims that the people who did this are 'like them'. They may have been once, they may be again; they may themselves have been abused. . . . But there still exists that place where one human being can look at another and encounter something utterly alien, cruel, implacable and terrifying. All our darkest images come from this source. . . .

There is no evidence that humankind can entirely exorcise the darker side from its consciousness. We can fight cruelty, hate and envy in ourselves as individuals; but to deny that they manifest themselves, horribly, in human experience is to create an illusion which is itself dangerous. [p. 248]

It might be argued that Morgoth corrupted the beings from which he fashioned the Orcs in such a way that they could only seek evil, and indeed, Tolkien never mentions any kind act on their part, or any hesitation in doing evil. If there is no hope that they might repent, or even cease to attack other races, then perhaps they should be considered as an analogy to a deadly virus or disease that mankind seeks to eradicate – though it should be pointed out that there is no evidence that Men and Elves set out to exterminate Orcs, although they offer Orcs no mercy when attacked by them.

Paul H. Kocher, commenting on the Orcs in the Third Age, suggests that 'the explanation of orc behavior . . . seems to be that Sauron (and Saruman) has carefully trained them to be what they are, continuing the training begun by Morgoth. Close under his thumb in Mordor, they have been educated to brutality and their social patterns set in a mold which will perpetuate it and its cognate qualities in generations to come.' They are 'plainly the toys of a mightier will than theirs. They have been conditioned to will whatever Sauron wills. . . . Never in Tolkien's tale are any orcs redeemed, but it would go against the grain of the whole to dismiss them as ultimately irredeemable' (*Master of Middle-earth: The Fiction of J.R.R. Tolkien*, 1972, pp. 70–1).

T.A. Shippey in 'Orcs, Wraiths, Wights: Tolkien's Images of Evil', *J.R.R. Tolkien and His Literary Resonances: Views of Middle-earth* (2000), analyses various conversations and actions of the Orcs and decides that

orcs are moral beings, with an underlying morality much the same as ours. But . . . it seems that an underlying morality has no effect at all on actual behavior. How, then, is an essentially correct theory of good and evil corrupted? If one starts from a sound moral basis, how can things go so disastrously wrong? It should require no demonstration to show that this is one of the vital questions raised with particular force during the twentieth century, in which the worst atrocities have often been committed by the most civilized people. Tolkien deserves credit for noting the problem, and refusing to turn his back on it, as so many of his more canonical literary contemporaries did. [p. 184]

He suggests that 'Orcish behavior, whether in orcs or in humans, has its root not in an inverted morality, which sees bad as good and vice versa, but in a kind of self-centeredness that sees indeed what is good . . . but is unable to set one's own behavior in the right place on this accepted scale' (p. 188) and he concludes 'there is in Tolkien's presentation of the orcs . . . a quite deliberate realism. Orcish behavior is human behavior, and their inability to judge their own actions by their own moral criteria is a problem all too sadly familiar' (p. 189).

Tolkien considered the question of whether any being was irredeemable in a draft letter of September 1954. If Morgoth had succeeded in creating 'rational' creatures, they 'would be creatures begotten of Sin and naturally bad. (I nearly wrote "irredeemably bad"; but that would be going too far. Because by accepting or tolerating their making – necessary to their actual existence – even Orcs would become part of the World, which is God's and ultimately good)' (letter to Peter Hastings, *Letters*, p. 195).

Princess Mee. Poem, first published in *The Adventures of Tom Bombadil and Other Verses from the Red Book* (1962), pp. 28–30. Based on the title character of the 1924 poem *The Princess Ní*, Princess Mee is lovely 'as in elven-song is told', dressed in pearls and gossamer, silver and 'diamond dew'. At night she dances in 'slippers frail / Of fishes' mail' on a 'mirror cool / Of windless water', while beneath her is 'A Princess Shee / As fair as Mee . . . dancing toe to toe' – her mirror image. Tolkien reinforces this idea of 'she' and 'me' by inverting the final four lines of the poem relative to the four that precede them.

Tolkien wrote *Princess Mee* no later than 15 November 1961, when he sent a copy to his *Aunt Jane Neave for her entertainment. In 1967 he made a recording of the poem, with others in the *Adventures of Tom Bombadil* volume, but it was not issued until 2001 as part of *The J.R.R. Tolkien Audio Collection* (*Recordings).

The Princess Ní. Poem, published in the collection *Leeds University Verse 1914–24* (1924), p. 58. Princess Ní is a slender elfin maid, 'wanly clad', girdled with fireflies, 'lighter than the air', who poses while we admire her frock and her smock of 'feathery pinafore' – the poem is no more than a brief *jeu d'esprit*. It served, however, as the basis for the longer, more developed poem *Princess Mee*.

The manuscript of the earliest version of *The Princess Ní* is dated 9 July 1915. Tolkien inscribed a later typescript '[written on the] Moseley B'ham [*Birmingham] Bus between Edgb[aston]. & Moseley July 1915'.

The Problem of Ros. Essay, published with commentary and notes in **The Peoples of Middle-earth* (1996), pp. 367–76.

It is one of several works in which Tolkien sought to explain 'in historical linguistic terms . . . names that went far back in the "legendarium" . . . and if such names had appeared in print he felt bound by them, and went to great pains to devise etymologies that were consonant with the now minutely refined historical development of Quenya and Sindarin [*Languages, Invented]' (p. 367). One of the most difficult of these names was *Elros*, mentioned in **The Lord of the Rings*. Though he had earlier explored its etymology, Tolkien returned to its study in 1968 or later. *The Problem of Ros*, so titled by *Christopher Tolkien, was written later than **The Shibboleth of Fëanor* in which Tolkien came to one conclusion on the matter.

Tolkien made several typescripts, each considering a different etymology, until he found one that satisfied him: in this he associated the name of Elros with that of his mother, Elwing. Only after writing several pages did he realize that his solution for the element *-ros* contradicted a published statement in *The Lord of the Rings*, which had to take precedence. 'So he was forced to accept that the element *-ros* in *Elros* must be the same as that in *Cair Andros*, the word must be Eldarin, not Atanic (Bëorian), and there could be no historical relationship between it and the Númenórean Adûnaic *Rothinzil*' (Christopher Tolkien, p. 371). In a related note, however, he tried to retain his proposed derivation of *-wing* from a Mannish tongue.

Like other late linguistic essays, *The Problem of* Ros also includes much information about the history of people and places: comment on the languages spoken by the various Houses of the Edain in the First Age; a brief conversation between Beren and Lúthien concerning her reasons for learning to speak his native tongue, and the reasons for the names of their descendants; the long dwelling of Folks of Hador and Bëor on opposite sides of a great sea during their movement west towards Beleriand; that Eärendil repeated his plea to Manwë in the tongues of the Elves and Men he represented. In connection with a statement that Eärendil did not use the language of the Folk of Haleth before Manwë, since that Folk and their tongue had perished, Christopher Tolkien summarizes the statements made in various texts concerning Túrin's fate after his death.

Progress in Bimble Town. Poem, first published as by 'K. Bagpuize' in the *Oxford Magazine* 50, no. 1 (15 October 1931), p. 22, one of a series of poems called **Tales and Songs of Bimble Bay*. 'Bimble Town' is an imaginary English seaside resort, exaggerated but of a kind Tolkien knew from some of his holidays. Once fair, it is now filled with shops selling 'sunburn-lotion / and picture-cards (of Godknowswhere, / and fat women dipped in ocean)', with motorcars making 'strong smells' and loud noises, litter on the grass and beach, and rubbish brought up with the tide.

Progress in Bimble Town was partly reprinted in the notes to **Roverandom* (1998), to illustrate the shared concern over pollution in the last part of that story; and fully reprinted in *The Annotated Hobbit* (1988, p. 212; rev. and expanded edn. 2002, p. 254). Douglas A. Anderson notes that it was written probably 'in the few years just prior to its publication', probably not before 1927. Its earliest extant manuscript, according to Anderson 'a clear copy with very few emendations' entitled *The Progress of Bimble*, is longer than the published poem by seventy-eight lines. Anderson speculates that its 'seaside setting may have been inspired by the [Tolkien] family's summer holidays in *Filey in North Yorkshire in 1923 [i.e. 1922] and 1925' (*The Annotated Hobbit* (2002), pp. 253–4), while its mock dedication 'to the Mayor and Corporation' may be indebted to Robert Browning's *The Pied Piper of Hamelin*.

Tolkien's pseudonym 'K. Bagpuize' plays on the name of Kingston Bagpuize, a village west of Oxford.

Publishers. Tolkien's earliest commercial publisher was **B.H. Blackwell**, established in *Oxford in 1879 by Benjamin Henry Blackwell, father of *Basil Blackwell. Its first book, actually a brochure, was *Mensae Secundae*, a collection of poetry produced by students at Balliol College, Oxford. The first volume in Blackwell's *Oxford Poetry* series appeared in 1913; Tolkien's poem *Goblin Feet* was published in *Oxford Poetry* for 1915. See also Rita Ricketts, *Adventurers All: Tales of Blackwellians, of Books, Bookmen, and Reading and Writing Folk* (2002).

The oldest publisher with which Tolkien was associated was the **Oxford University Press**, which traces its origins to the seventeenth century: the University of *Oxford first appointed Delegates, or directors, in 1633 to oversee the privilege to print books granted to the University by Star Chamber in 1586. Tolkien was first associated with the 'OUP' as an employee of the *Oxford English Dictionary* from 1919 to 1920. His first academic publication, *A Middle English Vocabulary*, was commissioned in 1919 and published under the Clarendon Press imprint – denoting a learned book of distinction – in 1922. The Tolkien-*E.V. Gordon edition of *Sir Gawain and the Green Knight* (1925; 2nd edn. 1967) was also a Clarendon Press book. Tolkien had dealings with the Press even into his later years, including co-editorship of the *Oxford English Monographs* and an aborted collaboration with *George S. Gordon on the 'Clarendon Chaucer' (see *Geoffrey Chaucer). See also Peter Sutcliffe, *The Oxford University Press: An Informal History* (1978).

His association with the London publisher **George Allen & Unwin Ltd** began probably in early 1936, in connection with the revision of John R. Clark Hall's translation of *Beowulf* and the 'Finnesburg Fragment' (see *Prefatory Remarks on Prose Translation of 'Beowulf'*), but his first publication by Allen & Unwin was *The Hobbit* in 1937. George Allen & Unwin was established by *Stanley Unwin in August 1914, after he acquired the assets of the publisher George Allen & Co. (begun 1871, merged with Swan Sonnenschein in 1911). Allen & Unwin published a wide variety of 'books that matter' (to quote their slogan), including works by influential thinkers such as Bertrand Russell, potentially controversial authors such as *Arthur Ransome (writing about

Russia immediately after the Revolution), and internationally famous figures such as Thor Heyerdahl (*The Kon-Tiki Expedition*, 1950). Tolkien frequently visited the firm's home office at 40 Museum Street, London.

Tolkien exchanged many letters with Stanley Unwin, with Unwin's youngest son *Rayner (who became a director in 1953, and head of the firm at his father's death in 1968), and with Unwin's cousin Philip Unwin (a director from 1949). Charles A. Furth, of the firm's production department, gave Tolkien valuable advice in regard to *The Hobbit* and *Mr. Bliss*; later Furth became an editor, and in 1949 a director. Art editor and designer Ronald Eames worked with Tolkien and *Pauline Baynes on *Farmer Giles of Ham* and *Smith of Wootton Major*, and in concert with production manager Walter N. Beard on *The Lord of the Rings*. Alina Dadlez, among others in the foreign rights department, corresponded with Tolkien on *translations of his works. *Susan Dagnall, in 1936 concerned with both editorial and advertising matters for Allen & Unwin, was instrumental in bringing *The Hobbit* to the publisher's attention. *Joy Hill, who served several functions at Allen & Unwin, also acted as Tolkien's secretary.

In 1986, to strengthen its financial position, Allen & Unwin merged with another small publisher, Bell and Hyman, to create Unwin Hyman; but profits declined, and in 1990 Unwin Hyman was sold in a takeover bid to Harper-Collins. Rayner Unwin resigned in protest, but was able to institute protections for the Tolkien Estate and to ensure the continued existence of the Allen & Unwin imprint in Australia. See also F.A. Mumby and Frances H.S. Stallybrass, *From Swan Sonnenschein to George Allen & Unwin Ltd.* (1955); Stanley Unwin, *The Truth about a Publisher: An Autobiographical Record* (1960); *Fifty Years of Publishing Books That Matter* (1964); Philip Unwin, *The Publishing Unwins* (1972); David Unwin, *Fifty Years with Father: A Relationship* (1982); and Rayner Unwin, *George Allen & Unwin: A Remembrancer* (1999).

The **Houghton Mifflin Company** has been Tolkien's principal hardcover and trade paperback publisher in the United States since they issued *The Hobbit* in 1938. The firm traces its history to the publisher Ticknor and Fields, established in Boston, Massachusetts in 1832; in 1880 Ticknor and Fields merged with the Riverside Press of Henry Houghton and George Mifflin to form Houghton, Mifflin and Company (the name later altered to its present form). Editors Anne Barrett, Paul Brooks, and Austin Olney helped to support the American publication of Tolkien's works during his lifetime, and originated *The Road Goes Ever On: A Song Cycle* (1967) by Tolkien and *Donald Swann. See also Paul Brooks, *Two Park Street: A Publishing Memoir* (1986).

Ballantine Books was the earliest paperback publisher of Tolkien's works in the United States, beginning with *The Hobbit* and the second edition of *The Lord of the Rings* in 1965 in response to the *Ace Books controversy. Ballantine Books was founded in 1952 by Ian Ballantine, a renowned figure in science fiction publishing. 'Ballantine Books' remains as an imprint under Random House, who acquired the firm in 1973. In 1977 Ballantine established the imprint 'Del Rey Books', under which later editions of Tolkien's works have appeared.

HarperCollins, Houghton Mifflin, and Ballantine/Del Rey remain Tolkien's primary English-language publishers. For the **Early English Text Society** as a publisher, see *Ancrene Riwle*. For **Puffin Books** (Penguin Books), see *The Hobbit*. For Tolkien's passing relationship with the publisher **Collins**, see *The Lord of the Rings* and *Milton Waldman.

Qenya: Descriptive Grammar of the Qenya Language. The first complete grammar of Tolkien's 'Elvish' language Qenya (later *Quenya*, see *Languages, Invented), with an associated phonology, published with commentary and notes in *Parma Eldalamberon* 14 (2003), pp. 35–86, as 'Early Qenya Grammar', ed. Carl F. Hostetter and Bill Welden.

The first two pages of the first, manuscript version of the grammar and an 'unnumbered slip', which contain 'a description of the Rúmilian letters used for written Qenya and notes on the sounds', were published as part of *The Alphabet of Rúmil* (*Writing systems), ed. Arden R. Smith, in *Parma Eldalamberon* 13 (2001), pp. 62–3. The grammar proper begins on the fourth page. This begins with a description of 'Qenya noun declension', then discusses numerals in Qenya (including cardinal and ordinal number-names and words for fractional values), Qenya pronouns, and the Qenya verb. Tolkien began, but did not complete, a much expanded second version, in typescript with manuscript additions and emendations. This includes sections on the definite and indefinite articles, nouns, declension, composition, loose compounds, duals, adjectives, adverbial suffixes or cases, comparison and formation of adverbs from adjectives, numerals, and (incomplete) pronouns.

The associated phonology survives in typescript with manuscript emendations, entitled *Qenya Phonology*. It is divided into two parts. The first 'briefly tabulates the "QENYA consonant system" and begins to explain its derivation from Primitive Eldarin by outlining the relationships between the various languages of the Three Kindreds and their distribution'. Its second part, entitled 'Qenya Development of the Eldarin Consonants', 'is concerned mostly with the development of the accentual system from the earliest period, and the reduction of final syllables, with the effects these had on the consonant system' (*Parma Eldalamberon* 14, p. 38).

On the envelope in which this text was preserved Tolkien wrote: 'Early Form of Qenya (done in Leeds)', that is, while he taught at the University of *Leeds from autumn 1920 until 1925. The *Parma Eldalamberon* editors date the work to *c.* 1923, following Humphrey Carpenter's statement in *Biography* (pp. 106–7) that it was while Tolkien was convalescing from pneumonia on his brother *Hilary's farm in summer 1923 that he turned again to his mythology (*'The Silmarillion') after a gap of time.

Hostetter and Welden conclude that the grammar and phonology postdate the *Qenyaqetsa* on which Tolkien worked from about 1915 to 1919, 'but the materials are closely related and largely complementary' (p. 40).

Qenya Lexicon *see* **Qenyaqetsa**

Qenya Phonology see Qenya: Descriptive Grammar of the Qenya Language

The Qenya Verb Forms. Description of the conjugation of the verb in Qenya (*Languages, Invented), published within 'Early Qenya Fragments' in *Parma Eldalamberon* 14 (2003), pp. 25–34, ed. Patrick Wynne and Christopher Gilson. Tolkien wrote it on four loose pages roughly contemporary with later writing in the *Qenyaqetsa (?1917–?1919).

Qenyaqetsa. A phonology and dictionary of Tolkien's 'Elvish' language Qenya (later *Quenya*, see *Languages, Invented), published in its entirety, with commentary and notes, in *Parma Eldalamberon* 12 (1998), ed. Christopher Gilson, Carl F. Hostetter, Patrick Wynne, and Arden R. Smith. The dictionary portion was first referred to by *Christopher Tolkien as the *Qenya Lexicon*, a name subsequently used elsewhere; some material from this is included in appendices on names in **The Book of Lost Tales, Part One* (1983) and **The Book of Lost Tales, Part Two* (1984).

Tolkien compiled a Qenya phonology and lexicon in a notebook beginning *c.* 1915. On the first page of the notebook as it survives is the title: 'Qenyaqetsa: The language of the Qendi who are the remnants of the Eldalie living now in Toleressea. (save only those Noldoli who cling yet to their own speech or Goldogrin.)'. The editors of *Parma Eldalamberon* suggest that *Qenyaqetsa* may mean '"Qenya language, Qenya speech" or perhaps "good speech in Qenya" including the ideas of correct pronunciation and diction, as the language was spoken by the Elves' (p. iv). On the back of the title-leaf is a table of contents for the phonology as originally written in pencil, as well as for a projected morphology that Tolkien never completed. Later he expanded and rearranged the phonology in ink, overwriting the pencil text and adding an introductory sketch of the origin and history of Qenya.

Following the phonology in the notebook is a lexicon, arranged according to 'roots', with the title 'Qenya dict[ionary]' added later on the first page so used. The *Parma Eldalamberon* editors note that in this 'the sections for roots beginning with the letters R through Y' come first, in reverse order, followed by sections for the roots in A through Q. 'Presumably Tolkien started the Lexicon at the beginning of the alphabet, and indeed the center of the page immediately preceding the A-section a title has been erased . . .' (p. viii). Some entries include references to very early forms of Tolkien's mythology, preceding **The Book of Lost Tales*. He continued to make entries during the writing of that work, until *c.* 1919. Many of the entries for the earlier part of the alphabet were made at one time and carefully written in pencil. Almost all of the entries in the second part of the alphabet are later than this first layer. Both the Qenya lexicon and the contemporaneous *Gnomish Lexicon show 'in the clearest possible way how deeply involved were the developments in the mythology and in the languages' (Christopher Tolkien, *The Book of Lost Tales, Part One*, p. 247).

In *Parma Eldalamberon* 14 (2003), p. 40, Carl F. Hostetter and Bill Welden describe the *Qenyaqetsa* and Tolkien's later Qenya grammar (**Qenya: Descriptive Grammar of the Qenya Language*) as 'closely related and largely complementary'.

Quantock Hills (Somerset). In April 1937, together with *Owen Barfield and *C.S. Lewis, Tolkien took a walking holiday in the Quantock Hills between Taunton and Bridgwater Bay. Although picturesque with 'clear springs, wild red deer, heather, and bilberries' (to quote the *Blue Guide*), Tolkien found the area to be rough country, hard going while walking more than twenty miles a day and carrying a pack.

Quendi and Eldar. Essay on Elvish names for incarnates, for the most part published, with commentary and notes, in **The War of the Jewels* (1994), pp. 359–424. Some omitted or associated material was published in **Morgoth's Ring* (1993) and in *Vinyar Tengwar* 39 (July 1998) and 41 (July 2000); see below.

A manuscript preamble describes the contents of the work: it is an 'enquiry into the origins of the Elvish names for Elves and their varieties clans and divisions: with Appendices on their names for the other Incarnates: Men, Dwarves, and Orcs; and on their analysis of their own language, Quenya: with a note on the "Language of the Valar"' (*The War of the Jewels*, p. 359). Although mainly linguistic in content, the essay also includes much background and historical information. The writing of the work and associated material is described by *Christopher Tolkien in *Morgoth's Ring*, p. 415, and by Carl F. Hostetter in *Vinyar Tengwar* 39, p. 4. Preliminary manuscript material was followed by a typescript and carbon copy of nearly fifty pages made by Tolkien with the title *Quendi and Eldar*, both of which he emended identically; and each of these copies is preceded by a page with the manuscript preamble and a parallel title in Quenya (see *Languages, Invented), *Essekenta Eldarinwa*. The essay probably dates to the period 1959–60, and as was common in his late works Tolkien included lengthy notes within the text, which for clarity Christopher Tolkien moved to the end.

The essay begins in *The War of the Jewels* with a lengthy section listing and commenting on the 'origin and meanings of the Elvish words referring to Elves and their varieties' (pp. 360–85, author's notes pp. 407–12). Appendices A and B describe the Elvish names for Men, and for the Dwarves with much information on the Petty-dwarves (pp. 386–9, author's notes pp. 412–15). The first part of Appendix C on Elvish names for Orcs was published in *Morgoth's Ring* (p. 416; see *Orcs), and the rest in *The War of the Jewels* (pp. 389–91, author's notes p. 415). Appendix D is on '*Kwen, Quenya, and the Elvish (especially Ñoldorin) words for "Language"' (pp. 391–7, author's notes pp. 415–16). Christopher Tolkien omitted from *The War of the Jewels* a substantial section from Appendix D, primarily for reasons of space, but also because 'the passage in question is a somewhat abstract account of the phonological theories of earlier linguistic Loremasters and the contributions of Fëanor, relying rather allusively on phonological data that are taken for granted . . .' (p. 359).

This omitted section (falling between pp. 395 and 396) was published in *Vinyar Tengwar* 39 (pp. 4–11), together with a preliminary manuscript text (pp. 15–20), ed. Carl F. Hostetter. In *The War of the Jewels* the remaining part of Appendix D is followed by a 'Note on the "Language of the Valar"' (pp. 397–407, author's notes pp. 416–17).

Tolkien subsequently added to one of the two title-pages of the essay: 'To which is added an abbreviation of the *Ósanwe-kenta* or "Communication of Thought" that Pengolodh set at the end of his *Lammas* or "Account of Tongues"', and an eight-page typescript of this work was added to both copies of *Quendi and Eldar*. Published in *Vinyar Tengwar* 39, ed. Carl F. Hostetter (pp. 21–34), supplemented in *Vinyar Tengwar* 41 with notes later discovered (pp. 5–6, as *Etymological Notes on the Ósanwe-kenta*), this discusses the communication of minds, considers at length how Morgoth managed to corrupt not only by the seed he planted in other minds but by his mastery of languages (which enabled him to deceive), and includes a lengthy defence of Manwë and the Valar against charges of 'folly' or weakness.

To the other two, Tolkien added a third element, a four-page typescript entitled *Orcs*, published in *Morgoth's Ring* (pp. 416–22). Christopher Tolkien notes that although 'the title *Quendi and Eldar* clearly belongs properly to the long essay' (*The War of the Jewels*, p. 359), his father used it also to include the other two works, *Ósanwe-kenta* and *Orcs*, all probably written in 1959–60.

For 'the legend of the awaking of the Quendi' mentioned in *Quendi and Eldar*, see **Cuivienyarna*.

Quenta Noldorinwa. A brief history of the Noldoli (later *Noldor*), published in **The Shaping of Middle-earth* (1986), pp. 76–218, as *The Quenta*.

According to a preamble, this work is meant to be 'drawn from the Book of Lost Tales which Eriol of Leithien wrote, having read the *Golden Book* . . . in Kortirion in Tol Eressëa, the Lonely Isle' (*The Shaping of Middle-earth*, p. 78). With the **Sketch of the Mythology* it is one of only two works to cover in narrative form the entire **'Silmarillion'* mythology from the arrival of the Valar in Arda to the overthrow of Morgoth. Neither the earlier **Book of Lost Tales* (c. 1916–20) nor the **Quenta Silmarillion* which followed (from the mid-1930s) were completed, and other texts dealing with the entire period are in the form of annals (**Annals of Valinor, *Annals of Beleriand*).

The *Quenta Noldorinwa* in fact is a reworking and expansion of the *Sketch of the Mythology* (c. 1926), as emended subsequent to its writing, with an additional section at the beginning describing the Valar. Tolkien composed most or all of it in 1930, almost certainly with the *Sketch* (but not *The Book of Lost Tales*) before him. It is extant in a typescript made apparently without any intervening notes or drafts. Tolkien abandoned the original typescript near the end, after the judgement of the Valar, and probably at once typed an expanded replacement for portions of the text covering the period from the foundation of Gondolin to the end of the work. Later he made further changes at different times, often in haste.

The opening page of the work is headed: 'The Quenta: herein is Qenta Noldorinwa or Pennas-na-Ngoelaidh'. In *The History of Middle-earth *Christopher Tolkien refers to it simply as the *Quenta*, but in the present book it is referenced as the *Quenta Noldorinwa*, the better to distinguish it from the later *Quenta Silmarillion*. Both typescripts are published in *The Shaping of Middle-earth*, with significant changes noted, as well as a fragment of the work translated into Old English with the title *Pennas*, presumably intended to be the work of Ælfwine or Eriol (*Eriol and Ælfwine), and lists of Elvish names for the Valar, places, kindreds of the Elves, and princes of the Noldoli, giving Old English equivalents. The latter includes an entry stating that (Quenya) *quenta* means 'story, tale', and Noldorin (later *Sindarin*) *pennas* means 'history'.

For the part played by the *Quenta Noldorinwa* in the evolution of Tolkien's mythology, see entries for the separate chapters of *The Silmarillion*.

Quenta Silmarillion. Narrative work, intended to be the centrepiece and main text of a published *'Silmarillion', recounting the history of Arda from the arrival of the Valar to the overthrow of Morgoth. Tolkien worked on it at various times: texts of the 1930s were published with commentary and notes in *The Lost Road and Other Writings* (1987), pp. 199–338; of the 1950s, dealing with events up to and including the creation of the Sun and the Moon, in *Morgoth's Ring* (1993), pp. 141–300; and of the 1950s, concerning the Years of the Sun and events after the return of the Noldor to Middle-earth, in *The War of the Jewels* (1994), pp. 173–247.

*Christopher Tolkien was unable to determine when his father began the *Quenta Silmarillion*, except in relation to other works. He dates to 1930 all or most of the original writing of the *Quenta Noldorinwa*, the work from which the *Quenta Silmarillion* was developed. Possibly around the same time, Tolkien wrote the first version of the 'earliest' *Annals of Beleriand*; these were followed by the 'earliest' *Annals of Valinor*, and the second version of the 'earliest' *Annals of Beleriand*, as well as the second 'Silmarillion' map. In *The Lost Road and Other Writings* Christopher Tolkien writes of the group of works he dated later than these, which he is inclined to place in the sequence: 'later' *Annals of Beleriand*; 'later' *Annals of Valinor*; the *Lhammas*; the *Ainulindalë* earlier than the *Quenta Silmarillion*; and the *Quenta Silmarillion* with the *Ambarkanta* after the 'later' *Annals of Beleriand* and before *The Fall of Númenor* (c. 1936-7). 'But a definitive and demonstrable sequence seems unattainable on the evidence; and the attempt may in any case be somewhat unreal, for my father did not necessarily complete one before beginning another' (p. 108).

In the *Quenta Silmarillion* Tolkien greatly expanded on his *legendarium* as told in the *Quenta Noldorinwa*. Christopher Tolkien comments:

> As originally written, the *Quenta Silmarillion* . . . was a beautiful and elegant manuscript; and when the first changes were made to it they were made with great care, usually by writing over erasures. It seems highly improbable that my father could have achieved this form without any

intermediate texts developing it from the *Quenta Noldorinwa* ... , and here and there in [the *Quenta Silmarillion*] it appears in any case that he was copying, for words necessary to the sense were missed out and then put in above the line. But there is now, remarkably, no trace of any such material, until the tale of Beren and Lúthien is reached: from that point preliminary drafts do exist. [*The Lost Road and Other Writings*, p. 199]

The title-page of the manuscript begins: 'The Quenta Silmarillion: Herein is *Qenta Noldorinwa* or *Pennas in Geleidh* or History of the Gnomes'. A preamble ascribes the compilation of tales to Pengolod of Gondolin rather than to Ælfwine (= Eriol, who wrote the *Quenta Noldorinwa*), who here is credited only with translating the *Quenta Silmarillion*.

Unlike the *Quenta Noldorinwa*, the *Quenta Silmarillion* is divided into a series of chapters: (1) 'Of the Valar'; (2) 'Of Valinor and the Two Trees'; (3) 'Of the Coming of the Elves', with two subsections headed 'Thingol' and 'Of Kôr and Alqualondë'; (4) 'Of the Silmarils and the Darkening of Valinor'; (5) 'Of the Flight of the Noldor'; (6) 'Of the Sun and the Moon and the Darkening of Valinor'; (7) 'Of Men'; (8) 'Of the Siege of Angband'; (9) 'Of Beleriand and Its Realms'; (10) 'Of Men and Dwarfs'; (11) 'Of the Ruin of Beleriand and the Fall of Fingolfin'; (12–15) 'Of Beren and Tinúviel' (general title), subdivided into 'Of the Meeting of Beren and Lúthien Tinúviel', 'The Quest of the Silmaril', 'The Quest of the Silmaril 2', and 'The Wolf-hunt of Carcharoth'; (16) 'Of the Fourth Battle: Nírnaith Arnediad'; (17) 'Of Túrin Turamarth or Túrin the Hapless' (abandoned as Túrin leaves Menegroth after killing Orgof); and a further, untitled section dealing with the arrival of Eärendel in Valinor and the end of the First Age. As Christopher Tolkien notes, the parts not dealt with in the *Quenta Silmarillion* are 'the greater part of the tale of Túrin, the destruction of Doriath, the fall of Gondolin, and the earlier part of the tale of Eärendel' (*The Lost Road and Other Writings*, p. 324).

Surviving preliminary material for the chapters telling the story of Beren and Lúthien (see *'Of Beren and Lúthien') shows that this part of the *Quenta Silmarillion* involved Tolkien in much preparatory work, mainly because of difficulty in reducing to a suitable length the long and detailed account of the story as it had developed in the *Lay of Leithian*. He began by making a rough draft 'in which the telling of the tale of Beren and Lúthien was very amply conceived' but 'soon abandoned' (p. 294). Using this as a basis, or perhaps a further (lost) draft, he added Chapter 12 and part of 13 to the finely written *Quenta Silmarillion* manuscript. But he abandoned the later text also, because he saw that it was going to be too long relative to the whole. He then made a rough draft of the whole story of Beren and Lúthien, and from this a more compressed version which continued almost to the end of Chapter 14, not yet at the end of the tale.

At this point, on 15 November 1937, Tolkien submitted the *Quenta Silmarillion* manuscript to George Allen & Unwin (*Publishers) for consideration as a successor to *The Hobbit*. During its absence for the next month he completed the tale of Beren and Lúthien as a separate text, wrote the chapter 'Of the Fourth Battle: Nírnaith Arnediad', and began the story of Túrin Turambar (see *'Of Túrin Turambar'). Christopher Tolkien comments that the new version of the story of Túrin as far as it went is told at such length, based on *The Children of Húrin, that his father would have had the same problem of length as with his first versions of the tale of Beren and Lúthien. Also in this period, rather than continue with the story of Túrin, Tolkien reworked a section from the end of the Quenta Noldorinwa; and on 20 November he made a list of changes to be made to the primary Quenta Silmarillion manuscript.

On 15 December 1937 Allen & Unwin returned the manuscript with advice that they needed, rather than 'The Silmarillion', another work about hobbits. Within days, Tolkien began to write *The Lord of the Rings, and (Christopher Tolkien feels certain) now 'abandoned (for good, as it turned out) the new "Silmarillion" narrative at the point he had reached' (The Lost Road and Other Writings, pp. 199–200). That is, he wrote no further chapters, but he did not abandon the work at once, before laying it aside for nearly thirteen years. He made the changes noted on his list of 20 November, copied the rest of Chapter 14 into the main manuscript, and at some time before 3 February 1938 made a typescript of the early part of the Quenta Silmarillion as far as the end of Chapter 3.

Associated with the latter are five sheets for The Silmarillion, a compilation of texts in which the Quenta Silmarillion was to be the first part, together with 'The Houses of the Princes of Men and Elves', 'The Tale of Years', and 'The Tale of Battles'. These were to be followed by the Annals of Valinor, the Annals of Beleriand, and (according to the earliest title-page only) the Lhammas. Tolkien copied the first, manuscript title-page in typescript, with Eldanyárë added to the title proper; then made an elaborate manuscript page in red, blue, and black based on the typescript, but with I·Eldanyárë ('The History of the Elves') as an alternative title to Silmarillion. With these are a preamble, in manuscript and typescript, which includes a note by Ælfwine that the histories had been written by Pengolod of Gondolin, which Ælfwine had translated into his own tongue (Old English), as well as a note by the unnamed 'translator' who had turned the words of Ælfwine into Modern English.

In The Lost Road and Other Writings Christopher Tolkien published the text of the typescript Quenta Silmarillion as far as it goes, with notes and comments on important differences from the earlier version, and from the point where the typescript was abandoned gave the text of the manuscript, except for the chapters on Beren and Lúthien.

Tolkien turned again to revision of the various parts of The Silmarillion in the period c. 1950–early 1952, when Collins showed an interest in publishing that work together with The Lord of the Rings. In addition to changes arising from the need to bring the 'Silmarillion' texts into accord with The Lord of the Rings, Tolkien also wanted to incorporate new ideas that had occurred to him in the years since 1937. So when he again took up the Quenta Silmarillion he did not complete the unwritten part, but revised what already existed, covering the original manuscript with additions and corrections. He reached the end of the tale of Beren and Lúthien on 10 May 1951. The amount of revision varied from chapter to chapter, from emendations on original manuscripts or typescripts of the 1930s to sections of new writing. The more significant rewriting included an addition to 'Of the Valar' concerning the Maiar; two successive typescripts of 'Of Valinor and the Two Trees'; a new typescript (changing to manuscript at the end) for the first part of 'Of the Coming of the Elves', continuing into the second section 'Of Thingol and Melian'; a new version of 'Of the Silmarils and the Darkening of Valinor', entitled 'Of Fëanor and the Silmarilli, and the Darkening of Valinor'; a three-page manuscript, much of it derived from the *Grey Annals*, with the title 'Of Turgon and the Building of Gondolin' (which later provided the first part of 'Of the Noldor in Beleriand' in *The Silmarillion*); and a revision of the first part of the chapter 'Of Men and Dwarfs', with a subheading 'Concerning the Dwarves' under a new title for the chapter, 'Of the Naugrim and the Edain'.

After Tolkien emended the original documents and made replacement manuscripts or typescripts, an amanuensis typescript of the whole was made *c.* 1951, taking up the changes. In some cases Tolkien made further changes to the earlier documents after this typescript was made, and some of these were lost when a second amanuensis typescript with carbon copy was made at the end of the 1950s, mainly from the earlier amanuensis typescript as later emended but in some cases from the original manuscript and with two chapters omitted altogether.

After the success of *The Lord of the Rings* made Allen & Unwin keen to publish *The Silmarillion*, Tolkien returned again to the *Quenta Silmarillion c.* 1958–60. At this stage the first chapter, 'Of the Valar', was detached from the *Quenta Silmarillion* and became a separate work, the **Valaquenta*. The most significant changes to the remaining part of the *Quenta Silmarillion* was that Finwë's first wife, Míriel, 'dies' after the birth of Fëanor and her spirit refuses to return to her body from Mandos; that Finwë wishes to marry again and after much debate is permitted to do so by the Valar; and that Fëanor resents his father's second wife, Indis, and her children. This change provided an explanation for Fëanor's character and his difficult relationship with his brothers, and indeed affected the interrelationships and behaviour of all the descendants of Finwë.

The development of this story involved Tolkien in considerable work. He began by adding a manuscript rider to the rewritten chapter 'Of Fëanor, the Silmarilli, and the Darkening of Valinor', but then felt the need to consider whether the nature of Elves who might be reborn if slain was compatible with remarriage after the death of a spouse, and the decisions of the Valar on this question: see **Of the Laws and Customs among the Eldar*. Tolkien then made a new typescript, 'Of Finwë and Míriel', followed by a further typescript (in January 1959 or later) with the title 'Of Fëanor and the Darkening of Valinor', changed to 'Of Finwë and Míriel'. But apparently he was still not satisfied, and made yet another, more substantial typescript of the whole chapter, with the title 'Of the Silmarils and the Darkening of Valinor' and the subtitle 'Of Finwë and Míriel'. This typescript continued into 'Of Fëanor and the Unchaining of Melko', 'Of the Silmarils and the Unrest of the Noldor', 'Of the Darkening of Valinor', 'Of the Rape of the Silmarils', and 'Of the Thieves' Quarrel'. Christopher Tolkien comments that 'in these substantially rewritten chapters of the "second phase"' his father

> was moving strongly into a new conception of the work, a new and much fuller mode of narrative – envisaging, as it appears, a thorough-going 're-expansion' from the still fairly condensed form (despite a good deal of enlargement in the 1951 revision) that went back through [the *Quenta Silmarillion* of the 1930s], and [the *Quenta Noldorinwa*] to the *'Sketch of the Mythology'* of 1926, which had made a brief summary from the amplitude of *The Book of Lost Tales.* . . . [*Morgoth's Ring*, p. 142]

In other late work of this period Tolkien rewrote part of the 1951 'Concerning the Dwarves', the first part of 'Of the Naugrim and the Edain', in two successive manuscripts; together with other material this became a separate chapter, 'Of Aulë and the Dwarves' (later used by Christopher Tolkien to form part of the chapter 'Of Aulë and Yavanna' in *The Silmarillion*). The second part of 'Of the Naugrim and the Edain', concerning Men, was now superseded by a new typescript entitled 'Of the Coming of Men into the West and the Meeting of the Edain and the Eldar'.

For the part played by the *Quenta Silmarillion* in the evolution of Tolkien's mythology, see entries for the separate chapters of *The Silmarillion*.

'Quenta Silmarillion'. The central and longest component of *The Silmarillion* (1977), pp. 33–255. Tolkien's unfinished *Quenta Silmarillion*, on which he had worked from the mid-1930s to early 1938, again *c.* 1951, and finally *c.* 1958–60, provided the structure and much of the content of the 'Quenta Silmarillion', but editor *Christopher Tolkien also incorporated material from other texts which contained additional information or later developments in the story. The latter include the *Annals of Aman* (see *Annals of Valinor*) and the *Grey Annals* (see *Annals of Beleriand*), and miscellaneous texts such as *Of Maeglin: Sister-son of Turgon, King of Gondolin*.

Each of the twenty-four chapters of the 'Quenta Silmarillion' is given a separate entry in the *Companion and Guide*, with a discussion of the evolution of the relevant section of the narrative and a brief note on the texts on which Christopher Tolkien drew to form the chapter.

Quenya see **Languages, Invented**; *see also titles beginning* **Qenya**

Quest. The quest is a common motif in literature. It appears not only in myth, legend, romance, and *fairy-stories, adapted suitably in mode and tone to the genre, but, transformed and mutated, sometimes underlies modern novels firmly set in the contemporary world. In the epic of Gilgamesh, dating back at least 5,000 years, the mythic hero's quest – to find a way to escape death – is archetypal, and all the more moving because it fails. In the later classical period quest stories more often recounted the deeds of legendary heroes, such as Jason and his quest for the Golden Fleece. The quest for the Holy Grail figured prominently in medieval romances, but other quests had more mundane objects, such as the rescue of an oppressed maiden. In fairy-stories the tone is often lighter but with a moral, as in 'The Black Bull of Norroway' (mentioned by Tolkien in *On Fairy-Stories*) where the heroine loses her husband when she disobeys an order and has to undertake a long journey to find him again. Also, whereas in myth, legend, or romance the quester is usually male, and usually a person of standing and repute – a king, hero, knight – in a fairy-story the focus may be on someone of lowly birth – the youngest son of a peasant, for instance – or on a female.

The object of the quest may be to win, find, or recover an object or person, or to fulfil a task imposed as a condition of gaining some desired reward, such as the hand of a princess; but almost all involve a journey through strange terrain. The quester may undertake this alone or with companions, or may acquire companions or helpers on the way. Quests demand that the hero or heroine persist and overcome all obstacles. In fairy-stories the quest may require certain moral behaviour for its successful achievement, and may depict personal growth or maturation.

Although different from each other in tone and depth, Tolkien's quest stories generally fit into the traditional patterns. The most mythic is the quest of Fëanor and the Noldor in *'The Silmarillion' to recover the stolen Silmarils in which 'the fates of Arda, earth, sea, and air, lay locked' (*The Silmarillion*, p. 67). Beren's quest to recover a Silmaril from Morgoth's crown as a bride-price for the hand of Lúthien moves in the various retellings from fairy-tale mode to the mythic as the Silmarils increase in significance. It is notable, though, that in all versions Lúthien rescues Beren from imprisonment and insists on accompanying him on his quest.

In *The Hobbit* the quest is mainly in the fairy-tale mode, with thirteen dwarves setting out to recover the gold stolen from their fathers by Smaug the dragon. On the advice of the wizard Gandalf they take the hobbit Bilbo Baggins with them, but at first do not welcome his company. During the journey, and especially after he acquires a ring of invisibility, Bilbo develops new strengths of character and gains the respect of the dwarves until 'he had become the real leader of their adventure' (ch. 12). Tolkien gave the title *The Quest of Erebor* to one version of his account of events before *The Hobbit* began, originally meant to be included in the Appendices to *The Lord of the Rings*.

The Lord of the Rings is also a quest story, though it differs from the archetype in that Frodo sets out not to find or gain, but to destroy the One Ring. Perhaps the closest precedent to this is Christian's journey to be rid of his burden in Bunyan's *Pilgrim's Progress*, though the resemblance is probably coincidental. Like many others on a quest, especially in fairy-stories, Frodo meets people on the way (such as Galadriel and Faramir) who give him aid, and he suffers when disobeying advice (such as when he puts on the Ring at Weathertop). After his capture and rescue Frodo becomes a passive figure, and it is Sam who plans the last stages of their journey to Mount Doom.

Another significant departure is that in the end, Frodo cannot fulfil the quest because he finds himself unable destroy the Ring; and even though the object of the quest is achieved through the agency of Gollum, Frodo is unable to enjoy the fruits of victory. Given the power of the Ring, his failure was inevitable, as Tolkien recognized in a letter to Michael Straight, end of 1955: 'The Quest [therefore] was bound to fail as a piece of world-plan. . . . Fail it would and did as far as Frodo considered alone was concerned. . . . But at this point the "salvation" of the world and Frodo's own "salvation" is achieved by his previous *pity* and forgiveness of injury' (*Letters*, p. 234; see also *Pity and Mercy). In another letter, to Amy Ronald on 27 July 1956, he commented: 'following the logic of the plot, it was clearly inevitable, as an event. And surely it is a more significant and real event than a mere "fairy-story" ending in which the hero is indomitable? It is possible for the good, even the saintly, to be subjected to a power of evil which is too great for them to overcome – in themselves. In this case the cause (not the "hero") was triumphant. . .' (*Letters*, pp. 252–3).

In his review of *The Return of the King* ('At the End of the Quest, Victory', *New York Times Book Review*, 22 January 1956) *W.H. Auden said that Tolkien 'has succeeded more completely than any previous writer in this genre in using the traditional properties of the Quest, the heroic journey, the Numinous Object, the conflict between Good and Evil while at the same time satisfying our sense of historical and social reality'. Auden also suggested that life was 'a succession of choices between alternatives. . . . For objectifying this experience, the natural image is that of a journey with a purpose' (p. 5). Tolkien later wrote some comments on this suggestion: 'Men do go, and have in history gone on journeys and quests, without any intention of acting out allegories of life. . . . (To a story-teller a journey is a marvellous device. It provides a strong thread on which a multitude of things that he has in mind may be strung to make a new thing, various, unpredictable, and yet coherent. My chief reason for using this form was simply technical.)' Since people do change or reveal themselves on journeys, it was 'another good reason for sending "hobbits" – a vision of a simple and calculable people in simple and long-settled circumstances – on a *journey* far from settled home into strange lands and dangers . . . provided with some strong motive for endurance and adaptation' (*Letters*, pp. 239–40).

In his article 'A World Imaginary, but Real', *Encounter* 3 (November 1954), written when he had read only *The Fellowship of the Ring*, Auden commented:

Perhaps Mr. Tolkien's greatest achievement is to have written a heroic romance which seems wholly relevant to the realities of concrete historical existence. When reading medieval examples of this genre, enjoyable as they are, one is sometimes tempted to ask the Knightly hero – 'Is your trip necessary?' Even in the Quest for the San Graal [Holy Grail], success or failure is only of importance to those who undertake it. One cannot altogether escape the suspicion that, in relation to such knights, the word 'vocation' is a high-faluting term for a game which gentlemen with private means are free to play while the real work of the real world is done by 'villains.'

In *The Fellowship of the Ring* ... the fate of the Ring will affect the daily lives of thousands who have never heard of its existence. Further, as in the Bible and many fairy stories, the hero is not a Knight, endowed by birth and breeding with exceptional *arete* [Greek = excellence, manly valour, prowess, nobility], but only a hobbit, pretty much like all other hobbits. [pp. 60, 62]

See also W.H. Auden 'The Quest Hero', *Texas Quarterly* 4, No. 4 (Winter, 1961), 81–93. Reprinted in *Tolkien and the Critics: Essays on J.R.R. Tolkien's The Lord of the Rings*, ed. Neil D. Isaacs and Rose A. Zimbardo (1968) pp. 40–61.

Randel Helms in *Tolkien's World* (HM 1974) thinks that Tolkien really wrote the same story in *The Hobbit* and *The Lord of the Rings* 'told first very simply, and then again very intricately. Both works have the same theme, a quest on which a most unheroic hobbit achieves heroic stature; they have the same structure, the "there and back again" of the quest romance. . . . The episodic structure of the two books are so closely parallel one says without exaggeration that *The Lord of the Rings* is *The Hobbit* writ large' (p. 21). He analyzes the similarities and then the more significant dissimilarities. He concludes that 'while both books are built upon the ancient structure of the quest, both concerned with the central plot of the maturation of an untried and apparently weak hero, they are differentiated in one great way: *The Hobbit* is a quest to *get* something, *The Lord of the Rings* a quest to *renounce* something' (p. 37) – though renunciation had appeared in a minor way in *The Hobbit*, in Thorin's words on his deathbed and Bilbo's handing over the Arkenstone.

Brian Rosebury, however, prefers to describe *The Lord of the Rings* as a journey rather as a quest. He points out in *J.R.R. Tolkien: A Cultural Phenomenon* (2003) that

Frodo's 'quest' is not formalised until the Council of Elrond meets at Rivendell, and that the journey which brings him to Elrond's House is at first a walking holiday, and then a flight from pursuit. If we are looking for structural unity conferred by the declared quest, these chapters must seem an anomalous, or at least over-protracted preamble. . . . But it is doubtful whether this notion of the post-Rivendell quest as the unifying concept is an apt one. As several critics have pointed out, whereas the purpose of most quests is to acquire a scared or precious object, such as the Holy Grail, the purpose of this quest is to get rid of something unholy, or more particularly to withhold it, first temporarily and then permanently from the malevolent quester who is 'the Lord of the Rings'. Frodo and his friends do not choose to pursue a quest, but have an unwelcome responsibility thrust upon them by ill-fate. [p. 28]

He notes that Frodo and Sam in Book IV refer generally to 'our course' or 'our road' and there is only one unobtrusive use of 'quest' by the narrator in chapter 5, just after the evening meal. He thinks that

'journey' . . . rather than the more narrowly defined 'quest', is the appropriate name for the image which unifies the heterogeneous narrative of *The Lord of the Rings*; the specific quest, Frodo's 'errand' as it is sometimes called, is merely the axis of the main action. The 'errand pertains to the plot, the journey to the story or 'history'. The difference is important. Whereas the quest as a unifying device is integrative, and relegates the locales to a subordinate status (every episode must represent a significant obstacle overcome, or a significant gain in enlightenment), the journey is expansive and exalts the locales: it permits diversions, loose ends, and celebrates the contingency and variety of the world. [p. 31]

The Quest of Erebor. An account of Gandalf's part in arranging the visit of Thorin and the other dwarves to Bilbo Baggins in the first chapter of *The Hobbit*, and persuading them to take Bilbo as one of their company on their quest to recover their lost treasure. Relevant material was published in *Unfinished Tales* (1980), *The Peoples of Middle-earth* (1996), and *The Annotated Hobbit* (rev. and expanded edn. 2002).

In a letter to Colonel Worskett on 20 September 1963 Tolkien wrote:

There are, of course, quite a lot of links between *The Hobbit* and [*The Lord of the Rings*] that are not clearly set out. They were mostly written or sketched out, but cut out to lighten the boat. . . . I actually wrote in full an account of what really happened before Gandalf's visit to Bilbo and the subsequent 'Unexpected Party', as seen by Gandalf himself. It was to have come in during a looking-back conversation in Minas Tirith; but it had to go, and is only represented in brief in App[endix] A . . . though the difficulties that Gandalf had with Thorin are omitted. [*Letters*, p. 334]

The idea of saying more about these events seems to have occurred to Tolkien while he was drafting a new version of 'Durin's Folk' for Appendix A. Most of the draft to the point where the dwarves settle in the Blue Mountains after the Battle of Azanulbizar is close to the published text, but there Tolkien drew a line 'as if the text were completed but the mention of the Ring of Thráin led him to say something further about it' (*Christopher Tolkien, *The Peoples of Middle-earth*, p. 280). In a rougher manuscript he continued with an account of the wanderings of Thráin, his capture by Sauron who took from him the last of the Seven Rings, and his death in Dol Guldur. Gandalf enters the story when he meets near Bree Thorin son of Thráin, who is eager for vengeance on the dragon Smaug, who had driven the Dwarves from their kingdom beneath Erebor and stolen their treasure. The unnamed writer of the text comments that great events resulted from this meeting, for it led to the finding of the One Ring by Bilbo, and as a consequence the involvement of the Hobbits in its destruction.

Some suppose that Gandalf foresaw what would happen, but this is contradicted by the account written by Frodo of what Gandalf told the hobbits in Minas Tirith. This is the link into the first version of *The Quest of Erebor*, but Christopher Tolkien was unaware of either link or first version when he edited *Unfinished Tales*, and thought that a manuscript with the title *The History of Gandalf's Dealings with Thráin and Thorin Oakenshield* was the original text rather than 'a (moderately) fair copy, much rewritten if not essentially changed' (*The Peoples of Middle-earth*, p. 282).

Neither the earliest version nor *The History of Gandalf's Dealings with Thráin and Thorin Oakenshield* has been published, apart from two preliminary notes, which show Tolkien's initial thoughts concerning the reasons for Gandalf's interest in Thorin's quest, and explain why Gandalf did not realize the identity of the dying dwarf he found in the dungeons of Dol Guldur; and a few short extracts from the earliest version in *The Peoples of Middle-earth* (pp. 282–4, and pp. 287–8, notes 10, 11, 13, 14). A few sentences from the second text were published in *Unfinished Tales* (pp. 329, 330), and an extract which might be from either of the first two versions was included in *The War of the Ring* (pp. 357–8, with notes).

Tolkien then made a ten-page typescript, with the titles *The Quest of Erebor* and *Gandalf's Account of How He Came to Arrange the Expedition to Erebor and Send Bilbo with the Dwarves*, incorporating further changes and emendations. Some extracts from this text were published in *Unfinished Tales* (pp. 328–6), and the complete text in an appendix to the second edition of *The Annotated Hobbit*. In this Gandalf is asked whether, when he planned the dwarves' quest to the Lonely Mountain and Bilbo's inclusion in the company, he saw beyond the destruction of Smaug to the fall of Sauron. He explains that his most immediate thought was to protect Rivendell and Lothlórien from attack by Sauron, by preventing the use of Smaug by the Dark Lord and by persuading the White Council to drive Sauron from Dol Guldur. Gandalf is said to have met Thorin by chance in Bree and, hearing of his desire for vengeance on Smaug, accepted an invitation to visit him in the Ered Luin. It was only when he heard more of Thorin's history that Gandalf realized that the dying dwarf he had found in Dol Guldur was Thorin's father, Thráin. He remembered the map and key that Thráin had given him, and suggested to Thorin that rather than wage open war he should deal with the dragon by stealth, with the help of a hobbit, whose smell would be unknown to Smaug. The dwarves, however, did not have a high opinion of Hobbits; and when Gandalf pointed out that Bilbo had courage and stealth (meaning the usual hobbit ability to disappear quietly and quickly), the dwarves leapt to the conclusion that Bilbo was a professional thief. Gandalf said that he would put the thief's mark on Bilbo's door, and with sudden foresight told Thorin that if he wanted to succeed he must persuade the hobbit to accompany them. In this Gandalf was relying on his memory of Bilbo as a child; upon seeing Bilbo as an adult, his confidence was shaken. After the bad initial impression Bilbo made on the dwarves, Gandalf had great difficulty in persuading Thorin to add Bilbo to his company.

In a fourth, untitled manuscript published in *Unfinished Tales* (pp. 321–6) Tolkien told the story 'in a more economical and tightly constructed form, omitting a good deal . . . and introducing some new elements' (*Unfinished Tales*, p. 327). In this version, when Gandalf hears Thorin's story he promises to help him if he can, but has no immediate plan. Then he visits the Shire and hears news of Bilbo: 'He was already growing a bit queer, they said, and went off for days by himself. He could be seen talking to strangers, even Dwarves.' Thus the plan for the quest of Erebor came suddenly into Gandalf's mind. He tried unsuccessfully to see Bilbo, who was away from home; and relying on what he had heard, Gandalf persuaded Thorin to accept his plan. Gandalf admits that this was a mistake: 'For Bilbo had changed. . . . He was altogether bewildered, and made a complete fool of himself . . . he did not realize at all how fatuous the Dwarves thought him, nor how angry they were with me' (*Unfinished Tales*, p. 323). Gandalf explains that it was only by producing the map and key at the right moment, and arguing with Thorin far into the night, that he persuaded him to accept the plan. The account of why the dwarves thought Bilbo was a professional burglar is omitted.

Among the papers associated with the earliest versions of *The Quest of Erebor* are calculations concerning the year of Bilbo's birth and the year of the dwarves' quest which refer to dates fixed in print, and which must have been written after the corrected page proofs of *The Fellowship of the Ring* went to the printer at the beginning of 1954. In a letter to *Naomi Mitchison on 25 April 1954 Tolkien offered to send her copies of various works including a 'Genealogy of Durin and the Dwarf-lords of *Moria*' (*Letters*, p. 177), but made no mention of *The Quest of Erebor*. None of the versions of that account can have been written earlier than 1954, and Tolkien may not have begun to write it until August, when he told *Katharine Farrer that he was working on the Appendices to *The Lord of the Rings*. The final, shorter version of *The Quest of Erebor* may date to early 1955, the result of an abortive attempt to reduce it sufficiently for inclusion in an Appendix. In a letter to *Rayner Unwin on 6 March 1955 Tolkien wrote of the need to compress into the available space unwritten sections of the Appendices, including information about the House of Durin, but in the event *The Quest of Erebor*, even in shortened form, was omitted from the material finally sent to George Allen & Unwin (*Publishers) in early April 1955. Only a very abridged version of the account appears in the published 'Durin's Folk'.

Raleigh, Walter Alexander (1861–1922). Educated at University College, London, and King's College, Cambridge, Raleigh was appointed in 1885 the first Professor of English Literature in the Mohammedan Anglo-Oriental College, Aligarh, but was invalided home in 1887. In the winter of 1888–9 he lectured for the Oxford University Extension Delegacy, and during 1889 worked briefly at Victoria University, Manchester. In 1890 he took up an appointment as Professor of Modern Literature at University College, Liverpool. While there he published the first of many critical works, including *The English Novel* (1894) and *Milton* (1900), the latter based on his Clark Lectures at Trinity College, Cambridge in 1899. In 1900 he moved to the chair of English Language and Literature at Glasgow, where he remained for four years, assisted by *David Nichol Smith. One of his pupils there was *George S. Gordon.

In 1904 Raleigh became the first holder of the new chair of English Literature at *Oxford, with a fellowship at Magdalen College. (In 1914 this was reconstituted as the Merton Professorship of English Literature.) Together with his colleagues C.H. Firth, *A.S. Napier, Ernest de Selincourt, and *Joseph Wright, Raleigh bifurcated the Oxford English syllabus to make it more attractive to students whose primary interest was literature rather than language: from 1908 only four out of ten papers were required in common of all students reading English, with the other six oriented to suit the language or literature specialty. In that year also, Raleigh was reunited with his Glasgow lieutenant, Nichol Smith, who had been named Goldsmith's Reader in English at Oxford, and together they made significant contributions to the further development of the English School (see D.J. Palmer, *The Rise of English Studies* (1965), especially ch. 8). Raleigh received a knighthood in 1911.

Tolkien attended Raleigh's lectures on 'Chaucer and His Contemporaries' in Michaelmas Term 1914, and on 'Drama in the Sixteenth and Seventeenth Centuries' in Hilary Term 1915. In summer 1920, when Tolkien was in Leeds to interview for the post of Reader in English Language, the subject of Raleigh came up in conversation with Professor George S. Gordon. As Tolkien later wrote: 'As (still) a stiff-necked young philologist, I did not in fact think much of Raleigh – he was not, of course, a good lecturer; but some kind spirit prompted me to say that he was "Olympian". It went well; though I only really meant that he reposed gracefully on a lofty pinnacle above my criticism' (draft letter to R.W. Chapman, 26 November 1941, *Letters*, p. 56).

Ransome, Arthur Michell (1884–1967). From an early age Arthur Ransome longed to write essays like Hazlitt and to produce books for children. He became a freelance writer of articles, stories, and reviews, learning his craft in the process. His first book of importance was the semi-autobiographical *Bohemia in London* (1907). His *History of Story-Telling* appeared in 1909, and critical works on Edgar Allan Poe and Oscar Wilde in 1910 and 1912 respectively. In 1913 Ransome went to Russia to study native folk-tales, some of which he retold in *Old Peter's Russian Tales* (1916). From 1915 to 1929 he worked as a newspaper correspondent in Russia, Latvia, and Estonia, reporting on the

First World War and on the Russian Revolution. Later he travelled on assignment for the *Manchester Guardian* to Russia, Egypt, Sudan, and China. An avid small-boat sailor and fisherman, he wrote notable books on both subjects. He is best known, however, for a popular series of novels for young readers which began with *Swallows and Amazons* in 1930, in which resourceful boys and girls sail, camp, and have adventures. The sixth book in the series, *Pigeon Post* (1936), won the first Carnegie Medal for excellence in children's literature. Ransome's masterpiece, however, was *We Didn't Mean to Go to Sea*, published in 1937, the same year as *The Hobbit*.

On 13 December 1937 Ransome wrote to Tolkien 'as a humble hobbit-fancier' but with the amiable complaint that Gandalf in *The Hobbit* should not call Bilbo 'an excitable little *man*' (since he is a Hobbit), and Thorin should not muse, if he is referring to Dwarves: 'If more *men* valued food and cheer and song above hoarded gold, it would be a merrier world.' Tolkien replied on 15 December, agreeing to change his text accordingly, pleased that Ransome (an author of some stature) had read *The Hobbit* so closely, and noting that his own reputation would now go up with his sons, who had not disposed of their copies of the 'Swallows and Amazons' books even though 'the eldest are now rather to be classed as "men"'. Ransome wrote again on 17 December, from hospital where he was recovering from an operation, that '*The Hobbit* has done a great deal to turn these weeks into a pleasure' (*Signalling from Mars: The Letters of Arthur Ransome* (1997), p. 251). Years later, at Tolkien's suggestion, Ransome was sent an advance copy of *The Lord of the Rings* for comment and read it enthusiastically.

See further, Hugh Brogan, *The Life of Arthur Ransome* (1984), and Wayne G. Hammond, *Arthur Ransome: A Bibliography* (2000).

Reade, Francis Vincent (*c.* 1895–1958). Father Vincent Reade of the *Birmingham Oratory was a friend of Tolkien since at least summer 1914 when they visited *Cornwall together. They took long walks every day around the Lizard peninsula, and stayed at the home of Father Vincent's mother. *Christopher Tolkien recalls a visit by Father Vincent to the Tolkien home at 20 Northmoor Road, *Oxford, not long before the beginning of the Second World War, when the priest described to Tolkien an eyewitness account of the maltreatment of Jews in Germany. On 6 May 1944, in response to 'grousing' by Christopher Tolkien in letters to his father, Tolkien replied that he 'used to write in just the same way or worse to poor old Fr. Vincent Reade' (*Letters*, p. 78).

Reading. Tolkien could read by the time he was four. In a paper written in the winter of 1914–15 he wrote:

> Most people are familiar from the days of their earliest books onwards with the general mould and type of mythological stories, legends, tales, romances that come from many sources, from Hellas by many channels, from the Celtic peoples, Irish and British, and from the Teutonic (I put

these in order of ascending appeal to myself) and which achieve for our youth their crowning glory in Stead's *Books for the Bairns*: that mine of ancient lore. [Tolkien Papers, Bodleian Library, Oxford]

(W.T. Stead began to publish his *Books for Bairns* in March 1896.) More specifically, Tolkien recalled that he had enjoyed the fairy-stories of the Brothers Grimm, and felt that he was not harmed by the beauty and horror of tales such as 'The Juniper Tree'. He liked stories of Red Indians, but even more, legends of the North, especially that of Sigurd in *Andrew Lang's *Red Fairy Book* (first published 1890). In drafts for *On Fairy-Stories* he said that he

liked my *magic in small purposeful doses (the proper way to take it); and I preferred the older tales that had not acquired the frippery and finery of the *Cabinet des fées* [French fairy-tales]. The *Story of Sigurd* (adapted by A. Lang himself from *[William] Morris's translation of *the Volsunga Saga*) was my favourite . . . . Even as it stands in the Red Book [i.e. *The Red Fairy Book*] that is no light matter: it is strong meat for nurseries. [Tolkien Papers, Bodleian Library, Oxford]

In addition to these retellings of old stories Tolkien also read some of the more recent books written for children. He was amused by Lewis Carroll's *Alice's Adventures in Wonderland* (1865) and *Through the Looking Glass* (1872); later in life he was also fond of Carroll's *Sylvie and Bruno* (1889) and *Sylvie and Bruno Concluded* (1893), and occasionally recited verses from them. Robert Louis Stevenson's *Treasure Island* (1883) did not interest him. The story 'Puss Cat Mew' in E.H. Knatchbull-Hugessen's *Stories for My Children* (1869) made a great impression on him, but he loathed Robert Browning's *The Pied Piper* (1845) and intensely disliked the fairy tales of Hans Christian Andersen. Some books he did enjoy were *The Princess and the Goblin* (1872) and *The Princess and Curdie* (1883) by *George MacDonald. It was probably in childhood that he read George Dasent's *Popular Tales from the Norse* (1858, 1859) which includes the story 'Soria Moria Castle' – which title, he later admitted, was 'echoed' in the name *Moria* casually introduced into *The Hobbit.

Whether he read *Kenneth Grahame's *The Wind in the Willows* soon after its publication in 1908 or discovered it later, it too made a great impression on him. When he heard in 1944 of the publication of *First Whispers of 'The Wind in the Willows'* edited by Grahame's widow, Elspeth, he wrote: 'I must get hold of a copy, if poss[ible]' (letter to *Christopher Tolkien, 31 July 1944, *Letters*, p. 90). He told C.A. Furth of George Allen & Unwin (*Publishers) in a letter in 1938 that *Edith Nesbit was 'an author I delight in' (courtesy of Christopher Tolkien). Her *Five Children – and It* (1902) inspired some elements in his own *Roverandom*, and in drafts for *On Fairy-Stories* he expressed admiration for Nesbit's *Phoenix and the Carpet* (1904) and *The Story of the Amulet* (1906). He had some reservations, though, about Andrew Lang's original fairy-story *Prince Prigio* (1889) and disliked its sequel, *Prince Ricardo of Pantouflia* (1893).

But in *On Fairy-Stories* he said that

a liking for fairy-stories was not a dominant characteristic of early taste.... I liked many other things as well, or better: such as history, astronomy, botany, grammar, and etymology.... I was ... insensitive to poetry, and skipped it if it came in tales. Poetry I discovered much later in Latin and Greek, and especially through being asked to translate English verse into classical verse. A real taste for fairy-stories was wakened by philology on the threshold of manhood, and quickened to full life by war. [*Tree and Leaf*, pp. 40–1; see further, *Languages, *Philology, *Poetry, *Science]

As a schoolboy and then an undergraduate, even before he transferred to the English School at *Oxford, Tolkien read the Norse Sagas, the Middle English *Sir Gawain and the Green Knight* and *Pearl*, and the works of *Chaucer. He read the Finnish *Kalevala* in translation while at school, and later tried to learn enough of the language to read the work in the original. In 1913 he bought a translation of the *Mabinogion*. He spent part of the Skeat Prize he won in Spring 1914 on William Morris's *Life and Death of Jason* (1867), Morris's translation of the *Völsunga Saga* (1870), and his prose and verse romance *The House of the Wolfings* (1889). Inspired by both the *Kalevala* and Morris, Tolkien tried to rewrite the *Kalevala* story of Kullervo in the style of *The House of the Wolfings*.

While he was living at Duchess Street, Birmingham (1908–early 1910) he probably read *John Inglesant* (1881), a best-selling novel written by a local author, John Henry Shorthouse. Tolkien later described it as 'a long book, which was queer, exciting, and debatable – or seemed so then, few now find it possible to read' (letter to Christopher Bretherton, 16 July 1964, *Letters*, p. 348). By 1913 he must have read Rudyard Kipling's *Kim* (1901), Arthur Conan Doyle's *The White Company* (1891), and *H. Rider Haggard's *King Solomon's Mines* (1886), since he confidently thought them suitable for the Mexican boys briefly in his care in Paris (*France). Other books he mentioned later in life but which he may have read in these years are Haggard's *She* (1887), S.R. Crockett's *The Black Douglas* (1899), and Lord Dunsany's *The Book of Wonder* (1912).

This list suggests a considerable range of reading in childhood and youth, and indicates that one should treat with caution some of Tolkien's remarks, such as one he made in a letter to Edith Bratt (*Edith Tolkien), *c.* 1913 – 'I so rarely read a novel, as you know' (quoted in *Biography*, p. 70) – or statements that he was not interested in 'literature'. The many books he mentioned in later letters, in interviews, and in miscellaneous writings refute the view held by some critics that Tolkien read almost nothing outside his professional field. Nonetheless, with many demands on his time, there was only so much time that Tolkien could devote to reading, and according to Humphrey Carpenter, when he did find 'the time or the inclination to read' fiction 'in general he preferred the lighter contemporary novels' (*Biography*, p. 165), such as the stories of John Buchan, to critically accepted 'Literature'. The authors of the present book have found no mention of Tolkien reading novels by writers such as Virginia Woolf, Joseph Conrad, and D.H. Lawrence, whose work is looked on with favour by critics and writers on 'literature'; but an unpublished note among Tolkien's papers in the Bodleian Library, Oxford, shows that he had, at the least, glanced at *Finnegan's Wake* (1939) by James Joyce. Considering the intense study of texts required by his professional work, it is perhaps not surprising that Tolkien preferred something less demanding and more relaxing in his few leisure hours.

Concerning literature, he wrote to *Robert Murray on 2 December 1953:

> Certainly I have not been nourished by English Literature, in which I do not suppose I am better read than you; for the simple reason that I have never found much there in which to rest my heart (or heart and head together). I was brought up in the Classics, and first discovered the sensation of literary pleasure in Homer. Also being a philologist, getting a large part of any aesthetic pleasure that I am capable of from the *form* of words (and especially from the *fresh* association of word-form with word-sense). I have always best enjoyed things in a foreign language, or one so remote as to feel like it (such as Anglo-Saxon). [*Letters*, p. 172]

On 8 February 1967 Tolkien wrote to Charlotte and Denis Plimmer: 'I read quite a lot – or more truly, try to read many books (notably so-called Science-Fiction and Fantasy). But I seldom find any modern books that hold my attention. I suppose because I am under "inner" pressure to complete my own work – and because ... "I am looking for something I can't find"' (*Letters*, p. 377). His interest in science-fiction and fantasy is confirmed by other references in letters, writings, and interviews. When he wrote to Stanley Unwin on 4 March 1938, refuting unfavourable readers' reports of *Out of the Silent Planet* by *C.S. Lewis (published later in 1938), Tolkien compared it to other works of science fiction he had read: 'I realize of course that to be even moderately marketable such a story must pass muster on its surface value, as a *vera historia* of a journey to a strange land. I am extremely fond of the genre, even having read *Land under England* [by Joseph O'Neill, 1935] with some pleasure (though it was a weak example, and distasteful to me in many points.' Later he says of *Out of the Silent Planet*:

> I at any rate should have bought this story at almost any price if I had found it in print, and loudly recommended it as a 'thriller' by (however and surprisingly) an intelligent man. But I know only too sadly from efforts to find anything to read even with an 'on demand' subscription at a library that my taste is not normal. I read 'Voyage to Arcturus' [*A Voyage to Arcturus* (1920) by David Lindsay] with avidity – the most comparable work, though it is both more powerful and more mythical (and less rational, and also less of a story – no one could read it merely as

a thriller and without interest in philosophy religion and morals). [*Letters*, pp. 33–4]

In *The Notion Club Papers*, which Tolkien wrote during the Christmas vacation of 1945 and during the first half of 1946, his characters discuss other works of science fiction and social comment involving a visit to a strange country: *The First Men in the Moon* (1901) and *The Time Machine* (1895) by H.G. Wells; *News from Nowhere* (1891) by William Morris; *Erewhon* (1872) by Samuel Butler; *Last Men in London* (1932) by Olaf Stapledon; and *Perelandra* (1943) by C.S. Lewis.

Tolkien enjoyed the works of *E.R. Eddison, *The Worm Ouroboros* (1922), *Mistress of Mistresses* (1935), *A Fish Dinner in Memison* (1941), and *The Mezentian Gate* (1958), and wrote of them:

> I read [Eddison's] works with great enjoyment for their sheer literary merit . . . [but] disliked his characters (always excepting the Lord Gro [in *The Worm Ouroboros*]) . . . [and] thought that, corrupted by an evil and indeed silly 'philosophy', he was coming to admire, more and more, arrogance and cruelty. Incidentally, I thought his nomenclature slipshod and often inept. In spite of all of which, I still think of him as the greatest and most convincing writer of 'invented worlds' that I have read. [letter to Caroline Everett, 24 June 1957, *Letters*, p. 258]

He was also 'greatly taken by' *The Death of Grass* (1956) by John Christopher, and enjoyed the science fiction of Isaac Asimov (letter to the Plimmers, 8 February 1967, *Letters*, p. 377). Although he read many of Edgar Rice Burroughs' earlier works, he developed a dislike for Tarzan.

Detective fiction featured in his reading as well. He liked the early Lord Peter Wimsey novels of Dorothy L. Sayers, but in 1944 commented that he could not stand *Gaudy Night* (1935) or *Busman's Honeymoon* (1937). In a letter to *Donald Swann on 18 November 1966 he mentioned reading a book written by his colleague *J.I.M. Stewart (as 'Michael Innes') which inspired him to look into the origin of the word *melody*, a problem he found 'much more complicated and less soluble than the murder' (Marion E. Wade Center, Wheaton College, Wheaton, Illinois).

On occasion he praised or alluded to other novels. He read Sinclair Lewis's *Babbitt* (1922) and later thought that its title might have influenced that of *The Hobbit*. He read T.H. White's *Sword in the Stone* soon after its publication in 1938. A reference to 'Joad' in a letter written in 1948 suggests that he knew John Steinbeck's *Grapes of Wrath* (1939). He was embarrassed to find that he disliked *Naomi Mitchison's *To the Chapel Perilous* (1955) and could not respond to a request by George Allen & Unwin (*Publishers) for a blurb. Also in 1955 *P.H. Newby sent him a copy of his new novel, *Picnic at Sakkara*, which Tolkien stayed up very late reading. In 1967 Tolkien wrote to the Plimmers that he 'was recently deeply engaged in the books of Mary Renault; especially the two about Theseus, *The King Must Die* [1958], and *The Bull from the Sea* [1962]', and had 'received a card of appreciation from her; perhaps the piece of "Fanmail" that gives me most pleasure' (8 February 1967, *Letters*, p. 377). He wrote to his son *Michael on 6 January 1965 of his surprise in receiving a fan-letter from Iris Murdoch, a more mainstream novelist, in terms which suggest that she was more than just a name to him. Other references in *Letters* indicate that Tolkien probably read some of the great novelists of the eighteenth and nineteenth centuries: a reference to 'Trollopean Society' (*Letters*, p. 61), a mention of 'the "manners" of life 150 years ago (nearly) as depicted by Jane Austen' (p. 72), a remark that he was unable 'to enjoy *Pickwick*' (p. 349, i.e. the *Pickwick Papers* by Charles Dickens).

He also read or heard a wide variety of works, fiction and non-fiction, written by fellow members of the *Inklings. *Owen Barfield's *Poetic Diction* (1928) was a significant influence on Tolkien and his writings. He 'actively disliked *Charles Williams's Arthurian-Byzantine mythology' (letter to Anne Barrett, 7 August 1964, *Letters*, p. 349), referring to the poems *Taliessin through Logres* (1938) and *The Region of the Summer Stars* (1944), and did not share C.S. Lewis's enthusiasm for Williams' novels. His reaction to Lewis's works varied: although he was very appreciative of *Out of the Silent Planet* and *Perelandra*, he was less so of *That Hideous Strength* (1945), which he thought had been spoiled by the influence of Charles Williams. He did not like the Narnia books, finding them 'outside the range of my sympathy', and described *Letters to Malcolm: Chiefly on Prayer* (1964) as 'a distressing and in parts horrifying work' (letter to David Kolb, 11 November 1964, *Letters*, p. 352). He read *Adam Fox's poem *Old King Coel*, and enjoyed hearing *W.H. Lewis read from the book he was writing on the reign of Louis XIV (published in 1953 as *The Splendid Century: Some Aspects of French Life in the Reign of Louis XIV*) even though it was not a subject of personal interest.

Despite his early 'insensitivity' to poetry, Tolkien came to read verse often, in particular once he had decided to make his own name as a poet, and was advised to read poems by his friend *G.B. Smith. In 1913 and 1914 Tolkien bought *The Works of Francis Thompson*, poet and literary critic, and gave a talk on him in March 1914 to the Exeter College Essay Club (*Societies and clubs). In May 1915 at *Oxford he read a paper to the Psittakoi (*Societies and clubs) on *The Quest of Beauty and Other Poems* (1915) by H.R. Freston, an Exeter College student who had recently enlisted and who would be killed in action in January 1916. Tolkien must have bought the book on or soon after its publication, and it was still in his library at his death. If he followed G.B. Smith's advice in July 1915, he bought and read all of Rupert Brooke's poems, and at least one of the volumes of *Georgian Poetry*. After a surprise meeting with *Roy Campbell in Oxford in October 1944 Tolkien described him in a letter to his son *Christopher as a 'powerful poet', author of *The Flaming Terrapin* (1924), *Flowering Rifle* (1939), and *Flaming Terrapin* (1939) among other works. When *Elizabeth Jennings, a friend and contemporary of Tolkien's children, sent him a copy of *A Way of Looking*, her first book of poetry in December

1955, he read it carefully and commented on it in detail. He told *W.H. Auden, after receiving a copy of his latest book of poetry, *About the House* (1965), that although Auden's writing did not arouse in him 'the same immediate response' as his own works did with Auden, 'I took it up to read one night when I was about to get into a warm bed (about midnight). At 2.30 a.m. I found myself, rather cold, still out of bed, reading and re-reading it' (23 February 1966, *Letters*, p. 368).

Occasionally a brief remark in a letter suggests an area of Tolkien's reading about which we have no other evidence. In January or February 1938 he wrote to the editor of *The Observer* that he had read 'several books on African exploration' (*Letters*, p. 30). In August 1967 he wrote to a Mr Rang: 'naturally, as one interested in antiquity and notably in the history of languages and "writing", I knew and had read a good deal about Mesopotamia' (*Letters*, p. 384). At least for a brief period he subscribed to the journal *Antiquity*.

*Priscilla Tolkien told Donald O'Brien in a letter in August 1992 that her father 'was steeped in the works of *[G.K.] Chesterton and [Hilaire] Belloc' (*Beyond Bree*, September 1992, p. 8). Tolkien bought Chesterton's *Coloured Lands* soon after its publication late in 1938, and used material from it several times in his lecture *On Fairy-Stories* delivered on 8 March 1939.

In preparing *On Fairy-Stories* Tolkien read widely. Among the works to which he refers either in the essay itself or in its working papers, and not mentioned elsewhere in this entry, are *Eros and Psyche* by Apuleius; *Egyptian Reading Book* by Wallace Budge; *Popular Tales of the West Highlands* by Joseph Campbell; *Brer Rabbit* by Uncle Remus; *The Everlasting Man* and *Orthodoxy* by G.K. Chesterton; *Progress and Religion* by Christopher Dawson; *Nymphidia* by Michael Drayton; various 'colour' fairy books by Andrew Lang; *Lilith* by George MacDonald; *The Blue Bird* by Maurice Maeterlinck; *Travels of Baron Münchhausen*; *In Northern Mists* by Fridtjof Nansen; *Contes de ma Mère l'Oye* by Charles Perrault; *The Tailor of Gloucester*, *The Tale of Peter Rabbit*, and *The Tale of Mrs Tiggywinkle* by Beatrix Potter; *Gulliver's Travels* by Jonathan Swift; *The Rose and the Ring* by W.M. Thackeray; and the *Ballad of Thomas the Rhymer*.

In later life Tolkien appreciated children's books as much for himself as for his children and grandchildren: books such as *E.A. Wyke-Smith's *Marvellous Land of Snergs*, which Tolkien himself said was a probable influence on *The Hobbit*; *Arthur Ransome's *Swallows and Amazons* and its successors; Hugh Lofting's 'Doctor Dolittle' books; and Mary Norton's *The Borrowers* and its sequels (his own copies of which Tolkien lent to his granddaughter, Joanna – see *Michael Tolkien). He did not think that Pompey in J.B.S. Haldane's *My Friend Mr Leakey* was a real dragon. Tolkien was ten when the first of Beatrix Potter's books for young children was published, so it was probably as an adult and a father that he came to appreciate her work. C.S. Lewis wrote in a letter on 30 November 1942 that Tolkien had pointed out to him that Beatrix Potter's 'art of putting about ten words on one page so as to have a perfect rhythm and to answer just the questions a child would ask, is almost as severe as that of lyric poetry. She has a secure place among the masters of English prose. He and I have often played with the idea of a pilgrimage to see her . . .' (*C.S. Lewis: Collected Letters*, vol. 2 (2004), pp. 537–8).

In 1956 Tolkien said to Mrs M. Wilson, in regard to children reading *The Lord of the Rings*, for whom it was not written, that he himself was 'a very "unvoracious" reader, and since I can seldom bring myself to read a work twice I think of the many things that I read – too soon! Nothing, not even a (possible) deeper appreciation, for me replaces the bloom on a book, the freshness of the unread. Still what we read and when goes, like the people we meet, by "fate"' (11 April 1956, *Letters*, p. 249). And when he re-read a book after a period of time, his opinion of it sometimes changed. Although he enjoyed G.K. Chesterton's poem *The Ballad of the White Horse* when he first read it, when he tried 'to explain the obscurer parts' to his daughter he found it 'not as good as I thought. The ending is absurd. The brilliant smash and glitter of the words and phrases (when they come off, and are not mere loud colours) cannot disguise the fact that G.K.C. knew nothing whatever about the "North", heathen or Christian' (letter to Christopher Tolkien, 3 September 1944, *Letters*, p. 92). In *On Fairy-Stories* he praised George MacDonald's 'The Golden Key', but when he read the story again in 1964 he 'found that a highly selective memory had retained only a few impressions of things that moved me, and re-reading [George MacDonald] critically filled me with distaste.' C.S. Lewis much admired MacDonald, but 'he was evidently born loving (moral) allegory, and I was born with an instinctive distaste for it'. MacDonald's *Phantastes* similarly 'afflicted me with profound dislike' (Tolkien Papers, Bodleian Library, Oxford).

As an academic Tolkien built up a personal reference library, much of which, while he was still teaching, he kept in college. *John and Priscilla Tolkien note in *The Tolkien Family Album* (1992) that the walls of their father's study at 20 Northmoor Road 'were lined with books from floor to ceiling' (p. 55). Tolkien began to collect books while still an undergraduate; in 1970 he wrote to *Neil Ker that 'the foundation of my library was laid by *[Kenneth] Sisam. He taught me not only to read texts, but to study second-hand book catalogues, of which I was not even aware. Some he marked for me' (22 November 1970, *Letters*, p. 406). When he lost his room at Merton College in 1959, moved to *Poole in 1968, and returned to Oxford in 1972, he had to cull his library for lack of space; even so, when he died he possessed a substantial collection. Some 280 of his books on Celtic, Icelandic, Anglo-Saxon, Middle English, and Germanic languages and literature were given to the English Faculty Library in Oxford. Many of these contain the inscribed dates that acquired them, which show that he was buying such books avidly in the early 1920s, especially Gaelic, Welsh, Breton and Irish works. Of the 200 volumes published in 1925 or earlier and not shown by inscriptions to have been acquired after 1925, Tolkien owned at least 15 already by 1919, and added 61 in 1920–25 while he was at *Leeds – over a third of the total. He added at least 29 of these books to his collection in 1922, almost all of them on the various Celtic languages and literature. His library also contained a large number of offprints from academic journals, most sent to him by admiring colleagues and former students. On 20 July 1965 Tolkien wrote to Zillah Sherring, who had bought second-hand the copy of *The Fifth Book of Thucydides* that Tolkien had once owned as a schoolboy, and in which he had written inscriptions in Gothic. 'I still feel no compunction in writing in my own books,' he said, 'though I now usually put only notes supposed to be of use – if I can later decipher them' (*Letters*, p. 358).

In March 1966 Henry Resnik interviewed Tolkien by telephone for an article in the *Saturday Evening Post*. A transcript of this interview was published in *Niekas* 18 (Spring 1967), in which Tolkien is reported to have said that he read newspapers every day and that 'we' (at this date, Tolkien and Edith) took three newspapers. Tolkien continued: 'I read newspapers . . . they're there, and I read them when I'm interested. I take a strong interest in what is going on, both in the university and in the country and in the world' (p. 39). Two of these were *The Times* and the *Daily Telegraph*. Among the Tolkien papers in the Bodleian are some two hundred pages or scraps torn from newspapers, preserved because Tolkien doodled on them while completing the crossword. The third paper was probably local to Oxford. He may also have taken the *Catholic Herald*, to which he wrote a letter in February 1945, and possibly on Sundays *The Observer*, to which he wrote a letter early in 1938 in reply to a letter about *The Hobbit*. For some period at least he took the *Sunday Times*: in November 1962 he told Rayner Unwin that he had given it up when it changed hands (it was purchased in 1959 by Roy Thomson).

See further, two articles by Nancy Martsch: 'Tolkien's Reading', *Beyond Bree*, April 1997; and 'Tolkien's Reading: "On Fairy-Stories"', *Beyond Bree*, August 1997. See also *Classical influences; *Northernness; *Science; and entries for asterisked authors in this article.

Recordings. The earliest recording of Tolkien's voice, as far as is known to us, was made by June 1930 for the *Linguaphone Conversational Course* in English, issued by the Linguaphone Institute of London as a set of 78 rpm records. Tolkien read the introduction to, and played one of two roles in, Lesson 20, 'At the Tobacconist's', and again was one of two readers for Lesson 30, 'Wireless'. In these he was joined by the author of the lessons, A. Lloyd James of the University of London. His *Oxford colleague *Professor H.C.K. Wyld also recorded for the course. See further, René van Rossenberg, 'Tolkien and Linguaphone', *Tolkien Collector* 5 (November 1993).

In late August 1952 Tolkien visited his friends *George and Moira Sayer at *Malvern. One evening, to entertain his guest, Sayer produced a tape recorder, into which Tolkien read some of the poems from *The Lord of the Rings*, an extract from 'The Ride of the Rohirrim' (Book V, Chapter 5), and the riddle scene from *The Hobbit* (Chapter 5). At least some of these recordings were issued by Caedmon Records of New York in 1975, as *J.R.R. Tolkien Reads and Sings His The Hobbit and The Fellowship of the Ring* and *J.R.R. Tolkien Reads* *and Sings His The Lord of the Rings: The Two Towers/The Return of the King.* An excerpt from the *Hobbit* tape was included on the recording *The Spoken Word: Children's Writers* (BBC, 2003). Two brief excerpts from the *Fellowship of the Ring* tape were included on the recording *The Spoken Word: Writers* (BBC, 2003). In 'Tales of the Ferrograph', *Minas Tirith Evening-Star* 9, no. 2 (January 1980), George Sayer wrote that as a lecturer Tolkien 'muttered and spoke very quietly. He had a very poor speaking voice, although we produced very good recordings of him with that old Ferrograph [tape recorder] by putting the microphone very close to him really. The speaking voice on the Caedmon records give one the impression that his voice was far stronger than it was in actual life' (p. 2). Tolkien hoped in 1953 to pay another visit to Sayer, so that they could record together, as two voices, but this seems never to have occurred.

Tolkien also made a private tape recording, by 3 May 1954, of his verse-drama **The Homecoming of Beorhtnoth Beorhthelm's Son*, speaking all of the voices and making his own sound effects. This was released, with other material recorded by *Christopher Tolkien, as an audio cassette tape by HarperCollins, London (*Publishers), in a complimentary limited edition for the Tolkien Centenary Conference at Oxford in 1992.

By mid-January 1966 *Joy Hill of George Allen & Unwin (*Publishers) began to promote the possibility that a long-playing record would be produced which would include the song cycle **The Road Goes Ever On* by *Donald Swann, together with extracts from Tolkien's works read by Swann's long-time partner, Michael Flanders. By April 1967, in conjunction with the book **The Road Goes Ever On: A Song Cycle* planned to be published by the Houghton Mifflin Company, Boston (*Publishers), and George Allen & Unwin, a scheme was put together for a record to be produced by Caedmon, with the song cycle performed by composer-pianist Donald Swann and singer William Elvin on one side, but now with Tolkien himself on the other, reading some of his poems. On 15 June 1967 Tolkien recorded at least eight of the poems in **The Adventures of Tom Bombadil and Other Verses from the Red Book*, as well as the Elvish verses *A Elbereth Gilthoniel* and *Namárië* from *The Lord of the Rings*. Most of these were first issued in 1967, together with the Swann-Elvin performance of the song cycle, on the Caedmon recording *Poems and Songs of Middle Earth* (*sic*).

The J.R.R. Tolkien Audio Collection, first released in 2001, includes the three Caedmon recordings of 1967 and 1975, excluding the Swann-Elvin performance of *The Road Goes Ever On*, but with the addition of four poems from Tolkien's 1967 recording session not included on the original album: *Errantry*, *Princess Mee*, *The Sea-Bell*, and *Namárië*. (The set also includes two recordings of selections from **The Silmarillion* read by Christopher Tolkien, originally released in 1977–8.)

In 1964 Tolkien was interviewed by Irene Slade for the programme 'Reluctant Olympians' in the British Broadcasting Corporation's radio series *A World of Sound*, and informally (with a midget tape recorder) by Denys Gueroult for the BBC Sound Archives (now the National Sound Archives). A portion of the former was included in *J.R.R. Tolkien: An Audio Portrait of the Author of The Hobbit and The Lord of the Rings* (2001), presented by Brian Sibley. An edited version of a second, professionally recorded interview by Gueroult was first issued in 1980 as a commercial audio cassette by BBC Cassettes, London, and Audio-Forum in Guilford, Connecticut. In February 1968 Tolkien was recorded in conjunction with the BBC television documentary *Tolkien in Oxford*; this has not been commercially released, but a portion of an interview done on that occasion is included in *J.R.R. Tolkien: An Audio Portrait*, and has appeared in other documentaries about Tolkien.

Other recordings made by the BBC of Tolkien's voice or image appear not to have been preserved.

For recordings of Tolkien's works by other voices, see individual entries, and *Adaptations.

Recovery. Tolkien considered *recovery* to be one of the most valuable functions of *fairy-stories or fantasy. In *On Fairy-Stories* he comments that because of our great inheritance of story from the past we may despair of being able to say something new, of being able to add to the 'Tree of Tales': 'It seems vain to add to the litter. Who can design a new leaf? The patterns from bud to unfolding, and the colours from spring to autumn were all discovered by men long ago. But that is not true. . . . Spring is, of course, not really less beautiful because we have seen or heard of other like events: like events, never from world's beginning to world's end the same event' (*Tree and Leaf*, p. 52). And always there are some witnessing the patterns for the first time. We are heirs to the works of many generations of artists, and there is a danger that through boredom or a desire to be original we may reject or distort their achievements. 'But the true road of escape from such weariness is not to be found in the wilfully awkward, clumsy, or misshapen, not in making all things dark or unremittingly violent; nor in the mixing of colours on through subtlety to drabness, and the fantastical complication of shapes to the point of silliness and on towards delirium' (p. 53).

Rather, we need to regain a clear view, look at familiar faces and things, and try to see them as if for the first time – 'to clean our windows; so that the things seen clearly may be freed from the drab blur of triteness or familiarity . . .' (p. 53). Fairy-stories can help us do this, for in them we meet familiar things in a different light and setting:

> Fantasy is made out of the Primary World, but a good craftsman loves his material, and has a knowledge and feeling for clay, stone and wood which only the art of making can give. By the forging of Gram cold iron was revealed; by the making of Pegasus horses were ennobled; in the Trees of the Sun and the Moon root and stock, flower and fruit are manifested in glory. [*Tree and Leaf*, pp. 54–5]

In *Splintered Light: Logos and Language in Tolkien's World* (2nd edn. 2002) Verlyn Flieger comments that

> Tolkien's concept of Recovery is not unlike the Platonic concept of recollection, the idea – best expressed in the *Timaeus* [by Plato] – that knowledge is recollection of things already learned, that we constantly rediscover and repossess what we have formerly known. . . . The Secondary World can and should redirect our attention to the Primary World and through that World to its Maker. It should enable us to regain, to recollect what we have always known but have forgotten how to see. Through imitation of God, man has the opportunity to recover His works. [p. 25]

Some characters in Tolkien's own writings have such an experience. In *The Lord of the Rings*, when Frodo looks around at Cerin Amroth in Lothlórien 'he saw no colour but those he knew, gold and white and blue and green, but they were fresh and poignant, as if he had at that moment first perceived them and made for them names new and wonderful' (bk. II, ch. 6). In *Smith of Wootton Major* Smith is able, because of his experiences in Faery, to create delicate and beautiful things, but even the plain, useful, everyday objects he makes – 'farm tools, carpenters' tools, kitchen tools and pots and pans, bars and bolts and hinges, pot-hooks fire-dogs, and horse-shoes, and the like' – have a special quality. They are not only 'strong and lasting, but they also had a grace about them, being shapely in their kinds, good to handle and to look at' (p. 21).

In *The Lord of the Rings* Tolkien devotes much attention to describing the scenery and weather, flowers and trees – some real, some imaginary – and portrays with horror and sadness the careless destruction of the natural environment. By producing vivid pictures in the reader's mind, he leads one to look more closely at features and issues in our own world (see also *Environment, *Nature). Many readers of *The Lord of the Rings* have been led, for instance, to look at trees in a different way after reading about the Ents and their reactions to Saruman's destruction of the trees in Fangorn Forest. Diane Duane writes in 'The Longest Sunday', in *Meditations on Middle-earth* (2001), that during a stay in Switzerland she thought of Tolkien's visit there in 1911: as she looked at the peaks the Misty Mountains came to mind, and as she noticed a little golden flower, she thought of *elanor* from *The Lord of the Rings*.

> When the words and images start insinuating themselves into unexpected parts of life, so that suddenly everything seems to refer back to that work, or remind you of things in it, then you know that a secondary creator of unusual skill has been at work *in* you. And when finding a concrete example of something 'real,' which the writer has drawn into his own world and made his own, suddenly makes the 'real' world seem more magical than it actually is, that's wizardry of the most potent kind.

The best magic is 'the ability to make reality itself more real, to add something to it that wouldn't ever have been there otherwise, without one man's heartbreakingly inclusive imagination' (p. 128).

Rednal (Worcestershire). Though the hamlet of Rednal is only a few miles from the centre of *Birmingham to the south-west, even today it has a rural appearance. Cardinal Newman, the founder of the *Birmingham Oratory, built the Oratory House nearby as a place of retreat for the Oratory clergy. Adjoining it is the cemetery where the Oratory fathers, including Newman and Tolkien's guardian *Francis Xavier Morgan, are buried. When Tolkien's mother *Mabel was released from hospital in late June 1904 following treatment for diabetes, Father Francis arranged for her and her sons to rent a bedroom and a sitting room from the local postman at Woodside Cottage, Rednal. Ronald and *Hilary Tolkien were given the freedom of the Oratory House grounds and ranged further afield to the **Lickey Hills**.

When there was no priest in residence at the Oratory retreat, the Tolkiens went to Mass at the Catholic church of St Peter in the town of **Bromsgrove** south-west of Rednal. The church, designed in the Gothic Revival style by Gilbert R. Blount, was completed in 1860. Mabel Tolkien died on 14 November 1904 at Rednal and was buried on 17 November in St Peter's churchyard.

The Reeve's Tale. Version by Tolkien of one of the *Canterbury Tales* by *Geoffrey Chaucer. A *reeve* is a manager of an estate; the tale told by Chaucer's reeve concerns a miller who cheats those whose corn he grinds, and of two clerks of Cambridge who take revenge upon him. Tolkien prepared a 'slightly abbreviated' version of the 'Reeve's Tale' based on the edition by Skeat for reading aloud – in Middle English, and with contemporary pronunciation – at the 'Summer Diversions' in Oxford on 28 July 1939. A booklet containing the text, with a brief introduction, was printed presumably for the use of the audience on the occasion. The abbreviations were made for length, but also served to omit or reduce the bawdier elements of the tale less suitable for public performance.

The 'Reeve's Tale', Tolkien wrote, 'is neither easy to shorten nor improved by the process' (p. 4). The *Oxford Mail* of 29 July 1939, reporting on Tolkien's reading of the tale, deeply regretted the omissions made to the text:

> It seems an unjust criticism of an Oxford audience to indicate with such bluntness that they are not broadminded enough to accept the distinctly broad humour of Chaucer in a story of his which can least afford to be cut because of the amazingly ingenious way in which the plot is worked out. Nobody would deny that the 'Reeve's Tale' loses by abbreviation. ['Canterbury Tale and Ballet: Oxford Performances of Summer Diversions', final page]

Tolkien had a special interest in the 'Reeve's Tale'. In this Chaucer 'gave new life to the *fabliau*, the plot of which he borrowed, with the English local colour that he devised; and he introduced the new joke of comic dialect. This does not seem to have been attempted in English literature before Chaucer, and has seldom been more successful since' (p. 3). Tolkien had discussed the same subject at greater length eight years earlier, in his paper *Chaucer as a Philologist: The Reeve's Tale* (1931, published 1934).

Reincarnation of Elves. 'A hastily written manuscript', extracted and discussed by *Christopher Tolkien in *Morgoth's Ring* (1993), pp. 363–6. It is one of a series of works written *c.* 1959–60 which show Tolkien changing his ideas on Elvish reincarnation.

From the writing of *The Book of Lost Tales* for decades it was a firm tenet of his mythology that Elves who were killed might be reborn in their children, and this was still the case when Tolkien wrote *Laws and Customs among the Eldar* in the late 1950s, in connection with the story of the Elf Míriel who 'died' and refused to reincarnate. But after writing that work he gave more thought to the question, and the situation in *The Converse of Manwë and Eru* is that none of the *fëar* (spirits, singular *fëa*) of Elves whose bodies (*hröar*, singular *hröa*) had been killed had been rehoused until Manwë consulted Eru after the 'death' of Míriel. Eru then told Manwë that he had the authority to shape new bodies for houseless *fëar*, but he should submit for Eru's judgement any *fëa* that desired re-birth as a child and which he considered fit to be re-born.

Although in both *Laws and Customs among the Eldar* and *The Converse of Manwë and Eru* Tolkien had begun to consider the problems of identity of a *fëa* reborn in the body of a child, in *Reincarnation of Elves* he finally abandoned this method of reincarnation because (as Christopher Tolkien summarizes)

> the difficulties on every level (including practical and psychological) in the idea of the reincarnation of the *fëa* as the newborn child of second parents, who as it grows up recaptures the memory of its previous life: 'the most fatal objection' being that 'it contradicts the fundamental notion that *fëa* and *hröa* were each *fitted* to the other: since *hröar* have a physical descent, the body of rebirth, having different parents, must be different' [*Morgoth's Ring*, p. 363]

According to this text, not until Manwë consulted Eru were any houseless *fëar* summoned to Mandos, and the Valar are given the authority to reincarnate them in bodies identical to those lost. The same idea appears in the commentary on the *Athrabeth Finrod ah Andreth* which probably followed this work in sequence of writing.

In *Reincarnation of Elves*, as a second thought, Tolkien considered whether, rather than the Valar making the new body, the houseless *fëa* might be able to rebuild its body from memory. In very late writings it is clear that this became his view of the matter.

Religion. Tolkien's parents were Anglicans, and he himself was baptised in the Church of England. His mother, *Mabel Tolkien, taking comfort in religion after the death of her husband, for a while attended 'high' Anglican services, but in June 1900 converted to Roman Catholicism, in which she found greater satisfaction. Some in the staunchly Protestant *Tolkien and *Suffield families were outraged, and some withdrew financial support they had been giving to the widowed Mabel and her sons. Despite their opposition she remained true to her choice, and brought up Ronald and *Hilary as Catholics. Referring to his mother's early death from diabetes, Tolkien later wrote to his son *Michael that she had been 'worn out with persecution, poverty, and, largely consequent, disease, in the effort to hand on to us small boys the Faith' (9–10 January 1965, *Letters*, pp. 353–4). Humphrey Carpenter has suggested that after Mabel died, Tolkien's religion 'took the place in his affections that she had previously occupied. The consolation that it provided was emotional as well as spiritual' (*Biography*, p. 31). Although his mother's death left him subject to bouts of despair, his faith gave him consolation for the future, if not in this fallen world (see *The Fall). He wrote to Amy Ronald on 15 December 1956: 'I am a Christian, and indeed a Roman Catholic, so that I do not expect "history" to be anything but a "long defeat" – though it contains . . . some samples or glimpses of final victory' (*Letters*, p. 255).

Before she died, Mabel Tolkien arranged that *Father Francis Morgan of the *Birmingham Oratory should act as her sons' guardian. It is notable that Father Francis did not move Ronald from *King Edward's School to St Philip's, the Catholic grammar school attached to the Oratory (which Mabel Tolkien had found inferior). Instead, as Tolkien wrote to his son Michael, Father Francis

> obtained permission for me to retain my scholarship at [King Edward's School] and continue there, and so I had the advantage of a (then) first rate school and that of a 'good Catholic home' – 'in excelsis': virtually a junior inmate in the Oratory house, which contained many learned fathers. . . . Observance of religion was strict. Hilary and I were supposed to, and usually did, serve Mass before getting on our bikes to go to school. . . . I was even allowed to attend the Headmaster's classes on the N[ew] T[estament] (in Greek). I certainly took no 'harm', and was better equipped ultimately to make my way in a non-Catholic professional society. I . . . made the acquaintance of the Wiseman family through my friendship with *Christopher Luke W[iseman]. . . . His father was one of the most delightful Christian men I have met . . . (whom Fr Francis always referred to as The Pope of Wesley, because he was the President of the Wesleyan Methodist Conference). . . . [after 25 August 1967, *Letters*, p. 395]

Although Ronald was Catholic and Christopher Wiseman a Methodist, they were able to discuss and argue about religion without harming their friendship. In a letter to Wiseman of 16 November 1914, Tolkien acknowledged this as an important link between the two friends, which did not exist with the other members of the *T.C.B.S. He also raised the question of what the 'subjects of supreme importance' would be to the T.C.B.S.: one was 'religion of course'. 'I personally for instance as long as [G.B. Smith] (say) remains unconvinced or not yet developed on the religious side can go on numbering him as a friend *and* as a TCBSian: his potentialities are simply as yet unknown: that is all: – but as soon as enthusiasms or beliefs do develop, I *demand* to know them and reweigh him. If he became an atheist or satanist, either he or I would leave the TCBS for ever' (Tolkien Papers, Bodleian Library, Oxford).

Years later, *C.S. Lewis described *The Inklings, in which Tolkien again was a core member, as 'a sort of informal club . . . the qualifications (as they have informally evolved) are a tendency to write, and Christianity' (letter to *Charles Williams, 11 March 1936, *Collected Letters*, vol. 2 (2004), p. 183). In fact, Lewis was an atheist when he and Tolkien first became friends, but they shared other interests. Tolkien, together with *Hugo Dyson, played a large part in Lewis's conversion from atheism, first for theism and then Christianity – though to Tolkien's disappointment, a Christian in the Church of England, not of Rome. Tolkien was sometimes hurt by what he considered the prejudices of Lewis's Ulster background; yet he himself was not entirely unprejudiced. He criticized Lewis for believing propaganda against Francisco Franco, the Spanish dictator, and disbelieving stories of the slaying of Catholic priests by Franco's opponents. He accepted *Roy Campbell's (inaccurate) account of his deeds in Spain uncritically, and perhaps only for effect remarked that 'hatred of our church is after all the real only foundation of the C[hurch] of E[ngland]' (letter to *Christopher Tolkien, 6 October 1944, *Letters*, p. 96), allowing no possibility of any genuine religious feeling.

Catholic orders associated with Oxford colleges were expelled in the Reformation, and for many years afterward, an important function of the University was the training of Anglican clergy. During the time that Tolkien was an undergraduate and then a professor, the presence of the Roman Catholic Church in Oxford became more prominent. Catholics in fact had officially returned to Oxford in 1896, after a papal prohibition which had prevented them from attending Oxford or Cambridge was rescinded. At first, all Catholic students attended existing colleges, but after the Jesuits, Benedictines, Franciscans, and Dominicans established halls in Oxford in the period 1896–1921, these were preferred by students intending to enter the priesthood. Oxford Roman Catholic students in general were guided in their faith and religious education by a Roman Catholic chaplaincy, a major institution of Oxford religious life, especially under Ronald Knox (1926–39).

Carpenter notes that when Tolkien went up to Oxford 'among the second-year men at his college were a couple of Catholics, who sought him out and made sure that he settled in' (*Biography*, p. 53). He was probably also contacted by the Catholic chaplain, and certainly was involved with the chaplaincy when he returned as a professor. Another institution of particular importance in his life was the convent at Cherwell Edge run by the Society of the Holy Child Jesus, to which was attached a hostel for Catholic women in the Society of Oxford Home-Students. Among these students were *Susan Dagnall and *M.E. Griffiths, through whom, with the Reverend Mother of the Convent, *St Teresa Gale, *The Hobbit came to the attention of George Allen & Unwin (*Publishers). Tolkien also had contact with the Sacred Heart Convent at 11 Norham Gardens, Oxford; his children went to parties there in the summer and at Christmas, at which Tolkien was 'a famous entertainer' (*Priscilla Tolkien, private correspondence). An early version of his poem *The Last Ship was published in the Chronicle of the Convents of the Sacred Heart.

Tolkien was also active in the Catenian Association (*Societies and clubs), an international brotherhood of Catholic business and professional men. He seems to have held office in the local circle. He took part in the Eighth Pax Romana Congress (an international organization for Catholic students) when it was held in Oxford in August 1928. His many Catholic friends and colleagues in Oxford included Helen Buckhurst, *Martin D'Arcy, *James Dundas-Grant, Elaine Griffiths, *Colin Hardie (after 1940), *R.E. Havard, the Jennings family (see *Elizabeth Jennings), *Gervase Mathew, and *C.L. Wrenn. There was, however, still some open hostility to Catholics: in a letter to his son Christopher on 31 May 1944, Tolkien reported that during a dinner at Pembroke College, the Master of Pembroke, sitting next to him, commented in a loud voice on the recent election of a new Rector of Lincoln College: 'Thank heaven they did not elect a Roman Catholic to the Rectorship anyway: disastrous, disastrous for the college', an opinion echoed by another of those present (Letters, p. 84).

At least twice Tolkien recommended the Blessed Sacrament to his son Michael, which 'like the act of Faith . . . must be continuous and grow by exercise'. He was 'convinced by the Petrine claims', nor looking round the world does there seem much doubt which (if Christianity is true) is the True Church . . . for me that Church of which the Pope is the acknowledged head on earth has as chief claim that it is the one that has (and still does) ever defended the Blessed Sacrament and given it most honour, and put it (as Christ plainly intended) in the prime place' (1 November 1963, Letters, p. 338–9). He was also rigorous about attending Confession before Mass: as *George Sayer recalled, Tolkien

> always liked to go to confession before receiving communion. I do not think that this was because he had on his conscience any sin that most people would regard as serious. True, he was what spiritual directors call 'scrupulous', that is, inclined to exaggerate the evil of the undisciplined and erring thoughts that plague most of us. But he was above all a devout and strict old-fashioned Catholic, who had been brought up to think that if possible one should go to confession first. This was the usual nineteenth-century attitude. ['Recollections of J.RR. Tolkien', Proceedings of the J.R.R. Tolkien Centenary Conference 1992 (1995), p. 23]

Tolkien was a firm believer in prayer for family and friends, and to glorify and praise God. He advised his son Christopher to

> make a habit of the 'praises'. I use them much (in Latin): the Gloria Patri, the Gloria in Excelsis, the Laudate Dominum; the Laudate Pueri Dominum (of which I am specially fond), one of the Sunday psalms; and the Magnificat; also the Litany of Loretto (with the prayer Sub tuum præsidium). If you have these by heart you never need for words of joy. It is also a good and admirable thing to know by heart the Canon of the Mass, for you can say this in your heart if ever hard circumstance keeps you from hearing Mass. [8 January 1944, *Letters*, p. 66]

He told Amy Ronald in a letter on 16 November 1969 that he prayed for her in her afflictions, 'because I have a feeling (more near a certainty) that God, for some ineffable reason which to us may seem almost like humour, is so curiously ready to answer the prayers of the *least* worthy of his suppliants – if they pray for others' (*Letters*, p. 401).

During the second half of the twentieth century, beginning under Pius XII and continuing with the Second Vatican Council (1962–5), significant reforms were made in Roman Catholic worship. Tolkien approved of these in the abstract, as 'more suitable to the ways of life of modern Christians'; but he felt 'a little dislocated and even a little sad at my age to know that the ceremonies and modes so long familiar and deeply associated with the season will never be heard again!' (letter to Patricia Kirke, 28 March 1956, Gerard A. Stodolski, *Catalogue 299* (1999), item 29). The entire liturgy for Holy Week was gradually changed, and for the sake of 'ecumenicalism', Roman Catholic experts were allowed (under strict conditions) to join with other Christians when discussing faith and morals. Most notably, the 'Latin rite' was replaced with the vernacular, and liturgical texts were extensively revised. Tolkien for his part could not see the point of abandoning Latin in the Mass: he knew the language, and would struggle to use the Latin missal while the Mass was spoken in English. His grandson Simon Tolkien (see *Christopher Tolkien) recalled going to church with him in *Bournemouth, where he 'made all the responses very loudly in Latin while the rest of the congregation answered in English' ('My Grandfather', *The Mail on Sunday*, 23 February 2003).

In 1967 Tolkien wrote to his son Michael:

> 'Trends' in the Church are . . . serious, especially to those accustomed to find in it a solace and a 'pax' in times of temporal trouble, and not just another arena of strife and change. But imagine the experience of those born (as I) between the Golden and the Diamond Jubilee of Victoria. Both senses or imaginations of security have been progressively stripped away from us. . . . The Church which once felt like a refuge, now often feels like a trap. There is nowhere else to go! (I wonder if this desperate feeling, the last state of loyalty hanging on, was not, even more

often than is actually recorded in the Gospels, felt by Our Lord's follow-ers in His earthly life-time?) I think there is nothing to do but to pray, for the Church, the Vicar of Christ, and for ourselves; and meanwhile to exercise the virtue of loyalty, which indeed only becomes a virtue when one is under pressure to desert it. . . . The 'protestant' search backwards for 'simplicity' and directness – which of course though it contains some good or at least intelligible motives is mistaken and indeed vain. Because 'primitive Christianity' is now and in spite of all 'research' will ever remain largely unknown; because 'primitiveness' is no guarantee of value, and is and was in great part a reflection of ignorance. Grave abuses were as much an element in Christian 'liturgical' behaviour from the beginning as now. . . . Still more because 'my church' was not intended by Our Lord to be static or remain in perpetual childhood; but to be a living organism (likened to a plant) which develops and changes in externals by the interaction of its bequeathed divine life and history – the particu-lar circumstances of the world into which it is set. . . .

I find myself in sympathy with those developments that are strictly 'ecumenical', that is concerned with other groups or churches that call themselves (and often truly are) 'Christian'. We have prayed endlessly for Christian re-union, but it is difficult to see, if one reflects, how that could possibly begin to come about except as it has, with all its inevita-ble minor absurdities. An increase in 'charity' is an enormous gain. As Christians those faithful to the Vicar of Christ must put aside the resent-ments that as mere humans they feel – e.g. at the 'cockiness' of our new friends (esp[ecially] C[hurch] of E[ngland]). One is now often patted on the back, as a representative of a church that has seen the error of its ways. . . . [*Letters*, pp. 393–4]

For discussion of Tolkien's religion as related to questions of marriage, see *Edith Tolkien; *Women and marriage.

RELIGION IN TOLKIEN'S WRITINGS

Events related in *'The Silmarillion' and *The Lord of the Rings are meant to occur in a fictional pre-Christian era of our world. But in the former work, an element of religion was always present: Arda (the Earth) was created by the One (Eru, Ilúvatar – that is, God), with the participation of the Ainur, themselves created by Eru. Some of the Ainur choose to enter Arda, the chief among whom are the Valar (the Powers or Authorities), appointed by Eru as the guardians and rulers of the world. In the earliest version of this mythology (*The Book of Lost Tales), the Valar were in many ways closer to the pan-theons of Olympus and Asgard than the more austere figures they would later become: they included Makar and Meássë, a quarrelsome pair who are con-cerned with battle and slaughter, and Ossë and Ulmo who were often at odds. Although they have sometimes been called 'gods', Tolkien explained in a draft letter to Peter Hastings, the Valar 'are only created spirits – of high angelic order we should say, with their attendant lesser angels – reverend therefore, but not worshipful'. Therefore in *The Lord of the Rings* there are

no temples or 'churches' or fanes in this 'world' among 'good' peoples. They had little or no 'religion' in the sense of worship. For help they may call on a *Vala* (as *Elbereth*), as a Catholic might on a Saint, though no doubt knowing in theory as well as he that the power of the Vala was limited and derivative. But this is a 'primitive age': and these folk may be said to view the Valar as children view their parents or immediate adult superiors, and though they know they are subjects of the King he does not live in their country nor have there any dwelling. I do not think Hobbits practised any form of worship or prayer (unless through exceptional contact with Elves). The Númenóreans (and others . . . that fought against Morgoth, even if they elected to remain in Middle-earth and did not go to Númenor: such as the Rohirrim) were pure monotheists. But there was no temple in Númenor (until Sauron introduced the cult of Morgoth). The top of the mountain, the Meneltarma or Pillar of Heaven, was dedicated to Eru, the One, and there at any time privately, and at certain times publicly, God was invoked, praised, and adored: in imitation of the Valar and the Mountain of Aman. But Númenor fell and was destroyed and the Mountain engulfed, and there was no substitute. Among the exiles, remnants of the Faithful who had not adopted the false religion nor taken part in the rebellion, religion as divine worship (though perhaps not as philosophy and metaphysics) seems to have played a small part. . . . [September 1954, *Letters*, pp. 193–4]

In *The Silmarillion* it is said that in Aman 'Yavanna set times for the flowering and the ripening of all things that grew in Valinor; and at each first gathering of fruits Manwë made a high feast for the praising of Eru, when all the peoples of Valinor poured forth their joy in music and song upon Taniquetil' (pp. 74–5). While in Númenor, the summit of the Meneltarma

was somewhat flattened and depressed, and could contain a great multitude; but it remained untouched by hands throughout the history of Númenor. No building, no raised altar, not even a pile of undressed stones, ever stood there. . . . Thrice only in each year the King spoke, offering prayer for the coming year at the *Erukyermë* in the first days of spring, praise of Eru Ilúvatar at the *Erulaitalë* in midsummer, and thanksgiving to him at the *Eruhantalë* at the end of autumn. At these times the King ascended the mountain on foot followed by a great concourse of the people, clad in white and garlanded, but silent. At other times the people were free to climb to the summit alone or in company. . . . [*A Description of the Island of Númenor*, in *Unfinished Tales*, p. 166]

In contrast, the temple which Sauron built to Melkor/Morgoth on Númenor was an imposing building, and the rituals performed there included human sacrifice. In his comments of 1956 on *W.H. Auden's review of *The Return of the King*, Tolkien makes it clear that the rejection of Eru and worship of another, Morgoth or Sauron, is the ultimate evil. 'In *The Lord of the Rings* the conflict is not basically about "freedom", though that is naturally involved. It is about God and His sole right to divine honour. The Eldar and the Númenóreans believed in The One, the true God, and held worship of any other person an abomination. Sauron desired to be a God-King, and was held to be this by his servants...' (*Letters*, p. 243).

In a draft letter to Robert Murray on 4 November 1954 Tolkien wrote that the 'hallow' in Númenor perished in the Downfall.

Also when the 'Kings' came to an end there was no 'priesthood': the two being identical in Númenórean ideas. So while God (Eru) was a datum of good Númenórean philosophy, and a prime fact in their conception of history, He had at the time of the War of the Ring no worship and no hallowed place. And that kind of negative truth was characteristic of the West, and all the area under Númenórean influence: the refusal to worship any 'creature', and above all no 'dark lord' or satanic demon, Sauron, or any other, was about as far as they got. They had (I imagine) no petitionary prayers to God; but preserved the vestige of thanksgiving.... It later appears that there had been a 'hallow' on Mindolluin, only approachable by the King, where he had anciently offered thanks and praise on behalf of his people; but it had been forgotten. It was re-entered by Aragorn, and there he found a sapling of the White Tree.... It is to be presumed that with the reemergence of the lineal priest kings (of whom Lúthien the Blessed Elf-maiden was a foremother) the worship of God would be renewed, and His Name (or title) be again more often heard. But there would be no *temple* of the True God while Númenórean influence lasted. [*Letters*, pp. 206–7]

The people of Gondor do, however, remember the loss of Númenor in the Standing Silence before meals, when they face west and 'look towards Númenor that was, and beyond to Elvenhome that is, and to that which is beyond Elvenhome and will ever be' (bk. IV, ch. 5).

In *The Lord of the Rings* the worship of Sauron and the hallow on Mindolluin are mentioned only briefly. The One (Eru) is referred to twice in Appendix A: the Valar called upon the One when Ar-Pharazôn, the last King of Númenor, invaded Aman; and Arwen declared 'the gift of the One to Men' as bitter. There is also an oblique reference in Book III, Chapter 5, when Gandalf speaks of his return from death. Tolkien makes it clear in his draft letter to Robert Murray that this was accomplished by Eru. Gandalf had been sent with the other Wizards to Middle-earth 'by a mere prudent plan of the angelic Valar or governors; but Authority had taken up this plan and enlarged it, at the moment of its failure. . . . Sent back by whom, an whence? Not by the 'gods' [the Valar] whose business is only with this embodied world and its time; for he passed "out of thought and time"' (*Letters*, p. 203).

Of greater significance are references throughout *The Lord of the Rings* to something being *meant*, to people being *called* or *chosen*, which convey the impression of an unidentified Providence who seems to guide the course of events: see further, *Free Will and Fate.

The most prominent references to religion in *The Lord of the Rings* are to the Valar, and in particular, to Varda, also known as Elbereth. She is honoured by the Elves above all the Valar, as the creator of the stars under which the Elves first awoke. The Elves sing her praises, and call upon her in need. In *The Lord of the Rings*, songs to Elbereth are sung when Frodo and his companions meet Gildor in the Woody End, and in the Hall of Fire at Rivendell. Galadriel also mentions Varda in her song of farewell. Frodo calls upon Elbereth when the Black Riders attack under Weathertop and at the Ford, and Sam, who knows no Elvish, is inspired to call her name when he is facing Shelob, and in Cirith Ungol. Mablung, of the Rangers of Ithilien, calls upon the Valar to turn the charging Mûmak aside. The Valar are also mentioned a few times in the Appendices. The second edition of *The Lord of the Rings* adds a reference in Gandalf's words as he sets the crown on Aragorn's head: 'Now come the days of the King, and may they be blessed while the thrones of the Valar endure!' (bk. VI, ch. 5). They are referred to more obliquely during the Council of Elrond, as 'they who dwell beyond the Sea (bk. II, ch. 1), and Théoden's charge into battle is compared 'to Oromë the Great in the battle of the Valar when the world was young' (bk. V, ch. 5).

Gandalf's statement to Denethor that 'only the heathen kings, under the Domination of the Dark Power, did thus, slaying themselves in pride and despair, murdering their kin to ease their own deaths' (bk. V, ch. 7) refers to some of the practices of the followers of Morgoth and Sauron. Paul H. Kocher points out in *Master of Middle-earth: The Fiction of J.R.R. Tolkien* (1972) that 'the flavor of this prohibition is distinctly religious, condemning the practice as "heathen" and ascribing it to pride and despair, moral offenses in the lexicon of Christianity and other religions. Nothing is added, however, about punishment in an afterlife for Denethor or any other among the free peoples' (pp. 51–2). For this and the question of how Denethor's suicide differed from Aragorn choosing to lay down his life, see *Mortality and Immortality.

Some early readers of *The Lord of the Rings* took note of these references and interpreted them as indicating the existence of some form of religion in Middle-earth; but others came to the opposite conclusion. In 1955 Tolkien wrote to the Houghton Mifflin Company (*Publishers):

The only criticism [of *The Lord of the Rings*] that annoyed me was one that it 'contained no religion'. . . . It is a monotheistic world of 'natural theology'. The odd fact that there are no churches, temples, or religious rites and ceremonies, is simply part of the historical climate depicted. It will be sufficiently explained if . . . the *Silmarillion* and other legends of the First and Second Ages are published. I am in any case myself a Christian; but the 'Third Age" was not a Christian world. [*Letters*, p. 220]

A survey of early reviews finds in fact many references to *The Lord of the Rings* depicting a conflict between *Good and Evil, and of the few that mention religion, more seem to feel its subtle presence than bemoan its absence. In his comment to Houghton Mifflin Tolkien was probably referring to J.W. Lambert's review of *The Fellowship of the Ring* in the *Sunday Times*: 'It has, as so far revealed, two odd characteristics: no religious spirit of any kind, and to all intents and purposes no women' ('New Fiction', 8 August 1954, p. 5). Against this, Derek Traversi wrote in 'The Realm of Gondor', *The Month* for June 1956: 'On both levels – the remotely heroic and the intimately human, if we may call them so – the fable combines the heroic pessimism of the pagan epics with a restrained hope that is the distinctive contribution of Christian faith. This combination of two great traditions confers upon the entire conception its distinctive originality' (p. 371). The anonymous reviewer of *The Fellowship of the Ring* in the *Church Times* saw it as 'a deeply, though never overtly, Christian book, with a subtle converting power. Being the product of that rare thing, an entirely Christian imagination, it forces one throughout to breathe and enjoy the climate of faith. It is neither allegory nor sermon, though both may be extracted at will. In itself, it simply fills and feeds the heart' ('Fable for To-day', 8 October 1954, p. 4).

Others paid more attention to this matter, especially with information provided by Tolkien in various published interviews and in *The Road Goes On: A Song Cycle* (1967), which says more about the songs to Elbereth and reveals *Eru* as the name of the One. Paul H. Kocher observed that 'despite the absence of churches, priests, formal liturgies, and the like' in *The Lord of the Rings*, 'Tolkien is not drawing a purely secular Middle-earth, as many critics prefer to believe. His cosmos in the epic may not be exactly Christian but it contains many of the transcendent elements of a more than pantheistic religion' (*Master of Middle-earth: The Fiction of J.R.R. Tolkien*, p. 231). For Lin Carter, however, ritual was everything. He complained in *Imaginary Worlds* (1973) that 'there is no religion at all in *The Lord of the Rings* – no temples, shrines, priests, prayers, amulets, scriptures, ikons, idols – *nothing!* None of the many characters, not even the heroic warriors, so much as swears by his gods. Obviously because they *have* no gods. Which is simply incredible in a primitive world of wizards and warriors and walled stone cities' (p. 124). Richard L. Purtill in *Lord of the Elves and Eldils: Fantasy and Philosophy in C.S. Lewis and J.R.R. Tolkien* (1974) devotes a chapter to 'Religion in Tolkien' (pp. 115–33), in which he reasons that if Tolkien had shown his characters worshiping a pantheon, it would have introduced false gods, while monotheism is not plausible among races who do not appear to have 'a philosophical bent'. 'Is he to give them a special revelation, like the Hebrews? But if so, how is this to connect with the Judeo-Christian revelation?' (p. 116).

The question remains, however, and has been much discussed, as to the extent that Tolkien intended Christianity to underlie *The Lord of the Rings*. His own remarks on the subject varied. On 2 December 1953 he wrote to Robert Murray that '*The Lord of the Rings* is of course a fundamentally religious and Catholic work; unconsciously so at first, but consciously in the revision. That is why I have not put in, or have cut out, practically all references to anything like "religion", to cults or practices, in the imaginary world. For the religious element is absorbed into the story and the symbolism.' On the other hand, he 'consciously planned very little' (*Letters*, p. 172), implying that *The Lord of the Rings* is a 'religious' work only because its author was a devout Christian, and the faith of an author inevitably (subtly, even unconsciously, if not overtly) influences his fiction. (In this regard, see also *Leaf by Niggle*.) In the Foreword to the second edition of *The Lord of the Rings* Tolkien stated that 'the prime motive' for writing that work 'was the desire of a tale-teller to try his hand at a really long story that would hold the attention of readers, amuse them, delight them, and at time maybe excite them or deeply move them'. And in his 1955 statement to the Houghton Mifflin Company he wrote that *The Lord of the Rings* 'is not "about" anything but itself' (*Letters*, p. 220). On 25 October 1958 he wrote to Deborah Webster:

> I am a Christian (which can be deduced from my stories), and in fact a Roman Catholic. The latter 'fact' perhaps cannot be deduced; though one critic . . . asserted that the invocations of Elbereth, and the character of Galadriel as directly described (or through the words of Gimli and Sam) were clearly related to Catholic devotion to Mary. Another saw in waybread (lembas) = viaticum and the reference to its feeding the *will* . . . and being more potent when fasting, a derivation from the Eucharist. (That is: far greater things may colour the mind in dealing with the lesser things of a fairy-story.) [*Letters*, p. 288]

In a letter to Mrs Ruth Austin on 25 January 1971 he thought it was 'true that I owe much of [Galadriel] to Christian and Catholic teaching and imagination about Mary . . .' (*Letters*, p. 407). And in a letter to W.H. Auden, 12 May 1965, discussing his notion of Orcs as creatures of Evil, he said that he did not 'feel under any obligation to make my story fit with formalized Christian theology, though I intended it to be consonant with Christian thought and belief . . .' (*Letters*, p. 355). Elsewhere he deflected readers' claims of parallels between Frodo and Christ – pointing out that one does not have to be a Christian to be a saviour of one's country – while his apparently deliberate choice of 25 December (Christmas Day) as the date for the departure of the Company of the Ring from Rivendell, and of 25 March (the Feast of the Annunciation) as the date of the destruction of the Ring, are shown in drafts and working papers for *The Lord of the Rings* instead to have been developments from entirely different dates as the writing progressed. See further, *Reader's Companion*, especially pp. 263–4.

George Sayer reported that Tolkien

very much objected to the view that he wrote his books as Christian propaganda or anything like it. He wrote them as stories. He would sometimes pull a bunch of American letters or reviews towards him and say, 'You know, they're now telling me that . . .' and then he would say some of the things they'd told him about *The Lord of the Rings*. He'd say, 'You know, I never thought of that. I thought I was writing it as pure story'. He came gradually to believe some of the things that, well, you were telling him. ['A Dialogue: Discussion by Humphrey Carpenter, Professor George Sayer and Dr. Clyde S. Kilby, recorded Sept. 29, 1979, Wheaton, Illinois', *Minas Tirith Evening-Star* 9, no. 2 (January 1980), pp. 16–17]

Apart from the influence of Christianity on Tolkien's world, some critics have focused more narrowly on the influence of Roman Catholicism, though sometimes not distinguishing between elements that are generally Christian and those which are specifically Catholic. Joseph Pearce has no doubt that *The Lord of the Rings* was written as a Catholic book. He finds it 'not merely erroneous but patently perverse to see Tolkien's epic as anything other than a specifically Christian myth' (foreword to *J.R.R. Tolkien's Sanctifying Myth: Understanding Middle-earth* by Bradley J. Birzer (2002), p. ix). He finds that

ultimately, *The Lord of the Rings* is a sublimely mystical Passion Play. The carrying of the Ring – the emblem of Sin – is the Carrying of the Cross. The mythological Quest is a veritable Via Dolorosa. Catholic theology, explicitly present in *The Silmarillion* and implicitly present in *The Lord of the Rings*, is omnipresent in both, breathing life into the tales as invisibly but as surely as oxygen. Unfortunately, those who are blind to theology will continue to be blind to that which is most beautiful in *The Lord of the Rings*. [p. xiii]

Charles A. Coulombe in 'The Lord of the Rings: A Catholic View' discusses significant cultural and doctrinal aspects of Catholicism, and relates these to *The Lord of the Rings*.

It has been said that the dominant note of the traditional Catholic liturgy was intense longing. This is also true of her art, literature, her whole life. It is a longing for things that cannot be in this world: unearthly truth, unearthly purity, unearthly justice, unearthly beauty. By all these earmarks *The Lord of the Rings* is indeed a Catholic work, as its author believed; but it is more. It is this age's great Catholic epic, fit to stand beside the Grail legends, *Le Morte D'Arthur*, and *The Canterbury Tales*. It is at once a great comfort to the individual Catholic, and a tribute to the enduring power and greatness of the Catholic tradition, that JRRT

created this work. In an age which has seen almost total rejection of the
Faith on the part of the civilization she created, the loss of the Faith on
the part of many lay Catholics, and apparent uncertainty among her
hierarchy, *The Lord of the Rings* assures us, both by its existence and its
message, that the darkness cannot triumph for ever. [*Tolkien: A Celebration: Collected Writings on a Literary Legacy* (1999), pp. 65–6]

Other critics have discussed Tolkien's world in a more theological context.
Paul H. Kocher wrote in *Master of Middle-earth*:

Without using blatantly theological terms [Tolkien's] ideas are often
clearly theological nonetheless, and are best viewed in the context of the
natural theology of Thomas Aquinas, whom it is reasonable to suppose
that Tolkien, as a medievalist and a Catholic, knows well. The same is
true in the area of metaphysics. Some of Thomas' less specifically Christian propositions about the nature of evil seem highly congruent with
those which Tolkien expresses or implies in laymen's terms in *The Lord
of the Rings*. We must be very tentative, of course, and alert not to force
a literary masterpiece into any tight philosophical mold, Thomistic or
otherwise. Middle-earth is avowedly pre-Christian. [p. 77]

Matthew A. Fisher, in 'Working at the Crossroads: Tolkien, St. Augustine,
and the *Beowulf*-poet', *The Lord of the Rings 1954–2004: Scholarship in Honor
of Richard E. Blackwelder* (2006), compares statements by Tolkien in his letters with some of the teachings of St Augustine of Hippo, and concludes 'that
it may be helpful to describe Tolkien as an "Augustinian Catholic". By using
this term, I don't mean to suggest that Tolkien *consciously* intended to base his
fictional works on the teaching of St. Augustine. Rather, there is evidence for
a clear affinity between Tolkien's thought and the theological tradition that originated with the Bishop of Hippo' (p. 225). Fisher lays great stress on Tolkien's
statement in a letter to C. Ouboter on 10 April 1958 that he had no 'conscious
purpose in writing *The Lord of the Rings*, of preaching, or of delivering myself
of a vision of truth specially revealed to me! I was primarily writing an exciting
story in an atmosphere and background such as I find personally attractive.
But in such a process inevitably one's own taste, ideas, and beliefs get taken up'
(*Letters*, p. 267). 'Given the importance of his Catholic faith to Tolkien,' Fisher
remarks, 'it should come as no surprise that elements of Catholicism were
taken up into *The Lord of the Rings*'. But he thinks it wise

to remember Tolkien's words about the difference between *allegory . . .
and applicability. . . . Applicability rests in the freedom of the reader to
connect the story at hand to the experiences and questions central to
his or her own life. As such, applicability is something that is decided
by each reader on an individual basis. Clearly [some] see a great deal of
applicability in *The Lord of the Rings* to the Catholic faith, and I will not

challenge or dismiss the right of readers to focus on such applicability. But we must be clear that applicability as discerned by the reader is *not* the same as authorial intent. [pp. 219–20]

In addition to his earlier book cited above, useful comments on the present topic may be found in Richard L. Purtill, *J.R.R. Tolkien: Myth, Morality and Religion* (1984). More recently a considerable number of books have been published mainly or entirely devoted to religion in Tolkien's life and works, and many articles on this subject have been published in journals. Some do little more than use examples from his writings to promote particular moral behaviour, but others are more substantive. See *Tolkien: Man and Myth* by Joseph Pearce (1998), though much of this is biographical and relies heavily on *Biography* and *Letters*; *Tolkien: A Celebration: Collected Writings on a Literary Legacy*, ed. Joseph Pearce (1999); *J.R.R. Tolkien's Sanctifying Myth: Understanding Middle-earth* by Bradley J. Birzer (2002); *Bilbo's Birthday and Frodo's Adventure of Faith* by Robert Morse (2002); *Celebrating Middle-earth: The Lord of the Rings as a Defense of Western Civilization*, ed. John G. West, Jr. (2002); *Tolkien's Ordinary Virtues: Exploring the Spiritual Themes of The Lord of the Rings* by Mark Eddy Smith (2002); *Following Gandalf: Epic Battles and Moral Victory in The Lord of the Rings* by Matthew T. Dickerson (2003); *The Battle for Middle-earth: Tolkien's Divine Design in The Lord of the Rings* by Fleming Rutledge (2004); and *The Power of the Ring: The Spiritual Vision behind The Lord of the Rings* by Stratford Caldecott (2005). A useful review by David Bratman of most of these, as well as other works, was published in 'The Years' Work in Tolkien Studies 2001–2002', *Tolkien Studies* 2 (2005), pp. 309–12.

Research v. Literature. Review of *English Literature at the Close of the Middle Ages* by E.K. Chambers, published in the London *Sunday Times* for 14 April 1946. See *Tolkien Collector* 7, p. 22.

Tolkien finds the book 'little more than a compendium of research'; its arguments, 'little seasoned with wit, make hard reading'. He takes Chambers to task for applying the term *Protestant* (as opposed to *Catholic*) to the pre-Reformation play *Everyman*, and for devoting his section on Sir Thomas Malory to textual and biographical questions rather than 'the beauty and virtue' of *Le Morte d'Arthur*. Despite the title of the book 'much that belongs to the close of the Middle Ages is omitted . . . and much that does not belong there is included.' Chambers' three essays are 'about literature . . . but hardly in themselves literary works.'

The Return of the King *see* **The Lord of the Rings**

'Of the Return of the Noldor'. The thirteenth chapter of the *'Quenta Sil-marillion', published in *The Silmarillion* (1977), pp. 106–17.

SUMMARY

Fëanor and the returning Noldor win the Battle-under-Stars against Morgoth. Outstripping his host as he follows the fleeing enemy, Fëanor is mortally wounded by Gothmog, Lord of Balrogs. Before he dies, Fëanor curses Morgoth and lays it upon his sons to keep their oath to recover the Silmarils, and to avenge his death. In Mithrim the Noldor meet the Grey-elves, who have never left Middle-earth and believe that the Noldor have been sent to their aid by the Valar. Morgoth sends messengers to the Noldor, acknowledging defeat and offering terms, including a Silmaril. Fëanor's eldest son, Maedhros, agrees to a meeting to discuss the settlement, but both sides arrive with greater force than agreed. Maedhros is ambushed and hung from the face of a precipice by a steel band around his wrist.

As Fingolfin and his host march into Mithrim, 'the Sun rose flaming in the West; and Fingolfin unfurled his blue and silver banners, and blew his horns, and flowers sprang beneath his marching feet, and the ages of the stars were ended' (p. 108). The servants of Morgoth flee into Angband. The two hosts of the Noldor camp on opposite sides of Lake Mithrim. Fingolfin's son, Fingon, resolves to heal the feud between the hosts, and with the help of Thorondor, King of Eagles, frees Maedhros from his bond by cutting off his hand above the wrist. Maedhros recognizes Fingolfin as King of all the Noldor, and united they set watch on Angband.

King Thingol of Doriath is wary of the returning Noldor, and will permit only the children of Finarfin, his relations, to pass the girdle of enchantment protecting his realm. He sends messages to the Noldor through Angrod, son of Finarfin, telling them as Lord of Beleriand in which parts of the land he gives them leave to dwell. Most of the sons of Fëanor resent Thingol's words, and this troubles many of the Noldor. But Maedhros leads his brothers east, and with their followers settle beyond the River Aros where they come in contact with Dwarves.

Twenty years after the first rising of the Sun, Fingolfin holds a Feast of Reuniting attended by Grey-elves and Green-elves as well as Noldor, but from Doriath only two messengers, Mablung and Daeron. Already by this time many of the Noldor have learned the language of the Grey-elves. Oaths are sworn, and in the following years all seems to go well, as Morgoth remains within his stronghold. But thirty years later, the Vala Ulmo sends messages in dreams to Turgon, son of Fingolfin, and to Finrod, son of Finarfin, inspiring them to seek places of refuge in case of need. Finrod and Galadriel visit Thingol, and Finrod decides that he should build an underground fortress similar to Thingol's Menegroth. At Thingol's suggestion he builds Nargothrond within caves in the deep gorge of the River Narog. He is aided by the Dwarves, who also make for him the Nauglamír or Necklace of the Dwarves. From the

Dwarves he also receives the name *Felagund* 'hewer of caves'. His sister, Galadriel, dwells in Doriath to be near Celeborn, a kinsman of Thingol, whom she loves, and there she learns much from Melian. Turgon discovers the hidden vale of Tumladen and begins to plan the city he will build there.

After some time, Morgoth tests the strength of his opponents, but is defeated in the Dagor Aglareb, or Glorious Battle. Thereafter the Noldor strengthen their watch and set the Siege of Angband, which lasts nearly four hundred years. But they are unable to take the fortress or recover the Silmarils. War never wholly ceases, as they cannot wholly encircle Angband, while Morgoth's spies can enter Beleriand: he learns much from captured elves. A hundred years after the Dagor Aglareb, he again tests the defence of the Noldor, with an army sent out from the north, but it is defeated. A hundred years after that, the half-grown fire-drake Glaurung comes forth from Angband without Morgoth's command, but he is not yet strong enough to endure the arrows of the Elves and flees back to the fortress. After that the peace endures with little interruption for another two hundred years. The Noldor prosper and in many places become one people with the Grey-elves (Sindar).

HISTORY

Tolkien barely began to write *Gilfanon's Tale: The Travail of the Noldoli and the Coming of Mankind* (c. 1919), which in *The Book of Lost Tales* would have covered the events of this chapter of *The Silmarillion*. Even if he had continued, there would have been many differences: in *Gilfanon's Tale* he had not yet, for instance, developed the intricate relationships of the leaders of the Noldor. Early forms of some of the events in 'Of the Return of the Noldor' appear nonetheless in the completed part of *Gilfanon's Tale*, and in outlines for unwritten parts. A leader of the Noldor, in some versions Fëanor, in others Finwë Nólemë, dies soon after the return to Middle-earth, but the details of these deaths are entirely different. The Noldor fight with orcs and meet with Ilkorins (Elves who had not left Middle-earth) and Men. Either Fëanor or Maidros is captured by Melko, tortured, and sent back maimed. Fëanor's sons swear an oath of enmity against Melko. The returning Noldor and some of the Elves who have not left Middle-earth meet at the Feast of Reunion, but Tinwelint (Thingol) refuses to attend. In one account, Noldor, Ilkorins, and Men march against Melko, but Tinwelint refuses to join them. *Christopher Tolkien summarizes the essential features in *The Book of Lost Tales, Part One*, pp. 241–4.

In '*The Gnomes Come to the Great Lands*', a brief, hastily pencilled prose fragment, written probably at the beginning of the 1920s (*The Shaping of Middle-earth*, pp. 6–9), the Gnomes (Noldor) under the leadership of Gelmir (possibly another name for Finwë) and his three sons, one named Golfin, dwell on the shores of Lake Mithrim. Fëanor is described as the 'gem-smith'.

In the *Sketch of the Mythology* (c. 1926) Fëanor is the son of Finn or Finwë, and has a brother Fingolfin. The Gnomes (Noldor) return in two hosts, one led by Fëanor, reaching Middle-earth in stolen ships, and the other by Fingolfin's son Finweg (Fingon) by crossing the Grinding Ice. The outline of much of the later story for this chapter now entered: the success of Fëanor's first battle with Morgoth; his death after a fight with Gothmog; the capture and brutal treatment of Maidros; the arrival of Finweg at the rising of the Sun; the encampment of the two hosts on opposite shores of Lake Mithrim; the retreat of the Orcs to Angband; Finweg's resolve to heal the breach, and his rescue of Maidros; the meeting of the Gnomes and the Elves who had not left Middle-earth (but here, at about the same time, they also meet Men). Thingol's enmity to the Noldor because of their deeds at Alqualondë has not yet entered, nor (except by later emendation) Felagund (Finrod), the founder of Nargothrond; indeed, many Noldor take service with Thingol in Doriath. Here, as in *The Children of Húrin* (c. 1919–25), Nargothrond is founded by two sons of Fëanor, Celegorm and Curufin (by emendation, by Felagund and his brothers with the aid of Celegorm and Curufin). The siege of Angband is dealt with briefly; Glórung (Glómund, Glaurung) does not emerge until later in the story.

New elements which entered in the *Quenta Noldorinwa* (c. 1930) included the dying Fëanor's curse of Morgoth; the leadership of the second host of the Noldor by Fingolfin, his son Fingon, and Felagund son of Finrod; the settle-ment of the sons of Fëanor in the East, where they wage war with the Dwarves; and the encounter of the Noldor first with the Dark-elves, with whom is held a Feast of Meeting, and later with Men. Felagund founds Nargothrond but after the breaking of the Siege of Angband, which seems to last longer than in earlier versions.

The 'earliest' *Annals of Valinor* and the 'earliest' *Annals of Beleriand*, writ-ten in the early 1930s, provided a chronological framework for events. Fëanor arrives back in Middle-earth in about Valian Year 2995; his first battle, now named the Battle under Star, and his death take place in 2996. Maidros is cap-tured in 2997, and hung by his wrist in 2998. In Valian Year 3000 the Moon and then the Sun arise as Fingolfin reaches Middle-earth, and the Years of the Sun begin. (This event also appears in the annal for Year 1 of the Sun in the 'earliest' *Annals of Beleriand*.) Fingon rescues Maidros in Year 2; the Feast and Games of Reuniting are held in Year 20 and attended by the Noldor, Dark-elves (both Wood-elves and Elves from the Havens), and ambassadors from Thingol. In Year 50 Turgon and Felagund are troubled by dreams and establish Gondolin and Nargothrond; in 51 the Noldor drive back orcs sent by Morgoth (the origin of the later Dagor Aglareb), and the Siege of Angband begins: this lasts to Year 155 and the Battle of Sudden Fire in which the young Glómund emerges from Angband but is driven back. In a second version of the 'earliest' *Annals of Beleriand* the Siege of Angband is extended by a hundred years; it is specifically said that Felagund modelled Nargothrond on Thingol's Mene-groth; the Orc attack in Year 51 becomes a full-scale battle, the Dagor Aglareb, after which Turgon moves his people to Gondolin; in 102 the building of Nargo-thrond and Gondolin is more or less complete; some of Fëanor's folk first meet the Dwarves in 104; and in 105 Morgoth tests the siege, but his army is driven into the sea.

In the 'later' *Annals of Valinor* and 'later' *Annals of Beleriand* of the mid-1930s Tolkien made minor changes in dates, both as originally written and through later emendation, but the only significant change (through emendation) was the further extension of the Siege of Angband from 200 to 400 years.

Most of the elements of this chapter were already in place when Tolkien began the *Quenta Silmarillion* in the mid-1930s, based on the *Quenta Noldorinwa* but incorporating information which had emerged in the *Annals*. This chapter, with the title 'Of the Siege of Angband', is written in a more leisurely and expansive style, with many extra details: for instance, Fingon's rescue of Maidros is about twice as long as in the *Quenta Noldorinwa*. New elements include Maidros asking Fingolfin's pardon for deserting him, and the waiving of any claim to the kingship; and Ulmo being responsible for sending Turgon and Inglor (Felagund) dreams regarding hidden refuges. One difference from both the preceding versions and *The Silmarillion* is that Morgoth drives the dragon Glómund out of Angband unwillingly, before he is fully grown.

When Tolkien turned again to 'The Silmarillion' after completing *The Lord of the Rings*, his work on this chapter of the *Quenta Silmarillion* (c. 1951) was restricted mainly to emendations, but included notable additions, among which were Galadriel's stay in Doriath, where she learned much from Melian, and more detailed accounts of the arrival of Fëanor and his host in Middle-earth, and of the founding of Nargothrond and Turgon's discovery of the hidden vale where he would build Gondolin. Also c. 1951 Tolkien added new elements to the more expansive *Grey Annals* (see *Annals of Beleriand*), including that the Noldor adopted the language of the Grey-elves for daily use, and that Thingol felt resentment of the Noldor from the beginning and would only allow the children of Finarfin to visit Doriath. Angrod's visit, and the message he carried from Thingol to the meeting of the Noldor, now entered, as well as the visit of Finrod and Galadriel to Thingol. By emendation, Turgon does not immediately remove to Gondolin, but sets some of his folk to build the city secretly while he and most of his people remain in Nevrast; and he leads his people to Gondolin only in Year 116.

Parts of the text of 'Of the Return of the Noldor' were derived from a subtle interweaving of elements from the *Grey Annals* and the *Quenta Silmarillion* (the latter not generally much altered from the 1930s text). Other parts were taken almost entirely from the *Grey Annals* (for instance, the wounding and death of Fëanor, Angrod's visit to Thingol, and the angry reaction of Caranthir to the message sent by Thingol) or from the *Quenta Silmarillion* (such as Fingon's rescue of Maedhros, the dreams of Turgon and Finrod, and that Finrod built Nargothrond in imitation of Menegroth). But here Christopher Tolkien needed to make editorial decisions apart from (as usual in *The Silmarillion*) substituting the latest form of names and removing some archaisms. The most significant of these resulted from his solution to problems concerning the overthrow of Doriath by Dwarves in a later chapter (in which he made the Nauglamír the sole treasure brought by Húrin from the ruin of Nargothrond, rather than being made in Doriath); see *The War of the Jewels*, pp. 354–5. He therefore added, after an account of the building of Nargothrond, that the Dwarves made the necklace for Finrod, and for *The Silmarillion* adapted the description of it in *The Book of Lost Tales*. At the same point, based on a note for the *Narn i Chîn Húrin* (see *The War of the Jewels*, p. 180), he added a sentence that Finrod was not the first to dwell in the caves beside the Narog. He also added that the main reason that Galadriel remained in Doriath and did not join her brother in Nargothrond was her love for Celeborn, kinsman of Thingol, selecting this from differing traditions (see *Unfinished Tales*, p. 234).

The Return of the Shadow: The History of The Lord of the Rings, Part One. The sixth volume of *The History of Middle-earth*, ed. *Christopher Tolkien, first published in Great Britain by Unwin Hyman, London, in August 1988, and in the United States by the Houghton Mifflin Company, October 1988 (actual; the official date of first publication is January 1989). See further, *Descriptive Bibliography* A26.

The Return of the Shadow is concerned with the earliest texts for *The Lord of the Rings*, written between December 1937 and the end of 1939. Divided into twenty-five chapters, the volume covers Tolkien's work on Book I and the beginning of Book II, which were rewritten several times, and the continuation of Book II as far as Balin's tomb in Moria. Christopher Tolkien divides this process into three 'phases'.

The 'first phase' began in December 1937, when Tolkien wrote the first chapter of a sequel to *The Hobbit*, requested by *Stanley Unwin. He continued the story, with stops and starts, until probably mid-September 1938, when it reached Frodo's arrival in Rivendell. His ideas for the story having evolved as he wrote, at this point he stopped to consider what he had drafted, decided that it needed revising, and went back to the beginning of the tale. This phase is divided into the chapters: 'A Long-Expected Party' (four different versions); 'From Hobbiton to the Woody End'; 'Of Gollum and the Ring'; 'To Maggot's Farm and Buckland'; 'The Old Forest and the Withywindle'; 'Tom Bombadil'; 'The Barrow-wight'; 'Arrival at Bree'; 'Trotter and the Journey to Weathertop'; 'The Attack on Weathertop'; 'From Weathertop to the Ford'; and 'At Rivendell'. A supplementary chapter, 'Queries and Alterations', ends the section.

The 'second phase', in which Tolkien revised what he had written as far as the hobbits' stay with Tom Bombadil, probably occurred in late September or early October 1938, before term began at *Oxford. This involved considerable rewriting and the addition of a new chapter, as described in 'Return to Hobbiton'; 'Ancient History'; 'Delays Are Dangerous'; 'A Short Cut to Mushrooms'; and 'Again from Buckland to the Withywindle'.

Christopher Tolkien guesses that the 'third phase' probably had not yet begun, or had not proceeded far, when his father referred to 'Chapter XI' in a letter of 13 October 1938; but Tolkien worked at rewriting and new writing during the autumn before he set the book aside in December. This phase mainly involved making a fair copy of the very confused and sometimes illegible manuscripts up to the point in the story where the 'first phase' ended.

Tolkien made improvements to the text as he wrote, and also added a 'Foreword' (precursor of the Prologue in the published book) in which he provided background information, mainly about Hobbits. Christopher Tolkien deals with this phase in the chapters 'The Journey to Bree', 'At the Sign of the Prancing Pony', and 'To Weathertop and Rivendell'.

Such evidence as exists suggests that Tolkien did no further work on *The Lord of the Rings* between the beginning of December 1938 and August 1939. When he again turned his attention to it, making various notes and outlines, it is clear that he was uncertain about elements in the story and considered making changes; see 'New Uncertainties and New Projections' following the 'third phase'. He then wrote an account of the Council of Elrond and the journey of the Fellowship as far as Balin's tomb in Moria, reaching this point towards the end of 1939. This work is considered in the final section of *The Return of the Shadow*, 'The Story Continued', comprising 'In the House of Elrond', 'The Ring Goes South', and 'The Mines of Moria'. (Concurrently with this new writing, Tolkien also revised most, possibly all, of the chapters to the hobbits' arrival in Rivendell. This 'fourth phase' is examined in *The Treason of Isengard*.)

The Return of the Shadow also contains, in black and white, reproductions of various pages of manuscript, inscriptions, a plan of Bree, and 'the earliest map of the lands south of the Map of Wilderland in *The Hobbit*'. The first British and American hardcover editions include as well a colour reproduction of the first map of the Shire.

Reynolds, Richard William (1867–1948). R.W. 'Dickie' Reynolds was a master at *King Edward's School, Birmingham during Tolkien's years as a pupil. He had himself attended King Edward's School, after which he went up to Balliol College, *Oxford to read Greats (B.A. 1890). Although briefly called to the Bar, he was more interested in politics, journalism, and literature. For a while he wrote literary criticism for the prestigious *National Observer*. He returned to King Edward's School in 1900. As a permanent master from 1901 to 1922 he taught Classics, History, and English Literature, and among numerous School offices served as Chairman of the Literary and Debating societies and of the Library Committee, Treasurer of the Officers Training Corps, and Vice President of the School Club.

On 9 January 1964 Tolkien wrote to the Reverend Denis Tyndall, a fellow old boy of King Edward's School:

> I do remember very clearly the old IVth class room and Dickie; indeed I even remember that we read with him a non-classical Greek text furbished up by a German (Willamowitz Möllendorf?) in usum scholarum which bored me extremely. I behaved very badly, together with the later model of rectitude and headmasterly seriousness *Christopher Wiseman, as did many of those released from the strict regime of the class below under [C.H.] Heath [master of the Fifth Class]. Dickie was not an inspiring form-master and made Greek and Roman history as boring as

I suspect he felt them to be; but he was immensely interesting as a person. I kept up with him and the Beak (*R.C. Gilson) until they died. . . . [In 1911] I was brought up to Oxford by car (then a novelty), together with [fellow student] L.K. Sands, by Dickie. . . . [*Letters*, pp. 342–3]

During the First World War Tolkien sent some of his early poems to his former master for comment. Reynolds found them 'charming', and felt that 'fairy' poems such as *Goblin Feet and You & Me and the Cottage of Lost Play (*The Little House of Lost Play: Mar Vanwa Tyaliéva) were Tolkien's strongest and most original work; but when offered a glimpse of Tolkien's nascent *'Silmarillion' mythology in Kortirion among the Trees (*The Trees of Kortirion), he was unimpressed by its content, though he praised the poem for the beauty of its words and as an advance in Tolkien's technique. In August 1915 Reynolds offered sound advice in response to Tolkien's desire to see a volume of his poetry in print: normally, Reynolds said, a young poet should build an audience for his work through individual poems published in weekly or monthly magazines, before seeking to issue a collection in book form. But as Tolkien was then on active duty in France and in no position to follow the usual course, Reynolds counselled him to publish a book if the opportunity presented itself, even though it would likely fall flat with readers whose attention was focused on the war. (See further, *Poetry.)

Reynolds also corresponded with Tolkien's friend *G.B. Smith, himself a promising poet from King Edward's School, and after Smith was killed in 1916 Reynolds was approached by Smith's mother to arrange the publication of her son's verses. By that time Tolkien had come to feel that Reynolds had influenced Smith towards an excess of aestheticism, and their friend *Christopher Wiseman thought that although Reynolds knew good poetry from bad, he might not understand Smith's later, more esoteric work. The two therefore involved themselves in the matter, becoming co-editors of Smith's works (*A Spring Harvest*, published 1918) while Reynolds seems to have had little to do with the final result beyond using his literary contacts to find a publisher.

In November 1917 Reynolds expressed an interest in Tolkien's *Book of Lost Tales. But in 1922 he and his wife retired to Capri, and his correspondence with Tolkien did not resume until the end of 1925, by which time the Lost Tales had been abandoned. In the first part of 1926 Tolkien sent Reynolds part of the *Lay of Leithian and the alliterative *Children of Húrin, together with a prose *Sketch of the Mythology to explain the latter. These received only qualified approval: Reynolds found the Lay to be too prolix, and he had little or nothing to say about Húrin (see *The Lays of Beleriand, p. 3). It may be that they were too different from the poetry with which he was familiar –the work of Keats or Kipling or Walter de la Mare – for Reynolds to be able to judge them adequately. Even so, as John Garth has said, 'the intervention of Reynolds had a radical effect on Tolkien's central mythological project', in that the Sketch (rather than the Lost Tales) became the new basis for further development of his legendarium (Tolkien and the Great War (2003), p. 279).

Rice-Oxley, Leonard (1892–1960). Leonard Rice-Oxley read History at Keble College, *Oxford; he received his B.A. in 1915. After war service he returned to Keble as a Lecturer in Modern History, but in 1921 changed to the English School, and for the rest of his life taught English Literature as a fellow, tutor, and lecturer. He served for many years, together with Tolkien, on the English Faculty Board. At his death he was also Sub-Warden of Keble College.

As an amateur poet he contributed to *Oxford Poetry* in 1914, 1915 (with Tolkien), and 1918. In 1922–3 he edited the *Oxford Magazine*. He also edited a number of books, including *Poetry of the Anti-Jacobin* (1924) and works by Henry Fielding and Tobias Smollett: his chief academic interest was in the novelists and essayists of the eighteenth century. A collection of his essays, *In a Mantle Blue*, appeared in 1921. His popular book on the University of Oxford, *Oxford Renowned*, was first published in 1925.

The Ride of Eorl
see **Cirion and Eorl and the Friendship of Gondor and Rohan**

Ridley, Maurice Roy (1890–1969). In 1920 M.R. Ridley was appointed the first Fellow and tutor of English at Balliol College, *Oxford, where he himself had been a brilliant undergraduate before the First World War. He remained at Balliol until 1945. From 1920 to 1931 he was also College Chaplain. In 1948 he moved to Bedford College, London as a Lecturer. An assiduous worker, he edited the whole of the New Temple Shakespeare (beginning 1934) and produced a Modern English translation of *Sir Gawain and the Green Knight* (1944). His other works include *Keats' Craftsmanship: A Study in Poetic Development* (1933). He is said to have been an exquisite speaker, and the physical model for Lord Peter Wimsey in novels by Dorothy L. Sayers.

Tolkien and Ridley shared duties on the Oxford English Faculty Board, and were both concerned with the teaching of armed forces cadets during the Second World War. On 20 April 1943 Tolkien wrote to *C.S. Lewis that 'the valuable Ridley' had been 'astounded at the ignorance of all 22 cadets, revealed in his first class' and was happy to take another class while Lewis was ill (*Letters*, p. 59). In March 1944 Ridley was appointed to succeed Tolkien as director of the English Course for Navy and R.A.F. Cadets.

Ridley admired *The Lord of the Rings*, to the extent that he wrote to Tolkien about it in Elvish and helped to promote it. On 28 October 1955 a brief notice by Ridley of *The Return of the King* appeared in the *Daily Telegraph*: 'It is absurd, even impertinent,' he wrote, 'to try to say anything of the book in a few words, and I should quickly run out of superlatives. I can only say that I think it is, in range and power, a great and an abiding work, and leave it at that' ('The Trials of Teaching in a Secondary Modern School', p. 8). In autumn 1971 Tolkien commented in a draft letter in reply to Carole Batten-Phelps, herself an enthusiast: 'Not until I got your letter did I learn that [Ridley] had done me the honour of placing the works of his old colleague in the ranks of "literature", and gaining me intelligent and well-equipped readers' (*Letters*, p. 412).

Of the Rings of Power and the Third Age. The final component of **The Silmarillion* (1977), pp. 285–304. Together with the **Akallabêth*, *Of the Rings of Power and the Third Age* 'is the link between the *Silmarillion* and the Hobbit world' as Tolkien wrote to **Katharine Farrer (15 June ?1948, *Letters*, p. 130).

SUMMARY

Much of Beleriand was destroyed in the battles at the end of the First Age and sank into the sea. Of the Eldar who remained in Middle-earth after the end of the First Age, some settled in the Grey Havens in Lindon, and some established realms among the Silvan Elves further east, while the Noldor established the realm of Eregion. The jewel-smiths of Eregion, among whom was Celebrimbor, grandson of Fëanor, surpassed in skill all others 'that have ever wrought, save only Fëanor himself' (*The Silmarillion*, p. 286).

For long there was peace in Middle-earth, but Sauron, the most trusted servant of Morgoth, now sought to establish his power. Gil-galad and Elrond in Lindon refused to listen to him, but elsewhere, particularly in Eregion, he had more success, offering to share his knowledge and skills. The smiths of Eregion made the Rings of Power with his assistance, but secretly Sauron made the One Ring to rule the other rings, and let much of his strength pass into it. When the Elves realized what Sauron had done, they no longer wore their rings. Sauron attacked Eregion and seized the rings he found there, except for the three that were made last, without his help, by Celebrimbor, and hidden by the Elves.

Sauron gave seven rings to Dwarves, and nine to Men, hoping to control the wearers. The Dwarves proved hard to tame, but he had better success with Men. 'One by one, sooner or later, according to their native strength and to the good or evil of their wills in the beginning, they fell under the thraldom of the ring that they bore and under the domination of the One. . . . The Nazgûl were they, the Ringwraiths, the Enemy's most terrible servants . . .' (p. 289).

Sauron 'determined to make himself master of all things in Middle-earth. . . . He brooked no freedom nor any rivalry, and he named himself Lord of the Earth . . . and he gathered again under his government all the evil things of the days of Morgoth that remained on earth or beneath it . . .' (p. 289). Many Elves fled over the sea, but Gil-galad remained and was aided by the Númenóreans. Elsewhere in Middle-earth Sauron reigned, and Men under his dominion regarded him as both king and god. When his power was challenged by the King of Númenor, he cunningly let himself be taken to that realm, where he corrupted the king and many of his people. Inciting them to attack the Valar, he achieved their ruin, for in response to the attack the world was changed and the island drowned.

While Sauron's spirit fled back to his fortress in the Black Land, Mordor, faithful Númenóreans led by Elendil and his sons Isildur and Anárion escaped the ruin, bringing many treasures including a sapling of the White Tree and the *palantíri*. The Númenóreans established realms in the North and the South of Middle-earth. When it became clear that Sauron was preparing for war, Elendil and Gil-galad created the League of the Last Alliance and were victorious in a battle fought before the gate of Mordor. Besieged in his stronghold for seven years, at last 'Sauron himself came forth; and he wrestled with Gil-galad and Elendil, and they both were slain. . . . But Sauron also was thrown down, and . . . Isildur cut the Ruling Ring from his hand' (p. 294). Isildur took the One Ring for his own instead of destroying it; but the Ring soon betrayed Isildur to his death in the river Anduin.

Thus ended the Second Age. The Third Age began with hope, though much had perished, and even though the Elves and the Númenóreans had the victory, Sauron and his evil had not been wholly destroyed. Isildur's descendants ruled for a while in the North, but their glory soon passed and they became a wandering people, the Dúnedain; yet the line of Isildur endured, and his heirs preserved the broken sword of Elendil with which Isildur had cut the Ring from Sauron's hand. Gondor in the South, the realm of the heirs of Anárion, enjoyed great splendour before it too declined and the line of Elendil failed. Elves still lived in Middle-earth, at Rivendell where Elrond provided a refuge, at the Havens where Círdan dwelled, and in Lothlórien under Galadriel. The whereabouts of the Three Rings of the Elves were kept secret, but their power could be used while Sauron no longer wore the One. 'Those were the Fading Years, and in them the last flowering of the Elves east of the Sea came to its winter' (p. 299), for the Dominion of Men drew near.

As the shadow of Sauron began to grow again, he established himself in Dol Guldur in Greenwood, whose name was accordingly changed to *Mirkwood*. At that time also the Istari or Wizards arrived in Middle-earth, sent in the form of old men by the Valar to contest the power of Sauron and inspire Men and Elves to resist him. The White Council of the Wise was formed, with the Wizard Curunír (Saruman) as its chief. Curunír began to study the lore of the Rings of Power. When the shadow continued to grow, Mithrandir (Gandalf) secretly entered Dol Guldur and discovered that it was held by Sauron, who was seeking the One and the other rings. Mithrandir urged the White Council to take immediate action, but Curunír, who now desired the Ring for himself, declared that Sauron would not find it, that it had been carried down the Anduin and lost in the sea. Establishing himself at Isengard, Curunír sought for the Ring, but discovered that Sauron's spies were also searching the river where Isildur had fallen. When the White Council again urged action, Curunír agreed, hoping to hinder Sauron; but their action against Dol Guldur was too late. Sauron now left Mirkwood for his ancient stronghold of Mordor.

In fact, the Ring had been found years earlier by one of the fisher-folk who lived by the river, and he had taken refuge with it beneath the Misty Mountains. But in the year that the White Council attacked Dol Guldur, the Ring was found by a Halfling who lived in lands west of the mountains. Mithrandir learned of the Ring's existence and kept watch on the land of the Halflings with the help of the Dúnedain. But Sauron heard a rumour that the Ring had been found, and sent his servants to take it. Thus the Third Age ended in war:

Curunír was overthrown, and after a great battle in Gondor, Aragorn, the heir of Isildur, led an army to the gates of Mordor. Victory was achieved, however, only with the success of Mithrandir's secret plan, by which Frodo the Halfling and his servant journeyed to Mount Doom and the Ring was cast into the fires. With the destruction of the Ring Sauron was vanquished beyond return. Aragorn was crowned King of Gondor and Arnor, and for a while the White Tree flowered again.

Only when the time came for him to sail from Middle-earth into the West was it revealed that Mithrandir himself had long been the bearer of one of the elven-rings, given him on his arrival in Middle-earth by Círdan. The last of the Noldor left Middle-earth with him, including Elrond and Galadriel, the bearers of the other elven-rings, whose power had ended with the destruction of the One Ring. 'In the twilight of autumn [their ship] sailed out of Mithlond, until the seas of the Bent World fell away beneath it . . . and borne upon the high airs above the mists of the world it passed into the Ancient West, and an end was come for the Eldar of story and of song' (p. 304).

HISTORY

*Christopher Tolkien comments in *The Peoples of Middle-earth* that he 'should have returned [in *Sauron Defeated*] at the end of describing the writing of *The Lord of the Rings*, to give some description, at least, of the later developments in the chapters *The Shadow of the Past* and *The Council of Elrond*, and the evolution in relation to these of the work *Of the Rings of Power and the Third Age*' (p. x) – beyond, that is, a few passing remarks. In writing about a section of the fifth version of 'The Council of Elrond' (*The Lord of the Rings*, Book II, Chapter 2, written ?1940) he said: 'It will be found that in this passage are the bones of a part of the narrative of the separate work *Of the Rings of Power and the Third Age*. . . . In the later development of "The Council of Elrond" the chapter became the vehicle of a far fuller account of the early Númenórean kingdoms in Middle-earth, and much of this is now found not in *The Lord of the Rings* but in *Of the Rings of Power and the Third Age*' (*The Treason of Isengard*, pp. 144–5). He also expressed his opinion that it was in a lengthy passage concerning the Rings on the verso of a page inserted into the chapter that became 'The Mirror of Galadriel' (Book II, Chapter 7, written towards the end of 1941) that 'the final conception of the relation of the Rings of Power to Sauron emerged, at least in this essential: the Rings of Power were made by the Elven-smiths under the guidance of Sauron, but he made the One in secret to govern all the rest'. 'Ultimately,' he continued, 'this passage foreshadows that in *Of the Rings of Power*. . . . My father at this stage probably intended it for "The Council of Elrond"' (*The Treason of Isengard*, pp. 259–60).

Christopher Tolkien seems to imply in *The Peoples of Middle-earth* that *Of the Rings of Power and the Third Age* did not take shape until a very late stage in the writing of *The Lord of the Rings*, perhaps soon after its completion in late summer 1948. Certainly some version of the work was in existence by autumn

1948, as Tolkien wanted to lend *Of the Rings of Power* with other 'Silmarillion' matter to Katharine Farrar, but was unable to find it. He mentioned the work again in a letter to *Milton Waldman in ?late 1951, and in April 1954 offered to lend a typed copy of the work to *Naomi Mitchison.

Christopher Tolkien notes in *The Peoples of Middle-earth* (p. 349) that he altered the name of Gil-galad's father from *Felagund* to *Fingon* in *Of the Rings of Power and the Third Age* in *The Silmarillion*, since his father had recorded elsewhere that Finrod Felagund had no children, and in the *Grey Annals* (*Annals of Beleriand*) Fingon is his father. In writings later than the *Grey Annals*, however, Gil-galad is given a different descent.

The Rivers and Beacon-hills of Gondor. Essay, parts of which were published in sections of *Unfinished Tales* (1980), and the greater part (excluding those already in *Unfinished Tales*) in *Vinyar Tengwar* 42 (July 2001), pp. 5–31, edited with commentary and notes by Carl F. Hostetter, and additional commentary and materials provided by *Christopher Tolkien.

SUMMARY

The essay begins, in *Unfinished Tales*, pp. 264–5, with a discussion of the Glanduin. In the Second Age it marked the southern border of Eregion, and in the Third Age 'with the Gwathló formed by its confluence with the Mitheithel, formed the southern boundary of the North Kingdom'. The North–South Road connecting Gondor and Arnor, and the bridge across the river at Tharbad, are mentioned, as well as the 'ancient port' on the estuary of the Gwathló originally established by Aldarion of Númenor. *Vinyar Tengwar*, p. 7, supplies a sentence omitted in *Unfinished Tales*, and some variations between Tolkien's original typescript and the published text. It continues on p. 8 with an etymological discussion of *Glanduin* and a note on the river Adorn.

The first part of the following entry, for the river Gwathló, is in *Unfinished Tales*, pp. 261–3, under the heading 'The Port of Lond Daer'. This gives a brief history of Minhiriath and Enedwaith on either side of the river, and tells of exploitation of the area by the Númenóreans in the Second Age as a source of timber, and of the useless resistance of the native people who were forced to flee. A comment that these people did not flee south into Andrast leads into a brief account of the Púkel-men in the Second Age; see *Unfinished Tales*, pp. 383–4. The entry also describes further deforestation during the wars of the Second Age, the building of the great river-port of Tharbad, the draining of nearby fens, and the origin of the name *Gwathló*. *Vinyar Tengwar*, pp. 8–10, records editorial changes made to the original text by Christopher Tolkien in *Unfinished Tales*, and provides notes omitted from that book, including an etymological statement on *Gwathló*, and the text of a passage deleted by Tolkien and replaced by one that appears in *Unfinished Tales*. Two versions of a note omitted in *Unfinished Tales* on the name *Ringló*, with the same *-ló* element as in *Gwathló*, are given on pp. 13–14.

Vinyar Tengwar continues, pp. 10–11, with comments on the rivers Erui (with a note by Tolkien on *ui* as an adjectival ending, and the formation of ordinals), Serni, Sirith, and Celos. Christopher Tolkien notes an error in the statement about *Serni* in the index to *Unfinished Tales*, pp. 463–4. Tolkien's note on the Celos was also published in the *Unfinished Tales* index, p. 426.

The following entry, for the river Gilrain, begins in *Vinyar Tengwar*, pp. 11–12. The resemblance of the river-name to the name of Aragorn's mother, Gilraen, is discussed. Continuing in *Unfinished Tales*, pp. 242–5, the discussion of *Gilrain* leads into the story of Nimrodel and Amroth, and thence to a brief history of Lórien. Some omitted material is given in *Vinyar Tengwar* (pp. 12–13). Part of *the Legend of Amroth and Nimrodel Recounted in Brief* in *Unfinished Tales* (see **The History of Galadriel and Celeborn and of Amroth King of Lórien*) was written as an offshoot.

The essay continues in *Vinyar Tengwar*, pp. 13–15, with entries for the rivers Ciril (or Kiril), Ringló, Morthond, and Levnui. Tolkien considered whether the last name could mean 'fifth' (river), then wrote as an appendix a lengthy discussion on Eldarin numerals (*Vinyar Tengwar*, pp. 24–7). This discussion is followed (*Vinyar Tengwar*, pp. 15–18) by more about the name *Adorn* and notes on other names possibly derived from one of the languages spoken in Gondor before the arrival of the Númenóreans. The element *Bel-* in *Belfalas* is considered, for which both a rejected text and an unfinished draft replacement appear in *Vinyar Tengwar* (pp. 15–16); a small part of the latter is also in *Unfinished Tales*, p. 247. *Lamedon*, *Arnach*, and *Lossarnach* are also discussed, completing the section on 'Rivers'.

Vinyar Tengwar, p. 18, gives the introduction to the following, unfinished section on the 'Names of the Beacon Hills', a part of which appeared previously in *Unfinished Tales*, p. 315, n. 35. The first entry, for Amon Dîn, is in *Unfinished Tales*, final paragraph of n. 51, p. 319; the earlier part of that note includes most of the entry for Eilenach and Eilenaer, but some omitted material is given in *Vinyar Tengwar*, p. 19. *Vinyar Tengwar*, pp. 19–23, continues with entries for Erelas and Calenhad, parts of which were used in the index to *Unfinished Tales*, pp. 436, 425, and a lengthy entry for the Halifirien marked for deletion, which includes information about the importance of the place as that where Eorl and Cirion swore their oath, and about the religious practices of the Dúnedain and the Men of Darkness. Tolkien abandoned the entry after writing that a structure on the Halifirien may have been a tomb; a note by Christopher Tolkien suggests that this was the moment at which his father decided that Elendil had been buried on the Halifirien, and discusses the steps by which he reached this idea and wrote the various texts included in **Cirion and Eorl and the Friendship of Gondor and Rohan*.

HISTORY

The Rivers and Beacon-hills of Gondor, so called in *Vinyar Tengwar* 42, was entitled by its author simply *Nomenclature*. It was inspired by a letter to Tolkien from Paul Bibire on 23 June 1969, asking if the river Glanduin was the same as the Swanfleet. Tolkien replied on 30 June, giving information about *Glanduin* and a few other names, Elvish (*Languages, Invented) words for 'swan', and information about the history of the region of the Glanduin; see *Vinyar Tengwar* 42, pp. 6–7. Christopher Tolkien hoped to include an edited version of the text, which survives as thirteen typescript pages and two manuscript sheets, in *The Peoples of Middle-earth*, but had to omit it for lack of space. Christopher's edition, Carl F. Hostetter comments,

> being intended for a more general audience and made under constraints of space, naturally omits a number of more technical and/or discursive philological passages and notes. In editing the text for the more specialized audience of *Vinyar Tengwar* [i.e. those interested in Tolkien's invented languages], I have of course restored all such philological matter. I have also retained . . . as much of Christopher Tolkien's own commentary on the essay as practicable . . . while providing some additional commentary and notes of my own, primarily on linguistic matters. [*Vinyar Tengwar*, p. 5]

The Road. The image of the Road recurs frequently in Tolkien's works, often in contrast with the security and comfort of home. As a literary motif it was common in poetry and story when he was young: the open road with the promise of freedom and adventure, but also of risk and uncertainty. In his early poem *Goblin Feet* (1915) the speaker is 'off down the road / Where the fairy lanterns glowed', and in *The Cottage of Lost Play* in *The Book of Lost Tales* (end of 1916–early 1917) the children of Men find their way to Valinor along the Olórë Mallë or Path of Dreams. Later a prominent feature in Tolkien's mythology is the 'straight road' from Middle-earth to Aman in the West, lost except to Elves, and to a few exceptional mortals, at the end of the Second Age. Compare, in the poem *Earendel at the Helm*, the 'road going on for ever . . . / To havens in the West'.

One of Tolkien's best known expressions of the Road is in Chapter 19 of *The Hobbit*, in which Bilbo, upon returning to his homeland after his *quest to the Lonely Mountain, speaks of roads that 'go ever ever on, / Over rock and under tree, / By caves where never sun has shone, / By streams that never find the sea . . .' and 'feet that wandering have gone / Turn at last to home afar'. But more famous still is the poem known (from its opening words) as *The Road Goes Ever On* in *The Lord of the Rings*, Book I, Chapter 1: there Bilbo sings not of roads but of the Road, which 'goes ever on and on' from his own door. In context this is specifically the great East Road which leads from the Shire to Rivendell and beyond, but it is also an obvious metaphor for life. Frodo says in Book I, Chapter 3: '[Bilbo] used often to say there was only one Road; that it was like a great river: its springs were at every doorstep, and every path was its tributary. "It's a dangerous business, Frodo, going out of your door," he used to say. "You step into the Road, and if you don't keep your feet, there is no knowing where you might be swept off to.' And in Book I, Chapter 11, as Frodo stands upon Weathertop: 'In that lonely place Frodo for the first time fully realized his homelessness and danger. He wished bitterly that his fortune had left him in the quiet and beloved Shire. He stared down at the hateful Road, leading back westward – to his home.' When the hobbits sing in Book I, Chapter 3, 'Home is behind, the world ahead, / And there are many paths to tread / Through shadows to the edge of night, / Until the stars are all alight', still they leave the Road and world behind and 'wander back to home and bed' where the darkness fades; whereas their fate in *The Lord of the Rings* is to pass literally through the dark, and to find darkness, in the form of evil and destruction, even when returning to the Shire. (See further, *Reader's Companion*, pp. 70–1, 96, 651.)

The Road, broadly considered, features also in Tolkien's pictorial art: good examples are *Rivendell*, *Bilbo Comes to the Huts of the Raft-elves*, and *The Hall at Bag-End*, all illustrations for *The Hobbit* (*Artist and Illustrator*, figs. 108, 124, 139). As we have said in *Artist and Illustrator* (p. 116), Tolkien's 'best pictures have some device to lead the eye into the scene' – a river, bridge, or lane – 'as well as a way out, over a hill, or around a bend, or through a door or a mountain gap. In this way he suggests depth, adds interest, and provides a sort of visual narration, deliberately guiding the viewer through the painting or drawing.'

T.A. Shippey remarks on the Road as image in his *Road to Middle-earth* (2nd edn. 1992), especially pp. 27ff., 167–71. Wayne G. Hammond has discussed the contrast of Home and the Road in 'All the Comforts: The Image of Home in *The Hobbit* and *The Lord of the Rings*', *Mythlore* 14, no. 1, whole no. 51 (Autumn 1987).

The Road Goes Ever On: A Song Cycle. Settings of poems by Tolkien to music by *Donald Swann, with an appendix of 'notes and translations' by Tolkien, first published in the United States by the Houghton Mifflin Company, Boston, in October 1967, and in Great Britain by George Allen & Unwin, London, in March 1968. See further, *Descriptive Bibliography* B28.

HISTORY

Early in 1965 Donald Swann set to music six songs from *The Lord of the Rings* while in Ramallah, outside Jerusalem. The book was one of his favourites, and some of its poems appealed to him as a composer. 'As I came to them,' he wrote,

> I was struck by their clarity and concision, and I began to feel their flavour as poems outside the narrative in which they appear.... The shorter ones looked as if they would enjoy musical accompaniment, and every creature in them was on the road – Bilbo, who sets the pace, Frodo and Sam journeying to the Mountains of Doom, Treebeard herding his

trees – everyone was moving. So I called the cycle *The Road Goes Ever On*. [foreword to *The Road Goes Ever On: A Song Cycle* (2nd edn., rev. 1978), p. vi]

On 8 March 1965 he wrote to George Allen & Unwin (*Publishers), suggesting a song cycle of Tolkien's poems. By now he had rejected the setting he had made of 'O Orofarnë, Lassemista, Carnimírië!', the ent Quickbeam's lament for the dead rowan (*The Lord of the Rings*, bk. III, ch. 4), as too similar to Purcell's *Dido and Aeneas*. On 30 May 1965 Tolkien heard and approved five other songs: *The Road Goes Ever On* (see *The Road), *Upon the Hearth the Fire Is Red*, *In the Willow-meads of Tasarinan*, *In Western Lands*, and *I Sit beside the Fire* (including *A Elbereth Gilthoniel*). He also heard a new setting, of *Namárië*, Galadriel's song of farewell (*The Lord of the Rings*, bk. II, ch. 8), but preferred the version in plainchant he himself had imagined. In the published *Namárië* Swann added to Tolkien's theme an introduction, interlude, and coda.

With the author and publisher's permission, Swann began to perform his song cycle in company with the baritone William Elvin (Tolkien thought the name 'Elvin' a good omen). On 23 March 1966 Swann and Elvin gave a private performance of the work at Merton College in honour of Ronald and Edith Tolkien's Golden Wedding anniversary. *Joy Hill, then responsible for rights and permissions at Allen & Unwin, promoted Swann's efforts as well as his desire to make a phonograph record of his settings. In 1966 Austin Olney, of Tolkien's American publisher Houghton Mifflin (*Publishers), having heard *I Sit beside the Fire* in *At the Drop of Another Hat*, a musical revue in which Swann performed with his long-time partner Michael Flanders, suggested that Caedmon Records of New York would be a suitable publisher for the recording (*Poems and Songs of Middle Earth*, see *Recordings), and through his interest Houghton Mifflin considered whether to publish Swann's settings as a booklet. On *Rayner Unwin's suggestion, the songs were fleshed out with calligraphic inscriptions in Elvish, decorations, and notes. Tolkien disregarded advice that he write for the book a note on the origins of his verse and on the peregrinations of *Errantry*, a setting of which Swann had added to the cycle, and instead chose to write brief linguistic analyses of the two Elvish texts *Namárië* and *A Elbereth Gilthoniel*. He also supplied Elvish calligraphy which in the published book runs continuously along the top and bottom of the pages, but was too busy to make decorations to fill in blank spaces: these were made instead by the American illustrator Samuel Hanks Bryant. At the eleventh hour, but too late to be used, Tolkien also contributed a calligraphic figure combining his and Swann's initials.

For the second edition of *The Road Goes Ever On* (1978) Swann rewrote his foreword, added performance directions to the music, and included a new, eighth setting, of *Bilbo's Last Song*. This came to be the song he loved most of all in the Tolkien cycle:

The lyric was handed to me at Tolkien's funeral by his dedicated secretary, Joy Hill, who is a close friend and neighbour of mine in Battersea. . . . I was stirred up that day and went off and wrote a tune for it, to be sung as a duet, although I often perform it solo. . . . The tune is based on a song from the Isle of Man . . . [and] also resembles a Cephallonian Greek melody' [*Swann's Way: A Life in Song* (1991), p. 208]

A later setting by Swann, of Beren's 'Song of Parting' from Lúthien Tinúviel in *The Silmarillion* (ch. 19), was published privately in 1992 and included in the third edition of *The Road Goes Ever On* (Germany, 1993; London, 2002).

A complete recording of all nine parts of the song cycle, performed by the composer with William Elvin and Clive McCrombie, was issued on a compact disc to accompany the 2002 HarperCollins edition of *The Road Goes Ever On*.

CRITICISM

Critical opinion of the song cycle is mixed. At one extreme among its earliest reviewers was Robert Johnson ('Prizewinner', *The Irish Press*, 30 March 1968, p. 6), who judged that 'the music is not only questionable, but even worse, it is the kind of questionable stuff that leads us to think that we have heard it all before. The quasi music-hall pastiche which sounds so very apposite in an intimate review . . . makes a poor foundation for an attempt at serious song writing.' But 'M. Ch.', writing for the *Hindustani Times* ('A Faery-like Loveliness', 23 June 1968), wrote that Swann had

succeeded in giving voice to the spirit of Tolkien's Middle-earth. . . . The tonal pattern of the songs is sturdily English. Yet there is none of the conscious striving after archaic effects that creeps into, say, some of Vaughan Williams' compositions, nor are the harmonies as artful as some of Martin Shaw. When the music becomes harmonically clever, as it does in places, it soon recovers its own four-square English style. The song 'In western lands' illustrates this well. Comparisons may be out of court, but the music-lover can detect the same kind of felicitous interweaving of the 'contemporary' and the 'traditional' in many of Benjamin Britten's songs.

Opinion among Tolkien enthusiasts, who over the years have had a increasing variety of musical impressions of his works available on record, is no less divided, and likely to remain so. To some listeners Swann's settings seem old-fashioned, or not sufficiently of a sort that hobbits themselves would sing; but others respond to the simple directness and clarity of the shorter pieces, to Swann's dexterous handling of *Errantry*, and to the emotions behind his music for *Bilbo's Last Song* and *Lúthien Tinúviel*. Tolkien himself thought very well of the original song cycle, and of its composer.

Roverandom. Story, first published in Great Britain by HarperCollins, London, in January 1998, and in the United States by the Houghton Mifflin Company, Boston, in April 1998. See further, Christina Scull and Wayne G. Hammond, introduction to *Roverandom*; and *Tolkien Collector* 17 (December 1997), p. 9, and *Tolkien Collector* 18 (June 1998), p. 8.

SUMMARY

A little dog named Rover angers a passing wizard, Artaxerxes. As punishment he is turned into a toy and put in a shop, where he is bought for a young boy. Rover escapes onto a beach, meets a 'sand-sorcerer' named Psamathos, and is sent to the moon on the back of a seagull, Mew, along the light-path the full moon shines upon the sea. The Man-in-the-Moon gives Rover a new name, 'Roverandom', to avoid confusion with his own dog, also named Rover. Equipped with wings, Roverandom and the moon-dog explore the moon, accidentally angering the Great White Dragon, which the Man-in-the-Moon defeats with a spell. The Man-in-the-Moon also takes Roverandom to a garden on the dark side of the moon where children come in their dreams to play.

In time Roverandom becomes homesick and wishes that he could go back, as a real dog again, to the little boy who owned him as a toy. He returns with Mew to Psamathos who, unable to restore him to his former state, advises him to apologize to Artaxerxes. The latter is now married to 'the rich mer-king's elderly but lovely daughter' and has become resident Magician in the ocean world. Aided by Uin, 'the oldest of the Right Whales', Roverandom travels to the mer-king's realm; Artaxerxes, however, although he magically adapts Roverandom for living underwater, out of pique is reluctant to reverse his original spell. Roverandom passes the time, until the wizard should change his mind, by exploring the oceans with Uin and with yet another Rover, a mer-dog. The sea-Rover confirms that the name 'Roverandom' is appropriate for his new friend, for 'you never do seem to know where you are going next!'

Through an act of mischief Roverandom causes a great Sea-serpent to wake and turn, wreaking havoc with the waters and the mer-folk. The blame falls on Artaxerxes, who is unable to produce a spell to keep the Sea-serpent quiet. He is removed from his post as Pacific and Atlantic Magician and returns to dry land with his wife and Roverandom. At last he restores the dog to his proper form and size, and Roverandom returns to the little boy – by coincidence, the grandson of Rover's original owner.

HISTORY

In the summer of 1925 Tolkien and his family went on holiday to *Filey on the Yorkshire coast. His second son, *Michael, then nearly five, lost a beloved toy dog on the beach and was heartbroken. Tolkien devised an 'explanation' for the loss: that the toy had been a real dog, named Rover, who had been turned into a toy by a wizard, and after being lost on the beach had met a comical 'sand-sorcerer' and later had adventures on the moon and under the sea – or so, at least, the story became in written form. It had another purpose as well, according to Tolkien's eldest son, *John, who recalled that it was first told to the two older boys to keep them calm during a terrific storm: no doubt the inspiration for the episode in *Roverandom* of the great Sea-serpent awakening ('When he undid a curl or two in his sleep, the water heaved and shook and bent people's houses and spoilt their repose for miles and miles around', p. 76). John Tolkien also retained a clear memory of the 'moon-path' that shone upon the sea when he and his family were at Filey.

Tolkien seems to have set *Roverandom* on paper in 1927, possibly in response to a revival of interest in the story by his sons earlier that year. Three of the five illustrations that Tolkien drew for his story are dated September 1927, when he and his family were on holiday at *Lyme Regis, while a fourth is dated '1927–8'. (The remaining picture dates from 1925.) Moreover, the episode of the Man-in-the-Moon and the Great White Dragon is related to Tolkien's *'Father Christmas' letter for 1927, in which the Man-in-the-Moon visits the North Pole, and apparently also to the real lunar eclipse that occurred on 8 December that year. It seems likely that Tolkien wrote out *Roverandom* in manuscript during the 1927 Christmas holidays. Later he revised the work in the course of three typescripts, the latest made probably in 1936 for submission to George Allen & Unwin (*Publishers).

*Stanley Unwin, chairman of the firm, gave the typescript to his young son *Rayner to read. Rayner found *Roverandom* 'well written and amusing' in his report of January 1937, it was returned to the author for the time being. It may be that Allen & Unwin first wanted to gauge the success of Tolkien's yet unpublished *Hobbit*, or did not want to distract him from the business of reading proofs of that book (in February–April 1937). Then, before the end of 1937, *The Hobbit* was so successful that Allen & Unwin wanted another story about hobbits above all else, and Tolkien's attention, as a writer of fiction, now turned chiefly to *The Lord of the Rings*. He seems to have abandoned *Roverandom* completely, never to return to it. It was published only in 1998, edited by Christina Scull and Wayne G. Hammond from Tolkien's final typescript.

Although Tolkien completed *Roverandom*, he never polished it, and there can be little doubt that if the work had been accepted for publication Tolkien would have revised it further, to make it more suitable for an audience beyond his immediate family. As it stands, *Roverandom* contains numerous references to its author, his wife, and his sons – naturally, given its origin in the events at Filey – wordplay and allusions of interest and delight to Tolkien personally, and modest borrowings from his private mythology (*'The Silmarillion'): the garden on the dark side of the moon recalls the Cottage of Lost Play in *The Book of Lost Tales* (see also *The Little House of Lost Play: Mar Vanwa Tyaliéva), and Uin – namesake of 'the mightiest and most ancient of whales' in *The Book of Lost Tales* (and Finnish for 'I swim') – carries Roverandom within sight of 'the Mountains of Elvenhome' in the far West of the world, by another name the Mountains of Valinor in Aman.

As we have said in our introduction to *Roverandom*, the work contains a 'wealth of references to myth and fairy-story, to Norse sagas, and to traditional and contemporary children's literature', from Arthurian legend to E. Nesbit, Lewis Carroll, and Gilbert and Sullivan (p. xvii). We also remark:

> It is not too much to say that *The Lord of the Rings* might not have come into being were it not for stories like *Roverandom*; for their popularity with the Tolkien children, and with Tolkien himself, led at last to a more ambitious work – *The Hobbit* – and so to its sequel.... As more of Tolkien's works have been published in the quarter-century since his death, it has become clear that nearly all of his writings are interrelated, if only in small ways, and that each sheds a welcome light upon the others. *Roverandom* illustrates ... how the *legendarium* that was Tolkien's life-work influenced his storytelling, and it looks forward (or laterally) to writings on which *Roverandom* itself may have been an influence – especially to *The Hobbit*, whose composition ... was contemporaneous with the writing down and revision of *Roverandom*. Few readers of *The Hobbit* indeed will fail to notice (*inter alia*) similarities between Rover's fearsome flight with Mew to his cliffside home and Bilbo's to the eagles' eyrie, and between the spiders Roverandom encounters on the moon and those of Mirkwood; that both the Great White Dragon and Smaug the dragon of Erebor have tender underbellies; and that the three crusty wizards in *Roverandom* – Artaxerxes, Psamathos, and the Man-in-the-Moon – each in his own way is a precursor of Gandalf. [pp. xv, xx]

A commercial recording of *Roverandom* read by Derek Jacobi was first issued in 1998.

CRITICISM

Roverandom achieved a high level of publicity as a previously unpublished book by the author of *The Hobbit* and *The Lord of the Rings*. That association, however, coloured the experience of some reviewers, who compared *Roverandom* with Tolkien's later, longer, and more sophisticated fiction, and inevitably found the earlier story wanting as literature. Michael Dirda in the *Washington Post*, for instance, judged it to be

> a perfectly agreeable fantasy – so long as one doesn't think of Tolkien's masterpieces. Against such comparison, however, the book simply has no bite. A bit of charm, yes, and occasional humor but none of that dark grandeur and mythic power that makes a Sauron [in *The Lord of the Rings*] or a Smaug [in *The Hobbit*] so unforgettable. On the other hand, *Roverandom* makes a pleasant bedtime read-aloud for kids under 8. And there will be no nightmares about Orcs or Black Riders. ['Under the Big Top and on the Road', 3 May 1998, *Book World* section, p. 16]

Adam Mars-Jones in *The Observer* was less charitable, describing the invention in *Roverandom* as

> short-winded and the characterisation rudimentary. In his descriptions Tolkien brings off the occasional effect worthy of epic (the rising sun 'red as if he had been drinking hot wine'), but more often he looks back to the *fin de siècle* for his poetic palette: 'The moon rose up out of the sea, and laid the silver path across the waters that is the way to places at the edge of the world and beyond, for those that can walk on it. . . .'

Mars-Jones noted 'sparks of humour in the story, of a schoolmasterly sort' and saw a didacticism underlying the tale. Ultimately, he thought, 'most admirers of Tolkien will want to turn down this chance . . . to explore his imagination before it came into its own' with *The Hobbit* and *The Lord of the Rings* ('Hobbit-forming', 11 January 1998, p. 18). In fact, many Tolkien enthusiasts embraced *Roverandom*, and the majority of reviewers, if sometimes grudgingly, found the book engaging.

'Of the Ruin of Beleriand and the Fall of Fingolfin'. The eighteenth chapter in the *'Quenta Silmarillion', published in *The Silmarillion* (1977), pp. 150–61.

SUMMARY

Fingolfin, High King of the Noldor, wishes to attack Angband, rather than merely contain Morgoth in his stronghold under siege. But this course receives little support. Meanwhile, Morgoth prepare his forces in secret, and 455 years after the coming of Fingolfin into Beleriand he launches his attack on a dark night in the middle of winter, when the watch is slackened. He sends forth from Thangorodrim rivers of flame, and the mountains belch fire and fumes, so that the green plain is destroyed and many of the Noldor are killed. In front of the fire come the dragon Glaurung, now fully grown, and behind him Balrogs and multitudes of Orcs. The Battle of Sudden Flame, which breaks the siege of Angband, lasts until the coming of spring, and after that the war never wholly ceases. Both Elves and Men suffer great losses and are scattered. Most of the Grey-elves flee to Doriath, the Havens, Nargothrond, or Ossiriand. Two of the sons of Finarfin are killed, as well as many men of the House of Bëor. Finarfin's eldest son, Finrod Felagund of Nargothrond, is saved by Barahir, now lord of the House of Bëor, and swears an oath of friendship and aid with him, in token of which he gives Bëor his ring.

Many other Men and Elves fall, and the strongholds that survive the assault leave the Noldor isolated within lands controlled by Morgoth. Celegorm and Curufin flee to Nargothrond. In despair, Fingolfin rides to the gates of Angband and challenges Morgoth to single combat. Morgoth comes forth unwillingly, 'climbing slowly from his subterranean throne . . . and he stood before the King like a tower, iron-crowned, and his vast shield, sable unblazoned, cast a shadow over him like a stormcloud' (p. 153). He crushes Fingolfin, but is himself wounded seven times; even as he dies, Fingolfin hews at Morgoth's foot. Morgoth takes the corpse of his foe to cast to the wolves, but Thorondor, King of the Eagles, swoops, strikes at Morgoth's face, and seizes Fingolfin's body. He takes it to a mountaintop overlooking Gondolin, and there Turgon raises a cairn. From that day Morgoth bears a scar on his face, is lame in one foot, and suffers pain from wounds that will not heal. Fingon succeeds his father as King of the Noldor, but sends his young son, Gil-galad, to the Havens.

Morgoth now controls Dorthonion. Its northern forests become a place of dread, called Taur-nu-Fuin. Barahir and his people resist until only few remain, and at last the women and children, led by Barahir's wife, seek refuge elsewhere. One by one the men left behind are hunted down and slain, until only twelve remain with Barahir, among them his son Beren.

The Noldor hold the pass near the source of the River Sirion for nearly two more years, until Morgoth's greatest servant, Sauron, takes the fortress of Minas Tirith on the isle of Tol Sirion from its warden, Orodreth, who flees to Nargothrond. Tol Sirion becomes known as Tol-in-Gaurhoth, the Isle of Werewolves. Orcs now roam freely. Many of the Noldor and Sindar are taken prisoner to Angband and become thralls of Morgoth. Even if they escape, they are feared by their kin, who suspect that they are still controlled by Morgoth, for he sends forth many spies to foment mistrust, fear, and jealousy.

Morgoth pretends to be a friend to Men and blames all their woes on the Noldor. Few Men of the Three Houses of the Edain will listen to him, and he hates them. He has more success with the Swarthy Men or Easterlings who come into Beleriand at this time. Maedhros makes alliances with these new-comers, but whereas Bór and his sons will be faithful, Ulfang and his sons will prove faithless. Of the Edain, the House of Bëor is all but destroyed, and the folk of Hador are confined in Hithlum. An Orc army comes south after the taking of Minas Tirith and attacks the Haladin, but a force sent by Thingol from Doriath destroys the army, and the Haladin continue to live in the forest of Brethil.

Húrin and Huor, sons of Galdor, head of the House of Hador, are being fostered by their kinsman in Brethil at the time of the Orc attack. Taking part in the battle, they are cut off and in danger of death, but the Vala Ulmo hides them in a mist, and Thorondor sends two eagles to carry them to Gondolin. There they stay nearly a year as the guests of Turgon, who teaches them much. But they wish to return to their family, and argue that the law forbidding any who found the secret way to Gondolin from leaving does not apply to them, for they had not found the way, nor seen the way they were brought. Turgon agrees to let them go if Thorondor is willing to help. Maeglin expresses his resentment of the King's decision, and the brothers swear to keep secret where they have been and what Turgon has told them. Carried home by eagles, they refuse to tell even their father where they have been, but many guess the truth, and the story eventually reaches Morgoth.

Turgon still will not lead his people to war, but fearing the downfall of the Noldor, secretly sends Elves from Gondolin to build ships and sail into the West to seek pardon and aid from the Valar. Most are lost; none reach their goal.

Seeking to learn the whereabouts of Nargothrond and Gondolin, Morgoth sends out many spies, but recalls the main hosts of Orcs to Angband while he gathers new strength, for he too has suffered great losses in the war. Thus there is a short period of uneasy peace in the south of Beleriand. Seven years after the Battle of Sudden Flame, Morgoth sends a force against Hithlum, and Fingon gains the victory only when Círdan and Elves from the Falas come to his aid. Galdor is slain defending the fortress of Eithel Sirion; his son Húrin succeeds to the leadership of the House of Hador, and weds Morwen of the House of Bëor. At this time all of Barahir's band except Beren are slain.

HISTORY

Even if Tolkien had completed *The Book of Lost Tales* (c. 1916–20), very little of the content of this chapter would have appeared in it, since he evidently envisioned that only a short time would elapse between the return of the Noldor and the Battle of Unnumbered Tears, with no intervening battles; nor did he develop the intricate relationships of the leaders of the Noldor until later. One of the outlines for *Gilfanon's Tale: The Travail of the Noldoli and the Coming of Mankind* mentions Morgoth fostering mistrust and spying, and elsewhere Úrin (Húrin) appears, though not yet as a visitor to Gondolin.

The first version of the story that Barahir, father of Beren, saved Finrod Felagund's life, and that Finrod swore an oath of friendship and gave Barahir his ring, appears in Canto II of the *Lay of Leithian*, written in the summer of 1925. In this Beren's father, Egnor, does some service for Celegorm (at this time one of the founders of Nargothrond) and receives a ring in return. In the typescript of the *Lay* begun in 1926, Beren's father is called Barahir, and the service is to Felagund. Also in this canto is an account of the outlaw life of Egnor/Barahir and his small band of followers hunted by the servants of Morgoth.

The *Sketch of the Mythology* (c. 1926) contains a brief account of the history of the Noldor in Beleriand. Morgoth sends out his armies and breaks the siege of Angband. From that time, the fortunes of Elves and Men decline. The lies of Morgoth's agents spread mistrust among those who remain. Barahir and Húrin (already married to Morwen) fight in the war; Celegorm and Curufin found Nargothrond. Many of the Noldor take service with Thingol. Barahir, a friend of Celegorm, is driven into hiding and slain. By emendation and addition, Fingolfin is slain when the siege is broken; Felegund, not Celegorm, is saved by Barahir and swears a vow of friendship to him and his race; and Felagund and his brothers, escaping south, establish Nargothrond with the help of Celegorm and Curufin. Although this sparse account contains little detail, *Christopher Tolkien thinks (*The Shaping of Middle-earth*, p. 39) that references in the earlier *Children of Húrin* to the 'dusty drouth of Dor-na-Fauglith' and the 'Thirsty Plain' indicate that his father already had a fuller picture in mind of the end of the Siege of Angband than appears in the *Sketch*.

Canto VI of the *Lay of Leithian*, written in March 1928, refers to the breaking of the Siege, the flames of Morgoth's vengeance, and the might he poured across the Thirsty Plain. It tells that two sons of Finrod (= Finarfin) fell, but Barahir aided the escape of Felagund, who swore an oath of friendship.

In the *Quenta Noldorinwa* (*c.* 1930) almost all of the elements of the *Silmarillion* chapter are present, if in less detail. Notable additions or expansions are: the breaking of the Siege of Angband with rivers of flame at night in winter, the burning, and the fumes; Morgoth's great armies of Orcs (but not Balrogs); the slaughter of many Elves and Men and the flight of others, many of whom go to Doriath; that the pine forests become a place of dread; the taking of the watchtower of the Sirion, and that Thû (Sauron), his chief servant, dwelt there (though this seems to take place as part of the main battle and not two years later); that Orodreth flees south with his friends Celegorm and Curufin; that Fingolfin challenges Morgoth to single combat and wounds him seven times before he himself falls, and pierces Morgoth's foot; that Thorondor rescues Fingolfin's body and scars Morgoth's face; that Finweg (emended to *Fingon*) becomes King of the Noldor; that the Orcs roam ever more widely, while Morgoth's emissaries spread fear and mistrust; and the long resistance of Barahir and his band. Emendations add the name 'Battle of Sudden Flame', and that Glómund (Glaurung) precedes Morgoth's forces. Important details still missing were the arrival of the Easterlings soon after the battle, and Húrin's visit to Gondolin.

In work on the *Lay of Leithian* in September 1930, Tolkien described the beginning of the (unnamed) Battle of Sudden Flame in Canto XI, and Fingolfin's challenge to Morgoth and their subsequent fight in Canto XII, at greater length than in the *Quenta Noldorinwa*.

The 'earliest' *Annals of Beleriand* (early 1930s) provided a chronological framework. The attack begins in midwinter in Year 155, and here is called the Battle of Sudden Fire. It is said that the attack falls heavily on the sons of Finrod (Finarfin) and their folk, that the greater part of the House of Bëor falls, and that Barahir saves both Felagund and Orodreth. A second entry for 155 (possibly a mistake for 156) contains the first account of Húrin's visit to Gondolin, but not in its final form. Here he is accompanied by Haleth, his foster-father, not his brother Huor, and they are taken there by some of Turgon's folk, not by eagles, and are welcomed by Turgon because dreams sent by Ulmo have warned him that the help of Men is needed. Turgon secretly arranges for ships to be built to sail to Valinor. In 157, Morgoth takes Tol Sirion; Felagund and Orodreth with Celegorm and Curufin retreat to Nargothrond, and there make a hidden palace similar to that of Thingol; and the wives and daughters of Barahir's two nephews are sent to safety in Hithlum. In 160, Barahir's band is betrayed, and all but Beren slain. In 162, Húrin's father is killed in an assault upon Eithel Sirion. The Swarthy Men come into Beleriand in 163, and while it is said that they were divided into two houses, nothing further is said of one, while the only indication of the future actions of the other is that the sons of the leader were afterwards called the Accursed. Tolkien also began a second version of these *Annals*, in which he extended the Siege of Angband by a hundred years, so that the Battle of Sudden Fire took place in Year 255.

In the 'later' *Annals of Beleriand* (mid-1930s) the breaking of the Siege of Angband originally takes place in 255, but Tolkien then extended the siege a further 200 years, so that the Battle of Sudden Fire took place in Year 455. All of the events described under the second entry for 155 in the 'earliest' *Annals* now took place in 256/456. The entry for 257/457 includes the capture or slaying of all the women of the House of Bëor, except for the wives of Barahir's two nephews and their daughters, who were in Hithlum when the war broke out. The victory of Haleth and his folk with the help of Doriath against an army of Orcs now enters in 258/248. The division of the Swarthy Men into those who allied with Maidros and Maglor and were faithful, and those who allied with Cranthir and were faithless, also enters the tale.

Tolkien began the *Quenta Silmarillion* in the mid-1930s and was probably working on the precursor of this chapter in 1937. The text now came close to the chapter in *The Silmarillion*. New material included Fingolfin's wish to take the offensive against Morgoth, which was not supported by most of the other Noldor. Much of the lengthy account of Fingolfin's battle with Morgoth is based on that in the *Lay of Leithian*.

When Tolkien returned to 'The Silmarillion' *c.* 1951 after completing *The Lord of the Rings* he made only a few changes, mainly of names, to this chapter in the *Quenta Silmarillion*, but additions in the contemporary *Grey Annals* (see *Annals of Beleriand*). There, in the entry for 455, it is expressly stated that the Battle of Sudden Flame started at midwinter at the year's beginning, and during the same year Morgoth also took Tol Sirion. The account of Húrin's visit to Gondolin in the same year was little changed from its first writing, but at the end of 1951 or early 1952 Tolkien struck through the relevant part of the entry for 455 and inserted new material into the entry for Year 458, bringing the account close to that finally published. The story of Emeldir, wife of Barahir, leading the women and children to safety in Brethil or Dorlómin now entered under Year 457. One matter introduced in this account which is not included in *The Silmarillion* is that Celegorm and Curufin came to Orodreth's aid when Sauron attacked Minas Tirith, and thus were welcomed in Nargothrond.

In the late 1950s, as part of the *Narn i Chîn Húrin*, Tolkien wrote an account of the visit of Húrin and Huor to Gondolin so close to that in the *Grey Annals*, on which the account in *The Silmarillion* was based, that *Christopher Tolkien omitted it from the *Narn* in *Unfinished Tales*. Two significant differences are described in *The War of the Jewels*, pp. 169–70.

The greater part of the *Silmarillion* chapter was derived from the relevant chapter in the *Quenta Silmarillion*, probably written in 1937, taking up some of the few emendations made *c.* 1951 or later, and incorporating elements from the *Grey Annals*. Some short sections taken mainly from the *Grey Annals* include Fingolfin's ride to challenge Morgoth; the desperate situation in Dorthonion and the departure of the women and children led by Emeldir; and Círdan coming to the aid of Fingon. Again, the lengthy account of Húrin's and Huor's visit to Gondolin was taken for the most part from the *Grey Annals*, but also incorporates elements of the similar text of the *Narn i Chîn Húrin*.

'Of the Ruin of Doriath'. The twenty-second chapter of the *'Quenta Silmaril-lion', published in *The Silmarillion* (1977), pp. 227–37.

SUMMARY

Morgoth's malice towards the House of Hador does not cease with the deaths of Túrin and Nienor. Húrin has witnessed all that has happened to his family, but the lies of Morgoth lead him to believe Thingol and Melian at fault. Released by Morgoth after twenty-eight years' captivity, he goes first to Hithlum, but is shunned by the remnant of his people, who believe that he is now in league with the enemy; and then, as he makes his way towards the Encircling Mountains of Gondolin, Turgon too at first thinks that he has surrendered to Morgoth. By the time Turgon changes his mind and sends eagles to fetch Húrin, it is too late. They cannot find him, but by crying out to Turgon he has revealed the whereabouts of Gondolin to Morgoth's spies. Húrin comes to the stone at Brethil where Túrin is buried and which marks the spot where Nienor leapt to her death. There he meets his wife, Morwen, now grey and old. She asks him how Nienor found her brother, but he does not reply. Morwen dies, and Húrin buries her by the stone.

Seeking revenge on those he believes responsible for the fates of his family, Húrin travels to Nargothrond, where the Petty-dwarf Mîm had taken possession of the halls and treasure after Túrin slew Glaurung. Húrin kills Mîm because he had betrayed Túrin. From the treasures of Nargothrond he takes only the Nauglamír, the Necklace of the Dwarves, made for Finrod Felagund by craftsmen of Nogrod and Belegost. At Doriath he casts it at the feet of Thingol, scornfully calling it 'thy fee for thy fair keeping of my children and my wife' (*The Silmarillion*, p. 231). Thingol restrains his anger, and Melian tells Húrin that he is seeing events as Morgoth wishes him to see them, that she and Thingol are guiltless. He looks into her eyes and sees the truth. He picks up the necklace and gives it to Thingol, asking him to receive it as 'a gift from one who has nothing, and as a memorial of Húrin of Dor-lómin. For now my fate is fulfilled, and the purpose of Morgoth achieved; but I am his thrall no longer' (p. 232). He leaves, and is believed to have cast himself into the western sea.

Dwarves of Nogrod are already in Menegroth working for Thingol. He asks them to remake the Nauglamír as a setting for the Silmaril won by Beren. They agree, but lust for the jewel. Thingol is with them when they complete the work, but when he wishes to place the necklace about his neck they dispute his claim. He answers them scornfully, and they slay him. They flee with the necklace but are pursued and overtaken. Most are slain, and the necklace is taken back to Melian; but two escape and rouse the Dwarves of Nogrod, declaring that their companions have been slain on Thingol's orders to cheat them of payment. After mourning Thingol, Melian returns to Valinor, and her protection is withdrawn from Doriath. The army of Dwarves overcome the elves of Doriath, sack the treasuries of Thingol, and seize the Nauglamír with the Silmaril. But Beren and Lúthien, who live in the east of Beleriand with their son Dior and his wife and children, hear what has happened, and together with the Green-elves and the Ents attack the Dwarf army as it is returning home. All of the dwarves are killed. Beren takes the Nauglamír, but drowns the rest of the treasure which has been cursed by the leader of the dwarves. Lúthien wears the necklace, and the land where they live becomes fair and fruitful. Dior and his family try to restore Doriath. When Beren and Lúthien again die and go beyond the world, the Nauglamír is brought to Dior. When he refuses the demand of the sons of Fëanor that he give the Silmaril to them, they attack, and finally destroy Doriath. Three of Fëanor's sons are killed, as well as Dior and his wife, while their young sons are left to starve in the forest. Only Dior's daughter Elwing survives, and with a few others escapes to the Havens, taking the Silmaril with her.

HISTORY

The story told in *The Book of Lost Tales* (c. 1916–20) differs considerably from the *Silmarillion* version summarized above. The first part appears at the end of *The Tale of Turambar*. Mavwin (Morwen) discovers the stone that records the death of her children and hears their story. Úrin (Húrin) believes Morgoth's words that but for the 'weakness and cravenhood' of Tinwelint (Thingol) 'how could my designs have come to pass' (*The Book of Lost Tales, Part Two*, p. 113). Since Úrin has never been to Gondolin, he cannot betray its whereabouts, nor does he meet his wife by their children's memorial. Instead, collecting a band of lawless elves, he goes to the caves of the Rodothlim (the precursor of Nargothrond), where he slays the dwarf Mîm; but Mîm has no connection with Túrin Turambar, and has been left to guard the treasure by Glorund the dragon. Mîm curses the gold. Úrin and his band carry the hoard to Tinwelint, and Úrin casts it at his feet in payment for the little he did for Úrin's wife and family. Tinwelint declares that he did all that he could for them, but shows disdain: 'Wherefore dost thou of the uncouth race of Men endure to upbraid a king of the Eldalië?' (p. 115). It is said that when Úrin dies, his spirit and that of his wife haunt the woods, bewailing their children, but their prayers come to Manwë, and the Valar show mercy.

Here Tolkien hesitated over events and abandoned earlier ideas for the story: that Úrin finds no one guarding the treasure; that the elves who accompany him are reluctant to leave the gold, and a fight breaks out from which only Úrin escapes, cursing the treasure which Tinwelint casts into a deep pool; that Tinwelint himself fetches the treasure, which is unguarded; that Úrin and his band find the caves and treasure lightly guarded because orcs are elsewhere, seeking Glorund; that they carry off the treasure and orcs curse it.

The story is continued in *The Book of Lost Tales* in *The Nauglafring: The Necklace of the Dwarves*. After Úrin departs, Tinwelint's elves and Úrin's band fight. The latter are all slain, as well as some of the elves, and the gold is drenched with blood. Gwenniel (also called Gwendelin later in the story = Melian) warns Tinwelint that the gold is trebly cursed, but he is tempted by it and agrees to the suggestion of Ufedhin, a Gnome (Noldo) who has long dwelt with the Dwarves, that he ask the Dwarves to use their skill to fashion the gold, which they will do for a small reward. Tinwelint makes an agreement with Ufedhin that he will send half the gold in the care to the Dwarves of Nogrod for them to fashion. They are to return in seven months, and if he is pleased with their work the Dwarves would make more things to adorn him and Gwenniel, and ask only small reward which they will name when the work is done. Tinwelint insists that Ufedhin stay with him as a hostage. A great company of Dwarves duly returns in seven months, bearing what they have made from the gold. Ufedhin, annoyed at having been kept hostage, counsels them to ask for a great payment. Tinwelint will not let them return home with more gold, and insists that they remain and work in his stronghold. From the last of the gold, at their suggestion, they make the Nauglafring to hold the Silmaril. Tinwelint watches its making, and when it is completed puts it on, at which the curse makes him resent his promise to reward the Dwarves – even more so, when the demands they make are beyond reason, including the provision of elven maidens, and elves as hostages to repay the holding of Ufedhin. Tinwelint gives them much less, beats them, and sends them on their way.

The Dwarves plot revenge, and are even angrier when they learn from the Dwarves of Belegost that Úrin killed Mîm for the gold. The two houses of the Dwarves prepare for war and ally with Orcs. One of Tinwelint's elves, lusting for the gold, offers to lead the Dwarf army through the magics of Gwendelin. They ambush Tinwelint as he rides out hunting, sack his palace, and insult Gwendelin, who wanders weeping in the forest. Huan the hound, who witnesses Tinwelint's death, takes the news to Beren and Tinúviel, and Beren summons a host of Brown and Green Elves. Yet even before they arrive, fighting breaks out among the Dwarves when Ufedhin and one of the Dwarf leaders both try to steal the Nauglafring. Many dwarves are killed, and when Beren waylays the survivors, many more are slain. Beren kills the leader of the Dwarves and takes the Nauglafring, but drowns the rest of the gold. Beren sets the Nauglafring around Tinúviel's neck. When the distraught Gwendelin finds them, she declares the necklace accursed, but Beren thinks that the power of the Silmaril might prevail over the curse. To please her mother, Tinúviel takes it off, but Beren guards it. It may be that the shortness of their second lives is due to the curse, for while their child Dior is still young, Tinúviel fades and vanishes; Beren searches for her in vain, then also fades. When Dior comes to manhood he wears the Nauglafring, and the sons of Fëanor demand the Silmaril. When he refuses, they kill Dior and his son, but his daughter Elwing escapes with the necklace.

In the *Sketch of the Mythology* (c. 1926) the outlaws are with Húrin when he plunders Nargothrond, but it is not stated (though it is implied) that they carry the hoard to Doriath, and there is no mention of any fight over it after Húrin leaves. The central part of the story seems to have been simplified. Ufedhin and his schemes have disappeared. Thingol under the spell of the gold summons the Dwarves of Nogrod and Belegost to work for him, and himself requests that the necklace be made. The Dwarves plot treachery, and Thingol denies them their reward and drives them out. With the aid of some Noldor they return, kill Thingol, and sack his stronghold, but are ambushed on their way home (with no quarrel between the Dwarves). There is no mention of Huan; it is probably Melian who informs Beren what has happened. Beren and his Brown and Green Elves ambush the Dwarves, and Beren takes the necklace. The rest of the story is similar to the previous version, though in a section rejected almost as soon as it was written the sons of Fëanor take the Nauglafring, but because of the curse quarrel over it until only one of them remains.

In the *Quenta Noldorinwa* (c. 1930) Mîm is not the only Dwarf in Nargothrond; he and his companions are slain by Húrin's outlaws, and as a result of Mîm's curse the outlaws die or are slain in quarrels. In this version Húrin seeks Thingol's aid in bringing the treasure to Doriath, and when Thingol's folk carry it in, Húrin insults Thingol, reproaching him for his treatment of his family. Húrin wanders looking for his wife Morwen, and is said to have cast himself into the sea. Thingol now stints on the reward he promised the Dwarves, and after bitter words there is a battle in his halls. Many Elves and Dwarves are killed, and the remaining Dwarves are driven out without any reward. The story from that point, with the returning Dwarf army aided by treacherous Elves (but whether Noldor or Elves of Doriath is not stated), is similar to earlier versions but with more detail. Beren's Elves are now the Green Elves. Melian informs Beren and Lúthien what has happened, and returns to Valinor. Although Melian still warns of a curse on the Nauglafring, Lúthien wears it. An emendation implies that it is no longer responsible for her early fading, indeed it seems to have brought beauty and fruitfulness to where Beren and Lúthien dwell.

The relevant events in the 'earliest' *Annals of Beleriand* (early 1930s) are recorded very briefly, with no significant changes. In Year 199 Morgoth sets Húrin free; in 200 Húrin and his men kill Mîm who curses the treasure, the treasure is brought (in what way is not mentioned) to Thingol, and after bitter words Húrin leaves; in 201 the Dwarves are summoned to fashion the treasure, and driven out when enmity awakes; in 202 they return, kill Thingol, and sack his halls, but are themselves waylaid by Beren and Lúthien; and in the same year Dior goes to Doriath, Beren and Lúthien depart but their death day is not known, and Melian returns to Valinor; in 203 the Nauglafring is brought at night to Dior in Doriath; in 205 the sons of Fëanor demand the Silmaril, and in 206 attack Doriath, killing Dior and his sons. If an unfinished second version of the *Annals* of this time had been continued, it would have made all of these dates 100 years later. In the 'later' *Annals of Beleriand* (mid-1930s), by emendation Tolkien placed events a further 200 years later, so that Húrin is released in 499 and the date of Beren's and Lúthien's departure is in 503. Otherwise the necklace was now called the *Nauglamír*, and more detail was given of the slaying of Dior's young sons – that they are deliberately left to starve in the woods. Tolkien did not reach this point in the story in the *Quenta Silmarillion* in either the 1930s nor the 1950s.

Tolkien returned to 'The Silmarillion' in 1950–1, after he had completed *The Lord of the Rings*, and again in the late 1950s, but only events at the beginning of this chapter received attention. The *Grey Annals* (*c*. 1951, see *Annals of Beleriand*) end with the death of Túrin and a mention of the stone raised over the mound where he is buried, to which Tolkien added much later in the margin what is written on the stone. Christopher Tolkien comments: 'It always seemed strange that my father should have abandoned the *Grey Annals* where he did, without at least writing the inscription that was carved on the stone, yet the fact that the amanuensis typescript ended at this point also, and that he added in the inscription in rough script on the manuscript at some later time seemed proof positive that this was the case' (*The War of the Jewels*, p. 103). When he came to prepare the lengthy prose narrative *The Wanderings of Húrin* (*c*. 1958–9) for publication, however, Christopher Tolkien found misplaced additional material in varying scripts and inks made at different times, which continues the *Annals* with an account of Morwen coming to the stone, Húrin's release, his return to Hithlum where he gathers a band of desperate men, and with seven of these, including Asgon, confronts the new Lord of Hithlum, then leaves that land. Húrin goes to Nargothrond with a band of fugitives and masterless men he has gathered to him. On another page, written later, Húrin first tries to find the way to Gondolin without success. Although the annals end at this point, on the same page is a synopsis for continuing the story of Húrin; but this played little part in the story told in *The Wanderings of Húrin* or in 'Of the Ruin of Doriath' in *The Silmarillion*, apart from Húrin wishing to enter Brethil, and a query as to how Mîm came to Nargothrond. Christopher Tolkien also notes a plot-synopsis made by his father while 'engaged on his later work on the *Narn i Chîn Húrin* . . . in annalistic form' (*The War of the Jewels*, p. 235). This says a little of Húrin's movements after his release, among which, in the Year 501, he seeks in vain to find an entrance to Gondolin and thus betrays its location to Morgoth, and he meets Morwen at the stone, where she dies. In two sentences it describes events in Brethil which Tolkien told at length in *The Wanderings of Húrin*; but of events beyond that, tells only that Húrin goes with the seven men from Hithlum to Nargothrond, where he slays Mîm, the Petty-dwarf, and 'he and his men carry off the treasure of Glaurung and bring it to Doriath. Húrin is admitted in pity' (*The War of the Jewels*, p. 258). The early part of *The Wanderings of Húrin* tells at much greater length of Húrin's visit to Hithlum, his attempt to find Gondolin, and his meeting with Morwen. After describing events in Brethil with much detail, the work concludes with the burial of Morwen.

In *The Tale of Years* (*c*. 1951) Melian takes the Nauglamír to Beren and Lúthien before departing to Valinor, and it is Celegorm and Curufin who destroy the army of returning Dwarves. But in a letter written on 20 September 1963 to Colonel Worskett, Tolkien said that it was Beren, with the aid of the Ents, who intercepted the army and recovered the Silmaril (*Letters*, p. 334).

Christopher Tolkien comments: 'My father never returned to follow the further wanderings of Húrin. We come here to the furthest point in the narrative of the Elder Days that he reached in his work on *The Silmarillion* (in the widest sense) after the Second [World] War and the completion of *The Lord of the Rings*' (*The War of the Jewels*, p. 297). Although a note on *The Wanderings of Húrin* suggests that it was to lead to 'the Necklace of the Dwarves, *Sigil Elunaeth*, Necklace of the Woe of Thingol' (p. 258), this part was never written, and 'it is as if we come to the brink of a great cliff, and look down from highlands raised in some later age onto an ancient plain far below. For the story of the Nauglamír and the destruction of Doriath . . . we must return through more than a quarter of a century to the *Quenta Noldorinwa*, or beyond' (p. 297). He excluded most of *The Wanderings of Húrin* from *The Silmarillion* because to have done otherwise

> would have entailed a huge reduction, indeed an entire re-telling of a kind that I did not wish to undertake; and since the story is intricate I was afraid that this would produce a dense tangle of narrative statement with all the subtlety gone, and above all that it would diminish the fearful figure of the old man, the great hero [Húrin] . . . , furthering still the purposes of Morgoth, as he was doomed to do. But it seems to me now, many years later, to have been an excessive tampering with my father's actual thought and intention. . . . [*The War of the Jewels*, p. 298]

Christopher Tolkien wrote in his foreword to *The Silmarillion* that 'the concluding chapters (from the death of Túrin Turambar) introduced peculiar difficulties, in that they had remained unchanged for many years and were in some respects in serious disharmony with more developed conceptions in other parts of the book' (p. 8). In a note in *The War of the Jewels* concerning 'Of the Ruin of Doriath' in *The Silmarillion*, he says that if the material he presented in *The History of Middle-earth* is 'compared with the story told in *The Silmarillion* it is seen at once that the latter is fundamentally changed, to a form for which in certain essential features there is no authority whatever in my father's own writings' (p. 354).

One problem posed by the old versions concerned the bringing of the treasure from Nargothrond to Thingol. In the *Quenta Noldorinwa* Húrin seeks help from Thingol, and as Christopher Tolkien comments,

> it ruins the gesture, if Húrin must get the king himself to send for the gold with which he is *then* to be humiliated. It seems to me most likely (but this is mere speculation) that my father would have reintroduced the outlaws from the old [*Book of Lost*] *Tales* . . . as the bearers of the treasure (though not the fierce battle between them and the Elves of the

Thousand Caves): in the scrappy writings at the end of *The Wanderings of Húrin* Asgon and his companions reappear after the disaster in Brethil and go with Húrin to Nargothrond. . . . [*The War of the Jewels*, p. 355]

The plot synopsis in annalistic form that Tolkien made while working on the *Narn i Chîn Húrin* tells the same story, but neither says what became of the outlaws after they carried the treasure to Thingol. It seems unlikely that they would have willingly given up all of the gold. In *The Silmarillion* Christopher Tolkien solved the problem of the carrying of the treasure by having the Nauglamír made much earlier by the Dwarves, for Finrod of Nargothrond rather than Thingol, and only this is taken from Nargothrond by Húrin.

Another problem concerned Thingol's dispute with the Dwarves. In the years since the writing of *The Book of Lost Tales*, Thingol became much nobler in character than in his earlier incarnation as Tinwelint, and Tolkien no longer conceived the Dwarves as basically untrustworthy and evil. Nor was it clear how an army of Dwarves could pass the protection of the Girdle of Melian into Doriath? The only hints given by Tolkien are a note, 'cannot', added later against an entry in *The Tale of Years*, recording the invasion of Doriath by the Dwarves of Belegost and Nogrod, and a brief note: 'Doriath cannot be entered by a hostile army! Somehow it must be contrived that Thingol is lured outside or induced to go to war beyond his borders and is there slain by the Dwarves. Then Melian departs, and the girdle being removed Doriath is ravaged by the Dwarves' (*The War of the Jewels*, p. 352).

The story that appears in *The Silmarillion*, Christopher Tolkien says,

> was not lightly or easily conceived, but was the outcome of long experimentation. . . . It seemed at that time that there were elements inherent in the story of the Ruin of Doriath as it stood that were radically incompatible with 'The Silmarillion' as projected, and that there was here an inescapable choice: either to abandon that conception, or else to alter the story. I think now that this was a mistaken view, and that the undoubted difficulties could have been, and should have been, surmounted without so far overstepping the bounds of the editorial function. [p. 356]

He was able to take the text for the first part of the *Silmarillion* chapter, as far as Húrin leaving Morwen's grave, from *The Wanderings of Húrin* and additions to the *Grey Annals*, but omitted any mention of Húrin gathering a band of homeless men, or of his visit to Brethil. Where possible, he used his father's words, including short pieces from the *Quenta Noldorinwa* and *The Tale of Years*; and he based Mîm's claim to Nargothrond on a plot-outline for the *Narn i Chîn Húrin*. Beren gazing in wonder at the jewel he had cut from Morgoth's crown and recovered from the leader of the Dwarves, and one or two other details, seem to go back to *The Book of Lost Tales*. The account of events after the death of Beren and Lúthien was derived from early sources, including the *Annals of Beleriand*, and some details from the latest version of *The Tale of Years*.

Salu, Mary Bertha. Having received her B.A. from King's College, Newcastle, M.B. Salu went up to Lady Margaret Hall, *Oxford in Michaelmas Term 1941 to work for a B.Litt. Tolkien was her supervisor from 1941 to 1949 while she wrote her thesis, *Grammar of Ancrene Wisse (Phonology and Accidence)*, and assisted him with his own work on the *Ancrene Wisse* (*Ancrene Riwle*). Later she taught at Edinburgh and Reading, and was principal lecturer in English at St Mary's College, Newcastle upon Tyne. A translation of the *Ancrene Riwle* by Salu into Modern English was published in 1955 with a brief preface by Tolkien (see *Descriptive Bibliography* B23). Salu also edited *Essays on Troilus and Criseyde* (1979) and with Robert T. Farrell co-edited *J.R.R. Tolkien, Scholar and Storyteller: Essays in Memoriam* (1979).

Sarehole (Warwickshire). The former hamlet of Sarehole, now part of the suburb of **Hall Green**, is located a few miles south of *Birmingham. Once part of Worcestershire, it was taken into Warwickshire (*West Midlands) when Birmingham extended its boundaries in 1911. Tolkien, his mother *Mabel, and his brother *Hilary moved there in summer 1896, to a semi-detached cottage at **5 Gracewell Road** (today **264a Wake Green Road**). Sarehole was then a rural area with little traffic other than the occasional farm cart or tradesman's wagon. A complete contrast to the open veldt of *South Africa and to Birmingham with its factory smoke, it became in Tolkien's memory an idyllic place, and an inspiration for the Shire in *The Lord of the Rings* ('more or less a Warwickshire village of about the time of the Diamond Jubilee [of Queen Victoria, 1897]', letter to George Allen & Unwin, 12 December 1955, *Letters*, p. 230). In an interview for the *Oxford Mail*, Tolkien said to John Ezard:

> I could draw you a map of every inch of [Sarehole]. . . . I loved it with an intensity of love that was a kind of nostalgia reversed. There was an old mill that really did grind corn [grain] with two millers . . . a great big pond with swans on it, a sandpit, a wonderful dell with flowers, a few old-fashioned village houses and further away a stream with another mill. . . . It was a kind of lost paradise and it was wonderful. ['The Hobbit Man', 3 August 1966, p. 4]

In spring 1968 he recalled in an interview with Keith Brace 'the great mill-pool fed by leats from the River Cole', and that Sarehole 'was a very tree-ish part [of the country], like open parkland. There was a willow hanging over the mill-pool, and I learned to climb it. . . . One day they cut it down. They didn't do anything with it; the log just lay there. I never forgot that' ('In the Footsteps of the Hobbits', *Birmingham Post Midland Magazine*, 25 May 1968, p. 1).

Hilary Tolkien too had golden memories of Sarehole. He and his brother 'would stare through the fence at the water-wheel [of the mill] turning in its dark cavern, or run round to the yard where the sacks were swung down on to a waiting cart. Sometimes they would venture through the gate and gaze into an open doorway, where they could see the great leather belts and pulleys and shafts and the men at work.' Ronald Tolkien nicknamed the younger of the two millers 'the White Ogre' because of his white dusty face, and when he yelled at them the boys

> would scamper away from the yard, and run round to a place behind the mill where there was a silent pool with swans swimming on it. At the foot of the pool the dark waters suddenly plunged over the sluice to the great wheel below. . . . Not far from Sarehole Mill, a little way up the hill towards Moseley, was a deep tree-lined sandpit that became another favourite haunt for the boys. . . . An old farmer who once chased Ronald for picking mushrooms was given the nickname 'the Black Ogre' by the boys. [Humphrey Carpenter, *Biography*, pp. 20–1]

Hilary also recalled that the boys

> spent lovely summers just picking flowers and trespassing. The Black Ogre used to take people's shoes and stockings from the bank where they'd left them to paddle and run away with them, make them go and ask for them. And then he'd thrash them! The White Ogre wasn't quite so bad. But in order to get to the place where we used to blackberry (called the Dell) we had to go through the white one's land, and he didn't like us very much because the path was very narrow through the field and we traipsed off after corncockles and other pretty things. [quoted in *Biography*, p. 21]

There has been a mill at Sarehole since at least 1542. The one Tolkien knew was built in the 1760s. At the end of the 1850s a steam engine was installed to supplement the power of the mill stream. Sarehole Mill on Cole Bank Road, the sole survivor of some fifty water-mills that once operated in Birmingham, is now a branch of the city Museums and Art Gallery and is open to the public. Tolkien subscribed in 1968 to an appeal for its restoration. Photographs of the mill appear in *Biography*, pl. 2, and in *The Tolkien Family Album*, p. 20, together with a photograph of Gracewell Road. Although Carpenter writes in *Biography*, p. 20, that in Tolkien's time 'the mill's chief work was the grinding of bones to make manure', an official brochure states that 'Sarehole Mill was used for corn milling right up until 1919' (*Sarehole Mill* (1986), p. 2).

After a visit to Sarehole with his family in September 1933 Tolkien wrote in his diary:

> I pass over the pangs to me of passing through Hall Green – become a huge tram-ridden meaningless suburb where I actually lost my way – and eventually down what is left of beloved lanes of childhood, and past the very gate of our cottage, now in the midst of a sea of new red-brick. The old mill still stands and Mrs Hunt's still sticks out into the road as it turns uphill; but the crossing beyond the now fenced-in pool, where the

bluebell lane ran down into the mill lane, is now a dangerous crossing alive with motors and red lights. The White Ogre's house (which the children were excited to see) is become a petrol station, and most of Short Avenue and the elms between it and the crossing have gone. How I envy those whose precious early scenery has not been exposed to such violent and peculiarly hideous change. [quoted in *Biography*, pp. 124–5]

Mabel Tolkien and her sons lived in Sarehole until, apparently, in September 1900, when they moved to Alcester Road in Moseley, closer to the centre of Birmingham.

Sauron Defeated: The End of the Third Age (The History of The Lord of the Rings, Part Four); The Notion Club Papers and The Drowning of Anadûnê. The ninth volume of *The History of Middle-earth*, edited with notes and commentary by *Christopher Tolkien, first published in Great Britain by HarperCollins, London, in January 1992, and in the United States by the Houghton Mifflin Company, Boston, in October 1992. See further, *Descriptive Bibliography* A29 and *Tolkien Collector* 2 (February 1993), p. 10.

Part One, 'The End of the Third Age', describes the writing of Book VI of *The Lord of the Rings*, including its previously unpublished Epilogue, probably in August–September 1948, and completes the history of that work apart from the Appendices (see *The Peoples of Middle-earth*). At the end of this text are reproduced two of three versions of the 'King's letter', texts in Tengwar (*Writing systems) written by King Elessar (Aragorn) to Sam Gamgee, and five sheets with multiple drawings by Tolkien of Orthanc and Dunharrow.

Part Two is *The Notion Club Papers*, Tolkien's second attempt to write a time-travel story. As with the first, *The Lost Road*, Númenor at the time of its destruction is a powerful influence; but this tale too was left unfinished. Here its original division into two parts is preserved. Tolkien began to write *The Notion Club Papers* at Christmas 1945, and seems to have continued to work on both it and the associated *Drowning of Anadûnê* (see below) until August 1946. Within the notes to the second part of *The Notion Club Papers* the poem *Imram* is reprinted. The first edition of *Sauron Defeated* includes two colour plates which reproduce a manuscript meant to be fragments of Adunaic, the language of Númenor, recorded by the character Alwin Arundel Lowdham; and three black and white reproductions of pages in 'Númenórean script' (Tengwar) written by Edwin Lowdham.

Part Three, *The Drowning of Anadûnê*, is concerned mainly with accounts of the end of Númenor. The first of these is the third version of *The Fall of Númenor*, written in the early 1940s, still close to the first two versions written c. 1936–7. Then follow three texts of *The Drowning of Anadûnê* which give a significantly different view of the founding and destruction of Númenor. Then in 'The theory of the work' Christopher Tolkien presents three sketches which preceded the writing of the earliest version of *The Drowning of Anadûnê*. He concludes that in that work his father was writing a version preserved in the traditions of later Men, as compared to *The Fall of Númenor* which records the tradition of the Elves.

Part Three also includes 'Lowdham's Report on the Adunaic Language', supposedly written by A.A. Lowdham of the Notion Club, which is a substantial if incomplete account of the phonology of Adunaic.

Sayer, George Sydney Benedict (1914–2005). George Sayer read English at Magdalen College, *Oxford; his tutor was *C.S. Lewis, who became a lifelong friend. In his biography of Lewis, *Jack: A Life of C.S. Lewis* (1988; 2nd edn. 1994), Sayer recalled having met Tolkien outside Lewis's rooms in Magdalen in 1934. Later he went to some of his lectures, but soon gave them up, disappointed in Tolkien's voice and manner of delivery. After leaving Oxford Sayer turned to writing and then teaching. In 1949 he became Senior English Master at Malvern College in Worcestershire, where he remained until his retirement in 1974.

Sayer came to know Tolkien better in August 1947, when the latter went to *Malvern on a walking tour with Lewis and his brother *Warnie. The Lewis brothers preferred to walk vigorously, but Sayer was happy to accompany Tolkien at a more leisurely pace.

Sayer also saw Tolkien at meetings of the *Inklings, to which Sayer was an occasional visitor. And he heard about him from Lewis, who praised *The Lord of the Rings*, then still unpublished. In August 1952 Tolkien lent the typescript of the work to Sayer and his wife Moira in two parts. Having read the first, Sayer returned it to Tolkien in Oxford and collected both the second part and its author for another visit to Malvern. On this occasion Tolkien stayed with the Sayers: they walked in the Malvern Hills, and drove in the Black Mountains on the borders of Wales, and joined them, fellow Roman Catholics, at Sunday Mass. Producing a tape recorder, Sayer captured Tolkien reading and singing excerpts from *The Hobbit* and from the typescript of *The Lord of the Rings*. Although Tolkien pretended to regard Sayer's machine with suspicion, reciting the Lord's Prayer in Gothic to cast out any devils that might be within, he enjoyed the recording session, at least some of which was released commercially in 1975 (see *Recordings).

In spring 1953, at Tolkien's request, Sayer wrote a blurb for *The Lord of the Rings*, then in production. The final publicity blurb issued by George Allen & Unwin (*Publishers) was evidently derived from comments by both Sayer and Tolkien.

Science. Tolkien said in *On Fairy-Stories* that the books that interested him most as a child or schoolboy were not fairy or adventure stories: 'I liked many other things as well, or better: such as history, astronomy, botany, grammar, and etymology' (*Tree and Leaf*, pp. 40–1). He added in Note D to *On Fairy-Stories* that he was introduced to zoology and palaeontology while quite young. Similarly, when asked *c.* 1970 to reply to the question 'Which book or books were your favorites or influenced you most as a teenager and why?'

Tolkien said that he was not interested in 'literature', but rather in his early teens the 'things I read with most pleasure were mostly scientific in reference, especially botany and astronomy. My most treasured book was [C.A.] Johns' *Flowers of the Field* [first published *c.* 1850]' (**Attacks of Taste* (1971), p. 43).

Tolkien's interest in botany was a lasting one. He wrote to his friend Amy Ronald in 1969, after she had sent him a book he had enjoyed, *Wild Flowers of the Cape Peninsula* by Mary Matham Kidd (1950):

> All illustrated botany books (or better, contact with an unfamiliar flora) have for me a special fascination. Not so much for the rare, unusual, or totally unrelated specimens, as in the variations and permutations of flowers that are the evident *kin* of those I know – but not the same. They rouse in me visions of kinship and descent through great ages, and also thoughts of the mystery of pattern/design as a thing other than its individual embodiment, and recognizable. [16 November 1969, *Letters*, p. 402]

In the same letter he recounts his delight in seeing in a botanical garden a 'missing link' between the Figwort and the Foxglove.

*Priscilla Tolkien once wrote that her father had a general interest in astronomy,

> as he did in a vast number of subjects, and he encouraged my brothers and myself to be interested in various ways: my brother Christopher had a telescope, and I was given a book when I was a child called *The Starry Heavens* [by Ellison Hawks, 1933] which was an admirably simple introduction to the subject. . . . My brother and I looked at the stars through the telescope and learnt their names and the constellations. My father also talked to us about eclipses of the sun and moon and about the planets and their satellites. [quoted in Emma Henry, 'A Star on His Brow: The Role of Astronomy in *The Lord of the Rings*', *The Southern Star* 2 (September 1985), p. 16]

Towards the end of his life Tolkien's interest in astronomy led him to consider drastically changing *'The Silmarillion' as he became more and more uncomfortable with the idea, of long standing in his mythology, of a flat earth made round, which could not be attributed to a change in perception with his development of the Elvish lore-masters who had learned the truth from the Valar.

During his early holidays at *Lyme Regis with *Father Francis Morgan he hunted for fossils along the cliffs. Later he used his knowledge of palaeontology when he gave a lecture on *dragons to children on 1 January 1938 in the University Museum, Oxford, and compared ideas about dragons with what was known about dinosaurs.

Scotland. In 1955 Tolkien wrote to the Houghton Mifflin Company (*Publishers) that he had 'often been in Scotland ([but] never north of the Tay)' (*Letters*, p. 219). The River Tay is just north of **St Andrews**, which Tolkien visited in 1910 or 1911, possibly to see his *Aunt Jane Neave. He made a drawing, *St Andrews from Kinkell Brake*, which is dated both '1910' and '1910 or 1911.' While in St Andrews again in 1912, probably in the summer vacation but possibly at Easter, he wrote a short poem, *The Grimness of the Sea* (later *The Horns of Ylmir*). He was also in St Andrews on 8 March 1939, to deliver the Andrew Lang Lecture at the University of St Andrews (*On Fairy-Stories). On that occasion he was entertained by T.M. Knox, Professor of Moral Philosophy at the University.

Tolkien visited **Edinburgh** in early April 1949, probably to attend an academic conference (to which Tolkien alludes in a letter to George Allen & Unwin (*Publishers) on 4 May 1949; but C.S. Lewis wrote to Edward A. Allen on 5 April 1949 that Tolkien was in Edinburgh to give a series of lectures). On 13 July 1973 Edinburgh University conferred upon Tolkien an honorary D.Litt. He travelled to Edinburgh accompanied by his daughter *Priscilla and stayed for a few days with a former pupil, Angus McIntosh, Professor of English at Edinburgh, and his wife Barbara.

On 14 April 1953 Tolkien travelled to **Glasgow** to give the W.P. Ker Memorial Lecture on *Sir Gawain and the Green Knight*. An audience of about 300 attended the lecture on 15 April.

The Sea. Tolkien was born in the Orange Free State (*South Africa), far from the sea, but retained vague memories of his first visit to the coast near Cape Town when he was not quite three. He recalled 'running back from the sea to a bathing hut on a wide flat sandy shore' (Humphrey Carpenter, *Biography*, p. 15). Only a few months later he saw the sea in earnest when he sailed with his mother and younger brother to England. Later he

> remembered two brilliantly sharp images: the first of looking down from the deck of the ship into the clear waters of the Indian Ocean far below, which was full of lithe brown and black bodies diving for coins thrown by the passengers; the second was of pulling into a harbour at sunrise and seeing a great city set on the hillside above, which he realised much later in life must have been Lisbon. [John and Priscilla Tolkien, *The Tolkien Family Album*, p. 18]

The death of his father meant that Tolkien never returned to Africa, but grew up in England, where no one lives much more than fifty miles from the sea, and most much nearer. Tolkien spent many childhood and adult holidays on the coast, as was the custom in the days before air travel encouraged people to travel further afield. Sometimes he stayed at popular tourist resorts such as *Filey, *Weston-super-Mare, *Sidmouth, *Bournemouth, and *Poole (his home for a few years near the end of his life), or at more remote locations such as Lamorna Cove in *Cornwall and Trywn Llanbedrog on the coast of Cardigan Bay in north *Wales. During many of these visits he spent time drawing, usually looking seawards, though in more picturesque places such as *Lyme Regis, St Andrews (*Scotland), and the fishing port of *Whitby in Yorkshire, he was tempted to draw the harbour or views of the town itself (see Artist and Illustrator, figs. 5, 6, 8, 9, 26).

At Filey in 1925 he conceived the story *Roverandom, in which the dog Rover 'had never either seen or smelt the sea before', but comes to experience it in all its fairy-tale strangeness: 'by the evening the place was full of mermen and mermaidens, not to speak of the smaller sea-goblins that rode their small sea-horses with bridles of green weed right up to the cliffs and left them lying in the foam at the edge of the water' (Roverandom (1998), pp. 9–10, 10–11). In the final third of the story, Rover is taken by the whale Uin – 'borrowed' by Tolkien from 'The Silmarillion' – to visit the mer-king's realm under the sea, for which Tolkien painted one of his most attractive illustrations (Artist and Illustrator, fig. 76).

But it was not the peaceful, tame, often belittered resorts of Britain, but rather wilder coasts, and the sea itself, which stimulated his imagination. In St Andrews in 1912 he wrote a twelve-line poem, The Grimness of the Sea, the germ of what would become a much longer poem fully integrated into his *'Silmarillion' mythology. In August 1914, while visiting the Lizard Peninsula in *Cornwall, a sparsely populated area with a rugged coastline which looks out across the Atlantic, he tried to draw what he saw there (see Cove Near the Lizard and Caerthilian Cove & Lion Rock in Artist and Illustrator, figs. 21, 20) and to describe it in words in a letter to his fiancée (*Edith Tolkien): 'The sun beats down on you and a huge Atlantic swell smashes and spouts over the snags and reefs. The sea has carved weird wind-holes and spouts into the cliffs which blow with trumpety noises or spout foam like a whale, and everywhere you see black and red rock and white foam against violet and transparent sea-green' (quoted in Biography, p. 70). Later that year he extended The Grimness of the Sea to forty lines as The Tides, and in March 1915 revised and enlarged the poem again, as Sea Chant of an Elder Day.

It is possible that in 1915 Tolkien was already envisioning the poem as the work of Tuor, as it became in a still later version, composed in spring 1917 at about the same time that Tolkien was working on The Fall of Gondolin in *The Book of Lost Tales. That version, The Horns of Ulmo (or *The Horns of Ylmir), becomes the song that Tuor tells to his son Eärendel, of how the Vala Ulmo, Lord of Waters and King of the Sea, appeared 'and played to him on his magic flute of hollow shells. Thereafter did Tuor hunger ever after the sea and had no peace in his heart did he dwell in pleasant inland places' (*The Shaping of Middle-earth, pp. 214–15). In The Fall of Gondolin Tuor comes to 'black cliffs by the sea and saw the ocean and its waves for the first time, and at that hour the sun sank beyond the rim of Earth far out to sea, and he stood on the cliff-top with outspread arms, and his heart was filled with a longing very great indeed. Now some say that he was the first of Men to reach the Sea and look upon it and know the desire that it brings . . .' (*The Book of Lost Tales, Part Two, p. 151). The retelling of Tuor's story which Tolkien began *c.* 1951 in *Of Tuor and His Coming to Gondolin repeats this account, but subtly alters it for even greater impact: in this Tuor

> came suddenly to the black brink of Middle-earth, and saw the Great Sea, Belegaer the Shoreless. And at that hour the sun went down beyond the rim of the world, as a mighty fire; and Tuor stood alone upon the cliff with outspread arms, and a great yearning filled his heart. It is said that he was the first of Men to reach the Great Sea, and that none, save the Eldar, have ever felt more deeply the longing that it brings. [*Unfinished Tales, pp. 24–5]

Tuor accepts a task from Ulmo which takes him inland, but is first given a vision of the sea in all its power: 'The Great Sea he saw through its unquiet regions teeming with strange forms, even to its lightless depths, in which amid the everlasting darkness there echoed voices terrible to mortal ears' (*Unfinished Tales*, p. 30).

Tuor's son Eärendil inherits his father's sea-longing, and both eventually sail into the West. Nor are they the only characters in Tolkien's writings who feel a powerful yearning for the sea. Ælfwine, successor to Eriol (see *Eriol and Ælfwine) as the voyager who heard and recorded the tales in *The Book of Lost Tales*, grew up inland, but in a bitter siege both his parents were slain and he was enslaved.

> But behold a wonder, for Ælfwine knew not and had never seen the sea, yet he heard its great voice speaking deeply in his heart, and its murmurous choirs sang ever in his secret ear between wake and sleep, that he was filled with longing. This was the magic of Éadgifu, maiden of the West, his mother, and this longing unquenchable had been hers all the days that she dwelt in the quiet inland places. . . . [*The Book of Lost Tales, Part Two*, p. 314]

At last Ælfwine's longing for the sea is so strong that he breaks his bonds and escapes. Legolas in *The Lord of the Rings feels a similar attraction, common to Elves, as he walks in Minas Tirith and sees 'white sea-birds beating up the River'. Gulls are a wonder to him 'and a trouble to my heart . . . for their wailing voices spoke to me of the Sea. . . . Alas! I have not yet beheld it. But deep in the hearts of all my kindred lies the sea-longing, which it is perilous to stir. . . . No peace shall I have again under beech or under elm' (bk. V, ch. 9).

In a letter to *W.H. Auden on 7 June 1955 Tolkien commented that as 'a man of the North-west of the Old World' he naturally set *The Lord of the Rings* 'in an imaginary world of that air, and that situation: with the Shoreless Sea of his innumerable ancestors to the West, and . . . his heart may remember, even if he has been cut off from all oral tradition, the rumour all along the coasts of the Men out of the Sea' (*Letters*, p. 212). Tolkien included one such legend of Men from the Sea in both *The Lost Road* and *The Notion Club Papers*, that of Scyld Scefing (King Sheaf, or Sheave) whose story is told in *Beowulf*, but he also wrote his own legends in his history of the Númenóreans. In a letter to Mrs E.C. Ossendrijver on 5 January 1961 he wrote that the stories of Númenor 'are my own use for my own purpose of the *Atlantis* legend', based 'on a special personal concern with this tradition of culture-bearing Men of the Sea, which so profoundly affected the imagination of peoples of Europe with west-ward-shores' (*Letters*, p. 303). In the Númenórean story *Aldarion and Erendis*, Tolkien created in Aldarion a character who could not be kept from the sea by wife or child or royal duties.

Richard Mathews in 'The Edges of Reality in Tolkien's Tale of Aldarion and Erendis', *Mythlore* 18, no. 3, whole no. 69 (Summer 1992), comments that

> while Tolkien's love of trees and land is well established in *The Lord of the Rings*, his elemental understanding of the sea, so important in the sailing of Eärendil the Mariner and the total mythos of Arda, is nowhere more strongly conveyed than in this tale in which Aldarion is pulled in two directions. The power of the sea is so strong upon him that it is physical: 'Then suddenly the sea-longing took him as though a great hand had been laid on his throat, and his heart hammered, and his breath was stopped' ([*Unfinished Tales*, p.] 185). The power is as strong as the power of love or death. [p. 28]

The Sea-Bell. Poem, first published in *The Adventures of Tom Bombadil and Other Verses from the Red Book* (1962), pp. 57–60. The poet, as if in a dream, hears within a sea-shell 'a buoy swinging, a call ringing / over endless seas, faint now and far.' He is carried in a boat 'to a forgotten strand in a strange land'; in 'a country fair' he hears dancing and music, which vanish whenever he comes near. He lives in a dark wood until, old, grey, and worn, he returns to the sea and is borne to a haven 'silent as snow, deep in the night'. Clutching a shell now 'silent and dead', he walks ragged through alley and street, talking to himself; 'for still they speak not, men that I meet.'

The Sea-Bell is a revision and expansion of an earlier poem, *Looney*, written probably in 1932 or 1933, and published in the *Oxford Magazine* 52, no. 9 (18 January 1934), p. 340. There the speaker is asked: 'Where have you been; what have you seen / Walking in rags down the street?' He replies with a similar strange tale of a land rich with flora and fauna but empty of people; he has returned to the world of men bearing 'a single shell, where I hear still the spell / Echoing far'. He talks to himself, 'for seldom they speak, men that I meet.' The 'Elvish' element, in which the inhabitants of the distant land are ever just out of reach, is not present, nor is the speaker utterly cut off either from his fellow man or from the paradise in which he journeyed 'for a year and a day'.

In his preface to the *Tom Bombadil* collection, in which he pretends that the volume contains examples of Hobbit poetry, Tolkien describes *The Sea-Bell* as an exception to the book's generally 'lighthearted or frivolous' verses. At the head of the poem is said to be a scrawled title, *Frodos Dreme*,

> associated with the dark and despairing dreams which visited [Frodo Baggins in *The Lord of the Rings*] in March and October during his last three years. But there were certainly other traditions concerning Hobbits that were taken by the 'wandering-madness', and if they ever returned, were afterwards queer and uncommunicable. The thought of the Sea was ever-present in the background of hobbit imagination; but fear of it and distrust of all Elvish lore, was the prevailing mood in the Shire at the end of the Third Age. . . . [1962 edn., p. 9]

T.A. Shippey in his *Road to Middle-earth* (1982; 2nd edn. 1992) points out the 'increasing darkness' between *Looney* and *The Sea-Bell*, both 'poems of "disenchantment"'. In the later work 'the return to Faërie, even in memory, is banned' (pp. 249–50). Verlyn Flieger includes a lengthy discussion of the two poems in *A Question of Time: J.R.R. Tolkien's Road to Faërie* (1997).

In a letter to Pauline Baynes of 6 December 1961 Tolkien said that *The Sea-Bell* was the 'poorest' of the poems he was then considering for the *Adventures of Tom Bombadil* volume. But no less a critic than *W.H. Auden wrote to Tolkien in 1967 in praise of the work, which 'greatly cheered' its author (letter to Auden, 29 March 1967, *Letters*, p. 379).

Tolkien made a recording of *The Sea-Bell* in 1967, with other poems in the *Adventures of Tom Bombadil* volume, but it was not issued until 2001, as part of *The J.R.R. Tolkien Audio Collection* (*Recordings).

A Secret Vice. Lecture. In manuscript it bears the title *A Hobby for the Home*, but Tolkien later referred to it as *A Secret Vice*, and under that title it was first published in *The Monsters and the Critics and Other Essays* (1983), pp. 198–223.

SUMMARY

The 'hobby' or 'vice' was that of inventing languages for personal enjoyment (see also *Languages, Invented). Tolkien tells of encountering a fellow soldier in the First World War whose interest in a training lecture was less than in how he should express the accusative case in whatever language he himself had devised. And he mentions the linguistic talent of children, in fact his *Incledon cousins Marjorie and Mary, 'who constructed a language called *Animalic* almost entirely out of English animal, bird, and fish names' (p. 200), and of others – Mary Incledon and himself – who devised 'an idiom called *Nevbosh*, or "New Nonsense"' (p. 202). But these were crude, and in Nevbosh there was 'no real breaking away from "English" or the native traditional language. Its notions – their associations with certain sounds, even their inherited and accidental confusions; there range and limits – are preserved' (p. 204).

Development of private languages beyond this level is rare:

> A few [creators] go on, but they become shy, ashamed of spending the precious commodity of time for their private pleasure, and higher developments are locked in secret places. The obviously unremunerative character of the hobby is against it – it can earn no prizes, win no competitions (as yet) – make no birthday presents for aunts (as a rule) – earn no scholarship, fellowship, or worship. It is also – like poetry – contrary to conscience, and duty; its pursuit is snatched from hours due to self-advancement, or to bread, or to employers. [p. 205]

But Tolkien admits that he did progress to the next stage, with a more sophisticated creation called 'Naffarin', influenced by Latin and Spanish, and later to those languages associated with his tales of Middle-earth and tied to its invented world. He writes that he

> originally embarked on this odd topic because I somewhat dimly grasped at questions which did seem to me to arise, of interest not only to students of language, but to those considering rather mythology, poetry, art. As one suggestion, I might fling out the view that for perfect construction of an art-language it is found necessary to construct at least in outline a mythology concomitant. Not solely because some pieces of verse will inevitably be part of the (more or less) completed structure, but because the making of language and mythology are related functions; to give your language an individual flavour, it must have woven into it the threads of an individual mythology, individual while working within the scheme of natural human mythopoeia, as your word-form may be individual while working within the hackneyed limits of human, even European, phonetics. The converse indeed is true, your language construction will *breed* a mythology. [pp. 210–11]

He concludes with remarks on his interest in word-form, 'and in word-form in relation to meaning' (p. 211), and with examples of poetry in 'Elvish' languages (with versions in English) related to his mythology: *Oilima Markirya* (**The Last Ark*), **Nieninque*, and *Earendel* (**Earendel at the Helm*) in Qenya, and a 'fragment' in Noldorin beginning 'Dir avosaith a gwaew hinar' ('Like a wind, dark through gloomy places . . .').

HISTORY

A Secret Vice was written apparently to be delivered at a meeting of a philological society (not identified), at least before an audience with sufficient knowledge and interest to follow its more technically linguistic passages. Since the Esperanto Congress in Oxford mentioned at the beginning of the lecture as having taken place 'a year or more ago' occurred in August 1930, the work can be dated to ?Autumn 1931. See also Tolkien's letter to Charlotte and Denis Plimmer, 8 February 1967, *Letters*, p. 374.

In *The Monsters and the Critics and Other Essays* editor *Christopher Tolkien appended to the lecture other versions of *Oilima Markirya* and variant readings. In his foreword to the collection he remarks that *A Secret Vice* is unique among his father's works 'in that only on this one occasion, as it seems, did the "invented world" appear publicly and in its own right in the "academic world" – and that was some six years before the publication of *The Hobbit* and nearly a quarter of a century before that of *The Lord of the Rings*. It is of great interest in the history of the invented languages, and . . . touches on themes developed in later essays [*English and Welsh* and *Valedictory Address to the University of Oxford*] . . .' (p. 1).

Shadow-Bride. Poem, first published in *The Adventures of Tom Bombadil and Other Verses from the Red Book* (1962), p. 52. A man who sits 'as still as carven stone', casting no shadow, upon the appearance of 'a lady clad in grey' wakes and breaks 'the spell that bound him'. He embraces the lady and wraps 'her shadow round him'. 'There never more she walks her ways' but 'dwells below', except for 'once a year when caverns yawn / and hidden things awake' when the man and lady dance 'till dawn / and a single shadow make.'

Tolkien wrote one version of the poem on the earliest extant manuscript that also contains his *Elvish Song in Rivendell*, which was written apparently in the early 1930s. But a version of *Shadow-Bride* seems to have been printed already in the 1920s, in a periodical possibly entitled *Abingdon Chronicle*, about which nothing more is known.

Paul H. Kocher in *Master of Middle-earth: The Fiction of J.R.R. Tolkien* (1972) notes a resemblance between *Shadow-Bride* and the legend of Proserpina (Persephone).

The Shaping of Middle-Earth: The Quenta, The Ambarkanta and the Annals Together with the Earliest 'Silmarillion' and the First Map. The fourth volume of *The History of Middle-earth*, edited with notes and commentary by *Christopher Tolkien, first published in Great Britain by George Allen & Unwin, London, in August 1986, and in the United States by the Houghton Mifflin Company, Boston, in November 1986. See further, *Descriptive Bibliography* A24. This volume contains prose works relating to *'The Silmarillion' later than *The Book of Lost Tales* (i.e. from the early 1920s up to and including the early 1930s). Poetic works from the same period were published and discussed in *The Lays of Beleriand*. The seven parts of *The Shaping of Middle-earth* are indicated by roman numerals:

I. Early, brief 'Prose Fragments Following the Lost Tales': *Turlin [i.e. Tuor] and the Exiles of Gondolin*; a text concerning the Gnomes (later Noldor) and Fëanor (*'The Gnomes Come to the Great Lands'); and an isolated slip, described in the entry *'Flight of the Gnomes'.

II. 'The Earliest "Silmarillion"' or *Sketch of the Mythology, a brief synopsis of the whole mythology written c. 1926 to be sent with *The Children of Húrin to *R.W. Reynolds to explain its background. It was heavily revised in the following years up to c. 1930.

III. The Quenta or *Quenta Noldorinwa, a 'brief history of the Noldoli or Gnomes', an expansion of the Sketch of the Mythology all or mostly written in 1930. This is the second, and last complete, narrative of the mythology. This section also contains as appendices the probably contemporary translation Tolkien made of just the beginning of the Quenta Noldorinwa into Old English, presumed to have been made by the Anglo-Saxon mariner Ælfwine or Eriol; a compilation of several lists of Old English equivalents of Elvish names, associated with this and other 'translations by Ælfwine' in the early 1930s; and texts of the poem ultimately called *The Horns of Ylmir.

IV. 'The First "Silmarillion" Map', reproductions and discussion of a map made by Tolkien at *Leeds, possibly in association with The Children of Húrin or the Sketch of the Mythology. In the Allen & Unwin and most later British editions, the map is reproduced in colour as two facing plates between pp. 220 and 221; in other editions these are in greyscale. Two supplementary maps, westward and eastward extensions, are printed in black and white only.

V. The *Ambarkanta. Although grouped in The Shaping of Middle-earth with works of the early 1930s, Christopher Tolkien decided when preparing *The Lost Road and Other Writings (1987) that the Ambarkanta belonged rather with works of the mid-thirties. Its brief text is associated with three diagrams of the world and two maps.

VI. The 'earliest' Annals of Valinor (*Annals of Valinor), from the early 1930s, a chronological record of events from the time the Valar entered Arda until the return of the Elves to Middle-earth, and the rising of the Sun and the Moon. Included as an appendix are 'Ælfwine's translations of the Annals of Valinor into Old English' (*Eriol and Ælfwine).

VII. The 'earliest' Annals of Beleriand (*Annals of Beleriand), also from the early 1930s, a summary of events which led to the return of the Elves to Middle-earth, leading into a chronological record from the rising of the Sun and Moon to the overthrow of Morgoth. Tolkien possibly made the first version while he was writing the Quenta Noldorinwa to help to keep track of events; a second version with much new material was not finished. Included as an appendix is 'Ælfwine's translation of the Annals of Beleriand into Old English'.

The Shibboleth of Fëanor. Essay, published with commentary and notes in *The Peoples of Middle-earth (1996), pp. 331–66, with a title assigned by *Christopher Tolkien. The work is concerned with the sound-change in Quenya (*Languages, Invented) from þ to s. Tolkien concludes that this must have been a 'conscious and deliberate change agreed to and accepted by the majority of the Ñoldor' for reasons of 'taste' and theory (The Peoples of Middle-earth, p. 332). But it was resisted by linguistic loremasters, including Fëanor, son of Finwë, who 'insisted that þ was the true pronunciation for all who cared for or fully understood their language' (p. 333). Fëanor was influenced by the fact that his late mother, Míriel, had been called Þerindë 'needlewoman', and by his resentment of his father's second wife, Indis of the Vanyar, who on joining the Ñoldor adopted their use of *s*. This is discussed in context of the death of Míriel (here not until Fëanor was fully grown, compare *'Of Fëanor and the Unchaining of Melkor'), the repercussions of her choice to die and not reincarnate, the later actions of Finwë, and the resulting division among his children. Also discussed here are Galadriel, the names she bore, her youth in Valinor and her relationship with Fëanor, her part in the revolt of the Ñoldor, and her refusal of the pardon of the Valar at the end of the First Age. (Extracts and summaries from this work as they concern Galadriel were previously published in *Unfinished Tales*, pp. 229–31, 266–7).

Three notes conclude the original essay. The first of these, concerning the reasons the Ñoldor made the sound change, was omitted in *The Peoples of Middle-earth* except for an extract (p. 401, note 3) but published in *Vinyar Tengwar* as *From The Shibboleth of Fëanor*, together with other omitted authorial notes of a phonological nature, edited by Carl F. Hostetter (41 (July 2000), pp. 7–10). The second note, 'Note on Mother-names', deals also with other names that might be given or acquired by Elves. The third note, 'The Names of Finwë's Descendants', is concerned with their various names in Quenya and Sindarin and provides information not given elsewhere, though most of the names are included in Elvish genealogies made by Tolkien at the end of 1959 (see *'Of Eldamar and the Princes of the Eldalië').

Tolkien abandoned the finished text of the *Shibboleth* before he reached a promised 'excursus' on the names of the sons of Fëanor, but some drafting for this exists, including a new story that the two youngest sons were twins; that their mother, Nerdanel, foresaw disaster for one of them and tried to persuade Fëanor to leave them in Valinor, but he refused; and that the youngest stayed on one of the ships to sleep when they reached Middle-earth, and was burnt to death when his father set fire to them.

Written in 1968 or later, *The Shibboleth of Fëanor* is an example of the close relationship in Tolkien's final writings between linguistic history and the history of persons and peoples, 'arising from his consideration of a problem of historical phonology, which records how the difference in pronunciation of a single consonantal element in Quenya played a significant part in the strife of the Noldorin princes in Valinor [in *'Of the Silmarils and the Unrest of the Noldor"]' (Christopher Tolkien, *The Peoples of Middle-earth*, p. 331).

The Shores of Faery. Poem. Its earliest extant version was published in *Biography* (1977), pp. 76–7, with errors of transcription, and more faithfully in *Artist and Illustrator* (1995), pp. 47–8, excepting one error of punctuation (line 23, for 'O' read 'O!'). (The poem as given in *Artist and Illustrator* was repeated without correction by John Garth in *Tolkien and the Great War* (2003), p. 84.) The latest version of the poem was published, with notes, commentary, and variant readings, in *The Book of Lost Tales, Part Two* (1984), pp. 271–3.

The Shores of Faery (or *Faëry*) describes, to use its earliest text and orthography, 'a lonely hill' (named in Tolkien's mythology *Kôr*), 'Beyond Taniquetil in Valinor', where 'the Two Trees naked grow / That bear Night's silver bloom; / That bear the globed fruit of Noon'. 'There are the shores of Faery' and 'the Haven of the Star' where 'Wingelot [> Vingelot] is harboured', ship of the mariner Earéndel, 'one alone / That hunted with the Moon'. Tolkien wrote its earliest extant manuscript in *The Book of Ishness* (see *Art), below the words 'The Shores of Faery' and opposite a related watercolour painting dated 10 May 1915. The latter depicts the Elvish city Kôr framed by two dying trees from whose branches grow a crescent Moon (framing a star) and a blazing Sun (see *Artist and Illustrator*, fig. 44).

Tolkien wrote a date of composition of the poem, 'July 8–9 1915', on the second of its four versions, contained in a notebook of fair copies. That manuscript, incorporating slight changes, was joined by a brief prose preface in which Tolkien describes Ëarendel (now spelled thus) as 'the Wanderer who beat about the Oceans of the World' and eventually launched his ship on 'the Oceans of the Firmament', but hunted by the Moon he fled back to Valinor where he gazed at the Oceans of the World from the towers of Kôr. (A subsequent version of the preface was published in *The Book of Lost Tales, Part Two*, p. 262.) Later Tolkien inscribed typescripts of the poem 'Moseley & Edgb[aston] July 1915 (walking and on bus). Retouched often since – esp 1924' and 'First poem of my mythology Valinor [?thought of about] 1910'.

In *Artist and Illustrator*, p. 47, we rashly stated that the date written on the fair copy manuscript was 'mistakenly assigned' by Tolkien; in the first reprint of our book this was emended to 'elsewhere assigned'. We felt, however, that since the earliest surviving version of the poem in *The Book of Ishness* was written opposite a painting dated 10 May 1915 which depicts many of the elements mentioned in the verses, both picture and poem may have been produced at roughly the same time in May, and the July dates on subsequent versions may reflect revision rather than original composition. On re-examination of the physical evidence (see further, **Chronology**), this still seems possible, even likely. The words 'The Shores of Faery' on the page facing the watercolour are centred in the same manner as the titles of two other watercolours in the same section of *The Book of Ishness*, from which one may easily infer that the phrase is meant to be the title of the facing picture. Below these words Tolkien wrote out the poem now known as *The Shores of Faery*, but whether he meant that to be the title of the poem as well as of the picture, or the verses simply have become associated with the title by proximity, is impossible to say. (It could be just as well that the first lines of the poem – 'WEST of the MOON | EAST of the SUN' – written in larger letters above the rest, were the intended title of this version, or rather 'East of the Moon, West of the Sun' as emended in the manuscript, recalling the title of a Norwegian fairy-tale; but 'The Shores of Faery' persisted.) The poem in fact appears not to have been written out at the same time as the title. Its verses are not centred under the words 'The Shores of Faery', and are written less carefully: Tolkien found that he did not have enough space for the last five lines, and placed them in a second column to the extreme right of the page.

It may be, then, that the picture *The Shores of Faery* preceded the poem of the same title, or at least preceded its earliest extant manuscript: for that appears to be a fair copy, which implies the existence of earlier workings (now lost). In any case, Tolkien was certainly pondering much of the content of the poem already in May, in order to depict it early that month in the watercolour.

Although the demonstrably earlier poem *The Voyage of Éarendel the Evening Star* (*Éalá Éarendel Engla Beorhtast*) contains elements that became part of Tolkien's *legendarium*, it was not written as part of that larger work, which may be why Tolkien gave chronological priority to *The Shores of Faery* in one of his inscriptions as the 'first poem of my mythology'. *The Shores of Faery* is, at least, one of several early poems by Tolkien concerning Eärendel (variously spelled), who figured prominently in his mythology (*'The Silmarillion') as it developed: see further, *'Of the Voyage of Eärendil and the War of Wrath'.

'Sí Qente Feanor'. Prose text in Qenya (*Languages, Invented), published with commentary and notes in *Parma Eldalamberon* 15 (2004), pp. 31–40, ed. Christopher Gilson. The thirteen-line passage in Qenya consists of two sentences spoken by Fëanor (the assigned title is Qenya 'thus spoke Fëanor') and a brief explanation of the circumstances. It is associated with *The Nauglafring: The Necklace of the Dwarves* (*The Book of Lost Tales*), and seems to date from the first half of 1919.

Sidmouth (Devon). A dignified seaside town on the south coast of Devon, where the Tolkien family took a summer holiday each year from 1934 to 1938. *John and *Priscilla Tolkien recalled that Sidmouth 'spread out from a core of elegant Regency and Victorian houses, but its hinterland consisted of the remains of the original fishing village. . . .' Their father would drive to Sidmouth with the family luggage, which left room for only himself in the car, while *Edith, *Christopher, and Priscilla travelled by train, and John and *Michael went down on their bicycles. Between 1934 and 1937 they stayed 'at a house called "Aurora" in the older part of the town, settling down to a routine of swimming, sitting on the beach, shopping in town, playing clock-golf on the green opposite and making expeditions to more distant beaches to collect beautiful, rare shells like cowries' (*The Tolkien Family Album*, pp. 64–5, with photographs).

In summer 1938 Tolkien wrote part of *The Lord of the Rings* at Sidmouth, the last holiday in that town for the entire Tolkien family, parents and four children. Michael Tolkien was appointed to coastal defence in Sidmouth in 1941. After the war, Tolkien and his wife continued to visit Sidmouth, sometimes with Priscilla. In a letter to Christopher written in June 1971 Tolkien described a late holiday in Sidmouth as very pleasant indeed. We were lucky in our time . . . and we came in for a 'spring explosion' of glory, with Devon passing from brown to brilliant yellow-green, and all the flowers leaping out of dead bracken or old grass. . . .

The Belmont proved a v[ery]g[ood] choice. Indeed the chief changes we observed in Sidmouth was the rise of this rather grim looking hotel (in spite of its perfect position) to be the best in the place – especially for *eating*. . . . Neither M[other] nor I have eaten so much in a week (without indigestion) for years. In addition our faithful cruise-friends (Boarland) of some six years ago, who recently moved to Sidmouth, and were so anxious to see us again that they vetted our rooms [at] the Belmont, provided us with a car, and took us drives nearly every day. So I saw again much of the country you (especially) and I used to explore in the old days of poor JO [their car]. . . . An added comfort was the fact that Sidmouth seemed practically unchanged, even the shops: many still having the same names. . . . [*Letters*, p. 408]

Tolkien and Priscilla took Christopher's son, Simon (see *Christopher Tolkien), for a week's holiday at Sidmouth during the last week of August 1972.

Sigelwara Land. Article, published in two parts in *Medium Ævum* 1, no. 3 (December 1932), pp. 183–96, and 3, no. 2 (June 1934), pp. 95–111.

The name *Sigelhearwan* (or *Sigelwaran*, i.e. Ethiopians) and its forms occur frequently in Old English manuscripts. These are remarkable because 'classical or biblical proper names are not usually translated [here from *Æthiopes*, *Æthiopia*, etc.] – by a word having no obvious connexion with the original. Even glosses by the learned, explaining the real or fancied meaning of names, are rare. But *Sigelhearwan* explains nothing and is itself obscure' (part 1, p. 183). Tolkien examines its elements, citing many examples: *sigel* = (chiefly) 'sun' but also 'jewel', and *hearwa* uncertain, but related to devils and blackness. But he admits that some of his analysis is guesswork and

naturally inconclusive. It seeks to probe a past probably faded even before the earliest documents, such as *Exodus*, which now preserve mention of the *Sigelhearwan*, were written. Yet it may not be pointless to have probed. Glimpses are caught, if dim and confused, of the background of English and northern tradition and imagination, which has coloured the verse-treatment of Scripture, and determined the diction of poems. *Sigel* may be taken as a symbol of the intricate blending of the Latin and Northern which makes the study of Old English peculiarly interesting and controversial. . . . [part 2, pp. 110–11]

Among other comments on *sigelhearwan* in *The Road to Middle-earth*, T.A. Shippey writes that Tolkien's speculation on the word 'offers some glimpses of a lost mythology', and in terms of Tolkien's mythology (*'The Silmarillion') it 'helped to naturalise the "Balrog" in the traditions of the North, and . . . to create (or corroborate) the image of the *silmaril*, that fusion of "sun" and "jewel" in physical form' (2nd edn. 1992, p. 39).

'The Silmarillion'. For almost sixty years, Tolkien wrote and revised a private 'mythology' or *legendarium*, which came to be called 'The Silmarillion' after the Elvish gems, the Silmarils, which are a central feature. (In the *Companion and Guide* the larger mythology is cited within quotation marks, as 'The Silmarillion', to distinguish it from the published *Silmarillion* of 1977, cited in italics. But Tolkien's own practice varied, which we have retained in quotations from his letters.) On 16 December 1937 Tolkien told *Stanley Unwin that 'the construction of elaborate and consistent mythology (and two languages [*Languages, Invented]) rather occupies the mind, and the Silmarils are in my heart'; while on 24 February 1950 he explained to Unwin how the *legendarium* affected almost everything he wrote: 'The *Silmarillion* and all that has refused to be suppressed. It has bubbled up, infiltrated, and probably spoiled everything (that even approached "Faery") which I have tried to write since. It was kept out of *Farmer Giles [of Ham]* with an effort, but stopped the continuation. Its shadow was deep on the later parts of *The Hobbit*. It has captured *The Lord of the Rings* so that that has become simply its continuation and completion' (*Letters*, pp. 136–7). He told *W.H. Auden on 23 February 1966 that he wished that the writing of any book about himself (such as Auden had proposed) 'could wait until I produce the *Silmarillion*' (*Letters*, p. 367), which was central to his life and thought. And on 25 August 1967 he wrote to *Joy Hill, asking her to decline a request for information for his '"interior" literary history', because 'there is a particular reason for not publishing anything at the present time: my work is not finished; an account of its progress and genesis is quite impossible without reference to The Silmarillion and all that which preceded what is published' (Tolkien-George Allen & Unwin archive, HarperCollins). Only with the publication of *Unfinished Tales* (1980) and *The History of Middle-earth* (1983–96) can one more fully appreciate the significance of 'The Silmarillion' in Tolkien's life.

In the **Reader's Guide** the texts that comprise 'The Silmarillion' are examined as individual entries, and as appropriate in analyses of the parts and chapters of the published *Silmarillion*. In the present entry, dates generally refer to the first writing of a work, and further dating is mentioned only where major rewriting of a significant text is concerned.

HISTORY

'The real seed' of his mythology, Tolkien told Henry Resnik, 'was starting when I was quite a child by inventing languages, largely to try and capture the esthetic mode of the languages I was learning, and I eventually made the discovery that language can't exist in a void. . . . It had to come alive – so really the languages came first and the country after' ('An Interview with Tolkien',

Niekas 18 (Spring 1967), p. 41). Tolkien makes it clear, however, in his famous letter to *Milton Waldman of ?late 1951, that 'The Silmarillion' was founded as much on a love of story-telling as on a love of language:

> An equally basic passion of mine *ab initio* was for myth (not *allegory!) and for fairy-story [*fairy-stories], and above all for heroic legend on the bring of fairy-tale and history, of which there is far too little in the world (accessible to me) for my appetite. . . . Also – and here I hope I shall not sound absurd – I was from early days grieved by the poverty of my own beloved country: it had no stories of its own (bound up with its tongue and soil), not of the quality that I sought, and found (as an ingredient) in legends of other lands. . . . [*Letters*, p. 144]

Tolkien also wrote to Milton Waldman:

> Do not laugh! But once upon a time (my crest has long since fallen) I had a mind to make a body of more or less connected legend, ranging from the large and cosmogonic, to the level of romantic fairy-story – the larger founded on the lesser in contact with the earth, the lesser drawing splendour from the vast backcloths – which I could dedicate simply to: to *England; to my country. It should possess the tone and quality that I desired, somewhat cool and clear, be redolent of our 'air' (the clime and soil of the North West, meaning Britain and the hither parts of Europe: not Italy or the Aegean, still less the East), and, while possessing (if I could achieve it) the fair elusive beauty that some call Celtic (though it is rarely found in genuine ancient Celtic things), it should be 'high', purged of the gross, and fit for the more adult mind of a land long now steeped in poetry. I would draw some of the great tales in fullness, and leave many only placed in the scheme, and sketched. The cycles should be linked to a majestic whole, and yet leave scope for other minds and hands, wielding paint and music and drama. Absurd.
>
> Of course, such an overweening purpose did not develop all at once. The mere stories were the thing. They arose in my mind as 'given' things, and as they came, separately, so too the links grew. An absorbing, though continually interrupted labour (especially since, even apart from the necessities of life, the mind would wing to the other pole and spend itself on the linguistics). . . . [*Letters*, pp. 144–5]

Here Tolkien may be excused for waxing eloquent: his letter was intended not only to explain his mythology to Waldman, but also to sell it to the publisher Collins, for whom Waldman worked and who had become reluctant to take a work as long as 'The Silmarillion', in addition to *The Lord of the Rings*. The literary origins of the mythology were much more modest and tentative. They may be traced back, on the one hand, to a series of poems Tolkien began to compose in autumn 1914 and continued to write and revise for the next few years. Not all were necessarily connected to 'The Silmarillion' when first written (in so far as a coherent mythology had even begun to exist), and some are connected only peripherally. The most significant of these are *The Voyage of Éarendel the Evening Star* (**Éalá Éarendel Engla Beorhtast*); *Sea-Chant of an Elder Day* (**The Horns of Ylmir*); **The Bidding of the Minstrel*; *Why the Man in the Moon Came Down Too Soon* (**The Man in the Moon Came Down Too Soon*); *You & Me and the Cottage of Lost Play* (**The Little House of Lost Play: Mar Vanwa Tyaliéva*); **Tinfang Warble*; *Kôr: In a City Lost and Dead* (**The City of the Gods*); **The Shores of Faery*; **The Happy Mariners*; **A Song of Aryador*; *Kortirion among the Trees* (**The Trees of Kortirion*); **Narqelion*; **Over the Hills and Far Away*; **The Lonely Isle*; and **Habbanan beneath the Stars* (see individual entries for comment). But Tolkien also, in the period March–?May 1915, made several watercolour paintings related to 'The Silmarillion', most of them illustrating poems: in three cases, *Water, Wind & Sand* (associated with *Sea-Chant of an Elder Day*), *The Shores of Faery*, and *Why the Man in the Moon Came Down Too Soon*, he may have depicted elements of the mythology in pictorial art first, and only later in words. A fourth watercolour, *Tanaqui*, is connected with the poem *Kôr: In a City Lost and Dead*. (See further, *Artist and Illustrator*, ch. 2.)

At this time Tolkien hoped to make his name as a poet, and was encouraged by his friends in the *T.C.B.S., especially *G.B. Smith, and by his former schoolmaster *R.W. Reynolds. Probably in early May 1915 he had copies of many of his poems professionally typed and made them into a booklet. He seems to have thought to submit them to a publisher, and asked his friends for advice. On 2 August 1915 R.W. Reynolds wrote to him:

> At ordinary times I should certainly counsel you to wait and get your name known a little to the public and the reviewers by publishing single poems in the weeklies and monthlies before embarking on a volume. It would stand a much better chance then of getting properly appreciated and noticed. . . . But these are not ordinary times. The odds are against your being able to have the leisure for some time to come to go bombarding editors and publishing verses. The poems are there, and you and your friends – among whom I hope I may count myself – would naturally like to see them put into a more permanent and accessible form from those scattered sheets of typescript. . . . It is hardly necessary to warn you that you must be prepared for the book to fall very very flat. Neither readers nor reviewers have any attention to give to poetry just now, nor are likely to for some time to come. [Tolkien Papers, Bodleian Library, Oxford]

On 5 October 1915 *R.Q. Gilson wrote that he and G.B. Smith thought that Tolkien should submit his poems to the London publisher Sidgwick & Jackson; and on 9 October Smith wrote suggesting the same, or else the publisher Hodder and Stoughton. Early in 1916 Tolkien sent the proposed volume to Sidgwick & Jackson, with the title *The Trumpets of Faerie*. After it was rejected on 31 March 1916, Tolkien seems to have made no further effort to publish it – no attempt, indeed, to publish 'The Silmarillion', except for a few independent poems, until 1937.

Instead he began to record, probably during 1916, in a notebook and on slips of paper, ideas for what would become *The Book of Lost Tales. He commenced actual writing of that lengthy prose text towards the end of 1916 or the beginning of 1917. The 'lost tales', told to the mariner Eriol by Elves living in Tol Eressëa, relate the greater part of the mythology except for an account of early events after the Noldoli return to Middle-earth, and of events after the fall of Gondolin, for which there are only brief notes. Tolkien was inspired to write one of the most important tales, that of Beren and Lúthien (*'Of Beren and Lúthien'), as well as the poem *Light as Leaf on Lindentree (1919–20), when his wife *Edith danced for him in a wood at Roos (*Yorkshire) probably in May or June 1917. After June 1919, however, he apparently did little work on the Lost Tales (see *A Middle English Vocabulary), and abandoned it c. 1920, at the last deciding to reorganize its framework, substituting Ælfwine for Eriol and writing an account of how Ælfwine came to Tol Eressëa (see *Eriol and Ælfwine).

Tolkien seems to have been uncertain whether to continue 'The Silmarillion' in prose or turn most of his attention to verse. A few prose fragments probably date from his first year at *Leeds, c. 1920–1: *Turlin and the Exiles of Gondolin, *'The Gnomes Come to the Great Lands', and *'Flight of the Gnomes'. An unfinished poem, *The Lay of the Fall of Gondolin, belongs to the same period. Tolkien may written a little of *The Children of Húrin in alliterative verse as early as 1919, but the bulk of it was composed at Leeds from c. 1921 to early 1925. Two short poems, Iumonna Gold Galdre Bewunden (*The Hoard) and *The Nameless Land, also date from this period (?end of 1922 and May 1924 respectively). Between abandoning The Children of Húrin early in 1925 and commencing work on the *Lay of Leithien during the summer examinations of that year (?July), Tolkien began but soon abandoned two poems in alliterative verse: *The Flight of the Noldoli from Valinor and a *'Lay of Earendel'. For the Lay of Leithian, on which he worked from summer 1925 to September 1931, he abandoned alliterative verse in favour of octosyllabic couplets.

In the first part of 1926 Tolkien lent The Children of Húrin and the beginning of the Lay of Leithian to R.W. Reynolds. At the same time, he wrote a prose *Sketch of the Mythology to set The Children of Húrin in the context of the entire legendarium. Although only a synopsis, the Sketch is important as the first complete account of the Elder Days, excepting only an account of Creation. Tolkien recorded of Reynolds' comments: 'Tinúviel [the Lay of Leithian] meets with qualified approval, it is too prolix, but how could I ever cut it down, and the specimen I sent of Túrin [The Children of Húrin] with little or none' (diary, quoted in *The Lays of Beleriand, p. 3). By this time he had already abandoned The Children of Húrin, but he continued to develop the Lay of Leithian, and at the end of 1929 lent a much longer section of that work to C.S. Lewis.

Probably between 1926 and 1930 Tolkien made the first 'Silmarillion' Map (see below). During summer holidays in 1927 and 1928 he made several paintings and drawings related to 'The Silmarillion', including *Glórund Sets Forth to Seek Túrin, Mithrim, Nargothrond* (two pictures), *Taur-na-Fúin, Halls of Manwë on the Mountains of the World above Faerie* (also known as *Taniquetil*), *The Vale of Tol Sirion, Gondolin & the Vale of Tumladin*, and a rough sketch of Hirilorn and Lúthien's hut; see *Artist and Illustrator*, ch. 2. In this period Tolkien also developed the *Sketch of the Mythology*, and *c.* 1930 wrote an expanded version, the **Quenta Noldorinwa*, incorporating changes in the story of Beren and Lúthien made in the *Lay of Leithian*. More fully, the *Quenta Noldorinwa* is 'the brief History of the Noldoli or Gnomes, drawn from the Book of Lost Tales which Eriol of Leithien wrote, having read the *Golden Book*, which the Eldar call *Parma Kuluina*, in Kortirion in Tol Eressëa, the Lonely Isle' (**The Shaping of Middle-earth*, pp. 77–8). **Christopher Tolkien has suggested that it was for his own use while working on the *Quenta Noldorinwa* that his father wrote the earliest versions of the **Annals of Beleriand* and **Annals of Valinor*, 'as a convenient way of driving abreast, and keeping track of, the different elements in the ever more complex narrative web' (*The Shaping of Middle-earth*, p. 294). At length, however, the *Annals* became more than an aid to the author, but part of 'The Silmarillion' itself.

Tolkien made more detailed versions of these works, as well as new texts, beginning in the mid-1930s. According to a manuscript title-page made at the end of 1937 or beginning of 1938, some were to be parts of a book with the overall title *The Silmarillion*: 'the history of the Three Jewels, the Silmarils of Fëanor, in which is told in brief the history of the Elves from their coming until the Change of the World'. Its contents are listed as the '*Qenta Silmarillion*, or *Pennas Hilevril*', a much enlarged, but unfinished, version of the *Qenta Noldorinwa* (see **Quenta Silmarillion*), 'to which is appended The houses of the princes of Men and Elves' (presumably emended versions of genealogies associated with the 'earliest' *Annals of Beleriand*), 'The tale of years' (a more concise form of the *Annals*, see **The Tale of Years*), and 'The tale of battles'; *The Annals of Valinor; The Annals of Beleriand*; and 'The **Lhammas* or Account of Tongues' (**The Lost Road and Other Writings*, p. 202). A later title-page excludes the *Lhammas*. Although during this period Tolkien also wrote the **Ainulindalë* (a retelling of the Creation myth, compare *The Music of the Ainur* in *The Book of Lost Tales*), the **Ambarkanta* (describing the shape or fashion of the world), and the **Etymologies* (a vocabulary of Elvish languages), these are not listed on any of the extant title-pages that Tolkien made for *The Silmarillion*.

In late 1937 Tolkien offered the *Ainulindalë* and *Ambarkanta*, with the *Lay of Leithian*, the *Quenta Silmarillion*, the story **The Lost Road* partly set in **Númenor*, and a new work, **The Fall of Númenor*, to George Allen & Unwin (**Publishers*) for consideration as possible successors to *The Hobbit*. He did not expect these to be accepted, but wondered whether 'The Silmarillion' had any value in itself, 'or as a marketable commodity' (letter to **Stanley Unwin, 15 October 1937). In the event, among these papers only the *Lay of Leithian* was given to a publisher's reader, and he found it to be 'of a very thin, if not always downright bad, quality' (Edward Crankshaw, report to Allen & Unwin, Tolkien-George Allen & Unwin archive). The other 'Silmarillion' works were apparently too disordered, or their relationship to one another too confused, to warrant (or permit) formal reading. The publisher's report to Tolkien was kind, but misleading in that it failed to convey how fully the 'Silmarillion' matter was rejected. Tolkien wrote to Stanley Unwin on 16 December 1937: 'I have suffered a sense of fear and bereavement, quite ridiculous, since I let this private and beloved nonsense out; and I think if it had seemed to you to be nonsense I should have felt really crushed. . . . I shall certainly now hope one day to be able, or to be able to afford, to publish the Silmarillion!' Convinced now that 'a sequel or successor to The Hobbit [was] called for' (*Letters*, p. 26), within days he began to write *The Lord of the Rings*.

It is tempting to wonder what would have happened if Allen & Unwin had found any part of 'The Silmarillion', as it stood at that stage, worthy of publication. If Stanley Unwin had not pressed Tolkien for another work about Hobbits, *The Lord of the Rings* might never have come to be. Instead, because Tolkien turned his thoughts to a *Hobbit* sequel, he set the *Quenta Silmarillion* aside; and by the time the success of *The Lord of the Rings* made Allen & Unwin keen to publish *The Silmarillion*, Tolkien found himself unable to complete the *Quenta Silmarillion* and prepare it for publication together with related texts.

For several years his attention as a writer of fiction was devoted mainly to *The Lord of the Rings*, and to the further development of the matter of Númenor in **The Notion Club Papers* and **The Drowning of Anadûnê*. Then in 1948 his friend *Katharine Farrer, who had heard of 'The Silmarillion', evidently asked to be allowed to read it. He collected for lending to her 'out of the unfinished mass such things as are more or less finished and readable (I mean legible). You may find the "compendious history" or [*Quenta*] *Silmarillion* tolerable – though it is only really half-revised' (letter of 15 June 1948, *Letters*, p. 130). In a draft for this letter Tolkien wrote: 'I have ventured to include, besides the "Silmarillion" or main chronicle [the *Quenta Silmarillion*], one or two other connected "myths": "The Music of the Ainur", the Beginning [the *Ainulindalë*]; and the Later Tales: "The Rings of Power" [**Of the Rings of Power and the Third Age*], and "The Fall of Númenor", which link up with Hobbit-lore of the later or "Third Age"' (quoted in **Morgoth's Ring*, p. 5). By this date, Tolkien's projected *Silmarillion* was to include two works, one dealing with the Second Age, and one with the Second and Third Ages, firmly linking the First Age of original 'Silmarillion' with *The Hobbit* and *The Lord of the Rings*. Another draft indicates that Tolkien sent Farrer alternative versions of two works which formed part of the larger *Silmarillion*: a 'Round World' version of the *Ainulindalë*, written *c*. 1946, in which the Earth is round from its creation, rather than made round through a later cataclysm; and 'A "Man's" version of the *Fall of Númenor* told from men's point of view. . . . ***"The Drowning of Anadûnë". This also is "Round World"' (quoted in *Morgoth's Ring*, p. 5).

Tolkien also mentioned in his letter to Katharine Farrer 'the long tales out of which [the *Silmarillion*] is drawn', which 'are either incomplete or not up to date' (*Letters*, p. 130). He identified these as *The Fall of Gondolin*, *The Lay of Beren and Lúthien* (i.e. the *Lay of Leithian*), and *The Children of Húrin*. By *The Fall of Gondolin* he must have meant the story as told in *The Book of Lost Tales*, the final version of which by this time was almost thirty years old.

In October 1948 Katharine Farrer wrote to Tolkien that she liked 'the Flat Earth versions best' (*Morgoth's Ring*, p. 6) – the earlier *Ainulindalë*. Possibly influenced by her opinion, Tolkien now produced a new version of the *Ainulindalë*, incorporating elements from both of its preceding versions. While working on the Appendices for *The Lord of the Rings*, *c.* 1948–51, he also wrote, in close association with the *Tale of Years* for the Second and Third Ages, *The Downfall of Númenor* or **Akallabêth*. For the latter, a third distinct account of the destruction of Númenor, Tolkien drew upon both *The Fall of Númenor* and *The Drowning of Anadûnê* to create a blend of Elvish and Mannish traditions. This seems to have been written to include in a published *Silmarillion*.

By now Tolkien had expressed to C.S. Lewis his agreement with Gerard Manley Hopkins 'that "recognition" with some understanding is in this world an essential part of authorship, and the want of it a suffering to be distinguished from (even when mixed with) mere desire for the pleasures of fame and praise' (25 January 1948, *Letters*, p. 128). Thus when, towards the end of 1949, the publisher Collins through their representative Milton Waldman showed an interest in publishing both *The Lord of the Rings* and *The Silmarillion*, if the latter could be completed, Tolkien responded eagerly. (See further, **The Lord of the Rings*.) For the next few years, he spent much time rewriting old 'Silmarillion' texts and beginning new ones. He revised and greatly expanded the *Annals of Valinor* (as the *Annals of Aman*) and the *Annals of Beleriand* (as the *Grey Annals*), so that for much of their length they became more narrative than annals, while a new version of *The Tale of Years* served the original purpose of the *Annals*. He also revised parts of the existing *Quenta Silmarillion*, but made no attempt to complete it. He began a revision of the *Lay of Leithian* and wrote a closely related prose version which does not extend far, perhaps uncertain whether verse or prose would be the most effective means of presenting the tale. Christopher Tolkien believes that after his father eventually reduced the story of Beren and Lúthien to a suitable length for the *Quenta Silmarillion*, 'he must still have felt that even if one day he could get "The Silmarillion" published, the story would still not be told as he wished to tell it' (*The Lost Road and Other Writings*, p. 295). Tolkien also began a new prose version of *The Fall of Gondolin* to be told at length, but left it unfinished (see **Of Tuor and His Coming to Gondolin*); related to this is a contemporary manuscript, *Of Meglin* (later **Of Maeglin: Sister-son of Turgon, King of Gondolin*). And he wrote much of an extensive prose version of the story of Túrin, beginning well into the story, after the fall of Nargothrond: the **Narn i Chîn Húrin*. The brief texts **Dangweth Pengoloð*, **Of Lembas*, and **Tar-Elmar* may also date from this time.

By the end of 1951, Collins not yet having committed to publication and concerned about the length of *The Silmarillion* and *The Lord of the Rings*, Tolkien wrote a long letter to Milton Waldman meant to demonstrate that the two works are interdependent and indivisible. In doing so, he provided a summary of the mythology from Creation to the end of the Third Age, which includes some indication of what Tolkien then thought *The Silmarillion* might contain: 'a cosmogonical myth: the *Music of the Ainur*' [the *Ainulindalë*]; 'the *History of the Elves*, or the *Silmarillion* proper' [the *Quenta Silmarillion*]; and for the Second Age, '[Of] The Rings of Power' [*Of the Rings of Power and the Third Age*, possibly not yet extending into the Third Age] and the *Downfall of Númenor* [the *Akallabêth*]'. He notes that if 'The Silmarillion' and other tales or links such as *The Downfall of Númenor* were published, much of the explanation of background events in *The Lord of the Rings*, especially in 'The Council of Elrond' (bk. II, ch. 2), could be omitted (?late 1951, *Letters*, pp. 146, 151, 161). He makes no mention of the *Annals*, maybe for reasons of space or clarity, but possibly because he had already realized how much in their rewritten form they overlapped with the *Quenta Silmarillion*. He mentions that 'the chief of the stories of the *Silmarillion*, and the one most fully treated is the *Story of Beren and Lúthien* the Elfmaiden', then adds a note: 'It exists indeed as a poem of considerable length, of which the prose version in *The Silmarillion* is only a reduced version' (*Letters*, p. 149). He also refers to 'other stories almost equally full in treatment, and equally independent and yet linked to the general history' (p. 150): the *Children of Húrin*, *The Fall of Gondolin*, and the tale or tales of *Earendil the Wanderer*.

Unless Tolkien was hoping to be able to complete the unfinished versions of the first three stories mentioned, and to write that of Earendil (*sic*) in a very short time, it seems unlikely that at this point he expected longer versions of these tales to be included in a Collins *Silmarillion*, as well as the account in the *Quenta Silmarillion*, or in replacement sections of that work. Indeed, he was hardly in a position to press Collins for early publication of the work if it intended their inclusion, given that his work on these longer versions had not progressed very far.

In the event, negotiations with Collins failed, and in 1952 Tolkien signed a contract with Allen & Unwin for the publication of *The Lord of the Rings* alone. Preparing that work for printing occupied most of his spare time until near the end of 1955; but even before the appearance of *The Return of the King* in October of that year, the success of *The Lord of the Rings* made *The Silmarillion* a very desirable property for Allen & Unwin. Readers of *The Lord of the Rings* looked forward to Tolkien's account of the Elder Days of Middle-earth, and wrote to ask of its progress. Some eighteen years were now left to Tolkien, in which to put his life's work at last into publishable form; but well before his death, it was clear to him that he would never finish the task.

There were many reasons for this. He did not retire from his chair at Oxford until mid-1959, and even after that he needed to spend time on his long overdue edition of the **Ancrene Wisse*. He was 'no longer young enough to pillage the night to make up for the deficit of hours in the day' (letter to Lord Halsbury, 10 November 1955, *Letters*, p. 228), and occasionally ill (see *Health). His wife's health too was a constant worry; and Tolkien and Edith moved house twice during the period, with attendant disruption. Although Allen & Unwin relieved him of as much correspondence as possible, there were many letters that they could not answer. In addition, Tolkien received frequent requests for interviews, autographs, and endorsements, and uninvited visitors and telephone calls. The *Ace Books controversy, and consequent revision of *The Lord of the Rings* and *The Hobbit*, occupied much of his time in 1965–6; later he was distracted by proposals for filming his works. Allen & Unwin themselves, anxious to keep Tolkien's name before his public, suggested or encouraged new projects which they thought would not involve Tolkien in much work, but in fact often did: thus *The Adventures of Tom Bombadil and Other Verses From the Red Book* was published in 1962, *Tree and Leaf* in 1964, and *Smith of Wootton Major* in 1967. Tolkien also worked on his translations of *Sir Gawain and the Green Knight* and *Pearl* (not published until after his death), and with Donald Swann on *The Road Goes Ever On: A Song Cycle* (1967).

When he did turn to 'The Silmarillion', matters were not as straightforward as they had been. In the 1930s Tolkien seems to have had a clear idea of the shape of a published *Silmarillion*; but now, 'Silmarillion' material had accumulated over the years, and most of its texts were unfinished or unrevised. Since, after the success of *The Lord of the Rings*, it was unlikely that Allen & Unwin would impose restrictions of length, Tolkien could consider the inclusion of longer versions of his major tales. Their revision was complicated, however, by the fact that Tolkien began to doubt some of the fundamental elements of his mythology, and considered whether to make drastic changes in its cosmology: the existence of the Sun and a round Earth from the beginning. As he worked on material, new ideas for stories or background material arose in his mind, and he considered whether to include some of these in *The Silmarillion*. He wondered even if the longer versions of the great stories (of Beren and Lúthien, Turin, Tuor, and Eärendil) should be included. Christopher Tolkien wrote: 'My father came to conceive *The Silmarillion* as a compilation, a compendious narrative, made long afterwards from sources of great diversity (poems, and annals, and oral tales) that had survived in agelong tradition' (*The Silmarillion*, p. 8). During these years, Tolkien made only a few statements of what he thought a published *Silmarillion* might include, and these were not in agreement with each other. His ideas seem to have changed frequently.

At the end of the 1950s he did more work on existing texts. After rewriting the first chapter of the *Quenta Silmarillion*, he decided to make it a separate work, the *Valaquenta*. He introduced some major changes elsewhere in parts of the *Quenta Silmarillion*, which involved substantial thought and rewriting. Christopher Tolkien has said that the rewritten chapters of this phase of work show his father 'moving strongly into a new conception of the work, a newer and much fuller mode of narrative – envisaging, as it appears, a thorough-going "re-expansion" from the still fairly condensed form (despite a good deal of enlargement in the 1951 revision) . . .' (*Morgoth's Ring*, p. 142). But to Christopher 'the most remarkable fact in the whole history of *The Silmarillion*' was that his father did no work on the last chapters of the *Quenta Silmarillion*: '(the tale of Húrin and the dragon-gold of Nargothrond, the Necklace of the Dwarves, the ruin of Doriath, the fall of Gondolin, the Kinslayings) remained in the form of the *Quenta Noldorinwa* of 1930 and were never touched again' (**The War of the Jewels*, p. viii). He suggests that his father may have wanted to write these stories at length before dealing with the relevant chapters in the *Quenta Silmarillion*.

Tolkien did return to the *Narn i Chîn Húrin* and write an account of Túrin's early years, but abandoned it long before he reached the end of Túrin's story which he had written at the beginning of the 1950s. He began *The Wanderings of Húrin*, which took up the story after the death of Túrin, a projected account of what happened to Húrin after he was released by Morgoth, but wrote only of Húrin's actions in Brethil and not the intended continuation of Húrin and Doriath and the story of the Necklace of the Dwarves. In association with the introduction of the remarriage of Finwë Tolkien also wrote **Laws and Customs among the Eldar*, **The Converse of Manwë and Eru*, and **Reincarnation of Elves*. Other texts connected to 'The Silmarillion' from the end of the decade (with varying degrees of certainty) include **Aman*; *Concerning Galadriel and Celeborn* and *The Elessar* (both, see **The History of Galadriel and Celeborn and of Amroth King of Lórien*); various works considering problems of cosmology and the nature of evil, among which are **Melkor Morgoth*, **Notes on Motives in the Silmarillion*, **Orcs*, and **Sun The Trees Silmarils*; and **Quendi and Eldar*, with the *Ósanwe-kenta*. In 1960 he devoted more time to Númenor, writing **Aldarion and Erendis*, **A Description of the Isle of Númenor*, and **The Line of Elros: Kings of Númenor*, and in the autumn produced watercolours depicting heraldic devices and elven and Númenórean artefacts. Later texts connected with the *legendarium* include **Of the Ents and the Eagles*, perhaps from autumn 1963; **The Problem of Ros*, **The Rivers and Beacon-hills of Gondor*, and **The Shibboleth of Fëanor*, from 1969; discussions of Círdan the Shipwright (**Círdan*) and of Elvish reincarnation leading to one on the 'reincarnation' of Dwarves (**'Elvish Reincarnation'*), a note on the landing of the Five Wizards (**The Five Wizards*), an account of Glorfindel (**Glorfindel*), and notes on the Istari (**The Istari*), from 1972 or 1973; and an account of Galadriel (see **The History of Galadriel and Celeborn and of Amroth King of Lórien*) written in August 1973, the last month of Tolkien's life.

In a memorandum, probably typed before 1959, concerning 'the three Great Tales', Tolkien asked: 'Should not these be given as Appendices to the *Silmarillion*?' (*Morgoth's Ring*, p. 373). The Tales in question were '(1) *Narn Beren ion Barahir* [Tale of Beren son of Barahir] also called *Narn e·Dinúviel* (Tale of the Nightingale). (2) *Narn e·mbar Hador* [Tale of the House of Hador] containing (a) *Narn i·Chîn Hurin* (or *Narn e·'Rach Morgoth* Tale of the Curse of Morgoth); and (b) *Narn en·Êl* [Tale of the Star] or (*Narn e·Dant Gondolin ar Orthad en·Êl* [Tale of the Fall of Gondolin and the Rising of the Star]' (*Morgoth's*

Ring, p. 373). This suggests that he was considering whether to make the tales of Túrin and Tuor (both great-grandsons of Hador) subdivisions of one long history of the descendants of Hador. The alternative title for the *Narn i Chîn Húrin* may indicate that he was thinking of extending the tale of Túrin to include *The Wanderings of Húrin*; but the titles of the final item leave no doubt that it would tell not only the story of Tuor and the fall of Gondolin, but also that of Eärendil.

On the newspaper of January 1960 in which he wrapped another work of the late 1950s, the **Athrabeth Finrod ah Andreth*, Tolkien wrote 'Addit. Silmarillion' and 'Should be last item in an appendix' (i.e. to *The Silmarillion*) (*Morgoth's Ring*, p. 329). On 12 September 1965 Tolkien wrote to Dick Plotz, referring to 'the "Silmarillion" and its appendages', and said that

> there is also a large amount of matter that is not strictly part of the [*Quenta*] *Silmarillion*: cosmogony [*Ainulindalë*] and matter concerning the Valar [*Valaquenta*]; and later matter concerning Númenor, and the War in Middle-earth (fall of Eregion and death of Celebrimbor, and the history of Celeborn and Galadriel) [*Of the Rings of Power and the Third Age*, and possibly *Concerning Galadriel and Celeborn*, see **The History of Galadriel and Celeborn and of Amroth King of Lórien*]. As for Númenor, the tale of the *Akallabêth* or Downfall is fully written. The rest of its internal history is only in Annal form, and will probably remain so, except for one long Númenórean tale: *The Mariner's Wife* [i.e. *Aldarion and Erendis*]. [*Letters*, pp. 359–60]

It is not clear from this if Tolkien meant to include *Aldarion and Erendis* in a published *Silmarillion*. In a note to *The Shibboleth of Fëanor*, 1968 or later, Tolkien refers to *The Silmarillion* as a 'compilation' which includes 'the four great tales or lays of the heroes of the Atani [Men]' (**The Peoples of Middle-earth*, p. 357). A few years earlier, he had referred to the *three* great tales, but the titles seem to suggest that the stories of Tuor and Eärendil might be told in one *Narn*. Earlier still, in his letter to Milton Waldman, he had mentioned these as separate tales.

Tolkien pondered how to present his *Silmarillion*, and took note of what appealed to readers in *The Lord of the Rings*. He wrote to Colonel Worskett on 20 September 1963 that

> the legends have to be worked over ... and made consistent; and they have to be integrated with [*The Lord of the Rings*]; and they have to be given some progressive shape. No simple device, like a journey and a quest, is available.
>
> I am doubtful myself about the undertaking. Part of the attraction of The L.R. is, I think, due to the glimpses of a large history in the background: an attraction like that of viewing far off an unvisited island, or seeing the towers of a distant city gleaming in a sunlit mist. To go there is

to destroy the magic, unless new unattainable vistas are again revealed. [*Letters*, p. 333]

In *The Book of Lost Tales, Part One* Christopher Tolkien quotes this letter and says that, nonetheless, 'in the latest writing there is no trace or suggestion of any "device" or "framework" in which it was to be set. I think that in the end [my father] concluded that nothing would serve, and no more would be said beyond an explanation of how (within the imagined world) it came to be recorded' (p. 5). He then comments on the *Translations from the Elvish* given by Bilbo to Frodo at the end of *The Lord of the Rings*, and on Robert Foster's assumption in *The Complete Guide to Middle-earth*, which Christopher Tolkien accepts (though it can be no more than supposition), that one of these was to be the *Quenta Silmarillion*. In support of this idea is a report by Dick Plotz that when he visited Tolkien on 1 November 1966,

he, half-heartedly I suppose, was thinking up schemes for rendering the *Silmarillion* publishable. So far, I think what he is doing is relating it to Bilbo's stay in Rivendell, which is what he said to me.

Now there is a hint of this somewhere in the *Lord of the Rings*. . . . But apparently when Bilbo went to Rivendell he was surrounded by Elves and all Elven records for seventeen years. Here was living history and he attempted to write it down, and this is what became the *Silmarillion*. ['An Edited Transcript of Remarks at the December 1966 TSA [Tolkien Society of America] Meeting', *Niekas* 19 (Spring 1967), p. 40]

Tolkien certainly did not intend everything he wrote in his later years to be included in a published *Silmarillion*. Much of it was a working out of theory or events behind a text which might be included, or often just to satisfy his own interest. This is not to say that he was against the publication of such writings: on 29 February 1960 he asked Rayner Unwin if he would 'have any objection to me publishing any separate or minor items belonging to the Ring cycle? . . . The things I have in mind are not integral parts of the Silmarillion, and for some of them it is very likely that no place will be found in that work, but I suppose I could publish them without in any way affecting the question of their inclusion in the major work if necessary' (Tolkien–George Allen & Unwin archive, HarperCollins). In the event, he himself published none of this material, and it was left to his son Christopher to do so, selecting from the great mass of 'Silmarillion' papers for *Unfinished Tales*, *The History of Middle-earth*, and *The Silmarillion* itself.

See **The Hobbit* for a discussion of its relationship to 'The Silmarillion'.

INTERNAL SOURCES

The history of 'The Silmarillion' may be expressed also in terms of how its texts cite internal 'sources': witnesses to events, written works and their authors, paths of transmission. The source of *The Book of Lost Tales* is a mariner from Western Europe, Eriol or Ælfwine, who was told stories of the Elves while in Tol Eressëa; but several of the story-tellers themselves have sources: Littleheart, for instance, who tells of the fall of Gondolin, is the son of Voronwë who accompanied Tuor to that city. Tolkien's notes for unwritten parts or proposed changes indicate that Eriol or Ælfwine would record all that he heard in the 'Golden Book', or perhaps the Golden Book would be compiled by Eriol's son from his father's writings.

Although Tolkien abandoned the framework of *The Book of Lost Tales* in later 'Silmarillion' writings, Eriol/Ælfwine continued to play a role in recording or transmitting the history of the Elves, as the Anglo-Saxon Ælfwine, called by the Elves *Eriol*. The writings of Eriol seem to be the source of the *Sketch of the Mythology* and (originally) the *Quenta Noldorinwa*. In 'Silmarillion' works of the 1930s he became merely the translator of works written by Pengolod the Wise of Gondolin, including the *Quenta Noldorinwa*, the *Annals of Valinor*, and the *Annals of Beleriand*; while Pengolod is said in turn to have derived material for the *Annals of Valinor* and the *Lhammas* from the writings of Rúmil the Elfsage of Valinor. The *Ambarkanta* and the *Ainulindalë* are said to have been written by Rúmil of Tûn, and transmitted to Ælfwine, and the *Quenta Silmarillion* was composed in brief by Pengolod, who drew on many older and fuller accounts, and translated by Ælfwine. This fictional account echoes fact, for behind the *Quenta Silmarillion* lie Tolkien's longer treatments of the stories in *The Book of Lost Tales*, *The Children of Húrin* and the *Lay of Leithian*. Later, preambles for a work called *The Silmarillion*, comprising both sets of *Annals*, the *Quenta Silmarillion*, and possibly the *Lhammas*, indicate that Ælfwine's Old English translation of Pengolod's work had now been 'translated' into Modern English.

The extension of the *legendarium* during the second half of the 1930s into a Second Age, with the history of the island of Númenor inhabited by Men in touch with both the Elves of Tol Eressëa and Men of Middle-earth, opened new possibilities for the transmission of the history of the Elves. Tolkien took these up at a later date, when he began to feel uneasy about presenting a cosmology in contravention of known scientific facts.

In new writing and revisions *c.* 1948–51, little change was made in the transmission of texts, but more emphasis laid on the sources of information. In the *Ainulindalë* Pengoloð provides extra information in response to Ælfwine's questions, and significantly, this includes a tale he had heard among the loremasters of the Noldor in ages past. In the *Quenta Silmarillion* Ælfwine cites additional written sources for certain material. In the *Annals of Aman* (successor to the *Annals of Valinor*) Rúmil is described as the 'most renowned of the masters of the lore of speech' (*Morgoth's Ring*, p. 92). A later typescript of the beginning of the *Annals* provides a different mode of transition from that of Rúmil > Pengolod > Ælfwine: 'Rúmil made them in the Elder Days, and they were held in memory by the Exiles [the Noldor in Middle-earth]. Those parts which we learned and remembered were thus set down in Númenor before the

Shadow fell upon it' (*Morgoth's Ring*, pp. 64–5). The *Grey Annals* (successor to the *Annals of Beleriand*) are said to have been made 'by the Sindar, the Grey Elves of Doriath and the Havens, and enlarged from the records and memories of the remnant of the Noldor of Nargothrond and Gondolin at the Mouths of Sirion, whence they were brought back into the West' (*The War of the Jewels*, p. 5). The *Dangweth Pengoloð*, and *Of Lembas*, are said to record Pengoloð's answers to queries from Ælfwine.

Towards the end of the 1950s Men began to play a more prominent part in the internal transmission of 'Silmarillion' texts. Christopher Tolkien comments of *Laws and Customs among the Eldar* that it is clearly 'presented as the work, not of one of the Eldar, but of a Man' (*Morgoth's Ring*, p. 208). Though the published *Athrabeth Finrod ah Andreth* is said to have been recorded in the ancient lore of the Eldar, other accounts, edited under Númenórean influence and derived from the traditions of the People of Marach, are also mentioned. In notes to the commentary on this work Tolkien stated that 'all Elvish traditions are presented as "histories", or as accounts of what once was' (*Morgoth's Ring*, p. 342). *Ælfwine and Dírhaval*, an introductory note to the *Narn i Chîn Húrin*, gives two accounts of its writing. One, written by its translator into Modern English, says that Ælfwine translated into prose the *Húrinien*, a lay written in Elvish by a Man, Dírhavel, who had 'lived at the Havens in the days of Ëarendel and there gathered all the tidings and lore that he could of the House of Hador, whether among Men or Elves, remnants and fugitives of Dorlómin, of Nargothrond, or of Doriath' (*The War of the Jewels*, p. 311). The other, written by Ælfwine, lists even more sources used by Dírhaval [*sic*], and says that he had help from the Elves in making his translation.

Various works written by Tolkien c. 1959–60 stress the importance of loremasters, the gathering of information, and the preservation or passing on of writings and knowledge. In *Quendi and Eldar* Fëanor 'is credited by tradition with the foundation of a school of *Lambengolmor* or "Loremasters of Tongues"' in Valinor, which 'continued in existence among the Ñoldor, even through the rigours and disasters of the Flight from Aman and the Wars in Beleriand, and it survived indeed to return to Eressëa'; and that 'the most eminent member after the founder was, or still is, Pengolodh, an Elf of mixed Sindarin and Ñoldorin ancestry. . . . He was one of the survivors of the destruction of Gondolin, from which he rescued a few ancient writings, and some of his own copies, compilations, and commentaries. It is due to this, and to his prodigious memory, that much of the knowledge of the Elder Days was preserved' (*The War of the Jewels*, p. 396).

But the existence of the Elvish loremasters made it impossible for the Elvish traditions to be anything but the 'truth'. Therefore Tolkien began to stress even more the part that Men played in the transmission of the stories and the inevitable confusion that arose over time. He wrote in a note c. 1958:

The Mythology must actually be a 'Mannish' affair. . . . The High Eldar living and being tutored by the demiurgic beings must have known, or

at least their writers and loremasters must have known, the 'truth'. . . .
What we have in the *Silmarillion* etc. are traditions (especially person-
alized, and centred upon *actors*, such as Fëanor) handed on by *Men* in
Númenor and later in Middle-earth (Arnor and Gondor); but already far
back – from the first association of the Dúnedain and Elf-friends with
the Eldar in Beleriand – blended and confused with their own Mannish
myths and cosmic ideas. [*Morgoth's Ring*, p. 370]

Another note says that 'the cosmogonic myths are Númenórean, blending
Elven-lore with human myth and imagination' (*Morgoth's Ring*, p. 374); and in
a note to *The Shibboleth of Fëanor* (1968 or later) Tolkien wrote that *The Sil-*
marillion 'is not an Eldarin title or work. It is a compilation, probably made in
Númenor, which includes (in prose) the four great tales or lays of the heroes of
the Atani, of which "The Children of Húrin" was probably composed already
in Beleriand in the First Age, but necessarily is preceded by an account of
Fëanor and his making of the Silmarils. All however are "Mannish" works'
(*The Peoples of Middle-earth*, p. 357). In another late work, discussing the question of Elvish reincarnation, Tolkien wrote that 'nearly all the matter of *The*
Silmarillion is contained in myths and legends that have passed through Men's
hands and minds, and are (in many points) plainly influenced by contact and
confusion with the myths, theories, and legends of Men' (*Peoples of Middle-*
earth, p. 390).

MAPS AND GEOGRAPHY

Although some of Tolkien's early poems mention places which survive in his
mythology, albeit sometimes with changed nomenclature (e.g. Taniquetil,
Valinor, and Eglamar in *The Shores of Faëry*, written in 1915), it was only in
The Book of Lost Tales that Arda began to take shape. In a section headed 'The
earliest conceptions of the Western Lands and the Oceans' in *The Book of*
Lost Tales, Part One, pp. 81–7, Christopher Tolkien discusses his father's earliest ideas as they appear both in the narrative and in a map and diagram, and
the possible meaning of various names. The earliest map is a rough sketch,
drawn in the middle of a page of the manuscript text of *The Theft of Melko*
and the Darkening of Valinor (written probably early in 1919); it is reproduced, redrawn, on p. 81 of *The Book of Lost Tales, Part One*. An early diagram,
entitled *I Vene Kemen* (?'The Shape of the Earth' or ?'The Vessel of the Earth'),
is a cross-section from west to east of the flat world of the mythology and the
Airs above it, with a mast, sail, and prow added (possibly later) to give the
appearance of a Viking ship (see frontispiece and p. 84 to *The Book of Lost*
Tales, Part One). For significant sections of geographical description within the
Lost Tales and other comments by Christopher Tolkien on geography, etc., see
Part One, pp. 68, 125, 134, 137, 166–7, 172, 214–5, 224, and 226–7, and *The Book of*
Lost Tales, Part Two, pp. 60–3, 140–1, 217, 248, 323–5. For the relationship of Tol
Eressëa and places in it to England, see *England, *Great Haywood, *'Heraldic

Devices of Tol Erethrin', *The Town of Dreams and the City of Present Sorrow, *The Trees of Kortirion, and *Warwick.

Christopher Tolkien thinks that his father may have made the first 'Silmarillion' map of part of Middle-earth in association with *The Children of Húrin* (c. 1919–25) or perhaps with the *Sketch of the Mythology* (c. 1926), but he notes that 'some names which seem to belong with the first making of the map do not appear in the texts before the *Quenta* [*Noldorinwa*, c. 1930]' (*The Shaping of Middle-earth*, p. 219). The map, reproduced in *The Shaping of Middle-earth* with commentary, cannot have been made earlier than autumn 1920, since it was drawn on a sheet of *Leeds examination paper. Christopher Tolkien describes it as a working map used by his father for many years, 'much handled and much altered. Names were emended and places re-sited; the writing is in red ink, black ink, green ink, pencil, and blue crayon, often overlaying each other. Lines representing contours and others representing streams tangle with lines for redirection and lines cancelling other lines. But it is striking that the river-courses as drawn on this first map were scarcely changed afterwards' (p. 219). As the story of 'The Silmarillion' progressed, Tolkien added two supplementary sheets to indicate areas to the west and east of the original map.

For commentary on geography in *The Children of Húrin* and in the *Lay of Leithian* (1925–31), see *The Lays of Beleriand*, pp. 86–9, 160, 170–1, 222–4, 234–5, 274, 314.

In the early 1930s Tolkien made a second 'Silmarillion' map, developed from the first, of Middle-earth west of the Blue Mountains. This was the basis of the map that Christopher Tolkien drew for the published *Silmarillion*. His father used this map for many years, during which it 'became covered all over with alterations and additions of names and features, not a few of them so hastily or faintly pencilled as to be more or less obscure' (Christopher Tolkien, *The Lost Road and Other Writings*, p. 407). Tolkien drew it on four sheets of paper pasted together; the original layer can be distinguished by its fine, careful penwork. For publication, Christopher Tolkien redrew the map to show it 'as it was originally drawn and lettered'; see *The Lost Road and Other Writings*, pp. 408–11, with discussion of points of interest, and developments that took place since the first map, on pp. 407, 412–13.

Tolkien discussed the shape (or fashion) of his invented world in the *Ambarkanta* of the mid-1930s (published, mistakenly as a work of the early thirties, with commentary by Christopher Tolkien in *The Shaping of Middle-earth*, pp. 235–61). The text is accompanied by three diagrams: *The World from Númen (West) to Rómen (East)*, *The World from Formen (North) to Harmen (South)*, and *The World after the Cataclysm and the Ruin of the Númenóreans*; and two maps: *The World about V[alian] Y[ear] 500 after the Fall of the Lamps . . . and the First Fortification of the North by Melko* and *After the War of the Gods (Arvalin Was Cast up by the Great Sea at the Foot of the Mts)*. Chapter 9 in the *Quenta Silmarillion* (mid-1930s), *'Of Beleriand and Its Realms'*, is devoted to a description of the geography of the area and the various spheres of influence;

see *The Lost Road and Other Writings*, pp. 258–72. Commentary by Christopher Tolkien makes frequent references to the two 'Silmarillion' maps.

The second of these, redrawn to show its final state after much emendation by Tolkien, was reproduced in *The War of the Jewels*, pp. 182–5. Christopher Tolkien discusses these emendations, together with changes made in the 1950s to 'Of Beleriand and its Realms', chapter 11 in the revised *Quenta Silmarillion* (pp. 180–98). While reworking the text *Of Meglin* (*c*. 1951) as *Of Maeglin: Sister-son of Turgon, King of Gondolin* (*c*. 1970–1), Tolkien added much detail concerning the 'geography, times, and distances of journeys on horseback' (*The War of the Jewels*, p. 330). As an aid, he had photocopies made of the relevant part of the second 'Silmarillion' map, then almost in its final form, and entered on it changes and additions arising from late work. Christopher Tolkien comments on this complicated material in *The War of the Jewels*, pp. 330–9. See further, his remarks on developments in the later writings, including Tolkien's changing conception of the place of the world within the wider cosmology, in *Morgoth's Ring*: the *Annals of Aman* (*c*. 1951), pp. 62–4, 76–7, 78–9, 89 (noting the influence of the geography of *The Lord of the Rings* on the account of the Elves' journey west), and 'Myths Transformed' pp. 370–90; and in the *Grey Annals* (*c*. 1951) in *The War of the Jewels*, pp. 111–2, 139–40, 157, 159–60. On p. 157 of the latter work Christopher Tolkien accepts a suggested modification to the sketch map published in *Unfinished Tales* (p. 149), drawn to explain references to the area where the dragon Glaurung was slain.

It should be noted that the term *Middle-earth* (also called *Outer Lands*, *Hither Lands*, and especially in earlier works, the *Great Lands*) properly used applies only to lands east of the Great Sea, and not to the world as a whole or to *Aman* in the West. Both *Aman* and *Valinor* are often used to refer to the lands west of the Great Sea, but more correctly, *Aman* is the entire land mass, and *Valinor* the area behind the Pelóri where the Valar dwelt. Occasionally in early writing Tolkien used *Outer Lands* to mean the Twilit Isles and Aman. In late writing, *Arda* came to mean our Solar System, not merely the world.

See further, Charles E. Noad, 'On the Construction of "The Silmarillion"', *Tolkien's Legendarium: Essays on The History of Middle-earth* (2000); and Karen Wynn Fonstad, *The Atlas of Middle-earth* (rev. edn. 1991).

The Silmarillion. Edition of Tolkien's unfinished *'Silmarillion'*, edited after his death by his youngest son and literary executor, *Christopher Tolkien, first published in Great Britain by George Allen & Unwin, London, and in the United States by the Houghton Mifflin Company, Boston, in September 1977. See further, *Descriptive Bibliography* A15.

CONTENTS

The Silmarillion contains five works, the contents and history of which are examined in separate entries in the **Reader's Guide**:

*Ainulindalë.
*Valaquenta.
*'Quenta Silmarillion'.
*Akallabeth.
*Of the Rings of Power and the Third Age.

The 'Quenta Silmarillion' (not to be confused with the earlier *Quenta Silmarillion, distinguished by italics) in turn is divided into twenty-four chapters:

I. * 'Of the Beginning of Days'.
II. *'Of Aulë and Yavanna'.
III. *'Of the Coming of the Elves and the Captivity of Melkor'.
IV. *'Of Thingol and Melian'.
V. *'Of Eldamar and the Princes of the Eldalië'.
VI. *'Of Fëanor and the Unchaining of Melkor'.
VII. *'Of the Silmarils and the Unrest of the Noldor'.
VIII. *'Of the Darkening of Valinor'.
IX. *'Of the Flight of the Noldor'.
X. *'Of the Sindar'.
XI. *'Of the Sun and Moon and the Hiding of Valinor'.
XII. *'Of Men'.
XIII. *'Of the Return of the Noldor'.
XIV. *'Of Beleriand and its Realms'.
XV. *'Of the Noldor in Beleriand'.
XVI. *'Of Maeglin'.
XVII. *'Of the Coming of Men into the West'.
XVIII. *'Of the Ruin of Beleriand and the Fall of Fingolfin'.
XIX. *'Of Beren and Lúthien'.
XX. *'Of the Fifth Battle: Nirnaeth Arnoediad'.
XXI. *'Of Túrin Turambar'.
XXII. *'Of the Ruin of Doriath'.
XXIII. *'Of Tuor and the Fall of Gondolin'.
XXIV. *'Of the Voyage of Eärendil and the War of Wrath'.

The Silmarillion also contains genealogies of Elves and Men, a chart of 'The Sundering of the Elves', a 'Note on Pronunciation', an 'Index of Names', an appendix of 'Elements in Quenya and Sindarin Names', a map of 'The Realms of the Noldor and Sindar' and a 'Map of Beleriand and the Lands to the North'.

HISTORY

In late 1937, when asked for a successor to his recently published *Hobbit, Tolkien could not think of anything more to say about Hobbits, but had 'only too much to say, and much already written, about the world into which [Bilbo Baggins] intruded. . . . I should rather like an opinion, other than that of Mr

*C.S. Lewis and my children, whether it has any value in itself, or as a marketable commodity . . .' (letter to *Stanley Unwin, 15 October 1937, *Letters*, p. 24). On 27 October he met with Stanley Unwin to discuss possibilities, after which Unwin made a rough list of material Tolkien had mentioned: this included 'a volume of short fairy stories in various styles practically ready for publication . . . (Sil Marillion) [*sic*]' and 'the typescript of a History of the Gnomes, and stories arising from it' (Tolkien-George Allen & Unwin archive, HarperCollins). On 15 November Tolkien delivered to Allen & Unwin for consideration, along with other writings, several parts of 'The Silmarillion': the *Lay of Leithian*, recorded on receipt as a 'Long Poem', and the *Quenta Silmarillion*, the *Ainulindalë*, the *Ambarkanta*, and *The Fall of Númenor*, together recorded as 'The Gnomes Material'.

The publisher's reader, Edward Crankshaw, found himself at a loss to know what to do with the *Lay of Leithian*. He presumed that it was an authentic Celtic *geste*, outside of his area of expertise, and thought poorly of it. He seems not to have been given any of the prose material. Christopher Tolkien has guessed 'that my father had not made it sufficiently clear at the outset what the Middle-earth prose works were and how they related to each other, and that as a result [they] had been set aside as altogether too peculiar and difficult' (*The Lays of Beleriand*, p. 365). Apparently to spare Tolkien's feelings when the manuscripts were returned on 15 December, Stanley Unwin implied that all of the 'Silmarillion' papers had been read. 'The Silmarillion', Unwin wrote, 'contains plenty of wonderful material; in fact it is a mine to be explored in writing further books like *The Hobbit* rather than a book in itself' (quoted in *The Lays of Beleriand*, p. 366). Tolkien replied on 16 December:

> My chief joy comes from learning that the *Silmarillion* is not rejected with scorn. I have suffered a sense of fear and bereavement, quite ridiculous, since I let this private and beloved nonsense out; and I think if it had seemed to you to be nonsense I should have felt really crushed. I do not mind about the verse-form [criticized by Edward Crankshaw], which in spite of certain virtuous passages has grave defects; for it is only for me the rough material. But I shall certainly now hope one day to be able, or to be able to afford, to publish the *Silmarillion*! [*Letters*, p. 26]

Within days, as Unwin wished, Tolkien began to write another story about Hobbits, *The Lord of the Rings*.

But that book, like so much else that Tolkien wrote, became strongly attracted to 'The Silmarillion', which provided a foundation of history and legend. By the late 1940s *The Lord of the Rings* was, to its author, so clearly an extension of the *legendarium* that Tolkien felt that both works deserved to be published together. When he wrote to *Naomi Mitchison on 18 December 1949 he optimistically hoped 'to give you soon two books. . . . One is a sequel to "The Hobbit" which I have just finished after 12 years (intermittent) labour. . . . The other is pure myth and legend of times already remote in

Bilbo's days' (*Letters*, p. 134). Tolkien recalled that Allen & Unwin had rejected 'The Silmarillion' in 1937; but towards the end of 1949 he was introduced to *Milton Waldman, an editor for the London publisher Collins, who expressed interest in publishing both *The Lord of the Rings* and *The Silmarillion*. On 24 February 1950 Tolkien wrote to Stanley Unwin that *The Silmarillion* had

> captured *The Lord of the Rings*, so that that has become simply its continuation and completion, requiring the *Silmarillion* to be fully intelligible – without a lot of references and explanations. . . .
>
> Ridiculous and tiresome as you may think me, I want to publish them both . . . in conjunction or in connexion. 'I want to' – it would be wiser to say 'I should like to', since a little packet of, say, a million words, of matter set out in extenso that Anglo-Saxons (or the English-speaking public) can only endure in moderation, is not very likely to see the light, even if paper [then still in short supply following the war] were available at will. [*Letters*, pp. 136–7]

Unwin suggested in reply that the two works might be divided into three or four self-contained volumes. But Tolkien pressed the issue, in fact wanting to free himself from any moral as well as legal obligation to Allen & Unwin so that he could deal with Collins instead. On 3 April Unwin unwisely forwarded to Tolkien a comment by *Rayner Unwin that 'any *really* relevant material from *The Silmarillion*' could be incorporated into *The Lord of the Rings*; but 'if this is not workable I would say publish *The Lord of the Rings* as a prestige book, and after having a second look at it, drop *The Silmarillion*' (quoted in *Letters*, p. 140). On 14 April 1950 Tolkien asked Unwin for an immediate decision whether to publish *The Lord of the Rings* and *The Silmarillion*, without divisions that Tolkien considered artificial. Unwin was forced to decline, in the absence of a final manuscript and considering the substantial cost of publishing two works of such great length. (See further, *The Lord of the Rings*.)

Tolkien had already begun to devote much time to 'The Silmarillion', to bring it to a publishable form. Before long, however, it became clear that Collins was not willing to publish *The Lord of the Rings* without cuts, and the length of the still unfinished *Silmarillion* was a serious concern. Evidently in late 1951, at Milton Waldman's request, Tolkien wrote a letter of some 10,000 words which explained his saga and illustrated the interdependence of *The Silmarillion* and *The Lord of the Rings* (see *Letters*, pp. 143–61, and *Reader's Companion*, pp. 742–9). But Waldman spent much of his time abroad, unable to influence events in person, and other staff at Collins were unsympathetic. Probably in March 1952 Tolkien demanded that *The Lord of the Rings* be published at once; in April Collins, alarmed by its length and the rising cost of paper, withdrew from negotiations. In the meantime, Tolkien had continued to correspond with Allen & Unwin, on matters concerning *The Hobbit* and *Farmer Giles of Ham*; and in November 1951 Rayner Unwin had written to enquire about *The Silmarillion* and *The Lord of the Rings*. On 22 June 1952 Tolkien replied, worried now about the passing of years and willing to have *The Lord of the Rings* published by itself.

Work on that book now took precedence; but as soon as its final volume was published in 1955 Rayner Unwin began to encourage Tolkien to complete *The Silmarillion*. Tolkien has already returned to work on the *legendarium*, as much as his other responsibilities allowed. The task proved to be massive: to decide between different versions of tales, and to produce a work consistent not only within itself but also with the published *Lord of the Rings*. Moreover, Tolkien began to feel that some of the more mythic elements of 'The Silmarillion', such as the creation of the Sun and Moon, should be abandoned if they contradicted scientific fact; but he failed to find satisfactory ways to deal with this problem, while also retaining elements important to him, such as the purity and significance of *light as provided by the Two Trees. Work on *The Silmarillion* was also hindered by problems of health, both his own and that of his wife (*Edith Tolkien), and the need to undertake many *domestic duties; by unfulfilled academic obligations, such as an edition of the *Ancrene Wisse* (**Ancrene Riwle*); by the success of *The Lord of the Rings*, which generated fan mail, requests for interviews, intrusive visitors, and requests to dramatize or illustrate his works; and by a challenge to his American copyrights (see *Ace Books controversy) which required revision of *The Lord of the Rings* and *The Hobbit*.

Although Tolkien continued to work on *The Silmarillion* until his death, in his later years, rather than concentrating on the work as a whole or on its least finished parts, he spent many hours writing essays on linguistic or philosophical questions. He was well aware that time was against him, and arranged that if the work was still unfinished when he died it should be edited by his youngest son, Christopher, whom he appointed his literary editor.

After Tolkien died on 2 September 1973 Allen & Unwin hastened to assure readers of *The Lord of the Rings* who been waiting patiently for *The Silmarillion* that the book would eventually appear, though perhaps not for some time. 'No decision has yet been taken about the professor's last book "The Silmarillion"', it was officially said; 'only part of the manuscript has been completed. It is hoped that Prof. Tolkien's son, Christopher . . . will be able to complete the two to three-volume novel. . . . Many of the legends to be used in the novel have not yet been put into narrative form. . . . Work to link the story together will have to be done' (statement of 3 September 1973, quoted in 'Another Book Still Awaits Completion', *Oxford Times*, 7 September 1973, p. 6). Another statement, issued with the publication of Tolkien's will on 21 December 1973, warned that it would take 'years of work to assemble' *The Silmarillion* 'into a coherent work', which Christopher Tolkien would undertake himself ('Tolkien's Will', *The Bookseller*, 5 January 1974). In the event, he did so with the assistance of Guy Gavriel Kay, later a noted writer of fantasy novels.

The difficulty, Christopher Tolkien wrote, was that although the mythology, 'considered simply as a large narrative structure, underwent relatively little radical change' throughout its long history of writing, it was far indeed from being a fixed text, and did not remain unchanged even in certain fundamental ideas concerning the nature of the world it portrays; while the same legends came to be retold in longer and shorter forms, and in different styles. As the years passed the changes and variants, both in detail and in larger perspectives, became so complex, so pervasive, and so many-layered that a final and definitive version seemed unattainable. Moreover the old legends ('old' now not only in their derivation from the remote First Age, but also in terms of my father's life) became the vehicle and depository of his profoundest reflections. In his later writing mythology and poetry sank down behind his theological and philosophical preoccupations: from which arose incompatibilites of tone.

On my father's death it fell to me to try to bring the work into publishable form. It became clear to me that to attempt to present, within the covers of a single book, the diversity of the materials – to show *The Silmarillion* as in truth a continuing and evolving creation extending over more than half a century – would in fact lead only to confusion and the submerging of what is essential. I set myself therefore to work out a single text, selecting and arranging in such a way as seemed to me to produce the most coherent and internally self-consistent narrative. [*The Silmarillion*, pp. 7–8]

Names, which sometimes differed between versions, had to be made consistent for the final text, as did the tone of the work, which in some writing had more archaic language (*thee* and *thou* rather than *you*, for instance) than Tolkien used otherwise.

The concluding chapters of the book posed the greatest problem, 'in that they had remained unchanged for many years, and were in some respects in serious disharmony with he more developed conceptions in other parts of the book'. Tolkien had come 'to conceive *The Silmarillion* as a compilation, a compendious narrative, made long afterwards from sources of great diversity', and from this derived a 'varying speed of the narrative and fullness of detail in different parts'. The *Ainulindalë* and *Valaquenta* were included in the published *Silmarillion* because they are closely associated with 'the *Quenta Silmarillion*, or *Silmarillion* proper'; the other two components, the *Akallabêth* and *Of the Rings of Power and the Third Age*, which are 'wholly separate and independent', were 'included according to my father's specific intention; and by their inclusion the entire history is set forth from the Music of the Ainur in which the world began to the passing of the Ringbearers from the Havens of Mithlond at the end of the Third Age' (p. 8).

In *The Silmarillion* [*by*] *J.R.R. Tolkien: A Brief Account of the Book and Its Making*, a promotional booklet published by Houghton Mifflin (1977), Christopher Tolkien wrote that in determining the form of *The Silmarillion* he worked for a time towards a book which would show something of its unfinished and many-branched growth. But it became clear to me that the result would be so complex as to require much study for its comprehension; and I feared to crush *The Silmarillion* under the weight of its own history. I set myself, therefore, to work out a single text, by selection and arrangement. To give even an impression of the way this has been done is scarcely possible in a short space, and it must suffice to say that in the result *The Silmarillion* is emphatically my father's book and in no sense mine. Here and there I had to develop the narrative out of notes and rough drafts; I had to make many choices between competing versions and to make many changes of detail; and in the last few chapters (which had been left almost untouched for many years) I had in places to modify the narrative to make it coherent. But essentially what I have done has been a work of organization, not of completion. [p. 6]

This decision was certainly wise, according to the expectations of readers and the practicalities of the market in 1977, both of which demanded a single coherent text to harmonize with Tolkien's other tales of Middle-earth. But Christopher Tolkien continued to doubt whether he had truly fulfilled his duty as his father's literary executor. Hence followed *Unfinished Tales* (1980) and the twelve volumes of *The History of Middle-earth* (1983–96), in which Christopher produced a full 'longitudinal' history of 'The Silmarillion' to complement the 'fixed' *Silmarillion*. The happy result is that readers now have the best of both worlds.

Two selections from *The Silmarillion*, read by Christopher Tolkien, were first issued as commercial recordings in 1977 (*The Silmarillion: Of Beren and Lúthien*) and 1978 (*Of the Darkening of Valinor and Of the Flight of the Noldor from The Silmarillion*). An unabridged recording of *The Silmarillion*, read by Martin Shaw, was first issued in 1998.

CRITICISM

When the long-awaited *Silmarillion* finally appeared it was a publishing event, and not surprisingly the book was widely reviewed. Critical response ranged from the positive, through the puzzled or unimpressed, to the actively hostile. It was frequently said that many readers would be disappointed, because *The Silmarillion* lacked the 'human element' provided by the hobbits in *The Lord of the Rings*; that the book was likely to appeal mainly to committed readers of Tolkien; that it was not Tolkien's own work at all, but that of its editor; and that many would abandon the book long before reaching the end.

Margaret Drabble, reviewing it in *The Listener* ('Rebels against Ilúvatar', 15 September 1977), stated that although she had once been an ardent Tolkien fan, but found *The Silmarillion* 'extremely dull'.

It is a curious book, uneven in style and pace, with none of the narrative drive of its predecessors. . . . But its most serious weakness seems to lie in the loftiness of its aspirations. It is pretentious. It is written in the high epic style . . . and there is not a flicker of either the homeliness or humour that enliven *The Hobbit*. . . .

There is certainly much that is Miltonic in Tolkien's liking for proper nouns and resounding lists, and the prose is full of biblical cadences. . . . Most of the name-making is successful, for Tolkien had a wonderful ear for mysterious and euphonious sounds. . . . [p. 346]

Jan Marsh in the *Daily Telegraph* also found *The Silmarillion* very different from *The Lord of the Rings*, 'employing an elevated style full of place names and genealogies, great deeds and stupendous battles, modelled on the manner of the Sagas or Arthurian legend. Although it displays a marvellous mastery of the problems of language inherent in any modern rendering of archaic material, it is not altogether easy to read and the characters tend to be remote' ('Tolkien's Source-book', 22 September 1977, p. 14).

In the *Church of England Newspaper* ('A Myth for Our Age', 2 October 1977), Eileen Mable in contrast thought that *The Silmarillion* fulfilled 'all expectations' and was 'a splendid achievement, a sustained and consistent work of imagination'. It tells how even something good and beautiful such as the Silmarils can become 'the means of mistrust, betrayal and death. The battle between good and evil is fought in a fallen world where no deed of heroism can finally thrust back the darkness. Even the Valar, the Guardians of the Earth, can only defeat evil by upheaving and remaking Middle-earth; and afterwards evil can still insinuate itself afresh into the hearts of Elves and Men.'

In the *Wall Street Journal* Edmund Fuller found *The Silmarillion* 'a work of power, eloquence, and noble vision that would be notable even if "The Hobbit" and "The Lord of the Rings" had never been', but recommended that new readers turn to those works first. *The Silmarillion* 'is the last structural block of [Tolkien's] edifice, among the noblest of its elements. Beware those hailed as his imitators, who try to conjure up the exotic with sound and fury but lack the deep underpinnings of J.R.R. Tolkien's theology, philosophy, scholarship and life commitment' ('A Superb Addition to Tolkien's Mythological Realm', 19 September 1977, p. 22).

Jessica Yates in *British Book News* for January 1978 thought that 'not all lovers of the *Rings* will like' *The Silmarillion*. 'They will miss the humour, suspense and variety of' *The Lord of the Rings*, and some will despise the new book's 'archaic biblical diction. . . . *The Silmarillion* will create admirers and enemies, neither of whom will listen to the other.'

Donald Bender in 'And Tolkien Begat the Silmarillion', *Independent Berkeley Gazette*, 14 October 1977, wrote that *The Silmarillion* might be 'on its way to becoming the most bought and least read book ever written', satisfying only 'professional philologists and Hobbit fanatics'. Compared with the Bible, *The Silmarillion* 'at its worst, and for the most part, . . . is as boring as the endless legalistic pedantries of Leviticus. At its best, and rarely, it contains phrases that for sheer brilliance and poetic force would not be markedly out of place in the

Songs of Solomon.' *The Silmarillion* is 'one long footnote to *The Lord of the Rings*. It is a scholar's book rather than a reader's book, a book to be studied, not a book to be read. It is a work that demands that you read it while holding a concordance in one hand and an Oxford Dictionary in the other' (p. 23).

The Silmarillion is indeed a book that needs time to be studied and digested. For a few years after its first publication it received little criticism other than reviews. *A Reader's Guide to The Silmarillion* by Paul H. Kocher (1980) is little more than a summary, with comment confined for the most part to a survey of sources and influences. A chapter on *The Silmarillion* in *J.R.R. Tolkien* by Katharyn W. Crabbe (1981; rev. and expanded edn. 1988) is more expansive in its analysis but still limited (in her second edition Crabbe adds a chapter on *Unfinished Tales* and *The History of Middle-earth*). Randal Helms in *Tolkien and the Silmarils* (1981) tried to provide some chronological framework for the writing of the components of *The Silmarillion*, relying mainly on the limited information provided in Carpenter's *Biography*; but just as Helms finished his final draft, *Unfinished Tales* was published, raising queries which Helms discussed in an afterword:

> Anyone interested, as I am, in the growth of *The Silmarillion* will want to study *Unfinished Tales*, not only for its intrinsic value but also because its relationship to the former provides what will become a classic example of a long-standing problem in literary criticism: what, really, *is* a literary work? Is it what the author intended (or may have intended) it to be, or is it what a later editor makes of it? The problem becomes especially intense for the practicing critic when, as happened with *The Silmarillion*, a writer dies before finishing his work and leaves more than one version of its parts, which then find publication elsewhere. Which version will the critic approach as the 'real' story? [*Tolkien and the Silmarils*, p. 93]

Helms followed this, however, by misinterpreting Christopher Tolkien's introduction to *The Silmarillion*, concluding: 'Christopher Tolkien has helped us in this instance by honestly pointing out that *The Silmarillion* in the shape that we have it is the invention of the son not the father. There is no "real" *Silmarillion*, it died as a dream and a plan in the mind of Tolkien' (p. 94).

As Christopher Tolkien ruefully comments in his foreword to *The Book of Lost Tales, Part One*, '*The Silmarillion* is commonly said to be a "difficult" book, needing explanation and guidance on how to "approach" it . . .' (p. 1). The 'difficulty' in truth – the wide chronological scope of the stories and multiplicity of character and place-names notwithstanding – is mostly one of perception rather than substance, but that seems to have been enough to put off at least critics, not to say general readers. And any difficulty in considering *The Silmarillion* was soon compounded by the publication (over a long period of years) in *Unfinished Tales* and *The History of Middle-earth* of the variant texts from which it was derived. This, surely, has been one reason why the published *Silmarillion*, let alone the larger, more complex 'Silmarillion', have generated little formal criticism even today. Only a small handful of writers have approached the work as a whole; a few more have addressed small portions of it, especially individual tales such as those of Túrin Turambar and of Beren and Lúthien.

Brian Rosebury, in his *Tolkien: A Critical Assessment* (1992), by way of a chapter title audaciously relegated 'The Silmarillion' to the status of a 'minor work'. For him *The Lord of the Rings* is the central work in Tolkien's career (a conclusion which can hardly be disputed, except to point out that 'The Silmarillion' was more prominent in Tolkien's imagination, and for a longer time), against which all else pales in comparison. In the revised edition of his work, retitled *Tolkien: A Cultural Phenomenon* (2003), Rosebury abandoned the tag of 'minor work' but repeated his view that

> the absence of the distinctive virtues of *The Lord of the Rings* – the exhilarating, expansive realisation of Middle-earth, the unified plot whose excitements are integrated with that realisation, the transparent prose which is the medium for both – has made *The Silmarillion* a confessed disappointment to many, perhaps most, of the admirers won for Tolkien by the earlier-published work. In view of the fact that its essential conception predates *The Lord of the Rings*, one is tempted to see its versions (up to 1937) as Tolkien's sketch-books, the evidences of his long and painful literary apprenticeship, through which he fumbled his way towards his true creative manner, that of *The Lord of the Rings*. According to this view, having accomplished *The Lord of the Rings* (for which *The Hobbit* is also an apprentice-piece), Tolkien proved incapable in his last years of bringing his mature mastery to bear upon transforming the recalcitrant material of 'The Silmarillion' into a comparably effective narrative. [p. 103]

And yet it must be said in reply that Rosebury is here imposing an interpretation of history ('apprenticeship') that did not actually occur. Tolkien did not himself see this sequence of events as a matter of maturing from one book to the next, but of writing according to time and purpose (*The Hobbit*, for instance, was invented for children), nor does it seem that he ever intended to rework 'The Silmarillion' into anything stylistically like *The Lord of the Rings*.

In *The Road to Middle-earth* (1982; 2nd edn. 1992) T.A. Shippey discusses *The Silmarillion* last, after *The Hobbit* and *The Lord of the Rings*, because most readers come to these books in that order, and 'it will probably always be hard' for them to understand Tolkien's posthumous works – *The Silmarillion* and *Unfinished Tales* – 'except after reading *The Lord of the Rings*' (2nd edn., p. 201). Thus, even though he accepted Christopher Tolkien's assertion in a private letter that 'a "very high proportion" even of the detailed wording' of the earlier *Quenta Silmarillion* remains in *The Silmarillion* (2nd edn., p. 201), he writes of that book as if it were a late work, and *The Hobbit* and *The Lord of the Rings* as 'earlier'. To a degree, this is a matter of practicality of expression, and when

Shippey wrote the first edition of *The Road to Middle-earth* the first volume of *The History of Middle-earth* had not yet appeared; but it confuses the issue, as Christopher Tolkien complained in his foreword to *The Book of Lost Tales, Part One*.

Shippey finds in *The Silmarillion* 'two of Tolkien's great strengths', inspiration and invention, but also a 'refusal to accept novelistic convention', whereby a story is told in relation to a central character and the novelist 'can explain, or show, what is "really" happening and contrast it with the limited perception of his character . . . . Against this *The Silmarillion* tries to preserve something much closer to the texture of reality, namely, that the full meaning of events can only ever be perceived retrospectively' (pp. 238–9). And like other critics, he remarks that *The Silmarillion* 'is all on the level of "high mimesis" or "romance", with no Gamgees [or other hobbits] in it' (p. 239). Tolkien was 'quite clearly, in the *Silmarillion* stories, recommending virtues to which most moderns no longer dare aspire: stoicism, nonchalance, piety, fidelity. In *The Lord of the Rings* he had learnt – by mixing hobbits in with heroes – to present them relatively unprovocatively' (pp. 239–40). Shippey concludes, in regard to 'ancient and modern modes of presentation, and . . . ancient and modern theories of virtue', that

> in his maturity, from the scenes at the end of *The Hobbit* almost all the way through *The Lord of the Rings*, Tolkien was able to hold a balance between them. In youth he had not learnt it, and in his later years he was unable to recover it – especially as recovering that balance would have meant what is notoriously one of the hardest jobs in the literary world, namely making a radical revision of something which has already taken a fixed shape of his own. Tolkien did not solve the problem of 'depth'; nor of 'novelising' romance; and in ignoring the one, as in brooding over the other, he showed himself out of step with his time, and exposed himself even more to lack of sympathy and careless reading. [p. 240]

Christopher Tolkien replied to some of Shippey's views in *The Book of Lost Tales, Part One*.

In the second edition of *The Road to Middle-earth* (1992) Shippey added a chapter, 'The Course of Actual Composition', in which he makes perceptive comments about 'The Silmarillion' as revealed in *The History of Middle-earth* as published to that date – not yet, however, later volumes such as *Morgoth's Ring* which revealed that Tolkien had indeed attempted 'radical revision' to his work, if ultimately in vain. Shippey returned to *The Silmarillion* in *J.R.R. Tolkien: Author of the Century* (2000), but there continued to maintain that the work 'can never be anything other than hard to read' (p. 261).

One of the most important studies of *The Silmarillion* is *Splintered Light: Logos and Language in Tolkien's World* by Verlyn Flieger (1983; 2nd edn. 2002). It is unsurpassed in its analysis of 'Tolkien's treatment of *light . . . [which] derives its primary image from his Catholicism [*Religion], its linguistic method from [*Owen] Barfield's theory' (2nd edn., p. 49). Flieger describes *The Silmarillion* as 'without doubt the most difficult and most problematic of Tolkien's major works', which 'strikes out into philosophical and theological territory seldom looked for by readers of [mythic fantasy]'. Whereas *The Hobbit* and *The Lord of the Rings* 'are tales of adventure with mythic overtones', '*The Silmarillion* is the parent myth that resonates in those overtones' (p. xiii).

'Of the Silmarils and the Unrest of the Noldor'. The seventh chapter of the 'Quenta Silmarillion', published in *The Silmarillion* (1977), pp. 67–72.

SUMMARY

Inspired to preserve the light of the Two Trees in an imperishable form, Fëanor uses all of his lore and power and skill to make three great jewels, the Silmarils. 'Even in the darkness of the deepest treasury the Silmarils of their own radiance shone like the stars of Varda; and yet, as were they indeed living things, they rejoiced in light and received it and gave it back in hues more marvellous than before' (p. 67). No one else knows the secret of their making. Varda hallows them, and Mandos foretells that the fate of Arda is locked within them. Melkor lusts for them and secretly sows dissension and mistrust among the Elves. His lies lead many of the Noldor to believe that the Valar have defrauded them of their rightful inheritance in Middle-earth by bringing them to Aman, and that they have done this so that the kingdoms of Middle-earth would pass to Men, whom they think will be easier to control. The Noldor begin to murmur against the Valar, and Fëanor becomes possessive of the Silmarils, keeping them locked away except when he wears them at great feasts, rarely letting others see them.

Melkor provokes division and suspicion between Fëanor and his half-brother Fingolfin, suggesting to each that the other wants to supplant him. He teaches the Noldor how to make weapons. Fëanor begins to speak openly against the Valar and of leading the Noldor out of servitude. Finwë, leader of the Noldor and the father of Fëanor and Fingolfin, is troubled by this unrest and summons a council. But Fingolfin hastens to his father and accuses Fëanor of acting as if he were the leader of the Noldor. Fëanor in turn accuses Fingolfin of usurping his place with his father and threatens him with his sword.

The Valar become aware of the unrest of the Noldor, though not that Melkor is behind it, but do nothing until Fëanor's attack on his brother. Now they question Fëanor and discover the part that Melkor has played. Because Fëanor has drawn a sword on his brother and broken the peace of Valinor, he is banished from Tirion for twelve years, and may return then only if the others involved pardon him. Fingolfin does so immediately, but Fëanor makes no response, and with his sons builds a stronghold, Formenos, for their treasures in the north of Valinor. Finwë joins him there, while Fingolfin rules the Noldor in Tirion. Through his actions Fëanor has made the lies of Melkor come true. Melkor flees, and the Valar are unable to find him. He makes an unexpected visit to Formenos and speaks to Fëanor, pretending friendship and warning him that even in his stronghold he cannot hold the Silmarils safe from the Valar. But Fëanor, perceiving that Melkor himself lusts for the Silmarils, turns him away with sharp words. Finwë sends news of this visit to the Valar, and as Oromë and Tulkas set off in pursuit of Melkor news comes that he has passed to the north, through a gap in the mountains. They are unable to find him, and a dread of the coming of an unknown evil spoils the joy of those who live in Valinor.

HISTORY

Much of the basic outline of this chapter is already present in *The Book of Lost Tales*, c. 1917–19, but much is also missing. The rivalry between the sons of Finwë, leader of the Noldor, does not enter the mythology until much later. In this first telling of the story neither Fingolfin nor any other son of Finwë plays a part; Fëanor is the greatest craftsman of the Noldoli, but no relation of Finwë. The Silmarils are of much less importance at this stage, merely the greatest of many jewels made by the Noldor. In *The Coming of the Elves and the Making of Kôr* in *The Book of Lost Tales, Part One* there is a detailed description of how Fëanor made the jewels, the ingredients including 'an urn full of the most luminous phosphor-light gathered in dark places' and 'the glint' of other gems 'by the light of white lamps and silver candles' (p. 128). There is no suggestion that Varda has hallowed them, or of any prophecy by Mandos, though they do begin to grow in significance in tales written later. Even Melko's desire is not so much for the Silmarils specifically, but more generally for jewels made by the Noldoli.

The earliest version of the rest of this chapter is found in the tale of *The Theft of Melko and the Darkening of Valinor* (*The Book of Lost Tales, Part One*). In this also Melko causes the Noldoli to question the motives of the Valar, but since the leader of the Noldoli, Nólemë, has no sons, Melko does not inflame family rivalry. Indeed, Nólemë becomes so worried by the discontent of his people, and realizing that Melko is at least partly responsible, goes to speak to Manwë. But Melko has been to Manwë before him, accusing the Noldoli of speaking against his lordship, and Manwë rebukes both of them. He sends Melko back to Mandos, and fearing that the unrest of the Noldoli will spread to other Elves, orders them to leave the city of Kôr, and they build a settlement further north in Valinor.

During the writing of *The Children of Húrin*, *The Lay of the Fall of Gondolin*, and *The Flight of the Noldoli from Valinor* in the first half of the 1920s, the Noldorin royal house moved towards its later form: Finwë now has two sons, Fëanor and Fingolfin, who are full-brothers; and in *The Flight of the Noldoli from Valinor* the Silmarils began to take on a greater significance. The story moved even closer to its final form in the next narrative, the *Sketch of the Mythology* (c. 1926): there the Silmarils combine the light of the Two Trees and burn impure hands that touch them; Morgoth desires the Silmarils most of all;

his lies lead Fëanor to believe that Fingolfin and Fingolfin's son are plotting to usurp the leadership of the Noldoli from Fëanor and his sons and take the Silmarils; and the brothers quarrel. (This seems to imply that Finwë has delegated at least part of his authority to Fëanor, but may be only due to compression. As first written, Fingolfin is the elder son, but this was soon changed, perhaps at the time of writing, to make Fëanor the elder.) Fëanor is summoned before the Valar, who discover the truth. Morgoth escapes their pursuit, and only Fëanor is banished from Tûn (Tirion), but his father and sons and many other Noldoli join him in exile. Fingolfin rules those who stay in Tûn, which seems to justify the words of Morgoth. In an early addition, Morgoth also tells the Noldoli of Men who are to come, and who because of the actions of the Valar will defraud the Elves of their kingdoms in Middle-earth.

In the next account, the *Quenta Noldorinwa (c. 1930), Finwë has three sons, Fëanor, Fingolfin, and Finrod, and Fingolfin has two sons and a daughter. The hallowing of, and prophecy concerning, the Silmarils now enter, but it is Manwë who hallows the jewels and Varda who makes the prophecy. The description of Morgoth's deceitful words about the Valar moved close to the final version. It is said that Fëanor kept the Silmarils locked away except when he wore them at great feasts, but not yet that he begrudged the sight of them to all save his father and sons. Melkor now escapes pursuit through a gap in the mountains. Additions made later introduce Fëanor's thoughts of leaving Valinor, and that at some time after Melkor's deceit is revealed news is brought to the Valar that he is moving north towards the dwelling of Finwë and Fëanor. *Christopher Tolkien considers this the first hint of Melkor's unexpected visit to Fëanor.

The 'earliest' *Annals of Valinor, written in the early 1930s, provided a chronological framework for events. At some time after Valian Year 2500 (one Valian year equals ten years of the Sun) but before Morgoth's release from Mandos in 2900 (changed to 2700 while writing), Fëanor makes the Silmarils. The judgement of the Valar takes place in 2950 (changed to 2900). An addition to the entry for 2900, which says that only Finwë and Fëanor knew that Morgoth was hiding in the north, is followed by the statement that the Valar attempted to apprehend him in 2950, but he escaped. There is little further change in the 'later' Annals of Valinor of the mid-1930s, except that it is stated that Morgoth visited Fëanor secretly in the north 'feigning friendship' (*The Lost Road and Other Writings, p. 114).

The story occupies the first part of Chapter 6 ('Of the Silmarils and the Darkening of Valinor') in the *Quenta Silmarillion begun in the mid-1930s. New elements which enter in this text are Morgoth teaching the Noldor to make weapons and armour; Fëanor beginning to grudge the sight of the Silmarils to all but himself and his sons; Fëanor shutting his doors against Morgoth; and Finwë sending to the Valar news of Morgoth's visit.

In revisions to Chapter 6 of the Quenta Silmarillion made by Tolkien after the completion of *The Lord of the Rings, the making of the Silmarils follows rather than precedes the release of Melkor from Mandos; Varda hallows the

Silmarils, and Mandos makes the prophecy that 'the fates of Arda, earth, sea, and air, lay locked within them' (*Morgoth's Ring, p. 187); Fingolfin seeks to restrain his brother when Fëanor speaks against the Valar and of leaving Valinor, and Fëanor draws his sword upon him. Fëanor's banishment is for ten (changed to twenty) years.

According to the Annals of Aman (see *The Annals of Valinor), written c. 1951, in which years are reckoned from the creation of the Trees, Fëanor begins to make the Silmarils in 1449 and completes his work in 1450, and it is said that no one knows of what substance he made the great jewels. Their description now reached the published form. Varda hallows them, but nothing is said about any prophecy. The Valar judge Fëanor in 1490, and the term of his banishment is extended in stages from three to twenty, and then to twelve Valian Years. In 1492 Morgoth fails in a further attempt to deceive Fëanor and flees south, escaping pursuit.

At the end of the 1950s Tolkien did more revision and expansion of parts of the Quenta Silmarillion, and reorganized some its chapters. This included the emergence of Chapter 7, 'Of the Silmarils and the Unrest of the Noldor', told in much more detail than before and taking up developments in the story which emerged only in this phase of writing, in particular the story of Finwë's two marriages, and that Fëanor and Fingolfin were half-brothers. The story of the council called by Finwë and the detailed account of the brothers' quarrel was now present.

The chapter in the published Silmarillion was drawn by *Christopher Tolkien mainly from Tolkien's c. 1958–60 revision of the Quenta Silmarillion, except with some phrases and sentences taken from the Annals of Aman (though in places these are identical). The description of the Silmarils near the beginning is almost entirely derived from the Annals.

Simpson, Percy (1865–1962). Percy Simpson read Classics at Selwyn College, Cambridge, and later taught there and at St Olave's Grammar School, then in Southwark. In 1913 he became a Lecturer in English at *Oxford at the invitation of *Sir Walter Raleigh. In 1921 he was made a Fellow of Oriel College, and from 1930 until his retirement in 1935 he was Goldsmiths' Reader in English at Oxford. His specialty was the Elizabethan period. With Tolkien, he served on the English Faculty Board and as an examiner. From 1914 to 1934 he was also Librarian of the English School. In 1946, though aged eighty, he took pupils once more in Oriel College, which had become crowded following the war.

Simpson's writings include Shakespearian Punctuation (1911), chapters in Shakespeare's England (1916), Proof-Reading in the Sixteenth, Seventeenth and Eighteenth Centuries (1935), and Studies in Elizabethan Drama (1955). He was also co-editor, with C.H. Herford and Evelyn Simpson, of an edition of the works of Ben Jonson (1925–1963).

'**Of the Sindar**'. The tenth chapter of the *'Quenta Silmarillion', published in *The Silmarillion* (1977), pp. 91–7.

SUMMARY

In Middle-earth, after the departure of the greater part of the Elves to Valinor, those in Beleriand, including the mariners at the Havens, acknowledge Thingol (Elwë) as their lord. These, the Sindar or Grey-elves, 'under the lordship of Thingol and the teaching of Melian [the Maia] . . . became the fairest and the most wise and skilful of all the Elves of Middle-earth' (*The Silmarillion*, p. 91). Although most of Middle-earth lies under the sleep of Yavanna, the power of Melian brings life and joy to Beleriand. At the end of the first age of the Chaining of Melkor, Lúthien, daughter of Thingol and Melian, is born, 'and the white flowers of *niphredil* came forth to greet her as stars from the earth' (p. 91).

During the following age Dwarves cross the Ered Luin into Beleriand. They delve halls in the Ered Luin, Belegost and Nogrod, but their greatest mansion, Khazad-dûm, is in the Misty Mountains far to the east of Beleriand. The Elves are amazed to meet other living beings. Few learn the language of the Dwarves or ever visit them, but the Dwarves learn the elven tongue and trade with the Elves. Thingol, on the advice of Melian who foresees that peace will not last for ever, employs the Dwarves of Belegost to make for him an underground stronghold, Menegroth, the Thousand Caves. In return Melian teaches them much that they are eager to learn, and Thingol gives them pearls he has received from Círdan at the Havens. With Dwarves and Elves using their skills to produce 'images of the wonder and beauty of Valinor', Menegroth becomes 'the fairest dwelling of any king that has ever been east of the Sea' (p. 93).

As the time of the captivity of Melkor draws on, dwarves bring news of fell beasts in the North and East, and soon evil wolves, Orcs, and other creatures begin to arrive in Beleriand. Thingol acquires weapons and armour from the Dwarves, and from the Sindar who have learned smithcraft. Thus armed, they drive off all creatures of evil.

Ages before, during the long march of the Elves to the Sea, some of the Teleri under the leadership of Lenwë left the main host when they halted by the River Anduin. These are the Nandor, who long wander without fear in Middle-earth. But with the coming of evil creatures many of the Nandor now make their way into Beleriand, led by Denethor son of Lenwë. They are welcomed by Thingol and settle in Ossiriand. Beleriand experiences a long period of untroubled peace, during which Daeron the Minstrel, Thingol's chief loremaster, devises runes, though these are used more by the Dwarves than by the Sindar. The peace comes to end when Morgoth (Melkor) returns to Middle-earth after the destruction of the Two Trees and rebuilds Angband. Ungoliant, after her quarrel with Morgoth, flees south into the realm of Thingol. The southern precipices of Dorthonion, where Ungoliant dwells for a time, become known as the Ered Gorgoroth, the Mountains of Terror; but the power of Melian prevents her from entering Neldoreth, the heart of Thingol's realm.

An army of Orcs comes secretly from Angband into Beleriand, plundering and attacking Thingol from two directions, so that he is cut off from the Havens. He requests aid from Denethor, and together they defeat the eastern host of Orcs. Those orcs that escape from the battle are slain by the Dwarves as they flee north; but Denethor and many of the Nandor die also. Thereafter the Nandor come either to avoid open war, living in secrecy in Ossiriand and becoming known as the Laiquendi or Green-elves, or to join the elves already living in the guarded realm of Thingol.

When Thingol returns from the East he learns that the Orcs in the West have been victorious, driving Círdan to the edge of the Sea. Thingol summons his people to the inner part of his realm, Neldoreth and Region, and Melian uses her power to fence that area with 'an unseen wall of shadow and bewilderment: the Girdle of Melian, that none thereafter could pass against her will or the will of King Thingol' (p. 97). Within this area, called Doriath, the guarded kingdom, there is peace. Outside the Girdle the servants of Morgoth roam freely except in the Havens.

But now, unexpected by any in Middle-earth, Fëanor and his followers arrive in the ships of the Teleri.

HISTORY

This chapter as an entity entered late into the 'Silmarillion' writings, though some of its content appeared already, if scattered, in *The Book of Lost Tales*. The later version of *The Tale of Tinúviel* (c. 1919) mentions briefly the elves who had not gone to Valinor (the Ilkorindi), who gather around Tinwelint (Thingol); his halls in a great cavern; the spells that Gwendeling (Melian) weaves to protect his realm; and Tinúviel (Lúthien), daughter of Tinwelint and Gwendeling. Dairon also appears as a maker of music and Tinúviel's brother. The Dwarves of Nogrod and Belegost are mentioned in *The Tale of the Nauglafring*. The alliterative *Children of Húrin* (c. 1919–25) calls Thingol's stronghold 'Thousand Caves'. It is noted in the early part of the *Lay of Leithian* (begun c. 1925) that Thingol has a store of weapons as well as precious jewels.

The *Sketch of the Mythology* (c. 1926) mentions the Elves lost on the march, and that Melian and Thingol rule the 'woodland Elves in Doriath, living in a hall called the Thousand Caves' (*The Shaping of Middle-earth*, p. 13), and that the Ilkorins who dwell in Doriath because of their association with Melian come near to matching the Elves who have dwelt in Valinor.

The *Quenta Noldorinwa* (c. 1930) added nothing to the story, but a few dates were provided by the 'earliest' and 'later' *Annals* of the early and mid-1930s. The events of this chapter occur during the period covered by the *Annals of Valinor* but take place in Beleriand; for some time Tolkien hesitated whether they should appear also in the *Annals of Beleriand* or in only one of the two. As first written the only relevant entry in the 'earliest' *Annals of Valinor* states that Fëanor arrived in Middle-earth in Valian Year 2995. A later addition records the arrival in 2700 of the Green-elves or Laiqeldar in Ossiriand and that they become allies of Thingol, but at this point they have a different history: they are not Teleri but Noldoli, and their leader is Denithor, son of Dan. Additions to Valian Year 2990–1 place the making of Menegroth and the protection of the Girdle of Melian at the time of Morgoth's return to Middle-earth, and state that most of the Elves of Beleriand withdrew behind its protection save those in the Havens and the Green-elves in Ossiriand; and that for a while Thingol with the help of Denithor (changed to *Denethor*) keeps the Orcs from the South, though Denithor is slain. In the first version of the 'earliest' *Annals of Beleriand* Elves do not meet Dwarves until the Year of the Sun 163. In the second version, the Noldor meet the Dwarves in 104. The information added to the 'earliest' *Annals of Valinor* appears in the 'later' *Annals of Valinor* as written, but the making of Menegroth follows the battle in which Denethor is slain. In the 'later' *Annals of Beleriand*, as part of a general adjustment of dates, the meeting of the Elves and Dwarves was changed from 104 to 154.

The *Quenta Silmarillion*, begun in the mid-1930s, still had no chapter comparable to that in *The Silmarillion*, only scattered references. It was now said that after Denethor was slain some of the Green-elves (or Danians) removed to Doriath and mingled with Thingol's people, while others remained in Ossiriand. More is said about the cities of the Dwarves, and that few Elves visited them.

According to the *Annals of Aman* (see *Annals of Valinor*), c. 1951, the Elves who desert the march in Valian Year of the Trees 1115 are now Teleri, not Noldor, and are called the Nandor. The entry for Valian Year 1152 describes Thingol as the ruler of all the Eldar of Beleriand – the Sindar – and mentions the birth of Lúthien, but this is not specifically stated as occurring in 1152. The Dwarves come into Beleriand in 1250, and Thingol welcomes them. They help him delve and build Menegroth. The Green-elves or Nandor came into Beleriand in 1350 and have the friendship of Thingol. Morgoth returns to Middle-earth in 1495, and after their quarrel Ungoliant flees south into Beleriand. Additions to the *Annals* record that in 1300 Daeron contrives runes, and in 1320 Orcs first appear in Beleriand.

Some of these entries were marked to be transferred to the new annals of Beleriand, the *Grey Annals*, and do appear there also, often in expanded form, together with additional entries. The entry for Valian Year 1200 records Lúthien's birth, but says that it is not known more precisely than at the end of the first age of the Chaining of Melkor. There are some variations in dating: Dairon's devising of the Runes is placed in 1350, and Orcs and other evil creatures first enter Beleriand in 1330. Rewriting of the *Quenta Silmarillion* c. 1951 added further information about the Dwarves (*The War of the Jewels*, pp. 202–15).

Almost the whole of the chapter 'Of the Sindar' in *The Silmarillion* was taken by *Christopher Tolkien from the *Grey Annals*. Some material on the Dwarves was derived from additions to the *Quenta Silmarillion* c. 1951.

Sindarin *see* **Languages, Invented**

Sir Gawain and the Green Knight. Alliterative poem in Middle English. It is attributed to the same anonymous late fourteenth-century poet who wrote **Pearl*, another of four works preserved in the same manuscript (British Library MS Cotton Nero A.x, with the poems *Patience* and *Cleanness*). *Sir Gawain* became a set text in the **Oxford English School in 1947, and every two years from 1946 Tolkien gave a series of lectures about it, usually spread across two or three terms. The number of lectures in the course increased over the years: in 1956–7 it was double that in 1946–7. During his time at **Oxford Tolkien also supervised or examined several B.Litt. theses on various Arthurian texts or topics, including two on *Sir Gawain.*

SUMMARY OF THE POEM

A New Year's feast at Camelot is interrupted by the arrival of a gigantic knight, bright green all over and mounted on a green horse. He challenges anyone in King Arthur's court to give him a stroke with his axe, and to take one in return. Sir Gawain accepts, and beheads the challenger with one blow; but the Green Knight picks up his head and departs, charging Gawain to meet him at the Green Chapel in twelve months' time. A year later, seeking the green man through Wales and beyond, Gawain is welcomed at a great castle: its lord promises to direct Gawain to the Green Chapel at the appointed time, and meanwhile they agree to exchange whatever fortune they may win each day. The lord duly gives Gawain the results of his hunting in the forest, while Gawain gives the lord kisses he has received from the lord's beautiful lady, by whom Gawain is tempted. Gawain also receives from the lady a magic girdle to make him invulnerable, but fearing for his life, he keeps this from his host. On New Year's Day Gawain meets the Green Knight as arranged and receives his stroke, only a slight wound. His foe reveals himself as the lord of the castle in other guise: he and his wife had tested Gawain at the bidding of Arthur's enemy, the sorceress Morgan le Fay, but Gawain successfully resisted temptation except in the matter of the girdle. Gawain confesses his faults and returns to Camelot, ashamed that he has succumbed to cowardice and covetousness.

EDITION IN MIDDLE ENGLISH

By August 1921 **C.T. Onions suggested to Tolkien that he should prepare, or help to prepare, an edition of *Sir Gawain* for students; and by early February 1922 Tolkien and his colleague at the University of **Leeds, **E.V. Gordon, agreed to produce one. Progress was slowed by their heavy teaching schedules and by Tolkien's work (by June 1923) also on the 'Clarendon **Chaucer'; and it was further complicated by **Kenneth Sisam at Oxford University Press (**Publishers), who asked that their book not exceed 160 pages for reasons of cost. By November 1923 Tolkien and Gordon concluded that *Sir Gawain*, a difficult work in the West Midlands dialect of Middle English (see **English language and **A Fourteenth-Century Romance), needed an additional forty pages to accommodate an extended glossary and notes. The language of the poem, they wrote (1925 edn., p. vi), 'is idiomatic, and the vocabulary rich. There are approximately as many distinct individual words as there are lines in the poem: a new word for every line.' Sisam accepted the greater length only on condition that Tolkien and Gordon submit a manuscript so clean that the cost of correction in proof would be negligible. The text of the poem went to Sisam on 14 December 1923, but several more months passed before Tolkien and Gordon finished their apparatus. In their edition of *Sir Gawain* as published by Oxford University Press at last in April 1925 (see further, *Descriptive Bibliography* B7) the text, notes, glossary, and index of names ran to 211 pages, in addition to preliminary matter.

Its 'first endeavour', Tolkien and Gordon wrote, was

> to provide the student with a text which, treating the unique manuscript [British Museum MS Nero A.x] with all due respect, is yet pleasant for the modern reader to look at, and is free (as are few Middle English texts) from a litter of italics, asterisks, and brackets, the trail of the passing editor. The second has been to provide a sufficient apparatus for reading this remarkable poem with an appreciation as far as possible of the sort which its author may be supposed to have desired. [1925 edn., p. v]

J.H.G. Grattan, writing in the *Review of English Studies* 1, no. 4 (October 1925), found the Tolkien-Gordon edition excellent. He praised its introduction and notes and its conservative text, and felt that its 'plan of keeping the printed page free from what the editors call "the trail of the passing editor" has much to recommend it in a book like this; but [the editors'] omission to state in the footnotes the authors of the emendations they have adopted, should be rectified in a second edition' (p. 485). Cyril Brett in *Modern Language Review* 22 (1927) praised the edition for its 'clearness, conciseness, scholarship, and common-sense' (p. 451), but like Grattan, suggested improvements. In *Modern Philology* 23 (1925–6) J.R. Hulbert commented that 'the edition is a good one; for it makes the poem available to readers who have not an extensive knowledge of Middle English and do not wish to spend hours hunting for information about rare words.' But Hulbert found the introduction 'not quite satisfactory', and criticized the editors' failure to acknowledge their indebtedness to other scholars (pp. 246).

Oliver Farrar Emerson wrote in the *Journal of English and Germanic Philology* 26 (1927): 'It goes without saying that all students of Middle English will welcome heartily this new edition of a great poem. It presents in reasonable compass a good introduction, a good text, a larger body of notes than in any previous edition, and a good glossary' (p. 248). But Emerson found it extraordinary for the editors to say that they had prepared the poem to be read 'with an appreciation as far as possible of the sort which its author may be supposed to have desired', and that 'much of the literature' of *Sir Gawain* 'has little bearing on this object' so has 'been passed over or lightly handled'. He too complained that no credit had been given to those who emended the text or whose scholarship informed the notes, and he disagreed with some of Tolkien and Gordon's interpretations.

In *Modern Language Notes* 41 (June 1926) Robert J. Menner called the Tolkien-Gordon edition 'a book of great importance for students of Middle English', whose 'glossary, which contains many new definitions and etymologies, is a valuable contribution to Middle English lexicography' (p. 400), but whose bibliography could have been longer.

*Priscilla Tolkien recalls having attended her father's lectures on *Sir Gawain* when she herself was a student at Oxford in the late 1940s, in which he delighted in pointing out errors Tolkien and Gordon had made in their edition. Some of these were corrected in later printings between 1930 and 1936. For the edition published by Alfred A. Knopf in 2003, W.S. Merwin used the original Tolkien-Gordon text as the basis of a Modern English verse translation, which appears on facing pages with the poem in Middle English.

By the end of the 1940s Tolkien and Oxford University Press (Gordon had died in 1938) discussed a revision of the book. Tolkien hoped to undertake this during sabbatical leave in Michaelmas Term 1949 and Hilary Term 1950, but in the event did not do so, distracted by other projects and by ill health. In 1951, still having made little or no progress with *Sir Gawain*, he judged that its text and notes needed only minor adjustment, but that its introduction should be rewritten and probably reset.

Much later, on 11 December 1959, Tolkien wrote to Oxford University Press that although he could send minor corrections for another printing, 'I am afraid any attempt to emend the book as a whole would be a major operation, requiring the re-writing of nearly everything except the text, and though I think I could do this and should like to, I cannot possibly do so for some time' (Oxford University Press archives).

*Norman Davis, Tolkien's successor in 1959 to the Merton chair of English Language and Literature at Oxford, agreed that much work needed to be done. *Gawain* scholarship by now had changed greatly, especially after the publication in 1940 of the Early English Text Society (*Societies and clubs) edition of *Sir Gawain* prepared by Sir Israel Gollancz. Davis himself wished to revise the Tolkien and Gordon edition, but was unable to do so officially until probably 1966. In his introduction to the second edition (Clarendon Press, October 1967) he wrote: 'Mrs. [E.V.] Gordon has consented to my attempting the task. J.R.R. Tolkien, long ago my teacher and now my much beloved friend, has allowed me a free hand in revising his work and has generously given me the use of his later notes. Many of these I have incorporated, but other changes are my own and for the final blend I am alone responsible' (p. v). Davis largely rewrote the introduction, notes, and appendix on language of the original edition.

A.R. Heiserman noted in a review in *Speculum* 44 (June 1969) that in his revision Davis doubled the number of notes, augmented the discussion of language, and modified the text. His new introduction, Heiserman felt, describes the manuscript more fully and accurately, 'but happily omits the first edition's long summary of the action'; but Davis does not always state all pertinent evidence for each emendation, his notes do not always cite contrary evidence, and his bibliography is 'cruelly selective' (pp. 176, 177).

W.P. KER LECTURE

In January 1952 Tolkien was chosen to be the 1952–3 W.P. Ker Lecturer at the University of Glasgow. He agreed to his selection around the end of January 1952, and suggested *Sir Gawain and the Green Knight* as his topic. Other matters, however, held his attention in 1952 and early 1953, so that when he left for Glasgow on 14 April 1953 to deliver the lecture, the work was still unfinished, or at least unpolished. Nonetheless he presented it on 15 April to an audience of 300. Although well received by his Glasgow listeners, Tolkien himself thought that the lecture was less good than it might have been, because he had not given it enough attention in the writing, but that it might improve when prepared for publication. A single typescript of the text is extant. *Christopher Tolkien edited this for inclusion in *The Monsters and the Critics and Other Essays* (1983), pp. 72–108, as his father's 'principal pronouncement on the poem to which he devoted so much thought and study' (foreword, p. 1).

Tolkien speaks on 'the movement of [the *Gawain*-poet's] mind, as he wrote and (I do not doubt) re-wrote the story, until it had the form that has come down to us', and on 'the kernel, the very nub of the poem as it was finally made, its great third "fit", and within that the temptation of Sir Gawain and his confession' (p. 73). The temptation is the *raison d'être* of the work, 'real and perilous in the extreme on the *moral* plane . . . ; yet hanging in the background, for those able to receive the air of "faerie" in a romance, is a terrible threat of disaster and destruction' (p. 83). From the very beginning of the poem the 'moral purpose of the poet' is at work. 'It is necessary to the temptation that Gawain's actions should be capable of moral approbation; and amidst all the "faerie" the poet is at pains to show that they were so. He takes up the challenge' of the Green Knight to his king 'as a matter of duty and humility and self-sacrifice' (pp. 74–5). Gawain's character is further established by the pentangle on his shield as he sets out for the Green Chapel: it is a symbol of perfection 'in religion (the Christian faith), in piety and morality, and the "courtesy" that flows therefrom into human relations' (p. 77).

At the castle, 'a courteous and Christian hall', Gawain finds himself 'in the midst of the life and society that he most liked, and where his very skill and pleasure in courteous converse would ensure him the highest honour' (p. 78). He is moved by the beauty of the lady of the castle, and tricked into the bargain with his host that each will exchange with the other what they gain during the day. Yet he cannot, out of courtesy, refuse to engage in the lady's play, nor can he insult the lord of the castle by leaving, having promised to accept his hospitality for a further three nights. 'Gawain is now in great peril. Wise flight has proved impossible without breaking his word and the rules of courtesy to his host. His sleep has been dark and troubled with the fear of death. And when the lady appears again he welcomes her with sheer pleasure and delight in her beauty' (p. 85). She leads him to the brink: 'he cared for his courtesy' to the lady, by which he must respond to her, but if he should sin thereby, he would be a 'traitor' to his host (p. 87).

Tolkien argues that 'the whole interpretation and valuation of *Sir Gawain and the Green Knight* depends on what one thinks of the thirtieth stanza of the Third Fit', stanza 75 all told, in which Gawain hides the magic girdle given him by the lady, then prays in a chapel and confesses to a priest. Tolkien considers 'arrant nonsense' Sir Israel Gollancz's statement in his edition of the poem, that Gawain's confession is sacrilegious, because he conceals from the priest the fact that he has accepted the girdle and intends to retain it. The text, Tolkien says, 'does not specify what Gawain confessed', and it is 'gratuitously silly to assert that he concealed anything'. Also, after his confession Gawain is seen to have a light heart, 'certainly not the mood induced by a bad confession and the wilful concealment of sin' (p. 88). The reader is driven, then, 'to consider the relation of all these rules of behaviour, these games and courtesies, to *sin*, morals, the saving of souls, to what the author would have held to be eternal and universal values. And that, surely, is precisely why the confession is introduced, and at this point. Gawain in his last perilous extremity was obliged to tear his "code" in two, and distinguish its components of good manners and good morals' (pp. 88–9). Tolkien discusses these matters at length. He concludes that the introduction of Gawain's confession and its precise place in the poem were deliberate, 'and that it is an indication of the author's opinion that *games* and *manners* were not important, ultimate (for "salvation" . . .), and were in any case on an inferior plane to real *virtue*, to which they must in the case of conflict give way' (p. 92).

Tolkien detects three planes to the tale: 'mere jesting pastimes', '"courtesy"', as a code of "gentle" or polite manners, which included a special mode of deference to women, and could be held to include . . . the more serious, and therefore more dangerous, "game" of courtly love-making', and 'real morals, virtues and sins'. If these compete with one another, 'the higher law must be obeyed. . . . The author is chiefly interested in the competition between "courtesy" and virtue (purity and loyalty); he shows us their increasing divergence, and shows us Gawain at the crisis of the temptation recognizing this, and choosing virtue rather than courtesy, yet preserving a graciousness of manner and a gentleness of speech belonging to the true spirit of courtesy' (p. 95). Each plane is judged by its own court: moral law by the Church, 'playing the game' by the Green Knight, and courtesy by its 'supreme court', that of King Arthur. But Gawain also judges himself, as guilty of cowardice and covetousness; and in this his excess of shame is true to his depicted character.

MODERN ENGLISH TRANSLATION

Within his April 1953 W.P. Ker Lecture Tolkien found occasion to quote from *Sir Gawain* in a Modern English translation he had 'just completed', and had made 'with two objects ... : to preserve the original metre and alliteration, without which translation is of little value except as a crib; and to preserve, to exhibit in an intelligible modern edition, the nobility and the courtesy of this poem, by a poet to whom "courtesy" meant so much' (*The Monsters and the Critics and Other Essays*, p. 74). At least part of a translation by Tolkien was in existence some thirty years earlier. On 15 November 1923 E.V. Gordon noted in a letter to Kenneth Sisam, who had asked for a sample translation of *Sir Gawain*, that Tolkien had prepared the requested lines of the poem (2000–2200) at some earlier time. Tolkien and Gordon planned to revise the sample for consideration by Oxford University Press, but nothing seems to have come of it. On 23 January 1947 a copy of a translation of *Sir Gawain* by Tolkien, presumably complete, was returned to him by his friend *Gwyn Jones, to whom it had been lent.

In 1950 Tolkien's Oxford colleague *John Bryson told the Controller of the BBC Third Programme about the translation, and in reply to an enquiry Tolkien wrote on 17 August 1950 that work on it was far advanced – probably, that is, it was complete but not yet revised to his satisfaction. He sent a portion to the BBC for a preliminary decision, commenting that with few exceptions the poem could not be cut without serious harm. The BBC quickly found the translation suitable for broadcast, but Tolkien did not finish a script until 1953, and sent it to the Third Programme in June of that year. On 15 July *P.H. Newby informed Tolkien that the BBC wished to broadcast his *Sir Gawain* around Christmas 1953, and suggested that it be read by a single voice – possibly by the poet Dylan Thomas. By 31 July Tolkien divided the work into six parts, the first of which he thought should be prefaced by a five-minute talk, and all of which he hoped to be allowed to read for broadcast himself. Aware that the BBC were not keen to have him as a performer, he hired a tape recorder with which to practice his delivery. On 1 September he auditioned for the BBC in a studio, and discussed practical matters of reading with Newby, at which the suggestion was made that the poem be read by several voices rather than only one.

On 3 September Tolkien wrote to Newby that he had reconsidered the division of the work, which he now felt would break better into five rather than six parts, with the Third (and longest) Fit divided in two. He suggested that he say a few preliminary words before the First Fit, and then speak the opening lines in Middle English as representing the voice of the medieval poet, after which a modern narrator should take over. In regard to his audition, he felt that

> it was very good for an elderly professor, who has been too long and too often in the position of critic, to be put through it. You are not very easy to please! If one can assume that the record you played back to me would, on an average [radio] set, come through with anything like the

clarity that it had in the studio, I can only say that it sounded to me better than most things I have listened to of the sort – more *interesting* (more variable and unexpectable [*sic*]). It could be improved, of course, quite apart from my voice-quality. I deliberately selected a passage that I had not practiced, and had seldom read aloud before; and I made one or two mistakes in the Middle English that pained me! [BBC Written Archives Centre]

As for the idea of using more than one voice, Tolkien stated that there are 1,790 narrative lines in the poem and 740 of direct speech, for which at least four voices would be needed. He calculated the number of lines for each character, and noted which parts could be doubled. He thought that the use of different voices would enliven and clarify the poem, and that he could increase the dialogue a little by making slight alterations. The BBC agreed that the work should be read by several performers, but in only four programmes, with a separate twenty-minute talk by Tolkien to make a fifth.

On 3 December 1953 Tolkien recorded his five-minute introduction to the broadcasts, and on 29 December his longer talk on *Sir Gawain*. The introduction and First Fit of the poem were first broadcast on 6 December 1953, with the remaining parts on 13, 20, and 30 December. Tolkien's longer talk, on the meaning of the poem and its place in the literature of the Chaucerian period, was first broadcast on 3 January 1954. On 4 December 1953 an article by Tolkien on *Sir Gawain*, *A Fourteenth-Century Romance*, was published in the *Radio Times*, who had commissioned it as a printed introduction to the broadcasts.

Despite efforts to bring it into print in his lifetime, Tolkien's Modern English *Sir Gawain* was not published until after his death, in *Sir Gawain and the Green Knight, Pearl and Sir Orfeo*, edited by Christopher Tolkien (1975). A slightly reduced version of his twenty-minute talk of 1953 was published as part of the introduction to the 1975 volume. A commercial recording of Tolkien's translation, read by Terry Jones, was first issued in 1997.

See further, Tom Shippey, 'Tolkien and the *Gawain*-poet', *Proceedings of the J.R.R. Tolkien Centenary Conference 1992* (1995); and numerous references in *Approaches to Teaching Sir Gawain and the Green Knight*, ed. Miriam Youngerman Miller and Jane Chance (1986).

Sir Gawain and the Green Knight, Pearl and Sir Orfeo. Modern English translations by Tolkien of these medieval works (see separate entries for summaries and history), with introductory material, ed. *Christopher Tolkien, first published in Great Britain by George Allen & Unwin, London, in September 1975, and in the United States by the Houghton Mifflin Company, Boston, in October 1975. See further, *Descriptive Bibliography* B30.

News of the existence of Tolkien's translation of *Sir Gawain and the Green Knight* reached *Stanley Unwin of George Allen & Unwin (*Publishers) by 6 November 1950. On that date Unwin wrote to Tolkien in the hope that he would allow Allen & Unwin the privilege of considering his work for publication. On 21 November 1950 Unwin wrote again, to express interest in 'a volume of non-Chaucerian Middle English translations' with an introductory essay by Tolkien (Tolkien-George Allen & Unwin archive, HarperCollins). Other work, notably the completion of *The Lord of the Rings, drew Tolkien's attention, as did the need to prepare or complete other translations to appear with Sir Gawain. In 1959 Tolkien briefly was at the point of signing a contract for Sir Gawain alone with the publisher William Heinemann, who wished to include it in the series Poetry Bookshelf, but at the last moment realized that he owed Allen & Unwin the right of first refusal. On 4 August 1959 he wrote to Rayner Unwin, apologizing for his lapse, and suggested that it was 'high time that Sir Gawain was published before some competitor (whether better or worse) spoils the field. Would you welcome it soon, or not?' (Tolkien-George Allen & Unwin archive, HarperCollins).

Rayner quickly agreed that Allen & Unwin would publish Sir Gawain on its own rather than as part of a collection. But Tolkien decided that Sir Gawain should be published with his translation of *Pearl, the rights to which were released by *Basil Blackwell, to whom the work had been promised long before. On 9 December 1959 he reported to Rayner Unwin that (despite lumbago) he had 'recently ordered and inspected' Sir Gawain and Pearl and did not think that the translations now needed much work, though he was 'still a little uncertain about what other matter to add to them by way of introduction or notes' (Letters, p. 301). Three years later he was still putting the work in order. On 2 November 1962 he told Rayner that the translations were completed,

> but they need a final revision before I can send them in. Pearl in particular has been subjected to a good deal of criticism, much of which is justified, by an expert in this field. These translations are of course on my list as the most urgent task before me, but the return to lecturing this term has proved a much greater burden than I expected. It has taken much more work than I guessed to shake the dust of seventeen years off matter which I once thought I knew. [Tolkien-George Allen & Unwin archive, HarperCollins]

He optimistically felt that the translations would be published early in the new year, but as time passed he continued to discover minor points in the work which led him astray, and then the issue of his American copyrights (see *Ace Books controversy) and of a revised edition of The Lord of the Rings demanded his attention. He wrote to Rayner Unwin on 8 November 1965:

> I expect you are getting anxious about [Sir Gawain and Pearl]. . . . It was rather disastrous that I had to put them aside, while I had them fully in mind. The work on the 'revision' of The Lord of the Rings took me clean away, and I now find work on anything else tiresome.

I am finding the selection of notes [for the translations], and com- pressing them, and the introduction difficult. Too much to say, and not sure of my target. The main target is, of course, the general reader of literary bent with no knowledge of Middle English; but it cannot be doubted that the book will be read by students, and by academic folk of 'English Departments'. Some of the latter have their pistols loose in the holsters. [*Letters*, p. 364]

The translations remained work in progress for Tolkien at the time of his death. Christopher Tolkien, as his father's literary executor, soon took them up, together with a Modern English version of *Sir Orfeo* of uncertain date which Tolkien apparently had long ago laid aside. In his preface Christopher Tolkien notes that his father had not decided on the final form of every line of the translations, nor did Tolkien ever write the commentary he wished to include, while 'the introduction did not get beyond the point of tentative beginnings' (*Sir Gawain and the Green Knight, Pearl and Sir Orfeo*, p. 7). The latter as published contains six parts. The first, on the author of *Sir Gawain*, was derived from Tolkien's notes. The second, on the poem itself, is a reduction of Tolkien's twenty-minute talk on the BBC Third Programme first broadcast in January 1954 (see **Sir Gawain and the Green Knight*). The third, on *Pearl*, is a reprint of Tolkien's contribution to the introduction of E.V. Gordon's edi- tion of the poem (see **Pearl*). The remaining sections are notes by Christopher Tolkien on *Sir Orfeo*, on editions of the three poems, and on the text of the translations. The glossary is also by Christopher Tolkien. An appendix, 'The Verse-forms of *Sir Gawain and the Green Knight* and *Pearl*', was drawn 'from drafts made for, but not used in, the introductory talk to the broadcasts of' *Sir Gawain*, and from unpublished notes on *Pearl* (p. 8).

Also appended to the volume is a short fourth work, *Gawain's Leave-taking*, a translation by Tolkien of four stanzas from another medieval English poem ('Nou Bernes, Buirdus, bolde and blyþe'), contained in the Vernon Manuscript in the Bodleian Library, Oxford. The poem originally had no connection with Sir Gawain, but was related to *Sir Gawain and the Green Knight* only in Tol- kien's thoughts.

Commercial recordings of Tolkien's translations, read by Terry Jones, were first issued in 1997.

CRITICISM

In a review of *Sir Gawain and the Green Knight, Pearl and Sir Orfeo* in the *Times Higher Educational Supplement* for 30 January 1976, A.C. Spearing found Tolkien's translations 'disappointing. Their chief merit is their skill in retaining the varying rhythms of the originals, but their style and diction have an archaic quality that produces a quite different effect from that of the originals – not of ancient grandeur, but of faded romanticism laced with awkwardness.' But 'the introduction to *Gawain* is a little masterpiece'. Roger Sale, writing in the *Times*

Literary Supplement for 12 March 1976, liked the 'jogging tetrameter couplets of *Sir Orfeo*' but the translation of *Sir Gawain*, 'read simply as a poem . . . is less good than either James L. Rosenberg's or Marie Boroff's [translations], because Tolkien was much more willing to keep (or even occasionally to adopt) constructions that are straightforward in Middle English but awkward now, much more willing, to fall into an idiom that is neither medieval nor twentieth-century, just as he does in *The Lord of the Rings*' ('Wonderful to Relate', p. 289; see also Sale, 'Tolkien as Translator', *Parnassus* 4 (1976)). The reviewer in *British Book News*, December 1975, found 'the versification . . . often slack and unimaginative; so many archaic words are used that a glossary to the translations has to be provided; the demands of the strict metres frequently cause both natural English word-order and the sense of the originals to be wrenched. This is not a book for the expert medievalist. As translations these are not very authoritative. . . .' Paul H. Kocher, in contrast, in his review in *Mythprint* 12, no. 4 (October 1975) praises Tolkien for translating *Sir Gawain* 'with practiced skill, born partly of his close acquaintance with the original text of the poem, and partly of his close affinity with its subject-matter'; and he notes that in the translation of *Pearl* Tolkien adhered to the customs of its verse-form 'without being slavish about it. Which is as much to say that Tolkien well knew how to balance on this thin edge between over-literal and over-free renditions, a problem that many translators never solve' (p. 3).

Sir Orfeo. Poem in Middle English, perhaps by way of a French original, composed probably in the late thirteenth or early fourteenth century. Its earliest known text, of three, is in the Auchinleck manuscript (made *c*. 1330) in the National Library of Scotland.

SUMMARY

Orfeo is an English king and a harper of sublime skill. His fair queen Heurodis having been taken away by magic, Orfeo leaves his realm in the care of a steward and flees into the wilderness, taking with him only a beggar's cloak and his harp. For ten years he lives in the wood, charming birds and beasts with his music. Then one day, as the king of Faërie rides by with his retinue, Orfeo sees among them Heurodis, and follows to their castle. Posing as a wandering minstrel, he gains entry and plays for the king:

> and all who were in palace found
> came unto him to hear the sound,
> and lay before his very feet,
> they thought his melody so sweet.
> He played, and silent sat the king
> for great delight in listening. . . .
> (**Sir Gawain and the Green Knight,*
> *Pearl and Sir Orfeo*, p. 133)

Thus pleased, the king grants Orfeo a gift. Orfeo chooses Heurodis, and returns with her to their city. Appearing at his own castle, he finds that his steward has ruled faithfully. Orfeo and Heurodis are crowned anew.

In *Sir Orfeo* the poet adapts the ancient Greek story of Orpheus and Eurydice to medieval England. Names are altered, and certain features changed or abandoned. Eurydice (as Heurodis) no longer dies; Orpheus (as Orfeo) does not seek her in Hades but in the Celtic underworld; he does not lose her with a forbidden backward glance, but returns home for a happy ending.

EDITION IN MIDDLE ENGLISH

In 1943 or 1944 Tolkien prepared an edition of *Sir Orfeo* for the use of Navy and Air Force cadets taking courses in the *Oxford English School. A typescript of this was reproduced by mimeograph by the Academic Copying Office, Oxford in 1944. Although this pamphlet is not credited to Tolkien by name, ample evidence exists to attribute the edition to him, including line numbers and corrections added in pencil manuscript by Tolkien to some of the extant copies. An afterword notes that most of the edition was based on the Auchinleck manuscript, except for a small portion based on the Harley manuscript in the British Library (where the Auchinleck version is wanting),

> though the spelling has in a few points been altered, and final *-e* has been restored or omitted in accordance with the grammar of earlier Southern English. In a few cases the lines have been emended by small changes, especially of word-order. The result is a much more metrical version than that offered even by [the Auchinleck manuscript], though several lines . . . remain obviously defective and corrupt. [p. 17]

Here Tolkien states that the poem was made probably in Essex, 'but it passed through several hands of copyists, or the mouths of reciters, between the author and the oldest surviving [manuscript], and these, in addition to the corruptions of error and forgetfulness, have infected it with the forms of later language and different dialect . . .' (pp. 17–18).

Tolkien's edition was re-presented, with an introduction and notes by Carl F. Hostetter, in *Tolkien Studies* 1 (2004), pp. 85–123. Hostetter demonstrates that Tolkien's version closely follows that in the collection *Fourteenth Century Verse & Prose* edited by *Kenneth Sisam, for which Tolkien provided *A Middle English Vocabulary*. Not only are these comparable in formatting and punctuation, they also share certain readings that are original to Sisam's edition, and the 1944 pamphlet includes most of Sisam's editorial revisions.

Beginning in 1947 Tolkien supervised the B.Litt. thesis of *A.J. Bliss, an edition of *Sir Orfeo* presenting the texts of all three extant manuscripts with introduction, notes, and glossary. With revision this was published in 1954 by Oxford University Press in the *Oxford English Monographs* series, of which Tolkien was an editor.

MODERN ENGLISH TRANSLATION

As also for *Pearl and *Sir Gawain and the Green Knight, Tolkien prepared a Modern English translation of Sir Orfeo. Since Carl F. Hostetter has shown that Tolkien's translation follows his edition prepared for cadets, the Modern English version cannot have been made earlier than c. 1944. On 28 April 1967 Tolkien wrote to Professor John Leyerle of the University of Toronto that he had written a 'reasonably successful translation of Sir Orfeo . . . some years ago'. It was first published in *Sir Gawain and the Green Knight, Pearl and Sir Orfeo (1975).

Sisam, Kenneth (1887–1971). Kenneth Sisam entered Merton College, *Oxford in 1910 as a Rhodes Scholar from New Zealand. In Hilary Term 1912 he became the personal assistant to *A.S. Napier, Merton Professor of English Language and Literature, Rawlinsonian Professor of Anglo-Saxon, and supervisor of Sisam's B.Litt. thesis, an edition of the Salisbury Psalter (Salisbury MS 150). With Napier in declining health, Sisam took on some of his academic burden: in a typical term he taught Sweet's Anglo-Saxon Reader (prose) on Mondays, Elementary Historical Grammar on Tuesdays, Morris and Skeat's Specimens of Early English on Wednesdays, Havelok on Thursdays, and the Anglo-Saxon Reader (verse) on Fridays. Tolkien attended some of these classes as an undergraduate, and when he moved from Classics to the English School Sisam became his tutor. 'He was an accurate and painstaking scholar, and Tolkien soon came to respect and like him' (Biography, p. 64). Tolkien once said that 'the foundation of my library was laid by Sisam. He taught me not only to read texts, but to study second-hand book catalogues, of which I was not even aware. Some he marked for me' (letter to *N.R. Ker, 22 November 1970, Letters, p. 406). Tolkien also felt indebted to Sisam for 'pointing out the chance to me' of becoming Reader in English Language at Leeds in 1920 (letter to R.W. Chapman, 26 November 1941, Letters, p. 56).

In 1915–16 Sisam worked for a brief time on the *Oxford English Dictionary under *Henry Bradley, and on light labours for the Oxford University Press – he was by this time a chronic invalid. In 1917 he entered the Ministry of Food, where he served for five years; during that period he edited the perennially useful anthology Fourteenth Century Verse & Prose (1921), to which Tolkien contributed a glossary (*A Middle English Vocabulary). In 1923 Sisam rejoined the Oxford University Press as Junior Assistant Secretary. In 1925 he applied for the Rawlinson and Bosworth Professorship in Anglo-Saxon, but the chair went to Tolkien. Sisam became instead Assistant Secretary to the Delegates of the Oxford University Press, and in 1942 Secretary.

His career in publishing was distinguished, his standards high. Some considered him a guide and friend to authors; others found him stern and parsimonious. Tolkien continued to be friendly with him, though they did not always agree about matters such as whether and to what extent notes were needed in a book, and Sisam complained about the length of time Tolkien took to complete work for the Press, and about the number of his corrections in proof.

After his retirement in 1948 Sisam found more time to write. Among his late works were *The Structure of Beowulf* (1965), in which he disagreed with some of Tolkien's conclusions in *Beowulf: The Monsters and the Critics*; and *The Oxford Book of Medieval Verse* (1971), one of several works he produced in collaboration with his daughter **Celia Sisam** (whose B.Litt. Tolkien supervised, and who became a Fellow of St Hilda's College, Oxford).

Sketch of the Mythology. A synopsis of the *'Silmarillion' mythology as it existed in Tolkien's mind from *c*. 1926, published with commentary and notes as 'The Earliest "Silmarillion"' in *The Shaping of Middle-earth* (1986), pp. 11–75.

Tolkien explained the purpose of the work in a later inscription on the envelope containing the manuscript: 'Original "Silmarillion". Form orig[inally] composed *c*. 1926–30 for R.W. Reynolds to explain background of "alliterative version" of Túrin & the Dragon: then in progress . . .' (*The Shaping of Middle-earth*, p. 11). At least during 1915–16 Tolkien had sent some of his early poems to *R.W. Reynolds, formerly a master at *King Edward's School, Birmingham, for criticism and advice about publication. At the end of 1925 they resumed correspondence, and subsequently Tolkien sent him many of his poems, including part of the unfinished alliterative *Children of Húrin*, the beginning of the *Lay of Leithian*, and the *Sketch of the Mythology*.

The *Sketch* is justifiably described as the 'original "Silmarillion"', as it was the basis of the *Quenta Noldorinwa* (*c*. 1930) from which the *Quenta Silmarillion* (mid-1930s–early 1938, revised *c*. 1951 and late 1950s) was derived. It was the first text to cover, if only briefly, almost the whole mythology (*The Book of Lost Tales* was abandoned before completion): it excludes the Creation, begins with the arrival of the Valar in Arda, and ends with the overthrow of Morgoth, prophecies of his eventual return, and final defeat and the recovery of the Silmarils and the rekindling of the Trees.

The story told in the *Sketch of the Mythology* had developed a great deal since *The Book of Lost Tales*, but no intervening texts survive. Christopher Tolkien thinks that there probably were none, but that his father developed his ideas in his head while at Leeds, and they were there when he came to write the *Sketch*; and he may even have written it from memory without even consulting the manuscripts of *The Book of Lost Tales*. Since it was only a synopsis, Tolkien had to omit much content. Christopher Tolkien comments that it was 'often extremely difficult, or impossible, to judge whether features in the *Tales* that are not present in the "Sketch" were omitted simply for the sake of compression, or whether they had been definitely abandoned' (p. 42).

The original twenty-eight page manuscript almost certainly dates from early in 1926 but it was subsequently heavily revised until probably 1930. Its full title is *Sketch of the Mythology with Especial Reference to 'The Children of Húrin'*.

For the part played by the *Sketch* in the evolution of Tolkien's mythology, see entries for the separate chapters of *The Silmarillion*.

Smith, Albert Hugh (1903–1967). A.H. Smith was a student of Tolkien at *Leeds; he received his B.A. in 1924, a Ph.D. in 1926, and a D.Litt. in 1937. He taught at the University of Leeds, at Saltley College in Birmingham, and at the University of Uppsala before settling at University College, London in 1930. Distinguished service in Intelligence during the Second World War, in part using new photographic techniques to examine captured enemy documents, earned him an O.B.E., one of numerous honours he ultimately received. After posts as Lecturer and then Reader in English at University College, from 1949 until his death he was Quain Professor of English Language and Literature, the successor to *R.W. Chambers. From 1945 to 1963 he was also Director of Scandinavian Studies at University College, London; from 1954 to 1964 Secretary of the Communication Research Centre at University College, reflecting his interest in general linguistics; and from 1951 Director of the English Place-Name Society.

His contributions to the history of place-names were many and important. Among his publications are *The Place-names of the North Riding* (1928, in which Tolkien is thanked for his encouragement and help with philological problems), *The Place-names of the East Riding of Yorkshire and York* (1937), *The Preparation of County Place-name Surveys* (1954), *English Place-name Elements* (2 vols., 1955), *The Place-names of the West Riding of Yorkshire* (1961–3, 8 vols.), *Place-names of Gloucestershire* (1964–5, 4 vols), and *The Place-names of Westmorland* (1967, 2 vols.). Smith took pains in every aspect of this work, whether consultation with experts in various fields from history to geology, or the making of maps, or the practical concerns of printing.

His interest in the latter dated at least from his student days at Leeds, when his booklet *The Merry Shire* (1923), containing six poems by Smith in the Yorkshire dialect and a foreword by *Lascelles Abercrombie, was published at the Swan Press. Arthur Brown (see reference below) speculates that if Smith did not print this himself, he was closely involved in all aspects of its production. (Around this time Smith published poetry as well in *A Northern Venture* (1923) and *Leeds University Verse 1914–24* (1924), to which Tolkien also contributed.) Two other booklets by Smith, certainly printed by the author, are recorded from 1925 and 1927. At University College, London he was concerned with the construction of a full-size working hand-press (destroyed in the war, but Smith and his colleagues built another), the cutting of punches to make type for printing Old English, and the making of further booklets, most notably *Songs for the Philologists* (1936) which includes verses by Tolkien and *E.V. Gordon.

With Professor Frederick Norman, Smith began *Methuen's Old English Library*, to provide undergraduates with reliable early English texts. The first volume of this series, *Three Northumbrian Poems*, edited by Smith, was published in 1933. Also in collaboration with Norman, Smith began in 1937 to publish the annual *London Medieval Studies*, which however was interrupted by the war and ceased in 1951. In this period he also collaborated with J.L.N. O'Loughlin in editing *Odhams Dictionary of the English Language*, published in 1946. In 1961 Tolkien consulted Smith about a point in British Library (British Museum) MS Cotton Cleopatra C. vi, the *Ancrene Riwle*, on which Smith was working at the time for the Early English Text Society (*Societies and clubs).

In a footnote to his article 'The Origin of the Name Wetwang', *Amon Hen* 63 (August 1983), J.S. Ryan says that Smith 'admitted' – perhaps 'speculated' would be more to the point – 'to the present writer in a private conversation in London in March 1966 that he had been a model for various hobbit antiquarian characteristics [in *The Lord of the Rings*]' (p. 13, n. 4).

See also Arthur Brown, 'Professor Albert Hugh Smith (1903–1967)', *Proceedings of the Ninth International Congress of Onomastic Sciences* (1969); and R.V. Jones, 'Wing Commander A.H. Smith, O.B.E.', in *Early English and Norse Studies Presented to Hugh Smith in Honour of His Sixtieth Birthday* (1963).

Smith, Geoffrey Bache (1894–1916). G.B. Smith, nearly three years junior to Tolkien, became acquainted with him as a fellow pupil at *King Edward's School, Birmingham. By all evidence he was witty and intelligent, a promising poet, and enthusiastic about literature and history. Tolkien and his friends *Rob Gilson and *Christopher Wiseman took Smith into their informal club, the *T.C.B.S., after he performed with them in a production of Sheridan's *The Rivals* at Christmas 1911. Within the school Debating Society, of which he was Secretary in 1912, Smith spoke frequently, and could not 'be induced, under any circumstances, to make a serious speech, but regales the house with tempestuous orations bubbling over with Bernard Shaw and G.K. Chesterton' ('Characters, 1911–12', *King Edward's School Chronicle* n.s. 27, no. 193 (June 1912), p. 40). In January 1913 he read a paper on King Arthur to the school Literary Society.

At the end of 1912 Smith won an exhibition at Corpus Christi College, *Oxford, and in October 1913 went up to read English. On 5 December 1913 Tolkien wrote in the *King Edward's School Chronicle* (as 'Oxon'):

> G.B. Smith is the proud possessor of rooms in Corpus Christi once occupied by R.B. Naish whom you may remember. His college often reminds him of this, but his tendency – self-confessed – to aesthetic intellectualism is outraging itself in a strange, if incomplete, scheme of decoration, so that the rooms now bear few marks of their former O.E. [Old Edwardian] occupant. We believe he was in the winning crew of some college fours and celebrated it magnificently, though the resplendent cup so obtained is now, but the receptacle for "Cape Gooseberries;" (or do you call them "Winter Cherries"?). [*Oxford Letter*, n.s. 28, no. 202 (December 1913), pp. 80–1]

War in Europe having broken out in August 1914, Smith enlisted that December in the Army. Although the quota of officers in the Oxfordshire and Buckinghamshire Light Infantry was complete, Smith was taken on as a supernumerary, and commissioned a temporary second lieutenant. By mid-April 1915 he applied to transfer to the recently formed 19th Battalion of the *Lancashire Fusiliers, the '3rd Salford Pals'. Tolkien later attempted to gain a commission in the same battalion, but instead was placed in the 13th (Reserve) Battalion, and later in the 11th. In June 1915 Smith was promoted to full lieutenant. He was posted to France in November that year.

Smith kept up a correspondence with Tolkien, congratulating him when he gained a first class degree at Oxford, advising him on his own entry into the Army – whom to contact, what equipment to bring and where to buy it – commenting on Tolkien's attempts at poetry, discussing their friends from Birmingham and Oxford. Widely read, he suggested that Tolkien should broaden his literary horizons by reading anything by Rupert Brooke and the Georgian Poets, Browne's *Religio Medici* and *Urn Burial*, Sir Philip Sidney's *Defence of Poesie*, and Sir Francis Bacon's *Essays*, the earlier books in editions with old spelling.

Also in 1915 one of Smith's poems, 'Songs on the Downs', was published in the annual volume of *Oxford Poetry*, in which Tolkien's *Goblin Feet*, and three poems by Smith's friend *H.T. Wade-Gery, also appeared. Smith felt that those works, by the three of them, were the best in the book; stylistically, they were among the more traditional, as opposed to Modern verse by poets such as *T.W. Earp. Smith consistently encouraged Tolkien to improve his poetry and to publish it, the latter with a sense of urgency hastened by the threat of death in battle. Tolkien sent Smith his poems as they were typed, and Smith responded with work of his own, including a long poem 'The Burial of Sophocles'.

Smith's letters preserved among the Tolkien papers in the Bodleian Library, Oxford (*Libraries and archives) suggest a writer with an easy-going manner combined with erudition, though not immune from boredom and depression. On 3 February 1916 he described the situation in France as an 'orgy of death and cruelty' (quoted in *Biography*, p. 86). In May 1916 he was able to visit Tolkien and his wife (*Edith Tolkien) while on leave, and in succeeding months the friends met occasionally in France, to which Tolkien himself had been posted in June.

By mid-November Smith was made Adjutant of his battalion. By then Tolkien had contracted 'trench fever' and been invalided home to England. On 29 November Smith's battalion came under fire, and he was hit by shrapnel. By 2 December gas gangrene set in, and he died in Warlincourt, France, early the next day. Tolkien heard the news in a letter of 16 December from Christopher Wiseman. On 22 December Smith's mother, Ruth, wrote to Tolkien with an account of Smith's death as she had learned it:

The village they were in was shelled. He was going down the road when two pieces of shell wounded him in the right arm & thigh. He walked to the Dressing Station & whilst waiting for the ambulance smoked a cigarette, cheerfully regretting being unable to play in a football match he had got up for the men that afternoon. He wrote himself to tell me not to be anscious [i.e. anxious], it was slight & he would soon be at the Base. In a day or two the thigh wound set up dangerous symptoms & an operation was necessary, after that he quickly sank. He dictated a letter to me saying I am doing famously & shall be in England soon after Christmas. He thought so, never realising the danger he was in. I am thankful, he would have troubled for me. The sisters who nursed him tell me they knew him before, & liked him so. He was so good & cheerful. [Tolkien Papers, Bodleian Library, Oxford]

That Christmas Tolkien wrote a poem, *GBS*, in memory of Smith, and the following August another poem, *Companions of the Rose*, in memory of Smith and of Rob Gilson, who had died in the Battle of the Somme; both works are unpublished.

An unsigned reminiscence in the *Oxford Magazine* for 23 February 1917 praised Smith as

one of the best undergraduate officers whom Oxford has sent out to France. The personal qualities which made his friendship a thing to treasure in the memory are not easily described in print. On these suffice it to say that he was always very popular in his battalion, and to some of his brother officers he was far more than the good companion. In his temporary profession he took the keenest intellectual interest, and at the time of his death had been acting for some months as intelligence officer. An officer is nowadays told in many lectures that he must always consider the welfare of his men before his own. To some this becomes more or less of a formula; but in G.B. Smith's work it was a living principle, and no sacrifice or labour that might further the welfare or comfort of his men was ever grudged by him.

He always hoped to return to Oxford and throw himself into advanced historical work. What his technical qualifications for this were I do not know; but he would not have failed for lack of a large-hearted enthusiasm. ['Oxford's Sacrifice', p. 173]

After Smith's death Tolkien inherited some of his books of Welsh literature, including *Hanes A Chan* by J.M. Edwards, *Gwaith: Twm o'r Nant* by Thomas Edwards, and *Gwaith* by Samuel Roberts, as well as *Essai sur la composition du Roman Gallois: Peredur* by Mary Rhionnan Williams. Ruth Smith wasted no time in contacting *R.W. Reynolds, one of her son's masters at King Edward's School, Birmingham, in connection with Smith's wish that a book of his poems be published. Reynolds in turn contacted Tolkien about the matter, and Tolkien consulted with Christopher Wiseman. Wiseman felt that Reynolds would do justice to Smith as a poet, but would see him 'as a poet and not a man, as something like a successful protégé . . . as a genius, as a prodigy, anything but a soul who is saying what it feels and how it thinks.' The T.C.B.S. should have a hand in the matter, Wiseman argued, but if so they – that is, effectively himself and Tolkien – must be 'cruelly honest and not allow sentiment to cloud judgement' (letter to Tolkien, 18 January 1917, Tolkien Papers, Bodleian Library, Oxford). He did not think that Smith's last poems were his best, but should probably go into a collection.

In April Tolkien lent Wiseman manuscripts of Smith's poems, together with a typewritten copy. A month later, Wiseman expressed his opinion that he and Tolkien should not aim to publish all of Smith's poetry, only a good book of verse. Probably between late June and early July Wiseman gave Tolkien a suggested arrangement for the book, according to the most effective order of poems rather than by strict order of writing, and suggested that some of the poems be accompanied by explanatory notes of the circumstances in which they were written. R.W. Reynolds seems to have arranged for the book to be considered by the London publishers Sidgwick and Jackson; in the event it was published, as *A Spring Harvest*, in June or July 1918 by Erskine Macdonald, London. Neither Tolkien nor Wiseman is credited in the book as editor, but a short introductory note is signed 'J.R.R.T.' The note explains that the order of poems 'is not chronological beyond the fact that the third part contains only poems written after the outbreak of the war. . . . "The Burial of Sophocles," which is here placed at the end, was begun before the war and continued at odd times and in various circumstances afterwards; the final version was sent me from the trenches' (p. 7).

Many of Smith's verses contain imagery of nature, of the sea, and wind, earth and sky, and ancient trees. Among those written at Oxford was 'Glastonbury', an unsuccessful entry for the Newdigate Prize for poetry:

> Thither through moaning woods came Bedivere,
> At gloomy breaking of a winter's day,
> Weary and travel-stained and sick at heart,
> With a great wound gotten in that last fray
> Ere he stood by, and watched the King depart
> Down the long, silent reaches of the mere:
> And all the earth was sad, and skies were drear,
> And the wind cried, and chased the relict leaves
> Like ships, that the storm-tossed ocean batters and heaves,
> And they fly before the gale, and the mariners fear.
> [etc.; *A Spring Harvest*, p. 13]

His earlier poems are lusty and positive, but in the war years his outlook became noticeably dark.

Tolkien continued to be in touch occasionally with Smith's mother, who was grateful for his attention. Her other son, Roger, was also killed in the war. *Priscilla Tolkien recalled visiting Mrs Smith with her parents in the 1930s, and in 1937 Tolkien sent her a copy of *The Hobbit.

A photograph of Smith in Army uniform was reproduced in *The Tolkien Family Album*, p. 41. The same photograph, as well as one of Smith in theatrical costume at King Edward's School, is reproduced in *Tolkien and the Great War* by John Garth (2003).

Smith of Wootton Major. Story, first published in Great Britain by George Allen & Unwin, London, in November 1967, and in the United States by the Houghton Mifflin Company, Boston, later in the same month. See further, *Descriptive Bibliography* A9.

SUMMARY

Once every twenty-four years a feast is held in the village of Wootton Major, to which twenty-four children are invited and for which the Master Cook makes a Great Cake. At the time of the story the Master Cook, a self-important villager named Nokes, decides to make the Cake 'pretty and fairylike', with 'a little doll on a pinnacle in the middle of the Cake, dressed all in white, with a little wand in her hand ending in a tinsel star, and *Fairy Queen* written in pink icing round her feet' (p. 11); and among its ingredients is a small silver star. Although Nokes thinks the star a mere trinket, his apprentice, Alf, warns that in fact 'it comes from Faery' (p. 13).

The star passes to a young boy, who for many years wears it on his forehead; but 'few people in the village noticed it though it was not invisible to attentive eyes' (p. 20). The boy grows to be a talented blacksmith, a maker of things in iron both plain and beautiful, but never weapons; and he journeys in Faery, where he was welcome, 'for the star shone bright on his brow, and he was as safe as a mortal can be in that perilous country' (p. 24). He becomes acquainted with some of its regions 'as well as any mortal can; though since too many had become like Nokes', dismissive of the existence of Faery, he speaks 'of this to few people, except his wife and children' (p. 22). In time he explores the deeper reaches of Faery, once coming upon the King's Tree, which 'bore at once leaves and flowers and fruits uncounted, and not one was the same as any other that grew on the Tree' (p. 28). He dances with elves, and is hunted by the Wind. At last he stands before the Queen of Faery, and his mind turns back 'until he came to the day of the Children's Feast and the coming of the star, and suddenly he saw again the little dancing figure with its wand, and in shame he lowered his eyes from the Queen's beauty' (p. 37). 'Better a little doll, maybe,' she tells him, 'than no memory of Faery at all. For some the only glimpse. For some the awaking.' She gives the smith a message for the King: 'The time has come. Let him choose' (p. 38).

Returning to his own land, the smith speaks with Alf, who encourages him to return the Faery star to the box that held it before it was put into the Cake, and tells the smith of his grandfather: Rider, the Master Cook before Nokes, who himself had travelled in Faery and brought back the star for his grandson. Now the smith chooses the child to whom the star will pass at the next Twenty-four Feast, while Alf is revealed as the King of Faery.

HISTORY

Smith of Wootton Major had its origin in an abandoned preface by Tolkien for an edition of 'The Golden Key' by *George MacDonald, commissioned by Pantheon Books, New York, in 1964. Tolkien supposed that he was asked to write about MacDonald's story because he had mentioned it with praise in *On Fairy-Stories*, the first part of *Tree and Leaf*, published earlier that year. (He had called the work one of MacDonald's successful 'stories of power and beauty', *Tree and Leaf*, p. 28). On 7 September 1964 Tolkien replied to an initial inquiry by Pantheon editor Michael di Capua that he would like to write the desired preface, but was hard pressed with other business, adding: 'I am not as warm an admirer of George MacDonald as *C.S. Lewis was; but I do think well of this story of his' (*Letters*, p. 351). Before long he agreed to deliver a preface by the beginning of February 1965.

As Tolkien noted on a sheet preserved in the Bodleian Library, however,

> the project fizzled out. It was in the course of trying to write an introduction (aimed at children!) to 'The Golden Key' – after re-reading that (and much else of G. MacDonald's) that I found how greatly selective memory had transmuted his 'F[airy] Stories' & how much I disliked them now. I think in any case I [should] have abandoned the effort. But [*Smith of Wootton Major*] arose out of my attempt (I tried to give an exemplar of 'fairy' magic). [Tolkien Papers, Bodleian Library, Oxford]

In fact, Michael di Capua had suggested that Tolkien might find it easier to address his preface to an adult rather than a child reader; and although 'the project fizzled out' as far as Tolkien was concerned, the new edition proceeded to appear in 1967 under the imprint of Farrar, Straus, and Giroux of New York, to which Michael di Capua moved in 1966. Instead of a preface by Tolkien, it included an afterword by *W.H. Auden.

In another account Tolkien recalled that

> when striving to say some useful things in a preface, I found it necessary to deal with the term 'fairy' – always necessary nowadays, whether talking to children or adults. . . .
>   In the course of this I tried to give an illustration of 'Faery', and said: 'this could be put into a short story like this' – and then proceeded in what is a first version of *Smith of W[ootton] M[ajor]* pp. 11–20. Then I stopped, realizing that the 'short story' had developed an independent

life and should be completed as a thing in itself. [Tolkien Papers, Bodleian Library, Oxford]

To that point Tolkien had written, in typescript, five pages of introduction to 'The Golden Key', followed by three pages of the illustrative story. The introduction proper was published in the 'extended edition' of *Smith of Wootton Major* (2005) edited by Verlyn Flieger, pp. 71–4. On p. 75 the text of the initial version of the story is said to break off only a few lines into the tale; in fact, it continues on the typescript pages reproduced and transcribed on pp. 108–13 of the 2005 edition.

The story having acquired a life of its own, Tolkien extended the initial typescript with eight pages of manuscript (reproduced in the extended edition, pp. 114–29). A complete second typescript followed, with the story fleshed out and revised (three pages of this are reproduced and transcribed in the 2005 edition, pp. 102–7 and colour plate facing p. 59), and then a third, with the title *The Great Cake*. By the time *Rayner Unwin read the work in May 1965 it had acquired the title *Smith of Wootton Major*. Unwin wished that Tolkien had more stories like it – like *Farmer Giles of Ham* years before, *Smith* was felt to be too short to warrant publication by itself – and urged him to 'keep it right on the surface so that if the spirit moves you to write three or four others we [George Allen & Unwin, *Publishers] might make a little collection of them' (letter of 19 May 1965, Tolkien-George Allen & Unwin archive, HarperCollins). Tolkien replied on 20 May: 'There is a lot of unfinished material there, but everything belongs definitely to the *Silmarillion* or all that world' (*Letters*, p. 355). In the first part of 1966 Tolkien learned that Ballantine Books (*Publishers) wished to publish a *Tolkien Reader*, which would include several of his short writings. On 29 March 1966 and again on 19 April Rayner Unwin advised Tolkien not to give up for the collection works of importance, like *Smith of Wootton Major*.

Tolkien completed the work by mid-February 1965, around which time he began to lend a typescript to relatives and friends. His cousin Marjorie Incledon (*Incledon family) returned it to him with praise on 1 March. On 26 October 1966 Tolkien read *Smith* at Blackfriars, the Dominican house of studies in St Giles, *Oxford. He introduced his talk thus:

> I must beg the pardon of any who may have come expecting me to talk about Poetry. Noting that poets might slip in by reading poetry of their own I asked permission as a story-teller to read a story. Not a saga! Rather tougher on the audience, perhaps. Though I have myself been subjected to lengthy poems read aloud to me, and even if enjoyable in print I usually found them in this mode a burden that closed the eyes. I have not found *stories* so afflicting. *If well read.*
>
> Alas! I cannot promise that. I have a poor voice. I read too fast. And I am suffering from the aftermath of a sore throat. So prick up your ears, but please close your eyes if it will help you to endure. I have known

people to snore when I was talking; on one occasion the chairman behind me led the chorus. But I will do my best.

This story is called *Smith of Wootton Major*. It was written recently and has not been published. It was not composed for the present purpose; but (I think or I would not read it now) it contains elements that are relevant to the consideration of Poetry, with a capital P, or that some may find so.

But it is *not* an allegory – properly so-called. Its primary purpose is itself, and any applications it or parts of it may have for individual hearers are incidental. I dislike real allegory in which the application is the author's own and is meant to dominate you – I prefer the freedom of the hearer or reader.

The story was (as often happens) the result of an *irritant*. And since the irritant will in some degree affect the presentation of the movement in the mind that it sets going I will just say what the *irritant* was in this case. George MacDonald. A writer for whom I have a sincere and humble – dislike. [Tolkien Papers, Bodleian Library, Oxford]

Two days after the event, Tolkien wrote to his grandson Michael George (see *Michael Tolkien):

I did not warn you of my talk on Wednesday night. I thought you would be too busy. I did not give a talk in fact, but read a short story recently written and yet unpublished; and that you can read when you have time: *Smith of Wootton Major*: if I have not already inflicted [it] on you. Though the title is intended to suggest an early Woodhouse [i.e. P.G. Wodehouse] or story in the B[oys'] O[wn] P[aper], it is of course nothing of the kind.

The event astonished me altogether, and also the promoters of the series: the Prior of Blackfriars and the Master of Pusey House. It was a nasty wet evening. But such a concourse poured into Blackfriars that the Refectory (a long hall as long as a church) had to be cleared and could not contain it. Arrangements for relay to passages outside had to be hastily made. I am told that more than 800 people gained admittance. It became very hot. . . . [28 October 1966, *Letters*, pp. 370–1]

Tolkien now evidently asked Allen & Unwin to sell serial rights to *Smith of Wootton Major* on his behalf. On 26 April 1967 Rayner Unwin informed him that *Redbook* magazine offered $2,000 for a single use of the story in their Christmas 1967 number, and pointed out that once *Smith* had appeared thus, there would be pressure to have it in a more permanent form. Abandoning his earlier position, he proposed that Allen & Unwin publish the story by itself as a small Christmas gift book, perhaps with pictures by *Pauline Baynes. Within a month, Baynes agreed to this plan. Galley proofs of the book were ready by the end of June, and page proofs with illustrations in place by early August.

On 2 August 1967 Tolkien replied to a letter from Allen & Unwin, informing him that the Houghton Mifflin Company (*Publishers), who were to issue *Smith of Wootton Major* in the United States, wanted to change its title. He could not understand why they should want to do so, 'though doubtless the mild joke of the title, vaguely suggesting a school story, is lost on an American' (Tolkien-George Allen & Unwin archive, HarperCollins). In the event, the book was published under the same title in Britain and abroad.

New editions in larger formats, repeating the Baynes pictures, were published in Britain and America in 1975 and 1978 respectively. *Smith of Wootton Major* was also reprinted in *Poems and Stories* (1980). An edition with illustrations by Roger Garland was first published in 1990. The 'extended edition' of 2005 includes an enlarged facsimile of the original 1967 setting illustrated in line by Pauline Baynes, as well as her later coloured picture (for *Poems and Stories*) of the Great Cake, with Tolkien's draft introduction to 'The Golden Key', a 'hybrid draft and transcription of "The Great Cake"', other drafts and transcriptions, one of three time schemes that Tolkien wrote for working reference, suggestions for the ending of the story, and most notably, an unfinished essay in which Tolkien discusses the content and meaning of the work.

ESSAY ON SMITH OF WOOTTON MAJOR

In this Tolkien pointedly comments that *Smith* is not an *allegory, though 'capable of course of allegorical interpretations at certain points. It is a "Fairy Story", of the kind in which beings that may be called "fairies" or "elves" play a part and are associated in action with human people, and are regarded as having a "real" existence, that is in their own right and independent of human imagination and invention.' Its setting is imaginary, but none the less meant to be the pre-industrial English countryside, in which the village of Wootton Major is prosperous and many of its people self-satisfied. Dancing, singing, and storytelling are little thought of, nor are there musical instruments. The village sits near the edge of an uncultivated forest, in which are the entrances to Faery. 'My symbol', Tolkien writes, referring to the common depiction of the fairy world as within a hill or mountain, 'is not the underground ... but the Forest: the regions still immune from human activities, not yet dominated by them (dominated! not conquered!). If Faery Time is at points contiguous with ours, the contiguity will also occur in related points in space – or that is the theory for the purpose of the story.'

Tolkien describes the government of the village, its traditional crafts, and the surnames of the villagers, such as *Smith*, derived from the family craft. He also details at length the family history of the Smith of the tale, beginning with his grandfather Rider. The background of Nokes is revealed; he indicates 'the vulgarization of Wootton'. Before the tale begins, 'history and legend and above all any tales touching on "faery", have become regarded as children's stuff' in the village, 'patronizingly tolerated for the amusement of the very young.' This situation 'aroused the concern of Faery':

The Elven Folk, the chief and ruling inhabitants of Faery, have an ultimate kinship with Men and have a permanent love for them in general. Though they are not bound by any moral obligation to assist Men, and do not need their help (except in human affairs), they do from time to time try to assist them, avert evil from them and have relations with them, especially through certain men and women whòm they find suitable.... Their good will is seen mainly in attempting to keep or restore relationships between the two worlds, since the Elves (and still some Men) realize that this love of Faery is essential to the full and proper human development.

Alf, the King of Faery, becomes apprentice to the Master Cook in an attempt to rescue Wootton from its decline. His plan is to use men who have explored Faery, and to enable them to do so he devises a mark of protection: the silver star passed to worthy children in the Great Cake.

Tolkien finally comments that no church or temple is said to be in the village, nor did its festivals any longer have religious significance. The Great Hall, however,

is evidently in a way an 'allegory' of the village church; the Master Cook with his house adjacent, and his office that is not hereditary, provides for its own instruction and succession but is not one of the 'secular' or profitable crafts, and yet is supported financially by the village, is plainly the Parson and the priesthood. 'Cooking' is a domestic affair practiced by men and women; personal religion and prayer. The Master Cook presides over and provides for all the religious festivals of the year, and also for all the religious occasions that are not universal: births, marriages, and deaths. [Tolkien Papers, Bodleian Library, Oxford]

The essay reflects the final version of *Smith of Wootton Major*, completed early in 1965, and may be contemporary with the reading of *Smith* at Blackfriars in October 1966, at which Tolkien made similar remarks about allegory (but cf. his denial of allegory in *The Lord of the Rings*, in the 1965 edition of that work). Tolkien mentioned the essay to Clyde S. Kilby in a letter of *c*. 3 December 1967.

Extracts from the essay on *Smith* were first published in 'Pitfalls of Faërie' by Verlyn Flieger, in *Mythos Journal* for Winter 1995, later incorporated in her book *A Question of Time: J.R.R. Tolkien's Road to Faërie* (1997). The greater part of the essay was published in the 2005 'extended edition' of *Smith of Wootton Major*, except for a few final pages of wandering philosophical comments unrelated to the story.

A commercial recording of *Smith of Wootton Major* read by Derek Jacobi was first issued in 1999, as part of *Farmer Giles of Ham and Other Stories*. It was later re-issued only with *Leaf by Niggle*. In 1992 a dramatization of *Smith of Wootton Major* by Brian Sibley was broadcast on BBC Radio as one part of the series *Tales from the Perilous Realm*. This series was issued as a commercial recording in 1993.

CRITICISM

Smith of Wootton Major was immediately popular and sold well. Critical response was generally positive: many found it a small gem of a book. But the occasional reviewer found it weak, even distressing. *Naomi Mitchison, for one, called it 'a very short glimpse of the Debateable Land on the outskirts of You-know-where. There are the Elven Folk at the far side, but I am less sure of the mortals and their medieval goings-on, which are a bit too Olde Worlde. Tolkien needs a bigger canvas and harder work on it if one is to become involved and convinced' ('Why Not Grown-Ups Too?', *Glasgow Herald*, 25 November 1967, p. 9). Of course neither she nor anyone else, until many years later, could have known about the depth of thought actually underlying the tale.

Many reviewers felt that *Smith* had meaning, whether or not that could be defined. Robert Phelps, writing in the *New York Times Book Review* ('For Young Readers', 4 February 1968, p. 26), found the work to be, 'like everything Tolkien has written, . . . an elegy – for the decline of our human capacity for awe.' But 'it is first and foremost a good tale, dense and engrossing, full of unexpected turns, worth telling for its own sake.' Brian Alderson, however, in his review in *Children's Book News* (January/February 1968) felt that it contained a weakness in 'the finely planned curve of the story', which upon introducing the word *fay*

> breaks away from its natural anchorage and takes on an artful, a cunningly worked didacticism. The whole central episode of Smith in Fairyland, for all the care of its writing, does not ring true – either to the traditional concept of fairy-tale or to the expectations aroused by the story's setting. . . . We are all too aware that an attempt is being made to tell us something about the genre and (like 'Leaf by Niggle' before it) what we have got is really a footnote to an essay [i.e. *On Fairy-Stories*] rather than a fairy-tale itself.

Christopher Derrick, writing in *The Tablet* ('And See Ye Not Yon Bonny Road?', 10 February 1968, p. 132), implied that *Smith* might have some relevance to the Catholic Church, only a few years after the Second Vatican Council in 1962–5. Although it offers 'sound direct nourishment' to its 'primary readership' – assuming that it was aimed at an audience of children – 'their elders may grope for a precise allegory, a *significacio* . . . and here and there clear hints will indeed be found, as when we hear that the ancient hall has been re-glazed and re-painted, "and there had been much debate on the Council about it. Some disliked it and called it "new-fangled", but some with more knowledge knew that it was a return to old custom."' And yet the reader should not see 'chiefly an explicit contribution to the arguments of the time': the story 'functions in its own right, as a diagram of inward experience'.

Jane Chance in *Tolkien's Art: A Mythology for England* (rev. edn. 2001) finds *Smith* heavy with symbolism, emphasizing 'Christian themes and concepts'; it 'provides the ultimate consolation for the good Christian – the reward of grace for humility and suffering' (p. 99). Paul H. Kocher in *Master of Middle-earth: The Fiction of J.R.R. Tolkien* (1972) sees *Smith* rather as a personal statement by the author: 'Tolkien apparently is saying that a man can become too old for wanderings in Faery. His powers of apprehending its marvels and translating them into art decay with age. . . . Reading "Smith of Wootton Major" as Tolkien's personal farewell to his art is tempting, and has at least as good an argument to support it as reading Shakespeare's *The Tempest* in the same auto-biographical light' (p. 203). In this, at least, there is some support from Tolkien himself: on 12 December 1967 he wrote to *Roger Lancelyn Green that *Smith* is 'an old man's book, already weighted with the presage of "bereavement"' (*Letters*, p. 389).

More recently and forcefully, T.A. Shippey has argued in *The Road to Middle-earth* (2nd edn. 1992) that the 'mode' of *Smith of Wootton Major* 'is allegorical, and its subject is the author himself, especially the relations between his job and his private sources of "inspiration"' (p. 241). 'If the old Cook is a philologist-figure', he continues, 'and Nokes a critic-figure, the suspicion must be that Smith is a Tolkien-figure. Smith himself never becomes Cook, never bakes a Great Cake. It is perhaps fair to remark that Tolkien never produced a major full-length work on medieval literature. Against that Smith's life is one of useful activity: pots, pans, bars, bolts, hinges, fire-dogs – or, one might say, lectures, tutorials, scripts, pupils' (p. 243). In *J.R.R. Tolkien: Author of the Century* (2000) Shippey states:

> Whatever one's detailed reading of the story, it is in general clear that *Smith of Wootton Major* is another *'Valedictory Address', or 'Farewell to Arms', in which Tolkien lays aside his star; defends the real-world utility of fantasy; insists that fantasy and faith are in harmony as visions of a higher world; hopes for a revival of both in a future in which the Nokeses of the world (the materialists the misologists) will have less power; and possibly, though this is my last and most tentative suggestion, expresses a veiled regret at his own denuding of the philological birch. . . . [p. 303]

Shippey suggests that the birch in *Smith*, which protects Smith from the Wind in Faërie but is left stripped of its leaves, may be seen as an allegory of scholarly study, of *philology, which Tolkien (in this view) neglected in favour of his fantasy fiction.

But already in the year of its publication Tolkien's friend Roger Lancelyn Green defended *Smith of Wootton Major* from the criticisms he evidently knew would be forthcoming. In a review for the *Sunday Telegraph* ('Slicing a Magical Cake', 3 December 1967) he famously wrote: 'To seek for the meaning is to cut open the ball in search of its bounce: those who read will certainly enjoy the cake, probably find the charms and possibly glimpse the star. But if one caught the star with a telescope it would not be there.' David Doughan, following on from Green in 'In Search of the Bounce: Tolkien Seen through Smith', *Leaves from the Tree: J.R.R. Tolkien's Shorter Fiction* (1991), disputed the arguments by Shippey and Kocher that *Smith of Wootton Major* is allegorical. Whereas Shippey wrote that 'Smith himself never becomes Cook, never bakes a Great Cake', Doughan observes that 'he is, after all, a Smith, not a cook' (p. 17); and whereas Kocher said that in *Smith* '"Tolkien broke his wand and drowned his magic books"' presumably returning to help Christopher [Tolkien] with the mundane but useful business of academic philology', Doughan counters that Tolkien did no such thing (p. 17). In *A Question of Time* Verlyn Flieger also took issue with Shippey, stating the 'mode' of *Smith* to be 'fairy tale, not allegory', and its subject not the author himself, but 'the experience of a human in the Faery world' (p. 187). She notes that 'there are at least demonstrable leftovers of an original allegorical intent' in *Smith*, but doubts 'whether a reading on that level comes closest to Tolkien's final intent and best serves the story as a work of art' (p. 186). The appeal of *Smith*, she argues, lies

> in what appears to be its effortless blend of simplicity and complexity, for the story's seemingly transparent surface covers unexpected depths of suggested meaning. The operative word here is 'suggested,' for the tale defies and defeats any one-to-one correlation or arbitrary signification, and the too-easy interpretations that its apparent simplicity encourages roll over it without denting the surface. [p. 230]

See also comments by Verlyn Flieger and T.A. Shippey in their joint article, 'Allegory Versus Bounce: Tolkien's Smith of Wootton Major', in *Journal of the Fantastic in the Arts* 12, no. 2 (Spring 2002).

Smithers, Geoffrey Victor (1909–2000). G.V. Smithers read English at *Oxford as a Rhodes Scholar from South Africa; he received his B.A. in 1933. Influenced by Tolkien and *C.T. Onions, he himself became a noted philologist and scholar of medieval English language and literature. He taught at King's College, London and University College, London before obtaining a University Lecturership at Oxford in 1940. He was appointed a Tutor at Merton College in 1947, and in 1954 was promoted to a Professorial Fellowship at Merton. During the 1950s Smithers served on the Oxford English Faculty Board with Tolkien, and they were sometimes co-examiners of B.Litt. candidates. In 1960 Smithers was elected to the chair of English Language at the University of Durham, where he created 'an intensive programme of philological and medieval study' ('Professor G.V. Smithers', *The Times* (London), 24 May 2000, p. 25).

Smithers produced editions of the medieval texts *King Alisaunder* (1952–7) and *Havelok* (1987), and was co-editor with *J.A.W. Bennett of *Early Middle English Verse and Prose* (1966; 2nd edn. 1968). His inaugural address at Durham, *The Making of Beowulf*, was published in 1961, but he left a larger study of *Beowulf* unfinished. His essays and shorter contributions mainly concerned 'the elucidation of texts and the understanding of medieval literature through a study of literary relationships, especially recurrent story patterns' (*Times* obituary).

Smoking. Tolkien was seldom without a pipe: he wondered if he had acquired the habit of pipe-smoking from the example of his guardian, *Father Francis Morgan. Interviewers noted that Tolkien almost clung to his pipe, cradling it in his hand, or speaking with it in his mouth, sometimes making him difficult to understand. In response to a draft of their article, in which they commented on this habit, Tolkien wrote to Charlotte and Denis Plimmer: 'I should forgo smoking on these occasions, but I have found being interviewed increasingly distasteful and distracting, and need some sedative' (8 February 1967, *Letters*, p. 372). Another interviewer, Richard Plotz, wrote that Tolkien 'took out a pipe as he entered his study, and all during the interview he held it clenched in his teeth, lighting and relighting it, talking through it; he never removed it from his mouth for more than five seconds' ('J.R.R. Tolkien Talks about the Discovery of Middle-earth, the Origins of Elvish', *Seventeen*, January 1967, p. 92).

Tolkien's granddaughter Joanna (see *Michael Tolkien) recalled that he always carried 'his penknife (in his inside jacket pocket), which was used to clean out his pipe, and the ritualistic process of filling the pipe, and the way he would light it. And the great concentration on the first few puffs, and the utter contentment in puffing away at his pipe' ('Joanna Tolkien Speaks at the Tolkien Society Annual Dinner', *Digging Potatoes, Growing Trees*, vol. 2 (1998), p. 34). E.L. Edmonds, a student of C.S. Lewis in the 1930s, recalled that Tolkien and Lewis had an 'inveterate habit of playing at smoke rings. Sometimes, each would try for the best sequence of rings, and it is still a source of wonderment to me how they manages to send up one ring and then put two or three more rings through very quickly before the first ring dissipated. Of such smoking habits were those of Gandalf formed?' ('C.S. Lewis, the Teacher', in *In Search of C.S. Lewis* (1983), p. 47).

Tolkien transferred his love of pipe-smoking to Bilbo Baggins and Gandalf in *The Hobbit*, and to a wide range of characters in *The Lord of the Rings*. On 'pipe-weed' (tobacco) in the latter, see *Reader's Companion*, p. 30. See also Anders Stenström (Beregond), 'Något om pipor, blad och rökning' ('Some Notes on Pipes, Leaf and Smoking'), *Arda* 4 (1988, for 1984), in Swedish with a summary in English; and Alan Smith, 'A Shire Pleasure', *Pipes and Tobacco* 5, no. 4 (Winter 2001).

Societies and clubs. At *King Edward's School, Birmingham Tolkien was an active member of the **Debating Society**: he made his maiden speech on 8 October 1909, on the motion 'That this house expresses its sympathy with the objects and its admiration of the tactics of the Militant Suffragette.' The Society seems to have met fortnightly on Fridays during the autumn and spring terms. The number of those in attendance at debates during Tolkien's years at the school, according to voting figures reported in the *King Edward's School Chronicle*, averaged about two dozen, except for the Annual Open Debate in March or April which parents and friends could attend. A printed programme for 1910–11 lists *R. Cary Gilson, the Chief Master, as President of the Society; two other masters, *R.W. Reynolds and A.E. Measures, as Vice-Presidents; Tolkien as Secretary; and four other pupils, including *Christopher Wiseman and *Robert Q. Gilson, as committee members. The office of Secretary seems to have involved the persuasion of members to open the debate: C.H. Richards, an Assistant Master who opposed the motion of 21 October 1910, is reported to have said that he 'regretted bitterly the weak moment in which he had capitulated to the highwaymanism of the Secretary' ('Debating Society', *King Edward's School Chronicle* n.s. 26, no. 183 (November 1910), p. 70). A report in the *King Edward's School Chronicle* for June 1911 described Tolkien as

> an energetic Secretary who does not consider his duties excuse him from speaking. Has displayed great zeal in arranging meetings throughout the session and considerable ingenuity in advertising them. He is an eccentric humorist who has made many excellent speeches, at times rather burdened with anacolutha [i.e. sentences or constructions lacking grammatical sequence]. Made one valiant effort to revive Beowulfic oratory. ['Debating Society', n.s. 26, no. 187, p. 46]

After he left King Edward's School Tolkien returned to take part in the Annual Open Debate in April 1912 and March 1913, and in the Annual Old Boys Debate in December 1912.

Although there is no direct evidence that Tolkien was a member of the King Edward's School **Literary Society**, it is hardly conceivable that he was not. Its programme for 1910–11 was printed on the same card as that of the Debating Society. The Chief Master was President of both organizations, in which pupils and masters alike participated. The Literary Society also met (at that time, in R.W. Reynolds' room) fortnightly on Fridays during the autumn and spring terms, but on alternate weeks to the Debating Society. Tolkien read a paper on the Norse sagas (*Northernness) to the Literary Society on 17 February 1911.

In 1907 a Cadet Corps was established at King Edward's School; in 1910 it was renamed the **Officers Training Corps**. Tolkien was a member by Summer Term 1909, and a corporal by autumn 1910. According to a printed booklet for January term, two of the masters held the ranks of captain and lieutenant, while the more senior cadets provided a colour sergeant, five sergeants, three corporals, and eight lance-corporals. The cadets were inspected annually by an officer of the Army. After a review by Major W.L. Loring on 15 June 1911 at the School fields, 'in marching, handling of arms, steadiness and turn-out, great progress was noticeable [in the cadets], while the section commanders had good control over their sections.... The attendance of parents of the cadets was meagre, considering the ideal weather conditions and the fact that this is practically the only "show" day in a normal Corps year' ('Officers' Training Corps', *King Edward's School Chronicle* n.s. 26, no. 188 (July 1911), p. 56). A selection of cadets, sometimes including Tolkien, also assembled on special occasions, as on 7 July 1909 when the King and Queen came to Birmingham to open the New Buildings of the University, and 21–23 June 1911 in London at the coronation of King George V.

In the summer term of 1911 Tolkien and some of the other senior boys at King Edward's School formed an unofficial Tea Club which met in the school library. Later they met in the Tea Room at Barrow's Stores in Birmingham, from which they coined the name 'Barrovian Society'. See further, separate entry under the abbreviation *T.C.B.S. (Tea Club, Barrovian Society).

During his undergraduate years Tolkien also participated in the **Old Edwardians**, a society of former students of King Edward's School, Birmingham. He attended the Oxford and Cambridge Old Edwardians Society Annual Dinner at the Midland Hotel, Birmingham, on 14 December 1911, and the London Old Edwardians Seventh Annual Dinner at the Holborn Restaurant on 20 February 1912. On 1 February 1913 he mentioned in a postcard to his fiancée (*Edith Tolkien) that he was on his way to an Old Edwardians meeting, though whether to a formal society meeting or to meet fellow Old Edwardians is not known. In December 1913 the *King Edward's School Chronicle* published a letter (*Oxford Letter) as by 'Oxon' – the author is identified as Tolkien in his papers – giving information about Old Edwardians at Oxford. They 'are a scattered community', he wrote, 'and seldom is any College honoured with the presence of more than one of us at a time'. He 'had the misfortune to "cut" two teas with Old Edwardians, and so we are in disgrace with them, rather than in possession of their secrets. Let us hint, though, that this probably is because there are not many deeds worthy of exoteric fame credited of late to the "Old Eds."' 'In the Old Edwardian Society ... much activity is, as always, shown by [members] in relentless criticism of their hapless officers' (n.s. 28, no. 202, p. 80). Tolkien played for the Old Edwardians or Old Boys in at least one rugby football match, in February or March 1914 when he captained the Oxford and Cambridge Old Boys in the annual match against King Edward's School. Much later, on 3 May 1972, Tolkien accepted an invitation to dine again with the London Old Edwardians, probably in December of that year, but poor health having prevented him from keeping the engagement he taped a short speech to be played to the members.

UNDERGRADUATE SOCIETIES AT OXFORD

At the University of *Oxford from 1911 to 1915 Tolkien found an even greater variety of social organizations. Their importance in Oxford life is suggested by the following, written not long after Tolkien's undergraduate years:

Within the college, social life (so far as it is organized) centres mainly in various clubs or societies – informal bodies having no special rooms, and meeting now and then in the rooms of the members. Every college has its debating society, with frequent meetings for debates which often call forth speakers with an astonishing amount of wit and fluency in discussing general subjects of wide variety. Then there is commonly a literary club, whose members read papers on Crashaw, Swinburne, Casanova, Butler, Poe, or other men of silver. After the paper, a general discussion will follow in which men just out of their teens become as confidently critical as a middle-aged reviewer. Some other college clubs are frankly convivial only, flockings of birds of a feather who delight in eating and drinking well. . . . An Oxford undergraduate will scarcely find another person also enthusiastically interested in the things he himself likes, before – presto – there is a club, with a president, secretary-treasurer, and minutes! The love of talk, and especially of witty talk, is strong. . . .

Debating and public discussion . . . is one of the chief and most popular activities of undergraduate University. . . . In Oxford . . . there is no instruction; there are no debating teams and no prize speaking contests, but scores of good and hundreds of mediocre debaters. The Oxford test of good debating is not the precise presentation of facts and figures, but the original and clever expression of ideas. An epigram outweighs the encyclopedia. [R.P. Coffin, 'Social Life and Activities at the University', *Oxford of Today: A Manual for Prospective Rhodes Scholars* (1927), pp. 152–5]

'Oxoniensis', the writer of 'Oxford Letter' in the *King Edward's School Chronicle* for December 1912, commented that 'Tolkien, if we are to be guided by the countless notices on his mantelpiece, has joined all the Exeter [College] Societies which are in existence . . .' (n.s. 27, no. 196, p. 85). See further, Lorise Topliffe, 'Tolkien as an Undergraduate, 1911–1915', *Exeter College Association Register* (1992).

First among these was the **Stapeldon Debating Society**, or simply the Stapeldon Society, begun as a private organization in 1869 but later opened to the College as a whole. By Tolkien's day it had added to its debating function and become a democratic assembly in which all matters affecting the interests of the College were discussed. The Society was influential, for instance, in the establishment of the Junior Common Room in 1887, and the placing of name-plates on the staircases and baths in 1908. Although there have always been standing jests, and supernumerary officials such as the Kitchen Committee, the College Jester, the Public Orator, and the 'Sergeant-Inspector-Ferret of the Rabbit Warren',

the Stapeldon has always realized its responsibilities. The College authorities have always felt that any question submitted to it will be fairly discussed, and that the decision of the Stapeldon represents the wishes of the undergraduates; and the Society has always condemned anything that offended against good taste and the best interests of the College.

['College Societies: 1. Stapeldon Debating Society', *Stapeldon Magazine* (December 1911), p. 101]

At that time its members assembled in the Undergraduates Reading Room or the Junior Common Room on Monday evenings, weekly in Michaelmas and Hilary Terms, fortnightly in Trinity Term. Tolkien is first recorded in the minutes of 4 March 1912, when he spoke for the motion: 'This House deplores the signs of degeneracy in the present age.' He is next recorded on 11 November 1912, and after that is mentioned frequently through Trinity Term 1915. He was active in Society matters and was elected or appointed to several offices, usually for one term only, including that of Secretary from 9 June 1913 (hence the minutes for Michaelmas Term 1913 are in his hand) and of President from 1 December 1913.

Tolkien was elected to the **Exeter College Essay Club** on 3 November 1912. In 1913 he and Colin Cullis helped to draw up a new constitution: the number of Ordinary Members was limited to fifteen, but became Honorary Members when they reached their fourth year, or had graduated, or were no longer in residence; and others could be elected to the status of Honorary Members. The officers were a President, a Secretary, and a Critic. The Club was to meet three times every Michaelmas and Hilary (then Lent) Term and twice every Trinity (then Summer) Term on Wednesday evenings. The officers were empowered to nominate readers of papers; the Secretary was to keep a list of members, note absences, supply new members with a list of the rules, and send members a printed list of meetings. Members were forbidden to miss two consecutive meetings without an adequate excuse. Before the last meeting of every term, members were to submit to the Critic original compositions in verse or prose, under a pseudonym, which the Critic would read out to the Club, and those judged of sufficient merit would be inscribed in a book kept for that purpose. (No such book survives.)

In 1914 Tolkien was elected Secretary of the Essay Club for Hilary Term, President for Trinity Term, and Critic for Michaelmas Term. In Trinity Term 1913 he read to the members a paper on Norse sagas, and in Hilary Term 1914 spoke on the poet Francis Thompson. Although by then its membership had been depleted by the First World War, at least three informal meetings of the Club were held in Tolkien's final year at Exeter. On 27 November 1914 he read his poem *The Voyage of Éarendel the Evening Star* (**Éalá Éarendel Engla Beorhtast*); in February 1915 he read an essay on the **Kalevala*; and in March 1915 he read his poem *Sea-Chant of an Elder Day* (**The Horns of Ylmir*).

In Hilary Term 1919 Tolkien was made an Honorary Member of the Essay Club, but did not attend meetings until Trinity Term that year. He was appointed Critic for Michaelmas Term 1919. At a meeting of the Club on 10 March 1920, not having found time to write a critical paper, he read his story *The Fall of Gondolin* (see **The Book of Lost Tales*).

While an undergraduate Tolkien helped to found at least two societies. Probably towards the end of Michaelmas Term 1911 he and several other students, mainly freshmen, formed the **Apolausticks**. Its membership seems to have been limited to twelve. A printed programme for Hilary Term 1912 lists Tolkien as President, with a Secretary and nine other members. During that term eight meetings were held, on Monday, 22 January, and then each Saturday until 9 March, in members' rooms, variously in the afternoon or evening. The evening meetings announced for Hilary Term 1912 were to be devoted to discussion of literary figures. A programme for Trinity Term 1912 lists twelve members, but apart from a dinner at the Randolph Hotel on 1 June there were to be only three meetings. A printed menu card for the dinner of 1 June suggests that the members had refined tastes: *hors d'oeuvres variées; petite marmite, crème à la Reine; suprême de sole au Chablis; foie gras en Belle Vue; petits filets de boeuf Parisienne, chouxfleur, haricots verts, pommes nouvelles; poulet de grain rôtis, salade; asperges verts, Sc. beurre fondu; pêches à la Melba, petits fours; soufflé au parmesan;* dessert, and coffee. Toasts were proposed to the King, the University, and the Club, the latter by Tolkien.

On 11 May 1912 Tolkien read a paper (subject not known) to the Apolausticks, and on 15 June proposed the subject of a debate: 'That a belief in ghosts is essential to the welfare of a people.' A photograph of the members at this time is reproduced in *Biography*, pl. 6b. In Michaelmas Term 1912 there were to be eight meetings, but the only programmed events were 'Swedish Punch' at the second meeting and a debate in Tolkien's rooms on 6 November. There is no record of the Apolausticks after that date, except for a dinner meeting on 31 May 1913.

Tolkien and Colin Cullis were also instrumental in founding the **Chequers Clubbe** at Exeter College. A dining society, it began in Hilary Term 1914 with permission from the Sub-Rector, dated 30 January 1914, for Tolkien and Cullis 'to have supper for nine on Sat[urday] nights in the rooms of one or the other this term' (Tolkien Papers, Bodleian Library, Oxford). The only direct record of a meeting of the Chequers Clubbe, however, is a printed menu card for a 'Chequers Clubbe Binge' on 18 June 1914, for which Tolkien designed the cover (*Life and Legend*, p. 26). The meal on that occasion was less elaborate than that of the Apolausticks on 1 June 1912, though it still comprised several courses: clear soup, salmon, chicken croquettes, roast lamb, salad, ice pudding, and wine jelly, served with Scotch Agra and Veuve Cliquot (1906). Twelve names are listed on the menu, but only eight signed Tolkien's preserved copy. As many of these men were also members of the Apolausticks, it seems possible that the Chequers Clubbe was a successor to that group.

While at Oxford Tolkien continued his military training as a member of the **King Edward's Horse**, an organization formerly known as the King's Colonials. He joined on 28 November 1911, a colonial himself by virtue of his birth in the Orange Free State (*South Africa). From 27 July to ?10 August 1912 Tolkien camped with the King Edward's Horse on Dibgate Plateau near *Folkestone. The historian Lieutenant-Colonel Lionel James reported that it was an altogether boisterous fortnight. The south-westerly gales were so severe, and the camping area so exposed, that on two nights the tents and marquees were nearly all levelled. The work done, however, was of quite a high standard for an irregular unit. For one night the Regiment practised billetting during field operations. The outpost scheme that necessitated the billetting was a foretaste of the actual service conditions which were soon to become the daily life of so many who were training that summer. There was not an officer or man out that night who was not drenched to the skin. [*The History of King Edward's Horse* (1921), p. 52]

Tolkien resigned on 28 February 1913.

In Michaelmas Term 1914 he joined the Oxford branch of the **Officers Training Corps**. The First World War having begun in August of that year, the Corps was now chiefly a recruiting and training organization. Cadets were divided into two classes: Class I for those eager to obtain a commission as soon as possible, and Class II for those who were unwilling or unable to undertake military duty at once. According to the *Stapeldon Magazine* for December 1914, Exeter College contributed seventeen students to Class I and twenty-five to Class II, Tolkien certainly among the latter. Membership in the Officer Training Corps obliged him to take part in drills in the University Parks on Mondays, Wednesdays, Fridays, and Saturdays, and usually to attend one lecture per week and classes in signalling and map-reading on free afternoons.

UNIVERSITY OF LEEDS

Probably in 1922 Tolkien and *E.V. Gordon founded the **Viking Club** at the University of Leeds to encourage interest in Old Icelandic, one of the Special Subjects offered to students in the English School. The Viking Club was mainly for undergraduates, but former students were also welcome to attend. Its meetings were both educational and social: members read sagas, sang comic songs, and drank beer. The comic songs were written mainly by Tolkien and Gordon, in languages such as Old English, Old Icelandic, Gothic, and Latin, as well as Modern English, set to well known tunes such as 'The Vicar of Bray'. At the time they were distributed by means of stencilled copies; later some of them were privately printed as *Songs for the Philologists* (1936).

LATER OXFORD SOCIETIES AND CLUBS

After Tolkien's return to Oxford in 1925 societies and clubs continued to play a significant part in his life. For convenience these are discussed below in alphabetical order.

The dining club **Ad Eundem** ('to the same [level]'), founded in the nineteenth century and still active, draws its members mainly from Oxford and Cambridge dons, but also from others associated with those universities. In Tolkien's time the members dined together about three times a year, alternately at different venues in Oxford and Cambridge. Membership was by election, with equal numbers from each university. Although the earliest definite evidence of Tolkien as a member of Ad Eundem is dated May 1949, a draft letter written by him between 1937 and 1940 suggests that he belonged to the club even earlier, and may already have been an organizer. For some years he seems to have been the secretary responsible for organizing at least the Oxford dinners and for agreeing dates with the Cambridge representatives. On 9 September 1955 he wrote to fellow member John Sparrow regarding subscriptions and membership in the Club, and disparities of financial support between Cambridge and Oxford; at this time other members included Lord David Cecil, Nevill Coghill, and the Warden of Merton College, Oxford, Geoffrey Mure. On 1 March 1957 he wrote to Lord Monckton, who had just been elevated to the peerage after holding a number of posts in the Cabinet, to inquire which dates for Ad Eundem dinners would suit him; Tolkien apologized for delaying the Oxford dinner and then giving short notice, and mourned that there always seemed to be more Cambridge members present at the dinners than those from Oxford. He last attended an Ad Eundem dinner shortly before his death, at St John's College, Cambridge, on 20 July 1973.

Tolkien was also active in the **Catenian Association**, an international brotherhood of Catholic business and professional men who meet socially at local branches or 'circles'. Founded in Manchester in 1908, its name is derived from Latin *catena* ('chain'). Today it has over 11,000 members in 300 Circles. New members must be practising Roman Catholics and sponsored by a Catenian. Tolkien served as Vice President of the Oxford Circle for some period of time beginning between 1930 and 1947, according to a Catenian Association letterhead listing him at 20 Northmoor Road. He was still a member, but probably no longer an officer, in 1951, when he received a letter from the Honourable Secretary, T.J. White, regarding a change in the date for 'President's Sunday'. In an undated draft reply, referring probably to a forthcoming dinner, Tolkien complained that 'the Catenians is already becoming very expensive for anyone with any limit of good income and many domestic commitments' (Tolkien Papers, Bodleian Library, Oxford).

Early in the 1930s members of the English School at Oxford with similar ideas for reforming its syllabus, led by Tolkien and *C.S. Lewis, formed a group called **The Cave**, after 'the Cave of Adullam in which David organised the conspiracy against Saul . . . , the implication being that Lewis' junto was conspiring against what had been, at least until 1931, the reigning party in the English School, and in particular David Nichol Smith, the Professor of English Literature' (Humphrey Carpenter, *The Inklings*, p. 56; cf. 1 Samuel 22:2 (Authorized Version): 'And every one that was in distress, and every one that was in debt, and every one that was discontented, gathered themselves unto him . . .'). The Cave allowed members more freely to exchange ideas; but after its members – notably including women as well as men – had achieved most of their initial goals, the group became more of a social and literary club which held informal dinners or met in members' rooms.

At one meeting, *c.* 1938–9, the members held a contest for the best reading, the prize to be the worst book that could be found. The winner on this occasion was *Leonard Rice-Oxley, who received a copy of *Would I Fight?* essays by Oxford undergraduates and recent graduates edited by Keith Briant and Lyall Wilkes (Blackwell, 1938), inscribed and signed by all those present: Tolkien, *H.F.B. Brett-Smith, *M.E. Griffiths, Rice-Oxley, *Dorothy Whitelock, F.C. Horwood, C.L. Morrison, *C.L. Wrenn, *Joan Blomfield, *Dorothy Everett, and C.S. Lewis. (According to its dust-jacket, '*Would I Fight* sets out to present the views of young men and young women and what they believe it is worth killing and being killed for. The Essayists have been chosen as representative of the various cross sections into which the youth of this country is divided. Behind each Essayist, it is claimed, stand thousands of others for whom he speaks, and it is well they should speak now.' Its contents include 'Would Christ Use a Bayonet?', 'Unwillingly Converted from Pacifism', 'It Is Natural to Die for One's Country', and 'Pacifism or Poison-Gas?') The inscription and signatures in Rice-Oxley's prize book were reproduced in *Catalogue 176: Oxford, Oxfordshire & the Cotswolds* issued by the Oxford bookseller Waterfield's, 1999, p. 14.

C.S. Lewis mentioned two other meetings of The Cave in letters to his brother: on 13 December 1939, in *M.R. Ridley's rooms at Balliol, where Ridley read poems by Swinburne and Kipling; and on 13 March 1940 at the Golden Cross, an ancient inn in Cornmarket Street, Oxford, with Tolkien, Lewis, Rice-Oxley, Brett-Smith, and *Hugo Dyson present. *Nevill Coghill was also a member.

In the early 1930s a University College, Oxford undergraduate named Edward Tangye Lean founded a literary or writers' club called in jest **The Inklings**. Tolkien later recalled to William Luther White that Tangye Lean

> was, I think, more aware than most undergraduates of the impermanence of their clubs and fashions, and had an ambition to found a club that would prove more lasting. Anyway, he asked some 'dons' to become members. . . . In the event both C.S.L. [C.S. Lewis] and I became members. The club met in T-L's rooms in University College; its procedure was that at each meeting members should read aloud, unpublished compositions. These were supposed to be open to immediate criticism. Also if the club thought fit a contribution might be voted to be worthy of an entry in a Record Book. (I was the scribe and keeper of the book).
>
> Tangye-Lean proved quite right. The Club soon died: the Record Book had very few entries. . . . Its name was then transferred (by C.S.L.) to the undetermined and unelected circle of friends who gathered about C.S.L., and met in his rooms in Magdalen. [11 September 1967, *Letters*, pp. 387–8; see further, *The Inklings]

Tangye Lean matriculated at Oxford in Michaelmas Term 1929 and graduated at the end of Trinity Term 1933.in summer 1933.

Tolkien also recalled, in a letter to *Rayner Unwin on 22 June 1952, that his poem *Errantry 'first appeared in its [the Inklings'] papers' (Letters, p. 162), which suggests that it may have been entered in the Record Book. Since Errantry was published in the 9 November 1933 issue of the Oxford Magazine, it must have been read to Tangye Lean's Inklings earlier than this date.

In Hilary Term 1926 Tolkien founded the **Kolbítar** or 'Coalbiters', 'those who lounge so close to the fire in winter that they "bite the coal"' (Humphrey Carpenter, Biography, pp. 119–20); the name comes from the Icelandic Kolbítr, a popular name of an idle youth always at the fireside. Each of its members was associated with Oxford; their common goal was to translate all of the major Icelandic sagas as well as the Prose or Younger Edda and the Poetic or Elder Edda. They met two or three times per term until finally achieving their aim in the early 1930s. Some members were already proficient in Icelandic: *G.E.K. Braunholtz, Professor of Comparative Philology; *R.M. Dawkins, Professor of Byzantine and Modern Greek; *John Fraser, Jesus Professor of Celtic; *C.T. Onions of the Oxford English Dictionary; and Tolkien himself. Others had little or no knowledge of the language, but after reading the works in translation wanted to know them in the original: among these were *John Bryson, the English tutor at Balliol College; Nevill Coghill, a Fellow at Exeter; *George S. Gordon, Merton Professor of English Literature; C.S. Lewis; and *Bruce McFarlane, a historian at Magdalen College.

At meetings each member in turn translated part of the relevant work according to his capabilities, the more proficient covering several pages, the less able just a paragraph or so, with assistance from others when necessary. After the reading, over drinks, the members discussed what had been read. C.S. Lewis wrote in his diary on 9 February 1927: 'Bought a copy of the Volsunga Saga, having had a card last night to say that the Kolbítar are reading it this term and I am put down for Chapter I and II at the next meeting. Began working on it. . . . Looked at Morris's translation of Volsunga Saga in the Union' (All My Road Before Me: The Diary of C.S. Lewis 1922–1927 (1991), p. 449). He noted doing more work on the Völsunga saga on 16 February, and commented about the meeting on 18 February: 'To the Kolbítar at Exeter in the evening. Very pleasant. Followed a good deal better than before' (p. 453). This meeting was probably in Coghill's rooms. Other places where the Kolbítar met, according to Coghill, were Bryson's rooms at Balliol, and on some occasions at the Eastgate Hotel or in back rooms of local pubs. John Bryson told Humphrey Carpenter that on one occasion 'a certain scholar, who must remain nameless, was actually caught using a printed "crib" under the table as he translated his passage apparently impromptu. He was not invited back again!' (The Inklings, p. 28).

The **Oxford Dante Society**, founded in 1876, met once a term, on the fifth Tuesday 'being entertained to dinner ("of an ordinary description") by members in turn'. The objects of the Society were defined as:

'to read papers and discuss subjects connected with Dante: to encourage mutual inquiry as to critical, historical and other points relating to his works: to interchange information as to new books, reviews, monographs, etc., and generally to stimulate and forward the study of the *Divina Commedia*, and other works of Dante and of his age.' A paper was to be read at each meeting by a member 'as far as possible in rotation in order of seniority'. [*Centenary Essays on Dante* by Members of the Oxford Dante Society (1965), p. 143]

The Secretary was the only officer of the Society, and the membership was limited to twelve, or for a time fifteen. *Colin Hardie, also one of the later *Inklings, was Secretary during the time that Tolkien was a member. Tolkien was elected as the fifty-eighth member on 20 February 1945, and resigned on 15 February 1955. C.S. Lewis had been a member since 1937; *Charles Williams was briefly a member from 15 February 1944 until his death on 15 May 1945.

After interviewing Tolkien, Charlotte and Denis Plimmer reported in a draft article that Dante did not attract him: 'He's full of spite and malice. I don't care for his petty relations with petty people in petty cities.' Tolkien replied on 8 February 1967: 'My reference to Dante was outrageous. I do not seriously dream of being measured against Dante, a supreme poet. At one time Lewis and I used to read him to one another. I was for a while a member of the Oxford Dante Society (I think at the proposal of Lewis, who over-estimated greatly my scholarship in Dante or Italian generally). It is true that I found the "pettiness" that I spoke of a sad blemish in places' (*Letters*, p. 377).

Tolkien's turn to read a paper to members may have come in Michaelmas Term 1947, as he placed a draft of it in an envelope postmarked 4 July 1947. Tolkien began the paper, *A Neck-Verse*, by quoting a rhyme by which, if he could recite it, an accused in the Middle Ages might be granted 'benefit of clergy' and be spared the hangman. He then continued:

> I wish I could get off as lightly. But what I have to offer this evening is, I fear, little more than a *neck-verse*; and whether it will suffice to satisfy the bishops of erudition here assembled, even on promise of later amendment, is very doubtful.
>
> I have, of course, hardly more claim to be included in this Society on grounds of learning in Dante than a villain who had conned the *Miserere* against an evil day has to be accounted a genuine *clerk*. But *lusinga* – for such is my theme – is a sweet snare to those less stern than Cato. And so it proved to me. The praise or honour that is not deserved has a special potency, a fatal charm. I accepted it, and have feasted since in your company (not without a grieving sense of guilt). Most enchanting it has been, but the awakening from such spells is often accompanied by a headache.
>
> If I had fully realized that *I* should be required to read a paper, however brief, in anyway connected with Dante, it would, I suppose, hardly have deterred me, for like many others I will promise such things, if only the date is far enough removed, and a dinner lies between. But now the hour has struck, and the neck verse must be read.

And what (I thought) can a man of Thule whose reading has been more upon the vision of the Northern Sibyl than on Albano or even upon Virgil or Dante. . . .

'A Northern look at Dante' should be my theme, I said in the early summer when the [?glass] of wine and the glow of the westering sun upon the Warden's garden of Wadham combined to make all things possible. But what effrontery! Dante would outstare me. . . .

For *tuestelle vel I am northern man* and find it difficult to deal in hard clarities, northern not only by descent (of little import) but by temper, taste, and such learning as I have scraped. There is a long gap between my first glimpses of the *Divina Commedia* in the embracing curiosity of earlier days and my return, too late to do more than stray in such regions, a chance visitor; tongue-tied – for my knowledge of the language of Tuscany is too slight for any profound converse with the inhabitants. And it is a hard – I do not mean difficult – but to me a flint-hard, gem-hard, glittering tongue, so unlike the soft northern tongues that I know better. . . . [Tolkien Papers, Bodleian Library, Oxford]

The **Oyster Club**, similar to The Cave in its later form, sometimes gathered to celebrate the end of examination-marking by eating oysters. Since at the most examinations took place only twice a year (the Preliminary Examination, and Finals; see entry for *Oxford English School), and examiners changed frequently, this may have been more a custom than a society.

The members of the dining club called **the Society** – its entire name – were generally though not exclusively resident in Oxford, associated with one or other of the colleges, and interested in Oxford education. Numbering twelve on average (though as many as nineteen), they tended to meet once each term for a dinner given by one of the members, typically at his college, at which the host was expected to read a paper – though these 'rules' were by no means always adhered to, especially in wartime and during postwar years. The origins of the Society seem to have been lost to history as early as the end of the nineteenth century, but the club was in existence from at least 1871, and was dissolved, for lack of enough members able to keep up its traditions, only in Michaelmas Term 1980. Tolkien was elected a member in Hilary Term 1935; other members at that time included *Nevill Coghill, *Kenneth Sisam, and the Society Secretary of long standing, *R.W. Chapman. Thereafter Tolkien was present at most of the Society dinners until he moved from Oxford, and was pleased to attend twice even in the year of his death. His son *Christopher was himself a member for a short time in the 1970s, when the Society minutes referred to 'Tolkien père et fils'.

PROFESSIONAL SOCIETIES AND ORGANIZATIONS

In some of these Tolkien played an active role, while others he seems to have joined mainly to receive their publications.

The **Arthurian Society** was formed on 27 November 1927 with the aims of fostering the study of Arthurian legend and romance by research and by the public discussion of such work. Two meetings were held each term, at which the Secretary furnished a list of studies in the field furnished since the last meeting. These were later published in the Society's annual publication *Arthuriana*, together with papers read to the Society. Tolkien is listed as a member in *Arthuriana: Proceedings of the Arthurian Society* 1, for January 1928–January 1929. Eugène Vinaver was the Honorary President and also joint editor of *Arthuriana*. There were thirty-two members, including the officials and three Honorary Members. The second volume of *Arthuriana*, covering the period January 1929 to January 1930, included some papers not given to the Society and some of more general interest, among them essays on medieval textual criticism. By then the membership had fallen to twenty-seven. Probably the falling membership and difficulty of obtaining enough purely Arthurian material led to its replacement by a society with a wider range of interests, the Society for the Study of Mediæval Languages and Literature (see below).

The **Early English Text Society** (EETS), as an official statement declares, 'was founded in 1864 by Frederick James Furnivall, with the help of Richard Morris, Walter Skeat, and others, to bring the mass of unprinted Early English literature within the reach of students and provide sound texts from which the New English Dictionary could quote'. Between 1867 and 1921 it also published an Extra Series of texts 'already printed, but not in satisfactory or readily obtainable editions'. Subscribers received the annual publication. Tolkien reviewed one of these, O. Cockayne's revision of F.J. Furnivall's edition of *Hali Meidenhad: An Alliterative Prose Homily of the Thirteenth Century*, in the *Times Literary Supplement* for 26 April 1923 (*Holy Maidenhood).

On 6 December 1938 Tolkien was appointed a member of the EETS Committee (from April 1949, the Early English Text Society Council). He attended meetings as his other duties permitted. From archived correspondence it seems that in some cases the Council actively sought editors of specific works, but also considered proposals submitted by prospective editors. In some cases these were suggesting texts on which they had worked for a B.Litt. or an M.Phil. One example was Tolkien's B.Litt. student M.Y. Offord, whose edition of *The Parlement of the Thre Ages* was published by EETS in 1959. Members of the Council with a knowledge of the texts in question were asked to study the proposals and report to the Council, who decided whether or not to accept a book for publication. At a meeting of 23 March 1956 *J.A.W. Bennett and C.L. Wrenn reported on *Meredith Thompson's edition of *Þe Wohunge ure Lauerd* and other pieces, presumably expressing some qualifications about accepting it, as Tolkien said that he thought that the edition should be accepted, and offered to read through its notes and help Thompson (a friend) make them conform to the requirements of the Society.

In addition, all Council members received proofs of works the Society published, and any comments they made were sent to the editor of the particular work. On 26 March 1957 *R.W. Burchfield, Secretary of EETS, asked Tolkien if he had had time to examine and comment on P. Clemoes's specimen homily (i.e. *Ælfric: Catholic Homilies*, ed. P. Clemoes, still forthcoming in 1962). In August 1961 Tolkien, who had been sent proofs of Frances M. Mack's edition of **Ancrene Riwle* (B.M. MS Cotton Titus D.XVIII), wrote to Burchfield that he had read the first section with care, 'as befits one who has received many valuable suggestions from other members of the Council' (Tolkien Papers, Bodleian Library, Oxford).

When Tolkien was a member, many of his fellow Officers and Council members were also professional associates, including J.A.W. Bennett (from 1956), R.W. Burchfield (Honorary Secretary from *c.* 1955), *W.A. Craigie (from *c.* 1933 to 1957), *Norman Davis (from *c.* 1955, Honorary Director from 1957), *Dorothy Everett (from *c.* 1946–1953), *N.R. Ker (from *c.* 1955), C.T. Onions (member *c.* 1941–*c.* 1963, Honorary Director 1946–57), *A.H. Smith (Honorary Treasurer 1938–40, member *c.* 1951–67), *Dorothy Whitelock (*c.* 1958–62), and C.L. Wrenn (*c.* 1949–66). Although she was not otherwise closely connected with Tolkien, much correspondence passed between Tolkien and *Mabel Day, Secretary of the EETS from 1931 to *c.* 1948.

On 10 July 1945 Tolkien became a member of the *Ancrene Riwle* subcommittee; the other members were Mabel Day, Dorothy Everett, C.T. Onions, and C.L. Wrenn. In April 1949 it was renamed the *Ancrene Riwle* Committee, and from April 1952 was incorporated into the ordinary meetings of the Council.

Tolkien's own involvement with editing a work for the Society began at a meeting of its Council on 2 December 1931, when the Secretary, Mabel Day, was commissioned to ask Professors Onions and Tolkien if they contemplated editing the *Ancrene Riwle*. It was over thirty years before Tolkien's edition of the Corpus Christi College Cambridge MS 402 of the *Ancrene Riwle* was published, in 1962 (for 1960, the 249th publication of the Society) under the title *Ancrene Wisse*. Although this was one of a series of editions of the English, French, and Latin texts of the *Ancrene Riwle* published by the EETS, Tolkien had his own views on approach, format, and typography: see **Chronology**.

Tolkien contributed to several publications by the **English Association** and was almost certainly a member. He wrote the section *Philology: General Works* in **The Year's Work in English Studies*, vols. 4–6 for the years 1923–5; and had writings included in the Association's annual volume of *Essays and Studies*, 14 (1929) and n.s. 6 (1953). On 20 January 1922 he talked to a joint meeting of the English Association, Leeds and District Branch, and to the Yorkshire Dialect Society on 'The New English Dictionary'.

The English Association was formed in 1906 by a group of English scholars and teachers, including A.C. Bradley and Sir Israel Gollancz, 'to foster and develop the study of English as an essential element of our national education'. It played a leading part in the movement to develop English studies in both schools and universities. Today its stated aim is 'to further knowledge, understanding and enjoyment of the English language and its literatures and to foster good practice in its teaching and learning at all levels'. In addition to its publications, it organizes conferences and lectures.

The **English Place-Name Society** was established to survey place-names in England county by county, to study the elements of such names, and to publish the results. Tolkien joined when the Society was founded in 1923, and remained a member until his death, but did not play an active role in its activities. One of his students at Leeds, *A.H. Smith, however, became a senior figure in the Society and a seminal name in English place-name studies. Tolkien wrote a review of the two volumes devoted to place-names in Devon, issued by the Society in 1931 and 1932, but apparently so long after the fact that it was never published.

According to the lists of members and officials published in the annual *Transactions* of the **Philological Society**, Tolkien apparently became a member in 1929; from 1930 to 1938 he was an ordinary member on the Council; and from 1939 until 1970–1 he was Vice President. The Philological Society was established in its present form in 1842, partly from members of a society of the same name established in 1830 at the University of London. One of its major projects, begun in 1857, was the *New English Dictionary on Historical Principles*, which became known as the *Oxford English Dictionary*, on which Tolkien worked from 1919 to 1920. 'As well as encouraging all aspects of the study of language, the Society has a particular interest in historical and comparative linguistics, and maintains its traditional interest in the structure, development and varieties of Modern English' (*ling.man.ac.uk*).

On 16 May 1931 Tolkien read a paper, *Chaucer's Use of Dialects*, to a meeting of the Society in Oxford. This was published as *Chaucer as Philologist: The Reeve's Tale* in *Transactions of the Philological Society* for 1934.

Tolkien was elected a Fellow of the **Royal Society of Literature** in April 1957. In a letter to his grandson Michael George (see *Michael Tolkien) he wrote of his election, which he assumed was due to *The Lord of the Rings*, and remarked that it was an honour that few on the Language side of his profession had received. The Society, founded by George IV, aims 'to sustain and encourage all that is perceived as best, whether traditional or experimental in English letters, and to strive for a catholic appreciation of literature' (*www.rslit.org*). It organizes lectures, discussions, and readings.

Tolkien was sent invitations to various lectures, but there is no evidence that he attended them. On 24 November 1966 *The Times* announced that the Royal Society of Literature had awarded the Benson Silver Medal to Dame Rebecca West and to Professor J.R.R. Tolkien, after a lapse of fourteen years since the last award. The Benson Medals were endowed by A.C. Benson at the beginning of the 20th century and are presented to authors of various types of work. The medals were presented on 19 July 1967 and lunches with Rayner beforehand.

The **Society of Authors** sent Tolkien an invitation to become a member on 7 March 1950, but he mislaid it, probably because he was in the middle of moving house. Over five years later, when the letter came to light in a general clean-up, he completed the form and applied for membership on 6 September 1955. The Society was founded in 1884 'to protect the rights and further the interests of authors'. On occasion Tolkien consulted the Society about various matters, including the sale of some of his manuscripts to Marquette.

He almost certainly attended the inaugural meeting of the **Society for the Study of Mediæval Languages and Literature** at 5.00 p.m. at the Taylor Institution, Oxford, since he was appointed to the Executive Committee for two years. The Executive Committee was made up of the President, the Secretary, the Treasurer, and the Editor, *ex officio* plus several ordinary members, but not the Vice-Presidents. Lists of officers published in the Society's journal, *Medium Ævum*, indicate that he remained on the Committee until at least February 1936; that from at least June 1936 until 1959 he was on the Editorial Board; that from at least June 1939 until 1949 he was again on the Executive Committee; from *c.* 1949 until *c.* 1952 he was President of the Society; and from *c.* 1953 until his death in 1973 he was a Vice-President. Some at least of these positions must have been more than honorary, and may have involved a considerable amount of work. Tolkien was probably also active in the Oxford branch of the Society.

The Society grew out of the Arthurian Society at Oxford (see above), and was founded to encourage research in medieval languages and literature and for the publication of the results of such research. One of the duties of the Executive Committee was to further the creation of Local Branches of the Society. Tolkien's *Sigelwara Land* was published in two parts in *Medium Ævum*, 1, no. 3 (December 1932) and 3, no. 2 (June 1934).

On 9 December 1936 Tolkien repeated his lecture *Beowulf: The Monsters and the Critics* to a meeting of the Manchester branch of the Society.

Tolkien gave a talk on 20 January 1922 to a joint meeting of the English Association, Leeds and District Branch, and the **Yorkshire Dialect Society** on 'The New English Dictionary'. He was probably a member of both at the time. He was still listed as a member in the *Transactions of the Yorkshire Dialect Society* for April 1939.

OTHER SOCIETIES

By May 1932, Tolkien became a member of the Board of Honorary Advisors of the Education Committee of the **British Esperanto Association**. In June 1933 he was elected an Honorary Member of **Hið íslenzka bókmenntafélag**, the Icelandic Literary Society. In a letter to Christopher Tolkien on 18 April 1944, he said that he had agreed to join the Oxford branch of 'a combined **Christian Council** of all denominations' (*Letters*, p. 73) being organized by Frank Pakenham, but refused the secretaryship. In August 1955 he mentioned that he was an official of the **International Congress of Linguists**. In 1966, when *Donald Swann began to perform musical settings of his poems, Tolkien joined the **Performing Rights Society**, which collected payments for him as the author. In a letter to Rayner Unwin in the same year, he mentioned that he was a member of **P.E.N.**, the international association of poets, playwrights, essayists, editors, and novelists.

On 22 November 1914 Tolkien read his paper on the *Kalevala* to the **Sundial Society** at Corpus Christi College, Oxford, with the title *The Finnish National Epic*; on 28 May 1915 he addressed the **Psittakoi** on *The Quest of Beauty and Other Poems* by H.R. Freston; and on 14 February 1938 he read a revised version of **Farmer Giles of Ham* to the **Lovelace Society** at Worcester College, Oxford. He was almost certainly not a member of any of these groups. The Psittakoi seems to have been based mainly at Exeter College; **T.W.* Earp was its president in 1915.

Tolkien very probably was a member of the **Newman Society** in Oxford, to which he gave a paper in 1928, but no conclusive evidence has come to light. Nor can it be shown that he was a member of the **Viking Society for Northern Research**, though he received several cards announcing forthcoming meetings.

See also **The Inklings; **T.C.B.S.*

Some Contributions to Middle-English Lexicography. Article, published in the *Review of English Studies* (London) 1, no. 2 (April 1925), pp. 210–15.

The 'only possible excuse' for the publication of these 'scraps of lexicographical and etymological information and suggestion', Tolkien writes, is that they may ultimately assist in the compilation of urgently needed Middle English dictionaries (p. 210). He notes uses of *long home* ('To go to one's long home' = 'to depart this life') older than those recorded in the **Oxford English Dictionary*, and through a discussion of *burde* 'lady, damsel' he investigates synonyms for 'man' and 'woman' in alliterative verse and speculates on Old English *byrde* 'embroideress'. Half of the article, however, is devoted to notes on the glossary to the Early English Text Society (**Societies and clubs) 1922 edition of *Hali Meidenhad* (see **Katherine Group).

A Song of Aryador. Poem, written by Tolkien on 12 September 1915 in an Army camp near Lichfield (**Staffordshire), published with commentary in **The Book of Lost Tales, Part One* (1983), pp. 138–9. 'In the vales of Aryador / By the wooded inland shore' there are goats on the fells and men kindling fires, where once 'shadow-folk' (Elves) sang 'ancient songs of olden gods'. The first of two extant copies has the title also in Old English, *Án léop Éargedores*. In both copies, a manuscript and a typescript, 'He' (the Sun) was emended to 'She'. In **The Book of Lost Tales* it was later said that when Men entered Hisilómë, which they called Aryador, some of the Elves who were lost on the march to Valinor still dwelt there and were feared by Men, who called them the Shadow Folk.

Songs for the Philologists. Booklet, privately printed by students in the Department of English, University College, London, in 1936. It began as mimeographed poems, the 'Leeds Songs', prepared by **E.V.* Gordon at the University of **Leeds in the 1920s (after his arrival in 1922) for the amusement of students in the English School. He included verses that he himself had written, and several by Tolkien, together with modern and traditional songs from

Icelandic student songbooks. In 1935 or 1936 *A.H. Smith of University College, London, formerly a student at Leeds, gave an uncorrected copy of the verses to a group of students to print as an exercise. Thirty poems, chiefly in Old, Middle, and Modern English, Gothic, Icelandic, and Latin, were assembled as *Songs for the Philologists*. Not all of the Leeds verses were set, some of them were altered to suit University College rather than Leeds conditions, and one new 'song' was added. Thirteen of the poems are by Tolkien:

From One to Five, a counting rhyme ('One old man of Durham', 'Two poor loons of London', etc.), altered in publication to suit University College (rather than Leeds) conditions, sung to the tune of 'Three Wise Men of Gotham';

Syx Mynet, an Old English rendering, and sung to the tune, of 'I Love Sixpence';

Ruddoc Hana, an Old English version of 'Who Killed Cock Robin?';

Ides Ælfscyne, sung to 'Daddy Neptune';

Bagme Bloma, sung to 'O Lazy Sheep!';

Eadig Beo Þu! sung to 'Twinkle, Twinkle, Little Star';

Ofer Widne Garsecg, sung to 'The Mermaid';

La, Huru, sung to 'O'Reilly';

I Sat upon a Bench, a robust drinking song, sung to 'The Carrion Crow';

Natura Apis, 'a sooth little song / Of the busy brown bee' (with the original concluding verse omitted), sung to 'O'Reilly';

The Root of the Boot (see *The Stone Troll*), sung to 'The Fox Went Out on a Winter's Night';

Frenchmen Froth, in praise of 'the English tongue fore all', sung to 'The Vicar of Bray';

Lit' and Lang', called in the table of contents 'Two Little Schemes', altered from its Leeds version (in such a way, Tolkien thought, as to break the rhyme), sung to 'Polly Put the Kettle On'.

As soon as *Songs for the Philologists* was ready, however, Smith realized that he had never asked permission of Tolkien and Gordon to publish their poems, and he restricted the number of copies of the booklet to be distributed. Most of the stock was later lost in a fire. On 25 April 1966 Tolkien commented to *Rayner Unwin that the collection contained, garbled and with many errors, 'some of the very songs and nonsense verses that I wrote for the amusement and encouragement of Leeds students. . . . It includes for instance a translation into Anglo Saxon of "The Mermaid" ([the traditional song] It was in the Broad Atlantic) which proved quite popular at the time' (Tolkien-George Allen & Unwin archive, HarperCollins).

Ides Ælfscyne ('Elf-fair Lady'), *Bagme Bloma* ('Flower of the Trees'), *Eadig Beo Þu!* ('Good Luck to You!'), and *Ofer Widne Garsecg* ('Across the Broad Ocean') were reprinted by T.A. Shippey in *The Road to Middle-earth* (1982; rev. edn. 1992) with Modern English translations.

Source-hunting. In his essay 'Real-world Myth in a Secondary World: Mythological Aspects in the Story of Beren and Lúthien', in *Tolkien the Medievalist* (2003), Richard C. West asks if there is anyone who, upon reading the *'Silmarillion' tale of Lúthien escaping from her tree house-prison by weaving a rope from her magically lengthened hair (see *'Of Beren and Lúthien), is not reminded of Rapunzel. 'Everybody mentions this fairy-tale resonance from what was probably the first published essay on this story on. . . . And I think rightly: certainly Tolkien was familiar with the *Märchen* of the Brothers Grimm.' Lúthien also having woven a shroud of darkness and cast a sleeping-spell on her guards,

> the situation is full of resonances from other traditional tales [as well]: the enchanted sleep in such stories as *Sleeping Beauty*; the cloak of invisibility in *The Twelve Dancing Princesses*, also suggestive of such magical devices as the Tarnhelm in *The Nibelungenlied*, or the Ring of Gyges in Plato's *Republic*, or the ring of invisibility in Chrétien's *Yvain*, or its analogue in *The Mabinogion*. . . .
>
> Tolkien is always teasing us with this sort of skein of almost-correspondences. Many articles and books have been written by authors who have become aware of yet another possible source for something in Tolkien's fiction, most of these sources being more or less plausible because Tolkien was so well and widely read. For many modern fantasy authors it is indeed valuable to study their direct sources to see how they have handled them, but with Tolkien what I think we get is more of a sense of an addition to the corpus in the same vein. . . .
>
> Indeed, with Tolkien we can be only be confident of a direct source when he has borrowed a feature that is unique to some particular story or he has told us what was in his mind, and both of those circumstances are rare. What I think we do get over and over are echoes, even when we cannot pinpoint an exact source. Tolkien studied and taught myths and legends and fairy tales all his life, and they were an integral part of his mental furniture and imaginative make-up. [pp. 263–4]

Tolkien's attitude to readers' and critics' attempts to find sources for his fiction was in some respects similar to his response to the suggestion that his works are allegorical: that there might be 'applicability', but not a one for one correspondence. He recognized that what he read and knew lay behind much that he wrote, but that his use was often not conscious. Referring to *The Lord of the Rings*, he said:

> One writes such a story not out of the leaves of trees still to be observed, nor by means of botany and soil-science; but it grows like a seed in the dark out of the leaf-mould of the mind: out of all that has been seen or thought or read, that has long ago been forgotten, descending into the deeps. No doubt there is much selection, as with a gardener: what one

throws on one's personal compost-heap; and my mould is evidently made largely of linguistic matter. [quoted in *Biography*, p. 126; cf. *Letters*, p. 409]

He also felt, as he wrote to a Mr Wrigley on 25 May 1972, that 'it is the particular use in a particular situation of any motive, whether invented, deliberately borrowed, or unconsciously remembered that is the most interesting thing to consider' (*Letters*, p. 418). Although he admitted, in respect to myth and fairy-stories, that he felt 'the fascination of the desire to unravel the intricately knotted and ramified history of the branches on the Tree of Tales', he had an even greater interest 'to consider what they are, what they have become for us, and what values the long alchemic processes of time have produced in them.' Basing his words on those of folklorist George Dasent, he said: 'We must be satisfied with the soup that is set before us, and not desire to see the bones of the ox out of which it has been boiled.' By 'the soup' Tolkien meant 'the story as it is served up by its author or teller, and by "the bones" its sources or material – even when (by rare luck) those can be with certainty discovered. But I do not, of course, forbid criticism of the soup as soup' (*On Fairy-Stories*, in *Tree and Leaf*, pp. 22–3).

In his long draft letter to Mr Rang, August 1967, concerning nomenclature in *The Lord of the Rings*, Tolkien refuted sources of names suggested by readers due to superficial similarities:

I remain puzzled, and indeed sometimes irritated, by the many guesses at the 'sources' of the nomenclature, and theories or fancies concerning hidden meanings. These seem to me no more than private amusements, and as such I have no right or power to object to them, though they are, I think, valueless for the elucidation or interpretation of my fiction. If published, I do object to them, when (as they usually do) they appear to be unauthentic embroideries on my work, throwing light only on the state of mind of their contrivers, not on me or on my actual intention and procedure. [*Letters*, pp. 379–80]

Even a name such as *Eärendil*, taken from an Anglo-Saxon poem and used for a prime figure in the *'Silmarillion'* mythology, 'had to be accommodated to the Elvish linguistic situation, at the same time as a place for this person was made in legend' (p. 385).

For discussion of some of the elements that went into the 'leaf-mould' of Tolkien's mind see *Atlantis; *Beowulf; *Celtic influences; *Classical influences; *Historical and cultural influences; *Kalevala;*Northernness.

South Africa. In this book 'South Africa' is used informally to refer to that part of the African continent at its southern extremity which became the Union of South Africa in 1910, and in particular to one of the colonies from which that nation was formed, the **Orange Free State**. Beginning in 1836, thousands of

Boers, descendants of the original Dutch settlers of the Cape of Good Hope colony, moved about 750 miles north of Cape Town into lands then occupied largely by Bantu tribes. In part their 'Great Trek' was in search of independence from British rule, the Cape colony having been ceded by the Dutch to Britain in 1814; but the British government insisted that they remain subject to its authority, and in 1848 annexed the country to which the settlers had moved, naming it the Orange River Sovereignty. In 1854, having found those lands to be of little value and wanting to limit its responsibilities in the region, Britain ceded governance of the territory to the Boers, who thereupon created a republic. The Oranje Vrystaat, or Orange Free State, between the Orange and Vaal rivers, thereafter enjoyed a period of prosperity, if not of peace with neighbouring native peoples, until it was re-annexed by Britain after the Boer War of 1899–1902.

Bloemfontein, the capital of the Orange Free State and the place of Tolkien's birth, was founded in 1852 and made a municipality in 1880. In 1892 its white population numbered about 3500 to 4000. An account of the city published only ten years later – probably drawn more from travel brochures than from first-hand experience – described it as 'more like a rural village, than the seat of government of an important state . . . a pleasant town on a high table-land, 4500 feet above the sea-level, and surrounded by low hills. The climate is dry and healthy, and much recommended to sufferers from lung-disease. . . . The town is well laid out; most of the public buildings are of red brick, and a white stone quarried in the neighbourhood, and the houses are surrounded by luxuriant gardens' (Harry Quilter, *What's What* (1902), pp. 246–7). Significant buildings included Parliament House, the Dutch Reformed Church, the Anglican Cathedral, and the hospital, clustered around the market square. There were shops and clubs and other amenities; but trees were sparse, and only a short distance outside the city was an open veldt, across which winds blew and wild animals roamed. Snakes and tarantulas lurked in wood-sheds and gardens. And while the climate was indeed dry, summers could be oppressively hot and winters bitterly cold.

Tolkien's father, *Arthur Tolkien, moved to South Africa in 1889 in the employ of the Bank of Africa. For the first year he held temporary postings in some of the principal towns between Cape Town and Johannesburg, then in 1890 was appointed manager of the branch in Bloemfontein, located at Bank House in Maitland Street near the market square. A photograph of Maitland Street reproduced in *Biography*, pl. 1b, shows the bank building (later demolished) on one side of a wide, dusty street near a shop selling linens and a photography studio. In 1891 Arthur and his fiancée Mabel Suffield (*Mabel Tolkien) were married in the Anglican Cathedral of St George in **Cape Town** and spent their honeymoon at nearby Sea Point. A photograph of the cathedral, *c.* 1890, is reproduced in *The Tolkien Family Album*, p. 15.

Bank House in Bloemfontein included accommodations for the manager and his family above the bank proper, and a large garden in which Arthur Tolkien made a small grove of cypresses, firs, and cedars. Photographs of

Arthur and his staff, and with his family, next to a vine-covered wall of Bank House, are reproduced in *The Tolkien Family Album*, pp. 15, 16; the second is also reproduced in *Biography*, pl. 1a. J.R.R. Tolkien was born in Bank House in 1892, and his brother *Hilary there also in 1894. At the end of January 1892 Ronald Tolkien was baptized in the Anglican Cathedral of St Andrew and St Michael, built in Bloemfontein in 1866, with a nave in the Gothic style added in 1885.

Many years later, Tolkien wrote to his son Christopher, who was then stationed in South Africa with the Royal Air Force:

> All you say about the dryness, dustiness, and smell of the satan-licked land reminds me of my mother; she hated it (as a land) and was alarmed to see symptoms of my father growing to like it. It used to be said that no English-born woman could ever get over this dislike or be more than an exile, but that Englishmen (under the freer conditions of peace) could and usually did get to love it (as a land; I am saying nothing of any of its inhabitants). [12 August 1944, *Letters*, p. 90]

On one occasion, Mabel Tolkien described Bloemfontein as ''Owlin' Wilderness! Horrid Waste!' (quoted in *Biography*, p. 11). Personal feelings aside, she was concerned about young Ronald, who suffered badly from the heat. In November 1894 she, Ronald, and Hilary went on holiday to the seaside at Cape Town, where the air was cooler; but this could be only a temporary measure. In April 1895 Mabel and her sons went to England on home leave, while Arthur continued with his work at the bank. In February 1896 Arthur died from rheumatic fever, and was buried in the President Brand cemetery in Bloemfontein.

Mabel, Ronald, and Hilary never returned to South Africa. Tolkien had the opportunity to do so in 1921 when he was offered the De Beers Chair in English Language at the University of Cape Town, but declined because he would have had to leave his wife and young children in England for a period of time. Later in life he felt a nostalgia for South Africa, though his earliest memories were of blazing heat. On 25 May 1944 he wrote to Christopher: 'I was disposed, at last, to envy you a little [for having been stationed in South Africa]; or rather wish I could be with you "in the hills". There is something in nativity, and though I have few pictorial memories, there is always a curious sense of reminiscence about any stories of Africa, which always move me deeply' (*Letters*, p. 82). And again to Christopher on 12 August 1944:

> Oddly enough all that you say, even to its detriment, only increases the longing I have always felt to see it [South Africa] again. Much though I love and admire little lanes and hedges and rustling trees and the soft rolling contours of a rich champain, the thing that stirs me most and comes nearest to heart's satisfaction for me is space, and I would be willing to barter barrenness for it; indeed I think I like barrenness itself, whenever I have seen it. [*Letters*, pp. 90–1]

Spiders. Spiders, or spider-like beings, figure in many of Tolkien's stories, usually unpleasant and menacing, or even fearsome, creatures of darkness. Some critics have associated this with the account in *Biography* in which Tolkien as a young child 'stumbled on a tarantula. It bit him, and he ran in terror across the garden until the nurse snatched him up and sucked out the poison. When he grew up he could remember a hot day and running in fear through long, dead grass, but the memory of the tarantula itself faded' (p. 13). Tolkien denied, however, that this encounter had any connection with the spiders in his stories, or that he had any special fear of spiders. He wrote to *W.H. Auden on 7 June 1955 that if people like to associate Shelob in *The Lord of the Rings* with the fact that he was stung by a tarantula as a small child, they 'are welcome to the notion. . . . I can only say that I remember nothing about it, should not know it if I had not been told; and I do not dislike spiders particularly, and have no urge to kill them. I usually rescue those whom I find in the bath!' (*Letters*, p. 217). But in a letter to his son *Michael, written in 1967–8, Tolkien recalled that while staying in a châlet inn in *Switzerland in 1911 he and his friends invented 'a method of dealing with . . . the harvestmen spiders, by dropping hot wax from a candle onto their fat bodies' (*Letters*, p. 392).

The spider sitting in a web and awaiting victims is of course an almost archetypal image, and potent because many people do have an inexplicable fear of spiders. In 'Tolkien and Spiders', *Orcrist* 4 = *Tolkien Journal* 4, no. 3, whole no. 13 (1969–70), Bob Mesibov comments on the success of 'Tolkien's giant spiders and spider imagery . . . their effect on his readers is strong and unambiguous'. He suggests various reasons why this is so:

> The first is that no one likes a predator, and spiders are notoriously predatory. Worse yet, they prefer living food. Thus Bilbo [*The Hobbit*, ch. 8] is attacked by a spider which tries 'to poison him to keep him quiet, as small spiders do to flies'. Sam abandons Frodo . . . because he doesn't realize . . . that Shelob '. . . doesn't eat dead meat, nor suck cold blood' [*The Lord of the Rings*, bk. IV, ch. 10]. Tolkien's spiders, and the spiders of our nightmares, hold commissions in that army of monsters bent on gobbling up the unwary. . . . But no one expects to be eaten by a *real* spider. . . .
>
> A second reason for disliking spiders is their sinister armament, the poison and the cunning snare with which they capture their prey. . . .
>
> A third common complaint about spiders is that they are ugly, and on this point Tolkien's feelings are apparently unmixed. [p. 4]

Mesibov also notes that Tolkien often uses a comparison to a spider in a negative way: for instance, Gandalf says of his imprisonment by Saruman: 'Gandalf the Grey caught like a fly in a spider's treacherous web!' (*The Lord of the Rings*, bk. II, ch. 2); Sam Gamgee describes Gollum as looking like 'a nasty crawling spider on a wall' (bk. IV, ch. 1); and Denethor 'sat in a grey gloom, like an old patient spider' (bk. V, ch. 4).

In cases where any indication is given, Tolkien's spiders are invariably female, possibly because spinning and weaving was usually a female occupation, and perhaps also because the notorious black widow spider is known for devouring her mate. The greatest of these is Ungoliant (or Ungoliantë), in Tolkien's mythology (*'The Silmarillion') the devourer of light and destroyer of the Two Trees of Valinor. In *The Silmarillion it is said that some believed that she had 'descended from the darkness that lies about Arda', and was one of those beings whom Melkor had 'corrupted to his service. . . . But she had disowned her Master, desiring to be mistress of her own lust, taking all things to herself to feed her emptiness'. She lived in a ravine, 'and took shape as a spider of monstrous form, weaving her black webs in a cleft of the mountains. There she sucked up all light that she could find, and spun it forth again in dark nets of strangling gloom, until no light more could come to her abode; and she was famished' (p. 73). When she fled with Melkor 'the Cloud of Ungoliant' confused even 'the riders of the Valar', who 'were blinded and dismayed, and they were scattered, and went they knew not whither. . . . And Tulkas was as one caught in a black net at night, and he stood powerless and beat the air in vain' (pp. 76–7). In Middle-earth Ungoliant demanded the Silmarils of Morgoth, and when he refused 'she rose against him, and her cloud closed about him, and she enmeshed him in a web of clinging thongs . . .' (p. 80). But his cry having brought balrogs to his aid, Ungoliant

> quailed, and turned to flight, belching black vapours to cover her; and fleeing from the north she . . . dwelt beneath Ered Gorgoroth, in that dark valley that was ever after called Nan Dungortheb, the Valley of Dreadful Death, because of the horror that she bred there. For other foul creatures of spider form had dwelt there . . . and she mated with them, and devoured them; and even after Ungoliant herself departed . . . her offspring abode there and wove their hideous webs. [p. 81]

Tolkien decided early in the writing of *The Lord of the Rings* that Frodo and Sam would encounter spiders on their journey to Mordor. The idea seems to have come to him in the outline called by Christopher Tolkien 'The Story Foreseen from Moria', when looking forward to the capture of Frodo. Tolkien wrote: '[Gollum] tries to utter horrible words over Frodo – incantation of sleep. A spider charm, or does Gollum get spiders' help? There is a ravine, a spiders' glen, they have to pass at entrance to Gorgoroth. Gollum gets spiders to put spell of sleep on Frodo. Sam drives them off. But cannot wake him' (*The Treason of Isengard*, p. 209). This is the germ of the story of Frodo's encounter with Shelob near Cirith Ungol. Several years later, only after Tolkien had proceeded quite far with the writing of the concluding chapters of Book IV did he realize that Frodo was attacked by not by several spiders but by one great spider, originally called Ungoliant. But Tolkien decided against reusing this name (or the original being so named) from 'The Silmarillion', and on 21 May 1944 wrote to his son Christopher: 'Do you think *Shelob* is a good name for a monstrous spider creature? It is of course only "she+lob" (= spider), but written as one, it seems to be quite noisome' (*Letters*, p. 81).

Of all of the spiders in Tolkien's works, Shelob in *The Lord of the Rings*, as seen through the eyes of Frodo and Sam, is the most vividly described and makes the most terrifying and loathsome impression:

> There [in the Mountains of Shadow] agelong she had dwelt, an evil thing in spider-form, even such . . . as Beren fought in the Mountains of Terror [Ered Gorgoroth] in Doriath. . . . How Shelob came there . . . no tale tells, for out of the Dark Years few tales have come. But still she was there, who was there before Sauron, and before the first stone of Barad-dûr; and she served none but herself, drinking the blood of Elves and Men, bloated and grown fat with endless brooding on her feasts, weaving webs of shadow; for all living things were her food, and her vomit darkness. Far and wide her lesser broods, bastards of the miserable mates, her own offspring, that she slew, spread from glen to glen, from the Ephel Dúath to the eastern hills, to Dol Guldur and the fastnesses of Mirkwood. But none could rival her, Shelob the Great, last child of Ungoliant to trouble the unhappy world. . . .
>
> Little she knew of or cared for towers, or rings, or anything devised by mind or hand, who only desired death for all others, mind and body, and for herself a glut of life, alone, swollen till the mountains could no longer hold her up and the darkness could not contain her. [bk. IV, ch. 9]

Tolkien's description of Shelob's history is a powerful piece of writing, both in its choice of vocabulary and its slow, relentless pace. Shelob seems to be able to sow seeds of darkness that are spiritual as well as physical. On the other hand, she is temporarily halted by the light from the phial given to Frodo by Galadriel, whereas Ungoliant desired light to devour it.

Though this description indicates that the spiders Bilbo encountered in Mirkwood in *The Hobbit* were also descendants of Ungoliant, there is no suggestion either that they devoured light or that their webs were webs of darkness. Moreover, Bilbo is able to understand their speech, and they understand his insulting songs. They are in fact treated in a partly humorous fashion, perhaps bearing in mind that Michael Tolkien, one of the original audience for the story, was afraid of spiders. His parents thought that this fear might be because a few months before he was born they had stayed in a cottage in north Wales, where spiders sometimes fell on their bed and upset *Edith Tolkien.

Several readers have pointed out that some aspects of Tolkien's depiction of Shelob are not characteristic of spiders: that spiders have no necks, and 'their eyes are simple, usually unclustered, and never more than eight in number' (Mesibov, p. 4). Tolkien, with his interest in natural history, was well aware of this, and in a late unpublished work noted that Shelob is not described 'in precise spider terms; but she was "most like a spider". As such she was enormously magnified; and she had two horns and two great clusters of eyes. But she had the characteristic tight constriction of spiders between the front section (head and thorax) and the rear (belly) – this is called . . . her "neck", because the rear portion is swollen and bloated out of proportion' (Tolkien Papers, Bodleian Library, Oxford). See further, *Reader's Companion*, pp. 490–3.

Spiders also appear in Tolkien's early children's story *Roverandom* (conceived 1925, published 1998), among creatures said to live on the moon. On the light side are 'fifty-seven varieties of spiders ready to eat anything they could catch' (p. 27), while on the dark side the spiders are poisonous and black.

Sports. When Tolkien attended *King Edward's School, Birmingham, all boys had to participate in physical exercise in the gymnasium unless excused for medical reasons. Organized games, however, were not compulsory. The only game that Tolkien is recorded as playing was Rugby Football, in autumn and spring terms. At first, because he lacked weight, he was not very successful, but as he later wrote to his son *Michael, 'one day I decided to make up for weight by (legitimate) ferocity, and I ended up a house-captain at the end of that season, & got my colours the next. But I got rather damaged – among things having my tongue nearly cut out . . .' (3 October 1937, *Letters*, p. 22). Tolkien played for the First XV during his last two years at King Edward's School, was Football Secretary during his final year, and returned at least once after he left Birmingham to play for the Old Edwardians against the School team. His abilities were described in the *King Edward's School Chronicle*: 'A light forward who possesses pace and dash, and is a good dribble. He has done much good individual work, especially in breaking away from the scrum to assist the three-quarters. His tackling is always reliable, he follows up hard' ('Football Characters 1910–11', n.s. 26, no. 187 (June 1911), p. 49). Tolkien also played Rugby Football for at least a short time while he was an undergraduate at Exeter College, *Oxford.

On 24 June 1957 Tolkien wrote to Caroline Everett that he did not dislike games, but it was fortunate that they were not compulsory 'as I have always found cricket a bore: chiefly though because I was not good at it' (*Letters*, p. 257). In later years he occasionally watched cricket matches, and in *On Fairy-Stories* remarked that 'a real enthusiast for cricket is in the enchanted state Secondary Belief. I, when I watch a match, am on the lower level. I can achieve (more or less) willing suspension of disbelief, when I am held there and supported by some other motive that will keep away boredom: for instance, a wild, heraldic, preference for dark blue rather than light' (*Tree and Leaf*, p. 37). (Oxford University players wear dark blue, Cambridge University players light blue.)

At various times Tolkien participated in individual sporting activities. At King Edward's School he took part at least twice in the annual Athletic Sports held near the end of summer term. In both 1910 and 1911 he came third in the One Mile Flat race. He probably learnt to swim at school, if not before, though his name is not mentioned in any reports; but in 1932 while on holiday at Lamorna Cove in *Cornwall he and his friend *C.L. Wrenn 'held a swimming race wearing panama hats and smoking pipes while they swam' (Humphrey Carpenter, *Biography*, p. 160).

For a short period during his undergraduate days at Oxford, between Michaelmas Term 1911 and Hilary Term 1913, Tolkien was enrolled in the King Edward's Horse, a territorial cavalry regiment similar to the Officers Training Corps. Also at Oxford he learned to punt, and would later take his family on the Cherwell 'floating in the family punt hired for the season down past the Parks to Magdalen Bridge, or better still polling up-river towards Water Eaton and Islip, where a picnic tea could be spread on the bank' (*Biography*, p. 160). In 1936 he damaged a ligament while playing squash, and was laid up for ten weeks.

As a spectator Tolkien could sometimes get carried away. *Priscilla Tolkien recalls her father's conflict of loyalties when Exeter College, where he had been an undergraduate, was rowing against Pembroke where he was then a Fellow: 'whilst having tea . . . on the Pembroke barge he shouted for their opponents' (*The Tolkien Family Album*, p. 77). Late in life Tolkien came to like watching sports on television. When he stayed with his brother Hilary after Edith's death, the brothers watched cricket and tennis. *Joy Hill from George Allen & Unwin (*Publishers) related in an interview that in the summer of 1973 she was worried when Tolkien failed to answer the phone several times, and when she was eventually successful he told her that he had been in the caretaker's flat watching Wimbledon tennis.

In 1966, writing to Charlotte and Denis Plimmer, Tolkien commented: 'Since my early sixties I have become "tubby". Not unusual in men who took their exercise in games and swimming, when opportunities for these things cease' (*Letters*, p. 373).

A *Spring Harvest* see **Smith, Geoffrey Bache**

Staffordshire. Tolkien spent most of the period from August 1915 through May 1916 in the central English county of Staffordshire, training with the 13th Battalion of the Lancashire Fusiliers. For three months he was stationed a few miles north of *Birmingham in the vicinity of **Lichfield**, known as the birthplace of Dr Samuel Johnson and for its cathedral (mainly thirteenth- and fourteenth century). Letters at this time were addressed to him at 'Whittington Heath' or 'Whittington Barracks'. According to a later inscription, while at this camp he wrote the poem **A Song of Aryador*, related to his *'Silmarillion' mythology by the invented place-name *Aryador* (= Hisilómë, Dor Lómin). On 25 and 26 September 1915 *R.Q. Gilson, *G.B. Smith, and *Christopher Wiseman joined Tolkien at the George Hotel in Lichfield for the final meeting of the four core members of the *T.C.B.S.

Sometime in November 1915 Tolkien's battalion was transferred to Rugeley, and in December to Brocton, the two large military training camps (not to be mistaken for the nearby villages of the same names) hastily established that year on **Cannock Chase**, an enormous moor between Lichfield and Stafford.

The two camps were separated by the Sherbrook Valley. Provided with their own water and power supplies, sewage, roads, and post offices, they were like small towns, even with branches of major banks and the stationer W.H. Smith and Son. Tolkien may have spent time at one or both already in October 1915: a letter posted to him on 21 October addressed to 'Brocton Camp, Stafford' was forwarded to 'Penkridge, Rugeley' – that is, the part of Rugeley Camp at Penkridge Bank – though another letter, dated 31 October, was addressed to him still at Whittington Heath. It was probably while stationed on Cannock Chase, once the hunting-forest of the Mercian kings, that Tolkien 'attended his troops' cutting up of a poached deer from the Pennine Uplands' (mentioned by Tolkien in a lecture given in 1955, according to J.S. Ryan, 'The Origin of the Name Wetwang', *Amon Hen* 63 (August 1983), p. 13, n. 7).

After moving to Brocton Camp in early December 1915 Tolkien seems to have remained there until 4 June 1916, apart from brief periods of leave and during April–May 1916 while on a signalling course in *Otley, Yorkshire. He was housed at 'P' Lines near Anson's Bank at the southern edge of the camp, and later at 'M' Lines near the camp post office – that is, specific groups of huts identified by letter. Photographs of quarters at 'M' Lines, and of Brocton and Rugeley Camps in general, are reproduced in *A Town for Four Winters* by C.J. and G.P. Whitehouse (1983): these show a bleak, windswept landscape with plain wooden buildings, later much changed soon after the war with the removal of the camps and the planting of trees.

Conditions in the Staffordshire camps were uncomfortable. According to Humphrey Carpenter,

> in the intervals between inedible meals, trench drill, and lectures on machine-guns, there was little to do except play bridge (which [Tolkien] enjoyed) and listen to ragtime on the gramophone (which he did not). Nor did he care for the majority of his fellow officers. 'Gentlemen are non-existent among the superiors,' he told Edith, 'and even human beings rare indeed.' He spent some of his time reading Icelandic . . . but the time passed slowly. 'These grey days,' he wrote, 'wasted in wearily going over, over and over again, the dreary topics, the dull backwaters of the art of killing, are not enjoyable.' [*Biography*, p. 78]

During this time Tolkien composed more poems related to his mythology. He later noted that *Habbanan beneath the Stars* was written in December 1915 at Brocton Camp or in June 1916 at Étaples (*France). He inscribed another poem, *Over the Hills and Far Away*, as written at Brocton Camp between December 1915 and February 1916. In March 1916 he revised his poem *Narqelion*. He also began or continued to compile a lexicon of his invented Elvish language then called Qenya (*Languages, Invented), which may have been near completion by the time he was posted to France in June 1916.

After his honeymoon in March 1916, Tolkien returned to Cannock Chase, while Edith moved to the nearby Staffordshire village of ***Great Haywood**.

Tolkien himself stayed there on sick leave from December 1916 through February 1917, having been sent home with trench fever following action on the Somme. In the spring of 1918, probably not long after a medical board on 10 April found him fit for general service, Tolkien was posted again to Penkridge Camp (Rugeley Camp). Edith, together with their baby son *John and Edith's cousin *Jennie Grove, now moved into rooms in **Gipsy Green**, a hamlet of two houses on the Teddesley Park estate, not far from Penkridge Camp and about four miles from Brocton Camp, to which Tolkien was later transferred. According to the Staffordshire Archives Service, at that time the two houses at Gipsy Green were inhabited by J.F. Newman and T. Husselbee.

Tolkien was sometimes able to stay with his family at Gipsy Green, travelling to and from camp on a motor bicycle. In an account of life at Gipsy Green, drawing upon stories told by her mother, *Priscilla Tolkien wrote that her parents

> woke up early one morning (it was fine and warm and the window was open) to hear a male voice saying, I'm coming up, I'm coming up! It got louder and eventually they were astonished to find a talking bird at the window! The bird [a jackdaw] was also mischievous and jealous. They were warned it might attack the baby and when John was put in the garden they had to cover his pram. . . . On another occasion they saw from their window their landlord bent down and planting onions in his vegetable garden. Unseen by him, the jackdaw followed behind, pulling out the onions as fast as he'd planted them. When he straightened up at the end of the row he saw what had happened and angrily chased off the bird. My parents said his language even at a distance came over very strongly, and even after many years they would re-tell this story with great amusement. ['J.R.R. Tolkien and Edith Tolkien's Stay in Staffordshire 1916, 1917 and 1918', *Angerthas* 34 (July 1993), p. 5]

Tolkien made several drawings at Gipsy Green. One is a view of the house seen through a row of trees (*Gipsy Green*, see *Artist and Illustrator*, fig. 22). Another, *High Life at Gipsy Green* (*Artist and Illustrator*, fig. 23) is a series of vignettes: Edith washing herself, fixing her hair, playing the piano, carrying John in the garden; John in his cot; cats that danced when Edith played the piano; the jackdaw in a tree; and Tolkien himself in uniform.

John Garth has suggested that the name *Gipsy Green* is reflected in *Fladweth Amrod* 'Nomad's Green', described in Tolkien's *Gnomish Lexicon* as 'a place in *Tol Erethrin* [= Tol Eressëa, the Lonely Isle of the Elves], where *Eriol* sojourned a while, nigh to *Tavrobel*' (*Parma Eldalamberon* 11 (1995), p. 35; see also John Garth, *Tolkien and the Great War* (2003), p. 246). Tavrobel in *The Book of Lost Tales* is associated with Great Haywood, a few miles to the north-east of Gipsy Green. In *Artist and Illustrator* we propose the Tolkiens' house at Gipsy Green, with its tall prominent chimneys, as a possible source for Gilfanon's 'House of the Hundred Chimneys' in *The Tale of the Sun and Moon*, though it is not 'nigh the bridge of Tavrobel', that is, Essex Bridge in Great Haywood (*The Book of Lost Tales, Part One*, p. 175).

Edith was happy at Gipsy Green, and seems to have stayed there until joining her husband in *Oxford at the end of 1918.

After he became a Catholic priest Tolkien's son John held a series of positions in Staffordshire. At the end of August 1960 his father spent a week with him in 'a small mining village looking like a shabby part of Mordor', as he referred to it in a letter to George Lewis Hersch (30 August 1960, quoted in Michael Silverman, *Catalogue No. 2* (1998), item 43). Tolkien visited John also from 20 to 28 June 1962, taking with him the galley proofs of *The Adventures of Tom Bombadil and Other Verses from the Red Book* for proofreading. On 1 October 1966 John was assigned to the important parish of Our Lady of the Angels in **Stoke-on-Trent**, a major centre of pottery production. Tolkien spent Christmas 1971, a few weeks after Edith's death, with John at Northcote House, 104 Hartshill Road, Stoke-on-Trent, and two weeks with him also in August 1972.

Stevens, Courtenay Edward (1905–1976). C.E. 'Tom Brown' Stevens was educated at New College, *Oxford, followed by postgraduate work at Oriel College and Magdalen College, Oxford. In 1933 he became a Fellow of Magdalen by special election. After the war he was an Official Fellow and Tutor in Ancient History at Magdalen, but tutored students from many other Oxford colleges as well. In 1950–1 he also served as Vice-President of Magdalen. Devoted to teaching, he nonetheless produced many articles and reviews, in particular on the history of Roman Britain.

An acquaintance of *C.S. Lewis and *Colin Hardie at Magdalen, Stevens joined the *Inklings in November 1947.

Stewart, John Innes Mackintosh (1906–1994). As a student at Oriel College, *Oxford, where he read English Language and Literature, J.I.M. Stewart was impressed by Tolkien's lectures: 'he would turn a lecture room into a mead hall in which he was the bard and we were the feasting, listening guests' (quoted in *Biography*, p. 133). Having received his B.A. in 1928, he studied Freudian psychoanalysis in Vienna, and held posts at *Leeds, Adelaide, and Belfast before returning to Oxford in 1949 as a Student of Christ Church. He remained on the Oxford English Faculty until 1973, the last four of those years as University Reader. In the 1950s he was one of several on the Faculty who shared examining duties with Tolkien for the English Final Honour School.

Stewart wrote several works of scholarship, including *Character and Motive in Shakespeare* (1949) and *Eight Modern Writers* (1963). He achieved greater fame, however, with the detective novels he wrote as 'Michael Innes', beginning with *Death at the President's Lodging* (1936), and with the five *romans à clef* collectively known as *A Staircase in Surrey* (1974–9). A character in the latter, J.B. Timbermill, is a notable scholar who produced a long book, *The Magic Quest*, which lured him away from academic labours. As Jessica Yates has said, Timbermill 'is not Tolkien under a pseudonym, and Stewart is not satirising the real Tolkien, but perhaps ridiculing those who imagined that [Tolkien] was an absent-minded bachelor who lived in an attic surrounded by thousands of books and a collection of Anglo-Saxon potsherds' ('Appetizers', *A Long-Expected Party: Progress Report* 6 (1992), p. 24).

The Stone Troll. Poem, first published in its final form and without a title as a comic song by Sam in *The Lord of the Rings*, Book I, Chapter 12 (1954), reprinted with the stated title in *The Adventures of Tom Bombadil and Other Verses from the Red Book* (1962), pp. 39–40. A troll sits 'alone on his seat of stone' where 'meat was hard to come by'. 'Tom' comes upon the troll and objects that he his gnawing on the shin-bone of Tom's uncle. The troll, 'tired o' gnawing old bones and skins', tries to catch his dinner, but Tom is too quick, and kicks the troll in the rump. 'But harder than stone' is a troll's flesh and bone: Tom returns home with an injured foot and leg.

The earliest version of the work, called *Pēro & Pōdex* ('Boot and Bottom'), dates from 1926, when Tolkien was at the University of *Leeds. In 1936 it was privately printed, as *The Root of the Boot*, in the booklet *Songs for the Philologists* along with other poems devised at *Leeds; this text was reprinted in *The Annotated Hobbit* (1988, p. 45; rev. and expanded edn. 2002, pp. 74–5), and again, with corrections and one revision, in *The Return of the Shadow* (1988), pp. 142–4. When a drinking song was needed for Bingo (later Frodo) to perform in the Prancing Pony in *The Lord of the Rings*, it was this work that first came to Tolkien's mind (later replaced, however, by *The Man in the Moon Stayed Up Too Late*).

In August 1952 Tolkien tape recorded a version of *The Stone Troll* at the home of his friend *George Sayer, sung to the tune of the English folk-song 'The Fox Went Out'. This was later issued on *J.R.R. Tolkien Reads and Sings His The Hobbit and The Fellowship of the Ring* (1975), and most recently reissued in *The J.R.R. Tolkien Audio Collection* (2001); see *Recordings.

Stonyhurst (Lancashire). On 16 May 1940 the Venerable English College left its traditional home in Rome, and for the duration of the Second World War relocated to England, first to Ambleside in the Lake District and then to the Jesuit seminary in Stonyhurst (St Mary's Hall, now the preparatory school for Stonyhurst College). During this period Tolkien's eldest son, *John, was at the College, training for the priesthood. Tolkien briefly visited Stonyhurst on several occasions for rest and relaxation, staying at a nearby guest house, New Lodge, where his son himself had stayed in earlier years. He first signed its guest book after a visit from 25 March to 1 April 1946. He returned to New Lodge with his wife *Edith on 26 June 1946, staying until 4 July, and with his daughter, *Priscilla, from 12 to 21 August 1947. On the latter occasion he made a drawing of the back of the Lodge as seen from the garden (*New Lodge, Stonyhurst*, see *Artist and Illustrator*, fig. 28). Priscilla Tolkien recalls that New Lodge 'was run and lived in as their home by Mr Tom Bailey (the College carpenter) and his wife, who was a superb cook, and we had wonderful home-grown food from the garden' (private correspondence). On 21 September 1947 Tolkien wrote to *Stanley Unwin: 'I have been no farther at farthest than Lanca-shire: the vales of Hodder and Ribble. For a few days my daughter and I had there blazing sun, a rare commodity in those parts, and abundant food, less rare there than in some other places' (Tolkien-George Allen & Unwin archive, HarperCollins).

Tolkien's second son, *Michael, taught at Stonyhurst from the mid-1960s to the 1970s.

Sub-creation. The 1987 supplement to the *Oxford English Dictionary* defines *sub-creation* as 'J.R.R. Tolkien's word for the process of inventing an imaginary or secondary world, different from the primary world but internally consist-ent', and refers to its use in *On Fairy-Stories*. In that work Tolkien defines when a 'sub-creator' succeeds: 'He makes a Secondary World which your mind can enter. Inside it, what he relates is "true": it accords with the laws of that world. You therefore believe it, while you are, as it were, inside. The moment disbelief arises, the spell is broken; the magic, or rather art, has failed. You are then out in the Primary World again, looking at the little abortive Secondary World from outside' (*Tree and Leaf*, pp. 36–7).

From various writings it seems clear that Tolkien thought that the spell could be broken by an obtrusive narrator's voice, or by any nod or wink or allusion to readers or hearers referring them back to the Primary World. As Richard L. Purtill has said, the author must take his own work seriously. 'Even a hint of a snigger behind the hand, of an attitude of "we can't *really* take this seriously, but let's pretend," is fatal to secondary belief. That is precisely what makes so many modern fantasies ultimately unsatisfactory: we cannot take them seriously because their authors do not' (*J.R.R. Tolkien: Myth, Morality and Religion* (1984), p. 12).

Tolkien thought that in such cases, 'if you are obliged, by kindliness or circumstance, to stay, then disbelief must be suspended (or stifled), other-wise listening and looking would become intolerable. But this suspension of disbelief is a substitute for the genuine thing, a subterfuge we use when con-descending to games or make-believe, or when trying (more or less willingly) to find what virtue we can in the work of an art that has for us failed' (*Tree and Leaf*, p. 37). With this he specifically rejects Coleridge's idea that a successful author procures for his 'shadows of imagination that willing suspension of dis-belief for the moment that constitutes poetic faith' (*Biographia Literaria*, ch. 14), since any effort, however 'willing', places the reader outside the Secondary World.

Tolkien points out that anyone can say *the green sun*, and 'many can then imagine or picture it'; but

> to make a Secondary World inside which the green sun will be cred-ible, commanding Secondary Belief, will probably require labour and

thought, and will certainly demand a special skill, a kind of elvish craft. Few attempt such difficult tasks. But when they are attempted and in any degree accomplished then we have a rare achievement of Art: indeed narrative art, story-making in its primary and most potent mode. [*Tree and Leaf*, p. 46]

Katharyn W. Crabbe comments in *J.R.R. Tolkien* (rev. and expanded edn. 1988) that 'the reader must never feel that the natural laws (or indeed the social or psychological laws) governing the secondary world are simply imposed in order to create special effects. The secondary world must be as consistent and as interconnected as tree and leaf' (p. 154).

In his poem *Mythopoeia Tolkien argues that because Man was made in God's image, and God was a Creator, Man has the right to try to create, or rather to 'sub-create'; and 'since the human imagination came from God, then its products must come from God too, must be fragments of some genuine if other-worldly truth, guaranteed by their own "inner consistency" and no more the author's own property than the star from Elfland was Smith's [in *Smith of Wootton Major*]' (T.A. Shippey, *The Road to Middle-earth* (2nd edn. 1992), p. 251). When Peter Hastings, a reader of *The Lord of the Rings, queried certain aspects of Tolkien's mythology, in particular the reincarnation of the Elves, because he felt that 'a sub-creator, when dealing with the relations between creator and created, should use those channels which he knows the creator to have used already', Tolkien strongly rose to the defence:

Since the whole matter from beginning to end is mainly concerned with the relation of Creation to making and sub-creation . . . it must be clear that references to these things are not casual, but fundamental: they may well be fundamentally 'wrong' from the point of view of Reality (external reality). But they cannot be wrong inside this imaginary world, since that is how it is made.

We differ entirely about the nature of the relation of sub-creation to Creation. I should have said that liberation 'from the channels the creator is known to have used already' is the fundamental function of 'sub-creation', a tribute to the infinity of His potential variety, one of the ways in which indeed is exhibited, as indeed I said in [*On Fairy-Stories*]. [September 1954, *Letters*, pp. 187–8]

In his story *Leaf by Niggle Tolkien describes how the sub-creation of Niggle, a not particularly skilful or very successful painter, 'came to be taken up into Creation in some plane' (letter to Peter Hastings, September 1954, *Letters*, p. 195). Niggle had begun a painting of an entire tree, though he was better at rendering single leaves, and had not finished the work when he was called to make a Journey. After spending time in a 'purgatorial' Workhouse he finds that his picture of the Tree has been given reality: 'All the leaves he had ever laboured at were there, as he had imagined them rather than as he had made them; and there were others that had only budded in his mind, and many that might have budded, if only he had had time' (*Tree and Leaf*, pp. 88–9). Tolkien suggests in *On Fairy-Stories* that 'every writer making a secondary world, a fantasy, every sub-creator, wishes in some measure to be a real maker' (*Tree and Leaf*, p. 64).

In *Master of Middle-earth: The Fiction of J.R.R. Tolkien* (1972) Paul H. Kocher comments on the relationship between *On Fairy-Stories* and *Leaf by Niggle*:

> The essay defines and analyzes subcreation as the process by which human imagination invents secondary worlds strange to the everyday primary world in which we live and move, but nevertheless possessed of an internal consistency of their own. Furthermore, and most significant for the Niggle story, the best of these imagined worlds reflect dimly a higher reality lying beyond the appearance of the primary world. . . .
>
> Tolkien means Niggle's fate to be a literary embodiment of this doctrine. For, when the Voice of mercy wins its traditionally required victory he finds himself standing in the middle of the very landscape in his painting. . . . [p. 165]

Sub-creation also lies at the heart of *'The Silmarillion', for as Tolkien explained to Peter Hastings, 'in this myth, it is "feigned" . . . that [Ilúvatar] gave special "sub-creative" powers to certain of His highest created beings: that is a guarantee that what they devised and made should be given the reality of Creation' (*Letters*, p. 195).

Tolkien spelled the word in question both as *sub-creation* and *subcreation*, but the hyphened form is predominant in his published writings.

Suffield family. 'Though a Tolkien by name,' Tolkien wrote to his son *Michael, 'I am a Suffield by tastes, talents and upbringing' (letter of 18 March 1941, *Letters*, p. 54). The family into which his mother (*Mabel Tolkien) was born lived for generations in the town of Evesham in Worcestershire (*West Midlands), but even well before Tolkien's birth was mainly to be found in *Birmingham and its environs. His maternal grandfather, **John Suffield** (1833–1930), born in Birmingham, was one of at least eight children of **John Suffield** (?1802–1891) and his first wife, **Jane** (*née* **Oliver**, ?1806–1859). Like his father he was a hosier and seller of lace, and in later years was a commercial traveller (salesman) for Jeyes' Disinfectant. With his wife **Emily Jane** (*née* **Sparrow**, *b*. ?1838 in *Oxford) he had at least seven children: **John** (*b*. ?1859); **Roland** (*b*. ?1865); **Edith Mary**, called 'May' (?1866–1936, see *Incledon family); **Mabel** (1870–1904); **Emily Jane** (1872–1963, see *Emily Jane Neave); **William** (1874–1904); and **Rose** (?1879–1886).

In *Biography* Humphrey Carpenter describes Tolkien's maternal grandfather as a jolly fellow with a long beard, who cracked jokes and made dreadful puns while his wife Emily was 'kind and understanding' (p. 16).

Sometimes he would take a sheet of paper and a pen with an extra fine nib. Then he would draw a circle around a sixpence, and in this little space would write in fine copperplate the words of the entire Lord's Prayer. His ancestors had been engravers and plate-makers, which was perhaps why he had inherited this skill; he would talk with pride about how King William IV had given the family a coat of arms because they did fine work for him, and how Lord Suffield was a distant relative (which was not true). [*Biography*, p. 18]

John Suffield had attended a Methodist school, Queen's College in Taunton, Somerset, but later became a Unitarian. He was outraged when his daughters May and Mabel converted to Roman Catholicism in June 1900. May abandoned the Catholic faith at her husband's insistence, but Mabel 'clung to her conversion and died young, largely through the hardships of poverty resulting from it' (letter by Tolkien to Robert Murray, 2 December 1953, *Letters*, p. 172). Walter Incledon, who had provided financial support for Mabel after her husband's death in 1896, now ceased to do so. But the wrath of the Suffield family said to have fallen on Mabel appears not to have extended to her sons. Hilary was sent to stay with his Suffield grandparents in spring 1904 when Mabel in hospital; and after Mabel's death in that year, her boys seem often to have visited their Incledon relatives, and for the rest of their lives were close to their Aunt Jane Neave.

Soon after their mother died, Ronald and Hilary Tolkien were placed by their guardian, *Father Francis Morgan, with their Aunt Beatrice Suffield (*née* Bartlett), widow of William Suffield who also passed away in 1904. Beatrice lived near the *Birmingham Oratory and had a room to let. But she showed the boys little or no affection, and burned their mother's letters and personal papers, apparently never considering that they might wish to keep them.

In May 1923, when Tolkien caught a severe cold which turned into pneumonia, John Suffield, aged ninety, stood by his grandson's bedside in *Leeds, 'a tall thin black-clad figure, . . . looking at me and speaking to me in contempt – to the effect that I and my generation were degenerate weaklings. There was I gasping for breath, but he must now say goodbye, as he was off to catch a boat to go a trip by sea around the British Isles!' (quoted in *Biography*, p. 106). He lived to the age of ninety-seven, having spent most of his remaining years visiting his daughter Jane.

Photographs of Tolkien's Suffield grandparents are reproduced in *The Tolkien Family Album*, p. 14.

See also the family trees printed as an appendix to the **Chronology**.

Suffield, Mabel *see* **Mabel Tolkien**

'Of the Sun and Moon and the Hiding of Valinor'. The eleventh chapter of the *'Quenta Silmarillion', published in *The Silmarillion (1977), pp. 98–102.

SUMMARY

The Valar sit long in silent council after the flight of Melkor, and grieve not only for the death of the Two Trees but also for the marring of Fëanor. The messenger Manwë had sent to Fëanor returns and tells them that Fëanor will not listen to his advice, and has declared that at least the Noldor would do deeds that will live in song. Manwë says: 'So shall it be! Dear-bought those songs shall be accounted, and yet shall be well-bought' (The Silmarillion, p. 98). Mandos prophesies that Fëanor will soon come to him.

At the bidding of Manwë when he learns that the Noldor have indeed departed, Yavanna and Nienna put forth their powers to try to heal the Trees. Their song and tears fail to heal the wounds inflicted by Melkor and Ungoliant, but before the Trees finally die Telperion bears one last silver flower and Laurelin one golden fruit. Manwë hallows these, Aulë and his people make vessels to hold them and preserve their radiance, and Varda sets them – the Moon and the Sun – to travel through the lower regions of heaven to the east and then return to the west, giving light to both Valinor and Middle-earth. The Valar fear to make war on Melkor, lest the resulting upheaval might harm not only the Elves but also Men who, Manwë knows, will come soon. The light of the Moon and the Sun will give hope to Elves and Men in Middle-earth and will hinder the deeds of Melkor.

Then follows an account of the names given to the Moon and the Sun, and of the two Maiar, Tilion and Arien, who are chosen to guide them. The vessel of the Moon rises first, and by its light many things in Middle-earth stir from the sleep of Yavanna. At the first rising of the Moon Fingolfin begins his march into Middle-earth. When the Moon guided by Tilion has crossed the sky seven times, the Sun guided by Arien rises into the sky. Varda's original intention was that each should journey from West to East and return, each leaving the West as the other turned back in the East, and their lights would mingle as they passed. But she changed this plan, not only because was Tilion was wayward and sought to approach Arien, but also to provide a time of shadows and half-light. Both then travel from East to West, and pass under the earth to reach the East again. Because Tilion is still wayward, the Valar reckon days by the movements of the Sun. The light in Valinor is still greater than in Middle-earth, since the Sun rests on the Outer Sea before beginning the journey beneath the earth. But the light of the Sun and Moon is not the same as the light of the Two Trees before they were poisoned; that light lives only in the Silmarils.

Morgoth hates these new lights. When he sends spirits to attack the Moon, Tilion is victorious, and Morgoth dares not attack Arien. He has been weakened by letting so much of his power pass into his creatures and be dispersed in Arda. He hides himself and his servants, and shrouds his strongholds with fumes and clouds.

Alarmed by the attack on Tilion, the Valar fortify Valinor, raising the mountain-walls of the Pelóri even higher and setting a guard on the only pass through them, the Calacirya, left open for the sake of the Elves. They also set the Enchanted Isles in the Shadowy Seas to the east of Valinor and Tol Eressëa to deter anyone trying to reach Valinor. Any mariner that reaches the Isles is entrapped in sleep until the Change of the World. Thus of all the messengers sent from Middle-earth in after days, only one reached Valinor.

HISTORY

Much of the story in this chapter was already present in *The Book of Lost Tales* (c. 1916–20), in *The Tale of the Sun and Moon*, where it is told at greater length, but with many differences. The early tale includes an account of how the Valar returned from the hunt for Melko, and of their vain attempts to revive the Trees. Manwë takes counsel with Varda, Aulë, and Yavanna, and inspired by the stars which Varda has set above the earth, suggests that they make a greater vessel, fill it with golden dew surviving from Laurelin, and launch it above the world to provide light to both Middle-earth and Valinor. But Aulë and Varda are unable to devise a substance for it. At length, at the urging of the other Valar, Yavanna makes a last attempt to revive the Trees. When this seems to fail, Vána weeps on the roots of Laurelin, which puts forth leaves and flowers and one great fruit, from which Aulë makes a vessel able to sail in the sky and carry the liquid light dropped from Laurelin. The making of this vessel, and how Urwendi (Arien) and her maidens by bathing in fire prepare themselves to undertake the task of guiding the Sun, are told in great detail. Once launched, the Sun gives forth such great light that many of the Valar are disturbed. Ulmo then declares that 'much of the great beauty of the Trees of old' lay 'in change, and in slow alternation of fair things, the passing blending sweetly with that which was to come' (*The Book of Lost Tales, Part One*, p. 190). This inspires Lórien to sit by Silpion (Telperion) and sing, whereupon the Tree bears one last pale flower with a heart of white flame, the Rose of Silpion.

The making of the Moon from this flower is also described. This vessel is guided by Ilinsor, 'but an aged Elf with hoary locks stepped upon the Moon unseen and hid him in the Rose, and there dwells he ever since and tends that flower, and a little white turret has he. . . . Some indeed have named him the Man in the Moon . . .' (*The Book of Lost Tales, Part One*, pp. 192–3). It was intended that in memory of the changing lights of the Trees the Sun and Moon should in turn leave Valinor and sail the heavens, but for various reasons, explained at length, their movements are more changeable.

Part of the story is told in *The Hiding of Valinor*. Since both Ilinsor and Urwendi prove wayward in the guidance of their vessels, Manwë calls a council to determine the courses of the Sun and Moon. But many of the Eldar and Valar are more concerned with protecting Valinor against a possible attack by Melko or with the return of the Noldoli, and will not listen. The Valar wrongly do not themselves challenge Melko, but instead raise a mountain barrier to protect Valinor and cast the webs of Ungweliantë into the Sea to entangle those who might try to find their way thence. The pass where Kôr stood is left open at the wish of the Teleri (the later Vanyar) and because Oromë has woods there, but against the wishes of the Solosimpi (the later Teleri). Ossë sets the Magic Isles to guard the Bay of Faery against any that may try to reach it.

This text is followed by a long account of how the Valar devised new courses for the Sun and Moon. They intended that both should travel from East to West and then pass under the earth to reach the East again, but when it was found that this route was unsafe for the galleon of the Sun, the Valar built in the Wall of Things which fenced the world the Gates of Morn in the East and the Door of Night in the West, and the Sun passed through the Door of Night and travelled through the Outer Dark to the Gates of Morn.

*Christopher Tolkien comments that the part of 'Of the Sun and Moon and the Hiding of Valinor' which deals with the making of the Sun and Moon, compared with *The Tale of the Sun and Moon* in *The Book of Lost Tales*,

is extremely brief. Despite many differences the later versions read in places almost as summaries of the early story, but it is often hard to say whether the shortening depends rather on my father's feeling . . . that the description was too long, was taking too large a place in the total structure, or an actual rejection of some of the ideas it contains, and a desire to diminish the extreme 'concreteness' of its images. Certainly there is here a revelling in materials of 'magic' property, gold, silver, crystal, glass, and above all light conceived as a liquid element, or as dew, as honey, an element that can be bathed in and gathered into vessels, that has quite largely disappeared from *The Silmarillion*. . . .

As a result of this fullness and intensity of description, the origin of the Sun and Moon in the last fruit and last flower of the Trees has less mystery than in the succinct and beautiful language of *The Silmarillion*; but also much is said here to emphasize the great size of the 'Fruit of Noon'. . . . In the early story the last outpourings of life from the dying Trees are utterly strange and 'enormous', those of Laurelin portentous, even ominous. . . . [*The Book of Lost Tales, Part One*, pp. 200–1]

The account in the *Sketch of the Mythology* (*c.* 1926) is also very brief, saying only that the Trees cannot be revived, but that they bear a last bloom and a last fruit from which the Moon and Sun are fashioned, and that the Valar find it safer to alter the courses they had originally designed for them, so that both now pass beneath the earth. The order in which they are mentioned suggests that the Moon was now made first. The account of the fortifying of Valinor mentions the raising of the mountains and the establishing of magic isles in the Shadowy Seas. The Elves that remain in Côr are commanded to guard ceaselessly the gap in the mountains. Some details were restored in later versions, but Tolkien omitted the liquid light from the Trees placed in the vessel formed from the fruit and that fashioned to carry the flower.

Tolkien restored some details in the *Quenta Noldorinwa* (*c.* 1930): some of the names given to the Sun and Moon, and that the vessels were guided by Árien and Tilion. The reason now given for changing the original design that the Sun and Moon should sail to the East and back to the West is not for safety, but because of the waywardness of Tilion (only) and the need for a time of peace and sleep. The light in Valinor is greater and fairer than elsewhere because the Sun and Moon rest there, but nonetheless their light is not the light of the Trees before they were poisoned, which lived only in the Silmarils. After describing the setting of the Magic Isles to prevent anyone reaching Valinor, it is said that only one of all the emissaries sent by the Noldor reached Valinor, and he came too late (changed to 'the mightiest mariner of song', *The Shaping of Middle-earth*, p. 99). This change marks the major development in the story which entered in the second version of the last part of the *Quenta Noldorinwa*, that Eärendil should plead with the Valar on behalf of Elves and Men and secure aid against Morgoth.

The 'earliest' *Annals of Valinor* (early 1930s) mention only that at the end of 3,000 Valian Years (the equivalent of 30,000 Years of the Sun) the Sun and Moon were sent forth, but it is made clear that the Moon arose before the Sun. The *Annals* also state that at the first moonrise Fingolfin set foot in the North of Middle-earth. The 'later' *Annals of Valinor* (mid-1930s) add nothing.

The story is told at greater length, though still in brief compared with *The Book of Lost Tales*, in the *Quenta Silmarillion* (mid-1930s–early 1938), Chapter 6, 'Of the Sun and the Moon and the Hiding of Valinor'. This closely approaches the chapter in *The Silmarillion*, not only in length and detail but also in much of its phrasing. Tolkien made only a few emendations to the text when he revised the *Quenta Silmarillion c.* 1951. This probably preceded the writing of the equivalent entries in the *Annals of Aman* (see **Annals of Valinor*, also *c.* 1951), which are closely based on the *Quenta Silmarillion* as revised, but with additions which include the silent council of the Valar; their grief not only for the loss of the Trees but for the marring of Fëanor; their reception of Fëanor's reply to Manwë's messenger; that they did not pursue Morgoth lest the resultant upheavals harm Men whose coming Manwë knew was near; that Morgoth attacked Tilion but was afraid of Arien, and indeed could not attack Arien since he had dispersed so much of his power; and that the attack on Tilion was the main reason for the fencing of Valinor.

The text of the chapter in *The Silmarillion* was almost entirely derived from the *Annals of Aman*, though much of that text is common with the *Quenta Silmarillion*. In a few cases Christopher Tolkien preferred the *Quenta Silmarillion* reading or added material omitted by his father, and also included a few fragments from the **Grey Annals, c.* 1951: the detail of Fingolfin blowing his silver trumpets, and the account of Morgoth sending forth reek and cloud to hide Angband from the Sun.

Although Tolkien was already doubting whether he could, or should, include an account of the Sun and Moon so remote from known scientific knowledge, he made no fundamental changes in 1951 but brought the account in line with other developments in the mythology since the 1930s. By the late 1950s, when he returned to the *Quenta Silmarillion* after publishing **The Lord of the Rings*, he seriously contemplated radical changes to the cosmology of his *legendarium* by which the Sun and Moon would have existed from the beginning of Arda. At the same time, he wished to preserve fundamental aspects of the earlier versions of the work: that the light of the Two Trees was purer than that of the Sun and Moon, and after the destruction of the Trees was only preserved in the Silmarils; and that the Elves awoke by starlight. But he made only a few revisions to the *Quenta Silmarillion* chapter *c*. 1951, and none thereafter. This may have been because he was uncertain how to achieve conflicting aims. The chapter in the *Quenta Silmarillion*, and the *Annals of Aman* largely derived from it, remain in many respects work of the 1930s. Christopher Tolkien says of a problem he faced in compiling *The Silmarillion*: 'As the mythology evolved and changed, the Making of the Sun and Moon became the element of greatest difficulty; and in the published *Silmarillion* this chapter does not seem of a piece with much of the rest of the work, and could not be made to be so '(*The Book of Lost Tales, Part One*, p. 202).

Several brief texts which show Tolkien wrestling with the problem are included in the section 'Myths Transformed' in **Morgoth's Ring*. See entries for that work and for **Sun The Trees Silmarils*.

Sun The Trees Silmarils. Brief 'comment', published as Text V in the section 'Myths Transformed' in **Morgoth's Ring* (1993), pp. 389–90, together with comments by **Christopher Tolkien.

Probably dating from the late 1950s, it is one of the writings in which Tolkien rejects the original cosmology of his mythology (**'The Silmarillion'*), on the grounds that the Eldar must have learned the truth about the structure of the universe from the Valar: 'The making of the Sun after the Death of the Tress is not only impossible "mythology" now . . . it is also impossible chronologically in the Narrative' (p. 389). But this change introduced the problem of how, in the circumstances, the Two Trees could be considered Blessed. In this one-page note Tolkien decided that although the Sun and Moon existed from the beginning of Arda, the Two Trees 'were kindled and illumined by the light of the Sun and Moon *before these were tainted*' by Morgoth. Hence after the destruction of the Trees the unmarred light was preserved only in the Silmarils.

Swann, Donald Ibrahim (1923–1994). Donald Swann went up to Christ Church, **Oxford in 1941 to read Modern Languages. By then music was already the focus of his life: he was proficient (if eccentric) at the piano, and had contributed to a revue written by fellow Westminster School pupil Michael Flanders. He was also a pacifist and, entering the Second World War, a conscientious objector. He joined the Friends Ambulance Unit and served in Egypt, Palestine, and Greece. On returning to Oxford he read Russian and Modern Greek; he received an Honours Degree in 1948. At the same time, he began to set to music words by poets such as Pushkin and Froissart, and he contributed to revues by Laurier Lister and Sandy Wilson. Chief among his collaborators was Michael Flanders, a gifted satirical lyricist; some of their many songs, such as 'The Hippopotamus Song' ('Mud, mud, glorious mud'), were first brought to public attention by Ian Wallace. In 1956 Swann and Flanders created a two-man show, *At the Drop of a Hat*: Swann played the piano and was usually the straight man. A 'sequel', *At the Drop of Another Hat*, began in 1963 and ended in 1967. Recordings were made of both productions, along with *The Bestiary of Flanders and Swann*, a selection of songs about animals.

Early in 1965 Swann set to music six songs from *The Lord of the Rings*, a work he greatly admired. Having written to Tolkien's publisher George Allen & Unwin (*Publishers) regarding his settings, on 30 May 1965 he played them for Tolkien on the piano at the home of the author's daughter, *Priscilla. By this time, he had abandoned a setting of the ent Quickbeam's lament for the dead rowan (*The Lord of the Rings*, bk. III, ch. 4), but added one of *Namárië* (bk. II, ch. 8). Tolkien approved all but the latter, for which he had his own plainchant setting in mind. Swann and Tolkien now began a warm and lively correspondence.

Through Allen & Unwin Swann met *Joy Hill, then in charge of rights and permissions, and she in turn introduced him to a music student friend, baritone William Elvin, with whom Swann began to perform the Tolkien songs publicly. One of these, *I Sit beside the Fire*, was included also in some performances of *At the Drop of Another Hat* (captured on *The Only Flanders and Swann Video* (1992)). On 18 September 1965 Tolkien and his wife *Edith attended a Flanders and Swann concert at the New Theatre, Oxford, and afterward spoke to the performers backstage. In his *Swann's Way: A Life in Song* (1991) Swann commented that Tolkien 'relished' the humorous Flanders and Swann song 'I Wish I Were Dead', and in general 'really respected Michael [Flanders]' word-play. In a way, they were birds of a feather, playing around with words' (p. 210). On 23 March 1966 Swann and Elvin gave a private performance of the Tolkien song cycle at Merton College in honour of Ronald and Edith Tolkien's Golden Wedding anniversary.

Plans were made for a recording of the cycle performed by Swann and Elvin, with readings from Tolkien's works by Michael Flanders; in the end, Tolkien himself did the reading, largely poems from the *Adventures of Tom Bombadil* collection (*Poems and Songs of Middle Earth* (1967), see *Recordings). By now Swann had also set to music Tolkien's *Errantry*, for single voice, after attempting to craft a duet with counterpoint by Michael Flanders. The Swann-Tolkien song cycle was first published as *The Road Goes Ever On: A Song Cycle* in October 1967. For its second edition (1978) Swann added a setting of *Bilbo's Last Song*, which he came to love in particular. His music for Beren's 'Song of Parting' from Lúthien Tinúviel in *The Silmarillion* (ch. 19) was published privately in 1992 and included in the third edition of the song cycle (Germany, 1993; London, 2002). A recording of the complete work, performed by the composer with William Elvin and Clive McCrombie, was issued on a compact disc to accompany the 2002 HarperCollins edition of *The Road Goes Ever On: A Song Cycle*. Swann recorded *Bilbo's Last Song* and *I Sit beside the Fire* also in his autobiographical recording *Donald Swann's Alphabetaphon* (1990), and *Bilbo's Last Song* also on the John Amis album *Amiscellany* (1992).

Swann wrote and performed a wide variety of songs and other musical compositions, apart from the Flanders and Swann productions and his Tolkien cycle, drawn from diverse influences. These include a dream musical, *Lucy and the Hunter*, libretto and lyrics by Sydney Carter; a three-act opera based on the novel *Perelandra* by *C.S. Lewis, with libretto and lyrics by David Marsh; the recorder concerto *Rhapsody from Within*; and a cycle based on his enduring love for Greek poetry and music, *The Isles of Greece*. Among his prose writings are *The Space between the Bars* (1968), *Swann's Way Out* (1975), and *Swann's Way: A Life in Song* (1991; rev. edn. 1993).

See also Alison Swann, *The Donald Swann Website*, at *www.donaldswann. co.uk*.

Switzerland. In summer 1911 Tolkien, his brother *Hilary, and their *Aunt Jane Neave visited Switzerland in a party organized by family friends, the *Brookes-Smiths. James and Ellen Brookes-Smith, enamoured of alpine scenery, had made many excursions to Switzerland, often in company with friends and relations. In 1911 their party seem to have numbered twelve at the start. They were dressed in light and waterproof Austrian Loden cloaks, hobnailed boots, and hats to ward off the sun. Each carried a spiked staff or alpenstock. Jane Neave was in charge of food and cooking (on methylated spirit stoves) while the party were on the march.

Colin Brookes-Smith, son of James and Ellen and at that time a young boy, in recounting the holiday many years later (unpublished account, Tolkien-George Allen & Unwin archive, HarperCollins), recalled that the party travelled by boat and train from Harwich to Ostend, then to Cologne, Frankfurt, Munich, and Innsbruck, and from there went on foot or by train to the Rhone Valley and into the mountains. Tolkien also remembered their journey long after the fact, in a letter written to his son *Michael after 25 August 1967, but described only the part that occurred after he and the others had reached Switzerland:

> Our wanderings mainly on foot in a party of 12 are not now clear in sequence, but leave many vivid pictures as clear as yesterday.... We went on foot carrying great packs practically all the way from **Interlaken**, mainly by mountain paths, to **Lauterbrunnen** and so to **Mürren** and eventually to the head of the Lauterbrunnenthal in a wilderness of morains. We slept rough – the men-folk – often in hayloft or cowbyre, since we were walking by map and avoided roads and never booked, and after a meagre breakfast fed ourselves in the open.... [*Letters*, pp. 391–2]

Colin Brookes-Smith recalled having slept once in a large barn, the men on a haystack and the ladies below it, but said that the party rarely failed to find accommodations at inns or minor hotels. In one of the latter, Tolkien spoke gibberish with a German accent which sent a maid into fits of laughter.

'We must then have gone eastward', wrote Tolkien, 'over the two Scheidegge to **Grindelwald**, with Eiger and Mönch on our right, and eventually reached **Meiringen**. I left the view of *Jungfrau* with deep regret: eternal snow, etched as it seemed against eternal sunshine, and the *Silberhorn* sharp against dark blue: the *Silvertine* (*Celebdil*) of my dreams' (*Letters*, p. 392). The 'two Scheidegge' are two high ridges east of Lauterbrunnen, the Grosse and Kleine Scheidegge, around 6,600 feet altitude. The Jungfrau is just south-east of the Kleine Scheidegge; the Silberhorn is adjacent to the Jungfrau to the north-east. Meiringen is north-east of Grindelwald. Celebdil, or the Silvertine, or Zirakzigil, is one of the three Mountains of Moria in *The Lord of the Rings*, where Gandalf throws down the balrog.

'We later crossed the Grimsel Pass', Tolkien wrote, 'down on to the dusty highway, beside the Rhône, on which horse 'diligences' still plied: but not for us. We reached **Brig** on foot, a mere memory of noise: then a network of trams that screeched on their rails for it seemed at least 20 hrs of the day' (*Letters*, p. 392). The Grimsel Pass (6,928 ft.) is at the eastern edge of the Aletsch glacier, and south-east of Meiringen. Brig is south-west of the Grimsel Pass, down the valley of the Rhône; there, according to Colin Brookes-Smith, the party was increased by two. 'After a night of that', Tolkien continued, 'we climbed up some thousands of feet to a village at the foot of the Aletsch glacier, and there spent some nights in a châlet inn under a roof and in beds (or rather under them: the *bett* being a shapeless bag under which you snuggled)' (*Letters*, p. 392). The village was **Belalp**. There Tolkien and his friends played a joke on the local residents by damming a stream and then letting the waters loose.

Later they marched up the Aletsch glacier, at 65 square miles (including tributaries) the largest in the Alps, where Tolkien

came near to perishing. We had guides, but either the effects of the hot summer were beyond their experience, or they did not much care, or we were late in starting. Any way at noon we were strung out in file along a narrow track with a snow-slope on the right going up to the horizon, and on the left a plunge down into a ravine. The summer of that year had melted away much snow, and stones and boulders were exposed that (I suppose) were normally covered. The heat of the day continued the melting and we were alarmed to see many of them starting to roll down the slope at gathering speed. . . . [*Letters*, pp. 392–3]

One missed Tolkien by 'a foot at most' (*Letters*, p. 393). A photograph of the party on the Aletsch glacier is reproduced in *The Tolkien Family Album*, p. 31.

According to Tolkien, the party then went on into the **Valais** region, but his memories of this stage were less clear. He recalled their arrival, and one evening in **Zermatt** (south-west of Brig). 'We climbed with guides up to

[a] high hut of the Alpine Club, roped (or I should have fallen into a snow-crevasse), and I remember the dazzling whiteness of the tumbled snow-desert between us and the black horn of the Matterhorn some miles away [to the south-west]' (*Letters*, p. 393). According to Colin Brookes-Smith, however, from Brig the party walked a few miles south-west to **Visp**, then south to **Stalden** where they spent the night. On the following day they went over a high pass into the next valley to the west, from **St-Niklaus** to **Gruben** in the **Turtman Thal**; then west over the Forcletta Pass to **Grimentz**; and after a day's rest, south-south-west to **Les Haudères** and **Arolla**. From the latter village, Brookes-Smith recalled, the party took a day trip to a high-altitude hut around 11,000 feet, roped for the more hazardous part. On their return to the village they were beset with an avalanche from which some members of the party had a narrow escape. The similarity of this story to Tolkien's tale of falling boulders naturally calls into question whether the incident occurred on the Aletsch glacier or above Arolla, or if there were two avalanches. If Brookes-Smith is correct, the party may have ascended Mont Collon, which rises to 11,955 feet (Baedeker's *Switzerland* for 1911 describes it as 'fit only for adepts with steady heads', p. 399).

From Arolla the party may have walked down the Val d'Herens to **Sion**, and from there took a train on the first leg of their return to England.

'It was a remarkable experience for me at 19, after a poor boy's childhood,' Tolkien wrote to his son Michael (*Letters*, p. 393). He recalled it with passion, and acknowledged its effect on his work. On 31 July 1947 he wrote to *Stanley Unwin, who was about to travel to Switzerland: 'How I long to see the snows and the great heights again!' (*Letters*, p. 123). In a letter to Joyce Reeves on 4 November 1961 he wrote of journeying

> with a mixed party of about the same size as the company in *The Hobbit* ... on foot with a heavy pack through much of Switzerland, and over many high passes. It was [while] approaching the Aletsch [glacier] that we were nearly destroyed by boulders loosened in the sun rolling down a snow-slope. ... That and the 'thunder-battle' – a bad night in which we lost our way and slept in a cattle-shed – appear in *The Hobbit*. [*Letters*, p. 309]

And to Michael Tolkien in 1967 he wrote: 'The hobbit's (Bilbo's) journey from Rivendell to the other side of the Misty Mountains, including the glissade down the slithering stones into the pine woods, is based on my adventures in 1911: the *annus mirabilis* of sunshine in which there was virtually no rain between April and the end of October' (*Letters*, p. 391). (Jim Ring recounts in *How the English Made the Alps* (2000), p. 193, that the summer of 1911 was one 'of peculiar brilliance, a season of seasons'.)

The Swiss Alps, with their distinctive peaks and valleys, were clearly a direct influence upon the mountains in all of Tolkien's paintings and drawings, most dramatically in the *Hobbit* illustration *Bilbo Woke Up with the Early Sun in His Eyes* (*Artist and Illustrator*, fig. 113). Marie Barnfield has convincingly argued in *Þe Lyfe and þe Auncestrye* 3 (Spring 1996) that Tolkien based his *Hobbit* illustration of Rivendell, the valley and the Last Homely House, on the Lauterbrunnenthal (the valley of Lauterbrunnen). She also believes that the Rottalhorn, a mountain near the Jungfrau and the Silberhorn, is memorialized in *The Lord of the Rings* as the Redhorn (Caradhras); however, there is an actual *Rothorn* which Tolkien might have seen near the Matterhorn towards the end of his holiday.

Physical similarities are strikingly evident as well between Mürren, in the southern part of the Lauterbrunnenthal, and Tolkien's drawing of Dunharrow (*Artist and Illustrator*, fig. 166).

'Synopsis of Pengoloð's *Eldarinwe Leperi are Notessi*'. Text, published with commentary and notes as part of '*Eldarin Hands, Fingers & Numerals* and Related Writings' in *Vinyar Tengwar* 48 (December 2005), pp. 4–22, ed. Patrick H. Wynne. Written *c.* 1968, it presents an 'abbreviation' of a 'document', *Eldarinwe Leperi are Notessi* ('The Elvish Fingers and Numerals'), attributed to the linguistic loremaster Pengoloð of Gondolin. It is related to, but postdates, **Eldarin Hands, Fingers & Numerals*, in which it is mentioned. *Vinyar Tengwar* editor Carl F. Hostetter comments that the 'synopsis' contains

> parallel Eldarin forms of the adult and children's finger-names and the numerals 1–12, and an account of this document's rescue from the destruction of Númenor; [it] also features two appendices, one presenting four brief texts on the etymology of the Quenya numerals 6, 11,and 12, and the other a late note on Quenya fractions. [p. 2]

Editorial notes draw extensively from Tolkien's unpublished writings.

Tal-Elmar. A fragment of a story set in the Second Age of Tolkien's mythology, published with commentary and notes in **The Peoples of Middle-earth* (1996), pp. 422–38. Tal-Elmar, the youngest son of a large family, is much loved by his father, Hazad, because he does not look like others in the village: he is broad, swarthy, and short, but resembles Hazad's mother who had been captured in war against a fair, tall, grey-eyed people coming out of the East. One morning, while Hazad sits with his son on a hill by the sea, Tal-Elmar sees strange shapes in the distance, three ships with white sails and one with black. Hazad fears this as 'a black vision out of the past' (*The Peoples of Middle-earth*, p. 426) and tells Tal-Elmar tales of the High Men of the Sea who had settled to the north and south of their village. Some had come to trade, but others took captives away in a ship with black sails, and it is believed that the captives were eaten or slain in worship of the Dark.

Tal-Elmar tries to warn his village, but the town-master, Mogru, does not believe him, and by the time Mogru looks for the ships they have disappeared. Tal-Elmar having suggested that the ships have sailed into a nearby inlet, he is sent by Mogru to spy on them if they are there. From a hill he sees three ships with sails lowered, and tall men on the shore. Although afraid, he walks towards the men and speaks to them in his own tongue. He is led before their captain, who thinks that Tal-Elmar, because of his appearance, must be of a people akin to the Númenórean race, and should be treated kindly.

At this point the narrative is interrupted by Tolkien with comments on the strangers, their motives, and how the story should continue. It resumes as Tal-Elmar realizes that he understood the strangers' language because he had heard it in dreams sent by the Eldar. When he asks about the black ship, fearing that it will take him away and give him to the Dark, the reply makes it clear that the ship with black sails he saw was not evil, for 'the black sails are to us a sign of honour, for they are the fair night before the coming of the Enemy, and upon the black are set the silver stars of Elbereth' (pp. 436–7). But the fragment ends as Tal-Elmar is told that the men of the West have decided to establish themselves in that place, and the people of his village must depart or be slain.

It is not known when Tolkien conceived the story of Tal-Elmar; Christopher Tolkien believes, however, that its first expression – a typescript of six sides which breaks off in mid-sentence, together with a rejected page that is part typescript and part manuscript – dates from the 1950s. If so, it was in the early part of that decade, for Tolkien continued the story as a rough manuscript draft, inscribed 'January 1955', which ends with questions how to continue. According to a note written by Tolkien in 1968, it was to be 'a tale that sees the Númenóreans from the point of view of the Wild Men' (*The Peoples of Middle-earth*, p. 422). When he began the story he did not consider how it might fit in with his other writings, and looking at it in retrospect 'it must recount the coming of the Númenóreans (Elf-friends) *before the Downfall* [of Númenor], and represent their choice of permanent havens. So the geography must be made to fit that of the mouths of the Anduin and the Langstrand [as presented in *The Lord of the Rings*]' (p. 422). But he never made the necessary alterations or additions.

The Tale of Years. Chronology of events in the Elder Days of Tolkien's *'Silmarillion'* mythology, partly published with commentary in *The War of the Jewels* (1994), pp. 342–56.

*Christopher Tolkien describes this as 'an evolving work that accompanied successive stages in the development of the *Annals*', but of small value until towards the end of the later version 'when it becomes a document of importance' for the last years of the First Age, not reached by other texts (*The War of the Jewels*, p. 342). Only this later part, the content of which is not duplicated in other works, is published in *The History of Middle-earth*.

Tolkien later transferred to *The Tale of Years* from the *Annals of Aman* (see *Annals of Valinor*) a section headed 'Of the Beginning of Time and Its Reckoning', attributed to Quennar Onótimo. Two fine manuscripts of *The Tale of Years* written out by Tolkien begin with this text; and the text together with a few entries from the chronological section of *The Tale of Years* were published in *Morgoth's Ring, pp. 49–51, and 56–7, notes 5–16. The first page of the second manuscript, which Christopher Tolkien describes as among the most beautiful that his father made, was reproduced in colour as a frontispiece to Morgoth's Ring.

The first version of The Tale of Years was written probably in the mid-1930s. Its dates agree with those of the 'later' Annals of Valinor and the 'later' *Annals of Beleriand, but nothing from it has been published. A second version was written c. 1951–2, contemporary with the Annals of Aman and the Grey Annals (see *Annals of Beleriand), with the original dates in each work agreeing with the other. This began as a good clear text, but in use as a working document it was 'heavily corrected, interpolated and rewritten in many stages' (The War of the Jewels, p. 342), especially in the part corresponding to the latter part of the Annals of Aman. Christopher Tolkien describes it as 'perhaps the most complex and difficult text of all that my father left behind him' (Morgoth's Ring, p. 49). Since, in general, it repeats information given in the contemporary Annals, Christopher Tolkien notes only a few interesting variations between the Annals and The Tale of Years, as well as some of the changes made in the part of the typescript which followed the manuscript of this Tale of Years.

From the point where Tolkien abandoned the Grey Annals, part way through an entry for Year 501, adding only a few notes for later events, The Tale of Years continuing to Year 600 'becomes a major source for the end of the Elder Days, and indeed in almost all respects the only source deriving from the time following the completion of *The Lord of the Rings, woefully inadequate as it is' (The War of the Jewels, pp. 344–5). For the period in question, as originally written this Tale of Years was little more than a fair copy of that made in the mid-1930s. In the next stage Tolkien made 'many corrections and interpolations and alterations of date' (p. 346). He then struck though 'the whole manuscript from Year 400 almost to the end' (p. 347) and replaced it with a new version, reaching only as far as Eärendil's arrival in Valinor (in 536 > 540 > 542), in which many of the entries with passages of narrative were expanded so that they began to approach the Annals in style. Christopher Tolkien also gives the relevant part of an incomplete typescript/manuscript of The Tale of Years which followed, extending as far as Year 527.

The Tale of Years described in this entry should not be confused with the chronologies of the Second and Third Ages in Appendix B of *The Lord of the Rings, also called The Tale of Years.

Tales and Songs of Bimble Bay. Series of poems, written by Tolkien c. 1928 (not in 1922, as implied in Biography, p. 106), incorporating fantasy and satire, and centred on an imaginary English coastal town and harbour. These include The Bumpus (revised as *Perry-the-Winkle), *The Dragon's Visit, *Glip, Old Grabbler (earlier Poor Old Grabbler), *Progress in Bimble Town, and A Song of Bimble Bay; those titles not asterisked are still unpublished. Both Old Grabbler and Progress in Bimble Town show Tolkien's concerns about pollution and industrialization (see *Environment).

Tales from the Perilous Realm. Collection of shorter works by Tolkien, first published by HarperCollins, London, in 1997. The volume contains **Farmer Giles of Ham*, **Leaf by Niggle*, **Smith of Wootton Major*, and the poems of **The Adventures of Tom Bombadil and Other Verses from the Red Book*. (See also ***Adaptations for the BBC Radio series of the same title.)

T.C.B.S. In summer term 1911 Tolkien succeeded to the office of Librarian at **King Edward's School, Birmingham, whose library was administered chiefly by senior boys. Tolkien had previously been one of six Sub-Librarians, also among whom were his friends **Christopher Wiseman, **R.Q. Gilson, and **Vincent Trought. As Wiseman later recalled, 'exams went on for six weeks, and if you were not having an exam you really had nothing to do; so we started having tea in the school library'. Unofficially calling themselves the Tea Club, the friends boiled a kettle on a spirit stove and disposed of tea-leaves in the school cleaners' buckets. According to Wiseman,

> those first teas were in the library cubby-hole. Then, as it was the summer term, we went out and had tea at Barrow's Stores in Corporation Street. In the Tea Room there was a sort of compartment, a table for six between two large settles, quite secluded; and it was known as the Railway Carriage. This became a favourite place for us, and we changed our title to the Barrovian Society, after Barrow's Stores. Later, I was editor of the School Chronicle [the *King Edward's School Chronicle*, the school magazine], and I had to print a list of people who had gained various distinctions; so against the people in the list who were members I put an asterisk, and at the bottom of the page by the asterisk it said 'Also members of the T.C., B.S., etc'. It was a seven-days wonder what it stood for!
> [quoted in *Biography*, pp. 45–6]

The 'Tea Club, Barrovian Society' was known to its members almost exclusively by its initials, written as both 'T.C.B.S.' and 'TCBS'.

The asterisked names in the list referred to by Wiseman (a list of Prefects who served during the 1911 autumn and summer terms, see 'Notes and News', *King Edward's School Chronicle* n.s. 26, no. 189 (October 1911), pp. 74–6) were those of **S. Barrowclough, R.Q. Gilson, **R.S. Payton, **W.H. Payton, J.R.R. Tolkien, Vincent Trought, and Wiseman himself. **T.K. 'Tea Cake' Barnsley was not a Prefect, but was a member of the T.C.B.S., as was **G.B. (Geoffrey Bache) Smith apparently by the end of autumn term 1911. Many years later, in a letter to Wiseman of 24 May 1973, Tolkien quoted from a letter sent by a former schoolmate, C.V.L. Lycett: 'As a boy you could not imagine how I looked up to you and admired and envied the wit of that select coterie of J.R.R.T., C.L. Wiseman, G.B. Smith, R.Q. Gilson, V. Trought, and Payton. I hovered on the outskirts to gather up the gems. You probably had no idea of this schoolboy worship.' Tolkien commented to Wiseman that they had 'certainly never meant to be' a select coterie (*Letters*, p. 429).

Tolkien's close friendship with *Christopher Wiseman, whom he first met in the Fifth Class of King Edward's School in autumn term 1905, predated the T.C.B.S. They shared many interests, including Latin and Greek, and rugby football. Although Wiseman was a Methodist and Tolkien a Roman Catholic, and each held strongly to his faith, they were able to discuss religion with no harm to their friendship; indeed, religion came to be an important link between them, which they did not share with the other core members of the T.C.B.S., R.Q. Gilson and G.B. Smith.

It seems likely that during their years at King Edward's School, and possibly for some time after, the members of the T.C.B.S. did little more than share their disparate interests. Tolkien 'delighted his friends with recitations from *Beowulf*, the *Pearl*, and *Sir Gawain and the Green Knight*, and recounted horrific episodes from the Norse *Völsungasaga*, with a passing jibe at Wagner whose interpretations of the myths he held in contempt' (Humphrey Carpenter, *Biography*, p. 46). Gilson's interests were Renaissance painting and the eighteenth century, Wiseman was interested in natural sciences and music, and Trought was a poet and artist.

In autumn term 1911 Gilson was Secretary of the Musical and Dramatic Society and planned a performance of *The Rivals* by Sheridan to be staged at the end of term. Tolkien, by then at *Oxford, was lured back to play Mrs Malaprop, while Wiseman played Sir Anthony Absolute, Gilson Captain Absolute, and T.K. Barnsley Bob Acres. It may have been the casting of G.B. Smith as Faulkland that brought him into the inner circle of the T.C.B.S. After the dress rehearsal, still in costume, the friends marched up Coronation Street in *Birmingham to have tea in Barrow's Stores.

After he left King Edward's School Tolkien continued to correspond with, and meet, Wiseman and Gilson. Vincent Trought, another particularly close friend, died on 20 January 1912 after a long illness. Wiseman collected money for a T.C.B.S. wreath in addition to the one sent by the School. In autumn 1912 both Wiseman and Gilson went up to Cambridge, where they were joined a year later by Barrowclough and R.S. Payton. At the end of 1912 G.B. Smith, still at King Edward's School, won an exhibition to Corpus Christi College, Oxford. The earliest surviving letter between Smith and Tolkien (which refers to previous letters) is one from Smith dated 9 June 1913, asking advice about coming up to Oxford. After Smith matriculated in Michaelmas Term 1913 he and Tolkien became close friends. In a letter written on 9 February 1916 Smith wrote: 'I never knew you until I went up to Oxford' (Tolkien Papers, Bodleian Library, Oxford).

Much of the early extant correspondence between Tolkien, Wiseman, Gilson, and Smith is lighthearted, and certainly does not suggest that these four had any joint programme or mission. Tolkien kept his engagement to Edith Bratt (*Edith Tolkien) secret from his friends for nearly a year, and when he did inform them, he did not even tell them her name. In autumn 1914 Wiseman began to feel that the four had lost some of their earlier closeness and ideals, and in part blamed T.K. Barnsley (now also at Cambridge) and his influence on Gilson. He wrote to Tolkien on 15 November 1914 that the current T.C.B.S. had begun to seem 'so far removed from the old, good T.C.B.S., that it had become a coterie with which under ordinary circumstances I should never have thought for one moment of joining myself', but a letter from Tolkien showed that he 'at any rate still felt for the old spirit. I think that for once we are in complete agreement.' In the same letter Wiseman wrote:

> Mind you, I think those old days will not easily come back to us two. If Oxford, as I once suspected, has altered you as much as it seems to have altered G.B.S[mith], & if, as is almost certain, Cambridge has done much the same for me, there is a good deal between us. However I don't think that either accursed institution . . . can really have destroyed what made you & me the Twin Brethren in the good old school days before there was a T.C.B.S. apart from us & V[incent] T[rought]. . . .
>
> I was at one time afraid that Oxford had killed your religion. I am not afraid now, for no man can be angry, used in the noblest sense, unless he is fundamentally religious, that is to say unless he has an honest & *living* conviction on the subject of the Divinity of Our Lord. I do not care for the moment whether he accepts it or denies it. You & I used to argue honestly on these matters. Since I left school never has any member of the T.C.B.S. ever approached the subject in my presence except on *one* occasion, when I talked about things with G.B.S. in Wales, & I am convinced he wasn't honest. I can only conclude that such things no longer interest the T.C.B.S., or that such a wedge has been driven in between us that we dare not mention them one to another. [Tolkien Papers, Bodleian Library, Oxford]

In his reply to Wiseman written the following day (16 November) Tolkien said that 'the joy of rediscovering the great twin brotherhood – after all the vitality and fount of energy from which the T.C.B.S. derived its origin! – has almost made me forget any hunger for the T.C.B.S.'

> The great twin-brotherhood must always remain an inner nucleus of the T.C.B.S. itself . . . having certain things esoteric to itself. I have been conscious of that from the beginning: there are some discussions – and some peculiar pastimes – which only the GTB [Great Twin Brotherhood] unobserved by other eyes would indulge in. The difference between this innermost nucleus is of course (or was) quite negligible when measured against the gulf between the T.C.B.S. as a whole and the outer void: but always existed.

He had 'never discussed fundamentals with Rob [Gilson]', and 'very seldom' and on only 'one or two points' with Smith. For himself, he 'simply cannot divorce morality ever from any of my conceptions, thoughts, or criticisms of any human activities at all', and he knew that for himself and Wiseman 'religion is the moving force and at the same time the foundation of both of us'. He thought that the T.C.B.S. had not yet decided what 'our subjects of supreme importance' were, and what were 'allowable distances' of opinion on these, matters to be discussed at their next meeting (Tolkien Papers, Bodleian Library, Oxford).

The friends evidently did so when they met in London at the Wiseman family house on 12–13 December 1914, and 'spent the weekend chiefly in sitting around the gas fire in the little upstairs room, smoking their pipes and talking. As Wiseman said, they felt "four times the intellectual size" when they were together' (*Biography*, p. 73). Tolkien later wrote about 'the hope and ambitions (inchoate and cloudy I know) that first became conscious at the Council of London. That Council was as you know followed in my own case with my finding a voice for all kinds of pent up things and a tremendous opening up of everything for me: – I have always laid that to the credit of the inspiration that even a few hours with the four always brought to all of us' (letter to G.B. Smith, 12 August 1916, *Letters*, p. 10). On 1 March 1915, in a letter urging Tolkien be present at another T.C.B.S. meeting, Gilson wrote: 'Do please move heaven and earth to come. . . . The 4 will meet & be for a few hours as absolutely undistracted by the outside world as when we met in London, and how perfectly magnificent that occasion was! Just think of those two days & the bliss of them. Our conversations & the vivid proof of the undimmed life & vigour of the T.C.B.S. I *never* spent happier hours' (Tolkien Papers, Bodleian Library, Oxford).

If any clear statement of the aims of the T.C.B.S. was ever written down, it does not appear to survive; but one may be deduced from references and allusions in correspondence, especially in letters to Tolkien after a second T.C.B.S. meeting in London in 1915, which he was unable to attend. The friends seem to have hoped that through their artistic achievements, including poetry, music, and architecture, they might bring about reform of what they saw as the corrupt state of arts and attitudes in England. In a letter of 24 October 1915 Smith said that the friends had sat up late and decided that the work of the T.C.B.S. after the war would be 'to drive from life, letters, the stage and society that dabbling in and hankering after the unpleasant sides and incidents in life and nature which have captured the larger and worser tastes in Oxford, London and the world: to be rid of A.J. Daw [?], Douglas Cole [probably George Douglas Cole, 1889–1959, a conscientious objector active in the Fabian Society], [George] Bernard Shaw and the rest of them: to reestablish sanity, cleanliness, and the love of real and true beauty in everybody's breast' (Tolkien Papers, Bodleian Library, Oxford). Wiseman wrote on 27 October that

> G.B.S[mith] confessed that [the] T.C.B.S. would have to leave [the] world better than it found it. His method [is] to be the presentation of a type of art strongly employing T.C.B.Sian principles. He suggested it as the general T.C.B.S. method. . . . I felt triumphant, for this is just the point of view I had longed to bring the T.C.B.S. to explicitly for a long time. . . . I

could offer no alternative method for myself; as I have repeatedly said, I do not intend to try to use art myself. You & G.B.S. have been given your weapon [poetry] early & are sharpening it. I don't know what mine is, but you shall see it one day. [Tolkien Papers, Bodleian Library, Oxford]

Gilson wrote on 31 October 1915 of their meeting in London:

We talked of many things in modern life and modern literature & poetry. Especially the horrible enjoyment of the sheer evil filth of immorality: an attitude that seems quite new to the world, & is certainly poles apart from the delight of the eighteenth century in the humour to be extracted from foulness – though I am no apologist for the obscenity of Tristram Shandy and the like. . . . There is the world – our England at least – unconsciously crying out for the TCBSian spirit. I believe we can never thank God enough for the purity of our school. On that night I suddenly saw the TCBS in a blaze of light as a great moral reformer. As GBS [G.B. Smith] said, all reformers have been moral reformers. However we set about it – I imagine that three of us will probably work through art – that remains the great task of the TCBS. England purified of this loathsome insidious disease by the TCBS spirit. It is an enormous task and we shall not see it accomplished in our lifetime. But we all have, and all must hold, our faith. [Tolkien Papers, Bodleian Library, Oxford]

Following the original 'Council of London' Tolkien began to write poetry more prolifically and to circulate it to the others for comment and criticism, especially to Smith who was also an aspiring poet. The other members gave Tolkien their honest opinions on his poems, and advice on trying to get them published. In response to a letter from Tolkien, evidently suggesting that he was imposing too much on his friends in asking them to read his verse, Smith wrote on 9 February 1916: 'You need never reproach yourself that you have taken up too much of our time and discourse. We believe in your work, we others, and recognise with pleasure our own finger in it. Christopher declares that he and Rob and I write your poems, and it is not altogether untrue, though not wholly true either' (Tolkien Papers, Bodleian Library, Oxford).

The last time all four of the friends met, and the last time that Tolkien saw Rob Gilson, was in Lichfield on 25–6 September 1915, but nothing is recorded of what they discussed there.

By early January 1916 Tolkien was the only T.C.B.S. member still in England: Smith and Gilson had been posted to France with the Army, and Wiseman, who had joined the Navy, was aboard ship off the coast of Scotland. While on leave at the end of May, Smith was able to visit Tolkien and Edith (now married) at *Great Haywood, Staffordshire. At the beginning of June Tolkien was himself posted to France, and on 22 June received a last letter from Gilson in which he said: 'I have never felt more forcibly than in the last few weeks, the truth of your words about the oasis of TCBSianism. Life just now is a veritable desert' (quoted in *Life and Legend*, p. 33). Gilson was killed on 1 July 1916, the first day of the Battle of the Somme, but his death was not confirmed for some time. G.B. Smith wrote to Tolkien with the news on 15 July: 'Now one realises in despair what the T.C.B.S. really was. O my dear John Ronald what ever are we going to do?' (quoted in *Life and Legend*, p. 33).

On 12–13 August 1916 Tolkien wrote a letter to Smith in which he referred to their hopes that the T.C.B.S. would be

> a great instrument in God's hands – a mover, a doer, even an achiever of great things, a beginner at the very least of large things. . . .
> What I meant . . . was that the TCBS had been granted some spark of fire – certainly as a body if not singly – that was destined to kindle a new light, or what is the same thing, rekindle an old light in the world; that the TCBS was destined to testify for God and Truth in a more direct way even than by laying down its several lives in this war.

After Gilson's death he no longer felt 'a member of a little complete body. . . . I honestly feel that the TCBS has ended. . . . Of course the TCBS may have been all we dreamt – and its work in the end be done by three or two or one survivor' (*Letters*, pp. 9–10). Smith replied on 19 August, rejecting the idea that the T.C.B.S. had ended:

> The T.C.B.S. is not so much a society as an influence on the state of being. . . . That such an influence on the state of being could come to an end with Rob's loss is to me a preposterous idea, a hideous idea. It (the influence) is a tradition, which forty years from now will still be as strong to us (if we are alive, and if we are not) as it is today. . . . The T.C.B.S. is not finished and never will be: there is something to write upon the face of dawn and cry to the uttermost corners of the skies. [Tolkien Papers, Bodleian Library, Oxford]

Tolkien and Smith were able to meet several times behind the front lines in July and August, the last occasion on 22 August 1916. At the beginning of the second week of November Tolkien was shipped home suffering from trench fever. Smith's last letter to Tolkien, sent to him in hospital in Birmingham, was dated 18 November 1916. Smith died on 3 December 1916 from wounds he had received on 29 November. In response to Smith's own wishes and those of his mother, Tolkien and *R.W. Reynolds, one of their masters at King Edward's School, edited a collection of Smith's poetry for publication. Christopher Wiseman made suggestions for possible arrangements, and argued for publication of only the best rather than all of Smith's poetry. This book, *A Spring Harvest*, was published by Erskine Macdonald in June or July 1918 with an introductory note by 'J.R.R.T'.

In 1965, in his Foreword to the second edition of *The Lord of the Rings*, Tolkien commented: 'As the years go by it seems now often forgotten that to be caught in youth by 1914 was no less hideous an experience than to be involved in 1939 and the following years. By 1918 all but one of my close friends were dead.' Wiseman, however, remained, with whom Tolkien continued to correspond regularly until at least 1919, and occasionally thereafter. Tolkien sent Wiseman copies of his poems for comment, and told him about the earliest stories of *The Book of Lost Tales*. In 1924 Tolkien named his youngest son, Christopher, after his old friend.

For a few years at least, *c.* 1911–18, the T.C.B.S. was clearly of great importance to Tolkien, and it is unfortunate that information about it is now so sparse. Of the four core members, only Christopher Wiseman was still alive when Humphrey Carpenter wrote his biography of Tolkien, and he was recalling events that happened some sixty years earlier. Correspondence preserved in the Tolkien Papers in the Bodleian Library (*Libraries and archives) consists almost entirely of letters from Gilson, Smith, and Wiseman to Tolkien (and certainly not all that were written); of Tolkien's own letters to the T.C.B.S., the present authors are aware of only two. He made only a few passing references to the group in later life. Although he probably would have followed the same literary path even without the fellowship and encouragement of the other members of the T.C.B.S., his works nonetheless embody some of the ideals of that group, especially *The Lord of the Rings* in which many have found a deep religious undercurrent, a moral and ethical tone, and above all, the ideals of friendship and fellowship.

'Of Thingol and Melian'. The fourth chapter of the *'Quenta Silmarillion', published in *The Silmarillion* (1977), pp. 55–6.

SUMMARY

Melian is a Maia dwelling in the gardens of Lórien, kin to Yavanna. She is skilled in songs of enchantment, and taught the nightingales their song. When the Elves awake, she leaves Valinor and fills 'the silence of Middle-earth before the dawn with her voice and the voices of her birds' (*The Silmarillion*, p. 55). During a rest on the great march of the Elves to Valinor, Thingol (Elwë), Lord of the Telerin Elves, visits his friend Finwë, Lord of the Noldor, and while travelling alone through the wood of Nan Elmoth, he is enchanted by the song of the nightingales and the voice of Melian, and forgets his people. When he finds Melian he sees the light of Aman on her face, 'and being filled with love Elwë came to her and took her hand, and straightway a spell was laid on him, so that they stood thus while long years were measured by the wheeling stars above them ...' (p. 55). The Teleri seek for him in vain, and depart for Valinor with Olwë, Thingol's brother. Although Thingol remains in Middle-earth, he had seen the Trees in Valinor when he went there as an ambassador of his people. He becomes King of the Elves of Beleriand, the Sindar, and Melian is his Queen. They dwell in Menegroth, the Thousand Caves, in Doriath. Through Melian the strain of the Ainur comes among Elves and Men. 'And of the love of Thingol and Melian there came into the world [Lúthien] the fairest of all the Children of Ilúvatar that was or shall ever be' (p. 56).

HISTORY

In *The Book of Lost Tales* this part of the story of Thingol (also called there Tintoglin, Linwë Tinto, Tinwë Linto, or Tinwelint) and Melian (also called Tindriel, Wendelin, Gwendeling, or Gwenniel) is told as part of *The Tale of Tinúviel*, the surviving version of which was probably written in mid-1919. The tale is similar to that in *The Silmarillion*, except that it is said that Tinwelint stands for many years listening to the nightingales before he comes to himself and finds Gwendeling, who at first dances away from him, as their daughter will do when she encounters Beren (see *'Of Beren and Lúthien'). Tinwelint follows, then falls into a very long sleep, during which time his kin depart for Valinor. Tinwelint had been one of the three ambassadors to Valinor.

Other parts of *The Book of Lost Tales* show that at this time Tolkien did not envision Wendelin and Tinwelint as the elevated characters they later became. Wendelin (Gwendeling) is a sprite from the gardens of Lórien, and also 'of the children of the gods', but has much less power and foresight than Melian. She is described as 'clad in filmy garments most lovely yet of black jet-spangled and girt with silver' (*The Book of Lost Tales, Part Two*, p. 8). Tinwelint is comparatively poor and, anxious for treasure, is not above resorting to trickery or swindling to get it. But in *The Children of Húrin* of *c.* 1919–25 Thingol is already noted as having great stores of Elven armour, and by the beginning of the *Lay of Leithian*, written in mid-1925, Thingol has become Lord of the Thousand Caves and possesses great wealth.

The story of the meeting of Thingol and Melian was also told at the beginning of Canto III of the *Lay of Leithian*, written in 1925, which describes the effect the singing of the birds and of Melian have on Thingol: 'Enchanted moments such as these / from gardens of the Lord of Sleep, / . . . do come, and count as many years / in mortal lands'. Long Thingol stays there. When he awakes after what seems an hour, he finds Melian 'upon a bed of leaves'. Thingol touches her hair, 'and his mind / was drowned in the forgetful deep, / and dark the years rolled o'er his sleep' (*The Lays of Beleriand*, pp. 172–3). This meeting no longer foreshadows that of Lúthien and Beren, with Thingol pursuing a dancing Melian.

In the *Sketch of the Mythology* (*c.* 1926) Melian is described as 'one of the divine maidens of the Vala Lórien' (*The Shaping of Middle-earth*, p. 13), and in the *Quenta Noldorinwa* (*c.* 1930) she is a 'fay', but the description of her powers of song approaches that in *The Silmarillion* even to some phrasing. Neither the 'earliest' nor the 'later' *Annals of Valinor* are specific as to the length of time Thingol was enchanted, but both (the former by emendation) indicate that Melian came to Middle-earth when Varda began to make stars.

In the *Quenta Silmarillion*, begun in the mid-1930s, Tolkien expanded the story from the *Quenta Noldorinwa* and formed a subsection of the third chapter, 'Of the Coming of the Elves'. In a typescript made by Tolkien c. December 1937–January 1938 of the beginning of the work, the subsection is headed 'Of Thingol'. Melian's kinship to Yavanna now appears, and the account of her meeting with Thingol is similar to that of *The Silmarillion* in that the singing draws him to her and only after he has looked on the light of Aman in her face is he enchanted. The reference that through Melian 'a strain of the immortal race of the Gods [Ainur] came among both Elves and Men' enters (*The Lost Road and Other Writings*, p. 220). But temporarily Thingol is *not* one of the ambassadors (confusingly, the ambassador was his brother, called Elwë).

Revision and writing of parts of the *Lay of Leithian* was one of Tolkien's earliest tasks when he returned to *'The Silmarillion' after completing *The Lord of the Rings. The account of the meeting of Thingol and Melian was rewritten, so that when Thingol hears a bird and then Melian's voice he forgets everything:

> One moment face to face they stand
> alone, beneath the wheeling sky,
> while starlit years on earth go by
> And in Nan Elmoth wood the trees
> grow dark and tall. . . . [*The Lays of Beleriand*, p. 347]

In revisions to the *Quenta Silmarillion* c. 1951 Melian is described as 'a *maia* of the race of the Valar', and of the folk of the Vala Lórien 'none was more beautiful than she, nor more wise, nor more skilled in songs of enchantment' (*Morgoth's Ring*, p. 172). Thingol, now called Elwë Singollo, is again one of the ambassadors who visits Valinor.

According to the *Annals of Aman* (see *Annals of Valinor*), also c. 1951, Melian went to Middle-earth when Varda made the stars and the Elves awoke in Valian year 1050 (each Valian year being roughly the equivalent of ten years of the Sun). In 1130 Thingol was enchanted by Melian, and in 1152 he awoke from his long trance. Some of this appears also in the *Grey Annals* (see *Annals of Beleriand*), and both state specifically that Thingol heard Melian *returning*, from a visit to Finwë.

The text published in *The Silmarillion* is basically that of the revised *Quenta Silmarillion*, but *Christopher Tolkien also incorporated information which appears in the *Annals*, including actual phrases and sentences.

Thompson, William Meredith. W. Meredith Thompson came from the University of Winnipeg in the 1930s to read English at Oriel College, *Oxford. With Tolkien's guidance he prepared, over a period of years, an edition of Þe Wohunge of Ure Lauerd ('The Wooing of Our Lord'), one of the so-called 'Wooing Group' of manuscript monologues or prayers, related to the *Ancrene Riwle and the *Katherine Group. It was published by the Early English Text Society (*Societies and clubs) in 1958. In this Thompson acknowledged 'the kind unfailing stimulus and advice of Professor J.R.R. Tolkien, who, wearing his own ring of power, is present in most of its best parts only' (p. vii).

In the course of his work, Thompson became a close friend of the Tolkien family, to whom he was known as 'Merry Tom'. *John and *Priscilla Tolkien note in *The Tolkien Family Album* that he took 'some of the best photos in the family collection' (p. 68, with a photograph of Thompson himself).

Thompson later became a distinguished teacher of English at universities in Los Angeles and Vancouver. He contributed 'Chaucer's Translation of the Bible' in the *Festschrift* *English and Medieval Studies Presented to J.R.R. Tolkien on the Occasion of His Seventieth Birthday* (1962).

Tidworth (Wiltshire). From 27 July to 4 August 1909 Tolkien attended a Public Schools Camp with the *King Edward's School Officers Training Corps (*Societies and clubs) at Tidworth Pennings on Salisbury Plain. Tidworth is one of a network of camps long used for military training. On this occasion, the students took part in exercises culminating in a grand field day with 20,000 troops.

Tinfang Warble. Poem, published probably in the mid-1920s; Tolkien preserved a copy of the leaf on which it was printed. A holograph list of his poems by Tolkien indicates the name of the publication as 'I U Mag'; John Garth in *Tolkien and the Great War* (2003) is correct that this was the *Inter-University Magazine*, published by the University Catholic Societies' Federation of Great Britain. See also *The Grey Bridge of Tavrobel*, which was published in the same magazine, though not in the same issue. *Tinfang Warble* was reprinted in *The Book of Lost Tales, Part One* (1983), p. 108.

Tinfang, or Timpinen, is a piper in *The Book of Lost Tales*, 'a wondrous wise and strange creature' (*The Book of Lost Tales, Part One*, p. 94) who plays and dances in summer dusks; children call him 'Tinfang Warble'. The poem suggests his music ('O the hoot! O the hoot! / How he trillups on his flute!') and his movements ('Dancing all alone, / Hopping on a stone, / Flitting like a faun'). Tinfang Warble is also featured in the poem *Over Old Hills and Far Away*. John Garth has suggested that the figure 'had a contemporary visual counterpart in a painting that [as a commercial print] found a mass-market' among British soldiers in the First World War: 'Eleanor Canziani's *Piper of Dreams*, which ... depicts a boy sitting alone in a springtime wood playing to a half-seen flight of fairies' (p. 77). And yet Tinfang Warble is consistently animated rather than seated, and clearly himself from the tradition of fairies and sprites (in the earliest version of the poem he is a 'leprawn', i.e. leprechaun), while the enticing sound of his flute recalls the piping of Pan: compare, for instance, 'the merry bubble and joy, the thin, clear happy call of the distant piping' of 'The Piper at the Gates of Dawn' in *Kenneth Grahame's *The Wind in the Willows* (1908).

Tinfang Warble exists in three versions, the earliest manuscript of which is dated 29–30 April (1915, though Tolkien indicated on a later typescript that the work was written at Oxford in 1914). He revised it at Leeds in 1920–3, and once again for publication.

Tolkien family. According to Tolkien's Aunt Grace Mountain (*née* Tolkien), the Tolkien family originally came from the Hohenzollern district of the Holy Roman Empire, and indeed their surname was originally *von Hohenzollern*; but this, like much else alleged by Aunt Grace, may be no more than family lore. It was also said in the family that some members emigrated to France and intermarried with nobility.

> Opinion differed among the Tolkiens as to why and when their ancestors had come to England. The more prosaic said it was in 1756 to escape the Prussian invasion of Saxony, where they had lands. Aunt Grace preferred the more romantic (if implausible) story of how one of the du Téméraires [in the French branch of the family] had fled across the Channel in 1794 to escape the guillotine, apparently then assuming a form of the old name 'Tolkien' [i.e. after *Tollkühn* 'foolhardy'; see *Names]. This gentle-man was reputedly an accomplished harpsichordist and clock-repairer. [Humphrey Carpenter, *Biography*, p. 19]

In an autobiographical statement written in 1955 Tolkien said that his Tolkien ancestors 'migrated to England more than 200 years ago, and became quickly intensely English (not British), though remaining musical – a talent that unfortunately did not descend to me' (*Letters*, p. 218).

In a letter to Amy Ronald on 2 January 1969 Tolkien referred to his father *Arthur as the 'eldest of my grandfather John Benjamin [Tolkien]'s second family; but his elder half-brother John had died leaving only 3 daughters. So John I had to be [so named as the eldest son of the eldest Tolkien son], and was dandled on the knee of old J[ohn] B[enjamin], as the heir, before he died' (*Letters*, p. 398). **John Benjamin Tolkien** (?1807–1896) was born in Clerkenwell, Middlesex, one of at least seven children of **George William Tolkien** (?1784–1840), a professor of music, and his wife **Eliza Lydia** (*née* Murrell, ?1787–1863). John Benjamin's first wife was **Jane Holmwood** (*b.* ?1806) of Fareham; in the 1851 Census they are listed with one son, **John Benjamin** (?1845–1883) but only two daughters, **Emily** (*b.* ?1838) and **Louise** (*b.* ?1840). After Jane's death, John Benjamin (the elder) married **Mary Jane Stowe** (?1834–1915) of *Birmingham.

As recounted in *Some Moseley Personalities Volume I* (1991), the Tolkien family

> had been piano makers, but John Tolkien had also become bankrupt and had turned to selling music. The publishing of music had been a family concern for at least a century; when Moseley Hall had been rebuilt in 1796, a great house-warming party was given by John Taylor II for which some music entitled *The Moseley Quadrilles* had been composed; the publisher of this music was called Tolkien. [p. 29]

Census records indicate numerous Tolkiens as pianoforte manufacturers, music dealers, and the like. Birmingham city directories list the Tolkiens' 'music and musical instrument warehouse' (or 'music and pianoforte warehouse') at 70 New Street, evidently also the home of John Benjamin and Jane Holmwood Tolkien, and the site of their son John's birth. In 1856, when John Benjamin married Mary Jane Stowe, he was recorded as living in the Birmingham suburb of Handsworth.

John Benjamin and Mary Jane Tolkien had at least eight children: *Arthur Reuel, Tolkien's father (1857–1896); Mabel (?1858–1937, not to be confused with *Mabel Tolkien, née Suffield, Tolkien's mother), who married Thomas Mitton; Grace Bindley (b. ?1861), who married William Mountain; Florence Mary (b. ?1863), who married Tom Hadley; Frank Winslow (?1864–?1867); Howard Charles (?1867–1867); Wilfred Henry (b. ?1870); and Laurence George H. (b. ?1873).

*King Edward's School, Birmingham recorded Tolkien's address immediately after his mother's death as care of Laurence Tolkien, his father's brother, in Kings Norton (*Birmingham and environs). As boys during their school holidays Tolkien and his brother *Hilary often stayed with their Aunt Grace and Uncle William Mountain, who lived in Newcastle upon Tyne, or with their Aunt Mabel and Uncle Tom Mitton in Moseley near Birmingham. In later years Tolkien stayed in touch with his Tolkien aunts and cousins: he was especially close to his Aunt Grace and her children Kenneth and Dorothy (known as 'Ding', later Dorothy Wood), and with his Aunt Florence Hadley, who moved to British Columbia, and her daughter Marjorie ('Midge').

See also the family trees printed as an appendix to the Chronology.

Tolkien, Arthur Reuel (1857–1896). Arthur Tolkien was one of eight children of John Benjamin and Mary Jane Tolkien (see *Tolkien family). He was born and raised in Moseley, near *Birmingham, and in his youth attended *King Edward's School. In 1888, at the age of thirty-one, he became engaged to Mabel Suffield (*Mabel Tolkien), but because she was only eighteen, Arthur was forbidden a formal betrothal by her father for a period of two years. For the next few months, Arthur and Mabel saw each other only at family parties and exchanged letters in secret.

By this time, Arthur had been employed for several years at Lloyd's Bank in Birmingham. Opportunities for advancement being poor, and with the financial requirements of marriage in mind, in 1889 he left England for the then commercially promising country of *South Africa, having taken a job with the Bank of Africa in the Cape colony. For the first year he held temporary postings in some of the principal towns between Cape Town and Johannesburg; then in 1890 he was appointed manager of the branch in Bloemfontein, capital of the Orange Free State. Mabel joined him in South Africa in April 1891. They were married in the cathedral in Cape Town, and lived in Bank House in Bloemfontein. Their two sons, Ronald and *Hilary, were born there in 1892 and 1894 respectively.

Life in South Africa agreed with Arthur: he was suited to the climate, and although he had to learn Dutch (the language of business in a land of Dutch settlers) and make social calls, and worry about competition from the rival National Bank, he enjoyed his work. In the garden of Bank House he planted a small grove of cypresses, firs, and cedars, and cultivated vines. He wrote to his father: 'I think I shall do well in this country and do not think I should settle down well in England again for a permanency' (quoted in *Biography*, p. 15). His wife however, despite her love for her husband, found much to dislike in Bloemfontein, and Ronald suffered from the heat. In April 1895 Mabel, Ronald, and Ronald's brother *Hilary went on home leave to England while Arthur stayed in Bloemfontein to attend to business; he could not, in any case, have afforded the cost of accompanying his family on leave at half pay.

In autumn 1895 Arthur contracted rheumatic fever. He partially recovered and returned to work, but suffered a relapse in January 1896, and died on 15 February of that year. As an obituary recounted, about three weeks before his death Arthur

> went to the Conquered Territory [in the south-east of the Orange Free State] to recruit, and, although on his return he was still weak, yet he appeared to be in good spirits until Friday evening, when he fell ill again. The patient did not at first surmise how bad his case was, and as late as Friday afternoon he expressed the hope that he would be able to resume his duties on Wednesday next, so as to enable his accountant to attend the cricket match on that day. But during the night haemorrhage set in, and on Saturday afternoon, after having received the sacrament, Mr. Tolkien breathed his last. . . . The funeral took place yesterday afternoon and was largely attended. There was a full choral service in the Cathedral. [reproduced in *The Tolkien Family Album*, p. 19]

Burial was in the President Brand cemetery in Bloemfontein.

Photographs of Arthur Tolkien with his staff outside Bank House, and with his family, are reproduced in *The Tolkien Family Album*, pp. 15 and 16 respectively. The latter is also reproduced in *Biography*, pl. 1a.

Tolkien, Christopher Reuel (*b.* 1924). The third child and youngest son of Ronald and *Edith Tolkien, Christopher Tolkien was named for his father's friend *Christopher Wiseman. (His initials on the maps of *The Lord of the Rings*, 'CJRT', include a confirmation name, John, which he does not customarily use.) He was born in *Leeds on 21 November 1924 and raised in *Oxford. As a boy he followed his brothers *John and *Michael to the Dragon School, Oxford, and the Oratory School in Caversham, *Berkshire. For a period of three years he remained at home with a heart ailment and worked with a private tutor. Given a telescope, he watched the stars, and with Michael Tolkien indulged a youthful passion for railways.

As a boy he was a frequent and attentive listener to his father's stories. Michael Tolkien recalled that Christopher, when between four and five years old, was greatly concerned with consistency as their father told the story of

The Hobbit in serial form, and on one occasion interrupted: 'Last time, *you said* Bilbo's front door was blue, and *you said* Thorin had a golden tassel on his hood, but you've just said that Bilbo's front door was green and that Thorin's hood was silver' (Christopher Tolkien, foreword to *The Hobbit* (Unwin Hyman, 1987), p. vii). Later Tolkien put him to work to find errors in the published *Hobbit*, at twopence a time.

Tolkien wrote in his diary that Christopher grew into 'a nervy, irritable, cross-grained, self-tormenting, cheeky person. Yet there is something intensely loveable about him, to me at any rate, from the very similarity between us' (quoted in *Biography*, p. 169). Christopher became a primary audience for *The Lord of the Rings*, for which he helped to make fair copies and typescripts and drew maps. He also read the *'Silmarillion' in manuscript.

In January 1942, aged only seventeen, he matriculated at Trinity College, *Oxford in order to complete some of his studies before being called up for war service. He entered the Royal Air Force in July 1943. In 1944 he went to *South Africa to train as a pilot; during this period of absence, his father wrote to him frequently, and periodically sent him parts of *The Lord of the Rings*. He returned to England in 1945 and was stationed in Shropshire; later that year, he returned to Oxford. On 9 October 1945 his father wrote to him that his friends in the *Inklings proposed 'to consider you a *permanent member*, with right of entry and what not quite independent of my presence or otherwise' (quoted in *Inklings*, p. 205). It now became Christopher's task to read aloud at Inklings meetings any new chapters of *The Lord of the Rings*, it having been generally agreed among the members that he read the work better than the author himself.

In April 1946 Christopher resumed his studies at Trinity College, where he read English. For a while his tutor was *C.S. Lewis. In 1949, having received his B.A., he was accepted as a B.Litt. student under the supervision of *E.O.G. Turville-Petre. His thesis was an critical edition and translation of an Old Icelandic work, *The Saga of King Heidrek the Wise* (published 1960). During the 1950s and early 1960s he was also a University Lecturer in Old and Middle English and Old Icelandic at Oxford. He worked with *Nevill Coghill to edit for separate publication three of *Chaucer's *Canterbury Tales*, the 'Pardoner's Tale' and the 'Nun's Priest's Tale' in 1958 and 1959 respectively, and the 'Man of Law's Tale' in 1969.

In 1963 Christopher was elected a Fellow of New College, Oxford. He resigned his fellowship in 1975, however, in order to devote himself to the administration of his father's literary affairs. Tolkien, who died in 1973, had named Christopher his literary executor, for whom a primary task was the publication of the 'Silmarillion' papers. Christopher assembled *The Silmarillion* (1977) from disparate manuscripts and typescripts, with the assistance of Guy Gavriel Kay, in only four years. In that time he also edited his father's translations of three medieval poems, *Sir Gawain and the Green Knight, Pearl and Sir Orfeo* (1975), and the *Nomenclature of The Lord of the Rings* (first published 1975 as *Guide to Names in The Lord of the Rings* in *A Tolkien Compass*).

In succeeding years, Christopher has balanced time-consuming responsibilities for the Tolkien Estate and the further study of his father's papers. In 1977 and 1978, portions of *The Silmarillion* recorded by Christopher were issued by Caedmon Records, New York. In 1979 notes he had written about his father's paintings and drawings for their publication in Tolkien calendars were reprinted in, or adapted for, the collection *Pictures by J.R.R. Tolkien*. The period 1980 to 1983 saw the publication of more important books edited or co-edited by Christopher: *Unfinished Tales*, *Letters of J.R.R. Tolkien* (with Humphrey Carpenter), *The Monsters and the Critics and Other Essays*, and *The Book of Lost Tales, Part One*. The last of these began a twelve-volume series, *The History of Middle-earth*, which ended in 1996. In 1988 Christopher also edited a new edition of *Tree and Leaf*, including the poem *Mythopoeia*.

Christopher's first wife, **Faith** (*née* **Faulconbridge**, *b.* 1928), took an English degree at Oxford and studied sculpture at the Oxford City Art School. They had one son, **Simon**. A bust of Tolkien by his daughter-in-law was exhibited at the Royal Academy. In 1966, when the English Faculty wished to buy a copy for their Library, Tolkien paid for its casting in bronze. Faith Tolkien has also sculpted his likeness on a commemorative plaque, as well as portraits of Roy Jenkins, Iris Murdoch, and *C.S. Lewis, and bronze reliefs on religious themes. See further, *Fr. Robert Murray, S.J., 'Faith Tolkien: A Theologian among Sculptors', *The Month* (August 1994).

Christopher's second wife, **Baillie** (*née* **Klass**, *b.* 1941), is the daughter of one of Tolkien's friends, Alan Klass, a surgeon and teacher in Manitoba. For a brief period Baillie (as Baillie Knapheis) was Tolkien's secretary, and was responsible for the section on poetry in the 1965 index to *The Lord of the Rings*. Later she edited the *'Father Christmas' letters for publication (1976 etc.). Christopher and Baillie Tolkien have had two children, **Adam** and **Rachel**.

See also *Children in the present volume; and Douglas A. Anderson, 'Christopher Tolkien: A Bibliography', in *Tolkien's Legendarium: Essays on The History of Middle-earth* (2000). Photographs of Christopher Tolkien are reproduced in *Biography*, pl. 9a and 10a; and on numerous pages in *The Tolkien Family Album*.

Tolkien, Edith Mary (*née* Bratt, 1889–1971). The future wife of J.R.R. Tolkien was born in Gloucester to Frances ('Fannie') Bratt of Wolverhampton and Alfred Frederick Warrilow, a paper dealer in the *Birmingham suburb of Handsworth. Frances, whose family owned a boot and shoe manufacturing business, was not married to Alfred, but a governess in the Warrilow household. Edith was brought up in Handsworth with her cousin *Jennie Grove; her mother died when Edith was fourteen.

Supported by a small income from land in Birmingham, Edith was sent to Dresden House, a boarding school in *Evesham run by the Watts sisters (who had received a musical education in Dresden; a photograph of the School is reproduced in *The Tolkien Family Album*, p. 27). There she developed a love of music and of playing the piano. At this time she had expectations of being a piano teacher or even a concert pianist. When, after leaving school, she lived with Mrs Louis Faulkner in Edgbaston, near Birmingham, her landlady was delighted to have a lodger who could play the piano at musical soirées; but Edith was not allowed to practise.

While at the Faulkners' she became friends with two fellow lodgers, Ronald and *Hilary Tolkien. She liked Ronald in particular:

> True, he was sixteen and she was nineteen. But he was old for his age and she looked young for hers, and she was neat and small and exception-ally pretty. Certainly she did not share his interest in languages, and she had received only a rather limited education. But her manner was very engaging. They became allies against 'the Old Lady', as they called Mrs Faulkner. [Humphrey Carpenter, *Biography*, p. 39]

Gradually their friendship blossomed into romance, as recounted more fully in **Chronology**. But their meetings, secret though they thought them, were observed, and gossip reached the ears of Ronald's guardian, *Father Francis Morgan. Father Francis, concerned both about his ward conducting a clandestine love affair and that such interest might distract from Ronald's school-work, forbade the romance and moved Ronald and Hilary to other lodgings. Before long Edith accepted an invitation to move to *Cheltenham to stay with two elderly family friends, 'Uncle' Charles and 'Auntie' Margaret Jessop (see photograph, *The Tolkien Family Album*, p. 29).

Edith now lived 'in comfort in a spacious house with several servants and could play to her heart's content on the grand piano. She also played the organ at the local Anglican church. . . . From playing the organ she developed a back injury, and to her lasting regret had to give up playing; nor did she ever fully recover' (*John and *Priscilla Tolkien, *The Tolkien Family Album*, p. 30). She spent hours copying music into albums, and she became engaged to George Field, the brother of a friend from school. When Ronald reached his twenty-first birthday in 1913 he wrote to Edith, learned of her engagement, and persuaded her to marry him instead.

During that same year Edith also agreed to convert to Ronald's faith, Roman Catholicism (see *Religion). In consequence, her Anglican 'Uncle' Jessop ordered her out of his home. She moved then with Jennie Grove to a rented house in *Warwick. On 22 March 1916 she married Ronald Tolkien, and in April moved to *Great Haywood, Staffordshire, near her husband's Army camp. There she enjoyed playing the piano while the local Catholic priest, *Father Augustine Emery, played the violin. But in June her husband was posted to *France, and for the next few months she followed his progress. She also acted as next of kin for her brother-in-law Hilary. On her husband's return from France with trench fever, she helped with his convalescence and made fair copies of parts of the mythology he had begun to write (**The Book of Lost Tales*).

Edith herself was an inspiration for Tolkien's story of the mortal Beren and his love, the elf-maiden Lúthien Tinúviel. As he wrote to his son *Christopher in 1972:

> I never called Edith *Lúthien* – but she was the source of the story that in time became the chief part of the *Silmarillion*. It was first conceived in a small woodland glade filled with hemlocks at Roos in *Yorkshire (where I was for a brief time in command of an outpost of the Humber Garrison in 1917, and she was able to live with me for a while). In those days her hair was raven, her skin clear, her eyes brighter than you have seen them, and she could sing – and *dance*. [11 July 1972, *Letters*, p. 420]

The lasting significance of this event to Tolkien is shown by the inscription on the gravestone he shares with Edith in Wolvercote Cemetery, Oxford: *Edith Mary Tolkien, Lúthien, 1889–1971. John Ronald Reuel Tolkien, Beren, 1892–1973*.

In November 1917 Edith gave birth to her first child, John. Tolkien was still in the Army, and moved from camp to camp; Edith, the baby, and Jennie Grove moved with him until doing so became too onerous. Her labour had been difficult, and Edith was often in pain even in the following year. At the end of the war in 1918, however, Tolkien was allowed to seek employment in *Oxford, and the family took up residence there. In 1919 they were able to rent their own small house.

Humphrey Carpenter comments in *Biography* that Edith had come from a non-intellectual background, had received only a limited education except in music, and had had little chance to improve her mind.

> More than this, she had lost a good deal of her independence. She had been set for a career as a piano teacher and just possibly as a soloist, but this prospect had simply faded away, first of all because there had been no immediate need for her to earn a living, and then because she had married Ronald Tolkien. In those days there was in normal circum-stances no question of a middle-class wife continuing to earn her living after marriage. . . . So piano playing was reduced to a mere hobby, although she continued to play regularly until old age, and her music delighted Ronald. He did not encourage her to pursue any intellectual activity, partly because he did not consider it to be a necessary part of her role as wife and mother, and partly because his attitude to her in court-ship . . . was not associated with his own intellectual life. . . . [*Biography*, pp. 153–4]

This, combined with an inclination to shyness, put Edith at a disadvantage at Oxford in 1918, with its formalities of social visits and the exchange of call-ing-cards. The university, she felt, 'was unapproachable in its eminence' (Carpenter, *Biography*, p. 154). She was not yet herself the wife of a don – Tol-kien was on the staff of the *Oxford English Dictionary* and an independent tutor – and was frightened of those who were.

What could she say to these people if she went into their imposing houses? What possible conversation could she have with these stately women, whose talk was all of people of whom she had never heard, of professors' daughters and titled cousins and other Oxford hostesses? . . . It became known that Mr Tolkien's wife *did not call* and must therefore be quietly excluded from the round of dinner-parties and At Homes. [*Biography*, pp. 154–5]

But she was in her own house, and could regularly play the piano. In October 1920 she gave birth to her second child, *Michael. By then Tolkien had accepted a teaching post at the University of *Leeds, and in 1921 Edith and her children moved north to join him. There she was pleased to find, in Humphrey Carpenter's words, that

people occupied ordinary modest houses, and there was no nonsense about calling-cards. Another university wife lived a few doors down in St Mark's Terrace and often called for a chat. Edith also began to see a good deal of Ronald's pupils who came in for tutorials or tea, and she liked many of them very much. . . . There were informal university dances which she enjoyed. . . . [*Biography*, p. 155]

On the whole she was happy in Leeds, though even with hired help it was difficult to keep her house and family clean in the 'dingy and soot-covered' city (*The Tolkien Family Album*, p. 45), and she had to take care with the family accounts, since her husband's post did not pay well.

In November 1924 the family was joined by a third son, Christopher. In 1926 they moved to a new house in Oxford, where Tolkien had been made Professor of Anglo-Saxon. In 1929 Edith gave birth to her fourth child, Priscilla. According to Carpenter, only in 1930, after the family moved from no. 22 to no. 20 Northmoor Road, into a larger house that could accommodate Ronald, Edith, and four children, 'could she feel settled' (*Biography*, p. 155).

Carpenter notes that Tolkien was loving and considerate of Edith, concerned about her health, and interested in household matters (see *Domestic duties). But he also argues that Edith sometimes felt ignored by her husband; that she was jealous of the time he spent in the company of his male friends, in particular *C.S. Lewis; that she cloaked uncertainty with authoritarian control of her home and its occupants; that she was often lonely,

without company other than the servants and the children during that part of the day when Ronald was out or in his study. During these years [the end of the 1920s and early 1930s] Oxford society was gradually becoming less rigid; but she did not trust it, and she made few friends among other dons' families, with the exception of *Charles Wrenn's wife, Agnes. She also suffered from severe headaches which could prostrate her for a day or more. [*Biography*, p. 156]

Furthermore, Carpenter says, Edith resented having been pressed to join the Catholic Church, a feeling which grew into anger which occasionally burst forth. Her husband, in contrast, had a true emotional connection to his faith, attended Mass often, and believed in frequent confession. 'After one such outburst in 1940 there was a true reconciliation between [Edith] and Ronald. . . . In the event she did not return to regular church-going, but for the rest of her life she showed no resentment of Catholicism, and indeed delighted to take an interest in church affairs . . .' (*Biography*, p. 157).

Despite such differences, Edith and her husband had a long and successful marriage. She was not a scholar, but took pride in Tolkien's achievements. Though not an expert in her husband's writings, she took a keen interest in them, and was the first person to whom he showed *Leaf by Niggle* and *Smith of Wootton Major*. She and Ronald shared many friends, such as the Wrenns, *Pauline Baynes and her husband Fritz Gasch, *Simonne d'Ardenne, *Joy Hill, *Robert Murray, and *Donald Swann; Edith never failed to ask about them and their families, and kept up her own correspondence. And both Edith and her husband were proud parents and grandparents.

In their later years Edith continued to be often in poor health. In particular she suffered from rheumatism and arthritis. So that Edith might spend her final years in greater comfort, away from the stress of Oxford society, with others of her own age with whom she felt at ease, after his retirement Tolkien willingly moved into a house without stairs in *Poole on the south coast of England, near the Hotel Miramar in *Bournemouth at which Ronald and Edith were frequent guests. There, Carpenter says, Edith 'ceased to be the shy, uncertain, sometimes troubled wife of an Oxford professor', and became 'herself once more, the sociable good-humoured Miss Bratt of the Cheltenham days' (*Biography*, p. 250). John and Priscilla Tolkien comment that their mother 'developed in her old age a kind of self-confidence, partly based on Ronald's success and prosperity, but to a great extent on her own inner strengths of character' (*The Tolkien Family Album*, p. 86).

Photographs of Edith Tolkien are reproduced in *Biography*, pl. 4a, 7, 10a, and 13, and on numerous pages in *The Tolkien Family Album*.

Tolkien, Hilary Arthur Reuel (1894–1976). Born in Bloemfontein (*South Africa) like his elder brother J.R.R. Tolkien, Hilary Tolkien was in contrast a healthy child who flourished in the climate of the Orange Free State. In April 1895 he sailed for England with his mother (*Mabel Tolkien) and brother on home leave, while his father, *Arthur Tolkien, remained in Bloemfontein; and upon Arthur's death they settled near *Birmingham. Like his brother, with whom he was close, Hilary attended St Philip's School for a short time, and at first failed the entrance examination to *King Edward's School, Birmingham. Of the latter his mother wrote to a relative: 'not my fault, or that he didn't know the things; but he is so dreamy and slow at writing' (quoted in *Biography*, p. 27). Not until after his mother's death in November 1904 did Hilary at last join his brother at King Edward's School, though he remained there only until

July 1910. Upon leaving he was given a post in the business of his uncle Walter Incledon (*Incledon family), but soon decided that he would rather work on the land. In 1911 he went on a walking tour of *Switzerland with his brother and members of the *Brookes-Smith family, for whom he was now working on a farm in Sussex.

Soon after the outbreak of war in Europe in August 1914 Hilary enlisted in the Army, as a private in the 16th Battalion of the Royal Warwickshire Regiment (originally the 3rd Birmingham 'City' Battalion, formed in September 1914). He saw long service in France from 1915 to 1918. A photograph of Hilary in 1914, as a bugler, is reproduced in *The Tolkien Family Album*, p. 39. In summer 1917 he received minor shrapnel wounds while helping to carry supplies over the Passchendaele Ridge near Ypres. Every time he was wounded, a telegram was sent to his designated next-of-kin, his sister-in-law *Edith Tolkien.

After the war, Hilary purchased a small orchard and market garden near Evesham (*West Midlands). When he was thirty-five he married **Magdalen Matthews**, whom he had met through the church choir in Evesham Catholic Church; they had three sons, **Gabriel**, born in 1931, **Julian**, born in 1935, and **Paul**, born in 1938.

Tolkien and family paid regular visits to Hilary, except in the period of petrol rationing during the Second World War. Tolkien's eldest son *John was also a regular visitor, and helped Hilary with fruit-picking during school and college vacations. Towards the end of their lives, when they were both widowers, Ronald and Hilary saw each other frequently. Humphrey Carpenter writes that

> Ronald and Hilary now resembled each other far more than they had ever done in their youth. Outside the window [at Evesham] the plum-trees whose crop Hilary had picked patiently for more than four decades had grown old and bore little fruit. They should be cut down, and fresh saplings planted in their place. But Hilary was past tackling such work, and the trees had been left standing. The two old brothers watched cricket and tennis on the television, and drank whisky. [*Biography*, p. 254]

Carpenter acknowledges assistance by Hilary, who told him much of Hilary and Ronald's early days, and corresponded with him at length during the writing of the *Biography*.

Additional photographs of Hilary Tolkien are reproduced in *Biography*, facing pl. 3a, and *The Tolkien Family Album*, p. 21.

Tolkien, John Francis Reuel (1917–2003). John Tolkien was the eldest of the four children of J.R.R. and *Edith Tolkien. Born in *Cheltenham, he was raised primarily in *Oxford and *Leeds. Some of his memories of childhood are related in *The Tolkien Family Album*, and helped to inform annotations to *Farmer Giles of Ham* and *Roverandom*, two of many stories devised by Tolkien partly for John's amusement (see also *The 'Father Christmas' letters). As a boy he attended the Dragon School, *Oxford, and the Oratory School, Caversham, *Berkshire; in his final year at the Oratory School he decided to become a Roman Catholic priest. From 1936 to 1939 he read English at Exeter College, *Oxford. In November 1939 he went to the Venerable English College in Rome to study and train for the priesthood. Although *Italy had not yet entered the war, she was an ally of Nazi Germany, and it was not long before the College determined that it was too dangerous to remain in Rome. On 11 May 1940 its priests and students, including John Tolkien, donned civilian clothes, journeyed north by train, and only just managed to board the last boat out of Le Havre. The College briefly settled at Ambleside in the Lake District, then for six years was in *Stonyhurst in Lancashire. There John's theological duties were combined with those of head gardener, in part to provide food for the staff and students.

John was ordained a priest on 10 February 1946 in the Church of St Gregory and St Augustine, Oxford, an achievement in which his parents felt great pride. He said his first Mass in the Church of St Aloysius, Oxford, later that some month. For the next forty-eight years he served in a succession of parishes: St Mary and St Benedict, Coventry; the English Martyrs at Sparkhill, Birmingham; Our Lady of Sorrows at Knutton, Staffordshire; the Church of Our Lady of the Angels and St Peter in Chains, Stoke-on-Trent; and St Peter's Church, Eynsham. Interested particularly in education, he oversaw the building of church schools. In North Staffordshire, in addition to his parish duties, he was chaplain to the University College (later Keele University), to the Catholic Teachers Association, to the Young Christian Students, and to area grammar schools. He was also concerned with ecumenism, which he attributed to his father; in Eynsham he furthered the close association of Catholics and Baptists. He retired to Oxford in 1994, but continued to be involved in Christian ministry as Chaplain of the De La Salle Brothers, a religious order of teachers living as religious brothers in community.

John Tolkien is buried in Wolvercote Cemetery, Oxford, near his parents.

With his sister *Priscilla, John wrote the text of *The Tolkien Family Album*, published in 1992.

See also *Children. Photographs of John Tolkien are reproduced in *Biography*, pl. 9a and 10a; and in *The Tolkien Family Album*, pp. 44 *et passim*.

Tolkien, Mabel (*née* Suffield, 1870–1904). The mother of J.R.R. Tolkien was one of six children of John and Emily Suffield (see *Suffield family) of Worcestershire. Unlike her younger sister Jane (*Emily Jane Neave), there is no record that Mabel attended King Edward VI High School for Girls in *Birmingham, but her letters reveal intelligence and wit beneath their idiosyncratic flourished script. One can also infer an active mind and a love of learning in the young Mabel from the many subjects in which she later instructed her sons: reading and writing, grammar, Latin, French, and German, botany, music, and art.

In 1888 she became engaged to *Arthur Tolkien, but because of her youth, her father forbade a formal betrothal for a period of two years. For the next few months, she and Arthur saw each other only at family parties and exchanged letters in secret. In 1889 Arthur left England for *South Africa to take a job with the Bank of Africa in the Cape colony; he became manager of the branch in Bloemfontein, capital of the Orange Free State, in 1890. In March 1891 Mabel, now twenty-one, sailed for South Africa on the *Roslin Castle*. She and Arthur were married in the cathedral in Cape Town in April 1891, and went to live in Bank House in Bloemfontein. Their two sons, Ronald and *Hilary, were born there in 1892 and 1894 respectively.

Although life in South Africa agreed with Arthur, Mabel found much to dislike. Writing home to her family, she described Bloemfontein as "Owlin' Wilderness! Horrid Waste!' (quoted in *Biography*, p. 11). A visit from her sister May (see *Incledon family) cheered her for a while in 1893, and she was bound by her love for Arthur; but she never came to enjoy the Bloemfontein climate or its social life, and was disturbed by colonists' racist treatment of the natives. Also she was concerned about young Ronald, who suffered badly from the heat. In April 1895 she, Ronald, and Hilary went to England at last on home leave, while Arthur continued with his work at the bank.

In February 1896 Arthur died from rheumatic fever. Mabel and her sons never returned to South Africa, and by summer 1896 moved from her parents' home in Kings Heath to the rural hamlet of *Sarehole. The dividend paid to Mabel by Arthur's legacy of shares in South African mines, supported by occasional help from relatives, could not support more than a low standard of living. For the time being Mabel herself educated her sons, except in geometry which was taught by her sister Jane. In 1955 Tolkien said that it was to his mother 'that I owe my tastes for philology, especially of Germanic languages, and for romance' (statement to the Houghton Mifflin Company, *Letters*, p. 218); and on 8 February 1967 he wrote to Charlotte and Denis Plimmer that his 'interest in languages was derived solely from my mother.... She knew German, and gave me my first lessons in it. She was also interested in etymology, and aroused my interest in this; and also in alphabets and handwriting' (*Letters*, p. 377). Nor did she neglect their religion: at first they attended a high Anglican church. Then in 1900 Mabel adopted the Roman Catholic faith, to which she had been increasingly drawn, and instructed her sons in it as well.

In that same year Mabel and the boys moved closer to the city. In 1902, after further moves of house, they settled in the suburb of Edgbaston, near the *Birmingham Oratory. There they were befriended by one of the priests, *Father Francis Morgan. Two years later, worn down by poverty, the opposition to her faith by some members of her family, and the strain of nursing her sons through serious illness, Mabel was admitted to hospital. She was found to have diabetes, for which there was not yet an effective treatment. Father Francis arranged for her to convalesce with her sons at *Rednal near the Oratory retreat. But her condition deteriorated, and she sank into a diabetic coma. She died in November 1904, and was buried in the Catholic churchyard in Bromsgrove, near Rednal.

Her death was a defining moment for Ronald Tolkien. He came to see her as a martyr to her faith, which strengthened his own devotion to the Catholic Church. In 1965 he wrote to his son *Michael:

> When I think of my mother's death . . . worn out with persecution, pov-
> erty, and, largely consequent, disease, in the effort to hand on to us small
> boys the Faith, and remember the tiny bedroom she shared with us in
> rented rooms in a postman's cottage in Rednal, where she died alone
> [in fact, her sister May and Father Francis Morgan were at her bedside],
> too ill for viaticum, I find it very hard and bitter, when my children stray
> away [from the Church]. [letter of 9–10 January 1965, *Letters*, pp. 353–4]

In Humphrey Carpenter's view, Mabel's death made Tolkien 'into two people', one with 'a deep sense of humour and a great capacity for making friends', the other 'more private . . . capable of bouts of profound despair' (*Biography*, p. 31).

A photograph of Mabel Tolkien is reproduced in *Biography*, pl. 1a, and *The Tolkien Family Album*, p. 16.

Tolkien, Michael Hilary Reuel (1920–1984). The second son of Ronald and *Edith Tolkien was born in *Oxford on 22 October 1920. Like his two broth-ers, he was educated at the Dragon School, Oxford, and the Oratory School in Caversham, *Berkshire. With his younger brother, *Christopher, he shared a passion for railways; and with Christopher and their elder brother *John he enjoyed the stories their father told them. While on holiday at *Filey, York-shire in summer 1925 Tolkien conceived the story of *Roverandom* to console Michael, then about five years old, when he lost a beloved toy dog. His father's drawings *Maddo* and *Owlamoo* (*Artist and Illustrator*, figs. 78–79) reflect fig-ures which haunted Michael's nightmares at about ages six through eight.

In 1939, early in the Second World War, Michael left the Oratory School and volunteered for Army service, but was ordered to first spend one year at university. Trinity College, *Oxford, allowed him to read History on reduced fees. During the Battle of Britain in 1940 he served as an anti-aircraft gunner in defence of aerodromes, for which he was awarded the George Medal. At the end of that year he was injured in a motor vehicle accident while on night training; but during his stay in hospital he met a nurse, **Joan Griffiths** (1916–1982), whom he married in November 1941.

According to his siblings John and *Priscilla in *The Tolkien Family Album*, Michael was 'appointed to coastal defence in Sidmouth in 1941', and while there 'persuaded his commanding officer to test the in situ guns. . . . The results were disastrous: the concrete gun emplacements were inadequate, and most of the guns collapsed!' (p. 65). Later that year, he transferred into the Royal Air Force, first as a gunner in night fighters, then as a rear-gunner in bombers, in which he saw action over France and Germany. In 1944 he was declared medic-ally unfit, and returned to Trinity College to complete his degree course. He took his finals in 1945. On 21 July 1946 Tolkien wrote to *Stanley Unwin:

My sons have survived [the war], though my second son, Michael, was much damaged in commando work, and returned still virtually a shell-shock case. . . . All he has got out of the war is the conversion of his certain 'first' in History into a gallant and very good 'second', since he had only two years to do the three years' work in, and started as a very sick man. I have still to find him a job. It is more difficult than I hoped – for a man with a George Medal, a good service record, a little business experience, and a year as a temporary Civil servant, and a good degree. [Tolkien-George Allen & Unwin archive, HarperCollins]

By then Michael and his wife had two children: **Michael George**, born in January 1943, and **Joanna** (**Joan Anne**), born in December 1944. (It was for Joanna that Tolkien later wrote the poem *Cat*.) A second daughter, **Judith**, was born in 1951.

For a brief time, Michael worked in Oxford on photographic research for the Admiralty, and for a year as a teacher at the Dragon School. From 1947 to the 1970s he taught successively at three prestigious Catholic boarding schools: the Oratory School, moved Woodcote in southern Oxfordshire; Ampleforth College in North Yorkshire; and *Stonyhurst in Lancashire.

Michael and his father frequently corresponded, and in later years spoke on the telephone, sometimes about difficult subjects such as the nature of marriage and changes in the Roman Catholic liturgy.

See also Derek Mills, 'An Interview with Michael Hilary Reuel Tolkien', conducted on Radio Blackburn in December 1975, transcribed by Gary Hunnewell with help from Sylvia Hunnewell, in *Minas Tirith Evening-Star* 18, no. 1 = *Ravenhill* 7, no. 4 (Spring 1989); and the entry *Children in the present volume. Photographs of Michael Tolkien are reproduced in *Biography*, pl. 9a, and on numerous pages of *The Tolkien Family Album*.

Tolkien, Priscilla Mary Reuel (*b.* 1929). The youngest child and only daughter of Ronald and *Edith Tolkien was born at home in 22 Northmoor Road, *Oxford. Her childhood fondness for toy bears and other soft toys inspired references in the *'Father Christmas' letters. From 1935 to 1939 she attended Rye St Antony, a small private school for girls run by two lay Catholic women, and from 1942 to 1947 the Oxford High School for Girls. Between 1939 and 1942 she was taught by a governess, her former piano teacher. From 1948 to 1951 she read English at Lady Margaret Hall, *Oxford, taking an honours degree; one of her tutors was Tolkien's colleague *Dorothy Everett.

In September 1952 Priscilla took a secretarial job in Bristol, where she remained until 1954. Later she worked as a secretary also in Birmingham. During this time she observed urban poverty, compounded by damage suffered in the war, such as she had never seen in Oxford; this led to an interest in social work. In 1956–8 she attended the London School of Economics, earning certificates in Social Science and Applied Social Studies, then returned to Oxford as a probation officer. In time she came to feel that her decision to put the academic world behind her while taking on a hard, demanding job was due partly to a desire to establish herself as an individual, not only as the daughter of a famous academic and author. Later she became a part-time tutor and lecturer in Social Work in the University of Oxford, then for five years (1966–71) was Tutor in Charge of the Social Work Training Course at High Wycombe College. For twelve years she taught English at Beechlawn Tutorial College. From 1982 to 2005 she conducted classes in Literature at her home.

As a trustee of the Tolkien Estate, Priscilla spends considerable time dealing with correspondence and other matters of business, and has represented the Tolkien family at public events such as the annual 'Oxonmoot' of the Tolkien Society (see *Fandom).

Priscilla lived with her parents after leaving university and while doing a secretarial course, but left home in 1952 when she took a job in Bristol. She went on holiday in *Ireland with her parents in 1951, and with her father to *Italy in 1955. Tolkien often depended upon Priscilla for help at home when Edith could not be left alone due to ill health. Priscilla's love of music was inherited from her mother, along with her mother's piano when Edith's arthritis no longer allowed her to play.

Priscilla has provided the present authors with much useful information about her family history, and has written numerous articles including 'My Father the Artist' in *Amon Hen* 23 (December 1976) and 'Memories of J.R.R. Tolkien in His Centenary Year' in *The Brown Book* (December 1992). See further, the bibliography to the present volume.

See also Janet McMeekin, 'Lady of the Rings', *Limited Edition: The Magazine of Oxfordshire* 77 (May/June 1993); and the entry *Children in the present volume. Photographs of Priscilla Tolkien are reproduced in *Biography*, pl. 9(a) and 10(a), and on numerous pages of *The Tolkien Family Album*.

Tolkien on Tolkien. Article, published in the magazine *Diplomat* (New York) for October 1966, p. 39. It is presented as if a single coherent work by Tolkien written especially for *Diplomat*, but in fact was assembled, by a person or persons unknown, from two sources written by Tolkien for other purposes.

The first of these was an autobiographical statement prepared by Tolkien for his American publisher, the Houghton Mifflin Company (*Publishers). Probably in May 1955 he had been asked to reply to a series of questions about himself and his works, to be used by Harvey Breit, the writer of the weekly column 'In and Out of Books' in the *New York Times Book Review*. When Tolkien saw what Breit had made of his answers, published on 5 June 1955, he wrote to Houghton Mifflin: 'Please do not blame me for what Breit made of my letter! . . . The original made sense . . .' (*Letters*, p. 218). With this he sent 'a few notes on points other than mere facts of my "curriculum vitae" (which can be got from reference books)'. Humphrey Carpenter comments in *Letters* (p. 218) that Houghton Mifflin made a typescript from Tolkien's notes, which 'was sent to a number of enquirers at different times, some of whom quoted from it in articles about Tolkien. Tolkien himself was given a copy of the typescript, and he made a number of annotations and corrections to it, which are incorporated into the text which is here printed.'

The second source was a letter written by Tolkien to Mrs Nancy Smith, begun Christmas Day 1963 and completed 2 January 1964. In December 1957 it had been agreed that George Allen & Unwin (*Publishers) would engage someone from among their regular indexers to compile an index of names in *The Lord of the Rings*, which Tolkien asked to have as an aid in dealing with translators of the work. The person hired for the task was Nancy Fisher Smith, coincidentally the wife of a former university roommate of *Christopher Tolkien. She completed her work by May 1958. Towards the end of 1963 Mrs Smith, now living in Cambridge, Massachusetts, wrote to Tolkien asking for biographical information, apparently for some Tolkien event she was to attend on 8 January 1964. Tolkien replied at length.

Some years later, Mrs Smith evidently showed his letter to whoever was preparing the Tolkien number of *Diplomat*, and gave permission for extracts from it to be published. When she realized that she had not asked Tolkien's permission to do this, she wrote to him. He replied on 30 May 1966, thanking her for the warning about the magazine: 'I hope the matter will not as distasteful and erroneous as most articles so far have been' (quoted in Christie's, *Fine Printed Books and Manuscripts*, New York, 24 May 2002, item 411). At the same time, the *Diplomat* editor obtained a copy of Tolkien's autobiographical statement, presumably from Houghton Mifflin's publicity department.

In *Tolkien on Tolkien* neither of these sources is credited, and material from them is freely intermingled. The full autobiographical statement sent by Tolkien to Houghton Mifflin, as later emended, was published in *Letters*, pp. 218–20, followed on p. 221 by the three paragraphs from Tolkien's first letter to Nancy Smith published in the *Diplomat* (but not so noted). The order in *Tolkien on Tolkien* with reference to *Letters* is: 'This business began ... Humber Garrison in 1913 [but see below]', *Letters*, p. 221 (letter to Smith); 'I think ... (as such)', *Letters*, p. 220 (statement); 'I came eventually ... stumbling blocks', *Letters*, p. 221 (letter to Smith); 'A primary "fact" ... this planet', *Letters*, pp. 219–20 (statement); 'Nothing has astonished ... comforting', *Letters*, p. 221 (letter to Smith).

Although the text was entirely written by Tolkien, his hope that it would not be erroneous went unrealized. The transcriber of the letter made several errors: *The Fall of Gandolin* instead of *The Fall of Gondolin*; *Deren* instead of *Beren*; 'while in the Humber Garrison in *1913*' instead of *1917*; and 'the sound of the *horses* of the Rohirrim at cockcrow' instead of 'the sound of the *horns*'. Humphrey Carpenter, who did not see the original letter, corrected the first two errors in *Letters*, but mistakenly altered the third to *1918* instead of *1917* – presumably because in *Biography* he had misdated the incident in Roos (*Yorkshire) – and overlooked the fourth error. In *Letters* he also corrected a further error in the section from the autobiographical statement, where *Middangeard* was given incorrectly as *Middangeart*.

In 2002 Tolkien's original letter to Nancy Smith was sold at Christie's, New

York, and is now in the possession of Marquette University (*Libraries and archives).

The Tolkien Reader. The first collection of shorter works by Tolkien, partly illustrated by *Pauline Baynes, first published by Ballantine Books, New York, in September 1966. See further, *Descriptive Bibliography* A8.

The volume contains *The Homecoming of Beorhtnoth Beorhthelm's Son*; *Tree and Leaf (i.e. *On Fairy-Stories and *Leaf by Niggle); *Farmer Giles of Ham*; and *The Adventures of Tom Bombadil and Other Verses from the Red Book. *Rayner Unwin reserved *Smith of Wootton Major for separate publication, and advised Tolkien that he should not include any of his academic works in a popular anthology. Tolkien felt, however, that *The Homecoming of Beorhtnoth Beorhthelm's Son*, with its accompanying essay on heroism ('Ofermod'), was 'very germane to the general division of sympathy exhibited in *The Lord of the Rings' (letter to Rayner Unwin, 25 April 1966, Tolkien-George Allen & Unwin archive, HarperCollins).

The Town of Dreams and the City of Present Sorrow. Poem, published with notes and associated texts in *The Book of Lost Tales, Part Two (1984), pp. 295–300.

In the first of its three parts ('Prelude') the poet looks back to days in which his 'fathers' sires' and their descendants 'took root / Among the orchards and the river-meads / And the long grasses of the fragrant plain', happy days of flowers and 'settled hours'. But 'now no more they sing, nor reap, nor sow', and the poet is an 'unsettled wanderer'. The second part, 'The Town of Dreams', is a picture of *Warwick (though not so named), 'this dear town of old forgetfulness' with its castle and 'mighty tower, / More lofty than the tiered elms'. In the third part, 'The City of Present Sorrow', the poet's attention turns to a distant city of willows on the river Thames, an 'agéd city of an all too brief sojourn' with a 'thousand pinnacles and fretted spires' – in fact, Oxford.

The earliest rough drafts of the poem were entitled *The Wanderer's Allegiance*. Later Tolkien gave it subtitles in three parts – 'Prelude', 'The Inland City', and 'The Sorrowful City' – and added the date 'March 16–17–18 1916'. A subsequent text bears the overall title *The Town of Dreams and the City of Present Sorrow* and the inscription 'March 1916, Oxford and Warwick; rewritten Birmingham November 1916'. Two texts are also extant which treat *The Town of Dreams* as a separate poem, with the subtitle *An Old Town Revisited*; in one of these Tolkien changed the title proper to *The Town of Dead Days. The City of Present Sorrow* was also treated as a separate poem in at least two texts, at first under the title *The Sorrowful City*, afterwards changed to *Winsele wéste, windge reste réte berofene* ('the hall of feasting empty, the resting places swept by the wind, robbed of laughter', a phrase adapted from *Beowulf*).

By March 1916 Tolkien had been in the Army for several months, training before his battalion was posted to the front lines in France. The happy days he had spent with his fiancée (*Edith Tolkien) in Warwick in 1913–15 were now a

treasured memory; the town had already been an inspiration to poetry (see
*The Trees of Kortirion). The City of Present Sorrow may have been inspired
by Tolkien's return to Oxford on 16 March 1916 for his long-delayed degree
ceremony.

Later, evidently at Easington in *Yorkshire c. 1917–18, Tolkien revised and
enlarged the 'Prelude' to The Town of Dreams and the City of Present Sorrow as
The Song of Eriol. Three manuscripts of this work are known, only the third of
which includes the second part of the poem. The pastoral imagery of the first
part (the former 'Prelude') was now followed by scenes of battle, 'Wars of great
kings and clash of armouries' rolling 'over all the Great Lands', armies burning 'fields and towns' and turning cities into 'flaming pyres'. There, the poet
says, his father fell 'on a field of blood' and his mother died 'in a hungry siege',
long ago.

> And now the dark bays and unknown waves I know,
> The twilight capes, the misty archipelago,
> And all the perilous sounds and salt wastes 'tween this isle
> Of magic and the coasts I knew awhile.

At this time Tolkien, still in Army service, was stationed with the Humber
Garrison near the shore of the North Sea. But the name Eriol (in the title of the
poem but nowhere in the text), and some of the narrative elements, link the
poem to the history of the mariner Eriol in *The Book of Lost Tales; see *Eriol
and Ælfwine.

The Tradition of Isildur
see Cirion and Eorl and the Friendship of Gondor and Rohan

Translations. The first translation of a work by Tolkien into another language
was evidently that of *Farmer Giles of Ham into French, made privately by
Tolkien's friend and colleague *Simonne d'Ardenne before 17 November 1937.
On that date Tolkien forwarded to his publisher, *Stanley Unwin, a letter from
a Mlle Tardivel, who wished to translate *The Hobbit into French. Tolkien
suggested d'Ardenne as a suitable translator as well; in the event, the first edition of The Hobbit in French, translated by Francis Ledoux, did not appear
until 1969. It was the aim of George Allen & Unwin (*Publishers) to interest
foreign commercial publishers in translations of Tolkien's works, and to this
end they worked industriously.

By July 1938 German translation rights in The Hobbit were negotiated, with
Rütten & Loening Verlag of Potsdam. On 22 July 1938, however, that publisher
wrote to Tolkien, stating that they had received approval for publication of
The Hobbit in German, subject to a declaration from the author of his Aryan
descent. Tolkien took issue with this (see *Prejudice and Racism), and also
expressed concern about the translation itself. On 10 February 1939 he wrote to
C.A. Furth at Allen & Unwin: 'The Germans promised to give me a chance of

reading and commenting on the translation before publication. Are they going to? I do not really mind very much; but certain expressions in their letters suggested that odd things might happen – e.g. to the nomenclature' (Tolkien-George Allen & Unwin archive, HarperCollins). In the event, because of the Second World War, the translation never materialized. On 21 July 1946 Tolkien sent to Furth a letter he had received from Horus Engels about a possible German translation of *The Hobbit*, and asked about the prospect of translations into other languages. Furth replied that the situation regarding German rights was still uncertain, only a year after the end of the war, but a Spanish publisher had shown an interest, and *The Hobbit* was on offer also to firms in Denmark and Czechoslovakia. A Dutch publisher had just declined it, saying that its peculiar charm and humour are of the type that Continental children, with their different tradition of children's books, are likely to miss. None of these efforts had any success, however, and thus the first translation of *The Hobbit* to be published was the Swedish *Hompen*, published in 1947.

There were no more translations of *The Hobbit* for some years, by which time the first translations of *The Lord of the Rings* had appeared. That work presented translators with a much more difficult problem, not only because of its length, but because of its complex and carefully constructed nomenclature. It was also a work about which Tolkien cared much more deeply. On 3 April 1956 he wrote to Mrs S. Newman, the foreign rights manager at Allen & Unwin, in regard to a proposed Dutch translation of *The Lord of the Rings*: 'I wish to avoid a repetition of my experience with the Swedish translation of *The Hobbit*. I discovered that this had taken unwarranted liberties with the text and other details, without consultation or approval' – most objectionably, from Tolkien's point of view, with the alteration of *Hobbit* to *Hompen*.

> It was also unfavourably criticized in general by a Swedish expert, familiar with the original, to whom I submitted it. I regard the text (in all its details) of *The Lord of the Rings* far more jealously. No alterations, major or minor, re-arrangements, or abridgements of this text will be approved by me – unless they proceed from myself or from direct consultation. [*Letters*, p. 249]

Tolkien was, in fact, surprised to learn that a translation of *The Lord of the Rings* was even to be attempted, 'in view of the bulk and difficulty of the book' (letter to Mrs Newman, 21 March 1956, Tolkien-George Allen & Unwin archive, HarperCollins). He also wrote on 3 April that it is

> surely intelligible that an author, while still alive, should feel a deep and immediate concern in *translation*. And this one is, unfortunately, also a professional linguist, a pedantic don, who has wide personal connexions and friendships with the chief English scholars of the continent.
> I am as eager as others for diffusion and profit, but I am also more strongly moved by linguistic considerations. The translation of *The Lord*

of the Rings will prove a formidable task, and I do not see how it can be performed satisfactorily without the assistance of the author. That assistance I am prepared to give, promptly, if I am consulted. . . .

By 'assistance' I do not, of course, mean interference, though the opportunity to consider specimens would be desirable. My linguistic knowledge seldom extends, beyond the detection of obvious errors and liberties, to the criticism of the niceties that would be required. But there are many special difficulties in this text. To mention one: there are a number of words not to be found in the dictionaries, or which require a knowledge of older English. On points such as these, and others that would inevitably arise, the author would be the most satisfactory, and the quickest, source of information. [Tolkien-George Allen & Unwin archive, HarperCollins, partly printed in *Letters*, pp. 248–9]

A few days later, on 6 April 1956, Tolkien referred to the question in a letter to *Rayner Unwin, again pointing out that *The Lord of the Rings* 'presents special problems, to some of which it is probable that I alone hold the key'. The Appendices, he said, presented 'a separate problem; and in their case at any rate reduction or even omission might in parts be a reasonable process. Only Appendix A v [*The Tale of Aragorn and Arwen*] is really essential to the story' (Tolkien-George Allen & Unwin archive, HarperCollins).

Daniël de Lange of the Dutch publisher Het Spectrum, who had been informed by Mrs Newman of Tolkien's comments, wrote to her on 24 May 1956 that the Dutch translation of the first half of *The Fellowship of the Ring* was nearly complete, and so far the translator, Max Schuchart, had not experienced particular difficulties, but had translated a few names into Dutch according to meaning or association. Schuchart had also suggested that Tolkien send him a list of points in the first volume where he thought a translator might go astray, and in reply would send Tolkien his solutions. Mrs Newman copied this letter to Tolkien, but before he could respond, he was sent Schuchart's proposed translations of various place-names on the map of the Shire ('Een Deel van de Streek') and the general map of Middle-earth ('Grote Kaart'). This reached him, unfortunately, during a busy part of term, so that he could not reply until 3 July: 'A glance was sufficient to show me that I should have to give careful consideration to the whole business, and to each item.' He did so by writing notes on six typed pages sent by Het Spectrum, which he elaborated in an eight-page commentary on Schuchart's lists sent with a long letter to Rayner Unwin. The matter, he said, 'disturbed and annoyed me greatly', and he hoped that Rayner could help him transmit his views to Het Spectrum in an appropriate tone and form.

Frankly, I do not understand how either the Dutch or your [foreign rights department] . . . could expect the versions of my place-names to have 'my approval' [which had been expected, or at least hoped]. Very slight acquaintance with the book, its structures, (or with me) should warn any one that I should regard it as an intolerable impertinence, and also stupidly unperceptive. . . . There must be some one in your [foreign rights department] that knows more Dutch than I, but even my knowledge of Dutch is enough to make it clear that the translator is stupid, and hasty, and, in this department of his work at any rate, incompetent to carry off his impertinence.

In principle I object as strongly as possible to the 'translation' of the *nomenclature* at all (even by a competent person). I wonder why a translator should think himself called on or entitled to do any such thing. That this is an 'imaginary' world does not give him any right to remodel it according to his fancy, even if he could in a few months create a new coherent structure which it took me years to work out.

I presume that if I had presented the Hobbits as speaking Italian, Russian, Chinese, or what you will, he would have left the names alone. Or, if I had pretended that 'the Shire' was some fictitious Loamshire of actual England. Yet actually in an imaginary country and period, as this one, coherently made, the nomenclature is a more important element than in an 'historical' novel. But, of course, if we drop the 'fiction' of long ago, 'The Shire' is based on rural England and not any other country in the world – least perhaps of any in Europe on Holland, which is topographically wholly dissimilar. (In fact so different is it, that in spite of the affinity of its language, and in many respects of its idiom, which should ease some parts of the translator's labour, its *toponymy* is specially unsuitable for the purpose.) The toponymy of *The Shire*, to take the first list, is a 'parody' of that of rural England, in much the same sense as are its inhabitants: they go together and are meant to. After all the book is English, and by an Englishman, and presumably even those who wish its narrative and dialogue turned into an idiom that they understand, will not ask of a translator that he should deliberately attempt to destroy the local colour. I do not ask that of a translator, though I might be glad of a glossary where (seldom) the meaning of the place-name is essential. I would not wish, in a book starting from an imaginary mirror of Holland, to meet *Hedge, Duke'sbush, Eaglehome,* or *Applethorn* even if these were 'translations' of 'sGravenHage, Hertogenbosch, Arnhem, or Apeldoorn! These 'translations' are not English, they are just homeless.

Actually the Shire Map plays a very small part in the narrative, and most of its purpose is a descriptive build-up. It is, of course, based on some acquaintance with English toponymical history, which the translator would appear not to possess (nor I guess does he know much of that of the Netherlands). But he *need not*, if he would leave it alone. The proper way to treat the first map is to change its title to *Een Deel von 'The Shire'* and no more; though I suppose *naar* for 'to' in such directions as '*To Little Delving*' w[oul]d do no harm.

The Translator has (on internal evidence) glanced at but not used the Appendices. He seems incidentally quite unaware of the difficulties he is creating for himself later. The 'Anglo-Saxon' of the Rohirrim is not much like Dutch! In fact he is pulling to bits with very clumsy fingers a web that he has made only a slight attempt to understand. His ignoring of actual pertinent parts of the *text* (see notes on *Haysend* and *Chetwood* . . .) also bode ill. If we turn to the actual list of Names, in the Small and Large Maps, that he submits – we shall see that (granted the right to remodel the nomenclature, which I deny) it is open to grave criticism.

The essential point missed, of course, is: even where a place-name is fully analysable by speakers of the language (usually not the case) this is not as a rule done. If in an imaginary land *real* place-names are used, or ones that are carefully constructed to fall into familiar patterns, these become integral names, 'sound real', and translating them by their ana-lysed senses is quite insufficient. This Dutchman's Dutch names should sound real Dutch. Well, actually I am no Dutch scholar at all, and know little of the peculiar history of Dutch toponymy, but I do not believe that as a rule they do. Anyway lots of them are *nonsense* or wholly erroneous, which I can only equal by supposing that you met Blooming, Newtown, Lake How, Documents, Baconbury, Blushing and then discovered the author had written Florence, Naples, (Lake or Lago di) Como, Chartres, Hamburg, and Flushing = Vlissingen!

In this regard, some critics have suggested that as *Florence* and *Naples* are actually Anglicized versions of *Firenze* and *Napoli*, Tolkien's case is invalid. Whichever name is used, however, it will be understood as referring to a place in Italy – the city on the Arno once ruled by the Medici, or that in the shadow of Vesuvius – and not some place in England or an unknown or imaginary place.

Tolkien continued:

I am sure the correct (as well as for publisher and translator the more economical?) way is to leave the maps and nomenclature alone as far as possible, but to substitute for some of the least-wanted Appendices a glossary of names (with meanings but no ref[erence]s). I could supply one for translation.

May I say now at once that I will *not* tolerate any similar tinkering with the *personal nomenclature*. Nor with the name/word *Hobbit*. I will not have any more [Swedish] *Hompen* (on which I was not consulted), nor any *Hobbel* [the translation of *Hobbit* in *Hobbiton* suggested by Schu-chart] or what not. Elves, Dwarfs/ves, Trolls, yes: they are mere modern equivalents of the correct terms. But *hobbit* (and *orc*) are of that world, and they must stay, whether they sound Dutch or not. . . .

I only venture to criticize the name-translation (or make suggestions) because I think it essential to indicate that this procedure is far more difficult than the translator supposes, is unnecessary as well as destruc-tive. I do not wish apart from this matter which concerns me deeply to pose as a 'translator'! My kn[owledge] of Dutch is quite insufficient, and I shall naturally bow to the translator's general competence in text and dialogue – unless his mistakes are glaring (as seems not beyond possibility) – and content myself with assisting with any difficulties which he wishes to refer to me. [3 July 1956, Tolkien-George Allen & Unwin archive, HarperCollins, partly printed in *Letters*, pp. 249–51]

On 9 July, as requested, Rayner Unwin wrote a letter to Het Spectrum, putting Tolkien's position more diplomatically. This was sent later in the month, with Tolkien's approval, accompanying his pages of comments:

Professor Tolkien is somewhat disturbed by the extent to which you intend to translate his nomenclature, and in certain cases questions the accuracy of the meaning that a Dutch reader would gather from your translator's version. In particular he feels most strongly that whenever an invented word – such as Hobbit, Orc, etc. has been used no attempt should be made to 'translate' it.

He suggests that your translator might be well advised to make the very minimum alterations to place names (obviously words of direction, explanation or words in common usage may safely be translated), but 'translation' can scarcely be justified in cases where no direct English significance is attached to a word, or where such significance is entirely dependent on an inter-association of purely English ideas. In such cases Professor Tolkien suggests you should leave his own carefully devised nomenclature, but add at the end, if you think appropriate, a glossary of Dutch parallels in the few cases where the meaning of a place name is essential (in the compiling of the English side of this Professor Tolkien has indicated his own willingness to help). . . .

That Professor Tolkien feels strongly on this subject of nomenclature will be appreciated when it is considered that he has devoted many years thought to the perfection of these names, and regards their retention, in essence, as an integral part of the structure of his book. In the case of words of his own invention, such as *Hobbit*, etc., he is firm in regarding them as unalterable, and he seriously recommends your translator to consider his treatment of proper names in general in the light of his own detailed comments which we attach. [George Allen & Unwin archive, University of Reading]

Daniël de Lange wrote a preliminary reply on 19 July 1956. Het Spectrum agreed that many of their suggested translations of names would have to be changed. They accepted that the names of Elves and Dwarves should remain unchanged, but on principle felt that names which have to Dutch ears an English ring should be translated – that is, all Hobbit names, including *Hobbit*, and names in the Common Speech. On 24 July de Lange wrote again at greater length, pointing to statements by Tolkien in the Appendices of *The Lord of the*

Rings which, he felt, justified translation. He cited from Appendix E II: 'The Westron or Common Speech has been entirely translated into English equivalents. All Hobbit names and special words are intended to be pronounced accordingly'; and from Appendix F II ('On Translation'), the most relevant extracts (here italicized) from Tolkien's explanation why the Common Speech had been 'translated' into English:

Only the languages alien to the Common Speech have been left in their original form; but these appear mainly in the names of persons and places.

The Common Speech, as the language of the Hobbits and their narratives, has inevitably been turned into modern English. . . .

I have also translated all Westron names according to their senses. When English names or titles appear in this book it is an indication that names in the Common Speech were current at the time, beside, or instead of, those in alien (usually Elvish) languages. . . .

It seemed to me that to present all the names in their original forms would obscure an essential feature of the times as perceived by the Hobbits (whose point of view I was mainly concerned to preserve): the contrast between *a wide-spread language, to them as ordinary and habitual as English is to us,* and the living remains of far older and more reverend tongues. All names if merely transcribed would seem to the modern reader equally remote. . . .

The name of the Shire (Sûza) and all other places of the Hobbits have thus been Englished.

De Lange further argued that Tolkien's imaginary world was not intrinsically English, but whole in and of itself. If the names were left untranslated, they would (he felt) appear alien to Dutch readers, and not 'ordinary and habitual'. Since *Hobbit*, to begin with, definitely sounded too English, Het Spectrum wished to use *Hobbel*.

Rayner Unwin replied at once on 25 July:

I feel a word of advice might be useful, particularly with regard to the name word Hobbit. Professor Tolkien, being by profession something of an expert on linguistics, feels deeply, and, perhaps you may say irrationally on this score, but I feel that in order to preserve his good will it would be wise to bow to his feelings in the spelling of this particular word [*Hobbit*]. Although the names in 'Common Speech' sound English, many of them are undefinable and cannot be transposed into Dutch or any other language without some harm to the fabric of the imagery. Neither you nor I would transpose the names in say, one of the great Russian novelists, into an English or Dutch version, we would accept the strangeness of the names of the characters as a part of the book. By the same analogy Professor Tolkien feels his created names, though somewhat strange to Dutch ears, should stand. [George Allen & Unwin archive, University of Reading]

In this he achieved at least one success: two days later, Het Spectrum agreed to yield on the name *Hobbit*. They felt, however, that Russian names in a Russian book set a known geographic environment were not a good analogy, and that the correct tone for Tolkien's book was one which suggests both indefiniteness and familiarity. (In fairness, it should be noted that, according to Max Schuchart in an interview conducted by Renée Vink, it was Daniël de Lange, and not the translator himself, who wished to 'Dutchify' Tolkien's nomenclature, at first in its entirety. See Renée Vink, 'Translation Troubles of an Author: Some Reflections on an Angry Letter by Tolkien', *Lembas-extra 93/94* [?1994].)

On 19 November 1956 Het Spectrum sent copies of the Dutch translation of *The Fellowship of the Ring* to Allen & Unwin and asked to be told what Tolkien thought about it. Tolkien wrote on 24 November 1956, before the book arrived:

> My knowledge of Dutch is not really adequate for general praise or blame. Nomenclature was a different & easier matter. I have *not* been consulted at all at any, or on any other point by the translator; so if he has made any minor 'howlers' of detail it will be his own fault. It is likely enough. There are quite a few things which even [his friend Professor P.N.U.] Harting of Amsterdam, the Dutchman with the most impeccable knowledge of English (and of *The Lord* &c.) would require to refer to the author. . . .
>
> As for myself I shall not have time to scrutinize the result very closely, & in any case have no intention of being unkind. I do not think that, even if merited, strong adverse criticism from me would do any good. . . .
>
> I still think the 'translation' of the nomenclature a primary blunder, indicative of a wrong attitude; and as I was not able to carry that point, I do not suppose I should be more successful in other points. [letter to Rayner Unwin, Tolkien-George Allen & Unwin archive, HarperCollins]

On receiving a copy, Tolkien noted that his name was incorrect on the dust-jacket: 'J.R. Tolkien'. On 30 January 1957 Rayner Unwin forwarded to Tolkien queries from Max Schuchart relating to *The Two Towers* and *The Return of the King*. On 3 February Tolkien replied, enclosing a long letter to be sent to Het Spectrum which dealt not only with queries, but also points he has noted during his reading of the Dutch *Fellowship of the Ring*. He asked Rayner to glance at them, and hoped that he had 'been sufficiently polite. After all they cannot expect me not to notice actual errors – and a close examination would show these to be fairly numerous . . .' (Tolkien-George Allen & Unwin archive, HarperCollins).

While dealing with the problems of the Dutch translation, Allen & Unwin had also been negotiating Swedish rights for *The Lord of the Rings* with Almqvist & Wiksell/Gebers Förlag. Disa Törngren wrote to Allen & Unwin on

3 July 1956 that the publisher had chosen Dr Åke Ohlmarks as translator but, because he was busy, publication might be delayed until 1958. Rayner Unwin replied on 15 August 1956 that Allen & Unwin would send a contract which

> will be normal in all respects except for one Clause which the author requires us to insert which concerns proper names of both people and things. The author does not wish these to be altered or 'translated' into another language without his prior consent. In effect he regards the invented and imaginary names for the most part non-translatable. If Dr Ohlmarks has any queries or doubts on this score, or on points that may arise, he will find Professor Tolkien most willing to help. [George Allen & Unwin archive, University of Reading]

It was not until the end of 1957 that anything further was heard of the Swedish translation. Early in December Rayner Unwin delivered to Tolkien in Oxford a letter and enclosures from Åke Ohlmarks. On 7 December Tolkien wrote to Rayner that this

> was both puzzling and irritating. A letter in Swedish from fil. dr. Åke Ohlmarks, and a huge list (9 pages foolscap) of names in [*The Lord of the Rings*] which he has altered. I hope that my inadequate knowledge of Swedish – no better than my kn[owledge] of Dutch, but I possess a very much better Dutch dictionary! – tends to exaggerate the impression I received. The impression remains, nonetheless, that Dr. Ohlmarks is a conceited person, less competent than charming if inadequate Max Schuchart, though he thinks much better of himself. In the course of his letter he lectures me on the Swedish language and its antipathy to borrowing foreign words (a matter which seems beside the point), a procedure made all the more ridiculous by the language of his letter, more than ⅓ of which consists of 'loan-words'. . . .
>
> I find this procedure puzzling; because the letter and the list seem totally pointless unless my opinion and criticism is invited. But if this is its object, then surely the timing is both unpractical and impolite, presented together with a pistol: 'We are going to start the composition now'. Neither is my convenience consulted: the communication comes out of the blue in the second most busy academic week of the year. I have had to sit up far into two nights to survey the list. Conceding the legitimacy or necessity of translation (which I do not, except in a limited degree) the translation does not seem to me to exhibit much skill, and contains a fair number of positive errors. Even if excusable, in view of the difficulty of the material, I think these regrettable, & they could have been avoided by earlier consultation. It seems to me fairly evident that Dr O. has stumbled along dealing with things as he comes to them, without much care for the future or co-ordination, and that he has not read the Appendices at all, in which he would have found many answers.

By now, Tolkien had written directly to the publisher, Almqvist, insisting that the word *hobbit* remain unaltered.

> I have also written to Ohlmarks, sending detailed criticism of his list. I have told him that, though unconvinced by his arguments, I concede the legitimacy of translating names that are cast in modern English form, and are or are meant to have an intelligible meaning for mod[ern] English readers; but all other names should be left alone – if they are not English there is no reason why they sh[oul]d be Swedish. I have insisted upon *hobbit*. (I do not suppose that I have any real power in the matter; but I hope the protest will be effective.) . . .
>
> I do hope that it can be arranged, if and when any further translations are negotiated, *that I should be consulted at an early stage.* . . .
>
> I see now that the lack of an 'index of names' is a serious handicap in dealing with these matters. If I had an index of names (even one with only reference to Vol. and chapter, not page) it would be a comparatively easy matter to indicate at once all names suitable for translation (as being themselves according to the fiction 'translated' into English), and to add a few notes on points where (I know now) translators are likely to trip. So far, though both eager to translate the toponymy into other terms, and deliberately to efface the references to England (which I regard as integral and essential) neither appear to be at all conversant with English toponymy, or even to be aware that there is anything to know. Nor do they consult large dictionaries when faced by anything that is not current. [letter to Rayner Unwin, 7 December 1957, Tolkien-George Allen & Unwin archive, HarperCollins, partly printed in *Letters*, pp. 263–4]

It would seem that the contract clause about altering or translating names mentioned in Rayner's letter to the Swedish publisher on 15 August 1956 was not clearly worded, or was interpreted to mean that if consulted, Tolkien would consent to such change.

In any case, Tolkien seems to have judged that he had no hope of preserving the Englishness of the names that he considered 'integral and essential', and decided that if the names were to be translated, they should be translated correctly. He tried to make a stand with *Hobbit*, but Almqvist or Ohlmarks refused to give way, and *Hobbit* became *Hob*, but at least not *Hompen*. Further correspondence between Ohlmarks and Tolkien took place directly rather than through Allen & Unwin, and copies of the letters are not preserved in the publisher's files. Apart from problems with the actual translation, Tolkien was offended when he received a copy of the Swedish *Fellowship of the Ring* and found that Ohlmarks had included a preface with an inaccurate biography of the author and his own interpretation of Tolkien's work, both of which Tolkien thought 'impertinent nonsense' (letter to Alina Dadlez, 16 January 1961, Tolkien-George Allen & Unwin archive, HarperCollins). See *Letters*, pp. 305–7.

Since Daniël de Lange of Het Spectrum cited Tolkien's own words in

Appendices E and F against him, it may be significant that soon after he laboured so hard to produce the Appendices for publication, Tolkien was willing to discard some or all of them in translation. Even before the battle with Het Spectrum, Tolkien suggested in his letter to Rayner Unwin of 6 April 1956 that some of the Appendices might be omitted from a translation, presumably because much of E and F was addressed to English-speaking readers. In March 1957, in a letter to Max Schuchart, he suggested that some parts of the Appendices might disappear, including F II, and D except for the section on the Shire Calendar. After an index of names in *The Lord of the Rings* was compiled for him by May 1958, he wrote to Rayner Unwin: 'I think some specific use should be made of it in some later edition and/or revision. . . . Some of what exists [in the Appendices] could be dropped without any damage at all, I think. I should say . . . most of Appendix D (other than [the Shire Calendar]); probably most of App[endix] E II, and most of F II, for a start: possibly some 15 pages' (27 May 1958, Tolkien-George Allen & Unwin archive, HarperCollins). When the Swedish publisher requested permission to omit the Appendices from *The Return of the King*, and possibly to publish them separately, Tolkien wrote to Alina Dadlez:

> I have no objection . . . to the omission of C, D (except for the Shire Calendar . . .), E ii and F ii. Omission of the remainder would be, in differing degrees, damaging to the book as a whole. In the case of Het Spectrum, A and B and the Shire Calendar were retained, and that is the arrangement that I favour. I feel strongly that the absolute minimum is retention of A (v) 'Of Aragorn and Arwen', and the Shire Calendar: two items essential to the understanding of the main text in many places. [24 January 1961, Tolkien-George Allen & Unwin archive, HarperCollins]

Following Tolkien's difficulties with the Swedish *Lord of the Rings*, contracts for translations of both *The Hobbit* and *The Lord of the Rings* stipulated that the word *Hobbit* be retained. Tolkien was, however, willing to accept another word in special circumstances. When a new Swedish translation of *The Hobbit* was being prepared, Tolkien wrote to Alina Dadlez that it might be best to use the same word which had appeared in the Swedish *Lord of the Rings* – but 'Hobbit' was used nonetheless. In a letter about the Spanish translation of *The Hobbit* on 20 July 1962 he wrote: 'In a Latin language *hobbits* looks dreadful, and if I had been earlier consulted I would have readily agreed to some naturalization of the form: e.g. *hobitos*, which consorts better with the long-adopted *elfos*, while having the good fortune to contain the normal Sp[anish] diminutive suffix, and a stem *hob-*, which as far as I know has no associations in Spanish' (Tolkien-George Allen & Unwin archive, HarperCollins). Dadlez passed Tolkien's comments to the publisher, Fabril, in Buenos Aires, who replied on 14 September 1962 that as *h* is mute in Spanish perhaps it should be *jobitos*. Dadlez put this to Tolkien, who wrote on 19 September: 'I prefer *hobitos* since it preserves to the eye more relationship to the original word. I do not much mind the *h* being "mute"; I am sure many hobbits drop their *h*s like most rural folk in England' (Tolkien-George Allen & Unwin archive, HarperCollins).

On 13 May 1968, André Bay of Editions Stock, who were about to publish a French translation of *The Hobbit*, wrote to Alina Dadlez that he was unhappy about the word *Hobbit*, which had unfortunate connotations in French – which, however, he did not dare explain to a woman. He suggested *Hopin* instead. When this was put to Tolkien he replied: 'I must rely on the objections raised by those who know more of the depths of the colloquial language! Anyway *hopin* seems to me a suitable and ingenious solution: *hopin/lapin* = *hobbit/rabbit*, I suppose. Not that I intended any such connexion. . . . So *hopin* let it be: as long as any illustrator is aware that this should not influence him unduly' (15 May 1968, Tolkien-George Allen & Unwin archive, HarperCollins). In the end, the French translation also used the form *hobbit*.

Tolkien may simply have been unlucky in dealings for the first translations of *The Lord of the Rings*. Later negotiations went more smoothly, possibly because those translators were more willing to listen; but in fact, Tolkien himself had more or less conceded that names could be translated, even if this was not what he really wished. He concentrated his efforts on promoting correct translation.

On 1 July 1959 Alina Dadlez forwarded to Tolkien a letter from Maria Skibniewska, who was to translate *The Lord of the Rings* into Polish for the publisher Czytelnik. Tolkien wrote to Dadlez on 3 July that he would try to answer Skibniewska as soon as possible.

> A proper answer will of course need a sketch of the general policy for her to follow (if she agrees), and that will require some thinking out. Though I have thought about the difficulties of name-translation in a language quite alien to English. . . .
>
> Do you think it would be useful if I cast my remarks in a form generally suitable? For instance, it might be then available for a Hebrew translation [a contract for one had just been signed]. Translators are of course of very different kinds. Not all are as humble as the Polish lady. [Tolkien-George Allen & Unwin archive, HarperCollins]

This might sound like a complete surrender, or even a change of opinion regarding the translation of names, but on 11 September 1959 Tolkien wrote to Alina Dadlez:

> As a general principle for [Mrs Skibniewska's] guidance, my preference is for as little translation or alteration of any names as possible. As she perceives, this is an English book and its Englishry should not be eradicated. That the Hobbits actually spoke an ancient language of their own is of course a pseudo-historical assertion made necessary by the nature of the narrative. . . . My own view is that the names of persons should all be left as they stand. I should prefer that the names of places were

left untouched also, including Shire. The proper way of treating these I think is for a list of those that have a meaning in English to be given at the end, with glosses or explanation in Polish. I think a suitable method or procedure would be that which was followed in the Dutch and Swedish versions, with Mrs. Skibniewska making a list of all the names in the book which she finds difficult or which she might for any reason wish to alter or translate. I will then be very happy to annotate this list and criticise it. [Tolkien-George Allen & Unwin archive, HarperCollins, partly printed in *Letters*, p. 299]

He asked Allen & Unwin for a spare copy of the index of names, so that he could mark on it all of those that are not English and therefore should not be translated.

Nothing more seems to have been heard of this until 12 December 1966, when Tolkien wrote to Alina Dadlez about a forthcoming Danish *Lord of the Rings*:

When I was reading the specimens of the proposed German translation, I began to prepare an annotated name list based on the index: indicating those names that were to be left unchanged and giving information of the meaning and origin of those that it was desirable to render into the language of translation, together with some tentative advice on how to proceed. I hope soon to complete this and be able to send you a copy or copies for the use of translators. . . . [Tolkien-George Allen & Unwin archive, HarperCollins]

Thus came into being the *Nomenclature to The Lord of the Rings*, which was sent to translators of Tolkien's works, and any question of retaining the original names was abandoned. Whether Tolkien came to feel that translation of the Common Speech names 'represented' by English was the best course, is another matter. Given the care he took to create a coherent structure of relationships based on English, and his strongly expressed opinions about the earliest translations of his works, it seems most likely that he simply abandoned a battle he saw that he could not win.

Renée Vink considers this problem in 'Translation Troubles of an Author', relying only on published material. She wonders if 'Tolkien had grown wiser by bitter experience' (p. 49), and concluded from the *Nomenclature* that Tolkien 'had changed his views about the translation of the English names'. But 'was it a choice between the least of two evils – if they have to translate things, let them do it according to my personal directions? Or did he change his principles, because he found his arguments of July 1956 no longer tenable?' (p. 50). After discussing the validity of the various objections to translation put forward by Tolkien, and his feelings for a work into which he put so much effort and thought, Vink concludes:

But if things are this way, it is not so very likely that Tolkien really changed his mind about the translation of his nomenclature. He was of course quite right when he stated that his network of names could not be translated undamaged in another language. But he could do nothing about it and will have chosen, for want of a better option, for the least of two evils: taking care by giving instructions that the translations would still come to something. . . .

Maybe, all in all, he was right. Rather an English map of the Shire than the present Dutch 'Shire'. Rather a not completely succeeded mythology for England than an Ardalogical no-man's land. Rather no translation than an erroneous one. [pp. 56–7]

A considerable amount of attention has been paid to how Tolkien's works have been translated, and to the discussion of problems faced by translators. See especially David Doughan, ed., *Translations of The Hobbit Reviewed* (1988), *Quettar Special Publication* 2; Natalia Grigorieva, 'Problems of Translating into Russian', *Proceedings of the J.R.R. Tolkien Centenary Conference 1992* (1995); Thomas Honegger, ed., *Tolkien in Translation*, Cormarë 4 (2003), containing six papers, five of them dealing with translations into Norwegian, French, Spanish, Esperanto, and Russian; Thomas Honegger, ed., *Translating Tolkien: Text and Film*, Cormarë 6 (2004), the first seven papers of which deal with Tolkien's conception of Westron and English, and translations into German, Hebrew, Latin, Dutch, and Swedish; Mark Hooker, *Tolkien through Russian Eyes*, Cormarë 5 (2003); Ron Pirson, ed., 'Schuchart vs. Mensink-van Warmelo: Round Two', *Lembas-extra 2004* (2004); Allan Turner, *Translating Tolkien: Philological Elements in The Lord of the Rings* (2005); and the column 'Transitions in Translations' by Arden R. Smith in some issues of *Vinyar Tengwar*.

Travel and transport. Tolkien retained only a few memories of his earliest journeys, a long train ride to the coast of *South Africa when he was not yet three, and about four months later, a voyage from South Africa to *England. He then spent several impressionable early years in the English countryside where he rarely saw a car. On 1 January 1904, when a law requiring motor-cars to be licensed came into effect, only 23,000 cars were registered in the whole of Great Britain.

In going to school from the various places he lived, Tolkien walked, or took a tram or train. When he began to attend *King Edward's School in *Birmingham in autumn 1900, still some months short of his ninth birthday, he and his family were still living in rural *Sarehole, some four miles from the centre of Birmingham, and 'for the first few weeks Ronald had to walk much of the way, for his mother could not afford the train fare and the trams did not run as far as his home' (Humphrey Carpenter, *Biography*, p. 24). At the end of 1900 he and his family moved to Moseley, which is nearer the centre of Birmingham and had better transport. As Tolkien told interviewer Keith Brace:

'I walked into the centre of the city every day; from the age of eight. Children walked long distances in those days' ('In the Footsteps of the Hobbits', *Birmingham Post*, 25 May 1968). Towards the end of his time at Sarehole Tolkien also took a long walk with his mother each Sunday to a 'high' Anglican church; and later to St Anne's, the Roman Catholic church in Alcester Street near the centre of Birmingham. In a reply to a letter from children at a primary school on 17 October 1966, Tolkien wrote that he used to walk from Sarehole to visit an uncle who lived in *Acocks Green, some two miles distant (quoted in Sotheby's, *English Literature, History, Children's Books and Illustrations*, London, 16 December 2004, p. 274).

During autumn 1904, when he and his brother *Hilary were living with their convalescent mother (*Mabel Tolkien) at *Rednal some distance from central Birmingham, 'Ronald had to rise early and walk more than a mile to the station to catch a train to school. It was growing dark by the time he came home, and Hilary sometimes met him with a lamp.' While staying in Rednal, if there was no priest resident at Oratory House, the Tolkien family would 'drive to mass in Bromsgrove [see *Rednal] sharing a hired carriage with . . . the gardener and caretaker for the Oratory fathers' (*Biography*, p. 30) – undoubtedly a carriage drawn by horses.

For greater distances, the train was the most used form of transport, and at the beginning of the twentieth century the rail network in England was extensive. Tolkien travelled by train to away matches for King Edward's School football, to courses with the Officers Training Corps (*Societies and clubs), to *London for the Coronation in 1911, and presumably to stay with Edwin and *Jane Neave in *Hove in 1904, to seaside holidays at *Lyme Regis and *Whitby, and to sit the entrance examination at *Oxford in 1909 and 1910.

When Tolkien went up to Oxford in 1911 he and a fellow scholar at King Edward's School were driven there by their teacher *R.W. Reynolds in a car, 'then a novelty' (letter to the Rev. Denis Tyndall, 9 January 1964, *Letters*, p. 343). In 1913, while acting as a chaperon to Mexican boys in *France, Tolkien had the experience of riding in a charabanc (motor-coach; see photograph in *The Tolkien Family Album*, p. 36). Although he frequently commented on the noise and pollution caused by the increasing numbers of cars, and the destruction of the countryside to provide roads for them (see *Environment), he himself bought a second-hand car in the autumn of 1932, and drove that and its successor until the introduction of petrol rationing in the Second World War. *John and *Priscilla Tolkien describe these cars, and their father as a driver, in *The Tolkien Family Album*:

Later that year Ronald purchased our first car – a dignified Morris known as Old Jo, followed shortly by an updated model known as Jo 2. There was no such thing as a driving test then, so Ronald was able to drive, but not always safely: as might be guessed from his tale of Mister Bliss [*Mr. Bliss]! The car – or rather the combination of the car and Ronald as driver – produced some adventures; notably an early outing to visit his brother Hilary on his small farm near Evesham. . . . This was no great distance away, yet in the space of a very few miles, not only did he drive off the road and demolish a wall, but also managed to get a puncture. It was not easy in those days to find a garage to mend it, and what with the accident and the long wait, only part of the family was willing to make the return trip in the car! [p. 63, with a photograph of 'Jo 2']

Tolkien drove his family on short excursions into the countryside around Oxford and, when the family spent a summer holiday in *Sidmouth, would drive there alone with the car packed with luggage and the soft toys Priscilla refused to leave behind, while Edith and the two younger children would travel by train, and the elder boys would ride to their destination on bicycles. Tolkien bought his second car in 1937 partly with money from *The Hobbit; it was evidently more comfortable than the first 'Jo', and it may be that by then Tolkien's driving had improved. He wrote to his son *Michael on 3 October 1937: 'Mummy seems to have taken to car-riding' (*Letters*, p. 23).

In 1915–16 Tolkien had a share in a second-hand motor bicycle which he used to visit his wife (*Edith Tolkien) or others when on leave from military training. Later he often rode a bicycle from his home in Oxford to his colleges or to give lectures, or to attend church in all weathers, even in heavy snow ('Indescribable mixture of ice and slush. I fell off [the bicycle] three times, and was, of course, hustled into the gutter and drenched . . . by those amiable people who drive "private cars"': letter to Christopher Tolkien, 30 January 1945, *Letters*, p. 109).

In 1911 Tolkien joined a party which included his brother Hilary and his aunt Jane Neave, on a walking tour in the Swiss Alps (*Switzerland) which had a considerable influence on *The Hobbit* and *The Lord of the Rings. Another seminal influence on his writing was a visit to the Lizard Peninsula (*Cornwall) in August 1914 with *Father Vincent Reade. Tolkien described one of their daily long walks in a letter to Edith: after a day exploring some inland villages,

> our walk home after tea started through rustic 'Warwickshire' scenery, dropped down to the banks of the Helford river (almost like a fjord), and then climbed through 'Devonshire' lanes up to the opposite bank, and then got into more open country, where it twisted and wiggled and wobbled and upped and downed until dusk was already coming on and the red sun was just dropping. Then after adventures and redirections we came out on the bleak bare 'Goonhilly' downs and had a four mile straight piece with turf for our sore feet. Then we got benighted in the neighbourhood of Ruan Minor, and got into the dips and waggles again. . . . The fourteen miles eventually drew to an end. . . . [quoted in *Biography*, p. 71]

He also accompanied *C.S. Lewis, his brother Warnie (*Warren H. Lewis), and other friends on walking holidays. From 15–?17 April 1937 he walked with C.S. Lewis and *Owen Barfield in the *Quantock Hills, Somerset. Barfield commented in an oral history for the Marion E. Wade Center (*Libraries and archives) that the holiday was 'not altogether a success because Tolkien wasn't very physically up to doing much walking'. Tolkien told Clyde S. Kilby in 1966 that only once had he accompanied Lewis on one of his longer walks: 'They had hiked in the neighbourhood of Minehead [in Somerset]. Tolkien concluded that twenty-five miles a day over rough country with a heavy pack on his shoulders was more than he preferred, so he had confined himself thereafter to shorter jaunts nearer Oxford with his friend' (*Tolkien & The Silmarillion* (1976), p. 11). One of the later occasions was a 'Victory Inklings' gathering at the end of 1945: Tolkien and Warnie Lewis formed an advance party, and were joined a day later by C.S. Lewis and *R.E. Havard. Since they stayed at the 'Bull' in *Fairford, Gloucestershire, and walked in different directions each day, there was no need to carry heavy packs.

In August 1947 Tolkien stayed with the Lewis brothers in *Malvern and were accompanied on some of their walks by *George Sayer. Comments made by Warnie Lewis in his journal reveal that Tolkien and the Lewises had different ideas about the objects of a walk: 'Tollers [Tolkien] fitted easily into our routine, and I think he enjoyed himself. His one fault turned out to be that he wouldn't trot at our pace in harness; he will keep going all day on a walk, but to him, with his botanical and entomological interests, a walk, no matter what its length, is what we would call an extended stroll, while he calls us "ruthless walkers"' (entry for 19 August 1947, *Brothers and Friends*, p. 207). George Sayer later recalled that C.S. Lewis asked him to walk with Tolkien while the brothers went ahead, because 'he's a great man, but not our sort of walker. He doesn't seem able to talk and walk at the same time. He dawdles and then stops completely when he has something interesting to say.' Sayer too found that Tolkien liked 'to stop to look at the trees, flowers, birds and insects' ('Recollections of J.R.R. Tolkien', *Proceedings of the J.R.R. Tolkien Centenary Conference 1992* (1995), p. 22).

Even in the years when Tolkien owned a car he seems to have used it mainly for leisure activities, preferring public transport, mainly the train, for other journeys within Britain. He crossed the English Channel and the Irish Sea by ferry on many occasions. In 1955, when he visited *Italy, he travelled there by train, as was common at the time. It was not until 1965 that he journeyed by air for the first time, from Birmingham to Dublin. In general he disliked aircraft as much as he did cars (see *Environment).

As he grew older, disabilities (see *Health) made it difficult for him to walk far or to ride a bicycle. Clyde S. Kilby recalled that one day during his visit to help Tolkien in 1966 'the idea arose of our taking a walk over some path which he and Lewis had once covered, but he said it was no longer possible for him to walk far. He reminisced about earlier years when he could ride his bicycle up the long, steep Headington Hill between his home and the university' (*Tolkien & The Silmarillion*, p. 27). Fortunately, by the time immobility became a serious problem, Tolkien's income from his writing enabled him to afford taxis for short journeys and a chauffeur-driven car for him and Edith to travel between Oxford and the Hotel Miramar in *Bournemouth.

In an autobiographical statement written in 1955 Tolkien said: 'I am very untravelled, though I know Wales, and have often been in Scotland (never north of the Tay), and know something of France, *Belgium, and *Ireland. I have spent a good deal of time in Ireland. . . . I first set foot in "Eire" in 1949 . . .' (*Letters*, p. 219). He forgot to include Switzerland in this list, and presumably wrote this statement before his visit to Italy in August 1955. He visited the *Netherlands in 1958, and went on a Mediterranean cruise in 1966, but planned visits to the U.S.A., Sweden, and Finland were abandoned for various reasons.

The Treason of Isengard: The History of The Lord of the Rings, Part Two. The seventh volume of *The History of Middle-earth*, edited with notes and commentary by *Christopher Tolkien, first published in Great Britain by Unwin Hyman, London, in September 1989, and in the United States by the Houghton Mifflin Company, Boston, in November 1989. See further, *Descriptive Bibliography* A27.

In this volume Christopher Tolkien examines texts for *The Lord of the Rings* written by his father between August 1939 and, probably, spring 1942, excluding material written in autumn 1939 already included in *The Return of the Shadow*. Divided into twenty-six chapters and an 'Appendix on Runes', it covers yet another revision of Book I, the rewriting of the part of Book II as far as Balin's tomb in Moria, and the continuation of the story to the end of Book II and into Book III, reaching the end of the chapter 'The King of the Golden Hall'.

In the later part of 1939 Tolkien continued to work on Book II and was also engaged in substantial revision of Book I, in part to explain the causes of Gandalf's delay in returning to Hobbiton. 'Gandalf's Delay' presents various outlines, notes, time-schemes, and chronologies, co-ordinating events and the movements of Gandalf, the Black Riders, and Frodo and his companions. This is followed 'The Fourth Phase (1): From Hobbiton to Bree' and 'The Fourth Phase (2): From Bree to the Ford of Rivendell', which summarize changes made in a 'fourth phase' fair copy, partly from new manuscript and partly from cannibalized pages of the 'third phase', which brought the text close to its published form.

Whether 'phase four' was finished by December 1939, as seems possible, or continued into the new year, there was almost certainly a considerable gap before Tolkien returned to *The Lord of the Rings* in August 1940. Various texts concerning Gandalf using Hamilcar Bolger as a decoy or rescuing him from the Black Riders, the emergence of the idea that Gandalf had been held prisoner by Saruman, and some changes now made to the 'fourth phase' Book I are presented in 'Of Hamilcar, Gandalf, and Saruman'. The evolution of Bilbo's song in Rivendell from the poem *Errantry* (c. 1930), through many versions to the text published in *The Lord of the Rings* and beyond, is presented together with some changes to the first chapter of Book II in 'Bilbo's Song at Rivendell: *Errantry* and *Eärendillinwë*'. Then follow chapters tracing the development of material first written in autumn 1939: 'The Council of Elrond (1)'; 'The Council of Elrond (2)'; 'The Ring Goes South'; and 'The Mines of Moria (1): The Lord of Moria'.

The next chapters continue the story to the end of Book II and part way through Book III, together with outlines and narratives considering the part of the story yet to be told and a survey of the first working map of *The Lord of the Rings*: 'The Mines of Moria (2): The Bridge'; 'The Story Foreseen from Moria'; 'Lothlórien'; 'Galadriel'; 'Farewell to Lórien'; 'The First Map of *The Lord of the Rings*', illustrated with redrawn diagrams; 'The Story Foreseen from Lórien'; 'The Great River'; 'The Breaking of the Fellowship'; 'The Departure of Boromir'; 'The Riders of Rohan'; 'The Uruk-hai'; 'Treebeard'; 'Notes on Various Topics'; 'The White Rider'; 'The Story Foreseen from Fangorn'; and 'The King of the Golden Hall'. Sparse evidence suggests that this writing proceeded slowly, with long gaps, in 1940–2.

The Treason of Isengard also contains, in black and white, reproductions of maps and of manuscript pages incorporating drawings. The first British and American hardcover editions include as well a colour reproduction of Tolkien's first drawing of Orthanc (*Artist and Illustrator*, fig. 162).

Tree and Leaf. Combined edition of *On Fairy-Stories* and *Leaf by Niggle*, first published in Great Britain by George Allen & Unwin, London, in May 1964 and in the United States by the Houghton Mifflin Company, Boston, in March 1965. See further, *Descriptive Bibliography* A7.

HISTORY

*Rayner Unwin suggested in 1955, as *The Lord of the Rings* was proving hugely popular, that the lecture *On Fairy-Stories* could be reprinted as a small book by itself if it were expanded by fifty per cent and framed as a long essay. This idea, however, lay dormant until spring 1963, when Unwin again suggested that *On Fairy-Stories* be reprinted, now together with the story *Leaf by Niggle*. Tolkien made a few additions, changes, and corrections to the lecture and wrote an introductory note for the new book. The two works, he said, were related 'by the symbols of Tree and Leaf, and by both touching in different ways on what is called in the essay *"sub-creation"*' (*Tree and Leaf*, p. 5). In a letter to *Stanley Unwin of 5 October 1963 (*Letters*, p. 335), with which he sent copy for the book, Tolkien noted that his suggested title *Tree and Leaf* alludes to passages in *On Fairy-Stories*, one of which includes the phrase 'the countless foliage of the Tree of Tales, with which the Forest of Days is carpeted', and the other the word *effoliation*. He received proofs of *Tree and Leaf* on 1 February 1964, and returned them corrected two days later.

Asked by Rayner Unwin to suggest suitable cover art – an illustration from one of *Andrew Lang's fairy-tale books, a tree or leaf from an illuminated manuscript, or a tree drawn by Tolkien himself – Tolkien replied that he had among his papers 'more than one version of a mythical "tree", which crops up regularly at those times when I feel driven to pattern-designing. They are elaborated and coloured and more suitable for embroidery than printing; and the tree bears besides various shapes of leaves many flowers small and large signifying poems and major legends.' He called this the 'Tree of Amalion': see *Artist and Illustrator*, pp. 64–5. With his reply, on 23 December 1963, he sent Rayner Unwin a 'hasty reduction of this pattern into leafy terms' (Tolkien-George Allen & Unwin archive, HarperCollins, partly printed in *Letters*, p. 342); and when this proved inadequate, he made a new drawing, double the earlier size and more elongated. This image appears on the cover of most copies of *Tree and Leaf*.

Tolkien states in his introductory note that *On Fairy-Stories* was reprinted from *Essays Presented to Charles Williams* (1947) 'with only a few minor alterations' (p. 5). In fact, there are many differences between the earlier and later texts, as detailed in *Descriptive Bibliography*, pp. 184, 186–90. There are only a few small differences in *Leaf by Niggle* between its *Dublin Review* (1945) version and that in *Tree and Leaf*.

Tree and Leaf has also been published in **The Tolkien Reader* (1966), **Poems and Stories* (1980), and other collections. Editions of *Tree and Leaf* published since 1988 have also included the poem **Mythopoeia*, from which Tolkien quotes in *On Fairy-Stories*.

CRITICISM

Tree and Leaf was widely reviewed at its first publication in both Britain and the United States. Invariably critics found more to say about *On Fairy-Stories*, in particular as it might shed light on **The Lord of the Rings*, while *Leaf by Niggle* received shorter notice. The lengthiest comments, perhaps, were 'Why Hobbits?' by D.H.V. (*Hugh) Brogan in the *Cambridge Review*, 23 January 1965; 'The Persistence of Light' by Guy Davenport in the *National Review*, 20 April 1965; 'The Elvish Art of Enchantment' by Loren Eiseley in the *Horn Book*, August 1965; and 'In the Soup' by John Yolton in the *Kenyon Review* (1965). See further, notes on criticism under **Leaf by Niggle* and **On Fairy-Stories*.

Trees *see* **Nature**

The Trees of Kortirion. Three versions of this poem, under two titles, were published with commentary in **The Book of Lost Tales, Part One* (1983), pp. 32–43. Its subject is Kortirion, the town at the centre of the Elvish isle Tol Eressëa in early workings of the **'Silmarillion'* mythology. In its earliest versions, as *Kortirion among the Trees*, Tolkien sings the praises of 'the city of the Land of Elms, / Alalminórë in the Faery Realms'. At one point in the writing of **The Book of Lost Tales* Kortirion was to be the site in later days of **Warwick, a place well loved by Tolkien and associated by him with his wife

*Edith: she lived there from early 1913 to April 1916, and they were married in Warwick in March 1916. The poem has a sentimental, yet hopeful tone (Kortirion is a 'fading town upon a little hill, / Old memory is waning in thine ancient gates', but the poet would find there 'a haunting ever-near content'), reflecting Tolkien's mood while undergoing army training, in preparation for service in the trenches during the First World War.

Inscriptions on various workings of the poem suggest that Tolkien began to compose *Kortirion among the Trees* while on leave in Warwick, continued to work on it after he returned to camp, and made at least two fair copies, all within the period 21–28 November 1915. He revised the poem significantly in 1937, and again early in 1962. The latest revision, as *Christopher Tolkien has said, is 'almost a different poem' (*The Book of Lost Tales, Part One*, p. 32). It was now divided into four sections, each with an Elvish title: 'Alalminórë', 'Narquelion' (cf. Quenya *Narquelië* 'sun-fading', the name of the tenth month given in *The Lord of the Rings*, Appendix D), *Hrívion* (cf. Quenya *hrívë* 'winter'), and 'Mettanyë' (cf. Quenya *metta* 'ending'), and the overall title became *The Trees of Kortirion*. Tolkien reworked it as a possible candidate for inclusion in *The Adventures of Tom Bombadil and Other Verses from the Red Book* (1962), though in the end he concluded that it was 'too long and too ambitious, and even if considered good enough would probably upset the boat' (letter to Rayner Unwin, 5 February 1962, quoted in *The Book of Lost Tales, Part One*, p. 32 note).

To one fair copy of the poem Tolkien later appended a prose introduction which explains that Kortirion was a city of the fairies (later Elves) in the Lonely Isle 'after the great wars with Melko and the ruin of Gondolin', built 'in memory of their ancient dwelling of Kôr in Valinor' (*The Book of Lost Tales, Part One*, p. 25).

Trought, Vincent (1893–1912). Vincent Trought was a close friend of Tolkien at *King Edward's School, Birmingham, and shared many of the same activities, including football, the School library, the Literary Society, and the Debating Society. As a member of the latter he 'spoke often in a dreamy, weary fashion and, though he never contributed much to a practical decision, his nightmare phantasies and grotesque conceits were one of the features of the Meetings. Our worst punster' ('Debating Characters'. *King Edward's School Chronicle* n.s. 26, no. 187 (June 1911), p. 46). He was also a member of the *T.C.B.S., one of the earliest, from a time when there was no T.C.B.S. apart from himself, Tolkien, and *Christopher Wiseman. Tolkien's friendship with Trought seems to have been deeply rooted, but was cut short: Trought died in January 1912 after a severe illness. He was eulogized in the *King Edward's School Chronicle*:

Everyone knew his grim tenacity on the football field and his quaint humour in debate. In poetry he found his most congenial means of expression, and some of his verses show great depth of feeling and control of language. But he was a true artist, with an artist's love of nature and keen sense of beauty as well in sculpture, painting and music as in literature. Though rather retiring and perhaps somewhat slow of thought, his singular depth of character stuck all who knew him. His influence was profound and widespread, and ever directed towards order, courtesy and honour. [n.s. 27, no. 191 (March 1912), p. 4]

Of Tuor and His Coming to Gondolin*. Narrative, published with commentary and notes in *Unfinished Tales (1980), pp. 17–56.

Tolkien original account of the story of Tuor (see *'Of Tuor and the Fall of Gondolin') was the first written tale (?end of 1916–first half of 1917) of *The Book of Lost Tales, though the events it relates come near the end of the history of the Elves as he then envisaged it. Usually called by Tolkien The Fall of Gondolin, though the title on the manuscript is Tuor and the Exiles of Gondolin, it was the only time he told the entire story at any length; both the *Quenta Silmarillion and the Grey Annals (*Annals of Beleriand) were abandoned before they reached that point. In ?1951–?2 he began a new narrative, which would have been of even greater length than that in The Book of Lost Tales, but abandoned it as Tuor has his first sight of Gondolin. *Christopher Tolkien comments in *The Book of Lost Tales, Part Two (p. 203): 'In places the later Tuor (the abandonment of which is one of the saddest facts in the whole history of incompletion) is so close in wording to The Fall of Gondolin, written more than thirty years before, as to make it almost certain that my father had it in front of him, or at least had recently reread it.' The actual title of this later work is Of Tuor and the Fall of Gondolin, but to avoid confusion with the chapter of the same name in *The Silmarillion, and because Tolkien abandoned the work before Tuor even set foot in Gondolin, Christopher Tolkien gave it a new title for publication.

Also included in Unfinished Tales are a few 'hasty jottings indicating the course of the story' (p. 56). A further note was published in The War of the Jewels, p. 323.

In 1951 Tolkien wrote another text relating to the story of Gondolin, *Of Meglin, to which he made additions and emendations on an amanuensis typescript of c. 1970. On the first page of a carbon copy of this typescript he wrote

that the text is 'An enlarged version of the coming of Maeglin to Gondolin, to be inserted in FG in its place', and noted that 'FG = Fall of Gondolin'. This can only be a reference to the abandoned Tale of Tuor (entitled Of Tuor and the Fall of Gondolin, but retitled Of Tuor and his Coming to Gondolin for inclusion in Unfinished Tales). . . . Thus at this very late date my father was still holding to the hope of an entirely rewritten story of the Fall of Gondolin, of which so little had been done. . . . [Christopher Tolkien, The War of the Jewels, p. 317]

It is indeed sad that Tolkien abandoned this late work, written when he had fully developed his narrative powers during the writing of *The Lord of the

Rings. Guy Gavriel Kay has said that 'this beautifully written piece comes closer than anything else in *Unfinished Tales* to evoking the qualities of awe and power that Tolkien at his best commanded. Tuor's encounter with the sea-god Ulmo, who speaks to him standing "knee-deep in the shadowy sea," is as good as anything he ever wrote' ('Dug Out of the Dust of Middle-earth', *Maclean's*, 26 January 1981, p. 46).

Brian Rosebury comments in *Tolkien: A Cultural Phenomenon* (2003) that this is 'the most tantalising piece in *Unfinished Tales*'.

> It has the lucid, austere style of the later-written parts of *The Silmarillion*, but also, at moments, a dream-like visual intensity and mystery largely absent from that volume. It twice uses a landscape motif also employed in *The Lord of the Rings*: the journey, first through a tunnel, then through a narrow ravine between towering hills, to a place of awe and wonder. A post-Freudian reader may be strongly tempted to interpret the imagery as symbolising birth: if this is so, the experience appears as tremendous and exhilarating, rather than traumatic. . . .
>
> Like too many dreams, however, the story breaks off abruptly [as Tuor sees Gondolin]. . . . The subsequent history of Gondolin might well . . . have provided further opportunities for visual splendour; and perhaps for counteracting the main weakness of the 1951 narrative, the uninterestingness of Tuor as an active character, as distinct from a consciousness to whom extraordinary images are revealed. [pp. 110–11]

'Of Tuor and the Fall of Gondolin'. The twenty-third chapter of the *'Quenta Silmarillion', published in *The Silmarillion (1977), pp. 238–45.

SUMMARY

Tuor is born after the death of his father, Huor, in the Battle of Unnumbered Tears, and fostered by Grey-elves in Mithrim. When he is sixteen these elves are attacked by Orcs and Easterlings, and Tuor is enslaved. After three years he escapes, and a year later, inspired by the Vala Ulmo, makes his way through a dark tunnel beneath the mountains and reaches the sea at Nevrast. After dwelling there a while, he follows swans south and comes to Vinyamar, deserted by Turgon when he led his people to the hidden city of Gondolin. Tuor takes up arms and armour that Turgon has left there on the instructions of Ulmo. On a night of storm Ulmo appears to Tuor and orders him to seek Gondolin. He gives Tuor a cloak to shield him from the eyes of enemies.

In the morning Tuor meets on the shore Voronwë, the sole survivor of the wreck of one of the ships Turgon has sent in vain into the West. On hearing Tuor's story, Voronwë agrees to guide Tuor to Gondolin. The chapter briefly describes their journey, noting that, as they reach the defiled Pools of Ivrin, a man in black (Túrin), passes them travelling north. By the power of Ulmo they find the hidden door and pass through the ravine to Gondolin. The arms

from Vinyamar reveal Tuor as the messenger of Ulmo. He is received with ceremony by Turgon, his daughter Idril, and his nephew Maeglin. Tuor delivers
Ulmo's message that Turgon should abandon Gondolin and travel to the sea,
but Turgon trusts in his city's strength and his people wish to have nothing to
do with the world outside. Maeglin also speaks against Ulmo's counsel. Eventually Turgon decides to reject it, and fearing treason, blocks the one entrance
to Gondolin. Tuor stays in the city and weds Idril, the second union of Men
and Elves. In the five hundred and third year since the return of the Noldor
to Middle-earth their son Eärendil is born. Although all seems full of joy and
peace in Gondolin, Idril has forebodings for the future, and causes to be built a
secret way beneath the city walls north onto the adjoining plain.

Húrin has inadvertently betrayed the general area of Gondolin to Morgoth,
who seeks for further knowledge of the city. Orcs capture Maeglin, who has
strayed beyond the hills against Turgon's orders. Maeglin buys his freedom by
revealing to Morgoth the exact location of Gondolin. He is also promised the
rule of the city as a vassal of Morgoth, and possession of Idril.

When Eärendil is seven Morgoth attacks Gondolin at a time of summer festival. The elves fight bravely but cannot prevail, even though Ecthelion of the
Fountain slays Gothmog, Lord of Balrogs. Ecthelion is himself slain in combat,
and Turgon is killed. Maeglin seizes Idril and Eärendil, but Tuor rescues them
and hurls Maeglin from the walls; they escape with other citizens of Gondolin
through Idril's secret way. When they emerge from the tunnel they are hidden
by the fumes and steams of the ravaged city, but are ambushed by orcs and a
balrog as they cross the pass of the Eagle's Cleft, Cirith Thoronath. They are
saved by Glorfindel, who fights the balrog and falls with him into the abyss,
and by the aid of eagles. They rest in the Land of Willows and hold a feast in
memory of those who have been slain, especially Glorfindel, and Tuor sings
to Eärendil of his meeting with Ulmo. They journey south to the mouths of
Sirion, and join elves who not long before had fled with Elwing from Doriath.
Gil-galad is named High King of the Noldor in Middle-earth, in succession to
Turgon. Morgoth pays little heed to these refugees, who learn the art of shipbuilding and sea-faring from Círdan.

Ulmo asks the Valar to forgive and rescue the Elves, and win back the
Silmarils in which was still the light of the Two Trees; but Manwë does not
respond. According to the wise, only one speaking in person on behalf of both
Elves and Men might move the Valar, and even Manwë could not free the sons
of Fëanor from their oath until it found its end.

As Tuor reaches old age a longing for the Sea grows ever greater. He builds a
great ship and with Idril sails into the sunset. Later it was sung that Tuor alone
of mortals was numbered among the Elves and joined with the Noldor, 'and
his fate is sundered from the fate of Men' (*The Silmarillion*, p. 245).

HISTORY

This chapter in *The Silmarillion* fills just over seven pages. The first (and only) telling of the story at length, *Tuor and the Exiles of Gondolin*, the first part of *The Book of Lost Tales* (c. 1916–20) to be written (usually referred to as *The Fall of Gondolin*), occupies nearly forty-eight pages in *The Book of Lost Tales, Part Two*. The basic story of the fall of Gondolin as told in *The Book of Lost Tales* is much the same as that published in *The Silmarillion* in most respects, but includes much more descriptive detail in every part. Some twelve pages, for instance, describe almost blow by blow the vain defence of Gondolin which in *The Silmarillion* is summarized in less than a paragraph; and more than three pages are devoted to the journey over the pass and Glorfindel's fight with the balrog, compared with only a half page in *The Silmarillion*. Typical of the style and detail is a description of one of the twelve houses of Gondolin as they assemble for battle: 'There stood the house of the Golden Flower who bare a rayed sun upon their shield, and their chief Glorfindel bare a mantle so broidered in threads of gold that it was diapered with celandine as a field in spring; and his arms were damascened with cunning gold' (*The Book of Lost Tales, Part Two*, p. 173).

The first version of the story does, however, differ in certain respects from the published version, due to the still undeveloped state of Tolkien's *legendarium* when he wrote *The Fall of Gondolin*. The account of Tuor's descent from the leaders of the House of Hador and his fostering by Elves after his father's death in the Battle of Unnumbered Tears is not present; instead Tuor tells Turgon that he is 'Tuor son of Peleg son of Indor of the house of the Swan of the Sons of the Men of the North' (p. 160). When he first reaches the Sea he builds a dwelling for himself at Falasquil, then journeys south as far as the Land of Willows. There is no mention of Vinyamar, or of the armour left there by Turgon. Ulmo appears to Tuor in the Land of Willows and tells him to seek for Gondolin, and there to speak words that would be put in his mouth, and that 'a child shall come of thee than whom no man shall know more of the uttermost deeps, be it of the sea or of the firmament of heaven' (p. 155). Ulmo tells Tuor that Noldoli will escort him, but after a while they desert him through fear of Melko. Tuor's movements are observed by spies of Melko until one of the Noldoli, Voronwë, returns and seeks with him for the hidden entrance to the Way of Escape, which leads to Gondolin and is protected by magic so that none but those of the blood of the Noldoli might find it; in this account Voronwë has not previously been in Gondolin. The Way of Escape is a dark tunnel made by the people of Gondolin, and only at the end is there a gate. The message that Ulmo gives to Turgon through Tuor is to prepare his people for battle, for the time is ripe, or if he is unwilling to do this, to build boats and send messengers to Valinor; but Turgon says that he has already done the latter for years with no success. Gondolin is described as being still unfinished though 'ages of years' had already been spent on its building (p. 163). In this account the marriage of Tuor and Idril is the first marriage of Man and Elf.

The secret way that Tuor builds at Idril's request leads south of the city, not north. When Meglin (spelled thus in this version) is captured he does not betray the situation of Gondolin, for Morgoth has already discovered it, but gives information about its defences and even advises Melko on how it might be overthrown. Melko now

> assembled all his most cunning smiths and sorcerers, and of iron and flame they wrought a host of monsters. . . . Some were all of iron so cunningly linked that they might flow like slow rivers of metal or coil themselves around and above all obstacles before them, and these were filled in their innermost depths with the grimmest of the Orcs with scimitars and spears; others of bronze and copper were given hearts and spirits of blazing fire, and they blasted all that stood before them with the terror of their snorting or trampled whatso escaped the ardour of their breath; yet others were creatures of pure flame that writhed like ropes of molten metal, and they brought to ruin whatever fabric they came nigh, and iron and stone melted before them and became as water, and upon them rode the Balrogs in hundreds. . . . [p. 170]

Meglin even sends messengers to advise Melko to guard the Way of Escape, and all who seek to flee that way perish.

Melko's attack at first was made at midwinter, not in summer, but Tolkien changed this in rewriting. The earlier account of the defence of Gondolin contains much that was omitted in later texts, probably because of the briefer format of the latter rather than because details were rejected. Turgon holds a council to discuss what should be done. Tuor and many others favour leaving the city, breaking out in one or more groups; but Meglin urges that they defend the city, counsel which Turgon accepts, for he loves both the city and the treasure it contains. Meglin reveals his cruel nature by attempting to throw Eärendel over the battlements into the fires below, and by dragging Idril to witness her son's death. When Tuor arrives unexpectedly to bid farewell to his family and tell them to escape by Idril's secret way, Meglin tries to stab Eärendel, but instead is thrown from the walls by Tuor. Tuor returns with his followers to the battle, leaving Voronwë to guard Idril. Although after a bitter fight the city is all but lost, Turgon refuses to leave. Tuor and his men, protecting a company of women and children, fight their way back to Tuor's house and Idril's secret tunnel. Idril, who has already sent Eärendel into the tunnel, meets them. They all follow and eventually come out onto the plain and meet those who had gone before, but Eärendel is not with them. Despite the advice of Idril some insist on seeking the Way of Escape. The rest turn towards Cristhorn, the Cleft of the Eagles, in the south, and on the way Tuor rescues Eärendel and his escort from orcs riding on wolves. Some time later, the refugees pass the outer end of the Way of Escape and see the remains of those who went that way and were killed by a monster sent there by Melko. The survivors of the passage of the Cristhorn settle at the mouth of the River Sirion.

At about the same time as he wrote the first version of *Tuor and the Exiles of Gondolin*, or a few months later, Tolkien also revised his poem *Sea-Chant of an Elder Day* (or *Sea-Song of an Elder Day*, see **The Horns of Ylmir*), making it 'the song that Tuor told to Eärendel his son what time the Exiles of Gondolin dwelt awhile in Dor Tathrin the Land of Willows' (**The Shaping of Middle-earth*, p. 214), of how Ulmo called to him in that land.

A brief unfinished prose text of the early 1920s, **Turlin and the Exiles of Gondolin*, describes Turlin's (= Tuor's) early years in Mithrim, but comes to an end as he makes his way through the hidden tunnel to the Sea. An unfinished metrical poem, **The Lay of the Fall of Gondolin*, probably dates to the same period. This follows the story and even the wording of *The Book of Lost Tales* closely, and contains the earliest account of Meglin's history which, as it evolved (and is related in **'Of Maeglin'* in *The Silmarillion*), explains some of his actions in 'Of Tuor and the Fall of Gondolin'. Probably early in 1925 Tolkien wrote a fragment of an alliterative poem, less than forty lines long, which **Christopher Tolkien thinks was probably the beginning of a projected **'Lay of Eärendel'*. This tells briefly of the escape of Tuor and others from the sack of Gondolin and introduces only minor changes to the story: Idril's secret tunnel leads north, not south, and the Cristhorn is also situated to the north.

In the **Sketch of the Mythology* (*c.* 1926) Tuor is the son of Huor killed in the Battle of Unnumbered Tears, and of Rían who died on the site of that battle after Tuor's birth. His thralldom now enters the story, but not his fostering by Elves. He meets Voronwë or Bronweg, who had previously visited Gondolin at the mouths of Sirion. They journey to the Land of Willows where Ylmir appears to Tuor and tells him messages he is to deliver to Turgon, which partly differ from those in the *Book of Lost Tales* version. If Turgon will not fight, the people of Gondolin are to go to Sirion's mouth where Ylmir will help them build ships and guide them back to Valinor. If Turgon will fight, Tuor is to draw Men into alliance with him. It is stated that Meglin supports Turgon's rejection of Ulmo's advice against the urging of Idril and Turgon's wisest counsellors. Since Tolkien had finally decided that Beren (see **'Of Beren and Lúthien'*) should be a Man and not an Elf, Tuor is now the second Man to wed an Elf, not the first. The wording used suggests that Meglin betrays the whereabouts of Gondolin to Morgoth rather than merely provide information about its defences.

The **Quenta Noldorinwa* (*c.* 1930) contains Tolkien's last narrative account of the whole of Tuor's story. A section of original typescript of this part of the tale was replaced, but with probably little time elapsed between the two texts. The story in the original version is close to the *Sketch of the Mythology*, but an emendation introduces Tuor's fostering by Elves. In the rewritten part Ulmo tells Tuor that if Turgon agrees to prepare for war, he should send Tuor to seek aid from Men in the East.

According to the 'earliest' *Annals of Beleriand* (early 1930s), Tuor was born in the Year 172; he left Hithlum in 195; the following year he met Bronweg, Ulmo appeared to him, and Tuor and Bronweg reached Gondolin; he married

Idril in 199 and Eärendel was born in 200; Meglin was captured and betrayed Gondolin in 206; Morgoth attacked the city in 207; the refugees from Gondolin reached the mouths of Sirion in 208; and Tuor set sail with Idril into the West in 224. Although the second version of the 'earliest' *Annals* did not reach to these entries, the extension there of the Siege of Angband by a hundred years meant that other dates had to be increased by that amount. The 'later' *Annals of Beleriand* of the mid-1930s by emendation extended the Siege a further 200 years, so that Tuor was born in 472 and the other dates were similarly adjusted.

Tolkien abandoned the *Quenta Silmarillion* before it reached the fall of Gondolin. The *Grey Annals* (*c.* 1951, see **Annals of Beleriand*) were also left unfinished, and contain only a few entries concerning Tuor's early years, including (as first written) that in 487 at the age of fifteen he came to Hithlum seeking his kin. By emendation he was enslaved by Easterlings, but escaped and became an outlaw. The message Ulmo sends to Turgon was no longer to prepare for battle but to leave Gondolin and go down to the Sea.

At about the same time or soon after, Tolkien began a new narrative with the title *Of Tuor and the Fall of Gondolin*, intending to tell the story at great length. This work is published in **Unfinished Tales* as **Of Tuor and His Coming to Gondolin*, a title chosen by Christopher Tolkien to avoid confusion with the chapter title in *The Silmarillion*, and also more suitable as Tolkien abandoned the work as Tuor has his first sight of Gondolin. Only a few rough notes beyond this refer to his reception in Gondolin. This work takes over thirty-four pages to cover events occupying only two pages in *The Silmarillion*, and not only adds much detail but also makes several significant changes. Tuor now no longer journeys to the mouths of Sirion when he leaves Hithlum, but less far, to Nevrast and then Vinyamar, where Turgon had dwelt before he removed to Gondolin. The story continues as in *The Silmarillion*, but with much more detail, including descriptions of each of the seven gates Tuor passes on his way through the ravine. Ulmo does not give Tuor a message, but says that when he sees Turgon 'the words shall arise in thy mind, and thy mouth shall speak as I would' (p. 30). Tolkien added some of the new material to the *Grey Annals* by emendation: in 488 Tuor was enslaved by Lorgan chief of the Easterlings; he escaped in 491 and lived four years as an outlaw; in 495 he left Mithrim and came to Nivrost, and was sent to Gondolin by Ulmo.

According to annalistic plot synopses which Tolkien made while working on **The Wanderings of Húrin* in the late 1950s, Tuor did not wed Idril until 502. **The Tale of Years* as first written agrees with the emended dates of the 'later' *Annals of Beleriand*, with the birth of Eärendil in 500 and the fall of Gondolin in 510. By emendations in various stages Tuor wed Idril in 502 > 504 > 502, Eärendil was born in 503 > 505 > 503, and Gondolin fell in 510 > 512 > 510.

Christopher Tolkien faced considerable problems in forming this chapter of *The Silmarillion*. The last full account of events was that in the *Quenta Noldorinwa*, but *Of Tuor and His Coming to Gondolin* from some twenty years later introduced important changes. Differences of scale and style between the two works made it impossible to use the later text as far as it went, and the earlier for the rest of the story. The first part of the chapter is an abridgement of *Of Tuor and His Coming to Gondolin*, using where possible material from the *Grey Annals* as emended and the *Qenta Noldorinwa* where suitable. It also takes in material from Tolkien's notes for the continuation of *Of Tuor and His Coming to Gondolin*. From the capture of Maeglin the chapter is almost entirely taken from the *Quenta Noldorinwa*, either from the replacement text or from the original text for the parts that were not rewritten.

Christopher Tolkien omitted a reference to the death of Rog in the defence of Gondolin because he was sure that his father would not have retained this name (*The Book of Lost Tales, Part Two*, p. 211). He added the blocking of the Way of Escape by Turgon after hearing Tuor's message from the late *Wanderings of Húrin* (*The Shaping of Middle-earth*, p. 194), and as a consequence omitted the fugitives who tried to escape by the Way and were destroyed by a dragon. The detail that when Tuor fought Maeglin and cast him from the walls 'his body as it fell smote the rocky slopes of Amon Gwareth thrice ere it pitched into the flames below' (*The Silmarillion*, p. 243) derives from *The Fall of Gondolin* (*The Book of Lost Tales, Part Two*, pp. 178, 212). The dating of the marriage of Tuor and Idril to 502, and the birth of Eärendil to 503, derive from synopses for *The Wanderings of Húrin* and *The Tale of Years*.

'Of Túrin Turambar'. The twenty-first (and longest) chapter of the **'Quenta Silmarillion'*, published in **The Silmarillion* (1977) pp. 198–226.

SUMMARY

In the Battle of Unnumbered Tears Huor, son of Galdor, was killed. His wife Rían, whom he had married only two months earlier, waited to give birth to their son and then lay down on the mound which covered the dead and herself died. Their son Tuor is fostered by Elves.

The previous chapter of *The Silmarillion* told how Húrin, Lord of Dor-lómin, when taken captive in the Battle of Unnumbered Tears defied Morgoth, who told him that 'evil and despair shall come upon those whom thou lovest' (*The Silmarillion*, p. 197), and that Húrin would witness all that happens. The present chapter describes the working of Morgoth's curse on Húrin's family. Húrin's wife is Morwen, kinswoman of Beren. At the time of Húrin's capture they have one child, an eight-year-old son, Túrin, for their daughter Lalaith had died young. After the battle, the lands that had belonged to Húrin and his people are given by Morgoth to the Easterlings, and Morwen is reduced to poverty. Fearing that Túrin will be enslaved, she sends him in the care of two servants to be fostered by Thingol, the elven King of Doriath. After he has left, she gives birth to Húrin's posthumous daughter, Nienor. She refuses Thingol's offer to join her son in Doriath, but sends the Dragon-helm of Dor-lómin for her son. After nine years, dangerous conditions prevent messengers from passing between Morwen and Doriath, and Túrin fears for his mother and sister.

He becomes a warrior and fights on the marches of Doriath, and is the companion at arms of Beleg Strongbow. In response to an insult from a Nandorin Elf, Saeros, he hurls a drinking vessel at him. The next day Túrin unintentionally causes his death, pursuing Saeros when he waylays him. Túrin refuses to return to the judgement of Thingol, flees from Doriath, and joins a band of outlaws. Thingol pardons him when he hears an account of what had happened. Beleg, who goes to find Túrin and inform him of the pardon, is captured by the outlaws and mistreated in Túrin's absence. Túrin frees him when he returns, but is too proud to accept Thingol's pardon. However, he is shamed into forsaking his lawless deeds and in future attacks only servants of Morgoth. Beleg returns to Thingol and gains his leave to join Túrin and guard him. As a gift for himself he chooses the sword Anglachel, though Melian warns that there is malice in it.

Túrin and his outlaws capture the Petty-Dwarf, Mîm, who as ransom leads them to his dwelling under the hill Amon Rûdh, which becomes their new stronghold. There they find one of Mîm's sons dead, killed by an arrow from one of the outlaws. Túrin promises that if he ever has wealth, he will pay Mîm a ransom of gold. From Mîm he hears the history of the Petty-Dwarves. When winter comes Beleg joins the band, bringing the Dragon-helm for Túrin. Morgoth is extending his power south, and Túrin's band opposes his armies, winning themselves fame. Because Túrin wears the Dragon-helm, Morgoth learns where he is and surrounds Amon Rûdh with spies. Mîm is captured and betrays Túrin and his companions, leading orcs secretly into the stronghold. Túrin is taken captive and all the others slain, save Beleg who is sorely wounded; as soon as he is able, he follows the orcs.

In the woods of Taur-nu-Fuin he comes upon Gwindor, an elf of Nargothrond, who has escaped from Angband. Together they rescue Beleg, carrying him still bound and asleep from a camp of sleeping orcs. But as Beleg is cutting his fetters with Anglachel, Túrin awakes and, thinking Beleg an orc, seizes the sword and kills him. A flash of lightning reveals the truth to him. It is long before Gwindor can rouse Túrin and lead him away. Not till they came to the springs of Eithel Ivrin and he drinks of the water is he able to weep and be healed of his madness. He makes a song for Beleg.

Gwindor leads Túrin to Nargothrond where he grows high in the favour of Orodreth, the king, but he conceals his true name and is known as the Mormegil, the Black Sword, after Anglachel which is reforged and given a new name, Gurthang, Iron of Death. Finduilas, the daughter of Orodreth, had loved Gwindor before his capture, but now gives her heart to Túrin though he does not realize it. Gwindor reveals to her Túrin's true name and warns her that a dark doom lies on him.

Túrin becomes great among the Elves of Nargothrond. On his advice, they abandon secrecy, attack the servants of Morgoth, and make a bridge over the River Narog from their stronghold to move more swiftly. During the time that Túrin dwells in Nargothrond, Morwen and Nienor leave Dor-lómin for Doriath, and remain there though they are grieved to hear that Túrin has gone.

In the year 495 two elves, Gelmir and Arminas, bring a warning to Orodreth from Ulmo that the people of Nargothrond should destroy the bridge and seek security behind their doors; but the counsel of Túrin prevails. When Morgoth sends a great host with the dragon Glaurung against Nargothrond, Orodreth's army marches to oppose it. The elves are defeated and most perish, including Orodreth and Gwindor, but before he dies the latter charges Túrin to save Finduilas, and warns that she alone stands between Túrin and his doom. Túrin speeds to Nargothrond, where he finds that the bridge had enabled the enemy to overcome the guards and enter the stronghold. Glaurung greets Túrin and, having bound him with a spell, taunts him with an account of those who have suffered because of him, and alleges that he has left his mother and sister to live as thralls. Túrin can do nothing to help Finduilas, who cries out to him as she is led away by orcs with other captives. Glaurung releases Túrin from the spell, but tells him that if he delays to help Finduilas he will never find Morwen and Nienor in Dor-lómin. Túrin hastens to find them, abandoning Finduilas to her fate. When he comes to Dor-lómin he learns from his father's kinswoman, Aerin, who has been taken to wife by Brodda the leader of the Easterlings, that Morwen and Nienor had left long before to seek him in Doriath. Aware now of the lies of Glaurung, in a rage he kills Brodda and other Easterlings, and flees from Dor-lómin. His one comfort is that his offensive as Mormegil had temporarily freed the lands from the followers of Morgoth and enabled his mother and sister to make their way to Doriath and safety.

Belatedly he seeks for Finduilas and learns from the woodmen of Brethil (defined elsewhere in *The Silmarillion* as the Haladin or people of Haleth) that when they had tried to rescue the prisoners from Nargothrond, orcs had slain all of the captives. The woodmen had buried Finduilas in a mound by the Crossings of Teiglin, which they named Haudh-en-Elleth, the Mound of the Elf-maid. They recognize Túrin as the Mormegil and tend him, though their lame ruler Brandir feels foreboding. Túrin stays with the Men of Brethil, defends the Crossings and the Haudh, and takes the name *Turambar*.

Meanwhile news of the fall of Nargothrond and that the Mormegil was in fact Túrin comes to Doriath, and against the advice of Melian Morwen and Nienor insist on riding to seek tidings. Glaurung, who is aware of their coming, frightens their horses and those of their escort into flight. Many are slain, and Morwen is lost. Nienor is thrown from her horse and finds herself looking straight into the eyes of Glaurung, who lays on her a spell of utter darkness and forgetfulness. She is led away by Mablung, the leader of their escort, with a few survivors; but when they are attacked by orcs she flees into the night. Mablung searches for her in vain.

After fleeing like a hunted beast, naked and in terror of a thunderstorm, Nienor flings herself down on the Haudh-en-Elleth and is found there by Turambar. Since she has no memory of her past he calls her Níniel, Tearmaiden. He takes her to the home of the woodmen, and on the way, as they pass Dimrost, the falls of Celebros, she suffers a strange shuddering. Although she feels love for Turambar she hesitates to marry him. Brandir, because of his forebodings rather than his own love for her, advises against the marriage and tells her Turambar's real name. But when she has been with the woodmen for nearly three years she and Turambar are married.

Orcs begin to attack Brethil. Turambar leads the Men of Brethil against them, thus revealing his presence to Glaurung. Níniel conceives a child. With Glaurung moving to attack Brethil, Turambar advises that it is useless to try to defeat the dragon by force, and offers to try to destroy it before it enters their land. The people should wait in Brethil, but if Turambar fails they should scatter until Glaurung leaves. Only two men respond to his request for companions. Níniel, refusing to stay behind, follows him. Brandir follows her, hoping to protect her but because he is lame is left far behind. One of Turambar's companions deserts him, and the other is killed by a falling stone. Turambar, however, clinging to the side of a ravine, kills Glaurung by thrusting his sword upwards into the dragon's soft belly as it begins to cross. In agony Glaurung reaches the far side. Turambar follows to withdraw his sword, but swoons, partly from the venom of the dragon's blood which falls on his hand, and partly from the malice of the dying beast.

Brandir thinks that Glaurung has triumphed and tries to lead Níniel away from the Dimrost, but she flees to find her husband. She cannot rouse Turambar but binds his injured hand. In Brandir's hearing, Glaurung reveals to Nienor-Níniel who she is, that she has married her brother, and that she carries the child of incest. As the dragon dies she recovers her memory and, distraught, casts herself into the ravine to her death. Brandir tells his people that Turambar, Níniel, and Glaurung have all perished, and that these tidings are good, but even when he explains their true identities the people think him crazed.

When Turambar recovers he refuses to believe Brandir and, accusing him of leading Níniel to her death and spreading lies, he kills him. But as Turambar sits by the Haudh-en Elleth Mablung passes by, and Turambar learns from him that Brandir had spoken truly. He goes to the place where Níniel had thrown herself to her death and asks his sword Gurthang to slay him quickly. The sword replies that it will do so in order to forget the blood of Beleg and Brandir. The body of Túrin is laid in a mound and a stone placed on it, recording the names Túrin Turambar and Nienor Níniel.

HISTORY

The following considers only the most significant points in the development of this story over forty years, the most complex of all the tales of the First Age. *Christopher Tolkien makes detailed comparisons of its several versions in *The History of Middle-earth.*

The seeds of the story seem to have been sown earlier than any other. During his final year at school, 1910–11, Tolkien discovered the *Kalevala; and in the autumn of 1914 he began to write in prose and verse *The Story of Kullervo* (see *Kalevala*), his own version of one of its tales. The original story in the *Kalevala* includes several elements which Tolkien incorporated into the story of Túrin, and some of the changes he made in *The Story of Kullervo* also reappear in it. Tolkien wrote years later that 'the germ of my attempt to write legends of my own to fit my private languages was the tragic tale of the hapless Kullervo in the Finnish *Kalevala*. It remains a major matter in the legends of the First Age ... though as "The Children of Húrin" it is entirely changed except in the tragic ending' (*Letters*, p. 345).

Tolkien made an entry in the *Qenyaqetsa, 'Fentor – the great worm slain by Ingilmo or Turambar', as early as 1915, certainly preceding the first written tale of Túrin, *The Tale of Turambar* (?1918), in *The Book of Lost Tales*. This first account, written out in pencil, was erased when overwritten by a revised version, apparently in the summer of 1919. A scrap of rejected outline (see *The Book of Lost Tales, Part Two*, pp. 138–9) shows some elements which appear in the surviving second version but also significant differences: for instance, Turambar's mother and sister (called Tirannë and Vainóni) *both* forget their names, and not through the malice of the Foalókë (dragon) but because they are given a baneful drink by an evil magician. Both Turambar and Vainóni learn the truth from the dying dragon.

The story in the surviving *Tale of Turambar* in turn differs from that in *The Silmarillion* at several points. Túrin's parents are Úrin and Mavwin, and his only sister, Nienóri, is born just before he is sent to be fostered by Tinwelint (Thingol), apparently because of Mavwin's poverty rather than from any fear of Túrin being enslaved. Although as originally written, Mavwin is kin to Beren, when in the rewritten *Tale of Tinúviel* Beren became an Elf, Húrin became a friend of Beren and his father. There is no mention of the Dragon-helm. Orgof the Elf at Tinwelint's court who mocks Túrin is killed by the drinking-vessel Túrin throws at him. When Túrin flees without waiting for Tinwelint's judgement, he gathers around him not outlaws but hunters, and Beleg is among them from the beginning. The story of Mîm and the stronghold in Amon Rûdh is absent, and Túrin is captured in a chance encounter with orcs. The elf who aids Beleg in the rescue of Túrin is called Flinding, and after Beleg's death he leads Túrin to the caves of the Rodothlim (the humble precursor of Nargothrond). Failivrin the Elf-maiden who loves Túrin is not the daughter of Orodreth the ruler of the Rodothlim, and in this and other early versions of the tale Túrin seems more inclined to return her feelings. The warning to the chiefs of the Rodothlim comes in dreams and not by messenger, and they are advised to depart rather than to shut themselves away. Túrin does not conceal his true name, and is only called Mormakil after the black sword Gurtholfin is made for him in Nargothrond. Although he persuades the Rodothlim to abandon their secrecy, there is no mention of the building of a bridge over the river. Túrin takes the name *Turambar* (meaning 'conqueror of fate') when Glorund the dragon taunts him and says that he will not slay him lest he escape his fate. When Túrin seeks his mother and sister he learns that they have departed, and that Brodda to whom Mavwin had entrusted her small herds had taken them as his own. When Túrin slays Brodda, by the judgement of Airin, Brodda's wife, friend and kinswoman of Mavwin, he is banished; he then joins not the Men of Brethil but a group of huntsmen or wood-rangers whose chieftain is Bethos. Nothing is told of Failivrin's fate after she is taken captive. When Mavwin who lives in safety and some prosperity hears long after of Túrin's departure from Doriath, she leaves her home and journeys there to seek Tinwelint's aid in finding her son. Both Mavwin and Nienóri encounter Glorund, are deprived of memory, and become separated. When Bethos dies Turambar is chosen to succeed him as chief, but the son of Bethos, Tamar Lamefoot, is bitter both because of this choice and because Turambar has wed Níniel. When Glorund moves to attack the settlement he leaves a guard under Mîm the Dwarf to watch his treasure. Níniel accompanies Turambar when he sets out to survey what might be done about the dragon, and he leaves her nearby with Tamar as her only companion. Only by an addition does Níniel conceive her brother's child; she does not fling herself into a ravine but over the water-fall of the Silver Bowl, where she had been seized with shuddering when she first saw it. Túrin slays Tamar on being told by him that Níniel was Nienóri, but knows in his heart that he speaks true and kills himself.

Tolkien began to tell the story at greater length in alliterative verse in *The Children of Húrin* (?1919–25) in two successive versions, both unfinished. The first version moves towards that in *The Silmarillion*: the Dragon-helm is introduced; Beleg and Túrin are companions in arms in Doriath; Túrin gathers outlaws around him when he flees Doriath; Beleg is captured and mistreated, but joins Túrin and the outlaws and persuades them to fight only evil creatures; they are betrayed by Blodrin, one of the outlaws, who resents this change; Nargothrond replaces the caves of the Rodothlim; and Failivrin is now the daughter of its ruler Orodreth. Tolkien abandoned the first version of the poem part way through Túrin's time in Nargothrond, but this includes the only detailed description of that place that Tolkien ever wrote. He abandoned the second version in turn before he reached the slaying of Orgof.

The *Sketch of the Mythology* (c. 1926) says that Morwen sent her son to Thingol before Nienor's birth, because faithless and hostile men had been settled by Morgoth in Hithlum where she is living. Túrin has Beleg's sword forged anew in Nargothrond, but the sword had not been given to Beleg by Thingol. An addition introduces Túrin's support for building a bridge over the Narog. Only when Morwen reaches Doriath does she learn that Túrin is no longer there; Túrin takes the name *Turambar* after the slaying of Brodda when he gathers a new people around him, among whom is Tamar the Lame; Nienor is alone when she is placed under a spell of forgetfulness by Glórung, and, by an addition, she is with child when Túrin sets out to slay the dragon.

Though Tolkien wrote the *Quenta Noldorinwa* (c. 1930) at greater length and with more detail than the *Sketch*, and some of its phrasing approaches that of *The Silmarillion*, he developed the story there in only a few aspects. The main reason for Morwen sending Túrin away is that hostile men driven into Hithlum enslave most of the women and children of the fallen faithful. After slaying Brodda Túrin meets woodmen who are survivors of the people of Haleth, who tell him how Finduilas perished. When the woodmen choose Túrin as their leader, the lame Brandir (replacing Tamar) who should have ruled yields to their choice.

These early texts include occasional references to the age of Túrin when certain events take place, and occasional indications of the length of time of certain events, as does *The Silmarillion*. According to the 'earliest' *Annals of Beleriand* (early 1930s), Túrin was born in the winter of Year 165 (an early change from 170); the Battle of Unnumbered Tears in which his father Húrin was captured took place in 172; Nienor was born at the beginning of 173, and Túrin (aged seven) sent to Doriath in that year; in 181 Morgoth's growing power prevented any further contact between Doriath and Morwen, and Túrin in the company of Beleg began to guard the marches of Doriath; in 184 Túrin killed Orgof, and he lived as an outlaw until 187, when the capture of Beleg shamed him into making war only on Orcs; in 189 the band was betrayed by Blodrin, Túrin was captured, and he killed Beleg by mistake; in 190 he was brought to Nargothrond by Flinding where he lived until its overthrow in 195; Morwen and Nienor left Hithlum for Doriath in 194; Túrin's visit to Hithlum and his slaying of Brodda, and the choice of Túrin as the lord of the woodmen, took place in 195–6; the ill-fated journey of Morwen and Nienor to Nargothrond and Nienor's rescue by Túrin occurred in 196; Túrin and Nienor were married in 198; in 199 Túrin killed Glómund and, on learning the truth of their relationship, both Nienor and Túrin committed suicide.

An unfinished second version of these annals added a hundred years to the Siege of Angband, which would have led to Túrin's birth taking place in 265, and so forth. In the 'later' *Annals of Beleriand* written in the mid-1930s Tolkien extended the Siege of Angband (by emendation) for a further 200 years, so that Túrin was born in the Year 465. No changes were made in the relationship of the various dates or the story.

In the mid-1930s Tolkien also began to write the **Quenta Silmarillion*, but left it unfinished in early 1938, after he had just begun (in late 1937) the story of Túrin with a chapter entitled 'Of Túrin Turamarth or Túrin the Hapless'. This extends only as far as Túrin's flight from Doriath after the slaying of Orgof, but the narrative was expanded to over five times the length of the same part of the story in the *Quenta Noldorinwa*. Tolkien took much of the extra detail from *The Children of Húrin*, and eventually this found its way also into the **Narn i Chîn Húrin*. The most significant change in the story is that Brodda had already taken most of Morwen's property and married Airin before Túrin was sent away.

At the beginning of the 1950s, when Tolkien turned again (from **The Lord of the Rings*) to work on 'The Silmarillion', among the works he began was the *Narn i Chîn Húrin*, telling the story of Túrin at great length as a prose narrative. This begins in the middle of the tale, after the fall of Nargothrond, as Túrin speeds north to find his mother and sister. Possibly Tolkien did so because he had already written at length of the earlier part of the story in *The Children of Húrin*. Every episode in Túrin's later life is described with much background information: whereas his return to Hithlum and slaying of Brodda is dealt with in only a brief paragraph in the *Quenta Noldorinwa*, it takes up five pages in the *Narn* as published in *Unfinished Tales*. The *Narn* includes an account of Túrin's meeting with the lame Sador Labadal whom he had known as a child, showing that Tolkien already had in mind details of Túrin's child-hood which he would not write about for nearly a decade. Tolkien also wrote a much longer and more detailed account to the expedition from Doriath to Nargothrond which shows the stubbornness of both Morwen and Nienor. This also introduces Mablung as their escort, who tries to save Nienor after she is held by the dragon's spell, but loses her when orcs attack.

In this the tale reverts to an earlier form in that Túrin does not become lord of the Men of Brethil, a position held by Brandir the Lame. Among the more interesting details added are that the woodmen buried Finduilas in the Haudh-en-Elleth, and that Túrin finds the naked, bespelled Nienor lying on that mound. Níniel no longer casts herself over the Dimrost, but into the nearby ravine. Christopher Tolkien comments on the attention his father paid in different versions to perfecting the details of the killing of Glaurung (see *The War of the Jewels*, pp. 152–6), and says of his own lengthy comments: 'This may seem much ado about a single episode, but it seems to me to illustrate in miniature the complex and subtle movement that is found in the history of the legends at large. It was, also, an episode of great importance: there are few "monsters" to rival Glaurung, and my father strove to perfect the tale of how Túrin earned the title of *Dagnir Glaurunga*' (p. 156). Tolkien was also con-cerned to provide a suitable means by which Túrin would realize that Brandir had told him the truth about Níniel's death: after considering various ideas, including one in which Túrin meets his mother, Tolkien decided that Túrin should learn from Mablung that Nienor and Níniel were indeed one and the same (see *The War of the Jewels*, pp. 161–5).

For the story of Túrin as far as the fall of Nargothrond the *Grey Annals* (c. 1951, see *Annals of Beleriand*) relate closely to the 'later' *Annals of Beleriand*, the *Quenta Silmarillion* (as far as it went), and the *Quenta Noldorinwa*. They did not add anything of great significance to the story, and remained basically annalistic in style and length except for the description of Túrin's encounter with Glaurung at Nargothrond. But the entries that relate Túrin's life after his departure from Nargothrond were much longer than before, Tolkien's own reduction of the *Narn i Chîn Húrin* to a suitable length. It is not clear whether the whole of this part of the *Narn* was completed first or whether Tolkien wrote the part of the *Grey Annals* concerning Túrin more or less simultaneously with the *Narn*. It should be noted that when Christopher Tolkien published the *Narn* in *Unfinished Tales* he thought that all of his father's work on it belonged to the end of the 1950s; after closer study, however, it was realized that the part of the *Narn* dealing with later events in Túrin's life in fact belonged rather to the beginning of the 1950s.

Towards the end of that decade Tolkien returned to the *Narn i Chîn Húrin* and began an extensive account of Túrin's earlier life, with many significant additions and developments. This was now a full narrative with much direct speech and well rounded characters, which indeed approaches parts of *The Lord of the Rings* in style. It includes an account of Túrin's childhood before he is cursed by Morgoth. It tells of his and his parents' grief when his much loved younger sister Urwen (or Lalaith) dies in a pestilence when she is only three. It also indicates traits in Túrin's character which may have been as much or more responsible for his ill-fate as Morgoth's curse: 'he was not merry . . . was slow to forget injustice or mockery; . . . he could be sudden and fierce' (*Unfinished Tales*, pp. 58–9). It also tells of his friendship with the lame Sador who is in the service of his family. Saeros (Orgof) is not killed by the drinking vessel thrown by Túrin, but when Saeros in anger the next day ambushes and attacks Túrin, he is overcome, stripped, and set to running through the forest. Saeros falls to his death while attempting to leap over a cleft. Túrin refuses to return to hear Thingol's judgement, and indeed Thingol is about to declare him banished when Beleg brings in as witness the maiden Nellas, who says that Saeros had attacked Túrin unawares, at which Thingol pardons Túrin. This text also develops the account of Túrin among the outlaws, his repentance after the capture of Beleg, the capture of Mîm who leads them to the stronghold of Amon Rûdh and feels some affection for Túrin but eventually betrays his band. The gift of the sword Anglachel by Thingol to Beleg also now entered.

Christopher Tolkien faced varying difficulties in editing this chapter for *The Silmarillion*. The part as far as Túrin's departure from Doriath after the slaying of Orgof existed in the *Quenta Silmarillion* text written in late 1937 and also in the *Grey Annals* of c. 1951. Tolkien however had greatly changed and developed the story of Túrin, from his early childhood to Morgoth's attack on Nargothrond, in the part of the *Narn i Chîn Húrin* written at the end of the 1950s. That work was too long to be used in *The Silmarillion* as it stood, and in places was disconnected and unfinished. Christopher Tolkien therefore combined elements from the *Quenta Silmarillion*, the *Grey Annals*, and the *Narn* and produced an abridged account of the latest version of the story.

For the middle portion of the tale, not reached in the *Quenta Silmarillion*, Christopher Tolkien turned to the *Narn*. That work, however,

> is here at its least finished, and in places diminishes to outlines of possible turns in the story. My father was still evolving this part when he ceased to work on it. . . . In preparing the text of *The Silmarillion* for publication I derived, by necessity, much of this section of the tale of Túrin from these very materials, which are of quite extraordinary complexity in their variety and interrelations. [*Unfinished Tales*, p. 6]

The *Grey Annals* seems to be the source for Gwindor's conversations with Finduilas and Túrin in Nargothrond, and for the visit of Gelmir and Arminas to Nargothrond. The rest was presumably formed from an abridgment of *Narn* texts published and unpublished.

As Christopher Tolkien notes in *The War of the Jewels*, 'virtually the sole source' for the latter part of the *Silmarillion* chapter 'Of Túrin Túrambar', from the defeat of the army of Nargothrond at the battle of Tumladen, was the *Grey Annals*, the narrative of which 'was *based directly on* the final text of that in the *Narn*, and was a *reduction* of that text' (p. 144). He did occasionally include short sections of text from the *Quenta Noldorinwa* and from the *Narn* itself (most notably from the latter Glaurung's last words to Nienor, and her farewell to Túrin). Christopher Tolkien himself noted (*The War of the Jewels*, p. 149) that for the journey of Morwen and Nienor to Nargothrond (p. 217 in *The Silmarillion*) he used the *Grey Annals*, the *Narn*, and the *Quenta Noldorinwa*.

One of the chronological outlines Tolkien made when working on the *Narn* in the late 1950s suggests that he was considering a further development in the story: that the reason for Morwen and Nienor leaving Hithlum was that Lorgan, the chief of the Easterlings, sought to take Nienor by force. Christopher Tolkien chose not to incorporate this idea.

Commenting on his father's failure to complete the *Quenta Silmarillion* in his later years, Christopher Tolkien wrote:

> There can be no simple explanation, but it seems to me that an important element was the centrality that my father accorded to the story of Húrin and Morwen and their children, Túrin Turambar and Niënor Níniel. This became for him, I believe, the dominant and absorbing story of the end of the Elder Days, in which complexity of motive and character, trapped in the mysterious workings of Morgoth's curse, sets it altogether apart. [*The War of the Jewels*, pp. viii–ix]

CRITICISM

Katharyn W. Crabbe comments in *J.R.R. Tolkien* (rev. and expanded edn. 1988) that 'most Tolkien characters who are on the side of the good are creators or life-givers', and that Túrin's one creative urge, the composition of the song in memory of Beleg, 'The Bowman's Friendship', provides him 'with a temporary cure for his despair'. She concludes that if Túrin really is cursed, he is

> a hero who, although he cannot triumph, can endure. . . . The one thing that one can say about Túrin is that he has courage. He may have bad judgment and bad timing, but he always has courage.
> The hero who is unfailingly courageous in the face of a hopeless situation allies Tolkien to a pre-Christian and nonromantic tradition – the ancient tradition of the hero whose virtue is not that he triumphs but that he endures. [pp. 186–7]

In *The Song of Middle-earth: J.R.R. Tolkien's Themes, Symbols and Myths* (1985) David Harvey comments that

> the incestuous relationship with Nienor is not the sole tragic element

in Túrin's history. It is one of the contributing factors to the spectacular downfall that he must suffer. It is perhaps because of the nature of incest and its use as a tragic theme in Oedipus and the *Kalevala* that it has a tendency to obscure the other equally important tragic aspects of Túrin's career. The fall of Túrin is continually associated with death. The death of Saeros is accidental. It is Túrin's anger, pride and fear of injustice that prevents him from returning to Thingol. But he cannot flee from the justice that pursues the tragic hero and which must inevitably overtake him. His major fault is his violent anger. This is set against his generosity, his love of justice and his obvious filial piety. He recognises in his self-naming the errors of his ways and the faults that beset him. Yet he cannot run from his own nature or from the violent anger that flares and results in the deaths of Beleg and Brandir. The curse upon Túrin lies within himself and is not laid upon him by Morgoth. [p. 76]

See also T.A. Shippey's discussion of the story and the causes or root of the tragedy – Túrin's character, bad luck, Morwen's ignoring the advice of Húrin, 'unfortunate' phrases and allusions, fate – in *J.R.R. Tolkien: Author of the Century* (2000), pp. 249–54.

Marie Barnfield in 'Túrin Turambar and the Tale of the Fosterling', *Mallorn* 31 (December 1994), discusses possible sources for the story of Turin. Gergely Nagy argues for a 'mythological' relationship between the Túrin texts in 'The Great Chain of Reading: (Inter-)textual Relations and the Technique of Mythopoesis in the Túrin Story', in *Tolkien the Medievalist* (2003). Richard C. West, in 'Túrin's *Ofermod*: An Old English Theme in the Development of the Story of Túrin', *Tolkien's Legendarium: Essays on The History of Middle-earth* (2000), considers the thirteenth-century *Völsunga Saga* 'at least as strong an influence on Túrin as the *Kalevala* and a good deal more pervasive. From it, supplemented perhaps by the *Nibelungenlied* and *Beowulf, Tolkien took much of his dragon lore. . . . In particular, the tactic by which Turin slays his worm . . . is very reminiscent of how Sigurd kills Fáfnir, different as the battles are in other respects . . .' (p. 239). West also compares Túrin's 'overmastering pride' with that discerned in Beorhtnoth in **The Homecoming of Beorhtnoth Beorhthelm's Son*: 'It is heroic to build a bridge over the Narog so that Elvish armies can march out against an evil enemy, but it also allows that enemy a means of access to the kingdom of Nargothrond. In maintaining the bridge, against the counsel of Ulmo the Vala, he is rash in the way Beorhtnoth was, permitting two armies to join battle for the sake of honor when one is far stronger' (p. 244).

See further, entry for **The Children of Húrin*.

Turlin and the Exiles of Gondolin. Prose fragment, published in **The Shaping of Middle-earth* (1986), pp. 3–5. Ilfiniol son of Bronweg (who as Littleheart the Gong-warden of the Cottage of Lost Play relates the story of *The Fall of Gondolin* in **The Book of Lost Tales*) tells first how Ulmo strove to help the

Gnomes (Noldorin Elves) and to stir them to send messengers to Valinor. When all who tried to do so failed because of Melko, Ulmo thought of a new plan. Ilfiniol then tells how a mighty house of Men who had arrived too late to take part in the Battle of Unnumbered Tears (see *'The Silmarillion') lived in Dor-Lómin. Among them was Turgon, who sought the company of Elves. One day he entered a cavern and was driven forward and could not retrace his steps, but Gnomes came and guided him through the passage.

The manuscript of *Turlin and the Exiles of Gondolin* breaks off at this point. It was probably written at the beginning of the 1920s, and seems to be the beginning of a new version of *The Fall of Gondolin*. In the text but not in its title, Tolkien emended *Turlin* to *Turgon*, but the name refers not to the King of Gondolin but rather to Tuor (see *'Of Tuor and the Fall of Gondolin').

Turville-Petre, Edward Oswald Gabriel (1908–1978). Gabriel Turville-Petre read English at Oxford, and 1931–4 completed a B.Litt. under Tolkien's supervision. In the course of his postgraduate study, in Trinity Term 1933, he taught a class in Old Norse on Tolkien's behalf. His thesis, an edition of the thirteenth-century *Víga-Glúms Saga*, was published in 1940 in the *Oxford English Monographs* series, of which Tolkien was a general editor. He wrote in its preface (p. vi): 'It would be difficult to overestimate all that I owe to Professor Tolkien; his sympathy and encouragement have been constant and, throughout the work, I have had the benefit of his wide scholarship.' Many other writings followed, including *The Heroic Age of Scandinavia* (1951), *Origins of Icelandic Literature* (1953; 2nd edn. 1967), an enlarged edition of *Víga-Glúms Saga* (1960), *Myth and Religion of the North* (1964), and articles for the *Saga-Book* of the Viking Society for Northern Research, of which journal Turville-Petre was joint editor from 1939 to 1963. He also contributed an essay on the Essex place-name *Thurstable* to the *Festschrift *English and Medieval Studies Presented to J.R.R. Tolkien on the Occasion of His Seventieth Birthday* (1962).

He made frequent visits to Iceland and other Northern lands to reinforce his studies. From 1936 to 1938 he was Lecturer in English at the University of Iceland, and from 1935 to 1950 Honorary Lecturer in Modern Icelandic at the University of Leeds. In 1941 he was appointed the first Vigfússon Reader in Ancient Icelandic Literature and Antiquities at the University of Oxford. In 1953 he was granted the title of Professor during the term of his Readership.

Beginning in December 1949 Turville-Petre supervised the Oxford B.Litt. thesis of *Christopher Tolkien. From this work resulted both *Hervarar saga ok Heiðreks* (1956), with notes and glossary by Turville-Petre and an introduction by Christopher Tolkien, and the latter's annotated translation *The Saga of King Heidrek the Wise* (1960).

In 1943 Turville-Petre married Joan Elizabeth Blomfield (*Joan Turville-Petre), with Tolkien and his wife in attendance.

Turville-Petre, Joan Elizabeth. Joan Turville-Petre (*née* Blomfield) of Somerville College, *Oxford studied for a B.Litt. under Tolkien from 1933 to 1935; her thesis was *The Origins of Old English Orthography, with Special Reference to the Representation of the Spirants and W*. Later she joined the Oxford English Faculty. Her 1938 essay 'The Style and Structure of *Beowulf*' (*Review of English Studies*) embraced Tolkien's remarks on the structure of **Beowulf* in **Beowulf: The Monsters and the Critics*. After Tolkien's death she prepared for publication (1981), as a 'salute [to] the memory of an inspiring teacher', his edited text and translation of the Old English *Exodus* (**The Old English Exodus*), with commentary and notes, that he had made for a series of lectures on the poem.

In 1943 Joan Blomfield married **E.O.G. Turville-Petre, with Tolkien and his wife in attendance.

The Two Towers *see* **The Lord of the Rings**

Unfinished Tales of Númenor and Middle-earth. Collection of miscellaneous writings, edited with notes and commentary by **Christopher Tolkien, first published in Great Britain by George Allen & Unwin, London, in October 1980, and in the United States by the Houghton Mifflin Company, Boston, in November 1980. See further, *Descriptive Bibliography* A17.

Part One, 'The First Age', contains **Of Tuor and His Coming to Gondolin* and *Narn i Hîn Húrin: The Tale of the Children of Húrin* (**Narn i Chîn Húrin*).

Part Two, 'The Second Age', contains **A Description of the Island of Númenor*, with a map redrawn by Christopher Tolkien; **Aldarion and Erendis: The Mariner's Wife*; **The Line of Elros: Kings of Númenor from the Founding of the City of Armenelos to the Downfall*; and **The History of Galadriel and Celeborn and of Amroth King of Lórien*.

Part Three, 'The Third Age', contains **The Disaster of the Gladden Fields*, with an appendix, *Númenórean Linear Measures*; **Cirion and Eorl and the Friendship of Gondor and Rohan*; **The Quest of Erebor*; **The Hunt for the Ring*; and **The Battles of the Fords of Isen*.

Part Four (no section title) contains *The Drúedain*, including *The Faithful Stone* (see **Of Dwarves and Men* and **The Rivers and Beacon-hills of Gondor*); **The Istari*; and **The Palantíri*.

Some of the titles in *Unfinished Tales* were assigned by Christopher Tolkien for convenience of reference.

HISTORY

The contents of the volume are 'unfinished' in different senses of the word. Some parts are incomplete narratives; some are rough drafts which never reached a final fair copy; some are fragments which Tolkien considered for inclusion in the Appendices to **The Lord of the Rings* but ultimately omitted, or which he wrote while working out the background to the Appendices; some are extracts from late philological essays or historical narratives; and a few were assembled by the editor from multiple sources. 'The narratives in this book', Christopher Tolkien writes in his introduction, 'constitute no whole, and the book is no more than a collection of writings, disparate in form, intent, finish, and date of composition (and in my own treatment of them), concerned with Númenor and Middle-earth.' As such it contrasts with *The Silmarillion (1977), in which variant texts were combined and edited to form 'a completed and cohesive entity', and it anticipates the more elaborate and systematic examination of Tolkien's writings, with more extensive commentary and notes, presented in *The History of Middle-earth (1983–96). Just as it was for Christopher Tolkien 'out of the question' that The Silmarillion 'should remain unknown . . . despite its disordered state', so the publication of other 'unfinished tales' was justified for the sake of their memorable moments and imagery, and for the rewards offered by the opportunity to further explore Tolkien's invented world (Unfinished Tales, p. 1).

At first Christopher Tolkien intended to include in Unfinished Tales the general map of Middle-earth he had drawn for The Lord of the Rings, 'but it seemed to me on reflection that it would be better to copy my original map and take the opportunity to remedy some of its minor defects' (p. 13). The redrawn map of 1980 contains additions and corrections: see further, Reader's Companion, pp. lxvi–lxvii.

CRITICISM

Many reviewers of Unfinished Tales disparaged its miscellaneous, fragmentary nature. Typical among these was Frederick Buechner in the New York Times Book Review, who described the book as 'a production less of Tolkien himself than of the Tolkien industry – a book for the specialist, the scholar of Middle-earth, the addict, who will doubtless revel in the wealth of lore that it provides. For the rest of us, I'm afraid, it cannot be more than a dim echo of glories past, a scattering of crumbs left over from a great and unforgettable feast' ('For Devotees of Middle-Earth', 16 November 1980, p. 20). In the British Fantasy Society Bulletin for March/April 1981, Martin D. Pay wrote that Unfinished Tales

> is a must for the serious Tolkien enthusiast, the person who wants to know more of the background to the creation of Middle-earth and the development of its history over a span of more than fifty years. The reader who accepts The Lord of the Rings and The Silmarillion as completed works entire unto themselves, however, will find the book, at best, boring and at worst, incomprehensible. . . .

And in Macleans magazine, fantasy novelist Guy Gavriel Kay, who had assisted Christopher Tolkien in editing The Silmarillion, wrote that 'for someone innocently seeking a good read, Unfinished Tales emerges as inaccessible, pedantic and perhaps ultimately saddening. Where has the magic gone? One feels at times like an archeologist, digging amongst the dusty rubble of a once-glorious civilization' ('Dug Out of the Dust of Middle-earth', 26 January 1981, p. 46).

In the *Washington Post*, however, Paul Piazza called *Unfinished Tales* 'an assemblage of brilliant fragments that gleam in scattered but splendid isolation. Though they lack context and thus lack full luster, the tales – perhaps because of their piecemeal nature – are all the more intriguing. Imaginative might-have-beens, they point to the vast cosmic scheme Tolkien envisaged, one of the boldest literary enterprises of the century' ('Mosaics from Middle-earth: Fragments of Tolkien's World', *Washington Post*, 8 December 1980, p. B7).

Unwin, Rayner Stephens (1925–2000). One of four children of publisher *Stanley Unwin, Rayner Unwin was educated at Trinity College, Oxford (B.A. 1949) and at Harvard University from 1949 to 1950 as a Fulbright Scholar, earning his Master's degree in English. In 1951 he formally entered the family firm, George Allen & Unwin (*Publishers); he had been involved in its operations, however, since he was a boy. At the age of ten he made, as he was later fond of saying, the best decision of his career in publishing when he wrote a favourable report on *The Hobbit*, ensuring its publication. A few months later he also read and recommended *Farmer Giles of Ham* and *Roverandom*.

Upon leaving school at seventeen Unwin worked briefly for Blackwell's Bookshop in Oxford, then as the representative of Allen & Unwin in the Midlands and East Anglia. Later he spent several months at Unwin Brothers, the family-owned printing works outside Woking, observing that side of book production, and then at the London offices of the Cambridge University Press, to learn the practice of book distribution. When at last he came to work at Allen & Unwin's offices in Museum Street, London, although the heir apparent to Stanley Unwin's chairmanship – David Unwin, Rayner's elder brother, having turned to writing children's books as 'David Severn' – he began in the trade department, answering booksellers' queries and with responsibility for salesmen and agents abroad. He continued in Sales during the 1950s, but also became a sponsoring editor.

Since Rayner's review of *The Hobbit* in 1936, Tolkien never failed to show affection towards him. When Rayner was a naval cadet at *Oxford in 1943 Tolkien visited him in his rooms in Trinity College, and Rayner visited Tolkien for tea at 20 Northmoor Road. They saw each other also after the war, when Rayner returned to Oxford to complete his B.A., and Tolkien took the opportunity to have him read parts of *The Lord of the Rings*, then in progress.

> Over tea, fussed over by *Edith [Tolkien], and subjected to cheerful monologues by the Professor on cruxes and variations that sometimes referred to what I had been reading, and sometimes to the totally unknown *Silmarillion*, I assumed that everything was proceeding slowly but in the right direction. We scarcely mentioned my academic work. . . . I did not even attend his lectures. He had adopted me as a friendly young initiate to Middle-earth, and I was unimaginatively content in that role.
> [Rayner Unwin, *George Allen & Unwin: A Remembrancer* (1999), p. 92]

In November 1951 and June 1952, now in a formal capacity at Allen & Unwin, Rayner wrote to Tolkien on routine matters and asked about the progress of *The Lord of the Rings* and *The Silmarillion*. Tolkien's negotiations with Collins to publish those works having failed, he was delighted to hear from Rayner, to whom he poured out his feelings. He wondered if Allen & Unwin was still interested in *The Lord of the Rings*, which earlier he had demanded be published together with the (unfinished) *Silmarillion*. Rayner replied at once, with characteristic diplomacy, and brought Tolkien back into the Allen & Unwin fold. Reading the complete *Lord of the Rings* (save for the Appendices), he found it a work of genius, and recommended its publication, though the firm risked a substantial loss if it did not sell.

The success of *The Lord of the Rings*, together with *The Hobbit* and shorter works by Tolkien, buoyed the fortunes of Allen & Unwin for decades. Rayner kept in frequent touch with Tolkien, telephoning, sending letters full of encouragement, visiting him in Oxford or lunching with him in London – not entirely for the sake of a completed *Silmarillion* or Tolkien's Modern English translation of *Sir Gawain and the Green Knight*, both perpetually delayed, but out of genuine friendship and admiration. Tolkien reciprocated. On 21 July 1967 he wrote to Rayner: 'I am singularly fortunate in having such a friend. I feel, if I may say so, that our relations are like that of Rohan and Gondor, and (as you know) for my part the oath of Eorl will never be broken, and I shall continue to rely on and be grateful for the wisdom and courtesy of Minas Tirith' (*Letters*, p. 379). In *George Allen & Unwin: A Remembrancer* Rayner wondered why he had been so privileged to have not only Tolkien's friendship but his trust: 'I was not of his generation and did not share his Faith; I was not in his league as a scholar, and I came to represent the humdrum, often unhelpful, side of the creative processes that impelled his life' (pp. 88–9).

Upon Stanley Unwin's death in 1968 Rayner succeeded him as chairman of Allen & Unwin. He also became an advisor to the Tolkien Estate and consulted closely with *Christopher Tolkien on new projects. He saw through the press the long-awaited *Silmarillion* and many other posthumous works by Tolkien, most notably the first volumes of *The History of Middle-earth*. His policy of reissues and periodic changes to book covers on the Tolkien line helped to keep it fresh in the public eye. The fortunes of Allen & Unwin were long buoyed by Tolkien's works; they declined, however, in the difficult economy of the 1970s and early 1980s, until in 1985 financial exigency forced Allen & Unwin to merge with Bell & Hyman, becoming Unwin Hyman. Five years later, Unwin Hyman was bought by HarperCollins, under circumstances that angered Rayner and led to his resignation from the Board of Unwin Hyman in protest.

In *George Allen & Unwin: A Remembrancer* Rayner placed upon himself much of the blame for the decline of the family firm, claiming that he 'never had the confidence, which my father instinctively possessed, to manage a Company with assurance'. But his account of the final years of Allen & Unwin makes it clear that the real blame must be attached to market forces beyond his control. In the end he worked hard to secure not only a measure of protection for the Tolkien Estate under the new owner of the publishing rights, but also the continued successful existence of the Allen & Unwin imprint by its former subsidiary in Australia.

Unwin long played active roles in organizations associated with books publishing. From 1965 to 1985 he was a member of the Publishers' Association council. From 1981 to 1988 he was chairman of the British Council publishers' advisory committee, and from 1989 to 1995 president of the Book Trade Benevolent Society. He also served as executive of the committee of the National Life Story Collection, the oral history archive at the British Library. As director of the Stanley Unwin Foundation, founded in 1968, he established Book House in Wandsworth, London, as the home of the Book Trust. He was awarded the CBE in 1977.

A promising author himself, Rayner Unwin published, in addition to the autobiographical *Remembrancer, The Gulf of Years* (1953), an edition of the letters of John Ruskin to Kathleen Olander; *The Rural Muse: Studies in the Peasant Poetry of England* (1954); *The Defeat of John Hawkins: A Biography of His Third Slaving Voyage* (1960); and *A Winter Away from Home: William Barents and the North-east Passage* (1995).

A photograph of Rayner Unwin is reproduced in *The Tolkien Family Album*, p. 81.

See also works by Rayner Unwin: 'The Hobbit 50th Anniversary' *The Bookseller*, 16 January 1987 (reprinted in *Science Fiction Chronicle*, June 1987, and in *Books for Keeps*, September 1987); 'Taming the Lord of the Rings', *The Bookseller*, 19 August 1988; 'Publishing Tolkien' in *Proceedings of the J.R.R. Tolkien Centenary Conference 1992* (1995); 'An At Last Finished Tale: The Genesis of *The Lord of the Rings*', *Lembas-extra 1998* (1998); and 'Early Days of Elder Days' in *Tolkien's Legendarium: Essays on The History of Middle-earth* (2000). His *George Allen & Unwin: A Remembrancer* is a significant resource for the biographical and bibliographical study of Tolkien. Jane Potter's article 'Rayner Stephens Unwin' in the *Oxford Dictionary of National Biography* (2004) is particularly useful. Among obituaries of Rayner Unwin, that by Philip Attenborough for *The Independent*, 23 December 2000, is the most sensitive to its subject.

Unwin, Stanley (1884–1968). Stanley Unwin was the son of the founder of the printing firm Unwin Brothers and of the daughter of papermaker James Spicer. His first employment was as an office boy in a London shipping office, but the foundations of his career in publishing were laid by nine months' work in a Leipzig bookshop, where he had his first experience with the European book trade. In 1904 he entered the publishing firm of T. Fisher Unwin, his father's younger stepbrother; there he specialized in contracts and the marketing of foreign rights. In 1912 he resigned, and with his brother-in-law Severn Storr toured British dominions and the Far East, studying important export markets; their journals of the experience were later published as *Two Young Men*

See the World (1934). In 1914 Unwin bought the firm of George Allen & Co. Ltd out of bankruptcy and created George Allen & Unwin Ltd (*Publishers).

Despite shortages during the First World War, Unwin was able to satisfy much of the public's greatly increased demand for books, and as virtually the only publisher at the time willing to print all points of view (Unwin himself leaned to the Left, and was a pacifist) Allen & Unwin attracted to its list noted intellects such as Bertrand Russell and works such as *Six Weeks in Russia in 1919* by *Arthur Ransome. This approach was characteristic of Unwin: support of the free flow of ideas despite the risk of controversy, opposition to censorship, the publication of 'books that matter'. As Director of the firm Stanley Unwin kept apprised of all of its operations, even to the extent of opening the daily post when he was not travelling.

Unwin himself was outspoken on subjects in which he was expert: the course of the British book trade, the economics of publishing, the inequities for foreign publishers under copyright law in the United States. His book *The Truth about Publishing* (1st edn. 1926) became a standard work. He was active in the Publishers' Association and the International Publishers' Congress, and served on the Executive Committee of the British Council. From time to time he was able to consolidate other publishers with Allen & Unwin, and 1937 worked with two of his competitors, J.M. Dent and Jonathan Cape, to co-operatively run the publisher the Bodley Head, which had been insolvent for more than a decade. He was knighted in 1946 and created KCMG in 1966.

In 1960 he published his autobiography, *The Truth about a Publisher*, a lengthy work which naturally says much also about the history of George Allen & Unwin. In this Unwin names *The Hobbit* as 'the best of its kind' and 'one of my favourite publications'. 'Now Allen & Unwin have never published many children's books, but those they do issue . . . are mostly outstanding. *The Hobbit* easily heads the list. My younger son [Rayner], as a boy, must have read it eight or nine times, so absorbing did he find it' (p. 233).

Tolkien and Unwin had a productive working relationship, despite differences of lifestyle – Unwin, a strict Noncomformist, neither smoked nor drank – and of opinion. They disagreed notably over Tolkien's demand in 1950 that *The Lord of the Rings* and *The Silmarillion* be published at the same time, though that was financially impossible and *The Silmarillion* was far from finished. In a draft letter to rival publisher *Milton Waldman, 5 February 1950, Tolkien said that he had 'friendly personal relations with Stanley (whom all the same I do not much like) and with his second son Rayner (whom I do like very much)' (*Letters*, p. 135). Even so, Tolkien was grateful for kindnesses shown to him by Stanley Unwin, especially in the promotion of his books. For the Golden Wedding anniversary of Tolkien and his wife *Edith in 1966 Unwin sent them fifty golden roses.

In an article by Nicolette Jones, 'Tolkien – "He was impossible, but a gent"', *Publishing News*, 20 February 1987, Rayner Unwin recalled the last meeting between his father and Tolkien: 'It was at the Garrick [Club in London]. They were both rather deaf. My father talked about the balance sheet, which Tolkien didn't understand, and he talked about *The Silmarillion*, which my father didn't understand. But they were full of goodwill. They knew they owed each other a lot – but they weren't sure what for' (p. 11).

See also Robin Denniston, 'Sir Stanley Unwin', *Oxford Dictionary of National Biography* (online edn.); and 'Sir Stanley Unwin: An Influential Publisher', *Times* (London), 15 October 1968.

Valaquenta. The second component of *The Silmarillion (1977), pp. 23–32. It includes an introduction and a text in three parts.

SUMMARY

The *Valaquenta* (Quenya 'account of the Valar') is a history of the Ainur – the Valar and the Maiar – according to the lore of the Eldar. Eru, the One, made the Ainur of his thought, and they participated in the Music of Creation. Some of them laboured long to achieve the vision they had seen in the Music, 'until in the time appointed was made Arda, the Kingdom of Earth. Then they put on the raiment of Earth and descended into it, and dwelt therein' (*The Silmarillion*, p. 25).

'Of the Valar' lists the greatest of the Ainur, the Powers, whom Men have often called gods: seven Lords – Manwë, Ulmo, Aulë, Oromë, Mandos, Irmo (also called Lórien), and Tulkas; and seven Queens – Varda, Yavanna, Vairë, Estë (the spouses of Manwë, Aulë, Mandos and Irmo respectively), Nienna the sister of Mandos and Irmo, Nessa the sister of Oromë and spouse of Tulkas, and Vána the younger sister of Yavanna and spouse of Oromë. The spheres of influence of each of these, their relationships with each other, and briefly their dwelling places are described. Originally nine of the Valar 'were of chief power and reverence', but Melkor was removed from their number, leaving eight, 'the Aratar, the High Ones of Arda: Manwë and Varda, Ulmo, Yavanna and Aulë, Mandos, Nienna, and Oromë' (p. 29).

'Of the Maiar' describes the spirits of lesser degree who accompanied the Valar, and names a few of them: Ilmarë the handmaid of Varda, Eönwë the herald of Manwë, Ossë and Uinen who are vassals of Ulmo, Melian of whom much is told in the **Quenta Silmarillion* (see *'Of Thingol and Melian'), and Olórin, who was later called Gandalf.

'Of the Enemies' discusses Melkor, the powerful Vala who turned to evil and was called Morgoth by the Elves, and those spirits whom he corrupted, some of whom became Balrogs. The greatest of his servants was Sauron, originally a Maia who served Aulë.

HISTORY

In the first account of Creation in Tolkien's mythology, *The Music of the Ainur*, c. 1919, Arda took shape during the making of the Music, and the Valar did not have to labour to achieve the vision. Unlike the remote and noble Valar of *The*

Silmarillion, those of *The Music of the Ainur* and *The Coming of the Valar and the Building of Valinor* (both published in *The Book of Lost Tales, Part One*) are much closer to the gods of Olympus or Asgard, with many faults and weaknesses. They have children, and even include among their number Makar and Meássë, a brother and sister whose main concern is strife and discord. In the earlier *'Silmarillion' the number of the Valar, their names, and some of their relationships differ from those published in *The Silmarillion*: they are named as Manwë and Varda, Melko, Ulmo, Aulë and Palúrien/Yavanna, Falman-Ossë and Ónen his consort, Salmar/Noldorin, Tulkas Poldórëa, Lórien Olofántur, Vefántur Mandos and Fui Nienna, Oromë and Vána, Makar, Meássë, and Ómar. Fui Nienna is there the spouse of Mandos and not his sister, and Oromë is the son of Aulë and Yavanna. Nessa is not named as one of the Valar, but appears in a later section of *The Book of Lost Tales* as the sister of Oromë and the wife of Tulkas.

The idea of the Maiar as Ainur, but less powerful than the Valar, was not at first present. Instead there were the 'lesser Vali . . . the sylphs of the airs and of the winds' who follow Manwë and Varda, and 'the sprites of trees and woods, of dale and forest and mountain-side . . . brownies, fays, pixies, leprawns' (*The Book of Lost Tales, Part One*, pp. 65–6) who follow Yavanna and Aulë. Fionwë Úrion and Erinti, the precursors of Eönwë and Ilmarë, are the children of Manwë and Varda. Though Ossë is subordinate to Ulmo with whom he is often in conflict, both he and Ónen are included among the Valar. Tindriel/Wendelin (Melian) is variously described as a 'lonely twilight spirit' (*The Book of Lost Tales, Part One*, p. 106) or 'a sprite . . . from the quiet gardens of Lórien' (p. 115) or 'the fay' (p. 120). The various dwelling places of the Valar are described in great detail. Elves who are slain go to Mandos, and Men who are slain to his wife Fui Nienna. Much is said also about their fates after death.

The 'Nine Valar' are mentioned in both the fragmentary poem *The Flight of the Noldoli from Valinor*, probably written in the earlier part of 1925, and in the *Sketch of the Mythology* (c. 1926), but not until the *Quenta Noldorinwa* written in 1930 are they listed. The nine chieftains of the Valar or Nine Gods and their spouses are Manwë and Varda, Ulmo, Ossë and Uinen, Aulë and Yavanna, Mandos and Nienna, Lórien, Tulkas, Oromë and Vana (described as the younger sister of both Varda and Yavanna and the mother of Nessa), and Melko. Makar, Meássë, and Ómar are no longer present; Salmar is not mentioned, and his omission presumably indicates that he was no longer counted among the Valar. The Valar still bring many spirits with them.

In the 'earliest' *Annals of Valinor*, written in the early 1930s, Nessa is again the sister of Oromë and is named as the wife of Tulkas. By an added note she is the daughter of Yavanna. Estë is introduced as the wife of Lórien, and by emendation Vairë becomes the wife of Mandos. Nienna now has no spouse, but is the sister of Manwë and Melko who are the most puissant of the Valar and brethren. With the Valar 'came many lesser spirits, their children, or beings of their own kind but of less might; these are the Valarindi' (*The Shaping of Middle-earth*, p. 263). The 'later' *Annals of Valinor* of the mid-1930s repeat much of what is said in the 'earliest' *Annals*, but now Oromë, Tulkas, Ossë, and Lórien 'are younger in the thought of Ilúvatar' than the other Valar, and Oromë is the son of Yavanna but not of Aulë, who were espoused only after they entered the world. With the Valar 'came many lesser spirits, beings of their own kind but of smaller might; these are the Vanimor, the Beautiful. And with them also were later numbered their children, begotten in the world, but of divine race, who were many and fair; these are the Valarindi' (*The Lost Road and Other Writings*, p. 110). Some of these changes also appear in versions of the 'earliest' *Annals* written in Old English.

In the mid-1930s Tolkien wrote an account of the Music of Creation, the *Ainulindalë*, a subject previously only described in *The Book of Lost Tales*. He includes in it an account of the Ainur who choose to enter Arda. It describes the powers of the four greatest: Melko, Manwë, Ulmo, and Aulë. Salmar, Ossë, and Uinen came with Ulmo. Varda is the spouse of Manwë, and their children are Fionwë Urion and Ilmarë. Mandos is mentioned in passing but none of the other Valar. The first chapter in the *Quenta Silmarillion* (also of the mid-1930s but later than the *Ainulindalë*), 'Of the Valar', is the precursor of the *Valaquenta* in *The Silmarillion*, though much shorter. It lists and comments on each of the Valar, among whom Ossë is still numbered, but there are no sections on the Maiar and the Enemies; Melko is described last after the other Valar.

The new versions of the *Ainulindalë* written in 1946 and 1951 introduced a major change: after the Music the Valar were shown a vision, not reality, and had to labour long to bring it into being. Both refer to the 'Seven Great Ones' (*Morgoth's Ring*, p. 15): Manwë, Ulmo, Aulë, Varda, Yavanna, Nienna, and Melkor. As in the earlier version, Salmar, Ossë, and Uinen come with Ulmo.

In *c.* 1951 Tolkien revised 'Of the Valar' in the *Quenta Silmarillion*, mainly with minor changes of wording. Fionwë and Ilmarë were now still the son and daughter of Manwë and Varda, but this was later struck through; and those who accompanied the Valar were still 'lesser spirits of their own kind' (p. 144). Estë is no longer numbered among the queens of the Valar, but she is still Lórien's wife. A paragraph added at the end of the text states there were nine Valar and seven queens of the Valar (specifically excluding Estë so Varda, Yavanna, Nienna, Vairë, Vána, Nessa, and Uinen) of which seven are pre-eminent, 'the Seven Great Ones of Arda' (*Morgoth's Ring*, p. 147): Manwë and Melkor, Varda, Ulmo, Yavanna, Aulë, and Nienna.

The *Annals of Aman* (*c.* 1951, see *Annals of Valinor*) was a new and expanded version of the *Annals of Valinor*. There only Oromë and Tulkas are said to be younger in the thought of Ilúvatar. The 'spirits of like kind but less might and authority' (p. 49) who accompany the Valar into the world are now called the Maiar, and the children of the Valar are numbered with them. Estë is not a Vala but the chief of the Maiar. Oromë is not stated to be Yavanna's son, but his wife Vána is the sister of Yavanna and Varda. Elsewhere in the *Annals* Melian is referred to as a Maia, and Sauron as the chief of the Maiar whom Melkor has perverted to his cause. Probably soon after the writing of the *Annals of Aman* Tolkien made a typescript with various changes: Vana is not said to be the sister of Yavanna, Nessa becomes a Maia rather than a Vala, and Nienna is said to be the sister of Manwë with no mention of Melkor. Contemporary emendations allow Nessa to remain a Vala but have no spouse, and the wife of Tulkas is Léa the Young.

Tolkien returned to 'Of the Valar' in the *Quenta Silmarillion c.* 1958–60 when his ideas about the Valar had changed. He replaced any use of 'wife' to describe a relationship of two Valar with 'spouse' and wrote a marginal comment: 'Note that "spouse" meant only an association. The Valar had no bodies but could assume shapes' (*Morgoth's Ring*, p. 151). At the same time he removed references to the Children of the Valar, and added three paragraphs describing the Maiar, including Eönwë (formerly Fionwë) and Ilmarë (no longer the children of Manwë and Varda), Melian and Olórin. He briefly notes that some Maiar followed Melkor, including Sauron.

Probably *c.* 1959 amanuensis typescripts were made of the *Annals of Aman* and the revised 'Of the Valar' in the *Quenta Silmarillion*, taking up early revisions. These were then further emended by Tolkien. Revisions made to the *Quenta Silmarillion* typescript include some changes in the relationships of the Valar: Yavanna and Varda are no longer sisters, and Vána is the sister only of Yavanna; Nienna is now the sister of Mandos, and not of Manwë. On a carbon copy Tolkien rewrote the description of Oromë, adding much new material, then made a typescript from the top copy which at first followed it closely but then diverged, becoming a draft with much new material added. Tolkien apparently abandoned it unfinished, and probably at once produced a second typescript, making more emendations. The first unfinished typescript was still headed 'Quenta Silmarillion', but a second, now headed 'Valaquenta', has become a separate work, no longer part of the *Quenta Silmarillion*. The number of the chieftains of the Valar becomes seven instead of nine by the removal of Melkor and Ossë; the queens of Valier remain seven, but Estë replaces Uinen; Ossë and Uinen are now Maiar. Similar late changes were made to the *Annals of Aman* and a note added that Ossë 'was not a Vala, but a chief of the Maiar, servant of Ulmo' (p. 91). The number eight of the Aratar or High Ones was achieved by removing Melkor and adding Mandos and Oromë.

The text of the *Valaquenta* in *The Silmarillion* is that of the second typescript. Various editorial changes by *Christopher Tolkien are noted in *Morgoth's Ring*, pp. 200–205, and *The Book of Lost Tales, Part One*, p. 82.

Valedictory Address to the University of Oxford. Although Tolkien was twice elected to chairs at the University of *Oxford, he never gave an inaugural lecture. Instead, on 5 June 1959, on the occasion of his retirement, he delivered a valedictory, of which he made several drafts. One was published in *J.R.R. Tolkien, Scholar and Storyteller: Essays in Memoriam*, ed. *Mary Salu and Robert T. Farrell (1979), pp. 16–32, and another, incorporating many alterations made by the author (either before or after delivery), was first published in *The Monsters and the Critics and Other Essays* (1983), pp. 224–40.

Tolkien reflects on his years in the Oxford Honour School of English Language and Literature. He regrets 'the loss of the M.A. as a genuine degree', and feels that the B.Litt. is 'the wrong tool' to address a 'real need . . . the desire for knowledge'. The B.Litt. is not a true 'research' degree: its 'proper scope . . . is much more limited' (*The Monsters and the Critics and Other Essays*, p. 227). Given the long history of English letters, there is much knowledge to be gained, and too little time for reading and learning. 'As far as my personal experience goes,' Tolkien says,

> if I had been allowed to guide the further reading and study of those for whom the Honour School had opened vistas and awakened curiosity, I could have done more good in *less time* than in the so-called supervision of research, done by candidates who had essential territories yet to explore, and who, in the breathless march from Prelim. to Final Schools, had also left much country in rear, only raided and not occupied. [pp. 228–9]

He suggests 'the possibility of taking a higher, or at least a further, degree for learning things, for acquiring more of the essential parts of the English field, or for digging deeper in some of them. . . .' As it is, students must contend with 'a four-year syllabus for the reading-time of two years and a bit' (p. 229).

Tolkien also regrets that 'sides' have been taken in the Oxford English School: 'Lang' (Language) and 'Lit' (Literature). But these are only aspects or emphases of a single subject, and should not be taken as 'parties', 'uneasy nest-fellows, each trying to grab more of the candidates' time' (p. 231). Tolkien argues that some exercise of linguistic effort and attention is needed 'in order to understand and enjoy literary or historical texts' (p. 234). Technical *philology and linguistic history is not confined to a single period; 'and if philology seems most exercised in the older periods, that is because any historical enquiry must begin with the earliest available evidence.' Philology, moreover, has rescued

> surviving documents from oblivion and ignorance, and presented to lovers of poetry and history fragments of a noble past that without it would have remained for ever dead and dark. But it can also rescue many things that it is valuable to know from a past nearer than the Old English period. . . . Which will bring more to life poetry, rhetoric, dramatic speech or even plain prose: some knowledge of the language, even of the pronunciation, of its period, or the typographical details of its printed form? [p. 235]

'Lang' and 'Lit' are artificial distinctions. The study of English letters is too large not to be divided, but the division 'should be primarily by period' (p. 236).

The address was heard by a capacity audience in Merton College Hall. Tolkien entered, as he is said to have done in some of his lectures, shouting the opening lines of *Beowulf*. The *Oxford Mail* reported that the address

> was a strictly academic farewell . . . and a very vigorous one. The Professor re-fought, with gusto, some of the historic battles of the English Faculty. Even that warlike corner of the learned world has seen few more redoubtable guerillas, and his resounding denunciation of old errors, alternating with deflating asides, or melodramatic declamations in Anglo-Saxons [*sic*], proved yesterday that he takes ample vigour to his retirement. ['Tolkien's Farewell', 6 June 1969, p. 4]

'Variation D/L in Common Eldarin'. Linguistic text, published with commentary as part of '*Eldarin Hands, Fingers & Numerals* and Related Writings' in *Vinyar Tengwar* 48 (December 2005), pp. 22–6, ed. Patrick H. Wynne. Written *c.* 1968, this two-page typescript is an expansion of briefer statements regarding Common Eldarin (*Languages, Invented) *d* and *l*. Considered with this, presented and discussed as 'The Problem of *Lhûn*', pp. 26–34, is a one-page manuscript written *c.* 1940, concerning the etymology of the river-name *Lhûn*. Wynne's analysis includes notes by Tolkien of later date.

'Of the Voyage of Eärendil and the War of Wrath'. The twenty-fourth chapter of the *'Quenta Silmarillion'*, published in *The Silmarillion* (1977), pp. 246–55.

SUMMARY

After his parents Tuor and Idril sail into the West, Eärendil becomes lord of the elves who live in the havens at the mouths of Sirion. He marries Elwing, with whom he has two sons, Elrond and Elros. But he longs for the open sea, to find his parents and to reach Valinor to plead for Men and Elves before the Valar. He sets sail in the ship *Vingilot* which Círdan the Shipwright has helped him build, leaving Elwing behind. After many adventures, he turns for home, driven by a sudden fear.

During his absence the four remaining sons of Fëanor demand from Elwing the Silmaril won by her grandparents, Beren and Lúthien. When she refuses, the sons attack the havens of Sirion. Most of the elves there are slain; the few who survive join Gil-galad. Elrond and Elros are taken prisoner, but Maglor, one of two sons of Fëanor to survive the attack, takes pity and cares for them. Elwing, wearing the Silmaril, throws herself into the sea, but Ulmo changes her into a white bird. In that form she flies to Eärendil's ship, 'and it is sung that she fell from the air upon the timbers of Vingilot, in a swoon, nigh unto death for the urgency of her speed, and Eärendil took her to his bosom; but in the morning with marvelling eyes he beheld his wife in her own form beside him with her hair upon his face, and she slept' (*The Silmarillion*, p. 247).

Elwing and Eärendil sail into the West. Eärendil now wears the Silmaril on his brow, and perhaps by means of its power they are able to escape the

Enchanted Isles and Shadowy Seas and reach the Bay of Eldamar. Eärendil wishes Elwing to stay in safety on the ship with the three mariners who sailed with them, fearing the anger of the Valar. She insists on landing but waits at the shore. Eärendil finds the city of Tirion empty, for it is a time of festival. 'He walked in the deserted ways of Tirion, and the dust upon his raiment and his shoes was a dust of diamonds. . . . He called aloud in many tongues . . . but there were none to answer him' (p. 248). But as he turns back he is hailed by Eönwë, the herald of Manwë: 'Hail Eärendil, of mariners most renowned, the looked for that cometh at unawares, the longed for that cometh beyond hope! Hail Eärendil, bearer of light before the Sun and Moon!' (pp. 248–9). Summoned to Valimar, his plea for pardon for the Noldor, and for help for Men and Elves against Morgoth, is granted by the Valar.

Eärendil is the son of a mortal man, but also a descendant of Finwë and of the Noldor who left Valinor. Manwë judges that he and Elwing should suffer no penalty for setting foot in the Undying Lands, but they cannot return to Middle-earth. He grants them and their sons leave to choose whether they should be joined in fate to Elves or Men. Eärendil finds that in his absence Elwing had come to Alqualondë and told the Teleri of the sorrowful events in Beleriand. They are both summoned to Valimar and told of Manwë's decree. Eärendil leaves the choice to Elwing; she chooses to be judged among the Elves.

Eärendil's three companions are sent back to Middle-earth in another ship, but the Valar hallow *Vingilot* and raise it to sail through the heavens. Eärendil sits at the helm with the Silmaril on his brow and glistening with the dust of elven-gems. Elwing lives in a white tower where many seabirds gather, and when Eärendil returns from his voyages she flies to meet him.

When the peoples of Middle-earth see the ship of Eärendil as a star in the sky they take it as a sign of hope. Morgoth does not believe that the Valar will ever attack him again, but the host of the Valar prepares for war, and with them come the Vanyar and those of the Noldor who had not left Valinor. The Teleri are unwilling to go into battle, but influenced by Elwing provide mariners to sail the ships that carry the host to Middle-earth.

In the Great Battle that follows the host of the Valar prevail, and most of Morgoth's Balrogs and Orcs are destroyed. The few remaining Men friendly to the Elves fight with the Valar, but most Men fight for Morgoth. Morgoth releases winged dragons, but these are attacked by Eärendil in *Vingilot* and by the great birds of the heavens. Eärendil himself slays the greatest of the dragons, Ancalagon the Black, who falls on Thangorodrim, destroying Morgoth's stronghold. The Valar bind Morgoth with the chain Angainor, beat his iron crown into a collar for his neck, and take its two remaining Silmarils. Much of Beleriand is destroyed and drowned in the tumult of the battle.

Eönwë now summons the Elves to depart from Middle-earth. Maedhros and his brother Maglor demand that Eönwë yield the two Silmarils to them, but Eönwë declares that they have forfeited all claim because of their evil deeds, and the Silmarils must return into the West where the brothers will be judged. Driven by their oath to recover the jewels stolen from their father, Maedhros and Maglor enter the camp of Eönwë, kill the guards, and steal the Silmarils. Burned by the jewel he holds and unable to bear the pain, Maedhros casts himself and his Silmaril into a fiery chasm, while Maglor casts his into the sea and wanders 'ever upon the shores, singing in pain and regret beside the waves'. Thus the three Silmarils pass into 'the airs of heaven', 'the fires in the heart of the world', and 'the deep waters' (p. 254).

Ships are built for the Eldar to sail into the West. The Vanyar return to Valinor, but their joy in victory is diminished because they return without the Silmarils. The Elves of Beleriand settle on Tol Eressëa. The Noldor are pardoned and permitted to visit Valinor. Some elves, however, are not willing to leave Middle-earth: among these are Círdan, Celeborn and Galadriel, Gil-galad, and Elrond, who chooses to be of elven-kind while his brother Elros chooses to be of Mankind. From these half-elven brothers the blood of the Elves and the strain of the divine spirits come among Men.

Morgoth is thrust into the Void, and watch is set on the Walls of the World to prevent his return, yet his lies still bear fruit in Arda.

HISTORY

Éarendel (variously spelled) appears in several of Tolkien's early poems (published in *The Book of Lost Tales, Part Two*) related to the *'Silmarillion' mythology, but only as a great mariner; it was not until years later that Tolkien developed the significance of the character as the descendant of both Men and Elves who could reach Valinor and plead with the Valar on behalf of both races. The first of these poems was The Voyage of Éarendel the Evening Star (*Éalá Éarendel Engla Beorhtast*), written in September 1914. Tolkien was inspired by the name 'Earendel' in the Old English poem Crist; the name means 'shining light, ray' in Old English, and was sometimes used to refer to the morning star. In the poem Tolkien sees Éarendel as a mariner who apparently sets sail in the sky, 'wandered far past many a star in his gleaming galleon', and fled from the Ship of the Moon. Looking at the poem in retrospect, it has hints of the mythology to come, but evidently this was not consciously planned: when his friend *G.B. Smith asked what the poem was about, Tolkien replied: 'I don't know. I'll try to find out' (quoted in Biography, p. 75).

Éarendel also appears in the poem later called *The Bidding of the Minstrel, from The Lay of Éarendel, possibly composed at the end of 1914, which refers to the story of Eärendel as 'a tale of immortal sea-yearning' (*The Book of Lost Tales, Part Two*, p. 270) but does not mention that he sailed in the sky. On the back of the sheet with the earliest workings of the poem is an outline of the voyage of Éarendel, which mentions places definitely in our world – Iceland, Greenland, the Mediterranean, the Atlantic – while others are out of myths or travellers' tales ('land of strange men, land of magic'). At the end of the voyage Éarendel 'sails west again to the lip of the world, just as the Sun is diving into the sea. He sets sail upon the sky and returns no more to earth' (p. 261).

The third poem, *The Shores of Faery*, written in May or July 1915, is the earliest poem, indeed the earliest written work, which is clearly part of the 'Silmarillion' mythology. Many details mentioned in the poem had already appeared in a watercolour by Tolkien, including a bright star framed by a crescent moon. In the poem it is said that to the lonely hill with white towers (the Elvish city of Kôr) 'Comes never there but one white star / That fled before the moon', and 'West of the Moon, East of the Sun' is 'the haven of the star' where 'Vingelot is harboured / While Eärendel looks afar' (pp. 271–2). A prose preface, written probably not much later than the poem, says that Eärendel on his final voyage passed Valinor, 'drew his bark over the bar at the margin of the world, and launched it into the Oceans of the Firmament' where he was 'hunted by the orbed Moon' (p. 262). Another poem, *The Happy Mariners*, written in July 1915, refers in passing to Earendel as a 'shining mariner' (p. 274).

Tolkien abandoned work on *The Book of Lost Tales c.* 1919–20 before writing a tale of Eärendel. We know from *The Fall of Gondolin* that the refugees from Gondolin, including Eärendel and his parents, dwelled at the mouth of Sirion, and *The Nauglafring* ends with the arrival there of Elwing and refugees from Doriath. In *The Book of Lost Tales, Part Two*, Chapter 5, *Christopher Tolkien assembled information from the poems and from miscellaneous notes and outlines written his father, and from these reconstructed as far as possible what the unwritten 'Tale of Eärendel' might have told. It was to last several evenings in the context of the *Lost Tales*. Many of the later elements of the story were already present: the love of Eärendel and Elwing; that he sailed to find his father; the building of *Wingilot*; the raid on Sirion; the reluctance of the Solosimpi (Teleri) to join the host against Morgoth, though here they are willing to go as far as the shores of Middle-earth. In one version Elwing comes to Eärendel in the form of a seabird, and Eärendel does eventually sail in the firmament. But the differences are greater than the similarities. The Elves still living in Valinor hear of the sorrows in Middle-earth from the birds of Gondolin, and against the wishes of the Valar go to the aid of their kin. Melko is overthrown and bound. Eärendel reaches Kôr only after the Elves have already sailed for Middle-earth. Elwing is captured in a raid on Sirion by agents of Melko, not by the sons of Fëanor, and Eärendel finds the former haven deserted when he returns. In one outline Elwing dies because of the curse of the Nauglafring, while in another she becomes a seabird and will not be reunited with Eärendel until the Faring Forth. The brightness with which Eärendel shines as a star is from the 'diamond dust of Kôr' and from his grief, not from a Silmaril. It is probably to search for Elwing that he sails into the sky, but he is hunted by the Moon through the Door of Night.

The first complete narrative of the tale is in the *Sketch of the Mythology* (*c.* 1926). Most of this work is a synopsis of events described at length in *The Book of Lost Tales* reflecting later developments in the mythology, but the last part is more an expansion of the outlines for the unwritten last tale. There Eärendel is still only a great mariner, not a messenger to the Valar. He does have many adventures, however, and even slays Ungoliant. Apparently even before he begins his voyages the Valar, at the urging of Ulmo, have already sent a force of 'the sons of the Valar' and the Eldar to the aid of the Noldor and to recover the Silmarils. Few of the Teleri are willing to join them. When the sons of Fëanor attack the haven at the mouth of Sirion Elwing throws the Nauglafring with the Silmaril into the sea and leaps after it, but is changed into a sea-bird and seeks for Eärendel on the shores of the world. When Eärendel learns what has happened, he sails in search of Elwing and Valinor. He finds Kôr empty, builds a tower on an isle where seabirds come, and 'sails by the aid of their wings even over the airs in search of Elwing, but is scorched by the Sun, and hunted from the sky by the Moon, and for a long while he wanders the sky as a fugitive star' (*The Shaping of Middle-earth, p. 38).

The account of the overthrow of Morgoth in this version is similar to that in The Silmarillion, but Eärendel does not take part in the defeat of the dragons. Only Maglor steals a Silmaril, and when it burns him he casts it into a pit in the earth. The Elves sail west, most to Tol Eressëa but some to Valinor. The Valar declare that Middle-earth should be left for Men, while any Elves who did not leave it will fade. Elwing and Eärendel's only son, Elrond, who was half-mortal and half-elven, is saved by Maidros from the wreck of the haven, and when the Elves depart, 'bound by his mortal half', chooses to stay in Middle-earth. Morgoth is thrust through the Door of Night beyond the Walls of the World, but his lies survive. Some believe that he or his shadow has returned, while others think that it is Thû, his former chief (later Sauron), who has escaped. There is also a prophecy that Morgoth will return and be defeated in a last battle, at which the two lost Silmarils will be recovered from the sea and the earth, and the Two Trees will be rekindled. Since in this version only one Silmaril is stolen by Maglor, one is taken back to Valinor and given by the Valar to Eärendel, who 'launches [his boat] into the outer darkness high above Sun and Moon. There he sails with the Silmaril upon his brow and Elwing at his side, the brightest of all stars, keeping watch upon Morgoth' (The Shaping of Middle-earth, p. 41).

Two texts exist for this part of the story in the *Quenta Noldorinwa (c. 1930). The earlier stops short after Morgoth is thrust into the Void; only the second continues to the end. In the first text the story of Eärendel and the overthrow of Morgoth is little changed from that told in the Sketch, but is expanded, and reads more like a narrative than a synopsis. Perhaps the most significant development is that Eärendel sails into the West not only in the hope of finding his parents, but also because he hopes to plead with the Valar to have pity 'on the world and the sorrows of Mankind' (The Shaping of Middle-earth, p. 149). Both Maidros and Maglor, after discussing their purpose, steal Silmarils, but Maidros is captured. Because the Silmaril he holds burns his hand, he casts it into the ground before Fionwë (the precursor of Eönwë) and kills himself.

At the foot of the page of the first text, where it is said that when Eärendel reached Kôr he found that the Elves had already left, Tolkien wrote a note: 'Make Eärendel move the Gods' (The Shaping of Middle-earth, p. 151). He took up this idea in the second Quenta Noldorinwa text, and made other changes as well. There Ulmo begs the Valar to help the Exiles, but Manwë says that 'only one speaking in person for the cause of both Elves and Men . . . might move the counsels of the Powers' (p. 151). This plea remains in *The Silmarillion* but is part of the preceding chapter, *'Of Tuor and the Fall of Gondolin'. The second text approaches that of *The Silmarillion*, even in many places in its phrasing. But Tolkien was still uncertain exactly what happened between Eärendel and Elwing after they arrived in Valinor. Elwing accepts Eärendel's desire that he alone should land in Valinor; there is no conversation in which she insists on leaving the ship but agrees to wait on the shore, and no account of her meeting with the Teleri. After his successful embassy to the Valar Eärendel is not allowed to return to Middle-earth, but he builds a white tower frequented by seabirds, and Elwing devises wings for his ship so that it is lifted into the heaven and shines as a new star lit by the Silmaril. Near the end (where the second text is the only text) it is said that after the Last Battle Eärendel was scorched by the Sun and hunted by the Moon, so the Valar hallowed his ship and sent it through the Door of Night to sail as a star above the Sun and Moon, and Elwing went with him – but this last is struck through. Tolkien then rewrote the earlier section, so that the Valar lift the ship in which Eärendel sails the sky but he is sundered from Elwing 'till the world endeth' (p. 156). She builds a white tower which is frequented by seabirds and makes wings for herself and tries to fly to his ship but fails. There is no discussion or judgement by the Valar concerning the fates of Eärendel and Elwing and their child; only by a later emendation does their second son Elros appear.

According to the 'earliest' *Annals of Beleriand* (early 1930s), in Year 224 Eärendel and Elwing wed; in 225 he sets out to seek Tuor and Valinor, Elrond is born, and the people of Sirion refuse the demand of the sons of Fëanor that they yield up the Silmaril; in 229 the sons of Fëanor ravage Sirion, Elrond is taken captive, and Elwing casts herself with the Silmaril into the sea and is reunited with Eärendel; in 230 Eärendel wears the Silmaril while he and Elwing search for Valinor; they reach Valinor in 233, and Eärendel speaks for both Elves and Men; Fionwë's host in Valinor prepares for war in 233–43; war in Middle-earth takes place 247–50; after the overthrow of Morgoth in 250, in which Eärendel defeats Ancalagon, Fionwë returns with his host and many of the Elves of Middle-earth travel to Valinor, but Elrond chooses not to go. Apart from his attack on Ancalagon in the sky, nothing is said about when and how Eärendel sailed the heavens. The dates of the 'later' *Annals of Beleriand* (mid-1930s) reflect *ab initio* an addition of 100 years to the Siege of Angband, following a change in an unfinished second version of the 'earliest' *Annals*; and then, by emendation, a further addition of 200 years to the Siege, with the result that Eärendel and Elwing are wed in 524 rather than 224. The 'later' *Annals* also took up a note written on the 'earliest' *Annals*, altering the span of the war against Morgoth from three to fifty years, now 547–97. Elros still only appears in a later change.

Tolkien never completed the *Quenta Silmarillion*, which he began in the mid-1930s and was still working on when he submitted the main manuscript to Allen & Unwin (*Publishers) in mid-November 1937. During the absence of the manuscript he continued to write, in part skipping ahead to a section dealing with the end of the First Age from the point where Eärendel and Elwing approach Valinor. An amanuensis typescript of this story was made *c.* 1958–60, on which Tolkien made a few emendations.

The first part of the chapter in *The Silmarillion* is based mainly on the second text of the *Quenta Noldorinwa* and on the emended *Quenta Silmarillion* where that text takes up the story. Since both of these are basically texts of the 1930s, *Christopher Tolkien not only had to regularize names or instances where his father failed to emend 'Gods' to 'Valar', but also to make changes to the tale to agree with later developments in the mythology. He comments in *The Peoples of Middle-earth* (p. 143) that one change in conception he had to take into account was that in later writings his father abandoned the idea of the Children of the Valar, in particular of the part played in the Great Battle by Fionwë/Eönwë, who when the *Quenta Silmarillion* account was written was the son of Manwë. This different status of Eönwë led him 'to doubt whether my father, had he ever returned to a real retelling of the story of the end of the Elder Days, would have retained Eönwë in so mighty and elemental a rôle'. Therefore in editing *The Silmarillion* Eönwë's 'part was in consequence somewhat diminished by omissions and ambiguous wording. . . . There is however no evidence for this supposition, and I now believe it to have been a mistaken treatment of the original text . . .' (p. 143).

The envoi, 'Here ends the SILMARILLION . . .' (*The Silmarillion*, p. 255), was originally written to close the *Valaquenta*.

The Voyage of Éarendel the Evening Star see Éalá Éarendel Engla Beorhtast

Wade-Gery, Henry Theodore (1888–1972). H.T. Wade-Gery read Classics at New College, Oxford, where he also studied Ancient History. In 1914 he was elected to a Tutorial Fellowship at Wadham College, Oxford, but could not take it up until after the war. Attached to the 19th Lancashire Fusiliers, eventually at the rank of Major, he was in the same battalion as *G.B. Smith, with whom he discussed poetry in general and Tolkien's poems in particular as they were sent to Smith. All three contributed to *Oxford Poetry 1915* (*Goblin Feet*). Wade-Gery's poetic style was conservative ('The grass is cold and wet, the dew is set / Where we together lie. / But love will keep us warm; we'll take no harm, / Belovèd, you and I.' – *Oxford Poetry 1915*, p. 71), more to the liking of Smith and Tolkien than the more Modern poetry of *T.W. Earp. On 22 December 1915 Smith wrote to Tolkien that he and Wade-Gery had

> talked of [*Oxford Poetry 1915*] and agreed (it sounds funny) that we three are much the best contributors! I mean that we have really got the right ideals and conceptions. Wade-Gery's things in there are really most frightfully good, you know. . . . I think it a great thing that the *T.C.B.S. is unanimous really in their preference of, say, W[ade]-G[ery] to Earp.

W-G seems to agree with many of the TCBSian principles, but not by any means all. . . . [Tolkien Papers, Bodleian Library, Oxford]

On 22 August 1916 Wade-Gery, Smith, and Tolkien, all by then serving in the Somme, met at Bouzincourt for dinner and were shelled while eating. After demobilization, Wade-Gery settled into life at Wadham College, among colleagues such as C.M. Bowra and *Lord David Cecil. A popular lecturer, he helped to revolutionize the study of Greek history at Oxford. In 1939 he became the Wykeham Professor of Ancient History and a Fellow of New College, to which the chair was attached. On his retirement in 1953 he was made a Fellow of Merton College. His writings include *Terpsichore and Other Poems* (1921), *The Athenian Tribute Lists* (with Benjamin Dean Meritt and Malcolm Francis McGregor, 1939–53), *The Poet of the Iliad* (1952), and *Essays in Greek History* (1958).

Wain, John Barrington (1925–1994). John Wain read English at St John's College, *Oxford, but due to wartime conditions was sent to Magdalen College for tuition by *C.S. Lewis. From 1946 to 1949 he was a Fellow of St John's, and from 1947 to 1955 Lecturer in English Literature at the University of Reading. He resigned from Reading in 1955 to devote himself to writing, editing, and criticism; by then he was already a published poet and novelist. Altogether he wrote a prodigious number of books, poems, essays, and stories, including *Mixed Feelings* (poetry, 1951), *Hurry on Down* (novel, 1953), the 'Oxford trilogy' of novels *Where Rivers Meet* (1988), *Comedies* (1990), and *Hungry Generations* (posthumous, 1994), and a well received biography of Samuel Johnson (1974). He was also a literary journalist and a radio and television broadcaster.

Wain was a late addition to the *Inklings, after the death of *Charles Williams in 1945. From 1946 to at least 1951 he attended many of their meetings, finding delight in their conviviality and much to admire in the participants. But he came to realize that he did not share their views of politics, religion, and art, which tended to be conservative and hostile to the 'modern'. Moreover, as Humphrey Carpenter has said, 'Wain did not share the belief, very precious to Tolkien and Lewis, that the practice of *"mythopoeia", the invention of myth-like stories, was a valuable (indeed invaluable) form of art' (*The Inklings*, p. 206). With mixed emotions Wain briefly recalled the Inklings, and the 'necessarily unfruitful part' he played in their discussions, in his *Sprightly Running: Part of an Autobiography* (1962):

> To me, it was all, in a sense, marginal and adventitious. My real development was going on in parts of my mind which simply did not come into play at these meetings. Still, I gained one valuable thing: sympathy with, and a certain amount of insight into, a set of attitudes which I should have been tempted to dismiss impatiently if I simply met them cold, on the printed page. I took no deep impress from those conversations; . . . I do not suppose I shall ever be able to read the romances of Lewis and

Tolkien. . . . But I am glad to have seen that corporate mind at work. [pp. 184, 185]

From 1971 to 1972 Wain was Fellow in Creative Arts at Brasenose College, Oxford, and from 1973 to 1978 Professor of Poetry at Oxford. Tolkien is recorded in the *Oxford Mail* (25 May 1973) as voting for Wain's opponent: 'It is high time', he said, that 'the chair came back to what it was originally intended for, scholars interested in poetry, but not practising poets, who are not in general very good lecturers on the subject' (Martin Halsall, 'Sheer Poetry as Green Velvet Sets the Scene', p. 13).

Waldman, Milton (1895–1976). Born in the United States and educated at Yale University and the Sorbonne, Milton Waldman had a long career as an adviser and editor for literary publishers in London. These included Longmans Green from 1919 to 1924 and William Collins from 1939 to 1953 and 1955 to 1968. From 1952 to 1955 Waldman was also a joint managing director of Rupert Hart-Davis Ltd, and from 1924 to 1927 an assistant editor for the magazine the *London Mercury*. In addition he himself was a writer, chiefly of history and biography; his works include *Sir Walter Raleigh* (1928), *Elizabeth, Queen of England* (1933), *Elizabeth and Leicester* (1944), and *The Lady Mary: A Biography of Mary Tudor* (1972).

According to Humphrey Carpenter in *Biography*, Waldman, a fellow Catholic, was introduced to Tolkien by *Father Gervase Mathew in late 1949. Aware of the success of *The Hobbit*, he expressed interest not only in its sequel, *The Lord of the Rings*, but also in *'The Silmarillion', parts of which Tolkien subsequently showed to him. Waldman offered to publish 'The Silmarillion' if Tolkien would finish it, and *The Lord of the Rings* if Tolkien had 'no commitment either moral or legal to [George] Allen & Unwin [*Publishers]' (quoted in *Letters*, p. 134). In April 1950 Tolkien pressed *Stanley Unwin to agree to publish the two works, which he argued are closely linked, and when this was refused he took them to Waldman. But to Tolkien's dismay, Waldman told him that *The Lord of the Rings* was too long; and before long Waldman went to Italy, where he lived for much of the year, leaving Tolkien's works in the hands of Collins staff who did not share his enthusiasm.

Evidently at Waldman's suggestion, in ?late 1951 Tolkien wrote a long letter explaining the two works, intended to demonstrate that they are interdependent and indivisible; but it did not have the desired effect. Most of this important statement was published in *Letters*, pp. 143–61. A description of *The Lord of the Rings*, omitted from *Letters*, is most readily found in *Reader's Companion*, pp. 742–9.

Tolkien had contact with Waldman at least once in later years, in 1956 when Waldman sought, unsuccessfully, to publish *The Hobbit* in Collins' Fontana paperback series.

Wales. Tolkien first became aware of the Welsh language (*Languages) in 1901 while living in Kings Heath (*Birmingham and environs), from the names of coal trucks that passed along the railway line behind his house: *Nantyglo, Senghenydd, Blaen-Rhondda, Penrhiwceiber, Tredegar.* Later in childhood he went on a railway journey to Wales; and in summer 1920 he and his family took a holiday in **Trywn Llanbedrog** on the coast of Cardigan Bay in north Wales. While there Tolkien drew at least two views of the coast. Part of *Farmer Giles of Ham* is set in north-west Wales: the home of the dragon Chrysophylax is said to be in the mountains of Venedotia. On 25 October 1958 Tolkien wrote to Deborah Webster: 'I love Wales (what is left of it, when mines, and the even more ghastly sea-side resorts have done their worst), and especially the Welsh language. But I have not in fact been in Wales for a long time (except for crossing it on the way to Ireland)' (*Letters*, p. 289).

The Wanderings of Húrin. Variant texts, published with commentary and notes in *The War of the Jewels* (1994), pp. 251–310, relating the movements of Húrin of the House of Hador, father of Túrin, in the period immediately following his release by Morgoth after twenty-eight years of captivity.

SUMMARY

As first written, Húrin returns to Hithlum, his former home, now occupied by the Easterlings, where he gathers a company of homeless men and outlaws, the chief of whom is Asgon; but he steals away at night, hoping to find his way to Gondolin. While seeking for Húrin, his men are captured by march-wardens of Brethil and brought before their master, Harathor. When he learns that they are followers of the House of Hador, Harathor spares their lives for the sake of Túrin, who had killed the dragon Glaurung, but keeps them prisoner because Túrin had also killed Brandir, the former ruler of Brethil. As they are led away, Asgon derides Harathor's justice and declares that Húrin will soon arrive.

Having written this far, Tolkien decided to make changes to avoid repetition and add a new dimension to the story: a division in the Haladin, the family from which the rulers of Brethil were elected. He decided that Hardang (the name replacing *Harathor*), the chieftain of Halad, should be hostile to the House of Hador, while Manthor, the Master of the North-march, also of the Haladin, should be friendly to the House of Hador, ambitious, and suspected by Hardang. Indications of these new relationships appear in replacement sections: instead of imprisoning Asgon and the others, Hardang expels them from Brethil, and only by the goodwill of Ebor, captain of the march-wardens and a follower of Manthor, are their weapons restored to them. Ebor also sends word to Manthor of what has happened, and news of Húrin.

When Húrin approaches Gondolin he is seen by watchful eagles who report his presence to Turgon. At first Turgon assumes that Húrin is now an agent of Morgoth, but changes his mind and sends the eagles to bring Húrin to the hidden city – too late, for Húrin has already departed. Húrin's presence and his cries to Turgon as he leaves, however, betray the location of Gondolin to Morgoth. Húrin then makes his way to the Crossings of Teiglin, where he knows that Túrin is buried. By the stone marking Túrin's grave he meets a haggard figure dressed in rags, his wife Morwen, and speaks with her before she dies. He is filled with a desire for vengeance on those he believes responsible for the wrongs done to his family. He is found sleeping by guards whom Hardang has set to watch for him. One of these, Avranc, who is close to Hardang, suggests that Húrin be killed as he sleeps, but is prevented from doing so. Manthor takes Húrin to Hardang, who receives the old man with discourtesy, not even offering him a seat. Húrin in anger hurls a stool at Hardang, hitting him on the forehead; he is bound and imprisoned. Hardang and Avranc want Húrin put to death, but instead a Folkmoot is summoned to judge the matter.

Manthor visits Húrin in prison, and with some difficulty wins his confidence. He goes again the following day, but Hardang's men will not admit him until evening. He finds Húrin so drowsy that he is unable to speak with him about his defence. Suspicious, Manthor takes away some of the food provided for Húrin and feeds it to a hound. At the Moot the following day nearly a thousand gather. Húrin is brought in fettered, and refuses to recognize the authority of the Moot while he is bound.

The trial is described at length, with frequent references to the laws and customs of the people of Brethil. When Hardang begins to recount the charge, Manthor intervenes, pointing out that, if he is the accuser, by law he cannot also be the judge. Hardang names Avranc as judge in his place, not a popular choice. Avranc charges that Húrin has come with evil intent, and had sought to slay Hardang. Húrin makes no answer until, as a result of Manthor appealing that it is not usual to bring to the Moot in fetters a man not yet condemned, Hardang orders the fetters removed, noting the feeling of the assembly on this matter. Húrin then declares who he is, but refuses to plead; rather, he accuses Hardang of insolence and discourtesy. Húrin is also accused of hating the people of Brethil because he spat on the food given to him by Manthor when he first found him, but Manthor declares that Húrin spat it out because he was so starved he could not swallow it. Manthor then accuses Hardang of having drugged the food sent to Húrin: the hound that ate it still lay fast asleep. He admits the throwing of a stool at Hardang, but declares that Húrin had been provoked by way Hardang had received an old man, head of a great house, his kinsman, without offering him a seat.

When the Moot calls for Húrin to be set free, he speaks. He had come to seek the graves of his children, he says, then accuses Hardang of casting Morwen out and doing nothing to succour her. He strides towards Harding as if to attack him, and battle breaks out between Hardang's supporters and opponents. Hardang flees. When he and his men refuse to surrender, Manthor's supporters set fire to the hall where they have sought refuge. Hardang is killed, but before he dies he rejects as a lie the charge that Húrin made against him. Manthor then tells Húrin that indeed, the Men of Brethil had had no knowledge of Morwen, or that she lay by the stone which they fear and avoid.

The next day, Manthor and others go with Húrin to bury Morwen and mourn her. As Manthor is about to return to Brethil, he is mortally wounded by an arrow shot by Avranc, who had escaped from the burning hall. Húrin praises Manthor as a valiant friend, but also comments that his help had not been entirely without self-interest. Manthor replies that Húrin's 'darkness touched me also. Now, alas! the Haladin are ended; for this wound is to the death. Was not this your true errand, Man of the North: to bring ruin upon us . . . ?' (p. 297). Manthor's body is carried away, and Húrin is left alone.

HISTORY

*Christopher Tolkien believes that one reason why his father in later years did little work on the last part of the *Quenta Silmarillion* was the 'centrality' that he 'accorded to the story of Húrin and Morwen and their children, Túrin Turambar and Niënor Níniel. This became for him . . . the dominant and absorbing story of the end of the Elder Days, in which complexity of motive and character, trapped in the mysterious workings of Morgoth's curse, sets it altogether apart' (*The War of the Jewels*, pp. viii–ix). In the 1950s Tolkien wrote an account at length of much of Túrin's story in the *Narn i Chîn Húrin*, the latter part of his life c. 1951 and the earlier part late in the decade. He also told the complete story in a shorter form, continuing into an account of Húrin's actions when first released, in the *Grey Annals* (c. 1951, see *Annals of Beleriand*). The *Wanderings of Húrin* begins by following closely the account of Húrin in the *Grey Annals* as far as it goes, and continues with another, entirely new to *'The Silmarillion'*, of Húrin's visit to Brethil and how, through the further working of Morgoth's curse, he brings destruction to that place and its people.

With the development of the story of Túrin as told in the *Narn i Chîn Húrin*, and its continuation into an unprecedented addition to the story of Húrin and to 'The Silmarillion' in the story of Húrin in Brethil, 'there entered an immediacy in the telling and a fullness in the recording of event and dialogue that must be described as a new narrative impulse: in relation to the mode of the "Quenta" [*Quenta Silmarillion*], it is as if the focus of the glass by which the remote ages were viewed had been sharply changed' (Christopher Tolkien, p. ix). But Tolkien did not continue with accounts of Húrin's visits to Nargothrond and Doriath, setting in train events leading to yet more disasters in Beleriand, nor did he even write a new chapter for the *Quenta Silmarillion* based on *The Wanderings of Húrin*. Christopher Tolkien felt unable to incorporate more than a few short sections from *The Wanderings of Húrin* in *'The Silmarillion* (his attempt to find Gondolin, and his meeting with his dying wife at the stone making their son's grave), because it was not compatible with other texts dealing with the end of the 'Silmarillion' matter.

My father never returned to follow the further wanderings of Húrin. We come here to the furthest point in the narrative that he reached in his work on *The Silmarillion* (in the widest sense) after the Second [World]

War and the completion of *The Lord of the Rings. . . . It is as if we were come to the brink of a great cliff, and look down from highlands raised in some later age onto an ancient plain far below. For the story of the Nauglamîr and the destruction of Doriath, the fall of Gondolin, the attack on the Havens, we must return through more than a quarter of a century to the *Quenta Noldorinwa . . . , or beyond. The huge abruptness of the divide is still more emphasised by the nature of this last story of the Elder Days, the Shadow that fell upon Brethil. In its portrayal of the life of Brethil into which Húrin came for its ruin, the intricacies of law and lineage, the history of ambition and conflicting sentiment within the ruling clan, it stands apart. . . .

To have included it [in *The Silmarillion*], as it seemed to me, would have entailed a huge reduction, indeed an entire re-telling of a kind that I did not wish to undertake; and since the story is intricate I was afraid that this would produce a dense tangle of narrative statement with all the subtlety gone, and above all it would diminish the fearful figure of the old man, the great hero, Thalion the Steadfast [Húrin], furthering still the purposes of Morgoth, as he was doomed to do. [*The War of the Jewels*, p. 297–8]

In retrospect, however, he felt its omission 'to have been an excessive tampering with my father's actual thought and intention, thus raising the question, whether the attempt to make a "unified" *Silmarillion* should have been embarked on' (p. 298).

Although Tolkien wrote some of the rough workings and draft of *The Wanderings of Húrin* on the backs of documents dated 1954 and 1957, he made the typescript that followed on the typewriter he first used in January 1959; therefore the work probably belongs at least to the end of the 1950s. When his ideas concerning the situation in Brethil and certain events in the story changed, he did not begin a new text but emended the completed part of this typescript, partly in manuscript and partly by replacing rejected passages with new typescript. In its original form the typescript had no title, but Tolkien later wrote in ink on the top copy 'Of the Fate of Húrin and Morwen, Link to the Necklace of the Dwarves, "Sigil Elu-naeth", Necklace of the Woe of Thingol', and still later 'The Wanderings of Húrin', a title which also appears on an amanuensis typescript. In *The War of the Jewels* Christopher Tolkien gives the final text, the sections replaced, and passages of interest in the draft, and notes other changes. According to a plot synopsis, Húrin is released in Year 500, and leaves Hithlum in 501, in which year his visit to Brethil also takes place.

Although this late work bears little or no resemblance in style or vocabulary to the romances of *William Morris which, as Tolkien wrote to his future wife in October 1914, inspired his earliest prose work, *The Story of Kullervo* (from the *Kalevala*), the social organization and the general air of *The Wanderings of Húrin* recall Morris's *House of the Wolfings* and *The Roots of the Mountains*.

War. Tolkien wrote to his friend *Christopher Wiseman on 16 November 1914: 'The duty of patriotism and a fierce belief in nationalism are to me of vital importance. . . . I think so. I am not of course a militarist. I no longer defend the Boer War! I am a more & more convinced Home Ruler (though I sympathised with the army in April). I don't defend "Deutschland über alles" but certainly do the Norwegian "alt for Norge" which translates itself (if I have it right?)' (Tolkien Papers, Bodleian Library, Oxford). Even taking part in one of the bloodiest battles in history, the Somme in 1916, did not turn him into a pacifist. He accepted that some wars might be just and necessary, though he deplored that this was so.

He believed that although 'right' might be on one side, on either side there would be individuals both good and bad. He wrote to his son *Christopher on 24 May 1944:

> Yes, I think the orcs as real a creation as anything in 'realistic' fiction . . . only in real life they are on both sides, of course. For 'romance' has grown out of *'allegory', and its wars are still derived from the 'inner war' of allegory in which good is on one side and various modes of badness on the other. In real (exterior) life men are on both sides: which means a motley alliance of orcs, beasts, demons, plain naturally honest men, and angels. But it does make some difference who are your captains and whether they are orc-like per se! And what it is all about (or thought to be). It is even in this world possible to be (more or less) in the wrong or in the right. [*Letters*, p. 82]

He recognized, though, that in our world it might not always be easy to decide where right and justice lay, and considered that evil deeds by men who had justice on their side did not make their cause evil, nor did good or heroic deeds by those in the wrong make their cause right. See further, his ?1956 comments on *W.H. Auden's review of *The Return of the King*, *Letters*, pp. 242–3.

Tolkien continued to consider aggressive, empire-building wars as unjust. On 31 July 1944 he wrote to Christopher: 'I should have hated the Roman Empire in its day (as I do), and remained a patriotic Roman citizen, while preferring a free Gaul and seeing good in Carthaginians. *Delenda est Carthago.* . . . I was actually taught at school that that was a fine saying; and I "reacted" . . . at once' (*Letters*, p. 89). On 25 May 1945, with victory in Europe achieved but war still continuing in the Far East, he wrote to Christopher: 'Though . . . I know nothing about British or American imperialism in the Far East that does not fill me with regret and disgust, I am afraid I am not even supported by a glimmer of patriotism in this remaining war. I would not subscribe a penny to it, let alone a son, were I a free man' (*Letters*, p. 115).

By the outbreak of the Second World War, Tolkien was too old for active service, but took part in home defence as an Air Raid Warden. Two of his sons, however, were actively at risk. He followed the course of events in newspapers and on the radio, and came into contact with refugees. His letters to his sons *Michael and Christopher show that he saw little glory in war, but much suffering by those both at the front and at home. On 9 June 1941 he wrote to Michael:

> One War is enough for any man. . . . Either the bitterness of youth or that of middle-age is enough for a life-time: both is too much. I suffered once what you are going through, if rather differently: because I was very inefficient and unmilitary (and we are alike only in sharing a deep sympathy and feeling for the 'tommy', especially the plain soldier from the agricultural counties). I did not then believe that the 'old folk' suffered much. Now I know. I tell you I feel like a lame canary in a cage. To carry on the old pre-war job – it is just poison. If only I could do something active! [*Letters*, pp. 54–5]

And in a letter to Christopher on 30 April 1944:

> The utter stupid waste of war, not only material but moral and spiritual, is so staggering to those who have to endure it. And always was (despite the poets), and always will be (despite the propagandists). . . . But so short is human memory and so evanescent are its generations that in only about 30 years there will be few or no people with that direct experience which alone goes really to the heart. The burnt hand teaches most about fire.
>
> I sometimes feel appalled at the thought of the sum total of human misery all over the world at the present moment: the millions parted, fretting, wasting in unprofitable days – quite apart from torture, pain, death, bereavement, injustice. If anguish were visible, almost the whole of this benighted planet would be enveloped in a dense dark vapour, shrouded from the amazed vision of the heavens! [*Letters*, pp. 75–6]

On 30–31 January 1945, with the Russians approaching Berlin and victory in sight, he wrote to Christopher:

> The appalling destruction and misery of this war mount hourly: destruction of what should be (indeed is) the common wealth of Europe, and the world, if mankind were not so besotted, wealth the loss of which will affect us all, victors or not. Yet people gloat to hear of the endless lines, 40 miles long, of miserable refugees, women and children pouring West, dying on the way. There seem no bowels of mercy or compassion, no imagination left in this dark diabolic hour. By which I do not mean that it may not all, in the present situation, mainly (not solely) created by Germany, be necessary and inevitable. But why gloat! We were supposed to have reached a stage of civilization in which it might still be necessary to execute a criminal, but not to gloat, or to hang his wife and child by him while the orc-crowd hooted. The destruction of Germany, be it 100 times

merited, is one of the most appalling world-catastrophes. . . . Well the first War of the Machines seems to be drawing to its final inconclusive chapter – leaving, alas, everyone the poorer, many bereaved or maimed and millions dead, and only one thing triumphant: the Machines. As the servants of the Machines are becoming a privileged class, the Machines are going to be enormously more powerful. What's their next move? [*Letters*, p. 111]

In the short term, he was not optimistic, even about victory. He wrote to Christopher on 3 June 1945 that he thought the stand-down parade for Civil Defence 'rather a mockery . . . for the War is not over (and the one that is, or the part of it, has largely been lost). But it is of course wrong to fall into such a mood, for Wars are always lost, and The War always goes on; and it is no good growing faint!' (*Letters*, pp. 115–16). Commenting to Michael Straight at the end of 1955, he felt that '"victors" never can enjoy "victory" – not in the terms that they envisaged: and in so far as they fought for something *to be enjoyed by themselves* (whether acquisition or mere preservation) the less satisfactory will "victory" seem' (*Letters*, p. 235). Yet in the longer term he still held on to hope: 'All we do know, and that to a large extent by direct experience, is that evil labours with vast power and perpetual success – in vain: preparing always only the soil for unexpected good to sprout. So it is in general, and so it is in our own lives' (letter to Christopher Tolkien, 30 April 1944, *Letters*, p. 76).

THE FIRST WORLD WAR ('THE GREAT WAR'), 1914–19

Tolkien's life and military service during this period are dealt with in detail in **Chronology**, which also includes general background information about the war; see also *Lancashire Fusiliers. Here, however, a few basic facts may be found useful.

By 1914 tensions between various nations in Europe had been growing for several years, but the catalyst which led to the 'Great War' (as it was called before 1939; in America it was the 'European War') was the assassination of the Austrian Archduke Francis Ferdinand and his wife in Sarajevo on 28 June by a Serbian nationalist. Austria-Hungary immediately declared war on Serbia. On 1 August, Germany declared war on Russia, an ally of France, and on 4 August invaded Belgium. Britain, a signatory to a treaty in 1839 guaranteeing the neutrality of Belgium, gave Germany an ultimatum that if its forces were not withdrawn by midnight German time on 4 August, Germany and Britain would be at war. In the absence of a response, Britain declared war, and the first units of the British Expeditionary Force crossed into France on 7 August. The guns finally fell silent on the Western front on 11 November 1918, with the signing of the German Armistice. The war cost the British Empire 947,000 dead, of whom 745,000 were from the United Kingdom. The war with Germany ended officially with the signing of the Peace Treaty of Versailles on 28 June 1919.

Neither the Germans nor the British expected the war to last long. Kaiser Wilhelm of Germany told his troops: 'You will be home before the leaves have fallen from the trees.' 'Almost everybody in Britain, except a few hard-headed realists like Lord Kitchener ... appeared to anticipate a brisk, spectacular and triumphant campaign. The worry of the would-be volunteer was that the war might be won before he got to it' (Malcolm Brown, *Tommy Goes To War* (2001), p. 5). Prime Minister Asquith declared in the House of Commons on 7 August: 'I do not think any nation ever entered into a great conflict ... with a clearer conscience or stronger conviction that it is fighting not for aggression, not for the maintenance of its own selfish ends, but in defence of principles the maintenance of which is vital to the civilization of the world' (quoted in Brown, p. 7).

Kitchener's initial call for 100,000 men between the ages of nineteen and thirty was soon answered, as was his further appeal, before the end of August 1914, for 100,000 more. Volunteers came forward in huge numbers, and continued to do so in 1915, so that some two million men had enlisted by the time conscription was introduced in early 1916. As Malcolm Brown has said, 'it is the particular tragedy of this story that so many of these men were to be savaged by the brutal, highly unromantic mode of warfare that was so soon to develop in France and Flanders, and which Churchill ... was to describe as "fighting machine-gun bullets with the breasts of gallant men". But all the horror and tragedy was hidden in the future during the buoyant summer weeks of 1914' (p. 7).

By winter 1914 the Western front evolved into two opposing trench systems extending some 400 miles through Belgium and France, one side occupied by German troops, the other by British and French. The front rarely shifted more than a few hundred yards one way or the other at a time. The British section usually had about 800 battalions of 1,000 men each. An excellent description of the trenches is supplied by Paul Fussell in *The Great War and Modern Memory* (1975):

There were normally three lines of trenches. The front-line trench was anywhere from fifty yards or so to a mile from its enemy counterpart. Several hundred yards behind it was the support trench line. And several hundred yards behind that was the reserve line. There were three kinds of trenches: firing trenches, like these; communication trenches, running roughly perpendicular to the line and connecting the three lines; and 'saps', shallower ditches thrust out into No Man's Land, providing access to forward observation posts, listening posts, grenade-throwing posts, and machine gun positions. The end of a sap was not usually manned all the time; night was the favourite time for going out. Coming up from the rear, one reached the trenches by following a communication trench sometimes a mile or more long. It often began in a town and gradually deepened. By the time pedestrians reached the reserve line, they were well below ground level.

A firing trench was supposed to be six to eight feet deep and four or five feet wide. On the enemy side a parapet of earth or sandbags rose about two or three feet above the ground. . . . Into the sides of the trenches were dug one- or two-man holes ('funk-holes'), and there were deeper dugouts, reached by dirt stairs, for use as command posts and officers' quarters. On the enemy side of the trench was a fire-step two feet high on which the defenders were supposed to stand, firing and throwing grenades, when repelling attack. . . . Every few yards a good trench zig-zagged. It had frequent traverses designed to contain damage within a limited space. . . . The floor of a proper trench was covered with wooden duckboards, beneath which were sumps a few feet deep designed to collect water. [pp. 41–2]

The total length of the British and French trenches may have been over 12,000 miles. Many of the British trenches were not well constructed, unlike those on the German side. Barbed wire was far enough to the front of them to prevent easy approach by the enemy. It was often difficult to recover the bodies of those killed in the area between the opposing front line trenches, called No Man's Land; but the situation was sometimes as bad in the trenches themselves. Captain Alfred Bundy wrote in his diary for 19 October 1916: 'Visited trenches to be taken over. . . . I have never seen such desolation. Mud thin, deep and black, shell holes full of water, corpses all around in every stage of decomposition, some partially devoid of flesh, some swollen and black . . .' (quoted in Malcolm Brown, *The Imperial War Museum Book of the Somme* (2002), p. 223).

For further information about the Battle of the Somme in which Tolkien took part, in addition to the books already mentioned, see Gerald Gliddon, *The Battle of the Somme: A Topographical History*, (1996), and Chris McCarthy, *The Somme: The Day-by-Day Account* (1998).

THE SECOND WORLD WAR, 1939–45

Tolkien considered Britain justified in declaring war on Germany on 3 September 1939 in response to Germany's invasion of Poland: it was a just war against an aggressor. The letter he wrote on 25 July 1938 to the prospective German publisher of a translation of *The Hobbit* shows that he had no sympathy with the racist ideas propagated by Adolf Hitler and his Nazi regime, and moreover found them based on false scholarship, and perverting ideals which he cared about deeply. He wrote to his son Michael on 9 June 1941:

I have spent most of my life . . . studying Germanic matters (in the general sense that includes England and Scandinavia). There is a great deal more force (and truth) than ignorant people imagine in the 'Germanic' ideal. . . . You have to understand the good in things, to detect the real evil. . . . I suppose I know better than most what is the truth about this 'Nordic' nonsense. Anyway, I have in this War a burning private grudge – which would probably make me a better soldier at 49 than I was at 22: against that ruddy little ignoramus Adolf Hitler.... Ruining, perverting, and making for ever accursed, that noble northern spirit, a supreme contribution to Europe, which I have ever loved, and tried to present in its true light. [*Letters*, pp. 55–6; see *Northernness]

In a letter to Christopher, written 23–25 September 1944, he called Hitler 'a vulgar and ignorant little cad' (*Letters*, p. 93).

Tolkien described the Second World War as the 'first War of the Machines' and was particularly unhappy that two of his sons, Michael (eventually) and Christopher, served in the Royal Air Force. He wrote to Christopher on 29 May 1945:

> It would not be easy for me to express to you the measure of my loathing for the Third Service [the RAF] – which can be nonetheless, and is for me, combined with admiration, gratitude, and above all pity, for the young men caught in it. But it is the aeroplane of war that is the real villain. And nothing can really amend my grief that you, my best beloved, have any connexion with it. My sentiments are more or less those that Frodo would have had if he discovered some Hobbits learning to ride Nazgûl-birds, 'for the liberation of the Shire'. [*Letters*, p. 115]

Some background about the Second World War, especially as it affected life at home, is included in **Chronology**, together with an account of Tolkien's life during those years. In addition, *When the Lights Went Out: Oxfordshire 1939 to 1945* by Malcolm Graham and Melanie Williams (1979) gives an interesting account of life in *Oxford and Oxfordshire during the war. There it is said that from March 1939 steps were taken to prepare for war, in particular air-raid precautions (ARP): the building of street air-raid shelters, the establishment of first aid posts, ambulance depots, auxiliary fire stations, the training of gas decontamination squads, and the planning of city-wide ARP organization. During August 1939, as war became more likely, the more valuable books in the Bodleian Library (*Libraries and archives) in Oxford were moved to safer premises within the Library, and much of the contents of the Ashmolean Museum were sent for storage in the country. 'The enforcement of the "blackout", the issue of gas masks, and the first wails of the air raid sirens brought the war into every home.... Those who failed to achieve perfection in masking their lights became accustomed to hammerings on the door and shouts from patrolling wardens...' (p. 3). To minimize the danger of driving at night, pavement edges, 'street trees, traffic islands and walls on bends were ... painted white.... Negotiating the dark pavements also called for some care, and pedestrians were urged to "Keep left" in order to avoid painful or embarrassing collisions. Despite all these difficulties, one man wrote to the *Oxford Mail* saying that it was very nearly worth a war to see Oxford in moonlight' (p. 3).

Individual families erected outdoor 'Anderson' shelters made of corrugated steel, usually sunk into the ground and covered with earth as a protection from debris. Graham and Williams comment that 'the race to the air raid shelter became a familiar part of life' (p. 4). Although Oxford itself received only a few stray bombs, there were raids on the thirty-six airfields in the surrounding countryside.

In June 1940, wishing to hinder the enemy should an invasion take place, the Government ordered the blacking out of railway station signs and the removal of signposts. Church bells, which were to be used to signal an invasion, remained silent.

V.E. (Victory in Europe) Day on 8 May 1945 was celebrated in Oxford with many bonfires, and with a torchlight procession which ended with the burning of Hitler's effigy opposite the Martyrs' Memorial.

WAR AND TOLKIEN'S WRITINGS

Tolkien's feelings about war are reflected notably in *The Lord of the Rings*. As he said to *Naomi Mitchison, 'the·story is cast in terms of a good side, and a bad side, beauty against ruthless ugliness, tyranny against kingship, moderated freedom with consent against compulsion that has long lost any object save mere power, and so on . . .' (25 April 1954, Letters, pp. 178–9). The attacks by Saruman on Rohan and by Sauron on Gondor are depicted as wars of aggression, aimed at domination, and are therefore unjust, even apart from the means used to attain the ends. Théoden tells Saruman, who had attacked Rohan unprovoked, 'even if your war on me was just – as it was not, for were you ten times as wise you would have had no right to rule me and mine for your own profit as you desired – even so, what will you say of your torches in Westfold and the children that lie dead there?' (bk. III, ch. 10). The terms that the Mouth of Sauron offers the West at the Black Gate are such that the men of the West would be little more than slaves, under his control as Sauron's lieutenant.

Nonetheless, Tolkien rejected on several occasions the allegation that those on the 'good side' in The Lord of the Rings were entirely good, pointing to Boromir and Denethor in particular (see *Good and Evil), and he also showed sympathy to those fighting for Sauron. Gandalf tells Denethor that he pities even Sauron's slaves. Sam sees the slain Southron as a man, not an enemy: 'He wondered what the man's name was and where he came from; and if he was really evil of heart, or what lies or threats had led him on the long march from his home; and if he would not really rather have stayed there in peace' (bk. IV, ch. 4). In general, the West is willing to pardon the enemy and set them free. The Rohirrim tell the Men of Dunland: 'Help now to repair the evil in which you have joined . . . and afterwards you shall take an oath never again to pass the Fords of Isen in arms, nor to march with the enemies of Men; and then you shall go free back to your land' (bk. III, ch. 8). Aragorn 'pardoned the Easterlings that had given themselves up, and sent them away free, and he made peace with the peoples of Harad; and the slaves of Mordor he released and gave to them all the lands about Lake Núrnen to be their own' (bk. VI, ch. 5).

Tolkien himself recognized that his personal experiences during the Battle of the Somme influenced his depiction of the Dead Marshes in *The Lord of the Rings*. He wrote to Professor L.W. Forster on 31 December 1960 that 'the Dead Marshes and the approaches to the Morannon owe something to Northern France after the Battle of the Somme' (*Letters*, p. 303). In a letter to *The Listener*, Graham Tayar, who like Tolkien had attended *King Edward's School, Birmingham, wrote that Tolkien 'once told me that the physical setting [of Mordor] derived directly from the trenches of World War One, the wasteland of shell-cratered battlefields where he fought in 1916' ('Tolkien's Mordor', 14 July 1977).

Paul H. Kocher thought that Tolkien's experiences influenced not only *The Lord of the Rings* but also *The Homecoming of Beorhtnoth Beorhthelm's Son*, in which he contrasts the attitudes to war of two men seeking the body of the Beorhtnoth, slain in battle by invading Vikings in AD 991:

> Looking back over Tolkien's poem . . . we may well be impressed by the crusading spirit with which he has Tídwald knock down every attempt by Torhthelm to idealize war. On the other hand he never hints that a fight with a determined enemy can or should be avoided. It would be nice if the Danes would stay home and stop ruining England, but since they will not they must be resisted by arms. . . . [Tídwald's] anguish after the Maldon fray is not that there has been a fray but that bad leadership has lost so many precious English lives without stopping enemy destruction of the land. If men must die in battle, let their deaths at least buy safety for their people. Tolkien, of course, writes here only about a specifically defensive war fought on English soil. The situation is essentially the same in *The Lord of the Rings* where the war against Sauron is again a war of defense waged in the home territories of the West against a foe implacably bent on invasion and enslavement. About other sorts of wars fought elsewhere for other reasons it is safe to deduce from the two works only that Tolkien's deep hatred of war and death would make him insist that they be plainly necessary to the defense of freedom at home.
> [*Master of Middle-earth: The Fiction of J.R.R. Tolkien* (1972), p. 194]

Some critics have seen *The Lord of the Rings* as a reflection of the Second World War, during which parts of the work were written. But Tolkien remarked in the Foreword to its second edition (1965) that it was 'neither allegorical nor topical'. Its crucial chapter 'The Shadow of the Past' (Book I, Chapter 2) 'was written long before the foreshadow of 1939 had yet become a threat of inevitable disaster, and from that point the story would have developed along essentially the same lines, if that disaster had been averted. Its sources are things long before in mind, or in some cases already written, and little or nothing in it was modified by the war that began in 1939 or its sequels.'

He did, however, comment to *Stanley Unwin in a letter of 13 October 1938 that 'the darkness of the present days has had some effect on [*The Lord of the Rings*]', a reference to the Munich Conference of the previous month; but still, 'it is not an allegory' (*Letters*, p. 41).

See also Nan C. Scott, 'War and Pacifism in *The Lord of the Rings*', *Tolkien Journal* 15 (Summer 1972); *Hugh Brogan, 'Tolkien's Great War', *Children and Their Books: A Celebration of the Work of Iona and Peter Opie* (1989); John Garth, *Tolkien and the Great War: The Threshold of Middle-earth* (2003); and Janet Brennan Croft, *War and the Works of J.R.R. Tolkien* (2004).

The War of the Jewels: The Later Silmarillion, Part Two: The Legends of Beleriand. The eleventh volume of *The History of Middle-earth*, edited with notes and commentary by *Christopher Tolkien, first published in Great Britain by HarperCollins, London, in October 1994, and in the United States by the Houghton Mifflin Company, Boston, in December 1994. See further, *Tolkien Collector* 9 (March 1995), pp. 8–9.

Part One, the *Grey Annals*, is a greatly expanded version of the *Annals of Beleriand*, written *c.* 1951.

Part Two, 'The Later *Quenta Silmarillion*', continuing the study begun in *Morgoth's Ring* (1993), contains additions and changes made *c.* 1951 and later to some of the chapters of the *Quenta Silmarillion*, dealing with events after the return of the Noldor to Middle-earth. Its chapters are: 'Of Men'; 'Of the Siege of Angband'; 'Of Beleriand and Its Realms'; 'Of Turgon and the Building of Gondolin' (a new chapter); 'Concerning the Dwarves'; 'Of the Coming of Men into the West' (this and the preceding chapter are almost entirely new writing, based on 'Of Men and Dwarfs' in the earlier *Quenta Silmarillion* examined in *The Lost Road and Other Writings*); 'Of the Ruin of Beleriand and the Fall of Fingolfin'; and 'The Last Chapters' (which Tolkien hardly touched).

Part Three, 'The Wanderings of Húrin and Other Writings not forming part of the *Quenta Silmarillion*', contains: *The Wanderings of Húrin; Ælfwine and Dírhaval* (see *Narn i Chîn Húrin*); *Maeglin* (see *Of Maeglin: Sister-son of Turgon, King of Gondolin*); *Of the Ents and the Eagles*; and *The Tale of Years*.

Part Four is *Quendi and Eldar*, an essay from *c.* 1959–60 mainly concerned with linguistic matters but also with much other information of interest, and as an appendix 'The Legend of the Awakening of the Quendi (*Cuivienyarna*)'.

Tolkien wrote the works examined in this volume in the years between the completion of *The Lord of the Rings* and his death in 1973. Most of them record events in the Elder Days of Arda, between the return of the Noldor and the overthrow of Morgoth at the end of the First Age. But the *Grey Annals* include events in Beleriand concerning the Elves before the return of the Noldor, and *Quendi and Eldar* is primarily linguistic.

The War of the Ring: The History of The Lord of the Rings, Part Three. The eighth volume of *The History of Middle-earth*, edited with notes and commentary by *Christopher Tolkien, first published in Great Britain by Unwin

Hyman, London, in September 1990, and in the United States by the Houghton Mifflin Company, Boston, in November 1990. See further, *Descriptive Bibliography* A28.

In this volume Christopher Tolkien examines texts for *The Lord of the Rings* written by his father between mid-1942 and autumn 1947. Part One, 'The Fall of Saruman', describes the writing of the last five chapters of Book III of *The Lord of the Rings*, probably during the summer vacation 1942. The chapters, here titled 'Helm's Deep', 'The Road to Isengard', 'Flotsam and Jetsam', 'The Voice of Saruman', and 'The Palantír', are preceded by a few pages on chronological problems ('The Destruction of Isengard'). Part Two, 'The Ring Goes East', deals with the writing of Book IV beginning in spring 1944. This is the best documented part of *The Lord of the Rings*, as Tolkien made frequent references to its writing in letters he wrote to his son Christopher in South Africa. The chapters are titled: 'The Taming of Sméagol'; 'The Passage of the Marshes'; 'The Black Gate Is Closed'; 'Of Herbs and Stewed Rabbit'; 'Faramir'; 'The Forbidden Pool'; 'Journey to the Cross-roads'; and 'Kirith Ungol'.

Part Three, 'Minas Tirith', is concerned with the writing of Book V. Christopher Tolkien first gives the continuation of an outline included in 'The Story Foreseen from Fangorn' in *The Treason of Isengard*, which he found only after the publication of that volume ('Addendum to "The Treason of Isengard"'). Then, in 'Book Five Begun and Abandoned', he discusses his father's statement in the Foreword to the second edition of *The Lord of the Rings*, that he wrote the first drafts of Book V, Chapters 1 and 3, in 1942. This is shown not to have been the case, since it is evident in the drafts that Book IV, written in 1944, was already in existence; and therefore Book V was begun also that year, in October. Tolkien did not proceed very far, however, before he laid *The Lord of the Rings* aside again and did not return to it until the summer vacation in 1946. The rest of Part Three describes this later writing, and the making of the second working map for *The Lord of the Rings*. The relevant chapters in *The War of the Ring* are: 'Minas Tirith'; 'Many Roads Lead Eastward (1)'; 'Many Roads Lead Eastward (2)'; 'The Siege of Gondor'; 'The Ride of the Rohirrim'; 'The Story Foreseen from Forannest'; 'The Battle of the Pelennor Fields'; 'The Pyre of Denethor'; 'The Houses of Healing'; 'The Last Debate'; 'The Black Gate Opens'; and 'The Second Map'.

The War of the Ring also contains, in black and white, reproductions of various drawings, maps, plans, and pages of manuscript. The first British and American hardcover editions include as well colour reproductions of Tolkien's drawings *Shelob's Lair* and *Dunharrow*.

Wardale, Edith Elizabeth (1863–1943). A distinguished scholar of Old English and related languages, Edith Wardale was intimately connected with the University of *Oxford and with women's education from 1887, when she entered Lady Margaret Hall. In the following year, she moved to St Hugh's Hall, then recently opened (later St Hugh's College), where she read Modern Languages. After receiving her degree she became a tutor and (for a few years) Vice-Principal of St Hugh's, and also tutor to the Association for the Higher Education of Women. At various times she was a lecturer at Lady Margaret Hall, St Hilda's College, Oxford, and Royal Holloway College, London. Tolkien may have attended her lectures on the Literature of the Old English Period during Hilary Term 1914. Some eleven years later, during summer 1925, he and Edith Wardale were fellow Examiners for the Oxford English School finals. Although she retired from tutoring at St Hugh's in 1923, she continued to serve on English Faculty Board committees, with some of which Tolkien was also involved.

Among Wardale's publications are *An Old English Grammar* (1922) and *An Introduction to Middle English* (1937). She reviewed 'Anglo-Saxon Studies' in the first four volumes of **The Year's Work in English Studies* (1919/20–23).

Warwick (Warwickshire). The town of Warwick, founded in 914 by Ethelfleda, daughter of Alfred the Great, is built on a hill north of the River Avon, close to *Birmingham and about forty miles north-east of *Oxford. Edith Bratt (*Edith Tolkien) moved there from *Cheltenham with her cousin *Jennie Grove in 1913. After a period of living in rooms, then rented a house at **15 Victoria Road**: a photograph of its façade is reproduced in *The Tolkien Family Album*, p. 37. Edith lived there until she married Ronald Tolkien in March 1916; in the meantime, Tolkien visited often. In August 1914 he stayed at The White House, Northgate, and in July 1915 was at 57 Emscott Road. He found the town beautiful, unspoiled by industry. Its old buildings, trees, and dramatically placed castle appealed to him. He took Edith punting on the river, and made at least two drawings: *Warwick Castle Seen from Under the Bridge*, drawn from a boat on the river or from Myton Fields (later dated '1913–14?'), and *Pageant House Gardens, Warwick* (18 June 1913; *Artist and Illustrator*, fig. 14). Pageant House is a late Georgian building in Jury Street.

On 8 January 1914 Edith was received into the Roman Catholic faith, and on 22 March 1916 she and Tolkien were married at the **Church of St Mary the Immaculate**, built in the mid-nineteenth century. A photograph of the interior of the church is reproduced in *The Tolkien Family Album*, p. 38.

Tolkien came to have deep emotional ties to Warwick because of its association with Edith, which are reflected in his early poetry and mythology. While visiting there in November 1915 he wrote *Kortirion among the Trees* (**The Trees of Kortirion*), dedicated to Warwick. Later, in a prose introduction to the poem and in the **The Book of Lost Tales* (begun in winter 1916–17), he conceived of Kortirion in Tol Eressëa, the isle of the Elves, as having been built in memory of the elven city of Kôr in Valinor, and like that city had a great tower. Tol Eressëa was to be drawn back in the Faring Forth and become England, and Warwick was to be built at its centre on the site of Kortirion. In a still later version, Kortirion in Tol Eressëa was built in imitation of Warwick. In mid-March 1916, at Warwick and Oxford, Tolkien wrote the poem *The Wanderer's Allegiance* (see **The Town of Dreams and the City of Present Sorrow*); its first part describes Warwick with no apparent connection at that time to the mythology.

See also *'Heraldic Devices of Tol Erethrin'.

West Midlands. Although he was born in *South Africa and spent most of his life in *Oxford, Tolkien felt that the West Midlands were his real home. This was the land of his *Suffield ancestors – that is, generally the area that was once Anglo-Saxon Mercia, and in particular in Tolkien's youth had been Worcestershire, together with adjoining parts of Herefordshire, Warwickshire, Shropshire, and *Staffordshire, as they were before county borders changed in the later twentieth century. Today one must distinguish the West Midlands that Tolkien knew from the present urban county of that name, created in 1973.

On 6 July 1955 he wrote to the Houghton Mifflin Company (*Publishers):

> I am in fact more of a Suffield (a family deriving from Evesham in Worcestershire) [than a Tolkien]. . . . I am indeed in English terms a West-midlander at home only in the counties upon the Welsh Marches; and it is, I believe, as much due to descent as to opportunity that Anglo-Saxon and Western Middle English and alliterative verse have been both a childhood attraction and my main professional sphere. [*Letters*, p. 218]

Indeed, the Middle English works with which he was most associated were products of the West Midlands: the *Ancrene Riwle*, the *'Katherine Group', *Pearl*, and *Sir Gawain and the Green Knight*. Earlier, on 18 March 1941, he had written to his son *Michael: 'Though a Tolkien by name, I am a Suffield by tastes, talents, and upbringing, and any corner of that county [Worcestershire] (however fair or squalid) is in an indefinable way "home" to me, as no other part of the world is' (*Letters*, p. 54). And on 18 January 1945 he wrote to his son *Christopher: 'For barring the Tolkien (which must long ago have become a pretty thin strand) you are a Mercian or Hwiccian (of Wychwood) on both sides' (*Letters*, p. 108).

On 12 December 1955 Tolkien wrote to George Allen & Unwin (*Publishers) that the Shire in *The Lord of the Rings* 'is in fact more or less a Warwickshire village [i.e. *Sarehole] of about the time of the Diamond Jubilee [of Queen Victoria, 1897]' (*Letters*, p. 230). Around the beginning of 1956 he also wrote, in a draft letter to Michael Straight: 'There is no special reference to England in the "Shire" – except of course that as an Englishman brought up in an "almost rural" village of Warwickshire on the edge of the prosperous bourgeoisie of Birmingham (about the time of the Diamond Jubilee!) I take my models like anyone else – from such "life" as I know' (*Letters*, p. 235). 'Bag End', the name of Bilbo and Frodo Baggins' home in the Shire, was also the local name for the Worcestershire farm of Tolkien's *Aunt Jane Neave.

After the First World War Tolkien's brother *Hilary bought a small orchard and market garden near **Evesham**. Tolkien and his family visited there on several occasions. In summer 1923 they 'were pressed into service to help on the land, and there were also hilarious games with giant kites, which the two brothers flew from the field opposite the house to amuse the children' (Humphrey Carpenter, *Biography*, p. 106). An allusion to Hilary's farm appears in

Roverandom, when the sand-sorcerer Psamathos says of the wizard Arta-xerxes: 'He comes from Persia. But he lost his way one day . . . and the first person he met on the road went and put him on the way to Pershore instead. He has lived in those parts, except on holidays, ever since. They say he is a nimble plum-gatherer for an old man' (p. 14). Hilary's orchard mainly con-sisted of plum trees, and was close to Pershore in Worcestershire.

In December 1940 and in early 1941 Tolkien went to **Worcester** several times to visit his son Michael, who had suffered a back injury, in the Worces-ter Royal Infirmary. Tolkien and his family also visited Worcester to see their *Incledon relatives, who lived there for four years during the Second World War. On 15 July 1960 Tolkien visited the cathedral library in **Hereford** to do research for his edition of the *Ancrene Wisse* (*Ancrene Riwle*).

See also *Barnt Green; *Birmingham and environs; *Malvern; *Rednal; *Sarehole; *Warwick.

Weston-super-Mare (Somerset). A resort in Somerset on the Bristol Chan-nel where the Tolkien family, except for *John, took a holiday in April 1940. A photograph of the Tolkiens on the esplanade is reproduced in *The Tolkien Family Album*, p. 65.

Whitby (Yorkshire). Tolkien visited Whitby, a town on the north-east coast of England built on two steep hills on either side of the River Eske, in summer 1910 and September 1945. On the first occasion, he made at least six drawings of its busy fishing port and one of the ruins of famed Whitby Abbey (see *Artist and Illustrator*, figs. 9–10, and *Life and Legend*, p. 19). The Abbey was founded as a double community, for both monks and nuns, c. 657; under its first abbess, later St Hild, it became an important centre of learning and culture, and in 664 was the site of a synod which decided that the Northumbrian Church would follow the Roman rather than the Irish method of calculating the date of Easter. The ruined church that Tolkien sketched, prominently located on a cliff two hundred feet above the sea, dates mainly to the twelfth and thirteenth centuries, the original building having been destroyed in 867.

Whitelock, Dorothy (1901–1982). Educated at Newnham College, Cambridge, Dorothy Whitelock came to St Hilda's College, *Oxford as a lecturer in Eng-lish Language in 1930. She was appointed Tutor in 1936 and a Fellow in 1937. A noted scholar of Anglo-Saxon poetry and history, she remained a colleague of Tolkien on the Oxford English Faculty until 1957, when she became Elrington and Bosworth Professor of Anglo-Saxon at Cambridge. She retired in 1969.

Her publications include *Anglo-Saxon Wills* (1930), *The Audience of Beowulf* (1951), *The Beginnings of English Society* (1952), the collection *English Historical Documents c. 500–1042* (1955), and a revision of Sweet's *Anglo-Saxon Reader* (1967). She also served as editor of the *Saga-Book* of the Viking Society for Northern Research, and on the Council of the Early English Text Society (*Societies and clubs).

Wilkinson, Cyril Hackett (1888–1960). C.H. Wilkinson read English at Worcester College, *Oxford, where he was much influenced by *Walter Raleigh. He received his B.A. in 1910. In 1913 he went to Eton as an assistant master. During the First World War he served in France with the Coldstream Guards, and in Italy as a General Staff Officer. In 1919 he returned to Worcester College as a Fellow and Dean, in which office he remained for thirty-four years. He also served at times as Senior Proctor and as Vice-Provost. He lectured on English Literature until 1956, and was concerned with both the College Library and the Bodleian. His military experience made him an obvious choice to command the Oxford University Officers' Training Corps, with the rank of Colonel, for a period between the wars and again during the Second World War.

On 14 February 1938 Wilkinson was present at a meeting of the Lovelace Society, a student organization at Worcester College, when Tolkien read *Farmer Giles of Ham* to the members' delight. On 30 September 1946 Tolkien wrote to *Stanley Unwin that 'Cyril Wilkinson (the old war-horse)' since the 1938 reading 'has always been at me to publish' the story. 'He returned to the charge on September 3rd when we met at the Election of [*David] Nichol Smith's successor to the Merton Chair of Literature . . .' (Tolkien–George Allen & Unwin archive, HarperCollins). In gratitude, Tolkien dedicated *Farmer Giles of Ham* when finally published in 1949 'To C.H. Wilkinson'.

Williams, Charles Walter Stansby (1886–1945). Educated from 1902 at University College, London, Charles Williams withdrew after only two years for financial reasons. He worked in the Methodist Bookroom in London, and enrolled in the Working Men's College. In 1908 he joined the Oxford University Press (*Publishers) as a proofreader, and remained a valued member of its staff until his death. He also taught English Literature in evening classes.

As a writer he was particularly devoted to poetry. His first book of verse, *The Silver Chair* (1912), was a sonnet sequence on romantic love, influenced by Dante. Other poetry followed, as well as plays, literary criticism, biography, and theology, and numerous reviews of detective fiction (collected 2003). His first novel, *Shadows of Ecstasy*, failed to find a publisher until 1933; by then four other novels – *War in Heaven* (1930), *Many Dimensions* (1931), *The Place of the Lion* (1931), and *The Greater Trumps* (1932) – had appeared. His approach in these, as in other writing, was out of the ordinary. Humphrey Carpenter refers to Williams'

> total disregard for the conventional distinctions of time and space, the natural and the supernatural, and his habit of setting extraordinary events against mundane backgrounds. If he wanted to talk about seeing Shakespeare [as he did in one poem], why should it not happen in a Tube railway station? If he wished to write a novel [*Many Dimensions*] about the magical properties of the Stone of Suleiman, then let it be set in modern London and let the participants include the Lord Chief Justice and his secretary. [*The Inklings*, p. 95]

Although he was a devout member of the Church of England, Williams was also deeply interested in magic and the supernatural. In 1917 he was inducted into the Order of the Golden Dawn, whose members concerned themselves with both Christianity and the occult. His life was as unconventional as his writings, ruled by ideas of 'co-inherence' (all beings are dependent on each other), romantic theology ('lovers should see in each other a reflection of God' – Carpenter, *The Inklings*, p. 103), and orthodox Christianity. But he had a personal magnetism which attracted admirers, especially females, and was an intelligent and captivating speaker.

In 1936 *Nevill Coghill praised *The Place of the Lion* to his friend *C.S. Lewis, who read and enjoyed it, and in turn recommended it to Tolkien. At the same time, Williams discovered Lewis's *Allegory of Love* in proof at Oxford University Press, and was delighted to read his comments on Dante. Letters were exchanged, and a friendship begun. Lewis was also enthusiastic about Williams' *Taliessin through Logres* (1938), a poetic cycle based on *Arthur and the Matter of Britain, with emphasis on the Grail. This, like his other works, met with little popular success; and because he wrote in different fields, he did not make his name as a specialist. His sixth novel, *Descent into Hell* (1937), was rejected by Gollancz, who had published his earlier fiction (to disappointing sales), but picked up by Faber & Faber with the encouragement of T.S. Eliot, a director of the firm.

In 1939, at the start of the war, Williams moved to *Oxford along with the London offices of Oxford University Press. At once Lewis persuaded him to join *The Inklings; by November 1939 he was a regular member. Lewis, together with Tolkien, also worked to bring Williams onto the Oxford English Faculty, whose numbers were depleted during the war. Williams' lectures on Milton were well attended. In 1943 he published one of his most significant works of criticism, *The Figure of Beatrice: A Study in Dante*, and the University awarded him an honorary MA.

Williams on his part enjoyed the stimulus of evenings with men who were his intellectual equals, often knew more than he did about a subject, and felt free to criticize his writings, especially their obscurity. The experience did not, however, fundamentally alter his ideas, and his writings continued to be highly personal and difficult to fathom. On 3 March 1955 Tolkien wrote to Dora Marshall that at Inklings gatherings he and Williams 'both listened . . . to large and largely unintelligible fragments of one another's works read aloud. . . . But I think we both found the other's mind (or rather mode of expression, and climate) as impenetrable when cast into "literature", as we found the other's presence and conversation delightful' (*Letters*, p. 209). Tolkien told Dick Plotz that he and Williams

> liked one another and enjoyed talking (mostly in jest) but we had nothing to say to one another at deeper (or higher) levels. I doubt if he had read anything of mine then available; I had read or heard a good deal of his work, but found it wholly alien, and sometimes very distasteful,

occasionally ridiculous. (This is perfectly true as a general statement, but is not intended as a criticism of Williams; rather it is an exhibition of my own limits of sympathy. And of course in so large a range of work I found lines, passages, scenes, and thoughts that I found striking.) I remained entirely unmoved. Lewis was bowled over. [12 September 1965, *Letters*, pp. 361–2]

And to Anne Barrett he wrote that he was 'a sort of assistant mid-wife at the birth of *All Hallows' Eve*', Williams' final novel (1945), read aloud to the Inklings 'as it was composed . . . and much enjoyed his company; but our minds remained poles apart. I actively disliked his Arthurian-Byzantine mythology . . .' (7 August 1964, *Letters*, p. 349; Williams' Arthurian cycle of poems continued with *The Region of the Summer Stars*, first published 1944). Williams on his part greatly enjoyed *The Lord of the Rings* as it was read by Tolkien to the Inklings, so much so that in 1944 he borrowed the typescript of the work as far as it had reached.

Humphrey Carpenter argues in *Biography* and *The Inklings* that Tolkien responded to Williams' move to Oxford, and membership in the Inklings, with at least faint jealousy, because Williams had attained a high place in the affections of C.S. Lewis, and this threatened, or at least diminished, Tolkien's own friendship with Lewis. John D. Rateliff discusses this view, and in general Tolkien's relationship with Williams, in '"And Something Yet Remains to Be Said": Tolkien and Williams', *Mythlore* 12, no. 3, whole no. 45 (Spring 1986). It seems clear at any rate that Williams was Tolkien's friend primarily because he was a friend of Lewis: as shown in **Chronology**, Williams and Tolkien seem rarely to have met when they were not also in Lewis's company.

In 1944, with the war winding down and the prospect of Williams returning to London came to mind, Lewis and Tolkien conceived of a *Festschrift* to honour Williams. Before this could be completed, however, in May 1945 Williams was taken ill, had an operation, and died. Tolkien wrote to his widow Florence 'Michal' Williams that 'in the (far too brief) years since I first met him I had grown to admire and love your husband deeply, and I am more grieved than I can express' (15 May 1945, *Letters*, p. 115). The *Festschrift* became a memorial volume, *Essays Presented to Charles Williams*, edited by C.S. Lewis and published in 1947.

In later years, as Tolkien's popularity rose, attention was focused also on his friends and on the Inklings. Critics often discussed Tolkien, Lewis, and Williams together, three Oxford Christians, in conjunction with one another as they read, heard, and influenced each other's works. Such views were sometimes forced – the three members were not alone among the Inklings, nor hardly inseparable – and it remains an issue how much cross-influence took place.

The Image of the City and Other Essays, ed. Anne Ridler (1958) and *Essential Writings in Spirituality and Theology*, ed. Charles Hefling (1993) are useful anthologies of Williams' writings. His wartime letters to his wife have been published as *To Michal from Serge*, ed. Roma A. King (2002), and his letters to a friend, Lois Lang-Sims, as *Letters to Lalage* (1989). The standard biography is *Charles Williams: An Exploration of His Life and Work* by Alice Mary Hadfield (1983); the major bibliography of works and criticism, though now dated, is still *Charles W.S. Williams: A Checklist* by Lois Glenn (1975). Substantive works of criticism include *Charles Williams: Poet of Theology* by Glen Cavaliero (1983); *Charles Williams: A Celebration*, ed. Brian Horne (1995); and *The Rhetoric of Vision: Essays on Charles Williams*, ed. Charles A. Huttar and Peter J. Schakel (1996). See also the biographical preface by C.S. Lewis to *Essays Presented to Charles Williams* (1947).

Photographs of Charles Williams are reproduced in *The Inklings*, pl. 5a, 6a, 7a, and 8a.

Wilson, Frank Percy (1889–1963). Like Tolkien, F.P. Wilson was a graduate of *King Edward's School, Birmingham (1908), and he too served on the Somme, where he was badly wounded in 1916. Before the war, he read English at the University of Birmingham and earned his B.Litt. at Lincoln College, *Oxford. In 1919 he returned to Birmingham to teach, but in 1921 accepted a lecturership in English Literature at Oxford, a post which in 1925 became a readership. He tutored for three of the men's colleges – among his pupils were *Nevill Coghill and *C.S. Lewis – and also many women while at Oxford. In 1929 he was elected to the chair of English at *Leeds, and in 1936 became Hildred Carlile Professor of English Literature at Bedford College, London, in each instance succeeding *Lascelles Abercrombie. He returned to Oxford in 1947 as the Merton Professor of English Literature, succeeding *David Nichol Smith.

Tolkien knew Wilson from at least the time of his own return to Oxford, in 1925, as a fellow member of the English Faculty Board. In addition to shared duties on Faculty committees, they were both general editors of the *Oxford English Monographs*, and both electors for the new chair of Medieval and Renaissance English at Cambridge, given to C.S. Lewis in 1954.

Wilson wrote widely on Shakespeare and Elizabethan literature. He edited the prose works of Thomas Dekker, and he was a co-editor of the *Oxford History of English Literature*.

Wiseman, Christopher Luke (1893–1987). Christopher Wiseman met Tolkien in the Fifth Class at *King Edward's School, Birmingham. Both excelled at their studies – at the end of autumn term 1905 Tolkien placed first in their class, and Wiseman second – and they shared interests in Latin and Greek, and rugby football. They became close friends and friendly rivals, able to discuss any subject honestly. *Religion was important to them both, and although Wiseman was a staunch Methodist, the son of a minister, and Tolkien a devout Roman Catholic, the differences in their faiths did not come between them. In Wiseman's words, they were the 'Twin Brethren', and together with *Vincent Trought the nucleus of the *T.C.B.S. (letter to Tolkien, 15 November 1914, Tolkien Papers, Bodleian Library, Oxford).

Active in many School activities, Wiseman served as Sports Secretary, Football Vice-Captain, House Swimming Captain, Sub-Librarian, Prefect, School Captain and General Secretary, and editor of the School magazine. A member as well of the Debating Society, it was said of Wiseman that he could 'make a good political speech but is frequently much too ponderous; while in his more frivolous speeches he is inclined to indulge in weird metaphors and similes altogether beyond the house's grasp. When at his best a formidable opponent, but at other times rather incoherent and irrational' ('Characters, 1911–12'. *King Edward's School Chronicle* n.s. 27, no. 193 (June 1912), p. 39).

In 1912 he went up to Peterhouse, Cambridge on a scholarship to read Mathematics. There he continued to excel in his studies and on the playing field, but found time also to pursue an interest in music composition. In 1913 his family moved to Wandsworth in *London, where a T.C.B.S. 'council' was held in December 1914. In June 1915 Wiseman joined the Royal Navy as an instructor in mathematics.

During the First World War, while serving on *HMS Superb*, he corresponded at length with Tolkien about poetry, art, faith, and the welfare of their friends *R.Q. Gilson and *G.B. Smith. On 1 March 1916, for instance, Tolkien having argued that Wiseman did not understand the 'intoxication' of the night and of stars – which, Wiseman admitted, he did not – he replied

> that you don't understand the grandeur of the glare of noon, of the sea, of the wonderful secrets that man is continually digging out in the most amazingly ingenious ways, out of the great sun, the great stars, the amazing greatness of mountains, of white & green & purple, the extraordinary & overwhelming greatness of men & children. You are fascinated by little, delicate, beautiful creatures; & when I am with you, I am too. So I do sympathize with you. But I feel more thrilled by enormous, slow moving, omnipotent things, & if I had greater artistic gifts I would make you feel the thrill too. And having been led by the hand of God into the borderland of the fringe of science that man has conquered, I can see that there are such enormous numbers of wonderful & beautiful things that really exist, that in my ordinary frame of mind I feel no need to search after things that man had used before these could fill a certain place in the sum of his desires. [Tolkien Papers, Bodleian Library, Oxford]

Wiseman enjoyed and generally praised Tolkien's poems as they were sent to him. Tolkien's *Wood-sunshine* (written 1910, rewritten 1914) inspired Wiseman to set it to music. Sometimes, however, he felt that Tolkien needed to show more restraint. On 25 April 1915 he wrote: 'I can't think where you get all your amazing words from. I think we are both afraid lest you should be carried away by them. I should point to the end of [the poem] "Copernicus & Ptolemy" which seems to me rather like a systematic & well thought out bombardment with asphyxiating bombs' (Tolkien Papers, Bodleian Library, Oxford). On 4 February 1916, having read *Kortirion among the Trees* (*The Trees of Kortirion*), he expressed his pleasure that Tolkien was no longer depicting 'underground caverns full of stalactites lit up with magnesium wire', that there had been a lessening of the 'arc-lamp' of overblown verse. 'I am not sufficiently analytical in matters of poetry to be able to offer any sort of criticism,' he said, 'but I used to be afraid you would never write anything but freak poetry, however clever it might be, & however beautiful the effect' (Tolkien Papers, Bodleian Library, Oxford). In 1918 Wiseman and Tolkien worked together to edit for publication the poems of their late friend G.B. Smith (*A Spring Harvest*, 1918).

After the war Wiseman returned to Cambridge, where he studied Physics and worked in the research laboratories with Professor Ernest Rutherford. From 1921 to 1926 he taught at Kingswood School, Bath, where he became Senior Mathematics Master. He was then appointed Headmaster at Queen's College in Taunton, Somerset, where he remained for more than a quarter-century. A great lover of music, he gave record recitals at Queen's College on Sunday nights, and was himself a composer of Methodist hymns.

Tolkien stayed in touch with Wiseman as the years passed, though their families and careers took them on different paths. Tolkien's youngest son, *Christopher, was named for Christopher Wiseman in 1924. Tolkien visited Wiseman in Milford-on-Sea, near *Bournemouth, in 1972, and wrote to him on 24 May 1973 as 'your most devoted friend' (*Letters*, p. 429).

A photograph of Christopher Wiseman (fourth from the left in the back row) is reproduced in *Biography*, pl. 5a, and *The Tolkien Family Album*, p. 26. This and two other photographs of Wiseman are reproduced in *Tolkien and the Great War* by John Garth (2003).

Women and marriage. From April 1895, when she left *South Africa with her sons, until her death on 14 November 1904, Tolkien's mother (*Mabel Tolkien) was the most important figure in his life. The death of her husband (*Arthur Tolkien) left her with the difficult task of caring for Ronald and his brother *Hilary, on her own and with only a small income. But she had been well educated, and was able to see to their education herself for several years.

During these years Mabel Tolkien did much to establish the future course of Ronald's life. In a biographical statement he sent to the Houghton Mifflin Company (*Publishers) on 30 June 1955 he wrote: 'It is to my mother . . . that I owe my tastes for philology, especially of Germanic languages, and for romance' (*Letters*, p. 218). In June 1900 she was received into the Church of Rome, and instructed her sons in the same faith; for this, she faced hostility from her family and a loss of financial support. Her death from diabetes in 1904 year may have been hastened by the strain of raising her sons under such difficult circumstances. In *Biography* Humphrey Carpenter quotes words that Tolkien wrote nine years later: 'My own dear mother was a martyr indeed, and it is not to everybody that God grants so easy a way to his great gifts as he did to Hilary and myself, giving us a mother who killed herself with labour and trouble to ensure us keeping the faith.' Carpenter comments that this is some indication of the way in which he associated her with his membership of the Catholic Church. Indeed it might be said that after she died his religion took the place in his affections that she had previously occupied. The consolation that it provided was emotional as well as spiritual. Perhaps her death also had a cementing effect on his study of languages. It was she, after all, who had been his first teacher and who had encouraged him to take an interest in words. [p. 31]

The only subject that Mabel did not teach Ronald was geometry. This he studied with her younger sister, Jane (*Jane Neave), who earned a Bachelor of Science degree at Mason College, the predecessor of the University of Birmingham, and became a schoolteacher. Tolkien proudly wrote in a letter to Joyce Reeves on 4 November 1961: 'The professional aunt is a fairly recent development, perhaps; but I was fortunate in having an early example: one of the first women to take a science degree' (*Letters*, p. 308). Tolkien stayed with his Aunt Jane and her husband, Edwin Neave, during part of 1904 while Mabel was in hospital. Jane was widowed in 1909, and apparently then spent a few years in St Andrews, *Scotland, during which time Tolkien visited her at least twice. In 1911 it was through Aunt Jane that he joined the *Brookes-Smith family on a walking tour of *Switzerland. In later years he sent her copies of his books and other writings, and it was in response to one of her suggestions that *The Adventures of Tom Bombadil and Other Verses from the Red Book* was conceived.

Biographies of Tolkien tend to suggest that while under the guardianship of *Father Francis Morgan he had little contact with relatives on either side of his family, and that between the *Oratory and *King Edward's School he lived in an almost entirely male society. In addition to contacts with Jane Neave, however – certainly more than we have noted – it is clear that he spent much time with the *Incledon family, his mother's elder sister May, her husband Walter, and their daughters Marjorie and Mary. Tolkien was close enough to Marjorie and Mary to share private languages with them (*Languages, Invented), as well as the writing and performance of amateur plays. Ronald and Hilary were also in frequent touch with three of their father's sisters and their families (see *Tolkien family): Mabel Mitton, Grace Mountain, and Florence Hadley. *Priscilla Tolkien has said that 'the Mittons were very important to my father as he was growing up. He spent holidays with them, and described taking his friend, *Christopher Wiseman, to visit and played quoits with him in the [Mitton] garden at Abbotsford' (private correspondence). The Mittons had three daughters. The Mountains, in Newcastle on Tyne, included Aunt Grace, her son Kenneth, and her daughter Dorothy ('Ding').

Early in 1908 Father Francis moved his wards Ronald and Hilary to lodgings in Edgbaston. There Ronald met his future wife, Edith Bratt. Their relationship is discussed at length in the entry for *Edith Tolkien and in **Chronology**, but one or two aspects are rightly considered here. The first of these concerns the reaction by Father Francis in autumn 1909 when he discovered that seventeen-year-old Ronald, still at school and supposedly working hard to win a scholarship to *Oxford, had formed an attachment to a girl three years his senior and had been meeting her secretly. Father Francis was well within his rights as Ronald's guardian to demand that this affair should cease.

It is worth noting, by analogy, that the courtship of Tolkien's parents also had not gone smoothly. Arthur Tolkien had proposed to Mabel Suffield in 1888, when she was only eighteen. Her father refused to allow a formal engagement for two years, during which time Arthur and Mabel might meet only at family gatherings; in fact, they managed to exchange secret letters. Even meetings in company ceased after a year, as Arthur left *England to take up a post with the Bank of Africa in Bloemfontein with good prospects for supporting a wife and family. Not until he could provide a house and had an adequate income did Mabel join him.

In 1909 it would be three years before Tolkien came of age. Even if he succeeded in winning a scholarship to Oxford, he would still need financial aid from his guardian, and it would be several more years after that before he could be in a position to support a wife. Humphrey Carpenter explains Father Francis Morgan's point of view and reactions: 'Ronald's guardian had been as a father to him, and his feelings can be imagined when he learnt that the ward on whom he had lavished so much affection, care, and money, was not concentrating his abilities on vital school-work but was . . . conducting a clandestine love affair . . .' (*Biography*, p. 41). It would have been natural to blame the affair as a distraction when Ronald failed in December 1909 on his first attempt to win an Oxford scholarship. Father Francis must have felt even more betrayed when he heard that Ronald and Edith had been seen together. His response was severe but understandable: 'Ronald must not meet or even write to Edith. He could only see her once more, to say good-bye on the day she left for *Cheltenham [where she had decided to move]. After that they must not communicate until he was twenty-one' (*Biography*, p. 43).

Tolkien's acceptance of his guardian's rules may seem strange to rebellious youth in the early twenty-first century, but as Carpenter comments, 'the social conventions of the time demanded that young people should obey their parents or guardian; moreover Ronald had great affection for Father Francis, and depended on him for money' (p. 41). In any case, there was no hope of marrying for years, unless Ronald was to give up a university education and an academic career.

For the most part, it was a male society that Tolkien entered as an Oxford undergraduate in 1911. Females were allowed to study, to attend lectures, and to take most examinations, but not yet to matriculate; contact between male and female students was restricted, and remained so for several years. Vera Chapman, founder of the Tolkien Society (*Fandom), while reminiscing about her time as an Oxford undergraduate (from 1918) commented on behaviour expected of women students:

The caps were to be worn soberly – not pushed to the back of the head with the point aspiring upward (as often seen now) but straight upon the head, with the point modestly lowered between the eyebrows. Nor must we give any cause for disapproval – we must sit together, apart from the men, and, if we had any acquaintances among them, not greet them or give any sign of recognition – coming out of the lecture we must not converse, or claim any friendship in the street – above all, no *new* friendships were to be formed – that was the very thing that was to be rigidly avoided.

Our colleges were rigidly cloistered. One man, and one man only, stood as guardian at our door – the porter – and he might admit fathers, or uncles, or brothers, but not, *not* cousins. . . . If one of us wished to entertain a young man, to tea, she required first a letter from a parent to the Principal – then a public sitting-room in the college must be booked, and then a senior member (or 'Don') must be engaged to join the party and act as chaperone. ['Reminiscences: Oxford in 1920, Meeting Tolkien and Becoming an Author at 77', *Proceedings of the J.R.R. Tolkien Centenary Conference 1992* (1995), pp. 12–13]

A male student might, however, often find himself in the company of female Faculty and the wives of dons, such as *Edith Wardale, whose lectures on Literature of the Old English period Tolkien may have attended, and Elizabeth Wright, the wife of Professor *Joseph Wright and herself a scholar, to whose house Tolkien sometimes went to tea.

A few years later, while on the staff of the *Oxford English Dictionary* in 1919 and 1920, Tolkien supplemented his work by tutoring undergraduates in his home. This was to the benefit of two of the Oxford women's colleges, Lady Margaret Hall and St Hugh's, which badly needed someone to teach Old English to their young ladies. Tolkien had the advantage of being married, which meant that a chaperone did not have to be sent to his home whenever he was teaching.

In May 1920 female students were granted full membership of the University, and were eligible for all degrees except the Bachelor of Divinity and the Doctor of Divinity. Women dons could now sit on Faculty boards and act as examiners. Miss Wardale was a member of the newly established English Faculty Board when it met for the first time on 5 November 1926, at which meeting she and Tolkien, with two others, were elected to the Library Committee. At the following meeting on 9 December, Miss Wardale and Tolkien were both appointed to committees to prepare lecture schedules for the following academic year, and to consider the question of a Preliminary Examination. Miss Wardale evidently completed her term of duty at the end of Trinity Term 1928, but another woman, *Helen Darbishire, was among those elected to serve from Michaelmas Term 1928. Miss Darbishire remained a member of the Board until the end of Trinity Term 1945, and from Michaelmas Term 1936 to Trinity Term 1939 was its first female chairman. From at least Hilary Term 1931, when *Dorothy Everett is first recorded as attending, there were at least two women dons on the Board (originally out of eight, but the size of the Board increased). For most of the period from Michaelmas Term 1949 there were three or four women on the Board, though men remained in the majority and filled all of the professorial chairs, those being associated with colleges for men only.

There were no co-educational colleges. The older colleges still accepted only male students, while females attended colleges established for women during the late nineteenth and early twentieth centuries. In 'Memories of J.R.R. Tolkien in His Centenary Year' (*The Brown Book*, December 1992) his daughter Priscilla wrote that 'of the five women's colleges in Oxford' at that time the one she herself attended, Lady Margaret Hall,

> was probably the one he knew best; he spoke with appreciation of his visits to the High Table in the days when Miss Grier was Principal and Miss Everett was his colleague on the language side of the English Faculty. One of the stories I remember from this time was his description of Miss Grier standing with her back to the fire in the Senior Common Room after dinner and smoking a pipe! . . . As a confirmed pipe-smoker himself this was no doubt an additional source of comradeship between himself and the Principal. [p. 12]

Her father's many years of friendship with Dorothy Everett was one of the reasons that Priscilla chose Lady Margaret Hall as her college. Later in the same article, she emphasizes that her father believed completely

> in higher education for girls; never at any time in my early life or since did I feel that any difference was made between me and my brothers, so far as our educational needs and opportunities were concerned.
> Perhaps in this he had been influenced by memories of his mother. . . . By the standards of her time and generation she had been highly educated. . . .
> It was therefore, I think, a source of pride and pleasure to him that he had a daughter as well as sons at the University, which was his scholarly and academic home for much of his working life. [pp. 12–13]

The Oxford English School was particularly popular with women. In the course of his career Tolkien supervised twenty-four females taking B.Litt. or D. Phil. degrees, almost half the total of his advanced degree students; and nine of the theses he examined, just under a third of the total, were submitted by women. Of the female students who became close friends of Tolkien and his family, perhaps the best known were *Simonne d'Ardenne, with whom he worked on *Seinte Iuliene* and other manuscripts in the *Katherine Group; *Mary Salu, a fellow student of the *Ancrene Riwle*; and *Elaine (M.E.) Griffiths, who helped to bring *The Hobbit* to the attention of George Allen & Unwin (*Publishers). Tolkien was appointed supervisor of Griffiths' B.Litt.

thesis in Michaelmas Term 1933; later, as a don in the English School, she was a fellow member of the English Faculty Board during the last years before Tolkien's retirement.

As Humphrey Carpenter has said (*The Inklings*, pp. 163–5), strong male friendships were characteristic of Oxford. Most of the dons were male, and it was customary for them to spend much of their time in their colleges, among each other. By extension, most of the *societies and clubs to which Tolkien belonged, as undergraduate and academic, were either exclusively male, or mostly so. The most famous of these was the *Inklings; The Cave, which included women as well as men from the Oxford English Faculty, was a notable exception. Although such segregation now would be considered objectionable, in Tolkien's day it was the norm – which is not to say, by any means, that he was a chauvinist. Indeed, it is evident from his friendships and professional relationships, of which there were many, with female students and dons at Oxford, and from personal accounts by female friends, that Tolkien respected women no less than men for their talents, and that he welcomed their company.

MARRIAGE

Tolkien's long letter to his son *Michael, written 6–8 March 1941 (*Letters*, pp. 48–54), has often been quoted as revealing his ideas about women, and about the relationship between men and women. It must be considered, however, in the context of the circumstances in which it was written, and in light of Tolkien's comment to Stanley Unwin on 21 July 1946 that Michael was 'prematurely married' (Tolkien-George Allen & Unwin archive, HarperCollins).

In early December 1940 Michael Tolkien was injured in an accident with an Army vehicle and admitted to Worcester Royal Infirmary. He apparently was still there in mid-March 1941. On 11 November 1941, three weeks after his twenty-first birthday, Michael married Joan Griffiths, a nurse at the Infirmary, who was four years his senior. It is clear that Tolkien's letter of 6–8 March 1941 was written in response to one from Michael, at the very least mentioning an interest in Joan Griffiths, and most likely expressing a wish to marry her. The heart of Tolkien's letter is the section beginning: 'My own history is so exceptional, so wrong and imprudent in nearly every point that it makes it difficult to counsel prudence. Yet hard cases make bad law; and exceptional cases are not always good guides for others. For what it is worth here is some autobiography – mainly on this occasion directed towards the points of *age*, and *finance*' (*Letters*, p. 52). He knows that any prohibition is likely to have the opposite effect, and as in his own case, harden 'the will enough' to give 'permanence' (p. 53) to an affair which might not otherwise last. In his account he points out that he *did* wait for many years, and finished his degree before marrying; the importance of obtaining that degree for future financial security; and the financial difficulties that he and Edith experienced during the war.

Looking at the earlier part of the letter in this light, it is evident that Tolkien's purpose – to caution a son who might be marrying in haste – has given it a deliberate slant, emphasizing difficulties which may arise in a relationship because of different interests and attitudes between men and women. He begins by suggesting that friendship between a man and a woman is virtually impossible without other feelings entering the relationship, and discusses the dangers of the 'romantic chivalric tradition' (*Letters*, p. 48) which lead men to see women other than they are. The paragraphs that follow, while probably exaggerated for the occasion, show that Tolkien's ideas were very much those of a man of the *early* twentieth century, in fact (by early twenty-first-century standards) with a certain romantic idealization combined with the idea that marriage and motherhood was the natural career for women. He holds that women are less moved by romantic love, but that

> the sexual impulse makes women (naturally when unspoiled more unselfish) very sympathetic and understanding, or specially desirous of being so (or seeming so), and very ready to enter into all the interests, as far as they can, from ties to religion, of the young man they are attracted to. No intent necessarily to deceive: sheer instinct: the servient, helpmeet instinct, generously warmed by desire and young blood. Under this impulse they can in fact often achieve very remarkable insight and understanding, even of things otherwise outside their natural range: for it is their gift to be receptive, stimulated, fertilized (in many other matters than the physical) by the male. . . . Before the young woman knows where she is . . . she may actually 'fall in love'. Which for her, an unspoiled natural young woman, means that she wants to become the mother of the young man's children, even if that desire is by no means clear to her or explicit. . . .
>
> Much though modern conditions have changed feminine circumstances, and the detail of what is considered propriety, they have not changed natural instinct. A man has a life-work, a career, (and male friends), all of which could . . . survive the shipwreck of 'love'. A young woman, even one 'economically independent', as they say now (it usually really means economic subservience to male commercial employers instead of a father or a family), begins to think of the 'bottom drawer' and dream of a home, almost at once. [pp. 49–50]

Today (in the West) few would suggest that all young women desire motherhood and cannot be happy otherwise, yet there are many who, in an attempt to satisfy this desire, go to great lengths to achieve it. Tolkien was not universally wrong in his statement (which, it must be appreciated, might have been expressed in a different way, or not at all, under less personal and pressing circumstances). And even though many women achieve success in a multitude of fields once considered unsuitable for females, there is still a great imbalance in fields such as politics and finance, and on the corporate boards of big business. In Britain, among some other countries, a woman has reached the highest political office, but this is always a matter for comment, and in most places the prospect still seems far off. Considering modern *mores*, Tolkien seems to have had an unrealistic view of women as being 'instinctively, when uncorrupt, monogamous' (p. 51), unlike men. He takes a somewhat doubting view of a man's ability to be faithful in thought as well as deed, and of the problems this poses in a Christian marriage, which for him as a Roman Catholic (*Religion) forbade divorce. 'Faithfulness in Christian marriage entails . . . denial, by suffering'.

> Marriage may help to sanctify & direct to its proper object his sexual desires; its grace may help him in the struggle; but the struggle remains. It will not satisfy him – as hunger may be kept off by regular meals. It will offer as many difficulties to the purity proper to that state, as it provides easements. No man, however truly he loved his betrothed and bride as a young man, has lived faithful to her as a wife in mind and body without deliberate conscious exercise of the *will*, without self-denial. [p. 51]

Marriage is not the end of a great romance, but too often leads to disillusionment and divorce.

> When the glamour wears off, or merely works a bit thin, they think they have made a mistake, and that the real soul-mate is still to find. The real soul-mate too often proves to be the next sexually attractive person that comes along. Someone whom they might indeed very profitably have married, if only—. Hence divorce. . . . Nearly all marriages, even happy ones, are mistakes: in the sense that almost certainly (in a more perfect world, or even with a little more care in this very imperfect one) both partners might have found more suitable mates. But the 'real soul-mate' is the one you are actually married to. You really do very little choosing: life and circumstances do most of it (though if there is a God these must be His instruments, or His appearances). [p. 51]

During this discussion Tolkien appears to comment on the relationship between a teacher and female students as an example of how responsive a woman can be to a man's interest: 'How quickly an intelligent woman can be taught, grasp his ideas, see his point – and how (with rare exceptions) they can go no further, when they leave his hand, or when they cease to take a *personal* interest in *him*' (p. 49). This seems a strange (and here, at least, a chauvinistic) remark, considering that a respectable number of Tolkien's female students subsequently took up academic careers, despite the obstacles to women in that regard. (At any rate, his male students on average do not seem to have done much better.)

In a further letter, on 12 March 1941, Tolkien discussed certain differences which might arise between a husband and wife. His main thrust is that one should be honest with one's partner.

There are many things that a man feels are legitimate even though they cause a fuss. Let him not lie about them to his wife or lover! Cut them out – or if worth a fight: just insist. Such matters may arise frequently – the glass of beer, the pipe, the non writing of letters, the other friend, etc., etc. If the other side's claims really are unreasonable (as they are at times between the dearest lovers and most loving married folk) they are much better met by above board refusal and 'fuss' than subterfuge. [*Biography*, pp. 156–7; *The Inklings*, p. 168]

Humphrey Carpenter cites this extract in both *Biography* and *The Inklings* as evidence that Edith Tolkien resented the time her husband spent with his male friends. According to Carpenter,

family affairs (though of great interest and importance to Tolkien) seemed to him to be quite apart from his life with his male friends. This division of his life into water-tight compartments inevitably caused a strain, and Edith Tolkien resented the fact that such a large part of her husband's affections were lavished on [*C.S.] Lewis and other men friends, while Tolkien himself felt that time spent with the Inklings and in other male company could only be gained by a deliberate and almost ruthless exclusion of attention to his wife. [*The Inklings*, p. 168]

And yet, this assertion of 'water-tight compartments' is not easy to defend. At least some of Tolkien's meetings in male company were expected of an Oxford professor; and he was demonstrably devoted to his wife. Whenever Edith was in poor health, as she was almost continuously in her later years, Tolkien put her first. Inklings meetings were missed, invitations were declined, opportunities to visit and lecture abroad were set aside because there was no one else to look after Edith, or she was not well enough to travel. Tolkien made frequent visits with her to *Bournemouth, where her health usually improved, though the company at the Miramar was not entirely to his taste; and in 1968 he abandoned *Oxford for *Poole for the sake of Edith's happiness and well-being.

Tolkien's thoughts on marriage may be found also in a presumably contemporary draft letter to C.S. Lewis, commenting on his book *Christian Behaviour* (1943). Tolkien found this to show Lewis

really committed (with the Christian Church as a whole) to the view that *Christian marriage* – monogamous, permanent, rigidly 'faithful' – is in fact the truth about sexual behaviour for *all humanity*: this is the only road of total health (including sex in its proper place) for all men and women. That this is dissonant with men's present sex-psychology does not disprove this, as you see: 'I think it is the instinct that has gone wrong,' you say. Indeed if this were not so, it would be an intolerable injustice to impose permanent monogamy even on Christians. [*Letters*, p. 60]

Tolkien clearly agrees with Lewis, but rejects some of his arguments before stating that 'the foundation of Christian marriage . . . is the correct way of "running the human machine"'. He adds a note that 'Christian marriage is not a prohibition of sexual intercourse, but the correct way of sexual temperance – in fact probably the best way of getting the most satisfying *sexual pleasure*, as alcoholic temperance is the best way of enjoying beer and wine' (p. 60). Therefore Tolkien states that 'toleration of divorce – if a Christian does tolerate it – is toleration of a human abuse, which it requires special local and temporary circumstances to justify (as does the toleration of usury) – if indeed either divorce or genuine usury should be tolerated as all, as a matter merely of expedient policy' (p. 61).

WOMEN IN TOLKIEN'S FICTION

Edith L. Crowe has said that 'the most problematic aspect of Tolkien is . . . the disappointingly low percentage of females that appear in his best-known and best-loved works, *The Hobbit* and *The Lord of the Rings*' ('Power in Arda: Sources, Uses and Misuses', *Proceedings of the J.R.R. Tolkien Centenary Conference 1992* (1995), p. 272). She is far from alone in making this point. Some have argued, in addition, that Tolkien included few female characters because his primary audience for story-telling, other than himself, was his three sons; his only daughter was not born until 1929. Nonetheless, in some of the stories he told to his boys Tolkien included females with strong personalities – minor characters, but memorable. In *Roverandom*, 'the rich mer-king's elderly but lovely daughter' (p. 51) knows exactly how to manage her husband, the wizard Artaxerxes. And in *Farmer Giles of Ham* is Giles' wife Agatha, who encourages her husband to 'be bold and quick' in facing the giant, and who at last becomes 'a queen of great size and majesty' and keeps 'a tight hand on the household accounts. There was no getting round Queen Agatha – at least it was a long walk' (p. 75).

In his 1955 autobiographical statement for the Houghton Mifflin Company Tolkien rejected the criticism, already levelled at him, that there are 'no Women' in *The Lord of the Rings*: 'that does not matter, and is not true anyway' (*Letters*, p. 220). Even so, there are not many, and most have only small parts (if developed personalities): Lobelia Sackville-Baggins, Mrs Maggot, Ioreth, Mrs Cotton, Rose. Lobelia is particularly interesting because she seems to have no redeeming features in the early chapters, but at the end is admired for her resistance to the Ruffians. Goldberry too is 'on stage' for only a brief time, but is of a different order: older than *The Lord of the Rings*, having already appeared in the poem *The Adventures of Tom Bombadil* (published 1934) as the 'River-woman's daughter' whom Tom marries, now with a power over water, with which she can summon rain with her singing. Tolkien once described her as representing 'the actual seasonal changes' in river-lands (letter to Forrest J. Ackerman, June 1958, *Letters*, p. 272).

Of the two more prominent female characters in *The Lord of the Rings*, Galadriel is the most difficult to understand. In Lothlórien Celeborn greets the Company first, and Galadriel tells them that 'the Lord of the Galadhrim is accounted the wisest of the Elves of Middle-earth' (bk. II, ch. 7), although she has just shown greater wisdom in refusing to judge Gandalf's actions and in winning the loyalty of Gimli. Elsewhere we have said that 'it is difficult to assess the relationship and relative positions of the two rulers of Lothlórien', and suggest that it may have taken Tolkien 'some time to appreciate fully the characters who had now entered the story, apparently unplanned; indeed, at first it was the Lord of Lothlórien (as "King Galdaran"), rather than the Lady, who was to show Frodo visions in a mirror' (*Reader's Companion*, p. 314). Galadriel soon becomes the more significant figure: she leads Frodo to her mirror, she wears one of the three elven rings, she gives Frodo the phial in which she has captured the light of Eärendil's star, and she seems to foresee that he will need it, just as later she foresees that Aragorn must take the Paths of the Dead. Her stature is increased by the respect with which Gimli and Sam later refer to her.

On the evidence of only *The Lord of the Rings*, many readers thought the Elves an unfallen, sinless race, and Galadriel perhaps the greatest of them. It was even suggested that Tolkien derived some of her aspects from the Virgin Mary. On 25 January 1971 he pointed out in a letter to Mrs Ruth Austin that while it was probably true that he owed 'much of this character to Christian and Catholic teaching and imagination about Mary . . . actually Galadriel was a penitent: in her youth a leader in the rebellion against the Valar . . .' (*Letters*, p. 407). Once conceived, Galadriel fascinated Tolkien, and when he returned to 'The Silmarillion' after the publication of *The Lord of the Rings* he constantly changed his ideas of her actions in both the First, Second and early Third Ages. See further, **The History of Galadriel and Celeborn and of Amroth King of Lórien*, and *Reader's Companion*, pp. 314–19.

Some have seen the spider-like Shelob (*Spiders) in *The Lord of the Rings* as a negative, devouring female figure of darkness, and contrast her with Galadriel as a figure of *light. But in the first versions of the last chapters of Book IV, Frodo was attacked by many great spiders, replaced only in rewriting by Shelob, obviously the descendant of the still more powerful Ungoliant in 'The Silmarillion'.

Although Galadriel is the most powerful female in *The Lord of the Rings*, Éowyn is the most carefully studied and developed. She has been trained to fight as a Rider, and the Rohirrim trust and respect her, asking that she lead them in the absence of Théoden and Éomer. Her action in riding secretly to war has been applauded by feminist critics as much as her decision to 'be a shieldmaiden no longer' (bk. VI, ch. 5) has been derided. Her acceptance of Faramir is seen as too sudden, when her love for Aragorn goes unrequited, a (supposed) life of domesticity a sad fate for one who has rode into battle and triumphed. But marriage and domesticity were what she would have had as Aragorn's wife, and indeed as Queen of Gondor her life no doubt would have been more restricted than as Faramir's wife in Ithilien. Tolkien drafted a letter *c.* 1963 to an unnamed correspondent concerning Éowyn:

> It is possible to love more than one person (of the other sex) at the same time, but in a different mode and intensity. I do not think that Éowyn's feelings for Aragorn really changed much; and when he was revealed as so lofty a figure, in descent and office, she was able to go on *loving* and admiring him. He was *old*, and that is not only a physical quality: when not accompanied by any physical decay age can be alarming or awe-inspiring. Also she was *not* herself ambitious in the true political sense. Though not a 'dry nurse' in temper, she was also not really a soldier or 'amazon', but like many brave women was capable of great military gallantry at a crisis. . . .
>
> Criticism of the speed of the relationship or 'love' of Faramir and Éowyn. In my experience feelings and decisions ripen very quickly (as measured by mere 'clock-time', which is actually not justly applicable) in periods of great stress, and especially under the expectation of imminent death. And I do *not* think that persons of high estate and breeding need all the petty fencing and approaches in matters of 'love'. This tale does not deal with a period of 'Courtly Love' and its pretences; but with a culture more primitive (sc. less corrupt) and nobler. [*Letters*, pp. 323–4]

For a brief time during the writing of Book III of *The Lord of the Rings*, Tolkien contemplated a marriage between Aragorn and Éowyn, but soon abandoned the idea. Apparently it was not until he was writing Book V that he decided to have Aragorn eventually marry Arwen, daughter of Elrond (or at least, here the first allusions to Arwen appeared), and that their story should in some respects echo that of their ancestors Beren and Lúthien (*'Of Beren and Lúthien'), though Arwen would not play such an active role in events as Lúthien, who had far more innate power. Tolkien then introduced Arwen into the feast at Rivendell in Book II and added other oblique references. Many first-time readers do not notice these, but this reticence is part of the basic structure of the story. Tolkien wrote in a draft letter to Joanna de Bortadano in April 1956 that *The Tale of Aragorn and Arwen* 'is placed in an appendix, because I have told the whole story more or less through "hobbits"' (*Letters*, p. 246). The arrival of Arwen at Minas Tirith in Book VI is just as much a surprise to Frodo and his friends as it is to readers.

In Book III, Chapter 4 Treebeard tells Merry and Pippin:

> When the world was young, and the woods were wide and wild, the Ents and the Entwives . . . they walked together and they housed together. But our hearts did not go on growing in the same way: the Ents gave their love to things that they met in the world, and the Entwives gave their thought to other things, for the Ents loved the great trees, and the wild woods, and the slopes of the high hills; and they drank of the mountain-

streams, and ate only such fruit as the trees let fall in their path; and they learned of the Elves and spoke with the Trees. But the Entwives gave their minds to the lesser trees, and to the meads in the sunshine beyond the feet of the forests; and they saw the sloe in the thicket, and the wild apple and the cherry blossoming in spring, and the green herbs in the waterlands in summer, and the seeding grasses in the autumn fields. They did not desire to speak with these things; but they wished them to hear and obey what was said to them. The Entwives ordered them to grow according to their wishes, and bear leaf and fruit to their liking; for the Entwives desired order, and plenty, and peace. . . .So the Entwives made gardens to live in. But we Ents went on wandering, and we only came to the gardens now and again.

Treebeard also sings a tale in which the points of view of both Ents and Entwives are equally treated; 'but the Ents could say more on their side, if they had time'. On 7 June 1955 Tolkien wrote to *W.H. Auden that into his depiction of the Ents 'crept a mere piece of experience, the difference of the "male" and "female" attitude to wild things, the difference between unpossessive love and gardening' (*Letters*, p. 212).

Nearly twenty years after writing of the Ents and Entwives, Tolkien began another account of what might be termed a dysfunctional relationship: *Aldarion and Erendis*, an unfinished story of the unhappy marriage of the sixth King of Númenor and his wife. It is significant in that Tolkien appears to sympathize with both parties in their discussion. Aldarion breaks his promises, and Erendis has good reason for feeling aggrieved; but she overreacts in her revenge, and mars her daughter's life as well as her own. In commenting to his father on the attitude of Erendis, Aldarion accepts that he was in some part responsible: 'She has dwindled; and if I have wrought this, then black is my blame. But do the large shrink in adversity? This was not the way, not even in hate or revenge! She should have . . . called for a Queen's escort. . . . I would rather have had it so: rather a beautiful Queen to thwart me and flout me, than freedom to rule while the Lady Elestirnë [Erendis] falls down dim into her own twilight' (*Unfinished Tales*, p. 205).

Tolkien keeps the balance with subtle touches. Because Aldarion sails to Middle-earth, he makes contact with Gil-galad, the Elven-king, at a time when the shadow of Sauron is beginning to rise again; the implication is that as king, Aldarion will aid the Elves in Middle-earth. But according to Christopher Tolkien, the notes for the continuation of the story say nothing of any alliance nor of any aid, but that all of Aldarion's works in Middle-earth are 'swept away' (p. 206). In old age, when Aldarion looks back on his life, he realizes that he had 'found more contentment' in the days he spent with Erendis just before their betrothal 'than in any others of his life' (p. 182); while Erendis in old age, neglected by her daughter, 'in bitter loneliness . . . longed once more for Aldarion' (p. 212).

Already in the list of rulers of Númenor in Appendix A of *The Lord of the*

Rings, written at least five years before *Aldarion and Erendis*, Tolkien stated that because the only child of the sixth King of Númenor was a daughter, 'it was then made a law of the royal house that the eldest child of the King, whether man or woman, should receive the sceptre' – a rule that began to be adopted in European royal houses only at the end of the twentieth century. Tolkien may have felt that no distinction should be made between sons and daughters, but it also possible that his aim was to enhance the stature of Elendil, descended from Silmariën, eldest child of the fourth king, who would have been Queen had this law then been in existence.

In a draft letter he wrote to A.C. Nunn, ?late 1958–early 1959, concerning Hobbit family customs Tolkien introduced another unusual inheritance pattern. The Hobbits were 'universally monogamous' and rarely married a second time, even if wife or husband died very young. Women took their husband's name, and children their father's. But while the titular head of a family or clan was usually the eldest male,

> the government of a 'family', as of the real unit: the 'household', was not a monarchy. . . . It was a 'dyarchy', in which master and mistress had equal status, if different functions. Either as held to be the proper representative of the other in the case of absence (including death). There were no 'dowagers'. If the master died first, his place was taken by his wife, and this included (if he had held that position) the titular headship of a large family or clan. This title thus did not descend to the son, or other heir, while she lived, unless she voluntarily resigned. ([Note:] We are here dealing only with titular 'headship' not with ownership of property, and its management. . . .) [*Letters*, pp. 293–4]

Those who criticize Tolkien for the paucity of women in his works have only slowly come to acknowledge that this is by no means true of *The Silmarillion*, nor was it true of the *legendarium* since Tolkien began **The Book of Lost Tales* around 1916. In that work, the earliest of the *'Silmarillion' narratives, Gwendeling (later Melian the Maia) is already a powerful figure. By her magics and spells she keeps the realm of Doriath hidden from Melko and ensures that only Elves can cross its borders. In later versions of the tales she is shown as having foresight and greater wisdom than her husband Thingol.

Their daughter, Tinúviel (later Lúthien), herself possesses inner strength, courage, and resourcefulness, which she uses to rescue her love, Beren, from Tevildo, Prince of Cats (later Sauron) – a reversal, as several critics have pointed out, of a common theme in fairy-tales in which the passive heroine is saved by the prince or hero. In all versions of her story she plays the greater role in gaining a Silmaril, an act of daring which has far-reaching consequences for Middle-earth.

In *The Fall of Gondolin*, the first of the 'Lost Tales' to be written, Idril, daughter of Turgon, King of Gondolin, is far wiser than her father, and it is only because of her foresight that she, Tuor, their son Eärendel, and other refugees from the city are able to escape when Morgoth's host attacks. She is described as having 'a great power of piercing with her thought the darkness of the hearts of Elves and Men, and the glooms of the future thereto – further even than is the common power of the kindreds of the Eldalië' (*The Book of Lost Tales, Part Two*, p. 167). It is she who conceives a plan to delve a secret way of escape out of Gondolin, under the walls and far out into the plain.

Women (Elves and Men) such as Melian, Lúthien, and Idril are joined in 'The Silmarillion' by others of special note. Nerdanel, who like her husband Fëanor 'was firm of will, but more patient', desired 'to understand minds rather than to master them, and at first she restrained [Fëanor] when the fire of his heart grew too hot; but his later deeds grieved her, and they became estranged' (*The Silmarillion*, p. 64). Emeldir the Manhearted, wife of Barahir, after the defeat of Elves and Men in the Battle of Sudden Flame would rather have stayed a fugitive with her husband and son and fought beside them, but instead 'gathered together all the women and children that were left, and gave arms to those that would bear them; and she led them into the mountains . . . and so by perilous paths, until they came at last with loss and misery to Brethil' (*The Silmarillion*, p. 155). Of particular interest are the Haladin, whose women take part at least in defensive fighting; among these is Haleth, 'a woman of great heart and strength' (*The Silmarillion*, p. 146) who fights beside her father and brother. When the men are killed, she is chosen as chief of her people. In the late *Of Dwarves and Men* Tolkien wrote that one of the 'strange practices' of the Haladin, the Folk of Haleth, was that 'many of their warriors were women, though few of these went abroad to fight in the great battles. This custom was evidently ancient; for their chieftainess Haleth was a renowned Amazon with a picked bodyguard of women' (*Unfinished Tales*, p. 377; *The Peoples of Middle-earth*, p. 309).

Eric Korn, reviewing *The Silmarillion* in the *Times Literary Supplement*, complained that the work (like *The Lord of the Rings*) had 'no women, but lots of female personages, all either Pallas Athene or Brunnhilde or Yseult, unnervingly large, healthy and clear-eyed, like John Buchan heroines' ('Doing Things by Elves', 30 September 1977, p. 1097). In this, however, he overlooked females such as Aredhel, who through wilfulness sets in motion events that lead to the fall of Gondolin (*Of Tuor and the Fall of Gondolin'), and Morwen, who through pride is partly responsible for the disasters that beset her son (*Of Túrin Turambar').

Although Eru, the One, in 'The Silmarillion' is referred to as male, the Valar to whom he entrusts the government of Arda assume both male and female forms. One of the most powerful of these, Melkor, the prime source of evil, is described as male, as is his most terrible servant, Sauron. The only evil female in 'The Silmarillion' (excepting Thuringwethil) is Ungoliant, who in spider-form devoured light and spun forth darkness. Her power is such that even Melkor has to summon Balrogs to free him from her webs.

Three of the Aratar, the eight most powerful of the Valar after Melkor has been cast out, are described as female. Of particular importance is Varda, the spouse of Manwë, who came to aid him against Melkor: each strengthens the other. When Manwë ascends his throne on Taniquetil,

> if Varda is beside him, he sees further than all other eyes, through mist, and through darkness, and over the leagues of the sea. And if Manwë is with her, Varda hears more clearly than all other ears the sound of voices that cry from east to west, from the hills and the valleys, and from the dark places that Melkor has made upon Earth. Of all the Great Ones who dwell in this world the Elves hold Varda most in reverence and love. Elbereth they name her, and they call upon her name out of the shadows of Middle-earth, and uplift it in song at the rising of the stars. [*The Silmarillion*, p. 26]

Many of the terms used to describe Varda and the position she occupies recall the devotion of Catholics, including Tolkien, to the Virgin Mary.

In *Laws and Customs among the Eldar* (c. 1958–60) Tolkien says of Elves that they 'wedded for the most part in their youth' and 'once only in life, and for love or at least by free will upon either part'; even when their hearts were 'darkened by the shadow that lies upon Arda, seldom is any tale told of deeds of lust among them'. Unless those to be married 'were of fitting age, the betrothal awaited the judgement of the parents of either party' and a year at least must elapse after the betrothal before the marriage could take place. He describes the usual ceremonies, but continues that these

> were not rites necessary to marriage; they were only a gracious mode by which the love of the parents was manifested, and the union was recognized which would join not only the betrothed but their two houses together. It was the act of bodily union that achieved marriage, and after which the indissoluble bond was complete. In happy days and times of peace it was held ungracious and contemptuous of kin to forgo the ceremonies, but it was at all times lawful for any of the Eldar, both being unwed, to marry thus of free consent one to another without ceremony or witness (save blessing exchanged and the naming of [Eru]; and the union so joined was alike indissoluble. . . .
>
> But at whatever age they married, their children were born within a short space of years after their wedding [as the Eldar reckoned time]. . . .
> The union of love is indeed to them great delight and joy, and the 'days of the children' as they call them, remain in their memory as the most merry in life; but they have many other powers of body and of mind which their natures urges them to fulfil.
>
> Thus, although the wedded remain so for ever, they do not necessarily dwell or house together at all times; for without considering the chances and separations of evil days, wife and husband, albeit united, remain persons individual having each gifts of mind and body that differ. [*Morgoth's Ring*, pp. 211–13]

See also Lisa Hopkins, 'Female Authority Figures in the Works of Tolkien, C.S. Lewis and Charles Williams', and Helen Armstrong, 'Good Guys, Bad Guys, Fantasy and Reality', in *Proceedings of the J.R.R. Tolkien Centenary Conference 1992* (1995). Edith L. Crowe, in 'Power in Arda: Sources, Uses and Misuses' cited above, demonstrates that 'feminine' characteristics (powers of nurturing and affirming life) are to be found in both male and female in Tolkien's works. Candice Frederick and Sam McBride in *Women among the Inklings: Gender, C.S. Lewis, J.R.R. Tolkien, and Charles Williams* (2001) include a useful bibliography, but unfortunately in this book-length study overlook significant figures such as Erendis and Idril.

'Words of Joy'. Five Roman Catholic prayers translated by Tolkien into Quenya (*Languages, Invented), published with commentary in *Vinyar Tengwar* 43 (January 2002), pp. 4–38, and 44 (June 2002), pp. 5–20, ed. by Patrick Wynne, Arden R. Smith, and Carl F. Hostetter. These comprise six texts of the *Pater Noster* (*Átaremma*), four of the *Ave Maria* (*Aia María*), and single texts of the *Gloria Patri* (unfinished), the *Sub Tuum Praesidium*, and the Litany of Loreto (unfinished). Tolkien wrote them apparently in two groups, the second (two each of the *Pater Noster* and *Ave Maria*, and the *Gloria Patri*) 'a significant period of time' after the first (*Vinyar Tengwar* 43, p. 6). The editors conclude that the translations altogether 'were probably written sometime in the 1950s'. Two of the associated manuscripts are reproduced in *Vinyar Tengwar* 43, p. 4, and 44, p. 6.

On 8 January 1944 Tolkien, a devout Roman Catholic, wrote to his son *Christopher that he frequently uses the 'praises', in Latin: 'the Gloria Patri, the Gloria in Excelsis, the Laudate Dominum; the Laudate Pueri Dominum (of which I am specially fond), one of the Sunday psalms; and the Magnificat; also the Litany of Loretto (with the prayer Sub tuum præsidium). If you have these by heart you never need for words of joy' (*Letters*, p. 66).

See also *Ae Adar Nín* and *Alcar mi Tarmenel na Erun*.

Wrenn, Charles Leslie (1895–1969). Educated at Queen's College, Oxford, C.L. Wrenn taught at Durham, Madras, and Dacca before becoming lecturer in English at the University of *Leeds from 1928 to 1930. From 1930 to 1939 he was University Lecturer in English Language at *Oxford, and from 1939 to 1946 Professor of English Language and Literature at King's College, the University of London. In 1946 he returned to Oxford as Rawlinson and Bosworth Professor of Anglo-Saxon at Oxford, succeeding Tolkien in that chair, which Wrenn held until 1963.

Jenifer Wayne recalled in *The Purple Dress: Growing Up in the Thirties* (1979) that Wrenn 'was quite as popular' as Tolkien and *C.S. Lewis as a lecturer at Oxford,

partly because he was a character, and nearly blind; partly because we felt convinced that he held the best key in the world to the mysteries of language. Occasionally he would hold a note about half an inch away from his eyes; but for the most part he ad-libbed with eccentrically abstracted ease and authority. Linguistic mutations, contractions, assimilations, corruptions, covering anything from Old Icelandic to Anglo-Saxon, Old French to Danish, Scandinavian to Oriental, came from him as readily as the twice-times table. . . . [pp. 65–6]

To Tolkien he was a valued colleague and friend, and his wife **Agnes** was one of the few friends Tolkien's wife *Edith made among the wives of Oxford dons. In 1932 their families shared a holiday at Lamorna Cove in *Cornwall, during which Wrenn and Tolkien held a swimming race while wearing panama hats and smoking pipes. John Lawlor in *C.S. Lewis: Memories and Reflections* (1998) recounts an anecdote of Wrenn and Tolkien walking home from a North Oxford party, each wearing a fur hat, claiming to be Russian bears. Both had a deep interest in Old English language and literature, and worked closely together in the English School during the two periods when Wrenn was at Oxford. In Michaelmas Term 1962 and Hilary Term 1963 Tolkien briefly returned from retirement to teach *Beowulf* while Wrenn was on leave. Wrenn was also a fellow committee member of the Early English Text Society (*Societies and clubs), and a member of the *Inklings.

In 1938, *Elaine Griffiths having failed to complete a revision of John R. Clark Hall's Modern English translation of *Beowulf, Tolkien recommended Wrenn to take her place. Wrenn revised Clark Hall's *Beowulf and the Finnesburg Fragment* in short order, but had to wait months before publication, until Tolkien completed a preface (*Prefatory Remarks on Prose Translation of 'Beowulf'). The book was first published in 1940 and revised in 1950. Wrenn's other writings include *The Poetry of Caedmon* (1947), *The English Language* (1949), an edition of *Beowulf* in Old English (1953; 2nd edn. 1958; 3rd edn., rev. W.F. Bolton, 1973; Tolkien and *R.W. Chambers are thanked for inspiring Wrenn's approach to the poem), *An Old English Grammar* (with Randolph Quirk, 1955), and *A Study of Old English Literature* (1967). He also published translations of Russian poets, including Pasternak. With *Norman Davis he edited the *Festschrift* *English and Medieval Studies Presented to J.R.R. Tolkien on the Occasion of His Seventieth Birthday* (1962), to which Wrenn contributed an essay, 'Magic in an Anglo-Saxon Cemetery'.

Recalling his student days at Oxford beginning in Trinity Term 1952, Peter Milward commented that Wrenn

specially singled out the work of his colleague at Merton College, Professor J.R.R. Tolkien, as the one man of genius then teaching in the English School. At that time there were many men of outstanding talent there, *C.S. Lewis himself, *Nevill Coghill, *H.V. Dyson, *Lord David Cecil and others; but only to Tolkien would my strict tutor [Wrenn] grant the title of genius. ['Perchance to Touch: Tolkien as Scholar', *Mythlore* 6, no. 4, whole no. 22 (Fall 1979), p. 31]

It was, perhaps, because of his high regard for Tolkien as a scholar that Wrenn was 'notably' one of the 'philological colleagues . . . shocked (cert[ainly] behind my back, sometimes to my face) at the fall of a philological into "Trivial literature"' with the publication of *The Lord of the Rings* (Tolkien, letter to Anne Barrett, 1956, *Letters*, p. 238).

Wright, Joseph (1855–1930). Joseph Wright raised himself through education from the life of a poor mill-worker in Yorkshire. Having taught himself to read and write, and other subjects besides, he used his savings to study in London, Heidelberg, and Leipzig, a course which led to an interest in philology. He earned a Ph.D. in 1885. In 1888 he came to *Oxford as a lecturer, and in 1891 was appointed deputy to Max Müller, the Professor of Comparative Philology. In 1901 Wright succeeded Müller in that chair. Talented and industrious, he gave far more than the number of lectures required by the Oxford statutes, on the comparative grammar of the Indo-Germanic languages in general and on comparative Greek and Latin grammar, while also publishing primers and grammars of historical German, Old English, and Gothic, and most notably the monumental *English Dialect Dictionary* in six volumes (completed 1905). Tolkien discovered Wright's *Primer of the Gothic Language* (1892) as a schoolboy, and experienced 'a sensation at least as full of delight as first looking into Chapman's *Homer*' (quoted in *Biography*, p. 37): this galvanized his interest in language, and once he had matriculated at Oxford it led him to attend Wright's lectures. Later he recalled that it was the acquisition of Wright's Gothic *Primer*

by accident that opened my eyes to a window on 'Gmc. [Germanic] philology'. No doubt it contributed to my poor performance in Hon. Mods. [Honour Moderations, intermediate examinations in Classics, which Tolkien read at Oxford before moving to the English School]; though it guided me to sit at the feet of old Joe in person. He proved a good friend and adviser. Also he grounded me in G[reek] and L[atin] philology. [letter to *Christopher Tolkien, 2 January 1969, *Letters*, p. 397]

Wright was both a demanding and an inspiring teacher. Having learned that Tolkien was interested in the Welsh language, Wright encouraged him to pursue it 'in a characteristically Yorkshire manner: "Go in for Celtic, lad, there's money in it"' (Humphrey Carpenter, *Biography*, p. 56). Tolkien sometimes visited Wright and his wife at home, and afterwards remembered 'the vastness of Joe Wright's dining room table (when I sat alone at one end learning the elements of Greek philology from glinting glasses in the further gloom)' (*Valedictory Address to the University of Oxford*, in *The Monsters and the Critics and Other Essays*, p. 238). Nor, writes Humphrey Carpenter, was Tolkien 'ever likely to forget the huge Yorkshire teas given by the Wrights on Sunday afternoons, when Joe would cut gargantuan slices from a heavyweight plum cake, and Jack the Aberdeen terrier would perform his party trick of licking his lips noisily when his master pronounced the Gothic word for fig-tree, *smakka-bagms'* (*Biography*, p. 56). Wright had married a former pupil, **Elizabeth Mary Lea** (1863–1957); herself an expert philologist, she assisted her husband, collaborated on several grammars, and also worked independently. After his death she wrote his biography, *The Life of Joseph Wright* (1932).

In 1925 Wright wrote in support of Tolkien's application for the Rawlinson and Bosworth chair of Anglo-Saxon:

> I have known Professor Tolkien intimately since the beginning of his undergraduate days at Oxford, and have greatly admired his keen interest in the philological study of Latin, Greek, and more especially the Germanic Languages. He regularly attended my classes and lectures for two years on Comparative Philology in general, and on Latin, Greek, and Gothic, and I formed a high opinion of his attainments in these subjects. . . . [*An Application for the Rawlinson and Bosworth Professorship of Anglo-Saxon in the University of Oxford by J.R.R. Tolkien, Professor of the English Language in the University of Leeds, June 25, 1925*]

Tolkien was later an executor of Wright's will.

A photograph of Joseph Wright is reproduced in *Biography*, pl. 5b, and in *The Tolkien Family Album*, p. 33. See also J.S. Ryan, 'An Important Influence, His Professor's Wife, Mrs. Elizabeth Mary (Lea) Wright', in *The Shaping of Middle-earth's Maker: Influences on the Life and Literature of J.R.R. Tolkien* (1992).

Writing systems. For one whose interest in *calligraphy was formed as early as his love of *languages, it was natural that Tolkien should devise alphabets and scripts of his own. The earliest of these seems to have been that used by him in 1909 in a notebook entitled the *Book of the Foxrook*, and called 'privata kodo skaŭta', Esperanto for 'private scout code'. This was 'a rune-like phonetic alphabet' with 'a sizable number of ideographic symbols called "monographs" by the young Tolkien, each monograph representing an entire word' (Arden R. Smith and Patrick Wynne, 'Tolkien and Esperanto', *Seven* 17 (2000), p. 29).

Around 1919 Tolkien invented a phonetic alphabet, which before long he linked to his *'Silmarillion' mythology as 'The Alphabet of Rúmil', named after an Elvish sage. The oldest of the Eldarin alphabets, it was described by Tolkien in a brief text, *The Elvish Alphabets* (*c.* 1937), as

> a final cursive elaboration of the oldest letters of the Noldor in Valinor. Only the completion and arrangement of this system was actually due to Rúmil of Túna; its author or authors are now forgotten. Though originating in Túna it is called 'Valinorian' because it was mainly used for writing of Qenya [*Languages, Invented], and was later ousted from use among the Noldor by the alphabet of Fëanor. [*The Treason of Isengard*, p. 453]

In Appendix E II of *The Lord of the Rings* the Rúmilian script is called 'the oldest Eldarin letters, the Tengwar of Rúmil'; but in the essay *Quendi and Eldar* its characters are said to be properly called *sarati*, from Qenya *SAR 'score, incise' > 'write', with the word *tengwar* applied only to the Fëanorian letters (see below). Tolkien wrote with the Rúmilian script chiefly from 1919 to the mid-1920s, with a few examples from after 1930. Most of the extant writing is in vertical rather than horizontal lines. A history of the Alphabet of Rúmil, with extensive reproductions, was published in *Parma Eldalamberon* 13 (2001), pp. 3–89, edited with an introduction and commentary by Arden R. Smith. An addendum followed in *Parma Eldalamberon* 15 (2004), pp. 85–8. See also Arden R. Smith, 'The Túrin Prose Fragment: An Analysis of a Rúmilian Document', *Vinyar Tengwar* 37 (December 1995), pp. 15–23.

In the *legendarium* the Rúmilian script is said to have been a source for a later Elvish writing system, that of Fëanor, maker also of the Silmarils. Called *Tengwar*, after the plural of Quenya *tengwa* 'letter', the 'Alphabet of Fëanor' was partly derived from the Rúmilian letters,

and partly devised afresh to fit a different system of writing (from left to right). Its actual author – in all forms except the later modifications to fit the changed conditions of Noldorin after the Exile, which were made after his death – was Fëanor. He constructed it both as a general phonetic alphabet, and devised special arrangements to fit the characteristics of Qenya, Noldorin, and Telerin. This alphabet is the one generally used for Qenya, and for all purposes by the surviving Qendi [Elves]. [*The Elvish Alphabets*, in *The Treason of Isengard*, p. 453]

In Appendix E II it is said that the Fëanorian letters were

not in origin an alphabet: that is, a haphazard series of letters, each with an independent value of its own, recited in a traditional order that has no reference either to their shapes or to their functions. It was, rather, a system of consonantal signs, of similar shapes and style, which could be adapted at choice or convenience to represent the consonants of languages observed (or devised) by the Eldar.

Tolkien represents such 'adaptation' – reflecting in his fiction the historical variation scripts undergo in our own world, though also his own changing ideas and preferences – as different 'modes'. In the 'mode of Beleriand', for instance, illustrated in the Moria Gate inscription (*The Lord of the Rings*, bk. II, ch. 4), vowels are represented by separate *tengwar*. In some other varieties, vowels are indicated by *tehtar* or vowel-signs above consonants or special 'vowel carriers'. Stylistic variants of Tengwar are shown (to give only a few instances) in the title-page inscriptions to *The Lord of the Rings* and other volumes of 'Middle-earth' fiction (written out by Tolkien himself and by *Christopher Tolkien), the Ring-verse in *The Lord of the Rings*, Book II, Chapter 2, the 'Book of Mazarbul' 'facsimiles' reproduced in *Pictures by J.R.R. Tolkien* (no. 23) and elsewhere, and inscriptions provided by Tolkien for *The Road Goes Ever On: A Song Cycle*. Tengwar is also used by the elf Ilbereth in the *'Father Christmas' letters (1937).

Signs for numerals in Tengwar are illustrated and discussed in Christopher Tolkien, 'The Tengwar Numerals', *Quettar* 13 (February 1982) and 14 (May 1982). On 23 November 1972 Tolkien wrote to Ed Meskys:

> I did devise numeral signs to go with the Fëanorian alphabet accommodated to both a decimal nomenclature and a duodecimal, but I never used them and no longer have an accurate memory of them. I am afraid the folder containing the numeral systems is not available and may be locked away in a strongroom. I remember that the numerals were written according to a positional system like the Arabic, beginning at the left with the lowest number and rising to the highest on the right. [*Letters*, pp. 422–3]

In the 1930s Tolkien wrote a seven-page essay, *The Feanorian Alphabet*, in which he compared Rúmilian and Fëanorian letterforms and considered various Fëanorian modes: see *The Alphabet of Rúmil, Parma Eldalamberon* 13 (2001), pp. 88–9.

Tolkien achieved the Tengwar of Fëanor in settled form around 1931, only after much experimentation with scripts of this style in the 1920s. 'The earliest of these', Arden R. Smith has said, 'appears with such names as *Qenya writing, Qenyatic, Qenyarinwa,* and *Valmaric*'; but Smith relates *Valmaric* only to this type of script, as *Qenyatic* 'is also applied to other Elvish alphabets' (*The Valmaric Script: Documents by J.R.R. Tolkien*, ed. with introduction and commentary by Arden R. Smith, *Parma Eldalamberon* 14 (2003), p. 89; see also addendum, *Parma Eldalamberon* 15 (2004), pp. 85–8). There are numerous variants of Valmaric, apparently confined to the period *c.* 1922–5; only one example is explicitly dated, the inscription on the picture *Lunar Landscape* drawn for *Roverandom* (1925). All known examples are reproduced and discussed in *Parma Eldalamberon* 14 and 15.

In Appendix E II of *The Lord of the Rings* Tolkien writes that the alphabets of the Third Age of Middle-earth 'were of two main, and in origin independent, kinds', one of which was the Tengwar. The other was the *Certar* or *Cirth* (Quenya and Sindarin plurals, respectively, of *certa, certh* 'cutting'), generally translated 'runes'. 'The *Tengwar* were devised for writing with brush or pen, and the squared forms of inscriptions were in their case derivative from the written forms. The *Certar* were devised and mostly used only for scratched or incised inscriptions.' In the fiction of *The Lord of the Rings* the Tengwar are 'the more ancient', developed by the Noldor before their exile from Valinor, while 'the Cirth were devised first in Beleriand by the Sindar, and were long used only for inscribing names and brief memorials upon wood or stone'. Tolkien was long familiar with runes from the Anglo-Saxon tradition, and indeed used real Anglo-Saxon runes (with additional characters) in illustrating *The Hobbit*, particularly in its dust-jacket inscription and on *Thror's Map*. He was pleased when readers were intrigued by the lettering, and at one point suggested that a runic alphabet be added to the book. To one of his readers interested in runes, he recommended *Runes: An Introduction* by Ralph W.V. Elliott (1959).

Tolkien himself had long been interested in runic alphabets, since at least November 1918. The Germanic *fuþark* of course was a matter of professional concern to him; but at least by the early 1920s, while he was at *Leeds, he experimented with invented runic lettering of his own. This included the 'Gnomic Letters' and the 'Gondolinic Runes', of which the latter are the earliest letters, linked with the Elves of Tolkien's mythology, which are truly runic in form. Examples of these and other writing are discussed by Arden R. Smith in *Early Runic Documents, Parma Eldalamberon* 15 (2004), pp. 89–121. In his 'Appendix on Runes' in *The Treason of Isengard* Christopher Tolkien notes that the values of the 'Gondolinic Runes' 'are almost totally different from the *Angerthas* [in *The Lord of the Rings*, Sindarin 'long rune-rows', i.e. runic alphabet], but . . . the principles of phonetic organisation in relation to letter-shape are strongly evident' (p. 452).

In *The 'Alphabet of Dairon'* (*c.* 1937) Tolkien wrote of the invention of that set of runes among the Danian Elves of Beleriand, and of

> a related alphabet . . . early in use among the eastern branch of the Danians, beyond the Blue Mountains, when it also spread to Men in those regions, becoming the foundation of the Taliskan *skirditaila* or 'runic series'. A related alphabet was also borrowed (from both Men and Elves) by the Dwarves; the western Dwarves early borrowed and adapted the full inscriptional 'Alphabet of Dairon', and most of the inscriptions in this form that survived the Great War in Eriador and elsewhere are of Dwarvish origin. . . . [*The Treason of Isengard*, pp. 454–5]

Christopher Tolkien remarks on the mention of the Mannish language Taliska as 'adumbrating a relationship between the runes of Beleriand and the ancient Germanic runes' (p. 455). See further, Arden R. Smith, 'Certhas, Skirditaila, Fuþark: A Feigned History of Runic Origins', *Tolkien's Legendarium: Essays on The History of Middle-earth* (2000); and Tolkien's *Runes of Beleriand* and *Dwarf-runes for Writing English (Phonetic)* in *The Treason of Isengard*, pp. 460–4.

Appendix E II refers to the 'Alphabet of Daeron' or *Certhas Daeron*, after its supposed inventor, a minstrel and loremaster of Doriath; and notes that 'the extension and elaboration of this *certhas* was called in its older form the *Angerthas Daeron*. . . .' Two other 'modes' are also described, the *Angerthas Moria*, as used by the Dwarves of Moria, and the mode used by the Dwarves of Erebor. Examples of Tolkien's more developed runic alphabets include, in *The Lord of the Rings*, the inscription on Balin's tomb (the *Angerthas Moria*), end of Book II, Chapter 4, and the upper title-page inscription.

Late in life, after the passing of *C.S. Lewis in November 1963, Tolkien again began to keep a diary, now utilizing another invention, a 'New English Alphabet'. This was intended as an improvement on 'the ridiculous alphabet propounded by persons competing for the money of that absurd man [George Bernard] Shaw', who had argued for language reforms. 'It used some conventional letters (though giving them different sound-values), some international phonetic signs, and some symbols from his own Fëanorian alphabet' (Tolkien quoted, and comment by Humphrey Carpenter, in *Biography*, p. 241). Examples are reproduced in *Artist and Illustrator*, figs. 185, 186.

Another alphabet by Tolkien, but wholly separate from the *legendarium*, is presented in the 'Father Christmas' letters, within that fiction invented by Karhu, the North Polar Bear, based on marks made on cave walls by Goblins. Some or all of these, however, in reality are elaborations of Tolkien's familiar 'JRRT' monogram.

Much useful information on Tolkien's writing systems may be found on the Internet, but for priority see Jim Allan, ed., *An Introduction to Elvish* (1978) and David Doughan and Julian Bradfield, *An Introduction to the Writing Systems of Middle-earth*, *Quettar Special Publication* nos. 1 and 2 (1987). Internet resources include *The Mellonath Daeron Index of Tengwar Specimina* (*www. forodrim.org/daeron/mdtci.html*) and *Index of Certh Specimina* (*www.forodrim. org/daeron/mdics.html*), and Måns Björkman's *Amanye Tenceli* (*at.mansbjork- man.net/*).

Wyke-Smith, Edward Augustine (1871–1935). The British author E.A. Wyke-Smith was a mining engineer and consultant by profession, and spent much of his life abroad. Towards the end of the First World War, in response to a request for a fairy-story from one of his three children, Wyke-Smith began to write *Bill of the Bustingforths* which he sent to his daughter Frances in instalments. These were preserved, and later reworked by Wyke-Smith into a book published in 1921. In that same year two more children's stories by Wyke-Smith also appeared, *The Last of the Barons* and *Some Pirates and Marmaduke*. His fourth, last, and most significant children's book, *The Marvellous Land of Snergs*, was published in 1927.

After a meeting with Tolkien on 27 October 1937 Stanley Unwin recorded that Tolkien had spoken 'enthusiastically of a children's book called *Marvellous Land of Snergs* illustrated by George Morrow and published by Benns some few years ago' (Tolkien-George Allen & Unwin archive, HarperCollins). In a draft for his lecture *On Fairy-Stories*, probably in 1938 or early 1939, Tolkien wrote: 'I should like to record my own love and my children's love of E.A. Wyke-Smith's *Marvellous Land of Snergs*, at any rate of the Snerg-element in that tale, and of Gorbo the gem of dunderheads, jewel of a companion in an escapade'. To which he added: 'I do not think the name *Snerg* happily invented, and I do not like the bogus "King Arthur" Land across the river' (Tolkien Papers, Bodleian Library, Oxford). Much later, in a letter to *W.H. Auden on 7 June 1955, he said that his children liked *The Hobbit* 'well enough' but 'not any better I think than *The Marvellous Land of Snergs*, Wyke-Smith, Ernest Benn 1927. Seeing the date, I should say that this was probably an unconscious source-book! for the Hobbits, not of anything else' (*Letters*, p. 215).

The main protagonists of *The Marvellous Land of Snergs* are two children, Joe and Sylvia, and Gorbo the Snerg. When Gorbo enters the story he is described as being fairly young for a Snerg, possibly two-hundred and fifty, 'utterly irresponsible . . . and though good-natured to excess he had little intelligence of the useful kind' (p. 35). He invites the children to go with him to see the Twisted Trees – a forest which may have had some influence on Mirkwood in *The Hobbit*. The friends lose their sense of direction among the tall trees, and the sky is 'hidden by a roof of matted leaves, and all sides and above them the thick smooth branches twisted and crossed and locked together' (p. 51). As Bilbo Baggins does in *The Hobbit*, Gorbo climbs one of the taller trees in the forest to try to see the way, but disturbs bats rather than spiders and butterflies. Gorbo leads the children into trouble and danger but, like Bilbo, as the story progresses he begins to think and act bravely. 'His sense of responsibility mingled with self-reproach brings out qualities he has never shown before, placing himself in front of the children when in danger (often incurred through their own thoughtlessness)' (Christina Scull, review in *Amon Hen* 113 (January 1992), p. 11). Gorbo rescues the children from the witch, Mother Meldrum, and the ogre Golithos. At the end of the story the Snerg has grown a great deal, if not quite as much as Bilbo.

In height the Snergs are similar to Hobbits, 'a race of people only slightly taller than the average table but broad in the shoulders and of great strength' (*The Marvellous Land of Snergs*, p. 7). Like Hobbits they are fond of food and parties:

> They are great on feasts, which they have in the open air at long tables joined end on and following the turns of the street. This is necessary because nearly everybody is invited – that is to say commanded to come, because the King gives the feasts, though each person has to bring his share of food and drink and put it in the general stock. Of late years the procedure has changed owing to the enormous number of invitations that had to be sent; the commands are now understood and only invitations to stay away are sent to people who are not wanted on the particular occasion. They are sometimes hard up for a reason for a feast, and then the Master of the Household, whose job it is, has to hunt for a reason, such as it being somebody's birthday. Once they had a feast because it was nobody's birthday that day. [p. 10]

From this extract it seems likely that some of the flavour of Wyke-Smith's book found its way not only into *The Hobbit* but also into the first chapter of *The Lord of the Rings*, with its elaborate 'long-expected party'.

In style, however, *The Marvellous Land of Snergs* is closer to *Farmer Giles of Ham* than to *The Hobbit*. It is written with tongue in cheek, frequently mocking fairy-tale and heroic traditions. One of its characters, Golithos, had supposedly reformed and no longer ate children, but lived on 'cabbage, turnip-tops, cucumbers, little sour apples and thin stuff like that' (p. 73); while the knight, Sir Percival, has a certain affinity with similarly ill-equipped Farmer Giles:

> He did not seem quite up to the standard of knights in books. It is true he had shining armour and the lance as long as a barge pole and so forth, but it seemed that his mail suit had not been made to measure. The breastplate was tied on to the back part with what looked like boot-laces, and they did not join well. The armour on his legs was on the large size and rattled when he moved. His helmet also was much too big and it wobbled. . . .
>
> He was out looking for adventures because he had become enam-oured of a young lady, and she had told him that if he would go forth as a knight-errant for one year and conquer a reasonable number of knights and caitiffs and slay some dragons and the like, she would have something to say to him, but she did not say what. So far he had not con-quered anybody because he hadn't met anybody who would fight, and as for dragons he really believed they had all left the country. [pp. 90–1, 95]

In objecting to 'a bogus "King Arthur" Land' Tolkien seems to disagree with Wyke-Smith's attempt to suggest a courtly medieval language with phrases and sentences such as 'In sooth', and 'a right winsome little lass' (p. 135).

A facsimile edition of *The Marvellous Land of Snergs*, with an introduction by Douglas A. Anderson, was published by Old Earth Books of Baltimore, Maryland in 1996.

Wyld, Henry Cecil Kennedy (1870–1945). H.C. Wyld was educated at Bonn and Heidelberg, and studied phonetics and linguistic theory with Henry Sweet at Corpus Christi College, *Oxford. In 1899 he was appointed an independ-ent lecturer in the English Language at University College, Liverpool. In 1904 he became Baines Professor of English Language and Philology at the Uni-versity of Liverpool, a post he held with distinction until returning to Oxford in 1920 as Merton Professor of English Language and Literature, succeeding *A.S. Napier. Long a colleague of Tolkien in the Oxford English School, Wyld earlier had been an external examiner at Oxford when Tolkien received his B.A., and an Elector for the Rawlinson and Bosworth Professorship of Anglo-Saxon when Tolkien was elected to that chair; and in 1945 Tolkien succeeded to the Merton Professorship following Wyld's death.

Among Wyld's writings works on the history of English predominated: these include *The Historical Study of the Mother Tongue: An Introduction to Philological Method* (1906), *A Short History of English* (1914), and *Studies in English Rhymes from Surrey to Pope* (1923). He also edited *The Universal Dic-tionary of the English Language* (1932). Before June 1930, like Tolkien, he was a participant in the *Linguaphone Conversational Course* in English (see *Recordings).

In his *Valedictory Address to the University of Oxford* Tolkien recalled 'seeing Henry Cecil Wyld wreck a table in the Cadena Café with the vigour of his representation of Finnish minstrels chanting the *Kalevala*' (*The Monsters and the Critics and Other Essays*, p. 238).

The Year's Work in English Studies. Annual review of scholarship in English studies by subject and period, sponsored by the English Association. Tolkien contributed three review essays in successive years for the section *Philology: General Works*: vol. 4, for 1923 (published in January 1925, despite an imprint date of 1924), pp. 20–37; vol. 5, for 1924 (published in March 1926), pp. 26–65; and vol. 6, for 1925 (published in February 1927), pp. 32–66. Each essay reflects wide and careful reading, expert judgement, and palpable enthusiasm for the subject, although he seems to have taken special delight in writing about new fascicles of the *Oxford English Dictionary* covering the letter W (on which he himself had worked) and about publications concerning place-names. In all three volumes he attempted not merely to inform but to entertain; in the latter two his humour may have been a means of making lighter tasks significantly greater than he had faced for 1923. In the volume for 1924, presented with numerous *Festschriften* and *Festgaben*, he began his essay:

> Philological studies, in common with other branches of organized scientific and historical research, have become so abundant in material, so varied in aspect, and at once so minute in detail and so far-reading in scope, that a general view and appreciation of recent work (even of one year's work) is already a task for a polymath of unusual leisure and voracity. As generals in command of modern millions may be imagined to have sighed for the simple little operations (and great renown) of Caesar, so now does a reviewer weakly sigh for the happy nineteenth century. [p. 26]

And in the volume for 1925, again with a wealth of publications to consider:

> It is merry in summer 'when shaws be sheen and shrads full fair and leaves both large and long'. Walking in that wood is full of solace. Its leaves require no reading. There is another and a denser wood where some are obliged to walk instead, where saws are wise and screeds are thick and the leaves too large and long. These leaves we must read (more or less), hapless vicarious readers, and not all we read is solace. The tree whereon these leaves grow thickest is the *Festschrift*, a kind of growth that has the property of bearing leaves of many diverse kinds. To add to the labour of inspecting them the task of sorting them under the departments of philology to which they belong would take too long. With a few exceptions we must take each tree as it comes. [p. 32]

J.S. Ryan discusses Tolkien's contributions to *The Year's Work in English Studies* at length in 'J.R.R. Tolkien: Lexicography and Other Early Linguistic Preferences', *Mallorn* 16 (May 1981).

Yorkshire. On 19 April 1917, having been ruled fit for light duty by an Army medical board, Tolkien took up a temporary posting to the 3rd Battalion of the Lancashire Fusiliers, part of the Humber Garrison in **Holderness**, a flat district in the north-east of England known for its grain crop and migratory birds. The 3rd Battalion, a reserve unit, was then located at **Thirtle Bridge**, near the resort town of **Withernsea**. Its duties were to train new recruits for active service, and to guard the coast of the North Sea against invasion. Tolkien's wife *Edith and her cousin *Jennie Grove probably moved at this time into furnished rooms in nearby **Hornsea**. For a brief time Tolkien was put in charge of an outpost and given quarters which allowed Edith to live with him for a while. The (later) inscription on a version of his poem *Sea-Song of an Elder Day* (*The Horns of Ylmir*), 'Present shape due to rewriting and adding introd[uction] and ending in a lonely house near Roos, Holderness (Thirtle Bridge Camp) Spring 1917', probably refers to the officer's quarters provided him as commander of the outpost. The village of **Roos** is just over a mile from Thirtle Bridge.

In late May or early June 1917 Tolkien and Edith visited a wood near Roos, where Edith danced for him. This was a seminal event in the development of his mythology, an inspiration for his tale of the warrior Beren and the elf-maiden Lúthien Tinúviel whom he first sees dancing in a wood. As Tolkien described it in 1964 in a letter to Christopher Bretherton: 'the original version of the "Tale of Lúthien Tinúviel and Beren" [*'Of Beren and Lúthien'] . . . was founded on a small wood with a great undergrowth of "hemlock" (no doubt many other related plants were also there) near Roos in Holderness, where I was for a while on the Humber Garrison' (*Letters*, p. 345); and in a letter to Nancy Smith, begun on Christmas day 1963, he wrote that 'the kernel of the mythology, the matter of *Lúthien Tinúviel* and *Beren*, arose from a small woodland glade filled with "hemlocks" (or other white umbellifers) near Roos on the Holderness peninsula – to which I occasionally went when free from regimental duties while in the Humber Garrison in 1917' (*Letters*, p. 221, where the last date is given incorrectly as '1918').

In mid-August 1917 Tolkien was admitted to 'Brooklands', a hospital in Cottingham Road, **Hull** (Kingston upon Hull), for treatment of persistent fever and pain. Hull is a major port city on the north bank of the Humber River, founded by Edward I at the end of the thirteenth century; the hospital had been established earlier in 1917 to accommodate officers from the Humber Garrison. There Tolkien began or continued to write *The Tale of Tinúviel*; he wrote two new poems, *The Companions of the Rose* and *The Grey Bridge of Tavrobel*; and he rewrote *Sea-Song of an Elder Day* to fit it explicitly within his mythology. During 1917 Tolkien also worked on a grammar and lexicon of his invented Gnomish language (*Gnomish Grammar*, *Gnomish Lexi-*

con): he noted on the final manuscript of the lexicon that it was written at 'Tol Withernon' and other places, the name inspired perhaps by the first element of 'Withernsea' and 'Winthernwick' (a town north of Thirtle Bridge, near the road to Hornsea).

Probably in late September 1917 Edith moved to *Cheltenham; she was now in an advanced state of pregnancy, and Cheltenham seemed to offer greater safety than Hornsea, as Zeppelin-bombers had been attacking the Yorkshire coast. On 16 October a medical board declared Tolkien fit for light duty and ordered him to rejoin the 3rd Lancashire Fusiliers at Thirtle Bridge. At some time in December he was transferred to the 9th Battalion, the Royal Defence Corps, based at **Easington**, some ten miles south of Thirtle Bridge near the tip of the Holderness peninsula. Tolkien resided a few miles still further south, in the town of **Kilnsea**, but received treatment from the regimental medical officer at Easington. While at this post he revised part of a poem of 1916, *The Town of Dreams and the City of Present Sorrow*, as *The Song of Eriol*, referring to the mariner in *The Book of Lost Tales*. By 19 March 1918 Tolkien returned again to Thirtle Bridge, where a medical board at last found him fit for general service and posted him back to Cannock Chase in *Staffordshire. He returned, however, to 'Brooklands' in Hull by 17 July 1918, having suffered severe gastritis in late June. On 11 September 1918 he was transferred to a convalescent hospital in Blackpool, Lancashire.

During 1918 Tolkien wrote the first version of *The Tale of Turambar* (see *'Of Túrin Turambar'*), part of *The Book of Lost Tales*, possibly while still in the Humber Garrison.

See also *Filey; *Harrogate; *Leeds; *Whitby.

You & Me and the Cottage of Lost Play
see The Little House of Lost Play: Mar Vanwa Tyaliéva

Works Consulted

FOLLOWING is a list of the books, articles, Web pages, and other materials used in the writing of *The J.R.R. Tolkien Companion and Guide* – among much else examined in the course of research – exclusive of works by Tolkien himself, which are listed separately (but occasionally cross-referenced from authors below), and writings mentioned in passing in entries in the **Reader's Guide**. Some of these resources are cited in the text as notable references or sources of quotations; others, cited only below, have provided general background and historical or chronological data. A dagger (†) preceding an entry indicates that we consider the source to be particularly useful for an appreciation of Tolkien's life and works. Although any such selection must be subjective, and necessarily omits much that is of interest and value, we hope that we have made it less according to taste or critical preference than by good judgement informed by decades of study. Many of the works so marked, it will be noticed, are collections of notable essays, some of which are also cited individually in this list. To these we would also add, for the study of Tolkien's invented languages, the journals *Parma Eldalamberon* and *Vinyar Tengwar*.

Some journals and newsletters listed here are (or were) connected with societies of Tolkien enthusiasts: *Amon Hen* and *Mallorn* (Tolkien Society); *Angerthas* (Arthedain, the Tolkien Society of Norway); *Anor* (Cambridge Tolkien Society); *Arda* (Arda-sällskapet and Tolkiensällskapet Forodrim, Sweden); *Beyond Bree* (American MENSA Tolkien Special Interest Group, published by Nancy Martsch); *Carandaith* (Australian Tolkien Society); *Inklings-Jahrbuch* (Inklings Gesellschaft für Literatur und Ästhetik, Germany); *Lembas* (Unquendor Tolkien Genootschap, the Dutch Tolkien Society); *Minas Tirith Evening-Star* (American Tolkien Society); *Mythprint* and *Mythlore* (Mythopoeic Society); *Orcrist* (University of Wisconsin Tolkien Society, Madison); *Parma Eldalamberon* and *Vinyar Tengwar* (Elvish Linguistic Fellowship); *The Southern Star* (Southfarthing Fellowship, Brighton); *Tolkien Journal* (Tolkien Society of America). *The Tolkien Collector* is an occasional publication of Christina Scull.

Corporate authors whose names include personal names, e.g. 'George Allen & Unwin', are alphabetized by the (first) surname. Dates and page numbers of newspaper and journal contributions are given when known, but we have not always been able to examine the original publication.

PUBLISHED SOURCES

'The Ace-Ballantine Storm of Competition over "Tarzan" and J.R.R. Tolkien Paperbacks'. *Book Production Industry*, September 1967.

Agøy, Nils Ivar. 'The Fall and Man's Mortality: An Investigation of Some Theological Themes in J.R.R. Tolkien's "Athrabeth Finrod ah Andreth"'. In Agøy, *Between Faith and Fiction*, pp. 16–30.

——, ed. *Between Faith and Fiction: Tolkien and the Powers of His World*. Arda Special 1. Oslo: Arthedain; Upsala: Arda-society, 1998.

Alderson, Brian. Review of *Smith of Wootton Major*. *Children's Book News*, January/February 1968.

Alexander, Peter. *Roy Campbell: A Critical Biography*. Oxford: Oxford University Press, 1982.

†Allan, Jim, ed. *An Introduction to Elvish*. Hayes, Middlesex: Bran's Head Books, 1978.

Allen, Carleton Kemp. 'College Life'. In *Handbook to the University of Oxford*, pp. 101–23.

George Allen & Unwin. *Fifty Years of Publishing Books That Matter*. London: George Allen & Unwin, 1964.

——. *Summer Announcements*. London: George Allen & Unwin, 1937.

Amis, John. 'Donald Swann'. *The Independent*, 25 March 1994, p. 30.

Anderson, Douglas A. 'Christopher Tolkien: A Bibliography'. In Flieger and Hostetter, *Tolkien's Legendarium*, pp. 247–52.

——. '"An Industrious Little Devil": E.V. Gordon as Friend and Collaborator with Tolkien'. In Chance, *Tolkien the Medievalist*, pp. 15–25.

†——. Introduction and notes to *The Annotated Hobbit* by J.R.R. Tolkien. Rev. and expanded edn. Boston: Houghton Mifflin, 2002.

——. 'J.R.R. Tolkien and W. Rhys Roberts's "Gerald of Wales on the Survival of Welsh"'. *Tolkien Studies* 2 (2005), pp. 230–4.

——. 'R.W. Chambers and *The Hobbit*'. *Tolkien Studies* 3 (2006), pp. 137–47.

——. 'Scholar Guest of Honor: Christopher Tolkien, Biographical and Bibliographical Sketch'. *The XVIIIth Mythopoeic Conference* [souvenir programme]. Milwaukee: Mythopoeic Society, 1987. pp. 8–9, 12.

'Andrew Lang's Unrivalled Fairy Stories: Oxford Professor's St Andrews Address'. *St Andrews Citizen*, 11 March 1939, p. 6.

Angles and Britons: O'Donnell Lectures. Cardiff: University of Wales Press, 1963.

'Another Book Still Awaits Completion'. *Oxford Times*, 7 September 1973, p. 6. Note on *The Silmarillion*.

Apeland, Kaj André. 'On Entering the Same River Twice: Mythology and Theology in the Silmarillion Corpus'. In Agøy, *Between Faith and Fiction*, pp. 44–51.

Armstrong, Helen. 'Good Guys, Bad Guys, Fantasy and Reality'. In Reynolds and GoodKnight, *Proceedings of the J.R.R. Tolkien Centenary Conference 1992*, pp. 247–52.

Ashmolean Museum and National Book League. *Catalogue of an Exhibition of Drawings by J.R.R. Tolkien.* Oxford: Ashmolean Museum; London: National Book League, 1976.

Atkins, Philip, and Michael Johnson. *A New Guidebook to the Heart of Oxford.* Stonefield, Oxfordshire: Dodo Publishing, 1999.

Attebery, Brian. *Strategies of Fantasy.* Bloomington: Indiana University Press, 1992.

Attenborough, Philip. 'Rayner Unwin'. *The Independent,* 23 December 2000, p. 4.

Auden, W.H. 'At the End of the Quest, Victory'. *New York Times Book Review,* 22 January 1956, p. 5. Review of *The Return of the King.*

——. 'Good and Evil in *The Lord of the Rings*'. *Tolkien Journal* 3, no. 1 (1967), pp. 5–8.

——. *Making, Knowing and Judging.* Oxford: Clarendon Press, 1956.

——. 'The Quest Hero'. *Texas Quarterly* 4, no. 4 (Winter 1961), pp. 81–93. Reprinted in Isaacs and Zimbardo, *Tolkien and the Critics,* pp. 40–61.

——. 'A World Imaginary, but Real'. *Encounter* 3 (November 1954), pp. 59–60, 62.

Baedeker, Karl. *Switzerland and the Adjacent Portions of Italy, Savoy, and Tyrol: Handbook for Travellers.* 24th edn. Leipzig: Karl Baedeker, 1911.

Baker, Chris. *The Long, Long Trail: The British Army in the Great War of 1914–1918. www.1914-1918.net/index.htm.*

Baker, D.C. Review of *The Old English Exodus. English Language Notes* 21, no. 3 (March 1984), pp. 58–60.

Baker, Peter S., ed. *Beowulf: Basic Readings.* New York: Garland, 1995. Reissued by Garland in 2000 as *The Beowulf Reader.*

Baldwin, Edea A. 'The Flag of Middle-earth: Tolkien's Use of Chesterton to Illustrate Hope and Despair in *The Lord of the Rings*'. 2003. *www.much-ado. net/flourish&blotts/main.php?p=tolkien.*

Barfield, Owen. *A Barfield Reader.* Ed. G.B. Tennyson. Hanover, New Hampshire: Wesleyan University Press/University Press of New England, 1999.

——. *A Barfield Sampler.* Ed. Jeanne Clayton Hunter and Thomas Kranidas. Albany: State University of New York Press, 1993.

——. 'Foreword'. *Seven* 1 (1980), p. 9.

——. 'The Inklings Remembered'. *The World & I* (April 1990), pp. 548–9.

Barnfield, Marie. 'Celtic Influences on the History of the First Age'. *Mallorn* 28 (September 1991), pp. 2–6.

——. 'More Celtic Influences: Númenor and the Second Age'. *Mallorn* 29 (August 1992), pp. 6–13.

——. 'The Roots of Rivendell'. *Þe Lyfe ant þe Auncestrye* 3 (Spring 1996), pp. 4–18.

——. 'Túrin Turambar and the Tale of the Fosterling'. *Mallorn* 31 (December 1994), pp. 29–36.

†Battarbee, K.J., ed. *Scholarship & Fantasy: Proceedings of The Tolkien Phenomenon, May 1992, Turku, Finland.* Turku: University of Turku, 1993. *Anglicana Turkuensia* 12.

Baxter, John. 'The Tolkien That Should Remain Decently Buried'. *Australian,* 11 February 1984. Review of *The Book of Lost Tales, Part One.*

Beach, Sarah. 'A Myth for Angle-land: J.R.R. Tolkien and Creative Mythology'. *Mythlore* 15, no. 4, whole no. 58 (Summer 1989), pp. 31–6.

Beagle, Peter S. 'A Fantasy Feast from Middle-earth'. *San Francisco Examiner,* 19 October 1980, pp. A13–14. Review of *Unfinished Tales.*

Beatie, Bruce. 'The Tolkien Phenomenon: 1954–1968'. *Journal of Popular Culture* 3, no. 3 (Spring 1970), pp. 689–703.

Bender, Donald. 'And Tolkien Begat the Silmarillion'. *Independent Berkeley Gazette,* 14 October 1977, p. 23. Review of *The Silmarillion.*

Walter R. Benjamin Autographs. *The Collector* 910 (1985).

Bennett, J.A.W. 'Charles Talbut Onions, 1873–1965'. *Proceedings of the British Academy* 65 (1979), pp. 743–58.

——. *Chaucer at Oxford and at Cambridge.* Toronto: University of Toronto Press, 1974.

——. 'Clive Staples Lewis (1898–1963)'. Rev. Emma Plaskitt. *Oxford Dictionary of National Biography.* Online edn.

Bentham, Martin. 'Literary Greats Exposed as Gossips and Snipes'. *Sunday Telegraph,* 7 February 1999.

Benton, Jill. *Naomi Mitchison: A Biography.* London: Pandora Press, 1990.

Bergman, Frank. 'The Roots of Tolkien's Tree: The Influence of George MacDonald and German Romanticism upon Tolkien's Essay "On Fairy-Stories"'. *Mosaic* 10, no. 2 (Winter 1977), pp. 5–14.

Bertenstam, Åke. 'Some Notes on the Reception of *The Hobbit*'. *Angerthas* 23 (16 August 1988), pp. 16–17, 20–5.

†—— (as Åke Jönsson). *En Tolkienbibliografi 1911–1980: verk av och om J.R.R. Tolkien = A Tolkien Bibliography 1911–1980: Works by and about J.R.R. Tolkien.* Rev. edn. Uppsala: Jönsson, 1986. Supplements have been published in *Arda.*

Bibire, Paul. 'By Stock or by Stone: Recurrent Imagery and Narrative Pattern in *The Hobbit*'. In Battarbee, *Scholarship & Fantasy,* pp. 203–15.

——. 'Sægde se þe cuþe: Tolkien as Anglo-Saxonist'. In Battarbee, *Scholarship & Fantasy,* pp. 111–31.

'Big Reduction in Paper Supply'. *The Times* (London), 15 April 1940, p. 8.

Birmingham Oratory. *The Birmingham Oratory. www.birmingham-oratory. org.uk/index.htm.*

†Birzer, Bradley J. *J.R.R. Tolkien's Sanctifying Myth: Understanding Middle-earth.* Foreword by Joseph Pearce. Wilmington, Delaware: ISI Books, 2002.

Bishop, Ian. *Pearl in Its Setting: A Critical Study of the Structure and Meaning of the Middle English Poem.* Oxford: Basil Blackwell, 1968.

Bissett, William. 'Elizabeth Jennings'. *Dictionary of Literary Biography* 27: *Poets of Great Britain and Ireland, 1945–1960*. Ed. Vincent B. Sherry, Jr. Detroit: Gale Research, 1984. pp. 163–70.

Bjork, Robert E., and John D. Niles, eds. *A Beowulf Handbook*. Lincoln: University of Nebraska Press, 1997.

Björkman, Måns. *Amanye Tenceli. at.mansbjorkman.net/*.

Blackburn, Bonnie, and Leofranc Holford-Strevens. *The Oxford Companion to the Year*. Oxford: Oxford University Press, 1999.

Blackwelder, Richard E. 'Dissertations from Middle-earth'. *Beyond Bree*, March 1990, pp. 4–5.

——. 'The Great Copyright Controversy'. *Beyond Bree*, September 1995, pp. 1–7.

——. *A Tolkien Thesaurus*. New York: Garland, 1990.

Bliss, A.J., ed. *Sir Orfeo*. Oxford: Oxford University Press, 1954.

Blomfield, Joan. 'The Style and Structure of *Beowulf*'. *Review of English Studies* 14 (1938), pp. 396–403.

Bloomfield, Leonard. 'Why a Linguistic Society'. *A Leonard Bloomfield Anthology*. Abridged edn. Ed. Charles F. Hockett. Chicago: University of Chicago Press, 1987. pp. 68–9. Originally published in *Language* 1 (1925).

Bodleian Library. *Drawings for 'The Hobbit' by J.R.R. Tolkien*. Oxford: Bodleian Library, 1987.

Bonhams. *Printed Books & Maps*. Auction catalogue (online). 24 February 2004. *www.bonhams.com*.

Bonjour, Adrien. *The Digressions in Beowulf*. Oxford: Basil Blackwell, 1950. *Medium Ævum Monographs* 5.

——. 'Monsters Crouching and Critics Rampant: or The *Beowulf* Dragon Debated'. *PMLA* 68 (March 1953), pp. 304–12.

Bowra, C.M. *Memories, 1898–1939*. London: Weidenfeld & Nicholson, 1966.

Boyd, J. 'Joseph Wright'. *Dictionary of National Biography 1922–1930*. pp. 923–5.

Brace, Keith. 'In the Footsteps of the Hobbits'. *Birmingham Post Midland Magazine*, 25 May 1968.

Bradfield, J.C. *A Dictionary of Quenya and Proto-Eldarin and Ante-Quenya*. Cambridge: J.C. Bradfield, 1982; rev. 1983.

Bratman, David S. 'A History of Tolkien Fandom'. *Gemini* 1, no. 2 (June 1976), pp. 13–19.

——. 'Hugo Dyson: Inkling, Teacher, Bon Vivant'. *Mythlore* 21, no. 4, whole no. 82 (Winter 1997), pp. 19–34.

——. 'In Search of the Shire: Tolkien and the Counties of England'. *Mallorn* 37 (December 1999), pp. 5–13.

——. 'The Literary Value of *The History of Middle-earth*'. In Flieger and Hostetter, *Tolkien's Legendarium*, pp. 69–91.

——. 'R.B. McCallum: The Master Inkling'. *Mythlore* 23, no. 3, whole no. 89 (Summer 2001), pp. 34–42.

——. Review of *The Book of Lost Tales, Part Two*. *Mythprint* 21, no. 12, whole no. 55 (December 1984), pp. 2–3.

——. Review of *The Lays of Beleriand*. *Mythprint* 22, no. 12, whole no. 67 (December 1985), pp. 2–3.

——. 'The Years' Work in Tolkien Studies 2001–2002'. *Tolkien Studies* 2 (2005), pp. 289–315.

Brazier, Reginald H., and Ernest Sandford. *Birmingham and the Great War, 1914–1919*. Birmingham: Cornish Brothers, 1921.

Brett, Cyril. Review of *Sir Gawain and the Green Knight* (ed. Tolkien and Gordon). *Modern Language Review* 22 (October 1927), pp. 451–8.

Brierly, J.L., and H.V. Hodson. 'The Constitution of the University'. *Handbook to the University of Oxford*, pp. 79–100.

Briggs, Julia. *A Woman of Passion: The Life of E. Nesbit, 1858–1924*. Harmondsworth: Penguin, 1989.

Briggs, K.M. Review of *Tree and Leaf*. *Folklore* 75 (Winter 1964), pp. 293–4.

Brock, M.G., and M.C. Curthoys, eds. *The History of the University of Oxford, Vol. VII: Nineteenth-Century Oxford, Part 2*. Oxford: Clarendon Press, 2000.

Brogan, Hugh. *The Life of Arthur Ransome*. London: Jonathan Cape, 1984.

——. 'Why Hobbits?' *Cambridge Review*, 23 January 1965, pp. 205–6.

——. 'Tolkien's Great War'. *Children and Their Books: A Celebration of the Work of Iona and Peter Opie*. Ed. Gillian Avery and Julia Briggs. Oxford: Clarendon Press, 1989. pp. 351–67.

Brooks, Paul. *Two Park Street*. Boston: Houghton Mifflin, 1986.

Brown, Arthur. 'Professor Albert Hugh Smith (1903–1967)'. *Proceedings of the Ninth International Congress of Onomastic Sciences*. Comp. J. McN. Dodgson and A.D. Mills. Ed. H. Draye. Louvain: International Centre of Onomastics, 1969. pp. 8–22.

Brown, Malcolm. *The Imperial War Museum Book of the Somme*. London: Pan Books, 2002.

——. *Tommy Goes to War*. New edn. Additional research by Shirley Seaton. Stroud, Gloucestershire: Tempus, 2001.

Brown, Ursula, ed. *Þorgils saga ok Hafliða*. Oxford: Oxford University Press, 1952. *Oxford English Monographs*.

Brunsdale, Mitzi M. 'Norse Mythological Elements in *The Hobbit*'. *Mythlore* 9, no. 4, whole no. 34 (Winter 1983), pp. 49–50.

Buechner, Frederick. 'For Devotees of Middle-Earth'. *New York Times Book Review*, 16 November 1980, pp. 15, 20.

Burchfield, R.W. 'My Hero: Robert Burchfield on J.R.R. Tolkien'. *Independent Magazine* (London), 4 March 1989, p. 50.

——. 'The *OED*: Past and Present'. *Unlocking the English Language*. New York: Hill and Wang, 1992. pp. 188–97.

Burkitt, M.C. *Prehistory: A Study of Early Cultures in Europe and the Mediterranean Basin*. 2nd edn. Cambridge: At the University Press, 1925.

Burns, Marjorie J. 'Echoes of William Morris's Icelandic Journals in J.R.R. Tolkien'. *Studies in Medievalism* 3, no. 3 (Winter 1991), pp. 367–73.

——. 'J.R.R. Tolkien and the Journey North'. *Mythlore* 15, no. 4, whole no. 58 (Summer 1989), pp. 5–9.

——. 'Norse and Christian Gods: The Integrative Theology of J.R.R. Tolkien'. In Chance, *Tolkien and the Invention of Myth*, pp. 163–78.

†——. *Perilous Realms: Celtic and Norse in Tolkien's Middle-earth*. Toronto: University of Toronto Press, 2005.

Caldecott, Stratford. *The Power of the Ring: The Spiritual Vision behind The Lord of the Rings*. New York: Crossroad, 2005.

Caluwé-Dor, Juliette de. 'Bibliographie de S.R.T.O. d'Ardenne'. *Revue des langues vivantes* 35 (1969), pp. 456–60.

Campbell, Roy. *Light on a Dark Horse: An Autobiography (1901–1935)*. Chicago: Henry Regnery, 1952.

'Canon Adam Fox'. *The Times* (London), 19 January 1977, p. 16.

'Canterbury Tale and Ballet: Oxford Performances of Summer Diversions'. *Oxford Mail*, 29 July 1939, final page.

Carpenter, Humphrey. *The Envy of the World: Fifty Years of the BBC Third Programme and Radio 3, 1946–1996*. With research by Jennifer Doctor. London: Weidenfeld and Nicolson, 1996.

†——. *The Inklings: C.S. Lewis, J.R.R. Tolkien, Charles Williams, and Their Friends*. London: George Allen & Unwin, 1978.

†——. *J.R.R. Tolkien: A Biography*. London: George Allen & Unwin, 1977. First published in the United States as *Tolkien: A Biography* (Boston: Houghton Mifflin, 1977). A revised edn. appeared in 1987 (London: Unwin Paperbacks).

——. 'Learning about Ourselves: Biography as Autobiography' (conversation with Lyndall Gordon). *The Art of Literary Biography*. Ed. John Batchelor. Oxford: Clarendon Press, 1995. pp. 267–79.

——. '". . . One Expected Him To Go On a Lot Longer": Humphrey Carpenter Remembers J.R.R. Tolkien', *Minas Tirith Evening-Star* 9, no. 2 (January 1980), pp. 10–13.

——. *OUDS: A Centenary History of the Oxford University Dramatic Society, 1885–1985*. Oxford: Oxford University Press, 1985.

——. *W.H. Auden: A Biography*. London: George Allen & Unwin, 1981.

—— and Mari Prichard. *The Oxford Companion to Children's Literature*. Oxford: Oxford University Press, 1984.

——, George Sayer, and Clyde S. Kilby. 'A Dialogue: Discussion . . . Recorded Sept. 29, 1979, Wheaton, Illinois'. *Minas Tirith Evening-Star* 9, no. 2 (January 1980), pp. 14–18, 8.

Carter, Lin. *Imaginary Worlds*. New York: Ballantine Books, 1973.

——. *Tolkien: A Look Behind 'The Lord of the Rings'*. New York: Ballantine Books, 1969.

Carter, Terry. *Birmingham Pals: 14th, 15th & 16th (Service) Battalions of the Royal Warwickshire Regiment: A History of the Three City Battalions Raised in Birmingham in World War One*. Barnsley, South Yorkshire: Pen & Sword, 1997.

Castell, Daphne. 'The Realms of Tolkien'. *New Worlds* 50 (November 1966), pp. 143–54.

Catenian Association. Web site. *thecatenianassociation.org*.

Cater, William. 'The Filial Duty of Christopher Tolkien'. *Sunday Times Magazine*, 25 September 1977.

——. 'Lord of the Hobbits'. *Daily Express* (London), 22 November 1966, p. 10.

——. 'The Lord of the Legends'. *Sunday Times* (London), 2 January 1972, pp. 24, 27–8.

Cavaliero, Glen. *Charles Williams: Poet of Theology*. Grand Rapids, Michigan: William B. Eerdmans, 1983.

Cecil, David. 'Oxford's Magic Circle'. *Books and Bookmen* 24, no. 4 (January 1979), pp. 10–12.

—— and Rachel Trickett. 'Is There an Oxford "School" of Writing?' *Twentieth Century*, June 1955, pp. 559–70.

Ch., M. 'A Faery-like Loveliness'. *Hindustani Times*, 23 June 1968. Review of *The Road Goes Ever On: A Song Cycle*.

Chabot, Caroline. 'Raymond Wilson Chambers (1874–1942)'. *Moreana* 24, no. 93 (February 1987), pp. 69–82, and no. 94 (June 1987), pp. 83–96.

Chambers, R.W. Review of *Beowulf: The Monsters and the Critics*. *Modern Language Review* 33, no. 2 (April 1938), pp. 272–3.

Chambers Biographical Dictionary. 5th edn. Edinburgh: Chambers, 1990.

Chance, Jane. *The Lord of the Rings: The Mythology of Power*. Rev. edn. Lexington: University Press of Kentucky, 2001.

——. *Tolkien's Art: A Mythology for England*. Rev. edn. Lexington: University Press of Kentucky, 2001.

†——, ed. *Tolkien and the Invention of Myth: A Reader*. Lexington: University Press of Kentucky, 2004.

†——, ed. *Tolkien the Medievalist*. London: Routledge, 2003.

—— and Alfred K. Siewers, eds. *Tolkien's Modern Middle Ages*. New York: Palgrave Macmillan, 2005.

—— and David D. Day. 'Medievalism in Tolkien: Two Decades of Criticism in Review'. *Studies in Medievalism* 3, no. 3 (Winter 1991), pp. 375–87.

Chapman, R.W. 'George Stuart Gordon'. *Dictionary of National Biography, 1941–1950*. pp. 307–9. Farrer obit *The Times* 30 December 1968, p. 10.

Chapman, Vera. 'Reminiscences: Oxford in 1920, Meeting Tolkien and Becoming an Author at 77'. In Reynolds and GoodKnight, *Proceedings of the J.R.R. Tolkien Centenary Conference 1992*, pp. 12–14.

'Characters, 1911–12'. *King Edward's School Chronicle* n.s. 27, no. 193 (June 1912), pp. 39–41.

Chaucer, Geoffrey. *The Works of Geoffrey Chaucer*. Ed. F.N. Robinson. 2nd edn. Boston: Houghton Mifflin, 1961.

Chavasse, Fr. Paul. *The Birmingham Oratory Church: A History and Guide*. Birmingham: Clarkeprint, [*c.* 1980].

Chesterton, G.K. *The Ballad of the White Horse*. 10th edn. London: Methuen, 1928. First published 1911.

——. *The Coloured Lands*. Introduction by Maisie Ward. London: Sheed & Ward, 1938.

——. *The Everlasting Man*. London: Burns & Oates, 1974. First published 1925.

——. *Heretics*. London: John Lane, the Bodley Head, 1905.

——. *Orthodoxy*. Ed. Craig M. Kibler. Lenoir, North Carolina: Reformation Press, 2002. First published 1908.

——. *The Outline of Sanity*. London: Methuen, 1926.

Christensen, Bonniejean. *Beowulf and The Hobbit: Elegy into Fantasy in J.R.R. Tolkien's Creative Technique*. Ph.D. dissertation, University of Southern California, 1969. Condensed as 'Tolkien's Creative Technique: *Beowulf* & *The Hobbit*' in *Orcrist* 7 (Summer 1973), pp. 16–20. See also her address with the same title published in *Mythlore* 15, no. 3, whole no. 57 (Spring 1989), pp. 4–10.

——. 'Gollum's Character Transformation in *The Hobbit*'. *A Tolkien Compass*. Ed. Jared C. Lobdell. La Salle, Illinois: Open Court, 1975. pp. 9–28.

——. 'Report from the West: Exploitation of *The Hobbit*'. *Orcrist* 4 = *Tolkien Journal* 4, no. 3, whole no. 13 (1969–70), pp. 15–16.

Christie's. *Autograph Letters and Printed Books, including First Editions*. Auction catalogue. London (South Kensington), 19 May 2000.

——. *Fine Printed Books and Manuscripts*. Auction catalogue. New York, 24 May 2002.

——. *Masterpieces of Modern Literature: The Library of Roger Rechler*. Auction catalogue. New York, 11 October 2002.

——. *20th Century Books and Manuscripts*. Auction catalogue. London (St James's), 2 December 2003.

——. *20th Century Books and Manuscripts*. Auction catalogue. London (St James's), 2 December 2004.

——. *20th-Century Books and Manuscripts*. Auction catalogue. London (South Kensington), 16 November 2001.

——. *20th-Century Books and Manuscripts*. Auction catalogue. London (South Kensington), 6 December 2002.

——. *Valuable Manuscripts and Printed Books*. Auction catalogue. London (St James's), 7 June 2006.

——. *Valuable Printed Books and Manuscripts*. Auction catalogue. London (St James's), 26 November 1997.

Christopher, Joe R. *C.S. Lewis*. Boston: Twayne, 1987.

——. 'Roy Campbell and the Inklings'. *Mythlore* 22, no. 1, whole no. 83 (Autumn 1997), pp. 33–4, 36–46.

——. 'Three Letters by J.R.R. Tolkien at the University of Texas'. *Mythlore* 7, no. 2, whole no. 24 (Summer 1980), p. 5.

Clark, George. *Beowulf*. Boston: Twayne, 1990.

†—— and Daniel Timmons, eds. *J.R.R. Tolkien and His Literary Resonances: Views of Middle-earth*. Westport, Connecticut: Greenwood Press, 2000.

'The *Clerkes Compleinte* Revisited'. *Arda* 1986 (1990), pp. 1–13.

Cofield, David. 'Changes in Hobbits: Textual Differences in Editions of *The Hobbit*'. *Beyond Bree*, April 1986, pp. 3–4.

——. Letter to the editor. *Beyond Bree*, September 1992, p. 8.

Coffin, R.P. 'Social Life and Activities at the University'. In Crosby, Aydelotte, and Valentine, *Oxford of Today*, pp. 151–87.

Coghill, Nevill. *The Collected Papers of Nevill Coghill, Shakespearian & Medievalist*. Ed. Douglas Gray. Brighton: Harvester Press, 1988.

Cohen, Morton. 'Roger Lancelyn Green'. *Independent* (London), 12 October 1987.

Cole, G.D.H., and T.W. Earp, eds. *Oxford Poetry 1915*. Oxford: B.H. Blackwell, 1915.

Coleridge, Samuel Taylor. *Biographia Literaria, or Biographical Sketches of My Literary Life and Opinions*. Ed. with an introduction by George Watson. London: J.M. Dent & Sons, 1956.

'Colin Hardie'. *Times* (London), 20 October 1998, p. 21.

'College Societies: 1. Stapeldon Debating Society'. *Stapeldon Magazine* (Exeter College, Oxford) 3, no. 16 (December 1911), pp. 97–101.

Collins, David R. *J.R.R. Tolkien: Master of Fantasy*. Minneapolis: Lerner Publications, 1992.

Collyer, Naomi. 'Recollections of Professor J.R.R. Tolkien'. *Arda* 5 (1988, for 1985), pp. 1–3.

Como, James T., ed. *C.S. Lewis at the Breakfast Table and Other Reminiscences*. New edn. San Diego: Harcourt Brace Jovanovich, 1992.

The Concise Oxford Dictionary of Current English. 8th edn. Ed. R.E. Allen. Oxford: Clarendon Press, 1990.

The Concise Oxford English Dictionary. 10th edn., rev. Ed. Judy Pearsall. Oxford: Oxford University Press, 2002.

Constable, John. 'C.S. Lewis: From Magdalen to Magdalene'. *Magdalene College Magazine and Record*, n.s. 32 (1987–88), pp. 42–6. Reprinted in *Anor* 26, n.s 1 (1995), pp. 15–19.

Cook, Irene Tolkien. Letter to the Editor. *Amon Hen* 162 (March 2000), pp. 24–5.

Coren, Michael. *J.R.R. Tolkien: The Man Who Created The Lord of the Rings*. Toronto: Stoddardt, 2001.

'The Coronation'. *King Edward's School Chronicle* n.s. 26, no. 188 (July 1911), pp. 59–60.

Corpus Christi College, Oxford. *Biographical Register, 1880–1974*. Comp. by P.A. Hunt. Ed. N.A. Flanagan. Oxford: Corpus Christi College, 1988.

Coulombe, Charles. 'The Lord of the Rings – A Catholic View'. In Pearce, *Tolkien: A Celebration*, pp. 53–66.

†Crabbe, Katharyn W. *J.R.R. Tolkien*. Rev. and expanded edn. New York: Continuum, 1988.

Craigie, W.A. 'Henry Bradley'. *Dictionary of National Biography, 1922–1930*. pp. 103–4.

Cranborne, Hannah, ed. *David Cecil: A Portrait by His Friends*. Stambridge, Wimborne, Dorset: Dovecote Press, 1990.

Croft, Janet Brennan. 'Three Rings for Hollywood: Scripts for *The Lord of the Rings* by Zimmerman, Boorman, and Beagle'. Unpublished paper, presented at the Mythopoeic Society Conference, Ann Arbor, Michigan, July 2004.

†——. *War and the Works of J.R.R. Tolkien*. Westport, Connecticut: Praeger, 2004.

——, ed. *Tolkien on Film: Essays on Peter Jackson's The Lord of the Rings*. Altadena, California: Mythopoeic Press, 2004.

Crosby, L.A. 'The Organization of the University and Colleges'. In Crosby, Aydelotte, and Valentine, *Oxford of Today*, pp. 29–39.

——. 'The Oxford System of Education'. In Crosby, Aydelotte, and Valentine, *Oxford of Today*, pp. 48–52.

——, Frank Aydelotte, and Alan C. Valentine, eds. *Oxford of Today: A Manual for Prospective Rhodes Scholars*. New York: Oxford University Press, 1927.

Cross, F.L., and E.A. Livingstone, eds. *The Oxford Dictionary of the Christian Church*. Oxford: Oxford University Press, 1997.

Crouch, Marcus. Review of *Farmer Giles of Ham*. *Junior Bookshelf*, January 1950, pp. 14–15.

Crowe, Edith L. 'Power in Arda: Sources, Uses and Misuses'. In Reynolds and GoodKnight, *Proceedings of the J.R.R. Tolkien Centenary Conference 1992*, pp. 272–7.

Curry, Patrick. *Defending Middle-earth: Tolkien, Myth and Modernity*. Edinburgh: Floris Books, 1997.

——. 'Tolkien and His Critics: A Critique'. *Root and Branch: Approaches towards Understanding Tolkien*. Ed. Thomas Honegger. *Comare Series* 2. Zurich: Walking Tree Publishers, 1999. pp. 81–148.

Curtis, Anthony. 'Hobbits and Heroes'. *Sunday Telegraph*, 10 November 1963, p. 16.

——. 'Remembering Tolkien and Lewis'. *British Book News*, June 1977, pp. 429–30.

Curtis, Philip. *A Hawk among Sparrows: A Biography of Austin Farrer*. London: SPCK, 1985.

'Daily Life in Middle Earth'. *The Bookseller*, 3 August 1968, p. 374.

Dale, Alzina Stone. *The Outline of Sanity: A Life of G.K. Chesterton*. Grand Rapids, Michigan: William B. Eerdmans, 1982.

'Dame Helen Gardner: Distinguished Contributions to Literary Studies'. *The Times* (London), 6 June 1986, p. 14.

D'Ardenne, S.R.T.O. 'The Editing of Middle English Texts'. In Wrenn and Bullough, *English Studies Today*, pp. 74–84.

——. 'The Man and the Scholar'. In Salu and Farrell, *J.R.R. Tolkien: Scholar and Storyteller*, pp. 33–7.

—— (as S.T.R.O.), ed. *The Katherine Group*. Paris: Société d'Edition 'Les Belles Lettres', 1977.

——, ed. *Þe Liflade ant to Passiun of Seinte Iuliene.* See THE PUBLISHED WRITINGS OF J.R.R. TOLKIEN in vol. 1.

—— and E.J. Dobson, eds. *Seinte Katerine: Re-Edited from MS Bodley 34 and the Other Manuscripts.* Oxford: Published for the Early English Text Society by the Oxford University Press, 1981.

Davenport, Guy. 'The Persistence of Light'. *National Review,* 20 April 1965, pp. 332, 334.

Davin, Dan. 'Norman Davis: The Growth of a Scholar'. *Middle English Studies Presented to Norman Davis in Honour of His Seventieth Birthday.* Ed. Douglas Gray and E.G. Stanley. Oxford: Clarendon Press, 1983. pp. 1–15.

Davis, Howard. 'The *Ainulindalë*: Music of Creation'. *Mythlore* 9, no. 2, whole no. 32 (Summer 1982), pp. 6–9.

Davis, Norman. 'Dr. Mabel Day: Early English Texts'. *The Times* (London), 24 September 1964, p. 18.

——. 'J.R.R. Tolkien'. *Postmaster* (Merton College, Oxford), January 1976, p. 10.

——. 'Jack Arthur Walter Bennett, 1911–1981'. *Proceedings of the British Academy* 68 (1982), pp. 481–94.

—— and C.L. Wrenn, eds. *English and Medieval Studies Presented to J.R.R. Tolkien on the Occasion of His Seventieth Birthday.* London: George Allen & Unwin, 1962.

De Camp, L. Sprague. Letter to the editor. *Andúril* 1 (April 1972), pp. 8–9.

——. Letter to the editor. *Mythlore* 13, no. 4, whole no. 50 (Summer 1987), p. 41.

'Deaths'. *The Times* (London), 16 March 1942, p. 6. Notice of the funeral of George S. Gordon.

'Deaths'. *The Times* (London), 14 October 1950, p. 1. Notice of the funeral of R.F.W. Fletcher.

'Deaths'. *The Times* (London), 5 July 1952, p. 1. Notice of the death of Susan Grindle *née* Dagnall.

'Debating Characters'. *King Edward's School Chronicle* n.s. 26, no. 187 (June 1911), pp. 45–7.

'Debating Society'. *King Edward's School Chronicle,* n.s. 24, no. 177 (November 1909), pp. 83–4; n.s. 24, no. 178 (December 1909), pp. 94–7; n.s. 26, no. 183 (November 1910), pp. 68–71; n.s. 26, no. 184 (December 1910), pp. 94–5; n.s. 26, no. 185 (February 1911), pp. 5–9; n.s. 26, no. 187 (June 1911), pp. 42–5; n.s. 27, no. 191 (March 1912), pp. 11–16; n.s. 27, no. 193 (June 1912), pp. 36–9; n.s. 28, no. 199 (May 1913), pp. 34–7.

'Deddington Court Now Library', *Oxford Mail,* 15 December 1956, p. 1.

Denniston, Robin. 'Sir Stanley Unwin'. *Oxford Dictionary of National Biography.* Online edn.

Derrick, Christopher. 'And See Ye Not Yon Bonny Road?' *The Tablet,* 10 February 1968, p. 132. Review of *Smith of Wootton Major.*

Deyo, Steven M. 'Niggle's Leaves: The Red Book of Westmarch and Related Minor Poetry of J.R.R. Tolkien'. *Mythlore* 12, no. 3, whole no. 45 (Spring 1986), pp. 28–31, 34–7.

†Dickerson, Matthew T. *Following Gandalf: Epic Battles and Moral Victory in The Lord of the Rings*. Grand Rapids, Michigan: Brazos Press, 2003.

'Dictionary Editors'. *Oxford English Dictionary* Web site. *www.oed.com/public/inside/editors.htm*.

Dirda, Michael. 'Under the Big Top and on the Road'. *Washington Post Book World*, 3 May 1998, p. 16. Review of *Roverandom*.

'Dr. C.T. Onions: The Making of O.E.D.' *The Times* (London), 12 January 1965, p. 11.

'Dr. George Gordon, President of Magdalen'. *The Times* (London), 13 March 1942, p. 7.

'Dr. J. Fraser, Professor of Celtic at Oxford'. *The Times* (London), 22 May 1945, p. 7.

'Dr. L.R. Farnell: Ancient Greek Religion'. *The Times* (London), 29 March 1934, p. 16.

'Dr. Percy Simpson, Editor of Ben Jonson'. *The Times* (London), 16 November 1962, p. 15.

'Dr. R.W. Chambers, English at University College, London'. *The Times* (London), 24 April 1942, p. 7.

Dolan, T.P. 'Alan J. Bliss, 1921–1985'. *Medieval English Studies Newsletter* 14 (1986), pp. 6–7.

'Donald Swann'. *The Times* (London), 25 March 1994, p. 21.

Doughan, David. 'Elvish and Welsh'. *Mallorn* 30 (September 1993), pp. 5–9.

——. 'An Ethnically Cleansed Faery?: Tolkien and the Matter of Britain'. *Mallorn* 32 (September 1995), pp. 21–4.

——. 'In Search of the Bounce: Tolkien Seen through Smith'. In *Leaves from the Tree: J.R.R. Tolkien's Shorter Fiction*, pp. 17–22.

——, ed. *Translations of The Hobbit Reviewed. Quettar Special Publication* 2. London: Quettar, 1988.

—— and Julian Bradfield. *An Introduction to the Writing Systems of Middle-earth. Quettar Special Publication* 1. London: Quettar, 1987.

Drabble, Margaret. 'Rebels against Ilúvatar'. *The Listener*, 15 September 1977, p. 346. Review of *The Silmarillion*.

Drawings for 'The Hobbit' by J.R.R. Tolkien. Oxford: Bodleian Library, 1987.

Drayton, Paul, and Humphrey Carpenter. 'A Preparatory School Approach'. *Music Drama in Schools*. Ed. Malcolm John. Cambridge: At the University Press, 1971. pp. 1–19.

Drout, Michael D.C. 'The Rhetorical Evolution of "*Beowulf: The Monsters and the Critics*"'. In Hammond and Scull, *The Lord of the Rings, 1954–2004: Scholarship in Honor of Richard E. Blackwelder*, pp. 183–215.

—— and Hilary Wynne. 'Tom Shippey's *J.R.R. Tolkien: Author of the Century* and a Look Back at Tolkien Criticism since 1982'. *Envoi: A Review Journal of Medieval Literature* 9, no. 1 (Fall 2000), pp. 101–67. A version in electronic form is at *members.aol.com/JamesIMcNelis/9_2/Drout_9_2.pdf*.

—— et al. 'A Bibliography of Scholarly Studies of J.R.R. Tolkien and His Works (through 2000)'. *acunix.wheatonma.edu/mdrout/TolkienBiblio/*.

Duane, Diane. 'The Longest Sunday'. In Haber, *Meditations on Middle-earth*, pp. 117–28.

Dubs, Kathleen E. 'Providence, Fate and Chance: Boethian Philosophy in *The Lord of the Rings*'. In Chance, *Tolkien and the Invention of Myth*, pp. 133–42.

Dunbabin, J.P.D. 'Finance since 1914'. In Harrison, *The History of the University of Oxford, Vol. VIII*, pp. 639–82.

Dundas-Grant, James. 'From an "Outsider"'. In Como, *C.S. Lewis at the Breakfast Table and Other Reminiscences*, pp. 229–33.

Dunsire, Brin. 'Of Ham, and What Became of It'. *Amon Hen* 98 (July 1989), pp. 14–17.

Duriez, Colin. 'Survey of Tolkien Literature'. *Seven* 20 (2003), pp. 105–14.

——. 'Tolkien and the Other Inklings'. In Reynolds and GoodKnight, *Proceedings of the J.R.R. Tolkien Centenary Conference 1992*, pp. 360–3.

E., A.B. 'R.F.W. Fletcher (1890–1950)'. *Oxford Magazine*, 26 October 1950, pp. 62, 64.

'The Earl of Halsbury'. *The Times* (London), 18 January 2000, p. 21.

Eddison, E.R. *The Worm Ouroboros*. Introduced and annotated by Paul Edmund Thomas. New York: Dell, 1991.

——. *Zimiamvia: A Trilogy*. Introduced and annotated by Paul Edmund Thomas. New York: Dell, 1992.

Eden, Bradford Lee. 'The "Music of the Spheres": Relationships between Tolkien's *The Silmarillion* and Medieval Cosmological and Religious Theory'. In Chance, *Tolkien the Medievalist*, pp. 183–93.

'An Edited Transcript of Remarks at the December 1966 TSA [Tolkien Society of America] Meeting'. *Niekas* 19 (Spring 1967), pp. 39–40.

'Editorial'. *King Edward's School Chronicle* n.s. 26, no. 186 (March 1911), pp. 17–18.

Edmonds, E.L. 'C.S. Lewis, the Teacher'. *In Search of C.S. Lewis*. Ed. Stephen Schofield. South Plainfield, New Jersey: Bridge Publishing, 1983. pp. 37–51.

Egan, Thomas M. 'Chesterton and Tolkien: The Road to Middle-earth'. *Seven* 4 (1983), pp. 45–53. Another version of this article was published as 'Tolkien and Chesterton: Some Analogies' in *Mythlore* 12, no. 1, whole no. 43 (Autumn 1985), pp. 29–30, 32–5.

——. 'Fragmentary Glimpses'. *Mythlore* 11, no. 1, whole no. 39 (Summer 1984), pp. 36–7. Review of *Finn and Hengest*.

——. 'Fragments of a World: Tolkien's Road to Middle-earth'. *The Terrier* (St Francis College, Brooklyn, N.Y) 48, no. 2 (Fall 1983), pp. 9–10.

——. 'Tolkien's Fantasy Universe Expands'. *New York City Tribune*, 25 March 1985, pp. 5B–6B.

——. 'Tolkien's Son Compiles Fascinating "Book of Lost Tales, Part I"'. *New York Tribune*, 8 March 1984, p. 5B.

Eiseley, Loren. 'The Elvish Art of Enchantment'. *Horn Book*, August 1965, pp. 364–7.

Ekwall, Eilart. *Concise Oxford Dictionary of Place-names*. 4th edn. Oxford: Clarendon Press, 1960.

'Elaine Griffiths'. *The Times* (London), 13 December 1996, p. 21.

'Elizabeth Jennings'. *Daily Telegraph*, 30 October 2001. *www.dailytelegraph. com/obituary*.

'Elizabeth Jennings'. *The Times* (London), 31 October 2001, p. 19.

Elliott, Ralph W.V. *Runes: An Introduction*. Manchester: Manchester University Press, 1959.

Ellison, John A. 'Editorial'. *Mallorn* 31 [December 1994], p. 5.

——. Review of *The Lays of Beleriand*. *Amon Hen* 75 (September 1985), pp. 11–12.

——. 'Tolkien's Art'. *Mallorn* 30 (September 1993), pp. 21–8.

——. 'The "Why", and the "How": Reflections on "Leaf by Niggle"'. In *Leaves from the Tree*, pp. 23–32.

Elton, Oliver. 'Lascelles Abercrombie'. *Dictionary of National Biography, 1931–1940*. pp. 1–2.

——. 'Lascelles Abercrombie, 1881–1938'. *Proceedings of the British Academy* 25 (1939), pp. 394–421.

'The Elvish Mode'. *New Yorker*, 15 January 1966, pp. 24–5.

Emerson, Oliver Farrar. Review of *Sir Gawain and the Green Knight* (ed. Tolkien and Gordon). *Journal of English and Germanic Philology* 26 (1927), pp. 248–58.

Encyclopædia Britannica. 14th edn. New York: Encyclopædia Britannica, 1938.

'The Epic of Westernesse', *Times Literary Supplement*, 17 December 1954, p. 817. Review of *The Two Towers*.

'Essay Club'. *Stapeldon Magazine* (Exeter College, Oxford) 5, no. 26 (June 1920), p. 87.

'Essay Club'. *Stapeldon Magazine* (Exeter College, Oxford) 7, no. 39 (December 1926), p. 96.

Etkin, Anne, ed. *Eglerio! In Praise of Tolkien*. Greencastle, Pennsylvania: Quest Communications, 1978.

Evans, Jonathan. 'The Dragon-Lore of Middle-earth: Tolkien and Old English and Old Norse Tradition'. In Clark and Timmons, *J.R.R. Tolkien and His Literary Resonances*, pp. 21–38.

Evans, Robley. *J.R.R. Tolkien*. New York: Thomas Y. Crowell, 1971.

Everett, Caroline Whitman. *The Imaginative Fiction of J.R.R. Tolkien*. MA thesis, Florida State University, 1957.

Everett, Dorothy. *Essays on Middle English Literature*. Edited by Patricia Kean. Memoir by Mary Lascelles. Oxford: Clarendon Press, 1955.

——. 'Raymond Wilson Chambers'. *Dictionary of National Biography, 1941–1950*. pp. 145–6.

Exeter College, Oxford. [Oxford: Exeter College, *c*. 1980].

Ezard, John. 'The Hobbit Man'. *Oxford Mail*, 3 August 1966, p. 4.

——. 'Successor to the Hobbits at Last'. *Oxford Mail*, 11 February 1966, p. 11 (late final edn.).

'Fable for To-day'. *Church Times*, 8 October 1954, p. 4. Review of *The Fellowship of the Ring*.

'Fantasy Award to Professor Tolkien', *The Bookseller*, 14 September 1957, p. 1074.

'Fantasy of the Year'. *Oxford Mail*, 11 September 1957, p. 4.

Finseth, Claudia Riiff. 'Tolkien's Trees'. *Mallorn* 35 (September 1997), pp. 37–44.

Firth, C.H. 'Joseph Wright, 1855–1930'. *Proceedings of the British Academy* 18 (1932), pp. 422–38.

Fisher, Matthew A. 'Working at the Crossroads: Tolkien, St. Augustine, and the *Beowulf*-poet'. In Hammond and Scull, *The Lord of the Rings 1954–2004: Scholarship in Honor of Richard E. Blackwelder*, pp. 217–30.

Flieger, Verlyn. 'J.R.R. Tolkien and the Matter of Britain'. *Mythlore* 23, no. 1, whole no. 87 (Summer/Fall 2000), pp. 47–58.

——. 'The Footsteps of Ælfwine'. In Flieger and Hostetter, *Tolkien's Legendarium*, pp. 183–98.

†——. *Interrupted Music: Tolkien and the Making of a Mythology*. Kent, Ohio: Kent State University Press, 2005.

——. 'Pitfalls of Faërie'. *Mythos Journal* 2, no. 1 (Winter 1995), pp. 3–11.

†——. *A Question of Time: J.R.R. Tolkien's Road to Faërie*. Kent, Ohio: Kent State University Press, 1997.

†——. *Splintered Light: Logos and Language in Tolkien's World*. 2nd edn. Kent, Ohio: Kent State University Press, 2002.

——. 'Taking the Part of Trees: Eco-Conflict in Middle-earth'. In Clark and Timmons, *J.R.R. Tolkien and His Literary Resonances*, pp. 147–58.

——. 'A Tale That Grew in the Telling'. In *Selections from the Marquette J.R.R. Tolkien Collection*, pp. 16–19.

——. '"There Would Always Be a Fairy-tale": J.R.R. Tolkien and the Folklore Controversy'. In Chance, *Tolkien the Medievalist*, pp. 26–35.

——. 'Tolkien's Experiment with Time: *The Lost Road*, "The Notion Club Papers", and J.W. Dunne'. In Reynolds and GoodKnight, *Proceedings of the J.R.R. Tolkien Centenary Conference 1992*, pp. 39–44.

——. 'Whose Myth Is It?' In Agøy, *Between Faith and Fiction*, pp. 32–42.

——, ed. *Smith of Wootton Major* by J.R.R. Tolkien. Extended edn. London: HarperCollins, 2005.

†—— and Carl F. Hostetter, eds. *Tolkien's Legendarium: Essays on The History of Middle-earth*. Westport, Connecticut: Greenwood Press, 2000.

—— and T.A. Shippey. 'Allegory versus Bounce: Tolkien's *Smith of Wootton Major*'. *Journal of the Fantastic in the Arts* 12, no. 2 (Spring 2002), pp. 186–200.

Flood, John. 'Power, Domination and Egocentrism in Tolkien and Orwell'. *Mallorn* 34 (December 1996), pp. 13–19.

†Fonstad, Karen Wynn. *The Atlas of Middle-earth*. Rev. edn. Boston: Houghton Mifflin, 1991.

'Football'. *King Edward's School Chronicle* n.s. 24, no. 177 (November 1909), pp. 85–8; n.s. 26, no. 183 (November 1910), pp. 82–4.

'Football Characters'. *King Edward's School Chronicle* n.s. 25, no. 180 (April 1910), pp. 35–6.

'Football Characters 1910–11'. *King Edward's School Chronicle* n.s. 26, no. 187 (June 1911), pp. 49–51.

Foote, Peter. 'Gabriel Turville-Petre, 1908–1978'. *Proceedings of the British Academy* 64 (1978), pp. 467–81.

'Forestry and Us'. *Daily Telegraph*, 29 June 1972, p. 18.

Foster, Michael. 'The Shire and Notting Hill'. *Mallorn* 35 (September 1997), pp. 45–53.

†Foster, Robert. *The Complete Guide to Middle-earth: From The Hobbit to The Silmarillion.* London: George Allen & Unwin, 1978. In this, page references, keyed to the standard hardcover editions of the time, are given within the entries. In the HarperCollins, 2003 edn., the references are gathered awkwardly at the end of the volume.

Foster, William. 'A Benevolent and Furry-footed People'. *Scotsman Week-end Magazine*, 25 March 1967.

Fox, Adam. 'At the Breakfast Table'. In Como, *C.S. Lewis at the Breakfast Table and Other Reminiscences*, pp. 89–95.

Frederick, Candice, and Sam McBride. *Women among the Inklings: Gender, C.S. Lewis, J.R.R. Tolkien, and Charles Williams.* Westport, Connecticut: Greenwood Press, 2001.

Freeman, Gwendolen. Review of *Farmer Giles of Ham. Spectator*, 18 November 1949, p. 718.

Freston, H. Rex. *The Quest of Beauty and Other Poems.* Oxford: B.H. Blackwell, 1915.

Frost, K.T. 'The *Critias* and Minoan Crete'. *Journal of Hellenic Studies* 33 (1913), pp. 189–206.

——. 'The Lost Continent'. *The Times* (London), 19 February 1909, p. 10.

Fulford, Roger, J.C. Masterman, and C.H. Wilkinson. *C.H. Wilkinson, 1888–1960.* Oxford: Oxford University Press, 1965.

Fulk, R.D., ed. *Interpretations of Beowulf: A Critical Anthology.* Bloomington: Indiana University Press, 1991.

Fuller, Edmund. 'The Lord of the Hobbits: J.R.R. Tolkien'. Originally published in *Books with Men behind Them* (1962), reprinted in Isaacs and Zimbardo, *Tolkien and the Critics*, pp. 17–39.

——. 'A Superb Addition to Tolkien's Mythological Realm'. *Wall Street Journal*, 19 September 1977, p. 22. Review of *The Silmarillion*.

Fuller, John. *W.H. Auden: A Commentary.* London: Faber & Faber, 1998.

'Funeral and Memorial Services'. *The Times* (London), 24 May 1945, p. 6. On the requiem Mass for John Fraser.

'Funerals'. *The Times* (London), 22 September 1934, p. 15. On the funeral of F.F. Urquhart.

'Funerals'. *The Times* (London), 14 January 1965, p. 12. On the funeral of C.T. Onions.

Fussell, Paul. *The Great War and Modern Memory*. Paperback edn. New York: Oxford University Press, 1977.

'"Gammer Gurton" at Oxford Diversions: with Chaucer's "Nonnes Preestes Tale," Spoken in Middle English by Prof. J.R.R. Tolkien'. *Oxford Mail*, 4 August 1938, p. 6.

Gang, T.M. 'Approaches to *Beowulf*'. *Review of English Studies* n.s. 3 (1952), pp. 1–12.

Gardner, Helen. 'Clive Staples Lewis, 1898–1963'. *Proceedings of the British Academy* 51 (1965), pp. 417–28.

——. 'Is Beowulf Needed?' *The Times* (London), 17 November 1965, p. 13. Letter to the editor.

†Garth, John. *Tolkien and the Great War: The Threshold of Middle-earth*. London: HarperCollins, 2003.

Gay, David Elton. 'J.R.R. Tolkien and the *Kalevala*: Some Thoughts on the Finnish Origins of Tom Bombadil and Treebeard'. In Chance, *Tolkien and the Invention of Myth*, pp. 295–304.

Gillett, Edward, and Kenneth A. MacMahon. *A History of Hull*. 2nd, expanded edn. Hull: Hull University Press, 1989.

Gilliver, Peter M. 'At the Wordface: J.R.R. Tolkien's Work on the *Oxford English Dictionary*'. In Reynolds and GoodKnight, *Proceedings of the J.R.R. Tolkien Centenary Conference 1992*, pp. 173–86.

†——, Jeremy Marshall, and Edmund Weiner. *The Ring of Words: Tolkien and the Oxford English Dictionary*. Oxford: Oxford University Press, 2006.

Gilson, Christopher. 'Elvish and Mannish'. *Vinyar Tengwar* 33 (January 1994), pp. 10–26.

——. 'Gnomish Is Sindarin: The Conceptual Evolution of an Elvish Language'. In Flieger and Hostetter, *Tolkien's Legendarium*, pp. 95–104.

——. '*Narqelion* and the Early Lexicons: Some Notes on the First Elvish Poem'. *Vinyar Tengwar* 40 (April 1999), pp. 6–32.

—— and Patrick Wynne. 'The Growth of Grammar in the Elven Tongues'. In Reynolds and GoodKnight, *Proceedings of the J.R.R. Tolkien Centenary Conference 1992*, pp. 187–94.

——, Bill Welden, Carl F. Hostetter, and Patrick Wynne, eds. 'Early Noldorin Fragments'. *Parma Eldalamberon* 13 (2001), pp. 92–165.

—— see also THE PUBLISHED WRITINGS OF J.R.R. TOLKIEN in vol. 1

Gleeson, Gill. 'Music in Middle-earth'. *Mallorn* 16 (May 1981), pp. 29–31.

Glenn, Lois. *Charles W.S. Williams: A Checklist*. Kent, Ohio: Kent State University Press, 1975.

Gliddon, Gerald. *The Battle of the Somme: A Topographical History*. Corrected edn. Thrupp, Stroud, Gloucestershire: Sutton, 1996.

Godden, Malcolm. 'From the Heroic to the Allegorical'. *Times Literary Supplement*, 8 July 1983, p. 736.

GoodKnight, Glen. 'Two Decades: Looking Back'. *Mythlore* 13, no. 4, whole no. 50 (Summer 1987), pp. 3–4, 57.

Goolden, Peter, ed. *The Old English Apollonius of Tyre*. Oxford: Oxford University Press, 1958. *Oxford English Monographs*.

Gordon, E.V. *An Introduction to Old Norse*. 2nd edn., rev. A.R. Taylor. Paperback edn., from corrected sheets. Oxford: Clarendon Press, 1981.

——, ed. *The Battle of Maldon*. London: Methuen, 1937.

——, ed. *Pearl*. Oxford: Clarendon Press, 1953.

Gordon, George S. *The Discipline of Letters*. Preface by Mary Gordon. Oxford: Clarendon Press, 1946. Includes 'Andrew Lang', pp. 131–51.

——. *The Letters of George S. Gordon, 1902–1942*. Oxford: Oxford University Press, 1943.

Gordon, I.L., ed. *The Seafarer*. London: Methuen, 1960.

Gordon, Mary C. *The Life of George S. Gordon, 1881–1942*. London: Oxford University Press, 1945.

Graham, Malcolm, and Melanie Williams. *When the Lights Went Out: Oxfordshire 1939 to 1945*. Holton, Oxford: Libraries' Department, Oxfordshire County Council, 1979.

Grahame, Kenneth. *First Whisper of 'The Wind in the Willows'*. Ed., with an introduction, by Elspeth Grahame. Philadelphia: J.B. Lippincott, 1945. First published 1944.

——. 'The Reluctant Dragon'. *Dream Days*. London: Bodley Head, 1973. First published 1898.

——. *The Wind in the Willows*. Introduction by Peter Green. Oxford: Oxford University Press, 1983. First published 1908.

Grattan, J.H.G. Review of *Sir Gawain and the Green Knight* (ed. Tolkien and Gordon). *Review of English Studies* 1, no. 4 (October 1925), pp. 484–7.

Gray, Douglas. 'Eric John Dobson, 1913–1984'. *Proceedings of the British Academy* 71 (1985), pp. 533–8.

——. 'Norman Davis, 1913–1989'. *Proceedings of the British Academy* 80 (1993), pp. 261–73.

——. 'A Tribute to J.A.W. Bennett (1911–1981)'. *Medium Ævum* 50, no. 2 (1981), pp. 205–14.

Green, Peter. *Kenneth Grahame, 1859–1932: A Study of His Life, Work and Times*. London: John Murray, 1959.

——. 'Outward Bound by Air to an Inappropriate Ending'. *Daily Telegraph*, 27 August 1954, p. 8. Review of *The Fellowship of the Ring*.

Green, Roger Lancelyn. *Andrew Lang: A Critical Biography*. Leicester: Edmund Ward, 1946.

——. 'Recollections'. *Amon Hen* 44 (May 1980), pp. 6–8.

——. 'Slicing a Magical Cake'. *Sunday Telegraph*, 3 December 1967. Review of *Smith of Wootton Major*.

——. *Tellers of Tales: Children's Books and Their Authors from 1800 to 1964*. Rewritten and rev. edn. London: Edmund Ward, 1965.

—— and Walter Hooper. *C.S. Lewis: A Biography*. Rev. and expanded edn. London: HarperCollins, 2002.

Green, William H. *The Hobbit: A Journey into Maturity*. New York: Twayne, 1995.

Greene, Deirdre. 'Tolkien's Dictionary Poetics: The Influence of the *OED*'s Defining Style on Tolkien's Fiction'. In Reynolds and GoodKnight, *Proceedings of the J.R.R. Tolkien Centenary Conference 1992*, pp. 195–9.

Greenfield, Stanley B. *A Critical History of Old English Literature*. New York: New York University Press, 1965.

Greenman, David. 'Aeneidic and Odyssean Patterns of Escape and Return in Tolkien's *The Fall of Gondolin* and *The Return of the King*'. *Mythlore* 18, no. 2, whole no. 68 (Spring 1992), pp. 4–9.

Grigorieva, Natalia. 'Problems of Translating into Russian'. In Reynolds and GoodKnight, *Proceedings of the J.R.R. Tolkien Centenary Conference 1992*, pp. 200–205.

Grotta-Kurska, Daniel. *J.R.R. Tolkien: Architect of Middle Earth*. Ed. Frank Wilson. Philadelphia: Running Press, 1976. A 2nd edn., as by Daniel Grotta, and with the title *The Biography of J.R.R. Tolkien: Architect of Middle-earth*, was published by Running Press in 1998, and a 3rd edn. by the same publisher in 1992.

Haas, Joseph. 'War over Middle-earth'. *Chicago Daily News*, 7 August 1965.

Haber, Karen, ed. *Meditations on Middle-earth*. New York: St. Martin's Press, 2001.

Hadfield, Alice Mary. *Charles Williams: An Exploration of His Life and Work*. New York: Oxford University Press, 1983.

Haggard, H. Rider. *The Annotated She: A Critical Edition of H. Rider Haggard's Victorian Romance*. Introduction and notes by Norman Etherington. Bloomington: Indiana University Press, 1991. First published 1887.

——. *Ayesha: The Return of She*. New York: Ballantine Books, 1978. First published 1905.

——. *King Solomon's Mines*. Introduction by Roger Lancelyn Green. London: Collins, 1955. First published 1885.

——. *She and Allan*. New York: Ballantine Books, 1978. First published 1921.

†Patrick & Beatrice Haggerty Museum of Art, Marquette University. *The Invented Worlds of J.R.R. Tolkien: Drawings and Original Manuscripts from the Marquette University Collection*. Milwaukee: The Museum, 2004.

——. *J.R.R. Tolkien: The Hobbit Drawings, Watercolors, and Manuscripts*. Milwaukee: The Museum, 1987.

Halliday, W.R. 'Richard McGillivray Dawkins'. *Dictionary of National Biography 1951–1960*. pp. 287–8.

Halsall, Martin. 'Sheer Poetry as Green Velvet Sets the Scene'. *Oxford Mail*, 25 May 1973, p. 13.

Hammond, Wayne G. 'All the Comforts: The Image of Home in *The Hobbit* and *The Lord of the Rings*'. *Mythlore* 14, no. 1, whole no. 51 (Autumn 1987), pp. 29–33.

——. *Arthur Ransome: A Bibliography*. Winchester: St Paul's Bibliographies; New Castle, Delaware: Oak Knoll Press, 2000.

——. 'The Critical Response to Tolkien's Fiction'. In Reynolds and Good-Knight, *Proceedings of the J.R.R. Tolkien Centenary Conference 1992*, pp. 226–32.

——. 'In Memoriam Joy Hill'. *Beyond Bree*, February 1992, p. 5.

——. 'The Nature of the Beast: Tolkien's Bestiary Poems'. Unpublished essay.

——. 'Pauline Baynes'. *British Children's Writers, 1914–1960*. Ed. Donald R. Hettinga and Gary D. Schmidt. Detroit: Gale Research, 1996. pp. 36–44.

——. 'Special Collections in the Service of Tolkien Studies'. In Hammond and Scull, *The Lord of the Rings, 1954–2004: Scholarship in Honor of Richard E. Blackwelder*, pp. 331–40.

——, ed. *C.S. Lewis & Owen Barfield: A Souvenir Book for the Centenary Celebration Held . . . by the Mythopoeic Society*. Wheaton, Illinois: Mythopoeic Society, 1998.

—— and Christina Scull. 'The History of Middle-earth'. *Seven* 12 (1995), pp. 105–10.

†—— ——. *J.R.R. Tolkien: Artist and Illustrator*. London: HarperCollins, 1995. A corrected paperback edn. was issued by HarperCollins in 1998.

—— ——. 'J.R.R. Tolkien: The Achievement of His Literary Life'. *Mythlore* 22, no. 3, whole no. 85 (Winter 1999), pp. 27–37.

†—— ——. *The Lord of the Rings: A Reader's Companion*. London: Harper-Collins, 2005.

†—— ——, eds. *The Lord of the Rings, 1954–2004: Scholarship in Honor of Richard E. Blackwelder*. Milwaukee: Marquette University Press, 2006.

†——, with the assistance of Douglas A. Anderson. *J.R.R. Tolkien: A Descriptive Bibliography*. Winchester: St Paul's Bibliographies; New Castle, Delaware: Oak Knoll Books, 1993. Addenda and corrigenda have appeared in *The Tolkien Collector*.

Handbook to the University of Oxford. Oxford: Clarendon Press, 1933.

Hardie, Colin. 'A Colleague's Note on C.S. Lewis.' *Inklings-Jahrbuch für Literatur und Ästhetik* 3 (1985), pp. 177–82.

Hargrove, Gene. 'Who Is Tom Bombadil'. *Mythlore* 13, no. 1, whole no. 47 (Autumn 1986), pp. 20–4.

Doris Harris Autographs. *Catalogue 36*. Los Angeles, June 1987.

Harris, John. *The Somme: Death of a Generation*. London: White Lion, 1966.

Harris, Jose. 'The Arts and Social Sciences, 1939–1970'. In Harrison, *The History of the University of Oxford, Vol. VIII*, pp. 217–49.

Harrison, Brian, ed. *The History of the University of Oxford, Vol. VIII: The Twentieth Century*. Oxford: Clarendon Press, 1994.

Harshaw, Ruth. 'Carnival of Books no. 70'. Interview with Tolkien, recorded 15 January 1957. Private transcription from tape recording in the Library of Congress.

——. 'When Carnival of Books Went to Europe'. *American Library Association Bulletin* 51 (February 1957), pp. 117–23.

Hartley, L.P. 'Lord David Cecil'. *Essays & Poems Presented to Lord David Cecil*. Ed. W.W. Robson. London: Constable, 1970. pp. 1–8.

Harvey, David. *The Song of Middle-earth: J.R.R. Tolkien's Themes, Symbols and Myths*. London: George Allen & Unwin, 1985.

Harvey, Paul. *The Oxford Companion to English Literature*. 4th edn., rev. Dorothy Eagle. Oxford: Clarendon Press, 1967.

Havard, Robert E. 'Philia: Jack at Ease'. In Como, *C.S. Lewis at the Breakfast Table and Other Reminiscences*, pp. 215–28.

——. 'Professor J.R.R. Tolkien: A Personal Memoir'. *Mythlore* 17, no. 2, whole no. 64 (Winter 1990), p. 61.

Hawtree, Christopher. 'Robert Burchfield'. *The Guardian*, 7 July 2004. *books. guardian.co.uk/obituaries*.

Heath, Charles H., ed. *Service Record of King Edward's School, Birmingham during the War 1914–1919*. Birmingham: Cornish Brothers, 1920; facsimile reprint, with 1931 additions and corrections, Uckfield, East Sussex: Naval & Military Press, (print-on-demand) 2003.

Heiserman, A.R. Review of *Sir Gawain and the Green Knight* (ed. Tolkien and Gordon, rev. Davis). *Speculum* 44 (June 1969), pp. 176–7.

Heinemann, Fredrik J. 'Tolkien and Old Icelandic Literature'. In Battarbee, *Scholarship & Fantasy*, pp. 99–109.

†Helms, Randel. *Tolkien and the Silmarils*. Boston: Houghton Mifflin, 1981.

——. *Tolkien's World*. Boston: Houghton Mifflin, 1974.

Henderson, Jim. 'Dear PROM: Memories of Plyn'. 2001. *www.prom-aber.com*. On Gwyn Jones.

Henry, Emma. 'A Star on His Brow: The Role of Astronomy in *The Lord of the Rings*'. *The Southern Star* 2 (September 1985), pp. 14–16.

Herbert, Kathleen. Review of *Finn and Hengest*. *Mallorn* 20 (September 1983), pp. 12–13, 22.

'Heroic Endeavour', *Times Literary Supplement*, 27 August 1954, p. 541. Review of *The Fellowship of the Ring*.

Heythrop College Faculty, for Robert Murray. *www.heythrop.ac.uk/fac/murray. html*.

Hibbert, Christopher, ed. *The Encyclopædia of Oxford*. Associate ed. Edward Hibbert. London: Macmillan, 1988.

Hieatt, Constance B. 'The Text of *The Hobbit*: Putting Tolkien's Notes in Order'. *English Studies in Canada* 7, no. 2 (Summer 1981), pp. 212–24.

Hill, Joy. 'Echoes of the Old Ringmaster'. *The Times* (London), 10 December 1990, p. 16.

——. Extract from a letter to the editor. *Carandaith* (journal of the Australian Tolkien Society) 2, no. 1 (January 1970), p. 67.

Hillegas, Mark R., ed. *Shadows of Imagination: The Fantasies of C.S. Lewis, J.R.R. Tolkien, and Charles Williams*. Carbondale: Southern Illinois University Press, 1969.

Melissa and Mark Hime. *Precious Stones*. Booksellers' catalogue. Idyllwild, California, 1980.

Himes, Jonathan B. 'What J.R.R. Tolkien Really Did with the Sampo?' *Mythlore* 22, no. 4, whole no. 86 (Spring 2000), pp. 69–85.

Hindle, Alan. 'Memories of Tolkien'. *Amon Hen* 32 [May 1978], pp. 4–6.

The Historical Register of the University of Cambridge: Supplement, 1911–20. Cambridge: Cambridge University Press, 1922.

Hollis, Richard, and Brian Sibley. *Walt Disney's Snow White and the Seven Dwarfs & the Making of the Classic Film.* New York: Hyperion, 1994.

David J. Holmes Autographs. *Catalogue 37: Books from a Private Library (with Additions).* Philadelphia, December 1991.

Homer. *The Iliad.* Trans. E.V. Rieu. Harmondsworth: Penguin, 1950.

Honegger, Thomas. 'The Man in the Moon: Structural Depth in Tolkien'. *Root and Branch: Approaches towards Understanding Tolkien.* Ed. Thomas Honegger. Zurich: Walking Tree, 1999. *Cormarë Series* 2. pp. 9–76.

——, ed., *Tolkien in Translation.* Zurich: Walking Tree, 2003. *Cormarë Series* 4.

——, ed. *Translating Tolkien: Text and Film.* Zurich: Walking Tree, 2004. *Cormarë Series* 6.

'Honours in English: Final School at Oxford'. *The Times* (London), 3 July 1915, p. 6. Notice of Tolkien's First Class in English Language and Literature.

Hooker, Mark. *Tolkien through Russian Eyes.* Zurich: Walking Tree, 2003. *Cormarë Series* 5.

Hooper, Walter. *C.S. Lewis: A Companion & Guide.* London: HarperCollins, 1996.

Hopkins, G.W.S. 'Charles Walter Stansby Williams'. *Dictionary of National Biography, 1941–1950.* pp. 958–9.

Hopkins, Lisa. 'Female Authority Figures in the Works of Tolkien, C.S. Lewis and Charles Williams'. In Reynolds and GoodKnight, *Proceedings of the J.R.R. Tolkien Centenary Conference 1992,* pp. 364–6.

Hornblower, Simon, and Antony Spawforth, eds. *The Oxford Classical Dictionary.* 3rd edn. Oxford: Oxford University Press, 1996.

Horne, Brian, ed. *Charles Williams: A Celebration.* Leominster, Herefordshire: Gracewing, 1995.

Horobin, S.C.P. 'J.R.R. Tolkien as a Philologist: A Reconsideration of the Northernisms in Chaucer's *Reeve's Tale'. English Studies* (Amsterdam) 82, no. 2 (2001), pp. 97–105.

Hostetter, Carl F. '"Elvish as She Is Spoke"'. In Hammond and Scull, *The Lord of the Rings, 1954–2004: Scholarship in Honor of Richard E. Blackwelder,* pp. 231–55.

——. 'Over Middle-earth Sent unto Men: On the Philological Origins of Tolkien's Eärendel Myth'. *Mythlore* 17, no. 3, whole no. 65 (Spring 1991), pp. 5–10.

—— see also THE PUBLISHED WRITINGS OF J.R.R. TOLKIEN in vol. 1

—— and Arden R. Smith. 'A Mythology for England'. In Reynolds and Good-Knight, *Proceedings of the J.R.R. Tolkien Centenary Conference 1992,* pp. 281–90.

—— and Patrick H. Wynne. 'Addenda and Corrigenda to the *Etymologies'. Vinyar Tengwar* 45 (November 2003) pp. 3–38; 46 (July 2004), pp. 3–34 (with an appendix by Arden R. Smith, below).

—— ——. 'An Adunaic Dictionary'. *Vinyar Tengwar* 25 (September 1992), pp. 8–26.

Houghton, Joe. Review of *Finn and Hengest*. *Amon Hen* 61 (May 1983), p. 4.

Houghton, John. 'Augustine and the *Ainulindalë*'. *Mythlore* 21, no. 1, whole no. 79 (Summer 1995), pp. 4–8.

Howarth, Janet. 'The Self-Governing University'. In Brock and Curthoys, *The History of the University of Oxford, Vol. VII*, pp. 599–643.

Hughes, Richard. 'Books for Pre-Adults'. *New Statesman and Nation*, 4 December 1937, pp. 944, 946.

Hulbert, J.R. Review of *Sir Gawain and the Green Knight* (ed. Tolkien and Gordon). *Modern Philology* 23 (1925–6), pp. 246–9.

Hume, R.H. 'O.T.C. Annual Camp, Aldershot, 1910'. *King Edward's School Chronicle*, n.s. 26, no. 183 (November 1910), pp. 73–4.

Hunnewell, S. Gary. '"Sauron Is Alive and Well in Argentina": The Evolution of Tolkien's Audience in America'. Unpublished essay, presented at the Marquette University Tolkien Conference on 16 September 1983.

Huttar, Charles A., and Peter J. Schakel, eds. *The Rhetoric of Vision: Essays on Charles Williams*. Lewisburg: Bucknell University Press, 1996.

Hutton, T.W. *King Edward's School, Birmingham, 1552–1952*. Oxford: Basil Blackwell, 1952.

Hyde, Paul Nolan. 'The "Gondolinic Rules": Another Picture'. *Mythlore* 18, no. 3, whole no. 69 (Summer 1992), pp. 20–5.

——. 'Leaf and Key'. *Mythlore* 12, no. 4, whole no. 46, pp. 27–29, 36.

——. 'Mythos: The Daughter of Mountains, the Mother of Pearls'. *Mythlore* 16, no. 1, whole no. 59 (Autumn 1989), pp. 27–33.

——. 'Narqelion: A Single, Falling Leaf at Sun-fading'. *Mythlore* 15, no. 2, whole no. 56 (Winter 1988), pp. 47–52.

Isaacs, Neil D. 'On the Need for Writing Tolkien Criticism'. In Isaacs and Zimbardo, *Tolkien: New Critical Perspectives*, pp. 1–7.

——. 'On the Pleasures of (Reading and Writing) Tolkien Criticism'. In Zimbardo and Isaacs, *Understanding The Lord of the Rings: The Best of Tolkien Criticism*, pp. 1–10.

——. 'On the Possibilities of Writing Tolkien Criticism'. In Isaacs and Zimbardo, *Tolkien and the Critics*, pp. 1–11.

†—— and Rose A. Zimbardo, eds. *Tolkien and the Critics: Essays on J.R.R. Tolkien's The Lord of the Rings*. Notre Dame, Indiana: University of Notre Dame Press, 1968.

†—— ——, eds. *Tolkien: New Critical Perspectives*. Lexington: University Press of Kentucky, 1981.

'J.I.M. Stewart'. *The Times* (London), 16 November 1994, p. 19.

†*J.R.R.T.: A Portrait of John Ronald Reuel Tolkien, 1892–1973*. Video; script by Helen Dickinson. London: Produced for the Tolkien Partnership by Landseer Film & Television Productions, 1992.

Jacobs, Alan. *The Narnian: The Life and Imagination of C.S. Lewis*. San Francisco: HarperSanFrancisco, 2005.

James, Lionel. *The History of King Edward's Horse*. London: Sifton, Praed, 1921.

Jellema, Rod. 'Auden on Tolkien: The Book That Isn't, and the House That Brought It Down'. *W.H. Auden: A Legacy*. Ed. David Garrett Izzo. West Cornwall, Conn.: Locust Hill Press, 2002. pp. 39–45.

Jenkins, R.J.H. 'Richard MacGillivray Dawkins, 1871–1955'. *Proceedings of the British Academy* 41 (1955), pp. 373–88.

Jennings, Elizabeth. *A Way of Looking*. London: Andre Deutsch, 1955.

Jensen, Todd. 'Aragorn and Arthur'. *Beyond Bree*, January 1993, pp. 2–3.

——. 'Arthurian Britain and Middle-earth'. *Beyond Bree*, April 1993, pp. 3–4.

——. 'The Historical Arthur'. *Beyond Bree*, March 1993, pp. 2–3.

——. 'Hobbits at the Round Table: A Comparison of Frodo Baggins to King Arthur'. *Beyond Bree*, September 1988, pp. 9–10.

——. 'Merlin and Gandalf'. *Beyond Bree*, November 1992, pp. 2–5.

——. 'Mordred and Maeglin'. *Beyond Bree*, September 1992, pp. 5–6.

——. 'The Sons of Fëanor and the Sons of Lot'. *Beyond Bree*, July 1992, pp. 1–2.

——. 'Tolkien and Arthurian Legend'. *Beyond Bree*, November 1988, pp. 1–3.

——. 'The Zimmerman Film Treatment of *The Lord of the Rings*'. *Beyond Bree*, December 1995, pp. 7–8.

The Jerusalem Bible. General editor, Alexander Jones. Garden City, New York: Doubleday, 1966.

'John Wain'. *The Times* (London), 25 May 1994, p. 19.

†Johnson, Judith A. *J.R.R. Tolkien: Six Decades of Criticism*. Westport, Connecticut: Greenwood Press, 1986.

Johnson, Robert. 'Prizewinner'. *The Irish Press*, 30 March 1968, p. 6.

Johnston, Edward. *Writing & Illuminating, & Lettering*. London: Pitman, 1977. First published 1906.

Johnston, George Burke. 'The Poetry of J.R.R. Tolkien'. *Mankato State University Studies* 2, no. 2 (February 1967), pp. 63–75. *Mankato Studies in English* 2 ('The Tolkien Papers').

Jones, Leslie Ellen. *J.R.R. Tolkien: A Biography*. Westport, Connecticut: Greenwood Press, 2003.

Jones, Nicolette. 'Tolkien – "He was impossible, but a gent"'. *Publishing News*, 20 February 1987, p. 11.

Jones, R.V. 'Wing Commander A.H. Smith, O.B.E.' *Early English and Norse Studies Presented to Hugh Smith in Honour of His Sixtieth Birthday*. Ed. Arthur Brown and Peter Foote. London: Methuen, 1963. pp. 217–25.

'Kathleen Lea'. *The Times* (London), 21 March 1995, p. 19.

Kay, Guy Gavriel. 'Dug Out of the Dust of Middle-earth'. *Macleans*, 29 January 1981, p. 46.

Keates, Jonathan. 'Just a Bash at Bilbo'. *The Observer*, 15 March 1987. Review of *The Hobbit*.

Kenny, Anthony. *A Path from Rome: An Autobiography*. London: Sidgwick & Jackson, 1985.

Ker, Neil. 'A.S. Napier, 1853–1916'. *Philological Essays: Studies in Old and Middle English Language and Literature in Honour of Herbert Dean Meritt.* Edited by James L. Rosier. The Hague: Mouton, 1970. pp. 152–73.

——. 'Kenneth Sisam, 1887–1971'. *Proceedings of the British Academy* 58 (1972), pp. 409–28.

Kerr, Fergus. 'David James Mathew'. *Dictionary of National Biography, 1971–1980.* Including Gervase Mathew, his brother, p. 584.

Kilby, Clyde S. *Tolkien and the Silmarillion.* Wheaton, Illinois: Harold Shaw, 1976.

'The King in Birmingham: Opening of the New University Buildings'. *The Times* (London), 8 July 1909, p. 12.

Knatchbull-Hugesson, E.H. *Stories for My Children.* London: Macmillan, 1869. 'Ernest' was reprinted in *Alternative Alices: Visions and Revisions of Lewis Carroll's Books*, ed. Carolyn Sigler (Lexington: University Press of Kentucky, 1997). 'Puss-Cat Mew' was reprinted (without illustration) in *Tales before Tolkien: The Roots of Modern Fantasy*, ed. Douglas A, Anderson (New York: Ballantine Books, 2003).

†Kocher, Paul H. *Master of Middle-earth: The Fiction of J.R.R. Tolkien.* Boston: Houghton Mifflin, 1972.

——. *A Reader's Guide to The Silmarillion.* Boston: Houghton Mifflin, 1980.

——. Review of *Sir Gawain and the Green Knight, Pearl and Sir Orfeo. Mythprint* 12, no. 4 (October 1975), pp. 2–4.

König, Helga, and Cordula Schütz, eds. *Kataloge der Universitätsbibliothek Eichstätt*, Bd. 1: *Die Bibliothek der Inklings-Gesellschaft.* Wiesbaden: Harrassowitz Verlag, 2001.

Korn, Eric. 'Doing Things by Elves'. *Times Literary Supplement*, 30 September 1977, p. 1097. Review of *The Silmarillion.*

Kuteeva, Maria. '"Old Human", or "The Voice in Our Hearts": J.R.R. Tolkien on the Origin of Language'. In Agøy, *Between Faith and Fiction: Tolkien and the Powers of His World*, pp. 72–90.

Kuznets, Lois R. 'Tolkien and the Rhetoric of Childhood'. In Isaacs and Zimbardo, *Tolkien: New Critical Perspectives*, pp. 150–62.

Lacy, Norris J., ed. *The New Arthurian Encyclopedia.* New York: Garland, 1996.

Lambert, J.W. 'New Fiction'. *Sunday Times* (London), 8 August 1954, p. 5. Review of *The Fellowship of the Ring.*

Lamont, Claire. 'Mary Madge Lascelles, 1900–1995'. *Proceedings of the British Academy* 111 (2002), pp. 575–91.

Lang, Andrew. *Prince Prigio & Prince Ricardo.* London: J.M. Dent & Sons, 1961. First published separately, 1889 and 1893.

——, ed. *The Blue Fairy Book.* 6th edn. London: Longmans, Green, 1893. First published 1889.

——, ed. *The Lilac Fairy Book.* London: Longmans, Green, 1914. First published 1910.

——, ed. *The Red Fairy Book.* 5th edn. London: Longmans, Green, 1895. First published 1890.

Langer, William L., comp. and ed. *An Encyclopedia of World History*. Rev. edn. Boston: Houghton Mifflin, 1948.

Latter, J.C. *The History of the Lancashire Fusiliers, 1914–1918*. Aldershot: Gale & Polden, 1949.

Lawhead, Stephen. 'J.R.R. Tolkien: Master of Middle-earth'. In Pearce, *Tolkien: A Celebration*, pp. 156–71.

Lawlor, John. *C.S. Lewis: Memories and Reflections*. Dallas: Spence Publishing Co., 1998.

—— and W.H. Auden, eds. *To Nevill Coghill from Friends*. London: Faber, 1966.

Lea, Kathleen M. 'Dame Helen Louise Gardner'. *Dictionary of National Biography 1986–1990*. pp. 153–4.

——. 'Helen Gardner 1908–1986'. *Proceedings of the British Academy* 76 (1990), pp. 395–409.

†*Leaves from the Tree: J.R.R. Tolkien's Shorter Fiction*. London: The Tolkien Society, 1991.

Lee, Billy C. 'The War over Middle Earth'. *Paperback Quarterly* 1, no. 4 (Winter 1978), pp. 37–42.

Lee, Margaret L. 'Middle English'. *The Year's Work in English Studies* 2 (1920–1), pp. 41–53.

University of Leeds Annual Report. 1920–1 to 1923–4.

University of Leeds Calendar. 1920–1 to 1925–6.

Lennie, Campbell. 'Roy Campbell: Poet and Polemicist'. *Book and Magazine Collector* 208 (July 2001), pp. 39–48.

Levick, Barbara, ed. *The Ancient Historian and His Materials: Essays in Honour of C.E. Stevens on His Seventieth Birthday*. Westmead, Farnborough, Hants: Gregg International, 1975.

Levine, Stuart P. *The Importance of J.R.R. Tolkien*. Farmington Hills, Michigan: Lucent Books, 2004.

Lewis, Alex. 'The Lost Heart of the Little Kingdom'. In *Leaves from the Tree: J.R.R. Tolkien's Shorter Fiction*, pp. 33–44.

Lewis, C.S. *All My Road Before Me: The Diary of C.S. Lewis 1922–1927*. Ed. Walter Hooper. London: Fount, 1991.

——. *Collected Letters*, vols. 1–2 (all published to date): *Family Letters, 1905–1931*; *Books, Broadcasts and War, 1931–1949*. Ed. Walter Hooper. London: HarperCollins, 2000, 2004.

——. 'The Dethronement of Power'. *Time and Tide*, 22 October 1955, p. 1373. Review of *The Two Towers* and *The Return of the King*.

——. 'The Gods Return to Earth'. *Time and Tide*, 14 August 1954, p. 1082. Review of *The Fellowship of the Ring*.

——. *Letters of C.S. Lewis*. Ed., with a memoir, by W.H. Lewis. London: Geoffrey Bles, 1966.

——. 'On Stories'. *Essays Presented to Charles Williams*. London: Oxford University Press, 1947. pp. 90–105.

——. *Out of the Silent Planet*. London: John Lane, the Bodley Head, 1938.

——. *A Preface to 'Paradise Lost'*. Oxford: Oxford University Press, 1942.

——. 'Professor Tolkien's "Hobbit"'. *The Times* (London), 8 October 1937, p. 20. Unsigned review of *The Hobbit*.

——. *Surprised by Joy: The Shape of My Early Life*. London: Geoffrey Bles, 1955.

——. *They Stand Together: The Letters of C.S. Lewis to Arthur Greeves (1914–1963)*. Ed. Walter Hooper. London: Collins, 1979.

——. 'A World for Children'. *Times Literary Supplement*, 2 October 1937, p. 714. Unsigned review of *The Hobbit*.

Lewis, W.H. *Brothers and Friends: The Diaries of Major Warren Hamilton Lewis*. Ed. Clyde S. Kilby and Marjorie Lamp Mead. San Francisco: Harper & Row, 1982.

Liberty Historic Manuscripts. Autumn auction catalogue, 1994.

Linley, Steve. 'Farmer Giles: *Beowulf* for the Critics?' *Amon Hen* 98 (July 1989), pp. 11–12.

——. 'Farmer Giles of Ham'. *Anor* 28 (1996), pp. 4–10.

——. 'Tolkien and Haggard: Some Thoughts on Galadriel'. *Anor* 23 (1991), pp. 11–16.

'Literary Society'. *King Edward's School Chronicle* n.s. 26, no. 186 (March 1911), pp. 19–20.

Lobdell, Jared C. 'Mr. *Bliss*: Notes on the Manuscript and Story'. In *Selections from the Marquette J.R.R. Tolkien Collection*, pp. 5–10.

†——, ed. *A Tolkien Compass*. LaSalle, Illinois: Open Court, 1975. A 2nd edn. was published by Open Court in 2003 with the same contents, except for Tolkien's *Guide to the Names in The Lord of the Rings*.

Location Register of 20th-century English Literary Manuscripts and Letters. www.library.rdg.ac.uk/colls/projects/locreg.html.

'The London Gazette'. *The Times* (London), 17 July 1915, p. 8.

'The London Gazette'. *The Times* (London), 26 November 1917, p. 2.

Lönnrot, Elias. *The Kalevala, or Poems of the Kaleva District*. Trans. with foreword and appendices by Francis Peabody Magoun, Jr. Cambridge, Massachusetts: Harvard University Press, 1963.

——. *Kalevala: The Land of Heroes*. Trans. W.F. Kirby. London: J.M. Dent & Sons, 1907 (1951 printing).

——. *The Old Kalevala and Certain Antecedents*. Trans. by Francis Peabody Magoun, Jr. Cambridge, Massachusetts: Harvard University Press, 1969.

'Lord David Cecil, Eminent Man of Letters'. *The Times* (London), 3 January 1986, p. 10.

Lowe, Shirley. 'Priscilla Tolkien Talks to Shirley Lowe'. *Over 21*, December 1976, pp. 32–3.

Loyn, Henry. 'Dorothy Whitelock, 1901–1982'. *Proceedings of the British Academy* 70 (1984), pp. 543–54.

Lucas, Peter J. Review of *The Old English Exodus*. *Notes and Queries* (June 1983), pp. 243–4.

——, ed. *Exodus*. Rev. edn. Exeter, Devon: University of Exeter Press, 1994.

Luling, Virginia. 'An Anthropologist in Middle-earth'. In Reynolds and Good-Knight, *Proceedings of the J.R.R. Tolkien Centenary Conference 1992*, pp. 53–7.

Lynch, Doris. *J.R.R. Tolkien: Creator of Languages and Legends*. New York: Franklin Watts, 2003.

Lynch, F. Philip. 'F. Francis Xavier Morgan'. *www.birmingham-oratory.org/uk/morgan.htm*.

Maas, Jeremy, et al. *Victorian Fairy Painting*. London: Merrell Holberton, 1997.

Mable, Eileen. 'A Myth for Our Age'. *Church of England Newspaper*, 2 October 1977. Review of *The Silmarillion*.

McCallum, R.B. 'Pembroke 1925–1967'. *Pembroke Record* (1966–7), pp. 13–17.

McCarthy, Chris. *The Somme: The Day-by-Day Account*. London: Brockhampton Press, 1998.

MacCarthy, Fiona. *William Morris: A Life for Our Time*. London: Faber and Faber, 1994.

MacDonald, George. *At the Back of the North Wind*. London: J.M. Dent, 1956.

——. 'The Fantastic Imagination'. *Fantasists on Fantasy: A Collection of Critical Reflections*, ed. Robert H. Boyer and Kenneth J. Zahorski. New York: Avon Discus, 1984. pp. 14–21.

——. *The Light Princess and Other Tales*. Introduction by Roger Lancelyn Green. London: Victor Gollancz, 1961.

——. *Lilith*. Introduction by Lin Carter. New York: Ballantine Books, 1969.

——. *Phantastes*. Introduction by Lin Carter. New York: Ballantine Books, 1970.

——. *The Princess and Curdie*. London: J.M. Dent, 1949.

——. *The Princess and the Goblin*. London: J.M. Dent, 1949.

Mackail, J.W. 'William Morris'. *Dictionary of National Biography*. Vol. 22 (Supplement), pp. 1069–75.

McMeekin, Janet. 'Lady of the Rings'. *Limited Edition: The Magazine of Oxfordshire* 77 (May/June 1993), pp. 12–13.

McNeil, Donald G., Jr. 'Heirs'. *People*, 26 Nov. 1984, pp. 79–81.

Maggs Bros. *Autograph Letters & Historical Documents* (Catalogue 1086). London, 1988.

'Major W.H. Lewis: Soldier and Writer'. *The Times* (London), 16 April 1973, p. 16.

Malory, Thomas. *The Works of Sir Thomas Malory*. Ed. Eugène Vinaver. Oxford: Clarendon Press, 1947.

Manlove, Colin. *Modern Fantasy: Five Studies*. Cambridge: Cambridge University Press, 1975.

Marinatos, Spyridon. 'The Volcanic Destruction of Minoan Crete'. *Antiquity* 13 (1939), pp. 423–39.

Marks, John. *Moseley and Kings Heath on Old Picture Postcards*. Keyworth, Nottingham: Reflections of a Bygone Age, 1991.

Mars-Jones, Adam. 'Hobbit-forming'. *The Observer*, 11 January 1998, p. 18. Review of *Roverandom*.

Marsh, Jan. 'Tolkien's Source-book'. *Daily Telegraph*, 22 September 1977, p. 14. Review of *The Silmarillion*.

Martsch, Nancy. *Basic Quenya*. Sherman Oaks, California: Beyond Bree, 1992.

——. 'The Poetry of J.R.R. Tolkien'. *Beyond Bree*, January 1983, p. 2.

——. 'Tolkien and William Morris'. *Beyond Bree*, September 1997 pp. 6–7.

——. 'Tolkien, Roman Catholicism, and the Birmingham Oratory'. *Beyond Bree*, March 2000, pp. 2–4.

——. 'Tolkien's Reading'. *Beyond Bree*, April 1997, pp. 4–6.

——. 'Tolkien's Reading: "On Fairy-Stories"'. *Beyond Bree*, August 1997, pp. 1–4.

——. 'The Use of Language in Tolkien's Poetry: Part 1 [*The Hoard*]'. *Beyond Bree*, December 2003, pp. 2–4.

——. 'The Use of Language in Tolkien's Poetry: Part 2 [*The Man in the Moon Came Down Too Soon* and *Errantry*]'. *Beyond Bree*, April 2004, pp. 2–4.

——, ed. *List of Tolkienalia*. Sherman Oaks, California: Beyond Bree, 1992.

Mascall, E.L. 'Austin Marsden Farrer, 1904–1968'. *Proceedings of the British Academy* 54 (1968), pp. 435–42.

Masefield, John. *Letters to Reyna*. Ed. William Buchan. London: Buchan and Enright, 1983.

——. *The Old Front Line, or The Beginning of the Battle of the Somme*. London: William Heinemann, 1917.

Masson, David. 'The Lord of the Rings'. *Times Literary Supplement*, 9 December 1955, p. 743.

Mathew, Gervase. 'Orator'. In Como, *C.S. Lewis at the Breakfast Table and Other Reminiscences*, pp. 96–7.

Mathews, Richard. 'The Edges of Reality in Tolkien's Tale of Aldarion and Erendis'. *Mythlore* 18, no. 3, whole no. 69 (Summer 1992), pp. 27–30.

——. *Fantasy: The Liberation of Imagination*. New York: Twayne, 1997.

Medcalf, Stephen. 'The Anxious Longing'. *Times Literary Supplement*, 23–9 December 1988, p. 1414. Review of *The Lost Road and Other Writings*.

——. 'The Coincidence of Myth and Fact'. *Ways of Reading the Bible*. Ed. Michael Wadsworth. Brighton: Harvester Press; Totowa, New Jersey: Barnes & Noble, 1981. pp. 55–78.

——. 'Hugo Dyson'. *Postmaster* (Merton College, Oxford), January 1976, pp. 13–17.

——. '"The Language Learned of Elves": Owen Barfield, *The Hobbit* and *The Lord of the Rings*'. *Seven* 16 (1999), pp. 31–53.

The Mellonath Daeron Index of Certh Specimina. www.forodrim.org/daeron/mdics.html.

The Mellonath Daeron Index of Tengwar Specimina. www.forodrim.org/daeron/mdtci.html.

Menner, Robert J. Review of *Sir Gawain and the Green Knight* (ed. Tolkien and Gordon). *Modern Language Notes* 41 (June 1926), pp. 397–400.

Mertens-Fonck, P. 'Les Études anglaises medievales à Liège'. *Revue des langues vivantes* (Liège) 35 (1969), pp. 452–6.

Merton College Register II, 1891–1989. Oxford: Merton College for private circulation, 1991.

Mesibov, Bob. 'Tolkien and Spiders'. *Orcrist* 4 = *Tolkien Journal* 4, no. 3, whole no. 13 (1969–70), pp. 3–4.

Meskys, Ed. 'Tolkien Notes from All Over'. *Tolkien Journal* 3, no. 3, whole no. 9 (late summer 1968), p. 3.

——. 'Tolkien Fandom'. *The View from Entropy Hall* 12. *www.worldpath.net/~bullsfan/entropy/issues/12.html.*

'Middle Earth Verse'. *Times Literary Supplement*, 23 November 1962, p. 892. Review of *The Adventures of Tom Bombadil and Other Verses from the Red Book.*

Miller, M.G. 'Lice and Men: Trench Fever and Trench Life in the AIF'. 1993. *raven.cc.ukans.edu/~kansite/ww_one/medical/liceand.htm.*

Miller, Miriam Youngerman. 'J.R.R. Tolkien's Merlin: An Old Man with a Staff: Gandalf and the Magus Tradition'. *The Figure of Merlin in the Nineteenth and Twentieth Centuries.* Ed. Jeanie Watson and Marueen Fries. Lewiston, New York: Edwin Mellen Press, 1989. pp. 121–42.

—— and Jane Chance, eds. *Approaches to Teaching Sir Gawain and the Green Knight.* New York: Modern Language Association of America, 1986.

Millett, Bella, and Jocelyn Wogan-Browne, eds. *Medieval English Prose for Women: Selections from the Katherine Group and Ancrene Wisse.* Rev. ed. Oxford: Oxford University Press, 1992.

Millin, Leslie. 'Books'. *Toronto Globe and Mail*, 17 September 1977, p. 37. Review of *The Silmarillion.*

Mills, Beth Ann. Review of *The Lays of Beleriand. Library Journal*, December 1985, p. 114.

Mills, Stella M. *The Saga of Hrolf Kraki.* Oxford: Basil Blackwell, 1933.

Mills, T.F. 'A Dictionary of Unit Nomenclature'. *Land Forces of Britain, the Empire and Commonwealth. www.regiments.org/regiments/nomencla.htm.*

Milward, Peter. 'Perchance to Touch: Tolkien as Scholar'. *Mythlore* 6, no. 4, whole no. 22 (Fall 1979), pp. 31–2.

'Miss D[orothy]. Everett: Studies in Medieval English'. *The Times* (London), 23 June 1953, p. 8.

'Miss Edith Wardale: Women's Education at Oxford'. *The Times* (London), 5 March 1963, p. 7.

'Miss Helen Darbishire: Wordsworth and His Circle'. *The Times* (London), 13 March 1961, p. 21.

'Mr C.E. Stevens: Distinguished Ancient Historian'. *The Times* (London), 2 September 1970, p. 4.

'Mr. C.H. Wilkinson: Former Vice-Provost of Worcester College'. *The Times* (London), 21 January 1960, p. 17.

'Mr. Charles Williams'. *The Times* (London), 17 May 1945, p. 7.

'Mr. E.R. Eddison, Civil Servant and Author'. *The Times* (London), 24 August 1945, p. 6. Eddison.

'Mr. H.S. Bennett, Scholar and Administrator'. *The Times* (London), 8 June 1972, p. 18.

'Mr. H.V.D. Dyson'. *The Times* (London), 11 June 1975, p. 17.

'Mr. J.N. Bryson, Teacher and Editor'. *The Times* (London), 20 August 1976, p. 14.

'Mr John Masefield: Writer of Ships and the Sea and Poet Laureate since 1930'. *The Times* (London), 13 May 1967, p. 12.

'Mr. K.B. McFarlane, Medieval Historian'. *The Times* (London), 18 July 1966, p. 12.

'Mr Kenneth Sisam, Publisher and Editor'. *The Times* (London), 28 August 1971, p. 14.

'Mr. L. Rice-Oxley'. *The Times* (London), 11 July 1960, p. 14

'Mr. L. Rice-Oxley'. *The Times* (London), 15 July 1960, p. 15.

'Mr. M.R. Ridley, Lecturer and Editor'. *The Times* (London), 13 June 1969, p. 12.

'Mr. R. Cary Gilson: A Great Birmingham Headmaster'. *The Times* (London), 20 February 1939, p. 14.

'Mr Roger Lancelyn Green: Treasures of Children's Literature'. *The Times* (London), 12 October 1987.

'Mr. Roy Campbell: Poet and Man of Action', *The Times* (London), 25 April 1957, p. 13.

'Mr. T.W. Earp: Art Critic and Author'. *The Times* (London), 9 May 1958, p. 15.

'Mrs. Joan Bennett'. *The Times* (London), 22 July 1986, p. 14.

Mitchison, Naomi. 'Maps of Middle Earth'. *Books and Bookmen*, October 1977, pp. 28–30. Review of *Biography* and *The Silmarillion*.

——. 'One Ring to Bind Them'. *New Statesman and Nation*, 18 September 1954, p. 331. Review of *The Fellowship of the Ring*.

——. 'Why Not Grown-ups Too?' *Glasgow Herald*, 25 November 1967, p. 9. Review of *Smith of Wootton Major*.

Morey, Dom Adrian. *Bartholomew of Exeter, Bishop and Canonist: A Study in the Twelfth Century*. Cambridge: Cambridge University Press, 1937.

Morris, Richard, ed. *An Old English Miscellany*. London: Published for the Early English Text Society by N. Trübner, 1872.

——, ed. *Specimens of Early English*. 2nd edn, rev. Oxford: Clarendon Press, 1898.

Morris, William. *The Earthly Paradise: A Poem*. London: Longmans, Green, 1918. First published 1868–70.

——. *Icelandic Journals*. Introduction by Magnus Magnusson. Foreword by Fiona MacCarthy. London: Mare's Nest, 1996. First published 1911.

——. *The Roots of the Mountains*. North Hollywood, California: Newcastle Publishing Co., 1979. First published 1889.

——. *A Tale of the House of the Wolfings and All the Kindreds of the Mark*. London: Longmans, Green, 1913. First published 1889 (i.e. 1888).

——. *William Morris: Selected Writings and Designs*. Ed. with an introduction by Asa Briggs. Harmondsworth: Penguin Books, 1962.

——. *The Wood beyond the World*. Introduction by Tom Shippey. Oxford: Oxford University Press, 1980.

Morse, Robert. *Bilbo's Birthday and Frodo's Adventure of Faith*. San Jose, California: Writers Club Press, 2002.

——. *Evocation of Virgil in Tolkien's Art: Geritol for the Classics*. Oak Park, Illinois: Bolchazy-Carducci, 1986.

Morus, Iwan Rhys. Letter to the editor. *Amon Hen* 42 (December 1979), p. 18.

——. 'The Tale of Beren and Lúthien'. *Mallorn* 20 (September 1983), pp. 19–22.

Mosley, Charles. *J.R.R. Tolkien*. Plymouth: Northcote House, in association with the British Council, 1997.

Mumby, F.A., and Frances H.S. Stallybrass. *From Swan Sonnenschein to George Allen & Unwin Ltd*. London: George Allen & Unwin, 1955.

Munro, Robert. *Les Stations lacustres d'Europe aux ages de la pierre et du bronze*. Trans. Paul Rodet. Paris: Schleicher frères, 1908.

Murphy, Jan. 'Another Fairy Tale for Adults'. *San Francisco Chronicle*, 10 November 1985. Review of *The Lays of Beleriand*.

Murray, Robert. 'Faith Tolkien: A Theologian among Sculptors'. *The Month*, August 1994, pp. 320–4.

——. 'Sermon at Thanksgiving Service, Keble College Chapel, 23rd August 1992'. In Reynolds and GoodKnight, *Proceedings of the J.R.R. Tolkien Centenary Conference 1992*, pp. 17–20.

——. 'A Tribute to Tolkien'. *The Tablet*, 15 September 1973, pp. 879–80.

'The Musical and Dramatic Society'. *King Edward's School Chronicle* n.s. 27, no. 191 (March 1912), pp. 9–11.

Nagy, Gergely. 'The Great Chain of Reading: (Inter-)textual Relations and the Technique of Mythopoesis in the Túrin Story'. In Chance, *Tolkien the Medievalist*, pp. 239–58.

'Naomi Mitchison'. *The Times* (London), 13 January 1999. Online edn.

Neimark, Anne E. *Myth Maker: J.R.R. Tolkien*. San Diego: Harcourt Brace, 1996.

Nelson, Graham. 'Seed-ground: *Oxford Poetry*, 1910–2000'. *Oxford Magazine*, second week, Trinity Term, 2000, pp. 4–5.

Nesbit, E. *Five Children and It*. London: T. Fisher Unwin, 1902.

Newbold, John. *A History of the Catholic Church in Bromsgrove*. Bromsgrove, Worcestershire: Chris Floate, 1992.

Nichol Smith, David. 'H.C.K. Wyld'. *Oxford Magazine*, 15 February 1945, pp. 149–50.

——. 'Sir Walter Alexander Raleigh'. *Dictionary of National Biography, 1922–1930*. pp. 701–4.

Noad, Charles E. 'The Natures of Tom Bombadil: A Summary'. In *Leaves from the Tree: J.R.R. Tolkien's Shorter Fiction*, pp. 79–83.

——. 'The Early Days of the Tolkien Society'. *A Long-expected Party: Progress Report* 1 (1990), pp. 9–11.

——. 'On the Construction of "The Silmarillion"'. In Flieger and Hostetter, *Tolkien's Legendarium*, pp. 31–68.

——. Review of *The Book of Lost Tales, Part One. Mallorn* 21 (June 1984), pp. 11–13.

——. Review of *The Lays of Beleriand. Mallorn* 23 (Summer 1986), pp. 14–16.

——. "'Tolkien Reconsidered': A Talk by Humphrey Carpenter Given at the Cheltenham Festival of Literature'. *Amon Hen* 91 (May 1988), pp. 12–14.

Norman, Philip. 'The Hobbit Man'. *Sunday Times Magazine* (London), 15 January 1967, pp. 34–6. Reprinted as 'The Prevalence of Hobbits', *New York Times Magazine*, 15 January 1967, pp. 30–1, 97, 100, 102.

'Note sur les travaux du Congrès'. *Essais de philologie moderne.* Paris: Société d'édition "Les belles lettres", 1953. pp. 9–12.

'Notes and News', *King Edward's School Chronicle* n.s. 26, no. 189 (October 1911), pp. 74–6

Notice concerning E.O.G. Turville-Petre. *Oxford Magazine* 60, no. 5 (13 November 1941), pp. 65–6.

Notice of George Brewerton's retirement. *King Edward's School Chronicle*, 1914, pp. 4–5.

Notice of R.W. Reynolds' retirement. *King Edward's School Chronicle*, November–December 1922, pp. 79–80.

Obituary of George Brewerton. *King Edward's School Chronicle*, March 1929, p. 4.

Obituary of R.W. Reynolds. *Old Edwardians Gazette*, 1948, pp. 9–10

Obituary of Vincent Trought. *King Edward's School Chronicle* n.s. 27, no. 191 (March 1912), p. 4.

'Officers' Training Corps'. *King Edward's School Chronicle*, n.s. 24, no. 177 (November 1909), pp. 80–2.

'Officers' Training Corps'. *King Edward's School Chronicle* n.s. 26, no. 188 (July 1911), pp. 56–7.

'The Officers Training Corps'. *The Times* (London), 3 July 1911, p. 7.

Orchard, Andy. *A Critical Companion to Beowulf.* Cambridge: D.S. Brewer, 2003.

University of Oxford. *The Examination Statutes.* Oxford: Clarendon Press. Volumes for 1912, 1917, 1925, 1937.

——. *Excerpta e Statutis Universitatis Oxoniensis.* Oxonii: E Prelo Clarendoniano, [1930].

——. *Statuta Universitatis Oxoniensis.* Oxonii: E Typographeo Clarendoniano. Volumes for 1912, 1925.

Oxford Dante Society. *Centenary Essays on Dante.* Oxford: Clarendon Press, 1965.

Oxford English Dictionary. Compact edn. Oxford: Oxford University Press, 1971 (1987 issue with supplement, in 3 vols.).

'Oxford Poetry'. *www.gnelson.demon.co.uk/oxpoetry.*

'The Oxford Summer Diversions'. *The Times* (London), 12 July 1938, p. 14.

Oxford University Gazette, 1911–1972.

Oxford University Calendar. 1911–12 to 1965–6.

'Oxford's Sacrifice'. *Oxford Magazine*, 23 February 1917, p. 173. On Geoffrey Bache Smith.

'Oxoniensis'. 'Oxford Letter'. *King Edward's School Chronicle* n.s. 27, no. 196 (December 1912), pp. 84–5.

Pace, David Paul. 'The Influence of Vergil's *Aeneid* on *The Lord of the Rings*'. *Mythlore* 6, no. 2, whole no. 20 (Spring 1979), pp. 37–8.

Palmer, Alan, and Veronica Palmer. *The Pimlico Chronology of British History*. Updated edn. London: Pimlico, 1996.

Palmer, D.J. *The Rise of English Studies*. London: Published for the University of Hull by Oxford University Press, 1965.

Parker, Douglass. 'Hwaet We Holbytla . . .' *Hudson Review* 9 (Winter 1956–7), pp. 598–609.

Parry, Linda, ed. *William Morris*. London: Philip Wilson, in association with the Victoria and Albert Museum, 1996.

'The Past Year at Oxford'. *The Times* (London), 8 October 1925, p. 10.

Patterson, Nancy-Lou. 'An Appreciation of Pauline Baynes'. *Mythlore* 7, no. 3, whole no. 25 (Autumn 1980), pp. 3–5.

——. 'Tree and Leaf: J.R.R. Tolkien and the Visual Image'. *English Quarterly* 7, no. 1 (Spring 1974), pp. 11–26.

Patry, William F. *Copyright Law and Practice*. *digital-law-online.info/patry/patry1.html*.

Pavlac, Diana Lynne. 'More than a Bandersnatch: Tolkien as a Collaborative Writer'. In Reynolds and GoodKnight, *Proceedings of the Tolkien Centenary Conference 1992*, pp. 367–74.

Pay, Martin D. 'Reviews'. *British Fantasy Society Bulletin* 8, no. 6 (March/April 1981).

Pearce, Joseph. *Bloomsbury and Beyond: The Friends and Enemies of Roy Campbell*. London: HarperCollins, 2001.

——. *Tolkien: Man and Myth*. London: HarperCollins, 1998.

——. *Wisdom and Innocence: A Life of G.K. Chesterton*. London: Hodder & Stoughton, 2001.

†——, ed. *Tolkien: A Celebration: Collected Writings on a Literary Legacy*. London: Fount, 1999.

Pedersen, Holger. *The Discovery of Language: Linguistic Science in the Nineteenth Century*. Bloomington: Indiana University Press, 1962.

Pentikäinen, Juha Y. *Kalevala Mythology*. Expanded edn. Trans. and ed. Ritva Poom. Bloomington: Indiana University Press, 1999.

Petty, Anne C. *Dragons of Fantasy*. Cold Spring Harbor, N.Y.: Cold Spring Press, 2004.

†——. *Tolkien in the Land of Heroes: Discovering the Human Spirit*. Cold Spring Harbor, New York: Cold Spring Press, 2003.

Phelps, Robert. 'For Young Readers'. *New York Times Book Review*, 4 February 1968, p. 26. Review of *Smith of Wootton Major*.

Phillips. *Books, Maps & Manuscripts*. Auction catalogue. London, 24 March 2000.

Piazza, Paul. 'Mosaics from Middle-earth: Fragments of Tolkien's World'. *Washington Post*, 8 December 1980, p. B7.

Pirson, Ron, ed. 'Schuchart vs. Mensink-van Warmelo: Round Two'. *Lembas-extra 2004*. Leiden: Tolkien Genootschap Unquendor, 2004. pp. 75–99.

Plato. *The Dialogues of Plato*. Trans. B. Jowett. New York: Charles Scribner's Sons, 1905. Vol. 2, including the *Timaeus* and *Critias*.

Plimmer, Charlotte, and Denis Plimmer. 'The Man Who Understands Hobbits'. *Daily Telegraph Magazine*, 22 March 1968, pp. 31–3.

Plotz, Richard. 'The Aims of the Society'. *Tolkien Journal* 1 (Spring 1965), p. 1.

——. 'J.R.R. Tolkien Talks about the Discovery of Middle-earth, the Origins of Elvish'. *Seventeen*, January 1967, pp. 92–3, 118.

The Poetic Edda. Trans. with an introduction and explanatory notes by Lee M. Hollander. 2nd edn., rev. Austin: University of Texas Press, 1962; paperback edn., 1994 printing.

Potter, Jane. 'Rayner Stephens Unwin'. *Oxford Dictionary of National Biography*. Online edn.

Power, Norman S. Letter to the editor. *Amon Hen* 28 (August 1977), p. 18.

——. 'Mists of Middle Earth'. *Birmingham Post*, 17 November 1983. Review of *The Book of Lost Tales, Part One*.

——. 'Recollections'. *The J.R.R. Tolkien Centenary Conference* [souvenir book]. [Oxford]: Tolkien Society and Mythopoeic Society, 1992.

Pratchett, Terry. Review of *The Father Christmas Letters*. *Bath and West Evening Chronicle*, 18 September 1976, p. 7.

Prest, John. 'The Asquith Commission, 1919–1922'. In Harrison, *The History of the University of Oxford, Vol. VIII*, pp. 27–43.

Price, Anthony. 'Fairy Story for Grown Ups Too'. *Oxford Mail*, 16 September 1954, p. 4. Review of *The Fellowship of the Ring*.

——. 'With Camera and Pen'. *Oxford Times*, 27 January 1956, p. 8.

†Priestman, Judith. *J.R.R. Tolkien: Life and Legend*. Oxford: Bodleian Library, 1992.

Prince, Alison. *Kenneth Grahame: An Innocent in the Wild Wood*. London: Allison & Busby, 1994.

'Prof. A.H. Smith: English Place Names'. *The Times* (London), 13 May 1967, p. 12.

'Prof A.J. Bliss'. *The Times* (London), 2 December 1985, p. 14.

'Prof Alistair Campbell: Anglo-Saxon at Oxford'. *The Times* (London), 11 February 1974, p. 16.

'Professor C.L. Wrenn: Noted Scholar of Anglo-Saxon'. *The Times* (London), 4 June 1969, p. 12.

'Professor Dorothy Whitelock: Major Contributions to Anglo-Saxon Studies'. *The Times* (London), 17 August 1982, p. 10.

'Professor E.J. Dobson: Studies in English Philology'. *The Times* (London), 5 April 1984, p. 16.

'Professor F.P. Wilson: Elizabethan Literature'. *The Times* (London), 30 May 1963, p. 18.

'Professor G.V. Smithers', *The Times* (London), 24 May 2000, p. 25.

'Prof Gabriel Turville-Petre'. *The Times* (London), 18 February 1978, p. 16.

'Professor H.C.K. Wyld: Contributions to English Philology'. *The Times* (London), 31 January 1945, p. 7.

'Professor Joseph Wright: A Great English Philologist'. *The Times* (London), 28 February 1930, p. 9.

'Professor Leaves Literary Legacy'. BBC News, 10 December 1999. *news.bbc. co.uk*. On Gwyn Jones.

'Professor Nevill Coghill, Notable Popularizer of the Works of Chaucer'. *The Times* (London), 10 November 1980, p. 14.

'Professor Norman Davis'. *The Times* (London), 5 December 1989, p. 18.

Pugh, Dylan. 'The Tree of Tales'. *Mallorn* 21 (June 1984), pp. 36–8.

†Purtill, Richard L. *J.R.R. Tolkien: Myth, Morality, and Religion*. San Francisco: Harper & Row, 1984.

——. *Lord of the Elves and Eldils: Fantasy and Philosophy in C.S. Lewis and J.R.R. Tolkien*. Grand Rapids, Michigan: Zondervan, 1974.

Pyles, Thomas. *The Origins and Development of the English Language*. 2nd edn. New York: Harcourt Brace Jovanovich, 1971.

Pym, Barbara. *A Very Private Eye: An Autobiography in Diaries and Letters*. Ed. Hazel Holt and Hilary Pym. New York: Dutton, 1984.

Quilter, Harry. *What's What*. London: Sonnenschein, 1902.

Quiñonez, Jorge. 'A Brief Note on the Background of the Letter from J.R.R. Tolkien to Dick Plotz Concerning the Declension of the High-elvish Noun'. *Vinyar Tengwar* 6 (July 1989), pp. 13–14.

'R.W. Burchfield 1923–2004'. *Oxford English Dictionary Newsletter*, September 2004. *oed.com/newsletters/2004-09/suppl.html*.

Raeper, William. *George MacDonald*. Tring, Herts: Lion, 1987.

Ransome, Arthur. *Signalling from Mars: The Letters of Arthur Ransome*. Ed. Hugh Brogan. London: Jonathan Cape, 1997.

Raps, Eduard. *Josef Madlener 1881 bis 1967*. Stadt Memmingen, 1981.

Rateliff, John D. '"And Something Yet Remains to Be Said": Tolkien and Williams'. *Mythlore* 12, no. 3, whole no. 45 (Spring 1986), pp. 48–54.

——. 'The Lost Road, The Dark Tower, and The Notion Club Papers: Tolkien and Lewis's Time Travel Triad'. In Flieger and Hostetter, *Tolkien's Legendarium*, pp. 199–218.

——. 'Owen Barfield: A Short Reading List'. In Hammond, *C.S. Lewis & Owen Barfield*, pp. 22–5.

——. 'She and Tolkien'. *Mythlore* 8, no. 2, whole no. 28 (Summer 1981), pp. 6–8.

Rautala, Helena. 'Familiarity and Distance: Quenya's Relation to Finnish'. In Battarbee, *Scholarship & Fantasy*, pp. 21–31.

Ready, William. *The Tolkien Relation: A Personal Inquiry*. Chicago: Henry Regnery, 1968. Reprinted as *Understanding Tolkien and The Lord of the Rings* (1969).

Reckford, Kenneth. 'Some Trees in Virgil and Tolkien'. *Perspectives of Roman Poetry: A Classics Symposium*. Ed. G. Karl Galinsky. Austin: University of Texas Press, 1974. pp. 57–91.

Reeves, Marjorie. *St Anne's College, Oxford: An Informal History*. Oxford: St Anne's College, 1979.

Reilly, R.J. *Romantic Religion: A Study of Barfield, Lewis, Williams, and Tolkien*. Athens: University of Georgia Press, 1971.

Reilly, Robert J. 'Tolkien and the Fairy Story'. In Isaacs and Zimbardo, *Tolkien and the Critics*, pp. 128–50.

Reinach, Salomon. Part 2 of 'Andrew Lang' by R.S. Rait, *et al. Quarterly Review* (London) 218, no. 435 (April 1913), pp. 309–19.

Kenneth W. Rendell. *Catalogue 248*. South Natick, Massachusetts, 1995.

Resnik, Henry. 'The Hobbit-forming World of J.R.R. Tolkien'. *Saturday Evening Post*, 2 July 1966, pp. 90–92, 94.

——. 'An Interview with Tolkien'. *Niekas* 18 (Spring 1967), pp. 37–47.

'The Rev A.G. Mathew, Scholar and Polymath'. *The Times* (London), 6 April 1976, p. 18.

'Rev A.M. Farrer, Warden of Keble College, Oxford'. *The Times* (London), 30 December 1968, p. 10.

'The Rev. R.F.W. Fletcher'. *The Times* (London), 17 October 1950, p. 8.

Review of *The Adventures of Tom Bombadil and Other Verses from the Red Book*. *Junior Bookshelf*, March 1963.

Review of *Sir Gawain and the Green Knight, Pearl and Sir Orfeo*. *British Book News*, December 1975.

Revue des langues vivantes (1951/2). Special number on Le Congrès du LXe anniversaire des sections de philologie romane et de philologie germanique de l'Université de Liège, 10–12 November 1950.

'Report for 1921'. *Transactions of the Yorkshire Dialect Society*, part 23, vol. 4 (January 1922), p. 5.

Reynolds, Barbara. *Dorothy L. Sayers: Her Life and Soul*. London: Hodder and Stoughton, 1993.

Reynolds, Patricia. 'A History of the Mythopoeic Society'. *A Long-expected Party: Progress Report* 1 (1990), pp. 12–13.

——. 'The Real Tom Bombadil'. In *Leaves from the Tree: J.R.R. Tolkien's Shorter Fiction*, pp. 85–8.

——. *Tolkien's Birmingham*. Milton Keynes: Forsaken Inn Press, 1992.

†—— and Glen H. GoodKnight, eds. *Proceedings of the Tolkien Centenary Conference 1992*. Milton Keynes: Tolkien Society; Altadena, California: Mythopoeic Press, 1995.

Reynolds, William. 'Poetry as Metaphor in *The Lord of the Rings*'. *Mythlore* 4, no. 4, whole no. 16 (June 1977), pp. 12, 14–16.

Richards, Jeffrey. 'Tiptop Tolkien?' *Daily Telegraph*, 1 February 1997, p. 11.

Paul C. Richards Autographs. *Catalogue 228*. Templeton, Massachusetts, 1988.

Richardson, Maurice. 'New Novels'. *New Statesman and Nation*, 18 December 1954, pp. 835–6.

Ricketts, Rita. *Adventurers All: Tales of Blackwellians, of Books, Bookmen, and Reading and Writing Folk*. Oxford: Blackwell's, 2002.

Ridley, M.R. 'The Trials of Teaching in a Secondary Modern School'. *Daily Telegraph*, 28 October 1955, p. 8.

Ring, Jim. *How the English Made the Alps*. London: John Murray, 2000.

Roberts, W. Rhys. 'Gerald of Wales on the Survival of Welsh'. *Transactions of the Honourable Society of Cymmrodorion: Session 1923-1924*. London: Issued by the Society, 1925. pp. 46-60.

Roche, Norma. 'Sailing West: Tolkien, the Saint Brendan Story, and the Idea of Paradise in the West'. *Mythlore* 17, no. 4, whole no. 66 (Summer 1991), pp. 16-20, 62.

Rogers, William N., and Michael R. Underwood. 'Gagool and Gollum: Exemplars of Degeneration in *King Solomon's Mines* and *The Hobbit*'. In Clark and Timmons, *J.R.R. Tolkien and His Literary Resonances*, pp. 121-31.

'Roman Catholic Ceremony at Oxford'. *The Times* (London), 19 May 1936, p. 28.

Rómenna Meeting Report, 26 October 1986, p. 1.

Rosebury, Brian. *Tolkien: A Critical Assessment*. Houndmills, Basingstoke, Hampshire: Macmillan; New York: St Martin's Press, 1992.

†——. *Tolkien: A Cultural Phenomenon*. Houndmills, Basingstoke, Hampshire: Palgrave Macmillan, 2003.

Rossenberg, René van. 'Dutch Tolkien Illustrators'. *Tolkien Collector* 3 (May 1993), pp. 17-19.

——. 'Tolkien and Linguaphone'. *Tolkien Collector* 5 (November 1993), pp. 18-20.

——. 'Tolkien's Exceptional Visit to Holland: A Reconstruction'. In Reynolds and GoodKnight, *Proceedings of the Tolkien Centenary Conference 1992*, pp. 301-9.

Rossiter, Stuart, ed. *England*. 9th edn. London: Ernest Benn, 1980. *Blue Guide*.

'Royal Review at Windsor: The King and Officers Training Corps'. *The Times* (London), 4 July 1911, pp. 9-10.

Royal Society of Literature. *Report*. 1966-7.

——. Web site. *www.rslit.org*.

Rutledge, Fleming. *The Battle for Middle-earth: Tolkien's Divine Design in The Lord of the Rings*. Grand Rapids, Michigan: William B. Eerdmans, 2004.

Ryan, J.S. 'J.R.R. Tolkien: Lexicography and Other Early Linguistic Preferences'. *Mallorn* 16 (May 1981), pp. 9-12, 14-15, 19-22, 24-6.

——. 'J.R.R. Tolkien's Formal Lecturing and Teaching at the University of Oxford, 1929-1959'. *Seven* 19 (2002), pp. 45-62.

——. 'Lexical Impacts'. *Amon Hen* 76 (November 1985), pp. 21-3; and 77 (January 1986), pp. 20-2.

——. 'The Origin of the Name Wetwang'. *Amon Hen* 63 (August 1983), pp. 10-13.

——. *The Shaping of Middle-earth's Maker: Influences on the Life and Literature of J.R.R. Tolkien*. Highland, Michigan: American Tolkien Society, 1992.

Includes 'An Important Influence, His Professor's Wife, Mrs. Elizabeth Mary (Lea) Wright', pp. 34–8; 'J.R.R. Tolkien, C.S. Lewis and Roy Campbell', pp. 25–9; 'Tolkien and George Gordon: or, A Close Colleague and His Notion of "Myth-maker" and of Historiographic Jeux d'esprit', pp. 30–3.

——. *Tolkien: Cult or Culture?* Armidale, New South Wales: University of New England, 1969.

——. 'Two Oxford Scholars' Perceptions of the Traditional Germanic Hall'. *Minas Tirith Evening-Star* 19, no. 1 (Spring 1990), pp. 8–11.

——. 'The Work and Preferences of the Professor of Old Norse at the University of Oxford from 1925 to 1945'. *Angerthas* 27 (May 1990), pp. 4–10. Reprinted in *Angerthas in English* 2 (i.e. *Angerthas* 31), July 1992, pp. 51–8.

Ryder, Rowland. 'Nevill Coghill'. *Exeter College Association Register 1992*, pp. 39–43.

S., P. 'H.F.B. Brett-Smith, 1884–1951, Editor of *The Oxford Magazine*, 1921–2'. *Oxford Magazine*, 1 February 1951, p. 233.

'The Saga of Middle-earth'. *Times Literary Supplement*, 25 November 1955, p. 704. Review of *The Return of the King*.

St. Clair, Gloria. 'An Overview of the Northern Influences on Tolkien's Works'. In Reynolds and GoodKnight, *Proceedings of the J.R.R. Tolkien Centenary Conference 1992*, pp. 63–7.

——. '*Volsunga Saga* and Narn: Some Analogies'. In Reynolds and Good-Knight, *Proceedings of the J.R.R. Tolkien Centenary Conference 1992*, pp. 68–72.

Sakers, Don. 'It Isn't "Lord of the Rings" but It Is Tolkien'. *The Sun* (Baltimore), 25 March 1984, p. C4. Review of *The Book of Lost Tales, Part One*.

Sale, Roger. *Fairy Tales and After: From Snow White to E.B. White*. Cambridge, Massachusetts: Harvard University Press, 1978.

——. 'Tolkien as Translator'. *Parnassus* 4 (1976), pp. 183–91.

——. 'Wonderful to Relate'. *Times Literary Supplement*, 12 March 1976, p. 289.

Salmon, Nicholas, with Derek Baker. *The William Morris Chronology*. Bristol: Thoemmes Press, 1996.

Salo, David. *A Gateway to Sindarin: A Grammar of an Elvish Language from J.R.R. Tolkien's Lord of the Rings*. Salt Lake City: University of Utah Press, 2004.

Salu, Mary, and Robert T. Farrell, eds. *J.R.R. Tolkien: Scholar and Storyteller: Essays in Memoriam*. Ithaca, New York: Cornell University Press, 1979.

Santoski, Taum (T.J.R.). 'The Boundaries of the Little Kingdom'. In *Selections from the Marquette J.R.R. Tolkien Collection*, pp. 11–15.

——. *Catalogue of an Exhibit of the Manuscripts of JRRT*. Milwaukee: Marquette University Memorial Library, Dept. of Special Collections and University Archives, 1983 [i.e. 1984].

Sarehole Mill. Birmingham: Birmingham Museums and Art Gallery, 1986.

Sayer, George. 'George Sayer'. *A Long-Expected Party: Progress Report* 6 (1992), p. 20.

——. *Jack: C.S. Lewis and His Times*. 2nd edn. Wheaton, Illinois: Crossway Books, 1994.

——. 'Recollections of J.R.R. Tolkien'. In Reynolds and GoodKnight, *Proceedings of the J.R.R. Tolkien Centenary Conference 1992*, pp. 21–5.

——. Sleeve notes for *J.R.R. Tolkien Reads and Sings His The Hobbit and The Fellowship of the Ring*. New York: Caedmon Records, 1975. The same text appears on the sleeve of *J.R.R. Tolkien Reads and Sings His Lord of the Rings: The Two Towers/The Return of the King* (Caedmon, 1975).

——. 'Tales of the Ferrograph'. *Minas Tirith Evening-Star* 9, no. 2 (January 1980), pp. 2–4.

Sayers, Frances Clarke. 'Walt Disney Accused'. *Horn Book* 41, no. 6 (December 1965), pp. 602–11.

Schall, James V., S.J., 'On the Realities of Fantasy'. In Pearce, *Tolkien: A Celebration*, pp. 67–72.

Schultz, Jeffrey D., and John G. West, Jr., eds. *The C.S. Lewis Readers' Encyclopedia*. Grand Rapids, Michigan: Zondervan, 1998.

Schultz, Steve. 'Hobbits in the House'. *Marquette Magazine* 19, no. 4 (Fall 2001), pp. 16–19.

Schweicher, Eric. 'Aspects of the Fall in *The Silmarillion*'. In Reynolds and GoodKnight, *Proceedings of the J.R.R. Tolkien Centenary Conference 1992*, pp. 167–71.

Scott, Nan C. 'No "Intermediary"'. *Saturday Review*, 23 October 1965, p. 56.

——. 'A Visit with Tolkien'. *The Living Church*, 5 February 1978, p. 11–12. Reprinted as 'Tolkien: Hobbit and Wizard' in Etkin, *Eglerio!: In Praise of Tolkien*, pp. 77–81.

——. 'War and Pacifism in *The Lord of the Rings*'. *Tolkien Journal* 15 (Summer 1972), pp. 23–5, 27–30.

Scoville, Chester N. 'Pastoralia and Perfectability in William Morris and J.R.R. Tolkien'. In Chance and Siewers, *Tolkien's Modern Middle Ages*, pp. 93–103.

Scull, Christina. 'The Development of Tolkien's *Legendarium*: Some Threads in the Tapestry of Middle-earth'. In Flieger and Hostetter, *Tolkien's Legendarium*, pp. 7–18.

——. 'Dragons from Andrew Lang's Retelling of Sigurd to Tolkien's Chrysophylax'. In *Leaves from the Tree: J.R.R. Tolkien's Shorter Fiction*, pp. 49–62.

——. 'The Fairy Tale Tradition'. *Mallorn* 23 (Summer 1986), pp. 30–6.

——. '*The Hobbit* Considered in Relation to Children's Literature Contemporary with Its Writing and Publication'. *Mythlore* 14, no. 2, whole no. 52 (Winter 1987), pp. 49–56.

——. 'The Influences of Archeology and History on Tolkien's World'. In Battarbee, *Scholarship & Fantasy*, pp. 33–51.

——. 'Margaret Joy Hill, 22 May 1936–21 December 1991'. *Amon Hen* 113 (January 1992), p. 5.

——. 'Open Minds, Closed Minds in *The Lord of the Rings*'. In Reynolds and GoodKnight, *Proceedings of the J.R.R. Tolkien Centenary Conference 1992*, pp. 151–6.

——. 'Rayner Unwin Speaks to the Cambridge Tolkien Society'. *Beyond Bree*, June 1986, pp. 1–2.

——. Review of *The Book of Lost Tales, Part Two. Beyond Bree*, November 1984, pp. 2–4.

——. Review of *The Lays of Beleriand. Beyond Bree*, November 1985, pp. 1–4.

——. 'Tom Bombadil and *The Lord of the Rings*'. In *Leaves from the Tree: J.R.R. Tolkien's Shorter Fiction*, pp. 73–7.

——. 'What Did He Know and When Did He Know It?: Planning, Inspiration, and *The Lord of the Rings*'. In Hammond and Scull, *The Lord of the Rings, 1954–2004: Scholarship in Honor of Richard E. Blackwelder*, pp. 101–12.

—— and Wayne G. Hammond, eds. *Farmer Giles of Ham* by J.R.R. Tolkien. Fiftieth anniversary edn. London: HarperCollins, 1999.

—— ——, eds. *Roverandom* by J.R.R. Tolkien. London: HarperCollins, 1998.

—— —— see also under *Wayne G. Hammond*

Seddon, Sue. 'The Return of Tolkien'. *Sunday Times* (London), 19 September 1982, pp. 82–3.

Seeman, Chris. 'Tolkien's Revision of the Romantic Tradition'. In Reynolds and GoodKnight, *Proceedings of the J.R.R. Tolkien Conference 1992*, pp. 72–83.

Selections from the Marquette J.R.R. Tolkien Collection. Milwaukee: Marquette University Library, 1987.

Senior, W.A. 'Loss Eternal in J.R.R. Tolkien's Middle-earth'. In Clark and Timmons, *J.R.R. Tolkien and His Literary Resonances*, pp. 173–82.

Shakespeare, William. *The Complete Works of Shakespeare*. Ed. Irving Ribner and George Lyman Kittredge. Waltham, Massachusetts: Ginn, 1971.

Sheppard, Thomas. *Kingston-upon-Hull before, during and after the Great War*. Hull: A. Brown & Sons, 1919.

Shimmin, A.N. *The University of Leeds: The First Half-Century*. Cambridge: Published for the University of Leeds at the University Press, Cambridge, 1954.

Shippey, T.A. (Tom). *Beowulf*. London: Edward Arnold, 1978.

——. 'Blunt Belligerence'. *Times Literary Supplement*, 26 November 1982, p. 1306. Review of *Mr. Bliss*.

——. 'Boar and Badger: An Old English Heroic Antithesis?' *Leeds Studies in English* 16 (1985), pp. 220–39.

†——. *J.R.R. Tolkien: Author of the Century*. London: HarperCollins, 2000.

——. 'Long Evolution: *The History of Middle-earth* and Its Merits'. *Arda* 1987 (1992), pp. 18–43.

——. 'A Look at *Exodus* and *Finn and Hengest*'. *Arda* 3 (1986, for 1982–83), pp. 72–82.

——. 'Orcs, Wraiths, Wights: Tolkien's Images of Evil'. In Clark and Timmons, *J.R.R. Tolkien and His Literary Resonances*, pp. 183–98.

†——. *The Road to Middle-earth*. 2nd edn. London: Grafton, 1992. We have found this the most convenient edition to cite, but our references may be found also in earlier and later editions. Except for a new final chapter, the text of the 1992 edn. is identical to that of the 1st edn. (1982), but

withdifferent pagination. A further 'revised and expanded edition', reset, was published by Houghton Mifflin, Boston, in 2003.

——. 'Structure and Unity'. *A Beowulf Handbook*. Ed. Robert E. Bjork and John D. Niles (1997). pp. 149–74.

——. 'Tolkien and Iceland: The Philology of Envy'. 2002. *www2.hi.is/Apps/WebObjects/HI.woa/wa/dp?detail=1004508&name=nordals_en_greinar_og_erindi*.

——. 'Tolkien and the *Gawain*-poet'. In Reynolds and GoodKnight, *Proceedings of the J.R.R. Tolkien Centenary Conference 1992*, pp. 213–19.

——. 'Tolkien and "The Homecoming of Beorhtnoth"'. In *Leaves from the Tree: J.R.R. Tolkien's Shorter Fiction*, pp. 5–16.

——. 'Tolkien as a Post-war Writer'. In Reynolds and GoodKnight, *Proceedings of the J.R.R. Tolkien Centenary Conference 1992*, pp. 84–93.

——. 'Tolkien's Academic Reputation Now'. *Amon Hen* 100 (November 1989), pp. 18–19, 21–2.

——. 'The Versions of "The Hoard"'. *Lembas* 100 (2001), pp. 3–7.

Shorto, Russell. *J.R.R. Tolkien: Man of Fantasy*. New York: Kipling Press, 1988.

Sibley, Brian. 'History for Hobbits'. *The Listener*, 2 October 1980, pp. 443–4.

——. 'The Ring Goes Ever On'. *www.briansibley.com/Broadcasts/RingGoesEverOn.htm*.

——, et al. *Microphones in Middle Earth: Radio 4's Serial 'The Lord of the Rings'*. Eastleigh, Hants: Ian D. Smith, 1982.

Signalling: Morse, Semaphore, Station Work, Despatch Riding, Telephone Cables, Map Reading. Written by an Officer of the Regular Army. Edited by E. John Solano. London: John Murray, 1915.

Michael Silverman. *Catalogue No. 2*. London, 1998.

——. *Catalogue Nine*. London, 1993.

——. *Catalogue Eleven*. London, 1994.

'Sir Basil Blackwell'. *The Times* (London), 11 April 1984, p. 16.

'Sir Charles Firth'. *The Times* (London), 20 February 1936, p. 16.

'Sir Stanley Unwin: An Influential Publisher', *The Times* (London), 15 October 1968, p. 13.

'Sir William Craigie: Lexicographer and Scholar'. *The Times* (London), 3 September 1957, p. 13.

Sisam, Kenneth. *The Structure of Beowulf*. Oxford: Clarendon Press, 1965 (corrected printing 1966).

——, ed. *Fourteenth Century Verse & Prose*. Oxford: Clarendon Press, 1921.

Sisson, C.J., and H. Winifred Husbands. 'Raymond Wilson Chambers, 1874–1942'. *Proceedings of the British Academy* 30 (1945), pp. 427–45.

Smith, Alan. 'A Shire Pleasure'. *Pipes and Tobacco* 5, no. 4 (Winter 2001).

Smith, Arden R. 'Certhas, Skirditaila, Fuþark: A Feigned History of Runic Origins'. In Flieger and Hostetter, *Tolkien's Legendarium: Essays on The History of Middle-earth*, pp. 105–11.

——. 'The *Tengwar* in the *Etymologies*'. *Vinyar Tengwar* 46 (July 2004), pp. 29–34.

——. 'Tolkienian Gothic'. In Hammond and Scull, *The Lord of the Rings, 1954–2004: Scholarship in Honor of Richard E. Blackwelder*, pp. 267–81.

——. 'Transitions in Translations'. *Vinyar Tengwar*, various numbers.

——. 'The Túrin Prose Fragment: An Analysis of a Rúmilian Document'. *Vinyar Tengwar* 37 (December 1995), pp. 15–23.

—— see also THE PUBLISHED WRITINGS OF J.R.R. TOLKIEN in vol. 1

—— and Patrick Wynne. 'Tolkien and Esperanto'. *Seven* 17 (2000), pp. 27–46.

Smith, Mark Eddy. *Tolkien's Ordinary Virtues: Exploring the Spiritual Themes of The Lord of the Rings*. Downers Grove, Illinois: InterVarsity Press, 2002.

R.M. Smythe. *Spring Autograph Auction*. Auction catalogue. New York, 10 May 2001.

Some Moseley Personalities, Volume I. Moseley: Moseley Local History Society, 1991.

Sotheby & Co. *Catalogue of Nineteenth Century and Modern First Editions, Presentation Copies, Autograph Letters and Literary Manuscripts*. Auction catalogue. London, 16–17 July 1973.

Sotheby Parke Bernet. *Catalogue of Autograph Letters, Literary Manuscripts and Historical Documents*. Auction catalogue. London, 16 October 1978.

——. *Catalogue of Nineteenth Century and Modern First Editions, Presentation Copies, Autograph Letters and Literary Manuscripts*. Auction catalogue. London, 28–9 July 1977.

Sotheby's. *Autograph Letters and Printed Books, including First Editions*. Auction catalogue. London, 19 May 2000.

——. *Catalogue of Valuable Autograph Letters, Literary Manuscripts and Historical Documents*. Auction catalogue. London, 21–22 July 1980.

——. *English Literature and English History*. Auction catalogue. London, 6–7 December 1984. See also *Beyond Bree*, May 1985, p. 4.

——. *English Literature and History, Private Press and Illustrated Books, Related Drawings and Animation Art*. Auction catalogue. London, 21–22 July 1992.

——. *English Literature, History, & Children's Books & Illustrations*. Auction catalogue. London, 16 December 2004.

——. *English Literature, History, Children's & Illustrated Books & Drawings*. Auction catalogue. London, 10 July 2001.

——. *English Literature, History, Children's Books and Illustrations*. Auction catalogue. London, 16 December 2004.

——. *English Literature, History, Children's Books and Illustrations*. Auction catalogue. London, 12 July 2005.

——. *English Literature, History, Children's Books, Illustrations and Photographs*. Auction catalogue. London, 8 July 2004.

——. *English Literature, History, Fine Bindings, Private Press Books, Children's Books, Illustrated Books, and Drawings*. Auction catalogue. London, 10 July 2003.

——. *English Literature, History, Private Press & Children's Books*. Auction catalogue. London, 12 December 2002.

——. *Fine Books and Manuscripts, including English and American Literature.* Auction catalogue. New York, 16–17 May 1984.

——. *Literature and Illustration.* Auction catalogue. London, 11–12 July 2002.

——. *Valuable Printed Books and Manuscripts.* Auction catalogue. London, 13 December 2001.

Spacks, Patricia Meyer. 'Ethical Pattern in *The Lord of the Rings*'. *Critique* 3 (Spring–Fall 1959), pp. 30–42. Revised as 'Power and Meaning in *The Lord of the Rings*', in Isaacs and Zimbardo, *Tolkien and the Critics*, pp. 81–99.

Spearing, A.C. Review of *Sir Gawain and the Green Knight, Pearl and Sir Orfeo. Times Higher Educational Supplement*, 30 January 1976.

'Speech Day', *King Edward's School Chronicle* n.s. 26, no. 189 (October 1911), pp. 71–2.

Spender, Stephen. 'Wystan Hugh Auden'. *Dictionary of National Biography, 1971–1980.* pp. 24–7.

Spurr, Barry. 'Expert beyond Experience'. *Oxford Today* 4, no. 3 (Trinity 1992), pp. 20, 22. Appreciation of Helen Gardner.

'Staying Home'. *The Times* (London), 9 February 1973, p. 14.

Stanley, E.G., and Douglas Gray, eds. *Five Hundred Years of Words and Sounds: A Festschrift for Eric Dobson.* Cambridge: D.S. Brewer; Totowa, New Jersey: Biblio, 1983.

Stapeldon Magazine 3, no. 16 (December 1911)–7, no. 42 (June 1928). Miscellaneous notes and articles.

Stedman, Michael. *La Boisselle, Ovieller, Contalmaison.* London: Leo Cooper, 1997.

——. *Thiepval.* London: Leo Cooper, 1995.

Steele, Robert. *The Story of Alexander.* London: David Nutt, 1894.

Stenström, Anders (Beregond). 'Något om pipor, blad och rökning' ('Some Notes on Pipes, Leaf and Smoking'). *Arda* 4 (1988, for 1984), pp. 32–93. In Swedish, with summary in English.

——. Review of *Finn and Hengest. Amon Hen* 66 (March 1984), pp. 5–7.

Stephens, Meic, comp. and ed. *The Oxford Companion to the Literature of Wales.* Oxford: Oxford University Press, 1986; reprinted with corrections 1990.

Sterling, Grant C. '"The Gift of Death": Tolkien's Philosophy of Mortality'. *Mythlore* 21, no. 4, whole no. 82 (Winter 1997), pp. 16–18, 38.

Stevenson, Jeffrey. 'T.B. or Not T.B.: That Is the Question'. *Amon Hen* 196 (November 2005), pp. 16–21.

Stimpson, Catharine R. *J.R.R. Tolkien.* New York: Columbia University Press, 1969.

Gerard A.J. Stodolski. *Catalogue 4.* Manchester, New Hampshire, August 1995.

——. *Catalogue 299.* Manchester, New Hampshire, June 1999.

†Strachey, Barbara. *Journeys of Frodo: An Atlas of J.R.R. Tolkien's The Lord of the Rings.* London: George Allen & Unwin, 1981.

Stringer, Jenny, ed. *The Oxford Companion to Twentieth Century Literature in English.* Oxford: Oxford University Press, 1996.

Stukeley, William. *Stonehenge: A Temple Restor'd to the British Druids*. London: Printed for W. Innys and R. Manby, 1740.

Sugerman, Shirley, ed. *Evolution of Consciousness: Studies in Polarity*. Middletown, Connecticut: Wesleyan University Press, 1976.

Sutcliffe, Peter. *The Oxford University Press: An Informal History*. Oxford: Clarendon Press, 1978.

Sutherland, James. 'David Nichol Smith'. *Dictionary of National Biography 1961–1970*. pp. 960–1.

——. 'David Nichol Smith, 1875–1962'. *Proceedings of the British Academy* 48 (1962), pp. 449–59.

Swann, Alison. *The Donald Swann Website. www.donaldswann.co.uk.*

Swann, Donald. Foreword to *The Road Goes Ever On: A Song Cycle* by J.R.R. Tolkien and Donald Swann. 2nd edn., rev. Boston: Houghton Mifflin, 1978.

——. *The Space between the Bars: A Book of Reflections*. New York: Simon and Schuster, 1968.

——. *Swann's Way: A Life in Song*. Recorded and ed. Lyn Smith. Rev. paperback edn. London: Arthur James, 1993.

Sweet, Henry. *An Anglo-Saxon Reader in Prose and Verse*. 8th edn., rev. Oxford: Clarendon Press, 1908.

Sykes, Peter. 'Tolkien's Fairies'. *Oxford Mail*, 28 May 1964, p. 6. Review of *Tree and Leaf*.

Tait, William H. Letter to the editor. *Old Edwardians Gazette*, June 1972, pp. 16–17.

Tayar, Graham. 'Tolkien's Mordor'. *The Listener*, 14 July 1977.

'Telling Stories'. *Times Literary Supplement*, 19 June 1948, p. 345. Review of *Essays Presented to Charles Williams*.

Tennyson, G.B. 'Owen Barfield: First and Last Inklings'. *The World and I* 5, no. 4 (April 1990), pp. 541–5.

Thomas, Paul Edmund. 'Some of Tolkien's Narrators'. In Flieger and Hostetter, *Tolkien's Legendarium*, pp. 161–81.

Thompson, Francis. *The Poems of Francis Thompson*. London: Hollis and Carter 1946.

Thompson, George H. 'Early Articles, Comments, Etcetera about J.R.R. Tolkien'. *Mythlore* 13, no. 3, whole no. 49 (Spring 1987), pp. 58–63.

——. 'Early Reviews of Books by J.R.R. Tolkien'. *Mythlore* 11, no. 2, whole no. 40 (Autumn 1984), pp. 56–60; 11, no. 3, whole no. 41 (Winter–Spring 1985), pp. 59–63; 12, no. 1, whole no. 43 (Autumn 1985), pp. 58–63; 12, no. 3, whole no. 45 (Spring 1986), pp. 61–2; 12, no. 4, whole no. 46 (Summer 1986), pp. 59–62; 13, no. 1, whole no. 47 (Autumn 1986), pp. 54–9.

——. 'Minor, Early References to Tolkien and His Works'. *Mythlore*, 14, no. 1, whole no. 51 (Autumn 1987), pp. 41–2, 55.

Thrall, William Flint, and Addison Hibbard. *A Handbook to Literature*. Rev. and enlarged by C. Hugh Holman. New York: Odyssey Press, 1960.

Thwaite, Anthony. 'Hobbitry'. *The Listener*, 22 November 1962, p. 831. Review of *The Adventures of Tom Bombadil and Other Verses from the Red Book*.

Tillotson, Kathleen. 'Helen Darbishire'. *Dictionary of National Biography 1961–1970*. pp. 270–1.

Timmons, Daniel. Introduction to Clark and Timmons, *J.R.R. Tolkien and His Literary Resonances*, pp. 1–10.

——. 'J.R.R. Tolkien: The "Monstrous" in the Mirror'. *Journal of the Fantastic in the Arts* 9, no. 3 (1998), pp. 229–46.

——. *Mirror on Middle-earth: J.R.R. Tolkien and the Critical Perspectives*. Ph.D. thesis, University of Toronto, 1998.

——. 'Tolkien-Related Dissertations and Theses in English'. *Tolkien Collector* 16 (July 1997), pp. 21–6.

Tolkien, Christopher. Foreword to *The Hobbit* by J.R.R. Tolkien. Fiftieth anniversary edn. London: Unwin Hyman, 1987. pp. i–xvi.

——. 'Notes on the Differences in Editions of *The Hobbit* Cited by Mr. David Cofield'. *Beyond Bree*, July 1986, pp. 1–3.

——. *The Silmarillion* [by] *J.R.R. Tolkien: A Brief Account of the Book and Its Making*. Boston: Houghton Mifflin, 1977.

——. 'The Tengwar Numerals'. *Quettar* (bulletin of the Linguistic Fellowship of The Tolkien Society) 13 (February 1982), pp. 8–9, with remarks by editor Steve Pillinger, p. 7; and 14 (May 1982), pp. 6–7.

Tolkien, Joan. Letter to the editor. *Sunday Times* (London), 10 October 1982, p. 25.

Tolkien, Joanna. 'Joanna Tolkien Speaks at the Tolkien Society Annual Dinner, Shrewsbury, April 16, 1994.' *Digging Potatoes, Growing Trees*, vol. 2. Ed. Helen Armstrong. Telford: The Tolkien Society, 1998. pp. 31–6.

†Tolkien, John, and Priscilla Tolkien. *A Tolkien Family Album*. London: HarperCollins, 1992.

Tolkien, Michael. 'An Interview with Michael Hilary Reuel Tolkien'. Conducted by Derek Mills on Radio Blackburn in December 1975, transcribed by Gary Hunnewell with help from Sylvia Hunnewell. *Minas Tirith Evening-Star* 18, no. 1 = *Ravenhill* 7, no. 4 (Spring 1989), pp. 5–9.

Tolkien, Priscilla. 'Beginnings and Endings'. *PN Review* 31, no. 1 (September–October 2004), pp. 9–10.

——. Foreword. *A Tribute to J.R.R. Tolkien, 3 January 1892–2 September 1973: Centenary*. Ed. Rosemary Gray. Pretoria: Unisa Medieval Association, 1992. pp. vii–x.

——. 'J.R.R. Tolkien and Edith Tolkien's Stay in Staffordshire 1916, 1917 and 1918'. *Angerthas* 34 (July 1993), p. 4–5.

——. 'Memories of J.R.R. Tolkien in His Centenary Year'. *The Brown Book* (December 1992), pp. 12–14.

——. 'My Father the Artist'. *Amon Hen* 23 (December 1976), pp. 6–7.

——. 'News from the North Pole'. *Oxford Today* 5, no. 1 (Michaelmas 1992), pp. 8–9.

——. 'Priscilla Tolkien Talks to Shirley Lowe'. *Over 21*, December 1976, p. 32.

——. 'Talk Given at the Church House Westminster on 16.9.77 by Priscilla Tolkien', *Amon Hen* 29 [?November 1977], pp. 4–6.

Tolkien, Simon. 'My Grandfather'. *The Mail on Sunday*, 23 February 2003.

'The Tolkien Affair: An Editorial'. *SFWA* [Science Fiction Writers of America] *Bulletin* 1, no. 3 (November 1965).

The Tolkien Collector 1–26 ([Autumn] 1992–December 2002).

'Tolkien Fandom'. *en.wikipedia.org/wiki/Tolkien_fandom*.

Tolkien in Oxford. British Broadcasting Corporation, 1968. Video.

'Tolkien Seeks the Quiet Life in Oxford'. *Oxford Mail*, 22 March 1972, p. 10.

†*Tolkien Studies* 1–3 (2004–6).

'Tolkien Talking'. *Sunday Times* (London), 27 November 1966.

'Tolkien's Farewell'. *Oxford Mail*, 6 June 1969, p. 4.

'Tolkien's Will', *The Bookseller*, 5 January 1974

Tolley, Clive. 'And the Word Was Made Flesh'. *Mallorn* 32 (September 1995), pp. 5–14.

——. 'The *Kalevala* and *The Silmarillion*'. *Mallorn* 15 (September 1980), pp. 13–15.

——. 'Tolkien and the Unfinished'. In Battarbee, *Scholarship & Fantasy*, pp. 151–64.

——. 'Tolkien's "Essay on Man": A Look at *Mythopoeia*'. *Inklings-Jahrbuch* 10 (1992), pp. 221–39.

Tolstoy, Nikolai. *The Quest for Merlin*. Sevenoaks: Coronet Books, 1986. First published London: Hamish Hamilton, 1985.

Topliffe, Lorise. 'Tolkien as an Undergraduate, 1911–1915'. *Exeter College Association Register* (1992), pp. 32–8.

Toynbee, Philip. 'Dissension among the Judges'. *The Observer*, 6 August 1961.

Tracey, Gerard. 'Tolkien and the Oratory'. *www.birmingham-oratory.org.uk/tolkien.htm*.

Traversi, Derek. 'The Realm of Gondor'. *The Month*, June 1956, pp. 370–1.

Treharne, Elaine, ed. *Old and Middle English: An Anthology*. Oxford: Blackwell, 2000.

Trott, Anthony. *No Place for Fop or Idler: The Story of King Edward's School, Birmingham*. London: James and James, 1992.

Trowbridge, Clinton W. *The Twentieth Century British Supernatural Novel*. Ph.D. thesis, University of Florida, 1958.

Turner, Allan. *Translating Tolkien: Philological Elements in The Lord of the Rings*. Frankfurt am Main: Peter Lang, 2005. *Duisburg Papers on Research in Language and Culture* 59.

Turner, F.M. 'Religion'. In Harrison, *The History of the University of Oxford, Vol. VIII*, pp. 293–316.

Turville-Petre, G., ed. *Víga-Glúms Saga*. Oxford: Oxford University Press, 1940. *Oxford English Monographs*.

Twiss, E.F. Obituary of Christopher Wiseman. *Old Edwardians Gazette*, April 1988.

'Two Benson Medals after 14 Years'. *The Times* (London), 24 November 1966, p. 14.

Tyack, Geoffrey. *Oxford and Cambridge*. 5th edn. London: A. & C. Black, 1999. *Blue Guide*.

Ulysses. *Catalogue 24: Modern First Editions & Illustrated Books*. London, November 1993.

'University Intelligence'. *The Times* (London), 8 April 1913, p. 6. Notice of Tolkien's Second Class in Classical (Honour) Moderations.

'University News'. *The Times* (London), 22 July 1925, p. 19. Notice of Tolkien's appointment as Rawlinson and Bosworth Professor of Anglo-Saxon.

'University News'. *The Times* (London), 2 January 1958, p. 8. Notice of Tolkien's appointment as Merton Professor of English Language and Literature.

Unwin, David. *Fifty Years with Father: A Relationship*. London: George Allen & Unwin, 1982.

Unwin, Philip. *The Publishing Unwins*. London: Heinemann, 1972.

Unwin, Rayner. 'Allen & Unwin Comments on Tolkien Reprints'. *Publishers Weekly*, 9 May 1966. Also printed in *Tolkien Journal* 2, no. 2 (Astron 1966), p. 5.

——. 'An At Last Finished Tale: The Genesis of *The Lord of the Rings*'. *Lembas-extra 1998*. Leiden: Tolkien Genootschap Unquendor, 1998. pp. 74–84.

——. 'Early Days of Elder Days'. In Flieger and Hostetter, *Tolkien's Legendarium*, pp. 3–6.

†——. *George Allen & Unwin: A Remembrancer*. Ludlow: Privately printed for the author by Merlin Unwin Books, 1999.

——. 'The Hobbit 50th Anniversary' *The Bookseller*, 16 January 1987, pp. 166–7.

——. "Publishing Tolkien". In Reynolds and GoodKnight, *Proceedings of the J.R.R. Tolkien Centenary Conference 1992*, pp. 26–9.

——. 'Taming the Lord of the Rings'. *The Bookseller*, 19 August 1988, pp. 647–50.

Unwin, Stanley. *The Truth about a Publisher: An Autobiographical Record*. London: George Allen & Unwin, 1960.

Van Meurs, J.C. 'Beowulf and Literary Criticism'. *Neophilologus* 39 (1955), pp. 114–30.

Veldman, Meredith. *Fantasy, the Bomb, and the Greening of Britain: Romantic Protest, 1945–1980*. New York: Cambridge University Press, 1994.

Venables, D.R., and R.E. Clifford, *Academic Dress of the University of Oxford*, 8th edn. Oxford: J. & P. Venables, 1998.

The Venerable English College, Rome. www.englishcollegerome.org/pages/frame1. htm.

Venice: An Illustrated Guide-book. Venezia: Renato Borgoni, [*c.* 1960].

Vergil. *Vergil's Works: The Aeneid, Eclogues, Georgics*. Trans. J.W. Mackail. New York: Modern Library, 1934.

'The Very Rev M.C. D'Arcy: Influential English Jesuit'. *The Times* (London), 22 November 1976, p. 14.

'The Vigfússon Readership', *Oxford Magazine* 60, no. 5 (13 November 1941), pp. 65–6.

Vinaver, Eugène. 'Mr Kenneth Sisam: Encouraging True Scholarship'. *The Times* (London), 2 September 1971, p. 14.

Vink, Renée. 'Translation Troubles of an Author: Some Reflections on an Angry Letter by Tolkien'. *Lembas-extra 93/94*. [Leiden]: Tolkien Genootschap 'Unquendor', [?1994]. pp. 45–57.

Wain, John. 'Push Bar to Open'. *Oxford Magazine*, Hilary Term 1988, pp. 3–5.

——. *Sprightly Running: Part of an Autobiography*. London: Macmillan, 1962.

Ward, Maisie. 'Gilbert Keith Chesterton'. *Dictionary of National Biography, 1931–1940*. pp. 171–5.

——. *Gilbert Keith Chesterton*. New York: Sheed and Ward, 1943.

Waterfield's. *Catalogue 176: Oxford, Oxfordshire & the Cotswolds*. Oxford, 1999.

Watson, J.R. 'The Hobbits and the Critics'. *Critical Quarterly* 13, no. 3 (Autumn 1971), pp. 252–8.

Watts, Janet. 'Bilbo Sings Again'. *The Guardian*, 19 September 1974.

Wawm, Andrew. *The Vikings and the Victorians: Inventing the Old North in 19th-Century Britain*. Woodbridge, Suffolk: D.S. Brewer, 2000.

Wayne, Jenifer. *The Purple Dress: Growing Up in the Thirties*. London: Victor Gollancz, 1979.

Webster's Geographical Dictionary. Rev. edn. Springfield, Massachusetts: G. & C. Merriam, 1957.

Weedon, Joan. *Father John Tolkien*. Eynsham: The Churches, 1994.

West, John G., Jr., ed. *Celebrating Middle-earth: The Lord of the Rings as a Defense of Western Civilization*. Seattle: Inkling Books, 2002.

West, Richard C. '"And She Named Her Own Name": Being True to One's Word in Tolkien's Middle-earth'. *Tolkien Studies* 2 (2005), pp. 1–10.

——. 'The Critics, and Tolkien, and C.S. Lewis: Reviews [of William Ready, *The Tolkien Relation*, etc.]'. *Orcrist* 5 = *Tolkien Journal* 4, no. 3, whole no. 14 (1970–1), pp. 4–9.

——. 'Real-world Myth in a Secondary World: Mythological Aspects in the Story of Beren and Lúthien'. In Chance, *Tolkien the Medievalist*, pp. 259–67.

——. 'The Status of Tolkien Scholarship'. *Tolkien Journal* 15 (Summer 1972), p. 21.

†——. 'A Tolkien Checklist: Selected Criticism 1981–2004'. *Modern Fiction Studies* 50, no. 4 (Winter 2004), pp. 1015–28.

†——. *Tolkien Criticism: An Annotated Checklist*. 2nd edn. Kent, Ohio: Kent State University Press, 1981.

——. 'Túrin's *Ofermod*: An Old English Theme in the Development of the Story of Túrin'. In Flieger and Hostetter, *Tolkien's Legendarium*, pp. 233–45.

——. 'W.H. Lewis: Historian of the Inklings and of Seventeenth-century France'. *Seven* 14 (1997), pp. 74–86.

White, Michael. *Tolkien: A Biography*. London: Little, Brown, 2001.

Whitehouse, C.J. and G.P. *A Town for Four Winters*. [Stafford?]: Staffordshire County Council, in association with the authors, 1983.

Who Was Who. Various volumes.

Who's Who. Various volumes.

Who's Who in Oxfordshire. London: 'Who's Who in the Counties', 1936.

Willett, Edward. *J.R.R. Tolkien: Master of Imaginary Worlds.* Berkeley Heights, New Jersey: Enslow, 2004.

Willey, Basil. 'Helen Darbishire, 1881–1961'. *Proceedings of the British Academy* 47 (1961), pp. 401–15.

——. 'Henry Stanley Bennett, 1889–1972'. *Proceedings of the British Academy* 58 (1972), pp. 551–67.

Williams, Charles. *Arthurian Torso.* With commentary by C.S. Lewis. London: Oxford University Press, 1948.

——. *Essential Writings in Spirituality and Theology.* Ed. Charles Hefling. Cambridge, Massachusetts: Cowley Publications, 1993.

——. *The Image of the City and Other Essays.* Ed. Anne Ridler. London: Oxford University Press, 1958.

——. *Letters to Lalage: The Letters of Charles Williams to Lois Lang-Sims.* Commentary by Lois Lang-Sims. Introduction and notes by Glen Cavaliero. Kent, Ohio: Kent State University Press, 1989.

——. *To Michal from Serge: Letters from Charles Williams to His Wife, Florence, 1939–1945.* Ed. Roma A. King, Jr. Kent, Ohio: Kent State University Press, 2002.

Wilson, A.N. *C.S. Lewis: A Biography.* London: Collins, 1990.

Wilson, Edmund. 'Oo, Those Awful Orcs'. *The Nation* 182 (14 April 1956), pp. 312–14. Review of *The Lord of the Rings.*

Winchester, Simon. *The Meaning of Everything: The Story of the Oxford English Dictionary.* Oxford: Oxford University Press, 2003.

Dominic Winter Book Auctions. *Printed Books, Maps & Ephemera.* Auction catalogue. South Cerney, Gloucestershire, 15 December 2004.

Wiseman, Christopher. 'Christopher Luke Wiseman'. *Old Edwardians Gazette,* April 1988, pp. 22, 24.

——. 'Notes and News'. *King Edward's School Chronicle* n.s. 26, no. 189 (October 1911), pp. 74–6.

Wollheim, Donald A. 'The Ace Tolkiens'. *Lighthouse* 13 (August 1965), pp. 16–18.

——. 'No "Intermediary"' (letter to the editor). *Saturday Review,* 23 October 1965, p. 56.

Wood, Anthony. 'Fireworks for the Author – and B.B.C. 2 Viewers'. *Oxford Mail,* 9 February 1968, p. 10.

Wrenn, C.L. 'Sir W. Craigie: Stimulus to Study of Germanic Languages'. *The Times* (London), 9 September 1957, p. 10.

——. *A Study of Old English Literature.* London: George G. Harrap, 1967.

——, ed. *Beowulf with the Finnesburg Fragment.* Rev. by W.F. Bolton. London: George G. Harrap, 1973.

—— and G. Bullough, eds. *English Studies Today.* Oxford: Oxford University Press, 1951.

Wright, Elizabeth Mary. *The Life of Joseph Wright.* London: Oxford University Press, 1932.

Wyllie, J.M. 'Sir William Craigie, 1867–1957'. *Proceedings of the British Academy* 48 (1962), pp. 272–91.

Wynne, Patrick, and Carl F. Hostetter. '"Verbs, Syntax! Hooray!": A Preliminary Assessment of Adunaic Grammar in *The Notion Club Papers*'. *Vinyar Tengwar* 24 (July 1992), pp. 14–38.

—— see also THE PUBLISHED WRITINGS OF J.R.R. TOLKIEN in vol. 1

—— and Christopher Gilson. 'Bird and Leaf: Image and Structure in *Narqelion*'. *Parma Eldalamberon* 3, no. 1, whole no. 9 (1990), pp. 6–19, 22–32.

Yamniuk, Stephanie. 'Klass and Tolkien Families' Program to Help Disadvantaged'. *On Manitoba*, April 2005, p. 29.

Yates, Jessica. 'Appetizers'. *A Long-Expected Party: Progress Report* 6 (Tolkien Society, 1992), pp. 23–6.

——. '"The Battle of the Eastern Field": A Commentary'. *Mallorn* 13 [1979], pp. 3–5.

——. 'The Other 50th Anniversary'. *Mythlore* 16, no. 3, whole no. 61 (Spring 1990), pp. 47–50.

—— (as Jessica Kemball-Cook). Review of *J.R.R. Tolkien: A Biography* by Humphrey Carpenter. *Amon Hen* 26 (May 1977), pp. 11–12.

——. 'Mr. Bliss in Context'. *Amon Hen* 59 (December 1982), pp. 6–7. Review of *Mr. Bliss*.

——. Review of *The Silmarillion*. *British Book News*, January 1978.

——. 'The Source of "The Lay of Aotrou and Itroun"'. In *Leaves from the Tree: J.R.R. Tolkien's Shorter Fiction*, pp. 63–71.

——. 'Tolkien the Anti-Totalitarian'. In Reynolds and GoodKnight, *Proceedings of the J.R.R. Tolkien Centenary Conference 1992*, pp. 233–45.

Yolton, John. 'In the Soup'. *Kenyon Review* (Summer 1965), pp. 565–7. Review of *Tree and Leaf*.

Zettersten, Arne. 'The AB Language Lives'. In Hammond and Scull, *The Lord of the Rings, 1954–2004: Scholarship in Honor of Richard E. Blackwelder*, pp. 13–24.

——. Review of *Ancrene Wisse*. *English Studies* 47 (1966), pp. 290–2.

Zimbardo, Rose A., and Neil D. Isaacs, eds. *Understanding The Lord of the Rings: The Best of Tolkien Criticism*. Boston: Houghton Mifflin, 2004.

Zimmermann, Manfred. 'The Origin of Gandalf and Josef Madlener'. *Mythlore* 23, no. 4, whole no. 34 (Winter 1983), pp. 22, 24.

Zocca, Emma. *Assisi e Dintorni*. 3rd edn. Roma: Istituto Poligrafico dello Stato, 1960.

ARCHIVAL SOURCES

Blackwell's Bookshops, Oxford
BBC Written Archives Centre, Caversham Park, Reading
University of Birmingham
Bloemfontein Cathedral
Bodleian Library, Oxford
British Library, London
Cambridge University Library
Centre for Oxfordshire Studies, Oxford Central Library
Corpus Christi College, Oxford
Early English Text Society
English Faculty Library, Oxford
English Place-Name Society
Exeter College Library, Oxford
Glasgow University Archive Services
HarperCollins, London
Hið íslenska bókmenntafélag (Icelandic Literary Society)
King Edward's School, Birmingham
Leeds University
Marquette University Libraries, Milwaukee, Wisconsin
Merton College, Oxford
National University of Ireland
Oxford University Archives
Oxford University Press, Oxford
Pembroke College, Oxford
National Archives, Kew (formerly Public Record Office)
National University of Ireland
Reading University Library
University of St Andrews Library
St Anne's College Library, Oxford
Simmons College, Boston, Massachusetts
Society for the Study of Mediaeval Languages and Literature
Society of the Holy Child Jesus
Staffordshire Archives Service
University College, London
Marion E. Wade Center, Wheaton College, Illinois
Worcester College, Oxford

Private collections

INDEX

Although each of the two volumes of *The J.R.R. Tolkien Companion and Guide* may be used independent of the other, they are designed to work in concert. To that end, we have prepared a common index, covering both the **Chronology** (Volume I) and the **Reader's Guide** (Volume II). This division is indicated by one or two asterisks on the title-page of each part, and by the roman numerals I and II below. The following is not meant to trace every mention of every person, place, or title in our text, but to point to those elements most pertinent to Tolkien's life and works, or otherwise likely to be of interest to readers, including the names of authorities and other writers. It follows the rules of style described in our preface, and the alphabetical structure of the Reader's Guide.

Andersen, Hans Christian I 5, II 272, 815
Anderson, Douglas A. II 104, 152, 214,
252, 335, 337, 347, 369, 372, 397–8, 401,
546–7, 796, 1012, 1132; see also The
Annotated Hobbit (ed. Anderson)
André, M. I 377
Andreas I 183, 204, 224, 247
Andúril II 287
Angerthas (Angerthas Daeron, Angerthas
Moria) II 1129
Angles and Britons: O'Donnell Lectures
I 586, 606, II 248
Anglo-Saxon see Old English language
and literature
Anglo-Saxon Verse I 206, 210, 211, 212,
II 85
Animalic I 11, 12, II 424, 475, 882
Annals of Aman I 356, 374, 380, 540–1,
773, II 50, 51, 52, 72, 80, 81, 183, 184,
206, 241–2, 302, 319, 517, 519, 595, 691,
806, 896, 897, 902–3, 920, 923, 989,
996, 997, 1006, 1073, 1074
Annals of Beleriand I 151, 156, 171, 355, 377,
II 49–51, 71, 82, 100, 186–7, 306–7, 318,
513, 565, 574, 606, 645–6, 671, 801, 802,
843–4, 864–5, 869–70, 872, 885, 894,
902, 922–3, 996–7, 1051–2, 1059, 1081;
see also Grey Annals
Annals of Valinor I 172, 373, 380, 974,
II 28, 42, 50, 51–2, 80, 182–3, 186, 206,
240–1, 301–2, 318, 512–13, 565, 801,
802, 843–4, 885, 894, 902, 919, 922–3,
989, 996–7, 1072–3; see also Annals of
Aman
Anne, Sister I 699
Annotated Hobbit, The (ed. D.A.
Anderson) II 214, 243, 252, 337, 340,
369, 372, 383, 397, 398, 401, 418, 419,
420, 421, 572, 796, 811, 981
Annúminas II 286
Aotrou and Itroun see The Lay of Aotrou
and Itroun
Apeland, Kaj André II 597
Apolausticks I 30–5 passim, 42, 777,
II 199, 320, 708, 956
Appearance, Tolkien's I 1, II 52–5
Appleton I 246
Applicability II 38–9, 40–1; see also
Allegory

Application for the Rawlinson and
Bosworth Professorship of Anglo-Saxon,
An I 126–7, 1301, II 1, 53, 139, 294, 349,
465–6, 499–500, 726, 759, 1126
Applications Committee (English Faculty
Board, Oxford) I 138, 139, 140, 142, 143,
147, 153–77 passim, 187, 191, 204, 214,
232, 244, 247, 295, 298, 310, 329, 342,
344, 346, 359, 362, 363, 369, 371, 372,
373, 378, 381, 382, 384, 385, 390, 393,
394, 414, 418, 429, 442, 451, 457, 477,
480, 492, 495, 502, 508, 512, 515, 534,
787, 795, II 741
Archer, Fred I 760
Archer, Jerome W. I 509, 512
Ardalambion II 482
Ardizzone, Edward I 334
Ariosto I 593, II 548
Aristophanes I 19, 26, II 226, 467
Ark!!! I 31
Armstrong, Helen II 792–3, 1123
Armstrong, Thomas I 496, 647, 721
Army, Tolkien enlists in I 69;
demobilization I 108–9; structure
of I 780
Armytage, Geoffrey Ayscough I 90
Arnell, Dora I 52
Arolla I 27, II 994
Art, Tolkien's interest in I 2; art by
Tolkien II 53–5, 162, 418, 515, 636–7,
899; see also titles of individual works
of art
Art nouveau II 55
Arthur and the Matter of Britain I 5,
II 56–60, 63, 148, 684
Arthurian Society I 143, 163, II 963
Arthuriana II 963
Arts and Crafts Movement II 598–9
Arundale, Justin I 615
As Two Fair Trees I 59, 61, 62, 64
Asbjørnsen, Peter Christen II 272
Ashmolean Museum II 55, 709
Asimov, Isaac II 818
Asquith, Lord II 1092
Assisi I 462, 468–73, II 435–6, 469
Associated Rediffusion I 608–9, 615
Astley, George D. I 733
Astronomy II 877
HMHS Asturias 95
Aðalsteinsdottir, Ungfrú I 772, II 469

to Cees Ouboter (in René van Rossenberg, 'Tolkien's Exceptional Visit to Holland: A Reconstruction', *Proceedings of the J.R.R. Tolkien Centenary Conference 1992*, 1995) © The J.R.R. Tolkien Copyright Trust 1995; letter by J.R.R. Tolkien to a class of primary school children (Sotheby's auction catalogue, 16 December 2004) © The J.R.R. Tolkien Copyright Trust 2004; letter by J.R.R. Tolkien to Eileen Elgar (Sotheby's auction catalogue, 6–7 December 1984) © The J.R.R. Tolkien Copyright Trust 1984; letter by J.R.R. Tolkien to Evelyn B. Byrne and Otto M. Penzler (*Attacks of Taste*, 1971) © The J.R.R. Tolkien Copyright Trust 1971; letter by J.R.R. Tolkien to G.E. Selby (Maggs Bros., *Catalogue 1086*) © The J.R.R. Tolkien Copyright Trust 1988; letter by J.R.R. Tolkien to G.E. Selby (Sotheby's auction catalogue, 28–29 July 1977) © The J.R.R. Tolkien Copyright Trust 1977; letter by J.R.R. Tolkien to G.E. Selby (Sotheby's auction catalogue, 16–17 May 1984) © The J.R.R. Tolkien Copyright Trust 1984; letter by J.R.R. Tolkien to George Lewis Hersch (Michael Silverman, *Catalogue No. 2*) © The J.R.R. Tolkien Copyright Trust 1998; letter by J.R.R. Tolkien to George Sayer (Christie's auction catalogue, 16 November 2001) © The J.R.R. Tolkien Copyright Trust 2001; letter by J.R.R. Tolkien to George Sayer (in Sayer, 'Recollections of J.R.R. Tolkien', *Proceedings of the J.R.R. Tolkien Centenary Conference 1992*, 1995) © The J.R.R. Tolkien Copyright Trust 1995; letter by J.R.R. Tolkien to H. Cotton Minchin (Christie's auction catalogue, 26 November 1997) © The J.R.R. Tolkien Copyright Trust 1997; letter by J.R.R. Tolkien to Humphrey Carpenter (University Archives, *Catalogue 116*) © The J.R.R. Tolkien Copyright Trust 1994; letter by J.R.R. Tolkien to J.L.N. O'Loughlin (Paul C. Richards Autographs, *Catalogue 228*) © The J.R.R. Tolkien Copyright Trust 1988; letter by J.R.R. Tolkien to James A.H. Murray (Sotheby's auction catalogue, 12 December 2002) © The J.R.R. Tolkien Copyright Trust 2002; letter by J.R.R. Tolkien to Jane Louise Curry (Sotheby's auction catalogue, 10 July 2001) © The J.R.R. Tolkien Copyright Trust 2001; letter by J.R.R. Tolkien to Jennifer Brookes-Smith (Christie's auction catalogue, 2 December 2003) © The J.R.R. Tolkien Copyright Trust 2003; letter by J.R.R. Tolkien to Joy Hill (quoted in Hammond and Scull, 'Note on the 50th Anniversary Edition', *The Lord of the Rings*, 2004) © The J.R.R. Tolkien Copyright Trust 2004; letter by J.R.R. Tolkien to 'King Ephedolos' (Sotheby's auction catalogue, 14–15 December 1992) © The J.R.R. Tolkien Copyright Trust 1992; letter by J.R.R. Tolkien to L.M. Cutts (Sotheby's auction catalogue, 10 July 2003) © The J.R.R. Tolkien Copyright Trust 2003; letter by J.R.R. Tolkien to L. Sprague de Camp, *Mythlore*, Summer 1987 © The J.R.R. Tolkien Copyright Trust 1987; letter by J.R.R. Tolkien to Milton Waldman, ?late 1951 (in *La Feuille de la Compagnie Cahier d'études tolkieniennes* 2, l'automne 2003) © The J.R.R. Tolkien Copyright Trust 2003; letter by J.R.R. Tolkien to Miss How (Sotheby's auction catalogue, 21–22 July 1980) © The J.R.R. Tolkien Copyright Trust 1980; letter by J.R.R. Tolkien to Miss Jaworski (Sotheby's auction catalogue, 16 October 1978) © The J.R.R. Tolkien Copyright Trust 1978; letter by J.R.R. Tolkien to Miss Morley (Dominic Winter Book Auctions catalogue, 15 December 2004) © The J.R.R. Tolkien Copyright Trust 1978; letter by J.R.R. Tolkien to Miss Perry (Michael Silverman, *Catalogue Nine*, 1993) © The J.R.R. Tolkien Copyright Trust 1978; letter by J.R.R. Tolkien to Mr Hodgson (Phillips auction catalogue, 24 March 2000) © The J.R.R. Tolkien Copyright Trust 2000; letter by J.R.R. Tolkien to Mrs Gill (eBay.com, December 2003) © The J.R.R. Tolkien Copyright Trust 2003; letter by J.R.R. Tolkien to Mrs Munby (Sotheby's auction catalogue, 11–12 July 2002) © The J.R.R. Tolkien Copyright Trust 1981, 2002; letter by J.R.R. Tolkien to Moira Sayer (Christie's auction catalogue, 13 November 2001) © The J.R.R. Tolkien Copyright Trust 2001; letter by J.R.R. Tolkien to Patricia Kirke (Gerard A.J. Stodolski, *Catalogue 4*, 1995) © The J.R.R. Tolkien Copyright Trust 1995; letter by J.R.R. Tolkien to Patricia Kirke (Gerard A.J. Stodolski, *Catalogue 299*, June 1999) © The J.R.R. Tolkien Copyright Trust 1999; letter by J.R.R. Tolkien to Paul Bibire (*Vinyar Tengwar*, July 2001) © The J.R.R. Tolkien Copyright Trust 2001; letter by J.R.R. Tolkien to Peter Alford (Sotheby's auction catalogue, 13 December 2001) © The J.R.R. Tolkien Copyright Trust 2001; letter by J.R.R. Tolkien to the President of the Tolkien Society of America (*Tolkien Journal*, 1968) © The J.R.R. Tolkien Copyright Trust 1968; letter by J.R.R. Tolkien to Professor Jongkees (R.M. Smythe, *Catalogue 10*, 2001) © The J.R.R. Tolkien Copyright Trust 2001; letter by J.R.R. Tolkien to R.W. Burchfield (Christie's auction catalogue, 7 June 2006) © The J.R.R. Tolkien Copyright Trust 2006; letters by J.R.R. Tolkien to R.W. Chapman (*Moreana*, February and June 1987) © The J.R.R. Tolkien Copyright Trust 1987; letter by J.R.R. Tolkien to 'Rosemary' (*Mallorn*, November 1998) © The J.R.R. Tolkien Copy-

Unwin archive); and René van Rossenberg. Quotations from George Allen & Unwin archives were made with permission of HarperCollins, successor to the publishers George Allen & Unwin and Unwin Hyman. Letters by or to Pauline Baynes were quoted with the permission of Mrs Pauline Gasch. Materials from the Pamela Chandler Archive were used with the permission of Mrs Diana Willson. Letters from the Early English Text Society archives were quoted with permission of the Council of the Early English Text Society. Material from the Exeter College Archives has been used with the permission of the Rector and Fellows of Exeter College, Oxford. Quotations from letters by Robert Q. Gilson were made with the permission of Ms Julia Margretts. Materials from the Oxford University Press Archives were quoted by permission of the Secretary to the Delegates of Oxford University Press. Quotations from letters by Christopher Wiseman were made with the permission of Ms Susan Wood.

The majority of quotations from Tolkien's writings have been made with the kind permission of the Tolkien Estate, and are acknowledged in detail in the preceding copyright statement. Quotations from the unrestricted Tolkien Papers in the Bodleian Library, University of Oxford, are documented below; all other citations in this book to the Tolkien Papers, Bodleian Library refer to materials currently with restricted access.

CHRONOLOGY

p. 183, 'our profit' (Tolkien A4/2, f. 10)
p. 184, 'once (lightheartedly) . . . several in use' (Tolkien A18/1, f. 8)
p. 185, 'grieved that . . . you have given' (Tolkien A4/2, f. 27)
p. 379, 'today . . . curious Chaucer usage' (Tolkien A18/1, f. 32)
p. 499, 'the emendations . . . to the class', 'I have not had time . . . translation' (Tolkien A22/1, f. 120)
p. 504, 'beginning to feel . . . two or three days', 'a first charge on what time is left', 'But work put aside . . . of this vacation' (Tolkien A7/7, f. 179)
pp. 531–2, 'of course' . . . (etc., extracts to) 'have no utility' (Tolkien A7/7, ff. 193–200)
p. 533, 'At the meeting . . . of your memo' (Tolkien A7/7, f. 185)
p. 557, 'that certain parts . . . of St. Katherine' (Tolkien A7/7, f. 208)
p. 563, 'Your notes on capitals . . . "very clear"' (Tolkien A4/2, f. 62)
p. 570, 'so that duplication . . . as we have agreed' (Tolkien A4/2, f. 106)
p. 570, 'As I said . . . admirable")' (Tolkien A4/2, f. 107)
p. 571, 'I am very much tied . . . on March 20' (Tolkien A4/2, f. 113)
pp. 572–3, 'if I had not had' . . . (etc., extracts to) 'proceed without me' (Tolkien A4/2, ff. 116–18)
p. 574, 'Forgive my chattiness . . . in the work' (Tolkien A4/2, ff. 124–5)
p. 577, 'as befits one' . . . (etc., extracts to) 'the threads of my other work' (Tolkien A4/2, ff. 146–8)
p. 586, 'I have had to do . . . is left alone' (Tolkien A4/2, f. 157)
p. 586, 'The alterations were . . . they deserve' (Tolkien A4/2, f. 162)
p. 586, 'May I thank you . . . "unauthorized"' (Tolkien A4/2, ff. 163)
p. 587, 'if I had fully understood . . . you and others', 'I had to think . . . if approved' (Tolkien A4/2, f. 178)
p. 594, 'This is the sort . . . give his all for' (MS Tolkien 19, f. 136)
p. 605, 'The faintest cloud . . . less trying than writing' (MS Tolkien 4, f. 76)
p. 623, 'but I am unfortunately . . . receive my contribution?' (MS Tolkien 9, fol. 164)
p. 687, 'should be given . . . might be cut down' (MS Tolkien 21, f. 3)

READER'S GUIDE

p. 40, 'is *not* an allegory . . . hearer or reader' (MS Tolkien 9, f. 108)
p. 45, 'enormous advantages . . . with the manuscript' (Tolkien A7/7, f. 170)
p. 47, 'the place of the line-ending . . . reasonable choice' (Tolkien A7/7, f. 200)
p. 56, 'hoped that some . . . not quite fair' (MS Tolkien 14, f. 105)

p. 224, 'the characters and even the places . . . limitations of plays' (MS Tolkien 6, f. 19)

p. 244, 'As the train . . . silent and furtive' (MS Tolkien 9, f. 7)

p. 254, 'It was fledged . . . mass-production of slaughter' (MS Tolkien 6, f. 22)

p. 255, 'So to save the life . . . just: no' (MS Tolkien 6, f. 22)

p. 255, 'it may have some practical uses . . . like locusts' (MS Tolkien 14, f. 161)

pp. 385–6, 'took long in first writing . . . than the Dragon' (MS Tolkien 21, f. 130)

p. 350, 'an almost perfect blend . . . explicit and revealed' (MS Tolkien 14, f. 119)

p. 457, 'Philology has been dethroned . . . *legend or myth*', 'higher or lower mythology as A.L. called them' (MS Tolkien 14, f. 91)

p. 458, 'six stories from Grimm . . . *The Red Etin*' (MS Tolkien 14, f. 132)

p. 525, 'The roof of Paddington Station . . . dome of heaven' (MS Tolkien 14, f. 110)

p. 555, 'In vain we regret . . . most of their tongue', 'the ruin of Gaul . . . the Cymric speaking peoples' (Tolkien A15/2, f. 149)

p. 567, 'For me at any rate . . . since childhood' (MS Tolkien 14, f. 74)

p. 568, 'get out B.Litt. on Macdonald' (MS Tolkien 14, f. 43)

p. 570, 'a gem – of the kind . . . Second part of Curdie.)' (MS Tolkien 6, f. 2)

p. 570, 'And beside *The Princess and the Goblin* . . . *The Golden Key*' (MS Tolkien 14, f. 119)

p. 570, 'Death is the theme . . . "romance of Lilith"' (MS Tolkien 14, f. 112)

p. 639, 'triumphant formula . . . Phoenix and the Carpet' (MS Tolkien 14, f. 119)

pp. 653–4, 'I must protest . . . impudence of a parasite' (Tolkien A30/1, f. 121)

p. 687, 'Grown-ups writing fairy-stories . . . "marketing problem"' (MS Tolkien 14, f. 119)

pp. 769–70, 'You of course go clean contrary . . . feeling and thought?' (Tolkien A35, f. 127)

p. 770, 'The making of translations . . . no other way', 'First of all . . . humble and loyal allegiance' (Tolkien A30, ff. 107–9)

p. 771, 'I have at present . . . no room to move' (Tolkien A35, f. 127)

p. 815, 'liked my magic . . . strong meat for nurseries' (MS Tolkien 14, f. 105)

p. 943, 'the project fizzed out . . . exemplar of "fairy" magic)' (MS Tolkien 9, f. 148)

pp. 943–4, 'when striving to say . . . thing in itself' (MS Tolkien 9, f. 3)

pp. 944–5, 'I must beg the pardon . . . sincere and humble – dislike' (MS Tolkien 9, f. 108)

p. 958, 'the Catenians . . . domestic commitments' (Tolkien A6/2, f. 145)

pp. 961–2, 'benefit of clergy', 'I wish I could get off as lightly . . . I know better' (Tolkien A13/1, ff. 168, 170)

p. 964, 'as befits . . . of the Council' (Tolkien A4/2, f. 146)

p. 1130, 'I should like to record . . . across the river' (MS Tolkien 14, f. 119).